BASEBALL PROSPECTUS 2019

The Essential Guide to the 2019 Season

Edited by Patrick Dubuque, Aaron Gleeman and Bret Sayre

Eddy Almaguer, Darius Austin, Mike Axisa, Emma Baccellieri, Mark Barry, Jonathan Bernhardt, Nathan Bishop, Paul Boye, Grant Brisbee, Craig Brown, Craig Calcaterra, Russell Carleton, Ben Carsley, Michael Clair, Roger Cormier, Zach Crizer, Chris Cwik, Matt Ellis, James Fegan, Chad Finn, Ken Funck, Brendan Gawlowski, Mike Gianella, Craig Goldstein, Bryan Grosnick, Jon Hegglund, Kevin Jebens, Jonathan Judge, Wilson Karaman, Justin Klugh, David Lee, Rob Mains, Rachael McDaniel, Whitney McIntosh, Jack Moore, Nick Nelson, Eric Nusbaum, Robert O'Connell, Nick Offerman, Jeffrey Paternostro, Kate Preusser, Matt Provenzano, Tommy Rancel, Dan Rathman, Sheryl Ring, David Roth, Meg Rowley, Nick Schaefer, Jarrett Seidler, Susan Slusser, Jesse Spector, Eric Stephen, Matt Sussman, David Temple, Matthew Trueblood, Ashley Varela, Levi Weaver, Collin Whitchurch, Jeff Wiser, Jason Wojciechowski, Nicholas Zettel

Craig Brown, Associate Editor
Jonathan Judge, Rob McQuown and Harry Pavlidis, Statistics Editors

Library of Congress Cataloging-in-Publication Data:
paperback
ISBN-10: 1732355509
ISBN-13: 978-1732355507

Project Credits
Cover Design: Kathleen Dyson
Interior Design and Production: Jeff Pease, Dave Pease
Layout: Jeff Pease, Dave Pease

Cover Photos
Front Cover: Shohei Ohtani. © Jay Biggerstaff-USA TODAY Sports
Back Cover: Shohei Ohtani. © Rick Osentoski-USA TODAY Sports

Baseball icon courtesy of Uberux, from https://www.shareicon.net/author/uberux

Manufactured in the United States of America
10 9 8 7 6 5 4 3 2 1

Table of Contents

Foreword

by Rob Mains

The nearly four pounds that you are holding in your hands—less, we hope, if you're reading this on an electronic device—represents the continuation of an evolution that had its roots in the rec.sport.baseball Usenet newsgroup from the early 1990s. In 1995, Gary Huckabay reached out to friends he met there, merging his "Vladimir" player projection system with Clay Davenport's minor league Translations and Rany Jazayerli's system for rating pitching depth with the writing talent of Joe Sheehan and Christina Kahrl to form Baseball Prospectus. The first *Annual*, published in 1996, cost $20, and accidentally omitted the Cardinals. Later that year, Dave Pease created the website baseballprospectus.com.

Let's take stock of where we've come. The year the first *Annual* arrived, the last *Bill James Baseball Abstract* had rolled off the presses eight years ago, and James' *Historical Baseball Abstract* was 11 years old. The last *Bill James Baseball Book* was printed in 1992. The main outlet for sabermetric analysis was Rob Neyer's fledgling column for ESPN.com, launched that year. There was no Statcast, no PITCHf/x, no PECOTA. The top two vote-getters in the 2018 National League Rookie of the Year balloting and the third baseman for the 2018 World Champions had not been born. There were 49 starting pitchers who logged more than 200 innings, and there were 290 complete games across the majors; the corresponding figures last season were 11 and 42. Position players laid down an average of 35 sacrifice bunts per team; last season there were fewer than 14. There was no major league baseball in St. Petersburg or Phoenix. Edwin Starr's soul single, "War" was a Sixties anti-war anthem, not a hackneyed go-to for boomer sportswriters railing against analytics. Barack Obama was an associate at a 13-attorney law firm in Chicago. Donald Trump was a real estate developer who'd just bought a share of the Miss Universe pageant.

Baseball Prospectus emerged as a leader in sabermetric analysis. We introduced our PECOTA projections in 2003. We pioneered the concept of pitch framing—the idea that catchers could help pitchers get borderline strike calls had been derided by traditionalists as well as analysts—a concept that has revolutionized ratings for catchers. Our Equivalent Average normalized hitting statistics for park and league. Our WARP (Wins Above Replacement Player) and its progenitor, VORP (Value Over Replacement Player) popularized the concept of the freely-available replacement player as the baseline for player valuation. Later, we introduced player ratings that used sophisticated mixed models to incorporate a wide gamut of factors affecting pitching (Deserved Run Average, in 2015) and hitting (Deserved Runs Created, introduced last fall and discussed in these pages).

Along the way, we've led the way. Baseball Prospectus, along with other outstanding sabermetrically-oriented websites like Baseball-Reference, FanGraphs, and Beyond the Box Score, has helped move sabermetrics into the mainstream. When we started, the 2002 *Moneyball* Oakland Athletics were six years away. Michael Lewis's book came out in 2003, and the movie in 2011, but the concepts it brought to the general public were the ones we'd been writing about for years. Now, as you'll see inside, Baseball Prospectus alumni are represented across MLB front offices. The scouts vs. stats narrative was always a false dichotomy, in part because there really wasn't a battle. Both sides won.

But the mission at BP has never been just about the numbers. For many of you, granted, that's largely why you're here: For the rankings, for the player summaries, and for the projections. But we've always prided ourselves for our writing as well. Baseball Prospectus authors have been nominated for SABR Analytics Conference Research Awards, the most prestigious award in our genre, every year since they were established. Our writers have moved on to major media outlets like ESPN (Christina Kahrl, Sam Miller) and Sports Illustrated (Joe Sheehan, Emma Baccellieri), with new talent taking their place. If you've read this book for a number of years, you've noticed a change of tone, as the snark has been dialed down now that managers are no longer putting batters with a sub-.300 OBP in the leadoff spot and teams aren't valuing free agent pitchers and hitters based on wins and RBI. But we feel we've maintained the wit, the cleverness, and above all, the analytical insights that you value in the *Annual*. And we deliver that every day on the website as well.

Many of you are familiar with the website. Our staff produces content for every baseball taste. Our daily features range from the statistically rigorous to the whimsical, written by many of the same writers whose work you'll read in these pages. Our prospect team spans the globe, from instructional leagues to AAA, and now includes analysts in Japan and Korea. They'll give you not only our Top Ten lists, details on call-ups and our annual Futures Guide, but also progress reports as tomorrow's stars advance through the minors. Our fantasy team offers expert advice on all formats, from mono to dynasty to H2H, with weekly updates on key topics like bullpens and likely starting pitchers and FAAB, preseason positional guides, and draft-day tools. Our Short Relief feature offers short takes on unexplored and often eccentric aspects of the game. And it's not just the game on the field; our writers have explored hot-button issues ranging from baseball economics to changes to the ball to the league's domestic violence policy. Subscribers to the site get all of this, plus our cutting-edge stats.

While much has changed since the first *Annual*, one thing that has not is our crusade to continually develop how we think about the game. Though the masthead of the company has been graced by some of the finest writers, analysts, and talent evaluators in the game today, the most indelible element of the company is its culture, how we've progressed from one era to another, sometimes changing in style or presentation, but always maintaining that same grassroots spirit of its early days. It's ironic to think, given how many of our alumni are now inside the game (and it is, without a doubt, a source of great pride), but Baseball Prospectus has always been, at its heart, a collection of outsiders: Writers and thinkers who examine the sport critically and externally. The stereotype of the blogger who doesn't watch baseball has never been true. We, like you, are people who love baseball and love thinking about it.

That's why we were excited and happy to announce last November that a group of the site's senior staff has purchased Baseball Prospectus. For the first time in a long time, BP is being run by BP again: By the people who have worked to make the site and this book what it is.

Over the course of this year, we'll be rolling out new features, new products, new tools, new contests and new products on the website. The evolving baseballprospectus.com will exist alongside a sport that serves as a capable metaphor for the next phase of the company, one of cyclical advancement, a shared team name seeing through shifting eras. Along the way, our mission will remain to give you the best baseball analysis and writing available, and to continue to make the Annual that you're holding in your hands the essential guide to the season. We're excited by the future for Baseball Prospectus, and look forward to sharing it with you. ▪

Statistical Introduction

by Bryan Grosnick

Sports are, fundamentally, a blend of athletic endeavor and storytelling. Baseball, like any other sport, tells its stories in so many ways: in the arc of a game from the stands or a season from the box scores, in photos, or even in numbers. At Baseball Prospectus, we understand that statistics don't replace observation or any of baseball's stories, but complement everything else that makes the game so much fun.

What stats help us with is with patterns and precision, variance and value. This book can help you learn things you may not see from watching a game or hundred, whether it's the path of a career over time or the breadth of the entire MLB. We'd also never ask you to choose between our numbers and the experience of viewing a game from the cheap seats or the comfort of your home; our publication combines running the numbers with observations and wisdom from some of the brightest minds we can find. But if you *do* want to learn more about the numbers beyond what's on the backs of player jerseys, let us help explain.

Offense

We've revised our methodology for determining batting value. Long-time readers of the book will notice that we've retired True Average in favor of a new metric: Deserved Runs Created Plus (DRC+). Developed by Jonathan Judge and our stats team, this statistic measures everything a player does at the plate–reaching base, hitting for power, making outs, and moving runners over–and puts it on a scale where 100 equals league-average performance. A DRC+ of 150 is terrific, a DRC+ of 100 is average and a DRC+ of 75 means you better be an excellent defender.

DRC+ also does a better job than any of our previous metrics in taking contextual factors into account. The model adjusts for how the park affects performance, but also for things like the talent of the opposing pitcher, value of different types of batted-ball events, league, temperature and other factors. It's able to describe a player's expected offensive contribution than any other statistic we've found over the years, and also does a better job of predicting future performance as well.

There's a lot more to DRC+'s story, and you can read all about it in greater depth near the end of this book.

The other aspect of run-scoring is baserunning, which we quantify using Baserunning Runs. BRR not only records the value of stolen bases (or getting caught in the act), but also accounts for all the stuff that doesn't show up on the back of a baseball card: a runner's ability to go first to third on a single, or advance on a fly ball.

Defense

Where offensive value is *relatively* easy to identify and understand, defensive value is...not. Over the past dozen years, the sabermetric community has focused mostly on stats based on zone data: a real-live human person records the type of batted ball and estimated landing location, and models are created that give expected outs. From there, you can compare fielders' actual outs to those expected ones. Simple, right?

Unfortunately, zone data has two major issues. First, zone data is recorded by commercial data providers who keep the raw data private unless you pay for it. (All the statistics we build in this book and on our website use public data as inputs.) That hurts our ability to test assumptions or duplicate results. Second, over the years it has become apparent that there's quite a bit of "noise" in zone-based fielding analysis. Sometimes the conclusions drawn from zone data don't hold up to scrutiny, and sometimes the different data provided by different providers don't look anything alike, giving wildly different results. Sometimes the hard-working professional stringers or scorers might unknowingly inflict unconscious bias into the mix: for example good fielders will often be credited with more expected outs despite the data, and ballparks with high press boxes tend to score more line drives than ones with a lower press box.

Enter our Fielding Runs Above Average (FRAA). For most positions, FRAA is built from play-by-play data, which allows us to avoid the subjectivity found in many other fielding metrics. The idea is this: count how many fielding plays are made by a given player and compare that to expected plays for an average fielder at their position (based on pitcher ground ball tendencies and batter handedness). Then we adjust for park and base-out situations.

When it comes to catchers, our methodology is a little different thanks to the laundry list of responsibilities they're tasked with beyond just, well, catching and throwing the ball.

By now you've probably heard about "framing" or the art of making umpires more likely to call balls outside the strike zone for strikes. To put this into one tidy number, we incorporate pitch tracking data (for the years it exists) and adjust for important factors like pitcher, umpire, batter and home-field advantage using a mixed-model approach. This grants us a number for how many strikes the catcher is personally adding to (or subtracting from) his pitchers' performance...which we then convert to runs added or lost using linear weights.

Framing is one of the biggest parts of determining catcher value, but we also take into account blocking balls from going past, whether a scorer deems it a passed ball or a wild pitch. We use a similar approach—one that really benefits from the pitch tracking data that tells us what ends up in the dirt and what doesn't. We also include a catcher's ability to prevent stolen bases and how well they field balls in play, and *finally* we come up with our FRAA for catchers.

Pitching

Both pitching and fielding make up the half of baseball that isn't run scoring: run prevention. Separating pitching from fielding is a tough task, and most recent pitching analysis has branched off from Voros McCracken's famous (and controversial) statement, "There is little if any difference among major-league pitchers in their ability to prevent hits on balls hit in the field of play." The research of the analytic community has validated this to some extent, and there are a host of "defense-independent" pitching measures that have been developed to try and extract the effect of the defense behind a hurler from the pitcher's work.

Our solution to this quandary is Deserved Run Average (DRA), our core pitching metric. DRA looks like earned run average (ERA), the tried-and-true pitching stat you've seen on every baseball broadcast or box score from the past century, but it's very different. To start, DRA takes an event-by-event look at what the pitchers does, and adjusts the value of that event based on different environmental factors like park, batter, catcher, umpire, base-out situation, run differential, inning, defense, home field advantage, pitcher role and temperature. That mixed model gives us a pitcher's expected contribution, similar to what we do for our DRC+ model for hitters and FRAA model for catchers. (Oh, and we also consider the pitcher's effect on basestealing and on balls getting past the catcher.)

It's important to note that DRA is set to the scale of runs allowed per nine innings (RA9) instead of ERA, which makes DRA's scale slightly higher than ERA's. The reason for this is because ERA tends to overrate three types of pitchers:

1. Pitchers who play in parks where scorers hand out more errors. Official scorers differ significantly in the frequency at which they assign errors to fielders.
2. Ground-ball pitchers, because a substantial proportion of errors occur on groundballs.

3. Pitchers who aren't very good. Better pitchers often allow fewer unearned runs than bad pitchers, because good pitchers tend to find ways to get out of jams.

Since the last time you picked up an edition of this book, we've also made a few minor changes to DRA to make it better. Recent research into "tunneling"—the act of throwing consecutive pitches that appear similar from a batter's point of view until after the swing decision point–data has given us a new contextual factor to account for in DRA: plate distance. This refers to the distance between successive pitches as they approach the plate, and while it has a smaller effect than factors like velocity or whiff rate, it still can help explain pitcher strikeout rate in our model.

New Pitching Metrics for 2019

We're including a few "new" pitching metrics in the book for the 2019 edition, though unlike last year, these numbers may be a little bit more familiar to those of you who have spent some time investigating baseball statistics.

Fastball Percentage

Our fastball percentage (FB%) statistic measures how frequently a pitcher throws a pitch classified as a "fastball," measured as a percentage of overall pitches thrown. We qualify three types of fastballs:

1. The traditional four-seam fastball;
2. The two-seam fastball or sinker;
3. "Hard cutters," which are pitches that have the movement profile of a cut fastball and are used as the pitcher's primary offering or in place of a more traditional fastball.

For example, a pitcher with a FB% of 67 throws any combination of these three pitches about two-thirds of the time.

Whiff Rate

Everybody loves a swing and a miss, and whiff rate (WHF) measures how frequently pitchers induce a swinging strike. To calculate WHF, we add up all the pitches thrown that ended with a swinging strike, then divide that number by a pitcher's total pitches thrown. Most often, high whiff rates correlate with high strikeout rates (and overall effective pitcher performance).

Called Strike Probability

Called Strike Probability (CSP) is a number that represents the likelihood that all of a pitcher's pitches will be called a strike while controlling for location, pitcher and batter handedness, umpire and count. Here's how it works: on each pitch, our model determines how many times (out of 100) that a similar pitch was called for a strike given those factors mentioned above, and when normalized for each batter's strike zone. Then we average the CSP for all pitches thrown by a pitcher in a season, and that gives us the yearly CSP percentage you see in the stats boxes.

As you might imagine, pitchers with a higher CSP are more likely to work in the zone, where pitchers with a lower CSP are likely locating their pitches outside the normal strike zone, for better or for worse.

Projections

Many of you aren't turning to this book just for a look at what a player has done, but for a look at what a player is going to do: the PECOTA projections. PECOTA, initially developed by Nate Silver (who has moved on to greater fame as a political analyst), consists of three parts:

1. Major-league equivalencies, which use minor-league statistics to project how a player will perform in the major leagues;

2. Baseline forecasts, which use weighted averages and regression to the mean to estimate a player's current true talent level; and

3. Aging curves, which uses the career paths of comparable players to estimate how a player's statistics are likely to change over time.

With all those important things covered, let's take a look at what's in the book this year.

Team Prospectus

Most of this book is composed of team chapters, with one for each of the 30 major-league franchises. On the first page of each chapter, you'll see a box that contains some of the key statistics for each team as well as a very inviting stadium diagram. (You can see an example of this for the Milwaukee Brewers on this very page!)

We start with the team name, their unadjusted 2018 win-loss record, and their divisional ranking. Beneath that are a host of other team statistics. **Pythag** presents an adjusted 2018 winning percentage, calculated by taking runs scored per game (**RS/G**) and runs allowed per game (**RA/G**) for the team, and running them through a version of Bill James' Pythagorean formula that was refined and improved by David Smyth and Brandon Heipp. (The formula is called "Pythagenpat," which is equally fun to type and to say.)

Next up is **DRC+**, described earlier, to indicate the overall hitting ability of the team either above or below league-average. Run prevention on the pitching side is covered by **DRA** (also mentioned earlier) and another metric: Fielding Independent Pitching (**FIP**), which calculates another ERA-like statistic based on strikeouts, walks, and home runs recorded. Defensive Efficiency Rating (**DER**) tells us the percentage of balls in play turned into outs for the team, and is a quick fielding shorthand that rounds out run prevention.

www.baseballprospectus.com

BREWERS PROSPECTUS
2018 W-L: 96-67, 1ST IN NL CENTRAL

Pythag	.562	9th	B-Age	28.9	24th
RS/G	4.63	12th	P-Age	28.7	17th
RA/G	4.04	8th	Salary	$91.0M	26th
DRC+	100	10th	M$/MW	$1.6M	28th
DRA	4.31	13th	DL Days	1025	13th
FIP	3.96	13th	$ on DL	16%	15th
DER	.721	4th			

400'
370'   374'
344'   345'

- Opened 2001
- Retractable roof
- Natural surface
- Fence profile: 8'

Three-Year Park Factors

Runs	Runs/RH	Runs/LH	HR/RH	HR/LH
102	102	100	102	112

Top Hitter WARP	5.1 Christian Yelich
Top Pitcher WARP	2.7 Josh Hader
Top Prospect	Keston Hiura

After that, we have several measures related to roster composition, as opposed to on-field performance. **B-Age** and **P-Age** tell us the average age of a team's batters and pitchers, respectively. **Salary** is the combined team payroll for all on-field players, and Doug Pappas' Marginal Dollars per Marginal Win (**M$/MW**) tells us how much money a team spent to earn production above replacement level.

Ending this batch of statistics is the number of disabled list days a team had over the season (**DL Days**) and the amount of salary paid to players on the disabled list (**$ on DL**); this final number is expressed as a percentage of total payroll.

Statistical Introduction - ix

Alex Bregman 3B Born: 03/30/94 Age: 25 Bats: R Throws: R Height: 6'0" Weight: 180 Origin: Round 1, 2015 Draft (#2 overall)

YEAR	TEAM	LVL	AGE	PA	R	2B	3B	HR	RBI	BB	K	SB	CS	AVG/OBP/SLG	DRC+	VORP	BABIP	BRR	FRAA	WARP
2016	CCH	AA	22	285	54	16	2	14	46	42	26	5	3	.297/.415/.559	170	38.9	.286	1.6	SS(51): -3.4, 3B(11): 1.4	3.7
2016	FRE	AAA	22	83	17	6	0	6	15	5	12	2	1	.333/.373/.641	138	10.0	.333	-1.2	SS(14): 2.1, LF(3): -0.1	0.8
2016	HOU	MLB	22	217	31	13	3	8	34	15	52	2	0	.264/.313/.478	99	9.6	.317	0.5	3B(40): 0.9, SS(6): -0.1	0.9
2017	HOU	MLB	23	626	88	39	5	19	71	55	97	17	5	.284/.352/.475	112	34.7	.311	-1.5	3B(132): 8.7, SS(30): -2.9	3.9
2018	HOU	MLB	24	705	105	51	1	31	103	96	85	10	4	.286/.394/.532	143	72.6	.289	-1.6	3B(136): 5.4, SS(28): -0.4	6.9
2019	HOU	MLB	25	682	98	39	4	23	82	73	108	12	4	.274/.363/.467	129	38.7	.303	-1.3	3B 7, SS 0	4.9

Breakout: 2%   Improve: 63%   Collapse: 2%   Attrition: 2%   MLB: 100%   *Comparables: Anthony Rendon, David Wright, Pablo Sandoval*

Next to each of these stats, we've listed each team's MLB rank in that category from first to 30th. In this, first always indicates a positive outcome and 30th a negative outcome, except in the case of salary—first is highest.

After the franchise statistics, we share a few items about the team's home ballpark. There's the aforementioned diagram of the park's dimensions (including distances to the outfield wall), a graphic showing the height of the wall from the left-field pole to the right-field pole, and a table showing three-year park factors for the stadium. The park factors are displayed as indexes where 100 is average, 110 means that the park inflates the statistic in question by 10 percent, and 90 means that the park deflates the statistic in question by 10 percent.

On the second page of each team chapter, you'll find three graphs. The first is the **2018 Hit List Ranking**. This shows our Hit List Rank for the team on each day of the 2018 season and is intended to give you a picture of the ups and downs of the team's season. Hit List Rank measures overall team performance and drives the Hit List Power Rankings at the baseballprospectus.com website.

The second graph is **Committed Payroll** and helps you see how the team's payroll has compared to the MLB and divisional average payrolls over time. Payroll figures are current as of January 1, 2019; with so many free agents still unsigned as of this writing, the final 2019 figure will likely be significantly different for many teams. (In the meantime, you can always find the most current data at Baseball Prospectus' Cot's Baseball Contracts page.)

The third graph is **Farm System Ranking** and displays how the Baseball Prospectus prospect team has ranked the organization's farm system since 2007.

After the graphs, we have a **Personnel** section that lists many of the important decision-makers and upper-level field and operations staff members for the franchise, as well as any former Baseball Prospectus staff members who are currently part of the organization. (In very rare circumstances, someone might be on both lists!)

Position Players

After all that information and a thoughtful bylined essay covering each team, we present our player comments. These are also bylined, but due to frequent franchise shifts during the offseason, our bylines are more a rough guide than a perfect accounting of who wrote what.

Each player is listed with the major-league team that employed him as of early January 2019. If a player changed teams after that point via free agency, trade, or any other method, you'll be able to find them in the chapter for their previous squad.

As an example, take a look at the player comment for Astros third baseman Alex Bregman: the stat block that accompanies his written comment is at the top of this page. First we cover biographical information (age is as of June 30, 2019) before moving onto the stats themselves. Our statistic columns include standard identifying information like **YEAR**, **TEAM**, **LVL** (level of affiliated play) and **AGE** before getting into the numbers. Next, we provide raw, untranslated numbers like you might find on the back of your dad's baseball cards: **PA** (plate appearances), **R** (runs), **2B** (doubles), **3B** (triples), **HR** (home runs), **RBI** (runs batted in), **BB** (walks), **K** (strikeouts), **SB** (stolen bases) and **CS** (caught stealing).

Next, we have unadjusted "slash" statistics: **AVG** (batting average), **OBP** (on-base percentage) and **SLG** (slugging percentage). Following the slash line is **DRC+** (Deserved Runs Created Plus), which we described earlier as total offensive expected contribution compared to the league average.

One of our oldest active metrics, **VORP** (Value Over Replacement Player), considers offensive production, position and plate appearances. In essence, it is the number of runs contributed beyond what a replacement-level player at the same position would contribute if given the same percentage of team plate appearances. VORP does not consider the quality of a player's defense.

BABIP (batting average on balls in play) tells us how often a ball in play fell for a hit, and can help us identify whether a batter may have been lucky or not...but note that high BABIPs also tend to follow the great hitters of our time, as well as speedy singles hitters who put the ball on the ground.

The next item is **BRR** (Baserunning Runs), which covers all of a player's baserunning accomplishments including (but not limited to) swiped bags and failed attempts. Next is **FRAA** (Fielding Runs Above Average), which also includes the number of games previously played at each position noted in parentheses. Multi-position players have only their two most frequent positions listed here, but their total FRAA number reflects all positions played.

Our last column here is **WARP** (Wins Above Replacement Player). WARP estimates the total value of a player, which means for hitters it takes into account hitting runs above average (calculated using the DRC+ model), BRR and FRAA. Then, it makes an adjustment for positions played and gives the player a credit for plate appearances based upon the difference between "replacement level"—which is derived from the quality of players added to a team's roster after the start of the season–and the league average.

The final line just below the stats box is **PECOTA** data, which is discussed further in a following section.

Catchers

Catchers are a special breed, and thus they have earned their own separate box which displays some of the defensive metrics that we've built just for them. As an example, let's check out J.T. Realmuto.

J.T. Realmuto

YEAR	TEAM	P. COUNT	FRM RUNS	BLK RUNS	THRW RUNS	TOT RUNS
2016	MIA	18935	-8.5	1.8	2.1	-5.6
2017	MIA	18959	5.3	1.7	1.0	9.1
2018	MIA	16399	-0.4	0.9	0.1	0.4
2019	MIA	18975	-1.4	1.5	0.7	0.8

The **YEAR** and **TEAM** columns match what you'd find in the other stat box. **P. COUNT** indicates the number of pitches thrown while the catcher was behind the plate, including swinging strikes, fouls and balls in play. **FRM RUNS** is the total run value the catcher provided (or cost) his team by influencing the umpire to call strikes where other catchers did not. **BLK RUNS** expresses the total run value above or below average for the catcher's ability to prevent wild pitches and passed balls. **THRW RUNS** is calculated using a similar model as the previous two statistics, and it measures a catcher's ability to throw out basestealers but also to dissuade them from testing his arm in the first place. It takes into account factors like the pitcher (including his delivery and pickoff move) and baserunner (who could be as fast as Billy Hamilton or as slow as Yonder Alonso). **TOT RUNS** is the sum of all of the previous three statistics.

Pitchers

Let's give our pitchers a turn, using 2018 NL Cy Young winner Jacob deGrom as our example. Take a look at his stat block: the first line and the **YEAR**, **TEAM**, **LVL** and **AGE** columns are the same as in the position player example earlier.

Here too, we have a series of columns that display raw, unadjusted statistics compiled by the pitcher over the course of a season: **W** (wins), **L** (losses), **SV** (saves), **G** (games pitched), **GS** (games started), **IP** (innings pitched), **H** (hits allowed) and **HR** (home runs allowed). Next we have two statistics that are rates: **BB/9** (walks per nine innings) and **K/9** (strikeouts per nine innings), before returning to the unadjusted K (strikeouts).

Next up is **GB%** (ground ball percentage), which is the percentage of all batted balls that were hit on the ground, including both outs and hits. Remember, this is based on observational data and subject to human error, so please approach this with a healthy dose of skepticism.

BABIP (batting average on balls in play) is calculated using the same methodology as it is for position players, but it often tells us more about a pitcher than it does a hitter. With pitchers, a high BABIP is often due to poor defense or bad luck, and can often be an indicator of potential rebound, and a low BABIP may be cause to expect performance regression. (A typical league-average BABIP is close to .290-.300.)

The metrics **WHIP** (walks plus hits per inning pitched) and **ERA** (earned run average) are old standbys: WHIP measures walks and hits allowed on a per-inning basis, while ERA measures earned runs on a nine-inning basis. Neither of these stats are translated or adjusted.

DRA (Deserved Run Average) was described at length earlier, and measures how many runs the pitcher "deserved" to allow per nine innings. Please note that since we lack all the data points that would make for a "real" DRA for minor-league events, the DRA displayed for minor league partial-seasons is based off of different data. (That data is a modified version of our cFIP metric, which you can find more information about on our website.)

Just like with hitters, **WARP** (Wins Above Replacement Player) is a total value metric that puts pitchers of all stripes on the same scale as position players. We use DRA as the primary input for our calculation of WARP. You might notice that relief pitchers (due to their limited innings) may have a lower WARP than you were expecting or than you might see in other WARP-like metrics. WARP does not take leverage into account, just the actions a pitcher performs and the expected value of those actions...which ends up judging high-leverage relief pitchers differently than you might imagine given their prestige and market value.

MPH gives you the pitcher's 95th percentile velocity for the noted season, in order to give you an idea of what the *peak* fastball velocity a pitcher possesses. Since this comes from our pitch-tracking data, it is not publicly available for minor-league pitchers.

Jacob deGrom RHP Born: 06/19/88 Age: 31 Bats: L Throws: R Height: 6'4" Weight: 180 Origin: Round 9, 2010 Draft (#272 overall)

YEAR	TEAM	LVL	AGE	W	L	SV	G	GS	IP	H	HR	BB/9	K/9	K	GB%	BABIP	WHIP	ERA	DRA	WARP	MPH	FB%	WHF	CSP
2016	NYN	MLB	28	7	8	0	24	24	148	142	15	2.2	8.7	143	47%	.312	1.20	3.04	3.30	3.5	96.3	59.6	12.1	47.2
2017	NYN	MLB	29	15	10	0	31	31	201¹	180	28	2.6	10.7	239	48%	.305	1.19	3.53	3.02	5.7	97.2	55.5	14.5	49.5
2018	NYN	MLB	30	10	9	0	32	32	217	152	10	1.9	11.2	269	48%	.281	0.91	1.70	2.09	8.0	98.2	52.1	16.3	48.4
2019	NYN	MLB	31	12	9	0	30	30	180	140	19	2.4	10.9	217	46%	.296	1.04	3.07	3.56	3.6	96.6	54.5	14.8	48.2

Breakout: 9%   Improve: 28%   Collapse: 28%   Attrition: 6%   MLB: 84%   *Comparables: Erik Bedard, CC Sabathia, A.J. Burnett*

Finally, we display the three new pitching metrics we described earlier. **FB%** (fastball percentage) gives you the percentage of fastballs thrown out of all pitches. **WHF** (whiff rate) tells you the percentage of swinging strikes induced out of all pitches. **CSS** (called strike probability) expresses the likelihood of all pitches thrown to result in a called strike, after controlling for factors like handedness, umpire, pitch type, count and location.

PECOTA

All players have PECOTA projections for 2019, as well as a set of other numbers that describe the performance of comparable players according to PECOTA. All projections for 2019 are for the player at the date we went to press in early January and are projected into the league and park context as indicated by the team abbreviation. (Note that players at very low levels of the minors are too unpredictable to assess using these numbers.) All PECOTA projected statistics represent a player's projected major-league performance.

The numbers beneath the player's stats—Breakout, Improve, Collapse, Attrition—are part and parcel of the PECOTA projections. They estimate the likelihood of changes in performance relative to the player's previously established level of production, based on the performance of comparable players:

Breakout Rate is the percent change that a player's production will improve by at least 20 percent relative to the weighted average of his performance over his most recent seasons.

Improve Rate is the percent chance that a player's production will improve at all relative to his baseline performance. A player who is expected to perform just the same as he has in the recent past will have an Improve Rate of 50 percent.

Collapse Rate is the percent chance that a position player's production will decline by at least 25 percent relative to his baseline performance.

Attrition Rate operates on playing time rather than performance. Specifically, it measures the likelihood that a player's playing time will decrease by at least 50 percent relative to his established level.

Breakout Rate and Collapse Rate can sometimes be counterintuitive for players who have already experienced a radical change in performance level. It's also worth noting that the projected decline in a player's rate performances might not be indicative of an expected decline in underlying ability or skill, but could just be an anticipated correction following a breakout season.

MLB% is the percentage of similar players who played in the major leagues in their relevant season.

The final pieces of information are the player's three highest-scoring comparable players as determined by PECOTA. All comparables represent a snapshot of how the listed player was performing at the same age as the current player, so if a 23-year-old pitcher is compared to Bartolo

Colon, he's actually being compared to a 23-year-old Colon, not the version that pitched for the Rangers in 2018, nor to Colon's career as a whole.

A few points about pitcher projections. First, we aren't yet projecting peak velocity, so that column will be blank in the PECOTA lines. Second, projecting DRA is trickier than evaluating past performance, because it is unclear how deserving each pitcher will be of his anticipated outcomes. However, we know that another DRA-related statistic–contextual FIP or cFIP–estimates future run scoring very well. So for PECOTA, the projected DRA figures you see are based on the past cFIPs generated by the pitcher and comparable players over time, along with the other factors described above.

Lineouts

In each chapter's Lineouts section, you'll find abbreviated text comments, as well as all the same information you'd find in our full player comments. The only difference is that we limit the stats boxes in this section to only including the 2018 information for each player.

Managers

After all those wonderful team chapters, we've got statistics for each big-league manager, all of whom are organized by alphabetical order. Here you'll find a block including an extraordinary amount of information collected from each manager's entire career. For more information on the acronyms and what they mean, please visit the Glossary at www.baseballprospectus.com.

There is one important metric that we'd like to call attention to, and you'll find it next to each manager's name: **wRM+** (weighted reliever management plus). Developed by Rob Arthur and Rian Watt, wRM+ investigates how good a manager is at using their best relievers during the moments of highest leverage, using both our proprietary DRA metric as well as Leverage Index. wRM+ is scaled to a league average of 100, and a wRM+ of 105 indicates that relievers were used approximately five percent "better" than average. On the other hand, a wRM+ of 95 would tell us the team used it's relievers five percent "worse" than the average team.

While wRM+ does not have an extremely strong correlation with a manager, it is statistically significant; this means that a manager is not *entirely* responsible for a team's wRM+, but does have some effect on that number.

PECOTA Leaderboards

If you're familiar with PECOTA, then you'll have noticed that the projection system often appears bullish on players coming off a bad year and bearish on players coming off a good year. (This is because the system weights several previous seasons, not just the most recent one.) In addition, we publish the 50th percentile projections for each player–which is smack in the middle of the range of projected production–which tends to mean PECOTA stat lines don't often have extreme results like 40 home runs or 250 strikeouts in a given season. In essence, PECOTA doesn't project very many extreme seasons.

At the end of the book, we've ranked the top players at each position based on their PECOTA projections. This might help you visualize just how a given player's projection compares to that of their peers, so that even if a dramatic stat line isn't projected, you can still imagine how they stack up against the rest of the league. ■

ARIZONA DIAMONDBACKS

Essay by Matthew Trueblood

Player comments by Jeff Wiser and BP staff

Diamondbacks closer Brad Boxberger had a 2.89 ERA, 24 saves in 28 tries and 52 strikeouts in 37 1/3 innings through July 24 of last season. Arizona was 56-46, just a half-game behind the Dodgers for first place in the NL West, and Boxberger was mowing batters down with his straightforward fastball-changeup mix despite that heater working much more at 91-92 miles per hour than at 93-94. The Diamondbacks had dealt for him on the eve of the non-tender deadline in November 2017, when the Rays were poised to cut him loose and in no position to demand anything meaningful in return. Now, it appeared, Arizona had shored up his shortcomings well enough to turn him back into the relief ace-caliber righty he'd been in 2014 and 2015.

On July 26, however, Boxberger gave up back-to-back homers to David Bote and Anthony Rizzo of the Cubs, blowing a two-run lead and sending the Diamondbacks to a walk-off loss on a getaway day in Chicago. Astutely sensing trouble (and needing to act on the lack of depth around Boxberger and setup man Archie Bradley, anyway), executive vice president and general manager Mike Hazen and the rest of the front office made two deals on the day of the trade deadline to bolster the bullpen, adding left-hander Jake Diekman and right-hander Brad Ziegler to the relief corps.

It worked, briefly, largely thanks to the jolt of another deadline acquisition, switch-hitting infielder Eduardo Escobar. Between August 25 and September 9, however, Boxberger blew (or aided in blowing) four more games, as the team began to spiral downward. Boxberger had a 7.88 ERA over his final 20 appearances, surrendering a .297/.418/.516 batting line. The Diamondbacks finished 8-19 in September, a fitting way to tumble from contention for a club plagued by inconsistency. They were utterly Jekyll and Hyde: 20-8 at the end of April, 8-19 in May, 19-9 in June. Boxberger was a microcosm of the team: surprising, impressive, then, when it mattered most, unable to come through.

As much as Boxberger embodied the Diamondbacks last season, the Diamondbacks also embody what it is to follow a baseball team right now. There's endless promise. There's always something by which to be impressed. Ultimately, though, there is inevitable frustration, and not in an only-one-team-can-win-the-championship kind of way, but in a

DIAMONDBACKS PROSPECTUS
2018 W-L: 82-80, 3RD IN NL WEST

Pythag	.534	13th	B-Age	29.2	26th
RS/G	4.28	20th	P-Age	29.6	26th
RA/G	3.98	4th	Salary	$131.6M	17th
DRC+	93	21st	M$/MW	$3.5M	20th
DRA	4.19	11th	DL Days	945	10th
FIP	3.87	8th	$ on DL	14%	11th
DER	.711	9th			

- Opened 1998
- Retractable roof
- Synthetic surface
- Fence profile: 7'6" to 25'

Three-Year Park Factors

Runs	Runs/RH	Runs/LH	HR/RH	HR/LH
107	108	106	108	102

Top Hitter WARP	4.1 Paul Goldschmidt
Top Pitcher WARP	5.9 Patrick Corbin
Top Prospect	Jazz Chisholm

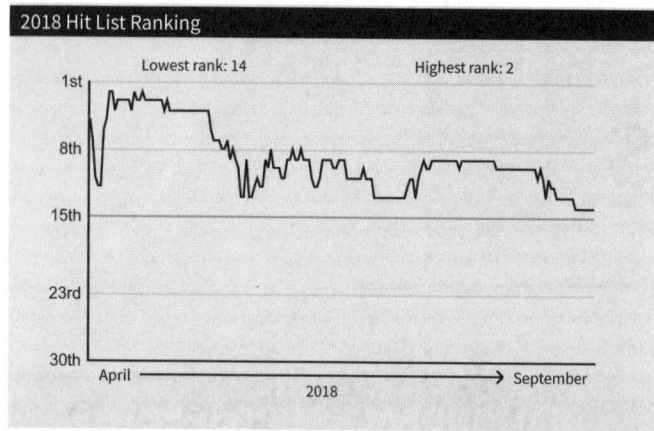

2018 Hit List Ranking

Lowest rank: 14   Highest rank: 2

April ————————————→ September
2018

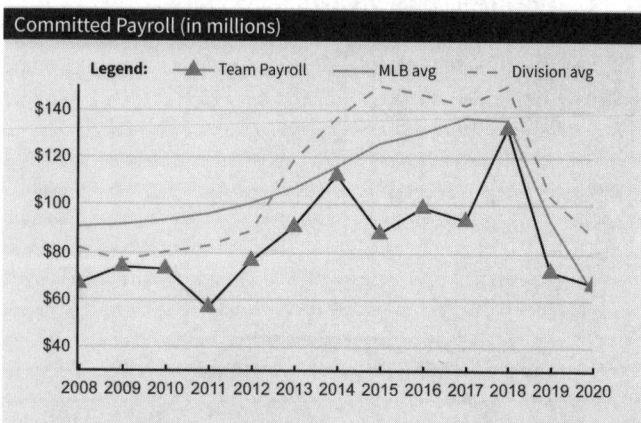

Committed Payroll (in millions)

Legend: ▲ Team Payroll   — MLB avg   - - - Division avg

2008 2009 2010 2011 2012 2013 2014 2015 2016 2017 2018 2019 2020

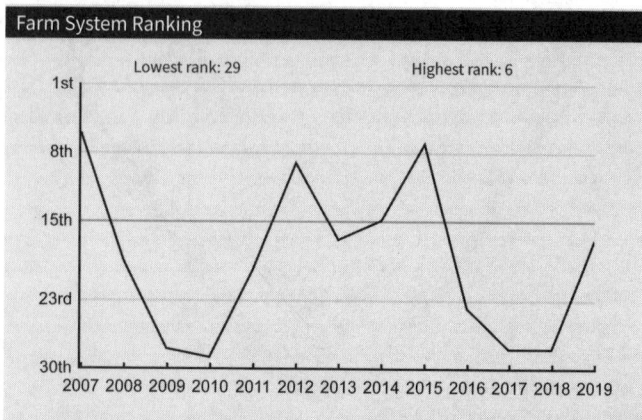

Farm System Ranking

Lowest rank: 29   Highest rank: 6

2007 2008 2009 2010 2011 2012 2013 2014 2015 2016 2017 2018 2019

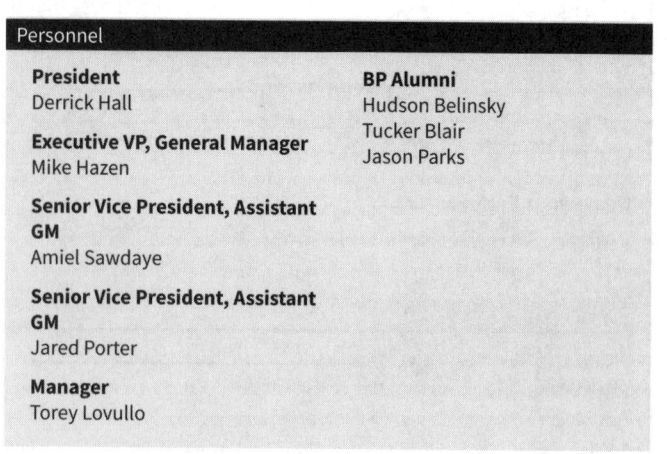

Personnel

President
Derrick Hall

Executive VP, General Manager
Mike Hazen

Senior Vice President, Assistant GM
Amiel Sawdaye

Senior Vice President, Assistant GM
Jared Porter

Manager
Torey Lovullo

BP Alumni
Hudson Belinsky
Tucker Blair
Jason Parks

troublesome, anti-competitive sense. Picking up Boxberger for pennies on the dollar was a neat trick, but if the Diamondbacks hadn't been engaged in careful shoestring budgeting, they never would have needed to rely on Boxberger the way they did. They could still have had him, but they could have had him in a lower-leverage role, surrounded by other, superior bullpen options.

That frustration only mounts now, as the team moves into a new phase without the two best homegrown players they've ever developed, Paul Goldschmidt and Patrick Corbin. The $131 million payroll the Diamondbacks ran in 2018 was a franchise record, by nearly $20 million, and owner Ken Kendrick viewed it as untenable. The team has paid more than $100 million for its MLB roster just three times in its history, and just twice since 2004, when Kendrick and his minority partners took over. It was no surprise when the marching orders came down and the baseball operations department was forced to find the best deal it could for Goldschmidt, owed $14.5 million in his final season before free agency, but that's only because baseball owners have so thoroughly accustomed their fans to view the situation through a distorted lens.

In late 2012, MLB rounded out its national television rights package for a total of $4.2 billion through 2021, an average annual per-team payout of more than $40 million. In February 2015, the Diamondbacks and FOX agreed to a 15-year local TV rights deal worth over $1.5 billion, which works out to $100 million or more per season. In early 2018, every MLB team received a one-time payment of $50 million for their share of the stake in MLB Advanced Media that the league sold to Disney. In November 2018, FOX extended its national TV rights deal with MLB for $5.1 billion through 2028, locking in a rate hike of more than 20 percent. Without selling a single ticket, Kendrick and company could pay that team-high payroll from 2018 every season from 2019 through at least 2030, even if that $50 million check went straight into their pockets and never came out.

Zack Greinke's contract provided unfortunate cover for Diamondbacks ownership, just as similar big-money free agent signings have done similar things for owners throughout the game. Greinke had his worst season since 2007 in the first year of that six-year, $206 million pact, and Kendrick and chief executive officer Derrick Hall fired general manager Dave Stewart at the end of that 2016 season. Shortly after that, a new Collective Bargaining Agreement was finalized, introducing harsher penalties for spending beyond the luxury-tax threshold and restrictions on various forms of amateur talent acquisition. All of which led to the team being able to encourage the development of a local narrative within the Phoenix sports scene, absolving them of further responsibility to spend aggressively and laying the blame for their potential inability to get over the hump at the feet of a Hall of Fame-caliber pitcher.

It also gave the Diamondbacks added leverage in an ongoing dispute with Maricopa County about the costs of repairs and upgrades to Chase Field. In May 2018, the

Diamondbacks essentially won that legal dispute. They gained control of funding allocation for stadium maintenance, increasing their leeway to spend those funds on non-structural things like a new scoreboard and improved air conditioning, and they secured the right to explore leaving Chase Field for a new stadium elsewhere in the Phoenix area five years earlier than their lease had otherwise allowed.

No thread should tie a big free agent deal to those kinds of negotiations, nor to high-level team strategy in a league as universally profitable as MLB is. However, because the owners have beaten the players as consistently in the court of public opinion as at the bargaining table, the partitions that ought to separate business decisions from baseball decisions have all but disappeared. Teams have no problem whatsoever selling cynical financial choices to their fan bases as on-field choices merely focused on long-term competitiveness and analytics.

Here enters Hazen and his troupe of erstwhile Theo Epstein and Ben Cherington disciples. They're among the best and fastest-improving front offices in baseball, having not only established a respected top-level brain trust, but cobbled together one of the more quietly effective and comprehensive baseball operations shops in the game. In 2016, under Stewart Diamondbacks catchers ranked 25th in Adjusted Fielding Runs Above, BP's defensive metric that bakes in pitch framing and pitch blocking as well as throwing and fielding. In 2017, after Hazen's crew signed veteran Jeff Mathis to anchor the catching unit, the team was eighth-best in Adjusted FRAA. In 2018, they were the best in baseball—edging out the Dodgers, who had led MLB in that category for two straight seasons.

It wasn't just about the front office's willingness to accept Mathis's poor offense as a tradeoff to carry his great glove, either. The on-field coaching staff, with help from the analytics department, also materially improved the pitch-framing performances of Chris Iannetta and Alex Avila during those two seasons. To help players improve in crucial, undervalued skills like framing is a very valuable organizational skill, and framing isn't the only area where Arizona has demonstrated it.

After a few of their players (A.J. Pollock, Chris Owings, Mitch Haniger) began to buy heavily into the air-ball revolution just before Stewart's departure, the new front office encouraged the same kinds of changes from other hitters in 2017, and redoubled their commitment to that approach in 2018 by hiring Robert Van Scoyoc as a hitting strategist, a non-coaching role in which he nonetheless provided frequent input and helped the team get the most out of the talent on hand. Consider Daniel Descalso. At age 31 and in his second year with the Diamondbacks, previously light-hitting utility man Descalso had by far the best season of his career, posting a .789 OPS and a 110 DRC+ in 423 plate appearances.

During the two previous seasons, Descalso had radically adjusted his approach, becoming far more selective and (thereby) boosting his on-base percentage. With the help of Van Scoyoc and Diamondbacks hitting coaches Dave Magadan and Tim Laker, he took his transformation a step farther. Swinging a bit more often but much more aggressively, Descalso brought his ground-ball rate down from just under 39 percent to under 31 percent—the sixth-lowest figure in MLB among all hitters with at least 300 plate appearances. He pulled the ball more and hit it harder. Though still not an elite power hitter, Descalso began generating enough pop to make his still-patient approach play up.

All over the roster, in every aspect of the game, the new front office made significant investments and demonstrated a nimble progressiveness typical of the Red Sox and Cubs organizations from which so many of them came. They've employed former pitcher Dan Haren as a pitching strategist, a role similar to that of Van Scoyoc (who has since been hired as the Dodgers' hitting coach). Through Haren's and other influences, the team has drawn impressive improvements out of talented pitchers like Patrick Corbin, Robbie Ray, Taijuan Walker and Archie Bradley.

They traded Haniger and shortstop Jean Segura for Walker and Ketel Marte, and turned Marte into both a more productive hitter and a vital piece of the National League's best defensive infield. They won 93 games in 2017 and 82 (with a third-order record of 87-75) in 2018, without damaging their farm system. They might even have strengthened it, despite their trade for J.D. Martinez in July 2017. This is what an exceptionally talented front office with a deep staff can accomplish, even during an era in which almost every front office is smarter than any front office was 20 years ago.

Yet, there that front office was, in early December, reluctantly dealing away its cornerstone, Goldschmidt, days after letting its co-ace, Corbin, sign elsewhere. They made a fine deal with the Cardinals, one very much in line with the points of strength and emphasis within the front office. They got a young, valuable starting pitcher (Luke Weaver) who might thrive in a move to relief the way Bradley did, a catcher (Carson Kelly) who can continue their defensive excellence behind the plate and a prospect (Andy Young) who's come out of nowhere on the strength of surprising power from a small frame. They also got a draft pick, and like any group descended from House Epstein, this front office knows how to maximize the value of extra draft picks. Arizona will also receive extra picks from the free agent departures of Corbin and A.J. Pollock.

For the hardcore baseball fan, immersed in the numbers and fascinated by the minutiae of team-building, the Diamondbacks will be fun to watch over the coming year. For most fans, though, and for anyone who enjoys the game on the field more than the behind-the-scenes details of its production, they might be something of a bummer. They're unlikely to be as good as they have been over the past two seasons, not because their top talent got old or because they weren't quick enough to evolve with an ever-changing game, but because their owners would rather pocket scores (rather than tens) of millions of dollars than retain the faces of their franchise, potentially creating a vacuum of production, leadership and fan affection that won't easily be filled. This isn't unique to the Diamondbacks. It's happening all over the league. But baseball fandom is provincial, so it's being felt only as it happens to each team, one by one. This season, it could be on display most vividly in Arizona. ■

—Matthew Trueblood is an author of Baseball Prospectus.

HITTERS

Nick Ahmed SS Born: 03/15/90 Age: 29 Bats: R Throws: R Height: 6'2" Weight: 195 Origin: Round 2, 2011 Draft (#85 overall)

YEAR	TEAM	LVL	AGE	PA	R	2B	3B	HR	RBI	BB	K	SB	CS	AVG/OBP/SLG	DRC+	VORP	BABIP	BRR	FRAA	WARP
2016	ARI	MLB	26	308	26	9	1	4	20	15	58	5	2	.218/.265/.299	76	-4.8	.258	2.3	SS(88): 9.4	1.7
2017	ARI	MLB	27	178	24	8	1	6	21	10	39	3	4	.251/.298/.419	91	1.7	.295	-0.8	SS(48): 3.9	0.9
2018	ARI	MLB	28	564	61	33	5	16	70	40	109	5	4	.234/.290/.411	94	17.1	.265	-0.4	SS(148): 15.1	3.7
2019	ARI	MLB	29	532	58	25	3	14	57	36	106	7	5	.246/.303/.393	89	13.1	.284	0.2	SS 11	2.5

Breakout: 2%   Improve: 45%   Collapse: 11%   Attrition: 23%   MLB: 90%   *Comparables: Angel Berroa, Brendan Ryan, Paul Janish*

For a while there, the Mendoza Line was dangerously close to being renamed. Calling it the "Hechavarria Line" was too much of a mouthful for most and the "Ahmed Line" seemed a better fit. At least until Ahmed broke his own mold by flirting with league-average offense for most of 2018. A mainstay in the lineup for his defensive chops, he finally made some headway by staying a bit more within himself at the plate. Ahmed chased less and produced more power than ever before. He nearly eclipsed his career total for home runs in just a single season and picked up some slack against right-handed pitching. He was again among the league leaders in FRAA and put together enough offense to avoid being a total black hole. It's been decided — the Hechavarria Line it is.

Alex Avila C Born: 01/29/87 Age: 32 Bats: L Throws: R Height: 5'11" Weight: 210 Origin: Round 5, 2008 Draft (#163 overall)

YEAR	TEAM	LVL	AGE	PA	R	2B	3B	HR	RBI	BB	K	SB	CS	AVG/OBP/SLG	DRC+	VORP	BABIP	BRR	FRAA	WARP
2016	CHA	MLB	29	209	19	6	0	7	11	38	78	0	0	.213/.359/.373	79	8.3	.341	-2.2	C(54): -5.7	-0.3
2017	DET	MLB	30	264	30	11	0	11	32	43	80	0	1	.274/.394/.475	106	16.2	.380	-1.5	C(50): -0.5, 1B(16): -0.9	1.0
2017	CHN	MLB	30	112	11	2	1	3	17	19	40	0	0	.239/.369/.380	112	5.6	.388	0.5	C(28): 0.2, 1B(3): 0.2	0.8
2018	ARI	MLB	31	234	13	6	0	7	20	37	90	0	0	.165/.299/.304	71	-0.2	.253	-1.4	C(61): 3.2, 1B(3): 0.0	0.5
2019	ARI	MLB	32	216	24	7	1	6	23	31	76	0	0	.204/.322/.346	90	6.0	.308	-0.8	C -3	0.3

Breakout: 3%   Improve: 33%   Collapse: 15%   Attrition: 26%   MLB: 91%   *Comparables: Chris Snyder, Jason LaRue, Jarrod Saltalamacchia*

Avila's career trajectory has been consistently up and down. One year he looks like an All-Star, the next a backup. The Diamondbacks received the latter in 2018 and it was so bad at times that fans were actively booing him in his own park. He managed just 17 hits in the first half while playing 50 games. The second half was better, but not exactly good. With Jeff Mathis and John Ryan Murphy around, Avila struggled to get consistent playing time and that's ... well, that's saying something. If there's a glimmer of hope, it might be that Avila has shown a knack for turning things around and never gave up over the course of a painful season. Can he salvage some value in 2019 before his deal runs out? He'd better, or he might just have a hard time finding employment beyond next season.

YEAR	TEAM	P. COUNT	FRM RUNS	BLK RUNS	THRW RUNS	TOT RUNS
2016	CHA	7394	-4.2	0.0	-0.6	-4.7
2017	DET	6716	-5.8	0.7	0.2	-4.8
2017	CHN	3507	-3.3	-0.2	0.0	-3.2
2018	ARI	7984	3.7	0.3	0.0	4.3
2019	ARI	6862	-2.6	0.1	-0.2	-2.6

Jazz Chisholm SS Born: 02/01/98 Age: 21 Bats: L Throws: R Height: 5'11" Weight: 165 Origin: International Free Agent, 2015

YEAR	TEAM	LVL	AGE	PA	R	2B	3B	HR	RBI	BB	K	SB	CS	AVG/OBP/SLG	DRC+	VORP	BABIP	BRR	FRAA	WARP
2016	MSO	RK	18	270	42	12	1	9	37	19	73	13	4	.281/.333/.446	90	15.4	.363	0.6	SS(60): 2.5, 2B(1): 0.0	1.1
2017	KNC	A	19	125	14	5	2	1	12	10	39	3	0	.248/.325/.358	74	6.4	.371	0.7	SS(29): 0.8	0.3
2018	KNC	A	20	341	52	17	4	15	43	30	97	8	2	.244/.311/.472	116	17.7	.303	-1.4	SS(75): -0.3	2.0
2018	VIS	A+	20	160	27	6	2	10	27	9	52	9	2	.329/.369/.597	125	21.0	.443	0.5	SS(36): -0.7	1.2
2019	ARI	MLB	21	251	29	7	0	9	26	12	87	3	1	.192/.231/.346	43	-7.6	.252	0.2	SS 1	-0.7

Breakout: 3%   Improve: 4%   Collapse: 3%   Attrition: 8%   MLB: 13%   *Comparables: Trevor Story, Javier Guerra, Joel Guzman*

Thelonious Monk once said, "You've got to dig it to dig it, you dig?" In Chisholm's case, most dig. There aren't many 20-year-olds jamming out 25 dingers. There are even fewer of them with the sweet, smooth actions to jive at shortstop. Chisholm missed much of the 2017 campaign with a knee injury, but returned in 2018 to do some serious damage. While his overall line wasn't great, he put the bass in baseball by making the most of his batted balls, especially once he reached Visalia. He's growing in his approach and admitted to trying too hard at times in Kane County. Jazz is supposed be a natural expression and Chisholm is still learning to let the game come to him. If the approach comes together, his crescendo could be transcendent.

Jarrod Dyson CF Born: 08/15/84 Age: 34 Bats: L Throws: R Height: 5'10" Weight: 165 Origin: Round 50, 2006 Draft (#1475 overall)

YEAR	TEAM	LVL	AGE	PA	R	2B	3B	HR	RBI	BB	K	SB	CS	AVG/OBP/SLG	DRC+	VORP	BABIP	BRR	FRAA	WARP
2016	KCA	MLB	31	337	46	14	8	1	25	26	39	30	7	.278/.340/.388	86	7.1	.315	1.7	CF(57): 0.4, RF(21): 3.7	1.2
2017	SEA	MLB	32	390	56	13	3	5	30	28	55	28	7	.251/.324/.350	82	3.0	.285	0.0	CF(96): 5.6, LF(12): 3.2	1.3
2018	ARI	MLB	33	237	29	4	2	2	12	27	34	16	3	.189/.282/.257	80	-3.7	.216	2.6	CF(41): 3.3, RF(18): 0.0	0.9
2019	ARI	MLB	34	497	63	19	4	7	40	43	73	38	8	.247/.324/.355	89	14.2	.276	1.6	CF 2	1.8

Breakout: 1%   Improve: 31%   Collapse: 5%   Attrition: 19%   MLB: 83%   *Comparables: Dave Roberts, Jacoby Ellsbury, Sam Fuld*

Dyson has never made his living as a hitter. That's just not his game, as his Twitter handle (@mrzoombiya) indicates. A move to the desert could have, in theory, given him a boost. Instead, he dried up even by his own standards. A jump in hard-hit balls weirdly didn't do his BABIP any favors before his season prematurely ended in early July. He'll enter 2019 as a 34-year-old bench outfielder recovering from a down season and groin surgery. Still, he has a year left on his deal and the Diamondbacks' cache of outfielders, particularly those capable of covering center field, instills little confidence. He'll get another shot to extend his playing days and hope for better results, even if just by a little.

Eduardo Escobar 3B Born: 01/05/89 Age: 30 Bats: B Throws: R Height: 5'10" Weight: 185 Origin: International Free Agent, 2006

YEAR	TEAM	LVL	AGE	PA	R	2B	3B	HR	RBI	BB	K	SB	CS	AVG/OBP/SLG	DRC+	VORP	BABIP	BRR	FRAA	WARP
2016	MIN	MLB	27	377	32	14	2	6	37	21	72	1	3	.236/.280/.338	77	-3.3	.280	1.7	SS(71): 1.0, 3B(23): -1.2	0.7
2017	MIN	MLB	28	499	62	16	5	21	73	33	98	5	1	.254/.309/.449	109	14.8	.279	2.3	3B(79): -5.1, SS(16): -0.5	1.9
2018	MIN	MLB	29	408	45	37	3	15	63	34	91	1	3	.274/.338/.514	113	26.7	.325	-0.1	3B(77): -2.1, SS(21): 0.0	2.0
2018	ARI	MLB	29	223	30	11	0	8	21	18	35	1	1	.268/.327/.444	115	12.0	.281	0.5	3B(54): -4.9	0.8
2019	ARI	MLB	30	633	71	36	3	20	81	47	122	4	3	.265/.326/.443	107	24.4	.303	1.6	3B -6, 2B -1	1.8

Breakout: 5% Improve: 47% Collapse: 8% Attrition: 7% MLB: 95% *Comparables: Joe Crede, Scott Brosius, Billy Johnson*

Two seasons ago, the Diamondbacks cashed in at the deadline on #JustDingers in J.D. Martinez. Last season, they cashed in at the deadline on #JustDoubles in Escobar. While the hashtag didn't take off, Escobar did during his time in Sedona Red. He filled in well for an injured Jake Lamb down the stretch and established his late-blooming excellence. He's roughly average at third base, but he hits well enough to justify everyday reps somewhere in the infield. After inking a three-year extension, he'll do just that for the Diamondbacks — a team that is always in need of inexpensive production. They'll hope his productive audition wasn't a fluke and that those doubles just keep coming, even if that requires moving him around defensively.

Jon Jay OF Born: 03/15/85 Age: 34 Bats: L Throws: L Height: 5'11" Weight: 195 Origin: Round 2, 2006 Draft (#74 overall)

YEAR	TEAM	LVL	AGE	PA	R	2B	3B	HR	RBI	BB	K	SB	CS	AVG/OBP/SLG	DRC+	VORP	BABIP	BRR	FRAA	WARP
2016	SDN	MLB	31	373	49	26	1	2	26	19	78	2	0	.291/.339/.389	76	18.0	.371	3.1	CF(72): -1.9, RF(9): 0.1	0.4
2017	CHN	MLB	32	433	65	18	3	2	34	37	80	6	2	.296/.374/.375	98	16.7	.368	2.4	LF(64): -3.6, CF(54): -4.8	0.4
2018	KCA	MLB	33	266	28	9	2	1	18	19	39	3	2	.307/.363/.374	82	6.1	.360	-0.5	LF(27): 1.2, CF(15): 1.8	0.4
2018	ARI	MLB	33	320	46	10	5	2	22	14	56	1	1	.235/.304/.325	84	-3.9	.284	-0.1	RF(45): 1.9, LF(14): -1.9	0.1
2019	ARI	MLB	34	522	56	23	4	5	41	36	103	4	2	.255/.329/.351	92	12.4	.319	1.3	RF 0, LF -1	1.1

Breakout: 0% Improve: 35% Collapse: 7% Attrition: 17% MLB: 77% *Comparables: Max Flack, Rip Radcliff, Tom McBride*

How was your day? Fine. Did anything exciting happen? Nah, not really. Did you have to manage any conflicts? Nope, things were fine. So your day really was just "fine" then? Yup, just fine. Ok ... This probably isn't exactly how conversations between GMs go when discussing Jay, but you wouldn't blame them if they did. Jay is just fine. He's a lefty batter who doesn't have splits. He's capable of covering center field but doesn't do it exceptionally well. He can get on base a little bit but won't be a major threat on the bases. And the Diamondbacks found this all out first-hand when they traded for him midseason. He's the epitome of just fine, but that's all.

Carson Kelly C Born: 07/14/94 Age: 24 Bats: R Throws: R Height: 6'2" Weight: 220 Origin: Round 2, 2012 Draft (#86 overall)

YEAR	TEAM	LVL	AGE	PA	R	2B	3B	HR	RBI	BB	K	SB	CS	AVG/OBP/SLG	DRC+	VORP	BABIP	BRR	FRAA	WARP
2016	SFD	AA	21	236	29	7	0	6	18	14	46	0	1	.287/.338/.403	101	14.4	.339	-0.9	C(60): 7.6	1.9
2016	MEM	AAA	21	126	14	10	0	0	14	11	17	0	0	.292/.352/.381	91	5.8	.340	-0.1	C(32): 2.4	0.7
2016	SLN	MLB	21	14	1	1	0	0	1	0	2	0	0	.154/.214/.231	89	-0.4	.182	-0.2	C(10): -0.1	0.0
2017	MEM	AAA	22	280	37	13	0	10	41	33	40	0	2	.283/.375/.459	118	22.1	.304	-1.9	C(68): 10.8	2.9
2017	SLN	MLB	22	75	5	3	0	0	6	5	11	0	0	.174/.240/.217	72	-4.0	.207	0.7	C(31): 3.0	0.5
2018	MEM	AAA	23	349	38	14	1	7	41	48	48	0	0	.269/.378/.395	113	24.7	.299	-0.6	C(83): 10.1, 1B(1): 0.0	3.4
2018	SLN	MLB	23	42	1	0	0	0	3	3	7	0	0	.114/.205/.114	76	-3.2	.143	-0.2	C(16): -0.9	0.0
2019	ARI	MLB	24	382	46	16	1	10	39	36	67	0	0	.246/.326/.391	93	12.9	.278	-0.6	C 4	1.8

Breakout: 5% Improve: 23% Collapse: 13% Attrition: 22% MLB: 58% *Comparables: Josh Thole, Victor Caratini, Christian Vazquez*

YEAR	TEAM	P. COUNT	FRM RUNS	BLK RUNS	THRW RUNS	TOT RUNS
2016	SLN	539	-0.2	0.2	0.0	0.2
2017	MEM	9388	11.5	1.2	-0.1	12.2
2017	SLN	2565	2.5	0.4	0.1	3.2
2018	MEM	11582	9.0	0.5	0.7	9.9
2018	SLN	1715	-0.8	-0.3	0.0	-1.1
2019	ARI	13584	4.6	0.9	-0.6	5.0

Kelly's long-term evaluation comes down to whether you believe in the long arc and late acceleration of catcher development. He's played seven pro seasons, five of them since making the transition from third base to catcher, and he's had offensive success only when seeing a league for a second time. He's gone sideways as a receiver, rather than making any great forward leap. In three tastes of the big leagues, he's looked utterly overmatched at the plate and just okay behind it. Pushing against all those red flags are the hit tool scouts have liked since he was in high school, an exceptionally polished approach and the fact that he's still just 24, at a position where 24 isn't all that old for a prospect.

Jake Lamb 3B Born: 10/09/90 Age: 28 Bats: L Throws: R Height: 6'3" Weight: 215 Origin: Round 6, 2012 Draft (#213 overall)

YEAR	TEAM	LVL	AGE	PA	R	2B	3B	HR	RBI	BB	K	SB	CS	AVG/OBP/SLG	DRC+	VORP	BABIP	BRR	FRAA	WARP
2016	ARI	MLB	25	594	81	31	9	29	91	64	154	6	1	.249/.332/.509	118	37.8	.294	2.3	3B(142): -5.0	3.3
2017	ARI	MLB	26	635	89	30	4	30	105	87	152	6	4	.248/.357/.487	120	44.8	.287	2.0	3B(144): -10.8	3.1
2018	ARI	MLB	27	238	34	8	0	6	31	26	65	1	2	.222/.307/.348	82	10.3	.286	1.6	3B(52): -3.7	0.1
2019	ARI	MLB	28	609	72	27	3	22	77	70	157	5	3	.234/.330/.416	107	18.4	.292	1.9	1B 0, 3B -4	1.6

Breakout: 0% Improve: 55% Collapse: 3% Attrition: 8% MLB: 96% *Comparables: Todd Frazier, Travis Shaw, Chase Headley*

Lamb is no longer a mystery. At his best, he's a low-to-medium-average hitter capable of sending pitches from righties into orbit and eking out a hit or two versus lefties. At his worst, he's not much more than a replacement-level player. He's run hot and cold for a few seasons now, often scorching the first half and going ice cold in the second. He didn't have a chance to tank in the second half of 2018, however, because a) he had already tanked to start the year and, b) got hurt just after the All-Star break, not to return. Shoulder injuries are weird and it's unclear how Lamb recovers. The Diamondbacks hedged their bets by signing the versatile, productive Eduardo Escobar to an extension. Lamb presumably has a short leash with the organization. He may end up being platooned (finally), or let go in some fashion as his salary rises through arbitration.

Ketel Marte 2B   Born: 10/12/93   Age: 25   Bats: B   Throws: R   Height: 6'1"   Weight: 165   Origin: International Free Agent, 2010

YEAR	TEAM	LVL	AGE	PA	R	2B	3B	HR	RBI	BB	K	SB	CS	AVG/OBP/SLG	DRC+	VORP	BABIP	BRR	FRAA	WARP
2016	SEA	MLB	22	466	55	21	2	1	33	18	84	11	5	.259/.287/.323	60	2.5	.313	2.6	SS(119): -1.5	0.0
2017	RNO	AAA	23	338	62	23	7	6	41	25	34	7	2	.338/.391/.514	121	31.4	.365	3.8	SS(59): 2.1, CF(5): 1.6	3.2
2017	ARI	MLB	23	255	30	11	2	5	18	29	37	3	1	.260/.345/.395	103	14.0	.290	1.5	SS(64): -0.1, 3B(3): 0.1	1.5
2018	ARI	MLB	24	580	68	26	12	14	59	54	79	6	1	.260/.332/.437	106	27.4	.282	0.6	2B(131): 4.5, SS(28): 1.8	3.2
2019	ARI	MLB	25	511	63	23	5	11	51	41	76	8	3	.264/.328/.409	103	21.0	.293	1.5	2B 5, SS 0	2.8

Breakout: 1%   Improve: 56%   Collapse: 7%   Attrition: 11%   MLB: 98%   *Comparables: Kolten Wong, Blake DeWitt, Aaron Hill*

It's easy to forget that Marte is still really young. With four seasons under his belt, he's coming off an age-24 season in which he put up his best numbers to date. He set career-highs in nearly every meaningful offensive category while also signing an extension that will guarantee that he remains affordable for years to come. His defensive versatility is a nice bonus, but perhaps more than anything, it's the way Marte plays that's most exciting. He's a tough dude who seems to think he's about six inches taller than he really is, battles every day and gives the kind of effort that has quickly made him a favorite among Diamondbacks fans. There's still room for improvement, and given his age, the #MartePartay might just be getting started.

Jake McCarthy CF   Born: 07/30/97   Age: 21   Bats: L   Throws: L   Height: 6'3"   Weight: 195   Origin: Round 1, 2018 Draft (#39 overall)

YEAR	TEAM	LVL	AGE	PA	R	2B	3B	HR	RBI	BB	K	SB	CS	AVG/OBP/SLG	DRC+	VORP	BABIP	BRR	FRAA	WARP
2018	YAK	A-	20	241	33	17	3	3	18	22	40	20	8	.288/.378/.442	108	20.3	.341	-0.5	CF(44): 8.0, LF(11): -2.3	1.5
2019	ARI	MLB	21	251	31	6	0	7	21	12	61	9	4	.191/.245/.306	45	-7.4	.228	0.4	CF 3, LF 0	-0.5

Breakout: 1%   Improve: 1%   Collapse: 1%   Attrition: 2%   MLB: 2%   *Comparables: Abraham Almonte, Xavier Avery, Ender Inciarte*

Michael Scott excitedly starts a Willy Wonka-inspired promotion by providing discounts to clients who receive golden tickets, then tries to blame the idea on Dwight Schrute when the promotion appears to cost the company an excessive amount of money. David Wallace comes to the Scranton branch and says the customer was so pleased with the discount they decided to make the company their exclusive provider of office supplies. Grateful, David congratulates Dwight for the idea and, after a moment's hesitation, Dwight accepts the credit. Michael is shocked and upset. McCarthy, a Scranton native, watches it all unravel from the outfield grass where he, and the Diamondbacks, hope he becomes a golden ticket in his own right.

John Ryan Murphy C   Born: 05/13/91   Age: 28   Bats: R   Throws: R   Height: 5'11"   Weight: 205   Origin: Round 2, 2009 Draft (#76 overall)

YEAR	TEAM	LVL	AGE	PA	R	2B	3B	HR	RBI	BB	K	SB	CS	AVG/OBP/SLG	DRC+	VORP	BABIP	BRR	FRAA	WARP
2016	ROC	AAA	25	290	24	14	0	3	39	21	51	0	0	.236/.286/.323	91	2.0	.274	-1.4	C(80): 17.8	2.7
2016	MIN	MLB	25	90	4	3	0	1	3	5	19	0	0	.146/.193/.220	77	-5.2	.175	-0.3	C(25): -0.6	0.1
2017	ROC	AAA	26	218	21	9	0	4	27	22	36	0	0	.222/.298/.330	98	2.5	.250	1.0	C(53): 1.2	1.1
2017	RNO	AAA	26	75	5	0	0	2	7	7	7	0	0	.284/.351/.373	114	2.2	.293	-0.4	C(19): -0.2	0.4
2017	ARI	MLB	26	7	0	1	0	0	1	0	1	0	0	.143/.143/.286	99	-1.3	.167	-0.1	C(5): 0.2	0.0
2018	ARI	MLB	27	223	19	9	0	9	24	11	71	0	0	.202/.244/.375	73	1.6	.256	-1.0	C(68): 10.2	1.3
2019	ARI	MLB	28	142	14	6	0	4	15	10	33	0	0	.227/.285/.364	70	0.8	.272	-0.3	C 5	0.7

Breakout: 4%   Improve: 26%   Collapse: 17%   Attrition: 42%   MLB: 78%   *Comparables: Mike Rabelo, Jason Jaramillo, Austin Romine*

Never trust a man with two first names. It's not clear if you can trust a man with *three* first names, but if Murphy provides any clues the answer is still probably no. He was an under-the-radar pickup by Mike Hazen toward the tail end of 2017 and started 2018 off with a bang, helping the Diamondbacks decide to carry three catchers all year. Seven of his nine home runs came in the first two months of the season and he eventually lost any semblance of significant playing time to the other two catchers on the roster. Murphy appeared to be capable of providing some offensive punch, but instead he broke the D-backs' heart and they may never trust him again.

YEAR	TEAM	P. COUNT	FRM RUNS	BLK RUNS	THRW RUNS	TOT RUNS
2016	MIN	3340	1.4	-1.7	0.1	-0.2
2017	ARI	249	0.1	0.1	0.0	0.2
2017	ROC	6992	21.3	-0.2	0.6	21.3
2017	RNO	2920	0.0	-0.6	0.7	-0.1
2018	ARI	7566	9.3	0.3	-0.1	9.9
2019	ARI	4811	5.7	-0.5	0.0	5.2

David Peralta LF   Born: 08/14/87   Age: 31   Bats: L   Throws: L   Height: 6'1"   Weight: 210   Origin: International Free Agent, 2005

YEAR	TEAM	LVL	AGE	PA	R	2B	3B	HR	RBI	BB	K	SB	CS	AVG/OBP/SLG	DRC+	VORP	BABIP	BRR	FRAA	WARP
2016	ARI	MLB	28	183	23	9	5	4	15	8	42	2	0	.251/.295/.433	89	4.7	.310	2.4	RF(44): 0.0, CF(8): -0.4	0.4
2017	ARI	MLB	29	577	82	31	3	14	57	43	94	8	4	.293/.352/.444	102	24.6	.333	-0.9	RF(78): 10.0, LF(50): 2.2	2.7
2018	ARI	MLB	30	614	75	25	5	30	87	48	124	4	0	.293/.352/.516	121	40.0	.328	1.2	LF(138): -11.0, RF(5): -0.5	2.2
2019	ARI	MLB	31	655	84	30	4	21	74	47	132	6	2	.262/.324/.429	108	25.4	.306	0.9	LF -5, RF 1	2.3

Breakout: 1%   Improve: 42%   Collapse: 5%   Attrition: 8%   MLB: 90%   Comparables: Carl Crawford, Juan Rivera, Kevin Mench

A winding career path for Peralta has brought plenty of surprises, not all of them good, but damn if he wasn't low-key excellent again in 2018. He often flies under the radar, but Peralta hit the 30-home run mark for the first time as neither opposing pitchers nor the humidor could hold him down. The defense isn't great, but it's fine for left field and he still has that cannon of an arm that once made him a prized pitching prospect. Peralta is a sneaky good player who has provided value beyond his compensation on multiple occasions—exactly what the Diamondbacks covet. He's on the wrong side of 30, however, and despite a delayed start to his big-league career, the real focus will be on how long he can keep it going. For now, the Freight Train appears to have plenty of momentum.

Geraldo Perdomo SS   Born: 10/22/99   Age: 19   Bats: B   Throws: R   Height: 6'2"   Weight: 184   Origin: International Free Agent, 2016

YEAR	TEAM	LVL	AGE	PA	R	2B	3B	HR	RBI	BB	K	SB	CS	AVG/OBP/SLG	DRC+	VORP	BABIP	BRR	FRAA	WARP
2017	DDI	RK	17	278	42	3	2	1	11	60	37	16	8	.238/.410/.285	132	20.0	.282	1.4	SS(63): 11.9	3.2
2018	DIA	RK	18	101	20	4	2	1	8	14	17	14	1	.314/.416/.442	135	14.9	.382	2.6	SS(14): 2.6, 2B(8): 0.5	1.3
2018	MSO	RK	18	29	3	0	1	0	2	7	4	1	1	.455/.586/.545	123	6.6	.556	0.4	SS(5): 0.3, 2B(1): -0.2	0.3
2018	YAK	A-	18	127	20	3	2	3	14	18	23	9	4	.301/.421/.456	124	16.1	.359	1.4	SS(30): 3.9	1.5
2019	ARI	MLB	19	251	28	3	0	5	19	25	62	6	2	.177/.257/.262	38	-9.7	.216	-0.1	SS 5, 2B 0	-0.5

Breakout: 0%   Improve: 7%   Collapse: 1%   Attrition: 11%   MLB: 18%   Comparables: Jurickson Profar, Carlos Correa, Elvis Andrus

Following prospects can be challenging. First of all, there are just *so many names.* You can't remember Steve from Accounting's name half the time. Wait, is it Tim? Pretty sure it's Tim. Anyways, it's also tough because prospects will break your heart. And let's be honest, there's only so much of your heart available for rent. Can you really give it to a teenager you've never seen before who plays half a continent away? You might want to do just that in the case of Perdomo, an under-the-radar international signing who's started to make significant noise. He's physical in the box, the bat speed is noteworthy and he can make all of the plays at shortstop look way too easy for a guy standing 6-foot-2. He popped up big time in 2018 and will get plenty of buzz moving forward.

A.J. Pollock CF   Born: 12/05/87   Age: 31   Bats: R   Throws: R   Height: 6'1"   Weight: 195   Origin: Round 1, 2009 Draft (#17 overall)

YEAR	TEAM	LVL	AGE	PA	R	2B	3B	HR	RBI	BB	K	SB	CS	AVG/OBP/SLG	DRC+	VORP	BABIP	BRR	FRAA	WARP
2016	ARI	MLB	28	46	9	0	0	2	4	5	8	4	0	.244/.326/.390	107	2.8	.258	1.8	CF(12): 1.5	0.5
2017	ARI	MLB	29	466	73	33	6	14	49	35	71	20	6	.266/.330/.471	105	28.2	.291	0.7	CF(109): 0.3	2.1
2018	ARI	MLB	30	460	61	21	5	21	65	31	100	13	2	.257/.316/.484	113	23.4	.284	1.1	CF(109): -7.6	1.7
2019	ARI	MLB	31	439	62	22	3	14	47	33	83	17	4	.256/.323/.430	106	21.5	.293	1.1	CF -1	2.2

Breakout: 0%   Improve: 53%   Collapse: 2%   Attrition: 4%   MLB: 96%   Comparables: Angel Pagan, Charlie Blackmon, Jacoby Ellsbury

Pollock is set for life either way and was one of this offseason's most coveted free agents, but if he'd just stayed healthy for one more season somewhere along the way he would have gotten *paid.* Instead, he's spent much of the time since his monster 2015 breakout campaign on the disabled list, and when healthy he's more often good rather than great. For now he's among the top 10-12 center fielders in the game, but Pollock seems unlikely to age particularly well and has already shown signs of slipping defensively.

Kristian Robinson CF   Born: 12/11/00   Age: 18   Bats: R   Throws: R   Height: 6'3"   Weight: 190   Origin: International Free Agent, 2017

YEAR	TEAM	LVL	AGE	PA	R	2B	3B	HR	RBI	BB	K	SB	CS	AVG/OBP/SLG	DRC+	VORP	BABIP	BRR	FRAA	WARP
2018	DIA	RK	17	182	35	11	0	4	31	16	46	7	5	.272/.341/.414	108	9.5	.351	1.3	CF(26): -5.3, LF(6): -0.9	0.4
2018	MSO	RK	17	74	13	1	0	3	10	11	21	5	3	.300/.419/.467	104	5.9	.405	0.5	CF(10): -2.3, LF(7): 0.4	0.1
2019	ARI	MLB	18	251	20	7	0	6	22	9	85	3	2	.177/.207/.268	26	-14.4	.243	-0.8	CF -1, LF 0	-1.7

Comparables: Adalberto Mondesi, Wilmer Flores, Tommy Brown

Kids these days. When they're not flossing or playing with their fidget spinners, they're apparently growing into large, explosive human beings. Robinson is built like a hybrid linebacker and flies like a wide receiver. His stateside debut didn't disappoint, though his youth showed at times, too. He didn't strike out at an extreme clip in either of the rookie leagues he graced, but did show some swing and miss. He also showed patience, walking at a strong clip while sprinkling in seven home runs over his first 57 professional games. More power will undoubtedly come as Robinson continues to learn how to control his at-bats. The biggest international signing for the franchise in recent history looks the part of a player to build around.

Pavin Smith 1B   Born: 02/06/96   Age: 23   Bats: L   Throws: L   Height: 6'2"   Weight: 210   Origin: Round 1, 2017 Draft (#7 overall)

YEAR	TEAM	LVL	AGE	PA	R	2B	3B	HR	RBI	BB	K	SB	CS	AVG/OBP/SLG	DRC+	VORP	BABIP	BRR	FRAA	WARP
2017	YAK	A-	21	223	34	15	2	0	27	27	24	2	1	.318/.401/.415	112	15.3	.363	-1.8	1B(42): 1.0	0.4
2018	VIS	A+	22	504	63	25	1	11	54	57	65	3	2	.255/.343/.392	108	9.5	.275	-1.1	1B(109): 9.0, RF(1): -0.1	1.8
2019	ARI	MLB	23	251	23	8	0	6	27	19	46	0	0	.216/.275/.334	58	-9.4	.240	-0.6	1B 2	-0.8

Breakout: 3%   Improve: 9%   Collapse: 1%   Attrition: 5%   MLB: 14%   Comparables: Alex Romero, David Cooper, James Loney

Smith's selection seventh overall came as a bit of a surprise. Sure, he profiled as one of the best pure hitters in the 2017 draft, but being limited entirely to first base puts a monumental amount of pressure on the bat. While the University of Virginia is notable for producing hitters with flat swings, Smith has developed some leverage in his. The problem is that it isn't producing. Scouts remain concerned about a lack of bat speed despite the leverage, and his overall power output has failed to live up to expectations. Smith continues to make plenty of contact, but a trade-off for more power would seem a worthy exchange. Without more pop and a revised plan of attack, he's in danger of losing whatever stock he has.

Steven Souza RF   Born: 04/24/89   Age: 30   Bats: R   Throws: R   Height: 6'4"   Weight: 225   Origin: Round 3, 2007 Draft (#100 overall)

YEAR	TEAM	LVL	AGE	PA	R	2B	3B	HR	RBI	BB	K	SB	CS	AVG/OBP/SLG	DRC+	VORP	BABIP	BRR	FRAA	WARP
2016	TBA	MLB	27	468	58	17	1	17	49	31	159	7	6	.247/.303/.409	79	6.8	.348	2.3	RF(111): -1.9, CF(3): 0.2	-0.1
2017	TBA	MLB	28	617	78	21	2	30	78	84	179	16	4	.239/.351/.459	109	27.3	.302	-1.9	RF(138): -6.8, CF(3): -0.5	1.2
2018	ARI	MLB	29	272	21	15	3	5	29	28	75	6	1	.220/.309/.369	82	-0.5	.298	0.1	RF(65): -5.9, CF(1): 0.0	-0.6
2019	ARI	MLB	30	544	64	22	3	17	63	56	155	13	4	.230/.319/.392	98	13.9	.304	0.2	RF -5	0.9

Breakout: 1%   Improve: 51%   Collapse: 10%   Attrition: 11%   MLB: 100%   *Comparables: Jayson Werth, Brad Hawpe, Will Venable*

In Charles Dickens' masterpiece *Great Expectations*, Pip rises to great wealth and leaves his old life behind before watching it all come crashing down due to his own arrogance. There's a metaphor in there somewhere in regard to the Diamondbacks' treatment of the outfield. They waved goodbye to J.D. Martinez and thought they had an adequate replacement in Souza before his season got downright weird. He hit to the opposite field more in 2018 and his fly balls lost a lot of their effectiveness, as his swing and approach produced new and damning results. All is not lost, however. Souza tried to revert back to form late in the season and the results picked up some. With two years of team control remaining, the Diamondbacks will hope to salvage something from their oft-criticized decision.

Chris Stewart C   Born: 02/19/82   Age: 37   Bats: R   Throws: R   Height: 6'4"   Weight: 215   Origin: Round 12, 2001 Draft (#373 overall)

YEAR	TEAM	LVL	AGE	PA	R	2B	3B	HR	RBI	BB	K	SB	CS	AVG/OBP/SLG	DRC+	VORP	BABIP	BRR	FRAA	WARP
2016	PIT	MLB	34	113	10	4	0	1	7	12	15	0	0	.214/.319/.286	94	2.9	.244	0.6	C(31): -2.9, 1B(1): 0.0	0.3
2017	PIT	MLB	35	144	8	1	2	0	4	9	22	0	0	.183/.241/.221	77	-6.0	.220	0.0	C(48): 3.3	0.6
2018	ATL	MLB	36	16	3	0	0	0	3	1	1	0	0	.214/.250/.214	95	0.3	.214	0.6	C(5): -0.4	0.1
2018	GWN	AAA	36	156	17	6	1	0	10	14	17	0	1	.219/.299/.277	85	0.1	.248	-0.3	C(45): -1.4	0.3
2018	ARI	MLB	36	1	0	0	0	0	0	0	0	0	0	.000/.000/.000	123	-0.1	.000	0.0	C(3): 0.0	0.0
2019	ARI	MLB	37	251	22	11	1	3	22	19	42	0	0	.232/.298/.332	70	2.8	.266	0.6	C -4	-0.1

Breakout: 2%   Improve: 34%   Collapse: 0%   Attrition: 14%   MLB: 64%   *Comparables: Ryan Hanigan, Brad Ausmus, Bob Boone*

You have no idea why you keep it around. Who are you kidding? You're not actually going to use that blender you got as a wedding gift all those years ago. You've used it, what, a handful of times over the last couple of years because you felt guilty? You're not a smoothie person and you prefer your margaritas on the rocks anyway. But what if you really did need it and didn't have it? Could you live without it? Probably, but if the in-laws show up and that thing isn't still taking up counter space you'd catch hell. And who knows — you might just need it one day after all. Best to hold onto that blender just in case. It does, technically, still work.

YEAR	TEAM	P. COUNT	FRM RUNS	BLK RUNS	THRW RUNS	TOT RUNS
2016	PIT	4077	-0.8	-1.5	0.0	-2.6
2017	PIT	5872	2.3	0.6	0.1	2.6
2018	ATL	632	-0.3	0.0	0.0	0.1
2018	GWN	6076	-1.7	-0.3	0.1	-1.7
2018	ARI	57	0.0	0.0	0.0	-0.6
2019	ARI	9665	-2.6	-0.9	-0.3	-3.8

Yasmany Tomas LF   Born: 11/14/90   Age: 28   Bats: R   Throws: R   Height: 6'2"   Weight: 250   Origin: International Free Agent, 2014

YEAR	TEAM	LVL	AGE	PA	R	2B	3B	HR	RBI	BB	K	SB	CS	AVG/OBP/SLG	DRC+	VORP	BABIP	BRR	FRAA	WARP
2016	ARI	MLB	25	563	72	30	1	31	83	31	136	2	4	.272/.313/.508	114	19.5	.310	-0.8	RF(91): -10.9, LF(60): -8.8	0.3
2017	ARI	MLB	26	180	19	11	1	8	32	13	50	0	0	.241/.294/.464	93	5.9	.294	-0.3	LF(42): -7.1	-0.4
2018	RNO	AAA	27	371	42	22	4	14	65	11	101	2	0	.262/.280/.465	89	-3.3	.322	-3.4	LF(44): -5.9, 1B(9): -0.3	-0.6
2019	ARI	MLB	28	251	26	12	1	9	31	13	70	1	1	.237/.280/.407	84	1.2	.297	0.0	LF -5, 1B 0	-0.5

Breakout: 1%   Improve: 49%   Collapse: 13%   Attrition: 19%   MLB: 91%   *Comparables: Chris Heisey, Xavier Nady, Ben Francisco*

Reno, Nevada is the biggest little city in America. Looking at their municipal brochure, it's easy to see why: there are ample opportunities to enjoy winter sports, fish Pyramid Lake and make $10 million playing for the Triple-A Reno Aces. There is no footage of Tomas on a snowboard or with a fly rod in his hands, but he did rake in the cash while notably *not* raking in the PCL. Demoted from the major-league roster, his line of trade suitors unsurprisingly did not materialize. His signing has been an unmitigated disaster considering the amount of payroll he assumes and the production he's never produced. But at least he can enjoy his time in the biggest little city in America, a setting that makes all of the sense in the world.

Ildemaro Vargas INF   Born: 07/16/91   Age: 27   Bats: B   Throws: R   Height: 6'0"   Weight: 170   Origin: International Free Agent, 2008

YEAR	TEAM	LVL	AGE	PA	R	2B	3B	HR	RBI	BB	K	SB	CS	AVG/OBP/SLG	DRC+	VORP	BABIP	BRR	FRAA	WARP
2016	MOB	AA	24	351	41	15	2	4	19	24	24	8	0	.276/.325/.372	107	12.9	.287	-0.7	SS(77): 7.5, 2B(4): -0.1	2.6
2016	RNO	AAA	24	224	35	13	0	2	18	20	13	13	1	.354/.418/.449	108	19.9	.372	1.3	2B(45): 4.0, SS(6): 1.5	1.7
2017	RNO	AAA	25	535	87	35	4	10	65	30	40	8	3	.312/.355/.462	109	33.4	.319	1.3	2B(93): 11.8, SS(8): -1.6	3.4
2017	ARI	MLB	25	13	4	1	0	0	4	0	3	0	0	.308/.308/.385	85	-0.2	.400	0.1	2B(3): 0.0, 3B(2): -0.1	0.0
2018	RNO	AAA	26	572	78	31	10	7	54	30	46	10	4	.311/.348/.445	103	19.8	.329	-3.8	SS(107): -6.0, 2B(17): -0.1	1.9
2018	ARI	MLB	26	20	2	0	0	1	4	1	4	1	0	.211/.250/.368	98	0.5	.214	0.0	3B(3): 0.3, 2B(2): 0.1	0.1
2019	ARI	MLB	27	124	14	6	1	3	12	6	15	2	0	.263/.304/.392	102	4.3	.282	0.1	3B 1, SS 0	0.6

Breakout: 6%   Improve: 16%   Collapse: 7%   Attrition: 18%   MLB: 39%   *Comparables: Christian Colon, Alex Mejia, Danny Sandoval*

As a society, we don't give Daniel Bernoulli enough credit. Sure, it's easy to overlook 18th century mathematicians, but we really shouldn't. Bernoulli is credited with a bunch of important stuff, like aerodynamics and the conservation of energy. He's also the creator of the economic term "utility." And in that very specific way, he's uniquely linked to Vargas — a guy with no carrying tool besides his utility. He — Vargas not Bernoulli — can play just about anywhere in the infield and basically never strikes out. He's your prototypical 27-year-old utility man who's still looking for a spot on the bench. Even if it's a working man's dream, Vargas' dream is a dream nonetheless.

Daulton Varsho C   Born: 07/02/96   Age: 22   Bats: L   Throws: R   Height: 5'10"   Weight: 190   Origin: Round 2, 2017 Draft (#68 overall)

YEAR	TEAM	LVL	AGE	PA	R	2B	3B	HR	RBI	BB	K	SB	CS	AVG/OBP/SLG	DRC+	VORP	BABIP	BRR	FRAA	WARP
2017	YAK	A-	20	212	36	16	3	7	39	17	30	7	2	.311/.368/.534	131	24.1	.338	2.4	C(36): 0.8	1.9
2018	VIS	A+	21	342	44	11	3	11	44	30	71	19	3	.286/.363/.451	116	30.4	.341	2.5	C(55): 1.4	2.3
2019	*ARI*	*MLB*	*22*	*251*	*29*	*8*	*1*	*10*	*31*	*14*	*61*	*6*	*1*	*.228/.272/.388*	*80*	*4.8*	*.263*	*0.5*	*C 0*	*0.6*

Breakout: 8%   Improve: 19%   Collapse: 9%   Attrition: 34%   MLB: 47%   *Comparables: Hank Conger, Francisco Mejia, Chance Sisco*

Black holes are pretty neat, just not when they're on your roster. They have the ability to distort the time and space of entities in their proximity, which sounds cool. Diamondbacks catchers over the last five years have seemed to have a similar quality. Buying low on Welington Castillo and, to a lesser extent, Chris Iannetta were shrewd opportunities, but they were never stars. Tuffy Gosewisch, Chris Herrmann, Jeff Mathis and Alex Avila have been, in a vacuum, devoid of any real impact. Meanwhile, Varsho has risen meteorically through the prospect rankings for good reason and he serves as the greatest opportunity for the organization to find a center to their solar system behind the plate. The VarShow isn't far off, as his athleticism has served as a platform for his improved receiving while he still shows plenty in the box to warrant near-top billing.

Andy Yerzy C   Born: 07/05/98   Age: 20   Bats: L   Throws: R   Height: 6'3"   Weight: 215   Origin: Round 2, 2016 Draft (#52 overall)

YEAR	TEAM	LVL	AGE	PA	R	2B	3B	HR	RBI	BB	K	SB	CS	AVG/OBP/SLG	DRC+	VORP	BABIP	BRR	FRAA	WARP
2016	DIA	RK	17	110	5	3	0	1	15	4	22	0	0	.196/.220/.255	93	-6.0	.232	-1.2	C(18): -0.3	0.1
2016	MSO	RK	17	62	2	2	0	0	1	0	16	0	1	.250/.274/.283	54	0.1	.341	0.0	C(15): -0.5	-0.1
2017	MSO	RK	18	249	36	12	0	13	45	24	45	0	0	.298/.365/.524	118	15.3	.323	-2.6	C(37): -0.4	1.1
2018	YAK	A-	19	276	30	11	1	8	34	28	67	0	0	.297/.382/.452	116	17.1	.380	-4.4	C(44): -1.0, 1B(8): -0.8	0.8
2019	*ARI*	*MLB*	*20*	*251*	*25*	*6*	*0*	*10*	*31*	*14*	*74*	*0*	*0*	*.202/.244/.354*	*54*	*-5.1*	*.242*	*-0.9*	*C -1, 1B 0*	*-0.6*

Breakout: 2%   Improve: 3%   Collapse: 0%   Attrition: 2%   MLB: 4%   *Comparables: Francisco Pena, Alex Liddi, Tommy Joseph*

Will he catch? Will he, uh, not catch? Those are the most pertinent questions when it comes to Yerzy. The answers haven't been entirely decided, but one would lean toward the latter. Yerzy has found some consistency and pounds the ball frequently while getting on base. He's not the quickest, most flexible or most fluid receiver, though. The arm plays and he's worked hard to improve, with some of that work paying off. And therein lies the third question: how much can a 20-year-old still improve his catching? Yerzy's bat would project as above average for a catcher, but trends below average if he has to play first base. It's an interesting experiment and the D-backs are unlikely to give up on the idea of him catching just yet.

PITCHERS

Matt Andriese RHP   Born: 08/28/89   Age: 29   Bats: R   Throws: R   Height: 6'2"   Weight: 225   Origin: Round 3, 2011 Draft (#112 overall)

YEAR	TEAM	LVL	AGE	W	L	SV	G	GS	IP	H	HR	BB/9	K/9	K	GB%	BABIP	WHIP	ERA	DRA	WARP	MPH	FB%	WHF	CSP
2016	DUR	AAA	26	1	2	0	6	6	34¹	32	2	1.8	11.5	44	48%	.345	1.14	3.41	2.37	1.2				
2016	TBA	MLB	26	8	8	1	29	19	127²	131	17	1.8	7.7	109	44%	.305	1.22	4.37	3.63	2.4	93.8	46	11.3	47.2
2017	TBA	MLB	27	5	5	1	18	17	86	90	16	2.9	8.0	76	46%	.296	1.37	4.50	4.10	1.4	93.5	44.3	11.8	48.2
2018	TBA	MLB	28	3	4	0	27	4	59²	55	7	2.7	8.9	59	52%	.291	1.22	4.07	4.89	0.1	93.8	48.9	12.8	48.5
2018	ARI	MLB	28	0	3	0	14	1	19	29	8	3.3	9.0	19	44%	.382	1.89	9.00	5.20	0.0	93.7	48.9	14.3	48
2019	*ARI*	*MLB*	*29*	*3*	*2*	*0*	*45*	*5*	*62²*	*57*	*7*	*2.9*	*9.0*	*63*	*46%*	*.308*	*1.24*	*3.79*	*4.37*	*0.7*	*93.0*	*46.5*	*12.1*	*48*

Breakout: 31%   Improve: 51%   Collapse: 19%   Attrition: 25%   MLB: 83%   *Comparables: Matt Belisle, Chase Anderson, Vidal Nuno*

When the Diamondbacks tried to address their needs at the 2018 trade deadline, they acquired Andriese from the Rays. He wasn't a clear upgrade and was coming from a non-traditional pitching scheme, but he made sense in a strange way. Other players on the roster were approaching free agency with demands that the Diamondbacks likely couldn't bargain for and Andriese was a long play to fill out the rotation in future. And while he didn't do much to help the team's postseason chances in the immediate, he should provide affordable depth moving forward.

Brad Boxberger RHP   Born: 05/27/88   Age: 31   Bats: R   Throws: R   Height: 6'2"   Weight: 205   Origin: Round 1, 2009 Draft (#43 overall)

YEAR	TEAM	LVL	AGE	W	L	SV	G	GS	IP	H	HR	BB/9	K/9	K	GB%	BABIP	WHIP	ERA	DRA	WARP	MPH	FB%	WHF	CSP
2016	TBA	MLB	28	4	3	0	27	0	24¹	23	3	7.0	8.1	22	49%	.294	1.73	4.81	6.17	-0.3	94.5	59.2	11.5	46.4
2017	TBA	MLB	29	4	4	0	30	0	29¹	23	4	3.4	12.3	40	46%	.292	1.16	3.38	2.89	0.7	94.2	65.6	14.3	49.4
2018	ARI	MLB	30	3	7	32	60	0	53¹	44	9	5.4	12.0	71	48%	.287	1.42	4.39	5.11	-0.1	93.4	66.3	11.5	46.7
2019	*ARI*	*MLB*	*31*	*2*	*1*	*14*	*43*	*0*	*46*	*37*	*6*	*4.8*	*10.6*	*54*	*45%*	*.299*	*1.34*	*4.13*	*4.74*	*0.1*	*92.9*	*64.5*	*12.1*	*47.3*

Breakout: 23%   Improve: 35%   Collapse: 28%   Attrition: 15%   MLB: 87%   *Comparables: Boone Logan, Sergio Santos, Mike Dunn*

Balling on a budget is great, but it's also important to remember you usually get what you pay for. Arizona has done plenty of bargain hunting in acquiring closers over the last five years. The Addison Reed experiment didn't really work. Brad Ziegler was reliable if not remarkable. Daniel Hudson got a few chances and then the Fernando Rodney Experience came to town. Digging into the depths yet again yielded Boxberger for 2018, and for a pitcher whose stuff is pretty meh, the results were pretty good ... for a while. Then reality set in and things took a steep dive, both on the mound and in the win column. He struck out plenty of hitters despite mediocre whiff rates, but walked more than his share and paid the price. His days as a closer may very well be over for good.

Silvino Bracho RHP   Born: 07/17/92   Age: 26   Bats: R   Throws: R   Height: 5'10"   Weight: 190   Origin: International Free Agent, 2011

YEAR	TEAM	LVL	AGE	W	L	SV	G	GS	IP	H	HR	BB/9	K/9	K	GB%	BABIP	WHIP	ERA	DRA	WARP	MPH	FB%	WHF	CSP
2016	RNO	AAA	23	0	2	15	36	0	33²	34	2	2.1	11.5	43	28%	.352	1.25	4.81	3.14	0.7				
2016	ARI	MLB	23	0	2	0	26	0	24²	31	7	3.6	6.2	17	29%	.293	1.66	7.30	7.46	-0.7	95.0	64.9	11.6	50.3
2017	RNO	AAA	24	3	2	8	33	0	35¹	25	8	4.3	12.2	48	34%	.239	1.19	4.08	3.57	0.7				
2017	ARI	MLB	24	0	0	0	21	0	20²	18	5	3.0	10.9	25	46%	.260	1.21	5.66	3.82	0.3	94.5	50.7	14.3	52
2018	RNO	AAA	25	2	2	8	27	0	34¹	39	3	2.1	13.6	52	39%	.450	1.37	4.46	2.10	1.2				
2018	ARI	MLB	25	2	0	0	31	0	31	25	2	3.5	9.9	34	38%	.295	1.19	3.19	4.12	0.3	94.5	55.6	16.5	49.1
2019	ARI	MLB	26	2	1	0	45	0	48	40	7	3.6	11.0	58	37%	.301	1.24	4.05	4.65	0.1	94.2	57.7	14.9	51.3

Breakout: 16%   Improve: 34%   Collapse: 21%   Attrition: 24%   MLB: 70%   Comparables: Chasen Shreve, Louis Coleman, Shawn Kelley

Do baseball players get to keep their own airline miles? Sure, most don't need the freebies given their paychecks, but Bracho may disagree. Over the past four seasons, he's been called up 22 times, usually making what must now be a familiar flight from Reno to wherever. Bracho has also yielded balls in play that might qualify for their own frequent flyer miles given his fly-ball tendencies. But after giving up nearly one home run for every four appearances through 2017, he was much more successful at keeping the ball in the park. He might just be in line for a future in the D-backs' bullpen this season, as he's finally out of options.

Archie Bradley RHP   Born: 08/10/92   Age: 26   Bats: R   Throws: R   Height: 6'4"   Weight: 225   Origin: Round 1, 2011 Draft (#7 overall)

YEAR	TEAM	LVL	AGE	W	L	SV	G	GS	IP	H	HR	BB/9	K/9	K	GB%	BABIP	WHIP	ERA	DRA	WARP	MPH	FB%	WHF	CSP
2016	RNO	AAA	23	5	1	0	7	7	40²	26	0	4.0	10.4	47	64%	.289	1.08	1.99	3.92	0.7				
2016	ARI	MLB	23	8	9	0	26	26	141²	154	16	4.3	9.1	143	47%	.338	1.56	5.02	5.68	-0.5	95.1	69.2	9.1	48.3
2017	ARI	MLB	24	3	3	1	63	0	73	55	4	2.6	9.7	79	49%	.276	1.04	1.73	3.88	1.1	98.0	75.6	10.9	52.7
2018	ARI	MLB	25	4	5	3	76	0	71²	62	9	2.5	9.4	75	50%	.282	1.14	3.64	4.48	0.4	97.3	81.7	10	51.3
2019	ARI	MLB	26	3	1	15	50	0	53¹	44	5	3.4	9.7	57	48%	.300	1.19	3.42	3.94	0.6	96.2	76.3	10	51.9

Breakout: 24%   Improve: 62%   Collapse: 13%   Attrition: 9%   MLB: 88%   Comparables: Yordano Ventura, Trevor Bauer, Gerrit Cole

The yin and the yang. The sun and the moon. Heads and tails. These things are meant to balance out. If you take Bradley's first and second halves, they balance themselves out, too. That "balance" makes for a reliever who hasn't quite turned the corner yet despite lofty expectations. A brilliant first half abruptly gave way to a miserable second half as Bradley took his untimely lumps down the stretch and let several key leads slip away. His command is still problematic and he used his fastball up plenty with occasionally catastrophic results. Problems with his curveball — a pitch that's been nasty in the past but was shelved at times — didn't help. He may still be the closer of the future, but what that future holds seems a toss-up.

Clay Buchholz RHP   Born: 08/14/84   Age: 34   Bats: L   Throws: R   Height: 6'3"   Weight: 190   Origin: Round 1, 2005 Draft (#42 overall)

YEAR	TEAM	LVL	AGE	W	L	SV	G	GS	IP	H	HR	BB/9	K/9	K	GB%	BABIP	WHIP	ERA	DRA	WARP	MPH	FB%	WHF	CSP
2016	BOS	MLB	31	8	10	0	37	21	139¹	130	21	3.6	6.0	93	42%	.263	1.33	4.78	5.29	0.0	94.4	63.4	10	45.7
2017	PHI	MLB	32	0	1	0	2	2	7¹	16	1	3.7	6.1	5	31%	.484	2.59	12.27	6.77	-0.1	92.1	65.2	6.5	49.7
2018	OMA	AAA	33	1	0	0	2	2	11¹	9	2	4.0	3.2	4	55%	.194	1.24	1.59	8.98	-0.4				
2018	RNO	AAA	33	0	1	0	2	2	11²	12	0	3.9	7.7	10	40%	.324	1.46	5.40	4.67	0.1				
2018	ARI	MLB	33	7	2	0	16	16	98¹	80	9	2.0	7.4	81	43%	.256	1.04	2.01	3.74	1.8	91.7	65.9	10.5	50.4
2019	ARI	MLB	34	5	6	0	15	15	87²	81	10	3.3	7.5	73	42%	.292	1.29	4.28	4.93	0.4	91.8	63.7	10	48.3

Breakout: 11%   Improve: 36%   Collapse: 22%   Attrition: 14%   MLB: 89%   Comparables: Doug Fister, Whitey Ford, Tim Hudson

Late last winter, Buchholz was enjoying a sojourn in Denmark when he was awoken to the sound of broken glass. He jolted from bed, grabbed an axe-handled bat with no idea of how to swing it and ventured downstairs in the dark. Seeing no intruders, he opened the front door to find a collection of broken dinner plates littered about. His elbow tinged and Buchholz wondered what kind of sick joke had just been played at his expense. He shut the door and turned to his favorite web browser, Altavista, searching for answers. He quickly found that the Danish throw broken dinner plates at houses on New Year's Eve as a wishing of good luck. Feeling renewed and, frankly, relieved, Buchholz went back to bed. "This year is going to be different," he said. Buchholz proceeded to pitch incredibly well for the Diamondbacks before finishing the season on the disabled list. It really was a different year, and also, it wasn't.

Andrew Chafin LHP   Born: 06/17/90   Age: 29   Bats: R   Throws: L   Height: 6'2"   Weight: 225   Origin: Round 1, 2011 Draft (#43 overall)

YEAR	TEAM	LVL	AGE	W	L	SV	G	GS	IP	H	HR	BB/9	K/9	K	GB%	BABIP	WHIP	ERA	DRA	WARP	MPH	FB%	WHF	CSP
2016	ARI	MLB	26	0	1	0	32	0	22²	22	1	4.4	11.1	28	52%	.368	1.46	6.75	5.65	-0.2	96.0	72	15.6	47
2017	ARI	MLB	27	1	0	0	71	0	51¹	48	5	3.7	10.7	61	58%	.326	1.34	3.51	3.51	0.9	95.1	61.2	11.9	41.8
2018	ARI	MLB	28	1	6	0	77	0	49¹	41	0	4.6	9.7	53	51%	.313	1.34	3.10	4.23	0.4	95.2	56.6	14.7	42.7
2019	ARI	MLB	29	3	1	0	50	0	53¹	42	5	4.2	10.0	59	50%	.295	1.26	3.67	4.23	0.3	94.6	60.2	13.7	43.5

Breakout: 29%   Improve: 56%   Collapse: 24%   Attrition: 21%   MLB: 94%   Comparables: Alex Colome, Justin Wilson, Zach Britton

Chafin is weird. Sure, he rocked a nasty mustache for much of 2018, once lived in a trailer behind Chase Field and he has a cow-milking title to his name, but he's weird on the mound, too. Chafin ran another good ERA, but it was a bit misleading. He struggled to limit inherited runners from scoring and walked a bunch of guys. He wasn't used as a LOOGY and lefties actually performed better against him than righties did. But he did something else weird: he made 77 appearances without allowing a home run. That's hard to do, even for someone not known for being taken deep. While he surely isn't the most efficient, Chafin has also avoided burning things down and that should keep him in the bullpen mix moving forward.

Taylor Clarke RHP Born: 05/13/93 Age: 26 Bats: R Throws: R Height: 6'4" Weight: 200 Origin: Round 3, 2015 Draft (#76 overall)

YEAR	TEAM	LVL	AGE	W	L	SV	G	GS	IP	H	HR	BB/9	K/9	K	GB%	BABIP	WHIP	ERA	DRA	WARP	MPH	FB%	WHF	CSP
2016	KNC	A	23	3	2	0	6	6	28²	24	1	1.6	7.5	24	32%	.277	1.01	2.83	3.50	0.5				
2016	VIS	A+	23	1	1	0	4	4	23	19	3	2.7	8.6	22	31%	.262	1.13	2.74	4.36	0.3				
2016	MOB	AA	23	8	6	0	17	17	97²	99	9	1.9	6.6	72	38%	.297	1.23	3.59	3.26	2.1				
2017	WTN	AA	24	9	7	0	21	21	111¹	94	7	3.2	8.6	107	40%	.292	1.19	2.91	4.52	0.9				
2017	RNO	AAA	24	3	2	0	6	6	33²	29	8	3.5	8.3	31	34%	.231	1.25	4.81	4.67	0.4				
2018	RNO	AAA	25	13	8	0	27	27	152	149	12	2.6	7.4	125	40%	.302	1.27	4.03	4.24	2.2				
2019	*ARI*	*MLB*	*26*	*1*	*1*	*0*	*3*	*3*	*17*	*16*	*2*	*2.9*	*8.0*	*15*	*38%*	*.288*	*1.24*	*4.25*	*4.90*	*0.1*				

Breakout: 7%   Improve: 17%   Collapse: 8%   Attrition: 18%   MLB: 41%   *Comparables: Kendry Flores, Chris Stratton, D.J. Mitchell*

It's Christmas morning and you're bursting at the seams with excitement. At 10 years old, you live for Christmas. It's the pinnacle of being a kid. You get a bunch of stuff you want and literally don't have to do anything to earn it besides show up. French toast breakfast? Check. RC car? Check. Diamondbacks shirsey? Check. The hits just keep coming, then you get the present left by grandma and it's ... a sweater? You've got five of these already and they're all scratchy as hell. Are they useful? Sure, they can be serviceable and there's an application when they're what you need, but like back-end starting pitchers, this sweater isn't getting you excited. You'll keep it and give it a try someday because you basically have to. Can't hurt to have an extra sweater around, even if it's your least exciting Christmas gift.

Jake Diekman LHP Born: 01/21/87 Age: 32 Bats: L Throws: L Height: 6'4" Weight: 200 Origin: Round 30, 2007 Draft (#923 overall)

YEAR	TEAM	LVL	AGE	W	L	SV	G	GS	IP	H	HR	BB/9	K/9	K	GB%	BABIP	WHIP	ERA	DRA	WARP	MPH	FB%	WHF	CSP
2016	TEX	MLB	29	4	2	4	66	0	53	36	4	4.4	10.0	59	50%	.248	1.17	3.40	4.73	0.1	97.7	73.6	12.1	42.1
2017	TEX	MLB	30	0	0	1	11	0	10²	4	1	8.4	11.0	13	59%	.143	1.31	2.53	7.02	-0.2	97.5	68.1	12.2	37.4
2018	TEX	MLB	31	1	1	2	47	0	39	31	2	5.3	11.1	48	48%	.302	1.38	3.69	6.34	-0.6	96.8	62.4	11.4	45.4
2018	ARI	MLB	31	0	1	0	24	0	14¹	18	2	5.0	11.3	18	57%	.400	1.81	7.53	6.25	-0.2	97.2	67.9	13.5	46.8
2019	*ARI*	*MLB*	*32*	*2*	*1*	*1*	*41*	*0*	*43*	*36*	*5*	*4.7*	*10.5*	*50*	*48%*	*.305*	*1.35*	*4.00*	*4.60*	*0.1*	*96.3*	*66.8*	*11.9*	*41.7*

Breakout: 21%   Improve: 41%   Collapse: 20%   Attrition: 9%   MLB: 86%   *Comparables: Adam Ottavino, Fernando Rodney, Jim Kern*

Strikeouts are good. Walks are bad. With Diekman, you get plenty of each. The Diamondbacks acquired him from the Rangers at the deadline, hoping to shore up a weakness in the bullpen against lefty swingers. Instead, they got a guy who weirdly struggled against same-handed hitters, including too many walks and some untimely long balls — just in time for the team's epic September collapse. Diekman has always walked a fine line between being dominant and disastrous, and his time in the desert was too much of the latter. On the right contract, he's a useful bullpen piece, but don't get your hopes up. He'll dash them quicker than he can issue four balls.

Jon Duplantier RHP Born: 07/11/94 Age: 24 Bats: L Throws: R Height: 6'4" Weight: 225 Origin: Round 3, 2016 Draft (#89 overall)

YEAR	TEAM	LVL	AGE	W	L	SV	G	GS	IP	H	HR	BB/9	K/9	K	GB%	BABIP	WHIP	ERA	DRA	WARP	MPH	FB%	WHF	CSP
2017	KNC	A	22	6	1	0	13	12	72²	45	4	1.9	9.7	78	52%	.240	0.83	1.24	3.41	1.6				
2017	VIS	A+	22	6	2	0	12	12	63¹	46	2	3.8	12.4	87	53%	.324	1.15	1.56	2.58	2.0				
2018	WTN	AA	23	5	1	0	14	14	67	52	4	3.8	9.1	68	56%	.282	1.19	2.69	4.70	0.5				
2019	*ARI*	*MLB*	*24*	*1*	*1*	*0*	*3*	*3*	*15*	*13*	*2*	*4.9*	*9.5*	*16*	*44%*	*.297*	*1.39*	*4.43*	*5.09*	*0.1*				

Breakout: 10%   Improve: 22%   Collapse: 22%   Attrition: 41%   MLB: 52%   *Comparables: P.J. Walters, Brian Johnson, Chris Reed*

Duplantier was the Diamondbacks' top prospect a year ago and is still regarded quite highly. But no one would blame you if you aren't totally excited about him. In the plus column, he's nearly big-league ready, has general command of his pitches and has yielded strong results. On the other side of the ledger, he missed time last season with an injury and his numbers weren't great, just good. The injury, of course, is the most worrisome. He pitched a bunch as a Rice Owl and dealt with shoulder issues there. He missed time right after he was drafted with a barking elbow, then suffered from biceps tendinitis in 2018. The latest entry into his injury history is the least concerning, but the whole of it remains a worry. TINSTAAPP is alive and well at the top of Arizona's prospect heap.

Zack Godley RHP Born: 04/21/90 Age: 29 Bats: R Throws: R Height: 6'3" Weight: 240 Origin: Round 10, 2013 Draft (#288 overall)

YEAR	TEAM	LVL	AGE	W	L	SV	G	GS	IP	H	HR	BB/9	K/9	K	GB%	BABIP	WHIP	ERA	DRA	WARP	MPH	FB%	WHF	CSP
2016	MOB	AA	26	2	5	0	8	8	49¹	48	4	2.0	5.7	31	56%	.291	1.20	3.83	3.65	0.9				
2016	RNO	AAA	26	2	1	0	7	6	32²	37	3	4.1	10.5	38	50%	.382	1.59	3.31	3.80	0.6				
2016	ARI	MLB	26	5	4	0	27	9	74²	86	13	3.0	7.2	60	55%	.313	1.49	6.39	4.34	0.8	92.8	64.4	12.7	44.3
2017	RNO	AAA	27	2	1	0	5	3	28	14	0	5.5	9.3	29	68%	.222	1.11	2.57	3.69	0.6				
2017	ARI	MLB	27	8	9	0	26	25	155	124	15	3.1	9.6	165	58%	.280	1.14	3.37	3.69	3.3	93.0	56.9	13.7	42.3
2018	ARI	MLB	28	15	11	0	33	32	178¹	177	16	4.1	9.3	185	50%	.324	1.45	4.74	4.78	1.1	91.5	54.4	12.2	43.4
2019	*ARI*	*MLB*	*29*	*11*	*10*	*0*	*30*	*30*	*180*	*154*	*17*	*3.4*	*9.2*	*185*	*51%*	*.303*	*1.24*	*3.64*	*4.19*	*2.3*	*91.6*	*56.5*	*12.7*	*43.2*

Breakout: 25%   Improve: 49%   Collapse: 15%   Attrition: 16%   MLB: 91%   *Comparables: Christian Friedrich, Aaron Heilman, Josh Outman*

It's amazing that a pitcher with Godley's stuff took so long to get drafted. He was 23 when he began his professional career, but reached the majors at 25, rushing through the Cubs' and Diamondbacks' systems with the kind of reckless abandon he's known for on the mound. He was a WTF trade target by Dave Stewart, then showed enough in his Diamondbacks debut to prove he belonged. A promotion from the bullpen to the rotation proved fruitful two years ago, but his 2018 was a bit rougher around the edges. He battled his mechanics for most of the season, falling off the mound like a drunken sailor at times. With pitches that have so much movement (a la Trevor Cahill), he struggles to throw strikes even when he's right, and when he's not, well, that's what 2018 was: too many walks, too many mistakes. Godley competes his ass off every time he takes the mound, but there's plenty of cleaning up to do before he can sparkle again.

Zack Greinke RHP Born: 10/21/83 Age: 35 Bats: R Throws: R Height: 6'2" Weight: 200 Origin: Round 1, 2002 Draft (#6 overall)

YEAR	TEAM	LVL	AGE	W	L	SV	G	GS	IP	H	HR	BB/9	K/9	K	GB%	BABIP	WHIP	ERA	DRA	WARP	MPH	FB%	WHF	CSP
2016	ARI	MLB	32	13	7	0	26	26	158²	161	23	2.3	7.6	134	47%	.294	1.27	4.37	4.23	2.1	93.8	48.3	11.2	43.1
2017	ARI	MLB	33	17	7	0	32	32	202¹	172	25	2.0	9.6	215	48%	.285	1.07	3.20	2.77	6.3	92.3	48.4	13.4	40.9
2018	ARI	MLB	34	15	11	0	33	33	207²	181	28	1.9	8.6	199	46%	.272	1.08	3.21	3.09	5.3	91.4	48.7	11.7	45.1
2019	*ARI*	*MLB*	*35*	*12*	*10*	*0*	*29*	*29*	*194¹*	*163*	*22*	*2.4*	*8.8*	*190*	*45%*	*.286*	*1.10*	*3.60*	*4.15*	*2.6*	*91.0*	*47.6*	*12*	*42.4*

Breakout: 17%   Improve: 38%   Collapse: 35%   Attrition: 8%   MLB: 91%   *Comparables: Adam Wainwright, Hiroki Kuroda, Bert Blyleven*

Greinke sat 94-95 mph and flirted with triple digits. A *decade* ago. While his velocity has dropped off in a major way in recent years, his strikeout rate has increased along the way. Greinke has leaned into that decline, as he used his slow curveball, which many have called an "eephus," more than ever in 2018. It's all smoke and mirrors these days for the former Cy Young winner and everybody knows it. While he was less ace-like in the season that was, it appears he's still on track to be a very good pitcher for years to come. His contract is surely burdensome, but he's maintained a productive pace into his mid-30s, defying Father Time in the process.

Yoshihisa Hirano RHP Born: 03/08/84 Age: 35 Bats: R Throws: R Height: 6'1" Weight: 185 Origin: International Free Agent, 2017

YEAR	TEAM	LVL	AGE	W	L	SV	G	GS	IP	H	HR	BB/9	K/9	K	GB%	BABIP	WHIP	ERA	DRA	WARP	MPH	FB%	WHF	CSP
2018	ARI	MLB	34	4	3	3	75	0	66¹	49	6	3.1	8.0	59	51%	.250	1.09	2.44	4.47	0.3	93.3	53.7	13.5	42.4
2019	*ARI*	*MLB*	*35*	*3*	*1*	*15*	*50*	*0*	*53¹*	*45*	*5*	*3.6*	*8.7*	*51*	*49%*	*.292*	*1.24*	*3.86*	*4.45*	*0.2*	*92.1*	*52.7*	*13.2*	*41.6*

Breakout: 23%   Improve: 51%   Collapse: 20%   Attrition: 17%   MLB: 88%   *Comparables: Trever Miller, Hideki Okajima, Mike Stanton*

Is magic real or is it just a trick to make the kids question reality? For non-believers, magic seems frivolous. For those who choose to accept the bounds of magic, anything is possible. For the Diamondbacks faithful, Hirano convinced many that magic is indeed alive and well among us. His splitter has Houdini-like properties and batters swung and missed at nearly 20 percent of them. His mediocre fastball was very real — almost too real — but the splitter was simply magic. Even if hitters managed to make contact, they routinely pounded it into the ground. While the profile is not closer-esque, he may find himself back in the closer conversation in 2019.

Merrill Kelly RHP Born: 10/14/88 Age: 30 Bats: R Throws: R Height: 6'2" Weight: 190 Origin: Round 8, 2010 Draft (#251 overall)

YEAR	TEAM	LVL	AGE	W	L	SV	G	GS	IP	H	HR	BB/9	K/9	K	GB%	BABIP	WHIP	ERA	DRA	WARP	MPH	FB%	WHF	CSP
2019	*ARI*	*MLB*	*30*	*7*	*7*	*0*	*21*	*21*	*119²*	*108*	*14*	*3.4*	*8.6*	*114*	*48%*	*.299*	*1.27*	*4.05*	*4.66*	*0.9*				

Breakout: 7%   Improve: 38%   Collapse: 31%   Attrition: 9%   MLB: 94%   *Comparables: Doug Davis, Yovani Gallardo, Travis Wood*

Tampa Bay's eighth-round pick in 2010, Kelly pitched reasonably well in the minors and advanced to Triple-A in 2014, but never received a call-up. He headed to Korea at age 26, putting together a three-season run as one of the top starting pitchers in the extremely hitter-friendly KBO. He topped 180 innings in all three seasons, posting a combined 3.80 ERA compared to a league average of 5.02. Now he'll hope to follow the path most recently taken by Miles Mikolas, returning to MLB after success in a foreign league turned more heads than previous work in the American minors. Kelly inked a two-year, $5.5 million deal with the Diamondbacks that includes cheap team options for 2021 and 2022. Expecting him to "replace" Patrick Corbin is beyond wishful thinking — Kelly was never considered a top prospect in America and there's nothing dominant about his numbers in Korea — but he has a chance to be a useful back-of-the-rotation starter for Arizona.

Matthew Koch RHP Born: 11/02/90 Age: 28 Bats: L Throws: R Height: 6'3" Weight: 215 Origin: Round 3, 2012 Draft (#107 overall)

YEAR	TEAM	LVL	AGE	W	L	SV	G	GS	IP	H	HR	BB/9	K/9	K	GB%	BABIP	WHIP	ERA	DRA	WARP	MPH	FB%	WHF	CSP
2016	MOB	AA	25	2	4	0	14	14	74²	87	7	1.6	5.9	49	42%	.324	1.34	4.70	4.31	0.7				
2016	RNO	AAA	25	4	2	0	7	7	46²	55	3	1.2	4.8	25	55%	.325	1.31	3.09	4.80	0.3				
2016	ARI	MLB	25	1	1	1	7	2	18	9	1	2.0	5.0	10	43%	.154	0.72	2.00	6.36	-0.2	94.2	49.6	9	53.1
2017	YAK	A-	26	1	0	0	2	2	11	13	2	0.8	7.4	9	41%	.344	1.27	4.91	4.92	0.0				
2017	ARI	MLB	26	0	0	0	1	0	0	2	0			0	0%	1.000					91.9	55.6	0	57
2017	RNO	AAA	26	2	2	0	10	10	45	68	11	3.0	5.0	25	45%	.350	1.84	8.40	8.81	-1.5				
2018	RNO	AAA	27	2	4	0	11	11	54¹	66	11	2.0	5.1	31	46%	.312	1.44	5.96	5.47	0.1				
2018	ARI	MLB	27	5	5	0	19	14	86²	88	19	2.3	5.2	50	45%	.262	1.27	4.15	5.80	-0.5	93.0	41.1	7.6	49.1
2019	*ARI*	*MLB*	*28*	*3*	*3*	*0*	*36*	*6*	*63²*	*66*	*10*	*2.8*	*6.3*	*45*	*43%*	*.298*	*1.34*	*4.93*	*5.68*	*-0.5*	*92.6*	*42.2*	*7.7*	*53.1*

Breakout: 7%   Improve: 19%   Collapse: 12%   Attrition: 24%   MLB: 37%   *Comparables: Josh Geer, Pat Dean, Christian Bergman*

Every kid plays with fire. Maybe it's hardwired into humans as part of our Neanderthal past. Maybe it's just stupid fascination and a resistance to being told not to do something. Either way, if you play with fire you'll get burned at some point and Koch did just that in 2018. It's hard to make your living as pitcher surrendering a lot of contact and Koch has no way around it. His stuff is just too hittable. Working as an up-and-down option for the Diamondbacks, things were more down than up in the majors, where he was mostly torched. He started hot but an unsustainable BABIP didn't hold and the rest went up in flames.

Yoan Lopez RHP Born: 01/02/93 Age: 26 Bats: R Throws: R Height: 6'3" Weight: 185 Origin: International Free Agent, 2015

YEAR	TEAM	LVL	AGE	W	L	SV	G	GS	IP	H	HR	BB/9	K/9	K	GB%	BABIP	WHIP	ERA	DRA	WARP	MPH	FB%	WHF	CSP
2016	MOB	AA	23	4	7	0	14	14	62	67	10	4.6	5.2	36	42%	.285	1.60	5.52	4.18	0.7				
2017	VIS	A+	24	2	0	4	20	0	30²	16	2	2.6	16.4	56	49%	.298	0.82	0.88	1.86	1.1				
2018	WTN	AA	25	2	6	12	45	0	61²	38	4	3.8	12.7	87	37%	.258	1.04	2.92	2.78	1.6				
2018	ARI	MLB	25	0	0	0	10	0	9	7	2	1.0	11.0	11	56%	.238	0.89	3.00	3.84	0.1	98.6	67.2	13.3	54.2
2019	*ARI*	*MLB*	*26*	*2*	*1*	*0*	*35*	*0*	*37¹*	*30*	*6*	*4.3*	*11.2*	*46*	*40%*	*.298*	*1.29*	*4.30*	*4.93*	*0.0*	*98.2*	*68.4*	*13.5*	*55.2*

Breakout: 11%   Improve: 24%   Collapse: 8%   Attrition: 18%   MLB: 34%   *Comparables: Daniel Stumpf, Barrett Astin, Ryan Brasier*

Can we just stop for a second and give Ziegler a hand for a fantastic career? It truly was remarkable, but it was also weird as hell. At 6-foot-4 and 220 pounds, he was built like a power pitcher but a power pitcher he was not. At least not the version that began his career with 39 scoreless innings. Despite debuting at the spry age of 28, he went on to average more than 67 appearances a season over his 11-year career. After four-plus years in the desert that featured perhaps the most consistently productive Ziegler, he found his way back to the Diamondbacks in late 2018 to cap it all off. He may have to pay for all of those worms he killed in the after-life given his nearly 67 percent ground-ball rate, but Ziegler won't care. He could inherit and clean up a mess with the best of them. Best of all, he defied convention and never backed down until it was time to call it a career. And what a career it was.

LINEOUTS

Hitters

HITTER	POS	TEAM	LVL	AGE	PA	R	2B	3B	HR	RBI	BB	K	SB	CS	AVG/OBP/SLG	DRC+	VORP	BABIP	BRR	FRAA	WARP
Blaze Alexander	SS	DIA	Rk	19	118	25	10	2	2	25	19	21	7	3	.362/.475/.574	140	21.5	.438	-0.9	2B(11): 0.5, SS(10): -3.5	0.6
	SS	MSO	Rk	19	129	27	9	3	3	17	12	31	3	0	.302/.364/.509	101	11.4	.386	1.5	SS(24): 3.6, 2B(4): 0.9	1.2
Jorge Barrosa	CF	DDI	Rk	17	241	57	8	3	3	21	25	34	37	6	.299/.402/.412	131	29.8	.345	6.8	CF(52): 8.0	3.1
	CF	DIA	Rk	17	47	4	0	2	0	1	3	6	2	2	.233/.298/.326	107	1.3	.270	-0.5	CF(9): 2.7, LF(2): -0.3	0.4
Socrates Brito	RF	RNO	AAA	25	478	85	34	5	17	69	44	104	15	4	.318/.383/.540	120	32.6	.384	2.1	RF(66): 5.3, CF(27): 0.3	3.7
	RF	ARI	MLB	25	44	3	0	0	1	3	3	9	0	1	.175/.227/.250	89	-1.6	.194	0.1	RF(11): -0.1, LF(3): -0.1	0.0
Kevin Cron	3B	RNO	AAA	25	438	57	28	1	22	97	36	100	1	0	.309/.368/.554	140	28.3	.359	0.0	3B(57): -3.7, 1B(46): 6.6	3.8
Drew Ellis	3B	VIS	A+	22	502	57	34	1	15	71	52	98	2	6	.246/.331/.429	112	15.7	.283	-4.2	3B(108): -10.6, 1B(2): 0.0	0.8
Domingo Leyba	2B	WTN	AA	22	358	43	17	2	5	30	35	46	5	2	.269/.344/.381	118	14.0	.300	-1.7	2B(72): -2.9, SS(8): 0.5	1.5
Rob Refsnyder	RF	TBA	MLB	27	103	10	3	0	2	5	18	26	0	2	.167/.314/.274	83	-4.2	.214	-1.3	LF(23): -0.2, RF(3): -0.2	-0.2
	RF	DUR	AAA	27	208	31	10	0	4	15	18	46	0	0	.283/.357/.402	102	5.7	.356	-0.5	RF(23): -2.2, CF(8): 0.0	0.2
Alek Thomas	CF	DIA	Rk	18	138	24	3	5	0	10	13	18	8	2	.325/.394/.431	130	15.2	.381	1.6	CF(13): -2.1, LF(11): -2.4	0.5
	CF	MSO	Rk	18	134	26	11	1	2	17	11	19	4	3	.341/.396/.496	110	7.8	.392	-1.0	CF(21): 0.1, LF(7): 0.5	0.6
Kelby Tomlinson	MI	SAC	AAA	28	204	15	2	0	0	10	18	44	7	4	.304/.365/.315	71	7.0	.399	0.9	SS(34): -0.9, 2B(10): -0.8	0.0
	MI	SFN	MLB	28	152	9	4	2	0	10	9	35	0	2	.207/.265/.264	57	-5.7	.276	-1.7	2B(35): -1.0, SS(13): 1.0	-0.4
Christian Walker	1B	RNO	AAA	27	359	68	25	4	18	71	26	86	1	0	.299/.354/.568	138	15.8	.351	-1.3	1B(64): 3.4, LF(18): -0.9	2.5
	1B	ARI	MLB	27	53	6	2	0	3	6	3	22	1	0	.163/.226/.388	65	-1.2	.208	0.2	1B(7): 0.2, LF(1): -0.1	-0.1
Marcus Wilson	CF	VIS	A+	21	502	60	26	2	10	48	44	141	16	6	.235/.309/.369	88	15.3	.316	0.9	CF(109): 4.8	1.4

Blaze Alexander's first name avails itself well to puns, but it's also a healthy descriptor for his game. He's got a cannon of an arm and is known for making loud, laser-like contact. An exciting prospect for his merits and his moniker. ⊗ Kristian Robinson got most of the buzz in Arizona's 2017 J2 class, but don't overlook the diminutive **Jorge Barrosa**. He's a lock to stick in center field and has potential as a leadoff hitter with on-base skills, a contact-oriented approach and enough speed to be a threat on the bases. Oh, and he started switch-hitting in 2018. ⊗ **Socrates Brito** isn't a prospect anymore. He was skipped over to fill J.D. Martinez's departure and has a murky future. He's 26 now and has done it all in Triple-A while mostly falling on his face in the majors. Philosophically, he's built for minor-league depth despite some interesting tools. ⊗ **Kevin Cron** continues to put up impressive minor-league numbers and even got some time at third base in Reno. He's also 26, has never taken a big-league at-bat and is blocked at both corners. ⊗ Drafted in 2017 out of a good Louisville program, nearly half of **Drew Ellis'** hits in 2018 were for extra bases. His defense at third base continues to draw skepticism, however. With questions about his ability to make contact as he climbs the ladder, he'll need to ensure that he's a capable defender because a move to first base may just sink his ship. ⊗ **Domingo Leyba** took to the field again in 2018 after missing most of the previous season with a shoulder injury. There's still potential here for a second-division starter, but anything short of that will turn him into a Quadruple-A player given a lack of defensive versatility. ⊗ Teams keeping picking up **Rob Refsnyder** and giving him a chance in the majors due to hypothetical versatility, but he's neither a good defender nor a good hitter. ⊗ **Alek Thomas'** pro debut was encouraging. He proved capable of hitting rookie-level pitching at two stops, notching strong averages while controlling the strike zone and making plenty of contact. His profile is that of a strong defender in center field with bat control, some on-base skills and enough speed to do additional damage. ⊗ Punch-and-Judy hitters like **Kelby Tomlinson** are unfashionable these days, and the bespectacled infielder doesn't play shortstop well enough to compensate for his powerless bat. ⊗ **Christian Walker** destroyed Triple-A pitching. *Again*. The righty-swinger has a ton of power and put it to use in Reno, but that output didn't exactly translate to the majors. *Again*. ⊗ **Marcus Wilson's** strong 2017 was a bright spot for a down system. A move to the California League in 2018 was supposed to cement his status, but the toolsy center fielder struggled against better pitching. A late-season surge helped salvage some value.

Pitchers

PITCHER	TEAM	LVL	AGE	W	L	SV	G	GS	IP	H	HR	BB/9	K/9	K	GB%	BABIP	WHIP	ERA	DRA	WARP	MPH	FB%	WHF	CSP
Jake Barrett	RNO	AAA	26	4	0	8	42	0	53¹	37	3	4.9	11.3	67	48%	.272	1.24	2.87	3.63	0.9				
	ARI	MLB	26	0	1	0	7	0	7	8	1	2.6	7.7	6	64%	.333	1.43	5.14	3.94	0.1	95.9	60.5	10.5	50.8
Randall Delgado	RNO	AAA	28	0	1	0	13	1	18	11	1	3.0	7.0	14	35%	.196	0.94	2.00	4.35	0.2				
	ARI	MLB	28	2	0	0	10	0	11¹	11	3	4.8	4.0	5	35%	.216	1.50	4.76	5.84	-0.1	93.5	54	10.9	43.5
Joseph Krehbiel	ARI	MLB	25	0	0	0	2	0	3	1	0	6.0	0.0	0	40%	.100	1.00	0.00	9.38	-0.2	98.0	53.1	4.1	47.4
	RNO	AAA	25	3	3	2	48	0	57¹	49	9	3.9	11.1	71	46%	.303	1.29	4.24	3.34	1.2				
Artie Lewicki	TOL	AAA	26	5	6	0	12	12	61²	64	5	2.3	8.0	55	42%	.328	1.30	4.67	3.88	1.2				
	DET	MLB	26	0	2	0	13	3	38²	48	4	3.3	7.0	30	42%	.364	1.60	4.89	5.45	-0.2	93.9	55.7	9.2	51.4
Matt Mercer	YAK	A-	21	0	0	0	12	12	27	19	1	2.0	12.3	37	48%	.295	0.93	3.00	1.95	1.0				
Jared Miller	RNO	AAA	24	1	3	0	38	0	42	46	6	13.5	11.1	52	47%	.374	2.60	7.71	4.15	0.5				
	WTN	AA	24	0	0	0	6	0	6	3	0	6.0	10.5	7	77%	.231	1.17	1.50	2.75	0.2				
Robby Scott	PAW	AAA	28	3	3	3	45	0	48¹	35	1	3.9	11.7	63	43%	.296	1.16	1.86	2.32	1.5				
	BOS	MLB	28	0	1	0	9	0	6²	10	2	6.8	10.8	8	23%	.400	2.25	8.10	8.96	-0.3	90.9	58.8	10.9	39.6
Braden Shipley	ARI	MLB	26	0	0	0	3	0	5	4	0	3.6	5.4	3	47%	.267	1.20	7.20	5.26	0.0	96.0	47.6	8.5	41.3
	RNO	AAA	26	6	4	1	30	6	74¹	93	13	4.4	7.0	58	38%	.340	1.74	5.81	7.30	-1.7				
Matt Tabor	YAK	A-	19	2	1	0	14	14	60²	59	4	1.9	6.8	46	45%	.296	1.19	3.26	3.92	0.9				
Emilio Vargas	VIS	A+	21	8	5	0	20	19	108	92	7	3.4	11.7	140	40%	.333	1.23	2.50	4.03	1.6				
	WTN	AA	21	1	3	0	6	6	35²	31	6	2.0	7.6	30	44%	.243	1.09	4.04	3.77	0.7				

Once upon a time, **Jake Barrett** looked like a bullpen fixture, but he did little to convince the Diamondbacks that he truly belongs. With just one minor-league option remaining, Barrett is running out of time to prove he's worthy of a 25-man roster spot. ⊗ **Randall Delgado**'s season was weird. He spent the first half continuing his recovery from shoulder and oblique injuries, made seven MLB appearances, was DFA'd, eventually re-signed, got sent to the minors and reappeared in the majors when rosters expanded. His issues, however, remained consistent: an inability to throw strikes and a penchant for giving up homers. ⊗ **Joseph Krehbiel** finally got his cup of coffee after a minor-league career full of decent seasons. He can run it up into the upper 90s, but it's a flat-ish fastball and the secondaries lack much depth. He appears destined for up-and-down work. ⊗ Swingman **Artie Lewicki** will miss all of 2019 following his second Tommy John surgery. ⊗ **Matt Mercer**'s pro debut flew under the radar after his fifth-round selection from the state of Oregon's second-best program. Pitching as a starter on a short leash, the delivery has some effort and violence to it. In the Northwest League playoffs he was running the heater up to 98, showing a get-me-over curve and flashing a good changeup. ⊗ **Jared Miller** is a poster boy for the "minor league relievers are hard to predict" movement. He looked like a real Dude for the vast majority of 2016 and 2017, before 2018 rolled around and he basically fell flat on his face. The hulking lefty has a lot to keep in check in the mechanics department and refinement is needed. ⊗ The "other" **Cody Reed** remains an enigma. The former second-round pick has posted up-and-down results without any semblance of stability as the scouting reports haven't matched the occasionally great stats. He missed all of 2018 with injury and the lefty will almost surely be moved to relief. ⊗ Looking for one New Englander who didn't love Alex Cora's managerial debut? Try LOOGY **Robby Scott**, who spent almost all year stuck in Pawtucket thanks to a roster crunch and spotty command. ⊗ **Braden Shipley**, a 2013 first-round pick, had a dismal 2018. He transitioned to a relief role and couldn't find any traction. He still fails to strike batters out while giving away too many free passes and round trips. It's hard to see how he fits, or rather *if* he fits at all. ⊗ **Matt Tabor** is an intelligent pitcher with some projection remaining. The projection is important because the stuff, in its current form, isn't exciting. He routinely sat 89-92 with inconsistent secondaries. He was able to generate some easy ground-ball outs, however, and was rarely hit hard. ⊗ **Emilio Vargas** was the California League pitcher of the year and his development as a pitcher, rather than a thrower, paid dividends. He can touch 96 when really humping it and mixes his secondaries (a slider and change) well. A jump to Double-A didn't go as smoothly, but there's hope here for a back-end starter.

ATLANTA BRAVES

Essay by Craig Calcaterra

Player comments by David Lee and BP staff

In 1997, I was a 24-year-old summer clerk at a law firm. I was between my second and third year of law school and, if I impressed the right people and didn't mess up that summer, I would probably get an offer for a full-time gig following graduation. It was the most pressure I had ever been under.

I worked hard that summer, but I also walked on eggshells for three months, desperately trying not to give the extraordinarily uptight partners at the firm a reason to hate me and tell me to pound sand come mid-August. Two weeks before the end of my clerkship, the firm's managing partner hosted a party at his lake house way out of town. All of the firm's lawyers and a good number of important clients would be there. Before the party even got started, however, I was certain that I had blown it.

I had blown it because the party started at seven o'clock and, because I was young and dumb and had grossly overestimated how long it would take to get there, I pulled up at 6:27. By the time I realized how early I was, my car had already kicked up a bunch of dust on the long gravel drive leading to the house. I assumed my car had been spotted and, as the only person at the firm who drove a 1987 Chevy Cavalier, they would know it was me. At that point, I figured turning around and high-tailing it out of there was a bad move that would lead to awkward questions later, so I drove on, parked the car and walked sheepishly to the front door. I was certain doom awaited me.

The 2018 Atlanta Braves showed up to the party early, too. Their party was not scheduled to begin until 2019, or maybe even 2020. Like me in 1997, a big reason for the Braves' early arrival was that they were too young to know better.

On May 1, the Braves faced the first-place Mets in New York. On the mound that day, making his big-league debut, was 20-year-old Mike Soroka. At second base and leading off was 21-year-old Ozzie Albies. In left field and batting second was 20-year-old Ronald Acuna Jr. They were, on that day, the three youngest players in Major League Baseball. Albies and Acuna combined for three hits. Soroka scattered six hits in six innings of one-run ball, striking out five and walking zero.

BRAVES PROSPECTUS
2018 W-L: 90-72, 1ST IN NL EAST

Pythag	.567	8th	B-Age	27.3	8th
RS/G	4.69	9th	P-Age	27.5	10th
RA/G	4.06	9th	Salary	$118.3M	21st
DRC+	98	12th	M$/MW	$2.5M	26th
DRA	3.91	6th	DL Days	1377	23rd
FIP	3.94	11th	$ on DL	11%	6th
DER	.722	2nd			

400'
385'   375'
335'   325'

- Opened 2017
- Open air
- Natural surface
- Fence profile: 6' to 16'

Three-Year Park Factors

Runs	Runs/RH	Runs/LH	HR/RH	HR/LH
101	99	104	89	96

Top Hitter WARP	4.0 Freddie Freeman
Top Pitcher WARP	4.0 Anibal Sanchez
Top Prospect	Ian Anderson

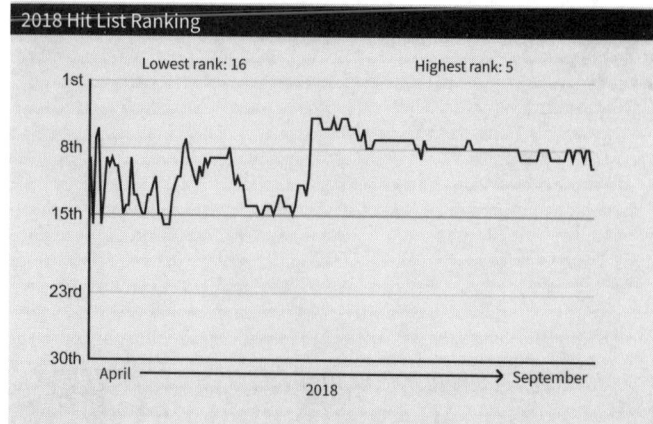

2018 Hit List Ranking

Lowest rank: 16   Highest rank: 5

April — 2018 → September

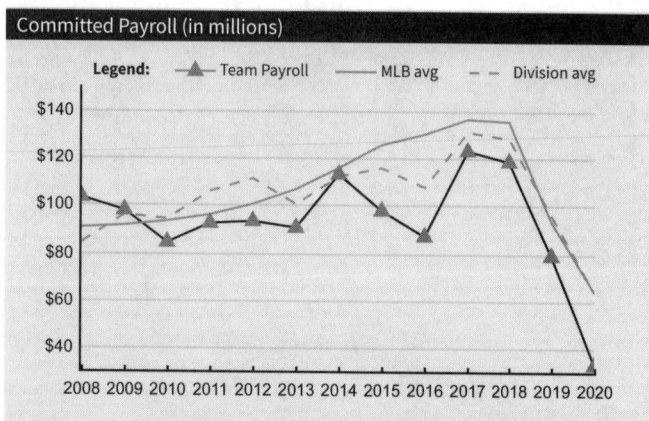

Committed Payroll (in millions)

Legend: —▲— Team Payroll   —— MLB avg   - - Division avg

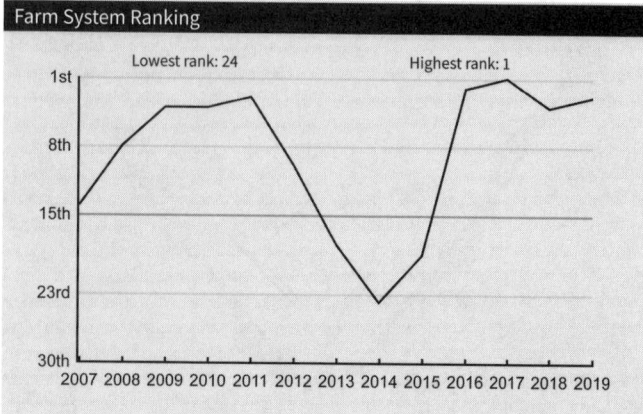

Farm System Ranking

Lowest rank: 24   Highest rank: 1

Personnel

Vice Chairman, Emeritus
John Schuerholz

Executive Vice President, General Manager
Alex Anthopoulos

Assistant General Manager, Research and Development
Jason Pare

VP, Baseball Operations & Assistant GM
Perry Minasian

Special Assistant to the General Manager
Mike Fast

Manager
Brian Snitker

BP Alumni
Mike Fast
Jason Paré
Ronit Shah
Noah Woodward

Soroka and the Braves won, 3-2. They beat the Mets again the next day and, for the first time all season, took first place for themselves.

The Braves played 133 more games after that, beginning 105 of them in first place or tied for it. Injuries kept Soroka from playing a big role, but Acuna and Albies certainly did, and they were joined as key contributors by 24-year-old Johan Camargo, 24-year-old A.J. Minter and 25-year-old Sean Newcomb. Atlanta won the division—arriving at the party too early—thanks in large part to those eager young go-getters who combined for nearly 12.0 WARP on a team that improved by 18 games, flipping their record from 72-90 to 90-72.

One key difference between the Braves in 2018 and me in 1997: It's good to get to the party early in baseball.

When the partner's wife opened the door to the lake house, spying the worst of all social creatures—an early party guest—something unexpected happened: she smiled. She was happy to see me because a lightbulb had burnt out in the fixture way up high in the foyer. She was too unsteady to climb 15 feet up a ladder to change it and she wasn't wild about her 60-something-year-old husband, my boss, doing it either. She directed me to the ladder in the garage and thanked me after I changed the bulb. When I got down, she asked if I'd help her handle a couple of other last-minute details.

While being treated as the help rather than as a guest may have irked some people, it saved me awkwardness and helped ingratiate me to the wife of the man who held my professional future in his hands. I was thrilled. I was impossibly lucky. The 2018 Braves were pretty lucky themselves, and not just because they had the good fortune of young stars performing right out of the gate. They were lucky in that several established players—meaning "players who had established themselves as not particularly valuable in recent years"—wildly exceeded expectations.

In 2017, Nick Markakis and Anibal Sanchez combined for -0.4 WARP, worse than replacement level. In 2018, they combined for 7.4 WARP, a pair of All-Star-caliber seasons. Meanwhile, two prominent young major leaguers, Dansby Swanson and Mike Foltynewicz, took big steps forward, combining for 6.3 WARP after mostly dragging the team down in 2017. To go from 90 losses to 90 wins, you need to catch a lot of breaks, and having four players—two afterthought veterans and two youngsters on the verge of bust status—take such significant leaps forward was a huge break.

After the bulb had been changed and the other tasks attended to, thankfully more guests began to show up to the party. Included in that group were the other four law clerks in my class that summer. I generally liked them, but one was kind of a problem. He was smart as a whip—he went to a way better law school than I did—but he was disorganized. He often rolled into the office late. He drank a bit too much at social functions and didn't always handle it well. He often gave off a vibe that suggested he believed he belonged at a more prestigious firm. Law clerks at that firm had no idea how many clerks would get permanent job offers, so we knew that we were in competition with each other. When I met this guy back in June, I figured his brains and credentials would bury me, but his self-sabotage allowed me to breathe a little bit easier.

The Washington Nationals were that law clerk in the 2018 NL East. They were loaded with talent and everyone reasonably assumed they'd run away with the division like some Ivy League-pedigreed summer law clerk. That didn't happen, with a new, often out-of-his-depth manager substituting for my fellow clerk's disorganization, their considerable injuries substituting for his excessive drinking, and their poor depth, bullpen issues and catching woes filling in for his late arrivals and snooty attitude. For the Braves it was even easier than that, though: Whereas the other three law clerks were good people and hard workers, Atlanta had to deal with only the Mets, Marlins and Phillies.

I'll drop this comparison now and cut to the end: I got an offer at the firm, although I don't know for certain if my good luck and my changing a lightbulb made up for my youthful *faux pas*. Mr. Ivy League ended up not getting a job offer that summer, but I'm not sure if him face-planting was the difference between me securing employment and scrambling for a job during my third year. I am comfortable saying that some combination of my hard work and those things were a part of me landing the gig, and that I'd always rather combine my hard work with good fortune than have to rely on my hard work alone.

Stuff happens that's out of your control sometimes, for bad and for good. Take any edge you can get. But what does that mean for the 2019 Atlanta Braves? They can certainly count on youth and talent again. Indeed, what we saw from them in that regard in 2018 was only the beginning, with more prospect waves on the way.

Right-hander Touki Toussaint, an afterthought of a prospect for a couple years, re-emerged in 2018 and is still just 22. Luiz Gohara faltered due to injury, personal struggles and lack of conditioning last year, but is said to have gotten into much better shape this offseason and seems poised to reclaim his status as a high-upside lefty. Right-hander Ian Anderson, the no. 3 pick in the 2016 draft, impressed moving up to Double-A as a 20-year-old. Soroka's shoulder issues are scary, but if healthy he's poised to help the rotation. Then there's Kyle Wright. There's Max Fried. There's a bunch of other guys. Pitching prospects will break your heart, but the Braves have such a mess of them that they can withstand some heartbreak and still be in great shape.

The good luck and the opposition doing themselves in again are another matter.

Acuna is a superstar in the making, so the Braves can reasonably expect him to continue to bring the thunder. Indeed, they can expect him to improve. Albies tailed off in the second half last year, but even if he's not quite the threat he looked to be early, second base is sorted for years. Swanson remains less of a hitter than many expected him to be when he was a prospect, but he took major defensive strides in 2018, sorting shortstop as well. Foltynewicz took the step forward long expected of him last year, making the All-Star team at 26. The young core—plus perennial MVP candidate Freddie Freeman, of course—has Atlanta positioned nicely for the foreseeable future.

But it'll take more than that core for the Braves to repeat as NL East champs, especially if the Phillies improve, the Nationals stop shooting themselves in the foot, and the Mets get semi-serious about contending. That's where Josh Donaldson comes in. Even while batting injuries in recent years the former MVP has been an impact player, and Donaldson's one-year, $23 million deal was the biggest upside play available to the Braves this offseason without having to add another comma to a contract offer. If healthy, or even mostly healthy, Donaldson will dramatically elevate the lineup with his power and, just as importantly, his plate discipline.

Braves batters swung early and often in 2018, seeing the fourth-fewest pitches per plate appearance and swinging at the third-most pitches outside the strike zone. Among NL teams, only the Pirates, Padres, Marlins and Giants—combined record of 284-362—drew fewer walks. Those early swings weren't all bad, as the Braves had one of the lowest strikeout rates in the league and that aggressiveness led to plenty of homers and doubles—it's a big reason Albies had such a hot first half, for instance—but the lineup's lack of patience was glaringly obvious in the NLDS loss to the Dodgers.

Dodgers batters took borderline pitches over and over again, extending plate appearances and forcing the Braves' young pitchers to work hard for their outs. Meanwhile, the Braves' hitters hacked their way out of potential run-scoring opportunities over and over again. Everything that went right for the Braves all season unraveled over the course of the four-game series. It was as if a better, more experienced team was showing them everything they'd have to become in order to not be one-season wonders. In the end, it caused the Braves to leave the party early. Which, in baseball, is far worse than arriving at the party too early. ■

—Craig Calcaterra is the lead baseball writer at NBC Sports.

HITTERS

Ronald Acuna LF   Born: 12/18/97   Age: 21   Bats: R   Throws: R   Height: 6'0"   Weight: 180   Origin: International Free Agent, 2014

YEAR	TEAM	LVL	AGE	PA	R	2B	3B	HR	RBI	BB	K	SB	CS	AVG/OBP/SLG	DRC+	VORP	BABIP	BRR	FRAA	WARP
2016	ROM	A	18	171	27	2	2	4	18	18	28	14	7	.311/.387/.432	112	17.3	.359	2.9	CF(34): 1.0	1.2
2017	BRV	A+	19	126	21	3	5	3	19	8	40	14	3	.287/.336/.478	107	7.4	.411	1.2	CF(19): -1.8, RF(9): 0.1	0.4
2017	MIS	AA	19	243	29	14	1	9	30	18	56	19	11	.326/.374/.520	127	21.7	.396	0.6	CF(34): -1.0, RF(14): -1.4	1.4
2017	GWN	AAA	19	243	38	14	2	9	33	17	48	11	6	.344/.393/.548	130	17.7	.404	0.0	CF(20): 1.7, RF(20): 2.8	2.0
2018	GWN	AAA	20	101	9	2	0	1	3	11	25	5	1	.211/.297/.267	86	-2.2	.281	1.0	LF(18): -3.1, CF(2): -0.6	-0.2
2018	ATL	MLB	20	487	78	26	4	26	64	45	123	16	5	.293/.366/.552	129	48.0	.352	3.1	LF(101): -10.8, CF(13): 1.0	2.4
2019	*ATL*	*MLB*	*21*	*675*	*103*	*32*	*4*	*28*	*83*	*57*	*159*	*25*	*10*	*.262/.332/.466*	*117*	*35.5*	*.310*	*1.7*	*RF -1, CF 0*	*3.5*

Breakout: 11%   Improve: 49%   Collapse: 8%   Attrition: 14%   MLB: 73%   *Comparables: Mike Trout, Bryce Harper, Jason Heyward*

When Acuna was 18 years old and getting his first full season underway, he showed up to Augusta's old ballpark for an April series. There were whispers about his abilities from those who saw him in short-season leagues, but there was little public knowledge about the former $100,000 signee. He proceeded to hit batting-practice tank after tank out of one of the most pitcher-friendly parks in professional baseball. The actions were explosive, the bat speed was plus, he tracked pitches at an advanced level and he got down the line with plus times. Scouts who saw him that year knew what he would become, and they knew it would happen quickly. It's already happening. Sure, Acuna won Rookie of the Year at 20, two years removed from that first full season. But it's just a stepping stone. He's already one of the best players in the game and is on his way to playing at an MVP level. Scouts love baseball. It's why they travel the majority of the year and spend most of their lives behind home plate. When an Acuna comes through, it makes all those long, summer nights breeze by. The Braves have a generational talent on their hands.

Ozzie Albies 2B   Born: 01/07/97   Age: 22   Bats: B   Throws: R   Height: 5'8"   Weight: 165   Origin: International Free Agent, 2013

YEAR	TEAM	LVL	AGE	PA	R	2B	3B	HR	RBI	BB	K	SB	CS	AVG/OBP/SLG	DRC+	VORP	BABIP	BRR	FRAA	WARP
2016	GWN	AAA	19	247	27	11	3	2	20	19	39	9	4	.248/.307/.351	94	4.9	.290	1.1	SS(33): 1.5, 2B(23): 2.3	1.3
2016	MIS	AA	19	371	56	22	7	4	33	33	57	21	9	.321/.391/.467	126	44.7	.376	4.5	2B(60): 3.3, SS(22): 2.9	3.6
2017	GWN	AAA	20	448	67	21	8	9	41	28	90	21	2	.285/.330/.440	111	28.0	.342	3.3	2B(82): 3.8, SS(14): -2.0	2.5
2017	ATL	MLB	20	244	34	9	5	6	28	21	36	8	1	.286/.354/.456	115	14.2	.316	0.6	2B(57): -2.9	1.0
2018	ATL	MLB	21	684	105	40	5	24	72	36	116	14	3	.261/.305/.452	103	32.5	.285	5.9	2B(157): 7.0	3.8
2019	*ATL*	*MLB*	*22*	*632*	*84*	*33*	*5*	*20*	*71*	*37*	*109*	*17*	*4*	*.264/.314/.441*	*106*	*28.9*	*.293*	*3.1*	*2B 6*	*3.7*

Breakout: 4%   Improve: 61%   Collapse: 3%   Attrition: 8%   MLB: 88%   *Comparables: Rougned Odor, Addison Russell, Xander Bogaerts*

Albies is far from being 6-foot-1, but he is tons of fun. He's a little guy who hits bombs with massive lift. What more could you want out of life? Add blazing speed, big hair and a helmet that flies off his head every time he's on the basepaths, and you have a winner, Bobby. Albies transformed from a slap-hitting speedster who might hit eighth to a launch-angle champion who's going to post 20-20 seasons. It's crazy to look at his home run totals by season and see how quickly he's changed, but it's proof of his aptitude at the plate. The bat is an extension of his body, it seems. The league caught up to him over the course of 158 games and started going up the ladder with success, but Albies has a potential plus hit tool.

Johan Camargo 3B   Born: 12/13/93   Age: 25   Bats: B   Throws: R   Height: 6'0"   Weight: 195   Origin: International Free Agent, 2010

YEAR	TEAM	LVL	AGE	PA	R	2B	3B	HR	RBI	BB	K	SB	CS	AVG/OBP/SLG	DRC+	VORP	BABIP	BRR	FRAA	WARP
2016	MIS	AA	22	491	46	26	6	4	43	24	82	1	2	.267/.304/.379	90	17.3	.317	1.2	2B(64): 2.5, SS(32): -0.4	1.4
2017	GWN	AAA	23	142	17	9	1	4	20	8	22	1	0	.295/.340/.473	112	9.0	.324	-0.2	SS(31): -6.4, 3B(2): 0.2	0.2
2017	ATL	MLB	23	256	30	21	2	4	27	12	51	0	0	.299/.331/.452	82	16.4	.364	3.0	3B(43): -0.4, SS(26): 0.6	0.7
2018	ATL	MLB	24	524	63	27	1	19	76	51	108	1	1	.272/.349/.457	111	33.7	.315	-1.6	3B(114): -9.8, SS(18): -1.5	1.4
2019	*ATL*	*MLB*	*25*	*561*	*64*	*27*	*2*	*17*	*67*	*45*	*115*	*1*	*0*	*.260/.326/.427*	*100*	*16.7*	*.301*	*0.8*	*LF 0, 3B -2*	*1.4*

Breakout: 2%   Improve: 57%   Collapse: 5%   Attrition: 16%   MLB: 97%   *Comparables: Lonnie Chisenhall, Cheslor Cuthbert, Kyle Seager*

Half a decade ago, Camargo was an aloof teenager who would eventually have to move off shortstop and wasn't getting anywhere with the bat. As Bob Wills told us in black and white many years ago, time changes everything. Camargo turned himself into a major leaguer with hard work and physical growth. His first full season was everything the Braves could've hoped for by getting consistent production at the plate and solid defense at third base. Is he the long-term answer at the position for a first-division team? Perhaps not after Josh Donaldson's arrival on a one-year deal. Can he carve out a long career as at least a super-utility guy or second-division regular? Why not?

Charlie Culberson UT   Born: 04/10/89   Age: 30   Bats: R   Throws: R   Height: 6'0"   Weight: 200   Origin: Round 1, 2007 Draft (#51 overall)

YEAR	TEAM	LVL	AGE	PA	R	2B	3B	HR	RBI	BB	K	SB	CS	AVG/OBP/SLG	DRC+	VORP	BABIP	BRR	FRAA	WARP
2016	OKL	AAA	27	285	32	17	2	4	33	18	61	6	5	.260/.310/.385	69	6.4	.325	-1.1	SS(57): 4.7, 2B(5): 0.5	0.6
2016	LAN	MLB	27	68	6	3	0	1	7	1	13	1	0	.299/.309/.388	81	3.8	.358	1.6	SS(11): -0.9, 2B(10): -0.8	0.1
2017	OKL	AAA	28	414	37	13	4	4	32	26	68	7	3	.250/.299/.336	75	-3.5	.294	-0.6	SS(97): 0.8, 3B(7): 0.9	0.8
2017	LAN	MLB	28	15	0	1	0	0	1	2	4	0	0	.154/.267/.231	79	-1.2	.222	0.0	SS(11): 0.2, 2B(2): 0.0	0.0
2018	ATL	MLB	29	322	47	18	2	12	45	21	85	4	2	.270/.326/.466	91	21.9	.340	2.3	LF(29): -2.1, 3B(20): -4.1	0.1
2019	*ATL*	*MLB*	*30*	*455*	*47*	*20*	*2*	*11*	*51*	*30*	*101*	*6*	*3*	*.246/.302/.386*	*85*	*8.2*	*.296*	*2.3*	*SS 0, 2B 0*	*0.8*

Breakout: 1%   Improve: 24%   Collapse: 14%   Attrition: 33%   MLB: 61%   *Comparables: David Lough, Trevor Crowe, Collin Cowgill*

Besides being a positive addition to the clubhouse and Dansby Swanson's twin, Culberson brought career-best production to Atlanta and became known as "Charlie Clutch." How one individual can come up with so many big moments over a short period of time is beyond reason or understanding. The brain tells us that the better players tend to come up in crucial situations more often because of their overall talent, but the heart tells us to shut up and love the fact that a utility guy can be the star so many times. He even added a career-high in home runs and played every position except catcher and center field last season. Culberson gave up a run in his inning on the mound, but he was probably forgiven.

Josh Donaldson 3B   Born: 12/08/85   Age: 33   Bats: R   Throws: R   Height: 6'1"   Weight: 210   Origin: Round 1, 2007 Draft (#48 overall)

YEAR	TEAM	LVL	AGE	PA	R	2B	3B	HR	RBI	BB	K	SB	CS	AVG/OBP/SLG	DRC+	VORP	BABIP	BRR	FRAA	WARP
2016	TOR	MLB	30	700	122	32	5	37	99	109	119	7	1	.284/.404/.549	147	64.6	.300	4.8	3B(136): -12.6	5.8
2017	TOR	MLB	31	496	65	21	0	33	78	76	111	2	2	.270/.385/.559	139	44.0	.289	1.3	3B(105): -5.9, SS(4): -0.2	3.8
2018	TOR	MLB	32	159	22	11	0	5	16	21	44	2	0	.234/.333/.423	101	4.2	.303	-0.4	3B(26): -0.9, 1B(1): 0.1	0.4
2018	CLE	MLB	32	60	8	3	0	3	7	10	10	0	0	.280/.400/.520	100	3.5	.297	-0.8	3B(12): -0.9	0.0
2019	*ATL*	*MLB*	*33*	*560*	*74*	*24*	*2*	*23*	*79*	*80*	*118*	*4*	*1*	*.254/.366/.461*	*125*	*32.0*	*.291*	*1.5*	*3B -8*	*2.6*

Breakout: 0%   Improve: 25%   Collapse: 2%   Attrition: 3%   MLB: 96%   *Comparables: Kevin Youkilis, George Brett, Chipper Jones*

We all have short memories. Donaldson spent 2013-2017 raining fire on the American League to the tune of .282/.377/.524 with excellent defense at third base. And sure, maybe Mike Trout deserved that MVP award in 2015, but the Bringer of Rain was right there with the elite players in either league. He missed half of 2017 due to injury and in 2018 he lost even more time to the disabled list, and suddenly we forgot he was in the small tier of position players who competed to be silver medalist to Trout in a given year. But, in both 2017 and 2018, he finished strong, hitting like his usual self after his midseason trade to Cleveland. Clearly, there's still top-grade hitting ability in here, so the questions are how often he'll be on the field and what those injuries may do to his ability to stay at third base. Atlanta hopes a one-year, $23 million bet pays off in a huge way.

Lucas Duda 1B   Born: 02/03/86   Age: 33   Bats: L   Throws: R   Height: 6'4"   Weight: 255   Origin: Round 7, 2007 Draft (#243 overall)

YEAR	TEAM	LVL	AGE	PA	R	2B	3B	HR	RBI	BB	K	SB	CS	AVG/OBP/SLG	DRC+	VORP	BABIP	BRR	FRAA	WARP
2016	NYN	MLB	30	172	20	7	0	7	23	15	36	0	0	.229/.302/.412	98	6.3	.250	0.7	1B(45): -3.4	0.0
2017	NYN	MLB	31	291	30	21	0	17	37	37	73	0	0	.246/.347/.532	114	13.1	.278	-3.4	1B(69): -1.7	0.5
2017	TBA	MLB	31	200	20	7	0	13	27	23	62	0	0	.175/.285/.444	104	0.3	.173	0.1	1B(24): -0.2	0.4
2018	KCA	MLB	32	345	34	12	1	13	48	24	95	1	0	.242/.310/.413	101	-0.1	.302	-2.4	1B(61): 2.4	0.6
2018	ATL	MLB	32	22	1	2	0	1	2	4	7	0	0	.222/.364/.500	96	0.7	.300	-0.6	1B(2): -0.7	-0.1
2019	*ATL*	*MLB*	*33*	*376*	*44*	*19*	*1*	*15*	*51*	*35*	*94*	*1*	*0*	*.246/.328/.443*	*108*	*7.7*	*.300*	*-1.6*	*1B 0*	*0.8*

Breakout: 1%   Improve: 36%   Collapse: 3%   Attrition: 9%   MLB: 93%   *Comparables: Andruw Jones, Pat Burrell, Adam LaRoche*

For years, Braves organist Matthew Kaminski played "Camptown Races" when Duda came to the plate in Atlanta. Duda was once quoted as saying it stopped being funny after the 300th time he heard it. He got some relief in August when he was dealt to the Braves and could pick his own music at SunTrust Park. He also did his part in Atlanta by offering some power off the bench, something the team needed down the stretch for its playoff push. Duda's days of mashing full time at first base are probably over, but his left-handed power can come in handy off the bench for teams and keep his career going a while longer. Five miles long? Somebody bet on the bay.

Adam Duvall LF   Born: 09/04/88   Age: 30   Bats: R   Throws: R   Height: 6'1"   Weight: 215   Origin: Round 11, 2010 Draft (#348 overall)

YEAR	TEAM	LVL	AGE	PA	R	2B	3B	HR	RBI	BB	K	SB	CS	AVG/OBP/SLG	DRC+	VORP	BABIP	BRR	FRAA	WARP
2016	CIN	MLB	27	608	85	31	6	33	103	41	164	6	5	.241/.297/.498	107	24.5	.275	-3.8	LF(137): 11.9, RF(6): -1.1	3.0
2017	CIN	MLB	28	647	78	37	3	31	99	39	170	5	3	.249/.301/.480	99	25.1	.290	-2.2	LF(151): 6.7, 1B(3): 0.0	2.1
2018	CIN	MLB	29	370	40	19	0	15	61	34	100	2	2	.205/.286/.399	86	3.1	.244	-0.6	LF(89): 6.9, 1B(10): 0.3	1.0
2018	ATL	MLB	29	57	8	1	0	0	0	3	17	0	0	.132/.193/.151	86	-4.2	.194	0.6	LF(12): 0.0, RF(2): 0.0	0.1
2019	*ATL*	*MLB*	*30*	*414*	*46*	*21*	*1*	*15*	*53*	*30*	*108*	*3*	*2*	*.234/.301/.416*	*91*	*6.1*	*.289*	*-1.1*	*LF 3, RF -1*	*0.9*

Breakout: 3%   Improve: 44%   Collapse: 9%   Attrition: 16%   MLB: 94%   *Comparables: Scott Hairston, Ryan Raburn, Rick Ankiel*

The Braves added Duvall in July to hit against lefties and offer some power off the bench on other days. It seemed like a good idea at the time, because his numbers suggested he was unlucky and would see a second-half turnaround. For that to work, he needed to hit, and he never hit. Instead, he kept doing what he was doing in Cincinnati and ended with a rather meager set of stats. His BABIP and batted-ball numbers say he was simply unlucky. He kept hitting baseballs hard and actually started walking more, but nothing fell for him when he found the barrel. He's a low-risk, medium-reward type going forward as someone who could see a slight bounceback. Don't call it a comeback.

Ryan Flaherty 3B   Born: 07/27/86   Age: 32   Bats: L   Throws: R   Height: 6'3"   Weight: 220   Origin: Round 1, 2008 Draft (#41 overall)

YEAR	TEAM	LVL	AGE	PA	R	2B	3B	HR	RBI	BB	K	SB	CS	AVG/OBP/SLG	DRC+	VORP	BABIP	BRR	FRAA	WARP
2016	BAL	MLB	29	176	16	7	0	3	15	17	48	2	0	.217/.291/.318	66	-0.7	.290	1.0	3B(40): 1.0, SS(13): -0.4	0.0
2017	BOW	AA	30	49	18	3	0	2	6	10	3	0	0	.395/.531/.632	147	7.8	.394	1.3	2B(4): -0.2, 3B(4): 0.1	0.6
2017	BAL	MLB	30	43	5	1	0	0	4	4	10	0	0	.211/.302/.237	80	0.5	.286	0.7	2B(12): 0.0, 3B(5): -0.6	0.1
2018	GWN	AAA	31	32	3	1	0	0	4	1	9	0	0	.267/.313/.300	74	0.5	.381	0.2	2B(3): -0.1, SS(2): 0.9	0.1
2018	ATL	MLB	31	182	17	6	0	2	13	18	41	4	2	.217/.298/.292	69	-1.0	.277	1.9	3B(40): -0.4, 1B(7): -0.1	0.1
2019	*ATL*	*MLB*	*32*	*251*	*25*	*10*	*1*	*5*	*23*	*22*	*60*	*3*	*1*	*.223/.301/.336*	*79*	*0.8*	*.281*	*1.4*	*3B -1, 1B 0*	*0.0*

Breakout: 5%   Improve: 43%   Collapse: 11%   Attrition: 15%   MLB: 88%   *Comparables: Ossie Bluege, Pinky Higgins, Chris Woodward*

The Braves picked up Flaherty for utility but instead got futility. Expectations surely weren't that high to begin with considering he hit as the same pace as every other season since 2012. Credit to the former first-rounder, though, for carving out a career and having the ability to play all over the field at a solid level. He'll probably keep filling holes for second-division teams until they no longer call him in the offseason.

Tyler Flowers C
Born: 01/24/86   Age: 33   Bats: R   Throws: R   Height: 6'4"   Weight: 260   Origin: Round 33, 2005 Draft (#1007 overall)

YEAR	TEAM	LVL	AGE	PA	R	2B	3B	HR	RBI	BB	K	SB	CS	AVG/OBP/SLG	DRC+	VORP	BABIP	BRR	FRAA	WARP
2016	ATL	MLB	30	325	27	18	0	8	41	29	91	0	0	.270/.357/.420	92	19.9	.366	-6.4	C(81): 6.5	1.4
2017	ATL	MLB	31	370	41	16	0	12	49	31	82	0	1	.281/.378/.445	113	35.8	.342	-0.2	C(85): 29.5	5.4
2018	ATL	MLB	32	296	34	9	0	8	30	35	76	0	0	.227/.341/.359	100	14.3	.292	0.3	C(76): 13.2	2.9
2019	ATL	MLB	33	377	42	17	1	10	43	35	95	0	0	.241/.349/.387	105	17.1	.321	-1.7	C 19	3.8

Breakout: 2%   Improve: 37%   Collapse: 11%   Attrition: 28%   MLB: 92%

Comparables: John Buck, Mike Macfarlane, Geovany Soto

YEAR	TEAM	P. COUNT	FRM RUNS	BLK RUNS	THRW RUNS	TOT RUNS
2016	ATL	11338	13.3	-0.8	-4.4	8.1
2017	ATL	12424	32.0	-0.8	-1.1	30.1
2018	ATL	10185	13.7	-0.4	-0.2	13.0
2019	ATL	12398	21.6	-0.8	-1.1	19.6

Watching Flowers frame behind the plate may not be Rembrandt level, but it's a work of art nonetheless. His receiving skills are what young catchers dream of attaining. He quietly had two very good seasons in 2016-2017 before the bat slowed a touch last season. Pitchers recognized it and attacked him with heat more often, causing him to lose some aggressiveness on pitches within the zone. That helped his walk rate tremendously, but didn't do much for his barrel awareness. Regardless, there's more than enough in the tank to contribute as a quality backup catcher in the future, and he's a good one to have for a young pitching staff.

Freddie Freeman 1B
Born: 09/12/89   Age: 29   Bats: L   Throws: R   Height: 6'5"   Weight: 220   Origin: Round 2, 2007 Draft (#78 overall)

YEAR	TEAM	LVL	AGE	PA	R	2B	3B	HR	RBI	BB	K	SB	CS	AVG/OBP/SLG	DRC+	VORP	BABIP	BRR	FRAA	WARP
2016	ATL	MLB	26	693	102	43	6	34	91	89	171	6	1	.302/.400/.569	140	69.6	.370	-0.9	1B(158): -2.9	4.2
2017	ATL	MLB	27	514	84	35	2	28	71	65	95	8	5	.307/.403/.586	143	53.6	.335	2.7	1B(105): -1.2, 3B(16): -2.4	3.6
2018	ATL	MLB	28	707	94	44	4	23	98	76	132	10	3	.309/.388/.505	131	52.8	.358	-1.7	1B(161): 3.5	4.0
2019	ATL	MLB	29	614	85	35	3	25	90	74	126	8	3	.286/.383/.507	142	40.6	.336	-0.1	1B 0	4.4

Breakout: 3%   Improve: 65%   Collapse: 1%   Attrition: 3%   MLB: 97%

Comparables: Mark Teixeira, Adrian Gonzalez, Joey Votto

Few in baseball deserve what could be an impending run of success for the Braves more than Freeman, who stuck through the lean years despite consistently offering monster production. There were times during the rebuild when no one had any business watching Atlanta's lineup except the four or so times he came to the plate each night. (It was usually four because it's not like his teammates hit enough to get to him more often.) Now, he's loving life in the middle of a lineup that features power, speed and on-base ability around him. If he stays healthy, it should only help his production as he continues to rake through his prime years. The wrist continues to be in the back of everyone's minds and has sapped some of his power lately, but he's still the same .300 hitter capable of anchoring a postseason lineup, probably with a better mood these days.

Ender Inciarte CF
Born: 10/29/90   Age: 28   Bats: L   Throws: L   Height: 5'11"   Weight: 190   Origin: International Free Agent, 2008

YEAR	TEAM	LVL	AGE	PA	R	2B	3B	HR	RBI	BB	K	SB	CS	AVG/OBP/SLG	DRC+	VORP	BABIP	BRR	FRAA	WARP
2016	ATL	MLB	25	578	85	24	7	3	29	45	68	16	7	.291/.351/.381	97	26.2	.329	0.4	CF(120): 20.9, LF(10): 3.3	4.4
2017	ATL	MLB	26	718	93	27	5	11	57	49	94	22	9	.304/.350/.409	102	35.6	.339	5.4	CF(156): 10.4	4.4
2018	ATL	MLB	27	660	83	27	6	10	61	49	86	28	14	.265/.325/.380	96	25.3	.293	2.3	CF(155): 9.6	3.3
2019	ATL	MLB	28	590	67	28	5	10	61	42	76	20	9	.282/.337/.408	106	29.0	.309	1.7	CF 12	4.3

Breakout: 6%   Improve: 48%   Collapse: 4%   Attrition: 5%   MLB: 96%

Comparables: Harvey Kuenn, Tom Oliver, Curt Flood

Inciarte saw the last of his days atop any sort of Atlanta lineup, but that's more the result of a better team than his own doing. Put simply, he's a second-division leadoff guy who should hit at the bottom of the order for a playoff team. Unlike your typical box of chocolates, you know what you're getting with Inciarte as a fringe-average hitter with plus speed and plus defense in center field. There's good value in that, but it tends to get overshadowed when you promote a player like Ronald Acuna Jr. Regardless of his future lineup spot or home, Inciarte should offer plenty more years of high-level defense, speed and decent on-base ability.

Ryan LaMarre CF
Born: 11/21/88   Age: 30   Bats: R   Throws: L   Height: 6'1"   Weight: 210   Origin: Round 2, 2010 Draft (#62 overall)

YEAR	TEAM	LVL	AGE	PA	R	2B	3B	HR	RBI	BB	K	SB	CS	AVG/OBP/SLG	DRC+	VORP	BABIP	BRR	FRAA	WARP
2016	BOS	MLB	27	6	1	0	0	0	0	1	2	0	0	.000/.167/.000	100	-1.2	.000	-0.1	LF(2): -0.1, RF(1): -0.1	0.0
2016	PAW	AAA	27	358	44	15	0	10	41	28	80	17	6	.303/.369/.445	114	23.6	.371	0.3	CF(46): 2.1, RF(31): 0.6	2.0
2017	SLC	AAA	28	48	6	1	1	0	7	6	11	4	1	.268/.375/.341	67	1.6	.367	0.3	LF(4): 0.4, CF(3): -0.2	0.0
2017	OAK	MLB	28	8	0	0	0	0	0	1	3	0	0	.000/.125/.000	60	-1.2	.000	0.0	CF(3): -0.3	0.0
2017	NAS	AAA	28	146	11	2	2	0	12	11	47	5	5	.240/.313/.287	56	-0.8	.373	-0.8	CF(24): 3.0, RF(10): 0.8	0.0
2018	MIN	MLB	29	109	7	5	0	0	8	8	33	1	1	.263/.321/.313	70	-0.8	.388	-0.5	CF(34): -2.8, LF(3): -0.4	-0.4
2018	ROC	AAA	29	54	5	4	1	0	5	5	15	1	0	.313/.389/.438	70	2.8	.455	-0.4	CF(5): 0.8, RF(5): -0.5	-0.1
2018	CHR	AAA	29	50	7	2	2	0	2	4	14	2	0	.222/.286/.356	69	-1.0	.323	0.0	RF(8): 1.5, LF(1): -0.1	0.0
2018	CHA	MLB	29	71	8	6	0	2	10	2	20	1	1	.303/.324/.485	67	4.0	.391	0.5	LF(26): 2.5, RF(4): -0.2	0.2
2019	ATL	MLB	30	90	9	3	0	1	8	7	26	2	1	.215/.283/.318	45	-3.0	.293	0.0	CF 0, RF 0	-0.3

Breakout: 2%   Improve: 4%   Collapse: 9%   Attrition: 17%   MLB: 31%

Comparables: Jason Repko, Bubba Crosby, George Lombard

The story told to LaMarre after the 29-year-old finally launched his first big-league home run, and in his home state of Michigan no less, was that one of his uncles in the stands caught the ball. While plenty of the LaMarre clan were in attendance, the truth is that his uncle had merely purchased the ball from the person who caught it, which in America basically means he caught himself. But another cold economic reality of this country is that right-handed-hitting fourth outfielders at his age must tolerate a transient existence. Despite a couple of banner performances in front of packed houses in Yankee Stadium and in the Crosstown series against the Cubs that surely made climbing through nine years in the minors and six different organizations feel worth it, LaMarre figures to have to scratch and claw for his next regular big-league opportunity.

Nick Markakis RF Born: 11/17/83 Age: 35 Bats: L Throws: L Height: 6'1" Weight: 210 Origin: Round 1, 2003 Draft (#7 overall)

YEAR	TEAM	LVL	AGE	PA	R	2B	3B	HR	RBI	BB	K	SB	CS	AVG/OBP/SLG	DRC+	VORP	BABIP	BRR	FRAA	WARP
2016	ATL	MLB	32	684	67	38	0	13	89	71	101	0	2	.269/.346/.397	103	19.6	.300	-3.1	RF(150): -3.1, 1B(1): 0.1	1.2
2017	ATL	MLB	33	670	76	39	1	8	76	68	110	0	2	.275/.354/.384	94	20.7	.324	2.1	RF(156): -9.0	0.4
2018	ATL	MLB	34	705	78	43	2	14	93	72	80	1	1	.297/.366/.440	115	33.7	.318	-1.6	RF(158): 6.9, LF(3): -0.4	3.4
2019	ATL	MLB	35	658	66	35	2	11	70	66	98	1	1	.269/.348/.394	103	20.3	.307	-0.4	RF -1, LF 0	2.0

Breakout: 1%   Improve: 28%   Collapse: 5%   Attrition: 18%   MLB: 78%   *Comparables: Taffy Wright, Billy Southworth, Tommy Griffith*

The Greek God of Woodstock, Ga. (that's not a thing, by the way) revitalized his career at age 34 and became the new poster child for the notion of a contract year. Not since 2012 has Markakis hit like he did last season, and he did it when most people had already written him off as a future backup or second-division regular. He actually posted the best hard-hit rate and second-highest line-drive rate of his career, which is crazy to think about at his age. He maintained a 10 percent walk rate and even dropped his strikeout totals to the point of almost walking more than he whiffed, something else that's unheard of now. It truly was the Markakis of old, and it was appropriate for the final year of a contract that served the Braves well, mostly off the field as a good clubhouse example for a young group.

Brian McCann C Born: 02/20/84 Age: 35 Bats: L Throws: R Height: 6'3" Weight: 225 Origin: Round 2, 2002 Draft (#64 overall)

YEAR	TEAM	LVL	AGE	PA	R	2B	3B	HR	RBI	BB	K	SB	CS	AVG/OBP/SLG	DRC+	VORP	BABIP	BRR	FRAA	WARP
2016	NYA	MLB	32	492	56	13	0	20	58	54	99	1	0	.242/.335/.413	111	11.7	.269	-3.9	C(92): 12.8, 1B(3): -0.6	3.6
2017	HOU	MLB	33	399	47	12	1	18	62	38	58	1	0	.241/.323/.436	110	19.2	.237	-0.2	C(95): -2.6	2.2
2018	HOU	MLB	34	216	22	3	0	7	23	19	40	0	1	.212/.301/.339	98	4.0	.229	-1.5	C(62): -3.4	0.5
2019	ATL	MLB	35	259	30	12	1	8	31	24	45	0	0	.252/.335/.414	107	12.4	.285	-1.0	C -1	1.3

Breakout: 1%   Improve: 31%   Collapse: 9%   Attrition: 22%   MLB: 87%   *Comparables: Ramon Hernandez, Ron Hassey, Mike Lieberthal*

YEAR	TEAM	P. COUNT	FRM RUNS	BLK RUNS	THRW RUNS	TOT RUNS
2016	NYA	12380	11.0	2.7	-0.5	13.2
2017	HOU	13673	1.4	-0.4	-2.5	-1.7
2018	HOU	7671	-3.0	-1.4	0.1	-4.5
2019	ATL	7734	-0.1	0.2	-0.6	-0.6

If Brian McCann were a material object, he would be a "Don't Tread On Me" flag. If Brian McCann were a baseball player, he'd be an aging catcher/designated hitter winding down a sizable career that should land him in the Hall of Very Good. There's no reason to believe that he can't be both. McCann brings his McCann-ness back to Atlanta on a one-year, $2 million deal, where he'll serve as the Sunday replacement to Tyler Flowers just like so many others provided him in his career. It's a reminder that not only can we go home again, from the dark metaphorical perspective, we have no other choice.

Cristian Pache CF Born: 11/19/98 Age: 20 Bats: R Throws: R Height: 6'2" Weight: 185 Origin: International Free Agent, 2015

YEAR	TEAM	LVL	AGE	PA	R	2B	3B	HR	RBI	BB	K	SB	CS	AVG/OBP/SLG	DRC+	VORP	BABIP	BRR	FRAA	WARP
2016	BRA	RK	17	114	16	2	4	0	11	6	11	7	3	.283/.325/.377	103	1.7	.313	-0.1	CF(25): 7.4, RF(1): 0.1	1.1
2016	DNV	RK	17	122	12	2	3	0	10	7	13	4	2	.333/.372/.404	96	10.1	.376	1.1	CF(27): 10.1, RF(2): -0.8	1.3
2017	ROM	A	18	514	60	13	8	0	42	39	104	32	14	.281/.335/.343	90	22.4	.360	5.8	CF(116): 27.8, RF(2): 0.0	4.5
2018	BRV	A+	19	387	46	20	5	8	40	15	69	7	6	.285/.311/.431	95	14.8	.330	-1.1	CF(93): 3.9	1.3
2018	MIS	AA	19	109	10	3	1	1	7	5	28	0	2	.260/.294/.337	82	-0.6	.347	-0.5	CF(28): 1.3	0.2
2019	ATL	MLB	20	251	22	5	1	6	24	9	62	4	2	.205/.233/.304	44	-7.3	.250	-0.1	CF 6	-0.2

Breakout: 2%   Improve: 7%   Collapse: 0%   Attrition: 3%   MLB: 8%   *Comparables: Anthony Gose, Gorkys Hernandez, Joe Benson*

A kid plays up the middle in center field and has elite potential on defense. OK. He reached Double-A as a 19-year-old and showed developmental signs at the plate. You had my curiosity. Now you have my attention. For a couple years, Pache was the guy with 70- to 80-grade potential as a defender in center but with an unknown future at the plate. He struggled keeping his lower half with him through extension and was often too aggressive. While his approach is still raw, Pache added a leg kick this past season and started to utilize his lower half better to stay with the swing and drive the ball. It's a long and confusing way of saying he's a better hitter now than a couple years ago. If Pache can be even a fringe-average hitter, he'll tap into average power potential and blazing speed to create a monster of a young player. Questions remain and his first full season in the upper levels will tell a lot, but beware, the thought of Pache reaching his potential as an impact up-the-middle player may cause giddy feelings beyond control.

Austin Riley 3B Born: 04/02/97 Age: 22 Bats: R Throws: R Height: 6'3" Weight: 220 Origin: Round 1, 2015 Draft (#41 overall)

YEAR	TEAM	LVL	AGE	PA	R	2B	3B	HR	RBI	BB	K	SB	CS	AVG/OBP/SLG	DRC+	VORP	BABIP	BRR	FRAA	WARP
2016	ROM	A	19	543	68	39	2	20	80	39	147	3	3	.271/.324/.479	124	33.9	.341	-2.6	3B(122): 3.1	3.4
2017	BRV	A+	20	339	43	10	1	12	47	23	74	0	2	.252/.310/.408	122	12.9	.289	-0.4	3B(80): -2.5	1.8
2017	MIS	AA	20	203	28	9	1	8	27	20	50	2	0	.315/.389/.511	128	20.1	.393	-0.5	3B(47): -1.6	1.2
2018	MIS	AA	21	109	17	10	3	6	20	8	28	0	0	.333/.394/.677	121	19.1	.415	1.0	3B(27): 1.2	0.9
2018	GWN	AAA	21	324	41	17	0	12	47	26	95	1	0	.282/.346/.464	117	24.1	.374	1.1	3B(71): -0.3	1.9
2019	ATL	MLB	22	49	5	2	0	2	6	3	16	0	0	.227/.290/.397	82	0.1	.313	-0.1	3B 0	0.0

Breakout: 1%   Improve: 27%   Collapse: 2%   Attrition: 15%   MLB: 47%   *Comparables: Chris Carter, Chris Davis, Andy Marte*

There's no denying what the Braves have felt internally about Riley. The power potential has been obvious and they saw the developmental strides coming for the glove, but they also believed in the bat. The 2018 season was a huge test for his bat and he passed with flying colors. Yes, the strikeouts are high, but Riley showed he belonged in the upper levels, mashing at Double-A before earning a promotion. To add to the positive season, Riley showed more strides at third base, where he's turned himself into someone who can stick there. He's always been a good athlete for his size and he has a plus arm, but his actions and glove have gotten even better. The hit grade should remain on the conservative side, possibly fringe-average potential, but that's a nice step from what it used to be for many scouts. He's now knocking on the door to third base, and that's pretty awesome for a guy who had to work hard just to get to the welcome mat.

Dansby Swanson SS   Born: 02/11/94   Age: 25   Bats: R   Throws: R   Height: 6'1"   Weight: 190   Origin: Round 1, 2015 Draft (#1 overall)

YEAR	TEAM	LVL	AGE	PA	R	2B	3B	HR	RBI	BB	K	SB	CS	AVG/OBP/SLG	DRC+	VORP	BABIP	BRR	FRAA	WARP
2016	CAR	A+	22	93	14	12	0	1	10	15	13	7	1	.333/.441/.526	116	14.9	.391	1.0	SS(21): 1.5	0.8
2016	MIS	AA	22	377	54	13	5	8	45	35	71	6	2	.261/.342/.402	117	29.9	.309	2.0	SS(83): 15.9	4.5
2016	ATL	MLB	22	145	20	7	1	3	17	13	34	3	0	.302/.361/.442	85	13.1	.383	0.8	SS(37): -2.3	0.3
2017	GWN	AAA	23	45	5	1	0	1	5	6	9	1	0	.237/.356/.342	99	1.6	.286	-0.9	SS(9): -0.9, 2B(2): -0.2	0.0
2017	ATL	MLB	23	551	59	23	2	6	51	59	120	3	3	.232/.312/.324	79	13.2	.292	3.2	SS(142): -10.1	0.4
2018	ATL	MLB	24	533	51	25	4	14	59	44	122	10	4	.238/.304/.395	89	22.7	.290	0.9	SS(136): 5.4	2.4
2019	ATL	MLB	25	445	50	20	2	10	46	47	99	6	2	.244/.327/.384	93	14.5	.300	1.4	SS 1	1.6

Breakout: 2%   Improve: 74%   Collapse: 6%   Attrition: 6%   MLB: 100%   *Comparables: Asdrubal Cabrera, Everth Cabrera, Yunel Escobar*

It's safe to say Swanson's major-league career hasn't gone as expected so far, and that continued last season with another inconsistent year at the plate that ended painfully with a torn ligament in his left wrist. It was poor timing for him and caused him to miss the postseason, but offseason surgery is said to have repaired it for 2019. The dashing young shortstop continued to lead the league in handsomeness over replacement level while improving enough at the plate to offer double-digit homers and steals. Combine that with solid defense up the middle and it really wasn't that terrible of a season, but it's not at the level scouts expected when he came out of Vanderbilt. He's going to be 25 years old in 2019 and is on track for further development, so staying on the course on this fellow is a good idea.

Preston Tucker LF   Born: 07/06/90   Age: 28   Bats: L   Throws: L   Height: 6'0"   Weight: 210   Origin: Round 7, 2012 Draft (#219 overall)

YEAR	TEAM	LVL	AGE	PA	R	2B	3B	HR	RBI	BB	K	SB	CS	AVG/OBP/SLG	DRC+	VORP	BABIP	BRR	FRAA	WARP
2016	FRE	AAA	25	229	35	14	3	8	29	15	49	1	1	.301/.349/.512	109	16.9	.355	0.5	RF(25): -4.0, LF(23): -0.3	0.4
2016	HOU	MLB	25	144	11	8	1	4	8	8	40	0	0	.164/.222/.328	64	-6.0	.200	0.2	LF(19): -1.5, RF(3): -0.2	-0.5
2017	FRE	AAA	26	569	84	20	7	24	96	65	102	2	3	.250/.333/.465	119	15.8	.263	-0.9	RF(54): -8.8, LF(35): 3.9	2.0
2018	GWN	AAA	27	62	7	4	1	0	6	2	5	0	0	.250/.274/.350	99	-0.6	.273	0.4	LF(14): 0.1	0.2
2018	CIN	MLB	27	42	4	1	0	2	5	4	9	0	0	.189/.286/.378	90	-0.1	.192	-0.2	LF(10): -2.6	-0.2
2018	ATL	MLB	27	142	15	10	0	4	22	9	34	0	0	.240/.303/.411	81	4.6	.293	0.4	LF(27): 1.2, RF(4): -0.2	0.2
2019	ATL	MLB	28	251	26	11	1	9	31	20	54	0	0	.231/.299/.399	91	4.3	.266	0.1	LF -1, RF 0	0.3

Breakout: 5%   Improve: 30%   Collapse: 13%   Attrition: 29%   MLB: 70%   *Comparables: Ryan Rua, Xavier Paul, Jorge Piedra*

Poor Tucker got thrown back and forth like a middle school dodgeball in P.E. class. He was dealt to Cincinnati in July as part of the Adam Duvall swap, only to be returned to Atlanta in September for cash. He actually didn't hit that badly in his Braves stints and gave them an outfield option they could confidently turn to in a pinch. He is what he is, though, further proof when he was outrighted on Halloween. Tucker is on track to be a useful outfield bench option for years to come, probably for multiple teams. May the yo-yo feeling commence.

PITCHERS

Kolby Allard LHP   Born: 08/13/97   Age: 21   Bats: L   Throws: L   Height: 6'1"   Weight: 190   Origin: Round 1, 2015 Draft (#14 overall)

YEAR	TEAM	LVL	AGE	W	L	SV	G	GS	IP	H	HR	BB/9	K/9	K	GB%	BABIP	WHIP	ERA	DRA	WARP	MPH	FB%	WHF	CSP
2016	DNV	RK	18	3	0	0	5	5	27¹	18	0	1.6	10.9	33	53%	.281	0.84	1.32	2.72	0.9				
2016	ROM	A	18	5	3	0	11	11	60¹	54	5	3.0	9.2	62	38%	.312	1.23	3.73	3.88	0.8				
2017	MIS	AA	19	8	11	0	27	27	150	146	11	2.7	7.7	129	44%	.310	1.27	3.18	3.42	3.1				
2018	ATL	MLB	20	1	1	0	3	1	8	19	3	4.5	3.4	3	36%	.444	2.88	12.38	8.43	-0.3	90.9	62.7	5.6	46.5
2018	GWN	AAA	20	6	4	0	19	19	112¹	102	6	2.7	7.1	89	39%	.296	1.21	2.72	4.71	1.1				
2019	ATL	MLB	21	1	1	0	3	3	15	14	2	3.4	8.1	13	39%	.300	1.32	4.18	4.91	0.1	91.1	65.7	5.9	48.7

Breakout: 4%   Improve: 7%   Collapse: 5%   Attrition: 12%   MLB: 15%   *Comparables: Zach Davies, Jameson Taillon, Will Smith*

Allard had about as much fun in the majors last year as a noseless dog in a manure pile. He got his shot but just couldn't do anything with it. A Braves team, looking for pitching options at that point in the season when everyone needs them, turned to the young left-hander, but he turned into a pumpkin by getting knocked around in three appearances. The stuff was flatter than previously seen, between an upper-80s fastball with little movement, a curveball that didn't show its usual plus depth and a previously plus-potential changeup that was as flat as the fastball. It doesn't elicit confidence, but he did have another strong minor-league season and there is still time for improvement considering he couldn't legally drink until August.

Ian Anderson RHP   Born: 05/02/98   Age: 21   Bats: R   Throws: R   Height: 6'3"   Weight: 170   Origin: Round 1, 2016 Draft (#3 overall)

YEAR	TEAM	LVL	AGE	W	L	SV	G	GS	IP	H	HR	BB/9	K/9	K	GB%	BABIP	WHIP	ERA	DRA	WARP	MPH	FB%	WHF	CSP
2016	BRA	RK	18	1	0	0	5	5	18	14	0	2.0	9.0	18	59%	.304	1.00	0.00	5.04	0.1				
2016	DNV	RK	18	0	2	0	5	5	21²	19	1	3.3	7.5	18	60%	.290	1.25	3.74	3.31	0.6				
2017	ROM	A	19	4	5	0	20	20	83	69	0	4.7	11.0	101	50%	.345	1.35	3.14	4.00	1.2				
2018	BRV	A+	20	2	6	0	20	20	100	73	2	3.6	10.6	118	47%	.282	1.13	2.52	3.25	2.4				
2018	MIS	AA	20	2	1	0	4	4	19¹	14	0	4.2	11.2	24	48%	.304	1.19	2.33	3.14	0.5				
2019	ATL	MLB	21	6	6	0	21	21	94²	83	12	4.7	9.5	100	46%	.301	1.39	4.37	5.12	0.2				

Breakout: 5%   Improve: 19%   Collapse: 5%   Attrition: 13%   MLB: 25%   *Comparables: Chris Tillman, Archie Bradley, Manny Banuelos*

Because the Braves needed more pitching prospects or something, they drafted Anderson third overall in 2016 and developed him into a notable prospect who could be in the majors in short order despite nearing only his 21st birthday. He's your prototypical mid-rotation-potential right-hander with a strong frame, three MLB-potential pitches and enough command to get there. The frame is one to dream on if you dream about projectable pitchers' frames. He gets good downhill plane and extension from his length, and he creates a tough angle with movement on his low-to-mid-90s fastball. The curveball and changeup both flash plus and should sit at least above average. Add average command potential and a strong work ethic, and you have your mid-rotation dude with a no. 2 ceiling.

Jesse Biddle LHP   Born: 10/22/91   Age: 27   Bats: L   Throws: L   Height: 6'5"   Weight: 220   Origin: Round 1, 2010 Draft (#27 overall)

YEAR	TEAM	LVL	AGE	W	L	SV	G	GS	IP	H	HR	BB/9	K/9	K	GB%	BABIP	WHIP	ERA	DRA	WARP	MPH	FB%	WHF	CSP
2017	MIS	AA	25	2	4	2	27	0	49²	48	3	2.9	9.6	53	45%	.328	1.29	2.90	3.42	0.8				
2018	GWN	AAA	26	0	0	1	4	0	6¹	3	0	1.4	11.4	8	23%	.231	0.63	0.00	2.08	0.2				
2018	ATL	MLB	26	6	1	1	60	0	63²	50	6	4.4	9.5	67	57%	.277	1.27	3.11	4.09	0.6	96.2	55.2	11.5	51.1
2019	ATL	MLB	27	2	1	0	41	0	43²	37	4	4.0	9.6	47	48%	.303	1.29	3.76	4.41	0.3	95.7	55.8	11.6	51.8

Breakout: 18%   Improve: 30%   Collapse: 21%   Attrition: 31%   MLB: 69%   *Comparables: Tyler Cravy, Tom Mastny, Matt Barnes*

Biddle rose from the ashes to finally put together the season the Phillies always knew was possible. Thing is, he did it for the Braves. Atlanta believed a rebound was possible if the lefty rehabbed in its organization, and a 2016 waiver claim, knowing he wouldn't pitch until 2017, paid off with a valuable season in relief for a bullpen that needed it. Biddle's stuff was lively, striking out 25 percent of batters faced. Although walks were an issue at times, he managed the walk rate enough to remain effective. Perhaps most importantly, he stayed healthy, and that's a win on its own after a period of uncertainty for a career that seemed promising but had barely gotten off the ground to that point.

Brad Brach RHP   Born: 04/12/86   Age: 33   Bats: R   Throws: R   Height: 6'6"   Weight: 215   Origin: Round 42, 2008 Draft (#1275 overall)

YEAR	TEAM	LVL	AGE	W	L	SV	G	GS	IP	H	HR	BB/9	K/9	K	GB%	BABIP	WHIP	ERA	DRA	WARP	MPH	FB%	WHF	CSP
2016	BAL	MLB	30	10	4	2	71	0	79	57	7	2.8	10.5	92	43%	.267	1.04	2.05	2.69	2.1	96.8	60	16	42.6
2017	BAL	MLB	31	4	5	18	67	0	68	51	7	3.4	9.3	70	42%	.256	1.13	3.18	3.39	1.3	96.4	62.9	12.9	46.6
2018	BAL	MLB	32	1	2	11	42	0	39	50	4	4.4	8.8	38	48%	.371	1.77	4.85	4.28	0.3	95.3	61.4	14	44.5
2018	ATL	MLB	32	1	2	1	27	0	23²	22	1	3.4	8.4	22	47%	.296	1.31	1.52	3.37	0.4	96.0	52.4	13.7	41.6
2019	ATL	MLB	33	3	1	9	57	0	60²	51	6	3.6	9.0	61	44%	.291	1.24	3.77	4.43	0.3	95.1	59.4	13.9	43.7

Breakout: 17%   Improve: 43%   Collapse: 29%   Attrition: 10%   MLB: 92%   *Comparables: Damaso Marte, Jason Frasor, Fernando Rodney*

It's as if Brach suddenly decided Baltimore was bad for his health. Going 47-115 will do that to a person. Brach's season did a 180 in late July when he was traded to the Braves. From there, he went on a string of seven scoreless appearances and allowed just four earned runs in 27 outings. While his strikeout totals remained similar, he received a big boost by cutting his walk rate by an entire walk per nine innings. You might say the move to the NL East would be behind the big change in numbers, but he was solid in important situations against playoff teams like the Red Sox and Brewers. Simply put, Brach was better in Atlanta. A better Brach behooved a better Braves.

Shane Carle RHP   Born: 08/30/91   Age: 27   Bats: R   Throws: R   Height: 6'4"   Weight: 210   Origin: Round 10, 2013 Draft (#299 overall)

YEAR	TEAM	LVL	AGE	W	L	SV	G	GS	IP	H	HR	BB/9	K/9	K	GB%	BABIP	WHIP	ERA	DRA	WARP	MPH	FB%	WHF	CSP
2016	ABQ	AAA	24	5	8	0	27	19	111¹	147	9	2.6	7.1	88	48%	.375	1.61	5.42	4.13	1.5				
2017	ABQ	AAA	25	3	5	1	36	3	62	74	8	3.2	7.3	50	45%	.344	1.55	5.37	4.16	0.8				
2017	COL	MLB	25	0	0	0	3	0	4	6	1	0.0	9.0	4	27%	.357	1.50	6.75	2.22	0.1	95.0	53.2	15.2	48.4
2018	ATL	MLB	26	4	1	1	53	0	63	50	2	3.9	6.1	43	48%	.258	1.22	2.86	3.70	0.9	96.5	47	13.4	44.5
2019	ATL	MLB	27	2	1	0	41	0	43²	42	5	3.5	7.6	37	45%	.302	1.33	4.13	4.85	0.0	95.9	48	13.7	46.8

Breakout: 12%   Improve: 19%   Collapse: 24%   Attrition: 37%   MLB: 67%   *Comparables: Jeremy Hefner, Sean Gilmartin, Blake Treinen*

The Braves have a track record of turning toiling pitchers into valuable relievers, and what was an overlooked January 2018 trade with Colorado turned into a nifty deal when Carle came into spring training with impressive stuff and carried it into the season. Suddenly, a former 10th-rounder who couldn't gain footing in the thin air found his groove with a sharp arsenal and turned in 63 innings of pure relief goodness in his first major-league season at 26 years old.

Grant Dayton LHP   Born: 11/25/87   Age: 31   Bats: L   Throws: L   Height: 6'2"   Weight: 210   Origin: Round 11, 2010 Draft (#347 overall)

YEAR	TEAM	LVL	AGE	W	L	SV	G	GS	IP	H	HR	BB/9	K/9	K	GB%	BABIP	WHIP	ERA	DRA	WARP	MPH	FB%	WHF	CSP
2016	TUL	AA	28	3	0	1	12	0	15²	8	0	1.7	16.1	28	46%	.308	0.70	2.30	0.72	0.8				
2016	OKL	AAA	28	2	2	4	26	0	36¹	22	2	2.0	15.6	63	34%	.303	0.83	2.48	0.96	1.7				
2016	LAN	MLB	28	0	1	0	25	0	26¹	14	4	2.1	13.3	39	29%	.196	0.76	2.05	2.61	0.7	94.6	77.5	16.8	44.2
2017	LAN	MLB	29	1	1	0	29	0	23²	19	5	4.6	7.6	20	33%	.215	1.31	4.94	6.00	-0.2	92.9	83.9	11.2	46.2
2019	ATL	MLB	31	1	0	0	10	0	11	9	2	3.7	10.8	13	37%	.295	1.25	4.08	4.77	0.0	92.8	80.4	13.7	45.1

Breakout: 11%   Improve: 20%   Collapse: 21%   Attrition: 18%   MLB: 44%   *Comparables: Edward Paredes, C.C. Lee, Jonathan Albaladejo*

President and U.S. General Ulysses S. Grant was born in Point Pleasant, Ohio, a little more than an hour from Dayton, Ohio. His first name at birth was Hiram, but a paperwork error at West Point listed him as Ulysses S. Grant, so he changed his name. The military didn't suit his eye and he soon was out of the picture, relegated to struggling with failed business ventures and ending up at his father's tannery. Within two years of selling firewood on the streets, Grant was major general over volunteers, and he eventually commanded the U.S. Army to victory in the Civil War. He later became the 18th president. Life comes at you fast. Grant Dayton was a waiver claim in November 2017 after undergoing Tommy John surgery three months prior. He had a solid season in relief for the Dodgers in 2016 but has yet to repeat it.

Mike Foltynewicz RHP   Born: 10/07/91   Age: 27   Bats: R   Throws: R   Height: 6'4"   Weight: 200   Origin: Round 1, 2010 Draft (#19 overall)

YEAR	TEAM	LVL	AGE	W	L	SV	G	GS	IP	H	HR	BB/9	K/9	K	GB%	BABIP	WHIP	ERA	DRA	WARP	MPH	FB%	WHF	CSP
2016	GWN	AAA	24	1	2	0	5	5	27	13	0	4.7	8.3	25	54%	.206	1.00	1.67	3.02	0.7				
2016	ATL	MLB	24	9	5	0	22	22	123¹	125	18	2.6	8.1	111	43%	.301	1.30	4.31	4.07	1.8	98.7	62.4	10.7	50.3
2017	ATL	MLB	25	10	13	0	29	28	154	169	20	3.4	8.4	143	42%	.324	1.48	4.79	5.52	0.1	97.9	60.7	10.3	46.6
2018	ATL	MLB	26	13	10	0	31	31	183	130	17	3.3	9.9	202	44%	.251	1.08	2.85	3.44	3.9	98.6	56.3	11.1	49
2019	ATL	MLB	27	10	8	0	28	28	159²	134	17	3.2	9.7	171	43%	.297	1.19	3.52	4.14	2.2	97.9	59.7	10.9	49.1

Breakout: 29%   Improve: 63%   Collapse: 15%   Attrition: 7%   MLB: 95%   *Comparables: Jordan Zimmermann, Kevin Gausman, Jason Hammel*

Everybody throws hard in the majors now. Even sitting 96 doesn't mean what it used to, although it'll still get a scout weak in the knees when it's commanded halfway decently. Foltynewicz always had the stuff and can sit 96 with the best of them. That line-drive rate, though, showed the stuff was hittable. Major-league batters were able to sit fastball and spit on the secondaries. Things change. Foltynewicz received a newfound confidence in his four-seam/slider combination to utilize it more often in 2018 and, overall, he started mixing up his secondaries more effectively. His walk percentage went up some but remained manageable, while he helped offset that with a nice boost in strikeouts. Sometimes all it takes is simplifying things. Foltynewicz went back to the basics of tunneling the four-seamer and slider to keep batters off the heat. It resulted in a major step toward what was always front-line potential.

Sam Freeman LHP   Born: 06/24/87   Age: 32   Bats: R   Throws: L   Height: 5'11"   Weight: 180   Origin: Round 32, 2008 Draft (#965 overall)

YEAR	TEAM	LVL	AGE	W	L	SV	G	GS	IP	H	HR	BB/9	K/9	K	GB%	BABIP	WHIP	ERA	DRA	WARP	MPH	FB%	WHF	CSP
2016	MIL	MLB	29	0	0	0	7	0	7²	13	2	10.6	9.4	8	37%	.440	2.87	12.91	6.05	-0.1	97.2	65.7	11.2	42
2016	CSP	AAA	29	2	1	2	30	3	55¹	63	4	4.6	7.5	46	59%	.351	1.64	5.20	4.20	0.5				
2017	GWN	AAA	30	3	1	1	9	0	10¹	5	1	5.2	7.0	8	54%	.160	1.06	0.87	3.37	0.2				
2017	ATL	MLB	30	2	0	0	58	0	60	48	3	4.1	8.9	59	58%	.278	1.25	2.55	3.61	1.0	96.7	57.3	12.2	44.7
2018	ATL	MLB	31	3	5	0	63	0	50¹	41	3	5.7	10.4	58	54%	.314	1.45	4.29	4.13	0.5	96.8	60.7	13.9	44.7
2019	ATL	MLB	32	2	1	0	31	0	33	27	3	4.6	9.7	36	51%	.296	1.32	3.84	4.51	0.1	95.8	59	12.9	43.6

Breakout: 26%   Improve: 42%   Collapse: 22%   Attrition: 19%   MLB: 80%   *Comparables: Tom Wilhelmsen, Al Alburquerque, Tommy Layne*

As further proof that parents should tie their child's right hand behind their back when throwing a baseball for the first time, Freeman had control issues for much of 2018, but the Braves stuck with him. After a stint on the disabled list for shoulder inflammation, he bounced back with 14 scoreless appearances to end the regular season. It was a nice reward for Atlanta's patience, but it helped that he had a solid 2017 campaign and saw a nice uptick in strikeout rate in 2018. Freeman is probably not a playoff team's answer as a main left-hander out of the bullpen, but he's starting to carve himself a nice career. No, seriously, don't even let your child pick their nose with their right hand.

Max Fried LHP   Born: 01/18/94   Age: 25   Bats: L   Throws: L   Height: 6'4"   Weight: 190   Origin: Round 1, 2012 Draft (#7 overall)

YEAR	TEAM	LVL	AGE	W	L	SV	G	GS	IP	H	HR	BB/9	K/9	K	GB%	BABIP	WHIP	ERA	DRA	WARP	MPH	FB%	WHF	CSP
2016	ROM	A	22	8	7	0	21	20	103	87	10	4.1	9.8	112	52%	.306	1.30	3.93	3.33	2.1				
2017	MIS	AA	23	2	11	0	19	19	86²	88	8	4.5	8.8	85	53%	.331	1.51	5.92	3.91	1.3				
2017	GWN	AAA	23	0	0	0	2	2	6	1	0	3.0	9.0	6	67%	.083	0.50	0.00	3.89	0.1				
2017	ATL	MLB	23	1	1	0	9	4	26	30	3	4.2	7.6	22	65%	.338	1.62	3.81	4.79	0.2	95.4	63	9.2	45.4
2018	MIS	AA	24	1	0	0	2	2	11¹	4	0	3.2	12.7	16	67%	.190	0.71	0.00	3.18	0.3				
2018	GWN	AAA	24	2	6	0	13	13	66¹	66	4	4.1	9.6	71	58%	.343	1.45	4.61	4.77	0.6				
2018	ATL	MLB	24	1	4	0	14	5	33²	26	3	5.3	11.8	44	53%	.315	1.37	2.94	3.31	0.7	96.3	58.7	14.4	48.1
2019	ATL	MLB	25	2	1	0	31	0	33	28	3	4.4	10.0	36	49%	.307	1.33	3.83	4.50	0.0	95.7	61.7	12.8	48

Breakout: 33%   Improve: 46%   Collapse: 19%   Attrition: 41%   MLB: 73%   *Comparables: Bobby Parnell, Cody Reed, Ross Detwiler*

Forget Fried's movie star-quality hair and smile. That curveball deserves its own star on the walk of fame. You'd be hard-pressed to find a better one from the left side in the minor leagues. You know the movie *Twister*? The original plot was centered on Fried's curveball and the destruction caused by all that spin. Fried got his first extended taste of the majors in 2018 and performed well aside from some control issues. Control has never been his greatest strength, but his command has average potential and should allow the stuff to play enough to be a long-term major leaguer. The fastball and changeup are enough to think he can be a viable starter. He was sort of put on the backburner in Atlanta with so many pitching prospects making debuts or knocking on the door, but tall lefties with double-plus curves don't grow on trees. If they do, please protect those trees.

Kevin Gausman RHP   Born: 01/06/91   Age: 28   Bats: L   Throws: R   Height: 6'3"   Weight: 190   Origin: Round 1, 2012 Draft (#4 overall)

YEAR	TEAM	LVL	AGE	W	L	SV	G	GS	IP	H	HR	BB/9	K/9	K	GB%	BABIP	WHIP	ERA	DRA	WARP	MPH	FB%	WHF	CSP
2016	BAL	MLB	25	9	12	0	30	30	179²	183	28	2.4	8.7	174	46%	.308	1.28	3.61	4.16	2.5	98.2	65.7	12.3	44
2017	BAL	MLB	26	11	12	0	34	34	186²	208	29	3.4	8.6	179	44%	.336	1.49	4.68	4.91	1.4	97.4	64.3	12	44.9
2018	BAL	MLB	27	5	8	0	21	21	124	139	21	2.3	7.5	104	48%	.317	1.38	4.43	4.42	1.3	96.7	58.8	12.1	47.2
2018	ATL	MLB	27	5	3	0	10	10	59²	50	5	2.7	6.6	44	43%	.260	1.14	2.87	3.13	1.5	96.1	56.9	12.1	45.9
2019	ATL	MLB	28	11	9	0	29	29	174	161	19	2.7	8.3	160	45%	.304	1.23	3.72	4.38	1.9	96.6	62.6	12.2	45.7

Breakout: 22%   Improve: 50%   Collapse: 17%   Attrition: 4%   MLB: 90%   *Comparables: Derek Holland, Erik Hanson, Dwight Gooden*

Gausman was on the path to another 4.00-plus ERA until the Orioles decided to get what they could at the deadline for him. The prospect package wasn't spectacular and Gausman turned a corner with much better numbers for the Braves down the stretch, even earning a playoff start. Add a much-improved Brad Brach to the mix and the Braves did well there. The drop in strikeouts is something to keep an eye on, but Gausman has always maintained very low walk numbers. The room for error tends to shrink when you work to contact while seeing your strikeouts go down, but Gausman has already proven himself capable of making adjustments.

Luiz Gohara LHP   Born: 07/31/96   Age: 22   Bats: L   Throws: L   Height: 6'3"   Weight: 265   Origin: International Free Agent, 2012

YEAR	TEAM	LVL	AGE	W	L	SV	G	GS	IP	H	HR	BB/9	K/9	K	GB%	BABIP	WHIP	ERA	DRA	WARP	MPH	FB%	WHF	CSP
2016	EVE	A-	19	2	0	0	3	3	15¹	13	1	1.8	12.3	21	68%	.333	1.04	1.76	1.56	0.7				
2016	CLN	A	19	5	2	0	10	10	54¹	44	1	3.3	9.9	60	52%	.314	1.18	1.82	2.91	1.4				
2017	BRV	A+	20	3	1	0	7	7	36¹	33	0	2.5	9.7	39	58%	.340	1.18	1.98	4.11	0.5				
2017	MIS	AA	20	2	1	0	12	11	52	42	2	3.1	10.4	60	46%	.299	1.15	2.60	3.46	1.1				
2017	GWN	AAA	20	2	2	0	7	7	35¹	31	4	4.1	12.2	48	43%	.318	1.33	3.31	3.27	0.9				
2017	ATL	MLB	20	1	3	0	5	5	29¹	32	2	2.5	9.5	31	37%	.366	1.36	4.91	4.40	0.4	98.7	56.9	14.1	50.5
2018	ATL	MLB	21	0	1	1	9	1	19²	16	3	3.7	8.2	18	27%	.245	1.22	5.95	3.45	0.4	95.9	57	12.9	51
2018	GWN	AAA	21	3	4	0	12	12	54²	54	9	2.5	9.1	55	41%	.302	1.26	4.94	5.36	0.1				
2019	*ATL*	*MLB*	*22*	*2*	*1*	*0*	*18*	*3*	*31¹*	*28*	*4*	*3.5*	*9.5*	*33*	*42%*	*.306*	*1.27*	*3.84*	*4.52*	*0.1*	*97.4*	*59.3*	*14.1*	*52.9*

Breakout: 15%   Improve: 25%   Collapse: 6%   Attrition: 16%   MLB: 36%   *Comparables: Lucas Giolito, Scott Olsen, Jonathan Broxton*

A lot went wrong for Gohara on and off the field in 2018, to the point of basically being a lost year. Much of it shouldn't be blamed on him, but there were also whispers of needing to develop more emotionally. The guy will always be big-bodied, but big bodies have proven capable on the mound in the past, so he just needs to stay on top of his conditioning. Gohara has seriously electric stuff from the left side. The fastball jumps out of his hand with ease in the mid-90s when he's feeling it, but his velocity was very inconsistent in 2018. The slider leaves hitters jelly-legged and is already a plus pitch, while the changeup flashes average. His command won't be more than average in his prime, but he shows enough feel to get by. It's a poor man's CC Sabathia profile here if he puts it together, but he needs to do that in more ways than one. For the sake of fans of great pitching, here's to hoping Gohara finds it.

Brandon McCarthy RHP   Born: 07/07/83   Age: 35   Bats: R   Throws: R   Height: 6'8"   Weight: 225   Origin: Round 17, 2002 Draft (#510 overall)

YEAR	TEAM	LVL	AGE	W	L	SV	G	GS	IP	H	HR	BB/9	K/9	K	GB%	BABIP	WHIP	ERA	DRA	WARP	MPH	FB%	WHF	CSP
2016	RCU	A+	32	0	2	0	4	4	14	21	6	1.3	7.7	12	48%	.326	1.64	7.07	3.66	0.3				
2016	LAN	MLB	32	2	3	0	10	9	40	29	2	5.8	9.9	44	35%	.278	1.38	4.95	5.04	0.1	94.7	69.9	8.4	49
2017	LAN	MLB	33	6	4	0	19	16	92²	89	5	2.6	7.0	72	44%	.303	1.25	3.98	3.60	2.0	94.5	74.7	9.1	48.3
2018	ATL	MLB	34	6	3	0	15	15	78²	94	15	2.4	7.4	65	49%	.332	1.46	4.92	3.76	1.4	94.3	69.4	8.1	54.2
2019	*ATL*	*MLB*	*35*	*5*	*4*	*0*	*14*	*14*	*71¹*	*69*	*7*	*3.3*	*7.8*	*62*	*44%*	*.311*	*1.34*	*3.97*	*4.67*	*0.5*	*93.2*	*70.4*	*8.4*	*50*

Breakout: 11%   Improve: 35%   Collapse: 20%   Attrition: 11%   MLB: 81%   *Comparables: Carl Pavano, John Lackey, Ricky Nolasco*

McCarthy went to the Braves in 2018 to keep the dream alive for another year while providing a bridge to the young guns. After a couple reliable months, the foundation to that bridge began to crumble, and the whole thing collapsed by the middle of summer. A few really rough outings marred his overall numbers, especially later when health became a factor. McCarthy called it a career, hanging it up with nice career totals that included a 4.20 ERA and 69 wins. He quickly joined the Rangers' front office, which is great news for them and probably bad news for everyone who loves his Twitter account (and his wife roasting him).

A.J. Minter LHP   Born: 09/02/93   Age: 25   Bats: L   Throws: L   Height: 6'0"   Weight: 215   Origin: Round 2, 2015 Draft (#75 overall)

YEAR	TEAM	LVL	AGE	W	L	SV	G	GS	IP	H	HR	BB/9	K/9	K	GB%	BABIP	WHIP	ERA	DRA	WARP	MPH	FB%	WHF	CSP
2016	ROM	A	22	0	0	2	5	0	6²	2	0	1.4	8.1	6	35%	.118	0.45	0.00	2.17	0.2				
2016	CAR	A+	22	0	0	0	8	0	9¹	3	0	3.9	9.6	10	75%	.150	0.75	0.00	3.63	0.2				
2016	MIS	AA	22	1	0	0	18	0	18²	13	0	2.9	14.9	31	46%	.333	1.02	2.41	2.04	0.6				
2017	GWN	AAA	23	1	2	0	17	0	15¹	15	1	5.9	10.0	17	30%	.326	1.63	4.70	5.21	0.0				
2017	ATL	MLB	23	0	1	0	16	0	15	13	1	1.2	15.6	26	34%	.387	1.00	3.00	2.15	0.5	97.0	50.8	19.5	43
2018	ATL	MLB	24	4	3	15	65	0	61¹	57	3	3.2	10.1	69	39%	.329	1.29	3.23	3.42	1.1	98.3	49	15.8	48
2019	*ATL*	*MLB*	*25*	*3*	*1*	*14*	*52*	*0*	*54²*	*45*	*6*	*3.7*	*10.7*	*65*	*41%*	*.302*	*1.23*	*3.55*	*4.17*	*0.4*	*97.8*	*50.5*	*16.8*	*46.9*

Breakout: 35%   Improve: 58%   Collapse: 17%   Attrition: 15%   MLB: 83%   *Comparables: Keone Kela, Cody Allen, Corey Knebel*

Minter may own the record for number of times being compared to another player. The whole lefty Craig Kimbrel thing was fun for a while, but let's be real, Minter's beard is much cleaner. The 2018 season was supposed to be Minter's breakout campaign at the back end of the bullpen. It happened for the most part, but there were stretches when Braves fans got a little nervous seeing him enter for the ninth. Part of that was health, which has been a little cloud hovering nearby throughout his career so far. A back issue midway through the season impacted his mechanics and cost him effectiveness for a while as he battled his release point. The stuff is obviously back-end material as either a stud setup type or closer. He has to hold up to the strain of a long season, though, and the jury is still out on that part. Minter's beard is solid and that case is closed.

Peter Moylan RHP   Born: 12/02/78   Age: 40   Bats: R   Throws: R   Height: 6'3"   Weight: 220   Origin: International Free Agent, 1996

YEAR	TEAM	LVL	AGE	W	L	SV	G	GS	IP	H	HR	BB/9	K/9	K	GB%	BABIP	WHIP	ERA	DRA	WARP	MPH	FB%	WHF	CSP
2016	OMA	AAA	37	1	1	5	12	0	12²	8	0	3.6	7.1	10	59%	.235	1.03	0.71	3.62	0.2				
2016	KCA	MLB	37	2	0	0	50	0	44²	42	4	3.2	6.9	34	63%	.281	1.30	3.43	5.33	-0.2	92.6	57	9.9	48.7
2017	KCA	MLB	38	0	0	0	79	0	59¹	40	4	3.8	7.0	46	62%	.221	1.10	3.49	4.54	0.4	91.8	49.8	11.6	44.8
2018	ATL	MLB	39	0	1	0	39	0	28¹	32	4	5.7	7.3	23	56%	.341	1.76	4.45	5.09	-0.1	91.0	58.3	11.6	41.1
2019	*ATL*	*MLB*	*40*	*2*	*1*	*0*	*34*	*0*	*36*	*31*	*3*	*4.2*	*7.7*	*31*	*54%*	*.283*	*1.32*	*4.20*	*4.93*	*0.0*	*90.1*	*52.4*	*10.8*	*42.8*

Breakout: 9%   Improve: 25%   Collapse: 19%   Attrition: 8%   MLB: 60%   *Comparables: Doug Brocail, Jamey Wright, Keiichi Yabu*

Moylan hung around in the majors so long in 2018 that the Braves should've had a no-loitering sign next to his locker. It's obviously not his fault that he got 28 innings of work before being stashed on the disabled list for a forearm strain. To his credit, he worked to become a reliable reliever again and kept his career going with a couple good seasons in Kansas City, but it was quickly apparent that he didn't have it in his third stint with Atlanta. That didn't stop the Braves from leaving him out there for a couple months and watching him serve taters from jimmy jack farms.

Kyle Muller LHP Born: 10/07/97 Age: 21 Bats: R Throws: L Height: 6'6" Weight: 225 Origin: Round 2, 2016 Draft (#44 overall)

YEAR	TEAM	LVL	AGE	W	L	SV	G	GS	IP	H	HR	BB/9	K/9	K	GB%	BABIP	WHIP	ERA	DRA	WARP	MPH	FB%	WHF	CSP
2016	BRA	RK	18	1	0	0	10	9	27²	14	0	3.9	12.4	38	55%	.233	0.94	0.65	1.50	1.3				
2017	DNV	RK	19	1	1	0	11	11	47²	43	5	3.4	9.3	49	40%	.284	1.28	4.15	4.93	0.6				
2018	ROM	A	20	3	0	0	6	6	30	24	3	2.4	6.9	23	54%	.253	1.07	2.40	4.86	0.1				
2018	BRV	A+	20	4	2	0	14	14	80²	80	2	3.6	8.8	79	42%	.350	1.39	3.24	4.73	0.6				
2018	MIS	AA	20	4	1	0	5	5	29	22	3	1.9	8.4	27	40%	.244	0.97	3.10	4.21	0.4				
2019	ATL	MLB	21	5	8	0	21	21	99¹	96	18	4.9	8.5	94	43%	.299	1.52	5.40	6.32	-1.2				

Breakout: 10%   Improve: 13%   Collapse: 6%   Attrition: 17%   MLB: 19%   *Comparables: Caleb Ferguson, Nick Adenhart, J.C. Ramirez*

The thing that immediately stands out about Muller, besides being a large human, is the above-average arm speed coming from such a big, left-handed kid. He found his arm slot in 2018 and regained his velocity in the low-to-mid-90s, and it jumps like the firecracker under Terry's wheels. He offers variations of breaking balls and a changeup, and the better pitch depends on when you see him, but all project at least average with average command potential. This is a young lefty throwing heat with an aggressive delivery, strong mound presence and rounded-out arsenal. But, sure, keep sleeping on that.

Sean Newcomb LHP Born: 06/12/93 Age: 26 Bats: L Throws: L Height: 6'5" Weight: 255 Origin: Round 1, 2014 Draft (#15 overall)

YEAR	TEAM	LVL	AGE	W	L	SV	G	GS	IP	H	HR	BB/9	K/9	K	GB%	BABIP	WHIP	ERA	DRA	WARP	MPH	FB%	WHF	CSP
2016	MIS	AA	23	8	7	0	27	27	140	113	4	4.6	9.8	152	46%	.302	1.31	3.86	3.12	3.3				
2017	GWN	AAA	24	3	3	0	11	11	57²	45	3	5.2	11.5	74	41%	.304	1.35	2.97	3.82	1.2				
2017	ATL	MLB	24	4	9	0	19	19	100	100	10	5.1	9.7	108	46%	.327	1.57	4.32	4.61	1.1	96.2	63.4	12.7	42.8
2018	ATL	MLB	25	12	9	0	31	30	164	137	18	4.4	8.8	160	44%	.273	1.33	3.90	3.83	2.8	95.3	62.4	11	46.3
2019	ATL	MLB	26	9	9	0	28	28	148¹	123	15	4.5	9.6	159	43%	.295	1.33	3.91	4.59	1.2	95.2	63.8	11.8	45.6

Breakout: 27%   Improve: 64%   Collapse: 14%   Attrition: 10%   MLB: 90%   *Comparables: Zack Wheeler, Chris Archer, Brad Hand*

Newcomb is the poster boy for patience. While he's far from a finished product, his first full season as a bonafide starting pitcher in the major leagues showed that, yes, you can actually reach The Show despite what Joe from down the street says. Control has been Newcomb's hold-up for a while now, and it's been talked about until everyone is blue in the face. Those who believe in the big left-hander are also blue in the face preaching patience for a kid with a plus fastball, plus curveball, much-improved changeup and prototypical strong frame. Sure, 81 walks in 164 innings isn't ideal, but it's the best walk rate of his career to this point, and he's shown positive development in his time in the majors. Is he the ace that scouts tabbed as a possibility? Probably not. Is he a long-term major leaguer who'll provide quality innings for years to come? Signs point to yes. Patience, young grasshopper.

Darren O'Day RHP Born: 10/22/82 Age: 36 Bats: R Throws: R Height: 6'4" Weight: 220 Origin: Undrafted Free Agent, 2006

YEAR	TEAM	LVL	AGE	W	L	SV	G	GS	IP	H	HR	BB/9	K/9	K	GB%	BABIP	WHIP	ERA	DRA	WARP	MPH	FB%	WHF	CSP
2016	BAL	MLB	33	3	1	3	34	0	31	25	6	3.8	11.0	38	34%	.260	1.23	3.77	3.00	0.7	88.3	55	15.5	45.9
2017	BAL	MLB	34	2	3	2	64	0	60¹	41	8	3.6	11.3	76	48%	.256	1.08	3.43	3.14	1.4	89.0	53.8	11.8	42.5
2018	BAL	MLB	35	0	2	2	20	0	20	18	3	1.8	12.1	27	26%	.326	1.10	3.60	3.67	0.3	88.1	52.3	13.2	51.7
2019	ATL	MLB	36	3	1	1	52	0	54²	43	8	3.8	10.7	65	38%	.283	1.20	4.12	4.81	0.1	87.4	52.6	12.7	46.2

Breakout: 34%   Improve: 47%   Collapse: 23%   Attrition: 4%   MLB: 82%   *Comparables: Joaquin Benoit, Tom Gordon, J.J. Putz*

When O'Day's season began, he probably didn't envision a season-ending hamstring injury or getting traded from the organization he's known for the past six years. To make it even more of a whirlwind, it all happened in the span of a couple weeks. The veteran went to the Braves as a way for the Orioles to unload some cash, but the sidearmer is still capable of being a valuable reliever when healthy. If that happens, he's worth the money being paid over the final year of his contract. If not, he's still capable of growing a crazy-awesome mustache. So, he's got that going for him, which is nice.

Chad Sobotka RHP Born: 07/10/93 Age: 25 Bats: R Throws: R Height: 6'7" Weight: 225 Origin: Round 4, 2014 Draft (#133 overall)

YEAR	TEAM	LVL	AGE	W	L	SV	G	GS	IP	H	HR	BB/9	K/9	K	GB%	BABIP	WHIP	ERA	DRA	WARP	MPH	FB%	WHF	CSP
2016	ROM	A	22	1	2	0	15	0	19	23	1	5.7	9.0	19	58%	.393	1.84	4.26	3.41	0.3				
2016	CAR	A+	22	1	1	3	13	0	17²	12	0	1.5	12.2	24	49%	.324	0.85	2.04	3.26	0.4				
2017	MIS	AA	23	3	1	0	18	0	31	29	1	5.5	6.7	23	56%	.295	1.55	5.52	4.17	0.2				
2017	BRV	A+	23	1	4	2	16	0	26²	32	3	4.4	9.8	29	44%	.403	1.69	6.75	3.62	0.4				
2018	BRV	A+	24	2	0	2	13	1	20¹	9	0	3.1	12.4	28	38%	.225	0.79	2.21	2.06	0.7				
2018	MIS	AA	24	2	3	6	22	0	28	16	1	4.2	11.9	37	32%	.254	1.04	1.93	2.12	0.9				
2018	GWN	AAA	24	0	0	3	9	0	9¹	5	0	8.7	11.6	12	38%	.238	1.50	1.93	3.87	0.1				
2018	ATL	MLB	24	1	0	0	14	0	14¹	5	2	5.7	13.2	21	32%	.115	0.98	1.88	2.39	0.4	98.2	63.6	13.6	47.2
2019	ATL	MLB	25	1	0	0	26	0	27¹	23	4	5.0	10.6	32	41%	.300	1.39	4.52	5.28	-0.1	97.9	65.1	13.9	48.4

Breakout: 18%   Improve: 20%   Collapse: 9%   Attrition: 28%   MLB: 42%   *Comparables: Angel Nesbitt, Jose Dominguez, Ben Heller*

Sobotka is a huge guy with an equally large fastball. He always had MLB-quality stuff, but finding the strike zone with it has been the issue. Sobotka seems to have cleared that hurdle by picking up newfound command and control. The result was a quick climb to the majors with dominance at every stop and, in the blink of an eye, getting important innings down the stretch for a playoff team. The big right-hander can hit triple digits when he's feeling frisky, and it comes at a hard, downhill angle, paired with a hard breaker. Sobotka has what it takes to give a major-league team quality innings late in games. It's going to happen soon, too.

Mike Soroka **RHP**   Born: 08/04/97   Age: 21   Bats: R   Throws: R   Height: 6'5"   Weight: 225   Origin: Round 1, 2015 Draft (#28 overall)

YEAR	TEAM	LVL	AGE	W	L	SV	G	GS	IP	H	HR	BB/9	K/9	K	GB%	BABIP	WHIP	ERA	DRA	WARP	MPH	FB%	WHF	CSP
2016	ROM	A	18	9	9	0	25	24	143	130	3	2.0	7.9	125	52%	.305	1.13	3.02	3.17	3.2				
2017	MIS	AA	19	11	8	0	26	26	153²	133	10	2.0	7.3	125	49%	.275	1.09	2.75	4.13	1.9				
2018	GWN	AAA	20	2	1	0	5	5	27	20	0	2.0	10.3	31	70%	.299	0.96	2.00	2.64	0.9				
2018	ATL	MLB	20	2	1	0	5	5	25²	30	1	2.5	7.4	21	45%	.345	1.44	3.51	4.64	0.2	94.4	68.9	10.4	48.9
2019	ATL	MLB	21	5	4	0	13	13	69	59	6	2.8	8.6	66	48%	.297	1.17	3.40	4.01	1.0	94.6	72.2	10.9	51.2

Breakout: 6%   Improve: 14%   Collapse: 12%   Attrition: 24%   MLB: 32%   *Comparables: David Holmberg, Jacob Turner, Tyler Skaggs*

The 2018 season was supposed to be Soroka's year to flourish, even though he was only 20 years old. Soroka's 20 turned out to be like most people's 30, though, both physically and mentally. Fate, being a fickle mistress and all, touched the Canadian kid's shoulder and limited him to five major-league starts. Luckily for him, it was a lingering inflammation and not something worse, so he avoided damage and is still on track for what should be a long and productive career. When he was on the field and healthy, Soroka showed why scouts love him even with less than amazing stuff, because of elite makeup, strong mound presence and a low-90s fastball that dives for days and has grown to bump mid-90s. It's still a mid-rotation profile, but as we've learned with shoulders, we haven't learned anything.

Julio Teheran **RHP**   Born: 01/27/91   Age: 28   Bats: R   Throws: R   Height: 6'2"   Weight: 205   Origin: International Free Agent, 2007

YEAR	TEAM	LVL	AGE	W	L	SV	G	GS	IP	H	HR	BB/9	K/9	K	GB%	BABIP	WHIP	ERA	DRA	WARP	MPH	FB%	WHF	CSP
2016	ATL	MLB	25	7	10	0	30	30	188	157	22	2.0	8.0	167	41%	.260	1.05	3.21	3.28	4.5	94.0	56	11.8	46.7
2017	ATL	MLB	26	11	13	0	32	32	188¹	186	31	3.4	7.2	151	41%	.281	1.37	4.49	5.07	1.1	93.7	64.3	10	46.3
2018	ATL	MLB	27	9	9	0	31	31	175²	122	26	4.3	8.3	162	40%	.217	1.17	3.94	4.06	2.5	92.3	61.9	12.3	44
2019	ATL	MLB	28	10	9	0	28	28	159²	129	20	3.2	8.6	152	40%	.270	1.16	4.03	4.72	1.1	92.7	61.6	11.4	45.7

Breakout: 19%   Improve: 61%   Collapse: 21%   Attrition: 5%   MLB: 94%   *Comparables: Brad Penny, Patrick Corbin, Chad Billingsley*

Can we just stop for a second and talk about the fact that Teheran is still a couple years away from his 30s? He's had to soldier his way through the Braves rebuild, and the workload that comes from being a team's no. 1 for several years, coupled with having a slight body, could be taking its toll earlier than usual. His average velocity has steadily decreased and took a pretty big hit in 2018. As tends to be the case for many pitchers, adjusting to the dip has been a process. Teheran's method of going up the ladder and inside with a four-seamer at 95 before snapping off a slider away doesn't have the same effectiveness when the bite becomes more bark. He's tried to offset it with sinking fastballs and changeups with varying results. Teheran still has his good days, which is crazy to say at his age, but it's increasingly apparent that his prime came early.

Touki Toussaint **RHP**   Born: 06/20/96   Age: 23   Bats: R   Throws: R   Height: 6'3"   Weight: 185   Origin: Round 1, 2014 Draft (#16 overall)

YEAR	TEAM	LVL	AGE	W	L	SV	G	GS	IP	H	HR	BB/9	K/9	K	GB%	BABIP	WHIP	ERA	DRA	WARP	MPH	FB%	WHF	CSP
2016	ROM	A	20	4	8	0	27	24	132¹	105	13	4.8	8.7	128	40%	.263	1.33	3.88	5.17	-0.3				
2017	BRV	A+	21	3	9	0	19	19	105¹	101	8	3.6	10.5	123	45%	.324	1.36	5.04	3.50	2.2				
2017	MIS	AA	21	3	4	0	7	7	39²	30	3	5.0	10.0	44	38%	.276	1.31	3.18	4.23	0.4				
2018	MIS	AA	22	4	6	0	16	16	86	66	7	3.8	11.2	107	48%	.284	1.19	2.93	3.93	1.4				
2018	GWN	AAA	22	5	0	0	8	8	50¹	35	0	3.0	10.0	56	44%	.280	1.03	1.43	3.37	1.2				
2018	ATL	MLB	22	2	1	0	7	5	29	18	1	6.5	9.9	32	47%	.254	1.34	4.03	4.69	0.2	95.7	53.4	9.9	43.6
2019	ATL	MLB	23	7	6	0	33	18	111²	89	13	4.6	9.8	122	41%	.284	1.30	4.15	4.86	0.5	95.6	55.3	10.3	45.2

Breakout: 12%   Improve: 23%   Collapse: 17%   Attrition: 34%   MLB: 54%   *Comparables: Mauricio Robles, Archie Bradley, Keyvius Sampson*

You won't find a better dude for a major-league clubhouse than Toussaint, who's the epitome of a team guy and fan favorite in the making. Toussaint had a career-altering season in 2018 and turned himself into an option for the Braves by working tirelessly to repeat his mechanics and improve his command. His elite athleticism and aptitude paid off by finding comfort in a lower release that produced a marked improvement in control and command. That's all it took. The guy was finally able to utilize his insane stuff like he wanted to and even added a devastating split-finger. He rocketed from Double-A to the majors. The results were mixed once he got there, but he firmly thrust himself into talks for a 2019 rotation spot. Bring up his name to evaluators, or basically anyone who's ever heard of him, and you'll still get the iffy-as-a-starter discussion. To Toussaint's credit, he had a monster season developmentally, and no one will take that away from him.

Jonny Venters **LHP**   Born: 03/20/85   Age: 34   Bats: L   Throws: L   Height: 6'3"   Weight: 200   Origin: Round 12, 2005 Draft (#379 overall)

YEAR	TEAM	LVL	AGE	W	L	SV	G	GS	IP	H	HR	BB/9	K/9	K	GB%	BABIP	WHIP	ERA	DRA	WARP	MPH	FB%	WHF	CSP
2017	PCH	A+	32	0	0	0	10	0	10	5	0	4.5	9.9	11	76%	.238	1.00	1.80	3.17	0.2				
2017	MNT	AA	32	0	0	0	8	0	7²	5	0	4.7	11.7	10	53%	.294	1.17	4.70	1.90	0.3				
2018	TBA	MLB	33	1	1	1	22	1	14	11	1	3.9	7.1	11	71%	.250	1.21	3.86	4.74	0.0	94.1	65.2	8.7	45.1
2018	ATL	MLB	33	4	1	2	28	0	20¹	15	0	4.4	7.1	16	72%	.250	1.23	3.54	5.02	0.0	94.7	81.8	11.3	42.6
2019	ATL	MLB	34	2	1	2	47	0	49¹	43	5	4.7	8.2	45	55%	.292	1.40	4.31	5.07	-0.1	93.3	74.2	10.1	42.9

Breakout: 12%   Improve: 22%   Collapse: 14%   Attrition: 11%   MLB: 48%   *Comparables: Zach Duke, Sean Burnett, Micah Bowie*

If you're looking for a good baseball movie script to write, or just simply want to open up all your feels, look into what Venters has been through to keep doing what he loves. The lefty worm-killer has had three Tommy John surgeries, a "half" Tommy John surgery and an injection for a flexor strain. He didn't pitch at all from 2013-2015 and threw four minor-league innings in 2016. He barely threw minor-league innings in 2017. Next thing you know, he's back where it all began with the Braves and giving a playoff team meaningful innings out of the bullpen for the first time since 2012. The long and rough rehab work, the desire, the determination, the work ethic, the multiple years without stepping foot on a mound, it's incredible what Venters has been through. If you suffer setbacks in life or in a career, and we all have, just look at what Venters did to overcome it all so many times. Pull a little determination from his story and keep fighting. Venters did to keep his dream alive. So can you.

Arodys Vizcaino RHP   Born: 11/13/90   Age: 28   Bats: R   Throws: R   Height: 6'0"   Weight: 245   Origin: International Free Agent, 2007

YEAR	TEAM	LVL	AGE	W	L	SV	G	GS	IP	H	HR	BB/9	K/9	K	GB%	BABIP	WHIP	ERA	DRA	WARP	MPH	FB%	WHF	CSP
2016	ATL	MLB	25	1	4	10	43	0	38²	37	3	6.1	11.6	50	56%	.333	1.63	4.42	3.76	0.5	100.1	61.6	14.6	46.8
2017	ATL	MLB	26	5	3	14	62	0	57¹	42	7	3.3	10.0	64	38%	.248	1.10	2.83	3.21	1.3	99.0	61.7	15.6	46.9
2018	ATL	MLB	27	2	2	16	39	0	38¹	30	4	3.5	9.4	40	34%	.268	1.17	2.11	4.38	0.2	99.1	66.9	15.2	48.4
2019	*ATL*	*MLB*	*28*	*3*	*1*	*19*	*52*	*0*	*54²*	*45*	*7*	*4.1*	*10.0*	*61*	*42%*	*.291*	*1.28*	*4.06*	*4.75*	*0.1*	*98.7*	*63.9*	*15.3*	*47.8*

Breakout: 32%   Improve: 56%   Collapse: 17%   Attrition: 9%   MLB: 87%   *Comparables: Boone Logan, C.J. Wilson, Brandon League*

Vizcaino was good when healthy last season. Copy, paste and save for every year for the rest of his career. You're welcome, future writers. He sat out a lengthy period with shoulder woes, which has typically been the case for him in the past when it wasn't elbow woes. When healthy, or relatively healthy, he was still pumping heat and throwing at closer-level. He's even cut down his walk rate to a very manageable level the past couple seasons. The Braves showed their trust by handing him the closer role down the stretch once he returned, and he picked up a save in a one-run playoff game. Having Vizcaino on the roster is an acknowledgement that you can live with the disabled list stints knowing he's going to be effective when active.

Bryse Wilson RHP   Born: 12/20/97   Age: 21   Bats: R   Throws: R   Height: 6'1"   Weight: 225   Origin: Round 4, 2016 Draft (#109 overall)

YEAR	TEAM	LVL	AGE	W	L	SV	G	GS	IP	H	HR	BB/9	K/9	K	GB%	BABIP	WHIP	ERA	DRA	WARP	MPH	FB%	WHF	CSP
2016	BRA	RK	18	1	1	0	9	6	26²	16	0	2.7	9.8	29	66%	.250	0.90	0.68	3.10	0.7				
2017	ROM	A	19	10	7	0	26	26	137	105	8	2.4	9.1	139	54%	.272	1.04	2.50	3.70	2.5				
2018	BRV	A+	20	2	0	0	5	5	26²	16	0	2.4	8.8	26	60%	.229	0.86	0.34	3.83	0.5				
2018	MIS	AA	20	3	5	0	15	15	77	77	3	3.0	10.4	89	44%	.347	1.34	3.97	3.82	1.4				
2018	GWN	AAA	20	3	0	0	5	3	22	20	6	1.2	11.5	28	45%	.280	1.05	5.32	3.15	0.6				
2018	ATL	MLB	20	1	0	0	3	1	7	8	0	7.7	7.7	6	29%	.381	2.00	6.43	5.37	0.0	96.4	71.1	15.6	45.4
2019	*ATL*	*MLB*	*21*	*1*	*1*	*0*	*2*	*2*	*10*	*9*	*1*	*3.9*	*9.1*	*10*	*48%*	*.298*	*1.31*	*4.26*	*5.00*	*0.0*	*96.6*	*74.5*	*16.3*	*47.6*

Breakout: 5%   Improve: 17%   Collapse: 5%   Attrition: 17%   MLB: 27%   *Comparables: Carlos Martinez, John Lamb, Jesse Biddle*

Wilson's season threw people into a tizzy almost as much as when they tried to spell his first name properly. Wilson and the Braves' development staff turned the fourth-rounder into a legitimate major-league starting option after he appeared to be another back-end starter/late-inning reliever type. He pushes mid-90s with aggressiveness and has two major-league-quality secondaries in a slider and changeup to go with solid-average command. His makeup is off the charts and his mound presence is exceptional. That should come as no surprise after he shot his way up the developmental ladder with 77 strong innings at Double-A. He's a bulldog type and has chewed his way into the picture for a rotation spot soon. The profile is more of a low no. 3, but that dog will hunt.

Daniel Winkler RHP   Born: 02/02/90   Age: 29   Bats: R   Throws: R   Height: 6'3"   Weight: 205   Origin: Round 20, 2011 Draft (#618 overall)

YEAR	TEAM	LVL	AGE	W	L	SV	G	GS	IP	H	HR	BB/9	K/9	K	GB%	BABIP	WHIP	ERA	DRA	WARP	MPH	FB%	WHF	CSP
2016	ATL	MLB	26	0	0	0	3	0	2¹	0	0	3.9	15.4	4	100%	.000	0.43	0.00	1.63	0.1	93.4	35.7	25	49.3
2017	GWN	AAA	27	1	0	0	10	0	10	14	2	0.9	10.8	12	39%	.414	1.50	6.30	4.12	0.1				
2017	ATL	MLB	27	1	1	0	16	0	14¹	7	1	3.8	11.3	18	38%	.214	0.91	2.51	3.91	0.2	94.7	43.2	12.4	40.5
2018	ATL	MLB	28	4	0	2	69	0	60¹	52	3	3.0	10.3	69	40%	.310	1.19	3.43	3.51	1.0	94.4	33.9	14	43.5
2019	*ATL*	*MLB*	*29*	*2*	*1*	*0*	*41*	*0*	*43²*	*35*	*5*	*4.2*	*10.1*	*49*	*44%*	*.283*	*1.26*	*4.05*	*4.74*	*0.1*	*93.8*	*35.3*	*13.9*	*44*

Breakout: 20%   Improve: 48%   Collapse: 21%   Attrition: 18%   MLB: 90%   *Comparables: Hector Neris, Cory Rasmus, Aaron Heilman*

The bullpen life can be unforgiving. You sit out there for hours at a time, they make you get up, they make you sit down, they make you get up again, they bring you in for maybe 10 pitches. Sometimes when you're young you carry a *Dora the Explorer* backpack full of gum. In the case of Winkler, you get worked for 69 games and you're spent by September, so you struggle and then get left off the postseason roster. For Winkler's part, simply having a career at this point should be considered a blessing after barely seeing a mound for several years because of Tommy John surgery and a nasty elbow fracture. For the first time in his career, at 28 years old, he had a full, successful season. That's worth the time spent carrying candy on your back.

Kyle Wright RHP   Born: 10/02/95   Age: 23   Bats: R   Throws: R   Height: 6'4"   Weight: 200   Origin: Round 1, 2017 Draft (#5 overall)

YEAR	TEAM	LVL	AGE	W	L	SV	G	GS	IP	H	HR	BB/9	K/9	K	GB%	BABIP	WHIP	ERA	DRA	WARP	MPH	FB%	WHF	CSP
2017	BRV	A+	21	0	1	0	6	6	11¹	8	0	3.2	7.9	10	61%	.258	1.06	3.18	4.53	0.1				
2018	MIS	AA	22	6	8	0	20	20	109¹	103	6	3.5	8.6	105	56%	.311	1.34	3.70	3.84	1.9				
2018	GWN	AAA	22	2	1	0	7	4	28²	15	2	2.5	8.8	28	51%	.183	0.80	2.51	4.19	0.4				
2018	ATL	MLB	22	0	0	0	4	0	6	4	2	9.0	7.5	5	41%	.133	1.67	4.50	4.98	0.0	95.3	51.6	10.2	37.6
2019	*ATL*	*MLB*	*23*	*3*	*3*	*0*	*18*	*8*	*51*	*43*	*5*	*3.7*	*8.6*	*48*	*51%*	*.286*	*1.26*	*3.98*	*4.67*	*0.3*	*95.2*	*53.4*	*10.5*	*39*

Breakout: 17%   Improve: 28%   Collapse: 20%   Attrition: 40%   MLB: 61%   *Comparables: Brett Marshall, Jake Thompson, Eddie Butler*

In a farm system loaded with pitching prospects throughout the 2018 season, it's not out of the question to say Wright was the best. The Braves were elated to see the right-hander fall to them at no. 5 the year prior, and he represented perhaps the best bet at having a solid major-league career from that class. A little over a year later, he was making his major-league debut. Wright has nothing left to prove in the minors and is easily one of the most polished prospect arms. He can pump mid-90s with heavy life and confidently mixes an array of secondaries, including a sharp, downward slider. There are occasional bouts of control concerns but, hey, we're all human and life is a big lack of control.

LINEOUTS

Hitters

HITTER	POS	TEAM	LVL	AGE	PA	R	2B	3B	HR	RBI	BB	K	SB	CS	AVG/OBP/SLG	DRC+	VORP	BABIP	BRR	FRAA	WARP
Lane Adams	CF	IOW	AAA	28	98	8	2	1	0	6	13	32	9	3	.136/.265/.185	64	-4.3	.216	0.3	CF(12): -1.1, LF(9): -1.5	-0.4
	CF	GWN	AAA	28	101	9	5	1	0	6	5	37	3	1	.191/.238/.266	50	-4.4	.310	-0.1	CF(15): 0.1, RF(11): 0.0	-0.4
	CF	ATL	MLB	28	29	10	1	0	2	6	4	8	1	0	.240/.345/.520	88	4.3	.267	1.7	RF(5): -0.2, CF(2): 0.0	0.2
William Contreras	C	ROM	A	20	342	54	17	1	11	39	29	73	1	1	.293/.360/.463	123	23.3	.351	-0.9	C(43): -0.3	2.0
	C	BRV	A+	20	90	3	7	0	0	10	6	16	0	0	.253/.300/.337	99	2.5	.309	-0.3	C(20): -0.4	0.3
Derian Cruz	2B	ROM	A	19	432	41	15	4	4	31	12	114	4	9	.222/.254/.308	74	-11.1	.298	-1.7	2B(111): 6.7	0.3
Travis Demeritte	LF	MIS	AA	23	494	69	22	5	17	63	57	140	6	2	.222/.316/.416	106	19.5	.284	-2.2	LF(119): -5.9, 3B(1): 0.1	0.7
Alex Jackson	C	MIS	AA	22	252	27	12	1	5	24	20	78	0	0	.200/.282/.329	83	3.7	.280	-0.9	C(61): -2.1	0.3
	C	GWN	AAA	22	125	15	11	2	3	17	12	42	0	0	.204/.296/.426	90	5.4	.292	0.2	C(29): 2.7	0.7
Greyson Jenista	RF	DNV	Rk	21	47	10	1	0	3	7	6	9	0	1	.250/.348/.500	114	2.2	.250	0.0	RF(7): 2.6, LF(2): 0.6	0.5
	RF	ROM	A	21	130	20	5	3	1	23	10	17	4	1	.333/.377/.453	117	7.5	.373	0.2	RF(30): -0.4	0.5
	RF	BRV	A+	21	74	3	3	1	0	4	7	15	0	0	.152/.230/.227	82	-5.8	.192	-0.6	RF(14): -0.8, CF(1): 0.0	-0.2
Rafael Lopez	C	SDN	MLB	30	117	11	2	0	3	13	13	43	1	0	.176/.265/.284	76	-1.8	.259	0.0	C(30): 3.2, 1B(1): 0.0	0.6
	C	ELP	AAA	30	202	27	12	1	9	38	18	56	0	0	.261/.328/.489	115	9.5	.325	0.9	C(34): 3.0	1.7
Rene Rivera	C	ANA	MLB	34	87	8	4	0	4	11	4	32	0	0	.244/.287/.439	75	2.2	.348	-1.1	C(26): 0.5, 1B(2): 0.0	0.1
	C	ATL	MLB	34	4	0	0	0	0	0	0	3	0	0	.000/.000/.000	65	-0.9	.000	0.0	C(3): 0.2	0.0
Drew Waters	CF	ROM	A	19	365	58	32	6	9	36	21	72	20	5	.303/.353/.513	111	31.6	.362	3.9	CF(83): -0.6	2.1
	CF	BRV	A+	19	133	14	7	3	0	3	8	33	3	0	.268/.316/.374	81	4.7	.363	0.0	CF(30): -1.5, RF(1): -0.1	0.0
Isranel Wilson	OF	ROM	A	20	257	38	10	2	6	25	28	77	11	4	.229/.316/.372	84	8.7	.319	2.5	RF(46): 2.3, CF(21): -1.7	0.4
	OF	BRV	A+	20	151	16	5	1	2	10	14	43	5	1	.215/.287/.311	82	0.1	.297	0.5	LF(30): -1.6, CF(6): -1.0	-0.2

Besides having a solid Twitter account and the ability to play all three outfield spots in a pinch, **Lane Adams** displays impressive business skills by offering advertising for your company in place of his walk-up music. ⓧ Squint and **William Contreras** looks a lot like older brother Willson on the field, and not just because of all the Ls in their names. A loud set of tools behind the plate and in the box could help a major-league team avoid taking Ls in the future. ⓧ A full-season assignment exposed **Derian Cruz**'s raw feel for the game, but he's still young and very fast. There's some utility potential, but the gap between present and potential is wider than the Gates of Lodore. ⓧ It took an eternity, but **Travis Demeritte** is finally at the age where it's now or never. A couple full seasons at Double-A have shown his easy power and defensive versatility come at a heavy price in terms of hit utility. ⓧ **Alex Jackson**'s career has as many twists and turns as his curly hair. Struggles with the bat in the high minors meant a curve in the wrong direction, but improvements behind the plate mean more chances. ⓧ **Greyson Jenista** can mash from the left side. He'll need to do it heavily if he wants to smash baseballs long term, because defense won't be his ticket on the tater train. ⓧ Despite catching 13 innings the night before, **Rafael Lopez** relished the chance to play again the following afternoon—his first chance to start on Mother's Day since his mom's passing in 2015. He said it was a very emotional day for him, and here at BP, we applaud his sentiment. ⓧ The Braves claimed **Rene Rivera** off waivers when their catchers were momentarily dropping like flies, marking his eighth organization. He's had a nice run as a defense-first depth guy and should soak in what's left of it. ⓧ Looking for the next big thing out of Atlanta's recent drafts? Your first thought may be to look at arms, but **Drew Waters** will turn your head with five tools that will all play at the major-league level. You can still look at Atlanta's arms, though. They're pretty. ⓧ **Isranel Wilson**'s numbers went down after he started going by Izzy. Coincidence? Probably, because his plate discipline is still very raw and he struggles tapping into his tools in games.

Pitchers

PITCHER	TEAM	LVL	AGE	W	L	SV	G	GS	IP	H	HR	BB/9	K/9	K	GB%	BABIP	WHIP	ERA	DRA	WARP	MPH	FB%	WHF	CSP
Thomas Burrows	BRV	A+	23	6	2	4	29	0	46²	38	0	5.8	10.6	55	42%	.322	1.46	3.28	4.26	0.4				
	MIS	AA	23	0	0	6	15	0	19	10	0	2.8	12.8	27	50%	.263	0.84	1.42	2.47	0.5				
Jasseel De La Cruz	ROM	A	21	3	4	0	15	13	69	65	6	4.4	8.5	65	64%	.309	1.43	4.83	4.14	0.8				
Josh Graham	BRV	A+	24	1	5	1	15	0	23¹	19	2	3.9	12.7	33	57%	.315	1.24	3.86	2.19	0.7				
	MIS	AA	24	5	3	2	32	0	39²	42	4	7.0	9.3	41	54%	.352	1.84	6.81	4.66	0.1				
Luke Jackson	GWN	AAA	26	2	1	0	10	1	21¹	11	0	4.2	14.3	34	45%	.289	0.98	1.69	2.23	0.7				
	ATL	MLB	26	1	2	1	35	0	40²	41	3	4.6	10.2	46	50%	.339	1.52	4.43	5.79	-0.4	96.0	41.7	11.7	42.7
Wes Parsons	MIS	AA	25	1	2	0	8	7	29¹	24	1	3.1	8.6	28	64%	.277	1.16	1.23	4.24	0.4				
	ATL	MLB	25	0	1	0	1	0	5	6	1	5.4	5.4	3	41%	.312	1.80	7.20	6.22	-0.1	92.7	61	8.5	44.8
	GWN	AAA	25	7	4	1	16	14	88	77	7	2.6	7.8	76	47%	.278	1.16	3.27	5.00	0.5				
Jose Ramirez	ATL	MLB	28	0	2	0	7	0	6¹	9	0	11.4	9.9	7	29%	.429	2.68	17.05	7.51	-0.2	96.3	62.6	9.7	43.7
Trey Riley	DNV	Rk	20	0	0	0	6	2	9	10	1	10.0	13.0	13	44%	.409	2.22	8.00	4.00	0.2				
Freddy Tarnok	ROM	A	19	5	5	0	27	11	77¹	70	5	4.8	9.7	83	40%	.297	1.44	3.96	3.97	1.0				
Joey Wentz	BRV	A+	20	3	4	0	16	16	67	49	3	3.2	7.1	53	46%	.250	1.09	2.28	4.15	0.9				
Huascar Ynoa	ROM	A	20	7	8	0	18	18	91²	69	7	4.1	9.8	100	47%	.264	1.21	3.63	3.99	1.3				
	BRV	A+	20	1	4	0	6	6	24²	33	1	4.4	11.3	31	46%	.438	1.82	8.03	3.86	0.4				

Tristan Beck, a polished righty with plus stuff, rejected the Braves' advances out of high school because of his strong commitment to Stanford. They got Mike Soroka with the pick instead, and ended up with Beck three years later anyway. ⊗ Aside from occasional control lapses, **Thomas Burrows** can be thrown into a big-league bullpen at any point and be one of its best left-handed specialist options. His last name is appropriate because of his fastball that burrows in on lefties, paired with a two-plane slider for an effective relief mix. ⊗ **Jasseel De La Cruz** hasn't garnered the fanfare of other prospects throwing 95 with a quick arm, but he also hasn't established himself in a full season yet, and there's volatility for days here. ⊗ **Josh Graham** went to Oregon, but he's no quack. The arm motion and corresponding amount of effort are a bit insane, but he throws in the upper 90s and flashes major-league potential. ⊗ **Luke Jackson**'s transaction page reads like Ross and Rachel's relationship on *Friends*. The Braves might like to say they were on a break a few times, but they couldn't quit their love for the hard-throwing middle reliever with the 4.00-plus ERA. ⊗ The elbow issues for **Jacob Lindgren** are seemingly endless and he's now lost almost three full seasons. Crazy thing is, he's still young and offers left-handed relief upside if he can regain some semblance of feel. ⊗ Seeing **Wes Parsons** make his debut was like watching an old friend's dream come true. The lanky right-hander had been at it a long time before that call came. Cups of coffee will probably be his long-term specialty. ⊗ After a couple solid seasons in the bullpen, **Jose Ramirez** went down with shoulder issues when the Braves needed him most. He has setup-type stuff when healthy, but it's unclear what he may have left in the tank after his shoulder responded negatively to his first heavy workload. ⊗ **Trey Riley** was a fifth-round pick, but the Braves were perhaps more excited about nabbing him than anyone not named Tristan Beck. Riley has a plus fastball into the mid-90s paired with a power slider, giving him the framework as a starting pitcher project with an easy power reliever backup plan. ⊗ A scout deemed **Freddy Tarnok** as Atlanta's white whale after he emerged from the cloak of darkness as a raw project for the development staff. The kid has athleticism and projection for days, and his stuff shows promise, but there are some baby-giraffe elements on the mound. ⊗ **Patrick Weigel** jumped on the scene tossing gas and turned himself into a strong prospect just in time to blow out his elbow, but he was already shoving again on the complex after 14 months and again offers electric starter potential. ⊗ Everything about **Joey Wentz** screams mid-rotation candidate, from the size and durability to the three-pitch mix and advanced feel. The low-90s fastball, above-average pair of secondaries and advanced polish will play in the majors. ⊗ Acquired from the Twins in a summer 2017 trade for Jaime Garcia, **Huascar Ynoa** is a legitimate prospect with a strong, lean frame and quick arm tossing mid-90s, but the secondaries still need to come along.

BALTIMORE ORIOLES

Essay by Jonathan Bernhardt

Player comments by Kate Preusser and BP staff

A clean break with the past can be a good thing. For a baseball franchise with a history of being a punching bag and a punchline, it should be the most important thing. But for the Baltimore Orioles, it might be fairly considered to be the only thing they had left.

Buck Showalter is gone. Dan Duquette is gone. Manny Machado, Jonathan Schoop, Zach Britton, Adam Jones, all of them are gone. Darren O'Day, Brad Brach, Kevin Gausman will be absent as well. The senior-ranking member of the 2019 Baltimore Orioles with any heavy association with the teams that went to the playoffs three times, won the American League East once, and finished in last place the past two seasons will be Dylan Bundy, and it's probably just a matter of time for him, too. The future is bright, and blindingly uncertain.

There have been a lot of words written about new general manager and executive vice president of baseball operations, Mike Elias, and his new field manager, Brandon Hyde; there's no need to repeat them here in full, but Elias was one of Jeff Luhnow's few seconds atop the Houston Astros front office during their rise through the American League, and Hyde served as bench coach and first base coach during the ascension of the Chicago Cubs before joining Baltimore. The Cubs won the Series in 2016; the Astros won it in 2017. Each franchise is seen as the class of its respective league in both process and results. If you wanted a series of hires to wipe away all doubts that the Orioles were joining the modern age, you quite literally could not have scripted them better than this. Elias even brought over Sig Mejdal, the analytics genius who turned Houston's program around. You might not have heard, but he used to work for NASA. The previous head of analytics for the Orioles, Sarah Gelles, has left for a new job with...the Houston Astros. Perhaps the issue before with Baltimore's analytics before wasn't the ideas, but the implementation—either way, Elias has an excellent history of ensuring that implementation.

Indeed, one of Elias's first and strongest promises was to overhaul the way the Orioles do business on a fundamental level, and unlike his predecessor, he was given the authority to clean house immediately. He's spent the offseason molding the Warehouse on Eutaw Street into the sort of machine that Houston used to achieve their championship

ORIOLES PROSPECTUS
2018 W-L: 47-115, 5TH IN AL EAST

Pythag	.335	30th	B-Age		28.4	20th
RS/G	3.84	27th	P-Age		27.0	6th
RA/G	5.51	30th	Salary		$148.6M	13th
DRC+	88	25th	M$/MW		$100.0M	1st
DRA	5.82	29th	DL Days		1248	16th
FIP	5.01	30th	$ on DL		19%	20th
DER	.690	30th				

- Opened 1992
- Open air
- Natural surface
- Fence profile: 7' to 21'

Three-Year Park Factors

Runs	Runs/RH	Runs/LH	HR/RH	HR/LH
99	100	98	107	103

Top Hitter WARP	3.6 Manny Machado
Top Pitcher WARP	1.3 Kevin Gausman
Top Prospect	Yusniel Diaz

2018 Hit List Ranking

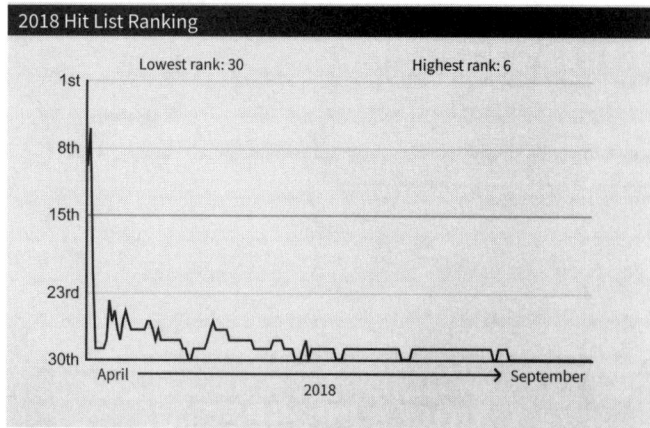

Lowest rank: 30   Highest rank: 6

Committed Payroll (in millions)

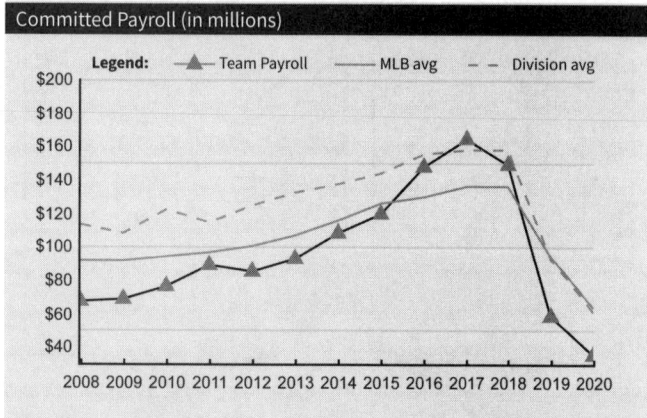

Legend: ▲ Team Payroll — MLB avg – – Division avg

Farm System Ranking

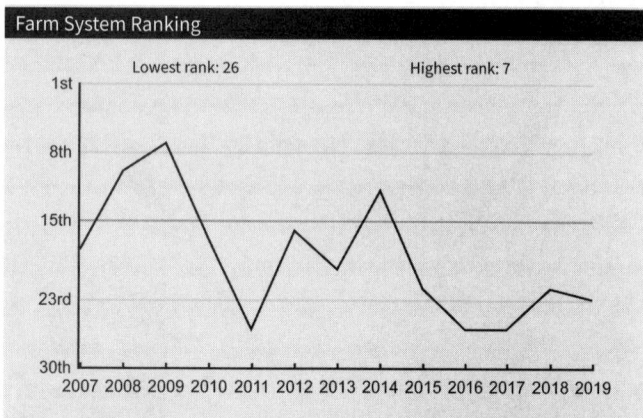

Lowest rank: 26   Highest rank: 7

Personnel

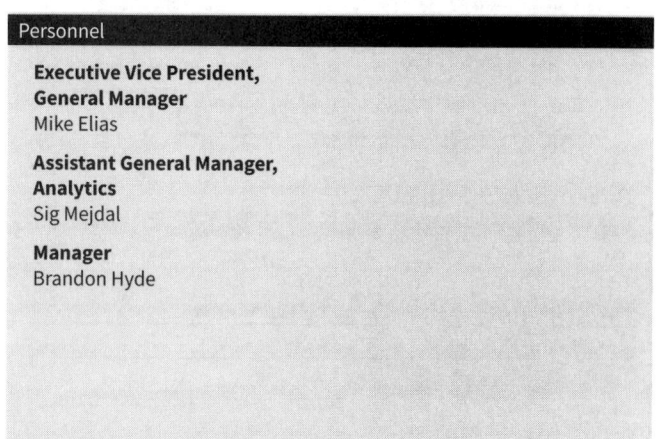

Executive Vice President, General Manager
Mike Elias

Assistant General Manager, Analytics
Sig Mejdal

Manager
Brandon Hyde

with maximum efficiency, and he will attend to that machine with a watchmaker's eye. Hyde will be his man on the field level, his most important work being done outside of the box scores and perhaps even outside of the season itself, developing raw players in spring training and then polishing the few of them that make his active roster in the majors. Baltimore will seize every advantage, exploit every rule, and take every inch they are given by rule and by law to make themselves into a lean, competitive organization; that is what the Angelos family is paying for, and as the conventional wisdom goes, that is what a club needs to do if they're sharing a division with the Red Sox and Yankees.

Baltimore will finally join the rest of the league in a healthy pursuit of teenagers from the global south via international free agency. They will hopefully avoid the pratfalls and outright criminal acts that have led to the Atlanta Braves getting a general manager banned from baseball for life, or to an FBI investigation into the Los Angeles Dodgers revealing a spreadsheet ranking overseas contractors by level of suspected criminality. The international market for amateur players is one of the few remaining true free markets in baseball, with all of the lawlessness that implies; Major League Baseball is thankfully getting that under control by degrees, the posting agreement with the Cuban league being the latest step in making sure players don't have to turn to human traffickers to get to America and play ball. If there's any time to be joining, it's now—but, at least in the past, perhaps this was one area that patriarch Peter Angelos was right to stay away from, even if it did hurt the team on the field. The Orioles have their slot money, however, and there's no sense in them not using it. One has to assume the new regime will find a better use to which to put it than mediocre relievers at the trade deadline.

The watchwords of the modern MLB team are "financial flexibility," and the good news for the incoming regime is they have it by...the truckload? By whatever means you judge a concept which embodies not action, but being in a state in which you could act. Elias entered the winter with three contracts worth over $10 million annually on his books, and only one of them—you know which one—being of such ludicrous negative value that it will remain there for at least another season or two. Alex Cobb and Mark Trumbo are both useful major league pieces with the chance to flash much, much brighter given the right run of luck and health, and even if Baltimore can't move them at the deadline, they're looking at a roster commitment of some $65 to $70 million for 2019. That's half (or less so, more likely) the player payroll for 2018. That's incredible financial flexibility...and it would be silly to use it on free agents on a team in the middle of a tear-down, so presumably those savings will be put back into the organization in the form of player development and facilities upgrades, rather than merely being pocketed. That's what the Los Angeles Dodgers did—not Elias's Astros or Hyde's Cubs, but the Dodgers—and it has paid dividends for them, even if it hasn't gotten them a ring yet.

The casual fan will likely know only a few of the players on Baltimore's Opening Day roster next season, but that's just an opportunity to grow to care about a whole host of brand new faces. The good ones will get traded away, of course, and the important ones won't show up until May or June. Even if your new favorite player makes it through the year on the active roster, that just makes it more likely he'll be dealt before spring rolls around, as teams have gravitated strongly away from the deadline and towards November for impact trades over the past few seasons. But the odds say that at least one or two of the guys on the field for the anthem the first time around next year will be on the next decent Orioles team. The odds point heavily towards one, however. Probably a catcher.

There is one unalloyed bit of good news: paying attention to Baltimore's minor league system will no longer be the exercise in masochism it was for...well, likely for as long as you can remember. The Orioles still don't have a good system, per se—it lacks credible superstar-grade talent at the top, and real depth at the bottom—but one or two more seasons should fix that, and for now, you can still pay attention to top prospect outfielder Yusniel Diaz as he works on his defense for the first couple months of the season, track Ryan Mountcastle as he figures out whether his position moving forward is left field or first base, and transfer all your dreams into the person of Dillon Tate, because the idea of a pitcher the Yankees traded to the Orioles becoming an ace for Baltimore would be something akin to riding into Camden Yards bearing the Holy Grail.

If you've detected a marked lack of enthusiasm for all this and instead the creeping hold of resignation, well, modern, efficient, maximally-impactful smart baseball is a whole lot more fun to think about than to watch during the first two or three years of the contention cycle. Both the Astros and the Cubs had to stress to fans through sustained PR campaigns that they were going to be bad for a while to be good—and now that both teams have held up their end of the bargain, many other fan bases are eager to sign on without the soft sell. They're not particularly wrong to do so, given the systemic rewards for accumulating cost-controlled young talent, but the first two seasons are brutal. Luhnow's Astros lost 107 and 111 games his first two years at the helm; Epstein's Cubs, 101 and 96. Baltimore lost 115 games last year, which has some fans thinking, "that wasn't so bad; I can do that again."

Perhaps so; history has allowed for braver acts. But you'll have to get through the first half of the season not just without Manny Machado or Kevin Gausman or Jonathan Schoop or any of the bullpen guys, but without something far more important: hope. It was easy to say you saw this all coming last September as the team blew past 100 losses on its way towards the cliff, looking out into that great big sky. In April and May, though, you were telling yourself and everyone who would listen that this team was one solid winning streak from turning things around; that Kevin Gausman was *this* close to figuring it out; that if they had a good year, the team could get Schoop to sign an extension; that if things broke right, maybe Showalter and his managerial magic could all drag this rattling train one more stop down the line.

Even if you suspected the wheels were about to come off and the engineer had jumped out a dozen mile markers back, there was always the possibility that the bridge wasn't actually out. The Orioles didn't look like a great team going into 2018, but they didn't look like a great team going into 2012 and 2015; what they did look like was a team that was trying to win, even if it didn't all line up on paper. As an Orioles fan going into those seasons, you knew that just because the Orioles shouldn't be a good team didn't mean they couldn't be. That's hope; it might be stupid, it might be overrated, and it certainly isn't compatible with a five-year plan, but it's absolutely necessary if you're going to watch 162 games of Major League Baseball in one calendar year. Few teams have provided that feeling this decade than the logic and PECOTA-defying Baltimore Orioles.

But you cannot have hope in 2019. All you are permitted is Chris Davis. ■

—Jonathan Bernhardt is an author of The Athletic.

HITTERS

Rylan Bannon 2B   Born: 04/22/96   Age: 23   Bats: R   Throws: R   Height: 5'10"   Weight: 180   Origin: Round 8, 2017 Draft (#250 overall)

YEAR	TEAM	LVL	AGE	PA	R	2B	3B	HR	RBI	BB	K	SB	CS	AVG/OBP/SLG	DRC+	VORP	BABIP	BRR	FRAA	WARP
2017	OGD	RK	21	175	39	8	0	10	30	19	29	5	0	.336/.425/.591	146	19.4	.360	0.8	3B(34): 5.9	2.1
2018	RCU	A+	22	403	58	17	6	20	61	59	103	4	4	.296/.402/.559	146	35.8	.367	0.0	3B(54): 2.9, 2B(22): 0.2	3.8
2018	BOW	AA	22	122	16	6	0	2	11	22	24	0	0	.204/.344/.327	106	2.5	.243	-1.4	2B(30): -0.9, 3B(2): -0.1	0.2
2019	BAL	MLB	23	251	33	9	0	11	32	23	66	0	0	.226/.297/.423	86	2.2	.264	-0.5	3B 1, 2B 0	0.3

Breakout: 7%   Improve: 21%   Collapse: 8%   Attrition: 18%   MLB: 41%   *Comparables: Vince Belnome, Adam Duvall, Brett Wallace*

Bannon was being developed as a utility bat toward the end of his tenure with the Dodgers, but the Orioles could use his defensive ability at his natural home of third. Bannon isn't a typical light-hitting utilityman, though; the former Big East Player of the Year stormed into rookie ball, and the Dodgers aggressively promoted Bannon to High-A this season. The Orioles were even more aggressive, forwarding Bannon to Double-A Bowie, where his power predictably fell off over a hundred or so plate appearances, but the excellent plate discipline that's been a hallmark of his game since college remains intact. Something to monitor is whether the 5'10/180-lb Bannon can maintain his power numbers away from the hitter-friendly California League, but even if the power dips slightly, his profile is brimming with tools.

Tim Beckham INF
Born: 01/27/90 Age: 29 Bats: R Throws: R Height: 6'1" Weight: 205 Origin: Round 1, 2008 Draft (#1 overall)

YEAR	TEAM	LVL	AGE	PA	R	2B	3B	HR	RBI	BB	K	SB	CS	AVG/OBP/SLG	DRC+	VORP	BABIP	BRR	FRAA	WARP
2016	TBA	MLB	26	215	25	12	5	5	16	14	67	2	1	.247/.300/.434	70	5.2	.349	-0.9	SS(25): 1.5, 2B(19): -0.2	-0.1
2017	TBA	MLB	27	345	31	5	3	12	36	24	110	5	4	.259/.314/.407	91	11.0	.357	-0.4	SS(70): -2.2, 2B(17): -0.8	0.8
2017	BAL	MLB	27	230	36	13	2	10	26	12	57	1	1	.306/.348/.523	98	18.2	.376	0.9	SS(49): 3.2	1.4
2018	BAL	MLB	28	402	45	17	0	12	35	27	100	1	2	.230/.287/.374	81	5.1	.282	0.8	SS(49): -3.7, 3B(40): -2.2	0.1
2019	*BAL*	*MLB*	*29*	*418*	*46*	*17*	*2*	*12*	*47*	*30*	*113*	*4*	*2*	*.239/.299/.393*	*84*	*4.3*	*.305*	*0.2*	*3B -3, SS 1*	*0.2*

Breakout: 1%   Improve: 53%   Collapse: 6%   Attrition: 14%   MLB: 99%   *Comparables: Ian Desmond, Luis Aguayo, Khalil Greene*

After the historically garbagetastic season the Orioles just had, it's hard to remember that in 2017, the team stood just one game out of a Wild Card spot as late as September 5. That late-season surge was spurred in part by trade deadline acquisition Beckham, whom the Rays flipped to their division rival in exchange for a short-season pitcher. He went on a tear that August, out-slugging Mike Trout for the month and making Tampa Bay look silly for essentially giving away a former #1 overall pick. However, Beckham came back to Earth in 2018; he suffered a groin strain in late April that kept him out until the end of June and never really got on track in the back half of the season. There are causes for optimism: his atrocious contact skills are growing less atrocious, and the quality of his contact doesn't explain the near-hundred-point drop in BABIP. Beckham, who made no secret of his desire to be an everyday shortstop while with Tampa Bay, will finally have a full season to do that in 2019, and perhaps shed the Buster Posey comparisons once and for all.

Chris Davis 1B
Born: 03/17/86 Age: 33 Bats: L Throws: R Height: 6'3" Weight: 230 Origin: Round 5, 2006 Draft (#148 overall)

YEAR	TEAM	LVL	AGE	PA	R	2B	3B	HR	RBI	BB	K	SB	CS	AVG/OBP/SLG	DRC+	VORP	BABIP	BRR	FRAA	WARP
2016	BAL	MLB	30	665	99	21	0	38	84	88	219	1	0	.221/.332/.459	113	14.6	.279	0.3	1B(152): 5.7, RF(3): -0.1	2.7
2017	BAL	MLB	31	524	65	15	1	26	61	61	195	1	1	.215/.309/.423	92	-2.0	.301	-2.0	1B(125): 4.2, 3B(2): -0.1	0.5
2018	BAL	MLB	32	522	40	12	0	16	49	41	192	2	0	.168/.243/.296	62	-28.5	.237	-4.6	1B(116): -5.4	-2.7
2019	*BAL*	*MLB*	*33*	*569*	*62*	*23*	*2*	*20*	*70*	*58*	*197*	*2*	*1*	*.212/.299/.381*	*87*	*-2.7*	*.301*	*-1.8*	*1B -2*	*-0.5*

Breakout: 2%   Improve: 27%   Collapse: 6%   Attrition: 14%   MLB: 86%   *Comparables: Richie Sexson, Brandon Moss, Mo Vaughn*

While most US schoolchildren learn about the Great Chicago Fire, little attention is paid to a much larger fire that occurred on the same day in 1871: the Peshtigo Fire in Wisconsin burned over a million acres of forest and killed scores more than in Chicago, its conditions so deadly that in WWII, US and British soldiers studied the so-called Peshtigo Paradigm to plan bombing campaigns against Axis strongholds. It remains to this day the deadliest wildfire in American history, and yet few outside of the region know about it. This is to say, historical memory is often a social construct, or so Chris Davis should hope it is. This may be the only way to leave the smoking ruin of his historically awful 2018 campaign behind, hoping that somewhere out there in baseball is the equivalent of Mrs. O'Leary's cow and one very tippy lantern.

Yusniel Diaz OF
Born: 10/07/96 Age: 22 Bats: R Throws: R Height: 6'1" Weight: 195 Origin: International Free Agent, 2015

YEAR	TEAM	LVL	AGE	PA	R	2B	3B	HR	RBI	BB	K	SB	CS	AVG/OBP/SLG	DRC+	VORP	BABIP	BRR	FRAA	WARP
2016	RCU	A+	19	348	47	8	7	8	54	29	71	7	8	.272/.333/.418	104	8.7	.326	-2.1	CF(34): -6.1, RF(15): -0.7	0.2
2017	RCU	A+	20	374	42	15	3	8	39	35	73	7	9	.278/.343/.414	108	8.9	.328	-1.0	CF(29): 1.8, RF(26): -1.2	1.2
2017	TUL	AA	20	118	15	8	0	3	13	10	29	2	5	.333/.390/.491	99	6.6	.434	-0.8	RF(26): -0.6, CF(5): -0.1	0.1
2018	TUL	AA	21	264	36	10	4	6	30	41	39	8	8	.314/.428/.477	140	21.5	.360	1.8	CF(29): -1.7, RF(28): -1.6	1.8
2018	BOW	AA	21	152	23	5	1	5	15	18	28	4	5	.239/.329/.403	115	4.6	.267	-0.5	RF(29): 0.3, CF(6): -0.5	0.5
2019	*BAL*	*MLB*	*22*	*251*	*27*	*9*	*1*	*8*	*28*	*20*	*57*	*4*	*4*	*.230/.289/.378*	*82*	*1.7*	*.271*	*-0.8*	*RF 0, CF -1*	*0.0*

Breakout: 6%   Improve: 26%   Collapse: 2%   Attrition: 21%   MLB: 36%   *Comparables: Domonic Brown, Billy McKinney, Caleb Gindl*

The crown jewel of the Machado deal, Diaz—who immediately rocketed to the top of Orioles top prospect lists the moment he buttoned up his Bowie Baysox jersey—is close to major-league ready. Scouts wonder when or if his raw power will translate into game power, although he's seen a significant uptick in that area over the past two seasons. Diaz is a well-rounded player who is average-to-good in all categories, even if no one skill jumps off the page. He's a very good contact hitter with advanced plate discipline and has a strong enough arm to man right field even if he has to move off center, and while he may not fit the traditional power-bat model of a corner OF, his ability to barrel line drives to all fields while taking walks and limiting his strikeouts will be a tremendous boost to the team with the worst OBP in the AL in 2018. When he makes the majors, Diaz's plate appearances will be a balm upon the eyes of O's fans who watched Chris Davis strike out 36.8 percent of the time this season.

Jean Carlos Encarnacion 3B
Born: 01/17/98 Age: 21 Bats: R Throws: R Height: 6'3" Weight: 195 Origin: International Free Agent, 2016

YEAR	TEAM	LVL	AGE	PA	R	2B	3B	HR	RBI	BB	K	SB	CS	AVG/OBP/SLG	DRC+	VORP	BABIP	BRR	FRAA	WARP
2016	DBR	RK	18	156	19	3	3	0	16	11	30	4	0	.264/.340/.329	91	6.5	.336	1.4	3B(19): -2.0, SS(16): 0.0	0.4
2017	BRA	RK	19	107	16	8	4	2	16	4	22	4	2	.350/.374/.563	99	10.6	.430	0.3	3B(15): -1.9, 1B(14): 1.0	0.2
2017	DNV	RK	19	98	14	3	0	1	6	3	21	3	5	.290/.316/.355	81	6.2	.361	0.9	3B(23): 4.1	0.6
2018	ROM	A	20	379	45	23	5	10	57	13	100	5	5	.288/.314/.463	97	24.8	.370	-0.2	3B(92): 5.0	1.6
2018	DEL	A	20	104	10	4	2	2	7	3	34	0	0	.218/.240/.356	92	2.6	.308	2.2	3B(21): 2.0	0.7
2019	*BAL*	*MLB*	*21*	*251*	*19*	*6*	*0*	*7*	*26*	*3*	*80*	*0*	*0*	*.192/.201/.304*	*25*	*-17.7*	*.249*	*-0.5*	*3B 2*	*-1.6*

Breakout: 2%   Improve: 2%   Collapse: 1%   Attrition: 8%   MLB: 8%   *Comparables: Josh Bell, Nick Castellanos, Neftali Soto*

One of four prospects obtained in the Gausman deal, the young, athletic Encarnacion is the kind of prospect the Braves have coming out of their ears and the Orioles...do not. Encarnacion's walk rate is nursery-rhyme puny, especially considering how often he strikes out, and he'll need to improve his plate discipline in order to tap into the raw power hidden in his 6'3" frame. He's shown flashes of it throughout his time in the low minors, and also a strong arm, fast-twitch muscles, and athletic ability that indicate he could stick at the hot corner if the Orioles are willing to take the time to work on the finer points of fielding with him, emphasis on *work*—Encarnacion had 30 errors at third in 92 games with the Rome Braves this season. Prospects with the kind of power upside Encarnacion possesses are few and far between in the Orioles system, and he'll play next season at just 21 years of age, so there's plenty of time for the Orioles to polish this particularly rough diamond.

Cadyn Grenier SS Born: 10/31/96 Age: 22 Bats: R Throws: R Height: 5'11" Weight: 188 Origin: Round 1, 2018 Draft (#37 overall)

YEAR	TEAM	LVL	AGE	PA	R	2B	3B	HR	RBI	BB	K	SB	CS	AVG/OBP/SLG	DRC+	VORP	BABIP	BRR	FRAA	WARP
2018	DEL	A	21	183	23	12	2	1	13	17	53	3	2	.216/.297/.333	80	9.9	.312	-0.5	SS(39): 2.7	0.5
2019	BAL	MLB	22	251	23	9	0	5	20	12	84	1	0	.178/.216/.281	26	-13.7	.246	-0.5	SS 2	-1.3

Breakout: 2% Improve: 4% Collapse: 3% Attrition: 6% MLB: 8%   *Comparables: Pete Kozma, Ian Desmond, Argenis Diaz*

Two things about the Orioles' second overall pick in 2018: First, he lists his favorite movie as Ace Ventura 2: When Nature Calls. Not the first one; the sequel, and full title only, please. Second, although he names Troy Tulowitzki as his favorite player, Grenier also shares traits with fellow Vegas native Bryce Harper. Sporting similar hair and similar insouciant swag, Grenier plays short like Harper hits bombs, a relentless barrage of highlight reel plays that earned him a Pac-12 DPOY award over teammate, and fellow defensive wizard, Nick Madrigal. His challenge in pro ball will be to translate that swag to his offensive game, although he steadily improved in all offensive categories each year at Oregon State. Grenier's quick hands and ability to hit to all fields, plus reflexes of a cat and the speed of a mongoose, are a solid base to work from. Alrighty then!

Austin Hays OF Born: 07/05/95 Age: 23 Bats: R Throws: R Height: 6'1" Weight: 195 Origin: Round 3, 2016 Draft (#91 overall)

YEAR	TEAM	LVL	AGE	PA	R	2B	3B	HR	RBI	BB	K	SB	CS	AVG/OBP/SLG	DRC+	VORP	BABIP	BRR	FRAA	WARP
2016	ABE	A-	20	153	14	9	2	4	21	11	32	4	3	.336/.386/.514	132	15.7	.410	-0.9	RF(20): 0.3, CF(5): 0.1	0.9
2017	FRD	A+	21	280	42	15	3	16	41	12	40	4	6	.328/.364/.592	152	26.0	.337	0.7	CF(57): 8.1, RF(4): -0.6	3.5
2017	BOW	AA	21	283	39	17	2	16	54	13	45	1	1	.330/.367/.594	135	31.3	.345	3.2	CF(31): -3.3, RF(29): -0.4	2.1
2017	BAL	MLB	21	63	4	3	0	1	8	2	16	0	0	.217/.238/.317	65	-3.2	.273	-0.4	RF(14): -1.6, CF(8): -1.3	-0.4
2018	BOW	AA	22	288	34	12	2	12	43	12	59	6	3	.242/.271/.432	104	8.3	.263	0.9	RF(36): 6.7, LF(16): -0.3	1.5
2019	BAL	MLB	23	241	26	11	1	10	32	8	54	2	1	.243/.270/.427	85	1.9	.274	-0.3	RF 0, LF 0	0.2

Breakout: 8% Improve: 29% Collapse: 9% Attrition: 20% MLB: 52%   *Comparables: Dayan Viciedo, Josh Kroeger, Anthony Santander*

The O's have been aggressive with their 2016 third-rounder, going so far as to call him up to the majors in his first full season to help with a potential playoff push. Hays fell flat in his brief exposure to the majors and was summarily returned to Double-A Bowie last year, where he struggled over the first two months of the season before wrenching an ankle. He returned to Bowie in August and put together a strong conclusion to his season, with numbers much more in line with the totals he'd posted that earned him spots on various top prospect lists. The team had hoped to send him to the AFL to continue building on his strong finish and make up for lost time, but the ankle issue persisted, eventually requiring surgery. Hays should be ready for spring training, but there won't be another playoff run to compel the team to rush him a second time.

Adam Jones CF Born: 08/01/85 Age: 33 Bats: R Throws: R Height: 6'2" Weight: 215 Origin: Round 1, 2003 Draft (#37 overall)

YEAR	TEAM	LVL	AGE	PA	R	2B	3B	HR	RBI	BB	K	SB	CS	AVG/OBP/SLG	DRC+	VORP	BABIP	BRR	FRAA	WARP
2016	BAL	MLB	30	672	86	19	0	29	83	39	115	2	0	.265/.310/.436	107	17.4	.280	2.7	CF(152): 4.4	3.8
2017	BAL	MLB	31	635	82	28	1	26	73	27	113	2	1	.285/.322/.466	105	28.1	.312	3.4	CF(147): -4.7	2.6
2018	BAL	MLB	32	613	54	35	0	15	63	24	93	7	1	.281/.313/.419	97	12.8	.311	1.0	CF(106): -11.8, RF(33): 2.0	0.9
2019	BAL	MLB	33	583	71	29	2	17	64	31	98	4	1	.269/.316/.423	98	21.7	.302	1.8	CF -4, RF 0	2.0

Breakout: 0% Improve: 38% Collapse: 12% Attrition: 13% MLB: 99%   *Comparables: Bing Miller, Willie Davis, Al Oliver*

There is only so much control a baseball player has. He can't control where he's drafted, or where he goes for first few years of his career. He can't control how much ownership spends, who his teammates are, or the conditions in which he plays. Only a select few can control whether or not they're traded. Adam Jones elected to exercise what control he has this year when he refused a deadline trade, opting instead to finish out his ten-year Orioles career on his terms. The 33-year-old will be able to control where he signs as a free agent this winter. While his days as a center fielder seem past him, Jones can still play a respectable corner outfield, and although his power numbers took an enormous dip in 2018, the decline was so steep as to suggest a resurgence is possible for a team willing to gamble that Jones is closer to the 25-home run player he's been over the past half-decade plus.

Trey Mancini LF Born: 03/18/92 Age: 27 Bats: R Throws: R Height: 6'4" Weight: 215 Origin: Round 8, 2013 Draft (#249 overall)

YEAR	TEAM	LVL	AGE	PA	R	2B	3B	HR	RBI	BB	K	SB	CS	AVG/OBP/SLG	DRC+	VORP	BABIP	BRR	FRAA	WARP
2016	BOW	AA	24	75	18	4	0	7	14	10	17	0	0	.302/.413/.698	137	7.8	.308	0.6	1B(15): 0.4	0.6
2016	NOR	AAA	24	536	60	22	5	13	54	48	123	2	2	.280/.349/.427	115	15.4	.351	-1.9	1B(121): 6.5	2.1
2016	BAL	MLB	24	15	3	1	0	3	5	0	4	0	0	.357/.400/1.071	108	2.7	.286	-0.1		0.0
2017	BAL	MLB	25	586	65	26	4	24	78	33	139	1	0	.293/.338/.488	101	21.8	.352	0.9	LF(88): 0.9, 1B(45): -2.1	1.3
2018	BAL	MLB	26	636	69	23	3	24	58	44	153	0	1	.242/.299/.416	90	3.0	.285	0.5	LF(98): 4.5, 1B(47): 2.7	1.4
2019	BAL	MLB	27	553	70	24	3	21	67	39	127	1	0	.254/.315/.436	105	15.7	.302	0.6	LF 1, 1B 0	1.8

Breakout: 1% Improve: 43% Collapse: 6% Attrition: 11% MLB: 92%   *Comparables: Brennan Boesch, J.D. Martinez, Cody Asche*

The greatest irony of Alanis Morissette's 1996 song "Ironic" is that none of the situations described therein are actually ironic, but instead just variations of spectacularly bad luck. That the 2018 Orioles paid Chris Davis and Mark Trumbo over 30 million dollars combined to do nothing other than hit home runs, and the fact that both of them were out-homered by Mancini, is a little bad luck, a lot of poor resource allocation, and significantly more ironic than a black fly in one's chardonnay. In order to manufacture playing time for the team leader in HRs, the O's wedged Mancini—who, of all the first basemen in the world, is the first-basiest—into left and hoped an aging Adam Jones could cover a little extra ground in the outfield, which led to predictably disastrous results (Predictably Disastrous Results: title of the 2018 Orioles' sextape). Perhaps a second year of playing out of position fueled Mancini's brutal first-half slump, but by August he was getting the ball into the air again and doing damage; his second-half slugging jumped 120 points.

Ryan McKenna CF   Born: 02/14/97   Age: 22   Bats: R   Throws: R   Height: 5'11"   Weight: 185   Origin: Round 4, 2015 Draft (#133 overall)

YEAR	TEAM	LVL	AGE	PA	R	2B	3B	HR	RBI	BB	K	SB	CS	AVG/OBP/SLG	DRC+	VORP	BABIP	BRR	FRAA	WARP
2016	ABE	A-	19	252	29	10	1	1	26	22	59	17	6	.241/.320/.309	101	8.0	.319	1.5	CF(57): 0.5	1.0
2017	DEL	A	20	530	62	33	2	7	42	43	128	20	2	.256/.331/.380	96	29.0	.336	-0.2	CF(124): -7.6	0.6
2018	FRD	A+	21	301	60	18	2	8	37	37	45	5	6	.377/.467/.556	153	46.2	.436	2.5	CF(64): -6.2, LF(2): -0.2	2.6
2018	BOW	AA	21	250	35	8	2	3	16	29	56	4	1	.239/.341/.338	93	10.6	.312	2.6	CF(55): 3.4, RF(3): 2.1	1.4
2019	BAL	MLB	22	251	28	9	0	6	23	19	64	2	1	.216/.285/.334	65	-1.5	.272	-0.4	CF -1, LF 0	-0.3

Breakout: 7%   Improve: 27%   Collapse: 3%   Attrition: 18%   MLB: 45%   *Comparables: Ryan Kalish, Andrew McCutchen, Dalton Pompey*

Moss campion, also called the compass plant, is a hardy wildflower that is able to tolerate a harsh Arctic climate by creating a dense interior space that is warm and sheltered from the wind, a mini-nursery that will issue shocking pink blooms in the summer. Like the moss campion, Maine native Ryan McKenna has been a slow-growing perennial since being drafted in 2015, but exploded in dazzling color this summer for High-A Frederick. Improved plate discipline, especially a better two-strike approach, has unlocked the potential in McKenna's bat, as have some mechanical refinements, such as adding a toe tap. While his frame doesn't foreshadow a lot of balls over the fence, McKenna can spray line drives all over the field and is quick enough to nab an extra base here and there. That speed also helps him in center, where his arm is graded by most scouts as average, to occasionally make a highlight-reel diving catch. After a promotion to Double-A, the Orioles assigned McKenna to the AFL, a somewhat more hospitable environment to which the former cold-weather prospect has quickly adapted.

Ryan Mountcastle 3B   Born: 02/18/97   Age: 22   Bats: R   Throws: R   Height: 6'3"   Weight: 195   Origin: Round 1, 2015 Draft (#36 overall)

YEAR	TEAM	LVL	AGE	PA	R	2B	3B	HR	RBI	BB	K	SB	CS	AVG/OBP/SLG	DRC+	VORP	BABIP	BRR	FRAA	WARP
2016	DEL	A	19	489	53	28	4	10	51	25	95	5	4	.281/.319/.426	105	25.2	.331	-1.7	SS(105): -21.1	-0.3
2017	FRD	A+	20	379	63	35	1	15	47	14	61	8	2	.314/.343/.542	133	28.9	.343	1.5	SS(76): -12.1	2.0
2017	BOW	AA	20	159	18	13	0	3	15	3	35	0	0	.222/.239/.366	76	-0.4	.265	0.5	3B(37): -1.1	0.0
2018	BOW	AA	21	428	63	19	4	13	59	26	79	2	0	.297/.341/.464	118	22.2	.339	-1.5	3B(81): -4.9	1.7
2019	BAL	MLB	22	251	25	13	1	8	31	9	56	0	0	.251/.279/.409	86	1.0	.293	-0.4	3B -3	-0.2

Breakout: 7%   Improve: 16%   Collapse: 11%   Attrition: 25%   MLB: 37%   *Comparables: Josh Vitters, Brandon Laird, Renato Nunez*

The Orioles have been stockpiling bat-first prospects and Mountcastle, a compensation pick for losing Nelson Cruz in 2015, is no exception. The team gave up on the illusion of Mountcastle playing shortstop this year, moving him to third, but many scouts see his eventual defensive home in left field. That adds to a logjam of bat-first, defensively-limited prospects in the O's system; with Mountcastle being one of the youngest of these, and not needing protection on the 40-man yet, look for him to spend time ripening in the minors as the O's sort out their major-league situation. If he can stick at third, that will accelerate the timeline significantly. Mountcastle has made an obvious attempt to take more walks and turned in a strong season at Double-A thanks to his ability to hit for average, but he'll need to maintain that selectivity at the plate to push his power numbers up if he wants to be the Mount in the high castle of Camden Yards.

Cedric Mullins CF   Born: 10/01/94   Age: 24   Bats: B   Throws: L   Height: 5'8"   Weight: 175   Origin: Round 13, 2015 Draft (#403 overall)

YEAR	TEAM	LVL	AGE	PA	R	2B	3B	HR	RBI	BB	K	SB	CS	AVG/OBP/SLG	DRC+	VORP	BABIP	BRR	FRAA	WARP
2016	DEL	A	21	559	79	37	10	14	55	37	101	30	6	.273/.321/.464	118	39.8	.314	2.2	CF(122): 5.0	3.8
2017	BOW	AA	22	350	53	19	1	13	37	27	58	9	7	.265/.319/.460	111	15.7	.283	0.9	CF(57): 7.2, LF(8): 1.1	2.5
2018	BOW	AA	23	218	36	12	5	6	28	15	28	9	1	.313/.362/.512	121	22.8	.339	2.4	CF(43): 0.4, LF(3): 0.5	1.6
2018	NOR	AAA	23	269	41	17	3	6	19	22	39	12	0	.269/.333/.438	103	15.0	.298	2.2	CF(60): 0.2	1.3
2018	BAL	MLB	23	191	23	9	0	4	11	17	37	2	3	.235/.312/.359	83	1.7	.279	-0.6	CF(45): -3.8, LF(1): 0.0	-0.2
2019	BAL	MLB	24	615	76	24	2	16	58	47	115	15	5	.227/.295/.364	78	8.0	.257	0.7	CF 3	1.2

Breakout: 11%   Improve: 38%   Collapse: 8%   Attrition: 29%   MLB: 63%   *Comparables: Raimel Tapia, Franklin Gutierrez, Felix Pie*

Mullins might have been the happiest player on a 108-loss team ever. After tearing up Double-A for the first couple months of the season, Baltimore promoted Mullins to Triple-A on June 1st. There he might have languished if not for Adam Jones, who willingly moved to left to accommodate Mullins, who has plus speed and a flair for dramatic diving catches. And Mullins made the most out of his brief major league tenure: During Player's Weekend, he got to wear a jersey with his chosen nickname ("The Entertainer") and custom kicks depicting his home state of Georgia. He participated in rookie dress-up day (costume: a child riding a dinosaur). He won the Orioles' Minor Leaguer of the Year award, with a special acknowledgement by Brooks Robinson, after whom the award is named. He robbed Giancarlo Stanton of a home run. He got a shoe deal. And he got to live out his dream of playing in the majors, and for a fanbase desperately looking for exactly the kind of player Cedric Mullins is: talented, young, fun, and contractually obligated to stick with them.

Renato Nunez 3B   Born: 04/04/94   Age: 25   Bats: R   Throws: R   Height: 6'1"   Weight: 220   Origin: International Free Agent, 2010

YEAR	TEAM	LVL	AGE	PA	R	2B	3B	HR	RBI	BB	K	SB	CS	AVG/OBP/SLG	DRC+	VORP	BABIP	BRR	FRAA	WARP
2016	NAS	AAA	22	550	61	20	2	23	75	31	119	2	0	.228/.278/.412	102	16.8	.249	0.9	3B(89): -1.2, LF(12): -0.5	1.9
2016	OAK	MLB	22	15	0	0	0	0	1	0	3	0	0	.133/.133/.133	71	-3.1	.167	-0.7		-0.1
2017	NAS	AAA	23	533	74	27	2	32	78	47	141	2	1	.249/.319/.518	113	24.6	.279	-1.5	LF(48): -7.0, 3B(44): -4.7	1.1
2017	OAK	MLB	23	16	1	0	0	1	3	1	8	0	0	.200/.250/.400	73	-0.5	.333	-0.2	LF(3): -0.2, 3B(1): 0.2	0.0
2018	NAS	AAA	24	30	3	0	0	0	4	2	6	0	0	.357/.400/.357	88	1.4	.455	-0.5	3B(2): -0.2, LF(2): -0.5	-0.1
2018	TEX	MLB	24	41	2	1	0	1	2	3	12	0	0	.167/.244/.278	89	-0.7	.208	-0.2	3B(8): 0.9, LF(4): -0.2	0.1
2018	NOR	AAA	24	228	25	14	1	5	25	23	49	1	0	.289/.361/.443	110	12.2	.356	0.8	3B(38): 0.1, 1B(6): 0.6	1.1
2018	BAL	MLB	24	220	26	13	0	7	20	16	50	0	0	.275/.336/.445	93	8.6	.333	-0.8	3B(59): -4.0	0.1
2019	BAL	MLB	25	482	55	20	1	19	61	37	116	0	0	.237/.301/.416	92	5.0	.279	-1.5	3B -4	0.1

Breakout: 7%   Improve: 29%   Collapse: 20%   Attrition: 38%   MLB: 75%   *Comparables: Brandon Wood, Mat Gamel, Josh Bell*

A prospect blocked at all his positions by various Matts and Marks, the A's tried to sneak Nunez through waivers while he was rehabbing a hamstring injury in Triple-A Nashville. He was claimed first by the Rangers before being DFA'd for Rougned Odor's return from the DL, at which point the Orioles picked him up, fixed him up a little bed in the garage, and gave him run of the backyard. The knock on Nunez is that he doesn't have strong enough plate discipline when he's not smashing dingers, and his glove probably isn't good enough to stick at third. That didn't stop Baltimore from playing him there exclusively, and as a non-contending team they have the luxury of seeing if Nunez's bat is powerful enough to make up for his other shortcomings.

Colby Rasmus OF Born: 08/11/86   Age: 32   Bats: L   Throws: L   Height: 6'2"   Weight: 195   Origin: Round 1, 2005 Draft (#28 overall)

YEAR	TEAM	LVL	AGE	PA	R	2B	3B	HR	RBI	BB	K	SB	CS	AVG/OBP/SLG	DRC+	VORP	BABIP	BRR	FRAA	WARP
2016	HOU	MLB	29	417	38	10	0	15	54	43	121	4	1	.206/.286/.355	86	-2.8	.257	-0.3	LF(87): 2.6, CF(21): 1.5	1.1
2017	TBA	MLB	30	129	17	7	1	9	23	7	45	1	0	.281/.318/.579	93	9.6	.368	0.5	LF(23): 4.2, RF(7): -0.3	0.7
2018	FRD	A+	31	40	8	3	1	1	8	2	7	0	0	.297/.325/.514	101	2.2	.333	0.4	RF(7): 0.4	0.2
2018	BAL	MLB	31	49	5	1	0	1	1	3	19	0	0	.133/.204/.222	59	-4.1	.200	-0.5	RF(11): 1.2, LF(4): -0.1	-0.1
2019	*BAL*	*MLB*	*32*	*251*	*27*	*11*	*1*	*9*	*31*	*19*	*74*	*2*	*0*	*.232/.295/.401*	*89*	*3.6*	*.303*	*-0.1*	*RF 1, CF 0*	*0.5*

Breakout: 4%   Improve: 39%   Collapse: 11%   Attrition: 21%   MLB: 90%   *Comparables: Geoff Jenkins, Brad Wilkerson, Matt Kemp*

"All ballplayers should quit when it starts to feel as if all the baselines run uphill" is a quote attributed, probably apocryphally, to Babe Ruth. Maybe Colby Rasmus felt like the baselines ran uphill with the Rays in Tampa Bay; maybe they ran even more steeply uphill in Baltimore. Or maybe Colby was just following in the footsteps of his brother, Casey, who quit baseball at the age of 24. Or his brother Cory, currently a free agent, or his brother Cyle, whose name is Cyle. Colby has a cattle ranch in his home state of Alabama and in 2016 bought a prize bull for more than the cost of a year's tuition at an Ivy-League school. Maybe the baselines run uphill in baseball, but in cattle ranching run to the cool river's bank.

Rio Ruiz 3B Born: 05/22/94   Age: 25   Bats: L   Throws: R   Height: 6'1"   Weight: 215   Origin: Round 4, 2012 Draft (#129 overall)

YEAR	TEAM	LVL	AGE	PA	R	2B	3B	HR	RBI	BB	K	SB	CS	AVG/OBP/SLG	DRC+	VORP	BABIP	BRR	FRAA	WARP
2016	GWN	AAA	22	533	52	24	3	10	62	61	116	1	4	.271/.355/.400	108	14.8	.337	-3.8	3B(119): -7.0	1.2
2016	ATL	MLB	22	7	1	0	1	0	2	0	2	1	0	.286/.286/.571	81	0.3	.400	0.2	3B(2): -0.1	0.0
2017	GWN	AAA	23	432	48	25	2	16	56	42	110	1	2	.247/.322/.446	111	13.9	.304	-0.2	3B(91): 2.0, 1B(5): 0.2	2.1
2017	ATL	MLB	23	173	22	5	0	4	19	19	41	1	0	.193/.283/.307	82	-0.9	.231	0.9	3B(41): 0.6, 1B(2): 0.0	0.4
2018	GWN	AAA	24	541	72	25	4	16	72	40	90	2	1	.269/.322/.390	111	9.9	.311	1.8	3B(49): 2.3, 1B(35): 1.5	2.3
2018	ATL	MLB	24	15	1	0	0	0	0	2	5	0	0	.083/.267/.083	71	0.3	.143	-0.1	3B(1): -0.2	0.0
2019	*BAL*	*MLB*	*25*	*70*	*7*	*3*	*0*	*2*	*8*	*5*	*16*	*0*	*0*	*.233/.296/.374*	*74*	*-0.7*	*.281*	*-0.1*	*3B 0*	*-0.1*

Breakout: 3%   Improve: 17%   Collapse: 13%   Attrition: 30%   MLB: 52%   *Comparables: Max Muncy, Colin Moran, Brian Anderson*

Ruiz was never considered a real option as the next long-term third baseman in Atlanta, but it's to the point now that he needs to start doing something in the majors to avoid the Quad-A label. He hasn't done much other than walk in his two short stints in the majors and he's fallen behind on the depth chart as younger whippersnappers make their moves. The realistic role was always something along the lines of a left-handed bench option with plate discipline as the main strength, while the ceiling was a platoon mate. He still has time to revive that, but someone is on call to perform CPR at a moment's notice.

Chance Sisco C Born: 02/24/95   Age: 24   Bats: L   Throws: R   Height: 6'2"   Weight: 195   Origin: Round 2, 2013 Draft (#61 overall)

YEAR	TEAM	LVL	AGE	PA	R	2B	3B	HR	RBI	BB	K	SB	CS	AVG/OBP/SLG	DRC+	VORP	BABIP	BRR	FRAA	WARP
2016	BOW	AA	21	479	53	28	1	4	44	59	83	2	2	.320/.406/.422	115	28.8	.387	-5.7	C(83): -9.8	1.1
2017	NOR	AAA	22	388	47	23	0	7	47	32	99	2	2	.267/.340/.395	94	22.5	.351	1.9	C(94): 3.2	2.1
2017	BAL	MLB	22	22	3	2	0	2	4	3	7	0	0	.333/.455/.778	90	3.9	.444	-0.3	C(10): -0.7	0.0
2018	NOR	AAA	23	151	22	5	0	3	12	16	36	0	0	.242/.344/.352	109	5.4	.308	-1.1	C(37): -2.8	0.5
2018	BAL	MLB	23	184	13	8	0	2	16	13	66	1	0	.181/.288/.269	59	-3.5	.293	-1.3	C(55): -2.8	-0.5
2019	*BAL*	*MLB*	*24*	*236*	*23*	*10*	*0*	*5*	*23*	*18*	*69*	*0*	*0*	*.208/.290/.329*	*66*	*0.0*	*.288*	*-0.8*	*C -5*	*-0.6*

Breakout: 8%   Improve: 28%   Collapse: 12%   Attrition: 26%   MLB: 62%   *Comparables: Chris Iannetta, Hank Conger, Josh Donaldson*

YEAR	TEAM	P. COUNT	FRM RUNS	BLK RUNS	THRW RUNS	TOT RUNS
2017	BAL	653	-0.6	-0.2	-0.1	-1.1
2017	NOR	13196	5.9	1.1	-1.7	4.6
2018	BAL	6491	-2.2	0.3	-0.1	-2.1
2018	NOR	5151	-1.3	0.0	-0.8	-2.0
2019	*BAL*	*8887*	*-3.3*	*0.3*	*-0.8*	*-3.9*

The Orioles treated Sisco like a trip to a mid-priced buffet this season, giving him a spot on the 25-man out of spring training, only to pile up trips between levels like salad bar-sticky plates. Sisco did strike out his share over the first two months of the season, but also showed off the discerning eye that's kept his OBP in the .330s or higher in every season of his minor league career. Sisco, who started playing catcher only late in high school, is still developing at the position, so perhaps the goal of shifting him between levels was to give him exposure to major-league pitching staffs without becoming overly fatigued by the fire-breathing but poor-commanding arms parading from the O's bullpen on a nightly basis. It's a notion supported by this curious quote from Buck Showalter after Sisco was optioned down: "I'm afraid he's coming down with...He hasn't slept in two or three days." Catching for the 2018 Baltimore Orioles pitching staff: literally a hazard to one's health.

D.J. Stewart OF Born: 11/30/93   Age: 25   Bats: L   Throws: R   Height: 6'0"   Weight: 230   Origin: Round 1, 2015 Draft (#25 overall)

YEAR	TEAM	LVL	AGE	PA	R	2B	3B	HR	RBI	BB	K	SB	CS	AVG/OBP/SLG	DRC+	VORP	BABIP	BRR	FRAA	WARP
2016	DEL	A	22	262	27	12	1	4	25	42	58	16	6	.230/.366/.352	106	7.3	.294	-1.2	LF(58): 0.2	0.6
2016	FRD	A+	22	240	41	12	2	6	30	36	46	10	3	.279/.389/.448	130	10.7	.333	0.0	LF(51): 1.0, CF(2): -0.2	1.4
2017	BOW	AA	23	540	80	26	2	21	79	65	87	20	4	.278/.378/.481	135	37.6	.299	2.1	LF(110): -0.6, RF(4): 0.7	4.1
2018	NOR	AAA	24	490	59	24	2	12	55	54	103	11	4	.235/.329/.387	106	14.4	.278	4.7	RF(88): -14.1, LF(24): 1.9	0.6
2018	BAL	MLB	24	47	8	3	0	3	10	4	12	2	1	.250/.340/.550	88	3.2	.269	0.5	LF(9): 4.4, RF(6): -0.4	0.5
2019	*BAL*	*MLB*	*25*	*443*	*51*	*17*	*1*	*13*	*46*	*40*	*102*	*9*	*3*	*.212/.296/.354*	*78*	*-0.1*	*.254*	*0.2*	*RF -10, LF 1*	*-1.0*

Breakout: 7%   Improve: 21%   Collapse: 12%   Attrition: 26%   MLB: 45%   *Comparables: Bronson Sardinha, Thomas Neal, Phil Ervin*

In 2017, Stewart changed his stance from "Albert Pujols with the Duomo strapped to his back" and, after a year of realigning his spine, had his most successful season as a pro. The former first-round pick didn't have quite as much success this season at Triple-A, where his strikeouts surged and his offense fell off across the board, but that didn't stop the Orioles from giving him a taste of MLB action. In just under 50 PAs, Stewart went deep three times, with three doubles, hinting that the bat will play in the majors. He also swiped two bags, reinforcing his reputation as an excellent base-runner. Unfortunately, like Mancini, the defensively-limited Stewart is marooned between the Scylla and Charybdis of Mark Trumbo and Chris Davis, so he might have to hang out and chew some lotus until the way forward reveals itself.

Mark Trumbo DH Born: 01/16/86 Age: 33 Bats: R Throws: R Height: 6'4" Weight: 225 Origin: Round 18, 2004 Draft (#533 overall)

YEAR	TEAM	LVL	AGE	PA	R	2B	3B	HR	RBI	BB	K	SB	CS	AVG/OBP/SLG	DRC+	VORP	BABIP	BRR	FRAA	WARP
2016	BAL	MLB	30	667	94	27	1	47	108	51	170	2	0	.256/.316/.533	123	18.5	.278	-2.6	RF(95): 2.2, 1B(6): 0.2	3.2
2017	BAL	MLB	31	603	79	22	0	23	65	42	149	1	0	.234/.289/.397	86	-9.2	.278	-2.3	RF(31): -4.6, 1B(2): 0.2	-0.7
2018	BAL	MLB	32	358	41	12	0	17	44	24	87	0	0	.261/.313/.452	103	6.4	.303	0.9	RF(19): -1.4, 1B(3): 0.2	0.7
2019	BAL	MLB	33	575	64	25	2	22	76	43	140	1	0	.244/.305/.425	96	3.6	.291	-1.2	RF -1, 1B 0	0.4

Breakout: 2%   Improve: 38%   Collapse: 8%   Attrition: 12%   MLB: 91%   *Comparables: Ryan Zimmerman, Xavier Nady, Glenn Davis*

Lingering knee pain shortened Trumbo's season, which had been trending in the right direction after a catastrophic 2017. Although he'll probably never scrape the lofty ceiling of his 47-home run season again, Trumbo's power numbers were well up, and not by a fluke—he was hitting the ball harder than ever, and finished the season in the top ten in all of baseball for average exit velocity. In the final year of his contract with the O's, Trumbo is slated to make $11M, and then a total of $4.5M in deferred payments after his contract ends. If Baltimore was willing to eat some of that money, they might find a willing trade partner in a contender who needs a power bat and has space at 1B/DH, thus clearing space for one of their more defensively-limited prospects. Trumbo will first need to prove that he's back to full health, and, more importantly, that his power resurgence is for real.

Danny Valencia 4C Born: 09/19/84 Age: 34 Bats: R Throws: R Height: 6'2" Weight: 210 Origin: Round 19, 2006 Draft (#576 overall)

YEAR	TEAM	LVL	AGE	PA	R	2B	3B	HR	RBI	BB	K	SB	CS	AVG/OBP/SLG	DRC+	VORP	BABIP	BRR	FRAA	WARP
2016	OAK	MLB	31	517	72	22	1	17	51	41	115	1	1	.287/.346/.446	102	24.4	.346	-2.5	3B(68): -3.9, RF(37): 1.8	1.2
2017	SEA	MLB	32	500	54	19	3	15	66	40	122	2	2	.256/.314/.411	88	2.9	.312	-1.7	1B(118): 8.9, RF(10): 0.0	0.8
2018	BAL	MLB	33	282	28	8	1	9	28	22	53	1	1	.263/.316/.408	101	5.7	.293	-0.9	3B(39): 2.8, RF(19): 0.1	1.1
2019	BAL	MLB	34	309	33	14	1	8	37	25	68	1	1	.257/.322/.408	93	3.7	.309	-0.9	3B -1, RF -1	0.3

Breakout: 1%   Improve: 40%   Collapse: 7%   Attrition: 9%   MLB: 90%   *Comparables: Ty Wigginton, David Freese, Michael Young*

For Player's Weekend this year, Valencia went with the nickname "Slugger," a bold move for a player with single-digit home runs on the season. Maybe Valencia was trying to invoke the magic of the law of attraction, but he might want to send that copy of *The Secret* to Goodwill, as he hit just one home run before being released by the Orioles in mid-August. There was speculation a contending team might pick up the lefty-masher as a bench piece; the Yankees, in particular, had noted offensive struggles down the stretch, and specifically struggled against left-handed pitching. But, just like at the trade deadline, no teams bit on the defensively-limited 33-year old, whose offensive numbers have trickled steadily downward over the past few seasons, and who carries a reputation—deserved or not—as a difficult clubhouse personality. Whatever the talent threshold is for annoying personality traits dismissed as quirks, Valencia isn't there anymore, if he ever was.

Breyvic Valera UT Born: 01/08/92 Age: 27 Bats: B Throws: R Height: 5'11" Weight: 160 Origin: International Free Agent, 2010

YEAR	TEAM	LVL	AGE	PA	R	2B	3B	HR	RBI	BB	K	SB	CS	AVG/OBP/SLG	DRC+	VORP	BABIP	BRR	FRAA	WARP
2016	SFD	AA	24	192	16	5	1	0	12	9	18	3	1	.258/.289/.298	84	-2.0	.282	0.8	SS(26): 1.1, 2B(15): 1.2	0.4
2016	MEM	AAA	24	257	32	14	1	0	31	31	22	8	4	.341/.417/.415	103	28.5	.370	1.6	2B(32): -1.9, 3B(21): 0.6	1.1
2017	MEM	AAA	25	470	68	22	6	8	41	38	34	11	11	.314/.368/.450	112	31.9	.324	1.5	2B(78): -1.3, LF(18): 0.5	2.3
2017	SLN	MLB	25	11	0	0	0	0	0	1	0	0	0	.100/.182/.100	93	-1.3	.100	0.0	2B(3): -0.2	0.0
2018	LAN	MLB	26	34	4	0	0	0	4	4	4	0	0	.172/.273/.172	88	-1.3	.200	0.3	2B(5): -0.4, 3B(3): -0.1	0.0
2018	OKL	AAA	26	223	36	8	2	6	25	21	20	4	6	.284/.350/.433	110	12.6	.290	0.7	SS(25): -0.4, 2B(16): -0.8	1.3
2018	NOR	AAA	26	160	14	6	2	3	14	16	14	3	2	.229/.310/.364	113	4.3	.234	-1.8	2B(25): 3.0, LF(7): -0.1	0.9
2018	BAL	MLB	26	41	4	0	1	0	4	3	9	1	0	.286/.325/.343	94	0.9	.357	0.1	2B(11): -1.3, SS(2): -0.1	0.0
2019	BAL	MLB	27	137	14	6	1	3	15	10	19	2	2	.256/.313/.395	95	3.2	.277	-0.3	2B -1, SS 0	0.3

Breakout: 3%   Improve: 23%   Collapse: 10%   Attrition: 24%   MLB: 50%   *Comparables: Jeff Keppinger, Jarrett Hoffpauir, Eric Sogard*

A long-time Cardinals prospect, Valera was picked up by the Dodgers this season as a stopgap measure after the Corey Seager injury, and then flipped to the O's in the Machado trade. Here are three interesting things about Valera, a switch-hitting infielder: 1) 10 separate times, at levels ranging from rookie ball to Triple-A, he has had a higher BB% than K%. 2) He hails from the Venezuelan state of Carabobo, or in literal translation from Spanish, "stupid face." 3) While candid photos are fine, every single posed photograph that has ever been taken of Breyvic Valera has made him look like a combination of Frankenstein's monster and a cliff face that has lured unsuspecting hikers to their deaths for years.

Engelb Vielma INF Born: 06/22/94 Age: 25 Bats: B Throws: R Height: 5'11" Weight: 155 Origin: International Free Agent, 2011

YEAR	TEAM	LVL	AGE	PA	R	2B	3B	HR	RBI	BB	K	SB	CS	AVG/OBP/SLG	DRC+	VORP	BABIP	BRR	FRAA	WARP
2016	FTM	A+	22	30	5	0	0	0	0	5	8	2	0	.200/.333/.200	92	0.1	.294	-0.6	SS(4): 0.9, 2B(3): -0.5	0.1
2016	CHT	AA	22	367	47	7	4	0	21	34	62	10	8	.271/.345/.318	90	12.1	.333	1.6	SS(57): -0.1, 3B(21): 2.8	1.3
2017	CHT	AA	23	141	7	5	0	0	18	14	13	1	3	.286/.362/.328	104	5.2	.312	-1.3	SS(19): -0.2, 2B(14): 0.2	0.5
2017	ROC	AAA	23	314	36	12	2	0	17	11	72	2	5	.206/.233/.260	51	-1.6	.266	3.2	SS(84): 3.8, 2B(2): -0.3	0.2
2018	BAL	MLB	24	8	1	0	0	0	0	1	4	0	0	.143/.250/.143	68	0.5	.333	1.0	2B(4): -0.3, SS(2): 0.0	0.1
2018	NOR	AAA	24	43	3	2	1	0	3	4	9	0	0	.184/.256/.289	88	-0.2	.233	0.3	SS(12): 0.0	0.2
2019	BAL	MLB	25	251	22	8	1	4	21	14	62	2	2	.202/.252/.293	47	-7.9	.250	-0.6	SS 1, 2B 0	-0.6

Breakout: 2%   Improve: 10%   Collapse: 8%   Attrition: 19%   MLB: 27%   *Comparables: Andrew Romine, Mike Freeman, Rafael Ynoa*

Whatever kind of a stinker you feel you've been handed in the last name derby, we feel confident in suggesting it's better than the lot that befell one Engelb Stalin Vielma. That's "Engelb," like someone got partway through writing "Engelbert" and got bored; "Stalin," like Stalin; and "Vielma," which would probably be fine on its own but in concert with the rest of the name summons images of food-borne parasites, Scooby-Doo characters, and/or mechanically reclaimed meat. All that said, thank goodness Vielma played for the 2018 Baltimore Orioles, for while the name Engelb Vielma is 80-grade, nothing else about the player is, and on a more competent team, the baseball record books might have been denied this glory.

Jonathan Villar SS   Born: 05/02/91   Age: 28   Bats: B   Throws: R   Height: 6'1"   Weight: 215   Origin: International Free Agent, 2008

YEAR	TEAM	LVL	AGE	PA	R	2B	3B	HR	RBI	BB	K	SB	CS	AVG/OBP/SLG	DRC+	VORP	BABIP	BRR	FRAA	WARP
2016	MIL	MLB	25	679	92	38	3	19	63	79	174	62	18	.285/.369/.457	100	44.9	.373	-2.4	SS(108): 5.5, 3B(42): -4.1	2.9
2017	MIL	MLB	26	436	49	18	1	11	40	30	132	23	8	.241/.293/.372	66	5.8	.330	1.6	2B(98): 2.7, CF(6): -0.1	-0.1
2018	MIL	MLB	27	279	26	10	1	6	22	19	80	14	2	.261/.315/.377	83	6.6	.355	0.5	2B(74): -6.1	-0.3
2018	BAL	MLB	27	236	28	4	0	8	24	22	58	21	3	.258/.336/.392	86	8.2	.319	2.4	2B(36): 1.0, SS(18): 0.5	0.8
2019	BAL	MLB	28	583	73	20	2	14	58	49	163	37	9	.234/.302/.363	79	5.3	.307	0.1	2B -3, SS 1	0.4

Breakout: 0%   Improve: 54%   Collapse: 10%   Attrition: 14%   MLB: 97%   *Comparables: Dan Uggla, Logan Forsythe, Danny Espinosa*

Villar is just two seasons removed from a year where he snuck up on the 20-homer threshold while playing middle infield, but an offensive stallout over the past two seasons cost him his job in Milwaukee, who opted to trade up by acquiring Jonathan Schoop. He may not be the toolsed-out prospect some dreamed on during his age-25 season, but he is a perfectly serviceable middle infield piece for a rebuilding club, someone who can man multiple positions and provide the occasional pop at the plate. He won't be swiping 60-plus bags, either, but Villar is still a real threat on the bases, which will be a lift for the leaden-footed Orioles. He isn't a free agent until 2021, so Baltimore has the flexibility of timing a hot stretch or a needy contender into an opportunity to flip him for prospects down the line.

Stephen Wilkerson INF   Born: 01/11/92   Age: 27   Bats: B   Throws: R   Height: 6'1"   Weight: 195   Origin: Round 8, 2014 Draft (#241 overall)

YEAR	TEAM	LVL	AGE	PA	R	2B	3B	HR	RBI	BB	K	SB	CS	AVG/OBP/SLG	DRC+	VORP	BABIP	BRR	FRAA	WARP
2016	FRD	A+	24	461	49	17	4	4	36	45	98	18	6	.251/.334/.343	90	4.2	.321	0.8	2B(112): -1.8, SS(1): 0.2	0.6
2017	FRD	A+	25	180	29	10	0	2	15	19	40	2	3	.323/.407/.426	101	11.3	.425	1.0	2B(26): -0.5, 3B(8): 0.6	0.7
2017	BOW	AA	25	273	34	13	0	6	30	20	53	5	2	.294/.354/.420	99	11.7	.351	-0.5	3B(35): -0.6, 2B(27): 0.8	0.9
2018	NOR	AAA	26	86	13	5	0	4	13	5	15	0	1	.270/.329/.500	110	6.0	.276	0.2	2B(10): 2.7, 3B(6): 0.3	0.7
2018	BAL	MLB	26	49	2	3	0	0	3	3	16	1	0	.174/.224/.239	62	-3.7	.267	-0.6	2B(9): 0.9, 3B(6): 0.2	0.0
2019	BAL	MLB	27	105	11	4	0	3	12	7	25	1	1	.228/.287/.372	67	-1.2	.274	-0.1	2B 1, 3B 0	0.0

Breakout: 4%   Improve: 16%   Collapse: 4%   Attrition: 16%   MLB: 29%   *Comparables: Hernan Iribarren, Kevin Russo, Chris Valaika*

It's not unheard of for organizations to send prospects on the back nine of 25 or those with major-league experience to the Arizona Fall League, but there's usually a specific reason behind it: an injured player who needs extra reps, or a mechanical change that needs to be worked out against non-instructional-league opposition. For Wilkerson, a repeat trip to the AFL is to make up time from his 50-game PED suspension last season, as the organization attempts to suss out what they have in the utility infielder. Wilkerson has shown a solid feel for hitting in the minors, but has fallen off some in plate discipline recently. With no power to speak of and average footspeed, Wilkerson has to prove he can both get on base and play an acceptable third base in order to carve out a spot as a bench player.

Austin Wynns C   Born: 12/10/90   Age: 28   Bats: R   Throws: R   Height: 6'2"   Weight: 205   Origin: Round 10, 2013 Draft (#309 overall)

YEAR	TEAM	LVL	AGE	PA	R	2B	3B	HR	RBI	BB	K	SB	CS	AVG/OBP/SLG	DRC+	VORP	BABIP	BRR	FRAA	WARP
2016	BOW	AA	25	82	11	7	0	0	10	7	12	1	0	.247/.309/.342	89	1.8	.290	0.1	C(20): 0.8	0.4
2016	FRD	A+	25	206	23	10	0	5	20	13	32	0	0	.303/.351/.436	111	8.4	.340	0.4	C(36): 1.8	1.2
2017	BOW	AA	26	434	54	19	1	10	46	52	64	1	0	.281/.377/.419	120	25.8	.314	0.6	C(90): 1.3	3.3
2018	NOR	AAA	27	153	19	4	0	4	16	11	38	0	0	.230/.288/.345	89	3.2	.283	0.5	C(39): -1.0	0.5
2018	BAL	MLB	27	118	16	2	0	4	11	5	25	0	0	.255/.287/.382	87	0.7	.296	-0.8	C(41): -0.5	0.3
2019	BAL	MLB	28	236	23	9	1	6	25	15	56	0	0	.227/.281/.364	72	2.2	.273	-0.4	C -4	-0.2

Breakout: 3%   Improve: 12%   Collapse: 14%   Attrition: 30%   MLB: 57%   *Comparables: Bobby Wilson, Kyle Phillips, Dustin Garneau*

In the seminal 1995 film *Showgirls*, Cristal Connors—played brilliantly by Gina Gershon, who knows exactly what kind of film she's in, even as the filmmakers apparently did not—intones from her hospital bed: "there's always someone younger and hungrier coming down the stairs after you." It's not any kind of philosophical statement; Cristal literally gets pushed down some stairs by another, younger showgirl. "Younger" is a relative term in the Orioles system, as Wynns is now 27, the same age fellow catcher Caleb Joseph was when he made his major league debut. Both players have been in the Orioles system for their

YEAR	TEAM	P. COUNT	FRM RUNS	BLK RUNS	THRW RUNS	TOT RUNS
2017	BOW	12803	-2.2	2.7	0.5	0.6
2018	BAL	5269	-2.3	0.5	0.1	-1.8
2018	NOR	5362	0.1	-0.1	0.0	-0.3
2019	BAL	9399	-4.7	0.4	-0.3	-4.5

entire pro careers, grinding their way up level by level with strong defensive play at a premium position and passable offense. This year, it was Wynns' turn to get his call to the Show, and with his plus set of defensive chops coupled with solid plate discipline, it looks like Wynns will be the Nomi Malone to Joseph's Cristal Connors next season.

PITCHERS

Keegan Akin LHP Born: 04/01/95 Age: 24 Bats: L Throws: L Height: 6'0" Weight: 225 Origin: Round 2, 2016 Draft (#54 overall)

YEAR	TEAM	LVL	AGE	W	L	SV	G	GS	IP	H	HR	BB/9	K/9	K	GB%	BABIP	WHIP	ERA	DRA	WARP	MPH	FB%	WHF	CSP
2016	ABE	A-	21	0	1	0	9	9	26	15	0	2.4	10.0	29	51%	.231	0.85	1.04	4.46	0.2				
2017	FRD	A+	22	7	8	0	21	21	100	89	12	4.1	10.0	111	38%	.307	1.35	4.14	5.88	-0.7				
2018	BOW	AA	23	14	7	0	25	25	137²	114	16	3.8	9.3	142	32%	.278	1.25	3.27	4.07	2.0				
2019	BAL	MLB	24	5	9	0	22	22	106	110	22	4.2	8.4	99	35%	.297	1.51	5.74	5.67	-0.2				

Breakout: 5%   Improve: 10%   Collapse: 5%   Attrition: 11%   MLB: 18%   Comparables: Caleb Smith, James Houser, Drew Anderson

Listed at six feet tall, Akin's stuff plays like he's much taller, thanks to the sharp downward plane the stocky lefty is able to generate with his mechanics. Akin has three solid pitches in a low-to-mid 90s fastball, a slider with some sharp movement, and a changeup that will make the difference as to whether he's a back-of-the-rotation piece or a Quad-A/swingman type. The Western Michigan grad has made steady progress through the system since being drafted in 2016 and shown an ability to miss bats at every level, including an impressive AFL stint in 2017. An oblique injury slowed him last season, but he returned to full health this year and posted one of the strongest seasons for a starting pitcher in the Eastern League. Akin won the Eastern League Pitcher of the Year Award with Double-A Bowie, the first time an Orioles pitcher has won the award in a decade.

Cameron Bishop LHP Born: 02/14/96 Age: 23 Bats: L Throws: L Height: 6'4" Weight: 215 Origin: Round 26, 2017 Draft (#788 overall)

YEAR	TEAM	LVL	AGE	W	L	SV	G	GS	IP	H	HR	BB/9	K/9	K	GB%	BABIP	WHIP	ERA	DRA	WARP	MPH	FB%	WHF	CSP
2017	ABE	A-	21	1	1	0	8	8	34²	20	1	4.2	9.9	38	51%	.232	1.04	0.78	3.11	0.9				
2018	DEL	A	22	9	7	0	22	22	125²	107	5	1.4	7.1	99	50%	.274	1.01	2.94	3.71	2.2				
2019	BAL	MLB	23	4	7	0	16	16	83	97	15	3.6	5.9	54	42%	.305	1.57	5.80	5.71	-0.2				

Breakout: 2%   Improve: 2%   Collapse: 3%   Attrition: 5%   MLB: 6%   Comparables: Jason Adam, Ryan Sherriff, Jalen Beeks

The Orioles almost Orioles'd themselves out of Bishop's services by submitting his draft paperwork late, but the kind overlords of MLB took pity on Bishop, if being drafted by the Orioles qualifies as being pitied. A strained oblique cost Bishop his junior year of college and subsequently his draft standing, but Baltimore, sensing a deal, took the big lefty in the 26th round and signed him well overslot. The Orioles built Bishop's innings slowly through 2017 and continued a middle-of-the-road approach in 2018, assigning him to Single-A Delmarva. For the Shorebirds, Bishop proved to be a durable, reliable starter who doesn't record eye-popping strikeout numbers but also doesn't walk anyone, elicits plenty of ground balls, and keeps the ball in the yard. Bishop has a simple, repeatable delivery out of a high overhand slot with some sharp downward plane action. Bishop also throws a slider, curve, and changeup, all of which need significant refinement before they are major-league quality pitches.

Richard Bleier LHP Born: 04/16/87 Age: 32 Bats: L Throws: L Height: 6'3" Weight: 215 Origin: Round 6, 2008 Draft (#183 overall)

YEAR	TEAM	LVL	AGE	W	L	SV	G	GS	IP	H	HR	BB/9	K/9	K	GB%	BABIP	WHIP	ERA	DRA	WARP	MPH	FB%	WHF	CSP
2016	SWB	AAA	29	2	3	1	12	10	58	66	2	1.7	3.9	25	64%	.318	1.33	3.72	3.85	1.0				
2016	NYA	MLB	29	0	0	0	23	0	23	20	0	1.6	5.1	13	55%	.270	1.04	1.96	5.93	-0.3	91.7	61.3	9.7	43.8
2017	NOR	AAA	30	0	0	1	8	0	14²	9	0	0.0	9.2	15	70%	.243	0.61	0.61	3.26	0.3				
2017	BAL	MLB	30	2	1	0	57	0	63¹	62	6	1.8	3.7	26	69%	.259	1.18	1.99	5.01	0.1	91.1	62.8	10	52.7
2018	BAL	MLB	31	3	0	0	31	0	32²	36	0	1.1	4.1	15	58%	.319	1.22	1.93	5.09	-0.1	89.7	61.2	10	53.6
2019	BAL	MLB	32	3	1	0	56	0	58²	64	6	3.0	5.3	34	56%	.299	1.42	4.76	4.63	0.3	89.8	61.5	9.9	50.4

Breakout: 15%   Improve: 27%   Collapse: 20%   Attrition: 14%   MLB: 57%   Comparables: Dana Eveland, Steven Wright, Dan Otero

It was a sunny day game in early June when Richard Bleier clutched his side immediately after throwing a pitch. At the time, the command-control lefty was one of the lone bright spots on an Orioles team already circling the drain. Prised from the division rival Yankees in early 2017 for cash considerations, Bleier added a cutter to his repertoire over the past two seasons. Said pitch has transformed him from an average low-velo lefty who doesn't strike anyone out to a soft-contact monster who still doesn't strike anyone out but induces a ton of groundballs and keeps the ball in the park, a valuable skill for any AL East pitcher. On that day, the Orioles were down 5-1 to the Red Sox, and the broadcast team was busy modeling the day's giveaway, an Orioles-branded bucket hat. It took them several minutes to discern something was seriously wrong with Bleier. The hat, it turned out, was reversible.

Dylan Bundy RHP Born: 11/15/92 Age: 26 Bats: B Throws: R Height: 6'1" Weight: 200 Origin: Round 1, 2011 Draft (#4 overall)

YEAR	TEAM	LVL	AGE	W	L	SV	G	GS	IP	H	HR	BB/9	K/9	K	GB%	BABIP	WHIP	ERA	DRA	WARP	MPH	FB%	WHF	CSP
2016	BAL	MLB	23	10	6	0	36	14	109²	109	18	3.4	8.5	104	37%	.299	1.38	4.02	5.58	-0.4	97.0	61.7	12.3	48.2
2017	BAL	MLB	24	13	9	0	28	28	169²	152	26	2.7	8.1	152	33%	.273	1.20	4.24	4.93	1.2	94.0	53.8	12.3	46.4
2018	BAL	MLB	25	8	16	0	31	31	171²	188	41	2.8	9.6	184	35%	.316	1.41	5.45	5.34	-0.1	93.4	55.8	13.5	50.2
2019	BAL	MLB	26	9	12	0	30	30	171	170	28	3.2	9.0	172	36%	.304	1.36	4.70	4.58	1.8	93.9	57.2	13.1	49.3

Breakout: 24%   Improve: 59%   Collapse: 17%   Attrition: 7%   MLB: 92%   Comparables: Oliver Perez, Floyd Bannister, Melido Perez

It's a cruelty typical of the capricious baseball gods that when Bundy wished on that monkey paw for a career-high strikeout rate, it would come along with a career-high home run rate. Pitcher wins are a poor metric, but Bundy's sharp drop in fastball velocity from 2016-2017 looks a little more worrisome when his W-L record from last season is reversed, along with the alarming spike in runs allowed. The path to the major leagues for an Orioles pitching prospect never did run smooth, but Bundy has always seemed more snakebit than most, having to battle both his own body and arcane roster construction rules to secure a place as a starter in the major leagues. He's still just 25 years old, and baseball will be a better place if the one-time Gatorade Male Athlete of the Year—the first baseball player to ever win the award—is able to deliver on his incredible promise.

Cody Carroll RHP Born: 10/15/92 Age: 26 Bats: R Throws: R Height: 6'5" Weight: 215 Origin: Round 22, 2015 Draft (#663 overall)

YEAR	TEAM	LVL	AGE	W	L	SV	G	GS	IP	H	HR	BB/9	K/9	K	GB%	BABIP	WHIP	ERA	DRA	WARP	MPH	FB%	WHF	CSP
2016	CSC	A	23	4	4	3	26	6	91¹	89	3	4.0	8.9	90	51%	.336	1.42	3.15	3.35	1.6				
2017	TAM	A+	24	1	0	2	13	0	20	10	1	3.6	13.5	30	39%	.225	0.90	2.25	3.00	0.4				
2017	TRN	AA	24	2	5	5	26	0	47¹	36	4	4.2	11.2	59	48%	.291	1.23	2.66	2.50	1.3				
2018	SWB	AAA	25	3	0	9	32	0	41²	27	0	3.9	11.9	55	34%	.287	1.08	2.38	2.64	1.2				
2018	BAL	MLB	25	0	2	0	15	0	17	21	6	6.9	8.5	16	33%	.306	2.00	9.00	8.32	-0.7	97.6	66.4	8.9	44.9
2019	BAL	MLB	26	2	1	0	44	0	47	47	8	5.1	9.6	50	41%	.307	1.57	5.37	5.28	-0.2	97.2	67.6	9	45.7

Breakout: 13% Improve: 22% Collapse: 11% Attrition: 22% MLB: 38% Comparables: Angel Nesbitt, Jose Valdez, Juan Minaya

The Orioles got three MLB-adjacent pitchers in return for Zach Britton, including big (6'5") righty Carroll. The 2015 22nd-rounder made steady progress through the Yankees system, although his walk rate has always been a slight concern. Carroll has a big fastball that regularly sits in the upper-90s and can graze triple digits, and he pairs that with a hard, tightly-spinning slider that profiles as a plus pitch. Carroll also throws a splitter that's less developed than his other two pitches. The Orioles are shaping up to have a bullpen full of hard-throwing, poor-command pitchers; AL East hitters might be well-served to invest in all manner of protective gear this off-season.

Andrew Cashner RHP Born: 09/11/86 Age: 32 Bats: R Throws: R Height: 6'6" Weight: 235 Origin: Round 1, 2008 Draft (#19 overall)

YEAR	TEAM	LVL	AGE	W	L	SV	G	GS	IP	H	HR	BB/9	K/9	K	GB%	BABIP	WHIP	ERA	DRA	WARP	MPH	FB%	WHF	CSP
2016	SDN	MLB	29	4	7	0	16	16	79¹	80	13	3.4	7.6	67	49%	.291	1.39	4.76	6.24	-0.8	97.2	66.6	7.8	46.6
2016	MIA	MLB	29	1	4	0	12	11	52²	62	6	5.1	7.7	45	47%	.352	1.75	5.98	6.04	-0.4	96.6	66.6	8.1	44.3
2017	TEX	MLB	30	11	11	0	28	28	166²	156	15	3.5	4.6	86	49%	.266	1.32	3.40	5.58	0.0	96.0	65.1	6.7	49.6
2018	BAL	MLB	31	4	15	0	28	28	153	177	25	3.8	5.8	99	42%	.311	1.58	5.29	6.69	-2.4	94.8	60.2	7.5	46.7
2019	BAL	MLB	32	6	10	0	24	24	127¹	145	19	4.0	6.0	85	45%	.306	1.58	5.43	5.33	0.2	94.7	62.8	7.2	47

Breakout: 6% Improve: 38% Collapse: 25% Attrition: 9% MLB: 87% Comparables: Yovani Gallardo, Jon Garland, Jason Marquis

Cashner parlayed a strong 2017 for the Rangers into a two-year, $16MM contract with Baltimore. At the time, the O's rotation consisted of Bundy, Gausman, and three tallboys of Natty Boh, so it was easy enough to paper over Cashner's poor peripherals and focus instead on his shiny 3.40 ERA. Unsurprisingly, that strategy has backfired, and Cashner's numbers look awful no matter which lens one chooses to apply. A special low point came in early August, when Cashner set an Orioles record by surrendering 10 runs in fewer than two innings, an impressive achievement in considering both the history of the Orioles and the history of Orioles pitching. Maybe Baltimore's FO knew exactly what they were doing in signing Cashner to be an innings sponge for two years of a rebuilding team, just like maybe Alexander Fleming knew exactly what he was doing when he left those dishes in the sink and discovered penicillin. Crazy like a fox, those Orioles.

Miguel Castro RHP Born: 12/24/94 Age: 24 Bats: R Throws: R Height: 6'7" Weight: 205 Origin: International Free Agent, 2012

YEAR	TEAM	LVL	AGE	W	L	SV	G	GS	IP	H	HR	BB/9	K/9	K	GB%	BABIP	WHIP	ERA	DRA	WARP	MPH	FB%	WHF	CSP
2016	COL	MLB	21	0	0	0	19	0	14²	18	3	3.1	7.4	12	55%	.326	1.57	6.14	4.96	0.0	98.9	57.3	11.7	46.5
2016	ABQ	AAA	21	2	3	0	16	0	15²	21	5	4.0	8.6	15	49%	.364	1.79	10.34	5.28	-0.1				
2017	BOW	AA	22	3	0	0	6	0	24¹	23	1	2.2	4.1	11	49%	.275	1.19	4.44	3.80	0.3				
2017	BAL	MLB	22	3	3	0	39	1	66¹	53	8	3.8	5.2	38	50%	.227	1.22	3.53	5.51	-0.2	98.3	61.4	10.5	45.9
2018	BAL	MLB	23	2	7	0	63	1	86¹	75	9	5.2	5.9	57	49%	.259	1.45	3.96	6.49	-1.5	98.2	58.1	10.4	47.8
2019	BAL	MLB	24	3	1	0	67	0	70²	67	8	4.8	7.0	55	48%	.281	1.49	5.12	5.03	0.0	98.1	61	10.8	48.3

Breakout: 24% Improve: 44% Collapse: 25% Attrition: 18% MLB: 89% Comparables: Anibal Sanchez, Trevor Gott, Oscar Villarreal

Cheap, fast, or quality: the old adage in sales is that you can have two, but never all three. Castro is cheap, having been acquired off waivers in 2017 from the Rockies, and he throws his fastball very fast, but this year he posted dismal peripherals, walking almost as many batters as he struck out. Castro has been in organized baseball since 2012, when a triple-digit fastball was more of a unicorn than it is today; he's no longer the youngest nor the hardest thrower, and if he can't solve his command issues, it's hard to project him in the back end of anyone's bullpen, even the lowly Orioles. Castro will hit arbitration in 2020, so the clock is ticking on the "cheap" part of the trifecta, which is, unfortunately, the only compelling part of his value until he learns to throw more quality strikes.

Alex Cobb RHP Born: 10/07/87 Age: 31 Bats: R Throws: R Height: 6'3" Weight: 205 Origin: Round 4, 2006 Draft (#109 overall)

YEAR	TEAM	LVL	AGE	W	L	SV	G	GS	IP	H	HR	BB/9	K/9	K	GB%	BABIP	WHIP	ERA	DRA	WARP	MPH	FB%	WHF	CSP
2016	DUR	AAA	28	0	1	0	4	4	15	24	3	3.0	6.0	10	44%	.389	1.93	6.60	6.57	-0.2				
2016	TBA	MLB	28	1	2	0	5	5	22	32	5	2.9	6.5	16	52%	.355	1.77	8.59	4.56	0.2	92.5	48.2	8	47.1
2017	TBA	MLB	29	12	10	0	29	29	179¹	175	22	2.2	6.4	128	49%	.282	1.22	3.66	4.07	3.0	93.0	51.5	7.5	47
2018	BAL	MLB	30	5	15	0	28	28	152¹	172	24	2.5	6.0	102	51%	.303	1.41	4.90	5.50	-0.3	93.2	51.5	8	47.6
2019	BAL	MLB	31	8	12	0	30	30	159	177	21	3.1	6.0	106	48%	.304	1.46	4.94	4.82	1.2	92.2	51	7.7	47

Breakout: 10% Improve: 56% Collapse: 22% Attrition: 8% MLB: 96% Comparables: Ivan Nova, Kyle Lohse, Homer Bailey

Tommy John surgery robbed Cobb of his elite split-change, which didn't have the same movement when he brought back the pitch in 2017. After a slow start to the season, Cobb steadily improved month to month as the pitch once nicknamed "The Thing" started showing signs of life; from June to August, he nearly tripled the number of whiffs induced on the splitter. Cobb's improvement wasn't as stark as his first half (6.41) vs. second half (2.56) ERA would have you believe, but the peripherals improved enough to call it a bounceback from his early-season struggles. It's almost like having a spring training matters. While other teams guarded their purse strings jealously last off-season, the Orioles handed Cobb the third-largest contract for a pitcher in free agency that year, so a return to form is important for both Cobb and for his future trade value if the Orioles continue to flounder.

Mychal Givens RHP Born: 05/13/90 Age: 29 Bats: R Throws: R Height: 6'0" Weight: 210 Origin: Round 2, 2009 Draft (#54 overall)

YEAR	TEAM	LVL	AGE	W	L	SV	G	GS	IP	H	HR	BB/9	K/9	K	GB%	BABIP	WHIP	ERA	DRA	WARP	MPH	FB%	WHF	CSP
2016	BAL	MLB	26	8	2	0	66	0	74²	59	6	4.3	11.6	96	38%	.314	1.27	3.13	3.51	1.3	97.3	63.5	16	49.9
2017	BAL	MLB	27	8	1	0	69	0	78²	57	10	2.9	10.1	88	43%	.251	1.04	2.75	3.69	1.3	97.8	72.2	13.1	50.3
2018	BAL	MLB	28	0	7	9	69	0	76²	61	4	3.5	9.3	79	38%	.284	1.19	3.99	4.84	0.1	97.3	76.8	12.5	53.1
2019	*BAL*	*MLB*	*29*	*3*	*1*	*28*	*61*	*0*	*64²*	*60*	*9*	*4.0*	*9.5*	*68*	*40%*	*.294*	*1.37*	*4.61*	*4.50*	*0.5*	*96.8*	*71.8*	*13.6*	*51.4*

Breakout: 19% Improve: 40% Collapse: 30% Attrition: 17% MLB: 90% *Comparables: Hunter Strickland, A.J. Ramos, Michael Gonzalez*

Baltimore is one of America's best, most underrated cities, so if Givens wanted to remain there this season—and who wouldn't, when the alternatives were Houston or Cleveland or Arizona—he went about it exactly the right way. By posting an almost perfectly average performance for an AL reliever, Givens did enough to ensure his job security, but not so much as to tempt other teams who came sniffing around at the trade deadline. Closer by default after the Orioles started selling off bullpen pieces, Givens is arbitration-eligible in 2019 in a system that rewards saves, and wound up as Baltimore's most valuable pitcher, which will inflate his price tag. Now that the Orioles have flipped the hyperdrive switch on a rebuild, it wouldn't be surprising to see the 28-year-old moved this off-season to a team that values his ability to keep the ball in the park and won't mind paying closer prices for him in arbitration. Hopefully, he likes the neighborhood.

DL Hall LHP Born: 09/19/98 Age: 20 Bats: L Throws: L Height: 6'2" Weight: 195 Origin: Round 1, 2017 Draft (#21 overall)

YEAR	TEAM	LVL	AGE	W	L	SV	G	GS	IP	H	HR	BB/9	K/9	K	GB%	BABIP	WHIP	ERA	DRA	WARP	MPH	FB%	WHF	CSP
2017	ORI	RK	18	0	0	0	5	5	10¹	10	1	8.7	10.5	12	58%	.360	1.94	6.97	4.79	0.1				
2018	DEL	A	19	2	7	0	22	20	94¹	68	6	4.0	9.5	100	46%	.262	1.17	2.10	3.69	1.7				
2019	*BAL*	*MLB*	*20*	*2*	*7*	*0*	*14*	*14*	*57¹*	*64*	*13*	*7.6*	*8.0*	*51*	*44%*	*.304*	*1.96*	*7.44*	*7.45*	*-1.3*				

Breakout: 2% Improve: 2% Collapse: 1% Attrition: 3% MLB: 4% *Comparables: Sean Gallagher, Josh Hader, Jeurys Familia*

Let you love anything like Baltimore loves taking a prep pitcher in the first round. Baltimore's 2017 first-rounder (#21 overall) garners high praise for his late-breaking power curve, especially effective out of a deceptive left-handed slot, and his mid-90s fastball gives him the floor of a back-end bullpen arm, although of course the Orioles are hoping for more. After a strong full first year of pro ball at Single-A, Hall's ceiling looks much higher than that, provided he can polish a third pitch and tweak his delivery to land more pitches in the strike zone. In the meantime, his ability to put batters away with either the fastball or the deadly curve should propel Hall onto some top-100 lists in the near future. Love what you love, kittens.

Brenan Hanifee RHP Born: 05/29/98 Age: 21 Bats: R Throws: R Height: 6'5" Weight: 180 Origin: Round 4, 2016 Draft (#121 overall)

YEAR	TEAM	LVL	AGE	W	L	SV	G	GS	IP	H	HR	BB/9	K/9	K	GB%	BABIP	WHIP	ERA	DRA	WARP	MPH	FB%	WHF	CSP
2017	ABE	A-	19	7	3	0	12	12	68²	65	2	1.6	5.8	44	59%	.289	1.12	2.75	3.57	1.4				
2018	DEL	A	20	8	6	0	23	23	132	120	8	1.5	5.8	85	55%	.275	1.08	2.86	3.91	2.0				
2019	*BAL*	*MLB*	*21*	*4*	*8*	*0*	*16*	*16*	*92¹*	*113*	*16*	*2.9*	*4.4*	*46*	*47%*	*.304*	*1.55*	*5.78*	*5.69*	*-0.2*				

Breakout: 6% Improve: 8% Collapse: 1% Attrition: 2% MLB: 9% *Comparables: Kohl Stewart, Alex Cobb, Jair Jurrjens*

Hanifee grew up playing baseball on a field his father built in Northern Virginia, and spent 2018 playing for the Delmarva Shorebirds, just over four hours from his hometown. Hanifee was listed at 6'5"/185 when he was drafted out of high school in 2016, and it doesn't look like he's added much bulk to his frame since. A back injury has forced the Orioles to build his innings slowly, but when he's been on the mound the results have been solid. So far, Hanifee doesn't miss many bats, but he also doesn't walk batters, and he's able to generate a high number of groundball outs and keep the ball in the park with a fastball that, despite below-average velocity, has plenty of armside run and sink. That's an appealing profile for any pitcher, but especially one based in the AL East.

Donnie Hart LHP Born: 09/06/90 Age: 28 Bats: L Throws: L Height: 5'11" Weight: 180 Origin: Round 27, 2013 Draft (#819 overall)

YEAR	TEAM	LVL	AGE	W	L	SV	G	GS	IP	H	HR	BB/9	K/9	K	GB%	BABIP	WHIP	ERA	DRA	WARP	MPH	FB%	WHF	CSP
2016	BOW	AA	25	3	1	4	40	0	46¹	41	1	1.4	9.7	50	50%	.325	1.04	2.72	2.48	1.2				
2016	BAL	MLB	25	0	0	0	22	0	18¹	12	1	2.9	5.9	12	60%	.212	0.98	0.49	4.64	0.1	89.7	46.1	9.7	45.4
2017	NOR	AAA	26	1	0	0	13	0	15¹	17	1	1.2	11.7	20	55%	.390	1.24	2.35	2.10	0.5				
2017	BAL	MLB	26	2	0	0	51	0	43²	48	5	2.7	6.0	29	54%	.309	1.40	3.71	5.56	-0.2	88.8	48	10.7	39.4
2018	NOR	AAA	27	3	2	6	32	3	41	42	1	2.2	9.9	45	62%	.360	1.27	2.41	3.16	1.0				
2018	BAL	MLB	27	0	0	0	20	0	19¹	31	2	5.6	6.1	13	46%	.403	2.22	5.59	7.84	-0.6	89.3	56.5	9.2	50.6
2019	*BAL*	*MLB*	*28*	*2*	*1*	*0*	*33*	*0*	*35¹*	*38*	*4*	*3.5*	*7.4*	*29*	*50%*	*.315*	*1.47*	*4.59*	*4.46*	*0.2*	*88.6*	*50.9*	*10.1*	*45.8*

Breakout: 20% Improve: 34% Collapse: 25% Attrition: 27% MLB: 65% *Comparables: Bryan Morris, Brian Wolfe, Royce Ring*

For many teams, a 27th-round draft pick making it to the major leagues would be a story of inspiration and triumph against adversity. Sadly, by his third turn in the majors, Hart's strong minor league numbers have been eclipsed by major-league struggles. On September 26th, in a game against the Red Sox, the Orioles decided to try out the newfangled "Opener" strategy popularized by the Rays. Why let the inconsequential detail that the Rays 'pen was top-five in the league and the Orioles' was bottom-five stop them? The O's-pener made it all of 20 pitches, allowing two runs and loading the bases again before being pulled for Hart, who promptly surrendered a bases-clearing double and inspired a spate of bad puns based on his last name on Twitter. Tom Petty was wrong; it's the punning that's the hardest part.

Hunter Harvey RHP Born: 12/09/94 Age: 24 Bats: R Throws: R Height: 6'3" Weight: 175 Origin: Round 1, 2013 Draft (#22 overall)

YEAR	TEAM	LVL	AGE	W	L	SV	G	GS	IP	H	HR	BB/9	K/9	K	GB%	BABIP	WHIP	ERA	DRA	WARP	MPH	FB%	WHF	CSP
2017	DEL	A	22	0	1	0	3	3	8²	4	0	3.1	14.5	14	31%	.250	0.81	2.08	2.57	0.3				
2018	BOW	AA	23	1	2	0	9	9	32¹	36	3	2.5	8.4	30	36%	.351	1.39	5.57	4.17	0.4				
2019	*BAL*	*MLB*	*24*	*1*	*2*	*0*	*5*	*5*	*26²*	*29*	*5*	*4.3*	*8.2*	*24*	*37%*	*.310*	*1.57*	*5.69*	*5.61*	*0.0*				

Breakout: 3% Improve: 7% Collapse: 3% Attrition: 8% MLB: 13% *Comparables: Daniel Poncedeleon, Rob Rasmussen, Spencer Turnbull*

When risk-averse front office execs give presentations about Why Picking High School Pitchers in the First Round is Bad, the first slide is a picture of Harvey. Five years after being drafted 22nd overall by the O's, Harvey has yet to throw a pitch above Double-A. His injuries have been of both the typical baseball pitcher variety, including a flexor mass strain and Tommy John surgery in 2016, and of the freakish bad luck variety, including a fractured fibula after being drilled by a line drive during Spring Training in 2015 and popping his shoulder trying to dodge a foul ball in the dugout. When he's been on the field, Harvey has posted strong results against low-level hitters. The team had to add Harvey to the 40-man this past off-season to protect him against the Rule 5 Draft, so if he holds it together against the upper minors early next season, expect pitching-starved Baltimore to be aggressive in promoting Harvey, as long as he's relatively whole.

David Hess RHP Born: 07/10/93 Age: 25 Bats: R Throws: R Height: 6'2" Weight: 180 Origin: Round 5, 2014 Draft (#151 overall)

YEAR	TEAM	LVL	AGE	W	L	SV	G	GS	IP	H	HR	BB/9	K/9	K	GB%	BABIP	WHIP	ERA	DRA	WARP	MPH	FB%	WHF	CSP
2016	BOW	AA	22	5	13	0	25	24	127¹	162	19	2.8	6.0	85	36%	.335	1.58	5.37	5.80	-1.1				
2017	BOW	AA	23	11	9	0	27	26	154¹	137	16	3.1	7.2	123	32%	.269	1.23	3.85	5.73	-1.1				
2018	NOR	AAA	24	3	2	0	9	9	45²	38	3	3.7	8.7	44	29%	.285	1.25	3.15	3.96	0.8				
2018	BAL	MLB	24	3	10	0	21	19	103¹	106	22	3.2	6.4	74	35%	.268	1.38	4.88	7.38	-2.5	94.1	58.7	9.1	47.9
2019	BAL	MLB	25	5	8	0	19	19	100²	109	18	3.4	7.0	78	34%	.294	1.46	5.48	5.39	0.1	93.8	60.1	9.3	49

Breakout: 8%   Improve: 18%   Collapse: 12%   Attrition: 15%   MLB: 35%   *Comparables: Shairon Martis, Barry Enright, Justin Grimm*

Hess was on his way to a solid start at Triple-A before being unceremoniously flung into the O's starting rotation. Unsurprisingly, the 25-year-old righty, who struggled to adjust to Double-A two seasons ago, struggled even more against major league hitters. The fringey nature of Hess's secondary offerings combined with the average velo on his fastball have led some scouts to ponder if he wouldn't be better suited to the bullpen, where his fastball might play up to the mid-90s. In a stronger system, he'd probably have already been converted to long relief. The key to Hess sticking as a starter will be developing his changeup into a major league-quality pitch, but he's still a flyball pitcher in the AL East, baseball's equivalent of the passenger pigeon.

Blaine Knight RHP Born: 06/28/96 Age: 23 Bats: R Throws: R Height: 6'3" Weight: 165 Origin: Round 3, 2018 Draft (#87 overall)

YEAR	TEAM	LVL	AGE	W	L	SV	G	GS	IP	H	HR	BB/9	K/9	K	GB%	BABIP	WHIP	ERA	DRA	WARP	MPH	FB%	WHF	CSP
2018	ABE	A-	22	0	1	0	4	4	10¹	13	1	2.6	7.0	8	34%	.353	1.55	2.61	2.75	0.3				
2019	BAL	MLB	23	1	4	0	7	7	31¹	41	8	4.2	5.2	18	32%	.314	1.79	7.15	7.12	-0.6				

Breakout: 1%   Improve: 1%   Collapse: 0%   Attrition: 0%   MLB: 1%   *Comparables: Joseph Mantiply, Tanner Rainey, Dillon Peters*

A 2018 draftee out of Arkansas, Knight went undefeated during the regular season and carried the Razorbacks into the postseason. After a heavy innings workload, he was soft-pedaled in his first summer of pro ball, tossing just 10 innings at short-season Aberdeen. When he's up to speed, the polished Knight should move quickly through the O's system thanks to his poise on the mound and plus command of a dynamic four-pitch mix, including a 91-95 mph fastball that can touch 97, a plus slider, and a passable curveball and changeup. Durability questions have dogged the slightly-built Knight since college, but a major-league conditioning program should help Knight add some good muscle to his 6'3"/170-pound frame. And even if he doesn't, being slight hasn't hurt Chris Sale (6'6"/180), Blake Snell (6'5"/180), Jacob DeGrom (6'4"/180), or Kyle Freeland (6'3"/170).

Dean Kremer RHP Born: 01/07/96 Age: 23 Bats: R Throws: R Height: 6'3" Weight: 180 Origin: Round 14, 2016 Draft (#431 overall)

YEAR	TEAM	LVL	AGE	W	L	SV	G	GS	IP	H	HR	BB/9	K/9	K	GB%	BABIP	WHIP	ERA	DRA	WARP	MPH	FB%	WHF	CSP
2016	OGD	RK	20	0	1	0	6	6	16¹	15	0	1.7	7.2	13	46%	.312	1.10	3.86	3.60	0.4				
2016	GRL	A	20	2	0	0	6	0	15¹	4	0	2.3	12.9	22	52%	.148	0.52	0.59	2.48	0.4				
2017	RCU	A+	21	1	4	3	33	6	80	86	6	3.8	10.8	96	43%	.369	1.50	5.18	3.90	1.0				
2018	RCU	A+	22	5	3	0	16	16	79	67	7	3.0	13.0	114	40%	.351	1.18	3.30	3.38	1.8				
2018	TUL	AA	22	1	0	0	1	1	7	3	0	3.9	14.1	11	75%	.250	0.86	0.00	1.84	0.3				
2018	BOW	AA	22	4	2	0	8	8	45¹	38	3	3.4	10.5	53	41%	.310	1.21	2.58	3.61	0.9				
2019	BAL	MLB	23	5	6	1	43	15	98²	97	16	4.1	9.8	108	41%	.311	1.44	4.80	4.69	0.9				

Breakout: 8%   Improve: 16%   Collapse: 9%   Attrition: 17%   MLB: 32%   *Comparables: Tanner Roark, Michael Blazek, Yefrey Ramirez*

If Yusniel Diaz headlined the Machado trade, Kremer neck-lined it. Or possibly stomach-lined it, depending on if his future is truly as a back-end starter or, as some scouts seem inclined to believe, a bullpen piece. Kremer has a four-pitch mix with two MLB-ready offerings: a slow, loopy curveball that induces lots of whiffs, and a fastball that is effective despite average velocity, perhaps as a result of an elite spin rate. Even the homer-happy California League couldn't depress his strong numbers, and Kremer's one game in the Texas League was a sterling performance before he was sent to the Eastern League. The velocity-loving Dodgers didn't have much use for a soft-tossing prospect, but Baltimore can't afford to be as picky, so the move to the Orioles' system might be Kremer's best chance to make that starter money in his baseball career. Notable: Kremer was the first Israeli drafted by a Major League Baseball team and a member of the memorable Team Israel in the 2017 World Baseball Classic.

Zac Lowther LHP Born: 04/30/96 Age: 23 Bats: L Throws: L Height: 6'2" Weight: 235 Origin: Round 2, 2017 Draft (#74 overall)

YEAR	TEAM	LVL	AGE	W	L	SV	G	GS	IP	H	HR	BB/9	K/9	K	GB%	BABIP	WHIP	ERA	DRA	WARP	MPH	FB%	WHF	CSP
2017	ABE	A-	21	2	2	0	12	11	54¹	35	1	1.8	12.4	75	47%	.283	0.85	1.66	2.59	1.7				
2018	DEL	A	22	3	1	0	6	6	31	12	2	2.6	14.8	51	33%	.192	0.68	1.16	2.38	1.0				
2018	FRD	A+	22	5	3	0	17	16	92²	74	6	2.5	9.7	100	40%	.288	1.08	2.53	3.88	1.5				
2019	BAL	MLB	23	4	7	0	17	17	86²	86	16	3.5	9.3	89	37%	.301	1.38	5.02	4.92	0.6				

Breakout: 3%   Improve: 7%   Collapse: 15%   Attrition: 12%   MLB: 26%   *Comparables: Aaron Blair, Jon Gray, Dylan Bundy*

If Lowther were a cheese, he'd be one of those cheeses carried only by specialty cheesemongers, with a lengthy handwritten card extolling his virtues and recommending you buy now, pay no attention to those ratings in Cheese Fancier Magazine that see only a low-level pitcher with a below-average fastball. After a strong pro debut after being drafted in the competitive balance round in 2017, Lowther plowed into Single-A Delmarva intent on splitting it back into three distinct states. After six dominant starts, the Orioles gleefully promoted Lowther to High-A Frederick, where he saw his strikeouts drop, but held his other peripherals in check. (A "drop" in strikeouts for Lowther meant that he went from striking out 44 percent of batters to a mere 27 percent. Yawn.) What makes the lanky, leggy lefty so difficult isn't the velocity on his fastball, but a highly deceptive delivery, with lots of whip and extension and funk. Zac Lowther, the Funky Cheese Man; you're welcome in advance, Orioles marketing department.

Luis Ortiz RHP   Born: 09/22/95   Age: 23   Bats: R   Throws: R   Height: 6'3"   Weight: 230   Origin: Round 1, 2014 Draft (#30 overall)

YEAR	TEAM	LVL	AGE	W	L	SV	G	GS	IP	H	HR	BB/9	K/9	K	GB%	BABIP	WHIP	ERA	DRA	WARP	MPH	FB%	WHF	CSP
2016	HDS	A+	20	3	2	0	7	6	27²	23	4	2.0	9.1	28	51%	.264	1.05	2.60	3.19	0.7				
2016	FRI	AA	20	1	4	1	9	8	39²	47	3	1.6	7.7	34	47%	.352	1.36	4.08	4.10	0.5				
2016	BLX	AA	20	2	2	0	6	6	23¹	26	2	3.9	6.2	16	33%	.316	1.54	1.93	3.41	0.5				
2017	BLX	AA	21	4	7	0	22	20	94¹	79	12	3.5	7.5	79	36%	.258	1.23	4.01	3.43	1.9				
2018	BLX	AA	22	3	4	2	16	11	68	63	7	2.4	8.6	65	48%	.289	1.19	3.71	3.49	1.4				
2018	NOR	AAA	22	2	1	0	6	6	31²	34	4	2.3	6.0	21	40%	.297	1.33	3.69	7.37	-0.6				
2018	BAL	MLB	22	0	1	0	2	1	2¹	7	0	11.6	0.0	0	53%	.467	4.29	15.43	7.94	-0.1	94.0	59.1	9.1	41.8
2019	BAL	MLB	23	2	3	0	17	6	43²	47	7	3.3	7.2	35	41%	.304	1.45	5.07	4.96	0.2	93.9	61.2	9.4	43.3

Breakout: 11%   Improve: 15%   Collapse: 13%   Attrition: 28%   MLB: 34%   *Comparables: Taylor Guerrieri, Alex Cobb, Walker Lockett*

Ortiz has now been the centerpiece of two high-profile trades, first acquired by the Brewers from the Rangers in the Jonathan Lucroy trade, and then flipped in the Jonathan Schoop trade. A hearty serving of a fellow at 6'3" and 230 pounds, Ortiz has been able to rely on overpowering minor-league hitters with pure velocity mixed with a nasty slider, but his production has become uneven as he's moved up into the high minors, and his cup of coffee in the majors was short and bitter. A recurrent hamstring injury has also slowed his progress, and scouting reports are filled with vague references to "conditioning," which is scout-speak for "likely candidate to slip on an empty bag of potato chips and throw out his back." His ability to throw strikes means Ortiz has an absolute floor of a back-end reliever, but the O's are counting on getting at least a back-end starter out of him.

Zach Pop RHP   Born: 09/20/96   Age: 22   Bats: R   Throws: R   Height: 6'4"   Weight: 220   Origin: Round 7, 2017 Draft (#220 overall)

YEAR	TEAM	LVL	AGE	W	L	SV	G	GS	IP	H	HR	BB/9	K/9	K	GB%	BABIP	WHIP	ERA	DRA	WARP	MPH	FB%	WHF	CSP
2018	GRL	A	21	0	2	0	11	0	16¹	12	1	3.9	13.2	24	60%	.297	1.16	2.20	2.40	0.5				
2018	RCU	A+	21	1	0	7	19	0	27	13	0	2.0	7.7	23	68%	.197	0.70	0.33	4.38	0.2				
2018	BOW	AA	21	1	1	1	14	0	21¹	14	0	2.5	7.2	17	70%	.246	0.94	2.53	4.07	0.2				
2019	BAL	MLB	22	2	1	1	37	0	38²	39	6	5.7	8.0	34	52%	.297	1.63	5.60	5.52	-0.3				

Breakout: 17%   Improve: 21%   Collapse: 0%   Attrition: 3%   MLB: 22%   *Comparables: Dominic Leone, Jake Barrett, Arnold Leon*

Besides having a name that sounds like a zippy 1950s soda, Pop made a good impression on his new team when he came over from the Dodgers in the Machado trade, basically replicating his performance at High-A in a more challenging environment at Double-A Bowie. Pop, like Maddux and Tewksbury before him, isn't necessarily trying to rack up strikeouts; rather, he wants to use his sinker-slider combo to induce weak contact, break bats, and get batters to put the ball on the ground, though we'll let you find what's different in the stat line between Pop and those other guys. Pop's nasty mid-90s sinker comes out of a tricky, almost sidearm, slot, and the crossfire action makes the pitch especially tough on righties. His slider also comes in at above-average speed, but could use more sharpness to be a truly plus pitch. Kentucky turns out polished major league prospects, and that's no different in the case of 2017 draftee Pop, who has sailed through the lower minors and seems poised to be contributing to a big-league bullpen soon, so everyone warm up your Magnitude from *Community* impressions.

Yefrey Ramirez RHP   Born: 11/28/93   Age: 25   Bats: R   Throws: R   Height: 6'2"   Weight: 215   Origin: International Free Agent, 2011

YEAR	TEAM	LVL	AGE	W	L	SV	G	GS	IP	H	HR	BB/9	K/9	K	GB%	BABIP	WHIP	ERA	DRA	WARP	MPH	FB%	WHF	CSP
2016	CSC	A	22	4	2	0	11	11	61	48	4	2.1	9.7	66	40%	.272	1.02	2.80	2.67	1.7				
2016	TAM	A+	22	3	7	0	11	11	63¹	34	5	2.6	9.4	66	42%	.195	0.82	2.84	2.46	2.2				
2017	TRN	AA	23	10	3	0	18	18	92¹	78	9	3.7	8.9	91	36%	.284	1.26	3.41	3.57	1.8				
2017	BOW	AA	23	5	0	0	6	6	32	27	6	3.1	7.3	26	28%	.250	1.19	3.66	4.06	0.4				
2018	NOR	AAA	24	3	5	0	14	14	72	62	7	2.8	9.0	72	35%	.282	1.17	3.88	4.39	0.9				
2018	BAL	MLB	24	1	8	0	17	12	65¹	64	11	5.0	8.5	62	36%	.293	1.53	5.92	6.93	-1.3	94.8	51.8	11.9	44.2
2019	BAL	MLB	25	2	3	0	17	6	41²	41	7	3.7	8.4	39	36%	.289	1.40	5.19	5.09	0.1	94.5	53.1	12.1	45.2

Breakout: 14%   Improve: 40%   Collapse: 28%   Attrition: 42%   MLB: 80%   *Comparables: Robert Stephenson, Tyler Thornburg, Aaron Blair*

Acquired from the Yankees but D-Backs raised
In Norfolk was where he spent most of his days
Chilling out max and relaxing all fine
Upping Ks and dropping his walks per nine
When a couple of starters, their arms got fatigued
And Yefry got called up to the big leagues
He had a few little scuffles against the Yankees
The Orioles didn't have options, to put it quite frankly
But the changeup is plus and the fastball's alive
And in the O's rotation, that's good enough for #5.

Grayson Rodriguez RHP   Born: 11/16/99   Age: 19   Bats: L   Throws: R   Height: 6'5"   Weight: 220   Origin: Round 1, 2018 Draft (#11 overall)

YEAR	TEAM	LVL	AGE	W	L	SV	G	GS	IP	H	HR	BB/9	K/9	K	GB%	BABIP	WHIP	ERA	DRA	WARP	MPH	FB%	WHF	CSP
2018	ORI	RK	18	0	2	0	9	8	19¹	17	0	3.3	9.3	20	43%	.321	1.24	1.40	2.91	0.7				
2019	BAL	MLB	19	1	3	0	11	8	31	37	7	6.2	7.0	24	42%	.314	1.89	6.95	6.92	-0.5				

Comparables: Jaime Barria, Bryse Wilson, Raul Alcantara

Edgar Allan Poe's "imp of the perverse" is the little devil that sits on our shoulders, willing us to do the one thing we know we should not do: sticking out a foot to trip someone down the stairs, punching a fist into the birthday cake, being the Orioles and selecting a high school arm with a first-round draft choice. Rodriguez, at least, looks big and durable: at 6'5" and 220, he dwarfed his high school contemporaries, even in Texas. The bigger question is whether he'll be able to create a sharp distinction between his curve and slider, previously thrown as one pitch. Rodriguez jumped up draft boards late in the season thanks to an ability to adjust, including improved conditioning that sent his fastball up to 96-98 at max effort, so there's an intriguing mix of tools here, and plenty of time for the Orioles to develop them, provided the imp of the perverse minds its own business.

Tanner Scott LHP Born: 07/22/94 Age: 24 Bats: R Throws: L Height: 6'2" Weight: 220 Origin: Round 6, 2014 Draft (#181 overall)

YEAR	TEAM	LVL	AGE	W	L	SV	G	GS	IP	H	HR	BB/9	K/9	K	GB%	BABIP	WHIP	ERA	DRA	WARP	MPH	FB%	WHF	CSP
2016	FRD	A+	21	4	2	5	29	0	48¹	22	1	7.8	11.7	63	59%	.198	1.32	4.47	5.88	-0.4				
2016	BOW	AA	21	1	2	0	14	0	16	18	0	8.4	10.1	18	64%	.429	2.06	5.62	3.64	0.2				
2017	BOW	AA	22	0	2	0	24	24	69	45	2	6.0	11.3	87	54%	.281	1.32	2.22	4.12	0.9				
2017	BAL	MLB	22	0	0	0	2	0	1²	2	0	10.8	10.8	2	20%	.400	2.40	10.80	2.36	0.1	100.1	70.3	10.8	29.6
2018	NOR	AAA	23	0	1	0	10	0	12	10	0	6.8	9.8	13	62%	.345	1.58	0.75	3.47	0.2				
2018	BAL	MLB	23	3	3	0	53	0	53¹	55	6	4.7	12.8	76	49%	.380	1.56	5.40	2.85	1.3	98.6	55.3	18	43.3
2019	BAL	MLB	24	3	1	0	56	0	58²	51	7	6.6	11.3	74	50%	.312	1.61	4.83	4.74	0.3	98.4	57.4	18.3	38.3

Breakout: 24% Improve: 32% Collapse: 14% Attrition: 21% MLB: 58%   *Comparables: Cam Bedrosian, Carlos Estevez, Manny Delcarmen*

Triple-digit hurlers with poor command are baseball's Furbys, but Scott adds a wrinkle in throwing from the left side. He's never had a BB% below double-digits, though his ability to miss bats has helped mitigate the high walk rate in the minors. In the majors, Scott surrendered six home runs in just over 50 innings, twice the number he gave up over his entire minor league career, and his willingness to hand out free passes means those big flies turned into Earl Weaver Specials. With his plus fastball and wipeout slider, Scott can get away with either an elevated walk rate or the occasional solo shot, but not both. There are worse arms to dream on, but the O's might be smart to deal Scott this off-season and let some other team work out the command problems that have plagued him throughout his pro career.

Dillon Tate RHP Born: 05/01/94 Age: 25 Bats: R Throws: R Height: 6'2" Weight: 195 Origin: Round 1, 2015 Draft (#4 overall)

YEAR	TEAM	LVL	AGE	W	L	SV	G	GS	IP	H	HR	BB/9	K/9	K	GB%	BABIP	WHIP	ERA	DRA	WARP	MPH	FB%	WHF	CSP
2016	HIC	A	22	3	3	0	17	16	65	78	5	3.7	7.6	55	44%	.376	1.62	5.12	3.36	1.2				
2016	CSC	A	22	1	0	0	7	0	17¹	21	1	3.1	7.8	15	57%	.351	1.56	3.12	4.77	0.0				
2017	TAM	A+	23	6	0	0	9	9	58¹	48	4	2.3	7.1	46	61%	.262	1.08	2.62	3.97	0.9				
2017	TRN	AA	23	1	2	0	4	4	25	23	3	3.2	6.1	17	56%	.270	1.28	3.24	5.19	0.0				
2018	TRN	AA	24	5	2	0	15	15	82²	67	7	2.7	8.2	75	48%	.263	1.11	3.38	3.18	2.1				
2018	BOW	AA	24	2	3	0	7	7	40²	48	3	2.0	4.6	21	63%	.324	1.40	5.75	4.28	0.5				
2019	BAL	MLB	25	2	2	0	16	5	36²	41	5	3.6	6.1	25	47%	.304	1.52	5.31	5.21	0.1				

Breakout: 10% Improve: 14% Collapse: 14% Attrition: 24% MLB: 33%   *Comparables: Alex Wilson, Sam Howard, Myles Jaye*

Trades can be a blow to the player's ego; Beyonce does not write songs about being replaceable. For Tate, however, the two times he's been traded might have put him on the best path for baseball success. First, he was acquired by the Yankees as Texas, unimpressed with the former first-round pick's numbers at Single-A, shipped him off in the Carlos Beltran trade. Without directly dragging his old organization, Tate has spoken about the amount of learning he did with the Yankees in understanding his delivery and the craft of pitching. In a second exposure to Double-A, Tate's peripherals improved across the board, even as his mid-3s ERA didn't budge. Now Tate gets a shot to enact what he's learned in a significantly lower-pressure environment a few hours down the road on I-95. One red flag: Tate, who has battled injuries in his career, was shut down with shoulder soreness in late September, a similar injury to the one that derailed his first season of pro ball.

Mike Wright RHP Born: 01/03/90 Age: 29 Bats: R Throws: R Height: 6'6" Weight: 215 Origin: Round 3, 2011 Draft (#94 overall)

YEAR	TEAM	LVL	AGE	W	L	SV	G	GS	IP	H	HR	BB/9	K/9	K	GB%	BABIP	WHIP	ERA	DRA	WARP	MPH	FB%	WHF	CSP
2016	NOR	AAA	26	4	4	0	13	13	76¹	72	8	1.7	5.7	48	45%	.272	1.13	3.07	3.86	1.3				
2016	BAL	MLB	26	3	4	0	18	12	74²	81	12	3.1	6.0	50	43%	.299	1.43	5.79	7.13	-1.6	96.5	70.1	7.4	47.9
2017	NOR	AAA	27	4	6	0	16	16	83	81	6	2.8	7.7	71	46%	.301	1.29	3.69	4.20	1.4				
2017	BAL	MLB	27	0	0	0	13	0	25	26	5	2.5	10.1	28	44%	.318	1.32	5.76	4.41	0.2	96.2	61.2	11.3	45.3
2018	BAL	MLB	28	4	2	0	48	2	84¹	101	12	3.8	7.9	74	37%	.344	1.62	5.55	6.60	-1.6	96.5	58.2	9.1	48.7
2019	BAL	MLB	29	3	1	0	56	0	58²	65	10	3.4	7.3	48	41%	.307	1.48	5.26	5.16	-0.1	95.8	62	8.9	47.4

Breakout: 19% Improve: 31% Collapse: 19% Attrition: 23% MLB: 56%   *Comparables: Jeremy Hefner, Josh Hancock, Tom Koehler*

At the dawn of the Industrial Revolution, the circumstances of one's birth determined one's fate. Hit the jackpot and get born into a wealthy family? Enjoy your Grand Tour, bedsheets warmed by your personal valet, and rerouting train lines so the smoke doesn't belch onto your personal golf course. Born into a poor family? Best develop a taste for gruel and get well-acquainted with the inner workings of a spinning jenny. The same, unfortunately, describes the lot of those drafted by clubs trapped in a cycle of futility. Wright has been in the Orioles system since 2011, bouncing between Triple-A and the big club for the past four seasons, and looks bound for the same sort of existence next season. Sometimes you're the spinning jenny, sometimes you're the pitching prospect that gets ground under its wheels for the better part of a decade.

Jimmy Yacabonis RHP Born: 03/21/92   Age: 27   Bats: R   Throws: R   Height: 6'3"   Weight: 205   Origin: Round 13, 2013 Draft (#399 overall)

YEAR	TEAM	LVL	AGE	W	L	SV	G	GS	IP	H	HR	BB/9	K/9	K	GB%	BABIP	WHIP	ERA	DRA	WARP	MPH	FB%	WHF	CSP
2016	FRD	A+	24	0	2	5	16	0	20¹	17	2	2.7	9.3	21	43%	.278	1.13	3.98	3.64	0.3				
2016	BOW	AA	24	2	2	6	34	0	44¹	34	2	2.8	9.3	46	57%	.271	1.08	2.03	2.50	1.2				
2017	NOR	AAA	25	4	0	11	41	0	61¹	30	0	4.1	7.0	48	49%	.184	0.95	1.32	4.00	0.9				
2017	BAL	MLB	25	2	0	0	14	0	20²	18	2	6.1	3.5	8	47%	.242	1.55	4.35	7.28	-0.5	96.9	72.9	6.2	46.4
2018	NOR	AAA	26	3	5	0	21	21	76	61	6	3.8	7.3	62	46%	.258	1.22	4.26	3.96	1.4				
2018	BAL	MLB	26	0	2	0	12	7	40	40	8	4.1	7.4	33	43%	.283	1.45	5.40	7.66	-1.1	95.1	62.8	10.8	47.3
2019	BAL	MLB	27	2	3	0	17	6	41²	41	5	4.2	7.5	35	46%	.288	1.45	5.03	4.93	0.2	95.1	66.4	9.6	47.5

Breakout: 10%   Improve: 18%   Collapse: 13%   Attrition: 15%   MLB: 33%   *Comparables: Kanekoa Texeira, Logan Ondrusek, Eury De La Rosa*

After relieving for his entire professional career, the O's transitioned Jimmy Yaks to starter this year in Triple-A before calling him up to serve as a spot starter/long reliever. The combined 116 innings he pitched this season were a career-high by over 30, so in evaluating Yacaboneyard's season, it might be more fair to give it an "in progress" rather than a harsh letter grade. The fastball still has a lot of late life and the carnival-ride slider that corkscrews in on lefties is a major league-quality weapon when it stays on the tracks. Despite the more extensive work, his peripherals are mostly trending in the right direction, except for that pesky home run rate. Given his career performance in the minors, it's likely the HR rate will regress, and with continued improvement in command, the Yak Attack should be able to stick on the 25-man, preferably as a late-inning option.

LINEOUTS

Hitters

HITTER	POS	TEAM	LVL	AGE	PA	R	2B	3B	HR	RBI	BB	K	SB	CS	AVG/OBP/SLG	DRC+	VORP	BABIP	BRR	FRAA	WARP
Jean Carmona	SS	HEL	Rk	18	172	28	8	3	4	24	13	45	5	3	.239/.298/.406	76	5.0	.306	-0.8	SS(27): 0.7, 3B(7): -2.3	-0.2
	SS	ABE	A-	18	100	9	7	0	0	7	6	25	0	1	.226/.280/.301	90	-1.8	.309	-1.5	2B(9): -0.4, SS(6): -1.6	-0.3
Brett Cumberland	C	BRV	A+	23	341	40	15	0	11	39	52	85	0	1	.236/.367/.407	128	19.3	.296	-3.2	C(57): 0.5	2.3
	C	BOW	AA	23	49	6	0	0	3	7	4	12	0	0	.190/.292/.405	105	1.1	.185	-0.2	C(13): 0.0	0.2
Craig Gentry	CF	BAL	MLB	34	169	13	5	2	1	11	11	31	12	3	.269/.321/.346	82	-1.1	.331	-0.8	LF(31): -1.3, RF(24): 2.3	0.0
Adam Hall	SS	ABE	A-	19	256	35	9	3	1	24	17	58	22	5	.293/.368/.374	91	24.9	.386	2.6	SS(59): -3.0, 2B(4): 0.4	0.8
Drew Jackson	2B	TUL	AA	24	410	57	20	1	15	46	45	93	22	7	.251/.356/.447	121	26.3	.298	3.4	2B(64): 2.8, SS(30): 2.6	3.3
Caleb Joseph	C	NOR	AAA	32	97	10	2	0	2	14	8	19	0	0	.273/.340/.364	112	6.5	.328	0.5	C(15): -0.7	0.5
	C	BAL	MLB	32	280	28	14	2	3	17	10	68	2	1	.219/.254/.321	69	-0.9	.282	0.0	C(81): -4.8, 1B(2): 0.1	-0.1
Richie Martin	SS	MID	AA	23	509	68	29	8	6	42	44	86	25	10	.300/.368/.439	104	28.4	.357	-0.3	SS(96): 9.1, 2B(21): 1.0	3.4
Jace Peterson	2B	NYA	MLB	28	11	0	0	0	0	0	1	3	0	1	.300/.364/.300	89	-0.3	.429	-0.3	LF(2): -0.2, RF(1): 0.0	0.0
	2B	BAL	MLB	28	235	21	13	2	3	28	30	55	13	2	.195/.308/.325	84	-2.7	.252	1.3	3B(35): 1.9, LF(21): -0.4	0.5
Joey Rickard	CF	NOR	AAA	27	185	25	13	1	2	27	26	28	3	0	.275/.384/.412	119	14.5	.317	-0.1	CF(32): 4.0, LF(8): 0.4	1.4
	CF	BAL	MLB	27	230	27	10	1	8	23	15	55	4	2	.244/.300/.413	92	1.5	.293	-0.4	RF(40): 3.8, LF(36): -1.4	0.6
Anthony Santander	RF	BAL	MLB	23	108	8	5	1	1	6	6	21	1	0	.198/.250/.297	75	-5.8	.241	0.0	RF(29): 0.8, LF(1): 0.0	0.0
	RF	BOW	AA	23	222	26	9	3	5	22	10	32	4	1	.258/.293/.402	99	4.8	.282	0.7	RF(35): -3.6, LF(14): -1.4	0.0
	RF	NOR	AAA	23	47	3	3	0	2	7	2	9	0	0	.182/.213/.386	112	-1.7	.176	-0.1	RF(8): 1.1, LF(2): -0.3	0.2
Andrew Susac	C	BAL	MLB	28	26	1	1	0	0	0	0	12	0	0	.115/.115/.154	55	-2.9	.214	0.1	C(7): -0.6	-0.1
	C	NOR	AAA	28	158	15	7	0	6	26	31	42	0	0	.256/.405/.456	131	16.0	.333	-0.8	C(36): 4.1	1.7

Jean Carmona is a low-level lottery ticket obtained from Milwaukee in the Scoop deal, an infielder with a plus arm who can help prop up a system that's gone less for Harlem Globetrotters and more for Harlem Meatpackers. Good bat speed and some natural loft to his swing suggest Carmona might have more power to show as the 18-year-old adds strength. ⓧ The Orioles are perilously low on catching prospects, so acquiring bat-first **Brett Cumberland** from the Braves in the Gausman deal wasn't a bad idea. His new team made the curious decision to send him to the instructional league rather than the AFL, where he'd face tougher competition and get reps with higher-level pitching, indicating they aren't as worried about his bat as the need to develop his receiving skills. ⓧ There is a Stanford computer scientist named **Craig Gentry** who specializes in cryptology and writes papers with inscrutable and yet saucy titles like "Noncommutative Determinant is Hard: A Simple Proof Using an Extension of Barrington's Theorem" and "The Geometry of Provable Security: Some Proofs of Security in Which Lattices Make a Surprise Appearance." Baseball's Craig Gentry, released by the Orioles in September, could do with borrowing some of this insouciant swag, the mark of someone who has such mastery over a subject as to be able to play with it. ⓧ Born in Bermuda, **Adam Hall** convinced his parents to let him move to Canada as a preteen so he could have a shot at a baseball career. A legitimate shortstop, Hall started off slow this season at short-season Aberdeen but finished strong, winning Minor League Player of the Month honors after a torrid August where he slashed .390/.462/.524. ⓧ **Drew Jackson** is a plus defender at either second base or shortstop and even showed that he could hit for some power outside of the California League for the first time. He could be one of the first names called on if the Dodgers need some middle infield reinforcements in 2019. ⓧ Inexplicably, **Caleb Joseph** went from one of baseball's best-rated defensive catchers in 2017 to one of the worst in 2018. With an offensive downturn across the board, it's not hard to see him on the short end of the platoon with Chance Sisco or even losing out the backup job to similar defensive standout Austin Wynns. ⓧ **Richie Martin** began hitting the ball with authority at Double-A in 2018, which is what you hope eventually happens when you draft a top defensive shortstop and throw him to the professional-pitching wolves. You don't have to hit *that* much if you've got Martin's defensive profile, so there's now a light at the end of his development tunnel. ⓧ Another inhabitant of Lord Baltimore's Home for Wayward Former Prospects, the Orioles picked **Jace Peterson** up off waivers from the Yankees to serve as the standard Gritty Veteran Utilityman for 2018. Peterson still possesses the excellent plate discipline he's shown throughout his minors career, but he's no more than a warm body in the O's infield. ⓧ After years of a Woodrow Wilson-esque isolationist approach to the international market, the Orioles decided to dip a toe in the birdbath and started hoarding international slot money towards the end of the 2018 season. Their first two signings were 16-year-old shortstop **Moises Ramirez** and 19-year-old RHP Carlos Del Rosario, both out of the Dominican Republic. Look for the O's to be much more active internationally now that the Angelos scions have more control of the club's activities. ⓧ **Joey Rickard** collecting almost 800 plate appearances for the Orioles over the last three seasons is irrefutable proof the Mandela Effect is real, even if it targets mostly light-hitting outfielders. ⓧ **Anthony Santander** made Baltimore's 25-man after a strong spring but failed to translate that to in-season production. He was optioned back to Double-A in mid-May and was not recalled from Triple-A when rosters expanded. ⓧ Former catching prospect **Andrew Susac** now has more trades (two) than healthy seasons (one) under his belt since 2016. He still might be Baltimore's best backstop?

Pitchers

PITCHER	TEAM	LVL	AGE	W	L	SV	G	GS	IP	H	HR	BB/9	K/9	K	GB%	BABIP	WHIP	ERA	DRA	WARP	MPH	FB%	WHF	CSP
Pedro Araujo	BAL	MLB	24	1	3	0	20	0	28	29	9	5.8	9.3	29	36%	.278	1.68	7.71	4.07	0.3	94.1	49	14.6	43.7
Michael Baumann	DEL	A	22	5	0	0	7	7	38	23	0	3.1	11.1	47	53%	.277	0.95	1.42	3.25	0.9				
	FRD	A+	22	8	5	0	17	17	92²	82	9	3.9	5.7	59	35%	.261	1.32	3.88	8.09	-3.0				
Tyler Erwin	FRD	A+	23	4	4	18	50	0	68¹	45	1	3.0	11.1	84	53%	.268	1.00	1.58	2.93	1.6				
Gray Fenter	DEL	A	22	3	3	0	14	2	26²	31	2	4.4	10.5	31	38%	.382	1.65	6.75	4.39	0.2				
	ABE	A-	22	5	3	0	13	11	57	41	5	3.9	9.5	60	39%	.255	1.16	3.95	3.63	1.0				
Paul Fry	BOW	AA	25	3	0	2	15	0	19	10	2	5.2	13.3	28	68%	.229	1.11	2.84	2.70	0.5				
	NOR	AAA	25	0	1	0	13	1	23¹	22	2	1.5	11.2	29	53%	.345	1.11	3.47	2.52	0.7				
	BAL	MLB	25	1	2	2	35	0	37²	33	1	3.6	8.6	36	58%	.311	1.27	3.35	4.17	0.3	93.1	56.5	10.8	44.6
Sean Gilmartin	MEM	AAA	28	4	2	0	24	6	46¹	48	6	3.1	6.4	33	36%	.294	1.38	4.66	3.40	1.0				
	NOR	AAA	28	2	0	0	7	3	14¹	13	1	1.3	7.5	12	37%	.300	1.05	3.14	4.21	0.2				
	BAL	MLB	28	1	1	0	12	0	27	23	4	3.7	5.0	15	46%	.235	1.26	3.00	6.15	-0.4	90.0	36.9	7.9	46
Branden Kline	FRD	A+	26	1	0	2	12	0	20²	20	0	1.3	10.0	23	36%	.357	1.11	1.31	3.27	0.4				
	BOW	AA	26	4	4	15	32	0	45	32	3	3.0	9.6	48	45%	.254	1.04	1.80	3.11	1.0				
Evan Phillips	ATL	MLB	23	0	0	0	4	0	6¹	6	3	5.7	4.3	3	41%	.158	1.58	8.53	5.71	-0.1	95.5	62.5	11.5	47.6
	GWN	AAA	23	4	4	8	31	0	40²	28	1	3.1	13.1	59	51%	.325	1.03	1.99	2.52	1.2				
	NOR	AAA	23	0	2	0	8	0	10²	6	1	2.5	11.0	13	32%	.208	0.84	3.38	3.39	0.2				
	BAL	MLB	23	0	1	0	5	1	5¹	7	2	10.1	8.4	5	39%	.312	2.44	18.56	9.68	-0.3	95.4	73	7	44.8
Josh Rogers	SWB	AAA	23	6	8	0	19	19	109¹	118	13	2.4	6.8	83	42%	.308	1.34	3.95	4.48	1.3				
	NOR	AAA	23	2	1	0	5	5	30¹	26	3	2.1	5.3	18	41%	.245	1.09	2.08	4.60	0.3				
	BAL	MLB	23	1	2	0	3	3	11²	17	2	3.9	4.6	6	40%	.349	1.89	8.49	7.73	-0.3	92.2	56.1	6.1	49.4
Alex Wells	FRD	A+	21	7	8	0	24	24	135	142	19	2.2	6.7	101	36%	.301	1.30	3.47	4.49	1.3				
Gabriel Ynoa	BOW	AA	25	0	0	0	2	2	7	6	1	0.0	7.7	6	45%	.263	0.86	2.57	5.18	0.0				

Dan Duquette Customary Rule 5 Pick **Pedro Araujo** went down with an elbow injury in early June and was never seen again. Rule 5 picks: a reminder that generally, you get what you pay for. ⓧ **Michael Baumann** was drafted in 2017 out of Jacksonville University, which is a real school and not the faux alma mater of Jason from *The Good Place*. Even though the school's Wikipedia page counts among its notable alumni Leonard Skinner, namesake of the band Lynryd Skynyrd; but somehow this is a real school, really. ⓧ **Tyler Erwin** is the great-great-great nephew of James K. Polk, a maniacally productive president who achieved all his major, sweeping goals in office in just one term. While it's unclear if Erwin will be as productive as his famous forbear, the 23rd-round pick was one of the best relievers in the Carolina League this season despite a fastball that averages in the high 80s thanks to excellent command, a funky three-quarters delivery, and a bulldog mentality on the mound. ⓧ Prep arm **Gray Fenter**, drafted and paid overslot in the seventh round in 2015, is now over a year removed from TJ surgery and able to mix in his curve and changeup with abandon. His low-90s fastball plays up in limited outings and might point to a future bullpen role, especially if the command doesn't sort itself out. ⓧ **Paul Fry** stepped in as the designated lefty after Richard Bleier went down with injury and was quietly effective whenever the Orioles happened to wander into a high-leverage situation. He still allows too many walks for a lefty who sits low-90s with his fastball, but the funky, sharp-breaking slider is an effective putaway pitch. ⓧ One way to explain **Sean Gilmartin's** itinerant career path is that he has a punch card where if he plays for eight different teams, he can turn it in for a long-term contract. The other is he's barely good enough to be on a major league roster. ⓧ **Branden Kline** is a 2012 draftee who's had trouble staying on the mound, missing a large chunk of 2013 with a broken ankle, and most of 2015-2017 with Tommy John. Now a reliever with a mid to upper-90s fastball, Kline has been working as a closer, converting 17-of-18 save opportunities this season, and looks on track to finally make it to Baltimore some time next season. ⓧ An under-the-radar pickup from Atlanta in the Gausman trade, **Evan Phillips** has a lively arm but has struggled with command issues. "One adjustment away" is the pitcher equivalent of "triple shy of the cycle," but if Phillips can figure out how to curtail his walks, the O's have a strong middle to back-end relief option. ⓧ It's never a good sign for anyone involved when a pitcher gets shut down twice in the same year, but that's where the Orioles wound up with **Josh Rogers**, fourth piece in the Britton trade. They actually sent him home in mid-September just to keep it from happening again. ⓧ Bespectacled Australian brothers **Alex** and Lachlan **Wells** are both in organized baseball; Lachlan, who has a couple more ticks on his fastball, signed with the Twins a year earlier than Alex signed with the Orioles. What Alex lacks in velocity he makes up for with 60-grade command and a plus changeup. ⓧ Acquired for cash from the Mets, the Orioles failed to read the part of the medical report that disclosed Fred Wilpon holding **Gabriel Ynoa** by the shin when dipping him in the East River. After a relatively productive 2017 for the O's, Ynoa pitched only seven innings at Double-A this year before being shut down with recurring shin splints, and a shoulder injury to boot.

BOSTON RED SOX

Essay by Chad Finn

Player comments by Ben Carsley and BP staff

The culture of Red Sox fandom was going to change for the so-much-better after the affirming events of October 2004. Hell yeah, it was. How could it not? Though so many sunny summers that inevitably chilled to anguished autumns during the franchise's 86-season World Series championship drought, the daydream of what life as a Boston baseball fan would be like if—no, when, for there was always at least a frayed thread of authentic hope—the Red Sox won a World Series was a constant one.

The years when all the Boston faithful had were dreams provided a vivid idea of what winning would be like, how catharsis and pure, life-changing joy would feel, before it finally and at last came to be. There would be sweet camaraderie among us, an irresistible turn toward tender sentimentality, a warm this-is-for-you nostalgia for friends and loved ones who didn't live long enough to see their beloved Red Sox win, or for the beloved Sox players themselves who couldn't quite get it done despite their valiance. (Namely: Yaz.) Also, we would definitely stop bitching about every minute thing that went wrong, or even hinted that it might. Man, were we ever master pre-bitchers. No more of that. The good times, as the ubiquitous Neil Diamond earworm played during every eighth inning at Fenway, win or lose, told us, never would be so good. (So good.)

Yessir, that's how it was supposed to go, those 15 years ago, after the 2004 Red Sox—a united, supremely talented, oblivious-to-pressure squad, or one possessing every attribute necessary to exorcise all perceived ghosts and lame narratives—showed us what a seemingly impossible dream looked like once fulfilled. It has not gone that way, despite three more Red Sox champions since, and eight more among New England's other major professional sports teams since the turn of the century. Oh, for a time it did, and we were chill and satisfied and appreciative. For a time when it seemed like there would be a multiyear grace period before fans would ever have a gripe or a woe-is-us mentality. That grace period lasted … well, maybe through that 2004-05 winter, but it was long over by the time Red Sox fans began booing '04 postseason stalwart Keith Foulke in his injury-plagued summer of '05.

RED SOX PROSPECTUS
2018 W-L: 108-54, 1ST IN AL EAST

Pythag	.640	2nd	B-Age	27.7	12th
RS/G	5.41	1st	P-Age	28.9	20th
RA/G	3.99	5th	Salary	$233.2M	1st
DRC+	111	1st	M$/MW	$3.7M	17th
DRA	4.17	9th	DL Days	1259	18th
FIP	3.85	6th	$ on DL	11%	6th
DER	.706	15th			

390'

379'

380'

310'

302'

- Opened 1912
- Open air
- Natural surface
- Fence profile: 3' to 37'

Three-Year Park Factors

Runs	Runs/RH	Runs/LH	HR/RH	HR/LH
105	107	101	102	90

Top Hitter WARP	8.7 Mookie Betts
Top Pitcher WARP	5.6 Chris Sale
Top Prospect	Bobby Dalbec

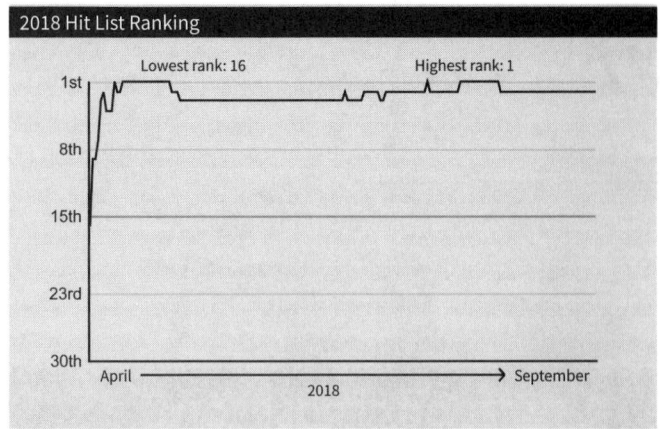

2018 Hit List Ranking

Lowest rank: 16   Highest rank: 1

April — 2018 → September

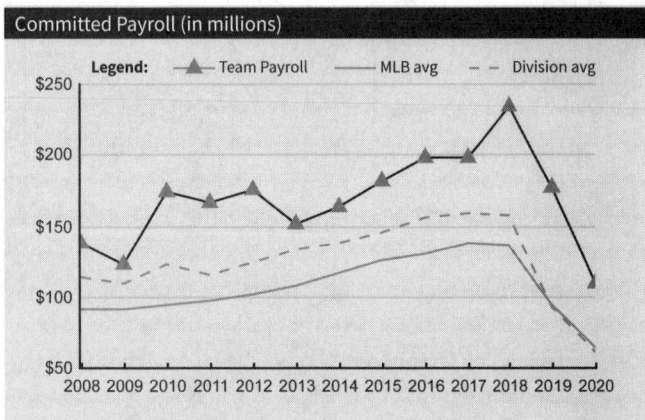

Committed Payroll (in millions)

Legend: ▲ Team Payroll — MLB avg – – Division avg

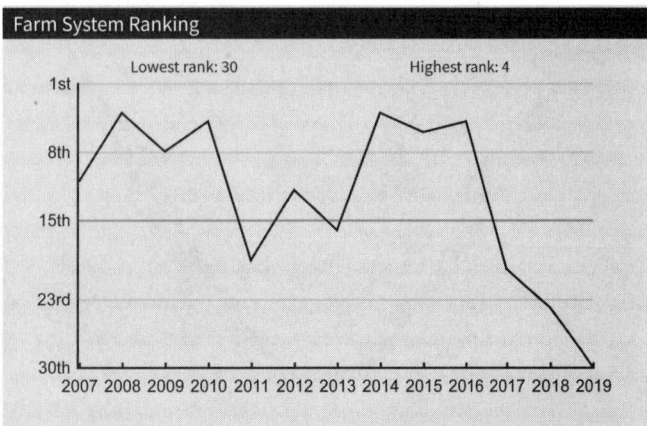

Farm System Ranking

Lowest rank: 30   Highest rank: 4

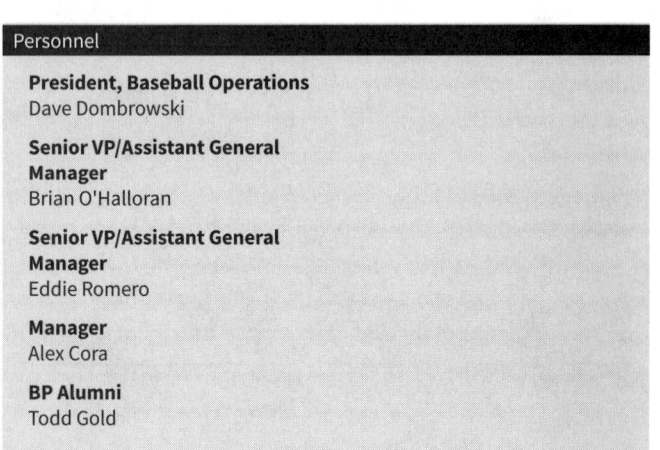

Personnel

President, Baseball Operations
Dave Dombrowski

Senior VP/Assistant General Manager
Brian O'Halloran

Senior VP/Assistant General Manager
Eddie Romero

Manager
Alex Cora

BP Alumni
Todd Gold

As exasperating as it can be, and as much as we should be accountable for our own actions as fans, I should stop suggesting that this is entirely on a vocal, negative segment of the fanbase because it is not entirely all their fault. It's the media culture that perpetrates it, shapes a bitter narrative, finds the negative needle a haystack of positives, conjures some negative conjecture when there is no real negative to be found, and then processes into hot takes for easy consumption.

I say this as a member of the media with the Marriott points to prove it. It's on us. And never more so than during the 2018 Red Sox season.

In retrospect, the '18 Red Sox played as close to a drama-free season of baseball excellence as there can be. They had the best record in spring training, sprinted out to a 17-2 regular-season start, never lost more than three games in a row, never won fewer than 15 games in a month, captured the American League East title by eight games, collected a franchise-record 108 regular season wins, and tore through the postseason, going 11-3 in the playoffs and World Series while wiping out the Yankees, Astros, and Dodgers along the way. The only team that has won more games and a World Series in a single season is the 1998 Yankees.

History will remember the 2018 Red Sox as one of the greatest teams ever. But few high-profile opinion makers in Boston—particularly in the aural cesspool that is sports radio—acknowledged it in real time. The most consistent talking points during the regular season weren't about Betts's all-around brilliance on a daily basis, rookie manager Alex Cora's charming candor and informed tactical boldness, or how J.D. Martinez was in every way the replacement for David Ortiz they so desperately lacked in 2017. No, they howled about Dave Dombrowski's checkered history of bullpen construction and his perceived failures to bolster the roster at the trade deadline. They told us time and time again that the regular season meant nothing, as if it were foolish and even wrong to enjoy the Red Sox' daily feats.

And they yapped about David Price. Everything about David Price that could be construed in the negative. His ignominious postseason history, his affinity for Fortnite, and his chronic struggles in New York.

I've often thought David Ortiz is the best thing ever to happen to the Red Sox; he delivered the big hits that all the legends before him could not. But Price, with his talent, defensiveness, flaws, and salary, might have been the greatest gift to happen to the Boston media. Much of the poison-tipped criticism aimed his way since signing a seven-year, $217 million free-agent deal with the Red Sox in December 2015 was earned. In his first two seasons, he brooded when he pitched poorly, carried himself with a sarcastic defiance on the occasions when he lived up to his ability and contract, and picked some strange battles to fight in what seemed a genuine but misguided quest to lead.

In June 2017, Price verbally ambushed Hall of Fame pitcher and Red Sox broadcaster Dennis Eckersley on the team plane, berating him for an innocuous comment he'd made about pitcher Eduardo Rodriguez's ugly pitching line during a rehab start. (Eck, ever candid, saw the line on a graphic and offered a one-word assessment: "Yuck.") Price later said Eckersley—who spent 24 years in the majors, endured two divorces, including one when his wife left him for a teammate, underwent alcohol rehabilitation, and was unfathomably gracious even after difficult on-field moments such as Kirk Gibson's home run in Game 1 of the 1988 World Series—didn't understand how hard it was to succeed in the major leagues. It was a jarring case-study in obliviousness.

But Price's latest failing—whether real or exaggerated—was too often the main story, when the real news was the unprecedented success of the ballclub; it's the first time I can recall seeing a dominating team also have a scapegoat.

The sports radio banshees didn't care to acknowledge that the Red Sox were cutting a path to history for a simple reason: preaching misery is lucrative. Negativity is proven to earn massive ratings in sports radio's targeted men 25-54 demographic in Boston, and with ratings come the coveted advertising dollars from every hair-replacement, weight-loss, and erectile dysfunction remedy hawker imaginable. Say this: They do know their audience.

One station, which happens to be the Red Sox radio rights holder, had internal discussions at the management level about turning its game broadcasts into more of a talk-show format. Imagine that. A broadcast booth that was once the home to Curt Gowdy, Ken Coleman, Ned Martin, and Jon Miller felt its broadcast might be enhanced by adding verbal fart-fest of contrived opinions. I could imagine hearing that on my car radio on a lovely New England summer night, sure—on the one AM radio with perfect reception in the deepest depths of hell.

A host on a competing station said during the World Series that he's tired of hearing about Dave Roberts's history-altering steal in Game 4 of the 2004 ALCS. Two days after Mookie Betts—as admirable a person as he is a ballplayer—won the American League Most Valuable Player award, the same host was yelping that the Red Sox should trade him now because he could leave as a free agent after 2020. This show has been rated No. 1 in its timeslot for six consecutive years.

Some criticism in real time is always justified, of course. Price's postseason record was abysmal. The bullpen had enough aggravating moments to wonder if they were harbingers for a fatally flawed postseason performance. The Red Sox had won back to back division titles in 2016-17, only to fizzle in the divisional round each time.

But the emphasis of the negative and only the negative makes for an aggravating experience for those Red Sox fans that are level-headed rather than fretting that the bandwagon is going to career off the highway eventually. Sports radio brainwashes too many fans into believing optimism makes you a Pollyanna. Too many fans are willing to go along with it without any critical thinking. It's not just

that they're chicken littles, telling you that the sky is falling. They tell you the sky was never that great, never especially bright or blue, in the first place.

The national perception is that the assorted titles have made Boston sports fans entitled. There's some truth there, but the landscape is more complicated than any smug t-shirt slogan like they hate-us-'cause-they-ain't-us might reveal. I'll admit it: As a columnist, I still want the local teams to win. It's good for business, your stories get read by a huge audience and, if you're lucky, saved in commemoration. It's more rewarding to cover memorable accomplishments than it is devastating disappointments, and your friends who truly care about the teams are happy, at least in the immediate days afterward. The Dunkin's tastes better the morning after a championship is won, you know?

But the chronic negativity via certain media brings a warped reality, too. An exceptional victory, like the one the Red Sox authored in 2018, can feel like two victories: One over the opponent on the ballfield, and one over the culture. That culture is long ingrained. A former Boston sports anchor, the cheeky Bob Lobel, was notorious for asking, "Why can't we get players like that?" whenever an ex-Red Sox would fare well. (It was usually Jeff Bagwell.) Lobel, not so cheekily, also told us to "be careful what we wish for" when the Red Sox won in '04, as if some meaningful part of the identity of being a Boston fan was lost. Yeah, I'll take the banners over the bummers, thanks.

That deep-seated instinct for negativity adds extra degrees of difficulty for the players. It can infect and permeate a team if it is not strong in every way. It was so critical for the 2004 Red Sox to possess an indefatigable mental toughness, a goofy, fearless defiance, because a weaker-minded team could not overcome … well, everything.

In the aftermath of the 2003 Red Sox' Game 7 loss to the Yankees in the ALCS, then-manager Grady Little acknowledged that there were players on the roster who were being crushed by the weight of history, fearful of being the next Bill Buckner. The 2018 team did not carry such a burden—it was a tight-knit and unfailingly professional clubhouse—but still, its mental toughness never wavered. They validated every belief and slaughtered every negative narrative along the way. It was incredibly impressive, and yet aggravating to that a team that won 108 regular season games had lousy narratives to slaughter at all.

I say this as someone who should have been the quintessential scarred and damaged Red Sox fan. The first year I followed baseball was 1978. I was 8. When Yaz popped up to Graig Nettles to end the one-game playoff and the Yankees commenced reveling on the Fenway lawn, I turned to my dad next to me on the couch and asked, "How do the Red Sox feel right now, dad?" It was the first dumb question in what would become a lifetime of asking dumb questions, but it elicited an answer I've never forgotten: "Well, Chad, they feel like [expletive]," he said, and then, in that eureka moment, so did I.

The 2018 season was the 40th anniversary of the Red Sox' collapse in '78, and there were no shortage of reminders of that this past season as the Red Sox built their lead over the Yankees. In a slight way, I do understand the misty watercolor nostalgia for the days of misery and disappointment. Perhaps those miserable times happened while you were watching the game with a loved one who is no longer with us or a friend who is no longer near. Perhaps it's not a longing for the time when the Red Sox would disappoint, but a longing for the time itself, when youth was still yours and days were more fulfilling. But in dwelling on days departed, so much is missed when these modern Red Sox rise to the magnitude of the moment.

During the 2018 postseason, I realized that it helps to get away from Boston to feel the spirit of true fandom. There were a thousand moments large and small through the Red Sox' championship run that felt pivotal and/or emboldening, including one that actually came in defeat: Nathan Eovaldi's six innings (and 97 pitches) of relief work on one day's rest in the 18-inning Game 3 epic.

The Red Sox tell you that defeat unified them even more, that they had tears in their eyes and steeled determination in their guts after Eovaldi's selflessness. But any claims that they were sure they were going to win the World Series at that point must be swallowed with a full shaker of salt.

After all, they trailed the Dodgers, 4-0, through six innings of Game 4. The Dodgers were nine outs from evening the series. Then, something extraordinary: Mitch Moreland connected for a three-run home run off of Pedro Baez in the seventh … and it was if a flipped switched at Chavez Ravine, as if every Dodger fan had been escorted out at that moment and replaced by a Red Sox fan. It remained Fenway West Coast for the rest of the series, through their eventual 9-6 victory in that Game 4, then the efficiently anticlimactic 5-1 victory in Game 5.

As the Red Sox rejoiced on the Dodger Stadium grass in the postgame chaos of their clinching victory, as the redeemed and beaming David Price hugged every non-reporter in sight, as Fox's David Ortiz swallowed his former teammate and understudy Mookie Betts in a bear hug, and as Alex Rodriguez tried to calculate the most authentic-seeming human emotion he could, thousands of Boston fans ringed the field, roaring deliriously, the picture of happiness, the sunshine without the clouds. The perfect picture of what being a Red Sox fan was supposed to look and feel like at the pinnacle was taken three-thousand miles away from Fenway.

In the final episode of the American version of The Office, the character Andy Bernard says, "I wish there was a way to tell you're in the good old days before you've actually left them." It's a sweet, sentimental line, but the reality is that there is a way to know—all it requires is a conscious effort and willingness to appreciate the good stuff as it is happening. I wish more Red Sox fans knew, or cared to do, this.

Sometimes it helps to get away from home to remember how fortunate we have become, to be reminded that even during the frustrating stretches that come every season that it's OK to assume things will be OK, to know that it doesn't make you soft or a Pollyanna or not a real fan because you believe in a team fully and without cynicism. The Red Sox have won four World Series titles in 15 years. Man, these are the good old days. I suppose there's some bonus satisfaction that comes in watching them silence the chronic and usually well-compensated cynics. But the greater satisfaction will come when the cynics' shrill wish-casting for disappointment stops registering at all. Maybe this will be the year. Doubt it, but crazier dreams have come true. ■

—Chad Finn is a columnist at the Boston Globe.

HITTERS

Andrew Benintendi LF
Born: 07/06/94 Age: 24 Bats: L Throws: L Height: 5'10" Weight: 170 Origin: Round 1, 2015 Draft (#7 overall)

YEAR	TEAM	LVL	AGE	PA	R	2B	3B	HR	RBI	BB	K	SB	CS	AVG/OBP/SLG	DRC+	VORP	BABIP	BRR	FRAA	WARP
2016	SLM	A+	21	155	30	13	7	1	32	15	9	8	2	.341/.413/.563	143	18.0	.354	-0.2	CF(30): 5.5	1.8
2016	PME	AA	21	263	40	18	5	8	44	24	30	8	7	.295/.357/.515	128	19.4	.308	0.7	CF(53): 0.2, LF(4): 1.9	1.9
2016	BOS	MLB	21	118	16	11	1	2	14	10	25	1	0	.295/.359/.476	90	5.0	.367	-0.6	LF(29): 0.9, CF(5): -0.2	0.2
2017	BOS	MLB	22	658	84	26	1	20	90	70	112	20	5	.271/.352/.424	108	18.4	.301	1.4	LF(123): -0.6, CF(30): 0.0	2.7
2018	BOS	MLB	23	661	103	41	6	16	87	71	106	21	3	.290/.366/.465	120	33.9	.328	-1.1	LF(129): 8.2, CF(24): -2.6	4.0
2019	BOS	MLB	24	608	84	32	4	16	65	62	104	17	4	.272/.353/.436	117	29.4	.308	-0.6	LF 2, CF 0	3.3

Breakout: 2% Improve: 53% Collapse: 7% Attrition: 9% MLB: 100%   *Comparables: Mookie Betts, Rafael Palmeiro, Bruce Bochte*

When a team wins 108 games—119 including the playoffs—it can be tough to come away with just one image that captures their historic greatness. But in the fifth inning of Game 2 of the World Series, Benintendi made a leaping catch in front of the Green Monster that will live on in Boston lore for many years. It was a good but not spectacular grab—in fact, it wasn't even Benintendi's most impressive catch of the postseason. But the visual was absolutely striking—an airborne Benintendi in the Air Jordan pose positioned directly in front of the iconic bright white standings that are manually entered on Fenway's great green wall. They read, in descending order: BOSTON—NEW YORK—TAMPA BAY—TORONTO—BALTIMORE, with each team's record following. That moment was the cherry on top of an outstanding sophomore season for Benintendi, who became a stronger hitter, better runner and smarter fielder in his second year. Despite some issues against same-side pitchers and a bit of a second-half swoon, Benintendi was very productive batting out of the two-spot in Boston's loaded order, and he excelled despite not turning 24 until July. He just narrowly missed out on his first All-Star selection, but if Benintendi stays on his current trajectory he'll be playing in quite a few before it's all said and done. He may never provide us with a better poster, though.

Mookie Betts RF   Born: 10/07/92   Age: 26   Bats: R   Throws: R   Height: 5'9"   Weight: 180   Origin: Round 5, 2011 Draft (#172 overall)

YEAR	TEAM	LVL	AGE	PA	R	2B	3B	HR	RBI	BB	K	SB	CS	AVG/OBP/SLG	DRC+	VORP	BABIP	BRR	FRAA	WARP
2016	BOS	MLB	23	730	122	42	5	31	113	49	80	26	4	.318/.363/.534	134	48.3	.322	8.7	RF(157): 24.8	8.2
2017	BOS	MLB	24	712	101	46	2	24	102	77	79	26	3	.264/.344/.459	111	31.4	.268	6.2	RF(153): 23.9	5.6
2018	BOS	MLB	25	614	129	47	5	32	80	81	91	30	6	.346/.438/.640	174	77.3	.368	3.8	RF(120): 10.7, CF(14): 0.4	8.7
2019	BOS	MLB	26	697	112	41	5	28	91	78	86	28	5	.300/.384/.518	149	66.6	.312	4.9	RF 15, CF 0	8.7

Breakout: 6%   Improve: 53%   Collapse: 3%   Attrition: 7%   MLB: 99%   *Comparables: Mike Greenwell, Gary Sheffield, Paul Waner*

We can argue until we're all blue in the face about who the *best* player in baseball is, but it seems fairly clear-cut that Betts is the game's most well-rounded player. Per our metrics, he was the game's second-best hitter, 14th-best defender (excluding catchers) and 20th-best base runner, which is why the BBWAA named him AL MVP. He had the best batting average, scored the most runs and had the best slugging percentage in the game. He also had the third-most doubles and stole the 10th-most bases. Betts became just the second Red Sox ever to join the 30-30 club. He won his third Gold Glove and his second Silver Slugger. Since our last Annual was published, Betts earned press for feeding the homeless outside the Boston Public Library, bowled a perfect game in the World Series of Bowling and became a father. It is entirely possible there's nothing he can't do on *or* off the baseball diamond. Betts only just turned 26 in October. There will be many more accolades in his future. He is tremendous for the game of baseball, and we are all lucky we get to watch him.

Xander Bogaerts SS   Born: 10/01/92   Age: 26   Bats: R   Throws: R   Height: 6'1"   Weight: 210   Origin: International Free Agent, 2009

YEAR	TEAM	LVL	AGE	PA	R	2B	3B	HR	RBI	BB	K	SB	CS	AVG/OBP/SLG	DRC+	VORP	BABIP	BRR	FRAA	WARP
2016	BOS	MLB	23	719	115	34	1	21	89	58	123	13	4	.294/.356/.446	110	38.4	.335	3.3	SS(157): -11.9	3.4
2017	BOS	MLB	24	635	94	32	6	10	62	56	116	15	1	.273/.343/.403	91	31.9	.327	5.5	SS(146): -9.2	1.9
2018	BOS	MLB	25	580	72	45	3	23	103	55	102	8	2	.288/.360/.522	123	50.2	.317	-0.2	SS(136): 1.5	4.5
2019	BOS	MLB	26	602	71	28	4	17	72	58	104	10	2	.267/.347/.427	115	35.9	.305	2.1	SS -8	3.0

Breakout: 4%   Improve: 57%   Collapse: 4%   Attrition: 9%   MLB: 98%   *Comparables: Jose Reyes, Yunel Escobar, J.J. Hardy*

Patience is not a strong suit among prospect lovers, or most Red Sox fans, for that matter. Some were ready to label Bogaerts a bust after his relatively disappointing 2017 season, ignoring his youth, pedigree and the wrist injury that clearly hampered his performance. But the more enlightened knew that with better health a breakout could be just around the corner, and in 2018, at the ripe old age of 25, Bogaerts finally delivered. The Sox shortstop set career-best marks in pretty much everything other than batting average and stolen bases. Among shortstops, he finished first in doubles, second in OBP, third in slugging and fifth in both total bases and home runs. He was among Boston's best hitters, steadiest defenders and most handsome players. And he was clutch, too, with a stout .333/.390/.563 effort in high-leverage situations. When it comes to long-term extensions, Mookie Betts obviously needs to be the Red Sox's top priority. But there's an argument that Bogaerts should come next, even among a crop of potential post-2019 free agents that also includes Chris Sale and Rick Porcello.

Jackie Bradley CF   Born: 04/19/90   Age: 29   Bats: L   Throws: R   Height: 5'10"   Weight: 200   Origin: Round 1, 2011 Draft (#40 overall)

YEAR	TEAM	LVL	AGE	PA	R	2B	3B	HR	RBI	BB	K	SB	CS	AVG/OBP/SLG	DRC+	VORP	BABIP	BRR	FRAA	WARP
2016	BOS	MLB	26	636	94	30	7	26	87	63	143	9	2	.267/.349/.486	114	31.1	.312	3.0	CF(156): 9.1	4.7
2017	BOS	MLB	27	541	58	19	3	17	63	48	124	8	3	.245/.323/.402	94	19.3	.294	3.8	CF(132): -7.4	1.2
2018	BOS	MLB	28	535	76	33	4	13	59	46	137	17	1	.234/.314/.403	88	15.3	.299	2.5	CF(135): 6.1, RF(15): 0.3	2.0
2019	BOS	MLB	29	539	65	24	3	16	60	50	125	11	2	.241/.326/.401	102	24.7	.297	2.3	CF 0	2.6

Breakout: 8%   Improve: 52%   Collapse: 5%   Attrition: 15%   MLB: 99%   *Comparables: Nate McLouth, Chris Young, Austin Jackson*

It took Leo 27 years to win an Oscar and Henry Winkler 43 years to win an Emmy, but the real crime is that Bradley had to wait five-plus seasons for his first Gold Glove. You have to watch Bradley for only a handful of games—say a playoff series or three—to understand that he should have a few such defensive honors by now. But ALCS MVP? Well, it was harder to see that award coming. JBJ earned his Hardware by driving in nine runs against the defending champs thanks in part to a game-clinching grand slam off Roberto Osuna at Minute Maid Park in Game 3. It's fitting that Bradley earned acclaim for his bat in a series in which he recorded only three hits, as it accurately represents who and what he is at the plate: often overmatched and streaky as all hell, yet capable of greatness in small spurts. He's found the perfect role in Boston as a down-the-order hitter who props up the pitching staff with his trademark brand of smooth-looking, spectacular defense.

Triston Casas 3B   Born: 01/15/00   Age: 19   Bats: L   Throws: R   Height: 6'4"   Weight: 238   Origin: Round 1, 2018 Draft (#26 overall)

Lots of things went right for Casas in 2018. He hit .385/.545/.884 with seven homers as a senior at American Heritage School in Florida. He was drafted 26th overall by the Red Sox in June. He signed a $2.55 million bonus, gave an adorable interview on MLB Network and got to visit Fenway for the first time. Are you waiting for the other shoe to drop? Here it is: just two games into his GCL career, Casas tore the UCL in his right thumb diving for a ball, meaning he was SOL for the rest of the season. While hand injuries can be scary for hitters, there shouldn't be any long-term ramifications for Casas. He still profiles as a plus-power hitter who's willing to go the other way, as well as a defender who's perhaps more likely to become a good first baseman than average across the diamond. Assuming he fully recovers, it should be fun to see which reliever Dave Dombrowski trades him for in three years.

Rusney Castillo CF   Born: 07/09/87   Age: 31   Bats: R   Throws: R   Height: 5'9"   Weight: 195   Origin: International Free Agent, 2014

YEAR	TEAM	LVL	AGE	PA	R	2B	3B	HR	RBI	BB	K	SB	CS	AVG/OBP/SLG	DRC+	VORP	BABIP	BRR	FRAA	WARP
2016	BOS	MLB	28	8	4	1	0	0	0	0	3	0	0	.250/.250/.375	83	0.2	.400	0.4	LF(2): -0.5, CF(1): 0.0	0.0
2016	PAW	AAA	28	429	55	20	5	2	34	24	68	9	3	.263/.309/.354	90	13.1	.310	4.6	CF(86): 10.1, LF(8): -1.8	2.3
2017	PAW	AAA	29	369	52	22	0	15	43	11	51	14	2	.314/.350/.507	129	29.5	.332	3.0	CF(73): 4.7, RF(7): 0.6	3.2
2018	PAW	AAA	30	511	56	31	0	5	59	29	80	13	7	.319/.360/.416	108	27.5	.372	1.2	CF(97): -4.6, RF(8): -0.4	1.7
2019	BOS	MLB	31	251	30	11	0	6	23	12	53	5	2	.245/.293/.370	77	2.0	.294	-0.1	CF 2, RF 0	0.4

Breakout: 4%   Improve: 16%   Collapse: 15%   Attrition: 27%   MLB: 45%   *Comparables: Jason Bourgeois, Lou Montanez, Jason Pridie*

Castillo is best known as a cautionary tale; an eight-figure international signee who has to date backfired more or less entirely. But is that really fair? In the four-plus years since Castillo signed with Boston, he's received 337 PA in the majors, and just eight of those have come since 2015. Castillo has proven definitively that he's too good for Triple-A, winning the International League batting title last season after thriving in 2017. So why no call up? Castillo's $10 million-plus AAV would count against the $237 million luxury tax threshold the Sox were desperately trying to stay under, at least until they splurged on Ian Kinsler in July. So why no call-up then? Perhaps because the Sox's four main outfielders consist of two MVP candidates, a 24-year-old stud and one of the game's best defenders. The Red Sox don't need and "can't afford" Castillo, but he's earned another shot to play in the big leagues. It's just unlikely to come in Boston.

C.J. Chatham SS   Born: 12/22/94   Age: 24   Bats: R   Throws: R   Height: 6'4"   Weight: 185   Origin: Round 2, 2016 Draft (#51 overall)

YEAR	TEAM	LVL	AGE	PA	R	2B	3B	HR	RBI	BB	K	SB	CS	AVG/OBP/SLG	DRC+	VORP	BABIP	BRR	FRAA	WARP
2016	RSX	RK	21	25	2	2	0	1	2	0	7	0	0	.167/.200/.375	85	-1.4	.188	-0.1	SS(7): -0.3	0.0
2016	LOW	A-	21	121	19	4	1	4	19	8	20	0	1	.259/.319/.426	111	5.0	.282	-0.7	SS(26): 0.3	0.6
2018	GRN	A	23	80	13	6	1	0	9	3	14	1	1	.307/.329/.413	103	1.6	.371	0.6	SS(4): -0.2	0.2
2018	SLM	A+	23	392	42	14	1	3	43	21	72	10	4	.315/.355/.384	102	16.4	.380	2.7	SS(67): -3.6	1.3
2019	BOS	MLB	24	251	22	8	0	5	24	10	60	2	1	.229/.261/.321	54	-5.8	.283	-0.5	SS -2	-0.9

Breakout: 2%   Improve: 7%   Collapse: 1%   Attrition: 19%   MLB: 19%   *Comparables: Yadiel Rivera, Angel Chavez, Blake Davis*

Listen, pretty much anyone who lives in New England knows to associate Chatham with delays and late arrivals, but C.J. here was taking that connection to the extreme. Boston's second-round pick from 2016 missed a ton of time in 2017 with leg issues and hit the DL last season thanks to a viral infection. That's the bad news. The good news? Whenever he's been on the field, Chatham has hit. Sure, High-A shouldn't be a super challenging environment for a 23-year-old with college experience, but Chatham showed good bat-to-ball skills and a strong approach at the plate. Combine that with solid-to-good shortstop defense and you get the makings of a second-division starter or solid backup infielder. That probably makes Chatham a top-10 Red Sox prospect right now, which...yikes.

Michael Chavis 3B   Born: 08/11/95   Age: 23   Bats: R   Throws: R   Height: 5'10"   Weight: 216   Origin: Round 1, 2014 Draft (#26 overall)

YEAR	TEAM	LVL	AGE	PA	R	2B	3B	HR	RBI	BB	K	SB	CS	AVG/OBP/SLG	DRC+	VORP	BABIP	BRR	FRAA	WARP
2016	GRN	A	20	312	30	11	3	8	35	22	74	3	1	.244/.321/.391	112	13.2	.303	1.3	3B(68): -0.4	1.5
2016	SLM	A+	20	27	5	0	0	0	1	2	7	1	0	.160/.222/.160	91	-0.8	.222	1.1	3B(2): -0.7	0.1
2017	SLM	A+	21	250	50	17	2	17	55	19	57	1	0	.318/.388/.641	153	28.8	.360	1.3	3B(24): -1.6	2.2
2017	PME	AA	21	274	39	18	0	14	39	20	56	1	0	.250/.310/.492	120	12.0	.265	0.1	3B(39): -0.5, SS(1): 0.0	1.5
2018	PME	AA	22	139	23	7	0	6	17	13	35	3	1	.303/.388/.508	121	13.3	.383	0.5	3B(18): 1.5, 1B(11): -0.5	0.9
2018	PAW	AAA	22	34	8	3	0	2	7	1	12	0	0	.273/.294/.545	82	4.7	.368	0.2	3B(4): -1.2, 1B(1): 0.0	-0.1
2019	BOS	MLB	23	34	4	2	0	1	4	2	10	0	0	.230/.288/.410	67	-0.7	.289	-0.1	3B 0	-0.1

Breakout: 7%   Improve: 20%   Collapse: 4%   Attrition: 14%   MLB: 46%   *Comparables: Alex Liddi, Paul DeJong, J.D. Davis*

When he was on the field in 2018, Chavis was pretty good. He continued to show promising game power and a willingness to take walks as he ascended the MiLB ladder, and he maintained an acceptable strikeout rate for good measure. But back to that "on the field" part... The oft-injured Chavis opened the year on the DL with an oblique issue. He had plenty of time to heal at least, as he was suspended 80 games for PED usage shortly thereafter. Chavis has more red flags than you like to see from a first-rounder, especially one with a likely defensive home at first. Still, his bat should make him a second-division starter or platoon corner bat at worst, and there's still some first-division upside if you squint. Though if the whole baseball thing *doesn't* work out, his status as a short, injury-prone steroid user could perhaps make him the next great Patriots receiver!

Bobby Dalbec 3B   Born: 06/29/95   Age: 24   Bats: R   Throws: R   Height: 6'4"   Weight: 225   Origin: Round 4, 2016 Draft (#118 overall)

YEAR	TEAM	LVL	AGE	PA	R	2B	3B	HR	RBI	BB	K	SB	CS	AVG/OBP/SLG	DRC+	VORP	BABIP	BRR	FRAA	WARP
2016	LOW	A-	21	143	25	13	2	7	33	9	33	2	2	.386/.427/.674	140	19.0	.473	1.3	3B(22): 2.5	1.5
2017	GRN	A	22	329	48	15	0	13	39	36	123	4	5	.246/.345/.437	111	12.9	.383	-2.0	3B(67): -2.3	1.0
2018	SLM	A+	23	419	59	27	2	26	85	60	130	3	1	.256/.372/.573	151	44.2	.318	0.9	3B(91): 5.2, SS(1): 0.0	4.7
2018	PME	AA	23	124	14	8	1	6	24	6	46	0	0	.261/.323/.514	88	7.1	.377	-0.1	3B(18): -3.9, 1B(2): -0.3	-0.3
2019	BOS	MLB	24	251	27	10	0	11	33	20	97	0	0	.190/.263/.375	71	-3.9	.267	-0.7	3B 0, 1B 0	-0.5

Breakout: 4%   Improve: 28%   Collapse: 10%   Attrition: 27%   MLB: 52%   *Comparables: Matt Chapman, J.D. Davis, Dylan Cozens*

As fun as this would be, it probably isn't going to work out. Dalbec struck out in about a third of his plate appearances last year despite spending the bulk of the season as a 23-year-old in High-A. Yes, he has prodigious power and yes, Dalbec's glove and arm are up to the task at third base. But when your swing-and-miss generates more energy than the Gansu Wind Farm, the utility of your other tools tends not to matter so much. Only four qualified hitters K'd in more than 30 percent of their plate appearances last year, and of that whiff-happy quartet, only two—Joey Gallo and former Sox prospect Yoan Moncada—had even moderately productive seasons. Those are the odds Dalbec is up against, but if we know anything about him, at the very least he'll go down swinging.

Rafael Devers 3B   Born: 10/24/96   Age: 22   Bats: L   Throws: R   Height: 6'0"   Weight: 237   Origin: International Free Agent, 2013

YEAR	TEAM	LVL	AGE	PA	R	2B	3B	HR	RBI	BB	K	SB	CS	AVG/OBP/SLG	DRC+	VORP	BABIP	BRR	FRAA	WARP
2016	SLM	A+	19	546	64	32	8	11	71	40	94	18	6	.282/.335/.443	112	25.1	.328	-1.2	3B(117): 22.2	4.6
2017	PME	AA	20	320	48	19	3	18	56	31	55	0	3	.300/.369/.575	135	26.8	.316	-0.7	3B(58): 4.6	3.0
2017	PAW	AAA	20	38	6	1	0	2	4	3	8	0	0	.400/.447/.600	110	5.6	.480	0.1	3B(8): -2.1	0.0
2017	BOS	MLB	20	240	34	14	0	10	30	18	57	3	1	.284/.338/.482	96	12.0	.342	0.2	3B(56): 4.9	1.3
2018	BOS	MLB	21	490	59	24	0	21	66	38	121	5	2	.240/.298/.433	95	13.6	.281	1.7	3B(116): 11.2	2.9
2019	BOS	MLB	22	482	57	22	1	19	64	41	110	4	2	.249/.317/.435	102	13.0	.291	0.7	3B 10	2.4

Breakout: 4%   Improve: 53%   Collapse: 1%   Attrition: 12%   MLB: 87%   *Comparables: Brett Lawrie, Ryan Zimmerman, Addison Russell*

Boston's favorite Large Adult Son had an up-and-down first full season in the majors. Let's start with the positives: Devers finished in the top 15 among third baseman in BWARP, homers and RBI. He remains adept at crushing premium velocity, can make the occasional spectacular play at third base and had some nice postseason moments. Unfortunately, there were some real growing pains, too. Devers hit just .229/.272/.347 against southpaws, had a worse overall OBP than Pablo Sandoval and will occasionally miss first base by...oh, let's say 50 feet or so when he rushes his throws from third. It's important to remember that Devers didn't turn 22 until Game 2 of the World Series. All the raw material required for him to emerge as a true middle-of-the-order hitter and tolerable third baseman (at least through his mid-20s) remains evident. But we call raw material "raw" for a reason, and Devers needs some refinement.

Gorkys Hernandez CF   Born: 09/07/87   Age: 31   Bats: R   Throws: R   Height: 6'1"   Weight: 196   Origin: International Free Agent, 2005

YEAR	TEAM	LVL	AGE	PA	R	2B	3B	HR	RBI	BB	K	SB	CS	AVG/OBP/SLG	DRC+	VORP	BABIP	BRR	FRAA	WARP
2016	SAC	AAA	28	503	74	22	3	8	51	52	77	20	13	.302/.382/.421	100	35.6	.349	2.1	CF(113): -0.2	2.1
2016	SFN	MLB	28	57	7	5	0	2	4	3	11	0	1	.259/.298/.463	95	2.2	.293	-0.1	CF(14): -0.1, RF(6): 1.0	0.2
2017	SFN	MLB	29	348	40	20	1	0	22	31	73	12	4	.255/.327/.326	72	6.4	.331	2.3	LF(57): -5.7, CF(50): 2.4	-0.3
2018	SFN	MLB	30	451	52	16	2	15	40	27	113	8	5	.234/.285/.391	78	7.9	.283	2.5	CF(86): -0.1, LF(37): -0.3	0.5
2019	BOS	MLB	31	405	49	17	2	8	36	31	90	10	5	.241/.306/.368	82	6.9	.294	1.4	CF 1, LF 0	0.8

Breakout: 1%   Improve: 27%   Collapse: 13%   Attrition: 22%   MLB: 70%   *Comparables: Alex Presley, Chris Burke, Chris Denorfia*

Ten pounds of muscle, 3.6 degrees of launch angle, 2.5 miles an hour of exit velocity and the intent to hit the ball up. Those four factors, along with a pain-free wrist, nearly tripled Hernandez's career home run total, yet the transformation hardly changed his offensive outlook overall. Gorkys the slugger was more entertaining than Gorkys the scrub, but the taters were virtually negated by a bushel of popups and a decrease in walks. While the Rockies—victims of seven Gorkys taters—never solved Hernandez, by the All-Star break, everyone else learned to steer clear of his down-and-in power alley, and he hit just .162/.220/.286 from that point on. Hernandez's true talent lies somewhere between the first and second halves, but he's still a fifth outfielder, just a more interesting one than he was before.

Brock Holt UT   Born: 06/11/88   Age: 31   Bats: L   Throws: R   Height: 5'10"   Weight: 180   Origin: Round 9, 2009 Draft (#265 overall)

YEAR	TEAM	LVL	AGE	PA	R	2B	3B	HR	RBI	BB	K	SB	CS	AVG/OBP/SLG	DRC+	VORP	BABIP	BRR	FRAA	WARP
2016	BOS	MLB	28	324	45	16	0	7	34	27	58	4	3	.255/.322/.383	89	5.1	.294	1.7	LF(64): 5.4, 3B(17): 1.9	1.4
2017	PAW	AAA	29	77	9	1	0	3	9	6	14	0	0	.214/.286/.357	93	0.6	.226	0.1	LF(7): 1.3, 3B(4): 0.1	0.3
2017	BOS	MLB	29	164	20	6	0	0	7	19	34	2	1	.200/.305/.243	68	-3.0	.259	0.6	2B(31): 0.1, LF(10): 0.7	0.0
2018	BOS	MLB	30	367	41	18	2	7	46	37	73	7	7	.277/.362/.411	101	13.6	.337	-1.9	2B(56): -5.3, SS(23): -2.0	0.1
2019	BOS	MLB	31	335	36	13	1	7	32	31	67	5	3	.235/.318/.354	87	5.3	.283	0.2	2B -2, RF 0	0.4

Breakout: 4%   Improve: 39%   Collapse: 6%   Attrition: 10%   MLB: 91%   *Comparables: Ryan Theriot, Dutch Meyer, Buddy Myer*

Major League Baseball was founded in 1903. There have been about two thousand playoff games since, which means many more thousands of players have participated in said battles. Holt became the first among them to hit for the cycle in a postseason game when he clubbed a ninth-inning homer off backup catcher Austin Romine in the Red Sox's ALDS Game 3 drubbing of their archrival Yankees. "WE ARE LIVING RENT-FREE IN THEIR HEADS," drunk New Yorkers in the bleachers screamed through tears as Holt rounded the bases. "RENT-FREE," they sobbed in unison. That moment—which also made Holt just the 26th player ever to hit for multiple cycles in a career—punctuated a nice bounceback season for Boston's favorite spark plug. Holt received his most playing time since 2015 thanks in large part to Dustin Pedroia's absence, and he responded by posting the best offensive year of his career. Would he be miscast as an everyday starter? Of course. Would Boston rather have anyone else as their super sub, clubhouse glue and resident Andrew Benintendi sidekick? Of course not. o/ forever.

Sandy Leon C   Born: 03/13/89   Age: 30   Bats: B   Throws: R   Height: 5'10"   Weight: 225   Origin: International Free Agent, 2007

YEAR	TEAM	LVL	AGE	PA	R	2B	3B	HR	RBI	BB	K	SB	CS	AVG/OBP/SLG	DRC+	VORP	BABIP	BRR	FRAA	WARP
2016	PAW	AAA	27	130	12	3	1	2	13	11	24	0	0	.243/.315/.339	86	1.4	.286	-0.1	C(29): 6.2, 1B(1): 0.0	1.0
2016	BOS	MLB	27	283	36	17	2	7	35	23	66	0	0	.310/.369/.476	96	20.7	.392	-1.5	C(74): -1.5	1.0
2017	BOS	MLB	28	301	32	14	0	7	39	25	74	0	0	.225/.290/.354	75	-1.9	.280	-5.2	C(84): 10.8	1.1
2018	BOS	MLB	29	288	30	12	0	5	22	15	75	1	0	.177/.232/.279	62	-1.3	.226	-0.7	C(87): 11.7	1.3
2019	BOS	MLB	30	256	25	11	1	6	26	20	62	0	0	.234/.300/.364	80	3.6	.290	-1.6	C 7	1.1

Breakout: 2%   Improve: 26%   Collapse: 9%   Attrition: 16%   MLB: 84%

Comparables: Geronimo Gil, Chris Herrmann, Jose Lobaton

In "The Power of Positive Thinking," author Norman Vincent Peale asserts that the keys to happiness are to clear your mind, focus on good things you can control and forgive yourself your imperfections. Leon is a tremendous defensive catcher. In fact, it's tough to determine what the best part about his glove work is. You could argue it's his ability to steal strikes, as our Framing Runs metrics had him as the seventh-best framer in the big leagues. You could make a case for his blocking ability, as Leon allowed just 13 passed balls in 685 innings caught. Hell, maybe you'll go old school and note the way Leon's pitchers talk about him,

YEAR	TEAM	P. COUNT	FRM RUNS	BLK RUNS	THRW RUNS	TOT RUNS
2016	BOS	9517	-2.1	-0.5	1.1	-1.0
2017	BOS	11373	9.7	0.4	2.0	10.7
2018	BOS	11108	11.6	0.1	0.1	11.7
2019	BOS	9531	6.7	-0.1	0.8	7.4

and how they adore the way he calls games and pounces on breaking balls in the dirt. Whenever Leon looks in the mirror next, a World Series champion with a great beard will be staring back at him. He accomplished something Barry Bonds, Ted Williams and Ernie Banks never could. He also just got on base at a worse clip than Carlos Martinez.

J.D. Martinez DH Born: 08/21/87   Age: 31   Bats: R   Throws: R   Height: 6'3"   Weight: 220   Origin: Round 20, 2009 Draft (#611 overall)

YEAR	TEAM	LVL	AGE	PA	R	2B	3B	HR	RBI	BB	K	SB	CS	AVG/OBP/SLG	DRC+	VORP	BABIP	BRR	FRAA	WARP
2016	DET	MLB	28	517	69	35	2	22	68	49	128	1	2	.307/.373/.535	117	24.0	.378	-7.3	RF(118): -11.2	0.4
2017	DET	MLB	29	232	38	13	2	16	39	29	54	2	0	.305/.388/.630	157	17.9	.338	-1.5	RF(53): -6.3	1.4
2017	ARI	MLB	29	257	47	13	1	29	65	24	74	2	0	.302/.366/.741	163	26.7	.315	-2.4	RF(60): -3.9	2.0
2018	BOS	MLB	30	649	111	37	2	43	130	69	146	6	1	.330/.402/.629	162	58.1	.375	-3.9	LF(32): -0.9, RF(25): 2.4	6.0
2019	BOS	MLB	31	657	99	35	2	40	116	74	163	5	1	.289/.373/.567	150	44.3	.338	-5.1	LF 0, RF 0	4.6

Breakout: 2%   Improve: 45%   Collapse: 5%   Attrition: 6%   MLB: 98%   *Comparables: Ryan Howard, Fred McGriff, Dick Allen*

Martinez did the unthinkable in his first year as a Red Sox; he hit so well that Boston shock jocks couldn't complain about his contract. Yes, Dave Dombrowski's $110-million man was worth every penny and then some in a dominant season that saw him win the 2018 AL Hank Aaron Award as the league's best hitter. Martinez finished in the top 10 in baseball among qualified batters in BWARP, homers, OBP and SLG, and first overall in total bases and RBI. He was devastatingly effective at the plate, lauded as a clubhouse leader and passable enough in the outfield to let Alex Cora occasionally give some other guys half-days off at DH. In this era of uber-athletes who are offensive threats as well as impact defenders, Martinez may never win an MVP award. But he's arguably one of the two or three best pure hitters in the game at present, and he's perhaps Boston's most fearsome right-handed hitter since Manny Ramirez. Oddly enough, giving the best players in the game a lot of money can still be a pretty solid roster-building strategy.

Mitch Moreland 1B Born: 09/06/85   Age: 33   Bats: L   Throws: L   Height: 6'2"   Weight: 230   Origin: Round 17, 2007 Draft (#530 overall)

YEAR	TEAM	LVL	AGE	PA	R	2B	3B	HR	RBI	BB	K	SB	CS	AVG/OBP/SLG	DRC+	VORP	BABIP	BRR	FRAA	WARP
2016	TEX	MLB	30	503	49	21	0	22	60	35	118	1	0	.233/.298/.422	96	-6.2	.266	-3.0	1B(139): 3.8	0.6
2017	BOS	MLB	31	576	73	34	0	22	79	57	120	0	1	.246/.326/.443	98	3.5	.278	-2.7	1B(138): 5.7, P(1): 0.0	1.0
2018	BOS	MLB	32	459	57	23	4	15	68	50	102	2	0	.245/.325/.433	106	3.8	.288	-2.5	1B(116): 2.4	1.0
2019	BOS	MLB	33	398	44	19	2	13	50	38	84	1	0	.246/.325/.419	105	6.5	.289	-1.8	1B 2	0.9

Breakout: 3%   Improve: 45%   Collapse: 4%   Attrition: 19%   MLB: 93%   *Comparables: Eddie Robinson, Jim Spencer, Don Mincher*

You know you've reached the final Galaxy Brain level of kvetching about sports contracts when Moreland's two-year, $13 million deal gets raked over the coals. A small sample of players who made more than Moreland last season: Drew Smyly, Michael Dunn, Brett Cecil, Michael Pineda and Joe Smith. Two of those guys didn't even pitch! But for the low, low price of $6.5 million, the Sox got a guy who hit .246/.331/.450 with 13 homers off righties, mashed one of the biggest homers of the championship run and continued to play a very solid first base. Moreland is a second-division starter/platoon option through and through, but *not* signing a guy like that for your $230 million-plus payroll is like opting not to insure your Mercedes-Benz. He should serve as a capable supporting cast member again in 2019, but even if he tanks all of a sudden, the Red Sox can cut him for the payroll equivalent of a parking ticket.

Eduardo Nunez INF Born: 06/15/87   Age: 32   Bats: R   Throws: R   Height: 6'0"   Weight: 195   Origin: International Free Agent, 2004

YEAR	TEAM	LVL	AGE	PA	R	2B	3B	HR	RBI	BB	K	SB	CS	AVG/OBP/SLG	DRC+	VORP	BABIP	BRR	FRAA	WARP
2016	MIN	MLB	29	396	49	15	1	12	47	15	58	27	6	.296/.325/.439	106	20.7	.320	4.8	SS(51): -1.8, 3B(33): -0.1	2.2
2016	SFN	MLB	29	199	24	9	3	4	20	14	30	13	4	.269/.327/.418	99	10.1	.302	1.4	3B(48): 3.8, SS(4): -0.3	1.3
2017	SFN	MLB	30	318	37	21	0	4	31	12	29	18	5	.308/.334/.417	96	18.8	.328	4.4	3B(49): -0.1, LF(19): 2.3	1.6
2017	BOS	MLB	30	173	23	12	0	8	27	6	25	6	2	.321/.353/.539	96	12.0	.341	-1.2	2B(26): -0.8, SS(5): 0.0	0.4
2018	BOS	MLB	31	502	56	23	3	10	44	16	69	7	2	.265/.289/.388	82	-1.0	.290	-2.6	2B(74): -2.0, 3B(45): 1.2	0.1
2019	BOS	MLB	32	302	36	14	2	7	31	15	42	11	3	.271/.313/.406	97	7.5	.295	0.8	3B 0, 2B -1	0.7

Breakout: 2%   Improve: 23%   Collapse: 10%   Attrition: 7%   MLB: 94%   *Comparables: Omar Infante, Freddy Sanchez, Ronnie Belliard*

Did Nunez have a good year or a bad year? On one hand, he was hurt constantly, his glove was a tire fire at second base and he basically stopped running altogether. He also posted his worst offensive season since 2014. By the time the World Series rolled around, Nunez was a collection of interconnected injured limbs, flailing about the diamond en route to spectacular plays, terrible plays and little in between. On the other hand, Nunez just won a ring! He also hit a big pinch-hit homer in Game 1 of the World Series and opted into a $5 million contact for 2019 to play for the defending champs. It's unclear as to exactly what his role will be—short-side platoon third baseman seems most likely—but what *is* clear is that we should all be so lucky as to have our rough stretches look like Nunie's.

Josh Ockimey 1B Born: 10/18/95   Age: 23   Bats: L   Throws: R   Height: 6'1"   Weight: 215   Origin: Round 5, 2014 Draft (#164 overall)

YEAR	TEAM	LVL	AGE	PA	R	2B	3B	HR	RBI	BB	K	SB	CS	AVG/OBP/SLG	DRC+	VORP	BABIP	BRR	FRAA	WARP
2016	GRN	A	20	499	60	25	1	18	62	88	129	3	1	.226/.367/.425	138	23.0	.284	1.8	1B(101): -3.2	2.8
2017	SLM	A+	21	425	56	20	2	11	63	66	110	1	4	.275/.388/.438	123	21.7	.362	-0.7	1B(82): -2.6	1.3
2017	PME	AA	21	121	12	7	0	3	11	17	33	0	0	.272/.372/.427	99	2.6	.368	-0.5	1B(21): 0.2	0.1
2018	PME	AA	22	376	43	19	2	15	56	59	112	0	1	.254/.370/.473	117	16.8	.339	-1.1	1B(71): -2.1	0.9
2018	PAW	AAA	22	105	10	2	0	5	15	11	37	1	0	.215/.305/.398	99	-1.6	.294	-0.9	1B(20): -1.2	-0.1
2019	BOS	MLB	23	251	26	9	0	9	30	28	81	0	0	.208/.296/.369	78	-3.6	.279	-0.6	1B -1	-0.5

Breakout: 6%   Improve: 21%   Collapse: 7%   Attrition: 20%   MLB: 40%   *Comparables: Ryan Lavarnway, Travis Shaw, Ike Davis*

Do you miss the big beefy sluggers of the early '90s? A time when half the first basemen in the league grew trucker goatees and couldn't field or run a lick but could hit the ball a country mile? If so, Ockimey is the throwback prospect for you. He does one thing and one thing well. He hits the ball very hard. And the ball subsequently travels very far. His prodigious raw pop plays on account of a decent approach, and that combination is the reason that Ockimey remains on the periphery of general baseball prospectdom despite no other discernible tools. For every one of these guys who turns into Jesus Aguilar there are dozens who never make meaningful progress past Double-A. That being said, Ockimey has already reached Pawtucket as a 22-year-old, so he doesn't just have power on his side; he's got time, too.

Steve Pearce 1B Born: 04/13/83   Age: 36   Bats: R   Throws: R   Height: 5'11"   Weight: 200   Origin: Round 8, 2005 Draft (#241 overall)

YEAR	TEAM	LVL	AGE	PA	R	2B	3B	HR	RBI	BB	K	SB	CS	AVG/OBP/SLG	DRC+	VORP	BABIP	BRR	FRAA	WARP
2016	TBA	MLB	33	232	26	11	1	10	29	26	40	0	3	.309/.388/.520	117	18.3	.342	0.0	1B(30): 1.7, 2B(14): 0.4	1.2
2016	BAL	MLB	33	70	9	2	0	3	6	8	14	0	0	.217/.329/.400	121	3.3	.233	1.5	1B(10): -0.3, LF(7): -0.1	0.5
2017	TOR	MLB	34	348	38	17	1	13	37	27	68	0	0	.252/.319/.438	100	7.4	.281	0.3	LF(85): 3.3, 1B(10): -0.4	1.2
2018	TOR	MLB	35	86	16	6	0	4	16	7	14	0	0	.291/.349/.519	126	5.2	.311	0.7	LF(9): -1.4, 1B(3): 0.4	0.4
2018	BOS	MLB	35	165	19	8	1	7	26	22	27	0	0	.279/.394/.507	130	10.8	.298	-1.4	1B(31): -1.0, RF(2): -0.1	0.6
2019	*BOS*	*MLB*	*36*	*403*	*46*	*20*	*2*	*13*	*51*	*40*	*73*	*1*	*1*	*.259/.345/.431*	*115*	*13.7*	*.296*	*0.7*	*1B 0*	*1.5*

Breakout: 2%   Improve: 24%   Collapse: 11%   Attrition: 11%   MLB: 87%   *Comparables: Rafael Palmeiro, Hideki Matsui, Travis Hafner*

Between the Red Sox and Dodgers, there were 50 total players who staked claim to World Series roster spots. There were probably 43 or 44 guys more likely to win Series MVP than Pearce. But when it comes to the weird, the unpredictable and the feel-good, baseball remains undefeated. Acquired from the Blue Jays in July for the low, low cost of historical footnote/middling infield prospect Santiago Espinal, Pearce went 4-for-12 and drove in eight runs in the Fall Classic. Three of those hits were homers, and two of them came off Kenley Jansen and Clayton Kershaw in Games 4 and 5, respectively. Joe Buck would like to interrupt this comment to let you know that Pearce grew up a Red Sox fan. Anyway, Pearce's postseason heroics capped a successful second-half stint with the Sox in which he served as the perfect right-handed complement to Mitch Moreland to add another lefty-killing presence to Boston's deep lineup. He'll turn 36 next April, but that didn't stop the Sox from giving him a one-year, $6.5 million reunion tour contract. Hey, can you really put a price on The Clutch Gene?

Dustin Pedroia 2B Born: 08/17/83   Age: 35   Bats: R   Throws: R   Height: 5'9"   Weight: 175   Origin: Round 2, 2004 Draft (#65 overall)

YEAR	TEAM	LVL	AGE	PA	R	2B	3B	HR	RBI	BB	K	SB	CS	AVG/OBP/SLG	DRC+	VORP	BABIP	BRR	FRAA	WARP
2016	BOS	MLB	32	698	105	36	1	15	74	61	73	7	4	.318/.376/.449	117	26.4	.339	-2.0	2B(152): -2.7	3.3
2017	BOS	MLB	33	463	46	19	0	7	62	49	48	4	3	.293/.369/.392	107	9.4	.315	-5.7	2B(98): -0.1	1.3
2018	BOS	MLB	34	13	1	0	0	0	0	2	1	0	0	.091/.231/.091	104	-1.3	.100	-0.1	2B(3): -0.4	0.0
2019	*BOS*	*MLB*	*35*	*327*	*35*	*16*	*1*	*7*	*36*	*31*	*47*	*3*	*2*	*.273/.346/.404*	*106*	*11.7*	*.305*	*-1.7*	*2B -1*	*1.2*

Breakout: 1%   Improve: 26%   Collapse: 4%   Attrition: 10%   MLB: 87%   *Comparables: Mark Loretta, Red Schoendienst, Frankie Frisch*

We always knew this might happen. The aging curve for second basemen is notoriously unkind, and knee injuries are scary for any player—nevermind one who puts his knees in jeopardy with every double play he turns. But this is *Dustin Freakin Pedroia* we're talking about here. The dude played through a torn UCL in 2013 and hit .301! Surely through sheer force of will he'd find a way to buck the trend, to beat the odds, to hit .290 and play Gold Glove defense until he was 50 on one damn leg if he had to. Unfortunately, Father Time doesn't care how scrappy you are. Pedroia played in just three games last year, his October 2017 knee cartilage restoration surgery ultimately necessitating July 2018 arthroscopic surgery to clean up scar tissue. Despite turning 35 a month after his latest procedure, Pedroia vowed to be ready to play come Spring Training. Hopefully, he can make good on that promise, as Pedroia deserves to go out on his own terms. But it's clear that the Red Sox need to count any production they glean from Pedroia moving forward as a bonus, even as he's due $40 million over the final three years of his extension.

Brandon Phillips 2B Born: 06/28/81   Age: 38   Bats: R   Throws: R   Height: 6'0"   Weight: 211   Origin: Round 2, 1999 Draft (#57 overall)

YEAR	TEAM	LVL	AGE	PA	R	2B	3B	HR	RBI	BB	K	SB	CS	AVG/OBP/SLG	DRC+	VORP	BABIP	BRR	FRAA	WARP
2016	CIN	MLB	35	584	74	34	1	11	64	18	68	14	8	.291/.320/.416	96	17.5	.312	-1.4	2B(138): -4.2	1.0
2017	ATL	MLB	36	499	68	27	1	11	52	19	57	10	8	.291/.329/.423	89	18.1	.313	2.2	2B(88): -3.4, 3B(25): -1.6	0.7
2017	ANA	MLB	36	105	13	7	0	2	8	2	16	1	0	.255/.269/.382	86	-0.7	.286	0.3	2B(24): -0.4	0.2
2018	LOW	A-	37	26	1	0	0	1	7	2	3	0	0	.318/.346/.455	129	1.4	.300	-0.1	2B(3): 0.3	0.2
2018	PAW	AAA	37	161	29	14	0	4	19	9	26	1	1	.302/.348/.477	102	12.4	.342	0.5	2B(19): 1.6, 3B(8): -0.7	0.6
2018	BOS	MLB	37	27	4	0	0	1	2	4	7	0	0	.130/.259/.261	75	1.4	.133	1.0	2B(5): -0.5, 3B(4): -0.3	0.0
2019	*BOS*	*MLB*	*38*	*251*	*26*	*12*	*1*	*5*	*26*	*11*	*43*	*5*	*2*	*.256/.299/.378*	*81*	*2.0*	*.293*	*0.5*	*2B -1, 3B -1*	*0.0*

Breakout: 2%   Improve: 22%   Collapse: 16%   Attrition: 20%   MLB: 70%   *Comparables: Mark Grudzielanek, Chris Gomez, Mark Ellis*

Get you a man who looks at you the way the Red Sox look at the elite second basemen of the last decade. It wasn't just Dustin Pedroia and Ian Kinsler who called Boston home in 2018; Phillips joined the fray as well, signing a minor-league contract in late June and earning a brief call up in September. That may seem like quite the fall from grace for a Hall of Very Good player, but Phillips sure seemed like he was having fun. He absolutely raked in 161 Triple-A plate appearances. Once he got the call, Phillips asked for the weirdest jersey number available since his preferred 4 was retired, thus becoming the first Red Sox in history to wear 0. And in his first game with the Sox, Phillips hit a go-ahead two-run homer in the ninth to cap a dramatic comeback in Atlanta. Yes, he'll turn 38 next season, but Dat Dude showed enough that a team could take a shot on him as a backup infielder if he decides to keep playing.

Hanley Ramirez DH Born: 12/23/83   Age: 35   Bats: R   Throws: R   Height: 6'2"   Weight: 235   Origin: International Free Agent, 2000

YEAR	TEAM	LVL	AGE	PA	R	2B	3B	HR	RBI	BB	K	SB	CS	AVG/OBP/SLG	DRC+	VORP	BABIP	BRR	FRAA	WARP
2016	BOS	MLB	32	620	81	28	1	30	111	60	120	9	3	.286/.361/.505	126	16.3	.315	-2.8	1B(133): -10.4	1.6
2017	BOS	MLB	33	553	58	24	0	23	62	51	116	1	3	.242/.320/.429	102	-0.1	.272	-1.8	1B(18): -1.1	0.7
2018	BOS	MLB	34	195	25	7	0	6	29	14	35	4	1	.254/.313/.395	91	-0.6	.283	-0.9	1B(25): -1.1	-0.2
2019	*BOS*	*MLB*	*35*	*256*	*30*	*11*	*1*	*8*	*31*	*24*	*50*	*3*	*1*	*.249/.329/.413*	*102*	*3.4*	*.288*	*-0.9*	*1B -3*	*0.0*

Breakout: 1%   Improve: 26%   Collapse: 4%   Attrition: 29%   MLB: 92%   *Comparables: Aubrey Huff, Kendrys Morales, Andre Ethier*

Ramirez has long been in the Tyson Zone—the phrase coined by Bill Simmons referring to athletes and celebrities about whom any story becomes believable—but in 2018 he reached a whole new level of bizarre. After claiming he wanted to rejoin the 30/30 club, Ramirez got off to a hot start in March and April, hitting .330/.400/.474 with three homers and steals apiece. That's when things got weird. He hit just .163/.200/.300 over the next three weeks en route to a surprising DFA from the Sox on May 25. It made some sense; Ramirez was getting squeezed out of playing time at DH and at first base, and was just 302 PA away from a $22 million vesting option for 2019. But the suddenness with which the Sox moved on from Ramirez was surprising; he'd batted third just two days before being designated. It was also odd that no team took a flier on him as a low-cost, all-upside acquisition. To make matters even stranger, in late June, reports surfaced that Ramirez's friend name-dropped him during a drug bust, and the rumors began to fly. It's important to note that Ramirez was never involved in a criminal investigation and that his name was fully cleared. But if this is truly it for Ramirez as a major leaguer, 2018 was perhaps the strangest possible way to close out an exciting, tumultuous and drama-filled career bookended by stints in Boston that ended abruptly.

Blake Swihart C   Born: 04/03/92   Age: 27   Bats: B   Throws: R   Height: 6'1"   Weight: 200   Origin: Round 1, 2011 Draft (#26 overall)

YEAR	TEAM	LVL	AGE	PA	R	2B	3B	HR	RBI	BB	K	SB	CS	AVG/OBP/SLG	DRC+	VORP	BABIP	BRR	FRAA	WARP
2016	PAW	AAA	24	122	13	4	0	1	8	17	17	2	1	.243/.344/.311	103	2.1	.276	-0.2	C(15): 0.3, LF(11): 1.4	0.6
2016	BOS	MLB	24	74	9	0	3	0	5	11	17	0	1	.258/.365/.355	89	0.5	.348	-0.6	LF(13): 1.0, C(6): -1.2	0.1
2017	PAW	AAA	25	212	22	6	1	4	23	13	54	1	0	.190/.246/.292	75	-7.7	.239	-1.7	C(43): 5.0, 1B(3): 0.2	0.6
2017	BOS	MLB	25	7	1	0	0	0	0	2	3	0	0	.200/.429/.200	67	-0.1	.500	-0.2	C(4): -0.4	-0.1
2018	BOS	MLB	26	207	28	10	0	3	18	15	57	6	1	.229/.285/.328	72	-2.9	.311	0.7	C(28): 1.1, RF(14): -1.9	-0.1
2019	BOS	MLB	27	188	19	7	1	4	17	14	48	3	1	.218/.284/.333	71	-1.3	.280	-0.1	C 0, LF 1	-0.1

Breakout: 6%   Improve: 41%   Collapse: 16%   Attrition: 27%   MLB: 90%

Comparables: *Martin Maldonado, Carlos Perez, Christian Vazquez*

YEAR	TEAM	P. COUNT	FRM RUNS	BLK RUNS	THRW RUNS	TOT RUNS
2016	BOS	908	-0.4	-0.7	0.0	-1.1
2017	BOS	187	0.1	-0.5	0.0	-0.4
2017	PAW	6033	6.0	-0.5	0.2	5.4
2018	BOS	2800	0.7	0.7	0.0	1.4
2019	BOS	2569	0.6	-0.2	0.0	0.3

Swihart was, to put it kindly, the vestigial organ of the 2018 Red Sox. Despite nominally appearing in just over half of the team's games, he received only 12 more plate appearances than Hanley Ramirez, who was released in May. He saw only 50 more innings in the field than Ian Kinsler, who was acquired as a part-time player on July 31. Swihart had one more post-season at-bat than Nate Eovaldi. He was the team's third-best catcher, fourth-best first baseman and sixth-best outfielder. He'll be 27 shortly after Opening Day 2019. There is no prospect shine left here. Men don't cut their nipples off just because they don't need them, but if a man could save only 25 body parts ...

Sam Travis 1B   Born: 08/27/93   Age: 25   Bats: R   Throws: R   Height: 6'0"   Weight: 205   Origin: Round 2, 2014 Draft (#67 overall)

YEAR	TEAM	LVL	AGE	PA	R	2B	3B	HR	RBI	BB	K	SB	CS	AVG/OBP/SLG	DRC+	VORP	BABIP	BRR	FRAA	WARP
2016	PAW	AAA	22	190	26	10	0	6	29	15	40	1	0	.272/.332/.434	105	7.8	.320	1.4	1B(34): 2.1	0.7
2017	PAW	AAA	23	342	40	14	0	6	24	37	57	6	2	.270/.351/.375	101	0.3	.315	-3.5	1B(58): -0.1	0.1
2017	BOS	MLB	23	83	13	6	0	0	1	6	23	1	0	.263/.325/.342	70	-3.8	.377	-1.0	1B(21): 0.2	-0.3
2018	PAW	AAA	24	398	35	13	0	8	43	29	89	1	2	.258/.317/.360	92	9.1	.317	1.3	1B(45): 0.5, LF(36): -2.7	0.2
2018	BOS	MLB	24	38	5	3	0	1	7	2	10	0	0	.222/.263/.389	81	-0.4	.280	0.0	LF(6): 0.0, 1B(3): -0.1	0.0
2019	BOS	MLB	25	34	3	1	0	1	3	2	8	0	0	.214/.276/.325	60	-1.2	.268	-0.1	1B 0	-0.1

Breakout: 5%   Improve: 13%   Collapse: 3%   Attrition: 18%   MLB: 30%

Comparables: *Chris Marrero, Scott Thorman, Gaby Sanchez*

Even die-hard Red Sox fans probably didn't hear much about Travis last year, and that's because there's relatively little to say. Boston's second-round pick from 2014 still can't stay healthy and still doesn't hit for power, and now his hit tool isn't impressing in Triple-A either. You always had to squint to look at Travis and see a starting first baseman, but it seemed like he'd at least be able to carve out a role as a platoon guy or bench bat. Maybe he still can but he's trending about as well as Papa John's stock right now. He probably makes better pizza at least.

Christian Vazquez C   Born: 08/21/90   Age: 28   Bats: R   Throws: R   Height: 5'9"   Weight: 195   Origin: Round 9, 2008 Draft (#292 overall)

YEAR	TEAM	LVL	AGE	PA	R	2B	3B	HR	RBI	BB	K	SB	CS	AVG/OBP/SLG	DRC+	VORP	BABIP	BRR	FRAA	WARP
2016	PAW	AAA	25	171	19	9	0	2	16	15	31	2	0	.270/.345/.368	97	9.4	.325	0.3	C(41): 5.2	1.3
2016	BOS	MLB	25	184	21	9	1	1	12	10	39	0	0	.227/.277/.308	67	-4.0	.288	-0.7	C(56): 7.8	0.9
2017	BOS	MLB	26	345	43	18	2	5	32	17	64	7	2	.290/.330/.404	89	7.0	.348	-3.3	C(95): 16.4, 3B(2): 0.0	2.6
2018	BOS	MLB	27	269	24	10	0	3	16	13	41	4	1	.207/.257/.283	76	-5.4	.237	-0.4	C(75): 8.3, 3B(2): 0.0	1.4
2019	BOS	MLB	28	320	33	15	1	6	30	21	55	4	1	.247/.305/.364	83	6.4	.287	-1.3	C 10	1.8

Breakout: 5%   Improve: 43%   Collapse: 8%   Attrition: 20%   MLB: 94%

Comparables: *Tony Cruz, Jordan Pacheco, Josh Thole*

YEAR	TEAM	P. COUNT	FRM RUNS	BLK RUNS	THRW RUNS	TOT RUNS
2016	BOS	7176	8.6	-0.8	-0.1	7.5
2017	BOS	13558	15.5	1.0	2.4	19.6
2018	BOS	10330	9.0	0.1	0.1	9.0
2019	BOS	12558	10.7	0.0	0.7	11.4

The Red Sox led the majors in a whole bunch of offensive categories last season, and the fact that they did so despite giving Vazquez north of 250 plate appearances is absolutely stunning. Vazquez placed 73rd *among catchers* in DRC+ last season. If that stat was a tweet, it'd get ratio-ed but still end up with a better line than Vazquez. His best offensive stint came between July 8 and September 1 when he was on the DL with a broken pinky. Ozzy Osbourne is more trustworthy with a bat in his hands. A super-low BABIP is partly to blame, but not as much to blame as Vazquez, who hits a few clutch bombs and almost literally nothing else every year. The eye test says Vazquez remains a wonderful defender, but Ivan Nova, Anibal Sanchez and Derek Holland were better at the plate last season. Vazquez doesn't need to do much offensively to justify his roster spot, but he needs to do more than nothing.

PITCHERS

Matt Barnes RHP Born: 06/17/90 Age: 29 Bats: R Throws: R Height: 6'4" Weight: 210 Origin: Round 1, 2011 Draft (#19 overall)

YEAR	TEAM	LVL	AGE	W	L	SV	G	GS	IP	H	HR	BB/9	K/9	K	GB%	BABIP	WHIP	ERA	DRA	WARP	MPH	FB%	WHF	CSP
2016	BOS	MLB	26	4	3	1	62	0	66²	62	6	4.2	9.6	71	46%	.318	1.39	4.05	4.68	0.2	99.1	65.4	11.9	43.6
2017	BOS	MLB	27	7	3	1	70	0	69²	57	7	3.6	10.7	83	50%	.298	1.22	3.88	3.30	1.5	96.8	55	13.2	42.7
2018	BOS	MLB	28	6	4	0	62	0	61²	47	5	4.5	14.0	96	53%	.321	1.26	3.65	2.21	1.9	98.4	54.8	15	42.7
2019	BOS	MLB	29	3	1	29	53	0	55²	46	6	4.0	11.7	72	48%	.307	1.28	3.46	3.62	0.9	97.3	57.6	13.6	42.9

Breakout: 28%   Improve: 61%   Collapse: 17%   Attrition: 20%   MLB: 96%   Comparables: *Nick Masset, Zach Putnam, Brett Cecil*

We might owe Barnes an apology. Barnes' last few Annual comments have judged his performance through the lens of a former first-round pick, and with that context he may still seem disappointing. But Barnes was drafted in 2011 and we should be over it by now. While the visions of a No. 3 starter that once danced in our heads may never come to be, we can appreciate Barnes for what he *has* become: a damn fine reliever. Barnes had easily the best season of his career in 2018, posting a slew of personal-best stats and whiffing well more than a third of the batters he faced. Whereas Barnes faded badly enough down the stretch in 2017 to get left off the postseason roster, he was a force for the Red Sox last fall, serving as Alex Cora's most reliable setup option. He still issues too many walks and loses feel for his curveball too often to be considered one of the game's truly elite relievers. But he no longer seems out of place serving as the Robin to a closer's Batman, and that makes him a valuable piece regardless of his draft pedigree.

Ryan Brasier RHP Born: 08/26/87 Age: 31 Bats: R Throws: R Height: 6'0" Weight: 225 Origin: Round 6, 2007 Draft (#208 overall)

YEAR	TEAM	LVL	AGE	W	L	SV	G	GS	IP	H	HR	BB/9	K/9	K	GB%	BABIP	WHIP	ERA	DRA	WARP	MPH	FB%	WHF	CSP
2016	NAS	AAA	28	5	3	1	46	0	60²	50	6	2.8	10.4	70	46%	.293	1.14	3.56	2.71	1.6				
2018	PAW	AAA	30	2	5	13	34	0	40¹	29	1	1.8	8.9	40	43%	.277	0.92	1.34	3.33	0.8				
2018	BOS	MLB	30	2	0	0	34	0	33²	19	2	1.9	7.8	29	43%	.198	0.77	1.60	3.57	0.5	98.3	62.6	17.3	45.8
2019	BOS	MLB	31	3	1	9	53	0	55²	51	7	3.4	8.8	54	43%	.287	1.29	4.21	4.44	0.4	97.4	62.2	17.2	45.5

Breakout: 13%   Improve: 27%   Collapse: 23%   Attrition: 21%   MLB: 56%   Comparables: *Dane De La Rosa, Adam Liberatore, Miguel Socolovich*

Every good team gets key performances from unexpected sources, but for the 2018 Red Sox no contributor was perhaps as unexpected as Brasier. The former Weatherford College Coyote went 49 months in between MLB appearances thanks in part to Tommy John surgery. The former Angel and Athletic spent 2017 in Japan pitching for the Hiroshima Carp, where he impressed enough that the Sox offered him a minor-league contract last offseason. After dominating Triple-A for three-plus months, Brasier got the call to the big leagues in early July and never looked back. He dealt down the stretch, touching 99 and missing bats with a nasty slider, ultimately sliding right into a shockingly high-leverage role in October. He was brilliant, allowing just one run across three series of heavy usage, but he really sealed the deal with Red Sox Nation when he barked at Gary Sanchez to "get in the f***ing box" during Game 2 of the ALDS, then promptly struck his ass out. Given Brasier's strange path and general reliever volatility, there's no real way to know who and what Brasier will be moving forward. But even if 2018 is the best we'll ever see from him, it makes for a hell of a comeback story.

Nathan Eovaldi RHP Born: 02/13/90 Age: 29 Bats: R Throws: R Height: 6'2" Weight: 225 Origin: Round 11, 2008 Draft (#337 overall)

YEAR	TEAM	LVL	AGE	W	L	SV	G	GS	IP	H	HR	BB/9	K/9	K	GB%	BABIP	WHIP	ERA	DRA	WARP	MPH	FB%	WHF	CSP
2016	NYA	MLB	26	9	8	0	24	21	124²	123	23	2.9	7.0	97	50%	.275	1.31	4.76	5.08	0.4	99.9	48.3	10.6	49.1
2018	TBA	MLB	28	3	4	0	10	10	57	48	11	1.3	8.4	53	48%	.245	0.98	4.26	3.19	1.4	98.5	38.2	12.7	54.7
2018	BOS	MLB	28	3	3	0	12	11	54	57	3	2.0	8.0	48	46%	.325	1.28	3.33	3.28	1.3	99.3	38.2	10.9	51.7
2019	BOS	MLB	29	9	8	0	26	26	148¹	153	19	2.8	8.2	135	46%	.311	1.34	4.13	4.35	1.9	98.6	42.3	11.3	51.7

Breakout: 13%   Improve: 34%   Collapse: 26%   Attrition: 8%   MLB: 99%   Comparables: *Joe Blanton, Rick Porcello, Mike Leake*

Pretty much every year, we end up talking about how Impending Free Agent X made himself a ton of money by performing well in the postseason. It's a narrative that tends to get overblown, but in Eovaldi's case it ended up being very real. Coming off of his second Tommy John surgery, Eovaldi quietly pitched really well in the season's first half, earning a July ticket to Boston, where he finally saw his pop-up stat boxes match his deserved contributions. That alone probably would've been enough to land him a two- or three-year pact in a down year for free agent pitching options, but what "Nasty Nate" did in October is truly the stuff of legend. Eovaldi made two starts and four relief appearances in Boston's 13 postseason matchups, allowing just four earned runs in 22.1 frequently-dominant innings. In Game 3 of the World Series, Eovaldi threw 97 pitches over six innings of shutout ball in relief before finally running out of gas and coughing up a walk-off homer to Max Muncy in the bottom of the 18th. Oh yeah, Eovaldi had already pitched in Games 1 and 2, and did we mention this was a guy coming off his second TJ? Clearly the Red Sox didn't see Eovaldi's excessive postseason work as a negative, even in light of those arm issues, as he'll now make big-boy money for the next four years in New England.

Durbin Feltman RHP Born: 04/18/97 Age: 22 Bats: R Throws: R Height: 6'0" Weight: 205 Origin: Round 3, 2018 Draft (#100 overall)

YEAR	TEAM	LVL	AGE	W	L	SV	G	GS	IP	H	HR	BB/9	K/9	K	GB%	BABIP	WHIP	ERA	DRA	WARP	MPH	FB%	WHF	CSP
2018	GRN	A	21	0	1	3	7	0	7	6	0	1.3	18.0	14	43%	.429	1.00	2.57	1.65	0.3				
2018	SLM	A+	21	1	0	1	11	0	12¹	12	0	2.9	10.9	15	58%	.364	1.30	2.19	2.64	0.3				
2019	BOS	MLB	22	1	0	0	24	0	25¹	24	3	4.4	9.7	27	44%	.307	1.44	4.50	4.74	0.1				

Breakout: 7%   Improve: 10%   Collapse: 2%   Attrition: 11%   MLB: 13%   Comparables: *Danny Barnes, Jacob Rhame, Ryan Burr*

After Feltman enjoyed a successful college career as TCU's closer, Boston popped the undersized right-hander with the 100th-overall selection last June. Armed with a 60-grade slider and 70-grade fastball, Feltman carved up low minors hitters with ease in limited action. His performance didn't come as much of a surprise, and there's not much development left here; Feltman looks ready to challenge MLB hitters sooner rather than later. As Boston's relievers stumbled down the stretch, there were whispers that the Sox might fast-track Feltman to help their beleaguered bullpen. That didn't come to pass, but assuming he stays healthy, he could log significant innings in the 2019 Red Sox bullpen once their depth is tested.

Jay Groome LHP Born: 08/23/98 Age: 20 Bats: L Throws: L Height: 6'6" Weight: 220 Origin: Round 1, 2016 Draft (#12 overall)

YEAR	TEAM	LVL	AGE	W	L	SV	G	GS	IP	H	HR	BB/9	K/9	K	GB%	BABIP	WHIP	ERA	DRA	WARP	MPH	FB%	WHF	CSP
2017	LOW	A-	18	0	2	0	3	3	11	5	0	4.1	11.5	14	58%	.208	0.91	1.64	3.33	0.2				
2017	GRN	A	18	3	7	0	11	11	44¹	44	6	5.1	11.8	58	55%	.355	1.56	6.70	3.80	0.8				
2019	BOS	MLB	20	2	3	0	8	8	32	34	6	5.7	8.8	31	45%	.310	1.69	5.79	6.12	-0.2				

Breakout: 0%   Improve: 2%   Collapse: 2%   Attrition: 2%   MLB: 4%   *Comparables: Timothy Melville, Michael Kopech, Miguel Castro*

When it comes to developing pitching prospects, the Red Sox are seemingly always the Groomsman and never the Groome. Our protagonist here was supposed to change all that after he was popped 12th overall in the 2016 draft, largely falling that far because of signability concerns. But pitching prospects have their own acronym for a reason, and two-plus years later, injuries and ineffectiveness have conspired to push Groome closer to "lottery ticket" than "blue-chipper" on the prospect scale. His recovery from mid-May Tommy John surgery figures to keep him off the mound for a solid portion of 2019. If he doesn't look sharper and healthier upon his return, he may not register on said prospect scale at all.

Heath Hembree RHP Born: 01/13/89 Age: 30 Bats: R Throws: R Height: 6'4" Weight: 210 Origin: Round 5, 2010 Draft (#168 overall)

YEAR	TEAM	LVL	AGE	W	L	SV	G	GS	IP	H	HR	BB/9	K/9	K	GB%	BABIP	WHIP	ERA	DRA	WARP	MPH	FB%	WHF	CSP
2016	PAW	AAA	27	0	0	8	13	0	13¹	6	0	2.0	14.9	22	38%	.250	0.68	0.68	2.23	0.4				
2016	BOS	MLB	27	4	1	0	38	0	51	51	6	3.0	8.3	47	38%	.294	1.33	2.65	4.92	0.0	96.5	60.4	10.4	52
2017	BOS	MLB	28	2	3	0	62	0	62	72	10	2.6	10.2	70	42%	.360	1.45	3.63	3.39	1.2	97.4	53.1	15.2	45.3
2018	BOS	MLB	29	4	1	0	67	0	60	53	10	4.1	11.4	76	40%	.295	1.33	4.20	3.87	0.7	96.6	54.9	15.5	45.3
2019	BOS	MLB	30	3	1	0	53	0	55²	52	8	3.6	10.1	62	40%	.300	1.33	4.21	4.43	0.4	96.1	55.2	14.3	46.8

Breakout: 18%   Improve: 48%   Collapse: 21%   Attrition: 17%   MLB: 83%   *Comparables: Fernando Abad, Junichi Tazawa, David Carpenter*

No pitcher better represents 2018 than Heath Hembree. He posted a 4.20 ERA, right on the nose. He struck out a ton of batters and gave up a ton of home runs. Plus, Hembree doesn't just look like Kenny Powers; he acts like him, too. When asked if he'd be visiting the White House post-World Series win, he replied "Hell Yeah! I F*** with Trump!" When asked what he likes best about the President, Hembree gave a thoughtful, measured response: "Everything!" There is a 90 percent chance Hembree believed Pizzagate. He's probably still worried about The Caravan. Unlike his voter-suppressing party, he still can't get lefties out. What a stupid time to be alive.

Darwinzon Hernandez LHP Born: 12/17/96 Age: 22 Bats: L Throws: L Height: 6'2" Weight: 245 Origin: International Free Agent, 2013

YEAR	TEAM	LVL	AGE	W	L	SV	G	GS	IP	H	HR	BB/9	K/9	K	GB%	BABIP	WHIP	ERA	DRA	WARP	MPH	FB%	WHF	CSP
2016	LOW	A-	19	3	5	0	14	14	48¹	39	1	6.7	10.8	58	51%	.304	1.55	4.10	3.71	0.9				
2017	GRN	A	20	4	5	0	23	23	103¹	85	8	4.3	10.1	116	50%	.292	1.30	4.01	3.71	1.9				
2018	SLM	A+	21	9	5	0	23	23	101	80	1	5.3	11.0	124	46%	.326	1.39	3.56	4.91	0.5				
2018	PME	AA	21	0	0	0	5	0	6	6	0	9.0	15.0	10	36%	.429	2.00	3.00	2.35	0.2				
2019	BOS	MLB	22	1	1	0	3	3	15	15	2	7.3	9.6	16	42%	.308	1.80	5.97	6.31	-0.1				

Breakout: 7%   Improve: 8%   Collapse: 3%   Attrition: 11%   MLB: 12%   *Comparables: Jimmy Barthmaier, Jose Cisnero, Dellin Betances*

For the ever-growing segment of the internuting baseball world that loves itself some good-ass names, Hernandez is a prospect to keep an eye on. The latest in a line of flame-throwing Venezuelan lefties to bless Boston's farm system, Hernandez boasts a mid-90s fastball with natural cut and run that should be murder on his fellow southpaws. Secondary offerings include a changeup that needs development, a slider that needs development, and...uh...a curveball that needs development. Add his control and command to the list, too, but all those imperfections didn't stop Hernandez from striking out a ton of guys in High-A, Double-A and the AFL. Hernandez has likely evolved into Boston's best pitching prospect, and while his ceiling may be only a mid-rotation piece, his floor is also solid as a wicked weapon out of the 'pen. That's not bad for a guy the Sox signed for a cool $7,500 back in 2013.

Tanner Houck RHP Born: 06/29/96 Age: 23 Bats: R Throws: R Height: 6'5" Weight: 210 Origin: Round 1, 2017 Draft (#24 overall)

YEAR	TEAM	LVL	AGE	W	L	SV	G	GS	IP	H	HR	BB/9	K/9	K	GB%	BABIP	WHIP	ERA	DRA	WARP	MPH	FB%	WHF	CSP
2017	LOW	A-	21	0	3	0	10	10	22¹	21	0	3.2	10.1	25	49%	.333	1.30	3.63	3.32	0.5				
2018	SLM	A+	22	7	11	0	23	23	119	110	11	4.5	8.4	111	50%	.298	1.43	4.24	5.61	-0.4				
2019	BOS	MLB	23	5	7	0	19	19	83¹	88	13	4.9	7.5	69	43%	.302	1.60	5.38	5.69	-0.2				

Breakout: 4%   Improve: 10%   Collapse: 5%   Attrition: 10%   MLB: 15%   *Comparables: Max Fried, Jimmy Barthmaier, Mike Hinckley*

Boston's first-round pick in 2017, Houck had an okay first full professional season in 2018. He still needs to develop his changeup if he wants to stick in the rotation, but scouting reports indicate he's made progress with his slider, and his heavy low-to-mid-90s fastball remains a potent weapon. There's a chance his lack of a third pitch and delivery conspire to push him to the bullpen, at which point he could be ready for the majors quickly. There's also a chance his ideal frame, lively fastball and makeup allow him to emerge as a mid-rotation arm. It's not the highest-ceiling profile, but it's one of the best in the Red Sox system—though that may say more about the organization than it does about Houck himself.

Brian Johnson LHP Born: 12/07/90 Age: 28 Bats: L Throws: L Height: 6'4" Weight: 235 Origin: Round 1, 2012 Draft (#31 overall)

YEAR	TEAM	LVL	AGE	W	L	SV	G	GS	IP	H	HR	BB/9	K/9	K	GB%	BABIP	WHIP	ERA	DRA	WARP	MPH	FB%	WHF	CSP
2016	LOW	A-	25	0	0	0	2	2	11	7	0	1.6	9.0	11	37%	.259	0.82	0.00	3.57	0.2				
2016	PAW	AAA	25	5	6	0	15	15	77	74	9	4.2	6.3	54	36%	.284	1.43	4.09	5.93	-0.5				
2017	BOS	MLB	26	2	0	0	5	5	27	32	5	2.7	7.0	21	38%	.310	1.48	4.33	5.98	-0.1	89.8	55.9	8.5	44.1
2017	PAW	AAA	26	3	4	0	17	17	90¹	82	10	2.8	7.0	70	39%	.271	1.22	3.09	5.25	0.5				
2018	BOS	MLB	27	4	5	0	38	13	99¹	104	16	3.4	7.9	87	38%	.301	1.43	4.17	6.16	-1.1	91.1	49	9.5	47
2019	BOS	MLB	28	4	4	0	24	10	65¹	65	10	3.7	7.6	55	38%	.287	1.41	4.90	5.17	0.2	90.3	50.5	9.4	46

Breakout: 13%   Improve: 26%   Collapse: 12%   Attrition: 25%   MLB: 53%   *Comparables: Allen Webster, Logan Verrett, Kyle Lobstein*

Life has not been terribly fair to Johnson since the Red Sox drafted him in the first round in 2012. A batted ball broke his face shortly after his professional debut. Shoulder and elbow injuries hampered him at various points. He's missed time with an anxiety disorder. Hell, he was even car-jacked at gunpoint back in 2016. We can all take some measure of happiness, then, in Johnson winning a ring in 2018. For the first time in his career, Johnson spent the entire season in the majors. He performed exactly as expected—not well, despite a decent looking ERA—while occupying the swingman role for the Red Sox, at some points serving as their primary southpaw out of the 'pen. This may very well be Johnson's ceiling, but at the same time it also seems like his floor.

Craig Kimbrel RHP   Born: 05/28/88   Age: 31   Bats: R   Throws: R   Height: 6'0"   Weight: 210   Origin: Round 3, 2008 Draft (#96 overall)

YEAR	TEAM	LVL	AGE	W	L	SV	G	GS	IP	H	HR	BB/9	K/9	K	GB%	BABIP	WHIP	ERA	DRA	WARP	MPH	FB%	WHF	CSP
2016	BOS	MLB	28	2	6	31	57	0	53	28	4	5.1	14.1	83	31%	.242	1.09	3.40	2.88	1.3	99.7	69	15.5	43.6
2017	BOS	MLB	29	5	0	35	67	0	69	33	6	1.8	16.4	126	37%	.260	0.68	1.43	1.94	2.5	99.8	68.5	21	47.8
2018	BOS	MLB	30	5	1	42	63	0	62¹	31	7	4.5	13.9	96	30%	.216	0.99	2.74	2.58	1.7	98.9	64.5	18.5	40.7
2019	BOS	MLB	31	3	1	29	49	0	52	37	7	4.0	13.1	75	34%	.275	1.15	3.66	3.83	0.7	98.5	66.5	18.6	43.6

Breakout: 30%   Improve: 39%   Collapse: 39%   Attrition: 18%   MLB: 96%   *Comparables: David Robertson, Brad Lidge, Ryne Duren*

Only five pitchers who threw at least 50 innings last year struck out a higher percentage of batters than Kimbrel. But only 19 walked hitters at a higher rate, and the wildness won the day more often than usual in pushing him to the second-worst season of his career. These stats seem incongruous, but they tell us a few things about this free-agent fireballer. First, Kimbrel doesn't need to be on his absolute A-game to dominate hitters. Second, Kimbrel's command and control are unquestionably getting worse. Third, Kimbrel's stuff is still worthy of one of the biggest reliever contracts in baseball. Fourth, whichever team signs him to that contract is gonna need some Xanax. Kimbrel is one of the best relievers in history, but he's not the best reliever in the game anymore. He's not great at going multiple innings. He's not great in non-save situations. He hasn't been great in the playoffs. Yet he's still pretty great most of the time.

Travis Lakins RHP   Born: 06/29/94   Age: 25   Bats: R   Throws: R   Height: 6'1"   Weight: 180   Origin: Round 6, 2015 Draft (#171 overall)

YEAR	TEAM	LVL	AGE	W	L	SV	G	GS	IP	H	HR	BB/9	K/9	K	GB%	BABIP	WHIP	ERA	DRA	WARP	MPH	FB%	WHF	CSP
2016	SLM	A+	22	6	3	0	19	18	91	111	8	3.6	7.8	79	41%	.355	1.62	5.93	4.61	0.9				
2017	SLM	A+	23	5	0	0	7	7	38	32	2	3.1	10.2	43	44%	.309	1.18	2.61	3.59	0.7				
2017	PME	AA	23	0	4	0	8	8	30¹	34	2	6.2	5.6	19	48%	.337	1.81	6.23	5.20	0.0				
2018	PME	AA	24	2	2	1	26	6	38	27	3	3.1	9.9	42	48%	.250	1.05	2.61	3.74	0.6				
2018	PAW	AAA	24	1	0	2	10	0	16¹	11	0	2.8	8.3	15	44%	.244	0.98	1.65	4.40	0.1				
2019	BOS	MLB	25	1	0	0	19	0	20¹	20	3	4.0	8.5	19	42%	.306	1.45	4.64	4.89	0.0				

Breakout: 9%   Improve: 13%   Collapse: 2%   Attrition: 12%   MLB: 19%   *Comparables: Daniel McCutchen, Parker Bridwell, David Goforth*

For years, scouts worried that Lakins' lean frame and injury history would conspire to force him to the bullpen. That fear became reality, as the Sox finally shifted Lakins into a relief role last June. The good news? Lakins was flat out dominant in his new role, striking out more than a batter per inning in Double-A thanks in part to an uptick in velo. He thrived in a shorter sample against Triple-A hitters, too. There probably isn't closer upside here, but if he stays healthy—and that's a very big if—Lakins could emerge as a mid-to-late-inning weapon for the Red Sox as soon as May or June.

Bryan Mata RHP   Born: 05/03/99   Age: 20   Bats: R   Throws: R   Height: 6'3"   Weight: 160   Origin: International Free Agent, 2016

YEAR	TEAM	LVL	AGE	W	L	SV	G	GS	IP	H	HR	BB/9	K/9	K	GB%	BABIP	WHIP	ERA	DRA	WARP	MPH	FB%	WHF	CSP
2016	DRX	RK	17	4	4	0	14	14	61	54	2	2.8	9.0	61	51%	.319	1.20	2.80	2.25	2.3				
2017	GRN	A	18	5	6	0	17	17	77	75	3	3.0	8.6	74	53%	.333	1.31	3.74	5.45	-0.1				
2018	SLM	A+	19	6	3	0	17	17	72	58	1	7.2	7.6	61	59%	.292	1.61	3.50	5.01	0.3				
2019	BOS	MLB	20	3	5	0	13	13	58²	63	8	6.5	7.0	46	49%	.306	1.81	6.04	6.40	-0.6				

Breakout: 0%   Improve: 0%   Collapse: 1%   Attrition: 1%   MLB: 1%   *Comparables: Tyler Matzek, Jair Jurrjens, Kohl Stewart*

The pessimist looks at Mata's 2018 line and thinks there's absolutely no way someone with this type of command profile can be a starter. The optimist looks past Mata's unsightly walk rate and sees a 19-year-old who just put up a good ERA in High-A despite having less control over his offerings than a slot machine. Mata has a good fastball and an advanced changeup for a pitcher his age, and he draws praise for his sequencing and feel for pitching. None of that will matter if Mata's K:BB rate remains close to flat, but time is on his side, and the general consensus is that he retains mid-rotation upside.

Drew Pomeranz LHP   Born: 11/22/88   Age: 30   Bats: R   Throws: L   Height: 6'6"   Weight: 240   Origin: Round 1, 2010 Draft (#5 overall)

YEAR	TEAM	LVL	AGE	W	L	SV	G	GS	IP	H	HR	BB/9	K/9	K	GB%	BABIP	WHIP	ERA	DRA	WARP	MPH	FB%	WHF	CSP
2016	SDN	MLB	27	8	7	0	17	17	102	67	8	3.6	10.1	115	50%	.240	1.06	2.47	3.08	2.7	93.5	58.4	12	44.7
2016	BOS	MLB	27	3	5	0	14	13	68²	70	14	3.1	9.3	71	47%	.306	1.37	4.59	3.82	1.2	94.0	58.4	11.5	46.6
2017	BOS	MLB	28	17	6	0	32	32	173²	166	19	3.6	9.0	174	45%	.310	1.35	3.32	4.17	2.7	93.5	61.6	10.6	43.1
2018	PAW	AAA	29	0	2	0	5	5	19²	16	7	5.9	5.5	12	58%	.173	1.47	5.49	4.17	0.3				
2018	BOS	MLB	29	2	6	0	26	11	74	87	12	5.4	8.0	66	39%	.344	1.77	6.08	7.90	-2.3	91.6	58.9	7.9	43.7
2019	BOS	MLB	30	6	6	0	28	16	99	97	13	4.0	7.7	85	44%	.290	1.43	4.78	5.05	0.4	92.4	59.7	10.3	43.8

Breakout: 7%   Improve: 43%   Collapse: 28%   Attrition: 11%   MLB: 90%   *Comparables: David Phelps, Jon Lester, Lance Lynn*

Last year's *Annual* comment noted that Pomeranz would be in for a big payday if he could just stay healthy in 2018. RON HOWARD VOICE: He couldn't. The artist formerly known as "Big Smooth" started the year on the DL with a left forearm flexor strain and ended up back on the DL in June with a combo biceps/neck issue. When he did manage to take the mound, Pomeranz was so ineffective that he finished last—yes, last—in the majors in DRA among pitchers with at least 70 IP. The Sox moved Pomeranz to the bullpen in early August in the hopes he'd at least emerge as a lefty matchup option. RON HOWARD VOICE: He didn't. Pomeranz allowed a .300/.394/.461 line as a reliever en route to getting left off two straight postseason rosters before quizzically making the cut for the World Series, where he was the only player on either roster who didn't appear in any games, 18-inning or otherwise. Instead of a lucrative multi-year deal, expect Pomeranz to settle for a pillow contract this offseason as he looks to rebuild some value.

Rick Porcello RHP   Born: 12/27/88   Age: 30   Bats: R   Throws: R   Height: 6'5"   Weight: 205   Origin: Round 1, 2007 Draft (#27 overall)

YEAR	TEAM	LVL	AGE	W	L	SV	G	GS	IP	H	HR	BB/9	K/9	K	GB%	BABIP	WHIP	ERA	DRA	WARP	MPH	FB%	WHF	CSP
2016	BOS	MLB	27	22	4	0	33	33	223	193	23	1.3	7.6	189	44%	.269	1.01	3.15	3.37	5.1	93.9	62.1	8.9	49.6
2017	BOS	MLB	28	11	17	0	33	33	203¹	236	38	2.1	8.0	181	40%	.322	1.40	4.65	4.84	1.7	93.9	59.4	10.4	49.1
2018	BOS	MLB	29	17	7	0	33	33	191¹	177	27	2.3	8.9	190	45%	.285	1.18	4.28	4.02	2.8	92.8	50	9.6	48.9
2019	BOS	MLB	30	11	9	0	28	28	168	165	22	2.3	8.0	150	43%	.296	1.24	4.13	4.35	2.2	92.7	56.2	9.7	49

Breakout: 11%   Improve: 48%   Collapse: 20%   Attrition: 5%   MLB: 97%   *Comparables: Don Drysdale, Wade Miley, Cliff Lee*

Porcello finally found the middle of the bell curve. In 2015, Porcello's first year with the Red Sox, he was terrible. In 2016, he won the Cy Young. In 2017, he was pretty bad. But in 2018, Pretty Ricky was the C+/B- version of himself, a guy whose results finally seemed to mesh with his stuff. There are three primary reasons Porcello got better last year. First, he did a better job keeping the ball in the yard, even if "better" still put him in a league with Kevin Gausman, Jason Hammel and Mike Wright. Second, Porcello threw his fastball and sinker a little less and his slider a little more, a mix that led to a career-best strikeout rate. Finally—and perhaps most importantly—he just had better luck. Porcello's 2017 BABIP and homer rates were always the good kind of unsustainable, and as they fell back to league average, so too did Porcello. Factor in some postseason heroics out of the bullpen and all things considered, Porcello had a really nice year. Whether he'll be great, average or terrible again in 2019 is anyone's guess.

David Price LHP   Born: 08/26/85   Age: 33   Bats: L   Throws: L   Height: 6'5"   Weight: 215   Origin: Round 1, 2007 Draft (#1 overall)

YEAR	TEAM	LVL	AGE	W	L	SV	G	GS	IP	H	HR	BB/9	K/9	K	GB%	BABIP	WHIP	ERA	DRA	WARP	MPH	FB%	WHF	CSP
2016	BOS	MLB	30	17	9	0	35	35	230	227	30	2.0	8.9	228	45%	.310	1.20	3.99	3.13	5.9	95.5	48.7	12.7	48.7
2017	BOS	MLB	31	6	3	0	16	11	74²	65	8	2.9	9.2	76	40%	.278	1.19	3.38	5.04	0.4	96.0	58.3	13.1	44.1
2018	BOS	MLB	32	16	7	0	30	30	176	151	25	2.6	9.1	177	41%	.274	1.14	3.58	3.72	3.2	94.2	46.5	10.8	49.9
2019	BOS	MLB	33	10	9	0	27	27	162	158	22	2.7	8.6	155	42%	.298	1.27	4.15	4.37	2.1	93.9	48.7	11.7	47.1

Breakout: 11%   Improve: 33%   Collapse: 35%   Attrition: 17%   MLB: 92%   *Comparables: Johan Santana, Josh Beckett, Cole Hamels*

If you sent a script outlining Price's postseason redemption arc to Hollywood, it'd get rejected as a fairy tale. Even as recently as October 6, it seemed unfathomable that we'd be talking about David Price: Postseason Hero. Price had just lost Game 2 of the ALDS against the Yankees, lasting only 1 2/3 innings while dropping his all-time playoff record to 0-10 with an ERA above 5.00. Had Alex Cora and Co. decided to withhold him from any further playoff starts, they wouldn't have received much pushback.

But Cora ignored the narrative, the small sample size and the noise, and trusted talent instead. Price got the nod to start ALCS Game 2 and held his own against a tough Astros lineup, earning a standing ovation from the Fenway Faithful despite pitching just 4.2 innings. Price took the ball again four days later and tossed an absolute gem in Game 5, holding Houston scoreless through six innings for his first playoff win. Add in two more outstanding World Series starts and one clutch relief appearance, and Price transformed from scapegoat to Boston's best overall postseason performer this side of Nate Eovaldi.

Make no mistake about it; many of the Sox fans who are singing his praises now will be quick to decry him once more if he struggles. That's especially true now that Price will make nearly $32 million per season over the next four years after declining his opt-out. But for the moment, let's all appreciate that the much-maligned Price has finally been accepted by his fan base, and that one of the best left-handers of his generation removed a King Kong-sized monkey from his back. Your move, Clayton!

Eduardo Rodriguez LHP   Born: 04/07/93   Age: 26   Bats: L   Throws: L   Height: 6'2"   Weight: 220   Origin: International Free Agent, 2010

YEAR	TEAM	LVL	AGE	W	L	SV	G	GS	IP	H	HR	BB/9	K/9	K	GB%	BABIP	WHIP	ERA	DRA	WARP	MPH	FB%	WHF	CSP
2016	PAW	AAA	23	0	4	0	7	7	38	33	6	1.7	5.7	24	43%	.233	1.05	3.08	3.52	0.8				
2016	BOS	MLB	23	3	7	0	20	20	107	99	16	3.4	8.4	100	33%	.278	1.30	4.71	5.81	-0.5	96.1	66.3	11.7	43.8
2017	PAW	AAA	24	0	1	0	2	2	10¹	10	0	4.4	10.5	12	38%	.385	1.45	4.35	3.36	0.3				
2017	BOS	MLB	24	6	7	0	25	24	137¹	126	19	3.3	9.8	150	36%	.299	1.28	4.19	4.37	1.8	95.0	65.3	12.4	44
2018	BOS	MLB	25	13	5	0	27	23	129²	119	16	3.1	10.1	146	39%	.301	1.26	3.82	3.77	2.3	95.1	51.6	12.4	46.4
2019	BOS	MLB	26	7	6	0	18	18	102²	94	13	3.2	9.6	110	38%	.296	1.27	3.93	4.13	1.6	94.9	60.7	12.5	45.8

Breakout: 28%   Improve: 68%   Collapse: 16%   Attrition: 8%   MLB: 96%   *Comparables: Tyler Skaggs, Matt Garza, Kevin Gausman*

Few people should be happier that the Red Sox won the World Series than Rodriguez, not just because of the ring and the history and playoff shares, but because he may have avoided infamy. Had the Dodgers prevailed, the image of Yasiel Puig triumphantly raising his hands as Rodriguez slammed his glove in the dirt after allowing a three-run homer in Game 4 might've gone down as one of the most iconic in postseason history. Instead, it's just a footnote in what was a wildly successful season for the Sox but yet another injury-marred one for Rodriguez. Rodriguez started the year strong enough after off-season knee surgery, posting a 3.44 ERA and striking out more than a batter per inning in his first 19 starts. But on July 15, E-Rod damaged the ligament in his ankle in a collision at first base, keeping him off the mound until September. The Sox tried to move him to the bullpen for their postseason run, but he was largely ineffective and he looked to be pitching hurt. Overall, it's a familiar tale for Rodriguez, who has the talent to become a mid-rotation mainstay but the overall leg integrity of an AT-AT. But hey, at least he avoided becoming a meme.

Chris Sale LHP   Born: 03/30/89   Age: 30   Bats: L   Throws: L   Height: 6'6"   Weight: 180   Origin: Round 1, 2010 Draft (#13 overall)

YEAR	TEAM	LVL	AGE	W	L	SV	G	GS	IP	H	HR	BB/9	K/9	K	GB%	BABIP	WHIP	ERA	DRA	WARP	MPH	FB%	WHF	CSP
2016	CHA	MLB	27	17	10	0	32	32	226²	190	27	1.8	9.3	233	42%	.279	1.04	3.34	3.13	5.8	97.0	60.9	12.2	49.3
2017	BOS	MLB	28	17	8	0	32	32	214¹	165	24	1.8	12.9	308	40%	.301	0.97	2.90	2.51	7.3	97.4	50.5	15.8	48.3
2018	BOS	MLB	29	12	4	0	27	27	158	102	11	1.9	13.5	237	45%	.283	0.86	2.11	2.24	5.6	99.1	50.1	16.9	49.4
2019	BOS	MLB	30	12	7	0	27	27	170	134	19	2.3	11.9	224	43%	.296	1.04	2.99	3.12	4.6	97.1	53.1	15.1	48.9

Breakout: 16%   Improve: 47%   Collapse: 20%   Attrition: 8%   MLB: 95%   *Comparables: Yu Darvish, David Price, Ron Guidry*

When Sale is at his best, he's the most dominant pitcher in baseball. Let's take his first 11 starts of 2018, for example: He posted a 2.17 ERA, struck out 96 batters in 70 2/3 innings and held batters to a .187/.252/.333 line. He started the All-Star game for the third straight year, and was in the catbird seat for his first-ever Cy Young award through the season's first half. But, as is often the case, Sale faded down the stretch. This time it was shoulder fatigue that derailed Sale's run, as the Sox put him on the DL twice due to his ailing joint. When he finally returned for good in September, Sale clearly wasn't himself, with diminished velocity and spotty command limiting his effectiveness even in short stints. Despite pitching at less than 100 percent, Sale enjoyed a solid postseason, gutting out three solid (albeit short) starts and two relief appearances, including the World Series-clinching ninth inning of Game 5. Sale is now entering his walk year, and there's an argument that a talent of his age (he'll turn 30 in March) and track record should threaten the record books when it comes to starting pitcher contracts. But given his whippet-thin frame, jerky delivery and history of relative second-half declines, Sale may fail to reach Kershaw-ian heights. That's putting the cart a bit before the horse, however, and for now Sale can keep his eye on a more immediate prize of helping the Sox repeat as World Champions.

Michael Shawaryn RHP   Born: 09/17/94   Age: 24   Bats: R   Throws: R   Height: 6'2"   Weight: 200   Origin: Round 5, 2016 Draft (#148 overall)

YEAR	TEAM	LVL	AGE	W	L	SV	G	GS	IP	H	HR	BB/9	K/9	K	GB%	BABIP	WHIP	ERA	DRA	WARP	MPH	FB%	WHF	CSP
2017	GRN	A	22	3	2	0	10	10	53¹	44	5	2.2	13.2	78	42%	.331	1.07	3.88	2.34	1.8				
2017	SLM	A+	22	5	5	0	16	16	81¹	71	10	3.9	10.1	91	34%	.289	1.30	3.76	3.76	1.4				
2018	PME	AA	23	6	8	0	19	19	112²	100	7	2.2	7.9	99	40%	.287	1.13	3.28	4.12	1.6				
2018	PAW	AAA	23	3	2	0	7	6	36²	30	6	2.7	8.1	33	34%	.247	1.12	3.93	3.21	1.0				
2019	BOS	MLB	24	1	1	0	3	3	15	15	3	3.3	8.4	14	36%	.295	1.38	4.90	5.18	0.1				

Breakout: 12%   Improve: 26%   Collapse: 18%   Attrition: 30%   MLB: 53%   *Comparables: Yefrey Ramirez, Thomas Pannone, Adam Plutko*

Not every pitching prospect is a potential future ace. Most of them profile more like Shawaryn: a guy who could be a back-end starter, a medium-leverage reliever or the type of multi-inning swingman with whom some of the league's more innovative teams are exploring the space. Shawaryn's main weapons are a low-to-mid 90s sinking fastball that induces a lot of weak grounders in spite of poor command, and a slider that could break its way to a plus grade. He's strong and sturdy, having thrown nearly 300 innings in two-plus seasons since being drafted. But his three-quarters delivery is high-stress, lending further credence to the notion that his future may be in the 'pen. He's already succeeded in Triple-A, and Shawaryn seems a safe bet to make the majors in some capacity. We just might not know in what role for a while.

Carson Smith RHP   Born: 10/19/89   Age: 29   Bats: R   Throws: R   Height: 6'6"   Weight: 215   Origin: Round 8, 2011 Draft (#243 overall)

YEAR	TEAM	LVL	AGE	W	L	SV	G	GS	IP	H	HR	BB/9	K/9	K	GB%	BABIP	WHIP	ERA	DRA	WARP	MPH	FB%	WHF	CSP
2016	BOS	MLB	26	0	0	0	3	0	2²	2	0	3.4	6.8	2	75%	.250	1.12	0.00	6.73	-0.1	94.5	52.1	4.2	48.3
2017	BOS	MLB	27	0	0	1	8	0	6²	7	0	2.7	9.4	7	61%	.389	1.35	1.35	3.42	0.1	93.5	49.1	9.7	51.5
2018	BOS	MLB	28	1	1	0	18	0	14¹	14	2	3.8	11.3	18	55%	.316	1.40	3.77	4.04	0.1	93.7	50.2	12.2	47.3
2019	BOS	MLB	29	2	1	1	32	0	33²	32	4	4.9	9.5	36	49%	.304	1.47	4.35	4.58	0.2	93.1	50.1	11	49

Breakout: 23%   Improve: 39%   Collapse: 31%   Attrition: 20%   MLB: 88%   *Comparables: Ryan Cook, Hunter Strickland, A.J. Ramos*

After missing most of 2017 recovering from Tommy John, Smith was okay-ish in 18 outings before three very bad throws derailed his season. The first one came on May 14, when Smith gave up a bomb to Khris Davis. The second one also came on May 14, when Smith hurt his shoulder chucking his glove in the dugout immediately after surrendering said Khrushjob. And the third bad toss? That came in mid-June, when Smith attempted to hurl Alex Cora under the bus, blaming overuse for his shoulder malady instead of, ya know, the whole glove-related temper tantrum. Smith eventually needed surgery to repair his labrum, and it's a toss-up as to whether he'll be ready for the start of 2019. The way those have gone for Smith lately it's hard to be very optimistic.

Tyler Thornburg RHP   Born: 09/29/88   Age: 30   Bats: R   Throws: R   Height: 5'11"   Weight: 190   Origin: Round 3, 2010 Draft (#96 overall)

YEAR	TEAM	LVL	AGE	W	L	SV	G	GS	IP	H	HR	BB/9	K/9	K	GB%	BABIP	WHIP	ERA	DRA	WARP	MPH	FB%	WHF	CSP
2016	MIL	MLB	27	8	5	13	67	0	67	38	6	3.4	12.1	90	36%	.229	0.94	2.15	3.05	1.5	96.4	66.3	13	46.9
2018	PAW	AAA	29	0	1	0	15	1	12²	11	3	4.3	7.8	11	20%	.216	1.34	4.26	4.45	0.1				
2018	BOS	MLB	29	2	0	0	25	0	24	28	6	3.8	7.9	21	37%	.319	1.58	5.62	5.01	0.0	94.4	55.6	9.5	46.2
2019	BOS	MLB	30	2	1	0	48	0	50²	49	9	4.0	8.4	47	37%	.286	1.42	5.08	5.37	-0.2	94.9	61.9	11.6	46.3

Breakout: 16%   Improve: 34%   Collapse: 18%   Attrition: 17%   MLB: 66%   *Comparables: Angel Guzman, Wesley Wright, Chris Resop*

By the time this book is published, it will have been more than two years since Dave Dombrowski traded Travis Shaw and some prospects to the Brewers for Thornburg. To date, it's a move that's cost the Red Sox about nine wins, per WARP. Thornburg finally threw his first pitch for Boston on July 6, a year-plus removed from thoracic outlet surgery on his right shoulder. In that debut outing Thornburg gave up a run to the lowly Royals, and his season didn't get better from there. The 29-year-old's velocity was down from his halcyon days of 2016, and while his breaking stuff occasionally had some bite to it, his fastball looked flat and his command went AWOL. The Sox shut Thornburg down for the season in late September with the hope that a full, healthy offseason gets him right. If not, the Thornburg deal will continue reading as a cautionary tale about trading for relief pitching.

Hector Velazquez RHP   Born: 11/26/88   Age: 30   Bats: R   Throws: R   Height: 6'0"   Weight: 180   Origin: International Free Agent, 2017

YEAR	TEAM	LVL	AGE	W	L	SV	G	GS	IP	H	HR	BB/9	K/9	K	GB%	BABIP	WHIP	ERA	DRA	WARP	MPH	FB%	WHF	CSP
2017	PAW	AAA	28	8	4	0	19	19	102	78	7	2.1	7.0	79	45%	.251	1.00	2.21	3.70	2.2				
2017	BOS	MLB	28	3	1	0	8	3	24²	21	4	2.6	6.9	19	44%	.258	1.14	2.92	4.88	0.1	92.0	68.9	8.6	51.2
2018	BOS	MLB	29	7	2	0	47	8	85	97	7	2.8	5.6	53	50%	.325	1.45	3.18	5.61	-0.5	93.1	59.2	9	46.7
2019	BOS	MLB	30	4	2	0	48	5	70²	74	8	3.0	6.1	48	46%	.296	1.38	4.61	4.87	0.3	92.1	60.8	8.9	48.5

Breakout: 12%   Improve: 28%   Collapse: 22%   Attrition: 19%   MLB: 64%   *Comparables: Christian Friedrich, Jeremy Guthrie, Clay Hensley*

In an era of strikeouts, homers and premium velocity, Velazquez seems like a traveler from the past. The former Mexican Leaguer averaged just 92 mph on his fastball. He struck out a lower percentage of batters faced than Mike Leake, Andrew Cashner or Wade Miley. He had no defined role, bouncing between starter, long reliever and medium-leverage fireman—he was basically a Ray. And yet, Velazquez succeeded. He didn't walk anyone. He induced some ground balls. He did a decent job suppressing homers. All told, he threw 85 boring, unremarkable, effective innings for the World Series champions. Contributions like Velazquez's will always go unnoticed on elite teams, but collectively, they make up much of the fabric of a successful 162-game season. Seriously though, how is he not a Ray?

Brandon Workman RHP Born: 08/13/88 Age: 30 Bats: R Throws: R Height: 6'5" Weight: 235 Origin: Round 2, 2010 Draft (#57 overall)

YEAR	TEAM	LVL	AGE	W	L	SV	G	GS	IP	H	HR	BB/9	K/9	K	GB%	BABIP	WHIP	ERA	DRA	WARP	MPH	FB%	WHF	CSP
2016	PME	AA	27	0	0	0	4	0	10	15	3	6.3	4.5	5	48%	.324	2.20	9.00	5.07	0.0				
2017	PAW	AAA	28	4	1	2	18	0	29	16	1	4.0	10.9	35	46%	.234	1.00	1.55	3.30	0.6				
2017	BOS	MLB	28	1	1	0	33	0	39²	37	7	2.5	8.4	37	44%	.283	1.21	3.18	3.68	0.7	94.7	51.4	11.3	45.9
2018	PAW	AAA	29	2	1	1	17	0	30	21	3	1.5	10.2	34	40%	.247	0.87	3.90	3.28	0.6				
2018	BOS	MLB	29	6	1	0	43	0	41¹	34	6	3.5	8.1	37	46%	.259	1.21	3.27	6.21	-0.6	93.2	38.9	11.1	48.1
2019	BOS	MLB	30	2	1	0	48	0	50²	48	7	4.1	8.4	47	43%	.289	1.40	4.70	4.96	0.1	93.1	44.1	11.2	47

Breakout: 11%   Improve: 26%   Collapse: 25%   Attrition: 27%   MLB: 60%   *Comparables: Josh Outman, Wil Ledezma, Tyler Yates*

What is the worst insult you can think of? Maybe it's a Winston Churchill quote? Or something in Piers Morgan's Twitter mentions? Or anything Peter MacNicol says to Jonah on "Veep?" Wrong; it's actually getting dropped from the World Series roster in favor of 2018 Drew Pomeranz. That indignity aside, Workman has to be fairly pleased with how his season went. He spent more than half the year in the majors, posted respectable surface-level stats and even made the postseason roster for a time. Let's just not talk about his DRA, or that homer rate, or all the "at least he can't bat this time" barbs following his pre-Fall Classic demotion. Workman is who he is at this point—a serviceable and unremarkable middle relief arm—but it's nice to see him healthy, happy and with another ring.

Steven Wright RHP Born: 08/30/84 Age: 34 Bats: R Throws: R Height: 6'2" Weight: 215 Origin: Round 2, 2006 Draft (#56 overall)

YEAR	TEAM	LVL	AGE	W	L	SV	G	GS	IP	H	HR	BB/9	K/9	K	GB%	BABIP	WHIP	ERA	DRA	WARP	MPH	FB%	WHF	CSP
2016	BOS	MLB	31	13	6	0	24	24	156²	138	12	3.3	7.3	127	46%	.279	1.24	3.33	3.22	3.8	87.7	13.9	11.2	48.6
2017	BOS	MLB	32	1	3	0	5	5	24	40	9	1.9	4.9	13	43%	.365	1.88	8.25	8.93	-0.9	86.9	8.2	7.2	48.3
2018	PAW	AAA	33	0	0	0	5	3	16²	20	0	2.2	4.9	9	48%	.333	1.44	3.78	5.13	0.0				
2018	BOS	MLB	33	3	1	1	20	4	53²	41	5	4.4	7.0	42	54%	.243	1.25	2.68	2.72	1.5	87.8	6.1	10	52.3
2019	BOS	MLB	34	4	4	0	24	10	72¹	75	11	3.7	6.6	53	46%	.288	1.45	5.18	5.48	-0.1	86.6	10.6	10.2	49.3

Breakout: 9%   Improve: 33%   Collapse: 16%   Attrition: 16%   MLB: 78%   *Comparables: Doug Fister, Jamey Wright, Whitey Ford*

Wright saw such limited MLB action in 2018 for two reasons: recovery from offseason knee surgery and a 15-game suspension for violating MLB's domestic violence policy. Per reporting from NBCSB's Evan Drellich and others, Wright was arrested at his Tennessee home in December 2017 and charged with domestic assault and preventing a 9-1-1 call. The case was later retired in court, and charges will be dropped if Wright goes a year without another incident. "It's really hard on a personal level to get past something that's constantly being thrown at you," Wright said. "But I did it to myself. It's one of those things that I've got to live with the consequences that came from my actions that night." Wright was effective when on the field, and figures to have a chance to carve out a role on the 2019 Red Sox assuming he can recover from yet another offseason knee procedure. If he does, any success he enjoys should be framed as yet another example of a team making on-field success their top priority.

LINEOUTS

Hitters

HITTER	POS	TEAM	LVL	AGE	PA	R	2B	3B	HR	RBI	BB	K	SB	CS	AVG/OBP/SLG	DRC+	VORP	BABIP	BRR	FRAA	WARP
Juan Centeno	C	TEX	MLB	28	38	3	1	0	1	3	1	7	0	0	.162/.184/.270	84	-2.7	.172	0.0	C(10): -0.7	0.0
	C	ROU	AAA	28	232	27	9	0	2	27	16	34	0	1	.234/.291/.307	74	-0.9	.266	-0.4	C(45): 1.8	0.4
Danny Diaz	3B	DRX	Rk	17	113	17	7	0	6	27	5	27	0	3	.238/.283/.476	120	3.2	.260	-1.3	3B(23): 2.9, 1B(1): -0.1	0.8
Jarren Duran	OF	LOW	A-	21	168	28	5	10	2	20	11	26	12	4	.348/.393/.548	142	19.6	.406	0.4	2B(20): 4.9, CF(15): 0.1	2.0
	OF	GRN	A	21	134	24	9	1	1	15	5	22	12	6	.367/.396/.477	109	12.2	.438	1.6	RF(30): 0.0	0.6
Antoni Flores	SS	DRX	Rk	17	57	10	3	1	1	14	8	7	0	1	.347/.439/.510	128	9.7	.390	0.3	SS(13): -1.7	0.3
Brandon Howlett	3B	RSX	Rk	18	163	24	15	0	5	25	22	38	0	1	.307/.405/.526	128	18.7	.385	0.3	3B(28): -2.6	0.7
Tzu-Wei Lin	SS	PAW	AAA	24	302	33	20	2	5	25	23	64	3	4	.307/.362/.448	105	25.0	.385	-0.4	SS(51): 1.6, CF(9): 0.9	1.7
	SS	BOS	MLB	24	73	15	6	1	1	6	8	17	0	1	.246/.329/.415	84	3.1	.319	0.2	SS(23): -0.3, CF(6): -0.6	0.1
Adam Lind	1B	TAM	A+	34	31	5	2	0	1	7	3	4	0	0	.429/.484/.607	123	3.0	.478	-0.8	1B(4): -0.4	0.0
	1B	SWB	AAA	34	63	7	4	0	2	7	5	13	0	1	.241/.302/.414	103	-0.4	.279	-0.1	1B(5): -0.5	0.0
	1B	PAW	AAA	34	189	21	7	0	8	32	14	36	0	0	.216/.270/.398	114	-2.0	.221	-1.0	1B(24): 1.3	0.6
Tony Renda	INF	PME	AA	27	108	19	11	0	3	16	9	13	4	1	.371/.435/.577	136	10.6	.407	-0.9	LF(9): -0.5, 3B(6): -0.4	0.5
	INF	PAW	AAA	27	184	30	8	1	2	11	11	31	6	1	.288/.337/.382	104	7.7	.341	2.3	2B(20): -1.2, LF(12): -0.8	0.7

Last year's book brought up the fact that "Centeno" is Spanish for "Rye," but failed to point out that **Juan Centeno** plays catcher. So that means at one point, a scout pointed to Juan and thought: "There's a catcher in the Rye." ⓧ Boston's most recent second-round pick, **Nick Decker** is an athletic, bat-first, prep school outfielder from New Jersey who...oh my god did the Red Sox just get the next Mike Trout? ⓧ One of Boston's big-ticket J2 signings from 2017, **Danny Diaz** has begun his transformation from lithe shortstop to big beefy third basemen. He was pretty bad in the DSL, but he's younger than the 21st century, so he's got time. ⓧ Even by the most generous estimates, Duran Duran had about eight major hits. **Jarren Duran**, Boston's seventh-round pick, had 101 between Salem and Greenville in his surprisingly potent professional debut. ⓧ A six-figure J2 signing out of Venezuela in 2017, **Antoni Flores** draws praise for his defensive chops at short, his advanced feel for hitting and his projectable body. He stands out from other Red Sox prospects in that he actually has some upside. ⓧ Utility man **Marco Hernandez** now has more shoulder surgeries (three) than homers (one) over the past two seasons. He's still on a better run than Felix Doubront, at least. ⓧ After falling to 640th overall in the 2018 draft, **Brandon Howlett** took his anger out on Rookie-ball pitchers, savaging them to the tune of a 128 DRC+. He's a steady defender with a decent enough arm at third, but he lacks a true Howlett-zer. ⓧ **Tzu-Wei Lin** logged time at second, short, third and center field for the Red Sox and Paw Sox, officially making him Brock Holt's faster understudy. ⓧ You think *you're* tired of the Yankees and the Red Sox? The formerly formidable **Adam Lind** was released by the two rivals three times last season amidst hitting like a pitcher in Triple-A, if they were permitted to hit. ⓧ The Red Sox signed athletic Dominican outfielder **Eduardo Lopez** to a $1,150,000 contract as part of their 2018 J2 class. He was born on May 8, 2002. You, person reading this, are old. ⓧ What can we say about **Tony Renda** that hasn't been said about a spare tire or a travel insurance policy? It's not the end of the world if you have to use him, but you'd sure rather not.

Pitchers

PITCHER	TEAM	LVL	AGE	W	L	SV	G	GS	IP	H	HR	BB/9	K/9	K	GB%	BABIP	WHIP	ERA	DRA	WARP	MPH	FB%	WHF	CSP
Colten Brewer	ELP	AAA	25	3	4	3	37	0	48	40	3	2.8	11.8	63	56%	.330	1.15	3.75	2.55	1.4				
	SDN	MLB	25	1	0	0	11	0	9²	15	0	6.5	9.3	10	50%	.469	2.28	5.59	2.71	0.2	95.0	68.6	10.8	48.6
Kutter Crawford	GRN	A	22	5	4	0	21	21	112¹	104	6	2.7	9.6	120	41%	.320	1.23	2.96	4.42	1.0				
	SLM	A+	22	2	3	0	6	6	31¹	28	0	4.0	10.6	37	43%	.346	1.34	4.31	3.96	0.5				
Jhonathan Diaz	GRN	A	21	11	8	0	26	26	153	123	6	2.3	8.6	147	55%	.287	1.06	3.00	4.46	1.3				
Justin Haley	BOS	MLB	27	0	0	0	4	0	7²	10	2	3.5	0.0	0	44%	.267	1.70	4.70	9.27	-0.4	93.7	58.1	4.7	49.5
	PAW	AAA	27	6	8	0	22	22	113²	124	10	2.6	8.5	107	45%	.342	1.38	3.80	4.23	1.7				
Bobby Poyner	PAW	AAA	25	0	0	6	33	0	43	43	4	2.3	7.3	35	26%	.300	1.26	3.14	5.35	-0.1				
	BOS	MLB	25	1	0	0	20	0	22¹	22	4	1.2	9.7	24	34%	.300	1.12	3.22	5.31	-0.1	91.2	59.9	13.9	44.9
Roniel Raudes	SLM	A+	20	2	5	0	11	11	54	58	2	3.2	5.8	35	37%	.322	1.43	3.67	4.18	0.7				
Alex Scherff	GRN	A	20	1	5	0	15	15	65	68	7	3.2	7.1	51	42%	.324	1.40	4.98	5.08	0.1				
Chandler Shepherd	PAW	AAA	25	7	10	0	25	25	129²	142	13	2.4	7.4	107	43%	.315	1.36	3.89	4.08	2.1				
Josh Taylor	VIS	A+	25	1	2	5	14	0	16	16	1	2.8	11.2	20	45%	.366	1.31	2.81	2.56	0.4				
	PME	AA	25	2	5	8	33	0	35²	42	1	4.5	9.3	37	54%	.376	1.68	3.79	3.78	0.5				
Marcus Walden	BOS	MLB	29	0	0	1	8	0	14²	14	0	1.8	8.6	14	58%	.341	1.16	3.68	3.18	0.3	95.6	45.1	12.7	49
	PAW	AAA	29	0	4	2	18	5	32²	44	2	4.7	6.6	24	53%	.365	1.87	4.96	4.36	0.3				

For **Colten Brewer**, the bad news is that he's the 10th best reliever on the 40-man roster. The good news is that there's never been a better time to be the 10th best reliever on a 40-man roster. ⓧ You'll never guess what generic back-end starter prospect **Kutter Crawford**'s best secondary pitch is. ⓧ Statistically speaking, 84 percent of all Red Sox prospects are left-handed starters from Venezuela. **Jhonathan Diaz** is among that group, though he lacks the upside of some of his younger countrymen. ⓧ Large adult right-hander **Justin Haley** remains a little too good for Triple-A and a little too bad for the majors. If only there was a term for this type of player... ⓧ Potential future up-and-down reliever **Austin Maddox** threw just 7.2 professional innings as he battled right shoulder inflammation, proving that a single vowel isn't all that separates him from one of baseball's great pitching families. ⓧ Prototypical LOOGY **Bobby Poyner** earned a surprise spot on the Opening Day roster, held opponents scoreless in four of his first six MLB appearances, and then got demoted to Triple-A anyway. He should probably get familiar with the Providence-to-Boston commuter rail line. ⓧ The Red Sox's farm system may not be great, but it's improved to the point where control artist/windup wonder **Roniel Raudes** isn't one of its best arms anymore. He added nearly as many DL stints (two) as quality starts (five) to his Salem resume in 2018. ⓧ Ok, close your eyes. Now imagine a non-elite hard-throwing righty pitching prospect from Texas. Congratulations, you just invented **Alex Scherff**! ⓧ We don't want to reduce **Chandler Shepherd**'s identity to that of a run-of-the-mill quad-A reliever, but let's just say that if he was a product, Costco would sell him in packs of 12. ⓧ **Josh Taylor** is left-handed enough that he was added to Boston's 40-man roster this offseason despite only occasionally knowing where the pitches he throws will be located. ⓧ When David Henry Thoreau writes about Walden Pond, it's inspirational. When we write about **Marcus Walden**, it's to let you know he doesn't miss enough bats.

CHICAGO CUBS

Essay by Nick Offerman

Player comments by Darius Austin and BP staff

"**W**ho led the Cubs in home runs two years ago?" asked Dad, shifting from second to third as we cleared the rickety, rust-riddled bridge over Aux Sable Creek. Our Suburban barreled on as the gravel dust it kicked up settled gently onto the fully matured corn leaves in the fields lining the road. We lived amongst the corn and soybean fields outside of Minooka, Illinois—the 50 miles separating it from Chicago felt more like 50 years. Rural life, it turns out, especially in decades past, was a great setting for baseball.

"1982? 'Bull' Durham. Twenty-two homers." answered my sister with a sigh, disappointed by any question that didn't refer to her heart's lifelong obsession, catcher Jody Davis.

I, for one, was relieved that Laurie had once again beaten me to the punch, as my guess was going to be everybody's favorite first baseman, Bill Buckner. I have always been prone to follow my heart more than my brain, but I mean, come on, black mitt, black cleats and a push-broom mustache? Badass. He may have later acquired fame of another shade in Boston, but in our town and at that time, Buckner was the bomb. All of that favorable evidence was notwithstanding, however, as he was the wrong answer to Dad's question.

On these frequent occasions when he would drive me and my sister home after school or baseball practice, we reveled in our Dad's invocation of the Cubby questions. Our lives were wonderfully less distracted then, before the internet and smartphones so completely usurped our collective attention. We (mostly) worked as required at school, sports and band, and then hungrily filled the remainder of our spare time and brain-pan real estate with the minutiae of the Cubs season and roster (ok, and some Dungeons and Dragons on my part, and Duran Duran on Laurie's…and maybe mine too. If you can't admit that John Taylor was and is a beautiful specimen then I declare that you are not in touch with your inner mammal).

Mom's team was the Cubs and Dad's team was the Cubs, so by God our team became the Cubs. Aunts, uncles, grandparents, cousins and pets: it was most assuredly in our blood. We were born breathers of oxygen, consumers of buttered sweet corn, drinkers of beer, players of Liverpool Rummy and mowers of grass, but above all we were born die-hard Cubs fans.

CUBS PROSPECTUS
2018 W-L: 95-68, 2ND IN NL CENTRAL

Pythag	.576	7th	B-Age	27.0	4th
RS/G	4.67	11th	P-Age	30.0	27th
RA/G	3.96	3rd	Salary	$183.2M	4th
DRC+	96	17th	M$/MW	$3.7M	18th
DRA	4.65	21st	DL Days	906	8th
FIP	4.09	17th	$ on DL	19%	20th
DER	.715	6th			

400'

368'   368'

355'   353'

- Opened 1914
- Open air
- Natural surface
- Fence profile: 11'6" to 15'

Three-Year Park Factors

Runs	Runs/RH	Runs/LH	HR/RH	HR/LH
102	104	98	104	90

Top Hitter WARP	4.6 Anthony Rizzo
Top Pitcher WARP	5.0 Kyle Hendricks
Top Prospect	Nico Hoerner

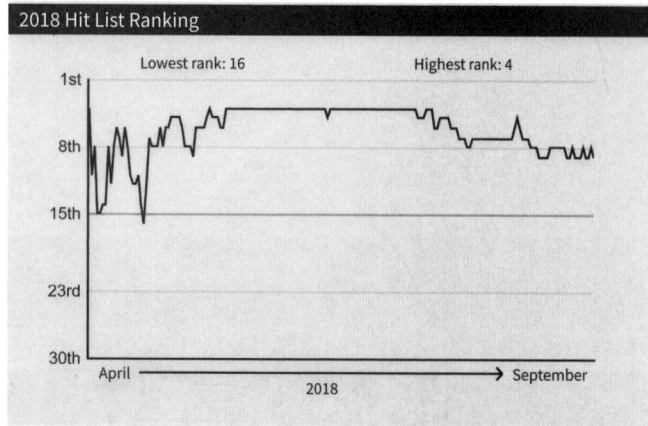

2018 Hit List Ranking

Lowest rank: 16   Highest rank: 4

April — 2018 → September

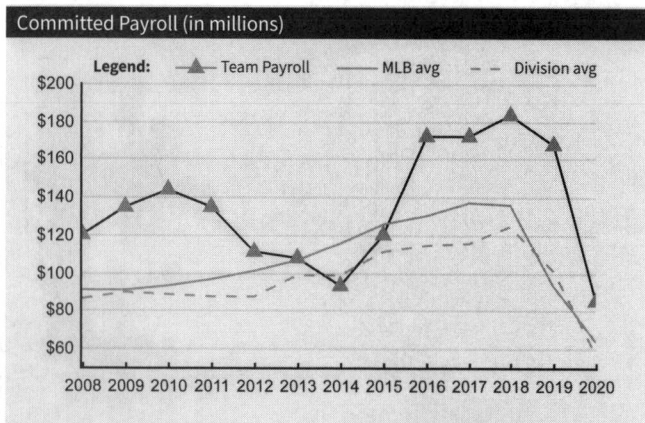

Committed Payroll (in millions)

Legend: — Team Payroll — MLB avg - - - Division avg

2008 2009 2010 2011 2012 2013 2014 2015 2016 2017 2018 2019 2020

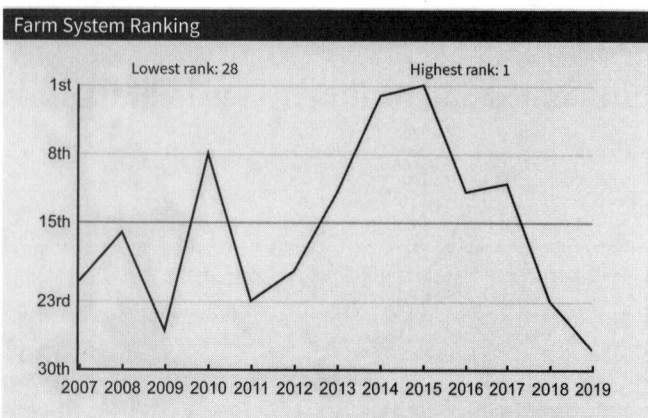

Farm System Ranking

Lowest rank: 28   Highest rank: 1

2007 2008 2009 2010 2011 2012 2013 2014 2015 2016 2017 2018 2019

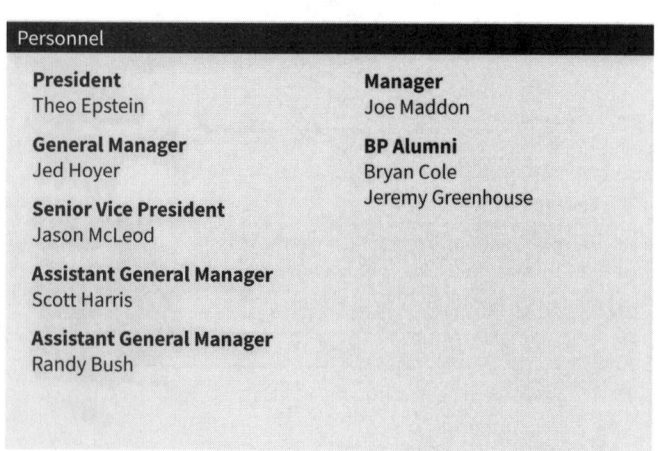

Personnel

President
Theo Epstein

General Manager
Jed Hoyer

Senior Vice President
Jason McLeod

Assistant General Manager
Scott Harris

Assistant General Manager
Randy Bush

Manager
Joe Maddon

BP Alumni
Bryan Cole
Jeremy Greenhouse

Our birthright indoctrination into Cubs fandom was not so much a conscious choice on the part of our folks as merely a continuation in the tradition of survival economy that is so imperative in farming families. We were taught to follow our charismatic baseball team in the same way we were instructed to garden, cook, sew, read, hammer and use good manners. It mattered not at all to us that the Cubs were the butt of every MLB rejoinder; famously ill-fated to forever fail, unfairly goat-cursed to never win another World Series, or to even get close.

Our fandom was unflappable. It was not to be flapped. Like anybody's hometown team, the Cubs were quite simply our fighting lads, and we gave them our adoration without question. Around 1978 or so, as I was playing with my G.I. Joe, the names I heard the announcers repeat on television or the radio began to stick and I began to wonder about these fellows. Buckner, Manny Trillo, Rick Reuschel, Bruce Sutter…but especially Trillo, who just sounded super-heroic in some way. When these names were broadcast, the specific attention that Dad would pay them made us pay attention, and thus we were hooked.

Baseball was a way of life in the Offerman household. Despite his ever-burgeoning work schedule, our Dad also found time to play catch, hit us grounders and coach us—throwing us "major-league pop-ups" that seemed to ascend until they gently smooched the very clouds before plummeting back down towards our eager, outstretched mitts. ("No, no. Let the ball come to you. Then give.") He understood fundamentals as a way of life and he patiently taught that to us in every possible instance. Mentally and physically, we learned that any success is merely a series of properly executed events strung together without dropping the ball, as it were. When Dad said "keep your eye on the ball; watch it all the way to the bat," we knew this could be applied to not only our actual hitting technique, but also metaphorically to life in general. Mom and Dad both were great adherents of the idea that in order to become better than oneself, a great deal of obstinate practice was required. You didn't just hit a home run or bake a perfect loaf of bread on the first try. You had to put your head down and work at it.

From the late seventies through the eighties, the Cubs generally had a scrappy good time of it, and we cheered them on like their lives depended on our scrutiny. Our front yard was about an acre and a half, and Laurie and I would drive the family tractor mower in simple laps from the house out to the road and back again. We learned to take turns of three laps each, while the other sibling would simultaneously watch the game in the living room and the progress of the mower out the window. Of course, we got good enough at it that we barely needed to stop the tractor when switching off every seven minutes or so, shouting any game developments to each other. Our enthusiasm was entirely unaffected by the fact that the Cubbies finished well below .500 in ten of the 12 years I was in the Minooka School System. Besides, when a team has had such thrilling MVP players in every era, like Ernie Banks, Ryne Sandberg, Rick

Sutcliffe, Mark Grace, Sammy Sosa, Fergie Jenkins, Billy Williams, Kerry Wood, Andre Dawson, Dave Kingman, Greg Maddux and Leon Durham, to name but a handful, it never felt like we were backing a team of losers regardless of the scoreboard.

It also doesn't hurt that the team talent and fan solidarity are intensely displayed in the crucible of the nation's greatest ballpark, Wrigley Field. My earliest memory is from 1980 or so, and the eldritch-seeming riveted steel girders comprising the skeleton of the stadium's innards with its wide ramp walkways and main concourse of souvenir stands, hot dogs, pretzels and beer taps. It was as magnificent to us as any pyramid Giza could provide. Emerging from the beehive of concessions below to the sunshine illuminating the cerulean sky, green outfield grass and ivy on the brick walls lent an immediate magic to the proceedings. Our annual trip to the "Friendly Confines" became an absolute highlight of the summer, and not just because our folks made sure to take us on a giveaway day. Jersey Day was my favorite—the greatest shirt of my youth was a three-quarters-sleeve jersey with a large Cubs logo on the front and a Keebler Elf-in-his-tree advertisement on the back.

Over the years, our familial attention spans have waxed and waned, but our fandom has burned true throughout. Our cheering section added two younger siblings, Matt and Carrie, who will forever hold a torch for Mark Grace and with good reason. Of all the teams in all the professional sports in the country, the Cubs have remained our household's only true love and we perhaps even began to take them a bit for granted in adulthood. That is, of course, until 2015. Thanks to a substantial rebuild, the Cubs were suddenly a contender in a way that we had not known in our lifetimes, and it's had a wonderfully rejuvenating effect on the world at large for Cubs fans. When they did break the curse (finally!) and win the World Series in 2016, the sensation was exquisitely climactic. If the ultimate sporting/sexual experience is achieved by the immense accumulation of tension due to incessant cycles of anticipation—arousal and denial, year after year, for *one hundred and eight years*—then the Cubs 2016 championship would have to unquestionably register as the greatest baseball orgasm in modern history.

These contemporary sluggers engender adoration in a substantial way that is based upon their actual league-leading performances, rather than just the handsome way they fill out their respective uniforms. Gold Glover Anthony Rizzo at first base is as dependable as a mountain, and he is also a flat-out hero when it comes to his generosity in charity work, specifically in the fight against cancer. The sense of moral character he displays, always with an easy smile, is all one could ever ask of a sports figure. Kris Bryant will likely bring his bat back to bear in the coming year, and he will be joined by fellow farm-raised standouts Kyle Schwarber, Albert Almora, Ian Happ and David Bote. All very exciting players who will dazzle you with their gloves and their wheels whilst only in their mid-twenties, which means they are only just beginning to realize their full potential on offense. And behind the plate, Wilson Contreras has developed the reputation of a very persnickety sheriff with his quick-draw talent for cutting down attempted base-stealers, as well as picking off dirty varmint runners with a lead he doesn't appreciate.

In baseball, winning requires talent and strategy, but timing and luck cannot be discounted (you also want to stay on the right side of any billy goat owners who might be attending the game). When the timing is right, the Cubs' starting rotation has the potential to be extremely dominant, depending upon the health of Yu Darvish or the couple of solid fellows available to take up his slack alongside Jon Lester, Kyle Hendricks, Jose Quintana and Cole Hamels. All four of these heartbreakers are more likely than not to befuddle opposing hitters, and they generally give off a sense of confidence going into their respective games. There is formidable strength in the bullpen as well, even with Brandon Morrow's uncertain future, and they score major bonus points for launching into a funky dance break every time a Cubs home run clears the fence.

With immense relish, this brings me to Javy Baez. Not since Sandberg's explosive MVP season of 1984 has a Cubs player provided such a consistent menu of delights to his disciples. His electricity at the plate is undeniable, his fielding is perhaps the best in the majors and the temerity with which he runs the bases is about as fun to watch as a Buster Keaton stunt. So physically impossible do his feats seem, particularly with regard to his defensive range, his cannon of an arm and his ability to literally tag base runners without even looking at them, that he has come to be nicknamed "El Mago," which means "The Magician."

Still, despite the immense triumph-tsunami manifested from the release of decades of dejection, the funny thing is that Wrigley Field doesn't feel terribly different to me today than it has over the years. Now that I am technically an adult, the ballpark doesn't feel quite so enormous or overwhelming. I am much more likely to raise an eyebrow at the price of a beer. Sometimes I get to throw out the first pitch or sing during the seventh-inning stretch, which I can only perhaps liken to the golden ticket that Charlie receives from Willy Wonka, especially because the view from the announcer's booth feels like you're floating above the park in a glass elevator.

It was magical then, as it is magical today, because it is the home of the Cubs. My family attendance has swelled to 24 souls in the seats—so substantial a group that we rent a bus to take us to the games. We have sat through two games in the last two seasons, both in rain, with a chill touching the upper forties, watching two underwhelming losses to mediocre teams, and we had the greatest time you could imagine. We're proper Midwesterners, so just the sheer sense of victory derived from consuming a bratwurst and a beer beneath a flimsy poncho without spoiling the bun is an accomplishment worthy of stoic celebration.

Only in hindsight do I realize that our family's deep enjoyment of the Cubs has to do with our adherence to the old saw, "it's not whether you win or lose, it's how you play the game." We love to track these particular north-side-of-Chicago players as their seasonal fortunes ebb and flow, so the number in the W column doesn't hold us in thrall nearly as much as the individual achievements of the players. All the tallies are a savory part of the meal—some for their rising, some for the opposite. We are equally impressed by "Wow, Jake Arrieta struck out nine today" and "Hey, Dad, Shawon Dunston struck out nine times in a double header!"

In eras past, the team has fielded pretty fun, but usually hit-or-miss, rosters with a few bright spots. What gives our family a new, warm feeling of confidence is this new idea wherein every position is manned by a fellow who might bring fireworks to the park on any given day. Our fortunes will undoubtedly wax and wane in the coming years, as they must, and the roster will turn over, as it will, but the lineup

of Offermans will continue to grow and put up consistently impressive numbers as we cheer on our north-side boys. With so much talent and personality to fascinate me and my family, this Cubs team will undoubtedly see us arguing over who is the cutest, fastest and most exciting player for years to come, and that is good news to this fan of gardening.

Postscript: In Hollywood, a rather inordinate percentage of Chicago actors have found success amongst a very competitive talent pool comprised of performers from all over the world. I have often been asked why I think this might be, and the clear answer now occurs to me: the vast majority of these male and female thespians were raised as Cubs fans, which means that they have been inculcated with an unparalleled stubbornness; a tenacity which is perhaps required above all other qualities to succeed in Tinsel Town. ▪

—Nick Offerman is an actor, writer and woodworker in Los Angeles.

HITTERS

Aramis Ademan SS   Born: 09/13/98   Age: 20   Bats: L   Throws: R   Height: 5'11"   Weight: 160   Origin: International Free Agent, 2015

YEAR	TEAM	LVL	AGE	PA	R	2B	3B	HR	RBI	BB	K	SB	CS	AVG/OBP/SLG	DRC+	VORP	BABIP	BRR	FRAA	WARP
2016	DCH	RK	17	248	37	5	4	0	16	34	28	17	9	.254/.366/.316	119	12.4	.293	1.1	SS(52): -1.6	1.6
2017	EUG	A-	18	183	23	9	4	4	27	14	30	10	6	.286/.365/.466	126	19.4	.331	-3.5	SS(38): -1.0	0.8
2017	SBN	A	18	134	13	6	1	3	15	4	24	4	2	.244/.269/.378	98	3.0	.275	0.1	SS(29): -5.0	0.0
2018	MYR	A+	19	452	49	11	3	3	38	38	95	9	5	.207/.291/.273	77	1.1	.264	0.0	SS(112): -8.9	-0.4
2019	*CHN*	*MLB*	*20*	*251*	*26*	*9*	*0*	*6*	*21*	*12*	*59*	*3*	*1*	*.202/.247/.313*	*48*	*-6.9*	*.241*	*-0.4*	*SS -4*	*-1.2*

Breakout: 1%   Improve: 6%   Collapse: 0%   Attrition: 2%   MLB: 7%   *Comparables: Amed Rosario, Ruben Tejada, Wilfredo Tovar*

If you missed the opportunity to get into Ademan before it was cool last season, you have another chance now. Granted, the Dominican shortstop was just 19 at High-A and displayed a good approach at the plate despite his other offensive struggles. Ademan has also drawn praise for his defensive skills. The chance to become an Ademan hipster still exists because of that ugly slash line, which will keep him from shooting up prospect lists. Of course, if he never really hits, it might never be cool, making him a perennial hipster dream.

Albert Almora CF   Born: 04/16/94   Age: 25   Bats: R   Throws: R   Height: 6'2"   Weight: 190   Origin: Round 1, 2012 Draft (#6 overall)

YEAR	TEAM	LVL	AGE	PA	R	2B	3B	HR	RBI	BB	K	SB	CS	AVG/OBP/SLG	DRC+	VORP	BABIP	BRR	FRAA	WARP
2016	IOW	AAA	22	336	46	18	3	4	43	9	44	10	3	.303/.317/.416	80	22.5	.336	3.8	CF(69): -0.5, LF(6): 1.5	0.8
2016	CHN	MLB	22	117	14	9	1	3	14	5	20	0	0	.277/.308/.455	90	5.2	.315	0.9	CF(33): -0.1, LF(8): 1.7	0.5
2017	CHN	MLB	23	323	39	18	1	8	46	19	53	1	0	.298/.338/.445	95	15.9	.338	3.2	CF(104): -1.1, RF(1): 0.0	1.2
2018	CHN	MLB	24	479	62	24	1	5	41	24	83	1	3	.286/.323/.378	82	10.7	.337	-0.1	CF(137): 2.5, LF(2): -0.1	0.8
2019	*CHN*	*MLB*	*25*	*398*	*39*	*19*	*2*	*9*	*44*	*25*	*71*	*2*	*1*	*.260/.310/.390*	*93*	*13.1*	*.298*	*1.4*	*CF 2*	*1.6*

Breakout: 3%   Improve: 61%   Collapse: 4%   Attrition: 9%   MLB: 98%   *Comparables: Odubel Herrera, Jacoby Ellsbury, Gil Flores*

Almora appeared in all but 11 Cubs games in 2018. He also started just 94 of them. No other player who appeared in at least 150 games was in the starting lineup for fewer than 125. In fact, only four other players in major league history have appeared in as many games in a single season without reaching 100 starts: early-career Shane Victorino and Andruw Jones, late-career Ichiro, and journeyman Jim Eisenreich. It's an unusual group, reflecting Almora's atypical role. He is something more than a fourth outfielder—fourth outfielders don't get almost 500 plate appearances—yet clearly short of a full-time regular. That's at least partly due to Joe Maddon's managerial tendencies and Chicago's roster construction. It's also an indication that Almora has not forced the issue with his performance. While evaluators and fans might talk about his glove as though he is an outfielder of Jones' caliber, the metrics do not agree, and he has yet to perform with the bat at a level that warrants 150 starts on a contender. Using Almora as a combination of fringe-average starter, platoon bat and defensive replacement is not inherently a problem for the team, but if he is to become a true full-time player, either his skills or his situation must change.

Miguel Amaya C   Born: 03/09/99   Age: 20   Bats: R   Throws: R   Height: 6'1"   Weight: 185   Origin: International Free Agent, 2015

YEAR	TEAM	LVL	AGE	PA	R	2B	3B	HR	RBI	BB	K	SB	CS	AVG/OBP/SLG	DRC+	VORP	BABIP	BRR	FRAA	WARP
2016	DCH	RK	17	242	29	12	0	1	22	21	27	9	3	.245/.344/.317	113	15.3	.276	2.4	C(33): -0.1, 1B(16): 3.0	1.7
2017	EUG	A-	18	244	21	14	1	3	26	11	49	1	0	.228/.266/.338	88	1.6	.274	-1.5	C(43): -0.5, 1B(8): -0.4	0.2
2018	SBN	A	19	479	54	21	2	12	52	50	91	1	0	.256/.349/.403	123	31.5	.298	0.6	C(95): 2.5, 1B(9): -0.7	3.5
2019	*CHN*	*MLB*	*20*	*251*	*23*	*8*	*0*	*8*	*28*	*14*	*61*	*0*	*0*	*.209/.254/.339*	*57*	*-3.3*	*.245*	*-0.6*	*C 0, 1B 0*	*-0.4*

Breakout: 2%   Improve: 9%   Collapse: 0%   Attrition: 6%   MLB: 11%   *Comparables: Carson Kelly, Jake Bauers, Freddie Freeman*

Of all the prospects in the Cubs system, Amaya's stock has risen the most over the past year. That might seem like damning with faint praise; a Futures Game appearance shows that it is anything but. An athletic backstop with the frame to handle the role, Amaya started to tap into his big raw power at South Bend without sacrificing contact. Add a strong arm and signs that he can be at least average behind the plate and it's clear the Panamanian has a rare combination of skills for a catcher that add up to at least a major league regular someday. Catcher development is smooth and uncomplicated, right?

Javier Baez INF   Born: 12/01/92   Age: 26   Bats: R   Throws: R   Height: 6'0"   Weight: 190   Origin: Round 1, 2011 Draft (#9 overall)

YEAR	TEAM	LVL	AGE	PA	R	2B	3B	HR	RBI	BB	K	SB	CS	AVG/OBP/SLG	DRC+	VORP	BABIP	BRR	FRAA	WARP
2016	CHN	MLB	23	450	50	19	1	14	59	15	108	12	3	.273/.314/.423	88	20.2	.336	-0.7	3B(62): 1.1, 2B(59): 2.7	1.3
2017	CHN	MLB	24	508	75	24	2	23	75	30	144	10	3	.273/.317/.480	95	30.0	.345	4.4	2B(80): -1.3, SS(73): -6.6	1.4
2018	CHN	MLB	25	645	101	40	9	34	111	29	167	21	9	.290/.326/.554	115	54.7	.347	3.2	2B(104): -0.6, SS(65): 1.3	4.3
2019	CHN	MLB	26	664	96	29	5	28	83	41	179	18	7	.261/.314/.463	109	32.7	.323	2.0	SS -1, 2B -1	3.3

Breakout: 7%   Improve: 55%   Collapse: 7%   Attrition: 12%   MLB: 98%   *Comparables: Danny Espinosa, Howie Kendrick, Starling Marte*

As soon as he arrived in the majors, Baez exuded talent in almost every facet of the game, from his prodigious bat speed to the outrageous flair of his glovework and a swim move that even Michael Phelps would envy. One issue seemed to be holding him back from becoming truly elite: patience. If Baez could just learn a little more restraint at the right time, surely he would join the game's elite. Instead, Baez did the opposite: he swung more than almost anyone in baseball, had one of the league's worst contact rates, and still became a legitimate MVP candidate. Mechanical changes, like moving his hands away from his body and adding a higher leg kick, have helped the Puerto Rico native make quality contact on a more regular basis, transforming him from the league's most spectacular average player into the star that his talent always promised.

David Bote UT   Born: 04/07/93   Age: 26   Bats: R   Throws: R   Height: 6'1"   Weight: 210   Origin: Round 18, 2012 Draft (#554 overall)

YEAR	TEAM	LVL	AGE	PA	R	2B	3B	HR	RBI	BB	K	SB	CS	AVG/OBP/SLG	DRC+	VORP	BABIP	BRR	FRAA	WARP
2016	TEN	AA	23	27	1	0	0	0	1	2	6	0	0	.200/.259/.200	78	-1.9	.263	0.2	3B(5): 0.3, 1B(2): 0.1	0.1
2016	MYR	A+	23	313	55	26	3	6	41	31	41	6	1	.337/.410/.518	128	39.6	.378	1.5	2B(31): -2.1, 3B(21): 0.7	1.9
2017	TEN	AA	24	536	65	30	3	14	59	49	101	5	2	.272/.353/.438	115	31.2	.318	1.0	2B(107): 5.7, RF(9): 1.2	3.3
2018	IOW	AAA	25	263	34	10	2	13	41	26	63	3	1	.268/.342/.494	112	16.4	.313	-0.2	2B(38): -2.9, SS(15): 1.3	1.3
2018	CHN	MLB	25	210	23	9	2	6	33	19	60	3	4	.239/.319/.408	79	7.3	.314	-1.0	3B(56): 2.4, 2B(13): -0.6	0.3
2019	CHN	MLB	26	208	24	8	1	7	25	19	58	2	1	.224/.304/.394	90	3.4	.285	0.0	3B 0, 2B 0	0.4

Breakout: 5%   Improve: 37%   Collapse: 16%   Attrition: 30%   MLB: 74%   *Comparables: Todd Frazier, Brendan Harris, Rob Refsnyder*

Get your towels ready, it's about to go down. There was a point in 2018 when it felt like Bote was finishing more games than most closers. He produced one of the most memorable moments of the season when he hit a walk-off grand slam in a 4-3 win over the Nationals in August. It was Bote's second walk-off of the season, rather more iconic than his walk-off walk in early July. Two weeks after the slam, he hit another game-ending blast, cementing his status as late-inning hero and ensuring that anyone who didn't already know how to pronounce his name would get the memo (it's Bow-dee, not Boaty or Boat, much to T-Pain's chagrin). Far less secure is a regular role going forward. Bote clearly has a ton of thunder in his bat, but his defensive utility is up for debate and beyond the heroics, the overall offensive production was simply average after he slumped in the final six weeks. That's not likely to get him on that big, blue watery road to regular playing time, no matter how many walk-offs he produces.

Kris Bryant 3B   Born: 01/04/92   Age: 27   Bats: R   Throws: R   Height: 6'5"   Weight: 230   Origin: Round 1, 2013 Draft (#2 overall)

YEAR	TEAM	LVL	AGE	PA	R	2B	3B	HR	RBI	BB	K	SB	CS	AVG/OBP/SLG	DRC+	VORP	BABIP	BRR	FRAA	WARP
2016	CHN	MLB	24	699	121	35	3	39	102	75	154	8	5	.292/.385/.554	141	86.5	.332	3.4	3B(107): 1.5, LF(60): 1.1	6.4
2017	CHN	MLB	25	665	111	38	4	29	73	95	128	7	5	.295/.409/.537	138	69.6	.334	1.9	3B(144): -3.9, RF(7): 0.2	5.5
2018	CHN	MLB	26	457	59	28	3	13	52	48	107	2	4	.272/.374/.460	109	31.3	.342	-2.2	3B(86): 0.8, RF(15): 0.0	1.9
2019	CHN	MLB	27	633	90	31	3	22	75	73	141	6	4	.259/.368/.448	126	36.0	.319		3B 1, LF 0	4.0

Breakout: 1%   Improve: 62%   Collapse: 2%   Attrition: 4%   MLB: 99%   *Comparables: Evan Longoria, David Wright, Bob Horner*

As Bryant goes, so do the Cubs. A stellar rookie campaign ended the franchise's six-year playoff drought, though his near 200 strikeouts foreshadowed an NLCS in which the team was blown away by Mets pitching. The triumphant MVP season followed, with a now 25-year-old Bryant leading Chicago to that historic World Series title. 2017 proved more challenging, as he battled through a hand injury. The team won the division comfortably in the end and Bryant, while diminished, was still one of the league's best players, but they both fell flat in the NLCS. 2018 was the team's most disappointing year since Bryant's debut, as shoulder inflammation limited him to 102 games and sapped his power when he was in the lineup. Just one more win would have ensured the division, a win their star third baseman would surely have provided if healthy. Instead the Cubs lost the division and then the Wild Card game. Theo Epstein and company probably didn't quite have this level of dependence in mind when they were building their franchise around Bryant.

Victor Caratini C   Born: 08/17/93   Age: 25   Bats: B   Throws: R   Height: 6'1"   Weight: 215   Origin: Round 2, 2013 Draft (#65 overall)

YEAR	TEAM	LVL	AGE	PA	R	2B	3B	HR	RBI	BB	K	SB	CS	AVG/OBP/SLG	DRC+	VORP	BABIP	BRR	FRAA	WARP
2016	TEN	AA	22	480	57	25	2	6	47	54	80	2	1	.291/.375/.405	108	29.3	.341	-1.5	C(82): -9.0, 1B(30): -0.1	1.2
2017	IOW	AAA	23	326	50	27	3	10	61	27	48	1	0	.342/.393/.558	114	34.4	.375	1.4	C(50): -3.9, 1B(30): 0.7	1.6
2017	CHN	MLB	23	66	6	3	0	1	2	4	13	0	0	.254/.333/.356	81	0.5	.311	-0.4	C(12): -0.6, 1B(8): 0.1	0.0
2018	IOW	AAA	24	137	13	7	0	4	22	18	25	0	0	.313/.409/.478	111	12.2	.364	-0.6	C(18): -2.2, 1B(12): 1.6	0.6
2018	CHN	MLB	24	200	21	7	0	2	21	12	42	0	0	.232/.293/.304	72	-1.4	.290	-0.6	C(37): -0.8, 1B(20): 0.5	0.0
2019	CHN	MLB	25	235	23	9	1	6	26	19	49	0	0	.238/.308/.375	86	3.7	.282	-0.4	C -4, 1B 0	0.0

Breakout: 2%   Improve: 39%   Collapse: 9%   Attrition: 27%   MLB: 85%   *Comparables: Hank Conger, J.R. Towles, Jonathan Lucroy*

Is Caratini a supporting cast member who never gets promoted to regular, or will he get a chance to play lead? After nearly 500 plate appearances of impressive offense in Triple-A, he was called upon to backup Willson Contreras and stretch out at a corner infield spot when needed. Unfortunately, American Airlines lost his bat on the 90-minute sojourn to Chicago. Instead of an above-average hitter who warranted that quasi-utility role but had some big questions behind the plate, the Cubs got passable defense and the worst offensive production of any player on the team by some margin. There are many ways to be a "tweener," and Caratini now fits multiple definitions of the term, but his flexibility and track record in the minors will give him more chances to shed all forms of that label.

YEAR	TEAM	P. COUNT	FRM RUNS	BLK RUNS	THRW RUNS	TOT RUNS
2017	CHN	1182	-1.0	0.5	0.0	-0.6
2017	IOW	7230	-3.9	0.6	0.1	-3.6
2018	CHN	4929	-1.0	0.3	0.1	-1.1
2018	IOW	2828	-1.9	0.0	-0.1	-1.5
2019	CHN	5024	-3.4	0.3	-0.2	-3.3

Willson Contreras C Born: 05/13/92 Age: 27 Bats: R Throws: R Height: 6'1" Weight: 210 Origin: International Free Agent, 2009

YEAR	TEAM	LVL	AGE	PA	R	2B	3B	HR	RBI	BB	K	SB	CS	AVG/OBP/SLG	DRC+	VORP	BABIP	BRR	FRAA	WARP
2016	IOW	AAA	24	240	40	16	3	9	43	28	32	4	4	.353/.442/.593	133	38.1	.382	-0.9	C(45): -4.5	1.5
2016	CHN	MLB	24	283	33	14	1	12	35	26	67	2	2	.282/.357/.488	99	21.5	.339	-0.9	C(57): 6.7, LF(24): -2.5	1.5
2017	CHN	MLB	25	428	50	21	0	21	74	45	98	5	4	.276/.356/.499	114	34.2	.319	-3.9	C(108): 0.7, 1B(5): 0.0	2.5
2018	CHN	MLB	26	544	50	27	5	10	54	53	121	4	1	.249/.339/.390	91	27.0	.313	0.6	C(133): -14.6, LF(5): -0.8	0.6
2019	CHN	MLB	27	517	60	20	3	17	63	51	120	5	2	.241/.328/.405	105	24.3	.293	-1.4	C -9	1.7

Breakout: 1%   Improve: 51%   Collapse: 4%   Attrition: 7%   MLB: 99%   *Comparables: Derek Norris, Wil Myers, Miguel Montero*

Contreras is one of the game's best backstops in a variety of ways. He caught 34 percent of attempted base stealers and picked off another seven runners, more than any other catcher in the majors. He's also one of the game's best blockers, ranking in the top five in Blocking Runs. There's just one issue: his presentation is worse than those PowerPoints with 50-word bullet points and completely incongruent animation that Jordan from Marketing makes you sit through in the team meetings every Monday morning. Contreras

YEAR	TEAM	P. COUNT	FRM RUNS	BLK RUNS	THRW RUNS	TOT RUNS
2016	CHN	6569	5.0	1.4	0.8	7.6
2017	CHN	14005	-2.8	0.6	-1.1	-1.1
2018	CHN	18508	-17.8	1.9	0.4	-15.0
2019	CHN	17556	-11.7	1.7	0.0	-10.0

cost his team dearly with his framing this year, negating all the runs he gained in the other defensive areas and then some. Add to that a relative power outage that Chili Davis is probably blaming on millennials right now and it wasn't quite the progression one might expect from a 26-year-old. Framing hasn't been such a big issue in the past, and it's possible that fatigue from playing in so many games cost him with both bat and glove. In fact, his 1,109 innings caught in 2018 were over 70 more than the next most used backstop. If MLB ever considers introducing an automated strike zone, Contreras should be leading the campaign, as it might make him the game's best overall catcher.

Daniel Descalso UT Born: 10/19/86 Age: 32 Bats: L Throws: R Height: 5'10" Weight: 190 Origin: Round 3, 2007 Draft (#112 overall)

YEAR	TEAM	LVL	AGE	PA	R	2B	3B	HR	RBI	BB	K	SB	CS	AVG/OBP/SLG	DRC+	VORP	BABIP	BRR	FRAA	WARP
2016	COL	MLB	29	289	38	12	2	8	38	34	56	3	0	.264/.349/.424	103	15.4	.305	3.4	SS(31): -6.0, 1B(16): 0.2	0.9
2017	ARI	MLB	30	398	47	16	5	10	51	48	89	4	0	.233/.332/.395	100	5.8	.283	-3.2	2B(45): 0.9, LF(36): -4.8	0.4
2018	ARI	MLB	31	423	54	22	4	13	57	64	110	0	1	.238/.353/.436	110	22.9	.300	-0.7	2B(52): 3.2, 3B(37): -0.8	2.0
2019	CHN	MLB	32	148	16	7	1	4	17	17	34	1	0	.246/.341/.404	108	6.1	.305	-0.1	SS -1, 3B -1	0.4

Breakout: 1%   Improve: 36%   Collapse: 5%   Attrition: 9%   MLB: 91%   *Comparables: Adam Kennedy, Dick McAuliffe, Orlando Hudson*

Descalso perennially struggled to provide even league-average offense and his days as a shortstop are all but over. But like a budget wine you decided to age despite the wildly affordable price tag, Descalso has improved over time. He's grown into the Old Player mold and embraced it, letting the strikeouts climb some as he takes more walks and hits for more power. He was a good offensive player in 2018 for the Diamondbacks when they needed one most. With Jake Lamb and Paul Goldschmidt struggling, Descalso carried the team at times early in the season. He did wither a bit down the stretch and his defense isn't what it once was, but he's still a useful piece for a team looking to bolster its bench.

Ian Happ UT Born: 08/12/94 Age: 24 Bats: B Throws: R Height: 6'0" Weight: 205 Origin: Round 1, 2015 Draft (#9 overall)

YEAR	TEAM	LVL	AGE	PA	R	2B	3B	HR	RBI	BB	K	SB	CS	AVG/OBP/SLG	DRC+	VORP	BABIP	BRR	FRAA	WARP
2016	MYR	A+	21	293	37	16	3	7	42	48	69	10	3	.296/.410/.475	122	26.1	.381	0.2	2B(50): -3.1, LF(6): 0.0	1.2
2016	TEN	AA	21	274	35	14	0	8	31	20	60	6	2	.262/.318/.415	104	9.8	.310	0.4	2B(42): -0.6, RF(7): -1.7	0.7
2017	IOW	AAA	22	116	21	6	0	9	25	11	27	2	1	.298/.362/.615	126	14.0	.319	0.0	2B(16): 1.2, CF(6): 1.0	1.0
2017	CHN	MLB	22	413	62	17	3	24	68	39	129	8	4	.253/.328/.514	111	25.2	.316	3.1	CF(54): 0.7, 2B(44): 0.1	1.9
2018	CHN	MLB	23	462	56	19	2	15	44	70	167	8	4	.233/.353/.408	94	23.0	.362	2.0	CF(63): -7.9, LF(59): -2.5	0.2
2019	CHN	MLB	24	471	66	19	2	18	54	59	162	8	4	.226/.328/.414	104	20.2	.324	2.0	CF -4, LF -2	1.4

Breakout: 4%   Improve: 51%   Collapse: 9%   Attrition: 14%   MLB: 95%   *Comparables: Oswaldo Arcia, Marcell Ozuna, Jorge Soler*

If Happ is Zobrist 2.0, there have been an awful lot of tweaks to the source code. Happ might walk like Zobrist, but he has struck out more in his first two seasons than Zobrist did in his first five, in almost 900 fewer plate appearances. He can't play the infield like Zobrist either, reflected by his diminished usage there in 2018. It's not like 'upgrading' from XP to Vista, but perhaps we should stop suggesting that Happ can fill the role of one of the most unique players in recent memory and instead recognize him on his own merits.

Jason Heyward RF Born: 08/09/89 Age: 29 Bats: L Throws: L Height: 6'5" Weight: 240 Origin: Round 1, 2007 Draft (#14 overall)

YEAR	TEAM	LVL	AGE	PA	R	2B	3B	HR	RBI	BB	K	SB	CS	AVG/OBP/SLG	DRC+	VORP	BABIP	BRR	FRAA	WARP
2016	CHN	MLB	26	592	61	27	1	7	49	54	93	11	4	.230/.306/.325	78	-2.6	.266	-0.4	RF(131): -0.2, CF(24): 2.8	0.1
2017	CHN	MLB	27	481	59	15	4	11	59	41	67	4	4	.259/.326/.389	95	8.6	.284	1.9	RF(120): 10.0, CF(13): 1.0	2.2
2018	CHN	MLB	28	489	67	23	4	8	57	42	60	1	1	.270/.335/.395	97	15.9	.297	3.0	RF(118): 11.5, CF(25): -2.7	2.2
2019	CHN	MLB	29	474	51	20	3	9	47	39	68	5	2	.252/.320/.378	92	11.0	.281	1.3	RF 4, CF 0	1.7

Breakout: 1%   Improve: 26%   Collapse: 13%   Attrition: 23%   MLB: 96%   *Comparables: Bob Molinaro, Randy Moore, Harvey Kuenn*

Heyward's offensive production improved again, albeit ever-so-slightly, and for the first time in a Cubs uniform he was an above-average hitter over the course of the season. The respectable but somewhat dull line is a stark contrast to the dizzying array of changes to both his swing and approach that he made to get here, and the oceans of virtual ink spilled over his efforts to discover an offensive formula that works. Much of the promise from the first half drifted away in the second, as the 28-year-old looked very much like the subpar hitter from his first two years on the North Side. Chicago will take an average Heyward at the plate if he is one of the game's best right fielders, a classification called into doubt by some comparatively pedestrian defensive ratings. The vagaries of fielding metrics allow us to handwave such single-season numbers with the combined weight of his exceptional track record, but it is telling that the first of his opt-out dates passed with barely a thought in November. It's even more telling that the kind of season it would take to imagine Heyward opting out of the final four years of his deal after 2019 feels impossibly far away.

Nico Hoerner SS   Born: 05/13/97   Age: 22   Bats: R   Throws: R   Height: 6'1"   Weight: 200   Origin: Round 1, 2018 Draft (#24 overall)

YEAR	TEAM	LVL	AGE	PA	R	2B	3B	HR	RBI	BB	K	SB	CS	AVG/OBP/SLG	DRC+	VORP	BABIP	BRR	FRAA	WARP
2018	EUG	A-	21	28	6	0	1	1	2	5	3	4	1	.318/.464/.545	108	4.1	.333	-0.5	SS(5): -0.4	0.0
2019	CHN	MLB	22	251	26	7	0	8	27	17	61	4	1	.199/.256/.330	55	-4.6	.232	0.0	SS 0, 2B 0	-0.5

Breakout: 2%   Improve: 15%   Collapse: 10%   Attrition: 18%   MLB: 26%   Comparables: Yamaico Navarro, Marcus Semien, Rosell Herrera

It was a little surprising to see Hoerner taken as early as 24th overall in the 2018 draft, and the Cubs first-rounder did not get much of a chance to show that the pick was justified, going down with a strained elbow ligament after just 14 pro games. The Stanford product was sent to the Arizona Fall League to make up for lost time, the first Cubs player to make that trip in his draft season since Kris Bryant. Although that might be setting expectations *a tad* high, Hoerner was one of the biggest stars in Arizona, showing the feel for hitting and excellent makeup that inspired the lofty pick. His ability to stick at short and the extent to which the power develops will determine whether he's more than an average regular at peak, but he might reach the majors even more quickly than Bryant, especially given that his service time will be less carefully...regulated.

Anthony Rizzo 1B   Born: 08/08/89   Age: 29   Bats: L   Throws: L   Height: 6'3"   Weight: 240   Origin: Round 6, 2007 Draft (#204 overall)

YEAR	TEAM	LVL	AGE	PA	R	2B	3B	HR	RBI	BB	K	SB	CS	AVG/OBP/SLG	DRC+	VORP	BABIP	BRR	FRAA	WARP
2016	CHN	MLB	26	676	94	43	4	32	109	74	108	3	5	.292/.385/.544	137	56.5	.309	-1.2	1B(154): 11.4, 2B(1): -0.2	5.2
2017	CHN	MLB	27	691	99	32	3	32	109	91	90	10	4	.273/.392/.507	137	36.3	.273	-3.2	1B(157): 14.4, 2B(10): -0.3	5.3
2018	CHN	MLB	28	665	74	29	1	25	101	70	80	6	4	.283/.376/.470	133	28.0	.287	-5.8	1B(153): 14.4, 2B(1): 0.0	4.6
2019	CHN	MLB	29	660	89	35	3	25	91	75	91	8	4	.273/.385/.472	140	39.1	.297	-2.8	1B 10	5.2

Breakout: 3%   Improve: 54%   Collapse: 4%   Attrition: 3%   MLB: 96%   Comparables: Todd Helton, Justin Morneau, Carlos Santana

It can be very disconcerting when even the most dependable players go through prolonged slumps. Even Amazon delivers a package to the wrong address, after all. Rizzo endured his worst month since he was a rookie to start the season, sporting a .149/.259/.189 line at the end of April, partly as the result of a back issue. Normal service soon resumed, as even with another relative slump in June, the first baseman hit a very Rizzo-esque .303/.393/.512 the rest of the way and was one of the few Cubs hitters to not disappear when needed late in the season. In this era of trading contact for power, only a handful of players combine Rizzo's power, patience and ability to avoid strikeouts so effectively. Only 11 hitters have reached 150 home runs over the past five seasons, and Rizzo is the only one to have struck out in fewer than 15 percent of his plate appearances.

Addison Russell SS   Born: 01/23/94   Age: 25   Bats: R   Throws: R   Height: 6'0"   Weight: 200   Origin: Round 1, 2012 Draft (#11 overall)

YEAR	TEAM	LVL	AGE	PA	R	2B	3B	HR	RBI	BB	K	SB	CS	AVG/OBP/SLG	DRC+	VORP	BABIP	BRR	FRAA	WARP
2016	CHN	MLB	22	598	67	25	3	21	95	55	135	5	1	.238/.321/.417	95	33.6	.277	-0.2	SS(148): 3.6	2.8
2017	CHN	MLB	23	385	52	21	3	12	43	29	91	2	1	.239/.304/.418	88	13.7	.289	-0.3	SS(101): 3.4	1.5
2018	CHN	MLB	24	465	52	21	1	5	38	40	99	4	0	.250/.317/.340	83	13.3	.314	-0.8	SS(129): 1.2	1.2
2019	CHN	MLB	25	296	31	14	1	7	31	25	67	2	1	.235/.310/.373	86	5.7	.290	-0.3	SS 3	0.9

Breakout: 2%   Improve: 66%   Collapse: 5%   Attrition: 3%   MLB: 96%   Comparables: Khalil Greene, Lyn Lary, Denis Menke

There is so much we could say about Russell, from his failure to live up to expectations on the field to the details of his abusive actions off it—actions which brought his immediate placement on administrative leave and a 40-game suspension. This shouldn't be about Russell, though—it should be about his ex-wife Melisa Reidy and the effects that the abuse had on her. We need to focus on the survivors, listen to them and change the way violence is discussed. We need to recognize that speaking out about domestic violence is incredibly difficult and that the appropriate first response to when a player is accused or suspended is not to dwell on that player, their trade value, contract status or how it might affect their career. Instead it should be to listen to the survivor, talk about the violence and do everything we can to prevent it happening again.

Kyle Schwarber LF   Born: 03/05/93   Age: 26   Bats: L   Throws: R   Height: 6'0"   Weight: 235   Origin: Round 1, 2014 Draft (#4 overall)

YEAR	TEAM	LVL	AGE	PA	R	2B	3B	HR	RBI	BB	K	SB	CS	AVG/OBP/SLG	DRC+	VORP	BABIP	BRR	FRAA	WARP
2016	CHN	MLB	23	5	0	0	0	0	0	1	2	0	0	.000/.200/.000	69	-0.7	.000	0.0	LF(2): 0.0	0.0
2017	IOW	AAA	24	44	9	1	0	4	9	8	12	0	0	.343/.477/.714	144	7.0	.421	-0.1	LF(9): -1.5	0.2
2017	CHN	MLB	24	486	67	16	1	30	59	59	150	1	1	.211/.315/.467	107	14.7	.244	0.6	LF(110): 2.7, C(4): 0.0	2.0
2018	CHN	MLB	25	510	64	14	3	26	61	78	140	4	3	.238/.356/.467	118	21.3	.288	-3.4	LF(120): 2.7	2.4
2019	CHN	MLB	26	507	64	20	2	22	70	61	137	3	2	.239/.338/.442	113	21.5	.296	-1.1	LF -2	2.1

Breakout: 1%   Improve: 55%   Collapse: 3%   Attrition: 5%   MLB: 98%   Comparables: Ryan Klesko, Mitchell Page, Carlos Gonzalez

Since it became clear that Schwarber was not going to catch in the majors, his fielding prowess has ranked almost equal with pitchers hitting on the list of reasons for the National League to adopt the DH. That all changed in 2018, as profiles which previously used the bat- prefix more than the headline writer at The Daily Gotham now have to account for an entirely competent defensive performance in left field.

To be fair to Schwarber, he did not previously rate as badly in left as the jokes might have led one to believe. Optics are important, and when a slimmed-down, fitter Schwarber emerged in spring looking far less like baseball's favorite Large Adult Son, the chatter about whether this would help his defense began. Some impressive plays with his arm helped, as he finished tied for the league lead in left with 11 assists. While most metrics agreed that he was above-average at the position by season's end, Statcast threw some shade on the improvements, suggesting that Schwarber was one of the game's ten worst outfielders at turning fly balls into outs. That might also suggest that the Cubs have simply used better positioning to address his shortcomings with regards to range, and it does not take away from the fact that his arm has turned into a legitimate weapon.

While poor range at 25 is not an encouraging sign for his long-term future at the position, Schwarber is still relatively inexperienced in the outfield and he doesn't need to be a Gold Glover in left to be a valuable regular on a contender. The primary concern now might be his struggles against southpaws, against whom he has a career .608 OPS. Figuring out how to be as passable against left-handers as he was in left field is the next step in unlocking his full offensive potential.

Mark Zagunis OF Born: 02/05/93 Age: 26 Bats: R Throws: R Height: 6'0" Weight: 215 Origin: Round 3, 2014 Draft (#78 overall)

YEAR	TEAM	LVL	AGE	PA	R	2B	3B	HR	RBI	BB	K	SB	CS	AVG/OBP/SLG	DRC+	VORP	BABIP	BRR	FRAA	WARP
2016	TEN	AA	23	211	30	13	1	4	24	30	36	1	2	.302/.408/.453	120	11.2	.360	-2.7	LF(40): 5.4, RF(8): -1.2	1.2
2016	IOW	AAA	23	211	31	12	4	6	25	22	42	4	0	.274/.360/.486	110	13.5	.316	0.4	RF(33): -0.2, LF(17): 0.2	0.8
2017	CHN	MLB	24	18	0	0	0	0	1	4	6	2	0	.000/.222/.000	78	-0.9	.000	0.6	RF(4): -0.3	0.0
2017	IOW	AAA	24	408	59	21	1	13	55	70	93	4	3	.267/.404/.455	117	24.8	.333	-1.7	LF(53): 1.1, RF(39): -3.4	1.5
2018	CHN	MLB	25	6	0	1	0	0	1	1	1	0	0	.400/.500/.600	96	0.9	.500	0.0	RF(1): 0.0	0.0
2018	IOW	AAA	25	453	63	17	0	7	40	70	101	11	1	.272/.395/.375	95	22.2	.353	-1.4	RF(63): -7.0, LF(44): -3.8	-0.3
2019	CHN	MLB	26	35	4	1	0	1	4	5	9	0	0	.218/.334/.354	79	0.1	.284	0.0	RF -1	-0.1

Breakout: 2%   Improve: 21%   Collapse: 15%   Attrition: 28%   MLB: 53%   *Comparables: Mike Baxter, Shane Peterson, Chad Huffman*

Zagunis has a .400 on-base percentage over more than 2000 plate appearances in the minors, demonstrating both his exceptional strike-zone judgement and his inability to force the issue in any other area. The problem is further highlighted by his increasingly lengthy stay at Triple-A. With a glove that plays only in a corner outfield spot and pop that would be more acceptable in center, the rest of the profile lags considerably behind the approach at the plate. In another organization, perhaps the walks alone would have been enough to earn Zagunis an extended look in the bigs. In Chicago, all it has earned him so far is the annual chance to battle Dan Vogelbach for the most free passes in the Pacific Coast League.

Ben Zobrist 2B Born: 05/26/81 Age: 38 Bats: B Throws: R Height: 6'3" Weight: 210 Origin: Round 6, 2004 Draft (#184 overall)

YEAR	TEAM	LVL	AGE	PA	R	2B	3B	HR	RBI	BB	K	SB	CS	AVG/OBP/SLG	DRC+	VORP	BABIP	BRR	FRAA	WARP
2016	CHN	MLB	35	631	94	31	3	18	76	96	82	6	4	.272/.386/.446	122	49.2	.290	3.9	2B(119): -7.2, LF(27): -1.6	3.1
2017	CHN	MLB	36	496	58	20	3	12	50	54	71	2	2	.232/.318/.375	97	5.2	.251	-1.3	2B(81): -2.0, LF(36): -0.2	0.8
2018	CHN	MLB	37	520	67	28	3	9	58	55	60	3	4	.305/.378/.440	118	36.0	.331	3.0	2B(63): 4.2, RF(61): 6.1	3.7
2019	CHN	MLB	38	567	67	28	3	11	54	59	80	4	3	.260/.342/.393	103	21.9	.289	1.6	2B -1, RF 0	2.3

Breakout: 0%   Improve: 26%   Collapse: 13%   Attrition: 29%   MLB: 76%   *Comparables: Brian Giles, Elmer Valo, Bernie Williams*

Zobrist's replacement-level season at the age of 36 had us wondering whether he was set to become the world's most expensive Willie Bloomquist impersonator. Instead he was a bargain version of his near-peak self, putting together his finest year since he was in Tampa Bay, ranking among the league's best in both batting average and on-base percentage while providing his trademark defensive versatility. That versatility is now officially unprecedented: Zobrist is the only player in major league history to play at least 200 games at second, short, and both outfield corners. He is keeping rare company on the offensive side too, as the only qualified hitters in the past decade to get on base more often in their age-37 season are Chipper Jones and David Ortiz.

PITCHERS

Adbert Alzolay RHP Born: 03/01/95 Age: 24 Bats: R Throws: R Height: 6'0" Weight: 179 Origin: International Free Agent, 2012

YEAR	TEAM	LVL	AGE	W	L	SV	G	GS	IP	H	HR	BB/9	K/9	K	GB%	BABIP	WHIP	ERA	DRA	WARP	MPH	FB%	WHF	CSP
2016	SBN	A	21	9	4	0	22	20	120¹	119	9	2.1	6.1	81	44%	.292	1.22	4.34	3.62	2.0				
2017	MYR	A+	22	7	1	0	15	15	81²	65	8	2.4	8.6	78	39%	.263	1.07	2.98	3.56	1.6				
2017	TEN	AA	22	0	3	0	7	7	32²	27	0	3.3	8.3	30	36%	.297	1.19	3.03	4.08	0.4				
2018	IOW	AAA	23	2	4	0	8	8	39²	43	4	2.9	6.1	27	37%	.307	1.41	4.76	4.19	0.6				
2019	CHN	MLB	24	1	0	0	15	0	15¹	16	2	3.2	7.2	12	38%	.300	1.37	4.73	5.24	-0.2				

Breakout: 3%   Improve: 3%   Collapse: 8%   Attrition: 9%   MLB: 15%   *Comparables: Jason Adam, Myles Jaye, Keury Mella*

A lofty ranking on Cubs prospect lists last offseason seemed to be more of a curse than a blessing for many of the unknowing recipients. Alzolay was at the top of the list and started the season just one step away from the majors. Instead of making his big-league debut, he struggled with his command at Triple-A before a severe lat strain finished his season in late May. Fortunately, it is unlikely to be a curse of Billy Goat proportions. Alzolay should have to wait only until 2019 for that debut, not 2089.

Tyler Chatwood RHP Born: 12/16/89 Age: 29 Bats: R Throws: R Height: 6'0" Weight: 185 Origin: Round 2, 2008 Draft (#74 overall)

YEAR	TEAM	LVL	AGE	W	L	SV	G	GS	IP	H	HR	BB/9	K/9	K	GB%	BABIP	WHIP	ERA	DRA	WARP	MPH	FB%	WHF	CSP
2016	COL	MLB	26	12	9	0	27	27	158	147	15	4.0	6.7	117	58%	.286	1.37	3.87	5.43	-0.1	94.8	71.7	8.7	43.3
2017	COL	MLB	27	8	15	1	33	25	147²	136	20	4.7	7.3	120	59%	.283	1.44	4.69	5.28	0.4	96.3	63.7	10.6	43.2
2018	CHN	MLB	28	4	6	0	24	20	103²	92	9	8.2	7.4	85	55%	.286	1.80	5.30	7.28	-2.4	94.9	58.9	8.6	43.4
2019	CHN	MLB	29	2	2	0	24	5	45²	40	5	5.6	7.9	40	54%	.288	1.50	4.85	5.38	0.0	94.7	64.2	9.3	43.3

Breakout: 15%   Improve: 42%   Collapse: 20%   Attrition: 14%   MLB: 93%   *Comparables: Darryl Kile, Bob Gibson, Jim Maloney*

Get him out of Coors, they said. He's so much better on the road, they said. Well, Chatwood did give up fewer home runs, and he did have a remarkable season—for all the wrong reasons. Chatwood's control, often lacking, deteriorated to such a point that he led the league in walks despite barely reaching triple digits in innings. It was so bad, in fact, that opposing hitters put up a .403 on-base percentage against Chatwood, a mark that would rank fifth in the majors, better than J.D. Martinez or Christian Yelich. Once Cole Hamels arrived, Chatwood was surplus to requirements, first joining the bullpen—where he walked everyone—then suffering a demotion to Triple-A—where he also walked everyone. We would say that things can presumably only get better from here, but then again, Chatwood seems quite adept at debunking baseball myths.

Steve Cishek RHP   Born: 06/18/86   Age: 33   Bats: R   Throws: R   Height: 6'6"   Weight: 215   Origin: Round 5, 2007 Draft (#166 overall)

YEAR	TEAM	LVL	AGE	W	L	SV	G	GS	IP	H	HR	BB/9	K/9	K	GB%	BABIP	WHIP	ERA	DRA	WARP	MPH	FB%	WHF	CSP
2016	SEA	MLB	30	4	6	25	62	0	64	44	8	3.0	10.7	76	45%	.242	1.02	2.81	3.08	1.4	93.9	48.7	11.9	44.5
2017	SEA	MLB	31	1	1	1	23	0	20	13	3	3.2	6.8	15	61%	.185	1.00	3.15	4.78	0.1	92.1	51.5	8.2	46.5
2017	TBA	MLB	31	2	1	0	26	0	24²	13	0	2.6	9.5	26	52%	.220	0.81	1.09	3.41	0.5	92.4	49.5	13.7	44.3
2018	CHN	MLB	32	4	3	4	80	0	70¹	45	5	3.6	10.0	78	49%	.238	1.04	2.18	4.68	0.2	92.3	61.6	12	46.7
2019	CHN	MLB	33	3	1	0	49	0	51²	42	6	3.7	9.9	56	47%	.290	1.23	3.85	4.27	0.3	91.7	54.7	11.6	45.2

Breakout: 17%   Improve: 40%   Collapse: 33%   Attrition: 10%   MLB: 93%   Comparables: Damaso Marte, Tyler Clippard, Fernando Rodney

Craig Kimbrel. Aroldis Chapman. Kenley Jansen. Dellin Betances. Clayton Kershaw. If one of the first names springing to mind in response is Cishek's, you probably have an unhealthy obsession with the veteran sidearmer, or simply spend a lot of time looking at leaderboards. Those players are the active career ERA leaders, among whom Cishek ranks eighth. Neither the peripherals nor the eye test suggest that he is in that class, and yet his delivery and arsenal clearly enable him to consistently induce poor contact, as his .232 BABIP over the past three seasons can attest. The command can waver and free passes can be a problem against left-handers, the constant nemesis of those with an arm slot as low as Cishek's. For righties, he genuinely is one of the most challenging pitchers to face in all of baseball, making that stellar company far less ridiculous than it seems.

Yu Darvish RHP   Born: 08/16/86   Age: 32   Bats: R   Throws: R   Height: 6'5"   Weight: 220   Origin: International Free Agent, 2012

YEAR	TEAM	LVL	AGE	W	L	SV	G	GS	IP	H	HR	BB/9	K/9	K	GB%	BABIP	WHIP	ERA	DRA	WARP	MPH	FB%	WHF	CSP
2016	FRI	AA	29	1	1	0	5	5	20	14	1	3.2	10.8	24	50%	.277	1.05	2.25	2.99	0.5				
2016	TEX	MLB	29	7	5	0	17	17	100¹	81	12	2.8	11.8	132	40%	.290	1.12	3.41	2.97	2.7	97.1	69	14	48.6
2017	TEX	MLB	30	6	9	0	22	22	137	115	20	3.0	9.7	148	42%	.275	1.17	4.01	3.95	2.5	96.5	66.6	12.7	49.3
2017	LAN	MLB	30	4	3	0	9	9	49²	44	7	2.4	11.1	61	45%	.308	1.15	3.44	2.47	1.7	96.4	66.6	14	46.6
2018	CHN	MLB	31	1	3	0	8	8	40	36	7	4.7	11.0	49	42%	.293	1.42	4.95	4.73	0.3	96.1	69.1	11.3	50.4
2019	CHN	MLB	32	9	8	0	43	24	157¹	140	23	3.5	10.0	175	42%	.302	1.28	4.14	4.58	1.2	95.6	67	12.9	48.9

Breakout: 17%   Improve: 52%   Collapse: 16%   Attrition: 2%   MLB: 94%   Comparables: Ron Guidry, Jakie May, Mickey Lolich

Of all the universes in which Darvish signed a six-year, $126 million deal, 2018 was surely the version of his first year plucked directly from the Darkest Timeline. His season wasn't quite over in the time it takes to go and collect some pizza, but Theo Epstein left the offseason with an apparently strengthened rotation and suddenly found that his acquisitions had turned into the pitching equivalent of a burning apartment. Darvish made just three good starts, struggled through several more before landing on the DL with triceps tightness, and was ultimately ruled out for the season after months of uncertainty. The final definitive diagnosis of Darvish's elbow woes, a stress reaction, also doubled as a comment on the likely response of Epstein and most Cubs fans every time another piece of news broke. At least the 32-year-old should be ready for Spring Training, in time for another roll of the dice.

Jorge De La Rosa LHP   Born: 04/05/81   Age: 38   Bats: L   Throws: L   Height: 6'1"   Weight: 215   Origin: International Free Agent, 1998

YEAR	TEAM	LVL	AGE	W	L	SV	G	GS	IP	H	HR	BB/9	K/9	K	GB%	BABIP	WHIP	ERA	DRA	WARP	MPH	FB%	WHF	CSP
2016	ABQ	AAA	35	0	0	0	3	3	14²	14	0	4.9	6.8	11	56%	.311	1.50	4.30	4.11	0.2				
2016	COL	MLB	35	8	9	0	27	24	134	157	23	4.2	7.3	108	49%	.325	1.64	5.51	7.41	-3.2	92.1	35.7	11.2	43.7
2017	ARI	MLB	36	3	1	0	65	0	51¹	46	7	3.7	7.9	45	49%	.273	1.31	4.21	4.32	0.5	94.8	48.1	15.2	43.7
2018	ARI	MLB	37	0	2	0	42	0	35	37	4	4.9	6.9	27	55%	.295	1.60	4.63	5.67	-0.3	93.7	45.5	11.6	45.1
2018	CHN	MLB	37	0	0	1	17	0	21	14	0	3.4	8.6	20	49%	.246	1.05	1.29	5.91	-0.2	93.2	45.5	13.1	44.7
2019	CHN	MLB	38	3	2	0	19	6	48¹	43	6	4.0	7.9	43	49%	.291	1.34	4.34	4.81	0.2	91.7	40.5	12.1	43

Breakout: 16%   Improve: 38%   Collapse: 20%   Attrition: 5%   MLB: 74%   Comparables: Sal Maglie, Chuck Finley, Fritz Ostermueller

De La Rosa has never really been in the right place. Most of his career was spent in Colorado, hardly the ideal setting for any pitcher. For the past two seasons, a 150-point split in OPS between same-side and opposite-side hitters has left the veteran southpaw wondering where all the LOOGYs have gone. Its golden age was in 2015, when left-handed relievers made a record 763 appearances in which they faced just one batter. Randy Choate and Javier Lopez made 92 of those appearances alone, with their 51 and 41 games respectively ranking first and second all-time in single-batter outings for a season. As approaches to pitcher usage have evolved and the innings burden shifts ever more from starters to relievers, the consequent decline of the LOOGY has been rapid. The 2018 season saw the fewest such appearances since 2003, and no single reliever making more than 20, a figure that does not even crack the top 100 all-time. In other words, De La Rosa is in the wrong place again, on this occasion in time rather than space.

Brian Duensing LHP   Born: 02/22/83   Age: 36   Bats: L   Throws: L   Height: 6'0"   Weight: 200   Origin: Round 3, 2005 Draft (#84 overall)

YEAR	TEAM	LVL	AGE	W	L	SV	G	GS	IP	H	HR	BB/9	K/9	K	GB%	BABIP	WHIP	ERA	DRA	WARP	MPH	FB%	WHF	CSP
2016	OMA	AAA	33	1	0	2	12	0	20¹	16	0	2.2	8.4	19	50%	.276	1.03	3.10	3.47	0.3				
2016	BAL	MLB	33	1	0	0	14	0	13¹	13	2	2.0	6.8	10	26%	.275	1.20	4.05	6.32	-0.2	94.4	55.1	9.8	50.9
2017	CHN	MLB	34	1	1	1	68	0	62¹	58	6	2.6	8.8	61	49%	.306	1.22	2.74	4.04	0.8	93.6	48.9	11.3	42.2
2018	CHN	MLB	35	3	0	1	48	0	37²	42	6	6.9	5.7	24	43%	.298	1.88	7.65	7.34	-1.0	92.9	54.6	9.5	46.9
2019	CHN	MLB	36	1	0	0	29	0	31	30	4	4.5	7.3	25	44%	.298	1.47	4.88	5.42	-0.2	92.1	50.7	10.2	45.3

Breakout: 25%   Improve: 37%   Collapse: 20%   Attrition: 4%   MLB: 64%   Comparables: Matt Lindstrom, Steve Kline, Bob Locker

As if we needed any more evidence to indicate that relievers are volatile, Duensing went directly from his best ever relief season to his worst. The increased changeup usage that helped him to neutralize righties persisted, while the results did not. It sounds like hyperbole to say that opposite-handed hitters got on base like Mike Trout against Duensing, when in reality that is insufficient: their OBP was ten points *higher* than Trout's in 2018. The right-handers have always been the bigger problem, yet the peripherals were far from impressive against lefties either. Although his numbers might suggest he simply lost the plate, Duensing threw more pitches in the zone than he did in 2017. Hitters simply went after those more, and weren't buying what he was selling when he tried to get them to chase. Whether the cause was the left shoulder inflammation that ultimately landed him on the DL in August or not, Duensing needs to demonstrate that volatility works both ways if he is to remain in the majors much longer.

Carl Edwards Jr. RHP   Born: 09/03/91   Age: 27   Bats: R   Throws: R   Height: 6'3"   Weight: 170   Origin: Round 48, 2011 Draft (#1464 overall)

YEAR	TEAM	LVL	AGE	W	L	SV	G	GS	IP	H	HR	BB/9	K/9	K	GB%	BABIP	WHIP	ERA	DRA	WARP	MPH	FB%	WHF	CSP
2016	IOW	AAA	24	1	1	1	24	0	25¹	17	1	6.0	12.4	35	40%	.286	1.34	4.26	2.24	0.8				
2016	CHN	MLB	24	0	1	2	36	0	36	15	4	3.5	13.0	52	51%	.162	0.81	3.75	2.34	1.1	97.6	73.2	18.6	41.4
2017	CHN	MLB	25	5	4	0	73	0	66¹	29	6	5.2	12.8	94	46%	.193	1.01	2.98	3.05	1.6	96.8	70	16.1	42.8
2018	CHN	MLB	26	3	2	0	58	0	52	36	2	5.5	11.6	67	32%	.281	1.31	2.60	4.39	0.3	96.2	75.8	15.6	42.6
2019	CHN	MLB	27	2	1	0	49	0	51²	37	7	4.8	11.4	65	41%	.276	1.25	4.01	4.44	0.3	96.2	73.9	16.5	42.9

Breakout: 30%   Improve: 50%   Collapse: 35%   Attrition: 11%   MLB: 94%   *Comparables: Daniel Bard, Carlos Marmol, Bobby Jenks*

The unprecedented levels of BABIP suppression that Edwards enjoyed through the first hundred-plus innings of his career finally normalized, yet hardly to his detriment. That good fortune instead manifested in a miniscule home run rate, which helped the slight right-hander to a career-best ERA. Somehow, this came about despite a fundamental change in the batted ball mix, as Edwards lost his ability to generate grounders and experienced a huge jump in both fly-ball and line-drive rate. With his premium velocity and the huge horizontal movement on his offerings, he should remain difficult to hit, borne out by that BABIP and the career ISO allowed of under .100. This tightrope act gets ever more precarious as the strikeout rate drops, though, and Edwards shows no signs of curtailing the walks.

Jaime Garcia LHP   Born: 07/08/86   Age: 32   Bats: L   Throws: L   Height: 6'2"   Weight: 215   Origin: Round 22, 2005 Draft (#680 overall)

YEAR	TEAM	LVL	AGE	W	L	SV	G	GS	IP	H	HR	BB/9	K/9	K	GB%	BABIP	WHIP	ERA	DRA	WARP	MPH	FB%	WHF	CSP
2016	SLN	MLB	29	10	13	0	32	30	171²	179	26	3.0	7.9	150	58%	.305	1.37	4.67	3.88	2.9	93.1	63	9.7	47.6
2017	ATL	MLB	30	4	7	0	18	18	113	108	12	3.3	6.8	85	56%	.287	1.32	4.30	4.22	1.7	92.6	64	12.6	45.6
2017	MIN	MLB	30	1	0	0	1	1	6²	8	0	4.1	9.4	7	47%	.421	1.65	4.05	5.23	0.0	92.5	76.5	12.2	49.2
2017	NYA	MLB	30	0	3	0	8	8	37¹	41	6	4.8	8.9	37	54%	.327	1.63	4.82	4.48	0.5	92.1	52	10.5	41.6
2018	TOR	MLB	31	3	6	0	25	13	74¹	76	13	4.6	8.4	69	43%	.297	1.53	5.93	6.34	-1.0	90.9	65.9	9.2	46
2018	CHN	MLB	31	0	1	0	8	1	7²	6	0	7.0	4.7	4	54%	.250	1.57	4.70	5.64	0.0	90.5	76.8	10.7	49.3
2019	CHN	MLB	32	5	5	0	16	16	86¹	81	11	3.8	8.1	77	49%	.300	1.35	4.38	4.85	0.5	91.3	62.8	10.4	45.7

Breakout: 23%   Improve: 49%   Collapse: 26%   Attrition: 19%   MLB: 93%   *Comparables: Wandy Rodriguez, Matt Garza, Scott Kazmir*

Three months of ineffective starts finally forced the Blue Jays into moving Garcia to the bullpen, a role he had not regularly occupied since his rookie season. Most starters see their stuff play up following the transition, yet Garcia went the other way, his peak velocity dipping down below 91 mph over the final month after he was picked up by the Cubs. The last time the veteran lefty threw that softly he was about to have his torn labrum repaired, and it should be noted that he was on the DL twice in Toronto with shoulder inflammation. That said, the results were much better in relief, even if they should not have been. Garcia walked a batter every other inning and struck out just 16 over 20.1 frames as a reliever, yet compiled a 3.54 ERA. Even the elite ground ball rate which has served him so well declined significantly, while career highs in both walk and home run rates are about as good a combination as wine and beer. All that's left at this point is the hangover.

Cole Hamels LHP   Born: 12/27/83   Age: 35   Bats: L   Throws: L   Height: 6'4"   Weight: 205   Origin: Round 1, 2002 Draft (#17 overall)

YEAR	TEAM	LVL	AGE	W	L	SV	G	GS	IP	H	HR	BB/9	K/9	K	GB%	BABIP	WHIP	ERA	DRA	WARP	MPH	FB%	WHF	CSP
2016	TEX	MLB	32	15	5	0	32	32	200²	185	24	3.5	9.0	200	50%	.299	1.31	3.32	3.91	3.3	94.9	66.7	13.1	42.3
2017	TEX	MLB	33	11	6	0	24	24	148	125	18	3.2	6.4	105	48%	.251	1.20	4.20	5.41	0.3	93.5	66.4	10	45.7
2018	TEX	MLB	34	5	9	0	20	20	114¹	115	23	3.3	9.0	114	45%	.296	1.37	4.72	5.17	0.2	93.3	60.4	13	45.7
2018	CHN	MLB	34	4	3	0	12	12	76¹	61	6	2.7	8.7	74	49%	.286	1.10	2.36	3.46	1.6	94.5	60.4	12.6	46.3
2019	CHN	MLB	35	11	10	0	29	29	174	157	22	3.3	8.5	164	46%	.297	1.27	4.21	4.66	1.3	92.8	62.7	11.9	44.1

Breakout: 18%   Improve: 37%   Collapse: 30%   Attrition: 12%   MLB: 87%   *Comparables: J.A. Happ, Jorge De La Rosa, Sam Jones*

Every now and again, decline phases seem to go almost exactly as we expect. The warning signs around Hamels had been flashing for a little while, so when the 34-year-old labored through four months with Texas it appeared that this was simply one of those cases. His chances of landing on a contender seemed to have been spectacularly torpedoed by a July in which he allowed 21 runs in just 17 innings. The Cubs were undeterred, though, and brought Hamels to Wrigley at the deadline, where he promptly looked like an ace again. It may have seemed as though Chicago fixed Hamels, when in truth the major changes—mechanical improvements that brought a velocity bump, and increased four-seam usage instead of the sinker—were both in progress well before he arrived in Illinois. He'll return in 2019 with the aim of staying ahead of the aging curve.

Kyle Hendricks RHP   Born: 12/07/89   Age: 29   Bats: R   Throws: R   Height: 6'3"   Weight: 190   Origin: Round 8, 2011 Draft (#264 overall)

YEAR	TEAM	LVL	AGE	W	L	SV	G	GS	IP	H	HR	BB/9	K/9	K	GB%	BABIP	WHIP	ERA	DRA	WARP	MPH	FB%	WHF	CSP
2016	CHN	MLB	26	16	8	0	31	30	190	142	15	2.1	8.1	170	50%	.250	0.98	2.13	2.62	6.0	90.2	65.1	10.5	45.3
2017	CHN	MLB	27	7	5	0	24	24	139²	126	17	2.6	7.9	123	52%	.281	1.19	3.03	3.45	3.3	87.6	64.1	9	46.7
2018	CHN	MLB	28	14	11	0	33	33	199	184	22	2.0	7.3	161	49%	.281	1.15	3.44	3.13	5.0	88.5	61.8	9.7	50.4
2019	CHN	MLB	29	10	9	0	29	29	165¹	147	18	2.6	7.9	145	48%	.290	1.18	3.83	4.23	2.1	88.1	63.3	9.7	47.9

Breakout: 17%   Improve: 45%   Collapse: 17%   Attrition: 10%   MLB: 96%   *Comparables: Garrett Richards, Dallas Keuchel, Johnny Cueto*

Only four active pitchers have started more than 100 games and still have a career ERA lower than Hendricks: Clayton Kershaw, Jacob deGrom, Chris Sale and Madison Bumgarner. Hendricks could not quite keep his career mark below 3.00, but the caliber of the company is a testament to the Professor's exceptional command and sequencing. It's even more impressive when you consider that the only two pitchers with lower average four-seam velocity were Brent Suter and Jason Vargas. There's always a temptation to point out how quickly things can go wrong for a player with an 88-mph fastball if everything is not exactly right, but Hendricks has spent most of his 789 major league innings getting everything exactly right.

Brandon Kintzler RHP   Born: 08/01/84   Age: 34   Bats: R   Throws: R   Height: 6'0"   Weight: 194   Origin: Round 40, 2004 Draft (#1182 overall)

YEAR	TEAM	LVL	AGE	W	L	SV	G	GS	IP	H	HR	BB/9	K/9	K	GB%	BABIP	WHIP	ERA	DRA	WARP	MPH	FB%	WHF	CSP
2016	ROC	AAA	31	4	1	0	10	0	15¹	15	0	1.8	6.5	11	56%	.326	1.17	3.52	3.20	0.3				
2016	MIN	MLB	31	0	2	17	54	0	54¹	59	5	1.3	5.8	35	63%	.310	1.23	3.15	5.06	-0.1	95.2	87.8	7.5	49.4
2017	MIN	MLB	32	2	2	28	45	0	45¹	41	3	2.2	5.4	27	54%	.273	1.15	2.78	4.76	0.2	95.1	80.9	6.5	46.9
2017	WAS	MLB	32	2	1	1	27	0	26	25	2	1.7	4.2	12	57%	.267	1.15	3.46	5.84	-0.2	94.7	83.2	4.8	54.7
2018	WAS	MLB	33	1	2	2	45	0	42²	40	2	2.7	6.5	31	49%	.302	1.24	3.59	6.36	-0.7	93.9	83.6	7.4	48.9
2018	CHN	MLB	33	2	1	0	25	0	18	27	3	4.5	6.0	12	53%	.381	2.00	7.00	6.40	-0.3	94.5	85.8	8.4	45.4
2019	CHN	MLB	34	1	1	0	29	0	31	31	3	3.3	6.7	23	51%	.307	1.37	4.32	4.79	0.0	93.5	82.8	6.9	48

Breakout: 19%   Improve: 32%   Collapse: 26%   Attrition: 9%   MLB: 78%   *Comparables: Brian Duensing, Paul Quantrill, Matt Albers*

Eyebrows were raised when the Nationals shipped Kintzler to Chicago for Jhon Romero, an unheralded reliever at High-A. The salacious rumors for the swap soon followed, with whispers that the real reason for the deal was that in a clubhouse leakier than the Oakland Coliseum's plumbing, Washington believed Kintzler was the prime source responsible for a Jeff Passan story on team unrest. By the time the season was over, one had to wonder whether the Nationals simply had perfect timing. Kintzler's spell in Chicago was a study in how one can pitch to contact with below-average command. To make matters worse, his ground-ball rate has dropped from elite to simply above-average. On his current trajectory (his DRA has now increased for the fourth straight season) it won't be leaks to the press that keep him out of a major-league clubhouse for good.

Jon Lester LHP   Born: 01/07/84   Age: 35   Bats: L   Throws: L   Height: 6'4"   Weight: 240   Origin: Round 2, 2002 Draft (#57 overall)

YEAR	TEAM	LVL	AGE	W	L	SV	G	GS	IP	H	HR	BB/9	K/9	K	GB%	BABIP	WHIP	ERA	DRA	WARP	MPH	FB%	WHF	CSP
2016	CHN	MLB	32	19	5	0	32	32	202²	154	21	2.3	8.7	197	48%	.256	1.02	2.44	2.77	6.0	94.4	58.5	11.2	44.3
2017	CHN	MLB	33	13	8	0	32	32	180²	179	26	3.0	9.0	180	48%	.310	1.32	4.33	3.71	3.8	92.7	50.6	11.3	42
2018	CHN	MLB	34	18	6	0	32	32	181²	174	24	3.2	7.4	149	40%	.290	1.31	3.32	4.44	1.8	92.5	50.3	8.9	47
2019	CHN	MLB	35	10	10	0	29	29	174	168	24	3.0	8.0	154	44%	.302	1.29	4.32	4.78	1.1	91.9	51.5	10.1	43.8

Breakout: 20%   Improve: 41%   Collapse: 25%   Attrition: 12%   MLB: 93%   *Comparables: Jeff Fassero, Koji Uehara, John Smoltz*

Another year, another 30-plus starts for Lester. 2018 took his annual streak of at least 31 starts to eleven, a number only two other active pitchers (Justin Verlander and James Shields) have reached at all, let alone consecutively. Despite the ERA, this was far from a vintage performance. The diminished innings total from 2017 was almost exactly replicated, only this time with a huge decline in strikeouts and grounders. Lester's primary whiff-inducing pitches, the changeup and curveball, both missed fewer bats than at any point since he arrived in Chicago. On the plus side, his well-documented inability to control the running game is barely an issue now with Willson Contreras behind the plate: for the second straight year, 39 percent of thieves were caught in the act with Lester on the mound, and he even picked off another runner for good measure. It seems increasingly likely that day Lester doesn't reach 30 starts will come only when he decides to hang up his cleats for good.

Dillon Maples RHP   Born: 05/09/92   Age: 27   Bats: R   Throws: R   Height: 6'2"   Weight: 225   Origin: Round 14, 2011 Draft (#429 overall)

YEAR	TEAM	LVL	AGE	W	L	SV	G	GS	IP	H	HR	BB/9	K/9	K	GB%	BABIP	WHIP	ERA	DRA	WARP	MPH	FB%	WHF	CSP
2016	MYR	A+	24	0	1	0	9	0	7	9	0	9.0	7.7	6	69%	.346	2.29	7.71	6.90	-0.1				
2016	SBN	A	24	1	2	9	19	0	25	18	1	3.6	6.1	17	76%	.233	1.12	3.24	3.86	0.2				
2017	MYR	A+	25	4	0	3	21	0	31¹	21	2	4.3	12.6	44	65%	.288	1.15	2.01	2.57	0.9				
2017	TEN	AA	25	1	1	6	14	0	13²	11	0	7.2	18.4	28	64%	.440	1.61	3.29	0.98	0.6				
2017	IOW	AAA	25	1	2	4	17	0	18¹	12	1	5.4	13.7	28	63%	.297	1.25	1.96	0.82	0.9				
2017	CHN	MLB	25	0	0	0	6	0	5¹	6	0	10.1	18.6	11	50%	.600	2.25	10.12	1.81	0.2	98.2	43.1	12.8	48.9
2018	IOW	AAA	26	2	3	10	41	0	38²	22	1	9.1	17.5	75	57%	.350	1.58	2.79	0.27	2.1				
2018	CHN	MLB	26	1	0	0	9	0	5¹	7	2	8.4	15.2	9	38%	.455	2.25	11.81	4.86	0.0	98.0	23.9	6.3	47.5
2019	CHN	MLB	27	1	0	0	19	0	20²	16	3	6.3	12.1	28	53%	.318	1.50	4.37	4.85	0.0	97.6	31.6	8.9	48.7

Breakout: 11%   Improve: 22%   Collapse: 20%   Attrition: 25%   MLB: 46%   *Comparables: Jack Leathersich, Cesar Cabral, Jaye Chapman*

For those of the opinion that there are not enough balls in play in modern baseball, Maples represents the epitome of the problem. He was practically a two-true outcomes player at Triple-A, with 64.6 percent of the batters he faced either walking or striking out. Unfortunately, the third true outcome also showed up in his second brief major league look. For someone who gets whiffs at almost unprecedented levels, Maples has been surprisingly hittable when batters actually accomplish the rare feat of putting the ball in play against him, an issue that is tied to how much he really knows where the ball is going. A step forward in control seems to be all that separates Maples from a late-inning role, but the magnitude of that step might be even greater than his strikeout rate.

Alec Mills   RHP   Born: 11/30/91   Age: 27   Bats: R   Throws: R   Height: 6'4"   Weight: 190   Origin: Round 22, 2012 Draft (#673 overall)

YEAR	TEAM	LVL	AGE	W	L	SV	G	GS	IP	H	HR	BB/9	K/9	K	GB%	BABIP	WHIP	ERA	DRA	WARP	MPH	FB%	WHF	CSP
2016	NWA	AA	24	1	2	0	12	12	67²	57	2	1.6	9.0	68	44%	.314	1.02	2.39	3.73	1.1				
2016	OMA	AAA	24	4	3	0	12	11	58	62	8	2.9	8.4	54	47%	.323	1.40	4.19	3.97	0.9				
2016	KCA	MLB	24	0	0	0	3	0	3¹	3	0	13.5	10.8	4	44%	.333	2.40	13.50	7.15	-0.1	94.2	70.9	8.1	34.2
2017	IOW	AAA	25	2	0	0	3	3	14	12	0	1.9	4.5	7	47%	.255	1.07	3.21	5.61	0.0				
2018	IOW	AAA	26	5	12	0	23	23	124²	121	10	3.0	7.8	108	42%	.303	1.30	4.84	3.78	2.5				
2018	CHN	MLB	26	0	1	0	7	2	18	11	1	3.5	11.5	23	51%	.250	1.00	4.00	2.42	0.6	92.3	58.9	12	47.1
2019	CHN	MLB	27	3	2	0	24	5	47	47	6	3.2	7.9	41	43%	.309	1.35	4.41	4.88	0.1	92.0	61.4	11.5	42.8

Breakout: 6%   Improve: 12%   Collapse: 30%   Attrition: 30%   MLB: 52%   *Comparables: Luke Farrell, Tyler Pill, Edwar Cabrera*

As a player primarily acquired for rotation depth, Mills has been called upon much less than he would have liked, especially given the issues Chicago had with their primary options. That might have something to do with the fact that his first scoreless outing of the year did not come until he made his Cubs debut as a reliever in late July. At least Mills was able to provide volume in the minors, frequently going six-plus innings, and he largely impressed in his major league work. Given that most of that work came out of the bullpen, a swingman role might be his best path to major league starts.

Mike Montgomery   LHP   Born: 07/01/89   Age: 29   Bats: L   Throws: L   Height: 6'5"   Weight: 215   Origin: Round 1, 2008 Draft (#36 overall)

YEAR	TEAM	LVL	AGE	W	L	SV	G	GS	IP	H	HR	BB/9	K/9	K	GB%	BABIP	WHIP	ERA	DRA	WARP	MPH	FB%	WHF	CSP
2016	SEA	MLB	26	3	4	0	32	2	61²	49	3	2.6	7.9	54	59%	.272	1.09	2.34	4.02	0.8	96.4	47.8	11.2	45.7
2016	CHN	MLB	26	1	1	0	17	5	38¹	30	5	4.7	8.9	38	61%	.258	1.30	2.82	2.48	1.2	95.5	47.8	13.6	45.1
2017	CHN	MLB	27	7	8	3	44	14	130²	103	10	3.8	6.9	100	59%	.253	1.21	3.38	4.31	1.6	94.1	53	8.9	44.6
2018	CHN	MLB	28	5	6	0	38	19	124	131	10	2.8	6.2	86	53%	.309	1.37	3.99	4.57	0.9	93.3	49.6	9.9	49.6
2019	CHN	MLB	29	4	3	0	45	6	73	66	7	3.4	7.5	61	54%	.293	1.29	4.08	4.52	0.6	93.5	50.5	10	46.9

Breakout: 26%   Improve: 51%   Collapse: 21%   Attrition: 14%   MLB: 92%   *Comparables: Jhoulys Chacin, Alex Colome, Clay Buchholz*

Nineteen starts. Nineteen relief appearances. Montgomery's numbers look like those of the quintessential swingman, making spot starts when needed and providing relief innings if the regular starters were healthy. That moniker implies more role changes than Montgomery really made: he started the year with 18 relief appearances before moving into the rotation in late May, with just a solitary bullpen outing in August interrupting that string of 19 starts. Surprisingly neat split aside, he did exactly what the Cubs have him on the roster for: fill in with solid innings wherever a gap arises. Contrary to his previous results, Montgomery was much better as starter than reliever in 2018, but it doesn't seem he'll get a chance to pitch a full season in the role with the Cubs.

Brandon Morrow   RHP   Born: 07/26/84   Age: 34   Bats: R   Throws: R   Height: 6'3"   Weight: 205   Origin: Round 1, 2006 Draft (#5 overall)

YEAR	TEAM	LVL	AGE	W	L	SV	G	GS	IP	H	HR	BB/9	K/9	K	GB%	BABIP	WHIP	ERA	DRA	WARP	MPH	FB%	WHF	CSP
2016	LEL	A+	31	0	1	0	2	2	11²	15	1	2.3	6.2	8	41%	.368	1.54	6.94	5.50	0.0				
2016	SAN	AA	31	1	1	0	2	2	10¹	18	3	3.5	3.5	4	40%	.375	2.13	7.84	5.42	0.0				
2016	ELP	AAA	31	0	0	2	12	2	21	29	2	3.9	9.0	21	52%	.403	1.81	6.43	4.55	0.1				
2016	SDN	MLB	31	1	0	0	18	0	16	19	2	1.7	4.5	8	47%	.309	1.38	1.69	5.03	0.0	97.1	48	11.9	50.7
2017	OKL	AAA	32	0	5	6	20	0	20	25	5	2.2	9.9	22	56%	.339	1.50	7.20	3.38	0.4				
2017	LAN	MLB	32	6	0	2	45	0	43²	31	0	1.9	10.3	50	46%	.282	0.92	2.06	2.98	1.1	99.6	59.5	16.8	47.1
2018	CHN	MLB	33	0	0	22	35	0	30²	24	2	2.6	9.1	31	53%	.278	1.08	1.47	3.66	0.4	99.2	72.8	14.1	48.2
2019	CHN	MLB	34	2	1	30	44	0	46¹	44	5	3.4	8.9	46	47%	.315	1.32	3.93	4.35	0.3	97.9	63	14.8	47.8

Breakout: 16%   Improve: 36%   Collapse: 16%   Attrition: 11%   MLB: 70%   *Comparables: Zach Duke, John Bale, Dale Thayer*

It looked as though Morrow had finally done the impossible and found a role that allowed him to both stay healthy and consistently perform at the elite level he has teased us with throughout his career. Naturally, it was too good to be true. Although Morrow proved that his 2017 dominance was no fluke, he also returned to a role that he is sadly more familiar with than any other: occupying a spot on the 60-day DL.

James Norwood   RHP   Born: 12/24/93   Age: 25   Bats: R   Throws: R   Height: 6'2"   Weight: 215   Origin: Round 7, 2014 Draft (#199 overall)

YEAR	TEAM	LVL	AGE	W	L	SV	G	GS	IP	H	HR	BB/9	K/9	K	GB%	BABIP	WHIP	ERA	DRA	WARP	MPH	FB%	WHF	CSP
2016	SBN	A	22	3	1	6	22	0	26²	30	0	2.7	11.8	35	47%	.400	1.42	3.71	2.10	0.8				
2016	MYR	A+	22	1	0	1	8	0	9¹	12	0	1.9	7.7	8	44%	.375	1.50	1.93	3.18	0.2				
2017	MYR	A+	23	3	0	6	27	0	39	32	1	3.7	9.5	41	37%	.313	1.23	2.31	3.14	0.8				
2017	TEN	AA	23	1	3	1	14	0	18²	22	1	4.3	9.2	19	46%	.362	1.66	5.30	3.66	0.3				
2018	TEN	AA	24	1	2	2	25	0	32²	25	2	3.3	9.9	36	40%	.277	1.13	2.48	3.53	0.5				
2018	IOW	AAA	24	1	1	0	15	0	17²	11	1	6.1	10.7	21	34%	.250	1.30	2.55	3.88	0.3				
2018	CHN	MLB	24	0	1	0	11	0	11	14	0	4.1	8.2	10	31%	.359	1.73	4.09	5.45	-0.1	99.7	71.4	8.4	48.7
2019	CHN	MLB	25	0	0	0	10	0	10¹	10	1	4.4	9.5	11	39%	.315	1.43	4.54	5.03	0.0	99.4	73.1	8.6	49.9

Breakout: 6%   Improve: 10%   Collapse: 6%   Attrition: 8%   MLB: 16%   *Comparables: Kevin McCarthy, Angel Nesbitt, Chad Smith*

Halfway through 2018, Norwood probably wasn't even the most famous James Norwood in sports: his British counterpart scored the goal that ensured Tranmere Rovers returned to the English Football League. If that seems like a particularly low bar to fail to clear, bear in mind that the American Norwood struggled to deal with Double-A hitters less than a year earlier and was yet to make his major league debut. The Cubs soon addressed that after his success at both Tennessee and Iowa, calling him up for a handful of games in early July and then bringing him back for good in late August. Norwood relies heavily on his big fastball, which sits 98 and touches 100, throwing it over 70 percent of the time. While that's not a terrible pitch to rely on, a lack of convincing alternatives leaves him vulnerable to hitters at the highest level.

Jose Quintana LHP Born: 01/24/89 Age: 30 Bats: R Throws: L Height: 6'1" Weight: 220 Origin: International Free Agent, 2006

YEAR	TEAM	LVL	AGE	W	L	SV	G	GS	IP	H	HR	BB/9	K/9	K	GB%	BABIP	WHIP	ERA	DRA	WARP	MPH	FB%	WHF	CSP
2016	CHA	MLB	27	13	12	0	32	32	208	192	22	2.2	7.8	181	41%	.293	1.16	3.20	4.13	2.9	94.6	66.8	8.5	47.7
2017	CHA	MLB	28	4	8	0	18	18	104¹	98	14	3.5	9.4	109	45%	.301	1.32	4.49	4.59	1.1	93.3	62.2	9.3	44.7
2017	CHN	MLB	28	7	3	0	14	14	84¹	72	9	2.2	10.5	98	48%	.300	1.10	3.74	3.94	1.5	94.0	63.7	9.3	46.4
2018	CHN	MLB	29	13	11	0	32	32	174¹	162	25	3.5	8.2	158	45%	.282	1.32	4.03	4.93	0.8	93.2	68.3	8.8	49
2019	*CHN*	*MLB*	*30*	*11*	*10*	*0*	*30*	*30*	*171*	*161*	*21*	*3.1*	*8.7*	*166*	*43%*	*.308*	*1.29*	*4.01*	*4.44*	*1.7*	*93.0*	*65.8*	*8.9*	*47.3*

Breakout: 5%   Improve: 37%   Collapse: 34%   Attrition: 11%   MLB: 96%   *Comparables: Gavin Floyd, Yovani Gallardo, Gaylord Perry*

You know when you keep telling someone how good something is, and then when they finally try it, it's just not quite right? A different chef was working the day you went back to a restaurant, the drink you tried on the beach on vacation just doesn't taste the same in your backyard, the band who blew you away in a small venue are underwhelming in an arena. For years, Quintana's talents went rather underappreciated on a White Sox team that never finished better than fourth in any of his full seasons, although Cubs fans got a half-season glimpse of the talent before a 2017 NLCS implosion. Finally given a whole campaign to showcase his talents on the North Side for the division favorites, Quintana had the worst season of his career, frequently losing his trademark command and getting crushed the third time through the order. Even if it's just for one year, it would be nice if Quintana was exactly as good as you've been telling everyone.

Randy Rosario LHP Born: 05/18/94 Age: 25 Bats: L Throws: L Height: 6'1" Weight: 200 Origin: International Free Agent, 2010

YEAR	TEAM	LVL	AGE	W	L	SV	G	GS	IP	H	HR	BB/9	K/9	K	GB%	BABIP	WHIP	ERA	DRA	WARP	MPH	FB%	WHF	CSP
2016	FTM	A+	22	6	6	1	21	16	94¹	102	3	3.2	6.5	68	58%	.330	1.44	3.34	3.76	1.8				
2016	CHT	AA	22	0	1	0	4	0	6	6	1	7.5	15.0	10	50%	.385	1.83	10.50	2.07	0.2				
2017	MIN	MLB	23	0	0	0	2	0	2¹	7	1	0.0	7.7	2	67%	.545	3.00	30.86	7.34	-0.1	96.2	67.2	6.2	41.6
2017	CHT	AA	23	1	0	1	32	0	57¹	57	4	3.6	7.1	45	51%	.312	1.40	4.08	3.53	0.9				
2018	IOW	AAA	24	0	0	0	15	0	22²	13	1	2.4	6.0	15	48%	.190	0.84	0.79	3.77	0.4				
2018	CHN	MLB	24	4	0	1	44	0	46²	47	5	4.2	5.8	30	53%	.294	1.48	3.66	5.16	-0.1	95.1	60	10.3	47.9
2019	*CHN*	*MLB*	*25*	*2*	*1*	*0*	*34*	*0*	*36*	*36*	*4*	*4.1*	*7.4*	*29*	*49%*	*.310*	*1.45*	*4.55*	*5.04*	*-0.1*	*94.9*	*61.9*	*10.2*	*46.2*

Breakout: 23%   Improve: 34%   Collapse: 26%   Attrition: 44%   MLB: 67%   *Comparables: Enrique Gonzalez, Dovydas Neverauskas, Carlos Frias*

Rosario keeps the infield grass well-trimmed with his four-seam/sinker/slider combo, all of which induce grounders at an above-average rate. It's a contact-focused profile that's tough on worms and left-handed hitters alike. Righties feel considerably more comfortable, a problem present throughout the minors and exacerbated by major-league competition, where an .876 OPS against sums up Rosario's struggles. He has toyed with incorporating a changeup, which would go a long way towards addressing such issues, although it is far from ready to feature on a regular basis. Until such an improvement is made, he realistically remains a lefty-only option unless a grounder is desperately needed and his manager is feeling lucky.

Pedro Strop RHP Born: 06/13/85 Age: 34 Bats: R Throws: R Height: 6'1" Weight: 220 Origin: International Free Agent, 2002

YEAR	TEAM	LVL	AGE	W	L	SV	G	GS	IP	H	HR	BB/9	K/9	K	GB%	BABIP	WHIP	ERA	DRA	WARP	MPH	FB%	WHF	CSP
2016	CHN	MLB	31	2	2	0	54	0	47¹	27	4	2.9	11.4	60	61%	.221	0.89	2.85	2.32	1.4	97.0	42.4	16.4	41.8
2017	CHN	MLB	32	5	4	0	69	0	60¹	45	4	3.9	9.7	65	61%	.270	1.18	2.83	3.23	1.3	97.2	55.7	16.3	43.1
2018	CHN	MLB	33	6	1	13	60	0	59²	38	4	3.2	8.6	57	48%	.222	0.99	2.26	3.67	0.9	96.4	38.6	17	42.7
2019	*CHN*	*MLB*	*34*	*3*	*1*	*5*	*53*	*0*	*56²*	*44*	*6*	*3.7*	*9.4*	*59*	*52%*	*.277*	*1.19*	*3.85*	*4.26*	*0.4*	*95.6*	*45.3*	*16.3*	*41.9*

Breakout: 9%   Improve: 29%   Collapse: 44%   Attrition: 7%   MLB: 91%   *Comparables: Heath Bell, Francisco Cordero, Billy Wagner*

There's a legitimate case to be made that Strop is one of the best Cubs relievers of all time. Those qualifiers might veer dangerously close to 'fun' fact territory, but consider that Strop's ERA ranks second all-time among Chicago relievers with at least 100 innings pitched, behind only Hall of Famer Bruce Sutter. Or what about his 28.2 percent strikeout rate, good for third on the same list? Orioles fans do not need more reasons to feel bad about the Jake Arrieta trade, so we can gloss over the fact that Strop is one of the twenty best relievers by WARP in the last half-decade. His lowest strikeout rate since arriving in Chicago suggests that age is starting to diminish the stuff just a little, but he remains extremely difficult to square up. He'll go into 2019 looking for a sixth straight year of an ERA beginning with two.

Jen-Ho Tseng RHP Born: 10/03/94 Age: 24 Bats: L Throws: R Height: 6'1" Weight: 210 Origin: International Free Agent, 2013

YEAR	TEAM	LVL	AGE	W	L	SV	G	GS	IP	H	HR	BB/9	K/9	K	GB%	BABIP	WHIP	ERA	DRA	WARP	MPH	FB%	WHF	CSP
2016	TEN	AA	21	6	8	0	22	22	113¹	138	12	2.5	5.5	69	49%	.327	1.50	4.29	3.59	2.0				
2017	TEN	AA	22	7	3	0	15	15	90¹	79	7	2.4	8.3	83	41%	.281	1.14	2.99	2.96	2.4				
2017	IOW	AAA	22	6	1	0	9	9	55	48	5	2.3	6.4	39	55%	.264	1.13	1.80	3.51	1.3				
2017	CHN	MLB	22	1	0	0	2	1	6	5	2	3.0	12.0	8	33%	.231	1.17	7.50	5.20	0.0	93.5	51.9	11.3	44.2
2018	CHN	MLB	23	0	0	0	1	1	2	4	1	0.0	13.5	3	57%	.500	2.00	13.50	2.19	0.1	91.8	53.9	17.9	45.2
2018	IOW	AAA	23	2	15	0	26	26	136¹	159	20	2.9	7.6	115	50%	.327	1.49	6.27	3.87	2.6				
2019	*CHN*	*MLB*	*24*	*1*	*1*	*0*	*3*	*3*	*15*	*15*	*2*	*3.0*	*7.3*	*12*	*46%*	*.305*	*1.33*	*4.29*	*4.75*	*0.1*	*92.8*	*54.1*	*13.8*	*46.1*

Breakout: 7%   Improve: 22%   Collapse: 13%   Attrition: 33%   MLB: 43%   *Comparables: Chad Jenkins, Richard Bleier, Nick Tepesch*

After his first run through the Pacific Coast League, Tseng must have wondered what all the fuss was about. He found out in unpleasant fashion during his second attempt. Many current major-league contributors have failed to conquer the PCL and its offensive demons, so Tseng's misfortune does not automatically condemn him to failure in the majors. It does provide a stark illustration of both the tightrope command-first types like Tseng have to walk and the risks of allowing so many balls in play, particularly in hitter-friendly parks. With four pitches that he can throw for strikes, including a plus change, a role as a number four or five is still realistic. There's a temptation to point to another command-first starter on this roster who is far more than simply the sum of his parts, but a huge spectrum of outcomes lies between not being able to start in the majors and Kyle Hendricks. Tseng could end up in the former category and although he certainly won't be the latter, the heights of his command will dictate exactly how far along that spectrum he moves, if at all.

Duane Underwood RHP Born: 07/20/94 Age: 24 Bats: R Throws: R Height: 6'2" Weight: 210 Origin: Round 2, 2012 Draft (#67 overall)

YEAR	TEAM	LVL	AGE	W	L	SV	G	GS	IP	H	HR	BB/9	K/9	K	GB%	BABIP	WHIP	ERA	DRA	WARP	MPH	FB%	WHF	CSP
2016	TEN	AA	21	0	5	0	13	13	58²	66	7	4.8	7.1	46	48%	.317	1.65	4.91	3.67	1.0				
2016	SBN	A	21	0	1	0	3	3	8²	5	0	4.2	12.5	12	44%	.278	1.04	2.08	2.35	0.3				
2017	TEN	AA	22	13	7	0	25	24	138	130	13	3.3	6.4	98	45%	.282	1.30	4.43	3.98	1.9				
2018	CHN	MLB	23	0	1	0	1	1	4	2	1	6.8	6.8	3	50%	.111	1.25	2.25	7.98	-0.1	94.8	53.3	5.2	46.1
2018	IOW	AAA	23	4	10	0	27	20	119¹	127	8	2.8	7.9	105	44%	.334	1.37	4.53	3.75	2.4				
2019	CHN	MLB	24	2	1	0	21	2	30²	29	4	3.6	7.9	27	43%	.302	1.36	4.51	5.00	0.0	94.6	54.8	5.3	47.5

Breakout: 13% Improve: 21% Collapse: 11% Attrition: 29% MLB: 38% *Comparables: Williams Perez, Anthony Ranaudo, Shawn Morimando*

For some time, there have been suggestions that Underwood might be better off in the bullpen, where his fastball could play up and his inconsistency represents less of an issue. After an unremarkable few months of starting at Triple-A, that transition finally happened, with his final seven appearances coming in relief. While Underwood's results weren't better in that small sample, it's one sign that the team might finally share that opinion. The fact that his major league debut was also the only start he made in 2018 despite several opportunities arising in Chicago is another hint that his prospects as a starter are fading.

Justin Wilson LHP Born: 08/18/87 Age: 31 Bats: L Throws: L Height: 6'2" Weight: 205 Origin: Round 5, 2008 Draft (#144 overall)

YEAR	TEAM	LVL	AGE	W	L	SV	G	GS	IP	H	HR	BB/9	K/9	K	GB%	BABIP	WHIP	ERA	DRA	WARP	MPH	FB%	WHF	CSP
2016	DET	MLB	28	4	5	1	66	0	58²	61	6	2.6	10.0	65	56%	.340	1.33	4.14	4.15	0.6	97.7	65.1	13.7	46.3
2017	DET	MLB	29	3	4	13	42	0	40¹	22	5	3.6	12.3	55	38%	.210	0.94	2.68	3.24	0.9	97.1	64.3	16	49.2
2017	CHN	MLB	29	1	0	0	23	0	17²	18	0	9.7	12.7	25	37%	.391	2.09	5.09	6.03	-0.2	97.0	64.3	9.2	46.5
2018	CHN	MLB	30	4	5	0	71	0	54²	45	5	5.4	11.4	69	37%	.310	1.43	3.46	4.65	0.2	96.0	75.4	13.4	51.9
2019	CHN	MLB	31	2	1	2	47	0	49¹	42	6	4.3	10.7	59	43%	.307	1.32	3.99	4.41	0.2	95.9	68.6	13.4	48.9

Breakout: 38% Improve: 48% Collapse: 32% Attrition: 18% MLB: 96% *Comparables: Francisco Rodriguez, Steve Cishek, Joel Hanrahan*

For some reason, Wilson and the Cubs have been about as good a combination as a Chicago hot dog and ketchup. His spell as one of the game's most devastating closers lasted only a few months with the Tigers, just long enough to convince the Cubs they were getting an elite bullpen arm. Any semblance of control fell off the back of the truck on I-94, even if the ERA might fool us into thinking 2018 was just fine. If this were a heartwarming sports movie, the lovable clubhouse attendant would have turned up at just the right time—just before Wilson entered Game 163 against the Brewers, for example—brandishing Wilson's magic glove, the source of all his control. Instead Orlando Arcia singled off a misplaced Wilson slider to start the game-winning rally and the Cubs were, once again, left wondering what happened to the guy they traded for.

LINEOUTS

Hitters

HITTER	POS	TEAM	LVL	AGE	PA	R	2B	3B	HR	RBI	BB	K	SB	CS	AVG/OBP/SLG	DRC+	VORP	BABIP	BRR	FRAA	WARP
Brennen Davis	CF	CUT	Rk	18	72	9	2	0	0	3	10	12	6	1	.298/.431/.333	121	4.4	.370	0.0	CF(10): 0.6, RF(4): -0.6	0.3
Taylor Davis	C	IOW	AAA	28	409	38	18	0	4	41	40	57	0	2	.275/.348/.360	85	13.8	.315	-2.7	C(67): 8.1, 1B(24): -1.3	1.4
	C	CHN	MLB	28	6	0	0	0	0	2	0	1	0	0	.400/.333/.400	90	0.5	.400	0.0	C(3): 0.1, 1B(1): 0.0	0.0
Johnny Field	RF	TBA	MLB	26	179	20	9	0	6	14	7	58	4	0	.213/.253/.373	63	-0.9	.286	0.5	RF(25): -0.5, LF(23): 1.4	-0.2
	RF	DUR	AAA	26	40	6	3	0	0	4	2	7	1	1	.351/.400/.432	88	3.3	.433	1.2	CF(6): -1.3, RF(2): 0.0	0.0
	RF	ROC	AAA	26	40	1	1	0	0	1	2	8	1	0	.135/.200/.162	93	-4.0	.172	0.1	RF(7): -0.5, LF(2): -0.6	0.1
	RF	MIN	MLB	26	54	8	4	0	3	7	0	14	0	0	.250/.259/.500	73	2.7	.278	0.5	LF(11): -0.7, RF(7): 0.1	-0.1
Cole Roederer	CF	CUT	Rk	18	161	30	4	4	5	24	18	37	13	4	.275/.354/.465	141	13.6	.337	2.1	CF(29): -1.3, RF(4): -1.1	1.1
Zack Short	SS	TEN	AA	23	524	68	28	2	17	59	82	136	8	3	.227/.356/.417	120	35.2	.290	-0.2	SS(117): 4.8, 2B(4): 0.4	4.2
D.J. Wilson	CF	MYR	A+	21	272	27	9	2	1	13	32	71	10	6	.219/.315/.287	83	1.6	.309	0.3	CF(58): 1.3, RF(3): -0.6	0.3

Second-round pick **Brennen Davis** helped his high school basketball team to an Arizona state championship in his junior year, so his profile is everything one might expect: tall, athletic, toolsy and filled with enough questions about the bat that the rest could be irrelevant. ⓧ **Taylor Davis** must have taken his eyes off you this season, as he has at least one on Theo Epstein, confessing his desire to move into the front office after his career is over. His solid approach and framing acumen might just be enough to make that a long-term goal rather than an imminent career move. ⓧ **Johnny Field** has the name, modestly toolsy profile and utter lack of control over the strike zone of someone going far out of their way to be a forgettable fringe outfielder. ⓧ Not content with one high school center fielder in the second round, the Cubs grabbed a second in **Cole Roederer**. He's following in some impressive recent footsteps: five Hart High School alumni played in the majors in 2018 alone, including Trevor Bauer. ⓧ Nominative determinism is on **Zack Short's** side, unlike his Double-A strikeout rate. He can definitely play short, and the on-base skills, power, and above-average performance at every level all point towards a future major league contributor, even if the batting average comes up a little...short. ⓧ As an outfield prospect with speed as his carrying tool, the onus has been on **D.J. Wilson** to show that he's more than a set of wheels with a future as a fourth outfielder. Injuries and poor performance have kept that tag dragging in the dust behind him.

Pitchers

PITCHER	TEAM	LVL	AGE	W	L	SV	G	GS	IP	H	HR	BB/9	K/9	K	GB%	BABIP	WHIP	ERA	DRA	WARP	MPH	FB%	WHF	CSP
Cory Abbott	SBN	A	22	4	1	0	9	9	47¹	35	5	2.5	10.8	57	39%	.275	1.01	2.47	2.86	1.3				
	MYR	A+	22	4	5	0	13	13	67²	59	3	3.5	9.8	74	46%	.316	1.26	2.53	4.94	0.3				
Jose Albertos	SBN	A	19	0	5	0	9	4	13	17	1	22.2	11.8	17	51%	.444	3.77	18.69	6.01	-0.2				
	EUG	A-	19	0	4	0	11	6	17¹	19	0	17.1	10.9	21	65%	.413	3.00	11.94	6.78	-0.3				
Anthony Bass	CHN	MLB	30	0	0	0	16	0	15¹	18	1	1.8	8.2	14	53%	.386	1.37	2.93	4.77	0.0	95.6	68.4	8.6	48.4
	IOW	AAA	30	0	3	3	27	0	32	34	3	1.7	7.0	25	53%	.307	1.25	3.38	3.63	0.5				
Trevor Clifton	TEN	AA	23	3	4	0	12	12	56²	41	0	3.7	7.1	45	36%	.255	1.13	2.86	6.63	-0.8				
	IOW	AAA	23	4	3	0	14	12	69¹	65	8	3.8	7.3	56	38%	.292	1.36	3.89	4.11	1.1				
Oscar De La Cruz	TEN	AA	23	6	7	0	16	16	77¹	76	8	3.6	8.5	73	36%	.313	1.38	5.24	5.09	0.2				
Justin Hancock	IOW	AAA	27	2	2	0	18	0	21²	25	2	3.3	11.2	27	58%	.397	1.52	4.57	3.24	0.5				
	CHN	MLB	27	0	0	0	10	0	12¹	5	1	6.6	8.0	11	41%	.143	1.14	1.46	6.10	-0.2	98.1	71.8	8.7	48.2
Danny Hultzen	CUB	Rk	28	0	0	0	8	3	6²	6	1	2.7	20.2	15	27%	.500	1.20	5.40	-0.29	0.4				
Alex Lange	MYR	A+	22	6	8	0	23	23	120¹	104	6	2.8	7.6	101	45%	.287	1.18	3.74	3.78	2.2				
Brendon Little	SBN	A	21	5	11	0	22	21	101¹	106	8	3.8	8.0	90	49%	.317	1.47	5.15	5.40	-0.2				
Brailyn Marquez	EUG	A-	19	1	4	0	10	10	47²	46	5	2.6	9.8	52	52%	.333	1.26	3.21	3.05	1.2				
	SBN	A	19	0	0	0	2	2	7	7	0	2.6	9.0	7	33%	.333	1.29	2.57	3.54	0.1				
Cory Mazzoni	CHN	MLB	28	1	0	0	8	0	8²	5	0	5.2	7.3	7	58%	.208	1.15	1.04	3.26	0.2	94.6	58.5	13.8	42.9
	IOW	AAA	28	4	3	4	29	0	38¹	37	5	2.6	8.0	34	39%	.281	1.25	4.46	3.65	0.7				
Michael Rucker	TEN	AA	24	9	6	0	26	26	132²	111	17	2.6	8.0	118	39%	.251	1.12	3.73	4.09	1.9				
Justin Steele	CUB	Rk	22	0	0	0	5	5	18¹	9	1	2.0	13.3	27	43%	.222	0.71	1.47	1.42	0.9				
	MYR	A+	22	2	1	0	4	4	18¹	12	0	2.9	9.3	19	41%	.261	0.98	2.45	4.03	0.3				
	TEN	AA	22	0	1	0	2	2	10	8	1	2.7	6.3	7	32%	.233	1.10	3.60	3.68	0.2				
Keegan Thompson	MYR	A+	23	3	3	0	12	12	67²	49	6	1.7	8.1	61	36%	.239	0.92	3.19	3.65	1.3				
	TEN	AA	23	6	3	0	13	13	62	66	3	3.0	7.8	54	36%	.333	1.40	4.06	4.53	0.6				
Erich Uelmen	SBN	A	22	5	5	0	11	11	56¹	54	0	2.4	9.3	58	67%	.344	1.22	3.51	3.62	1.1				
	MYR	A+	22	3	3	0	10	9	33	38	3	4.1	6.5	24	51%	.333	1.61	4.36	4.12	0.5				
Jerry Vasto	COL	MLB	26	0	0	0	1	0	0²	3	0	13.5	13.5	1	25%	.750	6.00	40.50	11.78	-0.1	93.4	65.2	4.3	58.7
	ABQ	AAA	26	2	1	3	37	0	37	32	3	4.4	10.7	44	46%	.309	1.35	3.16	4.44	0.3				
	KCA	MLB	26	0	1	0	5	0	3²	3	1	2.5	7.4	3	18%	.200	1.09	2.45	5.42	0.0	93.4	50.7	9.6	48.7
Allen Webster	CHN	MLB	28	1	0	0	3	0	3	2	1	3.0	9.0	3	33%	.125	1.00	6.00	3.00	0.1	96.8	32.7	18.2	42
Rowan Wick	SAN	AA	25	2	4	5	29	0	31¹	22	0	6.0	12.1	42	58%	.310	1.37	3.16	3.10	0.7				
	ELP	AAA	25	2	0	9	20	0	22²	16	3	4.0	8.7	22	48%	.224	1.15	1.99	4.71	0.1				
	SDN	MLB	25	0	1	0	10	0	8¹	13	1	1.1	7.6	7	43%	.414	1.68	6.48	4.10	0.1	96.1	67.7	12	56
Rob Zastryzny	CHN	MLB	26	1	0	0	6	0	5²	6	0	6.4	4.8	3	44%	.333	1.76	4.76	5.81	-0.1	90.9	68.5	11.1	48.1
	IOW	AAA	26	3	2	0	33	1	56	47	5	4.5	8.0	50	58%	.271	1.34	3.86	4.04	0.7				

Three months before he was drafted, **Cory Abbott** pitched the first perfect game in Loyola Marymount history. While his pro career has not been quite that impeccable, he is yet to find a level to truly challenge him. ⓧ Yes, **Jose Albertos** really went from consensus top-five prospect in this system to "oh my god that's his WHIP not his ERA" in just one season, and his continued presence on the mound throughout the season suggests the issue is mechanical, mental or both. ⓧ Called up in June after signing a minor-league deal in the offseason, **Anthony Bass** soon put together ten straight appearances in which he did not give up a walk or a run. Then he developed a back issue, got lit up and was placed on the DL, before being unceremoniously designated for assignment upon activation. Turning 30 is tough. ⓧ **Trevor Clifton** went from fourth on the Cubs prospect list after 2016 to vanishing completely following a woeful 2017, but he did halt the precipitous decline in his stock with a respectable showing at Triple-A and should be given a shot at a major league job in 2019. ⓧ Staying on the field has been a problem for **Oscar De La Cruz**. Until 2018 this was entirely an injury-based problem, so pitching an uninterrupted half-season before testing positive for a masking agent and promptly being suspended represents a step forward, for the glass half-full kind of person at least. ⓧ Signed at just 16, Venezuelan righty **Richard Gallardo** possesses a plus fastball, promising curveball and changeup and the kind of command that would be the envy of prospects several years his senior. ⓧ A move to the bullpen in 2017 provided the impetus for **Justin Hancock** to finally make his major league debut, seven years after he was drafted. His fastball now sits at 96 and touches 100, or at least it did before shoulder inflammation landed him on the DL in June. ⓧ Choosing a single poster boy for TINSTAAPP would be impossible, but **Danny Hultzen** would get his own month on the 2019 calendar. The former top prospect is still working to make it to the majors, the better part of a decade after he was drafted. ⓧ 2017 first-rounder **Alex Lange** had a rather average line that conceals a season of two halves. Through ten starts at High-A, he produced a 2.89 ERA and 45 strikeouts to just ten walks, while the next thirteen saw that strikeout-walk ratio halved and a 4.41 ERA. Combined, they still point to a likely back-end starter or bullpen role. ⓧ Seven of **Brendon Little**'s 22 starts were scoreless. Six of the remaining 15 saw him give up five or more earned runs, which is how his ERA also ended up starting with five. ⓧ As a 19-year-old lefty with a fastball that touches 98, **Brailyn Marquez** handled short-season ball in impressive fashion and was promoted to South Bend late in the year as a result. He throws both four- and two-seam fastballs and flashes with his curveball, although inconsistency is to be expected given his inexperience. ⓧ It would have been almost impossible for **Cory Mazzoni** to increase his major league ERA, as he came into the season at 17.28, but another season like 2018 and he'll finally be back in the single digits. ⓧ **Michael Rucker** successfully built on his 2017 transition from the bullpen to the starting rotation, developing his changeup and curve to back up a fastball that can hit 96 at times. ⓧ It would be better if **Justin Steele** was a speedy outfielder with a penchant for swiping bags. At least his recovery from Tommy John surgery was fast: it took him just 11 months to return to the mound, and he's right back on course to be a mid-rotation starter. ⓧ **Keegan Thompson** surrendered more than half of his total earned runs in just two Double-A starts. The rest were generally far more promising, although it's still not clear he has the fastball to be anything more than the name at the bottom of the depth chart. ⓧ If you played the delivery of a side-armer on double speed, it might look a little something like **Erich Uelmen**'s. That delivery has drawn plenty of grounders in his pro career so far, with mixed results beyond the glorious aesthetics. ⓧ As the return piece from Colorado for Drew Butera and his beloved hair flip, **Jerry Vasto** was unable to develop his own GIF-worthy moment during his short stay in Kansas City and will now compete for an bullpen spot with the Cubs, who claimed him on waivers. ⓧ Strangely, MLB does not hand out an award for Player You Were Most Surprised To See In The Majors. If they did, it would have gone to **Allen Webster**, who briefly reappeared after a three-year absence, a spell that covered trips to Reno, Round Rock and even the KBO. ⓧ A converted right fielder, **Rowan Wick** reached the Padres bullpen three years after switching over to the mound. He has the command you'd expect out of a right fielder, so even though he throws hard, middle relief is his ceiling. ① It's never a good sign when your major league innings total goes down every season. It's even worse when you started from 16, so **Rob Zastryzny** is hovering dangerously close to zero.

CHICAGO WHITE SOX

Essay by Brendan Gawlowski

Player comments by James Fegan and BP staff

"**T**odd's late with the deliverables and Carlos can't get his system running."

Work anywhere long enough, and the minor snags and hangups that characterize a typical day inevitably snowball into something more. The work was never tedious, and with proper clarity of thought, it still isn't. But after months and years of the same goals, always kept elusive by the familiar impediments, you begin to wonder if there's a better way to spend your day.

"Chris just chucked Dan's dinner into the whirlpool."

Sure, you like your colleagues well enough. But sometimes, too much familiarity breeds contempt. Minor quirks become major personality differences; small interruptions accumulate into unworkable distractions.

"Yeah, James is here, but, uh, are you sure this is the right guy for this project?"

Sometimes the new hand can't get anything done.

"And if I see Avi flail at one more curveball, so help me, I'm going to blow it all up."

Avi never stopped flailing at curveballs. And Rick Hahn blew it all up.

⚾   ⚾   ⚾

Jose Quintana and Chris Sale starred together for nearly five years, joined by Adam Eaton and Jose Abreu for the final three. Together, they established themselves as impact players and appeared set to lead the next great White Sox team.

2016 seemed like the long-awaited year. Over the winter, general manager Rick Hahn had bolstered his core with the acquisitions of Brett Lawrie and Todd Frazier. On paper, Hahn finally had a lineup that could keep the team in games on days his aces weren't pitching. For a while, it all clicked. The Pale Hose roared out to a 23-10 start and were six games above second place by mid-May.

It didn't last. Frazier's bat never caught fire, Lawrie regressed, and the incumbent role players did nothing to earn their keep. As Chicago faded, a bad season spiraled into a slapstick routine. Sale made like the Shrike and slashed the team's throwback jerseys ahead of Turn Back the Clock

---

WHITE SOX PROSPECTUS
2018 W-L: 62-100, 4TH IN AL CENTRAL

Pythag	.381	27th	B-Age	26.5	1st
RS/G	4.05	24th	P-Age	27.6	11th
RA/G	5.23	28th	Salary	$71.2M	29th
DRC+	86	27th	M$/MW	$4.3M	13th
DRA	5.55	27th	DL Days	834	4th
FIP	4.76	28th	$ on DL	18%	17th
DER	.708	12th			

- Opened 1991
- Open air
- Natural surface
- Fence profile: 8'

Three-Year Park Factors

Runs	Runs/RH	Runs/LH	HR/RH	HR/LH
97	97	97	102	110

Top Hitter WARP	3.3 Tim Anderson
Top Pitcher WARP	1.2 Jace Fry
Top Prospect	Eloy Jimenez

2018 Hit List Ranking

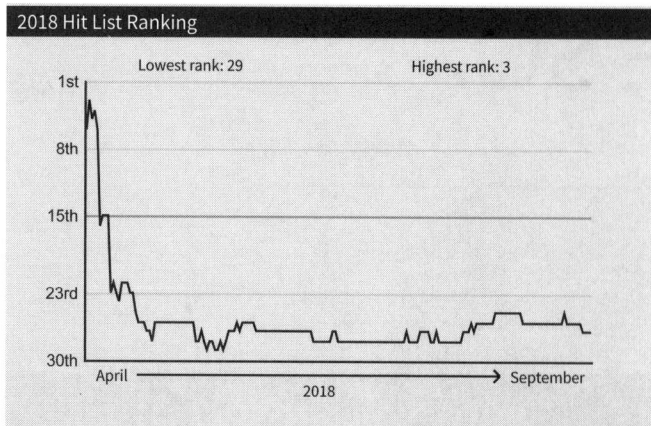

Lowest rank: 29   Highest rank: 3

Committed Payroll (in millions)

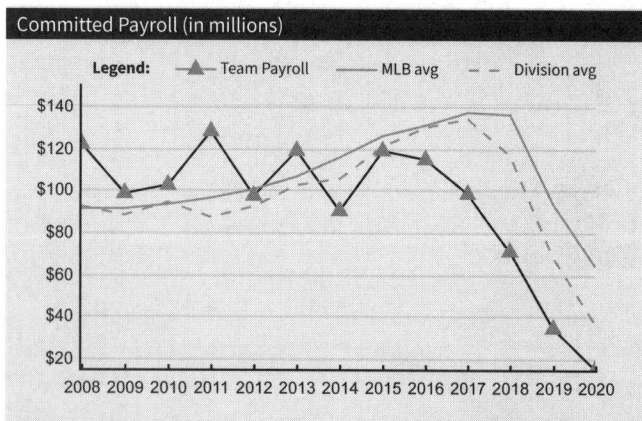

Legend: ▲ Team Payroll   MLB avg   Division avg

Farm System Ranking

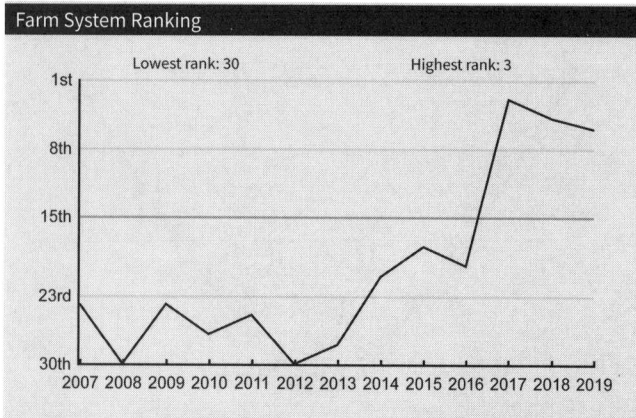

Lowest rank: 30   Highest rank: 3

Personnel

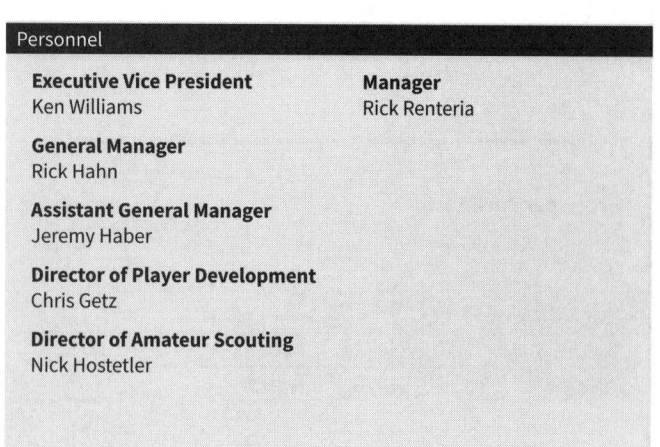

Executive Vice President
Ken Williams

General Manager
Rick Hahn

Assistant General Manager
Jeremy Haber

Director of Player Development
Chris Getz

Director of Amateur Scouting
Nick Hostetler

Manager
Rick Renteria

Night. Top prospect Tim Anderson took one walk in the month of July, rekindling a longstanding discussion about the organization's inability to develop young hitting talent. Chicago traded (now top prospect) Fernando Tatis Jr. for James Shields and the right-hander threw up a 6.77 ERA in 22 starts. The White Sox went 55-74 the rest of the way.

In response, Hahn did what every Twitter egg has begged for since the dawn of the platform, and dove headlong into a full rebuild. That winter, he dealt Sale to Boston and Eaton to Washington. The following July, he shipped Quintana across town to the Cubs.

To many, the moves were a breath of fresh air, the cathartic release that signals the arrival of a new dawn. In a flash, Chicago's long-moribund farm system transformed from one of baseball's worst to among the game's very best. From all appearances, Hahn had masterfully executed his rebuild. His three stars netted Lucas Giolito, Yoan Moncada, Eloy Jimenez, Michael Kopech, Dylan Cease, Reynaldo Lopez, and a handful of other interesting names. Giolito, Moncada and Jimenez were top 10 prospects, per BP's 2017 Top 101 list; Lopez and Kopech graced the top 40, and Cease soon entered their orbit.

It all feels so long ago.

⚾   ⚾   ⚾

It's still too early to call the rebuild a failure, although the preceding statement says much about how things are going. With the benefit of hindsight, it's clear that many of the first-wave prospects were overhyped.

The package for Eaton in particular proved a longstanding prospect axiom: If the return looks too good to be true, it probably is. Analysts covering the deal at the time—the author pleads guilty, your honor—lauded Giolito as the future ace evaluators gushed about in 2015. But by the time of the swap, Giolito no longer resembled that kind of impact talent. He was sitting several ticks lower with his fastball, with much loopier secondaries and only a basic grasp of where anything was going.

Giolito has regressed further in Chicago. He was arguably the worst pitcher in baseball last year, when he led the league in earned runs surrendered and walks allowed. That he also posted one of the lowest strikeout rates among all regular starters seems cruel to mention. At Baseball Prospectus, we annually run a list of the top 10 talents under the age of 26 in each organization as part of our top prospect series. Tellingly, Giolito not only failed to make the White Sox list, but was never part of the discussion.

Moncada did make that list, checking in at No. 2 just behind Anderson. Again though, he doesn't resemble the franchise-altering talent many had hoped for at the time of his acquisition. Moncada is still young and posted adequate numbers as a rookie, but he also proved, at least last year, to be a deeply flawed player. Every concern scouts had regarding his ability to make contact manifested. He led the league in whiffs—no small feat in 2018—and was also error-prone at second base.

While Giolito looks damaged beyond repair, Moncada is the dystopian avatar for Chicago's rebuild. Despite all his issues with baseball's fundamental components—hitting and catching the ball—the Cuban had his moments last year: He socked 17 homers and produced his share of jaw-dropping highlights. The disconnect should be worrisome for Chicago fans, because it's not that Moncada is *bad*. Despite grizzly WARP and FRAA totals, he clearly has the physical gifts to be a star. Amidst the empty hacks and booted grounders, his periodic successes look like the irrepressible spasms of pure, undistilled baseball talent. Compare his numbers to his raw abilities and you can't help but wonder how Chicago has made so little of so much.

The organization's recent inability to turn baseball protoplasm into steady production lingers like a cloud over the next wave of prospects. Jimenez and Nick Madrigal, the second overall pick in last year's draft, will presumably crack Chicago's lineup in 2019. They are two of the top hitters still loitering in the minor leagues and, as far as prospects go, are very likely to settle in as productive big leaguers. But that last caveat looms large in an organization bereft of recent player development success.

The White Sox haven't produced a consistent, first-division regular in more than a decade (Anderson could conceivably still get there; Avisail Garcia's juiced-ball fueled 2017 campaign may as well have been a dream). Part of that stems from a decades-long reluctance to spend big in Latin America or to splurge for talent in the draft. But the famously-miserly Sox have loosened the purse strings a bit recently and still don't have much to show for it. High-profile picks like Gordon Beckham, Courtney Hawkins and Zack Collins have sputtered in professional ball; toolsy athletes like Trayce Thompson and Marcus Semien have either withered on the vine or blossomed only after leaving town.

All failures point back to a player development operation that has lagged far behind its peers. As clubs throughout baseball spent the last few years experimenting with biomechanical research and the latest radar technology, Chicago's reliance on rote mechanical tinkering and traditional instruction methods was as stuck in the 80s as the red number on Carlton Fisk's left pant leg. The hiring of Chris Getz as director of player development was a breath of fresh air, and under his stewardship the club's development operation has entered the twenty-first century. But this is all more about keeping up with the Joneses than doing anything noticeably innovative, and there's a whole slew of organizational memory that could conceivably stunt well-intended new initiatives; not everyone wants to hear the new guy's pep talk about synergy.

Regardless of any changes at the top, the White Sox need to produce a few success stories before they can shed their reputation as a developmental backwater. Their ability to do so is an existential problem for the franchise—or at least the current administration in charge of it. Regardless of your recent draft picks, financial advantages, or abilities in the trade market, at some point you have to develop *somebody*. All the first-round picks and top prospect acquisitions in the world won't get a team to October if they keep hitting their thirtieth percentile outcomes. And at some point, there won't be a Quintana or Eaton left to flip for the benefit of the next rebuild, when it comes.

For now, a degree of pessimism is warranted in Chicago. If Hahn can't squeeze a good team out of this rebuild, the devastation fans feel will not solely stem from the failure of a promising cadre of prospects, but also from the sense that the organization was too slow to address the systemic problems that led to a rainy decade in the first place; Reds fans know this particular rodeo well. Already, it's fair to second guess the entire strategy.

Since leaving Chicago, Sale has been one of baseball's best pitchers. He's racked up 13 WARP and he very well might have walked home with last year's Cy Young award if he'd been healthy all year. A blown knee has limited Eaton to 120 games—and a footnote in the "what could have been" section of Washington's history books—though he's performed well when available. Quintana, more of a good player than a great one these days, has also been productive since leaving the South Side. Taken together, the group has earned nearly 20 WARP since the moves. Perhaps building around that core, Sisyphussian as it may have seemed at the time, would have provided a more realistic path to contention than trying to do so with volatile prospects and a subpar player development operation.

As the rebuild enters its third year, Hahn's decision must also be examined in the sport's broader economic context. In the past three years, the league's spending and competitive landscape has changed noticeably. The 2016 labor negotiations produced a joint bargaining agreement that, by nearly universal consensus, shifted power toward ownership. In the years since, teams have treated the luxury tax as a firm salary cap. Alongside, they have rushed to cut costs, leading to a depressed free agent market and widespread rebuilding and tanking; last year's American League campaign began with only seven or eight teams seriously trying to compete.

The White Sox, of course, were not one of them. The trades of Sale, Quintana, and Eaton—all of whom had multiple years remaining on team-friendly contracts when they were dealt—augured a period of austerity for the club. Fans of the 2018 White Sox were treated to the spectacle of a team playing in the nation's third largest city running one of the lowest payrolls in the league. Ostensibly, the purpose was to play the kids, and evaluate which players from this crop of rookies have the chops to contribute to the franchise's next competitive team. But the opportunity to strip tens of millions of dollars from the books was surely a pleasant happenstance for the man writing the checks as well.

You can make a case that the White Sox embody much of what is wrong with baseball in 2018. The fire sale (Sale?), the cost-cutting, the empty stadium, the focus on acquiring those sweet, sweet bargain-value prospects even absent a cohesive plan to turn them into major-league ballplayers: it's all here and it's frustrating.

It's all the more frustrating because, lurking beneath the cheap management and player development problems, there really is a decent amount of minor league talent present; the top prospects list at the back of this book sure isn't light on White Sox content. In a weak division, headlined by a Cleveland team that spent the winter openly questioning how much worse they could make their roster while still reaching the playoffs, Chicago isn't *that* far from contention. Develop a couple prize farmhands into solid big-

leaguers and augment the roster with a choice free agent or two (there's not a lot of money on the books these days) and this team could theoretically compete as soon as 2020.

2019 will tell us a lot about whether that's realistic. Any development from Moncada and Anderson would be welcome, of course, but it's Jimenez and Madrigal who seem poised to shape the franchise's future. Should they come up and succeed, their arrival could inject life into this dormant franchise. Should that crew falter? Well…

"Rick? This is Mr. Reinsdorf. I would like to have a word with you." ∎

—Brendan Gawlowski is an editor of Baseball Prospectus.

HITTERS

Jose Abreu 1B Born: 01/29/87 Age: 32 Bats: R Throws: R Height: 6'3" Weight: 255 Origin: International Free Agent, 2013

YEAR	TEAM	LVL	AGE	PA	R	2B	3B	HR	RBI	BB	K	SB	CS	AVG/OBP/SLG	DRC+	VORP	BABIP	BRR	FRAA	WARP
2016	CHA	MLB	29	695	67	32	1	25	100	47	125	0	2	.293/.353/.468	115	21.8	.327	-1.7	1B(152): 7.1	2.9
2017	CHA	MLB	30	675	95	43	6	33	102	35	119	3	0	.304/.354/.552	124	33.1	.330	0.8	1B(139): 5.5	3.7
2018	CHA	MLB	31	553	68	36	1	22	78	37	109	2	0	.265/.325/.473	106	15.1	.294	0.0	1B(114): 4.9	1.8
2019	CHA	MLB	32	605	74	32	3	23	83	48	110	2	1	.274/.351/.466	126	27.0	.313	-0.2	1B 2	3.1

Breakout: 1%   Improve: 28%   Collapse: 2%   Attrition: 9%   MLB: 95%   *Comparables: Ted Kluszewski, Bob Watson, Ernie Banks*

Perhaps to the layman outsider, Abreu's 2018 looks like a classic case of a hulking slugger hitting his thirties and promptly delivering the weakest and most injury-addled season of his proud career. A more uncomfortably insider view would reveal Abreu's strong second half was undone by a pair of injuries (testicular torsion, upper thigh infection brought on by an ingrown hair follicle) that are a bit difficult to link to the everyday wear and tear of salaried baseball. Of course, before all that, he also stumbled into the worst slump of his career fairly organically. Abreu is an odd duck: simultaneously consistent and measured while swinging at nearly everything as a matter of personal preference. His approach is too multifaceted to be relying on any one elite skill, but no more immune to the slow loss of strength and athleticism as anyone else. He will try to play 162 games in 2019, also as a matter of personal preference.

Micker Adolfo OF Born: 09/11/96 Age: 22 Bats: R Throws: R Height: 6'3" Weight: 200 Origin: International Free Agent, 2013

YEAR	TEAM	LVL	AGE	PA	R	2B	3B	HR	RBI	BB	K	SB	CS	AVG/OBP/SLG	DRC+	VORP	BABIP	BRR	FRAA	WARP
2016	KAN	A	19	265	30	13	1	5	21	14	88	0	1	.219/.269/.340	68	0.7	.318	0.0	RF(61): 8.9, CF(2): -0.2	0.4
2017	KAN	A	20	473	60	28	2	16	68	31	149	2	0	.264/.331/.453	111	17.5	.366	-4.1	RF(102): -12.1	-0.2
2018	WNS	A+	21	336	48	18	1	11	50	34	92	2	1	.282/.369/.464	117	14.6	.372	-1.5		0.9
2019	CHA	MLB	22	251	25	10	0	9	30	15	83	0	0	.204/.266/.359	67	-8.2	.275	-0.7		-0.9

Breakout: 0%   Improve: 5%   Collapse: 1%   Attrition: 8%   MLB: 12%   *Comparables: Chris Parmelee, Lars Anderson, Chris Marrero*

Watching Adolfo take batting practice with his best buddy Eloy Jimenez, it takes a studious eye to tell which one is the elite power-hitting prospect on the cusp of the major leagues, and which one is merely the prospect with elite raw power. The grind of annual injury (this year he was able to sneak in nearly 80 games of action between spraining his UCL in spring training and Tommy John surgery in July) has not prevented Adolfo in the least from adding muscle and strength. Against all odds, it has also not stalled the gradual progression of his once raw hitting approach, or the slow paring of his once-garish strikeout rate even as he advances through the lower minors. The real test of his approach and whether it holds up when he has to protect against top-level velocity is still on the way, and it will be years before he can hope to join Jimenez in Chicago, but he has exceeded expectations before.

Yonder Alonso 1B Born: 04/08/87 Age: 32 Bats: L Throws: R Height: 6'1" Weight: 230 Origin: Round 1, 2008 Draft (#7 overall)

YEAR	TEAM	LVL	AGE	PA	R	2B	3B	HR	RBI	BB	K	SB	CS	AVG/OBP/SLG	DRC+	VORP	BABIP	BRR	FRAA	WARP
2016	OAK	MLB	29	532	52	34	0	7	56	45	74	3	1	.253/.316/.367	83	-2.0	.284	0.2	1B(145): 6.5, 3B(7): -0.5	0.4
2017	OAK	MLB	30	371	52	17	0	22	49	50	88	1	0	.266/.369/.527	126	16.8	.301	-0.2	1B(96): -2.7	1.5
2017	SEA	MLB	30	150	20	5	0	6	18	18	30	1	0	.265/.353/.439	125	2.4	.302	-0.1	1B(39): -2.8	0.4
2018	CLE	MLB	31	574	64	19	0	23	83	51	123	0	0	.250/.317/.421	106	8.0	.283	1.1	1B(138): -0.6	1.4
2019	CHA	MLB	32	403	47	20	1	14	52	40	81	1	1	.261/.338/.438	110	10.4	.301	0.1	1B -1	1.0

Breakout: 4%   Improve: 40%   Collapse: 9%   Attrition: 13%   MLB: 84%   *Comparables: Wally Joyner, Doug Mientkiewicz, Ed Kranepool*

After sliding from top-10 pick to middling journeyman, Alonso appeared to enlist in the Launch Angle Revolution in an attempt to violently overthrow our ground-ball overlords in 2017. It worked for the first half, as he suddenly had more game power than he'd shown since the University of Miami. He turned almost all the way back into a pumpkin in the second half, and although he hit 23 homers in 2018, he managed only a .421 slugging percentage that's underwhelming at first base. Worse, his on-base rate, formerly his only asset at the plate, eroded to below league average. The power surge is increasingly looking like a small-sample blip rather than the new normal, which means Alonso is once again a mediocre stopgap.

Tim Anderson SS   Born: 06/23/93   Age: 26   Bats: R   Throws: R   Height: 6'1"   Weight: 185   Origin: Round 1, 2013 Draft (#17 overall)

YEAR	TEAM	LVL	AGE	PA	R	2B	3B	HR	RBI	BB	K	SB	CS	AVG/OBP/SLG	DRC+	VORP	BABIP	BRR	FRAA	WARP
2016	CHR	AAA	23	256	39	10	2	4	20	8	58	11	4	.304/.325/.409	89	10.9	.384	0.1	SS(52): -1.5	0.6
2016	CHA	MLB	23	431	57	22	6	9	30	13	117	10	2	.283/.306/.432	74	16.6	.375	4.0	SS(98): -4.7	0.5
2017	CHA	MLB	24	606	72	26	4	17	56	13	162	15	1	.257/.276/.402	73	10.6	.328	2.1	SS(145): -11.7	-0.2
2018	CHA	MLB	25	606	77	28	3	20	64	30	149	26	8	.240/.281/.406	85	19.9	.289	6.5	SS(151): 9.1	3.3
2019	*CHA*	*MLB*	*26*	*554*	*66*	*25*	*4*	*16*	*60*	*27*	*136*	*18*	*5*	*.250/.292/.403*	*90*	*17.2*	*.306*	*3.1*	*SS -3*	*1.5*

Breakout: 8%   Improve: 59%   Collapse: 5%   Attrition: 10%   MLB: 98%   *Comparables: Bill Hall, Ian Desmond, Glenn Wright*

The typical dog whistle sports radio caller critique, that Tim Anderson is more an athlete than a shortstop of yesteryear, is one the man himself is willing to reverse-engineer. Specifically, after his great leap forward defensively in the second half of 2018, now he feels he has proven himself a shortstop, rather than just an athlete. His profile going forward can be viewed the same way: rather than a collection of tools and upside with an uncertain destination, he has proven he will provide value defending the most difficult spot on the infield, and probably while snagging 20 or more stolen bases in the process. How much his offensive potential will be realized is still an open question after a season of incremental gains over a personally and professionally nightmarish 2017, but it's also less of a big deal. He can pick it.

Luis Alexander Basabe CF   Born: 08/26/96   Age: 22   Bats: B   Throws: R   Height: 6'0"   Weight: 160   Origin: International Free Agent, 2012

YEAR	TEAM	LVL	AGE	PA	R	2B	3B	HR	RBI	BB	K	SB	CS	AVG/OBP/SLG	DRC+	VORP	BABIP	BRR	FRAA	WARP
2016	GRN	A	19	451	61	24	8	12	52	40	116	25	5	.258/.325/.447	115	26.3	.330	2.7	CF(98): 11.6	3.8
2017	WNS	A+	20	435	52	12	5	5	36	49	104	17	6	.221/.320/.320	94	10.3	.292	4.4	CF(78): 0.1, RF(10): -0.4	1.4
2018	WNS	A+	21	245	36	12	5	9	30	34	64	7	8	.266/.370/.502	122	19.7	.341	-2.0	CF(28): 2.2, LF(16): 1.5	1.6
2018	BIR	AA	21	270	41	9	3	6	26	30	76	9	4	.251/.340/.394	94	13.3	.344	2.1	CF(42): -1.9, RF(15): 0.3	0.6
2019	*CHA*	*MLB*	*22*	*251*	*29*	*7*	*1*	*7*	*22*	*21*	*75*	*5*	*2*	*.197/.265/.324*	*62*	*-2.9*	*.257*	*0.1*	*CF 2, LF 0*	*0.0*

Breakout: 4%   Improve: 17%   Collapse: 3%   Attrition: 15%   MLB: 34%   *Comparables: Austin Jackson, Anthony Alford, Ryan Kalish*

At this stage of his career, Hunter Greene seems pretty darn predictable in his pitch mix and arm action, and he finished his 2018 season a full two levels below where Basabe ended up. Still, when it comes to announcing your legitimacy to the world, turning one of Greene's 102 mph fastballs on the outer half into a massive opposite-field home run serves pretty well. A surgically-repaired left knee allowed Basabe to drive off the leg and tap into his not insubstantial raw power, complementing a speedy center fielder profile. There was an understandable learning curve for him to deal with upon his midseason promotion, but he held his own despite not turning 22 until the end of August. With the swing-and-miss present, there's still plenty of room for Basabe to stumble down the fourth outfielder path, but he's already shown pretty clear evidence that he's willing to adjust. When he was on deck, and 102 mph flashed on the radar gun, Basabe's Futures Game manager David Ortiz popped his head out of the dugout and barked at him to shorten up his swing. Basabe complied.

Welington Castillo C   Born: 04/24/87   Age: 32   Bats: R   Throws: R   Height: 5'10"   Weight: 220   Origin: International Free Agent, 2004

YEAR	TEAM	LVL	AGE	PA	R	2B	3B	HR	RBI	BB	K	SB	CS	AVG/OBP/SLG	DRC+	VORP	BABIP	BRR	FRAA	WARP
2016	ARI	MLB	29	457	41	24	0	14	68	33	121	2	0	.264/.322/.423	96	18.6	.337	-4.5	C(107): -8.6	0.7
2017	BAL	MLB	30	365	44	11	0	20	53	22	97	0	0	.282/.323/.490	114	20.3	.336	-0.7	C(88): 10.8	3.5
2018	CHR	AAA	31	40	2	1	0	0	3	3	11	0	0	.189/.250/.216	77	-2.3	.269	-0.3	C(8): -0.5	0.0
2018	CHA	MLB	31	181	17	7	0	6	15	9	46	1	0	.259/.304/.406	88	4.8	.322	0.2	C(43): -6.5	-0.1
2019	*CHA*	*MLB*	*32*	*401*	*43*	*20*	*1*	*13*	*51*	*27*	*103*	*1*	*0*	*.255/.309/.421*	*95*	*14.0*	*.319*	*-1.6*	*C -4*	*1.1*

Breakout: 6%   Improve: 39%   Collapse: 10%   Attrition: 17%   MLB: 95%   *Comparables: John Buck, Ryan Doumit, Nick Hundley*

In the final weeks of the season as the White Sox were hurtling toward 100 losses, Castillo—as he is wont to do—hit a little bit. It was nothing life-changing, and his final season line settled in around "OK for a catcher." But when the White Sox reflect on Castillo's failure to provide the veteran stability they sought in free agency, they will probably focus less on the hitting, perhaps a bit more on his framing numbers' sudden dive from exceptional to exceptionally unacceptable, and a whole lot on the 80-game suspension for erythropoietin and what it means for projecting his role going forward. PED suspensions don't create the ripples in clubhouses for moral and ethical reasons like they used to, but

YEAR	TEAM	P. COUNT	FRM RUNS	BLK RUNS	THRW RUNS	TOT RUNS
2016	ARI	15918	-7.7	-1.5	3.1	-6.4
2017	BAL	13481	6.8	1.3	3.2	12.4
2018	CHA	6226	-5.5	-0.8	0.1	-6.4
2018	CHR	901	-0.6	0.0	0.2	-0.4
2019	*CHA*	*15013*	*-4.4*	*-0.5*	*2.1*	*-2.9*

like any workplace, it's one where showing up and being ready to contribute everyday is valued above all, and being caught with this very easily-tested for substance is not a particularly compelling reason for coming up short.

Zack Collins C   Born: 02/06/95   Age: 24   Bats: L   Throws: R   Height: 6'3"   Weight: 220   Origin: Round 1, 2016 Draft (#10 overall)

YEAR	TEAM	LVL	AGE	PA	R	2B	3B	HR	RBI	BB	K	SB	CS	AVG/OBP/SLG	DRC+	VORP	BABIP	BRR	FRAA	WARP
2016	WNS	A+	21	153	24	7	0	6	18	33	39	0	0	.258/.418/.467	144	10.8	.333	-0.4	C(18): -0.6	1.1
2017	WNS	A+	22	426	63	18	3	17	48	76	118	0	2	.223/.365/.443	130	22.9	.282	-2.6	C(63): 1.5	3.1
2017	BIR	AA	22	45	7	2	0	2	5	11	11	0	0	.235/.422/.471	113	4.8	.286	-0.1	C(11): -2.4	0.0
2018	BIR	AA	23	531	58	24	1	15	68	101	158	5	0	.234/.382/.404	113	33.7	.329	-3.2	C(74): -14.4	0.9
2019	*CHA*	*MLB*	*24*	*34*	*4*	*1*	*0*	*1*	*4*	*5*	*11*	*0*	*0*	*.196/.302/.356*	*67*	*0.0*	*.264*	*-0.1*	*C -2*	*-0.2*

Breakout: 3%   Improve: 12%   Collapse: 13%   Attrition: 17%   MLB: 35%   *Comparables: Carlos Santana, Derek Norris, Max Ramirez*

If Collins showed up around 10 years ago, this book might be touting him as a future star. He's a catcher who hits for decent power and walks more than literally any other player at his minor league level. But since this book costs too much to just regurgitate what could be gleaned from a stat line, and the last decade has dumped a lot of nuance into our laps, there are some hurdles between now and Collins putting his signature on a 15-year lease for a condo in Chicago worth noting: Strikeout rates looming on the fringes of acceptability

YEAR	TEAM	P. COUNT	FRM RUNS	BLK RUNS	THRW RUNS	TOT RUNS
2017	BIR	1559	-1.8	-0.3	0.0	-2.5
2018	BIR	10814	-12.2	-0.9	-0.7	-14.5
2019	CHA	1244	-1.9	-0.3	0.1	-2.1

in the minors tend to only worsen at higher levels. The still-present hitch in his swing figures to get tested by top velocity as he progresses. And the confidence with which advanced pitchers do so figures to have a sharp correlation with how sticky that elite walk rate proves to be. All these, and he still has to continue to progress defensively to prove he's a catcher, the biggest question mark he faced on his draft day. Still, though, power-hitting catcher who walks a ton: It's not a bad starter kit.

Ryan Cordell   OF   Born: 03/31/92   Age: 27   Bats: R   Throws: R   Height: 6'4"   Weight: 195   Origin: Round 11, 2013 Draft (#340 overall)

YEAR	TEAM	LVL	AGE	PA	R	2B	3B	HR	RBI	BB	K	SB	CS	AVG/OBP/SLG	DRC+	VORP	BABIP	BRR	FRAA	WARP
2016	FRI	AA	24	445	69	22	5	19	70	32	97	12	4	.264/.319/.484	117	24.7	.299	0.6	CF(42): 3.7, LF(35): 3.8	3.2
2017	CSP	AAA	25	292	49	18	5	10	45	25	65	9	4	.284/.349/.506	111	12.3	.339	1.6	RF(29): 0.0, LF(15): 0.2	1.4
2018	CHR	AAA	26	193	15	9	2	3	22	11	44	7	2	.239/.281/.364	86	-0.1	.293	0.4	CF(22): -0.2, RF(13): -0.4	0.5
2018	CHA	MLB	26	40	3	1	0	1	4	0	15	0	0	.108/.125/.216	62	-3.4	.130	0.4	RF(9): -0.3, CF(7): -0.6	-0.1
2019	CHA	MLB	27	140	14	6	1	4	15	8	36	3	1	.220/.272/.355	80	1.0	.274	0.1	RF 1, CF 0	0.4

Breakout: 6%   Improve: 24%   Collapse: 7%   Attrition: 25%   MLB: 43%   Comparables: Brandon Barnes, Matt Carson, Slade Heathcott

Getting traded into a White Sox rebuild that has witnessed some of the worst outfield production in recent memory should have been the equivalent of smashing open a window of opportunity with a sledgehammer. Instead, little hiccups like a fractured vertebrae and a broken collarbone conspired to limit Cordell to a 19-game major league cameo, and the rookie passed through eight of those 19 before his first career hit. That decisive blast into the mostly empty left field seats at Camden Yards served as one of the few triumphs in a season that saw Cordell struggle to stake any claim on a center field job that looked like it could have been his throughout spring training, and firmly place himself outside of the White Sox Opening Day roster picture going into 2019. With his 27th birthday coming near Opening Day, the promise of his all-around tools can spark only so much optimism.

Matt Davidson   DH   Born: 03/26/91   Age: 28   Bats: R   Throws: R   Height: 6'3"   Weight: 230   Origin: Round 1, 2009 Draft (#35 overall)

YEAR	TEAM	LVL	AGE	PA	R	2B	3B	HR	RBI	BB	K	SB	CS	AVG/OBP/SLG	DRC+	VORP	BABIP	BRR	FRAA	WARP
2016	CHR	AAA	25	326	35	20	0	10	46	32	86	0	0	.268/.349/.444	120	10.7	.346	-2.6	3B(66): 6.7, 1B(6): 0.1	2.3
2016	CHA	MLB	25	2	1	0	0	0	1	0	1	0	0	.500/.500/.500	99	0.1	1.000	-0.1		0.0
2017	CHA	MLB	26	443	43	16	1	26	68	19	165	0	1	.220/.260/.452	86	-7.8	.285	-3.4	3B(34): -1.9, 1B(19): -1.2	-0.5
2018	CHA	MLB	27	496	51	23	0	20	62	52	165	0	0	.228/.319/.419	92	3.7	.313	-3.9	1B(45): -3.1, 3B(14): 0.9	-0.3
2019	CHA	MLB	28	458	52	20	1	18	61	38	136	0	0	.238/.310/.425	96	2.1	.310	-2.6	1B -5, 3B 0	-0.3

Breakout: 5%   Improve: 54%   Collapse: 6%   Attrition: 19%   MLB: 93%   Comparables: Jonny Gomes, Carlos Pena, Mark Trumbo

When Earth is a microwaved wasteland sometime in the next 12-to-112 years, will historians/masochists seeking to understand our time focus more on Davidson completely revamping his plate approach to transform himself into a decent hitter, or the three scoreless innings he threw to spell a bad pitching staff for a team that lost 100 games? Strangely enough, probably the latter. The modern bullpen features few right-handers who sit 90-91 mph with a looping splitter-like thing, but if Davidson winds up ushering in a wave of part-time position players who earn their keep by contributing non-embarrassing innings, his place in history will be secure. Less secure is his positional role, since his third base work is increasingly occasional. A late-season slide and a struggle to reclaim his approach after back spasms left him with a campaign that will make a first base gig hard to hold. Non-tendered by the White Sox after the season, Davidson appears to be betting on being part of the wave of the future, training as a two-way player.

Nick Delmonico   LF   Born: 07/12/92   Age: 26   Bats: L   Throws: R   Height: 6'3"   Weight: 230   Origin: Round 6, 2011 Draft (#185 overall)

YEAR	TEAM	LVL	AGE	PA	R	2B	3B	HR	RBI	BB	K	SB	CS	AVG/OBP/SLG	DRC+	VORP	BABIP	BRR	FRAA	WARP
2016	BIR	AA	23	159	25	14	2	10	31	13	33	1	0	.338/.397/.676	137	15.7	.384	-4.3	1B(30): 0.4, 3B(3): 0.1	0.6
2016	CHR	AAA	23	295	32	16	0	7	30	29	74	2	0	.246/.320/.388	104	3.4	.311	-1.8	3B(39): 0.4, RF(17): 0.5	1.0
2017	CHR	AAA	24	429	55	18	3	12	45	46	73	4	2	.262/.347/.421	118	20.5	.296	2.9	3B(73): -1.4, LF(13): -0.6	2.4
2017	CHA	MLB	24	166	25	4	0	9	23	23	31	2	0	.262/.373/.482	120	10.0	.277	0.9	LF(27): 2.8, 1B(4): -0.6	1.1
2018	CHA	MLB	25	318	31	11	5	8	25	27	80	1	2	.215/.296/.373	87	-1.4	.269	-0.7	LF(76): -1.2, 1B(7): 0.6	0.1
2019	CHA	MLB	26	344	36	13	2	10	39	31	76	2	1	.229/.309/.379	90	3.3	.274	0.2	LF 1, 1B 1	0.5

Breakout: 7%   Improve: 39%   Collapse: 11%   Attrition: 22%   MLB: 84%   Comparables: Ben Gamel, Ryan Langerhans, Desmond Jennings

Surprise breakout performances from long-overlooked prospects are utterly delightful, undercut only by their unfortunate tendency to disappear back into obscurity as quickly as they arise. Delmonico was having a hard enough time repeating his surprising late-2017 power surge by mid-May, at the moment Matt Moore missed his target on a 1-2 count by matter of feet and broke the third metacarpal in Delmonico's right hand. Strangely enough, after missing two months of action with a hand injury, the week of his initial return was one of the few stretches where Delmonico flashed signs of carving out space for himself as a potential regular. The rest of the year he was a converted third baseman trying to make it work out in left field, providing decidedly below-average offense while Eloy Jimenez lingered a level below. It's a tenuous spot to be in.

Adam Engel CF Born: 12/09/91 Age: 27 Bats: R Throws: R Height: 6'2" Weight: 210 Origin: Round 19, 2013 Draft (#573 overall)

YEAR	TEAM	LVL	AGE	PA	R	2B	3B	HR	RBI	BB	K	SB	CS	AVG/OBP/SLG	DRC+	VORP	BABIP	BRR	FRAA	WARP
2016	WNS	A+	24	64	15	6	1	0	5	7	11	6	0	.327/.413/.473	96	9.6	.409	3.6	CF(12): -0.9, LF(2): -0.2	0.4
2016	BIR	AA	24	357	56	18	9	4	25	39	70	31	9	.255/.352/.412	110	26.1	.319	5.8	CF(71): -1.8	2.1
2016	CHR	AAA	24	161	19	6	2	3	16	10	50	8	5	.242/.298/.369	75	-0.1	.344	-0.1	CF(25): 4.9, LF(16): -2.1	0.3
2017	CHR	AAA	25	192	20	12	2	8	19	19	51	4	3	.218/.312/.461	105	10.0	.262	1.8	CF(33): -0.3, LF(13): 1.9	1.0
2017	CHA	MLB	25	336	34	11	3	6	21	19	117	8	1	.166/.235/.282	45	-9.3	.247	1.4	CF(95): 7.9, LF(1): 0.0	-0.2
2018	CHA	MLB	26	463	49	17	4	6	29	18	129	16	8	.235/.279/.336	63	-1.1	.322	1.5	CF(140): 10.0	0.7
2019	*CHA*	*MLB*	*27*	*443*	*49*	*16*	*3*	*9*	*39*	*26*	*123*	*15*	*6*	*.217/.280/.336*	*68*	*0.8*	*.286*	*0.7*	*CF 7*	*0.9*

Breakout: 4%   Improve: 40%   Collapse: 7%   Attrition: 15%   MLB: 82%   *Comparables: Brian Anderson, Jake Marisnick, Leury Garcia*

Even Adam Engel grew a little bit tired of talking about his home run robberies by the end of it all. They were three catches out of the 355 that he made during the 2018 season. They are a tiny fraction of his job. Yes, of course he practices them—just a little bit—but he also practices so many other things for all the other days and fielding chances that do not involve anything resembling a home run robbery. Still, if there's a better way to represent why Engel is on 240 major league games and counting despite accumulating one of the ten worst batting lines in baseball this past season—still a marked improvement over 2017—images of him flashing the speed, strength and athleticism to fly into a padded wall, absorb the impact and haul in a scorched deep drive all in one fluid motion, are about the most efficient way to communicate the appeal.

Avisail Garcia RF Born: 06/12/91 Age: 28 Bats: R Throws: R Height: 6'4" Weight: 240 Origin: International Free Agent, 2007

YEAR	TEAM	LVL	AGE	PA	R	2B	3B	HR	RBI	BB	K	SB	CS	AVG/OBP/SLG	DRC+	VORP	BABIP	BRR	FRAA	WARP
2016	CHA	MLB	25	453	59	18	2	12	51	34	115	4	4	.245/.307/.385	81	2.4	.309	2.0	RF(46): 6.1, LF(11): 0.0	0.6
2017	CHA	MLB	26	561	75	27	5	18	80	33	111	5	3	.330/.380/.506	118	29.2	.392	-0.5	RF(132): 7.2	3.2
2018	CHA	MLB	27	385	47	11	2	19	49	20	102	3	1	.236/.281/.438	91	4.3	.271	-1.4	RF(87): 6.3	0.9
2019	*CHA*	*MLB*	*28*	*403*	*47*	*18*	*2*	*14*	*52*	*30*	*92*	*4*	*2*	*.260/.327/.432*	*109*	*15.2*	*.314*	*0.0*	*RF 4*	*2.1*

Breakout: 3%   Improve: 55%   Collapse: 4%   Attrition: 11%   MLB: 98%   *Comparables: Hunter Pence, Delmon Young, Brennan Boesch*

The twinge Garcia felt in his right knee on Opening Day swiftly informed him that the follow-up to his All-Star breakout campaign would wind up landing somewhere between "unconventional," "troubled" and "downright hobbled." That trick knee would wind up taking the fall for inducing a pair of hamstring strains and persistent soreness, which conspired to limit Garcia to 93 games. There's no perfect accounting for how much a perturbed popliteal contributed to hampering a man who finished third in all of baseball in both infield hits and total batting average just a year before. But even with the knowledge that Garcia's tender bender was surgically repaired days after, pegging where his value falls between the elite corner outfielder performance he flashed in exactly one season and the oft-physically compromised mediocrity he's shown in his other four is literally something for an arbitrator to decide. The White Sox looked at that calculation and folded, opting instead to non-tender him.

Leury Garcia UT Born: 03/18/91 Age: 28 Bats: B Throws: R Height: 5'8" Weight: 180 Origin: International Free Agent, 2007

YEAR	TEAM	LVL	AGE	PA	R	2B	3B	HR	RBI	BB	K	SB	CS	AVG/OBP/SLG	DRC+	VORP	BABIP	BRR	FRAA	WARP
2016	CHR	AAA	25	342	45	9	4	6	35	24	64	18	8	.313/.367/.426	107	16.9	.378	1.3	LF(28): 1.2, SS(25): -1.1	1.9
2016	CHA	MLB	25	50	6	1	1	1	5	1	13	2	1	.229/.260/.354	73	-0.4	.294	0.4	CF(16): -1.1	-0.1
2017	CHA	MLB	26	326	41	15	2	9	33	13	69	8	5	.270/.316/.423	80	7.2	.321	0.5	CF(51): 3.4, LF(24): 0.2	0.8
2018	CHA	MLB	27	275	23	7	4	4	32	9	69	12	1	.271/.303/.376	72	5.0	.355	1.8	LF(40): 1.4, CF(26): -0.8	0.2
2019	*CHA*	*MLB*	*28*	*264*	*31*	*11*	*2*	*6*	*26*	*15*	*61*	*9*	*3*	*.245/.301/.380*	*87*	*5.1*	*.300*	*0.6*	*2B 1, CF 0*	*0.6*

Breakout: 3%   Improve: 30%   Collapse: 11%   Attrition: 29%   MLB: 73%   *Comparables: Eugenio Velez, Freddie Bynum, Josh Rutledge*

Albeit more subdued in recent years, Garcia was once one of the flashiest dressers in the White Sox clubhouse, flaunting a golden belt buckle that seemed to seek to be as large as his face and another similarly-sized gold plate on his hat to match. His manager—fluent and dexterous Spanish speaker Rick Renteria—refers to him as "Leroy" for reasons unknown. Garcia's most recent tweet was on Aug. 29, where he linked to a Wall Street Journal article about how President Trump's proposed tariffs might affect the Mexican auto industry (Garcia hails from the Dominican Republic). After being one of the worst even-occasional hitters in baseball in 2014 while appearing at seven positions (including pitcher), Garcia mostly disappeared from the major leagues for two seasons, before re-emerging in the opportunity afforded to him in the White Sox rebuild as a serviceable big league utility man. And all of these strange and promising developments surrounding him would be so much more interesting if he could just stay healthy.

Luis Gonzalez CF Born: 09/10/95 Age: 23 Bats: L Throws: L Height: 6'1" Weight: 185 Origin: Round 3, 2017 Draft (#87 overall)

YEAR	TEAM	LVL	AGE	PA	R	2B	3B	HR	RBI	BB	K	SB	CS	AVG/OBP/SLG	DRC+	VORP	BABIP	BRR	FRAA	WARP
2017	KAN	A	21	277	26	13	4	2	12	38	50	2	3	.245/.356/.361	114	11.3	.302	-0.2	CF(31): -2.9, LF(18): -0.1	0.8
2018	KAN	A	22	255	35	16	2	8	26	21	57	7	2	.300/.358/.491	109	19.8	.365	-0.6	CF(39): -1.0, RF(13): -1.9	0.7
2018	WNS	A+	22	288	50	24	3	6	45	27	46	3	5	.313/.376/.504	121	26.8	.354	5.8	CF(31): 3.9, LF(14): 0.2	2.5
2019	*CHA*	*MLB*	*23*	*251*	*27*	*9*	*0*	*6*	*23*	*18*	*58*	*1*	*1*	*.213/.268/.334*	*57*	*-5.0*	*.253*	*-0.6*	*CF 1, RF 0*	*-0.4*

Breakout: 1%   Improve: 14%   Collapse: 5%   Attrition: 11%   MLB: 28%   *Comparables: Jake Cave, Johnny Field, Gary Brown*

If his college run had ended more smoothly, Gonzalez might have been a first-round pick. Had he been a first-round pick in 2017, it's possible he would not have been buried in Low-A Kannapolis to start the season. Had he not started out there, perhaps his dominant 2018 campaign would be viewed less as a polished and mature college star nuking overwhelmed younger competition, and would have more unambiguously placed him on the prospect map with a clear role in the White Sox future plans. Instead, things are as they are, and the lefty-swinging center fielder who deserved a shot at Double-A this year will be only now be getting his first taste of the high minors. It's easy enough to see him in the majors one day not too long from now, but it's less certain how much his pop and center-field prowess will still be ahead of that of his peers by then.

Eloy Jimenez LF Born: 11/27/96 Age: 22 Bats: R Throws: R Height: 6'4" Weight: 205 Origin: International Free Agent, 2013

YEAR	TEAM	LVL	AGE	PA	R	2B	3B	HR	RBI	BB	K	SB	CS	AVG/OBP/SLG	DRC+	VORP	BABIP	BRR	FRAA	WARP
2016	SBN	A	19	464	65	40	3	14	81	25	94	8	3	.329/.369/.532	133	35.7	.391	-0.3	LF(86): -4.6, RF(11): 0.4	2.4
2017	MYR	A+	20	174	23	6	2	8	32	18	35	0	0	.271/.351/.490	143	10.1	.304	-0.3	LF(13): 0.3, RF(6): -0.1	1.2
2017	WNS	A+	20	122	20	11	1	8	26	12	21	0	2	.345/.410/.682	154	14.1	.370	0.4	RF(19): -0.6	1.0
2017	BIR	AA	20	73	11	5	0	3	7	5	16	1	1	.353/.397/.559	115	9.0	.429	0.1	RF(15): -1.1	0.2
2018	BIR	AA	21	228	36	15	2	10	42	18	39	0	0	.317/.368/.556	128	23.9	.344	-1.3	LF(30): -3.6, RF(13): -1.8	0.6
2018	CHR	AAA	21	228	28	13	1	12	33	14	30	0	1	.355/.399/.597	150	19.9	.371	-1.8	LF(41): -0.2, RF(6): 0.0	1.8
2019	*CHA*	*MLB*	*22*	*474*	*59*	*22*	*1*	*21*	*66*	*31*	*77*	*0*	*0*	*.272/.327/.469*	*115*	*20.2*	*.288*	*-1.0*	*RF -3, LF 0*	*1.8*

Breakout: 4%   Improve: 36%   Collapse: 1%   Attrition: 16%   MLB: 65%   *Comparables: Oswaldo Arcia, Austin Hays, Wil Myers*

Jimenez is not particularly fleet of foot. He's a large young man built like a Mack truck and no one expects those things to go from 0-to-60 mph particularly quickly either. As precocious as he is offensively, he's more of a normal large-bodied 22-year-old corner outfielder when it comes to his defense. He seemed to lose interest in walking during this past year against vastly inferior and overmatched minor league pitching, but also seemed to lose all interest in striking out, so call it even. If all these criticisms feel sort of like forced and insufficient explanations for why Jimenez—blatantly one of the most polished and big league-ready bats in the minors all season long—did not make his major league debut, then this served as a good synthesis of what it was like to follow his 2018 campaign. He is going to hit, hit and hit. He is going to do it nigh-immediately and he is not going to do much else, but he is going to do it enough that no one cares about much else either.

Nick Madrigal 2B Born: 03/05/97 Age: 22 Bats: R Throws: R Height: 5'7" Weight: 165 Origin: Round 1, 2018 Draft (#4 overall)

YEAR	TEAM	LVL	AGE	PA	R	2B	3B	HR	RBI	BB	K	SB	CS	AVG/OBP/SLG	DRC+	VORP	BABIP	BRR	FRAA	WARP
2018	KAN	A	21	49	9	3	0	0	6	1	0	2	2	.341/.347/.409	111	5.3	.319	1.1	2B(12): 0.9	0.4
2018	WNS	A+	21	107	14	4	0	0	9	5	5	6	3	.306/.355/.347	105	2.7	.319	0.0	2B(25): -1.8	0.2
2019	*CHA*	*MLB*	*22*	*251*	*25*	*7*	*0*	*5*	*24*	*10*	*36*	*6*	*3*	*.224/.265/.318*	*53*	*-6.3*	*.244*	*-0.3*	*2B -2, SS 0*	*-0.9*

Breakout: 7%   Improve: 11%   Collapse: 8%   Attrition: 18%   MLB: 26%   *Comparables: Breyvic Valera, Alexi Amarista, Yolmer Sanchez*

Despite being a do-everything, ego-less infielder generously listed at 5'7" and defined primarily by his categorical refusal to ever strike out, Madrigal was not actually created in a lab funded by a shady cabal of color commentators over 60 filled with resentment over the direction of the game these days. Despite being a diminutive figure with an increasingly unique quirk that defines his game, Madrigal is not a gimmick player, but rather the fourth-overall pick from last June's draft and a top-50 prospect in the game. His extreme contact ability is as clearly his carrying tool as light tower home run power or 100 mph fastball velocity would be for the average prospect, and even at the end of a long season filled with a broken wrist, a national championship at Oregon State, and a Carolina League playoff run in Winston-Salem, it was on display in his pro debut. Not much in the way of the extra-base pop the White Sox touted on draft night, nor the willingness to end a plate appearance with some other result than putting a ball in play were on display, but the cabal can wait for those details.

Yoan Moncada 2B Born: 05/27/95 Age: 24 Bats: B Throws: R Height: 6'2" Weight: 205 Origin: International Free Agent, 2015

YEAR	TEAM	LVL	AGE	PA	R	2B	3B	HR	RBI	BB	K	SB	CS	AVG/OBP/SLG	DRC+	VORP	BABIP	BRR	FRAA	WARP
2016	SLM	A+	21	284	57	25	3	4	34	45	60	36	8	.307/.427/.496	130	32.0	.395	6.2	2B(58): -1.7	2.2
2016	PME	AA	21	207	37	6	3	11	28	27	64	9	4	.277/.379/.531	108	16.4	.373	0.6	2B(34): -4.8, 3B(10): 0.8	0.4
2016	BOS	MLB	21	20	3	1	0	0	1	1	12	0	0	.211/.250/.263	44	-0.5	.571	0.3	3B(5): 0.2	0.0
2017	CHR	AAA	22	361	57	9	3	12	36	49	102	17	8	.282/.377/.447	131	17.1	.379	-0.1	2B(80): 1.4	2.5
2017	CHA	MLB	22	231	31	8	2	8	22	29	74	3	2	.231/.338/.412	88	4.2	.325	-0.7	2B(54): 5.8	0.9
2018	CHA	MLB	23	650	73	32	6	17	61	67	217	12	6	.235/.315/.400	87	15.5	.344	-0.4	2B(149): -12.7	-0.4
2019	*CHA*	*MLB*	*24*	*633*	*79*	*26*	*4*	*16*	*60*	*63*	*204*	*15*	*7*	*.221/.303/.368*	*84*	*7.6*	*.313*	*-0.6*	*2B -2, 3B 3*	*0.8*

Breakout: 3%   Improve: 46%   Collapse: 15%   Attrition: 23%   MLB: 94%   *Comparables: Javier Baez, Jorge Soler, Mark Reynolds*

Judging from interviews, Moncada's 2018 season was at least as confounding to experience as it was to observe. He was so terrible in the first few weeks of the year, which was immediately canceled out by how blisteringly amazing he was at the end of April. It was understandable when he couldn't relocate that rhythm at the plate immediately after a 10-day rehab-less disabled list stint for a minor hamstring strain. It was less so when he couldn't reproduce that power flourish for more or less the rest of the season, and barely avoided the all-time single-season strikeout record. Despite all that, he was never actually bad. You don't lead the league in strikeouts looking without drawing a healthy amount of walks. A strong finishing kick against September pitching helped, and the mental mistakes he made on defense never really threw into question his athletic ability to handle second base. It would have been a suitably promising—if aesthetically grueling—campaign for an athletic 23-year-old middle infield with dizzying tools and a good eye, if that 23-year-old were not former No. 1 global prospect and centerpiece of The Chris Sale Trade.

Daniel Palka OF Born: 10/28/91 Age: 27 Bats: L Throws: L Height: 6'2" Weight: 220 Origin: Round 3, 2013 Draft (#88 overall)

YEAR	TEAM	LVL	AGE	PA	R	2B	3B	HR	RBI	BB	K	SB	CS	AVG/OBP/SLG	DRC+	VORP	BABIP	BRR	FRAA	WARP
2016	CHT	AA	24	345	42	12	4	21	65	38	100	7	4	.270/.348/.547	136	25.4	.324	-1.4	RF(66): -11.3, 1B(3): -0.5	0.8
2016	ROC	AAA	24	223	31	12	0	13	25	18	86	2	1	.232/.296/.483	100	5.9	.324	-2.3	RF(47): -4.9	-0.3
2017	ROC	AAA	25	362	47	13	3	11	42	27	80	1	2	.274/.329/.431	104	10.0	.329	1.2	RF(61): 3.5, LF(25): 0.1	1.4
2018	CHR	AAA	26	73	11	3	0	3	7	10	21	1	2	.286/.384/.476	106	3.7	.385	0.1	RF(15): 0.5	0.3
2018	CHA	MLB	26	449	56	15	3	27	67	30	153	2	1	.240/.294/.484	99	11.8	.308	-0.8	RF(43): -3.0, LF(26): -0.5	0.4
2019	*CHA*	*MLB*	*27*	*547*	*61*	*20*	*2*	*22*	*72*	*40*	*161*	*3*	*2*	*.227/.288/.408*	*86*	*2.9*	*.286*	*-0.8*	*LF -4, RF -1*	*-0.3*

Breakout: 7%   Improve: 29%   Collapse: 4%   Attrition: 20%   MLB: 66%   *Comparables: Casper Wells, Nelson Cruz, Steven Souza*

Webster's defines Palkamania as:

—A specific sect of hedonism that values smoked home runs over equally valuable but less flashy concepts, such as outfield defense and taking the occasional pitch

—Recognition that home runs and rippling line drives are objectively fun and worth being celebrated even from fundamentally limited players

—A media phenomenon that is localized to the South Side of Chicago when there's an entertaining and quotable rookie on a 100-loss team

—Overexposure to intensely high exit velocities, and

—Not a real word

The BP Annual defines Palkamania as:

—A longtime minor leaguer thumper with one standout tool surprising everyone with his ability to actualize his double-plus raw power in games against major league pitching, even while defensive limitations and a hyper-aggressive approach perpetuate doubts about his long-term role

Luis Robert CF Born: 08/03/97 Age: 21 Bats: R Throws: R Height: 6'3" Weight: 185 Origin: International Free Agent, 2017

YEAR	TEAM	LVL	AGE	PA	R	2B	3B	HR	RBI	BB	K	SB	CS	AVG/OBP/SLG	DRC+	VORP	BABIP	BRR	FRAA	WARP
2017	DWS	RK	19	114	17	8	1	3	14	22	23	12	3	.310/.491/.536	168	21.7	.397	2.5	CF(19): -0.5	1.2
2018	KAN	A	20	50	5	3	1	0	4	4	12	4	2	.289/.360/.400	85	3.0	.394	-0.2	CF(10): 0.0	0.0
2018	WNS	A+	20	140	21	6	1	0	11	8	37	8	2	.244/.317/.309	82	2.7	.341	0.5	CF(27): 3.1, RF(4): -0.4	0.4
2019	CHA	MLB	21	251	29	9	0	4	18	18	75	9	3	.187/.269/.282	48	-6.6	.262	0.3	CF 2, RF 0	-0.5

Breakout: 2% Improve: 2% Collapse: 0% Attrition: 2% MLB: 2%   *Comparables: Joe Benson, Xavier Avery, Abraham Almonte*

When Luis Robert was signed to great fanfare, the public had little to identify him beyond nutty and precocious Serie Nacional stats, grainy batting practice video, and excited reports from clandestine showcases. And yet, more than a year later, Luis Robert's legend remains largely theoretical. Just the sight of his long, lean and muscled frame jogging around for five minutes gives a glimpse as why someone paid $26 million to bring him to their camp, and it takes only a couple batting practice cuts to see what the most standout offering of an electric toolset is. But after missing roughly three months of his first stateside season with two separate left thumb sprains, the wait for him to get in rhythm and show his in-game power has encompassed his entire professional career. It's been impressive to see how much he can make do with plus speed and no fear on the basepaths, and a strong Arizona Fall League quieted some concerns over the whiff-heavy nature of his Single-A struggles. But the primary hope for Luis Robert in 2019 is to actually see Luis Robert.

Blake Rutherford OF Born: 05/02/97 Age: 22 Bats: L Throws: R Height: 6'3" Weight: 195 Origin: Round 1, 2016 Draft (#18 overall)

YEAR	TEAM	LVL	AGE	PA	R	2B	3B	HR	RBI	BB	K	SB	CS	AVG/OBP/SLG	DRC+	VORP	BABIP	BRR	FRAA	WARP
2016	YAT	RK	19	30	3	1	0	1	3	4	6	0	0	.240/.333/.400	92	2.8	.263	0.0	CF(6): -1.1	-0.1
2016	PUL	RK	19	100	13	7	4	2	9	9	24	0	2	.382/.440/.618	104	14.7	.500	0.0	CF(14): -1.7, LF(2): -0.2	0.1
2017	CSC	A	20	304	41	20	2	2	30	25	55	9	4	.281/.342/.391	100	11.0	.341	-2.6	CF(39): -5.6, LF(13): -0.5	-0.2
2017	KAN	A	20	136	11	5	0	0	5	13	21	1	0	.213/.289/.254	100	-4.8	.257	-0.1	CF(13): -1.3, LF(10): -0.3	0.1
2018	WNS	A+	21	487	67	25	9	7	78	34	90	15	8	.293/.345/.436	106	18.7	.351	1.1	RF(74): -2.5, LF(15): -2.7	0.7
2019	CHA	MLB	22	251	22	9	1	5	25	12	57	3	1	.220/.255/.328	55	-6.5	.264	-0.2	RF 0, LF -1	-0.9

Breakout: 1% Improve: 5% Collapse: 1% Attrition: 6% MLB: 8%   *Comparables: Destin Hood, Jorge Bonifacio, Rymer Liriano*

All the smart baseball people out there seem to insist that context matters. As someone who entered 2018 coming off a truly abysmal second half at Low-A Kannapolis that nearly dragged him clear off every top-100 prospect list, Rutherford undertook an impressive bounce-back campaign. Moving to a more hitter-friendly ballpark, he more than tripled his previous year's home run output, flirted with a .300 average all year while showing actual gap power, as opposed to when we just say "gap power" to speak nicely about guys who can't hit home runs. He did this even though the Sox promoted him after a season that could have merited a repeat year in Kannapolis, at an age where most college prospects would be getting their first taste of professional baseball and would be happy to hold their own in the Carolina League. All of that is pretty good work for one year. In another context, as a lauded former first-round pick, as the centerpiece of a seven-player deal, as a top-100 prospect, he could be a corner outfielder with moderate power and a pedestrian on-base percentage. This would sound better if the downside was written first.

Yolmer Sanchez INF Born: 06/29/92 Age: 27 Bats: B Throws: R Height: 5'11" Weight: 185 Origin: International Free Agent, 2009

YEAR	TEAM	LVL	AGE	PA	R	2B	3B	HR	RBI	BB	K	SB	CS	AVG/OBP/SLG	DRC+	VORP	BABIP	BRR	FRAA	WARP
2016	CHR	AAA	24	260	31	11	2	8	29	17	55	10	4	.255/.309/.421	100	1.8	.299	-1.5	2B(45): -0.5, SS(16): 1.8	0.8
2016	CHA	MLB	24	163	15	9	1	4	21	5	42	0	1	.208/.236/.357	67	-4.9	.257	-1.2	2B(33): -1.8, 3B(6): 0.3	-0.4
2017	CHA	MLB	25	534	63	19	8	12	59	35	111	8	9	.267/.319/.413	91	13.2	.321	0.9	2B(78): -0.3, 3B(52): 3.2	1.5
2018	CHA	MLB	26	662	62	34	10	8	55	49	138	14	6	.242/.306/.372	78	11.8	.300	0.7	3B(141): -1.2, 2B(9): 0.2	0.6
2019	CHA	MLB	27	620	73	28	7	12	57	42	130	11	7	.247/.307/.387	91	8.3	.297	0.2	3B 2, 2B 0	1.0

Breakout: 6% Improve: 43% Collapse: 9% Attrition: 19% MLB: 90%   *Comparables: Cory Spangenberg, Lonnie Chisenhall, Andy LaRoche*

Only a few weeks after they displaced him with second baseman of the future Yoan Moncada in July of 2017, the White Sox conceded that Sanchez's spunky combination of adept glovework, gap power and borderline hyperactive energy actually made him the most capable third baseman on their major league roster, even if everything about his game has always screamed "utilityman on a good team." Sanchez probably drew the most national attention to himself for dunking a Gatorade bucket over his own head during celebrations of the White Sox' few walk-off wins. He's an unflinchingly positive presence on a team willfully enduring dire straits, who effortlessly blends a new school focus on enjoying the moment with old school bromides of constant hustle and has made himself into an affable avatar of the franchise. And as a second half power outage proved, he's still a utilityman filling in at third base, so his staying power will always be moment-to-moment, even as he's living in said moment.

Steele Walker CF Born: 07/30/96 Age: 22 Bats: L Throws: L Height: 5'11" Weight: 190 Origin: Round 2, 2018 Draft (#46 overall)

YEAR	TEAM	LVL	AGE	PA	R	2B	3B	HR	RBI	BB	K	SB	CS	AVG/OBP/SLG	DRC+	VORP	BABIP	BRR	FRAA	WARP
2018	GRF	RK	21	38	4	1	0	2	4	1	7	1	1	.206/.263/.412	111	0.9	.192	0.4	CF(8): -2.0	0.0
2018	KAN	A	21	126	13	5	0	3	17	8	29	5	1	.186/.246/.310	100	-1.3	.214	0.3	CF(21): 1.2	0.5
2019	CHA	MLB	22	251	23	11	0	7	26	9	63	4	1	.201/.231/.326	47	-7.1	.241	0.0	CF 0, RF 0	-0.7

Breakout: 0% Improve: 3% Collapse: 1% Attrition: 4% MLB: 4%   *Comparables: Darrell Ceciliani, Michael Taylor, Aaron Altherr*

Every year, there just has to be a Day 1 draft pick who perfectly embodies the principle of not judging college players by their immediate pro debuts. Placed into action after straining his right oblique near the tail end of a breakout junior season at Oklahoma, a rusty and weary Walker hit absolutely nothing across three separate stops. Given a fresh start in 2019, it'll be up to the 22-year-old to define which of his wide array of potentially average tools (power being the standout) will play up in games. He might not be a plus offensive contributor, he might not stick in center field, but if he shows progress toward at least one, he'll probably get another full writeup in the next version of this book.

Seby Zavala C Born: 08/28/93 Age: 25 Bats: R Throws: R Height: 5'11" Weight: 215 Origin: Round 12, 2015 Draft (#352 overall)

YEAR	TEAM	LVL	AGE	PA	R	2B	3B	HR	RBI	BB	K	SB	CS	AVG/OBP/SLG	DRC+	VORP	BABIP	BRR	FRAA	WARP
2016	KAN	A	22	404	40	19	3	7	49	35	108	1	1	.253/.330/.381	109	17.9	.341	-1.3	C(92): -1.3	2.0
2017	KAN	A	23	207	32	8	0	13	34	13	52	0	0	.259/.327/.514	139	17.6	.289	0.9	C(43): -1.5	1.9
2017	WNS	A+	23	228	31	13	0	8	38	24	52	1	0	.302/.376/.485	129	20.6	.373	3.0	C(31): 0.9	2.0
2018	BIR	AA	24	232	32	7	0	11	31	27	65	0	0	.271/.358/.472	120	18.4	.339	0.0	C(31): 4.0	1.8
2018	CHR	AAA	24	191	18	15	0	2	20	6	44	0	2	.243/.267/.359	86	-2.5	.304	-1.2	C(35): -3.0	0.0
2019	CHA	MLB	25	58	5	3	0	1	5	2	15	0	0	.222/.256/.336	45	-1.4	.281	-0.1	C -1	-0.3

Breakout: 4% Improve: 13% Collapse: 11% Attrition: 18% MLB: 29%   *Comparables: Andrew Knapp, Luke Montz, Johnny Monell*

As a San Diego State product of a certain era, Zavala has a requisite Tony Gwynn tattoo and a variety of oft-used phrases from his old college coach that he trots out when appropriate. One of them is "Know who you is," which probably sounded better coming from the mouth of a man with 3,141 career big league hits than it reads in print, but fits Zavala himself surprisingly well. As a short and stout, slow-footed catcher with a surgically repaired elbow, he's not in this book because he dazzles with tools, but more for his ability to actualize

YEAR	TEAM	P. COUNT	FRM RUNS	BLK RUNS	THRW RUNS	TOT RUNS
2018	BIR	4264	3.3	0.1	0.4	4.0
2018	CHR	4728	-2.6	0.0	-0.1	-2.3
2019	CHA	2122	-0.8	-0.1	-0.1	-1.0

everything he has in games. He doesn't have all-fields power, but is proficient at tucking in his wrists and yanking the ball to left with authority. He doesn't have a cannon or block pitches particularly well, but Zavala makes a concerted effort to frame and calls a game like someone who listened to Tony Gwynn talk a lot. At 25 years of age and having yet to solve Triple-A, it's hard to see him as the White Sox catcher of the future, but he'll likely be a White Sox catcher of the present before long.

PITCHERS

Spencer Adams RHP Born: 04/13/96 Age: 23 Bats: R Throws: R Height: 6'3" Weight: 171 Origin: Round 2, 2014 Draft (#44 overall)

YEAR	TEAM	LVL	AGE	W	L	SV	G	GS	IP	H	HR	BB/9	K/9	K	GB%	BABIP	WHIP	ERA	DRA	WARP	MPH	FB%	WHF	CSP
2016	WNS	A+	20	8	7	0	18	18	107²	120	7	1.8	6.2	74	55%	.313	1.31	4.01	3.57	2.3				
2016	BIR	AA	20	2	5	0	9	9	55¹	59	2	1.6	4.2	26	42%	.298	1.25	3.90	3.62	1.0				
2017	BIR	AA	21	7	15	0	26	26	152²	171	19	2.4	6.7	113	49%	.314	1.38	4.42	5.58	-0.8				
2018	BIR	AA	22	3	6	0	13	13	68²	80	10	2.6	6.9	53	44%	.329	1.46	4.59	7.01	-1.3				
2018	CHR	AAA	22	4	7	0	15	15	90¹	82	10	3.8	4.2	42	42%	.256	1.33	3.19	5.23	0.3				
2019	CHA	MLB	23	1	2	0	5	5	25	27	4	3.1	6.4	18	44%	.298	1.44	5.01	5.26	0.1				

Breakout: 2% Improve: 6% Collapse: 5% Attrition: 9% MLB: 10%   *Comparables: Adrian Sampson, Trevor Oaks, Steve Garrison*

For a year where he mostly pitched in a manner completely antithetical to his core principles as a ballplayer, Spencer Adams didn't have a half-bad 2018. Reaching Triple-A and not getting hammered there is fine work for a prospect defined by strike-throwing and pitchability more than overpowering stuff. That it came alongside a career-high and objectively high walk rate while his velocity languished in the low-90s was more worrisome. He never looked quite like his fluid, athletic, can-still-dunk-if-you-get-him-on-the-court self outside the month in Birmingham that got him promoted. Adams will not turn 23 until April and is already a step away from the majors, so 2019 is hardly a crossroads in his career. But prospects like him make their money by providing metronome-like consistency, not by suddenly having their command click to unlock wipeout stuff, so the control problems need to be a short blip in his ascent.

Ryan Burr RHP Born: 05/28/94 Age: 25 Bats: R Throws: R Height: 6'4" Weight: 225 Origin: Round 5, 2015 Draft (#136 overall)

YEAR	TEAM	LVL	AGE	W	L	SV	G	GS	IP	H	HR	BB/9	K/9	K	GB%	BABIP	WHIP	ERA	DRA	WARP	MPH	FB%	WHF	CSP
2016	KNC	A	22	1	2	0	14	0	21	22	0	3.9	7.7	18	43%	.328	1.48	3.86	4.98	-0.1				
2017	KNC	A	23	1	2	4	22	0	32	29	3	4.2	12.9	46	48%	.361	1.38	2.81	3.17	0.7				
2017	VIS	A+	23	1	0	1	17	0	25	13	0	2.2	10.4	29	74%	.245	0.76	0.72	3.68	0.4				
2017	WNS	A+	23	0	0	1	6	0	8¹	5	0	5.4	14.0	13	47%	.333	1.20	0.00	5.20	0.0				
2018	BIR	AA	24	4	2	2	30	0	43	30	3	4.8	9.0	43	51%	.248	1.23	2.72	3.48	0.7				
2018	CHR	AAA	24	0	1	0	7	0	8¹	4	0	2.2	8.6	8	80%	.200	0.72	1.08	3.42	0.2				
2018	CHA	MLB	24	0	0	0	8	0	9²	12	3	5.6	5.6	6	39%	.321	1.86	7.45	6.33	-0.2	96.1	67.5	11.5	52.4
2019	CHA	MLB	25	1	1	0	31	0	32²	31	5	5.3	9.1	33	45%	.294	1.53	5.07	5.32	-0.1	95.8	69.1	11.7	53.7

Breakout: 4% Improve: 8% Collapse: 8% Attrition: 13% MLB: 17%   *Comparables: Kevin McCarthy, Jose Ortega, Angel Nesbitt*

Burr was already 20 years old when Lin-Manuel Miranda's *Hamilton* premiered at The Public Theater in New York City. He was into his third professional season when he was traded into the White Sox organization and placed at the same affiliate as fellow relief prospect Ian Hamilton. He did not ask for this life, and all the jokes and themed promos for the team social media accounts that are likely coming with it. He also was taken a bit by surprise by his call-up at the end of 2018, a season that began with him struggling to command his 95 mph four-seamer/hard slider combination in Double-A until June, and ended with him struggling to regain the "hard" part of his slider as he adjusted to the seams on major league balls in September. In between those months, and all the Hamilton jokes, was a nice little (well, not little, he's 6'4", 225 pounds) relief prospect who should find his way into sixth and seventh innings in 2019.

Dylan Cease RHP   Born: 12/28/95   Age: 23   Bats: R   Throws: R   Height: 6'2"   Weight: 190   Origin: Round 6, 2014 Draft (#169 overall)

YEAR	TEAM	LVL	AGE	W	L	SV	G	GS	IP	H	HR	BB/9	K/9	K	GB%	BABIP	WHIP	ERA	DRA	WARP	MPH	FB%	WHF	CSP
2016	EUG	A-	20	2	0	0	12	12	44²	27	1	5.0	13.3	66	55%	.295	1.16	2.22	3.00	1.2				
2017	SBN	A	21	1	2	0	13	13	51²	39	2	4.5	12.9	74	46%	.339	1.26	2.79	3.50	1.1				
2017	KAN	A	21	0	8	0	9	9	41²	35	1	3.9	11.2	52	43%	.330	1.27	3.89	3.00	1.1				
2018	WNS	A+	22	9	2	0	13	13	71²	52	5	3.5	10.3	82	50%	.273	1.12	2.89	2.90	2.0				
2018	BIR	AA	22	3	0	0	10	10	52¹	30	3	3.8	13.4	78	50%	.273	0.99	1.72	2.77	1.6				
2019	*CHA*	*MLB*	*23*	*3*	*3*	*0*	*23*	*8*	*56¹*	*49*	*8*	*5.4*	*10.9*	*68*	*43%*	*.298*	*1.47*	*4.72*	*4.95*	*0.2*				

Breakout: 13%   Improve: 21%   Collapse: 16%   Attrition: 25%   MLB: 43%   *Comparables: Zack Wheeler, Stephen Gonsalves, Jacob Faria*

In his second to last start of the season, Dylan Cease needed 40 pitches to labor through the first inning on a rainy mid-August night. Since he was already near his season innings limit, the White Sox just pulled him. He got knocked around in his first game after being promoted to Double-A, even while striking out seven in less than five innings. He was absolutely torched for eight runs on nine hits in the middle of May when he was still at Winston-Salem—he explained that he just didn't have it that day. That's about half the comment space accounted for, but it was more concise to detail all the times Cease wasn't overpowering against minor league competition in 2018 rather than vice versa. Always blessed with top shelf velocity and an occasionally jaw-dropping curveball, Cease was finally challenged with a real starter's workload and responded with a dominant and healthy year. After a grip tip from James Shields in spring gave him more command of his curve, his best outings found him with an effective changeup, along with an occasional slider. There's still a gulf between his current command level and what will allow him to be consistent in the majors, and there's a logic that someone with his stuff was never going to be tested at the lower levels. But he'll be in the mix to be a top-50 prospect going into 2019, and he's earned it.

Alex Colome RHP   Born: 12/31/88   Age: 30   Bats: R   Throws: R   Height: 6'1"   Weight: 220   Origin: International Free Agent, 2007

YEAR	TEAM	LVL	AGE	W	L	SV	G	GS	IP	H	HR	BB/9	K/9	K	GB%	BABIP	WHIP	ERA	DRA	WARP	MPH	FB%	WHF	CSP
2016	TBA	MLB	27	2	4	37	57	0	56²	43	6	2.4	11.3	71	49%	.280	1.02	1.91	2.85	1.4	96.7	51.9	16.1	45.9
2017	TBA	MLB	28	2	3	47	65	0	66²	57	4	3.1	7.8	58	50%	.275	1.20	3.24	3.97	0.9	95.9	32.7	12.4	46.8
2018	TBA	MLB	29	2	5	11	23	0	21²	24	1	3.3	9.6	23	55%	.354	1.48	4.15	3.91	0.3	95.5	49.3	16	48.9
2018	SEA	MLB	29	5	0	1	47	0	46¹	35	6	2.5	9.5	49	42%	.254	1.04	2.53	3.97	0.5	96.5	49.3	15	45.5
2019	*CHA*	*MLB*	*30*	*3*	*1*	*20*	*52*	*0*	*54²*	*49*	*6*	*3.4*	*9.5*	*58*	*47%*	*.296*	*1.28*	*3.92*	*4.09*	*0.6*	*95.4*	*44.2*	*14.5*	*46.4*

Breakout: 25%   Improve: 60%   Collapse: 25%   Attrition: 10%   MLB: 97%   *Comparables: Chad Qualls, Blake Treinen, Phil Coke*

It's not so much that the game passed the recently age-30 Colome by so much as its tastes did. The work of a perfectly solid, one-inning-per-game, one-run-every-three setup man was en vogue a few years ago, when everyone was trying to stock deep, well-rounded bullpens. But then we fell in love with copying Andrew Miller, and now it's 15 K/9 closers or bust. Colome performed perfectly well after coming over to Seattle to assist Edwin Diaz in a salary cutting trade, and then that same salary propelled him to the South Side, where he'll compete for save chances with Nate Jones. He'll either win that job, or lose it. And afterwards, he'll pitch just fine.

Dylan Covey RHP   Born: 08/14/91   Age: 27   Bats: R   Throws: R   Height: 6'2"   Weight: 195   Origin: Round 4, 2013 Draft (#131 overall)

YEAR	TEAM	LVL	AGE	W	L	SV	G	GS	IP	H	HR	BB/9	K/9	K	GB%	BABIP	WHIP	ERA	DRA	WARP	MPH	FB%	WHF	CSP
2016	MID	AA	24	2	1	0	6	6	29¹	21	2	5.2	8.0	26	61%	.247	1.30	1.84	3.67	0.5				
2017	CHR	AAA	25	0	0	0	2	0	6	5	1	1.5	4.5	3	58%	.222	1.00	3.00	4.09	0.1				
2017	CHA	MLB	25	0	7	0	18	12	70	83	20	4.4	5.3	41	49%	.296	1.67	7.71	7.88	-1.9	94.6	60.5	6.8	45.5
2018	CHR	AAA	26	3	1	0	7	7	38²	32	3	3.5	8.1	35	57%	.282	1.22	2.33	4.62	0.4				
2018	CHA	MLB	26	5	14	0	27	21	121²	129	13	3.8	6.7	91	56%	.302	1.49	5.18	5.15	0.2	96.1	61.5	7.8	49.6
2019	*CHA*	*MLB*	*27*	*4*	*6*	*0*	*16*	*16*	*84²*	*85*	*11*	*4.3*	*7.4*	*70*	*52%*	*.294*	*1.47*	*4.93*	*5.17*	*0.3*	*95.1*	*62*	*7.6*	*48.4*

Breakout: 13%   Improve: 33%   Collapse: 15%   Attrition: 26%   MLB: 69%   *Comparables: Williams Perez, Colin Rea, Shawn Hill*

Year 2 of being pulled from the minors, dropped into a major league rotation only for a successive run of rough nights and harrowing days to route him to the bullpen went better for Covey than Year 1 of... more or less the same experience. Michael Kopech's torn UCL ushered him back into the White Sox rotation at year's end, and more importantly, he forged an identity on the mound as someone who is going to live and die with his sinker. The frequency of the dying after the first time through the order means he is probably well-advised to make his living out of the bullpen, where his two-seamer velocity can stay closer to the 95-96 mph band, but the state of the Sox rotation means a Year 3 could be in the works.

Dane Dunning RHP Born: 12/20/94 Age: 24 Bats: R Throws: R Height: 6'4" Weight: 200 Origin: Round 1, 2016 Draft (#29 overall)

YEAR	TEAM	LVL	AGE	W	L	SV	G	GS	IP	H	HR	BB/9	K/9	K	GB%	BABIP	WHIP	ERA	DRA	WARP	MPH	FB%	WHF	CSP
2016	AUB	A-	21	3	2	0	7	7	33²	26	1	1.9	7.8	29	65%	.263	0.98	2.14	3.92	0.5				
2017	KAN	A	22	2	0	0	4	4	26	13	0	0.7	11.4	33	64%	.224	0.58	0.35	3.10	0.7				
2017	WNS	A+	22	6	8	0	22	22	118	114	15	2.7	10.3	135	52%	.316	1.27	3.51	4.05	1.7				
2018	WNS	A+	23	1	1	0	4	4	24¹	20	2	1.1	11.5	31	61%	.300	0.95	2.59	3.51	0.5				
2018	BIR	AA	23	5	2	0	11	11	62	57	0	3.3	10.0	69	49%	.343	1.29	2.76	3.58	1.3				
2019	CHA	MLB	24	4	6	0	15	15	80	80	11	3.3	8.7	78	48%	.304	1.37	4.52	4.74	0.7				

Breakout: 11% Improve: 23% Collapse: 13% Attrition: 26% MLB: 42% *Comparables: Jordan Montgomery, Sean Nolin, Cody Martin*

Despite whatever notions his profile photo and thick-rimmed black glasses at the center of it might carry, despite what images the description of "back-end-to-mid-rotation starter who thrives on plus command" might conjure, Dunning is a physically imposing figure. He stands a strong, thickly-built 6'4" with all the muscle and athleticism to hold his delivery through the rigors of a full season. But despite his reputation as a safe and reliable starting pitching prospect—as safe and reliable as those can be—Dunning was still felled by the injury bug in 2018. He labored through whispers of elbow pain until they became a full-throated shout, and a sprain ended his season in late June, though he did complete a rehab circuit without any setbacks and still expects to avoid surgery. There may or may not be such a thing as a pitching prospect, but there's definitely no such thing as a hurt pitching prospect.

Danny Farquhar RHP Born: 02/17/87 Age: 32 Bats: R Throws: R Height: 5'9" Weight: 185 Origin: Round 10, 2008 Draft (#309 overall)

YEAR	TEAM	LVL	AGE	W	L	SV	G	GS	IP	H	HR	BB/9	K/9	K	GB%	BABIP	WHIP	ERA	DRA	WARP	MPH	FB%	WHF	CSP
2016	DUR	AAA	29	4	2	2	32	0	38	33	2	2.1	5.7	24	48%	.270	1.11	3.32	3.11	0.8				
2016	TBA	MLB	29	1	0	0	35	0	35¹	33	8	3.8	11.7	46	41%	.294	1.36	3.06	2.94	0.8	94.7	54.1	15.5	39.9
2017	TBA	MLB	30	2	2	0	37	0	35	28	2	5.7	8.5	33	47%	.280	1.43	4.11	3.94	0.5	94.5	58.1	14.6	44.1
2017	CHR	AAA	30	0	0	1	8	0	9	6	2	2.0	12.0	12	55%	.222	0.89	3.00	4.43	0.1				
2017	CHA	MLB	30	2	0	0	15	0	14¹	11	1	3.8	7.5	12	37%	.238	1.19	4.40	4.50	0.1	95.0	58.1	11.2	47.9
2018	CHA	MLB	31	1	1	0	8	0	8	6	3	0.0	10.1	9	35%	.176	0.75	5.62	3.04	0.2	93.9	56.9	16.4	47.1
2019	CHA	MLB	32	2	1	0	33	0	34¹	32	5	4.2	9.8	37	42%	.294	1.39	4.64	4.88	0.1	93.6	56.2	14.4	44.3

Breakout: 17% Improve: 38% Collapse: 19% Attrition: 10% MLB: 73% *Comparables: Justin Miller, Fernando Rodriguez, Matt Reynolds*

For whatever reason, there's just not a ton of prior precedent in major league baseball about comebacks from ruptured brain aneurysms and the associated near-death experiences that result. While the White Sox and the baseball community has spent the better part of 2018 just being very thrilled that Farquhar is alive after collapsing in the Guaranteed Rate Field home dugout on April 20, the journeyman reliever himself has been pretty set upon the idea of returning to pitching since walking out of the hospital a couple weeks later. Removed from the strain of a professional season for the first time in a decade, Farquhar is throwing harder than ever in his private sessions, but has been back and forth between the majors and Triple-A enough times to know that sticking in a big league bullpen is a battle every year, let alone after a setback of this magnitude.

Caleb Frare LHP Born: 07/08/93 Age: 25 Bats: L Throws: L Height: 6'1" Weight: 210 Origin: Round 11, 2012 Draft (#367 overall)

YEAR	TEAM	LVL	AGE	W	L	SV	G	GS	IP	H	HR	BB/9	K/9	K	GB%	BABIP	WHIP	ERA	DRA	WARP	MPH	FB%	WHF	CSP
2016	TAM	A+	22	3	3	0	32	0	49	33	0	4.2	9.6	52	56%	.275	1.14	0.92	2.16	1.6				
2017	TRN	AA	23	2	2	0	24	0	33²	19	2	9.1	11.2	42	48%	.254	1.57	4.28	3.82	0.4				
2017	TAM	A+	23	1	2	1	15	0	29	29	4	5.6	11.2	36	43%	.379	1.62	3.72	3.50	0.5				
2018	TRN	AA	24	4	1	5	31	0	43²	25	1	3.1	11.7	57	39%	.258	0.92	0.62	2.62	1.2				
2018	CHR	AAA	24	1	0	0	11	0	12²	5	0	5.0	13.5	19	42%	.208	0.95	0.71	2.50	0.4				
2018	CHA	MLB	24	0	1	0	11	0	7	6	0	5.1	11.6	9	29%	.353	1.43	5.14	2.03	0.2	96.3	54.3	17.8	42.6
2019	CHA	MLB	25	2	1	0	41	0	43²	39	7	5.6	11.1	54	43%	.301	1.51	5.03	5.29	-0.2	96.0	55.6	18.3	43.7

Breakout: 22% Improve: 29% Collapse: 10% Attrition: 27% MLB: 44% *Comparables: James Pazos, Kevin Quackenbush, Shawn Armstrong*

Frare's knowledge of R-rated movies that came out before he was 17 has proven strong in limited testing, but it's likely he's unfamiliar with Samuel L. Jackson's portrayal of Mitch Henessey in The Long Kiss Goodnight. Particularly so his line cautioning Charlie Baltimore, played by Geena Davis, that it isn't so easy to leave New Jersey: "Others have tried and failed. The entire population in fact." With that in mind, and that Frare walked 34 batters in 33 2/3 innings during his 2017 stint there, Frare's escape from Double-A Trenton is doubly impressive. Thanks to the revolutionary new method of "throwing the ball as hard as I can," he drastically cut his walk rate, and indeed, throws harder, sitting in the mid-90s and touching 97. Control eluded him during his big league cameo in September, but his deceptive arm action and slider could power him to a role as a lefty specialist for years to come.

Jace Fry LHP Born: 07/09/93 Age: 25 Bats: L Throws: L Height: 6'1" Weight: 190 Origin: Round 3, 2014 Draft (#77 overall)

YEAR	TEAM	LVL	AGE	W	L	SV	G	GS	IP	H	HR	BB/9	K/9	K	GB%	BABIP	WHIP	ERA	DRA	WARP	MPH	FB%	WHF	CSP
2017	BIR	AA	23	2	1	3	33	0	45¹	36	1	4.8	10.3	52	59%	.307	1.32	2.78	3.23	0.8				
2017	CHA	MLB	23	0	0	0	11	0	6²	12	1	6.8	4.1	3	39%	.407	2.55	10.80	5.83	0.0	95.5	68.2	10.8	41.1
2018	CHR	AAA	24	0	0	0	5	0	6²	3	1	0.0	14.9	11	54%	.167	0.45	1.35	2.02	0.2				
2018	CHA	MLB	24	2	3	4	59	1	51¹	37	4	3.5	12.3	70	47%	.277	1.11	4.38	2.96	1.2	95.2	34.2	15.3	43.7
2019	CHA	MLB	25	3	1	0	52	0	54²	45	6	4.3	11.4	69	48%	.298	1.31	3.84	4.01	0.6	94.9	38.6	15.2	43.6

Breakout: 36% Improve: 56% Collapse: 19% Attrition: 19% MLB: 85% *Comparables: Jensen Lewis, Cam Bedrosian, Jose Mijares*

Fry's triumphant recovery from a second Tommy John surgery and subsequent reallocation to the bullpen were undercut by the fact that his major league debut went, well, quite poorly. So it threw everyone for a loop that his return from yet another disabled list stint to start 2018—this time a humble oblique strain—spurred his emergence as arguably the most impressive member of the White Sox bullpen. He doesn't throw extremely hard, nor does he wield a dominant wipeout offering to point to as the fuel to his short relief success, and was absolutely not an overpowering strikeout pitcher as a starter in college. Apparently the whole thing where a crafty lefty mixes five pitches, all of out the same slot, and throws them all for strikes with good deception can be really effective out of the bullpen. Whether that means every soft-tossing southpaw is a relief ace in waiting is more doubtful, but it's certainly turned Fry into a valuable asset.

Carson Fulmer RHP   Born: 12/13/93   Age: 25   Bats: R   Throws: R   Height: 6'0"   Weight: 195   Origin: Round 1, 2015 Draft (#8 overall)

YEAR	TEAM	LVL	AGE	W	L	SV	G	GS	IP	H	HR	BB/9	K/9	K	GB%	BABIP	WHIP	ERA	DRA	WARP	MPH	FB%	WHF	CSP
2016	BIR	AA	22	4	9	0	17	17	87	82	7	5.3	9.3	90	45%	.310	1.53	4.76	3.49	1.7				
2016	CHA	MLB	22	0	2	0	8	0	11²	12	2	5.4	7.7	10	44%	.312	1.63	8.49	3.76	0.2	95.3	50.2	10.4	40.5
2016	CHR	AAA	22	2	1	0	4	4	16	14	1	2.8	7.9	14	61%	.289	1.19	3.94	6.18	-0.2				
2017	CHR	AAA	23	7	9	0	25	25	126	132	18	4.6	6.9	96	46%	.297	1.56	5.79	5.11	0.8				
2017	CHA	MLB	23	3	1	0	7	5	23¹	16	4	5.0	7.3	19	31%	.190	1.24	3.86	7.31	-0.5	94.6	51.8	9.6	46.1
2018	CHA	MLB	24	2	4	0	9	8	32¹	37	8	6.7	8.1	29	34%	.296	1.89	8.07	8.06	-1.0	94.3	55.3	7.3	44.8
2018	CHR	AAA	24	5	6	0	25	9	67²	70	10	5.5	8.2	62	40%	.316	1.64	5.32	4.97	0.3				
2019	CHA	MLB	25	2	1	0	52	0	54²	54	9	5.1	8.5	52	41%	.292	1.55	5.39	5.67	-0.5	94.2	54.9	8.6	45.3

Breakout: 27%   Improve: 38%   Collapse: 13%   Attrition: 38%   MLB: 60%   *Comparables: Zach Miner, Jose Cisnero, Josh Hall*

Well, the White Sox certainly tried. There were plenty of evaluators who felt Carson Fulmer was bound to be a reliever even when he was a star at Vanderbilt, and the Sox took him eighth overall. Despite minor league numbers always riddled with control problems, numerous tweaks to slow down his herky-jerky motion that didn't quite take, and struggles to maintain his college velocity and stuff, Chicago rewarded every hint of progress with a shot at the big league rotation. That continued despite a rocky spring training in 2018, but their ambitions for him couldn't survive watching him get blitzed out of the game before the fifth every other start under the big league lights. Despite a pledge that he would return to the majors soon after being optioned in May, Fulmer never gave the Sox a reason to recall him, and after a few more trying months in Triple-A, they finally conceded that he's a reliever. The question for him going forward is whether he can show signs of a being a good one.

Lucas Giolito RHP   Born: 07/14/94   Age: 24   Bats: R   Throws: R   Height: 6'6"   Weight: 245   Origin: Round 1, 2012 Draft (#16 overall)

YEAR	TEAM	LVL	AGE	W	L	SV	G	GS	IP	H	HR	BB/9	K/9	K	GB%	BABIP	WHIP	ERA	DRA	WARP	MPH	FB%	WHF	CSP
2016	HAR	AA	21	5	3	0	14	14	71	67	2	4.3	9.1	72	53%	.323	1.42	3.17	3.21	1.6				
2016	HAG	A	21	0	0	0	1	1	7	6	2	0.0	5.1	4	36%	.200	0.86	5.14	3.37	0.1				
2016	SYR	AAA	21	1	2	0	7	7	37¹	31	3	2.4	9.6	40	56%	.298	1.10	2.17	3.22	0.9				
2016	WAS	MLB	21	0	1	0	6	4	21¹	26	7	5.1	4.6	11	42%	.271	1.78	6.75	7.03	-0.4	96.1	71.1	6.3	48.1
2017	CHR	AAA	22	6	10	0	24	24	128²	122	17	4.1	9.4	134	45%	.312	1.41	4.48	4.32	2.0				
2017	CHA	MLB	22	3	3	0	7	7	45¹	31	8	2.4	6.8	34	47%	.189	0.95	2.38	4.27	0.7	94.1	59.8	11.1	46.2
2018	CHA	MLB	23	10	13	0	32	32	173¹	166	27	4.7	6.5	125	45%	.268	1.48	6.13	6.58	-2.5	94.7	59.5	9.2	46.8
2019	CHA	MLB	24	8	10	0	26	26	148¹	141	19	4.3	8.1	134	45%	.288	1.42	4.83	5.07	0.7	94.5	62.1	9.6	48.4

Breakout: 23%   Improve: 49%   Collapse: 16%   Attrition: 23%   MLB: 90%   *Comparables: Sean West, Martin Perez, Sean Marshall*

Giolito's 2018 was a search for a context other than "total disaster." For much of a grueling first half, it was about grinding without his best stuff, or without his best location, and competing even when unsteady mechanics robbed him of his command. As his second-half outings shaded more professional, his season drifted toward a story of growth, and the merits of letting a 24-year-old former top prospect work through his struggles, learn to make quicker adjustments and find the arm slot that allowed for the best balance between getting life on his fastball and actually putting it in the zone. Giolito's late-season success came from relying on his two-seamer, contradicting the carrying four-seamer and tumbling changeup approach that made him a success in spring training and the previous September. With how awful his 2018 season was in stretches, he just needed to show progress of any kind, which is why his disastrous close to the year was all the more discouraging. Starting in the majors requires consistency, and Giolito has still found preciously little.

Ian Hamilton RHP   Born: 06/16/95   Age: 24   Bats: R   Throws: R   Height: 6'0"   Weight: 200   Origin: Round 11, 2016 Draft (#326 overall)

YEAR	TEAM	LVL	AGE	W	L	SV	G	GS	IP	H	HR	BB/9	K/9	K	GB%	BABIP	WHIP	ERA	DRA	WARP	MPH	FB%	WHF	CSP
2016	KAN	A	21	1	1	8	21	0	31²	22	3	4.0	7.7	27	49%	.235	1.14	3.69	3.04	0.6				
2017	BIR	AA	22	1	3	1	14	0	19	26	0	3.8	10.4	22	52%	.419	1.79	5.21	4.95	0.0				
2017	WNS	A+	22	3	3	6	30	0	52²	33	1	1.4	8.9	52	46%	.241	0.78	1.71	2.82	1.3				
2018	BIR	AA	23	2	1	12	21	0	25¹	20	0	4.3	12.1	34	47%	.323	1.26	1.78	3.45	0.4				
2018	CHR	AAA	23	1	1	10	22	0	26¹	18	2	1.4	9.6	28	49%	.254	0.84	1.71	3.47	0.5				
2018	CHA	MLB	23	1	2	0	10	0	8	6	2	2.2	5.6	5	48%	.174	1.00	4.50	3.37	0.1	98.1	70.1	12	46.3
2019	CHA	MLB	24	2	1	0	41	0	43²	39	5	4.4	9.7	47	44%	.292	1.37	4.38	4.59	0.3	97.9	72.2	12.3	47.7

Breakout: 9%   Improve: 11%   Collapse: 9%   Attrition: 16%   MLB: 21%   *Comparables: Heath Hembree, Abel De Los Santos, Eury De La Rosa*

The short and unbelievably cut Ian Hamilton seems like he would be better suited leaking out of the backfield to catch screen passes, which would likely make better use of his plus speed than throwing off a mound. The thought definitely occurred to Hamilton, who was stopped from walking onto the Washington State football team only by the panicked efforts of a baseball coach anxious about seeing his closer getting laid out by 230-pound linebackers. Catching passes in the flat would be a waste of Hamilton's ability to sit 97-99 mph, a notable uptick from 2017, with command that sharpened over the course of the year. As he rapidly progressed from being a sorta-interesting reliever who threw sorta hard in High-A, to a completely dominant minor league closer, the scrutiny has heightened. With his short stature and arm action, Hamilton's fastball did not play as loud as its velocity in his big league debut, and he won't be able to survive stretches without feel for his slider like he did in Birmingham. But there's a real shot to carve out a big league relief future, where there was only a hint of one before.

Alec Hansen RHP Born: 10/10/94 Age: 24 Bats: R Throws: R Height: 6'7" Weight: 235 Origin: Round 2, 2016 Draft (#49 overall)

YEAR	TEAM	LVL	AGE	W	L	SV	G	GS	IP	H	HR	BB/9	K/9	K	GB%	BABIP	WHIP	ERA	DRA	WARP	MPH	FB%	WHF	CSP
2016	WSX	RK	21	0	0	0	3	3	7	1	0	5.1	14.1	11	70%	.100	0.71	0.00	2.03	0.3				
2016	GRF	RK	21	2	0	0	7	7	36²	12	3	2.9	14.5	59	52%	.161	0.65	1.23	1.92	1.5				
2016	KAN	A	21	0	1	0	2	2	11	11	0	3.3	9.0	11	53%	.344	1.36	2.45	2.40	0.4				
2017	KAN	A	22	7	3	0	13	13	72²	57	3	2.8	11.4	92	32%	.292	1.10	2.48	2.80	2.1				
2017	WNS	A+	22	4	5	0	11	11	58¹	42	5	3.9	12.7	82	38%	.296	1.15	2.93	3.42	1.3				
2017	BIR	AA	22	0	0	0	2	2	10¹	15	0	2.6	14.8	17	36%	.536	1.74	4.35	2.95	0.3				
2018	BIR	AA	23	0	4	0	9	9	35²	30	3	10.6	8.8	35	33%	.293	2.02	6.56	5.96	-0.3				
2018	WNS	A+	23	0	1	0	5	5	15²	14	0	9.8	11.5	20	27%	.378	1.98	5.74	4.53	0.1				
2019	CHA	MLB	24	2	5	0	12	12	56	55	11	7.1	10.0	62	38%	.304	1.78	6.11	6.45	-0.6				

Breakout: 6% Improve: 9% Collapse: 7% Attrition: 13% MLB: 19%   *Comparables: Humberto Sanchez, Josh Collmenter, Austin Brice*

"At least he stayed healthy" would be a decent qualifier to throw out after a year of disappointing performance for a top pitching prospect. Conversely, a season completely lost to injury would at least have preserved the optimism and dominance of Alec Hansen's 2017 campaign until February of 2019. Instead he was denied both silver linings, missing the first half of 2018 with a strangely nagging forearm issue and missing his spots for all of a nightmarish second half. The imposing right-hander was a top-50 prospect coming into the year, openly discussing his expectation to make it in the majors by September, and he ended the season still ineffective after a demotion to the Carolina League. Normally it would be fatuous to wonder if someone walking over a batter per inning at High-A at age 23 could turn it around and become a big league starter, but Hansen's biggest solace is that he's been here before, and worked his way back after a similarly walk-addled junior season at Oklahoma. That's if you consider that solace, though.

Nate Jones RHP Born: 01/28/86 Age: 33 Bats: R Throws: R Height: 6'5" Weight: 220 Origin: Round 5, 2007 Draft (#179 overall)

YEAR	TEAM	LVL	AGE	W	L	SV	G	GS	IP	H	HR	BB/9	K/9	K	GB%	BABIP	WHIP	ERA	DRA	WARP	MPH	FB%	WHF	CSP
2016	CHA	MLB	30	5	3	3	71	0	70²	48	7	1.9	10.2	80	47%	.243	0.89	2.29	2.84	1.7	99.2	63	15.3	48
2017	CHA	MLB	31	1	0	0	11	0	11²	9	1	4.6	11.6	15	59%	.308	1.29	2.31	4.95	0.0	98.3	52.5	13	41.5
2018	CHA	MLB	32	2	2	5	33	0	30	28	4	4.5	9.6	32	41%	.289	1.43	3.00	4.55	0.1	98.6	64.7	15.2	47.1
2019	CHA	MLB	33	3	1	10	52	0	54²	48	7	3.8	9.5	58	45%	.282	1.30	4.42	4.64	0.2	97.8	61.6	14.8	44.9

Breakout: 22% Improve: 42% Collapse: 30% Attrition: 17% MLB: 89%   *Comparables: Jose Valverde, Jay Witasick, Kiko Calero*

Nate Jones can still throw hard and miss bats when healthy. After missing three months in the middle of the 2018 with a pronator strain, sealing his fourth injury-marred season out of the last five, that was something he felt the need to work his way back and reaffirm, even at the end of a doomed campaign for a rebuilding team. Fastball-slider righties who can touch the upper-90s and strike out a batter per inning have become a lot more common since Jones first broke onto the scene in 2012, and he struggled with control problems that once seemed conquered in 2016 all while fighting off renewed elbow troubles. Still, there's a late-inning ceiling from a massive physical frame here, and as long as Jones continues to be willing to put the work in to get himself right, he'll get another chance to succeed.

Michael Kopech RHP Born: 04/30/96 Age: 23 Bats: R Throws: R Height: 6'3" Weight: 205 Origin: Round 1, 2014 Draft (#33 overall)

YEAR	TEAM	LVL	AGE	W	L	SV	G	GS	IP	H	HR	BB/9	K/9	K	GB%	BABIP	WHIP	ERA	DRA	WARP	MPH	FB%	WHF	CSP
2016	SLM	A+	20	4	1	0	11	11	52	25	1	5.0	14.2	82	45%	.273	1.04	2.25	2.78	1.6				
2017	BIR	AA	21	8	7	0	22	22	119¹	77	6	4.5	11.7	155	42%	.272	1.15	2.87	3.29	2.7				
2017	CHR	AAA	21	1	1	0	3	3	15	15	0	3.0	10.2	17	35%	.375	1.33	3.00	3.90	0.3				
2018	CHR	AAA	22	7	7	0	24	24	126¹	101	9	4.3	12.1	170	40%	.316	1.27	3.70	5.03	0.7				
2018	CHA	MLB	22	1	1	0	4	4	14¹	20	4	1.3	9.4	15	28%	.381	1.53	5.02	6.84	-0.3	97.7	62.5	10.9	50.9
2019	CHA	MLB	23	6	8	0	24	24	118¹	98	16	5.0	11.4	150	39%	.297	1.38	4.39	4.60	1.2	97.6	64.7	11.3	52.8

Breakout: 20% Improve: 31% Collapse: 12% Attrition: 28% MLB: 51%   *Comparables: Trevor May, Zack Wheeler, Tyler Thornburg*

Every time a marquee pitching prospect goes down with a torn ulnar collateral ligament, the reaction resembles being diagnosed with a terminal illness. But after a season defined by Kopech overcoming his control problems, dealing with personal tragedy, and even gaining some consistency killing some changeups as he finally earned his way toward his major league debut, Tommy John surgery was a particularly undeserved denouement. Before he went down with injury, Kopech's social media feeds were notable for their documentation of his grueling training regimen. Before he threw in the triple-digits, from the age of six, he spent his days in Texas working out and throwing sunup to sundown in an empty pasture under his father's watchful eye. To what degree the fate of rehab from Tommy John surgery can be swayed by sheer work ethic, Kopech should earn high marks. But the rest is beyond him.

Reynaldo Lopez RHP Born: 01/04/94 Age: 25 Bats: R Throws: R Height: 6'1" Weight: 200 Origin: International Free Agent, 2012

YEAR	TEAM	LVL	AGE	W	L	SV	G	GS	IP	H	HR	BB/9	K/9	K	GB%	BABIP	WHIP	ERA	DRA	WARP	MPH	FB%	WHF	CSP
2016	HAR	AA	22	3	5	0	14	14	76¹	69	7	2.9	11.8	100	43%	.320	1.23	3.18	2.32	2.5				
2016	SYR	AAA	22	2	2	0	5	5	33	21	6	2.7	7.1	26	33%	.174	0.94	3.27	4.87	0.2				
2016	WAS	MLB	22	5	3	0	11	6	44	47	4	4.5	8.6	42	43%	.326	1.57	4.91	4.86	0.2	98.7	64.3	10.4	47.8
2017	CHR	AAA	23	6	7	0	22	22	121	101	16	3.6	9.7	131	38%	.270	1.24	3.79	6.83	-1.5				
2017	CHA	MLB	23	3	3	0	8	8	47²	49	7	2.6	5.7	30	30%	.271	1.32	4.72	6.40	-0.4	97.6	60.9	9	48.8
2018	CHA	MLB	24	7	10	0	32	32	188²	165	25	3.6	7.2	151	34%	.260	1.27	3.91	5.65	-0.7	97.9	60.9	10	49.2
2019	CHA	MLB	25	8	10	0	26	26	148¹	139	23	3.6	8.5	139	37%	.279	1.34	4.81	5.05	0.7	97.6	62.7	10.1	49.9

Breakout: 14% Improve: 53% Collapse: 22% Attrition: 24% MLB: 94%   *Comparables: Kendall Graveman, Travis Wood, David Huff*

With the way Lopez's upper body leans back and then lurches forward in his three-quarters sling of a delivery, it would be wrong to say he comes by his top of the scale velocity easily, but it's certainly natural. And with the way he went from not throwing a slider at all in games in 2017 to leaning on it as a legit big league swing-and-miss offering in a year's time, he certainly is teachable. But despite the natural gifts, despite a curve and change that have also showed eye-opening potential at times, Lopez's overall performance remains less than the sum of its very intriguing parts, even as he grew better at avoiding the control lapses that marred his first half. Lopez edged closer to a future as a mid-to-back-end starter while many of his Sox teammates backflipped away from it, so he counts as a success story who earned the chance to continue progressing.

Juan Minaya RHP
Born: 09/18/90 Age: 28 Bats: R Throws: R Height: 6'4" Weight: 210 Origin: International Free Agent, 2008

YEAR	TEAM	LVL	AGE	W	L	SV	G	GS	IP	H	HR	BB/9	K/9	K	GB%	BABIP	WHIP	ERA	DRA	WARP	MPH	FB%	WHF	CSP
2016	FRE	AAA	25	1	3	0	17	0	25¹	25	1	3.6	6.8	19	51%	.308	1.38	3.91	3.53	0.4				
2016	CHR	AAA	25	4	3	1	17	0	26²	23	2	3.4	9.4	28	48%	.288	1.24	3.38	3.51	0.4				
2016	CHA	MLB	25	1	0	0	11	0	10¹	10	0	4.4	5.2	6	24%	.294	1.45	4.35	6.15	-0.1	96.6	65.6	10.6	46.9
2017	CHR	AAA	26	1	0	0	13	0	19	17	0	2.4	7.1	15	45%	.293	1.16	1.42	5.22	0.0				
2017	CHA	MLB	26	3	2	9	40	0	43²	38	7	4.1	10.5	51	34%	.304	1.33	4.53	5.52	-0.2	95.7	62.8	12.5	46.9
2018	CHR	AAA	27	1	3	2	19	0	23¹	18	4	3.1	10.4	27	44%	.264	1.11	4.24	3.98	0.3				
2018	CHA	MLB	27	2	2	1	52	0	46²	39	3	5.6	11.2	58	43%	.310	1.46	3.28	5.05	-0.1	96.5	61.2	12.4	45.2
2019	CHA	MLB	28	3	1	0	52	0	54²	49	7	4.4	10.0	61	42%	.298	1.39	4.47	4.69	0.3	95.6	62.5	12.4	46.5

Breakout: 13%   Improve: 29%   Collapse: 22%   Attrition: 22%   MLB: 63%   *Comparables: Clay Zavada, Brandon Cunniff, Jose Ramirez*

When Minaya staggered off the mound in disgust on April 7, it was fair to wonder how many more times he would be seen on a major league field again. He was offered up for a lopsided ninth inning and for a team unlikely to play a high-leverage game all year, and walked four hitters in a row. Before his manager sat down for his postgame media briefing, Minaya was optioned to boot. As a live-armed, walk-addled waiver claim clutching at a spot in a rebuilding bullpen, he will likely always be one step back in command from career-threatening peril. But by mid-June he was back in the majors and attacking the strike zone with a lively mid-90s fastball and slider combination, and by the end of the year, it was debatable whether the Sox had a more reliable right-handed reliever. That's not ideal, as his control will always give his high-leverage work a flair for the dramatic, but it's major league quality stuff from a major league body, which is a decent start.

Ivan Nova RHP
Born: 01/12/87 Age: 32 Bats: R Throws: R Height: 6'5" Weight: 250 Origin: International Free Agent, 2004

YEAR	TEAM	LVL	AGE	W	L	SV	G	GS	IP	H	HR	BB/9	K/9	K	GB%	BABIP	WHIP	ERA	DRA	WARP	MPH	FB%	WHF	CSP
2016	NYA	MLB	29	7	6	1	21	15	97¹	107	19	2.3	6.9	75	56%	.297	1.36	4.90	4.78	0.6	95.4	66.6	10.1	44.8
2016	PIT	MLB	29	5	2	0	11	11	64²	68	4	0.4	7.2	52	55%	.318	1.10	3.06	3.68	1.2	95.6	62.1	10.2	50.7
2017	PIT	MLB	30	11	14	0	31	31	187	203	29	1.7	6.3	131	48%	.299	1.28	4.14	4.71	1.8	94.7	68.1	9	49.5
2018	PIT	MLB	31	9	9	0	29	29	161	171	26	2.0	6.4	114	47%	.288	1.28	4.19	4.60	1.3	94.8	66.9	9.7	46.6
2019	CHA	MLB	32	9	11	0	28	28	159²	169	22	2.4	7.0	124	48%	.299	1.32	4.46	4.67	1.5	94.0	66.3	9.5	47.2

Breakout: 24%   Improve: 50%   Collapse: 20%   Attrition: 14%   MLB: 87%   *Comparables: Odalis Perez, Joe Blanton, Jon Lieber*

After he was acquired from the Yankees in the middle of 2016, Nova was quickly touted as Yet Another Ray Searage Success Story™ after 64.2 glittering innings at the tail end of that campaign. Since then, Nova has been…adequate. Detractors might look at Nova's WARP the last three seasons and shrug, but there's nothing wrong with an arm that can churn out a 1-2 WARP season like clockwork. Every staff needs guys like this, particularly when they can reliably eat 160-plus innings per season. Nova continues to be decent against righties but miserable against left-handers, and even his splits the last three seasons have been eerily similar. Nova is like a plain bagel with cream cheese. It hits the spot and keeps your stomach full all morning but isn't a meal you're going to remember when lunch rolls around.

Carlos Rodon LHP
Born: 12/10/92 Age: 26 Bats: L Throws: L Height: 6'3" Weight: 235 Origin: Round 1, 2014 Draft (#3 overall)

YEAR	TEAM	LVL	AGE	W	L	SV	G	GS	IP	H	HR	BB/9	K/9	K	GB%	BABIP	WHIP	ERA	DRA	WARP	MPH	FB%	WHF	CSP
2016	CHA	MLB	23	9	10	0	28	28	165	176	23	2.9	9.2	168	44%	.330	1.39	4.04	4.81	1.0	97.5	63.3	10.9	48.3
2017	CHR	AAA	24	0	3	0	3	3	13²	17	0	4.6	7.2	11	50%	.354	1.76	9.22	5.35	0.1				
2017	CHA	MLB	24	2	5	0	12	12	69¹	64	12	4.0	9.9	76	45%	.297	1.37	4.15	5.13	0.3	96.4	61.2	11.1	47.9
2018	CHR	AAA	25	1	0	0	3	3	12²	10	0	3.6	15.6	22	56%	.435	1.18	1.42	3.00	0.4				
2018	CHA	MLB	25	6	8	0	20	20	120²	97	15	4.1	6.7	90	42%	.243	1.26	4.18	6.57	-1.8	95.8	59.8	9.7	47.6
2019	CHA	MLB	26	8	10	0	26	26	156	149	20	3.7	8.8	153	43%	.298	1.36	4.47	4.68	1.4	96.1	62.5	10.6	48.7

Breakout: 17%   Improve: 53%   Collapse: 16%   Attrition: 11%   MLB: 99%   *Comparables: Johnny Cueto, John Danks, Vinegar Bend Mizell*

To paraphrase one longtime baseball man, Carlos Rodon's 2018 season was pretty good for someone who had their throwing shoulder cut open the previous season. When his peripheral-defying dominance ran dry all at once in September, the encouraging suffix of "and he's doing this without all his best stuff" morphed into "wait until he gets his best stuff back." Rodon spent a lot of his 2018 season sitting in the low-90s and struggling to prove to hitters he could command both versions of his slider—the wipeout destroyer and the early count strike-grabber—with the old level of snap and bite. He ended his year, after a disastrous outing that saw him yanked before the end of the second inning in Minnesota, very optimistic that the next step in his recovery would be on display in 2019. His experience of being a high-contact pitcher would indicate that he'll need it.

Hector Santiago LHP
Born: 12/16/87 Age: 31 Bats: R Throws: L Height: 6'0" Weight: 215 Origin: Round 30, 2006 Draft (#915 overall)

YEAR	TEAM	LVL	AGE	W	L	SV	G	GS	IP	H	HR	BB/9	K/9	K	GB%	BABIP	WHIP	ERA	DRA	WARP	MPH	FB%	WHF	CSP
2016	ANA	MLB	28	10	4	0	22	22	120²	104	20	4.3	8.0	107	40%	.257	1.33	4.25	5.51	-0.2	95.3	60.7	9.9	49.3
2016	MIN	MLB	28	3	6	0	11	11	61¹	65	13	3.2	5.4	37	28%	.264	1.42	5.58	7.77	-1.7	93.8	60.7	7.7	48.7
2017	MIN	MLB	29	4	8	0	15	14	70¹	70	15	4.0	6.5	51	32%	.263	1.44	5.63	7.41	-1.4	93.0	60.4	8.1	48.4
2017	ROC	AAA	29	1	2	0	7	7	23²	21	4	6.5	9.5	25	27%	.270	1.61	5.32	4.20	0.4				
2018	CHA	MLB	30	6	3	2	49	7	102	101	16	5.3	9.1	103	35%	.308	1.58	4.41	6.73	-2.0	93.0	68	9.4	49.3
2019	CHA	MLB	31	4	6	0	26	15	87¹	84	16	4.5	8.5	82	36%	.279	1.46	5.41	5.70	-0.3	92.9	63.2	9	48.6

Breakout: 20%   Improve: 55%   Collapse: 12%   Attrition: 13%   MLB: 87%   *Comparables: J.A. Happ, Todd Wellemeyer, Vicente Padilla*

It's fairly likely that Hector Santiago knows it's a little rough to watch him pitch. He knows his four-seam fastball moves a lot and moves strangely. Algorithms often mark it as a two-seamer (it isn't, he insists) but computer models' struggles to explain its movement mirrors the struggles of its handler. He knows he's always going to walk plenty of guys, he knows he's not going to generate easy ground ball outs with it, and he knows in turn that he will always allow plenty of home runs. But the thing moves, it's given life to a career that never was supposed to last this long, and it has allowed him to miss bats even as his velocity has declined. Back and shoulder problems made Santiago settle for a minor-league deal coming into 2018, and wildness plagued him as he pitched his way out of the Sox starting rotation, but he just kept throwing and trusting that darting four-seamer, through all the snags and scrapes, and he'll probably find his way to another major league job—however unglamorous—because of it.

James Shields RHP Born: 12/20/81   Age: 37   Bats: R   Throws: R   Height: 6'3"   Weight: 210   Origin: Round 16, 2000 Draft (#466 overall)

YEAR	TEAM	LVL	AGE	W	L	SV	G	GS	IP	H	HR	BB/9	K/9	K	GB%	BABIP	WHIP	ERA	DRA	WARP	MPH	FB%	WHF	CSP
2016	SDN	MLB	34	2	7	0	11	11	67¹	69	9	3.6	7.6	57	48%	.316	1.43	4.28	4.41	0.7	92.5	44.6	11.2	41.9
2016	CHA	MLB	34	4	12	0	22	22	114¹	139	31	4.3	6.1	78	38%	.296	1.70	6.77	6.68	-1.7	93.1	44.6	9	42.5
2017	CHR	AAA	35	0	3	0	3	3	14	13	0	1.9	9.0	14	48%	.325	1.14	3.21	3.77	0.3				
2017	CHA	MLB	35	5	7	0	21	21	117	116	27	4.1	7.9	103	40%	.270	1.44	5.23	5.05	0.7	91.9	38.4	10.9	45.4
2018	CHA	MLB	36	7	16	0	34	33	204²	190	34	3.4	6.8	154	37%	.262	1.31	4.53	5.44	-0.3	91.3	36.5	11	45.4
2019	CHA	MLB	37	8	12	0	27	27	159¹	162	28	3.8	7.6	134	39%	.288	1.44	5.32	5.61	-0.2	90.5	38.2	10.4	43.5

Breakout: 9%   Improve: 41%   Collapse: 8%   Attrition: 13%   MLB: 66%   *Comparables: Chris Capuano, Joe Nuxhall, Harvey Haddix*

Shields goes entire games without cracking 90 mph when it's cold out. In the middle of rough start in Boston in August 2017, he started dropping down in his delivery in a last-ditch grasp at more movement, and yet he's still coming off the lowest strikeout rate of his career. At the beginning of the 2018 season, he sagely noted that "if you swing a hammer 45,000 times, you're definitely not going to feel the same as you did the first time," and then proceeded to swing 3,300 more hammers. It is difficult to project what on Earth he is going to be able to provide, what his game will look like and how he will fare in 2019. But for James Shields—who bounced back from the two worst seasons of his career (by a lot) and the first disabled list trip of his life to face the second-most batters in the league—there's no doubt that he will fare, somehow.

Jordan Stephens RHP Born: 09/12/92   Age: 26   Bats: R   Throws: R   Height: 6'1"   Weight: 190   Origin: Round 5, 2015 Draft (#142 overall)

YEAR	TEAM	LVL	AGE	W	L	SV	G	GS	IP	H	HR	BB/9	K/9	K	GB%	BABIP	WHIP	ERA	DRA	WARP	MPH	FB%	WHF	CSP
2016	WNS	A+	23	7	10	0	27	27	141	129	12	3.1	9.9	155	46%	.319	1.26	3.45	2.98	4.0				
2017	BIR	AA	24	3	7	0	16	16	91²	84	4	3.4	8.1	83	43%	.309	1.30	3.14	4.06	1.2				
2018	BIR	AA	25	4	3	0	7	7	39²	37	1	2.7	9.1	40	37%	.340	1.24	2.95	3.79	0.7				
2018	CHR	AAA	25	4	7	0	21	21	107	114	11	3.5	8.3	99	34%	.328	1.46	4.71	4.77	0.9				
2019	CHA	MLB	26	3	3	0	23	8	56¹	59	9	3.7	8.2	51	39%	.306	1.46	5.00	5.25	0.1				

Breakout: 7%   Improve: 13%   Collapse: 6%   Attrition: 30%   MLB: 34%   *Comparables: Kyle McGowin, Sam LeCure, Hector Ambriz*

A good, hard overhand curveball and the knowledge of how to use it is a fine starter kit for a pitching prospect. Stephens' ability to spin it has carried the Rice product to the precipice of the majors despite a myriad of different injuries, a much slighter than typical physical frame, and a pedestrian fastball which can flatten out when he lets his back leg collapse in his delivery. He's 26, doesn't throw hard, his changeup is more of show-me offering and he spent most of 2018 hitting his head in Triple-A, so no one will be forecasting greatness out of the rotation even if he figures to get a crack at the White Sox starting mix in 2019. The beautiful simplicity of his attack when he's pairing high fastballs with the hard vertical drop of his spinner, and their waning effectiveness upon repeat viewings, gives you an idea of where the best moments of his career might take place.

Thyago Vieira RHP Born: 07/01/93   Age: 25   Bats: R   Throws: R   Height: 6'2"   Weight: 210   Origin: International Free Agent, 2010

YEAR	TEAM	LVL	AGE	W	L	SV	G	GS	IP	H	HR	BB/9	K/9	K	GB%	BABIP	WHIP	ERA	DRA	WARP	MPH	FB%	WHF	CSP
2016	BAK	A+	22	1	0	8	34	0	44¹	37	1	3.7	10.8	53	53%	.313	1.24	2.84	3.27	0.9				
2017	ARK	AA	23	2	3	2	29	0	36¹	30	1	3.7	8.7	35	49%	.293	1.24	3.72	3.42	0.6				
2017	SEA	MLB	23	0	0	0	1	0	1	0	0	0.0	9.0	1	50%	.000	0.00	0.00	4.46	0.0	100.7	70	0	42.4
2017	TAC	AAA	23	0	1	2	12	0	17²	18	1	3.6	5.6	11	53%	.298	1.42	4.58	3.84	0.3				
2018	CHR	AAA	24	0	4	6	36	0	41	40	2	5.3	11.0	50	43%	.349	1.56	5.05	4.00	0.5				
2018	CHA	MLB	24	1	1	1	16	0	17²	21	4	4.6	7.6	15	33%	.315	1.70	7.13	7.59	-0.5	99.0	80.3	11	50.6
2019	CHA	MLB	25	1	0	0	26	0	27¹	26	4	4.7	9.7	29	44%	.301	1.47	4.78	5.01	0.0	98.8	81.9	11	48.1

Breakout: 10%   Improve: 14%   Collapse: 6%   Attrition: 14%   MLB: 22%   *Comparables: Brian Ellington, Craig Breslow, Chad Smith*

Pitching the ninth inning of a Sept. 8 blowout home loss to Anaheim, Vieira's third wild pitch of the frame sailed so far high and wide of his target and struck the backstop so firmly and true, that it rebounded perfectly into the waiting glove of catcher Kevan Smith. The catcher merely pivoted in place behind home plate to retrieve it, laying a tag on a stunned and then resigned Kaleb Cowart trying to score from third. That would do pretty well as a summary of Vieira's season in a nutshell, but an ERA over 5.00 at Triple-A Charlotte would also do well to show how Vieira's raw tools and prospect reputation outstripped his effectiveness as a reliever. It's very long road between being able to hit 100 on the gun and delivering clean innings on a consistent basis, and it's paved with a lot more strikes than Vieira threw in 2018.

LINEOUTS

Hitters

HITTER	POS	TEAM	LVL	AGE	PA	R	2B	3B	HR	RBI	BB	K	SB	CS	AVG/OBP/SLG	DRC+	VORP	BABIP	BRR	FRAA	WARP
Bryce Bush	3B	WSX	Rk	18	52	8	4	0	1	8	8	4	1	2	.442/.538/.605	142	10.4	.474	0.4	3B(12): 2.3	0.7
	3B	GRF	Rk	18	108	16	5	1	2	10	10	21	3	0	.250/.327/.385	88	4.3	.301	1.0	3B(18): -2.1	0.1
Luis Curbelo	SS	KAN	A	20	343	35	19	2	3	31	18	87	0	0	.237/.282/.338	80	7.3	.314	0.3	SS(57): -4.6, 3B(20): -0.3	0.0
Lency Delgado	3B	WSX	Rk	19	150	20	4	1	1	22	9	40	4	0	.233/.309/.301	77	3.7	.323	1.7	SS(35): 0.4	0.4
Laz Rivera	SS	KAN	A	23	265	42	15	2	6	24	6	48	7	3	.346/.395/.502	119	27.2	.413	-0.7	SS(54): -3.5, 3B(5): -0.1	1.3
	SS	WNS	A+	23	250	38	15	2	7	37	7	44	10	7	.280/.325/.458	112	15.9	.318	1.4	SS(56): -0.1, 2B(1): 0.0	1.6
Jose Rondon	SS	CHR	AAA	24	336	41	15	4	18	38	16	82	5	6	.249/.290/.495	109	14.6	.278	0.9	SS(78): 10.9, 3B(2): 0.0	3.1
	SS	CHA	MLB	24	107	15	6	0	6	14	7	30	2	1	.230/.280/.470	87	2.4	.266	-1.0	SS(10): 0.8, 3B(8): 0.5	0.1
Gavin Sheets	1B	WNS	A+	22	497	58	28	2	6	61	52	81	1	0	.293/.368/.407	116	10.5	.344	-3.9	1B(108): -4.3	0.7
Charlie Tilson	CF	CHA	MLB	25	121	7	1	1	0	11	10	20	2	3	.264/.331/.292	75	-0.6	.322	0.7	LF(32): -0.3, CF(5): -0.2	0.0
	CF	CHR	AAA	25	292	27	12	0	0	25	16	52	10	2	.244/.288/.289	63	-5.1	.301	1.4	CF(49): -3.1, LF(17): -0.7	-0.7

Jake Burger entered 2018 ready to answer doubters about his ability to translate his plus raw power into game production and that his burly frame could stick at third base. Instead, he ruptured his left Achilles tendon on two separate occasions, which did little to address either concern. ⓧ The whole business about the $290,000 bonus that the White Sox offered **Bryce Bush** belies the underdog story of a low-round high schooler rolling in and torching complex league ball. He's a strong young man who can put the bat on the ball and hang with pitchers several years older than he is. He'll put those extra few years to good use in finding a defensive position. ⓧ Finally recovered from a meniscus tear than ended his 2017 season after just three games, **Luis Curbelo's** 2018 debut at a full-season affiliate wound up being an introduction to the age-old question: Is it better to be a toolsy but largely unseen prospect resigned to the backfields of the spring training complex, or a toolsy but underperforming prospect treading water in an aggressive assignment? ⓧ **Lency Delgado** proves that the White Sox as an organization are more enraptured by players born in Cuba than they are leery of spending high-round picks on high schoolers. Delgado is listed as a shortstop for now, but he's also listed as 6'3", 215 pounds at age 19, so, c'mon now. ⓧ The only way some 24-year-old pop-up prospect—who hasn't reached Double-A yet and came into pro ball as a 28th-round senior signing—is getting so much as a lineout in the Annual is if they did something drastic like slash .314/.361/.481 across two levels while showing the capability to handle a premium position. Luckily, **Laz Rivera** did that. ⓧ A review of **Jose Rondon**'s comments in previous versions of this publication reveals the story of an agile defender with some mentions of a solid hit tool and next to no home run power to speak of. Yet, in an organization that possessed Eloy Jimenez and Jose Abreu, his 24 home runs across Triple-A and a pair of stints in the majors was more than either one of those dudes managed. ⓧ It would be nice if a hitter as smart, multi-faceted and polished in his approach as **Gavin Sheets** could be appreciated beyond the bellows of "WHERE ARE THE DINGERS?" But unfortunately he's a first baseman, so no dice. ⓧ After losing the last two months of 2016 and all of 2017 to wave after wave of injuries and misfortune, everyone in the White Sox organization was pleased to see **Charlie Tilson** beat the odds to make it back to the majors. Eventually a sub-.300 slugging percentage caused the good feelings to wane.

Pitchers

PITCHER	TEAM	LVL	AGE	W	L	SV	G	GS	IP	H	HR	BB/9	K/9	K	GB%	BABIP	WHIP	ERA	DRA	WARP	MPH	FB%	WHF	CSP
Manny Banuelos	OKL	AAA	27	9	7	0	31	18	108²	109	10	3.5	10.5	127	45%	.349	1.39	3.73	2.82	3.3				
Aaron Bummer	CHR	AAA	24	2	3	0	31	0	30²	27	0	3.2	8.8	30	67%	.310	1.24	2.64	3.51	0.6				
	CHA	MLB	24	0	1	0	37	0	31²	40	1	2.8	9.9	35	62%	.402	1.58	4.26	3.71	0.4	94.8	65.9	10.5	48.5
Ian Clarkin	WNS	A+	23	0	0	0	4	0	7²	4	0	3.5	7.0	6	58%	.211	0.91	2.35	3.94	0.1				
	BIR	AA	23	4	5	0	18	10	68²	74	7	4.1	4.6	35	52%	.296	1.53	4.98	7.87	-2.1				
Bernardo Flores	WNS	A+	22	5	4	0	12	12	77²	75	5	2.0	6.7	58	56%	.294	1.18	2.55	3.40	1.7				
	BIR	AA	22	3	5	0	13	13	78¹	79	5	1.6	5.4	47	52%	.301	1.19	2.76	3.98	1.2				
Jeanmar Gomez	CHR	AAA	30	5	0	2	30	0	40	35	2	2.9	7.9	35	56%	.297	1.20	2.03	3.85	0.6				
	CHA	MLB	30	0	2	0	26	0	25	29	3	3.6	9.7	27	40%	.356	1.56	4.68	3.22	0.5	93.8	42.8	13.8	48.6
Miguel Gonzalez	CHA	MLB	34	0	3	0	3	3	12¹	24	4	4.4	3.6	5	38%	.392	2.43	12.41	6.53	-0.2	91.7	52.1	7.8	47.9
Jordan Guerrero	BIR	AA	24	3	6	0	14	13	65¹	84	6	2.6	8.0	58	43%	.377	1.58	6.06	4.46	0.7				
	CHR	AAA	24	7	2	0	12	12	65	64	4	3.9	8.6	62	52%	.316	1.42	3.46	4.12	1.0				
Lincoln Henzman	KAN	A	22	6	3	0	13	13	72²	68	5	1.0	7.4	60	62%	.288	1.05	2.23	3.30	1.6				
	WNS	A+	22	0	1	0	14	9	34²	34	1	2.6	5.2	20	56%	.289	1.27	2.60	3.71	0.6				
Tyler Johnson	KAN	A	22	5	0	7	20	0	27	16	1	3.3	15.3	46	56%	.306	0.96	1.33	1.96	0.9				
	WNS	A+	22	4	0	7	21	0	31	19	1	1.7	12.5	43	44%	.265	0.81	1.45	2.52	0.9				
Jimmy Lambert	WNS	A+	23	5	7	0	13	13	70²	57	5	2.7	10.2	80	46%	.292	1.10	3.95	3.18	1.8				
	BIR	AA	23	3	1	0	5	5	25	20	2	2.2	10.8	30	40%	.286	1.04	2.88	2.69	0.8				
Evan Marshall	CLE	MLB	28	0	0	0	10	0	7	12	0	5.1	11.6	9	56%	.522	2.29	7.71	3.65	0.1	94.9	54.7	17.3	43.1
	COH	AAA	28	1	1	4	20	0	24	18	1	1.1	7.9	21	68%	.254	0.88	1.12	4.06	0.3				
Kodi Medeiros	BLX	AA	22	7	5	0	20	15	103¹	90	9	3.9	9.3	107	50%	.298	1.31	3.14	4.35	1.1				
	BIR	AA	22	0	2	0	7	7	34¹	31	4	5.8	8.9	34	53%	.303	1.54	4.98	4.33	0.4				
Konnor Pilkington	GRF	Rk	20	0	1	0	6	6	12	14	1	3.0	6.8	9	52%	.333	1.50	5.25	4.36	0.2				
Jose Ruiz	WNS	A+	23	0	0	2	10	0	13¹	6	2	3.4	14.9	22	33%	.182	0.82	2.70	2.86	0.3				
	BIR	AA	23	3	1	14	33	0	45¹	33	2	3.8	10.9	55	41%	.290	1.15	3.18	3.05	1.0				
	CHA	MLB	23	0	0	0	6	0	4¹	5	1	6.2	12.5	6	42%	.364	1.85	4.15	2.40	0.1	97.7	58.4	16.9	44.7
Rob Scahill	CHR	AAA	31	3	4	5	52	0	60²	70	4	3.7	10.5	71	52%	.379	1.57	5.64	3.60	1.1				
	CHA	MLB	31	0	0	0	6	0	5	5	0	5.4	5.4	3	65%	.294	1.60	5.40	8.02	-0.2	93.6	64.9	7.8	47.5
Jonathan Stiever	GRF	Rk	21	0	1	0	13	13	28	23	3	2.9	12.5	39	48%	.323	1.14	4.18	3.59	0.8				

Much like the estate of Michael Jackson, **Manny Banuelos** gave up a ton of hits this season, before sliding into a bullpen role that led to a sub-3.00 DRA and Triple-A All-Star birth. Who's bad? ⊗ **Aaron Bummer's** funky left-handed sling of a delivery gives him enough movement to crack the Opening Day roster, and the strikeout-to-walk ratio to suggest he should stay there. It also seems to lead to enough command mistakes to push him toward the back of an increasingly long line of young White Sox lefty relievers. ⊗ **Zack Burdi** carried out the family tradition of undergoing Tommy John surgery in late July of 2017, so most of the cabin fever-inducing portions of rehab were over with by the start of the 2018 season. Still, his comeback appearances were not much more than a glorified rehab stint and did not feature his pre-injury, elite velocity. ⊗ A very prudent addition to the 40-man before 2018, recording more walks than strikeouts in Double-A Birmingham before he hit the disabled list with a groin strain in May was probably as deleterious for **Ian Clarkin's** hopes of starting as the missed development time. Scouts still like his curveball. ⊗ Of the two bespectacled strike-throwers who made their way through the Birmingham Barons rotation in 2018, **Bernardo Flores** is definitely the lesser-known. But while he currently lacks Dane Dunning's mid-rotation starter upside and swing-and-miss stuff, his feel for the changeup is already present and his lanky frame still allows for hope that he could regain his mid-90s college reliever velocity from the left side as he fills out. ⊗ Finding out that journeyman reliever **Jeanmar Gomez**—an avowed sinkerballer in the age of the letter-high four-seam fastball—posted the highest strikeout rate of his career in an otherwise unremarkable, up-and-down campaign for a 100-loss White Sox team: That's the kind of fun factoid you get in return for purchasing this book, provided you turned to this exact page. ⊗ Frank Sinatra once sang "Love is lovelier the second time around," which is the first of many hints that he never signed a one-year deal to eat innings with a team that had jettisoned him in an August waiver deal the previous season, only to tear a labrum after three starts. **Miguel Gonzalez**, however, did exactly that. ⊗ Getting pushed up a level to clear a path for better prospects is an unusual trigger for a jump forward in performance, but **Jordan Guerrero** surely wouldn't sneeze at any reason to finally be free of Double-A. It's a profile built on a plus changeup and avoiding mistakes, and maybe someday through it the tide will wash him up onto a big league roster for a while. ⊗ No one quite knows what baseball in 2020 and beyond will look like, or how well a converted college reliever turned into a low-90s sinkerballer like **Lincoln Henzman** will profile in a big league rotation. But so far, so good, as far as his ability to graze the bottom of bats rather than miss them in A-ball. ⊗ As a pure relief prospect who has not yet reached Double-A, there are rules about how excited you're allowed to get about crossfiring young righty **Tyler Johnson**. On the other hand, hachi machi, look at all those whiffs! ⊗ The low-90s fastball with a sweeping slider **Jimmy Lambert** of 2017 was not the most interesting prospect. The Jimmy Lambert who now touches 96 mph and pairs it with a hard overhand curveball and a fading changeup is several shades more intriguing, and it'd be polite not to hold it against him for taking his time to arrive at the latter. ⊗ Injuries and ineffectiveness have plagued **Evan Marshall**. With the caveat that hard-throwing relievers can randomly unlock success, he's now finished four straight years with ERAs beginning with the numbers 6, 7, 8 and 9. ⊗ The Brewers were willing to deal former first-round pick **Kodi Medeiros** because they lost faith in his ability to start, and the White Sox got a glimpse as to why. It's still a good slider, and it still comes out of his left hand, so he should have a career out of the bullpen ahead of him. Maybe it will end up in Milwaukee, given how many White Sox relievers end up there these days. ⊗ Sometimes the adage that a college starter can't be judged in his draft year is a cop out, and sometimes they spend the summer leading Mississippi State to the semifinals of the College World Series and get all of 14 scattershot pro innings. **Konnor Pilkington** is a command-over-stuff lefty whose goal will be to slide into the back end of a big league rotation one day, until further evidence is provided. ⊗ A six-game September cameo after being plucked from Double-A was never really going to be a clear opportunity for **Jose Ruiz** to distinguish himself beyond "young guy who throws hard." But for a converted catcher in just his third year pitching as a professional, his time in Chicago was more about placing a major league-prorated bow on a season that made the White Sox curious enough to get a look at what they had in their waiver claim gambit. ⊗ The White Sox called up **Rob Scahill** in September, narrowly pushing his streak of major league seasons to seven, despite less than 150 career innings pitched. Number eight might be his toughest challenge yet. ⊗ The universe itself does not revolve around the exploits of college starters in the Pioneer League. But for **Jonathan Stiever**, selected more for athleticism and control than raw stuff, striking out over 30 percent of opposing hitters in his pro debut is a positive development, if not so large as to wield its own gravitational force.

CINCINNATI REDS

Essay by Jack Moore

Player comments by Kevin Jebens, Ken Funck and BP staff

What exactly are they selling at Great American Ball Park these days? It sure isn't winning baseball. The Reds concluded 2018 with their fourth-straight last-place finish and 90-loss season. Cincinnati area baseball fans have responded as you would expect. Attendance fell to 1.6 million in 2018, the lowest mark not only in the Great American Ball Park era (since 2000), but the city's lowest mark since 1984.

Since the move to the new park, the Reds have made just three playoff appearances and won just two playoff games—none of which were won in their home city. The 2012 team was certainly the pinnacle of the Joey Votto Reds squads, a club that won 97 games and looked primed to make a run to the World Series after beating the San Francisco Giants twice at AT&T Park to open the NLDS. Instead, the Reds offense laid an egg in the two subsequent home games as they scored just four combined runs and allowed the series to return to San Francisco for a decisive Game 5, which the Giants won 6-4 en route to their second World Championship in three years. The next season's Wild Card Game appearance, in which Johnny Cueto lasted just 3.1 innings in a loss to division rival Pittsburgh, is the only playoff game they have played since.

With the absence of a present to sell fans, the Reds are left with two options: the future or the past. The past is rich for Cincinnati, at least. The town is the crucible of professional baseball, as next season marks the 150th anniversary of the Red Stockings. The club owns five World Championships and another four pennants. The Big Red Machine of the 1970s was one of baseball's most legendary dynasties, responsible for four of the 10 National League titles and the 1975 and 1976 World Series victories.

But now, a large portion of Reds fans—and Cincinnati area denizens in general—are too young to remember the Big Red Machine as anything but legend, and a substantial amount are too young to even remember the 1990 World Champions, the last great Reds team. A 35-year-old Reds fan experienced that one great Reds squad was when he was all of seven years old. Their kids? Forget it. Flags may technically fly forever, but history becomes a hard sell to those whose lived

REDS PROSPECTUS
2018 W-L: 67-95, 5TH IN NL CENTRAL

Pythag	.423	24th	B-Age	27.2	6th
RS/G	4.30	18th	P-Age	26.9	5th
RA/G	5.06	25th	Salary	$101.3M	22nd
DRC+	99	11th	M$/MW	$4.8M	11th
DRA	5.32	26th	DL Days	651	1st
FIP	4.62	25th	$ on DL	9%	4th
DER	.700	22nd			

- Opened 2003
- Open air
- Natural surface
- Fence profile: 8' to 12'

Three-Year Park Factors

Runs	Runs/RH	Runs/LH	HR/RH	HR/LH
101	99	104	110	111

Top Hitter WARP	4.6 Joey Votto
Top Pitcher WARP	1.2 Raisel Iglesias
Top Prospect	Nick Senzel

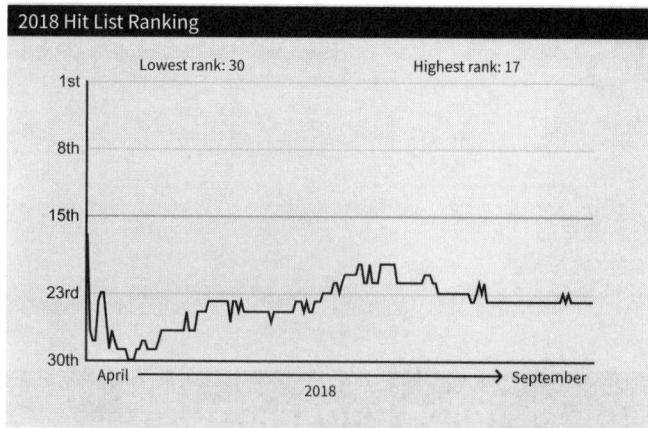

2018 Hit List Ranking

Lowest rank: 30   Highest rank: 17

April — 2018 — September

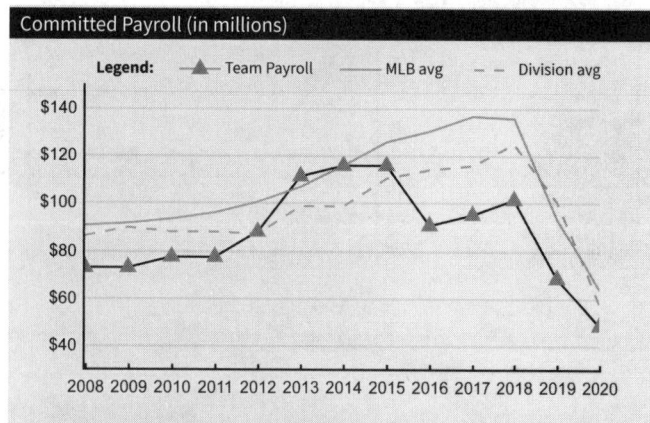

Committed Payroll (in millions)

Legend: — Team Payroll — MLB avg — Division avg

2008 2009 2010 2011 2012 2013 2014 2015 2016 2017 2018 2019 2020

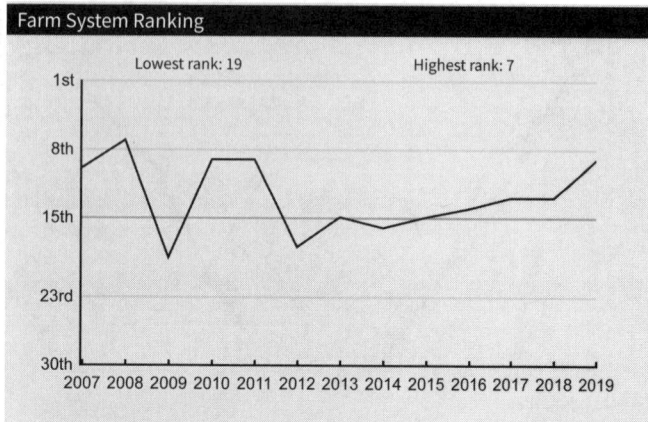

Farm System Ranking

Lowest rank: 19   Highest rank: 7

2007 2008 2009 2010 2011 2012 2013 2014 2015 2016 2017 2018 2019

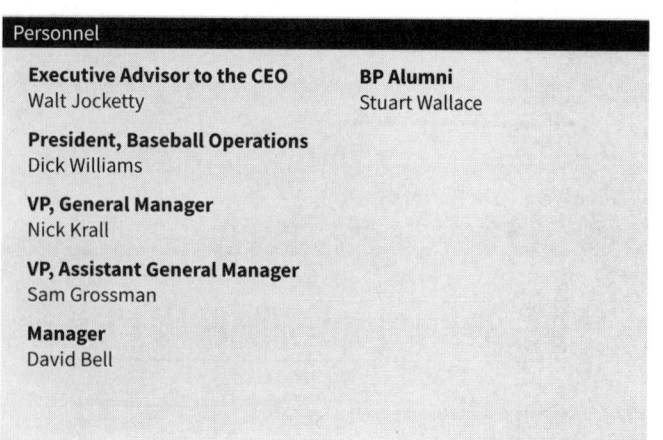

Personnel

Executive Advisor to the CEO
Walt Jocketty

President, Baseball Operations
Dick Williams

VP, General Manager
Nick Krall

VP, Assistant General Manager
Sam Grossman

Manager
David Bell

BP Alumni
Stuart Wallace

experiences tell them the Reds are an also-ran. The empty seats at GABP these days—sometimes half or more of the total capacity—represent a lost generation of Reds fans.

So the answer, really, is that they aren't selling much of anything at Great American Ball Park these days, unless you're a huge fan of Skyline Chili and $8 beers. Since 2005, when the ownership group led by Robert Castellini purchased the team from Carl Lindner for $270 million, the Reds have been the perfect example of how you don't actually need to sell baseball to make money off a baseball team. Only in 2013 and 2014, as the Reds tried desperately to hold the core of their early-decade success together, did the Reds get into the top half of MLB payrolls. Since then, the club's motto has been sell-sell-sell, as 2016 and 2017 marked their lowest payrolls of the decade (both under $100 million) and their lowest ranks in year-end payroll (28th and 25th, respectively) as far back as Cot's Contracts has tracked such data.

Lindner is a good example himself. He bought the Cincinnati Reds from Marge Schott in 1999 for $67 million. As owner, Lindner presided over six seasons, in which the Reds started as 96-win team and plummeted to losing at least 85 games in four straight campaigns. For those services rendered, Lindner walked away with a nearly 400 percent profit. Castellini's reign has been similarly lucrative. Even with attendance plummeting and the franchise stagnating, Forbes still pegs the value of the Reds at just over one billion dollars. Decent gig if you can get it.

A staggering amount of that value is entirely independent of the product the Reds put on the field. The terms of Cincinnati's new deal with Fox Sports Ohio were never disclosed, although we do know the team received an equity stake in the network. There are over 2 million cable households in Ohio, and thanks to bundled cable packages, most are subscribers to FSO. Even though Reds TV ratings were surprisingly high in 2018, they still reached all of 35,000 homes, meaning the rest of those cable TV households—roughly half the state—are footing that bill and contributing to the value of the Reds through that equity stake as well.

Revenue sharing checks also have no correlation with the win column, and league-wide revenue continues to balloon. The league passed the $10 billion mark for the first year in 2018. The MLB Players Association has already started coming after clubs for failing to use their revenue sharing checks for competitive purposes, namely the Rays, Marlins and Pirates. The Reds have only recently seen their payrolls reach similar lows to those culprits, and they don't have the history of cynical behavior the Rays and Marlins in particular have exhibited, but they could be next if the pattern doesn't change.

But the worst grift of all is the stadium. Of the $325 million price tag, $286 million came from a regressive sales tax on Hamilton County residents. The Reds insisted on a new stadium within three decades of the construction of Riverfront Stadium, Cincinnati's home beginning in 1970.

Was it even necessary? Riverfront's astroturf was always an eyesore, but the Cincinnati Business Courier reported in 1996 that the stadium's manager estimated it would take just $100 million to take the multi-purpose stadium (once home of both the Reds and the NFL's Cincinnati Bengals) and optimize it for baseball. The Reds declined that option, even though the city would have paid for all of Riverfront's renovations and was asking for a $45 million payment from the Reds for Great American Ball Park.

It makes sense, though, given that the stadium is the crown jewel of the Reds portfolio of assets. According to Forbes, Great American Ball Park accounts for $175 million of that $1.01 billion valuation of the Reds. Given that the Marlins sold for $1.2 billion and certainly offer nothing but their fancy new stadium, that estimate may be low. Between the passive value provided by the stadium, cable TV and revenue sharing, though, it's clear the Reds and other small-market teams around the country don't have to try to make money. When you profit simply by owning a baseball team, where is the incentive to push a rebuild?

I understand the competitive arguments for the protracted rebuilds like the one on which the Reds have embarked. I'm not convinced they will continue to work. The strategy breaks down when the strategy becomes en vogue. The Astros signed four top-five picks between 2012 and 2015, and two of them—Carlos Correa and Alex Bregman—have become franchise cornerstones. The Royals brief burst of success was fueled by four top-five picks between 2005 and 2008. All four—Alex Gordon, Mike Moustakas, Eric Hosmer and Luke Hochevar—were contributors to the 2015 World Champion Royals squad.

The Reds picked second in both 2016 and 2017, but they will pick just seventh in 2019 because nearly a third of the league threw in the towel on day one of the regular season, just as the Reds did. I don't think the Reds can reasonably compete in 2019, and if the goal is a championship, the focus has to be on the future. But waiting to lose and amass the draft picks necessary for the kind of Prospect Wave that is supposed to make those years of losing pay off becomes less and less viable the more teams are gunning—or falling flat on their faces—for those top picks.

Lest we forget, what made Moneyball compelling as a sports narrative isn't that it's possible to build a cheaper, more efficient baseball team. What was compelling was seeing the possibility of winning from an apparent losing position through intelligence and cunning, and through finding what nobody else even thought to look for. These copycat rebuilding efforts will proclaim their intelligent approach and how we must trust their Process, but they aren't doing anything we—or their opponents—haven't seen before.

Branch Rickey wrote in his 1965 autobiography that ownership must eliminate the signing bonus in order to curb competition among teams, competition Rickey thought would destroy the profitability of baseball. Thus, the draft, which more than succeeded in driving down the cost of amateur talent. The real problem Rickey was solving was the problem of competition. In 1964, the bidding on top prospect Rick Reichardt ended with the Angels signing him to a $205,000 bonus. The next year, Rick Monday received $100,000 from the Mets as the #1 draft pick. The effects of competition—or the lack thereof—are apparent.

What we have seen over the last 30 years or so since Bud Selig and his cohort of small-market allies rose to power is the erosion of avenues for teams to compete for talent. Want to sign top or mid-level free agents? Better be prepared to sacrifice draft picks. Want to get creative with leveraging free agent compensation for draft picks like the Rays and Blue Jays did? They'll restructure the compensation system to prevent it. Want to spend more on international free agents, amateur or otherwise? Better be prepared to pay huge taxes. Want to go over slot and add impact talent in the draft? More taxes.

Those strategies gave real hope that the system could be beaten. Naturally, major league owners—including the small market owners these rules restrict the most—have relentlessly struck them down over the last half-decade. Instead, these rules lead to a system where talent is passively distributed, according to slots and budgets and caps, rather than fought for.

It may sound counterintuitive, but this is the ideal setup for baseball owners—especially the small-market cohort. They, after all, are the ones who pushed hardest for these rules. These owners are happy to take their turns at competition whenever the prospect waves arrive as long as they can justify miniscule payrolls in the interim by calling it their Process. Want us to sign a free agent? Make a big splash in the draft or with international amateurs? Well, that wouldn't be prudent. Just don't ask us about how we made it that way.

For what Ohioans are paying—from ticket prices to the stadium cost to their cable bills—they deserve more than austerity-level baseball. Ohio is rich with other sports options for fans who are tired of the same-old same-old Reds, whether it's the other professional teams in Cincinnati or up the road in Cleveland, or the myriad college teams in the state and in nearby northern Kentucky or Indiana. The Reds, after nearly three decades of mediocrity, can't skate by on the clout of Major League Baseball. They have to offer something, or that lost generation of fans will turn into two as others ditch the Reds for the Indians, for hockey, for football, for basketball, or for something else entirely.

I hope, for the sake of Reds fans and for baseball fans in small markets everywhere, who are constantly being left behind by baseball's powers that be, that the system changes eventually, whether in the 2021 CBA or beyond. Cincinnati is a town with a nearly unparalleled baseball history and a thirst for winning. But as it exists right now, there is no incentive for Castellini or whatever hedge fund eventually buys the team from him to change the plan. It is working out quite well for him, and second lost generation of fans or not, the profits will keep flowing his way by design. Welcome to Major League Baseball, a magical world where failure is success and cities like Cincinnati are the losers because of it. ■

—Jack Moore is a freelance sports and video game writer in Minneapolis, MN.

HITTERS

Tucker Barnhart C   Born: 01/07/91   Age: 28   Bats: B   Throws: R   Height: 5'11"   Weight: 192   Origin: Round 10, 2009 Draft (#299 overall)

YEAR	TEAM	LVL	AGE	PA	R	2B	3B	HR	RBI	BB	K	SB	CS	AVG/OBP/SLG	DRC+	VORP	BABIP	BRR	FRAA	WARP
2016	CIN	MLB	25	420	34	23	1	7	51	36	72	1	0	.257/.323/.379	91	14.6	.299	-1.7	C(108): 3.4	1.9
2017	CIN	MLB	26	423	26	24	2	7	44	42	68	4	0	.270/.347/.403	95	20.8	.312	-1.6	C(110): 0.7	1.8
2018	CIN	MLB	27	522	50	21	3	10	46	54	96	0	4	.248/.328/.372	93	12.1	.291	-3.3	C(118): -9.6, 1B(11): -0.7	0.7
2019	CIN	MLB	28	451	48	22	2	8	46	44	77	2	1	.258/.336/.388	96	16.4	.297	-1.8	C -4	1.3

Breakout: 2%   Improve: 43%   Collapse: 8%   Attrition: 22%   MLB: 96%

Comparables: Dioner Navarro, Josh Thole, Clint Courtney

YEAR	TEAM	P. COUNT	FRM RUNS	BLK RUNS	THRW RUNS	TOT RUNS
2016	CIN	16074	-2.3	2.3	1.7	1.8
2017	CIN	15640	-8.2	2.7	4.9	-0.9
2018	CIN	16826	-11.5	3.6	-0.3	-8.4
2019	CIN	16716	-10.0	2.8	1.4	-5.9

A consistently above-average catcher over the three previous seasons, the Reds finally gave the full weight of catching duties to Barnhart in 2018. And while his offense remained as consistent as ever, the bottom fell out of his defense due to a combination of the third-worst framing in baseball and a precipitous drop from throwing out 44 percent of would-be stealers to a career-low 24 percent. Even a catcher of his 2018 pedigree is still a bargain at the rate at which he was extended, but a second year of depreciating skill behind the plate could turn the tables quickly. After all, Barnhart has never been even an average hitter by DRC+. A solid line-drive rate and improving contact quality means Barnhart has a good chance to mask his depreciation with a batting average bounce back, but he doesn't exactly excel in the sleight of hand.

Alex Blandino INF   Born: 11/06/92   Age: 26   Bats: R   Throws: R   Height: 6'0"   Weight: 190   Origin: Round 1, 2014 Draft (#29 overall)

YEAR	TEAM	LVL	AGE	PA	R	2B	3B	HR	RBI	BB	K	SB	CS	AVG/OBP/SLG	DRC+	VORP	BABIP	BRR	FRAA	WARP
2016	PEN	AA	23	465	52	18	0	8	37	55	114	14	5	.232/.333/.337	100	12.2	.302	-2.0	2B(74): -5.1, 3B(30): 1.2	0.9
2017	PEN	AA	24	236	31	22	0	6	31	32	49	3	4	.259/.374/.462	113	12.9	.315	-1.6	2B(39): 1.8, 3B(18): 2.1	1.4
2017	LOU	AAA	24	237	29	14	1	6	20	32	37	1	3	.270/.390/.444	129	11.9	.305	-2.8	2B(29): -1.8, 3B(26): 0.5	1.3
2018	CIN	MLB	25	147	14	4	0	1	8	13	41	0	0	.234/.324/.289	80	2.7	.337	2.3	2B(21): -1.4, 3B(15): -1.2	0.1
2019	CIN	MLB	26	66	7	3	0	1	7	6	16	1	0	.237/.326/.367	70	-0.1	.303	-0.1	SS 0, 2B 0	-0.1

Breakout: 5%   Improve: 19%   Collapse: 11%   Attrition: 22%   MLB: 42%

Comparables: Taylor Green, Travis Denker, Kory Casto

Blandino saw his season end early due to a knee injury, but given how often he takes a walk, he should be able to kick up his rehab by taking a lot of strolls to first base. In his short stint with the Reds, he was perhaps too passive, as he paired an extremely good ability to hold his swing on balls with an extremely bad swing rate on pitches in the zone. He does make a lot of contact when he chooses to engage the ball, but his power doesn't project to get to average and his speed won't be an asset. Defensively, he fits best at second base, but since he faces an uphill battle to stay in one spot, the fact that he can move around the infield will make help him get plate appearances and keep him from putting down roots in Louisville.

Curtis Casali C   Born: 11/09/88   Age: 30   Bats: R   Throws: R   Height: 6'3"   Weight: 235   Origin: Round 10, 2011 Draft (#317 overall)

YEAR	TEAM	LVL	AGE	PA	R	2B	3B	HR	RBI	BB	K	SB	CS	AVG/OBP/SLG	DRC+	VORP	BABIP	BRR	FRAA	WARP
2016	DUR	AAA	27	81	5	1	0	2	15	15	12	0	0	.254/.407/.365	135	3.6	.280	-1.1	C(13): 0.2	0.5
2016	TBA	MLB	27	256	23	10	0	8	25	25	82	0	0	.186/.273/.336	70	-0.4	.250	-2.6	C(76): 4.8	0.5
2017	DUR	AAA	28	343	36	10	0	5	48	37	65	0	0	.263/.351/.347	106	9.7	.320	-0.4	C(53): -2.1	1.2
2017	TBA	MLB	28	13	2	0	0	1	3	3	3	0	0	.333/.462/.667	92	3.0	.333	0.3	C(8): 0.6	0.1
2018	DUR	AAA	29	104	13	5	0	4	20	7	19	0	0	.274/.327/.453	112	4.5	.301	-0.1	C(26): 1.0	0.7
2018	CIN	MLB	29	156	15	10	0	4	16	12	32	0	2	.293/.355/.450	100	9.1	.352	0.1	C(38): -4.1, 1B(6): 0.1	0.3
2019	CIN	MLB	30	145	15	6	0	3	15	12	34	0	0	.227/.301/.355	68	0.3	.280	-0.3	C -2	-0.1

Breakout: 9%   Improve: 31%   Collapse: 6%   Attrition: 24%   MLB: 61%

Comparables: Chris Gimenez, Dustin Garneau, George Kottaras

YEAR	TEAM	P. COUNT	FRM RUNS	BLK RUNS	THRW RUNS	TOT RUNS
2016	TBA	9368	6.6	-1.3	0.9	5.5
2017	DUR	7761	2.3	-3.0	-1.0	-1.7
2017	TBA	486	0.6	-0.1	0.0	0.8
2018	CIN	4795	-2.1	-1.3	-0.2	-3.0
2018	DUR	3527	1.8	0.3	-0.3	1.9
2019	CIN	5036	-0.1	-1.0	-0.1	-1.2

After an inauspicious start to the offseason, one final change of scenery certainly looks to have done Casali some good, at least as far as his wallet is concerned. After being caught and released by two AL West teams, stashed in Triple-A by Tampa Bay, and dealt to the Reds for cash at the end of May, the former Commodore saw four straight months in the majors for only the second time in his career. His batting average may not be sustainable, but he made much more contact in the zone; his 86 percent in 2018 was nearly 10 percentage points higher than his career rate. Casali ranked among the top 20 hitters in baseball in line-drive rate. If he wants to get to arbitration and beyond, he'll need to make sure his framing doesn't slip again. Well, either that or transition full-time to first base, a position at which he accumulated a 1.467 OPS while he played there in 2018. Watch out, Joey Votto.

Phil Ervin OF Born: 07/15/92 Age: 26 Bats: R Throws: R Height: 5'10" Weight: 207 Origin: Round 1, 2013 Draft (#27 overall)

YEAR	TEAM	LVL	AGE	PA	R	2B	3B	HR	RBI	BB	K	SB	CS	AVG/OBP/SLG	DRC+	VORP	BABIP	BRR	FRAA	WARP
2016	PEN	AA	23	505	71	22	3	13	45	65	88	36	10	.239/.362/.399	132	38.8	.271	1.2	LF(76): 2.5, CF(31): -1.1	3.7
2017	LOU	AAA	24	408	46	20	2	7	40	37	83	23	6	.256/.328/.380	96	7.7	.315	0.6	LF(56): 8.7, CF(40): -3.1	1.4
2017	CIN	MLB	24	64	8	2	0	3	10	4	15	4	1	.259/.317/.448	95	4.6	.300	1.1	CF(9): -0.6, RF(5): -0.4	0.2
2018	LOU	AAA	25	202	25	12	4	5	38	20	39	10	7	.289/.373/.491	117	14.7	.341	-0.8	LF(37): 5.2, CF(8): -0.5	1.4
2018	CIN	MLB	25	247	27	10	1	7	31	20	60	6	1	.252/.324/.404	97	6.2	.310	1.0	LF(39): 0.2, RF(33): -2.7	0.4
2019	CIN	MLB	26	186	22	7	1	5	19	15	43	7	2	.230/.301/.367	85	3.1	.279	0.4	CF 0, LF 1	0.5

Breakout: 7% Improve: 32% Collapse: 12% Attrition: 25% MLB: 70% Comparables: Michael Choice, Max Muncy, Brandon Jones

The average National League center fielder hit .256/.326/.408 last year, a near-perfect match for Ervin's offensive numbers over half a season in Cincinnati. If he could also flash the defensive chops of an average big-league center fielder the Reds might have the heir to Billy Hamilton on their hands. Unfortunately, Ervin's plus speed has never been able to paper over the bad routes, inaccurate throws, and sketchy instincts that have made him a liability in the great grass sea. At 26 he's not likely to improve. Still, the first-round pick has enough juice in his bat to launch 20 bombs over a full season and would be a nice fourth outfielder on a contending squad, or a perfectly cromulent placeholder for the perpetually rebuilding Reds.

Scooter Gennett 2B Born: 05/01/90 Age: 29 Bats: L Throws: R Height: 5'10" Weight: 185 Origin: Round 16, 2009 Draft (#496 overall)

YEAR	TEAM	LVL	AGE	PA	R	2B	3B	HR	RBI	BB	K	SB	CS	AVG/OBP/SLG	DRC+	VORP	BABIP	BRR	FRAA	WARP
2016	MIL	MLB	26	542	58	30	1	14	56	38	114	8	1	.263/.317/.412	90	14.6	.315	-0.8	2B(127): 4.8	1.4
2017	CIN	MLB	27	497	80	22	3	27	97	30	114	3	2	.295/.342/.531	119	32.8	.339	-1.4	2B(99): -8.9, 3B(10): -0.2	1.7
2018	CIN	MLB	28	638	86	30	3	23	92	42	125	4	2	.310/.357/.490	121	41.8	.358	-0.1	2B(142): -4.5	3.2
2019	CIN	MLB	29	572	67	29	3	20	76	39	120	4	2	.276/.331/.455	115	28.5	.321	-0.9	2B -4	2.6

Breakout: 1% Improve: 48% Collapse: 4% Attrition: 8% MLB: 100% Comparables: Howie Kendrick, Aaron Hill, Jimmie Reese

"Gennett is still young enough to develop more power or refine his approach...with good contact skills, a low walk rate and an indifferent glove." That's what we wrote prior to his 2013 rookie season, so color us unsurprised that Scooter's refined approach has led to better pitches to drive, 50 bombs over the last two years, an All-Star berth and a perch among the league's best second sackers. (Okay, so we redacted the part where we compared Gennett to Aaron Miles and his 19 career home runs, so perhaps we're a little surprised.) Last year he stood in well against same-side pitchers and held his own in the field, gains that help to round out his portfolio as he nears free agency. The aging curve can be especially cruel to second basemen, but as long as he can barrel up a fastball he'll earn his keep.

Jonathan India 3B Born: 12/15/96 Age: 22 Bats: R Throws: R Height: 6'1" Weight: 200 Origin: Round 1, 2018 Draft (#5 overall)

YEAR	TEAM	LVL	AGE	PA	R	2B	3B	HR	RBI	BB	K	SB	CS	AVG/OBP/SLG	DRC+	VORP	BABIP	BRR	FRAA	WARP
2018	GRV	RK	21	62	11	2	1	3	12	15	12	1	0	.261/.452/.543	132	6.2	.290	0.6	3B(12): -0.6, SS(2): -0.2	0.4
2018	DYT	A	21	112	17	7	0	3	11	13	28	5	0	.229/.339/.396	102	7.0	.292	1.5	3B(21): 2.4, SS(4): -0.1	0.8
2019	CIN	MLB	22	251	24	8	0	8	26	19	75	3	1	.188/.251/.313	57	-7.1	.238	-0.4	3B 0, SS 0	-0.8

Breakout: 3% Improve: 8% Collapse: 1% Attrition: 10% MLB: 11% Comparables: Jesus Guzman, Kyle Kubitza, Kaleb Cowart

The word "kal" means both "yesterday" and "tomorrow" in Hindi, which seems appropriate when talking about India. A low-ceiling, high-floor college bat, India was chosen fifth overall in last year's draft based less on his potential to improve from yesterday to tomorrow than on his ability to continue the solid production of his Gator heyday. He's an advanced hitter with a solid approach, average power, decent speed and a capable if uninspiring glove at the hot corner. India's masala of average-or-better skills makes him a safe bet to be an everyday big leaguer, and a poor bet to become a superstar.

Matt Kemp RF Born: 09/23/84 Age: 34 Bats: R Throws: R Height: 6'4" Weight: 210 Origin: Round 6, 2003 Draft (#181 overall)

YEAR	TEAM	LVL	AGE	PA	R	2B	3B	HR	RBI	BB	K	SB	CS	AVG/OBP/SLG	DRC+	VORP	BABIP	BRR	FRAA	WARP
2016	SDN	MLB	31	431	54	24	0	23	69	16	100	0	0	.262/.285/.489	114	11.0	.288	-0.4	RF(97): -5.3	1.2
2016	ATL	MLB	31	241	35	15	0	12	39	20	56	1	0	.280/.336/.519	107	18.3	.316	1.5	LF(54): 0.0	1.0
2017	ATL	MLB	32	467	47	23	1	19	64	27	99	0	2	.276/.318/.463	100	7.4	.318	-3.4	LF(103): -14.6	-0.5
2018	LAN	MLB	33	506	62	25	0	21	85	36	115	0	0	.290/.338/.481	117	23.3	.339	-2.1	LF(75): -1.5, RF(51): -2.2	1.7
2019	CIN	MLB	34	295	33	16	1	11	39	20	66	1	0	.267/.318/.448	107	10.9	.315	-0.6	LF -3	0.8

Breakout: 0% Improve: 27% Collapse: 13% Attrition: 25% MLB: 91% Comparables: Jim Rice, Garret Anderson, Alfonso Soriano

When the Dodgers acquired Kemp in December 2017, it's unlikely they immediately started cutting a highlight video set to the popular Diddy ditty "Coming Home" to play on Opening Day. In reality, the deal was consummated as a swap of bad contracts with the hopes of lessening the team's luxury-tax burden. Rumors of a Spring Training release swirled, but Kemp responded in the best way, winning a roster spot and hitting .310/.352/.522 in the first half to earn his third All-Star appearance. The second half didn't go as well, but the former franchise cornerstone did manage to stay upright in the field, unlike the last handful of seasons. It's a luxury to be able to trade for a pricey slugger with the intention of handing out an immediate pink slip. It's an even bigger luxury when said slugger rejuvenates and turns into a legit asset, making the $22 million remaining on his 2019 contract infinitely more palatable—and for a middling-payroll squad no less.

Shed Long 2B   Born: 08/22/95   Age: 23   Bats: L   Throws: R   Height: 5'8"   Weight: 184   Origin: Round 12, 2013 Draft (#375 overall)

YEAR	TEAM	LVL	AGE	PA	R	2B	3B	HR	RBI	BB	K	SB	CS	AVG/OBP/SLG	DRC+	VORP	BABIP	BRR	FRAA	WARP
2016	DYT	A	20	389	47	24	1	11	45	44	85	16	3	.281/.371/.457	133	30.7	.346	3.2	2B(82): 2.0, 3B(3): -0.6	3.2
2016	DAY	A+	20	159	22	6	4	4	30	10	35	5	1	.322/.371/.503	115	12.2	.393	1.3	2B(38): 3.0	1.2
2017	DAY	A+	21	279	37	16	1	13	36	27	63	6	3	.312/.380/.543	141	21.5	.368	-1.1	2B(62): 5.4	2.7
2017	PEN	AA	21	160	13	6	2	3	14	19	31	3	1	.227/.319/.362	100	1.9	.271	-2.4	2B(39): -1.7	0.0
2018	PEN	AA	22	522	75	22	5	12	56	57	123	19	6	.261/.353/.412	107	32.1	.333	3.7	2B(123): -1.9	2.3
2019	CIN	MLB	23	37	5	1	0	1	4	3	10	1	0	.223/.286/.371	58	-0.6	.276	0.0	2B 0	-0.1

Breakout: 5%   Improve: 20%   Collapse: 7%   Attrition: 16%   MLB: 38%   *Comparables: Brandon Lowe, Dilson Herrera, Carlos Asuaje*

A former 12th round pick, Long succeeded in his second crack at Double-A and could soon be manning the keystone at GABP. He's an adequate defender with enough speed to post double-digit steal totals, but it's his skill with the lumber that will determine his future. Long draws walks and has a quick bat that can pack a wallop, but his swing can get long at times and leads to rafts of strikeouts. If he maintains his patient approach and makes enough contact he could launch 15 bombs and be a top-of-the order spark plug; if not, there are still enough tools in this Shed to build a career on a big league bench.

Jordan Patterson 1B   Born: 02/12/92   Age: 27   Bats: L   Throws: L   Height: 6'4"   Weight: 215   Origin: Round 4, 2013 Draft (#109 overall)

YEAR	TEAM	LVL	AGE	PA	R	2B	3B	HR	RBI	BB	K	SB	CS	AVG/OBP/SLG	DRC+	VORP	BABIP	BRR	FRAA	WARP
2016	ABQ	AAA	24	495	75	24	7	14	61	47	118	10	0	.293/.376/.480	120	19.6	.370	1.5	RF(76): 15.6, 1B(38): 0.4	4.1
2016	COL	MLB	24	19	1	1	0	0	2	1	1	0	1	.444/.474/.500	109	0.9	.471	-0.6	RF(5): -0.3, 1B(2): 0.1	0.0
2017	ABQ	AAA	25	542	78	32	7	26	92	36	128	3	5	.283/.348/.539	124	17.4	.330	-0.2	1B(84): 0.7, RF(39): -1.7	2.5
2018	ABQ	AAA	26	480	77	23	2	26	76	42	128	6	2	.271/.367/.525	137	21.0	.328	0.3	1B(71): 1.1, RF(44): -2.9	3.1
2019	CIN	MLB	27	251	31	12	1	10	34	18	63	2	1	.249/.328/.444	110	7.8	.307	-0.3	1B 0, RF 1	0.9

Breakout: 1%   Improve: 9%   Collapse: 9%   Attrition: 20%   MLB: 31%   *Comparables: Christian Walker, Daniel Dorn, Juan Miranda*

When you've got a type, you've got a type. The Rockies seem to produce a never-ending stream of corner guys with just enough bat to intrigue but not quite enough consistency or defensive value to grab firm hold of a spot on the 25-man roster. Exhibit infinity: Jordan Patterson. He crushed right-handed pitching again at Triple-A last year, ho-hummed his at-bats against lefties and managed to stand competently in both right field and at first base for a majority of the year. And speaking of types, if that sounds a lot like what Jay Bruce does, minus about $13.5 million in guaranteed salary commitment, congratulations! You're a Mets executive now. Wait...no. Now you're a Reds executive! Whew, the life of a journeyman minor leaguer can be confusing.

Jose Peraza SS   Born: 04/30/94   Age: 25   Bats: R   Throws: R   Height: 6'0"   Weight: 196   Origin: International Free Agent, 2010

YEAR	TEAM	LVL	AGE	PA	R	2B	3B	HR	RBI	BB	K	SB	CS	AVG/OBP/SLG	DRC+	VORP	BABIP	BRR	FRAA	WARP
2016	LOU	AAA	22	322	40	15	3	2	21	21	43	10	7	.281/.333/.375	103	14.8	.324	1.5	SS(58): -3.6, CF(6): -0.1	1.2
2016	CIN	MLB	22	256	25	8	2	3	25	7	33	21	10	.324/.352/.411	100	10.9	.361	-0.8	SS(31): -1.0, CF(13): -1.3	0.6
2017	CIN	MLB	23	518	50	9	4	5	37	20	70	23	8	.259/.297/.324	82	-0.1	.293	0.6	2B(77): 2.3, SS(55): 0.6	1.1
2018	CIN	MLB	24	683	85	31	4	14	58	29	75	23	6	.288/.326/.416	106	31.2	.307	2.4	SS(156): -3.4, RF(1): 0.0	3.6
2019	CIN	MLB	25	603	78	30	4	11	55	29	74	24	8	.285/.331/.412	102	24.6	.308	0.5	SS -4	2.2

Breakout: 3%   Improve: 68%   Collapse: 5%   Attrition: 14%   MLB: 99%   *Comparables: Yuniesky Betancourt, Erick Aybar, Alcides Escobar*

Peraza's first season as Cincinnati's full-time shortstop came in like a lamb (.243/.279/.317 through May 25), went out like a lion (.309/.348/.463 the rest of the way), and featured a surprising amount of gopher (14 home runs) in between. Long known as a free-swinging contact hitter with great speed and little thunder, Peraza made a concerted effort to avoid ground balls and raised his power profile from "non-existent" to "occasional." It's fair to question whether he can keep this up, as he continues to rank near the bottom of the league in exit velocity. If some of last year's wall-scrapers start dying at the track, Peraza's offensive value will die with them. Still, he's not yet 25, flashed a fringe-average glove and is worth another look to see if he can be the Reds long-term answer at the six.

Yasiel Puig RF
Born: 12/07/90 Age: 28 Bats: R Throws: R Height: 6'2" Weight: 240 Origin: International Free Agent, 2012

YEAR	TEAM	LVL	AGE	PA	R	2B	3B	HR	RBI	BB	K	SB	CS	AVG/OBP/SLG	DRC+	VORP	BABIP	BRR	FRAA	WARP
2016	OKL	AAA	25	75	12	3	1	4	12	6	8	0	1	.348/.400/.594	128	5.2	.351	-3.0	RF(17): 0.0	0.1
2016	LAN	MLB	25	368	45	14	2	11	45	24	74	5	2	.263/.323/.416	91	13.7	.306	1.4	RF(90): 5.3, LF(5): 0.0	1.2
2017	LAN	MLB	26	570	72	24	2	28	74	64	100	15	6	.263/.346/.487	118	27.9	.274	-4.3	RF(145): 9.0	3.1
2018	LAN	MLB	27	444	60	21	1	23	63	36	87	15	5	.267/.327/.494	121	23.3	.286	2.4	RF(118): -4.5	2.0
2019	CIN	MLB	28	493	68	22	2	20	65	46	91	12	5	.263/.336/.460	116	23.0	.289	-0.6	RF 2	2.7

Breakout: 3% Improve: 52% Collapse: 1% Attrition: 6% MLB: 97% Comparables: Andre Ethier, Chet Lemon, Nick Markakis

A Petrarchan sonnet for Yasiel Puig:

A wild horse gallops across the plains
Power, grace and speed, with limitless joy
In his world, never mistaken for coy
Lacking maturity was a refrain
Once flayed and maligned, now free from those reins
Playing a game made clear he enjoyed
Old unwritten rules, he surely destroyed
Teammates come and go, his passion remains
A wag of the tongue and taste of his bat
World Series home runs and jubilant flips
Try not to love him, you'll have to pretend
Catching runners with what some call a gat
Striding to the plate with a swag that drips
Exuberance is life for #PuigYourFriend

Scott Schebler OF
Born: 10/06/90 Age: 28 Bats: L Throws: R Height: 6'0" Weight: 228 Origin: Round 26, 2010 Draft (#802 overall)

YEAR	TEAM	LVL	AGE	PA	R	2B	3B	HR	RBI	BB	K	SB	CS	AVG/OBP/SLG	DRC+	VORP	BABIP	BRR	FRAA	WARP
2016	LOU	AAA	25	319	40	18	8	13	43	19	59	2	0	.311/.370/.564	148	29.9	.352	-1.7	CF(49): 3.1, LF(16): -1.1	2.8
2016	CIN	MLB	25	282	36	12	2	9	40	19	59	2	4	.265/.330/.432	93	10.0	.312	1.7	RF(41): 4.2, CF(18): -2.5	0.8
2017	CIN	MLB	26	531	63	25	2	30	67	39	125	5	3	.233/.307/.484	103	20.6	.248	-0.2	RF(120): -4.8, CF(15): 0.9	1.1
2018	CIN	MLB	27	430	55	19	0	17	49	39	99	4	2	.255/.337/.439	107	14.9	.301	-1.4	RF(86): -2.4, CF(16): 0.5	1.1
2019	CIN	MLB	28	457	54	19	2	17	59	37	101	5	2	.240/.322/.417	104	17.0	.284	0.3	LF 0, CF 2	2.1

Breakout: 0% Improve: 54% Collapse: 11% Attrition: 22% MLB: 91% Comparables: Nate Schierholtz, Will Venable, Kole Calhoun

On July 13, Schebler was proving those who thought his 2017 season a fluke wrong. He was hitting a cool .278/.351/.470, and while the power was being tampered by a career-low fly-ball rate, his newfound aggressiveness in the zone was helping him squeeze plenty of those extra grounders through the holes. The next day, his aggressiveness in the field would ultimately lead to his undoing. Giving chase to a Yadier Molina fly ball, Schebler ran his right shoulder directly into the outfield wall, sidelining him with a right AC joint sprain for the next six weeks. He limped to the finish line after returning, with a .674 OPS in the season's final month-plus. He'll man left field in 2019 for the Reds, as often as they'll allow him to given their newfound outfield depth.

Nick Senzel 3B
Born: 06/29/95 Age: 24 Bats: R Throws: R Height: 6'1" Weight: 205 Origin: Round 1, 2016 Draft (#2 overall)

YEAR	TEAM	LVL	AGE	PA	R	2B	3B	HR	RBI	BB	K	SB	CS	AVG/OBP/SLG	DRC+	VORP	BABIP	BRR	FRAA	WARP
2016	BIL	RK	21	41	3	1	0	0	4	6	5	3	0	.152/.293/.182	94	-1.5	.172	0.1	3B(10): 1.0	0.2
2016	DYT	A	21	251	38	23	3	7	36	32	49	15	7	.329/.415/.567	153	34.0	.392	1.6	3B(56): 3.2	3.0
2017	DAY	A+	22	272	41	26	2	4	31	23	54	9	2	.305/.371/.476	110	24.5	.378	1.3	3B(60): 5.1	1.9
2017	PEN	AA	22	235	40	14	1	10	34	26	43	5	4	.340/.413/.560	136	26.5	.391	-0.5	3B(56): 1.7	2.1
2018	LOU	AAA	23	193	23	12	2	6	25	19	39	8	2	.310/.378/.509	125	19.5	.367	1.9	2B(28): -0.8, 3B(14): 0.8	1.4
2019	CIN	MLB	24	454	55	22	1	14	51	39	105	10	4	.245/.315/.404	96	12.8	.296	-0.1		1.5

Breakout: 2% Improve: 30% Collapse: 15% Attrition: 26% MLB: 63% Comparables: Vince Belnome, Ryan Rua, Rob Refsnyder

Senzel's stock continued to rise as quickly as he did through the minor leagues until a series of injuries conspired to keep the 2016 first-rounder sidelined for the rest of the 2018 season. In May, it was vertigo. In June, it was a torn tendon in his right index finger. In October, it was surgery to remove bone spurs from his elbow. When healthy, he has consistently managed to do what we've come to expect from Senzel: all-around offensive success. He hit even more line drives and avoided repeating the ground-ball spike he saw in Double-A in 2017. The only question marks that remain are health-related and position-related. The Reds first sought to try him at the keystone with Eugenio Suarez entrenched at third in Cincinnati. And while that's still a possibility, they have also hinted at trying him at either center field or shortstop—and just the fact that they're trying it speaks volumes about his athleticism at the hot corner. However it shakes out, you don't have to worry about his bat nor do you have to worry about his defense. Save your worries for which God to pray to in order for Senzel to remain on the field long enough to establish himself as a star.

Jose Siri CF   Born: 07/22/95   Age: 23   Bats: R   Throws: R   Height: 6'2"   Weight: 175   Origin: International Free Agent, 2012

YEAR	TEAM	LVL	AGE	PA	R	2B	3B	HR	RBI	BB	K	SB	CS	AVG/OBP/SLG	DRC+	VORP	BABIP	BRR	FRAA	WARP
2016	DYT	A	20	87	5	3	0	0	3	2	34	3	2	.145/.163/.181	53	-8.9	.240	0.6	CF(17): 1.7, RF(9): -0.2	-0.1
2016	BIL	RK	20	255	52	12	8	10	35	8	66	17	4	.320/.348/.560	115	25.2	.404	3.9	RF(33): 4.6, CF(21): 5.4	2.4
2017	DYT	A	21	552	92	24	11	24	76	33	130	46	12	.293/.341/.530	131	49.1	.349	7.4	CF(103): 15.7, RF(9): 1.5	6.3
2018	DAY	A+	22	126	15	9	2	1	9	4	32	9	1	.261/.280/.395	82	2.2	.341	1.1	CF(26): 0.4	0.2
2018	PEN	AA	22	283	42	8	9	12	34	24	91	14	5	.229/.300/.474	121	15.0	.301	2.2	CF(59): -3.9	1.5
2019	CIN	MLB	23	171	22	7	2	7	20	8	52	7	2	.227/.263/.423	88	5.3	.285	1.2	CF 2	0.8

Breakout: 3%   Improve: 16%   Collapse: 2%   Attrition: 13%   MLB: 26%   Comparables: Teoscar Hernandez, Franchy Cordero, Trayce Thompson

We call them "tools," but in Siri's case it might be better to think of his tremendous natural gifts as "parts." His plus glove in center field? That's a part. His blazing speed, his cannon arm, the way his bat blurs as it whips through the zone? A bunch of parts. The easy power in his swing, the loft and backspin he generates as he launches a batting practice fastball into orbit? Those, too, are parts, all gleaming with a cold, sinister, yet strangely alluring light. His need to swing at every pitch in sight? That's not a part. That's the assembly line, and it's broken. Last year as a 23-year-old in Double-A, Siri struck out in nearly a third of his plate appearances. Until that gets fixed the sum of his parts will be infinitely greater than the whole. Raw talent and a bad approach can sometimes turn into Javier Baez; more frequently, it becomes Junior Lake.

Eugenio Suarez 3B   Born: 07/18/91   Age: 27   Bats: R   Throws: R   Height: 5'11"   Weight: 213   Origin: International Free Agent, 2008

YEAR	TEAM	LVL	AGE	PA	R	2B	3B	HR	RBI	BB	K	SB	CS	AVG/OBP/SLG	DRC+	VORP	BABIP	BRR	FRAA	WARP
2016	CIN	MLB	24	627	78	25	2	21	70	51	155	11	5	.248/.317/.411	97	19.8	.304	0.7	3B(151): 2.0, SS(2): -0.3	2.4
2017	CIN	MLB	25	632	87	25	2	26	82	84	147	4	5	.260/.367/.461	119	38.8	.309	-4.7	3B(153): -1.9, SS(1): 0.0	3.3
2018	CIN	MLB	26	606	79	22	2	34	104	64	142	1	1	.283/.366/.526	141	45.6	.322	-3.5	3B(143): -7.6, SS(3): 0.0	4.2
2019	CIN	MLB	27	565	72	27	2	23	79	60	128	4	3	.265/.355/.465	124	27.4	.315	-1.9	3B -2	2.7

Breakout: 7%   Improve: 45%   Collapse: 2%   Attrition: 9%   MLB: 99%   Comparables: Edwin Encarnacion, Michael Cuddyer, Kyle Seager

Pick your metric and Suarez has been improving it for several seasons, at least on offense. He saw gains for the second consecutive year in DRC+, batting average, OPS, line drives and hard-hit rate on fly balls. He's a star, but unfortunately for Suarez, he's about as well-hidden as The Secret Aquarium in Super Mario 64. He finds himself locked in baseball's version of the middle-child syndrome; this is a Reds team that loses too many games to have a second recognizable face, and Joey Votto is locked in at this spot for another half-decade. For the most part, the Venezuela native even went about his improvement in unspectacular fashion. His batted ball profile was nearly identical to 2017. His destruction of southpaws to the tune of a 1.020 OPS continued, but that wasn't not a new phenomenon either. Suarez did make one notable decision, however: he became more aggressive on pitches in the strike zone. Turns out, the trade-off of a handful of walks for reliably harder contact was a good one.

Taylor Trammell OF   Born: 09/13/97   Age: 21   Bats: L   Throws: L   Height: 6'2"   Weight: 195   Origin: Round 1, 2016 Draft (#35 overall)

YEAR	TEAM	LVL	AGE	PA	R	2B	3B	HR	RBI	BB	K	SB	CS	AVG/OBP/SLG	DRC+	VORP	BABIP	BRR	FRAA	WARP
2016	BIL	RK	18	254	39	9	6	2	34	23	57	24	7	.303/.374/.421	90	15.1	.396	2.7	LF(39): 0.5, CF(11): 2.1	0.7
2017	DYT	A	19	571	80	24	10	13	77	71	123	41	12	.281/.368/.450	123	41.6	.345	3.1	LF(104): -3.7, CF(17): -0.9	2.7
2018	DAY	A+	20	461	71	19	4	8	41	58	105	25	10	.277/.375/.406	124	26.4	.358	-0.8	CF(60): -1.7, LF(29): 4.5	2.8
2019	CIN	MLB	21	251	28	7	1	7	26	21	65	8	3	.218/.283/.344	72	0.2	.272	0.5	CF 0, LF 1	0.1

Breakout: 10%   Improve: 16%   Collapse: 2%   Attrition: 14%   MLB: 29%   Comparables: Anthony Gose, Austin Meadows, Victor Robles

The athletic, toolsy stereotype applies to Trammell, who's already shown double-plus speed and the potential for above-average power. Although his arm is a bit weak for center field and he takes routes in the outfield that make you think he accidentally set Waze to avoid highways, his combination of jaw-dropping raw skills is enough to make any national prospect writer fawn over him in GIF form. Trammell came away from the Futures Game with some Hardware and some notoriety as well: he celebrated a home run in the bottom of the eighth inning by flashing two fingers at the dugout, to represent his second bomb of the game, only it didn't actually clear the wall. He wasn't nearly as dynamic during his season in the FSL. We know there's clear star potential here, but whether he reaches that ceiling depends on how much consistency he can show on a game-to-game or week-to-week basis.

Joey Votto 1B   Born: 09/10/83   Age: 35   Bats: L   Throws: R   Height: 6'2"   Weight: 220   Origin: Round 2, 2002 Draft (#44 overall)

YEAR	TEAM	LVL	AGE	PA	R	2B	3B	HR	RBI	BB	K	SB	CS	AVG/OBP/SLG	DRC+	VORP	BABIP	BRR	FRAA	WARP
2016	CIN	MLB	32	677	101	34	2	29	97	108	120	8	1	.326/.434/.550	150	58.6	.366	-4.1	1B(154): -1.1	4.8
2017	CIN	MLB	33	707	106	34	1	36	100	134	83	5	1	.320/.454/.578	170	69.9	.321	-6.9	1B(162): 9.5	7.6
2018	CIN	MLB	34	623	67	28	2	12	67	108	101	2	0	.284/.417/.419	135	28.6	.333	-2.6	1B(139): 11.6	4.6
2019	CIN	MLB	35	622	83	34	2	18	80	102	98	4	1	.292/.417/.471	147	41.0	.333	-3.8	1B 7	5.1

Breakout: 1%   Improve: 31%   Collapse: 1%   Attrition: 6%   MLB: 98%   Comparables: Todd Helton, Edgar Martinez, Albert Pujols

Pitchers beware. Fresh off a disastrous season where Votto plummeted to near the bottom of the top 20 in all of baseball in most measures of offensive performance (including DRC+), the best batsman of his generation has dedicated his offseason to improving what he views as the current weak point in his game: hitting. Although he continued to reach base at a historic clip, last season Votto posted the lowest home run and slugging numbers of his career. His fly-ball rate dropped precipitously from the previous year but was still in line with his career norms, so the lack of thump could be luck, weather, swamp gas reflecting off a weather balloon or the fact Votto has now entered his late thirties. The Master himself blames his conditioning, saying he felt like he was "walking through mud" all season. Pro tip: You feel like that a lot after you turn 35, Joey. Experience tells us not to bet against him hitting 25 dingers this year, but even with diminished power Votto's peerless command of the strike zone will continue to make him an offensive force.

Mason Williams   RF   Born: 08/21/91   Age: 27   Bats: L   Throws: R   Height: 6'1"   Weight: 195   Origin: Round 4, 2010 Draft (#145 overall)

YEAR	TEAM	LVL	AGE	PA	R	2B	3B	HR	RBI	BB	K	SB	CS	AVG/OBP/SLG	DRC+	VORP	BABIP	BRR	FRAA	WARP
2016	TAM	A+	24	43	2	2	1	0	1	1	4	0	0	.333/.349/.429	106	0.6	.368	-1.1	CF(4): 0.3	0.0
2016	SWB	AAA	24	138	19	8	1	0	23	5	21	1	1	.296/.313/.376	84	4.1	.343	0.8	CF(18): -1.5, RF(3): -0.2	0.0
2016	NYA	MLB	24	29	4	1	0	0	2	1	12	0	0	.296/.321/.333	63	0.1	.533	0.3	RF(7): -0.3, LF(2): 0.4	0.0
2017	NYA	MLB	25	17	3	0	0	0	1	1	2	2	0	.250/.294/.250	98	0.0	.286	0.5	CF(5): -0.4, RF(1): -0.1	0.1
2017	SWB	AAA	25	437	44	10	3	2	30	28	66	19	5	.263/.309/.318	86	-4.7	.306	3.3	CF(64): 3.7, LF(19): 0.8	1.3
2018	LOU	AAA	26	356	52	18	4	6	30	29	57	5	8	.280/.341/.418	103	16.5	.324	-1.4	CF(85): -1.9	1.0
2018	CIN	MLB	26	132	10	5	1	2	6	7	29	1	2	.293/.331/.398	83	1.0	.370	0.4	RF(27): -1.7, CF(10): -0.1	-0.1
2019	*CIN*	*MLB*	*27*	*251*	*28*	*10*	*1*	*5*	*21*	*16*	*57*	*5*	*3*	*.230/.283/.341*	*68*	*-0.9*	*.280*	*-0.3*	*CF 0, RF 0*	*-0.1*

Breakout: 3%   Improve: 15%   Collapse: 10%   Attrition: 17%   MLB: 42%   *Comparables: Rafael Ortega, Reymond Fuentes, L.J. Hoes*

Williams continues to cling to a small chance of being the fifth outfielder on a roster. Don't be deceived by a high batting average in 2018, propped up by a lucky BABIP, because there's almost none of his prospect sheen remaining. The most he offers a major-league roster at this point is the ability to stand in center field without embarrassing himself. Apparently that wasn't quite good enough for the Reds, who outrighted him off the 40-man roster in November.

Jesse Winker   RF   Born: 08/17/93   Age: 25   Bats: L   Throws: L   Height: 6'3"   Weight: 215   Origin: Round 1, 2012 Draft (#49 overall)

YEAR	TEAM	LVL	AGE	PA	R	2B	3B	HR	RBI	BB	K	SB	CS	AVG/OBP/SLG	DRC+	VORP	BABIP	BRR	FRAA	WARP
2016	LOU	AAA	22	448	39	22	0	3	45	59	59	0	0	.303/.397/.384	128	20.4	.347	-1.0	RF(52): 1.0, LF(46): -2.3	2.3
2017	LOU	AAA	23	347	33	22	0	2	41	38	46	2	4	.314/.395/.408	120	14.7	.359	-3.2	RF(70): 2.7, LF(3): 0.4	1.5
2017	CIN	MLB	23	137	21	7	0	7	15	15	24	1	1	.298/.375/.529	116	9.7	.322	-0.6	RF(25): -1.4, LF(2): -0.3	0.4
2018	CIN	MLB	24	334	38	16	0	7	43	49	46	0	0	.299/.405/.431	126	17.2	.336	-2.6	RF(47): -1.0, LF(34): -3.5	1.1
2019	*CIN*	*MLB*	*25*	*365*	*46*	*17*	*1*	*8*	*37*	*43*	*55*	*1*	*1*	*.268/.363/.406*	*112*	*14.0*	*.302*	*-1.5*	*RF -1, LF -1*	*1.3*

Breakout: 9%   Improve: 46%   Collapse: 5%   Attrition: 15%   MLB: 88%   *Comparables: Carlos Quentin, Ramon Flores, Chris Coghlan*

Winker's rookie season was a resounding success cut short by surgery to correct a chronic shoulder problem. The former first-round pick proved that he can control the strike zone against major-league pitching by walking more than he whiffed and making consistent hard contact with his smooth lefty stroke. Winker's postage-stamp range confines him to an outfield corner and he rarely packs the wallop associated with success there. Yet there's plenty of reason to think more power will come: his shoulder and wrist may finally be healthy, he's about to enter his prime, launch-angle savants will be whispering in his ear, and he's got an open invitation to spit seeds and talk shop with Joey Votto, who grew into his own power at the same age. If Winker can continue to get on base at a 40-percent clip and starts launching 25 bombs per year, the Reds will have another top-20 bat on their hands.

PITCHERS

Luis Castillo   RHP   Born: 12/12/92   Age: 26   Bats: R   Throws: R   Height: 6'2"   Weight: 190   Origin: International Free Agent, 2012

YEAR	TEAM	LVL	AGE	W	L	SV	G	GS	IP	H	HR	BB/9	K/9	K	GB%	BABIP	WHIP	ERA	DRA	WARP	MPH	FB%	WHF	CSP
2016	JUP	A+	23	8	4	0	23	21	117²	95	2	1.4	7.0	91	50%	.271	0.96	2.07	2.76	3.6				
2016	JAX	AA	23	0	2	0	3	3	14	12	1	4.5	7.7	12	42%	.262	1.36	3.86	3.91	0.2				
2017	PEN	AA	24	4	4	0	14	14	80¹	68	5	1.5	9.1	81	42%	.293	1.01	2.58	2.81	2.3				
2017	CIN	MLB	24	3	7	0	15	15	89¹	64	11	3.2	9.9	98	60%	.247	1.07	3.12	3.41	2.2	98.7	62.1	13.5	47.9
2018	CIN	MLB	25	10	12	0	31	31	169²	158	28	2.6	8.8	165	48%	.282	1.22	4.30	4.76	1.1	97.8	57.2	14.2	48.9
2019	*CIN*	*MLB*	*26*	*10*	*8*	*0*	*27*	*27*	*154*	*137*	*19*	*2.7*	*9.4*	*160*	*46%*	*.305*	*1.20*	*3.75*	*4.05*	*2.2*	*97.7*	*59.7*	*14.3*	*49.3*

Breakout: 31%   Improve: 56%   Collapse: 16%   Attrition: 12%   MLB: 89%   *Comparables: Taylor Buchholz, Scott Baker, Anthony DeSclafani*

While he didn't blossom into an ace last summer, there were plenty of promising signs during Castillo's first full season in the Cincinnati rotation. Armed with a fastball that reaches into the high 90s and a filthy changeup, Castillo shrugged off a rocky April to post a 3.57 ERA thereafter. He held batters to a .232/.286/.408 line the rest of the way while lowering his walk rate and punching out a batter per inning. On the downside, his fly-ball and home run rates soared and lefties that were able to lay off the change tattooed him, slugging .671 against his fastball and sinker. If Castillo can find a way to stop handing out bleacher souvenirs and tame his opposite-handed foes, he has the goods to front the Reds rotation for a long time.

Anthony DeSclafani   RHP   Born: 04/18/90   Age: 29   Bats: R   Throws: R   Height: 6'1"   Weight: 195   Origin: Round 6, 2011 Draft (#199 overall)

YEAR	TEAM	LVL	AGE	W	L	SV	G	GS	IP	H	HR	BB/9	K/9	K	GB%	BABIP	WHIP	ERA	DRA	WARP	MPH	FB%	WHF	CSP
2016	LOU	AAA	26	0	1	0	3	3	13	12	4	0.0	7.6	11	46%	.229	0.92	5.54	3.20	0.3				
2016	CIN	MLB	26	9	5	0	20	20	123¹	120	16	2.2	7.7	105	44%	.295	1.22	3.28	4.32	1.5	95.1	55.9	10	47.2
2018	LOU	AAA	28	0	2	0	2	2	11¹	15	5	1.6	7.9	10	43%	.312	1.50	6.35	4.55	0.1				
2018	CIN	MLB	28	7	8	0	21	21	115	118	24	2.3	8.5	108	43%	.294	1.29	4.93	5.16	0.2	95.4	57.9	10.7	49.8
2019	*CIN*	*MLB*	*29*	*9*	*10*	*0*	*26*	*26*	*156*	*165*	*36*	*3.1*	*9.0*	*155*	*43%*	*.315*	*1.41*	*5.32*	*5.82*	*-0.9*	*94.6*	*57.1*	*10.4*	*48.8*

Breakout: 29%   Improve: 41%   Collapse: 30%   Attrition: 12%   MLB: 93%   *Comparables: Tommy Milone, Jason Vargas, Vance Worley*

DeSclafani returned from Tommy John surgery and pitched exactly like the mid-rotation starter he had been in 2016 except for, you know, all those extra runs. The culprit was a ridiculously high rate of home runs per fly ball, a notoriously fickle contagion that afflicted the entire Cincinnati rotation last summer. All of DeSclafani's other peripherals—swinging strike and contact rates; walk, whiff and ground-ball percentages; gum chews per minute—were uncannily similar to his 2016 season, a strange outcome as his pitch mix was notably different. The New Jersey native scrapped his cutter entirely and increased his slider usage by over 700 percent (no, that's not a typo, it jumped from under five percent to nearly 35 percent). Unfortunately, his slider and four-seamer didn't mesh well and hitters didn't let his speedball by them, smacking it around to the tune of a .698 slugging percentage. Like as not, DeSclafani will keep more balls in the park this year, as simply better luck will help return him to his glory days as a no. 4 starter, but a remix of his repertoire will be required to achieve anything more.

Brandon Finnegan LHP   Born: 04/14/93   Age: 26   Bats: L   Throws: L   Height: 5'11"   Weight: 212   Origin: Round 1, 2014 Draft (#17 overall)

YEAR	TEAM	LVL	AGE	W	L	SV	G	GS	IP	H	HR	BB/9	K/9	K	GB%	BABIP	WHIP	ERA	DRA	WARP	MPH	FB%	WHF	CSP
2016	CIN	MLB	23	10	11	0	31	31	172	150	29	4.4	7.6	145	41%	.256	1.36	3.98	5.90	-1.1	94.6	66.1	10.3	45.6
2017	CIN	MLB	24	1	1	0	4	4	13	9	1	9.0	11.1	16	53%	.276	1.69	4.15	5.31	0.0	96.0	69.8	13	42.1
2018	CIN	MLB	25	0	3	0	5	5	20²	27	5	6.5	6.1	14	40%	.319	2.03	7.40	7.64	-0.6	92.9	65.8	7.4	48.1
2018	LOU	AAA	25	2	10	0	28	9	67²	90	10	5.3	7.6	57	36%	.369	1.92	7.05	5.40	0.0				
2019	CIN	MLB	26	1	0	0	31	0	32¹	31	5	4.8	8.8	32	40%	.302	1.48	5.06	5.52	-0.3	94.1	67.5	10.2	46.3

Breakout: 22%   Improve: 57%   Collapse: 13%   Attrition: 19%   MLB: 85%   *Comparables: Andrew Miller, Jerome Williams, Danny Duffy*

Finnegan suffered another shoulder injury in 2017, but the Reds still held out some hope he could contribute as a starter at the outset of last season. After 14 mostly terrible starts spread between Cincinnati and Louisville, that dream finally died and he was shifted to the Triple-A bullpen. It would have been easy to imagine a scenario where the diminutive left-hander reclaimed his velocity in short bursts and started mowing down minor league bats on his way back to major-league redemption. Yet Finnegan struggled just as badly in the bullpen and wasn't heard from again—leaving his future up in the air, like so many of the batted balls hit against him.

Amir Garrett LHP   Born: 05/03/92   Age: 27   Bats: R   Throws: L   Height: 6'5"   Weight: 228   Origin: Round 22, 2011 Draft (#685 overall)

YEAR	TEAM	LVL	AGE	W	L	SV	G	GS	IP	H	HR	BB/9	K/9	K	GB%	BABIP	WHIP	ERA	DRA	WARP	MPH	FB%	WHF	CSP
2016	PEN	AA	24	5	3	0	13	12	77	51	4	3.3	9.1	78	50%	.252	1.03	1.75	2.95	2.0				
2016	LOU	AAA	24	2	5	0	12	11	67²	48	6	4.1	7.2	54	49%	.231	1.17	3.46	3.90	1.1				
2017	LOU	AAA	25	2	4	0	14	14	67²	79	7	3.2	8.1	61	41%	.346	1.52	5.72	4.57	0.8				
2017	CIN	MLB	25	3	8	0	16	14	70²	74	23	5.1	8.0	63	44%	.264	1.61	7.39	7.46	-1.5	94.4	62.1	9.1	47.7
2018	CIN	MLB	26	1	2	0	66	0	63	56	8	3.6	10.1	71	39%	.306	1.29	4.29	4.41	0.4	97.1	63.1	14.8	47.5
2019	CIN	MLB	27	3	1	0	51	0	53²	47	8	3.9	10.4	62	42%	.304	1.31	4.35	4.75	0.1	95.3	63.4	12.1	48.1

Breakout: 24%   Improve: 49%   Collapse: 7%   Attrition: 17%   MLB: 66%   *Comparables: Billy Buckner, Christian Friedrich, Buck Farmer*

Lots of pitching prospects have big fastballs, a bad third pitch and sketchy command, and when they inevitably move to the bullpen it feels like a failure. Not so for Garrett, who embraced his new role wholeheartedly when the Reds sent him to the 'pen last spring after struggling to carve out a niche in the rotation. He found instant success, as his mid-90s fastball played up in shorter stints and he was able to shelve his dodgy changeup and pitch with more emotion. Garrett faded somewhat down the stretch, but his stuff, temperament and experience as a starter make him well-suited to fill the high-leverage, multi-inning relief role all the cool teams have these days.

Hunter Greene RHP   Born: 08/06/99   Age: 19   Bats: R   Throws: R   Height: 6'4"   Weight: 215   Origin: Round 1, 2017 Draft (#2 overall)

YEAR	TEAM	LVL	AGE	W	L	SV	G	GS	IP	H	HR	BB/9	K/9	K	GB%	BABIP	WHIP	ERA	DRA	WARP	MPH	FB%	WHF	CSP
2018	DYT	A	18	3	7	0	18	18	68¹	66	6	3.0	11.7	89	43%	.353	1.30	4.48	3.69	1.2				
2019	CIN	MLB	19	3	4	0	13	13	48¹	50	10	4.3	9.5	51	40%	.322	1.52	5.52	6.06	-0.4				

Breakout: 1%   Improve: 1%   Collapse: 0%   Attrition: 1%   MLB: 1%   *Comparables: Kolby Allard, Vicente Campos, Roberto Osuna*

Greene, the Reds' top selection in the 2017 draft, has an electric fastball that can routinely top 100 mph and a slider that projects as plus. And despite that, he wasn't as dominant as was expected in his full-season debut. Ultimately, even 102 and 103 can be turned around with authority if it's true—and Spandau Ballet couldn't have laid in it there much more earnestness. As spring turned to summer, Greene turned up the heat on opposing batters, but unfortunately he inadvertently turned up the heat on his elbow ligament at the same time. After allowing one run or fewer in his last five starts, Greene was shut down for the season with a UCL sprain. Opting for rest and rehab, Greene will look to develop his secondary pitches and avoid the knife, in no particular order, during 2019.

Vladimir Gutierrez RHP   Born: 09/18/95   Age: 23   Bats: R   Throws: R   Height: 6'0"   Weight: 190   Origin: International Free Agent, 2016

YEAR	TEAM	LVL	AGE	W	L	SV	G	GS	IP	H	HR	BB/9	K/9	K	GB%	BABIP	WHIP	ERA	DRA	WARP	MPH	FB%	WHF	CSP
2017	DAY	A+	21	7	8	0	19	19	103	108	10	1.7	8.2	94	42%	.320	1.23	4.46	4.71	0.7				
2018	PEN	AA	22	9	10	0	27	27	147	139	18	2.3	8.9	145	46%	.298	1.20	4.35	3.75	2.7				
2019	CIN	MLB	23	1	0	0	10	0	10²	11	2	2.8	8.8	11	41%	.312	1.29	4.39	4.77	0.0				

Breakout: 9%   Improve: 15%   Collapse: 25%   Attrition: 34%   MLB: 45%   *Comparables: Felix Jorge, Chih-Wei Hu, Austin Gomber*

Gutierrez was signed out of Cuba, had no problem flashing dominance at High-A in 2017 and then held his own for a full season at Double-A in 2018. There's a lot to like if he can continue his steady climb, especially if he keeps maintaining (or improving) his walk and strikeout rates. He still struggles with consistency in his delivery, but he has the ceiling of a no. 4 starter and the durability to last in a rotation even if the results leave you wanting more. Worse comes to worst, his curve and a fastball that would hopefully play up in short bursts should guarantee him a spot in the bullpen.

David Hernandez RHP   Born: 05/13/85   Age: 34   Bats: R   Throws: R   Height: 6'3"   Weight: 245   Origin: Round 16, 2005 Draft (#483 overall)

YEAR	TEAM	LVL	AGE	W	L	SV	G	GS	IP	H	HR	BB/9	K/9	K	GB%	BABIP	WHIP	ERA	DRA	WARP	MPH	FB%	WHF	CSP
2016	PHI	MLB	31	3	4	1	70	0	72²	77	11	4.0	9.9	80	40%	.337	1.50	3.84	4.47	0.4	96.3	64.3	13.1	49.7
2017	GWN	AAA	32	1	0	4	7	0	8	4	0	2.2	10.1	9	44%	.222	0.75	1.12	3.39	0.2				
2017	ANA	MLB	32	1	0	1	38	0	36¹	29	0	2.0	9.2	37	49%	.309	1.02	2.23	2.56	1.1	95.0	55.1	14.2	49.6
2017	ARI	MLB	32	2	1	1	26	0	18²	19	4	0.5	7.2	15	36%	.278	1.07	4.82	3.80	0.3	95.0	55.1	12.4	49.4
2018	CIN	MLB	33	5	2	0	57	0	64	46	6	2.4	9.1	65	34%	.248	0.98	2.53	4.71	0.2	94.5	58.3	12.2	49.3
2019	CIN	MLB	34	3	1	0	51	0	53²	49	8	3.4	9.7	58	39%	.308	1.29	4.24	4.61	0.2	94.0	58.4	12.7	48.7

Breakout: 23%   Improve: 43%   Collapse: 26%   Attrition: 15%   MLB: 85%   *Comparables: Will Ohman, Joe Thatcher, Luis Vizcaino*

A veteran reliever who has cut down on his walks the last two years, Hernandez must have been extraordinarily nice to Lady Luck to come away with the 1.95 ERA he sported at Great American Ball Park last season given his highest fly-ball rate in five years. His back-of-the-baseball-card stats say that the Reds inking him to a two-year deal last year was a really slick move, while his underlying numbers suggest that it'll be something they end up regretting. The former Oriole, Diamondback, Phillie, Angel and Diamondback once more will slide into a setup role in front of Raisel Iglesias for as long as he can keep the ball out of the stands.

Jared Hughes RHP   Born: 07/04/85   Age: 33   Bats: R   Throws: R   Height: 6'7"   Weight: 240   Origin: Round 4, 2006 Draft (#110 overall)

YEAR	TEAM	LVL	AGE	W	L	SV	G	GS	IP	H	HR	BB/9	K/9	K	GB%	BABIP	WHIP	ERA	DRA	WARP	MPH	FB%	WHF	CSP
2016	PIT	MLB	30	1	1	1	67	0	59¹	62	6	3.3	5.2	34	59%	.295	1.42	3.03	6.40	-1.0	95.6	81.8	10.3	39.2
2017	MIL	MLB	31	5	3	1	67	0	59²	49	4	3.6	7.2	48	63%	.278	1.22	3.02	5.86	-0.5	95.1	77.4	12.5	41.9
2018	CIN	MLB	32	4	3	7	72	0	78²	57	4	2.6	6.8	59	66%	.252	1.02	1.94	4.59	0.3	93.4	86	12.8	42.2
2019	CIN	MLB	33	3	1	0	51	0	53²	47	5	3.7	8.1	49	58%	.294	1.28	3.99	4.31	0.3	93.3	81.4	12	40.9

Breakout: 26%   Improve: 42%   Collapse: 23%   Attrition: 8%   MLB: 83%   *Comparables: Brad Ziegler, Jim Johnson, Kent Tekulve*

Hughes doesn't strike out a lot of batters, but despite recent MLB trends, he's never had to in order to be effective. Another top-five ground-ball rate among relievers due to his heavy sinker use certainly helps. You can argue that his BABIP isn't sustainable, especially when he keeps the ball on the ground at such an extreme clip, but a career .275 BABIP is indicative of an arm batters just don't square up well. What's more, he had the best swinging strike rate of his career in 2018, but don't expect it to lead to an uptick in strikeouts as it came with an equal but opposite decrease in velocity. A veteran reliever who can go more than one inning when asked and dominates in save situations—Hughes had a pristine 1.03 ERA under such circumstances—is a valuable commodity for any team.

Raisel Iglesias RHP   Born: 01/04/90   Age: 29   Bats: R   Throws: R   Height: 6'2"   Weight: 188   Origin: International Free Agent, 2014

YEAR	TEAM	LVL	AGE	W	L	SV	G	GS	IP	H	HR	BB/9	K/9	K	GB%	BABIP	WHIP	ERA	DRA	WARP	MPH	FB%	WHF	CSP
2016	CIN	MLB	26	3	2	2	6	37	5	78¹	63	7	3.0	9.5	83	43%	.275	1.14	2.53	3.32	1.6	97.9	54.6	12.9	49.1
2017	CIN	MLB	27	3	3	28	63	0	76	57	5	3.2	10.9	92	43%	.287	1.11	2.49	3.34	1.6	98.6	57.1	15.1	50.2
2018	CIN	MLB	28	2	5	30	66	0	72	52	12	3.1	10.0	80	40%	.233	1.07	2.38	3.48	1.2	97.7	50.2	16.5	47.9
2019	CIN	MLB	29	3	1	30	56	0	59	48	8	3.4	10.7	70	41%	.294	1.18	3.74	4.06	0.7	97.4	53.7	15.1	49

Breakout: 14%   Improve: 42%   Collapse: 25%   Attrition: 9%   MLB: 98%   *Comparables: Ramon Ramirez, Frank Francisco, Scott Linebrink*

Another flame-throwing Cuban the Reds hoped would find success in the rotation, but instead has bowled over hitters out of the bullpen. Iglesias doesn't have the 100-mph fastball of Aroldis Chapman, but it's hard to quibble with the intensely consistent results from his three seasons in the Queen City. Yet despite the consistency, two things set Iglesias' season apart from the prior two: his touch of gopheritis and the development of his cambio. After allowing only 12 homers in his first two seasons, he matched that number in 2018—with most of the damage coming off his fastball. A relatively stable batted ball profile implies that this is a one-year blip. On the other side, he threw his changeup nearly twice as often last season, helping him narrow what was a 200-plus point platoon split differential to almost even. In fact, he pulled that string 231 times last season against left-handed hitters and allowed only one extra-base hit—a double to Colin Moran on the last day of the season. As reliable as a 3-Way at Skyline, Iglesias will again be the glue that holds together the Reds bullpen in 2019.

Michael Lorenzen RHP   Born: 01/04/92   Age: 27   Bats: R   Throws: R   Height: 6'3"   Weight: 217   Origin: Round 1, 2013 Draft (#38 overall)

YEAR	TEAM	LVL	AGE	W	L	SV	G	GS	IP	H	HR	BB/9	K/9	K	GB%	BABIP	WHIP	ERA	DRA	WARP	MPH	FB%	WHF	CSP
2016	CIN	MLB	24	2	1	0	35	0	50	41	5	2.3	8.6	48	64%	.277	1.08	2.88	3.61	0.8	98.6	47.8	10.5	47.4
2017	CIN	MLB	25	8	4	2	70	0	83	78	9	3.7	8.7	80	57%	.295	1.35	4.45	4.37	0.7	97.9	51.3	11.3	47.8
2018	CIN	MLB	26	4	2	1	45	3	81	78	6	3.8	6.0	54	52%	.291	1.38	3.11	5.87	-0.8	96.9	51.5	7.6	48.6
2019	CIN	MLB	27	6	5	0	54	13	112	106	13	3.7	8.2	102	53%	.308	1.36	4.22	4.57	0.8	97.1	51.5	9.6	48.6

Breakout: 19%   Improve: 37%   Collapse: 20%   Attrition: 12%   MLB: 81%   *Comparables: Erasmo Ramirez, Andrew Cashner, Noah Lowry*

Lorenzen isn't the most dominant of multi-inning relievers, but he may be the most interesting. He throws hard yet doesn't miss bats, relying on his mid-90s power sinker and worm-killing cutter to keep the ball in the yard and runs off the scoreboard. He has real skill at the plate, not "careful, he has some power" skill but "start him off with a breaking ball and then work the edges" skill. And his ability to move a full glass of water balanced on his forehead to the floor without spilling, involving a squat, a back roll and a two-knee pinch, belongs in the Stupid Human Tricks Hall of Fame (seriously, go watch that). The Reds have said they're open to him starting or relieving or even playing the outfield on occasion to get his bat in the lineup and save a roster spot. We love this, of course, but not as much as we love the idea of pairing Lorenzen with Amir Garrett as an athletic, lefty-righty, pitcher-outfield tandem, swapping them back and forth based on batter handedness. Betcha the Rays would do it.

Tyler Mahle RHP   Born: 09/29/94   Age: 24   Bats: R   Throws: R   Height: 6'3"   Weight: 210   Origin: Round 7, 2013 Draft (#225 overall)

YEAR	TEAM	LVL	AGE	W	L	SV	G	GS	IP	H	HR	BB/9	K/9	K	GB%	BABIP	WHIP	ERA	DRA	WARP	MPH	FB%	WHF	CSP
2016	DAY	A+	21	8	3	0	13	13	79¹	58	6	1.9	8.6	76	48%	.255	0.95	2.50	3.44	1.8				
2016	PEN	AA	21	6	3	0	14	14	71¹	78	12	2.5	8.2	65	42%	.320	1.37	4.92	3.04	1.8				
2017	PEN	AA	22	7	3	0	14	14	85	57	5	1.8	9.2	87	42%	.245	0.87	1.59	3.12	2.1				
2017	LOU	AAA	22	3	4	0	10	10	59¹	52	4	2.0	7.7	51	42%	.281	1.10	2.73	4.66	0.7				
2017	CIN	MLB	22	1	2	0	4	4	20	19	0	4.9	6.3	14	56%	.302	1.50	2.70	5.48	0.0	95.5	65.8	7.9	47.2
2018	LOU	AAA	23	2	1	0	5	5	29²	22	4	3.3	6.1	20	39%	.209	1.11	2.73	8.09	-0.8				
2018	CIN	MLB	23	7	9	0	23	23	112	125	22	4.3	8.8	110	41%	.324	1.59	4.98	6.30	-1.3	95.4	67.8	11.4	49.6
2019	*CIN*	*MLB*	*24*	*8*	*7*	*0*	*23*	*23*	*122*	*112*	*17*	*3.4*	*9.0*	*123*	*41%*	*.305*	*1.30*	*4.22*	*4.58*	*1.0*	*95.2*	*69.6*	*11.3*	*50*

Breakout: 19%   Improve: 43%   Collapse: 13%   Attrition: 26%   MLB: 72%   *Comparables: Daniel Mengden, Reynaldo Lopez, Robbie Ray*

"The lack of a special fastball could result in a bunch of homers at GABP," we said in our 2018 Cincinnati Top 10 Prospects article. Nailed it. Of the 22 long balls that helped torpedo Mahle's rookie season, 17 were launched at home. In related news, lefties took Mahle deep 15 times as part of the .300/.414/.576 hurtin' they laid on him. His low-90s heater and solid slider can miss bats, but spectral command and an inconsistent changeup produce too many walks and meatballs over the plate. None of this is to say Mahle isn't worth another look, but the young Californian will need to find a way to make hitters less comfortable if he wants to stick in a big-league rotation.

Keury Mella RHP   Born: 08/02/93   Age: 25   Bats: R   Throws: R   Height: 6'2"   Weight: 200   Origin: International Free Agent, 2012

YEAR	TEAM	LVL	AGE	W	L	SV	G	GS	IP	H	HR	BB/9	K/9	K	GB%	BABIP	WHIP	ERA	DRA	WARP	MPH	FB%	WHF	CSP
2016	DAY	A+	22	8	9	0	25	24	131²	150	7	3.8	6.5	95	47%	.340	1.56	3.90	6.32	-1.3				
2016	LOU	AAA	22	1	0	0	1	1	7	3	1	1.3	7.7	6	65%	.125	0.57	1.29	5.60	0.0				
2017	PEN	AA	23	4	10	1	27	26	134	135	14	2.9	7.3	109	47%	.300	1.33	4.30	3.68	2.4				
2017	CIN	MLB	23	0	0	0	2	0	4	5	1	4.5	2.2	1	31%	.267	1.75	6.75	8.01	-0.1	97.4	72.7	3.6	60.1
2018	PEN	AA	24	7	3	0	16	16	85	70	8	3.3	9.2	87	49%	.276	1.19	3.07	4.27	1.1				
2018	CIN	MLB	24	0	0	0	4	0	9¹	13	4	7.7	7.7	8	36%	.333	2.25	8.68	9.04	-0.4	96.7	70.8	9.4	51
2018	LOU	AAA	24	2	1	0	5	5	23	20	1	2.3	5.5	14	42%	.271	1.13	2.74	6.04	-0.1				
2019	*CIN*	*MLB*	*25*	*3*	*2*	*0*	*25*	*5*	*46²*	*47*	*7*	*3.9*	*8.3*	*43*	*44%*	*.314*	*1.44*	*4.81*	*5.24*	*0.0*	*96.6*	*72.8*	*8.6*	*56.4*

Breakout: 10%   Improve: 15%   Collapse: 9%   Attrition: 19%   MLB: 28%   *Comparables: Cesar Valdez, Thad Weber, Graham Godfrey*

Mella has taken steps forward for each of his seasons with the Reds. In 2017 he improved his strikeouts and walks while moving up to Double-A, and when he repeated that level in 2018, he missed even more bats. If Mella wants to be taken seriously as a member of the Reds bullpen in 2019, he'll need to work on getting batters to chase more out of the zone. Like seemingly everyone else who tried to pitch for the Reds last season, his tiny MLB sample in 2018 was one to forget. Of course, the 25-year-old still holds out some hope of being able to start as well, but one-pitch starters aren't the most successful breed.

Wandy Peralta LHP   Born: 07/27/91   Age: 27   Bats: L   Throws: L   Height: 6'0"   Weight: 220   Origin: International Free Agent, 2009

YEAR	TEAM	LVL	AGE	W	L	SV	G	GS	IP	H	HR	BB/9	K/9	K	GB%	BABIP	WHIP	ERA	DRA	WARP	MPH	FB%	WHF	CSP
2016	PEN	AA	24	0	1	0	13	6	17²	17	1	1.5	10.2	20	50%	.327	1.13	3.06	3.07	0.4				
2016	LOU	AAA	24	4	1	3	37	2	58	44	2	3.6	5.9	38	61%	.249	1.16	2.33	3.42	1.1				
2016	CIN	MLB	24	0	0	0	10	0	7¹	11	1	8.6	6.1	5	46%	.400	2.45	8.59	8.69	-0.3	97.5	62.9	14.4	44.5
2017	CIN	MLB	25	3	4	0	69	0	64²	53	8	3.3	7.9	57	56%	.260	1.19	3.76	4.38	0.6	98.0	53.3	15.5	45.2
2018	LOU	AAA	26	1	0	0	13	0	14¹	13	1	4.4	6.3	10	57%	.293	1.40	3.14	3.75	0.2				
2018	CIN	MLB	26	2	2	0	59	0	45¹	58	2	6.2	6.2	31	48%	.348	1.96	5.36	7.53	-1.4	97.1	48.8	10.7	48.2
2019	*CIN*	*MLB*	*27*	*3*	*1*	*0*	*51*	*0*	*53²*	*53*	*7*	*4.4*	*8.1*	*49*	*50%*	*.314*	*1.48*	*4.60*	*4.99*	*-0.1*	*97.1*	*52.1*	*13.3*	*46.8*

Breakout: 22%   Improve: 41%   Collapse: 16%   Attrition: 20%   MLB: 70%   *Comparables: Ryan Pressly, Chris Bassitt, Logan Ondrusek*

There's a lovely symmetry that goes along with finishing a season with the same number of both walks and strikeouts. If you're a hitter. In Peralta's case, it was a not-so-slow descent into accommodating the next wave of failing Reds' arms, as the southpaw took a step back in every facet of his performance. There's a slight glimmer of hope because he was better after he returned from his minor league demotion, but even an ERA around 4 and a middling strikeout rate isn't enough to lock him into a regular role on the 25-man roster.

Cody Reed LHP   Born: 04/15/93   Age: 26   Bats: L   Throws: L   Height: 6'5"   Weight: 230   Origin: Round 2, 2013 Draft (#46 overall)

YEAR	TEAM	LVL	AGE	W	L	SV	G	GS	IP	H	HR	BB/9	K/9	K	GB%	BABIP	WHIP	ERA	DRA	WARP	MPH	FB%	WHF	CSP
2016	CIN	MLB	23	0	7	0	10	10	47²	67	12	3.6	8.1	43	54%	.364	1.80	7.36	5.26	0.1	95.8	52.7	10.4	45.7
2016	LOU	AAA	23	6	4	0	13	13	73	71	6	2.5	8.0	65	52%	.314	1.25	3.08	3.41	1.6				
2017	LOU	AAA	24	4	9	0	21	20	106¹	105	7	5.2	8.6	102	50%	.328	1.56	3.55	4.84	1.0				
2017	CIN	MLB	24	1	1	1	12	1	17²	11	3	9.7	8.7	17	65%	.200	1.70	5.09	4.82	0.1	96.2	51.2	13.9	40.4
2018	LOU	AAA	25	4	8	0	18	17	105²	109	13	2.6	8.9	105	46%	.325	1.32	3.92	3.66	2.2				
2018	CIN	MLB	25	1	3	0	17	7	43	45	5	3.1	8.8	42	63%	.323	1.40	3.98	4.36	0.4	94.9	50.2	11	48.1
2019	*CIN*	*MLB*	*26*	*2*	*2*	*0*	*15*	*5*	*35²*	*35*	*4*	*3.6*	*9.3*	*37*	*49%*	*.326*	*1.37*	*4.06*	*4.41*	*0.3*	*95.0*	*52.2*	*11.5*	*45.7*

Breakout: 25%   Improve: 47%   Collapse: 21%   Attrition: 38%   MLB: 78%   *Comparables: J.R. Graham, Joe Saunders, Allen Webster*

It's been a couple of long years since Reed was the centerpiece in the deadline deal that sent Johnny Cueto to Kansas City. Hyped as a potential no. 3 starter with a plus-plus slider, Reed has been tattooed in 18 career starts for the Reds, giving up a .315/.387/.537 slash line and making him persona non grata when the team was given any other options. The slider was basically the pitch that was promised in 2018—he threw it over 40 percent of the time and allowed a .268 slugging percentage. Unfortunately, when you transform into a sinker/slider pitcher, it also implies that you throw a sinker. When Reed keeps the pitch down, it can work, but it didn't happen nearly enough and righties tore through the ticked-down version. The southpaw is now out of options and is likely to once again fill a swing role, but without improved command or rediscovered velocity, his days of starting are likely over.

Tanner Roark RHP Born: 10/05/86 Age: 32 Bats: R Throws: R Height: 6'2" Weight: 229 Origin: Round 25, 2008 Draft (#753 overall)

YEAR	TEAM	LVL	AGE	W	L	SV	G	GS	IP	H	HR	BB/9	K/9	K	GB%	BABIP	WHIP	ERA	DRA	WARP	MPH	FB%	WHF	CSP
2016	WAS	MLB	29	16	10	0	34	33	210	173	17	3.1	7.4	172	51%	.269	1.17	2.83	3.85	3.6	94.7	62.4	9.6	45.2
2017	WAS	MLB	30	13	11	0	32	30	181¹	178	23	3.2	8.2	166	49%	.300	1.33	4.67	3.89	3.4	94.3	56.2	10.7	45.3
2018	WAS	MLB	31	9	15	0	31	30	180¹	181	24	2.5	7.3	146	43%	.296	1.28	4.34	4.89	0.9	93.3	59.2	9.2	46.9
2019	CIN	MLB	32	10	9	0	26	26	156	146	22	3.1	8.2	143	46%	.299	1.28	4.37	4.74	1.0	93.1	58.5	9.7	45.5

Breakout: 9%   Improve: 37%   Collapse: 34%   Attrition: 14%   MLB: 93%   *Comparables: Clay Buchholz, Doug Fister, Kevin Millwood*

Roark did a new thing in 2018, which will catch your eye given his steady tendencies. Don't worry, you still need an electron microscope to detect pitch-mix changes, a pair of special jewelers' glasses to inspect variations in his peripheral numbers. But the naked eye will show, until the heat death of the internet, that he led the NL in losses last season. Roark has long been a contemporary prototype for that less-than-desirable black ink. Terrible pitchers don't pitch enough to rack up 15 losses. Very, very average pitchers, on the other hand, can go six innings per start, start 30 times in a season and post mid-4.00 ERAs while remaining useful to their teams but catching exactly the wrong wave of results. May Roark wear it as a badge of honor, now in Cincinnati.

Sal Romano RHP Born: 10/12/93 Age: 25 Bats: L Throws: R Height: 6'5" Weight: 270 Origin: Round 23, 2011 Draft (#715 overall)

YEAR	TEAM	LVL	AGE	W	L	SV	G	GS	IP	H	HR	BB/9	K/9	K	GB%	BABIP	WHIP	ERA	DRA	WARP	MPH	FB%	WHF	CSP
2016	PEN	AA	22	6	11	0	27	27	156	157	10	2.0	8.3	144	49%	.320	1.22	3.52	2.65	4.6				
2017	LOU	AAA	23	1	4	0	10	10	49¹	49	1	3.1	5.8	32	50%	.298	1.34	3.47	5.51	0.1				
2017	CIN	MLB	23	5	8	0	16	16	87	91	9	3.8	7.6	73	53%	.314	1.47	4.45	4.55	1.0	97.1	62.7	9.6	46.6
2018	CIN	MLB	24	8	11	0	39	25	145²	155	23	3.3	6.5	105	47%	.288	1.43	5.31	5.76	-0.8	95.8	65.6	8.6	49.1
2019	CIN	MLB	25	2	2	0	5	5	26²	27	3	3.2	8.1	24	46%	.324	1.39	4.15	4.49	0.3	95.9	66.1	9.2	49.1

Breakout: 22%   Improve: 52%   Collapse: 23%   Attrition: 36%   MLB: 92%   *Comparables: Mike Foltynewicz, Ricky Nolasco, Jeff Hoffman*

How acute were the Reds gopher ball woes last year? Of the six Whiplash Brigade members who worked at least 100 innings, Romano's rate of 1.4 home runs per nine innings was the best, yet still ranked as the 13th worst in the National League. Ye gods. Yet there's definitely hope for Romano, a massive right-hander with two bona fide big-league pitches: a slider and a mid-90s sinker that generates plenty of ground ball outs. He tinkered with a cutter last year but doesn't seem to trust it and his changeup is pretty much vaporware, so lefties sprinted to the plate to face him and posted a .303/.373/.528 line. If he can't get that sorted out soon, he'll be bullpen bound.

Antonio Santillan RHP Born: 04/15/97 Age: 22 Bats: R Throws: R Height: 6'3" Weight: 240 Origin: Round 2, 2015 Draft (#49 overall)

YEAR	TEAM	LVL	AGE	W	L	SV	G	GS	IP	H	HR	BB/9	K/9	K	GB%	BABIP	WHIP	ERA	DRA	WARP	MPH	FB%	WHF	CSP
2016	BIL	RK	19	1	0	0	8	8	39	32	4	3.7	10.6	46	46%	.292	1.23	3.92	2.36	1.5				
2016	DYT	A	19	2	3	0	7	7	30¹	27	3	7.1	11.3	38	38%	.338	1.68	6.82	3.51	0.6				
2017	DYT	A	20	9	8	0	25	24	128	104	9	3.9	9.0	128	45%	.281	1.25	3.38	4.17	1.6				
2018	DAY	A+	21	6	4	0	15	15	86²	81	5	2.3	7.6	73	44%	.298	1.19	2.70	5.03	0.3				
2018	PEN	AA	21	4	3	0	11	11	62¹	65	8	2.3	8.8	61	46%	.315	1.30	3.61	4.19	0.8				
2019	CIN	MLB	22	0	0	0	10	0	10²	11	2	4.5	8.7	10	40%	.312	1.50	5.14	5.61	0.0				

Breakout: 12%   Improve: 19%   Collapse: 8%   Attrition: 18%   MLB: 35%   *Comparables: Jake Thompson, Greg Reynolds, Alex Cobb*

Santillan has the name of a tertiary character in a Sopranos episode. And while the flamethrowing right-hander isn't from New Jersey or even New York, we can give him a mafioso nickname all the same. The Nutcracker hails from Seguin, TX, home to the world's largest nutcracker museum. He's been adding velocity and command to his heavy, sinking fastball, cracking more than a few bats along the way. He complements the heater with a hard slider, catching batters swinging over top as they anticipate the fastball. One thing he hasn't cracked thus far? The changeup. It flashes average but is inconsistent and often too firm. He might not miss enough bats to be more than an innings-eating middle of the rotation arm when it's all said and done, but that's not bad work for a character actor.

Lucas Sims RHP Born: 05/10/94 Age: 25 Bats: R Throws: R Height: 6'2" Weight: 230 Origin: Round 1, 2012 Draft (#21 overall)

YEAR	TEAM	LVL	AGE	W	L	SV	G	GS	IP	H	HR	BB/9	K/9	K	GB%	BABIP	WHIP	ERA	DRA	WARP	MPH	FB%	WHF	CSP
2016	GWN	AAA	22	2	6	0	11	10	50	56	12	6.7	10.4	58	42%	.333	1.86	7.56	3.97	0.8				
2016	MIS	AA	22	5	5	0	17	17	91	64	3	5.4	10.0	101	42%	.276	1.31	2.67	3.11	2.2				
2017	GWN	AAA	23	7	4	0	20	19	115¹	95	19	2.8	10.3	132	35%	.275	1.14	3.75	3.67	2.5				
2017	ATL	MLB	23	3	6	0	14	10	57²	64	9	3.6	6.9	44	40%	.314	1.51	5.62	6.13	-0.4	93.8	46.5	9	46.7
2018	ATL	MLB	24	0	0	0	6	0	10¹	12	2	7.0	8.7	10	42%	.323	1.94	7.84	6.38	-0.2	94.8	55	10	37.4
2018	GWN	AAA	24	4	3	0	15	14	73	66	6	4.2	10.2	83	44%	.330	1.37	2.84	4.83	0.6				
2018	LOU	AAA	24	0	2	0	5	5	28¹	20	5	1.6	10.2	32	29%	.224	0.88	3.81	3.84	0.5				
2018	CIN	MLB	24	0	0	0	3	0	5¹	3	1	8.4	10.1	6	23%	.167	1.50	6.75	3.59	0.1	93.9	55	15.3	49.3
2019	CIN	MLB	25	3	2	0	25	5	46²	41	7	4.4	10.1	52	39%	.304	1.37	4.59	5.01	0.1	93.7	50.1	10.1	44.9

Breakout: 16%   Improve: 34%   Collapse: 24%   Attrition: 45%   MLB: 71%   *Comparables: Fabio Castro, Aaron Blair, Keyvius Sampson*

Being traded from the organization whose prospect lists you once graced highly to one with which you have no history is freeing if you've yet to establish yourself as a notable contributor to date. It's akin to a celebrity putting on a fake mustache and roaming the streets of Los Angeles just doing things normal people do, like grabbing a double-double at In-N-Out or taking in a matinee at Century City. Sims celebrated that freedom by doing some walking of his own. The Georgia native certainly meshes well with his new team by simply being a formerly famous starting pitching prospect with little to no control, but just because you can fit in doesn't mean you should.

Matt Wisler RHP   Born: 09/12/92   Age: 26   Bats: R   Throws: R   Height: 6'3"   Weight: 210   Origin: Round 7, 2011 Draft (#233 overall)

YEAR	TEAM	LVL	AGE	W	L	SV	G	GS	IP	H	HR	BB/9	K/9	K	GB%	BABIP	WHIP	ERA	DRA	WARP	MPH	FB%	WHF	CSP
2016	GWN	AAA	23	2	1	0	4	4	26²	27	3	1.7	7.4	22	52%	.296	1.20	3.71	4.77	0.2				
2016	ATL	MLB	23	7	13	1	27	26	156²	159	26	2.8	6.6	115	42%	.279	1.33	5.00	4.62	1.3	95.1	59.3	10.1	45.6
2017	GWN	AAA	24	7	5	0	18	14	93²	101	7	1.9	6.1	64	44%	.310	1.29	3.56	4.04	1.7				
2017	ATL	MLB	24	0	1	0	20	1	32¹	43	5	3.6	6.1	22	33%	.342	1.73	8.35	7.24	-0.7	94.3	55.9	10.1	46.1
2018	ATL	MLB	25	1	1	0	7	3	26²	30	6	1.7	7.1	21	28%	.300	1.31	5.40	3.99	0.3	94.4	53.4	10.2	49.5
2018	GWN	AAA	25	4	4	0	13	13	70	79	6	1.8	8.4	65	48%	.348	1.33	4.37	3.25	1.8				
2018	LOU	AAA	25	1	1	0	8	2	19²	19	0	1.4	9.6	21	36%	.339	1.12	1.83	3.43	0.5				
2018	CIN	MLB	25	0	0	0	11	0	13¹	11	2	1.4	7.4	11	42%	.231	0.98	2.03	4.26	0.1	93.4	42.1	12.2	51.2
2019	CIN	MLB	26	2	1	0	41	0	43	42	6	2.8	8.6	41	41%	.311	1.29	4.15	4.50	0.3	94.3	57.4	10.4	48.5

Breakout: 27%   Improve: 46%   Collapse: 20%   Attrition: 22%   MLB: 85%   *Comparables: Justin Grimm, Gavin Floyd, Taylor Buchholz*

The twice-traded former prospect found himself in the Louisville bullpen after being a secondary piece in a trade for a secondary player. Air it out in short bursts, they said. Your stuff will play up, they said. Yet, try as he might, not only did Wisler's velocity not pick up out of the 'pen, it actually went down to the lowest level of his career. Faced with the specter of more long bus rides if he couldn't figure out a plan to get big league hitters out, Wisler did the only thing he could: He threw as many sliders as he possibly could. In his 11 appearances for the Reds between August and September, he threw the pitch nearly 55 percent of the time and it enough to save his 40-man spot for at least another offseason.

Alex Wood LHP   Born: 01/12/91   Age: 28   Bats: R   Throws: L   Height: 6'4"   Weight: 215   Origin: Round 2, 2012 Draft (#85 overall)

YEAR	TEAM	LVL	AGE	W	L	SV	G	GS	IP	H	HR	BB/9	K/9	K	GB%	BABIP	WHIP	ERA	DRA	WARP	MPH	FB%	WHF	CSP
2016	LAN	MLB	25	1	4	0	14	10	60¹	56	5	3.0	9.8	66	55%	.319	1.26	3.73	2.56	1.9	92.7	53	10.9	45.6
2017	LAN	MLB	26	16	3	0	27	25	152¹	123	15	2.2	8.9	151	54%	.267	1.06	2.72	2.89	4.5	94.0	50.4	12.5	45.1
2018	LAN	MLB	27	9	7	0	33	27	151²	143	14	2.4	8.0	135	50%	.293	1.21	3.68	3.41	3.3	91.4	43.1	11.6	47.2
2019	CIN	MLB	28	8	6	0	34	19	124¹	114	14	3.0	9.3	128	50%	.311	1.25	3.77	4.07	1.5	92.0	47.3	11.9	46.3

Breakout: 23%   Improve: 50%   Collapse: 22%   Attrition: 5%   MLB: 97%   *Comparables: Brandon Webb, Roy Halladay, Johnny Cueto*

At the risk of sounding lazy, you could probably CTRL+C everything from Wood's 2017 Annual comment and CTRL+V into this space, as the last two seasons worth of stats for the lefty's career have basically been the pitching version of the Spiderman meme. However instead of declining velocity leading to late season struggles, Wood's gas remained fairly consistent this year, and he managed to combat a second-half swoon by folding in his slider over a third of the time—the highest usage of his career. An ill-fated shift to the bullpen is a decision that manager Dave Roberts would like to have back, as Wood served up three taters in less than seven innings of work, ignominiously topping the reliever leaderboard (hmm click, hold and drag to trash). The former Georgia Bulldog will now have to spend his walk year in an environment more suited to giving up homers, after becoming collateral in a salary dump to the Reds.

LINEOUTS

Hitters

HITTER	POS	TEAM	LVL	AGE	PA	R	2B	3B	HR	RBI	BB	K	SB	CS	AVG/OBP/SLG	DRC+	VORP	BABIP	BRR	FRAA	WARP
Aristides Aquino	RF	CIN	MLB	24	1	0	0	0	0	0	0	0	1	0	.000/.000/.000	74	-0.9	--	-0.7	RF(1): -0.1	-0.1
	RF	PEN	AA	24	445	49	20	2	20	55	35	112	4	5	.240/.306/.448	113	8.2	.282	-1.3	RF(108): 7.7	2.3
Mariel Bautista	CF	BIL	Rk	20	233	43	12	4	8	37	16	29	16	3	.330/.386/.541	124	28.0	.349	2.3	CF(40): -4.4, LF(6): -1.3	1.0
Fidel Castro	RF	DRD	Rk	19	151	21	10	6	3	22	25	42	2	2	.262/.404/.516	115	9.5	.377	-1.7	RF(26): 3.1, CF(9): -2.0	0.5
	RF	CIN	Rk	19	63	9	4	2	1	5	8	23	2	1	.315/.413/.519	77	5.2	.533	0.3	RF(14): -3.7, LF(2): -0.5	-0.4
Stuart Fairchild	LF	DYT	A	22	276	40	12	5	7	37	31	65	17	4	.277/.377/.460	118	20.2	.352	2.3	CF(30): -2.3, LF(26): -0.4	1.3
	LF	DAY	A+	22	242	25	14	1	2	20	17	63	6	2	.250/.306/.350	100	-4.2	.335	-4.4	LF(31): 0.1, CF(30): -2.4	-0.1
Kyle Farmer	C	OKL	AAA	27	312	37	24	1	7	36	17	50	1	1	.288/.333/.451	98	13.8	.325	-2.2	3B(31): 3.2, C(29): -6.9	0.5
	C	LAN	MLB	27	77	1	4	1	0	9	5	15	0	0	.235/.312/.324	83	0.4	.296	-0.4	3B(22): 1.2, C(1): 0.0	0.2
Tim Federowicz	C	FRE	AAA	30	151	24	13	0	6	22	16	27	0	0	.328/.404/.560	126	15.9	.376	-1.1	C(33): 1.8, 1B(3): 0.0	1.3
	C	HOU	MLB	30	35	4	3	0	0	2	1	13	0	0	.206/.229/.294	74	-1.1	.333	0.3	C(10): -1.1	0.0
	C	LOU	AAA	30	88	10	6	0	1	9	9	20	0	0	.244/.318/.359	99	1.9	.310	-1.6	C(21): -0.3, 2B(1): 0.0	0.2
	C	CIN	MLB	30	7	1	1	0	1	2	1	3	0	0	.333/.429/1.000	78	1.1	.500	-0.6	C(4): 0.0	0.0
T.J. Friedl	OF	DAY	A+	22	274	40	10	4	3	35	38	44	11	4	.294/.405/.412	124	23.4	.350	4.7	LF(39): 2.0, CF(19): -1.0	2.2
	OF	PEN	AA	22	296	47	10	3	2	16	28	56	19	5	.276/.359/.360	104	12.7	.345	3.3	LF(53): 5.1, CF(9): -1.0	1.7
Jose Israel Garcia	SS	DYT	A	20	517	61	22	4	6	53	19	112	13	9	.245/.290/.344	82	10.3	.307	1.8	SS(93): -0.7, 2B(29): -1.8	0.7
Ibandel Isabel	1B	DAY	A+	23	420	62	11	0	35	75	36	152	1	1	.258/.333/.566	147	24.0	.326	1.1	1B(37): -1.3, RF(8): -1.8	2.7
Brian O'Grady	OF	PEN	AA	26	214	27	12	4	6	30	27	41	4	1	.258/.354/.472	126	13.5	.294	-1.5	LF(24): -2.8, 1B(12): -0.1	0.7
	OF	LOU	AAA	26	162	27	9	2	8	29	12	39	5	4	.306/.365/.563	124	13.6	.367	0.4	LF(29): -0.6, 1B(12): 0.6	0.9
Alfredo Rodriguez	SS	PEN	AA	24	29	4	0	0	0	0	2	7	0	0	.192/.276/.192	75	-1.0	.263	0.7	SS(9): -0.1	0.1
	SS	DAY	A+	24	122	12	5	1	2	12	8	22	4	0	.207/.270/.324	89	-2.9	.239	-0.7	SS(31): -0.4	0.3
Mike Siani	CF	GRV	Rk	18	205	24	6	3	2	13	16	35	6	4	.288/.351/.386	95	10.7	.342	-0.1	CF(45): 6.5	1.2
Tyler Stephenson	C	DAY	A+	21	450	60	20	1	11	59	45	98	1	0	.250/.338/.392	121	24.3	.301	0.2	C(97): -3.3	2.9
Blake Trahan	SS	LOU	AAA	24	510	55	17	1	2	31	49	104	6	3	.245/.327/.302	84	8.7	.317	0.5	SS(127): 6.6, 2B(2): -0.1	2.0
	SS	CIN	MLB	24	14	2	0	0	0	0	0	4	0	0	.214/.214/.214	78	-0.6	.300	-0.2	SS(5): 0.2, 2B(3): 0.0	0.0

If **Aristides Aquino** doesn't start adding more contact or on-base skills to his one redeeming tool, he's not going to make it much further than his own initials. ⊗ In his fourth rookie ball season between the Dominican and the States, **Mariel Bautista** had his most impressive campaign to date. He's not dripping with impact tools, but he doesn't strike out much and can at least fake it in center. ⊗ It's fitting that **Fidel Castro** gets to wear red, but he also hits plenty of missiles—a nearly 35 percent line-drive rate across two levels—causing a crisis for fielders. ⊗ **Stuart Fairchild** made quick work of Low-A in his first full minor-league season, but upon his promotion to the Florida State League, opposing pitchers made quick work of him due to an overly aggressive approach. ⊗ Depth is great for an organization, but perhaps not for guys like **Kyle Farmer**, who raked again in Triple-A, but can't seem to get a serious look at the big-league level. A career .295 hitter in the minors, the 28-year-old can credibly spend time at both catcher and third base. ⊗ **Tim Federowicz**, the perennial backup to the backup catcher, finds another team and nets another 15 games for his MLB career scrapbook. That's it. That's the whole story. ⊗ With plus speed, range enough for center and a smooth line-drive stroke, **T.J. Friedl** is a grindy Lenny Dykstra fan who fell out of the Nevada sky when teams discovered he had red-shirted as a sophomore and was eligible to be signed after the 2016 draft. ⊗ They say development isn't linear, but **Jose Israel Garcia** increased his OPS every month he was at Dayton in his stateside debut. His developing approach and ability to stick at shortstop makes him a good bet to take a step forward in 2019. ⊗ The good news: **Ibandel Isabel** does a good impression of "Hulk smash!" by hitting lots of home runs. The bad news: his hit tool is so poor that it'll be the pitchers in the upper minors yelling that at him if he doesn't make significant strides with his contact rate. ⊗ Twenty-five years ago, **Brian O'Grady** could have forged a career as a pinch-hitter and spare left fielder, but ever-growing bullpens leave him on the outside looking in at even getting the opportunity to be called a Quad-A hitter. ⊗ **Alfredo Rodriguez** is a defense-first shortstop who cost the Reds nearly $9 million to sign out of Cuba in 2016. If they'd taken that money and put it in an S&P 500 ETF, they'd have $11.4 million and lot fewer excuses to make for their poor investment. ⊗ There's a reason the Reds went well overslot on **Mike Siani** in the 2018 draft, and even if he never develops much power, the rest of his tools have enough upside to race him up their prospect list in short order. ⊗ Finally healthy after losing time to wrist, thumb and concussion problems, **Tyler Stephenson** flashed the plus arm and solid receiving skills of a big league backup and enough power projection to hope for more. ⊗ The first MLB All-Star from the University of Louisiana at Lafayette was Al Dark, who starred for the New York Giants in the early 1950's. If you add an extra L to his name, that basically sums up fellow Ragin' Cajun **Blake Trahan**'s offensive prowess.

Pitchers

PITCHER	TEAM	LVL	AGE	W	L	SV	G	GS	IP	H	HR	BB/9	K/9	K	GB%	BABIP	WHIP	ERA	DRA	WARP	MPH	FB%	WHF	CSP
Joel Bender	PEN	AA	26	0	1	0	19	0	28¹	22	2	1.9	8.3	26	51%	.256	0.99	1.59	4.14	0.3				
Matt Bowman	SLN	MLB	27	0	2	0	22	0	23	29	4	4.3	10.2	26	51%	.373	1.74	6.26	5.54	-0.2	93.8	60.1	9.1	47.8
	MEM	AAA	27	0	1	1	18	0	23	23	2	3.1	11.7	30	55%	.350	1.35	4.30	1.85	0.9				
Ryan Hendrix	DAY	A+	23	4	4	12	44	0	51	38	2	4.6	13.9	79	55%	.330	1.25	1.76	2.68	1.3				
Jimmy Herget	LOU	AAA	24	1	3	0	50	0	59²	59	5	3.2	9.8	65	36%	.327	1.34	3.47	3.69	1.0				
Jose Lopez	LOU	AAA	24	5	13	0	26	26	141	142	19	2.6	7.5	117	31%	.296	1.30	4.47	6.73	-1.9				
Jesus Reyes	LOU	AAA	25	1	2	0	9	0	13²	15	3	5.9	5.9	9	52%	.293	1.76	5.27	5.63	-0.1				
	PEN	AA	25	1	8	2	29	6	64	59	4	3.8	7.5	53	61%	.284	1.34	3.94	4.15	0.7				
	CIN	MLB	25	0	0	0	5	0	5²	4	1	3.2	3.2	2	63%	.167	1.06	3.18	6.68	-0.1	96.5	74.7	11.4	38.3
Lyon Richardson	GRV	Rk	18	0	5	0	11	11	29	37	3	5.0	7.4	24	41%	.362	1.83	7.14	5.20	0.3				
Kevin Shackelford	CIN	MLB	29	0	1	0	5	0	8	13	0	4.5	7.9	7	38%	.448	2.12	7.88	6.23	-0.1	95.6	66.1	8.6	46.5
Jackson Stephens	LOU	AAA	24	1	1	0	16	7	44	46	4	3.3	7.2	35	42%	.309	1.41	5.32	5.62	-0.1				
	CIN	MLB	24	2	3	0	29	0	38¹	50	7	3.5	7.7	33	41%	.344	1.70	4.93	5.43	-0.2	95.7	66.4	12	48.6
Robert Stephenson	LOU	AAA	25	11	6	0	20	20	113	74	12	4.5	10.8	135	38%	.239	1.16	2.87	3.65	2.4				
	CIN	MLB	25	0	2	0	4	3	11²	17	2	9.3	8.5	11	32%	.395	2.49	9.26	6.50	-0.2	94.6	36.4	11.3	47.2
Seth Varner	DAY	A+	26	1	0	0	1	1	6	3	1	0.0	4.5	3	44%	.133	0.50	1.50	4.84	0.0				
	PEN	AA	26	9	3	0	25	17	119¹	104	19	2.3	7.5	99	40%	.251	1.13	3.39	3.93	1.9				

After two seasons lost to elbow woes and a 50-game drug suspension, 26-year-old **Joel Bender** dominated in the Double-A 'pen but was as age-inappropriate there as Judd Nelson in The Breakfast Club. He might have found something last year that gives him LOOGY potential, unless it was just Claire's earring bringing him some long-needed good luck. ⦾ More movement off his sinker made **Matt Bowman's** slider a bat-misser, but he traded deception and control to achieve it. ⦾ Getting plenty of grounders and strikeouts are a good thing, but **Ryan Hendrix** is going to have to show that his improved control during the second half of 2018 is sustainable in the upper minors in order for him to be a realistic bullpen option for the Reds in the future. ⦾ **Jimmy Herget** was once again effective out of the Louisville pen and missed more bats than he did in his first tour of Triple-A. The Reds protected him from the Rule 5 draft last November, so expect him to start getting a taste of the majors in 2019. ⦾ While Reds pitchers were giving up homers at an incredible rate, **Jose Lopez** decided to get in on the action and make sure he fit in once he was given a shot at doing the same. He gave up nearly as many dingers in 2018 as he did in his entire pro career beforehand, and we'll see if that strategy of imitation pays off. ⦾ You know what the Midwest is? Young and restless. **Jesus Reyes** was yet another in a long line of relievers on the Reds you probably think we made up, but whether he gets an extended chance to stick in the bullpen will depend on how many batters Jesus Walks. ⦾ **Lyon Richardson** has near-elite fastball velocity and a decent breaking pitch, making expectations high for the 2018 second-round pick, which makes it a good thing he doesn't concern himself with the opinions of the sheep. ⦾ **Kevin Shackelford** started his career as a pitch-to-contact righty before seeing his strikeout rates spike in 2017. His deal with the devil finally ran out, as elbow surgery and a June release by the Reds puts his career in jeopardy. ⦾ If there were an award for the most generic reliever in baseball, **Jackson Stephens** has a good claim for it. Former starter? Check. Fastball-slider combo? Check. Always on the verge of being sent back to Triple-A? Check. ⦾ **Robert Stephenson** would be at home in an Imperial Stormtrooper's suit. His version of target practice may miss enough bats in the minors, but he won't fool MLB hitters with such a wild approach. ⦾ **Seth Varner** doesn't get a lot of accolades because he's gentler on the radar gun than most, but if he doesn't cut it as a back-end starter, his .494 OPS allowed against southpaws gives him a great chance of carving out a role as a lefty killer.

CLEVELAND INDIANS

Essay by Emma Baccellieri

Player comments by Nick Schaefer, Collin Whitchurch and BP staff

In baseball's pile of unwieldy and unanswerable questions, there's one that pokes out as most unwieldy and unanswerable of all: The question of baseball's purpose. It's far too messy and existential to unpack with any real satisfaction, and unlike many previously unanswerable questions, there's no help to be found in modern analysis and technology. But there are a few related inquiries that will get you pointing in the same general direction, without quite so much metaphysical pressure—the purpose of constructing a professional baseball roster, for instance. It might not seem like there's anything close to a universal answer for this one, but there are a couple starting points. *Winning* seems like an easy pick, but that's not quite specific enough; some teams are built to win this year and some teams are built to win in five years and some teams, really, aren't built to win at all. If that's out, then cost *efficiency* might sound like a more modern choice, but again, that's more of a common answer than a comprehensive one. (For now, at least.) No, the best option for a universal answer is somewhat related to both of these responses, but it's a little different: It's the defense against uncertainty.

No baseball team can ever fully protect itself against uncertainty; there will always be breakouts and breakdowns and blown-out elbows that can't be forecast. PECOTA's always going to miss *something*, and October is all uncertainty for all involved. But a team can still build a defense here, no matter what its precise greater goal might be. If the desired outcome is winning a championship, they can invest in the best players available. If it's winning a championship while spending the smallest sum necessary, they can try investing in everything other than the conventionally "best" players. If there's not enough around to set an immediate goal, you can zoom out a few years down the line and focus on the farm system—each individual prospect serves as his own hedge against uncertainty, after all, with his status decided by how strong of a hedge he can be. If the farm's beyond hope, they can sink their efforts into infrastructure, beefing up the operations department or, if all else fails, leasing that brand-new TV screen above center field. None of these is a guarantee; there is nothing that can

INDIANS PROSPECTUS
2018 W-L: 91-71, 1ST IN AL CENTRAL

Pythag	.608	5th	B-Age	29.3	27th
RS/G	5.05	3rd	P-Age	29.2	23rd
RA/G	4.00	7th	Salary	$134.9M	15th
DRC+	109	3rd	M$/MW	$2.9M	23rd
DRA	3.63	3rd	DL Days	1207	14th
FIP	3.82	5th	$ on DL	15%	13th
DER	.702	20th			

- Opened 1994
- Open air
- Natural surface
- Fence profile: 9' to 19'

Three-Year Park Factors

Runs	Runs/RH	Runs/LH	HR/RH	HR/LH
102	97	113	97	109

Top Hitter WARP	7.4 Jose Ramirez
Top Pitcher WARP	6.1 Corey Kluber
Top Prospect	Triston McKenzie

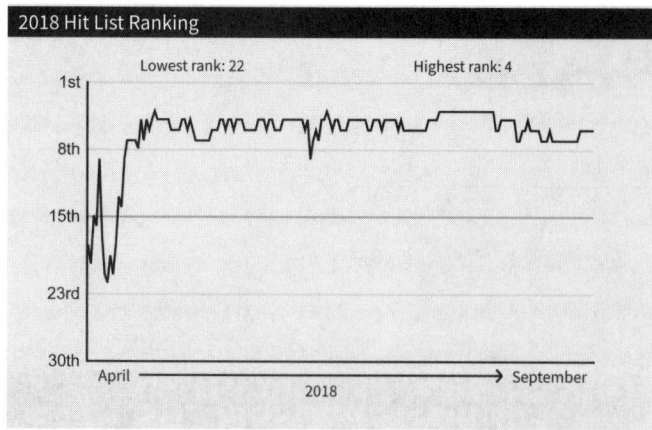

2018 Hit List Ranking

Lowest rank: 22   Highest rank: 4

April   2018   September

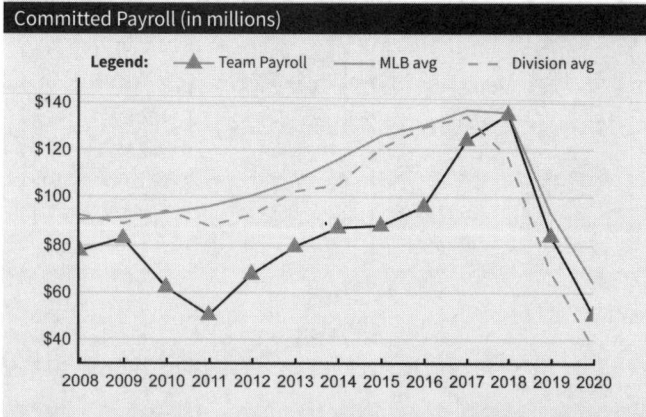

Committed Payroll (in millions)

Legend: Team Payroll — MLB avg — — Division avg

2008 2009 2010 2011 2012 2013 2014 2015 2016 2017 2018 2019 2020

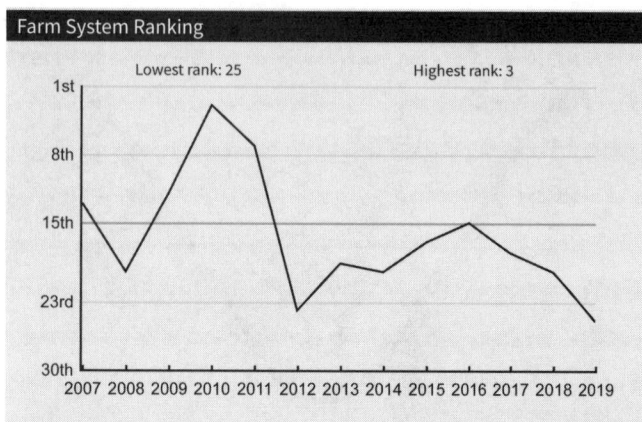

Farm System Ranking

Lowest rank: 25   Highest rank: 3

2007 2008 2009 2010 2011 2012 2013 2014 2015 2016 2017 2018 2019

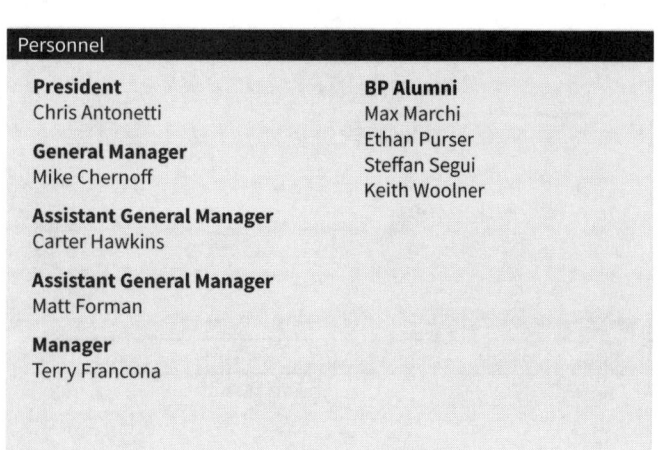

Personnel

President
Chris Antonetti

General Manager
Mike Chernoff

Assistant General Manager
Carter Hawkins

Assistant General Manager
Matt Forman

Manager
Terry Francona

BP Alumni
Max Marchi
Ethan Purser
Steffan Segui
Keith Woolner

be a guarantee. But they are all defenses, in one way or another. The uncertainty will always be there, and a team's goal is simply to guard against it.

There's a bit of a caveat here, though. There's no such thing as complete certainty—yet there's still relative certainty, imperfect certainty, a series of outcomes that are logically and realistically too likely not to bet on. This is all that a baseball team can hope for. But that kind of certainty is the product of a million factors, many outside the organization's control. A 100-win team could be perfectly constructed to achieve its goal, and it might still share the division with a 108-win team. Plans can be similarly ruined for a team at the other end of the standings; it's much more difficult to grab a high draft pick if there are multiple other clubs who have made their peace with losing. The best opportunity for certainty in baseball doesn't lie in a team's roster. It lies in a team's division.

By this logic, then, no team can be so certain as the Cleveland Indians. They've won three consecutive division titles; a fourth appears almost unavoidable. The AL Central isn't quite barren, but it's close: In 2018, Cleveland was the only team to win more than 78 games. A few green shoots are beginning to break through, and it wouldn't take an especially large investment to push these along even faster, but by and large, the division remains one great dry patch of cracked earth. It's easy to see how different the landscape might look in a few seasons—perhaps just one or two, even. But for now? Cleveland's set off in its own lush little space, and no other team is particularly close.

There's no greater luxury for a baseball team. It's certainty, but it's also *freedom*. Cleveland's front office entered this winter with the knowledge that they could do nothing, and they'd likely still walk to a division title. Flipped around, it's the knowledge that they could do just about *anything*, and they'd likely still win a division title. The ordinary winter checklist is there, sure—necessary replacements, preferred upgrades, whatever else can be tackled if money and energy and opportunity align. The list does not ever go away. But it does lose its weight. The list is now just a framework to build on; it's no longer a burden to bear. They can check off every single item and then go on to add a few more, just to have the joy of crossing them off. They can let all their free agents walk before crumpling the list into a tight little ball and shoving it in the back of a desk drawer. It doesn't matter. The initial outcome is, in all likelihood, going to be the same: They're going to win the division. But, of course, it does matter—very much. How is this freedom meant to be used, then?

They could treat it as freedom to go all the way in. *If we're all but guaranteed to win the division*, they could think, *we might as well be all but guaranteed to win the World Series*. It's permission to abandon caution and conservatism and just *go*. Again, there's no such thing as a guarantee here. But there's such a thing as a good chance, and if you have a chance as good as this one, why not take it? The conventional modern wisdom is that opportunities for contention arrive in carefully structured windows—opened with deliberate strategy, closed on a timed schedule. This, though, feels less like a window than a door. There is space to walk through, fully upright, without sacrifice or contortion or gimmickry. This is a cheesy inspirational poster brought to life: *What would you try if you knew you could not fail?* You are almost certainly going to be playing in October. Build a team that is as prepared as possible to *win* in October. Perhaps that's an exceptionally deep bullpen, or a modular defense, or an embrace of specialized roster roles like the designated runner. Perhaps it's all of these. There's plenty of space to experiment, because in the interim, there's plenty of space to do *anything*.

That's one line of thinking. Here is another: They could treat it as freedom to strip all the way down. *If we're all but guaranteed to win the division,* they could think, *we might as well sit back and let it happen.* This is very similar to the freedom to do nothing, and it is that, to a certain extent, but it's also the freedom to cut back. It's the freedom to get worse. They're going to win, after all, and that does not hinge on whether they project as a 95-win team or 90-win team or 85-win team. Why not let themselves get a little worse, then—or, in more practical terms, let themselves cut a few costs? They can let the free agents go. They can trade from an area of depth, without being particularly demanding about the return. (It's worth noting that this option does not necessarily mean saving money for its own sake. There's another path here—trading for top-tier prospects, which would likely mean taking on some money, too. It's a path that might feel like taking advantage of an isolated system to build a perpetual motion machine, rather than working to move as little as possible. But this path, it seems, isn't being taken here.) This is the opposite of the cheesy inspirational poster: *What would you do if you knew you didn't have to try?* There's no way to guarantee a win in October. Why try, then? The field will always have better odds than any single team, so what's the point? A division title gets preserved in the rafters, too.

These are different strategies, but they're also different philosophies. They point back to the original question posed here—the purpose of baseball, or, at least, the purpose of constructing a professional baseball roster. They get at the difference between *trying* and *winning*, and whether there is any virtue to be found in the space in between. If the true measure of a person's character is who he or she is when no one is watching, then, perhaps, the true measure of a front office's spirit is what its roster looks like when the division is bad. Of course, this can't be purely a philosophical question; any strategy here must first be filtered through practical constraints. There's the state of free agency, the landscape of trade opportunity, the threat of financial pressure from ownership—any or all of these might play a crucial role. But you can attempt to account for all of that behind the scenes, and you might still find it difficult to look at the result and see anything other than an endorsement of a particular ideology. It is, fundamentally, a measure of how much a team would like to bet on hope rather than against it.

Cleveland began the offseason by trading catcher Yan Gomes to Washington. His $7 million salary for 2019 was handed off for a minor-league outfielder and middling rookie reliever. Gomes' recent performance had been up-and-down, broken up by injuries and fallow stretches. The track record and outlook for his backup, Roberto Perez, was neither decidedly better nor decidedly worse. The obvious in-house replacement and number one prospect, Francisco Mejia, was shipped off at the deadline in 2018, leaving Eric Haase, the top young catcher in his stead, just about ready for the big leagues. The team hasn't shown any strong interest in looking elsewhere for a catcher. Perez and Haase—a decently capable duo, if not a particularly inspiring one—would be enough. The Gomes trade didn't make them better, then, but it didn't make them worse, either. Mostly, it just made them less expensive.

This set the tone for the winter. A three-team trade sent away slugger Edwin Encarnacion and third baseman Yandy Diaz for first baseman Carlos Santana and Jake Bauers. When Encarnacion was signed in 2016, he'd represented the biggest contract in Cleveland's history. Now, the relationship had been unceremoniously discontinued, in exchange for the slightly heftier contract of Santana. There was one key difference, though: Encarnacion's guaranteed money was stuck in 2019 (with a buyout for 2020), while Santana's went through 2019 and 2020 (with a smaller buyout for 2021). Cleveland couldn't dump a large contract outright, but they could spread out their costs over an extra year. Both Encarnacion and Santana have seen better days, though each kept the potential to function as a solid first baseman or DH; Diaz and Bauers similarly represent something close to a wash. Here, again, was a move that made the team not much better nor much worse. It just made them a little less expensive for the immediate future.

Cleveland freed up additional cash by trading first baseman Yonder Alonso to the Chicago White Sox, who agreed to pay in full his salary of $8 million for 2019. They watched one free agent walk after another: Michael Brantley, Andrew Miller, Lonnie Chisenhall. Their payroll cuts did not come with additions or extensions, with one exception. Pitcher Carlos Carrasco was kept on through 2022 on a remarkably team-friendly extension. The 31-year-old was evidently staying put for the long haul—which only served to fuel rumors about what might happen to the team's other starting pitchers, including Corey Kluber and Trevor Bauer. Both were reportedly put up on the trading block. Cleveland's greatest source of depth had been its rotation, and it was now at risk of being dismantled. It's a reasonable move for a team trying to survive, but that doesn't make it an exciting move for a team trying to win.

Cleveland's front office was apparently instructed to cut payroll, and they succeeded. A more optimistic view is that they've achieved financial flexibility; there's a crucial caveat, however, in that financial flexibility is only valuable insofar as it is used to stretch for anything. Given the nature of their trades—major-league salaries exchanged for minor-league talent—it seems that the team is more interested in investing in the future than for the present, without making a dramatic investment in either direction. The winter isn't just a question of philosophy. It's a practical exercise in money, in public relations, in balancing short-term and long-term need. Yet it can be all of that and still, at the same time, register as the picture of a team that didn't have to try and took that as a reason not to. ■

—Emma Baccellieri is a staff writer at Sports Illustrated.

HITTERS

Greg Allen CF   Born: 03/15/93   Age: 26   Bats: B   Throws: R   Height: 6'0"   Weight: 175   Origin: Round 6, 2014 Draft (#188 overall)

YEAR	TEAM	LVL	AGE	PA	R	2B	3B	HR	RBI	BB	K	SB	CS	AVG/OBP/SLG	DRC+	VORP	BABIP	BRR	FRAA	WARP
2016	LYN	A+	23	432	93	16	4	4	31	58	51	38	7	.298/.424/.402	129	49.4	.338	13.1	CF(92): 15.9	5.9
2016	AKR	AA	23	174	26	7	3	3	13	19	27	7	6	.290/.399/.441	129	16.1	.336	2.3	CF(36): 4.1	1.9
2017	AKR	AA	24	303	37	16	1	2	24	22	55	21	2	.264/.344/.357	88	12.9	.319	1.5	CF(67): -6.4, RF(1): -0.1	0.0
2017	CLE	MLB	24	39	7	1	0	1	6	2	8	1	0	.229/.282/.343	85	0.5	.259	0.7	CF(21): -0.9, LF(5): -0.1	0.0
2018	COH	AAA	25	205	31	13	0	2	14	19	44	12	6	.298/.395/.409	99	13.1	.389	0.3	CF(42): 2.3, LF(5): -0.4	0.9
2018	CLE	MLB	25	291	36	11	3	2	20	14	58	21	4	.257/.310/.343	84	4.1	.320	3.4	CF(78): 2.8, RF(16): -0.4	1.0
2019	*CLE*	*MLB*	*26*	*332*	*40*	*14*	*2*	*7*	*30*	*23*	*73*	*16*	*4*	*.237/.304/.360*	*85*	*7.0*	*.287*	*1.7*	*CF 1, LF 0*	*0.8*

Breakout: 4%   Improve: 39%   Collapse: 15%   Attrition: 24%   MLB: 71%   *Comparables: Brett Gardner, Trevor Crowe, Bryan Petersen*

Apply a rash of injuries to a Cleveland outfield group which was not very deep to begin with and you have a whole lot of opportunity. Enter Allen, a 25-year-old, speed-first center fielder who already had about 500 Double-A plate appearances heading into the year. Allen showed he can handle center in the bigs and that he can get at his speed in games, stealing 21 bases on 25 attempts and posting a BRR that was just outside the top 25 in baseball in only half a season. Those skills are going to keep buying him chances, but his bat will almost certainly limit him to a bench role barring unforeseen improvement.

Jake Bauers LF   Born: 10/06/95   Age: 23   Bats: L   Throws: L   Height: 6'1"   Weight: 195   Origin: Round 7, 2013 Draft (#208 overall)

YEAR	TEAM	LVL	AGE	PA	R	2B	3B	HR	RBI	BB	K	SB	CS	AVG/OBP/SLG	DRC+	VORP	BABIP	BRR	FRAA	WARP
2016	MNT	AA	20	581	79	28	1	14	78	73	89	10	6	.274/.370/.420	131	33.6	.305	2.1	RF(62): 7.2, 1B(57): 0.0	4.3
2017	DUR	AAA	21	575	79	31	1	13	63	78	112	20	3	.263/.368/.412	118	23.7	.314	0.5	LF(55): 4.7, 1B(52): -1.0	2.7
2018	DUR	AAA	22	222	31	14	0	5	24	23	47	10	6	.279/.357/.426	111	12.0	.345	0.9	1B(46): -0.4, LF(4): 0.3	0.7
2018	TBA	MLB	22	388	48	22	2	11	48	54	104	6	6	.201/.316/.384	86	8.5	.252	2.5	1B(76): -2.4, LF(16): 0.5	0.0
2019	*CLE*	*MLB*	*23*	*716*	*84*	*27*	*2*	*19*	*72*	*81*	*166*	*15*	*7*	*.218/.313/.358*	*84*	*2.1*	*.265*	*3.3*	*1B 0, LF 3*	*0.5*

Breakout: 8%   Improve: 34%   Collapse: 11%   Attrition: 27%   MLB: 59%   *Comparables: Casey Kotchman, Daric Barton, Ji-Man Choi*

Almost the son of Jack, Bauers made his debut in 2018 after being a figment of Rays fans' imagination since he was acquired from the Padres way back in the Wil Myers trade. Bauers is one of those guys who does a few things well but nothing great. He's an athletic defender at first base and can play the outfield corners competently. He's always shown the ability to hit at a solid clip with some power, although that profile is atypical for first base. Bauers was all of those things in the first half and did little in the second half. His strikeouts rose to an uncommon rate of 30 percent, which basically sunk all of his value at the plate. He was fine defensively, but when's the last time a team went defense first at the cold corner? On top of the strikeouts, he got a bit pull happy, resulting in more ground balls and more outs. The league adjusted to Bauers. He had the offseason to adjust back. Traded to the Indians, he'll look to be a cheap, team-controlled supporting player for the Lindor-Ramirez headliners.

Will Benson RF   Born: 06/16/98   Age: 21   Bats: L   Throws: L   Height: 6'5"   Weight: 225   Origin: Round 1, 2016 Draft (#14 overall)

YEAR	TEAM	LVL	AGE	PA	R	2B	3B	HR	RBI	BB	K	SB	CS	AVG/OBP/SLG	DRC+	VORP	BABIP	BRR	FRAA	WARP
2016	CLE	RK	18	184	31	10	3	6	27	22	60	10	2	.209/.321/.424	101	9.1	.293	2.5	RF(39): -2.0	0.4
2017	MHV	A-	19	236	29	8	5	10	36	31	80	7	1	.238/.347/.475	126	11.5	.339	0.1	RF(56): -2.5	1.0
2018	LKC	A	20	506	54	11	1	22	58	82	152	12	6	.180/.324/.370	117	5.6	.218	-0.4	RF(113): 5.4, CF(4): -0.2	2.5
2019	*CLE*	*MLB*	*21*	*251*	*26*	*7*	*0*	*10*	*30*	*24*	*89*	*2*	*1*	*.176/.253/.342*	*55*	*-7.1*	*.228*	*-0.4*	*RF 0, CF 0*	*-0.8*

Breakout: 0%   Improve: 3%   Collapse: 2%   Attrition: 3%   MLB: 7%   *Comparables: Caleb Gindl, Nomar Mazara, Trayce Thompson*

Power remains the calling card for Benson, the toolsy outfielder the Indians plucked with their first-round pick in 2016. In his first look at High-A in his age-20 season, he continued to show the skyscraping ability while questions about his hit tool remain. Benson is already a pretty strict Three True Outcomes guy, even at such a young age, with almost exactly 50 percent of his 2018 plate appearances resulting in either a home run, walk or strikeout. There's a model here for someone who reaches the majors as an above-average contributor, but we're still a few years away figuring out if he can put it all together.

Bobby Bradley 1B   Born: 05/29/96   Age: 23   Bats: L   Throws: R   Height: 6'1"   Weight: 225   Origin: Round 3, 2014 Draft (#97 overall)

YEAR	TEAM	LVL	AGE	PA	R	2B	3B	HR	RBI	BB	K	SB	CS	AVG/OBP/SLG	DRC+	VORP	BABIP	BRR	FRAA	WARP
2016	LYN	A+	20	572	82	23	1	29	102	75	170	3	0	.235/.344/.466	129	23.4	.293	0.2	1B(116): -6.4	1.9
2017	AKR	AA	21	532	66	25	3	23	89	55	122	3	3	.251/.331/.465	116	17.6	.287	-2.6	1B(123): -6.3	0.9
2018	AKR	AA	22	421	49	19	3	24	64	45	105	1	0	.214/.304/.477	109	17.0	.226	-2.3	1B(97): 1.4	0.9
2018	COH	AAA	22	128	11	7	2	3	19	11	43	0	0	.254/.323/.430	89	2.8	.377	0.3	1B(29): 1.5	0.2
2019	*CLE*	*MLB*	*23*	*103*	*12*	*4*	*0*	*5*	*14*	*8*	*29*	*0*	*0*	*.223/.285/.425*	*90*	*-0.3*	*.266*	*-0.2*	*1B 0*	*-0.1*

Breakout: 4%   Improve: 23%   Collapse: 5%   Attrition: 16%   MLB: 45%   *Comparables: Ryan O'Hearn, Paul Goldschmidt, Jerry Sands*

The large adult son made Akron his personal Dinger Town for the second straight season, showing off his one true calling card, power, as nearly 60 percent of his total hits went for extra bases. In an age where one-dimensional sluggers are becoming less and less valuable, Bradley will need to improve either his contact skills or his walk rate — and preferably both — to make the leap from interesting and fun prospect to a legitimately exciting one. That's especially true given that he's a non-factor defensively whose future lies at either first base or designated hitter. The power is real, though, so incremental improvements in any of those areas will likely bring BIG BOY SZN to Cleveland.

Melky Cabrera OF   Born: 08/11/84   Age: 34   Bats: B   Throws: L   Height: 5'10"   Weight: 210   Origin: International Free Agent, 2001

YEAR	TEAM	LVL	AGE	PA	R	2B	3B	HR	RBI	BB	K	SB	CS	AVG/OBP/SLG	DRC+	VORP	BABIP	BRR	FRAA	WARP
2016	CHA	MLB	31	646	70	42	5	14	86	47	69	2	0	.296/.345/.455	106	15.7	.314	-4.3	LF(147): -6.6	1.1
2017	CHA	MLB	32	428	54	17	0	13	56	25	52	0	0	.295/.336/.436	96	8.6	.310	-2.2	LF(92): -5.7	0.1
2017	KCA	MLB	32	238	24	13	2	4	29	11	22	1	2	.269/.303/.399	97	-0.3	.280	0.6	RF(46): -6.3, LF(12): -0.6	-0.2
2018	COH	AAA	33	80	7	6	1	0	8	2	10	2	0	.321/.338/.423	91	1.2	.368	-1.0	RF(10): 0.4, LF(6): 0.9	0.1
2018	CLE	MLB	33	278	28	17	0	6	39	20	38	1	1	.280/.335/.420	103	6.2	.303	-0.4	RF(68): 1.7, LF(4): 0.0	0.9
2019	*CLE*	*MLB*	*34*	*352*	*35*	*19*	*1*	*7*	*39*	*23*	*47*	*1*	*1*	*.272/.324/.406*	*96*	*6.9*	*.297*	*-1.1*	*RF -5, LF 0*	*0.2*

Breakout: 2%   Improve: 34%   Collapse: 8%   Attrition: 20%   MLB: 86%   *Comparables: Shane Victorino, Tommy Holmes, Rip Radcliff*

Cabrera looked like a potential casualty of the chilly 2017-2018 free agent market, another member of the fraternity of players who transitioned directly from "player the White Sox were counting on to get them into the playoffs" to "out of baseball." But with Cleveland's outfield woes, the veteran was pressed into service and he produced a classic Good Contact And Not Much Else Adequate season. ("GCANMEA" if you want to make a new statistic, it's what we do here. Melky will undoubtedly sign out this acronym with arm gestures from first base after a ringing single at some point.) He somehow turned only 34 in August and he plays with endearing joy, so he may keep producing this way for a little while longer.

Yu-Cheng Chang SS   Born: 08/18/95   Age: 23   Bats: R   Throws: R   Height: 6'1"   Weight: 175   Origin: International Free Agent, 2013

YEAR	TEAM	LVL	AGE	PA	R	2B	3B	HR	RBI	BB	K	SB	CS	AVG/OBP/SLG	DRC+	VORP	BABIP	BRR	FRAA	WARP
2016	LYN	A+	20	477	78	30	8	13	70	45	110	11	3	.259/.332/.463	115	35.1	.316	2.9	SS(104): 0.0	3.1
2017	AKR	AA	21	508	72	24	5	24	66	52	134	11	4	.220/.312/.461	117	33.8	.254	2.3	SS(119): 20.3	5.9
2018	COH	AAA	22	518	56	28	2	13	62	44	144	4	3	.256/.330/.411	102	16.6	.341	-3.3	SS(94): -7.3, 3B(23): -0.7	1.1
2019	*CLE*	*MLB*	*23*	*203*	*20*	*9*	*0*	*5*	*21*	*13*	*62*	*2*	*1*	*.212/.277/.346*	*61*	*-5.1*	*.288*	*-0.3*	*3B -3*	*-0.9*

Breakout: 8%   Improve: 21%   Collapse: 4%   Attrition: 13%   MLB: 40%   *Comparables: Todd Frazier, Trevor Story, Derek Dietrich*

Chang's biggest problem in 2018 was something he couldn't do anything about. He was a shortstop/third base prospect playing in the high minors for an organization that happens to have a pair of young 8s holding down those positions in the majors. They aren't going anywhere for awhile. Despite a power dip after moving to Triple-A, Chang possesses solid pull power and isn't afraid to take a walk. His hands should be good enough to stick at shortstop, but at the very least he should be able to handle third base. The question for Chang is whether he'll make enough contact to be a factor once he finally gets there (and whether "there" will be Cleveland).

Tyler Freeman SS   Born: 05/21/99   Age: 20   Bats: R   Throws: R   Height: 6'0"   Weight: 170   Origin: Round 2, 2017 Draft (#71 overall)

YEAR	TEAM	LVL	AGE	PA	R	2B	3B	HR	RBI	BB	K	SB	CS	AVG/OBP/SLG	DRC+	VORP	BABIP	BRR	FRAA	WARP
2017	CLE	RK	18	144	19	9	0	2	14	7	12	5	1	.297/.364/.414	131	12.8	.313	1.8	SS(29): -0.1, 2B(4): -0.9	1.1
2018	MHV	A-	19	301	49	29	4	2	38	8	22	14	3	.352/.405/.511	146	37.7	.372	3.5	SS(52): -0.1, 2B(10): -0.2	3.2
2019	*CLE*	*MLB*	*20*	*251*	*27*	*11*	*1*	*6*	*23*	*3*	*42*	*3*	*1*	*.227/.263/.344*	*69*	*-0.4*	*.258*	*-0.1*	*SS 0, 2B 0*	*-0.1*

Breakout: 1%   Improve: 7%   Collapse: 0%   Attrition: 2%   MLB: 9%   *Comparables: Amed Rosario, Orlando Arcia, Ruben Tejada*

Freeman's free-swinging approach helped him mash the New York-Penn League as a 19-year-old, living up to what many scouts saw in his hit tool when he was a second-round pick in 2017. He also drew just eight walks in 301 plate appearances, so he'll try to avoid being exposed once he begins facing more advanced competition. He was drafted as a shortstop, though he may get moved to second base before long. Wherever he's standing on the diamond, Freeman's bat will be the difference-maker.

Brandon Guyer OF   Born: 01/28/86   Age: 33   Bats: R   Throws: R   Height: 6'2"   Weight: 200   Origin: Round 5, 2007 Draft (#157 overall)

YEAR	TEAM	LVL	AGE	PA	R	2B	3B	HR	RBI	BB	K	SB	CS	AVG/OBP/SLG	DRC+	VORP	BABIP	BRR	FRAA	WARP
2016	TBA	MLB	30	249	27	12	1	7	18	12	42	2	1	.241/.347/.406	113	9.7	.268	-0.8	LF(25): 0.0, CF(18): -0.5	0.9
2016	CLE	MLB	30	96	12	5	0	2	14	7	13	1	1	.333/.438/.469	118	6.4	.379	0.2	LF(26): 2.1, RF(7): 0.1	0.7
2017	CLE	MLB	31	192	23	7	1	2	20	15	43	2	0	.236/.326/.327	77	0.8	.303	0.3	RF(37): 2.5, LF(33): -1.2	0.1
2018	CLE	MLB	32	221	25	11	0	7	27	15	48	1	1	.206/.300/.371	94	-0.7	.237	0.0	RF(76): -1.4, LF(21): -0.3	0.2
2019	*CLE*	*MLB*	*33*	*251*	*27*	*11*	*1*	*6*	*27*	*18*	*50*	*2*	*1*	*.236/.327/.371*	*96*	*5.8*	*.287*	*-0.1*	*RF 0, LF 0*	*0.6*

Breakout: 4%   Improve: 37%   Collapse: 7%   Attrition: 15%   MLB: 89%   *Comparables: Buddy Lewis, David Murphy, Gregor Blanco*

Guyer's non-trivial playing time in 2018 is probably more of an indictment of Cleveland's corner bat options than an endorsement of his current talents. His nice multi-year run is only a few years in the rearview mirror, but modern roster construction squeezes this particular profile — weak-side platoon bats without much defensive utility — harder than pretty much any other. After all, that 17th reliever has to take someone's spot. He still makes enough contact to scoop up playing time for desperate teams or to round out September rosters, but it doesn't look like he's capable of more than that anymore.

Daniel Johnson RF Born: 07/11/95   Age: 23   Bats: L   Throws: L   Height: 5'10"   Weight: 185   Origin: Round 5, 2016 Draft (#154 overall)

YEAR	TEAM	LVL	AGE	PA	R	2B	3B	HR	RBI	BB	K	SB	CS	AVG/OBP/SLG	DRC+	VORP	BABIP	BRR	FRAA	WARP
2016	AUB	A-	20	264	25	9	4	1	14	7	42	13	3	.265/.312/.347	97	8.7	.315	1.6	CF(24): -3.3, RF(24): 1.2	0.6
2017	HAG	A	21	364	61	16	4	17	52	22	70	12	9	.300/.361/.529	152	31.4	.333	-0.5	RF(51): -1.1, CF(15): 0.3	3.1
2017	POT	A+	21	185	22	13	0	5	20	13	30	10	2	.294/.346/.459	118	10.3	.331	1.7	CF(28): -3.2, RF(9): 3.5	1.1
2018	HAR	AA	22	391	48	19	7	6	31	23	90	21	4	.267/.321/.410	90	7.6	.338	-2.3	RF(54): 6.3, CF(33): -2.9	0.5
2019	CLE	MLB	23	251	31	11	1	7	25	9	63	7	2	.233/.269/.381	71	-0.2	.287	0.7	RF 0, CF -1	-0.2

Breakout: 1%   Improve: 7%   Collapse: 4%   Attrition: 5%   MLB: 11%   *Comparables: Mike Gerber, Andrew Lambo, Kyle Waldrop*

Were his desired big-league destination still Montreal, this high-variance, tooled-up outfielder might have been the third Daniel Johnson to serve as a Quebec premier ... attraction. His first taste of the advanced minors made for a more humble stat line than he's used to, but public Statcast data on his Arizona Fall League exploits raised eyebrows. Said a different way: He traffics in the exit velocity. All of the exit velocity. Shortly after that display, he exited Washington's plans in the Yan Gomes trade, but his power bat and showstopping arm are begging to be seen on a major-league stage.

Nolan Jones 3B Born: 05/07/98   Age: 21   Bats: L   Throws: R   Height: 6'4"   Weight: 185   Origin: Round 2, 2016 Draft (#55 overall)

YEAR	TEAM	LVL	AGE	PA	R	2B	3B	HR	RBI	BB	K	SB	CS	AVG/OBP/SLG	DRC+	VORP	BABIP	BRR	FRAA	WARP
2016	CLE	RK	18	134	10	5	2	0	9	23	49	3	1	.257/.388/.339	85	7.7	.459	0.2	3B(28): 4.6, SS(5): 0.2	0.7
2017	MHV	A-	19	265	41	18	3	4	33	43	60	1	0	.317/.430/.482	123	28.4	.417	1.7	3B(53): 0.0	1.7
2018	LKC	A	20	389	46	12	0	16	49	63	97	2	1	.279/.393/.464	142	33.5	.347	-0.9	3B(77): -4.1	2.7
2018	LYN	A+	20	130	23	9	0	3	17	26	34	0	0	.298/.438/.471	119	12.7	.418	0.1	3B(28): -0.3	0.7
2019	CLE	MLB	21	251	25	6	0	8	28	30	76	0	0	.191/.285/.325	66	-5.3	.245	-0.8	3B 0	-0.6

Breakout: 4%   Improve: 11%   Collapse: 4%   Attrition: 10%   MLB: 23%   *Comparables: Ryan McMahon, Willy Adames, Matt Dominguez*

Jones continued to develop in the exact way Cleveland likely envisioned when they nabbed the prep bat in the second round of the 2016 draft. In his first taste of full-season ball, he eviscerated the Midwest League and more than held his own in a late-season audition at High-A as a 20-year-old, showing patience rivaled by few hitters at the level. A converted shortstop, Jones' defense at the hot corner has been uneven — many believe he'll wind up at first base long term — but he's shown enough athleticism to go along with a plus arm that it's too early to give up on him there yet. If he does stick at third, he could turn into one of the more intriguing prospects in the game.

Jason Kipnis 2B Born: 04/03/87   Age: 32   Bats: L   Throws: R   Height: 5'11"   Weight: 195   Origin: Round 2, 2009 Draft (#63 overall)

YEAR	TEAM	LVL	AGE	PA	R	2B	3B	HR	RBI	BB	K	SB	CS	AVG/OBP/SLG	DRC+	VORP	BABIP	BRR	FRAA	WARP
2016	CLE	MLB	29	688	91	41	4	23	82	60	146	15	3	.275/.343/.469	110	24.1	.324	3.0	2B(151): 10.6	4.5
2017	CLE	MLB	30	373	43	25	0	12	35	28	71	6	2	.232/.291/.414	89	6.6	.256	-0.7	2B(75): 1.0, CF(11): -1.1	0.6
2018	CLE	MLB	31	601	65	28	1	18	75	60	112	7	1	.230/.315/.389	105	11.2	.258	-1.2	2B(131): -0.5, CF(14): -2.0	1.9
2019	CLE	MLB	32	489	61	26	2	13	50	41	98	8	2	.248/.318/.403	95	13.5	.290	-0.1	2B 3	1.8

Breakout: 1%   Improve: 29%   Collapse: 6%   Attrition: 8%   MLB: 93%   *Comparables: Orlando Hudson, Mark Ellis, Adam Kennedy*

We now have two subpar seasons worth of evidence that the best days of the grindy heart of the mid-2010s Indians may be behind him. Unlike a 2017 season that could optimistically be blamed on myriad injuries, Kipnis was mostly healthy in 2018, but found himself as the weak link in an infield that featured two MVP candidates. So what gives? Kipnis is now well onto the downward slope of an aging curve that's scarcely kind to anyone, let alone second basemen, and his defense there has become suspect enough that Cleveland has tried him in the outfield on occasion. His already deteriorating bat becomes a lot less appealing if moved to a corner outfield spot or first base.

Francisco Lindor SS Born: 11/14/93   Age: 25   Bats: B   Throws: R   Height: 5'11"   Weight: 190   Origin: Round 1, 2011 Draft (#8 overall)

YEAR	TEAM	LVL	AGE	PA	R	2B	3B	HR	RBI	BB	K	SB	CS	AVG/OBP/SLG	DRC+	VORP	BABIP	BRR	FRAA	WARP
2016	CLE	MLB	22	684	99	30	3	15	78	57	88	19	5	.301/.358/.435	112	40.4	.324	5.5	SS(155): 19.3	6.8
2017	CLE	MLB	23	723	99	44	4	33	89	60	93	15	3	.273/.337/.505	120	48.4	.275	2.1	SS(158): 3.8	5.8
2018	CLE	MLB	24	745	129	42	2	38	92	70	107	25	10	.277/.352/.519	135	58.6	.279	-0.5	SS(157): 5.9	7.3
2019	CLE	MLB	25	685	104	38	3	27	88	61	92	19	6	.289/.358/.497	127	49.8	.297	1.5	SS 9	6.3

Breakout: 2%   Improve: 65%   Collapse: 2%   Attrition: 0%   MLB: 98%   *Comparables: Jose Reyes, Troy Tulowitzki, George Brett*

Scouting the stat line would not have told you enough about Lindor as he approached the majors. He never cracked an .800 OPS in the minors, and scouts observed he had started to look almost bored in Triple-A. Credit to Cleveland for promoting him instead of letting him languish to teach him some sort of lesson. When he arrived, he was part of a trio of exciting rookies at shortstop along with Carlos Correa and Corey Seager, and there was fun debate about which would be the best. Lindor's ace in the hole seemed to be his elite defense, as set against Correa and Seager's middle-of-the-order thump. The elite defense was real, but as his power keeps blossoming without sacrificing too much of his contact ability, Lindor has clearly separated himself, posting back-to-back 30-plus-homer seasons on top of all the other things he does so magnificently. By the time you read this, he will be barely 25. If you could pick anyone in baseball to build a team around, he'd be in the mix for the no. 1 pick.

Jordan Luplow LF Born: 09/26/93 Age: 25 Bats: R Throws: R Height: 6'1" Weight: 195 Origin: Round 3, 2014 Draft (#100 overall)

YEAR	TEAM	LVL	AGE	PA	R	2B	3B	HR	RBI	BB	K	SB	CS	AVG/OBP/SLG	DRC+	VORP	BABIP	BRR	FRAA	WARP
2016	BRD	A+	22	425	63	23	3	10	54	60	78	6	2	.254/.363/.421	128	22.1	.294	0.2	LF(81): 7.5	3.0
2017	ALT	AA	23	288	45	15	0	16	37	29	45	1	3	.287/.368/.535	142	25.5	.294	1.5	LF(62): 4.3, 3B(1): 0.0	3.0
2017	IND	AAA	23	182	29	7	1	7	19	16	36	4	1	.325/.401/.513	132	18.2	.381	-0.8	LF(27): 3.4, RF(15): 0.9	1.4
2017	PIT	MLB	23	87	6	3	1	3	11	6	22	0	1	.205/.276/.385	80	-1.2	.241	-0.4	RF(14): 0.1, LF(10): 0.7	0.0
2018	IND	AAA	24	357	41	25	3	8	49	39	64	7	2	.287/.367/.462	124	20.4	.336	-1.7	LF(41): 4.3, RF(38): 1.4	2.3
2018	PIT	MLB	24	103	16	1	3	3	7	10	18	2	2	.185/.272/.359	87	-2.7	.197	-0.4	LF(16): 5.4, RF(11): -0.3	0.6
2019	CLE	MLB	25	310	35	14	1	9	37	29	65	3	2	.239/.320/.398	95	4.5	.281	-0.4	LF 2, RF -2	0.5

Breakout: 11% Improve: 39% Collapse: 11% Attrition: 29% MLB: 84%   Comparables: Matt LaPorta, Austin Slater, Yonder Alonso

Luplow's 2018 was a mirror image of his 2017. The Fresno State product terrorized pitchers in the minors, then struggled with the Pirates in a limited sample size. Outside of his discipline at the plate, nothing from Triple-A translated to the majors, which isn't good news for a player whose defensive utility is limited to a corner and who'll be more of an asset with the stick against southpaws than righties. In a different era, a right-handed masher with above-average power coming off the bench as a pinch-hitter and occasional starter would be an asset. In a world where pitchers take up 12-13 spot on a 25-man roster, Luplow runs the risk of becoming a Quad-A bat if he doesn't translate minor-league success to big-league performance in short order. Luplow could survive as a bench bat on a team that has the flexibility to move a corner-outfield starter into center when needed. Unfortunately, this is not that team.

Leonys Martin CF Born: 03/06/88 Age: 31 Bats: L Throws: R Height: 6'2" Weight: 200 Origin: International Free Agent, 2011

YEAR	TEAM	LVL	AGE	PA	R	2B	3B	HR	RBI	BB	K	SB	CS	AVG/OBP/SLG	DRC+	VORP	BABIP	BRR	FRAA	WARP
2016	SEA	MLB	28	576	72	17	3	15	47	44	149	24	6	.247/.306/.378	79	10.7	.313	2.5	CF(143): 9.6	1.8
2017	SEA	MLB	29	122	12	2	1	3	8	5	29	6	4	.174/.221/.287	67	-7.6	.205	-0.4	RF(15): 2.8, CF(15): -0.8	0.0
2017	TAC	AAA	29	388	63	24	5	11	39	21	89	25	6	.306/.346/.492	100	25.8	.376	1.1	CF(82): 16.2	3.1
2017	CHN	MLB	29	16	2	1	0	0	1	3	4	1	0	.154/.313/.231	72	-0.5	.222	0.1	CF(5): 0.0, RF(4): -0.4	0.0
2018	DET	MLB	30	336	45	15	3	9	29	29	75	7	3	.251/.321/.409	100	11.9	.305	0.7	CF(74): 18.5	3.2
2018	CLE	MLB	30	17	3	0	0	2	4	1	2	0	1	.333/.353/.733	109	2.3	.250	0.4	CF(5): 0.1, RF(1): 0.0	0.1
2019	CLE	MLB	31	543	72	24	3	15	54	38	132	20	7	.249/.308/.401	91	13.0	.308	1.0	CF 6, RF 2	2.1

Breakout: 2% Improve: 49% Collapse: 6% Attrition: 10% MLB: 86%   Comparables: Nyjer Morgan, Austin Jackson, Rajai Davis

The story of Martin's season was supposed to be one of reclamation. After years of unfulfilled potential bouncing from org to org as a speed/defense guy who couldn't handle the bat well enough to stay in the lineup, Martin signed with the rebuilding Tigers and combined elite defense in center field with a competent enough bat that the contending Indians traded for him. He played only 17 games with the Tribe before a bacterial infection that affected multiple internal organs nearly proved fatal. Thankfully, Martin is expected to make a full recovery and reportedly wanted to return before the season ended, though doctors advised against it. Continuing that progress he showed in 2018 would be a great story, but right now for Martin, baseball understandably takes a back seat.

Oscar Mercado CF Born: 12/16/94 Age: 24 Bats: R Throws: R Height: 6'2" Weight: 175 Origin: Round 2, 2013 Draft (#57 overall)

YEAR	TEAM	LVL	AGE	PA	R	2B	3B	HR	RBI	BB	K	SB	CS	AVG/OBP/SLG	DRC+	VORP	BABIP	BRR	FRAA	WARP
2016	PMB	A+	21	506	50	23	1	0	27	44	71	33	20	.215/.296/.271	87	5.3	.253	1.1	SS(81): 0.9, CF(38): 3.2	1.7
2017	SFD	AA	22	523	76	20	4	13	46	32	112	38	19	.287/.341/.428	110	32.9	.348	5.7	CF(108): -2.1, LF(7): -0.7	2.6
2018	MEM	AAA	23	427	73	21	1	8	42	36	64	31	8	.285/.351/.408	101	32.6	.323	8.1	CF(89): -2.6, LF(7): -0.5	2.1
2018	COH	AAA	23	119	12	5	1	0	5	13	23	6	4	.252/.342/.320	97	-2.3	.325	-2.2	CF(24): -0.8, RF(7): 0.3	0.1
2019	CLE	MLB	24	70	8	2	0	1	6	6	15	4	2	.212/.291/.310	56	-1.7	.260	0.1	LF 0, RF 0	-0.2

Breakout: 10% Improve: 19% Collapse: 4% Attrition: 29% MLB: 41%   Comparables: Jon Jay, Charlie Blackmon, Gary Brown

The Indians acquired the shortstop-turned-center fielder from the Cardinals in July and added him to the 40-man roster as additional outfield depth in Triple-A. The former second-round pick's specialty is speed, as he can make an impact on the basepaths and has looked the part tracking down fly balls in center. Mercado's bat remains a question and the offensive strides he seemed to make in Memphis weren't as prevalent once he moved to the International League. Mercado is still young enough to hope his hit tool comes around, but even if it doesn't his speed and defense make him an option as a fourth outfielder.

Tyler Naquin RF Born: 04/24/91 Age: 28 Bats: L Throws: R Height: 6'2" Weight: 195 Origin: Round 1, 2012 Draft (#15 overall)

YEAR	TEAM	LVL	AGE	PA	R	2B	3B	HR	RBI	BB	K	SB	CS	AVG/OBP/SLG	DRC+	VORP	BABIP	BRR	FRAA	WARP
2016	COH	AAA	25	79	6	3	1	1	8	8	15	1	2	.286/.354/.400	104	3.1	.345	-1.6	CF(15): 1.3, RF(2): -0.1	0.3
2016	CLE	MLB	25	365	52	18	5	14	43	36	112	6	3	.296/.372/.514	102	18.0	.411	-2.3	CF(105): -8.2, RF(4): -0.4	0.3
2017	COH	AAA	26	330	42	14	4	10	51	30	71	5	2	.298/.359/.475	119	18.7	.358	0.9	CF(49): 10.7, RF(23): -1.1	2.7
2017	CLE	MLB	26	40	4	2	0	0	1	2	9	0	1	.216/.250/.270	75	-1.4	.276	-0.2	CF(11): -0.4, RF(8): -0.5	-0.1
2018	CLE	MLB	27	183	22	7	0	3	23	6	42	1	1	.264/.295/.356	82	1.4	.331	1.0	RF(39): 5.2, CF(19): 0.2	0.7
2019	CLE	MLB	28	365	39	16	2	9	38	28	95	4	2	.237/.300/.376	86	3.5	.303	-0.6	RF 6, LF 0	1.0

Breakout: 0% Improve: 49% Collapse: 9% Attrition: 24% MLB: 88%   Comparables: Will Venable, Nate Schierholtz, Travis Buck

The former first rounder burst onto the scene in 2016 by hitting well enough to overlook his inadequate glove in center field. After his 2017 was lost to woeful ineffectiveness and injury, Naquin's age-27 season began to take on the look of a make-or-break one. While he hit better in his limited looks, his production was still nowhere near his rookie numbers. Perhaps it's fitting that, like Naquin, low-power outfielders who carry their profile with plus corner defense had a moment in 2016. Even if Naquin fights his way back into an everyday job, one suspects any team with real ambition will always be trying to upgrade him or shunt him to a bench role.

Bo Naylor C Born: 02/21/00 Age: 19 Bats: L Throws: R Height: 6'0" Weight: 195 Origin: Round 1, 2018 Draft (#29 overall)

YEAR	TEAM	LVL	AGE	PA	R	2B	3B	HR	RBI	BB	K	SB	CS	AVG/OBP/SLG	DRC+	VORP	BABIP	BRR	FRAA	WARP
2018	CLT	RK	18	139	17	3	3	2	17	21	28	5	1	.274/.381/.402	128	12.3	.341	0.3	C(19): -0.4, 3B(5): -0.7	0.8
2019	CLE	MLB	19	251	20	7	0	5	22	19	79	0	0	.178/.240/.268	35	-10.9	.242	-0.6	C 0, 3B 0	-1.2

Breakout: 0%   Improve: 6%   Collapse: 1%   Attrition: 4%   MLB: 11%   *Comparables: Francisco Pena, Nomar Mazara, Adalberto Mondesi*

Cleveland's 2018 first-round pick has a couple of general factors working against him. Naylor is a prep catcher and was taken at the very end of the first round, both demographics which tend to fare poorly. Still, he held his own in his brief rookie-ball debut and his best tool is probably his ability to make contact. In an era where bat-control hitters make swing-plane adjustments and start uncorking 20-30 home runs, perhaps this profile is worth monitoring more closely. Like his brother, Padres first base prospect Josh Naylor, he's stocky and already quite filled out. He's played some third base, but would likely be destined for first base if he can't stick behind the plate may not have the power to be very interesting over there.

Roberto Perez C Born: 12/23/88 Age: 30 Bats: R Throws: R Height: 5'11" Weight: 220 Origin: Round 33, 2008 Draft (#1011 overall)

YEAR	TEAM	LVL	AGE	PA	R	2B	3B	HR	RBI	BB	K	SB	CS	AVG/OBP/SLG	DRC+	VORP	BABIP	BRR	FRAA	WARP
2016	CLE	MLB	27	184	14	6	1	3	17	23	44	0	0	.183/.285/.294	74	0.2	.229	-0.2	C(61): 10.1	1.4
2017	CLE	MLB	28	248	22	12	0	8	38	26	71	0	1	.207/.291/.373	75	3.6	.266	-0.6	C(71): 19.8	2.4
2018	CLE	MLB	29	210	16	9	1	2	19	21	70	1	0	.168/.256/.263	53	-4.4	.257	-0.2	C(58): 11.1	0.9
2019	CLE	MLB	30	427	42	16	2	9	42	43	116	1	1	.215/.297/.344	73	4.6	.271	-0.4	C 26	3.2

Breakout: 3%   Improve: 31%   Collapse: 10%   Attrition: 19%   MLB: 88%   *Comparables: Landon Powell, Martin Maldonado, Jose Lobaton*

Over the past five seasons, the former 33rd-round pick has never appeared in even half of his team's games nor made 250 trips to the plate, but that may change in 2019 following the trade of Yan Gomes. Why has Perez never had a shot at starting? Well, he hits like a pitcher. But Perez sticks around because of his consistently solid pitch-framing and ability to stymie the running game. For a Cleveland team whose success has mostly been predicated on the success of its pitching staff, he's been more valuable than the raw numbers would indicate.

YEAR	TEAM	P. COUNT	FRM RUNS	BLK RUNS	THRW RUNS	TOT RUNS
2016	CLE	7261	7.7	1.3	1.2	10.8
2016	CLE	7261	7.7	1.3	1.2	10.8
2017	CLE	9658	17.6	2.2	0.4	19.7
2018	CLE	7861	10.9	1.6	-0.2	12.1
2019	CLE	16433	22.8	3.0	0.4	26.2

Jose Ramirez INF Born: 09/17/92 Age: 26 Bats: B Throws: R Height: 5'9" Weight: 165 Origin: International Free Agent, 2009

YEAR	TEAM	LVL	AGE	PA	R	2B	3B	HR	RBI	BB	K	SB	CS	AVG/OBP/SLG	DRC+	VORP	BABIP	BRR	FRAA	WARP
2016	CLE	MLB	23	618	84	46	3	11	76	44	62	22	7	.312/.363/.462	117	31.4	.333	4.7	3B(117): -2.6, LF(48): -0.8	3.6
2017	CLE	MLB	24	645	107	56	6	29	83	52	69	17	5	.318/.374/.583	132	57.1	.319	0.2	3B(88): 6.0, 2B(71): -0.1	5.6
2018	CLE	MLB	25	698	110	38	4	39	105	106	80	34	6	.270/.387/.552	155	70.7	.252	5.2	3B(137): -3.5, 2B(16): -0.7	7.4
2019	CLE	MLB	26	618	91	38	4	25	90	66	68	25	6	.302/.383/.529	147	53.5	.306	2.5	3B -4, 2B -1	5.2

Breakout: 1%   Improve: 62%   Collapse: 0%   Attrition: 3%   MLB: 99%   *Comparables: Dustin Pedroia, Wade Boggs, George Brett*

You know the old story: Do-everything utility player becomes a fan favorite thanks to his short stature, scrappy play and genuinely rosy demeanor. Those guys come around all the time, stick for a few years — maybe grabbing an everyday job for a year or two — and then spend the rest of their career bouncing around from org to org, the minors and the majors. You're left with your memories and little else. But what if that story turns out differently? What if your scrappy utility player morphs into a middle-of-the-order masher, a bonafide superstar and MVP candidate, terrorizing opposing pitching staffs with elite power to go along with one of the best eyes in the game? What if that power spike doesn't affect his strikeout rate at all? What if he becomes an elite base runner, too? What if he proves he can hold his own at the hot corner or second base? What if he does all that in his age-24 season, does even better in his age-25 season and is under team control for another five years after that? These questions are all rhetorical, of course, because things like that just never happen.

Carlos Santana 1B Born: 04/08/86 Age: 33 Bats: B Throws: R Height: 5'11" Weight: 210 Origin: International Free Agent, 2004

YEAR	TEAM	LVL	AGE	PA	R	2B	3B	HR	RBI	BB	K	SB	CS	AVG/OBP/SLG	DRC+	VORP	BABIP	BRR	FRAA	WARP
2016	CLE	MLB	30	688	89	31	3	34	87	99	99	5	2	.259/.366/.498	134	20.4	.258	-0.9	1B(64): 4.6	4.4
2017	CLE	MLB	31	667	90	37	3	23	79	88	94	5	1	.259/.363/.455	114	17.5	.274	-1.9	1B(140): 6.2, RF(7): 0.7	2.7
2018	PHI	MLB	32	679	82	28	2	24	86	110	93	2	1	.229/.352/.414	115	25.4	.231	0.2	1B(149): -0.7, 3B(19): 0.6	2.5
2019	CLE	MLB	33	682	83	32	2	22	85	94	97	5	2	.249/.359/.423	115	20.7	.266	-0.8	1B 2	2.4

Breakout: 2%   Improve: 30%   Collapse: 2%   Attrition: 10%   MLB: 90%   *Comparables: Prince Fielder, John Jaso, John Olerud*

It's weird to think of Santana as a risk. This is a guy who hit like a metronome for seven seasons, dependably getting on base in the mid-to-high-.300s and slugging in the mid-.400s while playing 150-plus games and saving a few runs on defense. As far as track records go, Santana's was about as low on the volatility scale as you can get, which certainly made him appealing as a free agent. But the Phillies raced ahead of the pack to sign Santana to a three-year deal, ostensibly and eventually displacing Rhys Hoskins to left field in the name of lowering the beta on their 2018 lineup's expected output. That ... didn't exactly play out according to those specs. Santana stayed healthy — 161 games! — but posted his second-worst OPS, while the butterfly effect of installing Hoskins in left field added extra weight to the yoke. Traded briefly to the Mariners and the back to the Indians, he can resume doing his usual thing without anyone worrying about what his presence means for the rest of the roster.

Bradley Zimmer CF Born: 11/27/92 Age: 26 Bats: L Throws: R Height: 6'5" Weight: 220 Origin: Round 1, 2014 Draft (#21 overall)

YEAR	TEAM	LVL	AGE	PA	R	2B	3B	HR	RBI	BB	K	SB	CS	AVG/OBP/SLG	DRC+	VORP	BABIP	BRR	FRAA	WARP
2016	AKR	AA	23	407	58	20	6	14	53	56	115	33	13	.253/.371/.471	114	30.6	.341	1.8	CF(76): -0.3, RF(9): 2.0	2.3
2016	COH	AAA	23	150	18	5	0	1	9	21	56	5	1	.242/.349/.305	69	1.4	.423	-0.7	CF(36): 1.2	0.0
2017	COH	AAA	24	144	22	11	2	5	14	14	43	9	3	.294/.371/.532	101	10.2	.405	-0.6	CF(26): 3.6, RF(8): 0.5	0.8
2017	CLE	MLB	24	332	41	15	2	8	39	26	99	18	1	.241/.307/.385	73	6.8	.328	1.6	CF(97): 9.5	1.2
2018	CLE	MLB	25	114	14	5	0	2	9	7	44	4	1	.226/.281/.330	53	-0.6	.367	1.4	CF(34): 5.4	0.4
2018	COH	AAA	25	28	1	0	0	1	1	1	11	1	0	.148/.179/.259	78	-2.4	.200	0.1	CF(5): -0.2	0.0
2019	*CLE*	*MLB*	*26*	*242*	*26*	*9*	*1*	*5*	*22*	*17*	*83*	*10*	*2*	*.201/.266/.319*	*58*	*-2.3*	*.292*	*0.6*	*CF 4*	*0.2*

Breakout: 7%   Improve: 48%   Collapse: 13%   Attrition: 24%   MLB: 84%   *Comparables: Drew Stubbs, Tyler Naquin, Curtis Granderson*

The electric start to Zimmer's major-league career sure does seem like a long time ago. After a 2017 season in which he conquered Triple-A and tore through the majors for the first two months after his promotion, the glaring hole in his hit tool showed up in a major way, first during the second half of the aforementioned rookie campaign and again during the first month of 2018. Handed the starting center fielder job out of spring training, what followed was a rib injury and demotion back to Triple-A, where he lasted only six more games before being shut down with what turned out to be an injured shoulder that required arthroscopic surgery. Zimmer's tool shed is still stocked with the parts that made him a top-101 prospect not all that long ago — speed, power and a solid approach at the plate — but the injury is a significant setback for someone who still needs to prove he can make enough contact to be relied on as an everyday player.

PITCHERS

Cody Allen RHP Born: 11/20/88 Age: 30 Bats: R Throws: R Height: 6'1" Weight: 210 Origin: Round 23, 2011 Draft (#698 overall)

YEAR	TEAM	LVL	AGE	W	L	SV	G	GS	IP	H	HR	BB/9	K/9	K	GB%	BABIP	WHIP	ERA	DRA	WARP	MPH	FB%	WHF	CSP
2016	CLE	MLB	27	3	5	32	67	0	68	41	8	3.6	11.5	87	48%	.232	1.00	2.51	2.90	1.6	96.5	63.3	14.4	45.9
2017	CLE	MLB	28	3	7	30	69	0	67[1]	57	9	2.8	12.3	92	34%	.304	1.16	2.94	2.64	1.9	95.5	55.5	15.5	41.8
2018	CLE	MLB	29	4	6	27	70	0	67	58	11	4.4	10.7	80	31%	.292	1.36	4.70	3.61	1.0	94.9	60.3	13.9	43.1
2019	*CLE*	*MLB*	*30*	*3*	*1*	*17*	*55*	*0*	*57[2]*	*52*	*9*	*4.0*	*10.5*	*68*	*38%*	*.295*	*1.34*	*4.44*	*4.74*	*0.2*	*94.7*	*59.2*	*14.5*	*43.2*

Breakout: 20%   Improve: 36%   Collapse: 38%   Attrition: 10%   MLB: 95%   *Comparables: Kyle Farnsworth, Brad Lidge, Armando Benitez*

Conventional wisdom says relievers are volatile year to year, and players in their primes tend to give their best performances in contract years. Allen is a bit of a contrarian, it seems. Since Barack Obama's first term, Allen had never had a season with an ERA over 3.00, and had only one year with a DRA over 3.00, pairing mid-90s heat with a vicious curveball to rack up nearly 100 strikeouts a year out of the bullpen. Unfortunately, Allen picked his contract year to let his run-prevention numbers spike. His velocity has now dropped five consecutive seasons, but there should still be enough for him to be effective. Although his peripherals also took a step backward last year, it wasn't as ugly as his ERA suggests. It's probably safe to guess his decline phase has arrived, but it may be a gentle slide from a very great height.

Trevor Bauer RHP Born: 01/17/91 Age: 28 Bats: R Throws: R Height: 6'1" Weight: 190 Origin: Round 1, 2011 Draft (#3 overall)

YEAR	TEAM	LVL	AGE	W	L	SV	G	GS	IP	H	HR	BB/9	K/9	K	GB%	BABIP	WHIP	ERA	DRA	WARP	MPH	FB%	WHF	CSP
2016	CLE	MLB	25	12	8	0	35	28	190	179	20	3.3	8.0	168	49%	.292	1.31	4.26	4.60	1.6	96.2	50.9	10.1	47.3
2017	CLE	MLB	26	17	9	0	32	31	176[1]	181	25	3.1	10.0	196	47%	.337	1.37	4.19	3.95	3.2	96.1	49.3	10.1	44
2018	CLE	MLB	27	12	6	1	28	27	175[1]	134	9	2.9	11.3	221	45%	.297	1.09	2.21	2.48	5.7	96.4	42.2	14.2	44.3
2019	*CLE*	*MLB*	*28*	*11*	*9*	*0*	*28*	*28*	*168*	*147*	*20*	*3.1*	*10.4*	*195*	*46%*	*.300*	*1.23*	*3.63*	*3.87*	*3.1*	*95.7*	*47.1*	*11.8*	*45.2*

Breakout: 20%   Improve: 56%   Collapse: 25%   Attrition: 6%   MLB: 95%   *Comparables: Gio Gonzalez, David Price, Justin Verlander*

Were it not for a fractured fibula that cost him six weeks toward the end of the season, it's entirely possible this comment could be about the defending Cy Young winner. Even with the injury, Bauer finished only five innings behind the ultimate winner and was downright dominant when he was on the mound. He proved his strikeout spike from a year earlier was no fluke and even improved upon it while simultaneously suppressing the home run numbers that have long been a nuisance. As someone who throughout the years was more likely to make headlines for what he said on Twitter or where he flew his drone, it was a welcome development for Cleveland. While those headlines didn't exactly disappear, they were accompanied by headlines talking about one of the best pitchers in baseball. After years of teasing with the potential of someone once drafted no. 3 overall, it appears Bauer has paired his consistently delete-your-account-worthy tweets with consistently dominant performances on the mound.

Shane Bieber RHP Born: 05/31/95 Age: 24 Bats: R Throws: R Height: 6'3" Weight: 195 Origin: Round 4, 2016 Draft (#122 overall)

YEAR	TEAM	LVL	AGE	W	L	SV	G	GS	IP	H	HR	BB/9	K/9	K	GB%	BABIP	WHIP	ERA	DRA	WARP	MPH	FB%	WHF	CSP
2016	MHV	A-	21	0	0	0	9	8	24	10	0	0.8	7.9	21	56%	.164	0.50	0.38	3.40	0.5				
2017	LKC	A	22	2	3	0	5	5	29	34	1	0.3	9.6	31	45%	.375	1.21	3.10	3.83	0.5				
2017	LYN	A+	22	6	1	0	14	14	90	95	5	0.4	8.2	82	50%	.340	1.10	3.10	3.30	2.1				
2017	AKR	AA	22	2	1	0	9	9	54[1]	56	2	0.8	8.1	49	50%	.331	1.12	2.32	3.04	1.4				
2018	AKR	AA	23	3	0	0	5	5	31	26	1	0.3	8.7	30	48%	.278	0.87	1.16	2.86	0.9				
2018	COH	AAA	23	3	1	0	8	8	48[2]	30	3	1.1	8.7	47	56%	.225	0.74	1.66	3.26	1.3				
2018	CLE	MLB	23	11	5	0	20	19	114[2]	130	13	1.8	9.3	118	46%	.356	1.33	4.55	3.32	2.6	94.7	57.4	12.3	51.2
2019	*CLE*	*MLB*	*24*	*6*	*6*	*0*	*19*	*19*	*100[2]*	*103*	*12*	*2.5*	*8.6*	*96*	*45%*	*.314*	*1.30*	*3.84*	*4.08*	*1.6*	*94.5*	*59.1*	*12.6*	*52.8*

Breakout: 18%   Improve: 53%   Collapse: 12%   Attrition: 17%   MLB: 83%   *Comparables: Luke Weaver, Mike Minor, Drew Smyly*

Like a mini Josh Tomlin, Bieber sprinted (definitely didn't walk) to the majors after barely 100 innings above High-A because of an adamant refusal to issue any free passes. In an abbreviated debut, he continued right along that path. The plus-plus command gives him a pretty high floor of capable innings eater, but the lack of advanced stuff or any true out-pitch is what keeps him from topping out as anything more than that. Bieber suddenly missing bats at an elite level would be almost as big of a surprise as making it through an entire comment about Bieber without making a bad reference to the musician with an identical surname.

Carlos Carrasco RHP Born: 03/21/87 Age: 32 Bats: R Throws: R Height: 6'3" Weight: 212 Origin: International Free Agent, 2003

YEAR	TEAM	LVL	AGE	W	L	SV	G	GS	IP	H	HR	BB/9	K/9	K	GB%	BABIP	WHIP	ERA	DRA	WARP	MPH	FB%	WHF	CSP
2016	CLE	MLB	29	11	8	0	25	25	146¹	134	21	2.1	9.2	150	50%	.289	1.15	3.32	3.01	3.9	96.8	53.3	13.4	47.1
2017	CLE	MLB	30	18	6	0	32	32	200	173	21	2.1	10.2	226	47%	.307	1.10	3.29	2.79	6.2	96.3	48.9	14.5	47.5
2018	CLE	MLB	31	17	10	0	32	30	192	173	21	2.0	10.8	231	48%	.315	1.12	3.38	2.91	5.3	95.6	44.9	16.5	45.9
2019	CLE	MLB	32	11	9	0	29	29	174	155	21	2.5	10.1	196	47%	.301	1.17	3.46	3.69	3.6	95.1	47.6	15	46.3

Breakout: 15%   Improve: 35%   Collapse: 30%   Attrition: 6%   MLB: 93%   *Comparables: Erik Bedard, Josh Beckett, A.J. Burnett*

Years ago, BP identified Carrasco as an elite prospect, with ace potential. Then he was bad for a long time and perhaps was lumped in with the multitude of busts who arrived in Cleveland with him as part of a teardown (think Matt LaPorta). Next, he got attention in a bad way for trying to bean some batters in the head. It was a long, weird, meandering journey, but then he just got right back on his path to being an elite pitcher, and for five seasons now he's been one of the best starters in the majors. He perhaps hasn't gotten the fanfare he deserves, as he's jockeyed with Trevor Bauer for the role of Kluber's Second Fiddle while Cleveland sleepwalked their way to multiple division titles, but a whole lot of teams would be happy to have him as their no. 1. Instead, Carrasco signed a below-market offseason extension that will keep him right where he is.

Aaron Civale RHP Born: 06/12/95 Age: 24 Bats: R Throws: R Height: 6'2" Weight: 215 Origin: Round 3, 2016 Draft (#92 overall)

YEAR	TEAM	LVL	AGE	W	L	SV	G	GS	IP	H	HR	BB/9	K/9	K	GB%	BABIP	WHIP	ERA	DRA	WARP	MPH	FB%	WHF	CSP
2016	MHV	A-	21	0	2	0	13	13	37²	23	0	1.9	6.7	28	62%	.225	0.82	1.67	3.16	0.9				
2017	LKC	A	22	2	4	0	10	10	57	64	2	0.8	8.4	53	55%	.358	1.21	4.58	3.49	1.2				
2017	LYN	A+	22	11	2	0	17	17	107²	96	11	0.8	7.4	88	49%	.276	0.98	2.59	3.55	2.2				
2018	AKR	AA	23	5	7	0	21	21	106¹	115	12	1.8	6.6	78	49%	.308	1.28	3.89	3.71	2.0				
2019	CLE	MLB	24	6	7	0	19	19	95	108	14	2.7	6.4	67	46%	.309	1.45	4.81	5.13	0.4				

Breakout: 10%   Improve: 19%   Collapse: 16%   Attrition: 35%   MLB: 42%   *Comparables: Ryan Merritt, Richard Bleier, Chad Jenkins*

With Shane Bieber reaching the majors and Josh Tomlin on his way out, Cleveland needed a new pitcher to join the Walk Resistance. Enter Civale. The former third-round pick got his first taste of the high minors in 2018 and saw his walk rate increase a bit, but not enough to make the other two furrow their brows in disapproval. Unfortunately for Civale, he's nearly as averse to strikeouts as he is to walks, and until he starts missing more bats it's unclear if he has a future in a big-league rotation.

Mike Clevinger RHP Born: 12/21/90 Age: 28 Bats: R Throws: R Height: 6'4" Weight: 210 Origin: Round 4, 2011 Draft (#135 overall)

YEAR	TEAM	LVL	AGE	W	L	SV	G	GS	IP	H	HR	BB/9	K/9	K	GB%	BABIP	WHIP	ERA	DRA	WARP	MPH	FB%	WHF	CSP
2016	COH	AAA	25	11	1	0	17	17	93	78	8	3.4	9.4	97	40%	.293	1.22	3.00	3.12	2.4				
2016	CLE	MLB	25	3	3	0	17	10	53	50	8	4.9	8.5	50	40%	.288	1.49	5.26	6.15	-0.5	96.1	58.4	10.2	44.9
2017	COH	AAA	26	3	2	0	7	7	34	28	3	3.7	10.1	38	40%	.298	1.24	2.65	3.80	0.7				
2017	CLE	MLB	26	12	6	0	27	21	121²	92	13	4.4	10.1	137	40%	.274	1.25	3.11	3.61	2.6	94.4	53.5	13.1	42.7
2018	CLE	MLB	27	13	8	0	32	32	200	164	21	3.0	9.3	207	41%	.280	1.15	3.02	3.52	4.1	95.9	52.9	12.8	48.8
2019	CLE	MLB	28	10	9	0	26	26	156	137	20	3.6	9.8	170	40%	.289	1.29	4.04	4.31	2.1	94.9	54	12.7	46.1

Breakout: 11%   Improve: 47%   Collapse: 24%   Attrition: 10%   MLB: 92%   *Comparables: Zack Godley, Jacob deGrom, Dan Straily*

Clevinger didn't so much break out in 2018 as he continued his breakout of 2017. His pitch mix was basically identical and the results were basically identical. He simply did it for 200 innings instead of 120. The most significant addition was that he added an extra 1.5 miles per hour on his fastball, although oddly his strikeout and walk rates both went down slightly with his newfound velocity. He's a late bloomer like Corey Kluber, but his peripherals show he's more of a no. 2/3 starter than an emergent ace. That said, it's an amazing outcome for a fourth-round pick who was once traded for 20-something innings of Vinnie Pestano.

Brad Hand LHP Born: 03/20/90 Age: 29 Bats: L Throws: L Height: 6'3" Weight: 228 Origin: Round 2, 2008 Draft (#52 overall)

YEAR	TEAM	LVL	AGE	W	L	SV	G	GS	IP	H	HR	BB/9	K/9	K	GB%	BABIP	WHIP	ERA	DRA	WARP	MPH	FB%	WHF	CSP
2016	SDN	MLB	26	4	4	1	82	0	89¹	63	8	3.6	11.2	111	47%	.264	1.11	2.92	3.58	1.4	95.6	61.1	12.9	46
2017	SDN	MLB	27	3	4	21	72	0	79¹	54	9	2.3	11.8	104	46%	.263	0.93	2.16	3.03	1.9	95.0	51.1	14.1	46.1
2018	SDN	MLB	28	2	4	24	41	0	44¹	33	5	3.0	13.2	65	48%	.298	1.08	3.05	3.15	0.9	95.9	44.2	13.6	50
2018	CLE	MLB	28	0	1	8	28	0	27²	19	3	4.2	13.3	41	44%	.286	1.16	2.28	3.47	0.5	95.6	48.1	13.2	52.7
2019	CLE	MLB	29	3	1	35	50	0	53¹	41	6	3.5	12.0	71	45%	.293	1.17	3.48	3.71	0.9	94.8	51.9	13.5	48.1

Breakout: 23%   Improve: 48%   Collapse: 28%   Attrition: 11%   MLB: 99%   *Comparables: Justin Grimm, Mark Davis, Drew Storen*

Once a replacement-level starter, Hand has now posted three straight years with 100-plus strikeouts, 70-plus innings and an ERA below 3.00 out of the bullpen. And, for a third year in a row, Hand significantly increased his slider usage, with the nasty offering accounting for more than half of the pitches he threw. In keeping with league trends, he's increasingly mothballed his sinker and basically doesn't throw his changeup at all anymore. In the land of the bullpenning, the one pitch Hand is king. Cleveland made a big bet on Hand being a late-inning stud, sending top catching prospect Francisco Mejia to San Diego for him at midseason.

Ethan Hankins RHP Born: 05/23/00   Age: 19   Bats: R   Throws: R   Height: 6'6"   Weight: 200   Origin: Round 1C, 2018 Draft (#35 overall)

YEAR	TEAM	LVL	AGE	W	L	SV	G	GS	IP	H	HR	BB/9	K/9	K	GB%	BABIP	WHIP	ERA	DRA	WARP	MPH	FB%	WHF	CSP
2019	CLE	MLB	19	1	3	0	7	7	30²	36	8	5.5	8.2	28	40%	.313	1.78	7.12	7.63	-0.8				

Comparables: Bryse Wilson, Jaime Barria, Jamie Callahan

A shoulder injury in his draft year dropped Hankins from a potential top pick to the end of the first round, where Cleveland scooped him up for slightly more than slot to spurn a commitment to Vanderbilt. His fastball can reach the high 90s and has good movement, and he easily blew away hitters with it at the low levels. Believe it or not, as a prep pitcher, he's a volatile prospect with overwhelming upside but high bust potential, but if he lives up to what teams saw out of him before and after his injury, Cleveland will be happy to make the Progressive Field pitcher's mound Hankins' Hill.

Chih-Wei Hu RHP Born: 11/04/93   Age: 25   Bats: R   Throws: R   Height: 6'0"   Weight: 220   Origin: International Free Agent, 2012

YEAR	TEAM	LVL	AGE	W	L	SV	G	GS	IP	H	HR	BB/9	K/9	K	GB%	BABIP	WHIP	ERA	DRA	WARP	MPH	FB%	WHF	CSP
2016	MNT	AA	22	7	8	0	24	24	142²	128	7	2.3	6.8	107	44%	.283	1.15	2.59	3.31	3.1				
2017	DUR	AAA	23	4	1	2	31	4	61²	59	9	1.8	8.3	57	46%	.292	1.15	3.06	3.55	1.3				
2017	TBA	MLB	23	1	1	0	6	0	10	5	2	3.6	8.1	9	37%	.120	0.90	2.70	5.64	-0.1	95.2	59.9	14.4	39
2018	DUR	AAA	24	5	7	0	24	19	102¹	113	14	2.5	8.1	92	38%	.321	1.38	4.66	4.20	1.5				
2018	TBA	MLB	24	0	0	0	5	0	13	7	2	2.1	8.3	12	23%	.152	0.77	4.15	4.27	0.1	94.7	47.7	10.8	50.6
2019	CLE	MLB	25	1	0	0	18	0	19¹	19	3	2.9	8.2	18	40%	.297	1.34	4.56	4.86	0.1	94.6	53.9	12.5	46.5

Breakout: 7%   Improve: 19%   Collapse: 17%   Attrition: 33%   MLB: 49%   *Comparables: Trevor Williams, Rob Zastryzny, Eric Jokisch*

Hu joined his third organization since turning pro at age 18 out of Taiwan, going from Minnesota to Tampa Bay and now to Cleveland following a 40-man-clearing offseason trade. Hu is a pitcher more than a thrower, with a low-90s fastball, a pair of breaking balls and a very good palmball. The latter has the best chance to miss bats at the highest level. He has above-average navigation, although his pitches can go off course once in the zone and his lack of height can leave the ball on a tee if not properly executed. He's worked mostly as a starter, although all 11 of his big-league appearances have come in relief.

Corey Kluber RHP Born: 04/10/86   Age: 33   Bats: R   Throws: R   Height: 6'4"   Weight: 215   Origin: Round 4, 2007 Draft (#134 overall)

YEAR	TEAM	LVL	AGE	W	L	SV	G	GS	IP	H	HR	BB/9	K/9	K	GB%	BABIP	WHIP	ERA	DRA	WARP	MPH	FB%	WHF	CSP
2016	CLE	MLB	30	18	9	0	32	32	215	170	22	2.4	9.5	227	46%	.271	1.06	3.14	3.33	5.0	94.8	51.2	13.7	46.1
2017	CLE	MLB	31	18	4	0	29	29	203²	141	21	1.6	11.7	265	46%	.267	0.87	2.25	2.28	7.5	94.0	42.4	16.4	47.2
2018	CLE	MLB	32	20	7	0	33	33	215	179	25	1.4	9.3	222	46%	.276	0.99	2.89	2.84	6.1	93.4	41.6	13	46.4
2019	CLE	MLB	33	13	9	0	29	29	194¹	171	24	2.3	9.5	204	45%	.290	1.14	3.56	3.79	3.8	92.9	43.8	14.1	46

Breakout: 11%   Improve: 39%   Collapse: 22%   Attrition: 14%   MLB: 96%   *Comparables: Pedro Martinez, Tom Seaver, Adam Wainwright*

Another year, another 200-plus innings with 220-plus strikeouts, which marks a fifth straight such season since he completed his full transformation into Klubot. For the second year in a row, he struggled at one point with a minor injury and then went right back to eviscerating hitters with his five-pitch mix. He turns 33 in April, he just had his second miserable postseason outing in a row and he lost a tiny shade off his four-seam fastball. This is obviously nitpicking, as Kluber is one of the best in the game and is an excellent bet to remain so. He did throw his four-seamer quite a bit less in favor of more cutters and sinkers, which might mean something, or it might mean Kluber is a smug jerk with way too many excellent pitches and he can use them as much or as little as he likes.

Triston McKenzie RHP Born: 08/02/97   Age: 21   Bats: R   Throws: R   Height: 6'5"   Weight: 165   Origin: Round 1, 2015 Draft (#42 overall)

YEAR	TEAM	LVL	AGE	W	L	SV	G	GS	IP	H	HR	BB/9	K/9	K	GB%	BABIP	WHIP	ERA	DRA	WARP	MPH	FB%	WHF	CSP
2016	MHV	A-	18	4	3	0	9	9	49¹	31	2	2.9	10.0	55	37%	.248	0.95	0.55	2.92	1.3				
2016	LKC	A	18	2	2	0	6	6	34	27	2	1.6	13.0	49	40%	.333	0.97	3.18	2.33	1.1				
2017	LYN	A+	19	12	6	0	25	25	143	105	14	2.8	11.7	186	43%	.283	1.05	3.46	2.60	4.5				
2018	AKR	AA	20	7	4	0	16	16	90²	63	8	2.8	8.6	87	34%	.234	1.00	2.68	4.03	1.4				
2019	CLE	MLB	21	5	5	0	15	15	79²	78	14	3.4	8.8	78	35%	.293	1.36	4.80	5.14	0.3				

Breakout: 6%   Improve: 17%   Collapse: 6%   Attrition: 17%   MLB: 29%   *Comparables: Chris Tillman, Jacob Turner, Chad Billingsley*

Height and weight listings are not permanent, but even if McKenzie isn't quite 6-foot-5 or weighs a few more pounds than 165, it's still safe to characterize him as "lanky." And 2018 gave doubters and believers alike plenty of ammunition. His velocity hasn't ticked up yet, as he continues to sit 88-92 with his fastball, he missed two months with the ever-ominous "forearm soreness" and his strikeout rate dropped significantly in his first look at Double-A. Detractors fear these issues are symptoms of his lack of physicality on the mound, questioning his durability and whether he'll make good on his projectability. Even so, McKenzie may have enough to be a good starting pitcher without a lot more. He uses his height to generate good plane on his pitches with above-average command, and has a genuine out-pitch in his high-70s curve. Even while fighting through injuries, at age 20, he kept his walks down, posted a sub-3.00 ERA against his highest competition yet and, hey, a guy with this build just struck out the side to win the World Series. McKenzie has held serve, failed to dispel the primary doubts about him and yet is now knocking on the door to the majors.

Tyler Olson LHP Born: 10/02/89   Age: 29   Bats: R   Throws: L   Height: 6'3"   Weight: 195   Origin: Round 7, 2013 Draft (#207 overall)

YEAR	TEAM	LVL	AGE	W	L	SV	G	GS	IP	H	HR	BB/9	K/9	K	GB%	BABIP	WHIP	ERA	DRA	WARP	MPH	FB%	WHF	CSP
2016	NYA	MLB	26	0	0	0	1	0	2²	3	0	6.8	0.0	0	27%	.273	1.88	6.75	7.53	-0.1	90.1	70.2	12.8	46.6
2016	SWB	AAA	26	1	2	0	11	3	27¹	31	2	2.6	6.9	21	53%	.341	1.43	5.27	4.81	0.1				
2016	OMA	AAA	26	0	0	0	5	0	6¹	10	1	2.8	2.8	2	48%	.346	1.89	2.84	4.44	0.0				
2016	COH	AAA	26	1	0	0	9	0	10²	12	1	5.1	8.4	10	29%	.333	1.69	5.91	3.68	0.2				
2017	COH	AAA	27	2	0	2	34	0	42	28	7	2.6	11.6	54	43%	.241	0.95	3.21	2.81	1.1				
2017	CLE	MLB	27	1	0	1	30	0	20	13	0	2.7	8.1	18	54%	.250	0.95	0.00	3.90	0.3	90.3	39.8	10.7	49.2
2018	COH	AAA	28	2	1	1	17	0	12¹	8	0	2.2	13.1	18	42%	.308	0.89	3.65	2.61	0.4				
2018	CLE	MLB	28	2	1	0	43	0	27¹	26	4	4.0	13.2	40	42%	.355	1.39	4.94	2.74	0.7	90.2	47.6	15.3	45.5
2019	*CLE*	*MLB*	*29*	*3*	*1*	*3*	*50*	*0*	*53¹*	*48*	*8*	*4.0*	*10.7*	*63*	*43%*	*.308*	*1.35*	*4.15*	*4.44*	*0.4*	*89.6*	*45.9*	*13.7*	*47*

Breakout: 15%   Improve: 23%   Collapse: 27%   Attrition: 24%   MLB: 61%   *Comparables: Darin Downs, Simon Castro, Rob Scahill*

Olson's composite numbers in 2018 numbers — his longest major-league look so far — are mediocre if not horrid. At a glance, he strikes out plenty of batters while also giving up walks and home runs at an unacceptable rate. A quick look at his splits, however, show Olson did not really change, he was just misused. As a pure LOOGY, he did his job pretty well, limiting lefties to a .182/.250/.345 line. But for some reason he faced as many right-handed batters (58) as he did lefties (60), and they hit like prime Albert Belle against him. Somewhere Randy Williams is weeping.

Dan Otero RHP Born: 02/19/85   Age: 34   Bats: R   Throws: R   Height: 6'3"   Weight: 205   Origin: Round 21, 2007 Draft (#644 overall)

YEAR	TEAM	LVL	AGE	W	L	SV	G	GS	IP	H	HR	BB/9	K/9	K	GB%	BABIP	WHIP	ERA	DRA	WARP	MPH	FB%	WHF	CSP
2016	CLE	MLB	31	5	1	1	62	0	70²	54	2	1.3	7.3	57	64%	.260	0.91	1.53	3.86	0.9	92.9	78.2	8.2	49.5
2017	CLE	MLB	32	3	0	0	52	0	60	63	6	1.4	5.7	38	65%	.302	1.20	2.85	4.46	0.5	91.6	80.3	8.2	51.4
2018	CLE	MLB	33	2	1	1	61	0	58²	69	12	0.8	6.6	43	61%	.310	1.26	5.22	4.26	0.4	91.5	79.7	9.1	49.2
2019	*CLE*	*MLB*	*34*	*2*	*1*	*0*	*46*	*0*	*48¹*	*49*	*5*	*2.8*	*7.0*	*38*	*58%*	*.299*	*1.32*	*4.11*	*4.37*	*0.4*	*90.8*	*78.3*	*8.5*	*49.2*

Breakout: 19%   Improve: 33%   Collapse: 30%   Attrition: 9%   MLB: 84%   *Comparables: Paul Quantrill, Doug Jones, Mark Eichhorn*

Otero has been many things: an old rookie, a waiver wire transient, a multi-team journeyman. And, for his first two seasons in Cleveland, a below-the-radar bullpen asset on the strength of a ground-ball rate above 60 percent. His third year in Cleveland was much rougher, as his strand rate dropped, a few more balls got hit in the air and uncharacteristically he allowed a boatload of home runs. His surface statistics turned out rather ugly as a result. DRA says it wasn't much to worry about, though, as his ground-ball rate was still excellent and he walked even fewer batters than before. However, as a high-contact sinker-baller, he's always going to be more prone to the whims of fortune than the flamethrowers of the world.

Oliver Perez LHP Born: 08/15/81   Age: 37   Bats: L   Throws: L   Height: 6'3"   Weight: 225   Origin: International Free Agent, 1999

YEAR	TEAM	LVL	AGE	W	L	SV	G	GS	IP	H	HR	BB/9	K/9	K	GB%	BABIP	WHIP	ERA	DRA	WARP	MPH	FB%	WHF	CSP
2016	WAS	MLB	34	2	3	0	64	0	40	38	4	4.5	10.4	46	43%	.324	1.45	4.95	4.68	0.1	94.3	57.3	9.9	50.3
2017	WAS	MLB	35	0	0	1	50	0	33	32	4	3.3	10.6	39	32%	.333	1.33	4.64	6.18	-0.4	94.6	57.3	11	53.6
2018	SWB	AAA	36	1	0	0	16	0	14	17	1	1.9	9.6	15	33%	.421	1.43	2.57	3.09	0.3				
2018	CLE	MLB	36	1	1	0	51	0	32¹	17	1	1.9	12.0	43	46%	.239	0.74	1.39	2.61	0.9	93.9	50.9	16	52.2
2019	*CLE*	*MLB*	*37*	*2*	*1*	*0*	*33*	*0*	*34¹*	*32*	*5*	*4.0*	*10.7*	*41*	*41%*	*.308*	*1.37*	*4.15*	*4.43*	*0.2*	*92.8*	*53.8*	*12.1*	*50.9*

Breakout: 24%   Improve: 42%   Collapse: 25%   Attrition: 6%   MLB: 86%   *Comparables: Scott Eyre, Trever Miller, Kyle Farnsworth*

Perez has been around for so long that the list of players he was in transactions with includes Roberto Hernandez. Not the Roberto Hernandez who was better known as Fausto Carmona, but the guy who closed for the White Sox in the mid-90s. It also includes Xavier Nady (remember Xavier Nady?!), Brian Giles and Jason Bay. The list of players who appeared in Perez's first career game includes Ruben Sierra, Ray Lankford, Ron Gant and a Jamie Moyer, who hadn't even turned 40 yet. Perez's existence as a competent part of a major-league bullpen in 2018 harkens memories of the famous quote from the cinematic masterpiece, *The Sandlot*: "Heroes get remembered, but lefties never die."

Neil Ramirez RHP   Born: 05/25/89   Age: 30   Bats: R   Throws: R   Height: 6'4"   Weight: 215   Origin: Round 1, 2007 Draft (#44 overall)

YEAR	TEAM	LVL	AGE	W	L	SV	G	GS	IP	H	HR	BB/9	K/9	K	GB%	BABIP	WHIP	ERA	DRA	WARP	MPH	FB%	WHF	CSP
2016	CHN	MLB	27	0	0	0	8	0	7²	5	1	9.4	11.7	10	29%	.250	1.70	4.70	4.09	0.1	94.3	50.7	13.2	44
2016	MIL	MLB	27	0	0	0	2	0	1²	2	2	0.0	16.2	3	25%	.000	1.20	10.80	1.49	0.1	94.1	76	24	42.1
2016	MIN	MLB	27	0	0	0	8	0	14²	15	5	6.1	6.8	11	25%	.256	1.70	6.14	5.76	-0.1	94.5	61.2	11.6	47.9
2016	ROC	AAA	27	0	0	0	16	0	20¹	14	2	3.1	12.0	27	26%	.267	1.03	3.10	3.08	0.4				
2017	SFN	MLB	28	0	0	0	9	0	10¹	15	2	3.5	15.7	18	27%	.464	1.84	8.71	3.73	0.2	94.6	55.9	12.6	42.3
2017	NYN	MLB	28	0	1	0	20	0	21	20	4	7.3	11.1	26	33%	.302	1.76	6.43	3.74	0.3	94.9	44.5	13.2	45
2017	SYR	AAA	28	2	1	1	14	0	14²	23	3	4.9	12.3	20	33%	.465	2.11	6.14	3.55	0.3				
2018	COH	AAA	29	2	1	3	14	0	18²	16	4	1.4	15.4	32	13%	.353	1.02	3.38	2.38	0.6				
2018	CLE	MLB	29	0	3	0	47	0	41²	36	9	3.9	11.0	51	36%	.273	1.30	4.54	3.64	0.6	96.8	57.1	16.3	47.5
2019	CLE	MLB	30	2	1	0	46	0	48¹	45	9	4.4	11.1	60	34%	.302	1.41	4.70	5.03	0.0	95.0	54.4	14.5	45.9

Breakout: 18%   Improve: 37%   Collapse: 27%   Attrition: 20%   MLB: 87%   *Comparables: J.J. Hoover, Mike Dunn, Boone Logan*

Did there really exist any such goal for this wandering mankind? That was a question to which he would have liked an answer before it was too late. Moses had not been allowed to enter the land of promise either. But he had been allowed to see it, from the top of the mountain, spread at his feet. Thus, it was easy to die, with the visible certainty of one's goal before one's eyes. He, Neil Andrew Ramirez, had not been taken to the top of a mountain; and wherever his eye looked, he saw nothing but waivers and the darkness of Triple-A. A dull blow struck the back of his slider. He had long expected it and yet it took him unawares. He felt, wondering, his knees give way and his body whirl round in a half-turn. How theatrical, he thought as he spun, and yet I feel nothing. He stood, gazing up on the mound, with his cheek on the cool glove leather. It got dark, the sea carried him rocking on its nocturnal surface. Walks passed through him, like streaks of mist over the water. Outside, someone was knocking on the clubhouse door, he dreamed that they were coming to release him; but on what team was he? He made an effort to slip his arm into his ice-compress sleeve. But whose color-print logo was hanging over his locker and looking at him? Was it the GM or was it the reporter — with the sympathetic smile or he with the same questions? A shapeless figure bent over him, he smelt the fresh leather of the iPhone case recording in front of him; but what insignia did his opponent wear on the sleeves and shoulder straps of his uniform? And in whose name did it raise the dark bat barrel? A second, smashing blow hit his belt-high four-seam. Then all became quiet. There was the sea again with its sounds. A wave slowly lifted him up. It came from afar and traveled sedately on, a shrug of eternity.

Danny Salazar RHP   Born: 01/11/90   Age: 29   Bats: R   Throws: R   Height: 6'0"   Weight: 195   Origin: International Free Agent, 2006

YEAR	TEAM	LVL	AGE	W	L	SV	G	GS	IP	H	HR	BB/9	K/9	K	GB%	BABIP	WHIP	ERA	DRA	WARP	MPH	FB%	WHF	CSP
2016	CLE	MLB	26	11	6	0	25	25	137¹	121	16	4.1	10.6	161	49%	.307	1.34	3.87	3.79	2.5	97.5	68.3	12	46.1
2017	CLE	MLB	27	5	6	0	23	19	103	94	14	3.8	12.7	145	39%	.343	1.34	4.28	3.54	2.3	97.2	59.7	17.3	45.8
2019	CLE	MLB	29	7	5	0	38	15	109²	98	15	4.0	11.0	134	44%	.308	1.34	3.97	4.23	1.2	96.7	64	14.7	45.9

Breakout: 14%   Improve: 35%   Collapse: 25%   Attrition: 5%   MLB: 87%   *Comparables: Lance Lynn, Max Scherzer, Tim Lincecum*

It wasn't all that long ago that Salazar was The Next Big Thing as a young right-hander with elite swing-and-miss stuff who seemed close to putting it all together. Bouts of wildness and an inability to stay healthy have kept him from living up to that potential, and he'd been passed in Cleveland's rotation pecking order by Carlos Carrasco and Trevor Bauer even before arthroscopic right shoulder surgery cost him the entirety of 2018. History is littered with guys robbed of what could've been brilliant careers by injuries, and Salazar fits firmly in that category until proven otherwise.

Josh Tomlin RHP   Born: 10/19/84   Age: 34   Bats: R   Throws: R   Height: 6'1"   Weight: 190   Origin: Round 19, 2006 Draft (#581 overall)

YEAR	TEAM	LVL	AGE	W	L	SV	G	GS	IP	H	HR	BB/9	K/9	K	GB%	BABIP	WHIP	ERA	DRA	WARP	MPH	FB%	WHF	CSP
2016	CLE	MLB	31	13	9	0	30	29	174	187	36	1.0	6.1	118	44%	.276	1.19	4.40	4.57	1.6	89.9	77.8	8.1	47.4
2017	CLE	MLB	32	10	9	0	26	26	141	166	23	0.9	7.0	109	42%	.329	1.28	4.98	4.44	1.8	89.1	71.8	9.6	49.1
2018	CLE	MLB	33	2	5	0	32	9	70¹	92	25	1.5	5.9	46	32%	.286	1.48	6.14	6.87	-1.4	89.6	72.7	9.4	49.9
2019	CLE	MLB	34	5	6	0	15	15	83¹	92	16	2.3	6.6	61	39%	.295	1.36	5.10	5.45	0.0	88.4	73.1	8.9	48.3

Breakout: 18%   Improve: 39%   Collapse: 15%   Attrition: 7%   MLB: 79%   *Comparables: Robin Roberts, Dan Haren, Fergie Jenkins*

Tomlin has always avoided walks to an almost hilarious degree. The approach has, of course, left him more susceptible to hard contact, as well as the more-than-occasional dinger, as evidenced by the fact that he's allowed more home runs than walks in every season since 2014. The problem in 2018 was that while his approach remained, he stopped missing bats almost entirely. He made seven starts from the beginning of the season through mid-May, when he was jettisoned from the rotation after allowing almost as many home runs (15) as he had strikeouts (18) in just 31 innings. He spent the rest of the year as a mop-up guy.

LINEOUTS

Hitters

HITTER	POS	TEAM	LVL	AGE	PA	R	2B	3B	HR	RBI	BB	K	SB	CS	AVG/OBP/SLG	DRC+	VORP	BABIP	BRR	FRAA	WARP
Brandon Barnes	OF	COH	AAA	32	566	75	39	2	14	81	47	152	19	5	.273/.347/.444	116	31.0	.362	3.5	CF(55): 0.9, LF(40): 2.2	3.8
	OF	CLE	MLB	32	21	2	0	0	1	2	2	5	0	0	.263/.333/.421	98	0.1	.308	-0.2	RF(16): 0.6, LF(2): -0.1	0.0
Jodd Carter	OF	LYN	A+	21	423	54	20	3	10	52	47	96	11	6	.244/.334/.397	110	16.5	.302	1.1	RF(46): 5.6, CF(42): -6.7	1.8
	OF	AKR	AA	21	75	6	0	1	1	4	3	12	0	0	.290/.338/.362	91	1.2	.339	-0.3	RF(15): -1.3, LF(3): -0.5	-0.2
Gavin Collins	C	LYN	A+	22	252	28	20	1	5	36	14	46	1	2	.232/.293/.395	94	7.7	.270	1.3	C(30): 0.0, 3B(26): 0.2	0.9
Raynel Delgado	SS	CLT	Rk	18	204	34	10	0	1	21	30	44	10	2	.306/.409/.382	119	14.1	.406	-1.0	SS(18): -0.2, 2B(13): 0.6	1.1
Mike Freeman	SS	IOW	AAA	30	331	51	15	2	6	38	25	66	6	6	.274/.330/.396	92	21.2	.332	1.8	SS(55): 2.7, 2B(16): -0.1	1.6
	SS	CHN	MLB	30	1	0	0	0	0	0	0	0	0	0		72	0.0	--	0.0	2B(1): 0.0	0.0
Eric Haase	C	COH	AAA	25	477	54	24	3	20	71	31	143	3	1	.236/.288/.443	100	17.5	.296	-0.7	C(90): -6.3	1.2
	C	CLE	MLB	25	17	0	0	0	0	1	0	6	0	0	.125/.176/.125	72	-2.1	.200	0.0	C(7): 0.2	0.0
Logan Ice	C	LYN	A+	23	166	15	5	1	1	21	18	46	0	0	.194/.289/.264	89	-0.1	.273	-0.6	C(38): -0.6	0.4
	C	AKR	AA	23	55	8	3	2	0	8	5	18	0	0	.250/.315/.396	72	5.4	.387	0.0	C(17): -1.3	-0.1
Max Moroff	SS	PIT	MLB	25	67	7	1	0	3	9	7	24	0	0	.186/.284/.356	79	0.3	.250	0.1	2B(17): -1.0, SS(6): -0.2	0.0
	SS	IND	AAA	25	297	38	14	2	8	38	43	68	5	0	.223/.334/.393	106	11.2	.270	-1.5	SS(29): -2.0, 3B(19): 0.7	1.0
Mike Papi	OF	COH	AAA	25	296	38	17	1	7	26	47	78	1	1	.247/.373/.412	105	14.6	.335	2.6	RF(65): 2.7, 1B(6): -0.1	1.3
Brayan Rocchio	INF	DIN	Rk	17	111	19	2	3	1	12	5	14	8	5	.323/.391/.434	134	9.7	.369	-1.0	SS(15): -0.2, 2B(8): 0.6	0.8
	INF	CLT	Rk	17	158	21	10	1	1	17	10	17	14	8	.343/.389/.448	139	15.0	.378	1.2	SS(26): 5.2, 3B(8): -1.1	1.8
Nellie Rodriguez	1B	COH	AAA	24	268	24	11	0	10	39	23	95	0	0	.204/.277/.375	88	-4.3	.285	0.9	1B(73): -0.1	0.0
	1B	AKR	AA	24	126	15	7	1	5	23	16	47	0	0	.283/.373/.509	92	8.5	.439	-1.1	1B(31): -2.9	-0.4
Adam Rosales	INF	COH	AAA	35	428	52	22	1	18	61	38	94	3	3	.239/.313/.445	120	11.1	.267	-2.1	2B(36): -0.8, 1B(32): 1.8	2.2
	INF	CLE	MLB	35	21	4	1	0	1	2	1	5	0	0	.211/.250/.421	89	0.0	.231	0.0	1B(5): 0.0, 2B(4): 0.2	0.1
Eric Stamets	INF	COH	AAA	26	269	22	10	2	5	16	18	63	5	2	.202/.272/.324	78	-1.6	.253	1.2	2B(40): 6.6, SS(38): 0.8	1.1

In 2013, **Brandon Barnes** was the starting center fielder for a Houston Astros team that went 51-111. In 2018, he was the guy you'd see when you took your family to a Columbus Clippers game and think "there's no way he's *that* Brandon Barnes." ⓧ A relatively undersized 24th-round pick whose parents named him "Jodd," he's plugged away in the low minors for five years and began scraping up against Double-A. Still, **Jodd Carter** of Mars has yet to demonstrate any specific carrying tool and he's likely org depth. ⓧ Evidently the Indians just love splitting their prospects between catching and third base. Unfortunately, 2018 represented a step backwards at the plate when **Gavin Collins** wasn't on the shelf with a back injury. ⓧ The Indians took the Cuban-born **Raynel Delgado** in the sixth round and gave him second-round money to bypass a commitment to Florida International. Early reports show an above-average command of the strike zone and a chance to stick at shortstop. ⓧ Minor-league journeyman **Mike Freeman** is probably getting jittery from all the cups of coffee he's had. His latest, clocking in at exactly one plate appearance, certainly did not satisfy his cravings. ⓧ **Erik Haase** flashed good power at Triple-A, proving the spike that earned him a 40-man roster spot in 2017 was no fluke. His lack of receiving skills might make it difficult for this Haase to find a long-term home in the majors. ⓧ Not to be confused with a limited release beer used to promote a Wolverine movie or the finance bro who always managed to smuggle Smirnoff into your desk, **Logan Ice** is a former college catcher who's yet to hit after three years the low minors. ⓧ A versatile fielder with a good batting eye, **Max Moroff** once again looked over-matched against big-league pitching, particularly against the hard stuff. ⓧ The former first-round pick and bat-first prospect forgot to bring his big stick with him in his second go at Triple-A. **Mike Papi**'s walk rate remains the calling card, but his power was virtually non-existent and he saw a significant uptick in strikeouts. ⓧ It may be passe to use batting average or prospect stat lines, but when a 17-year-old middle infielder hits .335 with decent walks and power it's worth taking notice. **Brayan Rocchio** may be an actual shortstop and has pretty good speed paired with potentially strong contact skills. ⓧ **Nellie Rodriguez** has spent two years mashing Double-A while failing to do the same at Triple-A. As a first base-only prospect nearing his mid-20s, it's unclear if any organization will be willing to take a ride with him. ⓧ **Adam Rosales** has stuck around a remarkably long time considering he's seemingly always changing teams and never really hitting, but the secret to utility-man success is often difficult to quantify. ⓧ The glove-first prospect isn't really a prospect any more, as **Eric Stamets** is older than the two MVP candidates on the left side of Cleveland's infield and his OPS in Triple-A started with the number 5. ⓧ **George Valera** signed for $1.3 million as an international free agent despite being born in New York and made his pro debut in 2018. It wound up being brief, as he broke a hamate bone, but the stats are pretty and there's a lot to like here in terms of projectable raw power.

Pitchers

PITCHER	TEAM	LVL	AGE	W	L	SV	G	GS	IP	H	HR	BB/9	K/9	K	GB%	BABIP	WHIP	ERA	DRA	WARP	MPH	FB%	WHF	CSP
Adam Cimber	SDN	MLB	27	3	5	0	42	0	48¹	42	2	1.9	9.5	51	53%	.315	1.08	3.17	3.92	0.6	88.7	75.8	12.7	59.1
	CLE	MLB	27	0	3	0	28	0	20	26	3	3.2	3.2	7	68%	.324	1.65	4.05	6.17	-0.3	89.4	73.5	7.4	50.4
Jon Edwards	AKR	AA	30	0	1	0	9	0	9²	6	1	5.6	13.0	14	45%	.263	1.24	3.72	1.84	0.3				
	COH	AAA	30	2	1	4	25	0	30	23	2	2.7	12.6	42	37%	.304	1.07	3.60	2.75	0.8				
	CLE	MLB	30	0	0	0	9	0	8²	6	2	4.2	10.4	10	48%	.190	1.15	3.12	2.51	0.2	96.8	57.6	17.3	48.6
Nick Goody	CLE	MLB	26	0	2	0	12	0	11²	15	4	3.9	9.3	12	30%	.306	1.71	6.94	5.33	-0.1	92.5	54.8	14.4	40.7
Sam Hentges	LYN	A+	21	6	6	0	23	23	118¹	114	4	4.0	9.3	122	41%	.343	1.41	3.27	3.99	1.9				
Juan Hillman	LKC	A	21	6	12	0	26	26	128²	140	7	3.6	7.7	110	46%	.327	1.49	5.18	5.10	0.2				
James Hoyt	HOU	MLB	31	0	0	0	1	0	0¹	1	0	27.0	0.0	0	100%	.500	6.00	0.00	2.07	0.0	94.7	66.7	6.7	33.6
	FRE	AAA	31	0	3	5	25	0	28	19	2	2.6	10.6	33	52%	.258	0.96	2.25	2.68	0.8				
Walker Lockett	SDN	MLB	24	0	3	0	4	3	15	22	4	6.0	7.2	12	56%	.360	2.13	9.60	6.05	-0.1	94.4	55.5	8.3	44.6
	ELP	AAA	24	5	9	0	23	23	133¹	145	17	2.2	8.0	118	48%	.323	1.34	4.72	4.18	2.1				
Alexi Ogando	CLE	MLB	34	0	1	0	1	0	1	2	0	27.0	9.0	1	25%	.500	5.00	18.00			94.7	67.7	6.4	53
	COH	AAA	34	2	0	0	14	6	34²	38	4	2.6	6.5	25	39%	.315	1.38	3.89	4.90	0.2				
Luis Oviedo	MHV	A-	19	4	2	0	9	9	48	34	3	1.9	11.4	61	52%	.274	0.92	1.88	3.31	1.1				
	LKC	A	19	1	0	0	2	2	9	5	0	7.0	6.0	6	44%	.217	1.33	3.00	4.44	0.1				
Adam Plutko	COH	AAA	26	7	3	0	14	14	84²	47	5	1.7	8.6	81	29%	.198	0.74	1.70	3.88	1.6				
	CLE	MLB	26	4	5	1	17	12	76²	78	21	2.7	7.0	60	29%	.258	1.32	5.28	7.22	-1.7	92.7	59.8	9.7	46.1
Jefry Rodriguez	HAR	AA	24	5	3	0	13	13	68	55	6	3.7	9.5	72	53%	.280	1.22	3.31	3.37	1.6				
	SYR	AAA	24	2	2	0	6	6	32²	32	0	4.1	8.3	30	47%	.333	1.44	3.58	4.45	0.4				
	WAS	MLB	24	3	3	0	14	8	52	43	8	6.4	6.8	39	46%	.240	1.54	5.71	7.35	-1.3	97.6	65	9.2	46.1
Nick Sandlin	LKC	A	21	0	0	1	10	0	10¹	9	0	0.0	13.1	15	52%	.391	0.87	1.74	1.08	0.5				
	LYN	A+	21	1	0	4	7	0	6¹	2	0	2.8	14.2	10	50%	.167	0.63	1.42	2.43	0.2				
Ben Taylor	CLE	MLB	25	0	0	0	6	0	6	6	2	1.5	12.0	8	50%	.286	1.17	6.00	4.80	0.0	95.0	67.7	11.1	58.3
	COH	AAA	25	7	2	11	46	0	57¹	42	5	1.4	11.0	70	42%	.274	0.89	2.51	3.07	1.3				
Lenny Torres	CLT	Rk	17	0	0	0	6	5	15¹	14	0	2.3	12.9	22	51%	.400	1.17	1.76	2.98	0.5				

Brady Aiken went no. 1 overall in the 2014 draft and has been relegated to Lineout status five years later, which says more about how his career has gone than anything. ⓪ Cleveland's lesser Cody A. had a brutal sophomore year in 2016 before missing all of 2017 and all but three innings of 2018 recovering from Tommy John surgery. We should see **Cody Anderson** back in 2019. After all, tell me, Mr. Anderson, what good is positive regression if you're unable to pitch? ⓪ When asked to describe the right-handed submariner's arm action, Ke$ha said, "It's going down, I'm yelling Cimber." She declined to comment on **Adam Cimber**'s peripherals. ⓪ **Oliver Drake** looked like a good fit for the Indians, at least until he ran into the Astros. Thirty minutes and two-thirds of an inning later, his ERA was three runs higher and he was heading off to his third team of the season. ⓪ O pitcher! Consider the fearful danger you are in. You hang by a slender thread, with the flames of awful command flashing about it, and ready every moment to singe it, and burn it asunder. (Jonathan Edwards. **Jon Edwards**. Whatever.) ⓪ After breaking through as a solid middle reliever in 2017, **Nick Goody** suffered an elbow injury early in 2018 and missed the remainder of the season, which is bad-y. ⓪ A fourth-round pick in 2014, **Sam Hentges** has been brought along slowly by Cleveland since undergoing Tommy John surgery, but put himself back on the radar with a strong showing in High-A. His fastball sits mid-90s and he his off-speed stuff shows enough potential to stick as a mid-rotation arm. ⓪ **Juan Hillman** repeated the Midwest League and showed the same command issues that plagued him a year earlier. His age and the fact that he has three potential above-average offerings still make the former second-round pick someone to wait on. ⓪ Spamming sliders is the new hotness, which is good news because that's basically all **James Hoyt** can do. Hoyt lost most of 2018 buried on the Astros' relief depth chart and on the disabled list, but there's a major-league reliever here. ⓪ **Walker Lockett**'s stuff and command are both at a point where if the other was slightly better, he could be a viable back-end starter. As they're each a little short, he's probably an up-and-down guy. ⓪ It's been five years since **Alexi Ogando** was anything resembling an effective major-league reliever, but he threw one inning in the majors in May for some reason so he qualifies for the book. ⓪ The projection Cleveland saw in **Luis Oviedo** when they signed him for $375,000 out of Venezuela in 2015 started to pay dividends in 2018, as he passed his first test at a level above complex ball, showing good velocity with his fastball to go along with three developing breaking pitches. ⓪ **Adam Plutko** spent most of 2018 riding back and forth on the Columbus-to-Cleveland shuttle, with the highlight being a Triple-A no-hitter on June 2. ⓪ Last seen returning from a PED suspension, 25-year-old **Jefry Rodriguez** hit the bigs after 13 good Double-A starts and turned every batter he faced into a plate discipline savant, walking 37 and striking out 39. ⓪ **Nick Sandlin** zoomed through the low minors before a late-season call-up to Double-A. With a mid-90s fastball and developing slider, he could see the majors as soon as 2019. ⓪ A team that shuffled through mediocre relievers like a family's White Elephant gift exchange couldn't find a spot for **Ben Taylor** outside of six random May appearances. With a generic name to go along with his generic stuff, he's about as anonymous a reliever as one can find. ⓪ The Indians took **Lenny Torres** no. 41 in the 2018 draft and handed him $1.35 million to bypass St. John's. He dominated at the prep level with a fastball that sat mid-90s, and will need to develop his slider and changeup to have a future in the rotation.

COLORADO ROCKIES

Essay by Jesse Spector

Player comments by Wilson Karaman and BP staff

The Rockies reached the playoffs in consecutive years for the first time in franchise history, have a young and self-developed starting rotation, boast arguably the best left side of the infield in baseball with Nolan Arenado and Trevor Story, and added a balls-in-play machine who should be perfect for Coors Field when they addressed their biggest need of the offseason with the signing of Daniel Murphy.

They've also won one playoff game in those two October appearances, have refused to either trade prospects for key upgrades or lean on positional prospects the way they have their young pitchers, hurled money at people named Ian Desmond, are a year away from possibly losing the best third baseman in the game as a free agent, and their big winter addition is an avatar for social division through the prism of baseball.

Whether you're an analyst or a fan, the side you take on the Rockies entering 2019 is not wrong. The Rockies are a team of opposites: one on the rise, whose time is almost up; playing with house money, but with twenty-five years of expectations heaped on them; and a group of lovable ragtag underdogs, and also...not so universally loveable. How this team looks at any moment depends entirely on the light. And yet there's one thing you can't say about this team that has been said about so many earlier iterations: that it's hopeless. The Dodgers still have their six-year run of division titles, and will be favored to make it seven, but the Rockies may have their best chance yet to overcome Los Angeles' baked-in advantages.

The Rockies' quarter-century existence has been all about overcoming everyone else's baked-in advantages, and it's possible that they have finally figured out the solution on the biggest one. The intense difference between playing in Colorado and playing everywhere else is something that no contemporary team has to deal with, with maybe the only comparison even approaching it being the Phillies, when they called Baker Bowl home. It's not just the ballpark, though, as I found last year when I wrote a piece for Rockies Magazine centered around asking players what people might not understand about Coors Life. The most interesting response belonged to Charlie Blackmon, who noted the

ROCKIES PROSPECTUS
2018 W-L: 91-72, 2ND IN NL WEST

Pythag	.522	14th	B-Age	28.7	23rd
RS/G	4.79	7th	P-Age	27.2	7th
RA/G	4.57	20th	Salary	$137.0M	14th
DRC+	103	7th	M$/MW	$2.9M	22nd
DRA	4.48	18th	DL Days	891	7th
FIP	4.02	14th	$ on DL	7%	1st
DER	.700	22nd			

- Opened 1995
- Open air
- Natural surface
- Fence profile: 8' to 16'6"

Three-Year Park Factors

Runs	Runs/RH	Runs/LH	HR/RH	HR/LH
112	113	110	110	109

Top Hitter WARP	7.0 Nolan Arenado
Top Pitcher WARP	4.7 German Marquez
Top Prospect	Brendan Rodgers

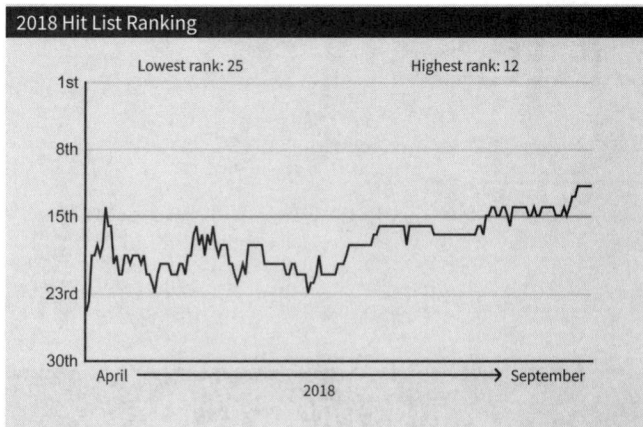

2018 Hit List Ranking

Lowest rank: 25   Highest rank: 12

April ——————→ September
2018

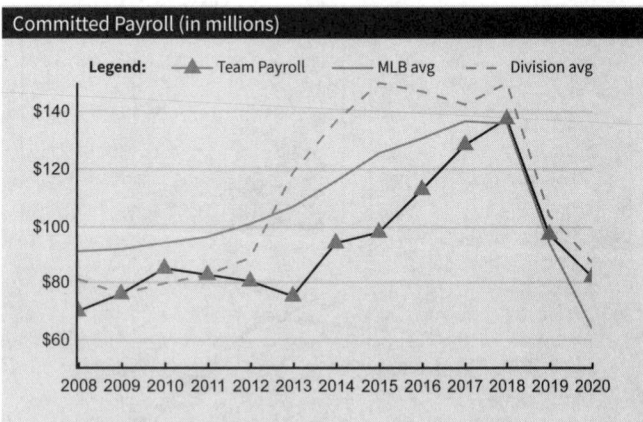

Committed Payroll (in millions)

Legend: —▲— Team Payroll   —— MLB avg   - - - Division avg

2008 2009 2010 2011 2012 2013 2014 2015 2016 2017 2018 2019 2020

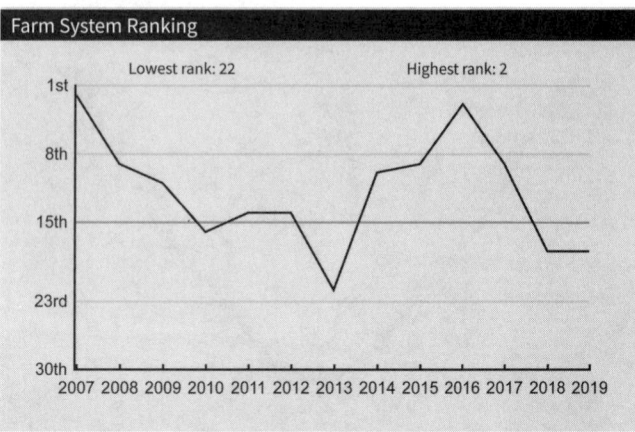

Farm System Ranking

Lowest rank: 22   Highest rank: 2

2007 2008 2009 2010 2011 2012 2013 2014 2015 2016 2017 2018 2019

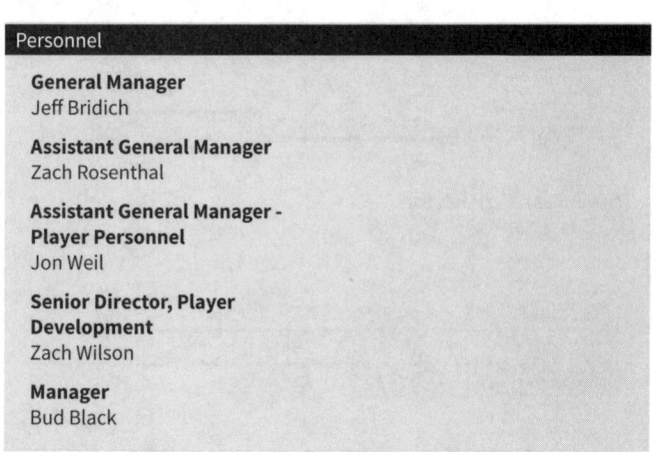

Personnel

General Manager
Jeff Bridich

Assistant General Manager
Zach Rosenthal

Assistant General Manager - Player Personnel
Jon Weil

Senior Director, Player Development
Zach Wilson

Manager
Bud Black

physical toll of spending six months traveling in and out of Denver and constantly adjusting to life at altitude, namely fatigue, sleep issues, and dehydration.

What Blackmon talked about is in addition to some things that get talked about often, namely when it comes to pitching. Catcher and wild card hero Tony Wolters brought up how pitches have a different shape to them in Denver, while erstwhile ace Jon Gray was open about the mental challenge of pitching in a huge park where lots of balls find grass but also plays like it has much shorter fences. No truism of baseball has held stronger than the suffocation of starting pitching in Coors, from Nied straight through Hampton and Neagle to Eddie Butler.

And now the Rockies are a pitching-first team that went 40-27 after last year's All-Star break, including 19-9 in September, to hold off the Dodgers and force a Game 163. Everything about the Rockies' position in the baseball universe says that should not be able to happen, yet it did.

It's not that the Rockies suddenly solved the issue of how to build a team that can succeed in Colorado. Instead, the unlikely success of Colorado's rotation was the culmination of long-term planning on multiple fronts, including having a farm system in which Double-A Hartford is the only affiliate that plays at an altitude of less than 2000 feet above sea level, with Triple-A Albuquerque clocking in 39 feet above Denver. The Rockies used seven starting pitchers in 2018. Tyler Anderson, Kyle Freeland, and Gray were Colorado's own first-round draft picks. Chad Bettis was a second-rounder. Antonio Senzatela signed with the Rockies as a 16-year-old out of Venezuela. German Marquez and Jeff Hoffman were acquired in trades as minor leaguers. Nearly all of them walked the same path up that metaphorical and very literal mountain.

It's not just the starting pitchers, though. From 2014-18, there were 25 different players who made Baseball Prospectus' annual top 10 lists of Rockies prospects. As of December, 21 remained in the organization. That includes every starter from last year other than Marquez, as well as Story, David Dahl, and Raimel Tapia. They also include Blackmon and Arenado, the Rockies' second-round picks in 2008 and 2009 who were well past prospect status by 2014 but clearly fit into the homegrown theme, not to mention the general manager, Jeff Bridich, who was promoted from farm director in 2014.

The strange thing about this is that the Rockies are more committed than any team since the reserve clause to winning with their own guys, yet they only really have been willing to stick with the young pitchers through their major league growing pains. Not so the position players. The Rockies played Ian Desmond at first base 138 times among his team-leading 160 appearances, not including starts at first base in all four of Colorado's playoff games, during which he went 2-for-17 with no extra-base hits, no walks, five strikeouts, and the flyout to center field that ended the season.

Desmond hit .236/.307/.422 for the season, and defied Rockies tradition by posting a higher slugging percentage on the road (.438) than at home (.404). His 22-homer campaign wasn't without highlights: a tiebreaking dinger off Sean Doolittle in Washington in April, a walkoff two-run shot off Kirby Yates in August, another two-run blast off Joe Ross to put the Rockies ahead to stay in the win that clinched a playoff spot. Still, Desmond's 619-plate appearance season clocked in at 0.4 WARP, the same figure Garrett Hampson posted in 48 trips to the plate.

The Rockies gave a combined 1,865 plate appearances in 2018 to Desmond and veterans Carlos Gonzalez, Gerardo Parra, and Chris Iannetta, and a combined 373 trips to the plate for Ryan McMahon, Hampson, Tapia, and Tom Murphy. The team with the worst VORP among the 10 playoff lineups in 2018 went through the summer and added two position players, signing age-38 Matt Holliday as a free agent on July 29 and trading for age-34 Drew Butera on August 31. While other teams picked up bench bats like Justin Bour and Lucas Duda, the Rockies saw no need to upgrade their woeful offense.

The bullpen was even more stark in the Rockies' prioritization of form over payroll space. Bryan Shaw, given a three-year, $27 million deal before last season, stunk for the better part of five months and was relegated in September to four extremely low-leverage appearances. Jake McGee, with the same contract, made 11 appearances from August 26 through the end of the season, and was asked to protect a lead only once: September 25, when he came in with a seven-run cushion and gave up two runs to the Phillies in one-third of an inning. By the end of the season, Bud Black's most trusted setup men were Adam Ottavino, Scott Oberg, and July acquisition Seunghwan Oh.

The failure to either let young players play or trade for lineup help almost certainly cost the Rockies what could have been their first ever National League West title in 2018, but the steadfast refusal to part with prospects may be what sets up Colorado to win in 2019 and beyond.

The Rockies tied a record in 2018 with 163 games started by pitchers with 150 or fewer games of major league experience, a year after doing the same thing in all 162 of their games. Sticking with young pitchers through their ups and downs has brought the Rockies to a place where, for the first time ever, the starting rotation is their greatest strength. What if they'd done the same with the position players, though? Their rotation is so good and still so young, with nobody even set to reach free agency until Bettis does after the 2020 season. At the same time, Arenado hits free agency after 2019, which will be an inflection point for the organization whether the third baseman stays or goes.

The shame is that it shouldn't have to be. In a way the Rockies are a distillation of the current economic climate of baseball: half a roster of underpaid, cost-controlled talents, sharing a locker room with overpaid, free-agent veterans. There will always be the latter (and they deserve it, they were underpaid themselves) but it's particularly painful to consider the possibility of a team not being able to afford their franchise player with so much misspent salary on the books.

But we are we are, which makes the 2019 so critical for the franchise. And the team approached it by making another veteran investment, though perhaps a more dramatic one than the Desmonds of the past, in three-time All-Star Daniel Murphy. In a way the acquisition is a culmination of everything Rockies, since he's as fractious as a player as the team itself. The team's new first baseman has made a career out of putting balls in play, and could easily be imagined following in the footsteps of Andres Galarraga, Michael Cuddyer, and Justin Morneau as late-career batting champions in Colorado. Then again, Murphy is entering his age 34 season, is coming off an injury-marred 2018 season, and has divided fanbases in multiple cities through his homophobic comments.

It's very easy to imagine Murphy being the story of the 2019 Colorado Rockies, and for that story to either end in triumph or shame. It's also very easy to imagine that story being the rise of Brendan Rodgers, or David Dahl, or the resurgence of Wade Davis. Or how German Marquez vanished as suddenly as he seemed to appear. As problematic as this team is, there are very few so interesting.

It's an exciting time to be a Rockies fan, a time when the second wild card was followed by getting to Game 163 and the NLDS, leading into a season with that whole young rotation hitting its stride, with an incredible left side of the infield, with a first baseman who fits exactly what the lineup needed, with a bunch of young players ready to show why Colorado was right not to trade them. The Rockies remain a fascinating, flawed franchise, but for perhaps the first time in a long time, it's a new flaw. And while the team may throw its money in the wrong direction sometimes, that's a much more interesting, and easily fixed, problem than watching flat curveballs get clubbed into the upper decks, year after year. It's by no means certain what fans will get with this team, but this may be the most exciting time for the Rockies since the initial joy of just having a major league team in Colorado. ■

—Jesse Spector is a freelance baseball and hockey writer in New York, NY.

HITTERS

Nolan Arenado 3B Born: 04/16/91 Age: 28 Bats: R Throws: R Height: 6'2" Weight: 205 Origin: Round 2, 2009 Draft (#59 overall)

YEAR	TEAM	LVL	AGE	PA	R	2B	3B	HR	RBI	BB	K	SB	CS	AVG/OBP/SLG	DRC+	VORP	BABIP	BRR	FRAA	WARP
2016	COL	MLB	25	696	116	35	6	41	133	68	103	2	3	.294/.362/.570	147	52.5	.293	-0.9	3B(160): 23.0	9.0
2017	COL	MLB	26	680	100	43	7	37	130	62	106	3	2	.309/.373/.586	142	63.0	.320	-0.5	3B(157): 5.0	6.6
2018	COL	MLB	27	673	104	38	2	38	110	73	122	2	2	.297/.374/.561	146	47.5	.314	-2.9	3B(152): 9.1	7.0
2019	COL	MLB	28	610	82	34	3	29	94	64	103	3	2	.286/.365/.518	141	42.9	.306	-1.1	3B 7	5.3

Breakout: 0%   Improve: 44%   Collapse: 2%   Attrition: 2%   MLB: 99%   *Comparables: Ryan Zimmerman, Eric Chavez, George Brett*

Arenado possesses one of the truly elite attack swings in baseball, his ferocious hacks sprung off a deep back-leg load with lightning-bolt hands guiding immense force. It is a swing that has now damaged baseballs in all directions of the atmospheric void in Denver for six seasons running, with the four most recent fusing to create a model of expert-level offensive consistency. And there's been plenty of elite defensive consistency, too. After a four-year run as one of the very best hot corner gloves in the world, the leather has held to very, very good over the last two. He'll have the opportunity to descend from the mile-high mountaintop and homestead in any of 29 other big-league valleys next winter coming off this, his age-28 season. When he does he'll probably be riding the wake of yet another brilliant effort and sitting on somewhere around 40 WARP for his career. Yet he'll inevitably stare down questions about sea-level adjusted production that'll cloud up the whole damn salary calculator, and that'll be a shame. That's next year, though. For now, we get another chance to admire an in-altitude, in-prime season of a player on a Hall-of-Fame track. And that's a fun thing to watch.

Charlie Blackmon CF Born: 07/01/86 Age: 32 Bats: L Throws: L Height: 6'3" Weight: 210 Origin: Round 2, 2008 Draft (#72 overall)

YEAR	TEAM	LVL	AGE	PA	R	2B	3B	HR	RBI	BB	K	SB	CS	AVG/OBP/SLG	DRC+	VORP	BABIP	BRR	FRAA	WARP
2016	COL	MLB	29	641	111	35	5	29	82	43	102	17	9	.324/.381/.552	141	57.4	.350	4.2	CF(138): -7.1	5.4
2017	COL	MLB	30	725	137	35	14	37	104	65	135	14	10	.331/.399/.601	153	79.2	.371	1.6	CF(158): -0.1	7.6
2018	COL	MLB	31	696	119	31	7	29	70	59	134	12	4	.291/.358/.502	128	37.7	.329	-0.6	CF(151): -21.7	2.6
2019	COL	MLB	32	637	96	34	5	26	83	52	120	15	7	.296/.365/.507	139	56.1	.334	1.4	CF -5	5.4

Breakout: 0%   Improve: 45%   Collapse: 1%   Attrition: 6%   MLB: 99%   *Comparables: Vernon Wells, Torii Hunter, Andre Ethier*

"We're encouraged by the process," Bud Black told reporters after the game. Charlie'd tested his tight, nearly-32-year-old April quad in the outfield before the game and felt pretty good. They didn't think he'd need to go on the disabled list. And in keeping with tradition, he never did; he hasn't since running into some turf toe in the spring of 2016. Offensive regression hit like a fat sack with a dollar sign on it for a long swath of the first half, but eventually Blackmon did, too. Not with quite the consistent oomph and sting as he had in his all-world 2017 campaign, mind you. But he again hit a bunch of dingers, got on base at a good clip, and led the league in runs. It was a very, very good offensive season.

To watch him in the field, however, is to know that lower half never quite got right, in April or any other month. The sprint speed and effort checked out, but the defensive metrics averted their eyes from a start-up explosion that was suddenly more of a light crackle. Greener corner pastures likely await, and with them about 95.5 million expectations for his bat to hold and carry his contract's load.

Drew Butera C Born: 08/09/83 Age: 35 Bats: R Throws: R Height: 6'1" Weight: 205 Origin: Round 5, 2005 Draft (#149 overall)

YEAR	TEAM	LVL	AGE	PA	R	2B	3B	HR	RBI	BB	K	SB	CS	AVG/OBP/SLG	DRC+	VORP	BABIP	BRR	FRAA	WARP
2016	KCA	MLB	32	133	18	10	1	4	16	8	36	0	0	.285/.328/.480	83	6.0	.373	-1.1	C(51): 0.5, P(2): 0.0	0.3
2017	KCA	MLB	33	177	18	4	1	3	14	12	41	0	0	.227/.284/.319	81	1.2	.286	-0.1	C(74): -3.4, 1B(4): -0.2	0.1
2018	KCA	MLB	34	166	11	9	0	2	18	13	37	0	0	.188/.259/.289	80	-0.4	.232	1.2	C(48): -6.9, 1B(2): 0.9	-0.1
2018	COL	MLB	34	16	2	0	0	1	3	2	2	0	0	.214/.313/.429	83	0.5	.182	0.1	C(6): -0.9, 1B(4): 0.0	-0.1
2019	COL	MLB	35	251	25	12	1	5	25	19	57	0	0	.242/.304/.372	80	4.7	.296	0.0	C -8, 1B 0	-0.3

Breakout: 3%   Improve: 27%   Collapse: 12%   Attrition: 37%   MLB: 86%   *Comparables: Mike Matheny, Ivey Wingo, Gus Mancuso*

"Failing upwards" isn't quite the correct turn of phrase, but anyone who's managed to post only three positive-WARP seasons this decade and still hang on to a big-league roster spot deserves our praise and admiration. Butera got right to work on making sure that number didn't rise in 2018, with a further slide in defensive efficiency joining his regular parades from dugout to dish and right back again. And somehow Kansas City managed to get a semi-interesting relief prospect back when they found a willing trade partner for him in Colorado at the end of August. Now 35 and buried among a deep free-agent class of catchers, Butera's days of guaranteed contractual cover may finally be at an end.

YEAR	TEAM	P. COUNT	FRM RUNS	BLK RUNS	THRW RUNS	TOT RUNS
2016	KCA	5369	1.8	-0.4	-0.1	1.0
2017	KCA	7350	-4.2	2.0	-0.2	-3.0
2018	KCA	6521	-6.4	0.0	-0.2	-6.8
2018	COL	730	-0.7	-0.1	0.0	-0.9
2019	COL	9578	-6.8	0.6	-0.4	-6.6

David Dahl LF Born: 04/01/94 Age: 25 Bats: L Throws: R Height: 6'2" Weight: 195 Origin: Round 1, 2012 Draft (#10 overall)

YEAR	TEAM	LVL	AGE	PA	R	2B	3B	HR	RBI	BB	K	SB	CS	AVG/OBP/SLG	DRC+	VORP	BABIP	BRR	FRAA	WARP
2016	NBR	AAX	22	332	53	21	2	13	45	39	85	16	5	.278/.367/.500	120	28.6	.351	3.7		2.2
2016	ABQ	AAA	22	68	17	6	2	5	16	6	11	1	2	.484/.529/.887	167	14.4	.543	0.8	CF(11): -1.3, LF(3): 0.8	0.8
2016	COL	MLB	22	237	42	12	4	7	24	15	59	5	0	.315/.359/.500	98	14.5	.404	2.1	LF(54): -2.4, CF(6): 0.3	0.6
2017	ABQ	AAA	23	74	12	2	2	2	14	3	17	1	1	.243/.274/.414	94	0.2	.294	0.7	LF(6): -0.2, CF(6): -0.3	0.1
2018	ABQ	AAA	24	78	7	7	0	2	9	1	19	1	0	.286/.295/.455	87	-0.4	.357	-0.6	CF(6): 0.4, RF(6): 0.2	0.3
2018	COL	MLB	24	271	31	11	3	16	48	19	68	5	3	.273/.325/.534	118	8.4	.311	-1.3	LF(34): 2.9, RF(30): -1.4	1.3
2019	COL	MLB	25	581	75	25	3	20	65	37	146	11	4	.246/.297/.417	92	10.9	.299	0.1	LF 1, RF 0	1.3

Breakout: 3%   Improve: 40%   Collapse: 7%   Attrition: 19%   MLB: 91%   *Comparables: Travis Snider, Wladimir Balentien, Chase Headley*

It's a tough thing, when one develops a bum rap. There's the perception, of course; impressions form in the blink of an eye, and once established they can be very difficult indeed to shake. But of perhaps greater salience, usually there's cause for it. Whither David Dahl, wearer still of the dreaded "injury prone" tag after yet *again* missing a big chunk of time, this time recovering from a broken foot that cost him two months. He returned with a roar to remind everyone of the top-shelf talent he's flashed periodically throughout his stop-and-start career. But the dynamite results came in spite of precious little progress beating back the other defining narrative of Dahl's still-young career, as he remained exceedingly willing to expand the zone and dangerously unlikely to make contact when doing so. With everyday at-bats penciled in, Colorado will hope for a reputation rehab.

Ian Desmond 1B Born: 09/20/85   Age: 33   Bats: R   Throws: R   Height: 6'3"   Weight: 215   Origin: Round 3, 2004 Draft (#84 overall)

YEAR	TEAM	LVL	AGE	PA	R	2B	3B	HR	RBI	BB	K	SB	CS	AVG/OBP/SLG	DRC+	VORP	BABIP	BRR	FRAA	WARP
2016	TEX	MLB	30	677	107	29	3	22	86	44	160	21	6	.285/.335/.446	98	26.2	.350	5.5	CF(130): -4.3, LF(29): -1.2	2.2
2017	COL	MLB	31	373	47	11	1	7	40	24	87	15	4	.274/.326/.375	79	3.7	.345	2.7	LF(66): -2.8, 1B(27): -2.5	-0.3
2018	COL	MLB	32	619	82	21	8	22	88	53	146	20	6	.236/.307/.422	98	4.3	.279	0.8	1B(138): -2.6, LF(18): 0.8	0.8
2019	COL	MLB	33	433	49	16	3	11	46	32	106	13	4	.241/.307/.376	90	5.3	.303	1.7	1B -1, LF -1	0.3

Breakout: 1%   Improve: 32%   Collapse: 14%   Attrition: 20%   MLB: 85%   *Comparables: Eli Marrero, Jeff Baker, Jim Fregosi*

There's this inventor from Sweden, Simone Giertz is her name. And she invents unnecessary robots. Robots that brush your teeth for you or fix you a bowl of soup. They're low on the hierarchy of robots because they don't really advance human productivity in meaningful ways. They do patch over the mundane, and that may be their greatest utility. They free up brain RAM that's otherwise committed to involuntary, procedural tasks, and that means more time to learn and create. It's not nothing, it's just not a lot of something.

Well, you'd find it easier to tie a Swedish useless robot inventor to an *Annual* comment about Ian Desmond than trying to explain the Ian Desmond contract to someone in 2019. It was one of the weirder deals anyone could remember when he signed it, and the returns have been every bit of a worst-case scenario through the first 40 percent. If Statcast is to be believed, he ran harder than any other player in the game on certain qualified plays last year and fantasy players still kind of enjoyed his 20/20 season. So all hope is not lost. But the 33-year-old is going to have to start cranking out that WARP right quick if he's going to make a run at returning any more than teeth-brushing robot value over the full five-year run.

Carlos Gonzalez RF Born: 10/17/85   Age: 33   Bats: L   Throws: L   Height: 6'1"   Weight: 220   Origin: International Free Agent, 2002

YEAR	TEAM	LVL	AGE	PA	R	2B	3B	HR	RBI	BB	K	SB	CS	AVG/OBP/SLG	DRC+	VORP	BABIP	BRR	FRAA	WARP
2016	COL	MLB	30	632	87	42	2	25	100	46	129	2	2	.298/.350/.505	110	23.0	.346	1.4	RF(148): -4.5	2.0
2017	COL	MLB	31	534	72	34	0	14	57	56	119	3	0	.262/.339/.423	90	10.7	.318	1.1	RF(125): -5.0	0.1
2018	COL	MLB	32	504	71	32	4	16	64	37	113	5	2	.276/.329/.467	100	18.2	.332	4.0	RF(117): 7.7	2.3
2019	COL	MLB	33	481	51	22	2	13	56	41	110	3	1	.246/.315/.396	93	11.0	.300	1.6	RF -1	1.0

Breakout: 1%   Improve: 39%   Collapse: 10%   Attrition: 14%   MLB: 92%   *Comparables: Casey Blake, Jose Guillen, Hunter Pence*

We all read the eulogies for Cargo's Colorado career last winter, and he had by and large earned the roundly effusive praise by carrying usually -terrible Rockies teams for nearly a decade. But the time had come. The speed was shot, the bat speed had slowed too much for good velocity, and there were younger options bubbling up from Triple-A. It was time to move on. Except it wasn't? A multi-year opportunity never materialized elsewhere, and that Triple-A talent probably shouldn't be counted on to produce out of the gate, you know? Gerardo Parra and Ian Desmond probably shouldn't be everyday players, either. Cargo had hit down the stretch in 2017, maybe...maybe it wouldn't be the worst idea to bring him back?

Well, he did come back on a Spring Training deal, and while he wasn't better than ever, he was better enough to contribute. He rediscovered his sea legs, his barrel started catching velocity again, and he earned himself 500 plate appearances. Now that is how you properly swan song. Or was it?

Garrett Hampson MI Born: 10/10/94   Age: 24   Bats: R   Throws: R   Height: 5'11"   Weight: 185   Origin: Round 3, 2016 Draft (#81 overall)

YEAR	TEAM	LVL	AGE	PA	R	2B	3B	HR	RBI	BB	K	SB	CS	AVG/OBP/SLG	DRC+	VORP	BABIP	BRR	FRAA	WARP
2016	BOI	A-	21	312	43	14	8	2	44	48	56	36	4	.301/.404/.441	136	36.7	.366	4.6	SS(64): 8.2, 2B(1): -0.2	3.9
2017	LNC	A+	22	603	113	24	12	8	70	56	77	51	14	.326/.387/.462	129	41.6	.364	7.5	2B(71): -0.4, SS(56): 7.3	5.9
2018	HFD	AA	23	172	28	8	2	4	15	21	17	19	1	.304/.391/.466	122	18.7	.323	3.5	SS(18): 0.4, 2B(17): 1.7	1.7
2018	ABQ	AAA	23	332	53	17	4	6	25	30	58	17	4	.314/.377/.459	96	16.8	.372	0.9	2B(44): -0.1, SS(23): -2.3	1.1
2018	COL	MLB	23	48	3	3	1	0	4	7	12	2	0	.275/.396/.400	84	3.5	.393	1.1	SS(8): 0.2, 2B(7): 0.6	0.3
2019	COL	MLB	24	354	41	12	2	8	33	28	77	16	3	.229/.295/.349	78	4.6	.275	2.1	2B 1, SS 0	0.6

Breakout: 7%   Improve: 14%   Collapse: 7%   Attrition: 23%   MLB: 39%   *Comparables: Jose Pirela, Matt Antonelli, Tim Locastro*

The High Plains stretch out and yawn across a huge swath of miles and tribes and states, over a mass of land that is vast in expanse and, for the purposes of its only resident big-league baseball club, elevation. The High Plains reside at an unusual height for plains, and a consequence of height on Earth is wind. Steady, consistent, flowing air, more robust in its bluster at some times, humming along unflinchingly from the west at most others. Hampson is going to fit right in. He grinds, he hums, he flows. He executes quality baseball plays over, and over, and over again. At every level he's stretched out, yawned, and played—up to and including a couple delicious cups of coffee last season. He hits, he runs, he defends well at multiple positions, and he gets every inch, every pebble, out of his game. DJ LeMahieu is going to walk out that door, Garrett Hampson is poised to walk in, and if history's any kind of a guide the winds will grumble on as the soundtrack to a most peaceful transfer of power.

Sam Hilliard RF Born: 02/21/94   Age: 25   Bats: L   Throws: L   Height: 6'5"   Weight: 225   Origin: Round 15, 2015 Draft (#437 overall)

YEAR	TEAM	LVL	AGE	PA	R	2B	3B	HR	RBI	BB	K	SB	CS	AVG/OBP/SLG	DRC+	VORP	BABIP	BRR	FRAA	WARP
2016	ASH	A	22	527	71	23	5	17	83	56	150	30	12	.267/.348/.449	118	20.3	.357	2.2	LF(62): 0.1, RF(56): -0.6	2.4
2017	LNC	A+	23	597	95	23	7	21	92	50	154	37	17	.300/.360/.487	117	25.2	.384	3.9	RF(85): 6.6, LF(30): 5.1	4.1
2018	HFD	AA	24	484	58	22	3	9	40	41	151	23	14	.262/.327/.389	84	9.1	.379	0.3	RF(70): 3.5, LF(29): -1.8	0.3
2019	COL	MLB	25	251	28	8	1	7	27	15	84	8	4	.223/.268/.360	64	-3.7	.306	0.1	RF 0, LF 0	-0.3

Breakout: 1%   Improve: 3%   Collapse: 1%   Attrition: 6%   MLB: 8%   *Comparables: Joey Butler, Brandon Barnes, Roger Kieschnick*

A results-heavy effort at Lancaster led to wait-and-see verdicts for Hilliard last winter, and it was Double-A pitchers who went and did the seeing. Hilliard's lagging swing got shot full of holes by more advanced arms, particularly the left-handed kind. The impressive speed for his size didn't play any finer against better batteries, either. He offers some outfield versatility, but that can only take him so far, and it can get late early for former 15th rounders with big whiff issues who are repeating Double-A at 25. On the plus side, he remains a physical specimen, and his bat has flickered enough that he toppled Jordan Patterson from the 40-man this winter. At the very least he should invite strong-side platoon auditions for a couple more years, and there remains a chance for big-league value despite a rough introduction to the high minors.

Matt Holliday LF   Born: 01/15/80   Age: 39   Bats: R   Throws: R   Height: 6'4"   Weight: 240   Origin: Round 7, 1998 Draft (#210 overall)

YEAR	TEAM	LVL	AGE	PA	R	2B	3B	HR	RBI	BB	K	SB	CS	AVG/OBP/SLG	DRC+	VORP	BABIP	BRR	FRAA	WARP
2016	SLN	MLB	36	426	48	20	1	20	62	35	71	0	0	.246/.322/.461	110	15.4	.253	-1.1	LF(84): -5.6, 1B(10): 0.8	1.0
2017	NYA	MLB	37	427	50	18	0	19	64	46	114	1	0	.231/.316/.432	95	2.8	.273	-1.3	1B(8): 0.5	0.3
2018	ABQ	AAA	38	62	12	4	0	3	14	9	9	0	0	.346/.452/.596	133	5.4	.375	0.8	LF(6): -1.5, 1B(2): -0.2	0.3
2018	COL	MLB	38	65	3	2	0	2	3	12	18	0	0	.283/.415/.434	102	3.6	.394	-0.2	LF(13): -0.5, 1B(1): 0.0	0.1
2019	COL	MLB	39	251	27	10	1	8	30	26	59	0	0	.233/.320/.390	96	4.6	.284	-0.5	LF -3, 1B 0	0.2

Breakout: 1%   Improve: 14%   Collapse: 5%   Attrition: 6%   MLB: 61%   *Comparables: Jayson Werth, Bobby Abreu, Johnny Damon*

When the Rockies went back to their roots and signed the 38-year-old, unemployed version of Holliday at the end of July, they did so for the sole purpose of adding some right-handed bench pop down the stretch. And for his part, Big Daddy more or less delivered. His trademark eagle eye trained quickly on big-league stuff after a brief energizer in Albuquerque, and he gave the Rockies solid-enough production in limited looks, even earning his way onto multiple postseason rosters. With an expressed intent to play again in 2019, he'll seek one last run at a ring before hanging 'em up on the sooner side of later.

Chris Iannetta C   Born: 04/08/83   Age: 36   Bats: R   Throws: R   Height: 6'0"   Weight: 230   Origin: Round 4, 2004 Draft (#110 overall)

YEAR	TEAM	LVL	AGE	PA	R	2B	3B	HR	RBI	BB	K	SB	CS	AVG/OBP/SLG	DRC+	VORP	BABIP	BRR	FRAA	WARP
2016	SEA	MLB	33	338	23	14	0	7	24	38	83	0	0	.210/.303/.329	80	0.2	.266	-5.1	C(93): -12.0	-0.9
2017	ARI	MLB	34	316	38	19	0	17	43	37	87	0	0	.254/.354/.511	116	26.2	.308	-2.0	C(78): 11.2, 3B(1): 0.0	3.1
2018	COL	MLB	35	360	36	13	1	11	36	50	87	0	0	.224/.345/.385	111	9.1	.275	-0.4	C(99): -0.5	2.2
2019	COL	MLB	36	349	40	16	1	10	40	40	88	0	0	.234/.334/.395	99	13.1	.297	-2.0	C -1	1.3

Breakout: 4%   Improve: 24%   Collapse: 7%   Attrition: 19%   MLB: 80%   *Comparables: Aaron Robinson, Ernie Whitt, Alan Ashby*

The Rockies stretched Iannetta a little further than most people stretch Iannetta these days. The 13-year veteran saw as much game action as he had since 2011, though his workload behind the dish stayed a relatively consistent half-time. The starved mile-high offense, on the other hand, desperately required more of his on-base skills. He obliged by crushing a four-digit OPS in a career-high 20 plate appearances in the pinch, sneaking his way to a third two-plus win season in the last four. It was a most welcome reunion in a season short on imported happy endings in Denver. Barring collapse, he's a solid bet to play out two more reasonable-rate contract years at elevation.

YEAR	TEAM	P. COUNT	FRM RUNS	BLK RUNS	THRW RUNS	TOT RUNS
2016	SEA	13011	-10.2	-1.4	0.8	-11.1
2017	ARI	10626	11.0	-1.1	0.2	10.0
2018	COL	12393	1.4	0.3	-0.4	1.2
2019	COL	12409	0.7	-0.8	0.0	-0.1

Grant Lavigne 1B   Born: 08/27/99   Age: 19   Bats: L   Throws: R   Height: 6'4"   Weight: 220   Origin: Round 1, 2018 Draft (#42 overall)

YEAR	TEAM	LVL	AGE	PA	R	2B	3B	HR	RBI	BB	K	SB	CS	AVG/OBP/SLG	DRC+	VORP	BABIP	BRR	FRAA	WARP
2018	GJR	RK	18	258	45	13	2	6	38	45	40	12	7	.350/.477/.519	153	27.3	.410	-0.6	1B(53): -6.8	1.2
2019	COL	MLB	19	251	26	8	0	7	27	29	64	2	1	.208/.297/.334	73	-5.4	.254	-0.9	1B -2	-0.8

Breakout: 0%   Improve: 8%   Collapse: 2%   Attrition: 5%   MLB: 14%   *Comparables: Nomar Mazara, Francisco Pena, Rougned Odor*

You can hear the drool puddling on the floor of the fantasy team's conference room from here. The Rockies popped Lavigne 42nd overall a few weeks after he graduated high school last summer, and it was a notable selection given his cold-weather roots and first base-only defensive profile. The earliest returns rewarded their resounding faith in his bat, however, as he pummeled Pioneer League pitching to a 98th percentile DRC+ among all Rookie ballers. A full-season debut should be on tap in 2019, with a subsequent promotion schedule that'll track pretty directly with his offensive progress from there.

DJ LeMahieu 2B   Born: 07/13/88   Age: 30   Bats: R   Throws: R   Height: 6'4"   Weight: 215   Origin: Round 2, 2009 Draft (#79 overall)

YEAR	TEAM	LVL	AGE	PA	R	2B	3B	HR	RBI	BB	K	SB	CS	AVG/OBP/SLG	DRC+	VORP	BABIP	BRR	FRAA	WARP
2016	COL	MLB	27	635	104	32	8	11	66	66	80	11	7	.348/.416/.495	133	44.1	.388	2.0	2B(146): -1.2	4.8
2017	COL	MLB	28	682	95	28	4	8	64	59	90	6	5	.310/.374/.409	106	27.8	.351	3.4	2B(153): 20.5	5.1
2018	COL	MLB	29	581	90	32	2	15	62	37	82	6	5	.276/.321/.428	105	17.2	.298	4.5	2B(128): 20.1	4.8
2019	COL	MLB	30	569	70	27	3	10	54	48	81	8	4	.284/.349/.409	108	27.6	.316	2.8	2B 12	4.2

Breakout: 7%   Improve: 44%   Collapse: 4%   Attrition: 10%   MLB: 97%   *Comparables: Bobby Avila, Alex Cora, Jerry Lumpe*

In days of yore, a guy like LeMahieu might set out into free agency off an injury-rattled "down" offensive season, rolling along on wheels that no longer moved down the track quickly enough to steal bases. The penalties would be exacerbated in the eyes of potential suitors by way of obedience to a vague Coors penalty, and we might be talking here about one-year contracts and the rebuilding of value. Unfortunately we're talking in vagaries because free agency is glacial and deadlines are deadlines. FRAA once again sniffed out a superior-to-all glove at the keystone. He produced among the league's best baserunning efforts, in spite of the inefficient thievery. And thanks to DRC+, we now know that the offensive drop-off, well, really wasn't much of a drop-off at all. He'll enter the next chapter of a solid, steady career as one of the better bets around to produce broad-based value.

Ryan McMahon INF Born: 12/14/94 Age: 24 Bats: L Throws: R Height: 6'2" Weight: 185 Origin: Round 2, 2013 Draft (#42 overall)

YEAR	TEAM	LVL	AGE	PA	R	2B	3B	HR	RBI	BB	K	SB	CS	AVG/OBP/SLG	DRC+	VORP	BABIP	BRR	FRAA	WARP
2016	NBR	AAX	21	535	49	27	5	12	75	55	161	11	6	.242/.325/.399	96	14.7	.338	1.3		1.2
2017	HFD	AA	22	205	28	16	2	6	32	20	39	7	0	.326/.390/.536	119	15.9	.381	0.0	1B(14): 0.4, 3B(9): 0.8	1.4
2017	ABQ	AAA	22	314	46	23	2	14	56	21	53	4	3	.374/.411/.612	140	24.7	.416	-2.9	1B(36): 1.1, 2B(24): 2.4	2.3
2017	COL	MLB	22	24	2	1	0	0	1	5	5	0	0	.158/.333/.211	91	0.3	.214	1.4	1B(7): 0.2, 2B(4): 0.0	0.2
2018	ABQ	AAA	23	242	40	15	3	11	48	15	61	3	2	.290/.339/.531	120	5.6	.353	1.9	1B(43): -1.9, 2B(10): -1.0	1.0
2018	COL	MLB	23	202	17	9	1	5	19	18	64	1	0	.232/.307/.376	77	-0.2	.327	0.9	1B(31): -1.1, 3B(17): 0.1	0.0
2019	COL	MLB	24	292	34	15	1	10	36	21	75	3	1	.254/.312/.431	99	8.6	.314	1.2	3B 1, 1B -1	1.0

Breakout: 5%   Improve: 25%   Collapse: 13%   Attrition: 30%   MLB: 51%   *Comparables: Nick Evans, Joey Votto, Brett Wallace*

McMahon's been a tough nut to crack at times, a shape-shifter in body, hitting skill development and defensive geography. It hasn't been linear, despite the straight and aggressive trajectory to Denver. Stop us if you've heard this before, but Colorado never quite committed to giving McMahon a shot at rolling into everyday reps. The bat bided time during its multiple exposures to more Triple-A pitching, and he can pick grounders at three different positions. He's still ready. There are enough questions about the hit tool and whether he can be better than fine anywhere off the coldest corner, but he remains a young player of considerable promise. So long as the Rockies continue signing veterans aging out of middle infield spots to occupy said corner, we may never truly find out.

Daniel Murphy 1B Born: 04/01/85 Age: 34 Bats: L Throws: R Height: 6'1" Weight: 221 Origin: Round 13, 2006 Draft (#394 overall)

YEAR	TEAM	LVL	AGE	PA	R	2B	3B	HR	RBI	BB	K	SB	CS	AVG/OBP/SLG	DRC+	VORP	BABIP	BRR	FRAA	WARP
2016	WAS	MLB	31	582	88	47	5	25	104	35	57	5	3	.347/.390/.595	145	70.7	.348	1.4	2B(117): -5.3, 1B(21): 0.7	4.7
2017	WAS	MLB	32	593	94	43	3	23	93	52	77	2	0	.322/.384/.543	132	51.5	.341	1.2	2B(139): 3.8	4.8
2018	HAR	AA	33	44	8	2	0	2	7	6	4	0	0	.243/.364/.459	125	3.6	.226	0.5	2B(8): -0.6, 1B(2): 0.3	0.3
2018	WAS	MLB	33	205	17	9	0	6	29	13	17	1	0	.300/.341/.442	118	8.1	.302	-1.0	2B(38): -2.9, 1B(14): -0.6	0.5
2018	CHN	MLB	33	146	23	6	0	6	13	7	23	2	0	.297/.329/.471	112	8.0	.318	0.7	2B(33): -1.1	0.6
2019	COL	MLB	34	600	81	40	2	20	74	46	77	4	1	.303/.361/.492	131	37.0	.323	0.8	1B 2, 2B -1	4.0

Breakout: 0%   Improve: 35%   Collapse: 8%   Attrition: 12%   MLB: 89%   *Comparables: Del Pratt, Robinson Cano, Ian Kinsler*

Murphy's recovery from offseason knee surgery turned out to be as frustrating as the teams he played for. Positive noises about his availability for Opening Day became muffled and then faded completely when it became apparent Murphy still wasn't able to run in March. Even when he finally did return in mid-June, he was still not starting games at second base due to concern over the knee. There aren't many major league roster spots available for bat-only players and Murphy's partial season, while respectable, was not the kind of stellar offensive output we have come to expect following his late 2015 transformation. The silver lining is that his DRC+ would still have ranked sixth among regular designated hitters, which would have been great if his next few years included a stay in the American League.

Tom Murphy C Born: 04/03/91 Age: 28 Bats: R Throws: R Height: 6'1" Weight: 220 Origin: Round 3, 2012 Draft (#105 overall)

YEAR	TEAM	LVL	AGE	PA	R	2B	3B	HR	RBI	BB	K	SB	CS	AVG/OBP/SLG	DRC+	VORP	BABIP	BRR	FRAA	WARP
2016	ABQ	AAA	25	322	53	26	7	19	59	16	78	1	1	.327/.361/.647	140	31.6	.386	-2.2	C(69): 2.0	3.2
2016	COL	MLB	25	49	8	2	0	5	13	4	19	1	0	.273/.347/.659	111	2.8	.350	-0.7	C(12): 0.5	0.3
2017	ABQ	AAA	26	154	22	10	1	4	19	9	56	0	0	.255/.312/.426	68	1.1	.390	-0.7	C(34): 0.9	0.1
2017	COL	MLB	26	26	1	1	0	0	1	2	9	0	0	.042/.115/.083	66	-2.7	.067	0.2	C(8): 0.5	0.1
2018	ABQ	AAA	27	264	40	16	3	17	49	22	76	4	2	.258/.333/.568	129	18.0	.306	-0.9	C(52): 6.9	2.8
2018	COL	MLB	27	96	5	7	1	2	11	3	44	0	1	.226/.250/.387	48	-2.1	.404	-0.7	C(22): -0.3	-0.3
2019	COL	MLB	28	70	7	3	0	2	8	5	24	0	0	.210/.273/.369	64	-0.1	.297	-0.1	C 0	0.0

Breakout: 3%   Improve: 19%   Collapse: 11%   Attrition: 25%   MLB: 45%   *Comparables: Brad Eldred, Carlos Peguero, Kelly Shoppach*

They say the first step is the hardest, and in Murphy's case they've been proven largely correct, at least insofar as his trips down the first base line are concerned. Once again the backstop's bat seasoned well at Triple-A, only to wither and crumble against big-league stuff. Nearly half of his limited plate appearances in The Show ended with a shaken head and slow trudge back to the dugout. With more accomplished leathermen around and available to battery there just wasn't much in the way of earned opportunity for ol' Tom Murphy. A date with his 28th birthday right around Opening Day confirms the urgency of the moment if he's going to establish himself in Colorado, as does the one solitary option left to dot his horizon.

YEAR	TEAM	P. COUNT	FRM RUNS	BLK RUNS	THRW RUNS	TOT RUNS
2016	COL	1415	0.3	0.1	0.1	0.4
2017	ABQ	4911	-0.8	0.1	0.4	-0.5
2017	COL	1031	-0.3	0.6	-0.1	0.1
2018	ABQ	7423	3.8	1.0	-0.2	4.6
2018	COL	2791	-0.3	0.0	0.0	-0.3
2019	COL	2623	-0.3	0.1	0.0	-0.2

Gerardo Parra RF Born: 05/06/87 Age: 32 Bats: L Throws: L Height: 5'11" Weight: 210 Origin: International Free Agent, 2004

YEAR	TEAM	LVL	AGE	PA	R	2B	3B	HR	RBI	BB	K	SB	CS	AVG/OBP/SLG	DRC+	VORP	BABIP	BRR	FRAA	WARP
2016	COL	MLB	29	381	45	27	3	7	39	9	73	6	4	.253/.271/.399	76	-1.7	.297	-1.1	LF(60): 1.8, 1B(19): 0.4	-0.3
2017	COL	MLB	30	425	56	24	1	10	71	20	67	2	5	.309/.341/.452	103	10.2	.343	-2.5	LF(82): 3.6, RF(22): -0.1	1.4
2018	COL	MLB	31	443	52	17	0	6	53	32	75	11	4	.284/.342/.372	97	10.9	.334	3.3	LF(111): 6.8, RF(10): 1.9	2.3
2019	COL	MLB	32	416	42	21	1	8	43	24	75	7	4	.263/.314/.386	87	5.1	.307	0.1	LF 4, RF 0	1.0

Breakout: 2%   Improve: 40%   Collapse: 4%   Attrition: 15%   MLB: 88%   *Comparables: Bama Rowell, Johnny Moore, Mike McCormick*

It's never a great thing when a player's Instagram feed is the most popular thing about him, and yet there we were with El Yolo in 2018. In a move that was perhaps over-reactive to Parra's scorching second half, and one that was definitely in spite of ample young organizational depth, Colorado turned over a set of everyday outfield keys to the career second-divisional stalwart. The bat didn't hold up to the increased exposure, but a draw-down to proper part-time status down the stretch resulted in some positively sublime pinch-hitting efforts. And a year after his bat bounced like a dead cat, it was his glove's turn. With the pinch-hitting prowess and some sneaky value added on the basepaths, he wound up producing a half-decent two-win season, public perception be damned. It wasn't enough to coax the club into exercising his $12.5 million team option, however, so he'll need to reacquaint himself with sea level once again.

Brendan Rodgers SS   Born: 08/09/96   Age: 22   Bats: R   Throws: R   Height: 6'0"   Weight: 180   Origin: Round 1, 2015 Draft (#3 overall)

YEAR	TEAM	LVL	AGE	PA	R	2B	3B	HR	RBI	BB	K	SB	CS	AVG/OBP/SLG	DRC+	VORP	BABIP	BRR	FRAA	WARP
2016	ASH	A	19	491	73	31	0	19	73	35	98	6	3	.281/.342/.480	145	21.9	.319	-2.5	SS(56): 0.0, 2B(24): 0.9	4.2
2017	HFD	AA	20	164	20	5	0	6	17	8	36	0	2	.260/.323/.413	105	6.5	.306	-0.5	SS(15): -1.2, 2B(3): 0.3	0.7
2017	LNC	A+	20	236	44	21	3	12	47	6	35	2	1	.387/.407/.671	155	26.5	.413	0.9	SS(47): -5.6, 2B(4): -0.6	2.1
2018	HFD	AA	21	402	49	23	2	17	62	30	76	12	3	.275/.342/.493	118	27.4	.301	0.6	SS(58): -6.7, 2B(21): -2.1	1.8
2018	ABQ	AAA	21	72	5	4	0	0	5	1	16	0	0	.232/.264/.290	79	-2.8	.302	-0.3	SS(11): -1.8, 3B(4): -0.2	-0.2
2019	COL	MLB	22	251	30	10	1	9	28	11	58	2	1	.233/.280/.393	84	3.5	.275	-0.2	SS -3, 2B 0	0.0

Breakout: 5%   Improve: 31%   Collapse: 8%   Attrition: 23%   MLB: 52%   *Comparables: Nick Franklin, Reid Brignac, Derek Dietrich*

It's always exciting when a long-touted prospect hops up the porch steps and sidles up to the door. All the more when the player's faults are evident but he might be so good that they don't matter. Rodgers' elite barrel skills have long been evident, especially given how frequently he has shown them off. The aggressiveness has been understandable: When an abundance of natural hitting talent and confidence gets dropped into bandbox after bandbox, sometimes very small walk rates and some bad habits happen. And sometimes a 150-ish DRC+ happens. Challenged by advanced assignments at every turn, Rodgers has thrived and marched on. Consensus remains that of a perfectly fine, okay, it'll do shortstop, though he probably works best with reps all over the dirt and the Rockies have increasingly nodded in that direction with his deployments. With their left side set for one more year the Rockies will have the luxury to oblige some additional high-minors seasoning, though an early forced entrance should not surprise.

Trevor Story SS   Born: 11/15/92   Age: 26   Bats: R   Throws: R   Height: 6'1"   Weight: 210   Origin: Round 1, 2011 Draft (#45 overall)

YEAR	TEAM	LVL	AGE	PA	R	2B	3B	HR	RBI	BB	K	SB	CS	AVG/OBP/SLG	DRC+	VORP	BABIP	BRR	FRAA	WARP
2016	COL	MLB	23	415	67	21	4	27	72	35	130	8	5	.272/.341/.567	129	31.2	.343	2.1	SS(96): 0.8	3.8
2017	COL	MLB	24	555	68	32	3	24	82	49	191	7	2	.239/.308/.457	93	28.7	.332	4.2	SS(142): -0.4	2.5
2018	COL	MLB	25	656	88	42	6	37	108	47	168	27	6	.291/.348/.567	136	51.9	.345	-0.8	SS(156): -2.0	5.7
2019	COL	MLB	26	591	78	29	3	26	82	49	178	16	5	.248/.316/.461	109	30.0	.320	1.6	SS -2	3.0

Breakout: 4%   Improve: 64%   Collapse: 1%   Attrition: 5%   MLB: 100%   *Comparables: Mark Reynolds, Alex Rodriguez, Jason Bay*

Well, now! Quite a different tale when told by a guy who's not battling a shoulder injury and striking out in over a third of his plate appearances, eh? Story hit the ball harder and did so much more frequently in 2018, shaving nearly nine percentage points off his whiff rate en route to a monster offensive campaign that was among the best in baseball, even when adjusted for the fictions of Coors. He authored significant adjustments, among them a new and pronounced early-count aggression and swing tweaks to get shorter into the zone again with the help of his longtime hitting coach. Near-elite speed gained novel utility on the bases, and the leather shone just shiny enough to justify the six and lock down some MVP votes. After dodging a late-season dagger that nearly spun Tommy John's yarn, Story will board his flight to Arizona this spring with nothing but a legend to grow.

Raimel Tapia OF   Born: 02/04/94   Age: 25   Bats: L   Throws: L   Height: 6'2"   Weight: 180   Origin: International Free Agent, 2010

YEAR	TEAM	LVL	AGE	PA	R	2B	3B	HR	RBI	BB	K	SB	CS	AVG/OBP/SLG	DRC+	VORP	BABIP	BRR	FRAA	WARP
2016	NBR	AAX	22	457	79	20	5	8	34	25	49	17	14	.323/.363/.450	116	25.2	.349	1.4		2.4
2016	ABQ	AAA	22	110	14	5	5	0	14	2	12	6	3	.346/.355/.490	111	2.9	.379	0.0	CF(12): 1.9, LF(8): 1.3	0.8
2016	COL	MLB	22	41	4	0	0	0	3	2	11	3	0	.263/.293/.263	90	-0.4	.357	1.2	CF(9): 0.2, LF(2): -0.2	0.2
2017	ABQ	AAA	23	277	45	20	8	2	30	13	42	12	2	.369/.397/.529	109	18.9	.432	-0.1	CF(48): 0.0, LF(5): -0.6	1.1
2017	COL	MLB	23	171	27	12	2	2	16	8	36	5	2	.288/.329/.425	80	4.0	.361	1.6	RF(22): -3.0, LF(18): -1.3	-0.3
2018	ABQ	AAA	24	473	81	33	9	11	62	32	85	21	3	.302/.352/.495	104	16.1	.354	1.4	CF(65): -5.2, RF(24): 0.0	1.2
2018	COL	MLB	24	27	6	2	1	1	6	2	7	0	0	.200/.259/.480	91	0.7	.235	0.7	CF(6): -0.4, LF(1): 0.0	0.1
2019	COL	MLB	25	466	50	20	4	10	48	29	102	14	4	.246/.298/.378	86	8.6	.298	2.9	RF 5, CF 0	1.4

Breakout: 10%   Improve: 50%   Collapse: 3%   Attrition: 38%   MLB: 73%   *Comparables: Kevin Pillar, Andrew Toles, A.J. Pollock*

Some players just kind of always are who you thought they were, and it's a path down which Tapia certainly appears poised to tread. While the stringbean frame isn't *quite* as stringy as it was once upon a time, the basic physicality appears set in stone. He's going to hit, potentially very well. He's going to hold his speed, and likely continue to refine it as he has throughout his development. It might be a bit of a tweener profile, but his glove should be more or less fine in whichever chunk of outfield grass it gets assigned. He's also out of options, and really it's just as well because the Pacific Coast League doesn't appear to have much else to teach him. Whether he'll learn more about big-league life in Colorado's everyday lineup remains to be seen, but one way or another it's nigh on time to see what the kid can do.

Mike Tauchman OF   Born: 12/03/90   Age: 28   Bats: L   Throws: L   Height: 6'2"   Weight: 200   Origin: Round 10, 2013 Draft (#289 overall)

YEAR	TEAM	LVL	AGE	PA	R	2B	3B	HR	RBI	BB	K	SB	CS	AVG/OBP/SLG	DRC+	VORP	BABIP	BRR	FRAA	WARP
2016	ABQ	AAA	25	527	72	24	7	1	51	40	77	23	10	.286/.342/.373	89	11.1	.337	5.4	CF(93): 2.4, LF(21): 5.1	2.3
2017	ABQ	AAA	26	475	82	30	8	16	80	40	73	16	7	.331/.386/.555	128	35.8	.361	2.5	CF(62): 1.3, LF(34): 5.7	4.0
2017	COL	MLB	26	32	2	0	1	0	2	5	10	1	2	.222/.344/.296	73	-1.0	.353	-0.5	CF(3): -0.3, RF(3): -0.1	-0.1
2018	COL	MLB	27	37	5	1	0	0	0	4	15	1	0	.094/.194/.125	62	-3.5	.176	0.1	CF(5): -0.1, LF(3): -0.9	-0.2
2018	ABQ	AAA	27	471	84	26	7	20	81	60	70	12	10	.323/.408/.571	152	39.6	.345	3.5	CF(65): 4.2, LF(30): 6.1	6.2
2019	COL	MLB	28	172	22	7	1	6	22	17	33	4	2	.258/.336/.436	109	7.2	.292	-0.1	RF 0, CF 1	0.8

Breakout: 6%   Improve: 18%   Collapse: 10%   Attrition: 23%   MLB: 39%   *Comparables: Kevin Thompson, Matt Angle, Jason Bourgeois*

Tauchman absolutely *crushed* baseballs all year in Albuquerque, again, going pretty much wire to wire showcasing an impressive ability to build off of successful adjustments made the season prior. He still batters it into the dirt a ton, but he'll also loft and drive the ball away from him now or turn it loose ahead in the count. There's legitimate pop and impressive underlying contact skills, too. That kind of a combination can make gold on the silver screen, and it can fight in the "Launch Angle Revolution" as a valuable late-bloomer, if only it is allowed. He's been roughly 40-percent better than a normal Triple-A hitter over the past two seasons, and he ain't getting any younger—both reasons it baffled and amazed that Colorado never gave him a proper trial run despite dire outfield straits for most of the year. He'll rinse, repeat and hope for the best.

Pat Valaika INF Born: 09/09/92 Age: 26 Bats: R Throws: R Height: 5'11" Weight: 200 Origin: Round 9, 2013 Draft (#259 overall)

YEAR	TEAM	LVL	AGE	PA	R	2B	3B	HR	RBI	BB	K	SB	CS	AVG/OBP/SLG	DRC+	VORP	BABIP	BRR	FRAA	WARP
2016	NBR	AAX	23	474	66	33	3	13	67	28	95	8	9	.269/.314/.450	109	25.9	.315	2.1		2.7
2016	ABQ	AAA	23	115	8	8	1	1	13	2	28	2	0	.209/.226/.327	85	-3.3	.265	0.6	SS(15): 0.7, 2B(9): 1.5	0.6
2016	COL	MLB	23	19	3	1	0	1	2	0	8	0	0	.263/.263/.474	80	0.5	.400	-0.4	3B(6): 0.1, 2B(5): -0.1	0.0
2017	ABQ	AAA	24	50	6	2	1	1	11	4	11	0	0	.267/.327/.422	93	1.2	.333	0.5	SS(9): 0.3, 1B(2): 0.0	0.3
2017	COL	MLB	24	195	28	11	0	13	40	7	53	0	0	.258/.284/.533	102	11.2	.291	2.1	SS(22): -0.6, 3B(19): -0.1	0.9
2018	ABQ	AAA	25	147	13	4	1	8	20	7	30	1	1	.216/.252/.432	115	-2.3	.216	-0.6	2B(9): 0.1, SS(9): 0.4	0.8
2018	COL	MLB	25	133	8	5	0	2	5	9	30	0	0	.156/.214/.246	72	-8.0	.189	0.3	2B(17): -0.6, 1B(15): -0.4	-0.1
2019	*COL*	*MLB*	*26*	*217*	*23*	*9*	*1*	*8*	*27*	*13*	*53*	*1*	*1*	*.239/.288/.407*	*87*	*4.7*	*.281*	*0.5*	*2B 0, SS 0*	*0.5*

Breakout: 2%   Improve: 10%   Collapse: 1%   Attrition: 8%   MLB: 19%   *Comparables: Wes Bankston, Kendrys Morales, Charlie Culberson*

Promise turned to panic for Pat in a disastrous 2018 campaign that more than halved his once-commanding lead on the Valaika career WARP leaderboard. Of course, retaining pole position off a down year is no small feat in a family with four brothers who all got drafted and have played professional ball. But after flashing provocative pinch-hitting pop in his rookie season, the third youngest of the bunch tumbled down well below true-talent level in all hitting contexts last season, posting the third-worst OPS of any player to amass at least his 133 plate appearances. It was a most unfortunate turn of events, given a window of opportunity that somehow never really quite closed for him in Colorado. Despite the hiccup, jack-of-all-trades infield utility should afford him another shake-it-off chance to prove his 25-man mettle in a final season of pre-arbitrated team control in 2019.

Ryan Vilade SS Born: 02/18/99 Age: 20 Bats: R Throws: R Height: 6'2" Weight: 194 Origin: Round 2, 2017 Draft (#48 overall)

YEAR	TEAM	LVL	AGE	PA	R	2B	3B	HR	RBI	BB	K	SB	CS	AVG/OBP/SLG	DRC+	VORP	BABIP	BRR	FRAA	WARP
2017	GJR	RK	18	146	23	3	2	5	21	27	31	5	5	.308/.438/.496	125	13.9	.378	0.4	SS(30): -2.1	0.8
2018	ASH	A	19	533	77	20	4	5	44	49	96	17	13	.274/.353/.368	111	25.8	.333	-1.9	SS(116): -6.3	2.1
2019	*COL*	*MLB*	*20*	*251*	*28*	*7*	*0*	*6*	*22*	*18*	*65*	*3*	*2*	*.209/.264/.321*	*53*	*-5.6*	*.255*	*-0.6*	*SS -2*	*-0.8*

Breakout: 1%   Improve: 10%   Collapse: 0%   Attrition: 2%   MLB: 10%   *Comparables: Ruben Tejada, Orlando Arcia, Wilfredo Tovar*

If this were a regular ol' column on the internet, this is the part where we would pause to insert a bunch of those flashing siren light emojis in order to broadcast to the world that Vilade is the proverbial SON OF A COACH. Blessed with all of the feels for the game, baseball instinct and #want that such progeny often exude, the former second-rounder rebounded after a tough start to the season at Low-A. There's a lot to like in his advanced hitting approach, and while precious little of his power has wandered into professional games as yet, it's in there, and there's likely to be more of it coming as he finishes filling out a platonic ideal of a baseball frame. It's likely he'll have to move off the six spot when that happens, but if the bat turns into what the Rockies think it will, that detail won't much matter.

Colton Welker 3B Born: 10/09/97 Age: 21 Bats: R Throws: R Height: 6'2" Weight: 195 Origin: Round 4, 2016 Draft (#110 overall)

YEAR	TEAM	LVL	AGE	PA	R	2B	3B	HR	RBI	BB	K	SB	CS	AVG/OBP/SLG	DRC+	VORP	BABIP	BRR	FRAA	WARP
2016	GJR	RK	18	227	38	15	2	5	36	13	28	6	4	.329/.366/.490	121	20.3	.356	-0.4	3B(48): -5.8	0.6
2017	ASH	A	19	279	32	18	1	6	33	18	42	5	7	.350/.401/.500	142	19.6	.399	-1.6	3B(52): -7.3	1.4
2018	LNC	A+	20	509	74	32	0	13	82	42	103	5	1	.333/.383/.489	127	30.0	.395	1.1	3B(92): -9.3, 1B(6): -0.7	2.3
2019	*COL*	*MLB*	*21*	*251*	*25*	*13*	*0*	*7*	*29*	*13*	*58*	*1*	*0*	*.251/.291/.392*	*80*	*-1.0*	*.301*	*-0.6*	*3B -6, 1B 0*	*-0.8*

Breakout: 1%   Improve: 3%   Collapse: 1%   Attrition: 12%   MLB: 14%   *Comparables: Cheslor Cuthbert, Wilmer Flores, Matt Dominguez*

To see the sheer violence in Welker's swing, especially when he's launching balls off the lunar reservation in Lancaster during batting practice, you'd be forgiven for having set the over/under on his High-A dingers at something approaching the Antelope Valley's 2,500-foot elevation. That didn't happen, though, despite a full season at the level. It hasn't happened anywhere for Welker, actually; the former fourth-rounder's raw power has thus far barked worse than it has bitten in games. And that's okay! He's hit at least .329 in each of his three professional seasons, displaying underlying hand-eye coordination and bat-to-ball skills that tickle the scouting senses. The hot corner defense has been a bit better than anticipated, too. It's an exciting package of talent moving through the minors on a just-as-exciting timeline.

Tony Wolters C Born: 06/09/92 Age: 27 Bats: L Throws: R Height: 5'10" Weight: 200 Origin: Round 3, 2010 Draft (#87 overall)

YEAR	TEAM	LVL	AGE	PA	R	2B	3B	HR	RBI	BB	K	SB	CS	AVG/OBP/SLG	DRC+	VORP	BABIP	BRR	FRAA	WARP
2016	COL	MLB	24	230	27	15	2	3	30	21	53	4	1	.259/.327/.395	84	8.4	.336	0.7	C(59): 8.9, 2B(7): -0.1	1.7
2017	ABQ	AAA	25	58	6	5	1	2	9	3	15	0	1	.259/.310/.500	82	3.7	.324	0.3	C(13): 1.9	0.4
2017	COL	MLB	25	266	30	8	1	0	16	33	55	0	1	.240/.341/.284	83	0.9	.316	0.5	C(77): -0.9, 2B(4): 0.1	0.8
2018	COL	MLB	26	216	19	4	4	3	27	26	33	2	0	.170/.292/.286	88	1.1	.189	2.5	C(64): 10.7, LF(2): 0.0	2.1
2019	*COL*	*MLB*	*27*	*263*	*28*	*10*	*2*	*4*	*25*	*29*	*52*	*2*	*1*	*.232/.328/.351*	*89*	*8.9*	*.281*	*0.9*	*C 6*	*1.6*

Breakout: 4%   Improve: 47%   Collapse: 7%   Attrition: 14%   MLB: 96%   *Comparables: Dioner Navarro, Mickey Owen, Tom Padden*

If you've ever wondered what a two-win player who hits a buck-seventy looks like, quest no further. Wolters rebounded from a concussed, sub-par effort in 2017 to post one of the league's best seasons behind the plate a year later. He's a Venus flytrap at the bottom of the zone, elite hand and wrist strength fueling a unique and devastating technique of pitch receipt that banks borderline strikes at an uncanny rate. And it's a good thing he does because when he's at the plate...well, that's usually about as far as things go. According to DRC+, the top-line numbers did overstate his struggles a bit, and he still managed to walk at an excellent rate. So there's some room to grow without even really growing. Alas, slugging under .300 for a couple years in a row despite calling Coors home'll only get you so far. The walking, framing definition of a back-up catcher, Wolters will be a fun test tube for the arbitration system over the next couple winters.

YEAR	TEAM	P. COUNT	FRM RUNS	BLK RUNS	THRW RUNS	TOT RUNS
2016	COL	8341	9.9	-0.1	0.5	9.8
2017	ABQ	1747	2.3	0.0	0.1	2.6
2017	COL	9693	-2.7	-0.6	1.1	-3.0
2018	COL	7924	10.2	-0.6	0.2	9.6
2019	COL	9456	5.8	-0.4	0.5	5.9

PITCHERS

Yency Almonte RHP Born: 06/04/94 Age: 25 Bats: B Throws: R Height: 6'3" Weight: 205 Origin: Round 17, 2012 Draft (#537 overall)

YEAR	TEAM	LVL	AGE	W	L	SV	G	GS	IP	H	HR	BB/9	K/9	K	GB%	BABIP	WHIP	ERA	DRA	WARP	MPH	FB%	WHF	CSP
2016	MOD	A+	22	8	9	0	22	22	138^1	124	14	2.5	8.7	134	47%	.285	1.18	3.71	3.36	3.3				
2016	NBR	AAX	22	3	1	0	5	5	30	22	4	4.8	6.6	22	37%	.212	1.27	3.00						
2017	HFD	AA	23	5	3	0	14	14	76^1	58	4	3.7	8.4	71	45%	.267	1.17	2.00	4.74	0.4				
2017	ABQ	AAA	23	3	1	0	8	7	35	41	7	5.4	5.7	22	50%	.321	1.77	4.89	6.51	-0.3				
2018	ABQ	AAA	24	3	5	1	18	10	43^2	44	8	2.9	7.0	34	45%	.283	1.33	5.56	4.43	0.5				
2018	COL	MLB	24	0	0	0	14	0	14^2	15	1	2.5	8.6	14	48%	.341	1.30	1.84	4.37	0.1	97.0	63	13.5	45.8
2019	COL	MLB	25	2	1	0	23	3	36^2	35	5	3.5	8.2	33	43%	.307	1.36	4.44	4.89	0.1	96.7	64.5	13.9	46.9

Breakout: 20%   Improve: 27%   Collapse: 14%   Attrition: 35%   MLB: 53%   *Comparables: Tyler Wagner, Tyler Anderson, Andrew Chafin*

Showtime, indeed. One of the great transitional periods of any pitcher's baseball life is the one from proverbial thrower to proverbial pitcher. The due course of time forces every arm to confront the dichotomy at some point, and those with aspirations of starting will typically face it that much sooner. Max effort tires and joggles the fine mechanics. Almonte crossed the first bridge in that journey back at Double-A in 2017, and that stat line at Triple-A belied further gains in this past season's first half. The Rockies were convinced and lined him up for a bullpen audition. He took to the role magnificently, at least from a results standpoint. It helps when the "paired-down" heater still sits 95 and sneaks late to get under barrels on the regular. He showed the ability to coax an awful lot of whiffs with the slider, too. It's a nice starting point, and he'll enter 2019 with the versatility to swing and the stuff to impact the big-league staff in big ways.

Tyler Anderson LHP Born: 12/30/89 Age: 29 Bats: L Throws: L Height: 6'4" Weight: 210 Origin: Round 1, 2011 Draft (#20 overall)

YEAR	TEAM	LVL	AGE	W	L	SV	G	GS	IP	H	HR	BB/9	K/9	K	GB%	BABIP	WHIP	ERA	DRA	WARP	MPH	FB%	WHF	CSP
2016	NBR	AAX	26	1	1	0	2	2	10	6	0	1.8	9.9	11	59%	.222	0.80	1.80						
2016	ABQ	AAA	26	1	1	0	3	3	17	15	1	3.2	6.9	13	48%	.286	1.24	2.12	3.90	0.3				
2016	COL	MLB	26	5	6	0	19	19	114^1	119	12	2.2	7.8	99	53%	.319	1.29	3.54	4.88	0.6	93.7	43.6	11.4	48.5
2017	ABQ	AAA	27	0	2	0	4	2	12^1	14	0	2.9	9.5	13	35%	.412	1.46	4.38	2.92	0.3				
2017	COL	MLB	27	6	6	0	17	15	86	88	16	2.7	8.5	81	46%	.304	1.33	4.81	4.15	1.3	93.9	47.1	12.4	47.6
2018	COL	MLB	28	7	9	0	32	32	176	165	30	3.0	8.4	164	38%	.281	1.27	4.55	4.82	1.0	93.7	44.6	12.3	50
2019	COL	MLB	29	10	9	0	28	28	159^2	158	25	2.9	8.6	152	43%	.312	1.31	4.30	4.72	1.1	93.1	44.9	12.2	48.8

Breakout: 31%   Improve: 47%   Collapse: 21%   Attrition: 7%   MLB: 87%   *Comparables: Tommy Milone, A.J. Griffin, Zach McAllister*

It took six full seasons as a professional, but Anderson finally managed to stay healthy enough to take 32 turns in Colorado's rotation. And he performed...okay! After toying with a two-seamed addition to the arsenal at season's beginning, he promptly reverted to the comfort of a three-pitch mix that includes a cutting version of both fastball and change. He found his groove in June, missed all of the barrels in July and missed none of them in August. It was a prototypical up-and-down performance from a prototypical back-end starter, the net result of which provided the Rockies 176 cheap, reasonably useful innings in sum. The arbitration clock has started ticking, so those innings will get increasingly more expensive, and a crop of higher-ceilinged young arms figures to push the former first-rounder for something a little better than "useful" in the year ahead.

Chad Bettis RHP Born: 04/26/89 Age: 30 Bats: R Throws: R Height: 6'1" Weight: 200 Origin: Round 2, 2010 Draft (#76 overall)

YEAR	TEAM	LVL	AGE	W	L	SV	G	GS	IP	H	HR	BB/9	K/9	K	GB%	BABIP	WHIP	ERA	DRA	WARP	MPH	FB%	WHF	CSP
2016	COL	MLB	27	14	8	0	32	32	186	204	22	2.9	6.7	138	54%	.310	1.41	4.79	5.17	0.4	94.8	56	9.7	44.4
2017	ABQ	AAA	28	0	3	0	4	4	18²	22	2	2.9	5.3	11	55%	.312	1.50	4.82	4.68	0.2				
2017	COL	MLB	28	2	4	0	9	9	46¹	52	8	2.1	5.8	30	50%	.293	1.36	5.05	4.39	0.6	92.4	51.9	9.7	43
2018	ABQ	AAA	29	0	0	0	3	3	14	16	2	1.9	6.4	10	51%	.311	1.36	5.14	4.97	0.1				
2018	COL	MLB	29	5	2	0	27	20	120¹	121	18	3.5	6.0	80	51%	.280	1.40	5.01	5.74	-0.6	93.0	41.4	9.2	46.9
2019	COL	MLB	30	4	3	0	42	6	69¹	73	9	3.2	6.8	52	50%	.312	1.41	4.53	4.98	0.1	92.9	48.8	9.4	44.8

Breakout: 6%   Improve: 40%   Collapse: 26%   Attrition: 14%   MLB: 80%   *Comparables: Chase Anderson, Mat Latos, Jeff Niemann*

A year removed from kicking cancer's ass, Bettis' single-minded focus returned to the only-marginally-less-daunting task of trying to get hitters out consistently at Coors Field. His calling card remains an ability to induce a nifty number of grounders, and best of all, the grounders he induces tend to be the weak, pulled kind that get converted into outs. Unfortunately, when hitters are able to get a little air under it these days, they lift balls harder against Bettis than just about any other pitcher in baseball. A nice April run gave way to May struggles, a horror show in middle months beset by blister issues and an eventual half-decent run of bullpen work down the stretch. That might just be a preview of coming attractions, though his barrel-scraping whiff rate suggests a treacherous path to holding down even that role.

Ben Bowden LHP Born: 10/21/94 Age: 24 Bats: L Throws: L Height: 6'4" Weight: 235 Origin: Round 2, 2016 Draft (#45 overall)

YEAR	TEAM	LVL	AGE	W	L	SV	G	GS	IP	H	HR	BB/9	K/9	K	GB%	BABIP	WHIP	ERA	DRA	WARP	MPH	FB%	WHF	CSP
2016	ASH	A	21	0	1	0	26	0	23²	23	1	5.7	11.0	29	43%	.373	1.61	3.04	3.99	0.2				
2018	ASH	A	23	3	0	0	15	0	15¹	17	2	2.9	14.7	25	43%	.429	1.43	3.52	3.21	0.3				
2018	LNC	A+	23	4	2	0	34	0	36²	35	6	3.7	13.0	53	35%	.337	1.36	4.17	4.64	0.1				
2019	COL	MLB	24	2	1	1	34	0	36¹	37	7	5.3	10.2	41	37%	.333	1.62	5.42	5.97	-0.4				

Breakout: 0%   Improve: 0%   Collapse: 2%   Attrition: 2%   MLB: 2%   *Comparables: Brian Schlitter, Neil Wagner, Josh Fields*

During the Great New England Shoemakers' Strike of 1860 in Bowden's home town of Lynn, Massachusetts, women protesting labor injustice marched through a blizzard with signs that read "Give Us a Fair Compensation and We Will Labor Cheerfully." Bowden got a head start on the former, inking an above-slot deal high in the second round back in 2016. Injuries prevented his labor, cheerful or otherwise, in 2017, but he got back on the bump for 52 solid innings out of a couple A-ball bullpens last year. It's a strong three-pitch mix from the left side, but the north-south nature of his sequencing and wandering in-zone command led to more squared offerings than ideal. The stuff was back, however, in all its bat-missing glory. And there's fast-track bullpen potential here if it's back for good.

Santiago Casilla RHP Born: 07/25/80 Age: 38 Bats: R Throws: R Height: 6'0" Weight: 210 Origin: International Free Agent, 2000

YEAR	TEAM	LVL	AGE	W	L	SV	G	GS	IP	H	HR	BB/9	K/9	K	GB%	BABIP	WHIP	ERA	DRA	WARP	MPH	FB%	WHF	CSP
2016	SFN	MLB	35	2	5	31	62	0	58	50	8	2.9	10.1	65	50%	.292	1.19	3.57	3.98	0.7	96.0	53.3	11.8	44.6
2017	OAK	MLB	36	4	5	16	63	0	59	58	8	3.4	8.7	57	40%	.301	1.36	4.27	5.80	-0.4	95.6	62.1	12.5	48.2
2018	OAK	MLB	37	0	0	1	26	0	31¹	18	0	5.7	6.3	22	44%	.209	1.21	3.16	6.44	-0.5	94.7	56.3	9.7	43.3
2018	ABQ	AAA	37	0	2	0	12	0	12¹	16	2	6.6	8.8	12	52%	.368	2.03	8.03	4.95	0.0				
2019	COL	MLB	38	2	1	5	40	0	42¹	41	6	4.1	7.9	37	44%	.306	1.42	4.66	5.13	-0.1	93.9	56.4	11.2	44

Breakout: 14%   Improve: 31%   Collapse: 20%   Attrition: 8%   MLB: 79%   *Comparables: Troy Percival, Ron Mahay, Kyle Farnsworth*

Five-pitch relievers aren't quite knuckleballer-level great white buffaloes, but they're a rare and precious breed all the same, and when one of 'em heads out to pasture it affects us all. Alas, if you watched Casilla pitch last year you saw a man wistfully if unwittingly staring out across the plains. None of those five pitches found the strike zone or eluded bats with nearly the consistency of days gone by, and while he managed to hold together the topline numbers reasonably well in Oakland, he did so only by stifling one of the largest DRA-ERA divergences of any pitcher to toe rubber in 2018. A mid-season migration to the Rockies' Triple-A ranks didn't help matters, and he figures to enter his age-38 season with no guaranteed deal and a beautiful sunset taking shape on the horizon.

Ryan Castellani RHP Born: 04/01/96 Age: 23 Bats: R Throws: R Height: 6'4" Weight: 220 Origin: Round 2, 2014 Draft (#48 overall)

YEAR	TEAM	LVL	AGE	W	L	SV	G	GS	IP	H	HR	BB/9	K/9	K	GB%	BABIP	WHIP	ERA	DRA	WARP	MPH	FB%	WHF	CSP
2016	MOD	A+	20	7	8	0	26	26	167²	156	8	2.7	7.6	142	55%	.302	1.23	3.81	3.63	3.5				
2017	HFD	AA	21	9	12	0	27	27	157¹	163	16	2.7	7.6	132	47%	.309	1.33	4.81	4.19	1.8				
2018	HFD	AA	22	7	9	0	26	26	134¹	135	15	4.7	6.1	91	39%	.291	1.53	5.49	5.32	0.0				
2019	COL	MLB	23	1	1	0	3	3	14	15	2	4.0	7.5	12	42%	.324	1.53	5.03	5.54	0.0				

Breakout: 15%   Improve: 22%   Collapse: 9%   Attrition: 26%   MLB: 36%   *Comparables: Duane Underwood, Jayson Aquino, Yency Almonte*

Colorado pushed their 2014 second-rounder aggressively up the low-minors ladder for a couple years after drafting him out of high school, but that trajectory ground to a screeching halt when Castellani struggled with his Double-A assignment in 2017. Given a second chance to try the level again in 2018, he struggled again. A full wind and stabbing, deep arm action are pages out of Max Scherzer's playbook, and it's a reminder that you have to be *Max Scherzer* to make those mechanics work. But he'll still show flashes of a three-pitch mix that looks real good in sporadic bursts of proper execution and location. An addition to the club's 40-man roster over the winter, he'll play at 23 with at least one more year to find it and force his way up the organizational depth chart.

Wade Davis RHP   Born: 09/07/85   Age: 33   Bats: R   Throws: R   Height: 6'5"   Weight: 225   Origin: Round 3, 2004 Draft (#75 overall)

YEAR	TEAM	LVL	AGE	W	L	SV	G	GS	IP	H	HR	BB/9	K/9	K	GB%	BABIP	WHIP	ERA	DRA	WARP	MPH	FB%	WHF	CSP
2016	KCA	MLB	30	2	1	27	45	0	43¹	33	0	3.3	9.8	47	48%	.300	1.13	1.87	2.99	1.0	97.8	50.1	13.6	43.5
2017	CHN	MLB	31	4	2	32	59	0	58²	39	6	4.3	12.1	79	42%	.262	1.14	2.30	2.78	1.6	96.1	47.6	16	41.8
2018	COL	MLB	32	3	6	43	69	0	65¹	43	8	3.6	10.7	78	42%	.238	1.06	4.13	3.90	0.8	95.5	49	12.7	40.1
2019	COL	MLB	33	3	1	35	56	0	59	49	8	3.6	10.3	67	43%	.296	1.23	3.88	4.27	0.4	95.1	48.1	13.9	41

Breakout: 22%   Improve: 40%   Collapse: 36%   Attrition: 7%   MLB: 96%   *Comparables: Pedro Strop, Brian Fuentes, Joe Nathan*

Things went pretty well for Davis in 2018, at least under the hood. His velocity basically held, which is perhaps the nicest peg on which any hurler can hang his after-30 hat. He continued to baffle with two elite whiff-generating pitches in his cutter and curve, the latter an especially deadly weapon. And hey, 43 saves are 43 saves. But more practically speaking, the season was a bit of a slog for the $52 million man. He received a standard and unceremonious mile-high treatment, paying a 150-point OPS tax on his adopted mound. And he blew a bunch of games at the top of a house-of-cards bullpen, including some higher-profile implosions amid the growing late-summer fire devil of an NL West race. So goes the life of the ninth-inning man. Colorado will hope the results part goes a bit better next year, and the year after for that matter, even if they'll likely be satisfied with another couple seasons of more or less the same, steady skill set.

Mike Dunn LHP   Born: 05/23/85   Age: 34   Bats: L   Throws: L   Height: 6'0"   Weight: 215   Origin: Round 33, 2004 Draft (#999 overall)

YEAR	TEAM	LVL	AGE	W	L	SV	G	GS	IP	H	HR	BB/9	K/9	K	GB%	BABIP	WHIP	ERA	DRA	WARP	MPH	FB%	WHF	CSP
2016	MIA	MLB	31	6	1	0	51	0	42¹	43	5	2.3	8.1	38	30%	.319	1.28	3.40	5.62	-0.3	95.8	62.9	12.8	49.2
2017	COL	MLB	32	5	1	0	68	0	50¹	43	8	5.0	10.2	57	34%	.276	1.41	4.47	5.29	-0.1	93.8	51.9	10.8	44.3
2018	COL	MLB	33	0	0	0	25	0	17	22	1	9.5	6.4	12	38%	.404	2.35	9.00	6.96	-0.4	93.3	56.1	10.6	43
2019	COL	MLB	34	1	1	0	31	0	32¹	34	5	4.5	7.9	28	37%	.318	1.56	4.96	5.46	-0.2	93.2	55.2	11.2	44.3

Breakout: 18%   Improve: 36%   Collapse: 25%   Attrition: 15%   MLB: 82%   *Comparables: Juan Cruz, John Axford, Will Ohman*

Mmmm, you forgot about Dunn when you were mentally Rolodexing all those bad Rockie reliever contracts, didn't you? These were dark days indeed in 2018, as the veteran southpaw tweaked his throwing shoulder in off-season workouts, tried (wildly unsuccessfully) to pitch through the pain, and ultimately succumbed to surgery that mercifully cut short his miserable campaign. When he's right he'll provide serviceable depth through the middle innings. But given his fly-ball tendencies and diminished velocity it seems unlikely that even in a return to good health he'll be able to pull off the late save on what has rapidly devolved into still more sunk cost in the Colorado 'pen.

Kyle Freeland LHP   Born: 05/14/93   Age: 26   Bats: L   Throws: L   Height: 6'3"   Weight: 170   Origin: Round 1, 2014 Draft (#8 overall)

YEAR	TEAM	LVL	AGE	W	L	SV	G	GS	IP	H	HR	BB/9	K/9	K	GB%	BABIP	WHIP	ERA	DRA	WARP	MPH	FB%	WHF	CSP
2016	NBR	AAX	23	5	7	0	14	14	88¹	84	9	2.5	5.2	51	53%	.268	1.23	3.87						
2016	ABQ	AAA	23	6	3	0	12	12	73²	81	7	2.3	7.0	57	55%	.330	1.36	3.91	3.97	1.2				
2017	COL	MLB	24	11	11	0	33	28	156	169	17	3.6	6.2	107	56%	.308	1.49	4.10	5.91	-0.6	93.6	64.5	8.2	46.1
2018	COL	MLB	25	17	7	0	33	33	202¹	182	17	3.1	7.7	173	48%	.285	1.25	2.85	3.89	3.3	93.6	52.5	9.9	47.9
2019	COL	MLB	26	11	9	0	29	29	174	167	18	3.0	7.8	150	49%	.310	1.30	3.91	4.30	2.0	93.2	58.2	9.4	48

Breakout: 28%   Improve: 62%   Collapse: 18%   Attrition: 8%   MLB: 90%   *Comparables: Sonny Gray, Martin Perez, Jesse Hahn*

Skepticism is a healthy part of evaluation, but it can create lag in appreciation. Freeland's debut the season prior had been very good, as far as most of the results went. But DRA was skeptical of a pitcher who whiffed so few in such an important place and time to whiff many. His game of keeping contact off the barrel doesn't tend to maintain as regularly, you see, especially at the height of rarefied air. Well, it translated in 2018, alright. Freeland shattered the all-time ERA mark for a pitcher at Coors, solving the impossibility of altitude across 15 excellent starts. The cutter cuts an obscene amount, and by year's end he was weaving hard stuff-heavy sequencing in and out of whichever quadrants he wanted. A dominant 11-game run tied off a rare 200-inning regular season and presaged electricity in October. The Rockies will gladly take four more sequels atop their rotation, though this next one will be his last before they have to start paying for the pleasure.

Jon Gray RHP   Born: 11/05/91   Age: 27   Bats: R   Throws: R   Height: 6'4"   Weight: 235   Origin: Round 1, 2013 Draft (#3 overall)

YEAR	TEAM	LVL	AGE	W	L	SV	G	GS	IP	H	HR	BB/9	K/9	K	GB%	BABIP	WHIP	ERA	DRA	WARP	MPH	FB%	WHF	CSP
2016	COL	MLB	24	10	10	0	29	29	168	153	18	3.2	9.9	185	45%	.309	1.26	4.61	4.54	1.6	97.9	55	13	48.2
2017	COL	MLB	25	10	4	0	20	20	110¹	113	10	2.4	9.1	112	49%	.336	1.30	3.67	3.32	2.8	97.8	57.4	9.9	49.8
2018	ABQ	AAA	26	1	0	0	2	2	10²	7	1	3.4	11.0	13	63%	.231	1.03	3.38	3.34	0.3				
2018	COL	MLB	26	12	9	0	31	31	172¹	180	27	2.7	9.6	183	49%	.323	1.35	5.12	4.45	1.7	96.8	49.7	13.3	48.7
2019	COL	MLB	27	11	8	0	28	28	159²	155	18	2.9	9.5	169	46%	.330	1.30	3.55	3.90	2.6	96.9	53.7	12.5	49.5

Breakout: 23%   Improve: 48%   Collapse: 16%   Attrition: 4%   MLB: 88%   *Comparables: Danny Salazar, Jordan Zimmermann, Jake Odorizzi*

The Rockies' erstwhile Ace walked through the gates at Talking Stick a leaner man after battling foot issues the season prior. But the trimmed-down Gray never really found a tighter groove, and a grooveless summer is no way to live. The velocity trailed off across the second half as his drive got stuck in traffic and his release point fluttered on up into the thin atmosphere. The spring in his step looked sprung. Playoff purgatory's a funky position for an Opening Day Starter, but a rocky homestretch tied a bow on it and bought him bleacher seats for October. DRA expected a better fate even in spite of the stretches of struggles, though there was an awful lot of hard contact along the way. The ceiling remains significant, but if it feels like an important season ahead for Gray, it is: The arbitration clock has started cha-chinging and the top of the rotation's been reserved for others.

Jeff Hoffman RHP   Born: 01/08/93   Age: 26   Bats: R   Throws: R   Height: 6'5"   Weight: 225   Origin: Round 1, 2014 Draft (#9 overall)

YEAR	TEAM	LVL	AGE	W	L	SV	G	GS	IP	H	HR	BB/9	K/9	K	GB%	BABIP	WHIP	ERA	DRA	WARP	MPH	FB%	WHF	CSP
2016	ABQ	AAA	23	6	9	0	22	22	118²	117	11	3.3	9.4	124	44%	.325	1.36	4.02	3.96	1.9				
2016	COL	MLB	23	0	4	0	8	6	31¹	37	7	4.9	6.3	22	51%	.297	1.72	4.88	7.05	-0.6	96.8	58.7	8.2	47.3
2017	ABQ	AAA	24	3	3	0	10	10	49²	44	3	3.4	8.5	47	46%	.304	1.47	5.89	6.08	-0.6	96.5	67	8.9	50.7
2017	COL	MLB	24	6	5	0	23	16	99¹	106	15	3.6	7.4	82	42%	.331	1.47	5.89	6.08	-0.6	96.5	67	8.9	50.7
2018	COL	MLB	25	0	0	0	6	1	8²	15	0	7.3	5.2	5	53%	.469	2.54	9.35	7.23	-0.2	94.7	53.9	8.9	42.8
2018	ABQ	AAA	25	6	8	0	21	21	105²	105	9	4.0	8.7	102	46%	.331	1.44	4.94	4.13	1.7				
2019	COL	MLB	26	2	3	0	8	8	40	40	5	3.7	8.1	36	44%	.318	1.42	4.35	4.79	0.2	96.0	65.3	8.9	47.4

Breakout: 24%   Improve: 45%   Collapse: 22%   Attrition: 31%   MLB: 76%   Comparables: Carlos Carrasco, Anthony Bass, Robbie Erlin

The Rockies did Toronto a big financial solid when they finally shipped Tulo in order to shop higher shelves and jumpstart their reboot. Hoffman was the spoils. Scouts loved the size, gas and hook, and Tommy John recovery was melting further into the past by the day. But it's been a minute now, and the stuff has backed up and dragged the control down with the ship. He made it back to the majors again in June, though the leash was short and he got walloped once again. From there on out he struggled back at Triple-A, and what he contributes from this here crossroads is anybody's guess.

D.J. Johnson RHP   Born: 08/30/89   Age: 29   Bats: L   Throws: R   Height: 6'4"   Weight: 235   Origin: Undrafted Free Agent, 2010

YEAR	TEAM	LVL	AGE	W	L	SV	G	GS	IP	H	HR	BB/9	K/9	K	GB%	BABIP	WHIP	ERA	DRA	WARP	MPH	FB%	WHF	CSP
2016	ARK	AA	26	4	4	6	47	1	69¹	78	1	4.2	8.7	67	51%	.374	1.59	4.02	4.14	0.5				
2017	HFD	AA	27	1	1	4	43	0	64¹	53	4	3.4	7.1	51	59%	.265	1.20	2.80	3.87	0.7				
2018	ABQ	AAA	28	3	5	18	50	0	55¹	56	5	2.4	13.7	84	44%	.398	1.28	3.90	2.74	1.5				
2018	COL	MLB	28	1	0	0	7	0	6¹	6	0	2.8	12.8	9	38%	.375	1.26	4.26	4.70	0.0	95.3	44.8	16.2	44.8
2019	COL	MLB	29	1	0	0	25	0	27	27	4	3.8	10.0	30	46%	.337	1.43	4.28	4.71	0.1	94.6	44.8	16.2	44.8

Breakout: 8%   Improve: 10%   Collapse: 7%   Attrition: 13%   MLB: 20%   Comparables: Layne Somsen, Jess Todd, Jose Valdez

Just your run-of-the-mill undrafted free agent who came out of minor-league bullpens for five different organizations across more than 270 affiliated appearances, beach bummed two tours of indy ball, tore his pitching shoulder apart, worked in a Scioto County lumber mill when it looked like he might not get another shot, got another shot, threw one season, then a full 32-game winter season in Mexico, then kept throwing right on into another season, and finally Beatrix Kiddo'ed his way onto a big-league mound a mile high in the sky. Johnson struck out both hitters he faced in his major league debut. Then he made the postseason roster instead of the club's Opening Day starter. He struck out a couple more hitters when he pitched in October, too. Unreal. He sits 94 with a wipeout slider and all the time in the world.

Peter Lambert RHP   Born: 04/18/97   Age: 22   Bats: R   Throws: R   Height: 6'2"   Weight: 185   Origin: Round 2, 2015 Draft (#44 overall)

YEAR	TEAM	LVL	AGE	W	L	SV	G	GS	IP	H	HR	BB/9	K/9	K	GB%	BABIP	WHIP	ERA	DRA	WARP	MPH	FB%	WHF	CSP
2016	ASH	A	19	5	8	0	26	26	126	125	7	2.4	7.7	108	47%	.324	1.25	3.93	6.30	-2.0				
2017	LNC	A+	20	9	8	0	26	26	142¹	147	18	1.9	8.3	131	43%	.321	1.24	4.17	3.92	2.2				
2018	HFD	AA	21	8	2	0	15	15	92²	80	6	1.2	7.3	75	50%	.282	0.99	2.23	4.53	0.9				
2018	ABQ	AAA	21	2	5	0	11	11	55¹	72	5	2.4	5.0	31	52%	.345	1.57	5.04	4.62	0.6				
2019	COL	MLB	22	7	7	0	23	23	118²	129	17	2.7	6.7	88	43%	.320	1.39	4.48	4.92	0.5				

Breakout: 14%   Improve: 22%   Collapse: 8%   Attrition: 23%   MLB: 41%   Comparables: Ariel Jurado, Enyel De Los Santos, Will Smith

With a spate of recent graduations and standard attrition around him, Lambert's claim as the organization's best pitching prospect isn't an especially controversial one. Whether the pedigree can translate to palatable big-league innings in the harshest of environments remains to be seen, though he's tamed such elements before. Eleven strikeout-challenged starts at Triple-A reminded us of his limitations, specifically the lack of a true bat-misser among his four pitches. But he made those starts at the same age as most college juniors, and his strike-throwing and tenacity are the stuff of a legitimate big-league starter. He should garner his first opportunity to fulfill that destiny in 2019.

German Marquez RHP   Born: 02/22/95   Age: 24   Bats: R   Throws: R   Height: 6'1"   Weight: 185   Origin: International Free Agent, 2011

YEAR	TEAM	LVL	AGE	W	L	SV	G	GS	IP	H	HR	BB/9	K/9	K	GB%	BABIP	WHIP	ERA	DRA	WARP	MPH	FB%	WHF	CSP
2016	NBR	AAX	21	9	6	0	21	21	135²	124	9	2.2	8.4	126	48%	.304	1.16	2.85						
2016	ABQ	AAA	21	2	0	0	5	5	31	30	5	1.7	8.4	29	45%	.298	1.16	4.35	4.18	0.4				
2016	COL	MLB	21	1	1	0	6	3	20²	28	2	2.6	6.5	15	55%	.361	1.65	5.23	5.71	-0.1	96.8	62.6	9.8	54.6
2017	ABQ	AAA	22	0	0	0	3	2	10	8	2	0.0	16.2	18	53%	.353	0.80	2.70	2.80	0.3				
2017	COL	MLB	22	11	7	0	29	29	162	174	25	2.7	8.2	147	47%	.316	1.38	4.39	5.08	0.9	97.5	65.5	10	53.7
2018	COL	MLB	23	14	11	0	33	33	196	179	24	2.6	10.6	230	48%	.312	1.20	3.77	3.23	4.7	97.5	54.9	13.4	49.9
2019	COL	MLB	24	11	8	0	29	29	165¹	151	18	2.8	10.2	187	46%	.325	1.22	3.31	3.65	3.2	97.3	61.1	12.3	53.9

Breakout: 27%   Improve: 66%   Collapse: 9%   Attrition: 14%   MLB: 96%   Comparables: Drew Smyly, Mike Minor, Matt Garza

It's weird to talk about the top of Colorado's rotation in glowing terms, but Marquez forced the issue after a stellar sophomore season. The evolution of his slider added a third lethal weapon to his arsenal, and with two well above-average spinners now in tow he left a trail of right-handed devastation in his wake. Lefties continued to see him pretty well, and if one were to pick non-Coors nits his lack of a reliable out pitch against the fairer-handed remains a heel fit for Achilles. The weakness wasn't nearly enough to derail one of the truly magnificent breakouts of 2018, however, and he even managed to offset his run prevention deficits with a Silver-Slugging effort at the dish. Still a year removed from arbitration eligibility, he'll enter the season as one of the most coveted assets in town.

Jake McGee LHP Born: 08/06/86   Age: 32   Bats: L   Throws: L   Height: 6'3"   Weight: 230   Origin: Round 5, 2004 Draft (#135 overall)

YEAR	TEAM	LVL	AGE	W	L	SV	G	GS	IP	H	HR	BB/9	K/9	K	GB%	BABIP	WHIP	ERA	DRA	WARP	MPH	FB%	WHF	CSP
2016	COL	MLB	29	2	3	15	57	0	45²	56	9	3.2	7.5	38	41%	.338	1.58	4.73	7.01	-1.1	96.5	84.3	10.3	50
2017	COL	MLB	30	0	2	3	62	0	57¹	47	4	2.5	9.1	58	40%	.287	1.10	3.61	4.26	0.6	97.2	93.4	10.2	51.9
2018	COL	MLB	31	2	4	1	61	0	51¹	59	10	2.8	8.2	47	42%	.322	1.46	6.49	6.15	-0.7	96.2	86.3	11.1	53.2
2019	COL	MLB	32	3	1	0	51	0	53²	53	7	3.2	8.4	50	41%	.314	1.35	4.21	4.63	0.1	95.7	87.5	10.5	51.5

Breakout: 22%   Improve: 37%   Collapse: 31%   Attrition: 6%   MLB: 93%   *Comparables: Joakim Soria, Rafael Betancourt, Mike Jackson*

Here's the thing about being a one-pitch reliever: if that pitch ain't working, you won't be for much longer, either. There is of course a caveat, as that calculus changes a bit when you've just put pen to paper and guaranteed yourself $27 million. But a season removed from salvaging his standing and earning that deal, McGee once again took a wander down the wrong block. His velocity crept down a tick, but of greater concern was the speed at which his pitched balls came screaming back in the other direction. His once-formidable heater increasingly looks miscast in the lift-and-launch era, as hitters routinely pummeled the pitch down in the zone en route to a 91st percentile exit velocity. A late-season flirtation with more sliders did little to stem the tide, and he'll continue his search for an adjustment that'll stick in 2019.

Harrison Musgrave LHP Born: 03/03/92   Age: 27   Bats: L   Throws: L   Height: 6'1"   Weight: 205   Origin: Round 8, 2014 Draft (#233 overall)

YEAR	TEAM	LVL	AGE	W	L	SV	G	GS	IP	H	HR	BB/9	K/9	K	GB%	BABIP	WHIP	ERA	DRA	WARP	MPH	FB%	WHF	CSP
2016	NBR	AAX	24	5	1	0	6	6	40¹	20	1	1.8	6.7	30	51%	.174	0.69	1.79						
2016	ABQ	AAA	24	8	7	0	19	19	113	118	17	3.2	6.3	79	43%	.292	1.40	4.30	4.24	1.4				
2017	ABQ	AAA	25	3	1	0	12	12	54¹	64	10	4.3	6.5	39	41%	.318	1.66	6.79	4.79	0.5				
2018	ABQ	AAA	26	0	1	0	8	3	16²	23	2	3.2	9.7	18	44%	.404	1.74	5.40	3.61	0.3				
2018	COL	MLB	26	2	3	0	35	0	44²	36	7	4.4	6.4	32	40%	.236	1.30	4.63	6.70	-0.9	92.9	59.5	10.7	42.7
2019	COL	MLB	27	1	1	0	31	0	32¹	33	5	3.7	7.6	27	42%	.304	1.42	4.88	5.37	-0.2	92.4	60.2	10.9	43.2

Breakout: 5%   Improve: 13%   Collapse: 21%   Attrition: 27%   MLB: 47%   *Comparables: Joe Biagini, Chris Stratton, Anthony Ranaudo*

Harrison Musgrave, pitcher, made the majors in 2018 and was about as interesting to watch as Harrison Musgrave, guest lecturer on the Teapot Dome Scandal. Back around the time Colorado drafted him in the round where teams draft polished Big 12 pitchers with limited upside, he projected for fringy big-league utility on the back of an average-ish fastball and a sure, okay, fine changeup from the left side. Well, here we are a handful of years later and you can chalk one up for the scouts. The cambio actually played a bit better than advertised in the bigs, but right-handers ruthlessly pummeled his spin and speed. There are probably still some useful days ahead of him—he *is* left-handed, after all—although that's what they used to say about ol' Warren G. Harding, too.

Scott Oberg RHP Born: 03/13/90   Age: 29   Bats: R   Throws: R   Height: 6'2"   Weight: 205   Origin: Round 15, 2012 Draft (#468 overall)

YEAR	TEAM	LVL	AGE	W	L	SV	G	GS	IP	H	HR	BB/9	K/9	K	GB%	BABIP	WHIP	ERA	DRA	WARP	MPH	FB%	WHF	CSP
2016	ABQ	AAA	26	1	0	9	27	0	29²	16	1	3.3	10.9	36	54%	.234	0.91	2.43	2.59	0.8				
2016	COL	MLB	26	1	1	1	24	0	26	26	3	3.8	6.9	20	56%	.295	1.42	5.19	5.34	-0.1	97.2	60	10.7	47.6
2017	COL	MLB	27	0	1	0	66	0	58¹	70	4	3.7	8.5	55	58%	.367	1.61	4.94	4.89	0.2	98.1	56.4	12.2	50.5
2018	ABQ	AAA	28	1	0	3	13	0	15¹	14	1	1.2	8.2	14	62%	.333	1.04	1.76	3.94	0.2				
2018	COL	MLB	28	8	1	0	56	0	58²	45	4	1.8	8.7	57	58%	.270	0.97	2.45	3.49	1.0	97.0	55.1	14.7	48.1
2019	COL	MLB	29	3	1	0	51	0	53²	49	5	3.4	9.1	54	52%	.315	1.28	3.59	3.96	0.6	96.8	56.3	13.2	48.8

Breakout: 28%   Improve: 46%   Collapse: 27%   Attrition: 20%   MLB: 92%   *Comparables: Ryan Pressly, Jared Burton, Hunter Strickland*

Step 1: sit 96 off an arm-strength delivery.
Step 2: start missing entirely or at least getting under the barrel of like four out of every five swinging bats with a high-80s, two-plane slider.
Step 3: stop throwing basically every other pitch.

So went the formula for Oberg's ascension from solid-if-unspectacular middle man to frothy highest-leverage October arm. By the time the Brewers cancelled Rocktober the right-hander was among the last reliable men standing in a ravaged bullpen, and even his uppins came in the decisive game. Despite the salty final bite, it was a dynamic rise for the former 15th-rounder, who survived a late-April meltdown and demotion to return a month later and yield five runs over the next nigh-on four months. As he'll arbitrate his first contract this winter, he should remain cheap enough for the Rockies to rely on for the next couple years.

Seung Hwan Oh RHP Born: 07/15/82   Age: 36   Bats: R   Throws: R   Height: 5'10"   Weight: 205   Origin: International Free Agent, 2016

YEAR	TEAM	LVL	AGE	W	L	SV	G	GS	IP	H	HR	BB/9	K/9	K	GB%	BABIP	WHIP	ERA	DRA	WARP	MPH	FB%	WHF	CSP
2016	SLN	MLB	33	6	3	19	76	0	79²	55	5	2.0	11.6	103	40%	.270	0.92	1.92	2.24	2.5	95.7	60.7	18.7	45.8
2017	SLN	MLB	34	1	6	20	62	0	59¹	68	10	2.3	8.2	54	30%	.319	1.40	4.10	5.70	-0.4	94.4	61.9	14.7	49.9
2018	TOR	MLB	35	4	3	2	48	0	47	37	5	1.9	10.5	55	31%	.276	1.00	2.68	4.31	0.3	93.1	57.5	15.2	46.6
2018	COL	MLB	35	2	0	1	25	0	21¹	15	3	3.0	10.1	24	30%	.240	1.03	2.53	4.81	0.0	93.2	43.6	17.6	42.9
2019	COL	MLB	36	3	1	0	51	0	53²	51	9	3.1	10.0	60	35%	.314	1.30	4.28	4.70	0.1	92.9	56.7	16	46

Breakout: 27%   Improve: 38%   Collapse: 29%   Attrition: 5%   MLB: 80%   *Comparables: Arthur Rhodes, Jim Brewer, Mike Adams*

The Final Boss morphed into more of a Middle Innings Boss in 2018, a Bald Bull for the modern era. His charge still hit hard, and he blew his four-seamer by hitters at a near-elite clip despite the pitch creaking down to 92. It was a nice return to form after his struggles during a second season in St. Louis, even if DRA wasn't convinced on the merits. The Rockies were, however, and imported him with his trusty translator Eugene Koo for the stretch run. They got what they bought, as Oh manufactured a bunch of outs at a time when that wasn't the cool thing to do in Colorado's bullpen. The club holds a no-brainer option on a full season of his services, and the greatest Korean reliever in the game's history should have opportunity to pitch for as long as he can and will.

www.baseballprospectus.com

Adam Ottavino RHP   Born: 11/22/85   Age: 33   Bats: B   Throws: R   Height: 6'5"   Weight: 220   Origin: Round 1, 2006 Draft (#30 overall)

YEAR	TEAM	LVL	AGE	W	L	SV	G	GS	IP	H	HR	BB/9	K/9	K	GB%	BABIP	WHIP	ERA	DRA	WARP	MPH	FB%	WHF	CSP
2016	COL	MLB	30	1	3	7	34	0	27	18	3	2.3	11.7	35	62%	.250	0.93	2.67	4.22	0.2	96.3	52.6	12.8	44.8
2017	COL	MLB	31	2	3	0	63	0	53¹	48	8	6.6	10.6	63	40%	.310	1.63	5.06	6.10	-0.6	96.3	50.2	9.9	46.3
2018	COL	MLB	32	6	4	6	75	0	77²	41	5	4.2	13.0	112	44%	.242	0.99	2.43	3.02	1.7	95.7	43.1	13	47.9
2019	COL	MLB	33	3	1	2	58	0	61²	51	8	4.3	11.4	78	45%	.310	1.29	3.90	4.30	0.4	94.9	46.2	11.7	46.1

Breakout: 20%   Improve: 44%   Collapse: 30%   Attrition: 9%   MLB: 91%   *Comparables: Pedro Strop, Damaso Marte, Brian Fuentes*

In a land of flat pitches, Ottavino's slider swept just about harder'n anybody else's slider last year. A diabolical delivery masked that filthy breaker, and it didn't help hitters that he sits 94 with a couple ticks on top from the extension and deception. He's older than you think he is, mostly because it took him a long time to stay healthy enough and find opportunity to dominate again. He's never really had a shot at sea-level home cooking. Then again, outside of a really poor two weeks in 2017, he hasn't ever really struggled to throw disgusting inning after disgusting inning at a mile high, either. Payment is due his way in free agency, and due it shall inevitably come. We've seen more than enough at this point to know that he'll be very, very good...if he's healthy.

Riley Pint RHP   Born: 11/06/97   Age: 21   Bats: R   Throws: R   Height: 6'4"   Weight: 195   Origin: Round 1, 2016 Draft (#4 overall)

YEAR	TEAM	LVL	AGE	W	L	SV	G	GS	IP	H	HR	BB/9	K/9	K	GB%	BABIP	WHIP	ERA	DRA	WARP	MPH	FB%	WHF	CSP
2016	GJR	RK	18	1	5	0	11	11	37	43	2	5.6	8.8	36	60%	.383	1.78	5.35	4.48	0.5				
2017	ASH	A	19	2	11	0	22	22	93	96	3	5.7	7.6	79	60%	.325	1.67	5.42	4.58	0.8				
2018	BOI	A-	20	0	2	0	3	3	8	4	0	10.1	9.0	8	47%	.235	1.62	1.12	4.88	0.0				
2019	COL	MLB	21	1	3	0	8	8	30²	36	6	7.9	7.2	25	46%	.330	2.04	6.77	7.50	-0.8				

Breakout: 1%   Improve: 1%   Collapse: 0%   Attrition: 2%   MLB: 2%   *Comparables: Elvin Ramirez, Greg Reynolds, James Houser*

Look, it was *always* going to be a process, from the moment Colorado popped Pint fourth overall a couple years back. He's a big dude, still growing into his big dude body, and his stuff moves just a disgusting amount. That's a recipe for lagging command and a slow growth curve if ever you've seen one. And sure enough, here we are where we are today. Pint made precious little progress refining his craft last year, staggering instead through a forearm scare and an oblique strain that combined to drink up just about the full season. The peaks of the Rocky Mountains themselves still look up at Pint's ceiling; pitchers with elite fastballs and the potential for three average-or-better secondaries don't grow on trees, after all. He'll hope for a healthy camp and healthier mechanics in 2019, while a thirsty pack of TINSTAAPP truthers gather and circle.

Ryan Rolison LHP   Born: 07/11/97   Age: 21   Bats: R   Throws: L   Height: 6'2"   Weight: 195   Origin: Round 1, 2018 Draft (#22 overall)

YEAR	TEAM	LVL	AGE	W	L	SV	G	GS	IP	H	HR	BB/9	K/9	K	GB%	BABIP	WHIP	ERA	DRA	WARP	MPH	FB%	WHF	CSP
2018	GJR	RK	20	0	1	0	9	9	29	15	2	2.5	10.6	34	66%	.200	0.79	1.86	3.40	0.8				
2019	COL	MLB	21	2	3	0	8	8	33²	37	5	5.0	8.1	30	56%	.331	1.65	5.26	5.79	-0.2				

Comparables: Thyago Vieira, Yency Almonte, Kendry Flores

The Rockies called Rolison's number with the 22nd overall pick last June, and when they did they brought on board one of the more polished arms in the draft class. The performance in a two-year career at Mississippi was more solid than spectacular, but the raw ingredients are much better than that, including one of the better curveballs in the collegiate ranks and a well-proportioned, athletic frame that should eventually allow repeatable mechanics to take hold. Each of the left-hander's four pitches already suggests average-or-better value down the line, and the combination proved much too difficult for Pioneer League hitters to handle during a brief slate of action after signing. He should see plenty of full-season ball in his first full year among professionals.

Chris Rusin LHP   Born: 10/22/86   Age: 32   Bats: L   Throws: L   Height: 6'2"   Weight: 195   Origin: Round 4, 2009 Draft (#140 overall)

YEAR	TEAM	LVL	AGE	W	L	SV	G	GS	IP	H	HR	BB/9	K/9	K	GB%	BABIP	WHIP	ERA	DRA	WARP	MPH	FB%	WHF	CSP
2016	COL	MLB	29	3	5	0	29	7	84¹	82	5	2.5	7.4	69	61%	.308	1.25	3.74	4.39	0.7	91.7	43.3	10.2	46.5
2017	COL	MLB	30	5	1	2	60	0	85	75	9	2.0	7.5	71	60%	.277	1.11	2.65	3.49	1.6	92.6	43.1	13.2	48.7
2018	COL	MLB	31	2	3	0	49	0	54²	56	7	4.3	7.7	47	57%	.308	1.50	6.09	5.62	-0.4	91.4	50.7	10	47.5
2019	COL	MLB	32	2	1	0	46	0	48¹	50	6	3.4	7.9	43	54%	.325	1.41	4.11	4.52	0.3	91.0	45.3	11.2	47.2

Breakout: 19%   Improve: 37%   Collapse: 20%   Attrition: 16%   MLB: 73%   *Comparables: Scott Downs, Casey Fossum, Dillon Gee*

Folks, we might as well call the Rockies' bullpen "American democracy" because a Rusin sure undermined the hell out of it in 2018. It's generally not a great sign when a player's high point for an entire season occurs in March, but there he was, inheriting a bases-loaded, no-out jam in a tight one on Opening Day. He got that left-left punchout they were looking for, the next-best-thing pop fly followed and then just the kind of harmless inning-ending rollover that affords time for proper histrionics heading off the mound. His reward? Two inherited runs on his tab the next inning and four consecutive months of injured, ineffective ugliness for his trouble. He found it in time for the real show, logging scoreless appearances in each one of the club's postseason games. It wasn't exactly a happy ending, but there was surely a satisfied nod to be seen. There's no hope for lifting the sanctions on him starting games, but lefties don't handle his sinker especially well and he's still cheap—both traits that tend to bode well for longevity.

Antonio Senzatela RHP   Born: 01/21/95   Age: 24   Bats: R   Throws: R   Height: 6'1"   Weight: 180   Origin: International Free Agent, 2011

YEAR	TEAM	LVL	AGE	W	L	SV	G	GS	IP	H	HR	BB/9	K/9	K	GB%	BABIP	WHIP	ERA	DRA	WARP	MPH	FB%	WHF	CSP
2016	NBR	AAX	21	4	1	0	7	7	34²	27	1	2.3	7.0	27	44%	.265	1.04	1.82						
2017	COL	MLB	22	10	5	0	36	20	134²	128	18	3.1	6.8	102	50%	.280	1.30	4.68	4.63	1.3	96.9	71.8	7.6	52.2
2018	ABQ	AAA	23	3	1	0	8	8	37²	29	1	2.9	10.0	42	48%	.298	1.09	2.15	4.27	0.5				
2018	COL	MLB	23	6	6	0	23	13	90¹	94	10	3.0	6.9	69	47%	.302	1.37	4.38	5.10	0.1	96.0	64.1	8.9	47.5
2019	COL	MLB	24	9	7	0	43	23	143¹	134	15	3.0	7.9	126	45%	.304	1.27	3.88	4.26	1.5	96.3	70.3	8.5	51.1

Breakout: 20%   Improve: 47%   Collapse: 21%   Attrition: 19%   MLB: 92%   *Comparables: Jeremy Sowers, Jarrod Parker, Joe Ross*

There's a certain responsibility that comes with being a not-enormous right-hander; certain assumptions to defy. Senzatela's up-and-over delivery helps his good fastball play better, but his career's path to date has been defined by a not-quite-successful quest to find things to throw with it. The slider's his strikeout pitch and a clear number two on his depth chart. But hitters slugged it like each and every one of 'em was Trevor Story last year. His change has always been a little too firm, and fly balls are dangerous balls (yes, especially so in Coors Field). The curve got decent results last year, but again, that thing about fly balls in Coors. His swing role on the cheap is a valuable one for every big-league team, and with arbitration still two years away it's a role that should suit him for the foreseeable future.

Bryan Shaw RHP Born: 11/08/87 Age: 31 Bats: B Throws: R Height: 6'1" Weight: 220 Origin: Round 2, 2008 Draft (#73 overall)

YEAR	TEAM	LVL	AGE	W	L	SV	G	GS	IP	H	HR	BB/9	K/9	K	GB%	BABIP	WHIP	ERA	DRA	WARP	MPH	FB%	WHF	CSP
2016	CLE	MLB	28	2	5	1	75	0	66²	56	8	3.8	9.3	69	56%	.284	1.26	3.24	3.49	1.1	95.9	81.4	12.9	47.5
2017	CLE	MLB	29	4	6	3	79	0	76²	71	5	2.6	8.6	73	57%	.311	1.21	3.52	2.73	2.1	96.5	88.2	13.1	48.4
2018	COL	MLB	30	4	6	0	61	0	54²	70	9	4.6	8.9	54	49%	.370	1.79	5.93	4.07	0.5	95.9	84.8	12.5	43.8
2019	COL	MLB	31	3	1	2	51	0	53²	52	6	3.9	8.6	51	50%	.315	1.39	4.10	4.52	0.2	95.3	84.7	12.8	46

Breakout: 31%   Improve: 57%   Collapse: 19%   Attrition: 10%   MLB: 90%   *Comparables: Mike MacDougal, Bob Locker, Rafael Perez*

Paying for past performance can be expensive, and sure enough, fresh off inking his first big-money deal Shaw looked anything but. Right from the jump in Spring Training he rather resembled the weathered part of a guy who led all of baseball in appearances over the previous five seasons. He never did get quite right in the season's first half, with a snowball of mid-season ineffectiveness culminating in the iron man getting put on ice for the first time in his career, a calf issue ostensibly to blame. The performance improved upon return, but the warning signs never stopped flashing; his patented cutter left a couple ticks of velocity in the trainer's room, he worked in back-to-back games but once more and Bud Black hailed his way just four times in September before leaving him off the playoff roster entirely. Like most of his bullpen-mates he'll look to hit the reset button this winter.

LINEOUTS

Hitters

HITTER	POS	TEAM	LVL	AGE	PA	R	2B	3B	HR	RBI	BB	K	SB	CS	AVG/OBP/SLG	DRC+	VORP	BABIP	BRR	FRAA	WARP
Willie Abreu	RF	BOI	A-	23	41	3	2	0	0	3	3	9	2	0	.162/.225/.216	100	-3.5	.214	-0.2	RF(8): 0.9	0.1
	RF	LNC	A+	23	277	41	12	2	7	27	20	62	19	9	.266/.322/.413	98	3.9	.328	1.9	RF(55): -5.9, CF(1): 0.0	0.0
Noel Cuevas	RF	ABQ	AAA	26	177	17	10	4	5	29	16	23	3	5	.331/.390/.538	122	11.2	.361	0.0	RF(26): -2.0, LF(17): -3.6	0.4
	RF	COL	MLB	26	153	16	4	1	2	10	6	24	1	0	.233/.268/.315	87	-5.8	.267	-0.4	RF(26): 0.9, LF(16): -3.4	-0.1
Yonathan Daza	CF	HFD	AA	24	228	27	18	2	4	29	7	24	4	5	.306/.330/.461	114	7.3	.330	-0.6	CF(30): 1.3, RF(16): 4.2	1.5
Eddy Diaz	SS	DCR	Rk	18	223	57	13	5	0	24	31	17	54	8	.309/.417/.436	139	33.4	.337	8.6	SS(39): -1.4, 2B(13): -0.7	2.5
Vince Fernandez	LF	LNC	A+	22	499	82	25	8	24	75	65	172	10	5	.265/.370/.532	134	30.6	.384	6.3	LF(70): 9.7, RF(38): 2.3	5.0
Josh Fuentes	3B	ABQ	AAA	25	586	93	39	12	14	95	21	103	3	5	.327/.354/.517	111	25.0	.376	2.5	3B(110): 6.2, 1B(21): 0.6	3.9
Daniel Montano	CF	DCR	Rk	19	51	4	2	0	1	8	5	5	2	0	.182/.275/.295	130	-1.0	.179	-0.4	RF(7): 0.3, CF(3): -0.4	0.2
	CF	GJR	Rk	19	264	32	15	5	4	29	21	57	9	5	.279/.338/.433	95	8.7	.350	-0.7	CF(58): -11.2, RF(1): 0.0	-0.4
Brian Mundell	1B	HFD	AA	24	506	49	25	1	7	41	53	77	1	3	.263/.345/.372	105	1.7	.301	-0.3	1B(92): 5.8, LF(24): 1.5	1.8
Tyler Nevin	1B	LNC	A+	21	417	59	25	1	13	62	34	77	4	3	.328/.386/.503	129	15.0	.383	-4.4	1B(67): -0.7, 3B(17): 1.0	1.7
Dom Nunez	C	HFD	AA	23	377	34	12	0	9	42	46	73	8	6	.222/.320/.343	100	6.3	.257	-1.0	C(70): 5.8	2.0
Roberto Ramos	1B	LNC	A+	23	255	44	15	3	17	43	32	65	3	1	.304/.411/.640	162	24.5	.364	1.2	1B(42): -0.8	2.3
	1B	HFD	AA	23	228	26	9	0	15	34	26	75	2	1	.231/.320/.503	124	7.2	.279	-1.1	1B(42): -0.4	0.8
Wes Rogers	OF	HFD	AA	24	197	17	4	1	2	15	15	44	14	4	.200/.269/.269	85	-4.5	.254	2.9	LF(31): 1.7, CF(14): -2.4	0.3
	OF	LNC	A+	24	206	30	8	0	6	34	17	48	10	3	.286/.345/.427	120	7.9	.351	1.4	LF(43): -4.1, CF(2): 0.1	0.7
Terrin Vavra	SS	BOI	A-	21	199	22	8	4	4	26	26	40	9	1	.302/.396/.467	126	15.7	.373	-0.5	SS(28): 0.8, 2B(16): -2.0	1.2

Willie Abreu looks and sometimes moves like a linebacker, but also doesn't quite hit with the oomph you'd expect from someone with his size and swing path. This concludes this test of the Future Fourth Outfielder Alert System. ⓧ The organization's highest-paid J2 signee last summer, **Warming Bernabel** has the chance to be a global superstar, though climate scientists might be warning about the waters rising to Denver by the time the 16-year-old reaches the majors. ⓧ A 21st-round selection presaged a journey of nearly eight years and almost 800 minor-league games before **Noel Cuevas** finally staggered onto a big-league field. But after his right-handed bat provided negative value against left-handed pitching (in Coors, no less), it might take that long for him to garner another shot. ⓧ Injuries dampened the follow-up to a breakout 2017 campaign, but **Yonathan Daza** continued to impress defensively at Double-A while flashing enough bat-to-ball to suggest a future 25-man role. ⓧ Colorado paid $750,000 to procure **Eddy Diaz**'s talents on the international market, and while DSL stats are overwhelmingly useless, his 84 stolen bases in 87 professional games at an 86-percent clip is some kinda alliterative something. He'll be stateside this year. ⓧ **Vince Fernandez** produced the most Lancaster season of any hitter last year, but a whole bunch of empty swings at fat pitches in the zone suggest we should temper expectations for him in Double-A. ⓧ Nolan Arenado's cousin went undrafted out of college, but here we are half a decade later and **Josh Fuentes** hasn't really ever stopped hitting, including all year at Albuquerque and throughout the Arizona Fall League. There's a decent chance he tags in for Nolan in his big-league debut, and that's just a plain old cool baseball thing. ⓧ A $2 million bonus baby once upon a time, **Daniel Montano** held his own in his stateside debut and might eventually, some day, grow old enough to hoist a pint to celebrate the performance. ⓧ The 24-year-old right-handed first base-only guys who slug .372 in Double-A do not, typically, top prospects make. And 25-year-olds who reprise that line tend more often than not to find themselves touring organizational depth charts from Hartford to Hanwha. So this year's a big one for **Brian Mundell**. ⓧ Patient and powerful like his dad, **Tyler Nevin** has battled significant injuries throughout his career, including two DL stints last season. He crushed California and Arizona Fall League pitching alike after returning from the most recent one though, and his bat might just be enough to carve out a big-league path if he can stay on the field. ⓧ On one hand, the bar for backup catcher offense has been set extremely low in Colorado (thanks, Tony Wolters). On the other, **Dom Nunez** might just test those limits if ever granted the opportunity. ⓧ **Roberto Ramos** won the Cal League home run derby and three-true-outcomed his way to Double-A, where he'll find long-term comfort unless the bat really maxes out. ⓧ It's Terrance Gore's world, and **Wes Rogers** is just hoping to one day live in it. ⓧ Back issues crunched his collegiate career, but third-rounder **Terrin Vavra** impressed with a broad base of skills in his pro debut.

Pitchers

PITCHER	TEAM	LVL	AGE	W	L	SV	G	GS	IP	H	HR	BB/9	K/9	K	GB%	BABIP	WHIP	ERA	DRA	WARP	MPH	FB%	WHF	CSP
Carlos Estevez	ABQ	AAA	25	0	1	1	28	0	28¹	37	6	3.5	11.1	35	39%	.397	1.69	6.35	3.44	0.5				
Rico Garcia	LNC	A+	24	7	7	0	16	15	100	99	12	2.0	9.1	101	46%	.315	1.21	3.42	4.28	1.2				
	HFD	AA	24	6	2	0	11	11	67	54	8	2.7	8.2	61	44%	.264	1.10	2.28	4.18	0.9				
Rayan Gonzalez	HFD	AA	27	0	1	0	19	0	17¹	19	4	4.2	8.8	17	44%	.300	1.56	5.19	5.09	0.0				
Sam Howard	ABQ	AAA	25	3	8	0	21	21	96	106	13	3.2	7.5	80	40%	.327	1.46	5.06	4.85	0.8				
	COL	MLB	25	0	0	0	4	0	4	5	0	6.8	2.2	1	53%	.333	2.00	2.25	8.49	-0.2	92.8	48.8	8.1	50.2
Reid Humphreys	LNC	A+	23	2	0	22	35	0	34¹	22	1	3.4	13.4	51	51%	.292	1.02	1.83	3.18	0.7				
Justin Lawrence	LNC	A+	23	0	2	11	55	0	54¹	36	2	4.5	10.3	62	63%	.264	1.16	2.65	3.41	1.0				
Mike Nikorak	BOI	A-	21	0	0	0	9	2	8¹	7	0	11.9	10.8	10	55%	.350	2.16	4.32	4.16	0.1				
Jesus Tinoco	HFD	AA	23	9	12	0	26	26	141	149	23	2.4	8.4	132	38%	.313	1.33	4.79	4.16	1.9				
Robert Tyler	ASH	A	23	4	2	8	34	0	38¹	37	5	1.6	12.2	52	62%	.323	1.15	3.99	2.85	0.9				
	LNC	A+	23	0	1	0	12	0	9¹	17	2	4.8	4.8	5	46%	.429	2.36	9.64	5.52	-0.1				

An anticipated piece of the bullpen puzzle entering the year, **Carlos Estevez** instead missed the first half of it with oblique and elbow issues, then got bit by the home run bug at Triple-A. The stuff remained intact on re-entry, and he'll try again to seize hold of a 25-man spot in 2019. ⊗ A former 30th-rounder, **Rico Garcia** up and tamed Lancaster for a hundred innings before holding his own in a half season of Double-A last year, and if that was his peak, he can lay claim to a better one than most. ⊗ The once-promising ascent of **Rayan Gonzalez** paused for the cause of a one-and-a-half-year Tommy John vacation, but he was back on the bump for a couple dozen rusty rehab runs in the season's second half. When healthy he'll pump mid-90s cheddar with cut and a boatload of groundballs on the back end. He could figure into the bullpen mix in Colorado this year. ⊗ Former third-rounder **Sam Howard**'s fringy fastball got knocked around again at Triple-A, and while he made his way to Denver for a couple cameos, the Rockies rewarded that debut with a post-season non-tender. ⊗ **Reid Humphreys'** nasty stuff—high-90s cheddar with a cutting cousin a few miles an hour slower—played its heart out at the launching pad in Lancaster, and if you can make it there, you can make it anywhere. ⊗ As if his funky delivery and the stilted visuals it produces for hitters weren't enough, **Justin Lawrence** sits high-90s with a wipeout slider. Nobody'll confuse him for Maddux, but it's effectively wild and a high-leverage profile in spite of it. ⊗ The Poconos sent its best to Colorado 27th overall in 2016, but **Mike Nikorak** famously left his control and a bunch of velocity back east after signing. A two-year vision quest in his elbow followed, spent mostly in recovery from Tommy John before finally getting back on a Pioneer League mound in August. ⊗ **Jesus Tinoco** has himself a heater and two hooks that can play nicely out of the 'pen. ⊗ A plus mid-90s fastball and solid, tumbling cambio highlight the arsenal for **Robert Tyler**, a former 38th-overall pick who spent the year in A-ball shaking off the rust of an injury-obliterated 2017.

DETROIT TIGERS

Essay by Zach Crizer

Player comments by Matt Sussman and BP staff

"**H**ow long are you willing to wait?"

"It's supposed to be really, really great. Everybody said they loved it, even though—yeah, it's going to take forever."

"So, get in line?"

"I think we have to."

Contemporary baseball decision-makers have lured fans into the mindset that fuels amusement parks: There's this ride. You're going to wait for it, bored and sweaty and not amused at all, but look at those people coming out the other side, smiling. It's all on purpose, all *worth it*. The euphoria, glimpsed vividly in several recent Novembers, sticks with people and provides license to start the whole process over; the all-important rush makes the next wait feel not just shorter, but *necessary*.

⚾   ⚾   ⚾

The 2018 Tigers didn't come close to mirroring the historically putrid 2003 Tigers, finishing third in a veritable wasteland of a division, but they existed in the same non-competitive fugue state that characterized the early Dave Dombrowski years in Detroit. However, their paths forward are unlikely to be similar.

The popular justification for suffering through terrible teams wasn't stated in its current form back then, and Tigers owner Mike Ilitch, who died in 2017, was refreshingly impatient with losing. Ilitch and Dombrowski dropped serious dollars on Ivan Rodriguez that winter, and on Magglio Ordonez the next offseason. They pumped money into the team in what many, today, would call "confusing" or "inefficient" moves that created incongruence between the utility of the highly paid stars and the young talent.

In 2006, Rodriguez and Ordonez were aging and merely average players, but Justin Verlander and Curtis Granderson arrived on the scene. That wasn't nearly enough to produce the World Series berth, though. Several other things were required. Namely:

- Jeremy Bonderman put forth his only good season.

TIGERS PROSPECTUS
2018 W-L: 64-98, 3RD IN AL CENTRAL

Pythag	.393	26th	B-Age	27.9	13th
RS/G	3.89	26th	P-Age	28.7	17th
RA/G	4.91	23rd	Salary	$125.3M	19th
DRC+	87	26th	M$/MW	$7.3M	4th
DRA	4.75	22nd	DL Days	865	6th
FIP	4.62	25th	$ on DL	24%	26th
DER	.709	10th			

- Opened 2000
- Open air
- Natural surface
- Fence profile: 6'10" to 14'

Three-Year Park Factors

Runs	Runs/RH	Runs/LH	HR/RH	HR/LH
102	103	99	102	104

Top Hitter WARP	3.2 Leonys Martin
Top Pitcher WARP	1.4 Joe Jimenez
Top Prospect	Casey Mize

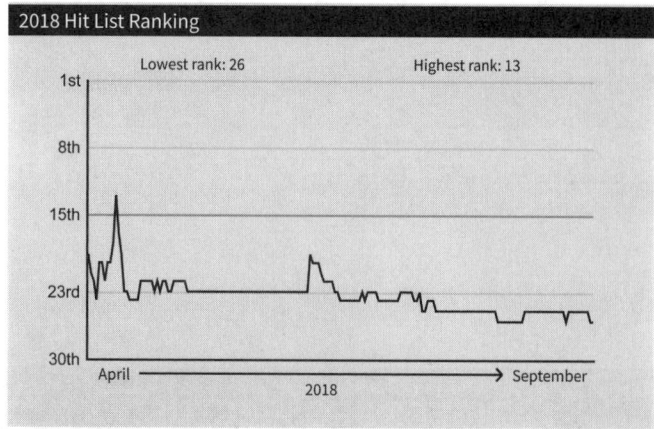

2018 Hit List Ranking

Lowest rank: 26   Highest rank: 13

(chart axis: 1st, 8th, 15th, 23rd, 30th; April — 2018 → September)

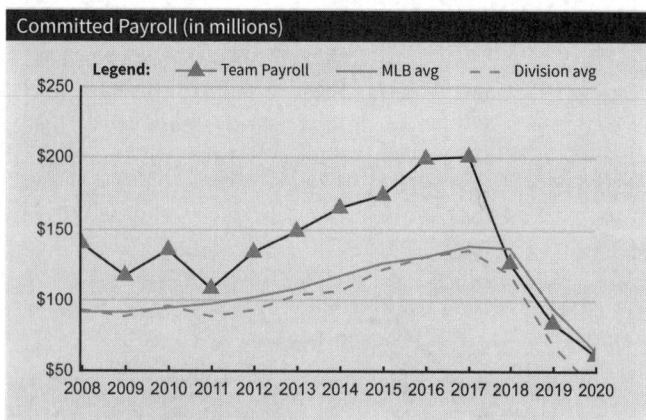

Committed Payroll (in millions)

Legend: Team Payroll — MLB avg — — Division avg

(chart axis: $250, $200, $150, $100, $50; 2008 2009 2010 2011 2012 2013 2014 2015 2016 2017 2018 2019 2020)

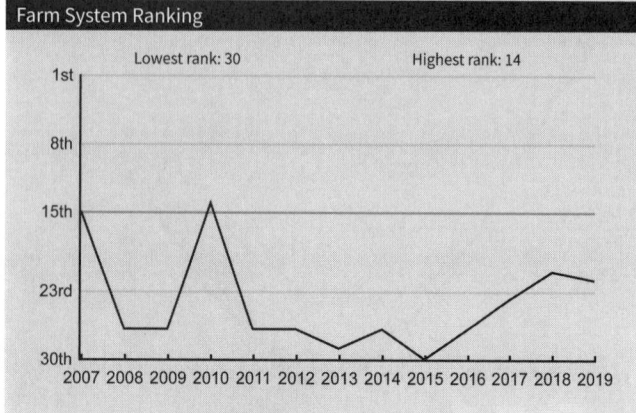

Farm System Ranking

Lowest rank: 30   Highest rank: 14

(chart axis: 1st, 8th, 15th, 23rd, 30th; 2007 2008 2009 2010 2011 2012 2013 2014 2015 2016 2017 2018 2019)

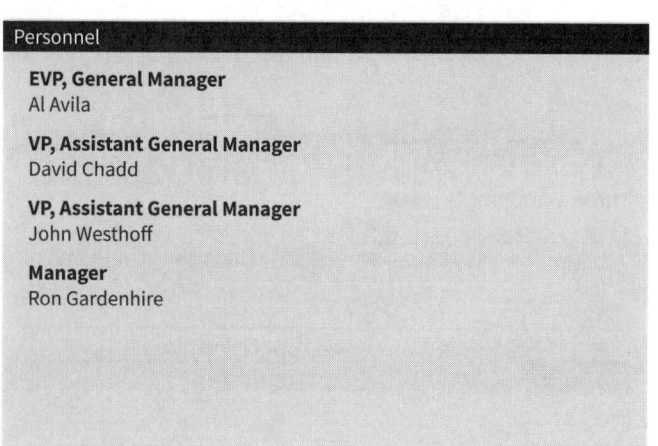

Personnel

EVP, General Manager
Al Avila

VP, Assistant General Manager
David Chadd

VP, Assistant General Manager
John Westhoff

Manager
Ron Gardenhire

- A 41-year-old Kenny Rogers signed for two years (two years!) and $16 million, pitching about as well as anyone could have reasonably hoped.
- Carlos Guillen put up a career-year at age 30, two years after being acquired for a prospect who'd never pan out and Ramon Santiago—who was already back on the Tigers after being released by the Mariners.
- Oh, and Brandon Inge posted a five-WARP season at third base.

None of those things held up. The team's main window of contention came later, after a couple more top-10 picks turned into Miguel Cabrera via trade. The Tigers, at that point, had officially reached the front of the line.

⚾   ⚾   ⚾

Even that Cabrera-led team didn't take off immediately, but the Tigers eventually ripped off four straight postseason appearances, including one trip to the World Series. Yet all of their Octobers ended in dry, quiet clubhouses. If hoisting the trophy was the payoff, then did Detroit wait for nothing? The notion feels blindingly dishonest.

Every other fan base has been waiting decades to see a Triple Crown winner. Certainly fans accepting a tanking plan would happily put in a wait to see such a thing. How long would you wait to see a pitching season so dominant it earned the Cy Young and MVP awards? Only the Dodgers have had the pleasure of seeing a season like Verlander's 2011 this millennium, and only the A's saw it in the 1990s. What amount of time is paid off by the chance to relish two Hall of Fame peaks fully and simultaneously? Since the strike, only the Yankees (pick your timeframe), the Braves of Chipper Jones, Tom Glavine and company, and the Tigers of Cabrera and Verlander are solid bets for multiple Cooperstown trips.

Those designations were all subject to the whims of the universe, deserved to differing degrees. Day by day, they become decreasingly relevant to the happiness of those who attach their feelings to a baseball team. It's true of a World Series win, too, but there is undeniably a greater release achieved when that trophy is handed over—one that Ilitch so clearly wanted, and that everyone around the team wanted for him.

In that sense, the gloom of the early 2000s and pre-Ilitch 1990s (when famed Michigan college football coach Bo Schembechler inexplicably ran the team) appear to be an interminable procession toward thrills set to fade in a fraction of the time.

⚾   ⚾   ⚾

Winning without *really* winning can feel like a singular, crushing sequence of events, mostly because of recent history's recency. It may remain crushing, but it won't be singular.

The Nationals have developed a talent pipeline that looks likely to keep their contention window open, but they exhausted the control years of Stephen Strasburg and Bryce Harper without winning a postseason series. The Pirates are toiling at transforming their roster for a longer haul, but just watched their former no. 1 overall pick, Gerrit Cole, go supernova in a different uniform.

The Braves, the Phillies, the White Sox, the post-championship Royals—some of these rebuilds are going to come up empty. This isn't a science despite the Cubs' and Astros' triumphant whole-hog teardowns. But the top-line disappointment of Detroit's last competitive cycle made for an easy reason to do things differently this time around. General manager Al Avila, embarking on his mission in 2016 after replacing Dombrowski, said he needed to make the club younger and leaner (read: cheaper).

So far, he's moving steadily along, staying within the roped-off path. They had the no. 1 overall pick in June, taking Auburn right-hander Casey Mize. They will have the no. 5 pick in the 2019 draft. A few prospects acquired in the sell-off have begun to pop, like Daz Cameron (son of Mike, acquired for Verlander) and Isaac Paredes (an infielder who came over from the Cubs). There's a void in premium position-player talent, but it's too early to be too worried; uncertainty is always going to be present in this phase of talent collection.

Still, it's worth noting that the biggest trade chips are used up, unless they plan to make the wait longer and the expectations subliminally bigger by dealing Michael Fulmer, a 26-year-old former first-round pick who was acquired as a prospect from the Mets for Yoenis Cespedes in mid-2015. The fact that it could end up looking like a good idea is reminder enough of why Ilitch and Dombrowski stalled as long as they could: Going to the back of the line is daunting.

Someone, multiple someones, eventually decided take the plunge. *I think we have to.*

⚾   ⚾   ⚾

But what if they didn't have to?

Say the Tigers had pursued a middle ground. They won't ever reach the carefree, uncommitted financial state of the pre-2018 Phillies or White Sox. They have Cabrera signed for huge money through 2023 and Jordan Zimmermann signed through 2020. In one fell swoop, they shaved 2017's top-tier $199.7 million Opening Day payroll to $125.3 million in 2018. After the 2018 season, another $24 million came off the books where the contracts of Victor Martinez and Jose Iglesias used to reside.

Could they have squeezed J.D. Martinez into the team's immediate and middle-term future with a backloaded deal? The $125 million payroll range could still have been achieved, just one year later, with a step in between. Even if Martinez didn't choose to stay—he seemed to really enjoy his first season in Boston, after all—might the draft-pick compensation have outstripped the trade return from Arizona? Might a commitment to Martinez have allowed them to turn the less established (but more controllable) Nicholas Castellanos into a trade chip for teams even more committed to restricting payroll?

It's become easier for front offices to sell good odds of being formidable in the future rather than middling with continuous chances of at least seeing October in the present. Stated differently, it sounds downright weird: Their job security is stronger if they lose indiscriminately for a few years.

What the tanking pitch fails to account for is the crowding on this recently blazed path to the bottom. Just as a glut of teams that "can never rebuild" will always end with multiple teams failing miserably, a bevy of teams that "gear up for the long term" will likely lead to multiple teams missing their marks. That's not to say the Tigers are destined to be standing up when the music stops, but someone surely will be.

There are other ways for the Tigers to escape or accelerate the procession, and they may well do it at some point—perhaps another Ivan Rodriguez-like signing, before the team is "ready" for such a move, or maybe a Dombrowski-like trade that packages multiple pieces for an in-his-prime mega-star. That doesn't change the questionable, financially driven decisions to hemorrhage talent and reasons to care without adding much intrigue up ahead.

At the start, rebuilding is accepted as an unquestioned, blank-check explanation, before everyone realizes what they've signed up for. Before the winding path ahead is even in view. The team was not obligated to join the increasingly long line of intentional losing any more than they are obligated to stay in it.

⚾   ⚾   ⚾

There are obvious benefits to decreasing the urgency of tomorrow's game. It opens opportunities for otherwise overlooked contributors, to build depth that can help support and eventually retain generational stars. That mindset can manifest in many forms, and doesn't require a bare-bones roster to flourish. Would employing J.D. Martinez or a third solid starting pitcher have eliminated the 40-man spot used to add discarded former Twins minor leaguer Niko Goodrum? Or blocked Joe Jimenez from running with a setup role?

Goodrum's average-hitting season in a super-utility role could be an aberration, or it could be the start of a useful career as a productive, flexible lineup stopgap. Jimenez may be the last Tigers All-Star you remember in a Sporcle quiz in 10 years, or he may be a contributor to the next Tigers contender. They are threads worth pulling on, and that's at least half the battle. Finding them, however, does not require clearing the deck of other attractions. Fans can justifiably wish young seasons were given as much chance to surprise as young careers. It's not too much to ask for a team to remain interesting through May.

While Ilitch's praiseworthy stewardship was sustaining consistent hope for a decade, other teams were mastering the rationalization of mind-numbing slogs through irrelevance. Detroit has arrived at the start again, enticed by this shiny sales pitch, but with no guarantee they're waiting for anything better than the 1990s. How Avila and company feel about the modern safety net of rebuilding, as opposed to the pins and needles of trying, well, that's a question that will define the next few years—and with it the rest of Cabrera's career, Fulmer's future in Detroit, etc.

History provides hope that the Tigers will reach for more than the basic rebuild, maybe sense opportunity in a down division. Even a return to some approximation of the Ordonez days could inspire envy in rival fans spending summer after summer dredging up muddy, metallic objects like Goodrum or Jimenez, telling themselves it's the only way. Those little joys are great, but they're anticipatory, pinned to promised memories from the future. Trying to sustain yourself on them is a fool's errand, like waiting for a ride that may never come. ■

—*Zach Crizer is an author of Baseball Prospectus.*

HITTERS

Miguel Cabrera 1B
Born: 04/18/83 Age: 36 Bats: R Throws: R Height: 6'4" Weight: 249 Origin: International Free Agent, 1999

YEAR	TEAM	LVL	AGE	PA	R	2B	3B	HR	RBI	BB	K	SB	CS	AVG/OBP/SLG	DRC+	VORP	BABIP	BRR	FRAA	WARP
2016	DET	MLB	33	679	92	31	1	38	108	75	116	0	0	.316/.393/.563	149	36.2	.336	-3.8	1B(147): 3.4, 3B(1): -0.1	5.2
2017	DET	MLB	34	529	50	22	0	16	60	54	110	0	1	.249/.329/.399	102	-1.3	.292	-6.6	1B(115): -1.7	0.1
2018	DET	MLB	35	157	17	11	0	3	22	22	27	0	0	.299/.395/.448	104	7.1	.352	0.5	1B(32): 0.0	0.4
2019	DET	MLB	36	574	65	29	2	15	69	74	109	0	0	.265/.364/.424	117	16.2	.312	-3.3	1B -1	1.6

Breakout: 1% Improve: 22% Collapse: 7% Attrition: 7% MLB: 91%   *Comparables: Paul Konerko, Mark Teixeira, Vladimir Guerrero*

If you learned nothing about Cabrera last year, you may have at least discovered that "biceps" is the singular version, not "bicep." That torn muscle is what kept him shelved for most of 2018, and with the biceps' mythical and physical link to power, the oft-hobbled Cabrera's career is finally starting to dovetail into a precarious roster dilemma. A torn biceps is not a common baseball injury — Dean Palmer had one early in his career, and he overcame it — and while Miggy could very well recover from this, there's always concern about the next one. When healthy, the future Hall of Famer is still a patient, intelligent hitter who can drive the ball to all fields. Given those concerns, it's high time to box him into what he does best and DH him more often than not. Cabrera, who'll turn 36 years old in April, is signed through his age-41 season in 2024 and is still owed at least $162 million.

Daz Cameron CF
Born: 01/15/97 Age: 22 Bats: R Throws: R Height: 6'2" Weight: 195 Origin: Round 1, 2015 Draft (#37 overall)

YEAR	TEAM	LVL	AGE	PA	R	2B	3B	HR	RBI	BB	K	SB	CS	AVG/OBP/SLG	DRC+	VORP	BABIP	BRR	FRAA	WARP
2016	QUD	A	19	87	5	2	2	0	6	8	33	4	3	.143/.221/.221	62	-5.6	.244	0.1	CF(10): -0.6, LF(6): -0.3	-0.3
2016	TCV	A-	19	89	13	3	1	2	14	6	26	8	2	.278/.352/.418	90	4.7	.392	0.0	CF(15): 0.0, LF(2): -0.3	0.1
2017	QUD	A	20	511	79	29	8	14	73	45	108	32	12	.271/.349/.466	127	38.4	.323	3.1	CF(110): 1.8, RF(4): 0.1	3.7
2018	LAK	A+	21	246	35	9	3	3	20	25	69	10	4	.259/.346/.370	101	9.9	.366	2.5	CF(38): 1.9, RF(18): 0.9	1.3
2018	ERI	AA	21	226	32	12	5	5	35	25	53	12	5	.285/.367/.470	111	11.4	.366	3.4	CF(34): -7.0, RF(16): 1.5	0.7
2018	TOL	AAA	21	62	8	4	1	0	6	2	15	2	2	.211/.246/.316	85	-1.1	.279	0.7	CF(14): 0.3, RF(1): 0.0	0.2
2019	DET	MLB	22	251	32	10	1	7	23	17	68	8	4	.222/.279/.364	73	1.1	.281	0.3	CF -1, RF 0	0.1

Breakout: 3% Improve: 12% Collapse: 1% Attrition: 10% MLB: 23%   *Comparables: Kirk Nieuwenhuis, Ryan Kalish, Michael Saunders*

Depending on how well he does in Triple-A this year, Cameron might force his way onto a major-league roster in September, reaching the bigs at the same age as Pops did for the White Sox in 1995. He moved quickly last year, thanks to playing an exceptional center field along with some plus speed. The bat-to-ball skills have always been the question mark for the former first-round pick acquired from the Astros in the Justin Verlander trade, but he checked that box as a 21-year-old in Double-A. While his tool mix likely won't put Cameron at the top of the lineup, his opportunity at the highest level should arrive sooner rather than later.

Jeimer Candelario 3B
Born: 11/24/93 Age: 25 Bats: B Throws: R Height: 6'1" Weight: 221 Origin: International Free Agent, 2010

YEAR	TEAM	LVL	AGE	PA	R	2B	3B	HR	RBI	BB	K	SB	CS	AVG/OBP/SLG	DRC+	VORP	BABIP	BRR	FRAA	WARP
2016	TEN	AA	22	244	30	17	1	4	23	32	46	0	0	.219/.324/.367	105	4.2	.261	0.0	3B(54): 2.7, 1B(2): -0.3	1.3
2016	CHN	MLB	22	14	0	0	0	0	0	2	5	0	0	.091/.286/.091	70	-0.5	.167	0.2	3B(3): -0.4	0.0
2016	IOW	AAA	22	309	44	22	3	9	54	38	53	0	2	.333/.417/.542	121	40.9	.383	1.7	3B(67): -0.8, 1B(10): 1.1	2.2
2017	CHN	MLB	23	36	2	2	0	1	3	1	12	0	0	.152/.222/.303	98	-1.1	.200	0.2	3B(9): 0.9, 1B(1): 0.0	0.2
2017	IOW	AAA	23	330	39	27	3	12	52	41	72	0	0	.266/.361/.507	108	23.4	.315	-4.5	3B(70): 5.0, 1B(16): -0.7	1.5
2017	TOL	AAA	23	128	13	9	1	3	19	5	32	1	0	.264/.297/.430	88	1.1	.333	-1.9	3B(28): -1.5	-0.1
2017	DET	MLB	23	106	16	7	0	2	13	12	18	0	0	.330/.406/.468	94	6.9	.392	0.2	3B(27): -2.4	0.1
2018	DET	MLB	24	619	78	28	3	19	54	66	160	3	2	.224/.317/.393	91	16.8	.279	-2.4	3B(140): -4.1	0.9
2019	DET	MLB	25	553	63	23	2	14	55	46	137	2	1	.228/.301/.368	82	-0.3	.286	-0.8	3B -2	-0.2

Breakout: 3% Improve: 53% Collapse: 8% Attrition: 16% MLB: 96%   *Comparables: Jake Lamb, Kyle Seager, Cody Asche*

Candelario is going to be a solid contributor hitting somewhere in the lower five spots in the lineup. Out of necessity he started 100 games at leadoff or second in 2018, and more than a dozen times in the cleanup spot. His team was bad, you see. Pitchers started figuring out the switch-hitter after a solid .275/.367/.526 two-month start. As one of the only decent bats in the Tigers' lineup, he chased and he pressed. There's little concern for his defense, at least compared to his positional predecessor Nick Castellanos. And the fact that he crushed nearly 20 homers in a full season shows Candelario can handle the day-to-day grind to some extent. Pencil him in at third base for a while, just don't expect him at the top of the lineup.

Nick Castellanos RF Born: 03/04/92 Age: 27 Bats: R Throws: R Height: 6'4" Weight: 203 Origin: Round 1, 2010 Draft (#44 overall)

YEAR	TEAM	LVL	AGE	PA	R	2B	3B	HR	RBI	BB	K	SB	CS	AVG/OBP/SLG	DRC+	VORP	BABIP	BRR	FRAA	WARP
2016	DET	MLB	24	447	54	25	4	18	58	28	111	1	1	.285/.331/.496	109	18.4	.345	-3.9	3B(108): -3.3	1.4
2017	DET	MLB	25	665	73	36	10	26	101	41	142	4	5	.272/.320/.490	110	22.6	.313	-2.6	3B(129): -7.7, RF(21): -6.0	1.6
2018	DET	MLB	26	678	88	46	5	23	89	49	151	2	1	.298/.354/.500	116	47.6	.361	3.4	RF(142): -2.8	2.9
2019	DET	MLB	27	606	70	37	4	21	82	46	136	3	2	.272/.334/.467	119	27.2	.327	-0.8	RF -5	2.4

Breakout: 0% Improve: 49% Collapse: 4% Attrition: 5% MLB: 93%   *Comparables: Del Ennis, Shawn Green, Harold Baines*

Castellanos is a terrific hitter, but it feels slightly misleading to call him one of the league's best right fielders. It's kind of like calling your mom's house your favorite restaurant. More accurately, he's a breakout middle-of-the-lineup hitter who just happens to be standing in right field on defense. He's a larval designated hitter still spry enough to play the field (and, as of last year, shared a roster with Victor Martinez). Third base didn't work out and right field isn't going much better. He could perhaps operate first base, the last bastion of dudes who rake but can't bag, but as long as defense matters, Nick the Stick couldn't be a more accurate moniker.

Brandon Dixon 2B Born: 01/29/92 Age: 27 Bats: R Throws: R Height: 6'2" Weight: 215 Origin: Round 3, 2013 Draft (#92 overall)

YEAR	TEAM	LVL	AGE	PA	R	2B	3B	HR	RBI	BB	K	SB	CS	AVG/OBP/SLG	DRC+	VORP	BABIP	BRR	FRAA	WARP
2016	PEN	AA	24	461	61	23	1	16	65	30	137	15	5	.260/.315/.434	106	28.9	.342	2.0	2B(62): 1.0, CF(20): -2.7	1.6
2017	LOU	AAA	25	491	58	31	3	16	64	37	125	18	8	.264/.327/.457	104	22.3	.328	1.0	3B(93): 5.2, 1B(17): -0.3	2.3
2018	LOU	AAA	26	193	28	18	2	6	23	12	54	9	3	.346/.389/.570	108	23.0	.467	2.9	1B(14): 0.1, 2B(14): -2.3	0.7
2018	CIN	MLB	26	124	14	6	0	5	10	6	43	0	0	.178/.218/.356	73	-5.4	.229	-0.5	1B(27): 0.0, RF(17): -1.1	-0.4
2019	DET	MLB	27	172	19	7	1	5	19	11	52	4	2	.215/.272/.363	77	-0.5	.284	0.1	2B 0, 1B 0	-0.1

Breakout: 3% Improve: 15% Collapse: 7% Attrition: 15% MLB: 31%   *Comparables: Russ Canzler, Ben Paulsen, Zach Walters*

In 2018, Brandon Dixon, a longtime theatrical actor and producer, played the role of Judas in NBC's live-action production of *Jesus Christ Superstar*, earning a Primetime Emmy nomination for his portrayal. In 2018, Brandon Dixon, a mildly-toolsy prospect with serious contact issues, played the role of Reds part-time first baseman while Joey Votto recovered from a lower-leg contusion. It's hard to discern which performance was more of a betrayal. A high strikeout rate has always portended struggles against the highest quality arms for Dixon, but he failed to live up to the low bar of replacement level. After being booted off the 40-man roster following the season, he was thrown to the Tigers (which will hopefully work better in the 21st century baseball sense than in the Roman-era punishment sense).

Niko Goodrum UT Born: 02/28/92 Age: 27 Bats: B Throws: R Height: 6'3" Weight: 198 Origin: Round 2, 2010 Draft (#71 overall)

YEAR	TEAM	LVL	AGE	PA	R	2B	3B	HR	RBI	BB	K	SB	CS	AVG/OBP/SLG	DRC+	VORP	BABIP	BRR	FRAA	WARP
2016	FTM	A+	24	26	3	4	0	1	5	1	7	1	0	.280/.308/.560	84	3.0	.353	-0.3	SS(2): 0.1, CF(2): -0.2	0.0
2016	CHT	AA	24	207	25	10	2	6	28	22	52	8	2	.275/.357/.451	111	12.3	.352	0.9	3B(24): 1.6, SS(12): 2.6	1.5
2017	ROC	AAA	25	499	71	25	5	13	66	30	119	11	7	.265/.309/.425	99	17.8	.326	4.4	RF(47): 3.3, 2B(37): -4.2	1.6
2017	MIN	MLB	25	18	1	0	0	0	0	1	10	0	0	.059/.111/.059	53	-2.9	.143	0.2	2B(8): -0.4, RF(1): 0.0	-0.1
2018	DET	MLB	26	492	55	29	3	16	53	42	132	12	4	.245/.315/.432	91	12.2	.312	-1.3	2B(64): 1.0, 1B(37): -0.8	0.6
2019	DET	MLB	27	341	38	15	2	10	39	26	90	7	3	.232/.295/.389	86	3.6	.292	-0.8	2B -2, 1B 0	0.2

Breakout: 2% Improve: 34% Collapse: 11% Attrition: 16% MLB: 85%   *Comparables: Ryan Flaherty, Dan Uggla, Luke Hughes*

Goodrum, a longtime Twins organizational soldier who joined the Tigers on a minor-league deal, took the lingering question mark surrounding his hit tool and deposited it into the right field seats, breaking out with a career-high in home runs for any season of his pro career. Ending camp last year as the Tigers' utility man, he ultimately won the regular second baseman job midseason and the club will keep his versatility as a contingency option. As a switch-hitter, he has an all-or-nothing approach batting lefty (15 of his homers were from that side) and effectively sprayed the field hitting right-handed. He's basically a younger, greener Marwin Gonzalez with a name more suited for an Agatha Christie character.

Grayson Greiner C Born: 10/11/92 Age: 26 Bats: R Throws: R Height: 6'6" Weight: 239 Origin: Round 3, 2014 Draft (#99 overall)

YEAR	TEAM	LVL	AGE	PA	R	2B	3B	HR	RBI	BB	K	SB	CS	AVG/OBP/SLG	DRC+	VORP	BABIP	BRR	FRAA	WARP
2016	LAK	A+	23	123	14	6	0	0	12	12	26	0	0	.312/.385/.367	101	5.1	.410	-3.0	C(27): -1.6	0.1
2016	ERI	AA	23	225	20	9	3	7	30	10	55	1	0	.288/.320/.462	102	9.7	.351	0.5	C(56): 5.1	1.7
2017	ERI	AA	24	371	34	20	1	14	42	38	72	0	0	.241/.323/.436	111	13.9	.266	-3.0	C(90): 27.5	5.0
2018	TOL	AAA	25	180	12	8	1	4	23	21	42	0	0	.266/.350/.405	109	10.9	.336	0.3	C(44): 11.2	2.3
2018	DET	MLB	25	116	9	6	0	0	12	17	32	0	1	.219/.328/.281	81	3.5	.313	0.3	C(30): -0.5	0.3
2019	DET	MLB	26	356	35	15	1	7	34	37	94	1	0	.220/.306/.343	76	5.1	.288	-0.6	C 10	1.6

Breakout: 3% Improve: 15% Collapse: 15% Attrition: 29% MLB: 54%   *Comparables: Tim Federowicz, Curtis Casali, Tony Sanchez*

Imagine being blessed with great height as well as uncanny athletic ability, and then you use that large frame to … crouch down for half the game. Greiner is the first 6-foot-6 dude to play catcher in the majors since Pete Koegel for the 1972 Phillies, and only the fourth such player on record. (He's also the first Grayson in the majors since the Chester A. Arthur administration.) Greiner already has more major-league starts at catcher than anyone that tall in history, by far, and that was just in his rookie season. Hopefully you're sitting down while reading this, but it may come as a shock that there's no real height advantage in

YEAR	TEAM	P. COUNT	FRM RUNS	BLK RUNS	THRW RUNS	TOT RUNS
2017	ERI	12250	22.4	5.5	0.2	27.3
2018	DET	4428	-0.6	-0.2	0.0	-0.9
2018	TOL	6014	9.5	0.5	0.3	10.0
2019	DET	13231	7.5	2.7	-0.7	9.4

catching and, some would insist, several disadvantages. He's certainly better at the plate, where the large frame has helped him establish hard contact more often than the league average, though the surface-level numbers didn't quite show that. One could say that his offensive numbers crouched down.

John Hicks 1B   Born: 08/31/89   Age: 29   Bats: R   Throws: R   Height: 6'2"   Weight: 230   Origin: Round 4, 2011 Draft (#123 overall)

YEAR	TEAM	LVL	AGE	PA	R	2B	3B	HR	RBI	BB	K	SB	CS	AVG/OBP/SLG	DRC+	VORP	BABIP	BRR	FRAA	WARP
2016	ROC	AAA	26	34	1	2	0	1	1	1	5	0	0	.242/.265/.394	102	-0.3	.259	-0.1	C(9): -0.1	0.2
2016	ERI	AA	26	54	7	1	1	1	4	4	9	1	0	.388/.426/.510	109	5.7	.450	0.4	C(11): 0.7, 1B(2): 0.2	0.4
2016	TOL	AAA	26	264	38	20	0	8	42	17	59	3	1	.303/.356/.485	108	20.2	.374	-1.3	C(66): -1.1, 3B(1): 0.0	1.3
2016	DET	MLB	26	2	1	1	0	0	0	0	0	0	0	.500/.500/1.000	76	0.2	.500	-0.2	1B(1): 0.0	0.0
2017	TOL	AAA	27	218	21	10	1	7	35	4	54	5	3	.269/.281/.428	87	5.8	.325	-0.5	C(37): 3.4, 1B(11): -0.8	0.6
2017	DET	MLB	27	190	25	12	0	6	22	13	51	2	1	.266/.326/.439	81	1.1	.342	-1.0	1B(26): -0.4, C(18): 0.8	0.0
2018	DET	MLB	28	312	35	12	1	9	32	22	84	0	1	.260/.312/.403	86	1.8	.337	-1.3	1B(59): 0.3, C(21): -2.3	-0.1
2019	DET	MLB	29	406	41	15	1	11	45	28	105	3	2	.234/.294/.371	76	-0.3	.295	-1.2	C -2, 1B -1	-0.3

Breakout: 2%   Improve: 10%   Collapse: 15%   Attrition: 22%   MLB: 39%   *Comparables: Ben Paulsen, Scott Thorman, Matt Downs*

Find you a man who looks at you the way a manager looks at a third catcher. That's Hicks, versatile enough to catch a game, play first base and possibly corner outfield. He's a streaky player with occasional power and disappears a bit in the lineup when a right-hander is throwing the sphere, which makes him better suited as the first option off the bench. He'll never be the best player from Goochland High School in Virginia, because Justin Verlander went there too, although Hicks did homer off Verlander in his first plate appearance. So, by transitive property, Goochland's field will eventually be Hicks Field.

YEAR	TEAM	P. COUNT	FRM RUNS	BLK RUNS	THRW RUNS	TOT RUNS
2017	DET	2077	0.9	-0.1	0.0	1.2
2017	TOL	4951	2.8	0.5	0.0	3.6
2018	DET	2984	-0.9	-0.9	-0.1	-1.9
2019	DET	8842	-1.2	-0.3	0.0	-1.5

Derek Hill CF   Born: 12/30/95   Age: 23   Bats: R   Throws: R   Height: 6'2"   Weight: 190   Origin: Round 1, 2014 Draft (#23 overall)

YEAR	TEAM	LVL	AGE	PA	R	2B	3B	HR	RBI	BB	K	SB	CS	AVG/OBP/SLG	DRC+	VORP	BABIP	BRR	FRAA	WARP
2016	WMI	A	20	415	66	17	6	1	31	24	105	35	6	.266/.312/.349	93	16.6	.361	6.6	CF(54): -6.7, RF(33): 5.1	1.2
2017	TGW	RK	21	61	11	1	1	1	7	10	15	7	0	.163/.300/.286	103	2.2	.206	1.2	CF(7): 0.6	0.3
2017	WMI	A	21	168	28	8	6	1	21	16	38	12	5	.285/.367/.444	106	15.0	.374	2.2	CF(23): 0.1	0.8
2017	LAK	A+	21	38	3	1	0	0	2	5	10	10	0	.194/.324/.226	84	3.0	.286	1.5	CF(6): -0.1	0.2
2018	LAK	A+	22	383	45	9	3	4	33	33	109	35	12	.239/.307/.318	79	5.4	.338	3.7	CF(55): -2.5, LF(27): -2.1	0.0
2019	DET	MLB	23	251	31	7	1	5	18	15	76	13	4	.196/.243/.296	47	-6.2	.262	1.5	CF -1, LF 0	-0.8

Breakout: 0%   Improve: 5%   Collapse: 2%   Attrition: 6%   MLB: 6%   *Comparables: Michael Taylor, Lane Adams, Keon Broxton*

So far it's been rough seas for Hill, a former first-round pick who's yet to reach Double-A and remains overmatched at the plate. If he can sneak one of those novelty wiffle ball bats to the plate — and it's unlikely he will, as umpires usually notice such gambits — he may fix that batting average. He did, however, lead the Florida State League in stolen bases, which has always been his meal ticket. His defense is also major league-ready and may have been ready when he was a teenager, which is why the team is going to stay patient.

Jose Iglesias SS   Born: 01/05/90   Age: 29   Bats: R   Throws: R   Height: 5'11"   Weight: 194   Origin: International Free Agent, 2009

YEAR	TEAM	LVL	AGE	PA	R	2B	3B	HR	RBI	BB	K	SB	CS	AVG/OBP/SLG	DRC+	VORP	BABIP	BRR	FRAA	WARP
2016	DET	MLB	26	513	57	26	0	4	32	28	50	7	4	.255/.306/.336	78	8.6	.276	1.2	SS(136): 14.2	2.6
2017	DET	MLB	27	489	56	33	1	6	54	21	65	7	4	.255/.288/.369	68	4.4	.285	3.7	SS(130): -4.8	0.2
2018	DET	MLB	28	464	43	31	3	5	48	19	47	15	6	.269/.310/.389	89	18.3	.291	1.6	SS(122): 4.7	2.2
2019	DET	MLB	29	443	46	21	2	7	41	26	54	10	5	.251/.303/.364	80	7.4	.272	1.4	SS 4	1.2

Breakout: 1%   Improve: 47%   Collapse: 3%   Attrition: 9%   MLB: 97%   *Comparables: Elvis Andrus, Luis Sojo, Cesar Izturis*

On paper, Iglesias is a second-division starter. He avoids strikeouts better than most (fifth-best in the majors last year), though does it without any meaningful line-drive power or a decent walk rate. He grades out fine on defense, although not as well as his reputation would suggest. Beyond the parchment, he's even money to make a breathtaking how-did-he-throw-that play at shortstop. He's right on the cusp of the style outweighing the substance because his level of defense is unteachable and makes the other side work for its outs. He falls somewhere between Rey Ordonez and Omar Vizquel on the one-dimensional shortstop spectrum. Keep in mind, not all players are built to win championships; highlight reels are almost as legendary. You may not remember who every World Series-winning shortstop was, but Tigers fans will sure as rain remember Iglesias throwing off balance to start a double play.

Jacoby Jones LF Born: 05/10/92 Age: 27 Bats: R Throws: R Height: 6'2" Weight: 201 Origin: Round 3, 2013 Draft (#87 overall)

YEAR	TEAM	LVL	AGE	PA	R	2B	3B	HR	RBI	BB	K	SB	CS	AVG/OBP/SLG	DRC+	VORP	BABIP	BRR	FRAA	WARP
2016	ERI	AA	24	89	11	6	2	4	20	10	23	2	1	.312/.393/.597	103	9.2	.392	-0.3	3B(9): -0.5, CF(9): 1.1	0.4
2016	TOL	AAA	24	324	33	14	5	3	23	25	97	11	4	.243/.309/.356	72	6.9	.349	1.8	CF(57): -5.3, 3B(22): -1.3	-0.5
2016	DET	MLB	24	28	3	3	0	0	2	0	12	0	0	.214/.214/.321	61	-1.2	.375	0.5	3B(6): 0.0, CF(5): -0.2	0.0
2017	TOL	AAA	25	393	57	19	2	9	44	33	104	12	4	.245/.314/.387	90	15.9	.322	3.6	CF(76): 3.2, LF(7): 0.2	1.5
2017	DET	MLB	25	154	14	3	1	3	13	9	65	6	2	.170/.240/.270	46	-8.0	.288	1.1	CF(51): 2.3, RF(1): 0.0	-0.2
2018	DET	MLB	26	467	54	22	6	11	34	24	142	13	5	.207/.266/.364	68	-1.2	.281	4.3	CF(67): 4.0, LF(55): 2.7	0.7
2019	DET	MLB	27	393	43	15	3	9	37	26	122	11	4	.209/.273/.342	71	3.6	.288	2.3	CF 5	0.9

Breakout: 4%   Improve: 32%   Collapse: 13%   Attrition: 20%   MLB: 77%   *Comparables: Brian Anderson, Trayce Thompson, Laynce Nix*

Jones still feels like a raw toolsy player, which isn't a positive quality for a 26-year-old. His rawness is mostly attributed to his hitting, which flashes occasional power with a strikeout percentage higher than his on-base percentage. His real value has been all things related to running fast. The zenith in his baserunning adventures came last September, when he scored from second base on a third-strike wild pitch. He remains a dangerous and smart runner, with plus-plus range in the outfield. He's exciting and athletic, but it all comes back to the maple. His inability to reach base is going to keep him from being anything beyond a second-division starter.

Dawel Lugo 2B Born: 12/31/94 Age: 24 Bats: R Throws: R Height: 6'0" Weight: 190 Origin: International Free Agent, 2012

YEAR	TEAM	LVL	AGE	PA	R	2B	3B	HR	RBI	BB	K	SB	CS	AVG/OBP/SLG	DRC+	VORP	BABIP	BRR	FRAA	WARP
2016	VIS	A+	21	333	61	14	5	13	42	15	41	2	1	.314/.348/.514	131	28.6	.328	2.5	3B(60): -3.5, SS(14): 2.0	2.5
2016	MOB	AA	21	177	24	9	2	4	20	4	15	1	1	.306/.322/.451	110	13.3	.318	2.7	3B(41): 4.7, SS(10): 0.4	1.7
2017	WTN	AA	22	369	40	21	4	7	43	21	51	1	0	.282/.325/.428	105	14.3	.310	-1.7	3B(77): 4.5, SS(10): -0.4	1.8
2017	ERI	AA	22	188	18	6	1	6	22	12	21	2	1	.269/.314/.417	110	3.4	.275	-1.5	3B(29): -1.1, 2B(13): 0.6	0.7
2018	TOL	AAA	23	523	56	26	3	3	59	9	66	12	4	.269/.283/.350	78	1.8	.302	-1.1	2B(80): -6.0, 3B(43): -2.0	-0.7
2018	DET	MLB	23	101	10	4	1	1	8	7	20	0	0	.213/.267/.309	75	-1.0	.260	-0.2	2B(27): -3.2	-0.4
2019	DET	MLB	24	373	32	13	1	6	33	12	63	3	1	.224/.254/.321	52	-10.6	.255	-0.2	2B -4, 3B 0	-1.5

Breakout: 4%   Improve: 20%   Collapse: 6%   Attrition: 21%   MLB: 45%   *Comparables: Scooter Gennett, Yangervis Solarte, Henry Rodriguez*

The expectations and machinations of Lugo's batting approach should dictate better numbers, yes. He has a line-drive swing and it's yet to translate to any meaningful power. Baseball is a game of precision, where large moments occur at imprecise times. Lugo's first month of major-league action was swallowing him whole until he finally smacked his first home run in one of the wildest scenes for a 98-loss team: pinch-hitting in playoff atmosphere versus Milwaukee, who needed the game to contend for their division, off Josh Hader, to tie the game and mute the lively crowd. If that's the best he'll do, then that's his story when he becomes a grandfather. For now he needs to further refine his hitting approach and scrape for playing time at second base to accumulate more stories.

Mikie Mahtook CF Born: 11/30/89 Age: 29 Bats: R Throws: R Height: 6'1" Weight: 216 Origin: Round 1, 2011 Draft (#31 overall)

YEAR	TEAM	LVL	AGE	PA	R	2B	3B	HR	RBI	BB	K	SB	CS	AVG/OBP/SLG	DRC+	VORP	BABIP	BRR	FRAA	WARP
2016	DUR	AAA	26	120	16	5	3	1	7	12	24	5	1	.305/.383/.438	108	6.9	.383	0.6	CF(11): -1.1, RF(9): 1.9	0.5
2016	TBA	MLB	26	196	16	9	0	3	11	7	68	0	1	.195/.231/.292	54	-11.6	.287	-1.2	LF(26): -0.9, RF(23): 0.5	-0.7
2017	DET	MLB	27	379	50	15	6	12	38	23	79	6	0	.276/.330/.457	101	15.7	.324	1.6	CF(67): -1.6, RF(25): -1.7	1.0
2018	TOL	AAA	28	316	40	12	6	11	35	25	82	6	4	.251/.321/.452	108	7.6	.313	-3.3	CF(36): 1.5, LF(24): 1.4	1.1
2018	DET	MLB	28	250	24	4	2	9	29	21	66	4	1	.202/.276/.359	85	0.8	.238	0.5	LF(54): 6.9, RF(6): -1.2	0.8
2019	DET	MLB	29	506	55	23	3	15	59	35	132	7	2	.238/.301/.397	92	7.6	.302	0.1	CF 0, RF -2	0.7

Breakout: 3%   Improve: 15%   Collapse: 15%   Attrition: 22%   MLB: 67%   *Comparables: Xavier Paul, Fred Lewis, Luis Terrero*

Rebuilds are, at least for players, opportunities to show teams what they can do with enough playing time. Mahtook leveraged Detroit's hard reset in 2017, but in 2018 he was nearly invisible. For the first time since his rookie year he spent more time honing his swing in Triple-A than he did holding down an outfield spot in the majors. Missing out on a rebuild is like oversleeping for class; you're going to try to cram and make up for it but you're not going to retain much long term. As a result he's becoming a one-dimensional hitter, basically a few homers or nothing at all. He's a fourth outfielder at best, fifth in a non-rebuilding year.

Victor Martinez DH   Born: 12/23/78   Age: 40   Bats: B   Throws: R   Height: 6'2"   Weight: 235   Origin: International Free Agent, 1996

YEAR	TEAM	LVL	AGE	PA	R	2B	3B	HR	RBI	BB	K	SB	CS	AVG/OBP/SLG	DRC+	VORP	BABIP	BRR	FRAA	WARP
2016	DET	MLB	37	610	65	22	0	27	86	50	90	0	0	.289/.351/.476	124	5.6	.303	-9.6	1B(5): 0.0	1.8
2017	DET	MLB	38	435	38	16	0	10	47	36	63	0	0	.255/.324/.372	100	-11.9	.280	-4.9		0.1
2018	DET	MLB	39	508	32	21	0	9	54	32	49	0	0	.251/.297/.353	95	-11.6	.260	-3.6	1B(1): 0.0	0.1
2019	DET	MLB	40	465	48	25	1	9	52	40	62	0	0	.271/.340/.405	101	0.6	.300	-4.5	1B 0	0.1

Breakout: 1%   Improve: 20%   Collapse: 8%   Attrition: 24%   MLB: 66%   *Comparables: Rusty Staub, Pete Rose, Todd Helton*

The Hall of Very Good just received another tenant. With a career of 2,000 hits and countless two-strike foul balls, Martinez spent years menacing the AL Central with base knocks and power to all fields. His twilight years were marred with injuries that prevented him from fielding, initially at catcher and then at first base, and finally even DHing during day games. Defensive shifts ate up the rest of his line drives, so he was left with what they call "professional at-bats."

He went out on his own terms — at his final home night game, showered with gifts from his teammates and bosses, and feeling good enough to play first base for the first time in 27 months. In his first plate appearance, he struck a weak ground ball directly into the shift. But on this evening, during this moment, none of that mattered. Martinez "ran" it out for an infield single, then was lifted for a pinch-runner. He never has to sprint again, for any reason, for the rest of his life.

James McCann C   Born: 06/13/90   Age: 29   Bats: R   Throws: R   Height: 6'3"   Weight: 225   Origin: Round 2, 2011 Draft (#76 overall)

YEAR	TEAM	LVL	AGE	PA	R	2B	3B	HR	RBI	BB	K	SB	CS	AVG/OBP/SLG	DRC+	VORP	BABIP	BRR	FRAA	WARP
2016	DET	MLB	26	373	31	9	1	12	48	23	109	0	1	.221/.272/.358	79	-4.3	.283	-2.0	C(99): 5.9	1.3
2017	DET	MLB	27	391	39	14	2	13	49	26	89	1	0	.253/.318/.415	97	13.4	.300	-0.9	C(103): -20.9	-0.3
2018	DET	MLB	28	457	31	16	0	8	39	26	116	0	3	.220/.267/.314	74	-4.8	.282	-4.2	C(114): -5.0	-0.2
2019	CHA	MLB	29	163	17	8	1	4	17	11	40	0	0	.239/.304/.380	88	4.3	.302	-0.7	C -4	0.1

Breakout: 2%   Improve: 37%   Collapse: 7%   Attrition: 17%   MLB: 88%

Comparables: Hank Conger, Tony Cruz, Ronny Paulino

A player who possesses leadership qualities through the roof but can't really hit a baseball is what you'd call, perhaps, a coach? Maybe a GM? Possibly a TED talker? McCann might wish he had a time machine to go back and Kenley Jansen-ize himself, because he ranks way down on the list of all sorts of catcher metrics — hitting, framing, blocking, running and also Best McCann. The lone exception: his throwing arm. He was no. 1 last year, the only catcher in baseball to save a whole run with his patent-pending trademarked "McCannon." That run doesn't nearly make up for his other deficiencies, yet he still gets a major-league paycheck, and *that*, my friends, is how you start a motivational seminar (perhaps something else that would suit him).

YEAR	TEAM	P. COUNT	FRM RUNS	BLK RUNS	THRW RUNS	TOT RUNS
2016	DET	13823	3.1	1.1	3.6	8.5
2017	DET	14626	-13.2	-3.4	-0.8	-18.6
2018	DET	16526	-2.3	-1.4	1.1	-2.9
2019	DET	6150	-2.4	-0.5	0.3	-2.6

Parker Meadows CF   Born: 11/02/99   Age: 19   Bats: L   Throws: R   Height: 6'5"   Weight: 185   Origin: Round 2, 2018 Draft (#44 overall)

YEAR	TEAM	LVL	AGE	PA	R	2B	3B	HR	RBI	BB	K	SB	CS	AVG/OBP/SLG	DRC+	VORP	BABIP	BRR	FRAA	WARP
2018	TGW	RK	18	85	16	2	1	4	8	8	25	3	1	.284/.376/.500	124	6.1	.378	0.0	CF(20): -3.1	0.2
2019	DET	MLB	19	251	21	9	0	8	27	7	94	1	0	.176/.201/.306	30	-12.4	.241	-0.8	CF -1	-1.4

Breakout: 0%   Improve: 6%   Collapse: 1%   Attrition: 3%   MLB: 11%   *Comparables: Engel Beltre, Nomar Mazara, Carlos Tocci*

Detroit drafted Meadows, who slipped to the second round due to his commitment to play college ball at Clemson. However, after being offered $2.5 million to skip class, he chose the Tigers instead of the Tigers. He wasn't drafted as high as his brother Austin (2013 first round, now with the Rays), but he did copy big bro in being a left-handed-hitting center fielder with some potentially next-level power and speed. Brotherly rivalries are always fun to watch blossom, so while Parker is behind his major-league big brother in several categories (except height), we have seen his story play out before: in six years they'll both wind up in the Braves outfield and it's going to go horribly wrong.

Jordy Mercer SS   Born: 08/27/86   Age: 32   Bats: R   Throws: R   Height: 6'3"   Weight: 210   Origin: Round 3, 2008 Draft (#79 overall)

YEAR	TEAM	LVL	AGE	PA	R	2B	3B	HR	RBI	BB	K	SB	CS	AVG/OBP/SLG	DRC+	VORP	BABIP	BRR	FRAA	WARP
2016	PIT	MLB	29	584	66	22	3	11	59	51	83	1	1	.256/.328/.374	97	25.8	.286	3.0	SS(146): -7.4	2.1
2017	PIT	MLB	30	558	52	24	5	14	58	51	88	0	4	.255/.326/.406	98	22.0	.284	-1.2	SS(144): -18.7	0.5
2018	PIT	MLB	31	436	43	29	2	6	39	32	87	2	0	.251/.315/.381	85	10.6	.306	-1.0	SS(117): -3.0	0.8
2019	DET	MLB	32	439	46	22	2	9	45	41	79	2	1	.256/.333/.390	98	15.9	.298	0.3	SS -7	0.9

Breakout: 1%   Improve: 34%   Collapse: 15%   Attrition: 19%   MLB: 97%   *Comparables: Zack Cozart, Jack Wilson, Brendan Ryan*

Appropriately, Mercer entered free agency this winter not with a bang but a whimper, sitting out most of September so the Pirates could get a long look at Kevin Newman. For the last three years Mercer was a cold streak away from losing his job, but somehow persevered despite subpar offense and defensive metrics that said he was pedestrian at best and outright bad/overmatched at shortstop at worst. While it's easy to point to how deep middle infield is now compared to 30 years ago, it still doesn't afford all 30 teams the ability to run a Francisco Lindor out there every day. We shouldn't wax poetically about Mercer's ordinariness, but surviving for six years as a major-league regular is worth something, even if that something is visible only under a magnifying glass.

Isaac Paredes 3B   Born: 02/18/99   Age: 20   Bats: R   Throws: R   Height: 5'11"   Weight: 225   Origin: International Free Agent, 2015

YEAR	TEAM	LVL	AGE	PA	R	2B	3B	HR	RBI	BB	K	SB	CS	AVG/OBP/SLG	DRC+	VORP	BABIP	BRR	FRAA	WARP
2016	CUB	RK	17	185	23	14	3	1	26	13	20	4	0	.305/.359/.443	124	15.6	.338	-0.3	SS(45): 6.6	1.9
2017	SBN	A	18	384	49	25	0	7	49	29	54	2	1	.264/.343/.401	107	17.4	.294	-1.0	SS(70): -2.7, 3B(7): 2.5	1.6
2017	WMI	A	18	133	16	3	0	4	21	13	13	0	0	.217/.323/.348	109	0.2	.214	-0.5	SS(22): -2.4, 3B(5): 1.4	0.5
2018	LAK	A+	19	347	50	19	2	12	48	32	54	1	0	.259/.338/.455	123	24.2	.274	0.3	SS(59): 3.2, 2B(22): 0.5	2.8
2018	ERI	AA	19	155	20	9	0	3	22	19	22	1	0	.321/.406/.458	127	13.7	.358	0.3	3B(18): 0.6, SS(15): 0.9	1.3
2019	*DET*	*MLB*	*20*	*251*	*25*	*10*	*0*	*8*	*29*	*16*	*46*	*0*	*0*	*.223/.286/.363*	*76*	*0.4*	*.248*	*-0.6*	*SS 0, 2B 0*	*0.1*

Breakout: 4%   Improve: 25%   Collapse: 0%   Attrition: 6%   MLB: 27%   *Comparables: Jurickson Profar, Francisco Lindor, Gleyber Torres*

Paredes was the "other" prospect, along with Jeimer Candelario, acquired in the deal that sent Alex Avila and Justin Wilson to the Cubs. He reached Double-A as a 19-year-old and thrived there for the final month-and-a-half of the season, showing the type of advanced hitting ability that may ultimately turn Candelario into the "other" prospect. He's unlikely to stick at shortstop given his stocky build and modest range, but should have more than enough arm for third base. Offensively he projects to have good, solid skills across the board, with plenty of time left to show that he has more upside than that.

Wenceel Perez SS   Born: 10/30/99   Age: 19   Bats: B   Throws: R   Height: 5'11"   Weight: 170   Origin: International Free Agent, 2016

YEAR	TEAM	LVL	AGE	PA	R	2B	3B	HR	RBI	BB	K	SB	CS	AVG/OBP/SLG	DRC+	VORP	BABIP	BRR	FRAA	WARP
2017	DTI	RK	17	258	31	8	1	0	22	27	21	16	6	.314/.387/.358	130	16.0	.343	2.6	SS(50): -6.8, 2B(11): 2.4	1.5
2018	TGW	RK	18	93	20	7	0	2	14	12	14	2	1	.383/.462/.543	150	14.4	.446	0.6	SS(19): 1.0	1.1
2018	ONE	A-	18	87	8	2	0	1	8	5	12	7	3	.244/.287/.305	115	2.0	.275	0.3	SS(21): -2.9	0.2
2018	WMI	A	18	71	8	3	3	0	9	2	8	4	1	.309/.324/.441	101	4.8	.344	0.1	SS(14): -0.6	0.2
2019	*DET*	*MLB*	*19*	*251*	*26*	*7*	*0*	*5*	*19*	*11*	*50*	*6*	*2*	*.207/.239/.291*	*42*	*-8.4*	*.239*	*0.0*	*SS -3*	*-1.2*

Breakout: 0%   Improve: 4%   Collapse: 1%   Attrition: 3%   MLB: 7%   *Comparables: Carlos Triunfel, Wilmer Flores, Adalberto Mondesi*

The Gulf Coast League was getting sick of Perez, the 18-year-old switch-hitting shortstop who signed into the Tigers organization in 2016 thanks to a cool half-mil bonus. He was hitting the ball everywhere, except beyond the fence and toward the fielders, and was rewarded with a push into full-season ball, where he still peppered the outfield. He should progress and maintain a high level of middle-infield defense and an exemplary bat-to-ball skill. And you've been very patient, so your reward for reading to the end: his first name rhymes with "pencil."

Dustin Peterson OF   Born: 09/10/94   Age: 24   Bats: R   Throws: R   Height: 6'2"   Weight: 210   Origin: Round 2, 2013 Draft (#50 overall)

YEAR	TEAM	LVL	AGE	PA	R	2B	3B	HR	RBI	BB	K	SB	CS	AVG/OBP/SLG	DRC+	VORP	BABIP	BRR	FRAA	WARP
2016	MIS	AA	21	578	65	38	2	12	88	45	100	4	1	.282/.343/.431	118	37.1	.327	0.1	LF(125): -1.1, CF(4): -1.2	2.5
2017	GWN	AAA	22	346	35	17	1	1	30	27	78	1	2	.248/.318/.318	75	-4.1	.328	0.1	LF(68): 6.4, RF(9): -0.4	0.3
2018	ATL	MLB	23	2	0	0	0	0	0	0	1	0	0	.000/.000/.000	87	-0.5	.000	0.0		0.0
2018	GWN	AAA	23	442	46	23	0	11	55	30	96	3	0	.268/.324/.406	101	11.1	.327	1.6	LF(65): -2.2, RF(34): 1.0	1.1
2019	*DET*	*MLB*	*24*	*105*	*9*	*3*	*0*	*2*	*10*	*6*	*26*	*0*	*0*	*.208/.265/.314*	*47*	*-4.7*	*.260*	*-0.2*	*LF 0, RF 0*	*-0.4*

Breakout: 3%   Improve: 18%   Collapse: 15%   Attrition: 28%   MLB: 39%   *Comparables: Thomas Neal, Bryan Petersen, Jake Cave*

It's been five years since Peterson was one of four players acquired for Justin Upton. It's also four years since a bus crash with the Carolina Mudcats put him on the disabled list and two years since hand surgery for a non-bus-related injury. In between doctor visits, he has neither blown away nor disappointed his superiors, which means he's steadily moved up the minor-league gauntlet and received exactly two major-league pinch-hit appearances. He also snagged the Gwinnett Stripers' "Most Competitive Player" award, which is a real thing, before being let go in a September waiver claim. He has just enough youth, power, speed, scars and bat-to-ball skills to warrant being a fifth outfielder.

Victor Reyes LF   Born: 10/05/94   Age: 24   Bats: B   Throws: R   Height: 6'5"   Weight: 194   Origin: International Free Agent, 2011

YEAR	TEAM	LVL	AGE	PA	R	2B	3B	HR	RBI	BB	K	SB	CS	AVG/OBP/SLG	DRC+	VORP	BABIP	BRR	FRAA	WARP
2016	VIS	A+	21	509	62	11	12	6	54	33	78	20	8	.303/.349/.416	106	24.6	.352	1.3	RF(89): -7.0, LF(20): -2.6	0.6
2017	WTN	AA	22	516	59	29	5	4	51	27	80	18	9	.292/.332/.399	100	10.7	.342	0.1	RF(83): 4.9, CF(57): 10.8	3.0
2018	DET	MLB	23	219	35	5	3	1	12	5	46	9	1	.222/.239/.288	62	-7.8	.277	0.1	LF(34): -3.2, CF(21): 2.2	-0.6
2019	*DET*	*MLB*	*24*	*353*	*36*	*14*	*3*	*6*	*31*	*17*	*73*	*10*	*3*	*.233/.275/.346*	*70*	*-3.9*	*.279*	*-0.5*	*CF 2, LF -2*	*-0.3*

Breakout: 6%   Improve: 23%   Collapse: 8%   Attrition: 20%   MLB: 43%   *Comparables: Raimel Tapia, Jake Marisnick, Felix Pie*

It certainly wouldn't hurt Reyes to start the year in Triple-A after being woefully overmatched as a backup center fielder, but Rule 5 picks are almost destined to be overmatched if they stick in the majors all year. Among those with his playing time or better, he had the second-worst walk rate, the third-highest swing rate and the second-worst chase rate. Oddly enough — and perhaps there's a lesson in all this — he had 18 three-ball counts and never got a hit on any of them, though did reach base seven times and scored each time. For a free-swinging large dude, he has stunningly little power, so he'll rely on line drives and speed.

Ronny Rodriguez 2B   Born: 04/17/92   Age: 27   Bats: R   Throws: R   Height: 6'0"   Weight: 170   Origin: International Free Agent, 2010

YEAR	TEAM	LVL	AGE	PA	R	2B	3B	HR	RBI	BB	K	SB	CS	AVG/OBP/SLG	DRC+	VORP	BABIP	BRR	FRAA	WARP
2016	COH	AAA	24	488	58	24	5	10	59	22	88	4	4	.258/.293/.400	90	8.4	.298	-0.2	2B(85): 1.4, 1B(17): 0.4	1.1
2017	COH	AAA	25	483	60	18	2	17	64	23	92	15	5	.291/.324/.454	110	11.5	.329	-1.4	2B(62): 7.9, 3B(25): 1.6	3.4
2018	TOL	AAA	26	275	42	20	5	9	40	10	47	10	8	.338/.365/.558	116	30.8	.383	-1.8	3B(34): 2.1, SS(26): -0.9	1.6
2018	DET	MLB	26	206	17	7	0	5	20	10	42	2	0	.220/.256/.335	76	-4.3	.253	-0.3	SS(24): -2.3, 2B(17): 0.1	-0.3
2019	*DET*	*MLB*	*27*	*262*	*28*	*10*	*1*	*8*	*30*	*13*	*55*	*5*	*2*	*.244/.283/.394*	*79*	*0.4*	*.277*	*-0.6*	*SS 0, 2B 1*	*0.1*

Breakout: 6%   Improve: 22%   Collapse: 12%   Attrition: 33%   MLB: 64%   *Comparables: Tyler Greene, Elliot Johnson, Phil Gosselin*

After 800 games as a minor leaguer followed by minor-league free agency, the toolsy Rodriguez finally reached the bigs, at which point his peculiar bat wielding — holding the bat vertical for a while, then parallel completely above his head — resulted in the Batting Stance Guy treatment. A midseason slump resulted in hitting coach Lloyd McClendon cleaning up the approach and ditching the idiosyncrasies, not unlike Wilson in *Cast Away*. He's an average hitter with double-digit-homer potential and can play anywhere, including shortstop, so he'll likely have a major-league job for now. But if things ever turn south, he can fall back on his winter gig: musician. As "El Felino," his YouTube record page has over 19,000 subscribers, with one song reaching 300,000 views, which is more than he'll ever get for his now-mundane but solid stance.

Jake Rogers C Born: 04/18/95 Age: 24 Bats: R Throws: R Height: 6'1" Weight: 190 Origin: Round 3, 2016 Draft (#97 overall)

YEAR	TEAM	LVL	AGE	PA	R	2B	3B	HR	RBI	BB	K	SB	CS	AVG/OBP/SLG	DRC+	VORP	BABIP	BRR	FRAA	WARP
2016	TCV	A-	21	104	11	7	1	2	12	13	18	0	2	.253/.369/.425	123	4.3	.299	-2.0	C(24): 0.1	0.6
2016	QUD	A	21	82	7	3	1	1	4	8	25	1	0	.208/.305/.319	84	1.6	.304	-0.7	C(19): -0.1	0.1
2017	QUD	A	22	116	17	7	1	6	15	9	28	1	0	.255/.336/.520	120	10.2	.290	0.3	C(21): 0.9	0.8
2017	BCA	A+	22	367	43	18	3	12	55	44	72	13	8	.265/.357/.457	127	30.2	.302	-0.8	C(24): 1.4	2.7
2018	ERI	AA	23	408	57	15	1	17	56	41	112	7	1	.219/.305/.412	113	20.8	.261	2.7	C(98): 29.4, 1B(1): 0.0	6.0
2019	DET	MLB	24	69	8	3	0	3	9	5	19	1	0	.220/.284/.394	79	1.2	.270	-0.1	C 2	0.4

Breakout: 5%   Improve: 8%   Collapse: 6%   Attrition: 14%   MLB: 20%

Comparables: *Andrew Knapp, Michael McKenry, Josh Donaldson*

YEAR	TEAM	P. COUNT	FRM RUNS	BLK RUNS	THRW RUNS	TOT RUNS
2018	ERI	13801	20.3	-0.4	7.2	28.0
2019	DET	2524	1.8	-0.3	0.6	2.1

Rogers is not here to make friends, which is why he was essentially the Eastern League's hall monitor, throwing out 50 baserunners on 90 steal attempts, 20 more than anyone else in the EL. (As a comparison, no *major*-league catcher has thrown out 50 baserunners in a season in 15 years.) His golden arm is accompanied by another arm, which when used in tandem is able to perform another fun baseball feat: home runs. His otherwise complete inability to make contact in any other fashion with regularity will keep him from becoming Buster Posey, but the defense will certainly be his hall pass to the majors.

Christin Stewart LF Born: 12/10/93 Age: 25 Bats: L Throws: R Height: 6'0" Weight: 205 Origin: Round 1, 2015 Draft (#34 overall)

YEAR	TEAM	LVL	AGE	PA	R	2B	3B	HR	RBI	BB	K	SB	CS	AVG/OBP/SLG	DRC+	VORP	BABIP	BRR	FRAA	WARP
2016	LAK	A+	22	442	60	22	1	24	68	74	105	3	1	.264/.403/.534	166	32.4	.306	-6.6	LF(94): -15.2	2.2
2016	ERI	AA	22	100	17	2	0	6	19	12	26	0	0	.218/.310/.448	130	4.1	.232	0.7	LF(22): 1.0	0.8
2017	ERI	AA	23	555	67	29	3	28	86	56	138	3	0	.256/.335/.501	127	31.3	.294	-0.8	LF(120): -10.6	2.1
2018	TOL	AAA	24	522	69	21	3	23	77	67	108	0	0	.264/.364/.480	141	36.1	.296	0.8	LF(97): 9.8, RF(12): -0.7	4.9
2018	DET	MLB	24	72	7	1	1	2	10	10	13	0	0	.267/.375/.417	110	3.4	.304	-0.3	LF(15): -0.9	0.1
2019	DET	MLB	25	514	68	24	1	20	63	53	115	0	0	.243/.329/.434	105	16.5	.282	-0.8	LF -1	1.7

Breakout: 10%   Improve: 30%   Collapse: 9%   Attrition: 31%   MLB: 70%

Comparables: *Khris Davis, Jerry Sands, Matt LaPorta*

Service-time manipulation be damned, the rebuilding Tigers did the unthinkable in a non-cost-saving move and gave their three-time minor-league player of the year the left field job for a month. The tryout checked all the boxes and Stewart is on the inside track to start the season in Detroit. With a homer every 20 minor-league plate appearances, his power will dictate his usefulness, since a young dude in left field is fine for now, but long term he's looking at 1B/DH. In fact, he'll probably be ready for that switch right around the time when Miguel Cabrera's contract strikes midnight.

PITCHERS

Victor Alcantara RHP Born: 04/03/93 Age: 26 Bats: R Throws: R Height: 6'2" Weight: 190 Origin: International Free Agent, 2011

YEAR	TEAM	LVL	AGE	W	L	SV	G	GS	IP	H	HR	BB/9	K/9	K	GB%	BABIP	WHIP	ERA	DRA	WARP	MPH	FB%	WHF	CSP
2016	ARK	AA	23	3	7	0	29	20	111	106	9	4.6	6.4	79	55%	.289	1.47	4.30	3.74	1.7				
2017	ERI	AA	24	1	2	1	30	2	54²	46	1	5.6	9.4	57	60%	.312	1.46	3.46	3.97	0.6				
2017	TOL	AAA	24	0	1	0	9	1	20	22	0	5.4	7.2	16	54%	.338	1.70	4.05	4.10	0.3				
2017	DET	MLB	24	0	0	0	6	0	7¹	12	1	4.9	6.1	5	54%	.407	2.18	8.59	5.22	0.0	94.6	76.1	12.7	45.3
2018	TOL	AAA	25	5	2	3	29	1	51¹	52	3	1.2	8.2	47	55%	.329	1.15	2.81	3.06	1.2				
2018	DET	MLB	25	1	1	0	27	0	30	25	5	1.8	6.3	21	51%	.230	1.03	2.40	4.35	0.2	95.2	72.5	10.9	48.5
2019	DET	MLB	26	2	1	0	48	0	50²	50	5	3.9	7.7	43	50%	.299	1.41	4.46	4.64	0.3	94.7	74.5	11.5	47.9

Breakout: 19%   Improve: 34%   Collapse: 11%   Attrition: 22%   MLB: 54%

Comparables: *Joely Rodriguez, Zach Phillips, Donn Roach*

"If he can figure out his control, he'll be a good pitcher" is the "thoughts and prayers" of relievers. Alcantara, the raw-power, salary-dump return for Cameron Maybin, struggled with command throughout his minor-league career, averaging about five free bases per nine innings at each rung. Last year, he cut it to below two per nine. He was still prone to allowing gopher balls and other hard contact, and given his velocity he has surprising trouble getting swings and misses when he needs it most, but his breakout year made him one of the most dependable Tigers relievers. That's admittedly a low bar, but his sudden ability to limit baserunners would make him a good late option for any team.

Sandy Baez   RHP   Born: 11/25/93   Age: 25   Bats: R   Throws: R   Height: 6'2"   Weight: 180   Origin: International Free Agent, 2011

YEAR	TEAM	LVL	AGE	W	L	SV	G	GS	IP	H	HR	BB/9	K/9	K	GB%	BABIP	WHIP	ERA	DRA	WARP	MPH	FB%	WHF	CSP
2016	WMI	A	22	7	9	0	21	21	113¹	125	7	2.2	7.0	88	40%	.337	1.35	3.81	3.71	1.8				
2017	LAK	A+	23	6	7	0	17	17	88²	88	7	2.4	9.3	92	39%	.328	1.26	3.86	3.32	2.0				
2017	ERI	AA	23	0	1	0	2	2	10	9	3	4.5	11.7	13	36%	.273	1.40	4.50	3.30	0.2				
2018	ERI	AA	24	1	9	1	33	15	103²	114	19	4.0	7.5	86	38%	.316	1.54	5.64	4.78	0.6				
2018	DET	MLB	24	0	0	0	9	0	14¹	12	2	5.7	6.3	10	31%	.233	1.47	5.02	6.65	-0.3	97.8	63.7	8.5	46.8
2019	*DET*	*MLB*	*25*	*2*	*1*	*0*	*53*	*0*	*56²*	*63*	*10*	*3.6*	*7.0*	*44*	*36%*	*.304*	*1.51*	*5.46*	*5.71*	*-0.5*	*97.5*	*65.2*	*8.7*	*48*

Breakout: 0%   Improve: 1%   Collapse: 0%   Attrition: 2%   MLB: 2%   *Comparables: Angel Sanchez, Francisco Cruceta, Sam LeCure*

Double-A was not kind to Baez, who was kindly asked to leave the rotation. However, existing on the 40-man roster of a team desperate for men with velocity allowed him to poke his head up as the 26th man for a doubleheader, no-hitting the Yankees over 4 1/3 innings in a mop-up appearance. His September sequel was less successful, and hitting his spots wasn't any easier under the bright lights. The closest Baez will be to becoming a successful reliever is being an anagram of Danys Baez, which is more than you can say for most struggling pitchers.

Matt Boyd   LHP   Born: 02/02/91   Age: 28   Bats: L   Throws: L   Height: 6'3"   Weight: 234   Origin: Round 6, 2013 Draft (#175 overall)

YEAR	TEAM	LVL	AGE	W	L	SV	G	GS	IP	H	HR	BB/9	K/9	K	GB%	BABIP	WHIP	ERA	DRA	WARP	MPH	FB%	WHF	CSP
2016	TOL	AAA	25	2	5	0	11	11	64	53	5	2.5	8.0	57	42%	.271	1.11	2.25	3.34	1.5				
2016	DET	MLB	25	6	5	0	20	18	97¹	97	17	2.7	7.6	82	39%	.286	1.29	4.53	5.94	-0.7	94.3	60.9	10.2	49.2
2017	TOL	AAA	26	3	3	0	8	8	51	35	7	2.3	9.4	53	39%	.224	0.94	2.82	3.53	1.2				
2017	DET	MLB	26	6	11	0	26	25	135	157	18	3.5	7.3	110	40%	.330	1.56	5.27	6.46	-1.3	94.3	50.7	11	48
2018	DET	MLB	27	9	13	0	31	31	170¹	146	27	2.7	8.4	159	30%	.258	1.16	4.39	5.22	0.2	93.5	48.9	10.9	49
2019	*DET*	*MLB*	*28*	*8*	*11*	*0*	*28*	*28*	*159²*	*152*	*25*	*2.9*	*8.2*	*145*	*36%*	*.283*	*1.28*	*4.67*	*4.86*	*1.1*	*93.3*	*51.9*	*10.9*	*49*

Breakout: 25%   Improve: 58%   Collapse: 10%   Attrition: 19%   MLB: 90%   *Comparables: Chris Young, Zach McAllister, John Maine*

When astronaut Scott Kelly spent 340 consecutive days in space — the longest such stint in the International Space Station — it's rumored that he finally wanted to come home because he was tired of finding Boyd's curveballs and changeups. When he takes the mound, birds are mobilized and asked to stay in their nests for security reasons. The United Nations routinely asks Boyd to throw bullpen sessions in areas of the world suffering from drought so he can seed the clouds. He's sort of a fly-ball pitcher, is what we're saying. Aerial assaults aside, Boyd still tosses a variety of pitches and is developing into an innings eater with a very average ERA. Expect anything more from him and your head is up in the clouds, which as mentioned, is the worst place to be when Boyd pitches.

Beau Burrows   RHP   Born: 09/18/96   Age: 22   Bats: R   Throws: R   Height: 6'2"   Weight: 200   Origin: Round 1, 2015 Draft (#22 overall)

YEAR	TEAM	LVL	AGE	W	L	SV	G	GS	IP	H	HR	BB/9	K/9	K	GB%	BABIP	WHIP	ERA	DRA	WARP	MPH	FB%	WHF	CSP
2016	WMI	A	19	6	4	0	21	20	97	87	2	2.8	6.2	67	42%	.283	1.21	3.15	3.87	1.3				
2017	LAK	A+	20	4	3	0	11	11	58²	45	3	1.7	9.5	62	45%	.298	0.95	1.23	3.14	1.5				
2017	ERI	AA	20	6	4	0	15	15	76¹	79	5	3.9	8.8	75	40%	.339	1.47	4.72	4.38	0.7				
2018	ERI	AA	21	10	9	0	26	26	134	126	12	3.8	8.5	127	32%	.310	1.36	4.10	6.93	-2.5				
2019	*DET*	*MLB*	*22*	*5*	*9*	*0*	*23*	*23*	*111*	*113*	*18*	*3.7*	*8.0*	*99*	*35%*	*.298*	*1.44*	*5.09*	*5.31*	*0.2*				

Breakout: 4%   Improve: 8%   Collapse: 7%   Attrition: 11%   MLB: 19%   *Comparables: Reynaldo Lopez, Chris Flexen, Merandy Gonzalez*

Burrows' lively fastball will propel him to the major leagues soon, and it's going to make him a starter. His Double-A numbers, while unspectacular, weren't too alarming, though his name does take us all the way back to the 1930s. The curveball plays well, and with changeups and sliders simmerin' in his crockpot, his secondary offerings will likely sustain success in the rotation. He plays often in the air, and has yet to get burned by the long ball (though it's the Eastern League, nobody does), but his floor potential is pretty lofty, about as lofty as having the name Beau in 2019.

Louis Coleman   RHP   Born: 04/04/86   Age: 33   Bats: R   Throws: R   Height: 6'4"   Weight: 205   Origin: Round 5, 2009 Draft (#152 overall)

YEAR	TEAM	LVL	AGE	W	L	SV	G	GS	IP	H	HR	BB/9	K/9	K	GB%	BABIP	WHIP	ERA	DRA	WARP	MPH	FB%	WHF	CSP
2016	LAN	MLB	30	2	1	0	61	0	48	45	5	4.5	8.4	45	37%	.299	1.44	4.69	4.05	0.5	91.9	39.5	12.9	40.9
2017	LOU	AAA	31	2	1	2	25	0	36²	28	1	3.9	10.8	44	33%	.303	1.20	2.21	3.90	0.6				
2017	RNO	AAA	31	2	1	0	25	0	27¹	16	2	5.3	10.9	33	35%	.230	1.17	2.30	4.05	0.4				
2018	TOL	AAA	32	0	0	8	13	0	15	8	1	3.0	9.0	15	43%	.194	0.87	2.40	2.41	0.5				
2018	DET	MLB	32	4	1	0	51	0	51¹	43	5	4.2	7.2	41	44%	.270	1.31	3.51	5.30	-0.2	91.2	54.3	12	40.5
2019	*DET*	*MLB*	*33*	*1*	*0*	*0*	*21*	*0*	*22²*	*21*	*3*	*4.4*	*7.9*	*20*	*40%*	*.283*	*1.44*	*5.03*	*5.25*	*-0.1*	*90.4*	*48*	*12.2*	*40.2*

Breakout: 18%   Improve: 24%   Collapse: 19%   Attrition: 18%   MLB: 48%   *Comparables: Tommy Layne, Dale Thayer, Jean Machi*

Coleman's sidearm-ish right-handed delivery has historically kept same-sided hitters silent. However, last year, in his first extended MLB playing time in a while, his platoon splits went tail over teakettle. Right-handers sat on his fastball while left-handers were thrown off balance with a new changeup. But no manager is going to call on him to retire lefties; he'll simply need to better hide that four-seamer so he can return to his specialty. Even if that happens, Coleman's command has always been too suspect to use him in high-leverage situations. He provides solid bullpen depth with a different look, and that's about it.

Alex Faedo RHP
Born: 11/12/95　Age: 23　Bats: R　Throws: R　Height: 6'5"　Weight: 230　Origin: Round 1, 2017 Draft (#18 overall)

YEAR	TEAM	LVL	AGE	W	L	SV	G	GS	IP	H	HR	BB/9	K/9	K	GB%	BABIP	WHIP	ERA	DRA	WARP	MPH	FB%	WHF	CSP
2018	LAK	A+	22	2	4	0	12	12	61	49	3	1.9	7.5	51	33%	.263	1.02	3.10	3.19	1.5				
2018	ERI	AA	22	3	6	0	12	12	60	54	15	3.3	8.9	59	28%	.250	1.27	4.95	4.38	0.7				
2019	DET	MLB	23	4	7	0	16	16	81	84	16	3.2	7.4	67	30%	.285	1.39	5.51	5.75	-0.3				

Breakout: 4%　Improve: 9%　Collapse: 16%　Attrition: 16%　MLB: 29%　　　　Comparables: Wes Parsons, Jon Gray, Brett Kennedy

Slight worry simmered throughout the coterie of prospect wonks when Faedo's velocity went from high to low 90s. The organizational brass was not so much concerned, because baseball is literally outdoors poker, though his numbers definitely went south as he moved north. Sometimes the simplest explanation is the most obvious one: Faedo recorded a video of him tasting one of the Erie Seawolves' featured concession stand items, a hot dog wrapped in cotton candy and Nerds. Well, yea, that'll cause anyone's fastball to shrivel up. He'll probably try Double-A again, though the 2017 first-round pick's ceiling remains as a very strong starting pitcher with multiple offerings.

Buck Farmer RHP
Born: 02/20/91　Age: 28　Bats: L　Throws: R　Height: 6'4"　Weight: 232　Origin: Round 5, 2013 Draft (#156 overall)

YEAR	TEAM	LVL	AGE	W	L	SV	G	GS	IP	H	HR	BB/9	K/9	K	GB%	BABIP	WHIP	ERA	DRA	WARP	MPH	FB%	WHF	CSP
2016	TOL	AAA	25	5	6	0	20	20	100	106	11	2.5	8.4	93	47%	.326	1.34	3.96	2.97	2.7				
2016	DET	MLB	25	0	1	0	14	1	29¹	25	4	6.1	8.3	27	52%	.266	1.53	4.60	4.78	0.1	95.5	61.4	11.5	41.4
2017	TOL	AAA	26	6	4	0	21	21	123²	133	9	2.3	8.3	114	43%	.343	1.33	3.93	3.79	2.6				
2017	DET	MLB	26	5	5	0	11	11	48	55	9	3.8	9.2	49	34%	.336	1.56	6.75	5.85	-0.1	93.9	61.2	11.7	45.7
2018	DET	MLB	27	3	4	0	66	1	69¹	67	6	5.3	7.4	57	41%	.300	1.56	4.15	5.49	-0.4	96.0	57.6	12	45.3
2019	DET	MLB	28	2	1	0	48	0	50²	53	7	3.8	7.6	43	42%	.307	1.47	4.76	4.95	0.1	94.7	59.6	11.9	44.7

Breakout: 34%　Improve: 56%　Collapse: 16%　Attrition: 24%　MLB: 83%　　　　Comparables: Dan Meyer, Craig Stammen, Shane Greene

Every good agricultural expert knows not to give out too many free samples, yet Farmer led last year's Tigers bullpen in free passes. Scarecrow malfunctions aside, his fastball-changeup combination kept the sphere in the park, even if that park was the cavernous Comerica. He might still have premonitions of being in the rotation someday, but relievers with two solid yet wild pitches are prone to travel from parcel to parcel, collecting several different souvenir uniforms along the way.

Michael Fulmer RHP
Born: 03/15/93　Age: 26　Bats: R　Throws: R　Height: 6'3"　Weight: 246　Origin: Round 1, 2011 Draft (#44 overall)

YEAR	TEAM	LVL	AGE	W	L	SV	G	GS	IP	H	HR	BB/9	K/9	K	GB%	BABIP	WHIP	ERA	DRA	WARP	MPH	FB%	WHF	CSP
2016	TOL	AAA	23	1	1	0	3	3	15¹	16	3	2.9	11.7	20	49%	.325	1.37	4.11	3.22	0.4				
2016	DET	MLB	23	11	7	0	26	26	159	136	16	2.4	7.5	132	51%	.268	1.12	3.06	4.30	1.9	97.3	56.8	11.5	45.8
2017	DET	MLB	24	10	12	0	25	25	164²	150	13	2.2	6.2	114	51%	.273	1.15	3.83	3.75	3.4	97.7	59.4	10.5	48.6
2018	DET	MLB	25	3	12	0	24	24	132¹	128	19	3.1	7.5	110	47%	.288	1.31	4.69	4.66	1.0	97.8	61	11.7	48.6
2019	DET	MLB	26	9	10	0	28	28	159²	146	16	2.8	7.7	137	47%	.285	1.23	4.00	4.15	2.4	97.2	60.4	11.4	48.7

Breakout: 20%　Improve: 59%　Collapse: 24%　Attrition: 10%　MLB: 93%　　　　Comparables: Sonny Gray, Marcus Stroman, Jesse Hahn

Fulmer was able to avoid the sophomore slump, but the junior jinx was right on schedule. He had two disabled list stints for different non-arm injuries, which never help, but he also tinkered with his signature slider. In 2017 it was one of the hardest-thrown sliders in baseball. Last year he brought the velocity down on purpose and added some more sweeping action, and it resulted in the ball flying out the park far too often. Needless to say, there's some figuring out to do with respect to his devastating breaking pitch, which will result in "senior slider" having either the good or bad connotation.

Kyle Funkhouser RHP
Born: 03/16/94　Age: 25　Bats: R　Throws: R　Height: 6'2"　Weight: 220　Origin: Round 4, 2016 Draft (#115 overall)

YEAR	TEAM	LVL	AGE	W	L	SV	G	GS	IP	H	HR	BB/9	K/9	K	GB%	BABIP	WHIP	ERA	DRA	WARP	MPH	FB%	WHF	CSP
2016	ONE	A-	22	0	2	0	13	13	37¹	34	0	1.9	8.2	34	53%	.324	1.12	2.65	3.04	1.0				
2017	WMI	A	23	4	1	0	7	7	31¹	30	3	3.7	14.1	49	56%	.403	1.37	3.16	3.18	0.8				
2017	LAK	A+	23	1	1	0	5	5	31¹	23	1	1.7	9.8	34	57%	.275	0.93	1.72	2.97	0.8				
2018	ERI	AA	24	4	5	0	17	17	89	88	10	3.9	9.0	89	44%	.326	1.43	3.74	4.01	1.4				
2018	TOL	AAA	24	0	2	0	2	2	8²	8	0	10.4	7.3	7	54%	.333	2.08	6.23	3.71	0.2				
2019	DET	MLB	25	4	6	0	17	17	76²	79	12	3.7	8.2	70	44%	.305	1.45	4.93	5.13	0.3				

Breakout: 11%　Improve: 19%　Collapse: 10%　Attrition: 30%　MLB: 36%　　　　Comparables: Matt Maloney, George Kontos, Jeff Niemann

The burly righty spent the year honing his secondary stuff to augment his upper-90s heat, earning a Double-A All-Star nod and a Triple-A promotion. Funkhouser's season ended abruptly when he fractured his foot on an uneven sidewalk walking home from Toledo's ballpark. Usually when coaches tell a minor-league pitcher to cut down on their walks, they don't mean it literally. It was the second physical setback in as many seasons for the former fourth-round pick, but his profile as a starter with three solid pitches remains unfunked.

Shane Greene RHP
Born: 11/17/88　Age: 30　Bats: R　Throws: R　Height: 6'4"　Weight: 197　Origin: Round 15, 2009 Draft (#465 overall)

YEAR	TEAM	LVL	AGE	W	L	SV	G	GS	IP	H	HR	BB/9	K/9	K	GB%	BABIP	WHIP	ERA	DRA	WARP	MPH	FB%	WHF	CSP
2016	DET	MLB	27	5	4	2	50	3	60¹	58	3	3.3	8.8	59	48%	.327	1.33	5.82	4.20	0.6	96.2	40.8	13.7	46.3
2017	DET	MLB	28	4	3	9	71	0	67²	50	6	4.5	9.7	73	49%	.265	1.24	2.66	4.56	0.5	96.4	56.2	9.8	52
2018	DET	MLB	29	4	6	32	66	0	63¹	68	12	2.7	9.2	65	42%	.311	1.37	5.12	3.94	0.7	95.9	50.8	9.9	51.1
2019	DET	MLB	30	3	1	28	53	0	56²	57	7	3.5	8.5	53	44%	.308	1.39	4.42	4.58	0.3	95.4	50.2	10.7	50.1

Breakout: 17%　Improve: 52%　Collapse: 15%　Attrition: 11%　MLB: 81%　　　　Comparables: Brian Matusz, Tom Gorzelanny, Trevor Cahill

In *Monsters University*, the plucky one-eyed green critter Mike Wazowski was well-read in the technical side of scaring but ultimately could not convince Dean Hardscrabble of his scaring ability for the simple fact that he just wasn't scary. Likewise, Greene has a closer's mentality but not a closer's stuff. As a result, he *is* scary with a tight lead. For a team way out of contention, he was used surprisingly often, twice pitching on four consecutive days and once in both ends of a double-header. The fatigue showed, especially at the end of the season, and taters were his undoing. He's embraced high-leverage situations but would be best used sparingly, probably not as a closer. However, a manager can rely on him to enter a game to strand some baserunners and put some rallies right to bed with nightmares.

Blaine Hardy LHP   Born: 03/14/87   Age: 32   Bats: L   Throws: L   Height: 6'2"   Weight: 218   Origin: Round 22, 2008 Draft (#655 overall)

YEAR	TEAM	LVL	AGE	W	L	SV	G	GS	IP	H	HR	BB/9	K/9	K	GB%	BABIP	WHIP	ERA	DRA	WARP	MPH	FB%	WHF	CSP
2016	TOL	AAA	29	1	0	1	32	0	31¹	20	1	1.4	5.5	19	56%	.213	0.80	1.72	3.08	0.7				
2016	DET	MLB	29	1	0	0	21	0	25²	25	2	4.2	7.0	20	49%	.295	1.44	3.51	4.99	0.0	91.1	49.2	10.5	47.4
2017	TOL	AAA	30	7	3	3	34	2	40²	32	1	1.1	10.0	45	48%	.304	0.91	3.10	1.77	1.6				
2017	DET	MLB	30	1	0	0	35	0	33¹	46	7	3.5	7.6	28	34%	.361	1.77	5.94	5.24	0.0	91.3	44.9	11.3	49.8
2018	TOL	AAA	31	3	0	0	9	4	26¹	14	0	1.4	11.6	34	39%	.250	0.68	1.03	2.40	0.9				
2018	DET	MLB	31	4	5	1	30	13	86	79	10	2.3	6.9	66	42%	.275	1.17	3.56	3.98	1.2	90.2	32.9	9.1	51.5
2019	DET	MLB	32	3	2	0	37	5	59	58	8	3.2	7.8	51	43%	.291	1.34	4.59	4.77	0.3	89.6	37.3	9.7	49.4

Breakout: 20%   Improve: 36%   Collapse: 26%   Attrition: 15%   MLB: 76%   *Comparables: Anthony Varvaro, Cesar Ramos, Brandon Kintzler*

After 164 big-league appearances — all in relief — the veteran lefty reinvigorated his career in 2018 by stretching out in the rotation, proving himself in Triple-A and then posting the second-best ERA by a Tigers starter. Hardy averaged about five innings per start and once took a no-hitter into the seventh, but was drastically more effective in his traditional role (0.98 ERA, in 18 1/3 innings of relief). He barely throws 90, but he's a lefty with control, a stellar curveball and newly discovered stamina. Those are all career-extending qualities. Platoon him with Yusmeiro Petit and send the rest of your bullpen home for the night.

Joe Jimenez RHP   Born: 01/17/95   Age: 24   Bats: R   Throws: R   Height: 6'3"   Weight: 272   Origin: Undrafted Free Agent, 2013

YEAR	TEAM	LVL	AGE	W	L	SV	G	GS	IP	H	HR	BB/9	K/9	K	GB%	BABIP	WHIP	ERA	DRA	WARP	MPH	FB%	WHF	CSP
2016	LAK	A+	21	0	0	10	17	0	17¹	5	0	2.6	14.5	28	36%	.179	0.58	0.00	2.11	0.6				
2016	ERI	AA	21	3	2	12	21	0	20²	12	0	3.5	14.8	34	24%	.316	0.97	2.18	1.86	0.7				
2016	TOL	AAA	21	0	1	8	17	0	15²	9	1	2.3	9.2	16	38%	.205	0.83	2.30	2.53	0.4				
2017	TOL	AAA	22	1	1	4	26	0	25	19	1	4.3	13.0	36	43%	.340	1.24	1.44	2.37	0.8				
2017	DET	MLB	22	0	2	0	24	0	19	31	4	4.3	8.1	17	37%	.403	2.11	12.32	5.25	0.0	97.2	63.1	12.8	52
2018	DET	MLB	23	5	4	3	68	0	62²	53	5	3.2	11.2	78	36%	.304	1.20	4.31	3.05	1.4	97.6	67.2	14.7	47.3
2019	DET	MLB	24	3	1	0	59	0	62	54	8	3.8	10.6	73	37%	.296	1.29	4.02	4.15	0.6	97.3	68.3	14.7	50.9

Breakout: 24%   Improve: 38%   Collapse: 24%   Attrition: 25%   MLB: 80%   *Comparables: Corey Knebel, Josh Spence, Keone Kela*

They said it couldn't happen. They said it was impossible. But you remember where you were — hopefully sitting down — the moment a Tigers homegrown reliever was named an All-Star. Jimenez's strong first half as a setup man made him Detroit's first non-closer reliever named to the Midseason Classic since Mike Henneman in 1989. The explosive fastball-slider two-step generates whiffs and weak contact. A high workload led to diminishing zip on the fastball and an ERA on the wrong side of seven for the last two months, because did we mention he was a Tigers reliever? Sometimes impossibility is mistaken for inevitability. However, Jimenez showed the work ethic and the results, and the 24-year-old will eventually be the ninth-inning stopper.

Francisco Liriano LHP   Born: 10/26/83   Age: 35   Bats: L   Throws: L   Height: 6'3"   Weight: 218   Origin: International Free Agent, 2000

YEAR	TEAM	LVL	AGE	W	L	SV	G	GS	IP	H	HR	BB/9	K/9	K	GB%	BABIP	WHIP	ERA	DRA	WARP	MPH	FB%	WHF	CSP
2016	PIT	MLB	32	6	11	0	21	21	113²	115	19	5.5	9.2	116	54%	.308	1.62	5.46	5.07	0.4	95.5	50.9	11.7	41.6
2016	TOR	MLB	32	2	2	0	10	8	49¹	42	7	2.9	9.5	52	52%	.267	1.18	2.92	4.77	0.3	95.9	51.1	13.1	42.3
2017	TOR	MLB	33	6	5	0	18	18	82²	91	11	4.7	8.1	74	44%	.327	1.62	5.88	5.75	-0.2	94.5	49.3	10.1	42.2
2017	HOU	MLB	33	0	2	0	20	0	14¹	14	0	6.3	6.9	11	54%	.341	1.67	4.40	6.59	-0.2	96.1	54.6	10	44
2018	DET	MLB	34	5	12	0	27	26	133²	127	19	4.9	7.4	110	49%	.285	1.50	4.58	5.36	-0.1	94.0	46.7	10.5	43.8
2019	DET	MLB	35	6	8	0	21	21	112²	111	14	4.6	7.8	98	48%	.296	1.49	4.86	5.06	0.5	93.5	48	10.7	42.1

Breakout: 13%   Improve: 36%   Collapse: 28%   Attrition: 14%   MLB: 87%   *Comparables: Doug Davis, Ryan Dempster, Bob Veale*

Liriano was once considered the top pitcher in baseball. That was 13 years ago, a unit of time longer than Sandy Koufax's entire career. Durability is a blessing and a curse; not everyone gets to pitch into a second decade. However, watching the 35-year-old Liriano gallivant about the circuit as a reduced shell of his electric rookie self is highly bittersweet. His attempt to reunite with Ron Gardenhire in Detroit to catalyze that 2006 magic brought us to the conclusion that it's not about location (although it is, in the other definition), he just can't retire righties. His last chance to provide meaningful outs is one at a time, as he did in the 2017 World Series, against lefties. (Both appearances were exclusively against Cody Bellinger, and he doesn't have to be that hyper-specialized, although Bellinger was 11 when Liriano was the talk of the league, and he would have struck him out then too.)

Matt Manning RHP Born: 01/28/98 Age: 21 Bats: R Throws: R Height: 6'6" Weight: 190 Origin: Round 1, 2016 Draft (#9 overall)

YEAR	TEAM	LVL	AGE	W	L	SV	G	GS	IP	H	HR	BB/9	K/9	K	GB%	BABIP	WHIP	ERA	DRA	WARP	MPH	FB%	WHF	CSP
2016	TGW	RK	18	0	2	0	10	10	29¹	27	2	2.1	14.1	46	38%	.379	1.16	3.99	2.54	1.0				
2017	ONE	A-	19	2	2	0	9	9	33¹	27	0	3.8	9.7	36	31%	.310	1.23	1.89	3.75	0.6				
2017	WMI	A	19	2	0	0	5	5	17²	14	0	5.6	13.2	26	49%	.341	1.42	5.60	3.43	0.4				
2018	WMI	A	20	3	3	0	11	11	55²	47	3	4.5	12.3	76	43%	.344	1.35	3.40	3.23	1.3				
2018	LAK	A+	20	4	4	0	9	9	51¹	32	4	3.3	11.4	65	47%	.241	0.99	2.98	3.69	1.0				
2018	ERI	AA	20	0	1	0	2	2	10²	11	0	3.4	11.0	13	46%	.393	1.41	4.22	3.06	0.3				
2019	DET	MLB	21	4	7	0	20	20	85¹	82	13	4.4	9.5	90	38%	.301	1.46	4.96	5.16	0.3				

Breakout: 6% Improve: 10% Collapse: 2% Attrition: 8% MLB: 16%   *Comparables: Sean Reid-Foley, Michael Kopech, Matt Magill*

The most polarizing Tigers prospect since Steven Moya, Manning will be given every chance to remain a starting pitcher. In only three of his 22 starts last year did he fail to record fewer than one strikeout per inning (and all three were barely below the threshold), because the fastball is a weapon and the curveball is becoming more consistent. He's going to be a major-league pitcher at some point, and especially these days there's no shame in carving out a niche as a reliever. However, the Tigers are going to force the former no. 9 overall pick to fail into the 'pen.

Casey Mize RHP Born: 05/01/97 Age: 22 Bats: R Throws: R Height: 6'3" Weight: 220 Origin: Round 1, 2018 Draft (#1 overall)

YEAR	TEAM	LVL	AGE	W	L	SV	G	GS	IP	H	HR	BB/9	K/9	K	GB%	BABIP	WHIP	ERA	DRA	WARP	MPH	FB%	WHF	CSP
2018	LAK	A+	21	0	1	0	4	4	11²	13	2	1.5	7.7	10	44%	.344	1.29	4.63	4.44	0.1				
2019	DET	MLB	22	2	3	0	8	8	33¹	36	6	3.6	7.5	28	42%	.301	1.46	5.41	5.64	-0.1				

Breakout: 1% Improve: 2% Collapse: 0% Attrition: 1% MLB: 2%   *Comparables: Michael Ynoa, Jace Fry, Chi Chi Gonzalez*

Mize was the no. 1 overall pick, which means he's going to be inserted into a major-league rotation at some point. He features a mid-90s fastball along with a very mature split-finger that kept SEC hitters honest for three years when he twirled the pitch at Auburn (including a no-hitter last year). Along with a retooled slider and newly-discovered cut fastball, he commands all four pitches with maturity. After Auburn was eliminated in the NCAA super regionals, he had amassed well over 110 innings, so after a taste of Single-A he'll go into his first full season learning all those life lessons that one does in professional baseball, such as: sometimes you don't pitch on Friday, and also there's no homework due the next day. Getting money for baseball rules!

Matt Moore LHP Born: 06/18/89 Age: 30 Bats: L Throws: L Height: 6'3" Weight: 210 Origin: Round 8, 2007 Draft (#245 overall)

YEAR	TEAM	LVL	AGE	W	L	SV	G	GS	IP	H	HR	BB/9	K/9	K	GB%	BABIP	WHIP	ERA	DRA	WARP	MPH	FB%	WHF	CSP
2016	TBA	MLB	27	7	7	0	21	21	130	125	20	2.8	7.5	109	38%	.280	1.27	4.08	4.63	1.1	95.3	63	10.7	49.6
2016	SFN	MLB	27	6	5	0	12	12	68¹	59	5	4.2	9.1	69	42%	.297	1.33	4.08	3.86	1.2	95.4	63	12.3	48.5
2017	SFN	MLB	28	6	15	0	32	31	174¹	200	27	3.5	7.6	148	39%	.320	1.53	5.52	5.34	0.4	93.6	51.7	9.4	49.7
2018	TEX	MLB	29	3	8	0	39	12	102	128	19	3.6	7.6	86	39%	.341	1.66	6.79	7.00	-2.2	94.4	58.7	10.7	52.5
2019	DET	MLB	30	4	6	0	16	16	84²	90	12	3.4	7.6	71	39%	.306	1.44	4.81	5.01	0.5	93.6	57.3	10.4	50.6

Breakout: 35% Improve: 54% Collapse: 6% Attrition: 10% MLB: 83%   *Comparables: Scott Kazmir, Tim Leary, Luke Hochevar*

The professor did not look up from his book, but simply held one finger aloft until, one by one, his students noticed, and lowered their voices until the room was silent. Only then did the old man's eyes spark to life as he looked into the room of hopeful young students. "In 2011," he began, "a rookie pitcher from Tampa Bay torpedoed the mighty Texas Rangers in the first game of the ALDS, holding them to no runs and just two hits over seven innings en route to a 9-0 blowout."

A flutter of whispers skittered around the room like autumn leaves. Baseball? Where was he going with this?

"Seven years later, that very pitcher, no longer a rookie, of course, no longer a prospect, was traded to the Texas Rangers, and again torpedoed them, this time notching just one win before June, when he was relegated to the bullpen. Of what, dear students, is this an example?"

He lowered his glasses and peered at the collected students until he spotted one confident soul, hand aloft. "Yes?"

"It's irony, sir." the freshman said, assuredly.

"No, you fool," the professor snapped, then scoffed again for effect as he paced around his lectern.

"Tragedy?"

"Perhaps, if you believe in such things," the professor allowed, still pacing. "He was, by all accounts, a good man with a kind heart. But no, that's not the answer I'm looking for."

The room went silent, and the professor stopped pacing, looking for another volunteer, but the room had gone still.

"It's NIHILISM!" he shouted with an enthusiasm that felt more like spite than joy. "The Rays lost that series to the Rangers in 2011; the rookie's performance was for naught! And the 2018 Rangers were careening head-first into a rebuild, anyway. They took a shot at a reclamation project and it didn't pan out. None of it matters. On that note, you're all being given a failing grade. If you're a true student of philosophy, you'll be back tomorrow because you want to learn anyway. The rest of you who were only here for a grade would have dropped the class in a month anyway. You're all dismissed."

Daniel Norris LHP   Born: 04/25/93   Age: 26   Bats: L   Throws: L   Height: 6'2"   Weight: 185   Origin: Round 2, 2011 Draft (#74 overall)

YEAR	TEAM	LVL	AGE	W	L	SV	G	GS	IP	H	HR	BB/9	K/9	K	GB%	BABIP	WHIP	ERA	DRA	WARP	MPH	FB%	WHF	CSP
2016	TOL	AAA	23	5	7	0	14	14	73¹	78	2	3.4	9.4	77	57%	.358	1.45	4.54	3.45	1.6				
2016	DET	MLB	23	4	2	0	14	13	69¹	75	10	2.9	9.2	71	38%	.327	1.40	3.38	5.31	0.0	96.0	61.8	11.6	46
2017	TOL	AAA	24	0	4	0	6	6	14	22	3	10.3	11.6	18	50%	.442	2.71	12.21	4.62	0.2				
2017	DET	MLB	24	5	8	0	22	18	101²	120	12	3.9	7.6	86	40%	.344	1.61	5.31	6.48	-1.1	94.8	55	10	45.1
2018	DET	MLB	25	0	5	0	11	8	44¹	46	8	3.9	10.4	51	33%	.317	1.47	5.68	5.12	0.1	92.1	52.7	11.4	49.4
2019	DET	MLB	26	5	7	0	18	18	90	91	12	3.7	9.3	93	41%	.313	1.42	4.42	4.59	0.9	94.0	57	11	48

Breakout: 26%   Improve: 57%   Collapse: 16%   Attrition: 13%   MLB: 94%   Comparables: *Luke Hochevar, Shaun Marcum, Jordan Zimmermann*

2014: Elbow surgery.
2015: Strained oblique. (And in the offseason, thyroid cancer treatment.)
2016: Strained oblique.
2017: Strained oblique, vertebral hairline fractures, groin injury.
2018: Groin injury.
2019: Oh, let's say, the mumps.
2020: Ingrown belly button.
2021: Grows a dorsal fin, and then the dorsal fin hurts a lot.
2022: Becomes one of us, stays in a padded room, forever, playing *Bases Loaded* on the NES until the pain is gone.

Franklin Perez RHP   Born: 12/06/97   Age: 21   Bats: R   Throws: R   Height: 6'3"   Weight: 197   Origin: International Free Agent, 2014

YEAR	TEAM	LVL	AGE	W	L	SV	G	GS	IP	H	HR	BB/9	K/9	K	GB%	BABIP	WHIP	ERA	DRA	WARP	MPH	FB%	WHF	CSP
2016	QUD	A	18	3	3	1	15	10	66²	63	1	2.6	10.1	75	39%	.344	1.23	2.84	3.40	1.2				
2017	BCA	A+	19	4	2	2	12	10	54¹	38	4	2.7	8.8	53	38%	.236	0.99	2.98	3.49	1.1				
2017	CCH	AA	19	2	1	1	7	6	32	33	2	3.1	7.0	25	35%	.316	1.38	3.09	3.51	0.6				
2018	LAK	A+	20	0	1	0	4	4	11¹	15	2	6.4	7.1	9	43%	.371	2.03	7.94	5.38	0.0				
2019	DET	MLB	21	2	2	0	13	6	33	37	5	3.9	6.4	23	37%	.301	1.55	5.48	5.73	-0.2				

Breakout: 1%   Improve: 3%   Collapse: 0%   Attrition: 5%   MLB: 7%   Comparables: *Jake Odorizzi, Matt Magill, Tyler Mahle*

There's still tons of potential in Perez, the centerpiece of the Justin Verlander trade. Worst-case scenario, we're copying and pasting this lead sentence into his next few *Annual* comments, because last year was all but lost for the young flamethrowing starter, from a three-month lat injury to a season-ending shoulder strain. We've yet to see a full workload, but he should impress with his above-average three pitches, the *coup de grace* being the changeup. Double-A is calling, and we'll see if he can stay on the line for a full season.

Tyson Ross RHP   Born: 04/22/87   Age: 32   Bats: R   Throws: R   Height: 6'6"   Weight: 245   Origin: Round 2, 2008 Draft (#58 overall)

YEAR	TEAM	LVL	AGE	W	L	SV	G	GS	IP	H	HR	BB/9	K/9	K	GB%	BABIP	WHIP	ERA	DRA	WARP	MPH	FB%	WHF	CSP
2016	SDN	MLB	29	0	1	0	1	1	5¹	9	0	1.7	8.4	5	47%	.474	1.88	11.81	3.40	0.1	95.2	53.3	14.4	40.4
2017	ROU	AAA	30	2	1	0	4	4	18²	23	3	5.3	5.3	11	46%	.345	1.82	7.71	5.26	0.1				
2017	FRI	AA	30	1	1	0	2	2	11²	11	0	3.1	7.7	10	62%	.324	1.29	2.31	3.59	0.2				
2017	TEX	MLB	30	3	3	0	12	10	49	53	7	6.8	6.6	36	48%	.305	1.84	7.71	8.24	-1.5	93.7	57.1	7.7	41.1
2018	SDN	MLB	31	6	9	0	22	22	123¹	112	16	3.8	7.8	107	45%	.276	1.33	4.45	4.94	0.5	92.9	41.7	9.3	43.9
2018	SLN	MLB	31	2	0	0	9	1	26¹	20	1	3.4	5.1	15	58%	.244	1.14	2.73	5.50	-0.1	93.8	41.7	8.3	46.1
2019	DET	MLB	32	5	9	0	21	21	111¹	115	14	4.2	7.1	88	46%	.299	1.50	5.00	5.22	0.3	92.3	45	8.8	41.9

Breakout: 8%   Improve: 41%   Collapse: 24%   Attrition: 12%   MLB: 84%   Comparables: *Doug Davis, Barry Zito, Carlos Zambrano*

Ross proved he can still make it through a season (mostly) healthy. That's a moral victory for a pitcher who has survived both Tommy John surgery and thoracic outlet syndrome. More concrete victories, however, seem mostly beyond his reach now. His fastball now sits 91-92 mph, with less hop than a Yugoslavian center, and his slider isn't the whipsaw it used to be. Ross hasn't been an average big-league hurler — let alone the budding ace he was at his peak — since 2015, and there's nothing left in his arm to suggest that's going to change. Still, that's the life of a major-league pitcher: plush velvet sometimes, sometimes just pretzels and beer. So far, he's still here.

Daniel Stumpf LHP   Born: 01/04/91   Age: 28   Bats: L   Throws: L   Height: 6'2"   Weight: 208   Origin: Round 9, 2012 Draft (#283 overall)

YEAR	TEAM	LVL	AGE	W	L	SV	G	GS	IP	H	HR	BB/9	K/9	K	GB%	BABIP	WHIP	ERA	DRA	WARP	MPH	FB%	WHF	CSP
2016	PHI	MLB	25	0	0	0	7	0	5	9	1	3.6	3.6	2	38%	.400	2.20	10.80	3.66	0.1	95.1	38	14	47.5
2016	NWA	AA	25	2	0	1	14	0	21¹	14	0	1.7	11.0	26	55%	.264	0.84	2.11	2.46	0.6				
2017	TOL	AAA	26	1	2	0	24	0	21¹	19	3	2.1	11.0	26	47%	.305	1.38	3.38	2.66	0.6				
2017	DET	MLB	26	0	1	0	55	0	37²	37	5	3.6	7.9	33	43%	.407	1.16	3.82	5.78	-0.3	95.2	60.2	8.2	48.3
2018	TOL	AAA	27	1	0	0	9	0	10¹	12	1	0.0	11.3	13	29%	.339	1.16	3.48	3.60	0.2				
2018	DET	MLB	27	1	5	0	56	0	38¹	44	5	3.8	8.7	37	38%	.306	1.57	4.93	3.44	0.7	95.4	53.7	12.4	46.2
2019	DET	MLB	28	2	1	0	43	0	45¹	46	6	3.7	8.4	42	42%	.306	1.42	4.70	4.88	0.1	94.7	55.9	10.8	47.5

Breakout: 22%   Improve: 37%   Collapse: 17%   Attrition: 22%   MLB: 65%   Comparables: *Mike Adams, Lucas Luetge, Jose Veras*

Stumpf could be useful if he simply faced mostly lefties, offering a fastball-slider combination and keeping everything low in the zone. His numbers suffered in part due to being the lone southpaw for a rebuilding team with neither luxury nor device for a one-out guy, so he faced foes of both handedness equally. Because, you never know, he might turn out to be one of those weird "good" left-handers. Spoiler alert: he's not. He's a specialist, and now for the bad news: there are better ones out there.

Spencer Turnbull RHP   Born: 09/18/92   Age: 26   Bats: R   Throws: R   Height: 6'3"   Weight: 215   Origin: Round 2, 2014 Draft (#63 overall)

YEAR	TEAM	LVL	AGE	W	L	SV	G	GS	IP	H	HR	BB/9	K/9	K	GB%	BABIP	WHIP	ERA	DRA	WARP	MPH	FB%	WHF	CSP
2016	TGW	RK	23	0	1	0	4	4	10²	3	0	4.2	5.9	7	69%	.115	0.75	3.38	4.54	0.1				
2016	LAK	A+	23	1	1	0	6	6	30	24	1	3.0	8.1	27	56%	.274	1.13	3.00	3.22	0.8				
2017	LAK	A+	24	7	3	0	15	15	82²	68	3	2.7	7.0	64	52%	.280	1.12	3.05	3.20	2.0				
2017	ERI	AA	24	0	3	0	4	4	20¹	22	1	3.5	9.7	22	58%	.356	1.48	6.20	4.48	0.2				
2018	ERI	AA	25	4	7	0	19	19	98²	92	4	3.6	9.6	105	56%	.332	1.34	4.47	3.73	1.8				
2018	TOL	AAA	25	1	1	0	2	2	13¹	8	0	2.0	12.8	19	57%	.267	0.82	2.03	2.57	0.4				
2018	DET	MLB	25	0	2	0	4	3	16¹	17	1	2.2	8.3	15	48%	.327	1.29	6.06	4.99	0.1	96.1	66.7	9.9	49.3
2019	DET	MLB	26	3	3	0	27	6	52²	52	7	3.9	8.4	49	50%	.302	1.42	4.60	4.78	0.2	95.7	67.9	10.1	50.2

Breakout: 11%   Improve: 29%   Collapse: 16%   Attrition: 36%   MLB: 55%   *Comparables: Sean Nolin, Samuel Gaviglio, Jack Egbert*

Prospects don't linearly traipse through an organization, as much as we'd like to pretend. Sometimes there's a setback, be it injury or self-inflicted struggle. Other times someone is rushed ahead to the finish line. Turnbull felt both sides of that progression, overcoming a midseason injury to scoot out of Double-A and into the majors by September. For funsies, he started the final game of the season against the playoff-bound Brewers, who needed the win to force an NL Central tiebreaker. They predictably broke him, but Turnbull will again rebound with a strong chance to start in 2019, featuring a power sinker and plenty of peripheral pitches that have caused off-balance swings throughout his career.

Jacob Turner RHP   Born: 05/21/91   Age: 28   Bats: R   Throws: R   Height: 6'5"   Weight: 215   Origin: Round 1, 2009 Draft (#9 overall)

YEAR	TEAM	LVL	AGE	W	L	SV	G	GS	IP	H	HR	BB/9	K/9	K	GB%	BABIP	WHIP	ERA	DRA	WARP	MPH	FB%	WHF	CSP
2016	CHR	AAA	25	4	7	0	18	18	107	125	10	2.4	7.1	85	49%	.342	1.44	4.71	5.78	-0.5				
2016	CHA	MLB	25	1	2	0	18	2	24²	33	5	5.8	6.6	18	49%	.346	1.99	6.57	8.16	-0.9	98.0	65.9	8	45.7
2017	WAS	MLB	26	2	3	0	18	2	39	43	8	3.5	5.3	23	44%	.285	1.49	5.08	6.54	-0.5	96.9	65.7	7	49.8
2017	SYR	AAA	26	2	6	0	14	14	65²	72	5	4.5	7.3	53	51%	.338	1.60	5.21	5.03	0.5				
2018	MIA	MLB	27	0	0	0	4	0	5²	13	1	7.9	3.2	2	39%	.444	3.18	15.88	8.25	-0.2	94.6	63.2	6.4	49.7
2018	NWO	AAA	27	1	0	1	11	0	21²	31	4	3.3	7.1	17	49%	.370	1.80	5.82	3.47	0.5				
2018	DET	MLB	27	0	1	0	1	1	1	6	1	9.0	9.0	1	44%	.625	7.00	45.00	10.81	-0.1	96.6	56.8	8.1	48.5
2018	TOL	AAA	27	3	4	0	15	15	82¹	74	6	3.2	6.3	58	54%	.283	1.25	3.50	4.23	1.2				
2019	DET	MLB	28	5	6	1	32	14	93¹	104	11	3.5	6.8	70	47%	.315	1.50	4.80	5.00	0.4	96.4	65.5	7.3	48.9

Breakout: 20%   Improve: 34%   Collapse: 19%   Attrition: 28%   MLB: 57%   *Comparables: Matt Chico, Jason Berken, Scott Diamond*

Turner, whose biopic would be called *Trouble With Everything But The Curve*, turns 28 this year but looks 43 in transaction years. He is not by any means major-league talent, but keeps getting opportunities because, y'know, he's Jacob Turner. Last year he found his way back to the team that drafted him and then traded him for Anibal Sanchez, though a dismal start resulted in being outrighted to Triple-A. Despite that, the Tigers announced his second chance, except he wasn't down the requisite 10 days, then never got the call-up. He'll likely tempt another team with a chance thanks to that curve, which means the only people he's getting to chase with two strikes are general managers.

Drew VerHagen RHP   Born: 10/22/90   Age: 28   Bats: R   Throws: R   Height: 6'6"   Weight: 230   Origin: Round 4, 2012 Draft (#154 overall)

YEAR	TEAM	LVL	AGE	W	L	SV	G	GS	IP	H	HR	BB/9	K/9	K	GB%	BABIP	WHIP	ERA	DRA	WARP	MPH	FB%	WHF	CSP
2016	DET	MLB	25	1	0	0	19	0	19	28	3	3.3	4.7	10	60%	.362	1.84	7.11	5.55	-0.1	97.0	62.7	7.6	46.6
2017	TOL	AAA	26	7	7	0	19	19	97¹	108	7	4.0	6.4	69	46%	.329	1.55	4.90	4.67	1.1				
2017	DET	MLB	26	0	3	0	24	2	34¹	42	10	2.4	6.6	25	51%	.317	1.49	5.77	4.95	0.1	95.5	60.5	9.6	50.2
2018	TOL	AAA	27	2	1	0	10	6	32²	18	0	2.8	14.1	51	52%	.273	0.86	1.65	2.89	1.0				
2018	DET	MLB	27	3	3	0	41	1	56¹	46	6	3.0	8.5	53	48%	.263	1.15	4.63	3.79	0.8	95.8	54	12.7	46.8
2019	DET	MLB	28	3	1	0	53	0	56²	52	7	3.6	8.7	54	48%	.294	1.32	4.31	4.47	0.5	95.3	57.3	11.2	48.1

Breakout: 21%   Improve: 41%   Collapse: 11%   Attrition: 21%   MLB: 71%   *Comparables: Troy Patton, Darrell Rasner, Tanner Roark*

The idea of VerHagen as a starter may never completely abandon him, as he can work multiple innings and keep the ball on the ground. That much we know. Yes, the big man works off his sinker, and his iffy additional pitches kept him away from the rotation, but the catch-22 is he was the Tigers' most useful middle reliever *because* of those other offerings, namely the slider and curve. Need more evidence? He was given one start last year, allowing three home runs — equal to his total in 52 2/3 reliever innings. Yeah, keep him in the bullpen.

Alex Wilson RHP   Born: 11/03/86   Age: 32   Bats: R   Throws: R   Height: 6'0"   Weight: 227   Origin: Round 2, 2009 Draft (#77 overall)

YEAR	TEAM	LVL	AGE	W	L	SV	G	GS	IP	H	HR	BB/9	K/9	K	GB%	BABIP	WHIP	ERA	DRA	WARP	MPH	FB%	WHF	CSP
2016	DET	MLB	29	4	0	0	62	0	73	68	5	2.6	6.0	49	45%	.285	1.22	2.96	5.20	-0.2	93.9	56.1	9.8	43
2017	DET	MLB	30	2	5	2	66	0	60	67	7	2.2	6.3	42	42%	.311	1.37	4.50	5.48	-0.2	94.0	58.3	9.5	46.7
2018	DET	MLB	31	2	4	0	59	0	61²	50	8	2.2	6.3	43	50%	.237	1.05	3.36	4.10	0.6	93.2	41.9	9.7	41.6
2019	DET	MLB	32	2	1	1	48	0	50²	50	6	3.2	6.5	36	45%	.282	1.33	4.64	4.84	0.1	92.7	50.7	9.6	43.3

Breakout: 22%   Improve: 43%   Collapse: 27%   Attrition: 17%   MLB: 86%   *Comparables: Burke Badenhop, Jared Hughes, Geoff Geary*

Making a living as a relief pitcher can be exhausting, especially since 649 different players made relief appearances last year. Take away about 100 that were swingmen or position players, and we're still left with about 17 different true relievers per team. Try naming them all. Some stand out with a crazy good breaking pitch. Some ramp up the velocity. Some are Carter Capps and do a weird delivery so they can go viral. Alex Wilson does none of this. He chooses to remain in the background. He's a flatly dull pitcher who doesn't strike out many batters, but limits baserunners across multiple innings. He's done this for four years and counting. The only thing he's done to stand out is sort of resemble Chris Pratt and become the only MLB pitcher born in Saudi Arabia, but those are really things his *parents* did.

Jordan Zimmermann RHP Born: 05/23/86 Age: 33 Bats: R Throws: R Height: 6'2" Weight: 225 Origin: Round 2, 2007 Draft (#67 overall)

YEAR	TEAM	LVL	AGE	W	L	SV	G	GS	IP	H	HR	BB/9	K/9	K	GB%	BABIP	WHIP	ERA	DRA	WARP	MPH	FB%	WHF	CSP
2016	TOL	AAA	30	0	1	0	5	5	20¹	19	2	1.8	4.9	11	46%	.270	1.13	1.33	3.53	0.4				
2016	DET	MLB	30	9	7	0	19	18	105¹	118	14	2.2	5.6	66	44%	.304	1.37	4.87	4.52	1.0	94.3	52.8	8.5	49.2
2017	DET	MLB	31	8	13	0	29	29	160	204	29	2.5	5.8	103	35%	.330	1.55	6.07	6.90	-2.4	93.5	54.2	8.8	51.3
2018	DET	MLB	32	7	8	0	25	25	131¹	140	28	1.8	7.6	111	37%	.288	1.26	4.52	4.76	0.8	92.5	45.3	9.9	48.2
2019	DET	MLB	33	8	11	0	27	27	154	169	25	2.5	6.7	115	39%	.302	1.38	4.89	5.09	0.7	92.2	49.8	9.1	48.9

Breakout: 25%   Improve: 46%   Collapse: 19%   Attrition: 11%   MLB: 86%   Comparables: Kyle Lohse, Rodrigo Lopez, Aaron Harang

He improved strongly last year, because it would have been difficult to sustain that awful 2017, though at this point Zimmermann and his contract are sunk costs. His fastball is in steady decline and is a favorite delicacy among those carrying baseball bats in the American League Central. It's rated highly on Yelp ("A must try! Goes high and far!") and there are plenty of portions to go around. His slider is workable, and on days it snaps like Michael rebooting *The Good Place* he'll go deep into the game and scribes will pine about his potential comeback. His strikeout and walk rates have stabilized, which means he can still operate as a fourth starter. He just needs to take the fastball off the menu or just garnish it with something.

LINEOUTS

Hitters

HITTER	POS	TEAM	LVL	AGE	PA	R	2B	3B	HR	RBI	BB	K	SB	CS	AVG/OBP/SLG	DRC+	VORP	BABIP	BRR	FRAA	WARP
Jim Adduci	LF	TOL	AAA	33	296	39	22	1	7	44	22	60	8	1	.309/.358/.474	117	18.8	.372	1.1	RF(45): -2.4, 1B(10): 0.8	1.1
	LF	DET	MLB	33	185	19	8	2	3	21	6	45	1	0	.267/.290/.386	71	-2.6	.341	-0.6	1B(48): -4.7	-0.9
Sergio Alcantara	SS	ERI	AA	21	494	53	18	3	1	37	42	95	8	5	.271/.335/.333	88	10.3	.342	-2.5	SS(93): -0.6, 2B(20): -0.3	0.9
Jose Azocar	OF	WMI	A	22	110	19	3	6	1	16	5	21	6	2	.317/.355/.490	113	10.6	.390	1.0	CF(24): -0.5, RF(2): -0.5	0.5
	OF	LAK	A+	22	318	34	14	3	1	34	9	64	5	2	.290/.308/.367	83	-0.1	.355	-1.7	RF(61): -0.7, CF(9): 0.7	-0.2
Willi Castro	SS	AKR	AA	21	410	55	20	2	5	39	28	84	13	4	.245/.303/.350	89	17.4	.304	1.3	SS(96): 7.5	2.2
	SS	ERI	AA	21	114	12	9	2	4	13	6	25	4	1	.324/.366/.562	101	10.0	.395	-0.8	SS(10): 0.7, 2B(9): -0.2	0.3
Kody Clemens	2B	WMI	A	22	174	18	10	2	4	17	21	27	3	1	.302/.387/.477	127	13.7	.342	-0.9	2B(39): -1.6	0.8
	2B	LAK	A+	22	46	6	2	0	1	3	2	12	1	0	.238/.283/.357	90	0.0	.300	0.3	2B(11): 0.2	0.1
Brock Deatherage	CF	WMI	A	22	195	25	7	5	2	18	14	50	15	3	.313/.369/.443	93	16.2	.421	3.2	CF(40): 4.0, RF(4): -0.3	1.1
	CF	LAK	A+	22	52	12	1	1	1	5	6	13	4	0	.333/.404/.467	97	6.0	.438	1.8	CF(9): -1.3, RF(2): -0.4	0.1
Pete Kozma	SS	TOL	AAA	30	296	23	18	2	1	17	19	52	6	1	.203/.260/.295	74	-2.4	.244	0.4	SS(64): -1.3, 3B(10): 0.3	0.2
	SS	DET	MLB	30	73	7	4	1	1	8	2	15	0	1	.217/.236/.348	81	0.3	.259	0.1	SS(15): 0.0, 3B(6): 0.3	0.2
Kingston Liniak	OF	TGR	Rk	18	166	14	7	0	0	9	7	51	5	4	.224/.259/.269	61	-5.2	.327	-1.0	CF(37): 10.8	0.7
	OF	TGW	Rk	18	34	5	1	0	0	4	0	7	2	0	.281/.324/.313	60	0.3	.360	0.9	CF(6): -0.7, RF(1): 1.0	0.1
Reynaldo Rivera	1B	WMI	A	21	454	41	28	4	9	62	36	119	3	2	.237/.295/.390	93	4.3	.304	2.0	1B(60): -2.0, LF(13): 0.2	0.1
Jake Robson	OF	ERI	AA	23	311	46	16	3	7	32	39	78	11	4	.286/.382/.450	94	22.8	.382	3.8	CF(27): -2.9, RF(25): 0.6	0.9
	OF	TOL	AAA	23	245	36	13	1	4	15	23	62	7	6	.305/.369/.427	91	16.8	.406	1.1	CF(28): -2.0, LF(16): 1.2	0.4
Jarrod Saltalamacchia	C	TOL	AAA	33	253	21	7	1	5	28	33	81	1	1	.174/.285/.284	86	-1.0	.248	0.4	C(63): 2.5	1.0
	C	DET	MLB	33	8	0	0	0	0	0	1	4	0	0	.000/.125/.000	69	-1.3	.000	0.0	C(1): 0.0, 1B(1): 0.0	0.0
Bobby Wilson	C	ROC	AAA	35	45	2	1	0	0	3	3	13	0	0	.125/.182/.150	70	-4.5	.179	-0.6	C(11): 0.3	0.0
	C	MIN	MLB	35	151	12	8	0	2	16	12	37	0	0	.178/.242/.281	67	-5.1	.224	-1.1	C(47): 4.1	0.5

Has this ever happened to you? Is your team 20 games out of first place in July and your roster is in dire need of a nap? You've tried the rest, now try starting **Jim Adduci** at first base for a while. ⓧ Scrawny infielder **Sergio Alcantara** doesn't have the frame or the bat for a starting shortstop gig in his future, but his plus speed, range and pitch recognition will make him a useful bench contributor in a few orbital revolutions. ⓧ Free-swinging **Jose Azocar** sputtered in High-A and took an unscheduled detour back a level before getting his GPS coordinates right to hit .330 in his second chance in Florida. ⓧ **Willi Castro** is a fringy middle-infield prospect playing beyond his age bracket with the promise of some power, which is why the Indians deemed him expendable in exchange for Leonys Martin. ⓧ The fourth and youngest Clemens progeny, **Kody Clemens** is already pigeonholed at second base but finished last season at High-A, so we'll quickly find out who gets to be the second-most-valuable Clemens. ⓧ The most metal of prospect names, speedy outfielder **Brock Deatherage** leapt into the mosh pit of professional baseball, thrashed three dingers in his first game and was carried all the way up to High-A. Ooh wa ah ah ah. ⓧ **Pete Kozma** keeps showing the youngsters in Triple-A how to play an elite defense, then in return the kids show *him* how to hit for power. The kids then get the call-up instead of him. ⓧ San Diego-area high schooler **Kingston Liniak** took the money and ran with the Tigers as a fourth-round pick. As is the case with young, toolsy high schoolers, he'll get all the time in the world to develop before the sun devours us all. ⓧ Geraldo Rivera looked in Al Capone's vault in search of treasure and left us all disappointed. **Reynaldo Rivera** will spend the next few years trying to tap into his mysterious vault of raw power, though untelevised. ⓧ They call **Jacob Robson** "Maple Hammer" because he is Canadian, but while "Hammer" seems anachronous for a 5-foot-10 outfielder, he's been quickly nailing every minor-league rung since the 2016 draft and may warrant a major-league appearance this year. ⓧ Okay, *now* we've likely seen the last of the longest name in sports, **Jarrod Saltalamacchia**, who mentored battery-mates for a Triple-A summer and was rewarded with one last September as a third catcher. ⓧ **Bobby Wilson** has never been even remotely close to average at the plate, so the fact that he just completed the 16th year of his professional career says a great deal about how teams value his work behind it.

Pitchers

PITCHER	TEAM	LVL	AGE	W	L	SV	G	GS	IP	H	HR	BB/9	K/9	K	GB%	BABIP	WHIP	ERA	DRA	WARP	MPH	FB%	WHF	CSP
Tyler Alexander	ERI	AA	23	3	2	0	9	9	48	64	7	1.7	6.6	35	45%	.358	1.52	3.75	3.91	0.8				
	TOL	AAA	23	3	6	0	17	15	92	120	9	1.3	5.9	60	47%	.354	1.45	4.79	4.22	1.4				
John Barbato	DET	MLB	25	0	0	0	7	0	6²	11	3	6.8	2.7	2	25%	.320	2.40	12.15	7.55	-0.2	95.5	58.3	7.6	42.8
	TOL	AAA	25	0	3	12	33	2	37¹	25	1	2.4	8.9	37	36%	.253	0.94	1.45	2.81	1.0				
Ryan Carpenter	DET	MLB	27	1	2	0	6	5	22¹	34	8	1.6	6.0	15	35%	.338	1.70	7.25	5.82	-0.1	91.8	51.8	9.9	50.9
	TOL	AAA	27	2	8	0	14	14	76¹	96	8	2.5	8.6	73	35%	.371	1.53	5.07	4.27	1.1				
Jose Fernandez	NHP	AA	25	3	1	2	23	0	31¹	23	5	6.6	9.5	33	28%	.240	1.47	3.45	7.22	-0.8				
	BUF	AAA	25	1	2	2	21	0	29¹	23	2	2.5	9.8	32	48%	.273	1.06	2.45	2.92	0.7				
	TOR	MLB	25	0	0	0	13	0	10¹	10	2	3.5	5.2	6	34%	.242	1.35	6.10	5.76	-0.1	95.9	44.8	9.9	47
Matt Hall	ERI	AA	24	5	2	0	27	4	57	33	1	3.9	12.0	76	54%	.256	1.02	1.58	2.92	1.4				
	TOL	AAA	24	4	0	0	10	10	57¹	46	1	3.1	9.3	59	44%	.294	1.15	2.67	3.90	1.1				
	DET	MLB	24	0	0	0	5	0	8	19	1	3.4	5.6	5	51%	.474	2.75	14.62	5.99	-0.1	91.1	63.3	6.5	46.9
Zac Houston	ERI	AA	23	1	1	0	13	0	17¹	8	1	4.7	13.0	25	40%	.206	0.98	2.60	2.35	0.5				
	TOL	AAA	23	0	1	10	33	0	38	20	2	3.8	13.0	55	48%	.254	0.95	1.18	2.21	1.3				
Eduardo Jimenez	LAK	A+	23	3	4	15	40	0	50	62	3	3.6	9.2	51	44%	.383	1.64	3.42	3.06	1.1				
Zac Reininger	TOL	AAA	25	5	1	6	37	0	51¹	46	3	2.8	9.3	53	34%	.305	1.21	2.63	4.43	0.4				
	DET	MLB	25	1	0	0	18	0	21¹	28	5	3.8	7.6	18	40%	.338	1.73	7.59	4.71	0.1	95.7	60.3	8.3	49.7
Warwick Saupold	DET	MLB	28	4	1	1	31	0	34¹	41	6	3.4	4.2	16	43%	.289	1.57	4.46	5.47	-0.2	92.9	40.1	6.3	41.4
	TOL	AAA	28	3	2	0	15	8	53¹	59	6	2.9	7.3	43	49%	.323	1.42	4.89	3.89	0.9				
Logan Shore	STO	A+	23	2	0	0	4	4	22¹	18	0	0.8	10.1	25	63%	.316	0.90	1.21	4.24	0.3				
	MID	AA	23	1	6	0	13	13	68²	85	7	2.5	6.4	49	50%	.342	1.51	5.50	4.81	0.4				
Josh Smoker	PIT	MLB	29	0	0	0	7	0	5²	11	2	7.9	3.2	2	25%	.409	2.82	11.12	9.90	-0.3	94.4	65	2.2	47.9
	IND	AAA	29	3	1	0	32	0	35	32	4	3.1	10.0	39	35%	.295	1.26	2.83	3.41	0.7				
	DET	MLB	29	0	0	0	1	0	1²	0	0	10.8	10.8	2	0%	.000	1.20	0.00	4.43	0.0	93.0	57.1	10.7	43.1
	TOL	AAA	29	0	1	0	10	0	10¹	13	0	3.5	9.6	11	28%	.406	1.65	5.23	3.22	0.2				
Gregory Soto	LAK	A+	23	8	8	0	25	23	113¹	101	4	5.6	9.1	115	47%	.306	1.51	4.45	4.00	1.7				

Drafted by the Tigers in 2013 and then again in 2015, **Tyler Alexander** has modest potential as a back-end starter and figures to make his big-league debut in 2019. ⓧ Spaghetti western villain/Triple-A reliever **Johnny Barbato** added a splitter to go with his fastball-slider revue. Anything to start silencing more bats, all of which currently act like Clint Eastwood protagonists against him. ⓧ Originally the Rays' seventh-round pick in 2011, **Ryan Carpenter** finally made his MLB debut at age 27 as part of the Tigers' clown car of a bullpen. ⓧ Everyone loves a lefty reliever, but **Jose Fernandez** pushed that trope to its natural limit in 2018 as he couldn't control his mid-90s heater and has yet to develop a proper breaking ball. ⓧ **Matt Hall**'s looping curveball won him the Tigers' minor-league pitcher of the year thanks to 21 straight shutout innings as well as a September cameo in the show. With a get-me-over fastball, that's enough for a smattering of innings, at least until Hall takes what's behind pitch no. 3. ⓧ **Zac Houston** is a one-pitch reliever who's demolished wood-based blunt instruments at every level with an enigmatic low-to-mid-90s fastball. He'll almost certainly get a bullpen cameo this year, where he will learn they're called "bats." ⓧ Credit to **Eduardo Jimenez**, who broke the mold of the Tigers' power pitching prospect who can't find the strike zone: he finds too much of it, as lefties hit .347 against him last year. ⓧ **Zac Reininger**'s biggest change last year was cutting his long hair because, hey, it worked for Jacob deGrom. The difference is deGrom has about eight different out-pitches, about nine more than Reininger. ⓧ Aussie hurler **Warwick Saupold** profiles better as a starter given his pitch-to-contact approach, but he was given the ol' didgeridoo off the roster last year (that means outrighted in "Australian," probably). ⓧ **Logan Shore** has been hampered by injuries and lack of stuff since being drafted out of the University of Florida in the second round in 2016. His upside is probably Mike Fiers, for whom he was traded as a PTBNL last year. ⓧ Lefty reliever **Josh Smoker** was designated for assignment by two teams and released by a third. He may not want a fourth opinion, but here it is: pretty cool name for a guy with a fastball. ⓧ It might be time for lefty starter **Gregory Soto** to see what his fastball can do in the bullpen, because if he remains a starter he might occasionally get called "Gregory Soso" and nobody can recover from a burn like that.

HOUSTON ASTROS

Essay by Robert O'Connell

Player comments by David Temple, Jarrett Seidler and BP staff

In the seventh game of the 2017 American League Championship Series against the New York Yankees, Alex Bregman made a perfect play. With one out in the fifth inning, Todd Frazier was at the plate, Greg Bird was 90 feet from home, and Bregman—then a salty and accomplished young player whose excellence was dimmed a bit by the brilliance of teammates Jose Altuve and Carlos Correa, now a salty and accomplished young MVP candidate—was offscreen, patrolling third. You can well enough imagine what he looked like before the pitch: a forward lean, a stare suggestive of distaste with all those moments in a game that don't directly involve him. Frazier hit a bouncer to shallow third and Bird took off. In one motion—weirdly slow-seeming even before the slo-mo replays that followed—Bregman collected the ball at his stomach and snapped it to Brian McCann at the plate. The throw had the trajectory of a landing plane, all downsloping speed, no gravitational slack. It got to McCann's glove an inch off the dirt, a foot in front of the plate, an instant before Bird's cleat.

The play was perfect in design, in timing and in all three dimensions: equal parts instinct and technique. Maybe the most pleasing part of its perfection, though, was that it wasn't at all rare, in the context of that Houston team. Those Astros—with a 101-win regular season behind them and a World Series championship en route—were the most refreshing kind of juggernaut, one whose quality didn't depend on predictability. They were the sport's daily best bet to show you something you hadn't seen before. Altuve hit his 39 doubles 39 different ways; Correa cast his bat out and pulled it in along every axis. Their lineup had the depth of an overstocked Yankee squad with none of the drudgery; their pitching staff featured Dallas Keuchel's foggy inventory and, by the end of the year, Justin Verlander's high heat. They stretched rallies and walloped homers and struck out sides and choreographed impromptu infield ballets, painting over their own not-yet-dry bits of impossibility. Bregman's fifth-inning geometry didn't even end up being The Thing from that ALCS closer; Lance McCullers came out of the bullpen to throw four innings of one-hit relief, finishing it off with 24 consecutive curveballs.

ASTROS PROSPECTUS
2018 W-L: 103-59, 1ST IN AL WEST

Pythag	.675	1st	B-Age		28.1	17th
RS/G	4.92	6th	P-Age		30.0	27th
RA/G	3.30	1st	Salary		$160.4M	9th
DRC+	104	6th	M$/MW		$2.7M	24th
DRA	3.16	1st	DL Days		859	5th
FIP	3.26	1st	$ on DL		7%	1st
DER	.717	5th				

- Opened 2000
- Retractable roof
- Natural surface
- Fence profile: 7' to 25'

Three-Year Park Factors

Runs	Runs/RH	Runs/LH	HR/RH	HR/LH
94	94	95	101	96

Top Hitter WARP	6.9 Alex Bregman
Top Pitcher WARP	7.3 Justin Verlander
Top Prospect	Forrest Whitley

2018 Hit List Ranking

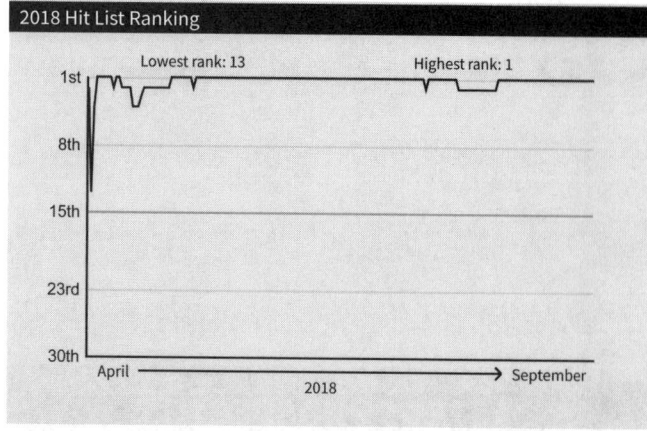

Lowest rank: 13   Highest rank: 1

Committed Payroll (in millions)

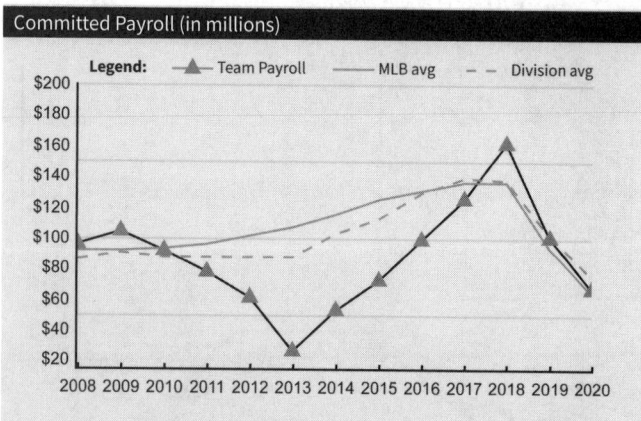

Legend: ▲ Team Payroll   — MLB avg   --- Division avg

Farm System Ranking

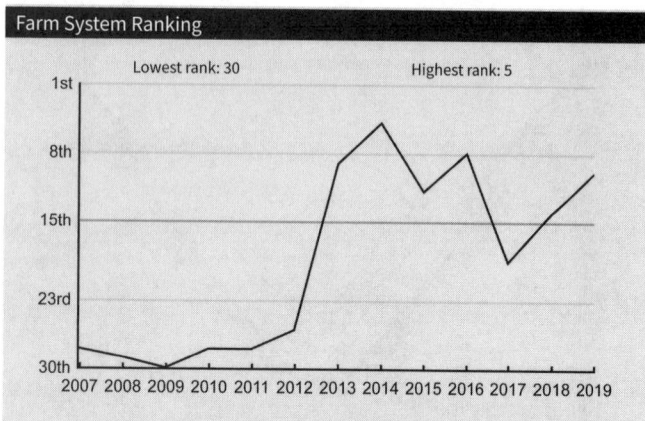

Lowest rank: 30   Highest rank: 5

Personnel

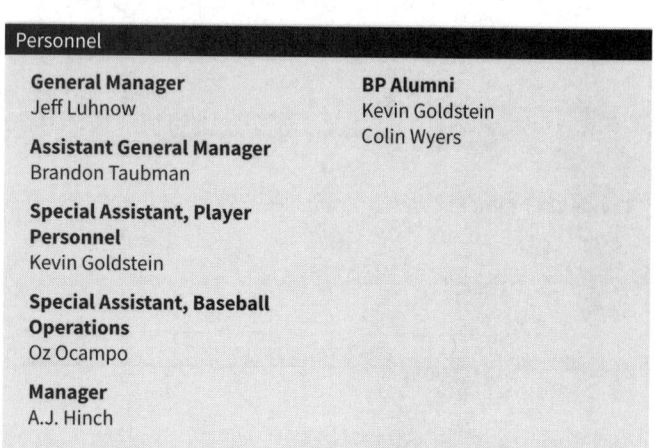

General Manager
Jeff Luhnow

Assistant General Manager
Brandon Taubman

Special Assistant, Player Personnel
Kevin Goldstein

Special Assistant, Baseball Operations
Oz Ocampo

Manager
A.J. Hinch

BP Alumni
Kevin Goldstein
Colin Wyers

I don't know why, then, Bregman's play is the one I think of when I think of the consistent newnesses the pre-championship Astros were made up of—or, more to the point, why it's the one I miss when I watch them now.

⚾   ⚾   ⚾

There's a small but crucial difference between trying to do something and trying to do it again. The 2018 Astros were a testament to this difference. They spent the offseason between title and title defense seemingly becoming only more themselves—adding Gerrit Cole's G-forces to their spin-rate-laden pitching staff last January, bringing back every offensive contributor of note, settling in for what looked like (what still looks like) a half-decade of comfortable contention. "That's been our goal all along," Houston general manager Jeff Luhnow said at the time of the Cole trade, "to get to the point of competitiveness and win a championship and hopefully win multiple championships."

But the GM-speak sterility in the above quote—the '17 Astros had gotten "to the point of competitiveness" in the way that Debussy "approached a viable melody"—seemed to manifest, at times, on the field. It's not that last season's Astros weren't excellent. They won two more regular-season games than the year before and rolled over the Cleveland Indians in the division series, the rotation missed bats and singed eyebrows, and the lineup piled up 797 runs against just 534 allowed. It's that, broadly, they seemed more dutiful in their approach. The sense of discovery that shot through the championship team gave way to one of recitation, of formulas followed and expected outcomes realized.

This is by far the preferable of the common trajectories for defending champions, of course, the other being a drowsy year-after letdown. And the Astros had some good excuses for being a little less fun: Altuve, Correa, and George Springer missed a combined 99 games. The greater source of displeasure, though, lay counterintuitively in just how well everything else *worked*. Verlander continued his late-career renaissance, putting up a 2.52 ERA over 34 starts, and Cole panned out spectacularly, with a 2.88 mark. Charlie Morton chipped in with the latest in a string of career years. The offense had enough margin for error to make up for the injuries to its stars and the regressions of nearly every major contributor. The illogical causation feels true: the Astros lost some of their magic because they didn't need it.

Back in 2017, the main drawback to that Houston team—that it was assembled via one of the more anti-competitive and cost-cutting spells of tanking in recent MLB history, that it marked a clear victory for the model of efficiency that now has even competitive teams selling off mid-career stars—was easy to ignore in favor of the plain lovability of the squad itself. Who could think of incentivized cynicism when Altuve and Correa were turning a double play, or when Marwin Gonzalez was slicing singles and filling in everywhere, or when Springer made the World Series the setting for the world's most indulgent physics experiment?

Even if the template was legible, with all those ill-gotten high picks turning into world-beaters right on schedule, the specifics were thrillingly non-formulaic.

Now, organizational shrewdness is the Astros' story. Idiosyncrasy remains—Altuve's somehow predictive swing, the apple-in-an-earthquake action of Verlander's breaking ball—but it is all folded into the perfection of the larger design. That Houston's 2017 title required feats as extreme as Altuve's MVP and Springer's Series breakout seems incongruous, in retrospect; this is a team that no longer needs anything out of the ordinary to happen in order to win.

⚾   ⚾   ⚾

So, Bregman. It is an odd thing to complain about a player's improvement, especially when the result is a Gold Glove-caliber infielder who slashes .286/.394/.532 with 31 homers, a league-leading 51 doubles, and more walks than strikeouts. But Bregman's transition from a figure of partially-realized potential to a source of clockwork line-drive-walloping dovetails in a not wholly pleasant way with the Astros' growth from baseball's upstarts to one of its constants.

The present Bregman is a nearly faultless player: quick glove, strong arm, clipped but potent swing, rapt attention. He hits homers and snares liners and studies Spanish to make for easier on-field communication. He's due for a pay increase when he becomes arbitration-eligible next year and a much more substantial one when he reaches free agency in 2023, but for now, he's as valuable an asset as any in the game. "He is baseball," his manager says.

It might be more accurate to say that he is the Houston Astros. His inefficiencies, like those of the organization, have been sanded away. His approach is not bland, but neither is it quite as fresh—as reliably surprising, in that old Astro way—as it used to be. In some ways, back in '17, Bregman seemed to stand in for the team as a whole even more than Altuve or Correa or Springer or Verlander. He was the youngest of the young stars and the least-known of the figures getting introduced to national audiences, the avatar of a precociousness that hadn't yet given way to unqualified, title-officialized greatness. He was still a revelation, maybe in a way that only players who haven't yet lifted the Commissioner's Trophy and received MVP votes can be.

That throw in Game 7 against the Yankees summed it up. The play was superb, like the Astros were and are, but it was also reckless. It was made by a 23-year-old still shouldering his way up the pecking order, on behalf of a team trying to win the title in front of them, not position itself for one or two more. It was a desperate play, in the finest sense of the word; it set aside caution to try for something perfect.

But the era of invention in Houston, and its assault on our reason, is complete. Originals come from the windblind fury of creation, sequels from care and management. Now, the Astros are doing what they were always supposed to do, what their architects drew up. A team designed for the long haul is settling into its purpose. Houston will rack up 100 wins again, or close to it, and play important games in October, and maybe win another championship. Altuve or Correa or Bregman might win an MVP; Verlander or Cole might win a Cy Young.

This is, of course, an enviable position. It is what teams and players alike work for—to turn fleeting success into something lasting, to find and then replicate lightning in a bottle. Baseball especially encourages its participants towards steadiness; its daily demands render that '17 kind of magic untenable, eventually. It is Bregman's job to become so good that he doesn't need to be so daring; it is the front office's job to assemble a roster complete enough that it doesn't need an iconic hitting season to pace it. The Astros are as close a thing as MLB has to an ideal team, and they figure to be so for some time. They're just a little different—a little more certain, a little less fun—than when they weren't quite there. ∎

—Robert O'Connell is a freelance sportswriter whose work has appeared in The Athletic and Deadspin.

HITTERS

Jose Altuve 2B   Born: 05/06/90   Age: 29   Bats: R   Throws: R   Height: 5'6"   Weight: 165   Origin: International Free Agent, 2007

YEAR	TEAM	LVL	AGE	PA	R	2B	3B	HR	RBI	BB	K	SB	CS	AVG/OBP/SLG	DRC+	VORP	BABIP	BRR	FRAA	WARP
2016	HOU	MLB	26	717	108	42	5	24	96	60	70	30	10	.338/.396/.531	138	66.3	.347	3.2	2B(148): -7.2, SS(1): 0.0	5.3
2017	HOU	MLB	27	662	112	39	4	24	81	58	84	32	6	.346/.410/.547	135	64.1	.370	2.7	2B(149): -0.1	5.3
2018	HOU	MLB	28	599	84	29	2	13	61	55	79	17	4	.316/.386/.451	120	41.9	.352	2.4	2B(130): -7.9	2.8
2019	HOU	MLB	29	635	86	33	4	18	79	64	82	25	7	.307/.387/.475	139	52.3	.335	1.9	2B -7	4.8

Breakout: 1%   Improve: 40%   Collapse: 4%   Attrition: 5%   MLB: 99%   *Comparables: Dustin Pedroia, Roberto Alomar, Frankie Frisch*

Despite a multitude of evidence to the contrary, it would appear that Altuve is, indeed, a human being. And human beings need at least two functioning knees to properly play the game of baseball. After fouling a pitch off his foot in April and stealing a single base all month, Altuve jammed one of his two human knees in July and his second half suffered for it. Of course, because he's Jose Altuve, he still performed a good deal above replacement level, but he certainly wasn't healthy enough to repeat his MVP numbers from the year prior. He should be ready to go come spring, and barring freak injury, the main question about his long-term future will be whether the power will rebound enough to offset his slowly-rising swinging strike percentage. He's Altuve, though. He's probably fine.

Yordan Alvarez LF Born: 06/27/97 Age: 22 Bats: L Throws: R Height: 6'5" Weight: 225 Origin: International Free Agent, 2016

YEAR	TEAM	LVL	AGE	PA	R	2B	3B	HR	RBI	BB	K	SB	CS	AVG/OBP/SLG	DRC+	VORP	BABIP	BRR	FRAA	WARP
2016	DAR	ROK	19	57	7	2	1	1	4	12	7	2	1	.341/.474/.500	131	8.1	.378	0.1		0.3
2017	QUD	A	20	139	26	6	0	9	33	23	36	2	0	.360/.468/.658	154	18.2	.449	-1.6	LF(13): -1.5, 1B(7): 0.0	0.8
2017	BCA	A+	20	252	19	11	3	3	36	19	41	6	1	.277/.329/.393	106	7.2	.316	-0.2	1B(9): -0.4, LF(6): 2.6	0.8
2018	CCH	AA	21	190	39	13	0	12	46	19	45	5	2	.325/.389/.615	131	21.5	.377	0.2	LF(31): 3.6, 1B(5): -0.1	1.5
2018	FRE	AAA	21	189	24	8	0	8	28	23	47	1	0	.259/.349/.452	111	5.3	.315	-2.0	LF(34): -6.3	-0.1
2019	HOU	MLB	22	66	8	3	0	3	8	6	18	0	0	.244/.313/.433	104	1.1	.303	-0.1	1B 0	0.1

Breakout: 2%   Improve: 33%   Collapse: 1%   Attrition: 13%   MLB: 52%   Comparables: Clint Frazier, Thomas Neal, Jesse Winker

The Astros play the One Red Paperclip game as well as anyone in baseball. With the first pick in the 2012 Rule 5 Draft, Houston selected reliever/former first-rounder/castoff Josh Fields from the Red Sox. There he found a measure of control to go along with his fastball and knuckle curve, but Boston didn't protect him on the 40-man. Fields spent the next few years in the Houston bullpen, sometimes dominating and often underperforming. Meanwhile, the Dodgers signed Alvarez for $2 million out of Cuba late in the 2015-16 signing period. They quickly flipped him to the Astros for Fields, before Alvarez even made his American pro debut. While Fields has pitched very well in Los Angeles, the real prize here turned out to be Alvarez, now one of baseball's best hitting prospects. Not bad for the $50,000 Rule 5 price and six years of careful work.

Seth Beer LF Born: 09/18/96 Age: 22 Bats: L Throws: R Height: 6'3" Weight: 195 Origin: Round 1, 2018 Draft (#28 overall)

YEAR	TEAM	LVL	AGE	PA	R	2B	3B	HR	RBI	BB	K	SB	CS	AVG/OBP/SLG	DRC+	VORP	BABIP	BRR	FRAA	WARP
2018	TCV	A-	21	51	9	3	0	4	7	6	10	0	0	.293/.431/.659	141	7.7	.296	-0.8	LF(7): -1.0, 1B(4): -0.1	0.2
2018	QUD	A	21	132	15	7	0	3	16	15	17	1	0	.348/.443/.491	136	11.6	.391	-1.2	RF(10): -0.9, LF(9): -1.1	0.4
2018	BCA	A+	21	114	15	4	0	5	19	4	22	0	1	.262/.307/.439	114	1.1	.288	-2.2	LF(13): -1.4, 1B(6): -0.2	0.0
2019	HOU	MLB	22	251	29	10	0	8	27	13	57	0	0	.228/.276/.374	70	-3.7	.266	-0.6	LF -1, 1B 0	-0.6

Breakout: 2%   Improve: 18%   Collapse: 2%   Attrition: 16%   MLB: 27%   Comparables: Austin Dean, Dustin Peterson, Andrew Lambo

After his monstrous freshman season at Clemson in 2016, Beer seemed like he was the inevitable first pick in the 2018 Draft. He would never quite hit as well again in college. With a dab of indifferent defense and a dash of prospect fatigue mixed in, he ultimately fell to the latter stages of the first round. Despite this, he's quite a hitting prospect, with strong batting average and power projection and a discerning eye. His defense ... well, it might turn out to be fortunate that he was drafted by an American League club, if he can't settle into left field or first base. A minor concern to keep tabs on: Beer's vaunted plate discipline disappeared after his promotion to High-A. It's a smallish sample and many college players have tuckered out late in their draft year, so it's just a minor concern for now.

Michael Brantley LF Born: 05/15/87 Age: 32 Bats: L Throws: L Height: 6'2" Weight: 200 Origin: Round 7, 2005 Draft (#205 overall)

YEAR	TEAM	LVL	AGE	PA	R	2B	3B	HR	RBI	BB	K	SB	CS	AVG/OBP/SLG	DRC+	VORP	BABIP	BRR	FRAA	WARP
2016	CLE	MLB	29	43	5	2	0	0	7	3	6	1	0	.231/.279/.282	94	-1.0	.265	0.4	LF(11): 0.3	0.2
2017	CLE	MLB	30	375	47	20	1	9	52	31	50	11	1	.299/.357/.444	108	13.7	.325	-0.6	LF(87): 5.2	1.9
2018	CLE	MLB	31	631	89	36	2	17	76	48	60	12	3	.309/.364/.468	124	31.8	.319	1.4	LF(134): -3.4	3.3
2019	HOU	MLB	32	508	57	27	2	11	57	41	71	10	2	.276/.341/.418	106	13.6	.306	0.3	LF -1	1.4

Breakout: 3%   Improve: 42%   Collapse: 3%   Attrition: 12%   MLB: 97%   Comparables: Tony Gwynn, Melky Cabrera, Shannon Stewart

Brantley cleared 600 plate appearances for the first time since 2014 and showed he might have a good amount left in the tank after all, pulling his strikeout rate back down after seeing it inflate in his two previous injury-shortened seasons. The result was a classic prime Brantley season chock full of contact and just enough power to keep pitchers honest. One of the all-time great players to be named later, Brantley turns 32 in May, but 2018 represented a serious reversal of some disturbing trends, and a welcome return to form for a fun, unusual player in the current era.

Alex Bregman 3B Born: 03/30/94 Age: 25 Bats: R Throws: R Height: 6'0" Weight: 180 Origin: Round 1, 2015 Draft (#2 overall)

YEAR	TEAM	LVL	AGE	PA	R	2B	3B	HR	RBI	BB	K	SB	CS	AVG/OBP/SLG	DRC+	VORP	BABIP	BRR	FRAA	WARP
2016	CCH	AA	22	285	54	16	2	14	46	42	26	5	3	.297/.415/.559	170	38.9	.286	1.6	SS(51): -3.4, 3B(11): 1.4	3.7
2016	FRE	AAA	22	83	17	6	0	6	15	5	12	2	1	.333/.373/.641	138	10.0	.333	-1.2	SS(14): 2.1, LF(3): -0.1	0.8
2016	HOU	MLB	22	217	31	13	3	8	34	15	52	2	0	.264/.313/.478	99	9.6	.317	0.5	3B(40): 0.9, SS(6): -0.1	0.9
2017	HOU	MLB	23	626	88	39	5	19	71	55	97	17	5	.284/.352/.475	112	34.7	.311	-1.5	3B(132): 8.7, SS(30): -2.9	3.9
2018	HOU	MLB	24	705	105	51	1	31	103	96	85	10	4	.286/.394/.532	143	72.6	.289	-1.6	3B(136): 5.4, SS(28): -0.4	6.9
2019	HOU	MLB	25	682	98	39	4	23	82	73	108	12	4	.274/.363/.467	129	38.7	.303	-1.3	3B 7, SS 0	4.9

Breakout: 2%   Improve: 63%   Collapse: 2%   Attrition: 2%   MLB: 100%   Comparables: Anthony Rendon, David Wright, Pablo Sandoval

The total package: He hits for average. He hits for power. He walks more than he strikes out. He plays a sterling third base. He's versatile enough to play the middle infield when Correa or Altuve isn't around. He hustles like a madman. He's funny on social media. He dunks on Trevor "Tyler" Bauer. He's one of the best interviews in the game. He's socially conscious. He's not exactly perfect as a player or a personality—I suppose he could run a little better, although he's certainly not slow, and sometimes his antics cross the imaginary line. But baseball is a far richer game when it has players this good and characters this fun. Bregman is a talent for any era, but also, he's a superstar that fits his time.

Robinson Chirinos C
Born: 06/05/84   Age: 35   Bats: R   Throws: R   Height: 6'1"   Weight: 210   Origin: International Free Agent, 2000

YEAR	TEAM	LVL	AGE	PA	R	2B	3B	HR	RBI	BB	K	SB	CS	AVG/OBP/SLG	DRC+	VORP	BABIP	BRR	FRAA	WARP
2016	TEX	MLB	32	170	21	11	0	9	20	15	44	0	1	.224/.314/.483	99	9.1	.250	0.2	C(54): -5.2	0.3
2017	TEX	MLB	33	309	46	13	1	17	38	34	79	1	0	.255/.360/.506	121	20.8	.298	-1.7	C(85): -0.2	2.2
2018	TEX	MLB	34	426	48	15	1	18	65	45	140	2	0	.222/.338/.419	105	22.0	.304	-1.4	C(108): -10.8	1.1
2019	*HOU*	*MLB*	*35*	*335*	*42*	*15*	*1*	*13*	*42*	*33*	*94*	*1*	*0*	*.233/.336/.421*	*108*	*17.6*	*.304*	*-0.8*	*C -8*	*1.0*

Breakout: 0%   Improve: 32%   Collapse: 15%   Attrition: 17%   MLB: 88%

Comparables: Doug Mirabelli, Jason Varitek, David Ross

YEAR	TEAM	P. COUNT	FRM RUNS	BLK RUNS	THRW RUNS	TOT RUNS
2016	TEX	6797	-7.4	1.9	0.0	-6.5
2017	TEX	11679	-1.6	2.4	-0.9	0.2
2018	TEX	15072	-11.2	0.7	-0.8	-11.0
2019	*HOU*	*12723*	*-8.8*	*1.7*	*-1.1*	*-8.2*

Chirinos caught more than 100 games in a season for the first time in 2018. That's great news for a well-loved clubhouse favorite who has battled concussions and other injuries for most of his career. The downside is that he threw out just 10 percent of runners attempting to steal, which is more commensurate with a teenage employee at Michael's craft store than it is a big-league catcher (league average in 2018 was 28 percent). Perhaps it was a one-off: Chirinos threw out 29, 27 and 25 percent, respectively, in 2015-2017. Or perhaps the greater workload was a bit much for the veteran. Whatever the case, Texas decided not to exercise their 2019 option on Chirinos, cutting him loose in favor of defensive guru Jeff Mathis.

Carlos Correa SS
Born: 09/22/94   Age: 24   Bats: R   Throws: R   Height: 6'4"   Weight: 215   Origin: Round 1, 2012 Draft (#1 overall)

YEAR	TEAM	LVL	AGE	PA	R	2B	3B	HR	RBI	BB	K	SB	CS	AVG/OBP/SLG	DRC+	VORP	BABIP	BRR	FRAA	WARP
2016	HOU	MLB	21	660	76	36	3	20	96	75	139	13	3	.274/.361/.451	109	53.7	.328	1.8	SS(153): -4.5	3.6
2017	HOU	MLB	22	481	82	25	1	24	84	53	92	2	1	.315/.391/.550	134	47.4	.352	-3.0	SS(108): -1.4	3.9
2018	HOU	MLB	23	468	60	20	1	15	65	53	111	3	0	.239/.323/.405	94	20.8	.282	0.8	SS(109): 7.2	2.6
2019	*HOU*	*MLB*	*24*	*609*	*77*	*28*	*2*	*22*	*80*	*73*	*127*	*8*	*2*	*.264/.358/.448*	*120*	*35.5*	*.309*	*-0.2*	*SS 2*	*4.0*

Breakout: 6%   Improve: 67%   Collapse: 0%   Attrition: 4%   MLB: 100%

Comparables: Hanley Ramirez, Corey Seager, David Wright

It's a testament to Houston's depth that they made it as far as they did in 2018 given all the key players that spent time on the disabled list. Along with such notable names as Altuve and Springer, Correa had his 2018 season diminished by injury, one that erased his July and ruined his batting line the rest of the season. Usually a mainstay in the heart of the Astros' lineup, Correa dealt with a lingering back issue that reduced him to ostensibly a below-average hitter in 2018. Backs are tricky things, but assuming he's healthy in 2019, there's no reason to expect he won't be back to his mashing ways again.

J.D. Davis 3B
Born: 04/27/93   Age: 26   Bats: R   Throws: R   Height: 6'3"   Weight: 225   Origin: Round 3, 2014 Draft (#75 overall)

YEAR	TEAM	LVL	AGE	PA	R	2B	3B	HR	RBI	BB	K	SB	CS	AVG/OBP/SLG	DRC+	VORP	BABIP	BRR	FRAA	WARP
2016	CCH	AA	23	539	61	34	1	23	81	45	143	1	3	.268/.334/.485	121	34.0	.331	-2.6	3B(101): -6.1, LF(4): 0.3	2.1
2017	CCH	AA	24	388	49	18	0	21	60	31	90	5	2	.279/.340/.510	133	30.0	.317	-0.5	3B(73): 6.1, LF(3): -0.5	3.5
2017	FRE	AAA	24	73	10	5	0	5	18	9	18	0	0	.295/.370/.623	126	7.9	.317	-0.4	3B(13): 2.1, 1B(4): 0.0	0.7
2017	HOU	MLB	24	68	8	4	0	4	7	4	20	1	1	.226/.279/.484	84	1.7	.256	-0.2	3B(22): 0.5, P(2): 0.0	0.2
2018	FRE	AAA	25	377	56	25	2	17	81	36	69	3	0	.342/.406/.583	137	39.4	.385	0.0	3B(51): 4.2, RF(11): -0.3	3.4
2018	HOU	MLB	25	113	9	2	0	1	5	10	29	0	0	.175/.248/.223	69	-7.3	.233	-0.5	3B(23): 0.9, 1B(13): 0.0	0.0
2019	*HOU*	*MLB*	*26*	*64*	*8*	*3*	*0*	*2*	*8*	*6*	*15*	*0*	*0*	*.246/.318/.431*	*98*	*0.9*	*.291*	*-0.1*	*3B 0, 1B 0*	*0.1*

Breakout: 3%   Improve: 31%   Collapse: 10%   Attrition: 25%   MLB: 69%

Comparables: Todd Frazier, Richie Shaffer, David Freese

The later years of "The Late Show with David Letterman" featured a bit called "Is This Anything?" in which the host would introduce the segment, the main curtain would rise, some oddball performer would do her or his shtick, the curtain would fall, and Dave and Paul would spend about 15 seconds debating whether what they just saw was anything or not. It was a perfect piece of irreverent humor done by the very people who were on the vanguard of that movement long before it became popular.

Davis never appeared on "The Late Show," but if roster machinations come to bear that he earns the starting job at first base in 2019, Houston will be playing a bit of a high-stakes game of "Is This Anything?" with a player that so far (albeit still at a young age) seems destined for Quad-A status.

Aledmys Diaz INF
Born: 08/01/90   Age: 28   Bats: R   Throws: R   Height: 6'1"   Weight: 195   Origin: International Free Agent, 2014

YEAR	TEAM	LVL	AGE	PA	R	2B	3B	HR	RBI	BB	K	SB	CS	AVG/OBP/SLG	DRC+	VORP	BABIP	BRR	FRAA	WARP
2016	SLN	MLB	25	460	71	28	3	17	65	41	60	4	4	.300/.369/.510	122	48.7	.312	1.4	SS(106): -9.6, 2B(1): 0.0	2.6
2017	MEM	AAA	26	187	19	9	1	4	26	10	30	3	3	.253/.305/.388	87	4.6	.281	-1.2	SS(28): 2.3, 3B(9): -0.6	0.7
2017	SLN	MLB	26	301	31	17	0	7	20	13	42	4	1	.259/.290/.392	77	2.3	.282	-1.3	SS(68): -10.6, 3B(4): -0.2	-0.7
2018	TOR	MLB	27	452	55	26	0	18	55	23	62	3	4	.263/.303/.453	108	19.2	.269	-1.8	SS(95): -5.8, 3B(38): -0.5	1.6
2019	*HOU*	*MLB*	*28*	*319*	*37*	*16*	*1*	*10*	*37*	*22*	*46*	*3*	*2*	*.261/.319/.423*	*101*	*10.7*	*.280*	*-0.4*	*SS -3, 2B 1*	*0.9*

Breakout: 2%   Improve: 52%   Collapse: 1%   Attrition: 6%   MLB: 97%

Comparables: Alexei Ramirez, Didi Gregorius, Erick Aybar

It can be difficult to divorce a seasoned player from his prospect profile. We want to believe the potential for greatness still lurks somewhere underneath a mediocre swing and lapsed velocity, and there's a certain defeat that comes with admitting the teenage superstar in the making is now little better than your garden-variety utility man. The Blue Jays scratched and scratched at that particular instant win ticket in 2018, but even given an everyday role (in the absence of Troy Tulowitzki, who lost the entire season to bone spurs in both heels), Diaz took only incremental steps forward to tweak his infield defense and on-base skills. You couldn't truthfully say that he excels at any one area of the game, but his positional flexibility and modest offensive totals were enough to intrigue the Astros, who will turn to him as their new Marwin Gonzalez come spring.

Derek Fisher OF
Born: 08/21/93   Age: 25   Bats: L   Throws: R   Height: 6'3"   Weight: 205   Origin: Round 1, 2014 Draft (#37 overall)

YEAR	TEAM	LVL	AGE	PA	R	2B	3B	HR	RBI	BB	K	SB	CS	AVG/OBP/SLG	DRC+	VORP	BABIP	BRR	FRAA	WARP
2016	CCH	AA	22	448	54	13	4	16	59	74	128	23	7	.245/.373/.431	119	30.0	.329	-0.5	CF(70): -7.7, RF(19): -1.2	1.3
2016	FRE	AAA	22	118	17	8	0	5	17	9	26	5	0	.290/.347/.505	93	8.2	.338	-0.6	CF(13): -0.9, RF(13): -1.6	-0.1
2017	FRE	AAA	23	384	63	26	1	21	66	35	74	16	10	.318/.384/.583	129	32.8	.352	-0.8	CF(53): -5.3, LF(17): 2.3	2.3
2017	HOU	MLB	23	166	21	4	1	5	17	17	54	3	3	.212/.307/.356	71	-1.4	.299	-0.5	LF(38): 1.2, RF(12): 0.0	-0.1
2018	HOU	MLB	24	86	13	2	2	4	11	5	42	2	0	.165/.209/.392	46	1.6	.257	1.6	LF(26): -1.3, CF(9): -0.4	-0.3
2018	FRE	AAA	24	281	44	12	1	10	34	39	85	11	1	.251/.363/.435	96	16.5	.347	2.2	CF(33): -2.7, LF(19): -0.7	0.6
2019	*HOU*	*MLB*	*25*	*122*	*15*	*4*	*0*	*5*	*14*	*12*	*39*	*3*	*1*	*.213/.298/.384*	*82*	*0.6*	*.284*	*0.3*	*RF 0, LF 0*	*0.1*

Breakout: 7%   Improve: 26%   Collapse: 13%   Attrition: 33%   MLB: 78%   *Comparables: Bradley Zimmer, Joe Benson, Trayvon Robinson*

Success in baseball can be measured in a thousand different ways. Getting drafted is a success. Being a first-round pick is an even bigger success. Showing up on a top prospect list is a success. Making the majors is a huge success. Getting your first major league hit, your first run, your first RBI, your first homer, all great successes. Making a playoff roster is a success. Scoring the game-winning run in one of the most memorable World Series games of all time is a success few others will ever achieve. Winning a World Series ring is one of the biggest successes you can have in all of sports. Derek Fisher's been an up-and-down fourth outfielder so far in the majors—an athletic guy who can play all three outfield spots and run a little, but hasn't hit much. He may well never be more than that. Yet he's already done all of the things listed above. He's experienced more success in his career to date than all but a small fraction of professional baseball players will. And you can't take any of those accomplishments away from him.

Evan Gattis C
Born: 08/18/86   Age: 32   Bats: R   Throws: R   Height: 6'4"   Weight: 270   Origin: Round 23, 2010 Draft (#704 overall)

YEAR	TEAM	LVL	AGE	PA	R	2B	3B	HR	RBI	BB	K	SB	CS	AVG/OBP/SLG	DRC+	VORP	BABIP	BRR	FRAA	WARP
2016	CCH	AA	29	42	8	2	0	5	10	1	4	0	0	.375/.405/.800	172	8.2	.323	0.1	C(4): 0.1	0.5
2016	HOU	MLB	29	499	58	19	0	32	72	43	127	2	1	.251/.319/.508	120	27.6	.273	-0.1	C(55): 0.5	2.8
2017	HOU	MLB	30	325	41	22	0	12	55	18	50	0	1	.263/.311/.457	98	8.6	.278	0.0	C(49): 0.8, 1B(1): 0.0	1.2
2018	HOU	MLB	31	451	49	17	0	25	78	33	101	1	0	.226/.284/.452	109	4.4	.232	-2.0	C(2): 0.0	1.0
2019	*HOU*	*MLB*	*32*	*401*	*47*	*20*	*1*	*17*	*56*	*32*	*81*	*1*	*0*	*.254/.321/.452*	*109*	*9.9*	*.285*	*-0.4*	*C 0*	*1.0*

Breakout: 2%   Improve: 34%   Collapse: 4%   Attrition: 11%   MLB: 95%   *Comparables: Dmitri Young, Ryan Zimmerman, Xavier Nady*

It seems fair to assume that Gattis' days as a catcher are over. In 2017, he started 47 games behind the dish. In 2018, that number went down by 47. He also may have seen his last days as a better-than-league-average hitter: His high-strikeout/high-power approach was lacking somewhat in the latter department, though surprisingly, it was the lack of singles and doubles that really undid his offensive line. Blame a tumbling exit velocity (an average of 87.5 mph in 2018, tied with Freddy Galvis) for the results. Unless the BABIP gods restore him to favor, he'll have to severely alter his approach (or miraculously become a slick-fielding shortstop) to continue to have much value going forward. Either would be equally surprising.

YEAR	TEAM	P. COUNT	FRM RUNS	BLK RUNS	THRW RUNS	TOT RUNS
2016	HOU	7151	3.9	-4.4	1.3	0.8
2017	HOU	7026	3.8	-0.7	-1.9	1.1
2019	*HOU*	*2048*	*0.9*	*-0.8*	*-0.1*	*0.1*

Marwin Gonzalez UT
Born: 03/14/89   Age: 30   Bats: B   Throws: R   Height: 6'1"   Weight: 205   Origin: International Free Agent, 2005

YEAR	TEAM	LVL	AGE	PA	R	2B	3B	HR	RBI	BB	K	SB	CS	AVG/OBP/SLG	DRC+	VORP	BABIP	BRR	FRAA	WARP
2016	HOU	MLB	27	518	55	26	3	13	51	22	118	12	6	.254/.293/.401	80	0.1	.311	-1.4	1B(92): 0.7, 3B(22): 0.6	-0.1
2017	HOU	MLB	28	515	67	34	0	23	90	49	99	8	3	.303/.377/.530	118	36.5	.343	-0.8	LF(47): -3.6, SS(38): -1.7	2.2
2018	HOU	MLB	29	552	61	25	3	16	68	53	126	2	3	.247/.324/.409	96	22.8	.301	1.5	LF(73): 0.7, SS(39): -2.7	1.3
2019	*HOU*	*MLB*	*30*	*513*	*60*	*25*	*2*	*16*	*64*	*44*	*109*	*6*	*4*	*.262/.334/.432*	*106*	*17.7*	*.307*	*-0.3*	*LF -2, SS -1*	*1.5*

Breakout: 1%   Improve: 43%   Collapse: 2%   Attrition: 8%   MLB: 94%   *Comparables: Hal McRae, Eric Byrnes, Del Ennis*

Marwin Gonzalez continued in his super-utility role in 2018, playing every position except pitcher and catcher. He also dabbled in beer concessions on off days, served as part-time tax consultant for fellow teammates, and hand-crafted every World Series ring the Astros handed out at the beginning of the year. His offensive production paled in comparison to his stellar 2017 output, primarily because the 2018 version is who he really is. But especially in an era of three-man benches, the real Gonzalez, with his average bat and positional flexibility, makes him valuable to every team on the market.

Yulieski Gurriel 1B
Born: 06/09/84   Age: 35   Bats: R   Throws: R   Height: 6'0"   Weight: 190   Origin: International Free Agent, 2016

YEAR	TEAM	LVL	AGE	PA	R	2B	3B	HR	RBI	BB	K	SB	CS	AVG/OBP/SLG	DRC+	VORP	BABIP	BRR	FRAA	WARP
2016	HOU	MLB	32	137	13	7	0	3	15	5	12	1	1	.262/.292/.385	94	-3.0	.267	-1.2	3B(21): -0.8, 1B(5): 0.1	0.1
2017	HOU	MLB	33	564	69	43	1	18	75	22	62	3	2	.299/.332/.486	105	18.0	.308	-1.7	1B(131): 8.4, 3B(7): -0.3	1.9
2018	HOU	MLB	34	573	70	33	1	13	85	23	63	5	1	.291/.323/.428	101	20.7	.306	1.1	1B(109): 1.5, 3B(21): 1.2	1.5
2019	*HOU*	*MLB*	*35*	*572*	*59*	*32*	*2*	*13*	*66*	*30*	*70*	*4*	*2*	*.274/.321/.418*	*99*	*7.1*	*.295*	*-0.6*	*1B 5*	*1.3*

Breakout: 3%   Improve: 26%   Collapse: 8%   Attrition: 26%   MLB: 84%   *Comparables: Bill Buckner, Ross Gload, Mike Sweeney*

In his second full season since defecting from Cuba, Gurriel wasn't able to repeat his 2017 output. Though the ball was softer for everyone, it wasn't helped by the fact that he hit into 22 double plays in 2018, as he chased (and succeeded in putting the bat on) more bad pitches in 2018. Somewhat paradoxically, most of those occurred in the first half of the season, the half in which he actually hit much better. Baseball, like life, is devoid of any understanding and this only proves it further. Gurriel also stunk up the joint in the 2018 postseason, and was arguably the worst hitter in the regular lineup (save for the catching position), so don't be surprised if he feels the pressure as early as Spring Training.

Tony Kemp **LF** Born: 10/31/91 Age: 27 Bats: L Throws: R Height: 5'6" Weight: 165 Origin: Round 5, 2013 Draft (#137 overall)

YEAR	TEAM	LVL	AGE	PA	R	2B	3B	HR	RBI	BB	K	SB	CS	AVG/OBP/SLG	DRC+	VORP	BABIP	BRR	FRAA	WARP
2016	FRE	AAA	24	301	36	9	4	2	24	34	34	10	8	.306/.389/.396	102	12.7	.344	0.2	2B(39): -0.1, LF(19): 2.3	1.2
2016	HOU	MLB	24	136	15	4	3	1	7	14	27	2	1	.217/.296/.325	83	-2.5	.269	-0.4	LF(37): -2.5, 2B(5): 0.0	-0.2
2017	FRE	AAA	25	554	95	23	9	10	62	35	43	24	7	.329/.375/.470	121	39.1	.344	0.4	2B(97): -10.2, LF(10): -1.4	2.1
2017	HOU	MLB	25	39	6	1	0	0	4	1	5	1	0	.216/.256/.243	92	-1.7	.250	0.9	LF(10): -0.4, CF(4): -0.2	0.1
2018	FRE	AAA	26	183	33	6	5	0	19	19	15	13	2	.335/.407/.435	110	14.6	.367	3.5	2B(25): -0.5, CF(14): -1.4	1.0
2018	HOU	MLB	26	295	37	15	6	6	30	32	44	9	3	.263/.351/.392	102	9.6	.296	-0.5	LF(61): -2.8, CF(32): 0.3	0.6
2019	*HOU*	*MLB*	*27*	*214*	*25*	*10*	*1*	*5*	*22*	*18*	*31*	*6*	*2*	*.268/.333/.407*	*102*	*7.4*	*.292*	*-0.1*	*LF -1, CF -1*	*0.5*

Breakout: 4%   Improve: 30%   Collapse: 11%   Attrition: 25%   MLB: 71%   *Comparables: Jeremy Reed, J.B. Shuck, Guillermo Heredia*

Kemp will always draw comparisons to Jose Altuve due to the facts that he is a smaller gentleman and he plays for the Houston Astros. Chances are he won't be able to change the former, and given his very respectable stint on the 2018 squad, the Astros might want to keep him around for a while. Kemp got the call in May to help an injury-plagued outfield and played serviceable defense while showing decent plate discipline and even knocked a handful of dingers. Like Altuve, he can put the bat on the ball quite well, and though he's not the same tier of hitter, he's at least a selective one. He can hold down the bottom end of a lineup, and will probably see plenty of left field unless Derek Fisher makes the leap, or one of Houston's stud prospects starts making a lot of noise.

Martin Maldonado **C** Born: 08/16/86 Age: 32 Bats: R Throws: R Height: 6'0" Weight: 230 Origin: Round 27, 2004 Draft (#803 overall)

YEAR	TEAM	LVL	AGE	PA	R	2B	3B	HR	RBI	BB	K	SB	CS	AVG/OBP/SLG	DRC+	VORP	BABIP	BRR	FRAA	WARP
2016	MIL	MLB	29	253	21	7	0	8	21	35	56	1	0	.202/.332/.351	100	6.5	.234	-1.1	C(69): 5.5	1.7
2017	ANA	MLB	30	471	43	19	1	14	38	15	119	0	2	.221/.276/.368	70	2.0	.273	-2.4	C(137): 32.1, 1B(1): 0.0	3.6
2018	ANA	MLB	31	290	24	14	0	5	32	13	73	0	1	.223/.284/.332	73	3.2	.287	-0.1	C(77): 1.1	0.6
2018	HOU	MLB	31	114	15	4	1	4	12	3	25	0	0	.231/.257/.398	73	-0.3	.263	-0.6	C(40): 2.0	0.3
2019	*HOU*	*MLB*	*32*	*395*	*41*	*17*	*2*	*9*	*40*	*28*	*93*	*1*	*1*	*.227/.309/.361*	*86*	*9.7*	*.285*	*-1.0*	*C 12*	*2.3*

Breakout: 1%   Improve: 42%   Collapse: 17%   Attrition: 21%   MLB: 98%   *Comparables: Al Evans, Matt Wieters, Hank Deberry*

Comedian Lewis Black had a joke long ago regarding being a weather reporter in San Diego, California, and how it was easily the best job in the country since all one had to do every day was proclaim "It's going to be nice. Back to you." While writing about Martin Maldonado full time would not put even the meagerest portion of bread on a table, the temptation is hard to resist: "Martin Maldonado is a solid defensive catcher who struggles to hit his weight. Back to you." Except that, entering his age-32 season, there's legitimate concern that the solid defense may be slipping away; framing may seem invisible, but it requires flexibility, and at some point a man can't just pluck those low strikes up with the same level of grace. I guess the point is that even in Southern California, the weather reporter is wrong once in a while.

YEAR	TEAM	P. COUNT	FRM RUNS	BLK RUNS	THRW RUNS	TOT RUNS
2016	MIL	9275	2.5	1.3	2.1	7.5
2017	ANA	18609	27.2	1.0	3.2	32.0
2018	ANA	11256	4.1	-0.8	0.3	4.0
2018	HOU	4686	1.7	-0.3	0.2	2.6
2019	*HOU*	*15333*	*10.1*	*0.3*	*1.8*	*12.2*

Jake Marisnick **CF** Born: 03/30/91 Age: 28 Bats: R Throws: R Height: 6'4" Weight: 220 Origin: Round 3, 2009 Draft (#104 overall)

YEAR	TEAM	LVL	AGE	PA	R	2B	3B	HR	RBI	BB	K	SB	CS	AVG/OBP/SLG	DRC+	VORP	BABIP	BRR	FRAA	WARP
2016	FRE	AAA	25	28	3	2	0	0	1	1	10	1	1	.185/.214/.259	65	-2.0	.294	-0.1	CF(6): 0.4, RF(2): 0.1	0.0
2016	HOU	MLB	25	311	40	18	1	5	21	16	83	10	5	.209/.257/.331	56	-6.2	.275	-1.1	CF(74): 8.8, LF(26): 1.4	0.3
2017	HOU	MLB	26	259	50	10	0	16	35	20	90	9	4	.243/.319/.496	97	13.8	.320	1.4	CF(93): -5.2, LF(6): 0.3	0.5
2018	FRE	AAA	27	82	18	8	2	4	13	6	17	3	1	.342/.402/.671	127	10.2	.396	-0.5	CF(12): -2.3, RF(6): 0.9	0.3
2018	HOU	MLB	27	235	34	8	1	10	28	15	84	6	2	.211/.275/.399	74	6.0	.292	2.3	CF(96): -5.7, LF(1): 0.0	-0.3
2019	*HOU*	*MLB*	*28*	*124*	*16*	*5*	*1*	*5*	*15*	*9*	*38*	*5*	*2*	*.227/.297/.407*	*99*	*4.8*	*.296*	*0.2*	*CF -1*	*0.4*

Breakout: 1%   Improve: 41%   Collapse: 7%   Attrition: 12%   MLB: 88%   *Comparables: Peter Bourjos, Mikie Mahtook, Franklin Gutierrez*

How can such a good-looking man have such ugly at-bats? Marisnick, who is very handsome, made a complete 180 on his promising 2017 campaign and fell flat on his very attractive face in 2018. Long regarded as an angelic defensive replacement, Marisnick looked to have gotten over a hump in 2017 when he complimented his poor plate discipline with some real power numbers. But much like Cinderella's carriage, this beautiful thing turned back into a pumpkin. He's very pleasing to look at, is what we're saying.

Freudis Nova **SS** Born: 01/12/00 Age: 19 Bats: R Throws: R Height: 6'1" Weight: 180 Origin: International Free Agent, 2016

YEAR	TEAM	LVL	AGE	PA	R	2B	3B	HR	RBI	BB	K	SB	CS	AVG/OBP/SLG	DRC+	VORP	BABIP	BRR	FRAA	WARP
2017	DAR	ROK	17	190	30	6	0	4	16	15	33	8	3	.247/.342/.355	128	10.6	.287	-2.1		0.7
2018	AST	RK	18	157	21	3	1	6	28	6	21	9	5	.308/.331/.466	129	9.8	.317	0.4	SS(24): -0.8, 2B(9): 0.0	1.0
2019	*HOU*	*MLB*	*19*	*251*	*25*	*8*	*0*	*7*	*22*	*3*	*59*	*3*	*2*	*.199/.212/.304*	*36*	*-11.3*	*.233*	*-0.6*	*SS -1, 2B 0*	*-1.3*

Breakout: 0%   Improve: 4%   Collapse: 1%   Attrition: 3%   MLB: 8%   *Comparables: Adalberto Mondesi, Wilmer Flores, Rougned Odor*

Nova's story is a fine example of the sinking feeling you often get when looking too closely at international signings. For some time before the 2016-17 signing period opened, Nova was "connected" to the Marlins for a bonus around $2.5 million. If you've been following prospects for any length of time, you already know that's a euphemism for a deal agreed to well, well ahead of July 2, the legal time to sign the year's new crop 16-year-olds. Nova tested positive for performance-enhancing drugs before signing, and the Marlins cancelled the deal, leaving him adrift in the international pool with most of that cycle's money long-since locked up, and no recourse against the team that spurned him. The Astros, who were blowing well past their pool restrictions that year anyway, swooped in and signed Nova for $1.2 million. Two seasons and a lot of big reports out of the complex leagues later, Nova is emerging as a top prospect with offensive tools to spare and a good chance to stick somewhere on the dirt. Unless you're Juan Soto, the road from the Gulf Coast League to the majors is lengthy and has a lot of potholes, so the story might go many different ways from here.

Josh Reddick RF   Born: 02/19/87   Age: 32   Bats: L   Throws: R   Height: 6'2"   Weight: 195   Origin: Round 17, 2006 Draft (#523 overall)

YEAR	TEAM	LVL	AGE	PA	R	2B	3B	HR	RBI	BB	K	SB	CS	AVG/OBP/SLG	DRC+	VORP	BABIP	BRR	FRAA	WARP
2016	OAK	MLB	29	272	33	11	1	8	28	28	34	5	0	.296/.368/.449	106	18.0	.317	2.1	RF(68): 3.0	1.3
2016	LAN	MLB	29	167	20	6	0	2	9	11	22	3	3	.258/.307/.335	114	-0.7	.290	-0.3	RF(42): 0.8	0.7
2017	HOU	MLB	30	540	77	34	4	13	82	43	72	7	3	.314/.363/.484	115	33.3	.339	2.5	RF(102): -1.6, LF(48): -1.2	2.2
2018	HOU	MLB	31	487	63	13	2	17	47	49	77	7	2	.242/.318/.400	108	10.7	.258	-1.0	RF(111): -2.0, LF(43): 0.4	1.4
2019	HOU	MLB	32	447	52	25	2	12	54	40	65	6	2	.283/.350/.443	117	22.2	.312	0.8	RF 0	2.4

Breakout: 1%   Improve: 35%   Collapse: 2%   Attrition: 11%   MLB: 98%   *Comparables: David DeJesus, Tommy Griffith, Dixie Walker*

Reddick's OPS sank by 129 points in 2018. Oddly enough, nothing about his plate discipline changed all that much, nor did his contact or walk rate. Most of the difference can be chalked up to a seemingly uncharacteristic .258 BABIP, despite nearly identical batted ball rates. In previous years, we'd see this as a harbinger for pending regression. However, there's another element now: Reddick's batted ball velocity, usually around the median for major leaguers, dropped to a tenth-percentile 85.2 mph, and he's barreling it up less often then he used to. Despite the red flags, Houston is forced to hope for a rebound, as they still owe him $26 million over the next two seasons.

A.J. Reed 1B   Born: 05/10/93   Age: 26   Bats: L   Throws: L   Height: 6'4"   Weight: 275   Origin: Round 2, 2014 Draft (#42 overall)

YEAR	TEAM	LVL	AGE	PA	R	2B	3B	HR	RBI	BB	K	SB	CS	AVG/OBP/SLG	DRC+	VORP	BABIP	BRR	FRAA	WARP
2016	FRE	AAA	23	296	42	22	1	15	50	32	67	0	0	.291/.368/.556	130	20.1	.337	-2.4	1B(46): 2.2	1.6
2016	HOU	MLB	23	141	11	3	0	3	8	18	48	0	0	.164/.270/.262	68	-7.2	.236	-0.2	1B(35): -2.0	-0.6
2017	HOU	MLB	24	6	0	0	0	0	0	0	1	0	0	.000/.000/.000	75	-1.5	.000	0.0	1B(1): 0.0	0.0
2017	FRE	AAA	24	556	89	24	0	34	104	72	146	0	0	.261/.358/.525	134	18.8	.299	-3.1	1B(109): -4.0	2.5
2018	HOU	MLB	25	3	0	0	0	0	0	0	1	0	0	.000/.000/.000	81	-0.8	.000	0.0	1B(1): 0.0	0.0
2018	FRE	AAA	25	540	72	24	4	28	108	64	128	0	0	.255/.344/.506	134	28.1	.285	-4.0	1B(90): -0.4	2.7
2019	HOU	MLB	26	117	16	5	0	6	16	12	32	0	0	.241/.323/.461	110	2.7	.290	-0.2	1B 0	0.2

Breakout: 3%   Improve: 27%   Collapse: 7%   Attrition: 29%   MLB: 64%   *Comparables: Tyler Austin, Mat Gamel, Tommy Medica*

The fall of a first base prospect can be swift and painful. Reed was our 55th-best prospect in baseball before the 2016 season, and likely would've ranked quite a bit higher on that year's midseason list were he not called up just before publication. To say that he was overmatched by major-league pitching would be putting it mildly. It's not like this sort of thing doesn't happen to good prospects in that small a sample—for example, Anthony Rizzo was just as bad in similar playing time as a rookie for the Padres in 2011. But Rizzo quickly got a change of scenery to a team that believed in him, whereas Reed's never gotten a clean opportunity for that second act, even when the Astros needed a power bat. He's dangerously close to falling into the Mike Hessman itinerant Quad-A slugger classification.

George Springer RF   Born: 09/19/89   Age: 29   Bats: R   Throws: R   Height: 6'3"   Weight: 215   Origin: Round 1, 2011 Draft (#11 overall)

YEAR	TEAM	LVL	AGE	PA	R	2B	3B	HR	RBI	BB	K	SB	CS	AVG/OBP/SLG	DRC+	VORP	BABIP	BRR	FRAA	WARP
2016	HOU	MLB	26	744	116	29	5	29	82	88	178	9	10	.261/.359/.457	113	29.4	.317	1.2	RF(147): 20.1, CF(1): 0.0	5.1
2017	HOU	MLB	27	629	112	29	0	34	85	64	111	5	7	.283/.367/.522	129	40.8	.297	0.5	CF(84): 2.6, RF(78): 0.6	4.6
2018	HOU	MLB	28	620	102	26	0	22	71	64	122	6	4	.265/.346/.434	110	30.6	.303	1.5	CF(80): -2.8, RF(77): 2.6	2.7
2019	HOU	MLB	29	661	95	28	2	26	81	73	132	8	6	.259/.354/.448	119	38.7	.298	1.3	CF -2, RF 2	4.1

Breakout: 8%   Improve: 50%   Collapse: 1%   Attrition: 6%   MLB: 96%   *Comparables: Carlos Beltran, Chet Lemon, Grady Sizemore*

There's a longstanding and highly-unsubstantiated theory that the one injury that can sap a batter's power more than any other is a hand injury. This seems a little weird given all the moving muscles, joints, bones and chitin that go into a baseball swing. But the hands are the body's connector to the bat and our world is built upon a bedrock of unanswerable questions, so here we are.

Regardless of the scientific reasoning behind said theory, Springer would a be a prime candidate in proving its validity. An early-August thumb sprain suffered while attempting to steal second stalled what was promising to be another highly productive year. All told, he missed only as many games as he did in his 2017 campaign, but when he returned he wasn't *George Springer* until the very end of the season. Assuming his hands are all healed up by next season, there isn't really any reason he shouldn't have another productive year in 2019. His age will catch up with him eventually—but it will for all of us and there's not much point in giving in to those kinds of thoughts.

Max Stassi C Born: 03/15/91 Age: 28 Bats: R Throws: R Height: 5'10" Weight: 200 Origin: Round 4, 2009 Draft (#123 overall)

YEAR	TEAM	LVL	AGE	PA	R	2B	3B	HR	RBI	BB	K	SB	CS	AVG/OBP/SLG	DRC+	VORP	BABIP	BRR	FRAA	WARP
2016	FRE	AAA	25	266	21	12	1	7	32	20	65	1	0	.230/.294/.374	83	5.1	.287	1.1	C(66): 8.5	1.8
2016	HOU	MLB	25	13	1	0	0	0	0	0	5	0	0	.077/.077/.077	61	-2.3	.125	-0.1	C(8): -0.3	0.0
2017	FRE	AAA	26	287	54	14	0	12	33	38	67	1	1	.266/.383/.473	118	26.3	.321	-0.2	C(65): 10.8	3.1
2017	HOU	MLB	26	31	5	1	0	2	4	6	4	0	0	.167/.323/.458	112	0.9	.105	0.0	C(11): 0.5, 1B(1): 0.0	0.2
2018	HOU	MLB	27	250	28	13	0	8	27	23	74	0	0	.226/.316/.394	79	9.8	.302	-0.1	C(82): 14.5	2.1
2019	HOU	MLB	28	263	29	10	1	8	30	25	69	0	0	.226/.314/.382	92	9.2	.286	0.0	C 8	1.8

Breakout: 4% Improve: 19% Collapse: 13% Attrition: 31% MLB: 52%

Comparables: Chris Gimenez, John Baker, Tony Sanchez

YEAR	TEAM	P. COUNT	FRM RUNS	BLK RUNS	THRW RUNS	TOT RUNS
2016	HOU	491	-0.3	0.1	0.0	0.2
2017	FRE	9878	11.4	0.0	-0.8	10.1
2017	HOU	1029	0.2	0.4	0.0	0.5
2018	HOU	9540	13.9	0.1	-0.1	14.0
2019	HOU	10111	8.9	-0.1	-0.4	8.4

What do we owe to a backup catcher? After five straight years spent mostly sitting around Triple-A as Houston's third catcher/Mindy St. Claire—getting MLB time every year but maxing out at 31 plate appearances in 2017—Stassi *finally* broke out of The Medium Place and established himself as a bona fide MLB backup catcher in 2018. He posted strong defensive numbers to go along with the sterling reputation he'd developed in the high minors, and surpassed the "greater than useless" offensive threshold for a reserve catcher. The good news for Stassi as he enters his late twenties is that once you're established as a viable backup catcher, you've got a shot to hang around in The Good Place long enough to fully vest your pension. The bad news is that Janet can always conjure up a Martin Maldonado in a trade if you don't keep accumulating those good person points, or if your framing slips a little.

Myles Straw OF Born: 10/17/94 Age: 24 Bats: R Throws: R Height: 5'10" Weight: 180 Origin: Round 12, 2015 Draft (#349 overall)

YEAR	TEAM	LVL	AGE	PA	R	2B	3B	HR	RBI	BB	K	SB	CS	AVG/OBP/SLG	DRC+	VORP	BABIP	BRR	FRAA	WARP
2016	QUD	A	21	307	40	14	6	0	22	29	58	17	10	.374/.432/.470	120	29.1	.472	0.3	RF(24): 4.4, CF(21): 2.5	2.9
2016	LNC	A+	21	90	21	4	0	1	5	11	17	4	2	.303/.393/.395	107	6.4	.373	2.7	CF(32): 6.9, RF(12): 7.2	0.8
2017	BCA	A+	22	533	81	17	7	1	41	87	70	36	9	.295/.412/.373	123	54.3	.347	5.5	CF(11): -1.1, LF(2): 0.7	5.3
2017	CCH	AA	22	54	9	0	0	0	3	7	9	2	0	.239/.340/.239	91	1.7	.297	0.6	CF(58): 6.0, RF(6): 2.0	0.1
2018	CCH	AA	23	294	47	7	3	1	17	35	42	35	6	.327/.414/.390	106	24.6	.386	4.4	CF(43): 4.9, RF(25): 1.4	2.4
2018	FRE	AAA	23	304	48	10	3	0	14	38	60	35	3	.257/.349/.317	80	8.1	.330	3.8	RF(5): -0.1, CF(3): 0.0	1.3
2018	HOU	MLB	23	10	4	0	0	1	1	1	0	2	0	.333/.400/.667	112	1.9	.250	0.7		0.1
2019	HOU	MLB	24	30	3	1	0	0	2	3	7	2	0	.223/.304/.323	35	-1.0	.282	0.2	CF 1	-0.1

Breakout: 4% Improve: 25% Collapse: 5% Attrition: 18% MLB: 48%

Comparables: Boog Powell, Ezequiel Carrera, J.B. Shuck

At first blush, Straw may have seemed like an odd choice for a September call-up. Just 23, and with a well-known penchant for being a slap hitter, it would have been easy to question Houston's decision to see how Straw's game played in the bigs. But a little more scrolling would have revealed the truth: Myles Straw is very, very fast. It's true that stolen base totals are not a terrific measure of a player's speed, but Straw swiped 70 bags in 131 games between AA and AAA in 2018. (Whit Merrifield led the majors last year with 45. Modern baseball, man.) It's doubtful he will develop much power given his frame, but slap hitters are people, too. A young outfielder with defensive prowess and tons of speed will always have some value, especially when the rosters expand, and Straw has shown he has just that.

Kyle Tucker OF Born: 01/17/97 Age: 22 Bats: L Throws: R Height: 6'4" Weight: 190 Origin: Round 1, 2015 Draft (#5 overall)

YEAR	TEAM	LVL	AGE	PA	R	2B	3B	HR	RBI	BB	K	SB	CS	AVG/OBP/SLG	DRC+	VORP	BABIP	BRR	FRAA	WARP
2016	QUD	A	19	428	43	19	5	6	56	40	75	31	9	.276/.348/.402	118	20.9	.322	1.3	CF(61): -5.2, LF(17): -0.3	1.7
2016	LNC	A+	19	69	13	6	2	3	13	10	6	1	3	.339/.435/.661	149	8.0	.340	0.2	RF(6): -0.1, LF(4): 0.2	0.6
2017	BCA	A+	20	206	31	12	4	9	43	24	45	13	5	.288/.379/.554	132	21.3	.336	-3.1	RF(16): -1.8, CF(7): 1.2	0.9
2017	CCH	AA	20	318	39	21	1	16	47	22	64	8	4	.265/.325/.512	130	19.6	.286	1.2	CF(37): -5.3, RF(18): -1.4	1.5
2018	FRE	AAA	21	465	86	27	3	24	93	48	84	20	4	.332/.400/.590	146	52.8	.364	1.7	RF(54): 0.3, LF(32): -0.4	4.0
2018	HOU	MLB	21	72	10	2	1	0	4	6	13	1	1	.141/.236/.203	75	-5.7	.176	-0.4	LF(20): -2.1, RF(3): 0.2	-0.3
2019	HOU	MLB	22	296	42	16	1	13	40	27	61	9	3	.271/.343/.482	123	16.7	.307	0.3	LF -4, RF 0	1.3

Breakout: 3% Improve: 36% Collapse: 2% Attrition: 15% MLB: 62%

Comparables: Oswaldo Arcia, Tyler Austin, Joc Pederson

Way back in 2015, the Astros signed Tucker to a below-slot deal to save money to sign fellow prep outfielder Daz Cameron with a supplemental pick. That decision has already paid off twice over, with Cameron as a key component in the Justin Verlander trade that led to a World Series win, and Tucker emerging into one of the top prospects in all the land. He didn't do a whole lot of damage in three short stints in the majors, but he hit the snot out of the ball as one of the youngest regular position players in Triple-A. The perceived bar for success for an elite prospect is higher than it's ever been right now because of all of the incredible hitting performances put up by top prospects graduating to the majors. This one just might clear it.

Tyler White 1B   Born: 10/29/90   Age: 28   Bats: R   Throws: R   Height: 5'11"   Weight: 225   Origin: Round 33, 2013 Draft (#977 overall)

YEAR	TEAM	LVL	AGE	PA	R	2B	3B	HR	RBI	BB	K	SB	CS	AVG/OBP/SLG	DRC+	VORP	BABIP	BRR	FRAA	WARP
2016	FRE	AAA	25	190	28	4	1	13	29	16	30	1	1	.241/.305/.500	141	5.8	.221	-1.2	1B(24): 0.9, SS(3): 0.3	1.3
2016	HOU	MLB	25	276	24	16	0	8	28	23	65	1	0	.217/.286/.378	82	-3.7	.258	-0.1	1B(58): -2.5, 3B(3): 0.0	-0.5
2017	FRE	AAA	26	497	84	22	1	25	89	47	101	7	3	.300/.371/.528	136	40.6	.334	0.5	3B(50): 8.3, 2B(21): -0.2	4.9
2017	HOU	MLB	26	67	7	6	0	3	10	4	16	0	1	.279/.328/.525	100	4.5	.326	0.4	1B(19): -1.5, 2B(4): 0.1	0.0
2018	FRE	AAA	27	313	55	18	0	14	53	46	39	1	1	.333/.444/.569	167	30.5	.345	-2.7	2B(26): 0.0, 3B(23): 1.5	3.5
2018	HOU	MLB	27	237	27	12	3	12	42	24	49	0	1	.276/.354/.533	119	16.9	.307	-2.2	1B(42): 0.6	0.7
2019	HOU	MLB	28	206	25	10	1	8	29	20	44	1	0	.261/.340/.462	118	6.6	.300	-0.4	1B -1	0.6

Breakout: 8%   Improve: 35%   Collapse: 13%   Attrition: 27%   MLB: 77%   *Comparables: Justin Bour, Chris Parmelee, Steve Pearce*

Back in the simpler days of 2016, White flamed out in an early-season shot at the MLB starting first base job. We said last year that the long-time minors masher deserved another shot to graduate to The Show, and he parlayed another hot first half in Triple-A into regular playing time after the Astros were struck by the injury bug. This time, he grabbed the brass ring and thrived. Even when all the regulars came back for the playoffs, he still had a role as a platoon DH and pinch-hitter. This is a fairly fungible profile these days, but he's still a few years away from arbitration. It doesn't hurt that he'll pitch in blowouts and stand at second base or even shortstop when you ask him, either. He's already made it further than you could've ever imagined for a 33rd-round senior sign from Western Carolina.

PITCHERS

Rogelio Armenteros RHP   Born: 06/30/94   Age: 25   Bats: R   Throws: R   Height: 6'1"   Weight: 215   Origin: International Free Agent, 2014

YEAR	TEAM	LVL	AGE	W	L	SV	G	GS	IP	H	HR	BB/9	K/9	K	GB%	BABIP	WHIP	ERA	DRA	WARP	MPH	FB%	WHF	CSP
2016	QUD	A	22	0	2	0	4	3	18²	12	0	1.4	9.6	20	67%	.245	0.80	1.93	3.02	0.4				
2016	LNC	A+	22	6	4	1	19	16	90¹	87	13	3.7	10.7	107	39%	.323	1.37	4.18	5.06	0.4				
2016	CCH	AA	22	2	0	0	3	3	18¹	17	1	2.0	6.4	13	36%	.308	1.15	1.96	3.71	0.3				
2017	CCH	AA	23	2	3	1	14	10	65¹	49	3	2.6	10.2	74	42%	.284	1.04	1.93	2.93	1.7				
2017	FRE	AAA	23	8	1	0	10	10	58¹	42	5	2.9	11.1	72	50%	.276	1.05	2.16	1.97	2.4				
2018	FRE	AAA	24	8	1	1	22	21	118	106	15	3.7	10.2	134	38%	.301	1.31	3.74	3.59	2.6				
2019	HOU	MLB	25	3	2	0	21	6	46¹	39	6	3.6	9.6	50	40%	.275	1.24	4.28	4.57	0.3				

Breakout: 10%   Improve: 31%   Collapse: 21%   Attrition: 24%   MLB: 62%   *Comparables: Brian Johnson, Austin Voth, Nick Tropeano*

Armenteros was not considered an elite Cuban prospect when the Astros took a $40,000 flier on him in 2014. Yet all he's done since is steadily march through the minors, racking up strikeouts, quality ERAs, and innings at every level. He's continued the trick in the upper levels, though his rates degraded a bit in the Pacific Coast League's tougher pitching environment. His spotty changeup has limited his ranking on prospect lists, but he's already shown durability, command of a useful fastball, and a big curveball. He's very close to being an MLB-quality pitcher right now, and how much his change improves will determine how high he can climb from there.

J.B. Bukauskas RHP   Born: 10/11/96   Age: 22   Bats: R   Throws: R   Height: 6'0"   Weight: 196   Origin: Round 1, 2017 Draft (#15 overall)

YEAR	TEAM	LVL	AGE	W	L	SV	G	GS	IP	H	HR	BB/9	K/9	K	GB%	BABIP	WHIP	ERA	DRA	WARP	MPH	FB%	WHF	CSP
2017	TCV	A-	20	0	0	0	2	2	6	4	0	6.0	9.0	6	53%	.267	1.33	4.50	3.27	0.1				
2018	TCV	A-	21	0	0	0	3	3	8¹	8	0	2.2	9.7	9	46%	.364	1.20	0.00	2.48	0.3				
2018	QUD	A	21	1	2	0	4	4	15	15	0	4.2	12.6	21	55%	.395	1.47	4.20	1.62	0.6				
2018	BCA	A+	21	3	0	0	5	5	28	13	1	4.2	10.0	31	59%	.194	0.93	1.61	3.13	0.7				
2018	CCH	AA	21	0	0	0	1	1	6	1	0	3.0	12.0	8	60%	.100	0.50	0.00	3.18	0.2				
2019	HOU	MLB	22	2	3	0	9	9	39²	36	6	4.9	8.9	39	45%	.284	1.45	5.04	5.41	0.0				

Breakout: 16%   Improve: 24%   Collapse: 6%   Attrition: 16%   MLB: 34%   *Comparables: Carl Edwards Jr., Matt Moore, Trevor May*

If this comment had been written right after the season, we might have made a joke about the dangers of saying his last name, and then segued into talk about another injury-plagued year for the flamethrower out of UNC. (This time, he missed half the season with an injured back from a car accident.) Instead, two far greater points of interest arose on Bukauskas as the leaves turned. First, he absolutely shoved in the Arizona Fall League, touching 98 mph with his fastball and reminding everyone that he still has one of the minors' best sliders. Then Ken Rosenthal of *The Athletic* reported that JBB was the proposed headliner in a deadline deal that would've sent Bryce Harper to the Astros, a trade that could've dramatically altered the American League playoffs. Both of those points hint at a buried lede: if Bukauskas can just stay healthy and throw strikes, he's one of the few pitchers in the minors with true top-of-the-rotation potential.

Gerrit Cole RHP   Born: 09/08/90   Age: 28   Bats: R   Throws: R   Height: 6'4"   Weight: 225   Origin: Round 1, 2011 Draft (#1 overall)

YEAR	TEAM	LVL	AGE	W	L	SV	G	GS	IP	H	HR	BB/9	K/9	K	GB%	BABIP	WHIP	ERA	DRA	WARP	MPH	FB%	WHF	CSP
2016	PIT	MLB	25	7	10	0	21	21	116	131	7	2.8	7.6	98	48%	.345	1.44	3.88	4.42	1.2	98.3	66.8	9.1	48.6
2017	PIT	MLB	26	12	12	0	33	33	203	199	31	2.4	8.7	196	47%	.298	1.25	4.26	3.84	3.9	98.0	60	10.1	49.5
2018	HOU	MLB	27	15	5	0	32	32	200¹	143	19	2.9	12.4	276	38%	.286	1.03	2.88	2.55	6.4	98.7	56.3	15.3	49.8
2019	HOU	MLB	28	13	9	0	30	30	189	156	24	2.9	10.9	229	42%	.290	1.15	3.66	3.90	3.4	97.8	59.8	12.4	49.7

Breakout: 21%   Improve: 59%   Collapse: 21%   Attrition: 4%   MLB: 95%   *Comparables: Josh Beckett, Madison Bumgarner, Yovani Gallardo*

The Astros gave up a hefty package—at least in terms of number of players and name recognition of said players—to acquire Cole prior to the 2018 season. Judging trades this early and judging trades in general is kind of a silly exercise, but it is safe to say that Houston was content with the pitcher they received in the form of 2018 Gerrit Cole.

Cole produced the highest strikeout rate of his major-league career—by a pretty big margin, actually. His underlying numbers didn't change all that much save for one thing: a more-utilized and faster fastball. An age-27 Gerrit Cole, who was not moved to the bullpen or coming off any kind of known injury, actually gained a half MPH on his fastball. And it doesn't take a highly respected and beloved publication like this one to tell you, the reader, that this is just kind of... strange. Perhaps it was a change of scenery, perhaps Cole has starting meddling in the dark arts. Regardless, his 2018 season was his best by pretty much every measure.

Chris Devenski RHP   Born: 11/13/90   Age: 28   Bats: R   Throws: R   Height: 6'3"   Weight: 210   Origin: Round 25, 2011 Draft (#771 overall)

YEAR	TEAM	LVL	AGE	W	L	SV	G	GS	IP	H	HR	BB/9	K/9	K	GB%	BABIP	WHIP	ERA	DRA	WARP	MPH	FB%	WHF	CSP
2016	HOU	MLB	25	4	4	1	48	5	108¹	79	4	1.7	8.6	104	34%	.271	0.91	2.16	2.78	2.8	95.6	45.8	14.5	47.2
2017	HOU	MLB	26	8	5	4	62	0	80²	50	11	2.9	11.2	100	41%	.220	0.94	2.68	3.09	1.9	95.5	39.7	17.7	45.9
2018	HOU	MLB	27	2	3	2	50	1	47¹	42	9	2.5	9.7	51	37%	.275	1.16	4.18	3.61	0.7	95.9	41.6	15.2	46.7
2019	HOU	MLB	28	3	1	0	52	0	54²	44	7	2.9	9.9	60	38%	.270	1.14	4.00	4.28	0.7	95.1	42.6	16	46.9

Breakout: 20%   Improve: 43%   Collapse: 27%   Attrition: 24%   MLB: 91%   *Comparables: Andrew Bailey, Hunter Strickland, Zack Godley*

Devenski's two-year run of being a dominant high-leverage reliever was foiled by a hamstring injury that put him on the shelf for over a month. When he returned late in the season, he found that his role had been filled by others, a fact that found him sitting out the entire 2018 postseason. Entering his age-28 season, he's still a young man, and has shown truly dominant stuff over the past couple of years. That stuff is unchanged, but there are a few worrying trends—a higher contact rate in the zone and an accompanying rise in homers—that he'll need to iron out to reclaim his status as the Right-Handed Andrew Miller.

Will Harris RHP   Born: 08/28/84   Age: 34   Bats: R   Throws: R   Height: 6'4"   Weight: 250   Origin: Round 9, 2006 Draft (#258 overall)

YEAR	TEAM	LVL	AGE	W	L	SV	G	GS	IP	H	HR	BB/9	K/9	K	GB%	BABIP	WHIP	ERA	DRA	WARP	MPH	FB%	WHF	CSP
2016	HOU	MLB	31	1	2	12	66	0	64	52	3	2.1	9.7	69	59%	.293	1.05	2.25	2.26	2.0	94.6	66.4	14.4	45
2017	HOU	MLB	32	3	2	2	46	0	45¹	37	7	1.4	10.3	52	49%	.270	0.97	2.98	2.45	1.4	93.2	68.7	13.9	46.9
2018	HOU	MLB	33	5	3	0	61	0	56²	48	3	2.2	10.2	64	54%	.306	1.09	3.49	2.32	1.7	93.5	62.3	14.5	42.5
2019	HOU	MLB	34	3	1	0	52	0	54²	43	6	2.9	9.8	59	51%	.270	1.12	3.67	3.90	0.7	92.6	64.3	14.1	43.9

Breakout: 12%   Improve: 29%   Collapse: 38%   Attrition: 8%   MLB: 87%   *Comparables: Heath Bell, Francisco Cordero, Scott Downs*

In 2018, Harris had a very similar season to his 2017 effort, which is to say it was very, very good. He stranded fewer batters, and his peripherals saw some light decay, but he made up for it by drastically reducing his home run rate. In the baseball roster equivalent of lighting cigars with hundred dollar bills, the reliever-rich Astros elected not to pick up Harris's very affordable $5.5 million option for 2019, but he remains under team control.

Josh James RHP   Born: 03/08/93   Age: 26   Bats: R   Throws: R   Height: 6'3"   Weight: 206   Origin: Round 34, 2014 Draft (#1006 overall)

YEAR	TEAM	LVL	AGE	W	L	SV	G	GS	IP	H	HR	BB/9	K/9	K	GB%	BABIP	WHIP	ERA	DRA	WARP	MPH	FB%	WHF	CSP
2016	LNC	A+	23	9	5	1	23	19	110¹	120	11	3.3	9.9	121	48%	.350	1.45	4.81	4.46	1.2				
2017	CCH	AA	24	4	8	3	21	11	76	79	1	3.8	8.5	72	53%	.338	1.46	4.38	3.59	1.3				
2018	CCH	AA	25	0	0	1	6	4	21²	17	1	4.2	15.8	38	58%	.364	1.25	2.49	1.73	0.9				
2018	FRE	AAA	25	6	4	0	17	17	92²	62	8	3.8	12.9	133	41%	.278	1.09	3.40	2.35	3.3				
2018	HOU	MLB	25	2	0	0	6	3	23	15	3	2.7	11.3	29	42%	.240	0.96	2.35	3.20	0.5	99.8	59.9	14.6	46.7
2019	HOU	MLB	26	6	5	0	26	16	91	75	11	3.8	10.8	109	44%	.287	1.24	3.95	4.21	1.5	99.4	61	14.9	47.5

Breakout: 17%   Improve: 32%   Collapse: 17%   Attrition: 33%   MLB: 60%   *Comparables: Tom Mastny, D.J. Snelten, Adam Conley*

Most of the world got introduced to James during the 2018 ALCS, and, well, it could have gone better for him. However, the young flamethrower had a good run during his late-season call up, save for a slight home run problem. James was almost exclusively a starter in the minors, but Houston may look to utilize his high-90s fastball and mid-80s changeup in the bullpen, depending on who ends up on the roster. If we can expect the usual velocity uptick when a pitcher migrates to the bullpen, James has the potential to be a dynamic asset late in games in 2019.

Dallas Keuchel LHP   Born: 01/01/88   Age: 31   Bats: L   Throws: L   Height: 6'3"   Weight: 205   Origin: Round 7, 2009 Draft (#221 overall)

YEAR	TEAM	LVL	AGE	W	L	SV	G	GS	IP	H	HR	BB/9	K/9	K	GB%	BABIP	WHIP	ERA	DRA	WARP	MPH	FB%	WHF	CSP
2016	HOU	MLB	28	9	12	0	26	26	168	168	20	2.6	7.7	144	58%	.304	1.29	4.55	3.36	3.9	90.6	64.3	10	42.8
2017	HOU	MLB	29	14	5	0	23	23	145²	116	15	2.9	7.7	125	68%	.256	1.12	2.90	3.64	3.1	90.4	68.2	12.3	38.9
2018	HOU	MLB	30	12	11	0	34	34	204²	211	18	2.6	6.7	153	55%	.300	1.31	3.74	3.87	3.4	90.9	69.1	8.9	45
2019	HOU	MLB	31	11	9	0	27	27	174¹	154	17	2.8	7.4	143	56%	.277	1.19	3.98	4.24	2.5	89.9	67.3	10	42.2

Breakout: 11%   Improve: 31%   Collapse: 26%   Attrition: 5%   MLB: 86%   *Comparables: Jake Westbrook, Tim Hudson, Roy Halladay*

Keuchel will always have a place in Houston Astros lore. A Cy Young Award and a World Series ring certainly help in that regard. However, we shouldn't forget that he was the resident old man on the team in 2018, at least in terms of tenure with Houston. Keuchel, along with Altuve, was one of the few holdovers from the not-so-distant days when the Astros were absolute garbage. In his first season with the team, he shared rotation duties with the likes of Lucas Harrell, Jordan Lyles, and Wandy Rodriguez. Trips down Memory Lane aside, Keuchel will still be only 31 when the 2019 season begins, and will be looking to keep his ground-ball-inducing ways going. PECOTA has never been enamored with his refusal to throw strikes, assuming that the magic has to end sometime, and batters made better contact on those not-quite-strikes than ever before. But so far, PECOTA has also always been wrong, to some extent. Regardless of whether he stays in Houston or moves on elsewhere, he'll still be able to regale youngsters with tales of what it was like to watch Brian Bogusevic take batting practice.

Francis Martes RHP Born: 11/24/95 Age: 23 Bats: R Throws: R Height: 6'1" Weight: 225 Origin: International Free Agent, 2012

YEAR	TEAM	LVL	AGE	W	L	SV	G	GS	IP	H	HR	BB/9	K/9	K	GB%	BABIP	WHIP	ERA	DRA	WARP	MPH	FB%	WHF	CSP
2016	CCH	AA	20	9	6	0	25	22	125¹	104	4	3.4	9.4	131	45%	.296	1.20	3.30	3.32	2.6				
2017	FRE	AAA	21	0	2	0	8	8	32¹	40	5	7.8	10.6	38	39%	.380	2.10	5.29	6.19	-0.2				
2017	HOU	MLB	21	5	2	0	32	4	54¹	51	7	5.1	11.4	69	44%	.328	1.51	5.80	4.39	0.6	97.8	55.4	13.5	46.7
2018	FRE	AAA	22	0	1	0	4	4	18²	25	2	8.2	7.7	16	40%	.397	2.25	6.75	6.90	-0.3				
2019	HOU	MLB	23	2	2	0	11	6	33²	31	4	4.9	8.9	33	41%	.292	1.47	4.80	5.14	0.1	97.7	57.4	14	48.3

Breakout: 23%   Improve: 38%   Collapse: 15%   Attrition: 30%   MLB: 62%   *Comparables: Randall Delgado, Dana Eveland, Marco Gonzales*

Sometimes the path to Tommy John surgery goes quickly—a pitcher starts shaking his arm out on the mound, the MRI reveals a torn UCL, and surgery is scheduled for a week or two later. More often, it meanders on for some time. A pitcher will initially present with elbow discomfort, forearm tightness, or a flexor issue. The team will claim there is no structural damage, but he'll still be out for weeks or months. He'll come back for a little bit after rehabbing it and probably won't pitch all that well or reach his initial level. Then another MRI reveals the torn UCL. Martes started this cycle early on in the season when he reported elbow discomfort, and ended it in mid-August with Tommy John surgery, hitting the usual notes in between. He might pop up for a token appearance in 2019, but he's going to miss most or all of the season. Losing two seasons of development like this strikes a cruel blow to hopes that he might stick in the rotation.

Corbin Martin RHP Born: 12/28/95 Age: 23 Bats: R Throws: R Height: 6'2" Weight: 200 Origin: Round 2, 2017 Draft (#56 overall)

YEAR	TEAM	LVL	AGE	W	L	SV	G	GS	IP	H	HR	BB/9	K/9	K	GB%	BABIP	WHIP	ERA	DRA	WARP	MPH	FB%	WHF	CSP
2017	TCV	A-	21	0	1	1	8	3	27²	20	1	2.6	12.4	38	63%	.297	1.01	2.60	2.54	0.8				
2018	BCA	A+	22	2	0	1	4	3	19	4	0	3.3	12.3	26	64%	.111	0.58	0.00	3.10	0.5				
2018	CCH	AA	22	7	2	0	21	18	103	84	7	2.4	8.4	96	48%	.277	1.09	2.97	3.41	2.3				
2019	HOU	MLB	23	3	2	0	8	8	40	34	6	3.5	8.9	40	47%	.272	1.24	4.43	4.75	0.3				

Breakout: 17%   Improve: 25%   Collapse: 21%   Attrition: 38%   MLB: 59%   *Comparables: Matt Magill, Giovanni Soto, Nestor Cortes*

Martin's stock has been on a steady rise since he burst onto the prospect scene as a reliever in the Cape Cod League in the summer of 2016. He made a smooth transition into the rotation midway through the 2017 college season at Texas A&M, and the Astros rewarded him with a second-round draft selection and a cool million dollars in bonus money. He quickly sliced through A-ball like a hot knife through cold butter, and spent most of his first full pro campaign beating up on the Double-A Texas League. Despite a history that might tilt you towards projecting a future in the bullpen, the makings of a four-pitch mid-rotation starter are all already present here. We'll have to see if he can keep exceeding our projections.

Lance McCullers RHP Born: 10/02/93 Age: 25 Bats: L Throws: R Height: 6'1" Weight: 205 Origin: Round 1, 2012 Draft (#41 overall)

YEAR	TEAM	LVL	AGE	W	L	SV	G	GS	IP	H	HR	BB/9	K/9	K	GB%	BABIP	WHIP	ERA	DRA	WARP	MPH	FB%	WHF	CSP
2016	HOU	MLB	22	6	5	0	14	14	81	80	5	5.0	11.8	106	59%	.383	1.54	3.22	3.65	1.6	97.0	43.2	13.7	43.4
2017	HOU	MLB	23	7	4	0	22	22	118²	114	8	3.0	10.0	132	62%	.330	1.30	4.25	4.13	1.9	96.5	40.4	12.8	45.4
2018	HOU	MLB	24	10	6	0	25	22	128¹	100	12	3.5	10.0	142	56%	.278	1.17	3.86	3.30	3.0	96.3	37.4	14.3	43.9
2019	HOU	MLB	25	8	5	0	20	20	110¹	88	9	3.7	10.4	127	54%	.290	1.21	3.51	3.72	2.2	96.2	40.4	14	45.3

Breakout: 27%   Improve: 62%   Collapse: 16%   Attrition: 11%   MLB: 99%   *Comparables: Chad Billingsley, Rich Harden, Yovani Gallardo*

American poet laureate Lil Jon eloquently summed up McCullers's approach to pitching when he asserted that one should "Shake What [Their] Mama Gave [Them]." In this particular case, what his mama gave him was a dastardly curveball that he employed to strike out fools left and right. Not unlike Icarus, however, McCullers pushed his body to unsustainable limits that caused him to come crashing back down to Earth, having thrown so many curveballs that he broke his dang elbow. Tommy John surgery was performed in the offseason, and McCullers is expected to return in 2020. Sadly, this is yet another cautionary tale of a life torn asunder by Lil Jon.

Collin McHugh RHP Born: 06/19/87 Age: 32 Bats: R Throws: R Height: 6'2" Weight: 190 Origin: Round 18, 2008 Draft (#554 overall)

YEAR	TEAM	LVL	AGE	W	L	SV	G	GS	IP	H	HR	BB/9	K/9	K	GB%	BABIP	WHIP	ERA	DRA	WARP	MPH	FB%	WHF	CSP
2016	HOU	MLB	29	13	10	0	33	33	184²	206	25	2.6	8.6	177	43%	.339	1.41	4.34	3.81	3.3	92.6	35.8	11.4	46.2
2017	CCH	AA	30	0	0	0	4	4	15	18	1	2.4	6.6	11	57%	.340	1.47	3.60	2.87	0.4				
2017	HOU	MLB	30	5	2	0	12	12	63¹	62	7	2.8	8.8	62	33%	.312	1.29	3.55	4.58	0.7	91.7	50.6	13.2	48.4
2018	HOU	MLB	31	6	2	0	58	0	72¹	45	6	2.6	11.7	94	35%	.248	0.91	1.99	2.70	1.9	93.5	49.6	14.1	47.1
2019	HOU	MLB	32	9	6	0	64	18	144²	122	20	3.0	10.5	169	39%	.288	1.18	3.93	4.20	2.0	91.8	42.8	12.5	46.9

Breakout: 10%   Improve: 34%   Collapse: 30%   Attrition: 12%   MLB: 88%   *Comparables: Jake Peavy, Kelvim Escobar, Johnny Cueto*

It's probably safe to assume that McHugh has started his last game, at least for the Houston Astros. The usually-good-never-great starter couldn't find a spot in the rotation in 2018, so off to the bullpen he went. There, he found another two ticks on his fastball and a knack for striking out hitters at an unprecedented (for him) rate. It's generally a good sign when batters are swinging more at your pitches out of the strike zone and swinging less at the ones in, showing that he was getting more life on his pitches than just pure velocity in short work. He can double as both a long relief and high-leverage pitcher and will no doubt have his place in the bullpen cemented come 2019.

Roberto Osuna RHP Born: 02/07/95 Age: 24 Bats: R Throws: R Height: 6'2" Weight: 215 Origin: International Free Agent, 2011

YEAR	TEAM	LVL	AGE	W	L	SV	G	GS	IP	H	HR	BB/9	K/9	K	GB%	BABIP	WHIP	ERA	DRA	WARP	MPH	FB%	WHF	CSP
2016	TOR	MLB	21	4	3	36	72	0	74	55	9	1.7	10.0	82	35%	.256	0.93	2.68	3.12	1.6	98.3	66.3	16.6	48.5
2017	TOR	MLB	22	3	4	39	66	0	64	46	3	1.3	11.7	83	47%	.285	0.86	3.38	2.41	2.0	95.9	48	17.6	41.9
2018	TOR	MLB	23	0	0	9	15	0	15¹	16	0	0.6	7.6	13	40%	.340	1.11	2.93	3.97	0.2	97.1	47.4	13.4	50.5
2018	HOU	MLB	23	2	2	12	23	0	22²	17	1	1.2	7.5	19	44%	.258	0.88	1.99	3.54	0.4	96.6	47.4	16.9	48.3
2019	*HOU*	*MLB*	*24*	*2*	*1*	*35*	*46*	*0*	*49¹*	*39*	*4*	*2.8*	*9.4*	*52*	*41%*	*.274*	*1.11*	*3.52*	*3.74*	*0.7*	*96.8*	*55.7*	*17.2*	*48*

Breakout: 29%   Improve: 50%   Collapse: 12%   Attrition: 10%   MLB: 97%   *Comparables: Huston Street, Joakim Soria, Drew Storen*

On May 8th, Osuna was arrested in Toronto on assault charges. Details remain mostly sealed, but the victim was the mother of Osuna's child, and he later reached a plea agreement that included a peace bond and no contact order. After six weeks on administrative leave, Osuna and Major League Baseball ultimately agreed that he would serve a 75-game suspension under the Joint Domestic Violence, Sexual Assault and Child Abuse policy, the second-longest suspension administered under the policy since its implementation in 2015. The Astros traded for the still-suspended Osuna at the deadline, sending banished former closer Ken Giles and two prospects to Toronto. General Manager Jeff Luhnow repeatedly defended acquiring Osuna, citing the team's "culture" and Osuna's "remorse," while sidestepping a claimed organizational "zero-tolerance" policy for domestic abuse. The suspension had the perverse effect of making Osuna a more valuable asset to a team morally bankrupt enough to profit off domestic violence: The Astros gained an extra year of control since players under suspension don't accrue service time, and despite the suspension he was eligible to pitch for his new team in the playoffs. Baseball needs to be better than this.

Brad Peacock RHP Born: 02/02/88 Age: 31 Bats: R Throws: R Height: 6'1" Weight: 210 Origin: Round 41, 2006 Draft (#1231 overall)

YEAR	TEAM	LVL	AGE	W	L	SV	G	GS	IP	H	HR	BB/9	K/9	K	GB%	BABIP	WHIP	ERA	DRA	WARP	MPH	FB%	WHF	CSP
2016	FRE	AAA	28	5	6	0	22	21	117	122	11	3.1	9.2	119	44%	.335	1.38	4.23	3.32	2.7				
2016	HOU	MLB	28	0	1	0	10	5	31²	21	6	4.0	8.0	28	41%	.190	1.11	3.69	4.84	0.2	94.1	52.6	8.7	49.7
2017	HOU	MLB	29	13	2	0	34	21	132	100	10	3.9	11.0	161	44%	.286	1.19	3.00	2.91	3.8	93.9	51.3	12.9	47.8
2018	HOU	MLB	30	3	5	3	61	1	65	56	11	2.8	13.3	96	37%	.317	1.17	3.46	2.54	1.8	94.6	54.6	13.9	45.4
2019	*HOU*	*MLB*	*31*	*7*	*4*	*0*	*54*	*13*	*108²*	*86*	*14*	*3.3*	*11.1*	*134*	*40%*	*.282*	*1.16*	*3.76*	*4.01*	*1.7*	*93.3*	*52.3*	*12.8*	*47*

Breakout: 34%   Improve: 62%   Collapse: 19%   Attrition: 16%   MLB: 94%   *Comparables: Glen Perkins, Juan Nicasio, Colby Lewis*

Much like Colin McHugh, it would seem as if Peacock's days as a starting pitcher are over. It's certainly not for a lack of chances, but history has seemed to prove that Peacock just doesn't have the longevity to last much farther than a run or two through the order. That will probably sit nicely with Houston, however, as his transition to the 'pen led to a drastic increase his strikeout rate and a significant drop in his walk rate. His overall durability doesn't seem to be an issue, either, as he was tied for the second-most games pitched on the team with 61. The promising starter who never quite produced has a new home in the Houston bullpen. In the past, this was seen as a demotion. In this new age of baseball, it's simply a new lease on life.

Cionel Perez LHP Born: 04/21/96 Age: 23 Bats: L Throws: L Height: 5'11" Weight: 170 Origin: International Free Agent, 2016

YEAR	TEAM	LVL	AGE	W	L	SV	G	GS	IP	H	HR	BB/9	K/9	K	GB%	BABIP	WHIP	ERA	DRA	WARP	MPH	FB%	WHF	CSP
2017	QUD	A	21	4	3	2	12	9	55¹	52	2	2.8	8.9	55	51%	.331	1.25	4.39	3.65	1.0				
2017	BCA	A+	21	2	1	0	5	4	25¹	27	1	1.8	6.4	18	46%	.325	1.26	2.84	3.58	0.5				
2017	CCH	AA	21	0	0	0	4	3	13	15	1	3.5	6.9	10	33%	.341	1.54	5.54	3.51	0.2				
2018	CCH	AA	22	6	1	1	16	11	68¹	54	3	2.9	10.9	83	47%	.304	1.11	1.98	3.08	1.7				
2018	HOU	MLB	22	0	0	0	8	0	11¹	6	3	5.6	9.5	12	58%	.130	1.15	3.97	4.58	0.0	96.9	63.2	11.8	41.6
2019	*HOU*	*MLB*	*23*	*4*	*3*	*0*	*39*	*8*	*72²*	*63*	*9*	*3.6*	*9.5*	*77*	*44%*	*.286*	*1.26*	*4.14*	*4.42*	*0.9*	*96.8*	*65.5*	*12.2*	*43.1*

Breakout: 10%   Improve: 13%   Collapse: 8%   Attrition: 15%   MLB: 29%   *Comparables: Matt Bowman, Buddy Baumann, Gio Gonzalez*

INTERIOR: *A kitchen in a middle-class home. A teenager enters and drops her backpack on the kitchen table.*

Mother: Hi Honey! How was school today?
Daughter: Fine.
Mother: Fine?
Daughter: Yep.
Mother: Just fine? Nothing interesting happened?
Daughter: No, Mom. I'd say my day was analogous to the pitching career of Houston prospect Cionel Perez. While nothing overtly promising developed, it also shouldn't be characterized as a failure or disappointment. It was ... fine. That is the most robust word that could be used to describe my day.
Mother: I don't like your tone.
Daughter: Well, I'm not crazy about Cionel Perez's walk rate during his admittedly short stint with the 2018 Astros. Yet, here we are. We cope.

Ryan Pressly RHP Born: 12/15/88 Age: 30 Bats: R Throws: R Height: 6'3" Weight: 210 Origin: Round 11, 2007 Draft (#354 overall)

YEAR	TEAM	LVL	AGE	W	L	SV	G	GS	IP	H	HR	BB/9	K/9	K	GB%	BABIP	WHIP	ERA	DRA	WARP	MPH	FB%	WHF	CSP
2016	MIN	MLB	27	6	7	1	72	0	75¹	79	8	2.7	8.0	67	41%	.311	1.35	3.70	3.90	0.9	98.0	54	12.3	47.6
2017	ROC	AAA	28	2	0	4	7	0	10	5	0	4.5	13.5	15	55%	.250	1.00	0.90	1.39	0.4				
2017	MIN	MLB	28	2	3	0	57	0	61¹	52	10	2.8	9.0	61	52%	.264	1.16	4.70	3.48	1.2	97.8	55	13.4	49.4
2018	MIN	MLB	29	1	1	0	51	0	47²	46	5	3.6	13.0	69	50%	.363	1.36	3.40	1.97	1.6	97.7	48.6	19.4	47.2
2018	HOU	MLB	29	1	0	2	26	0	23¹	11	1	1.2	12.3	32	62%	.213	0.60	0.77	1.73	0.9	97.5	34.7	17.7	47.6
2019	*HOU*	*MLB*	*30*	*3*	*1*	*5*	*57*	*0*	*60¹*	*46*	*6*	*3.3*	*11.2*	*75*	*48%*	*.282*	*1.14*	*3.47*	*3.69*	*0.9*	*97.0*	*50.1*	*15.4*	*47.9*

Breakout: 32%   Improve: 56%   Collapse: 18%   Attrition: 15%   MLB: 91%   *Comparables: Jason Frasor, Xavier Cedeno, Kevin Jepsen*

If you want definitive proof that saves are dead from an analytical standpoint, here you go. The Astros sent two prospects to Minnesota for Pressly's services, and it wasn't hard to see why when he landed in Houston. The long-time setup man honed his craft over the years, building up velocity and increasing the spin on his pitches, until he ultimately transformed himself into one of the best relievers in the game. Free from Minnesota's subpar overall defense, Pressly's numbers rose to meet his peripherals in spectacular fashion. He still has one more year of arbitration eligibility left, so expect Houston to utilize him and his extremely nasty slider as much as they can in 2019.

Hector Rondon   RHP   Born: 02/26/88   Age: 31   Bats: R   Throws: R   Height: 6'3"   Weight: 230   Origin: International Free Agent, 2004

YEAR	TEAM	LVL	AGE	W	L	SV	G	GS	IP	H	HR	BB/9	K/9	K	GB%	BABIP	WHIP	ERA	DRA	WARP	MPH	FB%	WHF	CSP
2016	CHN	MLB	28	2	3	18	54	0	51	42	8	1.4	10.2	58	49%	.274	0.98	3.53	2.52	1.4	98.5	63.3	11.7	50.1
2017	CHN	MLB	29	4	1	0	61	0	57¹	50	10	3.1	10.8	69	48%	.292	1.22	4.24	3.29	1.2	98.3	61.6	13	47.7
2018	HOU	MLB	30	2	5	15	63	0	59	58	4	3.1	10.2	67	48%	.340	1.32	3.20	2.81	1.4	98.8	61.7	14.7	48.9
2019	HOU	MLB	31	3	1	5	52	0	54²	46	7	3.1	9.9	60	47%	.280	1.18	3.81	4.07	0.6	97.7	61.6	13.4	48.5

Breakout: 27%   Improve: 42%   Collapse: 27%   Attrition: 6%   MLB: 89%   *Comparables: Bobby Jenks, Greg McMichael, Joakim Soria*

Former Cubs stalwart Hector Rondon was yet another addition for the 2018 Astros, a team desperate to address some surprising letdowns in their bullpen (or one with nothing else left to improve). Fallen from grace in Chicago, the Astros used him to bridge the gap between Giles and Osuna, and he turned in one of his better seasons to date despite battling some unlucky BABIP numbers. He'll be 31 as he plays the last of his two-year deal in 2019, and has shown no signs of stopping—even seeing an uptick in fastball velocity last season. Roster shuffling is always a factor, but Rondon should be in line to continue acting as a high-leverage reliever in the immediate future.

Tony Sipp   LHP   Born: 07/12/83   Age: 35   Bats: L   Throws: L   Height: 6'0"   Weight: 190   Origin: Round 45, 2004 Draft (#1333 overall)

YEAR	TEAM	LVL	AGE	W	L	SV	G	GS	IP	H	HR	BB/9	K/9	K	GB%	BABIP	WHIP	ERA	DRA	WARP	MPH	FB%	WHF	CSP
2016	HOU	MLB	32	1	2	1	60	0	43²	52	12	3.7	8.2	40	37%	.323	1.60	4.95	4.12	0.4	93.2	48.2	14	42.9
2017	HOU	MLB	33	0	1	0	46	0	37¹	36	8	3.9	9.4	39	50%	.277	1.39	5.79	4.77	0.2	92.2	49.4	13.5	43
2018	HOU	MLB	34	3	1	0	54	0	38²	27	1	3.0	9.8	42	42%	.277	1.03	1.86	2.69	1.0	93.5	52.7	14.7	48
2019	HOU	MLB	35	2	1	0	34	0	35²	30	5	3.8	9.5	38	42%	.275	1.27	4.37	4.68	0.1	91.8	49.4	13.9	44.2

Breakout: 21%   Improve: 40%   Collapse: 25%   Attrition: 10%   MLB: 88%   *Comparables: Kyle Farnsworth, Barney Schultz, Dan Miceli*

INTERIOR: *An overlit office at Baseball Gods headquarters.*
"Hey, Valerie. it's Dan down on the 188th floor. Hey…yeah, heck of a game. Anyway, hey, I'm calling about Tony Sipp. Sipp, two P's. Right, middle reliever. Hey, did he… did he make us angry in any way?…Well, it seems that after he signed his big deal with Houston, we made him a REALLY bad pitcher. Like worse than age or general attrition would explain even in the slightest. No…wait. Philip? The data entry guy we fired a while back? No Philip, two P's. Yeah, drunk on the job. No, I know we're always drunk. I mean way too drunk. I thought we caught all his mistakes, but I guess this one slipped through. Yeah. No, I'm just glad we figured it out. Yeah, this is gonna make for a weird stats page for him, but… right. We've done worse. I mean, we all remember Mike Norris. Ugh. OK, great, thanks Valerie. Still on for the Wild Card game tonight at O'Malleys? Great, see you there."

Joe Smith   RHP   Born: 03/22/84   Age: 35   Bats: R   Throws: R   Height: 6'2"   Weight: 205   Origin: Round 3, 2006 Draft (#94 overall)

YEAR	TEAM	LVL	AGE	W	L	SV	G	GS	IP	H	HR	BB/9	K/9	K	GB%	BABIP	WHIP	ERA	DRA	WARP	MPH	FB%	WHF	CSP
2016	ANA	MLB	32	1	4	6	38	0	37²	36	4	3.1	6.0	25	57%	.283	1.30	3.82	6.86	-0.8	90.6	63.5	9.2	44.8
2016	CHN	MLB	32	1	1	0	16	0	14¹	11	4	3.1	9.4	15	36%	.219	1.12	2.51	6.18	-0.2	90.6	57.8	9.4	47.7
2017	TOR	MLB	33	3	0	0	38	0	35²	30	3	2.5	12.9	51	44%	.342	1.12	3.28	3.28	0.8	90.6	67.7	13.4	52.8
2017	CLE	MLB	33	0	0	1	21	0	18¹	16	1	0.0	9.8	20	60%	.306	0.87	3.44	3.54	0.3	90.1	64.2	10.6	53.2
2018	HOU	MLB	34	5	1	0	56	0	45²	34	7	2.4	9.1	46	45%	.239	1.01	3.74	4.49	0.2	89.4	65.1	11.2	50.5
2019	HOU	MLB	35	1	1	0	26	0	27¹	23	3	3.4	9.1	28	46%	.277	1.22	4.11	4.39	0.2	88.9	63.6	10.9	49.2

Breakout: 22%   Improve: 43%   Collapse: 24%   Attrition: 11%   MLB: 87%   *Comparables: Akinori Otsuka, Scott Downs, Scott Eyre*

Joe Smith parlayed his penchant for embarrassing right-handed hitters into a two-year deal with Houston before the 2018 season. While it's unfair to say he regressed in 2018, in the sense that 2017 was probably the outlier, he didn't find the same successes due to a pretty significant dip in his strikeout rate and a bump in home run rate against righties. He did make the ALCS roster, which given the Astros' bullpen depth, is an achievement unto itself. If Smith can do some minor tweaking, he should bounce back as the righty-killer Houston hoped he'd be in 2019.

Jairo Solis   RHP   Born: 12/22/99   Age: 19   Bats: R   Throws: R   Height: 6'2"   Weight: 160   Origin: International Free Agent, 2016

YEAR	TEAM	LVL	AGE	W	L	SV	G	GS	IP	H	HR	BB/9	K/9	K	GB%	BABIP	WHIP	ERA	DRA	WARP	MPH	FB%	WHF	CSP
2017	DAR	ROK	17	1	1	0	6	4	26¹	20	2	2.7	9.6	28	57%	.277	1.06	2.73						
2017	AST	RK	17	1	0	0	5	4	21	19	1	3.0	10.3	24	43%	.305	1.24	3.00	3.88	0.5				
2017	GRV	RK	17	1	1	0	4	2	14	12	0	3.9	10.9	17	36%	.333	1.29	1.93	4.39	0.2				
2018	QUD	A	18	2	5	0	13	11	50²	49	1	5.7	9.1	51	47%	.345	1.60	3.55	5.34	-0.1				
2019	HOU	MLB	19	2	3	0	16	8	42	44	9	6.5	7.9	37	42%	.293	1.77	6.74	7.28	-1.2				

Comparables: Kelvin Herrera, Alex Sanabia, Wilfredo Boscan

The projectable Venezuelan righty Solis spent his age-18 summer pitching in full-season ball, which is quite a bit more than you can say for most teenagers summering in Davenport, Iowa. And that's the allure of our heroic young arm: not what he is, but what he might be, what he might end up weighing and how hard he might end up throwing. At the moment, he has a fastball he can place and a curve that he doesn't necessarily have to, given the count. That's not enough to finish the story, but it's more than enough reason to keep turning pages.

Framber Valdez LHP   Born: 11/19/93   Age: 25   Bats: L   Throws: L   Height: 5'11"   Weight: 170   Origin: International Free Agent, 2015

YEAR	TEAM	LVL	AGE	W	L	SV	G	GS	IP	H	HR	BB/9	K/9	K	GB%	BABIP	WHIP	ERA	DRA	WARP	MPH	FB%	WHF	CSP
2016	GRV	RK	22	1	0	0	2	2	10²	7	0	2.5	12.7	15	79%	.292	0.94	1.69	1.41	0.5				
2016	TCV	A-	22	2	1	0	5	2	21²	22	0	2.9	11.6	28	78%	.379	1.34	3.74	2.99	0.5				
2016	QUD	A	22	1	3	0	6	6	35¹	31	1	2.8	8.9	35	65%	.316	1.19	3.06	4.40	0.3				
2017	BCA	A+	23	2	3	1	13	9	61¹	41	3	4.3	10.7	73	57%	.257	1.14	2.79	3.54	1.2				
2017	CCH	AA	23	5	5	0	12	9	49	60	4	4.2	9.7	53	60%	.394	1.69	5.88	4.12	0.6				
2018	CCH	AA	24	4	5	1	20	13	94¹	92	7	2.8	11.4	120	58%	.363	1.28	4.10	3.58	1.8				
2018	FRE	AAA	24	2	0	0	2	1	8²	8	0	3.1	9.3	9	48%	.348	1.27	4.15	4.16	0.1				
2018	HOU	MLB	24	4	1	0	8	5	37	22	3	5.8	8.3	34	71%	.213	1.24	2.19	6.12	-0.4	94.3	69	8.9	43.9
2019	*HOU*	*MLB*	*25*	*5*	*4*	*0*	*37*	*11*	*82¹*	*73*	*9*	*3.9*	*9.5*	*87*	*54%*	*.296*	*1.31*	*4.09*	*4.36*	*1.3*	*94.0*	*70.7*	*9.1*	*44.9*

Breakout: 20%   Improve: 36%   Collapse: 24%   Attrition: 33%   MLB: 70%   *Comparables: Jeremy Jeffress, Luke Jackson, Enny Romero*

He's a short, beefy groundballin' lefty named Framber. (The listed weight might be, uh, a little light here.) Suffice to say, he's going to be a popular player for irony's sake if nothing else, but he's got a shot to be more than that. Valdez didn't make his pro debut until he was 21, downright ancient for a signing out of the Dominican, and is a testament to Houston knocking down every door to acquire talent. He got a lot of outs down the stretch for the Astros in a swingman role, although his characteristically good command deserted him and thus the rest of his line doesn't match the pretty ERA. The urge to make him a LOOGY as a small sinker/curveball lefty will be strong; that urge could limit a higher ceiling.

Justin Verlander RHP   Born: 02/20/83   Age: 36   Bats: R   Throws: R   Height: 6'5"   Weight: 225   Origin: Round 1, 2004 Draft (#2 overall)

YEAR	TEAM	LVL	AGE	W	L	SV	G	GS	IP	H	HR	BB/9	K/9	K	GB%	BABIP	WHIP	ERA	DRA	WARP	MPH	FB%	WHF	CSP
2016	DET	MLB	33	16	9	0	34	34	227²	171	30	2.3	10.0	254	35%	.255	1.00	3.04	3.40	5.1	96.8	57.3	13.4	45.8
2017	DET	MLB	34	10	8	0	28	28	172	153	23	3.5	9.2	176	34%	.283	1.28	3.82	4.03	3.0	97.3	58	11	47.8
2017	HOU	MLB	34	5	0	0	5	5	34	17	4	1.3	11.4	43	32%	.194	0.65	1.06	3.08	0.9	97.2	59.6	15.1	49.9
2018	HOU	MLB	35	16	9	0	34	34	214	156	28	1.6	12.2	290	31%	.272	0.90	2.52	2.33	7.3	97.1	61.2	16.2	51.6
2019	*HOU*	*MLB*	*36*	*12*	*9*	*0*	*29*	*29*	*182²*	*144*	*28*	*2.5*	*11.0*	*224*	*34%*	*.271*	*1.06*	*3.81*	*4.07*	*3.0*	*95.7*	*57.9*	*13.7*	*48*

Breakout: 15%   Improve: 38%   Collapse: 27%   Attrition: 10%   MLB: 89%   *Comparables: Jason Schmidt, Chris Carpenter, David Cone*

The Astros traded for Verlander at 11:59 PM on August 31, 2017, completing the deal literally two seconds before that season's waiver trade deadline. It's now pretty safe to say that one will go down as one of the best trades ever. Including two playoff runs, he's pitched to a 2.41 ERA over 302 innings as an Astro, with 388 strikeouts to only 58 walks. He's also added his seventh All-Star selection, the 2017 ALCS MVP trophy, and a World Series ring to a trophy case that already had a MVP, Cy Young, and Rookie of the Year from his Tigers days. He's Detroit's legend and Houston's hero, but he'll belong to Cooperstown six summers after he retires.

Forrest Whitley RHP   Born: 09/15/97   Age: 21   Bats: R   Throws: R   Height: 6'7"   Weight: 195   Origin: Round 1, 2016 Draft (#17 overall)

YEAR	TEAM	LVL	AGE	W	L	SV	G	GS	IP	H	HR	BB/9	K/9	K	GB%	BABIP	WHIP	ERA	DRA	WARP	MPH	FB%	WHF	CSP
2016	AST	RK	18	1	1	0	4	2	7¹	8	0	3.7	16.0	13	29%	.471	1.50	7.36	1.53	0.3				
2016	GRV	RK	18	0	1	0	4	4	11¹	11	0	2.4	10.3	13	53%	.344	1.24	3.18	2.34	0.4				
2017	QUD	A	19	2	3	0	12	10	46¹	42	2	4.1	13.0	67	37%	.388	1.36	2.91	3.10	1.2				
2017	BCA	A+	19	3	1	0	7	6	31¹	28	2	2.6	14.4	50	40%	.394	1.18	3.16	2.06	1.2				
2017	CCH	AA	19	0	0	0	4	2	14²	8	1	2.5	16.0	26	48%	.292	0.82	1.84	2.15	0.5				
2018	CCH	AA	20	0	2	0	8	8	26¹	15	2	3.8	11.6	34	39%	.220	0.99	3.76	3.49	0.6				
2019	*HOU*	*MLB*	*21*	*6*	*5*	*0*	*21*	*16*	*90¹*	*78*	*13*	*4.3*	*10.8*	*108*	*39%*	*.292*	*1.34*	*4.53*	*4.85*	*0.6*				

Breakout: 9%   Improve: 15%   Collapse: 8%   Attrition: 14%   MLB: 27%   *Comparables: Jake McGee, Robert Stephenson, Trevor May*

Baseball's top pitching prospect had the *Brooklyn Nine-Nine* of baseball seasons. Coming off a brilliant emergence, Whitley's first 50 games in 2018 were cancelled due to a drug suspension, and he later missed more time with oblique and lat problems. While it all combined to cost him his chance to make the majors before he could legally drink, the Arizona Fall League served as his NBC, a triumphant return just to remind everyone about all the plus pitches. He even touched triple digits in the Fall Stars game. He's only a handful of healthy and good starts away from The Show; exactly how many will depend on how aggressively his service time is manipulated. We can only hope *Nine-Nine*'s future is so bright.

LINEOUTS

Hitters

HITTER	POS	TEAM	LVL	AGE	PA	R	2B	3B	HR	RBI	BB	K	SB	CS	AVG/OBP/SLG	DRC+	VORP	BABIP	BRR	FRAA	WARP
Jose Alvarez	C	DAB	Rk	18	152	23	8	0	0	15	17	27	5	2	.359/.434/.420	102	19.8	.443	-1.3	C(32): 0.5, 1B(9): 0.1	0.5
Jonathan Arauz	SS	QUD	A	19	237	31	11	6	4	29	30	38	7	6	.299/.392/.471	132	22.0	.350	0.4	SS(33): 0.6, 2B(17): 0.4	1.9
	SS	BCA	A+	19	253	25	10	3	4	18	16	36	1	2	.167/.223/.288	80	-1.6	.180	-2.6	SS(70): -5.5, 2B(1): -0.1	-0.4
J.J. Matijevic	LF	QUD	A	22	56	8	6	1	3	5	8	10	3	0	.354/.446/.708	132	7.4	.400	0.0	LF(12): -1.6	0.2
	LF	BCA	A+	22	376	58	20	3	19	57	36	103	10	13	.266/.335/.513	127	25.3	.323	-2.0	LF(49): -2.1	1.5
Alex McKenna	CF	TCV	A-	20	137	14	7	1	5	21	11	24	6	5	.328/.423/.534	149	18.8	.375	0.6	CF(22): -1.4, RF(4): 1.4	1.3
	CF	QUD	A	20	51	5	1	1	2	7	3	16	0	0	.271/.314/.458	94	0.8	.367	-0.9	CF(8): -1.1	-0.1
Andy Pineda	LF	CCH	AA	21	71	9	2	6	2	4	6	16	3	3	.338/.394/.492	94	2.6	.426	-1.6	LF(15): -0.3	-0.1
	LF	TCV	A-	21	103	15	4	2	1	4	10	27	9	3	.253/.340/.374	85	3.6	.349	0.5	CF(10): 0.6, LF(9): -0.5	0.2
Garrett Stubbs	C	FRE	AAA	25	340	60	19	6	4	38	35	53	6	0	.310/.382/.455	111	30.6	.361	3.0	C(75): 10.5, RF(2): -0.2	3.5

HITTER	POS	TEAM	LVL	AGE	PA	R	2B	3B	HR	RBI	BB	K	SB	CS	AVG/OBP/SLG	DRC+	VORP	BABIP	BRR	FRAA	WARP
Abraham Toro-Hernandez	3B	BCA	A+	21	349	54	20	1	14	56	45	62	5	1	.257/.361/.473	133	31.1	.278	1.7	3B(81): 3.4	3.2
	3B	CCH	AA	21	202	16	15	2	2	22	17	46	3	3	.230/.317/.371	87	1.1	.298	-2.6	3B(43): -0.7	0.0

Jose Alvarez is a teenage catcher who hasn't been stateside yet, so in prospect terms, the light from him is so far away it hasn't reached earth. But what a fun batting line 2018 was! ⓧ Switch-hitting middle infielder **Jonathan Arauz** has a swing as graceful as the matador's cape, and carries about the same amount of weight behind it. ⓧ Astros 2017 second-rounder **J. J. Matijevic** swings a lot, shows a good deal of power, and offers the defensive value of someone who swings a lot and shows a good deal of power. Imagine if C.J. Cron were younger and had a name that was much harder to spell. ⓧ Big West Conference Player of the Year **Alex McKenna** raked nearly as much with wooden bats in his pro debut as he did with the composite bats at Cal Poly. ⓧ Houston drafted **Joe Perez** in 2017's second round knowing he'd need Tommy John surgery. He's only made a cameo appearance in the GCL to date, and the toolsy prepster could yet end up on the mound instead of in the infield. ⓧ **Andy Pineda** doesn't look like a power hitter (5 career home runs in a thousand plate appearances), but his outs go farther than you'd expect, and that combined with the hit tool marks him as perhaps the deepest sleeper in this book. ⓧ **Garrett Stubbs** is well-positioned to join the fraternity of long-term backup catchers, though he possesses sneaky athleticism and a sprinkle of hitting potential to go along with the pre-installed nickname and the usual strong defensive reputation. ⓧ Trilingual Montreal native **Abraham Toro-Hernandez** was drafted out of Seminole State College in Oklahoma, the same school as fellow Quebecer Eric Gagne. May he match Gagne's utter brilliance in the majors some day.

Pitchers

PITCHER	TEAM	LVL	AGE	W	L	SV	G	GS	IP	H	HR	BB/9	K/9	K	GB%	BABIP	WHIP	ERA	DRA	WARP	MPH	FB%	WHF	CSP
Brett Adcock	BCA	A+	22	5	3	1	16	9	67¹	32	1	4.8	9.0	67	49%	.189	1.01	2.54	3.21	1.6				
	CCH	AA	22	4	2	0	9	5	38²	34	2	5.1	6.5	28	35%	.281	1.45	3.49	4.44	0.3				
Brandon Bielak	BCA	A+	22	5	3	2	14	7	55²	44	2	2.7	12.0	74	43%	.331	1.10	2.10	2.50	1.7				
	CCH	AA	22	2	5	0	11	10	61¹	52	4	3.2	8.4	57	51%	.294	1.21	2.35	4.18	0.8				
Dean Deetz	FRE	AAA	24	2	0	0	21	0	34	22	1	4.8	13.2	50	49%	.304	1.18	0.79	2.52	1.0				
	HOU	MLB	24	0	0	0	4	0	3¹	4	1	2.7	8.1	3	30%	.333	1.50	5.40	6.63	-0.1	96.0	57.6	11.9	47.7
Reymin Guduan	FRE	AAA	26	3	3	2	43	0	55¹	46	5	5.2	13.5	83	55%	.328	1.41	3.74	1.82	2.1				
	HOU	MLB	26	0	0	0	3	0	3¹	1	1	0.0	10.8	4	14%	.000	0.30	2.70	2.91	0.1	97.6	55	17.5	43.8
Ryan Hartman	CCH	AA	24	11	4	0	25	18	120²	104	11	1.9	10.7	143	43%	.314	1.08	2.69	2.76	3.5				
Tyler Ivey	QUD	A	22	1	3	2	9	6	41²	36	2	1.7	11.4	53	50%	.315	1.06	3.46	2.29	1.4				
	BCA	A+	22	3	3	1	15	12	70¹	50	3	2.7	10.5	82	56%	.267	1.01	2.69	2.92	1.9				
Ernesto Jaquez	DAB	Rk	19	4	0	0	9	4	36	10	0	2.2	12.2	49	63%	.149	0.53	1.25	1.33	1.7				
	AST	Rk	19	0	0	0	5	1	17	9	1	2.6	11.1	21	46%	.211	0.82	1.06	2.65	0.6				
Cristian Javier	QUD	A	21	2	2	1	11	7	49¹	28	3	4.2	14.6	80	32%	.281	1.03	1.82	2.00	1.8				
	BCA	A+	21	5	4	0	14	11	60²	44	6	4.0	9.8	66	33%	.257	1.17	3.41	3.28	1.4				
Brady Rodgers	BCA	A+	27	0	0	0	4	4	12	12	0	0.0	5.2	7	59%	.308	1.00	1.50	2.55	0.4				
	FRE	AAA	27	3	3	0	8	8	41	48	4	2.2	6.6	30	38%	.333	1.41	5.49	4.43	0.5				
Jayson Schroeder	AST	Rk	18	0	0	0	7	5	18	13	0	4.5	9.0	18	49%	.302	1.22	1.50	4.02	0.4				

Brett Adcock has battled walks since he was a Michigan Man, but as a lefty with a good curve he'll get enough shots to need to Uber it home from the bar. ⓧ **Brandon Bielak** has better stuff than the usual late-round college pitcher shooting through the minors, and has a chance to contribute soon, likely in a relief role. ⓧ **Dean Deetz** returned from an 80-game PED suspension as a dominant Triple-A reliever, eventually making the majors in September. In so doing he fulfilled years of Wilson Karaman's predictions that he'd eventually figure out how to harness his big fastball and wipeout breaking ball. ⓧ It's hard to imagine the Astros actually needing **Reymin Guduan**, but he's here, he's left-handed and he throws hard. Some other team will eventually give him a chance to figure out the strike zone in some 8-3 losses. ⓧ **Jandel Gustave** spent the season recovering from Tommy John and will spend the offseason looking for work, having elected free agency. Recovering his command might take a while, but he's a worthwhile project for some team. ⓧ **Ryan Hartman** doesn't impress the scouts with his stuff, but that production at Double-A is just over the line of "let's wait and see how long it takes him to start failing." ⓧ **Tyler Ivey** has four pitches, throws strikes, and breezed through A-ball, but he'll need to pass that age-old Double-A test before we go all in. ⓧ **Ernesto Jaquez's** (very) brief taste of A-ball was a bit too spicy, but the teenager's prior performance and ability to command four pitches make his name one worth filing away. ⓧ These days on the minors beat you'll see a ton of young pitchers who clearly grew up watching either Pedro Martinez or Cole Hamels, and well, **Cristian Javier** is a Dominican righty with a change and a very familiar looking motion. He even wore number 45 for Quad Cities. ⓧ **Brady Rodgers** had just barely reached the top of the ladder when he was felled by a second TJS in 2017. He looked as good as ever in his late-2018 rehab, which is to say, he looked like a command-oriented, pitch-to-contact seventh starter. ⓧ If you've made it this far in, you can probably guess that the future for second-rounder **Jayson Schroeder** is pretty bright given Houston's wildly successful recent track record with identifying and developing projectable arms.

KANSAS CITY ROYALS

Essay by Craig Brown

Player comments by Jon Hegglund and BP staff

It's a good thing flags fly forever. The Royals' 2015 pennant feels like a lifetime ago.

Time is unforgiving, especially in baseball. Win a championship? That was great. Now, do it again. Yesterday was so much fun and we'll never forget the good times, but what are you going to do for me today? The fiscal realities of the game mean it's difficult to keep together a title-winning team for an extended period. That can go for double in baseball's smaller markets. This is nothing new. It's the economics of certainty.

After winning back-to-back American League pennants and reaching the summit in 2015, the goal in Kansas City was to keep their window of contention open as long as possible. Knowing their core players were under team control through at least the 2017 season, the Royals went for the ring again in 2016, spending $72 million to retain Alex Gordon and another $70 million and a first-round draft pick to add Ian Kennedy. For good measure, they splashed the cash on their bullpen, bringing back Joakim Soria on a $25 million deal. Payroll jumped to $131 million, rarefied air for a team of the Royals' means, and placing them firmly in baseball's middle class.

They won 81 games and finished in third place.

Undaunted, they went for it one final time the following season. They didn't make the same kind of noisy free agent signings, but the Royals did refuse to trade their most valuable assets in impending free agents Eric Hosmer, Mike Moustakas and Lorenzo Cain. Payroll increased to $143 million, which again placed the Royals in the middle of the fiscal pack.

They won 80 games and finished in third place.

And just like that, the Royals' window of contention slammed shut.

⚾   ⚾   ⚾

That quick rehash of the recent past wasn't meant as a direct history lesson, per se. Rather, it's a look into how the Royals' front office operates under general manager Dayton Moore, which is important when attempting to understand what comes next. Moore and his staff knew the reckoning was rapidly arriving, yet they still sought to delay the grim

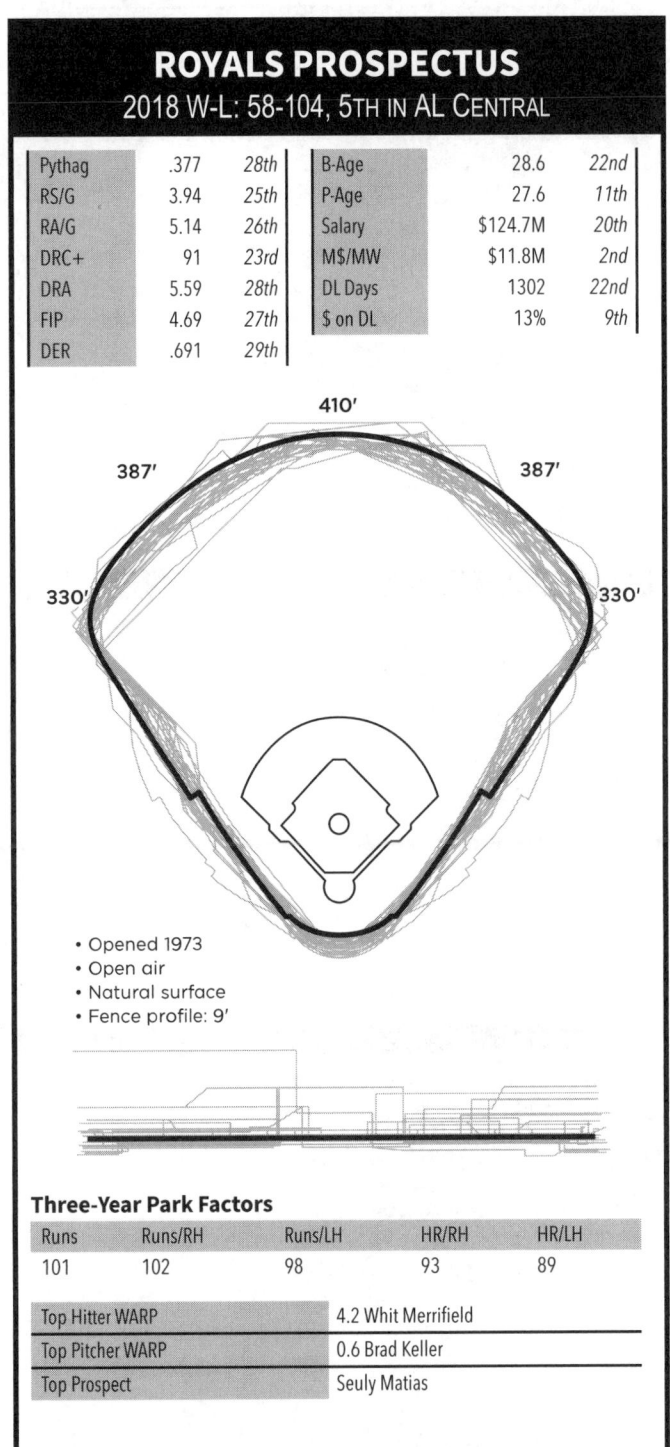

ROYALS PROSPECTUS
2018 W-L: 58-104, 5TH IN AL CENTRAL

Pythag	.377	28th	B-Age	28.6		22nd
RS/G	3.94	25th	P-Age	27.6		11th
RA/G	5.14	26th	Salary	$124.7M		20th
DRC+	91	23rd	M$/MW	$11.8M		2nd
DRA	5.59	28th	DL Days	1302		22nd
FIP	4.69	27th	$ on DL	13%		9th
DER	.691	29th				

410'
387'   387'
330'   330'

- Opened 1973
- Open air
- Natural surface
- Fence profile: 9'

Three-Year Park Factors

Runs	Runs/RH	Runs/LH	HR/RH	HR/LH
101	102	98	93	89

Top Hitter WARP	4.2 Whit Merrifield
Top Pitcher WARP	0.6 Brad Keller
Top Prospect	Seuly Matias

187

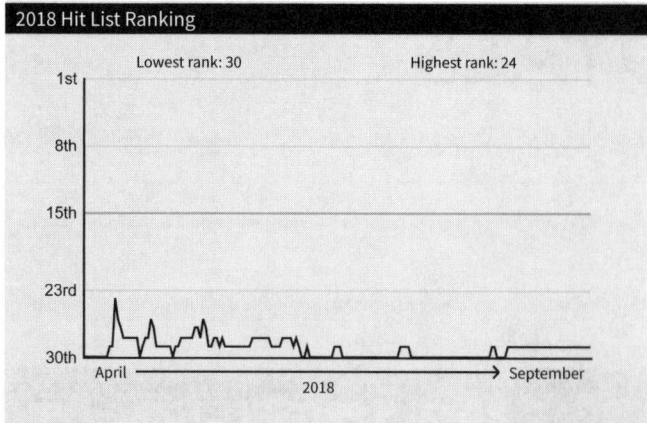

2018 Hit List Ranking

Lowest rank: 30   Highest rank: 24

April ——————————→ September
2018

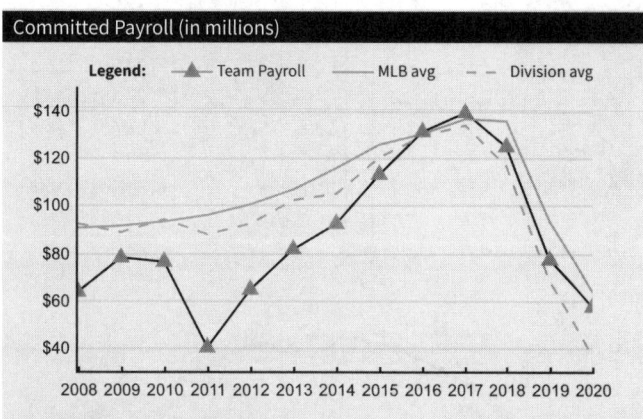

Committed Payroll (in millions)

Legend: ▲ Team Payroll   — MLB avg   - - Division avg

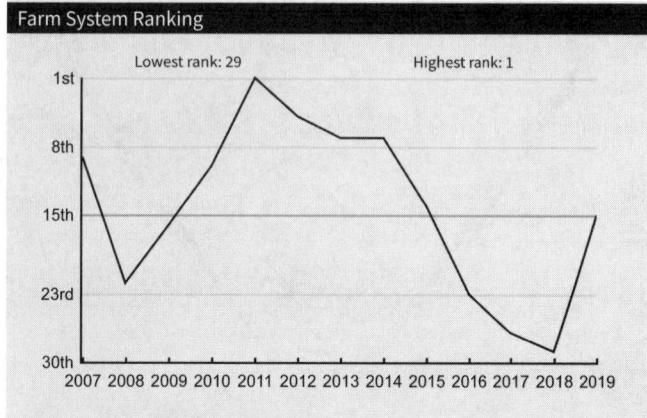

Farm System Ranking

Lowest rank: 29   Highest rank: 1

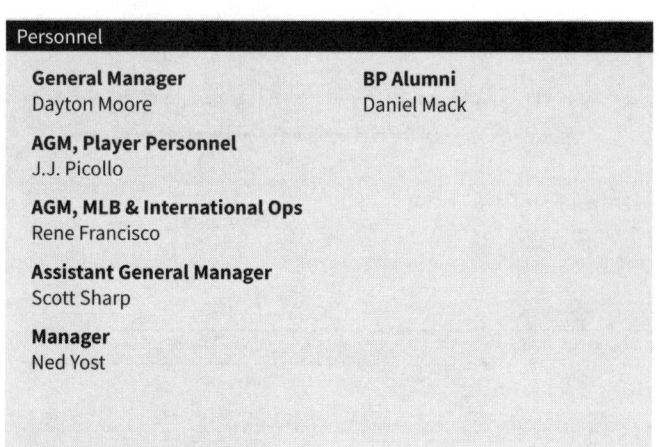

Personnel

General Manager
Dayton Moore

AGM, Player Personnel
J.J. Picollo

AGM, MLB & International Ops
Rene Francisco

Assistant General Manager
Scott Sharp

Manager
Ned Yost

BP Alumni
Daniel Mack

necessity of a rebuild as long as possible. They would spend money. They would trade prospects. They would attempt to compete. Damn the realities. They felt they owed at least that much to their players and their fans.

Sometimes, you can trip over sentimentality. Your head tells you to do one thing, while your heart pulls you in another direction. In this instance, neglecting the realities of the situation by chasing that elusive spot in the postseason, the Royals simply delayed the inevitable. They neglected the future because they were so focused on the present. By refusing to trade their most valuable players in exchange for cost-controlled prospects to stock the organization, they dug a deeper hole for themselves once the rebuild commenced. As Stinger once told Maverick, the Royals' ego was writing checks their body couldn't cash.

Most teams in the Royals' position would go for a full teardown. The middle ground—that area the Royals occupied in 2016 and 2017—is now considered the equivalent of baseball's Siberia. In this no-man's land, the abyss occupied between 75 and 89 wins is where a franchise isn't good enough to qualify for the postseason and not bad enough to restock the farm system with top-10 picks. Lather, rinse, repeat. It turns out there's a high price to pay for mediocrity.

⚾   ⚾   ⚾

Here's where things get tricky. Yes, it's obvious at this point that the Royals should tear everything down, absorb the losses on the field in the short term and begin constructing a plan to rebuild for the long term. Yet forget about losing today to build for tomorrow. Moore abhors the idea of losing, any time. That shapes his philosophy as a general manager more than just about anything else. They will not tank and they are loathe to use the term rebuild when describing where they are in their process. They pursued bringing back Hosmer. They took advantage of a stagnant free agent market and re-signed Moustakas. They were happy to stake out that middle ground. To Moore, tanking is cheating the paying customer and rebuilding is a three-syllable word for making excuses.

That's fine and all, but it ignored the harsh reality that the 2018 Royals just weren't going to be any good. They entered the season knowing wins would be difficult to come by, but they didn't expect the utter wretchedness that would define their team through the first five months. Internal expectations pegged them closer to 72 wins. Maybe 67 if they couldn't catch a few breaks. But 58? Somehow, they found that number to be unimaginable. It was the reality. They still insisted they were not among the teams tanking and losing on purpose, but how could you tell?

From June 1 to the All-Star break, they won seven times in 39 games. In August, they dropped to 52 games below .500, the furthest behind the break-even point in franchise history. They were, at one point, on pace to lose almost 115 games. They were giving the Baltimore Orioles a race to the bottom of the pile and the right to select first in the 2019 draft. They were boring and they were dreadful. It was, frankly, a chore to watch them play.

If they weren't tanking, then what the hell were they doing?

⚾ ⚾ ⚾

During the first go-around (known, now fondly, in Kansas City as simply, The Process) it took Moore and his staff close to five years to build a minor-league system that would be the envy of baseball. The Farm System Ranking in the sidebar shows the organization at no. 1 in 2011, but that doesn't quite do the overall strength of the system at that time proper justice. In that year's publication, Royals minor leaguers occupied 10 spots in BP's Top 101 Prospects list. By the time the Royals slammed into the end of their competitive window, the prospect cupboard was bare. (Again, refer to the Farm System Ranking that resembles a stockbroker's nightmare or an Austrian downhill course Lindsay Von would attack.)

Trades, player development busts and a few years of questionable drafting with later-round picks due to their major-league success conspired to strip a once-envied system into one most notable for an abyss of impact talent. So the Royals set about assembling depth. The ascent from close to rock bottom has begun. It's not a sexy farm system, but it's functional. The bad drafts and the trades made during the championship years mean there's little of potential impact in the upper levels, and it's likely to remain that way for another year or two. Indeed, the marrow of the minors was found last summer with the Single-A Lexington Legends. Six of the organization's current top 10 prospects spent some or all of 2018 playing for the Sally League champs.

The Royals will take most of that group and bump them a level this season. And they'll repeat the process for the next year, and then probably the next, keeping the majority together until they're ready to break into the majors. This is The Process 2.0. The blueprint of this rebuild can be found in the roots of the original Process when Hosmer, Moustakas, Danny Duffy and others joined forces at the lower levels of the organization and started charging to minor-league championships before arriving in Kansas City. It's about creating a culture of winning that's important to Moore. You undercut that culture when you lose on purpose to position yourself for future success. Moore has done it before. He has a ring. He trusts his process. But this time may be different.

The Process 2.0 is unique in that it abhors the losses generally marked by rebuilding. While restocking the minors is happening, the major-league team is looking for major-league players. Or in Royals parlance, action-type players. They spent $3 million on Chris Owings to be a utilityman. They tossed $5.25 million at Billy Hamilton. They gave Terrance Gore—owner of one hit and 27 steals spread over five big-league seasons—a major-league contract. These are the offseason moves of a marginal contender looking to fill

a few areas of need with moderately useful players. On the Royals, they will be counted on to save the team from 95 losses. They are not tanking.

The Process 2.0 cares not for conventional wisdom.

⚾ ⚾ ⚾

It's still a rebuild, damnit, even if the Royals don't want to use that word. For The Process 2.0 to work they'll need pitching, and the Royals know better than perhaps any other team how difficult it is to develop starting pitching.

Thanks to last offseason's free agents signing elsewhere after rejecting qualifying offers, the Royals entered the 2018 draft with the highest signing bonus pool available. They leveraged every dollar, going over-slot with their first-round selection, Florida Gators right-hander Brady Singer, and following that pick with four more college arms in the first two rounds. They broke that string to select a pair of college center fielders and then returned to the college pitching well for the next three picks. They didn't draft a high schooler until their 12th pick. Led by Singer, four of those pitchers (Jackson Kowar, Brady Lynch, Kris Bubic) are represented in the Royals' top 10 prospects, and Lynch and Bubic were instrumental in Lexington's title run.

The plan, it seems, is to inject the college draftees into a system where most of the talent resides in the bottom half. Add quantity to the quality that already exists. There are no sure things in prospecting, so hedge your bets and stock more high-upside prospects into your system. It just might work. Maybe this can accelerate the timetable of The Process 2.0. Moore, who once proclaimed that good decisions could accelerate a five-year plan into a three-year plan while bad decisions could turn a ten-year plan into no plan, is understandably hesitant to place a timetable on exactly when these Royals could return to relevance. From a strategic standpoint, it makes sense to manage expectations.

This is where the Royals front office ran afoul during their first rebuild. Nobody in Kansas City pines for the days of Jose Guillen, right fielder. Instead, Moore provides markers and suggested milestones. The plan for the next couple of years will be to shed expensive contracts while restocking the farm system. If it walks like a rebuild and talks like a rebuild, it's probably a rebuild. The problem is the bad contracts are so awful that it won't be easy to find willing partners to deal. The potential upside of gaining a decent prospect in exchange for someone like Kennedy comes with a more realistic downside in which the Royals would have to sweeten the offer by including a young, cost-controlled player of their own just to rid themselves of an odious contract. One step forward while taking two steps back is no way to gain ground.

Instead, Moore points to 2021 as the year where The Process 2.0 will come into clearer focus. By then, the Royals will have separated the wheat from the chaff of this current prospect crop and they will be clear of the heaviest of their financial obligations. The team will presumably lose plenty of games in the meantime, so they will have the advantage of high draft picks and the bonus pool that goes with those. It also means at least two more years of not-rebuilding.

☾   ☾   ☾

A funny thing happened down the stretch last summer: The Royals started winning, finishing the season by going 20-14. This coincided with the arrival of Adalberto Mondesi, who finally appeared ready to live up to the prospect expectations that have orbited around him since signing as a 16-year-old out of the Dominican Republic. The less unheralded Ryan O'Hearn got a late-season call-up and smashed 12 dingers in 170 plate appearances after homering only 11 times in Triple-A. They combined with Whit Merrifield—who at age 30 is the Royals' best player and most attractive trade chip—at the top of the order to bring back fond memories of the "Keep The Line Moving" days. The pitching was a little better. The hitting was timely. It also ran

parallel to what Moore said was a conscious decision to stop talking about the rebuild. One of these reasons is not like the other.

Beware the September paper tigers. The desire to drop payroll under $100 million is understandable given there's no sense in throwing good money after bad baseball. Still, they're not tanking! Things are not necessarily going to be worse than last year, but it's a stretch to see them being much better. This season will feel like last season, and judging by where the Royals' farm system stands, with the bulk of the talent in the lower minors, 2020 will be similar. They can avoid the word "rebuild" all they like, but that won't change the reality. The Process 2.0 is still in its infancy. It's going to be another long summer in Kansas City.

At least those flags remain just beyond the left field wall, still flying. ◼

—Craig Brown is an author of Baseball Prospectus.

HITTERS

Jorge Bonifacio RF
Born: 06/04/93   Age: 26   Bats: R   Throws: R   Height: 6'1"   Weight: 225   Origin: International Free Agent, 2009

YEAR	TEAM	LVL	AGE	PA	R	2B	3B	HR	RBI	BB	K	SB	CS	AVG/OBP/SLG	DRC+	VORP	BABIP	BRR	FRAA	WARP
2016	OMA	AAA	23	558	82	22	6	19	86	51	130	6	2	.277/.351/.461	116	29.3	.339	1.2	RF(72): 13.8, LF(50): 7.0	4.7
2017	OMA	AAA	24	57	6	2	2	3	12	6	8	0	0	.314/.386/.608	134	3.9	.325	-0.9	RF(9): 0.1, LF(3): 0.0	0.3
2017	KCA	MLB	24	422	55	15	1	17	40	35	118	1	1	.255/.320/.432	93	5.3	.324	-0.1	RF(92): -9.9, LF(9): -0.5	-0.5
2018	OMA	AAA	25	58	11	5	1	0	9	7	12	0	0	.392/.466/.529	100	5.4	.513	-0.2	RF(13): -1.2	0.0
2018	KCA	MLB	25	270	31	16	2	4	23	29	71	0	1	.225/.312/.360	81	2.1	.301	0.0	RF(55): -0.8, LF(7): -1.0	-0.2
2019	*KCA*	*MLB*	*26*	*354*	*39*	*17*	*2*	*10*	*39*	*34*	*91*	*1*	*1*	*.237/.317/.393*	*98*	*7.5*	*.302*	*0.2*	*RF -2, LF 0*	*0.7*

Breakout: 5%   Improve: 52%   Collapse: 10%   Attrition: 16%   MLB: 88%   *Comparables: Josh Reddick, Brandon Moss, Corey Hart*

The 2018 Royals posed the riddle: You have three outfield positions, but only fourth and fifth outfielders on your roster—what do you do? Part of the answer involved another long look at Bonifacio, who gave cause for encouragement with a 2017 season that held glimmers of promise. After an 80-game PED suspension nixed the first half of 2018, Bonifacio failed to impress in the second half, swiping the mantle of "Most Disappointing Outfield Jorge" from teammate Soler. On the brighter side, the Royals can certainly afford to dole out second (and third) chances, and the thin gruel of improving walk and strikeout rates may be enough to feed visions of mid-20s growth for Georgie Good Face.

Cheslor Cuthbert 3B
Born: 11/16/92   Age: 26   Bats: R   Throws: R   Height: 6'1"   Weight: 210   Origin: International Free Agent, 2009

YEAR	TEAM	LVL	AGE	PA	R	2B	3B	HR	RBI	BB	K	SB	CS	AVG/OBP/SLG	DRC+	VORP	BABIP	BRR	FRAA	WARP
2016	OMA	AAA	23	107	15	4	1	7	28	11	14	0	1	.333/.402/.624	143	14.8	.324	-1.4	3B(21): -2.0, 1B(3): 0.0	0.6
2016	KCA	MLB	23	510	49	28	1	12	46	32	96	2	0	.274/.318/.413	89	5.9	.320	-5.1	3B(127): -2.1	0.5
2017	OMA	AAA	24	68	10	3	1	4	9	7	11	0	0	.271/.353/.559	123	4.8	.267	0.0	3B(10): 0.6, 1B(2): -0.2	0.4
2017	KCA	MLB	24	153	10	7	0	2	18	9	39	0	0	.231/.275/.322	69	-1.7	.301	0.2	3B(44): 0.6, 1B(6): 0.0	0.0
2018	KCA	MLB	25	117	11	2	0	3	7	11	23	0	1	.194/.282/.301	92	-3.7	.218	0.6	3B(12): 0.1, 1B(10): -0.9	0.1
2019	*KCA*	*MLB*	*26*	*142*	*14*	*7*	*1*	*4*	*16*	*11*	*28*	*0*	*0*	*.248/.314/.391*	*101*	*1.6*	*.290*	*-0.6*	*1B -2*	*-0.1*

Breakout: 5%   Improve: 53%   Collapse: 8%   Attrition: 18%   MLB: 95%   *Comparables: Willy Aybar, Matt Duffy, Wilmer Flores*

A news item that may have escaped mainstream notice: shortly after the conclusion of the 2018 regular season, Royals GM Dayton Moore wrote a formal request to MLB Commissioner Rob Manfred "to retire the position of third base for the Kansas City Royals organization, such that the team will no longer have the responsibility of covering that position for the remainder of time that the franchise remains active in Major League Baseball." The irredeemable fall from the greatness of George Brett, and the okay-ness of Mike Moustakas, were cited in the request. The somewhat informal phrasing "have you even seen our org depth chart?!" was used in an otherwise blandly bureaucratic document. When that request was (unsurprisingly) rejected, Brett himself was called, Moore probing lightly as to the question of his physical fitness in a potential age-66 comeback season. A perfunctory search of the Rolodex for Mark Teahen's agent was conducted. Hunter Dozier reluctantly began taking grounders at the hot corner again, with mutterings about (expletive) Ryan (expletive) O'Hearn and "that was *my* job" overheard. For three days, Moore felt uneasy. He felt like he had forgotten where he put his keys, or temporarily blanked on his Social Security number. Then it came to him. "Cuthbert. We've still got Cuthbert, right?" He sighed audibly. "Yep, I guess we've still got Cuthbert."

Hunter Dozier 1B   Born: 08/22/91   Age: 27   Bats: R   Throws: R   Height: 6'4"   Weight: 220   Origin: Round 1, 2013 Draft (#8 overall)

YEAR	TEAM	LVL	AGE	PA	R	2B	3B	HR	RBI	BB	K	SB	CS	AVG/OBP/SLG	DRC+	VORP	BABIP	BRR	FRAA	WARP
2016	NWA	AA	24	110	14	8	0	8	21	14	23	4	0	.305/.400/.642	155	14.5	.328	0.1	3B(19): -0.3, LF(6): -1.2	0.9
2016	OMA	AAA	24	434	65	36	1	15	54	40	100	3	1	.294/.357/.506	107	31.6	.358	0.9	3B(63): -6.6, RF(14): 1.0	1.2
2016	KCA	MLB	24	21	4	1	0	0	1	2	8	0	0	.211/.286/.263	64	-0.2	.364	0.0	RF(7): -0.2	-0.1
2017	OMA	AAA	25	96	11	6	1	4	12	9	37	1	1	.226/.313/.464	62	4.0	.341	-0.3	RF(10): -0.1, 3B(7): -0.3	-0.3
2018	OMA	AAA	26	143	18	7	0	1	11	24	43	2	1	.254/.385/.339	86	5.4	.392	-0.2	3B(19): 0.6, RF(13): 1.2	0.3
2018	KCA	MLB	26	388	36	19	4	11	34	24	109	2	3	.229/.278/.395	77	-4.7	.296	-0.3	1B(51): -7.5, 3B(37): -5.9	-1.6
2019	KCA	MLB	27	533	52	19	2	15	58	41	169	4	2	.207/.276/.349	68	-9.2	.284	0.2	3B -9, 1B -1	-2.0

Breakout: 5%   Improve: 26%   Collapse: 13%   Attrition: 24%   MLB: 56%   *Comparables: Mike Carp, Jeff Baker, Mark Canha*

On February 4, 2017, Dozier posted a video to his Instagram account. You've seen these before, especially with baseball players: his partner tosses a plastic ball filled with colored powder, either pink or blue, indicating the biological sex of their unborn child. Amanda, his wife, gives him an underhand toss a bit inside, but Dozier keeps his hands in and squares up, the ball exploding blue powder. The first comment on the post, from "nsyndergaard": "Surprised you didn't whiff." Dozier and Thor are friends, but sometimes our pals can hide hard truths in levity: Dozier has run K rates around 30 percent across Triple-A and the majors over the past two seasons, and this, along with marginal defense, is keeping him from assuming the third-base mantle of the Moose. This season promises an opportunity—perhaps the final one—for Dozier to make memories on the baseball diamond that will be favorited beyond his circle of family and friends.

Alcides Escobar SS   Born: 12/16/86   Age: 32   Bats: R   Throws: R   Height: 6'1"   Weight: 205   Origin: International Free Agent, 2003

YEAR	TEAM	LVL	AGE	PA	R	2B	3B	HR	RBI	BB	K	SB	CS	AVG/OBP/SLG	DRC+	VORP	BABIP	BRR	FRAA	WARP
2016	KCA	MLB	29	682	57	24	6	7	55	27	96	17	4	.261/.292/.350	78	5.8	.295	0.4	SS(162): 0.8	1.5
2017	KCA	MLB	30	629	71	36	5	6	54	15	102	4	7	.250/.272/.357	66	3.1	.291	0.6	SS(162): 10.0	1.4
2018	KCA	MLB	31	531	54	22	3	4	34	29	74	8	2	.231/.279/.313	73	-1.3	.263	0.0	SS(104): -10.3, 3B(29): 1.3	-0.4
2019	KCA	MLB	32	520	50	25	3	7	46	26	79	8	4	.253/.297/.362	77	3.7	.284	0.1	SS -1, 3B -1	0.2

Breakout: 6%   Improve: 41%   Collapse: 6%   Attrition: 22%   MLB: 92%   *Comparables: Bill Russell, Jimmy Cooney, Bob Lillis*

INT. GENERAL MANAGER'S OFFICE. KAUFFMAN STADIUM. As we pan across the room, we see family photographs, framed awards, memorabilia. The camera lingers on a team photo, emblazoned with the legend: "2015 World Champions." We settle on a side view of DAYTON MOORE, well-tanned, middle-aged, wearing a blue polo shirt and sporting a tidy crew cut. As he picks up the office phone, the electronic desk calendar shows a monthly view: "January 2018." Moore's face brightens as he hears a voice on the other end of the line.

"Ned! Hey, it's Dayton. Yeah...you know I don't like texting. Old school, I guess, ha ha. Besides, I wanted to share some good news directly. Yup. So, hey, I got a box of those Esky bobbleheads you asked for... $350 on eBay, would you believe? Says 'Esky Magic' right there on the base. I was the only bidder, but they have this 'Buy It Now' button, and I figured why wait, right?...What?...What?...I don't underst— Oh. Ohhhh. You wanted *literally Alcides Escobar*? But you said 'good luck charm,' and I figured...OK, Ned, hold on...Yeah, I've got a, what you call 'em, one of them 'quants' here...Yeah, I'm being told that Alcides has, uh, not been very good. A .272 on-base percenta—Ned, stop yelling—walked only 15 times *all season*. I know, but I thought we'd try to get Mondesi in there, see what we've got going forward. Yes, of course I remember 2015. Yes, magic, I know. Ned, stop yelling...OK. OK. Yes, I'll call—or text. Yes, right now...Oh, Ned? One more thing. Looks like I'm out $350, so if your next per diem is a little light, it's becau—Ned? Ned?"

Cameron Gallagher C   Born: 12/06/92   Age: 26   Bats: R   Throws: R   Height: 6'3"   Weight: 230   Origin: Round 2, 2011 Draft (#65 overall)

YEAR	TEAM	LVL	AGE	PA	R	2B	3B	HR	RBI	BB	K	SB	CS	AVG/OBP/SLG	DRC+	VORP	BABIP	BRR	FRAA	WARP
2016	NWA	AA	23	346	23	16	1	4	24	37	52	2	2	.259/.348/.359	108	11.1	.300	-3.9	C(80): 17.0	3.3
2017	OMA	AAA	24	282	26	13	0	5	37	18	33	0	1	.292/.336/.400	96	5.5	.317	-4.1	C(71): 11.8	2.1
2017	KCA	MLB	24	27	2	1	0	1	5	3	4	0	0	.250/.333/.417	87	0.4	.263	-0.4	C(13): -0.2	0.0
2018	OMA	AAA	25	303	28	13	0	4	42	26	38	1	0	.265/.334/.358	91	11.3	.294	-2.0	C(72): 11.9	2.2
2018	KCA	MLB	25	69	5	3	0	1	7	3	15	0	0	.206/.250/.302	88	-1.9	.250	-1.6	C(20): 2.4	0.3
2019	KCA	MLB	26	121	12	5	0	3	12	8	20	0	0	.249/.305/.374	77	1.9	.278	-0.2	C 3	0.5

Breakout: 3%   Improve: 18%   Collapse: 13%   Attrition: 17%   MLB: 48%

Comparables: Jordan Pacheco, Sandy Leon, Bruce Maxwell

YEAR	TEAM	P. COUNT	FRM RUNS	BLK RUNS	THRW RUNS	TOT RUNS
2017	KCA	1026	-0.2	0.2	-0.1	0.6
2017	OMA	9981	11.1	1.6	1.0	14.1
2018	KCA	2387	1.5	1.0	0.0	2.6
2018	OMA	9812	11.3	0.3	0.1	11.4
2019	KCA	4492	2.6	0.4	0.0	3.1

You've got a reliable old truck that you seldom use except for that trip to the dump every few months, or when your buddy needs to move that absurdly heavy sofabed across town. You've been happy with your everyday car, and it starts pretty much every time you turn the key; you'll replace it someday, but probably not for a few years (after all, your contract—er, lease—doesn't end until 2021). The thing about your truck: it'll get you where you need to go, but man, you really thought it had more power. I mean, the ol' jalopy couldn't even manage an ISO over .100 in the hitter-friendly PCL. Given that Sal Perez is less likely to break down than this extended metaphor, the defense-only Gallagher should be an acceptable backup vehicle for 2019, at least.

Brian Goodwin OF Born: 11/02/90 Age: 28 Bats: L Throws: R Height: 6'0" Weight: 200 Origin: Round 1, 2011 Draft (#34 overall)

YEAR	TEAM	LVL	AGE	PA	R	2B	3B	HR	RBI	BB	K	SB	CS	AVG/OBP/SLG	DRC+	VORP	BABIP	BRR	FRAA	WARP
2016	SYR	AAA	25	492	51	25	1	14	68	46	106	15	3	.280/.349/.438	112	21.3	.336	-2.1	CF(85): -4.9, RF(18): 0.3	1.9
2016	WAS	MLB	25	44	1	4	1	0	5	2	14	0	0	.286/.318/.429	65	0.4	.429	-0.2	RF(8): -1.5, LF(5): -0.3	-0.3
2017	SYR	AAA	26	103	9	4	0	2	11	10	29	2	1	.256/.327/.367	95	0.4	.350	-1.6	RF(9): 0.8, CF(8): 0.0	0.1
2017	WAS	MLB	26	278	41	21	1	13	30	23	69	6	0	.251/.313/.498	97	13.2	.291	0.1	CF(34): -1.2, LF(31): -0.2	0.8
2018	WAS	MLB	27	79	9	1	0	3	12	10	26	3	1	.200/.321/.354	82	-0.6	.270	-1.8	LF(11): -0.2, RF(10): -0.7	-0.2
2018	OMA	AAA	27	44	6	4	0	2	9	4	11	0	0	.225/.295/.475	94	2.6	.259	0.1	CF(3): -0.5, RF(2): -0.4	0.1
2018	KCA	MLB	27	101	11	5	0	3	13	6	31	1	1	.266/.317/.415	84	3.6	.367	0.2	CF(25): -0.7, LF(1): -0.1	0.1
2019	KCA	MLB	28	185	21	8	1	5	20	14	51	3	1	.231/.297/.384	82	2.0	.297	-0.5	CF -2, RF 0	0.1

Breakout: 4%   Improve: 44%   Collapse: 12%   Attrition: 28%   MLB: 88%   *Comparables: Ryan Church, Kirk Nieuwenhuis, Scott Hairston*

So maybe Goodwin's mid-season trade to Kansas City didn't result in his raising his outstretched arms in the driving rain, *Shawshank*-style. But getting out of Washington's deep outfield and onto a team where opportunity abounds had to feel liberating for the former first-round pick. Goodwin held his own in his brief Royals debut, but as has been the case throughout his career, the swing-and-miss in his approach mitigates his power/speed upside. A fifth outfielder on a good team, a fourth outfielder on an average team, Goodwin projects to be the starting center fielder for the 2019 Royals, and perhaps beyond, depending on how the rebuild fares.

Alex Gordon LF Born: 02/10/84 Age: 35 Bats: L Throws: R Height: 6'1" Weight: 225 Origin: Round 1, 2005 Draft (#2 overall)

YEAR	TEAM	LVL	AGE	PA	R	2B	3B	HR	RBI	BB	K	SB	CS	AVG/OBP/SLG	DRC+	VORP	BABIP	BRR	FRAA	WARP
2016	KCA	MLB	32	506	62	16	2	17	40	52	148	8	1	.220/.312/.380	89	1.6	.288	1.2	LF(126): -3.1	0.4
2017	KCA	MLB	33	541	52	20	2	9	45	45	126	7	4	.208/.293/.315	71	-8.8	.261	-0.2	LF(140): 2.7, CF(15): -0.9	-0.3
2018	KCA	MLB	34	568	56	24	0	13	54	50	124	12	2	.245/.324/.370	91	4.3	.299	-1.9	LF(125): 3.3, CF(11): -0.9	0.9
2019	KCA	MLB	35	545	57	24	2	12	56	49	131	8	3	.226/.313/.352	87	6.3	.290	-0.6	LF 0	0.7

Breakout: 1%   Improve: 28%   Collapse: 15%   Attrition: 26%   MLB: 67%   *Comparables: Kevin McReynolds, Jason Michaels, Rube Bressler*

Baseball analysts always talk of the uneven developmental curve of prospects. We know that growth is anything but linear, with so many variables in play: changes in bodily composition, the increased difficulty of ascending levels, the acquisition of new skills or the significant improvement of existing ones. What often goes unnoticed is the uneven decline curve of major-leaguers; the Grim Reaper comes for us all, but sometimes he takes a coffee break between gathering our mortal coils. There's no question that Gordon is in decline—his yearly WARP had been plummeting since his 2011-14 peak—but he found a tiny ledge on the cliff in 2018, getting to double digits in both homers and steals and recording a WARP that was no longer in red ink. None of this portends a late-career renaissance, but it does make it slightly more palatable for the Royals to shell out $20 million for that one final hit of championship-era nostalgia.

Terrance Gore LF Born: 06/08/91 Age: 28 Bats: R Throws: R Height: 5'7" Weight: 165 Origin: Round 20, 2011 Draft (#606 overall)

YEAR	TEAM	LVL	AGE	PA	R	2B	3B	HR	RBI	BB	K	SB	CS	AVG/OBP/SLG	DRC+	VORP	BABIP	BRR	FRAA	WARP
2016	NWA	AA	25	302	31	2	1	0	11	26	58	44	5	.233/.314/.249	67	5.7	.303	5.4	CF(70): 5.2, LF(15): -0.1	0.8
2016	KCA	MLB	25	3	6	0	0	0	0	0	1	11	2	.000/.000/.000	94	-0.5	.000	0.1	LF(2): 0.0	0.0
2017	NWA	AA	26	62	9	1	0	0	1	2	13	8	0	.254/.279/.271	77	-1.2	.326	1.4	LF(10): 1.5, CF(7): -0.3	0.3
2017	OMA	AAA	26	192	29	3	3	1	10	16	38	13	3	.247/.321/.319	65	2.4	.310	2.5	LF(30): 1.1, CF(29): 0.7	0.2
2017	KCA	MLB	26	5	2	0	0	0	0	1	2	2	2	.000/.200/.000	73	-0.4	.000	0.3	LF(2): -0.2	0.0
2018	OMA	AAA	27	168	26	2	2	0	5	17	36	16	4	.211/.304/.254	49	-1.4	.283	2.0	LF(42): -0.2, CF(18): 1.4	-0.3
2018	IOW	AAA	27	37	6	0	0	0	0	2	13	5	1	.118/.189/.118	54	-3.8	.190	0.7	CF(6): -0.5, LF(5): -0.4	-0.1
2018	CHN	MLB	27	5	5	0	0	0	0	0	1	6	0	.200/.200/.200	73	0.2	.250	0.9	LF(7): -0.2	0.1
2019	KCA	MLB	28	251	32	8	1	4	20	18	61	20	3	.221/.284/.328	59	-1.5	.268	3.0	LF 2, CF 2	0.3

Breakout: 2%   Improve: 10%   Collapse: 8%   Attrition: 17%   MLB: 25%   *Comparables: Luis Durango, Norris Hopper, Freddy Guzman*

It's possible that Gore is both the best runner and worst hitter in pro ball. The Wild Card game was a microcosm of his utility, or lack thereof: he saved the Cubs from elimination in the eighth inning, stealing second and then hurtling home to tie the game on a single. In other words, Gore did exactly what he was there for. The problem was that the Cubs ran out of position players to replace him with, and so once again needing a single run to save their season in the bottom of the 13th, Gore was thrust back into the spotlight, this time with a bat in his hand. Gore's skillset represents a very specific tool that is monumentally useful in playoff baseball if deployed at the right time. At any other, it's like using a rubber duck when you need a hammer.

Billy Hamilton CF Born: 09/09/90 Age: 28 Bats: B Throws: R Height: 6'0" Weight: 160 Origin: Round 2, 2009 Draft (#57 overall)

YEAR	TEAM	LVL	AGE	PA	R	2B	3B	HR	RBI	BB	K	SB	CS	AVG/OBP/SLG	DRC+	VORP	BABIP	BRR	FRAA	WARP
2016	CIN	MLB	25	460	69	19	3	3	17	36	93	58	8	.260/.321/.343	77	13.4	.329	10.5	CF(115): 9.5	2.4
2017	CIN	MLB	26	633	85	17	11	4	38	44	133	59	13	.247/.299/.335	73	4.7	.313	6.6	CF(137): 5.1	1.3
2018	CIN	MLB	27	556	74	16	9	4	29	46	132	34	10	.236/.299/.327	78	8.2	.309	8.3	CF(150): 4.2	1.8
2019	KCA	MLB	28	433	54	17	5	5	33	31	92	36	8	.250/.305/.357	83	12.9	.304	4.9	CF 3	1.6

Breakout: 7%   Improve: 49%   Collapse: 8%   Attrition: 27%   MLB: 94%   *Comparables: Willy Taveras, Chuck Carr, Lance Johnson*

No player of recent vintage has made such modest contributions to winning a baseball game as scintillating as Hamilton. Few things on the diamond can match the excitement of watching him chase down a gapper with runners on base or dash first-to-third in a seeming heartbeat. In some ways his anemic bat makes him more of an entertainer than a ballplayer, and as fans and analysts ruminate over the effect fewer balls in play have on the game's appeal, keep in mind that players like Hamilton are the ones most affected. Fewer fly balls mean fewer opportunities to add value by hauling them in; more strikeouts and home runs mean getting to second or third base are less important to scoring runs than in the past. Hamilton's skill set is becoming less and less viable for an everyday player, and MLB will need to do some hard thinking on whether or not that is a good thing. In the meantime, hello, Kansas City! The speed, glove, and out-making ways should fit right in.

Kyle Isbel CF   Born: 03/03/97   Age: 22   Bats: L   Throws: R   Height: 5'11"   Weight: 183   Origin: Round 3, 2018 Draft (#94 overall)

YEAR	TEAM	LVL	AGE	PA	R	2B	3B	HR	RBI	BB	K	SB	CS	AVG/OBP/SLG	DRC+	VORP	BABIP	BRR	FRAA	WARP
2018	IDA	RK	21	119	27	10	1	4	18	14	17	12	3	.381/.454/.610	147	18.0	.429	-0.8	CF(19): 4.5, RF(2): 1.1	1.5
2018	LEX	A	21	174	30	12	1	3	14	12	43	12	3	.289/.345/.434	106	7.0	.377	2.8	CF(27): 0.8, LF(11): -0.5	1.0
2019	KCA	MLB	22	251	30	10	0	7	22	10	70	8	2	.214/.243/.335	53	-4.6	.269	0.6	CF 2, LF 0	-0.3

Breakout: 0%   Improve: 4%   Collapse: 1%   Attrition: 4%   MLB: 5%   *Comparables: Darrell Ceciliani, Xavier Avery, Roger Bernadina*

A bit undersized and perhaps destined for a corner outfield or second-base home, former UNLV center fielder Isbel did his best to justify his spot as the Royals' highest-drafted position player from the 2018 class. After ripping through the Northwest League, he finished the season at Low-A Lexington, where he continued to hit hard, run fast, and (in true Royals prospect tradition) swing often. There seem to be few roadblocks in Isbel's way as he hopes to do some drive-by truckin' through multiple minor-league levels in 2019.

Khalil Lee CF   Born: 06/26/98   Age: 21   Bats: L   Throws: L   Height: 5'10"   Weight: 170   Origin: Round 3, 2016 Draft (#103 overall)

YEAR	TEAM	LVL	AGE	PA	R	2B	3B	HR	RBI	BB	K	SB	CS	AVG/OBP/SLG	DRC+	VORP	BABIP	BRR	FRAA	WARP
2016	ROY	RK	18	222	43	9	6	6	29	33	57	8	4	.269/.396/.484	146	18.6	.358	-0.4	CF(23): -2.5, RF(15): -2.5	1.1
2017	LEX	A	19	532	71	24	6	17	61	65	171	20	18	.237/.344/.430	114	20.1	.338	-2.2	CF(67): -6.2, RF(52): 4.3	1.9
2018	WIL	A+	20	301	42	13	4	4	41	48	75	14	3	.270/.402/.406	108	26.4	.371	2.2	CF(57): 3.8, RF(9): 0.3	1.8
2018	NWA	AA	20	118	15	5	0	2	10	11	28	2	2	.245/.330/.353	77	1.2	.319	0.6	CF(17): 0.3, LF(9): 0.7	0.1
2019	KCA	MLB	21	251	25	7	0	7	25	21	80	4	2	.189/.266/.308	54	-5.6	.256	-0.4	CF -2, RF 0	-0.9

Breakout: 5%   Improve: 7%   Collapse: 1%   Attrition: 5%   MLB: 10%   *Comparables: Clint Frazier, Daniel Fields, Trayce Thompson*

Twenty-year-olds can go in so many different directions—that applies generally, but even more specifically to power-speed prospects. Lee flashed impressive amounts of both at Low-A but seemed to lose the power stroke at High-A Wilmington in 2018. Set to begin his age-21 season at Double-A, Lee has a future that is bright but not particularly clear. His plate approach still walks the line between patient and over-patient. Does the body fill out to 20-home-run power? Do the on-base skills mesh with the speed to create a run-scoring force? Or does the swing-and-miss begin to take center stage, dragging down the multi-tool upside? This should be the year when Lee's Magic 8-Ball comes up with something other than "Reply Hazy, Try Again."

Nicky Lopez MI   Born: 03/13/95   Age: 24   Bats: L   Throws: R   Height: 5'11"   Weight: 175   Origin: Round 5, 2016 Draft (#163 overall)

YEAR	TEAM	LVL	AGE	PA	R	2B	3B	HR	RBI	BB	K	SB	CS	AVG/OBP/SLG	DRC+	VORP	BABIP	BRR	FRAA	WARP
2016	BNC	RK	21	283	54	6	5	6	29	35	30	24	4	.281/.393/.429	136	34.1	.296	5.4	SS(62): 7.8	3.6
2017	WIL	A+	22	324	42	12	7	2	27	36	23	14	8	.295/.376/.407	123	26.0	.315	0.8	SS(58): 4.4	2.8
2017	NWA	AA	22	253	26	6	1	0	11	16	29	7	4	.259/.312/.293	85	4.5	.296	2.2	SS(33): -2.9, 2B(25): 2.5	0.7
2018	NWA	AA	23	325	42	8	5	2	27	33	23	9	4	.331/.397/.416	113	25.9	.351	2.8	SS(58): -4.8, 2B(14): 0.4	1.7
2018	OMA	AAA	23	256	33	6	2	7	26	27	29	6	2	.278/.364/.417	112	19.5	.294	0.0	SS(36): -1.0, 2B(18): 1.7	1.6
2019	KCA	MLB	24	105	13	4	0	3	13	9	15	2	1	.257/.332/.418	87	1.5	.271	-0.1	SS 0, 3B 0	0.2

Breakout: 10%   Improve: 16%   Collapse: 10%   Attrition: 23%   MLB: 42%   *Comparables: Kevin Newman, Jace Peterson, Greg Garcia*

Bad problems to have: Unidentified dark fluid pooling under your car engine. A power outage with a freezer full of fresh game. A rash only made worse by over-the-counter medication. Going the wrong way over tire spikes. Spotty internet when you just pressed "purchase now." That "stomach thing" going around your child's first-grade class. An upstairs neighbor who never got beyond his nu-metal phase. A paucity of middle-infield talent in your organization.

Good problems to have: A litter of cute puppies. A weekend with perfect weather and nothing to do. Frequent-flier miles that you need to use or lose. Halloween candy. A major-league-ready middle-infield prospect whose only apparent drawback is a lack of power, and a franchise building block who won't hit free agency until 2023.

Seuly Matias RF   Born: 09/04/98   Age: 20   Bats: R   Throws: R   Height: 6'3"   Weight: 200   Origin: International Free Agent, 2015

YEAR	TEAM	LVL	AGE	PA	R	2B	3B	HR	RBI	BB	K	SB	CS	AVG/OBP/SLG	DRC+	VORP	BABIP	BRR	FRAA	WARP
2016	DRY	RK	17	27	2	1	0	0	2	2	13	0	0	.125/.222/.167	67	-1.4	.273	0.0	CF(7): 0.6	0.1
2016	ROY	RK	17	198	32	11	2	8	29	22	73	2	4	.250/.348/.477	113	9.9	.385	0.0	CF(23): -1.6, RF(19): 0.6	0.6
2017	BNC	RK	18	246	27	13	3	7	36	16	72	2	1	.243/.297/.423	80	7.0	.318	0.7	RF(52): 9.0	0.8
2018	LEX	A	19	376	62	13	1	31	63	24	131	6	0	.231/.303/.550	146	18.8	.264	0.7	RF(75): -2.1	2.8
2019	KCA	MLB	20	251	23	7	0	11	31	7	98	0	0	.170/.195/.331	33	-14.6	.222	-0.9	RF -1	-1.6

Breakout: 7%   Improve: 25%   Collapse: 0%   Attrition: 4%   MLB: 26%   *Comparables: Giancarlo Stanton, Domingo Santana, Lewis Brinson*

Matias may be baseball's quality-control experiment as it tests just how much swing-and-miss a prospect can have while still succeeding on raw, brutal power. He clobbered Low-A as a 19-year-old, mashing a rich season's worth of home runs in a mere 376 plate appearances, with nearly identical strikeout and HR/FB rates in the mid-thirties. It helps Matias' case that he's an athletically-built right fielder with a cannon arm, so he should stick safely in the outfield. The question that Matias will pose: can a prospect make it on power alone even if that power is Straight Outta Stanton? Even Joey Gallo could take a walk now and again.

MJ Melendez C   Born: 11/29/98   Age: 20   Bats: L   Throws: R   Height: 6'1"   Weight: 185   Origin: Round 2, 2017 Draft (#52 overall)

YEAR	TEAM	LVL	AGE	PA	R	2B	3B	HR	RBI	BB	K	SB	CS	AVG/OBP/SLG	DRC+	VORP	BABIP	BRR	FRAA	WARP
2017	ROY	RK	18	198	25	8	3	4	30	26	60	4	2	.262/.374/.417	101	11.4	.385	0.1	C(28): 0.5	0.7
2018	LEX	A	19	472	52	26	9	19	73	43	143	4	6	.251/.322/.492	117	24.5	.327	-1.7	C(73): 1.4	2.7
2019	KCA	MLB	20	251	21	7	1	8	28	13	92	0	0	.178/.220/.321	38	-8.9	.245	-0.3	C 0	-1.0

Breakout: 2%   Improve: 5%   Collapse: 0%   Attrition: 4%   MLB: 7%   *Comparables: Gary Sanchez, Matt Olson, Tommy Joseph*

For all that has gone wrong with the Royals since 2015, things might be falling into place with respect to a worthy backstop successor to Sal Perez. Assuming that the hard-ridden Perez will loosen his death grip on the position sometime in the next half-decade, Melendez looks to be on a schedule that would deliver him to major-league relevance at the right time. A strong showing at Low-A suggests the power and defense are a worthy foundation; we'll have to wait and see how the hit tool comes along. But (CTRL+C, CTRL+V for every low-minors catching prospect) catchers, man. Who even knows?

Whit Merrifield 2B   Born: 01/24/89   Age: 30   Bats: R   Throws: R   Height: 6'0"   Weight: 195   Origin: Round 9, 2010 Draft (#269 overall)

YEAR	TEAM	LVL	AGE	PA	R	2B	3B	HR	RBI	BB	K	SB	CS	AVG/OBP/SLG	DRC+	VORP	BABIP	BRR	FRAA	WARP
2016	OMA	AAA	27	304	46	19	0	8	29	22	55	20	2	.266/.321/.423	102	14.4	.302	1.5	2B(40): 1.5, 1B(9): -0.5	1.1
2016	KCA	MLB	27	332	44	22	3	2	29	19	72	8	3	.283/.323/.392	81	6.0	.361	-0.2	2B(65): 2.2, LF(13): 1.9	0.7
2017	KCA	MLB	28	630	80	32	6	19	78	29	88	34	8	.288/.324/.460	108	26.8	.308	1.7	2B(132): -0.2, RF(10): -1.9	2.6
2018	KCA	MLB	29	707	88	43	3	12	60	61	114	45	10	.304/.367/.438	115	38.9	.352	3.5	2B(108): 2.3, CF(30): 1.4	4.2
2019	KCA	MLB	30	629	89	37	4	15	62	46	106	33	8	.282/.341/.434	115	33.3	.323	1.2	2B 3, RF -1	3.8

Breakout: 2%   Improve: 47%   Collapse: 2%   Attrition: 4%   MLB: 92%   *Comparables: Freddy Sanchez, Josh Harrison, Mike Aviles*

While it's true that one indeed can't spell "Whit" without "hit"—a category in which Merrifield improbably finished tops in the AL—it's equally true that one can't spell "Whit" without "WTH," as in, what the H-E-double-hockey-sticks happened to turn a low-ceiling org soldier into a four-win, black-ink-owning, bona fide star? Maybe we lay a bit of the power spike at the juicy baseball of 2017, but Merrifield has excelled in non-power aspects as well: he's improved his walk rates, he hits effectively to all fields, and he's stealing bases frequently and efficiently (leading the AL for two years running). Given his late blooming, Merrifield enters 2019 at age 30 with one more year at the league minimum before the arbitration clock starts, so the questions he poses are questions about the Royals' future writ large: hold at low cost, making him the cornerstone through the lean years; extend with a long-term deal, building a bridge to the next contending team and a face for the fans; or cash out via trade and keep filling the prospect tank? What does one do with found money?

Adalberto Mondesi SS   Born: 07/27/95   Age: 23   Bats: B   Throws: R   Height: 6'1"   Weight: 190   Origin: International Free Agent, 2011

YEAR	TEAM	LVL	AGE	PA	R	2B	3B	HR	RBI	BB	K	SB	CS	AVG/OBP/SLG	DRC+	VORP	BABIP	BRR	FRAA	WARP
2016	WIL	A+	20	39	5	2	1	1	4	2	11	2	0	.243/.282/.432	86	1.5	.320	0.9	SS(6): 0.5	0.2
2016	NWA	AA	20	131	20	5	1	5	17	13	30	17	1	.259/.331/.448	112	10.5	.305	1.0	SS(21): 2.1, 2B(6): 0.4	1.1
2016	OMA	AAA	20	61	9	2	4	1	9	2	19	5	0	.304/.328/.536	68	7.1	.444	1.4	SS(12): 0.6, 2B(2): 0.1	0.3
2016	KCA	MLB	20	149	16	1	3	2	13	6	48	9	1	.185/.231/.281	50	-5.1	.271	1.5	2B(42): -4.4, SS(7): -0.1	-0.7
2017	OMA	AAA	21	357	52	20	8	13	52	18	86	21	3	.305/.340/.539	96	31.3	.373	1.3	SS(71): 2.2, 2B(10): 0.1	1.8
2017	KCA	MLB	21	60	4	1	0	1	3	3	22	5	2	.170/.214/.245	55	-5.8	.267	-1.4	2B(14): 0.1, SS(9): 0.1	-0.2
2018	OMA	AAA	22	133	19	8	3	5	21	8	30	10	0	.250/.295/.492	89	7.6	.291	1.2	SS(18): 0.6, 2B(6): 0.8	0.6
2018	KCA	MLB	22	291	47	13	3	14	37	11	77	32	7	.276/.306/.498	98	18.6	.335	0.3	SS(61): 1.2, 2B(12): 0.9	1.5
2019	KCA	MLB	23	541	84	20	5	19	55	29	145	43	8	.240/.285/.415	87	12.4	.287	0.6	SS 5	1.8

Breakout: 12%   Improve: 54%   Collapse: 7%   Attrition: 16%   MLB: 89%   *Comparables: Adam Jones, Hanley Ramirez, Arismendy Alcantara*

For a team saved only by the historically dismal Orioles from being the worst in baseball, the second half of the Royals' season was surprisingly… not that depressing? The power explosion of Ryan O'Hearn, the quiet emergence of Brad Keller, and the burnishing of Whit Merrifield's excellence all made for good, happy stories. But any optimistic account of the Royals' 2018 has to begin with the breakout of Mondesi, who pulled a Joey/Albert Belle and proceeded to barnstorm the AL Central like an infield version of Byron Buxton (late 2017 edition). It was easy to gloss over the impatient plate approach when the eyes were blinded with blazing speed and surprising power. In the colder days of winter, a long, hard look at Mondesi's performance leaves a number of questions unanswered: Can he walk even just a bit more? The power was no doubt luck-driven, but how far will it regress? Is there a risk that the on-base skills plummet to the disastrous level of Buxton (2018 edition)? As the comparison to Buxton suggests, there's a natural pull for storylines to veer toward happy endings or darkest timelines. Reality tends to live between the poles, a region populated by uneven-but-productive players like Tim Anderson and Jonathan Villar. Prospects who flash star qualities usually won't end up being stars, and if Mondesi finds a home in the great, flawed middle, it will still count as a win for the Royals.

Ryan O'Hearn 1B   Born: 07/26/93   Age: 25   Bats: L   Throws: L   Height: 6'3"   Weight: 200   Origin: Round 8, 2014 Draft (#243 overall)

YEAR	TEAM	LVL	AGE	PA	R	2B	3B	HR	RBI	BB	K	SB	CS	AVG/OBP/SLG	DRC+	VORP	BABIP	BRR	FRAA	WARP
2016	WIL	A+	22	98	13	7	0	7	18	8	27	0	0	.352/.408/.670	132	13.7	.436	-0.3	1B(21): -0.7	0.4
2016	NWA	AA	22	466	49	25	2	15	60	48	131	3	5	.258/.339/.437	114	14.8	.342	-2.8	1B(61): 1.9, LF(39): -3.7	1.1
2017	OMA	AAA	23	463	48	26	1	18	53	45	119	1	0	.252/.325/.450	92	5.2	.309	-2.5	1B(75): -1.2, RF(5): -0.2	-0.1
2017	NWA	AA	23	76	7	1	1	4	11	10	20	0	0	.258/.355/.485	107	3.0	.310	0.1	1B(8): 0.3, LF(5): -0.6	0.1
2018	OMA	AAA	24	406	47	21	1	11	52	45	97	2	0	.232/.322/.391	91	6.0	.286	3.9	1B(69): -6.3, LF(13): -2.1	-0.2
2018	KCA	MLB	24	170	23	10	2	12	30	20	45	0	0	.262/.353/.597	129	9.0	.293	-3.6	1B(31): 0.4, LF(1): -0.1	0.5
2019	KCA	MLB	25	540	60	20	2	21	70	49	142	1	0	.225/.300/.404	90	0.4	.271	-0.8	1B -3	-0.2

Breakout: 4%   Improve: 29%   Collapse: 6%   Attrition: 22%   MLB: 55%   *Comparables: Brandon Allen, Travis Ishikawa, Tyler Austin*

A lefty power bat, O'Hearn hit an underwhelming 11 home runs in 406 plate appearances at Triple-A Omaha. After a late-July call-up to Kansas City, he proceeded to hit 12 bombs in only 170 times under the lights. (And they say there's nothing different about the major-league ball.) O'Hearn has his obvious strengths, starting with his… well… strength. He also knows how to take a free pass, walking in around 12 percent of his plate appearances across both

Triple-A and the majors. His weaknesses become apparent the moment you click on his splits: with a triple-slash of .108/.195/.270 against major-league lefties, you see the prototypical picture of a platoon first baseman. But there's a twist! O'Hearn's minor-league splits tilt the *other* way, so his first order of business in 2019 will be proving that he can handle major-league lefties. And if he can't, there's nothing wrong with being a strong-side platoon bat, provided the Royals don't fantasize about bigger things.

Chris Owings   UT   Born: 08/12/91   Age: 27   Bats: R   Throws: R   Height: 5'10"   Weight: 185   Origin: Round 1, 2009 Draft (#41 overall)

YEAR	TEAM	LVL	AGE	PA	R	2B	3B	HR	RBI	BB	K	SB	CS	AVG/OBP/SLG	DRC+	VORP	BABIP	BRR	FRAA	WARP
2016	ARI	MLB	24	466	52	24	11	5	49	20	87	21	2	.277/.315/.416	88	14.7	.334	1.9	SS(70): -3.5, CF(49): -1.9	0.9
2017	ARI	MLB	25	386	41	25	1	12	51	17	87	12	2	.268/.299/.442	90	14.9	.318	-0.6	SS(54): 4.2, RF(25): 1.5	1.6
2018	RNO	AAA	26	92	15	4	2	1	11	1	17	1	2	.286/.293/.407	100	-0.6	.342	1.4	2B(10): -0.2, 3B(6): 0.3	0.5
2018	ARI	MLB	26	309	34	15	0	4	22	24	75	11	4	.206/.272/.302	72	-6.4	.265	0.8	RF(43): -1.1, CF(16): 1.2	-0.3
2019	*KCA*	*MLB*	*27*	*362*	*45*	*17*	*2*	*8*	*33*	*23*	*79*	*12*	*3*	*.247/.299/.380*	*85*	*4.2*	*.298*	*-0.1*	*2B 1, 3B -1*	*0.5*

Breakout: 6%   Improve: 46%   Collapse: 9%   Attrition: 27%   MLB: 88%   *Comparables: Mel Clark, Roman Mejias, Alex Ochoa*

The Diamondbacks once seemed to choose Owings over Didi Gregorius. In their defense, Gregorius wasn't hitting yet and Owings was the sort of gritty, do-it-all, hard-nosed player coveted by the fallen regime of the past. That decision ultimately provided the opening seized by Nick Ahmed, leaving Owings on the outside looking in. Slowed by injuries and battling inconsistency, he assumed a super-utility role for 2018 but couldn't pass that test as he was dismal at the dish. Just 27, he moves on to an organization that always loves grit and gloves, inking a one-year deal with the Royals to replace Alcides Escobar.

Salvador Perez   C   Born: 05/10/90   Age: 29   Bats: R   Throws: R   Height: 6'4"   Weight: 240   Origin: International Free Agent, 2006

YEAR	TEAM	LVL	AGE	PA	R	2B	3B	HR	RBI	BB	K	SB	CS	AVG/OBP/SLG	DRC+	VORP	BABIP	BRR	FRAA	WARP
2016	KCA	MLB	26	546	57	28	2	22	64	22	119	0	0	.247/.288/.438	95	12.7	.280	-2.7	C(128): -1.9, 1B(1): 0.0	1.9
2017	KCA	MLB	27	499	57	24	1	27	80	17	95	1	0	.268/.297/.495	107	19.5	.280	-1.3	C(115): -10.2	1.7
2018	KCA	MLB	28	544	52	23	0	27	80	17	108	1	1	.235/.274/.439	107	9.5	.245	-3.7	C(96): -8.1, 1B(3): 0.0	1.5
2019	*KCA*	*MLB*	*29*	*561*	*67*	*32*	*2*	*25*	*82*	*27*	*109*	*1*	*0*	*.265/.313/.475*	*111*	*29.2*	*.293*	*-2.3*	*C -11*	*1.9*

Breakout: 1%   Improve: 37%   Collapse: 4%   Attrition: 12%   MLB: 95%

Perez will enter his ninth major-league season still not having blown out thirty candles. While teammate and relative major-league *arriviste* Whit Merrifield passed this magic milestone in January, the general sense of Salvy is that he long ago stepped out of a wagon train on the far edge of Missouri, gazed westward across the Kansas plains, donned his gear, and uttered: "Here. I will stay here." Perez and the Royals have been through a lot—futility, relevance, almost-championship, CHAMPIONSHIP, irrelevance, futility again—and Perez has played through nearly all of it, as he's one 2017 missed plate

Comparables: Wilson Ramos, Harry Danning, Walker Cooper

YEAR	TEAM	P. COUNT	FRM RUNS	BLK RUNS	THRW RUNS	TOT RUNS
2016	KCA	18379	-9.5	2.9	5.6	-1.4
2017	KCA	15629	-10.0	1.5	0.1	-8.4
2018	KCA	14052	-9.9	-0.6	0.8	-9.5
2019	*KCA*	*18606*	*-13.9*	*1.4*	*1.9*	*-10.6*

appearance from six straight seasons with at least 500. He's been around long enough that we know his strengths (durability, power, solid defense, charm) and weaknesses (won't take a walk, not a great framer, limits career opportunities of backup catchers). With a contract that keeps him in Kansas City through 2021, Perez represents the likeliest last link to the glory days of 2014-15. But for now his value to the club is still anchored in present value, rather than sepia-toned memories.

Brett Phillips   OF   Born: 05/30/94   Age: 25   Bats: L   Throws: R   Height: 6'0"   Weight: 185   Origin: Round 6, 2012 Draft (#189 overall)

YEAR	TEAM	LVL	AGE	PA	R	2B	3B	HR	RBI	BB	K	SB	CS	AVG/OBP/SLG	DRC+	VORP	BABIP	BRR	FRAA	WARP
2016	BLX	AA	22	517	60	14	6	16	62	67	154	12	7	.229/.332/.397	110	24.9	.311	1.5	CF(102): 0.8, RF(19): 0.0	2.6
2017	CSP	AAA	23	432	79	23	10	19	78	45	129	9	1	.305/.377/.567	124	30.5	.412	2.1	RF(52): -3.2, CF(49): 3.9	2.9
2017	MIL	MLB	23	98	9	3	0	4	12	9	34	5	0	.276/.351/.448	90	6.6	.408	0.3	CF(26): 4.8, RF(9): -0.3	0.7
2018	CSP	AAA	24	299	42	12	7	6	25	36	94	11	0	.240/.331/.411	90	10.7	.346	1.1	RF(34): 2.9, CF(20): -1.8	0.7
2018	MIL	MLB	24	24	2	0	1	0	4	2	11	0	0	.182/.250/.273	45	-1.0	.364	0.0	RF(7): -0.6, CF(5): 0.5	-0.1
2018	KCA	MLB	24	123	13	4	2	2	7	9	50	1	1	.188/.252/.313	48	-1.8	.311	0.3	CF(23): 4.4, RF(9): 0.3	0.1
2019	*KCA*	*MLB*	*25*	*344*	*39*	*15*	*3*	*10*	*38*	*32*	*117*	*6*	*1*	*.220/.296/.385*	*89*	*6.0*	*.314*	*0.4*	*RF 1, CF 1*	*0.8*

Breakout: 4%   Improve: 22%   Collapse: 9%   Attrition: 25%   MLB: 52%   *Comparables: Brent Clevlen, Rymer Liriano, Matt Joyce*

Here are two truths and a lie about Phillips, acquired by the Royals in the trade-deadline deal that sent Mike Moustakas to the Cream City. 1: He struck out in more than 40 percent of his major-league plate appearances in 2018. 2: His right arm is the stuff of legend, a missile launcher that leaves baserunners vaporized in the shape of their former bodies before they dissolve in a heap of smoldering ash, Wile E. Coyote-style. 3: He has a very soft, gentle, unassuming laugh. Answer: #3 is the lie. His laugh can range from piercing pterodactyl's screech to a guttural donkey's bray, stretching his face into a rictus so taut that one's own cheek muscles twinge in sympathetic pain. But as YouTube commenter "Wawa 123" noted about a video of said laugh, "Lol This guy is going to be known more for his laugh than his baseball abilities." Whether #1 improves will determine if major-league fans will get to enjoy #2 and #3. Laugh, and the world laughs with you; strike out, and you walk back to the dugout alone.

Nick Pratto 1B Born: 10/06/98 Age: 20 Bats: L Throws: L Height: 6'1" Weight: 195 Origin: Round 1, 2017 Draft (#14 overall)

YEAR	TEAM	LVL	AGE	PA	R	2B	3B	HR	RBI	BB	K	SB	CS	AVG/OBP/SLG	DRC+	VORP	BABIP	BRR	FRAA	WARP
2017	ROY	RK	18	230	25	15	3	4	34	24	58	10	4	.247/.330/.414	109	4.7	.319	-0.8	1B(48): 5.2	0.9
2018	LEX	A	19	537	79	33	2	14	62	45	150	22	5	.280/.343/.443	109	14.4	.375	1.4	1B(125): -0.6	1.3
2019	KCA	MLB	20	251	23	11	0	6	26	11	82	4	1	.201/.235/.326	43	-13.4	.273	0.0	1B 1	-1.3

Breakout: 2%   Improve: 4%   Collapse: 0%   Attrition: 4%   MLB: 7%   *Comparables: Jose Osuna, Chris Marrero, Chris Parmelee*

If you're going to be a first-base prospect, be a first-base prospect. Own it. Don't pretend you're a "third baseman who can make most of the throws" or a "left fielder who can cover most of the area"; just be the best doggone first-base prospect you can be. Pratto has never been anything but a first baseman, and this is not a veiled dig at defensive incompetence; he's a good first baseman. His 2018 season also hinted that he doesn't fall into the conventional slugger profile, displaying intriguing speed to go with gap power that should grow into more. As with nearly every Royals low-minors prospect, cutting down the strikeouts is the main challenge, but Pratto's advanced hit tool suggests that he might be better positioned than some of his organizational colleagues to meet it.

Jorge Soler RF Born: 02/25/92 Age: 27 Bats: R Throws: R Height: 6'4" Weight: 230 Origin: International Free Agent, 2012

YEAR	TEAM	LVL	AGE	PA	R	2B	3B	HR	RBI	BB	K	SB	CS	AVG/OBP/SLG	DRC+	VORP	BABIP	BRR	FRAA	WARP
2016	TEN	AA	24	42	4	0	0	0	2	11	11	0	0	.167/.381/.167	105	0.1	.250	0.0	LF(6): -0.5	0.1
2016	CHN	MLB	24	264	37	9	0	12	31	31	66	0	0	.238/.333/.436	105	13.9	.276	-0.4	LF(53): -2.7, RF(7): -1.1	0.4
2017	OMA	AAA	25	327	49	9	0	24	59	50	82	1	0	.267/.388/.564	147	25.8	.293	-2.0	RF(39): -0.4, LF(23): 3.0	2.7
2017	KCA	MLB	25	110	7	5	0	2	6	12	36	0	0	.144/.245/.258	62	-8.6	.203	-0.3	RF(15): -1.6, LF(7): 0.8	-0.4
2018	KCA	MLB	26	257	27	18	0	9	28	28	69	3	1	.265/.354/.466	94	11.9	.340	-0.5	RF(52): -1.0	0.2
2019	KCA	MLB	27	511	61	20	1	20	66	58	137	2	1	.230/.326/.413	101	6.2	.288	-0.6	RF 0	0.6

Breakout: 5%   Improve: 51%   Collapse: 5%   Attrition: 12%   MLB: 94%   *Comparables: Kyle Blanks, Shin-Soo Choo, Matt Joyce*

The wave of Cuban emigres into the major leagues over the past decade has tended to bifurcate pretty sharply along the curves of success and failure. Among the higher-profile signings, Yoenis Cespedes, Jose Abreu, Yasiel Puig, and Yuli Gurriel are the success stories. Yasmany Tomas, Rusney Castillo, Alex Guerrero, and Hector Olivera (you forgot about him, didn't you?) have to be counted as the opposite. Soler appeared to fall into the latter after two disappointing seasons with the Cubs and a trade to the Royals that led to nearly a full year of "meh" in the offense-friendly PCL in 2017. Cue 2018, when Soler began the season in Kansas City, doing a plausible impression of "middle-of-the-order bat." A broken big toe truncated his season in late May, leaving us to wonder if a small, productive sample portends anything bigger. He should be fully recovered by spring training and will try to make a case to be counted among the happier stories of recent Cuban imports.

Meibrys Viloria C Born: 02/15/97 Age: 22 Bats: L Throws: R Height: 5'11" Weight: 220 Origin: International Free Agent, 2013

YEAR	TEAM	LVL	AGE	PA	R	2B	3B	HR	RBI	BB	K	SB	CS	AVG/OBP/SLG	DRC+	VORP	BABIP	BRR	FRAA	WARP
2016	IDA	RK	19	259	54	28	3	6	55	20	36	1	1	.376/.436/.606	147	39.5	.418	2.3	C(50): -0.8	2.6
2017	LEX	A	20	398	42	25	0	8	52	25	79	4	3	.259/.313/.394	99	8.5	.310	-0.4	C(92): -0.4	1.6
2018	WIL	A+	21	407	34	16	1	6	44	40	75	2	1	.260/.342/.360	99	11.0	.313	-2.8	C(88): 2.8	1.7
2018	KCA	MLB	21	29	4	2	0	0	4	1	9	0	0	.259/.286/.333	70	0.2	.389	0.1	C(10): -1.0	0.0
2019	KCA	MLB	22	35	3	1	0	1	4	2	8	0	0	.209/.254/.318	55	-0.4	.248	-0.1	C -1	-0.2

Breakout: 5%   Improve: 10%   Collapse: 12%   Attrition: 19%   MLB: 26%   *Comparables: Blake Swihart, John Ryan Murphy, J.T. Realmuto*

Caught between the higher upside of M.J. Melendez and the major-league-backup readiness of Cam Gallagher, the Royals won't see much of Meibrys tomorrow but will they see Meibrys... someday? Viloria is on the 40-man roster and got a surprise September call-up after an age-appropriately decent year at High-A Wilmington, but he has not otherwise changed his place in this world. Of course, it never hurts to have extra young catchers in the organization, but Viloria may just be a Pretender to the throne that Sal Perez will eventually vacate.

YEAR	TEAM	P. COUNT	FRM RUNS	BLK RUNS	THRW RUNS	TOT RUNS
2018	KCA	1167	0.0	-0.8	0.0	-0.1
2019	KCA	1297	-0.1	-0.8	0.0	-0.9

PITCHERS

Jason Adam RHP Born: 08/04/91 Age: 27 Bats: R Throws: R Height: 6'4" Weight: 225 Origin: Round 5, 2010 Draft (#149 overall)

YEAR	TEAM	LVL	AGE	W	L	SV	G	GS	IP	H	HR	BB/9	K/9	K	GB%	BABIP	WHIP	ERA	DRA	WARP	MPH	FB%	WHF	CSP
2017	NWA	AA	25	0	0	0	5	0	6¹	3	0	5.7	15.6	11	27%	.273	1.11	7.11	2.58	0.2				
2018	NWA	AA	26	1	0	0	6	0	11¹	5	0	3.2	13.5	17	36%	.227	0.79	1.59	3.89	0.1				
2018	KCA	MLB	26	0	3	0	31	0	32¹	30	9	4.2	10.3	37	29%	.269	1.39	6.12	7.04	-0.8	96.0	61.1	13.1	45.6
2018	OMA	AAA	26	2	0	4	11	0	12²	6	0	5.0	10.7	15	34%	.207	1.03	1.42	2.80	0.3				
2019	KCA	MLB	27	2	1	1	37	0	39¹	38	7	5.1	10.2	45	36%	.307	1.54	5.33	5.57	-0.2	95.5	61.9	13.3	46.2

Breakout: 19%   Improve: 39%   Collapse: 8%   Attrition: 20%   MLB: 56%   *Comparables: Francisco Rosario, Gonzalez Germen, Scott Mathieson*

For most of a three-month stretch last summer, Adam was a useful righty bullpen arm, even if that arm was deployed in low-leverage situations (to be fair, the 2018 Royals rarely had any other type of leverage). On August 17, facing the White Sox, he surrendered five earned runs on two homers, two singles, and a walk. His ERA shot up from 4.78 to 6.12, where it will forever live on his 2018 stat line, as Adam was sent down to Omaha the next day never to return, even to an expanded September roster. (Oh, the statistical tragedy of small samples for fringy relief arms.) Dependent on a fastball-curve combo that yields both strikeouts and home runs in abundance, Adams should be once again in the mix for a bullpen role and have a chance to keep that unfortunate 2018 line from being the last one on the back of his baseball card.

Scott Barlow RHP
Born: 12/18/92   Age: 26   Bats: R   Throws: R   Height: 6'3"   Weight: 215   Origin: Round 6, 2011 Draft (#194 overall)

YEAR	TEAM	LVL	AGE	W	L	SV	G	GS	IP	H	HR	BB/9	K/9	K	GB%	BABIP	WHIP	ERA	DRA	WARP	MPH	FB%	WHF	CSP
2016	TUL	AA	23	4	7	0	24	23	124¹	125	9	3.8	7.4	102	45%	.306	1.42	3.98	3.40	2.5				
2017	OKL	AAA	24	1	3	0	7	7	32¹	37	6	6.4	10.0	36	37%	.333	1.86	7.24	4.48	0.4				
2017	TUL	AA	24	6	3	0	19	19	107¹	60	9	3.1	10.4	124	45%	.211	0.90	2.10	3.33	2.4				
2018	KCA	MLB	25	1	1	0	6	0	15	16	2	1.8	9.0	15	40%	.311	1.27	3.60	3.69	0.2	93.1	53	11.9	50.8
2018	OMA	AAA	25	1	4	1	13	10	45²	54	9	4.1	9.9	50	38%	.357	1.64	6.11	3.71	0.9				
2019	KCA	MLB	26	2	2	0	31	5	52¹	53	8	4.1	8.6	50	40%	.304	1.48	4.99	5.22	0.1	92.7	53.9	12.1	51.7

Breakout: 7%   Improve: 23%   Collapse: 9%   Attrition: 21%   MLB: 45%   *Comparables: Jeff Niemann, Tyler Anderson, Brian Johnson*

At this point, the Royals would be happy to have a player who ranks at the top of *any* list not beginning with "Most Disappointing..." or "Whatever Happened To..." As it happens, in former Dodger farmhand Barlow, they currently have 2017's #1 ranked minor-league free agent, according to Chris Mitchell's stat-line-scouting KATOH system. That might seem like damnation by faint praise, and it assuredly is, but the baseball intelligentsia loves these types (Wilmer Font and Willians Astudillo were on last year's list), so if you're looking for a player upon which to plant your hipster flag, Barlow is a deep-ballot candidate. The righty doesn't wow with raw stuff—hence the "minor-league free agent" part—but he acquitted himself well in his brief time in Kansas City and may have a chance to go mainstream in 2019.

Scott Blewett RHP
Born: 04/10/96   Age: 23   Bats: R   Throws: R   Height: 6'6"   Weight: 210   Origin: Round 2, 2014 Draft (#56 overall)

YEAR	TEAM	LVL	AGE	W	L	SV	G	GS	IP	H	HR	BB/9	K/9	K	GB%	BABIP	WHIP	ERA	DRA	WARP	MPH	FB%	WHF	CSP
2016	LEX	A	20	8	11	0	25	25	129¹	138	10	3.5	8.4	121	47%	.338	1.46	4.31	3.96	1.7				
2017	WIL	A+	21	7	10	0	27	27	152²	153	16	3.1	7.6	129	47%	.302	1.34	4.07	5.24	0.0				
2018	NWA	AA	22	8	6	0	26	25	148¹	164	12	3.0	6.1	100	42%	.319	1.44	4.79	7.52	-3.8				
2019	KCA	MLB	23	6	10	0	23	23	122²	145	19	3.9	5.9	80	41%	.313	1.61	5.51	5.79	-0.4				

Breakout: 4%   Improve: 5%   Collapse: 3%   Attrition: 4%   MLB: 9%   *Comparables: Danny Salazar, David Buchanan, Raul Alcantara*

It's tough when you're a prospect whose growth is decelerating and your name is a past-tense homonym for failure. The clock is ticking, but the 23-year-old has a bit more time to prove that he can overcome the magnetic pull of nominative determinism. Still being thought of as a starter by the Royals, his changeup will have to develop into a credible third pitch alongside his fastball-curve combo if he is to fulfill that destiny. And if not, the life of a middle reliever isn't the worst life to live. He didn't make great strides at Double-A, but his youth, size, and fastball still keep him in the present-tense conversation, assuming you aren't reading this far in the future.

Kris Bubic LHP
Born: 08/19/97   Age: 21   Bats: L   Throws: L   Height: 6'3"   Weight: 220   Origin: Round 1, 2018 Draft (#40 overall)

YEAR	TEAM	LVL	AGE	W	L	SV	G	GS	IP	H	HR	BB/9	K/9	K	GB%	BABIP	WHIP	ERA	DRA	WARP	MPH	FB%	WHF	CSP
2018	IDA	RK	20	2	3	0	10	10	38	38	2	4.5	12.6	53	47%	.379	1.50	4.03	2.95	1.3				
2019	KCA	MLB	21	1	3	0	7	7	30¹	34	6	7.5	8.1	27	44%	.317	1.96	6.87	7.21	-0.6				

Comparables: Bryan Mitchell, John Gant, Corey Oswalt

Though it may get you noticed, a Kershaw-esque stop-start delivery alone will not get you drafted 40th overall. An effective fastball-change combo with an identical arm slot and repeatability will, apparently. Even if Bubic's ceiling is more Alex Wood than Clayton Kershaw, the Royals have cause to be excited for anyone in their system who bears passing resemblance to a mid-rotation starter, much less a multiple-Cy Young winner. The foundation is there for the Stanford product; a credible curveball is the main missing piece.

Danny Duffy LHP
Born: 12/21/88   Age: 30   Bats: L   Throws: L   Height: 6'3"   Weight: 205   Origin: Round 3, 2007 Draft (#96 overall)

YEAR	TEAM	LVL	AGE	W	L	SV	G	GS	IP	H	HR	BB/9	K/9	K	GB%	BABIP	WHIP	ERA	DRA	WARP	MPH	FB%	WHF	CSP
2016	KCA	MLB	27	12	3	0	42	26	179²	163	27	2.1	9.4	188	37%	.291	1.14	3.51	3.65	3.5	97.8	59.4	14	49.4
2017	KCA	MLB	28	9	10	0	24	24	146¹	143	13	2.5	8.0	130	41%	.309	1.26	3.81	3.87	2.8	94.8	47.3	12.3	50.6
2018	KCA	MLB	29	8	12	0	28	28	155	161	23	4.1	8.2	141	36%	.304	1.49	4.88	5.54	-0.4	95.5	55.7	10.8	49.6
2019	KCA	MLB	30	9	11	0	28	28	159²	157	21	3.2	8.0	142	38%	.296	1.33	4.39	4.59	1.6	95.2	54.1	12	49.7

Breakout: 5%   Improve: 33%   Collapse: 36%   Attrition: 12%   MLB: 94%   *Comparables: Josh Johnson, Jason Hammel, Gavin Floyd*

Duffy would rather you not read these projections. The Royals' ace, struggling through his most trying season since his rookie year, has long been critical of baseball analytics and its inability to measure the heart within a person: their camaraderie, their mood, their focus. In one sense, he's correct: all projection systems inculcate a sense of over-certainty. That one line there looks like what he's supposed to do in 2019, but it's really only the most likely result, a plurality, barely more possible than any other. In another sense, though, he's also right, because PECOTA not only fails to see into Duffy's heart, it also can't investigate his left arm. He underwent elbow surgery after the end of 2017 and one could make the case, though again without certainty, that he simply never got right afterward, finally culminating in a September shutdown. While the pure numbers on his stuff looked fine, Duffy struggled badly to keep his breaking pitches down, leading to extra baserunners and extra home runs with baserunners on. We can make our best guess on his performance–really, it's our job–but when 2019 arrives and Duffy readies himself for a new season, we'll all find out together.

Heath Fillmyer   RHP   Born: 05/16/94   Age: 25   Bats: R   Throws: R   Height: 6'1"   Weight: 195   Origin: Round 5, 2014 Draft (#162 overall)

YEAR	TEAM	LVL	AGE	W	L	SV	G	GS	IP	H	HR	BB/9	K/9	K	GB%	BABIP	WHIP	ERA	DRA	WARP	MPH	FB%	WHF	CSP
2016	STO	A+	22	5	6	0	18	16	95	101	4	2.9	8.4	89	44%	.328	1.39	3.60	4.03	1.5				
2016	MID	AA	22	2	0	0	8	8	39	31	3	1.8	6.7	29	47%	.259	1.00	2.54	3.89	0.6				
2017	MID	AA	23	11	5	0	29	29	149²	158	19	3.1	6.9	115	45%	.310	1.40	3.49	3.77	2.5				
2018	OMA	AAA	24	4	5	0	13	13	67¹	82	5	3.7	6.3	47	44%	.342	1.63	5.75	4.19	1.0				
2018	KCA	MLB	24	4	2	0	17	13	82¹	78	11	3.5	6.2	57	46%	.277	1.34	4.26	5.47	-0.2	94.3	52.5	9.7	45.8
2019	KCA	MLB	25	4	4	0	49	8	83²	90	11	3.6	6.9	64	43%	.307	1.48	4.88	5.11	0.2	94.0	53.7	10	46.9

Breakout: 26%   Improve: 35%   Collapse: 23%   Attrition: 40%   MLB: 70%   *Comparables: T.J. McFarland, Wade Miley, Zach Jackson*

In the spring of 2018, radio station "New Jersey 101.5" ran a piece on their website: "Major League via Jersey: 2018 MLB Players Born in NJ." No surprises at the top: Trout, of course, then Todd Frazier, Rick Porcello, Brad Brach, and so on. Fillmyer, of Roebling, just across the Delaware River from Levittown, Pennsylvania, had not yet made his major-league debut and was thus not eligible for this list. Ranking him among the similarly fringy arms in the Royals system isn't much fun, but where would he fit on the New Jersey list after a competent-but-forgettable debut season? A quick eyeballing suggests right around #11, nestled just below fifth-outfielder Matt Szczur and Orioles hurler Jimmy Yacabonis (and if you think that ranking was determined by a desire to type the name "Jimmy Yacabonis" in this comment, you are correct). Fillmyer's fastball-slider profile may not be good enough to bring glory to the Garden State, but neither will he bring it shame.

Brian Flynn   LHP   Born: 04/19/90   Age: 29   Bats: L   Throws: L   Height: 6'7"   Weight: 255   Origin: Round 7, 2011 Draft (#227 overall)

YEAR	TEAM	LVL	AGE	W	L	SV	G	GS	IP	H	HR	BB/9	K/9	K	GB%	BABIP	WHIP	ERA	DRA	WARP	MPH	FB%	WHF	CSP
2016	OMA	AAA	26	2	1	0	9	4	23²	22	1	4.6	10.6	28	66%	.350	1.44	3.04	3.36	0.5				
2016	KCA	MLB	26	1	2	0	36	1	55¹	38	5	3.7	7.2	44	57%	.223	1.10	2.60	4.41	0.4	95.4	66.7	11.6	42
2017	OMA	AAA	27	5	3	0	22	4	50	68	10	2.2	9.0	50	46%	.369	1.60	5.40	2.82	1.4				
2017	KCA	MLB	27	0	0	0	1	0	2¹	3	0	0.0	0.0	0	38%	.375	1.29	3.86	7.08	0.0	94.2	65.5	0	58.1
2018	KCA	MLB	28	3	5	1	48	0	75²	87	5	4.2	5.6	47	51%	.333	1.61	4.04	6.59	-1.5	94.0	68.7	8.9	46.7
2019	KCA	MLB	29	3	1	5	57	0	59²	67	8	4.1	7.0	46	49%	.318	1.57	4.99	5.23	-0.2	93.8	68.1	9.5	49.3

Breakout: 28%   Improve: 36%   Collapse: 26%   Attrition: 25%   MLB: 69%   *Comparables: Vin Mazzaro, Jared Hughes, Alex Wilson*

If you Google "Brian Flynn serviceable reliever," you'll find roughly one page worth of hits, enough to suggest that Flynn has self-actualized to a rare and impressive degree. A groundballer with average velocity and average baseball facial hair who doesn't strike many folks out, the imposing 6'7" lefty logged the most relief innings for the Royals in 2018. Entering his first year of arbitration, he may be back for another 75 innings next year—not that you'd notice.

Jesse Hahn   RHP   Born: 07/30/89   Age: 29   Bats: R   Throws: R   Height: 6'4"   Weight: 215   Origin: Round 6, 2010 Draft (#191 overall)

YEAR	TEAM	LVL	AGE	W	L	SV	G	GS	IP	H	HR	BB/9	K/9	K	GB%	BABIP	WHIP	ERA	DRA	WARP	MPH	FB%	WHF	CSP
2016	OAK	MLB	26	2	4	0	9	9	46¹	57	8	3.7	4.5	23	51%	.320	1.64	6.02	6.21	-0.5	96.4	71.9	6.5	48.9
2016	NAS	AAA	26	1	7	0	15	15	66²	72	4	4.6	6.2	46	55%	.318	1.59	4.32	4.03	1.0				
2017	OAK	MLB	27	3	6	0	14	13	69²	78	4	3.5	7.1	55	47%	.327	1.51	5.30	5.94	-0.3	95.9	61.8	8	49.7
2017	NAS	AAA	27	2	0	0	6	5	25	28	1	5.0	6.5	18	54%	.342	1.68	4.32	4.68	0.3				
2019	KCA	MLB	29	1	0	0	15	0	16¹	18	2	4.8	6.3	11	46%	.308	1.64	5.48	5.75	0.0	95.4	64.9	7.5	49.4

Breakout: 28%   Improve: 47%   Collapse: 24%   Attrition: 20%   MLB: 84%   *Comparables: Roberto Hernandez, Jimmy Nelson, Jeff Locke*

A teammate of Matt Harvey's at Fitch Senior High School in Groton, Connecticut, Hahn has followed a career path with less fame and infamy than his former rotation partner. But the degree to which both righties have fallen on hard times and debilitating injuries makes you wonder if there was a late-night, disturbed-burial-ground prank that went wrong sometime back in the mid-aughts. The latest chapter in Hahn's book of misfortune: a wonky UCL that was fixed by a "primary repair" surgery—a non-Tommy John procedure requiring only six months of rehab. It's not exactly encouraging that the only other major-league pitcher to undergo this surgery, Seth Maness, enjoyed a mere 9 2/3 major-league innings (with the Royals!) before his release. For Hahn, a comeback of even that duration is beginning to feel like a positive outcome.

Jason Hammel   RHP   Born: 09/02/82   Age: 36   Bats: R   Throws: R   Height: 6'6"   Weight: 225   Origin: Round 10, 2002 Draft (#284 overall)

YEAR	TEAM	LVL	AGE	W	L	SV	G	GS	IP	H	HR	BB/9	K/9	K	GB%	BABIP	WHIP	ERA	DRA	WARP	MPH	FB%	WHF	CSP
2016	CHN	MLB	33	15	10	0	30	30	166²	148	25	2.9	7.8	144	44%	.267	1.21	3.83	4.51	1.6	94.3	51.8	10.9	46.7
2017	KCA	MLB	34	8	13	0	32	32	180¹	209	26	2.4	7.2	145	38%	.318	1.43	5.29	5.57	0.0	93.5	50	10.4	47.9
2018	KCA	MLB	35	4	14	0	39	18	127	168	18	2.8	6.5	92	38%	.349	1.63	6.02	6.22	-1.4	94.0	51.6	10.1	48.9
2019	KCA	MLB	36	6	9	0	22	22	121	136	17	3.1	6.7	90	40%	.309	1.46	4.86	5.10	0.5	92.6	50	10.2	47

Breakout: 23%   Improve: 47%   Collapse: 13%   Attrition: 11%   MLB: 78%   *Comparables: John Lackey, Dan Haren, James Shields*

There's a certain art in being able to ride the wave of just-good-enough to a thirteen-year career, and Hammel has been the Picasso of this particular metier. Or perhaps Thomas Kinkade offers a better analogy, as even Hammel's best moments evoke nothing particularly interesting, bold, or memorable. In Kansas City over the past two seasons, the brushwork has become a bit sloppy, and Hammel has morphed from paint-by-numbers rotation filler to full-fledged disaster artist. The Royals, whose tolerance of bad art has been too generous at times, played the role of mean critic and declined their side of a mutual option for 2019.

Jake Junis RHP Born: 09/16/92 Age: 26 Bats: R Throws: R Height: 6'2" Weight: 225 Origin: Round 29, 2011 Draft (#876 overall)

YEAR	TEAM	LVL	AGE	W	L	SV	G	GS	IP	H	HR	BB/9	K/9	K	GB%	BABIP	WHIP	ERA	DRA	WARP	MPH	FB%	WHF	CSP
2016	NWA	AA	23	9	7	0	21	21	119	110	12	2.0	8.8	117	43%	.302	1.15	3.25	3.21	2.7				
2016	OMA	AAA	23	1	3	0	6	6	30	39	6	2.1	7.8	26	41%	.367	1.53	7.20	4.84	0.2				
2017	OMA	AAA	24	3	5	0	12	12	71	61	6	1.9	10.9	86	37%	.307	1.07	2.92	3.16	2.0				
2017	KCA	MLB	24	9	3	0	20	16	98¹	101	15	2.3	7.3	80	42%	.294	1.28	4.30	4.88	0.7	93.1	55.3	9.9	51.8
2018	KCA	MLB	25	9	12	0	30	30	177	182	32	2.2	8.3	164	43%	.298	1.27	4.37	5.53	-0.4	93.0	53.3	10.3	49.2
2019	KCA	MLB	26	8	10	0	27	27	154	155	19	2.7	8.2	140	41%	.306	1.30	4.16	4.35	2.0	92.7	54.9	10.4	51.2

Breakout: 27% Improve: 44% Collapse: 20% Attrition: 19% MLB: 86% *Comparables: Matt Boyd, Taylor Buchholz, Wade LeBlanc*

Over the course of the season, Junis logged 177 innings, making him the de facto workhorse of a beleaguered staff. And while the limited light of national attention on the Royals shone on the breakout of Adalberto Mondesi, the second half of 2018 saw a step forward from Junis that may have gotten lost in the shadows. Struggling with control in the middle of the season, Junis heeded the advice of pitching coach Cal Eldred to get back to basics, throwing his four-seam fastball more often. The result: He dramatically cut both walks and home runs—but it remains to be seen if a fastball-slider combo is enough for Junis to thrive as a starter. On a rebuilding team, he'll certainly get every chance to prove it.

Nate Karns RHP Born: 11/25/87 Age: 31 Bats: R Throws: R Height: 6'3" Weight: 225 Origin: Round 12, 2009 Draft (#352 overall)

YEAR	TEAM	LVL	AGE	W	L	SV	G	GS	IP	H	HR	BB/9	K/9	K	GB%	BABIP	WHIP	ERA	DRA	WARP	MPH	FB%	WHF	CSP
2016	SEA	MLB	28	6	2	1	22	15	94¹	95	11	4.3	9.6	101	43%	.327	1.48	5.15	4.50	0.9	95.8	52.8	11.6	48.2
2017	KCA	MLB	29	2	2	0	9	8	45¹	41	9	2.6	10.1	51	48%	.283	1.19	4.17	4.94	0.3	95.1	49.4	13.6	47.7
2019	KCA	MLB	31	2	2	0	6	6	34¹	33	5	3.8	9.3	36	44%	.307	1.39	4.43	4.62	0.3	94.7	51.2	12.3	47.6

Breakout: 28% Improve: 52% Collapse: 21% Attrition: 20% MLB: 88% *Comparables: Chris Narveson, Matt Shoemaker, Tom Gorzelanny*

Karns last threw a competitive pitch on May 19, 2017, when Brian Dozier flied out to center to end the bottom of the fifth. That otherwise unremarkable at-bat only gains significance as it recedes in the rear-view mirror, with only pain, surgery, rehab and waiting filling the space between. After missing most of 2017 and all of 2018 with thoracic outlet surgery, Karns enters 2019 hoping that a random Friday night in May represents the end of a chapter rather than the end of a career.

Brad Keller RHP Born: 07/27/95 Age: 23 Bats: R Throws: R Height: 6'5" Weight: 230 Origin: Round 8, 2013 Draft (#240 overall)

YEAR	TEAM	LVL	AGE	W	L	SV	G	GS	IP	H	HR	BB/9	K/9	K	GB%	BABIP	WHIP	ERA	DRA	WARP	MPH	FB%	WHF	CSP
2016	VIS	A+	20	9	7	0	24	24	135	147	13	1.7	6.6	99	56%	.321	1.28	4.47	4.08	2.2				
2017	WTN	AA	21	10	9	0	26	26	130²	142	7	3.9	7.6	111	51%	.339	1.52	4.68	4.07	1.7				
2018	KCA	MLB	22	9	6	0	41	20	140¹	133	7	3.2	6.2	96	56%	.294	1.30	3.08	4.87	0.6	96.1	69.8	9.8	46.5
2019	KCA	MLB	23	9	10	0	28	28	159²	162	14	3.2	7.0	124	51%	.307	1.37	4.09	4.28	2.2	96.0	72.3	10.1	48.2

Breakout: 20% Improve: 39% Collapse: 26% Attrition: 32% MLB: 79% *Comparables: Aaron Sanchez, Antonio Senzatela, Robert Gsellman*

Hailing from the bucolic-sounding town of Flowery Branch, Georgia, Keller was nabbed by the Reds from Arizona in the 2018 Rule 5 draft and immediately flipped to the Royals. Once in Kansas City, his reliable ground-ball tendencies earned him a rotation spot by the end of May and made him the Royals' most valuable starter in the second half of the season. Keller's sinking fastball is designed not for whiffs but for downward contact, and while it's fair to be skeptical of the gaudy ERA, his profile suggests a solid mid-rotation arm in 2019 and beyond. The problem is that he might just be the Royals' best candidate for Opening Day starter.

Ian Kennedy RHP Born: 12/19/84 Age: 34 Bats: R Throws: R Height: 6'0" Weight: 205 Origin: Round 1, 2006 Draft (#21 overall)

YEAR	TEAM	LVL	AGE	W	L	SV	G	GS	IP	H	HR	BB/9	K/9	K	GB%	BABIP	WHIP	ERA	DRA	WARP	MPH	FB%	WHF	CSP
2016	KCA	MLB	31	11	11	0	33	33	195²	173	33	3.0	8.5	184	34%	.268	1.22	3.68	4.93	1.0	94.5	66.2	11.1	48
2017	KCA	MLB	32	5	13	0	30	30	154	143	34	3.6	7.7	131	36%	.257	1.32	5.38	6.18	-1.0	93.6	61.7	10.2	50.2
2018	KCA	MLB	33	3	9	0	22	22	119²	125	20	3.0	7.9	105	31%	.298	1.38	4.66	5.32	0.0	93.7	58.7	9	49.2
2019	KCA	MLB	34	7	11	0	26	26	148¹	159	27	3.4	7.4	122	35%	.297	1.45	5.32	5.58	-0.2	92.8	61.2	9.9	48.5

Breakout: 18% Improve: 49% Collapse: 13% Attrition: 10% MLB: 82% *Comparables: Aaron Harang, Jerry Koosman, Earl Wilson*

There's no easier sport in the world than playing 20/20 hindsight with long-term free-agent contracts for pitchers in their early thirties coming off a down season and no sustained record of consistency, but you didn't need a modded-out DeLorean to see how this one would end up. Arriving in KC in 2016, just in time to experience the championship hangover without any of the champagne showers, Kennedy has labored to a total of one (one!) WARP across the first three seasons of a five (five!) year contract. The question isn't really whether he'll recoup any value, but whether it's possible for one pitcher to single-handedly reverse Kauffman's long-standing position as one of the more homer-unfriendly environments in the majors.

Jorge Lopez RHP Born: 02/10/93 Age: 26 Bats: R Throws: R Height: 6'3" Weight: 195 Origin: Round 2, 2011 Draft (#70 overall)

YEAR	TEAM	LVL	AGE	W	L	SV	G	GS	IP	H	HR	BB/9	K/9	K	GB%	BABIP	WHIP	ERA	DRA	WARP	MPH	FB%	WHF	CSP
2016	CSP	AAA	23	1	7	0	17	16	79¹	101	12	6.2	7.5	66	58%	.355	1.97	6.81	7.06	-1.6				
2016	BLX	AA	23	2	4	0	8	8	45¹	45	5	3.2	9.3	47	48%	.323	1.35	3.97	3.94	0.6				
2017	MIL	MLB	24	0	0	0	1	0	2	4	0	4.5	0.0	0	44%	.444	2.50	4.50	9.45	-0.1	96.1	74.3	5.7	42.2
2017	BLX	AA	24	8	8	7	39	13	103²	92	7	3.3	9.1	105	49%	.301	1.25	4.25	3.33	2.1				
2018	CSP	AAA	25	3	3	5	24	0	28²	33	3	3.1	7.2	23	63%	.333	1.50	5.65	4.23	0.3				
2018	MIL	MLB	25	0	1	0	10	0	19²	16	1	5.9	6.9	15	56%	.268	1.47	2.75	3.84	0.3	95.6	53.5	11.5	43.8
2018	OMA	AAA	25	1	0	0	2	2	9	8	2	1.0	11.0	11	26%	.286	1.00	4.00	2.83	0.2				
2018	KCA	MLB	25	2	4	0	7	7	34	41	5	2.4	6.1	23	40%	.324	1.47	6.35	5.08	0.0	95.2	50.8	7.4	51.1
2019	KCA	MLB	26	5	5	0	52	11	98²	105	12	4.2	7.4	81	48%	.314	1.53	4.78	5.01	0.3	95.0	53.4	8.9	46.5

Breakout: 23%   Improve: 37%   Collapse: 14%   Attrition: 25%   MLB: 67%   *Comparables: Clay Hensley, Rafael Montero, Bryan Mitchell*

In dealing Mike Moustakas, the Royals did something that may prove to be sneaky smart; rather than getting back high-upside prospects who were years away from big-league contribution, they got two distressed assets who were potentially close to major-league contribution. While there was some prospect fatigue with former top-100 outfielder Brett Phillips, Lopez, the other piece in the trade, had been battered and bruised by the thin air of Colorado Springs, the unfortunately-chosen Triple-A outlet of the Brewers (and a city which has since been demoted to Rookie League affiliation). Lopez features a fringy fastball but excellent command of secondary pitches, including a plus curveball—precisely the profile to generate a 6.52 ERA across a season and a half with the Sky Sox. Some late-season work with the Royals proved inconclusive, but the lower-altitude Lopez should get a chance at a career reset in 2019.

Richard Lovelady LHP Born: 07/07/95 Age: 23 Bats: L Throws: L Height: 6'0" Weight: 175 Origin: Round 10, 2016 Draft (#313 overall)

YEAR	TEAM	LVL	AGE	W	L	SV	G	GS	IP	H	HR	BB/9	K/9	K	GB%	BABIP	WHIP	ERA	DRA	WARP	MPH	FB%	WHF	CSP
2016	ROY	RK	20	2	0	3	8	0	10¹	4	0	1.7	12.2	14	52%	.174	0.58	1.74	1.88	0.4				
2016	IDA	RK	20	0	1	6	13	0	14²	10	0	4.3	9.8	16	71%	.294	1.16	1.84	3.76	0.3				
2017	WIL	A+	21	1	0	7	21	0	33¹	18	0	1.1	11.1	41	70%	.237	0.66	1.08	2.99	0.7				
2017	NWA	AA	21	3	2	3	21	0	33¹	28	1	3.5	9.7	36	50%	.310	1.23	2.16	3.68	0.4				
2018	OMA	AAA	22	3	3	9	46	0	73	53	3	2.6	8.8	71	51%	.262	1.01	2.47	2.45	2.2				
2019	KCA	MLB	23	3	1	2	53	0	56	52	6	4.5	8.4	53	51%	.294	1.42	4.43	4.63	0.4				

Breakout: 12%   Improve: 23%   Collapse: 20%   Attrition: 28%   MLB: 48%   *Comparables: Corey Knebel, Eduardo Sanchez, Bruce Rondon*

Like first-base prospects, minor-league pitchers already placed in the "reliever" bucket have gotten a bad rap. But after a Brewers playoff run that saw every broadcaster and analyst breathlessly obsess over Josh Hader whether or not he was actually pitching, future bullpen arms can now step into the light and puff their chests with pride over their newfound importance. Lovelady is vaguely Haderesque in his high-90s velocity and low-slung arm slot, and after a season that saw him emerge from the abattoir of the PCL relatively bloodlessly, he should have the chance to arrive in the majors in 2019. Whether he becomes a LOOGY, a multi-inning stopper, or a closer, the opportunities—and the puerile nicknames—should be plentiful.

Daniel Lynch LHP Born: 11/17/96 Age: 22 Bats: L Throws: L Height: 6'6" Weight: 190 Origin: Round 1C, 2018 Draft (#34 overall)

YEAR	TEAM	LVL	AGE	W	L	SV	G	GS	IP	H	HR	BB/9	K/9	K	GB%	BABIP	WHIP	ERA	DRA	WARP	MPH	FB%	WHF	CSP
2018	BNC	RK	21	0	0	0	3	3	11¹	9	0	1.6	11.1	14	59%	.310	0.97	1.59	3.28	0.3				
2018	LEX	A	21	5	1	0	9	9	40	35	1	1.4	10.6	47	51%	.343	1.02	1.58	3.57	0.8				
2019	KCA	MLB	22	2	3	0	8	8	34¹	36	5	3.2	8.3	32	45%	.314	1.40	4.47	4.67	0.3				

Breakout: 4%   Improve: 7%   Collapse: 4%   Attrition: 6%   MLB: 11%   *Comparables: Nik Turley, Alex Wood, Frankie Montas*

After Florida's Brady Singer and Jackson Kowar, Lynch, a Virginia product, was the third piece of the big-college pitcher draft strategy for the Royals in 2018. While the race to the majors is long, even for advanced prospects such as these, Lynch jumped out to an early lead by breezing through rookie ball and logging a productive stretch at Low-A Lexington, where he displayed both turbo velocity and excellent control. Given his spotty secondary pitches and flying-bundle-of-sticks mechanics, the likeliest outcome for Lynch is as a power lefty out of the pen, which could put him on an even faster track to a major-league debut than the other members of his draft cohort.

Brandon Maurer RHP Born: 07/03/90 Age: 28 Bats: R Throws: R Height: 6'5" Weight: 225 Origin: Round 23, 2008 Draft (#702 overall)

YEAR	TEAM	LVL	AGE	W	L	SV	G	GS	IP	H	HR	BB/9	K/9	K	GB%	BABIP	WHIP	ERA	DRA	WARP	MPH	FB%	WHF	CSP
2016	SDN	MLB	25	0	5	13	71	0	69²	65	7	3.0	9.3	72	39%	.297	1.26	4.52	3.80	0.9	98.4	55.3	12.7	48.4
2017	SDN	MLB	26	1	4	20	42	0	39¹	39	4	1.8	8.7	38	44%	.315	1.19	5.72	4.61	0.2	98.6	58.2	11	52
2017	KCA	MLB	26	2	2	2	26	0	20	34	4	4.9	9.4	21	33%	.435	2.25	8.10	5.27	0.0	98.8	54.6	10.6	50
2018	OMA	AAA	27	1	3	5	19	0	23	23	1	5.1	9.4	24	54%	.333	1.57	5.48	2.61	0.7				
2018	KCA	MLB	27	0	4	1	37	0	31¹	42	7	7.2	8.9	31	43%	.365	2.14	7.76	6.45	-0.5	98.7	44.3	11	46
2019	KCA	MLB	28	2	1	8	48	0	51¹	53	6	4.3	8.3	47	42%	.312	1.52	4.66	4.87	0.1	98.0	52.8	11.5	48.6

Breakout: 25%   Improve: 54%   Collapse: 18%   Attrition: 5%   MLB: 96%   *Comparables: Mark Lowe, Dan Wheeler, Tony Castillo*

When mysteries are presented to the human mind, we will always speculate as to their answers, even in the absence of sufficient data or evidence. The mystery of Maurer's silent "r" is no different. The Padres, noting Maurer's spotty record as a starter, took it to stand for "reliever," and he became a usable closer over parts of two seasons. Kansas City may have interpreted it to mean "Royal," and they acquired him in a six-player deadline deal in 2017. Once in KC, the mystery of the silent "r" was solved beyond any doubt: it stood for "runs," of which Maurer gave up nearly one per inning in his two-season tenure. The Royals had the literal last "r" word, however, releasing the disappointing righty after the 2018 season.

Kevin McCarthy RHP Born: 02/22/92 Age: 27 Bats: R Throws: R Height: 6'3" Weight: 215 Origin: Round 16, 2013 Draft (#474 overall)

YEAR	TEAM	LVL	AGE	W	L	SV	G	GS	IP	H	HR	BB/9	K/9	K	GB%	BABIP	WHIP	ERA	DRA	WARP	MPH	FB%	WHF	CSP
2016	NWA	AA	24	3	2	11	22	0	34²	26	3	2.1	7.5	29	53%	.245	0.98	3.12	2.97	0.7				
2016	OMA	AAA	24	2	4	5	25	0	33¹	28	4	4.3	8.1	30	56%	.270	1.32	2.97	3.85	0.4				
2016	KCA	MLB	24	1	0	0	10	0	8¹	11	1	5.4	7.6	7	55%	.357	1.92	6.48	7.59	-0.2	96.1	61.5	4.8	48.5
2017	OMA	AAA	25	1	1	2	25	0	32	32	3	2.5	4.8	17	58%	.296	1.28	3.09	4.04	0.4				
2017	KCA	MLB	25	1	0	0	33	0	45	50	4	2.6	5.4	27	55%	.303	1.40	3.20	5.36	-0.1	94.3	60.8	9.7	52.3
2018	KCA	MLB	26	5	4	0	65	0	72	70	7	2.5	5.8	46	65%	.289	1.25	3.25	4.46	0.4	93.4	67	10.1	49.4
2019	*KCA*	*MLB*	*27*	*3*	*1*	*2*	*57*	*0*	*59²*	*60*	*5*	*3.6*	*6.6*	*44*	*54%*	*.299*	*1.41*	*4.24*	*4.44*	*0.5*	*93.3*	*65.3*	*9.8*	*50.7*

Breakout: 21%   Improve: 41%   Collapse: 20%   Attrition: 23%   MLB: 71%   *Comparables: Ramon Troncoso, Franquelis Osoria, Ryan Webb*

The answer to the never-to-be-asked trivia question, "Who was the 2018 Royals best reliever by BWARP?," McCarthy managed an impressively anonymous season of steady, unspectacular competence. Inducing ground-ball contact on nearly two-thirds of his hitters faced (which ranked him fourth in the majors among pitchers with at least 70 IP), McCarthy found a formula of sorts to become one of the only reliable arms in an otherwise shaky pen. His sinker/change combo is built for contact rather than strikeouts, however, which suggests a return to a middle-inning role.

Trevor Oaks RHP Born: 03/26/93 Age: 26 Bats: R Throws: R Height: 6'3" Weight: 225 Origin: Round 7, 2014 Draft (#219 overall)

YEAR	TEAM	LVL	AGE	W	L	SV	G	GS	IP	H	HR	BB/9	K/9	K	GB%	BABIP	WHIP	ERA	DRA	WARP	MPH	FB%	WHF	CSP
2016	RCU	A+	23	1	1	0	4	4	25	26	1	1.1	7.9	22	60%	.352	1.16	3.60	3.28	0.6				
2016	TUL	AA	23	8	1	0	10	10	63	56	1	1.3	5.4	38	65%	.276	1.03	2.14	2.99	1.6				
2016	OKL	AAA	23	5	1	0	10	10	63	64	7	1.3	6.9	48	58%	.300	1.16	3.00	3.50	1.3				
2017	OKL	AAA	24	4	3	0	16	15	84	87	5	1.9	7.7	72	52%	.336	1.25	3.64	4.07	1.5				
2018	KCA	MLB	25	0	2	0	4	2	13²	21	1	4.0	6.6	10	45%	.417	1.98	7.24	5.48	0.0	91.1	58.7	11.7	47.1
2018	OMA	AAA	25	8	8	0	22	22	128¹	130	5	3.1	4.9	70	51%	.298	1.36	3.23	5.40	0.2				
2019	*KCA*	*MLB*	*26*	*3*	*3*	*0*	*18*	*8*	*53¹*	*57*	*6*	*3.0*	*6.0*	*36*	*50%*	*.303*	*1.39*	*4.49*	*4.71*	*0.4*	*90.7*	*59.8*	*12*	*47.9*

Breakout: 11%   Improve: 20%   Collapse: 14%   Attrition: 26%   MLB: 47%   *Comparables: Jake Buchanan, Tyler Wagner, Myles Jaye*

One of the few things a pitcher can do to push back on the entropy and decay that attends the forward motion of time's arrow is to learn a new pitch, or significantly alter an existing one. Oaks, working with former major-leaguers Justin Masterson and some dude named Greg Maddux, modified his bread-and-butter sinker to return to the elite ground-ball rates he posted before an oblique injury cost him most of 2017. While the 2018 results were good at Triple-A, and earned him a few innings in the show, his only path to major-league relevance is by pitching to contact, and if that contact isn't both weak and downward, Oaks' career path will be.

Wily Peralta RHP Born: 05/08/89 Age: 30 Bats: R Throws: R Height: 6'1" Weight: 255 Origin: International Free Agent, 2005

YEAR	TEAM	LVL	AGE	W	L	SV	G	GS	IP	H	HR	BB/9	K/9	K	GB%	BABIP	WHIP	ERA	DRA	WARP	MPH	FB%	WHF	CSP
2016	CSP	AAA	27	1	3	0	10	10	41¹	55	5	3.7	8.5	39	56%	.391	1.74	6.31	4.92	0.2				
2016	MIL	MLB	27	7	11	0	23	23	127²	152	19	3.0	6.6	93	52%	.336	1.53	4.86	5.82	-0.7	97.6	62.7	9.4	41.5
2017	MIL	MLB	28	5	4	0	19	8	57¹	73	10	5.0	8.2	52	46%	.362	1.83	7.85	7.18	-1.1	97.8	58.4	9.3	42.4
2017	CSP	AAA	28	1	0	1	13	0	16	13	0	5.6	5.6	10	57%	.255	1.44	3.38	4.84	0.1				
2018	OMA	AAA	29	0	1	1	18	2	35	36	3	5.4	10.0	39	57%	.351	1.63	4.37	3.70	0.6				
2018	KCA	MLB	29	1	0	14	37	0	34¹	28	4	6.0	9.2	35	49%	.279	1.49	3.67	6.24	-0.5	97.8	49.6	10.5	43.7
2019	*KCA*	*MLB*	*30*	*3*	*1*	*30*	*57*	*0*	*59²*	*62*	*7*	*4.4*	*8.3*	*55*	*49%*	*.321*	*1.53*	*4.53*	*4.73*	*0.3*	*96.9*	*58.3*	*9.6*	*42.6*

Breakout: 18%   Improve: 55%   Collapse: 13%   Attrition: 12%   MLB: 84%   *Comparables: Victor Santos, Dillon Gee, Ross Detwiler*

For a bad team, the last few months of a baseball season must be a weird time. Summer drags on interminably; everyone has to find reasons to show up and care about making pitches, grinding out at bats, staying healthy, and generally trying to derive some purpose and pleasure from a game that must feel like a clock-punching exercise. For Peralta, earning and keeping the rarefied title of "major-league closer" may have held some motivation. By this criterion, Peralta was perfect: 14 save chances, all converted (the only other pitcher with more than ten saves not to blow a chance in 2018? Ken Giles). Peralta still walked far too many batters, and his role would likely have come under scrutiny on a team with more at stake, but for the Royals in 2018, the unblemished results were enough to transform him into a capital-C Closer and give him the inside track to continue the role in 2019.

Brady Singer RHP Born: 08/04/96 Age: 22 Bats: R Throws: R Height: 6'5" Weight: 210 Origin: Round 1, 2018 Draft (#18 overall)

It might not have been "Old Man Yells at Cloud," but the widely-circulated video of the Royals' 2018 first-round pick spitting expletives at a College World Series delay might be titled "Young Man Curses at Rain." In spite of the extremely audible F-bombs, clean-livin' advocate Dayton Moore took this as a sign of Singer's competitive fire and evidence of that indefinable aura of "makeup." Intangibles aside, what is very tangible is Singer's talent and arsenal: a mid-90s fastball, complementary slider, and emerging changeup—all burnished in the elite competitive environment of the SEC. Once mentioned as a possible first-overall pick, Singer seemed to suffer from prospect fatigue despite winning a Dick Howser Award (for the best college player) and the SEC Pitcher of the Year Award. The Royals were apparently so happy to get him at pick 18 that they ended up going nearly a million dollars over slot to sign the righty. Challenging overused abbreviations addressing the ontology of pitching prospects, Singer will be expected to move quickly through the minors and arrive as a main rotation piece of the next competitive Royals team.

Eric Skoglund LHP   Born: 10/26/92   Age: 26   Bats: L   Throws: L   Height: 6'7"   Weight: 210   Origin: Round 3, 2014 Draft (#92 overall)

YEAR	TEAM	LVL	AGE	W	L	SV	G	GS	IP	H	HR	BB/9	K/9	K	GB%	BABIP	WHIP	ERA	DRA	WARP	MPH	FB%	WHF	CSP
2016	NWA	AA	23	7	10	0	27	27	156¹	135	19	2.2	7.7	134	44%	.263	1.11	3.45	3.31	3.4				
2017	OMA	AAA	24	4	5	0	19	19	100²	110	14	2.6	9.1	102	42%	.331	1.38	4.11	3.75	2.2				
2017	KCA	MLB	24	1	2	0	7	5	18	30	2	6.0	7.0	14	39%	.431	2.33	9.50	8.05	-0.5	94.1	63.3	7.1	54
2018	KCA	MLB	25	1	6	0	14	13	70	66	12	2.4	6.3	49	44%	.261	1.21	5.14	6.20	-0.7	93.4	60.2	8	49.2
2019	KCA	MLB	26	4	5	0	23	13	85	90	11	3.1	6.9	65	42%	.301	1.40	4.67	4.89	0.5	93.1	62	8	52.2

Breakout: 21%   Improve: 39%   Collapse: 28%   Attrition: 39%   MLB: 77%   *Comparables: Marco Gonzales, Parker Bridwell, A.J. Cole*

One thing that defines the current pitching epoch: tall, skinny lefties will find work beyond the point where skill level ceases to merit continued employment. OK, that's been true since the dawn of the La Russa bullpen, but now those guys are starting, too. Maybe something about the visual echoes of Sale, Kershaw, and Hader work unconsciously on scouts, GMs and managers to project glimmers of something great where there is mere competence. This is just a theory, but it's one that may be tested by the role Skoglund assumes in 2019. The average fastball, low strikeout rates and home-run propensity put him in a very large and crowded bucket with other potential fifth-starter pieces in Kansas City, but everyone loves a limb-shaking southpaw, and Skoglund may well be chosen for rotation duty simply because Ned Yost can't see who's standing behind him.

Burch Smith RHP   Born: 04/12/90   Age: 29   Bats: R   Throws: R   Height: 6'4"   Weight: 225   Origin: Round 14, 2011 Draft (#443 overall)

YEAR	TEAM	LVL	AGE	W	L	SV	G	GS	IP	H	HR	BB/9	K/9	K	GB%	BABIP	WHIP	ERA	DRA	WARP	MPH	FB%	WHF	CSP
2017	PCH	A+	27	3	1	0	9	8	37	26	1	4.9	8.0	33	35%	.255	1.24	2.43	5.84	-0.3				
2017	DUR	AAA	27	2	1	0	3	3	16¹	9	2	2.2	10.5	19	46%	.200	0.80	1.65	1.95	0.7				
2018	KCA	MLB	28	1	6	0	38	6	78	90	15	4.6	8.9	77	41%	.338	1.67	6.92	6.28	-1.1	96.1	61.8	11.1	48.9
2019	KCA	MLB	29	3	3	0	35	8	63²	67	10	4.6	8.3	59	40%	.310	1.56	5.19	5.43	-0.2	95.4	61.8	11.1	48.9

Breakout: 22%   Improve: 37%   Collapse: 16%   Attrition: 17%   MLB: 65%   *Comparables: Jeff Samardzija, Jason Bergmann, Matt Kinney*

The accepted custom for the Comeback Player of the Year is that a candidate has to have fallen from great heights and returned to at least moderate success; it's never given to someone who wasn't an All-Star, much less to an anonymous swingman-type. But with his spondaic, arboreal name straight out of a Robert Frost poem, Smith doggedly labored his way back from an early 2014 injury that led to Tommy John surgery and the associated rehab, with a four-year lacuna in his major-league stat line. There was no fanfare for a return to a season that saw far too many walks and homers, but they were major-league walks and homers, at least. Pitchers who miss that much time almost never make it within a stone's throw of the majors; Smith, to his credit, has indeed taken the road less travelled. Whether it makes a difference to the Royals, or any team, is a verse yet unwritten.

Glenn Sparkman RHP   Born: 05/11/92   Age: 27   Bats: B   Throws: R   Height: 6'2"   Weight: 210   Origin: Round 20, 2013 Draft (#594 overall)

YEAR	TEAM	LVL	AGE	W	L	SV	G	GS	IP	H	HR	BB/9	K/9	K	GB%	BABIP	WHIP	ERA	DRA	WARP	MPH	FB%	WHF	CSP
2016	ROY	RK	24	1	3	0	7	7	16²	19	1	0.5	9.2	17	56%	.353	1.20	5.40	3.10	0.5				
2016	LEX	A	24	0	2	0	3	3	14¹	21	2	1.9	11.9	19	46%	.487	1.67	6.91	2.65	0.4				
2016	WIL	A+	24	1	0	0	2	2	11²	9	1	0.8	6.9	9	46%	.235	0.86	3.86	3.62	0.2				
2016	NWA	AA	24	0	2	0	4	4	17²	21	2	2.5	10.2	20	30%	.373	1.47	4.58	2.59	0.5				
2017	TOR	MLB	25	0	0	0	2	0	1	9	0	9.0	9.0	1	20%	.900	10.00	63.00	9.33	0.0	95.2	63.6	3.6	46.8
2018	NWA	AA	26	3	2	0	6	6	33²	35	4	0.3	7.0	26	45%	.321	1.07	2.94	4.47	0.3				
2018	OMA	AAA	26	5	1	0	12	12	67¹	76	10	1.5	6.4	48	46%	.314	1.29	4.01	3.74	1.4				
2018	KCA	MLB	26	0	3	0	15	3	38¹	47	3	3.5	6.3	27	47%	.338	1.62	4.46	5.21	-0.1	95.9	56.6	10.6	48.9
2019	KCA	MLB	27	1	1	0	31	0	32²	37	4	3.2	6.4	23	43%	.313	1.50	4.85	5.08	0.0	95.4	57.7	10.3	48.6

Breakout: 12%   Improve: 16%   Collapse: 30%   Attrition: 38%   MLB: 65%   *Comparables: Sean Gilmartin, Cody Martin, Seth Lugo*

The Rule 5 draft is a garage sale with a very liberal return policy. We all know about those Rule 5 picks who go on to great success: Dan Uggla. Johan Santana. Jose Bautista. R.A. Dickey. But what about the players returned to their original teams? How does a used suit feel when it doesn't even merit the forgotten spot at the dark end of the closet? After suffering a broken thumb in the spring of 2017, Sparkman was returned from the Blue Jays to the Royals. He worked his way into a midseason call-up in 2018 and did what swing men are built to do: ate some innings in blowout losses and earned a few starts when pitchers (Danny Duffy, in this instance) were sidelined. Sparkman has decent control, mid-90s velocity, and ground-ball tendencies, all of which are useful but none of which are exceptional enough to lift him out of swingman purgatory, or into a guaranteed job.

Josh Staumont RHP   Born: 12/21/93   Age: 25   Bats: R   Throws: R   Height: 6'3"   Weight: 200   Origin: Round 2, 2015 Draft (#64 overall)

YEAR	TEAM	LVL	AGE	W	L	SV	G	GS	IP	H	HR	BB/9	K/9	K	GB%	BABIP	WHIP	ERA	DRA	WARP	MPH	FB%	WHF	CSP
2016	WIL	A+	22	2	10	0	18	15	73	62	3	8.3	11.6	94	46%	.328	1.77	5.05	4.10	1.1				
2016	NWA	AA	22	2	1	0	11	11	50¹	42	2	6.6	13.1	73	42%	.364	1.57	3.04	3.38	1.0				
2017	OMA	AAA	23	3	8	0	16	15	76	64	14	7.5	11.0	93	41%	.279	1.67	6.28	4.72	0.8				
2017	NWA	AA	23	3	4	0	10	10	48²	42	2	6.3	8.3	45	36%	.308	1.56	4.44	4.74	0.2				
2018	OMA	AAA	24	2	5	1	41	5	74¹	59	4	6.3	12.5	103	44%	.327	1.49	3.51	3.77	1.2				
2019	KCA	MLB	25	1	0	0	31	0	32²	29	5	7.9	11.1	40	41%	.308	1.77	5.57	5.81	-0.4				

Breakout: 18%   Improve: 23%   Collapse: 10%   Attrition: 26%   MLB: 38%   *Comparables: Matt Magill, Esmerling Vasquez, Kyle Crick*

With his big, scary triple-digit fastball, Staumont stands out in a system in which command-control is the name of the game. Unfortunately, the fastball is, like, *really* scary, as no one in the park, much less Staumont himself, has any idea where it's going. It's a testament to his raw stuff that the power righty managed a Triple-A ERA that was little more than half of his BB/9. "Effectively wild" is often used as a backhanded compliment for a pitcher, but in Staumont's case, it's a life goal.

LINEOUTS

Hitters

HITTER	POS	TEAM	LVL	AGE	PA	R	2B	3B	HR	RBI	BB	K	SB	CS	AVG/OBP/SLG	DRC+	VORP	BABIP	BRR	FRAA	WARP
Gabriel Cancel	2B	WIL	A+	21	507	54	31	1	8	73	35	91	7	4	.259/.316/.385	97	15.5	.301	0.5	2B(87): 1.6, SS(12): 0.3	1.3
Donald Dewees	CF	NWA	AA	24	310	35	12	5	2	25	20	48	8	4	.253/.305/.351	92	3.0	.297	-0.6	CF(69): 5.3	1.2
	CF	OMA	AAA	24	241	31	11	3	6	29	15	45	8	2	.266/.315/.423	88	9.3	.310	2.2	CF(36): 5.8, RF(14): 3.9	1.7
Samir Duenez	1B	NWA	AA	22	328	44	18	2	10	60	35	68	5	0	.282/.357/.463	112	12.7	.332	-0.1	1B(76): -4.1	0.4
Kelvin Gutierrez	3B	HAR	AA	23	249	36	6	3	5	26	16	62	10	1	.274/.321/.391	87	9.2	.352	1.0	3B(56): 12.7, SS(1): 0.1	1.9
	3B	NWA	AA	23	264	29	8	3	6	40	20	46	10	3	.277/.337/.409	106	9.8	.321	1.3	3B(62): -0.7, SS(2): -0.2	1.1
Paulo Orlando	RF	KCA	MLB	32	93	6	3	0	0	5	3	25	0	0	.167/.194/.200	52	-7.8	.231	-0.1	CF(16): 0.2, LF(3): -0.2	-0.3
	RF	OMA	AAA	32	311	46	17	2	12	41	17	58	2	0	.270/.319/.467	107	16.2	.301	-2.1	RF(38): -1.1, LF(18): 0.3	0.7
Blake Perkins	CF	POT	A+	21	305	39	11	0	1	21	42	67	12	5	.234/.344/.290	94	7.9	.307	2.7	CF(62): -6.6, LF(1): 0.1	0.4
	CF	WIL	A+	21	291	48	11	1	2	18	50	67	17	4	.240/.381/.322	93	11.3	.329	0.4	CF(61): 11.9, LF(1): -0.1	2.0
Emmanuel Rivera	3B	WIL	A+	22	411	45	25	6	6	61	29	59	3	2	.280/.333/.427	105	16.8	.315	-2.0	3B(89): -5.8	0.7
Frank Schwindel	1B	OMA	AAA	26	556	65	38	1	24	93	34	71	2	2	.286/.336/.506	116	31.2	.290	-1.1	1B(63): -6.7	1.3
Bubba Starling	OF	OMA	AAA	25	41	5	2	0	0	2	5	6	1	0	.257/.350/.314	88	0.8	.310	-0.2	CF(10): -0.7, RF(1): -0.1	0.0
Ramon Torres	2B	KCA	MLB	25	29	4	1	0	0	1	1	3	0	0	.179/.207/.214	87	-2.5	.200	0.2	3B(6): 0.1, 2B(3): -0.2	0.1
	2B	OMA	AAA	25	405	44	20	2	6	27	25	59	6	3	.230/.279/.343	71	1.6	.257	0.7	2B(38): 1.3, 3B(30): 0.3	0.0

In a full season as a 21 year-old in High-A, **Gabriel Cancel** started slow and finished strong, which is better than the opposite. With time on his side, and some room for growth in both power and speed, he may yet develop into a middle infielder who can offer more than bupkus with the bat. ⓧ It's not optimal to be a fringy fourth-outfielder in a system particularly deep in fourth outfielders. **Donnie Dewees** offers a little bit of everything—power, speed, hit—but as you read that sentence to yourself, put the stress on the "little bit" rather than the "everything." ⓧ If describing **Samir Duenez** as the second-best first-base prospect in an organization sounds like damnation by faint praise, well, at least his developing power and patience are praiseworthy. 2018 was not an ideal year to lose a half season to a wrist injury, as Duenez now has the promising Nick Pratto looming in the rear view mirror. ⓧ After an impressive 2017 that ended in Low-A Lexington, center field prospect **Michael Gigliotti** began 2018 with a pop—unfortunately, of his ACL. Given that Gigliotti's value resides with speed and defense—things you'd ideally want two healthy knees for—the clock is on pause until we see how he comes out of the gate in 2019. ⓧ In a rare Kelvin-for-Kelvin swap, the Royals received third baseman **Kelvin Gutierrez** from the Nationals when they shipped closer Herrera in a midseason deal. The current Kelvin is a capable defender who lacks the power one would prefer at a corner position, but even if he's rushed to the majors, his offensive production won't be an absolute zero. ⓧ Being second-best at something is usually something to be proud of, but as the second-best Brazilian position player in major-league history, **Paulo Orlando** would prefer that this particular club held more members than him and Yan Gomes. Any chance to eclipse Gomes will have to come with another club, as the Royals have plenty of younger options for "offensively-challenged righty platoon bat" and cut ties with Orlando after the 2018 season. ⓧ **Blake Perkins** arrived in the Kelvin Herrera trade, providing the Royals another speedy centerfielder-type to their growing minor-league collection. Perkins stands out in this group for his patience at the plate and his switch-hitting, but if he makes it to the bigs, it will almost certainly be for defensive reasons. ⓧ Rare among Royals prospects for his advanced plate approach, **Emmanuel Rivera** is also a polished defender at the hot corner. While the big club has a desperate need for a third baseman, Rivera still needs some time in the oven, ideally to bake in more power. ⓧ After nearly a thousand Triple-A plate appearances with an .853 OPS and not even a sniff of the big club, the Royals seem to have decided that "King of Omaha" **Frank Schwindel** is organizational filler. The Royals will probably look elsewhere for a righty platoon partner for Ryan O'Hearn, but should they? ⓧ At this point, 2011 fifth-overall pick **Bubba Starling**, who lost last season to myriad injuries and has yet to see his major-league debut, would likely sell off parts of his soul to duplicate the five-win career of Bubba Trammell. ⓧ One definition of "utility" is "functional rather than attractive." Speaking in baseball terms, **Ramon Torres** is an archetypal utility player: functional middle-infield defense and hitting that—no, really, just look away.

Pitchers

PITCHER	TEAM	LVL	AGE	W	L	SV	G	GS	IP	H	HR	BB/9	K/9	K	GB%	BABIP	WHIP	ERA	DRA	WARP	MPH	FB%	WHF	CSP
Yefri Del Rosario	LEX	A	18	6	5	0	15	15	79	69	10	3.3	8.2	72	40%	.263	1.24	3.19	4.95	0.2				
Conner Greene	SFD	AA	23	4	3	0	11	10	48²	43	1	5.9	8.0	43	49%	.302	1.54	4.44	4.67	0.4				
	MEM	AAA	23	0	2	0	29	0	39¹	33	2	7.1	5.9	26	47%	.282	1.63	3.66	4.22	0.4				
Foster Griffin	NWA	AA	22	10	12	0	28	26	152²	197	20	2.4	6.9	117	39%	.357	1.55	5.13	5.11	0.4				
Carlos Hernandez	LEX	A	21	6	5	0	15	15	79¹	71	7	2.6	9.3	82	44%	.298	1.18	3.29	6.02	-0.8				
Tim Hill	KCA	MLB	28	1	4	2	70	0	45²	46	4	2.8	8.3	42	64%	.309	1.31	4.53	5.00	0.0	93.1	76.4	9.5	55.6
Jackson Kowar	LEX	A	21	0	1	0	9	9	26¹	19	2	4.1	7.5	22	59%	.239	1.18	3.42	3.90	0.4				
Ben Lively	PHI	MLB	26	0	2	0	5	5	23²	34	4	3.8	8.4	22	30%	.395	1.86	6.85	5.12	0.0	92.6	61.9	8.6	52.1
	LEH	AAA	26	3	2	0	11	8	52	37	3	2.6	8.1	47	43%	.250	1.00	2.42	3.85	1.0				
	KCA	MLB	26	0	1	0	5	0	6²	7	0	6.8	6.8	5	55%	.350	1.80	1.35	4.67	0.0	95.0	56.2	7.4	47.9
Andres Machado	OMA	AAA	25	0	4	0	7	6	25	41	4	5.8	9.0	25	51%	.435	2.28	9.72	5.87	-0.1				
	NWA	AA	25	2	3	9	30	6	58	60	5	3.4	7.3	47	45%	.314	1.41	3.72	4.50	0.4				
Jake Newberry	NWA	AA	23	2	0	12	25	0	29²	29	2	2.4	11.2	37	32%	.360	1.25	2.12	2.79	0.7				
	OMA	AAA	23	3	0	3	16	0	20	13	1	2.7	7.2	16	51%	.231	0.95	0.90	3.26	0.4				
	KCA	MLB	23	2	0	0	14	0	13¹	13	3	6.1	7.4	11	32%	.270	1.65	4.72	5.64	-0.1	95.3	54.8	10.3	47.1

Two things about **Yefri Del Rosario**: 1) He was an 18-year-old pitching in the Sally League. 2) He rejected better offers to sign with the Royals because of his respect for the late Yordano Ventura. His mid-90s fastball velocity is reminiscent of his idol, and he's got time on his side to develop his secondary offerings. ⚾ **Conner Greene** has a double consonant in one name, a double vowel in the other, flirts with triple digits on the fastball, and is doomed to a Quadruple A future in baseball. ⚾ The route from Arvest Ballpark in Springdale, Arkansas to Kauffman Stadium is pretty much a straight shot north on I-49—225 miles, according to Google Maps. With an underwhelming second year in Double-A, and a fastball that rarely touches 90 mph, **Foster Griffin** may as well measure that distance in light years. ⚾ Tall, slender, and projectable, **Carlos Hernandez** fared well in the better part of a season at Low-A. With an electric mid-90s sinker and (stop us if you've heard this before) still-developing secondary offerings, Hernandez has a future that falls in that Venn diagram intersection of "back-end starter" and "power reliever," which can be said of nearly every Royals pitching prospect not named Singer, Kowar, or Lynch. ⚾ **Tim Hill** shares a throwing side (left) and a last name with a certain pitcher who earned the nickname "Dick Mountain" from his Dodger teammates. Tim Hill can aspire to modest heights—Tim Rise, Tim Mound, Tim Butte, Tim Hummock—but he will never be Tim Mountain. ⚾ The Sundance Kid to Brady Singer's Butch Cassidy at the University of Florida, **Jackson Kowar** and his compadre will reprise their buddy-movie roles in the Royals system, having both been first-round picks of the club in 2018. Kowar has an angry fastball, but sometimes it shoots a little too straight, and rounding out the arsenal will be the primary quest for 2019. ⚾ The Royals claimed **Ben Lively** off of waivers from Philadelphia in September, because why not? The former prospect threw a handful of late-season innings out of the pen, jumping his four-seam velocity from the low- to mid-90s and possibly hinting at his future major-league role, if he is indeed to have one. ⚾ After a brief taste of the bigs in 2017, **Andres Machado** reversed course this past season. Demoted from Triple to Double-A in May and pushed into the bullpen shortly thereafter, the Venezuelan righty will need to re-discover his slider and his command before climbing back up the organizational ladder. ⚾ One instinctively roots for a 37th-round pick to make good, and if "making good" means pitching in the major leagues, then **Jake Newberry** realized a dream in August. Given a fringy fastball and middling secondary offerings, making a 25-man roster in 2019 might prove a second-level challenge.

LOS ANGELES ANGELS

Essay by Rachael McDaniel

Player comments by Matt Sussman, Craig Goldstein and BP staff

On April 3rd, Shohei Ohtani came to the plate for the Angels in the bottom of the first. There were two out. The bases were loaded. Mike Trout had already homered in the inning, turning what had been a 2-0 lead for Cleveland into a 2-1 lead; a Kole Calhoun RBI single brought the score to a 2-2 tie, where it stood as Ohtani walked slowly to the plate. It was his first home plate appearance as a major league baseball player. The fans packing Angels Stadium rose to their feet; the crush of photographers and reporters who had come from far and wide specifically to document this moment stood at attention. And around the world, the signal went out, through texts and tweets and push notifications. If you were a baseball fan—no matter which team you rooted for, no matter which continent you lived on—this was the moment you were paying attention to. It was April, and the center of the baseball universe was in Anaheim.

The first pitch from Cleveland's Josh Tomlin was a ball outside. The second was a cutter, down and in; Ohtani fouled it off. He swung over a low curveball. The count stood at 1-2; the crowd was a tremor of anxious anticipation. Tomlin's fourth pitch to Ohtani almost hit him. It rolled past Roberto Perez, allowing Calhoun to score from third. 3-2 Angels. Ohtani's first home plate appearance could no longer end in a grand slam.

And you began to feel a little foolish for expecting, even a little bit, that this plate appearance was ever really going to end in a grand slam. You try to inculcate yourself against such romantic high hopes in baseball. The perfect outcome is so rare. And for Ohtani to succeed—for Ohtani to succeed in this moment, in this way—would be too perfect of an outcome to hope for. You were warned when he decided to play in the major leagues, and you were warned when he signed with the Angels, donned that too-bright red jersey, and you were warned when spring training rolled around and the reports began to flow in. Don't hype the guy up so much. He was no Babe Ruth. There were injury concerns. The stuff was there, but not polished enough. The swing was too easily exploited. He would never hit in the major leagues. As Ohtani fouled off another pitch, still with two strikes on him, you tempered your hope, and with you, so did everyone else watching, the millions of eyes all turned to this one man, hoping.

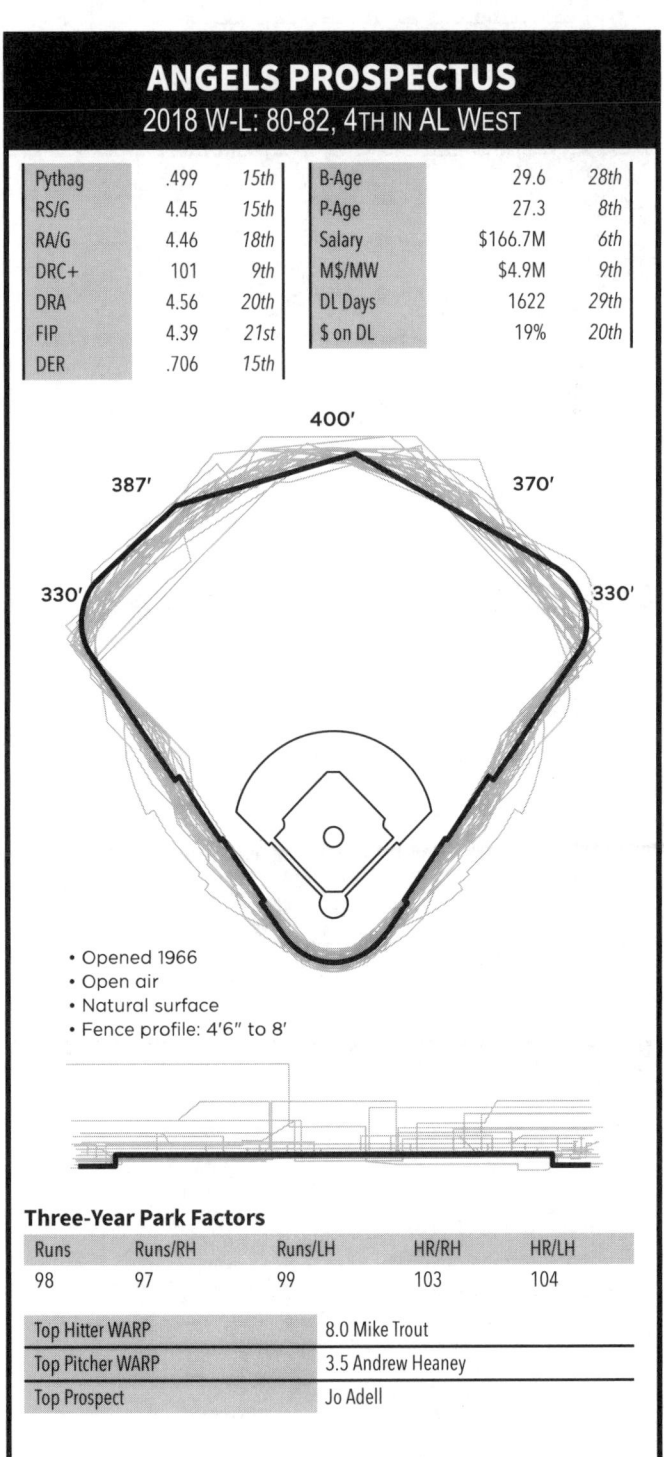

ANGELS PROSPECTUS
2018 W-L: 80-82, 4TH IN AL WEST

Pythag	.499	15th	B-Age	29.6	28th
RS/G	4.45	15th	P-Age	27.3	8th
RA/G	4.46	18th	Salary	$166.7M	6th
DRC+	101	9th	M$/MW	$4.9M	9th
DRA	4.56	20th	DL Days	1622	29th
FIP	4.39	21st	$ on DL	19%	20th
DER	.706	15th			

- Opened 1966
- Open air
- Natural surface
- Fence profile: 4'6" to 8'

Three-Year Park Factors

Runs	Runs/RH	Runs/LH	HR/RH	HR/LH
98	97	99	103	104

Top Hitter WARP	8.0 Mike Trout
Top Pitcher WARP	3.5 Andrew Heaney
Top Prospect	Jo Adell

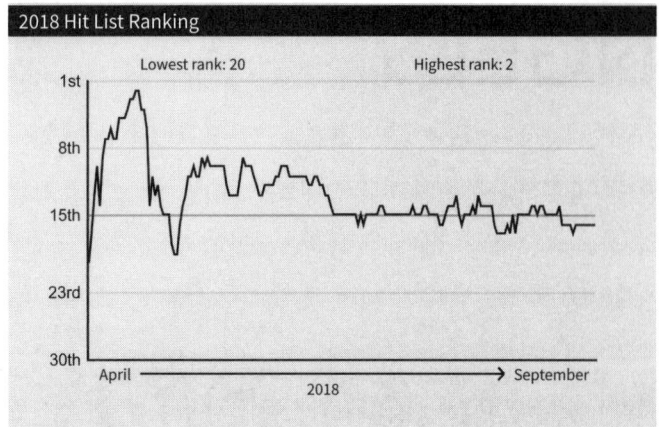

2018 Hit List Ranking

Lowest rank: 20 — Highest rank: 2

April ——— 2018 ———→ September

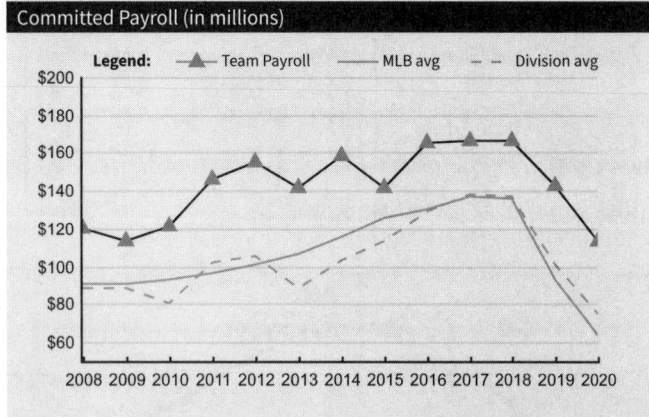

Committed Payroll (in millions)

Legend: ▲ Team Payroll — MLB avg - - - Division avg

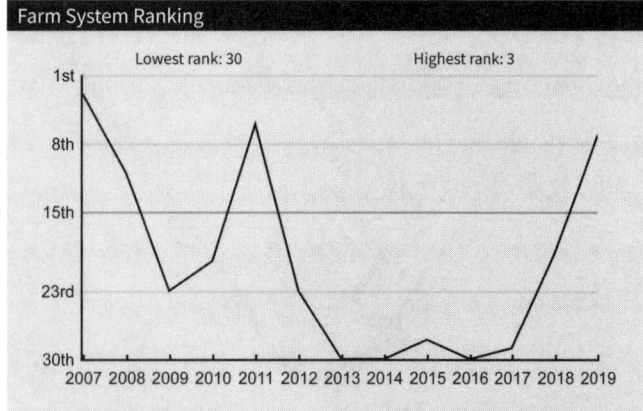

Farm System Ranking

Lowest rank: 30 — Highest rank: 3

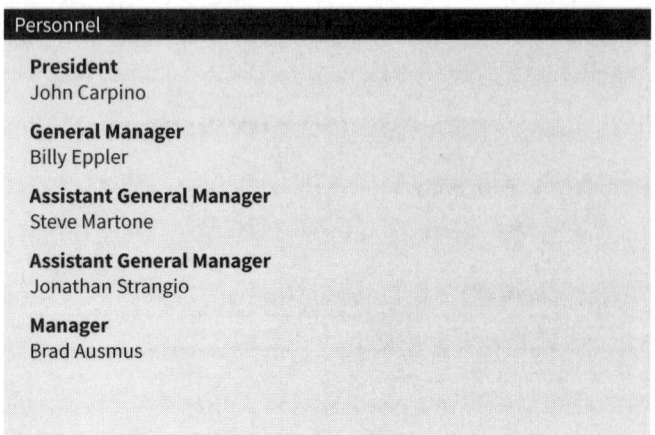

Personnel

President
John Carpino

General Manager
Billy Eppler

Assistant General Manager
Steve Martone

Assistant General Manager
Jonathan Strangio

Manager
Brad Ausmus

And then Tomlin threw a curveball down and in. A swing, a crack, the voice of the stadium rising. The ball arcing high into the air—is it gone? is it really gone?—coming down in the uplifted arms of some random, grinning fan. Ohtani rounded the bases, face serious, a hand on his helmet, holding it in place. When he reached the dugout, he took his helmet off and broke into a smile. His teammates gave him the silent treatment for as long as they could bear it. Then they converged upon him.

⚾   ⚾   ⚾

We all read the same baseball news at the end of the day, the big, important stories that have national columns written about them. We read analysis of specific player performances that we may not necessarily have seen ourselves, follow up on our fantasy rosters. But for the majority of people with a strong interest in baseball, whether they're fans or beat writers, that interest is filtered through one team, maybe two. Baseball is, after all, so vast. There are just so many teams, and so many games, and within those games dozens of batted ball events, hundreds of pitches. It's much easier to process that amount of information through the convenient narrative arc of a single team's season. It's a way of making it all make sense.

With the number of teams in baseball, and the number of games that each of those teams play, though, this means the collective consciousness of the baseball-watching public is largely fragmented. A hypothetical someone who is an exclusive devotee of the San Diego Padres, for example, might have very little overlap between the content of their baseball consumption and that of a die-hard Red Sox fan. The moments that make up the story of their respective seasons, the sounds and images of their day-to-day baseball interactions, will be almost completely different from each other. A large part of the appeal of the postseason, then, is the fact that it represents a convergence of all these perspectives. From the alternating chaos and numbness of September comes an expectant silence, a baseball-universal waiting for a single event. All the narratives flow into one; all of the disparate perspectives unite. Everyone is hanging on the same pitches, breathing in the same pauses, waiting for the narrative of the season to write its ending.

Moments like these are rare in the regular season. They often center around some historic milestone. Everyone will tune in when a pitcher is three outs away from a perfect game, or when a player is one home run away from an all-time landmark, but these kinds of universal must-watch events are few and far between. And for the Los Angeles Angels of the last decade, they have been almost non-existent. Yes, the Angels have had Mike Trout, who might end up being the best player ever. Trout's greatness, though, is a cumulative, consistent greatness. Trout's greatness is not composed of the kinds of distinct events around which the world of baseball can turn. You could make an argument for Trout being must-watch television whenever he takes the field, but the team around him as a whole has been undeniably uncompelling.

Even the Angels' one postseason appearance in the last years—a 98-win division-title campaign in 2014—was unmemorable at best. The Angels were swept by the wild-card Kansas City Royals. They scored six runs in three games. Since that season, the Angels have been on the losing end of mediocre, plagued by inconsistent pitching, even less consistent hitting, an apparently unfillable void in left field, and the ongoing burden of Albert Pujols' overwhelming contract and overwhelming age.

Billy Eppler's tenure as general manager has seen the improvement of a farm system bereft of talent to one featuring several top-end prospects, leaving it ranked somewhere in the middle of the road in terms of MLB-wide rankings. But a Jo Adell doesn't currently translate to an interesting Major League team; his Venn Diagram and Trout's may hardly overlap. The Angels have failed to bring one of the greatest players of all time anywhere close to a championship. And with the arrival of the dominant Astros, they have become not only an afterthought in their geographic area—the Dodgers, a team that already possessed of a pervasive cultural cachet that has eluded the Angels, have won six straight division titles—but an afterthought in the division as well. With three years of Mike Trout left, the Angels' best offseason efforts could only reasonably put them in contention for the second Wild Card spot alongside a slough of other not-great teams.

In 2018, though, they had Shohei Ohtani, by far the offseason's biggest topic of conversation. They added Zack Cozart and Ian Kinsler to shore up their infield. And for two weeks in April, the Angels were the undeniable center of the baseball universe. They were now not simply the team wasting Mike Trout's talent, but the team with Mike Trout and Shohei Ohtani. The Angels went 13-3 in their first 16 games, their best start to a season in franchise history. Trout had his first-ever 0-for-6 game on Opening Day and went through a 1-for-18 stretch, yet his line was still Troutian in its quality. Cozart performed well at the plate, while shoring up the left side of the Angels' infield. Andrelton Simmons continued to be Andrelton Simmons.

The contributions were far-ranging, but every conversation about the Angels' success ended up being about Ohtani. After that first homer, he hit two more homers in his next two games. In his first start, he pitched six innings, allowing three runs on a home run and striking out six. His next start—his first home start—was incredible. He cut through the Oakland A's lineup, a lineup that would end the year as one of baseball's best offenses, striking out 12 over seven scoreless innings. Through the first six of those, he was perfect.

⚾   ⚾   ⚾

Much is made of the grind of a 162-game season, the burden it puts on a player's mind and body. Significant injuries are a part of any team's journey from March to September, and the teams that survive are often the ones who have the good fortune and depth enough that the injuries don't become the story of the season. The Angels' injuries started early, and they didn't stop. First came Ian Kinsler, one of their key offseason acquisitions, who got a left adductor strain sliding into second on March 31st. Pitcher JC Ramirez went down with UCL damage on April 17th. Closer Keynan Middleton went down with the same injury on May 22nd, and so did reliever Blake Wood on May 30th. Most devastating of all was the UCL damage Ohtani suffered, taking him out of the rotation from early June onward — and as if that weren't enough, Garrett Richards, too, fell to Tommy John in mid-July. The Angels' rotation had already appeared to be a weakness of the team. That rotation itself being utterly and completely decimated by injury made it untenable.

And though the Angels' position players were less severely affected, they were far from immune. Kole Calhoun—who had to that point been posting historically terrible numbers at the plate—was placed on the DL in late May. Andrelton Simmons was sidelined with an ankle sprain in early June. Zack Cozart dislocated his shoulder—also in early June.

On Monday, May 15th, the Angels remained tied with the Mariners for the lead in the AL West. A month later, that tie had turned into a 7 1⁄2 game deficit.

⚾   ⚾   ⚾

The signal went out again on September 2nd. By this point, the Angels' postseason hopes had long since evaporated: They were four games under .500, 18 games back in the division. It had been months since they had played any baseball one might consider "meaningful"; they'd been sellers at the deadline, trading away catcher Martin Maldonado and the recently-acquired Kinsler. But as the Angels took the field in Houston, facing the Astros team that had so far lapped them in the division, the eyes of the baseball-watching public turned en masse once again in expectation of a Shohei Ohtani start. There was anticipation, but anticipation not of the stunning perfection that had seemed possible and then become fulfilled back in April. This time, the anticipation was tinged with anxiety. Ohtani was making his return to the mound. The range of realistic good options were somewhat limited. The range of realistic disasters was massive. For Ohtani to be pitching at all in September was far sooner than most had expected. The baseball-watching public was united not in hope, but in anxiety.

Ohtani's first pitch to George Springer came in at 96.9 mph—a fastball outside for ball one. His second, another fastball at 95.7, was poked into right field for a base hit. Ohtani got out of the inning without allowing a run to score. But the second inning was more concerning. His average fastball velocity fell from 97.4 mph in the first to 95.5 in the second. In the third, it fell all the way to 91.4 mph; he recorded one out, gave up a two-run homer to Springer, and was pulled from the game.

Both the Angels and Ohtani insisted that his elbow was fine. It wasn't. On September 30th, Ohtani underwent Tommy John surgery.

At season's end, Mike Scioscia announced his departure from the role of manager, after over two decades at the helm of the team—one of baseball's most distinctive figures finally ousted from his position, replaced by a non-descript Brad Ausmus. Because while this team has grown accustomed to losing over the last decade, 2018 was a different kind of loss. The world saw, for a few weeks, what this team could be when everything was going right, before everything went back to being wrong.

The Angels only have Mike Trout for a few more years. They won't have Shohei Ohtani the two-way player back for a while. In a division with the Astros, and now with the A's, the chances of them reaching anything close to the heights of competition in the foreseeable future are slim. But it is not even the dim hopes for a competitive team that constitutes the great disappointment of the 2018 Angels. For a few weeks at the beginning of the season, the Angels were the center of the baseball universe. For a few weeks, they were a manifestation of the wildest hopes and dreams any baseball fan could have coming true. There was Mike Trout, and there was a fully-realized Shohei Ohtani, playing on the same nearly-unbeatable team. The outcome, in the end, remained the same. They became another team struggling with injury, another losing team in the American League. Another losing season in Anaheim. The promise of the 2018 Angels faded once again into the expected outcomes of an uninteresting team, the afterthought of the AL West, too far removed from the glow of Hollywood's lights to catch any of their shine. The great disappointment is that the Angels couldn't hold that perfect moment together. They might not have another one any time soon. ∎

—Rachael McDaniel is an author of Baseball Prospectus.

HITTERS

Jordyn Adams CF   Born: 10/18/99   Age: 19   Bats: R   Throws: R   Height: 6'2"   Weight: 180   Origin: Round 1, 2018 Draft (#17 overall)

YEAR	TEAM	LVL	AGE	PA	R	2B	3B	HR	RBI	BB	K	SB	CS	AVG/OBP/SLG	DRC+	VORP	BABIP	BRR	FRAA	WARP
2018	ANG	RK	18	82	8	2	2	0	5	10	23	5	2	.243/.354/.329	84	2.3	.362	0.9	CF(14): -4.2, RF(1): 0.0	-0.3
2018	ORM	RK	18	40	5	4	1	0	8	4	7	0	1	.314/.375/.486	87	1.3	.379	-0.8	CF(8): 3.1	0.3
2019	*ANA*	*MLB*	*19*	*251*	*20*	*3*	*0*	*3*	*14*	*12*	*95*	*2*	*1*	*.135/.176/.192*	*-12*	*-24.9*	*.201*	*-0.2*	*CF -1, RF 0*	*-2.8*

Breakout: 0%   Improve: 6%   Collapse: 1%   Attrition: 3%   MLB: 11%   *Comparables: Carlos Tocci, Engel Beltre, Nomar Mazara*

Adams has a name like a pop star, the speed of a wideout, and one of the highest ceilings of anyone in the 2018 draft. A four-star football recruit with a commitment to North Carolina—where his dad is a coach—Adams showed last spring that he was more adept at the plate than many anticipated, landing him a selection in the middle of the first round. He boasts plus-plus speed, and has the bat speed and frame such that a plus power projection isn't irresponsible. Like many a high-beta prospect, Adams' future rests on the outcome of his hit tool, but if that comes around, the high notes are going to be quite something.

Jo Adell CF   Born: 04/08/99   Age: 20   Bats: R   Throws: R   Height: 6'3"   Weight: 208   Origin: Round 1, 2017 Draft (#10 overall)

YEAR	TEAM	LVL	AGE	PA	R	2B	3B	HR	RBI	BB	K	SB	CS	AVG/OBP/SLG	DRC+	VORP	BABIP	BRR	FRAA	WARP
2017	ANG	RK	18	132	18	6	6	4	21	10	32	5	0	.288/.351/.542	124	13.2	.361	1.9		0.7
2017	ORM	RK	18	90	25	5	2	1	9	4	17	3	2	.376/.411/.518	91	7.2	.463	0.4		0.0
2018	BUR	A	19	108	23	7	1	6	29	11	26	4	1	.326/.398/.611	121	12.4	.391	1.2	CF(16): -0.4, RF(3): -0.9	0.5
2018	INL	A+	19	262	46	19	3	12	42	15	63	9	2	.290/.345/.546	118	21.8	.345	2.0	CF(36): -5.6, RF(8): -1.1	0.8
2018	MOB	AA	19	71	14	6	0	2	6	6	22	2	0	.238/.324/.429	83	4.5	.333	-0.3	CF(17): -1.9	-0.1
2019	*ANA*	*MLB*	*20*	*251*	*29*	*9*	*1*	*9*	*27*	*11*	*78*	*3*	*1*	*.205/.239/.370*	*56*	*-4.0*	*.259*	*0.4*	*CF -4, RF -1*	*-0.9*

Breakout: 9%   Improve: 20%   Collapse: 0%   Attrition: 6%   MLB: 21%   *Comparables: Ronald Acuna, Domingo Santana, Xander Bogaerts*

While he didn't play the field after signing in 2017, Adell proved he was right as rain in 2018, manning center field in 69 of 99 games and scalding the ball across three different levels while firmly entrenching himself among the game's top prospects, all at the tender age of 19. His physique is enough to melt one's heart to stone, and his bat speed helps him generate prodigious power — enough to make him your first love among prospects. A-ball hurlers found that pitching to Adell was just chasing pavements, though he tired towards the end of the season, definitely not saving the best for last, as Double-A arms gave him the cold shoulder. Tepid end to the season aside, it wouldn't be crazy for you to see Adell in the majors by the end of the 2019 season, helping the Angels restore some hometown glory. What he'll be at 21 or 25? We'll leave that to the daydreamers.

Jabari Blash RF Born: 07/04/89 Age: 29 Bats: R Throws: R Height: 6'5" Weight: 235 Origin: Round 8, 2010 Draft (#252 overall)

YEAR	TEAM	LVL	AGE	PA	R	2B	3B	HR	RBI	BB	K	SB	CS	AVG/OBP/SLG	DRC+	VORP	BABIP	BRR	FRAA	WARP
2016	ELP	AAA	26	229	30	12	0	11	30	41	66	1	2	.260/.415/.514	138	17.6	.340	0.6	LF(31): 0.4, RF(18): 2.2	2.0
2016	SDN	MLB	26	84	7	2	0	3	5	11	34	1	0	.169/.298/.324	70	-2.4	.265	0.4	RF(18): 2.6, LF(4): -0.1	0.2
2017	ELP	AAA	27	291	53	16	1	20	62	48	88	3	2	.285/.419/.617	149	24.8	.367	0.2	RF(59): 8.3	3.3
2017	SDN	MLB	27	195	24	6	0	5	16	28	66	1	2	.213/.333/.341	80	3.6	.319	0.8	RF(33): 0.0, LF(18): -1.7	-0.1
2018	SLC	AAA	28	346	73	21	1	29	68	49	102	5	7	.317/.431/.700	179	36.7	.395	1.7	RF(54): 1.7, LF(16): 0.9	4.7
2018	ANA	MLB	28	45	4	1	0	0	1	5	24	2	1	.103/.200/.128	49	-4.2	.250	0.3	RF(14): -1.8, LF: 0.2	-0.3
2019	*ANA*	*MLB*	*29*	*251*	*32*	*9*	*0*	*12*	*35*	*30*	*87*	*2*	*2*	*.218/.325/.426*	*99*	*7.1*	*.302*	*0.5*	*RF 2, LF 0*	*1.0*

Breakout: 7%   Improve: 37%   Collapse: 6%   Attrition: 13%   MLB: 69%   *Comparables: Jarrett Parker, Calvin Pickering, Travis Taijeron*

Blash has terrific plate discipline and is a threat to go deep every at bat... in Triple-A. He owns a 1.000 career Triple-A OPS in nearly 1,300 PAs. He can play both corner outfield positions and even a skosh of center. It's just that the hit tool fails to translate to an average bench bat. He evokes Brad Eldred, another tall bad-ball basher who has spent the last seven years carving out a fine career in Nippon Professional Baseball. And after signing an early-December deal with the Rakuten Golden Eagles, Blash will follow in those promising footsteps. Quad-A depth is not way to make a living, after all.

Justin Bour 1B Born: 05/28/88 Age: 31 Bats: L Throws: R Height: 6'3" Weight: 265 Origin: Round 25, 2009 Draft (#770 overall)

YEAR	TEAM	LVL	AGE	PA	R	2B	3B	HR	RBI	BB	K	SB	CS	AVG/OBP/SLG	DRC+	VORP	BABIP	BRR	FRAA	WARP
2016	MIA	MLB	28	321	35	12	1	15	51	38	56	0	0	.264/.349/.475	120	17.7	.278	-1.1	1B(82): -5.1	0.7
2017	MIA	MLB	29	429	52	18	0	25	83	47	95	1	0	.289/.366/.536	124	30.2	.322	-1.8	1B(102): -10.0	0.8
2018	MIA	MLB	30	447	43	10	1	19	54	69	111	1	0	.227/.347/.412	103	14.3	.267	-3.1	1B(103): -6.3	-0.1
2018	PHI	MLB	30	54	6	3	0	1	5	4	13	1	0	.224/.296/.347	109	-0.9	.286	0.2	1B(10): -0.5	0.2
2019	*ANA*	*MLB*	*31*	*363*	*47*	*15*	*1*	*16*	*52*	*44*	*81*	*1*	*0*	*.260/.354/.468*	*122*	*13.8*	*.303*	*-1.4*	*1B -7*	*0.8*

Breakout: 2%   Improve: 40%   Collapse: 4%   Attrition: 8%   MLB: 84%   *Comparables: Allen Craig, Justin Smoak, Lucas Duda*

First basemen are weird, man. One year, you're OPSing .900 and swatting some megaton bombs in your home park during the Home Run Derby, the next your slugging percentage is 120 points in the red and you're getting traded within the division for a single prospect not even on a Top 20 list. So goes the saga of Justin Bour, whom the Phillies picked up to provide pure offensive depth and who...did not quite provide pure offensive depth. Hampered by an oblique injury and a depth chart already crammed with corner players, Bour made just 54 trips to the plate with his new team and did little to reverse what had already been, to that point, a disappointing season. After Philadelphia predictably cut ties the Angels swooped in to beef up a first base/designated hitter depth chart sagging under the weight of the back end of Pujols' contract. Bour should get some chances to reignite the stick while Ohtani mends, but his cheap contract and ever-present platoon issues signal a limited engagement if he starts slow.

Kole Calhoun RF Born: 10/14/87 Age: 31 Bats: L Throws: L Height: 5'10" Weight: 200 Origin: Round 8, 2010 Draft (#264 overall)

YEAR	TEAM	LVL	AGE	PA	R	2B	3B	HR	RBI	BB	K	SB	CS	AVG/OBP/SLG	DRC+	VORP	BABIP	BRR	FRAA	WARP
2016	ANA	MLB	28	672	91	35	5	18	75	67	118	2	3	.271/.348/.438	105	23.5	.309	0.1	RF(154): -6.7	1.3
2017	ANA	MLB	29	654	77	23	2	19	71	71	134	5	1	.244/.333/.392	98	10.9	.284	-0.6	RF(154): 10.0	2.3
2018	ANA	MLB	30	552	71	18	2	19	57	53	133	6	2	.208/.283/.369	89	-3.1	.241	-0.2	RF(136): -3.7, CF(4): -0.2	0.1
2019	*ANA*	*MLB*	*31*	*603*	*76*	*30*	*3*	*17*	*64*	*60*	*122*	*5*	*2*	*.251/.333/.410*	*107*	*21.6*	*.297*	*-0.1*	*RF -1*	*2.2*

Breakout: 2%   Improve: 39%   Collapse: 13%   Attrition: 20%   MLB: 91%   *Comparables: Curt Walker, Johnny Callison, Nate Schierholtz*

Calhoun had one of the worst months of May since Anne Boleyn's arrest and execution, spilling out a .314 OPS in considerable playing time. (The last time someone had a monthly OPS that low with 20 starts was 11 years ago.) He emerged from a brief DL stint with a brand new crouched stance, and the adjustment paid off big-time, as he rode significantly more aerial contact to an OPS nearly four times higher in July. So don't let the season stats fool you too much: He still has plenty of range in right field and is a strong candidate to return to a league-average leadoff hitter.

Zack Cozart INF Born: 08/12/85 Age: 33 Bats: R Throws: R Height: 6'0" Weight: 205 Origin: Round 2, 2007 Draft (#79 overall)

YEAR	TEAM	LVL	AGE	PA	R	2B	3B	HR	RBI	BB	K	SB	CS	AVG/OBP/SLG	DRC+	VORP	BABIP	BRR	FRAA	WARP
2016	CIN	MLB	30	508	67	28	2	16	50	37	84	4	1	.252/.308/.425	97	20.4	.274	3.1	SS(111): 2.6	2.8
2017	CIN	MLB	31	507	80	24	7	24	63	62	78	3	0	.297/.385/.548	138	51.2	.312	-2.8	SS(112): 1.3	4.6
2018	ANA	MLB	32	253	29	13	2	5	18	19	42	0	0	.219/.296/.362	89	3.5	.244	-0.2	3B(35): -0.7, 2B(16): -0.2	0.5
2019	*ANA*	*MLB*	*33*	*505*	*64*	*26*	*3*	*14*	*55*	*46*	*83*	*3*	*1*	*.262/.339/.429*	*109*	*17.4*	*.292*	*-0.1*	*3B -7, 2B 0*	*1.0*

Breakout: 3%   Improve: 35%   Collapse: 5%   Attrition: 15%   MLB: 89%   *Comparables: Pie Traynor, George Kell, Martin Prado*

Cozart broke out in 2017 and then broke in the more traditional sense last year amidst an ocean of change: new team, new league, new time zone, new position. He also missed half the year to shoulder surgery. He was probably never a 138 DRC+ guy to begin with, but moving around the diamond seemed difficult for him, or so the defensive metrics tell us. If healthy he should still be able to crank out enough extra-base hits to steady the bottom-third of a lineup, and two years of eight guaranteed figures apiece will certainly give Anaheim plenty of incentive to let him try.

David Fletcher INF
Born: 05/31/94   Age: 25   Bats: R   Throws: R   Height: 5'10"   Weight: 175   Origin: Round 6, 2015 Draft (#195 overall)

YEAR	TEAM	LVL	AGE	PA	R	2B	3B	HR	RBI	BB	K	SB	CS	AVG/OBP/SLG	DRC+	VORP	BABIP	BRR	FRAA	WARP
2016	INL	A+	22	355	42	12	1	3	31	22	43	15	3	.275/.321/.346	88	11.7	.307	1.6	SS(47): -6.2, 2B(28): -0.2	0.3
2016	ARK	AA	22	83	10	6	0	0	6	3	13	1	0	.300/.325/.375	85	5.0	.358	0.6	SS(18): 2.3	0.5
2017	MOB	AA	23	272	32	14	1	1	22	21	30	12	5	.276/.341/.354	95	10.1	.308	-1.5	2B(34): 1.0, SS(28): 0.0	0.7
2017	SLC	AAA	23	217	27	6	1	2	17	6	25	8	1	.254/.285/.322	75	-0.1	.281	2.3	SS(26): 0.2, 2B(22): 0.2	0.5
2018	SLC	AAA	24	275	55	25	5	6	37	16	21	7	2	.350/.394/.559	124	24.4	.364	3.4	SS(31): 3.4, 2B(18): -1.6	2.7
2018	ANA	MLB	24	307	35	18	2	1	25	15	34	3	0	.275/.316/.363	88	6.6	.307	3.5	2B(43): 1.8, 3B(33): 4.7	1.5
2019	*ANA*	*MLB*	*25*	*520*	*59*	*20*	*3*	*10*	*46*	*26*	*69*	*9*	*2*	*.250/.296/.364*	*80*	*7.5*	*.272*	*2.9*	*2B -1, 3B 2*	*0.9*

Breakout: 5%   Improve: 20%   Collapse: 17%   Attrition: 39%   MLB: 68%   *Comparables: Kevin Frandsen, Tyler Pastornicky, Donovan Solano*

It's impossible to hear about Fletcher without someone invoking another David: Eckstein. The latter also came up with the Angels with a papier-mache bat and the ability to play all over the infield. There are a few differences, of course. Eckstein was a true shortstop for the early part of his career, lessening the demand on his offense. Fletcher also struck out more in his inaugural 80 games than Eckstein ever did over the course of an entire season. Fletcher needs that kind of regular contact to get balls through the infield and get on base. It's a different era in terms of strikeouts, but it's also an era where teams carry fewer bench players. Fletcher has the tool set to be an end-of-the-bench guy—we'll just have to find out if he's in the right time period.

Michael Hermosillo OF
Born: 01/17/95   Age: 24   Bats: R   Throws: R   Height: 5'11"   Weight: 190   Origin: Round 28, 2013 Draft (#847 overall)

YEAR	TEAM	LVL	AGE	PA	R	2B	3B	HR	RBI	BB	K	SB	CS	AVG/OBP/SLG	DRC+	VORP	BABIP	BRR	FRAA	WARP
2016	BUR	A	21	160	22	8	1	2	22	18	22	4	3	.326/.411/.442	125	10.4	.377	0.2	CF(20): -4.9, LF(11): -0.6	0.2
2016	INL	A+	21	174	36	7	4	4	17	16	30	6	7	.309/.393/.490	122	22.5	.359	2.5	CF(25): -3.3, RF(8): -0.7	0.7
2017	INL	A+	22	64	5	6	0	0	2	9	15	5	2	.321/.438/.434	87	4.2	.447	-1.3	CF(9): -2.3, LF(3): -0.3	-0.3
2017	MOB	AA	22	340	40	13	2	4	26	40	73	21	9	.248/.361/.353	103	15.4	.316	-2.0	CF(52): -2.3, RF(13): 2.3	1.0
2017	SLC	AAA	22	129	20	6	1	5	16	7	28	9	2	.287/.341/.487	98	5.3	.337	0.3	LF(14): -0.1, CF(10): 0.6	0.5
2018	SLC	AAA	23	323	43	14	4	12	46	30	87	10	5	.267/.357/.480	116	11.6	.341	-0.4	CF(36): 5.5, RF(19): 0.3	2.5
2018	ANA	MLB	23	62	7	4	0	1	1	3	17	0	1	.211/.274/.333	62	-1.2	.282	-0.5	CF(12): 1.5, RF(12): 0.7	0.1
2019	*ANA*	*MLB*	*24*	*235*	*29*	*9*	*1*	*8*	*26*	*16*	*63*	*7*	*3*	*.227/.296/.387*	*83*	*3.0*	*.283*	*0.1*	*CF 0, LF -1*	*0.3*

Breakout: 9%   Improve: 31%   Collapse: 8%   Attrition: 20%   MLB: 49%   *Comparables: Brandon Nimmo, Brian Goodwin, Roman Quinn*

Just by making his debut, Hermosillo more than justified the 28th-round pick the Angels spent on him in 2013. The former three-star University of Illinois football recruit doesn't lack for athleticism, and showed it of at all three outfield positions. He doubled for his first major-league hit, but was never able to string together two hits in one game. It was a small sample, to be sure, but his ability with the stick is going to determine whether he's more—or less—than the fourth outfielder he currently projects to become.

Jeremiah Jackson SS
Born: 03/26/00   Age: 19   Bats: R   Throws: R   Height: 6'0"   Weight: 165   Origin: Round 2, 2018 Draft (#57 overall)

YEAR	TEAM	LVL	AGE	PA	R	2B	3B	HR	RBI	BB	K	SB	CS	AVG/OBP/SLG	DRC+	VORP	BABIP	BRR	FRAA	WARP
2018	ANG	RK	18	91	13	4	2	5	14	7	25	6	1	.317/.374/.598	137	13.9	.396	1.3	SS(21): -1.3	0.8
2018	ORM	RK	18	100	13	6	3	2	9	8	34	4	1	.198/.260/.396	63	-1.5	.286	-0.3	SS(21): -1.7, 2B(1): 0.0	-0.2
2019	*ANA*	*MLB*	*19*	*251*	*29*	*10*	*0*	*9*	*26*	*7*	*92*	*4*	*1*	*.201/.220/.357*	*44*	*-7.4*	*.272*	*0.2*	*SS -1, 2B 0*	*-0.9*

Breakout: 0%   Improve: 6%   Collapse: 1%   Attrition: 4%   MLB: 10%   *Comparables: Adalberto Mondesi, Elvis Andrus, Rougned Odor*

A second-round draft pick, Jackson boasts an exciting offensive skill set for a six-spotter, and it flashed aplenty in a first professional stop in Arizona before running into resistance in the Pioneer League. Jackson's hands do the work at the plate, generating dynamic bat speed that results in impressive raw power, especially for a middle infielder. They're less reliable in the field, however, where he was error prone at shortstop despite having enough arm strength for the position. He might be a second baseman or third baseman when it is all said and done, but he has the offensive projection to justify a position switch if it comes to that.

Jahmai Jones 2B
Born: 08/04/97   Age: 21   Bats: R   Throws: R   Height: 6'0"   Weight: 215   Origin: Round 2, 2015 Draft (#70 overall)

YEAR	TEAM	LVL	AGE	PA	R	2B	3B	HR	RBI	BB	K	SB	CS	AVG/OBP/SLG	DRC+	VORP	BABIP	BRR	FRAA	WARP
2016	ORM	RK	18	226	49	12	3	3	20	21	29	19	6	.321/.404/.459	109	23.1	.364	1.3	CF(41): -4.2, RF(4): -0.5	0.7
2016	BUR	A	18	70	8	1	0	1	10	5	13	1	0	.242/.294/.306	92	-1.3	.286	0.2	CF(8): -0.7, LF(4): -0.1	0.2
2017	BUR	A	19	387	54	18	4	9	30	32	63	18	7	.272/.338/.425	113	27.2	.309	5.7	CF(65): -3.4, LF(16): 0.5	2.0
2017	INL	A+	19	191	32	11	3	5	17	13	43	9	6	.302/.368/.488	112	17.7	.379	2.0	CF(37): -9.7, LF(3): -0.5	0.0
2018	INL	A+	20	347	47	10	5	8	35	43	63	13	3	.235/.338/.383	112	12.5	.272	1.5	2B(70): -6.9	0.9
2018	MOB	AA	20	212	33	10	4	2	20	24	51	11	1	.245/.335/.375	99	5.7	.323	-1.5	2B(45): -1.7	0.3
2019	*ANA*	*MLB*	*21*	*251*	*30*	*8*	*1*	*7*	*23*	*19*	*61*	*6*	*2*	*.219/.281/.354*	*71*	*0.1*	*.265*	*0.6*	*2B -2, CF 0*	*-0.2*

Breakout: 3%   Improve: 21%   Collapse: 0%   Attrition: 14%   MLB: 23%   *Comparables: Jonathan Schoop, Adrian Cardenas, Steve Lombardozzi*

Jones carried the torch for a starved Angel system over the first couple years of his career, as the club signed free agents and lost draft picks. But with an influx of talent into the system, and specifically in the outfield, Jones took on a transition to the keystone this season — a position he hadn't manned since high school. He acclimated to the role over the course of the season, but the process appeared to take a toll on his bat, as he struggled to make consistent contact at either stop. There are positives though: he walked more than ever before and his athleticism still shines. A mixed bag of a season has Jones a bit of a forgotten man in prospect circles, but it's not because he's lost any luster so much as there are finally additional stars in the Orange County sky around him.

D'Shawn Knowles OF   Born: 01/16/01   Age: 18   Bats: B   Throws: R   Height: 6'0"   Weight: 165   Origin: International Free Agent, 2017

YEAR	TEAM	LVL	AGE	PA	R	2B	3B	HR	RBI	BB	K	SB	CS	AVG/OBP/SLG	DRC+	VORP	BABIP	BRR	FRAA	WARP
2018	ANG	RK	17	130	19	4	1	1	14	15	27	7	4	.301/.385/.381	117	9.6	.384	1.1	LF(13): -3.1, CF(9): -0.5	0.3
2018	ORM	RK	17	123	27	9	2	4	15	13	38	2	3	.321/.398/.550	101	8.6	.463	0.3	CF(17): -1.2, RF(9): 1.8	0.4
2019	*ANA*	*MLB*	*18*	*251*	*19*	*6*	*0*	*4*	*21*	*13*	*76*	*2*	*1*	*.186/.227/.261*	*27*	*-14.5*	*.251*	*-0.6*	*CF 0, RF 0*	*-1.6*

Comparables: Adalberto Mondesi, Wilmer Flores, Tommy Brown

Part of the Bahamian wave of prospects (Jazz Chisholm, Lucius Fox, Trent Deveaux, Kristian Robinson, etc.), the switch-hitting Knowles stood out in his debut season. He's a small guy but the frame suggests average raw power may come in time, and his contact skills and approach impressed scouts and coaches alike. He's known for his speed, and natural feel in center field, and given the organization's penchant for pushing prospects, Knowles could see full-season ball at the tender age of 18. A competitive player with a strong work ethic, Knowles projects as a table-setting, top-of-the-order bat who should be able to remain in center for the long haul.

Tommy La Stella 2B   Born: 01/31/89   Age: 30   Bats: L   Throws: R   Height: 5'11"   Weight: 180   Origin: Round 8, 2011 Draft (#266 overall)

YEAR	TEAM	LVL	AGE	PA	R	2B	3B	HR	RBI	BB	K	SB	CS	AVG/OBP/SLG	DRC+	VORP	BABIP	BRR	FRAA	WARP
2016	IOW	AAA	27	46	6	2	0	1	3	2	9	0	0	.273/.304/.386	92	-0.2	.324	0.4	3B(6): 0.9, 2B(4): -0.6	0.2
2016	CHN	MLB	27	169	17	12	1	2	11	18	27	0	1	.270/.357/.405	99	8.0	.319	-1.8	3B(33): -3.3, 2B(9): -0.9	0.0
2017	IOW	AAA	28	121	14	2	0	1	6	10	22	0	1	.218/.281/.264	80	-3.6	.261	1.0	2B(22): 0.3, 3B(4): 0.0	0.2
2017	CHN	MLB	28	151	18	8	0	5	22	20	18	0	0	.288/.389/.472	120	11.6	.298	-0.7	2B(21): -2.4, 3B(18): -0.5	0.5
2018	CHN	MLB	29	192	23	8	0	1	19	17	27	0	1	.266/.340/.331	86	3.0	.312	0.7	3B(26): -1.8, 2B(15): 0.3	0.2
2019	*ANA*	*MLB*	*30*	*313*	*33*	*15*	*1*	*6*	*32*	*29*	*52*	*1*	*1*	*.254/.330/.380*	*94*	*6.5*	*.292*	*-0.5*	*2B -2, 3B -2*	*0.2*

Breakout: 1%   Improve: 29%   Collapse: 11%   Attrition: 18%   MLB: 83%   *Comparables: Jeff Keppinger, Luis Rodriguez, Eric Sogard*

After refusing an assignment to Triple-A in mid-2016 because he wanted to play only in Chicago, La Stella eventually got what he wanted: he was ever-present on the Cubs roster, appearing in over 75 percent of the team's games. At the same time, he was as peripheral as ever, starting just 24 times and seeing PH next to his name so often he might as well have been followed around by a GIF of Eleanor Shellstrop shouting "Ya Basic" at him. He hit well enough off the bench, though, and while the glove is more passable than remarkable at second and third, there's value in embodying replacement level. The Angels clearly think so, anyway, trading for him in a lo-fi deal that should provide him with a shot at reprising his performance in 2019.

Jonathan Lucroy C   Born: 06/13/86   Age: 33   Bats: R   Throws: R   Height: 6'0"   Weight: 200   Origin: Round 3, 2007 Draft (#101 overall)

YEAR	TEAM	LVL	AGE	PA	R	2B	3B	HR	RBI	BB	K	SB	CS	AVG/OBP/SLG	DRC+	VORP	BABIP	BRR	FRAA	WARP
2016	MIL	MLB	30	376	48	17	3	13	50	33	70	5	0	.299/.359/.482	121	32.1	.340	2.0	C(82): -1.2, 1B(6): -0.6	2.8
2016	TEX	MLB	30	168	19	7	0	11	31	14	30	0	0	.276/.345/.539	125	12.8	.279	-1.1	C(44): -0.4	1.2
2017	TEX	MLB	31	306	27	15	0	4	27	19	32	1	0	.242/.297/.338	94	0.0	.259	1.0	C(66): -0.7, 1B(1): 0.0	1.2
2017	COL	MLB	31	175	18	6	3	2	13	27	19	0	0	.310/.429/.437	101	13.8	.341	-0.2	C(44): 0.6	1.0
2018	OAK	MLB	32	454	41	21	1	4	51	29	65	0	0	.241/.291/.325	80	2.4	.273	-2.5	C(125): -9.7	-0.1
2019	*ANA*	*MLB*	*33*	*402*	*42*	*19*	*2*	*7*	*39*	*34*	*58*	*1*	*0*	*.257/.330/.377*	*95*	*15.4*	*.291*	*-0.3*	*C -9*	*0.7*

Breakout: 2%   Improve: 41%   Collapse: 9%   Attrition: 16%   MLB: 93%

Comparables: Del Crandall, Hank Severeid, Paul Lo Duca

YEAR	TEAM	P. COUNT	FRM RUNS	BLK RUNS	THRW RUNS	TOT RUNS
2016	MIL	11622	3.8	2.1	2.2	7.5
2016	TEX	5788	1.8	-0.2	2.2	3.5
2017	TEX	9640	-11.1	-1.2	0.6	-12.2
2017	COL	5958	-6.8	-1.8	0.1	-8.8
2018	OAK	16900	-3.7	-3.7	0.3	-7.3
2019	*ANA*	*14541*	*-8.0*	*-1.5*	*1.0*	*-8.4*

Lucroy signed a very late free-agent deal with the A's for less money (just $6.5 million) than you might expect after he averaged about 2.7 WARP over the prior three years. Sometimes, though, the market gets it right, as Lucroy replicated for Oakland the disastrous Texas portion of his 2017 season. Imitation is the sincerest form of flattery and all, but why he thought a replacement-level season needed flattering is beyond us. He's not the framer he once was behind the plate, and he lacks the punch to put any fear into opposing pitchers. Even if this is what he is now, he's still a playable backup, especially if you want him to do a Yoda routine with some hotshot youngster's defense, and there's always the chance that this is *not* what Lucroy is, since he's still only 33 (despite a very respectable amount of grizzle) and not far removed from being one of the better catchers in the league.

Kevin Maitan 3B   Born: 02/12/00   Age: 19   Bats: B   Throws: R   Height: 6'2"   Weight: 190   Origin: International Free Agent, 2016

YEAR	TEAM	LVL	AGE	PA	R	2B	3B	HR	RBI	BB	K	SB	CS	AVG/OBP/SLG	DRC+	VORP	BABIP	BRR	FRAA	WARP
2017	BRA	RK	17	37	5	3	0	0	3	2	10	1	0	.314/.351/.400	88	2.0	.440	0.3	SS(5): -1.7	-0.1
2017	DNV	RK	17	139	10	5	1	2	15	9	39	1	0	.220/.273/.323	78	0.2	.295	-0.7	SS(30): 0.9	0.2
2018	ORM	RK	18	284	42	13	1	8	26	19	66	1	2	.248/.306/.397	87	7.4	.303	1.1	3B(40): 3.3, SS(21): -3.1	0.8
2019	*ANA*	*MLB*	*19*	*251*	*21*	*6*	*0*	*7*	*21*	*4*	*85*	*0*	*0*	*.163/.176/.265*	*12*	*-20.9*	*.211*	*-1.2*	*3B 0, SS -1*	*-2.3*

Breakout: 0%   Improve: 7%   Collapse: 2%   Attrition: 4%   MLB: 12%   *Comparables: Francisco Pena, Adalberto Mondesi, Engel Beltre*

The Miguel Cabrera comparisons were never fair, and they've long since faded away. Even the standard top prospect luster has been coated by the patina of stagnant development. It's fair to put a parenthetical "or lack thereof" behind that last statement, but we've long told you that development isn't linear for a reason. Maitan still has a spate of potential league-average tools, but the distance between present and projection has gotten longer and bumpier. The bat lacks polish and his inability to make consistent, hard contact makes his power play down in-game. His weight has fluctuated, and hasn't really ended up in a good place. He's already moved off of short and there's a good chance he's a first baseman when it is all said and done, and while that worked for Miggy, they call them "generational talents" for a reason.

Brandon Marsh OF
Born: 12/18/97   Age: 21   Bats: L   Throws: R   Height: 6'4"   Weight: 210   Origin: Round 2, 2016 Draft (#60 overall)

YEAR	TEAM	LVL	AGE	PA	R	2B	3B	HR	RBI	BB	K	SB	CS	AVG/OBP/SLG	DRC+	VORP	BABIP	BRR	FRAA	WARP
2017	ORM	RK	19	192	47	13	5	4	44	9	35	10	2	.350/.396/.548	111	18.1	.417	3.2	RF(26): -1.9, CF(11): 1.5	0.9
2018	BUR	A	20	154	26	12	1	3	24	21	40	4	0	.295/.390/.470	97	12.2	.400	2.9	CF(14): 1.2, RF(13): -1.3	0.7
2018	INL	A+	20	426	59	15	6	7	46	52	118	10	4	.256/.348/.385	100	21.2	.356	4.3	CF(50): -0.8, RF(33): 3.0	1.8
2019	ANA	MLB	21	251	27	10	0	6	24	16	75	2	1	.215/.265/.346	54	-5.7	.285	-0.2	CF 0, RF 0	-0.5

Breakout: 2%   Improve: 3%   Collapse: 0%   Attrition: 2%   MLB: 6%   *Comparables: Michael Saunders, Daniel Fields, Domonic Brown*

Marsh put his bevy of tools on display in his first taste of full-season ball, splitting time between center and right field, and producing so well with the bat that he earned an early-season promotion to High-A Inland Empire. At 20 years old, it was an aggressive promotion, and his bat got bogged down facing the more advanced pitching of the California League. Marsh did make swing adjustments throughout the year, sacrificing some plane to keep the bat in the zone longer, and profiled as a gap-to-gap hitter who could grow into above-average home run pop by season's end. Variance swamps a lot, but one constant was Marsh's impressive approach across both levels. He's consistently posted high BABIPs throughout his brief career, but there's no reason to believe his production is inflated because of it: he has the speed and hard contact to justify it. There's a chance Marsh will have to move off center in the long term, but there's enough projection in the bat and the overall profile that he can be a regular in an outfield corner.

Shohei Ohtani DH
Born: 07/05/94   Age: 24   Bats: L   Throws: R   Height: 6'4"   Weight: 200   Origin: International Free Agent, 2017

YEAR	TEAM	LVL	AGE	PA	R	2B	3B	HR	RBI	BB	K	SB	CS	AVG/OBP/SLG	DRC+	VORP	BABIP	BRR	FRAA	WARP
2018	ANA	MLB	23	367	59	21	2	22	61	37	102	10	4	.285/.361/.564	122	23.2	.350	-2.3	P(10): 0.7	1.4
2019	ANA	MLB	24	454	62	21	2	23	69	48	118	6	2	.263/.345/.497	128	19.9	.316	-0.1		2.1

Breakout: 5%   Improve: 73%   Collapse: 2%   Attrition: 3%   MLB: 98%   *Comparables: Frank Robinson, Willie McCovey, Bob Robertson*

You, a baseball fan, have various circles of connections: friends and online acquaintances who are equally zealous about the sport; co-workers and neighbors who dabble in all the athletic prowesses; and those people you love but could (possibly?) identify a baseball among a lineup of other spheres. Baseball news stories flash by our lives and depending on the magnitude/nerdery of the story, you share it with one or more of those circles.

When the Ohtani scouting report hit the states, you told everyone, even your grandparents who stopped watching baseball in 1962 when players kept hot-doggin' it. So many paragraphs have been rendered based on his substance and his phenomenon, so place this in the simplest of contexts: Ohtani is one of the league's best hitters and one of the league's best pitchers and the last person to embody both roles was Babe Ruth. And he did it simultaneously for only a couple seasons. Everyone has heard of general baseball players existing, but Ohtani, or at least the idea of him, transcends generations.

You are painfully aware that this year Thomas Edward John surgery will keep him off the mound but not from the batter's box, so we'll still get to watch him mash, at least. And a year from now you can go back to being the herald that cries the wonders of the two-way player.

Albert Pujols 1B
Born: 01/16/80   Age: 39   Bats: R   Throws: R   Height: 6'3"   Weight: 240   Origin: Round 13, 1999 Draft (#402 overall)

YEAR	TEAM	LVL	AGE	PA	R	2B	3B	HR	RBI	BB	K	SB	CS	AVG/OBP/SLG	DRC+	VORP	BABIP	BRR	FRAA	WARP
2016	ANA	MLB	36	650	71	19	0	31	119	49	75	4	0	.268/.323/.457	119	11.8	.260	-3.8	1B(28): -1.1	2.1
2017	ANA	MLB	37	636	53	17	0	23	101	37	93	3	0	.241/.286/.386	92	-17.7	.249	-1.2	1B(6): -0.6	0.1
2018	ANA	MLB	38	498	50	20	0	19	64	28	65	1	0	.245/.289/.411	102	1.2	.247	-1.9	1B(70): 3.8	1.1
2019	ANA	MLB	39	500	54	26	2	15	62	35	69	2	0	.263/.319/.424	102	6.2	.281	-1.8	1B 1	0.8

Breakout: 1%   Improve: 14%   Collapse: 13%   Attrition: 13%   MLB: 71%   *Comparables: Victor Martinez, Eddie Murray, Hideki Matsui*

In Milton's epic poem *Paradise Lost*, we learn about the band of angels who rebelled against God, ultimately lost and were banished to Hell. Their leader, Satan, began to plot their revenge by tempting Adam and Eve into the most forbidden of fruits: a long-term contract for Pujols. They were warned of the grave consequences. Of course they shouldn't have done this, but mind you this poem takes place years ago, when we were all a bit naive. Eve, excited to get a Hall of Famer in his prime, signed Pujols to a 700-year contract. Adam was not without sin either, as he agreed to a full no-trade clause. The angels decided to honor the contract as penance for Adam and Eve's recklessness, and to this day Pujols still roams the roster and gets plenty of plate appearances. Satan, however, got the brunt of the punishment: he had Pujols in his keeper league.

Luis Rengifo INF
Born: 02/26/97   Age: 22   Bats: B   Throws: R   Height: 5'10"   Weight: 165   Origin: International Free Agent, 2013

YEAR	TEAM	LVL	AGE	PA	R	2B	3B	HR	RBI	BB	K	SB	CS	AVG/OBP/SLG	DRC+	VORP	BABIP	BRR	FRAA	WARP
2016	MRN	RK	19	124	16	7	2	1	9	13	31	22	3	.239/.325/.367	79	7.1	.325	3.3	3B(12): -0.5, 2B(10): 2.9	0.6
2017	CLN	A	20	450	65	24	4	11	44	33	80	29	14	.250/.318/.413	106	22.0	.285	4.3	SS(31): -2.8, 2B(25): 2.8	2.2
2017	BGR	A	20	104	14	3	1	1	8	8	17	5	3	.250/.308/.333	111	6.0	.295	0.4	SS(23): -1.5	0.5
2018	INL	A+	21	190	36	11	3	2	16	27	22	22	8	.323/.426/.466	127	28.1	.365	2.5	SS(36): 3.9, 2B(2): 0.0	2.1
2018	MOB	AA	21	181	37	10	5	2	21	23	22	13	2	.305/.420/.477	129	14.2	.346	-1.0	SS(30): -3.4, 2B(9): -0.8	0.9
2018	SLC	AAA	21	219	36	9	5	3	27	25	31	6	6	.274/.358/.421	106	12.0	.310	3.3	2B(31): -1.5, SS(16): 0.1	1.2
2019	ANA	MLB	22	134	16	4	1	3	13	12	25	5	2	.235/.311/.367	81	1.6	.270	0.3	SS -1, 3B 0	0.0

Breakout: 4%   Improve: 29%   Collapse: 10%   Attrition: 23%   MLB: 41%   *Comparables: Ivan De Jesus, Daniel Robertson, J.P. Crawford*

Rengifo didn't stay out of the AL West for long, departing the Mariners but landing in Anaheim by way of Tampa Bay. Like many of the other prospects in this system, Rengifo appeared at three levels, ravaging the High-A California League and then performing even better at Double-A, before stumbling slightly in Triple-A Salt Lake City, all at the age of 21. The switch-hitter lashed *13 triples* in 2018, en route to 50 extra-base hits. While not a powerful guy, he gets the most of his fringe-average raw power by dovetailing improved pitch selection with a contact-oriented swing. He's aggressive on the bases despite average speed, and while his raw number of stolen bases (41) might impress, he was caught 16 times on the year and was notably successful only 50 percent of the time at Triple-A. Rengifo has the traditional profile of a utility man, but his patience at the plate and newfound power could push him into a second-division starter role.

Andrelton Simmons SS Born: 09/04/89 Age: 29 Bats: R Throws: R Height: 6'2" Weight: 200 Origin: Round 2, 2010 Draft (#70 overall)

YEAR	TEAM	LVL	AGE	PA	R	2B	3B	HR	RBI	BB	K	SB	CS	AVG/OBP/SLG	DRC+	VORP	BABIP	BRR	FRAA	WARP
2016	ANA	MLB	26	483	48	22	2	4	44	28	38	10	1	.281/.324/.366	90	15.3	.298	0.8	SS(124): 6.2	2.4
2017	ANA	MLB	27	647	77	38	2	14	69	47	67	19	6	.278/.331/.421	94	31.8	.291	2.7	SS(158): 16.1	4.4
2018	ANA	MLB	28	600	68	26	5	11	75	35	44	10	2	.292/.337/.417	103	35.6	.300	3.8	SS(145): -6.8	2.7
2019	*ANA*	*MLB*	*29*	*591*	*65*	*29*	*4*	*12*	*65*	*44*	*56*	*12*	*3*	*.278/.337/.413*	*107*	*29.1*	*.292*	*1.7*	*SS 2*	*3.4*

Breakout: 1%   Improve: 41%   Collapse: 2%   Attrition: 9%   MLB: 96%   *Comparables: Elvis Andrus, Gil Garrido, Nellie Fox*

Simmons has won six straight Fielding Bible awards, most in that award's history, and he's played six-and-a-half seasons. His negative FRAA last year is a shocking outlier, but its explanation is a bit inside baseball, so ... oh, right, this is a baseball book. Essentially, the grounder rates for the Angels were very consistent year-to-year, and Simmons just made considerably fewer overall plays in 2018, namely assists, than one would estimate. That dinged the numbers, but feel free to chalk it up to single-season defensive metric wackiness. He remained tops in shortstop Defensive Runs Saved, putouts and double plays. He's the best active defensive shortstop and remains highly durable. And to further not compare him with Ozzie Smith, Simmons has improved as a hitter, setting career bests in average and on-base percentage, while maintaining incredibly good contact rates. He still has never been named to an All-Star team, but he seems to be finally entering his prime, as if ground-ball hitters needed to hear that.

Kevan Smith C Born: 06/28/88 Age: 31 Bats: R Throws: R Height: 6'4" Weight: 230 Origin: Round 7, 2011 Draft (#231 overall)

YEAR	TEAM	LVL	AGE	PA	R	2B	3B	HR	RBI	BB	K	SB	CS	AVG/OBP/SLG	DRC+	VORP	BABIP	BRR	FRAA	WARP
2016	CHR	AAA	28	205	18	9	6	8	24	16	36	0	0	.219/.291/.399	110	-0.2	.229	-1.1	C(43): -2.1	0.8
2016	CHA	MLB	28	16	2	0	0	0	0	0	6	0	0	.125/.125/.125	75	-1.0	.200	0.7	C(6): -0.1	0.1
2017	CHR	AAA	29	62	10	6	0	0	15	6	9	0	0	.377/.435/.491	109	5.5	.435	0.5	C(13): -0.2	0.4
2017	CHA	MLB	29	294	23	17	0	4	30	9	46	0	0	.283/.309/.388	77	6.4	.323	0.5	C(79): -6.2	0.0
2018	CHR	AAA	30	124	12	4	0	4	16	8	18	0	0	.268/.331/.411	111	2.6	.286	-1.0	C(22): -0.7	0.5
2018	CHA	MLB	30	187	21	6	0	3	21	10	18	1	0	.292/.348/.380	97	7.4	.311	0.2	C(47): 0.1	0.9
2019	*ANA*	*MLB*	*31*	*165*	*16*	*7*	*1*	*3*	*16*	*10*	*30*	*0*	*0*	*.243/.300/.363*	*81*	*3.8*	*.281*	*0.3*	*C -2*	*0.1*

Breakout: 1%   Improve: 28%   Collapse: 12%   Attrition: 21%   MLB: 82%   *Comparables: Brayan Pena, Steve Clevenger, Manny Pina*

Some inquisitive souls in Los Angeles finally grew curious on how sustainable Smith's above-average on-base percentage and average framing would be in a larger role. They would be right to follow their curiosity, since despite those merits, Smith has repeatedly found himself on the periphery of the White Sox catching picture, backing up the likes of Omar Narvaez. Give him credit for his tenacity: Smith continued to toil at self-improvement at an age when his bosses might have already given up looking for it. He'll need to continue to defy the odds as he enters his thirties just to maintain his average-hitting, average-running, average-defense production. But you've seen what catchers as a whole hit like these days, right?

YEAR	TEAM	P. COUNT	FRM RUNS	BLK RUNS	THRW RUNS	TOT RUNS
2016	CHA	396	-0.2	0.2	0.0	-0.2
2017	CHA	10862	1.6	-1.6	-3.9	-4.5
2017	CHR	1944	0.1	-0.4	-0.1	-0.4
2018	CHA	6961	1.5	-0.9	-0.3	0.7
2018	CHR	2973	0.4	-0.8	-0.2	-0.5
2019	*ANA*	*6384*	*-0.3*	*-1.0*	*-0.6*	*-1.9*

Matt Thaiss 1B Born: 05/06/95 Age: 24 Bats: L Throws: R Height: 6'0" Weight: 195 Origin: Round 1, 2016 Draft (#16 overall)

YEAR	TEAM	LVL	AGE	PA	R	2B	3B	HR	RBI	BB	K	SB	CS	AVG/OBP/SLG	DRC+	VORP	BABIP	BRR	FRAA	WARP
2016	ORM	RK	21	71	16	7	1	2	12	4	4	2	4	.338/.394/.569	131	4.7	.339	-1.0	1B(15): 0.7	0.3
2016	BUR	A	21	226	24	12	3	4	31	22	28	1	0	.276/.351/.427	128	5.2	.302	-3.6	1B(43): 5.5	1.2
2017	INL	A+	22	385	46	13	4	8	48	40	59	4	3	.265/.353/.399	114	13.4	.299	0.5	1B(78): 2.8	1.5
2017	MOB	AA	22	221	29	14	0	1	25	37	50	4	3	.292/.412/.388	108	12.2	.389	-1.2	1B(46): -1.5	0.2
2018	MOB	AA	23	176	24	10	2	6	25	16	35	2	1	.287/.352/.490	126	9.0	.331	-1.1	1B(36): 2.6	1.0
2018	SLC	AAA	23	400	54	24	6	10	51	28	68	6	3	.277/.328/.457	110	-0.6	.314	0.2	1B(77): 5.4	1.7
2019	*ANA*	*MLB*	*24*	*67*	*7*	*3*	*0*	*2*	*8*	*4*	*13*	*0*	*0*	*.256/.301/.418*	*76*	*-1.1*	*.294*	*-0.1*	*1B 1*	*0.0*

Breakout: 3%   Improve: 9%   Collapse: 1%   Attrition: 14%   MLB: 16%   *Comparables: O'Koyea Dickson, David Cooper, Chad Wallach*

Thaiss runs like a what, what, what? Okay, Sisqo wouldn't have made a useful scout. Running isn't part of Thaiss' game anyway and, concerningly, neither was power entering the 2018 season. He came out trying to change minds, sending a career-high 16 balls over the fence between two different levels. There was a tradeoff though, as Thaiss' trademark patience took a hit and his overall production relative to the league average didn't change too much despite the different shape of it. Limited to first base defensively, there's a lot of pressure on the bat. There's a good chance he's a major leaguer at some point, but he's more likely to be remembered as the guy who was taken one pick ahead of Forrest Whitley than anything else. That's okay though, Sisqo's only remembered for one thing too.

Mike Trout CF Born: 08/07/91 Age: 27 Bats: R Throws: R Height: 6'2" Weight: 235 Origin: Round 1, 2009 Draft (#25 overall)

YEAR	TEAM	LVL	AGE	PA	R	2B	3B	HR	RBI	BB	K	SB	CS	AVG/OBP/SLG	DRC+	VORP	BABIP	BRR	FRAA	WARP
2016	ANA	MLB	24	681	123	32	5	29	100	116	137	30	7	.315/.441/.550	152	90.7	.371	4.8	CF(148): -6.8	6.6
2017	ANA	MLB	25	507	92	25	3	33	72	94	90	22	4	.306/.442/.629	163	69.0	.318	0.0	CF(108): -3.3	5.5
2018	ANA	MLB	26	608	101	24	4	39	79	122	124	24	2	.312/.460/.628	180	92.0	.346	1.5	CF(125): -2.5	8.0
2019	*ANA*	*MLB*	*27*	*677*	*127*	*32*	*4*	*36*	*105*	*137*	*129*	*27*	*5*	*.302/.454/.579*	*185*	*95.8*	*.342*	*1.4*	*CF -6*	*9.6*

Breakout: 4%   Improve: 56%   Collapse: 2%   Attrition: 1%   MLB: 98%   *Comparables: Joe Dimaggio, Mickey Mantle, Frank Thomas*

Part of baseball's generational allure is the day-to-day grind, the struggle to persist in the face of adversity and how it relates to a fan's personal journey. Trout has faced adversity but he still hasn't struggled. This past year he achieved the Jay Jaffe JAWS threshold for a Hall of Fame center fielder, as if you were yet convinced, and is younger than 15 rookies who had 100 plate appearances in 2018, including Joey Wendle and Luke Voit and Nick Martini. He has struggled only to struggle. We can't relate, we can only venerate. He is the diamond standard, already standing alone with ghosts and Barry Bonds. He once again set a career high in OPS—baseball's best single-season mark since Bonds. At some point he may struggle, 30 years from now, when baseball is a mindless cacophony of robots, all modeled after this baseball player, all who dominate baseball yet keep short-circuiting when it rains. Which is why they keep the human Trout employed.

Justin Upton LF   Born: 08/25/87   Age: 31   Bats: R   Throws: R   Height: 6'2"   Weight: 205   Origin: Round 1, 2005 Draft (#1 overall)

YEAR	TEAM	LVL	AGE	PA	R	2B	3B	HR	RBI	BB	K	SB	CS	AVG/OBP/SLG	DRC+	VORP	BABIP	BRR	FRAA	WARP
2016	DET	MLB	28	626	81	28	2	31	87	50	179	9	4	.246/.310/.465	102	16.3	.301	2.4	LF(146): -5.4, CF(6): 0.0	1.6
2017	DET	MLB	29	520	81	37	0	28	94	57	147	10	5	.279/.362/.542	120	31.4	.351	-0.6	LF(124): 11.8	3.8
2017	ANA	MLB	29	115	19	7	0	7	15	17	33	4	0	.245/.357/.531	118	7.6	.293	1.1	LF(27): -2.6	0.4
2018	ANA	MLB	30	613	80	18	1	30	85	64	176	8	2	.257/.344/.463	115	33.1	.321	-1.6	LF(140): 17.0	4.4
2019	ANA	MLB	31	625	83	29	2	28	88	67	179	11	4	.248/.337/.459	116	29.8	.316	0.3	LF 11	4.3

Breakout: 3%   Improve: 50%   Collapse: 5%   Attrition: 7%   MLB: 99%   *Comparables: Jason Bay, Mack Jones, Jason Kubel*

It's easy to gloss over how much of a background staple Upton has been in the majors since his teens. He didn't set the game ablaze at 19 like Griffey or Soto, but in each season from ages 20 through 30 he's gently warmed the lineup to the core, achieving an above average OPS+. To cull a complete list of other players with that accomplishment in that age range, you'd end up with 12 Hall of Famers, Alex Rodriguez, and someone from the deadball era named Sherry Magee, which is probably made up. He's rarely an MVP candidate, sometimes an All-Star, and always consistent. The Hall of Very Good is going to have a stellar inductee in Upton when all is said and done.

Luis Valbuena 3B   Born: 11/30/85   Age: 33   Bats: L   Throws: R   Height: 5'10"   Weight: 215   Origin: International Free Agent, 2002

YEAR	TEAM	LVL	AGE	PA	R	2B	3B	HR	RBI	BB	K	SB	CS	AVG/OBP/SLG	DRC+	VORP	BABIP	BRR	FRAA	WARP
2016	HOU	MLB	30	342	38	17	1	13	40	44	81	1	1	.260/.357/.459	108	19.4	.315	-1.4	3B(81): 5.9, 1B(8): 0.3	2.1
2017	ANA	MLB	31	401	42	15	0	22	65	48	106	0	2	.199/.294/.432	97	4.5	.210	-0.6	3B(59): 1.6, 1B(48): -0.3	1.0
2018	ANA	MLB	32	288	23	9	0	9	33	19	100	3	0	.199/.253/.335	70	-6.5	.277	-0.8	3B(57): 1.3, 1B(39): -0.1	-0.2
2019	ANA	MLB	33	297	33	13	1	10	37	30	81	1	1	.231/.312/.405	94	3.2	.292	-0.5	3B 0, 1B -2	0.2

Breakout: 2%   Improve: 40%   Collapse: 3%   Attrition: 7%   MLB: 90%   *Comparables: Chase Headley, David Freese, Kelly Johnson*

Luis Valbuena and former big leaguer Jose Castillo were driving in a private car after a game in their native Venezuela when they were ambushed by bandits who had blocked the road. The practice is commonplace in the poverty-stricken country; most players travel by bus, protected by security. The driver swerved to avoid the blockade and crashed; both players were killed.

Taylor Ward 3B   Born: 12/14/93   Age: 25   Bats: R   Throws: R   Height: 6'1"   Weight: 200   Origin: Round 1, 2015 Draft (#26 overall)

YEAR	TEAM	LVL	AGE	PA	R	2B	3B	HR	RBI	BB	K	SB	CS	AVG/OBP/SLG	DRC+	VORP	BABIP	BRR	FRAA	WARP
2016	INL	A+	22	529	61	11	0	10	56	48	81	0	0	.249/.323/.337	97	9.4	.279	1.4	C(90): 4.2	2.5
2017	INL	A+	23	247	32	11	1	6	30	35	43	0	0	.242/.348/.391	115	11.2	.275	1.3	C(42): -0.8	1.5
2017	MOB	AA	23	145	14	3	0	3	19	22	17	0	0	.286/.400/.387	131	11.5	.307	0.3	C(21): -3.9	0.7
2018	MOB	AA	24	179	26	8	0	6	25	29	33	8	1	.345/.453/.520	137	19.7	.409	-1.6	3B(33): -2.8	1.0
2018	SLC	AAA	24	267	42	18	0	8	35	36	61	10	2	.352/.442/.537	121	16.9	.450	-4.4	3B(53): -10.4	0.2
2018	ANA	MLB	24	147	14	3	0	6	15	9	45	2	0	.178/.245/.333	79	-4.2	.214	-2.4	3B(40): -2.3	-0.3
2019	ANA	MLB	25	100	12	4	0	3	11	10	28	1	0	.227/.312/.380	84	0.4	.294	0.0	3B -3	-0.2

Breakout: 2%   Improve: 16%   Collapse: 12%   Attrition: 27%   MLB: 51%   *Comparables: Max Muncy, Yamaico Navarro, Matt Carpenter*

Three seasons after the Angels drafted him in the first round, Ward transitioned from light-hitting backstop to thumping third baseman. GM Billy Eppler and Director of Player Development Mike Gallego thought Ward would reach the majors faster if he was no longer burdened with the tools of ignorance, and boy were they right: Ward rocketed through Double-A and Triple-A, showing more power (and speed) than ever before. His transformation resulted from a series of swing tweaks to keep his bat in the zone longer and match pitch planes than through a wholesale change in approach. Always the owner of a cautious eye at the plate, Ward saw his approach exploited at the big-league level, where pitchers' elite stuff made two-strike counts more dangerous than ever. While the switch to the hot corner saw him improve at the plate, the his work at third could still use some editing. He doesn't lack for athleticism, but is still raw, resulting in 17 errors between the three levels he saw last year. Further refinement in the field to complement his progress at the plate could see Ward solidify himself as an everyday player.

YEAR	TEAM	P. COUNT	FRM RUNS	BLK RUNS	THRW RUNS	TOT RUNS
2017	MOB	3243	-3.4	0.1	-0.1	-4.0

PITCHERS

Justin Anderson RHP   Born: 09/28/92   Age: 26   Bats: L   Throws: R   Height: 6'3"   Weight: 220   Origin: Round 14, 2014 Draft (#419 overall)

YEAR	TEAM	LVL	AGE	W	L	SV	G	GS	IP	H	HR	BB/9	K/9	K	GB%	BABIP	WHIP	ERA	DRA	WARP	MPH	FB%	WHF	CSP
2016	INL	A+	23	8	12	0	28	27	145¹	193	15	3.0	6.6	107	44%	.368	1.66	5.70	6.73	-2.1				
2017	MOB	AA	24	3	2	1	42	0	58²	56	7	4.4	5.5	36	49%	.266	1.45	5.06	5.87	-0.8				
2018	ANA	MLB	25	3	4	4	57	0	55¹	42	3	6.5	10.9	67	54%	.310	1.48	4.07	4.52	0.3	99.2	44.7	14.4	42.2
2019	ANA	MLB	26	3	1	0	59	0	62²	57	8	4.8	9.8	68	46%	.301	1.45	4.69	4.77	0.3	98.8	45.5	14.6	42.9

Breakout: 22%   Improve: 32%   Collapse: 9%   Attrition: 25%   MLB: 47%   *Comparables: Matt Marksberry, J.D. Durbin, Frank Garces*

Two years ago, Anderson was a Double-A power righty with awful command who couldn't generate outs, so you can blame him for not being in our book. While we were copyediting, he was delivery-editing. His seven scoreless appearances in spring training turned heads (despite no official invite) and he followed it up with blanks in Double-A and Triple-A. He snuck into the Angels' bullpen by late April, much in part to those ahead of him visiting the infirmary. His fastball peaked at 99 (though not as often late in the season) and his slider transformed into a more deceptive out pitch. When all was said and done he had the best K/9 of any Angel except for that Ohtani guy. They came at a cost, however, as his BB/9 nearly doubled the league average. He limits extra-base hits and doesn't show much of a platoon preference, so he'll stick around long enough for attentive fans to remember the name.

Jaime Barria RHP   Born: 07/18/96   Age: 22   Bats: R   Throws: R   Height: 6'1"   Weight: 210   Origin: International Free Agent, 2013

YEAR	TEAM	LVL	AGE	W	L	SV	G	GS	IP	H	HR	BB/9	K/9	K	GB%	BABIP	WHIP	ERA	DRA	WARP	MPH	FB%	WHF	CSP
2016	BUR	A	19	8	6	0	25	25	117	133	6	1.6	6.0	78	44%	.323	1.32	3.85	3.72	1.8				
2017	INL	A+	20	4	3	0	11	11	65¹	48	6	1.8	7.9	57	35%	.236	0.93	2.48	4.31	0.7				
2017	MOB	AA	20	1	6	0	12	12	61²	62	8	2.2	6.9	47	29%	.284	1.25	3.21	3.25	1.4				
2017	SLC	AAA	20	2	0	0	3	3	14²	11	0	1.8	8.0	13	29%	.262	0.95	2.45	3.61	0.3				
2018	SLC	AAA	21	0	0	0	5	5	18	20	2	2.5	9.5	19	28%	.353	1.39	3.50	4.64	0.2				
2018	ANA	MLB	21	10	9	0	26	26	129¹	117	17	3.3	6.8	98	37%	.272	1.27	3.41	5.67	-0.5	92.8	49.6	11.2	45
2019	ANA	MLB	22	7	7	0	21	21	111¹	105	17	3.0	7.7	96	36%	.279	1.27	4.75	4.83	0.8	92.8	51.7	11.7	46.9

Breakout: 17%   Improve: 28%   Collapse: 11%   Attrition: 18%   MLB: 50%   Comparables: Mat Latos, Drew Hutchison, Jacob Turner

Be thankful you're not getting a riff on Santana's "Maria, Maria" here. This west coast story's stage was set last year when Barria blew through three levels of the minor leagues, priming him to make his major-league debut at the tender age of 21. Not bad for a $60,000 investment by the Angels. He pitched well despite riding the bus from Salt Lake City to Anaheim throughout the first half of the season, suppressing offense despite the lack of a bat-missing pitch. Barria wasn't the type of prospect to generate a ton of buzz, because he was more about location and weak contact than elite stuff. But with a bevy of average-or-better offerings and advanced control he more than held his own in his inaugural season as a major leaguer. He relied heavily on his slider to mask his non-elite heater, but he has the flexibility to mix in his change more often if the league adapts. He might not generate a ton of headlines, but Barria should find himself taking regular rotation turns for the foreseeable future.

Jeremy Beasley RHP   Born: 11/20/95   Age: 23   Bats: R   Throws: R   Height: 6'3"   Weight: 215   Origin: Round 30, 2017 Draft (#895 overall)

YEAR	TEAM	LVL	AGE	W	L	SV	G	GS	IP	H	HR	BB/9	K/9	K	GB%	BABIP	WHIP	ERA	DRA	WARP	MPH	FB%	WHF	CSP
2017	ORM	RK	21	2	1	1	13	0	26	21	3	4.2	10.7	31	48%	.290	1.27	3.12	3.04	0.7				
2018	BUR	A	22	0	2	0	6	5	23	16	0	2.7	7.4	19	40%	.254	1.00	2.35	3.68	0.4				
2018	INL	A+	22	3	2	1	9	6	44¹	48	4	2.2	9.7	48	42%	.358	1.33	3.05	4.67	0.3				
2018	MOB	AA	22	3	3	0	10	7	44¹	32	3	2.8	7.5	37	44%	.248	1.04	2.44	4.61	0.3				
2019	ANA	MLB	23	4	4	1	38	9	76	75	15	4.5	8.0	68	41%	.282	1.49	5.84	6.02	-0.9				

Breakout: 3%   Improve: 7%   Collapse: 7%   Attrition: 6%   MLB: 16%   Comparables: Jose Quintana, P.J. Walters, Tanner Roark

It's not easy to find value in the 30th round, but the Angels just might have pulled it off. Selected in 2017, Beasley mowed down hitters across three levels, turning in a composite 2.66 ERA. His stuff won't wow you, but he can fill up the zone with his low-90s fastball(s) and bevy of offspeed offerings. He was mostly a starter this past year, but his future is likely in the bullpen, where his pedestrian offerings won't get exposed over extended outings. No matter what role Beasley embodies, that he's already seen success in Double-A can be seen as a victory given his draft status.

Cam Bedrosian RHP   Born: 10/02/91   Age: 27   Bats: R   Throws: R   Height: 6'0"   Weight: 230   Origin: Round 1, 2010 Draft (#29 overall)

YEAR	TEAM	LVL	AGE	W	L	SV	G	GS	IP	H	HR	BB/9	K/9	K	GB%	BABIP	WHIP	ERA	DRA	WARP	MPH	FB%	WHF	CSP
2016	SLC	AAA	24	1	0	1	5	0	8¹	7	1	4.3	15.1	14	53%	.333	1.32	3.24	1.99	0.3				
2016	ANA	MLB	24	2	0	1	45	0	40¹	30	1	3.1	11.4	51	52%	.309	1.09	1.12	3.14	0.8	97.6	67.7	11.7	46.7
2017	ANA	MLB	25	6	5	6	48	0	44²	41	5	3.4	10.7	53	45%	.313	1.30	4.43	2.97	1.1	95.4	57.7	13.5	46.5
2018	ANA	MLB	26	5	4	1	71	0	64	63	7	3.7	8.0	57	50%	.315	1.39	3.80	4.21	0.5	95.1	55.5	8.6	47.9
2019	ANA	MLB	27	3	1	8	59	0	62²	58	7	3.9	9.0	63	47%	.298	1.37	4.35	4.40	0.4	95.2	59.2	10.8	47.7

Breakout: 35%   Improve: 54%   Collapse: 19%   Attrition: 17%   MLB: 93%   Comparables: Kyle McClellan, Brian Bruney, Manny Delcarmen

Steve's kid had by far his biggest workload, but perhaps not coincidentally, also his slowest fastball. It could still beat Jered Weaver's in a footrace with its seams tied behind its back, but Bedrosian averaged fewer than a punchout per frame for the first time in his career. That's a fireballer's worst nightmare this side of a changeup marrying their mother. Even if the heater stays a modest 93 he's a durable reliever, but his days as emergency-closer-in-waiting might be behind him.

Austin Brice RHP   Born: 06/19/92   Age: 27   Bats: R   Throws: R   Height: 6'4"   Weight: 235   Origin: Round 9, 2010 Draft (#287 overall)

YEAR	TEAM	LVL	AGE	W	L	SV	G	GS	IP	H	HR	BB/9	K/9	K	GB%	BABIP	WHIP	ERA	DRA	WARP	MPH	FB%	WHF	CSP
2016	JAX	AA	24	4	7	2	27	13	93¹	79	5	2.8	7.6	79	47%	.280	1.16	2.89	3.15	2.1				
2016	NWO	AAA	24	0	0	2	5	0	8²	3	1	1.0	10.4	10	59%	.125	0.46	1.04	1.86	0.3				
2016	MIA	MLB	24	0	1	0	15	0	14	9	2	3.2	9.0	14	53%	.194	1.00	7.07	4.60	0.1	96.6	66.3	12.4	47.1
2017	LOU	AAA	25	1	2	1	15	0	21¹	23	0	3.8	8.9	21	46%	.365	1.50	3.80	3.88	0.3				
2017	CIN	MLB	25	0	0	0	22	0	32²	33	6	1.9	7.2	26	50%	.284	1.22	4.96	4.76	0.2	95.6	62.4	11.9	51.1
2018	CIN	MLB	26	2	3	0	33	0	37¹	39	9	3.1	7.7	32	53%	.286	1.39	5.79	5.75	-0.4	95.4	68.4	10	50.1
2018	LOU	AAA	26	3	1	1	17	0	23¹	18	2	2.7	9.3	24	36%	.296	1.07	2.31	4.79	0.1				
2019	BAL	MLB	27	1	0	0	17	0	17²	18	2	3.8	8.1	16	45%	.302	1.43	4.85	4.74	0.1	95.1	66.8	11.1	50.3

Breakout: 19%   Improve: 29%   Collapse: 18%   Attrition: 33%   MLB: 65%   Comparables: Adam Ottavino, J.D. Martin, Seth Lugo

A decade ago, we almost certainly would have heard from the sabermetric community that Brice didn't deserve his poor ERA. His walks and strikeouts were acceptable, and he even managed to keep the ball on the ground at a strong clip. There would have been a lot of xFIP talk thrown around. Fortunately, we have better tools now. The main issue is something that seemed to plague many Reds pitchers: he can't help but give up the long ball. He was better across the board in Triple-A.

Ty Buttrey RHP   Born: 03/31/93   Age: 26   Bats: L   Throws: R   Height: 6'6"   Weight: 230   Origin: Round 4, 2012 Draft (#151 overall)

YEAR	TEAM	LVL	AGE	W	L	SV	G	GS	IP	H	HR	BB/9	K/9	K	GB%	BABIP	WHIP	ERA	DRA	WARP	MPH	FB%	WHF	CSP
2016	PME	AA	23	1	9	0	33	9	79	80	6	5.2	5.9	52	52%	.292	1.59	4.44	4.41	0.5				
2017	PAW	AAA	24	1	1	0	10	0	17²	21	2	5.1	9.2	18	53%	.358	1.75	7.64	3.41	0.4				
2017	PME	AA	24	1	4	4	30	0	46	39	1	4.5	11.0	56	50%	.339	1.35	3.72	3.56	0.7				
2018	PAW	AAA	25	1	1	1	32	0	44	36	4	2.9	13.1	64	45%	.320	1.14	2.25	2.65	1.2				
2018	ANA	MLB	25	0	1	4	16	0	16¹	15	0	2.8	11.0	20	58%	.333	1.22	3.31	2.90	0.4	98.2	58	14	47.3
2019	ANA	MLB	26	3	1	15	59	0	62²	55	8	4.4	10.2	71	47%	.296	1.36	4.38	4.43	0.6	97.8	59	14.3	48.1

Breakout: 15%   Improve: 31%   Collapse: 6%   Attrition: 20%   MLB: 45%   *Comparables: Tom Mastny, Davis Romero, Patrick Light*

If you flip through previous editions of the Annual to look at Boston's 2012 overslot signing, you'll note a common theme: Buttrey issues too many free passes. Just last year we said he'd be stuck in Triple-A until he could cut down on the walks, so we'll just go ahead and assume he read the book. He finally broke through in 2018, reaching the majors to buttress the Angels' crumbling bullpen. His insistent fastball cut through opposing lineups like a hot knife through one of those midwestern gelatin salads, and he did a great job of keeping the ball on the ground in a small sample. He missed bats with his changeup (14 percent whiff rate) and slider (24 percent), and if he can maintain his ground-ball and strikeout rates, he can expect to be a mainstay in the bullpen.

Trevor Cahill RHP   Born: 03/01/88   Age: 31   Bats: R   Throws: R   Height: 6'4"   Weight: 240   Origin: Round 2, 2006 Draft (#66 overall)

YEAR	TEAM	LVL	AGE	W	L	SV	G	GS	IP	H	HR	BB/9	K/9	K	GB%	BABIP	WHIP	ERA	DRA	WARP	MPH	FB%	WHF	CSP
2016	IOW	AAA	28	0	3	0	6	6	19²	25	3	5.5	11.4	25	53%	.407	1.88	4.58	2.32	0.7				
2016	CHN	MLB	28	4	4	0	50	1	65²	49	7	4.8	9.0	66	57%	.246	1.28	2.74	4.14	0.7	95.1	54.5	11.6	40.4
2017	SDN	MLB	29	4	3	0	11	11	61	58	6	3.5	10.6	72	58%	.329	1.34	3.69	3.51	1.4	93.1	45.7	13.4	42.4
2017	KCA	MLB	29	0	0	0	10	3	23	33	10	8.2	5.9	15	54%	.319	2.35	8.22	6.61	-0.3	93.3	50	7.3	41.7
2018	NAS	AAA	30	0	1	0	3	3	13²	7	0	5.3	11.2	17	81%	.226	1.10	2.63	1.65	0.6				
2018	OAK	MLB	30	7	4	0	21	20	110	90	8	3.4	8.2	100	54%	.278	1.19	3.76	3.48	2.3	93.8	41.1	12.1	44.5
2019	ANA	MLB	31	6	5	1	42	14	97²	88	12	4.1	8.8	95	53%	.289	1.35	4.49	4.56	0.9	93.0	45.3	11.7	42.4

Breakout: 24%   Improve: 49%   Collapse: 19%   Attrition: 14%   MLB: 87%   *Comparables: Tom Koehler, David Phelps, Sam LeCure*

Cahill was the other half of the prodigal duo brought back to Oakland last year, along with Brett Anderson. In his years in the wilderness, the only constant was inconsistency, which led to him being available in mid-March for $1.5 million after Jharel Cotton hurt his elbow. Cahill had seen the usual velocity bump upon his move to the bullpen, adding about two mph to his sinker; the most intriguing part of his 2018 performance was that he kept that bump in Oakland's rotation. This helped him place among the top quartile of starting pitchers in the Statcast "barrel" measures (which attempt to capture how often batters make solid contact), near pitchers like Patrick Corbin and Max Scherzer. Cahill would need to add whiffs or cut walks (or both) to reach that type of elite status overall, and that's not going to happen, but avoiding hard contact could keep him in the league for a few more years, especially if he keeps pitching in front of top-notch defensive infields.

Griffin Canning RHP   Born: 05/11/96   Age: 23   Bats: R   Throws: R   Height: 6'1"   Weight: 170   Origin: Round 2, 2017 Draft (#47 overall)

YEAR	TEAM	LVL	AGE	W	L	SV	G	GS	IP	H	HR	BB/9	K/9	K	GB%	BABIP	WHIP	ERA	DRA	WARP	MPH	FB%	WHF	CSP
2018	INL	A+	22	0	0	0	2	2	8²	4	0	3.1	12.5	12	56%	.222	0.81	0.00	0.79	0.5				
2018	MOB	AA	22	1	0	0	10	10	45²	27	2	3.7	9.7	49	48%	.229	1.01	1.97	3.86	0.8				
2018	SLC	AAA	22	3	3	0	13	13	59	68	6	3.4	9.8	64	42%	.376	1.53	5.49	3.95	1.1				
2019	ANA	MLB	23	2	2	0	5	5	25	22	3	3.6	9.3	26	42%	.283	1.27	4.36	4.41	0.3				

Breakout: 18%   Improve: 27%   Collapse: 16%   Attrition: 29%   MLB: 52%   *Comparables: Zack Wheeler, Stephen Gonsalves, Eddie Butler*

A second-round pick in 2017, Canning fell due to health concerns, and seemed to validate them as he sat out the remainder of the summer. The rest seems to have done him right, as he mowed down batters across three different levels in 2018, ending the year on the precipice of the major leagues. He attacks hitters with a four-pitch mix headlined by a fastball that saw a velo jump and regularly hit 95 mph in 2018. The heater can be flat, though, and upper-level hitters took advantage of it, as his ground ball percentage decreased with each step up the organizational ladder. He'll flash a plus slider, along with an average curve and change to round out his arsenal. Canning looks like a steal based on his draft position and could find himself in the middle of the rotation sooner rather than later. He isn't the biggest guy, though, and paired with his command concerns the whispers of a bullpen future still persist.

Taylor Cole RHP   Born: 08/20/89   Age: 29   Bats: R   Throws: R   Height: 6'1"   Weight: 200   Origin: Round 29, 2011 Draft (#889 overall)

YEAR	TEAM	LVL	AGE	W	L	SV	G	GS	IP	H	HR	BB/9	K/9	K	GB%	BABIP	WHIP	ERA	DRA	WARP	MPH	FB%	WHF	CSP
2016	DUN	A+	26	1	0	0	3	3	15¹	20	0	1.8	4.7	8	59%	.370	1.50	4.70	4.33	0.2				
2016	NHP	AA	26	3	4	0	12	11	61²	70	6	2.5	7.9	54	51%	.352	1.41	3.79	3.95	0.8				
2017	TOR	MLB	27	0	0	0	1	0	1	6	0	9.0	9.0	1	57%	.857	7.00	36.00	11.11	-0.1	95.3	58.5	9.8	43.2
2018	SLC	AAA	28	3	0	6	34	0	55¹	55	6	4.4	10.6	65	48%	.343	1.48	5.37	3.88	0.8				
2018	ANA	MLB	28	4	2	0	18	2	36	20	3	3.0	9.8	39	52%	.218	0.89	2.75	4.24	0.3	95.1	39.1	15.9	41.8
2019	ANA	MLB	29	3	2	0	38	6	64	59	9	3.9	9.6	68	47%	.299	1.35	4.56	4.64	0.5	94.4	40.1	15.6	42.4

Breakout: 8%   Improve: 11%   Collapse: 13%   Attrition: 13%   MLB: 34%   *Comparables: Ramon A. Ramirez, Brian Slocum, Alex Wimmers*

Cole spent seven nondescript seasons in the Blue Jays organization before being given the ol' Toronto Toodle-loo. Last year he shuttled between Anaheim and Salt Lake, posting some curiously minuscule numbers, in the good way, for a team desperate for a warm body that knew how to hurl hard spheres. It's an average three-pitch repertoire across the board, though he'll throw any of the three in any count, and the advanced mixology shook out to a solid count of whiffs and grounders alike. The low ERA might have been a bit fortuitous, given the BABIP, though if everything works out he could start some late-summer games as the infirmary fills up. For now, he's a multi-inning relief option.

Odrisamer Despaigne RHP   Born: 04/04/87   Age: 32   Bats: R   Throws: R   Height: 6'0"   Weight: 200   Origin: International Free Agent, 2014

YEAR	TEAM	LVL	AGE	W	L	SV	G	GS	IP	H	HR	BB/9	K/9	K	GB%	BABIP	WHIP	ERA	DRA	WARP	MPH	FB%	WHF	CSP
2016	BAL	MLB	29	0	2	0	16	0	27¹	32	3	4.9	5.6	17	38%	.337	1.72	5.60	7.83	-0.9	95.2	72.9	9.3	45.5
2016	NOR	AAA	29	1	9	0	18	17	88¹	91	5	2.8	7.1	70	53%	.319	1.34	3.87	5.51	-0.2				
2016	MIA	MLB	29	0	0	0	3	0	3	4	0	3.0	0.0	0	50%	.333	1.67	9.00	8.00	-0.1	94.3	72.9	4.2	41.6
2017	NWO	AAA	30	2	4	2	20	10	70	62	6	3.1	6.3	49	52%	.271	1.23	3.09	3.83	1.3				
2017	MIA	MLB	30	2	3	1	18	8	58¹	57	3	3.7	4.8	31	38%	.280	1.39	4.01	5.17	0.2	94.2	84.3	8	47.5
2018	MIA	MLB	31	2	0	0	11	1	20¹	22	1	3.5	8.0	18	41%	.333	1.48	5.31	4.61	0.1	94.1	67.4	14.6	43.2
2018	NWO	AAA	31	2	3	2	13	4	43¹	52	0	2.5	8.3	40	44%	.380	1.48	4.36	3.90	0.7				
2018	ANA	MLB	31	0	3	0	8	4	18²	30	3	5.3	8.2	17	44%	.415	2.20	8.20	6.74	-0.4	94.9	67.4	9.7	48.9
2019	*ANA*	*MLB*	*32*	*4*	*4*	*0*	*34*	*11*	*78²*	*79*	*11*	*3.6*	*7.3*	*64*	*44%*	*.292*	*1.40*	*4.90*	*4.99*	*0.3*	*93.5*	*74.7*	*9.7*	*46*

Breakout: 15%   Improve: 30%   Collapse: 17%   Attrition: 12%   MLB: 60%   *Comparables: Ryan Drese, John Maine, D.J. Carrasco*

Despaigne holds the all-time best anagram in baseball: his first and last name transform to "San Diego Padres." He can also rearrange his six different pitches in various sequences, though lately he hasn't quite managed to find a consistent formula to retire batters. His cutter posed the biggest issue among several last year, as his third pitch yielded an unspeakable .483 ISO. Stuck between the rotation, the bullpen and the wrong side of the aging curve, Despaigne will continue to get a handful of innings with his myriad pitches while donning an arrangement of baseball jerseys known only to Calvinists.

Luis Garcia RHP   Born: 01/30/87   Age: 32   Bats: R   Throws: R   Height: 6'3"   Weight: 230   Origin: International Free Agent, 2017

YEAR	TEAM	LVL	AGE	W	L	SV	G	GS	IP	H	HR	BB/9	K/9	K	GB%	BABIP	WHIP	ERA	DRA	WARP	MPH	FB%	WHF	CSP
2016	LEH	AAA	29	6	3	13	48	0	54²	38	3	4.0	8.7	53	63%	.261	1.13	2.14	3.40	1.0				
2016	PHI	MLB	29	1	1	0	17	0	15¹	21	2	4.7	8.2	14	55%	.373	1.89	6.46	4.65	0.1	99.0	57.3	11.8	44.1
2017	PHI	MLB	30	2	5	2	66	0	71¹	61	3	3.3	7.6	60	57%	.282	1.22	2.65	3.26	1.5	98.7	63.3	12.8	49
2018	PHI	MLB	31	3	1	1	59	0	46	49	4	3.5	10.0	51	50%	.354	1.46	6.07	3.25	0.9	99.2	48.4	15.5	44.8
2019	*ANA*	*MLB*	*32*	*3*	*1*	*0*	*54*	*0*	*57*	*51*	*7*	*4.3*	*9.2*	*58*	*51%*	*.293*	*1.37*	*4.42*	*4.47*	*0.4*	*97.9*	*55.6*	*13.7*	*45.6*

Breakout: 23%   Improve: 41%   Collapse: 23%   Attrition: 20%   MLB: 78%   *Comparables: Saul Rivera, Ryan Mattheus, Joe Beimel*

Luis Garcia—or, I should say, the *idea* of Luis Garcia—doesn't make any sense. Bakc in 2014, Garcia emerged from the minors with a high-90s heater and buckling splitter, the same two-pitch combo propelling Hector Neris to success. That he'd added five ticks on his fastball midseason was striking, and seemingly positioned him well to hold down a bullpen spot in 2015. And while the velocity has held in the years since, Garcia's performance has been anything but predictable. Garcia managed to trim his walk rate below nine percent while bumping his strikeouts up to 25 percent in 2018—career-best numbers in both cases—but also got hit harder than ever in exchange. The end result is a negative RE24 for the fifth time in six seasons. It was an unlucky turn given the under-the-hood indicators. He under-performed his DRA by a larger margin than any other pitcher in baseball who matched his innings, and the Angels made a big bet that his actual 2019 will look more like his theoretical 2018 when they shipped their only reliable lefty reliever to Philly to get him.

Matt Harvey RHP   Born: 03/27/89   Age: 30   Bats: R   Throws: R   Height: 6'4"   Weight: 215   Origin: Round 1, 2010 Draft (#7 overall)

YEAR	TEAM	LVL	AGE	W	L	SV	G	GS	IP	H	HR	BB/9	K/9	K	GB%	BABIP	WHIP	ERA	DRA	WARP	MPH	FB%	WHF	CSP
2016	NYN	MLB	27	4	10	0	17	17	92²	111	8	2.4	7.4	76	44%	.353	1.47	4.86	3.57	1.9	97.4	60	10.9	48.8
2017	BIN	AA	28	0	0	0	2	2	7²	9	1	2.3	5.9	5	33%	.308	1.43	5.87	6.43	-0.1				
2017	NYN	MLB	28	5	7	0	19	18	92²	110	21	4.6	6.5	67	46%	.307	1.69	6.70	6.63	-1.1	95.9	59.3	8.6	47
2018	NYN	MLB	29	0	2	0	8	4	27	33	6	3.0	6.7	20	43%	.310	1.56	7.00	4.18	0.3	94.4	61.2	8.2	49.7
2018	CIN	MLB	29	7	7	0	24	24	128	132	21	2.0	7.8	111	46%	.296	1.25	4.50	4.79	0.7	96.2	58.7	10.4	53
2019	*ANA*	*MLB*	*30*	*6*	*6*	*0*	*19*	*19*	*100²*	*102*	*15*	*3.0*	*7.7*	*86*	*44%*	*.295*	*1.35*	*4.79*	*4.87*	*0.7*	*95.4*	*59.2*	*9.8*	*49.5*

Breakout: 23%   Improve: 55%   Collapse: 7%   Attrition: 9%   MLB: 85%   *Comparables: Chris Capuano, Paul Derringer, Ricky Nolasco*

It's hard to watch Harvey today without reflecting on all that's come before: the flight and the fall, the scowls and scars and bitterness and whispers and general cussedness that's surrounded the man. Yet we shouldn't lose track of the odds that he has beaten to return from elbow ligament and thoracic outlet surgery as a usable major league starter. When he's right, Harvey can still dial his fastball into the mid-90s and his slider still darts and dives. When he's not right, and like most back-end starters that happens a lot, lefty power bats take him to the woodshed. He's a solid number four with some upside remaining, and there's a non-zero chance that putting another winter between Harvey and the operating room will tease out a little more of the old magic. The Angels, believing in magic, signed him for a year at $11 million.

Andrew Heaney LHP   Born: 06/05/91   Age: 28   Bats: L   Throws: L   Height: 6'2"   Weight: 185   Origin: Round 1, 2012 Draft (#9 overall)

YEAR	TEAM	LVL	AGE	W	L	SV	G	GS	IP	H	HR	BB/9	K/9	K	GB%	BABIP	WHIP	ERA	DRA	WARP	MPH	FB%	WHF	CSP
2016	ANA	MLB	25	0	1	0	1	1	6	7	2	0.0	10.5	7	44%	.312	1.17	6.00	5.15	0.0	94.3	58.6	14.9	46
2017	ANG	RK	26	0	1	0	3	3	10¹	11	0	0.9	13.1	15	42%	.423	1.16	1.74	1.56	0.5				
2017	SLC	AAA	26	1	1	0	3	3	17¹	17	2	2.1	7.3	14	39%	.306	1.21	3.12	4.38	0.3				
2017	ANA	MLB	26	1	2	0	5	5	21²	27	12	3.7	11.2	27	34%	.283	1.66	7.06	5.71	0.0	94.2	61.6	14.6	44.5
2018	ANA	MLB	27	9	10	0	30	30	180	171	27	2.2	9.0	180	44%	.294	1.20	4.15	3.63	3.5	94.2	58.1	12.7	50.8
2019	*ANA*	*MLB*	*28*	*10*	*10*	*0*	*28*	*28*	*159²*	*149*	*28*	*3.4*	*9.4*	*166*	*43%*	*.288*	*1.31*	*4.85*	*4.96*	*0.9*	*93.6*	*58.8*	*13.1*	*47.8*

Breakout: 29%   Improve: 59%   Collapse: 8%   Attrition: 16%   MLB: 90%   *Comparables: Zach McAllister, John Maine, Chase Anderson*

Heaney is a wiry left-hander who finally assembled a complete season without any screws flying out the side in comical Hanna-Barbera fashion. He was way up the charts in terms of limiting hard contact on average and even tossed a one-hitter for good measure. For someone who doesn't burn the radar guns (he sits mostly at 92), many of those strikeouts are attributed to his curveball, arguably the best breaking pitch from the sinister side except for perhaps Blake Snell's curve. His bugaboo, as is the case with many soft-tossers, is the longball: over half his runs allowed were via the dinger. It's hard to find patterns in a record as spotty as Heaney's, and you'd like to believe that he can improve on his mistakes, but baseball has swallowed whole the careers of those much better than him.

Jim Johnson   RHP   Born: 06/27/83   Age: 36   Bats: R   Throws: R   Height: 6'6"   Weight: 250   Origin: Round 5, 2001 Draft (#143 overall)

YEAR	TEAM	LVL	AGE	W	L	SV	G	GS	IP	H	HR	BB/9	K/9	K	GB%	BABIP	WHIP	ERA	DRA	WARP	MPH	FB%	WHF	CSP
2016	ATL	MLB	33	2	6	20	65	0	64²	57	3	2.8	9.5	68	56%	.314	1.19	3.06	3.39	1.2	96.1	68.8	8.3	48.2
2017	ATL	MLB	34	6	3	22	61	0	56²	59	8	4.0	9.7	61	49%	.317	1.48	5.56	4.58	0.4	95.0	68.1	10.2	45.6
2018	ANA	MLB	35	5	3	2	62	1	63¹	64	9	3.1	6.4	45	50%	.288	1.36	3.84	5.40	-0.3	94.7	68.2	7.9	49.5
2019	*ANA*	*MLB*	*36*	*3*	*1*	*7*	*52*	*0*	*55*	*56*	*7*	*3.7*	*7.6*	*46*	*49%*	*.301*	*1.44*	*4.83*	*4.91*	*0.1*	*93.8*	*66.9*	*8.5*	*46.9*

Breakout: 25%   Improve: 43%   Collapse: 23%   Attrition: 3%   MLB: 73%   *Comparables: Joey Eischen, Bob Locker, Gene Garber*

Johnson is definitely a World WAR III reliever. bWAR and fWAR grade his career with eight and six wins respectively, but DRA puts him in the negative. Groundball-dependent pitchers tend to scatter opinions, but at least everyone can agree on one thing: Johnson is one of the game's most durable middle men. He hasn't had an arm or shoulder injury since 2010, a stretch that spans over 500 big-league appearances. As his career begins to wind down, his numbers mirror those you also barely remember: David Weathers, Mark Guthrie, Steve Reed, Chad Qualls, and ol' whats his face. He's one of only two closers ever to post consecutive 50-save seasons (along with Eric Gagne), which feels like two analytical movements ago. He'll silently but respectably fade into retirement sooner rather than later.

Deck McGuire   RHP   Born: 06/23/89   Age: 30   Bats: R   Throws: R   Height: 6'6"   Weight: 220   Origin: Round 1, 2010 Draft (#11 overall)

YEAR	TEAM	LVL	AGE	W	L	SV	G	GS	IP	H	HR	BB/9	K/9	K	GB%	BABIP	WHIP	ERA	DRA	WARP	MPH	FB%	WHF	CSP
2016	SFD	AA	27	0	0	1	1	1	7	2	0	3.9	10.3	8	25%	.125	0.71	0.00	1.42	0.3				
2016	MEM	AAA	27	7	11	0	26	26	134	134	22	3.4	7.5	111	39%	.294	1.37	5.10	4.51	1.3				
2017	PEN	AA	28	9	9	0	28	27	168	125	13	3.1	9.1	170	40%	.263	1.08	2.79	3.81	2.7				
2017	CIN	MLB	28	1	1	0	6	2	13²	10	1	1.3	7.2	11	26%	.220	0.88	2.63	4.43	0.1	94.7	63.6	9.6	49.4
2018	TOR	MLB	29	0	0	0	4	0	8¹	9	2	5.4	7.6	7	26%	.280	1.68	6.48	6.62	-0.2	94.7	58.2	11	52.6
2018	BUF	AAA	29	4	2	0	8	8	44²	33	3	3.8	8.1	40	40%	.259	1.16	3.22	3.59	1.0				
2018	SLC	AAA	29	1	1	0	6	3	11	9	2	4.1	8.2	10	31%	.233	1.27	4.91	5.51	0.0				
2018	ANA	MLB	29	0	2	0	17	4	29²	29	7	6.4	7.9	26	41%	.278	1.69	6.07	8.04	-1.0	94.7	55.9	9.1	45.8
2019	*ANA*	*MLB*	*30*	*5*	*6*	*0*	*28*	*15*	*92²*	*88*	*16*	*4.1*	*7.8*	*81*	*38%*	*.278*	*1.41*	*5.40*	*5.54*	*-0.2*	*93.9*	*57.6*	*9.5*	*48*

Breakout: 1%   Improve: 4%   Collapse: 8%   Attrition: 9%   MLB: 14%   *Comparables: Chris Seddon, Mike Parisi, Hiram Burgos*

A tumultuous path to the majors faced the former first-rounder, but McGuire finally found a healthy serving of major-league playing time, largely in part to someone forgetting to padlock the bullpen doors in Anaheim. McGuire was optioned *eight* times across three franchises last year. Let that sink in. He spent four days in the Texas organization, two of them filling out orientation paperwork. At some point, "Hey, Aren't You Deck McGuire?" won't work on a gullible general manager once they see him hang another slider, but place your bets on which three teams claim him off waivers this year.

Keynan Middleton   RHP   Born: 09/12/93   Age: 25   Bats: R   Throws: R   Height: 6'2"   Weight: 215   Origin: Round 3, 2013 Draft (#95 overall)

YEAR	TEAM	LVL	AGE	W	L	SV	G	GS	IP	H	HR	BB/9	K/9	K	GB%	BABIP	WHIP	ERA	DRA	WARP	MPH	FB%	WHF	CSP
2016	INL	A+	22	1	1	0	25	0	36¹	22	7	5.0	13.9	56	34%	.227	1.16	3.72	1.53	1.5				
2016	ARK	AA	22	0	0	6	13	0	15	11	1	2.4	10.8	18	42%	.270	1.00	1.20	1.71	0.5				
2016	SLC	AAA	22	0	1	2	8	0	14²	14	1	2.5	8.6	14	48%	.302	1.23	4.91	4.39	0.1				
2017	SLC	AAA	23	0	0	0	10	0	12²	11	0	2.8	5.7	8	36%	.282	1.18	2.84	4.31	0.1				
2017	ANA	MLB	23	6	1	3	64	0	58¹	60	11	2.8	9.7	63	38%	.318	1.34	3.86	3.80	0.9	99.2	62.6	18.2	48.7
2018	ANA	MLB	24	0	0	6	16	0	17²	14	1	4.6	8.2	16	33%	.295	1.30	2.04	5.55	-0.1	98.4	64.4	11	44.7
2019	*ANA*	*MLB*	*25*	*2*	*1*	*6*	*32*	*0*	*34*	*31*	*5*	*4.6*	*9.5*	*36*	*38%*	*.292*	*1.42*	*4.82*	*4.91*	*0.1*	*98.7*	*64.7*	*16.6*	*47.6*

Breakout: 35%   Improve: 48%   Collapse: 14%   Attrition: 23%   MLB: 74%   *Comparables: Will Smith, Ian Krol, Logan Kensing*

Middleton's a classic fastball-slider combo pitcher against righties, and he'll turn over a viable changeup against those weird lefties, so he can retire batters in a number of ways. The man they call Key was clearly the Angels' most reliable bullpen option, tasked to lock down the ninth inning. He was slotted on an All-Star track until the inexorable fragility of tendons in pitchers reached a yowling climax for Middleton last May. The hope is that Key comes back with a fresh new UCL later this year and re-assumes the closer's role by 2020.

Shohei Ohtani   RHP   Born: 07/05/94   Age: 24   Bats: L   Throws: R   Height: 6'4"   Weight: 200   Origin: International Free Agent, 2017

YEAR	TEAM	LVL	AGE	W	L	SV	G	GS	IP	H	HR	BB/9	K/9	K	GB%	BABIP	WHIP	ERA	DRA	WARP	MPH	FB%	WHF	CSP
2018	ANA	MLB	23	4	2	0	10	10	51²	38	6	3.8	11.0	63	40%	.269	1.16	3.31	3.46	1.1	99.5	46.4	15.5	47.6
2019	*ANA*	*MLB*	*24*	*2*	*2*	*0*	*7*	*7*	*36*	*28*	*4*	*3.9*	*11.1*	*44*	*40%*	*.282*	*1.21*	*3.88*	*3.90*	*0.7*	*99.3*	*47.8*	*15.9*	*49.1*

Breakout: 27%   Improve: 54%   Collapse: 12%   Attrition: 5%   MLB: 97%   *Comparables: Mark Langston, Hal Newhouser, Vinegar Bend Mizell*

You, a baseball fan, have various circles of connections: friends and online acquaintances who are equally zealous about the sport; co-workers and neighbors who dabble in all the athletic prowesses; and those people you love but could (possibly?) identify a baseball among a lineup of other spheres. Baseball news stories flash by our lives and depending on the magnitude/nerdery of the story, you share it with one or more of those circles.

When the Ohtani scouting report hit the states, you told everyone, even your grandparents who stopped watching baseball in 1962 when players kept hot-doggin' it. So many paragraphs have been rendered based on his substance and his phenomenon, so place this in the simplest of contexts: Ohtani is one of the league's best hitters and one of the league's best pitchers and the last person to embody both roles was Babe Ruth. And he did it simultaneously for only a couple seasons. Everyone has heard of general baseball players existing, but Ohtani, or at least the idea of him, transcends generations.

You are painfully aware that this year Thomas Edward John surgery will keep him off the mound but not from the batter's box, so we'll still get to watch him mash, at least. And a year from now you can go back to being the herald that cries the wonders of the two-way player.

Blake Parker RHP
Born: 06/19/85　Age: 34　Bats: R　Throws: R　Height: 6'3"　Weight: 225　Origin: Round 16, 2006 Draft (#479 overall)

YEAR	TEAM	LVL	AGE	W	L	SV	G	GS	IP	H	HR	BB/9	K/9	K	GB%	BABIP	WHIP	ERA	DRA	WARP	MPH	FB%	WHF	CSP
2016	TAC	AAA	31	1	2	19	38	0	39²	24	4	2.5	12.7	56	44%	.256	0.88	2.72	1.72	1.5				
2016	SEA	MLB	31	0	0	0	1	0	1	1	0	9.0	0.0	0	75%	.250	2.00	0.00	12.02	-0.1	94.4	73.1	7.7	50
2016	NYA	MLB	31	1	0	1	16	0	16¹	16	1	4.4	8.3	15	49%	.312	1.47	4.96	4.44	0.1	94.2	55.8	11.9	45.3
2017	ANA	MLB	32	3	3	8	71	0	67¹	40	7	2.1	11.5	86	48%	.229	0.83	2.54	2.26	2.2	95.0	60	15.1	44.7
2018	ANA	MLB	33	2	1	14	67	0	66¹	63	12	2.6	9.5	70	35%	.297	1.24	3.26	5.19	-0.2	94.0	57.5	11.6	46.5
2019	ANA	MLB	34	3	1	4	53	0	56	49	9	3.4	9.7	61	41%	.279	1.25	4.49	4.56	0.3	93.3	57.6	12.8	45

Breakout: 14%　Improve: 27%　Collapse: 32%　Attrition: 9%　MLB: 80%　　　　*Comparables: Justin Miller, Kiko Calero, Tyler Walker*

If Parker bloomed any later he would be a toad lily. You know the deal about toad lilies: The distinctive white flower with purple spots typically blooms from July to September just as all other flowers are beginning to fade. Since being a four-time waiver pickup three years ago, Parker has thrown the vast majority of his major league innings in the last two seasons. As he enters his age-34 season, he has settled into high-leverage roles via fiery baptism. His fastball became way less effective last year, getting hit and launched further than before, perhaps signifying his bloom is near its end. Toad lily, we hardly knew ye.

Felix Pena RHP
Born: 02/25/90　Age: 29　Bats: R　Throws: R　Height: 6'2"　Weight: 185　Origin: International Free Agent, 2009

YEAR	TEAM	LVL	AGE	W	L	SV	G	GS	IP	H	HR	BB/9	K/9	K	GB%	BABIP	WHIP	ERA	DRA	WARP	MPH	FB%	WHF	CSP
2016	IOW	AAA	26	3	4	3	36	0	63¹	46	4	3.3	11.5	81	35%	.288	1.09	3.41	2.51	1.8				
2016	CHN	MLB	26	0	0	1	11	0	9	5	1	3.0	13.0	13	42%	.222	0.89	4.00	2.41	0.3	95.3	59.7	18.6	49.4
2017	IOW	AAA	27	2	1	6	24	0	39	42	6	3.2	10.6	46	42%	.346	1.44	5.54	2.72	1.1				
2017	CHN	MLB	27	1	0	0	25	0	34¹	35	8	4.7	9.7	37	35%	.300	1.54	5.24	5.46	-0.1	96.0	65.8	13.4	46.7
2018	SLC	AAA	28	1	2	0	10	9	33¹	30	2	4.3	10.3	38	39%	.346	1.38	3.51	4.10	0.5				
2018	ANA	MLB	28	3	5	0	19	17	92²	87	12	2.7	8.3	85	44%	.288	1.24	4.18	4.15	1.2	94.1	57.9	11.8	46.2
2019	ANA	MLB	29	5	5	0	15	15	79²	73	12	3.8	9.2	81	40%	.287	1.34	4.81	4.90	0.5	93.9	59.9	12.4	47.2

Breakout: 25%　Improve: 40%　Collapse: 21%　Attrition: 20%　MLB: 69%　　　　*Comparables: Mike Fiers, Mike Bolsinger, Tyler Lyons*

The Angels executed a minor heist when they acquired Pena, an extremely forgettable reliever, from the Cubs for peace of mind, then converted him to the Church of Sinkertology. The sinker was exactly what his polished secondaries needed, and he added a changeup for good measure. He's also now a starting pitcher, a role he abandoned in the Cubs minor league system. Given the quick transformation it's tough to project his 2019 but Pena has demonstrated that he can hold his own in a major-league rotation, and it's extremely easy to project the Cubs' faces right now.

Noe Ramirez RHP
Born: 12/22/89　Age: 29　Bats: R　Throws: R　Height: 6'3"　Weight: 195　Origin: Round 4, 2011 Draft (#142 overall)

YEAR	TEAM	LVL	AGE	W	L	SV	G	GS	IP	H	HR	BB/9	K/9	K	GB%	BABIP	WHIP	ERA	DRA	WARP	MPH	FB%	WHF	CSP
2016	PAW	AAA	26	2	3	7	30	0	43²	39	3	2.3	11.1	54	44%	.333	1.15	1.85	1.93	1.5				
2016	BOS	MLB	26	0	0	0	14	0	13	16	4	5.5	10.4	15	36%	.375	1.85	6.23	5.71	-0.1	91.9	47.5	13.2	46
2017	BOS	MLB	27	0	0	0	2	0	4²	3	2	1.9	7.7	4	23%	.091	0.86	3.86	9.83	-0.2	91.2	50.7	16.9	48.8
2017	PAW	AAA	27	3	3	5	33	0	48²	40	7	3.0	10.5	57	35%	.284	1.15	3.51	2.63	1.4				
2017	ANA	MLB	27	0	0	0	10	0	8¹	3	0	4.3	10.8	10	65%	.176	0.84	2.16	3.65	0.1	91.4	25.9	14.7	42.4
2018	ANA	MLB	28	7	5	1	69	1	83¹	75	15	3.2	10.3	95	44%	.290	1.26	4.54	3.36	1.5	91.6	41.9	12.3	46.4
2019	ANA	MLB	29	2	1	0	48	0	51¹	45	8	3.7	9.7	55	41%	.283	1.28	4.57	4.64	0.3	91.0	41.6	12.7	45.7

Breakout: 18%　Improve: 40%　Collapse: 16%　Attrition: 23%　MLB: 75%　　　　*Comparables: Jason Motte, Heath Bell, Brad Brach*

It's not often someone throws barely 90 while striking out over a quarter of the batters they face, but that's Ramirez for you. He finally broke through with a successful major-league season thanks to his oddball arsenal. Classified as a sinker, his fastball surprisingly acts more as a swing-and-miss pitch than your textbook ground-ball offering. It's the pitch that was always red flagged as one that could be easily belted into the seats, and that's no longer happening. That and a slidery-curve both lead the way for the changeup, his true out pitch. The crafty righty can get outs in any situation, but going into 2019 he'll probably be one of the first to jog out of the bullpen.

Hansel Robles RHP
Born: 08/13/90　Age: 28　Bats: R　Throws: R　Height: 5'11"　Weight: 185　Origin: International Free Agent, 2008

YEAR	TEAM	LVL	AGE	W	L	SV	G	GS	IP	H	HR	BB/9	K/9	K	GB%	BABIP	WHIP	ERA	DRA	WARP	MPH	FB%	WHF	CSP
2016	NYN	MLB	25	6	4	1	68	0	77²	69	7	4.2	9.8	85	31%	.307	1.35	3.48	4.25	0.6	98.8	63.9	12.3	49.1
2017	LVG	AAA	26	0	1	4	18	0	23¹	27	5	5.4	8.5	22	36%	.319	1.76	5.79	4.95	0.1				
2017	NYN	MLB	26	7	5	0	46	0	56²	47	10	4.6	9.5	60	35%	.259	1.34	4.92	5.63	-0.3	97.0	66.6	9.8	48
2018	LVG	AAA	27	0	0	2	8	0	7²	7	1	5.9	8.2	7	61%	.273	1.57	3.52	4.73	0.0				
2018	NYN	MLB	27	2	2	0	16	0	19²	21	7	4.6	10.5	23	28%	.298	1.58	5.03	3.75	0.3	97.4	69.1	11.6	50.7
2018	ANA	MLB	27	0	1	2	37	0	36¹	32	2	3.7	8.9	36	40%	.300	1.29	2.97	4.90	0.0	98.6	67.5	12.5	49.5
2019	ANA	MLB	28	3	1	0	59	0	62²	56	10	4.3	9.4	65	37%	.279	1.38	5.00	5.11	0.0	97.4	66.7	11.6	49.4

Breakout: 26%　Improve: 41%　Collapse: 26%　Attrition: 17%　MLB: 78%　　　　*Comparables: Jensen Lewis, Shawn Tolleson, Fernando Cabrera*

Robles was destined for the unrelenting journey of new uniforms in different cities. His phenomenal September put that journey on hold, however, as managers tend to like relievers that can strike out batters without giving up large quantities of home runs. He incorporated his changeup more to get him out of trouble, especially against lefties, who kept driving the ball out of town. His high-octane fastball and slider had always accelerated the fire in Flushing, which is why the Mets were more than eager to let him go on waivers. Anaheim helped him figure some things out, though, and the third pitch may be enough, given that staying in one place is the ultimate change.

Patrick Sandoval LHP   Born: 10/18/96   Age: 22   Bats: L   Throws: L   Height: 6'3"   Weight: 190   Origin: Round 11, 2015 Draft (#319 overall)

YEAR	TEAM	LVL	AGE	W	L	SV	G	GS	IP	H	HR	BB/9	K/9	K	GB%	BABIP	WHIP	ERA	DRA	WARP	MPH	FB%	WHF	CSP
2016	GRV	RK	19	2	3	0	13	8	52²	53	4	4.3	8.7	51	48%	.331	1.48	5.30	3.53	1.2				
2017	TCV	A-	20	1	1	0	4	4	19	19	0	2.8	13.3	28	47%	.404	1.32	3.79	2.83	0.5				
2017	QUD	A	20	2	2	1	9	7	40	38	1	3.6	10.8	48	48%	.333	1.35	3.83	3.29	0.9				
2018	QUD	A	21	7	1	1	14	10	65	58	4	1.5	9.8	71	48%	.305	1.06	2.49	3.25	1.4				
2018	BCA	A+	21	2	0	1	5	3	23	12	1	1.6	10.2	26	46%	.216	0.70	2.74	2.78	0.7				
2018	INL	A+	21	1	0	0	3	3	14²	6	0	3.7	12.9	21	47%	.200	0.82	0.00	2.59	0.5				
2018	MOB	AA	21	1	0	0	4	4	19²	12	0	3.7	12.4	27	40%	.286	1.02	1.37	2.48	0.7				
2019	ANA	MLB	22	5	5	1	31	14	87	81	14	4.5	9.1	88	42%	.290	1.43	5.03	5.14	0.2				

Breakout: 19%   Improve: 28%   Collapse: 7%   Attrition: 16%   MLB: 39%   *Comparables: Jay Jackson, Anibal Sanchez, Gerrit Cole*

Another Angels prospect who played at three different levels in 2018, Sandoval differentiated himself by also playing for five different teams. The lefty played most of the season at Low-A Quad Cities in Houston before receiving a promotion to High-A. He was then traded from Houston to Los Angeles for Martin Maldonado, and received another in-season promotion shortly after to Double-A Mobile. Sandoval attacks hitters with a straight over-the-top motion, limiting the damage right-handed batters can do to him. You might imagine Sandoval can get a lot of downer action on his curveball from that release point, and you'd be right, as the pitch flashes plus and is currently above-average. He's got a great pitcher's frame and can run his fastball into the lower-90s. Originally an overslot 11th-rounder, Sandoval projects as a backend starter or, more likely, an effective reliever.

Tyler Skaggs LHP   Born: 07/13/91   Age: 27   Bats: L   Throws: L   Height: 6'4"   Weight: 200   Origin: Round 1, 2009 Draft (#40 overall)

YEAR	TEAM	LVL	AGE	W	L	SV	G	GS	IP	H	HR	BB/9	K/9	K	GB%	BABIP	WHIP	ERA	DRA	WARP	MPH	FB%	WHF	CSP
2016	SLC	AAA	24	3	2	0	7	7	32¹	19	2	2.2	12.5	45	39%	.246	0.84	1.67	2.54	1.0				
2016	ANA	MLB	24	3	4	0	10	10	49²	51	5	4.2	9.1	50	44%	.331	1.49	4.17	5.45	-0.1	95.7	59.5	8.9	49.7
2017	SLC	AAA	25	0	1	0	3	3	10	14	0	5.4	6.3	7	54%	.400	2.00	8.10	5.40	0.0				
2017	ANA	MLB	25	2	6	0	16	16	85	90	13	3.0	8.0	76	42%	.318	1.39	4.55	5.12	0.4	94.0	60.2	8.6	45.9
2018	ANA	MLB	26	8	10	0	24	24	125¹	127	14	2.9	9.3	129	45%	.328	1.33	4.02	3.86	2.1	93.9	58.6	12	48.9
2019	ANA	MLB	27	10	9	0	28	28	159²	148	20	3.3	9.2	164	44%	.298	1.29	4.22	4.26	2.2	93.7	59.9	10.7	48.7

Breakout: 23%   Improve: 61%   Collapse: 19%   Attrition: 8%   MLB: 97%   *Comparables: Patrick Corbin, Kevin Gausman, John Lackey*

Skaggs seems to be good for a productive season every four years coinciding with the Winter Olympics, which works out since his injury status is one long event of skeleton. For a stretch he was the Angels' top starter until, yes, he missed over a month of the season, this time to an adductor muscle strain. For all the missed time, his ratios of good and bad outcomes have remained eerily constant, perhaps erring on the side of improving. He is, of course, due for his next career year in 2022, so book your hotels now.

Jose Soriano RHP   Born: 10/20/98   Age: 20   Bats: R   Throws: R   Height: 6'3"   Weight: 168   Origin: International Free Agent, 2016

YEAR	TEAM	LVL	AGE	W	L	SV	G	GS	IP	H	HR	BB/9	K/9	K	GB%	BABIP	WHIP	ERA	DRA	WARP	MPH	FB%	WHF	CSP
2016	DAN	RK	17	3	5	0	14	14	57	37	2	4.7	7.1	45	53%	.230	1.18	1.58	4.96	0.5				
2017	ANG	RK	18	2	2	0	12	10	49	43	2	2.6	6.8	37	57%	.281	1.16	2.94	4.12	1.0				
2018	BUR	A	19	1	6	0	14	14	46¹	34	1	6.8	8.2	42	45%	.284	1.49	4.47	4.21	0.5				
2019	ANA	MLB	20	1	4	0	9	9	35	38	8	8.4	7.1	28	45%	.289	2.01	7.75	8.09	-1.1				

Comparables: Drew Hutchison, Tyler Chatwood, Duane Underwood

Soriano is one of those "don't trust the stat line" guys. He walked 35 batters in just over 46 innings in his first taste of full season ball and paired it with an ERA in the mid-fours. It's not what you want. Still, he's just 19 years old and has a highly projectable frame. He's gone from throwing in the upper-80s/low-90s when he was signed to sitting ~94 miles per hour and touching higher in Low-A. He throws both a four-seamer and a two-seamer, and both of them have a lot of life, while his secondaries flash above-average or better but have the inconsistency you'd expect out of a Low-A arm. The curve is ahead of the changeup on raw stuff; the power breaker is a bat-misser that he's willing to back-foot to left-handed batters, while the change shows the same tail as the two-seamer, but arrives a little firm in the mid-80s. Soriano is one of the better arms you haven't heard much about, and while projection is always fraught with risk, the payoff here is a potential mid-rotation stalwart.

Jose Suarez LHP   Born: 01/03/98   Age: 21   Bats: L   Throws: L   Height: 5'10"   Weight: 170   Origin: International Free Agent, 2014

YEAR	TEAM	LVL	AGE	W	L	SV	G	GS	IP	H	HR	BB/9	K/9	K	GB%	BABIP	WHIP	ERA	DRA	WARP	MPH	FB%	WHF	CSP
2016	ANG	RK	18	1	3	0	11	5	40¹	48	1	2.9	10.3	46	42%	.395	1.51	5.36	2.91	1.2				
2017	ANG	RK	19	1	0	0	3	3	14	10	1	2.6	12.2	19	40%	.310	1.00	1.93	2.02	0.6				
2017	BUR	A	19	5	1	0	12	12	54²	49	7	3.0	11.7	71	48%	.333	1.23	3.62	2.85	1.6				
2018	INL	A+	20	0	1	0	2	2	9	6	0	1.0	18.0	18	67%	.400	0.78	2.00	0.89	0.5				
2018	MOB	AA	20	2	1	0	7	7	29²	34	0	2.4	15.5	51	37%	.500	1.42	3.03	2.56	1.0				
2018	SLC	AAA	20	1	4	0	17	17	78¹	81	5	4.0	8.4	73	48%	.336	1.48	4.48	4.44	1.0				
2019	ANA	MLB	21	1	1	0	14	3	26¹	25	4	4.2	9.9	29	42%	.300	1.40	4.90	5.01	0.1				

Breakout: 15%   Improve: 20%   Collapse: 9%   Attrition: 22%   MLB: 33%   *Comparables: Shelby Miller, Jake McGee, Robert Stephenson*

Say it with me now: Suarez pitched at [everyone chimes in] "three different levels" this year. The stocky southpaw has the potential for three above-average pitches in his fastball, changeup, and curveball. The former two flash plus while the curve is less consistent at present. The heater has multiple looks to it with cut, run and tail, and he'll touch the mid-90s, while sitting a tick below. Suarez is shorter than scouts prefer for a starting pitcher, and he's thick through the middle, so conditioning will be important. Still, he generates good extension and plane despite his smaller stature. He repeats his mechanics well, allowing for above-average command and control — enabling his stuff to play up. He's got a middle-of-the-rotation profile if his frame can handle the innings workload (increasingly less of a problem in today's five-and-dive game).

Nick Tropeano RHP Born: 08/27/90   Age: 28   Bats: R   Throws: R   Height: 6'4"   Weight: 200   Origin: Round 5, 2011 Draft (#160 overall)

YEAR	TEAM	LVL	AGE	W	L	SV	G	GS	IP	H	HR	BB/9	K/9	K	GB%	BABIP	WHIP	ERA	DRA	WARP	MPH	FB%	WHF	CSP
2016	SLC	AAA	25	1	0	0	1	1	6²	3	1	1.4	9.4	7	53%	.143	0.60	2.70	2.51	0.2				
2016	ANA	MLB	25	3	2	0	13	13	68¹	70	14	4.1	9.0	68	36%	.309	1.48	3.56	5.61	-0.2	93.4	49.5	12.8	45.8
2018	ANA	MLB	27	5	6	0	14	14	76	68	16	3.7	7.6	64	38%	.256	1.30	4.74	4.78	0.5	92.0	47.5	12	45.2
2019	*ANA*	*MLB*	*28*	*7*	*7*	*0*	*21*	*21*	*111¹*	*103*	*19*	*3.9*	*8.6*	*107*	*38%*	*.280*	*1.35*	*5.04*	*5.16*	*0.4*	*91.9*	*48.5*	*12.4*	*45.7*

Breakout: 25%   Improve: 58%   Collapse: 13%   Attrition: 22%   MLB: 93%   *Comparables: John Maine, Wade LeBlanc, Chase Anderson*

While most of the Angels pitching staff underwent the knife, because it's always smart to buy in bulk, Tropeano was the rare seraph who came *back* from Tommy John surgery and returned to his itinerant home run-donating ways. The one positive revelation was a new splitter that became an effective out pitch. His max-effort delivery produces min-effort velocity, and it remained largely good enough while it lasted. But once again he finished the year in the trainer's room, this time nursing his shoulder again. If it's not one thing, it's another.

LINEOUTS

Hitters

HITTER	POS	TEAM	LVL	AGE	PA	R	2B	3B	HR	RBI	BB	K	SB	CS	AVG/OBP/SLG	DRC+	VORP	BABIP	BRR	FRAA	WARP
Francisco Arcia	C	SLC	AAA	28	168	18	3	2	3	26	11	25	2	1	.283/.352/.393	102	6.3	.322	0.4	C(41): -6.4, P(1): 0.0	0.3
	C	ANA	MLB	28	106	10	5	0	6	23	1	27	1	0	.204/.226/.427	80	2.1	.214	1.9	C(34): -4.5, P(2): 0.0	0.0
Peter Bourjos	CF	GWN	AAA	31	105	16	6	5	2	9	10	19	1	0	.277/.352/.511	90	8.2	.329	1.1	CF(22): 0.1, LF(2): -0.4	0.3
	CF	ATL	MLB	31	47	5	2	1	1	4	2	15	0	0	.205/.239/.364	66	-0.3	.286	-0.3	LF(20): 0.6, CF(3): -0.1	0.0
	CF	SAC		31	173	20	7	4	2	14	7	35	0	2	.296/.335/.426	83	5.9	.365	-1.0	CF(39): 1.0	0.3
Jose Briceno	C	SLC	AAA	25	118	22	5	0	8	25	4	22	3	0	.277/.297/.536	135	6.8	.274	-0.5	C(29): -0.1	1.1
	C	ANA	MLB	25	128	12	2	0	5	10	8	35	0	1	.239/.299/.385	86	4.1	.299	0.4	C(41): 0.0, 1B(2): 0.0	0.5
Trent Deveaux	CF	ANG	Rk	18	194	20	5	0	1	11	24	68	7	4	.199/.309/.247	65	-1.4	.327	1.4	CF(26): -6.1, RF(14): -0.3	-0.7
William English	DH	ANG	Rk	17	117	13	4	0	0	8	11	34	4	0	.220/.325/.260	72	-2.2	.328	0.7		-0.2
Jose Fernandez	1B	SLC	AAA	30	394	66	19	1	17	59	33	34	2	2	.333/.396/.535	136	18.8	.333	-0.7	2B(33): 1.4, 1B(17): 1.9	2.9
	1B	ANA	MLB	30	123	9	8	0	2	11	6	15	1	0	.267/.309/.388	91	-0.5	.293	-2.5	1B(28): -3.0, 3B(2): -0.1	-0.5
Dustin Garneau	C	NAS	AAA	30	80	8	3	0	2	9	5	10	0	0	.208/.263/.333	94	-2.1	.210	-1.3	C(18): -2.2	0.0
	C	CHA	MLB	30	3	0	0	0	0	1	1	0	0	0	.500/.667/.500	91	0.7	.500	0.0	C(1): -0.3	0.0
	C	CHR		30	160	19	9	0	7	22	16	38	0	2	.252/.340/.468	119	8.8	.295	-0.3	C(39): -0.9, LF(1): -0.2	0.9
Sherman Johnson	2B	MOB	AA	27	79	8	5	1	0	6	11	17	1	2	.194/.316/.299	105	0.0	.260	0.7	3B(11): -2.2, 1B(3): -0.2	0.1
	2B	SLC	AAA	27	171	32	7	4	4	14	20	47	2	0	.277/.359/.459	105	7.7	.374	2.3	2B(16): 0.4, LF(13): 0.2	1.0
	2B	ANA	MLB	27	11	0	0	0	0	0	0	4	0	0	.000/.091/.000	64	-2.0	.000	0.0	2B(7): -0.4, 1B(2): 0.2	0.0
Jefry Marte	1B	ANA	MLB	27	209	28	7	1	7	22	13	41	1	1	.216/.273/.371	82	-0.4	.240	2.2	1B(71): -0.4, 3B(10): 0.8	0.2
Ryan Schimpf	3B	ANA	MLB	30	7	2	0	0	1	2	2	3	0	0	.200/.429/.800	84	1.4	.000	0.0	3B(1): 0.0, LF(1): 0.0	0.0
	3B	SLC	AAA	30	125	14	6	2	3	13	16	49	1	1	.178/.288/.355	78	-2.8	.286	-0.1	2B(18): 0.3, 3B(9): 0.8	0.1
Livan Soto	SS	ORM	Rk	18	200	31	10	0	0	11	24	24	9	3	.291/.385/.349	109	8.3	.336	1.6	SS(28): 2.7, 2B(18): -1.1	1.3
Jared Walsh	RF	INL	A+	24	178	28	8	1	13	36	24	50	0	1	.275/.365/.604	150	15.2	.308	-0.6	1B(26): 0.3, RF(5): 0.7	1.3
	RF	MOB	AA	24	173	26	13	0	8	26	21	48	1	0	.289/.382/.537	115	9.6	.372	-0.8	1B(37): 2.0, P(2): 0.0	0.7
	RF	SLC	AAA	24	198	32	13	0	8	37	16	56	0	0	.270/.333/.478	110	7.1	.345	1.8	RF(27): -5.7, LF(14): -1.7	0.2
Chris Young	LF	ANA	MLB	34	128	17	2	1	6	13	11	37	2	0	.168/.252/.363	82	1.0	.183	1.2	RF(20): -2.2, CF(17): -0.5	-0.2
Eric Young	LF	SLC	AAA	33	348	46	18	7	5	34	35	66	10	6	.300/.367/.453	101	10.9	.363	-0.4	CF(46): -9.5, LF(25): -0.6	0.0
	LF	ANA	MLB	33	117	12	4	2	1	8	6	28	5	1	.202/.248/.303	61	-6.7	.259	-0.8	CF(24): 1.2, LF(13): 0.5	-0.1

Francisco Arcia finally got the call after twelve minor-league seasons to backfill the Martin Maldonado trade. His major league-hitting and catching skills demonstrated why it took twelve seasons. ⓧ Still a handy pinch-runner and defensive sub for September contenders, **Peter Bourjos** was stranded in Sacramento when the Giants waved the white flag. ⓧ **Jose Briceno** is proof the best catching prospects shine thanks to their hitting, but scads more will surface due to persistence. His skill shines brightest when he squats, wiggles his fingers, and snatches extra strikes. (The description of what a catcher does on a daily basis is probably why they don't advertise for catchers on CareerBuilder.) ⓧ One of the hotter under-the-radar names out there, Bahamian speedster **Trent Deveaux** was training with the Olympic sprinting team before signing with the Angels. He's going to be a project but has a monster top-end outcome. ⓧ Is it possible the Angels have a type? Overslot fifth-rounder **William English** was selected as a two-way player, and was the youngest player in the 2018 draft. ⓧ There's not much of a ceiling for 31-year-old infielder **Jose Fernandez**, but he sports a bit of power, which helped him reach the big leagues after his tumultuous journey from Cuba. ⓧ The ocean waves beat endlessly on the rocks, but the rocks do not move. So it is with **Dustin Garneau**, professional baseball player, catcher, human edifice. ⓧ **Sherman Johnson** has hardly blazed a trail in his career, and his contact rate in a repeat at Triple-A is worrying, given that selectivity was once his (only) calling card. ⓧ **Jefry Marte** is a corner infielder and former ranked prospect who slowly but surely earned major-league playing time because he could hit lefties and hit with power. Fortunately for the lefties, they have figured out how to pitch to him, so he crossed the ocean to find some unfamiliarity in the NPB. ⓧ **Alex Ramirez**, a toolsy Venezuelan outfielder known for his raw power, was the club's top J2 signing in 2018. If he falls short of his major league dreams, the NPB might answer his calls. ⓧ If **Ryan Schimpf** retired tomorrow, we would replace him, the game would go on; in three years it would make no difference whatsoever. ⓧ One of the players stripped from the Braves, **Livan Soto** performed well in his first year with the Angels at short-season Orem. The shortstop prospect has great barrel control and defensive instincts, but generic-paper-towel strength. ⓧ We don't generally give 25-year-olds beating up on younger competition much ink, but when it's a 39th-rounder like **Jared Walsh**, we can make an exception. The 2015 selection cruised through three levels with power and patience, and ohbytheway he struck out 7 in 5 2/3 innings on the mound. ⓧ For the first time in four years, **Chris Young** The Outfielder did not appear on a baseball team that lost the first round of their postseason. Given his dimming production, it's safe to say that he will not begin another streak. ⓧ **Eric Young, Jr.** has a career 80 percent stolen base success rate, 50th best in the history of baseball. Since this is a family reference book, we will not mention any of the other numbers.

Pitchers

PITCHER	TEAM	LVL	AGE	W	L	SV	G	GS	IP	H	HR	BB/9	K/9	K	GB%	BABIP	WHIP	ERA	DRA	WARP	MPH	FB%	WHF	CSP
Miguel Almonte	SLC	AAA	25	1	1	0	25	0	20¹	34	4	6.6	9.7	22	57%	.441	2.41	10.18	6.43	-0.3				
	ANA	MLB	25	0	0	0	8	0	7	9	1	3.9	9.0	7	44%	.364	1.71	10.29	4.09	0.1	96.6	50.8	11.9	43.3
Parker Bridwell	SLC	AAA	26	1	1	0	6	6	28	50	4	2.9	6.1	19	38%	.430	2.11	8.68	9.36	-1.2				
	ANA	MLB	26	1	0	0	5	1	6²	14	5	2.7	4.1	3	36%	.346	2.40	17.55	4.61	0.0	93.4	51.3	12.2	45.5
Jesus Castillo	MOB	AA	22	9	5	0	21	20	98¹	97	7	2.8	5.5	60	47%	.292	1.30	4.94	4.75	0.7				
Luke Farrell	CHN	MLB	27	3	4	0	20	2	31¹	30	7	4.6	11.2	39	31%	.295	1.47	5.17	4.27	0.3	94.3	58.3	12.6	47.3
	IOW	AAA	27	1	4	0	12	12	54¹	40	4	4.6	10.1	61	40%	.267	1.25	3.64	3.58	1.2				
Williams Jerez	PAW	AAA	26	2	1	5	34	0	52	48	6	4.2	11.9	69	47%	.331	1.38	3.63	3.87	0.8				
	ANA	MLB	26	0	0	0	17	0	15	17	3	4.8	9.0	15	38%	.311	1.67	6.00	5.94	-0.2	96.9	61.5	12.2	43.9
Jake Jewell	MOB	AA	25	1	0	2	7	0	13	15	1	1.4	7.6	11	73%	.389	1.31	2.08	6.16	-0.2				
	SLC	AAA	25	2	4	3	19	0	25	23	2	6.1	8.6	24	56%	.300	1.60	3.60	5.49	-0.1				
	ANA	MLB	25	0	1	0	3	0	2	2	0	4.5	4.5	1	43%	.286	1.50	9.00	10.28	-0.1	97.4	73.1	3.8	47.7
John Lamb	SLC	AAA	27	1	0	0	13	13	49²	49	7	2.7	9.8	54	43%	.318	1.29	3.44	4.70	0.5				
	ANA	MLB	27	0	1	0	3	3	10	15	4	3.6	9.9	11	37%	.355	1.90	7.20	7.76	-0.3	90.9	41.1	9.4	48.4
Luis Madero	BUR	A	21	2	7	0	14	14	61¹	69	5	2.2	7.2	49	46%	.332	1.37	4.26	4.03	0.9				
	INL	A+	21	2	1	0	9	9	44¹	41	3	2.4	9.3	46	40%	.314	1.20	2.44	3.06	1.2				
Eduardo Paredes	ANA	MLB	23	0	0	0	14	0	18¹	25	5	3.4	7.4	15	41%	.345	1.75	6.87	6.27	-0.3	94.9	59	8.3	48.5
	SLC	AAA	23	2	1	5	38	0	42¹	44	5	4.0	7.4	35	35%	.322	1.49	4.68	7.15	-1.0				
Dillon Peters	MIA	MLB	25	2	2	0	7	5	27²	34	4	4.9	5.5	17	45%	.326	1.77	7.16	5.69	-0.1	92.7	52.2	7.8	50.2
	NWO	AAA	25	6	7	0	19	19	102²	129	15	2.5	7.5	85	46%	.355	1.54	5.61	3.93	1.9				
J.C. Ramirez	ANA	MLB	29	0	2	0	2	2	6²	7	3	9.4	5.4	4	23%	.211	2.10	9.45	8.57	-0.3	95.3	49.2	10.2	50.5
Junichi Tazawa	MIA	MLB	32	1	1	0	22	0	20	28	6	5.8	10.8	24	24%	.393	2.05	9.00	5.84	-0.2	92.8	58.5	8.7	49.3
	TOL	AAA	32	0	1	0	7	0	7²	11	1	5.9	11.7	10	26%	.455	2.09	9.39	6.40	-0.1				
	SLC	AAA	32	0	1	2	7	0	6¹	10	1	2.8	7.1	5	44%	.409	1.89	7.11	4.74	0.0				
	ANA	MLB	32	0	0	0	9	0	8	7	1	3.4	4.5	4	36%	.222	1.25	2.25	7.24	-0.2	92.7	55	5	49.3
Blake Wood	ANA	MLB	32	1	0	0	13	0	11²	8	1	5.4	7.7	10	59%	.250	1.29	2.31	5.13	0.0	96.7	47.7	10.9	44.5

As a prospect, **Miguel Almonte's** calling card was a double-plus changeup. If he's not careful, his calling card as a pro will be a double-digit ERA. ⓧ A double-digit ERA never feels good, even when it was a ludicrously small sample size in an injury-ravaged season. **Parker Bridwell's** elbow kept him out of four months (and didn't look quite right after that) but none of that matters to his baseball card, which will display that 17.55 for as long as he's in production. ⓧ Unless **Jesus Castillo** can add velocity by filling out his wiry frame, it is difficult to imagine he is long for the rotation. If a shift to the bullpen doesn't add a little spice to his repertoire, then he might not be long for the high minors, either. ⓧ The Angels accomplished something with **Oliver Drake** that no other team managed to do in 2018: clear him through waivers. ⓧ Further proof that all of us are a little imperfect, **Luke Farrell** has trouble getting his pitches in the desired spots. But when he does, the batter also misses the mark. The inconsistency both ways is why Farrell has become a prolific waiver selection. ⓧ Third-round selection **Aaron Hernandez** boasts a fastball that can touch the upper 90s with sink and flashes a biting slider. Refining the consistency of his secondaries and command will determine if he can stick in the rotation. ⓧ **Williams Jerez** will long (partially) answer the question of who was sent to Anaheim in return for Ian Kinsler and (fully) answer the question of who is the most "attorneys general" player of all time. ⓧ **Jake Jewell** made his major-league debut in 2018 but a gruesome injury suffered covering home plate caused the experience to lose most of its luster. ⓧ If Wooderson got his act together and could throw a fastball, you would have **John Lamb**. The ultimate finesse pitcher underwent his second Tommy John surgery, so he really will get older while the batters stay the same age. ⓧ Acquired from the Diamondbacks in 2017 for David Hernandez, **Luis Madero** saw his stuff and strikeout rate tick up in the second half of the season, finishing strong at High-A. ⓧ Very few active pitchers strike out every fourth batter and walk every seventh. Those who do make their mark in the bullpen. **Alex Meyer** is the lone exception that still boasts a starter profile, thanks to high-velocity stuff and increased use of a sinking fastball that keeps the ball in the infield. He's also the only one with an excused absence from the 2018 season. ⓧ Perhaps the nicest thing one can say about **Eduardo Paredes'** 2018 is that he finished .03 shy of 6.90 ERA. ⓧ At 5-foot-9, Peters is the shortest pitcher on the Angels' 40-man roster, depending on how strong David Fletcher's posture is on a given day. If he had been born a righty, there's a chance he doesn't even approach the sport of baseball. ⓧ **J.C. Ramirez** doubled down on science healing his partially torn UCL. Physiology rolled snake eyes, so it was Tommy John surgery for the high-velocity, weak-contact hurler. He'll likely be tardy to 2019 as well. ⓧ **Junichi Tazawa** will always have 2013, but currently his other possessions are a suitcase and a worsening fastball. ⓧ The extremely shareable flamethrower **Blake Wood** had the April of his life, followed promptly by the most recent UCL replacement surgery of his life.

LOS ANGELES DODGERS

Essay by Eric Stephen

Player comments by Mark Barry and BP staff

The Dodgers are traveling dual paths, as they're both in the middle of one of the most successful runs the team has had since moving to Los Angeles in 1958 and yet still searching for an end to a championship drought that has reached an even 30 years. This offseason presented an extra challenge for the franchise, one of transition, making this arguably the most important offseason under the current ownership group.

Guggenheim Partners took over the Dodgers in May 2012. The team has reached the playoffs in each of the six full seasons since, unprecedented in franchise history, and their 565 regular-season wins during that span are the most in baseball by 20 over the second-place Indians. The ultimate prize hasn't yet been claimed by Los Angeles, with the Dodgers getting tantalizingly close by losing the last two World Series, with the pain at times great enough to undermine the accomplishment of actually reaching the Fall Classic, something they hadn't done since winning it all in 1988.

An attempt at a third straight World Series trip for the Dodgers will be without general manager Farhan Zaidi, who took over as the president of baseball operations for the rival Giants. Zaidi's combination of knowledge, baseball acumen and communication skills are nearly unparalleled in the game. Replacing him could be the Dodgers' biggest challenge.

Since Zaidi and president of baseball operations Andrew Friedman joined the Dodgers in November 2014, the club has continued to both win at the major-league level—four straight NL West titles, three straight NLCS trips, and two World Series—and strengthen the infrastructure, regularly ranking among the top 10 farm systems in baseball during their tenure. Since manager Dave Roberts was hired by this group before the 2016 season, the Dodgers' 23 postseason wins are six more than the team had in the previous 27 seasons combined.

With success comes opportunities, and in many cases that means elsewhere. In addition to Zaidi leaving to run the Giants, third base coach and infield instructor Chris Woodward was hired to manage the Rangers, hitting coach Turner Ward left to take the same position with the Reds,

DODGERS PROSPECTUS
2018 W-L: 92-71, 1ST IN NL WEST

Pythag	.626	3rd	B-Age	28.0	15th
RS/G	4.93	5th	P-Age	29.1	21st
RA/G	3.74	2nd	Salary	$186.2M	3rd
DRC+	108	4th	M$/MW	$4.0M	14th
DRA	3.51	2nd	DL Days	1486	27th
FIP	3.56	2nd	$ on DL	17%	16th
DER	.715	6th			

- Opened 1962
- Open air
- Natural surface
- Fence profile: 4' to 8'

Three-Year Park Factors

Runs	Runs/RH	Runs/LH	HR/RH	HR/LH
95	94	99	97	109

Top Hitter WARP	5.1 Justin Turner
Top Pitcher WARP	4.1 Clayton Kershaw
Top Prospect	Alex Verdugo

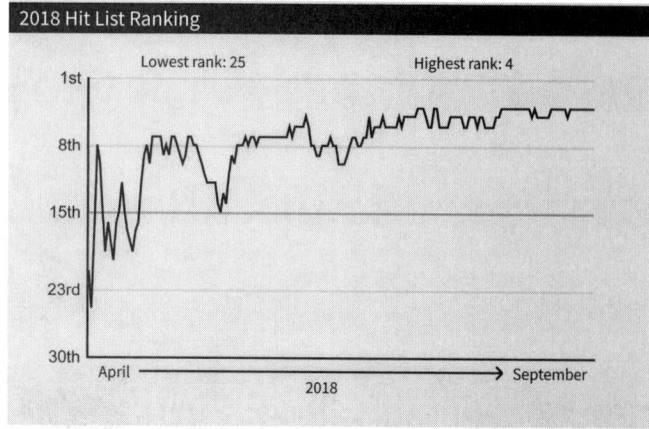

2018 Hit List Ranking

Lowest rank: 25   Highest rank: 4

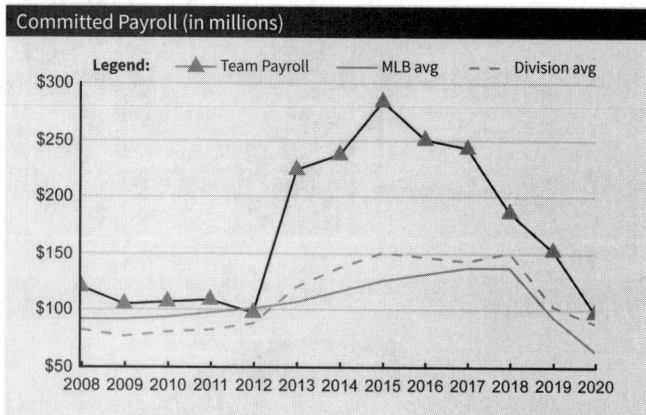

Committed Payroll (in millions)

Legend: ▲ Team Payroll — MLB avg --- Division avg

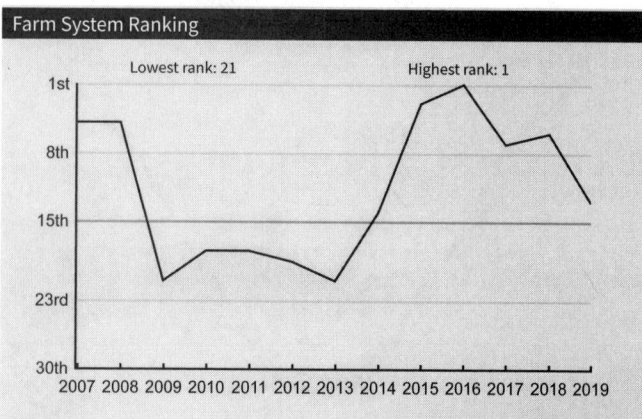

Farm System Ranking

Lowest rank: 21   Highest rank: 1

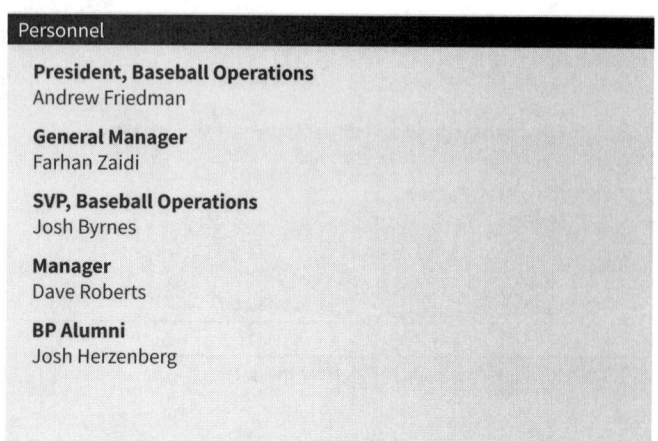

Personnel

President, Baseball Operations
Andrew Friedman

General Manager
Farhan Zaidi

SVP, Baseball Operations
Josh Byrnes

Manager
Dave Roberts

BP Alumni
Josh Herzenberg

assistant hitting coach Luis Ortiz got the hitting coach job on Woodward's staff in Texas and research and development analyst Ehsan Bokhari left after four years to run the baseball R&D department with the Astros.

All of those jobs were promotions except for Ward, who got to be closer to home with his move to Cincinnati. These departures followed last year, when Alex Anthopoulos left the Dodgers' front office to become the Braves' president of baseball operations, and farm director Gabe Kapler left to manage the Phillies. Those losses suggest the Dodgers have been doing something right, at least. The stated goal has always been to compete every year, and to put in place a system to keep the talent pipeline churning. Now they just have to keep it up, with some new cast members, and likely a tighter budget.

Friedman and Zaidi each came from smaller markets in Tampa Bay and Oakland, respectively, and they certainly enjoyed the trappings of a revenue behemoth in Los Angeles. In the first three seasons of the Friedman-Zaidi front office, the Dodgers averaged $268 million in annual payroll, paying a total of $111.7 million in competitive balance tax from 2015-2017. But it wasn't just money that fueled this Dodgers' run of success. The front office also proved adept at finding value in the margins.

Chris Taylor was plucked out of obscurity in Seattle, becoming a key lineup cog while playing all over the infield and outfield. He was acquired in a trade for former first-round pick Zach Lee, who has pitched only 12 1/3 major-league innings. Max Muncy was the shiny new diamond in the rough last season. After spending all of 2017 in the minors following mediocre major-league results with the A's in 2015-2016, Muncy controlled the strike zone and mashed in his breakout season. The 27-year-old infielder started the year in the minors, but still led the Dodgers in both walks (79) and home runs (35), the latter a total surpassed by only nine players in the 135-year history of the franchise. Not bad from a non-roster invitee to spring training signed to a minor-league deal.

Taylor and Muncy weren't alone. *Eighteen* different players (10 hitters, eight pitchers) amassed at least two WARP for the Dodgers last season, five more than any other team. The average MLB team had just shy of seven such players. The Dodgers' depth was a true strength.

Most 2-WARP players in 2018			
Team	Hitters	Pitchers	Total
Dodgers	10	8	18
Braves	9	4	13
A's	9	3	12
Astros	6	5	11

Friedman and Zaidi showed they could work under constraints, too. Last season's depth came with a payroll of just under the collectively bargained threshold of $197 million, which, given the previous five years of Dodgers payrolls, counted as austerity. This maneuver was only possible thanks to a creative trade between the Dodgers and former front office cohort Anthopoulos with the Braves. Mostly an accounting swap of undesirable contracts, the Dodgers reacquired Matt Kemp for Adrian Gonzalez, Brandon McCarthy, Scott Kazmir and Charlie Culberson. The cash-neutral deal shaved roughly $24 million off Los Angeles' competitive balance tax payroll for 2018, allowing them to get under the threshold.

Though the primary motivation for the trade was financial, the Dodgers also benefited from a bounce-back campaign from Kemp, who made the All-Star team and posted his highest DRC+ (117) since his first go-around with the Dodgers in 2014. In December, Kemp was part of yet another financially-motivated deal, traded to the Reds along with Yasiel Puig, Alex Wood and Kyle Farmer for Homer Bailey and a pair of prospects. This trimmed some excess and helped streamline the depth chart, but more notably shed roughly $16 million off the competitive balance tax payroll.

Much like with Gonzalez in the prior trade with the Braves, Bailey was immediately released as a condition of this deal. The Dodgers didn't so much trade for Bailey, but rather for the $28 million remaining on his contract to offset the salaries headed to Cincinnati. For the second year in a row, the Dodgers made a massive trade that was less about baseball and more about reallocating payroll. Welcome to Econ 101, with Professor Friedman.

Dodgers ownership chose to stay under the threshold in 2018 to both avoid paying competitive balance tax and to reset their penalty rate should they exceed again in the future. When or if the Dodgers decide to spend lavishly again remains to be seen. Per a November report in the *Los Angeles Times*, a document prepared by the team to lure potential investors in 2017 showed the Dodgers projected their payrolls to fall under the competitive balance tax every year through 2022. Even with the caveat that such a document presented projected profits in the strongest possible light and is in no way binding, it's clear there's at least some limit to the Dodgers' spending, which is a change from the first five years of the Guggenheim Partners ownership group.

Expecting another Muncy or another Taylor to come out of nowhere this season probably isn't wise, but there are many ways to add talent. In particular, the Dodgers have been excellent at incorporating young players into the mix in recent years. Last season, standout right-hander Walker Buehler followed the unanimous Rookie of the Year campaigns of Cody Bellinger (2017) and Corey Seager (2016), and even before that Joc Pederson was an impact starter as a rookie in 2015.

In all four years of this front office, the Dodgers have had at least one All-Star-caliber rookie (all but Buehler received made the actual All-Star team in their respective rookie seasons). Buehler, a 23-year-old rookie with all of 110 career minor-league innings under his belt, was the Dodgers' best pitcher in the second half, which means a lot on a team that's had Clayton Kershaw entrenched atop the rotation for nearly a decade. Buehler's 3.3 WARP was the highest by a 25-and-under Dodgers pitcher other than Kershaw since Chad Billingsley in 2010.

The system has developed and churned out young talent, the lifeblood of a successful team. Having key cogs making deflated pre-free agency salaries, including several near the league minimum, goes a long way in keeping a team's payroll below the competitive balance threshold. Building the infrastructure of the organization put the Dodgers at the forefront of improving the nutrition of their prospects, providing healthy and organic meal options at each minor-league level. Other teams followed suit, realizing that improving the odds of even one extra player contributing in the majors far exceeded the cost of implementing the program.

There are limits, self-imposed and otherwise, on major-league payroll and signing bonuses for amateur players, but there are no such limits on what a team can spend on its front office and development staff. The Dodgers have flexed their financial muscle in that infrastructure, adding to player development and beefing up an analytics department that team president Stan Kasten jokingly referred to as the "room of nerds."

Though the Dodgers didn't replace Zaidi this offseason, they did add an assistant general manager in Jeff Kingston, with more than a decade of experience in player development, analytics and various other front office disciplines in Seattle and San Diego. Kingston and a gaggle of others will try to find that next Seager, Bellinger or Buehler, or maybe even the next Taylor or Muncy. But there's a lot of talent already in the cupboard, with a pantry full enough to perhaps make another World Series run or two. One of these times, they might actually win it. ■

—Eric Stephen is a writer at SB Nation.

HITTERS

Austin Barnes C Born: 12/28/89 Age: 29 Bats: R Throws: R Height: 5'10" Weight: 190 Origin: Round 9, 2011 Draft (#283 overall)

YEAR	TEAM	LVL	AGE	PA	R	2B	3B	HR	RBI	BB	K	SB	CS	AVG/OBP/SLG	DRC+	VORP	BABIP	BRR	FRAA	WARP
2016	OKL	AAA	26	385	59	22	5	6	39	43	53	18	3	.295/.380/.443	111	38.3	.335	3.3	C(63): 16.1, 2B(15): 1.3	4.3
2016	LAN	MLB	26	37	3	1	0	0	2	5	9	0	0	.156/.270/.188	83	-1.0	.217	0.3	C(9): 0.2, 2B(7): -0.2	0.1
2017	LAN	MLB	27	262	35	15	2	8	38	39	43	4	1	.289/.408/.486	121	29.5	.329	0.5	C(55): 15.1, 2B(21): -0.1	3.5
2018	LAN	MLB	28	238	32	5	0	4	14	31	67	4	3	.205/.329/.290	75	5.5	.287	1.1	C(61): 10.0, 2B(19): 0.2	1.5
2019	LAN	MLB	29	421	50	17	2	9	42	51	96	8	3	.237/.343/.371	100	19.5	.298	1.1	C 22	4.5

Breakout: 4%   Improve: 35%   Collapse: 15%   Attrition: 28%   MLB: 89%   *Comparables: Carlos Ruiz, George Kottaras, Steve Holm*

In 1993, "Whoomp! (There It Is)" had its time in the sun. Unfortunately Tag Team wasn't back again with another hit, leaving the song as the only notable entry in the group's catalog. Barnes was great in 2017, pairing his unique-for-a-catcher athleticism with uncanny contact skills at the plate. The combination was enough to unseat Yasmani Grandal as the team's starter for the stretch run, and Barnes got the lion's share of the reps behind the dish in the postseason. His follow-up, however, was not inspiring. Barnes tanked offensively, adding almost 12 percentage points to his strikeout rate thanks to a crippling lack of aggression. Despite a paltry swinging strike rate below six percent, Barnes struck out almost a third of the time by saying "no thank you" to nearly half the strikes he saw. His framing numbers behind the plate remained strong, so Barnes should get plenty of chances, but he'll need to heat up the stick in order to avoid the fate of a one-hit wonder.

YEAR	TEAM	P. COUNT	FRM RUNS	BLK RUNS	THRW RUNS	TOT RUNS
2016	LAN	819	0.4	0.0	0.0	0.3
2017	LAN	7057	14.8	1.6	-0.5	15.8
2018	LAN	7013	8.3	1.0	-0.1	9.2
2019	LAN	14443	22.7	2.3	-1.0	24.0

Cody Bellinger 1B   Born: 07/13/95   Age: 23   Bats: L   Throws: L   Height: 6'4"   Weight: 210   Origin: Round 4, 2013 Draft (#124 overall)

YEAR	TEAM	LVL	AGE	PA	R	2B	3B	HR	RBI	BB	K	SB	CS	AVG/OBP/SLG	DRC+	VORP	BABIP	BRR	FRAA	WARP
2016	TUL	AA	20	465	61	17	1	23	65	59	94	8	2	.263/.359/.484	152	32.0	.287	1.0	1B(81): 0.7, LF(13): 1.2	4.0
2017	OKL	AAA	21	77	15	4	0	5	15	9	22	7	0	.343/.429/.627	104	9.0	.450	0.8	1B(16): 1.0, CF(2): -0.5	0.3
2017	LAN	MLB	21	548	87	26	4	39	97	64	146	10	3	.267/.352/.581	134	48.7	.299	-0.2	1B(93): 0.7, LF(39): -2.5	3.3
2018	LAN	MLB	22	632	84	28	7	25	76	69	151	14	1	.260/.343/.470	113	39.0	.313	3.3	1B(110): -0.9, CF(78): 2.0	2.9
2019	LAN	MLB	23	597	82	27	5	27	87	69	148	12	2	.259/.348/.484	130	42.0	.309	1.1	CF 3, 1B 0	4.8

Breakout: 2%   Improve: 58%   Collapse: 3%   Attrition: 6%   MLB: 98%   *Comparables: Yasiel Puig, Miguel Cabrera, Justin Upton*

Beauty is subjective. For some, you're talking about gazing upon the vast majesty of a Grand Canyon sunrise or marveling at the awe-inspiring natural classicism of Michelangelo's *Pieta* in St. Peter's Basilica. For others, it's watching a statuesque slugger uncorking a fluid, looping cut and launching dingers into the stratosphere from the left side. Since his 2017 call-up Bellinger has smashed 64 balls into oblivion, the fourth-highest total in the National League, despite playing around 20 fewer games than his counterparts. While his sophomore campaign didn't produce another top-five National League slugging percentage, Bellinger managed to shave another few percentage points from his strikeout rate, and even started 50 games in center field, contributing above-average defense up the middle. When the dust settles, you've got a versatile, athletic, former NLCS MVP that is one of the most prodigious power hitters in the game. And he's 23 years old. It's a sight to behold.

Brian Dozier 2B   Born: 05/15/87   Age: 32   Bats: R   Throws: R   Height: 5'11"   Weight: 200   Origin: Round 8, 2009 Draft (#252 overall)

YEAR	TEAM	LVL	AGE	PA	R	2B	3B	HR	RBI	BB	K	SB	CS	AVG/OBP/SLG	DRC+	VORP	BABIP	BRR	FRAA	WARP
2016	MIN	MLB	29	691	104	35	5	42	99	61	138	18	2	.268/.340/.546	133	41.4	.280	1.1	2B(151): -2.2	5.0
2017	MIN	MLB	30	705	106	30	4	34	93	78	141	16	7	.271/.359/.498	124	37.0	.300	2.2	2B(152): 9.7	5.6
2018	MIN	MLB	31	462	65	21	2	16	52	46	96	8	3	.227/.307/.405	96	11.6	.256	1.6	2B(103): 1.9	1.6
2018	LAN	MLB	31	170	16	9	0	5	20	24	33	4	0	.182/.300/.350	101	-1.6	.196	-1.6	2B(45): 0.1	0.4
2019	LAN	MLB	32	611	87	30	3	23	73	64	121	14	4	.253/.340/.446	115	32.3	.287	0.5	2B 0	3.5

Breakout: 5%   Improve: 39%   Collapse: 7%   Attrition: 11%   MLB: 100%   *Comparables: Rickie Weeks, Mark Ellis, Aaron Hill*

After flirting with the Dodgers for a couple years over Dozier's services, Minnesota finally succumbed to L.A.'s charm and sent the former All Star west in a July deal. The result was the biggest Minnesota-to-Hollywood disappointment since Fargo got passed over for Best Picture in 1996. A lingering knee injury drove Dozier to develop some bad habits at the plate, subsequently sapping the slugger's power and leading to his lowest DRC+ since his rookie year. While second basemen on the wrong side of 30 typically age like guacamole in the heat, Dozier has never spent a day on the disabled list and still smacked 21 dingers in a down season, so there's reason to believe his first free-agent contract won't end in disaster.

Omar Estevez MI   Born: 02/25/98   Age: 21   Bats: R   Throws: R   Height: 5'10"   Weight: 168   Origin: International Free Agent, 2015

YEAR	TEAM	LVL	AGE	PA	R	2B	3B	HR	RBI	BB	K	SB	CS	AVG/OBP/SLG	DRC+	VORP	BABIP	BRR	FRAA	WARP
2016	GRL	A	18	508	46	32	2	9	61	26	121	3	6	.255/.298/.389	95	10.6	.322	-2.7	2B(64): 3.0, SS(46): 6.5	2.1
2017	RCU	A+	19	502	56	24	3	4	47	33	97	2	2	.256/.309/.348	86	10.2	.314	1.0	SS(98): 2.7, 2B(22): 0.4	1.6
2018	RCU	A+	20	577	87	43	2	15	84	45	138	3	1	.278/.336/.456	107	36.1	.344	1.2	SS(74): 2.6, 2B(47): 1.7	3.1
2019	LAN	MLB	21	251	21	11	0	6	27	12	66	0	0	.212/.250/.338	50	-6.8	.262	-0.6	SS 2, 2B 1	-0.4

Breakout: 0%   Improve: 1%   Collapse: 0%   Attrition: 2%   MLB: 4%   *Comparables: Orlando Calixte, Christian Arroyo, Yamaico Navarro*

Blah blah blah development isn't linear blah blah. We've heard it before, and we've said it plenty of times before, but Estevez is the reason the cliche is always apropos. Signed for a cool $6 million bonus in 2015, the Cuban import finally started to put the pieces together during his second stint at High-A, leading the Cal League in doubles and runs, while clocking in at number three with 60 extra-base hits. Sure, hitting in the Cal League helps, but legitimate skill development carried a good bit of the numeric improvement. Estevez refined an already-sweet swing to create better, more consistent line-drive contact. He spent more time at the keystone, likely foreshadowing his eventual position, but he also continued to hold his own at short, a pleasant surprise to pair with his offense-heavy projected profile.

David Freese 3B   Born: 04/28/83   Age: 36   Bats: R   Throws: R   Height: 6'2"   Weight: 220   Origin: Round 9, 2006 Draft (#273 overall)

YEAR	TEAM	LVL	AGE	PA	R	2B	3B	HR	RBI	BB	K	SB	CS	AVG/OBP/SLG	DRC+	VORP	BABIP	BRR	FRAA	WARP
2016	PIT	MLB	33	492	63	23	0	13	55	45	142	0	0	.270/.352/.412	89	16.6	.372	-0.4	3B(78): 0.2, 1B(58): 3.0	1.1
2017	PIT	MLB	34	503	44	16	0	10	52	58	116	0	1	.263/.368/.371	95	17.5	.336	-4.7	3B(116): 5.3, 1B(3): 0.0	1.6
2018	PIT	MLB	35	265	29	10	1	9	42	18	56	0	0	.282/.336/.444	103	11.4	.330	-0.9	3B(55): 1.7, 1B(15): 1.0	1.2
2018	LAN	MLB	35	47	9	2	1	2	9	6	16	0	0	.385/.489/.641	111	7.0	.619	-0.5	1B(14): -0.4, 3B(3): 0.0	0.1
2019	LAN	MLB	36	246	26	9	1	6	27	23	65	0	0	.237/.328/.371	93	2.6	.316	-1.0	1B 2, 3B 0	0.6

Breakout: 0%   Improve: 31%   Collapse: 12%   Attrition: 25%   MLB: 74%   *Comparables: Melvin Mora, Ken Boyer, Casey Blake*

In the days of extreme shifts and openers, simple platoon players have somehow fallen by the wayside as far as trendy baseball topics are concerned. It's too bad for the lefty-mashing Freese, who will once again just have to rely on postseason heroics to create buzz for himself. Acquired at the August waiver deadline, Freese proceeded to hit a robust .464 against southpaws for his new club, bringing his career line against lefties to .305/.381/.467. In addition to providing the pop, Freese was an average-or-better defender for the third consecutive season, leaving the days of minus defense at both the hot and cold corners further in the rearview mirror. The Dodgers enjoyed the Freese experience so much, the team inked him to a new, one-year contract almost immediately upon the season's completion.

Yasmani Grandal C Born: 11/08/88 Age: 30 Bats: B Throws: R Height: 6'1" Weight: 235 Origin: Round 1, 2010 Draft (#12 overall)

YEAR	TEAM	LVL	AGE	PA	R	2B	3B	HR	RBI	BB	K	SB	CS	AVG/OBP/SLG	DRC+	VORP	BABIP	BRR	FRAA	WARP
2016	LAN	MLB	27	457	49	14	1	27	72	64	116	1	3	.228/.339/.477	119	33.1	.250	-5.1	C(115): 33.2, 1B(4): 0.4	6.3
2017	LAN	MLB	28	482	50	27	0	22	58	40	130	0	1	.247/.308/.459	93	25.8	.298	-2.6	C(117): 27.7	4.6
2018	LAN	MLB	29	518	65	23	2	24	68	72	124	2	1	.241/.349/.466	115	36.1	.278	-4.4	C(135): 17.7, 1B(2): 0.0	5.0
2019	LAN	MLB	30	481	57	21	1	20	65	53	121	1	1	.235/.323/.429	104	20.7	.281	-3.1	C 26, 1B 0	5.0

Breakout: 4%   Improve: 53%   Collapse: 2%   Attrition: 10%   MLB: 97%

Comparables: Geovany Soto, Chris Iannetta, Miguel Montero

YEAR	TEAM	P. COUNT	FRM RUNS	BLK RUNS	THRW RUNS	TOT RUNS
2016	LAN	15887	28.0	0.3	0.5	29.2
2017	LAN	16211	26.2	-1.4	1.3	26.2
2018	LAN	16615	15.7	0.8	0.1	16.3
2019	LAN	16752	23.4	-0.3	0.6	23.7

If you're wondering about big talent experiencing bumps in the road, always remember, James Cameron directed Piranha Part Two: The Spawning. And just like that sequel, Grandal's post-season once again burst into flames like a trash-filled dumpster. This year's nightmare extended to both sides of the ball, with uncharacteristic defensive miscues piling on top of terrible at-bats. The combination again led to an unceremonious October benching, this one at the worst possible time for the free-agent-to-be. Recency bias now clouds the fact that Grandal was again excellent, if inconsistent, for the boys in blue; He checked in as baseball's best defensive catcher according to FRAA, and the second most valuable backstop in the game by WARP. His easy double-digit walk rate returned after a brief hiatus, along with his plus power. Ultimately, the stick is a bonus, as Grandal makes his box office bank on the merits of that defense.

Enrique Hernandez UT Born: 08/24/91 Age: 27 Bats: R Throws: R Height: 5'11" Weight: 200 Origin: Round 6, 2009 Draft (#191 overall)

YEAR	TEAM	LVL	AGE	PA	R	2B	3B	HR	RBI	BB	K	SB	CS	AVG/OBP/SLG	DRC+	VORP	BABIP	BRR	FRAA	WARP
2016	LAN	MLB	24	244	25	8	0	7	18	28	64	2	0	.190/.283/.324	83	0.5	.234	-0.9	LF(41): 2.6, CF(22): -0.7	0.4
2017	LAN	MLB	25	342	46	24	2	11	37	41	80	3	0	.215/.308/.421	88	14.4	.254	2.6	CF(34): 5.8, LF(28): 0.7	1.8
2018	LAN	MLB	26	462	67	17	3	21	52	50	78	3	0	.256/.336/.470	115	29.0	.266	1.9	CF(63): -0.8, 2B(41): -0.3	2.4
2019	LAN	MLB	27	519	67	24	2	17	58	56	108	4	1	.238/.323/.413	99	18.1	.273	1.2	2B 0, CF 0	1.8

Breakout: 8%   Improve: 53%   Collapse: 6%   Attrition: 12%   MLB: 100%

Comparables: Nate McLouth, Ryan Sweeney, Chris Coghlan

Enrique, do you love me? Are you riding?
'Cause you're hitting righties now, and I like it
And I need ya, the pop and speed, yeah
You know I'm down for you always
KH, do you love me? I see you're playing
Out there at every single spot on the diamond
'Cause to me you're more than just UT, yeah
And I'm down for you always.

Jeren Kendall CF Born: 02/04/96 Age: 23 Bats: L Throws: R Height: 6'0" Weight: 190 Origin: Round 1, 2017 Draft (#23 overall)

YEAR	TEAM	LVL	AGE	PA	R	2B	3B	HR	RBI	BB	K	SB	CS	AVG/OBP/SLG	DRC+	VORP	BABIP	BRR	FRAA	WARP
2017	GRL	A	21	155	21	5	7	2	18	13	42	5	8	.221/.290/.400	93	2.0	.299	-0.6	CF(24): 3.5, RF(5): -0.4	0.5
2018	RCU	A+	22	494	68	20	3	12	42	52	158	37	14	.215/.300/.356	81	6.6	.305	2.5	CF(92): 1.1, RF(8): 0.8	0.7
2019	LAN	MLB	23	251	27	6	1	6	23	16	84	10	5	.182/.232/.303	37	-9.1	.246	0.8	CF 0, RF 0	-0.9

Breakout: 0%   Improve: 2%   Collapse: 1%   Attrition: 4%   MLB: 4%

Comparables: Keon Broxton, Drew Stubbs, Michael Taylor

Way back in the 90's, there were these things calls Magic Eye books, where readers could see 3D images by strenuously focusing on 2D patterns. For those too young to remember the phenomenon, it was a thing, seriously. Kendall has tools—oh so many tools—and you know what you're *supposed* to be seeing. But thus far those tools haven't started morphing into a clear, discernible picture of a big leaguer. It can be endlessly frustrating. Perhaps Kendall could use a magic eye of his own, as the former Vanderbilt Commodore had the fourth-highest strikeout rate in the Cal League, and is now hitting a meager .216 in 578 plate appearances since he graduated from rookie ball.

Gavin Lux SS Born: 11/23/97 Age: 21 Bats: L Throws: R Height: 6'2" Weight: 190 Origin: Round 1, 2016 Draft (#20 overall)

YEAR	TEAM	LVL	AGE	PA	R	2B	3B	HR	RBI	BB	K	SB	CS	AVG/OBP/SLG	DRC+	VORP	BABIP	BRR	FRAA	WARP
2016	DOD	RK	18	219	34	10	5	0	18	25	43	1	0	.281/.365/.385	118	16.6	.360	1.1	SS(43): -7.9	0.6
2016	OGD	RK	18	34	7	3	0	0	3	3	8	1	0	.387/.441/.484	75	4.1	.522	0.0	SS(8): -1.3	-0.1
2017	GRL	A	19	501	68	14	8	7	39	56	88	27	10	.244/.331/.362	105	19.5	.288	3.4	SS(65): 3.8, 2B(43): 4.0	3.3
2018	RCU	A+	20	404	64	23	7	11	48	43	68	11	7	.324/.396/.520	139	34.3	.374	-1.8	SS(66): -0.6, 2B(17): 0.8	3.4
2018	TUL	AA	20	120	21	4	1	4	9	14	20	2	2	.324/.408/.495	118	11.6	.370	1.3	SS(26): -0.6	0.9
2019	LAN	MLB	21	251	30	8	1	7	24	18	54	4	2	.226/.281/.361	72	0.5	.262	-0.1	SS 0, 2B 0	0.0

Breakout: 7%   Improve: 16%   Collapse: 1%   Attrition: 10%   MLB: 24%

Comparables: Daniel Robertson, Francisco Lindor, J.P. Crawford

The lineout for Lux last season indicated that the infielder would need a "strong showing to alleviate creeping doubts about his future." Well, consider those doubts alleviated. The only thing creeping up is Lux's stock as a prospect, with premium bat-to-ball skills, budding pop and a solid eye leading to domination across two levels and what we can only assume is a plaque for being the Dodgers' Minor League Hitter of the Year. A cold-weather product from Wisconsin, land of cheese and *Making a Murderer*, Lux's profile flipped on its head this season, combining his offensive outbreak with only fair defense up the middle. A decent arm and passable athleticism potentially calls his spot at the six into question, but even average defense to pair with a developing bat makes the 21-year-old an awfully interesting prospect.

Manny Machado 3B Born: 07/06/92 Age: 26 Bats: R Throws: R Height: 6'3" Weight: 185 Origin: Round 1, 2010 Draft (#3 overall)

YEAR	TEAM	LVL	AGE	PA	R	2B	3B	HR	RBI	BB	K	SB	CS	AVG/OBP/SLG	DRC+	VORP	BABIP	BRR	FRAA	WARP
2016	BAL	MLB	23	696	105	40	1	37	96	48	120	0	3	.294/.343/.533	123	46.7	.309	0.0	3B(114): 8.6, SS(45): -0.5	5.7
2017	BAL	MLB	24	690	81	33	1	33	95	50	115	9	4	.259/.310/.471	106	19.5	.265	-4.1	3B(156): -6.2	2.1
2018	BAL	MLB	25	413	48	21	1	24	65	45	51	8	1	.315/.387/.575	142	40.8	.311	-0.5	SS(96): -4.5	3.6
2018	LAN	MLB	25	296	36	14	2	13	42	25	53	6	1	.273/.338/.487	145	21.2	.296	1.4	SS(51): -4.5, 3B(16): 3.1	3.0
2019	LAN	MLB	26	665	89	36	3	30	99	62	102	10	3	.283/.353/.503	132	49.0	.298	-0.9	SS -8, 3B 0	4.4

Breakout: 9%   Improve: 62%   Collapse: 1%   Attrition: 6%   MLB: 100%   *Comparables: Nomar Garciaparra, Cal Ripken Jr., Troy Tulowitzki*

You either die the hero or you live long enough to become the villain. Machado was shipped west at the deadline, as a homegrown hero for Orioles fans. Sure, there were a few hiccups along the way, but ultimately memories of a .283/.335/.487 line with 162 homers and breathtaking, highlight-reel defense will always be associated with Machado's time on the left side at Camden Yards. If you go by the stat line, his stint in the City of Angels was pretty good, if not quite vintage Machado. But then the playoffs arrived, and along with them came overly aggressive slides (to be charitable), comments defending the lollygaggers of the world and a swing so long its Blu-ray required two discs. The truth is, everybody loves a villain. Whether it's the Joker, Hannibal Lecter or Marty Scurll, every great heel eventually turns babyface. Is Machado really a baseball villain? Time will tell. Is Machado a generational talent, halfway to Ernie Banks' career WARP by the age of 26? Yes, yes he is.

Max Muncy INF Born: 08/25/90 Age: 28 Bats: L Throws: R Height: 6'0" Weight: 210 Origin: Round 5, 2012 Draft (#169 overall)

YEAR	TEAM	LVL	AGE	PA	R	2B	3B	HR	RBI	BB	K	SB	CS	AVG/OBP/SLG	DRC+	VORP	BABIP	BRR	FRAA	WARP
2016	NAS	AAA	25	268	34	7	2	8	26	35	54	5	0	.251/.360/.408	113	15.1	.291	-0.5	LF(28): -1.3, 3B(13): -1.2	0.8
2016	OAK	MLB	25	133	13	2	0	2	8	20	24	0	0	.186/.308/.257	86	-2.5	.218	0.3	2B(21): 0.3, RF(17): 0.0	0.2
2017	OKL	AAA	26	379	62	20	1	12	44	54	84	3	6	.309/.414/.491	124	36.1	.387	2.0	3B(53): 0.3, 1B(22): 1.9	2.5
2018	OKL	AAA	27	38	7	2	0	2	4	6	5	0	0	.313/.421/.563	120	4.6	.320	0.7	1B(7): 0.1, 3B(3): 0.2	0.3
2018	LAN	MLB	27	481	75	17	2	35	79	79	131	3	0	.263/.391/.582	150	49.5	.299	2.3	1B(84): -0.5, 3B(38): 0.3	4.3
2019	LAN	MLB	28	501	67	21	1	21	67	68	120	3	1	.250/.359/.450	122	24.0	.301	1.1	1B -4, 2B -1	2.0

Breakout: 5%   Improve: 40%   Collapse: 10%   Attrition: 23%   MLB: 81%   *Comparables: Tyler Moore, Chris Shelton, Chris Parmelee*

Peter Parker. Bruce Banner. Bucky Barnes. Like his alliterative brethren, Max Muncy swooped to the rescue this season, transforming into an offensive superhero for the injury-riddled Dodgers. Muncy patiently waited seven years for a shot at regular playing time without riding buses, and that patience manifested itself in spades this season with the former Baylor Bear trailing only Mike Trout, Bryce Harper and Joey Votto in walk rate. While the free passes are nice, Muncy also added a shocking amount of thump with the lumber, smacking 24 of his 35 homers in his first 80 games with the team and leading the league in isolated power (min 450 PA). And he topped it all off by bailing the team out with his defensive flexibility, spending time at four defensive positions without embarrassing himself anywhere. With great power comes great responsibility, sure, and when that great power is attached to elite plate discipline, it's easy to get excited. Not too shabby for a mild-mannered, friendly neighborhood castoff.

Joc Pederson LF Born: 04/21/92 Age: 27 Bats: L Throws: L Height: 6'1" Weight: 220 Origin: Round 11, 2010 Draft (#352 overall)

YEAR	TEAM	LVL	AGE	PA	R	2B	3B	HR	RBI	BB	K	SB	CS	AVG/OBP/SLG	DRC+	VORP	BABIP	BRR	FRAA	WARP
2016	LAN	MLB	24	476	64	26	0	25	68	63	130	6	2	.246/.352/.495	115	35.5	.296	-3.6	CF(132): -2.2	2.0
2017	OKL	AAA	25	71	8	1	0	3	9	5	14	1	0	.169/.225/.323	101	-3.9	.163	-0.2	LF(10): 3.7, CF(4): 0.8	0.6
2017	LAN	MLB	25	323	44	20	0	11	35	39	68	4	3	.212/.331/.407	96	14.2	.241	1.8	CF(92): -9.1, LF(4): -0.4	0.2
2018	LAN	MLB	26	443	65	27	3	25	56	40	85	1	5	.248/.321/.522	119	26.4	.253	0.9	LF(116): -1.3, CF(32): -2.4	2.1
2019	LAN	MLB	27	413	51	18	2	17	55	43	90	4	4	.237/.332/.434	112	17.9	.272	-0.6	LF -1, CF -1	1.8

Breakout: 3%   Improve: 52%   Collapse: 3%   Attrition: 6%   MLB: 97%   *Comparables: Carlos Quentin, Alex Gordon, Nick Swisher*

Alexander Pope spoke on expectations: "Blessed is he who expects nothing, for he shall never be disappointed." The expectations were lofty for Pederson, especially after going 30/30 with a .300 batting average at Triple-A in 2014. The lefty followed suit by stealing 15 bases in his four subsequent seasons in the big leagues. No, Pederson would not be going 30/30 anytime soon, and it was probably unfair to expect him to (it's happened only eight times since 2010, and 62 times ever). Despite those inflated expectations, Yung Joc has turned into one of the better righty mashers in the game, putting up a .556 slugging percentage against right-handed pitching. Only about one of every eight Pederson plate appearances came against southpaws, the lowest number of his career, and one that should continue trending downward as Pederson ages. It's all about managing expectations, after all.

DJ Peters OF Born: 12/12/95 Age: 23 Bats: R Throws: R Height: 6'6" Weight: 225 Origin: Round 4, 2016 Draft (#131 overall)

YEAR	TEAM	LVL	AGE	PA	R	2B	3B	HR	RBI	BB	K	SB	CS	AVG/OBP/SLG	DRC+	VORP	BABIP	BRR	FRAA	WARP
2016	OGD	RK	20	302	63	24	3	13	48	35	66	5	3	.351/.437/.615	144	46.4	.432	0.5	CF(31): 4.5, RF(28): -3.6	2.2
2017	RCU	A+	21	587	91	29	5	27	82	64	189	3	3	.276/.372/.514	127	43.2	.385	0.9	CF(80): -3.5, LF(18): -1.0	3.2
2018	TUL	AA	22	559	79	23	3	29	60	45	192	1	2	.236/.320/.473	114	20.6	.316	-3.6	CF(96): -3.1, RF(29): 1.4	2.1
2019	LAN	MLB	23	251	27	10	0	11	33	15	96	0	0	.204/.271/.390	75	0.8	.294	-0.6	CF -1, RF 0	0.0

Breakout: 5%   Improve: 24%   Collapse: 5%   Attrition: 21%   MLB: 53%   *Comparables: Greg Halman, Joe Benson, Derek Fisher*

If pop artists from the 70s and 80s Frampton and Cetera started an MC duo, you'd likely get DJ Peters, who, as it turns out, is also a strong-armed and athletic outfielder in the Dodgers organization. In the mold of skyscraping sluggers like Aaron Judge and Jayson Werth, Peters does two things prodigiously—sock dingers and strike out. The native Californian achieved one of these two results in nearly 40 percent of his plate appearances, comfortably leading the Texas League this season in both categories. He has thus far defied the expectations for a man his size by holding his own in center, but a likely eventual move to right puts that much more pressure on his prodigious power to play more consistently.

Carlos Rincon RF Born: 10/14/97 Age: 21 Bats: R Throws: R Height: 6'3" Weight: 190 Origin: International Free Agent, 2015

YEAR	TEAM	LVL	AGE	PA	R	2B	3B	HR	RBI	BB	K	SB	CS	AVG/OBP/SLG	DRC+	VORP	BABIP	BRR	FRAA	WARP
2016	DDO	RK	18	96	19	5	2	6	26	15	23	8	2	.364/.458/.714	156	17.0	.431	1.0	RF(15): 1.7, CF(5): -0.2	1.1
2016	DOD	RK	18	105	13	6	3	7	23	2	30	0	2	.301/.314/.621	135	8.5	.364	-1.0	RF(23): 2.0	0.7
2017	GRL	A	19	370	41	13	1	18	48	32	143	6	1	.198/.270/.404	96	5.5	.274	1.1	RF(50): -7.6, LF(15): 2.2	-0.1
2017	OGD	RK	19	52	8	4	0	3	13	1	16	0	0	.275/.288/.529	90	2.9	.344	0.4	RF(2): -0.2, LF(1): 0.1	0.0
2018	GRL	A	20	338	28	13	2	7	33	41	91	5	1	.226/.331/.358	99	5.7	.301	0.6	RF(48): -0.9, LF(6): -0.7	0.3
2018	RCU	A+	20	131	36	9	0	15	35	16	31	0	1	.327/.427/.818	188	22.8	.323	1.7	RF(10): 0.5, LF(8): -0.5	1.9
2019	*LAN*	*MLB*	*21*	*251*	*27*	*8*	*0*	*12*	*33*	*18*	*85*	*0*	*0*	*.196/.251/.377*	*67*	*-4.1*	*.246*	*-0.7*	*RF -1, LF 0*	*-0.6*

Breakout: 4%   Improve: 7%   Collapse: 6%   Attrition: 8%   MLB: 16%   *Comparables: Domingo Santana, Caleb Gindl, Ryan McMahon*

Eyes are bleary and bloodshot. Handwritten scouting reports are strewn in every corner of the office; can recite them by heart. Raw power. High ceiling. Strong lower half. Forceful swing. Limited hit tool? The phrases flash like the neon casino lights, lighting up the Nevada desert like a Christmas tree. Another pull from the whiskey bottle as the old grandfather clock strikes something o'clock in the wee hours of the morning. Unspectacular stat lines littered Rincon's profile since his first rendezvous through rookie ball, making his progress and domination of High-A all the more intriguing and confounding. He walked more. He struck out less. He launched 15 homers in 29 games. It...it looked like progress. It looked like excitement. Just then, a silhouette crept into the doorway. He entered, the ghost of C.J. Retherford morphed with the ghost of Angelo Songco, two Dodger High-A legends. He spoke. "Forget it, Jake. It's Rancho."

Keibert Ruiz C Born: 07/20/98 Age: 20 Bats: B Throws: R Height: 6'0" Weight: 200 Origin: International Free Agent, 2015

YEAR	TEAM	LVL	AGE	PA	R	2B	3B	HR	RBI	BB	K	SB	CS	AVG/OBP/SLG	DRC+	VORP	BABIP	BRR	FRAA	WARP
2016	DOD	RK	17	39	5	4	1	0	15	3	4	0	0	.485/.513/.667	132	7.4	.516	-0.8	C(7): -0.1	0.2
2016	OGD	RK	17	206	28	18	2	2	33	12	23	0	0	.354/.393/.503	135	17.0	.389	-1.6	C(35): -1.2	1.3
2017	GRL	A	18	251	34	16	1	2	24	18	30	0	0	.317/.372/.423	109	15.7	.355	-3.2	C(49): -0.9	0.8
2017	RCU	A+	18	160	24	7	1	6	27	7	23	0	0	.315/.344/.497	128	13.2	.333	0.0	C(37): -0.3	1.3
2018	TUL	AA	19	415	44	14	0	12	47	26	33	0	1	.268/.328/.401	117	8.3	.266	-3.8	C(86): 3.5	2.6
2019	*LAN*	*MLB*	*20*	*251*	*25*	*11*	*0*	*8*	*30*	*11*	*37*	*0*	*0*	*.254/.291/.395*	*85*	*5.6*	*.272*	*-0.6*	*C -2*	*0.4*

Breakout: 4%   Improve: 16%   Collapse: 0%   Attrition: 6%   MLB: 18%   *Comparables: Carson Kelly, Jake Bauers, Freddie Freeman*

YEAR	TEAM	P. COUNT	FRM RUNS	BLK RUNS	THRW RUNS	TOT RUNS
2018	TUL	11928	5.3	-0.6	-0.4	3.9
2019	*LAN*	*8818*	*-1.8*	*0.0*	*0.0*	*-1.8*

A quick Google search for "contact" brings up pages and pages of results for a 1997 Jodie Foster and Matthew McConaughey flick that was, let's say decent if unspectacular. "Extreme contact" brings about plenty of Amazon reviews for tires. While both outcomes are certainly warranted, it's hard to not quibble with Ruiz's exclusion on either search. Sure, you might hope for a few more walks, but whip-quick wrists paired with an uncanny knack for, well, you know, and the Venezuelan wunderkind whiffed a staggeringly infrequent eight percent of the time. That's a hilariously low number for anyone in this baseball universe, and it's truly incredible for a 19-year-old switch-hitting catcher in Double-A. As if that wasn't enough, Ruiz even managed to pop a few more dingers this season to boot, avoiding the "empty average" moniker that usually accompanies high-contact hitters. While he didn't turn up in an extremely specific and limited search, the next option to try might be "super exciting catching prospects that could be really good for a long time." Ruiz would be all over that one.

Corey Seager SS Born: 04/27/94 Age: 25 Bats: L Throws: R Height: 6'4" Weight: 220 Origin: Round 1, 2012 Draft (#18 overall)

YEAR	TEAM	LVL	AGE	PA	R	2B	3B	HR	RBI	BB	K	SB	CS	AVG/OBP/SLG	DRC+	VORP	BABIP	BRR	FRAA	WARP
2016	LAN	MLB	22	687	105	40	5	26	72	54	133	3	3	.308/.365/.512	121	73.1	.355	2.7	SS(155): -8.8	4.4
2017	LAN	MLB	23	613	85	33	0	22	77	67	131	4	2	.295/.375/.479	118	58.5	.352	2.2	SS(138): -1.8	4.3
2018	LAN	MLB	24	115	13	5	1	2	13	11	17	0	0	.267/.348/.396	108	7.2	.301	0.8	SS(25): 0.3	0.8
2019	*LAN*	*MLB*	*25*	*617*	*71*	*32*	*3*	*18*	*77*	*59*	*120*	*3*	*2*	*.274/.351/.438*	*117*	*38.2*	*.322*	*2.2*	*SS -7*	*3.4*

Breakout: 2%   Improve: 71%   Collapse: 1%   Attrition: 2%   MLB: 100%   *Comparables: Troy Tulowitzki, Anthony Rendon, Hanley Ramirez*

There's nothing more brutal (from a sports standpoint) than seeing exciting young players lose huge chunks of time due to injury. Seager's 2018 campaign was riddled with more maladies than Cavity Sam from Operation. Lingering hip and elbow pain eventually led to separate surgeries, limiting the shortstop to only 26 games in what amounted to a lost season. While power numbers slowly creeping downward would typically be an alarming trend, we can probably just chalk that up to, you know, playing only 26 games. The injuries could cause whispers of an eventual move off the six to grow into a dull roar, but with a clean bill of health, Seager should once again resume his prodigious hitting, flirting with .300 and 30 homers on an annual basis.

Will Smith C   Born: 03/28/95   Age: 24   Bats: R   Throws: R   Height: 6'0"   Weight: 192   Origin: Round 1, 2016 Draft (#32 overall)

YEAR	TEAM	LVL	AGE	PA	R	2B	3B	HR	RBI	BB	K	SB	CS	AVG/OBP/SLG	DRC+	VORP	BABIP	BRR	FRAA	WARP
2016	OGD	RK	21	33	4	0	0	1	5	4	1	0	0	.321/.394/.429	120	3.2	.296	0.4	C(5): -0.1, 2B(1): 0.0	0.2
2016	GRL	A	21	97	12	1	0	1	7	11	18	2	1	.256/.371/.305	105	6.3	.317	2.0	C(18): 0.0, 2B(3): -0.2	0.6
2016	RCU	A+	21	115	13	4	0	2	12	14	31	1	0	.216/.330/.320	90	1.8	.292	-1.3	C(16): 0.4, 3B(6): 0.9	0.4
2017	RCU	A+	22	305	38	15	3	11	43	37	71	6	2	.232/.355/.448	126	16.8	.273	-2.0	C(55): 2.7, 3B(1): -1.0	2.2
2018	TUL	AA	23	307	48	14	0	19	53	36	75	4	0	.264/.358/.532	146	25.5	.295	-1.8	C(33): 7.4, 3B(33): -1.3	3.4
2018	OKL	AAA	23	98	9	4	0	1	6	7	37	1	0	.138/.206/.218	53	-3.8	.216	1.4	C(16): 1.4, 3B(10): 0.3	0.2
2019	LAN	MLB	24	69	7	3	0	2	8	5	21	0	0	.215/.290/.379	66	0.2	.281	-0.1	C 2	0.2

Breakout: 6%   Improve: 13%   Collapse: 9%   Attrition: 14%   MLB: 30%   *Comparables: Michael McKenry, Josh Donaldson, Andrew Knapp*

YEAR	TEAM	P. COUNT	FRM RUNS	BLK RUNS	THRW RUNS	TOT RUNS
2018	OKL	2087	1.2	0.0	0.0	2.1
2018	TUL	4187	7.0	0.1	0.6	8.4
2019	LAN	2524	1.5	-0.1	0.1	1.6

Now this is a story all about how this dude became one of the best framers around. And I'd like to take a minute, 'cause it ain't no myth, I'll tell you a little tale about a guy named Will Smith. Ahem. A beanball-induced broken hand cut short Smith's first foray into Double-A, but the former Louisville Cardinal picked his breakout right up where he left off, blending strong discipline with above-average contact skills, folding in a burst of pop for the first time in his young career. The backstop struggled with his first taste of the PCL, but the ugly abbreviated stint can likely be written off as a late-season small sample that shouldn't be used to damper this fresh prince's ultimate upside.

Chris Taylor UT   Born: 08/29/90   Age: 28   Bats: R   Throws: R   Height: 6'1"   Weight: 195   Origin: Round 5, 2012 Draft (#161 overall)

YEAR	TEAM	LVL	AGE	PA	R	2B	3B	HR	RBI	BB	K	SB	CS	AVG/OBP/SLG	DRC+	VORP	BABIP	BRR	FRAA	WARP
2016	SEA	MLB	25	3	0	0	0	0	0	0	2	0	0	.333/.333/.333	55	0.0	1.000	0.0	SS(1): -0.3	0.0
2016	TAC	AAA	25	280	41	19	4	3	29	29	49	12	5	.312/.387/.457	102	20.7	.378	0.0	SS(50): 2.1, 2B(7): -1.3	1.4
2016	OKL	AAA	25	64	7	6	2	0	8	6	16	5	0	.368/.438/.544	100	9.2	.512	1.0	SS(13): -1.2, 3B(2): -0.1	0.3
2016	LAN	MLB	25	62	8	2	2	1	7	4	13	0	0	.207/.258/.362	81	-0.7	.250	0.7	3B(10): -0.1, 2B(7): -0.5	0.1
2017	OKL	AAA	26	49	8	2	2	1	5	5	5	1	2	.233/.327/.442	91	2.9	.243	0.6	SS(5): 0.5, CF(3): 0.2	0.3
2017	LAN	MLB	26	568	85	34	5	21	72	50	142	17	4	.288/.354/.496	106	50.4	.361	4.4	CF(49): -2.2, LF(48): 6.6	3.4
2018	LAN	MLB	27	604	85	35	8	17	63	55	178	9	6	.254/.331/.444	100	34.9	.345	0.9	SS(81): 3.7, CF(50): -4.5	2.6
2019	LAN	MLB	28	612	81	29	6	18	65	53	156	14	6	.251/.324/.418	109	29.5	.319	1.9	2B 0, CF -1	3.3

Breakout: 4%   Improve: 50%   Collapse: 7%   Attrition: 20%   MLB: 92%   *Comparables: Sean Rodriguez, Brendan Harris, Tim Beckham*

After the baseball gods doused him with Dodger development dust upon his arrival, Taylor took a slight step back in his second year with the club. He ran a little, but not quite as much. He smacked a few dingers, but not quite at the torrid clip he set forth in his 2017 team debut. He led the National League in strikeouts (ok, maybe that last one isn't as spinnable). Even if Taylor's 2018 was regression to the mean, the end product was still extremely good. Year Two of the Taylor swing change experiment yielded even more line drives, at the expense of ground balls, and the offensive production paired with above-average defense from four spots on the diamond. Sure, the strikeouts aren't ideal, but the extra whiffs were often the product of working deep into counts, as only 13 National League hitters saw more pitches per plate appearances than Taylor. When a "down-ish" year looks like this, you're pretty close to a star.

Justin Turner 3B   Born: 11/23/84   Age: 34   Bats: R   Throws: R   Height: 5'11"   Weight: 205   Origin: Round 7, 2006 Draft (#204 overall)

YEAR	TEAM	LVL	AGE	PA	R	2B	3B	HR	RBI	BB	K	SB	CS	AVG/OBP/SLG	DRC+	VORP	BABIP	BRR	FRAA	WARP
2016	LAN	MLB	31	622	79	34	3	27	90	48	107	4	1	.275/.339/.493	120	49.2	.293	-1.7	3B(144): -4.8, 1B(1): 0.0	3.3
2017	LAN	MLB	32	543	72	32	0	21	71	59	56	7	1	.322/.415/.530	150	63.8	.326	-3.2	3B(121): -5.5	4.6
2018	LAN	MLB	33	426	62	31	1	14	52	47	54	2	1	.312/.406/.518	145	43.8	.334	0.3	3B(96): 11.1	5.1
2019	LAN	MLB	34	629	89	41	2	20	75	62	87	5	2	.290/.386/.476	139	42.8	.323	-1.7	3B 1	4.7

Breakout: 1%   Improve: 41%   Collapse: 2%   Attrition: 4%   MLB: 97%   *Comparables: George Brett, Aramis Ramirez, Chipper Jones*

If you ever wondered what might happen if a radioactive George Brett bit Gritty (and of course you have), you'd probably wind up with something like Turner, who continued his ascent up the list of the 30-40 biggest regrets for Mets fans with yet another strong season at the plate. For many hitters, a broken wrist suffered in Spring Training might be a decent excuse for a down year, especially when nicks to the shoulder, hip and groin all conspired to hold him down throughout the season's first half. Not for Turner, who rebounded with a scorching hot second-half line of .356/.447/.619. The ginger wonder was also a strong defender at the hot corner, a feat he hadn't accomplished since the 2014 season, his first in Tinseltown. This bodes well for Turner, as he hurtles into his mid-30s, and his profile combining minuscule strikeout totals with decent patience and a little pop is one that should age better than the opening metaphor for this comment.

Chase Utley 2B   Born: 12/17/78   Age: 40   Bats: L   Throws: R   Height: 6'1"   Weight: 195   Origin: Round 1, 2000 Draft (#15 overall)

YEAR	TEAM	LVL	AGE	PA	R	2B	3B	HR	RBI	BB	K	SB	CS	AVG/OBP/SLG	DRC+	VORP	BABIP	BRR	FRAA	WARP
2016	LAN	MLB	37	565	79	26	3	14	52	40	115	2	2	.252/.319/.396	91	21.6	.299	-1.1	2B(134): 1.1, 3B(1): 0.0	1.2
2017	LAN	MLB	38	353	43	20	4	8	34	32	57	6	1	.236/.324/.405	98	13.8	.264	2.0	2B(80): -1.7, 1B(17): 0.2	1.0
2018	LAN	MLB	39	187	18	10	1	1	14	17	34	3	1	.213/.305/.305	86	3.1	.262	1.9	2B(50): -3.4, 1B(2): -0.1	0.1
2019	LAN	MLB	40	251	28	13	1	4	22	21	49	3	1	.238/.319/.359	88	4.9	.290	0.5	2B -3, 1B 0	0.2

Breakout: 2%   Improve: 20%   Collapse: 10%   Attrition: 22%   MLB: 61%   *Comparables: Red Schoendienst, Brooks Robinson, Barry Larkin*

In one of the dumber "controversies" of the season, Braves color commentator and resident Old Man Yelling at Cloud, Joe Simpson, blasted the Dodgers for unprofessional attire during batting practice. The focus of Simpson's ire was a spunky, young upstart, the plucky 39-year-old Chase Utley. Damn millennials. The fact that this story was one of the bigger events of Utley's 2018 season reflects the anti-climactic culmination to the six-time All Star's career, as Utley announced his intention to retire at season's end. Thumb and wrist injuries kept the lefty from resuming his role as a platoon option at the keystone, but despite the time off, Utley seamlessly transitioned quite nicely from righty-masher to dugout purveyor of wisdom and presumed Ralph

Lauren model. The UCLA Bruin was the dominant force at second base for most of the 2000's, and it's honestly pretty shocking that he didn't add at least one MVP award to his trophy case. While the end may have come with a whimper rather than a bang, baseball will miss Utley (unless, you know, you're Ruben Tejada).

Alex Verdugo OF
Born: 05/15/96 Age: 23 Bats: L Throws: L Height: 6'0" Weight: 205 Origin: Round 2, 2014 Draft (#62 overall)

YEAR	TEAM	LVL	AGE	PA	R	2B	3B	HR	RBI	BB	K	SB	CS	AVG/OBP/SLG	DRC+	VORP	BABIP	BRR	FRAA	WARP
2016	TUL	AA	20	529	58	23	1	13	63	44	67	2	6	.273/.336/.407	114	20.8	.292	-1.2	CF(91): -1.0, RF(30): -0.1	2.3
2017	OKL	AAA	21	495	67	27	4	6	62	52	50	9	3	.314/.389/.436	115	32.4	.340	3.1	CF(59): -5.5, RF(46): 3.1	2.5
2017	LAN	MLB	21	25	1	0	0	1	1	2	4	0	1	.174/.240/.304	91	-1.2	.167	-0.1	CF(6): -0.7, LF(3): 0.3	0.0
2018	OKL	AAA	22	379	44	19	0	10	44	34	47	8	2	.329/.391/.472	112	24.0	.359	-0.5	CF(45): 2.0, RF(31): 2.4	2.1
2018	LAN	MLB	22	86	11	6	0	1	4	8	14	0	0	.260/.329/.377	85	3.2	.306	1.5	RF(16): -0.1, LF(12): 0.2	0.1
2019	LAN	MLB	23	558	63	24	2	14	61	47	86	4	2	.260/.327/.399	98	13.6	.287	-0.8	RF 2, LF 1	1.7

Breakout: 3% Improve: 35% Collapse: 8% Attrition: 20% MLB: 58%   *Comparables: L.J. Hoes, Michael Brantley, Desmond Jennings*

Per Wikipedia, vertigo can be described as a symptom where a person feels as if they or the objects around them are moving when they are not. Slow yourself down a bit phonetically, and you get Verdugo, an American baseball person that seems stagnant, at least in conjunction with his fellow prospects. It may feel like the Arizonan has been a blue chipper in the system forever, stuck in the minors as his colleagues whiz past him with promotions. However, Verdugo may have logged 874 plate appearances in Triple-A over the better part of two years—mashing to the tune of .321/.389/.452, by the way—but the 22-year-old has consistently been young for his level and still has plenty of time to capitalize on more than just a September call up. His superior contact skills and great eye at the plate should translate nicely to today's homerific game as well—provided that he improves on his ground-ball tendencies—and Verdugo's athleticism, combined with a plus arm, should offer plenty of flexibility in the outfield.

PITCHERS

Scott Alexander LHP
Born: 07/10/89 Age: 29 Bats: L Throws: L Height: 6'2" Weight: 190 Origin: Round 6, 2010 Draft (#179 overall)

YEAR	TEAM	LVL	AGE	W	L	SV	G	GS	IP	H	HR	BB/9	K/9	K	GB%	BABIP	WHIP	ERA	DRA	WARP	MPH	FB%	WHF	CSP
2016	OMA	AAA	26	2	0	1	22	0	30	32	2	3.0	7.2	24	67%	.323	1.40	3.00	3.47	0.5				
2016	KCA	MLB	26	0	0	0	17	0	19	24	1	3.3	7.6	16	69%	.383	1.63	3.32	5.33	-0.1	94.1	72.2	13.3	45.6
2017	KCA	MLB	27	5	4	4	58	0	69	62	3	3.7	7.7	59	73%	.306	1.30	2.48	4.64	0.4	95.0	93.9	14.3	45.6
2018	LAN	MLB	28	2	1	3	73	1	66	57	4	3.7	7.6	56	72%	.296	1.27	3.68	5.33	-0.3	95.1	85.6	12.4	46.5
2019	LAN	MLB	29	2	1	0	43	0	45²	38	4	3.6	8.4	43	62%	.295	1.24	3.63	4.05	0.5	94.3	87.8	13.3	46

Breakout: 36% Improve: 51% Collapse: 26% Attrition: 26% MLB: 88%   *Comparables: Sam Dyson, Jeremy Jeffress, Matt Grace*

Acquired by the Dodgers in a January three-team trade, Alexander wore out the path between the bullpen and the mound this season, pitching in almost half of all games for his new club; His 73 appearances ranked eighth in the National League. The southpaw tinkers with four pitches, but really he throws only one, a sinker he deploys roughly 85 percent of the time to coax an elite rate of ground balls. Despite handling right-handed bats in Kansas City, Alexander's reverse splits backed up a bit in 2018, and he still probably walks a few more guys than you'd prefer from a late-inning option. Nevertheless, with another year to go before arbitration, the Dodgers hope Alexander can age like a fine wine, a fitting desire for the Sonoma State University product.

Yadier Alvarez RHP
Born: 03/07/96 Age: 23 Bats: R Throws: R Height: 6'3" Weight: 175 Origin: International Free Agent, 2015

YEAR	TEAM	LVL	AGE	W	L	SV	G	GS	IP	H	HR	BB/9	K/9	K	GB%	BABIP	WHIP	ERA	DRA	WARP	MPH	FB%	WHF	CSP
2016	DOD	RK	20	1	1	0	5	5	20	9	0	4.5	11.7	26	64%	.200	0.95	1.80	2.11	0.8				
2016	GRL	A	20	3	2	0	9	9	39¹	31	1	2.5	12.6	55	50%	.326	1.07	2.29	2.49	1.2				
2017	RCU	A+	21	2	4	1	14	11	59¹	61	3	3.8	9.3	61	51%	.335	1.45	5.31	3.97	0.8				
2017	TUL	AA	21	2	2	0	7	7	33	29	1	6.8	9.8	36	56%	.318	1.64	3.55	4.42	0.3				
2018	DOD	RK	22	0	0	0	2	2	7	5	0	1.3	12.9	10	71%	.357	0.86	1.29	2.01	0.3				
2018	TUL	AA	22	1	2	1	17	8	48¹	37	2	8.0	9.7	52	54%	.285	1.66	4.66	4.53	0.4				
2019	LAN	MLB	23	3	3	0	19	11	55	47	7	5.6	9.8	60	48%	.301	1.48	4.57	5.15	0.0				

Breakout: 8% Improve: 19% Collapse: 6% Attrition: 20% MLB: 30%   *Comparables: Dan Cortes, Jose Cisnero, Zach Phillips*

So much has to go right for a blue-chip starting pitching prospect to reach his ceiling. Throwing hard is, well, hard. Developing pinpoint accuracy is harder, and then you have to deal with the possibility that every pitch brings with it the risk of a UCL explosion. It's sort of a marvel that any pitcher becomes good, ever. With Alvarez, all the physical tools are there. His electric fastball hits triple digits with ease, and his wipeout slider is still capable of inducing plenty of whiffs when it's biting. However, his horrific walk totals somehow got worse this year, and the former $16-million-man missed a good chunk of the season with a groin strain and made the majority of his appearances out of the bullpen upon his return. On top of that, Alvarez reportedly went AWOL before a scheduled start in September, which is um, never what you want. The talent is still there with Alvarez, but the days of him having unlimited potential as a starter are in their twilight.

John Axford RHP Born: 04/01/83 Age: 36 Bats: R Throws: R Height: 6'5" Weight: 220 Origin: Round 42, 2005 Draft (#1259 overall)

YEAR	TEAM	LVL	AGE	W	L	SV	G	GS	IP	H	HR	BB/9	K/9	K	GB%	BABIP	WHIP	ERA	DRA	WARP	MPH	FB%	WHF	CSP
2016	OAK	MLB	33	6	4	3	68	0	65²	65	6	4.1	8.2	60	56%	.311	1.45	3.97	5.00	0.0	98.3	73.2	11.5	45.5
2017	OAK	MLB	34	0	1	0	22	0	21	27	3	7.3	9.0	21	51%	.364	2.10	6.43	7.54	-0.6	96.8	66.2	8.1	45.7
2018	TOR	MLB	35	4	1	0	45	1	51	44	6	3.5	8.8	50	54%	.286	1.25	4.41	5.13	-0.1	97.1	76.1	9.3	46.7
2018	LAN	MLB	35	0	0	0	5	0	3²	8	0	4.9	9.8	4	67%	.533	2.73	17.18	6.82	-0.1	97.8	76.1	8.2	44.9
2019	LAN	MLB	36	2	1	0	41	0	44	40	5	3.9	8.9	43	51%	.303	1.34	4.18	4.68	0.1	96.1	71.7	9.6	45

Breakout: 23% Improve: 45% Collapse: 21% Attrition: 7% MLB: 75%   *Comparables: Scott Eyre, Trever Miller, Hoyt Wilhelm*

In 2011, Axford sponsored a local film festival in Milwaukee, the site of his major league origins. He has since become just as notable for his love of movies and uncanny Oscars predictions as his proclivity to shut down opposing hitters. A trade deadline move to the Dodgers was more art house horror flick than Hollywood ending, as the journeyman hurler surrendered seven earned runs in less than four innings. Oh well. At least we'll always have Milwaukee.

Pedro Baez RHP Born: 03/11/88 Age: 31 Bats: R Throws: R Height: 6'0" Weight: 230 Origin: International Free Agent, 2007

YEAR	TEAM	LVL	AGE	W	L	SV	G	GS	IP	H	HR	BB/9	K/9	K	GB%	BABIP	WHIP	ERA	DRA	WARP	MPH	FB%	WHF	CSP
2016	LAN	MLB	28	3	2	0	73	0	74	52	11	2.7	10.1	83	44%	.233	1.00	3.04	3.18	1.5	99.2	74.8	15.7	46.5
2017	LAN	MLB	29	3	6	0	66	0	64	56	9	4.1	9.0	64	35%	.267	1.33	2.95	4.81	0.3	98.6	72.7	17	44.8
2018	LAN	MLB	30	4	3	0	55	0	56¹	46	4	3.7	9.9	62	38%	.286	1.22	2.88	3.35	1.0	97.7	62.8	16.1	44
2019	LAN	MLB	31	3	1	0	53	0	55²	46	8	3.4	9.7	60	40%	.279	1.20	4.08	4.58	0.2	97.6	69.2	16.2	44.6

Breakout: 32% Improve: 47% Collapse: 26% Attrition: 16% MLB: 93%   *Comparables: Matt Bush, Brad Brach, Santiago Casilla*

As Mick Jagger famously belted, "Time is on my side, yes it is". It's fair to say that this lyric is likely crocheted onto a throw pillow in Baez's living room, as the hard-throwing righty was once again among the league's most deliberate hurlers on the bump. But really, what is time? People used to think that time was the same everywhere. But then Einstein got involved, and we...observer. It turns out that we, as humans, perceive time differently and relatively to the instruments used to measure time. So what if time is just an agreed upon social construct? And if that's the case, is Baez really that painfully slow, or are the reactions to his pace more of a commentary on where we're at as a society and our ever-shrinking attention spans? Either way, Baez is pitching high-leverage innings again, and is acquitting himself well. At least there's that.

Homer Bailey RHP Born: 05/03/86 Age: 33 Bats: R Throws: R Height: 6'4" Weight: 223 Origin: Round 1, 2004 Draft (#7 overall)

YEAR	TEAM	LVL	AGE	W	L	SV	G	GS	IP	H	HR	BB/9	K/9	K	GB%	BABIP	WHIP	ERA	DRA	WARP	MPH	FB%	WHF	CSP
2016	LOU	AAA	30	1	2	0	7	7	24	31	7	3.4	7.1	19	54%	.312	1.67	5.62	4.52	0.2				
2016	CIN	MLB	30	2	3	0	6	6	23	35	2	2.7	10.6	27	47%	.452	1.83	6.65	3.82	0.4	96.0	54.2	9.8	44.6
2017	CIN	MLB	31	6	9	0	18	18	91	112	11	4.2	6.6	67	46%	.346	1.69	6.43	7.38	-1.8	95.4	57	10.2	48
2018	LOU	AAA	32	2	2	0	7	6	37²	41	4	2.4	6.7	28	37%	.311	1.35	4.78	4.03	0.6				
2018	CIN	MLB	32	1	14	0	20	20	106¹	141	23	2.8	6.3	75	44%	.327	1.64	6.09	6.03	-0.9	95.2	56	9.8	49.6
2019	CIN	MLB	33	7	8	0	23	23	116	129	18	3.6	7.6	98	44%	.328	1.51	4.88	5.30	0.0	94.3	55.5	9.8	47.2

Breakout: 14% Improve: 32% Collapse: 19% Attrition: 13% MLB: 70%   *Comparables: Jerome Williams, Jeff Francis, Matt Cain*

If Bailey had reached free agency this year instead of next, his agent would take pains to show that the big Texan's arm was finally healthy, he reached the 100-inning plateau for the first time in ages and improved his ERA for the third straight season. That's why you should never listen to an agent talking about his player. Bailey missed two months with a sore knee but his arm was sound, making his horror show of a season all the more disappointing. He allowed a league-worst .901 OPS. Batters in the eight-hole hit .390/.490/.585 against him (the MLB average is .233/.302/370). The Reds lost 19 of the 20 games he started before mercifully pulling the plug in early September. The calls are coming from inside the house. One year. $28 million. Breathe deep. All but the major-league minimum will be picked up by the Dodgers, who immediately released him upon his trade from Cincinnati

Walker Buehler RHP Born: 07/28/94 Age: 24 Bats: R Throws: R Height: 6'2" Weight: 175 Origin: Round 1, 2015 Draft (#24 overall)

YEAR	TEAM	LVL	AGE	W	L	SV	G	GS	IP	H	HR	BB/9	K/9	K	GB%	BABIP	WHIP	ERA	DRA	WARP	MPH	FB%	WHF	CSP
2017	RCU	A+	22	0	0	0	5	5	16¹	8	0	2.8	14.9	27	57%	.267	0.80	1.10	1.77	0.7				
2017	TUL	AA	22	2	2	0	11	11	49	40	5	2.8	11.8	64	52%	.315	1.12	3.49	2.75	1.4				
2017	OKL	AAA	22	1	1	1	12	3	23¹	19	1	4.2	13.1	34	62%	.333	1.29	4.63	3.03	0.6				
2017	LAN	MLB	22	1	0	0	8	0	9¹	11	2	7.7	11.6	12	67%	.409	2.04	7.71	4.10	0.1	99.5	69.8	11.5	47.9
2018	OKL	AAA	23	1	0	0	3	3	13	10	0	2.8	11.1	16	61%	.303	1.08	2.08	3.07	0.4				
2018	LAN	MLB	23	8	5	0	24	23	137¹	95	12	2.4	9.9	151	50%	.248	0.96	2.62	3.21	3.3	98.2	59.6	12.6	49.5
2019	LAN	MLB	24	11	7	0	26	26	156	122	18	3.6	10.2	177	49%	.286	1.18	3.67	4.11	2.2	98.1	62.1	12.9	50.3

Breakout: 22% Improve: 62% Collapse: 6% Attrition: 10% MLB: 95%   *Comparables: Luis Severino, Lance McCullers, Carlos Martinez*

At the risk of running a reference into the ground, Buehler is very popular. The sportos, motorheads, geeks, wastoids, dweebies—they all adore him. They think he's a righteous dude. They're not wrong. Coming off an especially bitter cup of coffee in his first stint with the team down the stretch of 2017, Buehler was finally inserted into the rotation this season, and he didn't disappoint. Armed with a deep five-pitch mix including a heater that can run into triple digits, the rookie tossed 177 innings in 2018, including the playoffs—by far his heaviest workload as a professional. The stuff didn't fade, as the former Vanderbilt star finished strong, punching out 29 batters in 23.1 playoff innings, including seven dazzling and scoreless innings in Game 3 of the World Series. And after showing 80-grade proclivity for dropping public expletives during candid celebratory moments, it's safe to say that's Walker "F-ing" Buehler to you.

Tony Cingrani LHP   Born: 07/05/89   Age: 29   Bats: L   Throws: L   Height: 6'4"   Weight: 214   Origin: Round 3, 2011 Draft (#114 overall)

YEAR	TEAM	LVL	AGE	W	L	SV	G	GS	IP	H	HR	BB/9	K/9	K	GB%	BABIP	WHIP	ERA	DRA	WARP	MPH	FB%	WHF	CSP
2016	CIN	MLB	26	2	5	17	65	0	63	54	5	5.3	7.0	49	48%	.277	1.44	4.14	6.57	-1.2	96.7	87.4	9.6	47.6
2017	CIN	MLB	27	0	0	0	25	0	23¹	25	9	2.3	9.3	24	43%	.271	1.33	5.40	6.06	-0.2	95.9	90	14	52.4
2017	LAN	MLB	27	0	0	0	22	0	19¹	15	1	2.8	13.0	28	42%	.333	1.09	2.79	2.70	0.5	96.2	72	15.7	40.9
2018	LAN	MLB	28	1	2	0	30	0	22²	19	2	2.4	14.3	36	54%	.354	1.10	4.76	3.90	0.3	95.6	78	16.1	45.4
2019	LAN	MLB	29	1	1	0	24	0	25¹	20	3	3.7	11.6	32	47%	.296	1.19	3.73	4.18	0.2	95.5	83	13	46.4

Breakout: 30%   Improve: 47%   Collapse: 23%   Attrition: 10%   MLB: 89%   *Comparables: David Hernandez, Ken Howell, Dennys Reyes*

If Cingrani's season were a car, it wouldn't get very good gas mileage on account of all the starts and stops. The southpaw spent more time on the DL than off in 2018, which is a shame, as a career-high slider usage led to his best strikeout rate since an abbreviated 2012 cup of coffee. In the land of Priuses and Teslas, here's hoping Cingrani can find something a little more reliable moving forward.

Caleb Ferguson LHP   Born: 07/02/96   Age: 22   Bats: R   Throws: L   Height: 6'3"   Weight: 215   Origin: Round 38, 2014 Draft (#1149 overall)

YEAR	TEAM	LVL	AGE	W	L	SV	G	GS	IP	H	HR	BB/9	K/9	K	GB%	BABIP	WHIP	ERA	DRA	WARP	MPH	FB%	WHF	CSP
2016	DOD	RK	19	1	0	0	2	0	6	4	0	0.0	16.5	11	38%	.308	0.67	1.50	1.30	0.3				
2016	OGD	RK	19	1	0	0	2	2	10	4	0	1.8	9.9	11	67%	.167	0.60	0.90	3.15	0.3				
2016	GRL	A	19	1	4	0	10	10	50¹	49	3	0.5	7.3	41	60%	.309	1.03	2.68	4.03	0.6				
2017	RCU	A+	20	9	4	0	25	24	122¹	113	6	4.0	10.3	140	46%	.335	1.37	2.87	4.03	1.8				
2018	TUL	AA	21	3	0	0	8	8	39	31	2	2.3	9.2	40	42%	.284	1.05	1.38	4.07	0.6				
2018	OKL	AAA	21	0	0	0	2	2	8	6	0	7.9	13.5	12	21%	.316	1.62	2.25	3.79	0.2				
2018	LAN	MLB	21	7	2	2	29	3	49	43	8	2.2	10.8	59	47%	.292	1.12	3.49	3.17	1.0	96.1	71.9	12.5	54.7
2019	LAN	MLB	22	3	1	0	36	3	49²	43	6	2.8	9.6	53	44%	.298	1.18	3.80	4.25	0.5	96.1	75	13.1	57

Breakout: 22%   Improve: 31%   Collapse: 9%   Attrition: 25%   MLB: 51%   *Comparables: Tyler Skaggs, Lucas Giolito, Francis Martes*

While it surely stung to be left off the 25-man World Series roster, it's hard to call the 2018 season anything but a success for Ferguson, who started the campaign as a Double-A hurler, barely old enough to legally order a beer. Installed as a full-time, late-inning option in late June, the southpaw rode a fastball touching 97 mph and a biting curve to gaudy strikeout numbers. Ferguson's first foray into the postseason resulted in retiring nine of the 10 batters he faced, punching out three in three innings of work. The former 38th-round pick's future role as a big leaguer will likely be determined by curbing bouts of shaky control, and his changeup, which is still a work in progress.

Josh Fields RHP   Born: 08/19/85   Age: 33   Bats: R   Throws: R   Height: 6'0"   Weight: 195   Origin: Round 1, 2008 Draft (#20 overall)

YEAR	TEAM	LVL	AGE	W	L	SV	G	GS	IP	H	HR	BB/9	K/9	K	GB%	BABIP	WHIP	ERA	DRA	WARP	MPH	FB%	WHF	CSP
2016	HOU	MLB	30	0	0	0	15	0	15²	23	2	1.7	11.5	20	31%	.457	1.66	6.89	4.89	0.0	97.0	60.5	13.9	48.5
2016	FRE	AAA	30	1	0	1	23	0	27¹	19	0	2.3	10.5	32	46%	.279	0.95	1.65	2.36	0.8				
2016	LAN	MLB	30	1	0	0	22	0	19¹	20	2	3.7	10.2	22	41%	.333	1.45	2.79	2.60	0.5	97.4	60.5	15.2	49.9
2017	LAN	MLB	31	5	0	2	57	0	57	40	10	2.4	9.5	60	30%	.219	0.96	2.84	4.30	0.6	97	78.9	14.9	47.3
2018	LAN	MLB	32	2	2	2	45	0	41	28	4	2.4	7.2	33	26%	.226	0.95	2.20	4.94	0.0	96.6	72.9	13.3	45.5
2019	LAN	MLB	33	2	1	0	33	0	35¹	33	6	3.4	8.9	35	35%	.291	1.31	4.77	5.35	-0.2	95.8	71.9	14.1	46.5

Breakout: 19%   Improve: 38%   Collapse: 28%   Attrition: 15%   MLB: 87%   *Comparables: Kiko Calero, Jason Frasor, Joe Thatcher*

Thanks to Kenley Jansen's April struggles, Fields got a chance to earn his stripes as a Proven Closer (™), utilizing primarily a fastball-curve combo with an occasional changeup sprinkled in for good measure. It wasn't a roaring success, however, as a bout of shoulder inflammation led to slightly decreased velocity and the lowest strikeout rate of his career. In fact, DRA saw through the career-best ERA mostly because career-low ground-ball rates and home-run rates don't generally go hand-in-hand. It wasn't all bad in 2018 for Fields, however. His alma mater made the National Championship game in football and he and his wife welcomed their first child (you know, in no particular order). Glass half full!

Dylan Floro RHP   Born: 12/27/90   Age: 28   Bats: L   Throws: R   Height: 6'2"   Weight: 205   Origin: Round 13, 2012 Draft (#422 overall)

YEAR	TEAM	LVL	AGE	W	L	SV	G	GS	IP	H	HR	BB/9	K/9	K	GB%	BABIP	WHIP	ERA	DRA	WARP	MPH	FB%	WHF	CSP
2016	TBA	MLB	25	0	1	0	12	0	15	23	0	3.0	8.4	14	55%	.434	1.87	4.20	6.14	-0.2	95.1	73.8	10.2	49.9
2016	DUR	AAA	25	1	2	7	32	0	50	53	6	1.6	7.2	40	56%	.313	1.24	2.88	3.60	0.8				
2017	CHN	MLB	26	0	0	0	3	0	9²	15	2	1.9	5.6	6	53%	.382	1.76	6.52	6.19	-0.1	93.0	67.7	9.8	54.8
2017	IOW	AAA	26	3	2	1	25	2	48²	54	9	1.5	4.8	26	63%	.274	1.27	3.88	4.08	0.7				
2017	OKL	AAA	26	0	1	1	8	0	11¹	18	0	2.4	9.5	12	58%	.474	1.85	5.56	2.63	0.3				
2018	CIN	MLB	27	3	2	0	25	0	36¹	39	2	3.0	6.7	27	57%	.314	1.40	2.72	5.25	-0.1	94.7	62.4	9.8	48.1
2018	LAN	MLB	27	3	1	0	29	0	27²	18	1	3.6	10.1	31	55%	.250	1.05	1.63	3.14	0.6	95.5	64.8	15.3	45
2019	LAN	MLB	28	2	1	0	43	0	45²	45	5	3.0	8.2	41	53%	.314	1.32	4.02	4.49	0.3	94.3	65.4	11.8	50.5

Breakout: 13%   Improve: 23%   Collapse: 18%   Attrition: 20%   MLB: 54%   *Comparables: Matt Grace, Brian Flynn, Tyler Olson*

The journeyman right-hander went west in July, marking his fourth club in a two-year span. The move paid off handsomely, as Floro's ERA sparkled for the Dodgers, holding opposition hitters to a .522 OPS in the second half and punching out over 10 batters per nine, ultimately emerging as one of the team's lone trusted options out of the pen in late-inning situations. He also won the coveted Full Vogelsong Pitcher of the Year award, which is nice. However, the real tragedy of Floro's season was that the Dodgers traded Brandon McCarthy, depriving Dave Roberts of the opportunity to replace Brandon with Dylan.

Rich Hill   LHP   Born: 03/11/80   Age: 39   Bats: L   Throws: L   Height: 6'5"   Weight: 220   Origin: Round 4, 2002 Draft (#112 overall)

YEAR	TEAM	LVL	AGE	W	L	SV	G	GS	IP	H	HR	BB/9	K/9	K	GB%	BABIP	WHIP	ERA	DRA	WARP	MPH	FB%	WHF	CSP
2016	OAK	MLB	36	9	3	0	14	14	76	55	2	3.3	10.7	90	51%	.290	1.09	2.25	2.75	2.3	93.0	46.6	12.1	50.9
2016	LAN	MLB	36	3	2	0	6	6	34¹	22	2	1.3	10.2	39	38%	.244	0.79	1.83	2.89	1.0	92.2	48.3	11.6	50.9
2017	LAN	MLB	37	12	8	0	25	25	135²	99	18	3.3	11.0	166	39%	.261	1.09	3.32	3.35	3.4	90.7	54.8	12.7	49.2
2018	LAN	MLB	38	11	5	0	25	24	132²	108	20	2.8	10.2	150	40%	.268	1.12	3.66	3.92	2.1	91.2	58.8	11.6	54.5
2019	LAN	MLB	39	9	7	0	23	23	138	113	20	2.9	10.1	155	42%	.286	1.14	3.88	4.34	1.5	89.8	53.2	11.7	50.3

Breakout: 11%   Improve: 39%   Collapse: 13%   Attrition: 5%   MLB: 77%   *Comparables: Roger Clemens, Nolan Ryan, Allie Reynolds*

In 2017, MLB started promoting the Player's Weekend, a stretch of games where teams could wear fun uniforms (read: sell more merch) and players could flaunt their personalities by donning wacky monikers on the backs of their jerseys. If it sounds like a practice that a 38-year-old veteran hurler would find immature or distasteful, well, you'd be wrong. On August 24, "D. Mountain" took the bump for the Dodgers, and dominated a hapless Padres lineup, tossing a perfect game through four innings. Just when the possibility of Hill sending his nicknamed jersey to Cooperstown flickered in the distance, Hunter Renfroe doubled, ruining it for everyone. In the end, Hill punched out eight batters in six shutout innings, a vintage performance for the reinvented southpaw. The problem for Hill was that these outings were flanked by more clunkers—he allowed at least four earned runs in eight starts during 2018, compared to just three in 2017. As he enters his age-39 season, and the last season of his three-year contract, he'll be looking to recapture the ability to consistently baffle hitters with a steady diet of Uncle Charlies, and he'll do so in style.

Daniel Hudson   RHP   Born: 03/09/87   Age: 32   Bats: R   Throws: R   Height: 6'3"   Weight: 225   Origin: Round 5, 2008 Draft (#150 overall)

YEAR	TEAM	LVL	AGE	W	L	SV	G	GS	IP	H	HR	BB/9	K/9	K	GB%	BABIP	WHIP	ERA	DRA	WARP	MPH	FB%	WHF	CSP
2016	ARI	MLB	29	3	2	5	70	0	60¹	65	6	3.3	8.7	58	41%	.331	1.44	5.22	5.24	-0.2	97.7	62.8	13	44.5
2017	PIT	MLB	30	2	7	0	71	0	61²	57	7	4.8	9.6	66	44%	.312	1.46	4.38	4.74	0.3	96.7	60.2	12.8	47.3
2018	LAN	MLB	31	3	2	0	40	1	46	38	6	3.5	8.6	44	39%	.256	1.22	4.11	4.63	0.2	96.8	54.4	14	51.3
2019	LAN	MLB	32	2	1	1	44	0	46¹	41	7	3.6	9.2	47	42%	.292	1.28	4.34	4.87	0.0	96.0	58.6	13.1	47.8

Breakout: 23%   Improve: 41%   Collapse: 22%   Attrition: 7%   MLB: 85%   *Comparables: Tyler Yates, Santiago Casilla, Tippy Martinez*

Hudson's first month of the season was filled with more ups and downs than the newest attraction at Cedar Point. Jettisoned from the Pirates to the Rays in a swap for Corey Dickerson, the righty produced an ERA halfway to his age in Spring Training and found himself wandering between baseball cities once again. The Dodgers scooped him up and Hudson tossed 46 solid, unspectacular innings. After adding a sinker to his repertoire in 2017, Hudson all but scrapped the offering this year, sticking to his trusty four-seam-slider mix. The result was an extra tick on the heater, reverse platoon splits and the best swinging strike rate since his first full year as a reliever. The 31-year-old made fewer back-to-back appearances last season, however, and potential disaster nearly struck the two-time Tommy John survivor when an inflamed elbow cut his season short in August. He'll head into 2019 with both one of the more root-forable baseball biographies to pitch to prospective employers and an arm that perhaps more closely resembles the setting of a MacGruber sketch.

Kenley Jansen   RHP   Born: 09/30/87   Age: 31   Bats: B   Throws: R   Height: 6'5"   Weight: 275   Origin: International Free Agent, 2004

YEAR	TEAM	LVL	AGE	W	L	SV	G	GS	IP	H	HR	BB/9	K/9	K	GB%	BABIP	WHIP	ERA	DRA	WARP	MPH	FB%	WHF	CSP
2016	LAN	MLB	28	3	2	47	71	0	68²	35	4	1.4	13.6	104	33%	.238	0.67	1.83	1.93	2.4	96.6	93.8	18.8	53.3
2017	LAN	MLB	29	5	0	41	65	0	68¹	44	5	0.9	14.4	109	40%	.291	0.75	1.32	1.90	2.5	95.7	92	19.8	51.8
2018	LAN	MLB	30	1	5	38	69	0	71²	54	13	2.1	10.3	82	36%	.234	0.99	3.01	2.56	2.0	94.7	94.2	14.6	49
2019	LAN	MLB	31	3	1	31	53	0	55²	44	8	2.4	11.0	68	37%	.285	1.05	3.41	3.80	0.7	94.6	92.8	17.1	50.7

Breakout: 33%   Improve: 44%   Collapse: 34%   Attrition: 12%   MLB: 95%   *Comparables: Billy Wagner, David Robertson, Brad Lidge*

It wasn't a banner year for the Dodger closer, and it speaks to Jansen's brilliance that such a comment is even possible. The Curacao native's River-ian cutter remained potent, with eye-popping vertical and horizontal movement, once again ranking as one of the nastiest, liveliest pitches in the game. Having said that, Jansen started slow, barely touching 90 on the gun with an ERA approaching 6.00 in April. Homers were also a sore spot, as he served up nearly three times as many dingers than the previous three seasons combined. But those on-field woes don't matter, not really at least. During a series in Colorado, Jansen was rushed to the hospital, his heart in atrial fibrillation, an ailment he dealt with twice before in his career. His heart was shocked back into normal rhythm, and he was given medication to abate the symptoms. Fortunately Jansen escaped without further damage, and offseason surgery was performed to rectify the condition. In a rare instance of literalism, sappy or not, Jansen pitched his heart out for his team.

Joe Kelly   RHP   Born: 06/09/88   Age: 31   Bats: R   Throws: R   Height: 6'1"   Weight: 190   Origin: Round 3, 2009 Draft (#98 overall)

YEAR	TEAM	LVL	AGE	W	L	SV	G	GS	IP	H	HR	BB/9	K/9	K	GB%	BABIP	WHIP	ERA	DRA	WARP	MPH	FB%	WHF	CSP
2016	PAW	AAA	28	1	1	2	17	4	35	29	1	1.5	11.8	46	57%	.341	1.00	1.54	2.06	1.2				
2016	BOS	MLB	28	4	0	0	20	6	40	44	5	5.4	10.8	48	48%	.358	1.70	5.18	5.10	0.0	100.4	65.6	11.4	43.8
2017	BOS	MLB	29	4	1	0	54	0	58	42	3	4.2	8.1	52	51%	.252	1.19	2.79	4.00	0.8	100.9	64.4	11.6	45.2
2018	BOS	MLB	30	4	2	2	73	0	65²	57	4	4.4	9.3	68	49%	.301	1.36	4.39	4.56	0.3	100.2	55.4	11.4	45.8
2019	LAN	MLB	31	3	1	0	53	0	55²	47	6	3.6	9.4	58	48%	.294	1.25	3.86	4.32	0.4	99.6	59.9	11.4	44.9

Breakout: 22%   Improve: 46%   Collapse: 20%   Attrition: 11%   MLB: 92%   *Comparables: Ryan Dempster, Tyson Ross, Whitey Ford*

It's been only four-and-a-half years since the Red Sox acquired Kelly and his Great Stuff™, but it feels like he's been pitching in Boston for two decades. Kelly has given Sox fans some memorable moments, from his infamous and ill-fated Cy Young prediction in 2015 to his clutch performance against Tyler Austin in Fight Night at Fenway and even more clutch exclamation point on the eighth inning of the World Series clincher. In 2018, he was occasionally brilliant and often frustrating, because this is Joe Kelly we're talking about. He was dominant in April, May and August. He was dominated in June, July and September. He almost got left off the postseason roster. Then he threw 11 1/3 innings of one-run ball in the playoffs, fanning 13 of the 44 batters he faced and earning the W in Game 4 of the World Series. Anyone who claims to know what the future holds in store for him is lying. He could be a dominant bridge to Kenley Jansen. He could be another big reliever bust. He'll probably end up being both somehow? All we know for sure is Joe Kelly still has Great Stuff™. He just doesn't always know how to use it.

Clayton Kershaw LHP Born: 03/19/88 Age: 31 Bats: L Throws: L Height: 6'4" Weight: 228 Origin: Round 1, 2006 Draft (#7 overall)

YEAR	TEAM	LVL	AGE	W	L	SV	G	GS	IP	H	HR	BB/9	K/9	K	GB%	BABIP	WHIP	ERA	DRA	WARP	MPH	FB%	WHF	CSP
2016	LAN	MLB	28	12	4	0	21	21	149	97	8	0.7	10.4	172	51%	.254	0.72	1.69	2.01	5.7	95.1	50.8	16.1	49.6
2017	LAN	MLB	29	18	4	0	27	27	175	136	23	1.5	10.4	202	49%	.267	0.95	2.31	2.24	6.5	94.3	47.8	15.3	46.5
2018	LAN	MLB	30	9	5	0	26	26	161¹	139	17	1.6	8.6	155	50%	.274	1.04	2.73	3.11	4.1	92.4	41.2	11.8	50.6
2019	*LAN*	*MLB*	*31*	*11*	*7*	*0*	*25*	*25*	*157²*	*128*	*19*	*1.8*	*9.1*	*158*	*48%*	*.277*	*1.01*	*3.35*	*3.73*	*2.9*	*92.9*	*45.4*	*13.9*	*48.7*

Breakout: 10%　Improve: 30%　Collapse: 31%　Attrition: 7%　MLB: 85%　　　　*Comparables: Roger Clemens, CC Sabathia, Brandon Webb*

For the eighth time in his career, Kershaw pitched in the postseason, battling not only opposing lineups, but hot-take artists and straw men alike. And for the eighth time, he was mostly good, but also perhaps not at his peak. A weary fastball barely scraped 91 by October and yet again his bullpen crushed him.

Despite another dry final locker room, the former MVP and three-time Cy Young Award winner was still unquestionably great. For the 10th consecutive year, the ace posted an ERA under 3.00 and a WARP of at least 4.0. He's a surefire Hall-of-Famer. But for the fourth time in five seasons, Kershaw missed some time due to nagging injuries, and he lost nearly two ticks on his fastball—further narrowing the velocity gap between the heater and his secondaries. He struck out fewer than a batter per inning for the first time since 2013, and with the emergence of Walker Buehler, the days of Kershaw being the most dominant force on his own staff might be numbered. The team effectively bought out his opt-out with a one-year contract extension, so at least we know that the greatest Dodger lefty since Koufax will call L.A.'s rotation home for another three seasons.

Ryan Madson RHP Born: 08/28/80 Age: 38 Bats: L Throws: R Height: 6'6" Weight: 234 Origin: Round 9, 1998 Draft (#254 overall)

YEAR	TEAM	LVL	AGE	W	L	SV	G	GS	IP	H	HR	BB/9	K/9	K	GB%	BABIP	WHIP	ERA	DRA	WARP	MPH	FB%	WHF	CSP
2016	OAK	MLB	35	6	7	30	63	0	64²	63	7	2.8	6.8	49	48%	.292	1.28	3.62	4.80	0.1	96.9	72.9	12.5	45.1
2017	OAK	MLB	36	2	4	1	40	0	39¹	25	2	1.4	8.9	39	57%	.242	0.79	2.06	3.81	0.6	96.6	66.6	12.7	45.1
2017	WAS	MLB	36	3	0	1	20	0	19²	13	0	1.4	12.8	28	55%	.310	0.81	1.37	3.16	0.4	97.9	66.6	17.5	49
2018	WAS	MLB	37	2	5	4	49	0	44¹	48	6	3.0	8.3	41	47%	.326	1.42	5.28	5.82	-0.5	97.5	67	13.4	51.6
2018	LAN	MLB	37	0	0	0	9	0	8¹	10	1	1.1	14.0	13	27%	.429	1.32	6.48	1.67	0.3	97.2	67	21.1	45.1
2019	*LAN*	*MLB*	*38*	*2*	*1*	*2*	*46*	*0*	*49*	*42*	*6*	*3.0*	*9.1*	*49*	*47%*	*.294*	*1.19*	*3.82*	*4.27*	*0.3*	*95.6*	*66.7*	*13.6*	*46.5*

Breakout: 20%　Improve: 38%　Collapse: 29%　Attrition: 9%　MLB: 86%　　　　*Comparables: Tim Worrell, Matt Thornton, Bobby Shantz*

It's an unfortunate thing when your worst stretch plays out on the biggest stage, like that one summer Taylor Kitsch starred in two giant blockbusters. Madson tossed 2 1/3 innings in the World Series and allowed all seven of his inherited runners to score, an ignominious record the veteran hurler would surely love to forget. The debacle punctuated a largely disappointing season for the 38-year-old, whose campaign was speckled with extra homers, nagging injuries and his highest ERA since he shifted to the bullpen in 2007. On the bright side, Madson didn't see a ton of degradation to his stuff: His fastball still sat in the mid-to-high 90s and his bread-and-butter changeup still ranked among the league's best at missing bats. Despite his advanced age, Madson should still see late-inning action out of the bullpen, although it's likely to be in a supporting role.

Kenta Maeda RHP Born: 04/11/88 Age: 31 Bats: R Throws: R Height: 6'1" Weight: 175 Origin: International Free Agent, 2016

YEAR	TEAM	LVL	AGE	W	L	SV	G	GS	IP	H	HR	BB/9	K/9	K	GB%	BABIP	WHIP	ERA	DRA	WARP	MPH	FB%	WHF	CSP
2016	LAN	MLB	28	16	11	0	32	32	175²	150	20	2.6	9.2	179	45%	.283	1.14	3.48	3.01	4.7	92.5	42.9	12.6	43.1
2017	LAN	MLB	29	13	6	1	29	25	134¹	121	22	2.3	9.4	140	40%	.278	1.15	4.22	3.53	3.0	93.3	43.4	13	47.1
2018	LAN	MLB	30	8	10	2	39	20	125¹	115	13	3.1	11.0	153	42%	.321	1.26	3.81	2.78	3.6	93.5	44.4	15.8	46.1
2019	*LAN*	*MLB*	*31*	*10*	*7*	*0*	*52*	*23*	*161¹*	*137*	*23*	*2.8*	*10.1*	*182*	*42%*	*.296*	*1.16*	*3.78*	*4.22*	*1.6*	*92.3*	*43.3*	*13.8*	*45.4*

Breakout: 29%　Improve: 59%　Collapse: 22%　Attrition: 10%　MLB: 98%　　　　*Comparables: Zack Greinke, Josh Beckett, Bert Blyleven*

In what has become an annual tradition, much like the Macy's Thanksgiving Day Parade or denouncements of "today's game" from the postseason commentators, the Dodgers shifted Maeda to the bullpen for the final stretch of the season. Maybe they did this to keep him fresh for a playoff run. Perhaps to accommodate the club's abundance of starters. Or, if you're a conspiracy theorist, you might note that the move worked with shocking convenience against several rounds of nearly-triggered contract bonus clauses. Regardless, the Japanese import rode a six-pitch mix to gaudy strikeout totals and a career-best swinging strike rate. For pitchers with at least 125 innings, his DRA ranked 13th-best, ahead of Luis Severino and Corey Kluber. But a hip strain cost Maeda a couple of weeks in June, once again stoking the concerns of fragility that dominated his posting process. It will be interesting to see how the yo-yoing affects Maeda's relationship with the team (if at all), as the parties are betrothed to one another through the 2023 season.

Dustin May RHP Born: 09/06/97 Age: 21 Bats: R Throws: R Height: 6'6" Weight: 180 Origin: Round 3, 2016 Draft (#101 overall)

YEAR	TEAM	LVL	AGE	W	L	SV	G	GS	IP	H	HR	BB/9	K/9	K	GB%	BABIP	WHIP	ERA	DRA	WARP	MPH	FB%	WHF	CSP
2016	DOD	RK	18	0	1	1	10	6	30¹	37	0	1.2	10.1	34	57%	.394	1.35	3.86	4.29	0.4				
2017	GRL	A	19	9	6	0	23	23	123	121	8	1.9	8.3	113	52%	.306	1.20	3.88	4.81	0.7				
2017	RCU	A+	19	0	0	0	2	1	11	6	0	0.8	12.3	15	60%	.240	0.64	0.82	3.57	0.2				
2018	RCU	A+	20	7	3	0	17	17	98¹	91	9	1.6	8.6	94	58%	.294	1.10	3.29	4.47	1.0				
2018	TUL	AA	20	2	2	0	6	6	34¹	27	0	3.1	7.3	28	54%	.267	1.14	3.67	4.38	0.4				
2019	*LAN*	*MLB*	*21*	*8*	*7*	*0*	*22*	*22*	*115¹*	*108*	*15*	*2.8*	*7.7*	*99*	*50%*	*.294*	*1.25*	*4.29*	*4.80*	*0.7*				

Breakout: 4%　Improve: 10%　Collapse: 4%　Attrition: 13%　MLB: 17%　　　　*Comparables: Brad Keller, Antonio Senzatela, Jhoulys Chacin*

Lovingly bestowed the nickname "Gingergaard" on account of flowing locks that burn with the fire of 10,000 suns, May seeks to prove the theory that everything is better with a little ginger. He added a bit of butane to his heater this season, leaving a trail of broken bats and broken spirits in his wake, and he did so in the hitter's haven that is the PCL. Unlike his fellow pole-shaped peers, May has been adept at limiting walks, and while his crossfire delivery might be better served for 80's board games, the combination of deception, stuff and at least two plus pitches make the tall Texan one of the more exciting hurlers in the system.

Hyun-jin Ryu LHP   Born: 03/25/87   Age: 32   Bats: R   Throws: L   Height: 6'3"   Weight: 250   Origin: International Free Agent, 2013

YEAR	TEAM	LVL	AGE	W	L	SV	G	GS	IP	H	HR	BB/9	K/9	K	GB%	BABIP	WHIP	ERA	DRA	WARP	MPH	FB%	WHF	CSP
2016	OKL	AAA	29	0	1	0	3	3	9²	17	2	0.0	8.4	9	44%	.441	1.76	8.38	3.93	0.2				
2016	RCU	A+	29	1	1	0	5	5	18	15	2	0.5	7.0	14	45%	.241	0.89	2.00	2.94	0.5				
2016	LAN	MLB	29	0	1	0	1	1	4²	8	1	3.9	7.7	4	50%	.412	2.14	11.57	3.27	0.1	92.7	56.5	11.8	45.5
2017	LAN	MLB	30	5	9	1	25	24	126²	128	22	3.2	8.2	116	48%	.299	1.37	3.77	4.18	2.0	92.3	36.8	11.4	41
2018	LAN	MLB	31	7	3	0	15	15	82¹	68	9	1.6	9.7	89	47%	.281	1.01	1.97	2.45	2.7	91.9	37	12.6	49.8
2019	LAN	MLB	32	9	7	0	23	23	131	119	17	2.6	9.1	132	45%	.302	1.19	3.82	4.27	1.6	91.2	36.9	11.8	45.4

Breakout: 19%   Improve: 46%   Collapse: 28%   Attrition: 13%   MLB: 93%   *Comparables: Chris Capuano, Wandy Rodriguez, James Shields*

Just to qualify, injuries aren't good. Period. Having said that, when Ryu gruesomely tore his groin muscle right off the bone it reminded us all that some injuries are, in fact, way grosser than others. That said, it paved the way for rookie phenom Walker Buehler to join the rotation, so maybe there was a silver lining (well, at least for everyone other than Ryu himself). When the southpaw returned to the rotation, he dominated, making nine starts down the stretch, posting a 1.88 ERA and punching out a batter per inning. He also took the ball in Game 1 of the NLDS, tossing seven shutout innings and fanning eight Braves in the process. It was an impressive bounce-back season for Ryu, who spun that success into a qualifying offer from the Dodgers to kick off the hot stove.

Dennis Santana RHP   Born: 04/12/96   Age: 23   Bats: R   Throws: R   Height: 6'2"   Weight: 160   Origin: International Free Agent, 2013

YEAR	TEAM	LVL	AGE	W	L	SV	G	GS	IP	H	HR	BB/9	K/9	K	GB%	BABIP	WHIP	ERA	DRA	WARP	MPH	FB%	WHF	CSP
2016	GRL	A	20	5	9	0	25	14	111¹	84	2	4.5	10.0	124	56%	.290	1.26	3.07	3.56	1.8				
2017	RCU	A+	21	5	6	0	17	14	85²	87	5	2.3	9.7	92	50%	.340	1.27	3.57	3.54	1.7				
2017	TUL	AA	21	3	1	0	7	7	32²	32	2	6.3	10.2	37	52%	.337	1.68	5.51	3.48	0.7				
2018	TUL	AA	22	0	2	0	8	8	38²	26	3	3.3	11.9	51	56%	.258	1.03	2.56	2.72	1.2				
2018	OKL	AAA	22	1	1	0	2	2	11	10	0	1.6	11.5	14	45%	.345	1.09	2.45	2.58	0.4				
2018	LAN	MLB	22	1	0	0	1	0	3²	6	0	2.5	9.8	4	31%	.462	1.91	12.27	3.78	0.0	95.6	54.3	14.3	44.3
2019	LAN	MLB	23	2	1	0	5	5	25	21	3	3.9	10.3	29	48%	.304	1.28	3.99	4.48	0.2	95.5	56.2	14.8	45.9

Breakout: 10%   Improve: 13%   Collapse: 10%   Attrition: 21%   MLB: 28%   *Comparables: Max Scherzer, Chris Reed, Jordan Zimmermann*

Like an ACME rocket, Santana enjoyed a meteoric rise in the Dodger organization, exchanging his position at the six for a spot on the mound. After dominating Double- and Triple-A, the 22-year-old got the call to make his big-league debut. Like ACME's most famous customer, however, bad luck consumed the remainder of his campaign. His aforementioned debut came in Coors Field, where he clearly angered the BABIP gods en route to an ERA nearing a baker's dozen. A week later, Santana was scratched from his scheduled start with a balky shoulder. The next day he went on the DL, and the day after he was shifted to the 60-day DL. All that was missing was a handheld wooden sign with the word "Help" crudely written on its face. While a September return to the hill was certainly a welcome sight, it would still be wise for Santana to steer clear of Cal State-Bakersfield, home of the Roadrunners, during the offseason.

Ross Stripling RHP   Born: 11/23/89   Age: 29   Bats: R   Throws: R   Height: 6'3"   Weight: 210   Origin: Round 5, 2012 Draft (#176 overall)

YEAR	TEAM	LVL	AGE	W	L	SV	G	GS	IP	H	HR	BB/9	K/9	K	GB%	BABIP	WHIP	ERA	DRA	WARP	MPH	FB%	WHF	CSP
2016	OKL	AAA	26	0	2	0	5	4	16²	20	2	1.1	9.2	17	38%	.360	1.32	3.78	3.02	0.4				
2016	LAN	MLB	26	5	9	0	22	14	100	96	10	2.7	6.7	74	52%	.283	1.26	3.96	3.28	2.3	93.3	46.5	9.1	45.9
2017	LAN	MLB	27	3	5	2	49	2	74¹	69	10	2.3	9.0	74	51%	.294	1.18	3.75	3.23	1.6	94.5	38.4	12	44.1
2018	LAN	MLB	28	8	6	0	33	21	122	123	18	1.6	10.0	136	47%	.322	1.19	3.02	2.94	3.3	93.8	41.1	12.5	47.3
2019	LAN	MLB	29	10	7	0	52	23	161¹	140	20	2.5	9.3	168	48%	.298	1.15	3.62	4.04	2.4	93.2	41.8	11.5	45.9

Breakout: 25%   Improve: 50%   Collapse: 19%   Attrition: 4%   MLB: 91%   *Comparables: Taylor Buchholz, Shaun Marcum, Boof Bonser*

"I want you to hit me, as hard as you can." It's a notorious line from *Fight Club*, and it's also an instruction given to Stripling from Dodgers pitching coach Rick Honeycutt. Ok, fine, maybe it was more along the lines of "throw your curveball as hard as you can," but still. The result was stark, as the 28-year-old Texan's tunnel on the curve began to mirror that of his fastball, paving the way for more deception and more strikeouts. Stripling cruised to a 1.98 ERA in his first 11 starts, good enough for his first all-star berth. Minor injuries and staff depth limited him to only 10 mediocre starts and some time in the bullpen after July 1, but it was still a breakout campaign for Stripling, who also dabbles as a Series 7 licensed stockbroker. If he maintains this season's production, he'll have a much bigger portfolio to invest and play with in the very near future.

Julio Urias LHP   Born: 08/12/96   Age: 22   Bats: L   Throws: L   Height: 6'0"   Weight: 215   Origin: International Free Agent, 2012

YEAR	TEAM	LVL	AGE	W	L	SV	G	GS	IP	H	HR	BB/9	K/9	K	GB%	BABIP	WHIP	ERA	DRA	WARP	MPH	FB%	WHF	CSP
2016	OKL	AAA	19	5	1	0	11	7	45	31	2	1.6	9.8	49	54%	.269	0.87	1.40	2.66	1.4				
2016	LAN	MLB	19	5	2	0	18	15	77	81	5	3.6	9.8	84	45%	.358	1.45	3.39	3.42	1.7	95.4	55.8	11.7	44.3
2017	LAN	MLB	20	0	2	0	5	5	23¹	23	1	5.4	4.2	11	43%	.293	1.59	5.40	5.35	0.1	95.2	52	10.2	43.2
2017	OKL	AAA	20	3	0	0	6	6	31¹	20	1	4.3	9.2	32	47%	.253	1.12	2.59	2.97	0.9				
2018	LAN	MLB	21	0	0	0	3	0	4	1	0	0.0	15.8	7	50%	.167	0.25	0.00	1.89	0.1	95.4	69	22.4	58.6
2019	LAN	MLB	22	5	3	0	25	11	70¹	58	8	3.8	10.5	82	44%	.304	1.25	3.76	4.22	0.7	95.3	57.7	12.3	52

Breakout: 24%   Improve: 45%   Collapse: 12%   Attrition: 17%   MLB: 75%   *Comparables: Lance McCullers, Brett Cecil, Madison Bumgarner*

Everybody loves a comeback story. Everybody loves a heralded young phenom getting the chance to fulfill their potential. Affectionately dubbed "The Teenager," Urias has made fawning parents of us all, swelling with pride during his debut as a 19-year-old prodigy, and rooting unconditionally for a safe and healthy return to the bump after shoulder surgery limited him to 70 1/3 innings over the last two seasons. Well, the southpaw is back. No longer a teenager worrying about borrowing the car keys and going to the homecoming dance (those are still teenager things, right?), Urias can now shift his attention to full-on adult things like maintaining his fastball velocity and taking the ball every fifth day for the crown jewel of the country's second biggest media market. In his brief return to the big club, Urias ran his heater up to 97 mph, and showed enough in a small sample to surprise on both the NLCS and World Series rosters. Better yet, Dave Roberts declared that Urias would be built back up as a starter for 2019. So far, so good. And yet, we still worry.

Mitch White RHP Born: 12/28/94 Age: 24 Bats: R Throws: R Height: 6'4" Weight: 207 Origin: Round 2, 2016 Draft (#65 overall)

YEAR	TEAM	LVL	AGE	W	L	SV	G	GS	IP	H	HR	BB/9	K/9	K	GB%	BABIP	WHIP	ERA	DRA	WARP	MPH	FB%	WHF	CSP
2016	GRL	A	21	0	0	0	8	4	16	3	0	3.4	11.2	20	72%	.094	0.56	0.00	3.32	0.3				
2017	RCU	A+	22	-2	1	0	9	9	38²	26	0	3.7	11.4	49	64%	.286	1.09	3.72	2.78	1.1				
2017	TUL	AA	22	1	1	0	7	7	28	17	2	4.2	10.0	31	51%	.217	1.07	2.57	3.08	0.7				
2018	TUL	AA	23	6	7	0	22	22	105¹	114	12	2.9	7.5	88	49%	.317	1.41	4.53	5.32	0.0				
2019	LAN	MLB	24	6	6	0	21	21	87²	79	12	3.5	8.4	81	49%	.291	1.30	4.38	4.91	0.4				

Breakout: 10%   Improve: 19%   Collapse: 11%   Attrition: 24%   MLB: 41%   Comparables: *Kyle Weiland, Blake Wood, Scott Barlow*

Your assessment of White's 2018 might hinge on your outlook in life (you know, not to get too deep or anything). The sunshine and puppy dogs version of the former second rounder's campaign centers around his career high in innings. Meanwhile, on the glass-half-empty side sits basically everything else. White certainly got off on the wrong foot, logging an ERA touching 10.00 through five May starts, and his stat line and velocity both never really recovered. He's not particularly young and it's hard to envision him as anything more than a back-end starter the Dodgers don't have room for. It may be time for the Dodgers to pull the bullpen card and see if his stuff jumps (and his arm stays attached) in shorter bursts.

LINEOUTS

Hitters

HITTER	POS	TEAM	LVL	AGE	PA	R	2B	3B	HR	RBI	BB	K	SB	CS	AVG/OBP/SLG	DRC+	VORP	BABIP	BRR	FRAA	WARP
Ronny Brito	SS	OGD	Rk	19	244	37	11	0	11	52	21	74	1	6	.288/.352/.489	115	16.7	.382	-0.7	SS(38): 1.9, 2B(5): 0.3	1.5
Jeter Downs	2B	DYT	A	19	524	63	23	2	13	47	52	103	37	10	.257/.351/.402	121	23.2	.306	-1.6	2B(73): -2.9, SS(43): -9.3	1.6
Rocky Gale	C	OKL	AAA	30	318	24	14	2	4	34	12	50	1	2	.281/.305/.383	76	8.6	.322	-1.6	C(84): 14.1, 2B(1): 0.0	2.0
	C	LAN	MLB	30	2	0	0	0	0	0	0	1	0	0	.000/.000/.000	87	-0.5	.000	0.0	C(2): 0.0	0.0
Starling Heredia	OF	GRL	A	19	220	18	9	1	6	26	16	81	3	0	.182/.245/.325	65	-1.6	.267	-1.6	LF(33): -2.1, RF(6): -1.1	-1.1
Edwin Rios	3B	OKL	AAA	24	341	45	25	0	10	55	23	110	0	1	.304/.355/.482	81	16.5	.433	-2.4	3B(38): -4.2, 1B(28): -1.3	-0.8
Andrew Toles	LF	OKL	AAA	26	275	43	17	1	7	39	13	56	3	2	.306/.345/.461	92	12.3	.367	0.3	LF(37): -0.6, CF(19): 0.8	0.6
	LF	LAN	MLB	26	32	5	2	0	0	4	2	8	1	0	.233/.281/.300	83	0.1	.318	0.1	CF(8): -0.2, LF(2): -0.1	0.0
Connor Wong	C	RCU	A+	22	431	64	20	2	19	60	38	138	6	2	.269/.350/.480	116	27.8	.372	0.9	C(71): 0.7, 2B(11): -0.5	2.6

Signed for a cool $2 million out of the Dominican in 2015, **Ronny Brito** drove in eight runs in a July game for the Ogden Raptors. For all you math people out there, that comes out to a quarter mil per RBI. ⓧ As a promising defender behind the dish, **Diego Cartaya** signed a $2.5 million contract as a 16-year-old out of Venezuela, immediately making him one of the richest, let's say, 83,500 teenagers in Los Angeles. Reality show pending. ⓧ In his first full pro season **Jeter Downs** flashed his namesake's shortstop range, but not his namesake's blinkered refusal to move to a more appropriate defensive home; now fully ensconced at the keystone, the juice in his bat and a broad set of average tools will likely carry him to The Show. ⓧ Despite a name perhaps more fitting for an SEC defensive backs coach, **Rocky Gale** once again displayed extraordinary framing skills behind the dish. Those skills haven't translated to the batter's box, however, and a career .637 minor-league OPS likely keeps him relegated to third catcher status. ⓧ **Starling Heredia** followed up a breakout 2017 with a pretty middling 2018, a reminder that sometimes electric young superstars with unlimited potential turn into Shia Labeouf, and other times they turn into, well, Shia Labeouf. ⓧ As usual, **Edwin Rios** hit a lot this year, but he also hit for less power and started the season on the shelf due to an ominous, undisclosed injury. To boot, if his defense takes another step back, it might fall off the side of the boat. ⓧ A balky hammy and a crowded big-league outfield conspired to keep **Andrew Toles** from showing he can maintain above-average offensive performance more than 120 at-bats at a time. ⓧ The Dodgers saw an Austin Barnes-type when drafting athletic, positionally-flexible backstop **Connor Wong**, which has already made the major-league version very uncomfortable.

Pitchers

PITCHER	TEAM	LVL	AGE	W	L	SV	G	GS	IP	H	HR	BB/9	K/9	K	GB%	BABIP	WHIP	ERA	DRA	WARP	MPH	FB%	WHF	CSP
J.T. Chargois	OKL	AAA	27	1	0	0	11	0	15	13	0	4.2	5.4	9	47%	.289	1.33	1.80	3.74	0.2				
	LAN	MLB	27	2	4	0	39	0	32^1	26	4	4.2	11.1	40	63%	.297	1.27	3.34	3.33	0.6	97.1	47.9	13.9	47.8
Yimi Garcia	OKL	AAA	27	1	0	1	14	0	14^2	16	2	0.0	8.6	14	42%	.326	1.09	4.30	2.23	0.5				
	LAN	MLB	27	1	2	0	25	0	22^1	29	7	1.6	7.7	19	36%	.319	1.48	5.64	6.19	-0.3	96.6	56.4	12.4	51.5
Erik Goeddel	TAC	AAA	29	1	0	4	9	0	9	6	0	4.0	10.0	10	36%	.273	1.11	0.00	2.04	0.3				
	SEA	MLB	29	2	0	0	5	0	7^1	4	0	6.1	11.0	9	40%	.267	1.23	1.23	2.46	0.2	93.1	52.4	18.5	37.7
	LAN	MLB	29	1	0	0	26	0	29^1	22	4	4.6	10.7	35	48%	.254	1.26	3.38	3.60	0.4	93.7	49.8	16	42.3
Tony Gonsolin	RCU	A+	24	4	2	0	17	17	83^2	72	5	2.8	11.4	106	38%	.319	1.17	2.69	4.03	1.3				
	TUL	AA	24	6	0	0	9	9	44^1	32	3	3.2	9.9	49	39%	.261	1.08	2.44	3.45	1.0				
Marshall Kasowski	GRL	A	23	0	1	0	15	1	28	13	1	5.8	15.8	49	57%	.250	1.11	2.57	3.27	0.5				
	RCU	A+	23	2	0	4	16	0	23^2	10	1	4.2	16.7	44	44%	.273	0.89	1.14	1.80	0.9				
	TUL	AA	23	0	0	1	10	0	13	7	2	6.2	12.5	18	31%	.208	1.23	2.77	3.83	0.2				
Adam Liberatore	LAN	MLB	31	2	1	0	17	0	13	10	1	5.5	8.3	12	64%	.281	1.38	2.77	3.96	0.1	92.3	61.3	10.5	43.1
	OKL	AAA	31	2	2	0	18	0	17^1	29	3	3.1	8.8	17	41%	.413	2.02	5.19	2.68	0.5				
Zach McAllister	CLE	MLB	30	1	2	0	41	0	41^2	47	7	2.2	7.3	34	43%	.315	1.37	4.97	4.44	0.2	97.1	76.2	11.1	52.7
	DET	MLB	30	0	0	0	3	0	3^1	10	1	0.0	13.5	5	36%	.692	3.00	21.60	4.81	0.0	98.0	73.8	12.5	56.5
	OKL	AAA	30	1	1	0	5	0	6	6	0	3.0	13.5	9	40%	.400	1.33	9.00	3.46	0.1				
Adam McCreery	MIS	AA	25	2	5	2	34	0	47	48	1	6.3	11.7	61	57%	.376	1.72	3.83	3.43	0.8				
	ATL	MLB	25	0	0	0	1	0	1	4	0	0.0	18.0	2	40%	.800	4.00	18.00	8.51	0.0	93.3	43.3	13.3	54.6
	GWN	AAA	25	0	0	0	8	0	7^2	3	0	4.7	11.7	10	87%	.200	0.91	2.35	1.73	0.3				
Kevin Quackenbush	CIN	MLB	29	0	1	0	10	0	9	13	3	6.0	7.0	7	38%	.345	2.11	11.00	6.39	-0.2	91.8	68.6	11.1	47
	LOU	AAA	29	1	2	25	47	0	47	39	2	2.1	10.7	56	34%	.311	1.06	2.68	2.97	1.2				
Josh Sborz	TUL	AA	24	3	1	6	13	0	16^1	11	1	2.8	13.2	24	35%	.303	0.98	2.76	2.21	0.5				
	OKL	AAA	24	1	1	0	33	0	37	38	0	3.6	11.4	47	43%	.388	1.43	4.38	3.64	0.6				
Jordan Sheffield	RCU	A+	23	1	3	0	14	7	34	39	8	5.3	10.6	40	44%	.337	1.74	6.88	4.83	0.2				
Brock Stewart	LAN	MLB	26	0	1	0	9	2	17^2	23	4	4.6	7.1	14	47%	.317	1.81	6.11	5.35	-0.1	92.5	61.9	11.6	45.5
	OKL	AAA	26	3	3	0	19	19	96^1	83	7	2.7	7.5	80	41%	.274	1.16	2.99	3.42	2.3				

J.T. Chargois flirted with 99 mph and a slider that got grounders almost three-quarters of the time, but his return to the big leagues was spoiled by nerve irritation in his neck that cost the righty over a month of the season. ⓧ Two truths and a lie about **Yimi Garcia**: He pitched for the first time since 2016, his velocity was the highest since 2015 and he served up almost three dingers per nine innings. Oops, that's three truths. ⓧ One of the words to describe **Erik Goeddel's** 2018 season is "whiffy" (I know, but we're making it happen), as the righty tallied one of the better swinging strike rates in all of baseball. Sadly, the other descriptor is "injured" as frequent DL stints led to an August shut down. ⓧ A former two-way player at St. Mary's, **Tony Gonsolin** flew up prospect lists, carving up two levels thanks to a mid-90s fastball, sharp breaking ball and a sick mustache straight out of a 1970s B-movie. ⓧ The Dodgers failed to sign their first-rounder, leaving West Virginia power arm **Michael Grove** as the crown jewel of the draft class. He'll hope to reclaim his mid-90s heater and high-spin-rate slider upon his recovery from Tommy John surgery. ⓧ No hurler in the minor leagues averaged more strikeouts per nine innings than **Marshall Kasowski**, whose unorthodox delivery and significantly improved control helped the former 13th rounder mow through three levels in 2018. ⓧ The Dodgers took a $2 million flyer on **Tom Koehler** in what turned out to be their biggest offseason splurge. Sadly the New York native injured his shoulder in Spring Training and was shut down for good following surgery in July. ⓧ It was the best of times and it was the worst of times for **Adam Liberatore** this season. He closed out a team no-hitter in May, but nagging injuries shut him down for good in August, when he was released. He'll need that second city soon. ⓧ Not much went right in 2018 for **Zach McAllister**, but after two DFAs and three teams in the span of three weeks, at least he got to add a couple extra jerseys to his collection. ⓧ If massive lefties with stuff are your jam, **Adam McCreery**'s spot on the chart is somewhere between no. 1 hit and Pitbull. Control isn't his friend, but he definitely has a major-league arm. ⓧ **Kevin Quackenbush** could provide some bullpen depth, assuming he finds a way to transfer those minor league ratios to the majors again. The Dodgers will soon find out if they should have just stuck with one of their many birds in hand. ⓧ Righty **Josh Sborz** completed his first full season as a reliever, nearly doubling his strikeout rate in just over 50 innings across Double- and Triple-A. ⓧ **Jordan Sheffield** spent his season collecting strikeouts, walks, homers and days spent on the DL with a "mild" forearm strain. Since three of those four are less than ideal, Sheffield is the human version of the gritted teeth emoji. ⓧ Hop on the I-40 west for about 1,300 miles before taking the I-5 straight to Dodger Stadium. It's the road from Oklahoma City to Los Angeles that **Brock Stewart** travelled six times in 2018, with middling big-league results along the way.

MIAMI MARLINS

Essay by Michael Clair

Player comments by Eddy Almaguer and BP staff

The home run sculpture is gone. "Homer," designed by American artist Red Groom—which means it is capital-A Art—now resides outside the stadium and will be replaced in the park by a three-tier social game-watching area. While fans will get to mill around and sample food and beer, the seven-story home run sculpture will instead hang out on the street like a neon obelisk, marking the end of an era of Miami baseball.

And that's a bummer. The flipping dolphins and flamingos shown in a kaleidoscope of bright colors and flashing lights was such an insane and unique thing to reside in a baseball stadium. It's the kind of installation you'd imagine some megalomaniacal owner would have installed in the 1970s, like when Ewing Kauffman placed a crown over the Royals' center-field. That kind of un-focus-group-tested device seems to be the very opposite of what the Derek Jeter-fronted new Marlins ownership group now represents.

Of course, there could be one other reason why the new owners wanted it gone beyond merely tearing down the most obvious and unmistakable touch of Jeffrey Loria's tenure at the top of the team: The Marlins just didn't hit many home runs. The device exists to revel in the glory of 400-something-foot blasts, and in a post-Stanton world the Marlins hit the fewest in the Majors last year, with only 57 coming at home. Perhaps Jeter looked at the hulking monstrosity as if it were mocking him with its inaction. Maybe when he slept he dreamt of an oceanside pastiche of aquatic animals laughing at him.

But our dear, sweet friend "Homer" wasn't just something beautiful to look at it during a 98-loss Marlins season. It was a seven-story mirror held up to the Marlins' existence.

They are both bright and colorful, piscine, and largely taxpayer-funded. The reason why the art piece wasn't torn down for scrap parts or sent away for prospects was that Miami-Dade County paid $2.5 million for the obelisk. According to MarketWatch, because of bonds and other economics things I'll never understand, the county will have spent about $2.6 billion for Miami's stadium through 2049—which makes "Homer" an absolute steal.

MARLINS PROSPECTUS
2018 W-L: 63-98, 5TH IN NL EAST

Pythag	.357	29th	B-Age	27.5	10th
RS/G	3.66	30th	P-Age	27.3	8th
RA/G	5.02	24th	Salary	$99.5M	23rd
DRC+	81	29th	M$/MW	$5.9M	7th
DRA	4.78	23rd	DL Days	1013	12th
FIP	4.52	23rd	$ on DL	13%	9th
DER	.709	10th			

407'
386'
392'
344'
335'

- Opened 2012
- Retractable roof
- Natural surface
- Fence profile: 7' to 11'6"

Three-Year Park Factors

Runs	Runs/RH	Runs/LH	HR/RH	HR/LH
91	91	91	86	93

Top Hitter WARP	4.3 J.T. Realmuto
Top Pitcher WARP	2.6 Jose Urena
Top Prospect	Victor Victor Mesa

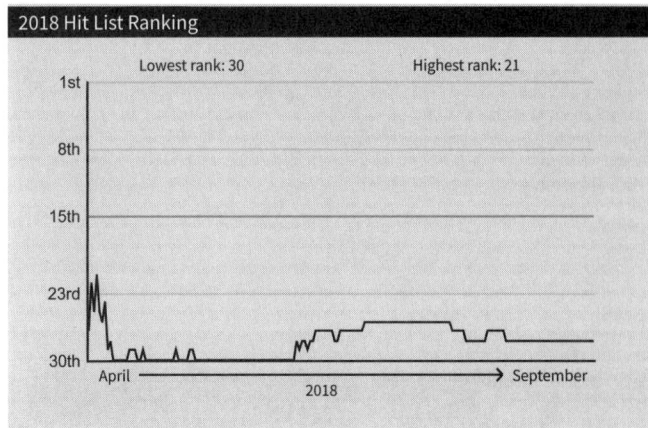

2018 Hit List Ranking

Lowest rank: 30   Highest rank: 21

April   2018   September

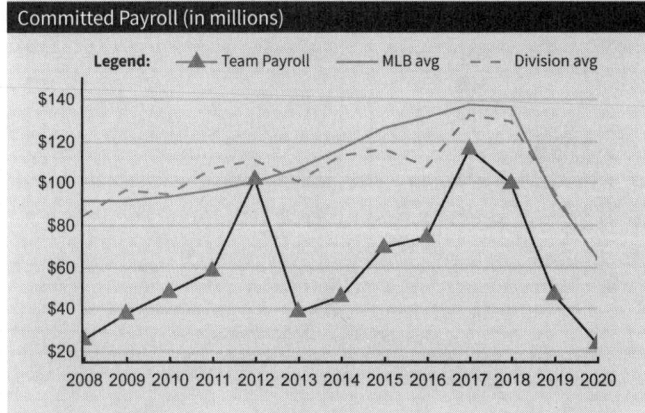

Committed Payroll (in millions)

Legend: ▲ Team Payroll — MLB avg - - - Division avg

2008 2009 2010 2011 2012 2013 2014 2015 2016 2017 2018 2019 2020

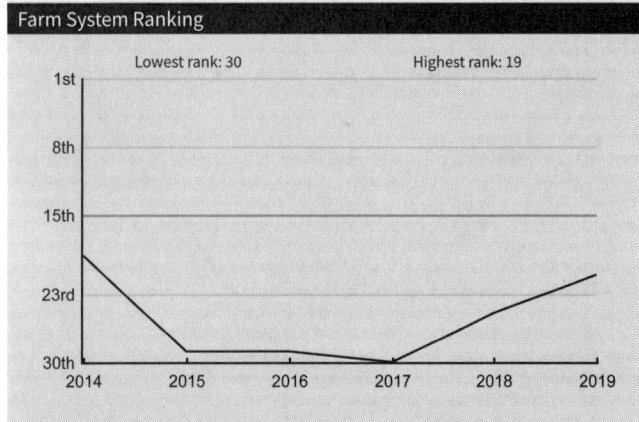

Farm System Ranking

Lowest rank: 30   Highest rank: 19

2014   2015   2016   2017   2018   2019

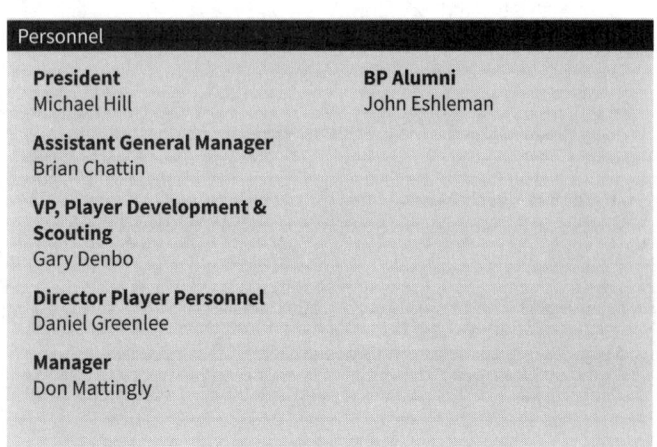

Personnel

President
Michael Hill

BP Alumni
John Eshleman

Assistant General Manager
Brian Chattin

VP, Player Development & Scouting
Gary Denbo

Director Player Personnel
Daniel Greenlee

Manager
Don Mattingly

Most importantly, both the team and the sculpture are trapped in an endlessly repeating cycle that can seemingly never be broken. Like Sisyphus pushing his rock up the hill, or Homer Simpson forever returning to Sector 7G no matter what transpired in the preceding half hour, so go the Marlins. Like the fish in "Homer," the Marlins rise, fall, disappear, rise again to win a World Series and then go back under the water to start again. If you believe in reincarnation, then perhaps the team just hasn't learned the lesson that will allow them to move to another stage of existence.

That doesn't just apply to their competitive windows, either. As soon as the postseason ended, the team started promoting their new uniforms with the hashtag #OurColores. While other teams were making moves, the Marlins unveiled a black-blue-and-pinkish rebrand that represented the team's *third* logo and uniform change in their short history. For comparison, the Rockies, who also joined the Majors in 1993, are still rocking the same unis, with a few alternates added to the set. (Oh, and as Craig Mish reported, Billy the Marlin will be getting an update with a smaller bill and thinner body. When you're in South Beach, even your mascot's gotta be fit.)

Unfortunately, while Miami attained the heights of World Series success in 1997 and 2003, they haven't reached the postseason since. Only Seattle has been caught in a longer drought. That's not going to end any time soon for the Marlins, with the team hopefully looking toward 2020—the time that once heralded the age of flying cars and robot maids—for its next competitive window. That's because it wasn't just the home run sculpture that the new owners kicked out of the stadium, but the team's best players, too. The jerseys may change with the whims of each new ownership group, but the prevailing team-building strategy has not.

Here, for those that don't spend every moment thinking of the Marlins rebuilds, is a brief history:

- The 1997 World Series-winning ballclub was dismantled so quickly, the trophy maker probably hadn't laser-etched the names in yet.

- They slashed payroll at the end of the 2005 season and traded Carlos Delgado, Paul Lo Duca, Mike Lowell, Juan Pierre and Josh Beckett in a single go.

- After moving into their new digs in 2011, the team flashed an impressive amount of cash as if to say "We're not the Florida Marlins anymore. We're the *Miami* Marlins." Mark Buehrle, Jose Reyes, and Heath Bell were all signed … and a year later, none of them were Miami Marlins.

And then last season came with the most WAR traded in a single offseason since the 1899 Louisville Colonels. Marcell Ozuna was sent to the Cardinals, Christian Yelich won the NL MVP and came a game shy of a World Series with the

Brewers, and Giancarlo Stanton fulfilled the prophecies when he was shipped to New York. And now, JT Realmuto-arguably the best catcher in the game—made it clear that he'd be out of Miami the moment free agency allowed it. It's not easy to rebuild when your next generation of stars don't want to be built around.

Those trades weren't the only moves that made it difficult for the local fan base to remember that they're Marlins fans. Despite having one of the most popular players in recent baseball history as the face of the group, one who managed to avoid almost every controversy possible throughout a playing career in a city that feasted on them, Jeter and Co. couldn't help but jump(throw) from scandal to scandal in the early going.

Longtime Marlins and Marlins employees like Jeff Conine were let go. A scout was fired while he was in the hospital receiving cancer treatment. And even Marlins Man, the second-most infamous orange man in America, got in a public fight with Jeter, arguing that he was paying Major League prices for Triple-A talent. He even threatened to wear another team's gear. Shockingly, Jeter didn't bite when he was offered a chance to ride in the "Marlins Car" with Marlins Man to help ingratiate himself to the local fans. Which, honestly, makes me wish there was a two-person sitcom about Jeter and Marlins Man solving petty crimes around Miami in hopes of developing the fanbase. Who wouldn't tune in?

Now that they've cleaned house, it's time to fill the stadium again. To that end, the Marlins seem committed to creating a unique (at least among Major League Baseball teams) fan atmosphere. The new logo is fun in a late-night "Miami Vice" kind of way. Loria may have brought in the Home Run Sculpture and filled the stadium with art (there was even a Roy Lichtenstein hanging on the walls—how many stadiums can claim that?), but now there will be the social area and a standing room only section with cheaper tickets. Looking to create the same atmosphere that has made English soccer and Caribbean Series games so much fun, the space will be replaced with a cheering section complete with fans encouraged to bring flags and musical instruments. It's all in the name of making something that cannot be duplicated from your couch or the bar or while staring at your phone and avoiding conversation at a cocktail party. If successful, this would put the Marlins ahead of the rest of the league, who will likely be trying similar tactics in hopes of getting fans through the turnstiles.

Interestingly enough, it's a kind of reversal from recent marketing efforts that seemed to showcase everything that *wasn't* on the field. Every ballpark features insane Man vs. Food dining options, Kidz Zonez, and enough shops to fill a suburban mall that seem to say, "Hey, there's plenty to do here even if you don't like baseball." Now the Marlins want the biggest fans, the ones who will wave flags and invent chants and songs for the entire lineup, to inspire others to do the same.

The question now is: Where are the fans going to come from?

Last year saw attendance drop to just over 10,000 fans a game. That was, in part, because the Marlins changed how they reported ticket sales, but it also was only 700 fans more per night than Loria's old 2004 Expos, who set the record for the lowest per-game attendance in the year before they moved to Washington. This is a new low for a team that has only finished in the top half of NL attendance once—1997—and has finished last for the previous six seasons.

Sure, the team has new ownership and new jerseys and the outfield wall will be painted a new color and fans will get sing to their heart's content, but more than any of that, fans tend to want to watch a winning baseball team. Some fanbases can rally behind a cry of "Trust the Process," but how does one do it when the process is all they've known?

It's not all doom and gloom, and you'll surely see articles soon saying that the Marlins are approaching winning the "right" way—whatever that is. While some may have argued that the teardown didn't need to happen—that a combination of Stanton, Yelich, and Ozuna represented one of the best outfields in the game and was only a few pieces away from contending—the Marlins are now in the league's toughest division. The Braves and Phillies have seen their rebuilds bear fruit and have begun adding the necessary star power to fill the gaps, while the Mets and Nationals are refusing to say goodbye to their own stranglehold atop the division. It's hard to imagine an 85-win team sneaking their way through the division.

So, while the returns for Miami's outfield trio may have been underwhelming, they at least gave the Marlins system plenty of quantity from which a star could emerge. Perhaps it will be Monte Harrison, who hit 19 home runs in Double-A (he also struck out 215 times.) Or maybe Lewis Brinson's abysmal 2017, that saw him hit .199 with a 120/17 K/BB ratio was only the growing pains of a future star. The team also loaded up on international pool money and, in the kind of thing that seems ripped from "Catch-22," landed Cuban star Victor Victor Mesa and his brother Victor Mesa Jr.

Unfortunately, there are no guarantees and prospects are still a crapshoot. For example, the Astros may have found stars in Alex Bregman and Carlos Correa, with Kyle Tucker looking every bit a top-flight prospect, but Jon Singleton, Mark Appel and Francis Martes didn't make the cut despite the once-glowing scouting reports. There are no guarantees that the Marlins' prospects will ever make an impact the way their three-headed home run-hitting monster of an outfield ever did. With more teams trying to create their own super team, the margins are slimmer than ever before, too.

The Marlins are rebuilding. The Marlins have new uniforms and a new direction. You have heard that before and it's happening again. While Marlins fans will hope a third World

Series ballclub is coalescing in the minors, the home run sculpture will be watching from outside the stadium. The team is hoping the fans will choose to do it from inside. ■

—Michael Clair writes for MLB's Cut4.

HITTERS

Brian Anderson   3B   Born: 05/19/93   Age: 26   Bats: R   Throws: R   Height: 6'3"   Weight: 185   Origin: Round 3, 2014 Draft (#76 overall)

YEAR	TEAM	LVL	AGE	PA	R	2B	3B	HR	RBI	BB	K	SB	CS	AVG/OBP/SLG	DRC+	VORP	BABIP	BRR	FRAA	WARP
2016	JUP	A+	23	207	27	12	2	3	25	22	38	3	0	.302/.377/.440	111	13.9	.364	-1.5	3B(47): 8.5	1.7
2016	JAX	AA	23	345	38	9	1	8	40	36	59	0	0	.243/.330/.359	112	13.7	.274	0.2	3B(85): 12.7	3.2
2017	JAX	AA	24	361	53	14	3	14	55	36	71	1	1	.251/.341/.450	125	19.8	.277	-1.3	3B(82): 9.0	3.3
2017	NWO	AAA	24	137	21	7	0	8	26	12	27	0	1	.339/.416/.602	128	20.8	.376	-0.4	3B(30): 5.0	1.1
2017	MIA	MLB	24	95	11	7	1	0	8	10	28	0	0	.262/.337/.369	68	4.6	.386	1.0	3B(25): -2.2	-0.1
2018	MIA	MLB	25	670	87	34	4	11	65	62	129	2	4	.273/.357/.400	100	43.2	.332	2.3	RF(91): -1.1, 3B(71): -9.0	1.2
2019	MIA	MLB	26	487	52	21	3	13	56	44	106	1	1	.247/.332/.394	104	18.0	.303	1.9	RF -2	1.7

Breakout: 4%   Improve: 41%   Collapse: 6%   Attrition: 13%   MLB: 86%   *Comparables: Stephen Piscotty, Chris Parmelee, Shin-Soo Choo*

There weren't many big-league bright spots for the Marlins last season, but Anderson was certainly one of them. He proved to be durable, starting all but six games on the season, and his bat, though lacking in thump, played consistently enough that he wasn't a detriment in the lineup. On a forgettable team, Anderson's rookie campaign became an afterthought, but his ability to play an average third base and a passable right field, walk at a slightly above-average rate and temper his strikeouts creates the foundation for a consistent regular. The one wish-list item would be to hit for more power, but with a ground-ball rate north of 50 percent and a cavernous ballpark to call home, a season with 15 home runs might be the best-case scenario.

Will Banfield   C   Born: 11/18/99   Age: 19   Bats: R   Throws: R   Height: 6'0"   Weight: 200   Origin: Round 2, 2018 Draft (#69 overall)

YEAR	TEAM	LVL	AGE	PA	R	2B	3B	HR	RBI	BB	K	SB	CS	AVG/OBP/SLG	DRC+	VORP	BABIP	BRR	FRAA	WARP
2018	MRL	RK	18	94	7	8	1	0	14	7	28	0	1	.256/.330/.378	87	1.8	.375	-0.9	C(22): 1.2	0.3
2018	GRB	A	18	52	5	0	0	3	4	4	15	0	0	.208/.269/.396	108	0.7	.233	0.1	C(14): 0.1	0.3
2019	MIA	MLB	19	251	18	8	0	6	24	9	84	0	0	.175/.203/.275	25	-12.5	.237	-0.8	C 0	-1.3

Breakout: 0%   Improve: 7%   Collapse: 1%   Attrition: 4%   MLB: 13%   *Comparables: Francisco Pena, Nomar Mazara, Adalberto Mondesi*

Taken with the nicest pick of the 2018 draft, Banfield is considered the Marlins' catcher of the future. He has everything you could want from the defensive spectrum: strong athleticism, the foundation for pitch-framing and a plus arm to nail runners. With that alone, Banfield is an easy pick to stay behind the plate. He exhibits plus raw power and has above-average bat speed, but his over-aggressiveness and lack of off-speed awareness raise questions about the future of the hit tool. He reached Low-A as an 18-year-old, but expect the Marlins to slow roll the rest of the way to ensure he properly develops.

Lewis Brinson   CF   Born: 05/08/94   Age: 25   Bats: R   Throws: R   Height: 6'3"   Weight: 195   Origin: Round 1, 2012 Draft (#29 overall)

YEAR	TEAM	LVL	AGE	PA	R	2B	3B	HR	RBI	BB	K	SB	CS	AVG/OBP/SLG	DRC+	VORP	BABIP	BRR	FRAA	WARP
2016	FRI	AA	22	326	46	14	6	11	40	17	64	11	4	.237/.280/.431	105	3.6	.264	-0.4	CF(65): -0.2, RF(5): -1.1	0.9
2016	CSP	AAA	22	93	14	9	0	4	20	2	21	4	2	.382/.387/.618	108	8.9	.455	-0.1	CF(23): 6.0	1.0
2017	MIL	MLB	23	55	2	0	1	2	3	7	17	1	0	.106/.236/.277	76	-3.4	.107	-0.5	CF(8): 0.4, LF(8): -0.1	0.0
2017	CSP	AAA	23	340	66	22	4	13	48	32	62	11	5	.331/.400/.562	136	27.2	.377	1.6	CF(61): 1.1, RF(6): 0.0	3.3
2018	MIA	MLB	24	406	31	10	5	11	42	17	120	2	1	.199/.240/.338	59	-5.2	.257	-0.9	CF(106): 3.3	-0.4
2019	MIA	MLB	25	471	53	20	4	14	53	31	123	7	3	.232/.292/.396	87	9.8	.291	-1.1	CF 7	1.8

Breakout: 6%   Improve: 41%   Collapse: 10%   Attrition: 33%   MLB: 84%   *Comparables: Brian Anderson, Ryan Kalish, Kirk Nieuwenhuis*

By all accounts, the Marlins did the right thing with Lewis Brinson — they let him play. But an OPS that couldn't cross the .600 mark stings more when you were the headliner of the trade that sent away the MVP. However, Brinson needed the major-league reps after showing he was done mastering Triple-A. The Florida native struggled mightily in every facet of the game, including defense, the part that was supposed to make up for his rawness at the plate. The impact profile is still there. His plus speed and power haven't disappeared and the ceiling remains a 25-25 player at peak. But even with a marginal improvement in the final month of 2018, Brinson is still very much a work in progress.

Starlin Castro   2B   Born: 03/24/90   Age: 29   Bats: R   Throws: R   Height: 6'2"   Weight: 230   Origin: International Free Agent, 2006

YEAR	TEAM	LVL	AGE	PA	R	2B	3B	HR	RBI	BB	K	SB	CS	AVG/OBP/SLG	DRC+	VORP	BABIP	BRR	FRAA	WARP
2016	NYA	MLB	26	610	63	29	1	21	70	24	118	4	0	.270/.300/.433	92	8.1	.305	-2.1	2B(150): 1.3, SS(3): -0.5	1.2
2017	NYA	MLB	27	473	66	18	1	16	63	23	93	2	0	.300/.338/.454	99	18.2	.347	0.5	2B(109): -4.9	1.0
2018	MIA	MLB	28	647	76	32	2	12	54	48	124	6	4	.278/.329/.400	92	31.4	.330	0.3	2B(150): -6.2	0.9
2019	MIA	MLB	29	597	63	27	3	16	70	40	116	4	2	.265/.320/.409	101	20.0	.311	-0.6	2B -3	1.8

Breakout: 3%   Improve: 51%   Collapse: 1%   Attrition: 4%   MLB: 100%   *Comparables: Jimmie Reese, Omar Infante, Howie Kendrick*

You likely forgot that Castro played for the Marlins last year. There were times where Castro himself surely wished he'd forget he was playing for the Marlins. He still punched his clock, racking up the second-most plate appearances on the team, splitting his time among the first three spots in the order. As expected, most of his counting stats suffered thanks to a barren lineup and a huge ballpark. Castro did marginally improve in one part of his game that caused a ripple effect, swinging less often overall and refusing to chase pitches while maintaining the same contact rate. He saw curveballs better than before, and as a result he ticked his walk rate to a career-best 7.4 percent.

Garrett Cooper LF
Born: 12/25/90   Age: 28   Bats: R   Throws: R   Height: 6'6"   Weight: 230   Origin: Round 6, 2013 Draft (#182 overall)

YEAR	TEAM	LVL	AGE	PA	R	2B	3B	HR	RBI	BB	K	SB	CS	AVG/OBP/SLG	DRC+	VORP	BABIP	BRR	FRAA	WARP
2016	BLX	AA	25	329	27	22	1	4	49	20	55	3	3	.299/.350/.419	104	16.5	.351	-2.5	1B(59): -0.3, RF(16): 0.7	0.3
2016	CSP	AAA	25	139	17	5	0	5	20	10	20	0	0	.276/.331/.433	114	-2.3	.291	0.1	1B(22): 0.1, LF(11): -1.1	0.4
2017	CSP	AAA	26	320	64	29	0	17	82	33	48	0	0	.366/.428/.652	155	26.3	.386	-2.3	1B(73): 4.3	2.9
2017	NYA	MLB	26	45	3	5	1	0	6	1	12	0	0	.326/.333/.488	78	1.3	.438	0.0	1B(13): 0.0	-0.1
2018	MIA	MLB	27	38	2	1	0	0	2	4	12	0	0	.212/.316/.242	63	0.3	.333	0.4	LF(6): 0.7, 1B(4): 1.1	0.1
2019	MIA	MLB	28	335	32	16	1	8	36	27	84	0	0	.234/.303/.370	83	0.3	.299	-0.5	1B 1, LF 0	0.2

Breakout: 9%   Improve: 23%   Collapse: 12%   Attrition: 25%   MLB: 48%   *Comparables: Jason Rogers, Russ Canzler, Jesus Guzman*

Persistent right wrist injuries turned 2018 into a lost year for Cooper, who was aiming to become at worst a platoon bat for the Fish and at best the everyday first baseman after Justin Bour's departure. The 6-foot-6 lefty bat showcased a 1.080 OPS in Triple-A Colorado Springs while with the Brewers in 2017, along with a 10 percent walk rate and just a 15 percent strikeout rate. He has 83 not-very-great MLB at-bats to his name, but a promising profile that should net positive returns in 2019.

Austin Dean LF
Born: 10/14/93   Age: 25   Bats: R   Throws: R   Height: 6'1"   Weight: 190   Origin: Round 4, 2012 Draft (#137 overall)

YEAR	TEAM	LVL	AGE	PA	R	2B	3B	HR	RBI	BB	K	SB	CS	AVG/OBP/SLG	DRC+	VORP	BABIP	BRR	FRAA	WARP
2016	JAX	AA	22	536	60	23	5	11	67	48	110	1	2	.238/.307/.375	102	8.6	.283	-0.5	LF(115): 3.3, RF(1): -0.1	1.7
2017	JAX	AA	23	251	29	14	4	4	30	14	46	3	1	.282/.323/.427	93	14.4	.333	0.9	LF(53): -2.8, RF(3): -0.5	0.1
2018	JAX	AA	24	88	13	8	1	3	14	6	7	0	0	.420/.466/.654	120	12.5	.437	-2.0	LF(21): 0.5	0.3
2018	NWO	AAA	24	358	58	12	4	9	54	33	49	2	2	.326/.397/.475	120	31.0	.360	0.5	LF(45): -2.2, RF(37): -0.8	1.6
2018	MIA	MLB	24	122	16	4	0	4	14	7	22	1	0	.221/.279/.363	90	1.5	.241	1.1	LF(31): 0.5	0.3
2019	MIA	MLB	25	360	38	16	2	10	43	26	63	1	0	.257/.324/.413	100	9.6	.293	-0.4	LF 0	1.0

Breakout: 5%   Improve: 32%   Collapse: 14%   Attrition: 34%   MLB: 69%   *Comparables: Austin Slater, Caleb Gindl, Zoilo Almonte*

Considering they assigned him to Double-A for a third straight year, the Marlins were likely unenthusiastic about Dean entering 2018. But after his absurd start in Double-A and an exceptional stint in Triple-A, the team finally felt he was worth the gamble and called him up. Dean, who exists in the unfortunate void where he isn't fast enough to be a center fielder and may not possesses enough game power to cut it as an everyday corner guy, will likely recede into the Land of Fourth Outfielder.

Jose Devers SS
Born: 12/07/99   Age: 19   Bats: L   Throws: R   Height: 6'0"   Weight: 155   Origin: International Free Agent, 2016

YEAR	TEAM	LVL	AGE	PA	R	2B	3B	HR	RBI	BB	K	SB	CS	AVG/OBP/SLG	DRC+	VORP	BABIP	BRR	FRAA	WARP
2017	DYA	RK	17	47	4	2	1	0	7	0	16	1	0	.239/.255/.326	57	-2.5	.367	-0.7	SS(7): 0.2, 2B(3): -0.1	-0.1
2017	YAN	RK	17	169	17	7	2	1	9	18	21	15	3	.246/.359/.348	118	10.4	.277	-2.9	SS(39): -0.4	0.7
2018	GRB	A	18	362	46	12	4	0	24	15	49	13	6	.273/.313/.332	91	4.0	.318	-2.6	SS(59): 2.2, 2B(15): 0.0	0.9
2019	MIA	MLB	19	251	21	4	0	4	17	4	63	3	1	.182/.195/.247	10	-18.3	.225	0.0	SS -1, 2B 0	-2.0

Breakout: 0%   Improve: 4%   Collapse: 1%   Attrition: 3%   MLB: 8%   *Comparables: Carlos Triunfel, Alcides Escobar, Elvis Andrus*

Rafael Devers' cousin doesn't possess the same kind of pedigree or boom in his bat. Instead, Jose is a glove-first player likely to remain at shortstop thanks to smooth footwork, slick transfers and a good enough arm that should stave off a move to second base. Because he'll stick up the middle, his light offensive game is still good enough to carry the profile. He shows good bat-to-ball skills, solid pitch recognition that lowers his strikeouts and enough speed to take advantage on the basepaths. His linear stroke sucks any punch out of his bat because he mashes everything into the ground. Becoming an average big-league regular is within reach.

Isan Diaz 2B
Born: 05/27/96   Age: 23   Bats: L   Throws: R   Height: 5'10"   Weight: 185   Origin: Round 2, 2014 Draft (#70 overall)

YEAR	TEAM	LVL	AGE	PA	R	2B	3B	HR	RBI	BB	K	SB	CS	AVG/OBP/SLG	DRC+	VORP	BABIP	BRR	FRAA	WARP
2016	WIS	A	20	587	71	34	5	20	75	72	148	11	8	.264/.358/.469	145	37.7	.332	2.5	SS(90): -0.1, 2B(41): 1.0	5.9
2017	CAR	A+	21	455	59	20	0	13	54	62	121	9	3	.222/.334/.376	110	14.8	.283	0.1	2B(58): -1.9, SS(32): -4.8	1.3
2018	JAX	AA	22	356	44	19	1	10	42	53	95	10	3	.245/.365/.418	99	22.5	.325	0.0	2B(82): 2.1	1.3
2018	NWO	AAA	22	155	19	4	4	3	14	15	45	4	0	.204/.281/.358	68	-2.0	.278	0.8	2B(35): -1.6	-0.2
2019	MIA	MLB	23	69	7	2	0	2	7	7	21	1	0	.197/.277/.335	61	-1.0	.259	0.0	2B 0	-0.1

Breakout: 4%   Improve: 11%   Collapse: 3%   Attrition: 8%   MLB: 19%   *Comparables: Carlos Asuaje, Brandon Lowe, Travis Denker*

Slowly but surely, Diaz is turning into someone who looks like a future starting second baseman. A shortstop while in Milwaukee, his poor range forced him to move to the keystone, where his bat should still play. And really, that's his main draw. Diaz features plus power, the kind that can scrape out 25 home runs in the majors in his better years. He's earning himself a reputation as a Three True Outcomes player thanks to excellent walk rates in the minors to go with strikeout rates that hover around 25 percent. There's still room to grow in the contact department, where he needs to stop expanding the zone and use his quick bat speed. There's a strong chance he debuts later this year.

Derek Dietrich LF
Born: 07/18/89   Age: 29   Bats: L   Throws: R   Height: 6'0"   Weight: 205   Origin: Round 2, 2010 Draft (#79 overall)

YEAR	TEAM	LVL	AGE	PA	R	2B	3B	HR	RBI	BB	K	SB	CS	AVG/OBP/SLG	DRC+	VORP	BABIP	BRR	FRAA	WARP
2016	MIA	MLB	26	412	39	20	5	7	42	32	84	1	0	.279/.374/.425	101	29.7	.343	-1.1	2B(75): -0.3, 1B(16): -0.1	1.1
2017	MIA	MLB	27	464	56	22	5	13	53	36	98	0	1	.249/.334/.424	97	22.6	.294	0.5	3B(103): -7.6, 1B(10): -0.3	0.8
2018	MIA	MLB	28	551	72	26	2	16	45	29	140	2	0	.265/.330/.421	92	24.8	.336	1.7	LF(97): -8.4, 1B(33): -1.9	-0.1
2019	MIA	MLB	29	502	54	23	3	14	58	36	115	1	1	.243/.333/.394	107	17.1	.309	0.3	LF -4, 1B -1	1.3

Breakout: 4%   Improve: 37%   Collapse: 3%   Attrition: 5%   MLB: 95%   *Comparables: Desmond Jennings, Alex Gordon, Andy Dirks*

What made Dietrich valuable in years past — his ability to play all over the infield while being shielded from left-handed pitchers like you shield your children from certain *Game of Thrones* scenes — evaporated. Roster construction and injuries forced Dietrich to play 98 percent of his innings at either first base or in the left field, and he topped 100 plate appearances versus lefties for the first time. Though he turned in an average-at-best season at the plate, he still suffered against lefties and was a legitimate defensive liability at his new positions, leading to a non-tender.

Joe Dunand SS   Born: 09/20/95   Age: 23   Bats: R   Throws: R   Height: 6'2"   Weight: 205   Origin: Round 2, 2017 Draft (#51 overall)

YEAR	TEAM	LVL	AGE	PA	R	2B	3B	HR	RBI	BB	K	SB	CS	AVG/OBP/SLG	DRC+	VORP	BABIP	BRR	FRAA	WARP
2018	JUP	A+	22	273	39	8	1	7	42	20	54	2	0	.263/.326/.391	114	14.8	.305	1.1	SS(62): 0.2	1.8
2018	JAX	AA	22	239	25	13	0	7	28	16	71	0	1	.212/.276/.369	86	9.4	.277	-0.8	SS(60): -0.6	0.5
2019	MIA	MLB	23	251	23	10	0	8	28	12	73	0	0	.210/.254/.347	59	-3.6	.269	-0.6	SS 0	-0.4

Breakout: 19%   Improve: 35%   Collapse: 5%   Attrition: 26%   MLB: 41%   *Comparables: Tim Beckham, Derek Dietrich, Zach Walters*

It was a tale of two seasons for Dunand. He walked with his chin up and a little pep in his step for 66 games at High-A, where he didn't outperform the league but certainly didn't flounder. A promotion to Double-A produced a record scratch and stopped him in his tracks. While he maintained his average power, his strikeouts soared and he cratered everywhere else. The Fish are insistent on keeping him at shortstop, which will help his bat play. But he has a lot of adjustments to make in order to keep moving on up. Oh, and something something nephew of Alex Rodriguez.

Isaac Galloway OF   Born: 10/10/89   Age: 29   Bats: R   Throws: R   Height: 6'2"   Weight: 205   Origin: Round 8, 2008 Draft (#238 overall)

YEAR	TEAM	LVL	AGE	PA	R	2B	3B	HR	RBI	BB	K	SB	CS	AVG/OBP/SLG	DRC+	VORP	BABIP	BRR	FRAA	WARP
2016	NWO	AAA	26	486	61	19	2	10	38	33	112	31	10	.254/.312/.374	76	19.1	.318	3.3	CF(57): -1.9, RF(48): 5.5	0.9
2017	JAX	AA	27	49	4	5	0	0	3	6	8	5	2	.405/.490/.524	99	6.8	.500	0.5	CF(5): -0.8, RF(2): -0.2	0.1
2017	NWO	AAA	27	83	12	0	0	7	16	7	21	5	0	.280/.349/.560	117	8.5	.298	0.4	CF(19): -0.6, LF(2): 0.0	0.5
2018	NWO	AAA	28	356	64	21	3	9	30	21	75	20	7	.262/.315/.429	84	22.9	.314	9.5	RF(59): -0.2, CF(22): -1.6	1.1
2018	MIA	MLB	28	74	7	3	0	3	7	9	21	1	1	.203/.301/.391	87	1.7	.250	0.4	LF(18): -0.8, RF(13): 1.3	0.2
2019	MIA	MLB	29	149	20	6	1	6	17	10	38	6	2	.231/.289/.405	97	4.3	.274	0.5	LF 3	0.7

Breakout: 1%   Improve: 4%   Collapse: 14%   Attrition: 20%   MLB: 26%   *Comparables: Jim Adduci, Moises Sierra, Reid Gorecki*

Isaac Galloway's name resembles that of a forlorn philosopher cast aside for his poppycock theories of Living Organisms on the Sun. Alas, the Galloway we know has also been cast aside in baseball, making a hard living in the minor leagues for the last 10 years. In fact, it wasn't until July 31 of last year that he made his major-league debut at the ripe age of 28. He even hit a walk-off double in late September. But it's memories like that Galloway must cling to because ultimately he's just there for organizational depth.

Monte Harrison CF   Born: 08/10/95   Age: 23   Bats: R   Throws: R   Height: 6'3"   Weight: 220   Origin: Round 2, 2014 Draft (#50 overall)

YEAR	TEAM	LVL	AGE	PA	R	2B	3B	HR	RBI	BB	K	SB	CS	AVG/OBP/SLG	DRC+	VORP	BABIP	BRR	FRAA	WARP
2016	WIS	A	20	298	34	11	1	6	37	20	97	8	3	.221/.294/.337	78	0.4	.321	1.0	CF(48): -0.7, RF(14): 1.0	0.1
2017	WIS	A	21	261	32	12	1	11	32	29	70	11	3	.265/.359/.475	121	21.9	.333	1.3	CF(62): 1.6	1.8
2017	CAR	A+	21	252	41	16	1	10	35	14	69	16	1	.278/.341/.487	110	21.4	.358	3.3	CF(27): -1.8, RF(18): 2.1	1.4
2018	JAX	AA	22	583	85	20	3	19	48	44	215	28	9	.240/.316/.399	86	28.5	.368	3.6	CF(121): -8.0, RF(14): 0.4	0.4
2019	MIA	MLB	23	73	9	2	0	3	7	4	27	2	1	.199/.255/.354	57	-1.7	.282	0.1	LF 0	-0.1

Breakout: 6%   Improve: 17%   Collapse: 3%   Attrition: 17%   MLB: 33%   *Comparables: Trayce Thompson, Joe Benson, Franchy Cordero*

It's drool-worthy to think of what Harrison could accomplish on a baseball field if his plate discipline is anything other than horrific. At 6-foot-3 and 220 pounds, he's a chiseled specimen, built like an NFL linebacker with plus power and speed as well a cannon for an arm. But in his first stint at Double-A he struggled mightily, with his 215 strikeouts pacing all of the minors. He has a bad habit of selling out for power and gets eaten alive by off-speed pitches as he still learns to time his massive leg kick. But he stayed healthy all season, which was a serious concern in the past. Harrison is the type of prospect to whom you give significant leash because the ceiling is an All-Star if it clicks.

Osiris Johnson SS   Born: 10/18/00   Age: 18   Bats: R   Throws: R   Height: 6'0"   Weight: 181   Origin: Round 2, 2018 Draft (#53 overall)

YEAR	TEAM	LVL	AGE	PA	R	2B	3B	HR	RBI	BB	K	SB	CS	AVG/OBP/SLG	DRC+	VORP	BABIP	BRR	FRAA	WARP
2018	MRL	RK	17	111	12	8	2	1	13	4	19	7	2	.301/.333/.447	115	8.7	.353	1.1	SS(23): 1.5	0.9
2018	GRB	A	17	88	4	3	0	2	6	1	34	0	2	.188/.205/.294	74	-5.1	.280	-1.3	SS(23): -6.3	-0.7
2019	MIA	MLB	18	251	18	8	0	5	23	3	87	2	1	.181/.189/.277	13	-17.8	.250	-0.7	SS -3	-2.3

Comparables: Adalberto Mondesi, Wilmer Flores, Tommy Brown

The 53rd overall pick in the 2018 draft impressed so much in his professional debut that the Marlins jumped him from rookie ball to Low-A as a 17-year-old. It was an aggressive (and likely unnecessary) promotion, but shows how much the organization likes Johnson. He won't be as good as cousin Jimmy Rollins, but Johnson does project to stay on the dirt after he improved his defense enough to avoid getting relegated to the outfield. Often described as twitchy, he has a habit of pulling the ball, which might hinder him down the line against more advanced pitching. The athleticism is there, as is the frame for perhaps a touch more power.

Victor Victor Mesa CF   Born: 07/20/96   Age: 22   Bats: R   Throws: R   Height: 6'0"   Weight: 185   Origin: International Free Agent, 2018

Being the top international prospect in a class brings with it lofty expectations. Signed by the Marlins for $5.25 million, the man with two first names raised those expectations even higher by holding out for weeks until the Marlins built up enough pool money to ensure he and his younger brother would have a home in the Cuban-centric Miami culture. Mesa, the son of legendary Cuban star Victor Mesa, joined the Serie Nacional, Cuba's top professional league, as a 16-year-old under the tutelage of his father. He struggled initially, but in his second year he acclimated and won the Gold Glove. It kick-started a strong career that saw him climb to the ranks of a young superstar. As a whole, the dynamic center fielder is a force on both sides of the ball. He's a plus defender with enough speed and arm to patrol center for the Marlins for years to come. At the plate, there are the makings of a future plus hit tool with enough pull-side power to get into double-digit home runs. He has the speed to notch 30 or more bases in a season. Though he'll be 22 when the season begins, expect him to get a full year of seasoning in the minors, likely jumping three or maybe four levels as he shakes off the rust of someone who hasn't played in over a year. The Fish won't debut him until 2020 at the earliest. He's no organizational savior, but he represents a major change for how the team operates going forward.

Brian Miller OF   Born: 08/20/95   Age: 23   Bats: L   Throws: R   Height: 6'1"   Weight: 186   Origin: Round 1, 2017 Draft (#36 overall)

YEAR	TEAM	LVL	AGE	PA	R	2B	3B	HR	RBI	BB	K	SB	CS	AVG/OBP/SLG	DRC+	VORP	BABIP	BRR	FRAA	WARP
2017	GRB	A	21	258	42	17	1	1	28	23	35	21	6	.322/.384/.416	108	15.7	.374	0.9	CF(35): 1.9, RF(13): -0.4	1.3
2018	JUP	A+	22	276	28	13	3	0	29	14	27	19	6	.324/.358/.398	109	17.0	.358	0.7	CF(33): -1.5, LF(19): 0.2	1.1
2018	JAX	AA	22	287	29	8	2	0	14	18	39	21	7	.267/.319/.313	91	4.1	.314	0.8	LF(49): 0.1, RF(12): 0.0	0.4
2019	MIA	MLB	23	251	29	7	1	4	19	11	46	11	3	.231/.264/.320	56	-4.7	.265	0.9	LF 1, CF 0	-0.3

Breakout: 3%   Improve: 5%   Collapse: 3%   Attrition: 7%   MLB: 11%   Comparables: Alex Romero, Ben Gamel, Whit Merrifield

Fresh off a 40-steal season split between High-A and Double-A, Miller showcased the type of player he could be in the majors. Though not an 80-grade burner, he maximizes his plus speed on the bases and in the outfield, where experience should allow him to overcome a fringy arm in center field. Miller has a knack for making contact, which leads to minimal strikeout rates, but his linear swing portends to 30-grade power in the future. If all breaks right, the former 36th overall pick in the 2016 draft can be an everyday player, but the influx of outfield prospects in the organization ensures he'll have to earn such a spot.

Tristan Pompey OF   Born: 03/23/97   Age: 22   Bats: B   Throws: R   Height: 6'4"   Weight: 200   Origin: Round 3, 2018 Draft (#89 overall)

YEAR	TEAM	LVL	AGE	PA	R	2B	3B	HR	RBI	BB	K	SB	CS	AVG/OBP/SLG	DRC+	VORP	BABIP	BRR	FRAA	WARP
2018	GRB	A	21	103	12	4	0	2	9	16	22	5	3	.314/.422/.430	110	6.5	.403	-0.8	LF(10): -1.4, RF(5): -1.1	-0.1
2018	JUP	A+	21	101	13	5	0	1	13	13	21	4	1	.291/.396/.384	105	6.6	.375	1.1	CF(16): -3.8	0.1
2019	MIA	MLB	22	251	24	8	0	6	24	21	68	4	2	.202/.269/.307	59	-4.7	.257	-0.4	CF -3, LF -1	-0.9

Breakout: 2%   Improve: 12%   Collapse: 2%   Attrition: 11%   MLB: 20%   Comparables: Aaron Hicks, Ryan Kalish, Daniel Fields

Brother of Blue Jays prospect Dalton Pompey, Tristan carries a more tantalizing all-around profile. The outfielder has played all three positions, but defensive limitations could point to a career in left field. The bat is good enough to play there, though. He's a switch-hitter who shows above-average raw power from both sides, exhibits a great eye at the plate and has enough speed to consistently reach double-digit steals early in his career. A 20-20 profile is not out of the question for the 2018 third-round pick.

Martin Prado 3B   Born: 10/27/83   Age: 35   Bats: R   Throws: R   Height: 6'0"   Weight: 215   Origin: International Free Agent, 2001

YEAR	TEAM	LVL	AGE	PA	R	2B	3B	HR	RBI	BB	K	SB	CS	AVG/OBP/SLG	DRC+	VORP	BABIP	BRR	FRAA	WARP
2016	MIA	MLB	32	658	70	37	3	8	75	49	69	2	2	.305/.359/.417	102	39.9	.331	0.2	3B(150): -3.1	2.4
2017	MIA	MLB	33	147	13	9	0	2	12	6	22	0	0	.250/.279/.357	79	-2.2	.282	-1.0	3B(34): -1.2	-0.1
2018	MIA	MLB	34	209	16	9	0	1	18	11	35	1	1	.244/.287/.305	81	1.2	.292	0.4	3B(48): -4.5, 1B(1): 0.1	-0.1
2019	MIA	MLB	35	481	44	25	2	8	49	31	77	2	1	.261/.313/.377	90	5.6	.300	0.1	3B -4	0.2

Breakout: 0%   Improve: 24%   Collapse: 12%   Attrition: 23%   MLB: 78%   Comparables: Aaron Hill, Yunel Escobar, Placido Polanco

It's been a horrid two seasons for Prado, one of the most beloved presences in the Marlins' clubhouse. He's amassed just 91 games since the start of 2017, battling myriad injuries that make the spotlight on his three-year, $40 million contract grow harsher and harsher. Last season, after recovering from right knee surgery in the offseason, he strained his left hamstring, his left quad, and for good measure, his right abdominal. With a deteriorating glove and a punchless bat, Prado has very little left to give. But with $15 million left on the final year of his contract, he'll have to provide value somewhere.

Harold Ramirez RF   Born: 09/06/94   Age: 24   Bats: R   Throws: R   Height: 5'10"   Weight: 220   Origin: International Free Agent, 2011

YEAR	TEAM	LVL	AGE	PA	R	2B	3B	HR	RBI	BB	K	SB	CS	AVG/OBP/SLG	DRC+	VORP	BABIP	BRR	FRAA	WARP
2016	ALT	AA	21	414	58	16	7	2	49	21	66	7	10	.306/.354/.401	101	17.2	.363	2.4	CF(67): -8.0, LF(14): 1.3	0.6
2017	NHP	AA	22	490	46	19	2	6	53	32	65	5	3	.266/.320/.358	89	-0.5	.296	-2.3	RF(69): 0.3, LF(23): -3.4	-0.2
2018	NHP	AA	23	505	60	37	0	11	70	27	88	16	2	.320/.365/.471	119	31.3	.371	2.5	RF(61): -2.7, LF(18): -0.5	2.0
2019	MIA	MLB	24	251	25	9	1	6	27	11	51	3	1	.243/.284/.363	75	-1.2	.284	-0.2	RF -1, LF 0	-0.2

Breakout: 2%   Improve: 8%   Collapse: 3%   Attrition: 15%   MLB: 22%   Comparables: Jamie Hoffmann, Ben Francisco, Mikie Mahtook

While there's no one tried-and-true path to major-league success, you'll rarely be steered wrong by a .300 batting average and double-digit stolen bases. Just ask Ramirez, who contested his indefinite exile in Double-A with a long-awaited breakout at the plate, and an MVP nod during the Fisher Cats' Eastern League championship run, to boot. Formerly a top prospect with the Pirates and allowed to walk as a minor-league free agent after last season by the Blue Jays, he hooked on with the Marlins and could fight his way onto the big-league roster at some point.

J.T. Realmuto C   Born: 03/18/91   Age: 28   Bats: R   Throws: R   Height: 6'1"   Weight: 210   Origin: Round 3, 2010 Draft (#104 overall)

YEAR	TEAM	LVL	AGE	PA	R	2B	3B	HR	RBI	BB	K	SB	CS	AVG/OBP/SLG	DRC+	VORP	BABIP	BRR	FRAA	WARP
2016	MIA	MLB	25	545	60	31	0	11	48	28	100	12	4	.303/.343/.428	93	38.0	.357	1.6	C(129): -0.1	2.4
2017	MIA	MLB	26	579	68	31	5	17	65	36	106	8	2	.278/.332/.451	99	37.9	.318	1.0	C(126): 15.8, 1B(9): 0.3	4.5
2018	MIA	MLB	27	531	74	30	3	21	74	38	104	3	2	.277/.340/.484	113	51.2	.312	4.1	C(112): 3.7, 1B(13): 0.6	4.3
2019	MIA	MLB	28	606	72	30	3	20	77	42	114	8	3	.272/.335/.444	114	36.8	.314	1.9	C 5, 1B 1	4.6

Breakout: 1%   Improve: 40%   Collapse: 10%   Attrition: 13%   MLB: 97%   Comparables: Jonathan Lucroy, Nick Hundley, Derek Norris

If 2017 was the year Realmuto announced his arrival to the baseball world, 2018 is the year he shouted to everyone that he's the best all-around catcher in the game. The 28-year-old generated value in a wide variety of ways. His traditional slash line categories ranked top two among catchers with a minimum of 400 plate appearances. He discovered newfound power after deciding to take to the skies with a new approach. He ranked as a plus defensively for the second straight season. He's also durable, one of just two catchers with at least 1,600 plate appearances since 2016. As the old guard of great catchers fades away, Realmuto has his grip firmly on the top spot.

YEAR	TEAM	P. COUNT	FRM RUNS	BLK RUNS	THRW RUNS	TOT RUNS
2016	MIA	18935	-8.5	1.8	2.1	-5.6
2017	MIA	18959	5.3	1.7	1.0	9.1
2018	MIA	16399	-0.4	0.9	0.1	0.4
2019	MIA	18975	-1.4	1.5	0.7	0.8

JT Riddle SS Born: 10/12/91 Age: 27 Bats: L Throws: R Height: 6'1" Weight: 180 Origin: Round 13, 2013 Draft (#382 overall)

YEAR	TEAM	LVL	AGE	PA	R	2B	3B	HR	RBI	BB	K	SB	CS	AVG/OBP/SLG	DRC+	VORP	BABIP	BRR	FRAA	WARP
2016	JAX	AA	24	429	49	18	4	3	51	33	72	5	1	.278/.332/.368	100	20.0	.331	1.0	SS(71): 1.0, 2B(21): -0.2	1.9
2016	NWO	AAA	24	57	4	2	0	1	2	1	9	1	0	.268/.281/.357	75	1.0	.304	-0.8	SS(13): -1.8, 2B(1): 0.0	-0.2
2017	NWO	AAA	25	64	9	4	1	2	6	1	8	1	0	.286/.297/.476	76	4.3	.302	-0.3	SS(16): 0.9	0.2
2017	MIA	MLB	25	247	20	13	1	3	31	12	50	0	2	.250/.282/.355	68	4.1	.300	0.7	SS(69): 1.5	0.4
2018	NWO	AAA	26	91	17	4	1	3	19	8	15	2	0	.346/.400/.531	99	14.1	.391	1.3	SS(21): 2.0	0.8
2018	MIA	MLB	26	332	28	10	4	9	36	20	67	0	3	.231/.277/.377	83	10.1	.266	1.7	SS(95): 8.1	1.8
2019	MIA	MLB	27	398	39	18	3	10	45	26	79	2	1	.247/.299/.392	90	11.8	.284	1.8	SS 2	1.5

Breakout: 6%   Improve: 36%   Collapse: 17%   Attrition: 25%   MLB: 90%   Comparables: Zack Cozart, Eduardo Escobar, Josh Wilson

Riddle stood at the plate in his final game of the season. His gaze wandered to the oversized scoreboard in Marlins Park, probably built to be that large to distract from the empty blue seats, he thought. His slash line, ranking as one of the worst in baseball for shortstops with at least 300 plate appearances, shone bright on the board. As the smattering of fans grew impatient with how long he was taking to begin his at-bat, he reached for his neck and began peeling away the silicone. It was a mask. The fans gasped once the man's identity had been revealed. All this time they had assumed this new player was traded from the organization more than a year ago. Adeiny Hechavarria breathed deeply and exhaled with a devilish smile. The madman had never left.

Miguel Rojas INF Born: 02/24/89 Age: 30 Bats: R Throws: R Height: 5'11" Weight: 195 Origin: International Free Agent, 2005

YEAR	TEAM	LVL	AGE	PA	R	2B	3B	HR	RBI	BB	K	SB	CS	AVG/OBP/SLG	DRC+	VORP	BABIP	BRR	FRAA	WARP
2016	MIA	MLB	27	214	27	12	0	1	14	11	27	2	1	.247/.288/.325	72	-2.1	.280	0.7	2B(45): -0.6, 1B(41): 1.8	0.5
2017	MIA	MLB	28	306	37	16	2	1	26	27	32	2	1	.290/.361/.375	92	21.0	.324	4.6	SS(77): -0.2, 3B(15): -0.2	1.5
2018	MIA	MLB	29	527	44	13	0	11	53	24	69	6	3	.252/.297/.346	86	8.8	.272	-2.5	SS(83): 5.4, 1B(49): -0.3	1.4
2019	MIA	MLB	30	460	48	20	2	8	45	34	61	4	2	.260/.325/.375	91	9.5	.285	0.8	SS 2, 3B 0	1.3

Breakout: 1%   Improve: 31%   Collapse: 12%   Attrition: 18%   MLB: 89%   Comparables: Ryan Theriot, Brendan Ryan, Paul Janish

One of the Marlins' fetishes is strong defensive infielders who are an active detriment when at the plate. For the last four years Rojas has been one of several phone calls the Fish make to satiate their needs, and last season his profile was on full display. Though most of his time came at shortstop and third base, he also saw time at first base and second base, showcasing an exceptional glove at each position. The light-hitting utility man has a knack for making contact and limiting strikeouts, but it doesn't help his production. But for the Marlins, his skills are always going to be just enough to make them bite their lower lip.

Connor Scott CF Born: 10/08/99 Age: 19 Bats: L Throws: L Height: 6'4" Weight: 180 Origin: Round 1, 2018 Draft (#13 overall)

YEAR	TEAM	LVL	AGE	PA	R	2B	3B	HR	RBI	BB	K	SB	CS	AVG/OBP/SLG	DRC+	VORP	BABIP	BRR	FRAA	WARP
2018	MRL	RK	18	119	15	1	4	0	8	14	29	8	5	.223/.319/.311	86	0.5	.307	-1.2	CF(22): -1.6	-0.1
2018	GRB	A	18	89	4	2	0	1	5	10	27	1	3	.211/.295/.276	78	-2.5	.300	-1.9	CF(22): -3.0	-0.5
2019	MIA	MLB	19	251	23	5	0	5	17	13	85	2	2	.154/.195/.236	10	-18.7	.209	-0.8	CF -3	-2.3

Breakout: 0%   Improve: 7%   Collapse: 1%   Attrition: 4%   MLB: 12%   Comparables: Engel Beltre, Nomar Mazara, Carlos Tocci

The 13th overall pick in 2018 and the first under the new Marlins regime, Scott has raw potential but a long way to go to achieve it. The center fielder's frame is very projectable, with the possibility of adding two grades of power with more muscle, an enticing thought for someone with plus speed. For now, he has strong plate discipline and contact problems, especially with off-speed stuff. However, considering his age (and an unusually aggressive promotion to the Sally), it's hard to criticize for now. Don't get stars in your eyes with the unfair Kyle Tucker comparisons, but the foundation is there for Scott to turn into a good defensive outfielder with enough bat to make him a future regular.

Magneuris Sierra CF Born: 04/07/96 Age: 23 Bats: L Throws: L Height: 5'11" Weight: 160 Origin: International Free Agent, 2012

YEAR	TEAM	LVL	AGE	PA	R	2B	3B	HR	RBI	BB	K	SB	CS	AVG/OBP/SLG	DRC+	VORP	BABIP	BRR	FRAA	WARP
2016	PEO	A	20	562	78	29	4	3	60	22	97	31	17	.307/.335/.395	101	28.9	.367	1.6	CF(121): 3.3	2.4
2017	PMB	A+	21	89	16	3	4	0	9	7	15	3	5	.272/.337/.407	100	4.2	.333	1.1	CF(19): 0.6	0.5
2017	SFD	AA	21	353	32	18	3	1	35	20	59	17	5	.269/.313/.352	74	3.6	.323	3.6	RF(34): 0.5, LF(26): 2.0	0.5
2017	SLN	MLB	21	64	10	0	0	0	5	4	14	2	2	.317/.359/.317	80	3.1	.413	0.8	RF(8): 0.7, CF(7): -1.3	0.0
2018	NWO	AAA	22	367	48	12	5	2	17	13	73	14	5	.260/.287/.341	58	5.8	.322	3.2	CF(81): 5.8, RF(1): 0.7	0.4
2018	MIA	MLB	22	156	10	3	0	0	7	6	39	3	2	.190/.222/.211	37	-1.2	.259	-0.4	CF(32): -0.3, RF(19): -0.1	-0.8
2019	MIA	MLB	23	312	36	12	2	6	26	16	73	8	4	.230/.275/.342	68	-1.5	.283	0.3	RF 3, CF 0	0.1

Breakout: 6%   Improve: 18%   Collapse: 6%   Attrition: 12%   MLB: 28%   Comparables: Eury Perez, Charlie Tilson, Engel Beltre

Last year was a significant step back for Sierra, one of the centerpieces in the Marcell Ozuna trade. Lauded for his speed and defense, he had a rough time showcasing either, especially during a major-league stint in which he hobbled to a .433 OPS, worst in baseball. The slapstick hitter managed just three extra-base hits in that span and showed that he had no self-restraint on pitches outside of the zone. Even when he did get on base, his instincts lacked polish, as he got caught seven times in 24 steal attempts across the minors and majors. He's still really young, and to make it to the majors at his age is an accomplishment on its own, but his current profile is best suited for a fourth or fifth outfielder role.

PITCHERS

Sandy Alcantara RHP Born: 09/07/95 Age: 23 Bats: R Throws: R Height: 6'4" Weight: 170 Origin: International Free Agent, 2013

YEAR	TEAM	LVL	AGE	W	L	SV	G	GS	IP	H	HR	BB/9	K/9	K	GB%	BABIP	WHIP	ERA	DRA	WARP	MPH	FB%	WHF	CSP
2016	PEO	A	20	5	7	0	17	17	90¹	78	4	4.5	11.9	119	46%	.333	1.36	4.08	3.09	2.1				
2016	PMB	A+	20	0	4	0	6	6	32¹	25	0	3.9	9.5	34	52%	.294	1.21	3.62	2.78	1.0				
2017	SFD	AA	21	7	5	0	25	22	125¹	125	13	3.9	7.6	106	46%	.305	1.43	4.31	4.95	0.3				
2017	SLN	MLB	21	0	0	0	8	0	8¹	9	2	6.5	10.8	10	26%	.333	1.80	4.32	6.58	-0.1	100.6	66.5	16.8	44.3
2018	JUP	A+	22	0	0	0	3	3	11¹	10	0	4.0	6.4	8	62%	.294	1.32	3.97	6.50	-0.2				
2018	NWO	AAA	22	6	3	0	19	19	115²	107	10	3.0	6.8	88	50%	.283	1.25	3.89	4.08	1.9				
2018	MIA	MLB	22	2	3	0	6	6	34	25	3	6.1	7.9	30	50%	.250	1.41	3.44	5.57	-0.1	97.9	60	11.8	45.2
2019	MIA	MLB	23	4	5	0	13	13	69	60	7	4.0	8.3	64	44%	.291	1.32	4.23	4.96	0.3	98.2	63.3	13.2	46.4

Breakout: 17%   Improve: 27%   Collapse: 15%   Attrition: 36%   MLB: 58%   *Comparables: Archie Bradley, Jake Thompson, Scott Barnes*

The same questions that dogged Alcantara a couple of years ago are still dogging him today. His big, upper-90s fastball is still a plus-plus pitch that has sink and run, and he deploys the four-seam and two-seam variety. His slider and changeup flash above average. Does he have the frame to grow into and become an innings eater? Yes. Does he have the raw stuff to become a no. 3 starter? Yes. Does he have the command and control to definitively say he can avoid the bullpen? Nope. There's no reason to sound an alarm on him yet, but the realistic outcome is perhaps less rosy than when the Marlins first acquired him.

Edward Cabrera RHP Born: 04/13/98 Age: 21 Bats: R Throws: R Height: 6'4" Weight: 175 Origin: International Free Agent, 2015

YEAR	TEAM	LVL	AGE	W	L	SV	G	GS	IP	H	HR	BB/9	K/9	K	GB%	BABIP	WHIP	ERA	DRA	WARP	MPH	FB%	WHF	CSP
2016	MRL	RK	18	2	6	0	11	7	47	54	1	1.9	5.4	28	41%	.331	1.36	4.21	2.80	1.5				
2017	BAT	A-	19	1	3	0	13	6	35²	42	1	2.0	8.1	32	55%	.350	1.40	5.30	4.64	0.2				
2018	GRB	A	20	4	8	0	22	22	100¹	105	11	3.8	8.3	93	44%	.329	1.47	4.22	6.61	-1.7				
2019	MIA	MLB	21	4	6	0	27	14	77	82	13	4.0	6.7	57	40%	.306	1.51	5.47	6.40	-1.3				

Breakout: 0%   Improve: 0%   Collapse: 0%   Attrition: 1%   MLB: 1%   *Comparables: Jamie Callahan, James Houser, Tyler Clippard*

Believe it or not, there is such a thing as a pop-up prospect in an organization like the Marlins, and with his size and arsenal Cabrera certainly qualifies. He projects to fill out and add durability and a touch more velocity. It's not like he needs more ticks on his fastball, though. He already added 2-3 mph last year and sits in the mid-90s, maxing out at 97. He complements his heater with a slider that flashes above average. Cabrera performed well nearly two years younger than the average competition in 2018, but he has a ways to go as the overall package is still raw. His changeup is almost nonexistent and inconsistencies in his make-you-lose-your-hat windup are holding back his command.

Wei-Yin Chen LHP Born: 07/21/85 Age: 33 Bats: R Throws: L Height: 6'0" Weight: 200 Origin: International Free Agent, 2012

YEAR	TEAM	LVL	AGE	W	L	SV	G	GS	IP	H	HR	BB/9	K/9	K	GB%	BABIP	WHIP	ERA	DRA	WARP	MPH	FB%	WHF	CSP
2016	MIA	MLB	30	5	5	0	22	22	123¹	134	22	1.8	7.3	100	42%	.302	1.28	4.96	3.88	2.1	93.5	60.4	10.1	49
2017	MIA	MLB	31	2	1	0	9	5	33	25	3	2.5	6.8	25	39%	.234	1.03	3.82	4.28	0.5	92.4	65	9.5	48.5
2018	MIA	MLB	32	6	12	0	26	26	133¹	131	19	3.2	7.5	111	38%	.285	1.34	4.79	4.88	0.7	93.1	55.9	9.2	49.1
2019	MIA	MLB	33	9	10	0	28	28	159²	150	21	2.8	7.6	134	40%	.292	1.25	4.20	4.92	0.7	92.1	57.6	9.4	48.3

Breakout: 26%   Improve: 49%   Collapse: 20%   Attrition: 9%   MLB: 87%   *Comparables: Ricky Nolasco, Aaron Harang, Kyle Lohse*

It's hard to tell what's more noteworthy: Chen's ability to escape Tommy John surgery or his 2018 home/road splits. The veteran lefty who began the season a month late with left elbow inflammation, the latest in a string of arm injuries, had an average year with the Fish. Fans might have wanted him to pitch less on the road, where he owned a whopping 9.27 ERA in 55 1/2 innings compared to a 1.62 mark in 78 innings at Marlins Park. Chen tweaked his repertoire, opting to decrease his fastball usage in favor of his slider, his best pitch, which he bumped up to nearly a quarter usage. With health, he should remain a league-average starter who helps anchor a poor rotation, but with the salary of a no.2. starter for the next two years.

Adam Conley LHP Born: 05/24/90 Age: 29 Bats: L Throws: L Height: 6'3" Weight: 200 Origin: Round 2, 2011 Draft (#72 overall)

YEAR	TEAM	LVL	AGE	W	L	SV	G	GS	IP	H	HR	BB/9	K/9	K	GB%	BABIP	WHIP	ERA	DRA	WARP	MPH	FB%	WHF	CSP
2016	MIA	MLB	26	8	6	0	25	25	133¹	125	13	4.2	8.4	124	41%	.300	1.40	3.85	5.05	0.5	94.3	65.5	10.9	46
2017	NWO	AAA	27	3	3	0	12	12	62¹	69	7	3.6	5.9	41	39%	.310	1.51	5.49	4.49	0.8				
2017	MIA	MLB	27	8	8	0	22	20	102²	114	19	3.7	6.3	72	42%	.295	1.52	6.14	6.64	-1.2	91.9	64.4	10.6	47.7
2018	NWO	AAA	28	2	4	0	8	8	40	45	6	3.2	5.6	25	50%	.300	1.48	5.18	4.29	0.6				
2018	MIA	MLB	28	3	4	3	52	0	50²	37	5	3.2	8.9	50	45%	.250	1.09	4.09	3.58	0.8	97.3	56.9	15.6	46.9
2019	MIA	MLB	29	3	1	6	54	0	57¹	51	7	3.6	7.9	50	43%	.291	1.30	4.27	4.99	-0.1	93.4	63.1	11.8	46.9

Breakout: 31%   Improve: 45%   Collapse: 18%   Attrition: 25%   MLB: 77%   *Comparables: Brian Duensing, Josh Outman, Jeff Niemann*

After coming to terms with the fact that Conley was a bad starter, the Marlins shifted him to the bullpen where his fastball went from 90 mph to a whopping 96 mph. He also dropped his release point and turned to his changeup a little more than before. As you might expect, his strikeout rate jumped, he limited home runs and he allowed much less hard contact. A couple of unfortunate second-half outings ballooned his ERA, but Conley's turned himself into an effective multi-inning reliever capable of some high-leverage work as well. As the game shifts toward a heavier reliance on bullpens, Conley's role is sure to prove vital.

Robert Dugger RHP   Born: 07/03/95   Age: 23   Bats: R   Throws: R   Height: 6'2"   Weight: 180   Origin: Round 18, 2016 Draft (#537 overall)

YEAR	TEAM	LVL	AGE	W	L	SV	G	GS	IP	H	HR	BB/9	K/9	K	GB%	BABIP	WHIP	ERA	DRA	WARP	MPH	FB%	WHF	CSP
2016	MRN	RK	20	0	0	2	4	0	8²	6	0	1.0	9.3	9	61%	.261	0.81	1.04	2.79	0.2				
2016	EVE	A-	20	2	1	0	6	6	26¹	25	5	3.4	8.5	25	75%	.282	1.33	5.47	3.86	0.4				
2017	CLN	A	21	4	1	2	22	9	72	55	4	2.0	8.6	69	51%	.263	0.99	2.00	3.29	1.6				
2017	MOD	A+	21	2	5	0	9	9	45²	49	4	3.2	9.3	47	40%	.341	1.42	3.94	4.06	0.6				
2018	JUP	A+	22	3	1	0	7	7	41¹	40	2	1.5	7.4	34	57%	.306	1.14	2.40	3.71	0.8				
2018	JAX	AA	22	7	6	0	18	18	109¹	100	13	3.0	8.8	107	36%	.296	1.24	3.79	5.46	-0.1				
2019	MIA	MLB	23	6	8	1	34	19	120²	113	17	3.5	8.1	108	45%	.293	1.32	4.56	5.33	-0.1				

Breakout: 5%   Improve: 9%   Collapse: 11%   Attrition: 17%   MLB: 24%   *Comparables: Chih-Wei Hu, Daniel Mengden, Sam Howard*

Part of the three-man return from Seattle for Dee Gordon, Dugger is shaping up to be a win for the Mariners' scouting department, except the Marlins are set to reap the benefits. A former 18th-round pick in 2016, on the mound he looks like he's pitching at 1.5X speed thanks to his extremely quick tempo and cross-body delivery. His fastball is his best pitch and clocks in at 92-93 mph with movement, but he lacks command of it. His slider is easily his second-best pitch, an above-average offering that he uses to put away lefties. It's now a question of whether Dugger's changeup or curveball can develop far enough so that he can stick in a rotation and become a fourth or fifth starter, or if he falters and is sent packing to the bullpen.

Tommy Eveld RHP   Born: 12/30/93   Age: 25   Bats: R   Throws: R   Height: 6'5"   Weight: 195   Origin: Round 9, 2016 Draft (#269 overall)

YEAR	TEAM	LVL	AGE	W	L	SV	G	GS	IP	H	HR	BB/9	K/9	K	GB%	BABIP	WHIP	ERA	DRA	WARP	MPH	FB%	WHF	CSP
2016	YAK	A-	22	2	1	2	24	0	29	17	0	2.5	9.6	31	51%	.243	0.86	1.86	3.64	0.4				
2017	KNC	A	23	1	0	14	22	0	27²	10	0	2.6	10.7	33	59%	.169	0.65	0.33	3.59	0.4				
2017	VIS	A+	23	0	5	2	19	0	22	22	1	4.5	10.6	26	64%	.350	1.50	5.73	3.26	0.4				
2018	VIS	A+	24	2	2	12	32	0	36¹	29	1	1.7	10.4	42	54%	.298	0.99	1.24	2.48	1.0				
2018	JAX	AA	24	1	1	3	10	0	9²	6	0	2.8	13.0	14	38%	.286	0.93	0.93	2.93	0.2				
2019	MIA	MLB	25	2	1	2	39	0	41²	35	5	3.9	9.3	43	46%	.291	1.28	4.11	4.81	0.0				

Breakout: 3%   Improve: 7%   Collapse: 7%   Attrition: 13%   MLB: 15%   *Comparables: Adam Kolarek, Rowan Wick, Edgar Santana*

Originally a quarterback at the University of South Florida, Eveld never saw a snap after tearing his ACL. The 6-foot-5 athlete then tried to juggle being a wide receiver instead, while also making the baseball team. Though a second ACL tear set him back, he played enough baseball to show that he had the goods on the mound. He has a four-pitch mix but relies heavily on his 92-95 mph fastball and a slider that sometimes mirrors a cutter thanks to how hard he throws it. He's a little on the older side but has a realistic chance at a setup role, perhaps by the end of 2019.

Riley Ferrell RHP   Born: 10/18/93   Age: 25   Bats: R   Throws: R   Height: 6'2"   Weight: 200   Origin: Round 3, 2015 Draft (#79 overall)

YEAR	TEAM	LVL	AGE	W	L	SV	G	GS	IP	H	HR	BB/9	K/9	K	GB%	BABIP	WHIP	ERA	DRA	WARP	MPH	FB%	WHF	CSP
2016	LNC	A+	22	0	1	4	8	0	10	9	1	1.8	12.6	14	62%	.348	1.10	1.80	3.43	0.2				
2017	CCH	AA	23	2	2	4	36	0	52	51	2	2.4	9.5	55	52%	.348	1.25	3.81	3.24	1.0				
2018	CCH	AA	24	2	2	7	21	0	23²	14	1	6.8	12.5	33	47%	.260	1.35	1.90	3.00	0.5				
2018	FRE	AAA	24	2	1	2	22	0	28	34	4	5.1	10.9	34	38%	.390	1.79	6.75	3.80	0.4				
2019	MIA	MLB	25	2	1	0	32	0	34¹	29	4	4.3	10.3	39	45%	.305	1.32	4.05	4.74	0.1				

Breakout: 15%   Improve: 18%   Collapse: 12%   Attrition: 25%   MLB: 33%   *Comparables: Jimmie Sherfy, Joe Paterson, Jaye Chapman*

Ferrell combines a plus fastball, a plus slider and a consistently high strikeout rate dating back to his college days. The next time you wonder why there are so many strikeouts in baseball, remember that this profile is now common enough that Ferrell was exposed to the Rule 5 draft, where the Marlins snagged the potential late-inning reliever from the Astros. He'll have to remain on the active roster all season to stick in Miami, but if any team has reason to show patience with a talented young pitcher no matter the growing pains, it's certainly the Marlins.

Zac Gallen RHP   Born: 08/03/95   Age: 23   Bats: R   Throws: R   Height: 6'2"   Weight: 191   Origin: Round 3, 2016 Draft (#106 overall)

YEAR	TEAM	LVL	AGE	W	L	SV	G	GS	IP	H	HR	BB/9	K/9	K	GB%	BABIP	WHIP	ERA	DRA	WARP	MPH	FB%	WHF	CSP
2016	CRD	RK	20	0	0	1	6	3	9²	7	0	0.0	14.0	15	48%	.333	0.72	1.86	1.29	0.5				
2017	PMB	A+	21	5	2	0	9	9	55²	44	1	1.6	9.1	56	48%	.283	0.97	1.62	3.39	1.2				
2017	SFD	AA	21	4	5	0	13	13	71¹	76	8	2.4	5.3	42	42%	.292	1.33	3.79	4.08	0.9				
2017	MEM	AAA	21	1	1	0	4	4	20²	18	2	2.6	10.0	23	47%	.314	1.16	3.48	4.02	0.4				
2018	NWO	AAA	22	8	9	0	25	25	133¹	148	14	3.2	9.2	136	41%	.351	1.47	3.64	3.95	2.4				
2019	MIA	MLB	23	7	8	0	22	22	119	109	14	3.2	8.7	115	42%	.302	1.27	4.04	4.73	0.8				

Breakout: 12%   Improve: 15%   Collapse: 8%   Attrition: 21%   MLB: 26%   *Comparables: Taylor Guerrieri, Alex Cobb, Brady Rodgers*

Despite being arguably only the third-best of four prospects acquired from St. Louis as the Marlins' return in the Marcell Ozuna trade, Gallen has the type of profile that could reasonably ensure he ends up producing the most value of the group. Gallen checks every box in the Not A Flamethrower But Has Command Starter Pack: A four-pitch mix (fastball, cutter, curveball, changeup) that doesn't feature any plus pitch, a chance at above-average command at peak, sequencing knowledge and a slightly undersized build. After an encouraging season at Triple-A, Gallen should see a fair amount of time in the major-league rotation this year at age 23.

Jarlin Garcia LHP   Born: 01/18/93   Age: 26   Bats: L   Throws: L   Height: 6'3"   Weight: 215   Origin: International Free Agent, 2010

YEAR	TEAM	LVL	AGE	W	L	SV	G	GS	IP	H	HR	BB/9	K/9	K	GB%	BABIP	WHIP	ERA	DRA	WARP	MPH	FB%	WHF	CSP
2016	JAX	AA	23	1	3	0	9	9	39²	38	4	2.5	6.1	27	48%	.274	1.24	4.54	3.19	0.9				
2016	JUP	A+	23	0	0	0	5	0	7	4	1	1.3	6.4	5	48%	.150	0.71	1.29	3.42	0.1				
2017	MIA	MLB	24	1	2	0	68	0	53¹	47	6	2.9	7.1	42	41%	.263	1.20	4.72	4.42	0.4	95.8	49.8	12.1	47.8
2018	NWO	AAA	25	2	2	0	10	9	48²	57	5	2.6	6.1	33	40%	.323	1.46	4.81	4.06	0.8				
2018	MIA	MLB	25	3	3	0	29	7	66	59	16	3.8	5.5	40	44%	.222	1.32	4.91	5.51	-0.3	93.9	52.5	8.4	49.3
2019	MIA	MLB	26	3	2	0	46	3	61²	58	7	3.3	6.9	48	42%	.290	1.31	4.31	5.06	0.0	94.3	52.3	10.1	49.5

Breakout: 23%   Improve: 37%   Collapse: 19%   Attrition: 26%   MLB: 62%   *Comparables: Brandon Workman, Zach Stewart, Liam Hendriks*

Sometimes you have to search deep to understand why a pitcher regressed. Other times, like in Garcia's case last season, you just have to look at his velocity. The southpaw lost two ticks across the board, leaving his fastball averaging 92 mph last season, and putting him right around the 50th percentile in velocity among lefty peers. Add a loss of control and he set new career-low marks in strikeout rate and walk rate. Even worse, he allowed the most home runs of any relief pitcher in baseball (16). About the only value he provides at the moment is name value, as the organization finally has someone whose name rhymes with the mascot.

Braxton Garrett LHP   Born: 08/05/97   Age: 21   Bats: L   Throws: L   Height: 6'3"   Weight: 190   Origin: Round 1, 2016 Draft (#7 overall)

YEAR	TEAM	LVL	AGE	W	L	SV	G	GS	IP	H	HR	BB/9	K/9	K	GB%	BABIP	WHIP	ERA	DRA	WARP	MPH	FB%	WHF	CSP
2017	GRB	A	19	1	0	0	4	4	15¹	13	3	3.5	9.4	16	49%	.250	1.24	2.93	2.87	0.4				
2019	MIA	MLB	21	2	3	0	8	8	35	35	6	4.2	8.1	31	42%	.300	1.46	5.22	6.09	-0.3				

Breakout: 1%   Improve: 2%   Collapse: 1%   Attrition: 3%   MLB: 5%   *Comparables: Tyrell Jenkins, Drew Anderson, Keury Mella*

It's been more than two years since the Marlins drafted Garrett seventh overall out of an Alabama high school and we barely know more about him now than we did back then. The southpaw underwent Tommy John surgery in July of 2017, setting him up for a second-half return this upcoming season. But in the 15 1/3 innings he pitched before going down, he showed glimpses of why the Marlins liked him so much as a prep arm. His curveball is a future plus pitch that hovers between 76-80 mph, the kind he can spot and play well off his average fastball. His changeup is a potential above-average offering, too. Because he was drafted out of high school time is still on his side, but he can ill afford any more loss of development.

Merandy Gonzalez RHP   Born: 10/09/95   Age: 23   Bats: R   Throws: R   Height: 6'0"   Weight: 216   Origin: International Free Agent, 2013

YEAR	TEAM	LVL	AGE	W	L	SV	G	GS	IP	H	HR	BB/9	K/9	K	GB%	BABIP	WHIP	ERA	DRA	WARP	MPH	FB%	WHF	CSP
2016	BRO	A-	20	6	3	0	14	14	69	65	2	3.5	9.3	71	54%	.337	1.33	2.87	3.42	1.5				
2017	COL	A	21	8	1	0	11	11	69²	50	3	1.7	8.4	65	43%	.253	0.90	1.55	3.10	1.8				
2017	SLU	A+	21	4	2	0	6	6	36¹	33	1	2.0	5.9	24	43%	.271	1.13	2.23	5.91	-0.3				
2017	JUP	A+	21	1	0	1	5	3	24¹	18	0	1.8	5.2	14	56%	.247	0.95	1.11	3.93	0.4				
2018	JAX	AA	22	3	6	0	14	14	73	68	7	4.1	5.8	47	41%	.282	1.38	4.32	4.92	0.4				
2018	MIA	MLB	22	2	1	0	8	1	22	31	4	3.3	7.8	19	34%	.375	1.77	5.73	7.39	-0.6	96.1	56.3	9.6	45.7
2019	MIA	MLB	23	4	6	1	23	14	85²	82	12	3.9	7.1	68	40%	.292	1.39	4.82	5.64	-0.5	96.0	58.3	10	47.3

Breakout: 4%   Improve: 8%   Collapse: 8%   Attrition: 10%   MLB: 18%   *Comparables: Tom Gorzelanny, Trevor Oaks, Yency Almonte*

It feels like the Marlins are hedging a bit with Gonzalez. Pegged by scouts to be a future reliever thanks to inconsistent fastball command and the lack of development on his changeup, the Fish insisted on keeping him as a starter. His strikeouts continued to wane and his walks doubled in his first taste of Double-A. Despite the mediocre results, the team surprisingly promoted him to the big-league bullpen in the early months, where he made seven appearances and struggled, though his strikeouts returned. His value to a major-league team remains in flux with his role questions, and he hasn't conquered either role recently.

Tayron Guerrero RHP   Born: 01/09/91   Age: 28   Bats: R   Throws: R   Height: 6'8"   Weight: 210   Origin: International Free Agent, 2009

YEAR	TEAM	LVL	AGE	W	L	SV	G	GS	IP	H	HR	BB/9	K/9	K	GB%	BABIP	WHIP	ERA	DRA	WARP	MPH	FB%	WHF	CSP
2016	SDN	MLB	25	0	0	0	1	0	2	3	0	4.5	0.0	0	50%	.375	2.00	4.50	6.75	0.0	96.2	86.4	0	39.5
2016	ELP	AAA	25	0	0	0	13	0	12	12	2	6.8	8.2	11	43%	.286	1.75	6.00	4.84	0.0				
2016	SAN	AA	25	0	3	0	19	0	23²	20	2	3.8	9.5	25	48%	.300	1.27	4.94	3.74	0.3				
2016	JAX	AA	25	1	1	4	12	0	14	11	0	1.9	9.6	15	27%	.297	1.00	1.93	2.51	0.4				
2017	JAX	AA	26	0	1	0	17	0	16	14	3	7.9	12.4	22	41%	.306	1.75	3.38	5.98	-0.2				
2017	NWO	AAA	26	3	2	0	13	0	15¹	12	2	7.0	6.5	11	44%	.217	1.57	5.87	4.47	0.1				
2018	MIA	MLB	27	1	3	0	60	0	58	64	8	4.7	10.6	68	45%	.354	1.62	5.43	4.80	0.1	101.5	79.2	12.4	49.4
2019	MIA	MLB	28	3	1	6	59	0	63	53	8	4.3	9.7	68	42%	.291	1.33	4.34	5.07	-0.1	100.8	79.7	12.3	46

Breakout: 12%   Improve: 25%   Collapse: 15%   Attrition: 21%   MLB: 47%   *Comparables: Royce Ring, Brandon Cunniff, Mark Malaska*

Guerrero burst onto the scenes on Opening Day against the Cubs, striking out his first four batters of the year. People wondered who the hell this 6-foot-8 dude averaging nearly 99 mph on his fastball was. Guerrero at times showed an above-average slider to pair with his heater, but he was very inconsistent in the zone, giving up too many free passes and ranking in the bottom five of reliever first-pitch strikes. Pair that with the fourth-worst BABIP in his class and it's easy to understand why just throwing a million miles an hour didn't work for him.

Jorge Guzman RHP Born: 01/28/96   Age: 23   Bats: R   Throws: R   Height: 6'2"   Weight: 182   Origin: International Free Agent, 2014

YEAR	TEAM	LVL	AGE	W	L	SV	G	GS	IP	H	HR	BB/9	K/9	K	GB%	BABIP	WHIP	ERA	DRA	WARP	MPH	FB%	WHF	CSP
2016	AST	RK	20	1	1	0	7	4	17¹	4	0	5.2	13.0	25	77%	.129	0.81	3.12	3.03	0.5				
2016	GRV	RK	20	2	3	0	6	4	22²	25	1	2.8	11.5	29	56%	.387	1.41	4.76	2.29	0.8				
2017	STA	A-	21	5	3	0	13	13	66²	51	4	2.4	11.9	88	55%	.311	1.03	2.30	2.14	2.4				
2018	JUP	A+	22	0	9	0	21	21	96	84	7	6.0	9.5	101	40%	.303	1.54	4.03	4.95	0.4				
2019	MIA	MLB	23	4	7	0	18	18	77²	73	14	5.8	9.1	78	44%	.301	1.59	5.56	6.48	-1.0				

Breakout: 2%   Improve: 2%   Collapse: 2%   Attrition: 2%   MLB: 4%   *Comparables: Steve Johnson, J.A. Happ, Josh Outman*

Not even Guzman's 99 mph fastball can distract you from realizing how much of a step back he took in 2018. The prized prospect acquired from the Yankees in the Giancarlo Stanton trade turned in a 15 percent walk rate in 96 innings, good for third-worst in the minors had he qualified. His strikeouts also regressed in his High-A debut; after easily crossing the 30 percent whiff mark in his past seasons, he finished at 23 percent. It was a rude awakening for Guzman, who tilted the scale a little closer to "future reliever" after showing he couldn't support his 80-grade fastball with a below-average changeup and average-at-best curveball. His control and command are still missing, and at 22 years old he can't fall back on age as an excuse.

Tyler Kolek RHP Born: 12/15/95   Age: 23   Bats: R   Throws: R   Height: 6'5"   Weight: 260   Origin: Round 1, 2014 Draft (#2 overall)

YEAR	TEAM	LVL	AGE	W	L	SV	G	GS	IP	H	HR	BB/9	K/9	K	GB%	BABIP	WHIP	ERA	DRA	WARP	MPH	FB%	WHF	CSP
2018	BAT	A-	22	1	2	0	8	0	14	12	0	4.5	7.7	12	44%	.279	1.36	4.50	4.11	0.1				
2019	MIA	MLB	23	0	4	0	9	6	27¹	30	6	13.2	6.4	20	43%	.303	2.58	9.49	11.14	-1.9				

Breakout: 1%   Improve: 2%   Collapse: 0%   Attrition: 2%   MLB: 2%   *Comparables: Kevin McGowan, Pedro Villarreal, Mike Parisi*

Have you ever decided to watch a movie only because it featured your favorite director or actor? Maybe you trusted the last piece of work they turned in and decided "screw it, I won't even care what this movie is about because it has their fingerprints!" This is what the Marlins did in the 2014 draft. The feature presentation *Tyler Kolek* was playing, directed by Josh Beckett and produced by "Large Texan Righty" studios. The movie bombed. After costing $6 million to produce, there's a chance Kolek will never be seen by a single member of the audience for which it was intended.

Nick Neidert RHP Born: 11/20/96   Age: 22   Bats: R   Throws: R   Height: 6'1"   Weight: 180   Origin: Round 2, 2015 Draft (#60 overall)

YEAR	TEAM	LVL	AGE	W	L	SV	G	GS	IP	H	HR	BB/9	K/9	K	GB%	BABIP	WHIP	ERA	DRA	WARP	MPH	FB%	WHF	CSP
2016	CLN	A	19	7	3	0	19	19	91	75	7	1.3	6.8	69	41%	.262	0.97	2.57	3.67	1.5				
2017	MOD	A+	20	10	3	0	19	19	104¹	95	7	1.5	9.4	109	43%	.318	1.07	2.76	3.16	2.6				
2017	ARK	AA	20	1	3	0	6	6	23¹	33	4	1.9	5.0	13	47%	.341	1.63	6.56	4.19	0.3				
2018	JAX	AA	21	12	7	0	26	26	152²	142	17	1.8	9.1	154	47%	.309	1.13	3.24	3.79	2.8				
2019	MIA	MLB	22	7	8	0	25	25	123¹	114	15	2.3	7.8	107	41%	.293	1.18	3.91	4.58	1.0				

Breakout: 16%   Improve: 32%   Collapse: 14%   Attrition: 28%   MLB: 55%   *Comparables: Alex White, Erasmo Ramirez, Aaron Poreda*

Neidert has old-man skills — the good kind that should lead him to a long and fruitful career in the majors. Living off advanced control and command, he takes his below-average fastball and masterfully sequences it with his nearly plus changeup and average curveball. It's how he's amassed a sub-2.0 BB/9 in his minor-league career. He peppers the fringes of the strike zone and induces weak contact. Neidert isn't just a pitch-to-contact guy, either, striking out more than a batter an inning last year. Don't be surprised if he takes on a significant role this upcoming season and ultimately becomes one of the more reliable no. 4 starters in baseball.

Trevor Richards RHP Born: 05/15/93   Age: 26   Bats: R   Throws: R   Height: 6'2"   Weight: 190   Origin: Undrafted Free Agent, 2016

YEAR	TEAM	LVL	AGE	W	L	SV	G	GS	IP	H	HR	BB/9	K/9	K	GB%	BABIP	WHIP	ERA	DRA	WARP	MPH	FB%	WHF	CSP
2016	BAT	A-	23	0	0	0	3	1	10²	9	1	1.7	12.7	15	28%	.333	1.03	1.69	1.26	0.5				
2016	GRB	A	23	2	3	0	8	8	43²	29	3	2.9	7.8	38	47%	.222	0.98	2.68	3.44	0.8				
2017	JUP	A+	24	7	4	0	13	11	70²	54	2	1.5	10.3	81	62%	.284	0.93	2.17	2.94	1.9				
2017	JAX	AA	24	5	7	0	14	14	75¹	67	4	2.2	9.2	77	50%	.297	1.13	2.87	2.93	2.0				
2018	NWO	AAA	25	3	2	0	6	6	39¹	31	4	0.9	8.5	37	50%	.260	0.89	2.06	2.64	1.3				
2018	MIA	MLB	25	4	9	0	25	25	126¹	121	15	3.8	9.3	130	38%	.309	1.39	4.42	3.57	2.5	92.2	54.8	11.7	44.4
2019	MIA	MLB	26	7	8	0	24	24	127¹	113	16	3.2	8.9	126	42%	.296	1.25	4.00	4.69	0.9	91.8	55.8	12	45.2

Breakout: 28%   Improve: 53%   Collapse: 18%   Attrition: 19%   MLB: 92%   *Comparables: Marc Rzepczynski, Angel Guzman, Anthony DeSclafani*

There can't be a Trevor Richards blurb without immediately mentioning his double-plus changeup that ranks as one of the best in baseball. It's an elite circle-change that he wields with aplomb, using it to rack up the 11th-best whiffs-per-swing rate among his peers thanks to its massive tumble. However, he neutralized that weapon by pairing it with one of the worst fastballs in baseball, a really hittable 91 mph offering that was below the 20th percentile in whiffs per swing. Overall, it was a solid rookie campaign for someone once seen as organizational depth. Richards is a good complement in the back end of a rotation.

Trevor Rogers LHP Born: 11/13/97   Age: 21   Bats: L   Throws: L   Height: 6'6"   Weight: 185   Origin: Round 1, 2017 Draft (#13 overall)

YEAR	TEAM	LVL	AGE	W	L	SV	G	GS	IP	H	HR	BB/9	K/9	K	GB%	BABIP	WHIP	ERA	DRA	WARP	MPH	FB%	WHF	CSP
2018	GRB	A	20	2	7	0	17	17	72²	86	4	3.3	10.5	85	48%	.394	1.56	5.82	4.46	0.6				
2019	MIA	MLB	21	3	4	0	12	12	54	53	8	3.9	8.4	51	41%	.312	1.42	4.61	5.39	0.0				

Comparables: Robbie Ross, Christian Friedrich, John Gant

Limbs. Limbs everywhere. Rogers' 6-foot-6 frame and three-quarters delivery from the left side display his long levers and allow him to get great extension as he delivers his pitches. His four-seamer sits 90-92 mph, but he can reach back for 95 when needed. His two-seamer is his ground-ball generator and his weapon against righties. His slider and changeup have nice velocity separation and project as future average offerings. As you might expect from someone so big on the mound, there are some command issues at present because of mechanics, but his low-effort delivery should aid in rectifying them. All in all it was a strong professional debut for Rogers in his first season after recovering from Tommy John surgery.

Caleb Smith LHP Born: 07/28/91 Age: 27 Bats: R Throws: L Height: 6'2" Weight: 205 Origin: Round 14, 2013 Draft (#434 overall)

YEAR	TEAM	LVL	AGE	W	L	SV	G	GS	IP	H	HR	BB/9	K/9	K	GB%	BABIP	WHIP	ERA	DRA	WARP	MPH	FB%	WHF	CSP
2016	TRN	AA	24	3	5	3	27	7	63²	66	4	2.8	9.9	70	45%	.344	1.35	3.96	3.04	1.4				
2017	SWB	AAA	25	9	1	0	18	17	98	75	7	2.6	8.9	97	42%	.264	1.05	2.39	4.04	1.8				
2017	NYA	MLB	25	0	1	0	9	2	18²	21	4	4.8	8.7	18	28%	.315	1.66	7.71	4.92	0.1	95.5	50.3	14.4	42.2
2018	MIA	MLB	26	5	6	0	16	16	77¹	63	10	3.8	10.2	88	31%	.276	1.24	4.19	4.05	1.1	94.3	59.1	13.3	48.7
2019	*MIA*	*MLB*	*27*	*4*	*5*	*0*	*15*	*15*	*75*	*63*	*10*	*3.3*	*9.8*	*82*	*37%*	*.290*	*1.21*	*4.01*	*4.69*	*0.5*	*94.0*	*58.4*	*13.7*	*46.4*

Breakout: 22% Improve: 38% Collapse: 16% Attrition: 24% MLB: 73%   *Comparables: Mark Leiter, Dustin Nippert, Adam Ottavino*

The most interesting pitcher in the rotation might be one who pitched for less than half a season after left lat surgery cut his year short in June. Smith rode one of the better sliders in baseball to success, neutralizing both righties and lefties and proving that it's a legitimate out-pitch. His fastball, which finished in the top 20th percentile in spin rate, elevates his mediocre changeup. While the swing and miss is there, concerns remain over his ability to command his pitches, as well as better utilize a changeup that was little more than a show-me offering. Health permitting, Smith should be a decent sleeper in a forgotten rotation.

Drew Steckenrider RHP Born: 01/10/91 Age: 28 Bats: R Throws: R Height: 6'5" Weight: 215 Origin: Round 8, 2012 Draft (#257 overall)

YEAR	TEAM	LVL	AGE	W	L	SV	G	GS	IP	H	HR	BB/9	K/9	K	GB%	BABIP	WHIP	ERA	DRA	WARP	MPH	FB%	WHF	CSP
2016	JUP	A+	25	0	0	1	6	0	10	2	0	1.8	15.3	17	64%	.143	0.40	0.00	2.00	0.4				
2016	JAX	AA	25	1	0	6	24	0	30¹	12	0	3.0	11.6	39	54%	.197	0.73	1.48	1.65	1.1				
2016	NWO	AAA	25	0	1	7	10	0	11²	11	1	5.4	11.6	15	52%	.333	1.54	5.40	2.96	0.3				
2017	NWO	AAA	26	0	1	5	26	0	33¹	18	3	2.2	11.9	44	43%	.217	0.78	1.62	1.67	1.3				
2017	MIA	MLB	26	1	1	1	37	0	34²	30	4	4.7	14.0	54	43%	.347	1.38	2.34	3.70	0.6	96.8	77.8	14.8	49.9
2018	MIA	MLB	27	4	4	5	71	0	64²	55	7	3.8	10.3	74	34%	.296	1.27	3.90	4.44	0.4	96.4	76.4	12.2	50.8
2019	*MIA*	*MLB*	*28*	*3*	*1*	*18*	*59*	*0*	*63*	*51*	*8*	*3.9*	*10.6*	*74*	*41%*	*.295*	*1.25*	*3.91*	*4.57*	*0.3*	*95.9*	*77.3*	*13.1*	*50.7*

Breakout: 24% Improve: 37% Collapse: 26% Attrition: 16% MLB: 73%   *Comparables: Michael Wuertz, Jerry Blevins, Zach Putnam*

Steckenrider took a step backward from an impressive rookie campaign in which he punched out nearly 36 percent of batters faced. While his 27 percent mark in 2018 is nothing to scoff at, his peripherals deteriorated and he turned into an extreme fly-ball pitcher after ditching his slider for a cutter. The whiffs remained the same on his new pitch, so it's not to blame for his loss of strikeouts. Instead, heatmaps showed he didn't elevate his fastball last year as much as in 2017, likely leading to the drop in whiff rate on his primary pitch. He improved his walk rate from bad to manageable, and he could be a candidate to close thanks to his raw stuff.

Dan Straily RHP Born: 12/01/88 Age: 30 Bats: R Throws: R Height: 6'2" Weight: 220 Origin: Round 24, 2009 Draft (#723 overall)

YEAR	TEAM	LVL	AGE	W	L	SV	G	GS	IP	H	HR	BB/9	K/9	K	GB%	BABIP	WHIP	ERA	DRA	WARP	MPH	FB%	WHF	CSP
2016	CIN	MLB	27	14	8	0	34	31	191¹	154	31	3.4	7.6	162	34%	.239	1.19	3.76	4.76	1.3	91.8	51	11.1	47.4
2017	MIA	MLB	28	10	9	0	33	33	181²	176	31	3.0	8.4	170	36%	.288	1.30	4.26	4.26	2.7	92.1	50.5	13.2	47.6
2018	MIA	MLB	29	5	6	0	23	23	122¹	107	20	3.8	7.3	99	34%	.256	1.30	4.12	5.19	0.2	91.9	49.3	11.2	46.5
2019	*MIA*	*MLB*	*30*	*7*	*10*	*0*	*26*	*26*	*137²*	*124*	*20*	*3.5*	*8.1*	*124*	*36%*	*.282*	*1.28*	*4.56*	*5.32*	*0.0*	*91.2*	*50.1*	*11.9*	*46.9*

Breakout: 17% Improve: 35% Collapse: 15% Attrition: 16% MLB: 71%   *Comparables: Byung-Hyun Kim, Scott Richmond, Jason Bergmann*

Straily led the 2017 Marlins in starts, but right forearm inflammation forced him to miss a month of last season. Whether or not he felt the side effects of that as the season wore on is more speculation than anything, but overall he regressed. His fastball, though it maintained similar velocity, induced fewer swings, and he began pitching it closer to the center of the zone rather than favoring the top like in the past. Throwing a 90 mph fastball down the middle more often is how you allow a .553 slugging on the pitch. Straily quietly has one of the more elite changeups in baseball, ranking in the top 15 in ground-ball rate and whiff rates last year, but he opted to turn more to his slider, enough that in his final start of the year he threw it more than his heater. It's an average pitch, but not one to prioritize. Still just 30 and under team control for two more seasons, Straily can be counted on to be an innings eater, but he's trending closer to the back of a rotation than the middle.

Jose Urena RHP Born: 09/12/91 Age: 27 Bats: R Throws: R Height: 6'2" Weight: 200 Origin: International Free Agent, 2008

YEAR	TEAM	LVL	AGE	W	L	SV	G	GS	IP	H	HR	BB/9	K/9	K	GB%	BABIP	WHIP	ERA	DRA	WARP	MPH	FB%	WHF	CSP
2016	NWO	AAA	24	3	3	0	12	12	48¹	41	4	3.9	7.6	41	46%	.278	1.28	3.17	3.36	1.1				
2016	MIA	MLB	24	4	9	1	28	12	83²	91	11	3.1	6.2	58	49%	.297	1.43	6.13	5.75	-0.5	97.7	66.2	10	43.1
2017	MIA	MLB	25	14	7	0	34	28	169²	152	26	3.4	6.0	113	44%	.249	1.27	3.82	5.25	0.5	97.3	56.2	9.1	45.2
2018	MIA	MLB	26	9	12	0	31	31	174	155	19	2.6	6.7	130	51%	.272	1.18	3.98	4.01	2.6	97.5	58.8	9.7	46.2
2019	*MIA*	*MLB*	*27*	*9*	*10*	*0*	*28*	*28*	*159²*	*138*	*16*	*3.1*	*7.6*	*134*	*47%*	*.284*	*1.21*	*3.97*	*4.65*	*1.2*	*97.0*	*59.6*	*9.6*	*45.6*

Breakout: 15% Improve: 35% Collapse: 22% Attrition: 19% MLB: 79%   *Comparables: Nick Martinez, Kendall Graveman, Chris Tillman*

Urena is a proud, card-carrying member of the Throw Hard, Strike No One Out club. Behind a fastball that averaged more than 96 mph, the righty posted yet another strikeout rate below 20 percent in 2018. He used one of those fastballs to hit Ronald Acuna Jr., who was on his leadoff home run tear in mid-August. His primarily value is eating innings at this point, as not much else about his game has the potential be above average.

Jordan Yamamoto RHP Born: 05/11/96 Age: 23 Bats: R Throws: R Height: 6'0" Weight: 185 Origin: Round 12, 2014 Draft (#356 overall)

YEAR	TEAM	LVL	AGE	W	L	SV	G	GS	IP	H	HR	BB/9	K/9	K	GB%	BABIP	WHIP	ERA	DRA	WARP	MPH	FB%	WHF	CSP
2016	WIS	A	20	7	8	0	27	18	134¹	130	6	2.1	10.2	152	48%	.343	1.20	3.82	2.99	3.2				
2017	CAR	A+	21	9	4	1	22	18	111	91	8	2.4	9.2	113	40%	.286	1.09	2.51	3.59	2.1				
2018	JUP	A+	22	4	1	0	7	7	40²	26	0	1.8	10.4	47	44%	.268	0.84	1.55	2.89	1.2				
2018	MRL	RK	22	1	0	0	3	3	11	5	1	1.6	12.3	15	64%	.190	0.64	2.45	1.77	0.5				
2018	JAX	AA	22	1	0	0	3	3	17	12	1	2.1	12.2	23	45%	.282	0.94	2.12	4.05	0.3				
2019	MIA	MLB	23	2	1	0	19	3	32¹	28	4	3.0	9.4	34	41%	.300	1.20	3.84	4.49	0.4				

Breakout: 6%   Improve: 10%   Collapse: 15%   Attrition: 18%   MLB: 33%   *Comparables: Austin Gomber, Miguel Almonte, Glenn Sparkman*

There's a non-zero chance that Yamamoto emerges as the best player acquired from the Brewers in the Christian Yelich trade, which included then-headliner Lewis Brinson, Monte Harrison and Isan Diaz. That's a loaded sentence to be sure, but also a testament to Yamamoto's arsenal and what he can do with it when healthy. He bookended the 2018 season with disabled list stints for his shoulder, but still carved some time in the Arizona Fall League. His above-average fastball and plus slider still play well with his short stride, and his strong control allows him to bust hitters in to rack up strikeouts. He's not a flashy guy, but the organization has to be thrilled with the returns on the former 12th rounder out of Hawaii.

LINEOUTS

Hitters

HITTER	POS	TEAM	LVL	AGE	PA	R	2B	3B	HR	RBI	BB	K	SB	CS	AVG/OBP/SLG	DRC+	VORP	BABIP	BRR	FRAA	WARP
Pedro Alvarez	3B	BAL	MLB	31	127	18	2	0	8	18	16	36	0	0	.180/.283/.414	98	-0.5	.179	-0.4	3B(8): -0.3, 1B(1): 0.0	0.1
	3B	NOR	AAA	31	178	21	6	0	8	32	11	42	0	0	.285/.331/.467	108	4.6	.336	0.5	1B(2): -0.1	0.5
Chris Bostick	CF	IND	AAA	25	327	32	24	3	4	32	24	66	6	3	.295/.351/.436	107	13.6	.367	-0.1	CF(52): -10.1, LF(15): 0.8	0.3
	CF	PIT	MLB	25	2	0	0	0	0	0	0	1	0	0	.000/.000/.000	77	-0.5	.000	0.0	LF(1): 0.0	0.0
	CF	NWO	AAA	25	71	6	1	0	0	6	5	19	1	1	.281/.338/.297	76	1.3	.391	0.8	LF(12): -0.6, 2B(3): -0.3	0.0
	CF	MIA	MLB	25	16	0	1	0	0	2	2	6	0	0	.214/.313/.286	70	-0.7	.375	-0.5	2B(2): -0.2, LF(1): 0.1	-0.1
Gabriel Guerrero	RF	PEN	AA	24	107	13	9	1	2	16	7	26	3	0	.296/.336/.469	87	6.7	.375	0.5	CF(24): 4.5	0.7
	RF	LOU	AAA	24	432	64	15	4	17	65	23	97	1	3	.292/.326/.475	115	20.1	.342	0.2	RF(88): -0.1, CF(16): 1.2	2.0
	RF	CIN	MLB	24	18	1	0	0	1	1	0	8	0	0	.167/.167/.333	73	-0.8	.222	0.0	CF(4): -0.2, RF(1): 0.0	0.0
Rosell Herrera	RF	CIN	MLB	25	13	0	0	0	0	0	0	5	0	1	.154/.154/.154	77	-1.5	.250	-0.1	LF(2): -0.1, 2B(1): -0.1	0.0
	RF	LOU	AAA	25	98	11	8	2	3	11	6	15	2	1	.267/.320/.500	116	6.9	.292	1.3	3B(7): -0.5, LF(6): -1.1	0.3
	RF	OMA	AAA	25	41	8	3	2	1	5	5	7	4	1	.278/.366/.556	104	5.4	.321	0.5	CF(6): 0.4, RF(2): 0.2	0.2
	RF	KCA	MLB	25	289	25	14	3	1	20	19	52	3	4	.238/.292/.325	69	-1.5	.290	1.7	RF(29): -0.4, 2B(17): 0.5	-0.3
Bryan Holaday	C	MIA	MLB	30	166	7	5	0	1	16	10	29	0	0	.205/.261/.258	82	-4.9	.244	-1.5	C(50): 4.5, P(2): 0.0	0.8
Dixon Machado	SS	DET	MLB	26	233	20	13	1	1	21	14	41	1	1	.206/.263/.290	73	-5.8	.249	1.5	2B(64): 0.8	0.2
	SS	TOL	AAA	26	171	19	5	0	1	8	18	28	4	2	.224/.321/.279	91	2.5	.271	0.0	SS(25): -0.2, 2B(16): 3.2	0.8
Deven Marrero	SS	ARI	MLB	27	85	11	1	1	0	7	6	23	3	0	.167/.224/.205	63	-6.6	.232	0.5	3B(33): 1.4, 2B(5): 0.0	0.1
	SS	RNO	AAA	27	76	10	4	1	1	7	7	20	0	0	.227/.297/.364	84	1.7	.304	1.1	3B(11): -0.8, SS(7): 0.0	0.2
Peter O'Brien	RF	TUL	AA	27	112	12	3	0	7	22	10	44	0	0	.150/.241/.390	97	-5.3	.163	0.3	1B(26): -3.3	-0.2
	RF	JAX	AA	27	174	22	4	0	13	31	28	49	0	0	.215/.345/.514	148	10.1	.217	-0.2	1B(23): -1.8, LF(7): -1.1	1.0
	RF	NWO	AAA	27	135	22	6	0	10	33	20	40	1	0	.277/.385/.598	126	18.0	.328	1.0	RF(17): 3.5, 1B(14): -1.3	1.1
	RF	MIA	MLB	27	74	8	5	0	4	10	7	22	0	0	.273/.338/.530	94	5.6	.341	0.7	1B(17): -1.9, RF(2): 2.4	0.2
Rafael Ortega	LF	NWO	AAA	27	328	51	10	10	2	28	44	31	12	1	.275/.375/.404	119	15.3	.304	2.5	LF(62): -7.0, RF(2): -0.3	1.2
	LF	MIA	MLB	27	143	10	3	1	0	7	10	23	5	2	.233/.287/.271	84	-5.5	.282	-0.6	RF(23): 0.7, LF(15): 2.7	0.3
Yadiel Rivera	3B	MIA	MLB	26	160	13	3	0	1	9	19	51	2	1	.173/.269/.216	56	-7.0	.258	-0.4	3B(29): 2.8, SS(28): -0.2	0.0
Chad Wallach	C	NWO	AAA	26	174	20	7	0	3	16	20	47	0	1	.224/.324/.333	79	1.9	.300	-2.6	C(40): 8.1	1.0
	C	MIA	MLB	26	52	4	1	0	1	5	4	23	0	0	.178/.275/.267	51	0.1	.333	0.1	C(14): 2.6	0.2

On a different but still terrible Orioles team, **Pedro Alvarez** might have had a role. Unfortunately the skill set of "hits for some power/poor defender" was filled many times over in 2018 by Baltimore's Stonehenge of Trumbo/Davis/Mancini. Not even an above-average walk rate could keep Alvarez safe from Norfolk, where an Achilles' tendon injury ended his season in late August. ⊗ Already traded three times before turning 23, **Chris Bostick**'s redeeming quality is his ability to play nearly every position. But without an outstanding glove, and with a forgettable, light bat, he's on his way to journeyman status. ⊗ **Gabriel Guerrero** is related to Vlad The Impaler, but he didn't get as lucky as his cousin, Vlad Jr., when it comes to the baseball genes. A bit of power returned last season, but the contact rate and strikeouts are too problematic for now. ⊗ A fringy, speed-based corner outfielder cut loose by the Reds (the Reds, for goodness sake!) in June, **Rosell Herrera** went on to accumulate over 300 plate appearances with the Royals, doing very poorly the two things he was supposed to do well: steal bases and take walks. ⊗ **Bryan Holaday**'s career OPS sank below .600 after a horrendous season at the plate, but he still provides defensive value thanks to being one of the better framing catchers in baseball. ⊗ If you're scavenging for Triple-A highlight reels, you're going to find **Dixon Machado** pick some crazy grounders. Because he can't hit worth a lick in the majors, the video quality is unlikely to be high-def. ⊗ Teams don't want to rely on a guy like **Deven Marrero**, but the Diamondbacks were forced to do so when early injuries pressed the journeyman into action. He provided solid defensive value, but he still can't hit. ⊗ Very little is known about the 17-year-old **Victor Mesa Jr.** He's a switch-hitter, he has a projectable body with below-average current offensive tools and his brother is rich now. ⊗ It's beginning to look like **Peter O'Brien** may not be the next great Yankees catcher. He could be the next Quad-A corner bat in Miami, though. ⊗ It's unfair to think **Rafael Ortega** has hit his apex just 179 games into his major-league career, but with nonexistent power, little speed, below-average defense and moderate plate discipline, he's a fifth outfielder at best. ⊗ Of 392 batters that accrued at least 150 plate appearances last year, **Yadiel Rivera**'s .485 OPS was second-worst in baseball. Rarely does one number summarize a player, but in Rivera's case, that's about all you need to know. ⊗ **Chad Wallach** will continue to be known as Tim's son until he shows he's more than a third-string catcher who can't hit.

Pitchers

PITCHER	TEAM	LVL	AGE	W	L	SV	G	GS	IP	H	HR	BB/9	K/9	K	GB%	BABIP	WHIP	ERA	DRA	WARP	MPH	FB%	WHF	CSP
Jeff Brigham	JAX	AA	26	4	1	0	7	7	38	27	1	2.1	9.7	41	41%	.299	0.95	1.18	4.43	0.4				
	NWO	AAA	26	5	2	0	9	9	52^1	53	7	2.2	8.3	48	30%	.315	1.26	3.44	4.17	0.8				
	MIA	MLB	26	0	4	0	4	4	16^1	16	2	7.2	6.6	12	20%	.292	1.78	6.06	7.19	-0.4	94.7	61.1	8.9	47.4
Tyler Cloyd	MIA	MLB	31	0	0	0	7	0	17^2	25	3	5.1	6.6	13	32%	.367	1.98	8.66	7.32	-0.5	91.8	82.1	8	49.5
	NWO	AAA	31	6	5	0	17	15	85^1	96	14	1.9	7.2	68	40%	.315	1.34	5.17	4.11	1.4				
Miguel Del Pozo	JAX	AA	25	5	0	1	28	0	34	37	3	4.0	9.0	34	39%	.343	1.53	3.97	4.50	0.2				
Brett Graves	JAX	AA	25	1	1	0	5	1	12^1	13	2	4.4	7.3	10	58%	.282	1.54	5.11	3.99	0.2				
	MIA	MLB	25	1	1	1	21	0	33^1	41	3	3.2	5.7	21	47%	.352	1.59	5.40	4.86	0.0	94.3	51.4	10.9	45.3
Javy Guerra	NWO	AAA	32	3	0	5	12	0	16^2	9	0	1.6	13.0	24	61%	.273	0.72	0.00	2.15	0.6				
	MIA	MLB	32	1	1	1	32	0	35^2	42	4	3.0	7.6	30	45%	.336	1.51	5.55	5.02	0.0	94.9	52.2	9.9	51.5
Elieser Hernandez	MIA	MLB	23	2	7	0	32	6	65^2	68	11	3.7	6.2	45	30%	.286	1.45	5.21	6.00	-0.7	92.7	62.1	9.3	49.7
Tyler Kinley	MIN	MLB	27	0	0	0	4	0	3^1	9	2	10.8	10.8	4	60%	.538	3.90	24.30	2.63	0.1	97.5	67.9	14.8	39
	NWO	AAA	27	2	2	8	40	0	40	32	2	4.9	12.6	56	38%	.326	1.35	2.92	2.42	1.2				
	MIA	MLB	27	0	0	0	9	0	7^2	6	0	4.7	10.6	9	55%	.300	1.30	7.04	2.30	0.2	98.5	56.2	15.4	45.7
Pablo Lopez	JAX	AA	22	1	2	0	8	8	43^2	30	3	1.6	10.5	51	42%	.245	0.87	0.62	3.62	0.9				
	NWO	AAA	22	1	1	0	4	4	18^2	16	3	1.9	7.2	15	47%	.236	1.07	3.38	3.93	0.3				
	MIA	MLB	22	2	4	0	10	10	58^2	56	8	2.8	7.1	46	50%	.281	1.26	4.14	4.58	0.5	94.7	60.4	11.7	46.5
Ben Meyer	NWO	AAA	25	5	4	0	15	11	63^2	67	4	2.7	6.9	49	43%	.320	1.35	4.24	3.83	1.2				
	MIA	MLB	25	0	0	0	13	0	19	26	2	6.6	4.3	9	44%	.353	2.11	10.42	8.00	-0.7	93.7	66.4	6	44.4
Chris O'Grady	MIA	MLB	28	0	1	0	8	0	7	7	2	5.1	10.3	8	20%	.278	1.57	6.43	4.34	0.0	89.0	41.6	10.9	48.7
Drew Rucinski	NWO	AAA	29	0	0	0	14	0	25	27	0	2.2	7.6	21	60%	.360	1.32	2.52	2.85	0.6				
	MIA	MLB	29	4	2	0	32	0	35^1	34	2	3.3	6.9	27	49%	.296	1.33	4.33	4.16	0.3	94.8	48.1	12.3	47.9
Nick Wittgren	NWO	AAA	27	0	5	2	25	0	29^1	34	4	2.5	10.4	34	46%	.353	1.43	5.22	2.94	0.7				
	MIA	MLB	27	2	1	0	32	0	33^2	29	1	4.0	8.3	31	46%	.280	1.31	2.94	3.81	0.4	93.8	70	10.7	49

Though **Jeff Brigham** has been a starter in the minors, he's limited by his over-reliance on a 91-94 mph fastball and a curveball, potentially pointing to a future as a reliever. ⓧ In the 2014 version of this tome, **Tyler Cloyd**'s usefulness was positioned as "a warm-blooded mammal capable of hurling a small sphere in the vicinity of a pentagon placed on the surface of the Earth, with little value beyond that." Not much has changed. ⓧ Hitting the mid-90s from the left side, **Miguel Del Pozo** uses good extension to get on top of hitters. Paired with his breaking stuff, he averages a strikeout an inning with average control. ⓧ The Giants were so enamored with **Julian Fernandez**'s triple-digit velocity in the 2017 Rule 5 draft that they didn't care he was already 22 and hadn't graduated A-ball. Now he's 23, recovering from elbow surgery and off to the Marlins on a waiver claim. ⓧ **Brett Graves** was a starter in the Athletics' farm system two years ago. Now, still armed with a poor strikeout rate and uninspiring fastball, slider, and curveball combo, he's another faceless reliever in the back end of a bullpen. ⓧ A below-average reliever for the past few years, there might be fewer than 10 people in the country who realized **Javy Guerra** pitched for the Marlins last season. ⓧ A Rule 5 pick last year, **Elieser Hernandez** bucked all expectations and became a star in the bullpen. Nah, just kidding. He stunk. What else did you think would happen when an organization rushes you from High-A to the majors? ⓧ Marlins fan weeping over the loss of Kyle Barraclough need to look no further than **Tyler Kinley**, a righty with a power fastball and big slider and Barraclough's trademark exorbitant walk rates. ⓧ With three average pitches and strong command, there's a path for **Pablo Lopez** to become a serviceable fifth starter. It's just a really boring one. ⓧ In 2017, **Ben Meyer** raised eyebrows with a sparkling strikeout-to-walk ratio, dominating the Sally and Florida State League. Given a new challenge in Triple-A and the majors last year, he flopped dramatically, losing the strikeouts and proving he couldn't cut it against left-handed batters. ⓧ **James Needy** earned a 40-man roster spot after being signed out of independent ball, but he missed all of 2018 with an injury and was promptly dropped from the roster. ⓧ **Chris O'Grady**'s 87 mph fastball from the left side makes it so he can't pitch to right-handed batters because they obliterate his offerings. If we're being honest, he shouldn't be pitching to lefties all that often either. ⓧ Overslot 2016 fourth-rounder **Chris Rodriguez** missed last season with a stress reaction in his lower back, and will likely see an innings limit heading into 2019. ⓧ When the season begins, **Drew Rucinski** will be a 30-year-old reliever with just 54 major-league innings under his belt, but several teams have been intrigued only to decide they didn't have the patience to give him a longer look. ⓧ **Nick Wittgren**'s three-pitch mix is good enough to let him carve a niche in the back end of a bullpen, but not good enough to let the world know he exists.

MILWAUKEE BREWERS

Essay by Russell Carleton

Player comments by Nick Zettel and BP staff

You've all read *Moneyball*, right? If you haven't, it's probably two shelves down from the shelf that you picked this book off. It's the story from back in the heyday of the Backstreet Boys about a team in a small market that managed to punch above its weight by finding value in places that no one else thought to look. At the time, the A's exploited the fact that everyone in baseball was too in love with batting average, when OBP was a much better stat. As (gasp!) both *Moneyball* and "I Want It That Way" are reaching the age where they would be legal to vote, it seems trite to talk about the problems of batting average, especially among the people who would be picking up a copy of *Baseball Prospectus*, but sometimes all you need is one decent idea.

The 2018 Milwaukee Brewers played in the smallest of all the 30 MLB media markets and yet somehow won the NL Central division and came within one game of the World Series and did it with one of the lowest payrolls in the game. And they seemed to do it on the back of one fairly simple idea. They found players that—for some strange reason—other teams didn't want. It's not that no one had ever figured this one out before. Baseball is filled with stories the ones who got away, and the Brewers seemed to have a knack for finding "perfectly respectable" players from the discard pile, to the point where it was almost seen as a weakness. If you have too many perfectly respectable players around, then the marginal upgrade that comes from a really good player isn't quite as large, and so finding a match between the marginal gain and the salary that the player commands on the open market becomes harder. Somehow though, the Brewers struck gold in the bargain pile.

When the Marlins inexplicably decided to trade their entire outfield, the Brewers staged the *coup* of the off-season. They ended up with Christian Yelich who was signed for several years at an entirely reasonable price, even if one believed that he was a good-but-not-great outfielder, which is what WARP suggested he had been to that point. Sure, he cost the team four prospects, but Yelich responded by nearly winning the Triple Crown. (And since this is *Baseball Prospectus*, let's throw in the obligatory note that he also led the National League in slugging percentage, OPS, WARP among position players, and came in third in OBP.)

BREWERS PROSPECTUS
2018 W-L: 96-67, 1ST IN NL CENTRAL

Pythag	.562	9th	B-Age	28.9	24th
RS/G	4.63	12th	P-Age	28.7	17th
RA/G	4.04	8th	Salary	$91.0M	26th
DRC+	100	10th	M$/MW	$1.6M	28th
DRA	4.31	13th	DL Days	1025	13th
FIP	3.96	13th	$ on DL	16%	15th
DER	.721	4th			

400'

370' 374'

344' 345'

- Opened 2001
- Retractable roof
- Natural surface
- Fence profile: 8'

Three-Year Park Factors

Runs	Runs/RH	Runs/LH	HR/RH	HR/LH
102	102	100	102	112

Top Hitter WARP	5.1 Christian Yelich
Top Pitcher WARP	2.7 Josh Hader
Top Prospect	Keston Hiura

2018 Hit List Ranking

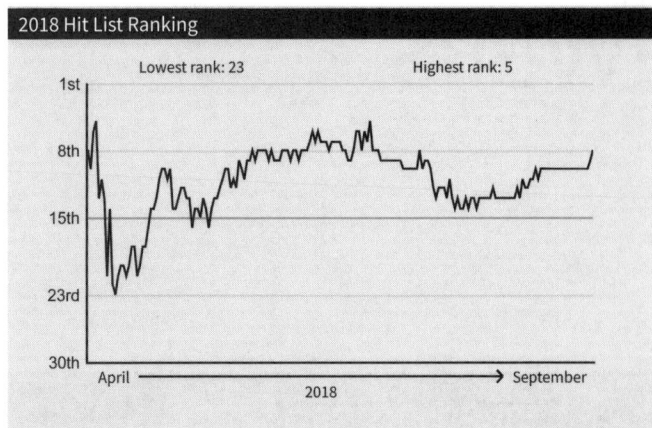

Lowest rank: 23   Highest rank: 5

1st
8th
15th
23rd
30th

April — 2018 → September

Committed Payroll (in millions)

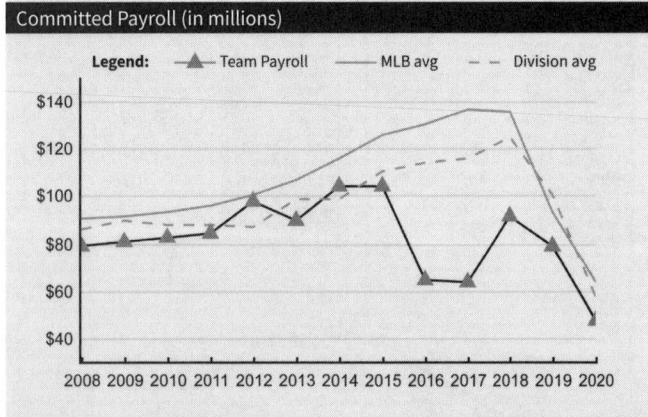

Legend: ▲ Team Payroll   — MLB avg   --- Division avg

$140
$120
$100
$80
$60
$40

2008 2009 2010 2011 2012 2013 2014 2015 2016 2017 2018 2019 2020

Farm System Ranking

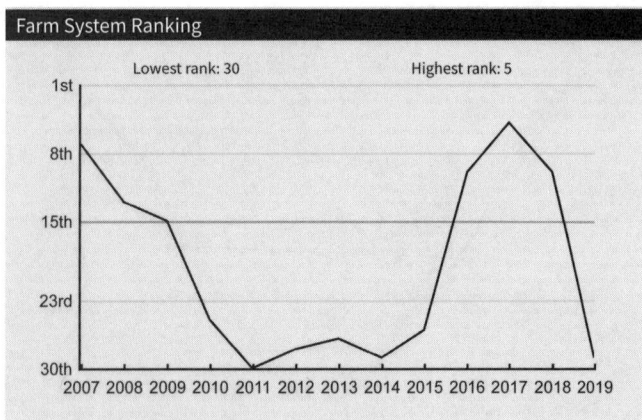

Lowest rank: 30   Highest rank: 5

1st
8th
15th
23rd
30th

2007 2008 2009 2010 2011 2012 2013 2014 2015 2016 2017 2018 2019

Personnel

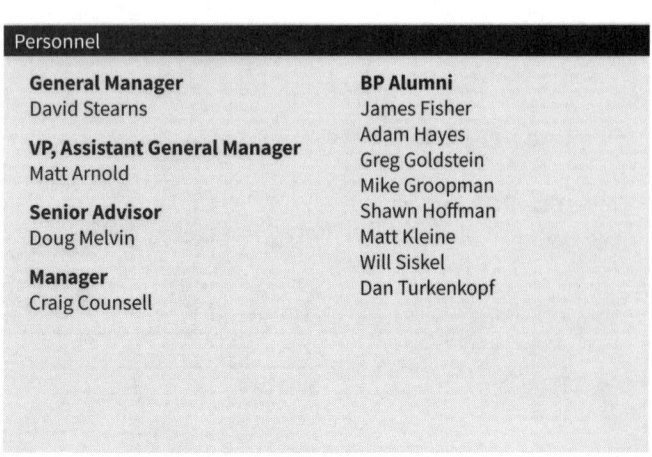

General Manager
David Stearns

VP, Assistant General Manager
Matt Arnold

Senior Advisor
Doug Melvin

Manager
Craig Counsell

BP Alumni
James Fisher
Adam Hayes
Greg Goldstein
Mike Groopman
Shawn Hoffman
Matt Kleine
Will Siskel
Dan Turkenkopf

There's even a case to be made that Yelich was even more valuable to the Brewers than his WARP would have suggested. Yelich played mostly in the corner outfield spots in 2018, and was compared to other corner outfielders when it came time to define "replacement level" for his performance. What WARP wasn't able to see was that in 2017, he was the Marlins' primary center fielder and acquitted himself decently well at the position. In 2018, he didn't need to play much center, as the Brewers also employed Lorenzo Cain, but he *could have* if the Brewers had needed him to. That extra glove in his locker, even though he rarely used it, meant that the Brewers could feel comfortable carrying Domingo Santana—a corner guy—as their fourth outfielder. Santana turned in a league-average performance with the bat, which is a nice thing to have coming off the bench. But for a moment, assume that Yelich had gotten hurt early in the year. The Brewers probably would have slid Santana into the starting lineup on a regular basis, but they would have had to replace Yelich on the roster with someone who could "handle center" because they didn't have their *de facto* backup center fielder any more. That probably would have meant more time on the roster for someone like Keon Broxton. So if Yelich would have practically had to be replaced by a center fielder on the roster and because he effectively allowed the Brewers to roster the better hitting Santana rather than Broxton, shouldn't his replacement level be the somewhat more forgiving center field one?

If Yelich wasn't enough, lightning struck twice in the Brewers outfield, when Lorenzo Cain landed (back) at Miller Park for a contract that was surprisingly affordable, given Cain's track record. Cain was widely known as an excellent defender in center, a good baserunner, and to have an above-average OBP, which is the sort of combination that a 5-win season is made of, but the "usual suspects" in free agency didn't really have an opening in center field and the 2017-2018 off-season was a winter of tan—we're not supposed to use the "T" word—rebuilding for a lot of teams. A lot of clubs were sitting on the sidelines. In a world where Sabermetric teams are always supposed to live for the future and hoard their dollars and prospects so that in three years they can hoard the same dollars and a new set of prospects, the Brewers realized that they had an opening. It's not like 5-win players grow on trees, and yet few teams seemed to want the one that was sitting right there in front of them. When everyone else is waiting, there is value in action.

But then if you look up and down the rest of the Brewers lineup from 2018, you see several other guys who were claimed and reclaimed from other teams, not because they were bad, but because the other team didn't have room. Jesus Aguilar hit 30 home runs for the Indians AAA team in 2016, but was stuck behind Carlos Santana and Edwin Encarnacion. The raw power was obviously there and there was enough OBP in the bat to make it work. At age 28, he blossomed. Travis Shaw had a perfectly respectable year for the Red Sox in 2016 when he was asked to fill-in for mega-signing Pablo Sandoval, but when Sandoval and his contract came back in 2017, Shaw was suddenly available and was gotten for Tyler Thornburg. Prototypical journeyman backup catcher Erik Kratz—the Brewers represented his 8th team in 9 years—logged the most plate appearances of his career at age-38 after someone realized that he was still one of the best pitch framers in baseball.

All you need is one good idea.

On the pitching side, the Brewers' big idea was that there were pitchers out in the universe who were under-valued because they were throwing the wrong pitches. Jhoulys Chacin, who had been the rare "pitcher who had a couple good years in Colorado" turned from castoff into the team's ace by doubling the usage of his slider, which the numbers showed had always been his best pitch. Jeremy Jeffress, back for his third tour of duty with the Brewers having been twice traded away previously, stopped relying primarily on his fastball and started throwing his curveball more. Junior Guerra came to the Brewers in 2016 and became less of a stinker by throwing a sinker. Wade Miley started throwing a cutter nearly half the time. Coupled with the emergence of Josh Hader in a throwback "let him throw two innings" relief role, the Brewers sewed together a silken pitching staff—and a decent one, they gave up the 8th fewest runs in baseball—out of what appeared to be a collection of sow's ears.

The Brewers aren't the only ones doing this. The ever-popular #NewMoneyball has moved from identifying players who are already doing something that people aren't valuing properly to identifying players who are not doing something (or doing it enough) but could and are being valued for what they have done rather than what they might become. The much-discussed "Launch Angle Revolution" was little more than hitting coaches talking to a few players and saying "Hey,

why don't you try hitting a few more fly balls. Some of them will leave the park" but it turned several floundering careers around. This is the pitching equivalent, though it's gotten less attention.

What the Brewers are doing is riding the shockwave caused by the collision of a couple of trends. Fastball usage has declined by nearly 10 percentage points between 2002 and 2018. It's not that pitchers have stopped throwing fastballs altogether, but now the ol' number 1 accounts for just a little more than half of the pitches thrown. Strangely though, the percentage of balls put into play that started their lives as fastballs has gone up. While most players will say that they "sit fastball" this is evidence that the fastball chair has gotten a lot more comfy for hitters. If hitters really are sitting fastball, why give them one? And if you have a pitcher who has an ineffective fastball and a better off-speed pitch of some sort, why not have him throw the pitch that is both better and not what the hitter is hoping for?

The fascinating piece about the Brewers' success story in 2018 wasn't that it heralded some new sort of thinking in baseball. The Brewers identified a couple of player types that were under-appreciated and loaded up on them. They found a couple of important trends and exploited them. They picked up little bits of extra value that even the "advanced" metrics didn't see. Add a little luck (no one gets by without a little bit of luck in baseball) and suddenly a team that was largely unfancied is knocking on the door of the World Series. In a world where Moneyball had never been written, but where some enterprising author wanted to write a book with the same message, they could have replaced the millennial A's with the 2018 Brew Crew.

—*Russell Carleton is an author of Baseball Prospectus.*

HITTERS

Jesus Aguilar 1B
Born: 06/30/90 Age: 29 Bats: R Throws: R Height: 6'3" Weight: 250 Origin: International Free Agent, 2007

YEAR	TEAM	LVL	AGE	PA	R	2B	3B	HR	RBI	BB	K	SB	CS	AVG/OBP/SLG	DRC+	VORP	BABIP	BRR	FRAA	WARP
2016	COH	AAA	26	578	62	26	0	30	92	53	110	0	0	.247/.319/.472	137	7.8	.255	-3.0	1B(120): -1.0, 3B(2): 0.3	3.0
2016	CLE	MLB	26	6	0	0	0	0	0	0	1	0	0	.000/.000/.000	74	-1.7	.000	0.0	1B(7): -0.3	0.0
2017	MIL	MLB	27	311	40	15	2	16	52	25	94	0	0	.265/.331/.505	100	12.8	.337	0.4	1B(77): 1.2, 3B(1): 0.0	0.7
2018	MIL	MLB	28	566	80	25	0	35	108	58	143	0	0	.274/.352/.539	134	35.0	.309	-1.1	1B(132): 3.6, 3B(5): 0.0	3.6
2019	MIL	MLB	29	561	69	26	2	25	81	51	140	0	0	.254/.330/.461	115	19.2	.304	-0.3	1B 0	2.1

Breakout: 7%   Improve: 20%   Collapse: 16%   Attrition: 21%   MLB: 55%   *Comparables: Darin Ruf, Jake Fox, Brandon Moss*

The best part about Aguilar is that he shouldn't be here. Of course, with logical scouting grades and assessments of potential career prototypes, the bulk of the comments in this here *Annual* could highlight shortcomings, reasons things shouldn't work. Aguilar is a great test of your threshold for this type of thinking; first as a surefire designated hitter who couldn't possibly find value on a National League bench that demands flexibility; then, as an everyday first baseman who stole a job and couldn't possibly be more than a one-year wonder (as evidenced by a brutal second-half in 2017); and now, as an All-Star who even mitigated the second-half collapse narrative with an excellent August and solid September in 2018.

Orlando Arcia SS Born: 08/04/94   Age: 24   Bats: R   Throws: R   Height: 6'0"   Weight: 165   Origin: International Free Agent, 2010

YEAR	TEAM	LVL	AGE	PA	R	2B	3B	HR	RBI	BB	K	SB	CS	AVG/OBP/SLG	DRC+	VORP	BABIP	BRR	FRAA	WARP
2016	CSP	AAA	21	440	59	19	6	8	53	29	77	15	8	.267/.320/.403	99	12.2	.312	-0.5	SS(92): 6.8, 2B(7): 0.7	2.7
2016	MIL	MLB	21	216	21	10	3	4	17	15	47	8	0	.219/.273/.358	74	-1.6	.267	-1.0	SS(53): 3.8	0.6
2017	MIL	MLB	22	548	56	17	2	15	53	36	100	14	7	.277/.324/.407	97	26.8	.317	2.1	SS(152): 6.8	3.3
2018	CSP	AAA	23	96	16	5	1	2	8	10	15	2	1	.341/.417/.494	110	10.8	.397	2.3	SS(22): 3.9	1.2
2018	MIL	MLB	23	366	32	16	0	3	30	15	87	7	4	.236/.268/.307	55	-0.3	.305	2.0	SS(116): 3.8	0.2
2019	MIL	MLB	24	435	47	17	2	9	42	30	90	10	4	.241/.298/.363	79	5.8	.288	0.5	SS 6	1.2

Breakout: 6%   Improve: 55%   Collapse: 2%   Attrition: 7%   MLB: 98%   Comparables: Ketel Marte, Asdrubal Cabrera, Everth Cabrera

Arcia could push the envelope as a throwback, defense-only shortstop even during an era that values defensive metrics. The glove was his only strength for the bulk of 2018, so much so that Arcia earned two demotions to Triple-A to figure out the bat. Judging Arcia by FRAA, he ranked in the 90th percentile of shortstops during each of his age-21 through age-23 seasons. Rare company shares this feat: Here lie legacy shortstops like Cal Ripken Jr. (1982-1984), current superstar Francisco Lindor, plus Roy McMillan (1951-1953), Milt Bolling (1952-1954) and Tim Foli (1972-1974). Should Arcia continue to bat according to his second-half slash of .290/.320/.386 he may have a chance to follow this category of defense-first shortstop comparison, transporting him to an era that challenges contemporary player valuations.

Ryan Braun LF Born: 11/17/83   Age: 35   Bats: R   Throws: R   Height: 6'2"   Weight: 205   Origin: Round 1, 2005 Draft (#5 overall)

YEAR	TEAM	LVL	AGE	PA	R	2B	3B	HR	RBI	BB	K	SB	CS	AVG/OBP/SLG	DRC+	VORP	BABIP	BRR	FRAA	WARP
2016	MIL	MLB	32	564	80	23	3	30	91	46	98	16	5	.305/.365/.538	130	45.7	.326	1.4	LF(127): -3.7, RF(2): -0.1	3.4
2017	MIL	MLB	33	425	58	28	2	17	52	38	76	12	4	.268/.336/.487	103	20.1	.292	0.5	LF(95): -3.7	1.0
2018	MIL	MLB	34	447	59	25	1	20	64	34	85	11	5	.254/.313/.469	107	17.5	.274	-0.8	LF(93): -4.9, 1B(18): -0.4	0.8
2019	MIL	MLB	35	466	59	21	2	17	59	40	87	13	5	.257/.327/.435	109	18.6	.288	0.2	LF -3	1.6

Breakout: 2%   Improve: 36%   Collapse: 8%   Attrition: 21%   MLB: 89%   Comparables: Steve Pearce, Dusty Baker, Monte Irvin

Thanks to a reported late-season mechanical adjustment which launched Braun into the fly-ball revolution, this wily veteran will receive one more player comment praising power and overall batting ability. Maybe he's born with it. In August, the superstar-turned-upstart leader began compiling the hits once more. The power placed an exclamation point on Milwaukee's improbable National League Central surge, and when it was all said and done those final two months read .283/.362/.538. The aging curve seemed to bend Braun out of his comfort zone, but don't count out the silver slugger if those swing mechanics stick.

Lorenzo Cain CF Born: 04/13/86   Age: 33   Bats: R   Throws: R   Height: 6'2"   Weight: 205   Origin: Round 17, 2004 Draft (#496 overall)

YEAR	TEAM	LVL	AGE	PA	R	2B	3B	HR	RBI	BB	K	SB	CS	AVG/OBP/SLG	DRC+	VORP	BABIP	BRR	FRAA	WARP
2016	KCA	MLB	30	434	56	19	1	9	56	31	84	14	5	.287/.339/.408	95	13.1	.341	2.2	CF(72): 7.9, RF(29): 0.4	2.3
2017	KCA	MLB	31	645	86	27	5	15	49	54	100	26	2	.300/.363/.440	111	36.6	.340	2.4	CF(151): 19.4	5.4
2018	MIL	MLB	32	620	90	25	2	10	38	71	94	30	7	.308/.395/.417	116	52.9	.357	4.3	CF(138): 2.1	4.2
2019	MIL	MLB	33	639	86	29	3	13	60	62	109	25	5	.277/.356/.407	111	35.9	.324	2.4	CF 13	5.2

Breakout: 1%   Improve: 38%   Collapse: 9%   Attrition: 16%   MLB: 94%   Comparables: Johnny Damon, Earle Combs, Chuck Hinton

When Cain broke out with the 2015 Royals, the elite center fielder served as Kansas City's third batter. Cain grew into a trusty veteran while serving in that run-production role, ultimately batting .299 with a 7.2 percent walk rate from 2015-2017. When the Brewers signed Cain to a reasonable $80 million deal during the ice cold offseason, they asked if Cain could serve as an on-base guy; Cain naturally responded with an 11.5 percent walk rate and .395 OBP. The veteran sacrificed some power for that discipline, but that's just splitting hairs as Cain produced arguably the best offensive season of his career during a low-key MVP campaign. Critics of Cain's contract point out that speed ages poorly, but they undersold the resolve of this shape-shifter; now Cain's elite plate discipline can help ease the other lumps on the aging curve.

Mauricio Dubon SS Born: 07/19/94   Age: 24   Bats: R   Throws: R   Height: 6'0"   Weight: 160   Origin: Round 26, 2013 Draft (#773 overall)

YEAR	TEAM	LVL	AGE	PA	R	2B	3B	HR	RBI	BB	K	SB	CS	AVG/OBP/SLG	DRC+	VORP	BABIP	BRR	FRAA	WARP
2016	SLM	A+	21	279	53	11	3	0	29	33	25	24	4	.306/.387/.379	111	25.6	.338	5.5	SS(61): -11.6	0.9
2016	PME	AA	21	270	48	20	6	6	40	11	36	6	3	.339/.371/.538	122	25.7	.374	4.1	SS(62): -5.7	1.7
2017	BLX	AA	22	304	34	14	0	2	24	25	42	31	9	.276/.338/.351	91	6.7	.319	0.3	SS(53): 5.4, 2B(20): 3.0	1.8
2017	CSP	AAA	22	244	40	15	0	6	33	14	34	7	6	.272/.320/.420	99	0.3	.297	-0.4	SS(30): -1.0, 2B(27): 3.5	1.2
2018	CSP	AAA	23	114	18	9	2	4	18	2	19	6	3	.343/.348/.574	99	10.6	.379	1.5	SS(23): 0.3, 2B(4): 0.6	0.8
2019	MIL	MLB	24	72	8	3	0	2	8	3	15	3	1	.243/.279/.386	70	0.2	.276	0.2	SS 0, 2B 1	0.1

Breakout: 4%   Improve: 21%   Collapse: 13%   Attrition: 30%   MLB: 54%   Comparables: Eduardo Nunez, Kevin Newman, Trevor Plouffe

Just when the Brewers needed a boost in the middle infield, this glove-first, high-floor shortstop tore his ACL and was finished until spring 2019. Rumor had it that Dubon was on the front office's radar at the time of the injury, which suggests that questions about the bat, or questions about his ultimate defensive location, can be tabled a bit as Dubon remains an advanced depth MLB roster consideration. The long view might stick Dubon as a second baseman, or perhaps as a high-end utility option; now we know that role is close to materializing.

Ben Gamel   LF   Born: 05/17/92   Age: 27   Bats: L   Throws: L   Height: 5'11"   Weight: 185   Origin: Round 10, 2010 Draft (#325 overall)

YEAR	TEAM	LVL	AGE	PA	R	2B	3B	HR	RBI	BB	K	SB	CS	AVG/OBP/SLG	DRC+	VORP	BABIP	BRR	FRAA	WARP
2016	NYA	MLB	24	10	1	0	0	0	0	1	1	0	0	.125/.222/.125	69	-0.4	.143	0.2	RF(5): -0.5	0.0
2016	SWB	AAA	24	533	80	26	5	6	51	43	94	19	8	.308/.365/.420	110	34.1	.370	4.6	CF(70): -7.3, LF(25): 0.3	1.8
2016	SEA	MLB	24	47	8	2	0	1	5	5	15	0	0	.200/.289/.325	68	0.5	.292	0.1	RF(24): -1.5, LF(2): -0.4	-0.2
2017	TAC	AAA	25	75	6	1	1	1	8	12	11	1	1	.300/.427/.400	113	5.9	.347	0.6	RF(11): -0.2, CF(7): -0.9	0.2
2017	SEA	MLB	25	550	68	27	5	11	59	36	122	4	1	.275/.322/.413	86	13.3	.340	1.1	LF(85): -3.5, RF(50): 3.1	0.5
2018	TAC	AAA	26	94	19	8	3	1	16	10	12	4	0	.349/.415/.554	102	10.7	.394	2.5	LF(8): -0.7, CF(6): -0.1	0.4
2018	SEA	MLB	26	293	37	14	4	1	19	31	61	7	3	.272/.358/.370	93	12.4	.352	3.3	LF(48): -1.4, RF(40): -1.9	0.5
2019	*MIL*	*MLB*	*27*	*266*	*29*	*12*	*2*	*5*	*26*	*24*	*57*	*4*	*2*	*.247/.321/.374*	*94*	*7.1*	*.304*	*1.0*	*LF -1, RF -1*	*0.5*

Breakout: 6%   Improve: 41%   Collapse: 9%   Attrition: 18%   MLB: 93%   *Comparables: Matt Murton, Robbie Grossman, Andy Dirks*

Rebounding from a disastrous second half in 2017, Gamel proved that he may indeed be a useful big leaguer. While his offensive contributions still rely more on the dark, fickle magic of BABIP than one would like, he nearly doubled his walk rate in 2018 and maintained his mysterious fielder-avoiding hitting skills. Not particularly fast, or strong-armed, Gamel's instincts and aggressiveness make him a perfectly adequate corner outfielder. His lack of power, or any true plus skill, means he's unlikely anything more than a fourth outfielder on a playoff contender, but he's still only 26. His frame and raw power tool would theoretically allow for more; he'll have fewer opportunities to demonstrate it this year after the Brewers obtained him in a trade to fill their fourth-outfielder role.

Jake Gatewood   INF   Born: 09/25/95   Age: 23   Bats: R   Throws: R   Height: 6'5"   Weight: 190   Origin: Round 1, 2014 Draft (#41 overall)

YEAR	TEAM	LVL	AGE	PA	R	2B	3B	HR	RBI	BB	K	SB	CS	AVG/OBP/SLG	DRC+	VORP	BABIP	BRR	FRAA	WARP
2016	WIS	A	20	524	70	33	0	14	64	18	141	3	2	.240/.268/.391	97	3.9	.303	0.6	3B(93): -1.2, 1B(26): 0.5	1.2
2017	CAR	A+	21	470	66	36	1	11	53	43	132	7	5	.269/.340/.438	108	15.8	.364	-0.7	1B(71): 0.4, 3B(10): -0.1	1.0
2017	BLX	AA	21	100	9	4	2	4	9	8	29	3	0	.239/.300/.457	100	2.7	.305	-0.1	3B(21): -0.4	0.3
2018	BLX	AA	21	388	45	19	1	19	59	28	114	2	0	.244/.302/.466	111	5.5	.299	-4.6	1B(87): 0.6, RF(2): -0.4	0.6
2019	*MIL*	*MLB*	*23*	*251*	*26*	*12*	*0*	*10*	*32*	*14*	*81*	*1*	*0*	*.218/.262/.397*	*71*	*-5.2*	*.282*	*-0.4*	*1B 0, RF 0*	*-0.5*

Breakout: 1%   Improve: 7%   Collapse: 0%   Attrition: 5%   MLB: 9%   *Comparables: Brandon Allen, Donald Lutz, Matt Clark*

Certainty is the last ingredient any prospect profile could possibly have, but it's the easiest ingredient to envision on the shelf. Gatewood gives this tempting promise, after the right-handed power bat acquitted himself well in his first full season attempt at the Southern League. Previously famous for retooling his swing and adding contact lenses to his repertoire, Gatewood went all-in with the game power, hitting for extra bases in more than 10 percent of his plate appearances. Only three other regular Southern League batters (300+ PA) accomplished that feat. The power will be crucial for Gatewood, as he played almost exclusively first base throughout 2018. Without a utility role, Gatewood must regularly tap into that power at the plate.

Curtis Granderson   RF   Born: 03/16/81   Age: 38   Bats: L   Throws: R   Height: 6'1"   Weight: 200   Origin: Round 3, 2002 Draft (#80 overall)

YEAR	TEAM	LVL	AGE	PA	R	2B	3B	HR	RBI	BB	K	SB	CS	AVG/OBP/SLG	DRC+	VORP	BABIP	BRR	FRAA	WARP
2016	NYN	MLB	35	633	88	24	5	30	59	74	130	4	2	.237/.335/.464	117	37.7	.254	1.3	RF(110): 3.1, CF(36): -4.4	3.1
2017	NYN	MLB	36	395	58	22	3	19	52	53	90	4	2	.228/.334/.481	112	26.5	.251	1.5	CF(59): -8.4, RF(30): 1.9	1.3
2017	LAN	MLB	36	132	16	2	0	7	12	18	33	2	0	.161/.288/.366	107	3.0	.153	0.2	LF(26): -3.2, RF(8): 0.2	0.2
2018	TOR	MLB	37	349	48	21	1	11	35	42	96	2	1	.245/.342/.430	101	8.2	.321	-2.3	LF(41): 0.5, RF(31): -1.9	0.5
2018	MIL	MLB	37	54	12	1	1	2	3	12	10	0	0	.220/.407/.439	111	3.3	.241	-0.5	RF(14): -0.5, LF(3): -0.1	0.1
2019	*MIL*	*MLB*	*38*	*405*	*53*	*19*	*2*	*14*	*46*	*46*	*96*	*4*	*2*	*.234/.329/.414*	*105*	*13.5*	*.283*	*0.0*	*LF -2, RF 1*	*1.3*

Breakout: 1%   Improve: 19%   Collapse: 12%   Attrition: 24%   MLB: 73%   *Comparables: Ken Griffey, Joe Harris, Larry Walker*

The "Curtis Granderson Scale" could update the "Kenny Lofton Scale": this scale weighs the point at which an elite player becomes less known for their overall career success and more for their desirable characteristics to help win a title through midseason acquisitions. Granderson has more than 40 career WARP, and Lofton was near a similar total when he began his playoff mercenary phase. Reaching this level of career achievement should be viewed as one of the highest honors in the game; teams want YOU! to contend. Granderson did not waste his shot to be a winner with Milwaukee, providing crucial walks and power during an improbable late-season stretch. Those desirable veteran traits wait in the balance once more, for trade or hire during the next playoff run.

Keston Hiura   2B   Born: 08/02/96   Age: 22   Bats: R   Throws: R   Height: 5'11"   Weight: 190   Origin: Round 1, 2017 Draft (#9 overall)

YEAR	TEAM	LVL	AGE	PA	R	2B	3B	HR	RBI	BB	K	SB	CS	AVG/OBP/SLG	DRC+	VORP	BABIP	BRR	FRAA	WARP
2017	BRR	RK	20	72	18	3	5	4	18	6	13	0	2	.435/.500/.839	164	17.1	.500	0.5		0.6
2017	WIS	A	20	115	14	11	2	0	15	7	24	2	0	.333/.374/.476	96	10.3	.422	1.1	2B(3): -0.4	0.1
2018	CAR	A+	21	228	38	16	3	7	23	14	47	4	6	.320/.382/.529	121	20.8	.386	0.6	2B(15): 0.6	1.1
2018	BLX	AA	21	307	36	18	2	6	20	22	56	11	5	.272/.339/.416	103	13.9	.323	0.6	2B(64): -3.5	0.7
2019	*MIL*	*MLB*	*22*	*172*	*17*	*6*	*1*	*4*	*18*	*8*	*44*	*3*	*1*	*.219/.261/.348*	*60*	*-2.6*	*.270*	*-0.1*	*2B -2*	*-0.5*

Breakout: 4%   Improve: 21%   Collapse: 6%   Attrition: 19%   MLB: 42%   *Comparables: Jonathan Schoop, Arismendy Alcantara, Ryan Brett*

Against the old adage "greed is good," risk is better. It's the assessment of risk that often leads to pricing discrepancies, such as Hiura falling to the ninth spot of the 2017 draft. This was fantastic luck for the Brewers, who in failing to "tank" during their rebuild had to gamble just as much as anyone else in the 2017 draft. So Hiura fell, on (reasonable) health and positional concerns, but 2018 helped Hiura to demonstrate the "advanced" in that advanced college bat. Meanwhile, the positional concerns slowly wound down; Hiura played almost twice as many games at the keystone as he did at designated hitter. The 22-year-old even had a chance to assuage other adversities, as a thumb injury derailed much of the second half of his minor-league season. Fortunately, the Arizona Fall League exists for elite MLB-bound prospects like Hiura, and the bat came all the way back in that friendly hitting environment. Here risk is reward, with Hiura placing an exclamation point on his midseason status as one of the top prospects in the industry.

Tristen Lutz RF   Born: 08/22/98   Age: 20   Bats: R   Throws: R   Height: 6'3"   Weight: 210   Origin: Round 1, 2017 Draft (#34 overall)

YEAR	TEAM	LVL	AGE	PA	R	2B	3B	HR	RBI	BB	K	SB	CS	AVG/OBP/SLG	DRC+	VORP	BABIP	BRR	FRAA	WARP
2017	HEL	RK	18	111	23	1	1	6	16	12	21	2	4	.333/.432/.559	133	11.5	.373	-1.1	CF(22): -1.7	0.5
2017	BRR	RK	18	76	12	4	3	3	11	4	21	1	0	.279/.347/.559	110	3.9	.364	0.1	CF(11): 0.5, LF(4): -1.2	0.2
2018	WIS	A	19	503	63	33	3	13	63	46	139	9	3	.245/.321/.421	96	13.1	.322	-0.9	RF(68): -11.4, LF(29): 1.9	-0.7
2019	MIL	MLB	20	251	25	7	1	8	25	11	84	1	0	.183/.217/.322	42	-10.6	.238	-0.2	RF -3, LF -1	-1.6

Breakout: 1%   Improve: 3%   Collapse: 0%   Attrition: 3%   MLB: 5%   *Comparables: Chris Parmelee, Caleb Gindl, Nomar Mazara*

The seasons of player development are plentiful. Clocks tick, leaves change and temperatures fluctuate as players wind toward their Overall Future Potential. Those seasons are often equally harsh judges: Lutz couldn't find the hit or power tools in the April cold of the Midwest League, and they vanished once more in the heat of August. Yet the hits sprung forward in May, and the mundane days of July were hardly monotonous for the big outfielder. These seasons change for an age-19 prospect playing their first full year, forging a path to a "true" right fielder. That path remains long, but thankfully the repetitions of player development can be as meaningful as seasonal returns; here, Lutz eagerly awaits April 2019.

Mike Moustakas 3B   Born: 09/11/88   Age: 30   Bats: L   Throws: R   Height: 6'0"   Weight: 225   Origin: Round 1, 2007 Draft (#2 overall)

YEAR	TEAM	LVL	AGE	PA	R	2B	3B	HR	RBI	BB	K	SB	CS	AVG/OBP/SLG	DRC+	VORP	BABIP	BRR	FRAA	WARP
2016	KCA	MLB	27	113	12	6	0	7	13	9	13	0	1	.240/.301/.500	117	5.4	.214	-0.7	3B(26): -0.4	0.6
2017	KCA	MLB	28	598	75	24	0	38	85	34	94	0	0	.272/.314/.521	122	26.5	.263	-1.6	3B(127): -7.4	2.9
2018	KCA	MLB	29	417	46	21	1	20	62	30	63	3	0	.249/.309/.468	109	14.2	.247	-2.6	3B(76): 11.3, 1B(4): -0.2	2.7
2018	MIL	MLB	29	218	20	12	0	8	33	19	40	1	1	.256/.326/.441	113	8.0	.282	-2.6	3B(52): 0.5	1.0
2019	MIL	MLB	30	592	75	31	2	27	89	44	91	2	1	.271/.332/.487	120	24.5	.282	-2.7	3B 1, 1B 0	2.7

Breakout: 1%   Improve: 35%   Collapse: 5%   Attrition: 9%   MLB: 95%   *Comparables: Kyle Seager, Garrett Atkins, Aubrey Huff*

From one small-market champion to another upstart contender, Moustakas had the opportunity to add a new line to his resume in 2018. The former Royals champion third baseman became a valuable midseason acquisition for the plucky Brewers, perhaps the veteran leadership profile for the Ivy League Analytics Age. That calling card power showed once again, and it was enough to carry the veteran's profile even if it was slightly diminished from a 2017 home run breakout. Moustakas is the type of productive player who can fade to a supporting role while doing just about everything right; this arrangement works because nothing categorically stands out among the walks, strikeouts, extra-base hits and glove. It's all there, enough to acquire Moustakas for a contending season and plug into the fifth or sixth batting spot.

Jacob Nottingham C   Born: 04/03/95   Age: 24   Bats: R   Throws: R   Height: 6'2"   Weight: 230   Origin: Round 6, 2013 Draft (#167 overall)

YEAR	TEAM	LVL	AGE	PA	R	2B	3B	HR	RBI	BB	K	SB	CS	AVG/OBP/SLG	DRC+	VORP	BABIP	BRR	FRAA	WARP
2016	BLX	AA	21	456	46	14	0	11	37	29	138	9	2	.234/.295/.347	89	12.2	.320	0.0	C(98): 4.2, 1B(3): 0.1	1.8
2017	BLX	AA	22	385	37	21	2	9	48	37	87	7	3	.209/.326/.369	110	13.2	.255	-3.0	C(83): 4.7, 1B(13): -0.8	2.3
2018	MIL	MLB	23	24	2	1	0	0	0	4	8	0	0	.200/.333/.250	75	0.7	.333	-0.1	C(8): -0.5	0.0
2018	CSP	AAA	23	196	33	10	2	10	36	14	59	2	1	.281/.347/.528	110	10.7	.367	-0.6	C(32): -0.3, 1B(9): 0.0	0.9
2019	MIL	MLB	24	107	12	5	0	4	13	7	34	1	0	.227/.286/.403	78	1.8	.303	-0.1	C -2	0.0

Breakout: 8%   Improve: 15%   Collapse: 7%   Attrition: 21%   MLB: 26%   *Comparables: Andrew Knapp, Luke Montz, Michael McKenry*

YEAR	TEAM	P. COUNT	FRM RUNS	BLK RUNS	THRW RUNS	TOT RUNS
2017	BLX	11440	7.2	-1.7	0.0	5.8
2018	CSP	4056	1.5	-1.1	0.2	0.7
2018	MIL	937	-0.7	0.2	0.0	-0.5
2019	MIL	3942	-0.6	-0.8	-0.1	-1.5

For all the effort a player makes to improve their shortcomings or solidify their strengths, then comes the certainty of the injury bug, trades or other role diversions. It was the injury bug that derailed Nottingham for much of 2018, especially disappointing given that the big catcher was on the verge of transferring his improved defensive profile to the MLB level. For years the scouting questions have narrowed in on Nottingham's ability to block pitches and perform behind the plate, and upon reaching the majors he looked the part. The power and plate discipline showed up at Triple-A in eye-popping form even suitable for the Pacific Coast League; Nottingham hardly had enough time in the big leagues to develop an approach, but he did walk twice and score a run in his April debut. This might be a first base profile when all is said and done, but entering his age-25 season Nottingham still has time to make some form of "catcher with pop" work.

Hernan Perez UT   Born: 03/26/91   Age: 28   Bats: R   Throws: R   Height: 6'1"   Weight: 215   Origin: International Free Agent, 2007

YEAR	TEAM	LVL	AGE	PA	R	2B	3B	HR	RBI	BB	K	SB	CS	AVG/OBP/SLG	DRC+	VORP	BABIP	BRR	FRAA	WARP
2016	CSP	AAA	25	67	10	4	1	1	11	3	10	2	0	.339/.364/.484	95	4.4	.385	0.4	2B(10): -0.8, 3B(6): 0.1	0.2
2016	MIL	MLB	25	430	50	18	3	13	56	18	94	34	7	.272/.302/.428	95	19.8	.322	3.0	3B(60): -0.5, RF(36): 3.6	1.8
2017	MIL	MLB	26	458	47	19	3	14	51	20	79	13	4	.259/.289/.414	86	9.4	.286	2.4	LF(53): 2.5, 3B(31): 3.4	1.3
2018	MIL	MLB	27	334	36	11	2	9	29	17	71	11	3	.253/.290/.386	90	9.7	.300	0.6	2B(51): -0.9, RF(27): 0.4	0.6
2019	MIL	MLB	28	394	46	18	2	11	45	21	77	15	4	.262/.304/.413	91	9.4	.300	1.2	2B -2, SS -1	0.8

Breakout: 4%   Improve: 44%   Collapse: 10%   Attrition: 20%   MLB: 95%   *Comparables: Brandon Phillips, Scooter Gennett, Tyler Saladino*

"If you can play shortstop, you can play anywhere" is a relatively common utterance on broadcasts, whispered in hushed tones befitting of a rumor so mundane as to be unquestionably true. Perez pushes this rumor to the extreme and is therefore a singular player. Whereas some might take an entire career to make those moves away from shortstop, down the defensive spectrum to third base, perhaps second base, maybe the outfield and first base, Perez makes those moves during a single season. According to the Baseball-Reference Play Index, Perez is the only player in recorded history to play 20 games each at 2B, 3B, SS and RF in one season. This level of sustained flexibility deserves analytical scrutiny for throwing the defensive spectrum into a blender. Perez is hardly a one-dimensional player either, as his modest power and speed makes his other shortcomings easier to forget. Piece it all together and a manager's best friend emerges, someone perfect for grinding through 162 games, up and down that defensive spectrum whenever and however it calls.

Manny Pina C Born: 06/05/87 Age: 32 Bats: R Throws: R Height: 6'0" Weight: 215 Origin: International Free Agent, 2004

YEAR	TEAM	LVL	AGE	PA	R	2B	3B	HR	RBI	BB	K	SB	CS	AVG/OBP/SLG	DRC+	VORP	BABIP	BRR	FRAA	WARP
2016	CSP	AAA	29	262	35	21	3	5	43	17	39	1	1	.329/.371/.506	115	17.8	.371	-3.4	C(57): -7.7	0.6
2016	MIL	MLB	29	81	4	4	0	2	12	10	15	0	1	.254/.346/.394	101	2.4	.296	-1.2	C(17): -0.8	0.2
2017	MIL	MLB	30	359	45	21	0	9	43	20	79	2	0	.279/.327/.424	95	16.8	.339	-0.6	C(102): 1.4	1.7
2018	MIL	MLB	31	337	39	13	2	9	28	21	62	2	0	.252/.307/.395	90	8.8	.285	-3.6	C(92): 7.0, 1B(1): 0.0	1.6
2019	MIL	MLB	32	355	38	17	2	8	38	27	72	2	1	.255/.322/.396	97	12.7	.304	-1.8	C 0	1.3

Breakout: 2%   Improve: 26%   Collapse: 13%   Attrition: 17%   MLB: 82%

Comparables: Ronny Paulino, John Baker, Dioner Navarro

YEAR	TEAM	P. COUNT	FRM RUNS	BLK RUNS	THRW RUNS	TOT RUNS
2016	MIL	2273	-0.5	-0.2	-0.1	-0.6
2017	MIL	12774	-2.9	0.7	2.0	3.0
2018	MIL	12411	4.8	1.3	0.5	6.3
2019	MIL	13105	-1.6	0.7	0.8	-0.1

The ostensible goal of a baseball season is to win as many games as possible, but the most effective manner of reaching that goal is debatable. Rather than outscoring an opponent as frequently as possible, which would be a clearly acceptable objective for winning frequently, a team can also work to bide time better than their opponents. For much of baseball is waiting for something to happen, to effectively (or at least competently) fill in the gaps while both teams are waiting for that never-ending something. It's why the sport can withstand profiles like Pina, who began as an age-29 rookie catcher by hitting just enough, walking a bit and playing passable defense. That profile may eventually morph into an age-31 catcher who can frame, block and throw, emerging as one of the best defensive catchers in the game, all the while balancing that line by hitting just enough. Value does not always need to loudly announce itself via big WARP and loud tools. Pina is not the big moment, but he assembles value in every little moment in-between.

Corey Ray CF Born: 09/22/94 Age: 24 Bats: L Throws: L Height: 6'0" Weight: 195 Origin: Round 1, 2016 Draft (#5 overall)

YEAR	TEAM	LVL	AGE	PA	R	2B	3B	HR	RBI	BB	K	SB	CS	AVG/OBP/SLG	DRC+	VORP	BABIP	BRR	FRAA	WARP
2016	BRV	A+	21	254	24	13	2	5	17	20	54	9	5	.247/.307/.385	94	2.4	.299	-1.9	CF(40): -3.3	0.0
2017	CAR	A+	22	503	56	29	4	7	48	48	156	24	10	.238/.311/.367	85	8.0	.346	-2.5	CF(69): 5.5, RF(21): 0.9	0.8
2018	BLX	AA	23	600	86	32	7	27	74	60	176	37	7	.239/.323/.477	117	35.8	.303	0.5	CF(126): 1.8, LF(6): 1.4	3.8
2019	MIL	MLB	24	251	34	9	1	9	25	18	84	10	2	.204/.262/.372	65	0.0	.274	1.2	CF 1, LF 0	0.1

Breakout: 13%   Improve: 14%   Collapse: 2%   Attrition: 11%   MLB: 23%

Comparables: Trayce Thompson, Melky Mesa, Matt Den Dekker

What's a fast-rising, no-questions-asked college bat anyway? Ray returned to the prospect scene in 2018 by producing a line that's impossible to ignore. Ray reportedly adjusted his swing and pitch recognition skills in order to unlock his big power, while also progressing in center field. It still looks like a risky profile in the advanced minors. Even with those developments, Ray is a big time swing-and-miss hitter, as that improved season at the plate found time for a strikeout rate near 30 percent. He's on track to debut at some point in 2019.

Domingo Santana LF Born: 08/05/92 Age: 26 Bats: R Throws: R Height: 6'5" Weight: 220 Origin: International Free Agent, 2009

YEAR	TEAM	LVL	AGE	PA	R	2B	3B	HR	RBI	BB	K	SB	CS	AVG/OBP/SLG	DRC+	VORP	BABIP	BRR	FRAA	WARP
2016	MIL	MLB	23	281	34	14	0	11	32	32	91	2	3	.256/.345/.447	92	14.8	.359	1.6	RF(62): -5.0, LF(4): -0.4	0.0
2017	MIL	MLB	24	607	88	29	0	30	85	73	178	15	4	.278/.371/.505	117	40.5	.363	0.2	RF(144): -7.7	2.0
2018	CSP	AAA	25	227	30	10	2	8	35	36	75	2	0	.283/.401/.487	104	10.8	.425	-2.6	RF(50): -10.4	-0.7
2018	MIL	MLB	25	235	21	14	1	5	20	20	77	1	1	.265/.328/.412	76	9.5	.386	-0.2	RF(55): -2.0	-0.4
2019	SEA	MLB	26	410	54	17	1	14	45	45	132	5	2	.230/.321/.397	97	10.3	.321	0.5	LF -5, RF -1	0.5

Breakout: 3%   Improve: 54%   Collapse: 9%   Attrition: 13%   MLB: 91%

Comparables: Jorge Soler, George Springer, Matt Joyce

Questions about Santana's swing-and-miss profile have been a staple on the prospect analysis scene since the big right fielder reached the majors. Last season was an adventure back to those questions, as Santana struck out in 33 percent of his plate appearances without doing much else during his first MLB stint, earning a demotion to Triple-A. It took another 17 games for Santana to hit a home run in the friendly environs of the Pacific Coast League. Then the power returned suddenly, getting Santana a September call-up. Brooks Baseball data shows that Santana redistributed the location of some of his whiffs during his successful recall, and his swings migrated to inside pitches. After falling out of the Brewers' plans, he'll get a chance to resurrect his solid-regular status with the rebuilding Mariners.

Travis Shaw INF Born: 04/16/90 Age: 29 Bats: L Throws: R Height: 6'4" Weight: 230 Origin: Round 9, 2011 Draft (#292 overall)

YEAR	TEAM	LVL	AGE	PA	R	2B	3B	HR	RBI	BB	K	SB	CS	AVG/OBP/SLG	DRC+	VORP	BABIP	BRR	FRAA	WARP
2016	BOS	MLB	26	530	63	34	2	16	71	43	133	5	1	.242/.306/.421	90	5.7	.299	-0.8	3B(105): 7.4, 1B(50): 2.3	2.0
2017	MIL	MLB	27	606	84	34	1	31	101	60	138	10	0	.273/.349/.513	117	41.5	.312	3.2	3B(143): 0.9, 1B(1): 0.0	4.0
2018	MIL	MLB	28	587	73	23	0	32	86	78	108	5	2	.241/.345/.480	132	42.9	.242	-0.7	3B(107): 1.8, 2B(39): -0.5	4.5
2019	MIL	MLB	29	561	71	28	2	24	79	57	119	6	1	.257/.338/.463	119	26.8	.293	0.2	3B 3, 2B 0	3.1

Breakout: 3%   Improve: 42%   Collapse: 4%   Attrition: 11%   MLB: 99%

Comparables: Chase Headley, Todd Frazier, Eric Chavez

If there were an award for Process-Oriented Vanguard, Shaw would be one of the frontrunners. The big third baseman tested fan perception of surface stats throughout the season, as the batting average (and, sometimes, slugging results) seemed to suggest a regression. Yet Shaw sliced his strikeout totals by roughly 20 percent, increased the walks, shredded line drives and lifted more batted balls into the air. Meanwhile in the field, the prototypical 3B-to-1B defensive spectrum prospect became the face of the Brewers' unorthodox defensive arrangements, willingly becoming a second baseman in Milwaukee's aggressive shifts once the club acquired Mike Moustakas. Thus the Vanguard, of fly balls, shifts and walks, Shaw represents one particularly intriguing mutation of MLB success.

Cory Spangenberg 2B Born: 03/16/91 Age: 28 Bats: L Throws: R Height: 6'0" Weight: 195 Origin: Round 1, 2011 Draft (#10 overall)

YEAR	TEAM	LVL	AGE	PA	R	2B	3B	HR	RBI	BB	K	SB	CS	AVG/OBP/SLG	DRC+	VORP	BABIP	BRR	FRAA	WARP
2016	SDN	MLB	25	53	6	1	1	1	8	4	13	1	0	.229/.302/.354	73	-0.2	.294	-0.2	2B(13): 0.4	0.0
2017	ELP	AAA	26	72	8	3	1	1	7	4	8	3	2	.348/.403/.470	99	3.3	.386	-0.2	3B(17): -3.3	-0.1
2017	SDN	MLB	26	486	57	18	2	13	46	34	128	11	3	.264/.322/.401	81	28.6	.342	5.3	3B(96): -0.8, LF(32): -3.0	0.8
2018	ELP	AAA	27	95	14	8	2	4	16	6	30	3	0	.341/.383/.614	102	6.4	.481	-0.4	3B(13): 0.8, 2B(5): -0.9	0.3
2018	SDN	MLB	27	329	35	9	4	7	25	25	108	6	1	.235/.298/.362	67	4.3	.344	-0.1	2B(49): -2.8, 3B(44): 0.3	-0.6
2019	MIL	MLB	28	219	24	8	1	5	22	16	61	4	1	.230/.295/.360	74	1.0	.299	0.8	2B -1, 3B 0	0.0

Breakout: 3%   Improve: 47%   Collapse: 9%   Attrition: 17%   MLB: 94%   *Comparables: Jayson Nix, Danny Valencia, Josh Rutledge*

Spangenberg has never done anything particularly well or badly, which more or less makes him the face of the franchise. He keeps hanging around, like a couch that's so ugly everyone just assumes it's comfortable, starting more often than not and whelming with inoffensive and unspectacular play. He's been a fine placeholder at second, but presuming that Luis Urias hits, Spangenberg will likely anchor the lineup for some other rebuilding club sooner rather than later.

Troy Stokes LF Born: 02/02/96 Age: 23 Bats: R Throws: R Height: 5'8" Weight: 182 Origin: Round 4, 2014 Draft (#116 overall)

YEAR	TEAM	LVL	AGE	PA	R	2B	3B	HR	RBI	BB	K	SB	CS	AVG/OBP/SLG	DRC+	VORP	BABIP	BRR	FRAA	WARP
2016	WIS	A	20	366	50	20	4	4	29	36	62	20	4	.268/.358/.395	118	11.3	.319	-1.2	LF(59): -2.3, CF(10): -0.3	1.4
2017	CAR	A+	21	426	60	19	5	14	56	47	77	21	9	.250/.344/.445	127	21.5	.278	0.5	LF(73): 5.5	2.9
2017	BLX	AA	21	153	19	9	0	6	18	16	34	9	3	.252/.333/.452	114	5.9	.292	-0.3	LF(34): 1.0, CF(1): 0.0	0.7
2018	BLX	AA	22	551	74	23	6	19	58	65	147	19	2	.233/.343/.430	119	28.5	.295	-1.5	LF(114): 4.1, CF(9): -1.5	2.8
2019	MIL	MLB	23	251	33	10	1	9	27	21	69	6	1	.217/.293/.389	84	3.1	.270	0.6	LF 3, CF 0	0.6

Breakout: 4%   Improve: 15%   Collapse: 5%   Attrition: 13%   MLB: 29%   *Comparables: Chad Huffman, Thomas Neal, Jordan Luplow*

The main knock on Stokes has been easy enough to recite in a way that lulls the observer into forecasting a supposedly crystal clear role: his hit tool leaves questions about MLB upside. But the speedy outfielder just doesn't quit, and it's worth citing the scouting knocks that have fallen by the wayside: what seemed a certain 'tweener outfield role years ago now looks like an average arm and glove that could hold down each outfield position. The power was absent years ago, but Stokes has refined that line-drive swing into a lofty effort that delivers game power in the advanced minors. The 23-year-old continues to place exclamation points on his ability to develop at every point in his career, giving him a chance to emerge from the shadows of that bench role.

Eric Thames 1B Born: 11/10/86 Age: 32 Bats: L Throws: R Height: 6'0" Weight: 210 Origin: Round 7, 2008 Draft (#219 overall)

YEAR	TEAM	LVL	AGE	PA	R	2B	3B	HR	RBI	BB	K	SB	CS	AVG/OBP/SLG	DRC+	VORP	BABIP	BRR	FRAA	WARP
2017	MIL	MLB	30	551	83	26	4	31	63	75	163	4	2	.247/.359/.518	121	29.5	.309	-2.7	1B(108): -2.2, 1B(25): -1.8	1.7
2018	MIL	MLB	31	278	41	10	3	16	37	29	97	7	0	.219/.306/.478	104	13.7	.284	2.3	RF(31): -0.3, 1B(29): -0.9	0.9
2019	MIL	MLB	32	230	32	11	1	10	29	24	74	3	1	.234/.322/.445	108	6.4	.315	-0.2	1B 1	0.8

Breakout: 0%   Improve: 27%   Collapse: 6%   Attrition: 8%   MLB: 100%   *Comparables: Mike Napoli, Richie Sexson, Fred McGriff*

Three True Outcomes, no waiting. Thames' massive power remained in his second season back from Korea, but his walks went down and his strikeouts went up, leaving him with a much lesser role for the Brewers. Among all left-handed hitters with at least 500 plate appearances in 2017-2018, his .267 isolated power ranked second to only Joey Gallo, but he also whiffed in a higher percentage of his at-bats than all lefties except Gallo, Chris Davis and Alex Avila. Thames' likely 2019 output is probably somewhere in between, but the Brewers may no longer need his strengths enough to live with more than 300-400 plate appearances of his weaknesses.

Brice Turang SS Born: 11/21/99 Age: 19 Bats: L Throws: R Height: 6'1" Weight: 165 Origin: Round 1, 2018 Draft (#21 overall)

YEAR	TEAM	LVL	AGE	PA	R	2B	3B	HR	RBI	BB	K	SB	CS	AVG/OBP/SLG	DRC+	VORP	BABIP	BRR	FRAA	WARP
2018	BRR	RK	18	57	11	2	0	0	7	9	6	8	1	.319/.421/.362	136	4.5	.357	0.0	SS(12): 2.0	0.6
2018	HEL	RK	18	135	26	4	1	1	11	22	28	6	1	.268/.385/.348	102	9.7	.345	1.7	SS(23): -0.1, 2B(5): -0.1	0.7
2019	MIL	MLB	19	251	25	7	0	4	18	17	59	4	1	.196/.249/.274	40	-9.1	.241	-0.1	SS 0, 2B 0	-1.0

Breakout: 0%   Improve: 6%   Collapse: 1%   Attrition: 4%   MLB: 11%   *Comparables: Adalberto Mondesi, Elvis Andrus, Carlos Triunfel*

There is nothing new under the sun. Ancient philosophers knew this even before divine figures walked the earth, so it stands to reason this lesson could be passed through generations to reach MLB scouts. Turang was a hype casualty in the 2018 draft, generator of much press about so-called "prospect fatigue," an indicator that the scouts took to the hills in search of the new and exciting, perhaps a new future to dream on, bigger tools or tools they had yet to see. But there is nothing new under the sun, as Turang demonstrated after falling to the 21st pick despite previously carrying a potential 1:1 pedigree as a prep standout. Turang might not necessarily have booming power or a flashy glove or phenomenal speed, but the polished prospect has enough of each to complement his hit tool and construct an overall middle infield future worth those big dreams.

Weston Wilson UT   Born: 09/11/94   Age: 24   Bats: R   Throws: R   Height: 6'3"   Weight: 195   Origin: Round 17, 2016 Draft (#501 overall)

YEAR	TEAM	LVL	AGE	PA	R	2B	3B	HR	RBI	BB	K	SB	CS	AVG/OBP/SLG	DRC+	VORP	BABIP	BRR	FRAA	WARP
2016	HEL	RK	21	269	38	16	7	4	38	23	33	5	4	.318/.390/.498	119	26.4	.350	0.6	3B(41): -1.8, 2B(11): -1.5	1.1
2017	WIS	A	22	162	22	9	2	5	26	16	29	1	5	.277/.366/.475	117	12.4	.318	-0.6	3B(26): 0.5, 1B(10): 1.4	0.8
2017	CAR	A+	22	288	26	11	1	3	27	16	80	3	0	.241/.298/.326	73	-5.9	.333	-2.3	1B(36): -0.3, 2B(6): -0.3	-0.8
2018	CAR	A+	23	424	60	23	2	13	62	31	93	7	4	.274/.330/.446	110	17.1	.325	3.1	1B(38): 0.9, LF(25): 4.7	2.5
2018	BLX	AA	23	49	5	1	0	1	3	3	7	1	1	.239/.286/.326	102	0.6	.263	0.4	3B(8): 0.1, 1B(4): 0.2	0.2
2019	MIL	MLB	24	251	23	7	0	7	27	13	66	1	1	.204/.248/.327	48	-10.7	.248	-0.6	1B 0, 3B 0	-1.0

Breakout: 0%   Improve: 0%   Collapse: 0%   Attrition: 1%   MLB: 1%   *Comparables: Russ Canzler, Joe Mahoney, Ben Paulsen*

The Arizona Fall League is regarded as a showcase for top prospects, and in October 2018 the league featured a utility player by design. Defensive flexibility is no longer a buzzword, which catapults prospects like Wilson into difficult territory for role projection. Looking at Wilson's profile, a scout could focus on that little bit of pop and some discipline at the plate, but nothing is necessarily jumping out with the hit tool. If one views the AFL as a potential bridge to MLB, Wilson's defensive flexibility leaps out, as the run down the defensive spectrum began primarily with third base and second base in 2016, the infield corners in 2017, and 1B/LF/3B/2B in 2018. Working in an MLB environment where more roster spots may be designated for pitchers, it's not hard to squint at Wilson's proven utility role and notch that Overall Future Potential slightly higher.

Christian Yelich LF   Born: 12/05/91   Age: 27   Bats: L   Throws: R   Height: 6'3"   Weight: 195   Origin: Round 1, 2010 Draft (#23 overall)

YEAR	TEAM	LVL	AGE	PA	R	2B	3B	HR	RBI	BB	K	SB	CS	AVG/OBP/SLG	DRC+	VORP	BABIP	BRR	FRAA	WARP
2016	MIA	MLB	24	659	78	38	3	21	98	72	138	9	4	.298/.376/.483	110	56.6	.356	2.2	LF(120): -5.0, CF(31): 0.0	2.4
2017	MIA	MLB	25	695	100	36	2	18	81	80	137	16	2	.282/.369/.439	103	46.3	.336	0.8	CF(155): -17.3	1.2
2018	MIL	MLB	26	651	118	34	7	36	110	68	135	22	4	.326/.402/.598	145	78.0	.373	2.4	LF(90): -7.3, RF(75): 2.1	5.1
2019	MIL	MLB	27	662	97	29	4	25	81	67	140	16	3	.272/.354/.463	125	39.5	.321	1.3	RF 4, LF -2	4.4

Breakout: 4%   Improve: 53%   Collapse: 7%   Attrition: 6%   MLB: 93%   *Comparables: Oscar Gamble, Enos Slaughter, Al Kaline*

During the playoffs, the *Los Angeles Times* reported that Yelich worked on several aspects of his offseason conditioning, and also lifted weights throughout the season for the first time in his career. When the closing bell rang on the first half, Yelich boasted a .292/.364/.459 line, a perfectly respectable debut in Milwaukee and a reasonable extension of his previous seasons in Miami. Yelich paired those physical tweaks with improved plate discipline throughout the second half, which catapulted the flexible outfielder into the MVP debate. It was evident during the last two weeks of July, when Yelich opened the second half with 12 extra-base hits in 12 games, it was evident in August when Yelich went deep 11 times in 124 plate appearances and it was evident when Yelich leveled up to lead the Brewers' unbelievable stretch run for the NL Central crown. The smooth-swinging bat unlocked the fullest extent of his scouting report, leaving potential areas of improvement for academic debates such as the aesthetics of a 1.000 OPS or whether Yelich can play right field defense for an entire season.

PITCHERS

Chase Anderson RHP   Born: 11/30/87   Age: 31   Bats: R   Throws: R   Height: 6'1"   Weight: 200   Origin: Round 9, 2009 Draft (#276 overall)

YEAR	TEAM	LVL	AGE	W	L	SV	G	GS	IP	H	HR	BB/9	K/9	K	GB%	BABIP	WHIP	ERA	DRA	WARP	MPH	FB%	WHF	CSP
2016	MIL	MLB	28	9	11	0	31	30	151²	155	28	3.1	7.1	120	38%	.287	1.37	4.39	5.34	0.0	93.6	56.7	9.2	46.9
2017	MIL	MLB	29	12	4	0	25	25	141¹	113	14	2.6	8.5	133	41%	.265	1.09	2.74	4.13	2.3	94.9	52.5	11.5	47.6
2018	MIL	MLB	30	9	8	0	30	30	158	131	30	3.2	7.3	128	36%	.239	1.19	3.93	5.52	-0.4	94.1	53.5	10.3	46.9
2019	MIL	MLB	31	9	9	0	25	25	142²	123	21	3.0	8.4	133	38%	.279	1.20	4.31	4.94	0.6	93.4	53.7	10.3	46.9

Breakout: 19%   Improve: 52%   Collapse: 16%   Attrition: 13%   MLB: 87%   *Comparables: Jeremy Hellickson, Jeff Francis, Brian Bannister*

The righty was inexplicably shut down during the Brewers' white-hot run in September despite a 15-start stretch featuring a strikeout-to-walk ratio near 3-to-1 and just 28 runs allowed in 77 innings. Anderson struggled with command and velocity vultures all season, as the fastball dipped below 93 mph during several months while demonstrating some monthly fluctuation patterns similar to 2017. Into August and September, Anderson sandwiched good and bad starts, placing a downward trend on that strong 15-start stretch and adding to the frustration of a season that never seemed bad but never delivered on the promise of the prior year's glory.

Luke Barker RHP   Born: 03/11/92   Age: 27   Bats: R   Throws: R   Height: 6'3"   Weight: 230   Origin: Undrafted Free Agent, 2016

YEAR	TEAM	LVL	AGE	W	L	SV	G	GS	IP	H	HR	BB/9	K/9	K	GB%	BABIP	WHIP	ERA	DRA	WARP	MPH	FB%	WHF	CSP
2017	WIS	A	25	1	4	5	22	0	31²	30	2	2.3	9.7	34	47%	.329	1.20	2.84	3.50	0.5				
2017	CAR	A+	25	1	1	1	12	0	22	24	2	2.5	5.7	14	35%	.306	1.36	3.68	3.90	0.3				
2018	CAR	A+	26	6	4	20	46	0	61	47	3	2.4	9.3	63	44%	.275	1.03	2.21	3.27	1.2				
2019	MIL	MLB	27	2	1	2	47	0	49²	47	8	3.5	8.4	46	40%	.297	1.34	4.72	5.42	-0.4				

Breakout: 4%   Improve: 5%   Collapse: 3%   Attrition: 5%   MLB: 9%   *Comparables: Rafael Martin, Guido Knudson, Brad Salmon*

The first thing that jumps out is how much Barker looks like Jake Arrieta, which is important because there are not many righties with this particular stature in MLB. The beard is a nice touch, too. Milwaukee purchased Barker's rights from independent ball, and debuted the five-pitch righty in Single-A for the 2017 season. Almost everything has gone right for Barker in the low minors. It's hard to ignore his command of the strike zone, even if he's old for the competition, a relatively polished product with three years at Chico State preceding his independent league play. Barker struck out 26 percent of batters faced in 2018, and features a fly ball-oriented approach to be carefully watched. It's hard to get past the minor-league level, age and relief role, but Barker sure looks like an MLB pitcher.

Zack Brown RHP Born: 12/15/94 Age: 24 Bats: R Throws: R Height: 6'1" Weight: 180 Origin: Round 5, 2016 Draft (#141 overall)

YEAR	TEAM	LVL	AGE	W	L	SV	G	GS	IP	H	HR	BB/9	K/9	K	GB%	BABIP	WHIP	ERA	DRA	WARP	MPH	FB%	WHF	CSP
2016	WIS	A	21	1	2	1	9	4	33	29	3	1.4	7.9	29	45%	.257	1.03	3.00	5.40	-0.2				
2017	WIS	A	22	4	5	0	18	13	85	78	7	3.6	8.9	84	47%	.316	1.32	3.39	4.78	0.4				
2017	CAR	A+	22	3	0	0	4	4	25	24	1	0.7	8.3	23	56%	.319	1.04	2.16	3.35	0.6				
2018	BLX	AA	23	9	1	0	22	21	125²	95	8	2.6	8.3	116	57%	.257	1.04	2.44	3.42	2.8				
2019	MIL	MLB	24	6	6	1	32	17	102²	91	13	3.2	8.2	93	46%	.289	1.25	4.20	4.82	0.5				

Breakout: 16%   Improve: 26%   Collapse: 16%   Attrition: 37%   MLB: 50%   *Comparables: Eric Jokisch, Steven Brault, Nick Kingham*

One of the ongoing stories for the 2018 Brewers was their elite bullpen and a national perception that they needed rotation help. All of this overshadowed the club's systemic development of high-floor minor-league arms into functional units, getting pitchers to stick with what works despite potential scouting flaws that would limit promulgation of elite rotation role fantasies. Brown is but one example of the type of arm the Brewers developed in 2018, a college prospect pushed quickly beyond A-ball and challenged in the advanced minors, where that floor becomes apparent. One wouldn't expect Brown's blend of a solid low-90s fastball, breakers with changing shapes and a change of pace to blow away the scouting scene, and the delivery might obscure the appearances of a frame that can withstand a starter's workload. Still, Brown worked two consecutive seasons with more than 100 innings, producing a profile that deserves extended looks and questions about what a pitching role is, anyway.

Corbin Burnes RHP Born: 10/22/94 Age: 24 Bats: R Throws: R Height: 6'3" Weight: 205 Origin: Round 4, 2016 Draft (#111 overall)

YEAR	TEAM	LVL	AGE	W	L	SV	G	GS	IP	H	HR	BB/9	K/9	K	GB%	BABIP	WHIP	ERA	DRA	WARP	MPH	FB%	WHF	CSP
2016	BRR	RK	21	0	0	0	3	1	7	3	0	2.6	12.9	10	64%	.214	0.71	1.29	2.74	0.2				
2016	WIS	A	21	3	0	0	9	5	28²	20	1	5.0	9.7	31	64%	.275	1.26	2.20	3.91	0.3				
2017	CAR	A+	22	5	0	0	10	10	60	37	1	2.4	8.4	56	54%	.243	0.88	1.05	4.48	0.5				
2017	BLX	AA	22	3	3	0	16	16	85²	66	2	2.1	8.8	84	51%	.279	1.00	2.10	2.97	2.2				
2018	CSP	AAA	23	3	4	0	19	13	78²	83	7	3.5	9.3	81	47%	.347	1.45	5.15	3.52	1.8				
2018	MIL	MLB	23	7	0	1	30	0	38	27	4	2.6	8.3	35	50%	.232	1.00	2.61	3.39	0.7	97.0	58.8	15.8	50.6
2019	MIL	MLB	24	5	4	0	32	11	77²	63	9	3.9	9.4	81	48%	.286	1.24	3.99	4.59	0.6	96.8	60.6	16.2	52.1

Breakout: 20%   Improve: 42%   Collapse: 21%   Attrition: 25%   MLB: 78%   *Comparables: Robbie Ross, Nick Tropeano, Alex Cobb*

Judging Burnes strictly by age, height and weight for his rookie season, one of the comps is Michael Fulmer. Burnes spent most of 2017 ramping up his stuff at a rate that seemed nearly impossible for evaluators to catch up; at each different locale, he seemed to offer something different. Fulmer followed a similar path as a surefire mid-rotation pitcher turned quasi-ace, and Burnes flashed signs of that brilliant potential in a bullpen stint with Milwaukee. But the bullpen will likely not be home for Burnes, who can no longer keep his hard-driving 96 mph fastball and two breaking pitches a secret.

Jhoulys Chacin RHP Born: 01/07/88 Age: 31 Bats: R Throws: R Height: 6'3" Weight: 215 Origin: International Free Agent, 2004

YEAR	TEAM	LVL	AGE	W	L	SV	G	GS	IP	H	HR	BB/9	K/9	K	GB%	BABIP	WHIP	ERA	DRA	WARP	MPH	FB%	WHF	CSP
2016	GWN	AAA	28	1	0	0	1	1	7²	5	0	2.3	8.2	7	53%	.263	0.91	0.00	2.90	0.2				
2016	ATL	MLB	28	1	2	0	5	5	26²	29	4	2.7	9.1	27	50%	.321	1.39	5.40	3.19	0.6	92.4	55.1	11.6	46.3
2016	ANA	MLB	28	5	6	0	29	17	117¹	124	10	3.6	7.1	92	52%	.316	1.46	4.68	5.27	0.0	93.9	55.1	8.1	47.5
2017	SDN	MLB	29	13	10	0	32	32	180¹	157	19	3.6	7.6	153	50%	.272	1.27	3.89	4.50	2.2	93.2	54.1	8.6	48.2
2018	MIL	MLB	30	15	8	0	35	35	192²	153	18	3.3	7.3	156	44%	.250	1.16	3.50	4.51	1.8	92.2	48.1	9.1	48.9
2019	MIL	MLB	31	10	10	0	30	30	171	143	20	3.4	8.4	160	47%	.279	1.21	4.11	4.71	1.2	92.0	51.3	8.8	48

Breakout: 14%   Improve: 40%   Collapse: 22%   Attrition: 12%   MLB: 88%   *Comparables: Tanner Roark, Andrew Cashner, Scott Feldman*

Everything wiggles; Chacin throws nothing flat. If you're watching him, look for a looping slider that defies definition of any breaking ball you know. In an era when so many pitchers insist on working hard velocity and sharp, darting sliders, Chacin's slider seems to chug up to the plate and bend in the same manner as its author dances on the mound. You'd dance, too, if you were a dependable, unsung rotation worker signed early during an austerity offseason, celebrating your success as opposed to so many more obvious free agent choices to boost a potential contender. It doesn't always work for the righty, and if you didn't want to have any fun you could write a book about his shortcomings, but none of that matters when Game 163 is on the line, or even some playoff games. Chacin dances like the ace you didn't know you needed.

Alex Claudio   LHP   Born: 01/31/92   Age: 27   Bats: L   Throws: L   Height: 6'3"   Weight: 180   Origin: Round 27, 2010 Draft (#826 overall)

YEAR	TEAM	LVL	AGE	W	L	SV	G	GS	IP	H	HR	BB/9	K/9	K	GB%	BABIP	WHIP	ERA	DRA	WARP	MPH	FB%	WHF	CSP
2016	ROU	AAA	24	0	0	1	6	0	16¹	7	0	2.2	4.4	8	71%	.156	0.67	0.55	3.15	0.3				
2016	TEX	MLB	24	4	1	0	39	0	51²	55	2	1.7	5.9	34	63%	.312	1.26	2.79	4.50	0.3	88.2	55.6	11	46.1
2017	TEX	MLB	25	4	2	11	70	1	82²	71	5	1.6	6.1	56	68%	.269	1.04	2.50	3.77	1.3	88.0	56.6	10.6	45.8
2018	TEX	MLB	26	4	2	1	66	1	68¹	91	4	1.7	5.4	41	64%	.366	1.52	4.48	4.69	0.2	87.6	52	12.3	45.1
2019	*MIL*	*MLB*	*27*	*2*	*1*	*0*	*48*	*0*	*50²*	*46*	*4*	*2.7*	*7.1*	*40*	*59%*	*.295*	*1.22*	*3.66*	*4.19*	*0.5*	*87.4*	*55.1*	*11.6*	*46.1*

Breakout: 25%   Improve: 51%   Collapse: 22%   Attrition: 13%   MLB: 92%   *Comparables: Jeremy Accardo, Luis Avilan, Bryan Shaw*

Claudio was never really expected to be a big-league pitcher, so the fact that he beat out Yu Darvish, Cole Hamels and everyone else to become the Rangers' pitcher of the year in 2017 is remarkable. In 2018, however, Claudio's performance matched his scouting reports a bit more closely. Rough year notwithstanding, there are few things in life that can prompt the sort of joy as watching hitters flail and miss at Claudio's high-60s changeup.

Here is an inclusive list; we will not be taking any more submissions: Watching guys with popped collars walk into a tree while looking at their phones. Cats chasing a laser pointer and falling into their water bowl. Drunk relatives dancing at a wedding and knocking over a whole table of cake. Martin Shkreli going to prison. When Charlie Brown tries to kick the football, but Lucy pulls it out and tricks him *yet again*. That GIF where Nick Young turns around with his arms up but the ball clangs off the rim. Watching a dude attempt to impress women with a double backflip dive but instead he does a super-loud belly-flop.

Zach Davies   RHP   Born: 02/07/93   Age: 26   Bats: R   Throws: R   Height: 6'0"   Weight: 155   Origin: Round 26, 2011 Draft (#785 overall)

YEAR	TEAM	LVL	AGE	W	L	SV	G	GS	IP	H	HR	BB/9	K/9	K	GB%	BABIP	WHIP	ERA	DRA	WARP	MPH	FB%	WHF	CSP
2016	CSP	AAA	23	0	0	0	2	2	9	6	0	2.0	11.0	11	44%	.261	0.89	2.00	2.14	0.3				
2016	MIL	MLB	23	11	7	0	28	28	163¹	166	20	2.1	7.4	135	47%	.302	1.25	3.97	3.77	3.0	91.4	56	8.9	42.8
2017	MIL	MLB	24	17	9	0	33	33	191¹	204	20	2.6	5.8	124	51%	.302	1.35	3.90	4.77	1.7	91.2	57.8	7.6	44.9
2018	CSP	AAA	25	0	3	0	5	5	17	18	0	6.4	6.9	13	44%	.333	1.76	6.35	4.74	0.2				
2018	BLX	AA	25	1	1	0	2	2	11	7	1	3.3	9.8	12	54%	.240	1.00	4.09	2.01	0.4				
2018	WIS	A	25	1	0	0	4	4	19	19	2	0.0	9.0	19	63%	.347	1.00	2.84	2.98	0.5				
2018	MIL	MLB	25	2	7	0	13	13	66	67	8	2.9	6.7	49	48%	.299	1.33	4.77	4.68	0.5	91.8	56.5	8.7	43.6
2019	*MIL*	*MLB*	*26*	*7*	*7*	*0*	*21*	*21*	*119²*	*112*	*13*	*2.8*	*7.8*	*104*	*47%*	*.302*	*1.24*	*3.88*	*4.45*	*1.2*	*91.0*	*57.9*	*8.4*	*44.6*

Breakout: 27%   Improve: 67%   Collapse: 10%   Attrition: 9%   MLB: 87%   *Comparables: Kendall Graveman, Erasmo Ramirez, Joe Blanton*

In the face of adversity, how does a pitcher respond? Davies lost much of the season to a series of rotator cuff and back injuries, and setbacks that necessitated lengthy rehab work in the minors. Curiously, at the MLB level Davies remained Davies, a true sinker-first pitcher who also works with variations of a cut fastball, looping curve and that gorgeous changeup. Davies basically threw his arsenal at a similar rate to his solid 2017 campaign, but he yielded more strikeouts thanks to his sinker and cutter. Despite the adversity, nothing major changed for Davies; the righty stuck with his arsenal, stuck with his general operation in the low strike zone and ticked up those whiffs at only moderate tradeoff to the ground balls. All of this is interesting because it's easy to imagine a counterfactual in which Davies is injured, the stuff backs up, the approach changes and a new pitcher emerges. Instead it seems that adversity hardly disrupted the Davies game plan.

Bubba Derby   RHP   Born: 02/24/94   Age: 25   Bats: L   Throws: R   Height: 5'11"   Weight: 185   Origin: Round 6, 2015 Draft (#188 overall)

YEAR	TEAM	LVL	AGE	W	L	SV	G	GS	IP	H	HR	BB/9	K/9	K	GB%	BABIP	WHIP	ERA	DRA	WARP	MPH	FB%	WHF	CSP
2016	BRV	A+	22	6	13	0	26	25	132	165	17	3.2	7.4	109	45%	.348	1.61	5.59	5.60	-0.2				
2017	BLX	AA	23	2	1	0	18	2	50	40	1	3.6	8.3	46	44%	.289	1.20	2.88	3.36	0.9				
2017	CSP	AAA	23	5	0	0	12	12	63¹	59	7	2.4	7.0	49	50%	.286	1.20	3.55	4.36	0.9				
2018	CSP	AAA	24	6	5	0	31	16	118¹	127	9	3.8	7.3	96	47%	.328	1.50	4.49	5.22	0.3				
2019	*MIL*	*MLB*	*25*	*6*	*6*	*1*	*38*	*17*	*100²*	*92*	*12*	*3.7*	*8.3*	*92*	*44%*	*.298*	*1.33*	*4.28*	*4.91*	*0.4*				

Breakout: 8%   Improve: 13%   Collapse: 14%   Attrition: 23%   MLB: 30%   *Comparables: Chad Bell, Stephen Fife, Justin Marks*

One of the interesting aspects of watching The Age of Velocity in baseball is seeing which *impossible* slow throwers reach the majors and establish serviceable roles. Derby is one candidate for this type of hobby, as the righty hardly tops out near the league-median fastball. When the Athletics traded him to the Brewers he might have been organizational depth, and then he might have been a reliever when he moved to Double-A. Since these developments, Derby has used a modest, command-oriented approach while the Brewers provided a solid slate of starts at Triple-A, reorienting the righty's org depth prospects. Milwaukee rewarded Derby with an Arizona Fall League appearance, following a recent set of moves in which depth-based arms are sent to the premier prospect showcase, which solidifies his prospect status even if the exact role is difficult to pinpoint.

Marcos Diplan   RHP   Born: 09/18/96   Age: 22   Bats: R   Throws: R   Height: 6'0"   Weight: 170   Origin: International Free Agent, 2013

YEAR	TEAM	LVL	AGE	W	L	SV	G	GS	IP	H	HR	BB/9	K/9	K	GB%	BABIP	WHIP	ERA	DRA	WARP	MPH	FB%	WHF	CSP
2016	WIS	A	19	6	2	1	17	11	70	49	3	4.1	11.4	89	51%	.274	1.16	1.80	2.91	1.7				
2016	BRV	A+	19	1	2	0	10	6	43¹	47	4	3.7	8.3	40	39%	.333	1.50	4.98	3.22	1.1				
2017	CAR	A+	20	7	8	0	26	22	125²	126	11	5.1	8.5	119	48%	.327	1.57	5.23	5.30	-0.1				
2018	CAR	A+	21	3	2	0	13	13	61¹	58	3	5.6	8.8	60	48%	.344	1.57	3.52	3.79	1.1				
2018	BLX	AA	21	2	6	0	12	11	57	58	6	5.7	9.0	57	41%	.325	1.65	4.58	4.91	0.3				
2019	*MIL*	*MLB*	*22*	*1*	*0*	*0*	*16*	*0*	*17*	*15*	*3*	*5.5*	*9.5*	*18*	*42%*	*.306*	*1.52*	*4.98*	*5.73*	*-0.5*				

Breakout: 7%   Improve: 10%   Collapse: 3%   Attrition: 11%   MLB: 13%   *Comparables: John Gant, Dallas Braden, Dellin Betances*

Milwaukee placed Diplan on the 40-man roster prior to the 2018 season, but the righty remained on a relatively slow path to the majors. We've been writing about him for years, so it's easy to forget that Diplan will work during his age-22 season in 2019, but the profile still seems stalled. He just completed three consecutive years with time in High-A, producing a total of 230 innings at that level. Once Diplan was promoted to Double-A, his ground-ball rate backed up while the whiffs and walks didn't budge much. The same caveats hold: command is the major concern with Diplan, even if the fastball is now more clearly grouped with a change and breaker.

Gio Gonzalez LHP   Born: 09/19/85   Age: 33   Bats: R   Throws: L   Height: 6'0"   Weight: 203   Origin: Round 1, 2004 Draft (#38 overall)

YEAR	TEAM	LVL	AGE	W	L	SV	G	GS	IP	H	HR	BB/9	K/9	K	GB%	BABIP	WHIP	ERA	DRA	WARP	MPH	FB%	WHF	CSP
2016	WAS	MLB	30	11	11	0	32	32	177¹	179	19	3.0	8.7	171	49%	.316	1.34	4.57	3.71	3.4	93.7	64.7	10.2	42.5
2017	WAS	MLB	31	15	9	0	32	32	201	158	21	3.5	8.4	188	48%	.258	1.18	2.96	3.60	4.4	91.4	56.8	9.4	42.3
2018	WAS	MLB	32	7	11	0	27	27	145²	153	15	4.3	7.8	126	47%	.319	1.53	4.57	4.33	1.7	91.7	56.4	9.8	45.8
2018	MIL	MLB	32	3	0	0	5	5	25¹	14	2	3.6	7.8	22	46%	.182	0.95	2.13	3.27	0.6	91.8	58.2	12.6	41.2
2019	MIL	MLB	33	9	9	0	26	26	149²	133	18	3.4	8.6	143	47%	.295	1.27	4.03	4.62	1.2	91.1	58	9.8	43

Breakout: 12%   Improve: 43%   Collapse: 17%   Attrition: 7%   MLB: 94%   *Comparables: Whitey Ford, Doug Davis, Clay Buchholz*

We eagerly await the *2028 BP Annual*, in which Gonzalez's 60 percent changeup selection from the ageless wonder is the talk of the league. In 2012, the southpaw could average 94 mph on his fastball, thus variations of rising and running, sinking fastballs comprised 70 percent of Gonzalez's pitch selections. Time eroded the velocity and the percentage of fastballs thrown, which Gonzalez selected only 56 percent of the time in 2018. There's less rise and run on both versions of the fastball, signs that would suggest a pitcher on their way out of the league in many cases. In this case, the changeup saves, and Gonzalez is entering the phase of his career in which he becomes a true junk-ball hero. Even if the surface stats suggest the former front-line starter is declining, it's evident that adjustments with the changeup are maintaining that useful rotational role.

Junior Guerra RHP   Born: 01/16/85   Age: 34   Bats: R   Throws: R   Height: 6'0"   Weight: 205   Origin: International Free Agent, 2001

YEAR	TEAM	LVL	AGE	W	L	SV	G	GS	IP	H	HR	BB/9	K/9	K	GB%	BABIP	WHIP	ERA	DRA	WARP	MPH	FB%	WHF	CSP
2016	CSP	AAA	31	0	2	0	5	5	26²	18	2	3.7	8.4	25	40%	.235	1.09	4.05	3.86	0.5				
2016	MIL	MLB	31	9	3	0	20	20	121²	94	10	3.2	7.4	100	47%	.250	1.13	2.81	4.19	1.6	95.5	61.6	11.6	45.5
2017	CSP	AAA	32	2	2	0	6	6	30	27	0	3.6	6.0	20	47%	.303	1.30	2.10	6.15	-0.1				
2017	MIL	MLB	32	1	4	0	21	14	70¹	61	18	5.5	8.6	67	36%	.236	1.48	5.12	6.31	-0.6	93.9	64.8	11.8	41.4
2018	MIL	MLB	33	6	9	0	31	26	141	143	19	3.5	8.7	136	45%	.313	1.40	4.09	4.50	1.3	95.1	69	11.6	46.5
2019	MIL	MLB	34	4	2	0	62	3	77	66	11	3.5	8.8	76	43%	.280	1.24	4.35	5.00	0.1	93.8	65.2	11.5	43.9

Breakout: 15%   Improve: 33%   Collapse: 27%   Attrition: 16%   MLB: 79%   *Comparables: Chris Narveson, Eric Stults, Jorge De La Rosa*

In the critically acclaimed film *The Aristocats*, it goes unspoken that everybody wants to be a cat because of their penchant for extra lives. Guerra can relate, as this cat just received *at least* his fourth go-round in professional ball. From catcher to international pitcher of intrigue to waiver fodder to surging ace, now Guerra has already turned a failed rotational stint into a bullpen reinvention. In September, the Brewers employed Guerra as part of their 40-man roster pitching depth squad, and to everyone's surprise the splitter-slider master emerged as a fastball-curveball relief ace. Guerra's got the guts to close, the guile to start and the brains to reinvent himself to seize every opportunity.

Josh Hader LHP   Born: 04/07/94   Age: 25   Bats: L   Throws: L   Height: 6'3"   Weight: 185   Origin: Round 19, 2012 Draft (#582 overall)

YEAR	TEAM	LVL	AGE	W	L	SV	G	GS	IP	H	HR	BB/9	K/9	K	GB%	BABIP	WHIP	ERA	DRA	WARP	MPH	FB%	WHF	CSP
2016	BLX	AA	22	2	1	0	11	11	57	38	1	3.0	11.5	73	41%	.291	1.00	0.95	2.31	1.9				
2016	CSP	AAA	22	1	7	0	14	14	69	63	5	4.7	11.5	88	43%	.345	1.43	5.22	4.55	0.6				
2017	CSP	AAA	23	3	4	0	12	12	52	49	14	5.4	8.8	51	37%	.265	1.54	5.37	5.19	0.3				
2017	MIL	MLB	23	2	3	0	35	0	47²	25	4	4.2	12.8	68	36%	.233	0.99	2.08	3.31	1.0	96.8	81.4	18.4	49.4
2018	MIL	MLB	24	6	1	12	55	0	81¹	36	9	3.3	15.8	143	31%	.220	0.81	2.43	2.00	2.7	96.9	79.1	20.5	51.7
2019	MIL	MLB	25	3	1	5	64	0	67²	42	10	3.7	14.1	106	36%	.280	1.03	3.21	3.72	1.3	96.6	81.7	20.3	51.9

Breakout: 29%   Improve: 58%   Collapse: 20%   Attrition: 15%   MLB: 87%   *Comparables: Carl Edwards Jr., Francisco Liriano, Kevin Siegrist*

This historic, role-bending strikeout reliever whiffed on social media content and damage control. Hader's 2018 was a brilliant demonstration of how quickly the tides can change in terms of baseball strategy and pitcher usage, but it was an equally devastating demonstration of the aloof privilege afforded many white, American baseball prospects. If you missed the unearthing of Hader's past racist, homophobic and sexist tweets, the fallout was what you'd expect. Hader issued an apology meant to assuage his clubhouse moreso than people impacted by his actions, a course that was also taken by Hader's parent organization and MLB. Brewers fans gave the young flamethrower a standing ovation at their first opportunity, demonstrating their approval to sweep this thing under the rug. "Boys will be boys, everyone makes stupid mistakes." People affected by these actions don't have it so easy, often carrying burdens from continued assaults against their identities that are heightened by the mundane return to "everyday life" enjoyed by everyone else. Hader will go on compiling three-inning saves and jaw-dropping strikeout totals, and more hate speech will be unearthed from a new group of MLB youngsters; hopefully next time MLB, teams and players orient their apologies and punishments in the proper direction.

Adrian Houser RHP   Born: 02/02/93   Age: 26   Bats: R   Throws: R   Height: 6'4"   Weight: 235   Origin: Round 2, 2011 Draft (#69 overall)

YEAR	TEAM	LVL	AGE	W	L	SV	G	GS	IP	H	HR	BB/9	K/9	K	GB%	BABIP	WHIP	ERA	DRA	WARP	MPH	FB%	WHF	CSP
2016	BLX	AA	23	3	7	0	13	13	70¹	76	5	2.8	7.2	56	62%	.326	1.39	5.25	4.75	0.3				
2017	WIS	A	24	1	0	0	3	2	9	5	0	0.0	11.0	11	71%	.238	0.56	1.00	4.05	0.1				
2018	BLX	AA	25	0	1	0	8	8	26²	30	3	2.4	10.1	30	51%	.365	1.39	4.72	4.45	0.3				
2018	MIL	MLB	25	0	0	0	7	0	13²	13	0	4.6	5.3	8	40%	.302	1.46	3.29	5.04	0.0	96.1	66.4	11.1	44.7
2018	CSP	AAA	25	2	3	0	13	13	52	66	6	3.1	6.4	37	54%	.357	1.62	5.19	4.56	0.6				
2019	MIL	MLB	26	3	2	0	37	5	57¹	56	9	3.4	8.1	52	51%	.304	1.35	4.62	5.31	-0.3	95.7	67.6	11.3	45.5

Breakout: 8%   Improve: 21%   Collapse: 9%   Attrition: 20%   MLB: 39%   *Comparables: Stephen Fife, Gus Schlosser, Chris Stratton*

For the Overall Future Potential files, the organizational depth role can be grueling. Milwaukee ran a real, live shuttle crew in 2018, and first recalled Houser from Double-A on April 6. On April 8, Houser allowed one hit and struck out three in two innings of work against the Cubs, averaging around 95 mph and showcasing both his change and curve. The big righty was promptly optioned back to Double-A, where he began a stretch of eight starts. May 26 was Houser's next recall, this time with two scoreless innings against the Mets also adorned with three strikeouts. The Brewers almost immediately optioned Houser to Triple-A, which is kind of a promotion in this context. On June 17, he was recalled again, and this time stayed for nearly two weeks before his Triple-A demotion. The Brewers used one-day recalls on July 12 and August 11; on July 12, the results weren't as good, but they were great in August. That's approximately 20 days of MLB service on a prorated 40-man roster contract, including at least 11 moves in six months, for a big fastball, big frame, high-floor MLB pitcher.

Thomas Jankins RHP   Born: 07/02/95   Age: 23   Bats: R   Throws: R   Height: 6'3"   Weight: 200   Origin: Round 13, 2016 Draft (#381 overall)

YEAR	TEAM	LVL	AGE	W	L	SV	G	GS	IP	H	HR	BB/9	K/9	K	GB%	BABIP	WHIP	ERA	DRA	WARP	MPH	FB%	WHF	CSP
2016	HEL	RK	20	0	0	0	4	2	11²	12	2	1.5	10.8	14	52%	.323	1.20	3.09	2.82	0.4				
2016	WIS	A	20	0	2	0	8	7	25¹	33	0	2.1	7.5	21	62%	.402	1.54	3.20	3.72	0.4				
2017	WIS	A	21	9	8	0	27	24	141²	141	14	2.0	7.7	121	55%	.305	1.22	3.62	3.97	2.1				
2018	BLX	AA	22	10	9	0	23	21	130¹	130	13	2.5	6.6	95	50%	.302	1.27	4.42	4.01	2.0				
2019	MIL	MLB	23	6	7	1	32	19	112²	111	17	3.1	7.5	94	47%	.301	1.33	4.62	5.30	-0.2				

Breakout: 6%   Improve: 9%   Collapse: 12%   Attrition: 20%   MLB: 23%   *Comparables: Zach Lee, Felix Jorge, Anthony Bass*

What is a sleeper? So many minor leaguers will fade off before they reach the majors, hitting a role ceiling, experiencing an injury or simply dropping off at the wrong time in their development cycle. It's easy to find sleepers, then: there are so many players who could succeed *if only this or that goes right*. Jankins, on the other hand, is a sleeper by leaping over High-A and posting a better-than-average DRA for Double-A Biloxi. The righty did all this with an unassuming sinker and slider combo, focusing on movement and command to succeed without velocity. This makes Jankins an intriguing high-floor depth arm, and when the attrition of 162 games wears down other louder arms that dot prospect lists, "unassuming" can morph into "valuable."

Jeremy Jeffress RHP   Born: 09/21/87   Age: 31   Bats: R   Throws: R   Height: 6'0"   Weight: 205   Origin: Round 1, 2006 Draft (#16 overall)

YEAR	TEAM	LVL	AGE	W	L	SV	G	GS	IP	H	HR	BB/9	K/9	K	GB%	BABIP	WHIP	ERA	DRA	WARP	MPH	FB%	WHF	CSP
2016	MIL	MLB	28	2	2	27	47	0	44²	45	2	2.2	7.1	35	59%	.312	1.25	2.22	4.45	0.3	98.3	73.7	11.2	50.3
2016	TEX	MLB	28	1	0	0	12	0	13¹	10	0	4.7	4.7	7	70%	.270	1.27	2.70	5.49	-0.1	96.9	83.3	7.8	49
2017	TEX	MLB	29	1	2	0	39	0	40²	49	8	4.2	6.4	29	56%	.328	1.67	5.31	6.45	-0.6	96.4	67.9	10.2	46.2
2017	MIL	MLB	29	4	0	0	22	1	24²	24	2	5.5	8.0	22	65%	.301	1.58	3.65	4.42	0.2	96.7	62	11.7	42.2
2018	MIL	MLB	30	8	1	15	73	0	76²	49	5	3.2	10.4	89	58%	.249	0.99	1.29	2.62	2.0	97.3	53.2	14.7	47.6
2019	MIL	MLB	31	3	1	5	59	0	62	49	6	3.6	10.0	69	55%	.295	1.20	3.54	4.07	0.6	96.3	61.5	12.5	46.9

Breakout: 23%   Improve: 47%   Collapse: 25%   Attrition: 12%   MLB: 91%   *Comparables: Peter Moylan, Chad Bradford, Pedro Feliciano*

Redemption is a difficult storyline because if you lean too hard on the moral, you'll miss the process. Jeffress' redemption is manifold, and his third go-round in Milwaukee demonstrated that some players just *belong* in some organizations. Player development takes a village, from the player to the front office and support staff. Jeffress is undoubtedly a success of the human side of the game. But don't let these morals write the full story. The high-leverage chameleon will work in any inning, splitting a plurality of appearances from the sixth through the ninth in 2018. He'll enter in tricky inherited runner situations. And, 55 percent of the time, he entered when the game was within one run. Stomping and huffing on the mound, glaring past the batter to get the sign, Jeffress became a curveball-first pitcher while also balancing usage between his electric sinker and traditional hard-riding fastball. This tweak helped multiply strikeouts without sacrificing excellent ground-ball abilities. Here the process was as important as the moral, which helps to explain why Jeffress' redemption placed him near the top of NL relief ranks, well beyond his previous profile as just another potential high-leverage reliever.

Corey Knebel RHP   Born: 11/26/91   Age: 27   Bats: R   Throws: R   Height: 6'4"   Weight: 220   Origin: Round 1, 2013 Draft (#39 overall)

YEAR	TEAM	LVL	AGE	W	L	SV	G	GS	IP	H	HR	BB/9	K/9	K	GB%	BABIP	WHIP	ERA	DRA	WARP	MPH	FB%	WHF	CSP
2016	CSP	AAA	24	1	0	2	11	2	13²	5	0	2.0	9.2	14	66%	.172	0.59	1.32	3.26	0.3				
2016	MIL	MLB	24	1	4	2	35	0	32²	32	3	4.4	10.5	38	43%	.333	1.47	4.68	5.45	-0.2	97.7	72.3	9.3	48
2017	MIL	MLB	25	1	4	39	76	0	76	48	6	4.7	14.9	126	39%	.311	1.16	1.78	3.09	1.8	98.9	71.8	15.4	47.4
2018	MIL	MLB	26	4	3	16	57	0	55¹	38	7	3.6	14.3	88	50%	.304	1.08	3.58	2.53	1.5	98.4	70.9	14.5	49.2
2019	MIL	MLB	27	3	1	30	59	0	62	42	6	3.9	12.9	89	45%	.293	1.11	3.05	3.53	0.9	98.0	72.4	14.3	48.9

Breakout: 32%   Improve: 57%   Collapse: 26%   Attrition: 14%   MLB: 97%   *Comparables: Cody Allen, Ken Giles, Jordan Walden*

It would be hard to believe a serious account of the 2018 season in which the Brewers won 96 games and Knebel might have been the fourth-best reliever on the staff. Yet Knebel battled injuries, command concerns and general ineffectiveness throughout much of the season. His overall stuff remained largely intact, with a hard fastball-curveball duo for the ex-closer. Refined command and mechanics means Knebel can throw the curve more than 35 percent of the time, however, and when that approach works, you can put the capital-"K" back in Knebel. He had a 5.01 ERA on September 1, but then tossed 16 1/3 scoreless innings with a 33/3 K/BB ratio in the final month and reclaimed a prominent role in the playoffs.

Wade Miley LHP   Born: 11/13/86   Age: 32   Bats: L   Throws: L   Height: 6'0"   Weight: 220   Origin: Round 1, 2008 Draft (#43 overall)

YEAR	TEAM	LVL	AGE	W	L	SV	G	GS	IP	H	HR	BB/9	K/9	K	GB%	BABIP	WHIP	ERA	DRA	WARP	MPH	FB%	WHF	CSP
2016	SEA	MLB	29	7	8	0	19	19	112	117	18	2.7	6.6	82	48%	.298	1.35	4.98	5.11	0.3	93.3	47	9.4	47.3
2016	BAL	MLB	29	2	5	0	11	11	54	70	7	2.5	9.2	55	50%	.389	1.57	6.17	4.06	0.8	92.8	47	9.8	42.6
2017	BAL	MLB	30	8	15	0	32	32	157¹	179	25	5.3	8.1	142	51%	.332	1.73	5.61	7.20	-2.9	93.3	53.4	9	36.9
2018	BLX	AA	31	1	2	0	7	7	25¹	27	3	1.4	9.9	28	59%	.393	1.22	3.55	3.61	0.5				
2018	MIL	MLB	31	5	2	0	16	16	80²	71	3	3.0	5.6	50	54%	.269	1.21	2.57	4.13	1.1	92.6	20	9.9	42.5
2019	MIL	MLB	32	6	6	0	18	18	97	94	11	3.2	7.8	84	50%	.307	1.32	4.12	4.73	0.6	92.1	43	9.3	41

Breakout: 15%   Improve: 45%   Collapse: 24%   Attrition: 16%   MLB: 86%   *Comparables: Gavin Floyd, Tom Koehler, Paul Maholm*

Revitalize your career in 10 steps: Cutter. Cutter. Change. Cutter. Curve. Cutter. Fastball. Curve. Cutter. Change. Miley deserves this pitch selection shoutout, as the struggling southpaw allegedly decided to throw cutters in the middle of a July 25, 2017 start against Tampa Bay because he was getting shelled. After that fateful decision, this veritable Paul Bunyan became a minor-league wizard for the Brewers, and dodged a couple of injuries to become a near-ace for the surprise contenders. The Legend of Wade Miley shows the tantalizing appeal of baseball's game of adjustments, but there's danger in merely leaning on the crutch of "learn a new pitch." Plus, it takes credit away from the difficulty of Miley's path: learn a new pitch, execute that pitch, take a minor-league contract, work in the minors, improve command, rehab injuries and throw that newfound pitch more and more as the season progresses. It only looks easy when it works. This one's a true legend for being so much more than a myth.

Jimmy Nelson RHP Born: 06/05/89 Age: 30 Bats: R Throws: R Height: 6'6" Weight: 250 Origin: Round 2, 2010 Draft (#64 overall)

YEAR	TEAM	LVL	AGE	W	L	SV	G	GS	IP	H	HR	BB/9	K/9	K	GB%	BABIP	WHIP	ERA	DRA	WARP	MPH	FB%	WHF	CSP
2016	MIL	MLB	27	8	16	0	32	32	179¹	186	25	4.3	7.0	140	51%	.299	1.52	4.62	6.23	-1.8	95.5	70.8	8.4	50.7
2017	MIL	MLB	28	12	6	0	29	29	175¹	171	16	2.5	10.2	199	51%	.340	1.25	3.49	3.32	4.4	95.5	61.2	12.3	50.7
2019	MIL	MLB	30	5	5	0	16	16	84²	72	9	3.3	9.4	89	49%	.300	1.22	3.68	4.23	1.1	94.7	65.3	10.5	50.6

Breakout: 14% Improve: 50% Collapse: 21% Attrition: 9% MLB: 92%   *Comparables: Tyson Ross, Jeff Locke, Trevor Cahill*

Nelson had hoped to return in the second half, which would have made the already fun Brewers an even better story, but instead he ended up missing the entire 2018 season recovering from a September 2017 shoulder injury suffered while running the bases. Prior to his career being derailed, Nelson had taken major strides to become a potential front-line starter, thriving in 2017 even while the BABIP gods did him dirty. However, it's hard to predict how he'll fare after what will be nearly 18 months off by the time spring training rolls around.

Freddy Peralta RHP Born: 06/04/96 Age: 23 Bats: R Throws: R Height: 5'11" Weight: 175 Origin: International Free Agent, 2013

YEAR	TEAM	LVL	AGE	W	L	SV	G	GS	IP	H	HR	BB/9	K/9	K	GB%	BABIP	WHIP	ERA	DRA	WARP	MPH	FB%	WHF	CSP
2016	WIS	A	20	4	1	2	16	8	60	45	3	3.6	11.6	77	35%	.292	1.15	2.85	3.06	1.3				
2016	BRV	A+	20	0	3	0	8	2	22	27	4	4.9	8.2	20	51%	.365	1.77	5.73	3.88	0.3				
2017	CAR	A+	21	1	3	0	12	8	56¹	39	6	5.0	12.5	78	39%	.268	1.24	3.04	3.55	1.1				
2017	BLX	AA	21	2	5	1	13	11	63²	38	2	4.4	12.9	91	44%	.267	1.08	2.26	2.68	1.9				
2018	CSP	AAA	22	6	2	0	13	13	61	49	1	4.1	12.8	87	48%	.343	1.26	3.10	2.96	1.8				
2018	MIL	MLB	22	6	4	0	16	14	78¹	49	8	4.6	11.0	96	33%	.237	1.14	4.25	5.21	0.1	93.8	77.6	12	49.2
2019	MIL	MLB	23	5	5	0	15	15	79²	59	10	4.3	11.7	103	38%	.290	1.22	3.79	4.37	0.9	93.7	80.4	12.5	51

Breakout: 18% Improve: 41% Collapse: 17% Attrition: 21% MLB: 68%   *Comparables: Alex Reyes, Zach Braddock, Rubby De La Rosa*

What makes Peralta's fastball special is that he throws several variations in one pitch, taking a little bit off when necessary, bending it like a cutter or trying to run it when he needs a different look. By the NLCS, Peralta was demonstrating increased velocity out of the bullpen while maintaining the velocity and movement variations that make the pitch tick. The easy money is on Peralta staying in a supporting role, but the lesson of 2018 should be loudly learned: the lack of a certain role and the existence of clear shortcomings will not stop Peralta from making an impact.

Cody Ponce RHP Born: 04/25/94 Age: 25 Bats: R Throws: R Height: 6'6" Weight: 240 Origin: Round 2, 2015 Draft (#55 overall)

YEAR	TEAM	LVL	AGE	W	L	SV	G	GS	IP	H	HR	BB/9	K/9	K	GB%	BABIP	WHIP	ERA	DRA	WARP	MPH	FB%	WHF	CSP
2016	BRV	A+	22	2	8	0	17	17	72	84	6	2.1	8.6	69	47%	.345	1.40	5.25	3.57	1.6				
2017	CAR	A+	23	8	8	0	22	22	120	130	14	1.9	7.1	94	42%	.312	1.29	3.38	4.08	1.7				
2017	BLX	AA	23	2	1	0	3	3	17²	10	0	2.5	4.6	9	54%	.200	0.85	1.53	5.39	0.0				
2018	BLX	AA	24	7	6	0	29	11	95	88	10	3.2	8.3	88	45%	.294	1.28	4.36	4.01	1.3				
2019	MIL	MLB	25	5	5	1	28	15	88¹	85	14	3.0	8.1	79	42%	.298	1.31	4.61	5.30	-0.1				

Breakout: 4% Improve: 6% Collapse: 7% Attrition: 14% MLB: 18%   *Comparables: Ryan Carpenter, Jason Wheeler, Mike Wright*

Witness the tortoise and the hare: Entering 2016, right handers Cody Ponce and Freddy Peralta represented two of the most divergent profiles in baseball. Peralta, a diminutive 20-year-old out of the Dominican Republic, made his first entry into full-season ball; Ponce, the definition of a big, advanced college arm, began the season in High-A and seemed poised to be a fast riser at age 22. The fast riser appeal seemed especially probable if one stuck with Ponce as a reliever or back-end starter. Ponce stalled. In 2017, the Brewers moved their High-A affiliate to Carolina, and so too moved Ponce, who finally earned a call to Double-A in late August of that year, catching up with the fast-rising Peralta. The slow-cooker continued with Ponce in 2018, when the underlying stats look solid, placing an exclamation point on the end of those fast-riser dreams. Now that back-end rotation role is a dream, but it feels entirely too soon to say that Ponce is close.

Trey Supak RHP Born: 05/31/96 Age: 23 Bats: R Throws: R Height: 6'5" Weight: 235 Origin: Round 2, 2014 Draft (#73 overall)

YEAR	TEAM	LVL	AGE	W	L	SV	G	GS	IP	H	HR	BB/9	K/9	K	GB%	BABIP	WHIP	ERA	DRA	WARP	MPH	FB%	WHF	CSP
2016	HEL	RK	20	1	1	0	4	2	14	10	0	0.6	7.1	11	54%	.256	0.79	1.29	2.75	0.4				
2016	WIS	A	20	2	3	1	11	6	44¹	48	3	3.5	8.1	40	41%	.338	1.47	3.86	3.75	0.6				
2017	WIS	A	21	2	2	0	8	7	41	21	1	2.2	11.6	53	36%	.235	0.76	1.76	2.74	1.2				
2017	CAR	A+	21	3	4	1	15	11	72¹	65	12	3.5	7.1	57	34%	.261	1.29	4.60	4.41	0.7				
2018	CAR	A+	22	2	1	0	9	9	51	37	2	2.8	8.5	48	38%	.269	1.04	1.76	4.69	0.4				
2018	BLX	AA	22	6	6	0	16	16	86²	74	4	2.9	7.8	75	45%	.286	1.18	2.91	3.73	1.6				
2019	MIL	MLB	23	2	2	0	6	6	31²	29	5	3.6	8.5	30	38%	.288	1.30	4.63	5.31	0.0				

Breakout: 2% Improve: 3% Collapse: 15% Attrition: 13% MLB: 19%   *Comparables: Adalberto Mejia, Steven Brault, Aaron Blair*

Let's have some fun with the mid-rotation starter! In 2018, 299 pitchers made at least two starts in the majors. The 70th percentile cutoff was 132 2/3 innings, 24 starts, a 3.99 DRA and a 3.68 ERA. Below that threshold, how many pitchers truly need more than two workable pitches? What type of command or mechanical shortcomings are exhibited below this threshold? We ask on behalf of Supak, who many view as a relief prospect given the unsightly walk totals, plus a profile that mostly hinges on two pitches. Yet this is not to oversell the questions on Supak, as the big righty also yielded more ground balls after making the leap to Double-A. With a strong fastball-curve profile and two consecutive seasons with more than 100 innings, Supak looks like a mid-rotation arm in a league starved for innings and settling on lower workloads to fill out their starts.

Brent Suter LHP Born: 08/29/89 Age: 29 Bats: L Throws: L Height: 6'5" Weight: 195 Origin: Round 31, 2012 Draft (#965 overall)

YEAR	TEAM	LVL	AGE	W	L	SV	G	GS	IP	H	HR	BB/9	K/9	K	GB%	BABIP	WHIP	ERA	DRA	WARP	MPH	FB%	WHF	CSP
2016	CSP	AAA	26	6	6	2	26	15	110²	129	5	1.1	6.1	75	41%	.348	1.29	3.50	5.47	-0.3				
2016	MIL	MLB	26	2	2	0	14	2	21²	25	3	2.1	6.2	15	44%	.328	1.38	3.32	6.45	-0.3	86.9	68.3	10.1	48.5
2017	CSP	AAA	27	3	1	0	10	8	36²	42	5	2.0	9.3	38	46%	.359	1.36	4.42	3.79	0.8				
2017	MIL	MLB	27	3	2	0	22	14	81²	83	8	2.4	7.1	64	46%	.306	1.29	3.42	4.72	0.7	88.2	70.6	10.3	49
2018	MIL	MLB	28	8	7	0	20	18	101¹	102	18	1.7	7.5	84	36%	.281	1.19	4.44	5.01	0.3	88.6	68.9	11.1	50.1
2019	MIL	MLB	29	1	0	0	11	0	11¹	10	2	2.4	8.2	10	40%	.295	1.19	4.08	4.68	0.0	87.7	69.5	10.7	49.3

Breakout: 24%   Improve: 34%   Collapse: 17%   Attrition: 18%   MLB: 61%   *Comparables: Pat Misch, J.D. Martin, Chris Rusin*

Don't let those velocity vultures tell you that hard-throwers have exclusive license to the Tommy John surgery! Suter's raptor delivery pumped up above 87 mph in 2018, even averaging 88 or better during some months. Be it the southpaw's herky-jerky mechanics, rapid-fire pace, the slider usage or the increased curveball, Suter succumbed to elbow surgery in August. Even without the ability to pitch, the Environmental Science and Public Policy graduate kept bringing his Eco Meal Kit to the park, emerging as a grade-80 hype man for the contending Brewers and one of the leaders of a raucous dugout celebration crew. Suter remains one to watch in 2019, both for his potential injury recovery and re-emergence as one of the fastest-working slow-throwers in MLB, and for his earnest, joyful support for the game.

Brandon Woodruff RHP Born: 02/10/93 Age: 26 Bats: L Throws: R Height: 6'4" Weight: 215 Origin: Round 11, 2014 Draft (#326 overall)

YEAR	TEAM	LVL	AGE	W	L	SV	G	GS	IP	H	HR	BB/9	K/9	K	GB%	BABIP	WHIP	ERA	DRA	WARP	MPH	FB%	WHF	CSP
2016	BRV	A+	23	4	1	0	8	8	44¹	33	2	2.0	9.9	49	52%	.277	0.97	1.83	2.11	1.7				
2016	BLX	AA	23	10	8	0	20	20	113²	88	4	2.4	9.8	124	49%	.286	1.04	3.01	2.29	3.8				
2017	CSP	AAA	24	6	5	0	16	16	75¹	78	8	3.0	8.4	70	49%	.323	1.37	4.30	4.01	1.4				
2017	MIL	MLB	24	2	3	0	8	8	43	43	5	2.9	6.7	32	50%	.292	1.33	4.81	5.65	0.0	96.3	60.5	9.8	46.2
2018	CSP	AAA	25	3	2	0	17	17	71¹	67	8	4.0	8.6	68	50%	.296	1.39	4.04	4.48	0.9				
2018	MIL	MLB	25	3	0	1	19	4	42¹	36	4	3.0	10.0	47	54%	.294	1.18	3.61	3.16	0.9	97.5	64.1	11.3	50.1
2019	MIL	MLB	26	9	7	0	35	24	138²	115	16	3.2	9.3	142	47%	.289	1.19	3.76	4.32	1.5	96.6	63.6	10.8	49.2

Breakout: 19%   Improve: 33%   Collapse: 24%   Attrition: 24%   MLB: 75%   *Comparables: Alfredo Aceves, David Phelps, Chris Devenski*

In another age, the Brewers would have simply plugged Woodruff into the rotation and allowed the big righty an opportunity to show mid-rotation potential, or at least eat innings. Only in 2018, Woodruff was not that, instead serving as a bizarre swingman between Triple-A and MLB, culminating in only four starts at the highest level. That development plan proved worthwhile as Woodruff emerged as an even harder-throwing, multi-inning arm out of the bullpen, with a new sinking fastball to run in on right-handed batters and a slower curve, too. This is the Woodruff who worked a pristine September, striking out 16 of 50 batters faced and yielding 18 ground balls against 12 fly outs. All of this makes Woodruff something of a chameleon, a flexible workhorse well-suited for an era of openers and longer relief.

LINEOUTS

Hitters

HITTER	POS	TEAM	LVL	AGE	PA	R	2B	3B	HR	RBI	BB	K	SB	CS	AVG/OBP/SLG	DRC+	VORP	BABIP	BRR	FRAA	WARP
Keon Broxton	CF	CSP	AAA	28	334	47	16	2	10	37	30	119	27	4	.254/.323/.421	76	10.2	.382	5.1	CF(61): -1.0, LF(8): 2.0	0.8
	CF	MIL	MLB	28	89	15	2	2	4	11	11	28	5	1	.179/.281/.410	80	6.0	.217	2.3	CF(24): 1.5, RF(20): 0.6	0.5
Larry Ernesto	RF	DBW	Rk	17	221	38	13	2	5	20	14	68	9	4	.236/.294/.394	78	4.5	.328	0.2	CF(28): 5.7, LF(15): 2.5	1.1
Nick Franklin	2B	BLX	AA	27	71	10	3	0	2	8	11	7	4	1	.288/.394/.441	109	5.6	.294	1.0	RF(6): 1.6, 3B(4): 0.7	0.6
	2B	MIL	MLB	27	2	0	0	0	0	0	0	0	0	0	.000/.000/.000	63	-0.4	.000	0.0	2B(1): 0.0	0.0
Trent Grisham	OF	BLX	AA	21	405	45	10	2	7	31	63	87	11	3	.233/.356/.337	108	7.1	.292	-1.8	RF(85): 3.5, LF(15): 1.1	1.9
Dustin Houle	C	BLX	AA	24	72	6	2	0	0	11	10	15	0	0	.197/.306/.230	92	0.4	.255	-1.8	C(24): -0.4	0.1
	C	CAR	A+	24	64	5	4	0	0	7	4	16	0	0	.296/.355/.370	94	3.0	.400	-0.8	C(17): -0.2	0.2
Erik Kratz	C	SWB	AAA	38	61	10	2	0	4	6	7	10	0	0	.269/.356/.538	130	5.1	.263	0.0	C(17): 1.6	0.7
	C	MIL	MLB	38	219	18	6	0	6	23	6	40	1	0	.236/.280/.355	93	2.9	.264	0.6	C(61): 10.2, P(3): 0.1	2.1
Robie Rojas	C	CAR	A+	23	44	7	2	0	0	5	6	15	0	0	.351/.455/.405	81	3.8	.591	0.1	C(8): -0.2	0.0
Tyler Saladino	SS	CHA	MLB	28	9	2	1	0	0	0	0	3	0	0	.250/.250/.375	60	0.0	.400	0.0	3B(2): 0.2	0.0
	SS	CSP	AAA	28	154	23	4	3	3	19	21	28	10	0	.262/.370/.408	112	8.9	.310	1.6	SS(25): -2.6, 2B(9): -0.7	0.8
	SS	MIL	MLB	28	130	11	3	0	5	16	9	38	2	2	.246/.302/.398	86	3.8	.316	0.1	SS(28): 1.7, 2B(6): 0.0	0.5
Eric Sogard	2B	MIL	MLB	32	113	7	3	0	0	2	12	23	3	0	.134/.241/.165	83	-5.4	.173	0.3	SS(24): 0.0, 2B(22): 0.1	0.2
	2B	CSP	AAA	32	101	10	4	0	0	11	10	16	0	1	.225/.297/.270	89	-2.0	.267	1.6	2B(18): 1.2, SS(5): 1.2	0.6
Tyrone Taylor	OF	CSP	AAA	24	481	73	23	9	20	80	27	74	13	4	.278/.321/.504	125	17.6	.292	2.3	CF(56): 0.5, LF(39): 7.2	4.2

Keon Broxton's incredible week between late June and early July should be entered as a candidate for the Ultimate Replacement Player (URP) leaderboard. Broxton demonstrated phenomenal game-saving defense while adding a few extra base hits for good measure. ⊗ After signing a big bonus during the summer of 2017, international prospect **Larry Ernesto** has already reached the continent and flashed that bat during a short stint in Arizona. ⊗ Milwaukee signed a couple of international prospects to identical deals in 2018, but **Eduarqui Fernandez** should not be confused for a bat-first play. This outfielder could build a name on defense up the middle, depending on how his 6-foot-2 frame ages and fills out. ⊗ Once a highly regarded prospect, now a utility-playing phoenix, **Nick Franklin** rebrands more frequently than a reality TV star. *Real Catchers of Biloxi* was the 2018 episode. ⓧ It was difficult not to lean on the name change for **Trent Grisham**, potentially a heartwarming narrative coupled with rejuvenation on the field. While climbing the ladder ever closer to MLB, the scouting knocks on the bat and power came along with Grisham. ⓧ Pour one out for the organizational catcher. **Dustin Houle** took five years to reach Double-A, bested that level, and absolutely shredded the Pacific Coast League for 13 plate appearances in 2018. How hard can you dream on a 50 arm? ⓧ Milwaukee is slowly increasing its presence around international baseball, with shortstop as their current success story. The club looks to **Branlyn Jaraba** as their next big-deal infielder, although this one probably moves down the defensive spectrum. ⓧ During the thrilling 2018 NLCS, a brief moment of organizational depth as performance art occurred when **Erik Kratz**'s college friends and teammates wore each of his previous MLB jerseys to Game 6. Kratz is truly blessed to have so many friends. ⓧ **Robie Rojas** dashed from the 38th round of the 2017 draft to Triple-A in 2018, which is about as thrilling as organizational depth gets. ⓧ The Brewers reacquainted **Tyler Saladino** with his leg kick in order to reclaim some of his previous power. While the homers resurfaced, Saladino's plate discipline leaves a new riddle for his next hitting coach. ⓧ Up next on *America's Got Talent*, **Eric Sogard** spun a .263/.404/.368 August 2017 into $2.4 million. With these monetary skills, rumor has it President Trump might nominate this shortstop to the Federal Reserve Board. ⓧ From athletic top prospect to forgotten minor leaguer and back, **Tyrone Taylor** is evidence of the length of player development cycles. Now, the age-25 outfielder is young for Triple-A and has a chance to answer org depth questions. ⓧ In the middle of August, the Brewers seemingly could not win a day game, so injured veteran **Stephen Vogt** began delivering day-game lineup cards. Milwaukee reversed fortunes immediately, making Vogt's feat the most interesting way to earn three million bucks.

Pitchers

PITCHER	TEAM	LVL	AGE	W	L	SV	G	GS	IP	H	HR	BB/9	K/9	K	GB%	BABIP	WHIP	ERA	DRA	WARP	MPH	FB%	WHF	CSP
Matt Albers	MIL	MLB	35	3	3	1	34	0	34^1	45	10	3.1	8.4	32	47%	.347	1.66	7.34	6.09	-0.5	93.9	64.6	11.6	44.1
Aaron Ashby	HEL	Rk	20	1	2	1	6	3	20^1	18	3	3.5	8.4	19	52%	.273	1.28	6.20	4.37	0.3				
	WIS	A	20	1	1	0	7	7	37^1	40	1	2.2	11.3	47	52%	.398	1.31	2.17	2.86	1.0				
Jacob Barnes	CSP	AAA	28	1	0	2	11	0	11^2	5	0	6.2	7.7	10	64%	.161	1.11	1.54	4.11	0.1				
	MIL	MLB	28	0	1	2	49	0	48^2	51	4	4.3	8.7	47	51%	.329	1.52	3.33	3.54	0.8	97.4	50.5	14.6	44.6
Xavier Cedeno	CHR	AAA	31	0	0	0	20	0	21^2	12	1	1.7	10.4	25	57%	.220	0.74	1.25	2.94	0.5				
	CHA	MLB	31	2	0	1	33	0	25^1	19	1	4.6	9.9	28	55%	.281	1.26	2.84	2.17	0.8	88.1	76.5	14.1	42.7
	MIL	MLB	31	0	0	0	15	0	8	7	0	3.4	6.8	6	52%	.280	1.25	1.12	3.12	0.2	88.9	76.5	12.1	42.4
Luis Gonzalez	BRR	Rk	19	1	2	0	7	2	11^1	15	2	10.3	4.8	6	43%	.325	2.47	6.35	5.82	0.0				
Dan Jennings	MIL	MLB	31	4	5	1	72	1	64^1	66	6	3.2	6.3	45	56%	.306	1.38	3.22	4.93	0.0	92.8	58.8	8.7	47
Jon Olczak	BLX	AA	24	10	3	4	42	0	56^1	36	1	2.9	9.6	60	41%	.252	0.96	1.44	3.48	1.0				
Miguel Sanchez	CAR	A+	24	1	0	1	10	0	21^1	14	4	2.5	12.7	30	53%	.233	0.94	2.53	2.12	0.7				
	BLX	AA	24	1	1	1	23	0	41	32	3	3.1	13.6	62	45%	.337	1.12	2.63	1.95	1.4				
Quintin Torres-Costa	BLX	AA	23	1	2	2	21	0	31	17	0	3.8	12.8	44	48%	.270	0.97	1.16	2.90	0.7				
	CSP	AAA	23	2	0	2	22	0	24	10	0	4.5	7.9	21	52%	.172	0.92	1.50	4.16	0.3				
Aaron Wilkerson	MIL	MLB	29	0	1	0	3	1	9	12	4	3.0	10.0	10	31%	.320	1.67	10.00	6.02	-0.1	90.5	54.8	10.2	44.2
	CSP	AAA	29	4	5	0	15	12	72^1	64	3	3.1	7.6	61	42%	.285	1.23	2.49	5.47	0.0				
Taylor Williams	MIL	MLB	26	1	3	0	56	0	53	53	6	4.2	9.7	57	39%	.320	1.47	4.25	4.34	0.4	97.1	64.9	14.9	44.6

Matt Albers had one of the most uneven run prevention seasons of 2018, shifting from elite early months to terrible performances after a run-in with the injury bug. ⓧ Emerging from Crowder College in Missouri, lefty **Aaron Ashby** had the Brewers' scouting department clicking their heels across the Midwest in an effort to repeat their Corbin Burnes magic. This wizard offers three high-floor pitches, making him a junior college sleeper. ⓧ Once compared to Chuck Crim for a bread-and-butter fastball-slider profile, righty **Jacob Barnes** seemingly disappeared in 2018. Things mostly clicked in September even if the command didn't, raising questions about repeating those high-leverage scenarios of years past. ⓧ It's stunning that someone with strikeout and ground-ball totals as strong as **Xavier Cedeno** has worked for four different teams in as many years. In an alternate universe, those peripherals made the 86 mph cutter specialist a relief ace. ⓧ Everything seemed on the up-and-up for **Oliver Drake** and the Brewers, until the Reds battered him for six runs on six hits, all on pitches outside the strike zone. It quickly became apparent that this might not have been his year. ⓧ A projection righty from Puerto Rico, **Luis Gonzalez** escaped the pre-draft hype machine but was promising enough to be drafted in the eighth round. Gonzalez was one of three players drafted out of PJ Education School in 2018. ⓧ Sparkling new Opener, available at The Leftorium! Acquire **Dan Jennings** now to record your first out! ⓧ Organizational righty **Jon Olczak** made the leap to the advanced minors in 2018, earning a spot in the Arizona Fall League to boot. DRA likes Olczak, and he was also a run-prevention sensation in a dozen AFL innings. ⓧ Rehabbing college right-hander **Drew Rasmussen** fell from the 31st pick in 2017 to a sixth-round gamble in 2018, providing the Brewers with one of the high-risk fliers to potentially define the high end of their class. ⓧ Don't scout the stat line unless an organizational depth reliever like **Miguel Sanchez** increases his strikeouts by 44 percent while moving from Single-A to Triple-A in one season. Then send that player to the Arizona Fall League, and join the nameless, faceless reliever revolution. ⓧ Isn't it ironic, don't you think? It's like **Quintin Torres-Costa** being scouted as a LOOGY from the get go, and then getting injured upon completing Triple-A. ⓧ When Michael Lewis writes a countercultural pitching tome *Brewers Guys*, **Aaron Wilkerson** will feature prominently. Perhaps a poor man's Mike Fiers, Wilkerson checks all the boxes: old prospect, taller than six feet, can't crack 90. ⓧ Once one of the most electric arms in the Brewers system, **Taylor Williams** has returned from an extended Tommy John episode to hold down the middle innings, from setup man to garbage time. When pitchers are throwing 120 mph in another decade or so, someone will fondly look back and ask, "Where have all the Taylor Williamses gone?"

MINNESOTA TWINS

Essay by Nick Nelson

Player comments by Matthew Trueblood and BP staff

Early on the morning of December 12, 2010, the roof of the Metrodome ripped open and gave way beneath the weight of a blizzard's heavy snow accumulation, which might be the most uniquely "Minnesota sports" thing that has ever happened. Caught on video by a news camera left running overnight, it was an astounding sight to behold.

A writeup in the *Minneapolis Star Tribune* described the aftermath: "Inside the bitterly cold stadium Sunday morning, a surreal scene emerged: Sunshine shimmered on seats and splattered snow covered the green turf. Lights and giant speakers hung perilously low above the field."

The Twins had called that giant inflated marshmallow home for 28 years before relocating across downtown in the spring. For baseball fans in a football-dominated market, there was a certain schadenfreude in seeing such misfortune fall upon the Vikings, who remained hapless inhabitants of The Dome.

Two months earlier, the Twins had capped their inaugural season at Target Field, a blissfully roofless marvel that instantly joined the ranks of baseball's finest yards. Yep, things were lookin' up for the Twins, fresh off their second straight American League Central title with a sparkling new ballpark, the reigning Manager of the Year in Ron Gardenhire and—most importantly—four-time All-Star catcher Joe Mauer locked up for many years to come.

Little did the Twins know they were about to experience their own deflating collapse.

In 2011, Gardenhire saw his team's win total drop from 94 to 63. As injuries and setbacks piled up, the roof caved in on the once-admired franchise, burying them under an ever-rising avalanche. That's more or less been the story of the past eight years, during which the Twins went 570-726 (.440) with zero division titles after going 708-589 (.546) with five division titles in the previous eight seasons. Minnesota has the worst record in baseball since 2011.

Any of the following names and terms are liable to trigger Twins fans who've seen their beautiful ballpark blighted by so much ugly baseball: *Matt Capps, pitch to contact, Tsuyoshi Nishioka, bilateral leg weakness, Total System Failure.* And last season, we saw another phrase added to this field of disdainful distinction: *This is how we baseball.*

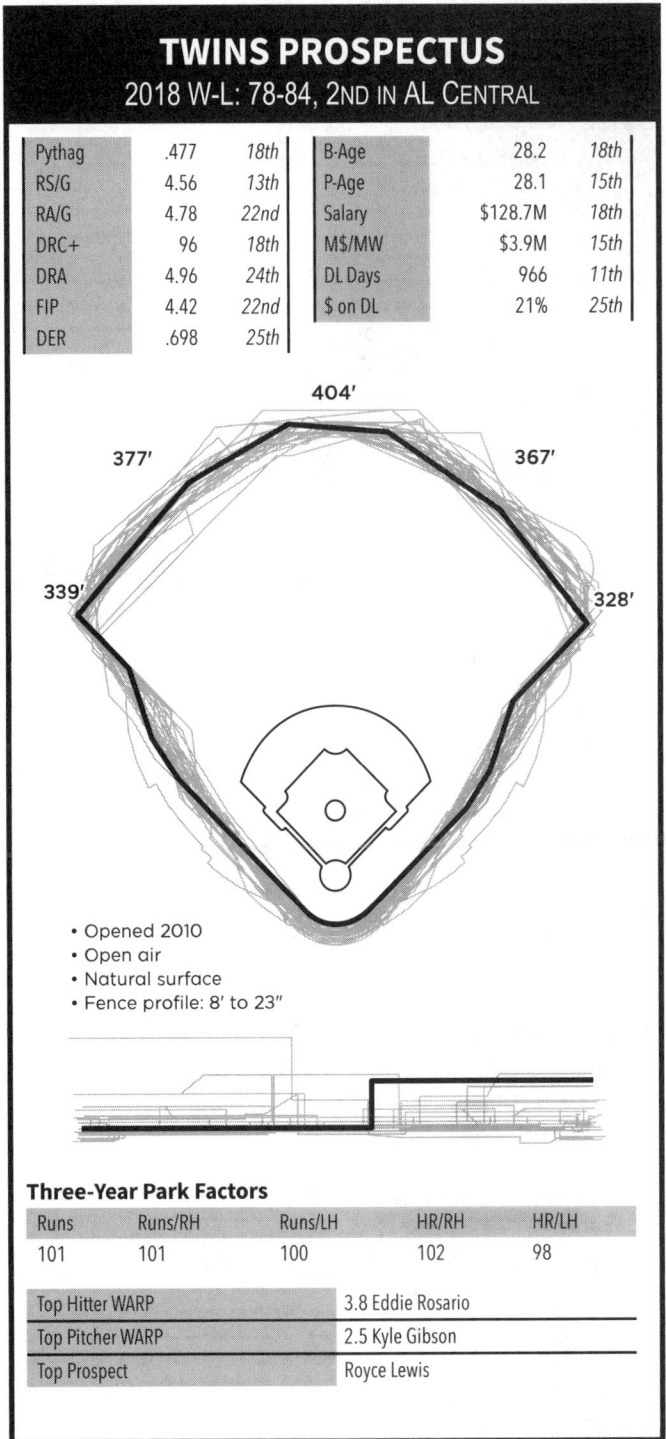

TWINS PROSPECTUS
2018 W-L: 78-84, 2ND IN AL CENTRAL

Pythag	.477	18th	B-Age	28.2	18th
RS/G	4.56	13th	P-Age	28.1	15th
RA/G	4.78	22nd	Salary	$128.7M	18th
DRC+	96	18th	M$/MW	$3.9M	15th
DRA	4.96	24th	DL Days	966	11th
FIP	4.42	22nd	$ on DL	21%	25th
DER	.698	25th			

404'
377'
367'
339'
328'

- Opened 2010
- Open air
- Natural surface
- Fence profile: 8' to 23"

Three-Year Park Factors

Runs	Runs/RH	Runs/LH	HR/RH	HR/LH
101	101	100	102	98

Top Hitter WARP	3.8 Eddie Rosario
Top Pitcher WARP	2.5 Kyle Gibson
Top Prospect	Royce Lewis

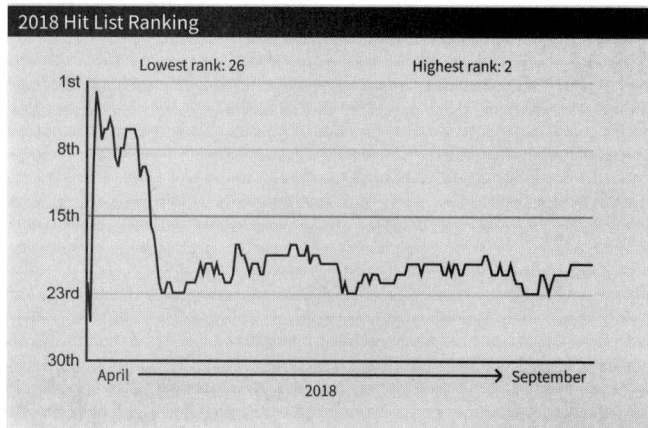

2018 Hit List Ranking

Lowest rank: 26   Highest rank: 2

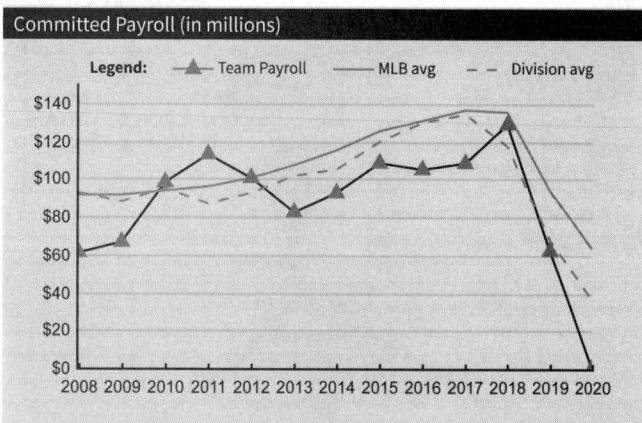

Committed Payroll (in millions)

Legend: —▲— Team Payroll   —— MLB avg   - - Division avg

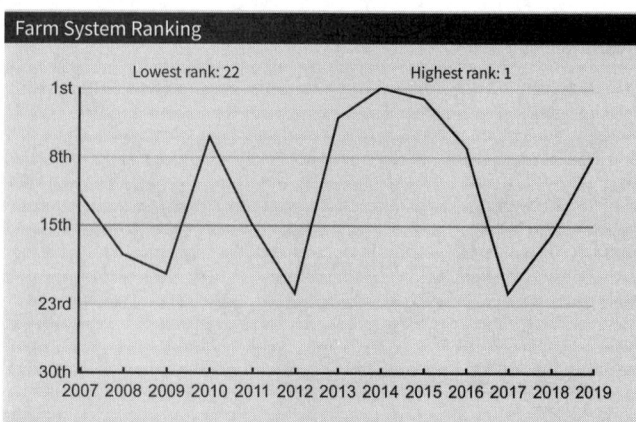

Farm System Ranking

Lowest rank: 22   Highest rank: 1

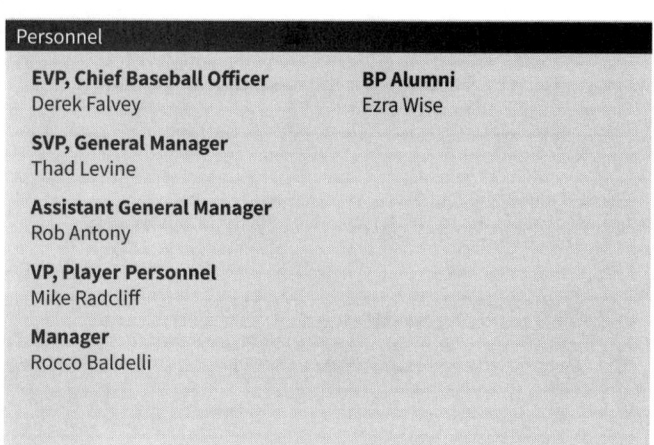

Personnel

EVP, Chief Baseball Officer
Derek Falvey

SVP, General Manager
Thad Levine

Assistant General Manager
Rob Antony

VP, Player Personnel
Mike Radcliff

Manager
Rocco Baldelli

BP Alumni
Ezra Wise

The team's grammatically painful marketing slogan drew plenty of Twitter guffaws when unveiled in the spring, but quickly became more sad than funny as the backdrop for a season full of grim developments and unmet promise. The Twins baseballed their way to a sub-.500 record in a division where three teams lost 98 or more games. After surging to a Wild Card spot in 2017, the freshly remodeled front office pumped record payroll into supplementing its electrifying young core with veteran free agent help, and then that core just…fizzled.

When Paul Molitor managed the Twins to 85 wins in 2017, sneaking into the postseason ever so briefly, it was primarily on the strength of five key contributors who combined for 16.3 WARP: Joe Mauer, Brian Dozier, Byron Buxton, Miguel Sano, Ervin Santana. In 2018, those same five players returned to produce 1.3 WARP for the Twins, with Mauer's miniscule 0.7 WARP ranking as the best of the sad bunch. That's the story in a nutshell. Given this astonishing drop-off, it's actually a minor miracle the team won 78 games last season. It wasn't enough to save Molitor, who was dismissed shortly after the season. The soft-spoken, cerebral skipper hadn't done much to merit firing—tribulations erased any chance at a successful outcome in 2018—but he also hadn't done much to merit keeping around, either.

A notoriously stable and loyal outfit, the Twins saw remarkably little churn in the quarter-century following their last championship in 1991. So when Gardenhire got the axe in 2014 following a fourth straight 90-loss season, it was a surprise. And when institutional general manager Terry Ryan was ousted two years later, in the wake of a 103-loss catastrophe, it came as a full-on shock to the system. But not necessarily the bad kind. More like the awakening, invigorating jolt of leaping into Lake Superior's chilly October embrace.

The Twins finally shook off insularity and embraced the game's changing tide. In a 180-degree pivot (a polar plunge?), they replaced the 62-year-old Ryan with 33-year-old Derek Falvey, plucked out of Cleveland's hotbed front office. Tossing out the old playbook, Minnesota created a new position for Falvey (chief baseball officer) and let him hire his own general manager, (Thad Levine, previously Jon Daniels' right-hand man in Texas). They've since dramatically expanded the research and development department, investing heavily in an area the previous regime viewed largely as an annoyance.

Of course, you can't put lipstick on a pig, and you can't just slap a new roof on a dingy, dilapidated Dome and call it good. The Vikings did replace and re-inflate the Metrodome's Teflon canopy, spending a couple more years in its confines, but ultimately they recognized what needed to be done: They tore down the entire dated structure and built anew in its place. That patch of land is now occupied by U.S. Bank Stadium, which is either a world-class entertainment venue or a billion-dollar eyesore depending on who you ask.

Similarly, revamping the Twins' baseball operations department was only the first step in a rebuild from the ground up. Molitor was deeply ingrained in the organization before taking over, as much a vestige of the past as his well-tenured veteran clubhouse stalwarts Dozier, Santana, and Mauer. Each moved on after 2018. Only one, however, was the subject of tearful on-field tributes.

Mauer was the face of Twins baseball, for better or worse. The locally sourced no. 1 overall draft pick blossomed into an MVP in his own backyard—a storybook tale of the modern era, complete with hideous comments section. The 2018 season was filled with milestones for the 15-year veteran, wrapping up his $184 million mega-deal, but still he was treated by many as a millstone. His hefty salary, lack of prototypical power and "aw shucks" personality made Mauer a magnet for misguided vitriol from fans, columnists and radio hosts alike.

No, he didn't hit many home runs. And if you called him milquetoast, he'd think you were talking about his favorite late-night snack. But whether or not you could revel in Mauer's unbridled Minnesotan docility, any true baseball diehard had to appreciate the absolute skill and precision with which he played the game. His smooth lefty swing was picture perfect, as if conjured into existence by an overzealous hitting coach. From his first day in the majors to his last, he understood the strike zone better than most umpires. He was as clutch as they come, retiring with the second-highest active batting average in RISP situations, behind only Joey Votto. Mauer played Gold Glove-caliber defense at catcher, and then, after a concussion forced him away from the position, he played Gold Glove-caliber defense at first base.

By the end, he wasn't producing much all-around value. That 2013 brain injury was a costly one for Mauer the player, turning him from elite catcher to middling first baseman and throwing a surefire Hall of Fame career drastically off course. In five years at first base, he produced a total of just 0.2 WARP more than he did in his final season at catcher alone. Yet for us hopeless purists, he remained a joy to watch until the very end. "The man was born to play baseball," tweeted teammate Mitch Garver shortly after an emotional 2018 season finale that saw Mauer suit up and receive one last pitch as catcher in the ninth inning.

Garver was the first rookie catcher for Minnesota since Mauer to give real cause for intrigue, posting a .749 OPS in 102 games after an outstanding 2017 season at Triple-A. He's among a new-look wave of talent that hopes to lead Minnesota back to the promised land; a youth-fueled group with a youthful new leader—Rocco Baldelli is now MLB's youngest manager, and Falvey and Levine are betting that the 37-year-old, fished out of Tampa's ranks, can take this talent-laden roster he's inheriting to the next level.

Unfortunately, Garver was one of the few on that roster to inspire much confidence last season. There were others, like Jose Berrios, Eddie Rosario, Jake Cave, Kyle Gibson and Taylor Rogers, but too many stumbled and scuffled—most vitally Buxton and Sano, two of the Twins' most critical assets. Each endured a nightmare season derailed by injuries, performance regressions and friction with the front office. It's hard to have much faith in Minnesota's short-term viability with that duo wandering by the wayside, but then it's also hard to forget the game-changing ability each displayed only one year earlier.

In 2017, Sano was an All-Star slugger and Buxton was among baseball's most valuable second-half contributors, winning a Gold Glove in center field. They're still young (both 25 as of Opening Day) and each possesses a signature skill—Sano's raw power, Buxton's straightaway speed—ranking at the highest of percentiles. Those are building-block tools for building-block players, and if the reconstruction of the Twins as a contender is to happen in short order, they'll need to bear weight.

Buxton and Sano are both down and out coming off campaigns more or less ruined by physical issues. Baldelli, whose own promising career was sabotaged by a rare muscle fatigue disorder, knows a thing or two about being at the helpless mercy of one's health. Perhaps he can bring to the table a relatability beyond that "under 45, recently retired" status now so in vogue around the league. He made a point to visit both Buxton and Sano for face-to-face meetings this offseason, traveling first to Georgia and then to the Dominican Republic in the hopes of getting to know his star pupils in a way Molitor never seemed to.

Cutting-edge trends are now guiding the Twins organization, a direct departure from the previous norm. The coupling of Falvey and Baldelli as figureheads creates strong parallels with Andy MacPhail and Tom Kelly, who took over as Minnesota's GM/manager duo in the mid-1980s, at even younger ages than the new regime. MacPhail and Kelly teamed up to win two World Series championships with a young core that blossomed together.

They also built an infrastructure that lasted three decades and yielded plenty of success, even if the final years were marked by decay. Now, the franchise fully presses restart, with fresh leadership and new faces all over the roster (including Nelson Cruz, the club's big-ticket offseason addition). Lying ahead is a potentially rapid rebuild, depending on the resilience of those entrenched foundational pieces and the speed at which the next big wave of talent—top-50 prospects Royce Lewis, Brusdar Graterol and Alex Kirilloff—can join them in the majors.

It's funny how history repeats itself. Granted, not as funny as the Vikings having to play a "home game" in Detroit. ∎

—Nick Nelson is a writer at Twins Daily.

HITTERS

Ehire Adrianza UT Born: 08/21/89 Age: 29 Bats: B Throws: R Height: 6'1" Weight: 170 Origin: International Free Agent, 2006

YEAR	TEAM	LVL	AGE	PA	R	2B	3B	HR	RBI	BB	K	SB	CS	AVG/OBP/SLG	DRC+	VORP	BABIP	BRR	FRAA	WARP
2016	SFN	MLB	26	71	3	2	0	2	7	2	13	0	1	.254/.299/.381	84	0.9	.292	-0.8	SS(13): 0.8, 3B(7): -0.2	0.1
2017	ROC	AAA	27	44	1	0	0	0	3	6	11	0	1	.216/.326/.216	86	-1.5	.308	-0.1	LF(4): 1.0, SS(2): 0.3	0.1
2017	MIN	MLB	27	186	30	9	2	2	24	16	25	8	1	.265/.324/.383	93	6.2	.291	1.6	SS(29): 3.0, LF(17): 1.5	1.2
2018	MIN	MLB	28	366	42	23	1	6	39	24	82	5	1	.251/.301/.379	81	7.6	.313	0.7	SS(64): -6.1, 3B(28): 0.6	-0.1
2019	MIN	MLB	29	187	20	9	1	4	18	14	36	4	1	.252/.311/.382	93	4.2	.290	0.1	2B -1, 3B 1	0.4

Breakout: 5%   Improve: 46%   Collapse: 14%   Attrition: 25%   MLB: 94%   *Comparables: Brendan Ryan, Jason Bartlett, Cliff Pennington*

Of the nine previous write-ups Adrianza has gotten in these pages, nine have used the exact phrases "good-glove/no-hit" or "utility player." That's a failure of imagination, an affliction Adrianza himself has nobly avoided. Over pieces of six big-league seasons, he's slowly organized an approach aimed at generating the consistent loft and authoritative contact on which hinge his chances of moving beyond those labels and into the realm of the regulars. Alas, he's not up to it. As he's more often generated what passes for high-value contact, he's lost the ability to draw walks and put the ball in play at an elite rate. Worse, the drives he does lift don't fly the way he imagines they might. Too many land relatively harmlessly in gloves or gaps, rather than bleachers. He's no longer so slick afield as to risk being called "good-glove," either.

Willians Astudillo C/UT Born: 10/14/91 Age: 27 Bats: R Throws: R Height: 5'9" Weight: 225 Origin: International Free Agent, 2008

YEAR	TEAM	LVL	AGE	PA	R	2B	3B	HR	RBI	BB	K	SB	CS	AVG/OBP/SLG	DRC+	VORP	BABIP	BRR	FRAA	WARP
2016	MIS	AA	24	342	24	9	0	4	30	5	11	1	1	.267/.293/.332	102	3.7	.263	-1.5	C(75): 12.0, 1B(8): -0.7	2.7
2017	RNO	AAA	25	128	22	14	0	4	22	4	5	0	1	.342/.370/.558	126	7.8	.330	-1.4	C(19): 0.9, 3B(14): 0.0	1.0
2018	ROC	AAA	26	307	30	17	1	12	38	10	14	7	4	.276/.314/.469	126	16.0	.255	-1.4	C(39): 2.5, 3B(28): 0.6	2.5
2018	MIN	MLB	26	97	9	4	1	3	21	2	3	0	0	.355/.371/.516	127	8.5	.341	0.4	C(16): 2.1, 3B(6): 0.0	1.0
2019	MIN	MLB	27	280	32	15	1	9	34	13	27	2	1	.274/.319/.439	105	11.0	.277	-0.4	C 1, 3B -1	1.2

Breakout: 6%   Improve: 23%   Collapse: 21%   Attrition: 37%   MLB: 65%   *Comparables: Jose Morales, Tomas Telis, Steve Clevenger*

For years, the man they call La Tortuga labored anonymously, buffeted by the breaks of the game, flipped onto his metaphorical shell time and time again. He was overlooked and underrated — out of mind, and often (thanks to persistent injury issues) out of sight. He became a baseball nomad, plodding through three organizations in as many seasons. Then, with just some good health and a slight adjustment, he found himself taking off. Astudillo has always been a good pitch framer; that skill is more appreciated than ever. He's always been a singular contact hitter; that skill is rarer than ever. When he added the

YEAR	TEAM	P. COUNT	FRM RUNS	BLK RUNS	THRW RUNS	TOT RUNS
2017	RNO	2571	1.4	0.0	-0.2	1.0
2018	MIN	2234	1.1	0.5	0.0	1.6
2018	ROC	5149	1.4	0.3	0.3	1.6
2019	MIN	5772	0.7	0.2	0.1	1.0

ability to hit the ball hard and get it in the air on occasion, without losing that extraordinary ability to avoid whiffs, he became too good to ignore. The numbers he put up during his brief big-league debut were eye-popping. His level of popularity rose to meet that of his utility, even as that level itself rose. He's not a turtle, really. He's just a fat, slow unicorn.

Tyler Austin 1B Born: 09/06/91 Age: 27 Bats: R Throws: R Height: 6'2" Weight: 220 Origin: Round 13, 2010 Draft (#415 overall)

YEAR	TEAM	LVL	AGE	PA	R	2B	3B	HR	RBI	BB	K	SB	CS	AVG/OBP/SLG	DRC+	VORP	BABIP	BRR	FRAA	WARP
2016	TRN	AA	24	210	22	10	1	4	29	30	46	1	1	.260/.367/.395	105	7.2	.326	1.2	1B(37): 0.1, LF(7): -1.5	0.4
2016	SWB	AAA	24	234	39	24	0	13	49	32	59	5	0	.323/.415/.637	152	26.9	.400	-0.2	1B(39): -3.5, RF(4): -0.3	1.5
2016	NYA	MLB	24	90	7	3	0	5	12	7	36	1	0	.241/.300/.458	77	1.4	.357	0.3	1B(27): 1.9, RF(3): 0.0	0.1
2017	SWB	AAA	25	190	29	14	1	10	32	18	52	0	0	.275/.342/.544	116	6.0	.336	-2.1	1B(23): 0.6, RF(4): 0.4	0.5
2017	NYA	MLB	25	46	4	2	0	2	8	4	17	0	1	.225/.283/.425	82	0.3	.304	-0.5	1B(8): 0.0, RF(7): -0.5	-0.1
2018	NYA	MLB	26	132	16	6	0	8	23	8	53	1	1	.223/.280/.471	101	0.0	.311	-0.1	1B(27): -1.3	0.1
2018	SWB	AAA	26	108	14	9	0	6	14	8	32	0	0	.253/.315/.525	119	3.1	.311	0.0	1B(17): -0.6, RF(2): -0.5	0.3
2018	ROC	AAA	26	40	6	2	1	3	8	1	10	0	0	.263/.300/.605	112	3.0	.280	-0.1	1B(7): -0.5	0.1
2018	MIN	MLB	26	136	18	4	0	9	24	11	42	0	1	.236/.294/.488	98	3.9	.270	-0.3	1B(15): 0.1	0.1
2019	MIN	MLB	27	131	14	5	0	5	17	10	42	1	0	.220/.282/.402	77	-1.9	.290	0.0	1B 0	-0.3

Breakout: 5%   Improve: 31%   Collapse: 6%   Attrition: 16%   MLB: 62%   *Comparables: Chris Carter, Tommy Medica, Juan Francisco*

No batter in baseball leaves less doubt about what he's in the box to do. Austin had a greater differential in average exit velocity between his air balls and his ground balls than any other hitter with at least 100 batted balls. When he connects, it can be really impressive. Unfortunately, he doesn't connect all that often. In fact, in 2018 only Jorge Alfaro and Joey Gallo whiffed on a higher percentage of their swings than Austin. Not being an insanely tooled-up former Rangers prospect, Austin is going to need to make more contact or draw more walks in order to be more than a second-division first baseman/designated hitter.

Akil Baddoo CF Born: 08/16/98 Age: 20 Bats: L Throws: L Height: 5'11" Weight: 195 Origin: Round 2, 2016 Draft (#74 overall)

YEAR	TEAM	LVL	AGE	PA	R	2B	3B	HR	RBI	BB	K	SB	CS	AVG/OBP/SLG	DRC+	VORP	BABIP	BRR	FRAA	WARP
2016	TWI	RK	17	128	15	0	2	2	15	18	36	8	1	.178/.299/.271	84	-0.6	.243	0.2	RF(23): -0.5, CF(11): -3.2	-0.3
2017	TWI	RK	18	86	18	4	3	1	10	9	13	4	0	.267/.360/.440	114	4.4	.311	0.9	CF(8): -0.7	0.3
2017	ELZ	RK	18	157	39	15	2	3	19	27	19	5	4	.357/.478/.579	160	26.4	.400	0.8	CF(28): -4.2	1.2
2018	CDR	A	19	517	83	22	11	11	40	74	124	24	5	.243/.351/.419	118	30.7	.311	4.7	CF(97): -12.1, LF(3): 0.1	1.9
2019	MIN	MLB	20	251	30	10	2	7	24	23	66	5	1	.214/.285/.361	81	4.2	.267	0.5	CF -4, LF 0	0.0

Breakout: 2%   Improve: 9%   Collapse: 0%   Attrition: 6%   MLB: 10%   *Comparables: Kyle Tucker, Victor Robles, Joe Benson*

Baddoo has been on the fast track since the day he was drafted, and because he's not Mike Trout, that meant some version of serious adjustment difficulty awaited him on his way through the low minors. The first half of 2018 was exactly that. A teenager tasked with figuring out his long swing and how to apply ample tools in a full-season league, Baddoo fanned roughly 30 percent of the time over the first two-plus months, and was limited by a hamstring injury. From June 16 on, however, he batted .263/.344/.449. He walked plenty, struck out less than 20 percent of the time, drove the ball to the gaps and became a terror on the bases. The ability to hang in there when challenged and to adjust that quickly make Baddoo a potential star.

Byron Buxton CF Born: 12/18/93 Age: 25 Bats: R Throws: R Height: 6'2" Weight: 190 Origin: Round 1, 2012 Draft (#2 overall)

YEAR	TEAM	LVL	AGE	PA	R	2B	3B	HR	RBI	BB	K	SB	CS	AVG/OBP/SLG	DRC+	VORP	BABIP	BRR	FRAA	WARP
2016	ROC	AAA	22	209	41	11	3	11	24	14	58	7	0	.305/.359/.568	121	23.7	.382	2.9	CF(47): -2.2	1.3
2016	MIN	MLB	22	331	44	19	6	10	38	23	118	10	2	.225/.284/.430	69	10.3	.329	4.9	CF(92): 6.4	1.1
2017	MIN	MLB	23	511	69	14	6	16	51	38	150	29	1	.253/.314/.413	87	17.0	.339	7.4	CF(137): 25.4	4.3
2018	MIN	MLB	24	94	8	4	0	0	4	3	28	5	0	.156/.183/.200	57	-7.6	.226	0.3	CF(27): 1.4	0.0
2018	ROC	AAA	24	148	22	11	1	4	14	9	42	4	1	.272/.331/.456	95	8.8	.367	1.4	CF(28): 9.0	1.4
2019	*MIN*	*MLB*	*25*	*408*	*47*	*17*	*2*	*10*	*40*	*29*	*120*	*17*	*2*	*.221/.284/.362*	*74*	*6.5*	*.294*	*3.8*	*CF 12*	*1.9*

Breakout: 4%   Improve: 51%   Collapse: 5%   Attrition: 18%   MLB: 95%   *Comparables: Austin Jackson, Cameron Maybin, Adam Jones*

Buxton has a truly unique skill set, and it sometimes makes him vulnerable to a unique set of problems. In 2018, those included a foot injury that (because his game relies so much on his speed, and because he even uses a toe tap to time the load phase of his swing) disproportionately wrecked his season; a crisis of offensive competence precipitated by the Twins' decision to rush him back from that injury, in order to save their season; and an unfair professional setback in September, when the club elected not to bring him back to the majors and lose a year of team control down the road, even as it remains an open question whether they'll want him when 2022 comes. Only an extraordinarily high-risk, high-reward player invites a decision like that one. At this point, that's exactly what Buxton is.

Jason Castro C Born: 06/18/87 Age: 32 Bats: L Throws: R Height: 6'3" Weight: 215 Origin: Round 1, 2008 Draft (#10 overall)

YEAR	TEAM	LVL	AGE	PA	R	2B	3B	HR	RBI	BB	K	SB	CS	AVG/OBP/SLG	DRC+	VORP	BABIP	BRR	FRAA	WARP
2016	HOU	MLB	29	376	41	16	3	11	32	45	123	2	1	.210/.307/.377	80	7.4	.297	-1.3	C(111): 18.0, 1B(3): -0.2	2.7
2017	MIN	MLB	30	407	49	22	0	10	47	45	108	0	0	.242/.333/.388	88	13.0	.318	-0.4	C(108): 7.7	2.2
2018	MIN	MLB	31	74	4	3	0	1	3	9	26	0	0	.143/.257/.238	63	-2.3	.216	-0.7	C(19): 2.5	0.2
2019	*MIN*	*MLB*	*32*	*300*	*30*	*13*	*1*	*6*	*29*	*31*	*88*	*1*	*0*	*.214/.303/.339*	*77*	*4.4*	*.295*	*-0.6*	*C 7*	*1.2*

Breakout: 3%   Improve: 38%   Collapse: 14%   Attrition: 25%   MLB: 91%   *Comparables: Brandon Inge, Vic Correll, Doug Mirabelli*

The second season of Castro's three-year deal with Minnesota was over almost before it began. He got off to a sluggish but typical start, hitting poorly but showing good enough plate discipline to at least make pitchers work, and continuing to frame pitches well behind the plate. When he went under the knife to have a portion of the torn meniscus in his knee removed, however, the surgeon decided Castro needed a full repair instead. That meant stretching the rehabilitation period from several weeks to several months, and Castro's a catcher and this is a knee injury, so it might stretch his true recovery period from a few months to eternity.

YEAR	TEAM	P. COUNT	FRM RUNS	BLK RUNS	THRW RUNS	TOT RUNS
2016	HOU	14976	18.5	0.0	-0.9	17.4
2017	MIN	14556	8.3	0.3	-0.2	8.1
2018	MIN	3132	1.4	0.9	0.1	2.2
2019	*MIN*	*11456*	*7.6*	*0.3*	*-0.6*	*7.3*

Jake Cave OF Born: 12/04/92 Age: 26 Bats: L Throws: L Height: 6'0" Weight: 200 Origin: Round 6, 2011 Draft (#209 overall)

YEAR	TEAM	LVL	AGE	PA	R	2B	3B	HR	RBI	BB	K	SB	CS	AVG/OBP/SLG	DRC+	VORP	BABIP	BRR	FRAA	WARP
2016	TRN	AA	23	116	12	8	3	3	17	10	28	3	4	.288/.353/.510	94	7.7	.365	-0.6	LF(24): 2.1, CF(3): -0.1	0.3
2016	SWB	AAA	23	354	47	18	6	5	38	26	78	3	3	.261/.323/.401	101	8.5	.329	-1.0	LF(43): -0.5, CF(28): 2.7	1.2
2017	TRN	AA	24	140	19	13	2	5	18	10	33	1	0	.266/.317/.516	92	6.5	.319	-1.0	LF(17): 0.7, CF(7): -0.5	0.1
2017	SWB	AAA	24	297	47	13	3	15	38	18	82	1	3	.324/.367/.554	124	25.5	.414	0.5	CF(30): -1.8, RF(25): 2.2	1.7
2018	ROC	AAA	25	250	26	9	1	6	28	26	55	4	2	.269/.352/.403	108	13.0	.327	-0.1	RF(36): 5.4, CF(17): -0.6	1.5
2018	MIN	MLB	25	309	54	16	2	13	45	18	102	2	1	.265/.313/.473	90	18.3	.363	3.1	CF(70): -7.5, RF(11): 0.3	0.2
2019	*MIN*	*MLB*	*26*	*258*	*30*	*12*	*1*	*10*	*32*	*17*	*79*	*2*	*1*	*.236/.293/.414*	*93*	*7.2*	*.309*	*1.2*	*RF 0, CF -1*	*0.7*

Breakout: 7%   Improve: 39%   Collapse: 15%   Attrition: 27%   MLB: 78%   *Comparables: Scott Schebler, Ben Johnson, Brett Carroll*

Everywhere, with Cave, the story is depth. No center fielder played deeper than he did in 2018. That's partially reflective of Minnesota's organizational philosophy about outfield positioning, but it served him well individually, too. Slightly stretched as a center fielder, given his merely average speed, Cave was better able to go back on long flies and to cut off hits to the gaps from his deeper starting point. He also hit some very deep home runs, demonstrating above-average power and generating some buzz based on sheer aesthetics. In the end, though, depth is probably all he is: his sky-high strikeout rate and failure to force big-league pitchers into the zone combine with the defensive questions to steer him toward a future as a fourth outfielder. Anything more, and Cave will likely be out of his depth.

Gilberto Celestino CF Born: 02/13/99 Age: 20 Bats: R Throws: L Height: 6'0" Weight: 170 Origin: International Free Agent, 2015

YEAR	TEAM	LVL	AGE	PA	R	2B	3B	HR	RBI	BB	K	SB	CS	AVG/OBP/SLG	DRC+	VORP	BABIP	BRR	FRAA	WARP
2016	DAR	ROK	17	165	22	9	3	2	17	25	23	9	2	.279/.388/.434	129	12.6	.316	-0.8		1.0
2016	AST	RK	17	65	7	3	1	0	2	8	16	6	1	.200/.308/.291	89	0.5	.275	-0.2	CF(16): -4.0	-0.3
2017	GRV	RK	18	261	38	10	2	4	24	22	59	10	2	.268/.331/.379	86	13.6	.339	5.3	CF(43): 2.6, RF(8): 0.1	1.0
2018	TCV	A-	19	142	18	8	0	4	21	10	25	14	0	.323/.387/.480	128	15.2	.374	1.6	CF(16): 0.9, RF(12): 2.6	1.3
2018	ELZ	RK	19	117	13	4	1	1	13	6	16	8	2	.266/.308/.349	90	-0.8	.301	1.1	CF(23): -1.0	0.2
2019	*MIN*	*MLB*	*20*	*251*	*26*	*6*	*0*	*7*	*21*	*9*	*67*	*5*	*1*	*.191/.219/.291*	*36*	*-10.8*	*.231*	*0.0*	*CF 0, RF 0*	*-1.1*

Comparables: Engel Beltre, Cedric Hunter, Joe Benson

When a team pays the kind of money the Astros paid Celestino in 2015, they're quietly hoping for a rapid breakout, a race up the minor-league ladder that culminates in a big-league debut before the guy turns 21. Those are extremely rare cases, though, and Celestino's career to date is still a positive outcome. He's flashed gap power, offensive polish, top-end speed and great instincts both afield and on the bases. He's advancing slowly, but by no means old for his level, and if he can start to put these pieces of a great profile together, he'll see his prospect stock rise rapidly. Celestino still has two or three tough tests of player development to pass, however, before things get serious.

C.J. Cron 1B   Born: 01/05/90   Age: 29   Bats: R   Throws: R   Height: 6'4"   Weight: 235   Origin: Round 1, 2011 Draft (#17 overall)

YEAR	TEAM	LVL	AGE	PA	R	2B	3B	HR	RBI	BB	K	SB	CS	AVG/OBP/SLG	DRC+	VORP	BABIP	BRR	FRAA	WARP
2016	ANA	MLB	26	445	51	25	2	16	69	24	75	2	3	.278/.325/.467	104	12.4	.302	-2.0	1B(97): 2.6	1.0
2017	SLC	AAA	27	96	11	6	0	4	23	7	15	1	0	.268/.344/.488	127	2.9	.273	0.0	1B(19): 0.9	0.6
2017	ANA	MLB	27	373	39	14	1	16	56	22	96	3	2	.248/.305/.437	96	2.3	.296	-2.1	1B(98): 4.1	0.6
2018	TBA	MLB	28	560	68	28	1	30	74	37	145	1	2	.253/.323/.493	109	18.0	.293	-3.5	1B(61): 2.6	1.4
2019	MIN	MLB	29	559	76	29	2	23	71	39	126	3	2	.258/.328/.455	113	14.9	.305	-2.3	1B 5	2.1

Breakout: 4%   Improve: 52%   Collapse: 10%   Attrition: 12%   MLB: 97%   Comparables: Adam Lind, Mike Jacobs, Mitch Moreland

Cron added a 30-homer season to his legacy while finally getting more than 500 plate appearances for the first time. Tampa Bay rewarded Cron by designating him for assignment and letting the Twins acquire his services for the cost of a waiver wire fee. Cron has legit power, but there's little else in the profile. Cron has sold out just a bit for the power, posting back-to-back seasons with at least 25 percent strikeouts. That number alone is not terrible, but the paltry walk rate does nothing to offset some ugly at-bats. Defensively, he's limited to first base and is typically passable there, making most routine plays. For a salary under $5 million, the 30-homer potential was certainly worth a shot for the Twins, who also have Cron under team control for 2020 via arbitration.

Nelson Cruz DH   Born: 07/01/80   Age: 38   Bats: R   Throws: R   Height: 6'2"   Weight: 230   Origin: International Free Agent, 1998

YEAR	TEAM	LVL	AGE	PA	R	2B	3B	HR	RBI	BB	K	SB	CS	AVG/OBP/SLG	DRC+	VORP	BABIP	BRR	FRAA	WARP
2016	SEA	MLB	35	667	96	27	1	43	105	62	159	2	0	.287/.360/.555	134	41.4	.320	-5.1	RF(48): -4.7	3.0
2017	SEA	MLB	36	645	91	28	0	39	119	70	140	1	1	.288/.375/.549	137	40.4	.315	-1.8	RF(5): -0.1	3.8
2018	SEA	MLB	37	591	70	18	1	37	97	55	122	1	0	.256/.342/.509	132	28.1	.264	-1.2	RF(4): 0.1	3.1
2019	MIN	MLB	38	598	82	29	2	30	93	62	127	1	1	.271/.363/.500	137	30.8	.311	-2.2		3.3

Breakout: 1%   Improve: 11%   Collapse: 10%   Attrition: 14%   MLB: 81%   Comparables: Johnny Mize, Hank Aaron, David Ortiz

Ozymandias gets a bad wrap, so let's clear a few things up. The "vast and trunkless legs of stone" were Cruz's old shoes. Shoes wear out, so he got new ones. Also, that ruined visage with the "sneer of cold command" lying in the desert? That is collectively the group of people who mocked the Mariners for giving him a four-year contract, a period over which he hit 163 home runs, the most of any hitter in the game.

Does this mean that Nelson Cruz is not human, but rather some sort of immortal Home Run Golem striding through history and baseball, programmed by devious magic to torment pitchers for all of time? Of course not. These are academic pages, and we would never reduce ourselves to such pithy indulgence. Clearly, the only logical explanation for Cruz's late career explosion is that he is, in fact, a vampire.

Logan Forsythe 2B   Born: 01/14/87   Age: 32   Bats: R   Throws: R   Height: 6'1"   Weight: 205   Origin: Round 1, 2008 Draft (#46 overall)

YEAR	TEAM	LVL	AGE	PA	R	2B	3B	HR	RBI	BB	K	SB	CS	AVG/OBP/SLG	DRC+	VORP	BABIP	BRR	FRAA	WARP
2016	TBA	MLB	29	567	76	24	4	20	52	46	127	6	6	.264/.333/.444	106	24.9	.314	0.6	2B(118): -7.9	1.4
2017	LAN	MLB	30	439	56	19	0	6	36	69	109	3	2	.224/.351/.327	91	14.1	.299	0.5	2B(80): 4.8, 3B(42): -0.1	1.5
2018	LAN	MLB	31	211	18	10	0	2	13	17	43	2	0	.207/.270/.290	80	-6.3	.255	0.0	2B(51): 5.7, 3B(12): 1.3	0.9
2018	MIN	MLB	31	205	19	6	0	0	14	24	40	1	0	.258/.356/.292	80	3.6	.333	1.5	2B(48): -5.5	-0.3
2019	MIN	MLB	32	401	46	19	1	6	34	44	89	4	2	.239/.330/.354	88	7.7	.302	0.8	2B -1, 3B 0	0.8

Breakout: 1%   Improve: 32%   Collapse: 7%   Attrition: 8%   MLB: 94%   Comparables: Orlando Hudson, Mark Ellis, Mike Sharperson

Forsythe saw 1,700 pitches in 2018, and 53.2 percent of them were in the strike zone. No batter who saw even 1,000 pitches had as many of them pass through the zone. That's who Forsythe is right now: the least-feared hitter in baseball. He's well past the line between patient and passive, and since he's managed just 45 extra-base hits over the last two seasons, that's probably the right strategy. Forsythe's best chance at retaining utility is to keep battling his way to the occasional walk. At this stage of his career, even that won't punch his ticket to Lineupville very often. He's not a good enough defender to make that profile work, especially if pitchers keep seeing a gigantic cartoon steak when they look in at him in the box.

Mitch Garver C   Born: 01/15/91   Age: 28   Bats: R   Throws: R   Height: 6'1"   Weight: 220   Origin: Round 9, 2013 Draft (#260 overall)

YEAR	TEAM	LVL	AGE	PA	R	2B	3B	HR	RBI	BB	K	SB	CS	AVG/OBP/SLG	DRC+	VORP	BABIP	BRR	FRAA	WARP
2016	CHT	AA	25	407	44	25	0	11	66	43	86	1	3	.257/.334/.419	117	18.4	.305	0.3	C(46): 7.3, 1B(14): -0.9	2.9
2016	ROC	AAA	25	84	6	5	0	1	8	7	21	0	0	.329/.381/.434	90	7.0	.436	0.4	C(14): 0.1, 1B(2): -0.1	0.2
2017	ROC	AAA	26	372	56	29	0	17	45	50	85	2	0	.291/.387/.541	130	40.4	.347	0.2	C(67): 3.6, 1B(14): 0.9	3.4
2017	MIN	MLB	26	52	5	1	3	0	3	6	15	0	0	.196/.288/.348	78	-1.0	.290	0.2	C(13): -1.1, 1B(3): 0.3	-0.1
2018	MIN	MLB	27	335	38	19	2	7	45	29	72	0	0	.268/.335/.414	94	14.3	.330	-1.3	C(86): -8.5, 1B(5): -0.1	0.3
2019	MIN	MLB	28	197	21	8	1	6	23	19	46	0	0	.238/.317/.394	95	6.4	.289	-0.3	C -3, 1B 0	0.3

Breakout: 8%   Improve: 32%   Collapse: 15%   Attrition: 34%   MLB: 74%   Comparables: Landon Powell, Ryan Lavarnway, Tommy Medica

His minor-league track record is tantalizing, but Garver raked there mostly as an overcooked prospect brought along too slowly. As a 27-year-old rookie in MLB, he was a slightly-below-average hitter, which is an acceptable level for a catcher. The problem is, Garver's not really a catcher. He's a dreadful pitch framer, ranking 27th of 33 regular catchers in Called Strikes Above Average. He's a poor stopper of the running game, ranking 58th of 67 qualifiers in pop time to second base. He does run like a catcher, and the bat isn't ever likely to play elsewhere, so he'll remain there as long as he's willing to take the abuse, but like the frat brother kept around only because he happily bears the brunt of everyone's jokes, Garver will forever be a second-string backstop in MLB.

YEAR	TEAM	P. COUNT	FRM RUNS	BLK RUNS	THRW RUNS	TOT RUNS
2017	MIN	832	-0.9	-0.1	0.0	-1.0
2017	ROC	8976	3.3	-0.9	0.4	2.5
2018	MIN	11726	-8.2	0.2	-0.4	-8.5
2019	MIN	6347	-2.9	-0.3	0.0	-3.2

Nick Gordon SS Born: 10/24/95 Age: 23 Bats: L Throws: R Height: 6'0" Weight: 160 Origin: Round 1, 2014 Draft (#5 overall)

YEAR	TEAM	LVL	AGE	PA	R	2B	3B	HR	RBI	BB	K	SB	CS	AVG/OBP/SLG	DRC+	VORP	BABIP	BRR	FRAA	WARP
2016	FTM	A+	20	494	56	23	6	3	52	23	87	19	13	.291/.335/.386	104	25.2	.353	-2.9	SS(103): 4.1, 2B(2): -0.1	2.3
2017	CHT	AA	21	578	80	29	8	9	66	53	134	13	7	.270/.341/.408	108	34.0	.347	1.1	SS(104): 0.4, 2B(14): 0.4	3.3
2018	CHT	AA	22	181	22	10	3	5	20	11	27	7	2	.333/.381/.525	133	13.8	.366	-1.4	SS(34): 2.4, 2B(6): -0.3	1.6
2018	ROC	AAA	22	410	40	13	4	2	29	23	82	13	3	.212/.262/.283	78	-7.1	.264	2.8	SS(69): 2.6, 2B(30): 4.1	1.5
2019	MIN	MLB	23	68	6	3	0	1	6	3	15	1	0	.214/.255/.315	53	-1.5	.265	0.0	SS 0, 2B 1	-0.1

Breakout: 16%   Improve: 32%   Collapse: 10%   Attrition: 29%   MLB: 44%   *Comparables: Yairo Munoz, Tim Beckham, Brad Miller*

If Tom was Flash and Gordon's brother Dee is Flash Jr., that still leaves Flash in the Pan as an available sobriquet, and the youngest Gordon in pro ball is circling it. He teases and inches toward real improvement every season, but the second half always seems to be a step backward. Gordon flashed power in his second trip through the Southern League, but a promotion to Triple-A saw the bat knocked out of his hands and a part-time move to second base. Though excruciatingly protracted, his development is by no means over. Gordon just needs to find a way to turn his foot speed into greater adjustment speed, because if he takes this long to adapt when he sees big-league pitching, he'll come to embody the original meaning of that new nickname: a misfire.

Robbie Grossman RF Born: 09/16/89 Age: 29 Bats: B Throws: L Height: 6'0" Weight: 215 Origin: Round 6, 2008 Draft (#174 overall)

YEAR	TEAM	LVL	AGE	PA	R	2B	3B	HR	RBI	BB	K	SB	CS	AVG/OBP/SLG	DRC+	VORP	BABIP	BRR	FRAA	WARP
2016	COH	AAA	26	139	14	5	0	6	13	21	25	3	1	.256/.370/.453	130	5.4	.279	-1.6	CF(19): -1.4, LF(10): 1.8	0.8
2016	MIN	MLB	26	389	49	19	1	11	37	55	96	2	3	.280/.386/.443	111	18.0	.364	-0.2	LF(75): -5.4, CF(1): 0.0	0.9
2017	MIN	MLB	27	456	62	22	1	9	45	67	79	3	1	.246/.361/.380	102	5.0	.287	-1.9	RF(35): -1.6, LF(18): -1.2	0.5
2018	MIN	MLB	28	465	50	27	1	5	48	60	83	0	1	.273/.367/.384	104	13.1	.329	-4.9	RF(52): -2.6, LF(34): 1.2	0.6
2019	MIN	MLB	29	440	47	22	2	8	47	57	85	2	2	.251/.354/.382	105	12.5	.302	-1.8	RF -2, LF -1	1.1

Breakout: 5%   Improve: 43%   Collapse: 9%   Attrition: 19%   MLB: 93%   *Comparables: Chris Coghlan, Gabe Gross, Chris Burke*

In one of the stories of *Winnie-the-Pooh*, Rabbit asks Pooh if he made up a particular song that Pooh had been singing. Pooh says he only sort of did — that sometimes, things just come to him. Rabbit waves away that answer, on his way to some other subject, because (as the narrator points out) Rabbit "never let things come to him, but rather went and fetched them." In today's game, Grossman is a Pooh, in a league full of Rabbits. He's excruciatingly patient, and when the right sequence of unworthy pitches comes along, he's quite good at going with them and creating something good, be it a walk, a double into the corner or a cheap homer. Most of the time, however, the competitive landscape of the league rewards Rabbit types, because today's pitchers don't make enough mistakes to let a Pooh like Grossman really thrive. He also plays the outfield like there's a honey pot over his head.

Max Kepler RF Born: 02/10/93 Age: 26 Bats: L Throws: L Height: 6'4" Weight: 205 Origin: International Free Agent, 2009

YEAR	TEAM	LVL	AGE	PA	R	2B	3B	HR	RBI	BB	K	SB	CS	AVG/OBP/SLG	DRC+	VORP	BABIP	BRR	FRAA	WARP
2016	ROC	AAA	23	128	16	4	6	1	19	16	14	1	1	.282/.367/.455	119	7.5	.309	0.7	RF(26): 1.9, CF(6): 0.4	0.9
2016	MIN	MLB	23	447	52	20	2	17	63	42	93	6	2	.235/.309/.424	99	6.3	.261	0.9	RF(108): 3.6, CF(4): -0.1	1.5
2017	MIN	MLB	24	568	67	32	2	19	69	47	114	6	1	.243/.312/.425	91	1.1	.276	-2.2	RF(138): 5.1, CF(13): 0.3	1.0
2018	MIN	MLB	25	611	80	30	4	20	58	71	96	4	5	.224/.319/.408	111	16.5	.236	2.7	RF(117): 10.2, CF(55): -1.3	3.6
2019	MIN	MLB	26	475	55	24	2	15	59	45	84	5	2	.247/.327/.420	102	15.6	.276	0.2	RF 4, CF 0	2.1

Breakout: 5%   Improve: 42%   Collapse: 7%   Attrition: 13%   MLB: 96%   *Comparables: Andre Ethier, Ryan Sweeney, Blake DeWitt*

On the surface, perhaps, Kepler had a frustrating season of non-progress. Dig deeper, though, and the signs point in all the right directions. In the absence of Byron Buxton, Kepler proved to be a perfectly cromulent center fielder. He swung significantly more often at pitches within the strike zone, and significantly less at those outside it. He made hard contact more frequently, but also swung and missed less often within the strike zone. For the second straight season, he embiggened his launch angle. He just hit too many balls that fell into the proverbial donut hole: too hard to become bloop singles, too high to get down between outfielders. He's one more set of small adjustments from hitting the homers he needs to round out his profile.

Alex Kirilloff RF Born: 11/09/97 Age: 21 Bats: L Throws: L Height: 6'2" Weight: 195 Origin: Round 1, 2016 Draft (#15 overall)

YEAR	TEAM	LVL	AGE	PA	R	2B	3B	HR	RBI	BB	K	SB	CS	AVG/OBP/SLG	DRC+	VORP	BABIP	BRR	FRAA	WARP
2016	ELZ	RK	18	232	33	9	1	7	33	11	32	0	1	.306/.341/.454	127	8.6	.328	0.8	RF(39): 5.2, CF(12): -2.7	1.5
2018	CDR	A	20	281	36	20	5	13	56	24	47	1	1	.333/.391/.607	147	27.2	.364	-0.8	RF(53): -4.0, CF(1): 0.0	1.6
2018	FTM	A+	20	280	39	24	2	7	45	14	39	3	2	.362/.393/.550	145	26.9	.399	-0.8	RF(51): 0.4, CF(3): 0.3	2.1
2019	MIN	MLB	21	251	26	14	1	9	33	11	50	0	0	.268/.298/.444	99	6.1	.302	-0.5	RF -2, CF 0	0.5

Breakout: 4% Improve: 14% Collapse: 5% Attrition: 16% MLB: 28% *Comparables: Nomar Mazara, Jorge Bonifacio, Caleb Gindl*

Confined to an outfield corner, Kirilloff has to hit for considerable power in order to deliver high-end value once he attains the majors. He demonstrated the potential to do just that in his return season from Tommy John surgery, blasting out 71 extra-base hits across the two least hitter-friendly full-season leagues in the minors. He also made plenty of contact and sprayed line drives all over the field. Kirilloff's midseason promotion to High-A was very aggressive, and his approach got a little less controlled there, but he still showed preternatural raw hitting talent. He'll get a chance to pass the Double-A test at 21, which would mean fully making up for the lost year of development, and all he needs to remember is to work for and punish his pitch.

Trevor Larnach OF Born: 02/26/97 Age: 22 Bats: L Throws: R Height: 6'4" Weight: 210 Origin: Round 1, 2018 Draft (#20 overall)

YEAR	TEAM	LVL	AGE	PA	R	2B	3B	HR	RBI	BB	K	SB	CS	AVG/OBP/SLG	DRC+	VORP	BABIP	BRR	FRAA	WARP
2018	ELZ	RK	21	75	10	5	0	2	16	10	11	2	0	.311/.413/.492	127	5.4	.340	-1.5	RF(14): 3.8	0.6
2018	CDR	A	21	102	17	8	1	3	10	11	17	1	0	.297/.373/.505	118	8.8	.338	0.7	RF(17): -1.5	0.3
2019	MIN	MLB	22	251	24	9	0	8	29	16	56	1	0	.222/.269/.358	67	-4.0	.256	-0.5	RF 0	-0.4

Breakout: 1% Improve: 3% Collapse: 1% Attrition: 5% MLB: 6% *Comparables: Destin Hood, Jorge Bonifacio, Rymer Liriano*

One of the clearest and most valuable lessons of the systematic study of baseball, from a baseball ops perspective, is that everyone should be drafting polished collegiate hitters more aggressively. Larnach has every tool but speed, and his power came on in a big way during his junior year at College World Series-winning Oregon State. He's a huge left-handed hitter with a solid approach and a gorgeous swing, and he won't hurt you in either outfield corner. He went out as a pro and smoothly swatted around low-minors pitching. That the Twins got him for well below slot value at the 20th pick in the first round is a reminder of how far many teams have to go in optimizing their draft strategies.

Royce Lewis SS Born: 06/05/99 Age: 20 Bats: R Throws: R Height: 6'2" Weight: 188 Origin: Round 1, 2017 Draft (#1 overall)

YEAR	TEAM	LVL	AGE	PA	R	2B	3B	HR	RBI	BB	K	SB	CS	AVG/OBP/SLG	DRC+	VORP	BABIP	BRR	FRAA	WARP
2017	TWI	RK	18	159	38	6	2	3	17	19	17	15	2	.271/.390/.414	138	17.3	.292	4.6	SS(32): -0.9	1.6
2017	CDR	A	18	80	16	2	1	1	10	6	16	3	1	.296/.363/.394	95	6.5	.364	1.0	SS(17): 1.9	0.6
2018	CDR	A	19	327	50	23	0	9	53	24	49	22	4	.315/.368/.485	129	31.3	.349	3.7	SS(67): 0.8	3.0
2018	FTM	A+	19	208	33	6	3	5	21	19	35	6	4	.255/.327/.399	103	11.6	.291	1.7	SS(45): -4.8	0.7
2019	MIN	MLB	20	251	30	8	0	7	23	14	55	6	2	.214/.261/.339	56	-3.8	.248	0.2	SS -1	-0.5

Breakout: 3% Improve: 19% Collapse: 0% Attrition: 6% MLB: 21% *Comparables: Alen Hanson, Gleyber Torres, Starlin Castro*

The first half of 2018 looked like a sure step on the path to superstardom for the top pick in the 2017 draft. The second half looked like a sideways step for an extremely polished and talented teenager who nonetheless has a lot to learn on his way to the majors. There's nothing wrong with the latter, unless one got carried away by the former. All five tools grade out well for Lewis, but none threaten the top of the scale. His aptitude and work ethic draw rave reviews, so there's always a chance his hit, power or glove plays up slightly. In the meantime, he'll ascend to Double-A, needing to demonstrate a bit more consistency but with plenty on which to build.

Joe Mauer 1B Born: 04/19/83 Age: 36 Bats: L Throws: R Height: 6'5" Weight: 225 Origin: Round 1, 2001 Draft (#1 overall)

YEAR	TEAM	LVL	AGE	PA	R	2B	3B	HR	RBI	BB	K	SB	CS	AVG/OBP/SLG	DRC+	VORP	BABIP	BRR	FRAA	WARP
2016	MIN	MLB	33	576	68	22	4	11	49	79	93	2	0	.261/.363/.389	106	3.1	.301	-2.2	1B(95): -2.7	0.8
2017	MIN	MLB	34	597	69	36	1	7	71	66	83	2	1	.305/.384/.417	108	8.3	.349	-6.6	1B(125): 1.6	1.0
2018	MIN	MLB	35	543	64	27	1	6	48	51	86	0	1	.282/.351/.379	97	4.2	.330	-1.5	1B(90): 2.0	0.7
2019	MIN	MLB	36	524	60	26	2	7	46	60	84	1	1	.266/.354/.375	105	8.2	.311	-2.7	1B 1, C 0	0.9

Breakout: 2% Improve: 20% Collapse: 12% Attrition: 26% MLB: 71% *Comparables: Charlie Grimm, Scott Hatteberg, Dave Bergman*

Five years after he last caught in a big-league game, Mauer still ordered catcher's mitts and equipment for the team's bullpen catcher (and longtime friend). He'd be there when it came, too, to try on the mitt, and he'd remark on how much he missed it. One of the greatest catchers ever didn't get to really catch for the final half-decade of his career. He played on a bit the way a person lives on after losing someone they love: with earnest effort and upright zeal, but with a bit less of the reckless joy that animated them at their very best. Mauer got on base at a .351 or better clip in every season of his career but one, and he finished 2018 red hot. Still, he was able to let the game go, partially because he lost the part of it he loved most in 2013 due to a concussion. When retirement started to look like a possibility, the people around him rallied to make sure that Mauer didn't have to leave without getting back that piece of it for one more moment. The result, a single pseudo-ceremonial pitch caught on a sun-soaked final Sunday, was a heartwarming culmination of a career well lived.

Logan Morrison 1B Born: 08/25/87 Age: 31 Bats: L Throws: L Height: 6'3" Weight: 245 Origin: Round 22, 2005 Draft (#666 overall)

YEAR	TEAM	LVL	AGE	PA	R	2B	3B	HR	RBI	BB	K	SB	CS	AVG/OBP/SLG	DRC+	VORP	BABIP	BRR	FRAA	WARP
2016	TBA	MLB	28	398	45	18	1	14	43	37	89	4	2	.238/.319/.414	94	4.5	.278	0.4	1B(83): -1.5	0.2
2017	TBA	MLB	29	601	75	22	1	38	85	81	149	2	0	.246/.353/.516	127	28.3	.268	0.4	1B(126): -0.6	2.9
2018	MIN	MLB	30	359	41	13	0	15	39	34	80	1	0	.186/.276/.368	94	-7.9	.196	0.0	1B(50): -1.8, LF(2): -0.1	0.1
2019	MIN	MLB	31	387	48	18	1	16	54	41	84	2	1	.245/.335/.447	111	10.8	.281	0.2	1B -1, LF 0	1.1

Breakout: 0% Improve: 46% Collapse: 4% Attrition: 7% MLB: 88% *Comparables: Lyle Overbay, Gaby Sanchez, Aubrey Huff*

Everything about Morrison is just a little bit off the mark. He's gregarious and outgoing in a way that is almost akin to Jonny Gomes, but which instead comes off, in turns, as either overbearing or uncaring. He's a power hitter who succeeds when he locks in on and attacks fastballs, but his eye for spin and his strike zone too often get a bit loose. In 2017, the Rays saw what he can do when he stays healthy, keeps his approach perfectly tuned and stays quick to the ball, thinking about hitting it hard. In 2018, the Twins saw what he can't do when he plays hurt, swings at too much off-speed stuff, jumps at the ball and lofts it too much.

Jorge Polanco SS Born: 07/05/93 Age: 25 Bats: B Throws: R Height: 5'11" Weight: 200 Origin: International Free Agent, 2009

YEAR	TEAM	LVL	AGE	PA	R	2B	3B	HR	RBI	BB	K	SB	CS	AVG/OBP/SLG	DRC+	VORP	BABIP	BRR	FRAA	WARP
2016	ROC	AAA	22	325	32	14	6	9	39	27	51	5	4	.276/.335/.457	126	17.5	.304	0.3	2B(64): 5.7, 3B(2): 0.2	2.6
2016	MIN	MLB	22	270	24	15	4	4	27	17	46	4	3	.282/.332/.424	96	9.3	.328	-0.7	SS(47): -1.9, 3B(9): -0.8	0.6
2017	MIN	MLB	23	544	60	30	3	13	74	41	78	13	5	.256/.313/.410	93	17.1	.278	0.8	SS(130): -9.2	1.2
2018	MIN	MLB	24	333	38	18	3	6	42	25	62	7	7	.288/.345/.427	97	12.9	.345	-3.0	SS(76): -9.7	0.1
2019	MIN	MLB	25	620	69	33	4	14	69	46	101	13	8	.266/.326/.414	101	22.6	.299	-1.5	SS -9	1.5

Breakout: 2%   Improve: 52%   Collapse: 7%   Attrition: 22%   MLB: 98%   *Comparables: Didi Gregorius, Jurickson Profar, Brad Miller*

Thanks to a rush-job of a minor-league career, Polanco has taken a long time to find his footing in the majors. The self-inflicted wound of an 80-game suspension for performance-enhancing drugs only exacerbated that problem last year. He continues to make progress in terms of controlling the zone; he attacks strikes and doesn't chase junk. There's still no sign that he'll develop real over-the-fence power, though. He's a fine athlete, but neither a good baserunner nor a viable shortstop. Polanco's chances to emerge as more than a second-division second baseman hinge on his ability to continue hitting line drives and forcing pitchers to throw strikes.

Brent Rooker LF Born: 11/01/94 Age: 24 Bats: R Throws: R Height: 6'3" Weight: 215 Origin: Round 1, 2017 Draft (#35 overall)

YEAR	TEAM	LVL	AGE	PA	R	2B	3B	HR	RBI	BB	K	SB	CS	AVG/OBP/SLG	DRC+	VORP	BABIP	BRR	FRAA	WARP
2017	ELZ	RK	22	99	19	5	0	7	17	11	21	2	2	.282/.364/.588	154	10.0	.288	0.6	LF(17): 0.4	0.9
2017	FTM	A+	22	162	23	6	0	11	35	16	47	0	0	.280/.364/.552	141	12.9	.341	-1.5	LF(16): -2.6, 3B(11): -0.4	0.6
2018	CHT	AA	23	568	72	32	4	22	79	56	150	6	1	.254/.333/.465	117	13.2	.316	-4.7	1B(47): -5.7, LF(44): -8.2	0.3
2019	MIN	MLB	24	251	32	11	0	11	32	17	78	1	0	.222/.278/.419	79	-1.7	.279	-0.4	1B -2, LF -3	-0.7

Breakout: 7%   Improve: 26%   Collapse: 7%   Attrition: 28%   MLB: 49%   *Comparables: Chris Shaw, Renato Nunez, Kyle Jensen*

Unapologetically focused on lifting and driving the ball, Rooker is more popular on Baseball Twitter than craft beer. Like craft beer, however, Rooker's commitment to a niche forces him to excel in certain areas. His 2018 campaign failed to prove conclusively that he's a future 35-homer slugger in the majors, but it *did* shatter any lingering dreams that he would be a useful fielder or baserunner. There's no shortage of power or patience here, but because his future impact hinges on both things translating neatly to the majors, the questions around him can't be answered until he sees big-league pitching for half a season or more.

Ben Rortvedt C Born: 09/25/97 Age: 21 Bats: L Throws: R Height: 5'10" Weight: 190 Origin: Round 2, 2016 Draft (#56 overall)

YEAR	TEAM	LVL	AGE	PA	R	2B	3B	HR	RBI	BB	K	SB	CS	AVG/OBP/SLG	DRC+	VORP	BABIP	BRR	FRAA	WARP
2016	TWI	RK	18	66	3	3	0	0	3	5	8	0	0	.203/.277/.254	101	-1.1	.235	-1.8	C(17): 0.4	0.2
2016	ELZ	RK	18	47	2	0	0	0	7	5	2	0	0	.250/.348/.250	112	2.6	.263	0.1	C(13): 0.1	0.3
2017	CDR	A	19	336	33	16	0	4	30	22	60	1	0	.224/.284/.315	85	3.0	.265	-1.1	C(86): 1.3	0.9
2018	CDR	A	20	157	14	9	2	1	16	10	35	1	0	.276/.325/.386	96	6.2	.355	1.1	C(29): 1.0	0.7
2018	FTM	A+	20	196	20	7	1	4	27	21	29	0	0	.250/.337/.372	106	10.2	.279	-0.4	C(45): -0.4	0.9
2019	MIN	MLB	21	251	22	7	0	6	24	12	55	0	0	.205/.244/.310	46	-6.1	.240	-0.5	C 0	-0.6

Breakout: 3%   Improve: 3%   Collapse: 2%   Attrition: 8%   MLB: 11%   *Comparables: Carson Kelly, Reese McGuire, Christian Vazquez*

The biggest problem with catching prospects — for the team, and for the prospects themselves — is that they tend to develop slowly. That means, with only extraordinary exceptions, a catcher will blossom into a viable big leaguer both at and behind the plate only just in time to slip him onto the 40-man roster, and if he becomes a star, it might not be for long, and he might be halfway out the door when it happens. For that reason, teams invest less in catching than they might, and we outsiders see that reflected in the evaluations of backstops. Rortvedt is a perfect example. An advanced hitter coming out of high school, he's slowed down at the plate, but he's figuring out receiving well. His approach is steady, though so far he's short on power. For a catcher, he's advancing pretty quickly.

Eddie Rosario LF   Born: 09/28/91   Age: 27   Bats: L   Throws: R   Height: 6'1"   Weight: 180   Origin: Round 4, 2010 Draft (#135 overall)

YEAR	TEAM	LVL	AGE	PA	R	2B	3B	HR	RBI	BB	K	SB	CS	AVG/OBP/SLG	DRC+	VORP	BABIP	BRR	FRAA	WARP
2016	ROC	AAA	24	169	26	14	0	7	25	7	25	5	3	.319/.343/.538	129	13.3	.338	1.1	CF(29): 2.6, RF(9): 3.0	1.8
2016	MIN	MLB	24	354	52	17	2	10	32	12	91	5	2	.269/.295/.421	80	9.0	.338	4.4	LF(57): 0.7, CF(37): -1.9	0.5
2017	MIN	MLB	25	589	79	33	2	27	78	35	106	9	8	.290/.328/.507	110	18.1	.312	-1.6	LF(138): -2.7, RF(16): 0.2	1.9
2018	MIN	MLB	26	592	87	31	2	24	77	30	104	8	2	.288/.323/.479	113	29.9	.316	6.8	LF(125): 5.9, RF(5): -0.2	3.8
2019	MIN	MLB	27	619	83	33	3	23	75	36	119	10	5	.273/.318/.458	110	27.8	.306	3.1	LF -1	2.8

Breakout: 6%   Improve: 62%   Collapse: 4%   Attrition: 11%   MLB: 96%   *Comparables: Marcell Ozuna, Yasmany Tomas, Joe Rudi*

To be a hitter is to perpetually maintain a fragile balance between staying within oneself and making the most of one's opportunities. It's a mental challenge and a physical one, and it's complicated by the opposition's constant effort to force an adjustment that might tip one out of balance. For a solid year, however, Rosario found that balance. From July 14, 2017 through July 15, 2018, he batted .303/.343/.546, with 44 doubles and 36 homers in 695 plate appearances. He did it in the heat of a pennant race, and in the cold of a bitter and disappointing spring. He did all that for a year, but on either side of that window were long stretches during which Rosario couldn't keep up with the adjustments opponents made, or wherein he was flummoxed by things like defensive shifts. (He saw 263 of those last season, more by a wide margin than he had seen in his three previous campaigns combined.) He's learned to use his aggressiveness, rather than being used by it. Now, he needs to learn to do it all the time.

Miguel Sano 3B   Born: 05/11/93   Age: 26   Bats: R   Throws: R   Height: 6'4"   Weight: 260   Origin: International Free Agent, 2009

YEAR	TEAM	LVL	AGE	PA	R	2B	3B	HR	RBI	BB	K	SB	CS	AVG/OBP/SLG	DRC+	VORP	BABIP	BRR	FRAA	WARP
2016	MIN	MLB	23	495	57	22	1	25	66	54	178	1	0	.236/.319/.462	104	13.6	.329	2.0	3B(42): 6.5, RF(38): -1.9	2.2
2017	MIN	MLB	24	483	75	15	2	28	77	54	173	0	0	.264/.352/.507	116	22.5	.375	-2.0	3B(82): -5.9, 1B(9): 1.2	1.8
2018	FTM	A+	25	77	11	2	0	2	12	13	21	0	0	.328/.442/.453	117	7.8	.463	0.2	3B(10): 0.4	0.4
2018	ROC	AAA	25	36	2	1	0	2	5	6	8	0	0	.267/.389/.500	128	2.7	.300	0.2	3B(4): 1.5, 1B(1): 0.0	0.4
2018	MIN	MLB	25	299	32	14	0	13	41	31	115	0	0	.199/.281/.398	77	-0.4	.286	-1.0	3B(56): 0.1, 1B(11): 0.1	0.0
2019	MIN	MLB	26	545	73	23	2	23	68	60	188	1	0	.230/.319/.431	103	13.3	.322	-0.4	3B 0, 1B 1	1.6

Breakout: 3%   Improve: 59%   Collapse: 4%   Attrition: 8%   MLB: 98%   *Comparables: Mark Reynolds, Pedro Alvarez, Mike Schmidt*

Sano handled his June demotion to the Florida State League as well as could be hoped under the circumstances. It's the only thing he's done right since late summer 2017. Plagued by very real questions of makeup and off-field comportment, he was unable even to answer the pressing on-field questions about his future in 2018. It's not clear whether his Brobdingnagian body will allow him to remain a third baseman, especially as injury issues persist (indeed, as symbolized by the permanent titanium rod in his shin, they seem to be going nowhere). It's not clear, even after over 1,600 trips to the plate in the majors, whether Sano can reel in his would-be historic strikeout rate, and the process-level numbers suggest he's already losing some of his would-have-been historic pop. He's at an off-field crossroads and an on-field nadir.

Jonathan Schoop 2B   Born: 10/16/91   Age: 27   Bats: R   Throws: R   Height: 6'1"   Weight: 225   Origin: International Free Agent, 2008

YEAR	TEAM	LVL	AGE	PA	R	2B	3B	HR	RBI	BB	K	SB	CS	AVG/OBP/SLG	DRC+	VORP	BABIP	BRR	FRAA	WARP
2016	BAL	MLB	24	647	82	38	1	25	82	21	137	1	2	.267/.298/.454	89	12.3	.305	1.5	2B(162): -2.4	1.1
2017	BAL	MLB	25	675	92	35	0	32	105	35	142	1	0	.293/.338/.503	112	37.6	.330	4.2	2B(159): 8.2, SS(5): 0.8	4.5
2018	BAL	MLB	26	367	45	18	1	17	40	12	74	0	1	.244/.273/.447	83	5.6	.262	-0.6	2B(85): 7.9, SS(2): 0.0	1.1
2018	MIL	MLB	26	134	16	4	0	4	21	7	41	1	0	.202/.246/.331	81	-1.1	.259	1.0	2B(31): 1.4, SS(15): 1.1	0.5
2019	MIN	MLB	27	475	53	22	2	18	64	25	99	1	1	.256/.307/.438	101	18.1	.293	1.5	2B 3	2.2

Breakout: 1%   Improve: 55%   Collapse: 1%   Attrition: 2%   MLB: 95%   *Comparables: Jeff Kent, Bret Boone, Jim Morrison*

Outside of a smoking hot July, Schoop batted .198/.242/.340 in 2018, crashing back down to earth after an All-Star campaign. He could not crack a .400 slugging percentage in any of those other spring or summer months. This marked a stunning reversal from an excellent 32-homer campaign in 2017. Schoop's power promise fully materialized that year, with the notable new-school and old-school trophies of a .500 slugging percentage and 100 RBI. The toughest aspect of Schoop's decline is explaining the prime age reversion; but entering 2019 as an age-27 batter, Schoop sees his strikeouts creeping up, walks dwindling away and ground balls increasing. Not every prime-age player has large margins for error, and Schoop demonstrates the hazards of one-dimensional power.

Ronald Torreyes INF   Born: 09/02/92   Age: 26   Bats: R   Throws: R   Height: 5'8"   Weight: 151   Origin: International Free Agent, 2010

YEAR	TEAM	LVL	AGE	PA	R	2B	3B	HR	RBI	BB	K	SB	CS	AVG/OBP/SLG	DRC+	VORP	BABIP	BRR	FRAA	WARP
2016	NYA	MLB	23	168	20	7	4	1	12	10	20	2	1	.258/.305/.374	82	4.6	.289	0.9	3B(34): 4.3, SS(15): -1.2	0.5
2017	NYA	MLB	24	336	35	15	1	3	36	11	43	2	0	.292/.314/.375	81	5.2	.326	1.3	2B(54): 0.8, SS(36): 0.5	0.9
2018	SWB	AAA	25	106	9	3	0	0	8	7	11	0	0	.247/.302/.278	98	-0.7	.276	-0.4	2B(11): -1.1, SS(6): 0.7	0.3
2018	NYA	MLB	25	102	9	7	1	0	7	2	16	0	0	.280/.294/.370	83	-0.5	.333	-0.4	2B(20): -0.4, 3B(11): 0.6	0.2
2019	MIN	MLB	26	148	14	7	1	2	14	9	21	1	0	.257/.305/.372	84	1.9	.284	0.3	3B 2, 2B 0	0.4

Breakout: 1%   Improve: 48%   Collapse: 17%   Attrition: 27%   MLB: 94%   *Comparables: Steve Lombardozzi, Darwin Barney, Donovan Solano*

Even when the Yankees are stocked with juggernaut after juggernaut, sometimes fan attention zeroes in on players with minimal statistical value but maximal "team" value, however that can be weighed. Luis Sojo comes to mind, though he did have 2000 World Series bonafides to hold up. Torreyes doesn't have those, though he possesses all of the Sojoian qualities to endear himself to fans — a dynamic and fun personality, solid defense and a high batting average. He was so highly touted that fans grumbled when he was sent down after the infield roster crunch, and some probably would even go so far that their second half slog was attributable to his intangibles missing from the team. That logic is clearly a stretch, but it's also true that every foot needs a Big Toe. Traded to the Cubs, released and then signed by the Twins, Torreyes will have the opportunity to build a new legion of over-enthusiastic fans at Target Field.

PITCHERS

Jorge Alcala RHP   Born: 07/28/95   Age: 23   Bats: R   Throws: R   Height: 6'3"   Weight: 180   Origin: International Free Agent, 2014

YEAR	TEAM	LVL	AGE	W	L	SV	G	GS	IP	H	HR	BB/9	K/9	K	GB%	BABIP	WHIP	ERA	DRA	WARP	MPH	FB%	WHF	CSP
2016	AST	RK	20	1	1	1	6	3	22¹	14	0	2.4	14.1	35	71%	.311	0.90	1.21	1.42	1.0				
2016	GRV	RK	20	2	1	0	6	4	20	12	0	3.6	9.0	20	55%	.245	1.00	1.80	2.67	0.6				
2016	TCV	A-	20	0	1	0	3	3	13²	20	1	2.6	9.9	15	49%	.432	1.76	5.27	2.80	0.4				
2017	QUD	A	21	2	0	0	6	4	31	16	3	3.5	10.2	35	51%	.194	0.90	2.03	2.79	0.9				
2017	BCA	A+	21	5	6	0	16	14	78¹	55	7	3.8	6.9	60	40%	.223	1.12	3.45	4.47	0.7				
2018	BCA	A+	22	1	4	2	10	7	38²	25	2	4.2	10.5	45	48%	.256	1.11	3.03	3.35	0.9				
2018	CCH	AA	22	2	3	1	9	5	40²	36	1	3.8	8.2	37	42%	.307	1.30	3.54	4.12	0.5				
2018	CHT	AA	22	0	4	0	5	4	20	23	4	6.3	9.9	22	35%	.339	1.85	5.85	5.08	0.0				
2019	MIN	MLB	23	4	5	1	34	13	82	80	13	4.9	8.6	79	43%	.293	1.53	5.28	5.54	-0.3				

Breakout: 13%   Improve: 20%   Collapse: 14%   Attrition: 29%   MLB: 42%   Comparables: *Brooks Brown, Shawn Morimando, Bobby Livingston*

What Alcala is depends entirely upon what you believe his miserable numbers after a midseason trade mean. In one reading, the fact that the Astros (with an analytical savvy that far outstrips that of any other team, one that has served them just as well in player development as in talent acquisition) gave up on Alcala might signal he's doomed never to find one good breaking ball among the two undistinguished ones he throws right now. In another, it might be a normal blip in the transition of a very talented pitching prospect to a new organization. Alcala's pro career has been spent in the rotation, but his future is in the bullpen, where his too-firm changeup isn't a problem and he can lean on just his high-90s heat and his slider. This season should see his first prolonged audition for that role.

Jose Berrios RHP   Born: 05/27/94   Age: 25   Bats: R   Throws: R   Height: 6'0"   Weight: 185   Origin: Round 1, 2012 Draft (#32 overall)

YEAR	TEAM	LVL	AGE	W	L	SV	G	GS	IP	H	HR	BB/9	K/9	K	GB%	BABIP	WHIP	ERA	DRA	WARP	MPH	FB%	WHF	CSP
2016	ROC	AAA	22	10	5	0	17	17	111¹	74	8	2.9	10.1	125	45%	.254	0.99	2.51	2.67	3.4				
2016	MIN	MLB	22	3	7	0	14	14	58¹	74	12	5.4	7.6	49	39%	.344	1.87	8.02	7.42	-1.4	95.9	64	9	43.8
2017	ROC	AAA	23	3	0	0	6	6	39²	24	2	1.8	8.8	39	40%	.214	0.81	1.13	3.49	1.0				
2017	MIN	MLB	23	14	8	0	26	25	145²	131	15	3.0	8.6	139	41%	.289	1.23	3.89	4.29	2.1	95.9	61.5	10.5	46.4
2018	MIN	MLB	24	12	11	0	32	32	192¹	159	25	2.9	9.5	202	43%	.270	1.14	3.84	4.25	2.4	95.2	60.4	12.3	46.7
2019	MIN	MLB	25	11	10	0	30	30	180	156	20	3.3	9.5	191	42%	.289	1.23	3.84	4.00	3.1	95.2	62.7	11.6	47

Breakout: 29%   Improve: 56%   Collapse: 23%   Attrition: 17%   MLB: 97%   Comparables: *Daniel Hudson, Michael Pineda, Clay Buchholz*

We live in an era of rapid player development, simplified approaches and a constantly changing set of quick-fix proposals to heal what ails any young player failing to live up to their billing. We also live in *the* era of the five-inning ace. The third time through the order is the danger zone for most starters, and rather than try to fix that in any way, teams have accepted it as the natural state of the game. Relievers are nearly equal partners with starters in the daily endeavor of winning games. As such, starters are expected to develop as rapidly as relievers do: to find two or three pitches that work for them, focus on the most dominant single offering in that mix and get the hell out of there before the opposing lineup figures them out.

Berrios violates all of those new norms. He's as true a throwback as any young starter in baseball. In 2018, opposing batters posted a .667 OPS the first time they saw him in a game. The second time through, that ticked up to only .679. The third time, it *dropped* to .637. Berrios uses four pitches, and is fairly dedicated to deploying all of them to advantage during each contest. He continues to tinker with his delivery, getting way to the third-base side of the rubber and lowering his arm angle, which has really allowed his sinker to take off to the arm side and has given his curveball a slider shape. He wore down and struggled with his control during the dog days in 2018, but in his third full season, he looks ready to be a consistent and often dominant workhorse.

Tyler Duffey RHP   Born: 12/27/90   Age: 28   Bats: R   Throws: R   Height: 6'3"   Weight: 220   Origin: Round 5, 2012 Draft (#160 overall)

YEAR	TEAM	LVL	AGE	W	L	SV	G	GS	IP	H	HR	BB/9	K/9	K	GB%	BABIP	WHIP	ERA	DRA	WARP	MPH	FB%	WHF	CSP
2016	ROC	AAA	25	1	1	0	5	5	30²	24	4	3.5	7.3	25	35%	.238	1.17	2.93	5.54	-0.1				
2016	MIN	MLB	25	9	12	0	26	26	133	167	25	2.2	7.7	114	49%	.339	1.50	6.43	6.01	-1.0	93.2	54.5	9.3	46.2
2017	MIN	MLB	26	2	3	1	56	0	71	79	9	2.3	8.5	67	50%	.326	1.37	4.94	3.65	1.2	93.8	59.4	11.8	48
2018	ROC	AAA	27	4	4	3	31	0	59	48	5	3.1	9.6	63	45%	.277	1.15	2.90	4.48	0.4				
2018	MIN	MLB	27	2	2	0	19	1	25	26	6	1.4	6.8	19	35%	.260	1.20	7.20	5.41	-0.1	95.2	61.2	11.3	48.5
2019	MIN	MLB	28	2	1	0	33	0	34²	35	5	3.2	8.3	32	44%	.304	1.36	4.32	4.51	0.3	93.2	57.5	10.5	48

Breakout: 22%   Improve: 47%   Collapse: 21%   Attrition: 28%   MLB: 90%   Comparables: *Billy Traber, Liam Hendriks, Christian Friedrich*

Bouncing between the rotation and the bullpen wasn't good for Duffey's development in the slightest. He spent his formative professional seasons focused on repeating his delivery, arm speed and release point, but doing so stole some of the natural electricity from his high-effort delivery and fastball-curveball combination. Starting meant working hard to remain unpredictable and emotionally steady, but the sturdy right-hander is a wild southpaw at heart. He's running out of chances to show it before becoming waiver wire fodder, but somewhere within Duffey's profile lurks a setup man whose intensity and sheer stuff make life difficult for opposing hitters.

Jhoan Duran   RHP   Born: 01/08/98   Age: 21   Bats: R   Throws: R   Height: 6'5"   Weight: 175   Origin: International Free Agent, 2014

YEAR	TEAM	LVL	AGE	W	L	SV	G	GS	IP	H	HR	BB/9	K/9	K	GB%	BABIP	WHIP	ERA	DRA	WARP	MPH	FB%	WHF	CSP
2016	DIA	RK	18	1	2	0	4	4	20	24	1	2.2	5.8	13	55%	.354	1.45	5.85	4.33	0.3				
2016	MSO	RK	18	0	1	0	3	3	12²	14	1	3.6	6.4	9	49%	.283	1.50	3.55	9.57	-0.5				
2017	DIA	RK	19	0	2	0	3	3	11¹	19	0	3.2	10.3	13	64%	.452	2.03	7.15	5.61	0.1				
2017	YAK	A-	19	6	3	0	11	11	51	44	5	3.0	6.4	36	54%	.253	1.20	4.24	4.32	0.6				
2018	KNC	A	20	5	4	0	15	15	64²	69	6	3.9	9.9	71	52%	.346	1.50	4.73	3.51	1.3				
2018	CDR	A	20	2	1	0	6	6	36	19	2	2.5	11.0	44	66%	.218	0.81	2.00	2.51	1.1				
2019	MIN	MLB	21	4	6	0	16	16	74²	82	13	4.6	7.6	63	47%	.308	1.62	5.55	5.82	-0.3				

Breakout: 5%   Improve: 9%   Collapse: 3%   Attrition: 11%   MLB: 14%   *Comparables: Jarrod Parker, Patrick Corbin, Jarred Cosart*

To bet on Duran is to bet on his changeup, and to bet on his changeup is an appealing proposition once you watch his delivery. He can ramp his fastball up into the high 90s in bursts, but it sits in the 95 mph range with life. Duran already possesses a curveball that flashes better than average, and has confidence in it. He's carved up the lower minors. The next step will be to see whether he can firm up his command, which can be loose within the zone. As with any pitching prospect yet to face advanced hitters and with the repertoire still in development, there's tons of risk here. If things fall together well, though, Duran will bloom into either a mid-rotation starter or a fiendish back-end reliever.

Blayne Enlow   RHP   Born: 03/21/99   Age: 20   Bats: R   Throws: R   Height: 6'3"   Weight: 170   Origin: Round 3, 2017 Draft (#76 overall)

YEAR	TEAM	LVL	AGE	W	L	SV	G	GS	IP	H	HR	BB/9	K/9	K	GB%	BABIP	WHIP	ERA	DRA	WARP	MPH	FB%	WHF	CSP
2017	TWI	RK	18	3	0	0	6	1	20¹	10	1	1.8	8.4	19	56%	.176	0.69	1.33	2.53	0.7				
2018	CDR	A	19	3	5	1	20	17	94	94	4	3.4	6.8	71	47%	.315	1.37	3.26	4.36	0.9				
2019	MIN	MLB	20	3	4	0	25	10	62²	76	13	4.9	6.0	42	44%	.309	1.75	6.55	6.89	-1.6				

Comparables: Robert Gsellman, James Parr, Raul Alcantara

Though he's yet to have any significant arm trouble, Enlow can't seem to stay healthy. He's gotten into a serious car accident in high school, slowing his pre-draft progress. In his first full pro season, he suffered ankle and back tweaks that sidelined him for several starts, though those recovery timetables were shaped by the Twins' preference to play it safe. After all, Enlow was already a teenager pitching in the Midwest League. When he was able to take the mound, however, he more than acquitted himself. With a fastball and a curve that each look to be plus offerings and a changeup he can throw for strikes when he needs to, Enlow will probably take the fastest track his body will permit. His size and mechanics suggest that he can stick in the rotation as he does so.

Kyle Gibson   RHP   Born: 10/23/87   Age: 31   Bats: R   Throws: R   Height: 6'6"   Weight: 215   Origin: Round 1, 2009 Draft (#22 overall)

YEAR	TEAM	LVL	AGE	W	L	SV	G	GS	IP	H	HR	BB/9	K/9	K	GB%	BABIP	WHIP	ERA	DRA	WARP	MPH	FB%	WHF	CSP
2016	MIN	MLB	28	6	11	0	25	25	147¹	175	20	3.4	6.4	104	50%	.330	1.56	5.07	6.31	-1.6	93.6	56.2	10.3	42.1
2017	ROC	AAA	29	1	2	0	3	3	17¹	13	1	2.6	11.9	23	60%	.308	1.04	2.08	2.75	0.6				
2017	MIN	MLB	29	12	10	0	29	29	158	182	24	3.4	6.9	121	52%	.328	1.53	5.07	5.20	0.7	94.4	56.7	10.6	42.2
2018	MIN	MLB	30	10	13	0	32	32	196²	177	23	3.6	8.2	179	51%	.285	1.30	3.62	4.21	2.5	95.1	57.8	12.1	40.4
2019	MIN	MLB	31	10	10	0	28	28	168	168	20	3.6	7.9	147	49%	.303	1.40	4.39	4.58	1.7	93.7	56.8	11.2	41.2

Breakout: 10%   Improve: 39%   Collapse: 30%   Attrition: 9%   MLB: 93%   *Comparables: Clay Buchholz, Yovani Gallardo, Andrew Cashner*

Of the 198 pitchers who threw 500 or more four-seam fastballs in 2018, Gibson had the second-lowest Called Strike Probability (CSProb) on those pitches. Of the 92 who threw at least 500 sinkers, he had the eighth-lowest CSProb. Of the 61 who threw at least 500 sliders, Gibson had the third-lowest CSProb. Almost no one in baseball is around the middle of the zone less often than Gibson, but his new formula is working. The four-seamer sets everything up and keeps opponents thinking about the whole zone, the sinker remains a worm-killer and the slider induced whiffs at by far the highest clip of his career. He walks more batters this way, but compared to the version of Gibson that tried to skate by with AstroTurf-era strikeout rates, he's way more effective.

Stephen Gonsalves   LHP   Born: 07/08/94   Age: 24   Bats: L   Throws: L   Height: 6'5"   Weight: 213   Origin: Round 4, 2013 Draft (#110 overall)

YEAR	TEAM	LVL	AGE	W	L	SV	G	GS	IP	H	HR	BB/9	K/9	K	GB%	BABIP	WHIP	ERA	DRA	WARP	MPH	FB%	WHF	CSP
2016	FTM	A+	21	5	4	0	11	11	65²	43	2	2.7	9.0	66	48%	.248	0.96	2.33	3.02	1.8				
2016	CHT	AA	21	8	1	0	13	13	74¹	43	1	4.5	10.8	89	38%	.255	1.08	1.82	3.31	1.6				
2017	CHT	AA	22	8	3	0	15	15	87¹	67	7	2.4	9.9	96	35%	.270	1.03	2.68	3.07	2.2				
2017	ROC	AAA	22	1	2	0	5	4	22²	27	4	3.2	8.7	22	34%	.343	1.54	5.56	4.13	0.4				
2018	CHT	AA	23	3	0	0	4	4	20¹	11	2	4.4	11.1	25	51%	.231	1.03	1.77	3.84	0.4				
2018	ROC	AAA	23	9	3	0	19	18	100¹	65	6	4.9	8.5	95	40%	.237	1.20	2.96	4.72	0.9				
2018	MIN	MLB	23	2	2	0	7	4	24²	28	2	8.0	5.8	16	40%	.321	2.03	6.57	8.22	-0.9	92.1	59	6.9	48.3
2019	MIN	MLB	24	3	4	0	11	11	55	50	8	4.4	9.0	55	39%	.284	1.40	4.76	4.99	0.3	91.9	60.8	7.1	49.7

Breakout: 16%   Improve: 30%   Collapse: 31%   Attrition: 38%   MLB: 72%   *Comparables: Henry Owens, Keyvius Sampson, Aaron Blair*

Overpowering opponents was never going to be much of an option for Gonsalves. That's not to say that dominating them was beyond his ability: he racked up impressive strikeout rates at several stops in the minors. To do so, however, he relied on the ability to repeat his delivery and execute with extraordinary consistency, giving all four of his fairly pedestrian pitches the advantage of an assailant who was off balance. His command was nowhere near good enough to make all that work in 2018, however, especially after his arrival in the majors. Gonsalves threw his four-seamer 60 percent of the time in 2018; his path to big-league success is having enough confidence in the rest of his arsenal to shrink that number by half.

Brusdar Graterol RHP   Born: 08/26/98   Age: 20   Bats: R   Throws: R   Height: 6'1"   Weight: 180   Origin: International Free Agent, 2014

YEAR	TEAM	LVL	AGE	W	L	SV	G	GS	IP	H	HR	BB/9	K/9	K	GB%	BABIP	WHIP	ERA	DRA	WARP	MPH	FB%	WHF	CSP
2017	TWI	RK	18	2	0	0	5	2	19¹	10	1	1.9	9.8	21	58%	.205	0.72	1.40	2.83	0.6				
2017	ELZ	RK	18	2	1	0	5	5	20²	16	1	3.9	10.5	24	59%	.300	1.21	3.92	3.76	0.5				
2018	CDR	A	19	3	2	0	8	8	41¹	30	3	2.0	11.1	51	64%	.270	0.94	2.18	3.57	0.8				
2018	FTM	A+	19	5	2	0	11	11	60²	59	0	2.8	8.3	56	49%	.343	1.29	3.12	4.21	0.8				
2019	MIN	MLB	20	4	6	0	15	15	70²	75	12	4.3	8.2	64	50%	.308	1.53	5.27	5.53	0.0				

Breakout: 4%   Improve: 5%   Collapse: 1%   Attrition: 3%   MLB: 7%   *Comparables: Brad Keller, Will Smith, Jenrry Mejia*

Some caution is in order where Graterol is concerned, because he won't turn 21 until August and he already has an elbow scar. His sheer stuff and ability to bully opposing batters tempted the Twins into a midseason level bump, and if he's not yet on the fast track he's one lane over from it. His fastball can touch 100 mph, and it's not without some wiggle. Pairing that with his plus slider would already make Graterol a holy terror in some future bullpen, but his arm action on the changeup gives him a chance to be more. Anything like ace status is off the table until he tightens his command, but he can already throw enough strikes to project as a mid-rotation hurler and an unhappy at-bat.

Trevor Hildenberger RHP   Born: 12/15/90   Age: 28   Bats: R   Throws: R   Height: 6'2"   Weight: 211   Origin: Round 22, 2014 Draft (#650 overall)

YEAR	TEAM	LVL	AGE	W	L	SV	G	GS	IP	H	HR	BB/9	K/9	K	GB%	BABIP	WHIP	ERA	DRA	WARP	MPH	FB%	WHF	CSP
2016	FTM	A+	25	1	1	3	6	0	9¹	11	0	0.0	7.7	8	64%	.355	1.18	0.96	3.03	0.2				
2016	CHT	AA	25	2	3	16	32	0	38²	21	2	1.4	10.5	45	61%	.211	0.70	0.70	2.09	1.2				
2017	ROC	AAA	26	2	1	6	21	0	30²	27	1	2.3	10.3	35	56%	.321	1.14	2.05	2.37	1.0				
2017	MIN	MLB	26	3	3	1	37	0	42	38	4	1.3	9.4	44	60%	.304	1.05	3.21	3.27	0.9	93.2	51	12.4	44.8
2018	MIN	MLB	27	4	6	7	73	0	73	75	12	3.2	8.6	70	48%	.301	1.38	5.42	5.28	-0.3	93.3	44.1	13.4	47.1
2019	MIN	MLB	28	3	1	4	55	0	57²	55	7	3.6	8.7	56	50%	.299	1.35	4.17	4.35	0.5	92.7	46.5	13.2	46.3

Breakout: 28%   Improve: 42%   Collapse: 27%   Attrition: 13%   MLB: 82%   *Comparables: Ryan Dull, Pedro Baez, Matt Reynolds*

Very few of the great things Hildenberger showed in his rookie campaign carried over to 2018. His control deserted him, largely because he lost the feel for both pitches (his sinker and his changeup) that move to the arm side. He did flash the grounder-inducing quasi-dominance of 2017 during the late spring and early summer, but he wore down from there and batters began sitting on his slider, then elevating and blistering it. At his best, Hildenberger is a four-pitch reliever with a non-existent platoon split and the command to consistently induce very weak contact, but it's possible the late bloomer's best is gone for good.

Zack Littell RHP   Born: 10/05/95   Age: 23   Bats: R   Throws: R   Height: 6'4"   Weight: 220   Origin: Round 11, 2013 Draft (#327 overall)

YEAR	TEAM	LVL	AGE	W	L	SV	G	GS	IP	H	HR	BB/9	K/9	K	GB%	BABIP	WHIP	ERA	DRA	WARP	MPH	FB%	WHF	CSP
2016	CLN	A	20	5	5	0	16	16	97²	94	5	1.9	8.8	95	51%	.332	1.18	2.76	3.64	1.6				
2016	BAK	A+	20	8	1	0	12	11	68	64	3	1.7	8.1	61	49%	.311	1.13	2.51	4.19	1.0				
2017	TAM	A+	21	9	1	0	13	11	71¹	65	4	1.9	7.2	57	55%	.302	1.12	1.77	4.32	0.8				
2017	TRN	AA	21	5	0	0	7	7	44	37	3	1.6	10.6	52	52%	.304	1.02	2.05	3.12	1.1				
2017	CHT	AA	21	5	0	0	7	7	41²	33	1	3.9	7.1	33	55%	.274	1.22	2.81	3.98	0.6				
2018	CHT	AA	22	0	3	0	6	5	23	28	3	2.7	12.5	32	38%	.431	1.52	5.87	3.72	0.4				
2018	ROC	AAA	22	6	6	0	19	15	106	100	5	3.4	8.3	98	40%	.310	1.32	3.57	4.02	1.7				
2018	MIN	MLB	22	0	2	0	8	2	20¹	25	3	4.9	6.2	14	44%	.319	1.77	6.20	6.71	-0.4	94.6	58.5	8	49.2
2019	MIN	MLB	23	3	2	0	32	5	54	57	7	3.3	8.0	48	44%	.312	1.42	4.52	4.72	0.2	94.5	60.6	8.3	51

Breakout: 7%   Improve: 16%   Collapse: 12%   Attrition: 25%   MLB: 30%   *Comparables: Abe Alvarez, Brady Rodgers, Justin Germano*

The only good way to approach Littell's first taste of the majors is to treat it as a mulligan. Still tall, young and polished, with five pitches and the athleticism to command them, Littell retains his back-of-the-rotation upside. Pitchers of his ilk — with so many weapons but no obviously optimal way to deploy them — bear a bit more risk than others of simply never putting everything together. Littell's repertoire's depth is mitigated by the absence of any offering that projects to facilitate a move to the bullpen. Risk certainly lurks with Littell, and it swells with each unsuccessful start he makes, but it's too early to count him out.

Matt Magill RHP   Born: 11/10/89   Age: 29   Bats: R   Throws: R   Height: 6'3"   Weight: 210   Origin: Round 31, 2008 Draft (#937 overall)

YEAR	TEAM	LVL	AGE	W	L	SV	G	GS	IP	H	HR	BB/9	K/9	K	GB%	BABIP	WHIP	ERA	DRA	WARP	MPH	FB%	WHF	CSP
2016	PEN	AA	26	0	0	1	9	0	9²	12	0	5.6	14.9	16	46%	.500	1.86	6.52	1.58	0.4				
2016	LOU	AAA	26	4	1	0	29	0	42¹	40	6	4.5	9.1	43	44%	.306	1.44	4.46	3.48	0.7				
2016	CIN	MLB	26	0	0	0	5	0	4¹	5	1	10.4	2.1	1	29%	.308	2.31	6.23	6.54	-0.1	94.9	68.3	7.3	45.4
2017	ELP	AAA	27	6	5	0	19	17	95²	105	13	3.9	6.9	73	45%	.316	1.53	3.95	4.81	0.9				
2018	ROC	AAA	28	0	0	2	5	0	8²	5	0	2.1	13.5	13	28%	.278	0.81	0.00	2.67	0.2				
2018	MIN	MLB	28	3	3	0	40	0	56²	58	11	3.7	8.9	56	35%	.301	1.43	3.81	5.42	-0.3	96.4	60.9	11.8	46
2019	MIN	MLB	29	2	1	0	49	0	52	53	9	4.3	8.9	51	40%	.305	1.50	5.12	5.37	-0.2	95.7	61.2	11.6	45.8

Breakout: 13%   Improve: 16%   Collapse: 14%   Attrition: 17%   MLB: 32%   *Comparables: Dusty Hughes, Rob Scahill, Joe Savery*

A minor-league journeyman, swingman and whack-a-mole big leaguer, Magill popped up for his longest stint in the majors throwing harder than ever. His mid-90s fastball is too straight and gets crushed, though, and he can't consistently throw strikes with his cutter or his curveball. He remains an extreme fly-ball guy, and is vulnerable to the long ball. By the end of 2018, the league brought its giant mallet down hard on Magill's head. In order to remain a useful reliever, he'll need to hone one of those breaking balls and continue the trend he used to survive September: throwing far fewer fastballs.

Trevor May RHP   Born: 09/23/89   Age: 29   Bats: R   Throws: R   Height: 6'5"   Weight: 240   Origin: Round 4, 2008 Draft (#136 overall)

YEAR	TEAM	LVL	AGE	W	L	SV	G	GS	IP	H	HR	BB/9	K/9	K	GB%	BABIP	WHIP	ERA	DRA	WARP	MPH	FB%	WHF	CSP
2016	MIN	MLB	26	2	2	0	44	0	42²	39	7	3.6	12.7	60	32%	.317	1.31	5.27	4.10	0.4	96.7	61	13.8	47.2
2018	ROC	AAA	28	0	4	2	13	4	27	24	2	5.3	8.3	25	40%	.293	1.48	4.00	3.55	0.5				
2018	MIN	MLB	28	4	1	3	24	1	25¹	21	4	1.8	12.8	36	41%	.298	1.03	3.20	2.98	0.6	95.5	59.2	15.6	46.7
2019	*MIN*	*MLB*	*29*	*3*	*1*	*25*	*55*	*0*	*57²*	*56*	*8*	*4.0*	*9.9*	*64*	*39%*	*.310*	*1.42*	*4.43*	*4.62*	*0.3*	*95.4*	*60.1*	*14.7*	*46.8*

Breakout: 28%   Improve: 56%   Collapse: 18%   Attrition: 15%   MLB: 85%   *Comparables: Brett Cecil, Charlie Furbush, Joel Hanrahan*

May has an average fastball, though it's played up from there during his past stints in the bullpen. He has a good changeup, though the movement differential from the fastball is almost all lateral, so it tends to generate ground balls more than whiffs (and when it's not executed well, batters can hit it a long way). His breaking stuff has always been a work in progress, but he did get more comfortable with his curveball last year even as he worked his way back from Tommy John surgery. Some modernization is in order for May's approach: he was absent from MLB for all of 2017 and most of 2018. During that relatively short time, the league underwent a significant shift toward fewer fastballs and more secondary pitches. May will benefit from mimicking that adjustment.

Adalberto Mejia LHP   Born: 06/20/93   Age: 26   Bats: R   Throws: L   Height: 6'3"   Weight: 195   Origin: International Free Agent, 2011

YEAR	TEAM	LVL	AGE	W	L	SV	G	GS	IP	H	HR	BB/9	K/9	K	GB%	BABIP	WHIP	ERA	DRA	WARP	MPH	FB%	WHF	CSP
2016	RIC	AA	23	3	2	0	11	11	65	48	4	2.2	8.0	58	48%	.251	0.98	1.94	2.96	1.7				
2016	SAC	AAA	23	4	1	0	7	7	40²	42	5	2.4	9.5	43	42%	.327	1.30	4.20	3.63	0.8				
2016	MIN	MLB	23	0	0	0	1	0	2¹	5	0	3.9	0.0	0	42%	.417	2.57	7.71	7.31	-0.1	93.2	45.2	7.1	45.8
2016	ROC	AAA	23	2	2	0	4	4	26¹	28	3	1.0	8.5	25	33%	.329	1.18	3.76	2.88	0.7				
2017	ROC	AAA	24	1	1	0	6	6	28²	26	1	1.9	6.9	22	51%	.294	1.12	2.83	3.90	0.6				
2017	MIN	MLB	24	4	7	0	21	21	98	110	13	4.0	7.8	85	41%	.328	1.57	4.50	6.02	-0.5	94.2	56.3	11.2	43.6
2018	ROC	AAA	25	5	3	0	15	12	63¹	55	3	2.8	8.8	62	43%	.294	1.18	3.27	4.10	1.0				
2018	MIN	MLB	25	2	0	0	5	4	22¹	17	1	3.6	5.2	13	40%	.239	1.16	2.01	6.86	-0.4	94.6	59.1	9.5	48
2019	*MIN*	*MLB*	*26*	*5*	*5*	*0*	*16*	*16*	*84²*	*85*	*10*	*3.3*	*8.2*	*77*	*42%*	*.304*	*1.37*	*4.27*	*4.45*	*1.0*	*93.9*	*57.7*	*11*	*46.8*

Breakout: 29%   Improve: 53%   Collapse: 19%   Attrition: 24%   MLB: 82%   *Comparables: Trevor Williams, Andrew Heaney, Cody Anderson*

Everywhere Mejia goes, frustration follows in his wake. He's blessed with a high-spin fastball, a hard, late-breaking slider and a fine changeup. He's never had great command, but the stuff should work better than it does. Mejia struggles to maintain a physique that keeps him balanced and strong on the mound, especially as he works past the first trip through the batting order. He doesn't even get ground balls, despite that mostly horizontal slider and a heavy sinker (a pitch he should, perhaps, throw more often). He's not embarrassingly out of shape, or a major makeup disaster, or a yips-afflicted wild horse. He's just a pitcher who seems like he should be decent but manages not to be.

Gabriel Moya LHP   Born: 01/09/95   Age: 24   Bats: L   Throws: L   Height: 6'0"   Weight: 175   Origin: International Free Agent, 2012

YEAR	TEAM	LVL	AGE	W	L	SV	G	GS	IP	H	HR	BB/9	K/9	K	GB%	BABIP	WHIP	ERA	DRA	WARP	MPH	FB%	WHF	CSP
2016	KNC	A	21	1	0	0	12	0	19	12	0	1.9	9.5	20	51%	.255	0.84	0.47	2.53	0.5				
2016	VIS	A+	21	5	1	5	40	0	44²	26	2	2.6	12.5	62	41%	.255	0.87	2.01	2.70	1.2				
2017	WTN	AA	22	4	1	17	34	0	43²	22	1	2.5	14.0	68	44%	.259	0.78	0.82	2.19	1.4				
2017	CHT	AA	22	2	0	7	13	0	14²	8	1	1.8	11.7	19	44%	.212	0.75	0.61	2.56	0.4				
2017	MIN	MLB	22	0	0	1	7	0	6¹	5	2	2.8	7.1	5	32%	.176	1.11	4.26	4.14	0.1	92.2	45.7	12.4	39.3
2018	ROC	AAA	23	1	1	4	26	4	42²	38	2	2.5	10.5	50	38%	.336	1.17	1.90	2.56	1.3				
2018	MIN	MLB	23	3	1	0	35	6	36¹	35	6	3.2	7.7	31	40%	.269	1.32	4.71	5.74	-0.3	91.6	42	10.5	48.5
2019	*MIN*	*MLB*	*24*	*3*	*2*	*0*	*52*	*8*	*54¹*	*48*	*7*	*3.7*	*10.1*	*61*	*40%*	*.292*	*1.29*	*4.11*	*4.28*	*0.6*	*91.5*	*43.7*	*11.1*	*45.8*

Breakout: 18%   Improve: 28%   Collapse: 18%   Attrition: 22%   MLB: 61%   *Comparables: Cody Allen, Shae Simmons, Manny Delcarmen*

Moya doesn't throw especially hard or have a truly nasty single pitch on which to lean. He succeeds, when he succeeds, by pitching as purely backward as any reliever in baseball. He would rather start a left-handed batter with a slider, or a right-handed one with a changeup, than throw them a fastball early in the count. When he falls behind, he uses the change to get back into the count or induce weak contact, even against fellow lefties. Then, he uses the fastball (which sits only in the low 90s) as his put-away pitch. That's a peculiar profile for a reliever, and it makes Moya tough to cast in a modern bullpen. He's not a matchup guy, per se, nor is he someone most teams want pitching full innings of high-leverage ball. Used as an opener at times in 2018, he does seem a good fit in that role.

Jake Odorizzi RHP   Born: 03/27/90   Age: 29   Bats: R   Throws: R   Height: 6'2"   Weight: 190   Origin: Round 1, 2008 Draft (#32 overall)

YEAR	TEAM	LVL	AGE	W	L	SV	G	GS	IP	H	HR	BB/9	K/9	K	GB%	BABIP	WHIP	ERA	DRA	WARP	MPH	FB%	WHF	CSP
2016	TBA	MLB	26	10	6	0	33	33	187²	170	29	2.6	8.0	166	38%	.271	1.19	3.69	4.88	1.0	94.1	60	10.7	45.7
2017	TBA	MLB	27	10	8	0	28	28	143¹	117	30	3.8	8.0	127	32%	.227	1.24	4.14	5.29	0.5	93.4	48.7	12.1	43.9
2018	MIN	MLB	28	7	10	0	32	32	164¹	151	20	3.8	8.9	162	31%	.290	1.34	4.49	5.62	-0.6	92.8	54.3	11.7	42.1
2019	*MIN*	*MLB*	*29*	*8*	*9*	*0*	*24*	*24*	*136²*	*134*	*24*	*3.5*	*8.5*	*129*	*34%*	*.286*	*1.37*	*4.97*	*5.21*	*0.4*	*92.7*	*54.2*	*11.5*	*43.6*

Breakout: 18%   Improve: 46%   Collapse: 18%   Attrition: 7%   MLB: 95%   *Comparables: Steve Carlton, Edwin Jackson, Don Drysdale*

All over MLB, 2018 saw sinkers disappear. Count that as another way in which Odorizzi is an outlier. He added a sinker back into his repertoire after being dealt to Minnesota, bringing the number of pitches he threw at least occasionally to six: four-seamer, splitter, curve, slider, cutter, sinker. He needs that ability to keep hitters guessing, because ever since his splitter ceased to be a bat-misser, he's been unable to consistently throw anything past opponents. Odorizzi pounds the top of the zone with his fastball, which sets up both his improved hook and that splitter, but he has yet to figure out how to induce the weak contact he's seeking with the other three pitches. Vulnerable to deep counts and short outings, he'll blossom if allowed to work behind an opener and avoid facing the meat of opposing lineups for a third time.

Michael Pineda RHP Born: 01/18/89 Age: 30 Bats: R Throws: R Height: 6'7" Weight: 260 Origin: International Free Agent, 2005

YEAR	TEAM	LVL	AGE	W	L	SV	G	GS	IP	H	HR	BB/9	K/9	K	GB%	BABIP	WHIP	ERA	DRA	WARP	MPH	FB%	WHF	CSP
2016	NYA	MLB	27	6	12	0	32	32	175²	184	27	2.7	10.6	207	46%	.340	1.35	4.82	3.30	4.2	96.9	51.4	15.3	44.6
2017	NYA	MLB	28	8	4	0	17	17	96¹	103	20	2.0	8.6	92	52%	.302	1.29	4.39	3.36	2.4	95.9	48.5	13.3	46.6
2019	*MIN*	*MLB*	*30*	*5*	*6*	*0*	*16*	*16*	*84²*	*98*	*15*	*3.5*	*7.3*	*69*	*44%*	*.316*	*1.54*	*5.13*	*5.38*	*0.1*	*95.7*	*50.1*	*14.5*	*45.6*

Breakout: 22% Improve: 55% Collapse: 9% Attrition: 5% MLB: 88% *Comparables: James Shields, Ricky Nolasco, Dutch Leonard*

When he's on the mound, there remains plenty to like about Pineda. He throws one of the hardest cutters in baseball, and because it's his primary fastball, he's pretty good at generating weak contact. The trouble is that there's no reason to believe he'll figure out how to stay on the mound. Huge and heavy and with scars all over the kinetic chain, Pineda almost made a late-season cameo in his comeback from Tommy John surgery, but had his campaign cut short by a torn meniscus in his knee. After avoiding a conversion to the bullpen for an improbably long time, he should ride the tide of the times and make the switch, even if his health limits his utility there.

Addison Reed RHP Born: 12/27/88 Age: 30 Bats: L Throws: R Height: 6'4" Weight: 230 Origin: Round 3, 2010 Draft (#95 overall)

YEAR	TEAM	LVL	AGE	W	L	SV	G	GS	IP	H	HR	BB/9	K/9	K	GB%	BABIP	WHIP	ERA	DRA	WARP	MPH	FB%	WHF	CSP
2016	NYN	MLB	27	4	2	1	80	0	77²	60	4	1.5	10.5	91	42%	.286	0.94	1.97	2.58	2.1	94.8	72.2	13.6	54
2017	NYN	MLB	28	1	2	19	48	0	49	49	6	1.1	8.8	48	38%	.307	1.12	2.57	3.86	0.7	93.7	69.1	13.5	55.2
2017	BOS	MLB	28	1	1	0	29	0	27	16	5	3.0	9.3	28	47%	.175	0.93	3.33	2.48	0.8	94.6	62.3	16.3	46.2
2018	MIN	MLB	29	1	6	0	55	0	56	65	11	2.4	7.1	44	32%	.320	1.43	4.50	5.61	-0.4	93.1	70.2	11.9	50.7
2019	*MIN*	*MLB*	*30*	*3*	*1*	*8*	*55*	*0*	*57²*	*60*	*10*	*3.3*	*8.2*	*53*	*38%*	*.298*	*1.39*	*4.82*	*5.04*	*0.0*	*93.2*	*69.2*	*13.3*	*51.8*

Breakout: 21% Improve: 52% Collapse: 22% Attrition: 8% MLB: 90% *Comparables: Hoyt Wilhelm, Jeff Montgomery, Joe Sambito*

Since 1947, 22 pitchers have appeared in at least 150 total games at ages 27 and 28. That might seem to mark extreme usage, but since the pitchers in this pool were already into their prime and physically mature, they've mostly held up better than one might expect. Sixteen of the first 21 pitched at least 100 innings across their age-29 and age-30 seasons, and most of them remained well above average. Reed, however, had a miserable 2018, and all signs point to fatigue, undiagnosed injury or some mixture of the two as the driving force. His velocity dropped precipitously, and his fastball straightened out in a way that made him far too easy to square up. There's no credible basis on which to project that his stuff will return to the level that allowed him to enjoy such success in the middle of the decade.

Taylor Rogers LHP Born: 12/17/90 Age: 28 Bats: L Throws: L Height: 6'3" Weight: 170 Origin: Round 11, 2012 Draft (#340 overall)

YEAR	TEAM	LVL	AGE	W	L	SV	G	GS	IP	H	HR	BB/9	K/9	K	GB%	BABIP	WHIP	ERA	DRA	WARP	MPH	FB%	WHF	CSP
2016	ROC	AAA	25	0	1	0	7	2	18	24	1	3.0	7.5	15	44%	.365	1.67	4.50	3.33	0.4				
2016	MIN	MLB	25	3	1	0	57	0	61¹	63	7	2.3	9.4	64	51%	.326	1.29	3.96	4.28	0.5	95.0	55.2	8	50.5
2017	MIN	MLB	26	7	3	0	69	0	55²	52	6	3.4	7.9	49	46%	.291	1.31	3.07	4.63	0.3	94.7	62.3	9.3	50
2018	MIN	MLB	27	1	2	2	72	0	68¹	49	3	2.1	9.9	75	46%	.280	0.95	2.63	3.33	1.3	95.2	52.9	12.3	51.5
2019	*MIN*	*MLB*	*28*	*3*	*1*	*3*	*55*	*0*	*57²*	*55*	*7*	*3.4*	*9.7*	*62*	*46%*	*.315*	*1.33*	*3.85*	*4.00*	*0.7*	*94.4*	*56.8*	*10.3*	*51*

Breakout: 21% Improve: 42% Collapse: 20% Attrition: 18% MLB: 86% *Comparables: Jose Alvarez, Blake Treinen, Joe Biagini*

Opposing hitters managed a pitcheresque .147/.206/.231 line against Rogers from June 1 through the end of the season, and that's not an arbitrarily drawn line. Starting very late in May, Rogers added a slider to a repertoire that had previously leaned heavily on an unimpressive sinker and a good curveball. The slider turned out to be a devastating partner in crime for the hook, such that by the end of the year, he was throwing one of his breaking balls nearly 60 percent of the time without the slightest loss of effectiveness. TrackMan rules the baseball world these days, because it makes improvements like Rogers' not only possible but repeatable, and often permanent.

Fernando Romero RHP Born: 12/24/94 Age: 24 Bats: R Throws: R Height: 6'0" Weight: 215 Origin: International Free Agent, 2011

YEAR	TEAM	LVL	AGE	W	L	SV	G	GS	IP	H	HR	BB/9	K/9	K	GB%	BABIP	WHIP	ERA	DRA	WARP	MPH	FB%	WHF	CSP
2016	CDR	A	21	4	1	0	5	5	28	18	0	1.6	8.0	25	53%	.250	0.82	1.93	3.31	0.6				
2016	FTM	A+	21	5	2	0	11	11	62¹	48	1	1.4	9.4	65	58%	.288	0.93	1.88	2.92	1.8				
2017	CHT	AA	22	11	9	0	24	23	125	124	4	3.2	8.6	120	54%	.328	1.35	3.53	3.79	2.0				
2018	MIN	MLB	23	3	3	0	11	11	55²	60	6	3.1	7.3	45	48%	.318	1.42	4.69	6.13	-0.5	97.1	63.3	11.3	48.4
2018	ROC	AAA	23	5	6	0	16	13	90²	85	5	3.2	6.8	69	50%	.294	1.29	3.57	4.14	1.4				
2019	*MIN*	*MLB*	*24*	*4*	*4*	*0*	*11*	*11*	*58¹*	*60*	*7*	*3.3*	*7.8*	*50*	*48%*	*.309*	*1.39*	*4.28*	*4.46*	*0.7*	*96.9*	*65.2*	*11.6*	*49.9*

Breakout: 14% Improve: 37% Collapse: 12% Attrition: 31% MLB: 64% *Comparables: Alex Sanabia, Chad Kuhl, Paul Maholm*

A classic case of a rookie learning the hard way what success in The Show requires, Romero's first taste of the big leagues looked really promising, only to crash and burn after five strong starts. At issue: Romero's attempt to rely on a heavy sinker as an equal partner to his four-seam fastball. He's more comfortable with the pitch, with aiming at low targets, with the matchup of his natural arm slot and the movement of the sinker. Unfortunately, the pitch just doesn't differentiate itself enough from his firm changeup or his sharp slider to make it (or them) effective. If he has a future in a big-league rotation, it's with that power sinker way up his sleeve. If he has a future in the bullpen, it might be as a turbo-sinker specialist.

Ervin Santana   RHP   Born: 12/12/82   Age: 36   Bats: R   Throws: R   Height: 6'2"   Weight: 175   Origin: International Free Agent, 2000

YEAR	TEAM	LVL	AGE	W	L	SV	G	GS	IP	H	HR	BB/9	K/9	K	GB%	BABIP	WHIP	ERA	DRA	WARP	MPH	FB%	WHF	CSP
2016	MIN	MLB	33	7	11	0	30	30	181¹	168	19	2.6	7.4	149	44%	.285	1.22	3.38	4.05	2.7	95.6	52.6	10.7	43.7
2017	MIN	MLB	34	16	8	0	33	33	211¹	177	31	2.6	7.1	167	43%	.245	1.13	3.28	4.06	3.6	95.0	52.7	11.3	44.3
2018	FTM	A+	35	0	2	0	3	3	10¹	7	1	0.9	6.1	7	32%	.200	0.77	3.48	4.05	0.2				
2018	ROC	AAA	35	0	1	0	2	2	11²	6	3	3.1	6.2	8	31%	.103	0.86	3.09	6.90	-0.2				
2018	MIN	MLB	35	0	1	0	5	5	24²	31	9	3.3	5.8	16	23%	.282	1.62	8.03	8.84	-1.0	90.9	50.7	4.9	45.9
2019	MIN	MLB	36	4	5	0	11	11	67	71	12	3.3	6.6	50	39%	.287	1.43	5.44	5.71	-0.2	93.6	51.4	10.3	43.9

Breakout: 10%   Improve: 40%   Collapse: 21%   Attrition: 10%   MLB: 81%   Comparables: Warren Spahn, Phil Niekro, Early Wynn

Santana proved ageless for about as long as a pitcher can do so. From 2009 through 2017, he threw 93 mph, leaned heavily on a slider that missed bats with the best of them and racked up as many innings as his managers were willing to give him. For all those years, he showed no sign of wearing down. Like most pitchers who never wear down, however, Santana eventually broke. Offseason finger surgery didn't wholly mend him, and even in his brief time with the big-league team, he was nowhere near himself. His fastball velocity tumbled by four miles per hour, forcing him to make more use of his changeup and sinker. His slider stopped missing bats. At 36, even perfect health might not bring back the electricity his arm has lost.

Lewis Thorpe   LHP   Born: 11/23/95   Age: 23   Bats: R   Throws: L   Height: 6'1"   Weight: 160   Origin: International Free Agent, 2012

YEAR	TEAM	LVL	AGE	W	L	SV	G	GS	IP	H	HR	BB/9	K/9	K	GB%	BABIP	WHIP	ERA	DRA	WARP	MPH	FB%	WHF	CSP
2017	CHT	AA	21	1	0	0	1	1	6	5	2	3.0	10.5	7	19%	.214	1.17	6.00	3.45	0.1				
2017	FTM	A+	21	3	4	0	16	15	77	62	3	3.6	9.8	84	39%	.304	1.21	2.69	3.59	1.5				
2018	CHT	AA	22	8	4	0	22	21	108	105	13	2.5	10.9	131	38%	.327	1.25	3.58	3.89	1.8				
2018	ROC	AAA	22	0	3	0	4	4	21²	20	3	2.5	10.8	26	45%	.321	1.20	3.32	3.69	0.5				
2019	MIN	MLB	23	1	0	0	22	0	23	22	3	3.5	9.9	25	37%	.306	1.35	4.32	4.51	0.0				

Breakout: 12%   Improve: 17%   Collapse: 10%   Attrition: 23%   MLB: 36%   Comparables: John Gant, Jake McGee, Charles Brewer

Finally healthy, Thorpe made the developmental leap for which scouts had long hoped (and for which they'd remained willing to wait, despite two-plus lost seasons). He employs a traditional four-pitch mix, but the improved consistency of his slider is especially encouraging. Any lefty who aspires to start in the majors needs a cutter or a changeup that really messes with right-handed batters, and Thorpe certainly has the latter. With enough confidence in his secondary stuff to consistently miss bats regardless of platoon matchups, he's essentially proved that he's ready for the test of big-league competition. If he passes it as impressively as he passed the Double-A test, he's a mid-rotation starter who will occasionally look even better than that.

Andrew Vasquez   LHP   Born: 09/14/93   Age: 25   Bats: L   Throws: L   Height: 6'6"   Weight: 228   Origin: Round 32, 2015 Draft (#950 overall)

YEAR	TEAM	LVL	AGE	W	L	SV	G	GS	IP	H	HR	BB/9	K/9	K	GB%	BABIP	WHIP	ERA	DRA	WARP	MPH	FB%	WHF	CSP
2016	ELZ	RK	22	2	0	0	4	0	10	6	0	3.6	13.5	15	67%	.333	1.00	0.90	1.86	0.4				
2016	CDR	A	22	1	0	1	13	0	28¹	13	0	3.8	11.4	36	64%	.210	0.88	1.59	2.32	0.8				
2017	CDR	A	23	1	0	0	14	0	22¹	15	0	4.0	13.3	33	70%	.326	1.12	1.61	3.05	0.5				
2017	FTM	A+	23	3	1	2	23	0	35²	32	0	2.8	13.1	52	62%	.390	1.21	1.51	2.53	1.0				
2018	FTM	A+	24	0	2	5	19	0	32²	24	1	3.6	10.2	37	60%	.280	1.13	1.38	5.92	-0.4				
2018	CHT	AA	24	1	0	0	17	1	31	21	1	1.2	17.1	59	50%	.408	0.81	1.16	0.77	1.5				
2018	MIN	MLB	24	1	0	0	9	0	5	5	0	3.6	12.6	7	57%	.357	1.40	5.40	4.48	0.0	92.5	34.7	11.9	42.9
2019	MIN	MLB	25	1	1	0	27	0	29	27	4	4.7	10.7	34	51%	.315	1.46	4.37	4.55	0.2	92.2	35.5	12.2	43.9

Breakout: 21%   Improve: 27%   Collapse: 4%   Attrition: 27%   MLB: 41%   Comparables: Donnie Joseph, Jack Leathersich, Shawn Armstrong

In eight stops over the last three seasons, Vasquez has put up video-game numbers (especially strikeouts) everywhere but MLB. Whether one calls his breaking ball a slider (it's pretty firm, relative to his below-average sinker velocity, and most of its movement is horizontal) or a curve (it's a really big breaker, with more lateral movement than all but a couple dozen other hurlers' breaking pitches), the pitch is nasty, and minor leaguers were consistently overmatched. In the big leagues, however, batters laid off it more often, and Vasquez didn't demonstrate the ability to throw it for a strike the way one must in order to succeed with his approach. His sinker has as much run as the curve has sweep, which can make it tough for him to remain deceptive against polished hitters and umpires who won't expand the plate. If he can firm up his command, though, he can make that a non-issue.

LINEOUTS

Hitters

HITTER	POS	TEAM	LVL	AGE	PA	R	2B	3B	HR	RBI	BB	K	SB	CS	AVG/OBP/SLG	DRC+	VORP	BABIP	BRR	FRAA	WARP
Luis Arraez	2B	FTM	A+	21	258	27	14	3	1	20	19	28	2	3	.320/.373/.421	110	14.2	.356	-2.4	2B(40): 1.7, 3B(6): 0.3	1.1
	2B	CHT	AA	21	195	25	6	0	2	16	13	16	2	0	.298/.345/.365	114	6.2	.315	0.0	2B(27): -1.0, 3B(10): 0.3	1.1
Randy Cesar	INF	CCH	AA	23	485	59	25	2	10	62	36	112	3	4	.296/.348/.428	96	20.3	.374	1.7	3B(50): 1.9, 1B(42): -2.2	0.9
Chris Gimenez	C	CHN	MLB	35	32	1	0	0	0	1	3	7	1	0	.143/.219/.143	78	-1.2	.182	-0.3	C(10): 1.6, P(1): 0.0	0.2
	C	IOW	AAA	35	227	15	12	1	2	18	20	67	1	1	.204/.282/.303	56	-2.6	.289	-2.5	C(38): -5.3, 1B(12): -0.4	-1.0
	C	MIN	MLB	35	34	6	1	0	2	6	3	9	0	0	.276/.353/.517	85	2.3	.316	-0.2	C(8): 0.6, 1B(3): 0.0	0.1
Zack Granite	OF	ROC	AAA	25	263	28	8	0	0	4	22	28	9	4	.211/.282/.245	79	-4.3	.238	1.5	CF(50): 6.6, LF(19): -0.5	0.9
Ryan Jeffers	C	ELZ	Rk	21	129	29	7	0	3	16	20	16	0	1	.422/.543/.578	158	19.7	.482	-1.0	C(10): 0.7	1.2
	C	CDR	A	21	155	19	10	0	4	17	14	30	0	0	.288/.361/.446	113	10.3	.343	0.4	C(22): 0.2	0.8
Gabriel Maciel	CF	KNC	A	19	313	44	10	0	1	16	30	50	14	5	.287/.362/.333	100	5.1	.346	0.2	CF(54): -7.1, RF(16): 0.0	0.1
	CF	CDR	A	19	126	16	4	2	2	7	5	21	2	5	.263/.302/.381	94	3.1	.302	-1.2	CF(15): -0.8, RF(9): -0.2	-0.1
Jose Miranda	3B	CDR	A	20	439	52	22	1	13	72	26	51	0	1	.277/.326/.434	122	20.2	.286	-0.5	2B(53): -2.8, 3B(41): 2.4	2.4
	3B	FTM	A+	20	113	9	5	0	3	10	5	11	0	2	.216/.292/.353	109	1.7	.216	-0.3	3B(19): -2.4, 2B(6): 0.3	0.3
Gregorio Petit	UT	ROC	AAA	33	312	31	12	1	1	29	17	47	4	1	.268/.313/.327	83	6.8	.314	2.6	SS(36): -0.3, 2B(28): 1.7	1.0
	UT	MIN	MLB	33	67	7	2	0	0	3	6	14	3	1	.246/.313/.279	81	-0.3	.319	0.6	2B(10): 1.0, SS(9): -0.7	0.2
Luke Raley	1B	TUL	AA	23	435	65	17	5	17	53	24	105	3	0	.275/.345/.477	120	21.2	.331	2.8	1B(44): -0.8, RF(28): -0.1	1.9
	1B	CHT	AA	23	116	15	2	3	3	16	12	32	1	0	.276/.371/.449	98	6.7	.369	0.7	LF(8): 0.7, RF(7): 0.5	0.5
Michael Reed	CF	MIS	AA	25	175	33	13	0	4	14	30	43	6	3	.314/.446/.493	116	23.0	.426	1.2	CF(30): -5.1, LF(8): -0.8	0.3
	CF	GWN	AAA	25	229	36	13	0	7	25	32	55	4	0	.363/.459/.539	139	26.2	.477	-2.3	CF(26): 1.1, RF(12): -1.2	1.5
	CF	ATL	MLB	25	7	1	0	0	0	0	0	3	0	0	.286/.286/.286	77	-0.3	.500	0.0	LF(1): 0.0	0.0
Yunior Severino	2B	ELZ	Rk	18	218	32	8	0	8	28	17	52	0	1	.263/.321/.424	96	5.9	.314	0.1	2B(38): 3.7, SS(10): 0.8	1.0
LaMonte Wade	LF	CHT	AA	24	201	30	2	1	7	27	26	20	5	2	.298/.393/.444	137	11.9	.301	1.5	LF(25): 1.1, CF(10): 1.1	1.8
	LF	ROC	AAA	24	294	24	9	3	4	21	38	54	5	1	.229/.337/.336	102	2.0	.277	0.2	LF(58): 2.8, RF(16): 0.5	1.1

Tremendous feel for putting the bat on the ball and for the strike zone make **Luis Arraez** an interesting prospect, but his lack of power and a serious knee injury have dimmed that star. ⓧ **Randy Cesar** broke a nice Texas League record last set in 1969 with a 42-game hitting streak, but he came well short of the nicest record in the minors, Joe Wilhoit's 69-gamer that has stood for a hundred seasons. ⓧ Beloved in every clubhouse he's occupied and formerly a fine defensive catcher, **Chris Gimenez** called it a career as a player and immediately joined the Dodgers' coaching staff. ⓧ **Zack Granite** hit rock bottom in 2018, in large part thanks to a shoulder injury, but still has plenty of speed and draws enough walks for a backup outfielder. ⓧ **Wander Javier** has yet to play above rookie-ball and didn't play at all in 2018 following shoulder surgery, yet still gets plenty of prospect hype thanks to a high-upside bat and the potential to remain a plus shortstop. ⓧ Second-round 2018 draftee **Ryan Jeffers** has a great stick for a catcher, but fell that far in June because most observers worry that he won't stick behind the dish. ⓧ If there's power coming, it's coming slowly, but svelte Brazilian outfielder **Gabriel Maciel** does everything else fast, including (so far) ascend the minor-league ladder. ⓧ A versatile infielder with plenty of pop and some control of the zone, **Jose Miranda** is now tasked with proving his bat can carry a likely move to third base. ⓧ **Gregorio Petit** has played in the majors for parts of six seasons, spread over 11 years, because general managers sometimes pick their utility infielders using random number generators. ⓧ First basemen nearly always need a better approach than **Luke Raley**'s, but he can fake it in the outfield if desperately needed and there's real pop in his bat. ⓧ **Michael Reed** apparently discovered the secret to hitting while in Triple-A, which angered the baseball gods into giving him a lower back strain that ended his successful season in early September. Claimed off waivers by the Twins in November, he warrants a look as someone's fourth outfielder. ⓧ Where the Braves saw only a second baseman and an opportunity to exploit the international signing system, the Twins saw **Yunior Severino**, whose stick and arm will play on either side of second base. ⓧ OBP is Life, Life is OBP, and that makes **LaMonte Wade** a bon vivant worth watching, despite his dearth of other tools.

Pitchers

PITCHER	TEAM	LVL	AGE	W	L	SV	G	GS	IP	H	HR	BB/9	K/9	K	GB%	BABIP	WHIP	ERA	DRA	WARP	MPH	FB%	WHF	CSP
Matt Belisle	CLE	MLB	38	0	0	0	8	0	10²	9	1	0.8	3.4	4	46%	.222	0.94	5.06	5.06	0.0	91.8	51.4	12.1	51.8
	COH	AAA	38	0	0	1	9	0	10²	10	1	0.8	9.3	11	55%	.321	1.03	4.22	3.92	0.1				
	MIN	MLB	38	1	1	0	25	0	23²	40	5	3.8	8.0	21	49%	.432	2.11	9.13	6.07	-0.3	93.1	55	12.9	45
Alan Busenitz	ROC	AAA	27	2	3	7	27	1	40	32	3	1.8	10.1	45	49%	.293	1.00	2.47	3.19	0.9				
	MIN	MLB	27	4	1	0	23	0	25¹	37	8	5.0	9.2	26	36%	.382	2.01	7.82	6.91	-0.6	97.1	63.9	11.4	46.7
John Curtiss	ROC	AAA	25	2	4	10	38	1	55¹	41	3	5.0	9.9	61	40%	.264	1.30	2.77	2.79	1.5				
	MIN	MLB	25	0	1	0	8	0	6¹	8	0	5.7	9.9	7	10%	.421	1.89	5.68	5.29	0.0	95.9	65.2	11.3	47.3
Chase De Jong	ARK	AA	24	5	5	0	21	21	120²	122	12	2.5	6.6	89	41%	.296	1.29	3.80	4.91	0.6				
	ROC	AAA	24	2	3	0	7	5	39¹	37	2	2.7	7.8	34	32%	.297	1.25	3.20	4.30	0.5				
	MIN	MLB	24	1	1	0	4	4	17²	18	3	3.1	6.6	13	31%	.288	1.36	3.57	5.23	0.0	91.3	52.9	9	47.7
Tyler Jay	CHT	AA	24	4	5	2	38	2	59²	74	7	3.0	7.4	49	42%	.349	1.58	4.22	5.67	-0.5				
Aaron Slegers	ROC	AAA	25	5	7	0	15	15	85¹	85	12	2.0	6.0	57	45%	.283	1.22	3.80	5.75	-0.2				
	MIN	MLB	25	1	1	0	4	2	13²	17	3	1.3	4.0	6	39%	.292	1.39	5.27	6.00	-0.1	91.9	68.5	7.4	48.6
Devin Smeltzer	TUL	AA	22	5	5	0	23	14	83²	94	9	2.0	7.2	67	39%	.321	1.35	4.73	4.22	1.0				
	CHT	AA	22	0	0	4	10	0	12	14	0	1.5	12.0	16	36%	.389	1.33	3.00	2.96	0.3				
Kohl Stewart	CHT	AA	23	3	4	0	14	14	68	84	3	2.8	9.4	71	58%	.389	1.54	4.76	4.63	0.6				
	ROC	AAA	23	0	3	0	7	5	40²	45	4	2.7	6.6	30	58%	.333	1.40	3.98	4.65	0.4				
	MIN	MLB	23	2	1	0	8	4	36²	34	1	4.4	5.9	24	56%	.292	1.42	3.68	5.88	-0.3	94.5	70.2	7.5	43.9

Professional teammate **Matt Belisle** can still soak up innings and be wrung for goodwill in the clubhouse, so if you can find room in your organization for a good towel, you can find room for him, too. ⓧ **Alan Busenitz** typifies the late-blooming, hard-throwing, forgettable and fungible reliever: a high-90s fastball that's already flattening out on him, and a breaking ball that doesn't miss bats. And now a trip to Japan. ⓧ A spring surgery and a summer trade for Fernando Rodney have eroded **Dakota Chalmers'** already-fading pedigree, but that pedigree existed for a reason. ⓧ Old-school #flow and a lovely fastball won't be enough to keep **John Curtiss** in a big-League bullpen, unless he much improves the command of his slider. ⓧ Pitchers long on pitchability and short on stuff, like **Chase De Jong**, can ill afford the tick down on everything that De Jong suffered in 2018. ⓧ Some other team won the World Series, but the Twins did what every other team tried to do and failed: unlock **Oliver Drake's** latent greatness, in the form of twenty strong late-season innings. Then, they cut him. ⓧ Former top-10 pick **Tyler Jay** was left off the 40-man roster and went unpicked in the Rule 5 draft, but there's still a potentially useful reliever here if his health holds up. ⓧ Built like a power forward, **Aaron Slegers** pitches too much like a point guard, dishing up meatballs so hittable he should get assists on all those home runs allowed. ⓧ Southpaw and cancer survivor **Devin Smeltzer** made a midseason move to the bullpen, and to the Twins in the Brian Dozier swap. He also saw everything take off, thanks in large part to streamlining his repertoire. ⓧ With a heavy sinker and nothing else of big-league quality, **Kohl Stewart** will try to carve out a fringe career based on the name value of his pedigree as a top-five draft pick.

NEW YORK METS

Essay by Roger Cormier

Player comments by Bryan Grosnick and BP staff

Are the Mets funny?

Their stadium literally caught fire. They lost a game 25-4 (it was 25-1 after eight innings). They lost another game 15-0 (it was 1-0 after seven innings). They hit out of order. They canceled a replica batting practice pullover giveaway hours before it was scheduled because of a "quality control issue". Their offense at one point cobbled together the lowest batting average by any major-league team in a homestand of at least seven games since 1900. One of their star pitchers missed time due to hand-foot-and-mouth disease, an illness most common with young children (he is 26 and does not have kids.) Their other star pitcher was the near unanimous National League Cy Young winner, but he won with a 10-9 record because of historically low run support. He broke a record by winning the Cy Young with the fewest wins ever. By three.

This all happened in 2018.

So far, yeah, this is fairly funny. Nobody died in the physical sense, so even better.

There is more, unfortunately.

The Mets play in New York, the largest media market on planet Earth, and they haven't even gotten their Amazon headquarters yet. There have always been and always will be literally millions of Mets fans that are willing to go to their games, even the day after they lose 25-4. The team owns 65 percent of SNY, the network that exclusively broadcasts their games locally. Each owner in Major League Baseball before 2018, which by definition includes Fred Wilpon, the principal owner of this team, received a reported $50 million from the BAMTech sale. Fred, his son Jeff (the team COO), and team president Saul Katz went from possibly needing to pony up over $1 billion to the victims of Bernie Madoff's Ponzi scheme in 2011 to being ordered to pay up $61 million five years later, in installments. It was estimated that ownership made $46 million in local TV revenues in 2016 alone. The $525 million national television contract is split among all 30 teams. There was enough money for Jeff to spend $20 million on an eSports team.

The Mets have money, is what I'm getting at here.

METS PROSPECTUS
2018 W-L: 77-85, 4TH IN NL EAST

Pythag	.479	17th	B-Age		28.4	20th
RS/G	4.17	23rd	P-Age		27.9	14th
RA/G	4.36	16th	Salary		$150.6M	12th
DRC+	89	24th	M$/MW		$4.8M	10th
DRA	3.82	4th	DL Days		1753	30th
FIP	3.93	9th	$ on DL		45%	30th
DER	.705	17th				

- Opened 2009
- Open air
- Natural surface
- Fence profile: 8'

Three-Year Park Factors

Runs	Runs/RH	Runs/LH	HR/RH	HR/LH
94	94	94	100	95

Top Hitter WARP	3.5 Brandon Nimmo
Top Pitcher WARP	8.0 Jacob deGrom
Top Prospect	Andres Gimenez

2018 Hit List Ranking

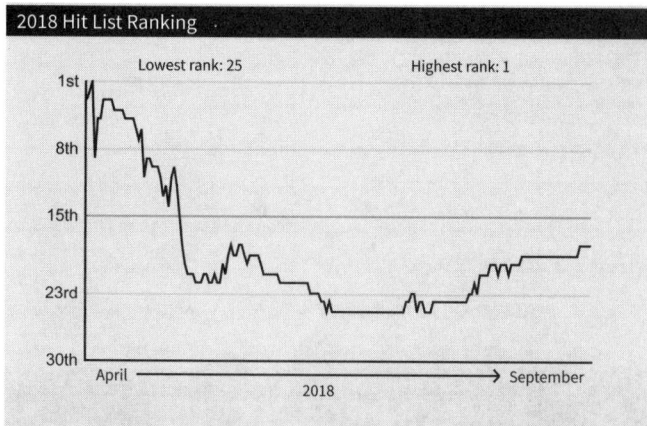

Lowest rank: 25   Highest rank: 1

April ⟶ September
2018

Committed Payroll (in millions)

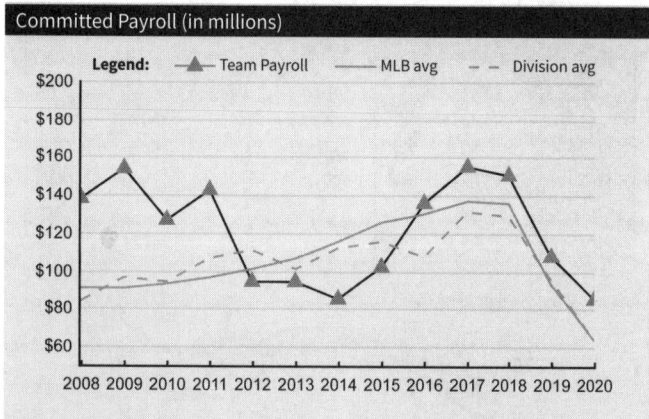

Legend: — Team Payroll — MLB avg - - - Division avg

2008 2009 2010 2011 2012 2013 2014 2015 2016 2017 2018 2019 2020

Farm System Ranking

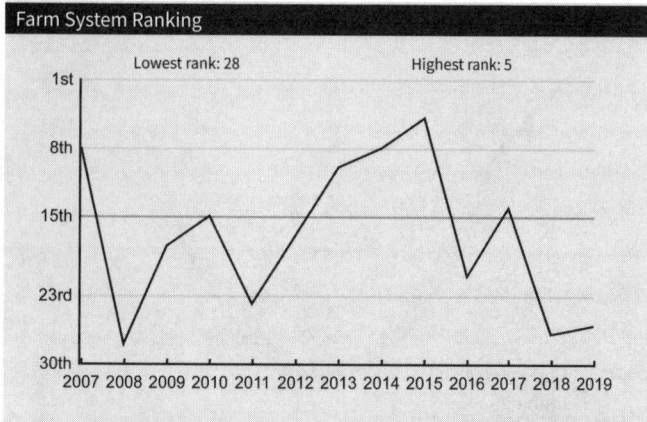

Lowest rank: 28   Highest rank: 5

2007 2008 2009 2010 2011 2012 2013 2014 2015 2016 2017 2018 2019

Personnel

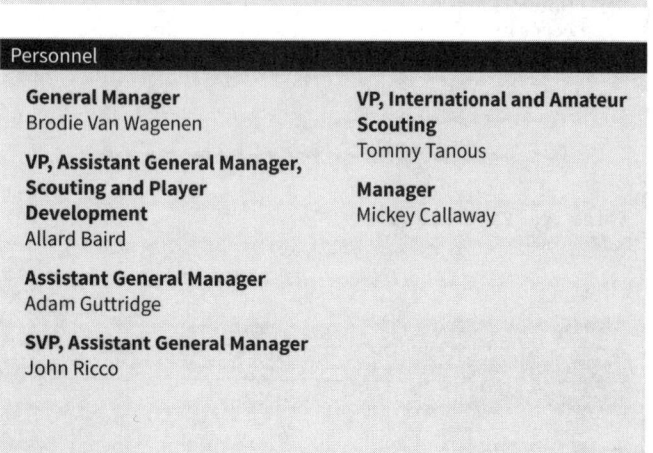

General Manager
Brodie Van Wagenen

VP, Assistant General Manager, Scouting and Player Development
Allard Baird

Assistant General Manager
Adam Guttridge

SVP, Assistant General Manager
John Ricco

VP, International and Amateur Scouting
Tommy Tanous

Manager
Mickey Callaway

Yet the team's Opening Day payroll in 2018 was about $150.5 million, down from the previous year. You would have needed to add more than $46 million to reach the luxury tax threshold. Even if you factor in the famous yearly installment they have to pay an old friend every July 1, they are more than $45 million away. The threshold is a soft salary cap. You could, technically, go over that number. The other professional baseball franchise in New York went over the luxury tax threshold every year since the tax's existence, up until 2018. That team almost always makes the postseason, unlike the Mets. Every owner in baseball now has become an industrial strength scoundrel and act as if the soft salary cap is a hard one, but the Wilpons are their heroes.

Ownership did not put their monies towards math. They had three full-time employees in their analytics department last season. The Yankees had 20. In a 2018 season post mortem, Jeff Wilpon claimed[1] the former general manager Sandy Alderson was cool with just the three. This was a particularly ridiculous and pathetic claim because he said this after Alderson resigned due to the return of his cancer, and Alderson was literally the mentor to Billy Beane, the man behind *Moneyball*. *The Athletic* reported that Jeff Wilpon's obvious lie was a lie within 24 hours of the statement.

Published reports claimed that the teeny tiny analytics department was not even listened to anyway. They were against[2] the Jay Bruce and Jason Vargas signings. Vargas finished with a 5.77 ERA. Bruce's WARP in 2018 was 0.12.

When Omar Minaya was GM of the Mets, according to a report that came out recently, he wanted one of his interns, a young man named David Stearns, promoted to a full-time analytics person. Fred and Jeff would not pony up the money[3]. David now runs the Milwaukee Brewers, who are really good without spending that much money.

It appears you are spitting out your beverage. This is funny to you. Good! I'll keep going.

Jeff also claimed Sandy Alderson's regime was responsible for the lack of big free agent spending. He then did not commit to signing a top tier free agent like Manny Machado. Jeff definitely did not bring up the fact that his father Fred more than once saved Terry Collins' job[4] when Sandy Alderson wanted to fire him, or that Fred rejected a trade Sandy had made with Cleveland for Jason Kipnis because of money[5], after refusing to tell Sandy Alderson how much money he could spend in the first place[6].

The Mets would have you know some other organizations do not spend to the limit and still succeed. Those organizations are able to identify their young talent and exploit those youths' talents before they reach free agency.

Yeah, the Mets do not do that. They have been blessed with good and potentially great young talent, one assumes usually by accident, based on how well they can evaluate their own talent. We all know The Tale of Justin Turner, and the Daniel Murphy Saga, but much less know of the following: Brandon Nimmo blossomed into an above-average everyday player in 2018, even though he was supposed to be blocked by Jay Bruce. It was revealed during this past season that when Wallace Matthews of Forbes asked the then-manager of the Mets, Terry Collins, why Nimmo wasn't playing regularly during the second half of the 2017 season when the Mets were comfortably out of playoff contention, Collins said, "Oh, we know what we got", and not in a fun, good vibes way. When Terry Collins was "reassigned" after the 2017 season, he became a special assistant to the General Manager. He was seen at various points during 2018 overlooking minor league games, growing increasingly certain of what they got.

The Mets featured Jose Reyes, a wayyyyyyy-past-his-prime former star player who had been suspended for 51 games for alleged domestic violence. Mickey Callaway started him eight games in a nine day stretch last July, instead of letting rookies show their potential worth. At least, that is what some of this team's fan base believed, because they mistakenly believed the manager was in charge of such decisions. Fred Wilpon loves the way-past-his-prime player, and more specifically loved how inexpensive he was for the team. And he loved these things while reportedly sitting in the manager's office before and after games after he said he would not do that anymore.

Reyes was so bad, and the usage of this player so egregious, that the critically acclaimed in-game announcers—Gary Cohen, Ron Darling, and Keith Hernandez—who it should again be noted work for a network 65 percent owned by Fred Wilpon—repeatedly noted with exasperation that Jose Reyes was starting, never once blaming the manager, but stopping short of saying who they all knew was really responsible. The final indignity was when everybody with a functioning brain asked the Mets why their sizzling hot second base prospect in Triple-A, Jeff McNeil, was in Triple-A, and were told with a straight face it was because the second base prospect could not possibly play other positions like, say, third base, where it just so happened Jose Reyes was currently playing. McNeil began to play third base in Triple-A almost immediately, and played there sometimes after he was eventually promoted, too. McNeil finished his rookie year 120th out of 1,270 players in bWARP. Reyes finished tied for 1,215th place.

Reyes was so unbelievably awful that he will surely not be signed yet again for 2019, but you never know. What we do know as of this writing is the Mets did bring back Jeurys Familia, when other relief pitchers who have never been suspended for a domestic incident were available, including Andrew Miller, a great pitcher who had his best seasons with Mickey Callaway as his pitching coach. Did I mention the first majority owner of the Mets was Joan Whitney Payson, the first female owner of a professional baseball franchise who did not inherit it?

You are shaking your head and looking disgusted. Fair enough.

Might as well bring up Brodie Van Wagenen. The Mets hired the prominent agent as their new general manager. This raised red flags around the game, since he might possess inside information with some former clients, some of whom are still on the team. Cynical thinking, sure. Maybe they just hired him because his father-in-law was Neil Armstrong, and that's cool. But then Noah Syndergaard, a client of Van Wagenen's old agency, was suddenly very much on the trading block.

Not that it matters. Peter Gammons said as far back as 10 years ago that Jeff Wilpon is the real general manager of the Mets[7]. Jeff has recently confirmed he has final say on all personnel matters[8].

Okay, I see you shaking your head and trying to moonwalk away from me. But you are also smirking. This is still kind of funny to you! Just definitely no longer ha ha funny.

Yes, I know I sound cynical. There's a new sheriff in town! And the gun the mayor gives his sheriffs is a gun made of newspaper from 1955.

Fine, Robinson Cano is still good. Edwin Diaz is exciting. Weird the Mets had to trade top prospects and did not spend money on players who won't be 40 years old when their contract expires but hey, Wilson Ramos is good when healthy.

Ah, "when healthy." I hate that phrase so.

David Wright, the one who discovered he suffered from spinal stenosis at the age of 32, played one final game in 2018 and had himself an emotional farewell. My television screen definitely got a little blurry that evening. He could not use the word "retire" though, out of ownership's fear insurance would stop paying 75 percent of his salary. While collecting those insurance funds (but not applying them back to the payroll budget), Jeff used one of the franchise's most beloved players ever as an excuse for their lack of spending. That was fun.

Yoenis Cespedes played hurt for a month and everybody with eyes knew it. He returned two months later to play one game, then announced after that game he needed surgery on both of his heels. He did not play another game in 2018, and is due out for at least half of 2019.

Oh goodness, I almost forgot Matt Harvey. After he was demoted to the bullpen he told the New York Times beat writer "I don't [expletive] want to" talk to the media about it. He was traded, and most fans were shocked he did not immediately become an ace again, because they've internalized this belief they are "snakebitten," as Fred Wilpon once confirmed to The New Yorker years ago.

A multi-millionaire wants the fans to believe this franchise's raison d'être is truly what it appeared to be since its 1962 inception as presented by Jimmy Breslin: a representation of New Yorkers of the lower and middle classes who could not relate to those Yankees who were compared to U.S. Steel and Coca-Cola. This Goofus and Gallant dynamic is ingrained, destined to play out in men hitting horsehide with wooden sticks until the end of civilized times, except we now do not bother mentioning the middle class because that disappeared, and we switch out the sugar water conglomerate with Amazon and keep telling that story.

Got it? Or maybe we factor in this team's ownership's constant hoodwinking and overall shadiness? Do we factor in both? Does it even matter?

Does any of this matter?

Because the Mets might be pretty good, despite all of *motions to the universe* this. They made the World Series not all that long ago! Their farm system is no longer considered one of the worst in the sport. This team, every damn spring, by virtue of always plotting and scheming their way to a projected .500 season but with a glossy sheen of

Pretty Decent *When Healthy*, is always on the cusp of Something Painfully Bad or Something Special. Usually, it's the former. Every so often, it proves to be the latter. It happens often enough to always keep you interested. God, it is always entertaining. They always get you in the end.

And now you are pointing and laughing at me. With me? It doesn't matter. ▪

—*Roger Cormier is an author of Baseball Prospectus.*

1. Anderson, R.J. "Mets ownership blamed Sandy Alderson for lack of spending and analytics staff." CBSSports.com. Accessed 26 December 2018. https://www.cbssports.com/mlb/news/mets-ownership-blamed-sandy-alderson-for-lack-of-spending-and-analytics-staff/

2. Ehalt, Matt. "NY Mets may be limiting GM field if they're not open to fully embracing analytics." Northjersey.com. Accessed 26 December 2018. https://www.northjersey.com/story/sports/mlb/mets/2018/10/04/ny-mets-may-limiting-gm-field-not-open-fully-embracing-analytics/1522928002/

3. Healey, Tim. "Mets experts at picking future executives but not keeping them." Newsday. Accessed 26 December 2018. https://www.newsday.com/sports/baseball/mets/mets-have-watched-homegrown-gm-candidates-blossom-elsewhere-1.21909689

4. Carig, Marc. "Sources: Mets owner Fred Wilpon protected Terry Collins from getting fired." Newsday. Accessed 26 December 2018. https://www.newsday.com/sports/baseball/mets/sources-mets-owner-fred-wilpon-protected-terry-collins-from-getting-fired-1.14297441

5. Carig, Marc. "Without another strong arm in the rotation, the Mets are doomed to mediocrity." The Athletic. Accessed 26 December 2018. https://theathletic.com/238391/2018/02/12/carig-without-another-strong-arm-in-the-rotation-the-mets-are-doomed-to-mediocrity/, January 5, 1952, p. 10.

6. Carig, Marc. "Mets analysis: Wilpons need to be more transparent about payroll, offseason moves." Newsday. Accessed 26 December 2018. https://www.newsday.com/sports/baseball/mets/mets-jeff-wilpon-1.15485312, January 5, 1952, p. 10.

7. Cerrone, Matthew. "Gammons: Jeff Wilpon is GM of the Mets." SNY Mets Blog. Accessed 26 December 2018. https://www.sny.tv/mets/news/gammons-jeff-wilpon-is-gm-of-the-mets/149375936

8. Ehalt, Matt. "Jeff Wilpon admits frustration with how the Mets have performed." Northjersey.com. Accessed 26 December 2018. https://www.northjersey.com/story/sports/mlb/mets/2018/06/26/ny-mets-coo-jeff-wilpon-says-mets-have-not-met-their-expectations/736653002/

HITTERS

Peter Alonso 1B   Born: 12/07/94   Age: 24   Bats: R   Throws: R   Height: 6'3"   Weight: 245   Origin: Round 2, 2016 Draft (#64 overall)

YEAR	TEAM	LVL	AGE	PA	R	2B	3B	HR	RBI	BB	K	SB	CS	AVG/OBP/SLG	DRC+	VORP	BABIP	BRR	FRAA	WARP
2016	BRO	A-	21	123	20	12	1	5	21	11	22	0	1	.321/.382/.587	121	14.1	.357	-0.5	1B(27): 2.3	0.6
2017	SLU	A+	22	346	45	23	0	16	58	25	64	3	4	.286/.361/.516	142	11.8	.314	-5.8	1B(78): 3.2	2.0
2017	BIN	AA	22	47	7	4	1	2	5	2	7	0	0	.311/.340/.578	111	3.3	.333	-0.1	1B(5): 0.1	0.1
2018	BIN	AA	23	273	42	12	0	15	52	43	50	0	2	.314/.440/.573	159	30.5	.344	-1.6	1B(51): 1.8	2.4
2018	LVG	AAA	23	301	50	19	1	21	67	33	78	0	1	.260/.355/.585	135	14.6	.284	1.2	1B(59): 5.0	2.5
2019	NYN	MLB	24	375	48	15	1	19	54	33	105	0	0	.230/.314/.451	105	7.3	.277	-0.8	1B 2	1.0

Breakout: 19%   Improve: 39%   Collapse: 17%   Attrition: 24%   MLB: 68%   Comparables: *Rhys Hoskins, Chris Carter, A.J. Reed*

When you hit at every level in the minor leagues, at some point you have to look past any flaws and give a man a chance. So nevermind that Alonso is a right-handed first baseman with little defensive value and no flexibility; he led the minor leagues in homers last season after ripping up both the Eastern and Pacific Coast League. By mid-season, it became fairly well-established that the former Gator was the best first baseman in the system, and that didn't just include rival prospect Dom Smith. The lack of a September call-up audibly frustrated Alonso, who took out his aggression on a few pitchers in the Arizona Fall League where he hit another half-dozen dingers. While there are precious few right-right first basemen worthy of everyday playing time at the game's highest level, Alonso has made it clear that he deserves his shot as a starter in 2019.

Robinson Cano 2B Born: 10/22/82 Age: 36 Bats: L Throws: R Height: 6'0" Weight: 210 Origin: International Free Agent, 2001

YEAR	TEAM	LVL	AGE	PA	R	2B	3B	HR	RBI	BB	K	SB	CS	AVG/OBP/SLG	DRC+	VORP	BABIP	BRR	FRAA	WARP
2016	SEA	MLB	33	715	107	33	2	39	103	47	100	0	1	.298/.350/.533	131	46.0	.299	-1.7	2B(157): 4.2	5.3
2017	SEA	MLB	34	648	79	33	0	23	97	49	85	1	0	.280/.338/.453	108	23.1	.294	-2.0	2B(150): -7.3	1.8
2018	SEA	MLB	35	348	44	22	0	10	50	32	47	0	0	.303/.374/.471	117	23.6	.329	-0.4	2B(69): -2.5, 1B(14): 0.3	1.5
2019	NYN	MLB	36	579	66	32	2	17	74	51	82	1	1	.280/.351/.447	119	30.6	.305	-1.3	2B -1, 1B 0	3.2

Breakout: 2% Improve: 30% Collapse: 6% Attrition: 6% MLB: 90% *Comparables: Del Pratt, Chase Utley, Carlos Guillen*

With a contract like Cano's, everything gets measured in the millions. How many millions left on the ledger? How many millions earned over the entire career? How many millions did the Mariners save over his 80-game suspension for the banned substance Furosemide? How many millions earned per win produced on the field? Perhaps that's one of the biggest dangers of the mega-contract, because to focus so intently on the financial aspect is to obscure what is rapidly becoming one of the greatest careers any second baseman has ever had. Despite playing only half a season in 2018, Cano was, once again, one of the most productive players at the keystone position. At 36 there's plenty of reason to speculate how long he can do it, but until he actually shows noticeable degradation of skills the Mets should not feel any pressing need to move him anywhere else. His career is already one of the greats, one whose direct path to Cooperstown is hopefully not marred by a lapse in judgment or misreading of a pharmaceutical bottle. If he can maintain healthy, near-peak production for a few more seasons, he will have cemented himself as one of the four or five greatest second basemen of the modern era. Of the millions who have played baseball, that's not bad company.

Yoenis Cespedes LF Born: 10/18/85 Age: 33 Bats: R Throws: R Height: 5'10" Weight: 220 Origin: International Free Agent, 2012

YEAR	TEAM	LVL	AGE	PA	R	2B	3B	HR	RBI	BB	K	SB	CS	AVG/OBP/SLG	DRC+	VORP	BABIP	BRR	FRAA	WARP
2016	NYN	MLB	30	543	72	25	1	31	86	51	108	3	1	.280/.354/.530	130	48.4	.298	-1.9	LF(80): 7.7, CF(63): -5.2	3.8
2017	NYN	MLB	31	321	46	17	2	17	42	26	61	0	1	.292/.352/.540	119	23.9	.316	-1.1	LF(74): 2.9	1.8
2018	NYN	MLB	32	157	20	6	0	9	29	13	50	3	0	.262/.325/.496	97	11.1	.333	0.5	LF(35): 1.8	0.6
2019	NYN	MLB	33	163	20	8	1	7	23	14	39	1	0	.262/.332/.464	119	8.2	.316	-0.3	LF 2	1.1

Breakout: 0% Improve: 25% Collapse: 7% Attrition: 6% MLB: 98% *Comparables: Ryan Braun, Scott Hairston, Alfonso Soriano*

For years, the Mets have played their brightest offensive star through a litany of injuries, both major and minor, in an attempt to get his potent bat into a sagging lineup. In 2018, the bill came due. Even as a hip flexor strain sucked months from his season, Cespedes was every bit the offensive dynamo advertised when the team acquired him. However, July brought with it the end of Cespedes' season. It will now be two heel surgeries and perhaps as much as a full year of rehab before he's likely to don a Mets uniform again. If he's back in the second half of 2019, expect him to be every bit the slugger he's always been: phenomenal raw power packed into a body that can barely contain it, bursting from the stress. He's already proven he can play through the pain, but the Mets are hoping there's less of it this year.

Michael Conforto OF Born: 03/01/93 Age: 26 Bats: L Throws: R Height: 6'1" Weight: 215 Origin: Round 1, 2014 Draft (#10 overall)

YEAR	TEAM	LVL	AGE	PA	R	2B	3B	HR	RBI	BB	K	SB	CS	AVG/OBP/SLG	DRC+	VORP	BABIP	BRR	FRAA	WARP
2016	LVG	AAA	23	144	30	8	2	9	28	13	18	2	2	.422/.483/.727	172	20.1	.446	-1.1	LF(18): 0.4, RF(6): 1.0	1.6
2016	NYN	MLB	23	348	38	21	1	12	42	36	89	2	1	.220/.310/.414	92	12.6	.267	1.2	LF(73): 0.8, RF(9): 0.7	0.8
2017	NYN	MLB	24	440	72	20	1	27	68	57	113	2	0	.279/.384/.555	132	47.8	.328	1.4	LF(52): 3.9, CF(43): -3.6	3.3
2018	NYN	MLB	25	638	78	25	1	28	82	84	159	3	4	.243/.350/.448	112	36.2	.289	-4.2	LF(84): 1.1, CF(58): -7.3	1.8
2019	NYN	MLB	26	588	77	27	2	26	85	69	145	3	2	.251/.352/.465	122	32.3	.304	-0.5	LF 1, RF 0	3.3

Breakout: 3% Improve: 62% Collapse: 1% Attrition: 4% MLB: 99% *Comparables: Carlos Quentin, Carlos Gonzalez, Justin Upton*

A miserable shoulder injury ended Conforto's All-Star 2017 season and threatened the start of his 2018 season as well. For well-trained Mets fans, it was quite a surprise how quickly he "recovered" and that he ended up seeing 153 games of duty last year, but the shoulder injury clearly affected his season throughout. He certainly did not appear healthy early in the year, and it showed in his offensive performance. Conforto couldn't regularly make his signature brand of loud contact, and he tried to adapt by being overly patient at the plate to find his way on base. By the second half of the season, his shoulder and stat line both looked a lot healthier. Scooter got more aggressive, the contact got louder, and balls started flying over the wall more regularly. A full season of total health should remind everyone just how rock-solid Conforto's offense can be.

Travis d'Arnaud C Born: 02/10/89 Age: 30 Bats: R Throws: R Height: 6'2" Weight: 210 Origin: Round 1, 2007 Draft (#37 overall)

YEAR	TEAM	LVL	AGE	PA	R	2B	3B	HR	RBI	BB	K	SB	CS	AVG/OBP/SLG	DRC+	VORP	BABIP	BRR	FRAA	WARP
2016	NYN	MLB	27	276	27	7	0	4	15	19	50	0	0	.247/.307/.323	79	6.2	.293	-0.3	C(73): 8.2	1.5
2017	NYN	MLB	28	376	39	19	1	16	57	23	59	0	0	.244/.293/.443	99	15.8	.250	-2.2	C(93): 11.5, 3B(1): -0.1	2.8
2018	NYN	MLB	29	16	1	0	0	1	3	1	5	0	0	.200/.250/.400	87	0.6	.222	-0.1	C(4): 1.0	0.1
2019	NYN	MLB	30	169	18	8	1	5	19	13	33	0	0	.251/.313/.403	99	6.5	.291	-0.4	C 4	1.1

Breakout: 0% Improve: 41% Collapse: 10% Attrition: 10% MLB: 94% *Comparables: Ramon Hernandez, Josh Bard, Michael Barrett*

YEAR	TEAM	P. COUNT	FRM RUNS	BLK RUNS	THRW RUNS	TOT RUNS
2016	NYN	10281	8.1	1.0	-2.5	6.2
2017	NYN	13404	11.2	0.9	-3.1	9.0
2018	NYN	689	1.0	0.1	0.0	1.0
2019	NYN	4799	3.6	0.3	-0.8	3.1

d'Arnaud's career has been one of qualified compliments—he's a good hitter *for a catcher*, or he's a potential All-Star *if he can stay healthy*—but now he'll likely never qualify for a big-league batting title. This go-round, it took just four games before he tore his UCL and knocked himself out for the season, out of the Mets' future plans and potentially out of a career behind the dish. Now what? His steady job is gone. His 20s are toast. And the position that granted him so much value is at risk, if not missing in action. If his patience and power haven't faded, then some squad will give him another chance once he hits free agency after the 2019 season. If he can resume a role as a backstop, his framing skills will make him valuable when he plays. But, for now, d'Arnaud will attempt to stay healthy in a supporting role and just doing that would qualify as a success at this point.

Rajai Davis LF Born: 10/19/80 Age: 38 Bats: R Throws: R Height: 5'10" Weight: 195 Origin: Round 38, 2001 Draft (#1134 overall)

YEAR	TEAM	LVL	AGE	PA	R	2B	3B	HR	RBI	BB	K	SB	CS	AVG/OBP/SLG	DRC+	VORP	BABIP	BRR	FRAA	WARP
2016	CLE	MLB	35	495	74	23	2	12	48	33	106	43	6	.249/.306/.388	88	6.3	.299	3.7	CF(80): 3.5, LF(66): 1.4	1.8
2017	OAK	MLB	36	328	49	17	2	5	18	26	70	26	6	.233/.294/.353	70	-1.5	.288	2.4	CF(79): -3.4, LF(19): -1.7	-0.4
2017	BOS	MLB	36	38	7	2	0	0	2	1	13	3	1	.250/.289/.306	71	-1.0	.391	0.1	LF(6): -0.5, RF(4): -0.2	-0.1
2018	CLE	MLB	37	216	33	6	1	1	6	11	48	21	7	.224/.278/.281	71	-4.4	.291	0.1	CF(47): 0.7, LF(30): -2.1	-0.2
2019	NYN	MLB	38	251	34	11	1	4	18	16	56	20	5	.233/.291/.339	70	-0.1	.292	0.6	CF 0, LF 0	-0.1

Breakout: 1% Improve: 23% Collapse: 16% Attrition: 27% MLB: 72%   Comparables: Al Nixon, Willie Wilson, Mike Kreevich

If you've tuned in to a national baseball broadcast in the last, oh, 15 years or so, you may have heard a former player lamenting the death of small ball and the vanishing of stolen bases. If Mr. Davis ever retires and becomes an announcer, he would certainly have more right to make the complaint than former first basemen or pitchers. Despite his advanced age, Davis still swiped more than 20 bags in part-time duty, as Cleveland brought back their World Series hero in a desperate attempt to throw anyone and anything at their outfield situation. He never possessed any real power or patience and his ability to hit for average looks like it might be cooked. His glove may not be too far behind. Even so, one suspects we will never see a Rajai Davis in the majors who can't steal a base.

Wilmer Flores INF Born: 08/06/91 Age: 27 Bats: R Throws: R Height: 6'3" Weight: 205 Origin: International Free Agent, 2007

YEAR	TEAM	LVL	AGE	PA	R	2B	3B	HR	RBI	BB	K	SB	CS	AVG/OBP/SLG	DRC+	VORP	BABIP	BRR	FRAA	WARP
2016	NYN	MLB	24	335	38	14	0	16	49	23	48	1	1	.267/.319/.469	118	21.9	.268	-2.4	3B(51): -4.0, 1B(27): 0.4	1.3
2017	NYN	MLB	25	362	42	17	1	18	52	17	54	1	1	.271/.307/.488	115	15.8	.270	-0.6	3B(55): 0.2, 1B(29): -0.2	1.7
2018	NYN	MLB	26	429	43	25	0	11	51	29	42	0	0	.267/.319/.417	104	13.0	.269	-3.2	1B(83): -2.6, 2B(13): 0.1	0.3
2019	NYN	MLB	27	395	45	23	2	14	53	26	50	1	0	.278/.333/.462	118	14.0	.290	-1.6	1B -2, 3B -1	1.2

Breakout: 5% Improve: 50% Collapse: 3% Attrition: 8% MLB: 97%   Comparables: James Loney, Eddie Waitkus, Eric Hosmer

This man is trying to break your heart. Despite playing for a team owned by, to put it bluntly, grifters and meddlers, Flores loves the New York Metropolitans in a way that puts most fans of the team to shame. He put up his typical season despite playing through various injuries. He continued to be jerked around in terms of playing time despite being the team's best right-handed hitting option at two or three positions. The Mets remained noncommittal about his future in blue and orange with free agency looming—all the way up until he received the diagnosis that he has early-onset arthritis in both of his knees, which ended his season early, and was likely why he was non-tendered. He does not deserve this.

Todd Frazier 3B Born: 02/12/86 Age: 33 Bats: R Throws: R Height: 6'3" Weight: 220 Origin: Round 1, 2007 Draft (#34 overall)

YEAR	TEAM	LVL	AGE	PA	R	2B	3B	HR	RBI	BB	K	SB	CS	AVG/OBP/SLG	DRC+	VORP	BABIP	BRR	FRAA	WARP
2016	CHA	MLB	30	666	89	21	0	40	98	64	163	15	5	.225/.302/.464	115	27.2	.236	2.4	3B(149): -2.4, 1B(7): -1.1	3.6
2017	CHA	MLB	31	335	41	15	0	16	44	48	71	4	3	.207/.328/.432	114	12.0	.214	-0.4	3B(67): 2.2, 1B(4): 0.5	2.0
2017	NYA	MLB	31	241	33	4	1	11	32	35	54	0	0	.222/.365/.423	114	10.2	.244	0.2	3B(66): 1.0	1.5
2018	NYN	MLB	32	472	54	18	0	18	59	48	112	9	4	.213/.303/.390	100	24.0	.241	2.5	3B(109): 5.9	2.6
2019	NYN	MLB	33	413	52	18	1	15	52	46	91	7	3	.233/.335/.414	105	12.7	.275	0.7	3B 1, 1B 0	1.4

Breakout: 1% Improve: 39% Collapse: 2% Attrition: 5% MLB: 94%   Comparables: David Freese, Scott Rolen, Carlos Guillen

The greatest trick the devil ever pulled was convincing the world he didn't exist. He's got nothing on Frazier, who fell into the stands to catch an Alex Verdugo pop fly, dropped the baseball, but swapped a nearby rubber toy ball to convince the umpires that he had pulled off an incredible diving grab. A second, less impressive trick has been the way Frazier has carried a reputation as a powerful slugger into the later stages of his career, when really he's getting by on his defense and near-average batting lines. Known for his durability, Frazier made the first two trips to the DL of his career in 2018 and flashed solid numbers both at the start of the season and after his second stint in August, but faded as those stretches of the season went on. He's a serviceable second-division starter and a convincing sleight-of-hand artist, but not the offensive threat he once was.

Andres Gimenez SS Born: 09/04/98 Age: 20 Bats: L Throws: R Height: 5'11" Weight: 161 Origin: International Free Agent, 2015

YEAR	TEAM	LVL	AGE	PA	R	2B	3B	HR	RBI	BB	K	SB	CS	AVG/OBP/SLG	DRC+	VORP	BABIP	BRR	FRAA	WARP
2016	MET	RK	17	141	24	10	4	1	17	21	13	7	1	.360/.461/.544	164	28.1	.388	2.1	SS(29): 7.1	2.4
2016	DME	RK	17	134	28	10	0	2	21	25	9	6	7	.340/.478/.500	166	20.0	.344	-0.9	SS(19): -2.9, 2B(12): -1.1	1.1
2017	COL	A	18	399	50	9	4	4	31	28	61	14	8	.265/.346/.349	104	22.5	.310	0.7	SS(89): 6.6	2.7
2018	SLU	A+	19	351	43	20	4	6	30	22	70	28	11	.282/.348/.432	102	24.9	.343	3.4	SS(83): 14.2, 2B(2): -0.1	3.5
2018	BIN	AA	19	153	19	9	1	0	16	9	22	10	3	.277/.344/.358	82	8.4	.330	1.2	SS(36): -1.3, 2B(1): 0.2	0.3
2019	NYN	MLB	20	251	30	6	1	6	20	10	54	9	4	.206/.259/.307	59	-2.6	.246	0.6	SS 3, 2B 0	0.1

Breakout: 2% Improve: 17% Collapse: 0% Attrition: 5% MLB: 19%   Comparables: Francisco Lindor, Elvis Andrus, Alen Hanson

Arguably the best prospect in the Mets' system, Gimenez isn't so much a star as he is a constellation; the whole surpasses the sum of the parts. He's possessed of many tiny points of light: the brightest might be the beginnings of a plus hit tool and better-than-average speed. Every piece of the picture matters. There's average leather at shortstop that could play up if he moves to second base, a hint at double-digit home-run power and a decidedly advanced approach for a guy who spent all of 2018 playing in both High-A and Double-A at 19 years old. If one light goes out, he could just be a utility player; if two dim, then he may not make it out of the minors. But if he continues on this path, the sky's the limit.

Luis Guillorme   INF   Born: 09/27/94   Age: 24   Bats: L   Throws: R   Height: 5'10"   Weight: 195   Origin: Round 10, 2013 Draft (#296 overall)

YEAR	TEAM	LVL	AGE	PA	R	2B	3B	HR	RBI	BB	K	SB	CS	AVG/OBP/SLG	DRC+	VORP	BABIP	BRR	FRAA	WARP
2016	SLU	A+	21	505	47	16	2	1	46	43	63	4	2	.263/.332/.315	94	9.9	.303	0.1	SS(72): -1.6, 2B(52): 4.0	1.7
2017	BIN	AA	22	558	70	20	0	1	43	72	55	4	3	.283/.376/.331	103	26.0	.316	3.4	2B(69): 4.1, SS(58): -2.1	2.9
2018	NYN	MLB	23	74	4	2	0	0	5	7	3	1	0	.209/.284/.239	94	-0.5	.219	0.7	3B(14): -1.8, 2B(8): -0.5	0.0
2018	LVG	AAA	23	281	41	15	2	3	33	30	39	2	1	.304/.380/.417	104	12.3	.350	0.3	SS(54): 1.9, 2B(9): -1.4	1.6
2019	*NYN*	*MLB*	*24*	*191*	*19*	*7*	*1*	*4*	*19*	*16*	*30*	*0*	*0*	*.244/.311/.361*	*85*	*2.8*	*.272*	*-0.2*	*SS 0, 3B -1*	*0.2*

Breakout: 7%   Improve: 14%   Collapse: 8%   Attrition: 20%   MLB: 35%   *Comparables: Jace Peterson, Dixon Machado, Kevin Newman*

Perhaps no player in the Mets' system was held down for as little reason as Guillorme, and that's saying something when Peter Alonso doesn't even get a September call-up. An exceptional defensive infielder, Guillorme has probably done all he needs to get a long look as a utility player … except figure out how to stop the Mets from rostering Jose Reyes. While Reyes was racking up negative value (and PR), Guillorme shuttled back and forth between Vegas and New York—which normally sounds like fun but isn't the best way to develop an infielder—and never got comfortable in his Flushing looks. No, he's not likely to hit for much game power (despite the occasional impressive BP round), but he has plenty of years left to prove his worth as an excellent gloveman in the Adam Everett mold.

Dilson Herrera   2B   Born: 03/03/94   Age: 25   Bats: R   Throws: R   Height: 5'10"   Weight: 210   Origin: International Free Agent, 2010

YEAR	TEAM	LVL	AGE	PA	R	2B	3B	HR	RBI	BB	K	SB	CS	AVG/OBP/SLG	DRC+	VORP	BABIP	BRR	FRAA	WARP
2016	LVG	AAA	22	389	61	24	2	13	55	27	72	6	7	.276/.327/.462	118	11.0	.313	0.5	2B(75): -4.7	1.7
2016	LOU	AAA	22	80	10	0	2	2	9	11	15	1	2	.266/.372/.422	112	6.4	.306	0.1	2B(16): -0.1	0.3
2017	LOU	AAA	23	265	31	9	1	7	42	15	61	2	4	.264/.312/.397	93	4.3	.322	-1.7	2B(55): 0.8, 3B(3): 0.2	0.4
2018	DAY	A+	24	92	18	3	1	2	8	7	19	1	1	.298/.359/.429	121	4.7	.365	1.0	2B(19): 3.1	0.9
2018	LOU	AAA	24	208	23	10	0	7	27	19	50	0	1	.297/.367/.465	116	10.1	.372	-2.8	2B(35): 0.6, 3B(11): 1.7	1.0
2018	CIN	MLB	24	97	11	5	0	5	11	8	39	0	0	.184/.268/.414	74	-0.4	.256	-0.6	2B(13): -0.7, LF(11): -0.2	-0.2
2019	*NYN*	*MLB*	*25*	*251*	*29*	*9*	*0*	*8*	*26*	*17*	*71*	*2*	*2*	*.217/.278/.364*	*67*	*-2.8*	*.277*	*-0.7*	*2B 0, 3B 1*	*-0.2*

Breakout: 4%   Improve: 26%   Collapse: 11%   Attrition: 23%   MLB: 70%   *Comparables: Jason Kipnis, Ryan Adams, Devon Travis*

Despite his youth and nearly-faded prospect sheen, Dilson Herrera hasn't shown much promise in recent years and his increasing lack of plate discipline doesn't give much hope that he'll rediscover any of that magic—not only was his strikeout rate obscene in his small sample with the Reds, but it has gone the wrong direction in each of his last three seasons in Triple-A. He'll play for a major-league team when there are injuries, but it's entirely possible that the 103 plate appearances with the Mets in 2015 are going to go down as his career high.

Austin Jackson   CF   Born: 02/01/87   Age: 32   Bats: R   Throws: R   Height: 6'1"   Weight: 198   Origin: Round 8, 2005 Draft (#259 overall)

YEAR	TEAM	LVL	AGE	PA	R	2B	3B	HR	RBI	BB	K	SB	CS	AVG/OBP/SLG	DRC+	VORP	BABIP	BRR	FRAA	WARP
2016	CHA	MLB	29	203	24	12	2	0	18	17	39	2	1	.254/.318/.343	84	0.4	.319	-0.4	CF(54): -1.2	0.2
2017	CLE	MLB	30	318	46	19	3	7	35	33	64	3	1	.318/.387/.482	108	20.9	.385	1.6	CF(38): -2.0, LF(38): 0.1	1.3
2018	SFN	MLB	31	165	12	8	0	0	13	14	59	2	1	.242/.309/.295	56	0.8	.396	0.9	CF(38): -4.5, LF(3): -0.2	-0.7
2018	NYN	MLB	31	210	17	9	1	3	19	12	74	1	2	.247/.290/.348	58	0.2	.380	-1.4	CF(53): 0.5	-0.4
2019	*NYN*	*MLB*	*32*	*346*	*35*	*17*	*2*	*5*	*32*	*30*	*91*	*4*	*2*	*.247/.315/.364*	*87*	*7.9*	*.329*	*0.0*	*CF -4, LF 0*	*0.5*

Breakout: 0%   Improve: 41%   Collapse: 3%   Attrition: 16%   MLB: 84%   *Comparables: Reed Johnson, Jacob Brumfield, Jack Smith*

A-Jax parlayed his 2017 resurgence into a nifty two-year deal with San Francisco and a host of compliments about being a "bargain" or a "great value." He promptly played his way out of a job in San Francisco's outfield—which is no mean feat—leading up to his release. He pulled off a neat trick afterwards, using his veteran presence and now-unfounded reputation for defense to broach a deeper outfield in New York, where he received plenty of playing time, sometimes at the expense of the team's two best position players: Brandon Nimmo and Michael Conforto. Did he play any better once he came to New York? Not really! But if there's one thing Jackson has figured out in his many years in the league, it's how to time a comeback.

Juan Lagares   CF   Born: 03/17/89   Age: 30   Bats: R   Throws: R   Height: 6'1"   Weight: 215   Origin: International Free Agent, 2006

YEAR	TEAM	LVL	AGE	PA	R	2B	3B	HR	RBI	BB	K	SB	CS	AVG/OBP/SLG	DRC+	VORP	BABIP	BRR	FRAA	WARP
2016	NYN	MLB	27	160	15	7	2	3	9	11	27	4	2	.239/.301/.380	82	2.4	.274	0.1	CF(68): 1.4, RF(2): 0.1	0.4
2017	NYN	MLB	28	272	37	16	2	3	15	14	56	7	3	.250/.296/.365	68	3.3	.309	1.9	CF(85): 6.2	0.7
2018	NYN	MLB	29	64	9	1	1	0	6	3	9	3	1	.339/.375/.390	82	5.7	.392	1.0	CF(20): 1.5	0.3
2019	*NYN*	*MLB*	*30*	*527*	*57*	*23*	*3*	*9*	*49*	*36*	*99*	*13*	*5*	*.245/.305/.364*	*81*	*10.3*	*.287*	*1.8*	*CF 4*	*1.5*

Breakout: 4%   Improve: 51%   Collapse: 7%   Attrition: 9%   MLB: 95%   *Comparables: Steve Finley, Ted Uhlaender, Harry Walker*

Over the past three years, Lagares has been injured often enough that you'd think the Mets are staging a revival of *Brigadoon* in the middle of their outfield. The team's fleet-of-foot and utterly platoonable center fielder only shows up once in a while, and with conditions. The thumb and oblique injuries that dogged him in '16 and '17 didn't recur, but he tore a toe ligament in May that required season-ending surgery. His sizzling start to the season proved that he can still be a valuable commodity when he takes the field, capable of providing excellent defense and the occasional run of hot hitting against lefties. But you're probably about as likely to find him spending regular time in the outfield as you are to find a magical, disappearing Scottish village, which is to say not very likely at all.

Ronny Mauricio SS

Born: 04/04/01   Age: 18   Bats: B   Throws: R   Height: 6'3"   Weight: 166   Origin: International Free Agent, 2017

YEAR	TEAM	LVL	AGE	PA	R	2B	3B	HR	RBI	BB	K	SB	CS	AVG/OBP/SLG	DRC+	VORP	BABIP	BRR	FRAA	WARP
2018	MTS	RK	17	212	26	13	3	3	31	10	31	1	6	.279/.307/.421	112	10.1	.310	-0.3	SS(45): 0.3	1.1
2018	KNG	RK	17	35	6	3	0	0	4	3	9	1	0	.233/.286/.333	77	1.9	.304	0.5	SS(8): -0.1	0.1
2019	NYN	MLB	18	251	17	6	0	5	21	10	81	0	0	.165/.198/.238	17	-17.4	.221	-1.5	SS 1	-1.8

Comparables: *Adalberto Mondesi, Wilmer Flores, Tommy Brown*

1. Mauricio has so much raw talent—he's a switch-hitting middle infielder that flashes power—that Lin-Manuel Miranda probably looks to *him* for inspiration.

2. Mauricio is just as likely to stick at shortstop—he's already 6'3"-6'4" and growing—as he is to get struck by lightning while getting eaten by a shark. *(Note that since he plays for the Mets, this is a legitimate, if unlikely, injury possibility.)*

3. Mauricio is so young—he played most of 2018 in the Gulf Coast League as a 17-year-old—that he's been around for less time than Outkast's *Stankonia*.

4. Mauricio is so far away from the majors that NASA just underwent a mission to land an unmanned probe on him.

Jeff McNeil 2B

Born: 04/08/92   Age: 27   Bats: L   Throws: R   Height: 6'1"   Weight: 195   Origin: Round 12, 2013 Draft (#356 overall)

YEAR	TEAM	LVL	AGE	PA	R	2B	3B	HR	RBI	BB	K	SB	CS	AVG/OBP/SLG	DRC+	VORP	BABIP	BRR	FRAA	WARP
2017	SLU	A+	25	116	13	7	0	3	15	7	19	2	2	.324/.388/.476	128	7.2	.373	-0.6	2B(18): -1.5, 3B(4): -0.3	0.4
2017	LVG	AAA	25	78	12	5	0	1	6	3	10	2	0	.254/.295/.366	99	0.4	.274	1.0	2B(17): 0.2, 3B(1): 0.6	0.4
2018	BIN	AA	26	241	49	16	3	14	43	22	23	3	0	.327/.402/.626	161	31.4	.316	1.7	2B(47): 3.9, 3B(9): -0.6	3.1
2018	LVG	AAA	26	143	23	10	2	5	28	14	19	3	0	.368/.427/.600	133	15.4	.394	0.4	2B(24): -3.3, 3B(3): -0.1	0.8
2018	NYN	MLB	26	248	35	11	6	3	19	14	24	7	1	.329/.381/.471	116	24.1	.359	0.8	2B(54): -2.6, 3B(3): 0.3	1.1
2019	NYN	MLB	27	576	63	28	5	14	67	39	84	8	2	.273/.333/.423	110	23.0	.303	0.6	3B -1, LF 1	2.3

Breakout: 8%   Improve: 45%   Collapse: 16%   Attrition: 28%   MLB: 95%

Comparables: *Rob Refsnyder, Jordany Valdespin, Justin Turner*

It wasn't supposed to be like this. A low-round draft pick, almost always old for his league, owner of just one preternatural skill: the ability to get hits. McNeil has been one of those players defined by his imperfections, including but not limited to a lack of pedigree and no ideal place to stand on the diamond except the batter's box. Year after year, McNeil put up big minor league numbers, until even a Mets organization who'd shown precious little faith in him as a big-leaguer was forced to give him a shot. McNeil took his opportunity and was as good a hitter on a rate basis as anyone on the Mets.

Here at BP, we know him by a number that isn't even on his jersey: *Six*. Coined by Jarrett Seidler, it refers to his opinion on McNeil's projected role in the big leagues as an above-average regular. McNeil may well be a first-division starter and a .300 hitter. After how good he's looked over the past couple of years, we're not allowed to be surprised by him anymore. Six has blossomed.

Devin Mesoraco C

Born: 06/19/88   Age: 31   Bats: R   Throws: R   Height: 6'1"   Weight: 229   Origin: Round 1, 2007 Draft (#15 overall)

YEAR	TEAM	LVL	AGE	PA	R	2B	3B	HR	RBI	BB	K	SB	CS	AVG/OBP/SLG	DRC+	VORP	BABIP	BRR	FRAA	WARP
2016	CIN	MLB	28	55	2	1	0	0	1	5	10	0	1	.140/.218/.160	72	-4.6	.175	-0.6	C(13): -1.8	-0.2
2017	PEN	AA	29	55	4	1	0	1	3	6	10	0	0	.170/.291/.255	96	-0.3	.194	-0.6	C(11): -0.5	0.1
2017	CIN	MLB	29	165	17	5	1	6	14	18	38	1	0	.213/.321/.390	90	5.2	.245	-0.8	C(40): -3.0	0.2
2018	CIN	MLB	30	45	1	2	0	1	3	2	10	0	0	.220/.289/.341	100	-0.5	.267	-0.1	C(10): -0.7, 1B(1): 0.0	0.1
2018	NYN	MLB	30	229	23	8	0	10	30	23	42	0	0	.222/.306/.409	99	8.8	.230	0.2	C(57): -6.6	0.4
2019	NYN	MLB	31	251	28	10	1	7	28	23	50	1	0	.237/.323/.385	93	8.8	.279	-0.3	C -8, 1B 0	0.1

Breakout: 2%   Improve: 29%   Collapse: 14%   Attrition: 19%   MLB: 95%

Comparables: *Ryan Doumit, Miguel Montero, Brian McCann*

Nothing beats a good challenge trade where both players improve after a move. While Matt Harvey's semi-renaissance was the bigger story of the Mets and Reds' headache-swap, Mesoraco had the second-best season of his career simply by staying moderately healthy. Sure, the multiple surgeries that derailed his career appear to have robbed him of some of his power and all of his reliability, but Mesoraco is still, put simply, a catcher with some pop. His defensive numbers were never good but now are exactly what you'd expect from someone with his litany of injuries, and yet the further out he gets from his latest surgery, the more one can dream on a slugger who was once among the best in the game at his position. He'll find another change of scenery in 2019, and if it comes with another run of health, he'll be an excellent value.

YEAR	TEAM	P. COUNT	FRM RUNS	BLK RUNS	THRW RUNS	TOT RUNS
2016	CIN	2035	-1.2	-0.2	0.0	-1.6
2017	CIN	5242	-5.5	1.6	-0.4	-4.9
2017	PEN	1408	-0.5	0.0	0.0	-0.7
2018	CIN	1378	-1.2	0.5	0.0	-0.7
2018	NYN	7897	-6.2	0.0	-0.4	-6.7
2019	NYN	9117	-8.6	0.6	-0.3	-8.4

Shervyen Newton SS

Born: 04/24/99   Age: 20   Bats: B   Throws: R   Height: 6'4"   Weight: 180   Origin: International Free Agent, 2015

YEAR	TEAM	LVL	AGE	PA	R	2B	3B	HR	RBI	BB	K	SB	CS	AVG/OBP/SLG	DRC+	VORP	BABIP	BRR	FRAA	WARP
2016	MET	RK	17	150	18	5	1	0	5	22	32	0	5	.169/.347/.229	101	3.6	.233	-1.2	SS(18): -0.5, 3B(11): -0.4	0.4
2017	MET	RK	18	303	51	11	9	1	31	50	57	10	4	.311/.433/.444	145	33.9	.398	-2.0	SS(60): 7.7, 3B(5): 0.8	3.0
2018	KNG	RK	19	266	50	16	2	5	41	46	84	4	0	.280/.408/.449	96	24.4	.421	2.2	SS(49): 10.8, 2B(3): 0.3	2.2
2019	NYN	MLB	20	251	23	5	0	5	18	25	93	0	0	.149/.233/.233	28	-13.7	.220	-0.9	SS 3, 2B 0	-1.2

Breakout: 0%   Improve: 3%   Collapse: 0%   Attrition: 1%   MLB: 4%

Comparables: *Amed Rosario, Tim Beckham, Andrew Velazquez*

After a couple of years getting his bearings in the Dominican Summer League, Newton came stateside in 2018 and impressed during his first taste of American pro ball. The numbers in Kingsport were fine, but the tools stand out; along with a tall, lean frame, the big infielder has lightning-quick bat speed fueling his legit raw power, and he can take a hack from both sides of the plate. In part because he shared a diamond with fellow high-test prospects Ronny

Mauricio and Mark Vientos, Newton spent a fair amount of time at second base, despite currently fitting in as a shortstop and perhaps lining up at the hot corner sometime in the future. He'll have every opportunity to figure out off-speed pitches—the kryptonite of so many young hitters—given the abundance of tools in his profile.

Tomas Nido C   Born: 04/12/94   Age: 25   Bats: R   Throws: R   Height: 6'0"   Weight: 210   Origin: Round 8, 2012 Draft (#260 overall)

YEAR	TEAM	LVL	AGE	PA	R	2B	3B	HR	RBI	BB	K	SB	CS	AVG/OBP/SLG	DRC+	VORP	BABIP	BRR	FRAA	WARP
2016	SLU	A+	22	370	38	23	2	7	46	19	42	0	1	.320/.357/.459	125	27.8	.344	-2.4	C(88): 4.8	3.0
2017	BIN	AA	23	404	41	19	1	8	60	30	63	0	0	.232/.287/.354	90	4.5	.255	2.4	C(82): 28.4	4.6
2017	NYN	MLB	23	10	0	1	0	0	3	0	2	0	0	.300/.300/.400	93	0.2	.375	-0.1	C(3): 0.3	0.1
2018	BIN	AA	24	228	23	18	1	5	30	7	36	0	0	.274/.298/.437	101	6.1	.303	-2.0	C(48): 8.5	1.7
2018	NYN	MLB	24	90	10	3	0	1	9	4	27	0	0	.167/.200/.238	59	-3.7	.224	0.2	C(30): 3.4	0.4
2019	NYN	MLB	25	33	3	2	0	1	4	2	8	0	0	.232/.289/.369	91	1.1	.291	0.0	C 1	0.3

Breakout: 4%   Improve: 9%   Collapse: 13%   Attrition: 22%   MLB: 40%

Comparables: Tony Cruz, Kyle Farmer, Josh Phegley

YEAR	TEAM	P. COUNT	FRM RUNS	BLK RUNS	THRW RUNS	TOT RUNS
2017	BIN	10148	27.4	2.3	0.6	30.8
2017	NYN	379	0.1	0.3	0.0	1.7
2018	BIN	6337	7.7	0.0	0.5	8.2
2018	LVG	727	0.4	-0.1	0.0	0.2
2018	NYN	3444	3.5	-0.1	0.0	3.3
2019	NYN	1255	1.3	0.1	0.0	1.4

The truth is a continuum, living somewhere between two points of objective reference. For example, in 2016, Nido was a minor-league batting champion, but in 2018 he hit .167 over 34 major-league games. Nearly every statistical possibility lies somewhere between those two goalposts, but here's the *truth*: Nido is almost certainly a defense-first backup catcher destined to flirt between the majors and minors for the next decade. He has solid bat control and a little raw power to supplement solid receiving chops—enough to help him ride a hot streak or two that masks his well-below-average approach. No future batting title is on the horizon, nor much of a chance to whiff his way out of the big leagues—*that's* the veracity of Nido.

Brandon Nimmo OF   Born: 03/27/93   Age: 26   Bats: L   Throws: R   Height: 6'3"   Weight: 207   Origin: Round 1, 2011 Draft (#13 overall)

YEAR	TEAM	LVL	AGE	PA	R	2B	3B	HR	RBI	BB	K	SB	CS	AVG/OBP/SLG	DRC+	VORP	BABIP	BRR	FRAA	WARP
2016	LVG	AAA	23	444	72	25	8	11	61	46	73	7	8	.352/.423/.541	139	35.3	.411	2.8	CF(65): 2.6, LF(23): 1.6	4.4
2016	NYN	MLB	23	80	12	1	0	1	6	6	20	0	0	.274/.338/.329	76	2.0	.365	-0.4	LF(13): -0.2, RF(7): -0.1	-0.1
2017	LVG	AAA	24	198	23	12	1	3	17	33	49	0	0	.227/.364/.368	88	5.4	.306	-1.0	CF(31): -4.8, RF(12): 2.2	0.0
2017	NYN	MLB	24	215	26	11	1	5	21	33	60	2	0	.260/.379/.418	96	12.1	.360	-0.9	LF(32): 3.0, CF(12): 0.5	0.8
2018	NYN	MLB	25	535	77	28	8	17	47	80	140	9	6	.263/.404/.483	119	56.5	.351	5.1	RF(62): 0.1, CF(44): -0.9	3.5
2019	NYN	MLB	26	641	83	26	5	17	65	77	167	7	4	.237/.345/.391	109	28.1	.313	2.0	RF 8, CF -1	3.7

Breakout: 4%   Improve: 49%   Collapse: 6%   Attrition: 9%   MLB: 95%

Comparables: Jorge Soler, Stephen Piscotty, Matt Joyce

For some, patience can feel like a chore. For Nimmo, it appears to be second nature. Smile and wait through the slow burn of the Mets' minor-league system. Smile and wait until the team can no longer deny your incredible on-base skills. Smile and wait for the perfect pitch, then drive it into the gap. Nimmo's practiced approach at the plate put him in the top 20 hitters in baseball in esoteric stats like strikes thrown, pitches per plate appearance and percentage of pitches taken without swinging. You'd think he were passive if it wasn't for the hustle on the basepaths and his penchant for attacking the first pitch. Of course there are still holes in the youngster's game: he's not much of a center fielder and southpaws give him trouble, but there's a chance he can still improve in at least one of those areas. In the meantime, during his plate appearances, Mets fans appear to have learned a thing or two from Nimmo—they tend to smile and wait until good things happen.

Kevin Plawecki C   Born: 02/26/91   Age: 28   Bats: R   Throws: R   Height: 6'2"   Weight: 210   Origin: Round 1, 2012 Draft (#35 overall)

YEAR	TEAM	LVL	AGE	PA	R	2B	3B	HR	RBI	BB	K	SB	CS	AVG/OBP/SLG	DRC+	VORP	BABIP	BRR	FRAA	WARP
2016	LVG	AAA	25	207	27	11	0	8	40	13	19	0	1	.300/.348/.484	125	9.9	.297	-1.9	C(41): 4.2, 1B(5): 0.2	1.8
2016	NYN	MLB	25	151	6	6	0	1	11	17	33	0	0	.197/.298/.265	70	2.3	.255	0.3	C(45): 7.4	1.0
2017	LVG	AAA	26	275	37	17	1	9	45	16	38	0	0	.328/.375/.514	123	22.0	.350	-1.4	C(63): 10.7	3.1
2017	NYN	MLB	26	118	11	5	0	3	13	14	17	1	0	.260/.364/.400	103	8.5	.284	-0.3	C(29): -3.3, 1B(2): 0.0	0.3
2018	NYN	MLB	27	277	33	13	2	7	30	28	65	0	1	.210/.315/.370	88	11.3	.257	-1.2	C(71): -2.0, 1B(3): 0.0	0.6
2019	NYN	MLB	28	139	15	6	1	4	15	13	28	0	0	.240/.327/.384	110	7.4	.286	-0.1	C 0	0.8

Breakout: 5%   Improve: 39%   Collapse: 6%   Attrition: 16%   MLB: 85%

Comparables: Ronny Paulino, Jett Bandy, Robbie Grossman

YEAR	TEAM	P. COUNT	FRM RUNS	BLK RUNS	THRW RUNS	TOT RUNS
2016	NYN	5670	7.1	0.9	-0.2	7.6
2017	LVG	9115	8.7	0.8	-0.4	8.6
2017	NYN	3842	-3.2	0.7	-0.6	-3.3
2018	NYN	9839	-4.6	2.0	0.0	-2.7
2019	NYN	3607	-0.5	0.4	-0.1	-0.2

For a slow-footed backstop, Plawecki sure can be elusive. Each time we think we've got him figured out, something in his numbers changes and blows our whole hypothesis to smithereens. In college, he was a contact machine, but those skills hid away for years before re-emerging in 2017. His calling card defensively was getting extra strikes and blocking errant balls—right up until his second consecutive poor season behind the plate this year. When his hit tool disappeared again in 2018, he upped his power production and put more and more batted balls on the ground (yes, simultaneously). He's been trying on a double-digit walk rate for size in Queens despite not having one at any minor-league stop. The only real consistency is that the numbers always point to Plawecki as a prototypical backup catcher. It's just tough to figure out what kind of backup catcher he is.

Wilson Ramos C Born: 08/10/87 Age: 31 Bats: R Throws: R Height: 6'1" Weight: 245 Origin: International Free Agent, 2004

YEAR	TEAM	LVL	AGE	PA	R	2B	3B	HR	RBI	BB	K	SB	CS	AVG/OBP/SLG	DRC+	VORP	BABIP	BRR	FRAA	WARP
2016	WAS	MLB	28	523	58	25	0	22	80	35	79	0	0	.307/.354/.496	116	43.2	.327	-4.3	C(128): 10.0	4.3
2017	TBA	MLB	29	224	19	6	0	11	35	10	36	0	0	.260/.290/.447	99	4.1	.262	-3.4	C(62): -3.1	0.4
2018	TBA	MLB	30	315	30	14	0	14	53	22	61	0	0	.297/.346/.488	109	15.9	.335	-4.4	C(73): -0.8	1.3
2018	PHI	MLB	30	101	9	8	1	1	17	10	19	0	0	.337/.396/.483	117	8.3	.408	-2.6	C(23): 0.0	0.4
2019	*NYN*	*MLB*	*31*	*421*	*48*	*20*	*2*	*15*	*57*	*31*	*71*	*0*	*0*	*.274/.332/.452*	*112*	*20.9*	*.302*	*-4.2*	*C -1*	*2.1*

Breakout: 0%   Improve: 27%   Collapse: 17%   Attrition: 18%   MLB: 91%

Comparables: Ramon Hernandez, Harry Danning, Matt Wieters

YEAR	TEAM	P. COUNT	FRM RUNS	BLK RUNS	THRW RUNS	TOT RUNS
2016	WAS	17715	10.7	-1.2	1.6	11.4
2017	DUR	799	0.3	0.1	0.0	0.3
2017	TBA	8203	1.4	-3.9	-0.8	-4.1
2018	TBA	9850	0.2	0.3	-0.2	· 0.6
2018	PHI	3106	0.1	-0.3	0.2	0.3
2019	*NYN*	*14732*	*2.0*	*-2.2*	*0.1*	*-0.1*

If the August and September Phillies were a quilt, Ramos could be thought of as the patch sewn in just left-of-center, prettily obscuring the hole that still exists behind it but not quite perfectly blending in. The Phils had rather ably made it to late July with a backstop tandem of Jorge Alfaro and Andrew Knapp, but as the latter grew increasingly untenable, a non-waiver deadline move like Ramos felt warranted. Really, it was one of a number of moves that was both philosophically and materially sound: The Phillies acquired Ramos on layaway at a player-to-be-named-or-cash discount—he was nursing an injured hamstring and was known to be on the shelf until mid-August—and his expiring contract meant he wouldn't obstruct the club's future plans to ride with Alfaro. For a while, Ramos was even better than expected, even if he probably could've been declared statuary on account of his obviously stiff lower body. But then, like the rest of the Phillies, his game went in the tank over the final two weeks, sucked into an eminently forgettable void that, mercifully, few of us will remember for long. That said, he traded one void for another by signing with the Mets in December to lead their group of almost-catchers.

Jose Reyes INF Born: 06/11/83 Age: 36 Bats: B Throws: R Height: 6'0" Weight: 195 Origin: International Free Agent, 1999

YEAR	TEAM	LVL	AGE	PA	R	2B	3B	HR	RBI	BB	K	SB	CS	AVG/OBP/SLG	DRC+	VORP	BABIP	BRR	FRAA	WARP
2016	ABQ	AAA	33	40	7	0	0	2	2	7	4	3	0	.303/.425/.485	130	4.0	.296	0.2	SS(9): -1.0	0.3
2016	BIN	AA	33	33	6	1	0	0	2	3	3	1	1	.207/.273/.241	101	-0.3	.222	-0.3	3B(7): -0.4	0.0
2016	NYN	MLB	33	279	45	13	4	8	24	23	49	9	2	.267/.326/.443	100	18.2	.302	1.6	3B(50): -2.6, SS(13): 0.1	1.0
2017	NYN	MLB	34	561	75	25	7	15	58	50	79	24	6	.246/.315/.413	97	27.0	.263	2.7	SS(80): -3.6, 3B(36): 1.3	1.8
2018	NYN	MLB	35	251	30	12	3	4	16	22	39	5	2	.189/.260/.320	74	-1.7	.211	0.5	3B(28): -3.2, SS(25): 0.6	-0.1
2019	*NYN*	*MLB*	*36*	*298*	*38*	*14*	*2*	*6*	*27*	*24*	*48*	*11*	*3*	*.247/.310/.389*	*87*	*5.5*	*.275*	*0.9*	*SS -1, 3B -1*	*0.2*

Breakout: 0%   Improve: 33%   Collapse: 16%   Attrition: 23%   MLB: 74%

Comparables: Jeff Cirillo, Jerry Hairston, Joe Stripp

The less said about Reyes' (hopefully) final season in New York, the better. Despite the team almost constantly talking up his veteran presence, he couldn't do anything right on the field. Don't let the triples fool you—he was a negative on the bases and both his contact and power tools disappeared. His fielding went from bad to worse even as the Mets played him out of position and—occasionally—ahead of Amed Rosario. Meanwhile, the Mets' front office and field staff committed to playing and rostering him longer than his performance warranted. And if that wasn't enough, he poisoned David Wright's retirement game for the fans who will not forgive him for his act of domestic violence and was a seemingly undeserving Marvin Miller Man of the Year finalist. Both as a man and a player, he's worn out his welcome in Queens.

Amed Rosario SS Born: 11/20/95 Age: 23 Bats: R Throws: R Height: 6'2" Weight: 189 Origin: International Free Agent, 2012

YEAR	TEAM	LVL	AGE	PA	R	2B	3B	HR	RBI	BB	K	SB	CS	AVG/OBP/SLG	DRC+	VORP	BABIP	BRR	FRAA	WARP
2016	SLU	A+	20	290	27	10	8	3	40	21	36	13	6	.309/.359/.442	123	24.0	.345	0.5	SS(60): -0.4	2.0
2016	BIN	AA	20	237	38	14	5	2	31	19	51	6	2	.341/.392/.481	90	20.9	.433	1.7	SS(53): -4.9	0.5
2017	LVG	AAA	21	425	66	19	7	7	58	23	67	19	6	.328/.367/.466	103	30.2	.377	1.4	SS(88): 2.0, 3B(6): -0.2	2.5
2017	NYN	MLB	21	170	16	4	4	4	10	3	49	7	3	.248/.271/.394	67	0.6	.330	1.0	SS(45): -0.3	0.2
2018	NYN	MLB	22	592	76	26	8	9	51	29	119	24	11	.256/.295/.381	78	22.2	.310	2.8	SS(146): -6.6	0.7
2019	*NYN*	*MLB*	*23*	*625*	*78*	*26*	*7*	*13*	*56*	*35*	*126*	*22*	*9*	*.252/.300/.387*	*92*	*19.7*	*.300*	*2.1*	*SS -4*	*1.7*

Breakout: 12%   Improve: 55%   Collapse: 5%   Attrition: 13%   MLB: 92%

Comparables: Orlando Arcia, Hanley Ramirez, Ketel Marte

The start to this past summer was cruel to Rosario's bat, but this electric youngster finally started to put his offensive tools together in August and September. Finally given regular playing time in the second half, Rosario started to look more comfortable at the plate. His plus contact skills started to translate into hits and his speed played up on the basepaths, though his swing-happy approach still kept his on-base percentage depressed. He's no finished product by far, even in the field where he's a sight better than many who've manned the dirt in Flushing, but not elite. It's tough being a work-in-progress in a league where almost half the shortstops can contend for MVP honors, but there's no need for discouragement—Rosario is already a solid regular with room to grow.

Dominic Smith 1B Born: 06/15/95 Age: 24 Bats: L Throws: L Height: 6'0" Weight: 239 Origin: Round 1, 2013 Draft (#11 overall)

YEAR	TEAM	LVL	AGE	PA	R	2B	3B	HR	RBI	BB	K	SB	CS	AVG/OBP/SLG	DRC+	VORP	BABIP	BRR	FRAA	WARP
2016	BIN	AA	21	542	64	29	2	14	91	50	74	2	1	.302/.367/.457	122	17.6	.329	-5.3	1B(106): 1.1	1.6
2017	LVG	AAA	22	500	77	34	2	16	76	39	87	1	1	.330/.386/.519	120	22.5	.380	-2.4	1B(107): 6.6	2.4
2017	NYN	MLB	22	183	17	6	0	9	26	14	49	0	0	.198/.262/.395	84	-3.4	.218	0.3	1B(46): -5.5	-0.6
2018	LVG	AAA	23	375	52	21	1	6	41	34	76	3	0	.258/.328/.380	100	3.6	.315	1.9	1B(53): 6.5, LF(22): -0.2	1.8
2018	NYN	MLB	23	149	14	11	1	5	11	4	47	0	0	.224/.255/.420	74	1.0	.297	0.3	1B(28): -0.5, LF(13): -1.9	-0.4
2019	*NYN*	*MLB*	*24*	*237*	*25*	*11*	*1*	*7*	*27*	*15*	*57*	*0*	*0*	*.240/.294/.390*	*87*	*1.8*	*.294*	*0.3*	*1B 1, LF 0*	*0.3*

Breakout: 7%   Improve: 29%   Collapse: 9%   Attrition: 26%   MLB: 53%

Comparables: Chris Marrero, Kendrys Morales, Joey Votto

Previous comments in this very Annual pegged Smith as an ill fit for first base; his bat-to-ball abilities always seemed better suited for a soft-handed second baseman or speedy left fielder. But 2018 was another year of the former top prospect's surprise conversion into all-or-nothing home run hitter. Instead of reaching base and driving the ball into the gap, he's now a longball hunter, and instead of being a *better* offensive player he's just a *different* one. Due to a logjam of cold-corner-only bats to start this past season, Smith did a bit of wandering. First, back to Vegas where there was nothing left to prove because Adrian Gonzalez was the team's first choice at the position. Later, the Mets tried him as an outfielder, which went exactly as poorly as everyone expected. Now that Peter Alonso has zoomed past him on the organization depth chart, Smith's best chance to establish himself in the majors might require a journey to another organization.

Mark Vientos 3B Born: 12/11/99 Age: 19 Bats: R Throws: R Height: 6'4" Weight: 185 Origin: Round 2, 2017 Draft (#59 overall)

YEAR	TEAM	LVL	AGE	PA	R	2B	3B	HR	RBI	BB	K	SB	CS	AVG/OBP/SLG	DRC+	VORP	BABIP	BRR	FRAA	WARP
2017	MTS	RK	17	193	22	12	0	4	24	14	42	0	2	.259/.316/.397	97	8.2	.313	0.8	SS(19): -1.6, 3B(14): 0.1	0.4
2018	KNG	RK	18	262	32	12	0	11	52	37	43	1	0	.287/.389/.489	145	17.4	.312	-3.0	3B(54): -1.7	1.7
2019	NYN	MLB	19	251	26	9	0	10	31	18	64	0	0	.207/.263/.357	72	-4.2	.237	-1.3	3B -1	-0.5

Breakout: 0%   Improve: 7%   Collapse: 2%   Attrition: 4%   MLB: 12%   Comparables: *Nomar Mazara, Adalberto Mondesi, Rougned Odor*

The Mets have a predilection for moving their position player prospects slowly through the ranks, so it wasn't exactly a surprise that Vientos spent the entire year at Kingsport despite proving he was more than capable against the throwers at the level. It also wasn't a surprise that the young Floridian hit for power, displayed a mature approach at the plate, and acquitted himself well in his first full season at third base; the former second-round draft pick had first-round talent from the jump. The shocks may come more as he progresses through full-season ball, as he'll need to catch up to premium velocity better, but he could force the Mets into promoting him more aggressively if the offensive barrage continues.

David Wright 3B Born: 12/20/82 Age: 36 Bats: R Throws: R Height: 6'0" Weight: 205 Origin: Round 1, 2001 Draft (#38 overall)

YEAR	TEAM	LVL	AGE	PA	R	2B	3B	HR	RBI	BB	K	SB	CS	AVG/OBP/SLG	DRC+	VORP	BABIP	BRR	FRAA	WARP
2016	NYN	MLB	33	164	18	8	0	7	14	26	55	3	2	.226/.350/.438	98	10.8	.320	-0.8	3B(36): -0.8	0.4
2018	NYN	MLB	35	3	0	0	0	0	0	1	0	0	0	.000/.333/.000	84	-0.2	.000	0.0	3B(1): 0.0	0.0
2019	NYN	MLB	36	251	28	11	0	6	23	22	66	3	2	.221/.293/.348	71	-3.5	.287	-0.4	3B -4	-0.8

Breakout: 0%   Improve: 30%   Collapse: 12%   Attrition: 29%   MLB: 70%   Comparables: *Jhonny Peralta, Joe Randa, Art Howe*

For almost 40 years, the Mets' third base position was a revolving door of inadequate hitters, short-term fixes and small-time hustlers. Don Zimmer was the inaugural third sacker, and he was just as representative of the '62 Mets' inadequacy as Marvelous Marv and the rest of the worst team in history. During the team's two World Series wins, the hot corner was manned by forgettable rookie Wayne Garrett and his -0.3 BWARP, then the talented but short-tenured Ray Knight. Not even 30-30 man Howard Johnson defined the position for the team, playing shortstop too often to really put his stamp on the seemingly cursed section of the Shea Stadium diamond. In 2004, Wright debuted for the Mets and changed the way the position would be viewed in New York forever.

On September 29, 2018, "Captain America" strode onto the field amidst an outpouring of support rarely seen in this sport, and likely played his last professional baseball game. Over his 15 years in uniform, he set the bar for every player to come after him, an elite combination of power, skill and smile that overshadows so many that came before and sets an unfair example for every person who will follow. He did everything that each of those previous players did. He had Johnson's combo of power and speed, Knight's flair for the clutch and the dramatic and Robin Ventura's quiet solidity. Only he was better than them all, and for a longer period of time. The injuries that robbed him of much of the last half-decade also likely swiped his Hall of Fame chances, but he'll long reside in the annals of team history, helping define the benchmarks against which all other Mets are held.

The New York Mets have a history of *should've* and *could've*, of wasted opportunity and squandered potential under the bright lights of the big city. Wright never fit that mold. With him on the field, the grass wasn't greener at Yankee Stadium; the Mets weren't second-class strivers. They, like Wright himself, were great just as they were.

PITCHERS

Tyler Bashlor RHP Born: 04/16/93 Age: 26 Bats: R Throws: R Height: 6'0" Weight: 195 Origin: Round 11, 2013 Draft (#326 overall)

YEAR	TEAM	LVL	AGE	W	L	SV	G	GS	IP	H	HR	BB/9	K/9	K	GB%	BABIP	WHIP	ERA	DRA	WARP	MPH	FB%	WHF	CSP
2016	COL	A	23	4	2	3	34	0	50¹	35	2	5.0	12.2	68	47%	.292	1.25	2.50	2.73	1.2				
2017	SLU	A+	24	2	2	10	34	0	35	33	1	5.4	15.7	61	39%	.438	1.54	4.89	2.24	1.1				
2017	BIN	AA	24	1	0	3	12	0	14²	7	0	2.5	14.1	23	41%	.259	0.75	0.00	2.34	0.4				
2018	BIN	AA	25	0	3	7	20	0	24	14	2	4.5	11.2	30	30%	.235	1.08	2.62	3.14	0.5				
2018	NYN	MLB	25	0	3	0	24	0	32	26	6	3.4	7.0	25	32%	.225	1.19	4.22	5.68	-0.3	98.3	68.9	11.9	45.7
2019	NYN	MLB	26	2	1	0	41	0	43²	37	7	4.9	10.5	51	37%	.297	1.40	4.72	5.47	-0.3	97.9	70.1	12.1	46.5

Breakout: 17%   Improve: 25%   Collapse: 14%   Attrition: 21%   MLB: 47%   Comparables: *Pedro Strop, David Carpenter, Brad Boxberger*

Bashlor, a late-developing strikeout artist, was bumped from Double-A to the majors in June due to the Mets' woeful bullpen situation. Already old for the Eastern League, this fireballer's shift to Queens wasn't nearly as smooth as either party would've liked. Command was once an issue for Bashlor, but in the majors he didn't have an issue there; the problem was mainly that major-league hitters did not flail at his slider as much as he was used to in the upper minors. In September, however, he looked a lot more like the dominant reliever that Met prospect hounds have dreamed on—he whiffed 10 of the 30 batters he faced and held opposing hitters to a .154 batting average. With his raw stuff, he'll certainly get another handful of chances to work his way into a leveraged role, even in an improved 2019 bullpen.

Jerry Blevins LHP   Born: 09/06/83   Age: 35   Bats: L   Throws: L   Height: 6'6"   Weight: 190   Origin: Round 17, 2004 Draft (#516 overall)

YEAR	TEAM	LVL	AGE	W	L	SV	G	GS	IP	H	HR	BB/9	K/9	K	GB%	BABIP	WHIP	ERA	DRA	WARP	MPH	FB%	WHF	CSP
2016	NYN	MLB	32	4	2	2	73	0	42	36	4	3.2	11.1	52	47%	.302	1.21	2.79	2.53	1.2	91.5	62.5	11.5	47.2
2017	NYN	MLB	33	6	0	1	75	0	49	43	4	4.4	12.7	69	42%	.336	1.37	2.94	2.94	1.2	90.4	45.7	13.2	39
2018	NYN	MLB	34	3	2	1	64	1	42²	36	6	4.6	8.6	41	22%	.263	1.36	4.85	7.12	-1.1	90.4	51.7	9.6	47
2019	NYN	MLB	35	2	1	1	37	0	39¹	35	6	4.1	9.9	43	37%	.296	1.35	4.68	5.43	-0.2	89.5	50.9	11.2	43.6

Breakout: 17%   Improve: 36%   Collapse: 29%   Attrition: 19%   MLB: 86%   *Comparables: Kerry Wood, George Sherrill, Damaso Marte*

For four seasons Blevins was a surprisingly steady and effective left-handed relief option, but he sure picked the wrong time to have his first bad season in a half-decade. This veteran southpaw went from bullpen lynchpin to two steps ahead of the lynch mob despite little change to his repertoire or velocity. His signature fastball lost some horizontal movement and hitters put it in the air much more than usual, but the underlying speed of the pitch never changed (except as it reverberated off left hitters' bats). And despite being asked to face more right-handed hitters than usual, it was the lefties who surprisingly beat up on him when he couldn't get swings and misses. He'll now go into his age-35 season bereft of contract and looking to make good rather than make bank. There's reason to think he'll rebound, but the damage to his wallet has been done.

Jacob deGrom RHP   Born: 06/19/88   Age: 31   Bats: L   Throws: R   Height: 6'4"   Weight: 180   Origin: Round 9, 2010 Draft (#272 overall)

YEAR	TEAM	LVL	AGE	W	L	SV	G	GS	IP	H	HR	BB/9	K/9	K	GB%	BABIP	WHIP	ERA	DRA	WARP	MPH	FB%	WHF	CSP
2016	NYN	MLB	28	7	8	0	24	24	148	142	15	2.2	8.7	143	47%	.312	1.20	3.04	3.30	3.5	96.3	59.6	12.1	47.2
2017	NYN	MLB	29	15	10	0	31	31	201¹	180	28	2.6	10.7	239	48%	.305	1.19	3.53	3.02	5.7	97.2	55.5	14.5	49.5
2018	NYN	MLB	30	10	9	0	32	32	217	152	10	1.9	11.2	269	48%	.281	0.91	1.70	2.09	8.0	98.2	52.1	16.3	48.4
2019	NYN	MLB	31	12	9	0	30	30	180	140	19	2.4	10.9	217	46%	.296	1.04	3.07	3.56	3.6	96.6	54.5	14.8	48.2

Breakout: 9%   Improve: 28%   Collapse: 28%   Attrition: 6%   MLB: 84%   *Comparables: Erik Bedard, CC Sabathia, A.J. Burnett*

I'm not sure how many superlatives are left to describe the reigning and defending National League Cy Young Award winner. deGrom's unbelievable 2018 season was the best in baseball over the past three years in terms of DRA-, and his 1.70 ERA underscored just how hard it was to mount an offense against his incredible right arm. In an era of Three True Outcomes, there's really only one that mattered against deGrom in 2018: the strikeout; the ace allowed just 10 dingers all season long despite throwing more innings than all but one pitcher. He was at his best against teams' best hitters and in the most pressure-packed situations. After years of being second fiddle behind Matt Harvey and Noah Syndergaard, the comparatively unassuming deGrom cut his long hair and got down to work. Now no Mets pitcher since Seaver can compare.

Edwin Diaz RHP   Born: 03/22/94   Age: 25   Bats: R   Throws: R   Height: 6'3"   Weight: 165   Origin: Round 3, 2012 Draft (#98 overall)

YEAR	TEAM	LVL	AGE	W	L	SV	G	GS	IP	H	HR	BB/9	K/9	K	GB%	BABIP	WHIP	ERA	DRA	WARP	MPH	FB%	WHF	CSP
2016	WTN	AA	22	3	3	1	16	6	40²	32	3	1.5	12.0	54	58%	.302	0.96	2.21	1.72	1.6				
2016	SEA	MLB	22	0	4	18	49	0	51²	45	5	2.6	15.3	88	48%	.377	1.16	2.79	1.84	1.9	101.0	67.5	20	51.1
2017	SEA	MLB	23	4	6	34	66	0	66	44	10	4.4	12.1	89	41%	.236	1.15	3.27	3.20	1.5	99.7	68.4	16.7	46
2018	SEA	MLB	24	0	4	57	73	0	73¹	41	5	2.1	15.2	124	47%	.281	0.79	1.96	1.77	2.7	99.3	62.4	20.7	48.4
2019	NYN	MLB	25	3	1	38	57	0	59²	39	6	2.8	13.9	93	45%	.301	0.97	2.50	2.92	1.3	99.5	67.1	19.6	49.4

Breakout: 36%   Improve: 60%   Collapse: 18%   Attrition: 14%   MLB: 90%   *Comparables: Jonathan Broxton, Francisco Liriano, Trevor Rosenthal*

If you were ever curious what, say, the Battle of Carthage would have looked like if just one Carthaginian magically had a fully operational flamethrower, you could have just watched the way Diaz treated hitters in 2018 and gotten a rough idea. Less abstractly, if you gave a pitcher a fastball that could blister Satan's catching hand, a 90-mph slider capable of trans-dimensional movement and wondered what would happen if he halved his walk and home runs rates, well then here is the merchant of death/baseball closer for you. While relievers are arguably the game's most fickle alchemy, Diaz's raw stuff, established track record of dominance, and youth should combine to make him one of baseball's elite closers for years to come.

Jeurys Familia RHP   Born: 10/10/89   Age: 29   Bats: R   Throws: R   Height: 6'3"   Weight: 240   Origin: International Free Agent, 2007

YEAR	TEAM	LVL	AGE	W	L	SV	G	GS	IP	H	HR	BB/9	K/9	K	GB%	BABIP	WHIP	ERA	DRA	WARP	MPH	FB%	WHF	CSP
2016	NYN	MLB	26	3	4	51	78	0	77²	63	1	3.6	9.7	84	66%	.304	1.21	2.55	3.49	1.3	98.8	78	16	45.2
2017	NYN	MLB	27	2	2	6	26	0	24²	21	1	5.5	9.1	25	61%	.290	1.46	4.38	6.48	-0.4	97.9	82.5	10.8	46.6
2018	NYN	MLB	28	4	4	17	40	0	40²	36	1	3.1	9.5	43	52%	.315	1.23	2.88	4.62	0.1	97.8	70.2	12.6	49.6
2018	OAK	MLB	28	4	2	1	30	0	31¹	24	2	4.0	11.5	40	40%	.293	1.21	3.45	3.06	0.7	98.4	66.8	17.5	47.3
2019	NYN	MLB	29	3	1	0	51	0	54¹	43	6	3.8	10.5	64	52%	.293	1.20	3.57	4.14	0.5	97.6	73.7	14.6	47.1

Breakout: 26%   Improve: 45%   Collapse: 34%   Attrition: 16%   MLB: 98%   *Comparables: Juan Rincon, Eric O'Flaherty, Peter Moylan*

Oakland bolstered its bullpen with Familia two months before his free agency in exchange for a couple of non-impact minor leaguers, and he did his job both down the stretch — fitting into a deep and sometimes invincible relief corps — and in the Wild Card game, where he set down three straight Yankees in the eighth inning (though the A's were already trailing by five at that point). The major change in Familia's approach last year was pushing his slider usage from 15 percent of his pitches up to 28, largely at the expense of sinkers. As you would expect, his slider gets more whiffs and fewer grounders than his sinker; as you would expect, he pushed his strikeout rate over 10 per nine innings for the first time in his career, but also saw his ground-ball rate drop below 50 percent for the first time. DRA prefers his early work; then again, DRA lives in Bed-Stuy and has insufferable facial hair.

Drew Gagnon **RHP**   Born: 06/26/90   Age: 29   Bats: R   Throws: R   Height: 6'4"   Weight: 215   Origin: Round 3, 2011 Draft (#100 overall)

YEAR	TEAM	LVL	AGE	W	L	SV	G	GS	IP	H	HR	BB/9	K/9	K	GB%	BABIP	WHIP	ERA	DRA	WARP	MPH	FB%	WHF	CSP
2016	BLX	AA	26	1	0	1	5	1	13¹	4	0	2.7	10.1	15	43%	.143	0.60	0.00	3.45	0.2				
2016	CSP	AAA	26	2	1	0	31	4	55	60	4	3.4	7.9	48	46%	.341	1.47	5.56	4.07	0.6				
2017	SLC	AAA	27	1	1	0	31	10	86¹	95	6	4.1	8.7	83	40%	.355	1.55	6.25	3.60	1.8				
2018	BIN	AA	28	1	0	0	1	1	6	2	0	1.5	7.5	5	62%	.125	0.50	0.00	3.86	0.1				
2018	LVG	AAA	28	6	6	0	27	27	157²	151	23	2.5	9.5	167	50%	.314	1.23	4.57	3.68	3.3				
2018	NYN	MLB	28	2	1	0	5	1	12	15	2	3.8	6.0	8	42%	.333	1.67	5.25	5.34	0.0	93.2	56.2	9	51.2
2019	*NYN*	*MLB*	*29*	*1*	*0*	*0*	*10*	*0*	*11*	*9*	*1*	*3.3*	*9.2*	*11*	*44%*	*.294*	*1.23*	*3.97*	*4.60*	*0.1*	*92.5*	*56.2*	*9*	*51.2*

Breakout: 8%   Improve: 12%   Collapse: 8%   Attrition: 13%   MLB: 26%   *Comparables: Red Patterson, Eddie Gamboa, Robert Ray*

Gagnon led the Mets' minor-league squads in games started, innings pitched and strikeouts last season, which earned him a mid-season spot start and a few late-season relief appearances—not to mention his first showing in these *Annual* pages since 2015. Even an improved strikeout rate doesn't change the ceiling we identified for him four years ago: he's likely either a pretty good Triple-A starter or a pretty bad big-league starter.

Robert Gsellman **RHP**   Born: 07/18/93   Age: 25   Bats: R   Throws: R   Height: 6'4"   Weight: 205   Origin: Round 13, 2011 Draft (#402 overall)

YEAR	TEAM	LVL	AGE	W	L	SV	G	GS	IP	H	HR	BB/9	K/9	K	GB%	BABIP	WHIP	ERA	DRA	WARP	MPH	FB%	WHF	CSP
2016	BIN	AA	22	3	4	0	11	11	66¹	57	2	2.0	6.5	48	57%	.282	1.09	2.71	3.63	1.2				
2016	LVG	AAA	22	1	5	0	9	9	48²	56	8	3.0	7.4	40	55%	.318	1.48	5.73	7.75	-1.3				
2016	NYN	MLB	22	4	2	0	8	7	44²	42	1	3.0	8.5	42	57%	.325	1.28	2.42	4.24	0.6	96.1	63.5	10.6	47.6
2017	BIN	AA	23	1	0	0	4	4	12¹	15	0	3.6	6.6	9	76%	.366	1.62	2.92	4.64	0.1				
2017	LVG	AAA	23	0	0	0	1	1	6	10	1	4.5	4.5	3	50%	.391	2.17	7.50	3.62	0.1				
2017	NYN	MLB	23	8	7	0	25	22	119²	138	17	3.2	6.2	82	51%	.303	1.50	5.19	5.77	-0.3	94.7	63.4	8.1	45.7
2018	NYN	MLB	24	6	3	13	68	0	80	76	8	3.2	7.9	70	52%	.291	1.30	4.28	4.38	0.5	96.1	62.8	10.8	49.3
2019	*NYN*	*MLB*	*25*	*3*	*1*	*6*	*67*	*0*	*70²*	*63*	*7*	*3.1*	*8.6*	*68*	*50%*	*.300*	*1.24*	*3.74*	*4.33*	*0.5*	*95.2*	*64.7*	*9.7*	*48.8*

Breakout: 19%   Improve: 50%   Collapse: 20%   Attrition: 26%   MLB: 95%   *Comparables: Kyle Freeland, Martin Perez, Chad Kuhl*

Noah Syndergaard's wingman went through a season of change. After converting to the 'pen full-time this year, Gsellman's year had more phases than Kitty Pryde. For the first month, he was a nightmare for opposing teams, a multi-inning relief ace capable of striking out the side or ripping through two or three innings. By the midpoint of May, he'd already thrown more than 26 innings and, perhaps starting to wear down a little, looked like a fairly average middle reliever. Finally, at the end of the year, he did a respectable impression of a one-and-done, second-division closer after incumbent Jeurys Familia was dealt away. Another year working out of the bullpen might see him gain a little more comfort, and hopefully see his velocity tick back up to the 2016 breakout levels, but the ceiling today isn't anything like the "7/6" that catapulted his profile years ago.

Eric Hanhold **RHP**   Born: 11/01/93   Age: 25   Bats: R   Throws: R   Height: 6'5"   Weight: 220   Origin: Round 6, 2015 Draft (#181 overall)

YEAR	TEAM	LVL	AGE	W	L	SV	G	GS	IP	H	HR	BB/9	K/9	K	GB%	BABIP	WHIP	ERA	DRA	WARP	MPH	FB%	WHF	CSP
2016	BRV	A+	22	2	12	0	19	19	101	120	12	2.9	5.7	64	54%	.327	1.51	4.81	5.55	-0.1				
2017	CAR	A+	23	8	3	2	30	3	64	71	3	3.0	8.4	60	60%	.364	1.44	3.94	4.03	0.7				
2018	BIN	AA	24	3	1	8	17	0	25¹	21	1	3.2	11.4	32	60%	.323	1.18	2.84	2.89	0.6				
2018	LVG	AAA	24	2	2	0	14	0	19	25	1	3.3	9.5	20	49%	.429	1.68	7.11	3.24	0.4				
2018	NYN	MLB	24	0	0	0	3	0	2¹	4	0	3.9	7.7	2	33%	.444	2.14	7.71	8.70	-0.1	96.7	71.2	6.8	46.1
2019	*NYN*	*MLB*	*25*	*1*	*0*	*0*	*15*	*0*	*16¹*	*15*	*2*	*3.8*	*9.3*	*17*	*50%*	*.319*	*1.37*	*4.21*	*4.88*	*0.0*	*96.4*	*72.9*	*6.9*	*47.2*

Breakout: 5%   Improve: 8%   Collapse: 6%   Attrition: 12%   MLB: 16%   *Comparables: Jeremy Horst, Ryan O'Rourke, Dan Meyer*

You might wonder why a guy with a 7.11 ERA over just 19 innings in Triple-A might be called up to a major-league bullpen role, but this is the Mets we're talking about. Not only was the team in desperate need of middle relief efficacy, but Hanhold's numbers distract from some solid underlying sparkles. His fastball comes in hard and has good movement, and at its best it can get both grounders and whiffs; much of his difficulty in Vegas seemed to spawn from a ridiculous BABIP over a short stretch. Though an early-season oblique injury slowed him down and a late-season recurrence prevented him from logging more innings with the big club in September, he's likely to pop back up with the Mets as they revamp their 'pen for 2019.

Franklyn Kilome RHP   Born: 06/25/95   Age: 24   Bats: R   Throws: R   Height: 6'6"   Weight: 175   Origin: International Free Agent, 2013

YEAR	TEAM	LVL	AGE	W	L	SV	G	GS	IP	H	HR	BB/9	K/9	K	GB%	BABIP	WHIP	ERA	DRA	WARP	MPH	FB%	WHF	CSP
2016	LWD	A	21	5	8	0	23	23	114²	113	6	3.9	10.2	130	49%	.346	1.42	3.85	3.14	2.6				
2017	CLR	A+	22	6	4	0	19	19	97¹	96	5	3.4	7.7	83	48%	.325	1.37	2.59	4.55	0.8				
2017	REA	AA	22	1	3	0	5	5	29²	25	2	4.6	6.1	20	43%	.267	1.35	3.64	4.00	0.4				
2018	REA	AA	23	4	6	0	19	19	102	96	7	4.5	7.3	83	46%	.305	1.44	4.24	4.65	0.8				
2018	BIN	AA	23	0	3	0	7	7	38	31	3	2.4	9.9	42	41%	.289	1.08	4.03	4.50	0.4				
2019	*NYN*	*MLB*	*24*	*7*	*8*	*0*	*22*	*22*	*115¹*	*108*	*15*	*4.2*	*8.7*	*111*	*42%*	*.305*	*1.40*	*4.59*	*5.32*	*0.0*				

Breakout: 4%   Improve: 5%   Collapse: 6%   Attrition: 11%   MLB: 17%   *Comparables: Scott Barlow, Caleb Smith, James Houser*

Since 2017, the Mets' stock-in-trade has been dealing big-league parts for middling relief arms in the hopes of stabilizing a shaky bullpen (not working!) and saving cash (working!) When the Mets pried Kilome loose from the Phillies in exchange for Asdrubal Cabrera last year, the fanbase seemed to breathe a sigh of relief. *Finally.* After all, Kilome was a top-100 prospect and a pitcher with legitimate middle-of-the-rotation upside. Sure, he's aging out of prospectdom and he'd worn out his welcome in a stacked Philadelphia farm system, but he has plus velocity on his fastball and a solid second offering in his curve. The stats haven't quite matched the projection as of yet, but there's real hope that Kilome could emerge as a legitimate starter in 2019. Or rather, there was that hope. During the World Series, the Mets announced that Kilome has become a true Met: he'll have Tommy John surgery and miss the 2019 season.

Seth Lugo RHP   Born: 11/17/89   Age: 29   Bats: R   Throws: R   Height: 6'4"   Weight: 225   Origin: Round 34, 2011 Draft (#1032 overall)

YEAR	TEAM	LVL	AGE	W	L	SV	G	GS	IP	H	HR	BB/9	K/9	K	GB%	BABIP	WHIP	ERA	DRA	WARP	MPH	FB%	WHF	CSP
2016	LVG	AAA	26	3	4	0	21	14	73¹	103	10	2.5	7.6	62	46%	.375	1.68	6.50	4.89	0.3				
2016	NYN	MLB	26	5	2	0	17	8	64	49	7	3.0	6.3	45	46%	.230	1.09	2.67	4.62	0.5	95.9	57.5	10.2	49
2017	BIN	AA	27	1	1	0	2	2	13	14	1	1.4	10.4	15	54%	.382	1.23	2.77	2.81	0.4				
2017	NYN	MLB	27	7	5	0	19	18	101¹	114	13	2.2	7.5	85	43%	.325	1.37	4.71	5.26	0.3	93.8	56.8	9.7	50.3
2018	NYN	MLB	28	3	4	3	54	5	101¹	81	9	2.5	9.1	103	47%	.269	1.08	2.66	3.82	1.4	96.6	48.8	10.8	50
2019	*NYN*	*MLB*	*29*	*5*	*3*	*0*	*68*	*6*	*95¹*	*84*	*11*	*2.8*	*9.1*	*96*	*45%*	*.300*	*1.20*	*3.70*	*4.29*	*1.0*	*94.8*	*53.2*	*10.3*	*49.8*

Breakout: 34%   Improve: 54%   Collapse: 17%   Attrition: 19%   MLB: 82%   *Comparables: Craig Stammen, Brandon Workman, Marco Estrada*

The Mets' best relief pitcher last season was a guy who would've started for many teams in the National League. The King of Spin Rate took to the bullpen like a fish to water and logged over 78 innings in relief while also popping up for five spot starts. In relief, the durability issues that have dogged him faded into the background, and his velocity spiked in shorter stints. Best of all, his well-regarded curveball added extra movement and stayed a premier out-pitch, allowing him to work as a multi-inning, multi-pitch Swiss Army knife for the Amazins. His underlying peripherals don't exactly reflect how good he's been at limiting runs, but he remains a solid example of the modern multi-faceted bullpen weapon every team needs.

Steven Matz LHP   Born: 05/29/91   Age: 28   Bats: R   Throws: L   Height: 6'2"   Weight: 200   Origin: Round 2, 2009 Draft (#72 overall)

YEAR	TEAM	LVL	AGE	W	L	SV	G	GS	IP	H	HR	BB/9	K/9	K	GB%	BABIP	WHIP	ERA	DRA	WARP	MPH	FB%	WHF	CSP
2016	NYN	MLB	25	9	8	0	22	22	132¹	129	14	2.1	8.8	129	54%	.312	1.21	3.40	3.34	3.1	96.0	61.5	10.4	50.4
2017	LVG	AAA	26	0	1	0	3	3	13¹	13	3	1.4	11.5	17	35%	.323	1.12	6.75	3.98	0.3				
2017	NYN	MLB	26	2	7	0	13	13	66²	83	12	2.6	6.5	48	49%	.329	1.53	6.07	6.03	-0.3	94.5	59.1	7.9	48.4
2018	NYN	MLB	27	5	11	0	30	30	154	134	25	3.4	8.9	152	50%	.267	1.25	3.97	3.62	3.0	95.0	60	10	52.6
2019	*NYN*	*MLB*	*28*	*8*	*8*	*0*	*26*	*26*	*130*	*113*	*15*	*2.8*	*9.3*	*135*	*49%*	*.299*	*1.18*	*3.74*	*4.34*	*1.5*	*94.6*	*60.6*	*9.8*	*51*

Breakout: 23%   Improve: 56%   Collapse: 11%   Attrition: 16%   MLB: 92%   *Comparables: Zach McAllister, John Maine, Carlos Carrasco*

He did it. Against all odds, Matz improbably made 30 starts in a Mets uniform, something few imagined given his perennial injury concerns. Given how dynamic this southpaw had previously been during his limited periods of health, did this lead him to a long-awaited, media-frenzied breakout? Nah. Not only was he eclipsed by his talented rotation-mates, he never seemed dominant or, for that matter, totally healthy in 2018. He managed only about five innings per outing over all of those starts, and that left the unpredictable Mets bullpen in play to ruin those games he did appear in. There were still MRIs and a brief DL stint that made everyone think he was about to fall apart, but in August and September the New York native churned out the best starts of his season, including a seven-inning, 11-strikeout performance you can dream on. Even after an improbable full season as a starter, Matz remains as risky and as tantalizing as ever.

Corey Oswalt RHP   Born: 09/03/93   Age: 25   Bats: R   Throws: R   Height: 6'5"   Weight: 250   Origin: Round 7, 2012 Draft (#230 overall)

YEAR	TEAM	LVL	AGE	W	L	SV	G	GS	IP	H	HR	BB/9	K/9	K	GB%	BABIP	WHIP	ERA	DRA	WARP	MPH	FB%	WHF	CSP
2016	SLU	A+	22	4	2	0	14	13	67²	73	4	2.4	9.0	68	60%	.348	1.34	4.12	3.35	1.6				
2017	BIN	AA	23	12	5	0	24	24	134¹	118	9	2.7	8.0	119	49%	.290	1.18	2.28	3.47	2.7				
2018	LVG	AAA	24	4	4	0	11	11	52¹	58	9	3.4	8.9	52	45%	.331	1.49	6.02	6.34	-0.5				
2018	NYN	MLB	24	3	3	0	17	12	64²	69	14	2.8	6.3	45	43%	.276	1.38	5.85	5.73	-0.4	92.5	67	8	47.8
2019	*NYN*	*MLB*	*25*	*3*	*4*	*0*	*11*	*11*	*58¹*	*56*	*8*	*3.0*	*8.2*	*53*	*46%*	*.304*	*1.29*	*4.25*	*4.93*	*0.3*	*92.2*	*68.6*	*8.2*	*49*

Breakout: 9%   Improve: 36%   Collapse: 20%   Attrition: 39%   MLB: 74%   *Comparables: Jarlin Garcia, Luis Cessa, Dillon Peters*

Despite very strong numbers in Double-A during 2017, this big right-hander was never really classified as a prospect. Oswalt's lack of helium was mostly due to the fact that his fastball lives in the (very) low 90s and his secondary pitches barely flash average. While that can get you far grinding it out in Binghamton, it's just not the profile of a regular starter in today's MLB. At his best, Oswalt's calling is as an emergency starter who can keep you in a game but will have trouble racking up whiffs. Every team needs one or two of those guys at the ready in Triple-A, but no team can afford to give him another 12 starts in a season.

David Peterson LHP   Born: 09/03/95   Age: 23   Bats: L   Throws: L   Height: 6'6"   Weight: 240   Origin: Round 1, 2017 Draft (#20 overall)

YEAR	TEAM	LVL	AGE	W	L	SV	G	GS	IP	H	HR	BB/9	K/9	K	GB%	BABIP	WHIP	ERA	DRA	WARP	MPH	FB%	WHF	CSP
2018	COL	A	22	1	4	0	9	9	59¹	46	1	1.7	8.6	57	68%	.283	0.96	1.82	3.50	1.2				
2018	SLU	A+	22	6	6	0	13	13	68²	74	1	2.5	7.6	58	64%	.335	1.35	4.33	3.99	1.1				
2019	*NYN*	*MLB*	*23*	*5*	*6*	*0*	*17*	*17*	*91*	*87*	*11*	*3.2*	*8.0*	*81*	*52%*	*.304*	*1.30*	*4.17*	*4.84*	*0.5*				

Breakout: 7%   Improve: 18%   Collapse: 12%   Attrition: 20%   MLB: 35%   *Comparables: Sal Romano, Brian Flynn, Fernando Romero*

As a college left-handed pitcher who was drafted in the first round, there's no reason Peterson shouldn't be chewing up hitters in the low minors as he barrels toward his true test in the upper echelons of minor league baseball. Instead, the Mets have moved methodically with him, starting his 2018 in Columbia before finally moving him to a more appropriate level at St. Lucie. While the tall lefty managed to maintain his incredible ground-ball rate at the more advanced level, he didn't put up the strikeout numbers one would hope for from a top-tier pitching prospect. You can chalk that up to his mediocre fastball, or maybe even his slow burn through the minors, but there's still a fair chance Peterson could become a reliable mid-rotation lefty or a LOOGY before it's all said and done.

A.J. Ramos RHP   Born: 09/20/86   Age: 32   Bats: R   Throws: R   Height: 5'10"   Weight: 200   Origin: Round 21, 2009 Draft (#638 overall)

YEAR	TEAM	LVL	AGE	W	L	SV	G	GS	IP	H	HR	BB/9	K/9	K	GB%	BABIP	WHIP	ERA	DRA	WARP	MPH	FB%	WHF	CSP
2016	MIA	MLB	29	1	4	40	67	0	64	52	1	4.9	10.3	73	39%	.309	1.36	2.81	4.03	0.7	95.4	39	12.7	44.2
2017	MIA	MLB	30	2	4	20	40	0	39²	30	4	5.0	10.7	47	42%	.271	1.31	3.63	4.36	0.4	94.5	39	12	43.2
2017	NYN	MLB	30	0	0	7	21	0	19	19	3	5.7	11.8	25	40%	.340	1.63	4.74	2.72	0.5	94.7	39	13.6	40.6
2018	NYN	MLB	31	2	2	0	28	0	19²	17	3	6.9	10.1	22	31%	.292	1.63	6.41	3.93	0.2	93.7	36.5	11.4	44.6
2019	*NYN*	*MLB*	*32*	*2*	*1*	*6*	*34*	*0*	*35²*	*29*	*5*	*4.8*	*10.2*	*40*	*38%*	*.285*	*1.35*	*4.54*	*5.26*	*-0.1*	*93.8*	*38.2*	*12.3*	*43.4*

Breakout: 23%   Improve: 43%   Collapse: 22%   Attrition: 9%   MLB: 89%   *Comparables: Tyler Clippard, Pedro Strop, Michael Gonzalez*

Coming into the season, the Mets' setup man and former Marlins closer had disappointed in his first turn in Flushing, but 2018 took an even steeper nosedive. Ramos wasn't on speaking terms with the strike zone, and by the end of May had been worked into a torn labrum that caused him to miss the rest of the season. The raw stuff and proven closer tag may make him a useful commodity in 2019, but the Mets spent a lot of money and prospect capital to bring him into the fold, and that investment certainly didn't pay off.

Paul Sewald RHP   Born: 05/26/90   Age: 29   Bats: R   Throws: R   Height: 6'3"   Weight: 207   Origin: Round 10, 2012 Draft (#320 overall)

YEAR	TEAM	LVL	AGE	W	L	SV	G	GS	IP	H	HR	BB/9	K/9	K	GB%	BABIP	WHIP	ERA	DRA	WARP	MPH	FB%	WHF	CSP
2016	LVG	AAA	26	5	3	19	56	0	65²	58	9	2.9	11.0	80	38%	.295	1.20	3.29	3.69	1.0				
2017	LVG	AAA	27	1	0	4	8	0	8²	7	1	2.1	12.5	12	27%	.286	1.04	2.08	2.02	0.3				
2017	NYN	MLB	27	0	6	0	57	0	65¹	58	8	2.9	9.5	69	35%	.287	1.21	4.55	3.59	1.2	93.2	64	12.3	50.4
2018	LVG	AAA	28	3	0	1	7	0	8	7	0	1.1	7.9	7	62%	.292	1.00	1.12	6.68	-0.1				
2018	NYN	MLB	28	0	7	2	46	0	56¹	62	8	3.7	9.3	58	32%	.331	1.51	6.07	4.24	0.4	92.4	63.4	10.3	50.6
2019	*NYN*	*MLB*	*29*	*2*	*1*	*0*	*36*	*0*	*38*	*33*	*5*	*3.4*	*9.4*	*40*	*37%*	*.292*	*1.25*	*4.16*	*4.82*	*0.0*	*92.1*	*63.6*	*11.2*	*50.5*

Breakout: 16%   Improve: 39%   Collapse: 21%   Attrition: 24%   MLB: 76%   *Comparables: Brad Brach, Josh Osich, Josh Fields*

Sewald the slider specialist is a unique convocation of a few extremely *Metsy* throughlines. First, he was once the poster boy for ridiculously low minor league salaries while working for a team owned by notorious spendthrifts. This year, he was worked exceptionally hard out of the bullpen during an excellent April and May, which left little in the tank for the rest of the season. (This is something new manager Mickey Callaway apparently learned from departing manager and expert relief-burner Terry Collins.) Now, after giving away more hits than the Neptunes at the end of 2018, Sewald is now 0-13 in two (almost) full big-league seasons despite projecting as an average middle reliever going forward. If that doesn't make him a lovable loser–and therefore a Met in the truest sense–I don't know what does.

Noah Syndergaard RHP   Born: 08/29/92   Age: 26   Bats: L   Throws: R   Height: 6'6"   Weight: 240   Origin: Round 1, 2010 Draft (#38 overall)

YEAR	TEAM	LVL	AGE	W	L	SV	G	GS	IP	H	HR	BB/9	K/9	K	GB%	BABIP	WHIP	ERA	DRA	WARP	MPH	FB%	WHF	CSP
2016	NYN	MLB	23	14	9	0	31	30	183²	168	11	2.1	10.7	218	52%	.334	1.15	2.60	2.28	6.5	100.5	59.1	15.3	47.5
2017	NYN	MLB	24	1	2	0	7	7	30¹	29	0	0.9	10.1	34	59%	.337	1.05	2.97	2.54	1.0	100.0	51.3	14.9	47
2018	NYN	MLB	25	13	4	0	25	25	154¹	148	9	2.3	9.0	155	50%	.320	1.21	3.03	2.47	5.0	99.3	53.7	14.4	47.5
2019	*NYN*	*MLB*	*26*	*11*	*8*	*0*	*28*	*28*	*168*	*147*	*15*	*2.5*	*10.2*	*190*	*50%*	*.318*	*1.16*	*3.06*	*3.56*	*3.4*	*99.4*	*56.6*	*15*	*48.2*

Breakout: 23%   Improve: 65%   Collapse: 17%   Attrition: 7%   MLB: 95%   *Comparables: Jaime Garcia, Alex Wood, Matt Garza*

Any season where Syndergaard doesn't strike out 15 hitters per game and win the Cy Young Award unanimously gets considered a disappointment. No, that's not fair, but that's how things tend to work when you're built like a Norse god, throw harder than any other starting pitcher, and play in New York. He pitched around a finger injury and a disease he picked up at a summer camp, but was mostly the same old Thor, a slight drop in his velocity and strikeout rate notwithstanding. Somehow this perturbed his team's front office enough to consider trading him in the offseason.

On a rate basis, Noah Syndergaard was the sixth-best starting pitcher in baseball last season, just behind AL Cy Young winner Blake Snell. In a "down year," Thor thrived on the strength of his velocity (yes it's still elite), his tenacity and a slider that can only be accurately described using swear words. If you want to consider his 2018 a disappointment, go ahead, but it's only because he's a run of good health and pinch of luck away from putting up the world-beating season everyone seems to be waiting for.

Jason Vargas LHP Born: 02/02/83 Age: 36 Bats: L Throws: L Height: 6'0" Weight: 215 Origin: Round 2, 2004 Draft (#68 overall)

YEAR	TEAM	LVL	AGE	W	L	SV	G	GS	IP	H	HR	BB/9	K/9	K	GB%	BABIP	WHIP	ERA	DRA	WARP	MPH	FB%	WHF	CSP
2016	OMA	AAA	33	0	2	0	3	3	13²	16	3	0.7	11.9	18	35%	.382	1.24	5.93	2.55	0.4				
2016	KCA	MLB	33	0	0	0	3	3	12	8	1	2.2	8.2	11	36%	.219	0.92	2.25	5.58	0.0	89.0	52.2	10.5	40.4
2017	KCA	MLB	34	18	11	0	32	32	179²	181	27	2.9	6.7	134	41%	.289	1.33	4.16	4.48	2.2	87.5	46.8	10.2	45
2018	BRO	A-	35	0	0	0	2	2	12	7	2	0.0	14.2	19	30%	.238	0.58	1.50	2.40	0.4				
2018	NYN	MLB	35	7	9	0	20	20	92	100	18	2.9	8.2	84	42%	.307	1.41	5.77	4.11	1.3	88.2	54.4	11.7	47.3
2019	NYN	MLB	36	7	8	0	23	23	122	110	17	3.0	8.9	121	41%	.297	1.24	4.18	4.84	0.7	86.6	48.8	10.5	43.9

Breakout: 15%   Improve: 34%   Collapse: 17%   Attrition: 14%   MLB: 71%   *Comparables: Kenshin Kawakami, Roy Oswalt, Cory Lidle*

You shouldn't sign Vargas expecting 18 wins, or even above-average performance; leading the AL in wins before signing his two-year deal with the Mets was a trick of the light, nothing more than a mirage. This lefty is best acquired to provide innings and the veneer of stability—if not in performance, at least in showing up on the regular. Every team needs innings, especially when you're the Mets, but 2018 started rough for Vargas and he barely held on to his rotation spot long enough to turn it around over the last two months of the season. The Mets will hope that his 3.60 ERA and a strikeout per inning over his last 10 starts was a glimmer of hope for 2019 and not a dead-cat bounce for a pitcher who may be viable only as a reliever at this phase of his career.

Zack Wheeler RHP Born: 05/30/90 Age: 29 Bats: L Throws: R Height: 6'4" Weight: 195 Origin: Round 1, 2009 Draft (#6 overall)

YEAR	TEAM	LVL	AGE	W	L	SV	G	GS	IP	H	HR	BB/9	K/9	K	GB%	BABIP	WHIP	ERA	DRA	WARP	MPH	FB%	WHF	CSP
2017	NYN	MLB	27	3	7	0	17	17	86¹	97	15	4.2	8.4	81	48%	.332	1.59	5.21	5.30	0.3	96.6	61.7	10	49.5
2018	NYN	MLB	28	12	7	0	29	29	182¹	150	14	2.7	8.8	179	46%	.279	1.12	3.31	3.01	4.8	98.3	58.3	12	48.2
2019	NYN	MLB	29	10	9	0	28	28	159²	141	19	3.3	9.2	163	44%	.302	1.25	3.92	4.54	1.4	97.1	59.3	11.4	48.8

Breakout: 17%   Improve: 38%   Collapse: 22%   Attrition: 10%   MLB: 96%   *Comparables: Matt Garza, Andy Messersmith, John Lackey*

Three long years separated Wheeler's impressive 2014 breakout and his equally stellar 2018. Between those bookends, the righty lost two full seasons to Tommy John surgery and its complications, then added an up-and-down 2017 marred by further injury and inconsistency. Until this year, his stock was in freefall—after all, what good is a hurler who can't stay healthy? Would all that time off hamper his already questionable command? It didn't appear so, as he finally harnessed his off-speed stuff, walked fewer batters than ever and grew into a full-on no. 2 starter. Usually it's the year before free agency where a pitcher really makes their money, but Wheeler has flashed enough top-end potential that all he needs to do is finish 2019 upright for him to get a very impressive payday when he hits free agency in nine months.

Daniel Zamora LHP Born: 04/15/93 Age: 26 Bats: L Throws: L Height: 6'3" Weight: 195 Origin: Round 40, 2015 Draft (#1207 overall)

YEAR	TEAM	LVL	AGE	W	L	SV	G	GS	IP	H	HR	BB/9	K/9	K	GB%	BABIP	WHIP	ERA	DRA	WARP	MPH	FB%	WHF	CSP
2016	WVA	A	23	3	2	1	21	0	39	32	2	3.5	10.4	45	47%	.294	1.21	3.46	2.96	0.8				
2017	BRD	A+	24	2	4	9	37	0	53¹	48	2	2.9	10.3	61	57%	.324	1.22	1.86	2.78	1.3				
2018	BIN	AA	25	1	1	2	40	1	51²	37	3	2.8	12.0	69	46%	.291	1.03	3.48	2.52	1.5				
2018	NYN	MLB	25	1	0	0	16	0	9	6	1	3.0	16.0	16	44%	.333	1.00	3.00	2.26	0.3	90.9	21.5	15.2	51.4
2019	NYN	MLB	26	2	1	0	31	0	32²	28	4	3.8	10.4	38	44%	.303	1.28	4.02	4.66	0.1	90.5	21.9	15.5	52.3

Breakout: 15%   Improve: 23%   Collapse: 10%   Attrition: 22%   MLB: 36%   *Comparables: Pat Venditte, Chris Rearick, Tyler Sturdevant*

There was an upside to the Mets' complete bullpen breakdown in 2018: desperation occasionally breeds opportunity for the unheralded. Few players who played as well as Zamora did at the end of the season were as anonymous heading into the year, but the funky left-hander has forced his way into the Mets' 2019 plans. He's ostensibly a lefty specialist on the strength of his only plus pitch—a frisbee slider that he throws frequently and in all counts. It's possible that a longer look at Zamora might allow opposing hitters to size up his breaker and sit on his below-average fastball, but the Stony Brook product has had statistical success at every level so far. Why should the big leagues be any different?

LINEOUTS

Hitters

HITTER	POS	TEAM	LVL	AGE	PA	R	2B	3B	HR	RBI	BB	K	SB	CS	AVG/OBP/SLG	DRC+	VORP	BABIP	BRR	FRAA	WARP
Ross Adolph	INF	BRO	A-	21	264	47	9	12	7	35	21	52	14	3	.276/.348/.509	144	26.3	.322	4.4	CF(27): 1.2, LF(18): -0.5	2.6
Gavin Cecchini	2B	LVG	AAA	24	119	14	11	1	2	9	7	15	1	1	.294/.342/.468	117	1.7	.326	-1.7	2B(18): -1.3, SS(11): 0.4	0.5
Christian Colon	INF	GWN	AAA	29	55	3	0	0	0	3	4	8	1	0	.204/.278/.204	82	-3.4	.244	-0.5	2B(14): 1.1	0.1
	INF	LVG	AAA	29	313	44	22	1	6	38	36	30	11	5	.304/.396/.459	128	14.9	.323	-0.9	2B(43): 4.5, 3B(25): 0.9	2.6
Carlos Cortes	2B	BRO	A-	21	202	26	5	2	4	24	17	34	1	0	.264/.338/.382	136	12.6	.303	1.1	2B(45): -1.8	1.4
Phillip Evans	UT	LVG	AAA	25	245	34	8	1	14	39	21	42	4	3	.256/.327/.493	133	4.2	.255	-1.0	3B(22): -0.6, SS(19): -1.0	1.5
	UT	NYN	MLB	25	23	1	0	0	0	1	2	8	1	0	.143/.217/.143	70	-2.4	.231	0.1	3B(3): -0.1, 2B(2): 0.0	0.0
Braxton Lee	CF	MIA	MLB	24	18	0	0	0	0	2	1	8	0	0	.176/.222/.176	54	-0.9	.333	0.0	RF(5): -0.3, LF(1): 0.0	-0.1
	CF	JUP	A+	24	29	6	0	0	0	3	3	3	0	1	.292/.393/.292	109	0.6	.333	-1.4	CF(4): -0.4, RF(2): -0.2	-0.1
	CF	JAX	AA	24	127	16	6	0	1	7	16	19	3	1	.218/.315/.300	102	4.1	.253	1.4	LF(13): 3.2, RF(9): -0.4	0.8
	CF	NWO	AAA	24	201	24	6	2	0	9	19	37	4	6	.235/.307/.291	64	-2.0	.294	0.5	CF(24): -2.8, RF(19): 0.2	-0.5
Desmond Lindsay	OF	SLU	A+	21	335	27	11	5	3	30	37	89	7	7	.218/.310/.320	90	0.3	.300	-0.7	CF(75): 6.0	1.2
Jose Lobaton	C	LVG	AAA	33	151	22	9	0	8	27	18	31	1	0	.348/.430/.598	139	15.5	.409	-0.7	C(37): -0.2	1.5
	C	NYN	MLB	33	57	3	2	1	0	4	7	15	0	0	.143/.246/.224	71	-1.1	.200	-0.1	C(18): -0.6	0.0
Ali Sanchez	C	COL	A	21	205	26	11	1	4	22	10	23	1	1	.259/.293/.389	107	6.5	.274	0.4	C(36): 1.4	1.1
	C	SLU	A+	21	142	11	9	0	2	16	5	15	1	1	.274/.296/.385	107	0.5	.292	-0.9	C(27): -0.1	0.5
Luis Santana	2B	KNG	Rk	18	242	34	13	0	4	35	27	23	8	3	.348/.446/.471	136	26.6	.376	-0.4	2B(51): -1.5, 3B(1): -0.1	1.5
Tim Tebow	LF	BIN	AA	30	298	32	14	1	6	36	22	103	1	0	.273/.336/.399	72	4.2	.417	-1.4	LF(59): -7.8	-1.4

Surprisingly athletic, leading the New York-Penn League in triples and isolated power—**Ross Adolph** wins both the award for best showing from the Mets' 2018 draft class and the Sterling Award for best player on the short-season Brooklyn Cyclones. ⓧ Just 16 years old, **Francisco Alvarez** is already 5'11", 220 pounds, and a multi-millionaire. After receiving the largest bonus in Mets international signing history, this young Venezuelan "catcher" will have a decade to learn how to improve his receiving game and tap into his substantial raw power. ⓧ Is it fair to say that his early-season foot injury derailed **Gavin Cecchini**'s forward progress, or was that already a lost cause despite solid numbers in his most recent Vegas go-round? Either way, he doesn't look like much of a major leaguer either at the dish or in the field. ⓧ Tetraphobia—fear of the number four—is a fairly common superstition in many East Asian countries, and might soon be moving into MLB front offices; **Christian Colon** is just the latest example of a fourth-overall draft pick who hasn't nearly lived up to the high expectations. Fortunately, or unfortunately, he's a fifth infielder at best now. ⓧ Recent third-round pick **Carlos Cortes** is both positionally dexterous and bilaterally ambidextrous: he throws left-handed when playing the infield and right-handed when playing the outfield. He packs some power in his diminutive frame, but he'll need a lot of polish before cracking a major-league roster. ⓧ Over the last few years, the Mets have had a habit of losing fringy middle infielders on hard takeout slides. This year, it was utility dude **Phil Evans** who followed in Ruben Tejada's unfortunate footsteps, and it wouldn't surprise us if the rest of his pro career goes about as well as Tejada's has. ⓧ **Braxton Lee** has received a decent amount of hype at various points along the way, but the Marlins declined to protect him from the *minor-league* phase of the Rule 5 draft. The Mets snatched him up, but that just means he'll be playing for a new Triple-A team in 2019. ⓧ Toolsy center fielder **Desmond Lindsay** is a lot like that film project that you saw on Kickstarter that looks amazing but you know will never hit its funding goal. ⓧ It's a minor miracle that **Jose Lobaton** snuck into 22 games last year, but he's quite the advertisement for the career security that comes with being a warm body who can wear a chest protector. ⓧ The *T.J.* in **T.J. Rivera** doesn't stand for "Tommy John," but it might as well. The eponymous surgery cost him the entire 2018 season, during which he saw Jeff McNeil basically doppelgang his 2017 breakout and push him down the org's depth chart. ⓧ Catching prospect **Ali Sanchez** tried out the Florida State League and the Arizona Fall League in 2018, but didn't impress much in either showing. He's got the glove for his position, but his bat is purely holographic. ⓧ So far, the only thing that 19-year-old **Luis Santana** has done consistently is make contact in the low minors. That's no small feat, but his bat-to-ball ability will have to carry him a long way, as his short stature and limited physical gifts make him a second-base-only prospect without other carrying tools. ⓧ Everything about the **Tim Tebow** Experience is vaguely surreal: he's a college football analyst who suits up for a team called the Rumble Ponies, draws large crowds of fans and admirers and hits just well enough to be a league-average hitter in the Eastern League.

Pitchers

PITCHER	TEAM	LVL	AGE	W	L	SV	G	GS	IP	H	HR	BB/9	K/9	K	GB%	BABIP	WHIP	ERA	DRA	WARP	MPH	FB%	WHF	CSP
Jamie Callahan	LVG	AAA	23	0	1	1	7	0	8¹	14		4.3	9.7	9	45%	.483	2.16	9.72	8.15	-0.3				
P.J. Conlon	NYN	MLB	24	0	0	0	3	2	7²	15	2	2.3	5.9	5	29%	.448	2.22	8.22	7.88	-0.2	88.9	60.7	7.4	48.7
	LVG	AAA	24	4	9	0	23	21	114	147	20	3.1	6.5	82	36%	.336	1.63	6.55	5.40	0.2				
Nabil Crismatt	LVG	AAA	23	3	4	0	9	9	38²	61	8	4.4	8.1	35	48%	.405	2.07	8.84	4.67	0.4				
	BIN	AA	23	8	6	0	18	18	105¹	95	8	3.2	9.0	105	47%	.304	1.25	3.59	3.70	2.0				
Chris Flexen	NYN	MLB	23	0	2	0	4	1	6¹	14	2	8.5	4.3	3	40%	.429	3.16	12.79	7.44	-0.2	94.3	62.3	6	45
	LVG	AAA	23	6	7	0	18	17	92	109	11	3.0	7.6	78	43%	.354	1.52	4.40	5.11	0.4				
Anthony Kay	COL	A	23	4	4	0	13	13	69¹	73	6	2.9	10.1	78	45%	.356	1.37	4.54	4.00	1.0				
	SLU	A+	23	3	7	0	10	10	53¹	51	1	4.6	7.6	45	41%	.321	1.46	3.88	4.21	0.7				
Timothy Peterson	LVG	AAA	27	0	1	8	32	0	38²	29	4	2.3	12.8	55	38%	.287	1.01	3.49	3.11	0.9				
	NYN	MLB	27	2	2	0	22	0	27²	29	8	1.6	8.1	25	34%	.266	1.23	6.18	5.51	-0.2	92.0	59.2	12.4	52.3
Jacob Rhame	LVG	AAA	25	1	2	11	25	0	32¹	22	4	2.2	11.4	41	32%	.250	0.93	3.06	3.42	0.6				
	NYN	MLB	25	1	2	1	30	0	32¹	38	8	2.2	7.8	28	30%	.316	1.42	5.85	4.84	0.0	97.3	68.5	15.2	50.9
Ryder Ryan	SLU	A+	23	1	0	2	16	0	20¹	14	0	2.2	10.2	23	47%	.286	0.93	1.77	2.66	0.5				
	BIN	AA	23	3	3	3	26	0	32²	27	5	2.8	9.9	36	38%	.265	1.13	4.13	2.85	0.8				
Drew Smith	LVG	AAA	24	5	1	2	23	1	32²	26	3	3.3	8.3	30	46%	.267	1.16	2.76	7.42	-0.8				
	NYN	MLB	24	1	1	0	27	0	28	34	2	1.9	5.8	18	39%	.348	1.43	3.54	5.07	0.0	97.7	69.3	9.9	50.1
Stephen Villines	COL	A	22	2	4	6	24	0	33¹	33	2	1.4	14.6	54	46%	.413	1.14	4.86	2.88	0.8				
	SLU	A+	22	2	0	4	16	0	22	7	0	2.5	10.2	25	44%	.152	0.59	0.41	2.99	0.5				
	BIN	AA	22	1	0	0	7	0	11¹	6	1	1.6	13.5	17	39%	.227	0.71	3.18	3.65	0.2				
Bobby Wahl	NAS	AAA	26	3	2	11	34	1	39²	17	2	3.9	14.7	65	42%	.224	0.86	2.27	1.43	1.7				
	NYN	MLB	26	0	1	0	7	0	5¹	9	2	6.8	11.8	7	17%	.438	2.44	10.12	4.11	0.0	97.6	72.3	14.3	51.7
Simeon Woods-Richardson	MTS	Rk	17	1	0	1	5	2	11¹	9	0	3.2	11.9	15	50%	.321	1.15	0.00	3.39	0.3				
	KNG	Rk	17	0	0	0	2	2	6	6	1	0.0	16.5	11	38%	.417	1.00	4.50	3.92	0.1				

Jamie Callahan didn't make the Mets' bullpen out of Spring Training and got off to a brutal start in Vegas, but when you're a Mets pitcher, things can always get worse. He went under the knife for shoulder surgery in June and missed the rest of the season. ⊗ Belfast-born **P.J. Conlon** came up with the woeful Mets, but was spirited away to the contending Dodgers on a waiver claim for four glorious days before being re-acquired by the Amazins. Perhaps the "luck of the Irish" only applies to leprechauns, and not LOOGYs. ⊗ **Nabil Crismatt** has an extremely *Star Wars* name but an earthbound prospect profile. His late start has him aging out of prospect status and his ceiling is more Stormtrooper than Skywalker. ⊗ It was hard to imagine that **Chris Flexen** could follow up an abysmal showing as the Mets' emergency starter in 2017 with an even worse 2018. Unfortunately, we don't need to imagine it—the homer-prone starter was throttled in a brief major-league cameo and looks to be stuck in the minors. ⊗ Signed as potential rotation depth, **A.J. Griffin** gave up 16 runs in three innings at Triple-A and the Mets released him before April had ended. The California native likely ends his pro career not with a whimper, but rather several resounding bangs. ⊗ Right-handed out machine **Jordan Humphreys** was having a nice low-minors breakout in 2017 before UCL surgery derailed his 2018 season. If his plus command comes back in 2019, he could quickly rise up both pref lists and minor league levels to catch up with his contemporaries. ⊗ Left-hander **Anthony Kay** made his pro debut in 2018, and put up solid numbers in a season split between Columbus and St. Lucie. Despite a solid changeup, he probably doesn't project as more than a back-of-the-rotation arm. ⊗ When we last saw **Jenrry Mejia**, he was dealing as an elite late-game reliever back in 2014 and 2015. Since then, he's had three PED suspensions and has recently been reinstated from his lifetime ban from MLB. The only thing more questionable than his judgement is his future performance. ⊗ Things went great for **Timothy Peterson**—whose eighth season in the Mets' organization was his first in which he cracked the majors—up until the calendar turned to July. From that point on, the command-and-control righty reliever gave up dinger after dinger and pitched his way back into a Triple-A role. ⊗ Somehow young fireballer **Jacob Rhame** spent exactly 32.1 innings thriving as closer for the Las Vegas 51s and exactly 32 1/3 innings getting shelled under better pitching conditions in Flushing. Perhaps it had something to do with the fact that he had *10* different stints with the big-league team; he went up and down so fast and frequently you'd think he was a Duncan Imperial. ⊗ Like almost every other relief prospect, **Ryder Ryan** has a mid-90s fastball and a potential plus slider. Maybe he'll be able to give his future bullpen-mate Edwin Diaz some advice about how to deal with the expectations that come with being the centerpiece of a Jay Bruce trade. ⊗ Good surface-level numbers and the ability to limit walks made **Drew Smith** an integral part of the Mets' late-season bullpen. The bad news? Smith hasn't shown enough underlying stuff to make him an integral part of a *good* team's bullpen. ⊗ When we last saw **Thomas Szapucki**, he was mowing down low-minors hitters with three interesting pitches and serious heat coming off the left side. Of course, that was right after a shoulder injury and right before Tommy John surgery, so 2019 will be a watershed year for his top-prospect status. ⊗ Over the past two years, former Jayhawk **Stephen Villines** has pitched 94 innings of pro ball, and in that time struck out 137 and walked just 14. Don't be shocked if he brings his low arm slot, pinpoint control and American Legion velocity to Queens as a situational reliever very soon. ⊗ The "prize" of the lopsided Jeurys Familia trade, **Bobby Wahl** has an injury history that would make Mets' trainers squeal, which puts a bit of a damper on his huge minor-league strikeout rates and triple-digit heat. ⊗ If **Simeon Woods-Richardson** was a filet, you'd send him back; he's that raw. Fortunately he's not a steak, he's a high-potential right-handed pitcher with a four-pitch arsenal, solid velocity and a nice start to his pro career. No one's sending him back.

NEW YORK YANKEES

Essay by Mike Axisa

Player comments by Matt Provenzano and BP staff

The current era of Yankees baseball, one in which a young team is led by a young manager, can be traced back to October 2005. The Yankees were one year removed from their embarrassing 2004 ALCS loss to the Red Sox and they'd just been ousted in the 2005 ALDS in five games by the Angels. Their top two starters in that series were 36-year-old Mike Mussina and 41-year-old Randy Johnson. Hall of Fame talents, both of them, but past their prime, like so many other Yankees. That way of doing business would soon end.

Following that 2005 ALDS loss general manager Brian Cashman signed a contract extension—he leveraged interest from the post-Ed Wade Phillies into a nice raise—after receiving assurances from George Steinbrenner that he would have autonomy over the baseball operations. Cashman didn't get it (no general manager truly has 100 percent autonomy), but he did get considerably more power, and he used it to overhaul the front office and ramp up the team's analytic and pro scouting efforts. He would begin to build the team in his image.

That's when the Yankees went from being the Evil Empire with a monster payroll to being a smart team with a monster payroll. Their farm system and player development improved, bolstered by improved drafting and prolific spending in the international market. They identified buy-low types and hit the jackpot with Nick Swisher, Didi Gregorius, and Aaron Hicks. The Yankees have had some high-profile misses since then (see: Ellsbury, Jacoby), but the spend spend spend team-building philosophy has been replaced by homegrown stars and shrewd pickups. The 2017 season ended a game short of the World Series, but it was clear: The *Yankees*, as a concept, were back.

And, in 2018, they handed the keys to this burgeoning modern baseball powerhouse over to a rookie manager. The successful and widely respected Joe Girardi was let go following the team's ALCS loss in 2017, and, soon after it was announced Girardi would not return, chairman Hal Steinbrenner said the managerial change would've been made even if the Yankees went to the World Series. Ouch. Girardi's fate had been decided long in advance.

YANKEES PROSPECTUS
2018 W-L: 100-62, 2ND IN AL EAST

Pythag	.612	4th	B-Age	27.2	6th
RS/G	5.25	2nd	P-Age	28.7	17th
RA/G	4.13	10th	Salary	$166.1M	7th
DRC+	111	2nd	M$/MW	$3.0M	21st
DRA	3.90	5th	DL Days	1283	20th
FIP	3.66	3rd	$ on DL	19%	20th
DER	.700	22nd			

408'
399'   385'
318'   314'

- Opened 2009
- Open air
- Natural surface
- Fence profile: 8'

Three-Year Park Factors

Runs	Runs/RH	Runs/LH	HR/RH	HR/LH
103	104	102	112	118

Top Hitter WARP	4.9 Didi Gregorius
Top Pitcher WARP	5.6 Luis Severino
Top Prospect	Jonathan Loaisiga

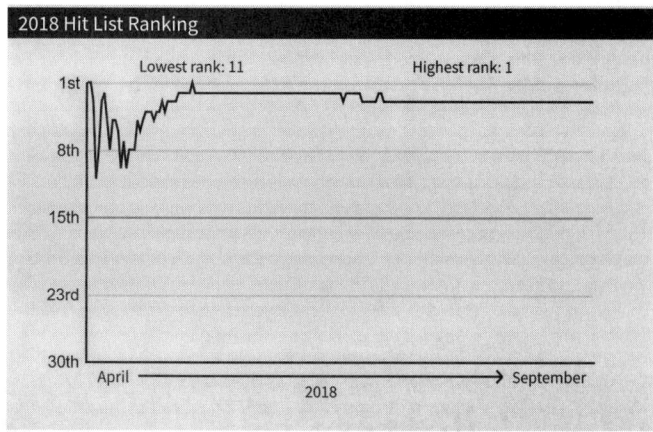

2018 Hit List Ranking

Lowest rank: 11   Highest rank: 1

1st
8th
15th
23rd
30th
April — 2018 → September

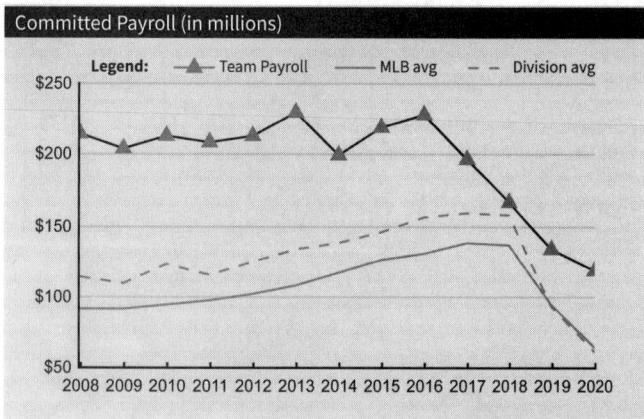

Committed Payroll (in millions)

Legend: ▲ Team Payroll   — MLB avg   - - Division avg

$250
$200
$150
$100
$50
2008 2009 2010 2011 2012 2013 2014 2015 2016 2017 2018 2019 2020

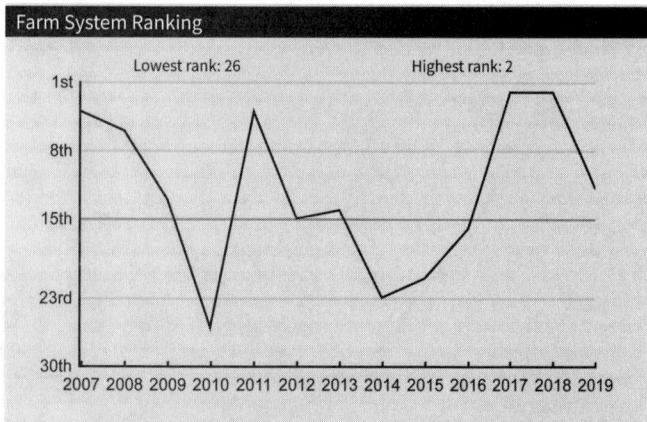

Farm System Ranking

Lowest rank: 26   Highest rank: 2

1st
8th
15th
23rd
30th
2007 2008 2009 2010 2011 2012 2013 2014 2015 2016 2017 2018 2019

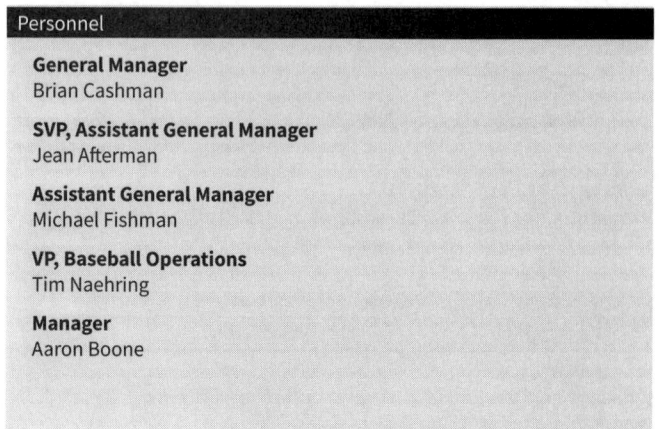

Personnel

General Manager
Brian Cashman

SVP, Assistant General Manager
Jean Afterman

Assistant General Manager
Michael Fishman

VP, Baseball Operations
Tim Naehring

Manager
Aaron Boone

To replace Girardi the Yankees hired Aaron Boone straight out of the broadcast booth. Boone spent 13 years in the big leagues from 1997-2009—he hit a rather notable home run in pinstripes, it's sometimes told—and had been in the broadcast booth since 2010. His brother, father, and grandfather were all big leaguers, but Boone had zero professional coaching or managerial experience. A team on the rise and in the game's largest market had just put a zero-experience manager in charge. To call it risky would be an understatement.

"Obviously, experience is very valuable and should be a check mark for somebody," Boone said during his introductory press conference. "But I would also say that I've been preparing for this job my entire life. I'm 44 years old now. I've been going to the ballpark since I was three and four years old. Going into broadcasting, I feel like so much of my job in the booth, especially the last few years, I find myself managing games all the time and thinking about strategies and thinking about situations."

Once Spring Training opened, Boone talked the talk. He talked about not having set bullpen roles and instead using guys like David Robertson, Chad Green, and Dellin Betances interchangeably. He talked about batting Aaron Judge leadoff to take advantage of his on-base skills. He talked about increased aggressiveness on the basepaths and treating the bench as an extension of the starting lineup rather than a bunch of dudes who only played when a regular needed a day. Boone appeared to be the platonic ideal of a saber-friendly manager.

A funny thing happened once the regular season started, however. Almost none of that stuff happened, and Boone and Girardi were damn near indistinguishable in terms of on-field strategy. Their lineups looked similar, which meant Brett Gardner in the leadoff spot even when better options (Hicks) existed, Judge married to the No. 2 spot, and using a lefty to break up a long string of right-handed batters (and vice versa) even if it meant using someone higher in the lineup than his production warranted. (Gregorius was often sandwiched between Judge and Giancarlo Stanton.)

That also meant fairly rigid bullpen roles. With Aroldis Chapman locked in at closer, Betances took over the eighth inning and Robertson was the primary seventh inning reliever. Green pitched in fifth and sixth inning situations, which arose quite often because, like Girardi, Boone rarely pushed his starting pitchers deep into the game. Only 35 times did a Yankees starter throw 100 pitches in a game in 2018, the 18th most in baseball. For years, they'd been consistently in the middle of the pack or below.

Girardi was often praised for his bullpen management and deservedly so. Year in and year out, the Yankees had a top flight bullpen under his watch. Girardi was also predictable with his regular season bullpen usage. He had set seventh and eighth inning relievers and rarely deviated. He also avoided using his relievers on back-to-back days whenever possible. In 2016 the Yankees had the ninth fewest instances of a reliever pitching on zero's day rest and they were a handful of games away from being bottom five. In 2017 they had the second fewest. Under Boone in 2018, they had the fifth fewest and were two games away from the third fewest.

Then there's the rest. Lordy, there's the rest. Every day around 3:30 p.m. ET is lineup complaining o'clock on social media. (It's that way for every team, but the Yankees have a larger social media presence than most, so yeah.) The daily lineup gets posted and the complaints begin. Why is that guy hitting so low? Why is that guy sitting a day after hitting a home run? Why is that guy in the lineup against a lefty? On and on it goes. The energy of those capable of nitpicking the lineup—the lineup of a great and high-scoring offense, at that—on a daily basis is admirable. It takes persistence.

The daily auditors could take note of at least one phenomenon. Stanton did something in 2018 no Yankee had done since Robinson Cano wore pinstripes: He played in 157 games. One-hundred-and-fifty-eight, to be exact. No other Yankee played in that many games over the last five seasons. There are lots of reasons for that (injuries, poor performance, etc.), including New York's apparent dedication to resting their regular position players. And in their case, that means predetermined rest. This guy is going to sit this day no matter what, even if he goes 3-for-4 with two homers the night before. The Yankees are big on rest, and have been for a few years. Fans hate it, as the lineup complainers remind us daily, but the Yankees believe in it.

The Yankees replaced a successful longtime veteran manager in Girardi with a neophyte in Boone and...nothing changed. At least not in terms of regular season strategy. Boone did have some noticeable gaffes in the postseason, no doubt about it. Most notably, he had too long a leash with Luis Severino and CC Sabathia in Games 3 and 4 of the ALDS, respectively, and he also brought Lance Lynn into a bases loaded, no outs situation in Game 3 rather than a high-strikeout guy like Robertson or Betances. Big mistakes, those were. Rookie mistakes? It's certainly seems that way. It's hard to imagine Girardi doing something like that, at least not toward the end of his tenure.

Despite those high-profile mishaps, not a whole lot changed on the field with the switch from Girardi to Boone. Almost nothing changed, really. The lineup was built the same way. The bullpen was used the same way when it came to defined roles and rest. Starters weren't pushed deep into games. Position players sat on predetermined days. Take a step back and examine things from high above, and it's awfully tough to look at the 2018 Yankees and the 2014-17 or so Yankees and see a meaningful difference in managerial strategy. Girardi and Boone were carbon copies.

That leads to two natural questions. One, why the managerial change then? Cashman cited communication issues when the Yankees announced Girardi would not return and, if nothing else, Boone is a great talker and very personable. He is several orders of magnitude more skilled at dealing with the media—no small thing in New York—and the Yankees believed he could foster better relationships with the players, particularly the young up-and-coming guys like

Judge and Severino and Gleyber Torres. That's why the change was made. To improve what happens behind closed doors in the clubhouse, on the plane, at the hotel, etc.

And two, if the on-field strategy is the same across two managers, who's really calling the shots? Is it all one giant coincidence that Girardi and Boone managed the same team exactly the same way? It's possible, but it seems incredibly unlikely. Chances are the directives are coming from upstairs, from the front office. It's no secret front offices, specifically analytical staffs, are more involved in the day-to-day operations across baseball than ever before. They provide data and information, and it's up to the manager and coaches to digest it and disseminate it. Some players like data. Others hate it. It's up to the manager and coaching staff to provide that individual touch and make best use of the information.

Front offices have been giving the coaching staff data for literally decades. The data is more sophisticated now, and better tailored to the recipient, but they've been doing it a long time. The next logical step in the analytical takeover is the front office weighing in on specific moves and strategies. We all read Moneyball, right? We all remember Billy Beane telling Art Howe to use Chad Bradford in high-leverage spots. The Yankees appear to have taken that a step further. This is the lineup construction we want. These are the bullpen roles we want. Rest these players on these days. So on and so forth. These directives, assuming they do actually exist, have remained in place across managers.

Teams across baseball are hiring younger, less experienced managers. The Yankees took it to the extreme with Boone, but the Phillies hired Gabe Kapler, the Mets hired Mickey Callaway, the Reds hired David Bell, and the Twins hired Rocco Baldelli, among others. Teams are hiring inexperienced managers en masse in part because they can develop them into the type of manager they want. Veteran skippers like Buck Showalter and Bruce Bochy and Bob Melvin are adaptable, they have to be to stick around as long as they have, but they're also set in their ways to some degree. Guys like Boone are not. They are a ball of managerial clay that can molded into whatever the front office wants in their dugout leader.

There are always going to be individual moves that stand out as different—again, few could see any way Girardi passes over Robertson or Green to go to Lynn with the bases loaded and no outs in a postseason game—but the overarching themes are the same. Strategically, the Yankees were very similar under Boone in 2018 as they were under Girardi in 2017 and earlier. The differences show up in the clubhouse, and in the way the information from Cashman's front office is used. It's been over a decade since Cashman was ostensibly given autonomy over the baseball operations. Now the fruits of that labor are extending into the dugout more than ever before. ■

—Mike Axisa is a writer at CBS.com.

HITTERS

Miguel Andujar 3B Born: 03/02/95 Age: 24 Bats: R Throws: R Height: 6'0" Weight: 215 Origin: International Free Agent, 2011

YEAR	TEAM	LVL	AGE	PA	R	2B	3B	HR	RBI	BB	K	SB	CS	AVG/OBP/SLG	DRC+	VORP	BABIP	BRR	FRAA	WARP
2016	TAM	A+	21	251	34	10	2	10	41	18	30	1	3	.283/.343/.474	132	14.6	.289	0.0	3B(51): 4.1	2.2
2016	TRN	AA	21	319	28	16	2	2	42	21	42	2	1	.266/.323/.358	93	12.3	.296	0.5	3B(64): -2.6	0.5
2017	TRN	AA	22	272	30	23	1	7	52	12	38	2	3	.312/.342/.494	99	19.2	.338	-1.6	3B(55): -4.5	0.3
2017	SWB	AAA	22	250	36	13	1	9	30	17	33	3	0	.317/.364/.502	115	20.3	.333	0.3	3B(57): -1.4	1.2
2017	NYA	MLB	22	8	0	2	0	0	4	1	0	1	0	.571/.625/.857	102	2.0	.571	0.0	3B(3): 0.0	0.0
2018	NYA	MLB	23	606	83	47	2	27	92	25	97	2	1	.297/.328/.527	114	38.1	.316	-0.1	3B(136): -15.2	1.6
2019	NYA	MLB	24	566	65	25	2	21	71	33	92	2	1	.254/.304/.428	97	10.8	.272	-0.1	3B -9	0.1

Breakout: 5%   Improve: 39%   Collapse: 8%   Attrition: 15%   MLB: 93%   *Comparables: Cheslor Cuthbert, Edwin Encarnacion, Maikel Franco*

Life during the George Steinbrenner era meant that any young player was always viewed with suspicion. Even when the highly-touted Derek Jeter was set to begin 1996 with the team, Steinbrenner infamously demanded to swap Mariano Rivera for a soon-to-be-retired Felix Fermin. It's still shocking to see prospect after prospect get a chance over the last three years, and even more shockingly, seeing Miguel Andujar announced as the starting third baseman sight unseen. All things considered, what a success it was. He broke Joe DiMaggio's Yankees record for doubles by a rookie, while putting up a .298 batting average and .855 OPS over 149 games. His performance will still be seen through fan double-vision. Older fans will probably see the player they wished was around more often in today's game—gap power, hitting for average, and a relatively low strikeout rate. Other analytically-inclined fans wince at the statuesque range at third. What that means for his future is up in the air. While the bat will carry him, will it be at third, which a certain free agent acquisition would complicate? Or at first, complicated by Luke Voit and extra offensive demands? It's difficult to succeed as one-half of a ballplayer, but that's often more of a rookie ballplayer than other teams can claim.

Greg Bird 1B Born: 11/09/92 Age: 26 Bats: L Throws: R Height: 6'4" Weight: 220 Origin: Round 5, 2011 Draft (#179 overall)

YEAR	TEAM	LVL	AGE	PA	R	2B	3B	HR	RBI	BB	K	SB	CS	AVG/OBP/SLG	DRC+	VORP	BABIP	BRR	FRAA	WARP
2017	SWB	AAA	24	59	12	4	0	3	7	11	9	0	0	.298/.424/.574	136	4.7	.306	-1.0	1B(10): 0.9	0.3
2017	NYA	MLB	24	170	20	7	0	9	28	19	42	0	0	.190/.288/.422	103	1.2	.194	-1.0	1B(46): -1.1	0.1
2018	NYA	MLB	25	311	23	16	1	11	38	30	78	0	0	.199/.286/.386	91	-7.7	.230	-1.8	1B(74): 1.4	0.1
2019	NYA	MLB	26	282	31	14	1	9	35	26	64	0	0	.233/.314/.408	94	1.0	.276	-1.0	1B 0	0.1

Breakout: 3%   Improve: 54%   Collapse: 4%   Attrition: 10%   MLB: 95%   *Comparables: Adam LaRoche, Matt LaPorta, Mike Jacobs*

Though he may be the owner of the cat related to Dr. Evil's Mr. Bigglesworth, it seems that Greg Bird has more in common with another *Austin Powers* character—Mustafa, who was responsible for Bigglesworth's hairless fate and had his chair collapsed from underneath him into a flaming dungeon. Bird may not be in a dungeon but he is riding the bench, losing a starting spot to Luke Voit after hitting to just a .327 wOBA from June 1st until the trade deadline. One would imagine he gets one more shot considering Brian Cashman, though three years past, called him "by far the best hitter (among prospects) in the organization," it seems his promising career in the Bronx is, in Mustafa's own words, "alive, but very badly burned."

Jacoby Ellsbury CF Born: 09/11/83 Age: 35 Bats: L Throws: L Height: 6'1" Weight: 195 Origin: Round 1, 2005 Draft (#23 overall)

YEAR	TEAM	LVL	AGE	PA	R	2B	3B	HR	RBI	BB	K	SB	CS	AVG/OBP/SLG	DRC+	VORP	BABIP	BRR	FRAA	WARP
2016	NYA	MLB	32	626	71	24	5	9	56	54	84	20	8	.263/.330/.374	94	12.3	.295	2.3	CF(148): -14.5	0.5
2017	NYA	MLB	33	409	65	20	4	7	39	41	63	22	3	.264/.348/.402	95	16.4	.304	1.4	CF(97): -5.8	0.7
2019	NYA	MLB	35	64	8	3	1	1	6	6	9	3	1	.263/.340/.387	125	4.5	.299	0.1	CF -1	0.4

Breakout: 0%   Improve: 17%   Collapse: 9%   Attrition: 27%   MLB: 79%   *Comparables: Mike Kingery, Lloyd Waner, Brady Clark*

On August 29th, it was announced that Yankee Stadium would soon feature a wine bar sporting a "cask-based aesthetic." One can only assume that it is of the Amontillado variety, and their unfortunate friend to live behind the cask is none other than Jacoby Ellsbury. The former All-Star might as well live in a wall behind the bar; he failed to appear in a single game due to a right oblique strain, which led to a left hip issue, and then plantar fasciitis, which then snowballed into a torn labrum in that same hip. With two years still remaining on his bloated deal, but the team skating under the luxury tax threshold, the front office is likely to reinvest the insurance money in more personnel... and a bigger bar.

Estevan Florial CF Born: 11/25/97 Age: 21 Bats: L Throws: R Height: 6'1" Weight: 185 Origin: International Free Agent, 2015

YEAR	TEAM	LVL	AGE	PA	R	2B	3B	HR	RBI	BB	K	SB	CS	AVG/OBP/SLG	DRC+	VORP	BABIP	BRR	FRAA	WARP
2016	PUL	RK	18	268	36	10	1	7	25	28	78	10	2	.225/.315/.364	88	5.1	.305	0.0	CF(43): 0.1, LF(6): -0.8	0.2
2017	CSC	A	19	389	64	21	5	11	43	41	124	17	7	.297/.373/.483	102	31.8	.431	-0.7	CF(62): -2.1, LF(13): 2.9	1.2
2017	TAM	A+	19	87	13	2	2	2	14	9	24	6	1	.303/.368/.461	100	7.4	.404	0.7	CF(18): 0.4	0.4
2018	TAM	A+	20	339	45	16	3	3	27	44	87	11	10	.255/.354/.361	93	10.5	.353	-0.9	CF(59): 1.8, RF(6): -0.2	0.8
2019	NYA	MLB	21	251	28	7	0	6	20	20	82	5	3	.189/.251/.297	45	-8.2	.260	-0.3	CF 1, LF 0	-0.8

Breakout: 7%   Improve: 10%   Collapse: 1%   Attrition: 9%   MLB: 18%   *Comparables: Clint Frazier, Anthony Gose, Christian Yelich*

With Stanton, Judge, Gardner and Frazier on the roster, it's an understatement to say that the Yankees have an embarrassment of riches in the outfield. What makes it truly a comical statement is when you consider Florial, who had a stunning AZL performance in 2017 and was poised to make the next jump in '18. The paths of prospects are circuitous, though, and Florial's might become more so after undergoing surgery on the hamate bone in his right wrist. You know the old saying with wrist injuries and power, and Florial missed a chunk of development time after being ranked 26th on BP's Top 101 last year. This won't impact his immense speed or the possible impact of his glove in center field, but even still at his young age, Florial needs more reps to nail down his issues with plate discipline and pitch recognition.

Clint Frazier OF   Born: 09/06/94   Age: 24   Bats: R   Throws: R   Height: 6'1"   Weight: 190   Origin: Round 1, 2013 Draft (#5 overall)

YEAR	TEAM	LVL	AGE	PA	R	2B	3B	HR	RBI	BB	K	SB	CS	AVG/OBP/SLG	DRC+	VORP	BABIP	BRR	FRAA	WARP
2016	AKR	AA	21	391	56	25	1	13	48	41	86	13	4	.276/.356/.469	113	24.2	.331	1.4	RF(31): -0.4, LF(26): 2.2	2.0
2016	SWB	AAA	21	108	17	2	3	3	7	7	30	0	0	.228/.278/.396	82	1.6	.294	0.8	LF(13): -0.7, RF(6): 1.5	0.2
2017	SWB	AAA	22	320	46	19	2	12	42	37	69	9	2	.256/.344/.473	118	14.9	.291	1.8	LF(38): 1.2, RF(29): -1.3	1.5
2017	NYA	MLB	22	142	16	9	4	4	17	7	43	1	0	.231/.268/.448	75	1.0	.307	0.8	LF(30): -3.1, RF(7): 0.4	-0.3
2018	NYA	MLB	23	41	9	3	0	0	1	5	13	0	0	.265/.390/.353	78	0.6	.429	0.2	LF(9): -0.7, CF(1): -0.2	-0.1
2018	SWB	AAA	23	216	38	14	3	10	21	23	52	4	2	.311/.389/.574	135	20.4	.380	0.9	CF(26): -2.9, LF(16): -0.3	1.3
2019	*NYA*	*MLB*	*24*	*151*	*17*	*7*	*1*	*5*	*17*	*13*	*40*	*2*	*1*	*.227/.302/.391*	*96*	*3.4*	*.285*	*0.0*	*LF 0, RF 0*	*0.3*

Breakout: 5%   Improve: 37%   Collapse: 13%   Attrition: 28%   MLB: 83%   *Comparables: Derek Fisher, Lewis Brinson, Joe Benson*

Chronic Traumatic Encephalopathy, commonly known as CTE, has been studied for nearly a century, and yet the implications of head injuries in baseball haven't been in team and fan lexicon for more than a decade or so. This is evident not only in how teams handle it, but how open players are in speaking up about their symptoms. When Clint Frazier suffered a concussion from a wall collision during spring training, the Yankees made sure to carefully inch him along, waiting until July to let him return full-time. After suffering migraines resulting from a collision with Jace Peterson, the Yankees once again shut him down, allowing him to creep back, this time as far as a minor league rehab stint. He was shut down—again—and his season was complete. Even though Michael Kay gave him flak for this, hearkening back to a time when that concussion lexicon didn't exist, saying, "Shame on [him] for not getting healthy." No one can blame Frazier for being frustrated, sniping back a "#ShameOnYouBro," especially considering this has truly been a lost season. Lost year or not, he is still a top prospect who can impress, and despite the grumbles, fans and Frazier alike should be rewarded with a healthy and concussion-free Red Lightning years down the road.

Brett Gardner LF   Born: 08/24/83   Age: 35   Bats: L   Throws: L   Height: 5'11"   Weight: 195   Origin: Round 3, 2005 Draft (#109 overall)

YEAR	TEAM	LVL	AGE	PA	R	2B	3B	HR	RBI	BB	K	SB	CS	AVG/OBP/SLG	DRC+	VORP	BABIP	BRR	FRAA	WARP
2016	NYA	MLB	32	634	80	22	6	7	41	70	106	16	4	.261/.351/.362	93	14.8	.310	5.2	LF(147): 14.3, CF(3): -0.1	3.1
2017	NYA	MLB	33	682	96	26	4	21	63	72	122	23	5	.264/.350/.428	106	25.7	.300	1.4	LF(122): 12.5, CF(22): 0.2	3.9
2018	NYA	MLB	34	609	95	20	7	12	45	65	107	16	2	.236/.322/.368	96	12.3	.272	4.1	LF(107): 11.8, CF(34): 0.0	3.1
2019	*NYA*	*MLB*	*35*	*569*	*73*	*25*	*5*	*11*	*53*	*56*	*98*	*16*	*3*	*.259/.341/.396*	*104*	*22.3*	*.297*	*2.5*	*LF 11, CF -2*	*3.4*

Breakout: 0%   Improve: 29%   Collapse: 10%   Attrition: 17%   MLB: 74%   *Comparables: Charlie Jamieson, Chone Figgins, Shannon Stewart*

The longest-tenured Yankee will get one more year as that namesake, as the team bought him out of his final contract year and settled on a one year, $7.5 million contract. By this point, Gardner is more fan favorite than useful player, as crazy as that may have sounded a year ago. Not long departed from his first 20/20 season, the markings of age and decline dominate the stat sheet. He hit just .209 in the second half with three home runs, and lost his everyday job to the trio of Andrew McCutchen, Aaron Hicks, and Aaron Judge. He still has his uses, of course, as not only Clint Frazier's future is in flux but a single injury could completely change the calculus. But as Gritty Gutty Gardner likely ends his career as rider of the bench, it will be bittersweet to see him in pinstripes not as the four-tool player he once was, but as a symbol of a bygone era where he himself was the Baby Bomber.

Didi Gregorius SS   Born: 02/18/90   Age: 29   Bats: L   Throws: R   Height: 6'3"   Weight: 205   Origin: International Free Agent, 2007

YEAR	TEAM	LVL	AGE	PA	R	2B	3B	HR	RBI	BB	K	SB	CS	AVG/OBP/SLG	DRC+	VORP	BABIP	BRR	FRAA	WARP
2016	NYA	MLB	26	597	68	32	2	20	70	19	82	7	1	.276/.304/.447	99	26.8	.290	4.2	SS(153): -5.6	2.6
2017	NYA	MLB	27	570	73	27	0	25	87	25	70	3	1	.287/.318/.478	113	39.0	.287	1.9	SS(135): 4.9	4.3
2018	NYA	MLB	28	569	89	23	5	27	86	48	69	10	6	.268/.335/.494	128	40.9	.259	2.3	SS(132): 0.4	4.9
2019	*NYA*	*MLB*	*29*	*218*	*27*	*12*	*1*	*8*	*30*	*13*	*27*	*3*	*1*	*.287/.338/.482*	*116*	*13.2*	*.296*	*0.8*	*SS 0*	*1.4*

Breakout: 4%   Improve: 51%   Collapse: 1%   Attrition: 5%   MLB: 96%   *Comparables: Edgar Renteria, Rafael Furcal, Tony Fernandez*

Very rarely does one get to pen the Annual comment for multiple seasons at once, but it seems like much of Gregorius' 2019 season is already written. After undergoing Tommy John surgery on his throwing hand on October 17th, the verdict was that he could return any time between June and August. It couldn't happen to a more exciting player: Of all of the stars of the new-look Baby Bombers, no one is a fan favorite quite like Gregorius. Not only he is one of the best shortstops in the league, a stellar defender with newly found power, but his array of dances, handshakes, and emoji-laden post-victory tweets help differentiate this Yankees team from the straight-laced teams of yore. His body will be missed, and the team will have to scramble to fill the performance. But the soul? That'll be missed more than anything.

Adeiny Hechavarria SS   Born: 04/15/89   Age: 30   Bats: R   Throws: R   Height: 6'0"   Weight: 195   Origin: International Free Agent, 2010

YEAR	TEAM	LVL	AGE	PA	R	2B	3B	HR	RBI	BB	K	SB	CS	AVG/OBP/SLG	DRC+	VORP	BABIP	BRR	FRAA	WARP
2016	MIA	MLB	27	547	52	17	6	3	38	33	73	1	0	.236/.283/.311	76	8.5	.269	6.5	SS(153): 2.3	1.8
2017	MIA	MLB	28	67	8	2	1	1	6	1	9	0	0	.277/.288/.385	84	0.6	.309	-0.9	SS(19): -1.1	0.0
2017	TBA	MLB	28	281	29	12	4	7	24	12	58	4	1	.257/.289/.411	79	5.7	.302	-1.3	SS(77): 3.4	0.8
2018	TBA	MLB	29	237	29	7	0	3	26	12	37	1	0	.258/.289/.332	87	6.7	.290	1.5	SS(61): -1.3	0.7
2018	PIT	MLB	29	47	2	4	0	1	3	3	11	0	0	.233/.277/.395	89	-1.2	.281	-1.3	SS(15): -1.1	-0.1
2018	NYA	MLB	29	37	3	0	0	2	2	1	10	1	0	.194/.216/.361	88	-0.2	.208	0.1	SS(16): -1.4, 3B(4): -0.3	-0.1
2019	*NYA*	*MLB*	*30*	*314*	*32*	*15*	*2*	*6*	*32*	*20*	*51*	*2*	*1*	*.261/.311/.392*	*90*	*8.9*	*.295*	*0.9*	*SS 0, 3B 0*	*1.0*

Breakout: 0%   Improve: 21%   Collapse: 8%   Attrition: 25%   MLB: 97%   *Comparables: Alex Cintron, Jack Wilson, Cristian Guzman*

When you're a potential playoff team with important games in September, defensive replacements become a near-necessity as the rosters expand. So it makes sense that the Yankees acquired Hechavarria at the waiver trade deadline for that very purpose. With Didi Gregorius dealing with injury and Miguel Andujar dealing with... his defense, Hechavarria was a more than capable backup, playing 18 games and four out of the five playoff games in just that short span, highlighted by a jaw-dropping leaping grab he made in the seventh inning of the Wild Card game. The bat never came around, and it likely never will, but those few saved runs on defense down the stretch could benefit a contending team in the future.

Aaron Hicks CF   Born: 10/02/89   Age: 29   Bats: B   Throws: R   Height: 6'1"   Weight: 202   Origin: Round 1, 2008 Draft (#14 overall)

YEAR	TEAM	LVL	AGE	PA	R	2B	3B	HR	RBI	BB	K	SB	CS	AVG/OBP/SLG	DRC+	VORP	BABIP	BRR	FRAA	WARP
2016	NYA	MLB	26	361	32	13	1	8	31	30	68	3	4	.217/.281/.336	81	-6.8	.248	0.3	RF(86): -0.7, LF(25): 2.7	0.5
2017	NYA	MLB	27	361	54	18	0	15	52	51	67	10	5	.266/.372/.475	115	22.1	.290	2.0	CF(52): -0.8, LF(22): 0.8	1.9
2018	NYA	MLB	28	581	90	18	3	27	79	90	111	11	2	.248/.366/.467	128	36.5	.264	2.3	CF(131): -8.6	3.5
2019	NYA	MLB	29	540	69	24	3	18	69	66	96	11	4	.256/.353/.437	118	33.7	.286	1.7	CF -4, RF -1	3.1

Breakout: 5%   Improve: 52%   Collapse: 5%   Attrition: 11%   MLB: 99%   *Comparables: David DeJesus, Shane Victorino, Jon Jay*

If your average baseball fan were asked to pick the ten best outfielders in baseball last year, would they even consider Aaron Hicks? You could make the argument that he's close to cracking the top five, as he set career records in home runs (27), walk percentage (15.5%), and conversely, strikeouts (111). His defense may have soured just a bit, ticking down six outs (3 to -3) in Statcast's Outs Above Average, but he has more than made up for that in power. It feels like ages ago when the front office was questioned for giving up John Ryan Murphy for an apparent platoon bench bat, but they've since been vindicated. While his splits have largely remained intact, still showing a weak spot against left-handers, he has more than made up in overall performance.

Kyle Higashioka C   Born: 04/20/90   Age: 29   Bats: R   Throws: R   Height: 6'1"   Weight: 205   Origin: Round 7, 2008 Draft (#230 overall)

YEAR	TEAM	LVL	AGE	PA	R	2B	3B	HR	RBI	BB	K	SB	CS	AVG/OBP/SLG	DRC+	VORP	BABIP	BRR	FRAA	WARP
2016	TRN	AA	26	256	31	15	0	11	51	26	42	0	1	.293/.355/.509	140	22.4	.305	-2.0	C(61): 12.2	3.6
2016	SWB	AAA	26	160	24	9	0	10	30	12	31	0	1	.250/.306/.514	136	7.3	.252	-1.9	C(36): 4.2	1.7
2017	NYA	MLB	27	20	2	0	0	0	0	2	6	0	0	.000/.100/.000	64	-1.7	.000	-0.1	C(8): 1.6	0.2
2017	SWB	AAA	27	57	5	4	0	2	11	4	7	0	0	.264/.316/.453	111	2.3	.273	-0.2	C(14): 4.5	0.8
2018	SWB	AAA	28	211	16	10	1	5	22	17	44	2	0	.202/.276/.346	102	-0.9	.234	-0.7	C(49): 6.6	1.6
2018	NYA	MLB	28	79	6	2	0	3	6	6	16	0	0	.167/.241/.319	106	-2.6	.170	-0.7	C(27): 3.8	0.8
2019	NYA	MLB	29	37	3	2	0	1	4	3	8	0	0	.225/.287/.354	81	0.7	.270	-0.1	C 1	0.2

Breakout: 2%   Improve: 18%   Collapse: 6%   Attrition: 19%   MLB: 45%   *Comparables: Stephen Vogt, Dustin Garneau, Brett Nicholas*

YEAR	TEAM	P. COUNT	FRM RUNS	BLK RUNS	THRW RUNS	TOT RUNS
2017	NYA	813	1.7	-0.1	0.0	1.5
2017	SWB	2153	4.3	-0.3	-0.1	3.8
2018	NYA	3384	3.2	0.8	-0.1	4.4
2018	SWB	6908	7.2	0.6	-0.2	7.6
2019	NYA	1439	1.0	0.0	-0.1	0.9

One usually doesn't think of the Yankees when they consider sabermetric advances, but the franchise has always been on the hunt for pitch framing. Jose Molina may have been a statistical oddity when he was on Tampa Bay, a case of valuing that skill over others, but the Yankees had him first, and it's not like he was tearing the cover off the ball in New York either. There was Chris Stewart, who was mocked by fans for his abysmal bat but collected 21 framing runs in 2013, and had 6+ WARP over a three year stretch that went largely unnoticed. There was Francisco Cervelli, who could never stay healthy, but ultimately put up similar framing numbers in his first season in Pittsburgh. Kyle Higashioka shouldn't be forgotten, either. He had just a .583 OPS, but his CSAA of 0.013 implies he could still be valuable in an extended stretch, if he can lift his offense to at least forgettable levels. If someone in the Bronx is sprinkling framing and defense fairy dust, the front office is betting it takes effect in short order.

Aaron Judge RF   Born: 04/26/92   Age: 27   Bats: R   Throws: R   Height: 6'7"   Weight: 282   Origin: Round 1, 2013 Draft (#32 overall)

YEAR	TEAM	LVL	AGE	PA	R	2B	3B	HR	RBI	BB	K	SB	CS	AVG/OBP/SLG	DRC+	VORP	BABIP	BRR	FRAA	WARP
2016	SWB	AAA	24	410	62	18	1	19	65	47	98	5	0	.270/.366/.489	138	31.4	.319	2.8	RF(66): 19.6, LF(7): -0.7	4.9
2016	NYA	MLB	24	95	10	2	0	4	10	9	42	0	1	.179/.263/.345	66	-2.5	.282	-0.5	RF(27): -3.2	-0.6
2017	NYA	MLB	25	678	128	24	3	52	114	127	208	9	4	.284/.422/.627	162	68.5	.357	-0.1	RF(141): 4.4	7.3
2018	NYA	MLB	26	498	77	22	0	27	67	76	152	6	3	.278/.392/.528	133	33.3	.368	1.0	RF(90): 12.6, CF(1): -0.1	4.5
2019	NYA	MLB	27	680	107	29	2	34	95	102	215	7	3	.249/.367/.485	132	43.6	.334	0.4	RF 5	5.2

Breakout: 2%   Improve: 59%   Collapse: 1%   Attrition: 0%   MLB: 99%   *Comparables: Giancarlo Stanton, Darryl Strawberry, Jose Canseco*

The Yankees' luck with injuries could be summed up by July 26th, when Jakob Junis drilled Aaron Judge on the ulnar styloid bone in his right wrist. What was expected to be a short DL stint dragged on until September 14th, and the team sagged, nearly losing their hold on the first wild card spot. If the team had not made the postseason then we'd probably be discussing whether his wrist was fully healed; he had just a .300 wOBA and one home run in September. Well, until they did make the postseason. He hit .421 in five games with three home runs, bringing his postseason total to seven in just 18 games. With that, the organization shouldn't be too worried that he's healthy, and he is still likely to be the most valuable player on the 2019 team. The Yankees' overall fortunes largely track with his performance, and if this past postseason was any indication, and the organization finally gets their other ducks in a row, then they are primed to put him in the position to achieve the playoff glory he seems destined to achieve.

Austin Romine C   Born: 11/22/88   Age: 30   Bats: R   Throws: R   Height: 6'1"   Weight: 220   Origin: Round 2, 2007 Draft (#94 overall)

YEAR	TEAM	LVL	AGE	PA	R	2B	3B	HR	RBI	BB	K	SB	CS	AVG/OBP/SLG	DRC+	VORP	BABIP	BRR	FRAA	WARP
2016	NYA	MLB	27	176	17	11	0	4	26	7	31	1	0	.242/.269/.382	81	-0.6	.271	-0.1	C(50): -3.2, 1B(6): -0.2	0.0
2017	NYA	MLB	28	252	19	9	1	2	21	16	57	0	0	.218/.272/.293	67	-4.9	.277	-1.8	C(67): 4.5, 1B(12): 0.7	0.5
2018	NYA	MLB	29	265	30	12	0	10	42	17	67	1	0	.244/.295/.417	87	4.5	.292	-3.1	C(76): 6.8	1.3
2019	NYA	MLB	30	159	16	7	1	4	17	11	34	0	0	.241/.299/.374	89	3.2	.288	-0.8	C 2, 1B 0	0.6

Breakout: 4%   Improve: 26%   Collapse: 8%   Attrition: 31%   MLB: 76%   *Comparables: Rob Johnson, Humberto Quintero, Chris Herrmann*

YEAR	TEAM	P. COUNT	FRM RUNS	BLK RUNS	THRW RUNS	TOT RUNS
2016	NYA	5754	-1.9	-0.1	-0.5	-2.7
2017	NYA	8705	6.3	-0.3	-1.3	4.3
2018	NYA	10341	4.2	2.2	0.0	6.3
2019	NYA	4871	1.6	0.2	-0.3	1.6

Jazayerli's Law of Backup Catchers is a powerful one, and Austin Romine looked like he would live up to reaching .300, or at least a .300 OBP, for once after Gary Sanchez missed time, hitting .270 with an .825 OPS in the first half. Unfortunately, Sanchez's absence stretched further in the second half with a groin issue, and so did Romine's regression to the mean. It doesn't mean his value was null, of course, as his framing netted them about four runs or so, and his blocking, while a minor skill in comparison to how much the media focuses on it, gave them a couple of runs here and there. With just one more year of team control, which amusingly makes him one of the longest tenured Yankees, he will get one more shot at that magic .300 mark.

Gary Sanchez C   Born: 12/02/92   Age: 26   Bats: R   Throws: R   Height: 6'2"   Weight: 230   Origin: International Free Agent, 2009

YEAR	TEAM	LVL	AGE	PA	R	2B	3B	HR	RBI	BB	K	SB	CS	AVG/OBP/SLG	DRC+	VORP	BABIP	BRR	FRAA	WARP
2016	SWB	AAA	23	313	39	21	1	10	50	21	45	7	1	.282/.339/.468	121	25.1	.302	-0.9	C(64): 10.8	3.2
2016	NYA	MLB	23	229	34	12	0	20	42	24	57	1	0	.299/.376/.657	141	23.5	.317	-1.2	C(36): 1.4	2.1
2017	NYA	MLB	24	525	79	20	0	33	90	40	120	2	1	.278/.345/.531	124	44.9	.304	2.3	C(104): 5.4, 1B(2): 0.0	4.8
2018	NYA	MLB	25	374	51	17	0	18	53	46	94	1	0	.186/.291/.406	97	5.7	.197	-1.4	C(76): -1.4	1.3
2019	NYA	MLB	26	598	79	25	2	30	90	59	135	3	1	.247/.335/.468	119	37.6	.280	-0.1	C 3	4.4

Breakout: 4%   Improve: 52%   Collapse: 1%   Attrition: 6%   MLB: 97%

Comparables: Buster Posey, Joey Votto, Justin Morneau

YEAR	TEAM	P. COUNT	FRM RUNS	BLK RUNS	THRW RUNS	TOT RUNS
2016	NYA	5290	1.0	-1.4	1.2	1.2
2017	NYA	14363	7.4	-3.1	2.3	7.2
2018	NYA	10822	3.3	-4.3	0.2	-0.9
2018	SWB	560	0.0	0.0	0.0	0.4
2019	NYA	17757	7.1	-5.0	2.0	4.1

If there was a nadir in a lowly season for Gary Sanchez, it occurred on July 23rd. The Yankees were in Tampa playing the Rays, and two costly mistakes arguably cost them the game. A cross-up from Luis Severino sent a pitch off his glove and into foul territory on the third base side, and Sanchez, slowly jogging to get the ball, misjudged Jake Bauers heading around third and watched him successfully steal home. Then, in the last play of the game, he hit a ground ball with the bases loaded that he didn't hustle on, and the game slipped away.

With Sanchez, there's always that cold, hard, lived reality, and then an underlying, mitigating truth. The mitigating truth in this instance was that Sanchez re-aggravated his groin injury during the cross-up, explaining that cringeworthy stroll down to first. In the case of his season, the mitigating truth was that he was limited physically. Not only did he miss much of the season due to that same groin injury, but it was revealed that Sanchez had been dealing with a shoulder issue since 2017; he had one cortisone shot then, and after this season was over, he underwent a left shoulder debridement, with a treatment schedule that should get him back before Opening Day.

Even when healthy, though, it seems that fans can't get over one thing: passed balls. Sanchez had 18 passed balls in just 76 games caught, which obviously looks bad! But here's that underlying truth again: His ability to frame pitches canceled out the damage he did by letting them roll by. Sanchez is an ugly catcher, and also, quantifiably, a good catcher, a man designed to be roasted on sports radio and celebrated in person. The latter became evident at very end of the season, when Sanchez hit two monstrous home runs in Game Two of the ALDS at Fenway Park, the last one silencing the crowd with a bat drop, and he hit a fly ball in Game Four that, if launched one degree lower, would have sent the series to a winner-take-all. And that was with surgery pending.

Even with all of the trials and tribulations, both with injury and the press dogging him over passed balls, it's humorous that there is probably not a catcher you would take over him if you were to start a franchise today. That's a testament to talent that isn't going away, even if people don't always notice it.

Anthony Seigler C   Born: 06/20/99   Age: 20   Bats: B   Throws: S   Height: 6'0"   Weight: 200   Origin: Round 1, 2018 Draft (#23 overall)

YEAR	TEAM	LVL	AGE	PA	R	2B	3B	HR	RBI	BB	K	SB	CS	AVG/OBP/SLG	DRC+	VORP	BABIP	BRR	FRAA	WARP
2018	YAT	RK	19	42	7	2	0	1	4	6	7	0	0	.333/.429/.472	123	4.7	.393	-0.3	C(10): -0.2	0.2
2018	PUL	RK	19	53	4	1	0	0	5	8	5	0	0	.209/.340/.233	119	0.4	.231	0.1	C(11): 0.0	0.4
2019	NYA	MLB	20	251	24	9	0	5	20	16	54	1	0	.204/.253/.293	50	-5.0	.240	-1.0	C 0	-0.6

Comparables: Francisco Pena, Carson Kelly, Brandon Drury

This century, the Yankees have drafted only one first-round position player that produced more than 0.5 WARP, and his name rhymes with fudge. Seigler isn't your typical first-round position player, though. In the age of two-way players, where Shohei Ohtani has set a trend carefully followed by draft prospects like Brendan McKay, he has followed suit... as baseball's first two-way pitcher/catcher. Not only can he do that, but he has somehow merged the powers of Pat Venditte, throwing both 90 mph as a right-hander and a shade lower out of the other hand. While the Yankees have sworn they'll exclusively use him behind the plate, we can dream. What matters most for his long-term prospects is his bat and his actual catching skills—despite how far we've come, the fundamentals are still of the utmost importance. Even if those don't fully hold, a switch-hitting, switch-pitching, catching pitcher is the kind of Rube Goldberg-esque utility player any team would love, and considering the organization's overall track record with these picks, they now have multiple vectors to succeed.

Giancarlo Stanton OF   Born: 11/08/89   Age: 29   Bats: R   Throws: R   Height: 6'6"   Weight: 245   Origin: Round 2, 2007 Draft (#76 overall)

YEAR	TEAM	LVL	AGE	PA	R	2B	3B	HR	RBI	BB	K	SB	CS	AVG/OBP/SLG	DRC+	VORP	BABIP	BRR	FRAA	WARP
2016	MIA	MLB	26	470	56	20	1	27	74	50	140	0	0	.240/.326/.489	110	31.2	.290	0.4	RF(106): 2.4	2.0
2017	MIA	MLB	27	692	123	32	0	59	132	85	163	2	2	.281/.376/.631	151	76.9	.288	-0.1	RF(149): 8.3	6.9
2018	NYA	MLB	28	705	102	34	1	38	100	70	211	5	0	.266/.343/.509	114	30.1	.333	0.0	RF(37): -1.1, LF(36): 0.0	2.5
2019	NYA	MLB	29	622	90	26	2	37	104	74	169	3	1	.256/.353/.515	136	38.0	.304	0.1	LF -1, RF 1	4.0

Breakout: 3%   Improve: 61%   Collapse: 1%   Attrition: 3%   MLB: 100%

Comparables: Fred McGriff, Dick Allen, Cecil Fielder

The tone of Giancarlo Stanton's season will be forever tarred by his Yankee Stadium debut, where he went 0 for 5 with five strikeouts. He redeemed himself in other ways; while Aaron Judge missed time, Stanton himself largely carried the offense, offering a .384 wOBA with 22 home runs from June 1st to September 1st. Yankee fans may remember only the end, though, where he finished with a .316 wOBA in September and hit just .238 in the postseason with seven strikeouts. In the eyes of said fans, there will always be a paradox: They believe in spending money on the best players, but that well-paid players become complacent. Complacency or no (the answer: no), 2018 was a clear disappointment for the slugger. He set a career high in strikeouts, and his chase rate was the highest it's been in over five years. While he expected his more closed stance to be advantageous for Yankee Stadium, pitchers took advantage by beating him with heat up-and-in. There's no reason to worry yet, but for the Yankees to hoist another trophy, they need Stanton to return to his South Beach self.

Gleyber Torres INF Born: 12/13/96 Age: 22 Bats: R Throws: R Height: 6'1" Weight: 200 Origin: International Free Agent, 2013

YEAR	TEAM	LVL	AGE	PA	R	2B	3B	HR	RBI	BB	K	SB	CS	AVG/OBP/SLG	DRC+	VORP	BABIP	BRR	FRAA	WARP
2016	MYR	A+	19	409	62	23	3	9	47	42	87	19	10	.275/.359/.433	109	26.1	.341	0.2	SS(87): 0.6	2.2
2016	TAM	A+	19	138	19	6	2	2	19	16	23	2	3	.254/.341/.385	114	5.2	.299	-2.9	SS(27): -0.9, 2B(1): 0.0	0.4
2017	TRN	AA	20	139	22	10	1	5	18	17	21	5	4	.273/.367/.496	126	15.5	.295	1.3	SS(19): 2.2, 3B(6): 0.8	1.5
2017	SWB	AAA	20	96	9	4	1	2	16	13	26	2	2	.309/.406/.457	101	7.2	.426	-1.8	3B(9): 1.8, SS(9): 1.0	0.4
2018	SWB	AAA	21	56	6	3	1	1	11	5	10	1	1	.347/.393/.510	110	4.7	.400	0.1	3B(8): 0.6, SS(3): 0.2	0.4
2018	NYA	MLB	21	484	54	16	1	24	77	42	122	6	2	.271/.340/.480	124	24.3	.321	0.8	2B(109): 5.4, SS(21): 1.5	3.9
2019	*NYA*	*MLB*	*22*	*540*	*69*	*22*	*2*	*22*	*69*	*51*	*140*	*8*	*4*	*.241/.322/.431*	*106*	*22.6*	*.294*	*-0.1*	*2B 3, SS 0*	*2.7*

Breakout: 2%   Improve: 49%   Collapse: 0%   Attrition: 8%   MLB: 74%   *Comparables: Addison Russell, Xander Bogaerts, Rougned Odor*

With all the talk of Miguel Andujar being snubbed in the Rookie of the Year voting, you'd forget that the Yankees have a rookie with even more promise, and arguably a better 2018 season, in Torres. His wOBA was just 12 points lower than Andujar, and he had just three fewer home runs. Yet the biggest difference was defense, where Torres was a whopping 24 (!!!) runs better by DRS. It's not like it was clutch hitting that made the difference in narrative, either, as Torres also had an edge in WPA by 1.58. In high leverage situations, however little predictability that carries, he had an other-worldly 1.387 OPS. Because Torres coincidentally made the team just after the service time cut-off, the Yankees will have six more years of team control. Another half-decade of well-above-average play at second base is exactly what the doctor ordered for a team that never really found an heir apparent to Robinson Cano.

Troy Tulowitzki SS Born: 10/10/84 Age: 34 Bats: R Throws: R Height: 6'3" Weight: 205 Origin: Round 1, 2005 Draft (#7 overall)

YEAR	TEAM	LVL	AGE	PA	R	2B	3B	HR	RBI	BB	K	SB	CS	AVG/OBP/SLG	DRC+	VORP	BABIP	BRR	FRAA	WARP
2016	TOR	MLB	31	544	54	21	0	24	79	43	101	1	0	.254/.318/.443	110	16.6	.272	-1.6	SS(128): 2.8	3.4
2017	TOR	MLB	32	260	16	10	0	7	26	17	40	0	1	.249/.300/.378	88	0.5	.272	-3.0	SS(64): 2.4	0.8
2019	*NYA*	*MLB*	*34*	*194*	*21*	*9*	*1*	*6*	*22*	*15*	*34*	*0*	*0*	*.254/.318/.408*	*105*	*7.6*	*.286*	*-0.8*	*SS 1*	*1.0*

Breakout: 0%   Improve: 28%   Collapse: 5%   Attrition: 9%   MLB: 92%   *Comparables: Jhonny Peralta, Miguel Tejada, Edgar Renteria*

For this game, we'll need a number—any number. Got it? Okay. Next, pick an adjective. Finally, think of a body part. The weirder, the better. Now, insert those words into this sentence: "Fazed by a career-worst performance in 2017, Troy Tulowitzki sought to reaffirm his place in the starting lineup once more, but was felled by [number] [adjective] [body part] and spent the entirety of his 2018 campaign watching Aledmys Diaz bobble ground balls at short." Rest assured that the words you chose have absolutely no bearing on this story; it's more or less the same one we've seen play out during each of his seasons in Toronto. Sure, he *could* work his way back from season-ending bone spur removal to a full workload in the spring, and sure, he *could* see a resurgence at the plate after three straight years of decline, but we should know better than to put our faith in fairy tales by now.

Luke Voit 1B Born: 02/13/91 Age: 28 Bats: R Throws: R Height: 6'3" Weight: 225 Origin: Round 22, 2013 Draft (#665 overall)

YEAR	TEAM	LVL	AGE	PA	R	2B	3B	HR	RBI	BB	K	SB	CS	AVG/OBP/SLG	DRC+	VORP	BABIP	BRR	FRAA	WARP
2016	SFD	AA	25	546	70	20	5	19	74	52	83	1	2	.297/.372/.477	142	34.1	.323	1.9	1B(104): 2.2, LF(12): 1.1	4.2
2017	MEM	AAA	26	307	35	23	1	13	50	29	53	1	1	.327/.407/.565	131	29.9	.368	-3.6	1B(62): 4.3	1.7
2017	SLN	MLB	26	124	18	9	0	4	18	7	31	0	0	.246/.306/.430	83	0.6	.304	-0.3	1B(31): 1.6	0.1
2018	SLN	MLB	27	13	2	0	0	1	3	2	4	0	0	.182/.308/.455	147	1.4	.167	0.1	1B(3): 0.3	0.2
2018	MEM	AAA	27	271	35	16	2	9	36	31	49	0	1	.299/.391/.500	122	17.0	.345	-1.3	1B(56): 2.1, LF(1): -0.1	1.3
2018	SWB	AAA	27	32	2	2	0	1	3	3	7	0	0	.310/.375/.483	133	1.3	.381	-0.1	1B(3): 0.2	0.2
2018	NYA	MLB	27	148	28	5	0	14	33	15	39	0	0	.333/.405/.689	154	18.4	.380	1.1	1B(32): -2.7	1.1
2019	*NYA*	*MLB*	*28*	*537*	*73*	*28*	*2*	*27*	*81*	*49*	*133*	*0*	*0*	*.267/.346/.499*	*130*	*27.9*	*.319*	*1.0*	*1B 2*	*3.2*

Breakout: 9%   Improve: 27%   Collapse: 13%   Attrition: 24%   MLB: 65%   *Comparables: Nate Freiman, Steve Pearce, Jesus Guzman*

If you were ever in the market for baseball paraphernalia centered on Luke Voit, you could head over on to his online shop, where he is selling "LV" shirts in the style of the Louis Vuitton logo. Brian Cashman certainly purchased designer, except it was the equivalent of buying a knock-off and discovering its authenticity after the fact. That being said, Cashman had some clue that he was the real thing, making the decision by the Cardinals to trade him all the more puzzling. He was one of the best hitters in the PCL last season—where the usual park factors caveats apply—and he, despite the small sample size in 2017, had eye-popping exit velocity numbers. He continued both upon arriving in New York, generating barrels at a higher rate than everyone not named Joey Gallo. While regression is a natural conclusion, the Yankees may have finally discovered their first basemen. That'd be Gucci.

Tyler Wade UT Born: 11/23/94 Age: 24 Bats: L Throws: R Height: 6'1" Weight: 185 Origin: Round 4, 2013 Draft (#134 overall)

YEAR	TEAM	LVL	AGE	PA	R	2B	3B	HR	RBI	BB	K	SB	CS	AVG/OBP/SLG	DRC+	VORP	BABIP	BRR	FRAA	WARP
2016	TRN	AA	21	583	90	16	7	5	27	66	103	27	8	.259/.352/.349	103	37.6	.317	11.0	SS(91): -5.6, 2B(38): 0.0	3.1
2017	SWB	AAA	22	388	68	22	4	7	31	38	75	26	5	.310/.382/.460	113	30.6	.375	3.0	SS(54): -2.3, 2B(13): 2.8	2.9
2017	NYA	MLB	22	63	7	4	0	0	2	5	19	1	1	.155/.222/.224	60	-3.3	.231	0.7	2B(15): -0.8, SS(7): 0.0	-0.2
2018	SWB	AAA	23	408	46	18	4	4	27	37	82	11	8	.255/.328/.360	89	8.5	.318	-2.1	SS(51): -0.2, LF(12): 2.1	1.3
2018	NYA	MLB	23	70	8	4	0	1	5	4	23	1	0	.167/.214/.273	62	-2.9	.238	1.7	2B(26): -0.6, RF(5): -0.1	0.0
2019	*NYA*	*MLB*	*24*	*194*	*21*	*7*	*1*	*4*	*17*	*15*	*46*	*6*	*2*	*.216/.285/.328*	*73*	*0.5*	*.270*	*0.3*	*2B 2*	*0.2*

Breakout: 4%   Improve: 18%   Collapse: 14%   Attrition: 29%   MLB: 54%   *Comparables: Matt Duffy, Chase d'Arnaud, Chris Taylor*

There's always one player who looks like they'd be a much better player on a different team, and for the Yankees, that's Wade. In most worlds he would have gotten more playing time; it seems eons ago that both Aaron Boone and Brian Cashman envisioned him as the everyday second baseman come Opening Day. That lasted just two and a half weeks, as Gleyber Torres supplanted both him and Neil Walker, and even with his ability to play second and shortstop, he played just 36 games at the big league level and hit .167. Though he struggled to find a fit, there is at least some role (or team) that would afford him the opportunity to get more plate appearances, something he needs dearly to become consistent. He's still that same Spring Training player, as mirage-like as that sometimes can be, and his dynamic speed and stellar defense will make him valuable sometime, or somewhere.

Neil Walker 2B Born: 09/10/85 Age: 33 Bats: B Throws: R Height: 6'3" Weight: 210 Origin: Round 1, 2004 Draft (#11 overall)

YEAR	TEAM	LVL	AGE	PA	R	2B	3B	HR	RBI	BB	K	SB	CS	AVG/OBP/SLG	DRC+	VORP	BABIP	BRR	FRAA	WARP
2016	NYN	MLB	30	458	57	9	1	23	55	42	84	3	1	.282/.347/.476	127	31.2	.302	0.3	2B(111): 2.6	3.3
2017	NYN	MLB	31	299	40	13	2	10	36	27	47	0	1	.264/.339/.442	111	12.6	.286	-1.5	2B(68): -5.0, 1B(3): 0.0	0.7
2017	MIL	MLB	31	149	19	8	0	4	13	28	30	0	1	.267/.409/.433	113	10.0	.326	-0.7	2B(27): -1.1, 1B(14): 0.0	0.5
2018	NYA	MLB	32	398	48	12	1	11	46	42	87	0	0	.219/.309/.354	96	-0.5	.257	-1.0	1B(42): 4.2, 2B(32): 0.7	1.1
2019	*NYA*	*MLB*	*33*	*388*	*43*	*19*	*2*	*11*	*47*	*39*	*74*	*1*	*1*	*.261/.343/.419*	*111*	*13.9*	*.305*	*-0.6*	*1B 3, 2B 0*	*1.8*

Breakout: 7% Improve: 41% Collapse: 2% Attrition: 13% MLB: 91% *Comparables: Aubrey Huff, Lyle Overbay, Tino Martinez*

The Yankees always have one move a year that could be classified as "good process, bad result." Last year was Matt Holliday, who was fairly competent until contracting Epstein-Barr, and this year the title goes to Neil Walker. The veteran was brought in late in spring training as insurance for resident neophytes Gleyber Torres and Miguel Andujar, and his $4 million deal fit the bill. Walker subsequently posted career lows in home runs, isolated power, hits, and a career high in his strikeout rate. Wherever he finds himself, Walker will be a prime rebound candidate to at least split the difference between his worst year and his baseline from 2014-16. He'll also likely be waiting for the call most of another winter.

PITCHERS

Domingo Acevedo RHP Born: 03/06/94 Age: 25 Bats: R Throws: R Height: 6'7" Weight: 250 Origin: International Free Agent, 2012

YEAR	TEAM	LVL	AGE	W	L	SV	G	GS	IP	H	HR	BB/9	K/9	K	GB%	BABIP	WHIP	ERA	DRA	WARP	MPH	FB%	WHF	CSP
2016	CSC	A	22	3	1	0	8	8	42²	34	1	1.5	10.1	48	49%	.308	0.96	1.90	1.84	1.7				
2016	TAM	A+	22	2	5	0	10	10	50¹	49	3	2.7	9.7	54	42%	.343	1.27	3.22	2.57	1.7				
2017	TAM	A+	23	0	4	0	7	7	41¹	49	5	2.0	11.3	52	54%	.393	1.40	4.57	2.28	1.4				
2017	SWB	AAA	23	1	1	0	2	2	12¹	12	0	5.8	5.8	8	35%	.300	1.62	4.38	3.79	0.3				
2017	TRN	AA	23	5	1	0	14	14	79¹	65	8	1.9	9.3	82	37%	.282	1.03	2.38	2.75	2.3				
2018	TRN	AA	24	3	3	0	14	10	64²	51	3	2.8	7.2	52	38%	.264	1.10	2.92	3.95	1.0				
2019	*NYA*	*MLB*	*25*	*1*	*0*	*0*	*14*	*0*	*15¹*	*16*	*3*	*3.4*	*7.9*	*13*	*39%*	*.304*	*1.46*	*5.05*	*5.08*	*0.0*				

Breakout: 9% Improve: 25% Collapse: 23% Attrition: 38% MLB: 58% *Comparables: Joey Lucchesi, Austin Voth, Trevor Richards*

Acevedo is nothing short of a physical specimen on the mound, a six-foot-seven behemoth with a triple-digit fastball. That hasn't come with the durability usually afforded to taller pitchers, as he missed most of this season dealing with both blisters and a biceps injury. His high point of the season might be the most symbolic: he earned a promotion to the majors on July 21, only to be sent back down that night, a so-called phantom player. He was removed from the Arizona Fall League roster with an unknown injury, so his 2019 is also in danger of being delayed. He's no longer as young—now entering his age-25 season—so the sun could be setting on his career as a starter. Health is the only thing standing in the way of what is, at bare minimum, a promising future in the back-end of the bullpen.

Chance Adams RHP Born: 08/10/94 Age: 24 Bats: R Throws: R Height: 6'1" Weight: 220 Origin: Round 5, 2015 Draft (#153 overall)

YEAR	TEAM	LVL	AGE	W	L	SV	G	GS	IP	H	HR	BB/9	K/9	K	GB%	BABIP	WHIP	ERA	DRA	WARP	MPH	FB%	WHF	CSP
2016	TAM	A+	21	5	0	0	12	12	57²	41	4	2.3	11.4	73	42%	.276	0.97	2.65	2.39	2.0				
2016	TRN	AA	21	8	1	0	13	12	69²	35	5	3.1	9.2	71	47%	.181	0.85	2.07	3.15	1.6				
2017	TRN	AA	22	4	0	0	6	6	35	23	2	3.9	8.2	32	43%	.228	1.09	1.03	3.57	0.7				
2017	SWB	AAA	22	11	5	0	21	21	115¹	81	9	3.4	8.0	103	42%	.236	1.08	2.89	4.14	2.0				
2018	SWB	AAA	23	4	5	0	27	23	113	101	16	4.6	9.0	113	42%	.282	1.41	4.78	4.15	1.8				
2018	NYA	MLB	23	0	1	0	3	1	7²	8	3	4.7	4.7	4	38%	.217	1.57	7.04	7.07	-0.2	94.2	66.7	5.2	41.6
2019	*NYA*	*MLB*	*24*	*2*	*1*	*0*	*22*	*3*	*35¹*	*31*	*5*	*4.1*	*8.3*	*33*	*41%*	*.268*	*1.34*	*4.82*	*4.85*	*0.2*	*94.0*	*68.7*	*5.4*	*42.9*

Breakout: 15% Improve: 29% Collapse: 33% Attrition: 37% MLB: 72% *Comparables: Aaron Blair, Keyvius Sampson, Adam Warren*

ABBA said you should *Take a Chance on Me,* but that wasn't so for Chance Adams. Formerly considered a sleeper pitching prospect, he gained some notice after pitching to the tune of a 2.89 ERA at Scranton in 2017. The thinking was that with one injury, Chance would be on his way. That didn't happen until August 4th, when he made his first major league start at Fenway Park. He lost the game, allowing home runs to Mitch Moreland and JD Martinez. That mirrored his minor league season, where his command suffered and his flyball tendencies became home run tendencies. The team has announced he will get an opportunity to make the team as a starter out of Spring Training, so he has just one more Chance at redemption.

Dellin Betances RHP Born: 03/23/88 Age: 31 Bats: R Throws: R Height: 6'8" Weight: 265 Origin: Round 8, 2006 Draft (#254 overall)

YEAR	TEAM	LVL	AGE	W	L	SV	G	GS	IP	H	HR	BB/9	K/9	K	GB%	BABIP	WHIP	ERA	DRA	WARP	MPH	FB%	WHF	CSP
2016	NYA	MLB	28	3	6	12	73	0	73	54	5	3.5	15.5	126	56%	.353	1.12	3.08	1.89	2.6	100.8	43.4	17.1	43.4
2017	NYA	MLB	29	3	6	10	66	0	59²	29	3	6.6	15.1	100	49%	.252	1.22	2.87	3.04	1.4	100.2	46.2	13.3	44.1
2018	NYA	MLB	30	4	6	4	66	0	66²	44	7	3.5	15.5	115	46%	.311	1.05	2.70	2.15	2.1	99.7	47.8	16	47.1
2019	*NYA*	*MLB*	*31*	*3*	*1*	*10*	*53*	*0*	*56*	*40*	*7*	*4.1*	*13.6*	*85*	*48%*	*.293*	*1.17*	*3.36*	*3.32*	*1.1*	*99.3*	*45.8*	*15.3*	*44.9*

Breakout: 28% Improve: 35% Collapse: 40% Attrition: 18% MLB: 93% *Comparables: David Robertson, Jonathan Papelbon, B.J. Ryan*

Watching Betances is very much like watching a world-class tightrope act. One moment you're swept up by the marvel of it, and the next, you're genuinely concerned that he is going to take a fall. The latter was the case early this season, when he had a 4.50 ERA through May, and his 2017 struggles to find the plate continued. He reclaimed his balance, though, pitching to a phenomenal 1.85 ERA with 75 strikeouts over 43 2/3 innings after June 1st. In totality, his resume is nothing short of impressive: not a single reliever has more innings pitched since 2014, and only one (Wade Davis) has more RA9-WAR.

Considering Davis just got $52 million, it's easy to imagine someone (likely another team, if he is still disgruntled with Yankees ownership after a tumultuous arbitration heading in 2017) will be salivating to add his services when he becomes a free agent next season. That's the thing about a tight-rope act: they must be good, or they'd have fallen before the night you saw the show.

Zach Britton LHP   Born: 12/22/87   Age: 31   Bats: L   Throws: L   Height: 6'3"   Weight: 195   Origin: Round 3, 2006 Draft (#85 overall)

YEAR	TEAM	LVL	AGE	W	L	SV	G	GS	IP	H	HR	BB/9	K/9	K	GB%	BABIP	WHIP	ERA	DRA	WARP	MPH	FB%	WHF	CSP
2016	BAL	MLB	28	2	1	47	69	0	67	38	1	2.4	9.9	74	80%	.230	0.84	0.54	3.29	1.3	98.6	92.1	18.1	40.6
2017	BAL	MLB	29	2	1	15	38	0	37¹	39	1	4.3	7.0	29	75%	.336	1.53	2.89	5.91	-0.3	97.3	94.7	12.4	42.2
2018	BAL	MLB	30	1	0	4	16	0	15²	11	1	5.7	7.5	13	64%	.263	1.34	3.45	7.71	-0.5	96.4	94.4	14.5	42.3
2018	NYA	MLB	30	1	0	3	25	0	25	18	2	4.0	7.6	21	78%	.229	1.16	2.88	6.55	-0.5	96.6	93.1	12.3	42.8
2019	NYA	MLB	31	2	1	6	37	0	39	34	4	4.1	8.2	36	65%	.283	1.33	4.18	4.17	0.4	96.6	92.8	14.6	41.7

Breakout: 14%   Improve: 38%   Collapse: 29%   Attrition: 12%   MLB: 92%   *Comparables: Joe Smith, Mariano Rivera, Francisco Cordero*

While Britton is best known for sitting in the bullpen during the 2016 AL Wild Card game, no one would have expected his next playoff appearance would come with the Yankees. Rumors of Manny Machado to the Yankees at the deadline were squashed by sources within the Angelos brain trust, as he would never trade a star to the Bronx. But Britton was fair game, and the O's were able to extract both Dillon Tate and Josh Rogers from their rival, a worthy haul for a rental. Britton lived up to his end of the bargain, but his peripherals are a source of concern. His velocity has taken a dive, and in 2018 his average sinker velocity of 95 mph was the lowest single-season mark since 2013, before he even made the jump to reliever. More worrisome, however, are how hitters are reacting: they've stopped swinging at as many of those pitches out of the zone, providing him fewer of those easy outs and putting him behind in the count more often: his first-strike percentage was a career-low 49.7 percent last season. He can still be serviceable, and any team would be happy to have him, particularly one with a strong framing catcher to reverse some of those worrisome trends. But the days of a 0.54 ERA are long gone.

Luis Cessa RHP   Born: 04/25/92   Age: 27   Bats: R   Throws: R   Height: 6'0"   Weight: 210   Origin: International Free Agent, 2008

YEAR	TEAM	LVL	AGE	W	L	SV	G	GS	IP	H	HR	BB/9	K/9	K	GB%	BABIP	WHIP	ERA	DRA	WARP	MPH	FB%	WHF	CSP
2016	SWB	AAA	24	6	3	0	15	14	77¹	66	8	2.7	8.0	69	47%	.278	1.15	3.03	3.24	1.9				
2016	NYA	MLB	24	4	4	0	17	9	70¹	64	16	1.8	5.9	46	45%	.233	1.11	4.35	4.95	0.2	97.5	50.2	11.1	45.8
2017	SWB	AAA	25	4	6	0	14	13	78¹	75	7	3.0	7.7	67	48%	.304	1.29	3.45	3.90	1.5				
2017	NYA	MLB	25	0	3	0	10	5	36	36	7	4.2	7.5	30	46%	.282	1.47	4.75	4.72	0.3	97.8	41.8	11.5	44.5
2018	TRN	AA	26	0	1	0	2	2	10	6	0	0.9	10.8	12	50%	.250	0.70	2.70	1.59	0.4				
2018	SWB	AAA	26	3	0	0	6	5	26¹	19	1	1.4	8.5	25	40%	.250	0.87	2.73	2.86	0.8				
2018	NYA	MLB	26	1	4	2	16	5	44²	51	5	2.6	7.9	39	48%	.333	1.43	5.24	3.23	1.0	96.9	41.6	12.6	45.7
2019	NYA	MLB	27	2	1	0	27	3	40²	41	6	3.3	8.1	36	45%	.300	1.37	4.49	4.49	0.5	96.9	45.2	12	45.9

Breakout: 30%   Improve: 48%   Collapse: 15%   Attrition: 24%   MLB: 80%   *Comparables: Brandon Workman, Jacob deGrom, Joe Saunders*

Explaining something like replacement level to an average fan sounds impossible; how could you illustrate such a vague archetype? You could start by following and watching Luis Cessa. He checks off most of the boxes: oft-traveled on the Scranton shuttle; a WARP consistently below 1.0; a nebulous mix of starts and relief, both instantly forgotten. Yet the question is always: "Well, then why is Brian Cashman keeping him around?" Partially because of convenience, but also because of peripherals that have made gentle, happy progress. Like the organization as a whole, he is leaning even more on a slider with an ever increasing whiff rate over the course of the season. Still a replacement archetype in the future? Probably. Something more? If he continues his current trend, very possibly.

Aroldis Chapman LHP   Born: 02/28/88   Age: 31   Bats: L   Throws: L   Height: 6'4"   Weight: 212   Origin: International Free Agent, 2010

YEAR	TEAM	LVL	AGE	W	L	SV	G	GS	IP	H	HR	BB/9	K/9	K	GB%	BABIP	WHIP	ERA	DRA	WARP	MPH	FB%	WHF	CSP
2016	NYA	MLB	28	3	0	20	31	0	31¹	20	2	2.3	12.6	44	38%	.273	0.89	2.01	2.37	0.9	104.1	80.4	19.2	51.3
2016	CHN	MLB	28	1	1	16	28	0	26²	12	0	3.4	15.5	46	59%	.261	0.82	1.01	2.04	0.9	104.2	81.9	20.1	47.5
2017	NYA	MLB	29	4	3	22	52	0	50¹	37	3	3.6	12.3	69	48%	.298	1.13	3.22	3.50	0.9	102.4	76.8	15.2	48.5
2018	NYA	MLB	30	3	0	32	55	0	51¹	24	2	5.3	16.3	93	46%	.268	1.05	2.45	2.13	1.7	102.3	73.8	16.8	45.8
2019	NYA	MLB	31	3	1	30	48	0	51	38	6	4.1	13.6	77	45%	.300	1.20	3.33	3.29	1.0	101.9	76.2	16.9	47.3

Breakout: 26%   Improve: 34%   Collapse: 40%   Attrition: 16%   MLB: 93%   *Comparables: David Robertson, A.J. Ramos, Jonathan Papelbon*

When the Yankees inked Aroldis Chapman to an $86 million deal, the largest ever given to a reliever, the argument against such a move was two-fold: it was a lot of luxury tax space devoted to one good reliever among a cadre of many, and that, frankly, the aging curve for a pitcher like Chapman might not look great. (There was also a third argument.) With the rise of flame-throwing relievers around the league, Chapman would, by this logic, become more pedestrian over time. When he broke into the league in 2010, the average reliever fastball velocity was 92.1 mph. In 2018, it was 93.4 mph. The Yankees' response to this trend was in line with their organizational philosophy, pushing him in the direction of fewer fastballs and more sliders. One positive side effect was his highest strikeout rate since 2014, but the negative one was that he had the highest walk rate (and most wild pitches) to go with it. That last wrinkle needs to be resolved for him to find an aging-curve-resistant form, but it's an encouraging development for a man often considered a one-trick pony.

A.J. Cole RHP   Born: 01/05/92   Age: 27   Bats: R   Throws: R   Height: 6'5"   Weight: 238   Origin: Round 4, 2010 Draft (#116 overall)

YEAR	TEAM	LVL	AGE	W	L	SV	G	GS	IP	H	HR	BB/9	K/9	K	GB%	BABIP	WHIP	ERA	DRA	WARP	MPH	FB%	WHF	CSP
2016	SYR	AAA	24	8	8	0	22	22	124²	131	16	2.5	7.9	109	43%	.310	1.33	4.26	3.89	2.1				
2016	WAS	MLB	24	1	2	0	8	8	38¹	37	7	3.3	9.2	39	32%	.283	1.33	5.17	4.92	0.2	93.4	57.3	10.9	44
2017	SYR	AAA	25	4	5	0	18	18	93¹	127	7	3.5	7.6	79	42%	.390	1.75	5.88	4.60	1.1				
2017	WAS	MLB	25	3	5	0	11	8	52	51	8	4.7	7.6	44	45%	.293	1.50	3.81	4.53	0.6	95.1	54.8	10.9	45.7
2018	WAS	MLB	26	1	1	0	4	2	10¹	16	6	5.2	8.7	10	27%	.323	2.13	13.06	7.82	-0.3	94.2	44.1	7.3	49.1
2018	NYA	MLB	26	3	1	0	28	0	38	39	9	3.8	11.6	49	37%	.319	1.45	4.26	2.88	0.9	95.7	30.9	16.9	43.2
2019	NYA	MLB	27	1	0	0	14	0	15¹	16	3	3.8	9.4	16	39%	.310	1.46	4.79	4.81	0.1	94.4	46.7	12.8	45.3

Breakout: 26%   Improve: 50%   Collapse: 6%   Attrition: 14%   MLB: 68%   *Comparables: Christian Friedrich, Billy Buckner, Chase Anderson*

Eight days. Five days. Ten days. Fourteen days. Fourteen days. Nine days. Five days. All represent gaps between consecutive outings, and likewise, all periods of time where fans and commentators alike wondered... why is Cole still on the 25-man roster? Brian Cashman is keeping the right-hander in his back pocket for a reason. After being acquired from the Nationals, the Yankees pushed upon Cole their patented slider-heavy focus, having him toss the pitch nearly *half* of the time. It seemed successful at first, generating whiffs on nearly a third of sliders in June, but it then declined month after month. That being said, overall, Cole had the third-highest swinging strike rate on the team, and when you combine a mid-90s fastball with that slider, you get the ingredients for a successful relief ace. His lack of opportunity, then, could be more of a symptom of one of the deepest bullpens in baseball than pure ability. Whether he remains with the team and stays a decent last option, or moves on to another and becomes something more like a middle reliever or a 7th inning guy, he will get a chance to prove his merit in a more consistent manner.

Roansy Contreras RHP   Born: 11/07/99   Age: 19   Bats: R   Throws: R   Height: 6'0"   Weight: 175   Origin: International Free Agent, 2016

YEAR	TEAM	LVL	AGE	W	L	SV	G	GS	IP	H	HR	BB/9	K/9	K	GB%	BABIP	WHIP	ERA	DRA	WARP	MPH	FB%	WHF	CSP
2017	DYA	RK	17	0	3	0	6	6	22	25	2	2.0	7.0	17	57%	.311	1.36	3.68	4.15	0.4				
2017	YAN	RK	17	4	1	0	8	5	31²	35	2	3.4	4.8	17	43%	.297	1.48	4.26	3.96	0.7				
2018	STA	A-	18	0	0	0	5	5	28²	15	1	2.8	10.0	32	49%	.219	0.84	1.26	3.91	0.4				
2018	CSC	A	18	0	2	0	7	7	34²	29	4	3.1	7.3	28	34%	.255	1.18	3.38	4.40	0.3				
2019	NYA	MLB	19	2	4	0	10	10	45¹	55	12	4.8	6.5	33	39%	.302	1.75	7.06	7.21	-0.9				

Comparables: Deolis Guerra, Kelvin Herrera, Vicente Campos

Contreras checks off every box for a teenage pitching prospect. Gained weight and started to fill out his frame? Check. Added velocity, up to the mid-90s? Check. A promising change and breaking ball? Check and check. Originally labeled the best Dominican prospect from the 2017 signing period, he is already living up to that title. While he threw in the high-80s to low-90s last season, he has subsequently exploded, and throws in the mid-90s with ease today. He has a plus change and a repeatable delivery. His six-foot and 175 pound frame is not on his side as far as health and durability is concerned, but he hasn't given them a reason to worry just yet. There's a long development road to go, but it fits directly in the mold of a long line of successful international amateurs pumped out of the Yankees' system.

Domingo German RHP   Born: 08/04/92   Age: 26   Bats: R   Throws: R   Height: 6'2"   Weight: 175   Origin: International Free Agent, 2009

YEAR	TEAM	LVL	AGE	W	L	SV	G	GS	IP	H	HR	BB/9	K/9	K	GB%	BABIP	WHIP	ERA	DRA	WARP	MPH	FB%	WHF	CSP
2016	CSC	A	23	1	1	0	5	5	26	15	2	0.7	6.2	18	43%	.186	0.65	3.12	3.56	0.5				
2016	TAM	A+	23	0	2	0	5	5	23²	26	1	3.4	7.6	20	45%	.342	1.48	3.04	2.51	0.8				
2017	TRN	AA	24	1	4	0	6	6	33	32	4	2.7	10.4	38	50%	.318	1.27	3.00	1.88	1.3				
2017	SWB	AAA	24	7	2	0	14	13	76¹	59	5	2.6	9.6	81	46%	.274	1.06	2.83	3.54	1.8				
2017	NYA	MLB	24	0	1	0	7	0	14¹	11	1	5.7	11.3	18	54%	.294	1.40	3.14	3.15	0.3	98.4	50.4	12.7	40
2018	NYA	MLB	25	2	6	0	21	14	85²	81	15	3.5	10.7	102	39%	.300	1.33	5.57	4.36	0.9	96.3	46.9	15.5	46.9
2019	NYA	MLB	26	3	3	0	10	10	50	47	8	3.5	9.5	53	41%	.297	1.34	4.46	4.47	0.6	96.2	48.1	15.4	44.6

Breakout: 21%   Improve: 39%   Collapse: 22%   Attrition: 23%   MLB: 86%   *Comparables: James McDonald, Trevor May, Jharel Cotton*

Like Jonathan Loaisiga, there are some pitching prospects that sprout up like weeds; so goes the Yankees pitching development machine. German may have been the biggest surprise, though, despite missing most of the season due to an ulnar nerve injury. The results may not have wowed, but the curve did, and people generally pay attention when you have a whiff rate higher than Justin Verlander. The concern is that he relies just on two pitches, not to mention his health; he also underwent Tommy John surgery in 2015. But one can't deny that he might be one of the most talented and overlooked pitchers on the 40-man, with enough talent to fit into, or even lead, an entire rotation. The bell curve of outcomes is wide and likely tends toward worse than better outcomes, but if he were to suddenly become a top-30 pitcher in baseball, not too many keen observers would be surprised.

Luis Gil RHP   Born: 06/03/98   Age: 21   Bats: R   Throws: R   Height: 6'3"   Weight: 176   Origin: International Free Agent, 2015

YEAR	TEAM	LVL	AGE	W	L	SV	G	GS	IP	H	HR	BB/9	K/9	K	GB%	BABIP	WHIP	ERA	DRA	WARP	MPH	FB%	WHF	CSP
2017	DTW	RK	19	0	2	0	14	14	41²	31	2	4.3	10.6	49	54%	.287	1.22	2.59	3.45	1.2				
2018	PUL	RK	20	2	1	0	10	10	39¹	21	1	5.7	13.3	58	35%	.256	1.17	1.37	3.34	1.2				
2018	STA	A-	20	0	2	0	2	2	6²	11	1	8.1	13.5	10	39%	.455	2.55	5.40	3.40	0.1				
2019	NYA	MLB	21	1	3	0	14	7	33	37	9	9.3	9.1	33	41%	.309	2.16	7.97	8.20	-1.1				

Comparables: Merandy Gonzalez, Nestor Cortes, Rafael Montero

Yet another helium prospect from a small deal, this one sending already-designated Jake Cave to Minnesota, Gil has the kind of stuff to make hitters stand and stare, and the kind of command that often rewards them for it. Never a buzzworthy prospect with the Twins, scouts began to take notice as Gil tossed triple-digit fastballs at Pulaski. Combine that with a high-spin curve and you have all of the ingredients for a reliever, at the bare minimum. Throw in a third pitch and more command, and as the thinking goes, there's a mid-rotation starter. For what was essentially a throwaway deal, it's looking more like a heist right about now.

Sonny Gray RHP   Born: 11/07/89   Age: 29   Bats: R   Throws: R   Height: 5'10"   Weight: 190   Origin: Round 1, 2011 Draft (#18 overall)

YEAR	TEAM	LVL	AGE	W	L	SV	G	GS	IP	H	HR	BB/9	K/9	K	GB%	BABIP	WHIP	ERA	DRA	WARP	MPH	FB%	WHF	CSP
2016	OAK	MLB	26	5	11	0	22	22	117	133	18	3.2	7.2	94	54%	.319	1.50	5.69	4.97	0.5	95.1	64.1	8.8	47.1
2017	OAK	MLB	27	6	5	0	16	16	97	84	8	2.8	8.7	94	58%	.285	1.18	3.43	4.22	1.5	94.8	63.7	13.1	45.5
2017	NYA	MLB	27	4	7	0	11	11	65¹	55	11	3.7	8.1	59	48%	.246	1.26	3.72	4.04	1.1	94.6	63.7	12	41.8
2018	NYA	MLB	28	11	9	0	30	23	130¹	138	14	3.9	8.5	123	52%	.326	1.50	4.90	5.00	0.4	95.2	57.2	10.8	45.2
2019	*NYA*	*MLB*	*29*	*3*	*2*	*0*	*46*	*3*	*61*	*58*	*8*	*3.5*	*8.1*	*55*	*51%*	*.293*	*1.35*	*4.37*	*4.36*	*0.2*	*94.3*	*61.1*	*11.1*	*45.3*

Breakout: 14%   Improve: 42%   Collapse: 22%   Attrition: 9%   MLB: 98%   *Comparables: Dean Chance, Orel Hershiser, Hyun-jin Ryu*

There was once an anonymous Yankees fan who would e-mail every Yankees-affiliated writer, posing as former Yankees to complain about Brian Cashman. It was largely cockamamie, ad hominem gibberish, but inside of almost every e-mail was mention of Cashman's last big flop, Carl Pavano. Even though criticisms have been a bit lighter considering fans got the homegrown "core" they have been clamoring for, one would imagine that a listserv like that today would contain complaints on Sonny Gray, the new teeth-grinder du jour. After being acquired last year for a trio of prospects that likely won't be missed too much, the consensus was that getting Gray was necessary to take them to all the way to the ALCS. Today, many wonder what the world would look like if they had acquired Justin Verlander instead.

Chad Green RHP   Born: 05/24/91   Age: 28   Bats: L   Throws: R   Height: 6'3"   Weight: 210   Origin: Round 11, 2013 Draft (#336 overall)

YEAR	TEAM	LVL	AGE	W	L	SV	G	GS	IP	H	HR	BB/9	K/9	K	GB%	BABIP	WHIP	ERA	DRA	WARP	MPH	FB%	WHF	CSP
2016	SWB	AAA	25	7	6	0	16	16	94²	68	3	2.0	9.5	100	50%	.271	0.94	1.52	3.03	2.5				
2016	NYA	MLB	25	2	4	1	12	8	45²	49	12	3.0	10.2	52	44%	.314	1.40	4.73	4.45	0.4	97.1	53	12.9	46.7
2017	SWB	AAA	26	2	1	0	5	5	26²	32	1	3.7	11.1	33	53%	.397	1.61	4.72	3.97	0.5				
2017	NYA	MLB	26	5	0	0	40	1	69	34	4	2.2	13.4	103	28%	.236	0.74	1.83	2.42	2.1	97.5	69.4	16.4	50.3
2018	NYA	MLB	27	8	3	0	63	0	75²	64	9	1.8	11.2	94	33%	.307	1.04	2.50	3.38	1.3	97.5	86.6	14.9	52.6
2019	*NYA*	*MLB*	*28*	*3*	*1*	*0*	*58*	*0*	*61¹*	*56*	*9*	*3.0*	*10.9*	*74*	*39%*	*.307*	*1.25*	*3.86*	*3.84*	*1.1*	*96.8*	*74.8*	*15.1*	*50.7*

Breakout: 28%   Improve: 50%   Collapse: 16%   Attrition: 13%   MLB: 83%   *Comparables: Cory Luebke, Charlie Furbush, Collin McHugh*

The only thing that was missing from Chad Green's 2017 season was high leverage opportunities, so it's still remarkable to think he accumulated 2.02 WPA (46th in baseball) working primarily in the sixth and seventh innings. That earned him some eighth inning work, so of course, he regressed all the way down to 1.85 WPA, ranking... 42nd. Green found his rhythm in the second half, allowing just seven earned runs over 29 2/3 innings, maintaining his status as the league's greatest anonymous reliever. Only two relievers have more RA9-WAR over the last two seasons: Blake Treinen and Craig Kimbrel. No one would have expected that from what is, essentially, a one-pitch pitcher; he threw his four-seamer a career high 86% of the time, and that trend likely won't abate.

J.A. Happ LHP   Born: 10/19/82   Age: 36   Bats: L   Throws: L   Height: 6'5"   Weight: 205   Origin: Round 3, 2004 Draft (#92 overall)

YEAR	TEAM	LVL	AGE	W	L	SV	G	GS	IP	H	HR	BB/9	K/9	K	GB%	BABIP	WHIP	ERA	DRA	WARP	MPH	FB%	WHF	CSP
2016	TOR	MLB	33	20	4	0	32	32	195	168	22	2.8	7.5	163	44%	.268	1.17	3.18	4.37	2.2	94.3	73.6	10.4	46.9
2017	TOR	MLB	34	10	11	0	25	25	145¹	145	18	2.8	8.8	142	48%	.302	1.31	3.53	4.07	2.4	94.0	71.3	10.5	43.8
2018	TOR	MLB	35	10	6	0	20	20	114	99	17	2.8	10.3	130	45%	.285	1.18	4.18	3.89	1.9	94.3	74.2	11.7	48
2018	NYA	MLB	35	7	0	0	11	11	63²	51	10	2.3	8.9	63	33%	.250	1.05	2.69	4.00	1.0	94.0	72.3	11.1	48.3
2019	*NYA*	*MLB*	*36*	*10*	*9*	*0*	*26*	*26*	*156*	*151*	*24*	*3.1*	*8.9*	*154*	*43%*	*.295*	*1.31*	*4.41*	*4.41*	*1.9*	*92.9*	*71.4*	*10.7*	*45.4*

Breakout: 12%   Improve: 40%   Collapse: 21%   Attrition: 11%   MLB: 86%   *Comparables: Whitey Ford, Jeff Fassero, Ryan Dempster*

The factoid tossed about when the Yankees acquired JA Happ was that he had 2.98 ERA against the Red Sox, so they would both block Boston from getting him themselves and they could use him in a potential playoff spot. Of course, the Yankees did play the Red Sox in the postseason, and... Happ allowed five runs in two innings. Yada yada can't predict baseball yada yada. That doesn't mean it was a poor idea; Happ proved invaluable as a patch for a tattered Yankees rotation into the second half. Even at the age of 36, he has been a consistent three-win pitcher going on a half-decade, the gold standard of third starters. Given the steadiness of his peripherals (even his increased flyball rate was mostly the infield variety), and his remarkable durability, there's little reason to think that he won't reinforce another rotation for a few more years.

Jonathan Holder RHP   Born: 06/09/93   Age: 26   Bats: R   Throws: R   Height: 6'2"   Weight: 235   Origin: Round 6, 2014 Draft (#182 overall)

YEAR	TEAM	LVL	AGE	W	L	SV	G	GS	IP	H	HR	BB/9	K/9	K	GB%	BABIP	WHIP	ERA	DRA	WARP	MPH	FB%	WHF	CSP
2016	TRN	AA	23	3	1	10	28	0	41	27	2	1.5	13.0	59	45%	.298	0.83	2.20	1.73	1.5				
2016	SWB	AAA	23	2	0	6	12	0	20¹	7	1	0.0	15.5	35	42%	.188	0.34	0.89	1.66	0.8				
2016	NYA	MLB	23	0	0	0	8	0	8¹	8	1	4.3	5.4	5	37%	.269	1.44	5.40	4.34	0.1	94.7	43.1	12.5	45.9
2017	SWB	AAA	24	0	0	1	12	0	16	15	1	4.5	11.8	21	40%	.359	1.44	1.69	2.49	0.5				
2017	NYA	MLB	24	1	1	0	37	0	39¹	45	5	1.8	9.2	40	42%	.348	1.35	3.89	3.11	0.9	93.5	37.2	13.2	47.9
2018	SWB	AAA	25	1	0	0	4	1	6	5	1	1.5	12.0	8	53%	.286	1.00	3.00	2.59	0.2				
2018	NYA	MLB	25	1	3	0	60	1	66	53	4	2.6	8.2	60	31%	.261	1.09	3.14	4.33	0.5	94.2	55.4	11.5	47.5
2019	*NYA*	*MLB*	*26*	*3*	*1*	*0*	*53*	*0*	*56*	*53*	*8*	*3.4*	*9.2*	*57*	*38%*	*.293*	*1.33*	*4.42*	*4.42*	*0.5*	*93.6*	*49.8*	*12.3*	*48.1*

Breakout: 30%   Improve: 51%   Collapse: 20%   Attrition: 16%   MLB: 84%   *Comparables: Jonathan Papelbon, Cory Wade, Daniel Herrera*

Another day, another solid reliever created out of thin air in Holder. While every other pitcher in the staff is zigging by backing off their fastball, Holder is one of the few pitchers on the staff who has zagged, throwing his fastball 55 percent of the time, up from about a third of the time a season before. It may have shown up in the results in his 73 ERA-, but it's possible he may adjust and lean more heavily on his new slider in 2019: he saw a decline in his strikeout rate, an increase in his walk rate, and no significant change in his whiff rate or quality of contact. His fastball has zip and is still a plus pitch, but he may benefit from a more backwards approach if he negatively regresses.

Tommy Kahnle   RHP   Born: 08/07/89   Age: 29   Bats: R   Throws: R   Height: 6'1"   Weight: 235   Origin: Round 5, 2010 Draft (#175 overall)

YEAR	TEAM	LVL	AGE	W	L	SV	G	GS	IP	H	HR	BB/9	K/9	K	GB%	BABIP	WHIP	ERA	DRA	WARP	MPH	FB%	WHF	CSP
2016	CHR	AAA	26	1	1	7	23	0	27	17	0	4.0	12.0	36	48%	.283	1.07	3.00	3.19	0.5				
2016	CHA	MLB	26	0	1	1	29	0	27¹	21	2	6.6	8.2	25	50%	.264	1.50	2.63	5.95	-0.3	99.3	73.6	11.5	49.8
2017	CHA	MLB	27	1	3	0	37	0	36	28	3	1.8	15.0	60	43%	.352	0.97	2.50	2.10	1.2	99.7	72.6	18.2	51.3
2017	NYA	MLB	27	1	1	0	32	0	26²	25	1	3.4	12.1	36	40%	.364	1.31	2.70	2.05	0.9	99.3	58.9	17.2	46.6
2018	SWB	AAA	28	2	2	1	25	0	24²	23	2	4.0	13.5	37	40%	.375	1.38	4.01	1.64	1.0				
2018	NYA	MLB	28	2	0	1	24	0	23¹	23	3	5.8	11.6	30	39%	.339	1.63	6.56	4.03	0.2	97.0	54.3	15.2	46
2019	NYA	MLB	29	2	1	0	48	0	51	44	7	4.5	10.7	61	42%	.295	1.37	4.30	4.31	0.4	98.1	64	15.8	48

Breakout: 18%   Improve: 50%   Collapse: 28%   Attrition: 13%   MLB: 95%   Comparables: Steve Cishek, Al Alburquerque, Boone Logan

The Yankees didn't give up Blake Rutherford and Ian Clarkin just because they were getting David Robertson and Todd Frazier. No, the hidden prize of that deal was Tommy Kahnle, who had a 165 ERA+ in a White Sox uniform and four and a half years of team control left. Now he's more of an afterthought, and his 2018 was an unmitigated disaster. He was plagued by injury and played just half the season, saw a 2.5 mph drop in velocity, and his command went completely out the window, as he walked 15 batters in just 23 1/3 innings. He was so unspectacular that he was left off the playoff roster entirely. 2019 will be a reset year, but make no mistake: if those negative trends don't reverse course, then one can likely close the book on that trade return's value. Sadly, in a league where starters are working harder and shorter, and relievers are overflowing the bullpen, Kahnle is the example of the risk involved: Relievers are still volatile and fragile creatures.

Jonathan Loaisiga   RHP   Born: 11/02/94   Age: 24   Bats: R   Throws: R   Height: 5'11"   Weight: 165   Origin: International Free Agent, 2012

YEAR	TEAM	LVL	AGE	W	L	SV	G	GS	IP	H	HR	BB/9	K/9	K	GB%	BABIP	WHIP	ERA	DRA	WARP	MPH	FB%	WHF	CSP
2017	YAN	RK	22	0	1	0	6	6	13²	10	1	1.3	9.9	15	58%	.257	0.88	2.63	2.59	0.5				
2017	STA	A-	22	1	0	0	4	4	17	7	0	0.5	9.5	18	51%	.171	0.47	0.53	2.82	0.5				
2018	TAM	A+	23	3	0	0	4	4	20	19	0	0.4	11.7	26	54%	.365	1.00	1.35	3.60	0.4				
2018	TRN	AA	23	3	1	0	9	9	34¹	37	6	1.6	10.5	40	39%	.356	1.25	3.93	3.08	0.9				
2018	NYA	MLB	23	2	0	0	9	4	24²	26	3	4.4	12.0	33	52%	.383	1.54	5.11	3.29	0.5	97.5	55.7	14.8	46.1
2019	NYA	MLB	24	3	4	0	11	11	55	57	10	3.6	9.1	56	42%	.311	1.44	4.90	4.93	0.3	97.3	57.4	15.3	47.5

Breakout: 27%   Improve: 48%   Collapse: 14%   Attrition: 27%   MLB: 75%   Comparables: David Paulino, Daniel Norris, Gio Gonzalez

They say that lasagna tastes the best the day after cooking, so it makes sense that Jonathan Loaisiga (with nom de guerre, "Johnny Lasagna") looks better start after start. And sure, there were only five major league starts to speak of, but the small sample raised a ton of eyebrows. His fastball not only touches the mid-to-high 90s, but it also has a phenomenal spin rate of 2,341 rpm. Meanwhile, his slider had a whopping 42% whiff rate, and his change could be deadly against left-handers. All of the ingredients are there for a fully fledged starting pitcher—or, ho-hum, just another high leverage reliever. The front office has bounced him around Trenton and Scranton, but you would imagine that in 2019 and beyond, he will get more trial runs at success. If he adds command to his existing repertoire, they will have manufactured a middle of the rotation starter out of whole cloth.

Jordan Montgomery   LHP   Born: 12/27/92   Age: 26   Bats: L   Throws: L   Height: 6'6"   Weight: 225   Origin: Round 4, 2014 Draft (#122 overall)

YEAR	TEAM	LVL	AGE	W	L	SV	G	GS	IP	H	HR	BB/9	K/9	K	GB%	BABIP	WHIP	ERA	DRA	WARP	MPH	FB%	WHF	CSP
2016	TRN	AA	23	9	4	0	19	19	102¹	94	5	3.2	8.5	97	45%	.299	1.27	2.55	3.23	2.3				
2016	SWB	AAA	23	5	1	0	6	6	37	28	0	2.2	9.0	37	56%	.286	1.00	0.97	2.30	1.3				
2017	NYA	MLB	24	9	7	0	29	29	155¹	140	21	3.0	8.3	144	42%	.275	1.23	3.88	4.51	1.8	93.4	41.8	12.7	43
2018	NYA	MLB	25	2	0	0	6	6	27¹	25	3	4.0	7.6	23	46%	.282	1.35	3.62	5.86	-0.2	91.7	41.1	11	45.3
2019	NYA	MLB	26	1	1	0	7	2	15	15	2	3.7	8.2	14	44%	.295	1.38	4.46	4.45	0.1	92.7	42.4	12.6	45.1

Breakout: 27%   Improve: 58%   Collapse: 23%   Attrition: 13%   MLB: 88%   Comparables: Alex Cobb, Steven Matz, Manny Parra

Would you be able to remember the Rookie of the Year voting from, say, five years ago? Did you know that vote-getters included JB Shuck and David Lough (with more notables like Chris Archer and the winner, Wil Myers)? Jordan Montgomery could be among those forgotten names, appearing out of nowhere to place sixth on the 2017 ballot. His sophomore effort proved a lost year, featuring just 27 1/3 innings, an elbow flexor strain, and the all-too-common Tommy John surgery. Where he goes from there is unknown. Armed with a mere 90 mph fastball, and with the very possible velocity decline most see in recovery, he could find himself unable to cope on just guile and command alone. We'll likely have to wait until 2020 to find out.

James Paxton   LHP   Born: 11/06/88   Age: 30   Bats: L   Throws: L   Height: 6'4"   Weight: 235   Origin: Round 4, 2010 Draft (#132 overall)

YEAR	TEAM	LVL	AGE	W	L	SV	G	GS	IP	H	HR	BB/9	K/9	K	GB%	BABIP	WHIP	ERA	DRA	WARP	MPH	FB%	WHF	CSP
2016	TAC	AAA	27	4	3	0	11	11	50²	43	6	2.7	9.4	53	52%	.285	1.14	3.73	3.17	1.3	99.7	62.4	12.8	50.4
2016	SEA	MLB	27	6	7	0	20	20	121	134	9	1.8	8.7	117	49%	.347	1.31	3.79	3.73	2.3	97.6	65.6	13.5	49.5
2017	SEA	MLB	28	12	5	0	24	24	136	113	9	2.4	10.3	156	46%	.300	1.10	2.98	2.63	4.5	97.5	63.7	15.8	53
2018	SEA	MLB	29	11	6	0	28	28	160¹	134	23	2.4	11.7	208	41%	.299	1.10	3.76	2.67	4.9	97.5	63.7	15.8	53
2019	NYA	MLB	30	10	8	0	26	26	156	140	21	2.9	10.9	190	44%	.309	1.22	3.62	3.58	3.4	97.2	63.8	14.4	51

Breakout: 14%   Improve: 53%   Collapse: 20%   Attrition: 6%   MLB: 97%   Comparables: Carlos Carrasco, Felix Hernandez, David Price

Let's talk for a moment about curses. It takes a special kind of talent to both throw a no-hitter and, in a separate start, strikeout 16 A's over 7 innings. To do that, and set a career high in innings and strike outs and STILL leave the season feeling somehow unfulfilled requires a special level of talent, and that's what Paxton is. Since the moment in 2016 when he dropped his arm slot and tacked 4-5 mph on his fastball, he has been one of the most gifted, sporadically-dominant pitchers on the planet. The levels of achievement possible for a 200-inning Paxton season are nearly as great as any in the game. That he can be just what he is—an incredible number two starter and the greatest left-hander Seattle has had since Randy Johnson - and still leave us expecting more is a testament to his ability. Oh yeah, and a curse.

CC Sabathia LHP   Born: 07/21/80   Age: 38   Bats: L   Throws: L   Height: 6'6"   Weight: 300   Origin: Round 1, 1998 Draft (#20 overall)

YEAR	TEAM	LVL	AGE	W	L	SV	G	GS	IP	H	HR	BB/9	K/9	K	GB%	BABIP	WHIP	ERA	DRA	WARP	MPH	FB%	WHF	CSP
2016	NYA	MLB	35	9	12	0	30	30	179²	172	22	3.3	7.6	152	52%	.288	1.32	3.91	4.52	1.7	93.4	63.6	10.6	44
2017	NYA	MLB	36	14	5	0	27	27	148²	139	21	3.0	7.3	120	51%	.276	1.27	3.69	3.92	2.7	92.9	53.2	9.6	45.3
2018	NYA	MLB	37	9	7	0	29	29	153	150	19	3.0	8.2	140	45%	.295	1.31	3.65	4.40	1.6	91.8	59	11.8	45.7
2019	NYA	MLB	38	7	7	0	21	21	119²	126	18	3.4	7.7	103	47%	.305	1.43	4.74	4.75	1.0	91.1	57	10.5	43.9

Breakout: 18%   Improve: 38%   Collapse: 16%   Attrition: 7%   MLB: 76%   *Comparables: John Lackey, Andy Pettitte, Derek Lowe*

Sabathia's 2018 season can be summed up by four words: "That's for you, [redacted]." With just two innings to go before reaching a $500,000 incentive for throwing 155 innings, he instead opted to plunk Jesus Sucre in retaliation for the Rays throwing at Austin Romine's head, leading to an ejection in his final start. It was a fiery moment, and it's how he will likely be remembered in pinstripes, putting his teammates above himself and remaining fiercely loyal and defensive for them. That isn't even to mention his performance. He now has a 117 ERA+ over his last three seasons, a marked turnaround from his 2013-2015 nadir. Overall, he had an illustrious Yankees career that will be nothing but fondly remembered: a 3.75 ERA over 1810 2/3 innings, three top-five Cy Young finishes, a World Series championship, and postseason performances in 2009, 2012, and 2017 that will be reminisced on for time immemorial. That's for you, New York.

Luis Severino RHP   Born: 02/20/94   Age: 25   Bats: R   Throws: R   Height: 6'2"   Weight: 215   Origin: International Free Agent, 2011

YEAR	TEAM	LVL	AGE	W	L	SV	G	GS	IP	H	HR	BB/9	K/9	K	GB%	BABIP	WHIP	ERA	DRA	WARP	MPH	FB%	WHF	CSP
2016	SWB	AAA	22	8	1	0	13	12	77¹	75	4	2.1	9.1	78	46%	.321	1.20	3.49	3.14	1.9				
2016	NYA	MLB	22	3	8	0	22	11	71	78	11	3.2	8.4	66	45%	.324	1.45	5.83	5.23	0.0	99.0	56	9.9	47.5
2017	NYA	MLB	23	14	6	0	31	31	193¹	150	21	2.4	10.7	230	50%	.272	1.04	2.98	2.68	6.2	99.5	51.4	13.7	49.4
2018	NYA	MLB	24	19	8	0	32	32	191¹	173	19	2.2	10.3	220	42%	.314	1.14	3.39	2.79	5.6	99.4	50.5	13.3	51.2
2019	NYA	MLB	25	12	8	0	29	29	174	153	21	2.8	10.2	197	44%	.297	1.19	3.62	3.58	3.8	99.1	52.7	13.4	50.9

Breakout: 23%   Improve: 57%   Collapse: 17%   Attrition: 11%   MLB: 98%   *Comparables: Gerrit Cole, Aaron Nola, Tommy Hanson*

One of the big question marks going into 2019 will be the Yankees' rotation, but up until a few months ago, people wouldn't have expected Luis Severino to be part of the problem. The postseason may have left a lasting impression because of his six earned runs in seven innings, though it could have been the result of tipping pitches. The bigger issue was his slider, though, which while nearly unhittable in the first half, lost about 150 RPM of spin from April to August. It featured less vertical drop and break. Barring any new information, this will likely confound analysts until he either figures it out or it becomes the new normal. Was the issue mechanics? Was it just fatigue? Whatever the reason, the Yankees will need first half Severino instead of the second half variety if they hope to patch together a competent rotation.

Masahiro Tanaka RHP   Born: 11/01/88   Age: 30   Bats: R   Throws: R   Height: 6'3"   Weight: 215   Origin: International Free Agent, 2014

YEAR	TEAM	LVL	AGE	W	L	SV	G	GS	IP	H	HR	BB/9	K/9	K	GB%	BABIP	WHIP	ERA	DRA	WARP	MPH	FB%	WHF	CSP
2016	NYA	MLB	27	14	4	0	31	31	199²	179	22	1.6	7.4	165	49%	.271	1.08	3.07	3.26	4.8	93.6	45	11.7	46.6
2017	NYA	MLB	28	13	12	0	30	30	178¹	180	35	2.1	9.8	194	50%	.306	1.24	4.74	3.91	3.3	94.0	37.6	15.8	41.7
2018	NYA	MLB	29	12	6	0	27	27	156	141	25	2.0	9.2	159	49%	.284	1.13	3.75	3.95	2.5	93.6	31.5	14.8	44
2019	NYA	MLB	30	11	9	0	28	28	168	158	24	2.4	8.6	160	48%	.287	1.21	4.17	4.16	2.5	93.0	37.3	14.3	43.7

Breakout: 10%   Improve: 50%   Collapse: 15%   Attrition: 3%   MLB: 96%   *Comparables: Jim Bunning, Aaron Harang, Billy Pierce*

When Masahiro Tanaka came over from NPB, a variety of his skills were seen as transferable to the big leagues: command, a deadly splitter, and the ability to pitch in high drama, cultivated from Koshien to sealing the deal in Game Six and Seven of the 2013 Japan Series. His Achilles heel was, and still is in 2018, his fastball and sinker. Those pitches had respective .594 and .560 opposing slugging percentages in 2018, but Larry Rothschild and the Yankees found a solution: stop throwing them. He had the second-lowest fastball percentage in baseball (only to CC Sabathia) and he rode it to a stellar second half (2.98 FIP). He followed up with a phenomenal October, putting his career postseason ERA at 1.80 in 30 innings. His PRP-injected elbow will always be a specter, but the organization is happy that they get two more years of Ma-kun.

LINEOUTS

Hitters

HITTER	POS	TEAM	LVL	AGE	PA	R	2B	3B	HR	RBI	BB	K	SB	CS	AVG/OBP/SLG	DRC+	VORP	BABIP	BRR	FRAA	WARP
Hanser Alberto	INF	ROU	AAA	25	384	45	17	3	7	58	9	28	0	3	.330/.346/.452	101	18.4	.337	-0.8	SS(44): 7.1, 1B(43): -3.5	1.7
	INF	TEX	MLB	25	30	0	2	0	0	0	2	4	0	1	.185/.241/.259	87	-1.3	.217	-0.4	SS(5): 0.1, 2B(4): -0.1	0.0
Josh Breaux	C	STA	A-	20	105	6	9	0	0	13	3	20	0	0	.280/.295/.370	79	3.4	.341	-2.1	C(21): -0.3	-0.1
Antonio Cabello	OF	DYA	Rk	17	30	5	0	1	0	1	6	6	5	1	.227/.433/.318	121	2.5	.313	0.5	CF(3): 0.1, LF(2): -0.3	0.2
	OF	YAT	Rk	17	162	21	9	4	5	20	21	34	5	5	.321/.426/.555	156	20.0	.398	-1.1	CF(28): 0.3, RF(4): 1.0	1.4
Oswaldo Cabrera	2B	CSC	A	19	526	48	24	1	6	48	28	66	4	9	.229/.273/.320	94	1.1	.251	-1.8	SS(55): 6.1, 2B(52): 6.4	2.7
Thairo Estrada	SS	TAM	A+	22	47	4	2	0	0	5	0	9	0	0	.222/.234/.267	85	-2.9	.270	-0.6	SS(8): -0.2	0.0
	SS	SWB	AAA	22	34	1	1	0	0	3	0	8	0	0	.152/.176/.182	80	-3.9	.200	-0.3	SS(5): 0.0, 2B(3): 0.9	0.1
Dermis Garcia	1B	CSC	A	20	363	37	17	2	15	50	36	111	3	2	.241/.320/.444	114	16.0	.317	-3.5	1B(44): -1.2, 3B(20): -1.0	0.6
Isiah Gilliam	OF	TAM	A+	21	520	59	22	2	13	71	36	151	4	5	.259/.313/.397	100	1.4	.348	-4.5	RF(65): 1.2, LF(39): -4.3	0.2
Ryder Green	OF	YAN	Rk	18	95	11	2	2	3	10	11	35	3	2	.203/.316/.392	98	3.9	.302	0.6	CF(19): -4.3, RF(4): 2.1	0.1
Ryan Lavarnway	C	IND	AAA	30	303	29	23	1	9	33	29	57	0	0	.288/.375/.485	128	26.5	.338	-3.0	C(60): -10.9, P(1): 0.0	1.0
	C	PIT	MLB	30	6	1	1	0	0	1	0	1	0	0	.667/.667/.833	80	2.0	.800	0.0		0.0
Everson Pereira	CF	PUL	Rk	17	183	21	8	2	3	26	15	60	3	2	.263/.322/.389	74	3.0	.390	-1.7	CF(36): 5.6	0.4
Giovanny Urshela	3B	COH	AAA	26	42	6	4	0	0	7	5	9	0	0	.324/.405/.432	105	3.1	.429	0.3	3B(4): 0.3, 2B(4): 0.3	0.2
	3B	TOR	MLB	26	46	7	1	0	1	3	2	10	0	0	.233/.283/.326	82	-1.4	.281	-0.2	3B(10): -0.8, SS(8): -0.3	0.0
	3B	BUF	AAA	26	91	7	3	0	0	5	4	9	0	0	.244/.275/.279	104	-3.4	.269	-0.1	3B(14): -1.4, 1B(7): 0.2	0.2
	3B	SWB	AAA	26	107	14	7	2	2	12	4	13	0	0	.307/.340/.475	110	5.2	.337	0.0	3B(20): 1.1, SS(8): -1.0	0.5

Hanser Alberto got back to the big leagues with the Rangers after battling a shoulder injury and then got claimed off waivers by the Yankees. His nickname is "Radio" because of a habit of calling play-by-play for games while playing in them. ⊗ The Yankees dropped serious cash in the international amateur market, signing four of the top 30 prospects, including Denny Larrondo (29th, $550k), Antonio Gomez (11th, $600k), Osiel Rodriguez (9th, $600k), and **Kevin Alcantara**, who signed for about $1 million. Sporting an above-average arm, plus speed, and a tall frame, he could be a formidable center fielder in a half-decade. ⊗ It's pronounced "Bro," and you know it, because this draft selection was announced by Nick Swisher. **Josh Breaux**, like fellow draftee Anthony Seigler, has pitching ability (to the tune of triple-digits), but hopes will rest on his raw power. ⊗ Venezuelan teenager **Antonio Cabello** moved from catcher to outfield to take advantage of his athleticism, and he put every ounce of it on display in his first stint stateside. He's the kind of prospect that makes prospects fun to track. ⊗ **Oswaldo Cabrera** was an unheralded prospect out of the 2014 international amateur class, and he did little to attract the attention of any nearby heralds. Youth is still on his side and his defense is a plus up the middle, but he still finds himself at the bottom of the offensive rung. ⊗ **Thairo Estrada** easily had the unluckiest season in the organization, both taking a bullet to the hip in a robbery attempt in Venezuela, and then missing most of the season with a back issue. ⊗ When **Dermis Garcia** knocked a few over the wall in a notoriously pitcher-friendly ballpark, it may not have been *spectacular*, per se. But as one of the more high profile 2014 international signings, all eyes will be on 2019, as the Yankees experiment with him as a two-way player. ⊗ **Isiah Gilliam** is part of a historic baseball bloodline; his grandfather, Jim, was the player that took over for Jackie Robinson with the Brooklyn Dodgers. Looking to skyrocket to a starting position on another historic franchise, his switch-hitting power should get him an extended look as he climbs the system. ⊗ **Ryder Green** may sound like the putting grounds of a golf championship, but this baseball name carries a bit more pop. Drafted over-slot in the third round last year, the organization is betting on his plus raw power translating to some long drives. ⊗ A one-time catching prospect thanks to his bat, **Ryan Lavarnway** has spent time in eight organizations over the last four seasons, in part because his defense isn't good enough to survive as a big league backup, but mostly because he keeps telling management "it's Lavarnway or the highway!" everywhere he goes. ⊗ Pegged as one of the top July 2nd amateurs last year and signed for a whopping $1.5 million, **Everson Pereira** completed his first full season with Pulaski, altogether skipping the Dominican Summer League. While the numbers may not be glowing, the reports are, and talk of his tremendous gap power could make him a consensus Top 100 prospect by year's end. ⊗ Now that he's a Yankees third baseman, **Giovanny Urshela** just has to hit a whole bunch of doubles and he'll earn some AL ROY votes.

Pitchers

PITCHER	TEAM	LVL	AGE	W	L	SV	G	GS	IP	H	HR	BB/9	K/9	K	GB%	BABIP	WHIP	ERA	DRA	WARP	MPH	FB%	WHF	CSP
Albert Abreu	TAM	A+	22	4	3	0	13	13	62²	54	9	4.2	9.3	65	45%	.274	1.32	4.16	4.00	1.0				
Phillip Diehl	TAM	A+	23	2	2	3	25	0	48²	37	2	2.2	14.6	79	43%	.357	1.01	3.14	2.34	1.5				
	TRN	AA	23	0	1	1	14	0	26²	18	2	3.7	9.8	29	35%	.254	1.09	1.35	2.49	0.8				
J.P. Feyereisen	SWB	AAA	25	6	6	1	37	0	60	56	5	3.8	8.9	59	36%	.317	1.35	3.45	4.84	0.2				
Deivi Garcia	CSC	A	19	2	4	0	8	8	40²	31	5	2.2	13.9	63	31%	.302	1.01	3.76	2.40	1.4				
	TAM	A+	19	2	0	0	5	5	28¹	19	0	2.5	11.1	35	37%	.292	0.95	1.27	3.18	0.7				
Nolan Martinez	STA	A-	20	4	0	0	8	5	36²	21	1	2.7	6.4	26	45%	.211	0.87	1.23	7.06	-0.8				
	CSC	A	20	0	4	0	5	5	25	24	2	5.0	5.4	15	36%	.293	1.52	6.48	8.27	-0.9				
Luis Medina	PUL	Rk	19	1	3	0	12	12	36	32	3	11.5	11.8	47	43%	.337	2.17	6.25	5.38	0.3				
Nick Nelson	CSC	A	22	1	1	0	5	5	24¹	18	1	2.6	12.8	35	56%	.304	1.01	3.65	3.49	0.5				
	TAM	A+	22	7	5	0	18	17	88¹	69	1	4.8	10.1	99	46%	.301	1.31	3.36	3.22	2.2				
	TRN	AA	22	0	0	0	3	3	8²	10	1	9.3	10.4	10	50%	.360	2.19	5.19	3.89	0.1				
Freicer Perez	TAM	A+	22	0	4	0	6	6	25	28	3	6.8	7.2	20	52%	.321	1.88	7.20	4.60	0.2				
Matt Sauer	STA	A-	19	3	6	0	13	13	67	60	3	2.4	6.0	45	46%	.274	1.16	3.90	7.29	-1.6				
Clarke Schmidt	STA	A-	22	0	1	0	2	2	8¹	4	0	2.2	10.8	10	37%	.211	0.72	1.08	3.04	0.2				
Trevor Stephan	TAM	A+	22	3	1	0	7	7	41	23	5	2.0	10.8	49	41%	.198	0.78	1.98	3.33	1.0				
	TRN	AA	22	3	8	0	17	17	83¹	80	5	3.1	9.8	91	36%	.336	1.31	4.54	3.90	1.4				
Stephen Tarpley	TRN	AA	25	5	0	2	19	0	35²	18	0	3.8	8.3	33	71%	.198	0.93	1.26	3.47	0.6				
	SWB	AAA	25	2	2	0	17	0	34	23	3	2.9	10.1	38	68%	.250	1.00	2.65	3.87	0.5				
	NYA	MLB	25	0	0	0	10	0	9	6	0	6.0	13.0	13	52%	.286	1.33	3.00	4.18	0.1	94.9	59.5	11.1	46.4
Juan Then	YAN	Rk	18	0	3	0	11	11	50	38	2	2.0	7.6	42	48%	.259	0.98	2.70	5.16	0.5				
Garrett Whitlock	CSC	A	22	2	2	0	7	7	40	23	1	1.6	9.9	44	63%	.234	0.75	1.12	3.61	0.8				
	TRN	AA	22	1	0	0	2	1	10²	10	0	5.9	3.4	4	56%	.294	1.59	0.84	5.42	0.0				
	TAM	A+	22	5	3	0	14	13	70	60	2	3.5	9.5	74	52%	.310	1.24	2.44	3.98	1.1				

After missing Spring Training due to appendix surgery, **Albert Abreu** is starting to look like a major haul in what was a salary dump in the Brian McCann trade. With a sometimes-triple-digits fastball and, overall, three plus pitches, he may be the definition of raw talent, but it's talent nonetheless. ⓧ Described as a "command guy" by Trenton Thunder manager Jay Bell, **Phillip Diehl** struggled a bit with said command at Double-A, walking 11 in 36 2/3 innings. That's not awful, though, and he featured sub-3 BB/9 walk rates in every other level of play. There was another unheralded "command guy" who snuck his way on to the big league roster in Jordan Montgomery, and Diehl could be another, albeit in the bullpen, before too long. ⓧ **J.P. Feyereisen**, with his consistent, underwhelming arsenal, isn't just a man destined to ride the bus back and forth from Scranton. He is a bus ride to Scranton. ⓧ Quickly becoming one of the best pitching prospects in the system, **Deivi Garcia** and his high-spin fastball-curve combination cracked Trenton this year. The Yankees are still waiting on the changeup to develop, but his two pitches are major-league ready out of the bullpen. ⓧ Supposedly the more immediate impact arm of the Andrew Miller trade, **Ben Heller** has tossed just 18 total innings, and underwent Tommy John surgery on April 6th. There's no immediacy now, but the team will have 2019 to determine the impact. ⓧ There's a certain ceiling for prospects like **Michael King**, and after a brilliant 2018 campaign, he's pushing against it. A finesse sinkerballer, his stock is at the point where even Brian Cashman admitted that, "We had a ton of requests on him [at the trade deadline]. We had a few teams tell us he would go into their rotation now." ⓧ **Tim Locastro** has four vowels in his name, but somehow they're not all "A", which would have been apropos of his status as a decent Quad-A hurler. ⓧ After missing most of 2017, lean right-hander **Nolan Martinez** finally returned to a full slate of action, picking up a NY-Penn League Player of the Week honor in August. ⓧ In terms of "stuff," **Luis Medina** has what it takes to be an elite big leaguer: mid-to-upper-90s heat, a plus curve, and a developing change that could be a plus in the future as well. There's just no consistency in his delivery. The risk is high with this dynamic 19 year-old, but so is the reward. ⓧ **Nick Nelson** is the definition of a sleeper with raw potential. He features a mid-90s fastball and a solid curve, but with absolutely no command of it. He has been moving up levels, but he will need to add a pitch, and a pinch of command, before he'll see even a cup of coffee. ⓧ Vague injuries are a constant in minor league reporting, and clouds the true direction of a player's development. **Freicer Perez** sits in true prospect limbo after the injury that cost him his 2018 was revealed to be shoulder inflammation. A year removed from rave reviews and Betances comparisons, now we wait for the fog of war to lift. ⓧ The team's 2017 second-rounder, **Matt Sauer** wields a mid-90s fastball, solid command, and a competent slider. With room on his frame for more velocity growth, his realistic floor is another high-powered arm in the bullpen. ⓧ The hardest part of making good on a first-round pick that just went underwent Tommy John surgery is getting through the recovery itself, which ends the careers of a solid chunk of pitchers. Now, the next hardest part for **Clarke Schmidt**: a full season of health. Well, that, and the waiting. ⓧ The Yankees love their fast-rising relievers, and **Trevor Stephan** was drafted in the third round last year to do exactly that. After just one year of development he finds himself knocking on Scranton's door, boasting a curve that could help him avoid same-side work. ⓧ Acquired as the player to be named later in the Ivan Nova trade, **Stephen Tarpley** was called up during roster expansion. A heavy groundball LOOGY isn't in high demand these days, but that one vector will put him among the big league bullpen's arsenal, or at least its reserves. ⓧ A return in the minor Nick Rumbelow deal with Seattle, **Juan Then** put up 11 starts with a 2.70 ERA in the GCL. Entering his age-19 season, and showcasing a fastball near the mid-90s, he's the example of how the Yankees will continue to revitalize their system as they compete: flip players from positions of strength, Then profit. ⓧ A former 18th-round pick, **Garrett Whitlock** continued his methodical rise to the upper minors, flashing that fabled combination of drawing both downward contact and whiffs. While reliever is a likely scenario, thanks to a flimsy third pitch, he'll likely muscle his way into the long Yankee bullpen queue soon.

OAKLAND ATHLETICS

Essay by Susan Slusser

Player comments by Jason Wojciechowski and BP staff

After three straight last-place finishes, the Oakland A's turned in a surprisingly successful 2018 season, winning 97 games and claiming the second Wild Card spot. But how?

Was the rebuilding team simply a year or two ahead of schedule? Did the "Moneyball" crew figure out some new market inefficiency? Considering the near complete rotation devastation the A's incurred, there was much more at work. It took a number of astute moves to patch things together. Sometimes, that's sheer luck, and Oakland certainly had some of that last season. More often, though, a lot of thought goes into moves: timing promotions and, just as important, demotions, and identifying good fits who might be easily obtained.

That's what the A's front office did so well in 2018, including laying some of the groundwork the previous November when they acquired minor-league outfielder Ramon Laureano from the Astros in exchange for minor-league pitcher Brandon Bailey. "We had asked about him prior to the 2017 season when we had explored some Sonny Gray trades, but he was off limits," A's general manager David Forst said. "We hadn't necessarily followed him closely throughout 2017 but we knew he had a hand injury. ... With what we had seen in 2016, it seemed like it was worth a roster spot for us."

The A's had extensive reports on Laureano from special assistant Billy Owens, as well as former Double-A Midland manager Ryan Christenson. Oakland has all minor-league managers turn in evaluations of opposing players, and according to assistant general manager Dan Feinstein, Christenson, now the A's bench coach, stands out when it comes to scouting opponents. Thumbs ups from Owens and Christenson were keys to adding Laureano, and the timing was perfect, with teams needing to protect prospects from the Rule 5 draft and the Astros having a number of top young outfielders—one element of luck for Oakland. Laureano hit .288/.358/.474 in 48 games for the A's.

A similar dynamic came into play with the A's biggest offseason addition. They'd been looking for a right-handed-hitting outfielder under multiple years of team control and the Cardinals, with a glut of outfielders, had a terrific fit: Stephen Piscotty, signed through 2022 with a club option for

ATHLETICS PROSPECTUS
2018 W-L: 97-65, 2ND IN AL WEST

Pythag	.588	6th	B-Age	28.0	15th
RS/G	5.02	4th	P-Age	29.1	21st
RA/G	4.16	11th	Salary	$66.0M	30th
DRC+	105	5th	M$/MW	$1.1M	30th
DRA	4.32	15th	DL Days	1469	26th
FIP	4.21	20th	$ on DL	12%	8th
DER	.730	1st			

400'

362'   362'

330'   330'

- Opened 1966
- Open air
- Natural surface
- Fence profile: 8' to 15'

Three-Year Park Factors

Runs	Runs/RH	Runs/LH	HR/RH	HR/LH
97	98	96	93	92

Top Hitter WARP	5.3 Matt Chapman
Top Pitcher WARP	2.5 Blake Treinen
Top Prospect	Jesus Luzardo

2018 Hit List Ranking

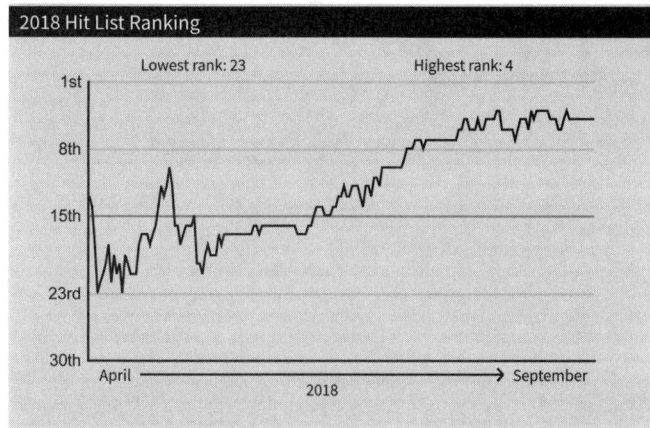

Lowest rank: 23   Highest rank: 4

Committed Payroll (in millions)

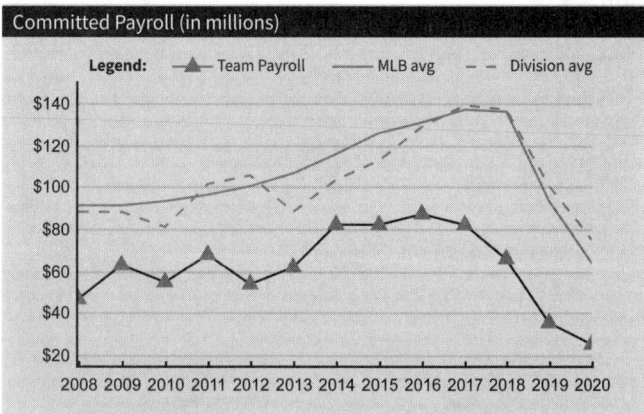

Legend: — ▲ — Team Payroll   —— MLB avg   – – – Division avg

Farm System Ranking

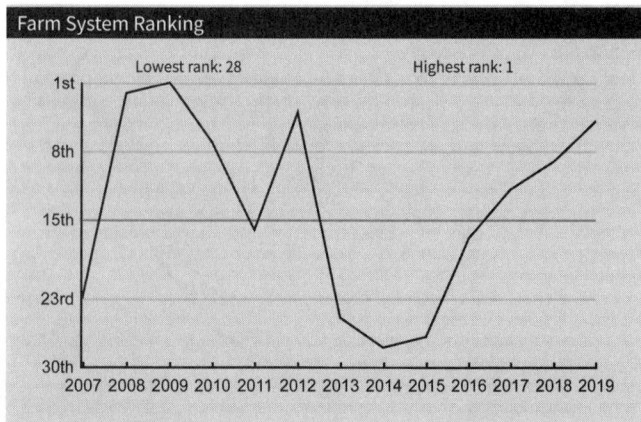

Lowest rank: 28   Highest rank: 1

Personnel

EVP, Baseball Operations
Billy Beane

General Manager
David Forst

Assistant General Manager
Dan Kantrovitz

Assistant General Manager
Billy Owens

Manager
Bob Melvin

BP Alumni
Al Skorupa

2023. There was so much more to this transaction, however. Piscotty is from Pleasanton, not far from Oakland, and his mother, Gretchen, had been diagnosed with ALS, in May. The Cardinals made it clear that if they could trade Piscotty, they'd try to do so to a team near his home. In a rare trade completed at least in part for benevolent reasons, the A's acquired Piscotty on December 14 in exchange for minor-league infielders Yairo Munoz and Max Schrock.

"I think our role in it was increased by the fact that [Cardinals president of baseball operations John Mozeliak] thought it was the right thing to get him closer to home," Forst said. "That being said, the Padres were there with us to the very end, at least that's what we heard. It's not like they were going to move him to us no matter what. ... Our analysis and what we knew of his personal situation led us to believe he could get back to what he did in 2016." Piscotty hit .267/.331/.491 with 27 homers and 41 doubles, topping his 2016 production.

Another outfielder from the St. Louis organization wound up in the A's plans in an under-the-radar deal: They signed Nick Martini as a six-year minor-league free agent based on multiple strong 2017 reports from special assistant Steve Sharpe. "We had him near or at the top of the minor-league free-agent list," Feinstein said. "We reached out to him as soon as we could and were as aggressive as we could be." Martini hit .296/.397/.414 in 55 games for the A's.

For a budget-conscious team, minor-league free agents can be a major plus, so the A's try to cover a lot of bases when looking at the crop each year. "There's one philosophy where we look for guys with upside, and you take some risks on guys who are young. You're looking for major leaguers, you're not just looking for Triple-A depth," Forst said. "We do also target areas of need in the system. With a guy like Martini and Anthony Garcia (another former St. Louis minor leaguer), we thought they could be big leaguers because of what they'd done."

The A's, like everyone else, stockpile as many starting pitchers as possible, but last season tested that almost immediately when Jharel Cotton and A.J. Puk went down with ulnar-collateral ligament tears in March. Oakland turned to two pitchers the front office knew well already, signing former A's Trevor Cahill and Brett Anderson. "There are so many unknowns when you bring players in in free agency or just outside the organization," Forst said. "If you can eliminate some of that uncertainty by dealing with a player who you know, it makes a difference."

Scout Tom Thomas had attended Cahill's February workout, and the A's were in touch with Cahill's agent long before there was a need. It was those two-and-a-half months of conversation that led up to the signing. The conversation with Anderson was more like two-and-a-half minutes. A's vice president of baseball operations Billy Beane simply ran into the left-hander at a Scottsdale gym just as the team was losing pitchers. "Billy assumed Brett had signed somewhere," Forst said. "He asked Brett 'Who are you with?'

He said, 'I'm not with anybody.' We know him, so some of that uncertainty is not there. We don't know if he's healthy because he hadn't been."

Once the season began, more starters landed on the disabled list. Daniel Gossett and Kendall Graveman needed Tommy John surgery, Andrew Triggs eventually had thoracic-outlet surgery, Paul Blackburn was out with a forearm issue most of the year, and Cahill and Anderson had a variety of small injuries. Even so, when the A's picked up Edwin Jackson on a minor-league deal after he asked for his release from the Nationals, few noticed. Oakland called up the veteran right-hander on June 25 and the team went 14-3 in his starts. His 3.33 ERA was the sixth-lowest in the league from June 25 on.

Another stroke of good fortune? No. "With Edwin, I wouldn't categorize that as luck because when he was released, Dan [Feinstein] had a relationship with the agent," Forst said. "[Trainer] Nick Paparesta had a relationship with him from Tampa. We knew what we were getting. The timing was really good. We were able to tell him that there might be a big-league opportunity, and we'll let you out if there's not. But … when I saw him throwing 97 at Detroit on TV, I had no idea."

With their depleted rotation, the front office realized the bullpen was the team's strength. Closer Blake Treinen—reacquired as part of the previous summer's Sean Doolittle deal—put up eye-popping numbers. And rookie Lou Trivino worked his way into the setup role, sporting an ERA as low as 1.16 on August 5 before some late-season struggles. "What Lou did, we didn't plan for that," Forst said. "It was such a huge part of our year. We were smart enough to protect him on the 40-man roster, but nobody in this office thought he was going to come up and be our setup guy."

When the trade deadline came around, knowing they didn't want to disrupt their rebuilding efforts by dealing top prospects for a major starter, the A's again looked at the bullpen and dealt for Mets closer Jeurys Familia, Twins closer Fernando Rodney, and Nationals setup man Shawn Kelley. "I think once we got into conversations about trades, we recognized that the acquisition costs and dollars on relievers were going to be more in our range than starters were," Forst said. "The Familia trade happened early. When we made that trade, we weren't yet canvasing everybody. … Rodney was a matter of, he shows up on waivers and we're still looking for help. He's really good, let's throw in a waiver claim and see what happens."

The Kelley move was unusual, as the A's took advantage of the fact that the Nationals had dumped him after an on-field snit-fit during a blowout. And then Oakland took a calculated risk, waiting him out on waivers. "With Kelley, we had talked to [Nationals general manager] Mike Rizzo about him before that incident," Forst said. "It was opportunistic when we saw what happened there and they designated him. We talked about him on trade waivers but we didn't put in the claim, hoping he would get through and we could get him for the minimum salary."

The A's also added starter Mike Fiers in a waiver deal with Detroit, with the team winning eight of his nine starts. They had held some talks with the Tigers before the deadline, but couldn't consummate a deal. The A's lucked out when Fiers fell to them on the waiver wire, surprising many around baseball who'd assumed the Mariners would claim him. "The fact that Fiers got to us on trade waivers, that was lucky," Forst said. "We had the foundation and the conversation in place because we talked about him before the deadline and we had also already talked to ownership about adding the money. All that stuff was in place when we did get the claim."

The biggest addition Oakland made that month, however, may have been Laureano, called up on August 3. Center field was the one unsettled spot in the A's lineup. They had fully intended for Dustin Fowler, acquired from the Yankees in the Sonny Gray deal, to fill the job long term, but he'd missed almost the entire year after a horrific knee injury and, after a promising start when first called up, he'd tailed off. Fowler's inexperience and the previous year's layoff was showing.

"That combination on Dustin was tough," Forst said. "Any time you have a young player, you want to bring them to the big leagues when they're over-ready and when they're performing really well so they can get off on the right foot. … It's not a science. You're just trying to figure out the right time. … We've talked about that going all the way back to Ben Grieve and Miguel Tejada and Eric Chavez. When you get someone here, you want them to stay. It doesn't always work out that way. It didn't with Matt Olson, for instance. Dustin was new to the organization effectively and you want to make sure you're respectful of his ego and feelings and all these things that go into those decisions when he's going up and down."

Laureano was batting .297 at Nashville, and his defensive work was off the charts. Every report the front office got was glowing. Nashville manager Fran Riordan was texting proof regularly. "Ramon was playing so well that we just couldn't keep him there any longer," Forst said. "Fran was sending us video on his assists from the outfield. From the minute he got there out of extended spring, they were raving about everything: How hard he plays, how great he is in the outfield. It was immediately noticed the impact he could make."

Laureano hit .288 the rest of the way, with five homers and seven steals in 32 starts. Most importantly: He turned in the best center-field defense the A's have seen in a long time and made one of the plays of the year on August 11, racing into the left-center gap for a Justin Upton drive and then turning and firing to first base—on the fly—to double off Eric Young Jr. Martini, too, turned out to be a nice fit as the team's left-handed-hitting leadoff man. He was playing so well, in fact, that it was surprising when he was optioned out on August 30 with the A's still trying to nail down a playoff spot.

As it turns out, this was one transaction the A's flubbed. They believed they could assign Martini to a minor-league team that was wrapping up its season and he would return before the 10-day limit was up. That rule, however, had changed in the most recent CBA—players optioned out before rosters expand in September can't return for 10 days, no matter where they're assigned. Forst took immediate responsibility for the gaffe—and, worse, he said in a November interview, A's travel secretary Mickey Morabito had warned the front office about the CBA change. "We screwed up," Forst said. "Mickey told me the rule five days before that, and I blew him off. I said, 'You're wrong,' without looking it up."

Ultimately, much of the A's success came down to that carefully constructed bullpen. They were undefeated when leading after seven innings into the final week of the season and finished 70-2 in such games. The bullpen's ERA was 3.00 from June 3 on. Oakland relievers earned 45 wins, the second-most in major-league history behind the 2018 Rays with 55—and when Manaea landed on the DL in August, the A's took a page from Tampa Bay's handbook and began using an "opener," reliever Liam Hendriks, when he was called up September 1. Hendriks was another oddity of a transaction. He'd been designated for assignment on June 25 with an ERA over 7.00, but he cleared waivers and got his act back together at Triple-A.

Once out of the picture, Hendriks was pitching the first inning for the A's once or twice a week in the middle of the pennant race. "Things were going so well at the back end of the bullpen with Rodney, Familia and Trivino. Everybody had a role," Forst said, adding that manager Bob Melvin didn't want to disrupt that dynamic. "The next-best place to get the most out of Liam was in the first inning. He was pitching really well. How do we fit him in because we don't want to use him just to mop up? We were down a starter, so let's get him in some high-leverage spots in the first inning."

Hendriks thrived, with a 1.38 ERA and a .178 opponents average. And somehow, someway, it was Hendriks, the once-abandoned Australian, opening in the Wild Card game at Yankee Stadium. New York got two quick runs off Hendriks when Aaron Judge smacked a two-run homer, but it was other relievers working much earlier than usual who really struggled; Rodney and Treinen combined to allow five runs.

"Right up until it didn't work, it was great," Forst said of the A's bullpenning experiment, adding that the team might continue to tinker with the strategy, depending on the personnel. "I think from the standpoint of the first inning, where scoring is the highest and you're facing the best hitters, it was really successful. Maybe the next part of the equation is making sure the mindset is right coming in after."

After the season, Beane was named the Major League Executive of the Year, reflecting the remarkable work by the entire front office. Forst received a four-year contract extension, through 2023, recognition that the story of the A's terrific season was one of many small transactions here and there, many under the radar. When lots of small decisions pay off, that can make all the difference for a team with limited resources, and in 2018 those moves fueled one of the more remarkable turnarounds in A's history. ■

—*Susan Slusser is a writer at the San Francisco Chronicle.*

HITTERS

Lazaro Armenteros LF Born: 05/22/99 Age: 20 Bats: R Throws: R Height: 6'0" Weight: 182 Origin: International Free Agent, 2016

YEAR	TEAM	LVL	AGE	PA	R	2B	3B	HR	RBI	BB	K	SB	CS	AVG/OBP/SLG	DRC+	VORP	BABIP	BRR	FRAA	WARP
2017	DAT	RK	18	26	6	0	0	0	1	3	9	2	2	.167/.385/.167	55	2.0	.300	0.9	CF(6): 1.5	0.2
2017	ATH	RK	18	181	24	9	4	4	22	16	48	10	1	.288/.376/.474	106	14.2	.387	2.8	LF(27): 4.2, CF(2): -0.5	1.0
2018	BLT	A	19	340	43	8	2	8	39	36	115	8	6	.277/.374/.401	99	21.6	.427	2.1	LF(69): -0.7	0.8
2019	OAK	MLB	20	251	26	7	0	7	23	15	96	1	1	.183/.237/.307	40	-11.8	.271	-0.5	LF 2	-1.1

Breakout: 1%   Improve: 3%   Collapse: 0%   Attrition: 2%   MLB: 4%   Comparables: *Caleb Gindl, Chris Parmelee, Matt Davidson*

Armenteros was one of just 11 teenage hitters in the Midwest League, yet he led his team in on-base percentage, a testament to the fact that he's a *hitter*, not merely a tools monster. Of course, he has tools, too: Analysts continue to talk up his future power, premised on excellent bat speed, but it hasn't shown up in games yet; it will need to, because he's already a left fielder, and is not likely to move back to center as he advances up the ladder. Armenteros missed a month of the season after appearing to injure his knee beating out an infield single. He departed with a .454 slugging percentage, and finished the year just a hair over .400. Correlation isn't causation, but considering how little information comes out of the minor leagues on injuries, one might wonder whether his base was fully stable under him (or whether he trusted it) after he came back.

Franklin Barreto MI Born: 02/27/96 Age: 23 Bats: R Throws: R Height: 5'10" Weight: 190 Origin: International Free Agent, 2012

YEAR	TEAM	LVL	AGE	PA	R	2B	3B	HR	RBI	BB	K	SB	CS	AVG/OBP/SLG	DRC+	VORP	BABIP	BRR	FRAA	WARP
2016	MID	AA	20	507	63	25	3	10	50	36	90	30	15	.281/.340/.413	108	27.5	.330	3.1	SS(81): -10.7, 2B(33): -3.1	1.3
2017	NAS	AAA	21	510	63	19	7	15	54	27	141	15	8	.290/.339/.456	88	34.6	.384	0.3	SS(83): -3.3, 2B(25): -2.6	0.9
2017	OAK	MLB	21	76	10	1	2	2	6	5	33	2	0	.197/.250/.352	59	0.2	.333	0.7	SS(11): 0.3, 2B(10): 0.2	0.0
2018	NAS	AAA	22	333	54	16	1	18	46	39	106	5	2	.259/.357/.514	117	35.6	.337	3.5	2B(60): -2.2, SS(11): 0.4	2.1
2018	OAK	MLB	22	75	10	4	0	5	16	1	29	0	0	.233/.253/.493	73	-0.8	.308	-1.1	2B(26): -1.7, SS(2): 0.0	-0.3
2019	OAK	MLB	23	262	32	10	1	11	34	18	86	5	2	.225/.291/.414	89	5.5	.300	0.0	2B -4, SS 0	0.1

Breakout: 9%   Improve: 32%   Collapse: 10%   Attrition: 20%   MLB: 64%   Comparables: *Arismendy Alcantara, Dilson Herrera, Yoan Moncada*

The five homers in 75 plate appearances Barreto put up in sporadic major-league time last year is around a 40-dinger pace for a full season, which is why everyone's still excited for him to arrive even though it seems like the wait has been forever. He's still just 23, though, and it's not his fault Jed Lowrie somehow figured out, in his mid-30s, how to stay healthy. Barreto was always a bat-to-ball prospect, but he seems to have traded that off (32 percent strikeout rate the last two years vs. 19 percent in 2013–16) in order to knock more balls out of the yard (a homer every 24 plate appearances vs. every 43). He is also a card-carrying member of the Fly Ball Revolution: The average launch angle of his balls in play last year was akin to Brian McCann's, who has a well-known affection for worms. That said, if Barreto is going to earn and keep a full-time job, he will need to start spitting on more pitches outside the zone, lest he find himself in Salvador Perez territory, simply not receiving enough hittable offerings to do damage.

Austin Beck CF Born: 11/21/98 Age: 20 Bats: R Throws: R Height: 6'1" Weight: 200 Origin: Round 1, 2017 Draft (#6 overall)

YEAR	TEAM	LVL	AGE	PA	R	2B	3B	HR	RBI	BB	K	SB	CS	AVG/OBP/SLG	DRC+	VORP	BABIP	BRR	FRAA	WARP
2017	ATH	RK	18	174	23	7	4	2	28	17	51	7	1	.211/.293/.349	81	2.6	.294	1.8	CF(33): 1.2	0.4
2018	BLT	A	19	534	58	29	4	2	60	30	117	8	6	.296/.335/.383	92	14.9	.377	-4.8	CF(113): 2.0	0.7
2019	OAK	MLB	20	251	18	6	0	5	23	8	76	1	0	.193/.218/.282	25	-13.5	.257	-0.4	CF -1	-1.6

Breakout: 1% Improve: 1% Collapse: 0% Attrition: 1% MLB: 2%   *Comparables: Engel Beltre, Carlos Tocci, Gorkys Hernandez*

Beck came into pro ball in 2017 with all the tools in the world and no idea what to do with them. In 2018, as one of the youngest hitters in the Midwest League (along with teammate Lazaro Armenteros), he started figuring out one piece: putting the wood bat on the pitched baseball. Over-the-fence power is the next hurdle, and there's every physical indication he'll clear it, though if he moves to the Cal League this year as expected, it may be tough to sort out the genuine improvement from the environmental help. He's still nowhere near the majors, and plenty of youngsters never translate strength into game pop, but Beck has at least checked the first box: not being overmatched by full-season ball.

Mark Canha OF Born: 02/15/89 Age: 30 Bats: R Throws: R Height: 6'2" Weight: 210 Origin: Round 7, 2010 Draft (#227 overall)

YEAR	TEAM	LVL	AGE	PA	R	2B	3B	HR	RBI	BB	K	SB	CS	AVG/OBP/SLG	DRC+	VORP	BABIP	BRR	FRAA	WARP
2016	OAK	MLB	27	44	4	0	0	3	6	0	20	0	1	.122/.140/.341	61	-3.6	.105	-0.1	1B(5): 0.2, 3B(3): -0.1	-0.2
2017	NAS	AAA	28	317	52	25	3	12	50	34	62	4	0	.283/.373/.529	114	33.0	.323	3.3	RF(61): -2.7, CF(8): 0.9	1.5
2017	OAK	MLB	28	187	16	13	1	5	14	7	56	2	0	.208/.262/.382	66	-2.9	.274	0.3	RF(22): -1.0, LF(20): -0.9	-0.6
2018	OAK	MLB	29	411	60	22	0	17	52	34	88	1	2	.249/.328/.449	108	19.2	.282	-0.3	CF(62): -5.9, LF(51): 1.4	1.1
2019	OAK	MLB	30	295	34	13	1	10	35	22	74	2	1	.232/.307/.403	92	4.6	.286	0.2	LF 1, CF -1	0.4

Breakout: 4% Improve: 44% Collapse: 6% Attrition: 11% MLB: 99%   *Comparables: Lorenzo Cain, Charlie Blackmon, Ben Francisco*

In last year's book, we posited that Canha did not have the requisite power to be a major-league player given that he was limited to the three easiest defensive positions. The obvious conclusion to draw from Canha's emergence last year is that he took motivation from us. You're welcome, A's fans. Canha's overall batting line ended just about even with the average major-league right fielder even as he took on a team-leading 466 innings of work in center field, where he performed somewhere in that nebulous "not unwatchable, but not exactly *capable* either" realm that signifies an unspoken "well, what the hell else do you want me to do?" from the manager while gesturing at the roster. Canha's hitting was driven by a .604 slugging percentage against lefties that was frightfully close to his .665 *OPS* against right-handers. That will probably keep him rosterable, or at least on the shuttle squad, for one more year, helped along by the A's burning only two of his option years so far.

Matt Chapman 3B Born: 04/28/93 Age: 26 Bats: R Throws: R Height: 6'0" Weight: 210 Origin: Round 1, 2014 Draft (#25 overall)

YEAR	TEAM	LVL	AGE	PA	R	2B	3B	HR	RBI	BB	K	SB	CS	AVG/OBP/SLG	DRC+	VORP	BABIP	BRR	FRAA	WARP
2016	MID	AA	23	504	78	26	4	29	83	59	147	7	4	.244/.335/.521	143	35.4	.293	1.8	3B(100): 14.6, SS(10): 3.6	6.6
2016	NAS	AAA	23	85	14	1	1	7	13	9	26	0	0	.197/.282/.513	122	6.7	.186	0.2	3B(18): 2.1	0.8
2017	NAS	AAA	24	204	30	6	2	16	30	25	63	5	4	.257/.348/.589	129	20.6	.293	-0.1	3B(49): 7.2	2.2
2017	OAK	MLB	24	326	39	23	2	14	40	32	92	0	3	.234/.313/.472	95	14.1	.290	-1.0	3B(84): 12.6	2.2
2018	OAK	MLB	25	616	100	42	6	24	68	58	146	1	2	.278/.356/.508	113	48.4	.338	3.8	3B(145): 15.6	5.3
2019	OAK	MLB	26	592	72	29	4	25	83	59	147	3	3	.247/.331/.456	117	27.5	.298	1.6	3B 18	4.9

Breakout: 4% Improve: 49% Collapse: 7% Attrition: 13% MLB: 95%   *Comparables: Chris Davis, Ian Stewart, Pedro Alvarez*

How was Chapman going to follow up a star-level half-season rookie performance that featured light-tower power, flashy defense and way too many whiffs? Why, by keeping the power and defense while chopping five percentage points off the strikeout rate, because everything always goes well and nothing is bad. Taking that step forward and doing it over a full season of playing time pushed Chapman to 11th in baseball in BWARP. Unfortunately for his notoriety, but fortunately for fans of great baseball, nine of the 10 ahead of him were 27 or younger and three of them were fellow third basemen (Jose Ramirez, Alex Bregman, Nolan Arenado, plus whatever Manny Machado is now). Chapman's season wound up strikingly similar to the 2014 line of the last Oakland superstar, Josh Donaldson; that name is bound to raise bitter feelings in A's fans because Donaldson was traded that winter. The difference, though, is that Chapman is two years younger than Donaldson was, and two years away from arbitration eligibility. Even if the A's cannot figure out their ballpark situation, or if they do get a new park but continue their bargain-basement ways anyway, there should still be another couple of years for the Oakland faithful to enjoy Chapman's cannon arm and balls-out, headlong sprints for foul popups.

Khris Davis DH
Born: 12/21/87   Age: 31   Bats: R   Throws: R   Height: 5'10"   Weight: 195   Origin: Round 7, 2009 Draft (#226 overall)

YEAR	TEAM	LVL	AGE	PA	R	2B	3B	HR	RBI	BB	K	SB	CS	AVG/OBP/SLG	DRC+	VORP	BABIP	BRR	FRAA	WARP
2016	OAK	MLB	28	610	85	24	2	42	102	42	166	1	2	.247/.307/.524	119	23.9	.270	-3.3	LF(93): 0.2	2.5
2017	OAK	MLB	29	652	91	28	1	43	110	73	195	4	0	.247/.336/.528	122	32.5	.290	-0.2	LF(116): -8.9	2.4
2018	OAK	MLB	30	654	98	28	1	48	123	59	175	0	0	.247/.326/.549	135	34.0	.261	-4.6	LF(11): -1.9	3.2
2019	OAK	MLB	31	632	88	30	2	38	105	60	172	2	1	.253/.334/.513	129	26.1	.298	-2.3		2.8

Breakout: 5%   Improve: 36%   Collapse: 7%   Attrition: 8%   MLB: 95%   *Comparables: Eric Thames, Fred McGriff, Richie Sexson*

The A's finally made Davis a full-time designated hitter last year, and reaped the reward, adding nearly a full win to Davis' WARP while running out a generally solid goulash of left fielders (Pinder, Joyce, Martini, Canha) in his place. Davis continued to do what he always does at the plate: hit .247 (his fourth straight year at that figure, indisputable proof of a benevolent higher power with a sharp sense of humor) and smack 40-plus dingers (his third straight season, and a new career high). He's the rare bat-only player worth a multi-year commitment, even though he costs you the ability to use the DH as a half-rest spot for other players, and even if we should look at Chris Davis' age-30 to -32 seasons for a sense of the downside.

Davis' Wild Card Game homer against the Yankees left him in a four-way tie for the best career homers-per-playoff-game rate in baseball history, with Eddie Rosario, Mark Trumbo and Mark Brouhard.

Dustin Fowler CF
Born: 12/29/94   Age: 24   Bats: L   Throws: L   Height: 6'0"   Weight: 195   Origin: Round 18, 2013 Draft (#554 overall)

YEAR	TEAM	LVL	AGE	PA	R	2B	3B	HR	RBI	BB	K	SB	CS	AVG/OBP/SLG	DRC+	VORP	BABIP	BRR	FRAA	WARP
2016	TRN	AA	21	574	67	30	15	12	88	22	86	25	11	.281/.311/.458	110	29.1	.313	3.5	CF(119): -9.7, LF(3): -0.3	1.8
2017	SWB	AAA	22	313	49	19	8	13	43	15	63	13	5	.293/.329/.542	127	18.5	.335	-0.7	CF(40): -4.5, RF(14): -1.1	1.4
2018	NAS	AAA	23	239	37	17	6	4	27	9	41	13	2	.341/.364/.520	95	24.4	.400	0.2	CF(51): -12.9, LF(2): 0.6	-0.5
2018	OAK	MLB	23	203	19	3	2	6	23	8	47	6	4	.224/.256/.354	84	-3.2	.262	-1.0	CF(57): -3.8, RF(3): -0.1	-0.2
2019	OAK	MLB	24	246	30	12	2	8	28	12	53	9	3	.254/.294/.422	98	6.8	.297	-0.3	LF 0, CF -2	0.5

Breakout: 10%   Improve: 49%   Collapse: 8%   Attrition: 30%   MLB: 76%   *Comparables: Josh Reddick, Nate Schierholtz, Raimel Tapia*

Fowler returned from the brutal knee injury that ended his 2017 season, but lost a spring battle for the A's center-field job to a Boog Powell-Jake Smolinski platoon. When Powell got hurt early on, and with Smolinski not hitting, Oakland turned largely to erstwhile first baseman Mark Canha to man the position. None of this speaks well of Fowler's standing with the A's brass. He came to the majors and joined a platoon with Canha in mid-May, but proceeded to justify the April decisions by putting up the batting line you see above. While Fowler had a reputation for aggression, and his walk rate appears to back that, the issue was less chasing bad pitches and more that pitchers weren't afraid of him: Among players with at least 100 plate appearances, he was in the top five percent of pitches seen in the strike zone. If Fowler can't figure out how to turn those strikes around for at *least* line-drive doubles, he's not going to be a major leaguer, not given that he's merely passable in center field, and especially now that Ramon Laureano took advantage of Fowler's struggles and seized the job in August and September.

Matt Joyce LF
Born: 08/03/84   Age: 34   Bats: L   Throws: R   Height: 6'2"   Weight: 205   Origin: Round 12, 2005 Draft (#360 overall)

YEAR	TEAM	LVL	AGE	PA	R	2B	3B	HR	RBI	BB	K	SB	CS	AVG/OBP/SLG	DRC+	VORP	BABIP	BRR	FRAA	WARP
2016	PIT	MLB	31	293	45	10	1	13	42	59	67	1	1	.242/.403/.463	129	22.6	.285	2.6	RF(43): -1.7, LF(26): -0.3	1.9
2017	OAK	MLB	32	544	78	33	0	25	68	66	113	4	1	.243/.335/.473	110	17.9	.263	1.9	RF(115): 0.6, LF(24): 2.4	2.4
2018	OAK	MLB	33	246	34	9	0	7	15	35	53	0	2	.208/.322/.353	96	4.6	.242	0.1	LF(49): 2.0, RF(6): -0.3	0.7
2019	OAK	MLB	34	297	39	14	1	9	33	38	64	1	1	.240/.343/.412	105	10.8	.284	0.9	LF 2, RF 0	1.4

Breakout: 1%   Improve: 34%   Collapse: 14%   Attrition: 16%   MLB: 91%   *Comparables: Willie Harris, Jose Cruz Jr., Alex Gordon*

Joyce suffered about as bad an entry to free agency as a player can, hitting the disabled list with a back problem twice, ultimately spending over 40 percent of the season inactive. He returned when rosters expanded, but was in the starting lineup just once in September as Nick Martini supplanted him as the A's main lefty left fielder. As miserable as "replaced by Nick Martini" sounds, and as bad as Joyce's final line looks, it's nowhere near the depths of his 2015 horror show in Anaheim, and he can probably still help a big-league team as long as it's willing to carry a platoon partner on the bench. That "probably" includes hedges for both age and back trouble, which means we're looking at "50.2 percent probably," not "75 percent probably."

Ramon Laureano CF
Born: 07/15/94   Age: 24   Bats: R   Throws: R   Height: 5'11"   Weight: 185   Origin: Round 16, 2014 Draft (#466 overall)

YEAR	TEAM	LVL	AGE	PA	R	2B	3B	HR	RBI	BB	K	SB	CS	AVG/OBP/SLG	DRC+	VORP	BABIP	BRR	FRAA	WARP
2016	LNC	A+	21	357	69	19	5	10	60	50	86	33	11	.317/.426/.519	132	35.2	.411	1.2	CF(30): 4.5, RF(23): 3.8	3.6
2016	CCH	AA	21	148	20	9	2	5	13	20	33	10	3	.323/.432/.548	123	18.9	.407	1.0	CF(20): 3.6, RF(15): 3.1	1.7
2017	CCH	AA	22	513	65	21	6	11	55	40	110	24	5	.227/.298/.369	91	11.6	.273	6.3	RF(95): 7.8, CF(31): -1.7	1.9
2018	NAS	AAA	23	284	44	12	1	14	35	31	70	11	2	.297/.380/.524	123	24.2	.358	1.7	RF(45): 6.2, CF(19): -0.5	2.4
2018	OAK	MLB	23	176	27	12	1	5	19	16	50	7	1	.288/.358/.474	85	16.2	.388	1.4	CF(47): 3.0	0.8
2019	OAK	MLB	24	507	68	23	2	19	61	45	141	18	4	.241/.318/.425	102	22.4	.308	1.6	CF 3	2.7

Breakout: 4%   Improve: 36%   Collapse: 12%   Attrition: 20%   MLB: 75%   *Comparables: Derek Fisher, Joe Benson, Lewis Brinson*

If Laureano is really a star, which is how he played over the last two months of 2018, here's who missed on him: the amateur scouts, who didn't draft him out of high school and popped him in the 16th round after two years in junior college; the Astros' talent evaluators, who added relief pitchers Cionel Perez and Dean Deetz to the 40-man roster rather than Laureano; 28 other teams, which weren't willing to give up more than the low-level pitching prospect the A's sent to Houston in trade; and every major public talent evaluator, including here at BP, none of whom put Laureano on a top-100 list. Stars do get missed! Jose Ramirez, J.D. Martinez, Matt Carpenter, Justin Turner and DJ LeMahieu all finished in the top 20 in BWARP last year without ever appearing on a top-100 prospect list. Turner, Martinez, Ramirez and LeMahieu scuffled for years in the majors before breaking out, though; it's the *immediate* impact by a non-elite prospect that makes the performance so hard to believe. (Though there's always Carpenter.) The point here is not that Laureano isn't a big leaguer: The defense is real, and he's always shown good command of the strike zone and enough power to make pitchers work. Just think more his September line (.269/.343/.441) than August (.317/.380/.524). That's more or less what George Springer hit in 2018, after all, and it meant he was a solidly above-average player.

Jed Lowrie 2B Born: 04/17/84 Age: 35 Bats: B Throws: R Height: 6'0" Weight: 180 Origin: Round 1, 2005 Draft (#45 overall)

YEAR	TEAM	LVL	AGE	PA	R	2B	3B	HR	RBI	BB	K	SB	CS	AVG/OBP/SLG	DRC+	VORP	BABIP	BRR	FRAA	WARP
2016	OAK	MLB	32	369	30	12	1	2	27	26	65	0	0	.263/.314/.322	83	-2.9	.316	-1.1	2B(82): 2.0, SS(2): 0.0	0.5
2017	OAK	MLB	33	645	86	49	3	14	69	73	100	0	1	.277/.360/.448	112	25.6	.314	-2.4	2B(136): -3.5, 3B(1): 0.2	2.4
2018	OAK	MLB	34	680	78	37	1	23	99	78	128	0	0	.267/.353/.448	121	38.5	.304	-3.0	2B(136): -0.4, 3B(14): -0.5	3.6
2019	OAK	MLB	35	635	68	39	2	14	74	65	110	0	0	.275/.353/.427	113	28.5	.319	-1.9	2B -2, 3B -1	2.7

Breakout: 1%   Improve: 28%   Collapse: 10%   Attrition: 12%   MLB: 80%   *Comparables: Orlando Hudson, Frankie Frisch, Ian Kinsler*

We opened last year's comment by pointing out that Lowrie was meant to be the A's placeholder for Franklin Barreto until he went out and had his best performance in years. Well, folks, he did it again, this time sending a few more balls over the wall that in 2017 had been doubles, resulting in the second-best WARP of his career, behind his 2012 season in Houston. PECOTA looks at Lowrie's age and sees a cliff coming, but that's what PECOTA said last winter, too. It's just as easy to see an injury-hastened fade into oblivion as it is to see him putting up above-average hitting lines with adequate defense until he's 40. "Give us a fun fact to end the comment!" you say? You got it. Lowrie attempted one steal in the last two years despite 1,325 plate appearances, easily the highest ratio in the league; the next-highest PA totals with zero or one attempts are Ryon Healy (1,129), Maikel Franco (1,088), Robinson Cano (996), Mark Trumbo (961) and Victor Martinez (943), all of whom have a listed weight at least 30 pounds higher than Lowrie.

Nick Martini OF Born: 06/27/90 Age: 29 Bats: L Throws: L Height: 5'11" Weight: 205 Origin: Round 7, 2011 Draft (#230 overall)

YEAR	TEAM	LVL	AGE	PA	R	2B	3B	HR	RBI	BB	K	SB	CS	AVG/OBP/SLG	DRC+	VORP	BABIP	BRR	FRAA	WARP
2016	SFD	AA	26	172	21	5	0	3	13	24	27	4	1	.234/.349/.331	111	4.6	.267	-0.8	CF(25): 0.9, RF(8): 0.4	0.7
2016	MEM	AAA	26	294	38	12	3	2	26	31	39	6	0	.273/.354/.367	98	13.6	.311	2.8	RF(38): 1.2, LF(20): -0.7	1.1
2017	SFD	AA	27	110	13	5	0	2	15	11	16	1	0	.263/.336/.374	110	5.0	.296	0.9	LF(16): 1.9, RF(3): 0.7	0.8
2017	MEM	AAA	27	426	60	20	5	6	55	55	77	5	1	.303/.394/.436	108	29.2	.363	1.2	LF(53): -0.3, RF(24): 0.6	1.7
2018	NAS	AAA	28	330	44	12	2	6	40	51	68	5	1	.297/.406/.420	109	23.3	.373	2.5	1B(41): 2.8, LF(22): 0.2	1.7
2018	OAK	MLB	28	179	26	9	3	1	19	21	36	0	0	.296/.397/.414	96	14.2	.379	1.1	LF(47): 2.1, CF(2): 0.2	0.8
2019	OAK	MLB	29	225	27	10	1	5	21	26	51	1	0	.243/.340/.375	100	6.1	.306	-0.1	LF 2	0.9

Breakout: 0%   Improve: 15%   Collapse: 13%   Attrition: 26%   MLB: 41%   *Comparables: Daniel Nava, Jake Goebbert, Mike Edwards*

Martini entered the A's system as a 28-year-old minor-league free agent who had never even sniffed a 40-man roster since being drafted in 2011 out of Kansas State. He ended the year as the starting left fielder for the A's in their Wild Card game loss to the Yankees. In between, he put up a Lorenzo Cain line at the plate. How had he slipped free so easily of his prior organization? Here's a hint: It was the Cardinals, who develop outfielders the way the rest of us develop carbon dioxide. Of course, the Cain comp is laughably incomplete: Martini gets on base and knocks some doubles, but that's all he does. He's not adding value with his glove or his legs, and his season-high in homers in the minors was eight. Bob Melvin also assiduously protected him from lefties, letting him face them just 11 times. For all that, a near-.400 OBP is a near-.400 OBP. As long as he doesn't mess with his glorious beard, he should be a perfectly nice corner-outfield option for the next few years.

Jorge Mateo SS Born: 06/23/95 Age: 24 Bats: R Throws: R Height: 6'0" Weight: 190 Origin: International Free Agent, 2012

YEAR	TEAM	LVL	AGE	PA	R	2B	3B	HR	RBI	BB	K	SB	CS	AVG/OBP/SLG	DRC+	VORP	BABIP	BRR	FRAA	WARP
2016	TAM	A+	21	507	65	16	9	8	47	33	108	36	15	.254/.306/.379	102	11.8	.313	3.2	SS(62): -5.1, 2B(40): -0.6	1.6
2017	TAM	A+	22	297	39	16	8	4	11	16	79	28	3	.240/.288/.400	92	15.4	.321	7.6	SS(42): 2.9, CF(22): -0.8	1.9
2017	TRN	AA	22	140	26	9	3	4	26	15	32	11	7	.300/.381/.525	106	17.0	.372	1.6	SS(16): 1.1, CF(5): -0.4	1.0
2017	MID	AA	22	147	25	5	7	4	20	9	33	13	3	.292/.333/.518	113	14.2	.356	2.2	SS(30): 0.8	1.2
2018	NAS	AAA	23	510	50	17	16	3	45	29	139	25	10	.230/.280/.353	65	3.7	.316	1.1	SS(123): -0.8, 2B(4): -0.5	0.1
2019	OAK	MLB	24	71	7	3	2	1	6	3	21	3	1	.217/.261/.347	91	2.4	.299	0.5	SS 0	0.3

Breakout: 3%   Improve: 13%   Collapse: 3%   Attrition: 17%   MLB: 25%   *Comparables: Grant Green, Brandon Crawford, Erik Gonzalez*

Spending a full year at Triple-A in your age-23 season is good; a .633 OPS, even from a shortstop, is substantially less so. Mateo is in danger of becoming a classic "can't steal first" player, though at the efficiency level he showed last year, he might get thrown out trying to do that, too. (Twenty-five steals in 35 attempts is not actually horrible; it's just striking when someone with 80-grade speed doesn't steal at a 90-percent-plus rate.) His plate discipline suffered against the advanced pitching he faced in the PCL, and his line is a good reminder that plate discipline doesn't just mean drawing walks; it also means waiting for pitches to drive. Mateo is young enough to spend another year at Triple-A trying to figure things out, but his roster situation means there's a clock on his development: He came stateside so long ago that he's already entering his *third* season on a 40-man roster (and therefore his third option year) without approaching the majors. Having just one fewer triple than double for the season is pretty cool, though.

Sean Murphy C Born: 10/10/94 Age: 24 Bats: R Throws: R Height: 6'3" Weight: 215 Origin: Round 3, 2016 Draft (#83 overall)

YEAR	TEAM	LVL	AGE	PA	R	2B	3B	HR	RBI	BB	K	SB	CS	AVG/OBP/SLG	DRC+	VORP	BABIP	BRR	FRAA	WARP
2016	VER	A-	21	85	10	1	0	2	7	9	12	1	0	.237/.318/.329	112	3.1	.258	0.4	C(20): 0.4	0.6
2017	STO	A+	22	178	22	11	0	9	26	11	33	0	0	.297/.343/.527	124	15.1	.323	0.2	C(40): -0.3	1.3
2017	MID	AA	22	217	25	7	0	4	22	21	34	0	0	.209/.288/.309	97	1.8	.232	0.6	C(51): 3.8	1.4
2018	MID	AA	23	289	51	26	2	8	43	23	47	3	0	.288/.358/.498	116	22.6	.324	2.1	C(65): 14.5	3.7
2019	OAK	MLB	24	71	7	3	0	2	8	4	14	0	0	.233/.283/.377	71	0.6	.263	-0.1	C 1	0.2

Breakout: 7%   Improve: 14%   Collapse: 14%   Attrition: 24%   MLB: 44%   *Comparables: Jonathan Lucroy, Josh Donaldson, John Jaso*

Murphy has now worked his way from undrafted walk-on to third-round pick to top-five catching prospect. The bat was suspect, but a return engagement in the Texas League saw him knock a ton of extra-base hits (though mostly inside the fences), at least until his second broken hamate in three years wiped out most of July and August. His arm remains the sexiest part of his toolkit, but we've learned in recent years that the arm is a small part of the overall catching package, and it's only gotten smaller as teams push station-to-station baseball to the outer limits of possibility. Murphy may not be a preternaturally gifted stealer of strikes with his pitch-receiving, but reports on that front are positive, and professional coaching can work wonders for players who have the athleticism and attitude to implement those lessons. His arrival in the major leagues has now become more "when" than "if." At this writing, the A's no. 1 catcher is Josh Phegley; if that doesn't change, the "when" might be answered by looking up the next Southwest flight from McCarran to Oakland.

YEAR	TEAM	P. COUNT	FRM RUNS	BLK RUNS	THRW RUNS	TOT RUNS
2017	MID	7267	3.6	-0.5	0.2	2.7
2018	MID	8864	13.6	1.4	0.6	15.6
2019	OAK	2597	1.1	-0.1	-0.2	0.9

Kyler Murray OF/QB Born: 08/07/97 Age: 21 Bats: R Throws: R Height: 5'11" Weight: 195 Origin: Round 1, 2018 Draft (#9 overall)

Murray was the A's first-round pick last year as a preposterously gifted athlete with an interesting background: He signed only on the condition that he be permitted to play the season as Oklahoma's quarterback before transitioning to baseball full time. (He has one more year of football eligibility but apparently no intention of using it.) Oakland acquiesced, and the result was a conference championship, a trip to the playoffs for OU and *the Heisman Trophy*. On the diamond, the hope is that Murray will become a power-speed-defense center fielder. He has played well against high-level competition, including in the wood-bat Cape Cod League, and he's only 21, but he's a two-sport 21, not the maniacal, year-round, travel-ball 21 that many of his competitors are. Every draft pick is a gamble, but some are blackjack and some are blindfolded darts after three beers and a dizzy bat race. When a bulls-eye is an All-Star center fielder, though, you chuck the darts first and worry about who might lose an eye later.

Sheldon Neuse 3B Born: 12/10/94 Age: 24 Bats: R Throws: R Height: 6'0" Weight: 195 Origin: Round 2, 2016 Draft (#58 overall)

YEAR	TEAM	LVL	AGE	PA	R	2B	3B	HR	RBI	BB	K	SB	CS	AVG/OBP/SLG	DRC+	VORP	BABIP	BRR	FRAA	WARP
2016	AUB	A-	21	141	16	5	3	1	11	13	26	2	2	.230/.305/.341	93	3.9	.280	-0.4	3B(26): 1.9, SS(6): 1.0	0.6
2017	HAG	A	22	321	40	19	3	9	51	25	66	12	5	.291/.349/.469	123	27.3	.347	-1.9	SS(43): -2.9, 3B(33): 6.6	2.4
2017	STO	A+	22	94	21	3	0	7	22	9	25	2	0	.386/.457/.675	140	16.9	.490	0.4	3B(10): -1.5, SS(8): -0.4	0.7
2017	MID	AA	22	75	9	4	0	0	6	6	21	0	0	.373/.427/.433	87	4.7	.532	0.3	3B(18): 1.4, 1B(1): -0.4	0.3
2018	NAS	AAA	23	537	48	26	3	5	55	32	172	4	1	.263/.304/.357	60	11.4	.385	-0.4	3B(130): -3.1, 2B(1): 0.0	-0.9
2019	OAK	MLB	24	251	20	11	1	4	23	13	86	1	0	.211/.252/.316	53	-8.7	.310	-0.3	3B 1, 2B 0	-0.8

Breakout: 2%   Improve: 7%   Collapse: 1%   Attrition: 8%   MLB: 10%   *Comparables: Patrick Wisdom, Russell Mitchell, Patrick Kivlehan*

After a 2017 breakout, Neuse simply failed his Triple-A test in 2018. There's plenty of time for him to try the PCL again, and plenty of reason to think his quick ascent to the high minors was not a fluke. (He was a major-college second-round pick, after all, not some up-from-nothing $2,500-bonus surprise case.) There's no real hurry because there's no place for him to play in Oakland anyway. He's going to have to force the issue, and a .357 slugging percentage doesn't force anything except gun jokes. Speaking of which, Neuse has a pistol right arm and might try relief pitching if the batting thing doesn't work out; it would only be appropriate, seeing how he came to the A's in the Sean Doolittle trade.

Matt Olson 1B Born: 03/29/94 Age: 25 Bats: L Throws: R Height: 6'5" Weight: 230 Origin: Round 1, 2012 Draft (#47 overall)

YEAR	TEAM	LVL	AGE	PA	R	2B	3B	HR	RBI	BB	K	SB	CS	AVG/OBP/SLG	DRC+	VORP	BABIP	BRR	FRAA	WARP
2016	NAS	AAA	22	540	69	34	1	17	60	71	132	1	0	.235/.335/.422	98	15.5	.289	-2.9	RF(81): -3.0, 1B(49): 3.9	0.8
2016	OAK	MLB	22	28	3	1	0	0	0	7	4	0	0	.095/.321/.143	92	-1.6	.118	-0.2	RF(5): -0.7, 1B(4): -0.1	-0.1
2017	NAS	AAA	23	343	56	16	1	23	60	45	83	3	0	.272/.367/.568	134	29.8	.298	-0.1	1B(73): -0.8, 3B(1): -0.2	1.9
2017	OAK	MLB	23	216	33	2	0	24	45	22	60	0	0	.259/.352/.651	152	15.5	.238	0.3	1B(43): 4.7, RF(12): 2.7	2.6
2018	OAK	MLB	24	660	85	33	0	29	84	70	163	2	1	.247/.335/.453	106	21.2	.292	-2.6	1B(162): 3.8	1.6
2019	OAK	MLB	25	580	78	26	1	30	89	64	131	1	0	.253/.345/.483	122	23.4	.286	-1.1	1B 2	2.7

Breakout: 2%   Improve: 56%   Collapse: 3%   Attrition: 9%   MLB: 97%   *Comparables: Ike Davis, Brandon Belt, Paul Goldschmidt*

So the 24:2 homers-to-doubles ratio from 2017 wasn't sustainable after all? Olson is a good illustration of what happens to first-base prospects: They can become perfectly fine major leaguers and very rarely end up anything special. That's even true when they win Gold Gloves, as Olson did last year with strong scoops and a good arm. The sorry state of first base in the American League means that Olson finished second in WARP at his position. Unsurprisingly for a player at his height, he did his best work on the low-and-away pitch, which he can golf out of the yard, but did absolutely nothing with offerings in the upper or inner thirds of the zone. Fortunately for him, even in a league in which the high pitch is ascendant, pitchers still worked more in the low-away quadrant than anywhere else.

Chad Pinder UT Born: 03/29/92 Age: 27 Bats: R Throws: R Height: 6'2" Weight: 195 Origin: Round 2, 2013 Draft (#71 overall)

YEAR	TEAM	LVL	AGE	PA	R	2B	3B	HR	RBI	BB	K	SB	CS	AVG/OBP/SLG	DRC+	VORP	BABIP	BRR	FRAA	WARP
2016	NAS	AAA	24	465	72	23	3	14	51	25	108	5	1	.258/.310/.425	94	31.4	.312	4.5	SS(98): -4.2, 2B(4): -0.9	1.7
2016	OAK	MLB	24	55	4	4	0	1	4	3	14	0	0	.235/.273/.373	73	0.4	.297	0.4	2B(13): 0.1, SS(7): -0.2	0.0
2017	NAS	AAA	25	71	3	2	1	1	2	6	23	2	1	.266/.338/.375	55	0.7	.400	-1.5	2B(8): 0.1, SS(4): -0.3	-0.4
2017	OAK	MLB	25	309	36	15	1	15	42	18	92	2	1	.238/.292/.457	93	6.9	.292	-1.8	RF(35): -0.5, SS(22): 1.6	0.7
2018	OAK	MLB	26	333	43	12	1	13	27	27	88	0	2	.258/.332/.436	105	15.7	.325	0.8	LF(64): 4.8, 2B(21): -1.3	1.6
2019	OAK	MLB	27	321	41	16	1	11	37	24	81	2	1	.247/.315/.422	98	8.1	.306	0.0	LF 2, 3B 1	1.2

Breakout: 3%   Improve: 35%   Collapse: 12%   Attrition: 19%   MLB: 88%   *Comparables: Brennan Boesch, Cody Asche, Ryan Rua*

In the 2000 edition of this book, Keith Woolner listed "quantifying the value of positional flexibility" as one of baseball's "Hilbert Problems," 23 critical areas for future research. Timothy C.Y. Chan and Douglas S. Fearing presented a paper at the 2013 MIT Sloan Sports Analytics Conference making inroads in this area by drawing on tools "from the theory of production flexibility in manufacturing networks," but this is hardly a solved problem in publicly available work, particularly at the individual level, and our own Russell A. Carleton has taken up on the cause in a series of recent articles. (Woolner himself has spent the last decade in the walled garden of Cleveland's front office, so who knows what kind of cool stuff he's figured out that we don't know about.)

What we can say with confidence is that extant WAR models do not account for the unique abilities of a player like Pinder, who drew at least one start in 2018 at every position but catcher, and did not embarrass himself defensively, even at shortstop (his main minor-league position) or center field. His cannon arm plays anywhere, and his overall batting line was above the MLB average at every position. He's not a starting-quality hitter against righties, even in the middle infield, but he'll run into enough homers against them that he doesn't need to immediately sit when the opposing team goes to its bullpen. Pinder isn't Tony Phillips, but he can absolutely be a winning team's 10th man. It's too bad he won't be eligible for free agency until 2023; it would be fascinating to see a player with this skill set hit the market with his powers intact.

Stephen Piscotty RF Born: 01/14/91 Age: 28 Bats: R Throws: R Height: 6'3" Weight: 210 Origin: Round 1, 2012 Draft (#36 overall)

YEAR	TEAM	LVL	AGE	PA	R	2B	3B	HR	RBI	BB	K	SB	CS	AVG/OBP/SLG	DRC+	VORP	BABIP	BRR	FRAA	WARP
2016	SLN	MLB	25	649	86	35	3	22	85	51	133	7	5	.273/.343/.457	107	30.1	.319	-2.1	RF(146): -2.3, CF(10): 0.1	1.6
2017	MEM	AAA	26	38	7	3	0	4	7	6	7	0	0	.313/.421/.781	124	6.9	.286	0.0	RF(6): -0.2	0.2
2017	SLN	MLB	26	401	40	16	1	9	39	52	87	3	6	.235/.342/.367	91	1.6	.286	-2.5	RF(99): -0.9	0.1
2018	OAK	MLB	27	605	78	41	0	27	88	42	114	2	0	.267/.331/.491	113	28.6	.290	-1.4	RF(151): -9.3	1.2
2019	OAK	MLB	28	553	67	26	2	19	67	52	111	4	3	.251/.334/.423	109	19.7	.291	-1.6	RF -2	1.8

Breakout: 1%   Improve: 57%   Collapse: 6%   Attrition: 18%   MLB: 95%   *Comparables: Corey Hart, Jeremy Hermida, Michael Saunders*

The Cardinals having their usual abundance of outfielders last winter allowed them to trade Piscotty to one of the two teams close enough to his hometown that he could spend his time off with his mother, Gretchen, who was in the late stages of a battle with ALS. She passed away in May, and one hopes that Piscotty's ability to spend April playing in Oakland rather than St. Louis gave him and his family some comfort in this difficult time. There remains some grace in the world.

On the field, physical health brought a welcome return to Piscotty's power stroke, though the early part of the season was rough, as you might imagine. His batting line bottomed out on May 27; from May 28 on, he hit .286/.352/.554, which is right around Jesus Aguilar's full-season figures. Even if you buy that he gave away nearly a win on defense, and even noting that he's now 28, the $28.5 million he's owed over the next four years looks like a bargain for a steady, "put him in the five hole and forget about him" right fielder.

Boog Powell OF Born: 01/14/93 Age: 26 Bats: L Throws: L Height: 5'10" Weight: 185 Origin: Round 20, 2012 Draft (#619 overall)

YEAR	TEAM	LVL	AGE	PA	R	2B	3B	HR	RBI	BB	K	SB	CS	AVG/OBP/SLG	DRC+	VORP	BABIP	BRR	FRAA	WARP
2016	TAC	AAA	23	277	39	9	2	3	27	22	42	10	6	.270/.326/.359	77	5.8	.311	0.5	CF(61): 1.4	0.4
2017	SEA	MLB	24	43	6	0	0	0	2	6	9	0	0	.194/.310/.194	91	-1.1	.259	0.0	LF(8): 0.7, RF(1): 0.0	0.1
2017	TAC	AAA	24	239	46	9	2	6	33	28	27	11	5	.340/.416/.490	117	23.3	.364	0.9	RF(25): -0.9, CF(24): -1.7	0.9
2017	OAK	MLB	24	92	18	5	0	3	10	9	21	0	1	.321/.380/.494	93	8.9	.390	1.7	CF(28): 2.0	0.6
2018	OAK	MLB	25	25	3	1	1	0	0	1	6	1	1	.167/.200/.292	62	-2.0	.222	-0.2	CF(7): -1.6	-0.2
2018	NAS	AAA	25	174	18	2	0	0	8	23	36	5	6	.224/.333/.238	71	-3.2	.297	-0.3	RF(21): 1.1, CF(14): 3.4	0.3
2019	OAK	MLB	26	251	30	10	1	5	22	24	60	5	4	.229/.307/.349	80	1.9	.286	-0.5	CF 0, RF 0	0.2

Breakout: 4%   Improve: 36%   Collapse: 16%   Attrition: 23%   MLB: 70%   *Comparables: Bryan Petersen, Trevor Crowe, Charlie Blackmon*

Powell began 2018 as the A's starting center fielder, but then sprained his knee, sprained his thumb while on a rehab assignment for the knee and got outrighted off the 40-man roster rather than called up when rosters expanded. He's still just 26, so if you write off 2018 as a lost season and start 2019 with a blank slate, there's still room for mild optimism; a second-division starter in center, with surprising pop for his size and enough athleticism to handle the position, is not out of the question.

Jurickson Profar INF Born: 02/20/93 Age: 26 Bats: B Throws: R Height: 6'0" Weight: 190 Origin: International Free Agent, 2009

YEAR	TEAM	LVL	AGE	PA	R	2B	3B	HR	RBI	BB	K	SB	CS	AVG/OBP/SLG	DRC+	VORP	BABIP	BRR	FRAA	WARP
2016	ROU	AAA	23	189	28	9	0	5	26	16	26	4	3	.284/.356/.426	109	13.9	.312	0.2	SS(31): 2.9, 2B(6): 0.1	1.3
2016	TEX	MLB	23	307	35	6	3	5	20	30	61	2	1	.239/.321/.338	84	-6.0	.291	-1.5	3B(25): -1.2, 2B(19): 1.9	0.2
2017	TEX	MLB	24	70	8	2	0	0	5	9	14	1	1	.172/.294/.207	78	-0.8	.227	0.8	LF(12): 1.2, SS(4): -0.6	0.1
2017	ROU	AAA	24	383	50	25	0	7	45	43	33	5	0	.287/.383/.428	111	32.9	.302	2.9	SS(78): -6.6, 2B(3): -0.2	1.9
2018	TEX	MLB	25	594	82	35	6	20	77	54	88	10	0	.254/.335/.458	112	29.0	.269	2.2	SS(68): -8.6, 3B(51): -3.7	2.1
2019	OAK	MLB	26	567	64	25	3	15	65	53	86	7	2	.250/.334/.401	103	19.3	.276	0.5	2B 7, LF 0	2.8

Breakout: 2%   Improve: 53%   Collapse: 7%   Attrition: 17%   MLB: 99%   *Comparables: Enrique Hernandez, Didi Gregorius, Jemile Weeks*

It feels weird to write about Profar without using the word "prospect," but all traditions must eventually come to an end. Years lost to shoulder injuries and a slow return to the big leagues have dashed expectations that once projected Profar to be a baseball demigod, but a 20-homer season certainly allowed for hope that he's still an above-average regular. The end of Profar's prospectdom did not, however, mean the end of the trade rumors that have swirled around him for *checks notes* the last 72 years. Rather than fill the massive shoes of Adrian Beltre at third base in Texas, he'll replace Jed Lowrie at second base in Oakland.

Marcus Semien SS   Born: 09/17/90   Age: 28   Bats: R   Throws: R   Height: 6'0"   Weight: 195   Origin: Round 6, 2011 Draft (#201 overall)

YEAR	TEAM	LVL	AGE	PA	R	2B	3B	HR	RBI	BB	K	SB	CS	AVG/OBP/SLG	DRC+	VORP	BABIP	BRR	FRAA	WARP
2016	OAK	MLB	25	621	72	27	2	27	75	51	139	10	2	.238/.300/.435	102	32.2	.268	2.6	SS(159): 1.0	3.5
2017	OAK	MLB	26	386	53	19	1	10	40	38	85	12	1	.249/.325/.398	96	18.2	.300	3.9	SS(85): -1.5	1.9
2018	OAK	MLB	27	703	89	35	2	15	70	61	131	14	6	.255/.318/.388	96	38.0	.296	5.4	SS(159): 16.2	5.1
2019	OAK	MLB	28	622	80	32	3	16	63	58	127	13	4	.252/.325/.406	100	26.4	.298	3.3	SS 5	3.3

Breakout: 2%   Improve: 45%   Collapse: 2%   Attrition: 8%   MLB: 97%   *Comparables: Stephen Drew, J.J. Hardy, Asdrubal Cabrera*

Semien had a wrist injury in 2017 that some (okay, it was us) speculated might have led to his trade of slugging for on-base percentage. Last year, though, at apparent full health, he kept 2017's balance at the plate (making his 27-dinger 2016 look more like a spike than a skill), while allegedly adding defense to the equation. All the metrics agree that he provided substantial value with the glove last year, though the enormous jump compared to years past is hard to swallow without any obvious physical changes. There's this, though: Semien was positioned more up the middle than any MLB shortstop except for Houston's trio. (Data from Semien's prior three years shows him in a league-average spot.) It's hard not to attribute this change to Matt Chapman playing every day a few feet to Semien's right. Even without the defense, though, Semien is probably the best shortstop whose name is never spoken outside of his team's fan base. But hey, it's an honor just to be invited and all that, right?

PITCHERS

Brett Anderson LHP   Born: 02/01/88   Age: 31   Bats: L   Throws: L   Height: 6'3"   Weight: 230   Origin: Round 2, 2006 Draft (#55 overall)

YEAR	TEAM	LVL	AGE	W	L	SV	G	GS	IP	H	HR	BB/9	K/9	K	GB%	BABIP	WHIP	ERA	DRA	WARP	MPH	FB%	WHF	CSP
2016	LAN	MLB	28	1	2	0	4	3	11¹	25	4	3.2	4.0	5	51%	.429	2.56	11.91	6.83	-0.2	94.2	58.7	5.8	47
2017	CHN	MLB	29	2	2	0	6	6	22	34	2	4.9	6.5	16	51%	.395	2.09	8.18	4.87	0.2	92.2	56.7	9	41.6
2017	TEN	AA	29	2	2	0	6	5	27¹	34	2	3.0	4.9	15	69%	.348	1.57	4.61	4.37	0.2				
2017	BUF	AAA	29	1	1	0	2	2	9²	4	0	1.9	2.8	3	53%	.133	0.62	0.93	4.18	0.2				
2017	TOR	MLB	29	2	2	0	7	7	33¹	39	3	2.4	5.9	22	50%	.340	1.44	5.13	5.88	-0.1	93.2	48.6	9.5	46.3
2018	NAS	AAA	30	2	1	0	7	7	32¹	32	0	1.7	10.0	36	60%	.333	1.18	2.78	3.21	0.9				
2018	OAK	MLB	30	4	5	0	17	17	80¹	90	10	1.5	5.3	47	57%	.307	1.28	4.48	3.98	1.2	92.6	49.5	8.1	49.2
2019	OAK	MLB	31	6	6	0	19	19	92²	92	9	2.9	6.4	66	51%	.292	1.32	4.13	4.60	0.9	91.9	50.7	8.3	46.7

Breakout: 22%   Improve: 44%   Collapse: 18%   Attrition: 13%   MLB: 76%   *Comparables: Tommy John, Andy Pettitte, Dillon Gee*

Anderson was once a tantalizing talent you'd employ with the expectation of injury and the hope for high-quality innings when healthy. If you had some money to burn and a good sixth man waiting in Triple-A, he could provide value. Now? With a 5.76 ERA over his last three seasons? While averaging well under five innings per start and throwing his fastball 90-92? Now it's hard to imagine another major-league contract for as long as he wants to hang on. (And if he signed one between the time we went to press and the time you read this, well, you know where to yell at us.) After he got absolutely pasted in the posterior by a 110 mph liner off the bat of Shohei Ohtani in his last start of the year, it's worth asking just how much longer Anderson wants that to be.

Chris Bassitt RHP   Born: 02/22/89   Age: 30   Bats: R   Throws: R   Height: 6'5"   Weight: 220   Origin: Round 16, 2011 Draft (#501 overall)

YEAR	TEAM	LVL	AGE	W	L	SV	G	GS	IP	H	HR	BB/9	K/9	K	GB%	BABIP	WHIP	ERA	DRA	WARP	MPH	FB%	WHF	CSP
2016	OAK	MLB	27	0	2	0	5	5	28	35	5	4.5	7.4	23	47%	.330	1.75	6.11	5.96	-0.2	96.0	59.2	9	49.7
2017	STO	A+	28	0	1	0	7	7	13	9	0	2.8	9.7	14	64%	.273	1.00	2.77	3.65	0.2				
2017	NAS	AAA	28	4	4	0	17	7	37²	41	3	3.8	7.4	31	36%	.336	1.51	6.21	4.53	0.4				
2018	NAS	AAA	29	5	5	0	18	14	81²	86	6	2.8	9.1	83	44%	.348	1.36	4.30	3.80	1.5				
2018	OAK	MLB	29	2	3	0	11	7	47²	40	4	3.6	7.7	41	44%	.265	1.24	3.02	5.24	0.0	94.2	57.4	7.6	51.8
2019	OAK	MLB	30	5	5	0	27	16	92	86	12	3.5	7.6	77	43%	.280	1.33	4.58	5.10	0.3	93.9	57.7	7.9	50.9

Breakout: 19%   Improve: 31%   Collapse: 17%   Attrition: 13%   MLB: 57%   *Comparables: Clay Hensley, Christian Friedrich, Chris Heston*

In his first full season back from a mid-2016 Tommy John surgery, Bassitt was optioned to Triple-A no fewer than seven times. It was his final option year, so props to the A's for making the most of it? (Two of his seven recalls resulted in no game action, so maybe it depends on your definition of "the most of it.") Bassitt's official stats show seven starts, but that omits three games pitching behind "opener" Liam Hendriks in September. He struck out 11 in 10 innings in those games, but the A's left him off their Wild Card game roster despite taking 10 relief pitchers (plus Edwin Jackson) to New York. All of that, plus stuff that simply isn't impressive in 2018 (much as the 20 mph differential between his fastball and curve is fun), spells a lot of "designated for assignment" in his future.

Ryan Buchter   LHP   Born: 02/13/87   Age: 32   Bats: L   Throws: L   Height: 6'4"   Weight: 258   Origin: Round 33, 2005 Draft (#984 overall)

YEAR	TEAM	LVL	AGE	W	L	SV	G	GS	IP	H	HR	BB/9	K/9	K	GB%	BABIP	WHIP	ERA	DRA	WARP	MPH	FB%	WHF	CSP
2016	SDN	MLB	29	3	0	1	67	0	63	34	4	4.4	11.1	78	21%	.227	1.03	2.86	5.61	-0.5	94.6	84.7	10.8	45.5
2017	SDN	MLB	30	3	3	1	42	0	38¹	28	7	4.2	11.0	47	33%	.239	1.20	3.05	5.03	0.1	94.3	72.1	12.7	47.3
2017	KCA	MLB	30	1	0	0	29	0	27	16	3	2.7	6.0	18	32%	.173	0.89	2.67	5.67	-0.2	94.0	72.1	10.3	49.8
2018	OAK	MLB	31	6	0	0	54	0	39¹	32	4	3.4	9.4	41	28%	.272	1.19	2.75	3.60	0.6	94.0	65.7	12.2	48.1
2019	OAK	MLB	32	3	1	0	52	0	54²	44	8	4.0	9.1	55	32%	.255	1.25	4.60	5.11	0.0	93.3	73.2	11.5	47.1

Breakout: 25%   Improve: 45%   Collapse: 17%   Attrition: 18%   MLB: 75%   *Comparables: Al Alburquerque, Cory Gearrin, Louis Coleman*

The A's picked Buchter up in a scrap-heap swap with the Royals that also saw Brandon Moss moving to Oakland in exchange for Heath Fillmyer and Jesse Hahn. Buchter spent the year as Oakland's main bullpen lefty (outside of a six-week stint on the DL with a shoulder strain), facing 92 same-side hitters against just 71 righties. He reincorporated a cutter and curve that he'd all but eliminated in 2016 and 2017, but the outcomes were essentially the same: solid strikeout numbers, scads of fly balls (and therefore more dong shots than you'd like) and something less than pinpoint control. Remember the old "if he could just cut one walk per nine while keeping everything else the same ..." game? Buchter did it, at least for 163 batters last year, and thereby made himself an employable big-league relief pitcher. On the one hand, that's right around the size of sample in which you can feel a little bit of confidence; on the other, he's spent the six months since he last pitched getting older, just like the rest of us. Go ahead and scribble his name in as your middle-relief lefty this year, but have a backup plan.

Mike Fiers   RHP   Born: 06/15/85   Age: 34   Bats: R   Throws: R   Height: 6'2"   Weight: 202   Origin: Round 22, 2009 Draft (#676 overall)

YEAR	TEAM	LVL	AGE	W	L	SV	G	GS	IP	H	HR	BB/9	K/9	K	GB%	BABIP	WHIP	ERA	DRA	WARP	MPH	FB%	WHF	CSP
2016	HOU	MLB	31	11	8	0	31	30	168²	187	26	2.2	7.2	134	44%	.313	1.36	4.48	4.46	1.7	91.9	41.1	9.9	46.7
2017	HOU	MLB	32	8	10	0	29	28	153¹	157	32	3.6	8.6	146	43%	.300	1.43	5.22	5.82	-0.4	91.5	47.5	9.9	46.6
2018	DET	MLB	33	7	6	0	21	21	119	121	20	2.0	6.6	87	39%	.277	1.24	3.48	4.87	0.6	91.2	46.7	8.8	49.1
2018	OAK	MLB	33	5	2	0	10	9	53	45	12	1.9	8.8	52	43%	.246	1.06	3.74	4.02	0.8	91.9	46.7	10.1	50.9
2019	OAK	MLB	34	9	9	0	25	25	142²	132	21	2.6	7.3	115	42%	.270	1.22	4.53	5.05	0.7	90.5	44.9	9.5	47.2

Breakout: 20%   Improve: 42%   Collapse: 18%   Attrition: 8%   MLB: 87%   *Comparables: Chris Capuano, Ben Sheets, Jake Peavy*

The A's didn't start the Fiers in the playoffs after a disastrous final game in the regular season when he followed an "opener" for the first time and got lit up for six runs in three-plus innings. Fiers had been a huge part of Oakland's burning-hot push to October, pitching in eight wins to just one loss, allowing two runs or fewer in seven of those eight. But since the world's been turning, pitchers with this kind of profile tend to fall off cliffs: He lives on low-velocity fastballs up in the zone and therefore gives up a ton of loud contact and fly balls, with one result being 90 dingers allowed over the last three years, second only to James Shields. PECOTA isn't buying the 2018 semi-resurgence at all, but the A's bought in for a two-year, $14 million deal, bringing back Fiers after initially non-tendering him.

Daniel Gossett   RHP   Born: 11/13/92   Age: 26   Bats: R   Throws: R   Height: 6'2"   Weight: 185   Origin: Round 2, 2014 Draft (#65 overall)

YEAR	TEAM	LVL	AGE	W	L	SV	G	GS	IP	H	HR	BB/9	K/9	K	GB%	BABIP	WHIP	ERA	DRA	WARP	MPH	FB%	WHF	CSP
2016	STO	A+	23	4	1	0	9	9	46	40	4	2.5	10.4	53	54%	.295	1.15	3.33	2.42	1.6				
2016	MID	AA	23	5	5	0	16	16	94	75	4	2.4	9.0	94	59%	.284	1.06	2.49	3.02	2.3				
2016	NAS	AAA	23	1	0	0	2	2	13²	10	0	2.0	2.6	4	57%	.227	0.95	1.98	3.30	0.3				
2017	NAS	AAA	24	4	4	0	14	14	76¹	70	6	2.8	8.4	71	52%	.292	1.23	3.66	3.35	2.0				
2017	OAK	MLB	24	4	11	0	18	18	91¹	116	21	3.1	7.1	72	45%	.328	1.61	6.11	5.76	-0.2	93.0	52.9	9.6	47.5
2018	NAS	AAA	25	4	0	0	7	5	38²	26	1	3.7	9.8	42	50%	.260	1.09	1.63	2.34	1.3				
2018	OAK	MLB	25	0	3	0	5	5	24¹	25	5	3.0	4.4	12	42%	.263	1.36	5.18	5.05	0.1	94.5	51.4	8.7	51
2019	OAK	MLB	26	4	4	0	13	13	71	62	8	3.3	8.1	64	47%	.274	1.24	4.15	4.62	0.7	93.0	53.5	9.6	50.3

Breakout: 24%   Improve: 45%   Collapse: 21%   Attrition: 38%   MLB: 79%   *Comparables: J.R. Graham, Luis Cessa, John Lamb*

The A's lost a bunch of starting pitchers to injury in 2018, from top prospect A.J. Puk to solid starters Kendall Graveman and Sean Manaea to young guy with upside Jharel Cotton to ... well, what is Gossett, exactly? You want to say "don't judge a guy by his performance in a season when he winds up needing Tommy John surgery" but then you realize he pitched just fine in Triple-A. So maybe Gossett simply isn't a big-league starter. He didn't have his surgery until August, so there's no reason to expect him back until 2020. Don't be surprised if the A's, or whichever team he's on by that point, try him out of the bullpen to see if he can add a few feet to his fastball and avoid the pounding that has typified his career to this point.

Kendall Graveman   RHP   Born: 12/21/90   Age: 28   Bats: R   Throws: R   Height: 6'2"   Weight: 200   Origin: Round 8, 2013 Draft (#235 overall)

YEAR	TEAM	LVL	AGE	W	L	SV	G	GS	IP	H	HR	BB/9	K/9	K	GB%	BABIP	WHIP	ERA	DRA	WARP	MPH	FB%	WHF	CSP
2016	OAK	MLB	25	10	11	0	31	31	186	196	22	2.3	5.2	108	53%	.290	1.31	4.11	4.94	0.9	95.3	61.8	8.1	48.6
2017	NAS	AAA	26	0	1	0	3	3	10	18	1	3.6	6.3	7	46%	.425	2.20	7.20	4.47	0.1				
2017	OAK	MLB	26	6	4	0	19	19	105¹	114	12	2.7	6.0	70	52%	.313	1.39	4.19	5.42	0.2	95.4	68.9	7.4	43.4
2018	OAK	MLB	27	1	5	0	7	7	34¹	44	9	3.4	7.1	27	57%	.324	1.66	7.60	5.38	0.0	95.5	57.2	8	44.4
2018	NAS	AAA	27	2	1	0	4	4	24	35	3	2.6	6.0	16	56%	.405	1.75	4.50	4.56	0.3				
2019	CHN	MLB	28	4	4	0	11	11	64	64	7	3.0	6.9	49	51%	.308	1.33	4.19	4.64	0.5	94.8	64	7.9	45.4

Breakout: 9%   Improve: 48%   Collapse: 17%   Attrition: 25%   MLB: 89%   *Comparables: Shawn Hill, Nick Blackburn, Sergio Mitre*

The list of good things that happened to Graveman in 2018 basically went "started on Opening Day." The list of bad things included two demotions to Triple-A, the unsightly performance you can see above, Tommy John surgery and being non-tendered. He's unlikely to pitch in 2019 given the timing of the surgery. Nothing we've seen so far indicates he'll be anything more than a fourth starter in 2020 even though he's out there throwing a heavy, mid-90s sinker. Maybe he'll add some kind of wrinkle, like taking his secondaries to a whole new level, in his time off; maybe, similarly, this cat will stop eating plastic bags.

Liam Hendriks RHP   Born: 02/10/89   Age: 30   Bats: R   Throws: R   Height: 6'0"   Weight: 200   Origin: International Free Agent, 2007

YEAR	TEAM	LVL	AGE	W	L	SV	G	GS	IP	H	HR	BB/9	K/9	K	GB%	BABIP	WHIP	ERA	DRA	WARP	MPH	FB%	WHF	CSP
2016	OAK	MLB	27	0	4	0	53	0	64²	69	6	1.9	9.9	71	42%	.344	1.28	3.76	3.89	0.8	96.8	75.6	12.5	50.7
2017	OAK	MLB	28	4	2	1	70	0	64	57	7	3.2	11.0	78	41%	.303	1.25	4.22	3.45	1.2	96.3	74.1	13.6	46.7
2018	NAS	AAA	29	4	1	6	23	1	25¹	21	1	1.4	15.3	43	41%	.364	0.99	2.84	2.31	0.8				
2018	OAK	MLB	29	0	1	0	25	8	24	25	3	3.8	8.2	22	41%	.324	1.46	4.12	4.70	0.1	97.2	70.1	12.1	47.1
2019	*OAK*	*MLB*	*30*	*3*	*1*	*0*	*57*	*0*	*60²*	*52*	*7*	*3.1*	*9.8*	*66*	*41%*	*.287*	*1.21*	*3.74*	*4.16*	*0.7*	*95.9*	*73.5*	*12.9*	*47.7*

Breakout: 25%   Improve: 51%   Collapse: 18%   Attrition: 16%   MLB: 84%   *Comparables: Kevin Gregg, Adam Ottavino, Tony Watson*

Meet your 2018 A's Wild Card game starter. Faced with injury after injury to what was a mediocre starting staff even at full health, Oakland decided to emulate the Rays and build the whole plane out of the black box, adding reliever after reliever to the roster in trades and trying out the "opener" thing in September. The maneuver was something of an obvious one, considering their other options, but the choice of personnel was substantially less obvious: Hendriks was designated for assignment in June and went unclaimed on waivers, leading to an outright assignment to Triple-A. He returned to the majors only when rosters expanded in September. Because of Bob Melvin's weird magic touch, Hendriks proceeded to post a 1.38 ERA in 13 September innings, salvaging his season. After all the noise, though, Hendriks is a 30-year-old middle reliever who throws hard but gives up a lot of fly balls, which is the same thing he was in 2018 (except he was 29 that year) and 2017 (28) and 2016 (27). Expect more of the same, which for Hendriks always includes the possibility of a bad three weeks when he allows four homers and gets cut.

Grant Holmes RHP   Born: 03/22/96   Age: 23   Bats: L   Throws: R   Height: 6'1"   Weight: 215   Origin: Round 1, 2014 Draft (#22 overall)

YEAR	TEAM	LVL	AGE	W	L	SV	G	GS	IP	H	HR	BB/9	K/9	K	GB%	BABIP	WHIP	ERA	DRA	WARP	MPH	FB%	WHF	CSP
2016	RCU	A+	20	8	4	1	20	18	105¹	103	6	3.7	8.5	100	53%	.316	1.39	4.02	3.64	2.2				
2016	STO	A+	20	3	3	0	6	5	28²	44	4	3.1	7.5	24	60%	.408	1.88	6.91	3.52	0.6				
2017	MID	AA	21	11	12	0	29	24	148¹	149	15	3.7	9.1	150	46%	.328	1.42	4.49	3.75	2.4				
2018	STO	A+	22	0	0	0	2	2	6	4	1	3.0	12.0	8	47%	.214	1.00	4.50	3.90	0.1				
2019	*OAK*	*MLB*	*23*	*3*	*3*	*0*	*10*	*10*	*50*	*45*	*7*	*3.9*	*8.7*	*49*	*45%*	*.283*	*1.34*	*4.75*	*5.27*	*0.1*				

Breakout: 18%   Improve: 28%   Collapse: 9%   Attrition: 36%   MLB: 47%   *Comparables: Justin Wilson, Scott Barnes, Wily Peralta*

Holmes pitched two High-A games in late August after missing the entire season with a rotator cuff injury; he was then shut down again and his 2019 status is unknown as of this writing. He left off 2017 with mid-rotation upside driven by intriguing command of his fastball and curve, but a strong possibility of a bullpen future due to a missing third pitch. Now, who knows. (The former first-round pick was added to the 40-man roster in November because he would have been eligible for the Rule 5 draft.) For all the criticism of the overly simplistic analysis that the term sometimes leads us toward, this is a big part of the reason Gary Huckabay started using "TINSTAAPP" in the first place.

Edwin Jackson RHP   Born: 09/09/83   Age: 35   Bats: R   Throws: R   Height: 6'2"   Weight: 215   Origin: Round 6, 2001 Draft (#190 overall)

YEAR	TEAM	LVL	AGE	W	L	SV	G	GS	IP	H	HR	BB/9	K/9	K	GB%	BABIP	WHIP	ERA	DRA	WARP	MPH	FB%	WHF	CSP
2016	MIA	MLB	32	0	1	0	8	0	10²	13	2	5.1	5.9	7	35%	.344	1.78	5.91	3.72	0.2	95.4	67.6	10.1	47
2016	ELP	AAA	32	0	1	0	3	3	12²	20	2	4.3	6.4	9	40%	.375	2.05	7.11	4.61	0.1				
2016	SDN	MLB	32	5	6	0	13	13	73¹	79	12	4.3	6.6	54	42%	.299	1.55	5.89	6.04	-0.6	94.6	67.6	10.1	47.5
2017	NOR	AAA	33	0	0	2	12	1	20¹	20	1	4.4	7.5	17	33%	.339	1.48	3.10	3.87	0.4				
2017	BAL	MLB	33	0	0	0	3	0	5	11	2	7.2	3.6	2	30%	.429	3.00	7.20	8.81	-0.2	93.6	76.9	8.3	42.3
2017	SYR	AAA	33	2	0	0	5	4	20¹	9	0	4.4	9.7	22	51%	.191	0.93	0.44	3.86	0.4				
2017	WAS	MLB	33	5	6	0	13	13	71	75	18	3.2	7.4	58	40%	.273	1.41	5.07	6.39	-0.7	95.7	76.9	10.9	48
2018	SYR	AAA	34	4	2	0	10	10	55²	51	4	3.6	7.6	47	42%	.285	1.31	3.40	4.27	0.8				
2018	NAS	AAA	34	0	1	0	3	3	15²	12	1	4.6	9.2	16	41%	.256	1.28	4.02	4.59	0.2				
2018	OAK	MLB	34	6	3	0	17	17	92	75	12	3.6	6.7	68	38%	.240	1.22	3.33	5.23	0.1	95.2	67	9.7	44.4
2019	*OAK*	*MLB*	*35*	*7*	*7*	*0*	*45*	*20*	*129¹*	*122*	*20*	*3.9*	*7.5*	*108*	*40%*	*.276*	*1.38*	*4.97*	*5.52*	*-0.2*	*93.9*	*68.9*	*9.9*	*45.4*

Breakout: 20%   Improve: 42%   Collapse: 8%   Attrition: 9%   MLB: 68%   *Comparables: Jose Lima, Brian Moehler, Eric Stults*

Jackson, who is somehow still just 35 and who somehow had not played for the A's yet, joined Oakland in June after catching his release from the Nationals. Over his first 10 starts in green and gold, eight of which the team won, he posted a 2.58 ERA, looking like a downright godsend for a rotation that went Montas-Bassitt-Manaea-Blackburn when he made his first appearance. (If you're reading this five years from now, first, how's the weather, and second, do you know more than one of the first names of these players? Hell, how about if you're reading this in March 2019?) Selective endpoints being what they are, you can guess that Jackson provided a 4.68 ERA over his last seven starts (which still resulted in six A's wins), almost precisely in line with his career ERA. Jackson's routine the last seven years went useful-bad-bad-good-bad-bad-good, so for the pattern-recognition aficionados out there, you can see where PECOTA's coming from. He's appeared in the majors for 13 different teams, though, so we're rooting for two more years of *any* quality so he can reach an even half.

Shawn Kelley RHP   Born: 04/26/84   Age: 35   Bats: R   Throws: R   Height: 6'2"   Weight: 237   Origin: Round 13, 2007 Draft (#405 overall)

YEAR	TEAM	LVL	AGE	W	L	SV	G	GS	IP	H	HR	BB/9	K/9	K	GB%	BABIP	WHIP	ERA	DRA	WARP	MPH	FB%	WHF	CSP
2016	WAS	MLB	32	3	2	7	67	0	58	41	9	1.7	12.4	80	37%	.258	0.90	2.64	2.30	1.8	95.2	56.2	17.1	51.2
2017	WAS	MLB	33	3	2	4	33	0	26	29	12	3.8	8.7	25	26%	.236	1.54	7.27	6.11	-0.3	93.9	59.2	15.4	46.9
2018	WAS	MLB	34	1	0	0	35	0	32¹	26	7	1.4	8.9	32	28%	.229	0.96	3.34	4.51	0.2	93.9	52.8	12.4	50.7
2018	OAK	MLB	34	1	0	0	19	0	16²	7	0	3.2	9.7	18	40%	.184	0.78	2.16	3.22	0.3	92.7	50.6	12.4	50.1
2019	*OAK*	*MLB*	*35*	*2*	*1*	*1*	*35*	*0*	*37¹*	*33*	*8*	*3.3*	*9.4*	*39*	*35%*	*.264*	*1.26*	*5.15*	*5.71*	*-0.2*	*92.9*	*54.1*	*14.4*	*48.6*

Breakout: 21%   Improve: 43%   Collapse: 27%   Attrition: 7%   MLB: 88%   *Comparables: Todd Worrell, Bill Henry, Dan Miceli*

Kelley was having a solid season in middle relief for Washington when Dave Martinez put him in for the ninth inning of a game the team led 25-1 over the Mets. An Austin Jackson two-run homer led to a glove slam and a look into the Nats' dugout, which in turn led to a designation for assignment, a very good 16 innings with the A's and his third postseason game pitched. That Kelley got cut for getting mad after he did a bad thing (and for *maybe* aiming some frustration at his manager, something he denied and that Martinez, at least publicly, said he did not take as showing him up) remains bizarre in a place of employment that features Angry Dudes on a daily basis. That the A's were the ones to jump in and extract value from a guy another team was unreasonably down on is enough to give you nostalgia. Remember when Billy Beane pulled off that kind of thing on a weekly basis? In any event, Kelley's a 35-year-old, two-pitch, fly-ball righty who's lost a mile and a half off his fastball over the last two years, so getting into a pissing match with Mike Rizzo might have been his last hurrah. At least he didn't go out with a whimper.

Jesus Luzardo LHP Born: 09/30/97 Age: 21 Bats: L Throws: L Height: 6'1" Weight: 205 Origin: Round 3, 2016 Draft (#94 overall)

YEAR	TEAM	LVL	AGE	W	L	SV	G	GS	IP	H	HR	BB/9	K/9	K	GB%	BABIP	WHIP	ERA	DRA	WARP	MPH	FB%	WHF	CSP
2017	NAT	RK	19	1	0	0	3	3	13²	14	1	0.0	9.9	15	33%	.342	1.02	1.32	2.01	0.6				
2017	ATH	RK	19	0	1	0	4	3	11²	9	0	0.8	10.0	13	58%	.290	0.86	1.54	2.73	0.4				
2017	VER	A-	19	1	0	0	5	5	18	12	1	2.0	10.0	20	53%	.250	0.89	2.00	2.56	0.6				
2018	STO	A+	20	2	1	0	3	3	14²	6	0	3.1	15.3	25	56%	.240	0.75	1.23	1.70	0.6				
2018	MID	AA	20	7	3	0	16	16	78²	58	5	2.1	9.8	86	46%	.268	0.97	2.29	3.40	1.8				
2018	NAS	AAA	20	1	1	0	4	4	16	25	2	3.9	10.1	18	51%	.469	2.00	7.31	2.90	0.5				
2019	*OAK*	*MLB*	*21*	*3*	*3*	*0*	*10*	*10*	*50*	*42*	*7*	*2.9*	*9.4*	*52*	*43%*	*.274*	*1.17*	*4.12*	*4.58*	*0.5*				

Breakout: 9%   Improve: 16%   Collapse: 8%   Attrition: 17%   MLB: 31%   *Comparables: Henry Owens, Drew Hutchison, Shelby Miller*

Last year, we told you not to "expect to see Luzardo set loose on the Midwest League" because 2016 Tommy John surgery meant his pro experience to that point had been limited and carefully managed. We were right, in the sense that Luzardo was instead set loose on the *Texas League* en route to a brief PCL experience after dumping the Cal League straight in the trash. (He still averaged less than five innings per start, though.) He's now in the proverbial conversation for best pitching prospect in the game, which is what happens when you bring mid-90s heat from the left side, a plus changeup to combat righties, an improving curveball and, most importantly, beyond-his-years knowledge of how convert his arsenal into outs. The difficult reality of Major League Baseball is that even no. 2 and 3 starters used to be extremely good prospects, and that's probably what Luzardo is in the majors, not a no. 1. He could start reaching that ceiling as soon as this year, minus the requisite few weeks to "work on some things" (read: ensure seven years until free agency rather than six) that will surely be imposed just as they are on every prospect who should be on an Opening Day roster until something is changed to create incentives for teams to always use their best available players in the major leagues.

Sean Manaea LHP Born: 02/01/92 Age: 27 Bats: R Throws: L Height: 6'5" Weight: 245 Origin: Round 1, 2013 Draft (#34 overall)

YEAR	TEAM	LVL	AGE	W	L	SV	G	GS	IP	H	HR	BB/9	K/9	K	GB%	BABIP	WHIP	ERA	DRA	WARP	MPH	FB%	WHF	CSP
2016	NAS	AAA	24	2	0	0	3	3	18	16	1	2.0	10.5	21	54%	.319	1.11	1.50	3.12	0.5				
2016	OAK	MLB	24	7	9	0	25	24	144²	135	20	2.3	7.7	124	46%	.281	1.19	3.86	4.17	2.0	95.2	58.2	12.8	47.3
2017	OAK	MLB	25	12	10	0	29	29	158²	167	18	3.1	7.9	140	44%	.318	1.40	4.37	5.17	0.7	93.7	58.3	12.1	46
2018	OAK	MLB	26	12	9	0	27	27	160²	141	21	1.8	6.0	108	46%	.247	1.08	3.59	4.04	2.4	92.5	56.2	10.2	53.4
2019	*OAK*	*MLB*	*27*	*9*	*8*	*0*	*24*	*24*	*137*	*124*	*14*	*2.6*	*7.3*	*111*	*45%*	*.274*	*1.19*	*3.95*	*4.40*	*1.7*	*93.1*	*58.1*	*11.6*	*50*

Breakout: 25%   Improve: 58%   Collapse: 13%   Attrition: 10%   MLB: 90%   *Comparables: Manny Parra, Paul Maholm, Dallas Braden*

Manaea had a very solid mid-rotation season, with fewer strikeouts and more homers than you'd like offset by an elite walk rate. DRA's overall reaction is summed up by that GIF of Robert Redford as Jeremiah Johnson, nodding his understated approval. Then Manaea had shoulder surgery in September that is expected to keep him out for all of 2019. A's fans' overall reaction is summed up by that GIF of Tobias Funke sobbing in the shower. It isn't so much that Manaea is Justin Verlander as that relative to the rest of the A's starting pitching the last few years, Manaea is ... well, Justin Verlander. See you in 2020, big fella.

Daniel Mengden RHP Born: 02/19/93 Age: 26 Bats: R Throws: R Height: 6'2" Weight: 190 Origin: Round 4, 2014 Draft (#106 overall)

YEAR	TEAM	LVL	AGE	W	L	SV	G	GS	IP	H	HR	BB/9	K/9	K	GB%	BABIP	WHIP	ERA	DRA	WARP	MPH	FB%	WHF	CSP
2016	MID	AA	23	2	0	0	4	4	23	15	0	4.7	11.0	28	51%	.283	1.17	0.78	3.65	0.4				
2016	NAS	AAA	23	8	2	0	13	13	75¹	54	4	2.0	8.0	67	50%	.246	0.94	1.67	3.33	1.7				
2016	OAK	MLB	23	2	9	0	14	14	72	83	9	4.1	8.9	71	42%	.344	1.61	6.50	5.67	-0.3	95.5	55.7	9.9	49.5
2017	NAS	AAA	24	2	4	0	9	9	41	40	5	4.0	8.8	40	43%	.307	1.41	4.17	3.49	1.0				
2017	OAK	MLB	24	3	2	0	7	7	43	36	6	1.9	6.1	29	40%	.240	1.05	3.14	4.82	0.4	94.0	56	9.3	47.6
2018	NAS	AAA	25	4	1	0	9	8	45¹	39	2	1.4	6.8	34	44%	.272	1.01	2.98	3.72	0.9				
2018	OAK	MLB	25	7	6	0	22	17	115²	103	18	2.0	5.6	72	40%	.238	1.12	4.05	5.41	-0.2	94.2	53	8.7	51.6
2019	*OAK*	*MLB*	*26*	*9*	*8*	*0*	*26*	*26*	*137²*	*122*	*16*	*2.9*	*7.0*	*107*	*42%*	*.262*	*1.20*	*4.33*	*4.82*	*1.0*	*94.1*	*55.2*	*9.3*	*50.6*

Breakout: 27%   Improve: 60%   Collapse: 15%   Attrition: 13%   MLB: 86%   *Comparables: Jose Urena, Brett Oberholtzer, Erasmo Ramirez*

Mengden entered last year in a battle for a back-end rotation spot, but found himself a starter by attrition after the A's injury troubles kicked off in camp. Then, through May, he posted a 2.91 ERA, and even managed a shutout. (Only 11 pitchers pitched a shutout in the AL last year.) A disastrous June led to an option to Triple-A after rehab from a foot injury rather than a return to the rotation. Mengden complicated the narrative with a 2.52 ERA in 25 innings over six games after his return to the majors in late August, pitching multiple times behind "opener" Liam Hendriks. Where does this leave him? June could have been an aberration, maybe even the result of a low-grade foot problem Mengden didn't tell anyone about until it blew up into a full-on sprain (though there's no *evidence* of this). You could therefore squint your way into seeing Mengden as a big-league starter who figured out how to be successful without impressive stuff, missing bats, getting ground balls or avoiding hard contact. Or you can avoid crow's feet, open your eyes wide, remember that the A's had the best defense in the league and regard his results with skepticism. The mustache is still aces, though.

Frankie Montas RHP Born: 03/21/93 Age: 26 Bats: R Throws: R Height: 6'2" Weight: 255 Origin: International Free Agent, 2009

YEAR	TEAM	LVL	AGE	W	L	SV	G	GS	IP	H	HR	BB/9	K/9	K	GB%	BABIP	WHIP	ERA	DRA	WARP	MPH	FB%	WHF	CSP
2016	OKL	AAA	23	0	0	0	4	3	11¹	12	1	1.6	11.9	15	63%	.400	1.24	2.38	2.55	0.4				
2017	OAK	MLB	24	1	1	0	23	0	32	39	10	5.6	10.1	36	36%	.349	1.84	7.03	6.69	-0.5	100.1	66.3	12.3	49.9
2017	NAS	AAA	24	0	2	0	9	8	29¹	25	4	2.1	11.4	37	53%	.296	1.09	5.22	2.84	0.9				
2018	NAS	AAA	25	4	5	0	15	15	71²	69	7	3.3	7.7	61	48%	.300	1.33	4.65	4.01	1.2				
2018	OAK	MLB	25	5	4	0	13	11	65	74	5	2.9	6.0	43	44%	.325	1.46	3.88	5.59	-0.2	97.6	72.5	9.4	51.3
2019	OAK	MLB	26	6	6	0	35	18	108¹	97	13	3.3	8.0	96	46%	.277	1.26	4.28	4.76	0.8	97.9	71.7	10.5	51.6

Breakout: 28%   Improve: 54%   Collapse: 19%   Attrition: 26%   MLB: 82%   *Comparables: Trevor Williams, Tyler Duffey, Sergio Mitre*

The A's picked up Montas in the Rich Hill/Josh Reddick trade with the Dodgers in 2016. Hill was 36; Montas was 23. It would have been fair to assume that by 2018, Montas would be out-pitching his counterpart. It would also have been dead wrong. Montas has transitioned from a triple-digit four-seamer to a 95 mph sinker in his quest for major-league results, and he did keep the ball down last year, but he lost so many whiffs that the end product wasn't meaningfully better than he'd shown out of the bullpen in 2017. We said he was out of options last year, and that also turned out dead wrong (because his injury-marred 2016 meant he had four option seasons rather than the usual three), but this year, we swear, he's really out of options. If Montas doesn't find a way to consolidate 2018's walks with 2017's whiffs, he could spend more time on waivers than on rosters this season.

Yusmeiro Petit RHP Born: 11/22/84 Age: 34 Bats: R Throws: R Height: 6'1" Weight: 255 Origin: International Free Agent, 2001

YEAR	TEAM	LVL	AGE	W	L	SV	G	GS	IP	H	HR	BB/9	K/9	K	GB%	BABIP	WHIP	ERA	DRA	WARP	MPH	FB%	WHF	CSP
2016	WAS	MLB	31	3	5	1	36	1	62	67	12	2.2	7.1	49	44%	.291	1.32	4.50	4.28	0.5	90.9	49.5	9.7	50.7
2017	ANA	MLB	32	5	2	4	60	1	91¹	69	9	1.8	10.0	101	34%	.267	0.95	2.76	2.83	2.4	91.2	47.8	11.6	48.5
2018	OAK	MLB	33	7	3	0	74	0	93	76	13	1.7	7.4	76	36%	.241	1.01	3.00	3.74	1.3	90.8	47.5	10	51.1
2019	OAK	MLB	34	3	1	0	63	0	66²	58	9	2.8	7.5	55	39%	.260	1.18	4.27	4.75	0.3	89.9	47.3	10.4	49.4

Breakout: 24%   Improve: 41%   Collapse: 27%   Attrition: 10%   MLB: 88%   *Comparables: Roy Face, Rollie Fingers, Rick Aguilera*

Petit, whose name belies his distinctly undainty build, parlayed a wildly successful 2017 in Anaheim into a two-year contract (with a team option) with Oakland. He took a step back last year but held onto enough of his performance that the A's may have already gotten their money's worth in a crude dollars-per-win sense. Petit remains the same soft-tossing, zone-pounding righty we've been writing about in these pages for over a decade, but as he enters his mid-30s, he's actually throwing slightly *harder* than he did when the first pitch-tracking systems came online in 2007. His curveball remains a weapon, deployed largely against righties and resulting in whiffs and weak contact, and his changeup, which he now uses almost as often as his fastball against lefties, keep hitters off balance enough to allow Petit to gobble the middle innings of close games; just under half his appearances over the last two years have gone past one inning. His stuff leaves him living on a razor's edge, but after five years of effective work, it's hard to imagine him falling off a cliff. Famous last words.

A.J. Puk LHP Born: 04/25/95 Age: 24 Bats: L Throws: L Height: 6'7" Weight: 220 Origin: Round 1, 2016 Draft (#6 overall)

YEAR	TEAM	LVL	AGE	W	L	SV	G	GS	IP	H	HR	BB/9	K/9	K	GB%	BABIP	WHIP	ERA	DRA	WARP	MPH	FB%	WHF	CSP
2016	VER	A-	21	0	4	0	10	10	32²	23	0	3.3	11.0	40	51%	.271	1.07	3.03	2.67	1.0				
2017	STO	A+	22	4	5	0	14	11	61	44	1	3.4	14.5	98	42%	.336	1.10	3.69	2.11	2.2				
2017	MID	AA	22	2	5	0	13	13	64	64	2	3.5	12.1	86	48%	.380	1.39	4.36	2.91	1.7				
2019	OAK	MLB	24	5	5	0	15	15	79²	69	10	4.0	9.6	85	41%	.287	1.31	4.19	4.65	0.8				

Breakout: 14%   Improve: 26%   Collapse: 12%   Attrition: 24%   MLB: 41%   *Comparables: Edwar Cabrera, Dan Meyer, Matt Barnes*

Puk entered 2018 as the A's best prospect, a hard-throwing lefty with a wipeout slider and a real shot at joining the rotation after a few phantom "development" weeks in Triple-A. He ended March on the shelf and had Tommy John surgery in early April. Puk had finished 2017 still needing to show the kind of mechanical consistency that will let him attack the zone or miss it with intent rather than throwing his best stuff in the general vicinity of the catcher and seeing what happens. A healthy camp might have shown us that a winter of work had leveled him up in that area; instead, it remains a question mark. Even if he never applies those finishing touches, though, the downside may not be what it once was: Rather than a boring traditional eighth-inning guy, one could dream of a Josh Hader/Andrew Miller-style weapon.

Fernando Rodney RHP Born: 03/18/77 Age: 42 Bats: R Throws: R Height: 5'11" Weight: 230 Origin: International Free Agent, 1997

YEAR	TEAM	LVL	AGE	W	L	SV	G	GS	IP	H	HR	BB/9	K/9	K	GB%	BABIP	WHIP	ERA	DRA	WARP	MPH	FB%	WHF	CSP
2016	SDN	MLB	39	0	1	17	28	0	28²	13	0	3.8	10.4	33	60%	.210	0.87	0.31	4.21	0.3	97.3	58.4	14.7	45.6
2016	MIA	MLB	39	2	3	8	39	0	36²	41	5	6.1	10.1	41	54%	.360	1.80	5.89	5.41	-0.2	97.6	57.1	12.6	41.9
2017	ARI	MLB	40	5	4	39	61	0	55¹	40	3	4.2	10.6	65	54%	.274	1.19	4.23	3.63	1.0	96.7	59.5	13.2	45.4
2018	MIN	MLB	41	3	2	25	46	0	43²	42	5	3.9	10.3	50	45%	.319	1.40	3.09	3.85	0.5	97.0	71.8	13.1	46.8
2018	OAK	MLB	41	1	1	0	22	0	20²	20	2	5.7	8.7	20	46%	.316	1.60	3.92	4.52	0.1	96.6	68.7	9.5	43.9
2019	OAK	MLB	42	3	1	5	52	0	54²	46	6	4.4	9.4	57	48%	.281	1.33	4.11	4.56	0.3	95.0	61.5	12.1	43.3

Breakout: 11%   Improve: 25%   Collapse: 24%   Attrition: 13%   MLB: 66%   *Comparables: Darren Oliver, Arthur Rhodes, Roberto Hernandez*

Rodney joined the A's Bullpen of Death in a mid-year trade for Low-A pitcher Dakota Chalmers and pitched well for two weeks before forgetting that the rules delimit a strike zone and permit the batter to decline to swing if the ball is not thrown in it; 13 walks in 14 2/3 innings from August 24 to the end of the year were the result. (He then added insult to insult with a disastrously brief appearance in the A's Wild Card game loss to the Yankees.) Oakland picked up his 2019 option at $5.25 million anyway, likely figuring that even in some of Rodney's good years (e.g. 2013 with Tampa Bay, 2017 with Arizona), he wasn't exactly Dennis Eckersley with the control. The much more alarming sign is the sharp fall-off in ground-ball rate. The pitch-tracking stats say that neither his sinker nor his changeup drop the way they used to; the difference, maybe an inch and a half for each, is surely imperceptible to the eye, but when the bat is only two and a half inches in diameter, an inch here and there can make a world of difference. Rodney's 42, old enough to make it extremely unlikely that he's going to get back anything he's lost.

Joakim Soria   RHP   Born: 05/18/84   Age: 35   Bats: R   Throws: R   Height: 6'3"   Weight: 200   Origin: International Free Agent, 2001

YEAR	TEAM	LVL	AGE	W	L	SV	G	GS	IP	H	HR	BB/9	K/9	K	GB%	BABIP	WHIP	ERA	DRA	WARP	MPH	FB%	WHF	CSP
2016	KCA	MLB	32	5	8	1	70	0	66²	70	10	3.6	9.2	68	52%	.323	1.46	4.05	3.47	1.1	95.2	62.2	12.5	48.6
2017	KCA	MLB	33	4	3	1	59	0	56	49	1	3.2	10.3	64	58%	.329	1.23	3.70	3.62	1.0	94.7	49.3	13.5	46.6
2018	CHA	MLB	34	0	3	16	40	0	38²	35	2	2.3	11.4	49	35%	.324	1.16	2.56	2.35	1.1	94.2	63	15.4	45.8
2018	MIL	MLB	34	3	1	0	26	0	22	18	2	2.5	10.6	26	48%	.286	1.09	4.09	2.94	0.5	94.4	71.2	14.2	50.1
2019	OAK	MLB	35	3	1	5	57	0	60²	50	6	3.2	9.6	65	46%	.279	1.18	3.62	4.02	0.6	93.4	58.6	13.6	46.6

Breakout: 19%   Improve: 38%   Collapse: 28%   Attrition: 17%   MLB: 93%   *Comparables: Jim Brewer, George Sherrill, Ryan Madson*

The era of the nameless, faceless elite reliever results from clear motivation of MLB teams: as the price of relief pitching increases, it's beneficial to take chances on some of those mid-90s fastballs or flawed two-pitch profiles reserved under minimum contracts. This ideal also leans on the thought that relievers are volatile, and there are very few who'll repeat elite, high-leverage performances on an annual basis. Soria straddled both edges of this thinking in 2018, recovering his status as an excellent closer after converting just two saves in 2016-2017, while also reinventing himself in a manner that almost makes him unrecognizable to the classic Soria of yore. The former changeup savant dropped his release point and embraced a slider, giving a new look to batters and producing his best results in years. A slider-heavy Soria may be nameless, faceless after all, for he's now swimming in uncharted waters as a wily, inventive veteran.

Blake Treinen   RHP   Born: 06/30/88   Age: 31   Bats: R   Throws: R   Height: 6'5"   Weight: 225   Origin: Round 7, 2011 Draft (#226 overall)

YEAR	TEAM	LVL	AGE	W	L	SV	G	GS	IP	H	HR	BB/9	K/9	K	GB%	BABIP	WHIP	ERA	DRA	WARP	MPH	FB%	WHF	CSP
2016	WAS	MLB	28	4	1	1	73	0	67	51	5	4.2	8.5	63	67%	.280	1.22	2.28	4.59	0.3	98.1	68.7	11.6	47.1
2017	WAS	MLB	29	0	2	3	37	0	37²	48	3	3.1	7.6	32	62%	.381	1.62	5.73	4.79	0.2	99.0	72.6	13.1	46.9
2017	OAK	MLB	29	3	4	13	35	0	38	32	3	2.8	9.9	42	60%	.299	1.16	2.13	3.96	0.5	98.9	61.8	14.3	48.3
2018	OAK	MLB	30	9	2	38	68	0	80¹	46	2	2.4	11.2	100	53%	.232	0.83	0.78	2.22	2.5	99.1	67.1	19.2	47.7
2019	OAK	MLB	31	3	1	30	57	0	60²	45	5	3.5	10.4	70	55%	.278	1.14	3.32	3.67	1.0	97.9	67.1	15.5	47.2

Breakout: 16%   Improve: 38%   Collapse: 30%   Attrition: 10%   MLB: 90%   *Comparables: Tony Watson, Francisco Cordero, Mark Melancon*

Treinen, who still has two more years of team control before free agency, built on his excellent half-season in the A's closer role in 2017 with the kind of performance that might have won him a Cy Young award in less enlightened times. As it is, he finished sixth in the AL voting, powered by the fifth-best reliever ERA (min. 50 IP) since 1946. He gets the job done largely with an unbarrelable, nigh untouchable 96–99 mph sinker; the only pitcher in baseball with a similar combination of whiffs and grounders on a high-usage sinker is Zach Britton. Treinen didn't reach pro ball until he was 23, and the majors at 26, so while it seems like he's just arrived, he's only a month younger than, to pick a name out of a hat, Craig Kimbrel. Odds are, then, that 2018 was a peak, not a plateau, but Edmund Hillary didn't make his home atop Everest and you know who he is anyway, so what's the difference in the long run?

Andrew Triggs   RHP   Born: 03/16/89   Age: 30   Bats: R   Throws: R   Height: 6'4"   Weight: 220   Origin: Round 19, 2012 Draft (#583 overall)

YEAR	TEAM	LVL	AGE	W	L	SV	G	GS	IP	H	HR	BB/9	K/9	K	GB%	BABIP	WHIP	ERA	DRA	WARP	MPH	FB%	WHF	CSP
2016	NAS	AAA	27	2	1	2	16	0	18¹	16	0	2.5	10.3	21	59%	.314	1.15	2.95	2.19	0.6				
2016	OAK	MLB	27	1	1	0	24	6	56¹	56	5	2.1	8.8	55	52%	.315	1.22	4.31	3.63	1.0	92.8	55.4	10.7	48.1
2017	OAK	MLB	28	5	6	0	12	12	65¹	68	9	2.6	6.9	50	49%	.294	1.33	4.27	4.53	0.8	91.1	43.9	10.6	46.8
2018	OAK	MLB	29	3	1	0	9	9	41¹	37	7	3.9	9.4	43	49%	.270	1.33	5.23	5.57	-0.1	91.2	48.5	10.6	45.1
2019	OAK	MLB	30	5	5	0	16	16	84²	73	10	3.3	8.5	80	48%	.275	1.23	4.07	4.52	0.9	90.9	48.3	10.6	46.3

Breakout: 20%   Improve: 42%   Collapse: 23%   Attrition: 20%   MLB: 75%   *Comparables: Kevin Gregg, Phil Coke, Adam Ottavino*

Keeping Triggs healthy has proven harder than remembering whether it's the cosecant or the secant that's the inverse of the sine. Last year's injury was nerve irritation in his pitching arm, which kept him out after mid-May (aside from a single rehab appearance in Stockton in September) and resulted in surgery to relieve thoracic outlet syndrome in late September. His outlook for 2019, or indeed his career, is unknown as this book goes to press. If Triggs does get back on the mound, he'll resume his attempt at a fifth-starter career, or maybe find himself as a useful multi-inning pitcher on one of these "no starters" pitching staffs we seem to be barreling toward.

Lou Trivino   RHP   Born: 10/01/91   Age: 27   Bats: R   Throws: R   Height: 6'5"   Weight: 225   Origin: Round 11, 2013 Draft (#341 overall)

YEAR	TEAM	LVL	AGE	W	L	SV	G	GS	IP	H	HR	BB/9	K/9	K	GB%	BABIP	WHIP	ERA	DRA	WARP	MPH	FB%	WHF	CSP
2016	STO	A+	24	1	3	2	33	0	41²	38	0	3.9	10.6	49	61%	.342	1.34	3.02	3.46	0.8				
2016	MID	AA	24	1	1	1	12	0	18¹	14	1	3.4	5.9	12	48%	.236	1.15	2.45	3.09	0.4				
2017	MID	AA	25	7	1	1	23	0	33¹	31	0	2.7	9.2	34	57%	.333	1.23	2.43	3.34	0.6				
2017	NAS	AAA	25	1	2	4	25	0	35	33	0	2.8	8.0	31	54%	.308	1.26	3.60	2.94	0.9				
2018	OAK	MLB	26	8	3	4	69	1	74	53	8	3.8	10.0	82	47%	.256	1.14	2.92	3.10	1.6	98.9	53.7	15.1	47.8
2019	OAK	MLB	27	3	1	0	57	0	60²	49	6	4.1	9.7	65	48%	.277	1.26	3.91	4.33	0.6	98.4	54.3	15.3	48.4

Breakout: 15%   Improve: 35%   Collapse: 22%   Attrition: 20%   MLB: 69%   *Comparables: Michael Blazek, Tom Mastny, Ryan Cook*

Any decent Hell Bullpen needs one guy like Trivino to leap out of the minors with no prospect pedigree and throw untouchable smoke while steadily earning a more central role than could have been anticipated in spring training. Trivino brings heat at 97 mph about half the time, split between a sinking and a straight fastball. His main secondary pitch is classified as a cutter, and comes in at 92, but in the context of his other fastballs, it comes across more like a very tight slider. His whiff rate on the pitch is elite, in the top 10 percent of the league, and of the pitchers in his vicinity, only Alex Colome throws his as often as Trivino does. The resulting three-fastballs, no-secondaries, lots-of-strikeouts approach is not *unique* (check out Ryan Tepera, for instance, or Dominic Leone), but it's still unusual and should make Trivino one of the more intriguing setup men in the league.

LINEOUTS

Hitters

HITTER	POS	TEAM	LVL	AGE	PA	R	2B	3B	HR	RBI	BB	K	SB	CS	AVG/OBP/SLG	DRC+	VORP	BABIP	BRR	FRAA	WARP
Nick Allen	SS	BLT	A	19	512	51	17	6	0	34	34	85	24	8	.239/.301/.302	86	15.2	.289	3.7	SS(121): 5.2	2.2
Greg Deichmann	OF	ATH	Rk	23	43	9	2	2	1	7	5	8	0	0	.289/.372/.526	118	3.3	.345	-0.1	RF(11): -0.4	0.1
	OF	STO	A+	23	185	18	14	0	6	21	17	63	0	0	.199/.276/.392	80	-0.7	.276	-0.1	RF(28): 0.7, LF(8): -0.8	-0.2
Jeremy Eierman	SS	VER	A-	21	267	36	8	2	8	26	13	70	10	4	.235/.283/.381	95	5.6	.294	-0.1	SS(56): 0.3, 2B(2): 0.9	1.0
Jameson Hannah	OF	VER	A-	20	95	14	4	1	1	10	9	24	6	0	.279/.347/.384	98	7.6	.377	1.1	CF(18): -2.4	0.1
Chris Herrmann	RF	TAC	AAA	30	174	26	3	1	6	24	36	42	0	0	.257/.416/.426	119	15.2	.330	-2.5	C(28): 0.5	1.0
	RF	SEA	MLB	30	87	6	4	2	2	7	10	24	0	0	.237/.322/.421	86	4.3	.314	0.0	C(28): 0.1, 1B(1): 0.0	0.3
Corban Joseph	INF	BOW	AA	29	523	73	30	2	17	68	52	43	8	2	.312/.381/.497	145	45.5	.311	2.0	2B(52): -8.6, 1B(21): 0.1	3.3
	INF	BAL	MLB	29	19	1	1	0	0	3	1	5	0	0	.222/.263/.278	81	-1.0	.308	0.0	1B(5): -0.2, 2B(2): -0.7	-0.1
Bruce Maxwell	C	OAK	MLB	27	58	5	4	0	1	6	2	13	0	0	.182/.207/.309	71	-1.9	.214	-0.3	C(16): -1.9	-0.2
	C	NAS	AAA	27	200	9	8	0	1	17	21	61	0	0	.219/.300/.281	65	-8.2	.325	-4.3	C(38): -0.4	-0.5
Kevin Merrell	SS	STO	A+	22	290	38	10	3	0	24	15	66	5	4	.267/.308/.326	71	9.1	.353	1.3	SS(59): -5.3	-0.3
Josh Phegley	C	NAS	AAA	30	139	12	6	3	3	18	15	31	0	0	.235/.331/.412	94	7.8	.287	-0.1	C(19): 2.8	0.7
	C	OAK	MLB	30	102	13	7	0	2	15	6	27	0	0	.204/.255/.344	77	0.9	.258	-0.1	C(39): -1.3	0.1
Tyler Ramirez	OF	MID	AA	23	594	73	35	4	10	79	62	148	5	4	.287/.370/.430	104	23.5	.378	2.0	LF(82): -7.8, CF(28): 3.6	1.5
Beau Taylor	C	NAS	AAA	28	356	39	15	3	3	39	50	89	2	0	.248/.360/.348	80	15.1	.341	-1.8	C(69): 1.8	0.7
	C	OAK	MLB	28	6	0	1	0	0	0	1	2	0	0	.200/.333/.400	89	0.2	.333	0.0	C(6): 0.2	0.0

Nick Allen got the bat knocked out of his hands in Low-A, which is what you expect from an undersized, teenage defensive wizard. David Eckstein played in 1,311 big-league games. ⊗ **Greg Deichmann** suffered an early-season wrist injury, which makes it hard to judge his results at High-A even after he did come back. A power-hitting right fielder lives within him. ⊗ **Jeremy Eierman** was the 70th overall pick last year as a major-college, power-speed shortstop, though he's probably a power-hitting third baseman long term if he's anything. His brother Johnny washed out after three rookie-ball seasons despite being a Rays third-round pick, if you need another reminder that "if he's anything" is a huge mountain to climb. ⊗ **Jameson Hannah** is a lefty outfielder who the A's took in the second round last year. His speed should keep him in center field, which is where his power profile also belongs. ⊗ **Chris Herrmann** is a fine baseball player with underrated athleticism and defensive utility. He deserves better than a pithy comment in this space. If he didn't then why would his name not literally be German for "Mr. Man?" ⊗ **Corban Joseph** has been in organized baseball for the past ten years, and in that span, he has a grand total of 26 major-league plate appearances. Based on his pattern, look for his next appearance in the 2024 Annual. ⊗ It's not clear whether **Bruce Maxwell** lost his presumptive 2018 starting catcher job *because* he pointed a gun at a delivery person over the winter, but it's hard to believe it wasn't on Oakland's mind when Jonathan Lucroy was still available early in the spring. In any event, Maxwell shouldn't even be a starter on a bad team, much less a good one. ⊗ **Kevin Merrell** runs like the dickens, but he hits like the mckittrick ros. ⊗ **Josh Phegley** doesn't hit, catch or stay healthy, and such small portions! (We know he's #actually quite large, don't @ us.) ⊗ **Tyler Ramirez**'s on-base ability should get him some big-league time, and soon, but his corner defensive profile and doubles power mark him as an up-and-down guy, not a true fourth outfielder. Guys like this used to have the careers that now go to extra pitchers. ⊗ **Beau Taylor** is a catcher who stands on the left side, so he'll get as many chances on minor-league deals as he wants even though he can't really hit. He's in this book for the first and perhaps last time because he made a brief big-league debut last year and notched a double and a walk, which puts him three bases up on the lot of youse.

Pitchers

PITCHER	TEAM	LVL	AGE	W	L	SV	G	GS	IP	H	HR	BB/9	K/9	K	GB%	BABIP	WHIP	ERA	DRA	WARP	MPH	FB%	WHF	CSP
Tanner Anderson	IND	AAA	25	3	2	6	39	0	61¹	65	2	2.2	7.2	49	63%	.337	1.30	2.64	4.11	0.7				
	PIT	MLB	25	1	0	0	6	0	11¹	15	1	6.4	4.8	6	58%	.350	2.03	6.35	6.40	-0.2	94.7	60.2	9.9	54.4
Paul Blackburn	OAK	MLB	24	2	3	0	6	6	27²	33	2	2.0	6.2	19	48%	.344	1.41	7.16	3.88	0.5	91.2	40.4	9.1	42.8
Aaron Brooks	CSP	AAA	28	9	4	0	26	15	99¹	100	8	2.5	6.7	74	56%	.307	1.29	3.35	4.68	0.9				
	OAK	MLB	28	0	0	0	3	0	2²	1	0	6.8	3.4	1	71%	.143	1.12	0.00	4.72	0.0	93.9	45.2	0	43.4
Daniel Coulombe	NAS	AAA	28	2	1	0	23	1	28¹	30	3	1.9	8.9	28	44%	.333	1.27	2.54	4.09	0.3				
	OAK	MLB	28	1	1	0	27	0	23²	24	5	4.2	9.9	26	56%	.339	1.48	4.56	2.77	0.6	91.0	33.8	13.7	46.5
Ryan Dull	NAS	AAA	28	3	2	1	23	0	28	27	5	2.6	11.6	36	45%	.367	1.25	3.54	2.86	0.7				
	OAK	MLB	28	0	0	0	28	0	25¹	22	3	2.5	7.5	21	35%	.275	1.14	4.26	3.83	0.3	92.1	52.9	11.5	44.9
Parker Dunshee	STO	A+	23	6	2	0	12	10	70	61	7	2.2	10.5	82	35%	.314	1.11	2.70	4.07	1.0				
	MID	AA	23	7	4	0	12	12	80²	59	5	1.6	9.0	81	34%	.266	0.90	2.01	3.52	1.7				
Brady Feigl	VER	A-	22	1	1	0	8	5	20	6	0	3.2	12.1	27	59%	.154	0.65	1.35	3.50	0.4				
	BLT	A	22	0	1	0	3	3	6	5	1	1.5	10.5	7	56%	.267	1.00	3.00	2.68	0.2				
Cory Gearrin	SFN	MLB	32	1	1	1	35	0	30	33	5	3.9	9.3	31	34%	.329	1.53	4.20	4.57	0.1	93.6	48.9	12.2	44.3
	TEX	MLB	32	1	0	0	21	0	21¹	13	2	2.5	8.4	20	52%	.212	0.89	2.53	4.97	0.0	93.4	49	12.4	46.6
	OAK	MLB	32	0	0	0	6	0	6	10	0	3.0	3.0	2	50%	.417	2.00	6.00	3.91	0.1	93.3	60	7.6	51.4
Chris Hatcher	NAS	AAA	33	0	1	0	5	0	8²	10	0	4.2	7.3	7	39%	.357	1.62	2.08	3.49	0.2				
	OAK	MLB	33	3	3	0	34	0	36¹	43	7	4.2	7.4	30	44%	.321	1.65	4.95	4.96	0.0	95.1	48.8	8.5	44.5
Dean Kiekhefer	PEN	AA	29	0	0	0	8	0	8	7	0	1.1	11.2	10	45%	.350	1.00	1.12	4.22	0.1				
	NAS	AAA	29	8	1	0	32	1	44²	50	4	1.2	7.3	36	54%	.322	1.25	3.83	3.03	1.1				
	OAK	MLB	29	0	0	0	4	0	2	7	1	4.5	4.5	1	67%	.545	4.00	18.00	3.81	0.0	89.4	53.3	8.9	41.6
J.B. Wendelken	MID	AA	25	0	1	3	11	0	13¹	11	3	6.8	15.5	23	43%	.320	1.58	3.38	2.78	0.3				
	NAS	AAA	25	1	1	3	22	1	35¹	29	2	2.5	13.2	52	49%	.342	1.10	2.80	1.72	1.4				
	OAK	MLB	25	0	0	0	13	0	16²	8	1	2.7	7.6	14	40%	.167	0.78	0.54	4.16	0.1	97.0	60.9	14	51.8

The Pirates featured an all-Ivy League battery four times in September, with **Tanner Anderson** (Harvard) pitching to Ryan Lavarnway (Yale). Rumors that scientists were working to harness this smart battery in an attempt to reduce worldwide energy use and global emissions could not be confirmed. ⓧ **Paul Blackburn** was healthy only for a month last season, sandwiched between a forearm strain to start the year and tennis elbow to end it, though neither required surgery. He's still just 25 and remains a solid back-of-the-rotation option if he can stay on the mound. ⓧ **Aaron Brooks** doesn't miss enough bats to pitch in the big leagues, which may not prevent him from being Oakland's fourth starter in 2019. ⓧ **Jharel Cotton** entered spring training last year hoping to prove he belongs in the majors after a miserable 2017; instead, he had Tommy John surgery in late March. ⓧ **Danny Coulombe** suffered the indignity of being designated for assignment in favor of Aaron Brooks in September. He's a pint-size lefty junkballer, which is a lot of fun, except when he falls behind and has to throw his "fast"balls. ⓧ **Ryan Dull** is an undersized slider artist whose spring shoulder strain and rough May took him out of the A's bullpen mix. His final season line contained a critical drop in strikeout rate, reflecting a substantially more hittable slider that will need to regain its previous form to make him a middle-relief option going forward. ⓧ **Parker "Crocodile" Dunshee** spent 2018 doing what he did in 2017: out-pitching his lack of stuff by changing speeds and throwing strikes, this time up to a successful half-season at Double-A. On a Pitching Staff of the Future, he could throw 150 solid frames without ever sniffing the first or seventh inning. ⓧ **Brady Feigl** is in this book to ensure that you Google his name and marvel at the weirdness of his simultaneous existence with the Brady Feigl in the Rangers' minor-league system. We're not living in a sophisticated simulation run by some unfathomable higher power; we're living in a beta test. ⓧ In the Kevin Smith movie *Dogma*, Jay, Silent Bob and Linda Fiorentino's Bethany are motoring down a dark highway at 95 mph with Jay at the wheel. Bethany shouts over the noise of the engine and the music, "What gear are you in?" Jay responds, bewildered, "Geeearrr??" Cut to the three peering into the smoking engine. This is a Lineout, so we have to say a name now: **Cory Gearrin**. ⓧ **Chris Hatcher** gave up a three-run walk-off dinger to Taylor Ward in the A's last regular-season game of 2018. It can't get *worse*, so why not keep pitching? ⓧ **Daulton Jefferies** missed essentially all of 2017–2018 after Tommy John surgery, but threw in instructional league and is expected to start 2019 in full health. Who knows what the lost development time will cost him, but he had a mid-rotation ceiling once upon a time. ⓧ **James Kaprielian**'s upside is worth more than 41 words in this book, but 29 regular-season innings since being drafted in 2015 (and 27 more in the Arizona Fall League) means there's simply no data. Dammit, Jim, we're baseball analysts, not doctors. ⓧ Run-of-the-mill lefty reliever **Dean Kiekhefer** has the name of a man who belongs in Cooperstown and the strikeout rate of a man who belongs in Triple-A. ⓧ **J.B. Wendelken** probably pitch in middle relief with a 95 mph fastball, but **J.B. Wendelken**'t be counted on for much more than that.

PHILADELPHIA PHILLIES

Essay by Justin Klugh

Player comments by Paul Boye and BP staff

There was once a young, inexperienced baseball man who came to Philadelphia to win it all.

He showed up and began unpacking some wacky ideas to gain a series of tiny advantages against his opponents that confused and enraged everyone watching. People thought him smug or strange; overcomplicating the game's purity by twisting knobs and pushing buttons. But it was in these narrow strategic margins that games were won or lost. One of his plans was to swap the placement of the Phillies' bullpen with their opponents' in order to increase their home field advantage. The idea was that it would allow his relievers a better angle to alert the third base coach if a batted ball was catchable or not by waving towels, gaining precious seconds for a runner.

As the legend goes, four years later, he proved his doubters wrong by managing one of the best Phillies teams of all time. As the legend continues, several weeks later, he proved his doubters right when that same team crumbled down the stretch and lost its playoff spot in the most baffling, demoralizing, and damaging collapse in the history of Philadelphia sports.

The point here, as Gene Mauch learned during that magical and then terrible 1964 season, is that in baseball, change is as inevitable as failure.

This past season, in 2018, another young, inexperienced baseball man arrived in Philadelphia with a monosyllabic name that starts with "G." Gabe Kapler brought some pretty wacky ideas with him, too. And once again, everything changed. Right before everything failed.

Over the winter, the Phillies had become ready to put a face on their franchise. They sent young slugger Rhys Hoskins across the street, with jackrabbit shortstop J.P. Crawford in tow, to ring the pregame bell at a Sixers game and wave to the crowd. "Here he is," the Phillies were saying, gesturing theatrically at Hoskins. "Philly's next baseball guy. Take down the faded Utley posters, gang; this one hits 'em long and walks a lot. Look at that smile. All right, have fun."

And then, the season began. Hoskins finished April hitting over .300, then plummeted from relevance. He then fouled a pitch off his jaw to close out May and came back with all of his power, crushing eight home runs with a .688 SLG in

PHILLIES PROSPECTUS
2018 W-L: 80-82, 3RD IN NL EAST

Pythag	.466	20th	B-Age	26.7	2nd
RS/G	4.18	21st	P-Age	26.6	3rd
RA/G	4.49	19th	Salary	$95.3M	24th
DRC+	92	22nd	M$/MW	$2.6M	25th
DRA	3.97	7th	DL Days	924	9th
FIP	3.79	4th	$ on DL	15%	13th
DER	.697	26th			

401'
374'
369'
329'
330'

- Opened 2004
- Open air
- Natural surface
- Fence profile: 6' to 19'

Three-Year Park Factors

Runs	Runs/RH	Runs/LH	HR/RH	HR/LH
100	101	97	111	112

Top Hitter WARP	4.0 Rhys Hoskins
Top Pitcher WARP	6.6 Aaron Nola
Top Prospect	Sixto Sanchez

2018 Hit List Ranking

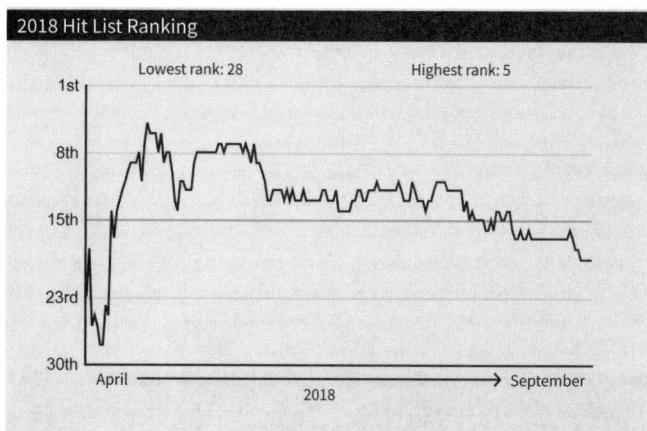

Lowest rank: 28   Highest rank: 5

Committed Payroll (in millions)

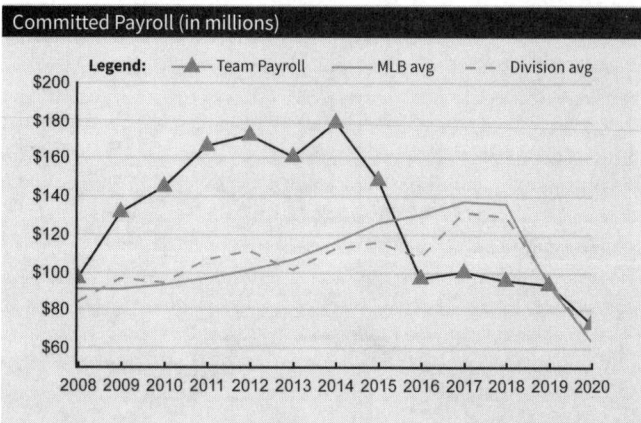

Legend: ▲— Team Payroll   —— MLB avg   – – – Division avg

Farm System Ranking

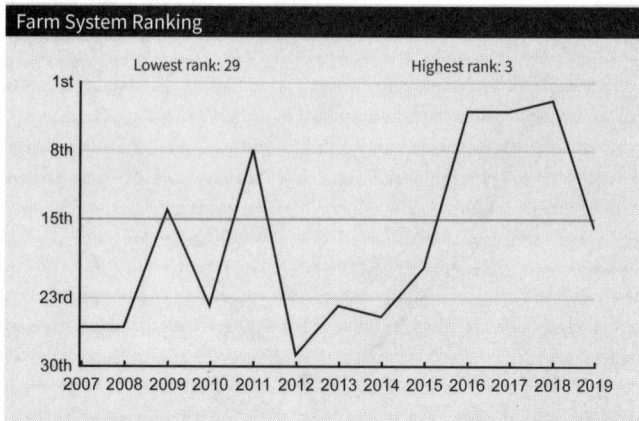

Lowest rank: 29   Highest rank: 3

Personnel

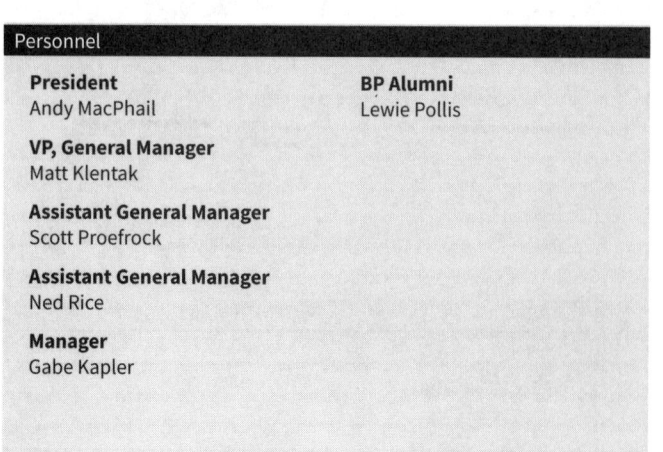

President
Andy MacPhail

VP, General Manager
Matt Klentak

Assistant General Manager
Scott Proefrock

Assistant General Manager
Ned Rice

Manager
Gabe Kapler

BP Alumni
Lewie Pollis

June. In July he went warm, in August he went cold, and in September he, like the rest of his teammates, was about as effective a hitter as Gene Mauch, who'd been dead for 13 years.

It wasn't just Hoskins. There was no impassioned speech or closed-door meeting that could rally this team by the season's final six weeks. The powerless offense waved feebly at pitches; the penetrable defense tumbled out of the way of ground balls; the roster lauded for its youthful outlook was now dotted with more veterans every night as extra parts like Asdrubal Cabrera, Jose Bautista, Wilson Ramos, and Justin Bour were added mid-season. Scott Kingery was tossed into a 24-4 August loss to the Mets for a garbage time pitching appearance and lobbed the ball so pathetically the stadium radar gun couldn't even pick it up. Focus wilted with each passing loss; just before the Phillies' penultimate game, Odubel Herrera and Dylan Cozens realized a moment before first pitch that they were in the wrong positions and had to switch spots.

The long baseball season chewed up this team, and exposed more of their weaknesses than there may have surfaced during a year in which they weren't simultaneously trying out new players, a new manager, and a new organizational mindset, all while John Middleton casually let it slip from the owner's box how much money he was going to spend in the most intimidating free agency class in franchise history.

Blame, in Philadelphia, flows hotter than the cheese steak grease. It splattered all over the Phillies, on the maddeningly inconsistent Odubel Herrera, on the maddeningly consistent Carlos Santana, on the consistently maddening Scott Kingery, on the bullpen, on the starters, on the front office, on math, on coconut oil—but the most hoarsely shouted name belonged to Gabe Kapler, the 43-year-old first-time manager with a penchant for analytics.

Once Kapler had been hired, he had voluntarily climbed into the mandibles of the Philadelphia sports scene without hesitation. While a coconut-scented breeze gently wafted through the palm trees of his former home in Malibu, Philadelphia was being thrashed by ice storms that filled the air with knives and left behind rivers of slush, quickly defiled by the city's boot prints and dog leavings. Kapler moved right in, and could be found lingering outside locally sourced restaurants in Northern Liberties and Fishtown, Apple products in hand, for most of the winter. As part of his introductory tour, Kapler, too, had gotten to attend a Sixers game and take part in the pregame bell-ringing ritual, doing so with an aggressive hammer strike that drew satisfied roars from the assembled sports fans.

By the Phillies' home opener, they were boos. He became the face the Phillies had sought for their franchise, but not in the way they had wanted.

"No, no!" the Phillies tried shouting over the boos. "Not him! Focus on *this* one!" they cried, desperately pointing at Rhys Hoskins stretching in the on-deck circle.

We don't have to relive the whole thing to understand what happened. Rather, there are three moments that do a pretty good job of painting the picture of Kapler's first year.

- **March 31:** With fans still heated over Kapler prematurely removing Aaron Nola from his opening day start and triggering a gut-punching loss, Kapler tries to bring reliever Hoby Milner into the game before the pitcher has warmed up in the bullpen. This leads to an uproar from players, analysts, umpires, and fans, who now have definitive proof that Kapler is the baseball antichrist. It was very clear very early that Kapler was not the kind of manager fans were used to seeing, and he was playing a kind of baseball they might not want to see. He also may not have fully understood the rules.

- **May 26:** Nola gives the Phillies six and two thirds of his best stuff, Maikel Franco crushes a deep line drive, and Nick Williams breaks a 1-1 tie in the eighth with a solo shot. The Phillies hold back the Blue Jays for a 2-1 win and slide into first place for the first time in seven years. They weren't there long, just a day, and only by a half-game margin. But it was enough that, after the Braves climbed back over the Phillies the next night, people wanted it back.

- **September 9:** Kapler says his team is in a "really good spot to strike," twitching the nose hairs of anyone who had just watched the downward spiraling Phillies lose four of six on a crucial road trip, further scattering their once promising playoff chances. Kapler has come under fire not just for the losing, but for the relentless positivity with which he chooses to face each downfall. If the Phillies were planning on striking, they did not do so, and lost 20 of 28 games in the regular season's final month.

There was a philosophical shift going on for the Phillies in 2018. The front office was focusing on accruing players who could take control of the strike zone, allowing for a deep pool of on-base threats from which Kapler, a strong advocate of these analytics himself, could select the best in-game matchups. Experimenting with this process, while also determining which young players were skilled enough for full-time jobs with the team—as well as determining what exactly a "full-time job" *meant* on this team—led to a clunky first season with Kapler at the helm. His management style, in which he employed such measures while refusing to denigrate his players in public and claimed to remain open to new ideas, drew the fire of rabid traditionalists, smirking columnists, and talking heads looking for a polarizing target.

And Kapler took them for a ride. This was a developmental season for the Phillies, so parts of it were always going to be a mess. The problem was, by reaching first place, his Phillies briefly became something else, as well: Contenders.

You could find fault with his methods, but with a first place team, you couldn't argue with Kapler's results (people *did*, though—just because the Phillies were changing doesn't mean Philadelphia was).

An 80-win team in Philadelphia was quite the quantifiable improvement, compared to their 66-win squad of the previous year (more commonly known as a "96-loss" squad). And your typical 80-win team is going to climb and stumble without every getting too far from the ground: a good month here, a bad stretch there, a power surge, a team-wide slump, somebody forgets to check the expiration date on post-game spread, etc. If the Phillies had lost their 82 games proportionally throughout the season, this page you're reading would be covered in an essay about how the Phillies laid a foundation from which they can build. Instead, they won in clumps, lost in batches, and played themselves right into and out of the contention that had caught everyone by pleasant surprise.

Kapler being a rookie himself played into this. His belief in the numbers cost him on a few occasions, trusting them over what he could see with his eyes when it came to relievers. His lineup was never the same twice, and the front office seemed convinced they could turn Kingery into Ben Zobrist just by writing new positions next to his name. They wanted so badly to be a team of 25 super utility on-base machines, taking pitches and slapping singles, but they just didn't have the tools for it. One of their two big off-season acquisitions, Carlos Santana, embodied this perfectly: A veteran player brought in to duplicate the role already filled by the team's face, Hoskins. A solid idea, bringing in one of the best players in the league at getting on base, and at a reasonable rate, but without an established bat in the lineup to knock him in, all he could do was stand out there.

In the clubhouse, there was no one for Kapler to rely on. He had Nola, the sole All-Star, a steadfast presence on the roster for the entire season. He had Hoskins, who was ready to be crowned the leader in the locker room but didn't quite have his own swing figured out and was still playing in his first full big league season. He had Santana, who just wasn't the type of player the Phillies needed, he had Jake Arrieta, whose patience wore thin, as did veteran Pat Neshek's. Beyond that, Kapler's roster was full of young players trying to rise to the occasion but kept bonking their heads on low ceilings.

The Phillies fell into an identity crisis. They looked in the mirror every morning and saw, what, exactly? A rebuilding team? A developing team? A National League contender? Carlos Santana playing shortstop in one of Kapler's shifts?

A team that improves by 14 wins gets to ask itself, "How do we build from this?"

A team that falls out of playoff contention over the season's last eight weeks has to answer... other questions. And one of them is, "Where did this team go?"

If development is about finding out what you have, then the Phillies found out plenty in 2018: Chiefly, that there *is* talent on this team, but plenty of room for more. The talent they do have could use support in order to be sustained through a full 162-game slog. True progress, as it occurs, can be hard to watch, and nobody was harder to watch in the second half of 2018 than the Phillies. Their failures were amplified by their earlier success, and as the team cratered come September, it left a lot of people wondering: In a development year, is it *possible* to fail? Or do you just learn things you didn't want to know?

The Phillies sealed themselves off, letting little information about their future plans squeak out. This follows a trend started by a 2017 preseason incident involving a "sensitivity bus" in the clubhouse that created a stir and Kapler squelched without incident. Throughout the season, Kapler delivered robust, flowery monologues after games and GM Matt Klentak gave empty, diplomatic responses during infrequent appearances, both of which explained nothing. Combined with the team's lackluster performances, it created a frustration among fans, amplified by the team's early season success and ultimate deflation. We've now latched onto Middleton's comment that he would "even be a little bit stupid about" spending money to improve the team,

and created a world in which the Phillies are a failure in 2019 if they don't build a monstrosity so heavy with talent that it crushes both the NL East and the luxury tax threshold into dust.

"Losing streaks are funny," Gene Mauch, author of one of the least funny losing streaks of all time, once said. "If you lose at the beginning you got off to a bad start. If you lose in the middle of the season, you're in a slump. If you lose at the end, you're choking."

The 2018 Phillies, it was widely presumed, were always going to lose around 82 games. They just picked the wrong time to lose them.

Mauch also once said, "Baseball and malaria keep coming back." In the end, the Phillies finding the sort of persistence at the heart of both America's pastime and a mosquito-borne tropical disease will be what achieves them the relevance they seek. That, and the talented established players they can afford to acquire. Those will help. And with these attainable qualities, the Phillies can keep up with—and potentially outpace—the growing competitiveness of the NL East.

Along the way, they'll keep changing, keep failing, and keep learning from the failing. And if things really get hairy, they can always try switching the bullpens. ∎

—*Justin Klugh is an author of Baseball Prospectus.*

HITTERS

Jorge Alfaro C
Born: 06/11/93   Age: 26   Bats: R   Throws: R   Height: 6'2"   Weight: 225   Origin: International Free Agent, 2010

YEAR	TEAM	LVL	AGE	PA	R	2B	3B	HR	RBI	BB	K	SB	CS	AVG/OBP/SLG	DRC+	VORP	BABIP	BRR	FRAA	WARP
2016	REA	AA	23	435	68	21	2	15	67	22	105	3	2	.285/.325/.458	105	20.9	.347	-1.5	C(95): 14.8	3.8
2016	PHI	MLB	23	17	0	0	0	0	0	1	8	0	0	.125/.176/.125	60	-2.5	.250	-0.1	C(4): -0.6	-0.1
2017	LEH	AAA	24	350	34	13	2	7	43	16	113	1	1	.241/.291/.358	65	4.4	.345	-1.4	C(77): 4.8	0.4
2017	PHI	MLB	24	114	12	6	0	5	14	3	33	0	0	.318/.360/.514	90	10.7	.420	-1.5	C(28): -2.5, 1B(2): 0.1	0.0
2018	PHI	MLB	25	377	35	16	2	10	37	18	138	3	0	.262/.324/.407	77	24.2	.406	0.5	C(104): 12.2, 3B(1): 0.0	2.2
2019	PHI	MLB	26	378	37	13	1	9	38	23	126	1	0	.213/.282/.339	65	0.3	.310	-0.7	C 5	0.6

Breakout: 5%   Improve: 37%   Collapse: 8%   Attrition: 19%   MLB: 77%   *Comparables: Nick Hundley, J.P. Arencibia, Yan Gomes*

You're likely to read a lot of "if he could only..." in this chapter. You're bound to come across a few variations on "you can see the potential." It's really only fitting that all of that kicks off with Alfaro, who might be the most tantalizingly talented player on the Phillies roster. No, he hasn't put the whole jigsaw puzzle together yet and, no, he might not put it all together in 2019. It's some comfort knowing that all those pieces are definitely there, even if some are on the other end of the table, a few more are underneath the table, and you just can't seem to find that fourth corner. But improvement was there in 2018 in the form of framing and receiving, along with a more accurate throwing arm, and even some slight decreases in

YEAR	TEAM	P. COUNT	FRM RUNS	BLK RUNS	THRW RUNS	TOT RUNS
2016	PHI	576	0.0	-0.6	0.0	-0.4
2017	LEH	10516	2.0	-0.5	0.3	0.9
2017	PHI	4051	-2.6	0.2	-0.1	-2.9
2018	PHI	14100	12.3	-2.4	0.0	10.2
2019	PHI	14164	5.1	-1.4	0.3	4.0

that monstrous K% as the months went by. Alfaro has the raw talent to be an absolute force on both sides of the ball, but it's fair to wonder if he'll realize it before it's too late.

Aaron Altherr OF
Born: 01/14/91   Age: 28   Bats: R   Throws: R   Height: 6'5"   Weight: 215   Origin: Round 9, 2009 Draft (#287 overall)

YEAR	TEAM	LVL	AGE	PA	R	2B	3B	HR	RBI	BB	K	SB	CS	AVG/OBP/SLG	DRC+	VORP	BABIP	BRR	FRAA	WARP
2016	PHI	MLB	25	227	23	6	0	4	22	23	69	7	2	.197/.300/.288	70	-0.7	.280	0.3	RF(42): -2.6, LF(20): 3.0	-0.3
2017	PHI	MLB	26	412	58	24	5	19	65	32	104	5	4	.272/.340/.516	104	23.4	.328	0.4	LF(52): 4.3, RF(50): 1.6	2.1
2018	LEH	AAA	27	134	15	5	0	2	12	14	37	4	0	.244/.321/.336	90	-0.2	.333	-0.6	CF(21): -0.6, LF(8): 2.7	0.4
2018	PHI	MLB	27	285	28	11	1	8	38	36	91	3	2	.181/.295/.333	76	-5.0	.247	-1.2	RF(68): -4.2, CF(11): -0.4	-0.7
2019	PHI	MLB	28	275	31	11	1	8	31	27	77	5	2	.221/.309/.372	87	4.3	.290	0.0	LF 2, CF 0	0.7

Breakout: 4%   Improve: 38%   Collapse: 13%   Attrition: 34%   MLB: 81%   *Comparables: Travis Buck, Gabe Gross, Brent Lillibridge*

Altherr's kidnapping was an underreported story in 2018. Not a lot of media attention was paid to the case of a guy who had simply vanished, and the decoy put in his place was a poor imitation. I mean, sure, the doppelganger **looked** like Aaron Altherr, but this other fellow couldn't play baseball nearly as well. He had a huge spike in K rate, couldn't hit for nearly as much power, and took way more pitches (probably to try and limit the chances of exposing himself as a fake, the clever devil). The Phillies finally got wise to the ruse and optioned the impostor to Triple-A in late July, executed a covert black ops mission to find the original Altherr, and brought him back in September. How the club managed to miss the signs of Altherr's disappearance for so many months may forever remain an unsolved mystery, but they're probably just as happy as the rest of us to have seen the real thing finally find his way home after months of struggle.

Jose Bautista OF Born: 10/19/80 Age: 38 Bats: R Throws: R Height: 6'0" Weight: 205 Origin: Round 20, 2000 Draft (#599 overall)

YEAR	TEAM	LVL	AGE	PA	R	2B	3B	HR	RBI	BB	K	SB	CS	AVG/OBP/SLG	DRC+	VORP	BABIP	BRR	FRAA	WARP
2016	TOR	MLB	35	517	68	24	1	22	69	87	103	2	2	.234/.366/.452	119	11.3	.255	-2.0	RF(91): -6.1, 1B(1): 0.0	1.5
2017	TOR	MLB	36	686	92	27	0	23	65	84	170	6	3	.203/.308/.366	89	-4.4	.239	-0.3	RF(143): 12.9, 3B(8): 1.3	2.0
2018	GWN	AAA	37	44	6	1	0	1	5	6	8	1	1	.250/.386/.361	112	1.8	.296	0.2	3B(9): 0.8	0.3
2018	ATL	MLB	37	40	3	1	0	2	5	5	12	0	0	.143/.250/.343	107	-1.1	.143	-0.6	3B(8): -0.9	0.0
2018	NYN	MLB	37	302	37	13	0	9	37	51	84	2	2	.204/.351/.367	101	15.1	.268	0.0	RF(45): 0.4, LF(14): -0.6	0.9
2018	PHI	MLB	37	57	12	4	0	2	6	11	15	2	1	.244/.404/.467	110	5.1	.321	0.9	RF(19): 1.2, 3B(2): -0.2	0.4
2019	PHI	MLB	38	442	49	19	1	12	49	60	104	4	2	.219/.335/.367	97	9.4	.274	-0.5	RF 1, 3B 1	1.1

Breakout: 1%   Improve: 16%   Collapse: 8%   Attrition: 19%   MLB: 75%   *Comparables: Al Kaline, Larry Walker, Magglio Ordonez*

Amidst the death knell of the 2018 season, toward the end of August, the Phillies still clung faintly to the hope of resuscitation. Despite tumbling out of first and losing series after series, they were still just close enough to justify one more attempt. Why not, especially at the "meal at Mendy's" price of a player-to-be-named or cash? Ultimately, it made no difference, and since all folks are going to remember about the last gasps of 2018 is how mad they got over it all, it's easy to forget that this story's embodiment of Kenny Bania's favor—Bautista, of course—was actually pretty good! A triple slash of .244/.404/.467 for a month of part-time work ranks pretty low on the list of grievances about the late-stage 2018 Phillies. Whether that ends up being justification for one more go in 2019 for the now-38-year-old, or a swan song to a unique career arc of fourth chances and iconic moments crammed into a relatively short time, is mostly irrelevant. Either way, it bookends a Major League career with an ending like its beginning, even though each belies the magic that lay in between.

Alec Bohm 3B Born: 08/03/96 Age: 22 Bats: R Throws: R Height: 6'5" Weight: 225 Origin: Round 1, 2018 Draft (#3 overall)

YEAR	TEAM	LVL	AGE	PA	R	2B	3B	HR	RBI	BB	K	SB	CS	AVG/OBP/SLG	DRC+	VORP	BABIP	BRR	FRAA	WARP
2018	WPT	A-	21	121	9	5	1	0	12	10	19	1	0	.224/.314/.290	101	-0.4	.273	-0.9	3B(20): -2.7	0.0
2019	PHI	MLB	22	251	19	6	0	5	23	12	60	1	0	.179/.224/.268	30	-16.3	.215	-0.5	3B -1	-1.8

Breakout: 0%   Improve: 1%   Collapse: 0%   Attrition: 1%   MLB: 1%   *Comparables: Ryder Jones, Mitch Walding, Erik Gonzalez*

If you follow sports besides baseball and, deeper still, the Philadelphia teams within, you'll probably sense the comparisons about to come here. For those uninitiated, allow me to present a quick primer. Top Philly draftees, across all sports, have kicked off their careers in Philadelphia by being hurt within a year or so. From Joel Embiid and Ben Simmons with the 76ers to Carson Wentz with the Eagles to seemingly anybody who tries to play goalie for the Flyers, dudes just seem to get banged up right as they're getting started in their new home. Which brings us to Bohm, the third overall pick in the 2018 Draft out of Wichita State, who made it roughly three weeks before getting plunked in the knee by a pitch and missing a month. It *felt* inevitable. The good news is that Bohm made it back before the end of the season, a welcome divergence from the tales of Embiid, Simmons, and Jones. The crystal ball forecasts Bohm as a contact/power combo that's becoming more and more rare in this age of baseball, and though he didn't hit for a ton of power in his pro debut, there seems to be little doubt he could poke 20-plus homers with an average in the .300 area and, probably, garner some All-Star votes along the way. If he can make all of that work while sticking at third base, the Phillies may finally have the hot corner mainstay they've been in search of for so many years.

Asdrubal Cabrera INF Born: 11/13/85 Age: 33 Bats: B Throws: R Height: 6'0" Weight: 205 Origin: International Free Agent, 2002

YEAR	TEAM	LVL	AGE	PA	R	2B	3B	HR	RBI	BB	K	SB	CS	AVG/OBP/SLG	DRC+	VORP	BABIP	BRR	FRAA	WARP
2016	NYN	MLB	30	568	65	30	1	23	62	38	103	5	1	.280/.336/.474	111	45.7	.310	0.1	SS(135): -4.2	3.0
2017	NYN	MLB	31	540	66	32	0	14	59	50	83	3	2	.280/.351/.434	104	31.1	.310	-2.2	SS(45): -0.2, 3B(44): -1.1	1.9
2018	NYN	MLB	32	407	48	23	1	18	58	29	81	0	0	.277/.329/.488	101	28.9	.309	1.9	2B(90): -10.8	0.4
2018	PHI	MLB	32	185	20	13	0	5	17	12	38	0	0	.228/.286/.392	108	4.2	.266	0.5	SS(31): -0.6, 3B(22): -0.5	0.9
2019	PHI	MLB	33	550	69	30	2	17	62	41	101	3	1	.265/.327/.431	106	22.5	.303	0.0	2B -9, SS -1	1.3

Breakout: 3%   Improve: 45%   Collapse: 6%   Attrition: 7%   MLB: 95%   *Comparables: Brandon Phillips, Aaron Hill, Orlando Hudson*

Picking up Cabrera was a less-than-tacit admission by the Phillies' front office that starting shortstop Scott Kingery was no longer tolerable for 2018. The messaging was unavoidable. At least, if it had been Manny Machado, the upgrade could've been justified with a sentence as simple as "because it's Manny Machado." Asdrubal Cabrera, though? That one's different. Cabrera was imported because he stood to provide an offensive upgrade for a team stuck eternally making left turns in a whirlpool, inching closer to the trough by the game. His poor defense at shortstop would be palatable, so long as he provided the expected lift in the lineup his Mets numbers indicated. Well, he too fell into the black pit of despair that entombed the rest of the Phillies offense over the last two months, with the traditional Asdrubalian defense intact. Cabrera enters free agency for the third time as a 33-year-old infielder without a clear position but, apart from being a bit of a drag for the Phils, has been reliable with the bat for some time now. He's probably best tolerated by a team with a good glove to bring off the bench, but could probably be expected to post a SLG-heavy high-.700s OPS no matter where he ends up playing in 2019.

Maikel Franco 3B   Born: 08/26/92   Age: 26   Bats: R   Throws: R   Height: 6'1"   Weight: 215   Origin: International Free Agent, 2010

YEAR	TEAM	LVL	AGE	PA	R	2B	3B	HR	RBI	BB	K	SB	CS	AVG/OBP/SLG	DRC+	VORP	BABIP	BRR	FRAA	WARP
2016	PHI	MLB	23	630	67	23	1	25	88	40	106	1	1	.255/.306/.427	102	23.3	.271	-1.6	3B(148): -7.2	1.7
2017	PHI	MLB	24	623	66	29	1	24	76	41	95	0	0	.230/.281/.409	88	2.2	.234	-1.8	3B(144): -9.2, 1B(2): -0.1	0.3
2018	PHI	MLB	25	465	48	17	1	22	68	29	62	1	0	.270/.314/.467	112	21.7	.270	1.5	3B(117): -2.7	2.3
2019	PHI	MLB	26	502	57	23	2	19	67	36	72	1	0	.259/.317/.441	104	13.3	.271	-0.4	3B -7	0.7

Breakout: 4%   Improve: 53%   Collapse: 2%   Attrition: 9%   MLB: 93%   *Comparables: Wilmer Flores, Matt Duffy, Kyle Seager*

Fans have now spent three years awaiting the return of the 2015 version of Franco. The then-22-year-old's excellent half-season has never been replicated, much to the chagrin of those not content to continue waiting to see if roster lottery tickets can be cashed in, but 2018 provided the closest imitation and brightest glimmer of hope for an eventual reprisal. Franco, still just 26, was having a better season than his final line suggests, hitting .281/.321/.490 as late as August 22 before losing time to a wrist injury and, shortly thereafter, neck and shoulder problems sustained from a fall into a camera well. He still possesses the arm for third base, and an above-average hitter is by no means a **bad** thing to have handy. But the flaws of sub-par pitch recognition—saved only by a rather surprisingly exceptional ability to make contact—and lead-footed defensive range offset a lot of his offensive value, even in the face of a potential resurgence. What do you do with a player like that? A move to first subtracts his arm's value, and a move to a corner outfield spot does little to help a team beset by defensive issues. Such is the tragedy of players with plenty of talent, none of it supernatural.

Luis Garcia SS   Born: 10/01/00   Age: 18   Bats: B   Throws: R   Height: 5'11"   Weight: 170   Origin: International Free Agent, 2017

YEAR	TEAM	LVL	AGE	PA	R	2B	3B	HR	RBI	BB	K	SB	CS	AVG/OBP/SLG	DRC+	VORP	BABIP	BRR	FRAA	WARP
2018	PLL	RK	17	187	33	11	3	1	32	15	21	12	8	.369/.433/.488	130	22.6	.418	-0.1	SS(43): -2.1	1.2
2019	PHI	MLB	18	251	25	7	0	4	18	9	56	5	3	.211/.236/.287	37	-10.0	.255	-0.3	SS -1	-1.2

Comparables: Adalberto Mondesi, Wilmer Flores, Tommy Brown

No, no, not *that* **Luis Garcia**. This is a new one, and he plays shortstop. The Phillies signed Garcia with $2.5 million of their pool money in July 2017, and if a club with a history of finding diamonds in the rough for a fraction of that amount goes all-in for multiple millions, you figure they must really like this guy. The switch-hitter produced some satisfying numbers in the Gulf Coast League in 2018, and if he adds a little strength to his relatively lithe 5'11", 170-pound frame, there might even be a teensy bit of power projection to look forward to as he rounds out his teenage years. As it stands, Garcia was regarded as one of the top defenders in his J2 class, and a skilled defensive shortstop will always find a home.

Adam Haseley OF   Born: 04/12/96   Age: 23   Bats: L   Throws: L   Height: 6'1"   Weight: 195   Origin: Round 1, 2017 Draft (#8 overall)

YEAR	TEAM	LVL	AGE	PA	R	2B	3B	HR	RBI	BB	K	SB	CS	AVG/OBP/SLG	DRC+	VORP	BABIP	BRR	FRAA	WARP
2017	WPT	A-	21	158	18	9	0	2	18	14	28	5	3	.270/.350/.380	110	12.9	.321	2.6	CF(31): 0.1	0.9
2017	LWD	A	21	74	15	3	1	1	6	6	13	0	1	.258/.315/.379	97	6.1	.302	1.6	LF(12): 1.3, CF(4): 0.8	0.6
2018	CLR	A+	22	354	54	13	5	5	38	19	54	7	3	.300/.343/.415	110	15.2	.346	2.9	LF(39): -2.5, CF(30): -2.2	1.5
2018	REA	AA	22	159	23	4	0	6	17	16	19	0	1	.316/.403/.478	140	13.1	.327	-0.5	CF(28): -2.3, RF(5): -0.5	0.9
2019	PHI	MLB	23	251	27	8	0	7	24	13	52	1	0	.229/.271/.350	64	-3.1	.264	-0.4	CF 0, LF 0	-0.4

Breakout: 1%   Improve: 14%   Collapse: 4%   Attrition: 8%   MLB: 22%   *Comparables: Gary Brown, Matt Szczur, Logan Schafer*

Finally! A Phillies position prospect who didn't immediately begin to regress in his second pro year! Haseley's quick movement through the minor leagues has some wondering whether he might force his way into some Major League time later in 2019, though proving himself across more than 159 Double-A PAs has to happen first. With an ability to play any outfield position—LF is probably his best spot, even as the bulk of his starts have come in CF—and minimal platoon splits at the plate, the likes of Aaron Altherr and Nick Williams might be on the clock to show whether they can keep Haseley at arm's length from their share of playing time. Haseley loads like Bryce Harper at the plate, with a follow-through that packs only a portion of the latter's violence, but what he defers in the power department, he makes up for with still-quick hands, good plate coverage, and an ever-improving sense of the strike zone. It allows him to make consistent contact and avoid high-K output, and although that might transform him into something more like Denard Span than Harper, it's hard to find fault with anything that falls between either of those outcomes.

Cesar Hernandez 2B   Born: 05/23/90   Age: 29   Bats: B   Throws: R   Height: 5'10"   Weight: 160   Origin: International Free Agent, 2006

YEAR	TEAM	LVL	AGE	PA	R	2B	3B	HR	RBI	BB	K	SB	CS	AVG/OBP/SLG	DRC+	VORP	BABIP	BRR	FRAA	WARP
2016	PHI	MLB	26	622	67	14	11	6	39	66	116	17	13	.294/.371/.393	99	33.4	.363	-0.9	2B(149): -0.4, SS(4): -0.2	1.8
2017	PHI	MLB	27	577	85	26	6	9	34	61	104	15	5	.294/.373/.421	104	37.3	.353	4.2	2B(127): -2.4, SS(1): 0.0	2.4
2018	PHI	MLB	28	708	91	15	3	15	60	95	155	19	6	.253/.356/.362	105	30.1	.315	2.0	2B(154): 3.7	3.3
2019	PHI	MLB	29	594	76	23	4	11	54	66	118	15	6	.265/.353/.385	108	27.1	.322	1.6	2B 0	2.9

Breakout: 2%   Improve: 50%   Collapse: 5%   Attrition: 7%   MLB: 99%   *Comparables: Craig Biggio, Eddie Moore, Buddy Myer*

What happens when a player enters a season among the most underrated in the league and exits it with a step back in nearly every offensive category—save for home runs, weirdly enough—and a whole lot of roster redundancy staring him down? After steady improvement from 2015-17, Cesar seemed like a guy who'd enter his age 28 season ready to lock 'n' load. In the first half, things mostly went according to plan until, like a lot of other players on this Philly roster, the entire thing fell apart for some reason. Some surmise Hernandez played the latter half of the year on a bum foot after fouling a pitch off it, but whatever the cause, a .657 post-All-Star OPS can't quite be the star turn the Phillies might have hoped for.

Odubel Herrera CF Born: 12/29/91 Age: 27 Bats: L Throws: R Height: 5'11" Weight: 205 Origin: International Free Agent, 2008

YEAR	TEAM	LVL	AGE	PA	R	2B	3B	HR	RBI	BB	K	SB	CS	AVG/OBP/SLG	DRC+	VORP	BABIP	BRR	FRAA	WARP
2016	PHI	MLB	24	656	87	21	6	15	49	63	134	25	7	.286/.361/.420	106	45.7	.349	3.1	CF(155): 8.3	4.1
2017	PHI	MLB	25	563	67	42	3	14	56	31	126	8	5	.281/.325/.452	84	22.7	.345	-1.8	CF(133): 10.5	1.8
2018	PHI	MLB	26	597	64	19	3	22	71	38	122	5	2	.255/.310/.420	98	20.8	.290	0.8	CF(133): -1.1, RF(9): -1.2	1.8
2019	PHI	MLB	27	561	64	25	3	16	66	41	116	10	4	.260/.322/.412	102	21.4	.308	0.3	CF 3, LF -1	2.5

Breakout: 5%   Improve: 56%   Collapse: 3%   Attrition: 7%   MLB: 97%   *Comparables: Mickey Brantley, Carl Furillo, Marquis Grissom*

If one single player could embody all of the characteristics needed to bifurcate an entire fan base, well, you're reading about him. Herrera exists at the crossroads between Fun Street, Potential Avenue, Infuriating Boulevard, and Unique Lane, the four main thoroughfares of the planet he inhabits. For the first three years of his career, it was easier to soothe the nerves of everyone frustrated by his mercurial play by pointing to the overall numbers and saying "Hey, look, this isn't so bad!" When the ability to make that argument evaporates in the wake of a .215/.265/.368 stretch from May 22 on, it becomes tougher to keep the sports radio hosts at bay. There's plenty of talent contained in this alien's body, but if his downward trend continues on into 2019, more folks might start wondering how long it'd take to fuel his spaceship up.

Rhys Hoskins LF Born: 03/17/93 Age: 26 Bats: R Throws: R Height: 6'4" Weight: 225 Origin: Round 5, 2014 Draft (#142 overall)

YEAR	TEAM	LVL	AGE	PA	R	2B	3B	HR	RBI	BB	K	SB	CS	AVG/OBP/SLG	DRC+	VORP	BABIP	BRR	FRAA	WARP
2016	REA	AA	23	589	95	26	1	38	116	71	125	8	3	.281/.377/.566	162	38.2	.297	-1.1	1B(129): -0.6	5.0
2017	LEH	AAA	24	475	78	24	4	29	91	64	75	4	2	.284/.385/.581	168	37.6	.281	-0.6	1B(105): -9.8, LF(3): 0.2	3.5
2017	PHI	MLB	24	212	37	7	0	18	48	37	46	2	0	.259/.396/.618	157	27.4	.241	-0.1	LF(30): -0.8, 1B(27): -0.3	1.9
2018	PHI	MLB	25	660	89	38	0	34	96	87	150	5	3	.246/.354/.496	129	47.4	.272	0.2	LF(135): -0.7, 1B(17): 0.2	4.0
2019	PHI	MLB	26	616	94	33	2	30	86	79	127	4	2	.258/.363/.495	134	34.8	.288	0.0	1B -3	3.4

Breakout: 1%   Improve: 52%   Collapse: 5%   Attrition: 7%   MLB: 98%   *Comparables: Matt Joyce, Derek Dietrich, Carlos Santana*

Hoskins has played a lot of baseball these last two years. This past season, the only games he missed were the nine he was forced to miss immediately after breaking his jaw on a foul ball, and he rather promptly made up for it by flying to Japan to take part in the six-game Japan Series exhibition in November. In 2017, between the Majors and minors, Hoskins played in a combined **165** games. It's a testament to his durability that Hoskins didn't really show signs of wear and tear or fatigue at the end of either marathon season, though '18 did contain a handful of cold streaks sprinkled throughout. And while 2018 seemed to position him more as the next Pat Burrell than Paul Goldschmidt, we've all evolved in our baseball knowledge enough to understand that any player who falls anywhere between those two endpoints provides plenty of offensive value. Defense, on the other hand, is something of a problem. It certainly would've made Matt Klentak's job a bit easier if Hoskins had adapted to left field the way the club hoped he would entering the year, but...well, he didn't, and the Phillies were left with a glut of corner-only players who couldn't handle the corners. It's a comfort to know that Hoskins's bat will play in any lineup, no matter where his glove gets stuck, but his pitchers are likely to appreciate him more now that his home is at first base.

Scott Kingery SS Born: 04/29/94 Age: 25 Bats: R Throws: R Height: 5'10" Weight: 180 Origin: Round 2, 2015 Draft (#48 overall)

YEAR	TEAM	LVL	AGE	PA	R	2B	3B	HR	RBI	BB	K	SB	CS	AVG/OBP/SLG	DRC+	VORP	BABIP	BRR	FRAA	WARP
2016	CLR	A+	22	420	60	29	3	3	28	33	54	26	5	.293/.360/.411	113	26.0	.334	1.6	2B(88): 7.7	2.7
2016	REA	AA	22	166	16	7	0	2	18	5	36	4	2	.250/.273/.333	79	-0.6	.306	1.9	2B(37): -1.4	0.1
2017	REA	AA	23	317	62	18	5	18	44	28	51	19	3	.313/.379/.608	148	35.0	.324	2.7	2B(59): 1.7	3.4
2017	LEH	AAA	23	286	41	11	3	8	21	13	58	10	2	.294/.337/.449	105	10.2	.348	-1.2	2B(54): 0.9, 3B(4): 0.3	1.0
2018	PHI	MLB	24	484	55	23	2	8	35	24	126	10	3	.226/.267/.338	72	4.3	.291	2.1	SS(119): -3.9, 3B(10): -0.2	0.3
2019	PHI	MLB	25	472	51	20	2	11	46	25	116	12	3	.232/.281/.361	73	0.8	.289	1.5	2B 1, 3B -1	0.1

Breakout: 6%   Improve: 45%   Collapse: 14%   Attrition: 39%   MLB: 93%   *Comparables: Eduardo Nunez, Eduardo Escobar, Cory Spangenberg*

There were risks. There were reasons to be skeptical. There were causes for caution. Presumably cognizant of them all, the Phillies gave Scott Kingery a six-year Major League deal before he'd played a single MLB game, and he responded by having one of the worst offensive performances of any regular in the league. Kingery grabbed the attention of the greater Philadelphia area thanks to a scorching-hot half-season in Double-A in 2017 and little else; he'd dropped a .606 OPS in 37 games at the same level just a year prior. It's hard enough adjusting to Major League pitching on its own, but Kingery was also tasked with learning how to be the everyday shortstop on-the-fly and on the heels of an attempt to play him at third base that failed spectacularly. Kingery was adequate at short, thanks in large part to clearly being a gifted athlete whose range was up to the challenge but whose arm clearly belongs at second. Everything about Kingery's 2018 felt forced: the contract, the position, the steadfast refusal to option him even as his struggles deepened. There's no reason to think Kingery couldn't be an elite defensive second baseman given his athletic toolset, and he'd be put in a position to succeed by playing there regularly, but he and incumbent Cesar Hernandez will have to coexist for another season.

Andrew Knapp C Born: 11/09/91 Age: 27 Bats: B Throws: R Height: 6'1" Weight: 195 Origin: Round 2, 2013 Draft (#53 overall)

YEAR	TEAM	LVL	AGE	PA	R	2B	3B	HR	RBI	BB	K	SB	CS	AVG/OBP/SLG	DRC+	VORP	BABIP	BRR	FRAA	WARP
2016	LEH	AAA	24	443	55	24	1	8	46	37	107	2	2	.266/.330/.390	100	22.3	.343	0.9	C(104): 12.2, 1B(1): 0.0	3.4
2017	PHI	MLB	25	204	26	8	1	3	13	31	56	1	0	.257/.368/.368	85	12.1	.360	0.1	C(53): -10.2, 1B(1): 0.0	-0.4
2018	LEH	AAA	26	25	2	1	0	0	1	5	6	0	0	.250/.400/.300	94	1.3	.357	-0.2	C(4): 0.2, 3B(1): -0.6	0.0
2018	PHI	MLB	26	215	19	6	2	4	15	24	75	1	0	.198/.294/.316	72	5.6	.303	1.2	C(53): -5.4, 1B(1): 0.0	-0.2
2019	PHI	MLB	27	283	29	11	1	6	27	33	84	1	0	.215/.311/.334	83	5.9	.301	0.4	C -5, 1B 0	0.0

Breakout: 4%   Improve: 36%   Collapse: 12%   Attrition: 24%   MLB: 87%   *Comparables: Martin Maldonado, Hank Conger, JD Closser*

If you squint or tilt your head just right while looking at Knapp's 2017 numbers, you could almost start to see a silhouette of early Stephen Vogt appear out of the negative space like some sort of apparition. Here was a catcher by title—if not in proficiency—who could work a count, keep the strikeout totals manageable, and even provide a hint of pop. With a little luck, you'd think, that Vogt Ghost could become a little more corporeal in 2018, and the Phillies could have a neat little contingency in their back pocket for 2018. Well, you know

YEAR	TEAM	P. COUNT	FRM RUNS	BLK RUNS	THRW RUNS	TOT RUNS
2017	PHI	7630	-6.1	-1.6	-1.2	-8.8
2018	PHI	6630	-3.5	-0.4	-0.3	-4.3
2019	PHI	8398	-4.0	-1.1	-0.2	-5.3

what they say about the best-laid plans of Phanatics and men. Instead of breaking out, Knapp fell backward in nearly every aspect of his game: His strikeout rate soared as his walk rate plummeted, he whiffed more, and his FRAA ranked 99th among 117 qualified catchers. Given the Phillies' dearth of upper-level catching depth, Knapp was still the team's second-best catching option. But with a clear preference for cultivating Jorge Alfaro's game and an intriguing farmhand in Deivi Grullon waiting in the wings, don't expect the Phillies to have many qualms about seeking out an upgrade over Knapp for the backup backstop post.

Andrew McCutchen RF Born: 10/10/86 Age: 32 Bats: R Throws: R Height: 5'11" Weight: 195 Origin: Round 1, 2005 Draft (#11 overall)

YEAR	TEAM	LVL	AGE	PA	R	2B	3B	HR	RBI	BB	K	SB	CS	AVG/OBP/SLG	DRC+	VORP	BABIP	BRR	FRAA	WARP
2016	PIT	MLB	29	675	81	26	3	24	79	69	143	6	7	.256/.336/.430	111	30.5	.297	-0.3	CF(151): -9.4	2.4
2017	PIT	MLB	30	650	94	30	2	28	88	73	116	11	5	.279/.363/.486	122	50.0	.305	1.0	CF(139): -10.4, RF(13): -0.8	3.1
2018	SFN	MLB	31	568	65	28	2	15	55	73	123	13	6	.255/.357/.415	116	22.3	.309	-3.7	RF(128): -4.9	1.5
2018	NYA	MLB	31	114	18	2	1	5	10	22	22	1	3	.253/.421/.471	120	9.0	.279	0.3	RF(15): -1.9, LF(12): 0.0	0.4
2019	PHI	MLB	32	625	87	30	3	20	71	74	129	10	6	.261/.357/.437	120	31.5	.310	-0.7	RF -7	2.6

Breakout: 0%   Improve: 32%   Collapse: 2%   Attrition: 5%   MLB: 97%   *Comparables: Ben Zobrist, Milton Bradley, J.D. Drew*

Andrew McCutchen and Giancarlo Stanton in the same Yankees outfield sounds like a 2013 Yankees fan message board fever dream, and yet here it was in 2018. Stanton is mostly the same player as then, but McCutchen most certainly is not, despite his usefulness in the Bronx. Necessitated by Aaron Judge's injury, Brian Cashman waited until the latest possible moment to both get his bat and minimize the bill, acquiring him on the last day before the trade waiver deadline. McCutchen rewarded the move with an .892 OPS in the month of September. If his short stint showed anything, it's that he is not going to fall off the map after becoming merely serviceable after his time in Pittsburgh. The defense will become completely untenable soon, but by hitting about 20% better than your average player, a team would be more than happy to take that trade-off in the short term.

Mickey Moniak CF Born: 05/13/98 Age: 21 Bats: L Throws: R Height: 6'2" Weight: 185 Origin: Round 1, 2016 Draft (#1 overall)

YEAR	TEAM	LVL	AGE	PA	R	2B	3B	HR	RBI	BB	K	SB	CS	AVG/OBP/SLG	DRC+	VORP	BABIP	BRR	FRAA	WARP
2016	PHL	RK	18	194	27	11	4	1	28	11	35	10	4	.284/.340/.409	112	9.0	.345	3.0	CF(30): 4.6, LF(2): 0.1	1.5
2017	LWD	A	19	509	53	22	6	5	44	28	109	11	7	.236/.284/.341	84	13.3	.292	-0.1	CF(115): -9.8	-0.5
2018	CLR	A+	20	465	50	28	3	5	55	22	100	6	5	.270/.304/.383	97	6.6	.334	-0.1	CF(99): -7.3, LF(9): -0.3	0.5
2019	PHI	MLB	21	251	20	8	0	5	24	6	62	2	1	.211/.230/.307	33	-11.4	.260	-0.5	CF -3, LF 0	-1.5

Breakout: 2%   Improve: 2%   Collapse: 0%   Attrition: 2%   MLB: 2%   *Comparables: Xavier Avery, Abraham Almonte, Rafael Ortega*

On the surface, it looks like Moniak made only slight improvements from 2017 into 2018. You look at the sub-.700 OPS and grimace a little, thinking the former No. 1 overall pick is still falling well short of expectations. But Moniak's year requires a closer look, and upon that further examination, it seems like there's a legitimate reason to be excited about what he can do in 2019. From late May through the end of the season, Moniak slashed .301/.342/.460, dramatically reducing his strikeout rate along the way. He might not be beating down the door for a spot with the Big League club anytime soon, nor is he all that likely to even return to Top Prospect lists heading into '19. But seeing as he doesn't turn 21 until May, it remains far too soon to call him a bust or rule him out of the Phillies' future plans altogether, assuming the adjustments he made from May onward prove sustainable.

Jose Pujols RF Born: 09/29/95 Age: 23 Bats: R Throws: R Height: 6'3" Weight: 175 Origin: International Free Agent, 2012

YEAR	TEAM	LVL	AGE	PA	R	2B	3B	HR	RBI	BB	K	SB	CS	AVG/OBP/SLG	DRC+	VORP	BABIP	BRR	FRAA	WARP
2016	LWD	A	20	549	67	21	3	24	82	44	179	5	3	.241/.306/.440	110	18.5	.322	-2.7	RF(113): 4.7	1.8
2017	CLR	A+	21	352	24	10	1	8	29	23	150	2	2	.194/.247/.305	60	-11.7	.324	-1.7	RF(63): 1.4, LF(1): -0.2	-1.3
2018	CLR	A+	22	387	56	16	4	18	58	33	127	1	1	.301/.364/.523	129	23.7	.425	-3.0	RF(88): 3.9	2.2
2018	REA	AA	22	104	11	2	0	4	18	14	35	2	2	.270/.365/.427	92	5.0	.392	0.2	RF(24): -2.1, CF(1): -0.2	-0.1
2019	PHI	MLB	23	251	23	7	0	8	28	15	97	1	0	.193/.240/.331	46	-10.0	.281	-0.6	RF 1, CF 0	-1.0

Breakout: 4%   Improve: 9%   Collapse: 2%   Attrition: 10%   MLB: 17%   *Comparables: Willy Garcia, Jamie Romak, Dylan Cozens*

What makes Pujols's 2018 breakout surprising isn't necessarily that it happened in the first place, but the magnitude by which his numbers jumped. After a washout 2017, Pujols returned to the Florida State League with a steadied hand and improved approach that helped him make more out of the moments he made contact. He still has a long road to travel in that whole "make contact" journey, and it isn't surprising to see so much of his slash line's improvement attributed to a BABIP spike, but things appear to finally be moving in the right direction nonetheless. If he's going to have any shot at the Bigs, it nearly goes without saying that striking out 35 percent of the time at every level has to stop. Even as Pujols was punched out in 35 of his 104 Double-A PAs, though, he nudged his walk rate to the highest point it's ever been, and it's clear there's far more to work with entering a pivotal 2019 than there was at this same point last year. The Phillies slipped him through the Rule 5 Draft once again, but this will be his last chance to prove worthy of a 40-man spot before he accrues enough pro time to hit free agency next offseason.

Roman Quinn CF   Born: 05/14/93   Age: 26   Bats: B   Throws: R   Height: 5'10"   Weight: 170   Origin: Round 2, 2011 Draft (#66 overall)

YEAR	TEAM	LVL	AGE	PA	R	2B	3B	HR	RBI	BB	K	SB	CS	AVG/OBP/SLG	DRC+	VORP	BABIP	BRR	FRAA	WARP
2016	REA	AA	23	322	58	14	6	6	25	30	68	31	8	.287/.361/.441	102	24.5	.357	9.6	CF(62): -6.6, LF(4): -0.8	1.9
2016	PHI	MLB	23	69	10	4	0	0	6	8	19	5	1	.263/.373/.333	72	3.9	.395	3.8	LF(12): -0.1, RF(4): 0.1	0.2
2017	LEH	AAA	24	197	24	8	3	2	13	18	49	10	4	.274/.344/.389	82	10.2	.368	3.8	CF(38): -0.4, LF(4): -0.2	0.5
2018	LEH	AAA	25	107	14	2	3	2	11	8	19	13	1	.296/.349/.439	92	6.7	.351	3.5	CF(21): 0.3, RF(2): -0.2	0.6
2018	PHI	MLB	25	143	13	6	4	2	12	10	35	10	4	.260/.317/.412	83	4.0	.340	-0.9	CF(30): 0.9, RF(5): 1.3	0.3
2019	PHI	MLB	26	259	31	9	2	5	22	20	66	16	4	.217/.285/.333	71	0.9	.277	0.1	CF 0	0.1

Breakout: 6%   Improve: 38%   Collapse: 16%   Attrition: 23%   MLB: 74%   *Comparables: Abraham Almonte, Lorenzo Cain, James Jones*

For a hot minute, among the flurry of trades they made in July and August, it seemed like the Phillies' best acquisition was going to come from within. Quinn figuratively—and almost nearly literally—flew out of the gate, going 18-for-40 in the second half of August. He then hit .145 in September, and even though that cold spell somehow wasn't enough to quiet calls for his supplanting of incumbent center fielder Odubel Herrera, it certainly tempered thoughts of Quinn being a favorite to land a starting job in 2019. Assuming he can ever put his injury issues behind him, or at least catch up to and run alongside them, Quinn should provide a good deal of value as a quick switch-hitter without much of a platoon split. Those injury issues can't simply be hand-waved away, as they've limited him to fewer than 90 games in every one of his seven professional seasons, so the Phillies signed Andrew McCutchen, happy to spread out Quinn's playing time as the team's fourth outfielder.

Jean Segura SS   Born: 03/17/90   Age: 29   Bats: R   Throws: R   Height: 5'10"   Weight: 205   Origin: International Free Agent, 2007

YEAR	TEAM	LVL	AGE	PA	R	2B	3B	HR	RBI	BB	K	SB	CS	AVG/OBP/SLG	DRC+	VORP	BABIP	BRR	FRAA	WARP
2016	ARI	MLB	26	694	102	41	7	20	64	39	101	33	10	.319/.368/.499	120	54.8	.353	6.5	2B(142): 5.3, SS(23): 0.2	5.4
2017	SEA	MLB	27	566	80	30	2	11	45	34	83	22	8	.300/.349/.427	97	27.6	.339	2.1	SS(124): -8.9	1.8
2018	SEA	MLB	28	632	91	29	3	10	63	32	69	20	11	.304/.341/.415	99	35.9	.327	-1.0	SS(144): 3.4	3.1
2019	PHI	MLB	29	616	72	30	4	12	66	40	83	22	9	.283/.339/.415	107	29.7	.312	1.7	SS -3	2.9

Breakout: 3%   Improve: 42%   Collapse: 2%   Attrition: 6%   MLB: 100%   *Comparables: Erick Aybar, Elvis Andrus, Rafael Furcal*

Segura was good again in 2018. Really just quite good at playing shortstop, and hitting, and running around out there. He was just really good and absolutely not even a little bit better than that. It's possible that calling him a slightly above-average shortstop on a reasonable contract sounds like faint praise, but unless your team is blessed with a Lindor or a Correa, chances are Segura would be a big improvement over your in-house options. More than any other position on the diamond, perhaps, we tend to think of shortstop as wizards or failures, but for a Phillies fanbase, "fine" will feel awfully refreshing. At 29, his hit tool will carry him anywhere in the middle infield his team needs him for at least the foreseeable future. He's really just quite good.

Nick Williams RF   Born: 09/08/93   Age: 25   Bats: L   Throws: L   Height: 6'3"   Weight: 195   Origin: Round 2, 2012 Draft (#93 overall)

YEAR	TEAM	LVL	AGE	PA	R	2B	3B	HR	RBI	BB	K	SB	CS	AVG/OBP/SLG	DRC+	VORP	BABIP	BRR	FRAA	WARP
2016	LEH	AAA	22	527	78	33	6	13	64	19	136	6	4	.258/.287/.427	90	10.7	.325	-0.7	LF(50): 1.9, CF(38): 2.0	1.0
2017	LEH	AAA	23	306	43	16	2	15	44	16	90	5	4	.280/.328/.511	110	14.6	.358	0.4	RF(37): 6.2, LF(17): 1.5	1.7
2017	PHI	MLB	23	343	45	14	4	12	55	20	97	1	2	.288/.338/.473	93	19.3	.375	-0.8	RF(58): -5.9, CF(16): -2.0	-0.3
2018	PHI	MLB	24	448	53	12	3	17	50	32	111	3	2	.256/.324/.425	102	11.0	.312	-1.4	RF(95): -9.8, LF(19): -1.5	-0.1
2019	PHI	MLB	25	413	47	18	2	15	52	28	106	3	2	.246/.311/.416	102	12.2	.307	-0.8	LF -3, RF -1	0.9

Breakout: 2%   Improve: 47%   Collapse: 8%   Attrition: 18%   MLB: 94%   *Comparables: Oswaldo Arcia, Travis Snider, Jorge Bonifacio*

How do you properly describe a single season in which one player experiences both the "Eureka!" moment of things beginning to click and, later, the forlorn walking back of that same revelation? Whatever phrase you deem best, it's likely some form of the word "uncertain" will be lurking nearby. So it goes for Williams, who looked to be experiencing a breakthrough with regular starts from late May through the end of August: His .270/.339/.457 line in 307 plate appearances is awfully close to the slash Williams put up in his stellar rookie season. Then September hit, shoulder and finger injuries surfaced, and Williams barely (but successfully) played enough to tank his batting line. In spite of all that, it feels reasonable to take heart in Williams's overall improvements in pitch recognition and plate discipline. He remains a bit messy in right field, and his arm might be better suited to left field than right, but adjusting Williams's position is rather low on the Phillies' list of priorities right now. He's a mid-division regular who'll command more respect at the plate if his disciplinary adjustments are for real, with the potential to surprise those who may have missed or dismissed his midsummer hot streak.

PITCHERS

Jose Alvarez LHP   Born: 05/06/89   Age: 30   Bats: L   Throws: L   Height: 5'11"   Weight: 180   Origin: International Free Agent, 2005

YEAR	TEAM	LVL	AGE	W	L	SV	G	GS	IP	H	HR	BB/9	K/9	K	GB%	BABIP	WHIP	ERA	DRA	WARP	MPH	FB%	WHF	CSP
2016	SLC	AAA	27	1	0	0	5	0	7¹	5	0	6.1	8.6	7	50%	.278	1.36	2.45	2.93	0.2				
2016	ANA	MLB	27	1	3	0	64	0	57¹	71	4	2.4	8.0	51	46%	.362	1.50	3.45	4.87	0.1	92.9	45.8	11.6	47.1
2017	SLC	AAA	28	0	0	0	9	0	11²	10	0	1.5	7.7	10	44%	.294	1.03	2.31	4.27	0.1				
2017	ANA	MLB	28	0	3	1	64	0	48²	50	7	2.2	8.3	45	39%	.309	1.27	3.88	4.35	0.4	92.8	55.9	12	45.6
2018	ANA	MLB	29	6	4	1	76	0	63	51	3	3.1	8.4	59	48%	.274	1.16	2.71	3.82	0.8	93.3	57	11.5	47.9
2019	PHI	MLB	30	2	1	0	36	0	38¹	35	5	3.4	9.2	39	44%	.308	1.30	4.03	4.48	0.2	92.3	53.7	11.6	46.8

Breakout: 28%   Improve: 55%   Collapse: 23%   Attrition: 13%   MLB: 92%   *Comparables: Burke Badenhop, Jeremy Jeffress, Brandon League*

Alvarez is a low-ceiling, high-floor middle-inning option. There is nothing incredible to say about him other than he does his job decently. He is so dull, his clubhouse nickname is Jose Alvarez. His favorite spice is oxygen. His fastball tops out at 92 mph. He wrote his dissertation on the practical applications of linoleum. He's a left-handed reliever and has been perfectly dependable for four years, and will continue to be dependable for a couple more. Middle relievers are like umpires; the ones you recognize are usually the ones with major flaws. When the bases are loaded and the manager needs some sanity in the game, sometimes you want a pitcher out there with a proclivity for watching paint dry.

Victor Arano RHP Born: 02/07/95   Age: 24   Bats: R   Throws: R   Height: 6'2"   Weight: 200   Origin: International Free Agent, 2013

YEAR	TEAM	LVL	AGE	W	L	SV	G	GS	IP	H	HR	BB/9	K/9	K	GB%	BABIP	WHIP	ERA	DRA	WARP	MPH	FB%	WHF	CSP
2016	CLR	A+	21	4	1	4	35	0	63	52	4	2.1	10.1	71	38%	.296	1.06	2.29	2.87	1.6				
2016	REA	AA	21	1	1	1	11	0	16²	11	2	2.2	13.0	24	47%	.250	0.90	2.16	1.43	0.7				
2017	REA	AA	22	1	2	9	32	0	38²	39	7	2.6	8.8	38	40%	.296	1.29	4.19	3.39	0.6				
2017	PHI	MLB	22	1	0	0	10	0	10²	6	0	3.4	11.0	13	44%	.240	0.94	1.69	2.82	0.3	95.5	44.2	20.4	46.1
2018	PHI	MLB	23	1	2	3	60	0	59¹	54	6	2.6	9.1	60	40%	.296	1.20	2.73	3.56	0.9	95.8	40.2	16.9	45.7
2019	PHI	MLB	24	2	1	0	36	0	38¹	34	5	3.3	10.2	43	40%	.310	1.26	3.98	4.44	0.2	95.6	41.9	17.9	47.3

Breakout: 31%   Improve: 48%   Collapse: 9%   Attrition: 19%   MLB: 69%   *Comparables: Manny Corpas, Brandon Beachy, Chris Ray*

It's not a stretch to consider Arano the best reliever in the entire Phillies organization. The 24-year-old may not have the best pure stuff—that title belongs to Seranthony Dominguez—but Arano's total package of lively four-seam and two-seam fastballs with a disappearing slider have made him awfully tough to square up thus far. He wasn't quite as dominant over a full season as he was in his short time up in 2017, but he was still awfully effective. He'll even show some multi-inning flexibility when needed, which feels more and more like a critical characteristic of a bullpen piece in this age. The Phillies aren't light on vibrant relief arms, but not only is Arano already arguably the best among them, better things might still be in store.

Jake Arrieta RHP Born: 03/06/86   Age: 33   Bats: R   Throws: R   Height: 6'4"   Weight: 225   Origin: Round 5, 2007 Draft (#159 overall)

YEAR	TEAM	LVL	AGE	W	L	SV	G	GS	IP	H	HR	BB/9	K/9	K	GB%	BABIP	WHIP	ERA	DRA	WARP	MPH	FB%	WHF	CSP
2016	CHN	MLB	30	18	8	0	31	31	197¹	138	16	3.5	8.7	190	54%	.241	1.08	3.10	2.76	5.9	96.3	65.7	11.4	46.2
2017	CHN	MLB	31	14	10	0	30	30	168¹	150	23	2.9	8.7	163	46%	.279	1.22	3.53	4.09	2.8	93.8	64.3	9.3	49.1
2018	PHI	MLB	32	10	11	0	31	31	172²	165	21	3.0	7.2	138	52%	.289	1.29	3.96	4.08	2.4	94.8	55.8	8.8	50.1
2019	PHI	MLB	33	10	10	0	30	30	171	145	21	3.1	8.4	160	49%	.281	1.19	4.07	4.51	1.6	93.9	60.5	9.6	48.2

Breakout: 13%   Improve: 45%   Collapse: 17%   Attrition: 10%   MLB: 96%   *Comparables: Zack Greinke, Tim Hudson, Clay Buchholz*

Compared to 2017, Arrieta had a higher ERA, lower K%, higher BB%, fewer swinging strikes, fewer quality starts, and permitted more and harder contact across 4.1 more innings...but saw increases over his 2017 WARP and rWAR. It's hard to discern which is more true: That Arrieta is in the midst of a continuing decline, or that he's still above-average in the eyes of a league whose attitudes toward starting pitchers continues to shift rapidly around him. (Or that going from the Cubs' defense to the Phillies interpretation is an act of courage worthy of a medal.) Make no mistake: His drops in power metrics like strikeouts and whiffs were even sharper this year than last, and the Snake of 2015-16 isn't walking through that door. But his velocity recovered, and his health held up through 30-plus starts for a fourth consecutive year, and there's something to be said for both of those accomplishments in the face of pointed offseason skepticism even as he appeared to lose steam over his final four starts in September. However much he has left in the tank, he'll need better backup from his defense if he's to stand any chance of successfully completing this late-stage metamorphosis into a pitch-to-contact style.

Luis Avilan LHP Born: 07/19/89   Age: 29   Bats: L   Throws: L   Height: 6'2"   Weight: 220   Origin: International Free Agent, 2005

YEAR	TEAM	LVL	AGE	W	L	SV	G	GS	IP	H	HR	BB/9	K/9	K	GB%	BABIP	WHIP	ERA	DRA	WARP	MPH	FB%	WHF	CSP
2016	OKL	AAA	26	0	3	4	33	0	34	35	3	4.2	9.8	37	49%	.337	1.50	4.24	3.07	0.7				
2016	LAN	MLB	26	3	0	0	27	0	19²	12	0	4.6	12.8	28	55%	.286	1.12	3.20	3.07	0.4	94.4	45.7	18.6	37.4
2017	LAN	MLB	27	2	3	0	61	0	46	42	2	4.3	10.2	52	56%	.342	1.39	2.93	3.33	0.9	94.3	41.7	15.1	33
2018	CHA	MLB	28	2	1	2	58	0	39²	40	2	3.2	10.4	46	37%	.352	1.36	3.86	4.83	0.0	92.3	35.5	10.8	42.3
2018	PHI	MLB	28	0	0	0	12	0	5²	4	1	6.4	7.9	5	38%	.200	1.41	3.18	5.26	0.0	91.9	41.8	13.3	43.6
2019	PHI	MLB	29	2	1	1	38	0	40²	36	5	4.3	10.4	47	44%	.314	1.36	4.16	4.64	0.1	92.7	39.4	13.5	38

Breakout: 33%   Improve: 46%   Collapse: 24%   Attrition: 20%   MLB: 91%   *Comparables: Brandon League, Bobby Parnell, Jared Burton*

There are a number of side effects to the new wave of pitcher management. Most have thus far simply been growing pains, the products of stirring a tablespoon of discomfort into the drink of expectation and predictability that had come to define the starter-setup-closer paradigm of the modern game. The past twenty years gently pushed those walls out, slowly, with match-up play and one-batter specialists finding more frequent—if still necessarily brief—time in the spotlight. But while relief appearances of one single batter faced rose above 1,400 league-wide in 2015, they have dropped back below 1,200 in each of the past three seasons as teams lean toward stretch types who can handle wraparound appearances and multiple innings. All of this brings us to Avilan: A lefty specialist in a world that, suddenly, teams might lean on less and less. How does a pitcher of limited utility fit on staffs that might regularly ask for more and more coverage from their relievers? Avilan, to his credit, is good at what he does. A premature end would be a plight of circumstance, not ability. But as the game reshapes itself around him, it's fair to wonder how much longer Avilan and his specialist kin can reliably find homes in Major League bullpens.

Austin Davis LHP Born: 02/03/93 Age: 26 Bats: L Throws: L Height: 6'4" Weight: 245 Origin: Round 12, 2014 Draft (#352 overall)

YEAR	TEAM	LVL	AGE	W	L	SV	G	GS	IP	H	HR	BB/9	K/9	K	GB%	BABIP	WHIP	ERA	DRA	WARP	MPH	FB%	WHF	CSP
2016	LWD	A	23	1	0	1	7	0	13	6	0	1.4	11.8	17	45%	.207	0.62	0.00	2.20	0.4				
2016	CLR	A+	23	0	1	1	11	1	15¹	16	0	2.3	10.6	18	40%	.356	1.30	5.28	2.07	0.5				
2017	CLR	A+	24	2	0	1	10	0	22¹	19	1	1.2	11.7	29	39%	.327	0.99	2.01	2.12	0.7				
2017	REA	AA	24	4	2	1	32	0	47	45	3	3.8	8.8	46	44%	.328	1.38	2.87	4.07	0.4				
2018	REA	AA	25	1	1	0	4	0	7	7	1	2.6	12.9	10	68%	.333	1.29	3.86	2.72	0.2				
2018	LEH	AAA	25	0	1	0	24	0	31¹	23	2	2.3	11.5	40	37%	.284	0.99	2.59	3.17	0.7				
2018	PHI	MLB	25	1	2	0	32	0	34²	35	4	3.1	9.9	38	42%	.326	1.36	4.15	4.29	0.3	95.5	47.9	12.4	47.6
2019	*PHI*	*MLB*	*26*	*1*	*1*	*0*	*26*	*0*	*27¹*	*24*	*4*	*3.8*	*10.3*	*31*	*41%*	*.310*	*1.31*	*4.19*	*4.67*	*0.1*	*95.1*	*48.7*	*12.6*	*48.4*

Breakout: 17%   Improve: 24%   Collapse: 8%   Attrition: 18%   MLB: 44%   *Comparables: Lucas Luetge, Royce Ring, Mayckol Guaipe*

You don't have to look too closely at Davis's game logs to see where it all began to crumble for the 25-year-old rookie. On July 24, Davis pitched in his third straight game and threw 35 pitches, holding down the 14th and 15th innings of a game that eventually went 16. It was the first time Davis had worked three straight as a pro, and the remainder of his season—directly or indirectly—bore the effects of that effort. Davis would eventually miss two weeks in August with a lower back issue, the same ailment that felled him in 2016, and opponents teed off on him (.940 OPS) even when he was healthy. When everything's going right, Davis will sit 94 with a slider and good separation on his tumbling changeup, and he carries a minor league usage pedigree geared toward higher pitch counts and multiple innings of work. The 2014 12th-rounder has some durability concerns to shake, but otherwise shows all the makings of a reliable bullpen piece after the winter allows for a hard reset.

Enyel De Los Santos RHP Born: 12/25/95 Age: 23 Bats: R Throws: R Height: 6'3" Weight: 170 Origin: International Free Agent, 2014

YEAR	TEAM	LVL	AGE	W	L	SV	G	GS	IP	H	HR	BB/9	K/9	K	GB%	BABIP	WHIP	ERA	DRA	WARP	MPH	FB%	WHF	CSP
2016	FTW	A	20	3	2	0	11	7	52²	38	2	2.4	7.7	45	41%	.242	0.99	2.91	3.50	0.9				
2016	LEL	A+	20	5	3	0	15	15	68¹	70	11	3.2	6.8	52	38%	.291	1.38	4.35	4.19	1.0				
2017	SAN	AA	21	10	6	0	26	24	150	131	12	2.9	8.3	138	45%	.290	1.19	3.78	3.25	3.4				
2018	LEH	AAA	22	10	5	0	22	22	126²	104	12	3.1	7.8	110	42%	.264	1.16	2.63	3.78	2.5				
2018	PHI	MLB	22	1	0	0	7	2	19	19	2	3.8	7.1	15	51%	.309	1.42	4.74	4.97	0.0	97.1	60.3	10.8	50.2
2019	*PHI*	*MLB*	*23*	*2*	*3*	*0*	*8*	*8*	*40*	*36*	*5*	*3.3*	*8.7*	*38*	*40%*	*.296*	*1.27*	*4.31*	*4.79*	*0.2*	*97.0*	*62.5*	*11.1*	*52*

Breakout: 13%   Improve: 22%   Collapse: 17%   Attrition: 34%   MLB: 55%   *Comparables: Tyler Mahle, Eddie Butler, Jake Thompson*

What they've long lacked in stars, the Phillies have compensated for in acquiring useful players in trades for their rentals. Count EDLS among those. The 23-year-old—acquired before the 2018 season for Freddy Galvis—pumps 95 with a solid changeup as a starter, but lacks a quality third pitch. That, coupled with the Phillies' relatively strong starting pitching depth in the upper minors, may make De Los Santos an appealing candidate for the Seranthony Dominguez Treatment. It's too early to assume or even to try to quantify his already live arm in short stints, but with Nola, Arrieta, and Pivetta firmly holding three rotation spots while other organizational favorites like Cole Irvin, Ranger Suarez and JoJo Romero are nearly ready to compete with Vince Velasquez and Zach Eflin, De Los Santos's best option for holding down a Major League job might just be in the bullpen. It helps to think he just might flourish in that role.

Seranthony Dominguez RHP Born: 11/25/94 Age: 24 Bats: R Throws: R Height: 6'1" Weight: 185 Origin: International Free Agent, 2011

YEAR	TEAM	LVL	AGE	W	L	SV	G	GS	IP	H	HR	BB/9	K/9	K	GB%	BABIP	WHIP	ERA	DRA	WARP	MPH	FB%	WHF	CSP
2016	WPT	A-	21	1	1	0	3	3	17	8	0	2.1	7.9	15	57%	.170	0.71	2.12	3.14	0.4				
2016	LWD	A	21	5	2	0	10	10	48¹	34	2	3.7	9.3	50	58%	.271	1.12	2.42	3.74	0.8				
2017	CLR	A+	22	4	4	0	15	13	62¹	51	6	4.3	10.8	75	45%	.306	1.30	3.61	3.28	1.4				
2018	REA	AA	23	1	2	0	8	0	13	8	0	1.4	12.5	18	52%	.296	0.77	2.08	3.09	0.3				
2018	PHI	MLB	23	2	5	16	53	0	58	32	4	3.4	11.5	74	56%	.220	0.93	2.95	3.00	1.3	99.5	66.6	16.3	49.1
2019	*PHI*	*MLB*	*24*	*3*	*1*	*20*	*52*	*0*	*55*	*43*	*7*	*4.0*	*11.1*	*68*	*48%*	*.297*	*1.22*	*3.85*	*4.29*	*0.4*	*99.3*	*68.6*	*16.8*	*50.6*

Breakout: 25%   Improve: 55%   Collapse: 12%   Attrition: 13%   MLB: 91%   *Comparables: Rubby De La Rosa, Matt Moore, Edwin Diaz*

There's something beautifully chaotic about watching Seranthony Dominguez pitch. What starts as a simple, compact wind-up gradually transforms and unfurls into a pinwheeling trebuchet of a delivery, an explosion of arm action that allows him to throw 99 MPH cutters and wipeout sliders. The changeup is still a bit of a work in progress—a reason he was converted from a starter to a reliever before the 2018 season began—but the established two-pitch mix is more than good enough to build on. That being said, whoever's doing the catching while Seranthony is on the mound will need to be sure they've limbered up while trying to corral the pitches that are simply too nasty to travel the full 60.5 feet; any time more than 1 percent of your pitches go down as wild pitches, well, that's a lot of runner movement that could be prevented. Really, though, in the context of his first professional season as a full-time reliever, it's hard to see 2018 as anything but a successful effort for Dominguez, and goes a long way toward stabilizing the club's 2019 relief outlook.

Zach Eflin RHP Born: 04/08/94 Age: 25 Bats: R Throws: R Height: 6'6" Weight: 215 Origin: Round 1, 2012 Draft (#33 overall)

YEAR	TEAM	LVL	AGE	W	L	SV	G	GS	IP	H	HR	BB/9	K/9	K	GB%	BABIP	WHIP	ERA	DRA	WARP	MPH	FB%	WHF	CSP
2016	LEH	AAA	22	5	2	0	11	11	68¹	49	2	1.4	7.2	55	47%	.245	0.88	2.90	4.01	1.0				
2016	PHI	MLB	22	3	5	0	11	11	63¹	67	12	2.4	4.4	31	37%	.261	1.33	5.54	6.62	-0.9	96.0	63.5	6.7	51.1
2017	LEH	AAA	23	1	4	0	8	7	43¹	48	3	3.1	7.9	38	41%	.346	1.45	4.57	4.38	0.6				
2017	PHI	MLB	23	1	5	0	11	11	64¹	79	16	1.7	4.9	35	46%	.297	1.41	6.16	5.62	0.0	95.5	68.1	7.6	51
2018	LEH	AAA	24	2	2	0	4	4	20	20	0	2.2	6.8	15	46%	.317	1.25	4.05	3.69	0.4				
2018	PHI	MLB	24	11	8	0	24	24	128	130	16	2.6	8.6	123	43%	.309	1.30	4.36	4.67	1.0	96.4	58.2	11.5	51.4
2019	*PHI*	*MLB*	*25*	*8*	*8*	*0*	*24*	*24*	*127¹*	*118*	*17*	*2.7*	*8.9*	*125*	*43%*	*.305*	*1.23*	*4.02*	*4.46*	*1.2*	*95.8*	*62.9*	*10*	*52.4*

Breakout: 14%   Improve: 45%   Collapse: 24%   Attrition: 35%   MLB: 86%   *Comparables: Matt Wisler, Brett Oberholtzer, Vance Worley*

When you're 6'6", it's pretty important to have healthy knees. They do a lot of work supporting that much human body! And when you're a 6'6" pitcher who needs strong knees to hold up to hours of standing and driving and planting, the demand is even greater. Given the trouble Eflin's knees gave him for years—finally addressed with surgery on both in late 2016—it's both understandable and convenient that a lot the struggles in his first two seasons could at least partially be blamed on them. Eflin started well, stringing together five consecutive wonderful starts in June against tough competition: The Cubs, Milwaukee twice, the Nationals, and the Yankees. He started leaking oil in mid-August, though, and had to putter his way through September before eventually admitting his side had been bothering him. Thus ended another intriguing but confusing season. Can Eflin's body hold up for 30 starts? Can he do what he did this past June for more than one month at a time? Will he be squeezed out in favor of the next batch of starters? As it stands right now, Eflin packs plenty of enticement into his stuff and should find Major League work for a few years if his body doesn't continue to betray him. It's just a shame his body didn't come with a warranty.

Jerad Eickhoff RHP Born: 07/02/90 Age: 28 Bats: R Throws: R Height: 6'4" Weight: 245 Origin: Round 15, 2011 Draft (#474 overall)

YEAR	TEAM	LVL	AGE	W	L	SV	G	GS	IP	H	HR	BB/9	K/9	K	GB%	BABIP	WHIP	ERA	DRA	WARP	MPH	FB%	WHF	CSP
2016	PHI	MLB	25	11	14	0	33	33	197¹	187	30	1.9	7.6	167	43%	.278	1.16	3.65	3.83	3.5	93.4	52.8	9.9	46.2
2017	PHI	MLB	26	4	8	0	24	24	128	142	16	3.7	8.3	118	39%	.328	1.52	4.71	5.24	0.5	92.2	50.2	9.7	48.4
2018	LEH	AAA	27	0	0	0	4	4	18²	17	1	3.9	4.8	10	52%	.267	1.34	2.41	6.78	-0.3				
2018	PHI	MLB	27	0	1	0	3	1	5¹	10	1	0.0	18.6	11	20%	.643	1.88	6.75	3.07	0.1	92.0	52	19.4	49
2019	PHI	MLB	28	5	5	0	16	16	80	74	11	3.1	8.6	77	42%	.299	1.27	4.25	4.73	0.5	92.3	51.8	10.1	48.4

Breakout: 21%   Improve: 53%   Collapse: 11%   Attrition: 22%   MLB: 89%   *Comparables: Chase Anderson, Vidal Nuno, Dan Straily*

For a time, it seemed like Eickhoff would be the surprise crown jewel of the Cole Hamels trade: The name no one in Philadelphia recognized in July 2015 eventually turning into one that regularly made starts alongside Aaron Nola for years to come. Would that baseball were that fair. First, it was a strained lat in mid-March. Then, numbness and tingling in the fingers of his pitching hand apparently **not** caused by Thoracic Outlet Syndrome, though the origin remains mostly mysterious. After that, a cortisone shot for his shoulder in June and his right wrist in July, all eventually culminating in a triumphant return to Philadelphia for three September appearances, including eight strikeouts in an abbreviated 3.1-inning start on September 28. For all we know, Eickhoff still has a long road to travel in his recovery. Maybe he never makes 30 starts in a season again. But the trials of 2018 have left little doubt about Eick's determination to get past whatever it is that ails him, and Phillies fans will always appreciate that.

Tommy Hunter RHP Born: 07/03/86 Age: 32 Bats: R Throws: R Height: 6'3" Weight: 250 Origin: Round 1, 2007 Draft (#54 overall)

YEAR	TEAM	LVL	AGE	W	L	SV	G	GS	IP	H	HR	BB/9	K/9	K	GB%	BABIP	WHIP	ERA	DRA	WARP	MPH	FB%	WHF	CSP
2016	CLE	MLB	29	2	2	0	21	0	21²	21	1	2.1	7.1	17	53%	.308	1.20	3.74	5.09	0.0	96.7	84.4	10	51.2
2016	COH	AAA	29	2	1	1	14	2	15	14	2	1.2	6.0	10	46%	.261	1.07	3.00	3.48	0.3				
2016	BAL	MLB	29	0	0	0	12	0	12¹	14	0	2.2	4.4	6	45%	.350	1.38	2.19	4.98	0.0	96.9	84.4	11.9	51.1
2017	TBA	MLB	30	3	5	1	61	0	58²	43	6	2.1	9.8	64	46%	.259	0.97	2.61	2.99	1.4	97.6	74.2	12.9	46.6
2018	PHI	MLB	31	5	4	4	65	0	64	65	6	2.1	7.2	51	51%	.303	1.25	3.80	4.54	0.3	97.2	86.2	11.5	49.1
2019	PHI	MLB	32	2	1	0	47	0	49¹	46	6	3.0	8.5	47	47%	.304	1.26	4.02	4.45	0.2	96.3	80.9	11.8	48.4

Breakout: 19%   Improve: 38%   Collapse: 32%   Attrition: 13%   MLB: 92%   *Comparables: Matt Wise, Anthony Swarzak, Luke Gregerson*

Almost immediately, Hunter became the focal point of Philly fans' angst. He tweaked his hamstring at the end of Spring Training and missed the first three weeks of April, pitching through May as if starting from scratch. Though he could never erase the early numbers, from June through September, things calmed down considerably. While he was by no means spectacular, Hunter did hold opponents to a .297 OBP in the season's final four months, and did a fine job keeping the ball in the park. None of his last nine inherited runners scored, either. It's hard to explain *why* it continued to feel like every appearance Hunter made—even in the good months—felt like it teetered on the brink of disaster, but we'd be willing to excuse that on account of the Negadelphia-colored glasses. It does, however, appear that Hunter's huge K% spike in Tampa Bay in 2017 was more fluke than foreshadowing, and anyone who pitches to more contact in this day and age walks a fine tightrope.

Cole Irvin LHP Born: 01/31/94 Age: 25 Bats: L Throws: L Height: 6'4" Weight: 180 Origin: Round 5, 2016 Draft (#137 overall)

YEAR	TEAM	LVL	AGE	W	L	SV	G	GS	IP	H	HR	BB/9	K/9	K	GB%	BABIP	WHIP	ERA	DRA	WARP	MPH	FB%	WHF	CSP
2016	WPT	A-	22	5	1	0	10	7	45²	36	2	1.6	7.3	37	49%	.248	0.96	1.97	2.83	1.3				
2017	CLR	A+	23	4	6	0	12	11	67	68	2	1.9	7.0	52	55%	.317	1.22	2.55	3.54	1.3				
2017	REA	AA	23	5	3	0	13	13	84¹	72	12	2.6	7.0	66	46%	.248	1.14	4.06	4.28	0.9				
2018	LEH	AAA	24	14	4	0	26	25	161¹	135	11	2.0	7.3	131	47%	.270	1.05	2.57	3.65	3.4				
2019	PHI	MLB	25	8	8	0	22	22	132¹	126	18	2.6	7.6	111	44%	.294	1.24	4.31	4.78	0.8				

Breakout: 11%   Improve: 28%   Collapse: 12%   Attrition: 31%   MLB: 46%   *Comparables: Matt Bowman, Taylor Rogers, Simon Castro*

It's been a few years now since the last time a Phillies player won a major award at the MLB level, but as far as the International League Pitcher of the Year Award is concerned, they've got that market cornered. Irvin became the latest member of the Phillies organization—the second in three years and sixth since 2001—to take home the crown after posting a sparkling record for the Lehigh Valley IronPigs. The 2016 5th-rounder out of the University of Oregon has been pretty remarkably consistent with his rate stats as a pro, regularly striking out around 17-20 percent while keeping walks and homers to a minimum. Irvin features a four-pitch mix of fastball, change, curve, and slider without a glaring weakness in the bunch, even if none of the four rates out as particularly flashy. He seems like a modest-floor, low-ceiling rotation option who will find his way onto the 40-man roster for the coming season, and a Major League debut won't be too far behind that.

Aaron Loup **LHP** Born: 12/19/87 Age: 31 Bats: L Throws: L Height: 5'11" Weight: 210 Origin: Round 9, 2009 Draft (#280 overall)

YEAR	TEAM	LVL	AGE	W	L	SV	G	GS	IP	H	HR	BB/9	K/9	K	GB%	BABIP	WHIP	ERA	DRA	WARP	MPH	FB%	WHF	CSP
2016	BUF	AAA	28	3	0	1	20	0	19²	21	0	1.4	11.9	26	54%	.404	1.22	1.83	2.62	0.5				
2016	TOR	MLB	28	0	0	0	21	0	14¹	15	2	2.5	9.4	15	40%	.342	1.33	5.02	4.76	0.0	94.8	66.7	8.8	52.4
2017	TOR	MLB	29	2	3	0	70	0	57²	59	4	4.5	10.0	64	56%	.340	1.53	3.75	5.68	-0.3	93.7	65.6	10.7	47.1
2018	TOR	MLB	30	0	0	0	50	0	35²	44	4	3.3	10.6	42	50%	.385	1.60	4.54	4.60	0.1	93.7	66.1	12.5	49.6
2018	PHI	MLB	30	0	0	0	9	0	4	4	0	2.2	4.5	2	69%	.308	1.25	4.50	6.95	-0.1	92.4	66.1	6.8	51.5
2019	*PHI*	*MLB*	*31*	*2*	*1*	*1*	*39*	*0*	*40²*	*37*	*5*	*3.7*	*10.0*	*45*	*49%*	*.323*	*1.33*	*3.90*	*4.34*	*0.2*	*92.9*	*65.5*	*11*	*49.3*

Breakout: 27%   Improve: 46%   Collapse: 22%   Attrition: 18%   MLB: 85%   *Comparables: Joba Chamberlain, Tyler Yates, Daniel Hudson*

It made sense to acquire Loup for their stretch run. The reliable lefty was posting a career-best K rate and inducing more whiffs than ever in his age-30 season, and the Phillies were desperate for someone, *anyone*, to get LHBs out. A forearm strain after two innings of work scuttled those plans, but his run of success with Toronto positions him as a mid-tier first-time free agent. We may not equate Loup with the likes of prime Andrew Miller or Aroldis Chapman or any other member of the elite southpaw relievers for good reason, but a team in search of some left-handed depth that misses out on Miller or Zach Britton in free agency may find Loup to be a worthy consolation prize.

Adonis Medina **RHP** Born: 12/18/96 Age: 22 Bats: R Throws: R Height: 6'1" Weight: 185 Origin: International Free Agent, 2014

YEAR	TEAM	LVL	AGE	W	L	SV	G	GS	IP	H	HR	BB/9	K/9	K	GB%	BABIP	WHIP	ERA	DRA	WARP	MPH	FB%	WHF	CSP
2016	WPT	A-	19	5	3	0	13	13	64²	47	5	3.3	4.7	34	57%	.214	1.10	2.92	3.89	1.0				
2017	LWD	A	20	4	9	0	22	22	119²	103	7	2.9	10.0	133	49%	.306	1.19	3.01	2.93	3.3				
2018	CLR	A+	21	10	4	0	22	21	111¹	103	11	2.9	9.9	123	51%	.316	1.25	4.12	4.72	0.8				
2019	*PHI*	*MLB*	*22*	*5*	*7*	*0*	*19*	*19*	*96¹*	*95*	*14*	*3.9*	*8.9*	*95*	*45%*	*.315*	*1.41*	*4.71*	*5.26*	*0.1*				

Breakout: 3%   Improve: 6%   Collapse: 6%   Attrition: 10%   MLB: 13%   *Comparables: Anthony Swarzak, Brett Kennedy, John Gant*

We may never know if Medina was actually offered to the Baltimore Orioles—or if it was the O's who requested him—for Manny Machado in July. The tricky thing about labels, though, is that they tend to linger, and the label Medina has now been branded with in Philadelphia is "Guy Who Could've Landed Us Machado." Part of the problem is that Medina lacks many other distinctions as a prospect: He climbs rungs and improves his pitches methodically and almost imperceptibly. At his best, Medina will be absolutely overpowering—he had multiple starts with 12 strikeouts and zero walks—but just as easily will be puzzlingly ineffective at his worst. Something is still yet to click for the 22-year-old, and he'll have to figure out what's missing while facing his most advanced opposition yet at Double-A Reading in 2019.

Adam Morgan **LHP** Born: 02/27/90 Age: 29 Bats: L Throws: L Height: 6'1" Weight: 200 Origin: Round 3, 2011 Draft (#120 overall)

YEAR	TEAM	LVL	AGE	W	L	SV	G	GS	IP	H	HR	BB/9	K/9	K	GB%	BABIP	WHIP	ERA	DRA	WARP	MPH	FB%	WHF	CSP
2016	LEH	AAA	26	6	1	0	8	7	50¹	43	4	1.8	9.3	52	42%	.293	1.05	3.04	2.19	1.8				
2016	PHI	MLB	26	2	11	0	23	21	113¹	141	23	2.3	7.5	95	40%	.331	1.50	6.04	4.83	0.7	93.6	49.3	11.6	43.6
2017	LEH	AAA	27	0	1	0	12	0	17¹	19	1	2.6	7.3	14	44%	.340	1.38	4.67	3.21	0.4				
2017	PHI	MLB	27	3	3	0	37	0	54²	51	10	3.0	10.4	63	45%	.297	1.26	4.12	3.12	1.2	96.3	33.2	17.5	44.8
2018	PHI	MLB	28	0	2	1	67	0	49¹	49	5	4.0	9.1	50	54%	.324	1.44	3.83	4.31	0.4	95.7	34.9	13.1	48.5
2019	*PHI*	*MLB*	*29*	*2*	*1*	*0*	*31*	*0*	*33*	*30*	*4*	*3.2*	*9.6*	*35*	*46%*	*.316*	*1.28*	*3.83*	*4.26*	*0.3*	*94.3*	*40.5*	*13.6*	*46*

Breakout: 26%   Improve: 52%   Collapse: 13%   Attrition: 12%   MLB: 79%   *Comparables: Boof Bonser, Glen Perkins, Brian Matusz*

You thought you had us fooled, Morgan. You thought we'd all bit on your 2017 second half as The Real Deal, a Platonic Leftiness that would solidify your place in the Phillies' bullpen for multiple years. Instead, you pulled off your mask to reveal that you were actually J.C. Romero all along. Sure, sure, you kept opponents' slugging numbers down and allowed only one homer to a lefty all year, but your walk totals took off as your strikeout tallies slipped backward, and next thing we all knew LHBs had a .350 OBP against you. Maybe your late-season velocity slip was to blame; maybe it was the disproportionate amount of batted balls that dropped in for hits; maybe hitters just had a better feel for your approach in your second season of full-time relieving. Or maybe you just need that mask back.

Hector Neris **RHP** Born: 06/14/89 Age: 30 Bats: R Throws: R Height: 6'2" Weight: 215 Origin: International Free Agent, 2010

YEAR	TEAM	LVL	AGE	W	L	SV	G	GS	IP	H	HR	BB/9	K/9	K	GB%	BABIP	WHIP	ERA	DRA	WARP	MPH	FB%	WHF	CSP
2016	PHI	MLB	27	4	4	2	79	0	80¹	59	9	3.4	11.4	102	44%	.272	1.11	2.58	3.15	1.7	96.9	45.3	16.7	45.7
2017	PHI	MLB	28	4	5	26	74	0	74²	68	9	3.1	10.4	86	35%	.306	1.26	3.01	4.25	0.8	96.0	48.6	17.8	48.3
2018	LEH	AAA	29	2	0	1	19	0	18²	9	0	3.4	14.9	31	46%	.257	0.86	1.45	2.34	0.6				
2018	PHI	MLB	29	1	3	11	53	0	47²	46	11	3.0	14.3	76	33%	.354	1.30	5.10	2.36	1.4	96.6	47.1	20.5	46.5
2019	*PHI*	*MLB*	*30*	*2*	*1*	*0*	*36*	*0*	*38¹*	*30*	*6*	*3.4*	*12.5*	*53*	*39%*	*.304*	*1.14*	*3.57*	*3.98*	*0.4*	*95.7*	*47*	*18.2*	*46.7*

Breakout: 23%   Improve: 43%   Collapse: 25%   Attrition: 13%   MLB: 83%   *Comparables: Pat Neshek, Vinnie Pestano, Danny Farquhar*

Okay, what did we just watch? What happened out there? Who was that man wearing 50 in red pinstripes through June, and what did he do with the reliable dude who'd previously inhabited his body? Even better, who was the *other* man who emerged in August, striking everyone out like he was Craig Kimbrel? There are two clear-cut, distinct parts to Hector Neris's season pre- and post-option on June 29, and neither was much like the guy who pitched the previous three seasons. The first three months were agony, and the longer they drew on, the more it became reasonable to question whether Neris, somehow, had burned out. The Phillies have said a big part of Neris's disastrous first three months was due to hand placement at set, and pitch tipping, a nasty combo if you're a two-pitch guy. With a fix in place, Neris returned to strike out 35 of the final 69 batters, giving up just a .172 opp. AVG despite a .379 BABIP and zero home runs. He looked unstoppable, but more than that, he might just have saved his career.

Pat Neshek RHP Born: 09/04/80 Age: 38 Bats: B Throws: R Height: 6'3" Weight: 220 Origin: Round 6, 2002 Draft (#182 overall)

YEAR	TEAM	LVL	AGE	W	L	SV	G	GS	IP	H	HR	BB/9	K/9	K	GB%	BABIP	WHIP	ERA	DRA	WARP	MPH	FB%	WHF	CSP
2016	HOU	MLB	35	2	2	0	60	0	47	33	6	2.1	8.2	43	37%	.216	0.94	3.06	3.56	0.8	92.0	38.9	11.9	54
2017	PHI	MLB	36	3	2	1	43	0	40¹	28	2	1.1	10.0	45	37%	.271	0.82	1.12	3.00	1.0	92.3	49.4	14.7	56.7
2017	COL	MLB	36	2	1	0	28	0	22	20	1	0.4	9.8	24	36%	.311	0.95	2.45	3.56	0.4	92.2	37.9	15	54.5
2018	PHI	MLB	37	3	2	5	30	0	24¹	23	2	1.8	5.5	15	41%	.266	1.15	2.59	4.73	0.1	90.9	39.5	11.3	56
2019	PHI	MLB	38	2	1	2	41	0	44	40	6	3.1	8.2	40	39%	.289	1.25	4.20	4.66	0.1	90.4	41	12.8	54

Breakout: 24% Improve: 38% Collapse: 30% Attrition: 8% MLB: 87% *Comparables: Rollie Fingers, Larry Andersen, Trevor Hoffman*

You wouldn't be at fault if you thought Neshek could finish Darren Oliver-ing his way through his late thirties, suppressing opposing hitters in short bursts of exposure without being overpowering. At the very least, the 2017 season was a strong point of evidence in favor, as Neshek made 71 mostly excellent appearances between Philadelphia and Colorado. His K rate spiked (at age 37, no less), his walk rate took a tumble in parallel, and his home run rate even *decreased* after joining the Rockies. Neshek publicly expressed an affinity for pitching in Philadelphia, and so a reunion for 2018 made perfect sense. That was about the extent of the fairy tale, though: Neshek got hurt toward the end of Spring Training and missed the first three months of the year. Upon his return, he threw 11 consecutive scoreless appearances, but once that streak ended on August 3, the sidearmer limped through the end of the season. Whether that's a harbinger of a crash to come or merely a blip during what's been a remarkable stretch of pitching from the sideswiping righty is a question only because of his age.

Juan Nicasio RHP Born: 08/31/86 Age: 32 Bats: R Throws: R Height: 6'4" Weight: 252 Origin: International Free Agent, 2006

YEAR	TEAM	LVL	AGE	W	L	SV	G	GS	IP	H	HR	BB/9	K/9	K	GB%	BABIP	WHIP	ERA	DRA	WARP	MPH	FB%	WHF	CSP
2016	PIT	MLB	29	10	7	0	52	12	118	117	15	3.4	10.5	138	45%	.331	1.37	4.50	3.94	1.7	97.2	69.2	11.4	46.1
2017	PIT	MLB	30	2	5	2	65	0	60	49	4	2.7	9.0	60	47%	.285	1.12	2.85	3.63	1.0	97.3	72.8	12	51.5
2017	PHI	MLB	30	1	0	0	2	0	1¹	0	0	0.0	6.8	1	100%	.000	0.00	0.00	5.22	0.0	98.3	45	20	59.7
2017	SLN	MLB	30	2	0	4	9	0	11	9	1	1.6	9.0	11	39%	.267	1.00	1.64	4.12	0.1	97.6	71.7	13.4	50.3
2018	SEA	MLB	31	1	6	1	46	0	42	53	6	1.1	11.4	53	37%	.402	1.38	6.00	2.73	1.1	96.0	70.7	12.2	51
2019	PHI	MLB	32	2	1	0	36	0	38¹	35	5	2.9	10.5	45	42%	.323	1.25	3.78	4.21	0.3	96.0	69.9	11.8	49.5

Breakout: 26% Improve: 49% Collapse: 22% Attrition: 3% MLB: 90% *Comparables: Jakie May, Manny Parra, Luke Hochevar*

There's one every year, and Nicasio may just have been 2018's King of Small Sample Size Weirdness. Signed to a two-year deal to provide a bridge to Edwin Diaz, Nicasio's peripheral results were exactly what you would hope. He struck out batters at a fast rate than he ever had, and walked fewer. Unfortunately for Nicasio and pitchers everywhere, as long as hitters continue to be pests and not strike out 100% of the time, there will always be balls in play, and when the ball is in play wacky things can happen. In this case, for Nicasio and the Mariners, "wacky" was a bit like Wile E. Coyote with a stick of dynamite. The strength of his velocity and track record of success says that we should expect positive regression in 2019, and if so he can still be a highly effective bridge-inning reliever. If not, well, most people like rooting for the Road Runner anyway.

Aaron Nola RHP Born: 06/04/93 Age: 26 Bats: R Throws: R Height: 6'2" Weight: 195 Origin: Round 1, 2014 Draft (#7 overall)

YEAR	TEAM	LVL	AGE	W	L	SV	G	GS	IP	H	HR	BB/9	K/9	K	GB%	BABIP	WHIP	ERA	DRA	WARP	MPH	FB%	WHF	CSP
2016	PHI	MLB	23	6	9	0	20	20	111	116	10	2.4	9.8	121	57%	.334	1.31	4.78	2.74	3.3	93.0	57.7	10.4	48.1
2017	LEH	AAA	24	1	0	0	2	2	10¹	6	0	0.9	8.7	10	65%	.231	0.68	0.87	3.48	0.3				
2017	PHI	MLB	24	12	11	0	27	27	168	154	18	2.6	9.9	184	50%	.309	1.21	3.54	3.22	4.4	94.1	53.3	11.8	49.1
2018	PHI	MLB	25	17	6	0	33	33	212¹	149	17	2.5	9.5	224	52%	.251	0.97	2.37	2.60	6.6	94.7	49.5	13.1	48.4
2019	PHI	MLB	26	12	9	0	30	30	189	155	19	2.6	10.4	217	51%	.304	1.11	3.18	3.52	3.9	93.9	53.1	12.4	49.4

Breakout: 20% Improve: 65% Collapse: 16% Attrition: 6% MLB: 95% *Comparables: Jon Lester, Gerrit Cole, Alex Wood*

Nola made The Leap, the fabled ascendance from "nice player" to "star" that so many yearn for and few achieve. Finally healthy for a full season, Nola sliced his opponents' HR rates and regularly drew poor contact when he wasn't striking guys out. That middle point is crucial, given how notoriously poor the 2018 Phillies were at playing defense, and Nola certainly did his part to make their jobs that much easier. It also helps the bullpen to know that Nola is becoming "Opener"-proof: The .540 OPS he allowed on the third time through the order was second only to Seattle's James Paxton in all of baseball, among pitchers who faced 150-plus batters for the third time. Some might say this version of Nola was lurking all along, shrouded by misleading ERAs that didn't tell the full story. Either way, he'll turn 26 in June, and the best still may be yet to come.

James Pazos LHP Born: 05/05/91 Age: 28 Bats: R Throws: L Height: 6'2" Weight: 235 Origin: Round 13, 2012 Draft (#427 overall)

YEAR	TEAM	LVL	AGE	W	L	SV	G	GS	IP	H	HR	BB/9	K/9	K	GB%	BABIP	WHIP	ERA	DRA	WARP	MPH	FB%	WHF	CSP
2016	SWB	AAA	25	2	2	1	23	0	27¹	19	1	6.3	13.5	41	57%	.316	1.39	2.63	2.74	0.7				
2016	NYA	MLB	25	1	0	0	7	0	3¹	7	2	2.7	8.1	3	46%	.455	2.40	13.50	7.70	-0.1	97.9	65.5	12.1	47.6
2017	SEA	MLB	26	4	5	0	59	0	53²	51	7	4.0	10.9	65	51%	.317	1.40	3.86	3.75	0.9	97.5	74.1	13.1	49.3
2018	SEA	MLB	27	4	1	0	60	0	50	47	4	2.7	8.1	45	47%	.303	1.24	2.88	4.66	0.2	96.4	91.8	10.8	52.3
2019	PHI	MLB	28	2	1	0	41	0	44	39	5	4.0	9.9	49	47%	.309	1.33	4.14	4.61	0.1	96.3	83.4	12	50.4

Breakout: 26% Improve: 44% Collapse: 20% Attrition: 24% MLB: 84% *Comparables: Evan Meek, Zach Putnam, Brandon Medders*

The velocity gains that helped vault Pazos to the majors largely disappeared in 2018, but his effectiveness did not. Although his fastball-slider arsenal and track record appear to peg him as a LOOGY, the Mariners actually let Pazos face significantly more right-handers than left last year, and he responded by running significant reverse-splits. While that result is probably more statistical oddity than predictive of future results, and his stuff and command are not close to elite in the modern game, Pazos can now boast a mid-90s fastball and a two-year track record of stable, dependable, big league production. Lengthy careers can and have been made on far less. He's also a reliever, so he could be out of baseball in 24 months.

Nick Pivetta RHP Born: 02/14/93 Age: 26 Bats: R Throws: R Height: 6'5" Weight: 220 Origin: Round 4, 2013 Draft (#136 overall)

YEAR	TEAM	LVL	AGE	W	L	SV	G	GS	IP	H	HR	BB/9	K/9	K	GB%	BABIP	WHIP	ERA	DRA	WARP	MPH	FB%	WHF	CSP
2016	REA	AA	23	11	6	0	22	22	124	108	10	3.0	8.1	111	45%	.283	1.20	3.41	3.43	2.5				
2016	LEH	AAA	23	1	2	0	5	5	24²	20	2	3.6	9.9	27	48%	.300	1.22	2.55	3.87	0.4				
2017	LEH	AAA	24	5	0	0	5	5	32	25	1	0.6	10.4	37	40%	.293	0.84	1.41	3.22	0.9				
2017	PHI	MLB	24	8	10	0	26	26	133	144	25	3.9	9.5	140	45%	.332	1.51	6.02	4.66	1.4	96.5	66	10.1	50.2
2018	PHI	MLB	25	7	14	0	33	32	164	163	24	2.8	10.3	188	50%	.327	1.30	4.77	3.40	3.6	96.6	58.9	13.2	49.1
2019	PHI	MLB	26	9	8	0	26	26	148¹	131	17	3.0	10.4	171	46%	.319	1.21	3.56	3.96	2.3	96.2	62.9	12.1	50.5

Breakout: 26%   Improve: 46%   Collapse: 14%   Attrition: 16%   MLB: 88%   *Comparables: Felipe Paulino, Boof Bonser, Justin Grimm*

The Phillies' legendarily poor defense in 2018 probably hurt no single pitcher more than Pivetta, whose peripherals bordered on outstanding while his key traditionals—W/L, ERA, opponents' AVG—provided a mediocre back of a baseball card. Cases like these make it difficult at the surface to explain why Pivetta actually made massive improvements over his rough 2017—a 2017 that, by the way, was also better than a 6.02 ERA would lead you to believe. But this sort of profile is exactly the type of thing you expect to see on lists of breakout candidates: Mid-90s heat, exceptional curveball, an improving change, and a hard slider for a show-me Plan D if all else fails. All of that sure seemed like it meshed well enough for stretches that 2018 should have been the foretold breakout year, but that peskily porous defense and seemingly every mistake pitch not just getting hit but *crushed* kept a lid on that breakout talk. Still, the stuff, body frame, and durability keep hope alive that Pivetta is more than just a back-end innings eater, and maybe 2019 is the season that finally transforms that belief into truth.

Edubray Ramos RHP Born: 12/19/92 Age: 26 Bats: R Throws: R Height: 6'0" Weight: 160 Origin: International Free Agent, 2010

YEAR	TEAM	LVL	AGE	W	L	SV	G	GS	IP	H	HR	BB/9	K/9	K	GB%	BABIP	WHIP	ERA	DRA	WARP	MPH	FB%	WHF	CSP
2016	REA	AA	23	1	1	7	11	0	15	9	1	0.6	9.0	15	51%	.211	0.67	2.40	2.65	0.4				
2016	LEH	AAA	23	1	0	3	15	0	23²	15	0	1.1	9.9	26	32%	.250	0.76	0.38	2.78	0.6				
2016	PHI	MLB	23	1	3	0	42	0	40	36	5	2.5	9.0	40	38%	.298	1.17	3.83	4.80	0.1	98.0	53.8	11.8	51.4
2017	LEH	AAA	24	2	0	1	10	0	11²	7	0	3.1	7.7	10	38%	.219	0.94	1.54	2.49	0.4				
2017	PHI	MLB	24	2	7	0	59	0	57²	57	4	4.4	11.7	75	39%	.356	1.47	4.21	4.00	0.8	96.2	42.2	12.2	48.3
2018	LEH	AAA	25	0	0	0	6	0	6	8	1	1.5	7.5	5	26%	.389	1.50	9.00	6.15	-0.1				
2018	PHI	MLB	25	3	1	1	52	0	42²	34	4	3.2	8.9	42	34%	.268	1.15	2.32	4.54	0.2	95.1	38.2	11.2	48.6
2019	PHI	MLB	26	2	1	0	31	0	33	28	4	3.6	10.0	37	38%	.304	1.25	3.95	4.39	0.2	95.8	43.6	11.9	50

Breakout: 27%   Improve: 43%   Collapse: 25%   Attrition: 21%   MLB: 81%   *Comparables: Clay Zavada, Manny Delcarmen, Cam Bedrosian*

Through June, Ramos was having a true shutdown season: ERA just above 1.00, opponents OPSing below .600, and everything looking hunky-dory. Then, a wave of injuries crashed on his shores, and Ramos's performance began to wobble. First, a shoulder impingement at the end of June; then, a patella tendon strain in late July; finally, a blister in late August. Over the season's final three months, Ramos was still effective as he pitched through and around his nagging injuries. He remains a touch too generous with the free passes, but has proven himself to be reliable in late-game pressure situations...at least in the ones that don't involve Asdrubal Cabrera. When he's pitching on healthy legs and with unblistered fingers, he'll find most of his success on the back of a sharply-humped low-to-mid-80s slider that can divebomb out of the bottom of the zone.

Yacksel Rios RHP Born: 06/27/93 Age: 26 Bats: R Throws: R Height: 6'3" Weight: 185 Origin: Round 12, 2011 Draft (#391 overall)

YEAR	TEAM	LVL	AGE	W	L	SV	G	GS	IP	H	HR	BB/9	K/9	K	GB%	BABIP	WHIP	ERA	DRA	WARP	MPH	FB%	WHF	CSP
2016	REA	AA	23	1	1	0	13	1	17²	20	0	7.1	10.7	21	47%	.392	1.92	4.58	2.80	0.4				
2016	CLR	A+	23	4	3	1	22	6	58²	59	4	3.5	6.4	42	44%	.306	1.40	6.14	3.75	1.0				
2017	REA	AA	24	1	2	2	24	0	38	22	2	2.4	11.1	47	40%	.235	0.84	1.89	3.02	0.8				
2017	LEH	AAA	24	0	1	1	13	1	18¹	10	3	2.0	8.3	17	36%	.159	0.76	1.96	3.25	0.4				
2017	PHI	MLB	24	1	0	0	13	0	16¹	15	4	5.0	9.4	17	36%	.256	1.47	4.41	6.52	-0.2	95.6	64.1	11.6	48.3
2018	LEH	AAA	25	0	0	1	22	0	22²	18	2	6.8	10.3	26	54%	.281	1.54	3.97	4.33	0.2				
2018	PHI	MLB	25	3	2	0	36	0	36	43	6	3.8	9.0	36	47%	.349	1.61	6.75	4.14	0.3	98.6	64.3	12.2	48.6
2019	PHI	MLB	26	1	0	0	10	0	11	10	1	4.4	9.8	12	43%	.304	1.37	4.38	4.88	0.0	97.4	65.4	12.3	49.3

Breakout: 15%   Improve: 25%   Collapse: 5%   Attrition: 15%   MLB: 38%   *Comparables: Mayckol Guaipe, Lucas Luetge, Randor Bierd*

Somewhere in the 2017-18 offseason, Rios must have unearthed some sort of enchanted totem or magic lamp that allowed him to add four MPH to his fastball, an overnight bump from 93-94 to 97 with semi-regular touches of 99 and 100. As we've all seen, however, pure raw velo does not a pitcher make. Rios is clearly more powerful now, but that doesn't mean he was overwhelming opposing hitters as a result. For what it's worth, Rios's new cannon delivers this enhanced heat with as much ease as his old 93-94 MPH self, and his slider vexed plenty of right-handed hitters. His bugaboo pretty clearly remains left-handed batters, though, and any hope of hanging on to a bullpen role lies pretty squarely on improving his splitter and locating his fastball better when attacking them.

David Robertson RHP Born: 04/09/85 Age: 34 Bats: R Throws: R Height: 5'11" Weight: 195 Origin: Round 17, 2006 Draft (#524 overall)

YEAR	TEAM	LVL	AGE	W	L	SV	G	GS	IP	H	HR	BB/9	K/9	K	GB%	BABIP	WHIP	ERA	DRA	WARP	MPH	FB%	WHF	CSP
2016	CHA	MLB	31	5	3	37	62	0	62¹	53	6	4.6	10.8	75	47%	.307	1.36	3.47	2.57	1.7	94.5	68.1	13.7	45.6
2017	CHA	MLB	32	4	2	13	31	0	33¹	21	4	3.0	12.7	47	43%	.250	0.96	2.70	1.98	1.2	93.2	56.1	16.5	46.9
2017	NYA	MLB	32	5	0	1	30	0	35	14	2	3.1	13.1	51	56%	.182	0.74	1.03	1.86	1.3	93.7	56.1	18.4	43.2
2018	NYA	MLB	33	8	3	5	69	0	69²	46	7	3.4	11.8	91	47%	.245	1.03	3.23	3.03	1.5	94.1	42.5	14.4	43.3
2019	PHI	MLB	34	3	1	15	52	0	55	42	7	3.8	11.7	71	46%	.293	1.18	3.56	3.97	0.6	92.8	52	14.9	43.8

Breakout: 15%   Improve: 28%   Collapse: 45%   Attrition: 7%   MLB: 94%   *Comparables: Seung Hwan Oh, Darren O'Day, J.J. Putz*

This decade, only two relievers have more Win Probability Added than David Robertson: Kenley Jansen and Craig Kimbrel. Dig further: Robertson's average Leverage Index upon entering the game is always lower than those two; he played behind Mariano Rivera to start his career, then as a closer on an underperforming White Sox crew, and now he is a relief ace among many. What's even more remarkable than his career numbers is the sheer consistency of it all. Here are things he has done in every single season since 2010: pitched more than 60 innings, struck out at least ten batters per nine innings, and allowed fewer than one home run per nine innings. Even he knows it: for the first time in his career, he represented himself in free agency, stating in a self-penned letter to MLB Trade Rumors that he "know[s] what [he] can offer a team." We do too—just look at his baseball card.

JoJo Romero LHP   Born: 09/09/96   Age: 22   Bats: L   Throws: L   Height: 6'0"   Weight: 190   Origin: Round 4, 2016 Draft (#107 overall)

YEAR	TEAM	LVL	AGE	W	L	SV	G	GS	IP	H	HR	BB/9	K/9	K	GB%	BABIP	WHIP	ERA	DRA	WARP	MPH	FB%	WHF	CSP
2016	WPT	A-	19	2	2	0	10	10	45²	44	2	2.2	6.1	31	58%	.303	1.20	2.56	3.64	0.9				
2017	LWD	A	20	5	1	0	13	13	76²	61	2	2.5	9.3	79	60%	.299	1.07	2.11	2.95	2.1				
2017	CLR	A+	20	5	2	0	10	10	52¹	43	2	2.6	8.4	49	52%	.289	1.11	2.24	3.28	1.2				
2018	REA	AA	21	7	6	0	18	18	106²	97	13	3.5	8.4	100	53%	.286	1.29	3.80	4.61	0.9				
2019	*PHI*	*MLB*	*22*	*1*	*1*	*0*	*3*	*3*	*15*	*14*	*2*	*3.4*	*8.4*	*14*	*48%*	*.305*	*1.32*	*4.32*	*4.80*	*0.1*				

Breakout: 12%   Improve: 18%   Collapse: 13%   Attrition: 23%   MLB: 38%   *Comparables: Scott Barnes, Keyvius Sampson, Jarred Cosart*

Sometimes, less is more. In Romero's case, shortening and simplifying his arsenal made a huge difference. From May 9 until a season-ending oblique injury in late July, Romero averaged more than six innings per start and held hitters to a .604 OPS, thanks in large part to an early emphasis on fastball-cutter attacks the first time through, followed by an introduction of changeups into the mix. Romero's run from May through July was good enough to earn him Player of the Year honors for the Reading Fightin' Phils and, thankfully, his injury isn't expected to linger into 2019. It wouldn't be unreasonable to see Romero start this season repeating Double-A, nor would it be a shock to see him quickly promoted if his new approach still proves effective.

Sixto Sanchez RHP   Born: 07/29/98   Age: 20   Bats: R   Throws: R   Height: 6'0"   Weight: 185   Origin: International Free Agent, 2015

YEAR	TEAM	LVL	AGE	W	L	SV	G	GS	IP	H	HR	BB/9	K/9	K	GB%	BABIP	WHIP	ERA	DRA	WARP	MPH	FB%	WHF	CSP
2016	PHL	RK	17	5	0	0	11	11	54	33	0	1.3	7.3	44	57%	.236	0.76	0.50	2.61	1.9				
2017	LWD	A	18	5	3	0	13	13	67¹	46	1	1.2	8.6	64	49%	.251	0.82	2.41	2.93	1.9				
2017	CLR	A+	18	0	4	0	5	5	27²	27	1	2.9	6.5	20	42%	.295	1.30	4.55	3.61	0.5				
2018	CLR	A+	19	4	3	0	8	8	46²	39	1	2.1	8.7	45	52%	.295	1.07	2.51	3.67	0.9				
2019	*PHI*	*MLB*	*20*	*3*	*3*	*0*	*9*	*9*	*46¹*	*44*	*6*	*3.1*	*8.4*	*43*	*47%*	*.307*	*1.30*	*4.32*	*4.80*	*0.3*				

Breakout: 5%   Improve: 8%   Collapse: 5%   Attrition: 14%   MLB: 18%   *Comparables: Jacob Turner, Francis Martes, Ian Krol*

It's prescriptivist to claim Sixto was destined to get hurt eventually, but reports of a teenager touching 102 with his fastball (while thrilling) are enough to plant a small seed of worry. Those worries grew and bore fruit in 2018, when Sanchez was forced to miss the majority of the season with elbow inflammation, assigned to the Arizona Fall League to make up for some of those lost outings, and then had to bail on that due to collarbone discomfort. It's no secret that Sixto's got impossibly powerful stuff for his or any age, but a healthy 2019 will go a long way toward assuaging doubts that his advanced arm will have shot its best bullets before he even gets to make his Phillies debut. Sanchez won't even turn 21 until the end of July, so any talk of his being "broken" or "damaged" on the heels of a lost half-season are far too premature. At the very least, we absolutely cannot be deprived of a second "Sixto" entry in the annals of baseball history. It's only just.

Ranger Suarez LHP   Born: 08/26/95   Age: 23   Bats: L   Throws: L   Height: 6'1"   Weight: 180   Origin: International Free Agent, 2012

YEAR	TEAM	LVL	AGE	W	L	SV	G	GS	IP	H	HR	BB/9	K/9	K	GB%	BABIP	WHIP	ERA	DRA	WARP	MPH	FB%	WHF	CSP
2016	WPT	A-	20	6	4	0	13	13	73²	61	4	2.9	6.5	53	53%	.260	1.15	2.81	3.62	1.4				
2017	LWD	A	21	6	2	0	14	14	85	52	4	2.5	9.5	90	58%	.233	0.89	1.59	3.05	2.2				
2017	CLR	A+	21	2	4	0	8	8	37²	43	1	2.6	9.1	38	50%	.382	1.43	3.82	3.76	0.7				
2018	REA	AA	22	4	3	0	12	12	75	64	2	2.4	6.5	54	51%	.283	1.12	2.76	4.71	0.6				
2018	LEH	AAA	22	2	0	0	9	9	49¹	48	2	2.7	5.7	31	50%	.297	1.28	2.74	4.02	0.9				
2018	PHI	MLB	22	1	1	0	4	3	15	21	3	3.6	6.6	11	52%	.367	1.80	5.40	5.73	-0.1	93.7	60.4	7.6	51.1
2019	*PHI*	*MLB*	*23*	*2*	*2*	*0*	*6*	*6*	*30*	*30*	*4*	*3.4*	*7.5*	*25*	*46%*	*.305*	*1.37*	*4.56*	*5.06*	*0.1*	*93.6*	*62.6*	*7.8*	*53*

Breakout: 15%   Improve: 19%   Collapse: 11%   Attrition: 28%   MLB: 41%   *Comparables: Troy Patton, Michael Bowden, Jorge Lopez*

When he made his Major League debut on July 26, Suarez snapped one of the most peculiar streaks in all of baseball: The Phillies, as a team, had not had a left-handed pitcher start a game since Adam Morgan in late September 2016. Further, Suarez was the first lefty younger than 24 to start for the Fightins since Antonio Bastardo way back in 2009. In that way, Suarez is emblematic of an organizational deficiency that lasted for years and is only just now being rectified as some starting southpaws finally claw their way through the system. He's unlikely to draw any Cole Hamels comparisons, and the vanishing of his strikeouts from 2017 to 2018 is borderline alarming, but Suarez, by all accounts, isn't done improving. He's consistently added velocity since coming to the U.S. in 2015, features a strong changeup to offset his low-90s fastball, and has made strides to sharpen his curveball. If that curve continues to get better and solidifies itself as a legitimate third pitch in Suarez's arsenal, there's something more than just "viable" at work here. There's still a good distance between that future and the present, but expect Suarez to get his fair shake of chances to have it all come together.

Vincent Velasquez RHP   Born: 06/07/92   Age: 27   Bats: R   Throws: R   Height: 6'3"   Weight: 205   Origin: Round 2, 2010 Draft (#58 overall)

YEAR	TEAM	LVL	AGE	W	L	SV	G	GS	IP	H	HR	BB/9	K/9	K	GB%	BABIP	WHIP	ERA	DRA	WARP	MPH	FB%	WHF	CSP
2016	PHI	MLB	24	8	6	0	24	24	131	129	21	3.1	10.4	152	37%	.325	1.33	4.12	3.54	2.7	96.8	64.9	12.7	49.1
2017	PHI	MLB	25	2	7	0	15	15	72	74	15	4.2	8.5	68	45%	.303	1.50	5.12	5.66	-0.1	96.2	68.5	10.1	51.7
2018	PHI	MLB	26	9	12	0	31	30	146²	138	16	3.6	9.9	161	41%	.316	1.34	4.85	4.20	1.9	96.2	64	12.5	50.3
2019	*PHI*	*MLB*	*27*	*6*	*5*	*0*	*32*	*16*	*96²*	*86*	*14*	*3.3*	*10.4*	*111*	*40%*	*.314*	*1.26*	*4.01*	*4.47*	*0.8*	*95.9*	*66*	*12.2*	*51.1*

Breakout: 32%   Improve: 63%   Collapse: 19%   Attrition: 11%   MLB: 93%   *Comparables: Ian Snell, Max Scherzer, Mike Minor*

Give Velasquez this: He had the conditioning to make 30 starts (plus one relief appearance) for the first time. Now, those starts were severely abbreviated—VV became the first pitcher ever to reach that mark throwing fewer than 150 innings—so we're no closer to understanding if Velasquez can really hack it as a SP or not. We're now roughly four years deep into this exploration, rapidly approaching the point of no return, and the only thing getting clearer is the worry that simply shifting Velasquez to a relief role won't fix what ails him. Does he still throw hard? Sure. But erratic command and gopheritis aren't things that typically get fixed simply by letting a guy throw harder for a shorter (on purpose, in this scenario) amount of time. It's still pretty plain that Velasquez has a top-tier arm, but no coach in Philadelphia has, thus far, been able to help him fully harness its capabilities for more than a scattered start here or there. It's not for lack of effort, nor work ethic, nor athleticism—I mean, did you *see* him get hit by a liner and recover to throw a bullet to first with his *left hand* to record the out?!—but something just isn't working. The Phillies figure to give him another look in 2019, but he may find himself in another uniform soon.

LINEOUTS

Hitters

HITTER	POS	TEAM	LVL	AGE	PA	R	2B	3B	HR	RBI	BB	K	SB	CS	AVG/OBP/SLG	DRC+	VORP	BABIP	BRR	FRAA	WARP
Daniel Brito	2B	LWD	A	20	368	33	13	2	4	31	27	64	15	6	.252/.309/.340	96	11.1	.297	0.8	2B(92): 3.7	1.3
	2B	CLR	A+	20	100	8	5	2	0	7	6	19	1	1	.250/.300/.348	97	1.8	.311	0.0	2B(24): 1.1	0.4
Dylan Cozens	RF	LEH	AAA	24	348	49	17	2	21	58	46	124	9	6	.246/.345/.529	131	26.4	.333	0.4	RF(70): 2.9, CF(9): -2.2	2.2
	RF	PHI	MLB	24	44	2	2	0	1	2	6	24	1	0	.158/.273/.289	48	-1.5	.385	0.1	LF(9): -1.0, RF(5): -0.1	-0.3
Pedro Florimon	SS	PHI	MLB	31	76	13	6	1	2	5	5	30	1	2	.225/.276/.423	59	4.0	.359	0.8	SS(21): 2.8, 2B(4): 0.2	0.3
Arquimedes Gamboa	SS	CLR	A+	20	497	49	14	4	2	37	53	111	6	4	.214/.304/.279	86	2.1	.281	-1.0	SS(109): -2.0	0.9
Deivi Grullon	C	REA	AA	22	353	36	14	1	21	59	18	81	0	0	.273/.310/.515	116	20.9	.296	-2.9	C(87): 2.7	0.0
Rafael Marchan	C	WPT	A-	19	210	28	8	2	0	12	11	18	9	6	.301/.343/.362	107	14.5	.330	0.3	C(47): 2.7	1.4
Simon Muzziotti	CF	LWD	A	19	299	33	12	2	1	20	14	40	18	4	.263/.299/.331	91	6.2	.303	1.7	CF(66): 4.6, RF(1): 0.0	1.3
Jhailyn Ortiz	RF	LWD	A	19	454	51	18	2	13	47	35	148	2	2	.225/.297/.375	86	12.5	.313	3.1	RF(96): -4.0	-0.1
Trevor Plouffe	INF	PHI	MLB	32	12	1	0	0	1	3	0	6	0	0	.250/.250/.500	74	0.5	.400	0.0	3B(2): 0.0, RF(1): 0.0	0.0
	INF	LEH	AAA	32	274	31	16	0	12	37	41	68	2	0	.230/.347/.460	127	11.2	.265	-0.8	2B(22): 0.3, 1B(15): 0.4	1.5
Cornelius Randolph	LF	REA	AA	21	465	52	18	0	5	40	48	92	3	3	.241/.324/.322	90	3.3	.298	2.2	LF(103): -5.1	0.2
Mitch Walding	3B	LEH	AAA	25	472	70	20	2	19	69	73	148	2	0	.265/.390/.474	132	40.8	.375	0.8	3B(108): 8.0, 1B(4): 0.0	4.4
	3B	PHI	MLB	25	19	1	0	0	1	2	2	12	0	0	.059/.158/.235	59	-1.7	.000	0.0	3B(7): 0.0	0.0

Daniel Brito has seemingly slipped from "sleeper" back to "pipe dream," as his offensive abilities have yet to overcome the challenges of post-rookie league ball. ⓧ If he's going to help reprise the Double-A Reading "Bash Brothers" tandem he and Hoskins formed in 2016, **Dylan Cozens** will need to find a way to put the bat on the ball more often. ⓧ **Pedro Florimon** played lots of positions—none exceptionally well—and struck out too much. In other words, he was the quintessential 2018 Phillies player. ⓧ Still raw in nearly every sense of the word, **Arquimedes Gamboa**'s most likely future is one of a defensive super-sub, with any shred of offensive value simply considered a bonus. ⓧ **Deivi Grullon** really likes to swing, and his career-doubling 21 home runs can only reinforce that particular habit. ⓧ **Rafael Marchan** has yet to homer as a pro, but has a strong throwing arm and struck out just 18 times in 210 plate appearances in his first season stateside. Is it too soon to start hunting for the next Willians Astudillo? (Yes.) ⓧ Out with Carlos Tocci, in with **Simon Muzziotti** as the torch-bearer for athletic Phillies minor league center fielders in need of some beefier arms. ⓧ **Jhailyn Ortiz** ranked ahead of Vladimir Guerrero, Jr., in the 2015 international class, which just seems cruel at this point. The athleticism remains, though at the moment it's most evident on empty follow-throughs. ⓧ **Trevor Plouffe**'s 16th-inning walk-off home run in late July proved that Enrique Hernandez can't actually play *every* position well. ⓧ Another even year, another hundred-point OPS drop from the previous season for **Cornelius Randolph**, who could only muster 23 extra-base hits with a full season of FirstEnergy Stadium as his home park in 2018. ⓧ **Mitch Walding** eventually delivered a home run for his first career hit after 14 empty trips to start his career. Did it come against a position player pitching? Sure. Was it still a real Major League homer that counted for two actual runs? You bet!

Pitchers

PITCHER	TEAM	LVL	AGE	W	L	SV	G	GS	IP	H	HR	BB/9	K/9	K	GB%	BABIP	WHIP	ERA	DRA	WARP	MPH	FB%	WHF	CSP
Drew Anderson	LEH	AAA	24	9	4	0	19	19	104²	92	14	2.5	7.2	84	37%	.258	1.16	3.87	4.13	1.7				
	PHI	MLB	24	0	1	0	5	1	12²	17	0	1.4	7.8	11	43%	.386	1.50	4.97	4.85	0.0	94.5	60.2	10.4	49.8
Kyle Dohy	LWD	A	21	3	3	7	24	0	33²	16	1	4.5	16.8	63	46%	.306	0.98	0.80	1.56	1.3				
	CLR	A+	21	2	1	2	7	0	11	5	1	2.5	14.7	18	42%	.222	0.73	1.64	1.21	0.5				
	REA	AA	21	2	5	1	18	0	22²	13	3	8.7	11.9	30	37%	.217	1.54	5.56	4.80	0.0				
Bailey Falter	CLR	A+	21	8	4	0	17	17	93²	87	6	1.4	8.0	83	50%	.302	1.09	2.69	4.66	0.7				
Spencer Howard	LWD	A	21	9	8	0	23	23	112	101	6	3.2	11.8	147	40%	.349	1.26	3.78	3.46	2.3				
Mauricio Llovera	CLR	A+	22	8	7	0	23	22	121	100	14	2.5	10.2	137	42%	.279	1.11	3.72	3.43	2.7				
Francisco Morales	WPT	A-	18	4	5	0	13	13	56¹	54	6	5.3	10.9	68	42%	.324	1.54	5.27	3.82	0.9				
David Parkinson	LWD	A	22	8	1	0	17	17	95¹	74	4	2.5	10.9	115	46%	.297	1.05	1.51	3.04	2.4				
	CLR	A+	22	3	0	0	5	4	29	17	1	2.8	8.1	26	42%	.225	0.90	1.24	3.85	0.5				
Ramon Rosso	LWD	A	22	5	1	0	12	12	67²	45	3	2.7	10.8	81	51%	.275	0.96	1.33	3.29	1.5				
	CLR	A+	22	6	2	0	11	10	55²	49	1	3.2	9.4	58	50%	.320	1.24	2.91	3.65	1.1				
Connor Seabold	CLR	A+	22	4	4	0	12	12	71²	57	6	1.8	8.5	68	47%	.260	0.99	3.77	3.31	1.7				
	REA	AA	22	1	4	0	11	11	58²	55	10	2.9	9.8	64	36%	.290	1.26	4.91	3.46	1.3				
Kyle Young	LWD	A	20	3	3	0	9	9	52¹	46	2	1.2	7.6	44	64%	.295	1.01	3.10	2.90	1.4				

Drew Anderson neither improved nor worsened his outlook as a potential depth option in the rotation or the bullpen. That we're saying this about the last pick of the 21st round of the 2012 draft means Anderson is already a success, no matter the ultimate outcome. ⊗ Striking out 81 of 172 batters is a performance that will raise eyebrows in any organization, and **Kyle Dohy** deserved a quick promotion with those eye-popping numbers. Alas, walking 22 of 101 hitters in Double-A only managed to raise a single eyebrow. ⊗ Considered a project when the Phillies took him in the fifth round, **Bailey Falter** has instead moved quickly. The concern is that he's aging straight into a fifth starter before his time, unless he can find some heat or an out pitch. ⊗ 2017 2nd-round pick **Spencer Howard** struck out 67 of the last 190 batters he faced in 2018, and capped off the year with a postseason no-hitter. The fastball and slider are sharp, so there's floor for days here. ⊗ In English, *Llovera* means "will rain." As far as **Mauricio Llovera** is concerned, the Phillies certainly hope he keeps making his mid-90s heat and those low-80s curves rain down for Ks. ⊗ 2016 J2 pickup **Francisco Morales**, only just turned 19, is already touching mid-90s with his fastball. His is a name to remember and forget and remember three or four more times in the coming years. ⊗ Over his first 157 professional innings, **David Parkinson** has a 1.55 ERA with a K/BB ratio over 4, and has only given up 7 homers. Greater tests of validity await him in Double-A, but it's hard not to be impressed with this start. ⊗ **Ramon Rosso** has been a little old for each level he's played at in two pro seasons, but at least he's making use of his advantage, via a 1.76 ERA and 244 strikeouts in 199 innings. ⊗ With flowing locks and a high leg kick from the right side, you'd be forgiven mistaking **Connor Seabold** for Bronson Arroyo. When the ball jumps upward off the bat, you'd be equally forgiven then, too. ⊗ If **Kyle Young** were any taller, he'd probably be able to reach the catcher's mitt from the mound, which would result in a pretty interesting morality experiment for hitters swinging at a ball still in a pitcher's hand as it crossed the plate.

PITTSBURGH PIRATES

Essay by David Roth

Player comments by Mike Gianella and BP staff

There were some names I expected to hear, and I did indeed hear them. I asked the population of Pittsburgh Pirates-adjacent people in my life—some coworkers and a comedy writer and some bloggers and an attorney with a podcast, a representation of my social circle at this point in my life such so distressingly apt that I feel compelled to mention it myself—about the bleakest moment in their last 15 or so years as fans of this team. This was not a scientific poll, of course, but writing an essay like this about a team like the Pirates is not a scientific pursuit. It is about a specific type of dread, and there is nothing scientific about dread. The broader vibe of the Pirates is not something that can be quantified, really. It is, as it has been for decades, a fact as obvious and inarguable as weather.

But yes, if you were wondering, Matt Morris came up more than once. In one of the last moves of his disastrous and implausibly long tenure as the team's GM, Dave Littlefield acquired the last $13.5 million of Morris's contract from San Francisco at the trade deadline in 2007, seemingly on a whim; the Bucs sent back a young Rajai Davis and a minor-leaguer-to-be-named who will also remain unnamed here. Littlefield was fired six weeks later, and Morris was released in late April of 2008 after allowing six homers in 22-and-a-third innings. There were also multiple mentions of Daniel Moskos, who was more valuable to the Pirates in a shorter stint with the club than Morris was—which is to say that he was more or less replacement level in the only 31 games he'd ever spend as a big leaguer—but whose legacy is even doomier. Littlefield drafted Moskos, a reliever out of Clemson, fourth overall in 2007's June Draft, because ownership declined to pay the bonus due to Georgia Tech phenom and eventual fifth-overall Matt Wieters; the team subsequently issued a press release noting that Moskos "was ranked by Baseball America as the fifth-best *pitcher* available in the draft."[1]

Derek Bell came up, too, as Derek Bell does; he was the worst of the many veteran free agents that Littlefield reliably snagged on the eve of their expiration dates. Aramis Ramirez, a homegrown star who was dealt away at the beginning of his prime for Bobby Hill—not the pudgy goofus from *King Of The Hill*, but no more valuable during his brief time with the Pirates—was mentioned. So was the Pirates having players from their organization selected with five of the first six picks

PIRATES PROSPECTUS
2018 W-L: 82-79, 4TH IN NL CENTRAL

Pythag	.499	15th	B-Age	27.9	13th
RS/G	4.30	18th	P-Age	26.5	2nd
RA/G	4.30	14th	Salary	$86.3M	27th
DRC+	94	19th	M$/MW	$2.2M	27th
DRA	4.18	10th	DL Days	696	2nd
FIP	4.02	14th	$ on DL	9%	4th
DER	.704	19th			

- Opened 2001
- Open air
- Natural surface
- Fence profile: 6' to 21'

Three-Year Park Factors

Runs	Runs/RH	Runs/LH	HR/RH	HR/LH
96	94	100	87	100

Top Hitter WARP	3.1 Starling Marte
Top Pitcher WARP	4.2 Jameson Taillon
Top Prospect	Mitch Keller

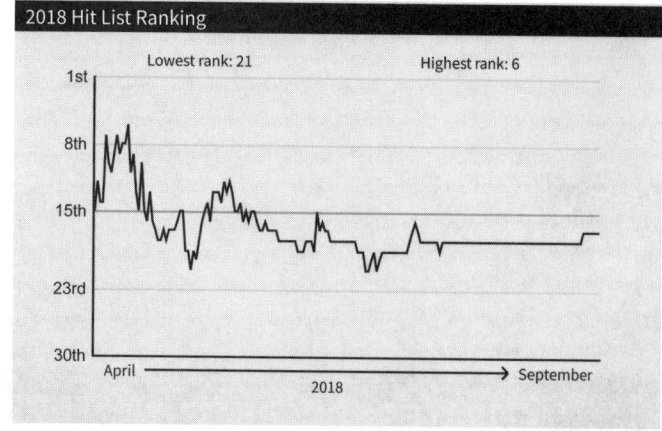

2018 Hit List Ranking

Lowest rank: 21   Highest rank: 6

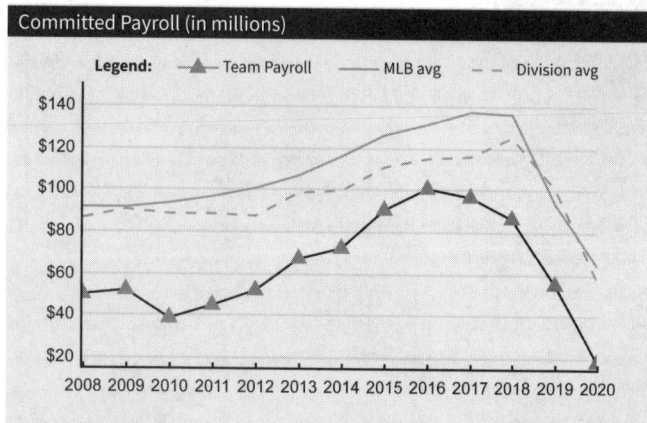

Committed Payroll (in millions)

Legend: —▲— Team Payroll   —— MLB avg   - - - Division avg

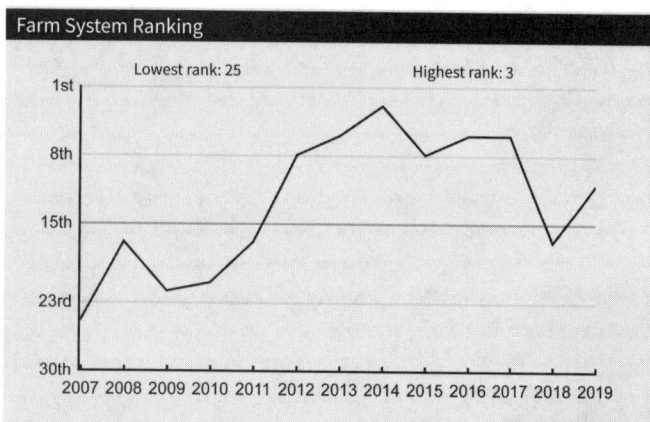

Farm System Ranking

Lowest rank: 25   Highest rank: 3

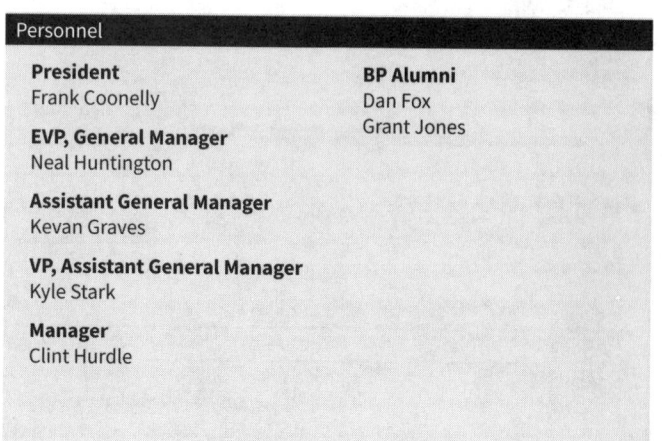

Personnel

President
Frank Coonelly

EVP, General Manager
Neal Huntington

Assistant General Manager
Kevan Graves

VP, Assistant General Manager
Kyle Stark

Manager
Clint Hurdle

BP Alumni
Dan Fox
Grant Jones

of the 2003 Rule Five Draft, "resulting in audible laughter in the New Orleans hotel meeting room" as the AP noted in its postmortem on Littlefield's six years with the team[2]; the best of those players was Jose Bautista, whom the team would later re-acquire and then trade again, for a catcher named Robinzon Diaz. No one mentioned Pat Meares, although I long ago got used to people not mentioning Pat Meares as often as I think they should. You are probably getting it by now.

All of this is well-known, not subtext but the actual lurid text itself, for people that care to know things about the Pirates. It also seemed just a few years ago to be something like ancient history. First Cam Bonifay and then Littlefield got some smallish things right and a great many bigger things wrong during their respective unconscionably long stints as GM, but were persistently hamstrung by two different but equally cheap owners; neither did especially well in the job, but both were set up to fail. Neil Huntington, who has been on the job since 2007 and was given a four-year contract extension back in 2017, is different. He got some of the big things right that his predecessors had always gotten wrong and a number of smaller things as well, and subsequently built teams that didn't just win but ranged from endearingly spunky to nearly sublime—few teams have been less well-served by the Wild Card system than the 98-win Pirates of 2015, whose postseason consisted entirely of one brisk manhandling by Jake Arrieta. It was not nearly as long ago as it seems that the Pirates were not just *competitive*, which is the current baseball slang for Decent Enough That No One Is Bringing Guillotines To The Stadium, but actually *good*.

But *good* is expensive, and difficult, and fleeting, and so after the team peaked at 98 wins in 2015 and then declined to pay the necessary cost to get even better Huntington was tasked with taking those teams apart, which he has done in his typical workmanlike fashion since the team's last brief postseason appearance in 2016. Huntington's name came up, too, in the messages I got back from my emissaries to Pirates nation. So, unsurprisingly, did that of Bob Nutting, who has owned the team since 2007. It couldn't have been any other way.

Owners are owners, and problematic for both intrinsic and obvious reasons; Huntington's job, given the constraints placed upon him by ownership, is to do the best he can with whatever chance ownership deigns to give him. He's proven to be pretty good at that fundamentally impossible job, and the Pirates bounced back to a winning record in 2018 and made some trades that promise to keep them both affordable and *competitive* in years to come. None of the players Huntington has recently acquired—affordable demi-ace Chris Archer, reliably cromulent slugger Corey Dickerson, live-armed reliever Keone Kela—came up, and neither did the franchise mainstays he dealt away under ownership-induced duress in exchange for notably less compelling players. The Pirates are back where they've spent these last lost decades, in pursuit of *competitive*, which means that the players are somewhere between incidental and academic. Mostly, of course, they are fungible. They are not there for bigger things, really, but also bigger things are not in play.

On the ghost roster that my correspondents gave back, one name surprised me more than the others, if only because I'd mostly forgotten that he was even with the team. Juan Nicasio was with the Pirates only briefly, but also he has played for six teams in eight big league seasons. He came aboard as a bit of classic Pirates arbitrage, a busted starter with an electric arm and negligible salary who might possibly figure things out under pitching coach Ray Searage. It took a year, but Nicasio did indeed figure it out, just in time for the team's 2017 stretch collapse.

Nicasio was one of the more effective relievers in the National League that year, even as the team slid out of contention. Instead of trading him at the deadline, the Pirates mysteriously let him go to the Phillies on waivers, where he made just two appearances before being dealt to the Cardinals, the team to which Huntington and his ownership had declined to trade him at the deadline. The machinations saved the Pirates about half a million dollars, cost them a pitcher they'd decided they couldn't re-sign—Nicasio, now established as a quality reliever, went on to sign a two-year, $17 million deal with the Mariners—and a shot at the fringe-y prospect that the Phillies got for their role in facilitating the deal. More than that, though, the specific circumstances of his departure clarified a deeper bleakness that fans had long dreaded looking in the face.

When the team declined to improve that nascent juggernaut between 2015 and 2016, it was clear that while the Pirates would do their level best to be *competitive*, they were not quite willing to take the risks required to actually win. This was a slight, but the pettiness of the Nicasio goofery was somehow worse. "It was a small moment, but I think for even a lot of hardcore Pirates fans that was a breaking point," a correspondent wrote. It wasn't just that they weren't trying to win. It was that it wasn't at all clear what they were trying to do, period. The team had given away a player that it had made valuable, and to a divisional rival through an opportunistic proxy team, for "just the most petty, meaningless amount of savings" and nothing else. Those were the comedy writer's words, if you were wondering. So that's about where we are.

⚾   ⚾   ⚾

It's something of a cliché among wised-up sports fans that the worst place for a team to be is in the middle. If you're on top, then you're on top; if you're on the bottom, there's at least some draft-driven opportunity to rebuild and, if the tank is branded properly, to build some perverse-ish Stockholm Syndrome spirit among the fans. The wide space between is not quite the wasteland it's cracked up to be, but it is also vast enough for a team to get lost in and certainly no place to take out a mortgage. After a budget-minded semi-teardown over the winter sent erstwhile cornerstones

Andrew McCutchen and Gerrit Cole out of town and brought back a collection of big league-ready but otherwise unremarkable young players, the Pirates won 82 games in 2018, good for fourth place in the National League Central and not really within hailing distance of the second Wild Card. They were competitive enough, late enough to justify a pair of July moves that brought in actual big league contributors in the bullpen and the rotation. In sum, the team was busy and better than mediocre, and in retrospect significantly less depressing than might have been expected after its offseason sell-off. That's about the size of the team's accomplishments in 2018, but it's not nothing. But also what is it, really?

Or, to reel back the doom and pull in the focus a bit, what is it that the Pittsburgh Pirates are trying to do, let alone trying to *be*, in 2019 and beyond? When the team seemed poised to break through after that brilliant 2015 season—a season in which no regular member of the starting lineup was older than 29 and the team's farm system was rated by BP as eighth-best in the game—the organization instead busily stood pat and so began to decline. They remained *competitive*—they will continue to be competitive, because Huntington is competent in the ways his predecessors were not and because the organization's best homegrown prospects are nearing the bigs—but they made clear that they were not aiming any higher than that.

For much of the Pirates' time in the wilderness it was not really clear what the team was even trying to do. One high draft pick after another flamed out or topped out or disappeared quietly during their umpteenth desolate Gulf Coast League rehab assignment; the players that survived represented the team with dignity as its sole All-Star selection until it came time to pay them what they were worth. The old Littlefieldian illogic—eagerly picking up the millions left on Matt Morris's contract while flipping homegrown stars for Groupons and Bobby Fucking Hill—is blessedly by the boards. It is clear what Huntington is doing, for the most part, and clear that he knows how to do it decently well. The Pirates will develop players, sometimes better and sometimes worse, and then seek to lock them up to team-friendly deals through their arbitration years; they will chase arbitrage opportunities wherever and whenever they find them, with an emphasis on versatility and depth and cost control. More or less every team does this now, of course. The question is whether the Pirates are willing to do more than that, and whether there's any institutional appetite to do more than compete.

In 2019, the Opening Day payroll is expected to once again be among the lowest in the league. Some help is on the way from within the system. Mitch Keller is the only real elite pitching prospect the team has at the moment, but he is indeed an elite pitching prospect. Despite the fact that he hasn't yet hit for much power in games, 2015 first-rounder Ke'Bryan Hayes drew a Josh Donaldson comp from a talent evaluator I spoke to and there are intriguing prospects studded throughout the system. The Major League roster still features a healthy amount of affordable, high-quality talent, and Huntington has done well at adding more of that on the cheap when he can. This is not always about buying low and seeing things other teams don't; the Pirates have stood by the affordable and versatile Korean infielder Jung-Ho Kang despite serial drunk-driving arrests and a sexual assault accusation, seemingly mostly because of how affordable and versatile he is. Cynicism at the top—owner Bob Nutting's family fortune has been estimated at $1.1 billion, which makes him both one of the richer owners in baseball[3] and someone who should be embarrassed to run the payrolls he does—shows up with unpredictable toxicity downstream. That's always the way it works.

The Pirates are not alone in this. Major League Baseball's unofficial Ennui Division has never been more crowded or competitive, with something like a third of MLB teams are not trying any harder or aiming any higher than the Pirates. Some of them are actively trying to get worse, in the hope that this will later make them better. Some are hoping to improve without spending any money on improvements, which is at least ambitious, or to stay roughly the same without upsetting anyone, which is maybe even more so. All of them are trying, very hard, not to get any more expensive. Many of those teams are much less competent in their pursuit of those lustily hedged goals, and led by ownership that's cheaper or more cynical than Nutting. This likely isn't really much comfort to Pirates fans, though. While they're at the top end of the Ennui Division, the Pirates will play their baseball in the National League Central once the weather gets nice enough, and that division is stocked with teams that have shown more organizational will and capacity to go for it.

The Pirates could be both a decent-to-good team and the fourth-best team in their five-team division. They could also be roughly that good and still finish last. It's a good division and baseball is weird like that, but also that doesn't really seem to be the point. Since it is by now quite clear what the Pirates are willing to do as an organization, and more painfully what they are not willing to do, the usual work of setting expectations seems both drearier and easier. All those decades of towering ineptitude have been exorcised, and what's replaced all that strange failure is something more rational and efficient and infinitely better executed, but finally not all that much more satisfying. Everyone involved unquestionably knows what they're doing, but it is also obvious what that is. The Pirates will be competitive, and lord knows they've certainly been much worse. It's the just barely unspoken willingness to leave it all there that stings. ∎

—David Roth is a senior editor at Deadspin.

1. Starkey, Joe. "Pirates Must Be Kidding." Trib Live. Accessed 26 December 2018. https://triblive.com/x/pittsburghtrib/sports/columnists/starkey/s_511615.html#axzz2dxVvGEK6

2. AP. "GM Littlefield Out After Another Lost Pirates Season. Accessed 26 December 2018. http://www.espn.com/mlb/news/story?id=3008832

3. Anonymous. "The Ten Richest MLB Owners." CNBC. Accessed 26 December 2018. https://www.cnbc.com/2012/04/03/The-10-Richest-MLB-Owners.html?slide=2

HITTERS

Josh Bell 1B   Born: 08/14/92   Age: 26   Bats: B   Throws: R   Height: 6'4"   Weight: 235   Origin: Round 2, 2011 Draft (#61 overall)

YEAR	TEAM	LVL	AGE	PA	R	2B	3B	HR	RBI	BB	K	SB	CS	AVG/OBP/SLG	DRC+	VORP	BABIP	BRR	FRAA	WARP
2016	IND	AAA	23	484	57	23	4	14	60	57	74	3	7	.295/.382/.468	139	24.1	.328	-4.0	1B(96): -3.4, RF(4): 1.3	2.3
2016	PIT	MLB	23	152	18	8	0	3	19	21	19	0	1	.273/.368/.406	109	6.4	.294	0.2	1B(23): -0.3, RF(16): -2.3	0.2
2017	PIT	MLB	24	620	75	26	6	26	90	66	117	2	4	.255/.334/.466	110	19.2	.278	-3.7	1B(147): -6.5	0.7
2018	PIT	MLB	25	583	74	31	4	12	62	77	104	2	5	.261/.357/.411	105	19.2	.305	-0.8	1B(137): -6.8	0.4
2019	PIT	MLB	26	609	69	27	4	18	74	71	106	3	4	.256/.345/.421	114	18.3	.288	-1.4	1B -5	1.4

Breakout: 5%   Improve: 50%   Collapse: 2%   Attrition: 8%   MLB: 98%   Comparables: Logan Morrison, Conor Jackson, James Loney

At first glance, Bell stagnated in 2018. The power he showed in 2017 disappeared. Although he made up for it in other areas, his overall offensive production, while acceptable, was slightly below average for a major-league first baseman. However, after struggling early, Bell was able to make a mechanical adjustment that turned his season around in the second half. Then-Pirates hitting coach Jeff Branson identified a timing issue and coaxed Bell to get his front foot down earlier, allowing him to make contact sooner and drive the ball like he was doing in 2017. There isn't enough data to know if the change will stick, but the talent is there. If Bell can combine his superb batting eye with a sustainable power stroke, Pittsburgh could finally see Bell's immense potential translate to on-the-field results for a full season.

Francisco Cervelli C   Born: 03/06/86   Age: 33   Bats: R   Throws: R   Height: 6'1"   Weight: 210   Origin: International Free Agent, 2003

YEAR	TEAM	LVL	AGE	PA	R	2B	3B	HR	RBI	BB	K	SB	CS	AVG/OBP/SLG	DRC+	VORP	BABIP	BRR	FRAA	WARP
2016	PIT	MLB	30	393	42	14	1	1	33	56	72	6	2	.264/.377/.322	95	16.6	.329	-2.9	C(95): 10.5, 1B(2): -0.1	2.5
2017	PIT	MLB	31	304	31	13	2	5	31	32	65	0	2	.249/.342/.370	90	12.1	.311	-2.9	C(78): -5.6	0.3
2018	PIT	MLB	32	404	39	15	3	12	57	51	84	2	3	.259/.378/.431	117	33.3	.308	0.7	C(94): -3.9, 1B(5): -0.1	2.5
2019	PIT	MLB	33	480	52	20	2	10	51	54	104	3	2	.243/.347/.373	102	19.8	.304	-1.6	C -5, 1B 0	1.6

Breakout: 1%   Improve: 44%   Collapse: 5%   Attrition: 8%   MLB: 92%   Comparables: Sherm Lollar, Miguel Montero, Bob Brenly

Even by catching standards, Cervelli is a late bloomer, so it should come as no surprise that he was late to the most recent hip trend. A ground-ball hitter throughout his Pittsburgh tenure—Cervelli had more than two grounders for each fly ball from 2015 to 2017—he started lifting the ball last year. The early returns were impressive, but after eight home runs in his first 42 games, Cervelli regressed, hitting only four in his final 234 plate appearances. No matter how much power Cervelli does or doesn't provide, or whether he's truly lost the ability to be an above-average framer, his excellent batting eye continued to elevate him above the backstop bourgeoisie in 2018. Entering the last year of a three-year, $31 million contract extension, Cervelli has been a bargain by any yardstick. Because of his long injury history, Cervelli can't be relied upon for 130-plus games, but even at 100 or so he should see another top-10 WARP season at the position.

YEAR	TEAM	P. COUNT	FRM RUNS	BLK RUNS	THRW RUNS	TOT RUNS
2016	PIT	13232	13.0	-1.9	-2.4	7.4
2017	PIT	10368	-6.0	0.5	-1.0	-6.8
2018	PIT	13072	-5.8	-1.1	0.6	-6.5
2019	PIT	15688	-5.0	-1.2	-0.9	-7.1

Lonnie Chisenhall RF Born: 10/04/88 Age: 30 Bats: L Throws: R Height: 6'2" Weight: 190 Origin: Round 1, 2008 Draft (#29 overall)

YEAR	TEAM	LVL	AGE	PA	R	2B	3B	HR	RBI	BB	K	SB	CS	AVG/OBP/SLG	DRC+	VORP	BABIP	BRR	FRAA	WARP
2016	CLE	MLB	27	418	43	25	5	8	57	23	70	6	0	.286/.328/.439	99	7.5	.328	-0.3	RF(118): 1.2, 1B(3): 0.0	1.0
2017	CLE	MLB	28	270	34	17	1	12	53	25	55	2	2	.288/.360/.521	113	12.6	.326	-1.5	RF(45): -1.6, CF(19): -0.2	1.0
2018	CLE	MLB	29	95	11	6	1	1	9	8	12	1	0	.321/.394/.452	109	5.1	.366	-0.2	RF(28): 2.1	0.5
2019	PIT	MLB	30	244	27	13	1	6	29	20	46	2	1	.269/.339/.428	104	7.7	.312	-0.5	RF -1, LF 0	0.8

Breakout: 1%   Improve: 49%   Collapse: 9%   Attrition: 15%   MLB: 91%   *Comparables: David Peralta, Roger Bernadina, Gabe Kapler*

For years, it seemed, Cleveland was waiting for Chisenhall to put it all together. For random spurts, he'd display the offensive skills to make you confident he could hold down an everyday job, only for everything to crater. Every year was the year Chisenhall was supposed to break out, but it never happened. He was a fine glove at the hot corner whose bat was sure to come around, until he wasn't fine there anymore. Then he was a corner outfielder, briefly (and failingly) a center fielder and then back to the corners again. Chisenhall was Cleveland's ultimate enigma, and you thought you'd go gray in the beard waiting for him to become the player many projected when he sat alongside Jason Kipnis atop the pecking order of Indians' prospects. He's been limited to just 365 plate appearances the last two seasons because of calf injuries that cut his season in half in 2017 and lingered throughout 2018. However, on the rare occasion he was healthy enough to swing the bat, he was better than ever before. Now on the wrong side of 30, Chisenhall's small-sample-size success the last two seasons still provides enough promise for him to continue receiving opportunities, but the question becomes whether the calf issues will prevent him from becoming the horse many thought he was meant to be.

Will Craig 1B Born: 11/16/94 Age: 24 Bats: R Throws: R Height: 6'3" Weight: 212 Origin: Round 1, 2016 Draft (#22 overall)

YEAR	TEAM	LVL	AGE	PA	R	2B	3B	HR	RBI	BB	K	SB	CS	AVG/OBP/SLG	DRC+	VORP	BABIP	BRR	FRAA	WARP
2016	WEV	A-	21	274	28	12	0	2	23	41	37	2	0	.280/.412/.362	142	18.3	.322	-2.7	3B(46): 0.1	1.9
2017	BRD	A+	22	542	59	26	1	6	61	62	106	1	3	.271/.373/.371	112	10.8	.335	-7.8	1B(93): 9.4	1.6
2018	ALT	AA	23	549	73	30	3	20	102	42	128	6	3	.248/.321/.448	105	28.6	.288	0.6	1B(122): 8.8	2.0
2019	PIT	MLB	24	251	25	9	0	8	29	17	65	1	0	.208/.280/.351	69	-6.2	.257	-0.5	1B 4	-0.3

Breakout: 2%   Improve: 6%   Collapse: 8%   Attrition: 16%   MLB: 21%   *Comparables: Mark Canha, Brock Peterson, Lars Anderson*

Entering last year, the knock on Craig was a glove limiting him to first base and not enough power to start there in the majors. The good news is Craig added the thump he was lacking, easily besting his professional highs in home runs and extra-base hits. The bad news is this improvement led to much more of an all-or-nothing approach, featuring a higher strikeout rate and an extreme fly-ball profile that isn't a template for long term success. His infield fly rate of 28 percent exposes a severe uppercut swing that worked in the minors but will be toyed with by major-league pitching. Craig should eventually make it to the majors but, barring a change in approach, he's likely to pad his minor-league home run totals more than he'd want.

Oneil Cruz SS Born: 10/04/98 Age: 20 Bats: L Throws: R Height: 6'6" Weight: 175 Origin: International Free Agent, 2015

YEAR	TEAM	LVL	AGE	PA	R	2B	3B	HR	RBI	BB	K	SB	CS	AVG/OBP/SLG	DRC+	VORP	BABIP	BRR	FRAA	WARP
2016	DDO	RK	17	211	28	18	5	0	23	22	44	11	5	.294/.367/.444	106	14.8	.382	0.0	3B(32): 4.5, SS(13): -0.7	1.3
2017	GRL	A	18	375	51	9	1	8	36	28	110	8	7	.240/.293/.342	77	13.5	.323	3.2	3B(47): -9.3, SS(30): 0.2	-0.5
2017	WVA	A	18	63	9	2	1	2	8	8	22	0	0	.218/.317/.400	89	3.5	.323	1.0	3B(15): 0.6, SS(1): 0.0	0.3
2018	WVA	A	19	443	66	25	7	14	59	34	100	11	5	.286/.343/.488	117	37.7	.346	2.5	SS(102): -5.9	2.5
2019	PIT	MLB	20	251	23	6	0	8	28	10	74	2	1	.200/.231/.329	41	-8.9	.250	-0.3	SS -1	-1.0

Breakout: 3%   Improve: 10%   Collapse: 0%   Attrition: 5%   MLB: 12%   *Comparables: Alen Hanson, Trevor Story, Gleyber Torres*

When scouts talk about a prospect towering over his opponents, it's usually a figure of speech complimenting how much better he is than the competition. Listed at 6'6" but actually closer to 6'8", Cruz literally stands out as a giant among men. Acquired from the Dodgers as part of a package for Tony Watson in 2017, Cruz elevated his prospect status last year with a strong campaign in the Sally League as a teenager facing older competition. Cruz will eventually move off short once he fills out, but it's unclear which corner he'll eventually call home. The larger question revolved around his ability to handle advanced pitching, and whether his large strike zone and gangly frame will be exposed as he moves up the ladder.

Elias Diaz C Born: 11/17/90 Age: 28 Bats: R Throws: R Height: 6'1" Weight: 215 Origin: International Free Agent, 2008

YEAR	TEAM	LVL	AGE	PA	R	2B	3B	HR	RBI	BB	K	SB	CS	AVG/OBP/SLG	DRC+	VORP	BABIP	BRR	FRAA	WARP
2016	PIT	MLB	25	4	0	0	0	0	1	0	1	0	0	.000/.000/.000	91	-0.9	.000	0.0	C(1): 0.1	0.0
2016	IND	AAA	25	97	4	3	0	0	10	3	17	1	0	.266/.289/.298	79	-1.1	.325	-1.0	C(25): -2.2	-0.1
2017	IND	AAA	26	229	19	10	0	2	27	9	36	3	0	.266/.298/.339	84	2.2	.311	-1.2	C(50): 6.3	1.1
2017	PIT	MLB	26	200	18	14	0	1	19	11	38	1	0	.223/.265/.314	62	-4.8	.273	-0.9	C(55): -3.8	-0.4
2018	PIT	MLB	27	277	33	20	0	10	34	21	40	0	1	.286/.339/.452	111	21.0	.302	0.5	C(70): 0.6	1.9
2019	PIT	MLB	28	198	20	9	1	5	23	14	35	1	0	.248/.306/.392	89	5.9	.279	0.0	C -1	0.5

Breakout: 4%   Improve: 27%   Collapse: 13%   Attrition: 35%   MLB: 83%   *Comparables: Brayan Pena, Jason Jaramillo, Jett Bandy*

Gushing write-ups and purple prose about player breakouts are typically reserved for high-profile prospects who took longer than expected to develop and eventually turned into superstars. Diaz's metamorphosis from a marginal backup into a quality major-league receiver barely registered any notice, even in the Steel City, but he went from being a punchless backup with mediocre receiving skills to a catcher with pop and, um, mediocre receiving skills. Despite amassing a mere 277 plate appearances and rating as an average defender, Diaz was the 15th-best catcher in baseball by WARP thanks to his newfound power. An adjustment led to a cleaner approach at the plate, with a slight uppercut replacing Diaz's previously level swing. These one-year changes can be ephemeral, but while framing is the contemporary buzzword for catcher value, having someone who can swing the lumber at a weak position helps as well.

YEAR	TEAM	P. COUNT	FRM RUNS	BLK RUNS	THRW RUNS	TOT RUNS
2016	PIT	141	0.0	0.0	0.0	0.5
2017	IND	7000	1.3	-0.4	0.8	1.2
2017	PIT	6832	-5.1	-0.7	0.2	-6.2
2018	PIT	9111	-1.2	-2.0	0.1	-3.2
2019	PIT	6172	-2.5	-0.7	0.1	-3.1

Corey Dickerson LF
Born: 05/22/89   Age: 30   Bats: L   Throws: R   Height: 6'1"   Weight: 200   Origin: Round 8, 2010 Draft (#260 overall)

YEAR	TEAM	LVL	AGE	PA	R	2B	3B	HR	RBI	BB	K	SB	CS	AVG/OBP/SLG	DRC+	VORP	BABIP	BRR	FRAA	WARP
2016	TBA	MLB	27	548	57	36	3	24	70	33	134	0	2	.245/.293/.469	95	7.5	.285	-1.5	LF(76): 4.2, RF(2): -0.3	1.1
2017	TBA	MLB	28	629	84	33	4	27	62	35	152	4	3	.282/.325/.490	100	25.0	.338	-1.9	LF(93): 13.4	2.6
2018	PIT	MLB	29	533	65	35	7	13	55	21	80	8	3	.300/.330/.474	108	16.7	.333	-4.1	LF(124): 10.7	2.7
2019	PIT	MLB	30	556	62	30	4	18	71	34	115	5	3	.267/.318/.447	108	19.2	.313	-2.0	LF 11	3.2

Breakout: 2%   Improve: 43%   Collapse: 3%   Attrition: 9%   MLB: 100%   *Comparables: Yoenis Cespedes, Irish Meusel, George Bell*

If you blinked, you might have missed it when Dickerson was designated for assignment by the Rays last winter, taking them off the hook for paying him $5.95 million. Conventional wisdom suggested some team would claim Dickerson at that price, and the Pirates bit, flipping Daniel Hudson's contract and $1 million for Dickerson's services. Known as a free-swinging, bad-ball hitter, Dickerson radically changed his approach in Pittsburgh, laying off high fastballs and cutting his strikeout rate by nine percentage points as a result. He made significant changes on the other side of the ball as well, winning a Gold Glove backed up by both the scouting reports and the defensive metrics. This would have made for an excellent star turn had Dickerson maintained his power, but leaves him as a solid contributor who seldom gets the respect he deserves.

Adam Frazier 2B
Born: 12/14/91   Age: 27   Bats: L   Throws: R   Height: 5'10"   Weight: 180   Origin: Round 6, 2013 Draft (#179 overall)

YEAR	TEAM	LVL	AGE	PA	R	2B	3B	HR	RBI	BB	K	SB	CS	AVG/OBP/SLG	DRC+	VORP	BABIP	BRR	FRAA	WARP
2016	IND	AAA	24	299	34	16	4	0	22	29	27	17	15	.333/.401/.425	122	26.5	.369	-1.3	LF(44): 2.0, CF(17): -3.1	1.4
2016	PIT	MLB	24	160	21	8	1	2	11	12	26	4	1	.301/.356/.411	99	6.4	.353	-2.3	LF(20): -0.7, 2B(17): -0.7	0.1
2017	PIT	MLB	25	454	55	20	6	6	53	36	57	9	5	.276/.344/.399	100	18.0	.306	1.3	LF(52): 2.8, 2B(42): -2.6	1.4
2018	IND	AAA	26	137	10	5	2	0	18	11	20	1	3	.223/.289/.298	93	-2.3	.262	-0.9	2B(17): 0.0, RF(7): -0.6	0.1
2018	PIT	MLB	26	352	52	23	2	10	35	29	53	1	3	.277/.342/.456	107	21.3	.305	1.7	2B(55): 2.5, LF(14): 0.7	1.8
2019	PIT	MLB	27	607	75	31	4	13	59	48	95	10	7	.265/.334/.406	105	23.4	.300	-0.5	2B 0, CF -2	2.3

Breakout: 6%   Improve: 44%   Collapse: 7%   Attrition: 16%   MLB: 98%   *Comparables: Alberto Callaspo, Kolten Wong, Jemile Weeks*

It's difficult to shed a label or move past a commonly held belief long after it has outlived its usefulness. Mention Frazier and the word "scrappy" comes to mind, primarily because he was never seen as much of a prospect despite decent minor-league results and because his size makes him look like a utility infielder out of central casting in 1975. Frazier was that guy during a minor-league career where he stole a few bases every year but failed to pop more than two dingers at any minor-league level. After hinting at it in 121 games during 2017, he flipped that script in 2018, claiming the Pirates' second base job after Josh Harrison got hurt and nearly matching his professional career home run total in barely 350 PA. Frazier will never be mistaken for a superstar, but every now and then someone cast as a permanent substitute rises to the occasion and becomes more.

Erik Gonzalez INF
Born: 08/31/91   Age: 27   Bats: R   Throws: R   Height: 6'3"   Weight: 195   Origin: International Free Agent, 2008

YEAR	TEAM	LVL	AGE	PA	R	2B	3B	HR	RBI	BB	K	SB	CS	AVG/OBP/SLG	DRC+	VORP	BABIP	BRR	FRAA	WARP
2016	COH	AAA	24	460	62	31	1	11	53	19	88	12	10	.296/.329/.450	101	27.3	.349	0.5	SS(90): 0.2, 2B(8): -1.5	1.9
2016	CLE	MLB	24	17	2	0	0	0	0	1	8	0	1	.313/.353/.313	55	0.2	.625	0.1	SS(8): 0.0, 2B(5): -0.1	-0.1
2017	COH	AAA	25	170	21	4	3	6	13	7	53	5	1	.256/.286/.431	72	2.7	.343	0.3	SS(26): -0.7, 2B(9): -0.5	0.0
2017	CLE	MLB	25	115	18	6	0	4	11	3	37	1	2	.255/.272/.418	64	-1.3	.343	-1.0	2B(36): -0.5, SS(11): 0.1	-0.3
2018	CLE	MLB	26	143	17	10	1	1	16	5	34	3	0	.265/.301/.375	68	3.8	.347	1.9	2B(30): 2.0, 3B(20): 0.9	0.4
2019	PIT	MLB	27	418	43	15	2	10	40	25	120	8	4	.216/.268/.343	64	-3.7	.281	0.7	SS 0, 2B 0	-0.3

Breakout: 7%   Improve: 30%   Collapse: 12%   Attrition: 32%   MLB: 77%   *Comparables: Tim Beckham, Tyler Greene, Jason Donald*

Gonzalez is the epitome of a stopgap utility player, as he bounced between Cleveland and Columbus for a majority of the last three seasons. He can play all four infield positions as well as the corner outfield spots in a pinch while not killing you with the bat, which is more valuable than ever with shortened benches. But utility will only get you so far, particularly when he's as allergic to taking walks as he's been, and that role is probably as far as he can be stretched him unless he's a last resort for a really rough shortstop situation.

Josh Harrison INF
Born: 07/08/87   Age: 31   Bats: R   Throws: R   Height: 5'8"   Weight: 185   Origin: Round 6, 2008 Draft (#191 overall)

YEAR	TEAM	LVL	AGE	PA	R	2B	3B	HR	RBI	BB	K	SB	CS	AVG/OBP/SLG	DRC+	VORP	BABIP	BRR	FRAA	WARP
2016	PIT	MLB	28	522	57	25	7	4	59	18	76	19	4	.283/.311/.388	89	14.2	.323	3.1	2B(128): -0.1, RF(1): -0.2	1.2
2017	PIT	MLB	29	542	66	26	2	16	47	28	90	12	4	.272/.339/.432	106	32.5	.303	1.7	2B(83): -2.6, 3B(49): 2.6	2.4
2018	PIT	MLB	30	374	41	13	1	8	37	18	68	3	0	.250/.293/.363	89	3.0	.286	0.5	2B(87): -5.6, 3B(2): 0.0	0.2
2019	PIT	MLB	31	389	49	20	2	9	38	21	69	8	2	.264/.328/.403	103	15.4	.309	0.8	2B -2, 3B 0	1.4

Breakout: 6%   Improve: 41%   Collapse: 3%   Attrition: 8%   MLB: 92%   *Comparables: Omar Infante, Ronnie Belliard, Dutch Meyer*

When Pittsburgh parted ways with Andrew McCutchen last winter, Harrison became the ersatz face of the franchise (albeit reluctantly; he requested a trade during Spring Training if the reloading Pirates weren't committed to winning in the short term). In some ways, Harrison is a more apt face of the franchise than Cutch was. A tough-as-nails player who isn't afraid to give up his body on both sides of the ball, Harrison has been a solid, if unspectacular, contributor outside of his career year in 2014.

Both Harrison and the Pirates reached a crossroads in 2018. He took the field for a mere 97 games, his lowest total since 2013, and the team took a long look at the next generation of up-and-coming Bucs in September. It has been a long, winding road since May 31, 2011, when Harrison debuted alongside a James McDonald/Dusty Brown battery in a lineup that included Lyle Overbay, Garrett Jones and Ronny Cedeno. The Pirates declined Harrison's $10.5 million option, making 2018 feel even more like a swan song, the torch handed gently to another generation of up-and-comers, much like Harrison when he made his Bucs debut.

Ke'Bryan Hayes 3B   Born: 01/28/97   Age: 22   Bats: R   Throws: R   Height: 6'1"   Weight: 210   Origin: Round 1, 2015 Draft (#32 overall)

YEAR	TEAM	LVL	AGE	PA	R	2B	3B	HR	RBI	BB	K	SB	CS	AVG/OBP/SLG	DRC+	VORP	BABIP	BRR	FRAA	WARP
2016	WVA	A	19	276	27	12	1	6	37	16	51	6	5	.263/.319/.393	103	12.4	.304	-1.5	3B(64): 2.0	1.0
2017	BRD	A+	20	482	66	16	7	2	43	41	76	27	5	.278/.345/.363	109	18.0	.331	0.8	3B(108): 20.7	4.4
2018	ALT	AA	21	508	64	31	7	7	47	57	84	12	5	.293/.375/.444	113	38.7	.344	-0.8	3B(116): 9.0	3.5
2019	PIT	MLB	22	251	29	8	2	5	22	18	51	4	1	.234/.291/.354	75	-1.4	.273	0.3	3B 4	0.3

Breakout: 6%   Improve: 28%   Collapse: 4%   Attrition: 28%   MLB: 38%   *Comparables: Taylor Green, Matt Dominguez, Rio Ruiz*

Hayes' numbers won't ever leap off the page, but the 21-year-old phenom continued to impress in his climb up the Pirates' organizational ladder. This year, Hayes passed the Double-A test with flying colors, not only holding his own as one of the youngest regulars in the circuit but posting numbers better than many of the older players in the Eastern League. Hayes already projects as a future major league third baseman; the question is if he will provide enough power to be a valuable contributor with the bat. The instincts and glovework continue to improve, and Hayes already looks like he has a higher ceiling than his ex-major-league dad Charlie ever did.

Jung-ho Kang 3B   Born: 04/05/87   Age: 32   Bats: R   Throws: R   Height: 6'0"   Weight: 210   Origin: International Free Agent, 2015

YEAR	TEAM	LVL	AGE	PA	R	2B	3B	HR	RBI	BB	K	SB	CS	AVG/OBP/SLG	DRC+	VORP	BABIP	BRR	FRAA	WARP
2016	IND	AAA	29	57	5	0	0	2	7	7	11	0	1	.146/.246/.271	94	-0.8	.135	-0.2	3B(13): -0.7	0.1
2016	PIT	MLB	29	370	45	19	0	21	62	36	79	3	1	.255/.354/.513	126	26.9	.273	-3.7	3B(92): 8.5	3.1
2018	BRD	A+	31	32	5	2	0	3	11	6	3	1	0	.417/.531/.875	157	7.2	.368	0.5	SS(4): -0.6, 3B(2): 0.1	0.4
2018	IND	AAA	31	39	4	1	0	0	5	3	5	0	1	.235/.308/.265	89	-2.7	.267	-1.9	3B(5): -0.6, SS(4): 0.2	-0.1
2018	PIT	MLB	31	6	0	0	0	0	0	0	1	0	0	.333/.333/.333	98	-0.4	.400	-0.4	3B(1): 0.0	0.0
2019	PIT	MLB	32	314	35	13	1	10	35	24	68	2	1	.227/.304/.376	89	2.6	.270	-2.1	3B 4, SS 0	0.6

Breakout: 3%   Improve: 32%   Collapse: 5%   Attrition: 9%   MLB: 97%   *Comparables: Troy Tulowitzki, Carlos Guillen, Vern Stephens*

Kang's legal troubles may have ended when he was granted a work visa by the United States in April, but 2018 was yet another lost season for the Korean third baseman. Kang fared terribly in the Dominican Winter League, so the Pirates took their sweet time getting him ready for game action once he came back to the States, sending Kang to instructs in late April before gradually easing him into minor-league action in June. Kang tore up High-A ball and then struggled at Triple-A before a wrist injury sidelined him and knocked him out until the last week of the regular season. The Pirates then inexplicably promoted him for three meaningless major-league contests in September. While he could return in 2019 and be the hitter he was in 2015-2016, there's no historical comp for this sort of comeback. The Pirates declined Kang's $5.5 million option, but quickly brought him back on a bonus-laden one-year deal for $3 million, multiple off-the-field transgressions be damned.

Kevin Kramer 2B   Born: 10/03/93   Age: 25   Bats: L   Throws: R   Height: 6'0"   Weight: 200   Origin: Round 2, 2015 Draft (#62 overall)

YEAR	TEAM	LVL	AGE	PA	R	2B	3B	HR	RBI	BB	K	SB	CS	AVG/OBP/SLG	DRC+	VORP	BABIP	BRR	FRAA	WARP
2016	BRD	A+	22	513	56	29	2	4	57	48	63	3	9	.277/.352/.378	104	18.0	.312	0.8	2B(103): 9.7	2.7
2017	ALT	AA	23	234	31	17	3	6	27	17	50	7	2	.297/.380/.500	110	20.5	.362	1.7	2B(48): -1.6	1.0
2018	IND	AAA	24	527	73	35	3	15	59	38	127	13	5	.311/.365/.492	118	42.2	.392	1.7	2B(82): -6.3, 3B(19): 0.9	2.6
2018	PIT	MLB	24	40	5	0	0	0	4	2	20	0	0	.135/.175/.135	64	-3.3	.278	0.5	3B(7): -0.3, 2B(4): -0.6	-0.1
2019	PIT	MLB	25	145	15	7	0	4	17	9	41	2	1	.241/.296/.393	77	0.5	.312	-0.1	2B 0, SS 0	0.0

Breakout: 4%   Improve: 23%   Collapse: 13%   Attrition: 26%   MLB: 55%   *Comparables: David Bote, Ryan Raburn, Ryan Adams*

After years of being profiled as a gap hitter without home run power, Kramer changed his hand positioning on the bat and started popping balls over the fence at Triple-A, with 10 of his 13 home runs at Indianapolis coming in his final 328 plate appearances. The Pirates rewarded Kramer with a September promotion and a healthy portion of playing time. It could have gone better. Kramer has hit at every level but is going to have to maintain the power he showed in 2018 to carve out a big-league future. Defensively, he is likely limited to second base; he doesn't have enough range for short or enough arm for third. Kramer will get a long look in 2019.

Starling Marte CF   Born: 10/09/88   Age: 30   Bats: R   Throws: R   Height: 6'1"   Weight: 190   Origin: International Free Agent, 2007

YEAR	TEAM	LVL	AGE	PA	R	2B	3B	HR	RBI	BB	K	SB	CS	AVG/OBP/SLG	DRC+	VORP	BABIP	BRR	FRAA	WARP
2016	PIT	MLB	27	529	71	34	5	9	46	23	104	47	12	.311/.362/.456	100	32.2	.380	4.9	LF(114): 7.5, CF(16): -0.4	2.7
2017	IND	AAA	28	40	4	1	0	1	3	2	8	3	0	.333/.400/.444	88	4.7	.407	0.9	LF(6): -0.4, CF(1): 0.1	0.1
2017	PIT	MLB	28	339	48	7	2	7	31	20	63	21	4	.275/.333/.379	91	10.9	.324	3.4	LF(56): 5.9, CF(25): 3.1	1.8
2018	PIT	MLB	29	606	81	32	5	20	72	35	109	33	14	.277/.327/.460	102	36.7	.312	0.1	CF(139): 7.0	3.1
2019	PIT	MLB	30	657	85	29	5	17	72	41	130	38	12	.262/.325/.409	104	30.9	.312	2.1	CF 6	3.9

Breakout: 1%   Improve: 49%   Collapse: 2%   Attrition: 7%   MLB: 100%   *Comparables: Shane Mack, Aaron Rowand, Adam Jones*

The overwrought narrative surrounding performance-enhancing drugs arguably took another hit last year, as Marte delivered the same level of performance in his first full season post-suspension as he has throughout his major-league career. Marte even reached a career high in home runs, something you're not supposed to be able to do after you've been pinched for juicing. Even factoring in the 80 games he missed in 2017 for ingesting something called Nandrolone, Marte has been one of the ten best outfielders in baseball since his first full season in 2013. He isn't off the charts in any particular area, but his all-around game puts him the next rung right below baseball's best. Marte moved to center field full-time this year and didn't miss a beat, continuing to deliver above-average defense but now from a premium position. Pittsburgh wisely locked him into a club-friendly, option-laden deal back in 2014, making it certain he'll be surefire bargain into his 30s.

Jason Martin CF Born: 09/05/95 Age: 23 Bats: L Throws: R Height: 5'10" Weight: 185 Origin: Round 8, 2013 Draft (#227 overall)

YEAR	TEAM	LVL	AGE	PA	R	2B	3B	HR	RBI	BB	K	SB	CS	AVG/OBP/SLG	DRC+	VORP	BABIP	BRR	FRAA	WARP
2016	LNC	A+	20	462	74	22	7	23	75	55	108	20	12	.270/.357/.533	143	27.8	.310	1.2	CF(54): -8.7, LF(26): -5.8	1.8
2017	BCA	A+	21	198	34	11	2	7	29	20	42	9	5	.287/.354/.494	120	13.7	.333	-1.6	LF(14): 1.1, CF(8): -2.2	0.7
2017	CCH	AA	21	320	38	24	3	11	37	19	82	7	6	.273/.319/.483	99	14.1	.343	1.1	LF(57): -6.9	0.0
2018	ALT	AA	22	289	49	13	5	9	34	28	61	7	8	.325/.392/.522	112	31.7	.396	-0.7	CF(62): -2.4, LF(6): -0.6	1.0
2018	IND	AAA	22	234	20	5	3	4	21	17	52	5	4	.211/.270/.319	83	-5.5	.261	-0.6	CF(53): -6.5, LF(6): -0.3	-0.5
2019	PIT	MLB	23	33	3	1	0	1	3	2	8	1	0	.200/.254/.318	48	-1.2	.243	0.0	RF -1	-0.2

Breakout: 11%   Improve: 28%   Collapse: 10%   Attrition: 33%   MLB: 58%   *Comparables: Brett Phillips, Michael Choice, Lewis Brinson*

If he hadn't been included as part of the Astros' four-player package for Gerrit Cole last winter, Martin would be another face in the crowd, a solid but unspectacular outfielder in Houston's seemingly never-ending plethora of prospects. Instead, Martin's interesting, albeit non-elite, mix of skills makes him someone to watch in Pittsburgh as a potential future starter. He picked up at Double-A Altoona where he left off in the Astros organization, showing decent plate discipline, generating power in a park that eats lefties alive and running enough to keep pitchers honest. Martin had a worse time in Indianapolis than Ron Swanson when he found a shuttered Charles Mulligan's Steakhouse, but he gets a pass given it was his first poor performance as a professional at any level.

Calvin Mitchell RF Born: 03/08/99 Age: 20 Bats: L Throws: L Height: 6'0" Weight: 209 Origin: Round 2, 2017 Draft (#50 overall)

YEAR	TEAM	LVL	AGE	PA	R	2B	3B	HR	RBI	BB	K	SB	CS	AVG/OBP/SLG	DRC+	VORP	BABIP	BRR	FRAA	WARP
2017	PIR	RK	18	185	17	11	0	2	20	24	35	2	3	.245/.351/.352	117	4.4	.303	-0.9	LF(35): 2.6, CF(3): 0.5	0.9
2018	WVA	A	19	495	55	29	3	10	65	41	109	4	5	.280/.344/.427	113	20.4	.347	-4.4	RF(100): 0.5, LF(11): -1.6	1.2
2019	PIT	MLB	20	251	21	10	0	6	25	14	68	0	0	.205/.246/.317	51	-8.9	.257	-0.8	RF 1, LF 0	-0.9

Breakout: 2%   Improve: 6%   Collapse: 0%   Attrition: 4%   MLB: 8%   *Comparables: Franmil Reyes, Caleb Gindl, Nomar Mazara*

In 2018, the Pirates decided to be aggressive with the 2017 second-round pick and start him in full-season ball. For two months, Mitchell was one best hitters in the circuit, then slowly faded as the season wore on—par for the course the first time a prep bat faces a full season of pro ball. Mitchell doesn't possess a sweet swing that generates ooohs and aaahs at the ol' ballyard, but he has a sound approach and knows how to hit, both unusual and coveted traits in a teenager.

Colin Moran 3B Born: 10/01/92 Age: 26 Bats: L Throws: R Height: 6'4" Weight: 205 Origin: Round 1, 2013 Draft (#6 overall)

YEAR	TEAM	LVL	AGE	PA	R	2B	3B	HR	RBI	BB	K	SB	CS	AVG/OBP/SLG	DRC+	VORP	BABIP	BRR	FRAA	WARP
2016	FRE	AAA	23	511	50	18	1	10	69	47	124	3	2	.259/.329/.368	87	5.0	.332	-4.6	3B(109): 5.1, SS(2): -0.3	1.1
2016	HOU	MLB	23	25	1	1	0	0	2	1	8	0	0	.130/.200/.174	68	-3.4	.200	0.1	3B(8): 0.8	0.1
2017	FRE	AAA	24	338	53	15	1	18	63	31	55	0	3	.308/.373/.543	139	27.8	.323	-0.3	3B(57): 0.3, 1B(15): -1.7	2.5
2017	HOU	MLB	24	12	3	0	1	1	3	1	1	0	0	.364/.417/.818	106	2.5	.333	0.6	1B(4): -0.1, 3B(3): -0.2	0.1
2018	PIT	MLB	25	465	49	19	1	11	58	39	82	0	2	.277/.340/.407	106	22.3	.316	-1.5	3B(116): -2.7	1.6
2019	PIT	MLB	26	366	41	19	1	12	47	30	73	1	1	.259/.326/.435	104	10.5	.298	-0.1	3B -1	1.1

Breakout: 4%   Improve: 39%   Collapse: 5%   Attrition: 18%   MLB: 73%   *Comparables: Andy Marte, Conor Gillaspie, Michael Morse*

Moran was freed from what we described as "purgatory" in last winter's *Annual* when the Pirates acquired him as part of an underwhelming package for Gerrit Cole. Moran wasn't supplanting Alex Bregman at the hot corner in Houston unless Bregman fell down a large well—and perhaps not even then—so the trade gave him what he has always needed: an opportunity to play. Ultimately, Moran was a second-division regular at third base whose defensive prowess is only going to get worse from here, just as the scouts foretold. Moran should continue to get opportunities, but he's likely to be the kind of player whose role is questioned if he finds himself on a contending team. For better or worse, that likely buys him some time.

Kevin Newman SS Born: 08/04/93 Age: 25 Bats: R Throws: R Height: 6'1" Weight: 180 Origin: Round 1, 2015 Draft (#19 overall)

YEAR	TEAM	LVL	AGE	PA	R	2B	3B	HR	RBI	BB	K	SB	CS	AVG/OBP/SLG	DRC+	VORP	BABIP	BRR	FRAA	WARP
2016	BRD	A+	22	189	24	10	1	3	24	17	12	4	1	.366/.428/.494	138	28.1	.375	1.4	SS(38): 1.4	1.9
2016	ALT	AA	22	268	41	11	2	2	28	26	24	6	3	.288/.361/.378	110	14.8	.308	2.3	SS(60): 0.3	1.8
2017	ALT	AA	23	375	42	18	2	4	30	22	40	4	2	.259/.310/.359	93	14.2	.282	1.4	SS(78): 0.6	1.6
2017	IND	AAA	23	178	23	11	2	0	11	7	22	7	1	.283/.314/.373	89	4.9	.324	-1.3	SS(38): 0.4	0.5
2018	IND	AAA	24	477	74	30	2	4	35	31	50	28	11	.302/.350/.407	117	32.8	.333	3.2	SS(83): 2.9, 2B(21): -0.6	3.6
2018	PIT	MLB	24	97	7	2	0	0	6	4	23	0	1	.209/.247/.231	65	-4.2	.275	-0.6	SS(24): -1.4, 2B(8): -0.7	-0.3
2019	PIT	MLB	25	382	39	16	1	6	34	21	63	9	4	.242/.289/.348	68	-0.4	.274	0.1	SS 0, 2B 0	-0.1

Breakout: 5%   Improve: 25%   Collapse: 17%   Attrition: 43%   MLB: 72%   *Comparables: Brock Holt, Dixon Machado, Brian Dozier*

Hello, Newman. After three and a half years in the minors, he finally made it to the Pirates for a September cup of coffee and a Drake's Coffee Cake (not the Junior. This was your big boy). The profile hasn't changed since Newman was drafted in the first round back in 2015. He has an excellent feel for hitting but his swing generates virtually no power. The defense is acceptable at shortstop, but if you're going to run an empty .275 batting average out there every day you want Ozzie Smith with the glove as opposed to "acceptable." Newman has the high floor and low ceiling that, like many young Pirates, fits the mold of a complementary player. If he's lucky, his career will last long enough to get a "nice game, pretty boy" from an angry fan on the gravely road behind PNC Park.

Jose Osuna 4C
Born: 12/12/92 Age: 26 Bats: R Throws: R Height: 6'3" Weight: 240 Origin: International Free Agent, 2009

YEAR	TEAM	LVL	AGE	PA	R	2B	3B	HR	RBI	BB	K	SB	CS	AVG/OBP/SLG	DRC+	VORP	BABIP	BRR	FRAA	WARP
2016	ALT	AA	23	283	34	18	3	6	38	23	44	1	1	.269/.329/.435	98	8.3	.298	0.3	1B(55): -3.2, RF(9): -0.4	0.0
2016	IND	AAA	23	234	27	19	1	7	31	13	36	2	3	.291/.333/.482	115	8.8	.322	0.3	1B(27): 0.9, LF(24): 3.9	1.3
2017	IND	AAA	24	41	6	5	0	0	1	5	9	1	1	.250/.341/.389	85	1.2	.333	0.1	1B(6): -0.2, RF(2): 0.0	0.0
2017	PIT	MLB	24	227	31	13	4	7	30	9	40	0	0	.233/.269/.428	80	-1.3	.254	-0.7	RF(25): -0.4, 1B(23): -1.1	-0.2
2018	IND	AAA	25	342	45	26	0	9	59	31	51	5	3	.321/.378/.497	129	30.5	.353	1.4	3B(47): 4.6, 1B(24): -0.7	3.0
2018	PIT	MLB	25	111	14	9	0	3	11	3	22	0	0	.226/.252/.396	76	0.6	.256	0.8	1B(12): 1.9, 3B(7): -0.2	0.2
2019	*PIT*	*MLB*	*26*	*177*	*21*	*8*	*1*	*5*	*19*	*12*	*33*	*1*	*1*	*.242/.300/.394*	*92*	*2.4*	*.274*	*-0.1*	*1B -1, RF 1*	*0.3*

Breakout: 5%   Improve: 33%   Collapse: 11%   Attrition: 26%   MLB: 72%   *Comparables: Danny Valencia, Michael Morse, Andy Marte*

Throughout his career, the knock on Osuna has been he's limited to first base on the defensive side of the spectrum and his bat can't carry him there. The Pirates decided to throw caution to the wind and tried Osuna out at third base, first in the minors and then in September as part of a platoon with Colin Moran. The experiment partially worked. Moran and Osuna both hit well, but their defense at the hot corner resembled Roger Dorn's in the first half of *Major League*. While versatility will never hurt any player's chances at landing a bench job, Osuna needs to show far more with the bat for the Pirates to overlook his deficiencies with the leather.

Gregory Polanco RF
Born: 09/14/91 Age: 27 Bats: L Throws: L Height: 6'5" Weight: 235 Origin: International Free Agent, 2009

YEAR	TEAM	LVL	AGE	PA	R	2B	3B	HR	RBI	BB	K	SB	CS	AVG/OBP/SLG	DRC+	VORP	BABIP	BRR	FRAA	WARP
2016	PIT	MLB	24	587	79	34	4	22	86	53	119	17	6	.258/.323/.463	106	19.6	.291	-1.0	RF(111): 9.8, LF(29): 0.1	2.7
2017	PIT	MLB	25	411	39	20	0	11	35	27	60	8	1	.251/.305/.391	92	3.4	.272	0.5	RF(68): 4.1, LF(25): -2.6	0.8
2018	PIT	MLB	26	535	75	32	6	23	81	61	117	12	2	.254/.340/.499	114	29.2	.287	0.7	RF(124): 1.3	2.3
2019	*PIT*	*MLB*	*27*	*431*	*59*	*21*	*3*	*14*	*48*	*39*	*83*	*11*	*3*	*.254/.328/.431*	*109*	*16.7*	*.291*	*-0.1*	*RF 2*	*2.0*

Breakout: 0%   Improve: 48%   Collapse: 4%   Attrition: 12%   MLB: 97%   *Comparables: Alex Rios, Gerardo Parra, Jason Heyward*

Some high-end prospects show up in the majors and take the world by storm. Others take years to convert their considerable promise into results. Polanco fell in the latter camp, mixing flashes of brilliance with stretches of disappointing performance that made some wonder if he would ever live up to the hype that made him a top-25 prospect heading into his rookie season. In 2018, he didn't exactly struggle out of the gate, but a .201 batting average and league-average production through May 30 didn't inspire confidence, either. Then Polanco took off, with a .287/.359/.557 slash from May 31 until his season ended on September 7 with a bone bruise in his left knee. Polanco then became the personification of the game Operation. Doctors repaired a dislocated shoulder and, in the process, discovered a damaged labrum that required surgery. We won't find out if Polanco's strong finish in 2018 was the beginning of his star turn until the 2019 season is well under way.

Pablo Reyes OF
Born: 09/05/93 Age: 25 Bats: R Throws: R Height: 5'8" Weight: 170 Origin: International Free Agent, 2012

YEAR	TEAM	LVL	AGE	PA	R	2B	3B	HR	RBI	BB	K	SB	CS	AVG/OBP/SLG	DRC+	VORP	BABIP	BRR	FRAA	WARP
2016	BRD	A+	22	355	41	20	1	5	45	37	47	13	8	.265/.341/.386	114	15.8	.293	1.5	SS(36): 3.8, 2B(35): -2.2	2.1
2017	ALT	AA	23	483	62	21	3	10	50	51	70	21	14	.274/.356/.410	110	27.6	.306	-0.4	2B(67): 3.9, CF(31): 1.6	2.7
2018	ALT	AA	24	49	3	3	0	0	5	4	5	3	0	.244/.306/.311	79	-0.3	.275	-0.2	CF(7): -0.7, 2B(3): 0.0	-0.1
2018	IND	AAA	24	398	52	20	4	8	36	28	71	13	7	.289/.341/.435	112	18.5	.338	1.2	LF(42): 3.6, 3B(27): 2.1	1.9
2018	PIT	MLB	24	63	9	2	0	3	7	5	11	0	1	.293/.349/.483	102	4.2	.318	0.4	RF(8): 2.0, LF(6): 0.7	0.5
2019	*PIT*	*MLB*	*25*	*104*	*13*	*5*	*0*	*3*	*10*	*7*	*21*	*3*	*1*	*.253/.306/.402*	*88*	*1.3*	*.290*	*-0.1*	*3B 0, LF 1*	*0.2*

Breakout: 8%   Improve: 27%   Collapse: 8%   Attrition: 28%   MLB: 52%   *Comparables: Phil Ervin, Chris Pettit, Trevor Crowe*

Reyes is an organizational soldier who marched on Pittsburgh, defying long odds as an unheralded and undrafted free agent out of the Dominican Republic in 2012 to make his major league debut last September. Reyes is the kind of player both scouts and projection systems see as "future replacement level," but all he has done since his professional debut as a 17-year-old is rake. Add some decent base-stealing ability and the versatility to play almost any position on the diamond and you've got a player who is deservedly banging on the door. Reyes was being groomed as a utility player in the minors last year, both during the regular season and in winter ball, and will get the opportunity to do the same in the majors.

Bryan Reynolds OF
Born: 01/27/95 Age: 24 Bats: B Throws: R Height: 6'3" Weight: 205 Origin: Round 2, 2016 Draft (#59 overall)

YEAR	TEAM	LVL	AGE	PA	R	2B	3B	HR	RBI	BB	K	SB	CS	AVG/OBP/SLG	DRC+	VORP	BABIP	BRR	FRAA	WARP
2016	SLO	A-	21	171	28	12	1	5	30	11	41	2	0	.312/.368/.500	118	11.7	.391	1.3	CF(33): -4.1	0.5
2016	AUG	A	21	66	11	5	0	1	8	3	20	1	0	.317/.348/.444	79	5.5	.452	0.2	CF(11): 1.5	0.2
2017	SJO	A+	22	541	72	26	9	10	63	37	106	5	3	.312/.364/.462	114	35.8	.376	-0.9	CF(50): -4.3, RF(42): -2.9	1.4
2018	ALT	AA	23	383	56	18	3	7	46	43	73	4	4	.302/.381/.438	119	33.4	.362	-0.2	CF(43): -3.2, LF(42): -3.6	1.5
2019	*PIT*	*MLB*	*24*	*33*	*4*	*1*	*0*	*1*	*4*	*3*	*8*	*0*	*0*	*.252/.310/.393*	*80*	*0.1*	*.309*	*0.0*	*LF 0*	*0.0*

Breakout: 3%   Improve: 17%   Collapse: 10%   Attrition: 22%   MLB: 33%   *Comparables: Bryan Petersen, Jake Cave, Austin Dean*

When the Pirates finally said their sad, perhaps inevitable goodbye to franchise icon Andrew McCutchen, many fans were underwhelmed by the return for the heart and soul of their team. From a fan perspective, it was difficult to fall in love with a trade that didn't have a true centerpiece, a potential gamechanger who might someday become the next Cutch. It is unfair to compare Reynolds to Cutch, but since he has a higher ceiling than Kyle Crick and you can't scout international slot money without a finance degree, those comparisons will be inevitable. Reynolds is the kind of prospect who underwhelms scouts but has done nothing but perform since being drafted by the Giants in 2016. He falls into that tired "tweener" profile (not good enough defensively for center field, not good enough with the bat for a corner slot), but if he keeps hitting, Reynolds will be in the Pirates' outfield plans sometime in late 2019 or early 2020.

Lolo Sanchez OF
Born: 04/23/99 Age: 20 Bats: R Throws: R Height: 5'11" Weight: 168 Origin: International Free Agent, 2015

YEAR	TEAM	LVL	AGE	PA	R	2B	3B	HR	RBI	BB	K	SB	CS	AVG/OBP/SLG	DRC+	VORP	BABIP	BRR	FRAA	WARP
2016	DPI	RK	17	190	19	4	1	0	10	24	18	4	8	.235/.359/.275	112	5.7	.265	0.0	CF(42): 3.2	1.2
2017	PIR	RK	18	234	42	11	2	4	20	21	19	14	7	.284/.359/.417	115	14.5	.295	-0.9	CF(49): 7.6	1.7
2018	WVA	A	19	441	57	18	1	4	34	41	72	30	13	.243/.322/.328	105	14.2	.287	2.7	CF(88): 8.4, LF(19): -2.1	2.6
2019	PIT	MLB	20	251	28	5	0	5	18	12	50	9	4	.193/.230/.277	30	-12.3	.217	-0.1	CF 3, LF 0	-1.0

Breakout: 1% Improve: 5% Collapse: 0% Attrition: 2% MLB: 5%   *Comparables: Cedric Hunter, Carlos Tocci, Ramon Flores*

Signed as a 16-year-old for a $450,000 bonus out of the Dominican Republic in 2015, Sanchez has impressed scouts with his overall athleticism but lacks any particular tool that stands out. He is a plus runner and advanced defender, but like many of the Pirates prospects profiled on these pages, might never develop the power most hitters need to be an acceptable option in today's game. Sanchez stumbled last year in his first taste of full-season ball, but was only 19 and will get many more opportunities to refine his game against more advanced competition. Sanchez could still grow into his frame but, even if he doesn't, his speed and defense give him a floor as a reliable future backup with the ability to play all three positions in the outfield.

Travis Swaggerty CF
Born: 08/19/97 Age: 21 Bats: L Throws: L Height: 5'11" Weight: 180 Origin: Round 1, 2018 Draft (#10 overall)

YEAR	TEAM	LVL	AGE	PA	R	2B	3B	HR	RBI	BB	K	SB	CS	AVG/OBP/SLG	DRC+	VORP	BABIP	BRR	FRAA	WARP
2018	WEV	A-	20	158	22	9	1	4	15	15	40	9	3	.288/.365/.453	111	12.5	.379	0.9	CF(36): -0.6	0.8
2018	WVA	A	20	71	6	1	1	1	5	7	18	0	0	.129/.225/.226	90	-1.2	.159	-0.6	CF(16): 0.7	0.2
2019	PIT	MLB	21	251	26	8	0	7	23	12	76	2	1	.194/.232/.317	41	-8.6	.249	-0.4	CF -1	-1.1

Breakout: 1% Improve: 1% Collapse: 0% Attrition: 1% MLB: 1%   *Comparables: Abraham Almonte, Xavier Avery, Joe Benson*

The 10th overall pick in the 2018 draft, Swaggerty inked a $4.4 million deal days after the draft was completed and reported to West Virginia. He didn't miss a beat in his professional debut, showing off the athleticism, defense and speed that made scouts drool over the University of South Alabama product in the first place—though his hits didn't quite drop when he moved up to the Sally League. The primary question about Swaggerty's long-term projection is how much power he'll ultimately develop. There is a lot of swing and miss in his bat, and some analysts believe an all-fields approach will serve him better than a swing-for-the-fences mentality that will pump up his strikeouts and expose him against more advanced pitching. Swaggerty's defense is potentially elite, so regardless of how the bat rounds out, he's a likely future major-league center fielder.

Cole Tucker SS
Born: 07/03/96 Age: 22 Bats: B Throws: R Height: 6'3" Weight: 200 Origin: Round 1, 2014 Draft (#24 overall)

YEAR	TEAM	LVL	AGE	PA	R	2B	3B	HR	RBI	BB	K	SB	CS	AVG/OBP/SLG	DRC+	VORP	BABIP	BRR	FRAA	WARP
2016	WVA	A	19	67	9	4	2	1	2	4	9	1	1	.262/.308/.443	104	6.5	.294	0.5	SS(15): 2.8	0.7
2016	BRD	A+	19	304	36	12	1	1	25	29	62	5	6	.238/.312/.301	85	3.1	.306	-1.1	SS(61): 12.6	1.9
2017	BRD	A+	20	316	46	15	6	4	32	34	70	36	12	.285/.364/.426	111	29.9	.368	1.5	SS(66): -0.4	1.9
2017	ALT	AA	20	194	25	4	5	2	18	21	31	11	3	.257/.349/.377	105	11.4	.304	1.3	SS(39): 0.9	1.3
2018	ALT	AA	21	589	77	21	7	5	44	55	104	35	12	.259/.333/.356	96	37.5	.310	3.4	SS(131): -0.6	2.6
2019	PIT	MLB	22	33	4	1	0	1	3	2	7	1	0	.231/.285/.350	66	0.0	.279	0.1	SS 0	0.0

Breakout: 6% Improve: 23% Collapse: 10% Attrition: 20% MLB: 35%   *Comparables: Tyler Wade, Daniel Robertson, Ivan De Jesus*

The stat line wasn't impressive outside of the stolen bases, but Tucker continued to improve his rising prospect stock thanks to a full season of health to go along with all-around improvements in his game. While his home run declined, Tucker displayed more lift in his swing and signs that his raw power will translate more into game action. While no one expects 30+ steals in the majors, 20 is a possibility even if Tucker grows into his 6'3" frame. Questions about whether Tucker will remain at short remain, but even if this is the finished product, he projects as a decent defender on the dirt with good on-base skills. Tucker could arrive on the scene in Pittsburgh in 2019 and will be a mainstay wherever or whenever he plays.

PITCHERS

Chris Archer RHP
Born: 09/26/88 Age: 30 Bats: R Throws: R Height: 6'2" Weight: 195 Origin: Round 5, 2006 Draft (#161 overall)

YEAR	TEAM	LVL	AGE	W	L	SV	G	GS	IP	H	HR	BB/9	K/9	K	GB%	BABIP	WHIP	ERA	DRA	WARP	MPH	FB%	WHF	CSP
2016	TBA	MLB	27	9	19	0	33	33	201¹	183	30	3.0	10.4	233	49%	.297	1.24	4.02	3.38	4.6	97.1	48.5	13.4	45.4
2017	TBA	MLB	28	10	12	0	34	34	201	193	27	2.7	11.1	249	43%	.325	1.26	4.07	3.53	4.6	97.4	47.4	14.6	47.4
2018	TBA	MLB	29	3	5	0	17	17	96	102	11	2.9	9.6	102	46%	.343	1.39	4.31	4.12	1.3	96.5	45.6	14.3	48.6
2018	PIT	MLB	29	3	3	0	10	10	52¹	53	8	3.1	10.3	60	48%	.328	1.36	4.30	4.30	0.6	96.6	49.3	13.2	45.6
2019	PIT	MLB	30	10	9	0	28	28	159²	146	18	2.9	9.7	172	45%	.319	1.23	3.51	4.06	2.3	96.2	47.4	14	46.8

Breakout: 15% Improve: 50% Collapse: 23% Attrition: 5% MLB: 98%   *Comparables: Tim Lincecum, Kenta Maeda, Matt Garza*

It's impossible to discuss Archer without the obligatory mention of how much better his DRA is than his ERA, and to desperately search for reasons why. As was the case when Charlie Day ranted about the existence of Pepe Silvia, reason frequently gives way to irrationality and dubious connections are established that make no sense whatsoever to the informed observer. While Archer has frequently outperformed his peripherals, he finally went from being somewhat unlucky to simply having a less-than-stellar season in 2018. The high strikeout rate we've come to expect from Archer wasn't there, and for the first time since his rookie season, his DRA jumped over four. An abdominal strain sidelined the right-hander in June, but there wasn't a discernable performance improvement when he returned in July. A change of scenery via a trade to Pittsburgh didn't help either. It's tempting to go full Charlie and cover a wall with reams of paper, bright red lines and arrows to figure out if 2018 was the new normal for Archer, but it's more likely it was a blip on the radar and Archer continues to perform like the reliable no. 2 starter that he always has been.

Braxton Ashcraft RHP   Born: 10/05/99   Age: 19   Bats: L   Throws: R   Height: 6'5"   Weight: 195   Origin: Round 2, 2018 Draft (#51 overall)

YEAR	TEAM	LVL	AGE	W	L	SV	G	GS	IP	H	HR	BB/9	K/9	K	GB%	BABIP	WHIP	ERA	DRA	WARP	MPH	FB%	WHF	CSP
2018	PIR	RK	18	0	1	0	5	5	17²	16	2	2.5	6.1	12	52%	.259	1.19	4.58	4.42	0.3				
2019	PIT	MLB	19	1	3	0	7	7	31²	39	7	5.1	5.1	18	46%	.317	1.81	6.93	7.96	-1.0				

Comparables: Antonio Senzatela, Tyrell Jenkins, Sal Romano

The Pirates' second-round pick in the 2018 draft, Ashcraft was lured away from a commitment to Baylor University with a $1.825 million, over-slot bonus. The 18-year-old hurler throws a 92-mph fastball that can scrape 95, and the sinking action on the heater combined with Ashcraft's imposing frame gave Texas prep school hitters fits. His other pitches need refinement, but that's to be expected from a teenager who has plenty of room to grow, both in physicality and consistency. Ashcraft's five starts in rookie ball were unremarkable, but the Pirates are understandably taking the long view.

Steven Brault LHP   Born: 04/29/92   Age: 27   Bats: L   Throws: L   Height: 6'0"   Weight: 200   Origin: Round 11, 2013 Draft (#339 overall)

YEAR	TEAM	LVL	AGE	W	L	SV	G	GS	IP	H	HR	BB/9	K/9	K	GB%	BABIP	WHIP	ERA	DRA	WARP	MPH	FB%	WHF	CSP
2016	IND	AAA	24	2	7	0	16	15	71¹	66	6	4.4	10.2	81	39%	.319	1.42	3.91	3.46	1.5				
2016	PIT	MLB	24	0	3	0	8	7	33¹	45	5	4.6	7.8	29	47%	.354	1.86	4.86	5.13	0.1	93.8	67.3	11.1	44.6
2017	IND	AAA	25	10	5	0	21	20	120¹	85	5	3.3	8.2	109	53%	.252	1.07	1.94	4.01	2.2				
2017	PIT	MLB	25	1	0	1	11	4	34²	41	3	3.6	6.0	23	45%	.317	1.59	4.67	6.17	-0.3	93.6	72	8.8	46.8
2018	PIT	MLB	26	6	3	0	45	5	91²	84	10	5.6	8.1	82	50%	.289	1.54	4.61	5.66	-0.7	94.7	65	10.8	46.9
2019	PIT	MLB	27	3	1	0	57	0	59²	52	6	4.4	8.8	59	46%	.300	1.36	4.09	4.72	0.2	93.9	67.6	10.6	46.8

Breakout: 23%   Improve: 39%   Collapse: 18%   Attrition: 21%   MLB: 76%   *Comparables: Alex Colome, Chris Bassitt, Adam Warren*

The highlight of Brault's season came on June 19 against the Milwaukee Brewers. Brault didn't take the mound that day but the microphone, belting out a beautiful rendition of the national anthem in full uniform. Unfortunately for the Pirates, very little about Brault's 2018 was pitch perfect. He picked up some velocity on his fastball but not enough to keep hitters guessing. On August 3, Brault's season struck a minor key, as the Pirates demoted him to Triple-A. It's been the same sad song for Brault throughout his big-league career, and unless something changes his appearances for Pittsburgh will be nothing but music to opposing batters' ears.

Kyle Crick RHP   Born: 11/30/92   Age: 26   Bats: L   Throws: R   Height: 6'4"   Weight: 220   Origin: Round 1, 2011 Draft (#49 overall)

YEAR	TEAM	LVL	AGE	W	L	SV	G	GS	IP	H	HR	BB/9	K/9	K	GB%	BABIP	WHIP	ERA	DRA	WARP	MPH	FB%	WHF	CSP
2016	RIC	AA	23	4	11	0	23	23	109	110	8	5.5	7.1	86	46%	.311	1.62	5.04	3.79	1.7				
2017	SAC	AAA	24	1	2	6	24	0	29¹	24	1	4.0	12.0	39	45%	.329	1.26	2.76	2.74	0.8				
2017	SFN	MLB	24	0	0	0	30	0	32¹	22	2	4.7	7.8	28	39%	.233	1.21	3.06	4.29	0.3	96.7	74.5	12.1	45.7
2018	PIT	MLB	25	3	2	2	64	0	60¹	45	3	3.4	9.7	65	43%	.268	1.13	2.39	4.41	0.4	97.4	72.9	12.6	47.9
2019	PIT	MLB	26	2	1	0	46	0	49	43	5	4.4	9.7	53	42%	.309	1.36	3.97	4.58	0.2	96.8	74.7	12.7	47.8

Breakout: 21%   Improve: 47%   Collapse: 15%   Attrition: 17%   MLB: 70%   *Comparables: Esmerling Vasquez, Jeremy Jeffress, Keyvius Sampson*

As sometimes happens with pitchers drafted out of high school, Crick devolved from a high-upside arm scouts and fantasy players dream on to a long-term project only a pitching coach could love. The Pirates inherited that project from the Giants last winter, grabbing Crick as part of the package for Andrew McCutchen. The results in his first full major-league season were okay. Literally. Despite a glittering ERA, cFIP pegged Crick as a league-average reliever. Though, for him, 2018 wasn't about a miraculous turnaround but rather about establishing himself as a viable major-league option both now and in the future. Crick did exactly that, harnessing more control than he's ever shown while still touching in the mid-90s on the gun and turning into a bit of a righty killer. Maybe Ray Searage will coax more than this out of Crick, but the 2018 version of Crick remains more than anyone was expecting at the end of his Giants tenure.

Luis Escobar RHP   Born: 05/30/96   Age: 23   Bats: R   Throws: R   Height: 6'2"   Weight: 210   Origin: International Free Agent, 2013

YEAR	TEAM	LVL	AGE	W	L	SV	G	GS	IP	H	HR	BB/9	K/9	K	GB%	BABIP	WHIP	ERA	DRA	WARP	MPH	FB%	WHF	CSP
2016	WEV	A-	20	6	5	0	15	12	67²	50	4	3.7	8.1	61	43%	.254	1.15	2.93	2.87	1.8				
2017	WVA	A	21	10	7	0	26	25	131²	97	9	4.1	11.5	168	44%	.282	1.19	3.83	2.93	3.6				
2018	BRD	A+	22	7	6	0	17	16	92²	76	9	3.7	8.3	85	48%	.272	1.23	3.98	3.93	1.5				
2018	ALT	AA	22	4	0	0	7	7	35²	30	4	5.3	6.3	25	43%	.248	1.43	4.54	4.05	0.5				
2019	PIT	MLB	23	1	0	0	21	0	21²	21	3	4.7	7.9	19	39%	.299	1.48	5.07	5.82	0.0				

Breakout: 6%   Improve: 16%   Collapse: 11%   Attrition: 17%   MLB: 32%   *Comparables: Aaron Blair, Jon Gray, Lucas Sims*

In a system that isn't pitching rich, Escobar is arguably Pittsburgh's best pitching prospect this side of Mitch Keller. Escobar throws in the mid-90s with ease and possesses a curve that could become a plus pitch as well. The issues that plagued Escobar in 2017—lack of command and the need for a consistent third pitch—dogged him in 2018 as well. Escobar struggled in his first taste of the upper minors before being suspended by the organization at the end of the year for "violating club policies." How much Escobar can develop his command and improve the change will determine if his future is as a mid-tier starting pitcher or in the bullpen.

Michael Feliz RHP   Born: 06/28/93   Age: 26   Bats: R   Throws: R   Height: 6'4"   Weight: 230   Origin: International Free Agent, 2010

YEAR	TEAM	LVL	AGE	W	L	SV	G	GS	IP	H	HR	BB/9	K/9	K	GB%	BABIP	WHIP	ERA	DRA	WARP	MPH	FB%	WHF	CSP
2016	FRE	AAA	23	1	0	0	2	2	8¹	8	1	7.6	7.6	7	44%	.292	1.80	9.72	4.20	0.1				
2016	HOU	MLB	23	8	1	0	47	0	65	55	10	3.0	13.2	95	42%	.315	1.18	4.43	2.44	1.9	98.1	63.3	14.5	46.2
2017	HOU	MLB	24	4	2	0	46	0	48	53	8	4.1	13.1	70	31%	.381	1.56	5.62	3.18	1.1	98.1	71.9	15.4	50.4
2018	IND	AAA	25	2	1	2	9	0	10	13	2	0.9	10.8	12	40%	.393	1.40	7.20	2.74	0.3				
2018	PIT	MLB	25	1	2	0	47	0	47²	49	6	4.3	10.4	55	33%	.331	1.51	5.66	5.20	-0.1	97.0	73.6	11	46.1
2019	PIT	MLB	26	2	1	0	46	0	49	44	6	3.6	10.2	56	38%	.315	1.30	3.87	4.46	0.3	97.3	71.3	13.6	48.4

Breakout: 32%   Improve: 49%   Collapse: 9%   Attrition: 14%   MLB: 82%   *Comparables: Hong-Chih Kuo, Fernando Cabrera, Jensen Lewis*

"Closer stuff." Even in the metrics-driven world of 2018, this is still shorthand for a high relief ceiling. Feliz has been tagged with this label ever since he was a teenager in the Astros' system. The problem is that while his raw stuff is drool-worthy, he is consistently inconsistent. Feliz's slider is a wipeout pitch, but when he can't throw it for strikes, hitters simply wait for ball four or a meaty fastball. His inaugural season as a Pirate was a lost one, and he has now struggled with his command/consistency for a season and a half. He has the talent to turn it around, but this can be said for any of the gazillion relievers on the cusp of a big-league roster with one superb pitch.

Clay Holmes RHP   Born: 03/27/93   Age: 26   Bats: R   Throws: R   Height: 6'5"   Weight: 230   Origin: Round 9, 2011 Draft (#272 overall)

YEAR	TEAM	LVL	AGE	W	L	SV	G	GS	IP	H	HR	BB/9	K/9	K	GB%	BABIP	WHIP	ERA	DRA	WARP	MPH	FB%	WHF	CSP
2016	ALT	AA	23	10	9	0	26	26	136¹	138	10	4.2	6.7	101	63%	.314	1.48	4.22	3.80	2.1				
2017	IND	AAA	24	10	5	0	25	24	112²	96	4	4.7	7.9	99	62%	.302	1.38	3.36	4.51	1.5				
2018	BRD	A+	25	0	0	0	1	1	6	4	0	0.0	12.0	8	79%	.286	0.67	1.50	1.44	0.3				
2018	IND	AAA	25	8	3	0	22	16	95¹	94	4	3.8	9.4	100	61%	.346	1.41	3.40	5.05	0.5				
2018	PIT	MLB	25	1	3	0	11	4	26¹	30	2	7.9	7.2	21	58%	.346	2.01	6.84	6.25	-0.3	97.2	70.1	7.8	43.3
2019	PIT	MLB	26	3	3	0	23	8	56¹	53	5	4.3	8.5	53	56%	.318	1.41	3.95	4.57	0.3	96.8	71.4	8	44

Breakout: 18%   Improve: 30%   Collapse: 19%   Attrition: 28%   MLB: 56%   *Comparables: Dallas Beeler, Jimmy Nelson, Jesse Biddle*

(exasperated sigh)

"How many times do I have to go through this? My name is Clay Holmes. I am a pitching prospect for the Pittsburgh Pirates. I made my major-league debut in 2018. The Pirates primarily used me as a reliever, although I started three times. I throw baseballs, not stones. The baseballs I throw can touch 99 mph, although it is more common for them to travel in the mid-90s. I sometimes have difficulty controlling those baseballs and hand out a lot of walks when that happens. My future is most likely going to be as a reliever, hopefully in a major-league bullpen. But your joke about 'people in glass houses shouldn't throw stones' is idiotic. My name isn't Glass Houses. It's Clay Holmes. And even if my name were 'Glass Houses,' I'd be the glass house, not the person inside of the glass house throwing stones. Your joke would work if there were little people inside me controlling everything I say and do, just like there were for Herman Brooks, the beloved title character in the witty yet short-lived early 1990s sitcom *Herman's Head*. Otherwise, your attempt at cheap humor at the expense of my perfectly NORMAL NAME simply doesn't make any sense."

Steven Jennings RHP   Born: 11/13/98   Age: 20   Bats: R   Throws: R   Height: 6'2"   Weight: 175   Origin: Round 2, 2017 Draft (#42 overall)

YEAR	TEAM	LVL	AGE	W	L	SV	G	GS	IP	H	HR	BB/9	K/9	K	GB%	BABIP	WHIP	ERA	DRA	WARP	MPH	FB%	WHF	CSP
2017	PIR	RK	18	0	2	0	10	10	26¹	31	2	3.4	4.4	13	57%	.305	1.56	4.10	6.12	0.0				
2018	BRI	RK	19	3	4	0	13	13	65¹	68	5	3.7	7.3	53	46%	.307	1.45	4.82	4.36	1.2				
2019	PIT	MLB	20	2	5	0	11	11	47¹	59	10	5.9	4.7	25	46%	.318	1.91	6.94	7.98	-1.5				

Comparables: Jordan Hicks, Clay Holmes, Sandy Alcantara

Jennings threw for 2,131 yards and rushed for another 908 as a junior quarterback before being selected in the second round of the 2017 draft. But this was in high school, not college, and the draft in question was for baseball, not football. That's right, Jennings is one of those athletic, projectable types who hasn't done anything noteworthy as a professional to date. Scouts project a mid-rotation ceiling for Jennings, thanks to a good feel for two breaking pitches and a fastball that hit 96 on the gun even though he was wearing a knee brace because of a torn ACL suffered on the gridiron. The raw numbers across two short seasons look rough, but a $1.9 million bonus and a high ceiling will give Jennings oodles of chances.

Keone Kela RHP   Born: 04/16/93   Age: 26   Bats: R   Throws: R   Height: 6'1"   Weight: 215   Origin: Round 12, 2012 Draft (#396 overall)

YEAR	TEAM	LVL	AGE	W	L	SV	G	GS	IP	H	HR	BB/9	K/9	K	GB%	BABIP	WHIP	ERA	DRA	WARP	MPH	FB%	WHF	CSP
2016	TEX	MLB	23	5	1	0	35	0	34	30	6	4.5	11.9	45	46%	.304	1.38	6.09	4.33	0.3	98.0	62.2	12.9	47.1
2017	TEX	MLB	24	4	1	2	39	0	38²	18	4	4.0	11.9	51	32%	.179	0.91	2.79	4.75	0.2	98.2	57.9	12.2	49.6
2018	TEX	MLB	25	3	3	24	38	0	36²	28	3	3.4	10.8	44	40%	.275	1.15	3.44	3.50	0.6	98.5	64.3	12.7	49.5
2018	PIT	MLB	25	0	1	0	16	0	15¹	10	2	2.9	12.9	22	27%	.258	0.98	2.93	2.37	0.5	98.2	58.7	16.1	50.3
2019	PIT	MLB	26	3	1	0	57	0	59²	47	7	3.7	11.2	74	40%	.299	1.19	3.44	3.97	0.6	97.9	62.4	13.3	49.9

Breakout: 29%   Improve: 55%   Collapse: 21%   Attrition: 8%   MLB: 93%   *Comparables: Corey Knebel, Rex Brothers, Ken Giles*

It took far longer than anticipated, but Kela ascended to the top of the Rangers' bullpen and took over as closer at the beginning of 2018. As is the case with many young stoppers, Kela failed to make it through the year as closer, but in his case it wasn't injury or ineffectiveness but rather a trade that removed him from the role. Kela picked up right where he left off after joining the Pirates but was never going to supplant Felipe Vazquez regardless of how either hurler performed. Kela is almost exclusively a two-pitch pitcher but it's his hard, biting curveball that makes him so devastating, especially against right-handers. Pittsburgh shut Kela down due to "workload concerns" in September, but he is expected to be ready to answer the bell on Opening Day.

Mitch Keller RHP   Born: 04/04/96   Age: 23   Bats: R   Throws: R   Height: 6'3"   Weight: 195   Origin: Round 2, 2014 Draft (#64 overall)

YEAR	TEAM	LVL	AGE	W	L	SV	G	GS	IP	H	HR	BB/9	K/9	K	GB%	BABIP	WHIP	ERA	DRA	WARP	MPH	FB%	WHF	CSP
2016	WVA	A	20	8	5	0	23	23	124¹	96	4	1.3	9.5	131	48%	.284	0.92	2.46	2.86	3.3				
2016	BRD	A+	20	1	0	0	1	1	6	5	0	1.5	10.5	7	47%	.333	1.00	0.00	2.80	0.2				
2017	BRD	A+	21	6	3	0	15	15	77¹	57	5	2.3	7.4	64	55%	.248	1.00	3.14	5.75	-0.4				
2017	ALT	AA	21	2	2	0	6	6	34²	25	2	2.9	11.7	45	48%	.280	1.04	3.12	3.36	0.8				
2018	ALT	AA	22	9	2	0	14	14	86	64	7	3.3	8.0	76	55%	.251	1.12	2.72	3.82	1.5				
2018	IND	AAA	22	3	2	0	10	10	52¹	59	3	3.8	9.8	57	35%	.366	1.55	4.82	3.71	1.1				
2019	*PIT*	*MLB*	*23*	*2*	*2*	*0*	*8*	*8*	*40*	*37*	*4*	*3.0*	*8.3*	*37*	*44%*	*.304*	*1.26*	*3.91*	*4.51*	*0.4*				

Breakout: 13%   Improve: 17%   Collapse: 14%   Attrition: 31%   MLB: 41%   *Comparables: J.R. Graham, Nick Martinez, Corbin Burnes*

As teams get more aggressive about saving money and maximizing player control, service time shenanigans are keeping more and more top-tier prospects in the minors even when they're clearly ready. Although he's the best prospect in Pittsburgh's system, this wasn't the case for Keller. His lack of a third pitch—a slow-to-develop change—has been a story for Keller for his entire career, and his improvement on this front has been incrementally slow. On the plus side, this is the only knock on an otherwise strong profile. His durability and consistency combined with a mid-90s fastball and plus curve rate him a future major league starter with a mid-rotation floor. Keller is almost definitely going to be part of the Pirates plans in 2019, and while the scouting reports keep hammering home the concept of a no. 2 or 3 starter, the clean delivery and confidence give him ace potential down the road.

Nick Kingham RHP   Born: 11/08/91   Age: 27   Bats: R   Throws: R   Height: 6'5"   Weight: 225   Origin: Round 4, 2010 Draft (#117 overall)

YEAR	TEAM	LVL	AGE	W	L	SV	G	GS	IP	H	HR	BB/9	K/9	K	GB%	BABIP	WHIP	ERA	DRA	WARP	MPH	FB%	WHF	CSP
2016	PIR	RK	24	0	4	0	6	6	24	23	0	0.4	6.0	16	46%	.291	1.00	3.00	2.90	0.8				
2016	BRD	A+	24	2	0	0	2	2	11	8	0	0.8	8.2	10	68%	.286	0.82	0.00	4.18	0.2				
2016	ALT	AA	24	1	1	0	2	2	11	6	1	3.3	8.2	10	48%	.179	0.91	5.73	2.41	0.4				
2017	IND	AAA	25	9	6	0	20	19	113¹	119	8	2.3	7.4	93	46%	.324	1.31	4.13	3.91	2.2				
2018	IND	AAA	26	4	2	0	12	12	62¹	57	5	2.3	8.4	58	42%	.301	1.17	3.61	3.27	1.6				
2018	PIT	MLB	26	5	7	0	18	15	76	79	18	3.1	8.2	69	40%	.272	1.38	5.21	5.63	-0.3	93.9	56.4	11.8	46.4
2019	*PIT*	*MLB*	*27*	*7*	*7*	*0*	*34*	*19*	*117*	*112*	*14*	*2.9*	*7.7*	*100*	*43%*	*.299*	*1.28*	*4.20*	*4.85*	*0.5*	*93.4*	*57.1*	*12*	*46.9*

Breakout: 19%   Improve: 29%   Collapse: 23%   Attrition: 33%   MLB: 69%   *Comparables: Albert Suarez, Mark Leiter, Kyle Lobstein*

Success stories are uplifting, but often inure us to the fact that they're outliers. Kingham went under the knife for Tommy John surgery in 2015, struggled to make it back to the majors, and when he finally did arrive in 2018 his results were poor. The temptation is to write him off as a washout, but despite the lousy ERA and DRA, he showed some signs of life, a few positive indicators that could be a harbinger of hope. When he was on, Kingham commanded a low-90s fastball well on both sides of the plate, harnessed an excellent slider with a whiff rate over 20 percent and used his changeup as an out pitch to neutralize lefties. None of this sweeps his poor 2018 under the rug but reminds us that Kingham could eventually emerge as a no. 4 starter, and that injury recovery is art, not science.

Chad Kuhl RHP   Born: 09/10/92   Age: 26   Bats: R   Throws: R   Height: 6'3"   Weight: 216   Origin: Round 9, 2013 Draft (#269 overall)

YEAR	TEAM	LVL	AGE	W	L	SV	G	GS	IP	H	HR	BB/9	K/9	K	GB%	BABIP	WHIP	ERA	DRA	WARP	MPH	FB%	WHF	CSP
2016	IND	AAA	23	6	3	0	16	16	83²	81	9	1.7	7.1	66	48%	.295	1.16	2.37	3.10	2.2				
2016	PIT	MLB	23	5	4	0	14	14	70²	73	7	2.5	6.8	53	46%	.304	1.32	4.20	4.87	0.4	96.1	61.4	9.1	48.4
2017	PIT	MLB	24	8	11	0	31	31	157¹	159	17	4.1	8.1	142	43%	.321	1.47	4.35	5.35	0.4	97.8	63.5	10.3	47.7
2018	PIT	MLB	25	5	5	0	16	16	85	89	14	3.5	8.6	81	41%	.311	1.44	4.55	4.24	1.0	97.2	59	10.3	49.3
2019	*PIT*	*MLB*	*26*	*5*	*5*	*0*	*16*	*16*	*83²*	*77*	*9*	*3.2*	*8.6*	*80*	*43%*	*.309*	*1.28*	*3.84*	*4.44*	*0.8*	*96.9*	*62.8*	*10.3*	*49.4*

Breakout: 34%   Improve: 62%   Collapse: 16%   Attrition: 14%   MLB: 92%   *Comparables: Anthony DeSclafani, Mike Foltynewicz, Gavin Floyd*

Ever since his major league debut in 2016, Kuhl looked a back-of-the-rotation arm, an innings eater who was unlikely to ever post an ERA under four. He was following the same script for most of 2018 until he started relying on his slider more and his heater less. For a brief period, Kuhl appeared to have shed that fifth-starter label, but a forearm strain in late June ended his season. Multiple attempts to get back on a mound led to additional pain and discomfort, and a medical exam in September led to a worst-case diagnosis and Tommy John surgery. Kuhl won't return until 2020. It's unknown what his recovery path will look like, and the Pirates have given no indications if they'll use an aggressive recovery path or keep Kuhl on ice.

Jordan Lyles RHP   Born: 10/19/90   Age: 28   Bats: R   Throws: R   Height: 6'4"   Weight: 230   Origin: Round 1, 2008 Draft (#38 overall)

YEAR	TEAM	LVL	AGE	W	L	SV	G	GS	IP	H	HR	BB/9	K/9	K	GB%	BABIP	WHIP	ERA	DRA	WARP	MPH	FB%	WHF	CSP
2016	ABQ	AAA	25	4	2	0	8	8	44²	57	5	3.6	5.8	29	42%	.361	1.68	5.44	4.73	0.3				
2016	COL	MLB	25	4	5	1	40	5	58²	69	4	4.3	4.9	32	52%	.319	1.65	5.83	7.64	-1.7	95.7	59.3	8.3	45.7
2017	COL	MLB	26	0	2	0	33	0	46²	61	11	2.3	6.4	33	52%	.331	1.56	6.94	5.61	-0.2	96.1	56.7	10.1	48.5
2017	ELP	AAA	26	1	1	0	5	5	20	20	1	3.6	9.0	20	48%	.333	1.40	4.50	3.10	0.6				
2017	SDN	MLB	26	1	3	0	5	5	23	35	5	3.9	8.6	22	46%	.395	1.96	9.39	4.14	0.3	94.5	53.3	10.9	43.3
2018	SDN	MLB	27	2	4	0	24	8	71¹	71	12	2.4	7.8	62	47%	.286	1.26	4.29	5.91	-0.6	95.6	48.8	10.2	50.2
2018	MIL	MLB	27	1	0	0	11	0	16¹	12	0	5.0	12.1	22	42%	.316	1.29	3.31	2.57	0.5	96.1	47.6	14.5	46.6
2019	PIT	MLB	28	4	3	0	49	8	83²	81	10	3.3	8.2	76	46%	.313	1.34	4.18	4.82	0.3	95.1	53.2	10.3	47.9

Breakout: 18%   Improve: 54%   Collapse: 14%   Attrition: 18%   MLB: 91%   *Comparables: Wily Peralta, Paul Maholm, Ivan Nova*

Induced demand is the dream of both regulators and pitching coaches. In public policy, if you wish for folks to drive less frequently in the future, you might not write any regulations about cars, but instead design land-use policies encouraging dense housing without parking spots. In coaching, if you hope to rehab a scuffling pitcher into a strikeout machine, you might not make any adjustment to his fastball, instead opting to shuffle those secondaries. Such is the case with Lyles, a middling, five-pitch journeyman who struck out 14 percent of batters faced in Colorado and 20 percent in San Diego. As soon as Lyles came to Milwaukee, the curveball became his primary pitch, but the extra whiffs didn't occur with the breaking ball. By simplifying Lyles' approach and placing focus on the fastball and curve, the whiffs on the fastball suddenly began piling up. This creates a new decision tree for the veteran, who can further induce those strikeouts by doubling down on simple two-pitch approach, or now slowly tinker with his other pitches to refine his starting value.

Travis MacGregor RHP   Born: 10/15/97   Age: 21   Bats: R   Throws: R   Height: 6'3"   Weight: 180   Origin: Round 2, 2016 Draft (#68 overall)

YEAR	TEAM	LVL	AGE	W	L	SV	G	GS	IP	H	HR	BB/9	K/9	K	GB%	BABIP	WHIP	ERA	DRA	WARP	MPH	FB%	WHF	CSP
2016	PIR	RK	18	1	1	0	9	9	31²	29	1	2.8	5.4	19	57%	.286	1.23	3.13	3.99	0.6				
2017	BRI	RK	19	1	4	0	12	12	41¹	61	3	4.4	7.0	32	48%	.389	1.96	7.84	5.18	0.4				
2018	WVA	A	20	1	4	0	15	15	63²	58	7	3.0	10.5	74	47%	.307	1.24	3.25	3.69	1.1				
2019	PIT	MLB	21	3	5	0	14	14	55¹	60	10	4.6	7.5	46	45%	.317	1.60	5.63	6.47	-0.7				

Breakout: 1%   Improve: 1%   Collapse: 1%   Attrition: 2%   MLB: 3%   *Comparables: Jayson Aquino, Zach Phillips, Jeremy Hellickson*

In recent drafts, the Pirates have taken a fair share of projectable, high-ceiling, prep school arms in the hopes of hitting the jackpot on at least one. At 6-foot-3 and with a lean, lanky frame, MacGregor fits this mold. The mechanics are clean and the fastball already has enough cheddar to be considered major-league ready. As is the case with many minor-league arms, the off-speed stuff is what will make or break MacGregor. The good news is both the curve and change showed signs of improvement. The bad news is MacGregor couldn't stay healthy thanks to a nagging shoulder injury that limited him to 70 2/3 innings. If healthy, MacGregor could take a big step forward in 2019, but shoulder problems have a way of lingering and ruining careers.

Joe Musgrove RHP   Born: 12/04/92   Age: 26   Bats: R   Throws: R   Height: 6'5"   Weight: 260   Origin: Round 1, 2011 Draft (#46 overall)

YEAR	TEAM	LVL	AGE	W	L	SV	G	GS	IP	H	HR	BB/9	K/9	K	GB%	BABIP	WHIP	ERA	DRA	WARP	MPH	FB%	WHF	CSP
2016	CCH	AA	23	2	1	0	6	4	26¹	19	1	1.0	10.3	30	49%	.265	0.84	0.34	2.44	0.8				
2016	FRE	AAA	23	5	3	0	10	10	59	60	8	1.1	8.7	57	55%	.317	1.14	3.81	2.82	1.7				
2016	HOU	MLB	23	4	4	0	11	10	62	59	9	2.3	8.0	55	43%	.289	1.21	4.06	4.43	0.6	94.6	45.6	10.4	48.7
2017	FRE	AAA	24	1	0	0	1	1	7	1	0	2.6	9.0	7	54%	.077	0.43	0.00	3.52	0.2				
2017	HOU	MLB	24	7	8	2	38	15	109¹	117	18	2.3	8.1	98	46%	.316	1.33	4.77	4.49	1.2	95.7	48	13	51.6
2018	IND	AAA	25	1	1	0	2	2	10²	10	0	1.7	9.3	11	41%	.312	1.12	5.06	3.41	0.3				
2018	PIT	MLB	25	6	9	0	19	19	115¹	113	12	1.8	7.8	100	48%	.294	1.18	4.06	3.43	2.5	95.0	50.3	12.5	53.5
2019	PIT	MLB	26	9	8	0	24	24	136²	124	14	2.5	8.5	129	46%	.303	1.19	3.58	4.14	1.8	94.8	49.5	12.6	52.6

Breakout: 31%   Improve: 54%   Collapse: 17%   Attrition: 4%   MLB: 92%   *Comparables: Jake Odorizzi, Patrick Corbin, Jordan Zimmermann*

If you're reading this chapter beginning-to-end, you're probably tired of hearing about Gerrit Cole, especially if you're a Pirates fan. That's right, Musgrove was part of the four-player package Pittsburgh received in exchange for their young, cost-controlled ace. When he was able to take the hill, Musgrove put together a solid season. He increased his use of a cutter he picked up from former major leaguer Jerome Williams in 2016, relying less on his slider and dropping his curve almost entirely. Musgrove's DRA was a notable improvement over his previous seasons, but the problem was he couldn't stay on the mound. The big right-hander missed time due to a shoulder strain, a finger infection and an abdominal strain. There's more ceiling here than the naysayers expected when the Pirates acquired Musgrove, but he'll need to stay healthy for a full season for that potential to be realized.

Richard Rodriguez RHP   Born: 03/04/90   Age: 29   Bats: R   Throws: R   Height: 6'4"   Weight: 205   Origin: International Free Agent, 2010

YEAR	TEAM	LVL	AGE	W	L	SV	G	GS	IP	H	HR	BB/9	K/9	K	GB%	BABIP	WHIP	ERA	DRA	WARP	MPH	FB%	WHF	CSP
2016	NOR	AAA	26	6	2	2	48	2	81²	65	5	2.8	8.9	81	34%	.276	1.10	2.53	3.10	1.8				
2017	NOR	AAA	27	4	4	10	42	1	70²	56	5	2.3	10.2	80	29%	.285	1.05	2.42	2.79	2.0				
2017	BAL	MLB	27	0	0	0	5	0	5²	12	4	4.8	4.8	3	46%	.400	2.65	14.29	8.32	-0.2	95.3	65.8	6.7	50.2
2018	PIT	MLB	28	4	3	0	63	0	69¹	55	5	2.5	11.4	88	40%	.309	1.07	2.47	2.82	1.7	94.4	75.1	15.2	50.7
2019	PIT	MLB	29	3	1	0	57	0	59²	49	7	3.2	10.4	69	37%	.296	1.17	3.68	4.23	0.7	93.8	74.3	14.5	50.5

Breakout: 7%   Improve: 17%   Collapse: 28%   Attrition: 31%   MLB: 54%   *Comparables: Miguel Socolovich, Justin Miller, Spencer Patton*

An anonymous minor-league journeyman who looked like he was one-and-done in the majors after an awful Orioles stint in 2017, Rodriguez not only survived in his new Pittsburgh home; he thrived. Rodriguez throws a decent enough fastball and slider, but his success came thanks to a newfound ability with location that would make Cookie Kwan envious. Only seven relievers (minimum 50 IP) threw more strikes in the zone than Rodriguez, but despite this, he ranked in the bottom third on contact for pitches in the zone as a result of improved command. Late-blooming relievers are sometimes one-year wonders, but Rodriguez's Days of Obligation working his way up to the majors are probably over, and he'll rely on the Hunger of Memory as inspiration to avoid getting demoted. Richard Rodriguez, autobiographical author and Emmy and Peabody Award winner? Nothing? Doesn't anyone listen to NPR anymore?

Edgar Santana RHP Born: 10/16/91 Age: 27 Bats: R Throws: R Height: 6'2" Weight: 195 Origin: International Free Agent, 2013

YEAR	TEAM	LVL	AGE	W	L	SV	G	GS	IP	H	HR	BB/9	K/9	K	GB%	BABIP	WHIP	ERA	DRA	WARP	MPH	FB%	WHF	CSP
2016	BRD	A+	24	2	0	0	9	0	22¹	13	0	0.8	8.1	20	61%	.220	0.67	0.81	2.69	0.6				
2016	ALT	AA	24	2	1	2	21	0	41¹	32	4	2.4	8.5	39	57%	.264	1.04	2.83	3.17	0.8				
2016	IND	AAA	24	0	0	1	13	0	16	22	1	3.4	6.8	12	53%	.389	1.75	5.06	3.43	0.3				
2017	IND	AAA	25	1	3	8	44	0	58	62	4	1.9	8.4	54	44%	.343	1.28	2.79	3.24	1.3				
2017	PIT	MLB	25	0	0	0	19	0	18	16	2	6.0	10.0	20	46%	.304	1.56	3.50	4.47	0.1	96.7	61.2	15.2	46.2
2018	PIT	MLB	26	3	4	0	69	0	66¹	61	7	1.6	7.3	54	47%	.277	1.10	3.26	3.56	1.0	96.0	57.6	12.6	51.5
2019	PIT	MLB	27	3	1	1	55	0	58¹	54	6	2.9	8.2	53	46%	.306	1.25	3.80	4.40	0.4	95.6	59	13.3	49.7

Breakout: 16%   Improve: 28%   Collapse: 29%   Attrition: 31%   MLB: 73%   *Comparables: Donnie Hart, Derek Law, Nick Wittgren*

Closers aren't born but rather invented, so when Felipe Vazquez complained of forearm discomfort in May, it appeared Santana might step into the ninth inning role for the Bucs. Vazquez's pain turned out to be much ado about nothing, so Santana quietly trudged along in a set-up role. He struggled in the first half but went through a 27.1-inning stretch in July and August where his tailing mid-90s fastball and mid-80s slider were almost unhittable. The wheels came off late in the season. Santana's strikeouts plummeted and after a posting a 12.60 ERA in five miserable September innings, and an examination with Dr. James Andrews led to Tommy John surgery at the end of the season. Santana won't return until 2020.

Jameson Taillon RHP Born: 11/18/91 Age: 27 Bats: R Throws: R Height: 6'5" Weight: 230 Origin: Round 1, 2010 Draft (#2 overall)

YEAR	TEAM	LVL	AGE	W	L	SV	G	GS	IP	H	HR	BB/9	K/9	K	GB%	BABIP	WHIP	ERA	DRA	WARP	MPH	FB%	WHF	CSP
2016	IND	AAA	24	4	2	0	10	10	61²	44	2	0.9	8.9	61	49%	.253	0.81	2.04	3.17	1.5				
2016	PIT	MLB	24	5	4	0	18	18	104	99	13	1.5	7.4	85	55%	.287	1.12	3.38	3.89	1.7	96.5	63.1	9.1	46.6
2017	IND	AAA	25	0	1	0	2	2	11	12	0	1.6	12.3	15	58%	.387	1.27	4.09	2.00	0.4				
2017	PIT	MLB	25	8	7	0	25	25	133²	152	11	3.1	8.4	125	49%	.352	1.48	4.44	4.08	2.2	96.7	64.1	9.6	48
2018	PIT	MLB	26	14	10	0	32	32	191	179	20	2.2	8.4	179	48%	.298	1.18	3.20	3.41	4.2	96.7	57.3	11.8	48.6
2019	PIT	MLB	27	11	9	0	30	30	180	165	17	2.5	8.7	173	48%	.311	1.19	3.36	3.90	2.9	96.2	61.2	10.8	48.5

Breakout: 21%   Improve: 59%   Collapse: 19%   Attrition: 6%   MLB: 96%   *Comparables: Kevin Gausman, Patrick Corbin, Ricky Nolasco*

Drafted as the second overall pick way back in 2010, Taillon has seen fellow first-rounders Chris Sale, Bryce Harper, Manny Machado and Christian Yelich blossom into superstars while he took a more methodical path to the majors. To be fair, pitchers drafted out of high school have a longer development cycle, but Taillon also took a detour down Tommy John Way in 2014 and survived testicular cancer in 2017. Nearly a decade after he was drafted, Taillon finally turned potential into a full season of high-end results. Taillon's 191 innings easily topped his career high. He added a 90-mph slider to his already devastating fastball-curve combo, resulting in a top-20 season by WARP. While it seems like he has been around forever, Taillon is only 27, and still young enough to be as much of a star as those other names who were part of his illustrious draft class.

Felipe Vazquez LHP Born: 07/05/91 Age: 27 Bats: L Throws: L Height: 6'2" Weight: 210 Origin: International Free Agent, 2008

YEAR	TEAM	LVL	AGE	W	L	SV	G	GS	IP	H	HR	BB/9	K/9	K	GB%	BABIP	WHIP	ERA	DRA	WARP	MPH	FB%	WHF	CSP
2016	WAS	MLB	24	0	3	1	47	0	49²	43	4	2.7	9.6	53	48%	.310	1.17	4.53	3.02	1.1	98.5	62.3	15.9	48.2
2016	PIT	MLB	24	1	3	0	28	0	27¹	23	3	5.9	12.8	39	48%	.317	1.50	3.29	2.96	0.6	99.8	61.1	15.8	47.7
2017	PIT	MLB	25	5	3	21	73	0	75¹	47	4	2.4	10.5	88	53%	.234	0.89	1.67	2.59	2.2	100.7	61	16.3	51.8
2018	PIT	MLB	26	4	2	37	70	0	70	63	4	3.1	11.4	89	44%	.331	1.24	2.70	2.64	1.8	100.5	65.6	15.8	53.8
2019	PIT	MLB	27	3	1	38	57	0	59²	47	6	3.3	10.8	72	46%	.300	1.15	3.16	3.66	0.8	99.7	63.9	16.2	52.3

Breakout: 24%   Improve: 50%   Collapse: 34%   Attrition: 9%   MLB: 99%   *Comparables: Juan Rincon, Kelvin Herrera, Manny Delcarmen*

In April 2018, he decided to legally change his surname from Rivero to Vazquez to honor his sister's influence on both his life and career. Shakespeare said that a rose by any other name smells just as sweet. In Vazquez's case, it didn't matter what he called himself because he kept delivering the same filth to batters that he had since becoming a Pirate in 2016. A case of forearm discomfort in May turned out to be nothing serious. The control issues that plagued him at the beginning of his Pirates' tenure are a memory, and health is the only thing potentially standing between Vazquez and a string of elite seasons at closer.

Trevor Williams RHP Born: 04/25/92 Age: 27 Bats: R Throws: R Height: 6'3" Weight: 230 Origin: Round 2, 2013 Draft (#44 overall)

YEAR	TEAM	LVL	AGE	W	L	SV	G	GS	IP	H	HR	BB/9	K/9	K	GB%	BABIP	WHIP	ERA	DRA	WARP	MPH	FB%	WHF	CSP
2016	IND	AAA	24	9	6	0	20	19	110¹	103	5	2.4	6.0	74	53%	.284	1.21	2.53	4.69	0.8				
2016	PIT	MLB	24	1	1	0	7	1	12²	19	4	3.6	7.8	11	49%	.366	1.89	7.82	5.39	0.0	96.7	66.5	9.8	48.2
2017	PIT	MLB	25	7	9	0	31	25	150¹	145	14	3.1	7.0	117	50%	.292	1.31	4.07	4.49	1.8	94.6	71.6	9.1	46.4
2018	PIT	MLB	26	14	10	0	31	31	170²	146	15	2.9	6.6	126	43%	.261	1.18	3.11	4.28	2.0	93.1	69.4	8.8	46
2019	PIT	MLB	27	9	9	0	26	26	148¹	143	15	3.0	7.3	121	46%	.304	1.30	3.95	4.57	1.3	93.3	71	9.1	47.3

Breakout: 17%   Improve: 43%   Collapse: 16%   Attrition: 12%   MLB: 80%   *Comparables: Sergio Mitre, Dillon Gee, Steven Matz*

On July 6, Williams allowed five runs in 2 1/3 innings to the Philadelphia Phillies. His ERA jumped to 4.60, and he didn't appear to be long for the Pirates rotation. Williams turned his season around after that start, although saying he turned it around is like saying Abraham Lincoln gave a little speech in Gettysburg. In his last 13 starts, Williams posted a ridiculous 1.29 ERA, looking like a world beater in the process. An absurdly great strand rate was tabbed as the primary reason for Williams' good fortune, but it wasn't all a matter of random batted-ball luck. Williams' usual masterful command of all his pitches was on display, but he also started pitching lower in the zone, making it more difficult to lift any of his offerings, especially his sinker. It also helped that he took a little something off his slider, creating more separation between it and his fastball. The odds of another season with an ERA near three is as likely as Williams arriving to Spring Training tattoo-free, but the year wasn't an entire fluke. The former Sun Devil is a smart pitcher with a strong fastball who knows how to command everything else in order to maximize his otherwise average stuff.

LINEOUTS

Hitters

HITTER	POS	TEAM	LVL	AGE	PA	R	2B	3B	HR	RBI	BB	K	SB	CS	AVG/OBP/SLG	DRC+	VORP	BABIP	BRR	FRAA	WARP
Jonah Davis	CF	BRI	Rk	20	241	46	15	6	12	34	27	59	6	5	.306/.398/.612	144	32.6	.372	-0.3	CF(51): -8.3	1.2
Patrick Kivlehan	OF	LOU	AAA	28	47	3	0	0	0	4	2	15	1	0	.167/.255/.167	75	-2.7	.259	-0.2	1B(7): 0.0, 3B(2): -0.3	-0.1
	OF	LVG	AAA	28	390	59	29	4	20	67	30	84	4	3	.314/.372/.588	134	23.8	.361	0.0	RF(41): 6.0, 1B(21): -2.4	3.1
	OF	ARI	MLB	28	14	3	0	2	0	0	0	6	0	0	.231/.286/.538	72	0.5	.429	0.1	LF(4): -0.3	0.0
Sean Rodriguez	2B	IND	AAA	33	42	5	1	0	2	7	5	10	1	1	.250/.357/.444	100	2.8	.292	0.1	3B(2): 0.0, SS(2): -0.2	0.3
	2B	PIT	MLB	33	173	21	5	1	5	19	22	60	1	0	.167/.277/.313	68	-1.5	.235	0.8	2B(26): -0.3, SS(16): 0.8	0.1
Jacob Stallings	C	IND	AAA	28	278	37	22	1	3	40	15	51	1	2	.285/.335/.414	93	15.4	.343	-1.4	C(63): -4.7	0.5
	C	PIT	MLB	28	41	2	0	0	0	5	3	9	0	0	.216/.268/.216	77	-0.1	.276	0.5	C(13): 0.1	0.1
Conner Uselton	RF	BRI	Rk	20	175	15	2	1	0	14	12	31	0	2	.225/.280/.250	81	-6.5	.275	-0.4	RF(41): -4.2	-0.5

The son of musicians, **Jonah Davis** is accustomed to performing on a big stage; at the age of nine he sang in an opera penned by his father. He has exceeded expectations ever since he was "graded" as a future Division III player at a baseball camp in high school and continued the trend with an impressive Rookie Ball campaign. ⓧ **Patrick Kivlehan** played for three organizations in 2018 and got just a handful of MLB plate appearances as a depth piece for the Diamondbacks down the stretch. That appears to be the type of role he's destined to keep. ⓧ At 29.4 seconds per pitch, **Daniel Nava** was the slowest hitter in baseball in 2017. You can't prove that Nava's absence from the majors in 2018 was the reason the median time of games was five minutes faster than they were in 2017, but then again you can't disprove it either. ⓧ Seventy days after "**Sean Rodriguez** Bobblehead Day" at PNC Park, the Pirates granted Rodriguez his unconditional release. The Pirates did not commemorate a bobblehead to mark the occasion. ⓧ A capable backstop, **Jacob Stallings** could be a backup for more than a few teams but was stuck behind two talented catchers in Pittsburgh. He's 29 years old, so he's already in a position where he's going to be Stallings for Time. ⓧ Subpar stats in short-season ball are no kiss of death, but **Conner Uselton** spent most of his year in the circuit as a 20-year-old and has already lost an entire season to a hamstring issue.

Pitchers

PITCHER	TEAM	LVL	AGE	W	L	SV	G	GS	IP	H	HR	BB/9	K/9	K	GB%	BABIP	WHIP	ERA	DRA	WARP	MPH	FB%	WHF	CSP
Dario Agrazal	BRD	A+	23	0	0	0	2	2	8	3	0	0.0	4.5	4	57%	.143	0.38	0.00	4.11	0.1				
	ALT	AA	23	5	6	0	15	14	85^2	91	9	1.4	5.5	52	50%	.298	1.21	3.99	4.56	0.8				
J.T. Brubaker	ALT	AA	24	2	2	0	6	6	35	29	1	2.1	9.0	35	63%	.289	1.06	1.80	2.88	1.0				
	IND	AAA	24	8	4	0	22	22	119	121	7	2.7	7.3	96	51%	.320	1.32	3.10	4.27	1.7				
Nick Burdi	PIT	MLB	25	0	0	0	2	0	1^1	3	1	13.5	13.5	2	33%	.400	3.75	20.25	1.82	0.0	98.4	71.4	14.3	46.9
Johnny Hellweg	IND	AAA	29	1	1	11	24	0	27	18	0	4.3	8.3	25	68%	.261	1.15	1.33	3.91	0.4				
Jesus Liranzo	ALT	AA	23	0	0	4	9	0	12	7	0	2.2	13.5	18	44%	.280	0.83	0.00	1.70	0.5				
	IND	AAA	23	2	3	3	32	0	45	31	7	6.2	9.4	47	30%	.220	1.38	5.00	4.33	0.4				
Alex McRae	PIT	MLB	25	0	1	0	2	0	6^1	8	0	7.1	7.1	5	57%	.381	2.05	5.68	7.80	-0.2	94.4	56	6	39.7
	IND	AAA	25	3	10	1	26	19	117	134	9	3.8	8.0	104	47%	.356	1.57	4.77	4.51	1.3				
Dovydas Neverauskas	IND	AAA	25	2	3	4	34	0	46^1	31	2	5.8	11.3	58	52%	.287	1.32	2.53	3.10	1.1				
	PIT	MLB	25	0	0	0	25	0	27	30	9	3.3	9.0	27	37%	.292	1.48	8.00	4.83	0.0	98.5	48.1	12.5	49.4
Braeden Ogle	WVA	A	20	2	0	0	4	4	17	16	1	5.3	11.1	21	40%	.366	1.53	2.65	3.57	0.3				
Casey Sadler	PIT	MLB	27	0	0	0	2	0	4^1	9	0	6.2	6.2	3	58%	.474	2.77	8.31	5.04	0.0	93.8	59.3	8.1	48.2
	IND	AAA	27	6	5	1	27	8	77	79	7	3.0	7.1	61	46%	.306	1.36	3.39	4.16	1.1				
A.J. Schugel	IND	AAA	29	0	0	0	12	0	13	18	4	2.8	8.3	12	44%	.359	1.69	6.23	3.31	0.3				
Bo Schultz	BRD	A+	32	0	0	0	8	0	10^2	2	0	3.4	8.4	10	65%	.087	0.56	0.00	3.77	0.1				
	IND	AAA	32	0	1	3	24	0	27	29	0	3.3	7.3	22	54%	.337	1.44	2.00	3.67	0.5				

In an era when every pitcher throws hard and gets strikeouts, **Dario Agrazal** is a pleasant throwback to a simpler world. A control artist who generates contact and allows fans to enjoy batted-ball results, he is going to make baseball better one grumpy, ex-major-league broadcaster at a time. ⓧ **J.T. Brubaker** was a fringy organizational arm until he started touching 97 on the gun in the 2017 Arizona Fall League. If he can keep getting hitters to pound the ball into the ground, Brubaker has a future as a back-end starter or in middle relief. ⓧ Tagged with the "future closer label" ever since he was drafted in 2014, **Nick Burdi** was taken by the Phillies last winter in the Rule 5 draft, traded to the Pirates immediately and spent most of 2018 on the DL recovering from Tommy John surgery, making it next to impossible to watch the Burdi. ⓧ Four years after Tommy John surgery, **Johnny Hellweg** still hasn't been able to find the plate or any semblance of control, for that matter. The Pirates released Hellweg in June so he could sign a contract with the Hiroshima Carp. ⓧ The Pirates nabbed **Jesus Liranzo** off waivers from the Orioles in April. He excites scouts because of a heavy fastball that can hit the upper 90s but needs a refined secondary pitch and improved command if he wants to do more than repeatedly tour the great cities of the International League. ⓧ After three and a half years toiling in the minors, **Alex McRae** made his major league debut as an emergency fill-in middle reliever, logging two appearances before unceremoniously being removed from the 40-man roster. ⓧ **Dovdas Neverauskas** hails from Vilnius, Lithuania, which claims both Chicago and Madison as sister cities, making it difficult for Vilnius natives who want to root for Neverauskas but must cheer for the Cubs and Brewers due to the complicated, byzantine rules and regulations of sister cities as established during the Paderborn/Le Mans Convention of 836. ⓧ **Braeden Ogle**'s season was cut short after four starts with shoulder inflammation; the promising Pirates prospect hopes to be fully healthy and ready to pitch in 2019. ⓧ **Casey Sadler** missed all of 2016 after Tommy John surgery and spent almost two full seasons working his way back to form in the minors. He could still be a useful major-league piece but, at 28, time is running out. ⓧ **A.J. Schugel** missed nearly all of 2018 with shoulder pain and struggled in the minors after he came back. This was his second shoulder ailment in three years and could mean the end of the line. ⓧ An aspiring journalist in college way back in 2004, **Bo Schultz** says he might go back to journalism when his career is over. He might have to put that dream on hold, since he was good enough to be organizational depth for the Pirates until forearm soreness shut him down in July. ⓧ There are lost seasons, and then there are Lost series finale seasons. **Nik Turley** followed up his ten-year trek to the majors with a PED suspension, a blown elbow, and a DFA. Hopefully he can re-write his own ending to be a little more satisfying.

SAN DIEGO PADRES

Essay by Eric Nusbaum

Player comments by Brendan Gawlowski and BP staff

The 2019 season will mark fifty years of National League baseball in San Diego. Five decades from Nate Colbert to Tony Gwynn to Chase Headley to, well, Chase Headley again. Hard to believe right? They grow up so fast. It feels like just yesterday that Dick Selma was walking out to the mound to throw the first pitch in Padres franchise history glaring out from under the brim of his brown and yellow cap at a half-full San Diego Stadium. Looking on from the home dugout as Selma tossed a complete game victory was Preston Gomez, the first full-time Latino manager in MLB history. Baseball in San Diego. The future held endless possibility.

No man could have felt that possibility more tangibly than the Padres' owner, C. Arnholt Smith. The tall self-made millionaire from Walla Walla, Washington had risen from bank teller to bank owner. They called him Mr. San Diego. It feels like just yesterday that Smith, deep into all sorts of legal trouble after just a few years as a baseball owner, was enlisting the help of his friend, the recently impeached President Richard M. Nixon, in a desperate attempt to sell the Padres to prospective buyers in Washington D.C.

It almost ended right there. In 1974, Topps printed a set of cards that said, instead of San Diego Padres: Washington (NL). The new team was going to be called the Washington Stars. They even made up uniforms. That could have been it. But, as we know, it wasn't. So let's take a moment to appreciate the Padres at 50. The mere existence of this franchise—the last remaining major sports team in San Diego!—is something of a miracle. And it's even more impressive when you consider how terrible they have been.

In fifty years, the Padres have put up:

- 14 winning seasons
- 2 .500 seasons
- 34 losing seasons.

They have made the playoffs just five times, including in 2005 when they won the NL West despite going 82-80. They have made the World Series twice: in 1984 and 1998. Both times they lost convincingly despite the best efforts of Tony Gwynn who hit a combined .371 over nine games.

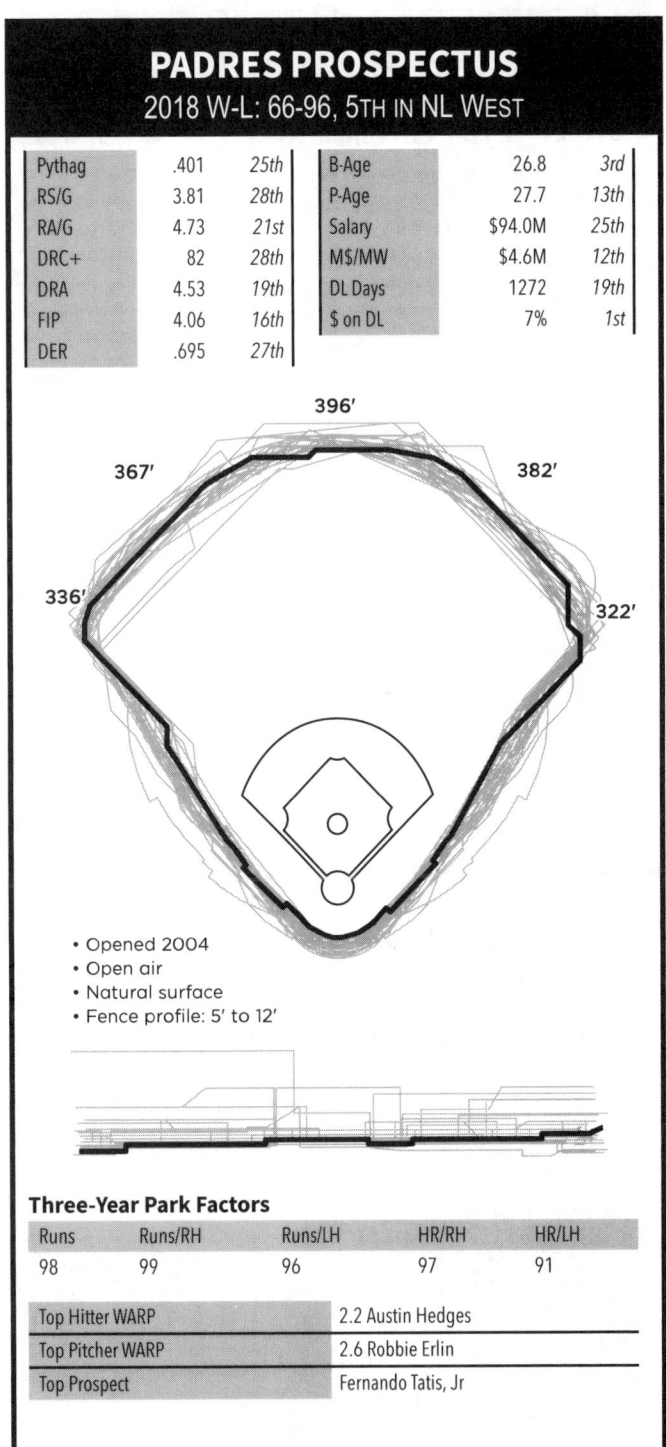

PADRES PROSPECTUS
2018 W-L: 66-96, 5TH IN NL WEST

Pythag	.401	25th	B-Age	26.8	3rd
RS/G	3.81	28th	P-Age	27.7	13th
RA/G	4.73	21st	Salary	$94.0M	25th
DRC+	82	28th	M$/MW	$4.6M	12th
DRA	4.53	19th	DL Days	1272	19th
FIP	4.06	16th	$ on DL	7%	1st
DER	.695	27th			

396'
367'
382'
336'
322'

- Opened 2004
- Open air
- Natural surface
- Fence profile: 5' to 12'

Three-Year Park Factors

Runs	Runs/RH	Runs/LH	HR/RH	HR/LH
98	99	96	97	91

Top Hitter WARP	2.2 Austin Hedges
Top Pitcher WARP	2.6 Robbie Erlin
Top Prospect	Fernando Tatis, Jr

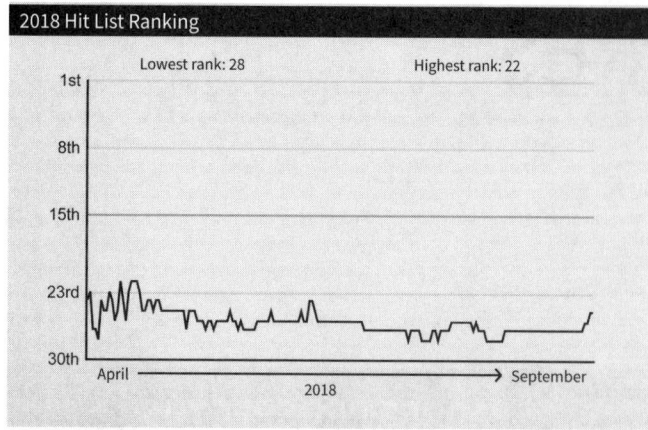

2018 Hit List Ranking

Lowest rank: 28   Highest rank: 22

(vertical axis: 1st, 8th, 15th, 23rd, 30th; horizontal: April — 2018 — September)

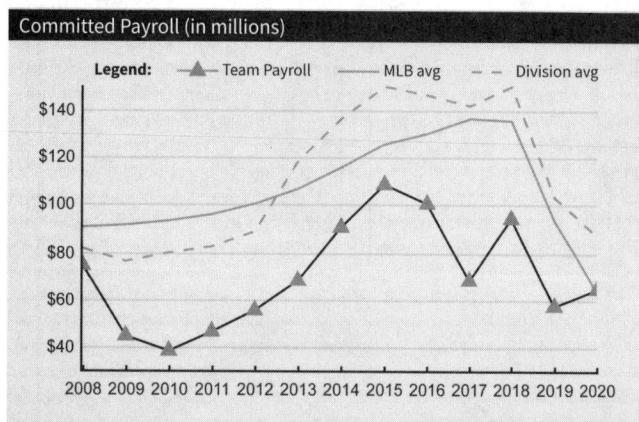

Committed Payroll (in millions)

Legend: Team Payroll — MLB avg — Division avg

(vertical axis: $140, $120, $100, $80, $60, $40; horizontal: 2008 2009 2010 2011 2012 2013 2014 2015 2016 2017 2018 2019 2020)

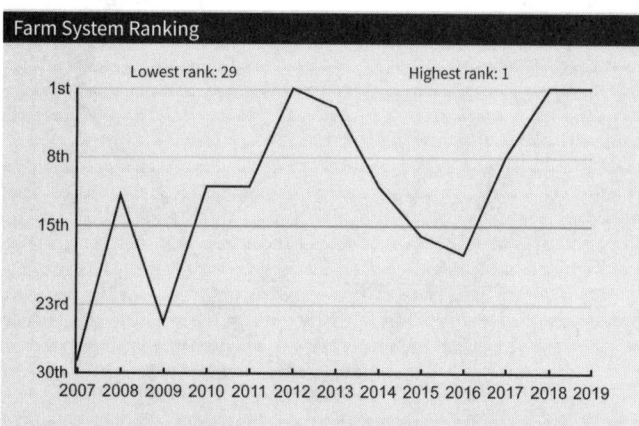

Farm System Ranking

Lowest rank: 29   Highest rank: 1

(vertical axis: 1st, 8th, 15th, 23rd, 30th; horizontal: 2007 2008 2009 2010 2011 2012 2013 2014 2015 2016 2017 2018 2019)

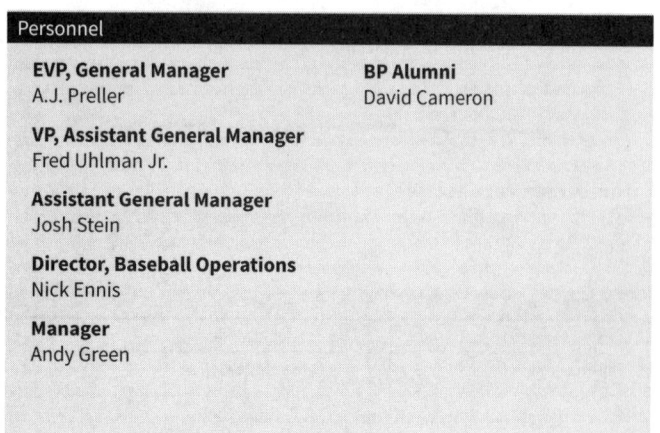

Personnel

EVP, General Manager
A.J. Preller

VP, Assistant General Manager
Fred Uhlman Jr.

Assistant General Manager
Josh Stein

Director, Baseball Operations
Nick Ennis

Manager
Andy Green

BP Alumni
David Cameron

Two of the Padres' fellow 1969 expansion clubs, the Montreal Expos and Seattle Pilots no longer exist. The Pilots only lasted a season before heading to Milwaukee. So all things considered, fifty years of mostly uneventful baseball really is an achievement. The on-field product might have been largely mediocre, but simply existing through all that mediocrity—well, that is a triumph.

Back in 1974, the Padres were rescued by a court injunction, and then by a fast food millionaire. C. Arnholt Smith was forced to sell the team, and the man who stepped in to buy it was McDonald's founder Ray Kroc, who made an immediate impression. During the eighth inning of his very first home game as owner, Kroc commandeered the public address system and declared, "I have never seen such stupid ballplaying in my life."

This scene, which did not make the Michael Keaton biopic, basically sums up the philosophical quandary that is the Padres. On one hand, it's great that there is a baseball team in San Diego. On the other, isn't it fair for Padres fans to ask for something better than stupid ballplaying? Doesn't the city of San Diego deserve something more than fourth place in the NL West, and the specter of a good team somewhere on the horizon?

If Ray Kroc was the first savior of the Padres, Tony Gwynn was the second. No team's legacy is as singularly defined by one player, locally or nationally. All due respect to Trevor Hoffman, Dave Winfield, Adrian Gonzalez, Randy Jones, Fred McGriff, Roberto Alomar, Ken Caminiti et. al but San Diego baseball is, and always has been Tony Gwynn. He has more than twice as many plate appearances in the uniform as the next closest Padre (that would be Randy Templeton).

But the thing about Tony Gwynn is that for as wonderful as he was—as a ballplayer and a person—he was one man. As Mike Trout can tell you, one man does not a baseball franchise make. The two times the Padres made the World Series, it was because they surrounded Gwynn with good players. In 1984 it was a dominant bullpen led by Goose Gossage, Dave Dravecky, and Craig Lefferts; in 1998 it was a balanced lineup (as Sosa and McGwire mashed their way into the record books, Greg Vaughn hit the quietest 50 homers in baseball history), an out-of-his-mind Kevin Brown, and an unstoppable Trevor Hoffman.

The Padres of today don't have a Tony Gwynn or a Trevor Hoffman or even a Greg Vaughn to buoy the franchise with star power and staying power. Although, if you are inclined, you can squint at Eric Hosmer and see the vague outline of Wally Joyner. Ever since general manager AJ Preller U-turned after his initial let's-go-crazy stab at contention in 2015, his teams have been Spangenberg-and-Jankowski-ing their way to 90-loss seasons. Last year, they lost 96.

"From a lineup standpoint," said Preller in a radio interview shortly after the conclusion of 2018 World Series, "it wasn't the '27 Yankees we ran out." But what the Padres have, in addition to a lovely, understated downtown ballpark, is potential. Not the squishy, ultimately meaningless notion of potential that C. Arnholt Smith sold his investors on before going to jail for tax fraud—but the real thing. They have a bunch of really good, and really fun young ballplayers with the capacity to become a really good, and really fun young team.

Yeah, it's easy to say that. It's easy to read all the professional prospect watchers and draw the line between a "loaded system" that is "stocked with talent" and a successful major league team. Obviously it doesn't work that way. Obviously not all the players fans are dreaming about now will become part of the next winning Padres team, or hell, the first World Series winning Padres team. After all, they have a billion corner outfielders. Manuel Margot, their leadoff man of the future, struggled mightily in 2018. Hosmer's contract is massive. They have about twenty starting pitching prospects and two actual starting pitchers.

But the signs are there. After years of plodding along, Hunter Renfroe and Austin Hedges took meaningful steps in the direction of repeatable MLB success last year. It's a *good* thing that Renfroe will have to battle for continued playing time with Myers and with rookie outfielders Franmil Reyes and Franchy Cordero, who both look like players too. It's a *good* thing that Hedges will have to compete with Francisco Mejia, the prospect acquired from Cleveland in last season's Brad Hand trade. All of a sudden the Padres' depth chart problem is that they actually have depth. Plus, despite trading Hand, they bring back one of the best bullpens in the majors. Kirby Yates and Craig Stammen were dominant last season. If the Padres are good, Yates and Stammen will anchor a bullpen that will be crucial to their success. If the Padres are bad again, they will probably be flipped for more prospects.

More prospects—which at this point might be redundant. It's too early to credit Preller for a successful rebuild, but there's something beautiful and balanced about how the Padres' farm system, baseball's deepest, has come together. There have been the usual high draft picks that follow repeated losing, like the touted lefty Mackenzie Gore. There have been big international signings like Cuban pitching prospects Michel Baez and Adrian Morejon, and second baseman Luis Urias out of Mexico. (Signings that vindicate the Padres' efforts to claim an identity as a scouting savvy, internationally-minded franchise.) And most importantly, there have been trades.

Preller, who caught flack for his seemingly reckless dealing when he first came on board, has turned in some masterworks in the intervening years. The crown jewel of the Padres system is shortstop Fernando Tatis Jr—the kind of player who you only need to look at once to understand is special. He's still a teenager. The Padres got him for James Shields. Chris Paddack, a rising star who has never pitched above Double-A, but whom projection systems see as their best starting pitcher right now, came over from the Marlins in exchange for a 39-year-old Fernando Rodney. Mejia came in the Hand trade. The list goes on and on: Logan Allen, Anderson Espinoza, Josh Naylor.

The Padres have managed to build their farm system without totally sacrificing culture at the major league level. Yes, the teams have been lousy, and yes the last five decades have resulted in very low institutional expectations, but San Diego has not tanked like Houston or Chicago. They went from being a bad team, to a bad team with a purpose, tending carefully, patiently to its soil, waiting for a garden to grow. (Perhaps this speaks to how little pressure the organization actually faces). Manager Andy Green is by all accounts forward-thinking and liked by all. If you watch the Padres, you get the sense that he is teasing out new strategies, working to develop his young players. What you don't get, is the sense that the Padres will go the way of the Cubs, Astros, and Braves, and fire their manager when it's time to compete. Rather, it appears they are building something with Green, sort of like (horrible cross-sport metaphor alert) the NBA's Philadelphia 76ers did with Brett Brown.

Which brings us to 2019. This is the year, Preller has said, that the Padres expect to take a step forward. Perhaps it will be led by Tatis, who is the only player in the system who makes you think, hmm, okay, maybe somebody *can* inherit Gwynn's mantle. Or perhaps this is simply the year that the explosive talent of Tatis and Urias and Paddack, and the still simmering potential of Margot, Reyes, Cordero, and Joey Lucchesi begins to coalesce. The Padres may not be a contender right now—but they can and should begin to resemble one.

Is it likely that now, fifty years into their existence, the core of the first Padres World Series winner is finally taking shape? If we've learned anything from Dick Selma and C. Arnholt Smith, it should be that the answer to this question is a resounding no. But it is possible: more possible than it has been since Gwynn was spraying line drives around Jack Murphy Stadium. The time is always right for appreciating the triumph of the Padres existence. But now the time is also right for fans to finally expect something more than stupid ballplaying, and more than optimism about the farm system.

And hell, they have Eric Hosmer. These Padres may not be the '27 Yankees. But maybe they can look to the only other surviving franchise from the expansion class of 1969. Maybe the '15 Kansas City Royals are within dreaming distance. ▪

—Eric Nusbaum is a freelance writer and former editor at VICE Sports.

HITTERS

Franchy Cordero LF   Born: 09/02/94   Age: 24   Bats: L   Throws: R   Height: 6'3"   Weight: 175   Origin: International Free Agent, 2011

YEAR	TEAM	LVL	AGE	PA	R	2B	3B	HR	RBI	BB	K	SB	CS	AVG/OBP/SLG	DRC+	VORP	BABIP	BRR	FRAA	WARP
2016	LEL	A+	21	322	47	16	8	5	35	19	83	11	8	.286/.339/.444	83	21.4	.381	3.1	CF(68): -3.9, LF(2): -0.4	0.3
2016	SAN	AA	21	264	31	8	8	6	19	17	67	12	6	.306/.356/.478	100	20.8	.401	-0.7	CF(59): 3.1	1.1
2017	SDN	MLB	22	99	15	3	3	3	9	6	44	1	1	.228/.276/.424	54	3.8	.400	1.2	CF(25): 0.8, LF(1): -0.1	0.0
2017	ELP	AAA	22	419	68	21	18	17	64	23	118	15	4	.326/.369/.603	124	37.2	.431	1.7	CF(61): -2.5, LF(22): 1.5	2.8
2018	SDN	MLB	23	154	19	5	1	7	19	14	55	5	2	.237/.307/.439	80	4.6	.338	0.6	LF(22): 0.4, CF(11): -1.3	-0.1
2019	SDN	MLB	24	335	39	13	3	12	40	24	113	9	3	.222/.284/.393	88	8.6	.307	1.2	CF -3, LF 1	0.7

Breakout: 4%   Improve: 39%   Collapse: 13%   Attrition: 28%   MLB: 69%   *Comparables: David Dahl, Randal Grichuk, Trayvon Robinson*

To call Cordero a shaky defender is to say Ignatius Reilly was a lousy frankfurter salesman; it's true, but also blandly understated. Last year, Cordero slipped and fell on his butt trying to field a single, clanged a flyball off his knee and somehow parlayed 70 speed into a 40 glove. As has long been the case, there's a canyon between his raw abilities and how they translate in games. Cordero can hit a ball 500 feet and run faster than just about anyone in the organization but he hasn't figured out how to productively apply those tools with any consistency. Instead, he'll follow up a four-hit weekend with a four-strikeout game, a nifty sliding catch with a slide that distinctly *prevents* a catch. Cordero isn't too old for a breakthrough, though he's more likely to become the league's toolsiest extra outfielder than a future regular.

Xavier Edwards SS   Born: 08/09/99   Age: 19   Bats: B   Throws: R   Height: 5'10"   Weight: 155   Origin: Round 1, 2018 Draft (#38 overall)

YEAR	TEAM	LVL	AGE	PA	R	2B	3B	HR	RBI	BB	K	SB	CS	AVG/OBP/SLG	DRC+	VORP	BABIP	BRR	FRAA	WARP
2018	PDR	RK	18	88	19	4	1	0	11	13	10	12	1	.384/.471/.466	119	13.5	.438	1.9	SS(15): 3.1	0.9
2018	TRI	A-	18	107	21	4	0	0	5	18	15	10	0	.314/.438/.360	102	9.9	.380	-0.3	SS(19): -1.1, 2B(5): 0.0	0.3
2019	SDN	MLB	19	251	28	4	0	5	19	22	58	7	1	.179/.251/.268	36	-10.0	.211	0.5	SS 0, 2B 0	-1.1

Breakout: 0%   Improve: 6%   Collapse: 1%   Attrition: 6%   MLB: 12%   *Comparables: Elvis Andrus, Carlos Triunfel, Adalberto Mondesi*

Edwards fell in the draft last June, and the Padres snapped him up with their second first-round selection. He has electric speed and a consistent track record of hitting pretty good amateur competition with a smooth and well-honed line drive swing. At 5-foot-10 and 155 pounds, he's smaller than most draft picks in his orbit, but he's a sure middle infielder with a lot of baseball ability. He doesn't project to hit for much power, but in the Altuve-Betts era, you've got to be at least mildly bullish that an athletic and deceptively strong kid with a great swing and terrific eye finds a way to add that to his game too. Potential oozes everywhere.

Freddy Galvis SS   Born: 11/14/89   Age: 29   Bats: B   Throws: R   Height: 5'10"   Weight: 185   Origin: International Free Agent, 2006

YEAR	TEAM	LVL	AGE	PA	R	2B	3B	HR	RBI	BB	K	SB	CS	AVG/OBP/SLG	DRC+	VORP	BABIP	BRR	FRAA	WARP
2016	PHI	MLB	26	624	61	26	3	20	67	25	136	17	6	.241/.274/.399	82	8.6	.280	-3.5	SS(156): 0.5	1.2
2017	PHI	MLB	27	663	71	29	6	12	61	45	111	14	5	.255/.309/.382	90	27.3	.292	1.6	SS(155): 1.7, LF(1): 0.0	2.6
2018	SDN	MLB	28	656	62	31	5	13	67	45	147	8	6	.248/.299/.380	87	18.5	.304	-1.2	SS(160): -8.9, 2B(5): -0.5	0.9
2019	SDN	MLB	29	621	73	31	4	13	58	39	123	11	5	.253/.305/.390	88	12.9	.298	-1.0	SS -3, 2B 0	1.1

Breakout: 5%   Improve: 53%   Collapse: 4%   Attrition: 12%   MLB: 94%   *Comparables: Jack Wilson, Rich Aurilia, Adam Everett*

Coming up, Galvis was the classic punchless but slick-fielding shortstop (and he's still very good there, despite what FRAA thought of his 2018 performance). Each of his early BP annual comments features some variation of that analysis, best encapsulated by Kevin Goldstein in 2012: "When discussing Galvis's hitting, it's worth noting that he has an excellent glove." But a funny thing happened when the league rolled out a new ball. Once anemic, Galvis's bat suddenly had 20-homer pop, and in 2018 he reached double-digits for the third year running. He's not *good* at the dish: he's still a .250 hitter who rarely walks and he doesn't have enough power to compensate for the first two problems. It's nonetheless interesting to note that even the glove-first shortstops in 2018 can run into a homer every couple of weeks.

Austin Hedges C   Born: 08/18/92   Age: 26   Bats: R   Throws: R   Height: 6'1"   Weight: 206   Origin: Round 2, 2011 Draft (#82 overall)

YEAR	TEAM	LVL	AGE	PA	R	2B	3B	HR	RBI	BB	K	SB	CS	AVG/OBP/SLG	DRC+	VORP	BABIP	BRR	FRAA	WARP
2016	ELP	AAA	23	334	55	20	1	21	82	13	51	1	1	.326/.353/.597	153	28.3	.329	-0.4	C(73): 5.2	4.4
2016	SDN	MLB	23	26	2	1	0	0	1	0	7	0	1	.125/.154/.167	80	-2.7	.167	-0.1	C(7): 0.0	0.1
2017	SDN	MLB	24	417	36	17	0	18	55	23	122	4	1	.214/.262/.398	75	8.3	.260	0.6	C(115): 34.1	4.3
2018	SDN	MLB	25	326	29	14	2	14	37	21	90	3	0	.231/.282/.429	90	7.9	.280	-2.1	C(83): 11.8	2.2
2019	SDN	MLB	26	348	39	15	1	12	41	24	89	3	1	.237/.294/.405	86	9.2	.289	-0.5	C 17	2.7

Breakout: 8%   Improve: 58%   Collapse: 3%   Attrition: 8%   MLB: 94%   *Comparables: Jarrod Saltalamacchia, Wilin Rosario, Mike Zunino*

For years, scouts gushed about Hedges's defense, wistfully saying he could be a franchise catcher, "if only he could hit..." In 2018, he finally hit. Amidst a slightly lower run scoring environment across baseball, Hedges notched modest improvements in most major categories. In theory, his development from a poor hitter to a below-average one with enough pop to keep pitchers honest should have sufficiently cleared the path to a contract extension and a decade in the bucket for San Diego. Instead, the Padres traded for Francisco Mejia, one of baseball's top catching prospects.

YEAR	TEAM	P. COUNT	FRM RUNS	BLK RUNS	THRW RUNS	TOT RUNS
2016	SDN	901	-0.3	0.2	0.0	2.1
2017	SDN	15353	28.0	1.3	2.2	30.3
2018	ELP	784	0.4	0.0	0.0	0.4
2018	SDN	11915	13.0	0.1	-0.4	12.6
2019	SDN	13054	15.1	0.7	0.3	16.1

Hedges is the more established backstop and Mejia has already seen time at other positions; if both play well in 2019, it's the import who will have to move out from behind the plate. Still, it's notable that San Diego made this trade in a year where his defensive statistics fell from stratospheric to merely excellent. His framing numbers in particular dropped, and there's evidence that the rest of the league's catchers have already begun to narrow the gap, sapping some of his value. As far as 2019 goes, if Hedges returns to form, the job is his. But if the glove is only great instead of special, he may well lose out to Mejia.

Eric Hosmer 1B Born: 10/24/89 Age: 29 Bats: L Throws: L Height: 6'4" Weight: 225 Origin: Round 1, 2008 Draft (#3 overall)

YEAR	TEAM	LVL	AGE	PA	R	2B	3B	HR	RBI	BB	K	SB	CS	AVG/OBP/SLG	DRC+	VORP	BABIP	BRR	FRAA	WARP
2016	KCA	MLB	26	667	80	24	1	25	104	57	132	5	3	.266/.328/.433	102	7.6	.301	0.1	1B(154): -2.2	1.0
2017	KCA	MLB	27	671	98	31	1	25	94	66	104	6	1	.318/.385/.498	122	35.1	.351	-1.3	1B(157): 0.6	2.8
2018	SDN	MLB	28	677	72	31	2	18	69	62	142	7	4	.253/.322/.398	87	-1.8	.302	-2.6	1B(157): 7.8	0.4
2019	SDN	MLB	29	640	75	26	2	20	79	62	120	6	3	.264/.338/.423	107	13.7	.302	-1.1	1B -1	1.4

Breakout: 3%   Improve: 63%   Collapse: 7%   Attrition: 8%   MLB: 97%   *Comparables: Don Baylor, Ted Kluszewski, Cesar Cedeno*

Hosmer is baseball's version of J.D. Salinger, in that there's a sizable gap between his production and reputation, and that it's uncouth to say so. The disconnect lurks at every turn. Despite shaky defensive metrics, he's always been considered a premier first baseman, and has won four Gold Gloves. He made the All-Star team and took home a trophy for the game's MVP award in a season where he wasn't much better than a replacement level player. And when just about everyone else signed for dimes on the dollar last winter, Hosmer inked a deal for $144 million. For Padres fans worried that Hosmer is a lemon, it's too early to panic. He's only 29 and has always had a weirdly large production disparity between odd and even years. While he hits the ball on the ground too often to be a great player, he's a decent bet to remind us why so many consider him a very good one in 2019.

Travis Jankowski RF Born: 06/15/91 Age: 28 Bats: L Throws: R Height: 6'2" Weight: 185 Origin: Round 1, 2012 Draft (#44 overall)

YEAR	TEAM	LVL	AGE	PA	R	2B	3B	HR	RBI	BB	K	SB	CS	AVG/OBP/SLG	DRC+	VORP	BABIP	BRR	FRAA	WARP
2016	SDN	MLB	25	383	53	13	2	2	12	42	100	30	12	.245/.332/.313	72	10.0	.343	7.1	CF(87): -2.2, RF(22): -0.5	0.4
2017	ELP	AAA	26	157	20	5	1	0	11	18	28	8	1	.266/.350/.317	86	1.2	.333	0.1	CF(22): -1.7, LF(7): -0.3	0.0
2017	SDN	MLB	26	87	10	2	0	0	1	9	28	4	0	.187/.282/.213	60	-3.1	.298	0.9	LF(19): -0.4, CF(4): 0.3	-0.1
2018	ELP	AAA	27	94	17	4	0	1	11	11	21	4	3	.363/.452/.450	95	8.8	.483	1.5	CF(20): 2.5	0.7
2018	SDN	MLB	27	387	45	12	3	4	17	37	73	24	7	.259/.332/.346	84	8.3	.319	4.5	RF(58): 3.3, CF(34): -1.7	0.7
2019	SDN	MLB	28	301	38	10	2	5	22	28	71	15	5	.228/.304/.329	78	4.7	.288	3.0	RF 6, CF 0	1.1

Breakout: 3%   Improve: 45%   Collapse: 7%   Attrition: 21%   MLB: 87%   *Comparables: Joey Gathright, Tony Gwynn, Eric Young*

Jankowski is a man out of his time. Called up a month after the unofficial start of the Juiced Ball Era, he's been among baseball's feeblest hitters ever since: Just one regular in that span has a lower slugging percentage and only a handful of guys have fewer home runs. Jankowski still has his uses, but you wonder how much more valuable he'd have been a few decades ago, when his slash-n-dash style would've been perfect on Astroturf. Perhaps he and Jerry Turner can get together and swap careers.

Ian Kinsler 2B Born: 06/22/82 Age: 37 Bats: R Throws: R Height: 6'0" Weight: 200 Origin: Round 17, 2003 Draft (#496 overall)

YEAR	TEAM	LVL	AGE	PA	R	2B	3B	HR	RBI	BB	K	SB	CS	AVG/OBP/SLG	DRC+	VORP	BABIP	BRR	FRAA	WARP
2016	DET	MLB	34	679	117	29	4	28	83	45	115	14	6	.288/.348/.484	123	40.2	.314	4.7	2B(151): 3.0	5.0
2017	DET	MLB	35	613	90	25	3	22	52	55	86	14	5	.236/.313/.412	105	9.0	.244	4.7	2B(135): 1.0	2.9
2018	ANA	MLB	36	391	49	20	0	13	32	30	40	9	4	.239/.304/.406	99	8.1	.237	-0.9	2B(91): 4.0	1.5
2018	BOS	MLB	36	143	17	6	0	1	16	10	24	7	3	.242/.294/.311	100	-3.1	.287	0.6	2B(37): -1.3	0.4
2019	SDN	MLB	37	232	28	13	1	6	26	18	33	6	2	.261/.329/.418	103	8.6	.286	0.9	3B 0, 2B 0	0.9

Breakout: 1%   Improve: 23%   Collapse: 16%   Attrition: 21%   MLB: 64%   *Comparables: Del Pratt, Jerry Hairston, Mark Ellis*

We should all feel happy that Kinsler, a Damn Fine Baseballer, was finally able to grab a ring with Boston last season after close calls with Texas and Detroit earlier in his career. It likely came at the perfect time, as it's tough to see a contender trusting him again. The once-dynamic talent is down to one remaining skill: defense. Our metrics may not love him, but that didn't stop him from winning his second Gold Glove. About that bat, though. Kinsler posted a lower ISO than Sean Rodriguez and a lower OBP than the ambulatory remains of Chase Utley. His running days are also behind him, as evidenced by his World Series pinch-running adventure that more closely resembled a Billy Joel drive home than anything approaching good base running. Could the 36-year-old sneak his way onto a roster as a defensive-minded bench piece? Sure. But at this point he'd be miscast as anything more.

Manuel Margot CF Born: 09/28/94 Age: 24 Bats: R Throws: R Height: 5'11" Weight: 180 Origin: International Free Agent, 2011

YEAR	TEAM	LVL	AGE	PA	R	2B	3B	HR	RBI	BB	K	SB	CS	AVG/OBP/SLG	DRC+	VORP	BABIP	BRR	FRAA	WARP
2016	ELP	AAA	21	566	98	21	12	6	55	36	64	30	11	.304/.351/.426	111	30.8	.335	7.9	CF(121): 19.3, RF(1): 0.2	5.7
2016	SDN	MLB	21	37	4	4	1	0	3	0	7	2	0	.243/.243/.405	81	2.4	.300	0.8	CF(9): 0.6, RF(1): 0.1	0.2
2017	SDN	MLB	22	529	53	18	7	13	39	35	106	17	7	.263/.313/.409	92	23.6	.309	1.3	CF(123): -1.0	1.4
2018	SDN	MLB	23	519	50	26	8	8	51	32	88	11	10	.245/.292/.384	87	10.1	.281	0.9	CF(136): -4.9	0.6
2019	SDN	MLB	24	342	43	15	4	7	32	23	63	10	5	.252/.306/.395	94	11.5	.291	0.6	CF 2	1.5

Breakout: 3%   Improve: 58%   Collapse: 1%   Attrition: 6%   MLB: 95%   *Comparables: Melky Cabrera, Lastings Milledge, Alejandro De Aza*

There's no way to twist the splits in good faith and come to a different conclusion: Margot had a bad year at the plate. Following a competent but unspectacular rookie season, his offensive regression was arguably the worst development of the year for the Friars. He's still as athletic and rangy in the outfield as ever and he'll put a charge into the ball just often enough to make you think his hitting ability is more latent than dormant. But while it's too early to say anything definitive, his first 1,000 plate appearances suggest he's more like Cameron Maybin than Lorenzo Cain. That's not the end of the world, even if it is disappointing given his prospect pedigree.

Francisco Mejia C Born: 10/27/95 Age: 23 Bats: B Throws: R Height: 5'10" Weight: 180 Origin: International Free Agent, 2012

YEAR	TEAM	LVL	AGE	PA	R	2B	3B	HR	RBI	BB	K	SB	CS	AVG/OBP/SLG	DRC+	VORP	BABIP	BRR	FRAA	WARP
2016	LKC	A	20	259	41	17	3	7	51	15	39	1	0	.347/.384/.531	135	29.7	.388	2.3	C(52): 1.5	2.7
2016	LYN	A+	20	184	22	12	1	4	29	13	24	1	2	.333/.380/.488	109	16.8	.366	-0.1	C(35): 0.6	1.0
2017	AKR	AA	21	383	52	21	2	14	52	24	53	7	2	.297/.346/.490	119	32.5	.311	1.5	C(71): 1.6, 3B(1): -0.1	3.0
2017	CLE	MLB	21	14	1	0	0	0	1	1	3	0	0	.154/.214/.154	84	-1.7	.200	-0.3	C(3): 0.0	0.0
2018	CLE	MLB	22	4	0	0	0	0	0	2	0	0	0	.000/.500/.000	56	0.1	.000	0.0		0.0
2018	COH	AAA	22	336	32	22	1	7	45	18	58	0	0	.279/.328/.426	99	9.4	.321	-1.2	C(41): 4.6, LF(22): -3.2	1.1
2018	ELP	AAA	22	132	22	8	1	7	23	7	25	0	0	.328/.364/.582	118	11.8	.359	0.7	C(26): 1.3	1.1
2018	SDN	MLB	22	58	6	2	0	3	8	3	19	0	0	.185/.241/.389	79	-0.3	.219	0.2	C(10): -1.7	0.0
2019	SDN	MLB	23	472	52	20	1	12	46	32	101	1	0	.228/.289/.362	75	4.1	.270	-0.7	C -5, LF -1	-0.1

Breakout: 7% Improve: 30% Collapse: 8% Attrition: 22% MLB: 57%

Comparables: Hank Conger, Travis d'Arnaud, Jeff Mathis

YEAR	TEAM	P. COUNT	FRM RUNS	BLK RUNS	THRW RUNS	TOT RUNS
2017	AKR	9761	-0.5	-0.8	-0.1	0.7
2017	CLE	40	0.0	0.0	0.0	3.2
2018	COH	5559	2.6	0.7	0.3	3.8
2018	ELP	3547	0.0	0.0	0.2	0.6
2018	SDN	1484	-0.7	-0.8	0.0	-0.7
2019	SDN	11703	-3.9	-1.2	-0.6	-5.7

You don't often see trades like this anymore: A premium prospect at a critical position dealt for two (admittedly good) relievers. But between Cleveland's desperate need to reshape the bullpen and Mejia's desire to catch full-time, San Diego landed an enticing young player at a great price. With Austin Hedges also in tow and Austin Allen charging through the minors, the Padres are flush with catchers, and Mejia's route to a starting job isn't quite as obvious as it would be in most rebuilding organizations. His arm is top-notch, but he's just an okay receiver and lacks Hedges' defensive chops; a shift down the defensive spectrum is a possibility. He'll have to hit regardless of where he plays, and despite less-than-sterling pitch selection skills, the consensus is that he will: He's a potential plus hitter who has the pop to blast 20+ homers annually at maturity. He's very adept at making contact, and he's hit at every minor league stop. Like any hit tool-reliant player though, it's hard to feel comfortable calling him a lineup anchor until he actually performs. As a prospect, Mejia is practically the first name below the "can't miss" tier.

Wil Myers LF Born: 12/10/90 Age: 28 Bats: R Throws: R Height: 6'3" Weight: 205 Origin: Round 3, 2009 Draft (#91 overall)

YEAR	TEAM	LVL	AGE	PA	R	2B	3B	HR	RBI	BB	K	SB	CS	AVG/OBP/SLG	DRC+	VORP	BABIP	BRR	FRAA	WARP
2016	SDN	MLB	25	676	99	29	4	28	94	68	160	28	6	.259/.336/.461	113	33.2	.305	5.2	1B(149): 1.8, RF(7): -0.3	2.8
2017	SDN	MLB	26	649	80	29	3	30	74	70	180	20	6	.243/.328/.464	105	28.7	.297	1.1	1B(154): -1.8	1.3
2018	SDN	MLB	27	343	39	25	1	11	39	30	94	13	1	.253/.318/.446	86	14.4	.327	1.3	3B(36): -4.3, LF(31): 0.8	0.4
2019	SDN	MLB	28	576	81	25	3	20	63	57	152	20	4	.240/.321/.415	101	15.7	.301	1.9	3B -18, 1B 0	-0.2

Breakout: 2% Improve: 47% Collapse: 4% Attrition: 7% MLB: 98%

Comparables: Dave Hollins, Jhonny Peralta, Morgan Ensberg

It's one thing for a top prospect to bust. To have talent and hope and potential and still fall short may be difficult to swallow, but it's also common and understandable. We all know at least one of those folks from high school. Far more perplexing are the blue chippers who turn into Phil Hughes or Jay Bruce. Back in 2016, when he made the All-Star team and hit .286/.351/.522 in the first half, Myers looked like he was finally developing into the star we'd long expected. But after a second-half slump and two years of solid but hardly special production, it increasingly appears that he's more of a good player than a building block. That the Padres have asked him to switch positions for the fifth time this decade—third base on your bingo cards, folks—all but confirms as much. Perhaps it's the lingering hype from his time as one of baseball's top prospects, or the notoriety that surrounded him throughout the endless litigation of the James Shields trade, but that feels like a bit of a letdown. That's not necessarily fair, but neither was expecting your Ivy League buddy to cure cancer.

Josh Naylor LF Born: 06/22/97 Age: 22 Bats: L Throws: L Height: 5'11" Weight: 250 Origin: Round 1, 2015 Draft (#12 overall)

YEAR	TEAM	LVL	AGE	PA	R	2B	3B	HR	RBI	BB	K	SB	CS	AVG/OBP/SLG	DRC+	VORP	BABIP	BRR	FRAA	WARP
2016	GRB	A	19	370	42	24	2	9	54	22	62	10	3	.269/.317/.430	112	10.5	.304	-1.9	1B(81): -2.3	0.5
2016	LEL	A+	19	144	17	5	0	3	21	3	22	1	1	.252/.264/.353	98	-2.9	.276	-0.6	1B(32): -3.4	-0.3
2017	LEL	A+	20	313	41	16	2	8	45	27	48	7	1	.297/.361/.452	116	14.6	.333	-0.1	1B(42): -0.6	0.9
2017	SAN	AA	20	175	18	9	0	2	19	16	36	2	1	.250/.320/.346	86	0.6	.308	-0.9	1B(40): 1.9	0.0
2018	SAN	AA	21	574	72	22	1	17	74	64	69	5	5	.297/.383/.447	127	27.4	.317	-5.1	LF(89): -20.4, 1B(29): 0.6	0.5
2019	SDN	MLB	22	251	28	10	0	9	32	19	45	1	0	.255/.314/.412	95	4.1	.281	-0.5	LF -5, 1B 0	-0.1

Breakout: 6% Improve: 22% Collapse: 3% Attrition: 18% MLB: 33%

Comparables: Ramon Flores, Jake Bauers, Alex Romero

Naylor has several promising traits that haven't quite clicked in games yet. The 21-year-old has 70-grade raw power, good barrel control, a decent understanding of the strike zone and a feel for contact. It all plays down, however, because his swing is relatively flat and he's too easily coaxed into weak contact on pitches outside his wheelhouse. There are signs he's snapping out of that to some extent—he hit a career high 17 bombs last year and added a bit of loft to his swing plane—but it's unclear whether San Diego will ever reap the benefits even if he hits: Naylor's physique and lack of speed suggest he's a first basemen all the way. But with Eric Hosmer in tow, he saw plenty of action in left last year, where he (not surprisingly) isn't up to snuff. The ingredients here are good, but you can't make cookies with pizza dough and marinara sauce. Whether that means Naylor needs a change of scenery or something else is for the chefs to determine.

Jose Pirela 2B Born: 11/21/89 Age: 29 Bats: R Throws: R Height: 6'0" Weight: 220 Origin: Undrafted Free Agent, 2006

YEAR	TEAM	LVL	AGE	PA	R	2B	3B	HR	RBI	BB	K	SB	CS	AVG/OBP/SLG	DRC+	VORP	BABIP	BRR	FRAA	WARP
2016	SDN	MLB	26	41	2	2	0	0	0	1	9	0	1	.154/.175/.205	66	-3.9	.200	-0.7	2B(12): -1.5, RF(1): 0.0	-0.3
2016	ELP	AAA	26	146	19	7	3	2	16	9	21	1	1	.248/.295/.387	89	-4.2	.281	0.4	LF(17): -0.9, RF(8): -0.7	0.1
2017	ELP	AAA	27	201	37	10	3	13	42	15	26	8	3	.331/.387/.635	145	17.5	.329	-1.4	1B(26): 3.1, LF(12): 2.0	1.8
2017	SDN	MLB	27	344	43	25	4	10	40	27	71	4	3	.288/.347/.490	99	22.8	.343	0.3	LF(68): 6.3, 2B(7): -0.1	1.4
2018	SDN	MLB	28	473	54	23	2	5	32	30	89	6	3	.249/.300/.345	72	-5.9	.301	-1.5	2B(77): 0.3, LF(31): -1.3	-0.6
2019	SDN	MLB	29	230	24	10	1	5	25	16	46	3	2	.242/.303/.378	82	2.4	.284	-0.3	2B -1, LF 0	0.2

Breakout: 4%   Improve: 28%   Collapse: 19%   Attrition: 25%   MLB: 74%   *Comparables: Whit Merrifield, Ramiro Pena, Russ Adams*

Pirela was one of the earliest fringe prospects to land in San Diego following the club's decision to rebuild. After hitting well in limited action back in 2017, he cratered last year, losing more than 150 points off his slugging percentage; by year's end, he'd fallen out of the lineup. In hindsight, his 2017 power surge almost certainly said more about the worst excesses of the juiced ball than about Pirela himself. Regardless, entering his age-29 season and coming off a replacement-level campaign, it appears that Pirela has missed his best chance to establish himself on the roster.

Hudson Potts 3B Born: 10/28/98 Age: 20 Bats: R Throws: R Height: 6'3" Weight: 205 Origin: Round 1, 2016 Draft (#24 overall)

YEAR	TEAM	LVL	AGE	PA	R	2B	3B	HR	RBI	BB	K	SB	CS	AVG/OBP/SLG	DRC+	VORP	BABIP	BRR	FRAA	WARP
2016	PDR	RK	17	195	35	12	2	1	21	9	34	8	4	.295/.333/.399	101	14.1	.356	1.4	SS(14): -1.1, 3B(4): 0.8	0.6
2016	TRI	A-	17	72	7	0	1	0	6	9	13	2	1	.233/.352/.267	86	5.0	.298	0.8	SS(10): 1.1, 3B(3): -0.2	0.3
2017	FTW	A	18	522	67	23	4	20	69	23	140	0	1	.253/.293/.438	104	9.8	.312	-0.5	3B(116): -6.9, SS(2): 0.2	1.1
2018	LEL	A+	19	453	66	35	1	17	58	37	112	3	1	.281/.350/.498	110	36.6	.348	0.3	3B(99): 0.7, 1B(8): 0.1	2.1
2018	SAN	AA	19	89	5	0	0	2	5	10	33	1	0	.154/.258/.231	62	-2.9	.233	-0.2	3B(21): 0.3	-0.1
2019	SDN	MLB	20	251	25	9	0	10	32	11	79	0	0	.210/.245/.376	61	-6.9	.264	-0.6	3B -1, 1B 0	-0.9

Breakout: 5%   Improve: 10%   Collapse: 0%   Attrition: 4%   MLB: 12%   *Comparables: Matt Davidson, Rafael Devers, Renato Nunez*

If you wanted to design a third base prospect starter set, Potts would make an effective model. San Diego's first-round pick in 2016 is a good athlete who lacks the lateral range required to play up the middle. He's not slow, but you wouldn't quite call him fast. His above-average arm is more than strong enough for the hot corner. At the plate, he has plenty of raw power but doesn't project to hit for a high average.

As is often the case with these player types, Potts's ultimate role will be shaped by whether he can make enough hard contact to facilitate the power. He's an aggressive hitter prone to expanding the strike zone, and his pitch recognition needs refinement. Provided that he stays healthy, we should learn quite a bit about Potts this season; the Double-A test looms large.

Buddy Reed CF Born: 04/27/95 Age: 24 Bats: B Throws: R Height: 6'4" Weight: 210 Origin: Round 2, 2016 Draft (#48 overall)

YEAR	TEAM	LVL	AGE	PA	R	2B	3B	HR	RBI	BB	K	SB	CS	AVG/OBP/SLG	DRC+	VORP	BABIP	BRR	FRAA	WARP
2016	TRI	A-	21	231	31	9	4	0	13	22	53	15	5	.254/.326/.337	86	8.3	.338	3.5	CF(50): 3.9	1.1
2017	FTW	A	22	347	48	17	8	6	35	23	97	12	8	.234/.290/.396	92	6.1	.315	1.1	CF(85): 1.0	0.9
2018	LEL	A+	23	343	54	21	7	12	47	24	84	33	7	.324/.371/.549	111	39.6	.407	6.5	LF(54): -6.1, CF(15): 1.8	1.5
2018	SAN	AA	23	195	21	7	0	1	15	12	63	18	3	.179/.227/.235	52	-9.0	.263	2.6	CF(39): 8.1, LF(3): 0.5	0.6
2019	SDN	MLB	24	251	32	8	1	7	21	10	79	13	3	.205/.237/.337	47	-6.0	.270	1.9	LF -1, CF 2	-0.5

Breakout: 0%   Improve: 1%   Collapse: 0%   Attrition: 2%   MLB: 2%   *Comparables: Noel Cuevas, Paulo Orlando, Jared Hoying*

Nobody doubts Reed's speed or ability to run 'em down in center, but scouts have long questioned whether his stiff and slappy swing would ultimately limit his upside. After a year-and-a-half of modest production, Reed finally hit a little bit last year, posting career highs across the board and earning a trip to the Futures Game for his efforts. It should take more than a sky-high BABIP and uncharacteristic power in the Cal League, however, before Padres fans get excited. Double-A arms carved Reed up after a late-season promotion, and the guess here is that he'll plateau as a defensive-minded fourth outfielder.

Hunter Renfroe LF Born: 01/28/92 Age: 27 Bats: R Throws: R Height: 6'1" Weight: 220 Origin: Round 1, 2013 Draft (#13 overall)

YEAR	TEAM	LVL	AGE	PA	R	2B	3B	HR	RBI	BB	K	SB	CS	AVG/OBP/SLG	DRC+	VORP	BABIP	BRR	FRAA	WARP
2016	ELP	AAA	24	563	95	34	5	30	105	22	115	5	2	.306/.336/.557	134	22.2	.339	1.8	RF(111): 5.8, CF(12): -0.9	4.5
2016	SDN	MLB	24	36	8	3	0	4	14	1	5	0	0	.371/.389/.800	127	6.1	.346	0.2	RF(9): 0.7	0.3
2017	ELP	AAA	25	61	18	7	1	4	18	6	7	1	0	.509/.557/.891	140	16.8	.545	0.8	RF(12): 1.9	0.7
2017	SDN	MLB	25	479	51	25	1	26	58	27	140	3	0	.231/.284/.467	91	16.0	.275	-0.9	RF(120): -2.1	0.3
2018	ELP	AAA	26	43	6	1	0	2	4	2	10	0	0	.220/.256/.390	85	-0.8	.241	-0.1	RF(9): 2.4	0.3
2018	SDN	MLB	26	441	53	23	1	26	68	30	109	2	1	.248/.302/.504	110	18.4	.271	-1.2	LF(58): -1.3, RF(50): 6.6	2.1
2019	SDN	MLB	27	517	64	24	2	25	76	36	123	3	1	.252/.314/.466	112	21.1	.293	-0.9	LF 0	2.3

Breakout: 6%   Improve: 44%   Collapse: 4%   Attrition: 10%   MLB: 89%   *Comparables: Mark Trumbo, Corey Dickerson, Khris Davis*

It took a long time for Renfroe—who was considered an advanced college bat when the Padres drafted him back in 2013—to establish himself as a big-leaguer. Throughout his minor league career and first season in San Diego, Renfroe's undisciplined hacking threatened to undercut prodigious in-game power. But while he's never going to win a batting title or post a great walk rate, he's managed to sand down the roughest edges in his game, fine-tuning his approach just enough to make everything work. The .248/.302/.504 slash line he posted last year seems like a reasonable approximation of his talent going forward. There will be slumps but also 480-foot homers, and enough of the latter to justify his spot in the middle of the order. He's like a recent grad who finally found a reliable job after a few false starts: You knew he had the talent, it took a long time to get here, you're not entirely sure he'll show up to work every day, but he's definitely in a better place now than six months ago.

Franmil Reyes RF Born: 07/07/95 Age: 23 Bats: R Throws: R Height: 6'5" Weight: 275 Origin: International Free Agent, 2011

YEAR	TEAM	LVL	AGE	PA	R	2B	3B	HR	RBI	BB	K	SB	CS	AVG/OBP/SLG	DRC+	VORP	BABIP	BRR	FRAA	WARP
2016	LEL	A+	20	547	63	32	3	16	83	47	108	2	3	.278/.340/.452	109	23.2	.324	-0.2	RF(112): 17.3, LF(1): -0.1	3.4
2017	SAN	AA	21	566	79	27	1	25	102	48	134	4	4	.258/.322/.464	117	25.5	.298	-1.1	RF(89): 3.2	2.5
2018	ELP	AAA	22	250	50	11	1	16	52	37	59	0	0	.324/.428/.614	154	20.3	.382	1.9	RF(46): -2.2	2.2
2018	SDN	MLB	22	285	36	9	0	16	31	24	80	0	0	.280/.340/.498	110	14.5	.345	0.3	RF(75): -7.1	0.3
2019	SDN	MLB	23	553	71	22	2	27	83	58	148	1	0	.251/.334/.470	117	26.9	.303	0.3	RF -2	2.7

Breakout: 1%   Improve: 28%   Collapse: 7%   Attrition: 16%   MLB: 65%   *Comparables: Jorge Soler, Wil Myers, Domonic Brown*

Hey look, another a power-hitting corner outfielder with strikeout issues and a shaky glove! It's a fairly common prototype in this organization, and as a profile, it's generally a bit of a tease; in many cases, plus (or plus-plus) power is the only carrying tool here and you're just sorta hoping the guy turns into Adam Duvall. Once in a while though, there's a bit more bat to go with that power, and the question is whether Reyes's torrid finish indicates that he's become one of those special cases.

After struggling and striking out in nearly 40 percent of his plate appearances in his first 40 big league games, Reyes caught fire over the last two months of the season. He hit .318/.385/.548 down the stretch, with shockingly acceptable walk and strikeout rates and a handful of monster home runs. His career trajectory and minor league body of work suggests he was just running hot, but he suddenly stopped missing fastballs in August and if that holds true, pitchers have an adjustment to make. Reyes's career could go in a lot of directions from here, depending on how he adjusts to the adjustments, but regardless, he's emerged as a real part of the team's present. On a long list of compelling Padres to follow in 2019, he's near the top of the heap.

Esteury Ruiz 2B Born: 02/15/99 Age: 20 Bats: R Throws: R Height: 6'0" Weight: 169 Origin: International Free Agent, 2015

YEAR	TEAM	LVL	AGE	PA	R	2B	3B	HR	RBI	BB	K	SB	CS	AVG/OBP/SLG	DRC+	VORP	BABIP	BRR	FRAA	WARP
2016	DRY	RK	17	244	44	18	5	5	26	19	35	13	10	.313/.378/.512	141	31.2	.354	2.2	2B(26): -0.8, SS(10): -1.8	1.6
2017	ROY	RK	18	91	22	10	6	3	23	4	20	9	0	.419/.440/.779	137	22.3	.516	3.3	2B(17): 3.8	1.3
2017	PDR	RK	18	134	23	10	4	1	16	9	34	17	6	.300/.364/.475	140	11.9	.412	1.8	2B(27): -0.9	1.0
2018	FTW	A	19	493	63	20	5	12	53	38	141	49	11	.253/.324/.403	101	21.3	.345	5.8	2B(74): -1.2, 3B(16): -2.6	1.5
2019	SDN	MLB	20	251	33	12	2	7	23	9	83	12	3	.215/.242/.374	62	-2.1	.290	2.0	2B 0, 3B -1	-0.3

Breakout: 2%   Improve: 9%   Collapse: 0%   Attrition: 7%   MLB: 11%   *Comparables: Dilson Herrera, Nick Noonan, Renato Nunez*

For the first time in his life, Ruiz struggled on the baseball field. "Struggle" is a relative word here: As a 19-year-old amid his first taste of full-season ball—and presumably first exposure to April in the Midwest—he was an above-average hitter, and his 49 steals paced the circuit. After dominating the complex leagues, though, Ruiz's 2018 campaign was a small step back. He struck out in nearly 30 percent of his plate appearances and chased far too many pitches out of the zone, undercutting his above-average raw power. He also did little to assuage concerns that he'll slip down the defensive spectrum. We're not big fans of fielding percentage at Baseball Prospectus, but any time you flirt with .900, things can't be going well. Ruiz's power-speed combo can still work if he has to transition from the keystone to left field, but there's much more pressure on his bat out there, and it's fair to speculate that his grip-N-rip approach will leave him too exposed against upper-level arms for the profile to actualize.

Fernando Tatis Jr. SS Born: 01/02/99 Age: 20 Bats: R Throws: R Height: 6'3" Weight: 185 Origin: International Free Agent, 2015

YEAR	TEAM	LVL	AGE	PA	R	2B	3B	HR	RBI	BB	K	SB	CS	AVG/OBP/SLG	DRC+	VORP	BABIP	BRR	FRAA	WARP
2016	PDR	RK	17	188	35	13	1	4	20	10	44	14	2	.273/.312/.426	105	13.0	.344	2.4	SS(29): -0.1, 2B(8): -1.3	0.8
2016	TRI	A-	17	49	4	4	2	0	5	3	13	1	1	.273/.306/.455	87	4.5	.364	0.4	SS(7): -1.4, 3B(3): -0.7	-0.2
2017	FTW	A	18	518	78	26	7	21	69	75	124	29	15	.281/.390/.520	144	51.2	.342	0.1	SS(109): -5.6	4.3
2017	SAN	AA	18	57	6	1	0	1	6	2	17	3	0	.255/.281/.327	72	0.4	.351	0.9	SS(9): -0.3, 3B(3): -0.5	0.0
2018	SAN	AA	19	394	77	22	4	16	43	33	109	16	5	.286/.355/.507	116	35.8	.370	3.0	SS(83): -1.9	2.6
2019	SDN	MLB	20	286	36	11	1	12	35	20	87	8	3	.226/.284/.405	86	6.3	.290	0.4	SS -1	0.5

Breakout: 17%   Improve: 30%   Collapse: 0%   Attrition: 14%   MLB: 31%   *Comparables: Xander Bogaerts, Addison Russell, Miguel Sano*

It's almost inconceivable that, less than three years ago, the Padres were able to acquire Tatis in exchange for James Shields (that the White Sox absorbed nearly $30 million is a hilarious footnote). Now entering his age-20 season, Fernando the Younger is the crown jewel in San Diego's sterling collection of young talent. Scouts project that he'll be a .270 hitter who can bash 25 homers per year in his prime, with room for more if his pitch recognition and plate discipline improve. If Tatis were a first baseman, he'd be an interesting prospect. As a shortstop? Well, he's one of the two or three best in the game.

It's worth mentioning that, for a top prospect, the delta of outcomes here is quite large. Tatis is young, super athletic and toolsy, which suggests that he has room to grow. But his youth also means that his track record isn't real long, and he hasn't faced many elite pitchers; we don't know how big leaguers will be able to exploit the one weakness in his game (plate discipline). There's a world where Tatis turns into a third basemen with contact issues that sap some of the power everyone expects out of him, like the best version of his father. But there's also a future where Tatis stays at short, works better counts and adds strength without sacrificing athleticism. That guy is a superstar, and the kind of franchise player you can build a team around. We won't know where Tatis fits along that spectrum for a few years, but Padres fans may get their first look at him as soon as this summer.

Luis Urias 2B Born: 06/03/97 Age: 22 Bats: R Throws: R Height: 5'9" Weight: 185 Origin: International Free Agent, 2013

YEAR	TEAM	LVL	AGE	PA	R	2B	3B	HR	RBI	BB	K	SB	CS	AVG/OBP/SLG	DRC+	VORP	BABIP	BRR	FRAA	WARP
2016	LEL	A+	19	531	71	26	5	5	52	40	36	7	13	.330/.397/.440	120	41.6	.348	-5.9	2B(80): 6.2, SS(22): -3.2	2.7
2017	SAN	AA	20	526	77	20	4	3	38	68	65	7	5	.296/.398/.380	112	40.3	.340	2.6	SS(60): 4.7, 2B(55): -1.1	3.4
2018	ELP	AAA	21	533	83	30	7	8	45	67	109	2	1	.296/.398/.447	103	27.3	.373	1.4	2B(90): 10.2, SS(20): 3.4	3.8
2018	SDN	MLB	21	53	5	1	0	2	5	3	10	1	0	.208/.264/.354	90	0.6	.216	0.3	2B(12): -0.2	0.1
2019	SDN	MLB	22	490	50	17	4	10	51	52	114	2	1	.226/.324/.355	92	12.1	.284	-0.3	2B 5, SS 0	1.8

Breakout: 7%   Improve: 33%   Collapse: 10%   Attrition: 25%   MLB: 52%   *Comparables: Kolten Wong, Steve Lombardozzi, J.P. Crawford*

Another of the cornerstone prospects in San Diego's rebuild, Urias is a high-floor second baseman. He's a good defender at the keystone—he can handle short in a pinch—but it's his bat that carries the profile. His athleticism, bat speed and feel for contact portends a future as a .300 hitter; his short frame and high leg kick suggests he could do so in style. He'll need to hit for average to have value, and most scouts think he's up to the task. The big question is whether there's juice in the profile beyond that.

Between a lively ball and the launch angle revolution, we've seen a much wider range of outcomes from the "good hit, low power" profile in recent years. Some players have been able to add loft to their swings, and combine excellent hand/eye coordination with their new bat path to unlock previously untapped power; others never get the hang of the new mechanics and take a step back. It's too early to tell where Urias will fit on this elongated spectrum, and it's not fair to project an attribute he's scarcely shown in the minors. Whether any power comes or not, Urias should play good D and get on base quite a bit. All that this is meant to say is that he's very likely to be a productive player, and that there's also a glimmer of star potential.

Christian Villanueva 3B · Born: 06/19/91 · Age: 28 · Bats: R · Throws: R · Height: 5'11" · Weight: 210 · Origin: International Free Agent, 2008

YEAR	TEAM	LVL	AGE	PA	R	2B	3B	HR	RBI	BB	K	SB	CS	AVG/OBP/SLG	DRC+	VORP	BABIP	BRR	FRAA	WARP
2017	ELP	AAA	26	454	69	28	2	20	86	43	83	4	2	.296/.369/.528	126	26.1	.326	-1.1	3B(59): -2.9, 1B(43): 2.1	2.5
2017	SDN	MLB	26	32	5	1	0	4	7	0	10	0	0	.344/.344/.750	90	7.1	.389	-0.4	3B(9): -0.9	-0.1
2018	SDN	MLB	27	384	42	15	0	20	46	23	104	3	0	.236/.299/.450	103	12.5	.276	0.4	3B(96): -1.8, SS(4): 0.1	1.4
2019	SDN	MLB	28	347	41	17	1	15	48	24	85	2	1	.247/.312/.444	104	9.4	.293	-0.2	3B -5, 1B 0	0.5

Breakout: 4%   Improve: 53%   Collapse: 7%   Attrition: 18%   MLB: 85%   *Comparables: Josh Donaldson, Josh Fields, David Freese*

One of the merits of a non-contending season is that managers can give 400 at-bats to the long-overlooked but vaguely-appealing fringe prospect. The job often proves too much for the player, but at least teams can say they kicked the tires on the Asuajes and Pirelas of the world. Occasionally though, you get a year like Villanueva's 2018 season, one that raises more questions than it resolves. The Mexican third baseman smoked the ball for two months out of the chute, bashing 15 homers in the season's first 50 games. He cooled considerably from there though, and both his minor league track record and lofty whiff rate suggest he was playing a bit above his head early on. The Padres evidently decided that Villanueva was a riddle not worth solving, as they sold his rights to the Yomiuri Giants of NPB.

PITCHERS

Logan Allen LHP · Born: 05/23/97 · Age: 22 · Bats: R · Throws: L · Height: 6'3" · Weight: 200 · Origin: Round 8, 2015 Draft (#231 overall)

YEAR	TEAM	LVL	AGE	W	L	SV	G	GS	IP	H	HR	BB/9	K/9	K	GB%	BABIP	WHIP	ERA	DRA	WARP	MPH	FB%	WHF	CSP
2016	FTW	A	19	3	4	0	15	11	54	48	2	3.7	7.8	47	38%	.301	1.30	3.33	3.85	0.7				
2017	FTW	A	20	5	4	0	13	13	68¹	49	1	3.4	11.2	85	43%	.294	1.10	2.11	3.86	1.1				
2017	LEL	A+	20	2	5	0	11	10	56²	60	2	2.9	9.1	57	50%	.352	1.38	3.97	3.84	0.9				
2018	SAN	AA	21	10	6	0	20	19	121	89	7	2.8	9.3	125	43%	.269	1.05	2.75	3.35	2.8				
2018	ELP	AAA	21	4	0	0	5	5	27²	21	4	4.2	8.5	26	38%	.236	1.23	1.63	6.12	-0.2				
2019	SDN	MLB	22	1	1	0	3	3	15	14	2	3.9	8.9	15	39%	.303	1.36	4.47	4.89	0.1				

Breakout: 10%   Improve: 19%   Collapse: 10%   Attrition: 18%   MLB: 43%   *Comparables: Mike Montgomery, Giovanni Soto, Josh Hader*

Allen's five-word scouting report is "lefty with a plus change," a description that implies an undersized, crafty southpaw getting by on guile rather than velocity. But Allen defies the stereotype. Listed at 6-foot-3 and 200 pounds, Allen can rush his fastball into the mid-90s and his command is actually one of the weaker attributes in the profile. Still, most evaluators project an average grade in that department at maturity, which makes him a strike-thrower without pinpoint accuracy. Between all that and an average curveball, Allen has the ingredients to be a mid-rotation starter, the kind who always seems to be pitching the day you decide to go the park.

Michel Baez RHP · Born: 01/21/96 · Age: 23 · Bats: R · Throws: R · Height: 6'8" · Weight: 220 · Origin: International Free Agent, 2016

YEAR	TEAM	LVL	AGE	W	L	SV	G	GS	IP	H	HR	BB/9	K/9	K	GB%	BABIP	WHIP	ERA	DRA	WARP	MPH	FB%	WHF	CSP
2017	FTW	A	21	6	2	0	10	10	58²	41	8	1.2	12.6	82	36%	.264	0.84	2.45	2.60	1.8				
2018	LEL	A+	22	4	7	0	17	17	86²	73	5	3.4	9.6	92	37%	.297	1.22	2.91	4.01	1.3				
2018	SAN	AA	22	0	3	0	4	4	18¹	22	4	5.9	10.3	21	31%	.375	1.85	7.36	3.22	0.5				
2019	SDN	MLB	23	4	6	0	16	16	83¹	83	16	3.7	9.4	87	34%	.313	1.40	5.07	5.55	-0.2				

Breakout: 9%   Improve: 18%   Collapse: 13%   Attrition: 25%   MLB: 41%   *Comparables: Jon Gray, Jake Odorizzi, Aaron Blair*

On BP's top 10 prospect list for San Diego, Wilson Karman aptly likened Baez's appearance to "a cardboard cutout of Dellin Betances." Blessed with all of the height and none of the girth of the Yankees fireballer, Baez is an interesting arm in his own right. He reaches the upper 90s with his fastball and complements the pitch with a tumbling change that plays up because of the unusually high angle he throws from. He also works with two breaking balls, and the slider in particular looks like a potential bat-misser.

But Baez's stature is a mixed blessing. While there isn't a magic line separating pitchers taller and shorter than six-and-a-half feet, that height is a tipping point at which the taller pitchers almost universally struggle with repeating their mechanics. It's just much harder for a 6-foot-8 pitcher to marshal his limbs toward the plate than it is for someone shorter. While he repeats his motion pretty well for a giant, things get ugly when he's out of sync, and it happens often enough to give evaluators pause. Baez is a very promising young arm, but there's a lot of reliever risk in the profile.

Jose Castillo LHP Born: 01/10/96 Age: 23 Bats: L Throws: L Height: 6'5" Weight: 246 Origin: International Free Agent, 2012

YEAR	TEAM	LVL	AGE	W	L	SV	G	GS	IP	H	HR	BB/9	K/9	K	GB%	BABIP	WHIP	ERA	DRA	WARP	MPH	FB%	WHF	CSP
2016	FTW	A	20	1	1	1	9	0	23²	23	0	1.5	13.3	35	47%	.397	1.14	2.28	2.36	0.7				
2016	LEL	A+	20	1	0	0	7	0	11¹	15	1	4.0	5.6	7	51%	.368	1.76	1.59	4.70	0.0				
2017	LEL	A+	21	3	2	1	39	0	47	38	0	4.2	9.4	49	42%	.297	1.28	2.87	5.24	-0.2				
2017	SAN	AA	21	1	0	0	8	0	9¹	8	1	3.9	9.6	10	28%	.292	1.29	2.89	2.57	0.2				
2018	SAN	AA	22	2	1	5	12	0	15	14	0	4.8	15.6	26	38%	.438	1.47	3.00	2.17	0.5				
2018	ELP	AAA	22	1	0	3	10	0	11¹	6	1	1.6	10.3	13	43%	.185	0.71	0.79	3.33	0.2				
2018	SDN	MLB	22	3	3	0	37	0	38¹	23	3	2.8	12.2	52	39%	.250	0.91	3.29	3.02	0.8	97.1	55.2	15.5	48.7
2019	SDN	MLB	23	3	1	0	60	0	63	53	8	4.2	11.2	79	40%	.314	1.30	3.88	4.23	0.6	97.0	57.2	16.1	50.4

Breakout: 15%   Improve: 23%   Collapse: 19%   Attrition: 28%   MLB: 48%   *Comparables: Zach Braddock, Jose Alvarado, Jon Meloan*

It's been a long six years since Castillo signed the fourth-largest J2 deal of the 2012 class. In that time, he's lost the velocity that initially excited scouts, got traded from Tampa Bay to San Diego, moved to the bullpen, re-discovered some of that missing gas, and made his major league debut. Along the way, he's thoughtfully and candidly spoke about the difficulties that Latin American kids have leaving home and living in an entirely different culture as a teenager. Castillo is one to root for, and given that his fastball-slider combination is electric enough to miss plenty of bats, you'll presumably have several years to do so.

Miguel Diaz RHP Born: 11/28/94 Age: 24 Bats: R Throws: R Height: 6'0" Weight: 214 Origin: International Free Agent, 2011

YEAR	TEAM	LVL	AGE	W	L	SV	G	GS	IP	H	HR	BB/9	K/9	K	GB%	BABIP	WHIP	ERA	DRA	WARP	MPH	FB%	WHF	CSP
2016	WIS	A	21	1	8	3	26	15	94²	83	7	2.8	8.7	91	47%	.279	1.18	3.71	3.47	1.6				
2017	SDN	MLB	22	1	1	0	31	3	41²	44	11	5.4	7.1	33	41%	.275	1.66	7.34	7.15	-0.9	97.6	65.5	9.3	47.1
2018	ELP	AAA	23	0	3	0	5	2	13¹	17	2	8.8	10.1	15	40%	.375	2.25	8.10	4.74	0.1				
2018	SAN	AA	23	5	2	2	19	9	65	45	4	4.2	9.1	66	57%	.253	1.15	2.35	3.73	1.1				
2018	SDN	MLB	23	1	0	0	11	0	18²	16	2	5.8	14.5	30	35%	.341	1.50	4.82	3.24	0.4	97.4	55.3	17.9	45.5
2019	SDN	MLB	24	2	1	0	42	0	44	40	5	4.4	9.3	46	44%	.304	1.39	4.35	4.76	0.1	97.3	63.7	12.7	47.6

Breakout: 24%   Improve: 33%   Collapse: 12%   Attrition: 20%   MLB: 54%   *Comparables: Chris Ray, Keynan Middleton, Ian Krol*

Diaz struck out more than a third of the batters he faced last year, which makes him about the 11th most exciting arm in San Diego's absurdly deep relief corps. He can reach the mid-90s without breaking a sweat and he's the rare reliever who misses bats with three distinct offerings. The problem is that he has no clue where any of them are going. While he doesn't employ the kind of grunting, full-effort, high-octane delivery we normally associate with control issues, his herky-jerk motion is very difficult to repeat and he's always struggled to throw strikes. There's enough arm strength here for him to keep getting chances, but given the Padres' bullpen depth, he'll have to make the most of them soon.

Robbie Erlin LHP Born: 10/08/90 Age: 28 Bats: R Throws: L Height: 6'0" Weight: 190 Origin: Round 3, 2009 Draft (#93 overall)

YEAR	TEAM	LVL	AGE	W	L	SV	G	GS	IP	H	HR	BB/9	K/9	K	GB%	BABIP	WHIP	ERA	DRA	WARP	MPH	FB%	WHF	CSP
2016	SDN	MLB	25	1	2	0	3	2	15²	12	3	1.7	7.5	13	43%	.231	0.96	4.02	4.10	0.2	91.4	54.4	9.8	48.2
2018	SDN	MLB	27	4	7	0	39	12	109	112	12	1.0	7.3	88	48%	.306	1.14	4.21	3.05	2.6	91.8	59.2	10.3	52
2019	SDN	MLB	28	9	9	0	44	26	149	147	17	2.8	8.3	138	45%	.317	1.30	3.89	4.24	1.8	91.2	59.2	10.3	50.9

Breakout: 16%   Improve: 45%   Collapse: 17%   Attrition: 19%   MLB: 93%   *Comparables: Doug Fister, Anthony DeSclafani, Liam Hendriks*

Coming up through the minors, Erlin universally earned praise as a smart and polished, if unspectacular, starter. He was the safest kind of arm, a low-effort pitchability southpaw who could spin a curve and keep hitters off balance with his changeup. But the Volvo of pitching prospects has been anything but reliable as a big leaguer. Now 28, Erlin has battled various ailments over the last four years, most seriously a torn UCL that cost him most of 2016 and all of 2017.

Just when he looked like the afterthought of the 40-man roster, Erlin turned in a sneaky good campaign last year, leading the rotation in DRA and all Padres pitchers in WARP. Befitting his reputation as a control pitcher, he walked only 12 hitters across 100 innings while generating far more grounders than flies. Strikes and weak contact have always been a winning combination and by years end, he'd bounced from long relief into the starting five. A stable slot in the back of a rotation has long seemed like Erlin's destiny, and with good health, he may finally fulfill it in 2019.

Anderson Espinoza RHP Born: 03/09/98 Age: 21 Bats: R Throws: R Height: 6'0" Weight: 160 Origin: International Free Agent, 2014

YEAR	TEAM	LVL	AGE	W	L	SV	G	GS	IP	H	HR	BB/9	K/9	K	GB%	BABIP	WHIP	ERA	DRA	WARP	MPH	FB%	WHF	CSP
2016	GRN	A	18	5	8	0	17	17	76	77	2	3.2	8.5	72	49%	.342	1.37	4.38	3.71	1.2				
2016	FTW	A	18	1	3	0	8	7	32¹	38	1	2.2	7.8	28	44%	.363	1.42	4.73	3.84	0.5				
2019	SDN	MLB	21	2	3	0	8	8	34	38	5	3.9	7.1	27	41%	.324	1.55	5.12	5.62	-0.1				

Breakout: 3%   Improve: 3%   Collapse: 1%   Attrition: 3%   MLB: 5%   *Comparables: Robert Gsellman, Taylor Guerrieri, Tyler Clippard*

The enigma of San Diego's talented farm system, Espinoza has started only seven minor-league games since arriving in 2016's Drew Pomeranz deal. Elbow discomfort in early 2017 begat Tommy John surgery that August, and the recovery process effectively sidelined him for two full years. That's a blow for someone like Espinoza, who has enticing tools but little feel for using them. It's possible that he comes back fully intact, looking like a future No. 2 starter and throwing 95-97 while flashing a plus curve and changeup. He's still only 21, and if he's in the Cal League this summer, he'll be ahead of schedule. But with all the missed reps, a bit of rust seems inevitable. A healthy season would do him a world of good but even if he manages to start 25 games, we'll learn more about him in 2020 than 2019.

MacKenzie Gore LHP   Born: 02/24/99   Age: 20   Bats: L   Throws: L   Height: 6'3"   Weight: 191   Origin: Round 1, 2017 Draft (#3 overall)

YEAR	TEAM	LVL	AGE	W	L	SV	G	GS	IP	H	HR	BB/9	K/9	K	GB%	BABIP	WHIP	ERA	DRA	WARP	MPH	FB%	WHF	CSP
2017	PDR	RK	18	0	1	0	7	7	21¹	14	0	3.0	14.3	34	69%	.333	0.98	1.27	2.99	0.7				
2018	FTW	A	19	2	5	0	16	16	60²	61	5	2.7	11.0	74	41%	.354	1.30	4.45	2.81	1.7				
2019	SDN	MLB	20	2	4	0	12	12	45	46	9	4.3	9.6	48	45%	.323	1.50	5.31	5.83	-0.3				

Breakout: 5%   Improve: 7%   Collapse: 1%   Attrition: 3%   MLB: 10%   *Comparables: Henry Owens, Matt Wisler, Michael Fulmer*

Several hurlers have a case to be San Diego's top pitching prospect, but Gore is our pick here at BP. He's just two years removed from high school ball and already flashing four above average pitches with plus command. Headlined by a sinking fastball that touches 96 and a fading change, Gore is advanced for his age. Still, there are risks. He's already battling recurring blister issues, he's never pitched above A-ball, and from all photographic evidence, his next shave will be his first. Still, he throws hard, knows where it's going and has multiple secondaries to miss a bat with. This is what a No. 2 starter looks like at 19-years-old.

Brett Kennedy RHP   Born: 08/04/94   Age: 24   Bats: R   Throws: R   Height: 6'0"   Weight: 200   Origin: Round 11, 2015 Draft (#327 overall)

YEAR	TEAM	LVL	AGE	W	L	SV	G	GS	IP	H	HR	BB/9	K/9	K	GB%	BABIP	WHIP	ERA	DRA	WARP	MPH	FB%	WHF	CSP
2016	FTW	A	21	2	1	0	6	6	28¹	29	2	2.2	12.1	38	54%	.391	1.27	2.54	2.90	0.7				
2016	LEL	A+	21	6	10	0	22	22	113²	114	9	3.5	8.6	109	48%	.325	1.39	3.80	3.88	2.1				
2017	SAN	AA	22	13	7	0	26	26	141	133	16	2.4	8.6	134	41%	.298	1.21	3.70	4.07	1.8				
2018	ELP	AAA	23	10	0	0	16	16	89¹	77	6	2.3	8.1	80	54%	.285	1.12	2.72	4.09	1.5				
2018	SDN	MLB	23	1	2	0	6	6	26²	36	6	4.1	6.1	18	43%	.333	1.80	6.75	6.98	-0.5	94.4	67.6	9.3	44.6
2019	SDN	MLB	24	4	4	0	28	10	69	68	8	3.4	8.2	63	45%	.315	1.36	4.27	4.67	0.4	94.2	69.6	9.6	46

Breakout: 10%   Improve: 21%   Collapse: 11%   Attrition: 25%   MLB: 44%   *Comparables: Ricardo Pinto, David Phelps, J.R. Graham*

We've reached the point in baseball's history where a righty throwing 92 mph with two functional secondaries isn't a potential No. 3 or 4 starter, but instead nearly an afterthought on top prospect lists, like the jar of Cheerios at a continental breakfast. Kennedy has actually done pretty well to make it this far, rising from 11th-round obscurity to the big leagues in only three seasons. The rookie out of Fordham is a bulldog on the mound, and he brings plenty of moxie and pretty good command out to the hill. Whether that's sufficient is for the fates to sort out, but his chances were better 10 years ago.

Eric Lauer LHP   Born: 06/03/95   Age: 24   Bats: R   Throws: L   Height: 6'3"   Weight: 205   Origin: Round 1, 2016 Draft (#25 overall)

YEAR	TEAM	LVL	AGE	W	L	SV	G	GS	IP	H	HR	BB/9	K/9	K	GB%	BABIP	WHIP	ERA	DRA	WARP	MPH	FB%	WHF	CSP
2016	TRI	A-	21	1	0	0	7	7	25	17	0	2.5	10.1	28	52%	.279	0.96	1.44	2.91	0.7				
2017	LEL	A+	22	2	5	0	12	12	67²	65	4	2.5	11.2	84	42%	.351	1.24	2.79	3.52	1.4				
2017	SAN	AA	22	4	3	0	10	9	55	52	6	2.8	7.9	48	38%	.295	1.25	3.93	3.31	1.2				
2018	ELP	AAA	23	2	1	0	4	4	21¹	13	1	3.8	9.3	22	48%	.226	1.03	2.53	6.31	-0.2				
2018	SDN	MLB	23	6	7	0	23	23	112	127	15	3.7	8.0	100	39%	.332	1.54	4.34	5.27	0.1	93.6	57.9	9.7	51.5
2019	SDN	MLB	24	7	9	0	26	26	130	128	18	3.8	9.2	133	40%	.320	1.41	4.38	4.80	0.8	93.4	59.6	10	53.1

Breakout: 22%   Improve: 50%   Collapse: 11%   Attrition: 26%   MLB: 81%   *Comparables: Derek Holland, Jacob Turner, Ricky Nolasco*

Lauer was the second of many rookies to take a turn in San Diego's rotation last year. Over 23 starts, he pitched to his billing as a low-90s lefty with three distinct offspeed pitches and decent control, but nothing to consistently miss bats with. But after a rough May, he was actually pretty good over his final 16 starts, posting a 3.16 ERA and generating more swings and misses with his slider. He played around with his pitch mix throughout the year, incorporating a cutter and changing his grip on the slider, which now moves a bit slower but with more depth. The result is a more well-rounded arsenal that gives hitters a greater variety of looks to stew over. It's hard to be bullish about a guy like this—he still doesn't have a true out pitch—but it's possible that the overall numbers slightly undersell Lauer's chances to hang around as a back-end starter for a few years.

Joey Lucchesi LHP   Born: 06/06/93   Age: 26   Bats: L   Throws: L   Height: 6'5"   Weight: 204   Origin: Round 4, 2016 Draft (#114 overall)

YEAR	TEAM	LVL	AGE	W	L	SV	G	GS	IP	H	HR	BB/9	K/9	K	GB%	BABIP	WHIP	ERA	DRA	WARP	MPH	FB%	WHF	CSP
2016	TRI	A-	23	0	2	1	14	10	40	27	0	0.4	11.9	53	58%	.293	0.73	1.35	1.59	1.7				
2017	LEL	A+	24	6	4	0	14	14	78²	56	9	2.2	10.9	95	53%	.251	0.95	2.52	2.21	2.8				
2017	SAN	AA	24	5	3	1	10	9	60¹	46	3	2.1	7.9	53	50%	.259	0.99	1.79	4.09	0.8				
2018	SDN	MLB	25	8	9	0	26	26	130	125	23	3.0	10.0	145	47%	.307	1.29	4.08	3.79	2.3	92.3	64.1	11.5	49.9
2019	SDN	MLB	26	8	8	0	26	26	130	116	17	2.9	9.7	141	46%	.306	1.21	3.88	4.23	1.6	91.9	65.3	11.7	50.8

Breakout: 27%   Improve: 51%   Collapse: 15%   Attrition: 15%   MLB: 92%   *Comparables: Shaun Marcum, Felipe Paulino, Angel Guzman*

Lucchesi is an odd duck on the mound. He's very flexible, and his delivery has a Gumby-like flavor to it, as he twists his shoulders, rocks back and slings himself toward the plate. The weird doesn't stop there. His primary offspeed pitch is what he calls a "churve," a unique cross between a change and curveball that nobody else throws. He grips and throws it like a changeup, but the ball's flight pattern more closely resembles a slider, with modest two-plane action that moves slightly away from lefties and into righties.

It's fair to call the churve a bit of a trick, as long as we also acknowledge that it's a pretty good one. Last year, Lucchesi enticed a whiff 20 percent of the time he threw his trademark, and he rode that and a low-90s fastball to a very effective rookie campaign. Oftentimes, pitchers with one trick face much tougher sledding the second time around the league (think Tony Cingrani and his ubiquitous four-seamer). The onus is on Lucchesi to prove his churve can still miss bats when hitters have first-hand knowledge of how it behaves.

Phil Maton **RHP** Born: 03/25/93 Age: 26 Bats: R Throws: R Height: 6'3" Weight: 220 Origin: Round 20, 2015 Draft (#597 overall)

YEAR	TEAM	LVL	AGE	W	L	SV	G	GS	IP	H	HR	BB/9	K/9	K	GB%	BABIP	WHIP	ERA	DRA	WARP	MPH	FB%	WHF	CSP
2016	FTW	A	23	1	1	1	8	0	12²	14	0	0.7	13.5	19	33%	.424	1.18	1.42	1.53	0.5				
2016	LEL	A+	23	3	2	9	25	0	33	17	2	2.2	12.8	47	39%	.217	0.76	1.91	2.47	1.0				
2016	ELP	AAA	23	1	0	1	5	0	6	1	1	3.0	18.0	12	14%	.000	0.50	1.50	1.83	0.2				
2017	ELP	AAA	24	1	1	13	23	0	25¹	22	1	2.8	11.0	31	38%	.328	1.18	2.84	3.87	0.4				
2017	SDN	MLB	24	3	2	1	46	0	43	41	10	2.9	9.6	46	47%	.284	1.28	4.19	3.99	0.6	94.4	76	14.1	50.9
2018	ELP	AAA	25	0	0	2	6	0	6¹	5	0	1.4	14.2	10	40%	.333	0.95	2.84	2.62	0.2				
2018	SDN	MLB	25	0	2	0	45	0	47¹	50	3	4.4	10.5	55	37%	.359	1.54	4.37	4.42	0.3	92.9	61.2	15.3	43.5
2019	SDN	MLB	26	3	1	0	54	0	56²	51	8	3.9	10.5	66	39%	.315	1.33	4.06	4.43	0.3	93.2	68.5	15.1	47.6

Breakout: 22%   Improve: 41%   Collapse: 19%   Attrition: 27%   MLB: 73%   *Comparables: Nick Goody, Chasen Shreve, Jordan Walden*

Analysts and scouts have long sought to identify why some pitchers with mediocre velocity survive in the big leagues while most of their peers peak in A-ball. The answer is typically some alchemical combination of elite command, deception, and guts. Recently, another explanation has come into vogue: spin. To simplify, the more a breaking ball or four-seamer spins (rotates) on its way to the plate, the harder these pitches are to hit. Maton's spin rates are off the charts for a guy who sits in the low-90s, and he's able to entice far more whiffs than most hurlers in his velo band. Tenuous as it sounds, the amount of rotation Maton is able to put on the ball when it leaves his fingers has helped him develop from a 20th-round pick to the 24th man on a big league roster. Youngsters understandably want to ask the stars of the game for tips; perhaps they should be asking Maton how he holds and throws his fastball instead.

Bryan Mitchell **RHP** Born: 04/19/91 Age: 28 Bats: L Throws: R Height: 6'3" Weight: 210 Origin: Round 16, 2009 Draft (#495 overall)

YEAR	TEAM	LVL	AGE	W	L	SV	G	GS	IP	H	HR	BB/9	K/9	K	GB%	BABIP	WHIP	ERA	DRA	WARP	MPH	FB%	WHF	CSP
2016	SWB	AAA	25	0	0	0	2	2	9	8	0	2.0	14.0	14	50%	.400	1.11	1.00	3.37	0.2				
2016	NYA	MLB	25	1	2	0	5	5	25	26	1	4.3	4.0	11	49%	.301	1.52	3.24	6.85	-0.4	96.9	50.5	6.7	48.2
2017	SWB	AAA	26	3	3	0	14	13	63²	59	1	1.8	9.3	66	54%	.326	1.13	3.25	3.98	1.2				
2017	NYA	MLB	26	1	1	1	20	1	32²	42	2	3.6	4.7	17	55%	.333	1.68	5.79	5.87	-0.2	97.2	48	7.6	50.3
2018	LEL	A+	27	1	3	0	6	6	28¹	23	6	3.8	8.9	28	44%	.239	1.24	4.13	4.56	0.3				
2018	SDN	MLB	27	2	4	0	16	11	73	85	12	5.3	4.7	38	49%	.302	1.75	5.42	7.10	-1.6	95.5	59.2	6.6	49.1
2019	SDN	MLB	28	4	6	0	16	16	80	84	9	4.1	7.0	63	47%	.319	1.51	4.69	5.14	0.2	95.5	55.8	6.9	49.6

Breakout: 12%   Improve: 28%   Collapse: 13%   Attrition: 33%   MLB: 59%   *Comparables: Darrell Rasner, Clay Hensley, Chris Bassitt*

Have you ever watched a swimming race until the very end, and noticed how long it takes for the last guy or gal to tap the wall? On some level, you know that that person is an amazing swimmer, one of the best in the world at a pretty difficult task. But, also, they finished last, by a good distance, crawling across the screen much slower than Mr. Phelps or Ms. Ledecky, conspicuous only in how badly they have failed relative to their peers.

Mitchell is the pitching equivalent of that swimmer. He posted a DRA north of 7, a FIP above 6. His earned run average looks merely bad, but if you adjust for a righty pitching in Petco, a 5.42 ERA is pretty ghastly as well. He was one of only two pitchers (minimum 50 innings) to walk more hitters than he struck out. That Mitchell was still starting games in September suggests a science experiment, or at least a concession to draft position. You know he isn't *bad* at this; his presence on a big league roster at all says as much. Sometimes though, being "one of the best in the world" isn't quite good enough.

Adrian Morejon **LHP** Born: 02/27/99 Age: 20 Bats: L Throws: L Height: 6'0" Weight: 175 Origin: International Free Agent, 2016

YEAR	TEAM	LVL	AGE	W	L	SV	G	GS	IP	H	HR	BB/9	K/9	K	GB%	BABIP	WHIP	ERA	DRA	WARP	MPH	FB%	WHF	CSP
2017	TRI	A-	18	2	2	0	7	7	35¹	37	2	0.8	8.9	35	41%	.337	1.13	3.57	3.94	0.6				
2017	FTW	A	18	1	2	0	6	6	27²	28	2	4.2	7.5	23	34%	.321	1.48	4.23	4.83	0.1				
2018	LEL	A+	19	4	4	0	13	13	62²	54	6	3.4	10.1	70	55%	.302	1.24	3.30	3.86	1.1				
2019	SDN	MLB	20	3	4	0	12	12	55	55	8	4.0	8.7	53	42%	.316	1.44	4.81	5.27	0.0				

Breakout: 2%   Improve: 2%   Collapse: 1%   Attrition: 2%   MLB: 4%   *Comparables: Casey Kelly, Brad Keller, Jeurys Familia*

Morejon's prospect profile hasn't changed much since San Diego signed him three years ago. The Cuban still works into the mid-90s with a biting two-plane curve. He's still succeeding against much older competition, still earning plaudits for his pitchability and command. He's still undersized and still working on that changeup.

There are positives and negatives to this sort of continuity. On the plus side, he remains on track to reach San Diego in his early-20s. But one big reason why Morejon appeared prominently on top prospect lists throughout his career was because he was so advanced so young, which gave him ample developmental time to iron out the wrinkles. That hasn't happened—at least not to the degree required to become one of baseball's very best pitching prospects. The change still looks fringy, his arm strength never took a step forward and the concerns evaluators raised about his small frame have manifested as well, first with a missed start here and there and then with his first trip to the disabled list in 2018. This probably reads more negatively than it should. Morejon still has every chance of becoming a good big league starter. He is, however, perhaps less likely to be a great one than he was this time two years ago.

Jacob Nix RHP Born: 01/09/96 Age: 23 Bats: R Throws: R Height: 6'4" Weight: 220 Origin: Round 3, 2015 Draft (#86 overall)

YEAR	TEAM	LVL	AGE	W	L	SV	G	GS	IP	H	HR	BB/9	K/9	K	GB%	BABIP	WHIP	ERA	DRA	WARP	MPH	FB%	WHF	CSP
2016	FTW	A	20	3	7	0	25	25	105¹	115	5	1.7	7.7	90	48%	.340	1.28	3.93	4.23	1.0				
2017	LEL	A+	21	4	3	0	11	10	66²	78	5	1.4	6.9	51	48%	.344	1.32	4.32	5.01	0.2				
2017	SAN	AA	21	1	2	0	6	6	27²	32	0	2.9	7.2	22	45%	.340	1.48	5.53	6.85	-0.6				
2018	SAN	AA	22	2	3	0	9	9	52²	39	3	1.5	7.0	41	46%	.250	0.91	2.05	3.86	0.9				
2018	ELP	AAA	22	1	0	0	1	1	6	5	0	0.0	4.5	3	44%	.278	0.83	0.00	4.12	0.1				
2018	SDN	MLB	22	2	5	0	9	9	42¹	52	8	2.8	4.5	21	42%	.306	1.54	7.02	6.94	-0.8	94.6	62.5	6.7	49.7
2019	SDN	MLB	23	6	8	0	23	23	115	123	15	2.9	6.9	88	42%	.316	1.39	4.51	4.93	0.5	94.5	64.7	7	51.5

Breakout: 9%   Improve: 17%   Collapse: 13%   Attrition: 25%   MLB: 33%   *Comparables: Zach Eflin, Blake Beavan, Will Smith*

On August 28, Nix threw one of the weirdest games in recent memory. Through 8.1 shutout innings, Nix had neither struck out a batter nor allowed a walk, an almost impossible accomplishment in modern baseball. Alas, a ninth-inning homer prompted Andy Green to lift Nix before he could get his shutout. It's not like Nix was fatigued—he'd only thrown 79(!) pitches when he came out of the game—but perhaps Green sensed that the guy who can't miss a bat isn't the best option for a one-run game in the ninth. To that last point: Nix struck out less than a batter every two innings, and posted the lowest K/9 of any National Leaguer who threw at least 40 frames. That won't work in the long run. He throws four pitches, all of which have their merits, but if he can't find a way to entice a few more whiffs, he'll be short for this world.

Chris Paddack RHP Born: 01/08/96 Age: 23 Bats: R Throws: R Height: 6'4" Weight: 195 Origin: Round 8, 2015 Draft (#236 overall)

YEAR	TEAM	LVL	AGE	W	L	SV	G	GS	IP	H	HR	BB/9	K/9	K	GB%	BABIP	WHIP	ERA	DRA	WARP	MPH	FB%	WHF	CSP
2016	GRB	A	20	2	0	0	6	6	28¹	9	2	0.6	15.2	48	51%	.163	0.39	0.95	0.89	1.4				
2016	FTW	A	20	0	0	0	3	3	14	11	0	1.9	14.8	23	45%	.379	1.00	0.64	2.51	0.4				
2018	LEL	A+	22	4	1	0	10	10	52¹	43	3	0.7	14.3	83	47%	.370	0.90	2.24	2.40	1.8				
2018	SAN	AA	22	3	2	0	7	7	37²	23	1	1.0	8.8	37	45%	.239	0.72	1.91	2.87	1.1				
2019	SDN	MLB	23	2	2	0	6	6	30	26	4	2.5	10.9	36	42%	.312	1.13	3.50	3.80	0.5				

Breakout: 13%   Improve: 29%   Collapse: 13%   Attrition: 19%   MLB: 50%   *Comparables: Drew Smyly, David Paulino, Marcus Stroman*

As a prospect, Paddack is mature beyond his years, like a teen who finishes his homework early and still gets to go out on the weekends. He has better control than just about any other prospect in baseball, and he didn't miss a beat after returning from Tommy John surgery. In 90 innings across two levels, he posted an absurd 15:1 strikeout-to-walk ratio while allowing only four homers. Given that he spent most of the season in the hitter-friendly California League, those numbers are all the more impressive. At 92-94 mph, Paddack won't blow anyone away but he's not a soft-tosser either, and the changeup is his bread and butter anyway. The change features late, tumbling action, and he throws it while maintaining the same arm speed as his fastball. It gives everyone fits, and could help Paddack shine as a mid-rotation starter as soon as 2019.

Luis Patino RHP Born: 10/26/99 Age: 19 Bats: R Throws: R Height: 6'0" Weight: 192 Origin: International Free Agent, 2016

YEAR	TEAM	LVL	AGE	W	L	SV	G	GS	IP	H	HR	BB/9	K/9	K	GB%	BABIP	WHIP	ERA	DRA	WARP	MPH	FB%	WHF	CSP
2017	DPA	RK	17	2	1	0	4	4	16	11	0	1.1	8.4	15	58%	.256	0.81	1.69	3.72	0.4				
2017	PDR	RK	17	2	1	0	9	8	40	32	2	3.6	9.7	43	50%	.286	1.20	2.47	3.35	1.1				
2018	FTW	A	18	6	3	0	17	17	83¹	65	1	2.6	10.6	98	45%	.320	1.07	2.16	3.53	1.6				
2019	SDN	MLB	19	3	5	0	13	13	61²	63	12	4.3	9.2	63	43%	.318	1.50	5.40	5.92	-0.4				

Breakout: 8%   Improve: 12%   Collapse: 0%   Attrition: 8%   MLB: 12%   *Comparables: Madison Bumgarner, Jordan Lyles, Roberto Osuna*

Few teams are lucky enough to have an 18-year-old who mixes premium athleticism, a high-90s fastball and a potentially plus breaking ball; only the Padres can credibly claim their system has 10 superior prospects. To be sure, Patino is no sure thing: He needs to develop a third pitch, his mechanics are a little violent for a starter and there's a long way between his present workload and the innings he'll need to eat in a big-league rotation. But even with those developmental hurdles ahead, he's one of the real sleepers in all of baseball. Patino is as projectable as they come, and don't be surprised if his prospect stock soars in 2019.

Luis Perdomo RHP Born: 05/09/93 Age: 26 Bats: R Throws: R Height: 6'2" Weight: 185 Origin: International Free Agent, 2003

YEAR	TEAM	LVL	AGE	W	L	SV	G	GS	IP	H	HR	BB/9	K/9	K	GB%	BABIP	WHIP	ERA	DRA	WARP	MPH	FB%	WHF	CSP
2016	SDN	MLB	23	9	10	0	35	20	146²	187	23	2.8	6.4	105	60%	.342	1.59	5.71	5.29	0.0	96.4	68.3	9	48.6
2017	SDN	MLB	24	8	11	0	29	29	163²	182	17	3.6	6.5	118	62%	.325	1.51	4.67	4.96	1.1	95.9	62.8	9.6	47.1
2018	ELP	AAA	25	6	3	0	13	13	75	72	12	2.5	7.3	61	57%	.284	1.24	3.72	3.91	1.4				
2018	SDN	MLB	25	1	6	0	12	10	44²	62	4	4.4	7.9	39	44%	.389	1.88	7.05	6.52	-0.6	95.0	63	8	47.1
2019	SDN	MLB	26	5	5	0	31	13	87²	92	9	3.4	7.9	77	53%	.334	1.43	4.09	4.47	0.7	95.5	65.8	9.3	48.3

Breakout: 31%   Improve: 63%   Collapse: 17%   Attrition: 15%   MLB: 89%   *Comparables: Jacob Turner, Billy Traber, Luke Hochevar*

For anyone wondering why baseball doesn't have more pitchers like Mike Leake or Jose Fernandez, guys who can skip from college or A-ball to the majors, just look at Perdomo. Tall, athletic, and armed with a nasty mid-90s two-seamer and a wipeout slider, Perdomo has most of the ingredients a major league pitcher needs. If any Rule 5 pick could jump from High-A to the majors, he seemed like a decent bet.

Unfortunately for Perdomo, it takes more than an ideal frame and good stuff to get big leaguers out. Back in A-ball, Perdomo was still learning how to deploy his arsenal: The art of sequencing, the finer points of the changeup, when to nibble. How to *pitch*, basically. Those are hard lessons to learn on the big stage, and the Padres finally ran out of patience. It's possible that last year's demotion gave him the reset he badly needs; it's perhaps more likely that the lost developmental time has already sunk his hopes of a lasting big league career.

Cal Quantrill RHP
Born: 02/10/95   Age: 24   Bats: L   Throws: R   Height: 6'3"   Weight: 208   Origin: Round 1, 2016 Draft (#8 overall)

YEAR	TEAM	LVL	AGE	W	L	SV	G	GS	IP	H	HR	BB/9	K/9	K	GB%	BABIP	WHIP	ERA	DRA	WARP	MPH	FB%	WHF	CSP
2016	PDR	RK	21	0	2	0	5	5	13²	12	0	1.3	10.5	16	49%	.324	1.02	5.27	2.63	0.5				
2016	TRI	A-	21	0	2	0	5	5	18²	15	0	1.0	13.5	28	56%	.333	0.91	1.93	1.69	0.8				
2017	LEL	A+	22	6	5	0	14	14	73²	78	5	2.9	9.3	76	42%	.353	1.38	3.67	3.65	1.4				
2017	SAN	AA	22	1	5	0	8	8	42¹	52	5	3.4	7.2	34	39%	.341	1.61	4.04	3.75	0.7				
2018	SAN	AA	23	6	5	0	22	22	117	135	12	2.9	7.8	101	45%	.336	1.48	5.15	4.18	1.6				
2018	ELP	AAA	23	3	1	0	6	6	31	39	4	1.5	6.4	22	50%	.333	1.42	3.48	3.97	0.6				
2019	*SDN*	*MLB*	*24*	*1*	*1*	*0*	*3*	*3*	*15*	*16*	*2*	*3.5*	*8.0*	*13*	*42%*	*.327*	*1.46*	*4.59*	*5.02*	*0.1*				

Breakout: 11%   Improve: 18%   Collapse: 5%   Attrition: 17%   MLB: 24%   *Comparables: Scott Diamond, Sam Howard, Wade Miley*

Another year, another season in which Quantrill's prospect stock sagged mildly, like a shirt slowly losing its vibrancy with repeated washings. Once a legitimate 1:1 candidate, Quantrill had Tommy John surgery in 2015, and his stuff never quite made it to the other side. After tossing 150 innings last year, he seems to be healthy, or at least stable, but his pedestrian whiff numbers reflect the degradation of his arsenal. That's not to say he isn't a viable big leaguer: Quantrill can locate his fastball, and the pitch scrapes the mid-90s with quite a bit of movement. His changeup isn't as nasty as it was in college, but both that and his breaking balls are usable secondaries. It all adds up to a perfectly serviceable No. 4 starter. That's nothing to scoff at, even if it isn't quite the career path we envisioned for him three years ago.

Garrett Richards RHP
Born: 05/27/88   Age: 31   Bats: R   Throws: R   Height: 6'3"   Weight: 210   Origin: Round 1, 2009 Draft (#42 overall)

YEAR	TEAM	LVL	AGE	W	L	SV	G	GS	IP	H	HR	BB/9	K/9	K	GB%	BABIP	WHIP	ERA	DRA	WARP	MPH	FB%	WHF	CSP
2016	ANA	MLB	28	1	3	0	6	6	34²	31	2	3.9	8.8	34	47%	.302	1.33	2.34	4.42	0.4	98.5	62.4	11.3	43.5
2017	ANA	MLB	29	0	2	0	6	6	27²	18	1	2.3	8.8	27	55%	.233	0.90	2.28	3.12	0.8	97.2	58.2	13.2	43.8
2018	ANA	MLB	30	5	4	0	16	16	76¹	64	11	4.0	10.3	87	50%	.277	1.28	3.66	3.73	1.4	97.5	50.4	12.3	47.5
2019	*SDN*	*MLB*	*31*	*4*	*4*	*0*	*11*	*11*	*63*	*53*	*7*	*3.8*	*9.8*	*69*	*48%*	*.300*	*1.26*	*3.76*	*4.10*	*0.9*	*96.7*	*53.6*	*12.2*	*45*

Breakout: 10%   Improve: 32%   Collapse: 28%   Attrition: 6%   MLB: 88%   *Comparables: C.J. Wilson, Tim Hudson, Bob Veale*

The general knowledge trivia website LearnedLeague has a term for players who forfeit so many times in a season that they are ineligible to play the next season: it's called a pavano, named after the pitcher who threw 26 games in his four years with the Yankees. Richards effectively pavanoed the completion of his Angels tenure, managing 28 starts in a four-year span. That total includes 2019, which he will miss to Tommy John surgery—his first (though his second UCL injury; the team tried to avoid surgery the first time around). Unlike Pavano, who was ineffective even when active, Richards' absence made the Angels' heart grow fonder. The Padres, reading the winds on their voyage to contention, decided to make Richards part of their 2020 playoff run, signing him to a two-year, $15.5 million deal.

Craig Stammen RHP
Born: 03/09/84   Age: 35   Bats: R   Throws: R   Height: 6'4"   Weight: 230   Origin: Round 12, 2005 Draft (#354 overall)

YEAR	TEAM	LVL	AGE	W	L	SV	G	GS	IP	H	HR	BB/9	K/9	K	GB%	BABIP	WHIP	ERA	DRA	WARP	MPH	FB%	WHF	CSP
2016	AKR	AA	32	0	1	0	10	0	11¹	9	1	2.4	7.1	9	69%	.235	1.06	0.79	2.64	0.3				
2016	COH	AAA	32	0	3	0	10	0	13	16	2	1.4	7.6	11	57%	.333	1.38	5.54	3.73	0.2				
2017	SDN	MLB	33	2	3	0	60	0	80¹	68	12	3.1	8.3	74	52%	.263	1.20	3.14	3.76	1.3	92.7	63.3	12.2	44.1
2018	SDN	MLB	34	8	3	0	73	0	79	65	3	1.9	10.0	88	51%	.301	1.04	2.73	2.86	1.9	93.4	67.6	14.6	47
2019	*SDN*	*MLB*	*35*	*3*	*1*	*2*	*60*	*0*	*63*	*56*	*7*	*3.4*	*9.4*	*66*	*50%*	*.309*	*1.27*	*3.85*	*4.20*	*0.6*	*91.9*	*64.4*	*13.3*	*44.9*

Breakout: 22%   Improve: 40%   Collapse: 26%   Attrition: 13%   MLB: 83%   *Comparables: Scott Downs, Brian Duensing, Ryan Madson*

Ever watched someone play and had a sudden impulse to see what their Twitter feed looked like? Such was the case for this humble author one summer night in 2012. Turns out, it was a pretty standard athlete profile—quotes from Scripture, some golf, shoutouts to the fans and the troops—not substantively different from his more famous teammates, just at two percent of the volume. Six years later, his posting habits haven't changed much and he's still quietly running an ERA in the mid-2s. In between he's had Tommy John surgery, got married, watched his wife go viral after notching a hole in one on their honeymoon, signed the first two-year deal of his life and sired a child. Not to get overly meta here, but the whole experience has me reflecting on just how little we really know about these people we share so much of our time with.

Robert Stock RHP
Born: 11/21/89   Age: 29   Bats: L   Throws: R   Height: 6'1"   Weight: 214   Origin: Round 2, 2009 Draft (#67 overall)

YEAR	TEAM	LVL	AGE	W	L	SV	G	GS	IP	H	HR	BB/9	K/9	K	GB%	BABIP	WHIP	ERA	DRA	WARP	MPH	FB%	WHF	CSP
2017	DAY	A+	27	1	3	2	16	0	25	18	1	2.9	9.0	25	55%	.279	1.04	2.52	3.22	0.5				
2017	PEN	AA	27	8	2	0	25	0	45¹	39	0	4.2	7.1	36	55%	.307	1.32	2.98	4.84	0.0				
2018	SAN	AA	28	1	0	1	8	0	9	7	1	3.0	15.0	15	40%	.316	1.11	2.00	2.38	0.3				
2018	ELP	AAA	28	0	0	8	24	0	28¹	15	2	3.5	8.6	27	59%	.183	0.92	1.59	2.95	0.7				
2018	SDN	MLB	28	1	1	0	32	0	39²	37	1	2.9	8.6	38	51%	.321	1.26	2.50	3.51	0.6	99.4	59	10.8	50.4
2019	*SDN*	*MLB*	*29*	*3*	*1*	*0*	*60*	*0*	*63*	*58*	*7*	*4.2*	*8.8*	*62*	*49%*	*.308*	*1.39*	*4.33*	*4.73*	*0.2*	*98.7*	*59*	*10.8*	*50.4*

Breakout: 12%   Improve: 22%   Collapse: 16%   Attrition: 19%   MLB: 39%   *Comparables: Josh Roenicke, Joe Paterson, Blake Parker*

A minor league journeyman with indy ball experience on his resume, Stock emerged from obscurity toting a triple-digit fastball; he soon established himself as one of San Diego's most reliable relievers. Stock is one of a growing number of pitchers who have dramatically altered their career trajectory by trying to throw every pitch through a brick wall and letting the chips fall where they may from there. These players, easily identifiable by their violent deliveries and velo-evangelizing tweets, are often too wild to be effective. Stock throws plenty of strikes though, and while his command needs refinement, hitters weren't able to regularly barrel his elite gas. It appears the Padres found a legitimate late-inning arm out of nowhere.

Matt Strahm LHP Born: 11/12/91 Age: 27 Bats: R Throws: L Height: 6'3" Weight: 185 Origin: Round 21, 2012 Draft (#643 overall)

YEAR	TEAM	LVL	AGE	W	L	SV	G	GS	IP	H	HR	BB/9	K/9	K	GB%	BABIP	WHIP	ERA	DRA	WARP	MPH	FB%	WHF	CSP
2016	NWA	AA	24	3	8	0	22	18	102¹	102	14	2.0	9.4	107	40%	.320	1.22	3.43	4.73	0.4				
2016	KCA	MLB	24	2	2	0	21	0	22	13	0	4.5	12.3	30	50%	.283	1.09	1.23	4.13	0.2	96.8	77.9	14.1	43.2
2017	KCA	MLB	25	2	5	0	24	3	34²	30	6	5.7	9.6	37	42%	.279	1.50	5.45	5.80	-0.2	95.7	67.3	11.2	49.1
2018	SAN	AA	26	1	0	0	9	2	14¹	14	1	2.5	13.8	22	42%	.406	1.26	2.51	3.54	0.3				
2018	SDN	MLB	26	3	4	0	41	5	61¹	39	6	3.1	10.1	69	37%	.226	0.98	2.05	3.96	0.7	95.5	58	13.3	52.9
2019	SDN	MLB	27	3	1	0	60	0	63	55	8	3.6	10.1	71	40%	.305	1.27	4.04	4.41	0.5	95.2	64.4	13	49.8

Breakout: 23%   Improve: 46%   Collapse: 17%   Attrition: 20%   MLB: 81%   *Comparables: Scott Elbert, Jose Capellan, Trevor May*

If it seems like you've read about a dozen or so quality relievers by this point, you're not mistaken. San Diego upheld its reputation as a reliever factory by producing one of the best bullpens in the league last year and the club didn't miss a beat after dealing Adam Cimber and closer Brad Hand to Cleveland last summer. Part of that is because of Strahm, who ran with his new role after a promotion to late-inning duty in August. Over the final two months, Strahm posted a 1.25 ERA with 30 punchouts and only six walks in 21 innings. Both Kansas City and San Diego have experimented with stretching him out but after last year's success in relief, it appears he's found his home.

Ryan Weathers LHP Born: 12/17/99 Age: 19 Bats: L Throws: L Height: 6'1" Weight: 200 Origin: Round 1, 2018 Draft (#7 overall)

YEAR	TEAM	LVL	AGE	W	L	SV	G	GS	IP	H	HR	BB/9	K/9	K	GB%	BABIP	WHIP	ERA	DRA	WARP	MPH	FB%	WHF	CSP
2018	SDP	RK	18	0	2	0	4	4	9¹	8	2	2.9	8.7	9	69%	.222	1.18	3.86	4.59	0.2				
2018	FTW	A	18	0	1	0	3	3	11	11	0	1.0	9.0	9	58%	.355	1.33	3.00	4.61	0.1				
2019	SDN	MLB	19	2	3	0	9	9	33²	38	6	4.4	7.0	26	50%	.318	1.61	5.74	6.31	-0.4				

Comparables: John Barbato, Wilfredo Boscan, Jaime Barria

Like anxious parents nervously giving a spoiled child bad news, teams tend to baby their first-round pitchers, introducing them to professional baseball slowly. If they pitch at all that first year, they'll get a cushy assignment to the complex leagues or short-season ball, where they'll overmatch hitters far below their talent level. Not so with Weathers. San Diego signed him quickly and he wound up making a few starts at Low-A Fort Wayne, a league that rarely sees a pitcher fresh out of high school.

The aggressive development path speaks to Weathers' maturity on the mound. The son of 19-year big-league vet David Weathers, Weathers the Younger works with a low-to-mid-90s fastball, a power curve, and a changeup that's already above average. He's athletic for a kid his size and he repeats his delivery well. His ceiling may ultimately not be as high as some of the other players taken in the top 10 last year, but for a high school pitcher, he's a pretty safe bet. No junk stock jokes, please.

Trey Wingenter RHP Born: 04/15/94 Age: 25 Bats: R Throws: R Height: 6'7" Weight: 200 Origin: Round 17, 2015 Draft (#507 overall)

YEAR	TEAM	LVL	AGE	W	L	SV	G	GS	IP	H	HR	BB/9	K/9	K	GB%	BABIP	WHIP	ERA	DRA	WARP	MPH	FB%	WHF	CSP
2016	FTW	A	22	1	0	4	8	0	11	6	0	1.6	11.5	14	46%	.250	0.73	0.82	2.85	0.2				
2016	LEL	A+	22	2	1	4	30	0	44¹	36	0	3.5	9.3	46	59%	.321	1.20	2.03	3.81	0.6				
2017	SAN	AA	23	2	1	20	49	0	47²	33	6	3.6	12.1	64	52%	.262	1.09	2.45	2.44	1.3				
2018	ELP	AAA	24	3	3	4	40	0	44¹	29	4	4.9	10.8	53	48%	.250	1.20	3.45	3.56	0.8				
2018	SDN	MLB	24	0	0	0	22	0	19	13	3	5.2	12.8	27	40%	.256	1.26	3.79	2.84	0.5	99.1	68.6	18.3	49.5
2019	SDN	MLB	25	3	1	0	60	0	63	52	8	4.6	10.8	76	46%	.303	1.34	4.31	4.71	0.2	98.8	70.3	18.8	50.6

Breakout: 17%   Improve: 21%   Collapse: 29%   Attrition: 35%   MLB: 53%   *Comparables: Keith Butler, Akeel Morris, Joseph Krehbiel*

In every rebuilding season, there comes a point when prospect saturation kicks in, when even plugged in fans no longer know anything about the new yannigan trotting in from the bullpen. Wingenter debuted on August 7th, the tenth Padre to do so in 2018, and it would have been easy to gloss over this big-bodied, long-haired, multisyllabic reliever. Wingenter, though, is actually pretty interesting. He sits in the high-90s, regularly touching triple digits, and he pairs the pitch with a sweeping slider. He needs to throw more strikes, but after posting elite whiff rates with both pitches, it looks like he has the raw stuff for late-inning duty.

Kirby Yates RHP Born: 03/25/87 Age: 32 Bats: L Throws: R Height: 5'10" Weight: 210 Origin: Round 26, 2005 Draft (#798 overall)

YEAR	TEAM	LVL	AGE	W	L	SV	G	GS	IP	H	HR	BB/9	K/9	K	GB%	BABIP	WHIP	ERA	DRA	WARP	MPH	FB%	WHF	CSP
2016	SWB	AAA	29	0	0	4	14	0	16²	12	0	3.2	10.3	19	46%	.279	1.08	1.62	2.17	0.5				
2016	NYA	MLB	29	2	1	0	41	0	41¹	41	5	4.1	10.9	50	44%	.340	1.45	5.23	4.07	0.4	95.3	59.9	12.4	45.3
2017	SLC	AAA	30	0	0	1	6	0	7	8	0	3.9	18.0	14	60%	.533	1.57	2.57	0.20	0.4				
2017	ANA	MLB	30	0	0	0	1	0	1	2	2	0.0	9.0	1	0%	.000	2.00	18.00	9.07	0.0	94.7	50	12.5	53.8
2017	SDN	MLB	30	4	5	1	61	0	55²	42	10	3.1	14.1	87	30%	.296	1.10	3.72	3.10	1.3	95.0	62.9	18.8	48.3
2018	SDN	MLB	31	5	3	12	65	0	63	41	6	2.4	12.9	90	43%	.263	0.92	2.14	1.92	2.2	95.3	58.3	18.6	43.2
2019	SDN	MLB	32	3	1	35	60	0	63	52	9	3.6	12.0	84	41%	.313	1.22	3.71	4.04	0.6	94.2	59.6	17.2	45

Breakout: 15%   Improve: 34%   Collapse: 24%   Attrition: 7%   MLB: 70%   *Comparables: Sergio Santos, Paul Assenmacher, Brian Sikorski*

Yates wasn't drafted out of college, needed four years of minor league seasoning and didn't assume closing duties until he was 31. And yet he was born for the role. You can see it in his fiery enthusiasm, populist forename, funky delivery and elite strikeout rate. His splitter is a closer's pitch, enticing an absurd whiff rate (27 percent last year) with late, vanishing action that makes it the kind of pro-wrestling move every fireman needs. That he also has a bit of a homer problem—he surrendered five over the last two months—makes him the best kind of closer, or at least the most watchable for neutrals. If he can limit the gopher balls, he should hang on to his new gig for a few years.

LINEOUTS

Hitters

HITTER	POS	TEAM	LVL	AGE	PA	R	2B	3B	HR	RBI	BB	K	SB	CS	AVG/OBP/SLG	DRC+	VORP	BABIP	BRR	FRAA	WARP
Austin Allen	C	SAN	AA	24	498	59	31	0	22	56	37	97	0	3	.290/.351/.506	123	34.8	.325	-2.1	C(91): 14.6, 1B(19): -1.5	4.6
Gabriel Arias	SS	FTW	A	18	504	54	27	3	6	55	41	149	3	3	.240/.302/.352	76	8.8	.340	-0.5	SS(111): 6.2, 3B(6): 0.2	1.1
Luis Campusano	C	FTW	A	19	284	26	11	0	3	40	19	43	0	1	.288/.345/.365	108	6.1	.335	-1.1	C(38): -0.8, 1B(4): 0.2	1.0
Allen Cordoba	INF	LEL	A+	22	164	15	6	2	2	16	4	46	3	4	.206/.233/.310	65	-4.6	.275	-0.3	SS(32): -2.7, LF(4): 0.1	-0.5
Allen Craig	1B	ELP	AAA	33	363	52	18	1	13	59	39	73	0	0	.293/.375/.479	119	12.4	.342	-1.2	1B(63): -1.2, LF(8): 0.2	1.3
A.J. Ellis	C	SDN	MLB	37	183	19	8	0	1	15	26	37	0	0	.272/.378/.344	98	7.9	.348	-1.4	C(44): -8.9, LF(1): 0.0	-0.2
Ty France	3B	SAN	AA	23	479	66	22	2	17	77	33	70	3	4	.263/.349/.448	123	23.8	.276	1.3	3B(101): -7.7, 1B(1): 0.0	2.3
	3B	ELP	AAA	23	110	18	8	0	5	19	13	19	0	0	.287/.382/.532	122	7.8	.310	0.6	3B(19): 2.8, 1B(9): 0.1	1.0
Greg Garcia	PH	SLN	MLB	28	208	15	6	0	3	15	20	37	3	1	.221/.309/.304	83	0.1	.259	0.2	2B(31): -0.4, SS(17): 1.9	0.5
Javier Guerra	SS	ELP	AAA	22	464	52	18	9	13	55	27	166	2	0	.223/.269/.398	63	-0.5	.329	1.1	SS(118): -7.6, 2B(2): -0.1	-0.6
	SS	SDN	MLB	22	19	2	0	0	0	1	3	9	0	0	.125/.263/.125	68	-0.8	.286	0.3	SS(7): -0.7, 3B(1): 0.0	0.0
Edward Olivares	CF	LEL	A+	22	575	79	25	10	12	62	29	102	21	8	.277/.321/.429	103	27.6	.319	2.8	CF(115): 0.6, RF(7): 0.5	2.6
Tirso Ornelas	RF	FTW	A	18	355	45	13	3	8	40	40	68	5	1	.252/.341/.392	108	9.3	.297	1.2	RF(63): -1.8, CF(5): 1.8	1.0
Jeisson Rosario	CF	FTW	A	18	521	79	17	5	3	34	66	108	18	12	.271/.368/.353	105	25.9	.347	3.5	CF(113): -1.2, RF(1): -0.2	2.2
Matt Szczur	OF	SDN	MLB	28	84	11	3	0	1	6	8	24	3	0	.187/.265/.267	65	-3.1	.260	0.5	LF(16): -0.7, RF(12): -0.8	-0.2
	OF	ELP	AAA	28	43	4	3	1	0	6	4	7	0	0	.316/.372/.447	105	1.1	.375	0.0	CF(7): 0.0, RF(2): 0.1	0.1
Luis Torrens	C	LEL	A+	22	515	62	36	3	6	73	26	77	1	1	.280/.320/.406	99	26.1	.318	1.8	C(85): 1.0, 1B(3): 0.0	2.1

Austin Allen proved that his strong 2018 numbers were no Cal League mirage, essentially replicating that production in Double-A. He's 25 now, though, and he's still a below average receiver without enough stick to project as a first baseman. Sometimes these types keep hitting all the way up, but there are a lot of tweener indicators here. ⓧ A marquee Latin American signing three years ago, **Gabriel Arias** struggled in 2018. He whiffed in nearly 30 percent of his plate appearances without flashing any of his once-coveted offensive tools in the other 70 percent. He was very young for the Midwest League, so there remains a chance everything comes back around against people (closer to) his own age. ⓧ San Diego's second round pick in 2017, **Luis Campusano** is a fringy defender behind the plate who may grow into plus raw power at maturity. A midseason concussion ended his season just when he was getting hot. ⓧ The Padres were chuffed when Rule 5 draftee **Allen Cordoba** batted .208 in surprisingly regular playing time in 2017; they were considerably less so when he hit .206 in the Cal League last summer. ⓧ It's been six years since **Allen Craig** and Everth Cabrera were All-Star teammates, four since their last big league game, and at least two since you've thought about either one of them. ⓧ The summer of 2016 must seem like a decade ago to **Alex Dickerson**. The late-bloomer cracked San Diego's lineup that July and notched surprisingly productive numbers. Injuries knocked him out for all of the past two years though, and given that he'll be 29 in May, he may have missed his opportunity to contribute in San Diego. ⓧ **A.J. Ellis** put together his best season at the plate since 2015 and lost playing time to Austin Hedges and Francisco Mejia down the stretch regardless. He had more job security back when he was Clayton Kershaw's personal catcher. ⓧ It's good to tie France when you're a World Cup underdog or engaged in trench warfare, but it's not great to **Ty France** if you need an impact first base prospect. ⓧ Always light on power and no longer a viable shortstop, **Greg Garcia** has become a bench bat with too little bat and a utility infielder with too little utility. ⓧ Once a consensus top 100 prospect, this once-promising shortstop will go down as baseball's second-most famous **Javy Guerra**. ⓧ A speedy outfielder with projectable power and a chance to stay in center, **Edward Olivares** would be a top prospect in many organizations. For San Diego, he's one of many enticing young talents. To stand out in this crowded pasture, he must prove he can square up advanced arms and hit for more power in games. ⓧ As baseball itself drifts increasingly toward the Three True Outcomes, **Tirso Ornelas** goes against the grain. Still a teenager, the Mexican corner outfielder has a great eye and approach at the plate and a knack for making solid, line drive contact. Expect him to destroy the Cal League and vault up prospect lists accordingly. ⓧ **Jeisson Rosario** has a strange profile. He's wiry to the point of being thin but he has a very projectable hit tool because of his elite hand-eye coordination and feel for contact. While quick, he's not as much of a burner as you'd think from looking at him, so to make good, the most fickle tool of all has to play to potential. ⓧ **Matt Szczur** was designated for assignment last summer, the latest casualty in baseball's march to vanquish fifth outfielders from big-league rosters. When he's not busy painting or punning his name on Twitter, he'll probably be giving Triple-A lefties and announcers fits in equal measure. ⓧ A member of San Diego's Rule 5 trio of 2017, **Luis Torrens** batted 139 times as a 21-year-old. He's safely back where he belongs, but with so many promising catchers throughout the system, he's almost entirely off the radar now.

Pitchers

PITCHER	TEAM	LVL	AGE	W	L	SV	G	GS	IP	H	HR	BB/9	K/9	K	GB%	BABIP	WHIP	ERA	DRA	WARP	MPH	FB%	WHF	CSP
Carter Capps	TRI	A-	27	0	1	1	6	0	7	5	0	2.6	12.9	10	53%	.333	1.00	1.29	2.12	0.2				
	LEL	A+	27	0	0	1	13	0	22	21	4	3.3	8.2	20	38%	.279	1.32	5.73	3.66	0.3				
	ELP	AAA	27	1	1	1	8	0	9	4	0	7.0	9.0	9	46%	.167	1.22	1.00	3.95	0.1				
Reggie Lawson	LEL	A+	20	8	5	0	24	22	117	130	11	3.9	9.0	117	43%	.348	1.55	4.69	5.57	-0.4				
Kazuhisa Makita	ELP	AAA	33	1	1	0	24	0	26¹	23	1	3.4	7.5	22	36%	.286	1.25	3.76	4.85	0.1				
	SDN	MLB	33	0	1	0	27	0	35	32	7	3.1	9.5	37	24%	.275	1.26	5.40	5.69	-0.3	82.3	74.3	13.1	52.8
Andres Munoz	SAN	AA	19	2	1	7	20	0	19	11	0	5.2	9.0	19	55%	.250	1.16	0.95	3.35	0.4				
Colin Rea	SAN	AA	27	0	3	0	6	6	24	32	3	4.9	7.9	21	39%	.367	1.88	7.12	3.98	0.4				
	ELP	AAA	27	3	2	0	12	9	51¹	58	11	4.0	8.6	49	44%	.333	1.58	5.08	4.84	0.4				
Brad Wieck	SAN	AA	26	1	2	10	27	0	28	20	1	2.6	11.6	36	29%	.279	1.00	1.93	2.62	0.8				
	ELP	AAA	26	3	0	2	17	0	18¹	16	2	4.4	16.7	34	50%	.389	1.36	3.44	1.88	0.7				
	SDN	MLB	26	0	0	0	5	0	7	3	1	0.0	12.9	10	29%	.154	0.43	1.29	2.68	0.2	93.4	64.5	12.9	55.2

Carter Capps is still hopping on his way to the plate—and still getting himself and his manager kicked out of the game once in a blue moon when an umpire decides that his delivery is just too weird to be street legal. Unless (until?) he gets his good fastball back, though, he'll fight these battles in Triple-A. ⓧ The long 2018 Padres season was the perfect time for a young hurler to hone his craft, but **Dinelson Lamet** missed all the fun recuperating from Tommy John surgery. Despite a strong strikeout rate in 2017, Lamet was already showing a lot of reliever traits, and all the time on the shelf certainly hasn't made that outcome any less likely. ⓧ **Reggie Lawson** is a great guy to have as your seventh-best pitching prospect. He's young and athletic enough to dream on better command and an improved changeup. But even if those never come around, he's added velocity as he's grown and his curveball flashes plus, giving him a potent combination if he's forced into relief work. ⓧ Just the third Japanese player to suit up for the Padres, **Kazuhisa Makita** is an odd fit for the roster. He's on a two-year deal, and it's unclear what his role will be on a team with a plethora of younger and better relief options. ⓧ At long last, a Padres pitching prospect with no chance to start. **Andres Munoz** is the only such player who earned a mention in these pages, but as long as you can hit 103 mph and flash a plus slider, you get your name in the paper. ⓧ **Colin Rea**, famous for being untraded from the Marlins, left a little of his right elbow behind. His rehab from Tommy John proved unsuccessful, and now he'll have to find his form and his income at the same time. ⓧ Just what the Padres need, another monster in the bullpen. **Brad Wieck** was 26 when he made his debut, but the gargantuan—he's 6-foot-9—lefty made a heck of an impression, striking out 10 without any walks across seven late-season innings.

SAN FRANCISCO GIANTS

Essay by Grant Brisbee

Player comments by Dan Rathman and BP staff

The biggest myth about the Brian Sabean-era Giants was that they weren't into analytics. They were, but it wasn't just the analytics found in a *Bill James Baseball Abstract* that they cared about. When the Giants traded for Jose Vizcaino to be a low-cost stopgap at shortstop in 1996, OBP-fetishists howled (he was worth 1.9 WARP that season). When they signed Rey Sanchez to be a part-time shortstop, the RC/27 crowd shrieked (he was worth 1.4 WARP that season). The Giants understood the importance of defense before dWAR, and it doesn't matter if they were using the eyeball test or scrawling scratch marks on the wall after every catch. They knew that a run saved was roughly as valuable as a run earned, and they built their roster around this truism.

A couple of months after the Giants started playing at Oracle Park in 2000, they noticed something about how the park played, and adjusted their outfield defenses accordingly. Other teams were slower to catch on, and the result was the Giants blowing away the competition in the second half of the season. They soared to the best record in baseball as the pitching staff enjoyed one of the best league-adjusted halves in franchise history. That it wasn't Statcast giving them this information about outfield positioning is beside the point. They were still analyzing the game better than their opponents that season. They were cracking the shell of baseball and feasting on the sweet, sweet nut inside.

And, yes, there were honest-to-goodness stats involved, too. After Aubrey Huff finished seventh in the 2010 NL MVP voting, the Giants' director of quantitative analysis, Yeshayah Goldfarb, explicitly referenced a deep-dive into advanced metrics as the primary reason he was acquired on the cheap. The Giants had a functioning, thriving quantitative analysis department while they were contending, and it helped them win three championships.

So, no, the hiring of a numbers wonk like Farhan Zaidi isn't exactly a revolution in San Francisco. It's more like the organization is taking its array of SETI dishes and pointing them at a different spot in the same sky. The Giants have been into analytics for a long time.

But, holy hell, have they been bad at it for the last couple years.

GIANTS PROSPECTUS
2018 W-L: 73-89, 4TH IN NL WEST

Pythag	.433	21st	B-Age	29.9	30th
RS/G	3.72	29th	P-Age	28.4	16th
RA/G	4.31	15th	Salary	$200.5M	2nd
DRC+	81	30th	M$/MW	$7.7M	3rd
DRA	4.37	17th	DL Days	1398	25th
FIP	3.94	11th	$ on DL	28%	28th
DER	.707	13th			

399'
364'
421'
339'
309'

- Opened 2000
- Open air
- Natural surface
- Fence profile: 8' to 25'

Three-Year Park Factors

Runs	Runs/RH	Runs/LH	HR/RH	HR/LH
96	97	94	88	82

Top Hitter WARP	4.0 Brandon Crawford
Top Pitcher WARP	2.9 Derek Holland
Top Prospect	Joey Bart

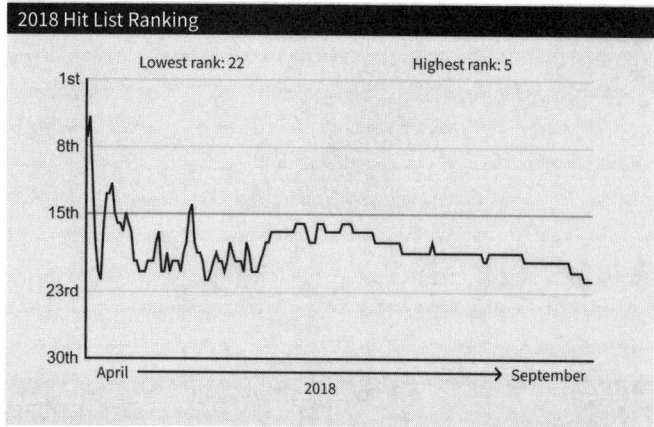

2018 Hit List Ranking

Lowest rank: 22   Highest rank: 5

April ———————————————→ September
2018

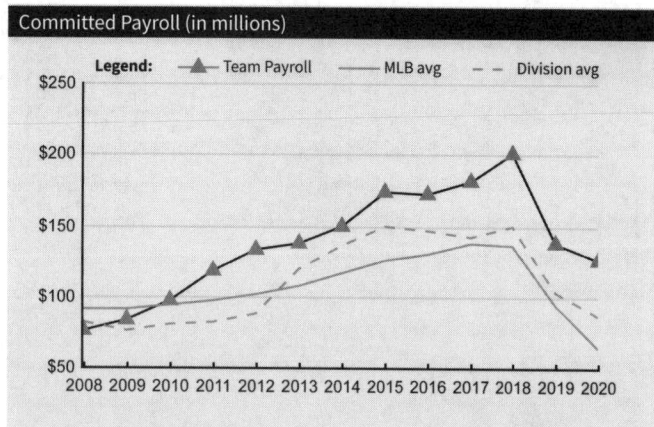

Committed Payroll (in millions)

Legend: ▲ Team Payroll — MLB avg - - Division avg

2008 2009 2010 2011 2012 2013 2014 2015 2016 2017 2018 2019 2020

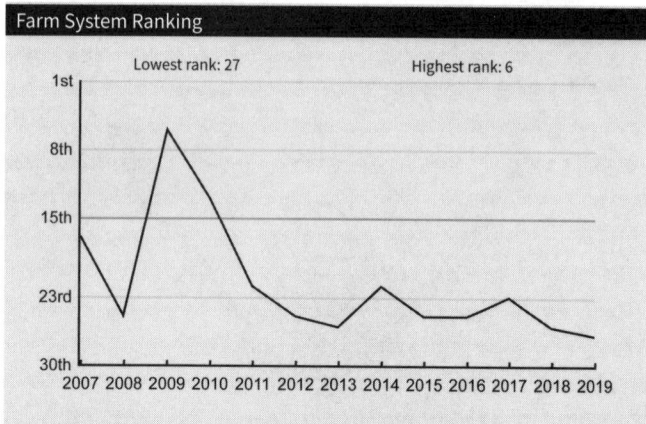

Farm System Ranking

Lowest rank: 27   Highest rank: 6

2007 2008 2009 2010 2011 2012 2013 2014 2015 2016 2017 2018 2019

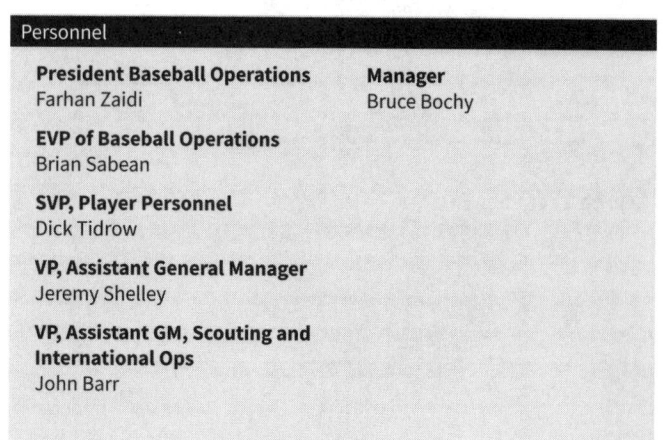

Personnel

President Baseball Operations
Farhan Zaidi

Manager
Bruce Bochy

EVP of Baseball Operations
Brian Sabean

SVP, Player Personnel
Dick Tidrow

VP, Assistant General Manager
Jeremy Shelley

VP, Assistant GM, Scouting and International Ops
John Barr

You can probably find the analogy in your own life. Maybe you were swimming along in your math career, acing algebra and geometry, only to get to calculus and fall into a viper pit. Maybe you followed my path and were a fine baseball player until the kids started throwing hard enough to break bones, at which point you punched the eject button and focused on theater. This is what happened with the Giants, who were analyzing their analytics with analytically sound analysis, and then woke up and found out the teacher was using an entirely different textbook. It was in Cyrillic and kept at the top of a mountain about a day's ride from here. They had no chance.

They've had to readjust before. Back in the early-to-mid-2000s, veterans would stay surprisingly fresh until their late-30s and avoid decline—a testament to hard work and good genes, surely—and the Giants figured out they were often undervalued. They would slap them onto their Winchester Mystery House of a roster, and it worked. Then the Mitchell Report came out, and, that's weird, the strategy stopped working and older veterans weren't as reliable.

When the Giants had to readjust that time, though, the front office found the state of baseball analytics more or less where they left it. Get good players. Develop them if you can, sign them if you have the money, or trade for them if you're creative enough. The Giants lost enough to net the draft picks that became Tim Lincecum, Buster Posey, and Madison Bumgarner, and the Golden Era began. Simple.

That's all still applicable to 2018, but the waterfall of information pouring into every front office changes everything. Now it's all of the above, while also sifting through the data and figuring out how to make your players better, how to make players on other teams better after you bamboozle them away, how to make your prospects better, and how to keep up with your opponents. The same stuff that baseball teams have always done, sure, but it used to be done with bows and arrows, and if you somehow got your hands on a musket, Brad Pitt would play you in the movie. Now it's all F-22 Raptors and nuclear submarines, and the arms race left teams like the Giants behind. They were still evaluating teams the way that they had been for the last two (very successful) decades, and it showed.

Consider the players the Giants employed in 2018. Everyone in the infield was an All-Star at one point. Other than Hunter Pence, everyone was 32 or younger—not exactly pups, but not the age when you expect everyone to fall down an elevator shaft.

They all fell down an elevator shaft.

The Giants finished the second half with a .598 OPS. Their adjusted OPS relative to the league's in the second half was the worst since the 1972 Texas Rangers and the sixth-worst in baseball history. Their .272 on-base percentage in the second half was the eighth worst in baseball history. Everyone was affected. There were no survivors.

Year	Team	2nd half OBP
1908	Superbas	.266
1965	Mets	.268
1972	Rangers	.268
1908	Cardinals	.269
1908	Highlanders	.269
1909	Superbas	.271
1910	Browns	.271
2018	Giants	.272
1910	White Sox	.275
1974	Padres	.278

Now, you can blame a poison cloud hanging over the roster, a contagious malady where everyone starts to tense up just a little bit more because the rest of the team isn't successful, and it all spirals down from there. There had to have been a bit of that going on, you would think.

It can't explain it all away, though. These were all once good players, sometimes as recently as a couple months before. Brandon Crawford had just started the All-Star Game, and Brandon Belt was a candidate for the final vote. But for the third year in a row, the entire Giants lineup absolutely cratered in the second half.

I'm not smart enough to prove this theory myself, but it sure looks like other teams are constantly figuring out the Giants like a collection of *Mike Tyson's Punch Out* opponents. Punch when the ruby flashes. Hit them with a left-right-left combination until you get the TKO. Watch for the uppercut after he blinks. Meanwhile, the Giants were trying to plug a Genesis controller into the NES and saying, "Wait, wait, wait!" They were overmatched.

This theory—this shred of a security blanket—is the only thing keeping me from thinking the Giants will go full Orioles next year. It's not as if Brandon Belt hitting like one of the better first basemen in the National League would be worthy of a feature-length how-did-this-happen breakdown in *Sports Illustrated*. If Evan Longoria suddenly hit at a league-average clip and continued to provide strong defense, it wouldn't make us rethink how we evaluate the game. These would all be the kinds of baseball things that happen in a baseball season with baseball players who are a known quantity. Who were a known quantity, at least.

They just need a different set of eyes. They need several dozen different sets of eyes. The Giants need to rely on analysis, just like they always have. It just needs to be a much, much different analysis. It needs to be the kind of analysis that the cool kids around the league are doing these days. Forget about trying to find the next Max Muncy. They need to find the old Joe Panik.

The need to reevaluate their current roster is of the utmost importance because most of these players are likely to stick around. By the time this article is published, it's possible this will look supremely silly, but I just don't see how this lineup is reinvented. Longoria makes too much money. Posey makes a lot of money and he's coming off hip surgery. Belt makes a lot of money, and his value is unfortunately tethered to his abominable second half. Crawford is a beloved fan favorite, but he has a full no-trade clause and is also compensated fairly.

None of these players will bring back the kinds of prospects needed for a full rebuild. They're all of the "toss in $15 million to get a B- prospect back" variety. It's probably more sensible to see if a new mechanic can get this sucker running again.

Probably not. But nobody expects Zaidi to work miracles in his first offseason, so trying one more time with the bulk of this lineup returning might be the plan. It's also important to note that the Giants are convinced that a full rebuild would set the organization back a decade in the public relations department. They've been one of the top draws in the league, and they're convinced that a screw-this-see-you-in-2022 philosophy would turn the park from a destination into a ghost town. If you think they're being paranoid, just look at the Phillies' attendance over the last five years.

If the Giants are going to threaten .500 next year, they'll be doing it with (mostly) the same hitters because there's no sense paying another team to take them away, get lower-end raffle tickets back, and alienate the casual fan at the same time.

But this has all been about hitting to this point. All the talk about the analytics arms race, all the talk about what has gone wrong since the 2016 All-Star Game has been focused on the lineup. If there was a bright spot to the Giants (and whatever analytics they're using) in 2018, it was the pitching. There aren't a lot of teams that could have survived the loss of Bumgarner, Johnny Cueto, and Jeff Samardzija for the bulk of 2018, but the Giants smoothly adapted. Derek Holland was a revelation, shepherded along nicely in his renaissance season. A couple of disastrous outings made Andrew Suarez's ERA swell, but he was an overwhelming positive for most of the year, a backend rotation piece who made the Giants believe his ceiling might be a little higher than he gets credit for. And, of course, there was Dereck Rodriguez, who probably won't have an ERA under 3.00 again, but gave the organization confidence that they can still scout undervalued contributors with the best of them.

All of this, combined with their rediscovered ability to build a bullpen, should give Zaidi and Giants fans at least some confidence that the organization isn't an unsalvageable Superfund site. They were able to polish pitchers last year. They were keeping up with the arms race in at least one way. They aren't completely hopeless. Mostly hopeless, sure, but don't be a pedant.

This is the state of the 2019 Giants, then. They might have traded Madison Bumgarner by the time you've read this, or they might trade him in July. They might empty the bullpen at the deadline, like the Padres have been so adept at doing in recent years. But you're probably going to see a lot of the same players back. They've likely spent a lot of money on reinforcements by the time you're reading this, whether for the rotation or the outfield or both, and they'll be the butt of a lot of jokes for doing so.

This is all they can do now, though. Figure out how to make their hitters hit. Figure out how to make Oracle Park work for them again. Continue to find and develop pitchers. Build the farm system like they haven't been. Hope they don't threaten 100 losses again, but collect the Posey-high draft picks if they do.

And, above all, hope that they can keep up with the state of baseball analytics in 2019. Hiring an architect away from one of the most advanced organizations in baseball—their blood rival, no less—is a fantastic, necessary start. Just don't be surprised if this new perspective, this new focus on analytics, helps the Giants be much better than you think, much sooner than you think. It's possible that it wasn't the roster or the poor injury luck that was ailing them this whole time. They were just studying for an Analytics 201 midterm while the rest of the league was already finished with their master's thesis, and it's not impossible for them to catch up quickly with the rest of the class. ■

—Grant Brisbee is a senior writer at SB Nation.

HITTERS

Abiatal Avelino MI
Born: 02/14/95 Age: 24 Bats: R Throws: R Height: 5'11" Weight: 195 Origin: International Free Agent, 2011

YEAR	TEAM	LVL	AGE	PA	R	2B	3B	HR	RBI	BB	K	SB	CS	AVG/OBP/SLG	DRC+	VORP	BABIP	BRR	FRAA	WARP
2016	TAM	A+	21	394	54	17	2	6	34	29	63	20	13	.266/.325/.375	95	10.1	.305	0.4	2B(44): 1.0, SS(43): -1.0	1.2
2016	TRN	AA	21	141	15	11	0	0	14	10	19	1	2	.244/.307/.331	82	1.8	.284	0.8	2B(23): 0.4, SS(9): -0.8	0.2
2017	TAM	A+	22	34	1	1	0	0	2	2	5	4	0	.219/.265/.250	81	-0.8	.259	0.6	3B(8): 0.5, 2B(2): 0.0	0.1
2017	SWB	AAA	22	68	5	1	1	0	6	5	10	3	1	.213/.284/.262	72	-1.6	.255	0.1	SS(11): 0.0, 3B(6): -0.4	0.0
2017	TRN	AA	22	249	35	12	4	3	28	14	33	4	0	.270/.315/.396	83	12.7	.301	4.4	2B(37): 1.7, SS(15): 0.5	1.0
2018	TRN	AA	23	211	32	7	2	10	28	18	37	15	4	.337/.392/.553	126	26.5	.375	-0.2	SS(44): 3.4, 2B(2): 0.3	2.0
2018	SWB	AAA	23	290	33	6	6	5	38	14	61	10	2	.252/.291/.372	82	1.3	.308	1.7	SS(52): 3.4, 2B(16): 2.2	1.3
2018	SFN	MLB	23	11	1	0	0	0	0	0	3	0	0	.273/.273/.273	73	0.0	.375	0.2	SS(3): 0.0, 2B(1): -0.1	0.0
2019	*SFN*	*MLB*	*24*	*126*	*14*	*3*	*1*	*2*	*10*	*7*	*29*	*3*	*1*	*.198/.248/.299*	*48*	*-3.2*	*.240*	*0.4*	*2B 1, SS 1*	*-0.2*

Breakout: 4%   Improve: 19%   Collapse: 12%   Attrition: 29%   MLB: 46%   *Comparables: Trevor Plouffe, T.J. Rivera, Tim Beckham*

A glove-first prospect until 2018, Avelino exploded offensively after a restart in Double-A, showing previously unseen power in his second stint with Trenton. Intrigued by the apparent breakout, the Giants targeted the infielder in the Andrew McCutchen trade and gave him a sip of coffee in the majors last September. Avelino's modest frame has little room for added muscle, but the newfound pop stemmed from a retooled approach, which saw the San Pedro De Macoris native reduce his ground-ball rate by 15 percentage points between his two stops in Double-A. Couple that with Avelino's plus arm and slick infield actions, and you can see the makings of a second-division regular at short. If the launch-angle gains don't hold up to major-league pitching, Avelino can always fall back on his versatility, serving as a capable backup anywhere on the dirt.

Joey Bart C
Born: 12/15/96 Age: 22 Bats: R Throws: R Height: 6'3" Weight: 220 Origin: Round 1, 2018 Draft (#2 overall)

YEAR	TEAM	LVL	AGE	PA	R	2B	3B	HR	RBI	BB	K	SB	CS	AVG/OBP/SLG	DRC+	VORP	BABIP	BRR	FRAA	WARP
2018	GNT	RK	21	25	3	1	1	0	1	1	7	0	0	.261/.320/.391	76	0.6	.375	-0.1	C(4): -0.1	0.0
2018	SLO	A-	21	203	35	14	2	13	39	12	40	2	1	.298/.369/.613	137	21.6	.318	1.2	C(32): -1.0	1.7
2019	*SFN*	*MLB*	*22*	*251*	*27*	*8*	*0*	*13*	*35*	*8*	*69*	*0*	*0*	*.194/.239/.389*	*62*	*-1.8*	*.215*	*-0.5*	*C -1*	*-0.3*

Breakout: 2%   Improve: 3%   Collapse: 6%   Attrition: 8%   MLB: 11%   *Comparables: J.T. Realmuto, Blake Swihart, Christian Vazquez*

John Barr, a 33-year veteran of baseball front offices, led the Giants' amateur draft room for 11 years, beginning with the first-round selection of Buster Posey in 2008. Since the 2013 draft, however, only 10 of Barr's choices have even reached the majors, and the leading WARP-getter among them was Andrew Suarez, who just debuted last year. In what would be his last draft at the helm, Barr held the Giants' earliest selection since 1985 at second overall. There, Barr chose another potential franchise cornerstone catcher: Bart, whose combination of power at the plate and polish behind it earned him a spot atop the team's board. Signed to a record $7.025 million bonus, Bart tormented short-season arms, but his true offensive potential won't be known until he proves his contact skills in Double-A. With little doubt about his bat speed or aptitude in the squat, Bart's hit tool—below average at present with average potential—will determine whether he's a rich or poor man's Mike Zunino.

Brandon Belt 1B
Born: 04/20/88 Age: 31 Bats: L Throws: L Height: 6'4" Weight: 235 Origin: Round 5, 2009 Draft (#147 overall)

YEAR	TEAM	LVL	AGE	PA	R	2B	3B	HR	RBI	BB	K	SB	CS	AVG/OBP/SLG	DRC+	VORP	BABIP	BRR	FRAA	WARP
2016	SFN	MLB	28	655	77	41	8	17	82	104	148	0	4	.275/.394/.474	122	37.8	.346	-6.4	1B(151): 0.9, LF(3): 0.0	2.3
2017	SFN	MLB	29	451	63	27	3	18	51	66	104	3	2	.241/.355/.469	110	25.6	.284	0.3	1B(98): 9.0, LF(15): -0.3	2.2
2018	SFN	MLB	30	456	50	18	2	14	46	49	107	4	0	.253/.342/.414	109	14.5	.311	-0.6	1B(104): 9.9, LF(8): 0.3	2.2
2019	*SFN*	*MLB*	*31*	*599*	*71*	*31*	*2*	*19*	*74*	*76*	*140*	*4*	*2*	*.250/.351/.425*	*115*	*18.6*	*.308*	*-1.9*	*1B 8, LF -1*	*2.7*

Breakout: 4%   Improve: 40%   Collapse: 5%   Attrition: 11%   MLB: 95%   *Comparables: Milton Bradley, Derrek Lee, Ryan Klesko*

Belt is baseball's ultimate schlimazel. Despite his best efforts to earn love and respect—from a .954 OPS through two months of play to an MLB record 21-pitch plate appearance in May—he's destined for the disabled list and ripe for scapegoating on local radio. This time, it wasn't Belt's proneness to head trauma that snapped his groove. Instead, he left his first June contest and went straight to the hospital for an emergency appendectomy. Belt returned after only two weeks off, but he hit just .203/.280/.290 in his remaining 230 trips to the plate, nursing a bad knee and wasting all the goodwill he'd built up in the spring. He's been a four-win player in his last three healthy seasons, but he's been healthy just twice in his last five. Supporters are certain his luck will turn; detractors will tell you he's a schlimazel for good.

Alexander Canario CF Born: 05/07/00 Age: 19 Bats: R Throws: R Height: 6'1" Weight: 165 Origin: International Free Agent, 2016

YEAR	TEAM	LVL	AGE	PA	R	2B	3B	HR	RBI	BB	K	SB	CS	AVG/OBP/SLG	DRC+	VORP	BABIP	BRR	FRAA	WARP
2017	DGI	RK	17	274	42	17	4	5	45	33	40	18	10	.294/.391/.464	151	24.0	.335	-1.0	RF(50): 4.0, CF(7): 0.7	2.1
2018	GIA	RK	18	208	36	5	2	6	19	27	51	8	5	.250/.357/.403	111	13.2	.317	-0.5	CF(44): 1.0	0.9
2019	SFN	MLB	19	251	22	7	0	6	24	15	77	4	2	.178/.227/.286	31	-11.7	.230	-0.4	CF -1	-1.3

Breakout: 0%   Improve: 7%   Collapse: 1%   Attrition: 4%   MLB: 12%   Comparables: Nomar Mazara, Engel Beltre, Adalberto Mondesi

The league's best farm systems have a flock of Canarios, and sometimes, a couple soar above the crowd. As one of the few tooled-up teenagers on the Giants farm, the 18-year-old was the headliner on the club's two Arizona League affiliates, and he didn't disappoint. Signed for just $60,000 three years ago, he's athletic and swings the bat with authority, projecting for above-average power while showing the speed to handle center. The latter may diminish with increased age and muscle but added strength might push his raw pop to plus, enough for everyday work in a corner. Canario's hit tool is nascent, his offense entirely based around punishing fastballs, but the ingredients of an impact bat are present, and that's more than scouts could say for his AZL teammates. He has star-level upside as a center fielder, with the extreme volatility that makes you wish you had more birds of his feather.

Brandon Crawford SS Born: 01/21/87 Age: 32 Bats: L Throws: R Height: 6'2" Weight: 227 Origin: Round 4, 2008 Draft (#117 overall)

YEAR	TEAM	LVL	AGE	PA	R	2B	3B	HR	RBI	BB	K	SB	CS	AVG/OBP/SLG	DRC+	VORP	BABIP	BRR	FRAA	WARP
2016	SFN	MLB	29	623	67	28	11	12	84	57	115	7	0	.275/.342/.430	103	36.6	.322	-1.8	SS(155): 3.9	3.4
2017	SFN	MLB	30	570	58	34	1	14	77	42	113	3	5	.253/.305/.403	83	24.4	.293	-1.4	SS(138): 4.1	1.7
2018	SFN	MLB	31	594	63	28	2	14	54	50	122	4	5	.254/.325/.394	95	26.5	.303	0.5	SS(146): 15.3	4.0
2019	SFN	MLB	32	574	60	28	2	13	64	51	116	5	4	.253/.325/.393	95	17.1	.302	-1.0	SS 4	2.2

Breakout: 0%   Improve: 43%   Collapse: 7%   Attrition: 8%   MLB: 96%   Comparables: Jhonny Peralta, Asdrubal Cabrera, Stephen Drew

Adjustments and ailments are inevitable parts of a long season, but their impacts don't always jump off the game log like they did for Crawford last year. In the 35 games spanning May 2nd through June 10th, he hit .445/.490/.711, as a tweak to his hand position triggered the best stretch of his career. In the 88 games before and after, he hit a combined .194/.273/.293, nagged by a left knee injury that ruined his balance at the plate. The slump-surge-slump pattern makes it easy to wonder what might have been if Crawford had stayed healthy, but players in their 30s rarely complete a season unscathed. His overall offensive numbers in 2018 were remarkably similar to his 2017 output, and the most likely outcome this year is a repeat of his previous two. Paired with Crawford's perennially exceptional defense, another Gold Glove bid is virtually certain, and he'll vie to start his second straight All-Star Game if he gets hot at the right time again.

Steven Duggar CF Born: 11/04/93 Age: 25 Bats: L Throws: R Height: 6'2" Weight: 189 Origin: Round 6, 2015 Draft (#186 overall)

YEAR	TEAM	LVL	AGE	PA	R	2B	3B	HR	RBI	BB	K	SB	CS	AVG/OBP/SLG	DRC+	VORP	BABIP	BRR	FRAA	WARP
2016	SJO	A+	22	311	43	12	4	9	30	44	66	6	7	.284/.386/.462	122	24.5	.346	-2.2	RF(60): 6.3, CF(5): -0.1	1.9
2016	RIC	AA	22	276	35	16	4	1	24	28	51	9	7	.321/.391/.432	107	27.7	.397	1.0	CF(59): 8.4	2.2
2017	SJO	A+	23	133	22	11	0	4	20	17	42	7	0	.270/.361/.470	90	9.9	.386	2.0	RF(22): -2.3, CF(1): -0.2	0.0
2017	SAC	AAA	23	54	7	1	0	2	6	8	12	3	2	.261/.370/.413	114	2.9	.313	0.1	CF(12): 1.7	0.5
2018	SAC	AAA	24	356	52	27	4	4	21	39	103	11	4	.272/.354/.421	81	13.1	.392	-0.1	CF(74): 9.6	1.4
2018	SFN	MLB	24	152	20	11	1	2	17	10	44	5	1	.255/.303/.390	67	8.2	.354	3.6	CF(40): -3.4	-0.1
2019	SFN	MLB	25	522	59	24	2	13	52	47	146	12	5	.226/.299/.365	83	9.4	.298	0.2	CF 10	2.0

Breakout: 8%   Improve: 37%   Collapse: 8%   Attrition: 35%   MLB: 73%   Comparables: Curtis Granderson, Drew Stubbs, Trayce Thompson

Minor-league scouts occasionally take in big-league contests to restore their perception of the traits and instincts young'uns must develop to succeed. After years of watching veterans on squeaky wheels flunk the eye test in center, Giants fans and Duggar's own teammates needed a similar refresher on major-league-caliber glove work up the middle. Duggar is no Billy Hamilton or Lorenzo Cain, but he's also not late-career Angel Pagan or Denard Span, and he so impressed Madison Bumgarner that the left-hander quipped, "I don't care if he ever gets a hit." That's good news, because the 2015 sixth-rounder will need time to adapt to major-league sequencing, and the torn shoulder labrum that ended his rookie season won't help. Still, Duggar is the most dynamic outfielder borne from the Giants' farm in years, and his range on the pasture might warrant patience with his growing pains at the plate.

Sandro Fabian RF Born: 03/06/98 Age: 21 Bats: R Throws: R Height: 6'1" Weight: 180 Origin: International Free Agent, 2015

YEAR	TEAM	LVL	AGE	PA	R	2B	3B	HR	RBI	BB	K	SB	CS	AVG/OBP/SLG	DRC+	VORP	BABIP	BRR	FRAA	WARP
2016	GIA	RK	18	174	30	13	5	2	35	7	28	3	1	.340/.364/.522	143	15.9	.388	-1.3	RF(40): 2.9, LF(1): -0.1	1.3
2017	AUG	A	19	504	51	30	0	11	61	10	88	5	4	.277/.297/.408	103	10.0	.317	-1.5	RF(111): 21.5, CF(2): -0.7	3.1
2018	SJO	A+	20	450	47	19	1	10	35	26	107	1	2	.200/.260/.325	74	-8.7	.241	-1.7	RF(112): 3.7	-0.4
2019	SFN	MLB	21	251	21	9	0	8	28	7	64	0	0	.210/.234/.344	47	-9.7	.249	-0.6	RF 4	-0.6

Breakout: 2%   Improve: 2%   Collapse: 1%   Attrition: 4%   MLB: 4%   Comparables: Kyle Waldrop, Moises Sierra, Destin Hood

Sending Fabian to High-A at the start of 2018 was tantamount to throwing a toddler into the ocean the moment he stops screaming in the tub. The Giants' overzealous parenting, prompted by Fabian treading water in the Sally League at 19, left one of their top outfield prospects flailing like a wounded fish in San Jose. Fabian's slump was predictable based on his chase rate in the box and, considering the Giants never threw him a life preserver, perhaps they felt the kid outfielder needed to learn selectivity the hard way. He didn't, and the struggles highlighted both his distance from the majors and the significant risk tied to his approach. Fabian may yet surface as a second-division regular whose batting average compensates for his low walk totals, but both the odds and the timeframe are much longer than they seemed last year.

Aramis Garcia C Born: 01/12/93 Age: 26 Bats: R Throws: R Height: 6'2" Weight: 220 Origin: Round 2, 2014 Draft (#52 overall)

YEAR	TEAM	LVL	AGE	PA	R	2B	3B	HR	RBI	BB	K	SB	CS	AVG/OBP/SLG	DRC+	VORP	BABIP	BRR	FRAA	WARP
2016	SJO	A+	23	160	20	6	0	2	20	14	42	1	0	.257/.323/.340	76	4.7	.350	-1.7	C(41): 1.8	0.3
2017	SJO	A+	24	347	43	20	1	17	65	15	73	0	0	.272/.314/.497	121	21.0	.301	-1.3	C(50): 0.7, 1B(17): 0.3	2.1
2017	RIC	AA	24	89	11	12	0	0	8	9	21	0	0	.282/.360/.436	81	6.6	.379	1.0	C(20): -0.5, 1B(2): 0.0	0.3
2018	RIC	AA	25	328	36	14	1	11	33	20	76	0	1	.233/.287/.395	93	10.4	.272	-2.0	C(69): 10.3, 1B(11): -0.5	2.0
2018	SAC	AAA	25	41	5	1	0	0	4	2	12	0	0	.237/.268/.263	78	-1.6	.333	0.3	C(10): 0.5	0.2
2018	SFN	MLB	25	65	8	1	0	4	9	2	31	0	0	.286/.308/.492	54	2.9	.500	0.2	1B(10): -0.6, C(7): 0.7	-0.2
2019	SFN	MLB	26	244	24	10	0	8	28	11	72	0	0	.221/.261/.379	60	-1.4	.280	-0.4	C 1	0.0

Breakout: 2% Improve: 13% Collapse: 6% Attrition: 21% MLB: 31%

Comparables: Cameron Rupp, John Hester, Lucas May

YEAR	TEAM	P. COUNT	FRM RUNS	BLK RUNS	THRW RUNS	TOT RUNS
2017	RIC	2761	-0.4	0.2	-0.1	-0.7
2018	RIC	9457	13.6	-0.6	-1.5	11.3
2018	SAC	1487	-0.2	0.0	0.0	0.3
2018	SFN	874	0.4	0.3	0.0	0.7
2019	SFN	7895	2.8	-0.7	-0.7	1.4

After two years of trudging through the upper minors in hopes of becoming an everyday catcher, Garcia arrived instead as a part-time first baseman who occasionally caught. The late-August promotion was prompted more by injuries than by Garcia's own performance, but the 2014 second-rounder acquitted himself well, putting his plus raw power to use from the jump. On the downside, Garcia struggled to catch up to elevated fastballs, which exposed other holes in his approach. Catchers can take time to blossom with the stick, but at 26, Garcia is stretching the late-bloomer limits. He looks like a tweener, even by backup standards, neither bat-first nor glove-first, offering a little of both but not enough of either.

Mike Gerber RF Born: 07/08/92 Age: 26 Bats: L Throws: R Height: 6'0" Weight: 190 Origin: Round 15, 2014 Draft (#460 overall)

YEAR	TEAM	LVL	AGE	PA	R	2B	3B	HR	RBI	BB	K	SB	CS	AVG/OBP/SLG	DRC+	VORP	BABIP	BRR	FRAA	WARP
2016	LAK	A+	23	388	52	22	3	14	60	32	111	2	3	.282/.343/.481	118	13.3	.371	-0.6	RF(61): 1.3, CF(16): -0.9	1.6
2016	ERI	AA	23	175	17	8	3	4	20	20	41	6	0	.261/.349/.431	95	7.9	.330	0.8	CF(20): -2.1, RF(19): 2.0	0.5
2017	ERI	AA	24	394	62	22	2	13	45	39	85	10	6	.291/.363/.477	117	27.5	.349	1.2	CF(83): -6.8	1.7
2018	DET	MLB	25	47	2	1	0	0	2	4	21	0	0	.095/.170/.119	57	-5.7	.182	-0.2	LF(7): -1.2, CF(4): 2.3	0.0
2018	TOL	AAA	25	316	35	14	2	13	34	22	103	2	2	.213/.277/.411	89	1.1	.279	-0.9	CF(40): -3.4, RF(28): 0.2	0.0
2019	SFN	MLB	26	120	12	5	0	4	14	7	41	1	0	.189/.245/.342	51	-3.3	.255	-0.1	CF 0, LF 0	-0.4

Breakout: 6% Improve: 28% Collapse: 10% Attrition: 29% MLB: 55%

Comparables: Blake Tekotte, Corey Brown, Matt Den Dekker

Gerber hangs right on the bell curve across the breadth of the outfielder skill set. He might remind you of Andy Dirks in that regard, or the Valkyrie from *Gauntlet*, reliable for any purpose but not for one. If you hold up his numbers, his minor-league progression looked quite promising, assuming you held your thumb over the 2018 line, which was a clever parlor trick on your part. Gerber's first taste of the majors ate him alive (as if the 50 percent strikeout rate wasn't telling enough) and he was understandably not recalled when rosters expanded in September. He's still a power threat who can play some center field, which is always enough to contend for a fourth outfielder spot.

Jacob Gonzalez 3B Born: 06/26/98 Age: 21 Bats: R Throws: R Height: 6'3" Weight: 190 Origin: Round 2, 2017 Draft (#58 overall)

YEAR	TEAM	LVL	AGE	PA	R	2B	3B	HR	RBI	BB	K	SB	CS	AVG/OBP/SLG	DRC+	VORP	BABIP	BRR	FRAA	WARP
2017	GIA	RK	19	194	23	15	1	1	21	16	23	0	1	.339/.418/.458	125	17.6	.384	-2.1	3B(37): -6.2	0.3
2018	AUG	A	20	507	54	20	2	8	45	31	107	7	5	.227/.296/.331	97	3.4	.277	-3.4	3B(94): -6.4	0.2
2019	SFN	MLB	21	251	20	8	0	6	24	9	60	0	0	.198/.239/.298	45	-11.9	.243	-0.7	3B -3	-1.6

Breakout: 0% Improve: 0% Collapse: 0% Attrition: 1% MLB: 1%

Comparables: Jefry Marte, Jeimer Candelario, Cheslor Cuthbert

A polished hitter for his age, Gonzalez is young enough that his Sally League stumble is more cause for caution than concern. The son of former slugger Luis Gonzalez, Jacob gears his swing for maximum power, using a high knee-lift to gather and explosive hip rotation to hammer the ball to left. While his raw pop is undeniable, its utility is tempered by a tendency to pull off of pitches away, a hole that Low-A arms gladly exposed. Gonzalez is a hard worker who should improve with time, but effort may not be enough to keep him at third base, where his awkward actions portend a move to first or left. Either would amplify the pressure on his hit tool, making Gonzalez a high-risk potential average regular who's more likely to end up a four-corners reserve.

Alen Hanson UT Born: 10/22/92 Age: 26 Bats: B Throws: R Height: 6'0" Weight: 170 Origin: International Free Agent, 2009

YEAR	TEAM	LVL	AGE	PA	R	2B	3B	HR	RBI	BB	K	SB	CS	AVG/OBP/SLG	DRC+	VORP	BABIP	BRR	FRAA	WARP
2016	IND	AAA	23	478	58	15	7	8	32	32	78	36	15	.266/.318/.389	95	12.3	.307	2.2	2B(67): -8.5, LF(26): -0.3	0.5
2016	PIT	MLB	23	33	5	1	0	0	1	2	5	2	1	.226/.273/.258	83	-0.4	.269	0.5	2B(8): -0.4	0.0
2017	PIT	MLB	24	59	8	0	2	0	1	2	9	2	1	.193/.220/.263	70	-4.5	.229	-0.9	2B(15): 0.0, SS(2): -0.1	-0.1
2017	CHA	MLB	24	175	28	9	1	4	10	10	43	9	2	.231/.276/.375	67	-0.5	.284	1.7	RF(18): -1.6, 2B(13): -0.1	-0.1
2018	SAC	AAA	25	71	17	5	1	3	9	8	7	6	1	.403/.479/.661	129	14.8	.423	3.2	2B(15): -0.6, SS(2): -0.1	0.8
2018	SFN	MLB	25	310	36	17	5	8	39	9	71	7	3	.252/.274/.425	77	7.2	.303	0.5	2B(45): -1.6, LF(18): -0.8	-0.1
2019	SFN	MLB	26	393	47	17	3	9	39	24	81	17	6	.243/.294/.385	83	5.1	.283	0.5	CF 1, RF -1	0.3

Breakout: 5% Improve: 60% Collapse: 7% Attrition: 23% MLB: 94%

Comparables: Cory Spangenberg, Josh Harrison, Devon Travis

Once on the periphery of the league's top 100 prospects, Hanson remains a maddening player with million-dollar tools and ten-cent instincts. The former Pirate is a make-things-happen baserunner, as demonstrated when he scored from first on an errant pickoff attempt in July. That said, he's also a TOOTBLAN connoisseur, prone to running on contact with less than two outs or turning the wrong way after reaching first on a throwing error—mistakes that cost his team in consecutive September games. Those might be excusable if Hanson excelled at getting aboard, but his injudicious approach betrays his innate ability to hit, to the tune of 41 strikeouts to one walk in 56 second-half games. Defensively, it's more of the same: Hanson has the athleticism and arm to lead the highlights, but his internal clock is a sundial, so he's liable to front the blooper reel the next day. The whole is far less than the sum of the five-tool parts, and the same flair that makes Hanson one of the game's flashiest utility men will leave you wondering why he can't be so much more.

Ryan Howard INF Born: 07/25/94 Age: 24 Bats: R Throws: R Height: 6'2" Weight: 195 Origin: Round 5, 2016 Draft (#155 overall)

YEAR	TEAM	LVL	AGE	PA	R	2B	3B	HR	RBI	BB	K	SB	CS	AVG/OBP/SLG	DRC+	VORP	BABIP	BRR	FRAA	WARP
2016	SLO	A-	21	246	33	10	0	4	31	13	24	2	2	.272/.313/.371	105	7.4	.285	0.0	SS(58): -12.0	-0.2
2017	SJO	A+	22	565	59	21	0	9	50	23	81	7	2	.306/.342/.397	104	29.4	.345	-0.3	SS(101): -9.7, 3B(23): -4.6	1.0
2018	RIC	AA	23	475	44	32	4	4	50	39	55	9	5	.273/.336/.396	97	27.3	.302	0.5	SS(93): -7.6, 2B(21): -5.7	0.5
2019	*SFN*	*MLB*	*24*	*74*	*8*	*3*	*0*	*2*	*7*	*4*	*13*	*1*	*0*	*.239/.285/.354*	*73*	*0.1*	*.267*	*-0.1*	*SS -1, 2B -1*	*-0.2*

Breakout: 6% Improve: 19% Collapse: 14% Attrition: 35% MLB: 52%   *Comparables: Kevin Newman, Adam Frazier, David Fletcher*

Promoted from hitter-friendly San Jose to the pitchers' haven of Richmond, Howard doubled his walk rate while reducing his strikeouts, displaying the sort of strike-zone management that catches scouts' attention when one's physical tools don't. The Mizzou product can shoot the gaps, placing third in the Eastern League in doubles, but he's content to punch the ball the other way, missing the approach and lower-half explosiveness to bop more than a handful of homers a year. In the field, Howard has just enough range at short but fits better at second, where his solid-average arm would be an asset in various defensive shifts. If that reads like a utility profile, well, it is, and Howard could be in line for such work by midyear.

Nick Hundley C Born: 09/08/83 Age: 35 Bats: R Throws: R Height: 6'0" Weight: 203 Origin: Round 2, 2005 Draft (#76 overall)

YEAR	TEAM	LVL	AGE	PA	R	2B	3B	HR	RBI	BB	K	SB	CS	AVG/OBP/SLG	DRC+	VORP	BABIP	BRR	FRAA	WARP
2016	COL	MLB	32	317	30	20	1	10	48	25	65	0	0	.260/.320/.439	103	12.8	.302	-0.3	C(79): -12.8	0.4
2017	SFN	MLB	33	303	27	23	0	9	35	12	81	0	0	.244/.272/.418	70	8.8	.307	-2.8	C(82): -0.9	0.0
2018	SFN	MLB	34	305	34	13	2	10	31	22	85	2	1	.241/.298/.408	88	10.3	.310	0.1	C(83): -14.0	-0.4
2019	*SFN*	*MLB*	*35*	*287*	*28*	*14*	*1*	*8*	*33*	*19*	*74*	*1*	*1*	*.238/.293/.386*	*85*	*6.9*	*.301*	*-0.8*	*C -11*	*-0.4*

Breakout: 3% Improve: 21% Collapse: 13% Attrition: 22% MLB: 89%

Comparables: Terry Steinbach, Benito Santiago, Ivan Rodriguez

YEAR	TEAM	P. COUNT	FRM RUNS	BLK RUNS	THRW RUNS	TOT RUNS
2016	COL	11523	-9.3	0.0	-3.2	-13.2
2017	SFN	10101	-1.1	0.0	0.6	-1.1
2018	SFN	10802	-13.2	-0.5	-0.3	-14.1
2019	*SFN*	*10549*	*-9.5*	*-0.2*	*-0.8*	*-10.5*

Hundley is a master of the intangible. He calls a good game. He gives you a quality at-bat. He steers his batterymates through trouble, be it a bases-loaded jam or a benches-clearing brawl. Revered in the press box and the broadcast booth, he's a pro's pro, a future manager, the preferred backup catcher of a bygone era when his shortcomings were as immeasurable as his strengths. As catching moves from art to science, each new metric stains Hundley's reputation. He's below average in every quantifiable facet of catcher defense: a poor blocker, a weak thrower, one of the very worst framers in the league. We'd feel worse if Hundley were 25 and not 35, for at least his skills are being devalued near the sunset of his playing career. It won't be long before today's Nick Hundleys are managing tomorrow's Sandy Leons. He'll be well prepared for that next chapter when he's ready to turn the page.

Evan Longoria 3B Born: 10/07/85 Age: 33 Bats: R Throws: R Height: 6'1" Weight: 215 Origin: Round 1, 2006 Draft (#3 overall)

YEAR	TEAM	LVL	AGE	PA	R	2B	3B	HR	RBI	BB	K	SB	CS	AVG/OBP/SLG	DRC+	VORP	BABIP	BRR	FRAA	WARP
2016	TBA	MLB	30	685	81	41	4	36	98	42	144	0	3	.273/.318/.521	118	41.6	.298	-2.3	3B(152): -5.4	3.3
2017	TBA	MLB	31	677	71	36	2	20	86	46	109	6	1	.261/.313/.424	91	22.4	.282	-1.9	3B(142): 3.8	1.9
2018	SFN	MLB	32	512	51	25	4	16	54	22	101	3	1	.244/.281/.413	88	6.5	.274	-5.2	3B(123): -10.5	-0.5
2019	*SFN*	*MLB*	*33*	*589*	*63*	*32*	*3*	*18*	*73*	*39*	*107*	*3*	*1*	*.257/.314/.425*	*101*	*12.1*	*.292*	*-2.4*	*3B -5*	*0.7*

Breakout: 3% Improve: 30% Collapse: 9% Attrition: 11% MLB: 91%   *Comparables: Michael Young, Mike Lamb, Juan Uribe*

Longoria's walk rate over the past half-decade tracks the stock price of your favorite office-supply chain in the age of Amazon Prime. No one enjoys seeing the kind folks at Office Depot or Staples lose their jobs, and it's no fun watching a player of Longoria's character have his plate discipline erode. Alas, the trends are largely irreversible, and the third baseman's sinking walk rate has taken his value down with it. Still owed more than $71 million over the next four seasons with a club option for a fifth, the aging Longoria is hurtling toward replacement level. He's a drag on any portfolio, even with the Rays retaining a 15 percent share.

Jalen Miller 2B Born: 12/19/96 Age: 22 Bats: R Throws: R Height: 5'11" Weight: 190 Origin: Round 3, 2015 Draft (#95 overall)

YEAR	TEAM	LVL	AGE	PA	R	2B	3B	HR	RBI	BB	K	SB	CS	AVG/OBP/SLG	DRC+	VORP	BABIP	BRR	FRAA	WARP
2016	AUG	A	19	500	65	20	5	5	44	26	107	11	5	.223/.271/.322	83	3.5	.277	3.8	2B(104): -6.2, SS(7): -0.6	0.0
2017	SJO	A+	20	470	61	25	4	6	44	31	100	6	4	.227/.283/.346	74	2.4	.281	1.2	2B(83): -9.0, SS(28): -0.6	-1.0
2018	SJO	A+	21	554	73	35	2	14	62	27	121	11	4	.276/.321/.434	96	34.4	.335	1.5	2B(119): -9.7	0.4
2019	*SFN*	*MLB*	*22*	*251*	*25*	*8*	*0*	*6*	*23*	*10*	*65*	*2*	*1*	*.209/.240/.327*	*41*	*-9.9*	*.254*	*-0.3*	*2B -3*	*-1.4*

Breakout: 3% Improve: 4% Collapse: 1% Attrition: 5% MLB: 8%   *Comparables: Nick Noonan, Charlie Culberson, Rey Navarro*

Miller announced his breakout intentions by hitting for the cycle in his seventh game of the season, an 18-6 Lancaster special in which his teammate, Gio Brusa, did the same. By year's end, the athletic infielder led all Giants farmhands in extra-base hits and was named High-A San Jose's team MVP. There are plenty of caveats to Miller's newfound power—he was repeating the level as a 21-year-old, it was the Cal League, he struggled with spin—but the glass-half-full view shows a toolsy young player finding his bearings at the plate. Miller is already a nifty defender at the keystone and he runs well underway, so if the bat blooms late, he could play every day. He'll be out to prove the legitimacy of his power as he advances to Double-A.

Joe Panik 2B Born: 10/30/90 Age: 28 Bats: L Throws: R Height: 6'1" Weight: 200 Origin: Round 1, 2011 Draft (#29 overall)

YEAR	TEAM	LVL	AGE	PA	R	2B	3B	HR	RBI	BB	K	SB	CS	AVG/OBP/SLG	DRC+	VORP	BABIP	BRR	FRAA	WARP
2016	SFN	MLB	25	526	67	21	7	10	62	50	47	5	0	.239/.315/.379	97	13.2	.245	1.3	2B(126): 12.7	3.0
2017	SFN	MLB	26	573	60	28	5	10	53	46	54	4	1	.288/.347/.421	105	27.2	.301	0.9	2B(137): -7.5	1.5
2018	SFN	MLB	27	392	38	14	1	4	24	26	30	4	2	.254/.307/.332	91	1.3	.265	1.0	2B(94): 4.3, 1B(1): 0.1	1.3
2019	*SFN*	*MLB*	*28*	*549*	*64*	*27*	*3*	*10*	*52*	*44*	*52*	*4*	*2*	*.265/.331/.392*	*98*	*17.8*	*.278*	*0.7*	*2B 3*	*2.2*

Breakout: 1% Improve: 41% Collapse: 5% Attrition: 8% MLB: 96%   *Comparables: Nellie Fox, Felix Millan, Johnny Ray*

On Opening Day of the 2018 season, Panik homered and the Giants won 1-0. The next day, Panik homered again and the Giants won 1-0 once more. Beyond their historical significance—no team had ever won back-to-back games on the same player's solo shots—those swings offered hope that the National League's feistiest contact hitter might have developed a power stroke to augment his game. Not so. Addled by a torn thumb ligament and a groin strain, Panik clubbed only two more homers the rest of the way, scuffling through the worst offensive season of his career. Panik's appeal used to be his stability—you could pencil him in for two WARP at the keystone and worry about everything else. But putting the ball in play ain't what it used to be, and after four years of rolling with the whims of the BABIP gods, he enters his late-20s searching for a sturdier foundation at the plate.

Hunter Pence RF   Born: 04/13/83   Age: 36   Bats: R   Throws: R   Height: 6'4"   Weight: 230   Origin: Round 2, 2004 Draft (#64 overall)

YEAR	TEAM	LVL	AGE	PA	R	2B	3B	HR	RBI	BB	K	SB	CS	AVG/OBP/SLG	DRC+	VORP	BABIP	BRR	FRAA	WARP
2016	SFN	MLB	33	442	58	23	1	13	57	43	95	1	1	.289/.357/.451	104	25.8	.348	-1.8	RF(102): -1.2	0.9
2017	SFN	MLB	34	539	55	13	5	13	67	40	102	2	3	.260/.315/.385	90	17.3	.301	4.4	RF(125): 2.0	1.2
2018	SAC	AAA	35	111	11	4	0	1	13	6	24	0	0	.301/.342/.369	75	1.9	.380	-0.1	RF(12): 0.1, LF(11): 0.2	0.0
2018	SFN	MLB	35	248	19	11	1	4	24	11	59	5	1	.226/.258/.332	63	-2.7	.282	0.4	LF(44): -3.1, RF(12): -1.2	-0.9
2019	SFN	MLB	36	310	30	12	1	6	32	22	69	2	1	.239/.298/.360	74	-0.4	.294	0.7	LF 1, RF 0	0.1

Breakout: 0%   Improve: 31%   Collapse: 7%   Attrition: 14%   MLB: 76%   *Comparables: Johnny Dickshot, Jose Cruz, Brian Jordan*

Desperate times call for desperate measures, so when a slumping Pence found himself rehabbing a thumb injury with Triple-A Sacramento in May, he seized the opportunity to alter his distinctive swing. The long-time fan favorite for lumbering movements and wacky faces that belied outstanding athleticism and dynamic tools, Pence stood more upright in the box, lowered his hands and used a more deliberate knee-lift stride reminiscent of Justin Turner's. Although the change didn't manifest in an offensive revival, Pence led the Giants with five batted balls over 110 mph, showing there's plenty of thunder left in his stick. He went all-in on the Turnerization in the offseason, visiting with Turner's coach Doug Latta, a last-ditch effort to prolong his career as he tests free agency for the first time. Pence's legs aren't what they once were, but his intangibles should net him an opportunity as an extra outfielder if he rediscovers some of his old pop.

Buster Posey C   Born: 03/27/87   Age: 32   Bats: R   Throws: R   Height: 6'1"   Weight: 210   Origin: Round 1, 2008 Draft (#5 overall)

YEAR	TEAM	LVL	AGE	PA	R	2B	3B	HR	RBI	BB	K	SB	CS	AVG/OBP/SLG	DRC+	VORP	BABIP	BRR	FRAA	WARP
2016	SFN	MLB	29	614	82	33	2	14	80	64	68	6	1	.288/.362/.434	112	40.5	.303	-3.3	C(123): 37.0, 1B(15): -0.7	7.3
2017	SFN	MLB	30	568	62	34	0	12	67	61	66	6	1	.320/.400/.462	122	50.2	.347	-1.5	C(99): 7.0, 1B(38): 3.5	4.8
2018	SFN	MLB	31	448	47	22	1	5	41	45	53	3	2	.284/.359/.382	107	20.1	.316	-1.3	C(88): 0.1, 1B(13): 1.5	2.5
2019	SFN	MLB	32	573	64	31	2	10	63	63	72	5	1	.282/.369/.412	117	32.1	.313	-2.0	C 10, 1B 3	4.8

Breakout: 0%   Improve: 30%   Collapse: 8%   Attrition: 10%   MLB: 95%   *Comparables: Yadier Molina, Victor Martinez, Jonathan Lucroy*

While the shoulders and arms control the bat, the back hip is the most important joint in hitting. Any weakness there, any decrease in mobility, can sap a hitter's power and prevent him from staying back against offspeed and spin. In Posey's case, it was both: A torn labrum and microfracture turned the one-time slugger into a slapper who could barely threaten the gaps, much less the fence. Despite the pain and the wear, Posey remained unimpressed with the fastest of fastballs, but sliders and changeups exposed his wobbly base. By late August, he relented and went under the knife. Like any major surgery, hip

YEAR	TEAM	P. COUNT	FRM RUNS	BLK RUNS	THRW RUNS	TOT RUNS
2016	SFN	17017	28.9	2.0	2.2	32.9
2017	SFN	13474	4.8	0.2	2.3	7.4
2018	SFN	12224	0.9	0.7	0.1	2.0
2019	SFN	15310	7.8	1.0	1.1	9.9

procedures are risky, and Posey's readiness for Opening Day is no sure thing—it falls squarely in the middle of his six-to-eight-month recovery estimate. Still, if the former MVP can restore even a fraction of his vintage power without the injury rendering him unable to catch, he could rejoin the National League's elite.

Heath Quinn OF   Born: 06/07/95   Age: 24   Bats: R   Throws: R   Height: 6'3"   Weight: 220   Origin: Round 3, 2016 Draft (#95 overall)

YEAR	TEAM	LVL	AGE	PA	R	2B	3B	HR	RBI	BB	K	SB	CS	AVG/OBP/SLG	DRC+	VORP	BABIP	BRR	FRAA	WARP
2016	SLO	A-	21	239	37	19	1	9	34	26	50	3	0	.337/.423/.571	151	26.9	.405	1.7	RF(49): 11.2	3.2
2017	SJO	A+	22	297	24	9	0	10	29	20	86	0	0	.228/.290/.371	93	-2.6	.294	-2.8	RF(35): -0.5, LF(26): -7.4	-0.9
2018	SJO	A+	23	407	53	24	0	14	51	42	98	4	1	.300/.376/.485	125	30.9	.373	0.3	LF(58): -11.4	0.8
2019	SFN	MLB	24	251	25	10	0	9	30	17	74	0	0	.217/.271/.369	72	-2.6	.276	-0.6	LF -7, RF 0	-1.0

Breakout: 2%   Improve: 6%   Collapse: 3%   Attrition: 9%   MLB: 13%   *Comparables: Jake Cave, Bryan Petersen, Jaycob Brugman*

A fractured hamate and a bum shoulder are any power hitter's worst nightmare, and Quinn endured both in 2017. Healthy again to begin last season, he excelled in a repeat tour of the Cal League, exhibiting the physicality and all-fields thunder that made him a third-round pick three years ago. With a plus arm accompanying his pop, Quinn checks the boxes that a right-field prospect must, and though he's more strongman than speedster, he won't be a hindrance on the grass. Assuming the injury bug flies away, Quinn's strikeout rate will dictate if he's a second-division regular or a short-end platooner who stars in BP.

Heliot Ramos CF   Born: 09/07/99   Age: 19   Bats: R   Throws: R   Height: 6'2"   Weight: 185   Origin: Round 1, 2017 Draft (#19 overall)

YEAR	TEAM	LVL	AGE	PA	R	2B	3B	HR	RBI	BB	K	SB	CS	AVG/OBP/SLG	DRC+	VORP	BABIP	BRR	FRAA	WARP
2017	GIA	RK	17	151	33	11	6	6	27	10	48	10	2	.348/.404/.645	130	20.8	.500	2.2	CF(28): -2.3	0.9
2018	AUG	A	18	535	61	24	8	11	52	35	136	8	7	.245/.313/.396	98	21.5	.319	1.8	CF(113): -4.5	1.2
2019	SFN	MLB	19	251	26	10	2	8	26	7	85	1	1	.206/.228/.366	56	-3.9	.275	-0.1	CF -1	-0.5

Breakout: 0%   Improve: 8%   Collapse: 1%   Attrition: 4%   MLB: 12%   *Comparables: Engel Beltre, Nomar Mazara, Adalberto Mondesi*

The Giants prefer to challenge rather than coddle their prospects, so a stellar pro debut in the Arizona League netted Ramos a chance to impress as the youngest player in the Sally. That context is critical when evaluating his performance, and while the topline numbers were pedestrian, his tools are anything but. Ramos converted his plus raw power into 43 extra-base hits and he placed fourth in the circuit with eight triples, utilizing the speed that will also enable him to stay in center field. While the Puerto Rican has bat speed to spare, his nascent approach is an area for improvement. A gap-to-gap hitter at present, scouts believe Ramos will develop selective aggression, learning to identify pitches he can pull over the fence and ones he's better off watching go by. Like any teenager, Ramos will need a few years of trial and error to find his place in the world. He could be a first-division regular if all breaks right.

Pablo Sandoval 3B Born: 08/11/86 Age: 32 Bats: B Throws: R Height: 5'11" Weight: 268 Origin: International Free Agent, 2003

YEAR	TEAM	LVL	AGE	PA	R	2B	3B	HR	RBI	BB	K	SB	CS	AVG/OBP/SLG	DRC+	VORP	BABIP	BRR	FRAA	WARP
2016	BOS	MLB	29	7	0	0	0	0	0	1	4	0	0	.000/.143/.000	77	-1.0	.000	0.0	3B(2): 0.1	0.0
2017	BOS	MLB	30	108	10	2	0	4	12	8	24	0	1	.212/.269/.354	84	-1.9	.236	-0.2	3B(29): -1.4, 2B(1): 0.0	0.0
2017	PAW	AAA	30	81	7	3	0	1	4	4	16	0	0	.221/.259/.299	88	-2.8	.267	-0.5	3B(15): -1.6	-0.1
2017	SAC	AAA	30	37	4	1	0	1	3	5	3	0	0	.207/.324/.345	111	1.3	.185	-0.1	3B(7): 1.2	0.3
2017	SFN	MLB	30	171	17	9	0	5	20	8	29	0	0	.225/.263/.375	81	-0.8	.242	-0.4	3B(38): -2.6, 1B(9): -0.1	-0.1
2018	SFN	MLB	31	252	22	10	1	9	40	19	52	0	0	.248/.310/.417	94	1.4	.282	-2.8	3B(36): -1.8, 1B(24): -1.4	-0.2
2019	SFN	MLB	32	150	15	7	1	4	17	11	33	0	0	.236/.297/.383	90	2.1	.282	-0.5	3B -1	0.1

Breakout: 4%   Improve: 45%   Collapse: 11%   Attrition: 12%   MLB: 91%   Comparables: Casey McGehee, B.J. Surhoff, Russ Wrightstone

When the Red Sox released Sandoval in July 2017, his career hung in the balance, imperiled by poor conditioning, a shoulder injury that sapped his power and a bad-ball approach known to accelerate the expiration dates of major-league bats. Granted a second chance by his first employer, he came to Spring Training looking slimmer, swinging easier and, most notably, swinging less. Players rarely make a mid-career U-turn at the plate, but Sandoval—once one of the league's leading first-pitch-hackers—became one of the most willing to let the 0-0 offering go by. In 252 plate appearances, he put the first pitch in play only four times. His 1.6 percent was a stark contrast to both the league average of 10.9 percent and his own career rate of 15.1 percent. The result was a productive corner-infield reserve, well worth the league-minimum balance of a contract on the Red Sox' books through 2019. A hamstring injury cut Sandoval's season two months short, but assuming he keeps the patient approach, he'll be a fine fill-in at first and third again this year.

Chris Shaw LF Born: 10/20/93 Age: 25 Bats: L Throws: R Height: 6'3" Weight: 226 Origin: Round 1, 2015 Draft (#31 overall)

YEAR	TEAM	LVL	AGE	PA	R	2B	3B	HR	RBI	BB	K	SB	CS	AVG/OBP/SLG	DRC+	VORP	BABIP	BRR	FRAA	WARP
2016	SJO	A+	22	305	47	22	0	16	55	28	70	0	0	.285/.357/.544	131	24.7	.326	-2.4	1B(52): -0.9	1.2
2016	RIC	AA	22	256	26	16	4	5	30	20	55	0	0	.246/.309/.414	88	1.6	.299	-3.5	1B(48): -2.3	-0.7
2017	RIC	AA	23	154	16	10	0	6	29	18	26	0	0	.301/.390/.511	122	10.5	.333	-1.5	LF(17): -1.1, 1B(16): -0.9	0.4
2017	SAC	AAA	23	360	42	25	1	18	50	20	106	0	0	.289/.328/.530	106	13.4	.367	-5.3	LF(76): -14.5	-0.7
2018	SAC	AAA	24	422	55	21	2	24	65	21	144	0	0	.259/.308/.505	96	14.4	.345	-2.0	LF(86): -10.4	-0.3
2018	SFN	MLB	24	62	2	2	0	1	7	7	23	1	0	.185/.274/.278	69	-1.8	.290	-0.1	LF(15): -1.9	-0.3
2019	SFN	MLB	25	440	56	20	1	21	58	22	149	1	0	.230/.273/.436	86	4.5	.302	-0.7	LF -9	-0.5

Breakout: 5%   Improve: 22%   Collapse: 12%   Attrition: 27%   MLB: 48%   Comparables: Matt Clark, Andrew Lambo, Peter O'Brien

In Shaw's case, power isn't everything … it's the only thing. The Boston College product can top the light-tower, but he's a 30-grade runner, merely acceptable at first base and unable to cover the outfield gaps. For players with this profile, contact rate draws the line between Quad-A slugger and second-division player in the bigs. Shaw toed the wrong side of it last season, both in Triple-A and in his major-league debut, where he swung at 42 percent of pitches outside of the strike zone. While jumpiness is normal for a rookie trying too hard to impress, pitchers were thrilled to find him equally willing to expand on fastballs up and sliders down, and the prolific chase rate poses a grave threat to Shaw's primary tool. The former first-round pick can be productive if he just strikes out one-fourth of the time instead of one-third, but he's yet to put bat on ball consistently above Double-A.

Austin Slater OF Born: 12/13/92 Age: 26 Bats: R Throws: R Height: 6'2" Weight: 197 Origin: Round 8, 2014 Draft (#238 overall)

YEAR	TEAM	LVL	AGE	PA	R	2B	3B	HR	RBI	BB	K	SB	CS	AVG/OBP/SLG	DRC+	VORP	BABIP	BRR	FRAA	WARP
2016	RIC	AA	23	172	20	8	1	5	25	24	36	6	1	.317/.413/.490	121	19.5	.387	1.1	CF(33): -10.0, LF(7): -0.4	0.0
2016	SAC	AAA	23	278	36	12	0	13	42	33	53	2	6	.298/.381/.506	123	26.1	.335	-0.5	LF(48): 0.4, CF(15): -1.3	1.6
2017	SAC	AAA	24	206	28	12	0	5	27	15	39	4	3	.321/.377/.467	90	9.1	.380	-2.7	RF(22): -0.9, LF(17): -0.1	0.0
2017	SFN	MLB	24	127	15	3	1	3	16	8	29	0	0	.282/.339/.402	84	4.9	.353	0.2	LF(30): -1.0, RF(3): -0.2	0.0
2018	SAC	AAA	25	223	32	24	2	5	32	21	39	8	2	.344/.417/.564	110	22.2	.405	1.4	RF(29): 0.6, 1B(13): -0.1	0.9
2018	SFN	MLB	25	225	21	6	1	1	23	20	69	7	0	.251/.333/.307	61	1.8	.377	1.3	LF(25): 1.8, 1B(21): 0.1	-0.3
2019	SFN	MLB	26	422	45	16	2	9	41	35	109	7	2	.228/.304/.352	81	1.7	.297	0.4	RF -5, 1B 0	-0.4

Breakout: 7%   Improve: 38%   Collapse: 12%   Attrition: 24%   MLB: 80%   Comparables: John Bowker, Shin-Soo Choo, Wladimir Balentien

There's some benefit to zagging while everyone zigs, but Slater's batted-ball profile tests the limits of bucking conventional wisdom. As nearly all his brethren aim to lift the ball pull-side, Slater doggedly filets even the meatiest pitches the other way. He sent 36 percent of his balls in play to the opposite field, more than any other right-handed hitter with 200 or more trips to the plate. His 63.1 percent ground-ball rate led the same group, as did his 3.9 grounders-per-fly. That spray chart made the former Stanford standout unshiftable, allowing him to bat .317 on grounders despite not being very fast and .724 on liners despite not hitting them especially hard. The downside is evident in Slater's ISO, the lowest of anyone with his volume of at-bats. That simply won't do for a corner outfielder or first baseman, relegating Slater to backup duty until he updates his approach.

Mac Williamson LF   Born: 07/15/90   Age: 28   Bats: R   Throws: R   Height: 6'4"   Weight: 237   Origin: Round 3, 2012 Draft (#115 overall)

YEAR	TEAM	LVL	AGE	PA	R	2B	3B	HR	RBI	BB	K	SB	CS	AVG/OBP/SLG	DRC+	VORP	BABIP	BRR	FRAA	WARP
2016	SAC	AAA	25	226	35	14	0	11	42	12	53	2	1	.269/.314/.495	106	14.9	.306	0.5	LF(25): 1.8, RF(23): -1.0	0.9
2016	SFN	MLB	25	127	14	3	0	6	15	13	35	0	1	.223/.315/.411	94	1.8	.268	0.0	RF(23): -0.9, LF(13): 2.2	0.4
2017	SAC	AAA	26	382	54	21	0	14	50	25	100	4	1	.244/.301/.423	78	2.5	.301	1.8	RF(56): -2.0, LF(27): -2.5	-0.4
2017	SFN	MLB	26	73	8	2	0	3	6	5	25	1	1	.235/.288/.397	63	3.3	.325	1.3	RF(12): -0.1, LF(9): -0.3	-0.1
2018	SFN	MLB	27	105	14	4	0	4	11	11	27	1	1	.213/.295/.383	84	1.6	.254	0.3	LF(25): -0.6, RF(2): -0.1	0.0
2018	SAC	AAA	27	215	31	7	1	13	44	23	44	1	0	.269/.372/.533	121	14.8	.283	0.0	RF(31): -0.2, LF(13): 0.9	1.2
2019	SFN	MLB	28	371	41	13	1	14	46	30	99	2	1	.224/.296/.391	85	5.4	.276	1.5	RF -1, LF -1	0.4

Breakout: 6%   Improve: 24%   Collapse: 14%   Attrition: 25%   MLB: 54%   *Comparables: John Rodriguez, Todd Linden, Matt Tuiasosopo*

Blessed with the most raw power in the organization, Williamson struggled to actualize his strength because of subpar contact rates and a propensity to pound the ball into the ground. While at Triple-A Sacramento in 2017, journeyman catcher Tim Federowicz referred him to Justin Turner's hitting instructor Doug Latta, and Williamson returned last spring with unmistakably Turner-ish movements in his swing. You know the ones: a lowered hand-set meant to increase the loft in his stroke and a more patient leg-lift to better store energy in his back hip. The effects came together on a cool April night at AT&T Park, when Williamson launched a mammoth, 464-foot blast to right-center, a head-turning homer that left fans wanting more. Alas, in addition to thumping another bomb, Williamson crashed head-first into a wall the next day, and concussion symptoms ruined the remainder of his season. Assuming he's healthy, Williamson will come to spring training out of options and with considerable intrigue still surrounding his new swing. That should secure his roster spot and give him a chance to shed the Quad-A tag for good.

PITCHERS

Shaun Anderson RHP   Born: 10/29/94   Age: 24   Bats: R   Throws: R   Height: 6'4"   Weight: 225   Origin: Round 3, 2016 Draft (#88 overall)

YEAR	TEAM	LVL	AGE	W	L	SV	G	GS	IP	H	HR	BB/9	K/9	K	GB%	BABIP	WHIP	ERA	DRA	WARP	MPH	FB%	WHF	CSP
2017	GRN	A	22	3	0	0	7	7	38²	30	2	2.6	8.6	37	52%	.272	1.06	2.56	3.62	0.8				
2017	SLM	A+	22	3	3	0	11	11	58²	53	6	2.8	7.4	48	43%	.270	1.21	3.99	3.80	1.0				
2017	SJO	A+	22	3	3	0	6	5	25²	19	1	1.4	7.7	22	51%	.247	0.90	3.51	4.63	0.2				
2018	RIC	AA	23	6	5	0	17	16	94	93	9	2.1	8.9	93	49%	.316	1.22	3.45	2.88	2.7				
2018	SAC	AAA	23	2	2	0	8	8	47¹	48	5	2.1	6.5	34	47%	.287	1.25	4.18	4.09	0.8				
2019	SFN	MLB	24	2	2	0	5	5	26²	25	3	2.8	7.8	23	44%	.301	1.27	4.13	4.78	0.2				

Breakout: 11%   Improve: 23%   Collapse: 20%   Attrition: 40%   MLB: 52%   *Comparables: Walker Lockett, Matt Andriese, Simon Castro*

During his junior year at the University of Florida, Anderson shared a roster with six future first- or second-rounders. That collection of arms relegated him to the bullpen as a collegian, his four-pitch repertoire and starter's motion notwithstanding. The Red Sox saw a mid-rotation arm when they chose Anderson in the third round in 2016, and the Giants, who obtained the right-hander in the Eduardo Nunez trade, heartily agree. While Anderson doesn't have a putaway pitch, he manipulates the shape of his slider and the depth of his changeup, keeping each offering in a distinct velocity band to turn over lineups multiple times. Add an ideal pitcher's frame and easy mechanics, and you've got a near-ready fourth starter. Anderson should shed the "near" part this year.

Tyler Beede RHP   Born: 05/23/93   Age: 26   Bats: R   Throws: R   Height: 6'3"   Weight: 211   Origin: Round 1, 2014 Draft (#14 overall)

YEAR	TEAM	LVL	AGE	W	L	SV	G	GS	IP	H	HR	BB/9	K/9	K	GB%	BABIP	WHIP	ERA	DRA	WARP	MPH	FB%	WHF	CSP
2016	RIC	AA	23	8	7	0	24	24	147¹	136	9	3.2	8.2	135	49%	.309	1.28	2.81	3.17	3.4				
2017	SAC	AAA	24	6	7	0	19	19	109	121	14	3.2	6.9	83	52%	.316	1.47	4.79	5.50	0.2				
2018	SFN	MLB	25	0	1	0	2	2	7²	9	0	9.4	10.6	9	46%	.409	2.22	8.22	4.22	0.1	94.3	51.8	11.5	41.3
2018	SAC	AAA	25	4	9	0	33	10	74	82	10	6.8	9.1	75	41%	.346	1.86	7.05	5.04	0.3				
2019	SFN	MLB	26	2	3	0	8	8	40	37	5	4.4	8.9	39	44%	.311	1.43	4.59	5.29	0.0	93.9	52.7	11.7	42.1

Breakout: 10%   Improve: 17%   Collapse: 7%   Attrition: 22%   MLB: 33%   *Comparables: Justin Haley, Tom Koehler, Chris Stratton*

On draft day in 2014, most saw Beede and the Giants as a match made in heaven: a wayward ace meeting a team known for getting lost arms back on track. But instead of finding the straight and narrow up to San Fran, Beede wound up on a winding road to the Triple-A bullpen, travel time four years, severe traffic along his route. At alternating times in his pro career, Beede's control, stuff, confidence and mechanics have abandoned him. When they seemed to gel in 2016, the acquisition of Matt Moore blocked his path. That all reads like the prelude to a change of scenery, which would be a bitterly ironic ending to a marriage that seemed perfect at the start.

Ty Blach LHP   Born: 10/20/90   Age: 28   Bats: R   Throws: L   Height: 6'1"   Weight: 213   Origin: Round 5, 2012 Draft (#178 overall)

YEAR	TEAM	LVL	AGE	W	L	SV	G	GS	IP	H	HR	BB/9	K/9	K	GB%	BABIP	WHIP	ERA	DRA	WARP	MPH	FB%	WHF	CSP
2016	SAC	AAA	25	14	7	0	26	26	162²	147	9	2.1	6.3	113	50%	.280	1.14	3.43	4.08	2.4				
2016	SFN	MLB	25	1	0	0	4	2	17	8	1	2.6	5.3	10	60%	.152	0.76	1.06	5.57	-0.1	93.1	61.5	7.1	46.3
2017	SFN	MLB	26	8	12	0	34	24	163²	179	17	2.4	4.0	73	48%	.290	1.36	4.78	4.75	1.5	91.5	60.1	7	50.5
2018	SFN	MLB	27	6	7	0	47	13	118²	133	8	3.1	5.7	75	55%	.323	1.47	4.25	4.79	0.5	91.5	57.6	7.9	50.3
2019	SFN	MLB	28	5	4	0	52	11	98¹	96	8	2.8	6.3	68	49%	.300	1.28	3.87	4.50	0.8	91.0	59.3	7.5	49.7

Breakout: 7%   Improve: 25%   Collapse: 21%   Attrition: 18%   MLB: 63%   *Comparables: Joe Biagini, Taylor Jordan, Jose Alvarez*

"Utility man" applies exclusively to position players, but if there were an analogous job description for pitchers, Blach would fit that role to a T. He worked in almost every capacity in 2018, from starter to specialist, long guy to setup man, appearing at least once in every frame from the first through the 16th. Like a true utility man, Blach wasn't particularly adept at any job, but he was always up for the task at hand. And, since the little things set the best utility men apart, Blach made sure to field his position and hold runners, recording 24 assists without an error while holding foes to just three steals in six tries. Managers typically deploy utility men to keep their key regulars fresh, and the same usage best suits Blach. When a veteran starter needs an extra day, it's 10-to-nothing in the fifth inning or it's #weirdbaseball time in the 14th, Blach's there to do the job so his teammates don't have to.

Ray Black RHP   Born: 06/26/90   Age: 29   Bats: R   Throws: R   Height: 6'5"   Weight: 225   Origin: Round 7, 2011 Draft (#237 overall)

YEAR	TEAM	LVL	AGE	W	L	SV	G	GS	IP	H	HR	BB/9	K/9	K	GB%	BABIP	WHIP	ERA	DRA	WARP	MPH	FB%	WHF	CSP
2016	RIC	AA	26	1	4	6	35	0	31¹	17	1	9.2	15.2	53	39%	.286	1.56	4.88	1.61	1.2				
2018	RIC	AA	28	0	0	4	10	0	10	4	0	3.6	18.0	20	7%	.286	0.80	0.90	1.37	0.4				
2018	SAC	AAA	28	3	0	1	26	0	25²	15	2	2.8	16.1	46	25%	.310	0.90	3.16	1.49	1.1				
2018	SFN	MLB	28	2	2	0	26	0	23¹	17	4	3.9	12.7	33	41%	.277	1.16	6.17	2.66	0.6	100.0	64	17.1	45.7
2019	SFN	MLB	29	2	1	0	46	0	48²	39	10	6.9	13.5	73	38%	.314	1.57	5.31	6.06	-0.6	99.3	64	17.1	45.7

Breakout: 10%   Improve: 30%   Collapse: 21%   Attrition: 25%   MLB: 64%   *Comparables: Ryan O'Rourke, Steve Delabar, James Hoyt*

Tommy John surgery. A torn throwing-shoulder labrum. Bone spurs in the elbow. If there's an arm injury, Black's had it. From high school through his major-league debut at the age of 28, the right-hander tantalized scouts with a power fastball and devilish slider, and frequented surgeons with the medical consequences of throwing them. A seventh-round pick in 2011, he was the sort of prospect you rush to the majors as soon as his control passes muster, in hopes of extracting value before his arm gives in. But Black hit the disabled list with the aforementioned labrum tear in his very first Spring Training, and good control didn't coincide with good health until seven years later. He arrived with his arm scarred but still working, his fastball still electric, his slider still darting. The stuff will play in the late innings for as long as his arm is able to deliver it.

Madison Bumgarner LHP   Born: 08/01/89   Age: 29   Bats: R   Throws: L   Height: 6'4"   Weight: 242   Origin: Round 1, 2007 Draft (#10 overall)

YEAR	TEAM	LVL	AGE	W	L	SV	G	GS	IP	H	HR	BB/9	K/9	K	GB%	BABIP	WHIP	ERA	DRA	WARP	MPH	FB%	WHF	CSP
2016	SFN	MLB	26	15	9	0	34	34	226²	179	26	2.1	10.0	251	41%	.267	1.03	2.74	2.70	6.9	92.6	48.2	12.4	45.4
2017	SJO	A+	27	0	1	0	2	2	10	11	4	1.8	11.7	13	29%	.292	1.30	8.10	3.23	0.2				
2017	SFN	MLB	27	4	9	0	17	17	111	101	17	1.6	8.2	101	42%	.272	1.09	3.32	3.66	2.4	92.7	43	11.1	46
2018	SFN	MLB	28	6	7	0	21	21	129²	118	14	3.0	7.6	109	43%	.274	1.24	3.26	4.47	1.3	91.9	34.4	10.1	49
2019	SFN	MLB	29	10	11	0	30	30	180	163	22	2.7	8.3	167	42%	.293	1.20	3.92	4.53	1.6	91.7	41.8	11.2	47.1

Breakout: 12%   Improve: 35%   Collapse: 21%   Attrition: 4%   MLB: 95%   *Comparables: Masahiro Tanaka, David Price, Len Barker*

When Bumgarner signed a long-term extension before the 2012 season, he secured the largest guarantee ever paid to a pitcher with less than two years of service time while delaying his free agency from 2018 to 2020. Had the left-hander hit the market after 2017, he would have been 28, still in the prime of his career, an ace whose sterling reputation was tainted only by poor judgment in riding a dirt bike. Instead, Bumgarner enters 2019 needing to shake his second straight freak-injury-shortened year, allay concerns about diminishing velocity and reestablish his standing as a frontline arm. A workhorse's workhorse, Bumgarner should flirt with 1,800 career innings before his 30th birthday, mileage that has taken a toll on his fastball. Opponents slugged .571 against his now-average four-seamer and struck out just 19 times in the 147 at-bats that ended with it. Bumgarner responded by throwing more curveballs and cutters, pitches that miss more bats but also miss the strike zone more often, yielding the highest walk rate of his career. Unless reversed, these trends threaten to cost a would-be $200 million pitcher half his earning potential. Among the top players in next winter's free agent class, Bumgarner may face the most pivotal contract year.

Seth Corry LHP   Born: 11/03/98   Age: 20   Bats: L   Throws: L   Height: 6'2"   Weight: 195   Origin: Round 3, 2017 Draft (#96 overall)

YEAR	TEAM	LVL	AGE	W	L	SV	G	GS	IP	H	HR	BB/9	K/9	K	GB%	BABIP	WHIP	ERA	DRA	WARP	MPH	FB%	WHF	CSP
2017	GIA	RK	18	0	2	0	13	10	24¹	14	1	8.1	7.8	21	46%	.203	1.48	5.55	4.49	0.4				
2018	GNT	RK	19	3	1	0	9	9	38	38	1	4.0	9.9	42	46%	.349	1.45	2.61	3.69	1.0				
2018	SLO	A-	19	1	2	0	5	5	19²	14	1	6.9	7.8	17	54%	.245	1.47	5.49	4.82	0.1				
2019	SFN	MLB	20	1	5	0	11	11	39²	43	8	9.5	7.6	33	43%	.317	2.16	7.57	8.72	-1.6				

Comparables: Jordan Hicks, Paul Blackburn, Jeanmar Gomez

From the unique rock formations of Bryce Canyon to the breathtaking red cliffs of Zion, Utah has a national park for every outdoorsman. Indeed, it claims more national parks (five) than drafted pitchers who've eclipsed 5.0 career WARP in the major leagues. Chosen in the third round in 2017, Corry came equipped with a cutting mid-90s fastball and a plus curve, a fine starter kit to which he recently added a promising change. Now, consistency is the steepest hill the southpaw must climb—game to game, inning to inning, even pitch to pitch. There's a mountain of switchbacks between Corry and a big-league rotation, but sometimes the view at the top is worth the grueling hike.

Johnny Cueto RHP   Born: 02/15/86   Age: 33   Bats: R   Throws: R   Height: 5'11"   Weight: 229   Origin: International Free Agent, 2004

YEAR	TEAM	LVL	AGE	W	L	SV	G	GS	IP	H	HR	BB/9	K/9	K	GB%	BABIP	WHIP	ERA	DRA	WARP	MPH	FB%	WHF	CSP
2016	SFN	MLB	30	18	5	0	32	32	219²	195	15	1.8	8.1	198	52%	.293	1.09	2.79	2.93	6.1	94.3	50.1	10.5	46.2
2017	SFN	MLB	31	8	8	0	25	25	147¹	160	22	3.2	8.3	136	41%	.322	1.45	4.52	4.57	1.7	93.2	51.2	11.4	42.7
2018	SFN	MLB	32	3	2	0	9	9	53	46	8	2.2	6.5	38	45%	.253	1.11	3.23	4.56	0.5	92.0	46.8	10	46.4
2019	SFN	MLB	33	4	4	0	10	10	64²	60	8	2.6	7.7	55	45%	.294	1.22	4.11	4.74	0.4	92.4	49.4	10.6	44.6

Breakout: 12%   Improve: 41%   Collapse: 21%   Attrition: 15%   MLB: 96%   *Comparables: Kelvim Escobar, Roy Oswalt, Cole Hamels*

The opportunity to rehab an arm injury in lieu of surgery, to sit out two months instead of two years, is a glimmer of hope in a dark hour at the office of Dr. James Andrews. Coming off a five-start stretch of 0.84 ERA ball to start the season, Cueto took the rehab route, hopeful that if he could pitch so effectively through the soreness of a sprained UCL, it must not be so serious after all. Alas, the same pitcher who was nearly unhittable in April became a punching bag when he returned in July, and with his fastball scarcely touching 90 on the gun, Cueto gave in to Tommy John surgery that will sideline him until 2020. The right-hander will be 34 when he next shimmies and deals from a big-league rubber, amplifying the risk in a recovery that's not automatic even for pitchers 10 years younger. His guile and savvy should sustain him into the '20s, but his days as an ace have likely passed.

Camilo Doval RHP   Born: 07/04/97   Age: 21   Bats: R   Throws: R   Height: 6'2"   Weight: 185   Origin: International Free Agent, 2015

YEAR	TEAM	LVL	AGE	W	L	SV	G	GS	IP	H	HR	BB/9	K/9	K	GB%	BABIP	WHIP	ERA	DRA	WARP	MPH	FB%	WHF	CSP
2016	DGI	RK	18	2	0	1	12	0	21²	13	0	4.6	10.0	24	64%	.260	1.11	1.66	1.88	0.8				
2017	GIA	RK	19	1	2	1	17	0	32¹	23	0	3.6	14.2	51	65%	.348	1.11	3.90	1.58	1.4				
2018	AUG	A	20	0	3	11	44	0	53	40	2	4.6	13.2	78	42%	.322	1.26	3.06	2.85	1.2				
2019	SFN	MLB	21	2	1	1	38	0	40	38	7	6.8	10.3	46	47%	.318	1.70	5.73	6.57	-1.0				

Breakout: 0%   Improve: 0%   Collapse: 1%   Attrition: 2%   MLB: 2%   *Comparables: Craig Kimbrel, Nick Goody, Alejandro Chacin*

Everyone's entitled to a bad day or three, and if you forgive Doval's awful beginning of 2018, which saw him walk eight of his first 19 foes, you'll uncover one of the most exciting relievers to grace a Low-A roster last year. The Dominican's lightning-quick arm unfurls high-90s velocity and a wicked cutter, along with a slider that could tighten into a third out pitch. What holds Doval back is a slender frame that's incompatible with his max-effort motion, the source of the command deficiency and velocity variance that give scouts pause. Having just turned 21 on the Fourth of July, Doval has plenty of time to add good weight and find an answer for left-handed opponents. With a 70-grade cutter in hand, he could soar to the big leagues as soon as everything clicks.

Sam Dyson RHP   Born: 05/07/88   Age: 31   Bats: R   Throws: R   Height: 6'1"   Weight: 212   Origin: Round 4, 2010 Draft (#126 overall)

YEAR	TEAM	LVL	AGE	W	L	SV	G	GS	IP	H	HR	BB/9	K/9	K	GB%	BABIP	WHIP	ERA	DRA	WARP	MPH	FB%	WHF	CSP
2016	TEX	MLB	28	3	2	38	73	0	70¹	63	5	2.9	7.0	55	65%	.291	1.22	2.43	4.48	0.4	98.2	70.5	8.7	49.9
2017	TEX	MLB	29	1	6	0	17	0	16²	31	6	6.5	3.8	7	62%	.379	2.58	10.80	8.89	-0.7	96.6	73.8	6	47.2
2017	SFN	MLB	29	3	4	14	38	0	38	36	2	4.3	6.4	27	67%	.286	1.42	4.03	6.27	-0.5	96.7	73.8	10	48.3
2018	SFN	MLB	30	4	3	3	74	0	70¹	56	5	2.6	7.2	56	62%	.270	1.08	2.69	4.01	0.7	95.6	65.4	11.9	48.8
2019	SFN	MLB	31	3	1	0	56	0	59²	54	5	3.5	7.8	52	59%	.302	1.29	3.81	4.42	0.3	95.7	69	10	48.5

Breakout: 25%   Improve: 48%   Collapse: 24%   Attrition: 13%   MLB: 88%   *Comparables: Chad Bradford, Eric O'Flaherty, Rafael Perez*

The importance of getting ahead in the count is one of baseball's few undisputed truths. In 2017, Dyson's first-pitch-strike rate plunged eight points to 53.1 percent, 17th-worst in the majors, and his opponents hit a Bonds-ian .364/.479/.636 after 1-0 counts. Having seen his career flash before his eyes, Dyson resolved to attack hitters with his best pitch, throwing his turbo sinker to start nearly three-fourths of the batters he faced. With renewed confidence in the heater, the right-hander restored his first-pitch-strike clip to its previous norm around 60 percent while retaining his place among the premier ground-ball generators in the league. A middling strikeout rate and trouble holding runners still make Dyson a dubious choice for saves, but he should be a quality middle-inning man as long as he can earn strike one.

Sean Hjelle RHP   Born: 05/07/97   Age: 22   Bats: R   Throws: R   Height: 6'11"   Weight: 225   Origin: Round 2, 2018 Draft (#45 overall)

YEAR	TEAM	LVL	AGE	W	L	SV	G	GS	IP	H	HR	BB/9	K/9	K	GB%	BABIP	WHIP	ERA	DRA	WARP	MPH	FB%	WHF	CSP
2018	SLO	A-	21	0	0	0	12	12	21¹	24	4	1.7	9.3	22	49%	.317	1.31	5.06	2.92	0.6				
2019	SFN	MLB	22	2	4	0	10	10	34²	39	7	3.3	7.1	27	39%	.316	1.50	5.60	6.44	-0.4				

Comparables: Eric Lauer, Matt Hall, Madison Younginer

Hoping to boost a system with few standout prospects, the Giants spent their second-round selection on a potential mid-rotation starter who literally stands out in any crowd. Hjelle—whose Norwegian surname is pronounced "jelly"—generates extraordinary extension toward the plate thanks to his beanstalk physique without exhibiting the mechanical volatility that often fells pitchers his height. Little else about the Minnesotan is exceptional, however, and he'll need to progress his modest pitch mix through further gains in the weight room. Without another tick or two across the board, Hjelle might be just an ordinary pitcher who happens to tower over his peers.

Derek Holland LHP   Born: 10/09/86   Age: 32   Bats: B   Throws: L   Height: 6'2"   Weight: 213   Origin: Round 25, 2006 Draft (#748 overall)

YEAR	TEAM	LVL	AGE	W	L	SV	G	GS	IP	H	HR	BB/9	K/9	K	GB%	BABIP	WHIP	ERA	DRA	WARP	MPH	FB%	WHF	CSP
2016	ROU	AAA	29	0	0	0	3	3	10	11	1	3.6	7.2	8	58%	.312	1.50	4.50	3.83	0.2				
2016	TEX	MLB	29	7	9	0	22	20	107¹	116	15	2.9	5.6	67	38%	.295	1.41	4.95	6.48	-1.4	94.5	61.4	8.3	46.7
2017	CHA	MLB	30	7	14	0	29	26	135	156	31	5.0	6.9	104	39%	.307	1.71	6.20	8.59	-4.6	93.1	55.1	7.8	45.1
2018	SFN	MLB	31	7	9	0	36	30	171¹	154	19	3.5	8.9	169	42%	.288	1.29	3.57	3.80	2.9	93.3	56.9	11.2	49.5
2019	SFN	MLB	32	8	9	0	26	26	136²	132	19	3.6	8.5	129	41%	.309	1.37	4.42	5.09	0.3	92.5	56.6	9.4	46.9

Breakout: 28%   Improve: 52%   Collapse: 17%   Attrition: 11%   MLB: 86%   *Comparables: Edwin Jackson, Claudio Vargas, Odalis Perez*

In 2017, Holland was the very worst pitcher in baseball, below replacement level by any value metric and buried deep beneath it by DRA. With his career hanging by a thread, the lefty chose San Francisco for his revival, betting on himself to win a roster spot, and on the cushy ballpark and savvy coaching staff to perform CPR. Injuries afforded Holland the opportunity he sought, and after just gobbling innings for two months and change, he turned a corner with two midseason adjustments. After working from the third-base edge of the rubber through June 15th, Holland shifted to the first-base side, giving hitters a sharper angle. At the same time, he swapped many of his curveballs for sliders, and the change in his positioning gave the breaking ball more room to work back toward the plate. By year's end, Holland boasted a career-high whiff rate while throwing his highest share of pitches in the zone since 2012. Those improvements came at a price—right-handed foes posted a .798 OPS to lefties' .440—but on balance, he was much better for them. Back on the right side of the replacement-level bar, Holland should have value in a swing role again this year.

Mark Melancon RHP Born: 03/28/85 Age: 34 Bats: R Throws: R Height: 6'2" Weight: 215 Origin: Round 9, 2006 Draft (#284 overall)

YEAR	TEAM	LVL	AGE	W	L	SV	G	GS	IP	H	HR	BB/9	K/9	K	GB%	BABIP	WHIP	ERA	DRA	WARP	MPH	FB%	WHF	CSP
2016	PIT	MLB	31	1	1	30	45	0	41²	31	2	1.9	8.2	38	49%	.257	0.96	1.51	2.64	1.1	93.3	73.3	11	43.7
2016	WAS	MLB	31	1	1	17	30	0	29²	21	1	0.9	8.2	27	65%	.263	0.81	1.82	2.47	0.9	93.7	73.3	12.3	44.9
2017	SFN	MLB	32	1	2	11	32	0	30	37	3	1.8	8.7	29	54%	.374	1.43	4.50	2.75	0.8	93.1	74.7	10.6	43.9
2018	SFN	MLB	33	1	4	3	41	0	39	48	2	3.2	7.2	31	52%	.365	1.59	3.23	3.62	0.6	92.9	68.3	10.6	46.2
2019	SFN	MLB	34	3	1	0	51	0	54¹	50	5	3.0	7.8	47	50%	.298	1.24	3.84	4.45	0.3	92.1	70.6	10.8	44.3

Breakout: 15% Improve: 35% Collapse: 33% Attrition: 8% MLB: 89%   Comparables: Mariano Rivera, Heath Bell, Bob Howry

The Giants have a long list of real good reasons for all the things they've done—even briefly making Melancon the highest-paid reliever (by average annual value) in baseball history. You could cry for the money they've wasted, but that's a waste of time and tears. So instead of dwelling on the $62 million lost, note that Melancon—dogged by forearm woes in his first two seasons out west—ended 2018 with a healthy right arm. Note, also, his velocity climbed over the year, more than half the balls in play against him were on the ground and the advanced metrics saw an above-average pitcher, albeit not a dominant one. If you cast the financial baggage aside, you'll find that Melancon enters 2019 as a decent seventh-inning arm, and you do need those. So forgive everything that forgiveness will allow; there's nothing you or the Giants can do about it now.

Reyes Moronta RHP Born: 01/06/93 Age: 26 Bats: R Throws: R Height: 5'11" Weight: 241 Origin: International Free Agent, 2011

YEAR	TEAM	LVL	AGE	W	L	SV	G	GS	IP	H	HR	BB/9	K/9	K	GB%	BABIP	WHIP	ERA	DRA	WARP	MPH	FB%	WHF	CSP
2016	SJO	A+	23	0	3	14	60	0	59	43	7	3.1	14.2	93	34%	.295	1.07	2.59	2.03	2.1				
2017	RIC	AA	24	0	1	5	19	0	18	15	1	6.0	13.0	26	42%	.333	1.50	4.00	2.63	0.5				
2017	SAC	AAA	24	3	0	0	13	0	17	13	1	4.2	9.0	17	33%	.273	1.24	2.12	4.04	0.2				
2017	SFN	MLB	24	0	0	0	7	0	6²	6	1	4.1	14.9	11	47%	.357	1.35	2.70	2.60	0.2	97.5	52.7	16.4	50.2
2018	SFN	MLB	25	5	2	1	69	0	65	34	4	5.1	10.9	79	43%	.211	1.09	2.49	3.09	1.4	98.4	51	14.8	47.2
2019	SFN	MLB	26	3	1	0	51	0	54¹	43	6	4.6	11.4	69	39%	.306	1.30	3.73	4.29	0.4	97.9	52	15.2	49.4

Breakout: 19% Improve: 36% Collapse: 26% Attrition: 28% MLB: 76%   Comparables: Enrique Burgos, Tommy Kahnle, Bruce Rondon

If there were a GIF dictionary for scouting terms, you'd find one of Moronta pitching under the listing for "max-effort delivery." The short, squat right-hander kicks his leg high, whirls back, loads his right arm deep and throws his weight around in a ferocious uncoiling of his body that sends electric stuff in the general direction of home plate. When his high-90s heaters cross over the white, setting up Moronta's hard diving slider, the tandem rivals those of the game's top closers. But with Moronta's strenuous motion and below-average athleticism come the sort of control woes that would bind fans and managers together in fear if they arose in the ninth. Moronta tunnels his fastball and slider well, racking up whiffs with both, but his inability to massage the breaker in for looking strikes frequently leaves him behind in the count. Already a weapon in middle-inning jams, the Dominican is a few more sliders in the zone from joining the most feared late-game arms in the league.

Aaron Phillips RHP Born: 10/11/96 Age: 22 Bats: R Throws: R Height: 6'5" Weight: 215 Origin: Round 9, 2017 Draft (#276 overall)

YEAR	TEAM	LVL	AGE	W	L	SV	G	GS	IP	H	HR	BB/9	K/9	K	GB%	BABIP	WHIP	ERA	DRA	WARP	MPH	FB%	WHF	CSP
2017	SLO	A-	20	3	0	1	14	0	28¹	20	2	4.1	11.4	36	47%	.265	1.16	4.45	2.68	0.7				
2018	AUG	A	21	6	7	0	19	18	101²	94	13	1.4	10.6	120	46%	.301	1.08	3.72	3.09	2.5				
2019	SFN	MLB	22	4	4	1	29	11	76	76	13	3.3	8.7	74	40%	.312	1.37	4.73	5.45	-0.3				

Breakout: 16% Improve: 23% Collapse: 5% Attrition: 13% MLB: 30%   Comparables: Alec Asher, Johnny Cueto, Simon Castro

Phillips hails from upstate New York, where he endured snowy winters from birth through college. He was a three-sport high-school athlete who also played football and hoops. Even after settling on baseball at St. Bonaventure, he split his time between the outfield and the mound. In other words, this 2017 ninth-rounder checks all the boxes of a potential late-bloomer. While his changeup and command are works in progress, Phillips has the frame and mechanics of a starter, and his two best pitches—a fastball that rides above barrels and a curveball that dives below them—are increasingly en vogue. The chief constraint here is velocity, since the 91s on top-100 lists are sliders nowadays, but Phillips could settle into the back of a rotation after a few more years of focus on his primary craft.

Dereck Rodriguez RHP Born: 06/05/92 Age: 27 Bats: R Throws: R Height: 6'1" Weight: 215 Origin: Round 6, 2011 Draft (#208 overall)

YEAR	TEAM	LVL	AGE	W	L	SV	G	GS	IP	H	HR	BB/9	K/9	K	GB%	BABIP	WHIP	ERA	DRA	WARP	MPH	FB%	WHF	CSP
2016	CDR	A	24	4	11	0	18	18	101	98	7	3.4	8.3	93	41%	.311	1.35	5.08	3.61	1.7				
2016	FTM	A+	24	1	2	0	5	5	31²	29	4	0.6	5.1	18	41%	.250	0.98	2.56	3.81	0.6				
2017	FTM	A+	25	5	2	0	11	11	68	59	7	1.5	7.8	59	43%	.278	1.03	2.51	3.89	1.1				
2017	CHT	AA	25	5	4	0	15	13	75¹	74	9	3.2	7.4	62	41%	.294	1.34	3.94	3.88	1.1				
2018	SAC	AAA	26	4	1	0	9	9	50¹	49	11	2.0	9.5	53	39%	.284	1.19	3.40	4.31	0.7				
2018	SFN	MLB	26	6	4	0	21	19	118¹	98	9	2.7	6.8	89	41%	.257	1.13	2.81	5.18	0.1	94.3	53.3	9.9	48
2019	SFN	MLB	27	7	9	0	24	24	136²	130	19	3.1	7.7	117	39%	.293	1.29	4.50	5.19	0.2	93.8	53.9	10.1	48.6

Breakout: 13% Improve: 21% Collapse: 21% Attrition: 32% MLB: 63%   Comparables: Tyler Wilson, Kyle Lobstein, Albert Suarez

While the outgoing Giants regime fell short in many areas of roster building, its enduring strength was mining gems in minor-league free agency, where they found Rodriguez last winter. A converted outfielder who moved to the mound with the Twins only in 2014, the right-hander was Bobby Evans' parting gift to Farhan Zaidi, who inherited at least a durable back-end starter and potentially much more. Armed with Hall of Fame bloodlines, a sturdy lower half and four pitches he could throw for strikes, Pudge's son defied middling peripherals to rank 10th in ERA among pitchers with at least as many innings. Caution flags—from a .257 BABIP to a 6.9 percent HR/FB rate—abound in his rookie campaign, but so did causes for optimism; his inexperience and low mileage leave ample room for growth on the bump. With gobs of problems to solve and limited financial resources at his disposal, Zaidi will be happy to have a controllable mid-rotation arm in Rodriguez.

Jeff Samardzija RHP Born: 01/23/85 Age: 34 Bats: R Throws: R Height: 6'5" Weight: 240 Origin: Round 5, 2006 Draft (#149 overall)

YEAR	TEAM	LVL	AGE	W	L	SV	G	GS	IP	H	HR	BB/9	K/9	K	GB%	BABIP	WHIP	ERA	DRA	WARP	MPH	FB%	WHF	CSP
2016	SFN	MLB	31	12	11	0	32	32	203¹	190	24	2.4	7.4	167	47%	.285	1.20	3.81	3.44	4.5	96.7	67.3	10	49.5
2017	SFN	MLB	32	9	15	0	32	32	207²	204	30	1.4	8.9	205	43%	.303	1.14	4.42	3.43	5.0	96.3	56.8	11.1	50.5
2018	SAC	AAA	33	0	2	0	4	4	17	17	5	1.6	10.6	20	40%	.286	1.18	5.29	3.86	0.3				
2018	SFN	MLB	33	1	5	0	10	10	44²	47	6	5.2	6.0	30	32%	.287	1.63	6.25	7.20	-1.0	95.1	63.2	9.2	46.3
2019	SFN	MLB	34	9	11	0	28	28	159²	157	23	2.9	7.6	136	41%	.302	1.31	4.52	5.22	0.2	95.1	60.6	10.3	47.8

Breakout: 17%   Improve: 40%   Collapse: 15%   Attrition: 4%   MLB: 85%   Comparables: Ben Sheets, Jake Peavy, Ted Lilly

After leading the National League in innings in 2017, Samardzija ceded his reputation for durability to shoulder inflammation that wouldn't subside. The right-hander made three separate trips to the disabled list, had pain-killing injections and tried various rehab protocols, none of which got the workhorse's arm in working order. His 10 starts came in three separate spurts, all marred by a diminished fastball and trouble getting loose. The same pitcher who struck out nearly 6.5 batters for every walk in 2017 could barely keep the ratio above water a year later. On the bright side, doctors agreed that surgery was unnecessary and rest would eventually get Samardzija ready to pitch again. Assuming that happens, he'll be a fine innings-chewer, the sort of mid-rotation starter who can keep the relievers fresh for bullpenning when the no. 5 spot in the rotation comes around.

Gregory Santos RHP Born: 08/28/99 Age: 19 Bats: R Throws: R Height: 6'2" Weight: 190 Origin: International Free Agent, 2015

YEAR	TEAM	LVL	AGE	W	L	SV	G	GS	IP	H	HR	BB/9	K/9	K	GB%	BABIP	WHIP	ERA	DRA	WARP	MPH	FB%	WHF	CSP
2016	DRX	RK	16	3	3	1	16	10	41	40	1	5.7	5.5	25	62%	.300	1.61	4.17	6.71	-0.5				
2017	DRS	RK	17	2	0	0	8	8	30¹	22	0	4.5	7.1	24	83%	.265	1.22	0.89	4.88	0.4				
2017	DGI	RK	17	1	0	0	4	4	18²	21	2	2.4	8.2	17	59%	.322	1.39	1.93	4.32	0.4				
2018	SLO	A-	18	2	5	0	12	12	49²	64	3	2.7	8.3	46	63%	.379	1.59	4.53	5.00	0.1				
2019	SFN	MLB	19	2	4	0	10	10	41²	48	7	5.8	6.1	28	55%	.318	1.79	6.16	7.11	-0.9				

Comparables: Jenrry Mejia, John Barbato, Alberto Cabrera

Whereas most teams favor athletic, projectable pitchers on the international market, the Giants love them some arm strength, so they jumped at the chance to acquire Santos in the Eduardo Nunez trade two summers ago. Originally signed by the Red Sox, the teenage righty wields a world-class cannon, sitting in the mid-90s while spinning a plus vertical slider to boot. That tandem alone could put Santos on the express train to the big-league bullpen, but some see a future starter if he stops to find a changeup and refine his command on the way. Like most hurlers with elite arm talent and only average athleticism, Santos is prone to losing his delivery; his particular vice is throwing across his front side. Scouts are mixed on whether it's curable, but they're unanimously fond of the arm either way.

Will Smith LHP Born: 07/10/89 Age: 29 Bats: R Throws: L Height: 6'5" Weight: 248 Origin: Round 7, 2008 Draft (#229 overall)

YEAR	TEAM	LVL	AGE	W	L	SV	G	GS	IP	H	HR	BB/9	K/9	K	GB%	BABIP	WHIP	ERA	DRA	WARP	MPH	FB%	WHF	CSP
2016	MIL	MLB	26	1	3	0	27	0	22	18	3	3.7	9.0	22	42%	.263	1.23	3.68	4.57	0.1	94.2	55.4	9.7	45.5
2016	SFN	MLB	26	1	1	0	26	0	18¹	13	0	4.4	12.8	26	40%	.325	1.20	2.95	2.20	0.6	95.0	43.9	14.7	42.1
2018	SFN	MLB	28	2	3	14	54	0	53	37	3	2.5	12.1	71	41%	.281	0.98	2.55	3.34	1.0	94.4	46.1	15.8	50.7
2019	SFN	MLB	29	3	1	30	51	0	54¹	44	6	3.7	11.2	68	41%	.312	1.23	3.38	3.91	0.5	93.8	47.4	14.6	48.1

Breakout: 21%   Improve: 49%   Collapse: 37%   Attrition: 11%   MLB: 97%   Comparables: Francisco Rodriguez, Antonio Bastardo, Jonathan Broxto

If you didn't get Smith on the first or second pitch of your at-bat last season, chances are, you were doomed. His foes hit .378 and slugged .600 on 0-0, 1-0 and 0-1 counts; those who waited longer hit .137 and slugged .185. The ex-Brewer returned from Tommy John surgery with a bulldog mindset and an unhittable slider, the former getting him ahead, the latter putting opponents away. Promoted to closer at the end of June, he thrived in high-leverage spots, trailing only Josh Hader, Aroldis Chapman and Brad Hand in strikeout rate among southpaw relievers with at least 50 innings. A free agent after the 2019 season, Smith is poised to be the market's most coveted bullpen lefty if he repeats that body of work.

Chris Stratton RHP Born: 08/22/90 Age: 28 Bats: R Throws: R Height: 6'2" Weight: 211 Origin: Round 1, 2012 Draft (#20 overall)

YEAR	TEAM	LVL	AGE	W	L	SV	G	GS	IP	H	HR	BB/9	K/9	K	GB%	BABIP	WHIP	ERA	DRA	WARP	MPH	FB%	WHF	CSP
2016	SFN	MLB	25	1	0	0	7	0	10	11	1	4.5	5.4	6	38%	.323	1.60	3.60	5.01	0.0	94.1	61.7	8.4	45.2
2016	SAC	AAA	25	12	6	0	21	20	125²	120	6	2.8	7.4	103	45%	.305	1.27	3.87	3.38	2.8				
2017	SAC	AAA	26	4	5	0	15	15	79¹	94	10	2.5	8.1	71	53%	.340	1.46	5.11	3.86	1.6				
2017	SFN	MLB	26	4	4	1	13	10	58²	59	5	4.3	7.8	51	46%	.316	1.48	3.68	4.62	0.6	93.3	62.4	9.9	45.5
2018	SAC	AAA	27	3	0	0	4	4	24	25	3	3.0	9.0	24	44%	.324	1.38	3.00	3.83	0.5				
2018	SFN	MLB	27	10	10	0	28	26	145	153	19	3.4	7.0	112	44%	.306	1.43	5.09	4.99	0.5	92.6	62.2	9.6	49.9
2019	SFN	MLB	28	7	8	0	24	24	127¹	125	15	3.2	7.7	108	44%	.309	1.33	4.15	4.81	0.7	92.3	62.6	9.7	47.5

Breakout: 17%   Improve: 38%   Collapse: 14%   Attrition: 26%   MLB: 69%   Comparables: Darrell Rasner, Tanner Roark, Cha Seung Baek

Complete-game shutouts are a dying breed in the era of bullpenning, but 20 pitchers earned their managers' trust to record 27 outs last season. The list was a who's who of Cy Young contenders and breakout flamethrowers, plus a few randos like Stratton, who two-hit the Rockies in the midst of their September surge. One of the league's leaders in curveball spin rate for two years running, the right-hander is oddly reluctant to lean on the hook, placing his faith in a fringy fastball that requires pinpoint command. When he has it, he can silence a powerful lineup. When he doesn't, he's just a serviceable fifth starter, another endangered species that openers and multi-inning relievers might soon supplant for good.

Hunter Strickland RHP   Born: 09/24/88   Age: 30   Bats: R   Throws: R   Height: 6'3"   Weight: 225   Origin: Round 18, 2007 Draft (#564 overall)

YEAR	TEAM	LVL	AGE	W	L	SV	G	GS	IP	H	HR	BB/9	K/9	K	GB%	BABIP	WHIP	ERA	DRA	WARP	MPH	FB%	WHF	CSP
2016	SFN	MLB	27	3	3	3	72	0	61	50	4	2.8	8.4	57	47%	.274	1.13	3.10	4.00	0.7	99.5	73.1	12.7	49.5
2017	SFN	MLB	28	4	3	1	68	0	61¹	59	4	4.3	8.5	58	38%	.314	1.43	2.64	5.11	0.0	97.5	68.5	11.7	49.2
2018	SFN	MLB	29	3	5	14	49	0	45¹	43	5	4.2	7.3	37	40%	.277	1.41	3.97	4.49	0.2	97.0	64.3	11.8	46.9
2019	SFN	MLB	30	2	1	3	45	0	47²	42	5	3.8	8.3	44	42%	.293	1.31	4.13	4.77	0.1	97.1	68.1	12	48.2

Breakout: 25%   Improve: 53%   Collapse: 23%   Attrition: 12%   MLB: 91%   *Comparables: Darren O'Day, Jason Frasor, Kevin Jepsen*

The growth of social media has given fans a clearer window into players' lives away from the field than ever before in the game's history. Follow Strickland on Instagram, for instance, and you'll quickly learn that Hunter is, fittingly, an avid hunter who even created his own line of hunting gear. Stay a while, and you'll see pictures of his daughter, Kinsey, throwbacks to his high-school days in Georgia and, of course, his latest 10-point buck. But while it's increasingly hard for players to keep their private lives private, there's a lot about our favorite hitters and pitchers that we don't know until they tell us.

Strickland's anger issues are well documented, and they've boiled over twice in as many seasons. First, there was the culmination of his long-held grudge against Bryce Harper; then there was his losing battle against a dugout door. Those blow-ups have cost the right-hander his reputation, the closer role and two months of the 2018 season. And through all that, he kept a secret.

Last September, Strickland finally revealed that he's spent two years battling ulcerative colitis, cycling through myriad medications that contributed to his fits of rage. He opened up about the condition not to beg for sympathy, but to use his platform to help others afflicted by the same disease. The pain and frustration that come with colitis excuse neither Strickland's behavior nor the dip in his performance. But they do lend context to both, and perspective for those who ripped him on talk radio or Twitter without knowing all the facts.

Strickland's season began with saves in consecutive 1-0 wins over the Dodgers. He was throwing his slider with more conviction after seeking John Smoltz's advice in the offseason, and collecting more whiffs on the breaking ball as a result. Then, after a meltdown in June, he broke his hand. Strickland's velocity and command weren't the same when he returned in August, and a year that started so brightly became a letdown, perhaps prompting his disclosure.

Whatever you now think of Strickland the pitcher—closer or righty specialist—or Strickland the person—real tough guy or fake—you can render a more informed verdict because he opened up. Other players may choose to keep their off-field matters and maladies to themselves. Before judging them, remember that there's usually more to the men than their work and antics on the field.

Andrew Suarez LHP   Born: 09/11/92   Age: 26   Bats: L   Throws: L   Height: 6'0"   Weight: 187   Origin: Round 2, 2015 Draft (#61 overall)

YEAR	TEAM	LVL	AGE	W	L	SV	G	GS	IP	H	HR	BB/9	K/9	K	GB%	BABIP	WHIP	ERA	DRA	WARP	MPH	FB%	WHF	CSP
2016	SJO	A+	23	2	1	0	5	5	29²	25	2	1.5	10.3	34	61%	.299	1.01	2.43	3.38	0.7				
2016	RIC	AA	23	7	7	0	19	19	114	129	11	1.9	7.1	90	48%	.332	1.34	3.95	2.90	3.0				
2017	RIC	AA	24	4	4	0	11	11	67	72	3	2.0	7.4	55	49%	.332	1.30	2.96	3.89	1.0				
2017	SAC	AAA	24	6	6	0	15	13	88²	94	7	2.7	8.1	80	51%	.328	1.36	3.55	3.82	1.8				
2018	SJO	A+	25	0	0	0	1	1	6²	8	0	2.7	9.4	7	43%	.381	1.50	1.35	7.07	-0.1				
2018	SAC	AAA	25	2	0	0	3	3	16²	10	0	3.8	8.6	16	48%	.238	1.02	1.08	3.57	0.4				
2018	SFN	MLB	25	7	13	0	29	29	160¹	163	23	2.5	7.3	130	53%	.302	1.30	4.49	4.08	2.3	93.5	51.2	8.3	49.5
2019	SFN	MLB	26	8	8	0	24	24	136²	135	13	2.6	7.7	117	48%	.318	1.28	3.72	4.32	1.6	93.1	52.1	8.4	50.4

Breakout: 27%   Improve: 42%   Collapse: 21%   Attrition: 29%   MLB: 80%   *Comparables: Robbie Erlin, Juan Nicasio, Tyler Duffey*

The easiest way to meet expectations is to never set them too high. With four pitches, none of them plus, and solid-but-unspectacular command of the lot, Suarez was billed as a back-end starter, nothing more, nothing less. He fulfilled that promise swiftly in his first big-league year, pitching to league-average results for most of the season before fatigue set in down the stretch. Suarez compensates for his lack of swing-and-miss stuff by pounding the bottom of the zone, inducing enough ground balls to keep his home-run rates in check. While his misses above the belt are vulnerable to glove-side opponents and in hitter-friendly environs, the depth of his arsenal is an asset on his third tour through the order. The former Miami Hurricane will never be mistaken for an ace, but as long as the expectations don't rise above what he was as a rookie, Suarez won't disappoint in his sophomore year.

Tony Watson LHP Born: 05/30/85 Age: 34 Bats: L Throws: L Height: 6'3" Weight: 218 Origin: Round 9, 2007 Draft (#278 overall)

YEAR	TEAM	LVL	AGE	W	L	SV	G	GS	IP	H	HR	BB/9	K/9	K	GB%	BABIP	WHIP	ERA	DRA	WARP	MPH	FB%	WHF	CSP
2016	PIT	MLB	31	2	5	15	70	0	67²	52	10	2.7	7.7	58	46%	.232	1.06	3.06	4.35	0.5	95.5	66.5	13.5	46.3
2017	PIT	MLB	32	5	3	10	47	0	46²	57	7	2.7	6.8	35	46%	.333	1.52	3.66	5.55	-0.2	95.0	65.1	14	50.8
2017	LAN	MLB	32	2	1	0	24	0	20	15	2	2.7	8.1	18	62%	.241	1.05	2.70	5.14	0.0	95.2	64.9	13.3	46.7
2018	SFN	MLB	33	4	6	0	72	0	66	54	4	1.9	9.8	72	47%	.294	1.03	2.59	3.31	1.2	94.2	51.2	13.9	54.4
2019	SFN	MLB	34	3	1	0	51	0	54¹	45	6	3.0	9.2	55	46%	.291	1.17	3.65	4.22	0.4	93.7	58.9	13.6	50

Breakout: 9%   Improve: 27%   Collapse: 47%   Attrition: 6%   MLB: 89%   *Comparables: Hideki Okajima, Joe Smith, Scot Shields*

Caught up in the deflated free-agent market of 2017-2018, Watson signed for pennies on the dollar just days after pitchers and catchers reported to camp. The southpaw's financial loss was the Giants' gain, both in the bullpen and on the books, as his creatively structured deal kept his new team from incurring the luxury tax. On the mound, Watson stayed a step ahead of his opponents by tweaking his pitch mix. The 2018 edition featured fewer sinkers and more sliders, along with career-high changeup usage, all of which yielded his best strikeout rate in eight years. An impressively nimble reliever who's thrived regardless of foe, role or setting, he'll be a top setup option again this year.

Logan Webb RHP Born: 11/18/96 Age: 22 Bats: R Throws: R Height: 6'2" Weight: 220 Origin: Round 4, 2014 Draft (#118 overall)

YEAR	TEAM	LVL	AGE	W	L	SV	G	GS	IP	H	HR	BB/9	K/9	K	GB%	BABIP	WHIP	ERA	DRA	WARP	MPH	FB%	WHF	CSP
2016	AUG	A	19	2	3	0	9	9	42	54	7	2.6	6.4	30	57%	.326	1.57	6.21	3.72	0.7				
2017	SLO	A-	20	2	0	0	15	0	28	26	1	2.2	10.0	31	68%	.325	1.18	2.89	3.10	0.6				
2018	SJO	A+	21	1	3	0	21	20	74	54	2	4.4	9.0	74	48%	.274	1.22	1.82	6.27	-0.8				
2018	RIC	AA	21	1	2	0	6	6	30²	30	4	3.2	7.6	26	52%	.289	1.34	3.82	3.80	0.5				
2019	SFN	MLB	22	1	2	0	5	5	25	25	3	3.9	8.0	22	47%	.309	1.42	4.61	5.32	0.0				

Breakout: 15%   Improve: 21%   Collapse: 7%   Attrition: 14%   MLB: 30%   *Comparables: Greg Reynolds, Jonathan Pettibone, Paul Blackburn*

Seventeen-year-olds who can chuck it 96 mph don't grow on trees, so when Webb lit up scouts' guns six weeks before the 2014 draft, he went from an anonymous high-schooler bound for Cal Poly to a coveted prospect in the blink of an eye. The Giants plucked the country-strong right-hander out of their Central Valley backyard, handed him $600,000, and then watched him flounder in the low minors before undergoing Tommy John surgery. Four years into his career, Webb suddenly popped back onto prospect radars last summer, touching 97 while fearlessly pounding hitters inside. The command and secondary stuff lag behind the plus fastball, as you might expect given Webb's resume, but he has the makings of at least a seventh-inning arm, an outcome that seemed remote not too long ago.

Garrett Williams LHP Born: 09/15/94 Age: 24 Bats: L Throws: L Height: 6'1" Weight: 200 Origin: Round 7, 2016 Draft (#215 overall)

YEAR	TEAM	LVL	AGE	W	L	SV	G	GS	IP	H	HR	BB/9	K/9	K	GB%	BABIP	WHIP	ERA	DRA	WARP	MPH	FB%	WHF	CSP
2016	GIA	RK	21	1	0	0	3	1	7	4	0	3.9	6.4	5	63%	.211	1.00	2.57	3.64	0.1				
2016	SLO	A-	21	1	2	0	7	7	25¹	28	1	5.0	7.8	22	59%	.342	1.66	5.68	4.18	0.3				
2017	AUG	A	22	4	3	0	12	11	64	59	0	3.5	8.2	58	63%	.296	1.31	2.25	3.76	1.1				
2017	SJO	A+	22	2	2	0	6	5	33	28	3	2.7	10.4	38	58%	.287	1.15	2.45	3.58	0.6				
2018	RIC	AA	23	3	9	1	33	15	81²	96	6	6.7	8.0	73	55%	.353	1.92	6.06	5.22	0.0				
2019	SFN	MLB	24	4	6	0	25	14	76¹	77	9	5.8	7.8	66	50%	.319	1.66	5.16	5.96	-0.7				

Breakout: 6%   Improve: 9%   Collapse: 4%   Attrition: 10%   MLB: 16%   *Comparables: Ricky Romero, Curtis Partch, Jonny Venters*

Yo-yo'd between the rotation and bullpen at Double-A Richmond, Williams never found a groove during the regular season, so the Giants gave the lefty a second chance in the Arizona Fall League. There, Williams showcased the plus fastball and curveball that keep scouts coming despite the poor control and foul body language that turns them off. The former Oklahoma State Cowboy struggles to throw strikes because of a wacky delivery that he can't repeat, and his changeup is two full grades behind his heater and breaker. With two plus offerings, Williams should at least find work as a specialist, and at 24, he's much closer to settling for that floor than he is to reaching his mid-rotation ceiling.

LINEOUTS

Hitters

HITTER	POS	TEAM	LVL	AGE	PA	R	2B	3B	HR	RBI	BB	K	SB	CS	AVG/OBP/SLG	DRC+	VORP	BABIP	BRR	FRAA	WARP
Gregor Blanco	CF	SAC	AAA	34	194	20	7	2	4	13	23	40	2	1	.247/.337/.382	99	0.1	.302	-4.0	CF(19): -4.2, RF(16): -2.6	-0.6
	CF	SFN	MLB	34	203	19	7	3	2	12	12	58	6	2	.217/.262/.317	63	-3.9	.300	0.9	LF(34): -1.2, CF(23): -1.8	-0.6
Aaron Bond	CF	AUG	A	21	94	12	1	0	0	6	12	29	3	1	.205/.301/.218	71	-1.7	.308	0.5	RF(12): 0.4, LF(11): 0.1	-0.1
	CF	SLO	A-	21	201	38	6	5	14	39	14	58	8	1	.268/.320/.585	126	15.5	.310	3.2	CF(26): -1.4, RF(12): 0.9	1.4
Chase d'Arnaud	INF	SAC	AAA	31	300	54	14	4	12	43	40	65	15	3	.292/.393/.522	127	27.7	.346	2.2	2B(32): -3.9, SS(23): -0.6	1.8
	INF	SFN	MLB	31	100	9	5	0	3	9	4	37	2	1	.215/.253/.366	70	-1.5	.315	-1.0	2B(17): -0.2, 3B(10): -0.1	-0.2
Miguel Gomez	2B	SFN	MLB	25	15	3	0	0	0	1	0	5	0	0	.267/.267/.267	73	-0.7	.400	-0.2	2B(3): -0.1	0.0
	2B	RIC	AA	25	201	16	12	4	4	25	7	28	1	0	.313/.333/.479	110	14.2	.346	-0.1	2B(46): 0.2	0.9
	2B	SAC	AAA	25	236	20	14	1	2	23	2	35	0	0	.273/.280/.368	72	-3.9	.311	0.8	2B(57): -2.9	-0.3
Ryder Jones	4C	SAC	AAA	24	482	57	22	4	11	59	30	106	2	2	.274/.328/.417	99	13.2	.335	-1.0	3B(103): 3.1, 1B(6): -0.2	1.9
	4C	SFN	MLB	24	8	2	0	0	2	3	0	5	0	0	.375/.375/1.125	77	2.3	1.000	0.0	1B(2): 0.0, 3B(1): -0.1	0.0
Brock Stassi	1B	ROC	AAA	28	133	14	6	0	2	13	15	28	0	1	.211/.316/.316	88	-1.8	.259	-0.2	1B(20): 0.7, RF(1): 0.1	0.0
	1B	SAC	AAA	28	84	11	10	0	0	11	19	14	0	0	.391/.536/.547	118	7.2	.500	-1.2	1B(19): 1.0, LF(1): -0.1	0.3
Luis Toribio	3B	DGI	Rk	17	274	44	13	1	10	39	51	62	4	1	.270/.423/.479	160	23.9	.333	-1.8	3B(47): -5.6	1.9

A minor-league free agent find before 2012, **Gregor Blanco** saved a perfect game, caught the final out of a no-hitter and contributed to two World Series championships. If this is the end, he's enjoyed a dream career for a fourth outfielder, and a bright future in coaching awaits him. ⊗ A lithe athlete who looks the part, **Aaron Bond** has the power and speed to be rated AAA someday, but he'll need to smooth his choppy swing path to rise above junk status first. ⊗ There's a little Justin Turner in **Chase d'Arnaud**'s new lift-oriented swing, but it was undone by all the Chase d'Arnaud in his old whiff-prone approach. ⊗ **Miguel Gomez** and CB Bucknor share a common understanding of the strike zone, only Gomez's major-league employment actually depends on his professional development. ⊗ Despite logging only eight plate appearances in the majors last season, **Ryder Jones** experienced the Three True Outcomes and a great deal of pain. He homered twice, struck out five times and gave way to a Brandon Belt walk after dislocating his left knee on a swing. ⊗ Signed for $2.6 million last summer, Dominican shortstop **Marco Luciano** has an explosive swing with precocious all-fields power, which gives him a chance to hit in the heart of the order. The athletic teenager may outgrow the six spot, but his offensive tools project favorably even with a move to third base or right field. ⊗ **Brock Stassi**'s baseball travels took him out to Williamsport and down to Caracas, from the Mexican Pacific Winter League to indy ball in the Atlantic, before a stop with Triple-A Sacramento brought him to within 40 miles of his hometown. The journeyman can resume his odyssey with renewed confidence after a 21-game star turn with the River Cats. ⊗ If you're looking for a diamond in the rough that is the Giants' system, look no further than **Luis Toribio**, whose hitting tools awed DSL scouts last summer. The third baseman will be the main attraction on the complex when he comes stateside this year.

Pitchers

PITCHER	TEAM	LVL	AGE	W	L	SV	G	GS	IP	H	HR	BB/9	K/9	K	GB%	BABIP	WHIP	ERA	DRA	WARP	MPH	FB%	WHF	CSP
Melvin Adon	SJO	A+	24	2	5	0	16	15	77²	82	6	3.9	8.2	71	57%	.338	1.49	4.87	5.91	-0.5				
Juan De Paula	STA	A-	20	2	2	0	10	9	47¹	35	1	4.9	8.7	46	46%	.274	1.29	1.71	5.84	-0.4				
Roberto Gomez	SFN	MLB	28	1	0	0	5	0	9¹	20	0	1.0	7.7	8	51%	.513	2.25	7.71	5.59	-0.1	96.6	58.8	9	54.1
	SAC	AAA	28	1	3	2	14	0	18	23	3	3.5	6.5	13	42%	.339	1.67	5.00	4.12	0.2				
Tyler Herb	GIA	Rk	26	1	1	0	4	4	12²	13	0	2.8	5.7	8	50%	.283	1.34	5.68	3.75	0.3				
	SAC	AAA	26	2	8	0	13	13	70²	85	9	3.6	7.5	59	39%	.357	1.60	5.35	4.53	0.8				
Chase Johnson	RIC	AA	26	2	5	0	18	18	58¹	52	3	3.2	5.7	37	55%	.269	1.25	3.86	4.21	0.8				
Pierce Johnson	SAC	AAA	27	0	0	4	17	0	22²	15	1	4.0	11.9	30	35%	.275	1.10	3.57	3.09	0.5				
	SFN	MLB	27	3	2	0	37	0	43²	38	5	4.5	7.4	36	40%	.268	1.37	5.56	5.06	-0.1	95.2	50.2	11.2	46.2
Casey Kelly	SAC	AAA	28	10	9	0	24	24	136	155	19	2.5	7.3	111	42%	.325	1.42	4.76	4.30	1.9				
	SFN	MLB	28	0	3	0	7	3	23²	28	3	1.9	6.1	16	50%	.316	1.39	3.04	3.49	0.5	93.5	52.7	11.6	49.6
Derek Law	SFN	MLB	27	1	0	0	7	0	13¹	16	2	5.4	8.1	12	42%	.326	1.80	7.43	3.72	0.2	95.9	51.6	11.3	44.7
	SAC	AAA	27	1	3	8	33	0	40²	34	2	2.0	9.5	43	49%	.305	1.06	4.20	2.61	1.2				
Steven Okert	SAC	AAA	26	2	1	1	33	0	31²	37	3	2.3	12.2	43	29%	.395	1.42	4.55	3.16	0.7				
	SFN	MLB	26	0	0	0	10	0	7¹	4	1	0.0	9.8	8	42%	.167	0.55	1.23	2.89	0.2	93.2	41.9	17.2	57.7
Josh Osich	SFN	MLB	29	0	0	0	12	0	12	20	2	5.2	7.5	10	45%	.450	2.25	8.25	6.64	-0.2	96.7	48.5	14.1	49.6
	SAC	AAA	29	0	0	0	37	2	45¹	56	2	3.6	8.3	42	47%	.365	1.63	4.96	3.99	0.6				
Tyler Rogers	SAC	AAA	27	3	2	3	51	0	67²	50	4	3.1	8.0	60	62%	.254	1.08	2.13	3.41	1.3				
Patrick Ruotolo	SJO	A+	23	3	0	6	14	0	18¹	12	0	3.4	12.8	26	40%	.300	1.04	1.47	3.46	0.3				
	RIC	AA	23	1	1	4	23	0	26	18	5	3.5	12.5	36	31%	.245	1.08	2.42	2.95	0.6				
Jose Valdez	SFN	MLB	28	0	0	0	4	0	5	8	3	1.8	7.2	4	47%	.312	1.80	12.60	5.37	0.0	97.0	62.3	7.8	54.5
	SAC	AAA	28	3	4	1	37	0	49¹	44	3	6.4	10.6	58	35%	.331	1.60	4.93	3.94	0.7				
Pat Venditte	OKL	AAA	33	4	2	4	45	0	51¹	30	1	2.5	10.9	62	44%	.244	0.86	1.75	2.78	1.4				
	LAN	MLB	33	0	0	0	15	0	14	11	1	1.9	5.8	9	40%	.238	1.00	2.57	3.15	0.3	90.2	40.2	11.6	51.5
Jake Wong	SLO	A-	21	0	2	0	11	11	27¹	28	1	2.0	8.9	27	53%	.329	1.24	2.30	4.26	0.3				

An all-gas thrower for most of his career, **Melvin Adon** opened eyes in the Arizona Fall League with a sharp slider and improved control. He'll work the late innings in short order if those gains hold up. ⓧ Acquired from the Yankees in the Andrew McCutchen trade, **Juan De Paula** flashes three above-average pitches and has ample velocity projection, making him a potential riser on prospect lists as he matures. ⓧ **Roberto Gomez** is tall and chucks a healthy heater, but neither of his breaking balls is up to snuff. ⓧ Among the many inconveniences of shuttling between Triple-A and the majors, potential up-and-down arm **Tyler Herb** would need to have two barbers on call to maintain his flow. ⓧ Perhaps the most anonymous 40-man roster member in the league, **Chase Johnson** has held the distinction since November of 2016 without anyone noticing. He has a plus fastball and solid changeup, but doesn't miss enough bats. ⓧ A former top-100 prospect, **Pierce Johnson** still has the dandy curveball that earned him that status, but shoddy fastball command keeps him from leveraging his bender into a stable big-league role. He'll spend 2019 in Japan. ⓧ **Casey Kelly** never lived up to his first-round draft position, but last year, he got to start a major-league game with his dad bench-coaching in the other dugout. That's a cooler experience than many of his highly touted peers will ever enjoy. ⓧ With the right-hander's career in a tailspin since 2017, it seems the Trump administration is a real threat to the rule of **Derek Law**. ⓧ Buried on the depth chart by veteran imports, **Steven Okert** still has the slider and deception to reemerge as a useful specialist. ⓧ Last July, FiveThirtyEight published a cheat sheet to help fans determine when to leave a baseball game. ICYMI, it's when **Josh Osich** comes in to pitch. ⓧ **Tyler Rogers** doesn't throw as hard as fellow submariners Brad Ziegler and Darren O'Day, but he's shaved his walk rate over three tours in Triple-A and might have novelty value as a specialist. ⓧ Stocky right-hander **Patrick Ruotolo** uses a deceptive motion to play up his solid-average fastball and curve. He's trending toward a late-inning role with a 37 percent strikeout rate through two-plus seasons in the minors. ⓧ **Jose Valdez** owns a high-90s fastball, a tight slider and the highest HR/9 rate of any Modern Era pitcher with at least 50 career innings in the major leagues. ⓧ Ambidextrous marvel **Pat Venditte** has proven that he's probably overqualified for Triple-A, but his offerings haven't yet translated to sustained, big-league success. That last sentence also reads the same from right to left as from left to right. Just kidding. That would've been cool, though. ⓧ Third-rounder **Jake Wong** ran his fastball up to 97 as a Cape Cod League reliever, but with a handful of average to solid offerings, the Grand Canyon University product deserves a fair chance to start.

SEATTLE MARINERS

Essay by Matt Ellis

Player comments by Nathan Bishop and BP staff

It is Tuesday, May 6th, 2008. Miguel Batista cuts through the fifty-two-degree air as he earns the Mariners' first out of the game, which just so happens to score Ian Kinsler from third base. It isn't quite *foggy*, but there is certainly something heavy sitting in the air. Maybe it's the brisk Pacific Northwest twilight, illuminated by the pale yellow of the LED scoreboard, causing Safeco Field to look like a helipad awaiting yet another nightly delivery of failure. Perhaps it was the carbon dioxide indifference of the 15,000 gathered in the stands on a Tuesday night; always a *Tuesday*, it seems. Nevertheless, it is one of *those* games which would come to define, if not just an era, perhaps the essence of Seattle's long-tortured ballclub. An operating theater of errors, surrounded by folded green plastic seats. A cool breeze.

Mariners fans are a wealthy bunch, in that they have such bountiful options to choose from in finding that one game to sum up what it has all been like. The elders point to the first decade of the franchise, which featured all from the above paragraph save for the frigid air and the live grass. That team found themselves aiming for the ceiling of a fourth-place finish under a concrete sky, but more often than not slipping to sixth, or seventh, the September conversation centering on just how soon the manager will be fired. *Wednesday, June 12th, 1985: White Sox 6, Mariners 3. 9,808 in attendance.* Switch the year out for one that begins with the number 2, and you wouldn't even think twice.

The anomaly, of course, are the Griffey nineties, the Ichiro early 2000s. '95 has become a groan-inducing signifier amidst the faithful, that year which saw the Mariners rally over a thirteen-game deficit to earn their first playoff berth. Both the elders and new blood would be quick to point out the irony that the most hapless team in Major League Baseball is *also* the team which tied the all-time single-season win total in 2001 with 116. Three years later it would be back to the Tuesdays and the 9,808s. The years since have brought with them endless cycles of tinkering, retooling, re-envisioning, re-marketing, each iteration promising that the lessons of the past had finally been learned: GM Bill Bavasi was fired in 2008 after he literally locked the team in the closet for a stern talking to, and ownership caught up with the times in appointing Brewers' Special Assistant to the GM Jack Zduriencik to the position. But promises of a cutting-

MARINERS PROSPECTUS
2018 W-L: 89-73, 3RD IN AL WEST

Pythag	.477	18th	B-Age	29.8	29th
RS/G	4.18	21st	P-Age	29.3	25th
RA/G	4.39	17th	Salary	$157.9M	11th
DRC+	96	16th	M$/MW	$3.6M	19th
DRA	4.31	13th	DL Days	764	3rd
FIP	4.09	17th	$ on DL	20%	24th
DER	.705	17th			

401'
378'   381'
331'   326'

- Opened 1999
- Retractable roof
- Natural surface
- Fence profile: 8'

Three-Year Park Factors

Runs	Runs/RH	Runs/LH	HR/RH	HR/LH
96	96	94	102	100

Top Hitter WARP	3.3 Mitch Haniger
Top Pitcher WARP	4.9 James Paxton
Top Prospect	Justus Sheffield

2018 Hit List Ranking

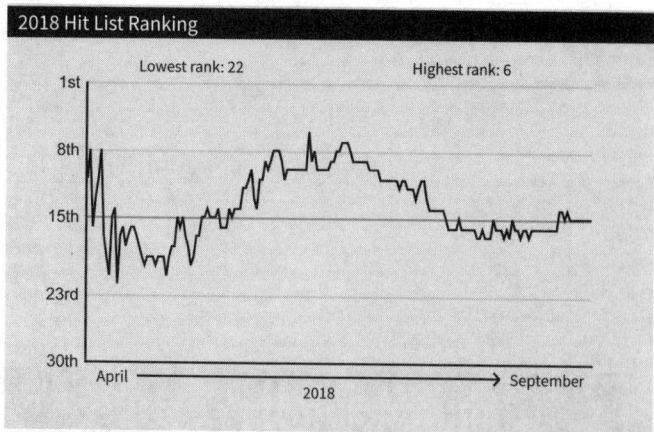

Lowest rank: 22   Highest rank: 6

April — 2018 → September

Committed Payroll (in millions)

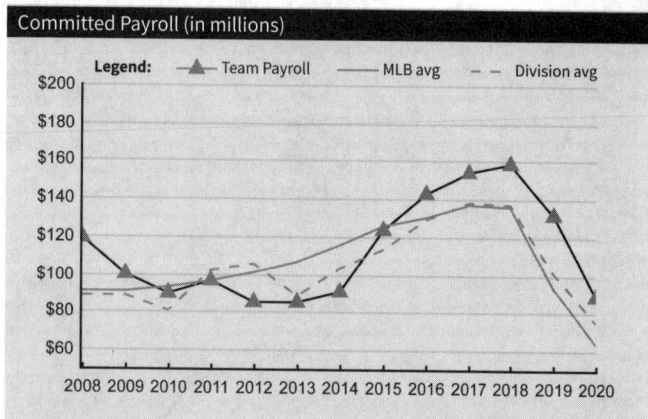

Legend: Team Payroll — MLB avg – – Division avg

2008 2009 2010 2011 2012 2013 2014 2015 2016 2017 2018 2019 2020

Farm System Ranking

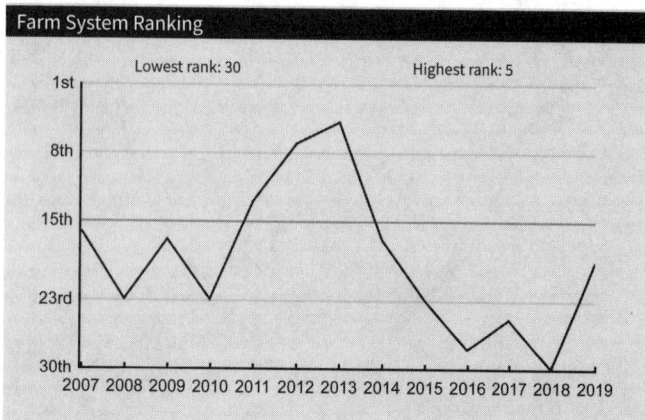

Lowest rank: 30   Highest rank: 5

2007 2008 2009 2010 2011 2012 2013 2014 2015 2016 2017 2018 2019

Personnel

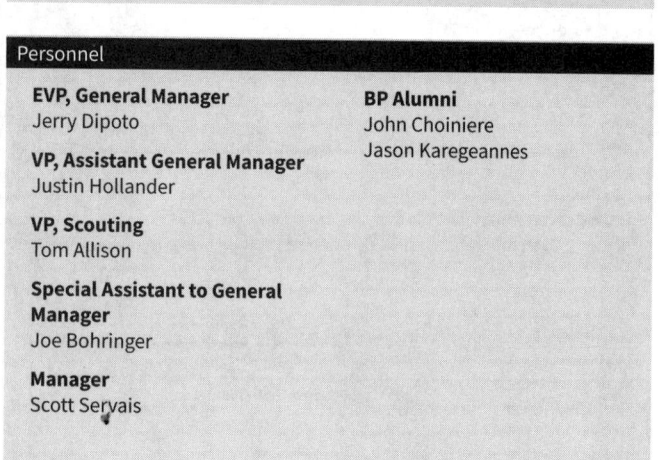

EVP, General Manager
Jerry Dipoto

VP, Assistant General Manager
Justin Hollander

VP, Scouting
Tom Allison

Special Assistant to General Manager
Joe Bohringer

Manager
Scott Servais

BP Alumni
John Choiniere
Jason Karegeannes

edge scout/stat combo soon gave way to arguments over fonts in backroom powerpoint presentations, and so he had to go, too.

Jerry Dipoto arrived in Seattle in the final days of a losing 2015 season, inheriting eight years of Robinson Cano, an aging once-ace Felix Hernandez, a seemingly ageless Nelson Cruz, and a coterie of young-ish homegrown players who managed to stand out amidst seven years of drafting and busting: Kyle Seager, Mike Zunino, James Paxton, Taijuan Walker, Brad Miller, Chris Taylor, and so on. Despite the family tradition of failure, it wasn't the worst situation a new GM could be adopted into. A relatively stable core which only missed the playoffs by a game in 2014, and an opportunity to clean house and implement a vertically-integrated culture in the farm system.

But it soon became clear that Dipoto wasn't planning on implementing only a few small tweaks. He let go baseball's greatest tantrum auteur since Lou Piniella, manager Lloyd McClendon, replacing him with Jerry Lundegaard impersonator Scott Servais. He hired a sports psychologist to run the entire farm system, and invented a new job for a PhD Exercise Physiologist, Dr. Lorena Martin, who was set to be the first-ever Director of High Performance. This was a club that was going to have #synergy, run top to bottom with a Silicon Valley ethos of #disruption set to finally get the Mariners over that hurdle so frustratingly out of reach for so long.

Soon, everyone but the established core was shipped out in an attempt to re-imagine the roster Dipoto had inherited from Zduriencik in a new image. Some moves worked out quite well: Taijuan Walker and Ketel Marte were sent to the Diamondbacks to acquire Jean Segura and Mitch Haniger, both of whom would soon be representing Seattle in the All Star Game. He bought low on a few bounce-back candidates, and designed what was supposed to be one of the best defensive outfields in the club's history to mitigate a fly-ball pitching staff. But the tinkering and the tossing in left the Mariners with the worst farm system in the game. Yet still, on he went, *Trader Jerry*, gutting the system for marginal upgrades with an apparent goal of sneaking into the second Wild Card. Each autumn, the team's momentum appeared spent, and each winter, the team refused to go gentle.

Then, 2018: the Mariners came out of the gates with their best start in over a decade, at one point owning an 88.3 percent chance to make the playoffs. Vindication was in the air, vindication on behalf of a front office whose main goal always seemed to be less winning than *inventing new ways to win*. Dee Gordon, recently acquired from Miami, was sent out to roam centerfield because he was fast, and had a Gold Glove. Wade LeBlanc, who had nearly pitched himself out of a career, earned a multi-year extension after being picked up on a minor league contract. Edwin Diaz, a starter throughout his career in the minor leagues, torched the league as the club's first-ever 57-save closer.

Servais and Dipoto were extended mid-season. It was finally going to happen. But the Mariners were radically overplaying their Pythagorean record, and it caught up to them. First, it was Cano, suspended for 80 games in May after testing positive for a PED masking agent. Then, a fight in the clubhouse that spilled out right in front of the awaiting press. Tensions were mounting. Servais left Hernandez out to die for six innings in a brutal loss to the Rangers, then moved him to the bullpen to send a message. The trade deadline offered few reinforcements, as Dipoto had already given away just about everything he had short of starting a rebuild. In the final series of the season, Segura was benched for lack of hustle. You could read it in their faces, all of them, that they just wanted this whole thing to be over. And as soon as it was, Dr. Martin publicly accused the front office of racism and sexism after her contract wasn't renewed, culminating in a lawsuit and evoking a PR nightmare as the club began planning what to do for 2019. They still had no real prospects.

Amidst all this, or perhaps as a result, Jerry decided the only thing left to do was to tear it down to the foundation, put up a few earthquake-proof walls, and hope the new house stands stronger than the last. It remains to be seen just which warm bodies they will find to fill the double-digits required to field a team by the official rulebook over the next couple of years, but of course, the goal isn't next year. In essence, Dipoto's five-year plan is both a Nietzschean eternal return and a rebirth, an acknowledgement that the driver had the map upside-down. It is a realization that taking the right exit would require backtracking a few miles on the other side of the concrete divider, showing all those same road signs previously seen on the drive up. After stripping the roster down to its bare bones—sending their ace James Paxton to the Yankees, Cano and Diaz to the Mets, amongst others—the Mariners will once again be playing baseball on *Tuesday*. They will be lucky to win 80 games. None of that is new. But at the same time, it *will* be new: There are prospects again, for the first time since 2013, with new names, and new hopes. The system is far from elite, and they will have to strike gold in just about every last one of them for this to work. But it's a system, nonetheless.

By saying they aim to compete by 2021, Dipoto has given the Mariners an aggressive timeline which theoretically will allow them to compete with declining Astros, Yankees, and Red Sox cores. He has overturned his roster for a farm system in the matter of weeks, giving himself that opportunity at full synergy he dreamt of while playing out the hand of Jack Zduriencik. This will be the real test of his front office: not whether they can innovate or sell technocratic expertise, but to see if they can build a winning baseball team from the ground up. They certainly think they can do it.

For fans, however, the hope is unearned, as many Mariners faithful have begun to question just how many This Times they have the patience to sit through. They have sat through many a Tuesday, and you can't quite blame them for wanting something different for once, even if they know deep down inside the Astros are unbeatable, that Felix doesn't have it anymore, that *nobody* is coming through the pipeline for reinforcements. And even with a new set of prospects ready to blossom in the minor leagues, the past decade of Mariner player development hasn't exactly earned the benefit of the doubt by fans skeptical or not—see: Dustin Ackley, Justin Smoak, or Jesus Montero. Why trust them now? Fans want results, not more press conferences.

So the Mariners will play, they will play baseball on Tuesday, June 18th, 2019, and there will be 9,808 fans in attendance. This time, however, they will do it without a concrete dome, they will do it without an exciting young fireballer from Venezuela, the only thing worth watching while the rest of the club withers into oblivion. They will play in 2020 and they will play in 2021, and a young outfielder named Jarred Kelenic might make his major league debut as a pinch-hitter in the bottom of the eighth in a 6-0 loss to the Padres. He might stare at a few balls in the dirt and then make weak contact, dribbling the ball up the middle as he beats out the throw with his freshman legs. Fans might see this and think that thought that they had so many times before, *I was there for his first at-bat*, or *when will the store have his shirsey in*. They might see a 24-year old pitcher who did not spend the 2019 season on the Mariners notch eleven strikeouts in a meaningless start, and they might feel like their good faith has been rewarded, because they were there that day, that Tuesday, September 14th, 2021.

The Mariners will play, because the end of Tuesday brings yet another day. ■

—*Matt Ellis is an author of Baseball Prospectus.*

HITTERS

Braden Bishop   CF   Born: 08/22/93   Age: 25   Bats: R   Throws: R   Height: 6'1"   Weight: 190   Origin: Round 3, 2015 Draft (#94 overall)

YEAR	TEAM	LVL	AGE	PA	R	2B	3B	HR	RBI	BB	K	SB	CS	AVG/OBP/SLG	DRC+	VORP	BABIP	BRR	FRAA	WARP
2016	CLN	A	22	284	38	5	1	1	21	25	48	6	1	.290/.363/.331	96	13.8	.355	1.5	CF(40): -0.8, LF(14): -1.1	0.6
2016	BAK	A+	22	184	19	6	0	2	22	11	39	2	0	.247/.300/.319	80	4.6	.310	-1.1	CF(34): -3.6, RF(7): -0.8	-0.4
2017	MOD	A+	23	412	71	25	3	2	32	45	65	16	4	.296/.385/.400	100	23.2	.356	0.8	CF(70): -1.8, LF(14): 2.1	1.3
2017	ARK	AA	23	145	18	9	1	1	11	15	15	6	1	.336/.417/.448	110	14.3	.373	-1.5	CF(31): 1.5	0.7
2018	ARK	AA	24	394	70	20	0	8	33	37	68	5	2	.284/.361/.412	113	17.1	.331	-1.9	CF(81): -0.9, RF(2): -0.1	1.6
2019	SEA	MLB	25	36	4	1	0	1	4	3	7	0	0	.240/.302/.361	80	0.5	.279	0.0	CF 0	0.0

Breakout: 10%   Improve: 35%   Collapse: 10%   Attrition: 37%   MLB: 58%   *Comparables: Tim Locastro, Darin Mastroianni, Adron Chambers*

Bishop's 2018 was a familiar tale for the organization. A (for the Mariners) Top-10 prospect, the 25-year old was pushing for his first promotion to Triple-A, winning the Texas League Player of the Month award in June by hitting .379. Then, just as real hope for something good and enjoyable began to manifest, Bishop had a fastball crack his forearm in half, and his dreams of becoming a big league fourth outfielder were put on hold.

It was another frustrating setback for the farm system, which has produced more tales of woe than big leaguers this decade. Bishop will most likely start next season back in the high minors, chasing fly balls and lost time in the cavernous center fields of Arkansas or Tacoma.

Jay Bruce RF Born: 04/03/87 Age: 32 Bats: L Throws: L Height: 6'3" Weight: 225 Origin: Round 1, 2005 Draft (#12 overall)

YEAR	TEAM	LVL	AGE	PA	R	2B	3B	HR	RBI	BB	K	SB	CS	AVG/OBP/SLG	DRC+	VORP	BABIP	BRR	FRAA	WARP
2016	CIN	MLB	29	402	60	22	6	25	80	27	83	4	2	.265/.316/.559	117	24.4	.275	0.5	RF(95): -2.8, CF(1): 0.0	1.6
2016	NYN	MLB	29	187	14	5	0	8	19	17	43	0	0	.219/.294/.391	118	-0.5	.246	-2.1	RF(43): -2.3	0.4
2017	NYN	MLB	30	448	61	20	0	29	75	39	102	0	1	.256/.321/.520	119	25.6	.271	0.1	RF(92): 2.3, 1B(11): -0.1	2.3
2017	CLE	MLB	30	169	21	9	2	7	26	18	37	1	0	.248/.331/.477	122	6.6	.283	0.4	RF(41): -2.7, 1B(1): 0.0	0.6
2018	NYN	MLB	31	361	31	18	1	9	37	41	75	2	3	.223/.310/.370	95	1.9	.263	-1.8	RF(64): -0.6, 1B(21): -0.2	0.3
2019	SEA	MLB	32	574	67	31	2	21	76	52	125	4	3	.253/.323/.445	106	16.3	.294	-0.9		1.8

Breakout: 0%   Improve: 41%   Collapse: 8%   Attrition: 13%   MLB: 92%   *Comparables: Jermaine Dye, Cody Ross, Eric Hinske*

When the Mets brought Jay Bruce back before the 2018 season, they must've expected him to be the same steadfast slugger he'd almost always been, good for 30 homers and a mildly disappointing on-base percentage. But last year was a disappointment for all parties, as Bruce spent extended time on the DL while dealing with nagging plantar fasciitis and hip injuries, the kinds of maladies that tend to linger for an entire season and beyond. These injuries sapped his signature power, which, paired with his awkward fit on the New York roster, forced the veteran to make a few adjustments. After learning to play first base and changing his approach to draw more walks, there's one more adjustment on the horizon: he'll now be suiting up for Seattle as the team's latest beefy corner slugger, a human reminder of the Robinson Cano era.

J.P. Crawford SS Born: 01/11/95 Age: 24 Bats: L Throws: R Height: 6'2" Weight: 180 Origin: Round 1, 2013 Draft (#16 overall)

YEAR	TEAM	LVL	AGE	PA	R	2B	3B	HR	RBI	BB	K	SB	CS	AVG/OBP/SLG	DRC+	VORP	BABIP	BRR	FRAA	WARP
2016	REA	AA	21	166	23	8	0	3	13	30	21	5	3	.265/.398/.390	119	11.7	.295	1.3	SS(36): 6.0	1.9
2016	LEH	AAA	21	385	40	11	1	4	30	42	59	7	4	.244/.328/.318	99	10.4	.284	2.1	SS(87): -3.2	1.6
2017	LEH	AAA	22	556	75	20	6	15	63	79	97	5	4	.243/.351/.405	121	28.4	.275	1.6	SS(113): -6.0, 3B(6): -0.7	3.2
2017	PHI	MLB	22	87	8	4	1	0	6	16	22	1	0	.214/.356/.300	89	3.2	.306	-0.2	3B(13): 2.3, SS(6): 0.4	0.5
2018	CLR	A+	23	49	8	1	0	1	4	7	14	0	0	.143/.265/.238	104	-1.5	.185	0.0	SS(8): -0.6, 3B(3): 0.5	0.2
2018	LEH	AAA	23	68	6	2	1	1	7	5	17	1	0	.259/.358/.379	86	2.8	.350	-1.7	SS(16): 0.2	0.0
2018	PHI	MLB	23	138	17	6	3	3	12	13	37	2	0	.214/.319/.393	84	4.7	.286	0.2	SS(30): 0.6, 3B(13): -0.6	0.3
2019	SEA	MLB	24	405	43	15	2	10	41	38	97	3	1	.218/.301/.353	80	4.7	.270	-0.4	SS 0	0.6

Breakout: 4%   Improve: 28%   Collapse: 12%   Attrition: 29%   MLB: 66%   *Comparables: Greg Garcia, Aaron Hill, Daniel Robertson*

After a couple of years of riding a player's hype train once it gets rolling, Philadelphia fans get restless and antsy as passengers, wondering how much longer it'll be before they finally arrive at Realization Station. They'll forever be scarred by the rocky trips aboard the Carlton Loewer and Domonic Brown locomotives, let down by top prospects after years of stockpiling hope as they traveled uphill through the minor leagues. You can only preach patience for so long, and people get tired of varying excuses. In Crawford's case, this season's excuses were two significant injuries that limited him to 49 MLB games and 29 minor league and rehab games, and a slow April that masks a .245/.394/.472 line over 67 PA spread across June and September. All this is to say that there were fewer of the typical prospect-hugging lamentations in Philadelphia when the Phillies sent the rookie to Seattle in the Jean Segura trade. If there's good news in all this, J.P. Crawford will now just get to be J.P. Crawford, not Former Number One Prospect J.P. Crawford. Now we just have to sit back and wait to see what that looks like.

Edwin Encarnacion DH Born: 01/07/83 Age: 36 Bats: R Throws: R Height: 6'1" Weight: 230 Origin: Round 9, 2000 Draft (#274 overall)

YEAR	TEAM	LVL	AGE	PA	R	2B	3B	HR	RBI	BB	K	SB	CS	AVG/OBP/SLG	DRC+	VORP	BABIP	BRR	FRAA	WARP
2016	TOR	MLB	33	702	99	34	0	42	127	87	138	2	0	.263/.357/.529	135	28.7	.270	-0.4	1B(75): -2.8	3.9
2017	CLE	MLB	34	669	96	20	1	38	107	104	133	2	0	.258/.377/.504	137	27.5	.271	-5.2	1B(23): -0.6	3.6
2018	CLE	MLB	35	579	74	16	1	32	107	63	132	3	0	.246/.336/.474	123	12.9	.265	-5.1	1B(23): 0.8	2.0
2019	SEA	MLB	36	601	82	28	1	29	92	76	124	2	0	.259/.361/.489	128	23.8	.288	-3.0	1B 0	2.5

Breakout: 0%   Improve: 28%   Collapse: 4%   Attrition: 7%   MLB: 91%   *Comparables: Paul Konerko, David Ortiz, Stan Musial*

It took him a while to get going, but this late bloomer has been as steady as they come since finding his footing in Toronto. Last season was Encarnacion's seventh straight with at least 30 home runs and an OPS above .800. Sadly, it was also a decline year. His ISO dropped for the fourth year in a row, he posted his highest strikeout rate since his rookie year and his walk rate sagged. It's hard to find hitters with Encarnacion's power who whiff as rarely as he does, so there's reason to believe he could age more gracefully than most 1B/DH masher types, but it looks like age is finally catching up to him. That said, the parrot should still have a good amount of rides to look forward to in 2019.

Eric Filia RF Born: 07/06/92 Age: 26 Bats: L Throws: R Height: 6'0" Weight: 189 Origin: Round 20, 2016 Draft (#597 overall)

YEAR	TEAM	LVL	AGE	PA	R	2B	3B	HR	RBI	BB	K	SB	CS	AVG/OBP/SLG	DRC+	VORP	BABIP	BRR	FRAA	WARP
2016	EVE	A-	23	292	43	19	1	4	46	39	19	10	5	.362/.450/.496	147	28.9	.376	0.6	RF(43): -2.2, CF(7): -0.3	1.9
2017	MOD	A+	24	567	63	28	5	5	59	65	45	9	6	.326/.407/.434	131	39.7	.348	-0.6	RF(106): -11.7, 1B(12): -1.0	1.9
2018	ARK	AA	25	345	44	14	1	2	38	44	30	1	0	.274/.371/.348	111	5.1	.297	-1.1	RF(44): -0.9, LF(11): -0.8	0.8
2019	SEA	MLB	26	251	25	10	0	5	27	24	33	0	0	.259/.332/.373	90	2.9	.282	-0.5	RF -1, LF 0	0.2

Breakout: 0%   Improve: 14%   Collapse: 6%   Attrition: 16%   MLB: 29%   *Comparables: Cole Figueroa, Jermaine Curtis, Daniel Robertson*

Filia is the answer to the question: What if we just make the entire player out of hit tool? With almost no draft or scout pedigree, the 2016 20th-round pick nonetheless spent his first two years in the low minors hitting like a Lumberjack Ichiro. After two years of running out of conversation topics with opposing first basemen, 2018 was poised to be Filia's opportunity to finally gain traction as a legitimate prospect.

Instead, what he earned was a 50-game suspension for a "drug of abuse" before the season started. Within weeks of returning to the field, he was traded to the Red Sox as a PTNBL. 2018, though, was not done tormenting Eric Filia. Like a reverse-Jesus, three days after being granted new life in a new system, he was returned to the Mariners as damaged goods, where his complete lack of power may have forever planted his prospect status in the tomb.

Dee Gordon 2B Born: 04/22/88 Age: 31 Bats: L Throws: R Height: 5'11" Weight: 170 Origin: Round 4, 2008 Draft (#127 overall)

YEAR	TEAM	LVL	AGE	PA	R	2B	3B	HR	RBI	BB	K	SB	CS	AVG/OBP/SLG	DRC+	VORP	BABIP	BRR	FRAA	WARP
2016	MIA	MLB	28	345	47	7	6	1	14	18	55	30	7	.268/.305/.335	77	7.2	.319	3.4	2B(78): -6.3	-0.2
2017	MIA	MLB	29	695	114	20	9	2	33	25	93	60	16	.308/.341/.375	89	26.7	.354	8.4	2B(153): -0.6, SS(3): 0.0	2.1
2018	SEA	MLB	30	588	62	17	8	4	36	9	80	30	12	.268/.288/.349	73	5.0	.304	4.2	2B(81): 2.5, CF(53): 0.7	0.7
2019	SEA	MLB	31	584	75	22	6	6	42	24	86	38	12	.268/.309/.363	86	13.9	.306	3.9	2B -3, CF 0	1.2

Breakout: 3%   Improve: 32%   Collapse: 2%   Attrition: 11%   MLB: 85%   *Comparables: Jimmie Reese, Hughie Critz, Emilio Bonifacio*

Gordon was pressed into starting the season in center field, despite having zero outfield experience in professional baseball. Perhaps it's not surprising, then, that his early-season defense looked a lot like the Contra Code: Up, up, down, down, left, right, left, right. After a mid-May toe injury, followed by Robinson Cano's suspension, the experiment was tabled, and Gordon returned to the keystone, where he proceeded to put up the worst full offensive season of his career.

Always a low walk, BABIP-dependent offensive profile, Gordon spent the summer of 2018 attempting to reach the limits of the hacky slap-hitter profile, setting a career high in swinging outside the zone and a career low in making contact out there. What he found at the edge of that space was a black hole, a .268 batting average, and the lowest walk rate of any qualified hitter in decades. After the addition of Mallex Smith and departure of Cano, Gordon's spot is as secure as any in the lineup. Given his track record, and historically late-aging skillset, he seems a relatively safe bet for a significant bounce back in 2019.

Mitch Haniger RF Born: 12/23/90 Age: 28 Bats: R Throws: R Height: 6'2" Weight: 215 Origin: Round 1, 2012 Draft (#38 overall)

YEAR	TEAM	LVL	AGE	PA	R	2B	3B	HR	RBI	BB	K	SB	CS	AVG/OBP/SLG	DRC+	VORP	BABIP	BRR	FRAA	WARP
2016	MOB	AA	25	236	21	14	2	5	30	30	37	4	3	.294/.407/.462	130	17.9	.340	-0.9	LF(32): 1.4, CF(16): -0.4	1.7
2016	RNO	AAA	25	312	58	20	3	20	64	39	62	8	1	.341/.428/.670	168	43.5	.373	3.4	RF(34): 3.3, CF(34): -0.4	4.3
2016	ARI	MLB	25	123	9	2	1	5	17	12	27	0	0	.229/.309/.404	108	2.3	.256	0.2	CF(22): 1.5, LF(9): 0.1	0.7
2017	TAC	AAA	26	48	6	2	0	3	6	7	5	0	0	.256/.375/.538	123	6.3	.219	-1.0	RF(6): 1.4	0.3
2017	SEA	MLB	26	410	58	25	2	16	47	31	93	5	4	.282/.352/.491	104	16.8	.338	-1.4	RF(94): 4.7, CF(6): 0.2	1.5
2018	SEA	MLB	27	683	90	38	4	26	93	70	148	8	2	.285/.366/.493	120	49.3	.336	-3.5	RF(144): 5.0, CF(35): -2.8	3.3
2019	SEA	MLB	28	613	75	30	3	21	80	58	130	7	3	.263/.347/.445	117	28.4	.314	-1.9	RF 5, CF 0	3.5

Breakout: 2%   Improve: 57%   Collapse: 4%   Attrition: 8%   MLB: 100%   *Comparables: Matt Joyce, Shin-Soo Choo, Carlos Quentin*

Mediocrity has been a constant for Mariner fans, but a steady stream of superstar talent has, since the arrival of Ken Griffey Jr. in 1989, through Randy Johnson, Alex Rodriguez, Ichiro, Adrian Beltre, and finally Felix Hernandez, helped make the experience tolerable. Seventy-six wins or so a year for all eternity isn't so bad when within them flickers some of the greatest individual talent the game has ever seen. With Haniger's acquisition in 2016, Dipoto may have also ensured the team continues its run of having at least one truly elite player.

The mildest praise one can offer the Mariners' right fielder is that he is, by far, the greatest proponent of Dipoto's ballyhooed and seemingly disregarded "Control the Zone" approach. In a hypothetical fantasy draft, where all MLB players are available for all teams to select, Haniger would almost certainly be the first Seattle player picked. Entering his age-28 season, and under club control through 2022, his all-around good-to-great game renders him an above-average player at worst, and one of the game's best outfielders at best. Regardless of wins and losses, Mariner fans have a good chance of at least one truly great player to make the ballpark an enjoyable place to spend summer evenings.

Ryon Healy 1B Born: 01/10/92 Age: 27 Bats: R Throws: R Height: 6'5" Weight: 225 Origin: Round 3, 2013 Draft (#100 overall)

YEAR	TEAM	LVL	AGE	PA	R	2B	3B	HR	RBI	BB	K	SB	CS	AVG/OBP/SLG	DRC+	VORP	BABIP	BRR	FRAA	WARP
2016	MID	AA	24	164	27	12	3	8	34	18	35	1	0	.338/.409/.628	142	18.6	.398	-0.5	1B(25): 0.5, 3B(7): -0.5	1.1
2016	NAS	AAA	24	210	33	16	1	6	30	13	40	0	1	.318/.362/.505	108	17.5	.369	0.0	1B(19): -1.2, 3B(15): -3.5	0.2
2016	OAK	MLB	24	283	36	20	0	13	37	12	60	0	0	.305/.337/.524	105	19.0	.352	-2.4	3B(72): -0.2	1.0
2017	OAK	MLB	25	605	66	29	0	25	78	23	142	0	1	.271/.302/.451	96	5.5	.319	-2.1	1B(39): 0.9, 3B(34): -1.4	0.7
2018	SEA	MLB	26	524	51	15	0	24	73	27	113	0	0	.235/.277/.412	93	-4.9	.257	-2.9	1B(131): -4.3, 3B(2): 0.0	-0.4
2019	SEA	MLB	27	505	56	25	2	20	69	28	108	0	0	.263/.311/.448	105	8.6	.304	-2.1	1B -1	0.8

Breakout: 2%   Improve: 54%   Collapse: 3%   Attrition: 5%   MLB: 93%   *Comparables: Matt Adams, C.J. Cron, Adam Lind*

Have you ever driven a truly fast car out into the middle of nowhere and let it eat? Just settled that bad boy on a level, straight, empty stretch of road and punched the gas? Did you feel that sudden jolt of terror as you realized all the millions of man-hours and expertise that have gone into developing the combustion engine to make it capable of such pure savagery? Did you grip the wheel in terror as you realized none of those man-hours, not even one, went into teaching you how to use all that power the slightest bit? That your very life is literally being held in your hands, and the slightest miscalculation or lapse in concentration will send you flying off the road?

Healy hit 24 home runs last year, and had a lower DRC+ than Alex Gordon.

Jarred Kelenic CF   Born: 07/16/99   Age: 19   Bats: L   Throws: L   Height: 6'1"   Weight: 196   Origin: Round 1, 2018 Draft (#6 overall)

YEAR	TEAM	LVL	AGE	PA	R	2B	3B	HR	RBI	BB	K	SB	CS	AVG/OBP/SLG	DRC+	VORP	BABIP	BRR	FRAA	WARP
2018	MTS	RK	18	51	9	2	2	1	9	4	11	4	0	.413/.451/.609	117	8.0	.514	-0.1	CF(9): 2.0	0.4
2018	KNG	RK	18	200	33	8	4	5	33	22	39	11	1	.253/.350/.431	124	15.2	.300	2.5	CF(43): 5.8	2.0
2019	SEA	MLB	19	251	23	8	1	7	27	13	68	3	1	.199/.240/.333	51	-5.2	.242	0.2	CF 0	-0.6

Breakout: 0%   Improve: 6%   Collapse: 1%   Attrition: 3%   MLB: 10%   Comparables: Engel Beltre, Carlos Tocci, Nomar Mazara

Kelenic, the Mets' first-round selection in the 2018 draft, impressed in his pro debut, laying waste to the rookie leagues despite being a touch old for a prep prospect. Given the limited sample and unlimited hype, it's perhaps no surprise that opinions vary on the athletic outfielder: While the Baseball Prospectus in-house reports see him as a player with five average-or-better tools but perhaps without an elite carrying tool, other voices in the industry see superstar potential. The Mariners fall in the latter camp, targeting him as the prize return of the Robinson Cano blockbuster. They'll have to hope that the hit tool, power and approach all continue to develop in their system, because if they do Kelenic could grow into a well-rounded, dynamic outfield cornerstone.

Kyle Lewis CF   Born: 07/13/95   Age: 23   Bats: R   Throws: R   Height: 6'4"   Weight: 210   Origin: Round 1, 2016 Draft (#11 overall)

YEAR	TEAM	LVL	AGE	PA	R	2B	3B	HR	RBI	BB	K	SB	CS	AVG/OBP/SLG	DRC+	VORP	BABIP	BRR	FRAA	WARP
2016	EVE	A-	20	135	26	8	5	3	26	16	22	3	0	.299/.385/.530	133	12.1	.344	-1.2	CF(27): -0.9	0.7
2017	MRN	RK	21	46	9	2	1	1	7	4	14	1	0	.263/.348/.447	93	4.0	.360	1.4	CF(6): -1.0	0.1
2017	MOD	A+	21	167	20	4	0	6	24	15	38	2	1	.255/.323/.403	105	1.9	.299	-1.5	CF(13): 0.1	0.3
2018	MOD	A+	22	211	21	18	0	5	32	11	55	0	0	.260/.303/.429	87	8.9	.333	0.3	CF(23): -3.1, RF(11): -0.7	-0.2
2018	ARK	AA	22	152	18	8	0	4	20	17	32	1	0	.220/.309/.371	104	0.2	.255	-2.0	CF(29): -2.6, RF(1): 0.0	0.0
2019	SEA	MLB	23	251	24	9	0	8	29	15	67	0	0	.216/.263/.357	62	-3.3	.262	-0.5	CF -1, RF 0	-0.5

Breakout: 1%   Improve: 9%   Collapse: 3%   Attrition: 7%   MLB: 17%   Comparables: Bryan Petersen, Daniel Fields, Jake Cave

The good first: Two year removed from a catastrophic knee injury, Lewis appeared healthy in 2018. His future home on the field remains a corner outfield spot, but the knee allowed him to play nearly a full season without significant issue. Scouts indicate the tools that got him drafted 11th overall in 2016—athleticism, natural power and lift, as well as a rounded approach at the plate, remain. The tools and health combined as Lewis finished the year strong at Double-A Arkansas, hitting .253/.340/.470 over the final month of the season.

Now, the bad: Despite the fog of war that lingers over his performance because of his injuries, Lewis's tools have not yet translated to the performance worthy of a top prospect rating. The offense is going to have to improve significantly in order to justify a projection of anything but a part-time player on a below-average major league roster. While it's too early to make sweeping declarations, Lewis will be entering his age-24 season. It won't be too early much longer.

Noelvi Marte SS   Born: 10/16/01   Age: 17   Bats: R   Throws: R   Height: 6'1"   Weight: 181   Origin: International Free Agent, 2018

As it says in The Good Book, there is a season for everything under the sun; a time to laugh, and a time to weep. A time to sow, and a time to give millions of dollars to teenagers from Latin America. The Mariners have been hesitant to enter that last season, but whatever their scouts saw in Marte was sufficient to offer him $1.55 million, and he became the biggest international free agent purchase of the Dipoto Era. Like all age-16 prospects, Marte is essentially a rough sketch of a person capable of hitting a baseball very far. His size (6'1" 180 lbs) at his age could easily mean he'll grow out of his current shortstop position. More than getting too worked up about the particulars of where and how he plays for the next year or two, his signing is an encouraging sign that Seattle intends to more seriously invest in the international market, something they have done very little of recently.

Cameron Maybin OF   Born: 04/04/87   Age: 32   Bats: R   Throws: R   Height: 6'3"   Weight: 215   Origin: Round 1, 2005 Draft (#10 overall)

YEAR	TEAM	LVL	AGE	PA	R	2B	3B	HR	RBI	BB	K	SB	CS	AVG/OBP/SLG	DRC+	VORP	BABIP	BRR	FRAA	WARP
2016	TOL	AAA	29	100	14	9	0	2	11	14	17	4	1	.188/.310/.365	109	0.0	.212	0.8	CF(9): 0.3	0.4
2016	DET	MLB	29	391	65	14	5	4	43	36	69	15	6	.315/.383/.418	100	23.9	.383	5.1	CF(91): -1.1	1.9
2017	ANA	MLB	30	387	57	19	1	6	22	48	78	29	6	.235/.333/.351	79	9.9	.289	4.9	LF(45): 2.6, CF(42): 1.5	1.0
2017	HOU	MLB	30	63	6	1	1	4	13	3	16	4	3	.186/.226/.441	85	0.0	.179	-0.4	CF(15): -0.4, LF(5): -0.3	-0.1
2018	MIA	MLB	31	287	20	12	1	3	20	32	55	8	5	.251/.338/.343	85	7.9	.308	-2.7	LF(44): 2.1, CF(30): -0.7	0.2
2018	SEA	MLB	31	97	12	2	1	1	8	6	20	2	0	.242/.289/.319	86	-0.5	.300	-0.2	CF(20): -1.6, LF(12): 0.4	0.0
2019	SEA	MLB	32	377	49	15	2	6	31	39	76	16	5	.244/.327/.361	90	8.7	.298	1.4	LF 3, CF 1	1.4

Breakout: 1%   Improve: 37%   Collapse: 4%   Attrition: 14%   MLB: 86%   Comparables: Ryan Freel, Jon Jay, Nyjer Morgan

With a long track record of being useful at every aspect of the sport but the part that involves holding a bat, Maybin was a trade deadline acquisition designed to shore up center field. Unfortunately both for him and the Mariners he was still forced, on occasion, to hold the aforementioned bat. A .600 OPS in Seattle coupled with the team's fall from postseason grace led to diminished playing time, until by season's end he was all but replaced by Guillermo Heredia, the very player whose substandard offense he had been brought in to replace. Much like a two-seamer on the hands, life comes at you fast.

Omar Narvaez C   Born: 02/10/92   Age: 27   Bats: L   Throws: R   Height: 5'11"   Weight: 220   Origin: International Free Agent, 2008

YEAR	TEAM	LVL	AGE	PA	R	2B	3B	HR	RBI	BB	K	SB	CS	AVG/OBP/SLG	DRC+	VORP	BABIP	BRR	FRAA	WARP
2016	BIR	AA	24	49	4	2	0	0	5	4	8	0	0	.222/.286/.267	92	-1.6	.270	-1.1	C(13): -0.2	0.0
2016	CHR	AAA	24	156	14	6	0	2	11	9	17	0	0	.245/.292/.329	101	0.1	.264	1.5	C(39): -4.4	0.4
2016	CHA	MLB	24	117	13	4	0	1	10	14	14	0	0	.267/.350/.337	103	5.0	.295	-0.5	C(34): -3.5	0.2
2017	CHA	MLB	25	295	23	10	0	2	14	38	45	0	0	.277/.373/.340	98	8.2	.330	-1.0	C(83): -9.5, 1B(1): 0.0	0.3
2018	CHA	MLB	26	322	30	14	1	9	30	38	65	0	2	.275/.366/.429	109	21.3	.330	0.0	C(85): -17.6	0.1
2019	SEA	MLB	27	424	48	21	2	9	45	48	69	1	1	.272/.360/.409	113	25.5	.311	-0.3	C -18	0.8

Breakout: 4%   Improve: 38%   Collapse: 5%   Attrition: 11%   MLB: 99%   Comparables: Tucker Barnhart, Josh Thole, Kurt Suzuki

It doesn't seem particularly fair to fret over an on-base machine catcher once available in the minor league phase of the Rule 5 draft, but there comes a time when "incredible bargain catcher" becomes just "catcher." Narvaez found some charge in his bat during his third pro season, curiously right in line with Welington Castillo's PED suspension, and his moderate power and eagle eye combined to make the lefty hitter one of the best offensive catchers in the American League. (Note incredibly low bar, but proceed.) That's an impressive down payment on a long-time starting catcher, but the 2018 White Sox pitching

YEAR	TEAM	P. COUNT	FRM RUNS	BLK RUNS	THRW RUNS	TOT RUNS
2016	CHA	4399	-1.0	-0.8	-1.0	-2.9
2017	CHA	11422	-6.3	-1.5	-0.6	-9.3
2018	CHA	11231	-10.8	-4.6	-0.1	-15.7
2019	SEA	16578	-12.4	-3.5	-0.2	-16.1

staff was not the sort of cast that was going to let Narvaez's defensive flaws go unexposed. It's hard to frame and block pitches that miss their spots by feet, but Narvaez graded out near the bottom of the league in both, and this means he'll likely split time with similar on-base enthusiast David Freitas next year.

Cal Raleigh C   Born: 11/26/96   Age: 22   Bats: B   Throws: R   Height: 6'3"   Weight: 215   Origin: Round 3, 2018 Draft (#90 overall)

YEAR	TEAM	LVL	AGE	PA	R	2B	3B	HR	RBI	BB	K	SB	CS	AVG/OBP/SLG	DRC+	VORP	BABIP	BRR	FRAA	WARP
2018	EVE	A-	21	167	25	10	1	8	29	18	29	1	1	.288/.367/.534	137	11.6	.309	0.3	C(25): -0.2	1.3
2019	SEA	MLB	22	251	26	9	0	10	33	14	62	0	0	.219/.261/.390	67	-0.5	.247	-0.6	C 0	-0.1

Breakout: 4%   Improve: 5%   Collapse: 7%   Attrition: 10%   MLB: 15%   *Comparables: Blake Swihart, Austin Hedges, Christian Vazquez*

If you're an offense-first catcher, you better provide some offense, and that's exactly what Raleigh did in his first season of professional ball. A third-round pick, the Florida State product presents a big silhouette behind the dish, and his pop times will require a lot of slide-stepping from whoever is pitching to him. Still, his receiving skills are solid to above-average and the possibility, even if small, that he can turn into a plus bat at catcher will keep him back there until he definitively proves he can't handle it. Given the Mariners organization-wide concerns at the position, Raleigh should advance quickly, provided that the bat leads.

Julio Rodriguez RF   Born: 12/29/00   Age: 18   Bats: R   Throws: R   Height: 6'3"   Weight: 180   Origin: International Free Agent, 2017

YEAR	TEAM	LVL	AGE	PA	R	2B	3B	HR	RBI	BB	K	SB	CS	AVG/OBP/SLG	DRC+	VORP	BABIP	BRR	FRAA	WARP
2018	DMR	RK	17	255	50	13	9	5	36	30	40	10	0	.315/.404/.525	146	33.9	.364	0.6	RF(45): 8.1, CF(6): -0.1	2.6
2019	SEA	MLB	18	251	19	6	4	4	24	17	66	0	0	.189/.243/.312	51	-7.3	.240	0.5	RF 2, CF 0	-0.6

Comparables: Adalberto Mondesi, Wilmer Flores, Tommy Brown

It's too early to get excited about Rodriguez, logically. Teenagers dominating other teenagers in the DSL is a world away from a star on the big league level. Trying to extrapolate something meaningful from the stats is a foolish, empty endeavor. Fortunately, there are professionals whose job it is to watch those same teenagers play baseball, and tell us which ones they think are going to be very, very good. We call them "scouts," and a good portion of them are very high on Rodriguez, to the point that he just may have the highest ceiling of any prospect in Seattle's farm. Of course even if he pans out perfectly he won't be a Mariner until practically the entire current big league roster is gone (or will get traded away for their sake), and there are far more ways a player this young can wash out than succeed, but if you have followed Seattle's farm system over the past 3-5 years you're readily acquainted with many of them. So, for 2019, Rodriguez will be a shiny beacon of hope and possibility. The Mariners and their fans can certainly use it.

Kyle Seager 3B   Born: 11/03/87   Age: 31   Bats: L   Throws: R   Height: 6'0"   Weight: 210   Origin: Round 3, 2009 Draft (#82 overall)

YEAR	TEAM	LVL	AGE	PA	R	2B	3B	HR	RBI	BB	K	SB	CS	AVG/OBP/SLG	DRC+	VORP	BABIP	BRR	FRAA	WARP
2016	SEA	MLB	28	676	89	36	3	30	99	69	108	3	1	.278/.359/.499	125	46.5	.295	1.8	3B(156): 21.5	7.1
2017	SEA	MLB	29	650	72	33	1	27	88	58	110	2	1	.249/.323/.450	108	21.1	.262	-5.6	3B(154): 7.4	3.3
2018	SEA	MLB	30	630	62	36	1	22	78	38	138	2	2	.221/.273/.400	87	8.1	.251	-1.6	3B(154): 11.2, 2B(1): 0.0	2.3
2019	SEA	MLB	31	553	64	32	2	19	72	49	98	3	2	.258/.333/.441	112	19.6	.289	-1.5	3B 9	3.1

Breakout: 0%   Improve: 45%   Collapse: 4%   Attrition: 4%   MLB: 95%   *Comparables: Mike Lowell, Eric Soderholm, Brooks Robinson*

When your entire identity and value is built upon being practically the same player year after year after year, what do you do when it's clear you have to change? Since his first full season in 2012, Seager has been one of baseball's most dependable second-level stars, good for 25+ home runs, and solid-to-great defense at third base. He's also been remarkably durable, having never played in fewer than 154 games in a full season. That foundational dependability began to erode with a bad slump in the second half of 2017, and careened into a near full-on offensive collapse in 2018. Career-worst walk and strikeout rates are rarely a successful combination, and the question now is: What comes next? Seager is only 31 in 2019, and conversations with scouts back up observation: His physical skills are intact. With a batted ball profile completely in line with the rest of his career, and an increasing number of defensive shifts that nullify that profile, the Mariners and their third baseman are at a crossroads. With $58 million still left on his contract, everyone involved needs to hope for a significant bounceback.

Mallex Smith OF   Born: 05/06/93   Age: 26   Bats: L   Throws: R   Height: 5'10"   Weight: 180   Origin: Round 5, 2012 Draft (#165 overall)

YEAR	TEAM	LVL	AGE	PA	R	2B	3B	HR	RBI	BB	K	SB	CS	AVG/OBP/SLG	DRC+	VORP	BABIP	BRR	FRAA	WARP
2016	ATL	MLB	23	215	28	7	4	3	22	20	48	16	8	.238/.316/.365	75	5.0	.302	0.2	CF(35): 2.9, LF(22): 0.2	0.4
2017	DUR	AAA	24	205	26	7	4	3	10	17	45	21	8	.263/.325/.392	92	5.7	.333	2.3	CF(33): 5.1, LF(7): 0.5	1.1
2017	TBA	MLB	24	282	33	8	4	2	12	23	62	16	5	.270/.329/.355	76	10.8	.347	2.1	CF(51): -5.2, LF(24): 0.2	-0.1
2018	TBA	MLB	25	544	65	27	10	2	40	47	98	40	12	.296/.367/.406	95	28.8	.366	4.4	CF(71): -7.0, RF(47): -1.9	0.7
2019	SEA	MLB	26	552	68	20	6	8	47	46	112	34	12	.244/.315/.361	88	15.5	.295	2.3	CF -2	1.4

Breakout: 3%   Improve: 56%   Collapse: 11%   Attrition: 19%   MLB: 95%   *Comparables: Jacoby Ellsbury, Denard Span, Wally Moses*

After spending a few hours as a member of Mariners in early 2017, Seattle decided to acquire Smith again a year later. The club missed out on a fantastic season that saw Smith become one of the more dynamic offensive players in the American League. He led the league with 10 triples and finished second behind Whit Merrifield with 40 steals. He showed good plate discipline and used his speed to propel his average around .300 despite hitting half of his balls in play on the ground. Smith manned the outfield corners most days, playing alongside Kevin Kiermaier, but also had to play a lot of center field due to his former teammate's fragility; the defensive metrics, FRAA in particular, didn't consider his performance to match what you'd expect from his tools.

Denard Span LF Born: 02/27/84 Age: 35 Bats: L Throws: L Height: 6'0" Weight: 210 Origin: Round 1, 2002 Draft (#20 overall)

YEAR	TEAM	LVL	AGE	PA	R	2B	3B	HR	RBI	BB	K	SB	CS	AVG/OBP/SLG	DRC+	VORP	BABIP	BRR	FRAA	WARP
2016	SFN	MLB	32	637	70	23	5	11	53	53	79	12	7	.266/.331/.381	97	21.5	.291	-0.2	CF(137): -14.9	0.5
2017	SFN	MLB	33	542	73	31	5	12	43	40	69	12	7	.272/.329/.427	95	24.4	.295	0.3	CF(123): -11.3	0.5
2018	TBA	MLB	34	173	27	7	1	4	28	28	24	6	2	.238/.364/.385	108	5.4	.259	1.5	LF(34): 1.8	0.9
2018	SEA	MLB	34	328	36	15	6	7	30	23	55	3	2	.272/.329/.435	101	13.9	.307	-0.6	LF(86): -0.8, CF(1): 0.1	0.8
2019	SEA	MLB	35	482	60	23	4	10	46	39	70	10	4	.263/.330/.404	103	15.5	.291	0.3	LF 3, CF 0	1.9

Breakout: 1%   Improve: 27%   Collapse: 7%   Attrition: 11%   MLB: 72%   Comparables: Shannon Stewart, Rip Radcliff, Harvey Kuenn

Every workplace has a person who has been there forever, shows up on time, and leaves their station impeccably clean at quitting time. Span is that worker. Happily raising his family near his hometown of Tampa, a May trade sent him to Seattle, as far away from Florida as Major League Baseball can take a person. Whatever effect is had on his mindset or personal life, it had zero on his ability to continue to be what he always has been: a perfectly fine baseball player. Aged 34 and with a beard aged 44, Span produced his usual above-average offense with the Mariners, played an adequate left field, and seemed to fit himself perfectly into whatever role the team needed him to fill. He is very good at his job, and there's little reason to expect one year or a little more gray to change that.

Josh Stowers CF Born: 02/25/97 Age: 22 Bats: R Throws: R Height: 6'1" Weight: 200 Origin: Round 2, 2018 Draft (#54 overall)

YEAR	TEAM	LVL	AGE	PA	R	2B	3B	HR	RBI	BB	K	SB	CS	AVG/OBP/SLG	DRC+	VORP	BABIP	BRR	FRAA	WARP
2018	EVE	A-	21	244	32	15	0	5	28	37	57	20	4	.260/.380/.410	115	12.1	.336	0.5	CF(47): -2.8	0.9
2019	SEA	MLB	22	251	27	7	0	7	25	22	72	9	2	.192/.260/.314	54	-4.3	.240	0.3	CF -2	-0.6

Breakout: 0%   Improve: 2%   Collapse: 1%   Attrition: 3%   MLB: 3%   Comparables: Roger Bernadina, Darrell Ceciliani, Michael Taylor

Seattle's second-round pick in last year's draft, Stowers had a thoroughly encouraging, if unspectacular, debut in professional baseball. A gifted runner and defender in center field, the Louisville product also features a sound knowledge of the strike zone, and the combination of bat speed and swing plane that could provide the current game's preferred offensive profile, AKA fly balls all over the place. Whether the fly balls travel far enough to turn into dingers, or if his range allows him to stay in center or elicits a move to left field, Stowers' athleticism is a shot of adrenaline to one of the game's least athletic farm systems.

Ichiro Suzuki RF Born: 10/22/73 Age: 45 Bats: L Throws: R Height: 5'11" Weight: 175 Origin: International Free Agent, 2000

YEAR	TEAM	LVL	AGE	PA	R	2B	3B	HR	RBI	BB	K	SB	CS	AVG/OBP/SLG	DRC+	VORP	BABIP	BRR	FRAA	WARP
2016	MIA	MLB	42	365	48	15	5	1	22	30	42	10	2	.291/.354/.376	94	8.5	.329	-1.7	RF(54): -1.9, CF(14): -0.7	0.6
2017	MIA	MLB	43	215	19	6	0	3	20	17	35	1	1	.255/.318/.332	79	-3.0	.297	-2.7	RF(16): -0.1, CF(10): -1.3	-0.1
2018	SEA	MLB	44	47	5	0	0	0	0	3	7	0	0	.205/.255/.205	73	-2.6	.243	0.9	LF(11): -0.2, RF(1): 0.1	0.0
2019	SEA	MLB	45	251	28	10	1	3	20	22	43	4	1	.252/.322/.351	83	0.5	.297	-1.1	LF 1, RF 0	0.2

Breakout: 0%   Improve: 10%   Collapse: 5%   Attrition: 5%   MLB: 57%   Comparables: Omar Vizquel, Sam Rice, Pete Rose

What then to make of this man; this slap-hitting, fence-climbing, quote-generating world conqueror? His in-game achievements—the infield single, the broken bat looper parachuted over the third baseman's head, the stolen base—are, by design, performed in second, and at incredible speed. By contrast his career accomplishments have taken a full lifetime to accumulate.

This comment should serve as an attempt to summarize that lifetime. It should flail and sputter as it somehow attempts to describe one our sport's truly unique athletes, and men. It should try to put a bow on the records, the pressure his game put on a defense, his ability to dominate the sport without hitting a ball out of the infield. It would fail to do all that, but it should try.

It will not try, however, because Ichiro will not let it. He is 45 years old, and will not stop playing baseball. In 2018 he exercised every bit of the cache his legendary career allowed him, and, after a few months of replacement-level play for the Mariners, built his own job title and duties out of thin air. At every turn he, and anyone associated with Seattle, pointed out that he "is not retired".

The Mariners open the 2019 season in Ichiro's native Japan. He will play, at least a bit, and the duty of writing his career's summary in these pages will pass to next year's annual. This is good because, like the man himself, it is impossible.

Dan Vogelbach 1B   Born: 12/17/92   Age: 26   Bats: L   Throws: R   Height: 6'0"   Weight: 250   Origin: Round 2, 2011 Draft (#68 overall)

YEAR	TEAM	LVL	AGE	PA	R	2B	3B	HR	RBI	BB	K	SB	CS	AVG/OBP/SLG	DRC+	VORP	BABIP	BRR	FRAA	WARP
2016	IOW	AAA	23	365	53	18	2	16	64	55	67	0	0	.318/.425/.548	140	35.7	.362	-1.8	1B(76): -3.0	1.9
2016	TAC	AAA	23	198	26	7	0	7	32	42	34	0	0	.240/.404/.422	144	8.9	.263	-3.1	1B(25): -0.9	1.0
2016	SEA	MLB	23	13	0	0	0	0	0	1	6	0	0	.083/.154/.083	63	-2.3	.167	-0.4	1B(4): -0.3	-0.1
2017	TAC	AAA	24	541	65	25	0	17	83	76	98	3	1	.290/.388/.455	113	20.9	.332	-7.3	1B(81): -8.3	0.2
2017	SEA	MLB	24	31	0	1	0	0	2	3	9	0	0	.214/.290/.250	86	-3.0	.316	-1.2	1B(7): -0.3	-0.2
2018	TAC	AAA	25	378	54	16	0	20	60	77	59	0	1	.290/.434/.545	161	27.8	.299	-6.0	1B(53): -2.9	2.7
2018	SEA	MLB	25	102	9	2	0	4	13	13	26	0	0	.207/.324/.368	91	1.0	.246	0.6	1B(20): -1.1	0.0
2019	SEA	MLB	26	66	8	3	0	2	8	8	15	0	0	.246/.340/.421	98	0.6	.288	-0.1	1B -1	0.0

Breakout: 4%   Improve: 26%   Collapse: 11%   Attrition: 27%   MLB: 73%   *Comparables: Kila Ka'aihue, Tyler White, Vince Belnome*

The Mariners traded for Vogelbach late in 2016 believing two things: Firstly, that his polished, disciplined approach at the plate and unique frame could translate into an above-average offensive bat, and secondly, that their player development staff could coax a passable defensive first basemen out of him. They were, it seems, half-right. Over more than two seasons in Triple-A Tacoma, Vogelbach has abused pitchers who throw him strikes, and been content to lope to first base when they have not. His defense, despite sincere effort from all parties, has remained decidedly inadequate, if not quite at Dae-Ho Lee levels, to the point that the Mariners acquired Ryon Healy (on purpose even!) before the 2018 season. Vogelbach's future in the majors, if he is to have one, is almost certainly at designated hitter. The rumors, it turns out, are true. First base is incredibly hard.

Evan White 1B   Born: 04/26/96   Age: 23   Bats: R   Throws: L   Height: 6'3"   Weight: 205   Origin: Round 1, 2017 Draft (#17 overall)

YEAR	TEAM	LVL	AGE	PA	R	2B	3B	HR	RBI	BB	K	SB	CS	AVG/OBP/SLG	DRC+	VORP	BABIP	BRR	FRAA	WARP
2017	EVE	A-	21	55	6	1	1	3	12	6	6	1	1	.277/.345/.532	139	3.7	.250	-0.1	1B(8): -0.6	0.2
2018	MOD	A+	22	538	72	27	7	11	66	52	103	4	3	.303/.375/.458	114	38.3	.363	-0.5	1B(106): 5.5	2.0
2019	SEA	MLB	23	251	25	8	1	8	30	16	57	0	0	.231/.280/.379	74	-4.6	.268	-0.3	1B 1	-0.3

Breakout: 4%   Improve: 11%   Collapse: 2%   Attrition: 7%   MLB: 16%   *Comparables: Shane Peterson, Ronald Guzman, David Cooper*

The Mariners farm system has long been a trash-filled, post-apocalyptic wasteland, but White may just be the plant from WALL-E, poking his head above the rubble, telling us it's safe to return. A superb athlete for a first baseman, White lowered his hands to generate a better swing plane. The result was a very encouraging power explosion in August. White slugged over .700 in the season's final month, while continuing to show promising contact and on-base skills. It's still a little weird that the M's haven't at least tried out his athleticism at a corner outfield spot, but this new version of his bat might hold up even at first.

For a 22-year-old, first-round draft pick, destroying High-A pitching doesn't put White exceptionally far ahead on the development curve, though he built upon the performance in the Arizona Fall League. However, it also doesn't put him woefully, distressingly behind, and for the Mariners, that's an accomplishment in and of itself.

PITCHERS

Dan Altavilla RHP   Born: 09/08/92   Age: 26   Bats: R   Throws: R   Height: 5'11"   Weight: 200   Origin: Round 5, 2014 Draft (#141 overall)

YEAR	TEAM	LVL	AGE	W	L	SV	G	GS	IP	H	HR	BB/9	K/9	K	GB%	BABIP	WHIP	ERA	DRA	WARP	MPH	FB%	WHF	CSP
2016	WTN	AA	23	7	3	16	43	0	56²	40	3	3.5	10.3	65	48%	.261	1.09	1.91	3.63	0.7				
2016	SEA	MLB	23	0	0	0	15	0	12¹	11	0	0.7	7.3	10	50%	.306	0.97	0.73	3.38	0.2	99.2	66.3	12.8	53.3
2017	TAC	AAA	24	2	0	6	20	0	23¹	17	1	5.8	13.9	36	44%	.340	1.37	1.54	2.26	0.8				
2017	SEA	MLB	24	1	1	0	41	0	46²	43	9	3.9	10.0	52	38%	.281	1.35	4.24	3.88	0.7	98.8	62.4	13.9	48.5
2018	SEA	MLB	25	3	2	0	22	0	20²	11	2	6.5	10.0	23	40%	.209	1.26	2.61	3.45	0.4	98.4	52.8	13.4	44.3
2018	TAC	AAA	25	0	2	0	9	1	6²	9	2	5.4	9.4	7	35%	.333	1.95	9.45	2.97	0.2				
2019	SEA	MLB	26	3	1	5	57	0	60	52	8	4.6	10.0	67	42%	.285	1.37	4.57	4.93	0.1	98.3	60.7	13.9	48.8

Breakout: 29%   Improve: 39%   Collapse: 18%   Attrition: 21%   MLB: 76%   *Comparables: Fernando Nieve, Michael Stutes, Hansel Robles*

It's a hard fact of life that things change. It used to be when a fella had a fastball that averaged 96 mph and a slider that moved through the multiverse on its way to home, he could count on them. Getting through life one eighth inning at a time wasn't easy, but it got one by, and that was more than many relievers with slower fastballs could say. (Pause here to spit dramatically into a spittoon, the chaw echoing loudly in an empty saloon.) These days, though, seems everybody everywhere has a 96 mph heater, and what made someone like Altavilla a few years ago now is just keeping him from being left behind. When the world's caught up to you and you're no longer special, the real trick is learning to survive. That's Altavilla's challenge for 2019.

Sam Carlson RHP   Born: 12/03/98   Age: 20   Bats: R   Throws: R   Height: 6'4"   Weight: 195   Origin: Round 2, 2017 Draft (#55 overall)

YEAR	TEAM	LVL	AGE	W	L	SV	G	GS	IP	H	HR	BB/9	K/9	K	GB%	BABIP	WHIP	ERA	DRA	WARP	MPH	FB%	WHF	CSP
2019	SEA	MLB	20	2	3	0	7	7	31²	32	5	4.8	7.0	25	53%	.274	1.54	6.07	6.55	-0.4				

Comparables: Deolis Guerra, Alex Burnett, Juan Minaya

For someone a year from being old enough to legally drink, Carlson is awfully young to feel so behind. After spending high school pitching in the brief Minnesota spring, Seattle's second-round pick from 2017 threw three innings in the AZL before being shut down with elbow discomfort. When an offseason of rest did not provide healing, further investigation revealed a torn UCL. Tommy John surgery last July means Carlson may not pitch until 2020. He may be able to order that beer before he steps on a mound again.

Ryan Cook RHP   Born: 06/30/87   Age: 32   Bats: R   Throws: R   Height: 6'2"   Weight: 215   Origin: Round 27, 2008 Draft (#828 overall)

YEAR	TEAM	LVL	AGE	W	L	SV	G	GS	IP	H	HR	BB/9	K/9	K	GB%	BABIP	WHIP	ERA	DRA	WARP	MPH	FB%	WHF	CSP
2018	TAC	AAA	31	0	2	3	34	0	33¹	28	2	4.6	10.0	37	58%	.302	1.35	2.16	2.93	0.8				
2018	SEA	MLB	31	2	1	0	19	0	17	15	4	3.7	12.2	23	56%	.282	1.29	5.29	3.85	0.2	96.0	67.3	10.6	46.7
2019	SEA	MLB	32	2	1	0	33	0	35	32	5	4.9	8.8	34	49%	.284	1.46	5.06	5.46	-0.2	95.0	66.7	10.5	46.3

Breakout: 19%   Improve: 35%   Collapse: 9%   Attrition: 19%   MLB: 56%   *Comparables: Blake Wood, Brandon Gomes, Chris Hatcher*

A player's statistical summary reduces seasons missed with injury to nothing. As far as fans and analysts are concerned the season—or in Cook's case, seasons—simply do not exist. For the player of course, our informational gaps are filled with surgery, painful rehab, potential lost earning potential, and questioning whether one's chosen vocation is still a viable career.

Cook returned to a major league mound last season for the first time since 2015. His results-based numbers are skewed by some small sample size weirdness and obscure encouraging factors, like a career-high strike rate, and a fastball velocity higher than it has ever been. Whatever months and years of toil, pain, and doubt filled his recent years seem to have staved off the one thing we fans notice less than a lost season: An end.

Zach Duke LHP   Born: 04/19/83   Age: 36   Bats: L   Throws: L   Height: 6'2"   Weight: 210   Origin: Round 20, 2001 Draft (#594 overall)

YEAR	TEAM	LVL	AGE	W	L	SV	G	GS	IP	H	HR	BB/9	K/9	K	GB%	BABIP	WHIP	ERA	DRA	WARP	MPH	FB%	WHF	CSP
2016	CHA	MLB	33	2	0	1	53	0	37²	31	2	3.8	10.0	42	65%	.299	1.25	2.63	3.92	0.5	92.4	56.9	12.4	45.2
2016	SLN	MLB	33	0	1	1	28	0	23¹	17	0	5.0	10.0	26	60%	.293	1.29	1.93	4.65	0.1	92.1	67.4	9.5	48.4
2017	SLN	MLB	34	1	1	0	27	0	18¹	13	3	2.9	5.9	12	52%	.196	1.04	3.93	5.47	-0.1	89.7	57.3	13	47.9
2018	MIN	MLB	35	3	4	0	45	0	37¹	44	0	3.6	9.4	39	60%	.370	1.58	3.62	3.73	0.5	89.9	47.2	10.9	45.8
2018	SEA	MLB	35	2	1	0	27	0	14²	13	1	3.7	7.4	12	60%	.286	1.30	5.52	3.65	0.2	90.4	53.9	11	43.7
2019	SEA	MLB	36	2	1	1	41	0	43	39	5	4.2	8.7	41	55%	.293	1.38	4.39	4.73	0.1	89.5	53.1	11.1	45.4

Breakout: 23%   Improve: 43%   Collapse: 26%   Attrition: 5%   MLB: 78%   *Comparables: Fernando Rodney, Francisco Cordero, Scott Eyre*

Informed baseball fans are familiar with the process/results matrix: "Good process/good result", "Bad process/Good result", etc. Fans of specific baseball teams root for "good/good" at all times, but for fans of sport and chaos, "bad process/good result", and "good process/bad result" are the very lifeblood the courses through the heart of sports itself.

When healthy, Duke—LOOGY Edition—has spent years performing with minimal variance. The Mariners acquired what appeared to be a very standard, perhaps even above-average Zach Duke at the trade deadline for two non-prospects. It was a fine trade, and naturally what the Mariners received was the worst of all possible Zach Dukes, with nearly a quarter of his appearances resulting in meltdowns. It was a tragic, maybe even unfair result for Seattle. But while small sample size is terrible for analysis, its volatility is maybe one of the reasons we come back to sports again and again. As baseball executives go, Jerry Dipoto seems to be a fairly world-conscious guy. Nonetheless, I doubt he takes comfort that Duke's miserable performance in Seattle fuels the hurricane-causing-butterfly factor that makes the game fun. That doesn't mean we can't, though.

Justin Dunn RHP   Born: 09/22/95   Age: 23   Bats: R   Throws: R   Height: 6'2"   Weight: 185   Origin: Round 1, 2016 Draft (#19 overall)

YEAR	TEAM	LVL	AGE	W	L	SV	G	GS	IP	H	HR	BB/9	K/9	K	GB%	BABIP	WHIP	ERA	DRA	WARP	MPH	FB%	WHF	CSP
2016	BRO	A-	20	1	1	0	11	8	30	25	1	3.0	10.5	35	46%	.320	1.17	1.50	2.19	1.1				
2017	SLU	A+	21	5	6	0	20	16	95¹	101	5	4.5	7.1	75	44%	.322	1.56	5.00	4.27	1.0				
2018	SLU	A+	22	2	3	0	9	9	45²	43	2	3.0	10.1	51	42%	.325	1.27	2.36	3.43	1.0				
2018	BIN	AA	22	6	5	0	15	15	89²	85	7	3.7	10.5	105	47%	.345	1.36	4.22	3.48	1.9				
2019	SEA	MLB	23	6	7	0	21	21	105	103	14	4.3	8.9	104	40%	.305	1.45	4.72	5.09	0.5				

Breakout: 8%   Improve: 15%   Collapse: 5%   Attrition: 16%   MLB: 25%   *Comparables: Glen Perkins, D.J. Mitchell, Cody Reed*

An uninspiring full-season debut in 2017 led more than a few to prematurely apply the "bust" tag to this former first-round pick out of Boston College, but last season saw Dunn turn around some of the naysayers. He still has trouble with consistency—whether it's keeping his velocity steady, retaining his control or smoothing performance from start to start—but his fastball-slider combo is good enough to make him either a bullpen weapon if nothing changes or a no. 3 starter if a third pitch ever comes along. It will now be on the Mariners to finish off his development and see if there's any chance he might one day replace the now-departed James Paxton or Edwin Diaz.

Matthew Festa RHP   Born: 03/11/93   Age: 26   Bats: R   Throws: R   Height: 6'2"   Weight: 195   Origin: Round 7, 2016 Draft (#207 overall)

YEAR	TEAM	LVL	AGE	W	L	SV	G	GS	IP	H	HR	BB/9	K/9	K	GB%	BABIP	WHIP	ERA	DRA	WARP	MPH	FB%	WHF	CSP
2016	EVE	A-	23	6	2	0	14	8	60¹	60	3	2.1	8.7	58	49%	.324	1.23	3.73	3.10	1.4				
2017	MOD	A+	24	4	2	6	42	1	69²	61	7	2.5	12.8	99	44%	.327	1.15	3.23	2.55	1.9				
2018	ARK	AA	25	5	2	20	44	0	49	50	6	2.2	12.3	67	47%	.364	1.27	2.76	2.58	1.4				
2018	SEA	MLB	25	0	0	0	8	1	8¹	13	0	2.2	4.3	4	33%	.394	1.80	2.16	7.26	-0.2	94.0	47.8	7.5	51.2
2019	SEA	MLB	26	2	1	0	33	2	34²	34	5	3.4	9.5	37	41%	.303	1.34	4.48	4.83	0.1	93.6	48.7	7.7	52.1

Breakout: 13%   Improve: 21%   Collapse: 8%   Attrition: 18%   MLB: 33%   *Comparables: Evan Scribner, Cody Ege, Tyler Webb*

Life itself is a resplendent, kaleidoscopic, orgy of variety. Here we see one of its rarest, and most exotic strains: The Jerry Dipoto Draft Pick in the Major Leagues. Although typically found in abundance in the mid-minors, where they serve largely as a sort of feudal working class for their larger and more gifted brethren, there is a micro-species that breaks free from the ball fields of Appalachia and plains of Texas and migrates to the big leagues. Festa represents the first sighting of this evolutionary oddity in Seattle. While his fastball-slider combination aren't at the elite level, his polish and command should make him a viable bullpen contributor, and an enduring testament to the evolutionary power of our species. Velocity finds a way.

Logan Gilbert RHP Born: 05/05/97 Age: 22 Bats: R Throws: R Height: 6'6" Weight: 225 Origin: Round 1, 2018 Draft (#14 overall)

From the same college that brought you smash hits Corey Kluber and Jacob deGrom, Seattle is betting they have another winner on their hands with the 6'6" Gilbert, drafting him 14th overall in last year's draft. The right-hander saw his stock dip along with his velocity in midseason, only to see both return by draft time. It's that fastball, which reportedly averaged 94-97 MPH in the Cape Cod League, along with his large frame and athleticism, that rounds out the profile of a quality mid-rotation starter. Even though a long college season and mid-summer illness kept him from throwing even one professional inning in 2018, he is arguably already Seattle's top pitching prospect, and a player theoretically primed to move quickly should all go according to plan.

Marco Gonzales LHP Born: 02/16/92 Age: 27 Bats: L Throws: L Height: 6'1" Weight: 195 Origin: Round 1, 2013 Draft (#19 overall)

YEAR	TEAM	LVL	AGE	W	L	SV	G	GS	IP	H	HR	BB/9	K/9	K	GB%	BABIP	WHIP	ERA	DRA	WARP	MPH	FB%	WHF	CSP
2017	PMB	A+	25	0	0	0	1	1	6	2	1	0.0	10.5	7	38%	.083	0.33	1.50	2.94	0.2				
2017	SLN	MLB	25	0	0	0	1	1	3¹	6	3	0.0	5.4	2	50%	.273	1.80	13.50	3.83	0.1	92.4	69	13.8	43
2017	MEM	AAA	25	6	4	0	11	11	68¹	54	6	2.2	7.5	57	45%	.255	1.04	2.90	3.67	1.5				
2017	TAC	AAA	25	2	0	0	2	2	12	8	0	3.8	6.8	9	56%	.235	1.08	4.50	3.28	0.3				
2017	SEA	MLB	25	1	1	0	10	7	36²	53	5	2.7	7.4	30	45%	.393	1.75	5.40	4.51	0.4	93.1	51	9.8	44.5
2018	SEA	MLB	26	13	9	0	29	29	166²	172	17	1.7	7.8	145	45%	.319	1.22	4.00	3.58	3.3	91.5	32.5	10.2	49.4
2019	*SEA*	*MLB*	*27*	*10*	*9*	*0*	*28*	*28*	*159²*	*157*	*19*	*2.6*	*8.1*	*144*	*44%*	*.301*	*1.27*	*4.05*	*4.37*	*2.0*	*91.3*	*36.5*	*10.3*	*47.7*

Breakout: 29% Improve: 62% Collapse: 9% Attrition: 11% MLB: 85%   *Comparables: Anthony DeSclafani, Tyler Duffey, Liam Hendriks*

Coming into 2018, Gonzales was one of the key factors to the Mariners' success: handed a rotation spot despite a rough 2017 effort, and with little help in the wings, there was perhaps an unrealistic expectation for him to succeed. And yet everything came together for the southpaw in 2018, as he recaptured much of the high-command, high-polish skillset that made him a first-round draft pick. While the raw velocity in today's game is below average, an improved curveball coupled with the addition of a superb cutter (unavailable while recovering from Tommy John) resulted in exactly the mid-rotation performance Jerry Dipoto envisioned when he acquired him from St. Louis in 2017. While it's fair to question whether Gonzales' ceiling is much higher than what he showed last year, for an organization as thin in pitching as Seattle, they will happily take an approximate repeat of 2018 next year. If healthy, given his contract status, Mariner fans can hope for it for many more years than that.

Felix Hernandez RHP Born: 04/08/86 Age: 33 Bats: R Throws: R Height: 6'3" Weight: 225 Origin: International Free Agent, 2002

YEAR	TEAM	LVL	AGE	W	L	SV	G	GS	IP	H	HR	BB/9	K/9	K	GB%	BABIP	WHIP	ERA	DRA	WARP	MPH	FB%	WHF	CSP
2016	SEA	MLB	30	11	8	0	25	25	153¹	138	19	3.8	7.2	122	52%	.271	1.32	3.82	5.74	-0.7	92.9	47	10.4	43.1
2017	TAC	AAA	31	2	0	0	3	3	13	9	1	2.1	11.1	16	42%	.267	0.92	4.15	3.13	0.4				
2017	SEA	MLB	31	6	5	0	16	16	86²	86	17	2.7	8.1	78	49%	.287	1.29	4.36	5.72	-0.1	92.2	44.5	10.2	46.5
2018	SEA	MLB	32	8	14	0	29	28	155²	159	27	3.4	7.2	125	48%	.286	1.40	5.55	5.30	0.0	91.1	43.3	8.8	45.3
2019	*SEA*	*MLB*	*33*	*7*	*8*	*0*	*31*	*21*	*130²*	*123*	*18*	*3.3*	*7.5*	*109*	*47%*	*.281*	*1.31*	*4.70*	*5.07*	*0.6*	*90.9*	*44.1*	*9.4*	*44.6*

Breakout: 14% Improve: 39% Collapse: 22% Attrition: 12% MLB: 89%   *Comparables: Scott Kazmir, Gavin Floyd, Kevin Millwood*

Hernandez burst into the bigs seemingly fully formed at 19, an age where even the best prospects are fortunate to find themselves in Double-A. While even Mike Trout spent his age-19 season allowing baseball the illusion that he would need to grow into his godlike ability, Hernandez did no such thing. He threw 7+ innings in 10 of his 12 starts after his 2005 callup. He struck out 11 against the Royals in his third start, tossed a complete game against Texas a month later. For a fan who didn't follow the minor leagues, there was no development for this pitcher. He simply was not, and then very much was.

The tragedies of Hernandez, then, are twofold. He has built a borderline Hall-of-Fame resume, and made hundreds of millions of dollars. He is one of the most successful, dynamic, beloved, memorable starters of his era. But he famously never played on a Mariner team that made the postseason. While no fault of his own, his career and our appreciation of it are lessened having never seen such an imposing ace toe the rubber in October.

More (or at least more presently) disappointing is the way in which Hernandez's career has fallen off. His age at the beginning of his career, combined with that seemingly unnecessary development period, allowed anyone interested in seeing a starting pitcher reach the counting totals of yesteryear's greats to hope. Could we see 300 wins? Top-10 in strikeouts? How many Cy Youngs? Anything seems possible when you're an ace by 23.

It's hard not to mourn for Hernandez's career. The decline was inevitable, if unscheduled. But the true greats are marked by an ability to gently glide downward during it, and Hernandez plummeted. He has lost his status as ace, team's best pitcher, quality major league starter, back end filler, competent major leaguer. In 2018 he was one of the worst starting pitchers in the game. He enters 2019, at 33—still so young for one who seems so old—in the final year of his contract. It's not hard to imagine where things go after this year, but it's entirely unpleasant. A kingdom mourns its once-mighty king.

Hisashi Iwakuma RHP Born: 04/12/81 Age: 38 Bats: R Throws: R Height: 6'3" Weight: 210 Origin: International Free Agent, 2012

YEAR	TEAM	LVL	AGE	W	L	SV	G	GS	IP	H	HR	BB/9	K/9	K	GB%	BABIP	WHIP	ERA	DRA	WARP	MPH	FB%	WHF	CSP
2016	SEA	MLB	35	16	12	0	33	33	199	218	28	2.1	6.6	147	42%	.311	1.33	4.12	4.49	2.0	90.6	46.3	8.6	50.1
2017	SEA	MLB	36	0	2	0	6	6	31	27	7	3.5	4.6	16	41%	.220	1.26	4.35	6.21	-0.2	88.0	42.9	8.7	47.4
2019	*SEA*	*MLB*	*38*	*2*	*3*	*0*	*6*	*6*	*33²*	*38*	*7*	*3.6*	*5.8*	*22*	*38%*	*.293*	*1.53*	*6.01*	*6.51*	*-0.4*	*88.7*	*44.5*	*8.4*	*47.2*

Breakout: 11% Improve: 33% Collapse: 16% Attrition: 9% MLB: 69%   *Comparables: Kyle Lohse, Jon Lieber, Paul Byrd*

Iwakuma should have been an Athletic. Oakland won the posting bid in 2010, and the rights to negotiate with the Rakuten Golden Eagles, but a combination of thriftiness and principles kept Iwakuma in Japan. Two years later, this time as a free agent, Iwakuma allegedly turned down higher offers to sign with the Mariners, citing his "comfort level with the organization and the city." He signed a one-year contract for just $1.5 million.

He waited 15 games to make his major league debut: four innings of mop-up duty against the Tigers, amid one of Seattle's indistinguishable lost seasons. Besides then-manager Eric Wedge, nobody really knows why it took so long for Iwakuma to appear. After his debut, he waited eight days to pitch again. Then, nine days. Then, two weeks. By June 1st, a man with more than a thousand NPL innings in his past, and a third place Cy Young finish and no-hitter in his future, had made five appearances in the major leagues. He had not yet started a game; Blake Beavan and Hector Noesi had 20 starts between them.

Iwakuma should have been a Dodger. Technically, he was a Dodger. Iwakuma and Los Angeles agreed to a three-year, $45 million dollar deal during the winter of 2015. Before Iwakuma could put pen to paper, a doctor somewhere looked at some kind of scan of Iwakuma's shoulder, slowly removed his glasses, made a baleful, hound dog look at Farhan Zaidi, and shook his head. Thanks to that head shake, new Mariner GM Jerry Dipoto pulled off a rockstar move, announcing his return to Seattle at the Mariners Employee Christmas Party in the winter of 2015. In 2016, as Felix Hernandez, James Paxton, and every other Mariner starting pitcher deteriorated over the season, Iwakuma and his Grim Shoulder made every start, throwing 199 quality innings.

Hisashi Iwakuma should not have been an Everett Aquasock. A 36-year old man, a devoted husband and father and an accomplished pitcher on both sides of the globe, he didn't belong with teenagers on a short-season roster. Yet, there he was, starting Game One in the Northwest League playoffs. Iwakuma threw two innings, and allowed three runs to the Spokane Indians. It was only his third appearance of the year.

With his contract fulfilled, Iwakuma is walking away from Major League Baseball. He announced he will return home and attempt to pitch in the NPL. His career has taken him around the world, through multiple surgeries and rehabs, and across the professional and personal crossroads that confront us all. He is many things, and with different timing and circumstance could have perhaps been many more. His baseball card, however, says one thing, and one thing only: Pitcher — Seattle Mariners

Yusei Kikuchi LHP Born: 06/17/91 Age: 28 Bats: L Throws: L Height: 6'0" Weight: 194 Origin: International Free Agent, 2018

YEAR	TEAM	LVL	AGE	W	L	SV	G	GS	IP	H	HR	BB/9	K/9	K	GB%	BABIP	WHIP	ERA	DRA	WARP	MPH	FB%	WHF	CSP
2019	SEA	MLB	28	9	9	0	26	26	148¹	139	19	3.1	8.5	139	47%	.291	1.28	4.20	4.53	1.6				

Breakout: 24%   Improve: 58%   Collapse: 20%   Attrition: 4%   MLB: 93%   *Comparables: Patrick Corbin, Mat Latos, Matt Garza*

This could have been Kikuchi's ninth entry in the BP Annual: In 2009, he considered becoming the first major Japanese high school prospect to circumnavigate the NPB and sign with an MLB team. He opted not to, and instead enjoyed a successful career with the Seibu Lions, making three All-Star games and throwing the league's hardest fastball, sitting in the low-to-mid nineties. He pairs it with an excellent hard slider, as well as a changeup and slow curve that technically exist. Scouts generally agree that Kikuchi looks like a solid number two starter, which makes him Seattle's clear number one starter, which means that his first major league start will ironically be in Japan against the Athletics. The main concern, and the price he paid for his national loyalty, is an overworked shoulder that diminished his 2018 season, though he appeared to finish the year healthy. The Mariners are likely to be more cautious with their newest star, especially given the level of stakes they're likely to offer him the next couple of years.

Casey Lawrence RHP Born: 10/28/87 Age: 31 Bats: R Throws: R Height: 6'2" Weight: 170 Origin: Undrafted Free Agent, 2010

YEAR	TEAM	LVL	AGE	W	L	SV	G	GS	IP	H	HR	BB/9	K/9	K	GB%	BABIP	WHIP	ERA	DRA	WARP	MPH	FB%	WHF	CSP
2016	NHP	AA	28	3	6	0	13	13	75	92	8	1.6	6.0	50	54%	.341	1.40	4.56	3.56	1.4				
2016	BUF	AAA	28	5	6	0	15	15	87	87	5	2.5	6.0	58	51%	.293	1.28	3.83	3.62	1.7				
2017	TOR	MLB	29	0	3	0	4	2	13¹	21	2	7.4	4.7	7	59%	.365	2.40	8.77	7.90	-0.4	92.2	63.6	7.6	51.1
2017	BUF	AAA	29	1	0	0	3	3	10	9	1	0.9	6.3	7	50%	.258	1.00	0.90	2.50	0.3				
2017	TAC	AAA	29	2	4	0	11	7	57¹	50	7	1.6	6.4	41	40%	.256	1.05	4.08	3.96	1.0				
2017	SEA	MLB	29	2	0	0	23	0	42	56	9	3.0	9.6	45	44%	.382	1.67	5.57	5.49	-0.1	92.7	57.9	13.1	43.2
2018	TAC	AAA	30	7	5	1	19	16	98	98	11	1.2	8.2	89	42%	.302	1.13	3.31	3.10	2.6				
2018	SEA	MLB	30	1	0	0	11	0	23¹	28	2	3.9	5.4	14	48%	.333	1.63	7.33	6.46	-0.4	92.0	50.3	10.8	43
2019	SEA	MLB	31	6	6	0	30	15	102²	111	15	2.7	7.2	82	44%	.305	1.38	4.68	5.06	0.4	91.5	55.9	11.4	43.7

Breakout: 8%   Improve: 18%   Collapse: 7%   Attrition: 19%   MLB: 28%   *Comparables: Bobby Cramer, Stephen Fife, Andrew Albers*

You don't really care about a comment about Lawrence, and that's fine. He's over thirty, has thrown a few dozen big league innings, and has a fastball significantly slower than Noah Syndergaard's slider. After consecutive regrettable tours of duty, it's unlikely Lawrence will have much more of a major league career, in Seattle or elsewhere. Baseball's legends stand atop the bones of the legions of foot soldier relievers like him, their endorsement ads filled with benign-looking men, with benign-facial hair, standing in another team's generic uniform. You can absolutely move along reading this book as an informed fan without worrying that you're missing anything important. Just know that Lawrence wasn't drafted out of high school, and, after walking on at a Division III school, wasn't drafted out of college either. The only signing bonus he received as an undrafted free agent was the money for a plane ticket to Spring Training. If you're going to lodge one small bookmark in your head about Lawrence, let it be that he spent more than seven seasons and appeared in almost two hundred games before he donned a major league uniform. Make a mental note that he took the loss in that debut, and was DFA'd a few days later. Just know that he came back later that year to strike out nine Rockies in five innings, a Mariner record for a single relief appearance.

Or don't. Just go ahead and forget about all that. There's a lot of players, and most of them, from a fan perspective, matter a whole lot more. Whether you remember any of this or not though, know that regardless of your decision, or his 2018 ERA, Lawrence probably feels pretty good about where he's ended up, and he probably should. This year, he gets to live in Japan.

Mike Leake RHP Born: 11/12/87 Age: 31 Bats: R Throws: R Height: 5'10" Weight: 170 Origin: Round 1, 2009 Draft (#8 overall)

YEAR	TEAM	LVL	AGE	W	L	SV	G	GS	IP	H	HR	BB/9	K/9	K	GB%	BABIP	WHIP	ERA	DRA	WARP	MPH	FB%	WHF	CSP
2016	SLN	MLB	28	9	12	0	30	30	176²	203	20	1.5	6.4	125	55%	.318	1.32	4.69	3.43	3.9	93.0	77.4	7.6	46.9
2017	SLN	MLB	29	7	12	0	26	26	154	169	19	2.0	6.0	103	55%	.306	1.32	4.21	4.20	2.4	91.6	70.9	8.5	48.8
2017	SEA	MLB	29	3	1	0	5	5	32	32	1	0.6	7.6	27	50%	.323	1.06	2.53	3.64	0.7	92.1	70.9	9.7	47.9
2018	SEA	MLB	30	10	10	0	31	31	185²	207	23	1.6	5.8	119	50%	.306	1.30	4.36	4.46	1.8	90.5	59.4	8.3	50.7
2019	SEA	MLB	31	10	10	0	28	28	168	172	19	2.3	6.5	120	50%	.294	1.27	4.18	4.51	1.9	90.7	67.2	8.2	48.8

Breakout: 12%   Improve: 38%   Collapse: 31%   Attrition: 10%   MLB: 96%   *Comparables: Ivan Nova, Bob Friend, Joel Pineiro*

The oceans may rise, cities may fall, and fires may rain from the heavens. Still, there will be Leake. He will throw 170-200 innings. He will not allow walks, nor home runs. That is good because he will not get strikeouts. He will have two or three starts in a row where BABIP is friendly to him, and someone somewhere will write about him "taking his career to the next level". That notion will be disproved immediately, when the hits string together and he allows five or more runs in his next three starts. He will do this forever. Your children's children's children's great grandchildren will sit in their holoseats, and watch Leake go six and a third, allowing three runs, and striking out two. World without end. Amen.

Wade LeBlanc LHP   Born: 08/07/84   Age: 34   Bats: L   Throws: L   Height: 6'3"   Weight: 205   Origin: Round 2, 2006 Draft (#61 overall)

YEAR	TEAM	LVL	AGE	W	L	SV	G	GS	IP	H	HR	BB/9	K/9	K	GB%	BABIP	WHIP	ERA	DRA	WARP	MPH	FB%	WHF	CSP
2016	BUF	AAA	31	7	2	0	14	14	89²	84	3	2.1	8.5	85	43%	.315	1.17	1.71	2.82	2.6				
2016	SEA	MLB	31	3	0	1	11	8	50	52	14	1.6	7.4	41	34%	.264	1.22	4.50	5.65	-0.2	89.0	62.9	10.1	46.7
2016	PIT	MLB	31	1	0	1	8	0	12	7	0	1.5	7.5	10	41%	.219	0.75	0.75	3.91	0.2	88.7	62.9	13.8	47.8
2017	PIT	MLB	32	5	2	1	50	0	68	64	10	2.2	7.1	54	47%	.269	1.19	4.50	3.77	1.1	88.4	62.9	10.3	46.1
2018	SEA	MLB	33	9	5	0	32	27	162	151	24	2.2	7.2	130	37%	.273	1.18	3.72	5.07	0.4	87.5	61.1	10.1	47.7
2019	SEA	MLB	34	7	8	0	24	24	127¹	124	19	2.7	7.7	110	40%	.286	1.27	4.51	4.87	0.9	86.8	60.8	10.1	46.2

Breakout: 13%   Improve: 30%   Collapse: 22%   Attrition: 17%   MLB: 74%   *Comparables: Eric Stults, Chris Narveson, Claudio Vargas*

If you ever wanted an elevator pitch for caring about the game of baseball, you could do a lot worse than LeBlanc's 2018 season. After a decade hovering around the fringes of big league rosters as a near replacement-level pitcher, the soft-tossing lefty found unprecedented success in his second stint in Seattle. Posting a career high in innings and strikeouts, the Mariners rewarded LeBlanc with his first ever multi-year contract, a team option deal that could theoretically keep him in Seattle through 2022. So, how did he do it? How did a 33-year old man with an 86 mph fastball and ten seasons telling us he barely belonged in the league spend 166 innings surviving Mike Trout, Mookie Betts and the rest of the American League? Did he add a new pitch? A new windup that concealed the ball longer from the hitter? Combing the data, the answer seems to be: Nothing. LeBlanc threw the same pitch mix, at the same speed, from the same arm slots. Amazingly, most of his results were perfectly in line with career norms. He just... did them longer... and the results proved slightly better. He'll almost certainly never repeat last season, but that's not the point. By all accounts last season never should have happened in the first place. As analytics press us ever onward towards a fully optimized future, baseball's ability to still produce season-long accidents like LeBlanc's 2018 is something to cherish.

Wyatt Mills RHP   Born: 01/25/95   Age: 24   Bats: R   Throws: R   Height: 6'3"   Weight: 175   Origin: Round 3, 2017 Draft (#93 overall)

YEAR	TEAM	LVL	AGE	W	L	SV	G	GS	IP	H	HR	BB/9	K/9	K	GB%	BABIP	WHIP	ERA	DRA	WARP	MPH	FB%	WHF	CSP
2017	EVE	A-	22	0	1	2	7	0	7	3	0	3.9	14.1	11	50%	.214	0.86	2.57	3.01	0.2				
2017	CLN	A	22	0	1	4	11	0	13¹	5	0	4.1	12.1	18	57%	.179	0.82	1.35	4.14	0.1				
2018	MOD	A+	23	6	0	11	35	0	42¹	29	1	1.9	10.4	49	54%	.277	0.90	1.91	3.59	0.7				
2018	ARK	AA	23	0	2	9	9	0	10²	18	0	3.4	8.4	10	42%	.450	2.06	10.12	3.98	0.1				
2019	SEA	MLB	24	2	1	1	36	0	38¹	35	5	4.3	9.3	40	45%	.295	1.40	4.68	5.05	0.0				

Breakout: 0%   Improve: 0%   Collapse: 1%   Attrition: 1%   MLB: 1%   *Comparables: Colton Murray, Adam Kolarek, Branden Pinder*

There are a lot of words in the English language for the act of throwing a baseball: toss, heave, fling, whip, fire, lob, sidearm, underhand, flip, and on. What Mills does is, in the opinion of these pages, best described as "slanging." His near-sidearm delivery results in good arm side run, which when coupled with 92-94 mph velocity, project him as a tough at-bat for right-handers. While he struggled in his short stint in Double-A last year, look for Mills to start there in 2019. If he stays on track the stuff and record appears to have him ticketed for a major league bullpen no later than 2020.

Ariel Miranda LHP   Born: 01/10/89   Age: 30   Bats: L   Throws: L   Height: 6'2"   Weight: 190   Origin: International Free Agent, 2015

YEAR	TEAM	LVL	AGE	W	L	SV	G	GS	IP	H	HR	BB/9	K/9	K	GB%	BABIP	WHIP	ERA	DRA	WARP	MPH	FB%	WHF	CSP
2016	BAL	MLB	27	0	0	0	1	0	2	4	0	0.0	18.0	4	43%	.571	2.00	13.50	8.60	-0.1	95.4	56	6	45.2
2016	NOR	AAA	27	4	7	0	19	19	100²	95	11	2.8	7.8	87	38%	.291	1.25	3.93	3.61	2.0				
2016	SEA	MLB	27	5	2	0	11	10	56	43	12	2.9	6.4	40	31%	.205	1.09	3.54	5.73	-0.3	95.5	58.3	9	49
2017	SEA	MLB	28	8	7	0	31	29	160	140	37	3.5	7.7	137	34%	.236	1.27	5.12	5.95	-0.7	93.9	57.6	12.3	46
2018	SEA	MLB	29	0	0	0	1	1	5	6	0	7.2	9.0	5	40%	.400	2.00	1.80	5.93	0.0	92.9	59.8	12	51.2
2018	TAC	AAA	29	5	0	0	10	9	45¹	44	3	4.8	7.9	40	35%	.318	1.50	3.97	4.81	0.4				
2019	SEA	MLB	30	4	5	0	12	12	65	60	11	3.7	8.0	58	36%	.271	1.34	5.07	5.48	0.0	93.4	57.6	11.6	48.7

Breakout: 12%   Improve: 22%   Collapse: 16%   Attrition: 18%   MLB: 44%   *Comparables: Wade LeBlanc, Scott Richmond, Jason Bergmann*

As brutal and cutthroat as professional baseball can be, it can also see acts of surprisingly sincere kindness. Despite leading the 2017 Mariners in innings pitched (or perhaps because of the home runs that resulted), Miranda was squeezed out of Seattle's 2018 big league roster, and began the year in Triple-A. When it became clear the organization had no place for him at the big league level, Jerry Dipoto granted Miranda his release, allowing him to help the Fukuoka Hawks capture a Japan Series championship.

That shortly thereafter Seattle's rotation disintegrated into a morass of spot starts, roster shuffling, and "Openers" does not diminish the thoughtfulness of the act, but perhaps shows why it's relatively rare in high level athletics. Nice guys may not finish last, but they also don't tend to make the playoffs.

Erasmo Ramirez RHP   Born: 05/02/90   Age: 29   Bats: R   Throws: R   Height: 5'10"   Weight: 215   Origin: International Free Agent, 2007

YEAR	TEAM	LVL	AGE	W	L	SV	G	GS	IP	H	HR	BB/9	K/9	K	GB%	BABIP	WHIP	ERA	DRA	WARP	MPH	FB%	WHF	CSP
2016	TBA	MLB	26	7	11	2	64	1	90²	90	14	2.6	6.3	63	55%	.280	1.28	3.77	4.48	0.5	94.3	63	9.9	48
2017	TBA	MLB	27	4	3	1	26	8	69¹	66	10	2.1	7.1	55	49%	.280	1.18	4.80	4.23	1.0	93.2	42.2	11	51.5
2017	SEA	MLB	27	1	3	0	11	11	62	57	12	2.2	7.8	54	39%	.257	1.16	3.92	4.52	0.7	93.4	42.2	10.6	45.3
2018	TAC	AAA	28	0	2	0	5	5	18²	14	1	1.4	8.2	17	46%	.245	0.91	2.41	3.85	0.4				
2018	SEA	MLB	28	2	4	0	10	10	45²	52	14	2.4	6.5	33	40%	.271	1.40	6.50	6.55	-0.7	91.6	40.8	9.6	49.4
2019	BOS	MLB	29	4	4	1	28	10	69¹	71	10	3.0	7.0	54	45%	.291	1.35	4.70	4.97	0.3	92.5	47.1	10.3	48.8

Breakout: 34%   Improve: 49%   Collapse: 23%   Attrition: 13%   MLB: 93%   *Comparables: Jae Weong Seo, Wade Miley, Josh Towers*

One of the encouraging trends in baseball the past few years has been the move away from the baseball player as spreadsheet abstraction, and towards a more humanistic, holistic appraisal of the men in uniform. As such, when a player suffers a poor game, week, month, or season, it is no longer en vogue to take turns slinging acerbic witticisms. Instead, perhaps, our better angels demand we consider the truth of all baseball players: They are human, and they try hard. When discussing Ramirez's 2018, it is probably best if we acknowledge those two facts, and, in absence of anything else positive to say, move on to 2019.

Justus Sheffield LHP   Born: 05/13/96   Age: 23   Bats: L   Throws: L   Height: 6'0"   Weight: 200   Origin: Round 1, 2014 Draft (#31 overall)

YEAR	TEAM	LVL	AGE	W	L	SV	G	GS	IP	H	HR	BB/9	K/9	K	GB%	BABIP	WHIP	ERA	DRA	WARP	MPH	FB%	WHF	CSP
2016	LYN	A+	20	7	5	0	19	19	95¹	91	6	3.8	8.8	93	45%	.321	1.37	3.59	3.57	2.1				
2016	TAM	A+	20	3	1	0	5	5	26	14	0	3.5	9.3	27	45%	.226	0.92	1.73	2.95	0.7				
2017	TRN	AA	21	7	6	0	17	17	93¹	94	14	3.2	7.9	82	48%	.293	1.36	3.18	3.54	1.8				
2018	TRN	AA	22	1	2	0	5	5	28	16	1	4.5	12.5	39	44%	.259	1.07	2.25	3.47	0.6				
2018	SWB	AAA	22	6	4	0	20	15	88	66	3	3.7	8.6	84	46%	.264	1.16	2.56	4.27	1.2				
2018	NYA	MLB	22	0	0	0	3	0	2²	4	1	10.1	0.0	0	55%	.300	2.62	10.12	6.56	-0.1	95.7	54.4	1.8	38.3
2019	*SEA*	*MLB*	*23*	*4*	*5*	*0*	*13*	*13*	*74*	*66*	*10*	*4.1*	*9.6*	*79*	*43%*	*.288*	*1.34*	*4.37*	*4.71*	*0.7*	*95.6*	*56.3*	*1.8*	*39.7*

Breakout: 21%   Improve: 26%   Collapse: 14%   Attrition: 32%   MLB: 48%   *Comparables: Michael Fulmer, Matt Magill, Giovanni Soto*

There's nothing quite like the post-trade prospect re-evaluation. Ranked as the 57th best prospect according to BP last year, Sheffield built upon past success, albeit unsteadily, culminating in his brief, nerve-wracking major league debut, where he said his "legs felt like Jell-O." He appeared to be a brisk, contract-extending April tune-up away from a rotation spot when he was shipped to Seattle as the headliner in the James Paxton trade. Suddenly there were all sorts of concerns about his makeup, his command, and the floor of "talented but inconsistent relief arm" flew up at him. He'll get a chance to prove his worth in Seattle, after the usual six-week period of reflection, during which time he switches from "good prospect in overcrowded system" to Seattle's obvious No. 1. The key will be his ability to find the strike zone, and the Mariners obviously feel that they, unlike the organization that produces an elite arm every three weeks, can unlock the secrets to control the zone.

Erik Swanson RHP   Born: 09/04/93   Age: 25   Bats: R   Throws: R   Height: 6'3"   Weight: 235   Origin: Round 8, 2014 Draft (#246 overall)

YEAR	TEAM	LVL	AGE	W	L	SV	G	GS	IP	H	HR	BB/9	K/9	K	GB%	BABIP	WHIP	ERA	DRA	WARP	MPH	FB%	WHF	CSP
2016	HIC	A	22	6	4	1	19	15	81¹	77	4	2.8	8.6	78	53%	.319	1.25	3.43	3.26	1.7				
2016	CSC	A	22	0	1	0	5	2	15	14	0	3.0	9.0	15	50%	.333	1.27	3.60	2.65	0.4				
2017	TAM	A+	23	7	3	0	20	20	100¹	115	10	1.3	7.5	84	42%	.344	1.29	3.95	4.34	1.1				
2018	TRN	AA	24	5	0	0	8	7	42²	22	0	3.2	11.6	55	36%	.253	0.87	0.42	3.54	0.9				
2018	SWB	AAA	24	3	2	0	14	13	72¹	63	10	1.7	9.7	78	37%	.283	1.06	3.86	3.55	1.6				
2019	*SEA*	*MLB*	*25*	*3*	*3*	*0*	*10*	*10*	*50*	*49*	*8*	*3.0*	*8.9*	*49*	*40%*	*.295*	*1.31*	*4.62*	*4.99*	*0.3*				

Breakout: 14%   Improve: 22%   Collapse: 11%   Attrition: 29%   MLB: 37%   *Comparables: Sean Gilmartin, Jeremy Hefner, Cory Luebke*

Swanson likely wouldn't have warranted much discussion in any other year, but that changes when you're part of a trade for James Paxton alongside Justus Sheffield. While Sheffield may be the headliner, Swanson compared favorably from a statistical standpoint, actually outperforming the top prospect between Double- and Triple-A by DRA. That fun fact will probably get employed more as an indictment on the former than credit to the latter, who looks every bit the part of a stodgy fourth or fifth starter. While he was blocked by what is now a stocked rotation, Swanson now gets the chance to put that performance to the test at the big leagues, on a rebuilding ball club that will give him a leash to sink or swim. If his fastball is for real, as Jerry Dipoto likely believes, then Seattle's front office may have smuggled a full-time starter behind a possibly more risky high-upside headliner.

Anthony Swarzak RHP   Born: 09/10/85   Age: 33   Bats: R   Throws: R   Height: 6'4"   Weight: 215   Origin: Round 2, 2004 Draft (#61 overall)

YEAR	TEAM	LVL	AGE	W	L	SV	G	GS	IP	H	HR	BB/9	K/9	K	GB%	BABIP	WHIP	ERA	DRA	WARP	MPH	FB%	WHF	CSP
2016	SWB	AAA	30	1	4	7	15	6	46²	47	4	1.5	8.3	43	45%	.323	1.18	3.86	2.64	1.4				
2016	NYA	MLB	30	1	2	0	26	0	31	28	10	2.0	9.0	31	46%	.240	1.13	5.52	4.39	0.2	95.8	48.2	10.2	43.4
2017	CHA	MLB	31	4	3	1	41	0	48¹	37	2	2.4	9.7	52	40%	.294	1.03	2.23	2.92	1.2	95.9	48.8	15.5	47.3
2017	MIL	MLB	31	2	1	1	29	0	29	21	4	2.8	12.1	39	51%	.270	1.03	2.48	3.37	0.6	96.3	48.2	15.3	46.8
2018	NYN	MLB	32	0	2	4	29	0	26¹	28	6	4.8	10.6	31	31%	.344	1.59	6.15	5.71	-0.2	95.7	53.5	9.8	46.9
2019	*SEA*	*MLB*	*33*	*3*	*1*	*25*	*57*	*0*	*60*	*55*	*9*	*3.6*	*9.4*	*63*	*40%*	*.297*	*1.33*	*4.41*	*4.76*	*0.2*	*94.9*	*49.3*	*12.9*	*45.5*

Breakout: 25%   Improve: 36%   Collapse: 29%   Attrition: 22%   MLB: 84%   *Comparables: Tyler Walker, Justin Miller, Casey Fien*

Exactly how many things need to go right for a journeyman starting pitcher pathologically incapable of getting whiffs to transform into a shutdown end-of-game ace? And how many things need to go wrong for that newly-minted fireman to revert to imperfect performance? When Swarzak signed after his emergent 2017, it was far from a sure thing that he'd remain magical indefinitely; when his 2018 began with a litany of injuries (calf, oblique, and shoulder) things looked appropriately dire. By the end of the year, his fastball and slider were down a tick, his command went AWOL and he was salary ballast in a blockbuster trade instead of the reliever in demand. A change of scenery to the West Coast should give Swarzak the opportunity to remain in a late-game relief role, but it's more realistic to see him as a middle reliever. Not everything breaks right forever.

Nick Vincent RHP   Born: 07/12/86   Age: 32   Bats: R   Throws: R   Height: 6'0"   Weight: 185   Origin: Round 18, 2008 Draft (#555 overall)

YEAR	TEAM	LVL	AGE	W	L	SV	G	GS	IP	H	HR	BB/9	K/9	K	GB%	BABIP	WHIP	ERA	DRA	WARP	MPH	FB%	WHF	CSP
2016	SEA	MLB	29	4	4	3	60	0	60¹	53	11	2.2	9.7	65	34%	.271	1.13	3.73	3.16	1.3	92.0	94.8	16.2	48.4
2017	SEA	MLB	30	3	3	0	69	0	64²	62	3	1.8	7.0	50	35%	.301	1.16	3.20	4.11	0.8	91.3	94.4	11.2	49.3
2018	SEA	MLB	31	4	4	0	62	1	56¹	50	7	2.4	8.9	56	31%	.272	1.15	3.99	3.55	0.9	90.7	96	13.2	50.9
2019	*SEA*	*MLB*	*32*	*2*	*1*	*0*	*47*	*0*	*50*	*47*	*7*	*3.3*	*8.8*	*49*	*35%*	*.292*	*1.30*	*4.33*	*4.68*	*0.2*	*90.3*	*94.3*	*13.1*	*49.3*

Breakout: 16%   Improve: 34%   Collapse: 28%   Attrition: 9%   MLB: 83%   *Comparables: Casey Janssen, Matt Bush, Todd Coffey*

Armed with the pitch arsenal, physique, and at times facial hair of a bygone era, Vincent is something like baseball's third-best bar mitzvah magician. He throws a fastball that tops out around 90 mph, a cutter about two ticks below that, and that's about it. He throws them near the top of the strike zone, to any and all manner of terrifying opposing hitter. When the magic is on, and the fly balls stay in the park, he rides those two pitches and that approach to years like 2017, when he erased eighth innings so effectively you hardly noticed them. When the balls carry over the fence, he'll still provide adequate relief, if even the mere appearance of him warming up will chill your very soul. Either way, the audience will be on the edge of their seats the entire time.

Adam Warren RHP Born: 08/25/87 Age: 31 Bats: R Throws: R Height: 6'1" Weight: 224 Origin: Round 4, 2009 Draft (#135 overall)

YEAR	TEAM	LVL	AGE	W	L	SV	G	GS	IP	H	HR	BB/9	K/9	K	GB%	BABIP	WHIP	ERA	DRA	WARP	MPH	FB%	WHF	CSP
2016	IOW	AAA	28	0	0	0	2	2	8²	6	1	4.2	6.2	6	38%	.217	1.15	4.15	4.63	0.1				
2016	CHN	MLB	28	3	2	0	29	1	35	31	7	4.9	6.9	27	44%	.242	1.43	5.91	4.16	0.3	95.3	45	11.9	43.1
2016	NYA	MLB	28	4	2	0	29	0	30¹	28	4	3.0	7.4	25	45%	.282	1.25	3.26	6.46	-0.5	94.9	42	10.2	44.6
2017	NYA	MLB	29	3	2	1	46	0	57¹	35	4	2.4	8.5	54	44%	.208	0.87	2.35	3.01	1.4	94.1	38.9	10.7	42.5
2018	NYA	MLB	30	0	1	0	24	0	30	26	3	3.6	11.1	37	37%	.307	1.27	2.70	3.27	0.6	93.0	39	12	38.6
2018	SEA	MLB	30	3	1	0	23	0	21²	22	3	3.3	6.2	15	39%	.279	1.38	3.74	5.44	-0.1	93.7	41.7	10.4	44.2
2019	SEA	MLB	31	2	2	1	33	3	48¹	42	6	3.7	8.8	47	42%	.275	1.28	4.37	4.71	0.3	93.2	40.5	11	41.9

Breakout: 18%   Improve: 42%   Collapse: 27%   Attrition: 11%   MLB: 90%   *Comparables: Ramon Ramirez, Justin Duchscherer, Jim Johnson*

History has no record of Warren prior to his appearance in the Yankees' bullpen in 2012. There are claims that he played college baseball with Kyle Seager and Dustin Ackley at North Carolina, but witnesses couldn't corroborate. Seager was unavailable for comment, while Ackley simply responded with an eternally blank stare and silence. Still, consider the facts: Since his debut Warren has been largely effective as long as he wears the black pinstripes. The second he dons another uniform, as he did in 2016 for the Cubs, and last year for the Mariners, everything falls apart. Does this mean the Yankees, with all their immense wealth and access to technology, have begun manufacturing smooth-shaven androids, nefarious sleeper agents designed to malfunction and fail the second they leave the Bronx? Is this baseball's next great conspiracy? Unfortunately, for the purposes of this player comment, Brian Cashman did not return our calls, and also barred us from his favorite restaurant, the TGI Fridays in Times Square.

LINEOUTS

Hitters

HITTER	POS	TEAM	LVL	AGE	PA	R	2B	3B	HR	RBI	BB	K	SB	CS	AVG/OBP/SLG	DRC+	VORP	BABIP	BRR	FRAA	WARP
John Andreoli	RF	SEA	MLB	28	6	0	0	0	0	0	1	2	0	0	.200/.333/.200	77	-0.3	.333	-0.1	RF(1): 0.0, LF(1): 0.0	0.0
	RF	TAC	AAA	28	388	54	18	5	3	36	55	86	19	5	.287/.397/.401	99	18.0	.381	-2.5	RF(35): 0.1, LF(30): 5.6	1.1
	RF	BAL	MLB	28	61	4	2	0	0	4	4	17	2	0	.232/.279/.268	71	-1.5	.325	0.1	LF(13): -0.4, RF(5): -0.4	-0.1
Gordon Beckham	2B	TAC	AAA	31	425	64	24	1	10	51	57	52	6	2	.302/.400/.458	124	28.9	.326	1.6	2B(32): -0.6, SS(27): -0.5	3.2
	2B	SEA	MLB	31	50	3	1	0	0	1	4	11	1	0	.182/.250/.205	82	-1.6	.242	0.3	2B(13): 1.4, 3B(6): 0.2	0.3
Kaleb Cowart	SS	SLC	AAA	26	279	36	20	3	6	45	18	52	8	1	.287/.333/.457	103	5.1	.337	0.7	SS(28): -4.6, RF(12): -2.5	0.6
	SS	ANA	MLB	26	124	7	7	1	1	10	10	44	1	0	.134/.210/.241	52	-7.4	.206	0.2	3B(24): 0.5, 2B(14): 0.9	-0.2
Joey Curletta	1B	ARK	AA	24	556	70	24	0	23	94	81	130	1	1	.282/.383/.482	132	38.1	.336	-1.3	1B(118): -7.0	2.0
David Freitas	C	TAC	AAA	29	167	15	12	1	4	23	17	27	0	0	.349/.428/.527	119	16.1	.409	-1.6	C(29): 2.6	1.2
	C	SEA	MLB	29	106	9	6	0	1	5	8	25	0	0	.215/.277/.312	74	-0.9	.284	-1.2	C(35): 0.9, 1B(1): 0.0	0.2
Cesar Izturis	SS	MRN	Rk	18	206	28	7	0	1	12	12	44	5	3	.245/.304/.298	71	3.6	.315	0.0	SS(38): -1.8, 2B(12): -1.0	-0.2
Luis Liberato	LF	MOD	A+	22	370	48	20	2	11	44	34	63	2	5	.250/.317/.424	103	19.6	.275	1.0	LF(43): 3.1, CF(27): 1.5	1.6
Ian Miller	CF	TAC	AAA	26	478	60	16	3	2	41	43	89	33	9	.261/.333/.327	74	10.2	.322	3.1	CF(71): 0.4, LF(41): -1.8	0.3
Kris Negron	3B	ARI	MLB	32	3	0	0	0	0	1	0	0	0	0	.333/.333/.333	82	0.1	.333	0.1	RF(1): 0.0	0.0
	3B	RNO	AAA	32	425	71	17	5	15	45	43	121	10	3	.283/.368/.477	106	27.4	.380	5.4	2B(43): 2.0, RF(24): -0.8	2.9
	3B	SEA	MLB	32	30	6	0	0	1	3	1	9	2	0	.207/.233/.310	80	-1.4	.263	0.2	LF(4): 0.2, 3B(4): -0.6	0.1
Juan Querecuto	SS	DMR	Rk	17	280	37	8	2	3	29	25	54	3	6	.243/.331/.329	106	12.2	.298	-1.7	SS(62): -2.1, 2B(3): 0.6	1.1
Joe Rizzo	3B	MOD	A+	20	508	46	21	2	4	55	40	108	6	1	.241/.303/.321	86	-2.2	.303	-0.9	3B(99): 0.5, 2B(6): -0.1	0.6
Andrew Romine	SS	SEA	MLB	32	131	15	2	1	0	2	7	39	1	0	.210/.260/.244	54	-3.6	.313	1.0	2B(18): -0.9, SS(18): 0.3	-0.2
Dom Thompson-Williams	OF	CSC	A	23	40	7	1	0	5	9	2	7	3	2	.378/.425/.811	151	6.7	.360	-0.4	CF(7): -1.2, LF(2): -0.1	0.2
	OF	TAM	A+	23	375	56	16	4	17	65	31	95	17	7	.290/.356/.517	134	26.4	.354	1.3	CF(35): -1.9, LF(27): -0.5	2.3
Donnie Walton	2B	MOD	A+	24	256	35	12	3	3	19	30	37	8	3	.309/.402/.433	112	24.1	.358	-0.3	2B(36): -4.2, SS(19): 1.0	0.8
	2B	ARK	AA	24	238	22	14	1	1	22	21	34	3	1	.236/.325/.327	91	1.8	.276	-1.4	2B(62): 6.2	0.9
Nick Zammarelli	RF	MOD	A+	23	508	60	30	6	10	60	39	136	5	1	.274/.336/.431	97	21.7	.365	-3.1	RF(55): -8.7, 1B(25): -3.1	-1.3

As anyone who read Colm Toibin's Brooklyn (or the many, many more people who saw the movie) could tell you: any given AL East roster has room for either Darren Christopher O'Day or **John Francis Andreoli**. Not both. Never both. ⊗ In a new tradition, the Mariners have taken to holding **Gordon Beckham** up to the big league roster every July 1st. If he runs back to Tacoma and hides it's six more weeks of contention. If not, well... ⊗ Fielding yeoman **Kaleb Cowart** is a decent utility option, since nowhere in this rulebook does it say the DH has to bat for the pitc— never mind, found it. ⊗ **Joey Curletta** sounds like a name you would give to a bodybuilder NPC in a bad JRPG, but if the organization's Minor League Hitter of the Year can continue to control the zone, he may graduate to playable DLC. ⊗ **David Freitas** has kind eyes, soft hands, and unfortunately for his baseball career, a softer bat. It is recommended he look into a low-emissions, high-MPG automobile for that Tacoma-Seattle commute. ⊗ By 2100, if our earth remains, all baseball players will be the offspring of former big leaguers. Mack Trout will be the game's best player, Krys Sale its most dominating pitcher, and Cesar Izturis V, **Cesar Izturis Jr**'s great-grandson, will hit .240 in AA while playing slightly above-average defense at shortstop. ⊗ Repeating High-A, **Luis Liberato's** offensive 2018 was a near carbon copy of his previous year. The ability to punish mistakes is a good starting point, but he'll need to start occasionally being good against opponents who are also being good. ⊗ **Ian Miller** has a negative scouting report as his headline image on Twitter, presumably to serve as inspiration to beat the haters. The report is worth reading, as it's largely very accurate. ⊗ The Mariners largely wasted a roster spot on Andrew Romine in 2018, which makes the idea of **Kris Negron** so appealing moving forward. He has a very nice mustache, you see. ⊗ *You swung so fast at that hanger / Only eighteen but just hit a banger / And* *it goes back, back, back, to the trees / Didn't you, **Juan Querecuto**?* ⊗ Any prospect shine has almost completely worn off **Joe Rizzo**. At only twenty-one there's still plenty of time for the former 2nd-round pick, but he'll need to start showing he can slug higher than the mid-.300's if he wants to find himself on organizational top-10 lists, and/or move into the mid-minors. ⊗ The Mariners let **Andrew Romine** spend all of 2018 on the big league roster. As he was both very bad at baseball and exceedingly quiet, we can only assume he positioned himself behind Nelson Cruz whenever the team's executives were around, and they forgot he was there. You can always tell a Romine Man. ⊗ The Dipoto Collective loves nothing more than a swing adjustment, and none were bigger than that of **Dom Thompson-Williams**, who put it together at age 23 in Low and High-A ball. The toolsy former Yankee product makes lots of easy outs, but a high HR/FB rate and low infield fly rate suggests he might be onto something. ⊗ How to make **Donnie Walton** at home: Start with two quarts of Bloomquist stock, simmering at 200 degrees. Add two cups chopped Ryan Theriot, a peel of Brooks Conrad, and two-thirds cup of melted Kelby Tomlinson. Stir until fully mixed, add powdered David Eckstein to flavor. Serve, and enjoy. ⊗ Every baseball player needs a standout tool to get noticed. Joey Gallo had power. Billy Hamilton had speed. In **Nick Zammarelli's** case his, uh, well, his name is very fun to say loudly and dramatically.

Pitchers

PITCHER	TEAM	LVL	AGE	W	L	SV	G	GS	IP	H	HR	BB/9	K/9	K	GB%	BABIP	WHIP	ERA	DRA	WARP	MPH	FB%	WHF	CSP
Shawn Armstrong	TAC	AAA	27	2	5	15	49	0	56	38	3	4.2	13.2	82	35%	.294	1.14	1.77	2.16	1.9				
	SEA	MLB	27	0	1	1	14	0	14²	9	1	1.8	9.2	15	44%	.229	0.82	1.23	4.40	0.1	95.3	39.2	12.7	52.1
Gerson Bautista	BIN	AA	23	1	0	0	6	0	9¹	12	0	0.0	14.5	15	42%	.500	1.29	4.82	1.88	0.3				
	NYN	MLB	23	0	1	0	5	0	4¹	8	2	10.4	6.2	3	35%	.400	3.00	12.46	7.18	-0.1	99.6	81.1	8.9	52
	LVG	AAA	23	3	1	3	31	0	39²	54	3	4.1	12.3	54	24%	.443	1.82	5.22	4.74	0.2				
Chasen Bradford	TAC	AAA	28	0	0	1	7	0	6²	5	0		5.4	4	48%	.238	0.75	0.00	3.69	0.1				
	SEA	MLB	28	5	0	0	46	0	53²	55	9	2.3	6.4	38	46%	.279	1.29	3.69	5.46	-0.3	92.5	55.1	11.8	47.9
Roenis Elias	PAW	AAA	29	1	0	1	4	0	7¹	2	1	2.5	11.0	9	47%	.071	0.55	1.23	2.61	0.2				
	TAC	AAA	29	2	4	0	10	7	33²	32	1	4.0	8.3	31	44%	.313	1.40	4.54	4.30	0.4				
	SEA	MLB	29	3	1	0	23	4	51	46	1	2.8	6.0	34	35%	.285	1.22	2.65	5.35	-0.2	95.6	55	9.8	46.9
Joey Gerber	EVE	A-	21	1	0	6	13	0	14	9	0	3.9	13.5	21	59%	.333	1.07	1.93	2.71	0.4				
	CLN	A	21	0	0	2	9	0	11²	9	0	3.9	17.0	22	35%	.450	1.20	2.31	2.00	0.4				
Justin Grimm	KCA	MLB	29	1	3	0	16	0	12²	17	2	9.9	5.7	8	44%	.349	2.45	13.50	7.86	-0.4	94.6	52.1	7.1	44.8
	SEA	MLB	29	0	0	0	5	0	4²	2	1	0.0	5.8	3	23%	.083	0.43	1.93	3.50	0.1	95.5	43.6	14.6	53.1
Max Povse	TAC	AAA	24	1	6	0	8	8	36²	40	6	6.9	11.0	45	43%	.362	1.85	8.84	4.52	0.4				
	ARK	AA	24	4	3	0	10	10	60²	62	2	2.8	8.9	60	47%	.347	1.34	3.41	4.20	0.8				
Zac Rosscup	LAN	MLB	30	0	1	0	17	0	11¹	9	3	3.2	15.9	20	30%	.300	1.15	4.76	3.75	0.2	93.8	49.5	21	40.2
Nick Rumbelow	TAC	AAA	26	1	0	2	13	0	17²	13	1	4.1	12.7	25	38%	.308	1.19	2.04	2.76	0.5				
	SEA	MLB	26	0	0	0	13	0	17²	19	6	3.1	8.2	16	33%	.271	1.42	6.11	5.95	-0.2	95.0	50.9	11.3	49
Marc Rzepczynski	SEA	MLB	32	0	1	0	18	0	7²	13	2	10.6	11.7	10	61%	.423	2.87	9.39	3.36	0.1	93.2	52.8	14.2	42.2
	CLE	MLB	32	0	0	0	5	0	2²	3	0	3.4	3.4	1	62%	.375	1.50	0.00	5.48	0.0	92.8	59.5	10.8	52.8
	TAC	AAA	32	0	0	0	12	0	9¹	15	2	7.7	9.6	10	66%	.433	2.46	9.64	4.18	0.1				
Ricardo Sanchez	DNV	Rk	21	1	0	0	2	2	11²	11	1	2.3	6.9	9	54%	.278	1.20	3.09	3.72	0.3				
	MIS	AA	21	2	5	0	13	13	57²	65	3	3.7	6.9	44	41%	.333	1.54	4.06	6.19	-0.6				
Sam Tuivailala	SLN	MLB	25	3	3	0	31	0	31²	35	3	3.1	7.4	26	50%	.314	1.45	3.69	4.77	0.1	97.3	58.7	10.6	52.3
	SEA	MLB	25	1	0	0	5	0	5¹	6	0	1.7	6.8	4	56%	.375	1.31	1.69	2.93	0.1	96.6	63	13.6	53.9
Art Warren	ARK	AA	25	1	2	2	14	0	15²	10	0	8.0	12.6	22	39%	.303	1.53	1.72	3.37	0.3				
Rob Whalen	SEA	MLB	24	0	0	0	1	0	4	1	0	2.2	0.0	0	46%	.077	0.50	0.00	6.80	-0.1	91.9	59.6	6.4	48.1
	TAC	AAA	24	7	7	0	20	20	99¹	119	5	3.4	8.3	92	48%	.360	1.57	5.16	4.38	1.3				
	ARK	AA	24	0	2	0	2	2	6	10	1	4.5	12.0	8	52%	.450	2.17	7.50	3.71	0.1				

It is tempting to ridicule **Shawn Armstrong** for letting nominative determinisim direct his vocational pursuits. But as long as he can keep that walk rate down, the Mariners won't have to worry about his low-90s fastball making him liable in a suit for false advertising. ⊗ Relief prospect **Gerson Bautista** was able to top 101 miles per hour during one of his extremely brief and ineffective stints with the Mets last year. Because said fastball is arrow-straight, this is likely the last time "Gerson Bautista" and "top 101" will ever be found in the same sentence. ⊗ From June 17th until August 31st, the Mariners went 1-13 in games **Chasen Bradford** appeared in. This is probably an indication that he's simply a mop-up reliever, but we should at least consider the possibility that he's the human equivalent of a mummy's curse. ⊗ It may not be as catchy, but "Life is like a **Roenis Elias** Curveball: Slow, loopy, and prone to massive failure" is much more authentic to the human condition. ⊗ **Joey Gerber** struck out a ridiculous number of batters—over 40 percent—in his abbreviated introduction to pro ball. A late bloomer in college, he's a relief prospect only, but on the bright side, Mariners fans: He's a prospect. ⊗ For years **Justin Grimm** built his success in large part on his ability to get hitters to chase pitches out of the strike zone. His stuff has degraded to the point where that they don't do that much anymore, and now his name serves as a very full and complete self-scouting report. ⊗ "**David Phelps**", the Mariners answered when asked who would get the ball to Edwin Diaz. "Dave Phelps, Dave Phelps, Dave Phelps." Instead his year was lost to injury and rehab. One certainly hopes he fully recovers. After all, people say he has a cannon for an arm. ⊗ The term for a player who succeeds in AAA but struggles in MLB is "AAAA player". **Max Povse**, however, succeeds in AA but struggles in AAA. Scholars are split on whether this makes him a "AA.5" or "AAa" player. ⊗ **Zac Rosscup** tossed an immaculate inning in late August against the Mariners, making him one of only 87 pitchers to ever achieve such a feat. So that's cool. ⊗ Jerry Dipoto asked the Yankees for **Nick Rumbelow** on purpose, meaning that he knew his name, and didn't have to awkwardly google how to spell it. This is high praise for both men. Excellent work, gents. ⊗ In 2018 **Marc Rzepczynski** lost his command, lost his job, lost his spot in Seattle, and for all we know lost his dog too. What he didn't lose was his contract, which paid $5.5 million dollars last year. Admittedly that part doesn't make for a great country song. ⊗ The Braves were high enough on **Ricardo Sanchez** to protect him from the Rule 5 draft, but their reward was a mediocre season at Double-A and more health concerns. ⊗ Every Mariners season, no matter how promising or postseason-destined it may appear, is doomed to end in misery and pain. Still, losing **Sam Tuivailala** to a snapped Achilles in August seemed a little too on the nose, even for whichever hamfisted hack Fate employs to write out the script for the cursed franchise. ⊗ In EMPIRE RECORDS (1995), young record store employee Lucas responds to an inquiry as to his purpose behind gluing quarters to the floor with, "I don't feel I need to explain my art to you, Warren." This serves as good an explanation for **Art Warren's** 2018 walk rate as we can conceive. ⊗ **Rob Whalen** is a strong arm from the right, and despite the incredible advantage society gives someone from that position, he's floundered in large part due to his own failures.

ST. LOUIS CARDINALS

Essay by Russell Carleton

Player comments by Matthew Trueblood and BP staff

Flash back to the warm glow of 2011. The Cardinals had just won the World Series, surely not suspecting that it would be the last time that they did so for a while. Cardinals fans know what happened next. Albert Pujols, a man who had spent most of the previous decade winning MVPs, terrorizing opposing pitchers, and authoring a career already worthy of the Hall of Fame, was a free agent. At the time, he was about to enter his age-32 season, but was coming off a season in which he had produced 6.3 WARP.

What if the Cardinals had signed just signed Albert Pujols? The conventional wisdom is that the Cardinals dodged a bullet when they let Pujols decamp for the West Coast, and that Pujols's contract is now one of the most un-tradeable assets in baseball. There had even been talk that the Angels would release him before his contract expired. He still has 20 HR power, but with a sub-.300 OBP and limited defensive and baserunning value, he's starting to look like the kind of guy who would be replaced quickly if he were making $500,000.

Here's Pujols's contract that he actually signed with the Los Angeles, California Angels of Anaheim, California, and the WARP that he's produced since then.

Year	Salary	WARP
2012	$12,000,000	4.0
2013	$16,000,000	2.1
2014	$23,000,000	2.8
2015	$24,000,000	2.6
2016	$25,000,000	1.1
2017	$26,000,000	-1.8
2018	$27,000,000	0.5
2019	$28,000,000	?
2020	$29,000,000	?
2021	$30,000,000	?
2022-2031	$10,000,000 (personal services contract)	--

Let's go back in time and erase the word "Angels" on that contract and replace it with "Cardinals." How might recent Cardinal history have been different? It's a question that gets harder to answer the further that we get from 2012, when Pujols's contract with the Angels started. After all, a baseball team is an array of moving parts, and when you change one piece, the effects ripple through the system. It is fortunate

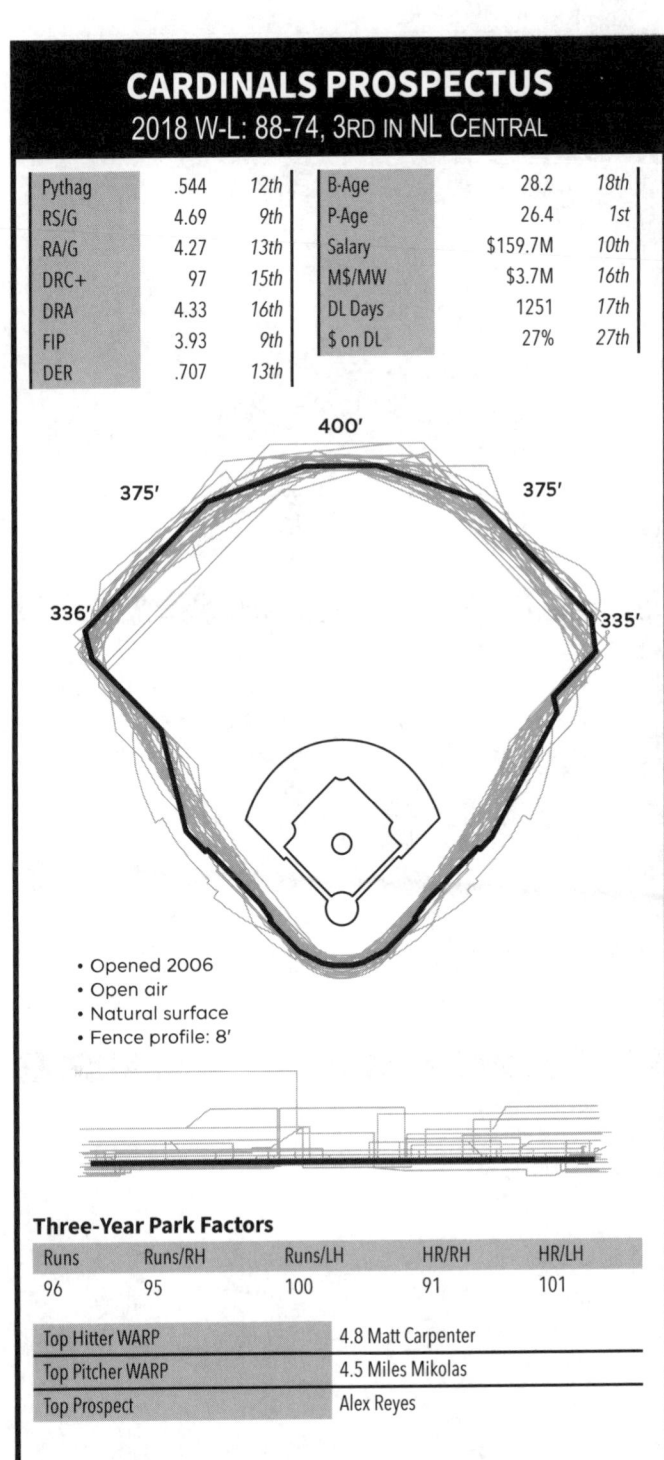

CARDINALS PROSPECTUS
2018 W-L: 88-74, 3RD IN NL CENTRAL

Pythag	.544	12th	B-Age	28.2	18th
RS/G	4.69	9th	P-Age	26.4	1st
RA/G	4.27	13th	Salary	$159.7M	10th
DRC+	97	15th	M$/MW	$3.7M	16th
DRA	4.33	16th	DL Days	1251	17th
FIP	3.93	9th	$ on DL	27%	27th
DER	.707	13th			

400'

375'   375'

336'   335'

- Opened 2006
- Open air
- Natural surface
- Fence profile: 8'

Three-Year Park Factors

Runs	Runs/RH	Runs/LH	HR/RH	HR/LH
96	95	100	91	101

Top Hitter WARP	4.8 Matt Carpenter
Top Pitcher WARP	4.5 Miles Mikolas
Top Prospect	Alex Reyes

2018 Hit List Ranking

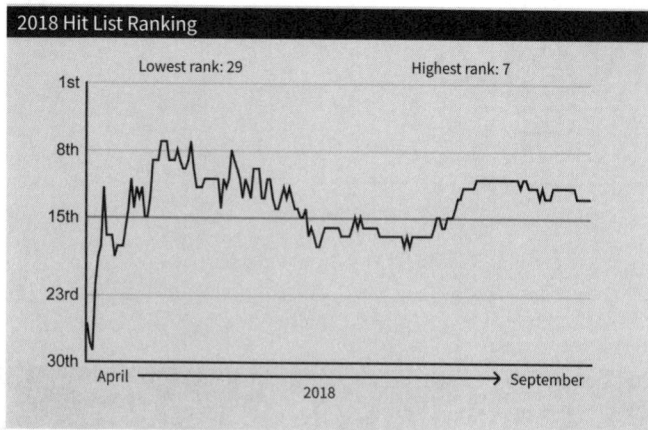

Committed Payroll (in millions)

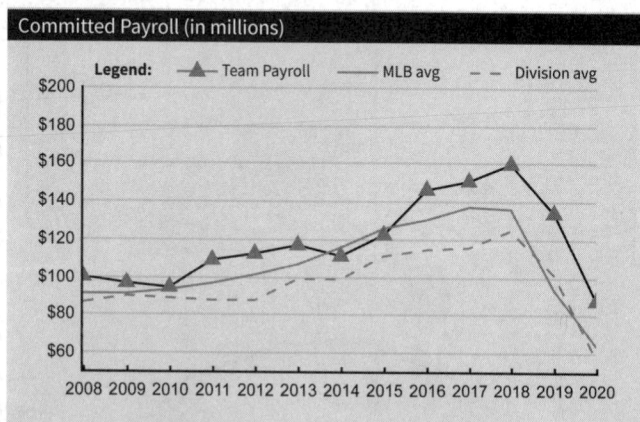

Farm System Ranking

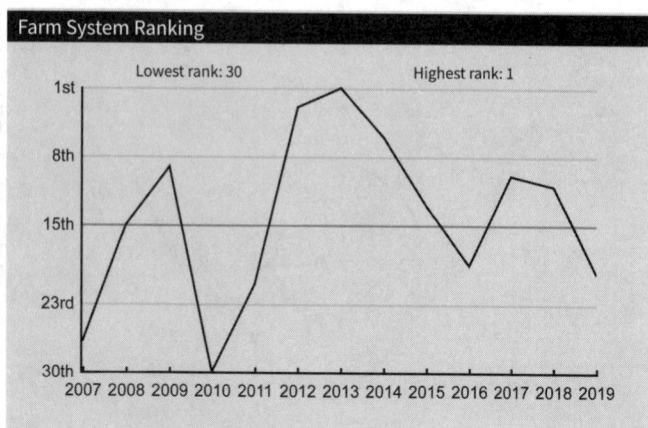

Personnel

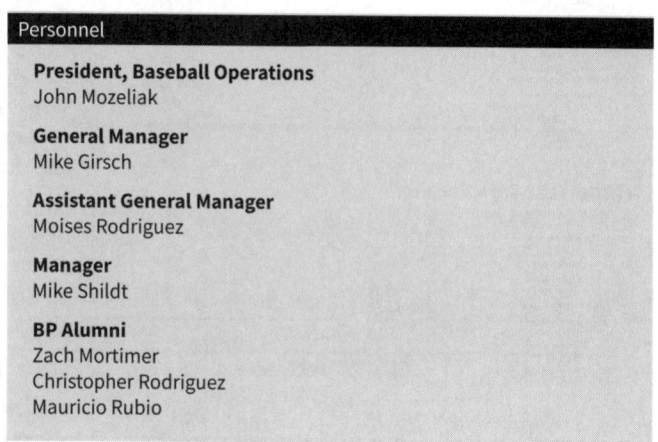

President, Baseball Operations
John Mozeliak

General Manager
Mike Girsch

Assistant General Manager
Moises Rodriguez

Manager
Mike Shildt

BP Alumni
Zach Mortimer
Christopher Rodriguez
Mauricio Rubio

for us that the Cardinals began their post-Pujols era by doing something which was obviously meant as a 1-to-1 compensatory move.

2012

On December 23rd, 2011, the Cardinals signed Carlos Beltrán to a 2-year contract and slid him into right field. Fortunately for this exercise, his salaries in 2012 and 2013 ($13 million in both years) are pretty close to what Pujols got from the Angels. In the meantime, regular Cardinals 2011 right fielder Lance Berkman grabbed a first baseman's glove from Pujols's vacated locker returning to a spot that had been his primary hangout since 2005. At least that was the plan. Berkman eventually hurt his knee in 2012 and only appeared in 32 games for the Cardinals. It's impossible to know whether Berkman would have been injured if he had been patrolling right field while Pujols had been stretching for infield throws at first. We know from Berkman's 2011 performance that he probably would have been a below average right fielder, but his performance at first base in what parts of 2012 (and eventually, 2013 and 2014) he did play shows that his defense at first wasn't much better.

Berkman's injury did reveal Allen Craig to the world—this was back when Allen Craig actually got MVP votes—and had Pujols been on the roster, Craig would have likely played in a corner outfield position. Advanced defensive metrics rated Craig as a somewhat below average first baseman in 2012 (and 2013), but slightly worse still in the outfield. The Cardinals probably would have lost some value there.

Verdict: In 2012, had the Cardinals signed Albert Pujols, they likely wouldn't have signed Carlos Beltrán (2.8 WARP for the year), and would have lost some of Allen Craig's defensive value. Compared to Pujols's 4.0 WARP, the Cardinals came out losers by something like 1.5 to 2 wins. Giving those two wins back to the 88-74 Cardinals wouldn't have made much difference in the standings. They still would have visited Atlanta for the Wild Card game (which they won), and the Nationals in the NLDS (which they won). Could Pujols, rather than Beltrán, have won them the extra game against the Giants in the NLCS that they would have needed to make the World Series? It's at least plausible that the answer is "yes."

2013

In 2013, for the second straight year, Carlos Beltrán made $13,000,000 and provided 2.8 WARP for the Cardinals. This time, under-earning Pujols by $3 million and out-performing him by 0.7 WARP. The biggest "moves" that the Cardinals made in the 2012-13 offseason involved signing lefty reliever Randy Choate (0.2 WARP) and utility guy Ty Wigginton (-0.6 WARP in 63 PA!) to contracts which paid them a combined $4 million in 2013. There's your cost-savings from not signing Pujols.

In the "signed Pujols" world, again, Beltrán, Choate, and Wigginton would have been elsewhere, with Allen Craig likely in a corner outfield spot for most of the season. But the biggest casualty of the counterfactual would have been Matt Adams, who emerged as the Cardinals' first baseman of choice (and actually did push Craig to the corners) while providing 1.1 WARP in value. Had Pujols been on the cold corner, the Cardinals would have likely been forced to use either Craig or Adams strictly in a pinch hitting role. It's reasonable to say that the Cardinals ended up a win or so better off for the fact that Albert Pujols wasn't there.

Verdict: The Cardinals had the best record in the National League in 2013 and made the World Series. Removing a win of value from that team by re-inserting Albert Pujols probably doesn't derail that train, but it wouldn't have helped. In the same wishy-washy way that Pujols might have helped the Cardinals a bit in 2012, he probably would have hurt the Cardinals a bit in 2013.

2014 and 2015

Now, we begin the post-Beltrán era of Cardinals history and the era where Fat Albert started to have a particularly fat contract ($23 million in 2014; $24 million in 2015). We also begin the part of the exercise where it's harder to nail down what moves the Cardinals made because they weren't committed to paying Albert Pujols that money. Other players (and their salaries) had since come off the books and some of the surrounding cast had changed. The closest thing to a replacement for Beltrán that the Cardinals committed to on the free agent market was Jhonny Peralta who checked in at a tidy $15 million salary in 2014 and 2015. Peralta responded by putting up 4.4 and 4.1 WARP in those seasons, respectively, besting Pujols by roughly a win and a half each season, with some change left over.

Had Pujols been on the Cardinals' roster, Peralta likely would have taken his talents elsewhere, and it's questionable whether the Cardinals would have felt as comfortable as they did in extending franchise icons Adam Wainwright and Yadier Molina with the contracts that they got. In 2014 and 2015, Molina made $15 million and Wainwright made $19.5 million, and both made sizeable contributions to the team. Maybe the Cardinals would have kept Waino and Yadi around, and some other contributor (Jon Jay?) would have been sent away. Then again, a more charitable read would be that Pujols's presence on the Cardinals' roster would have created a logjam at first base and would have forced the Cardinals to trade away either Craig or Adams for what at the time would have been considered a loss. Given that both men turned into pumpkins shortly thereafter, it might have actually been a blessing in disguise.

Verdict: In both 2014 and 2015, the Cardinals finished in first place in the Central, two games ahead of the Pittsburgh Pirates in each year. In our alternate universe with El Hombre still a Redbird, it's likely that Jhonny Peralta and at least one other contributor would have been lacking in the Cards' lineup, which would have been a difference of 2 or 3 wins. In 2014, three fewer wins would have knocked the Cardinals out of the playoffs, while in 2015, it would have knocked them into the second Wild Card spot. It's probably a good thing

that Albert Pujols was no longer around. If the Cardinals cleared any value from their decision to let Albert walk (slowly) away, it was during these years.

2016-2018

And so we enter the modern era of Cardinal malaise. There's no glory (or high draft picks) in 80-something wins and no playoff appearances, but that's pretty much been the Cards for the last three seasons. Meanwhile, Albert Pujols made 25, then 26, then 27 million dollars (and on the whole functioned below replacement level) during the last three years with the Angels. His poor showing in the American League would have been exacerbated by the fact that the Cardinals, lacking the DH option, would either have to play him in the field—something that he stopped doing full time in 2016—or relegate him to a bench bat. Realistically, even the modest Jose Martinez would have been a better everyday option at first. Pujols might have already been politely asked to leave by this point.

On the banks of the Mississippi River though, the guys on whom the Cardinals seem to have spent the "Pujols money" haven't exactly covered themselves in glory. In 2016 and 2017, Jhonny Peralta suddenly forgot how to play baseball and turned in seasons of -0.3 and -0.5 WARP. Wainwright and Molina, once perennial All-Stars, turned into guys who are worthy of a roster spot, but nothing special. Still, that's better than a negative number, so the Cardinals were likely better off without Pujols than they would have been with him, but the Cardinals were still spending money on late career players in decline.

Verdict: Signing Albert Pujols probably would have meant that Adam Wainwright would have been slinging curveballs in San Diego by now. Even though the Cardinals were probably better for not having signed Pujols, they didn't make the playoffs with him, so it's not like things would be that much different.

2019 and beyond

This is the part where it becomes a team preview. It's tempting to look back on not signing Albert Pujols, seeing his dwindling WARP over the past half-decade, and figuring that the Cardinals now have "so much extra payroll flexibility" because they aren't responsible for paying him nearly $90 million over the next three years. Someone out there is tying the Cardinals trade for the last year of Paul Goldschmidt's contract to that fact right now. (He isn't blocked at first by Pujols!)

That's now how things work. An honest look at the Cardinals' payroll sheet tells a different story. Had the Cardinals signed Pujols and promised to pay him $28 and $29 million over the next two years for what everyone would have correctly predicted—even in 2011—would be "decline" years, it's very likely that they wouldn't have signed Yadier Molina to a contract that pays him $20 million in each of the next two years for what are likely to be Molina's "decline" years. (Yes, Molina gave the Cards 3.0 WARP last year, but 36-year-old catchers tend to be bad bets going forward.)

There seems to be a piece of every team's payroll which is reserved for keeping around fan favorites and paying off the back ends of contracts given to star players signed five years earlier.

In a world where a win above replacement is allegedly worth $10 million, but the highest paid players in baseball are just now reaching toward the $40 million mark, we know that the real currency of the game at the high end of the free agent market is extra years on a contract. Partisans who lauded the Cardinals non-decision in the Winter of 2011 because it would allow the Cardinals to have more flexibility once 2019 rolled around are probably miffed to realize that the Cardinals just made a junior varsity version of the same—is mistake the correct word here?

In retrospect, the Cardinals probably did get the better of the decision not to sign Pujols to that ten-year deal that he wanted (and got from the Angels). Instead, they got two years of Carlos Beltrán who turned out to be Pujols's equal in value, then two years of good Jhonny Peralta and the ability to extend a couple of other guys, then two years of bad Jhonny Peralta, and finally, the back end of Yadier Molina's career. They got four years of pretty good performance, followed by a tailing off. The tailing off wasn't as severe as Pujols, nor was the cash outlay quite as much, and the net effect was a couple of wins of value—a phrase which by its construction under-sells how tremendously impactful "a couple wins of value" are—but it's funny to note that the arc of Pujols's replacements have tended to follow a somewhat less odious version of the path that contracts like Pujols's usually take.

If you want to look back on Cardinals management over the last decade and make some statement about their general abilities at navigating this whole baseball thing, the decision not to sign Albert Pujols was not a sign that they had somehow transcended the usual pratfalls of modern baseball free agency signings. They still did most of the same things that drive people crazy, but they had the good sense to do it a little bit at a time. ∎

—Russell Carleton is an author of Baseball Prospectus.

HITTERS

Randy Arozarena LF Born: 02/28/95 Age: 24 Bats: R Throws: R Height: 5'11" Weight: 170 Origin: International Free Agent, 2016

YEAR	TEAM	LVL	AGE	PA	R	2B	3B	HR	RBI	BB	K	SB	CS	AVG/OBP/SLG	DRC+	VORP	BABIP	BRR	FRAA	WARP
2017	PMB	A+	22	295	38	22	3	8	40	13	53	10	4	.275/.333/.472	116	23.4	.313	-2.5	LF(47): 4.3, CF(13): -0.5	1.6
2017	SFD	AA	22	195	34	10	1	3	9	27	34	8	3	.252/.366/.380	106	8.2	.299	2.7	LF(40): 0.1, CF(4): -0.9	0.8
2018	SFD	AA	23	102	22	5	0	7	21	6	25	9	3	.396/.455/.681	125	15.4	.492	1.0	RF(12): 1.6, CF(6): -0.4	0.8
2018	MEM	AAA	23	311	42	16	0	5	28	28	59	17	5	.232/.328/.348	77	9.3	.278	0.8	LF(49): -2.7, RF(18): 0.2	-0.3
2019	SLN	MLB	24	251	31	7	1	5	20	20	58	9	3	.201/.288/.308	66	-2.3	.250	0.6	LF 0, RF 0	-0.4

Breakout: 3%   Improve: 26%   Collapse: 12%   Attrition: 22%   MLB: 47%   *Comparables: Austin Slater, Chad Huffman, Alex Hassan*

There's more strength to Arozarena, from the hands and wrists up through the shoulders and down into his legs, than in most players of his size. It's not translating into consistent or intimidating power, however, and the way his swing works, it might not ever do so. As he's not ever likely to become a viable everyday center fielder, that puts real pressure on Arozarena's pure hit tool. His approach is polished, though he's still learning to adjust at the incredibly rapid pace the upper levels of professional baseball require. With plenty of speed and arm for either corner, he will get numerous chances to carve out a role, but without a studied change to that swing to generate more natural pop, it might be a strictly complementary one.

Harrison Bader CF Born: 06/03/94 Age: 25 Bats: R Throws: R Height: 6'0" Weight: 195 Origin: Round 3, 2015 Draft (#100 overall)

YEAR	TEAM	LVL	AGE	PA	R	2B	3B	HR	RBI	BB	K	SB	CS	AVG/OBP/SLG	DRC+	VORP	BABIP	BRR	FRAA	WARP
2016	MEM	AAA	22	161	22	7	1	3	17	11	38	2	3	.231/.298/.354	77	2.5	.292	-0.1	CF(26): 1.5, LF(16): 0.7	0.3
2016	SFD	AA	22	356	48	12	4	16	41	25	93	11	10	.283/.351/.497	119	29.5	.349	0.7	CF(77): 0.9, RF(4): -0.4	2.1
2017	MEM	AAA	23	479	74	18	1	20	55	34	118	15	9	.283/.347/.469	105	40.8	.345	5.3	CF(111): 13.7, LF(3): -0.4	3.9
2017	SLN	MLB	23	92	10	3	0	3	10	5	24	2	1	.235/.283/.376	80	1.3	.288	0.3	CF(20): 2.0, LF(7): -0.1	0.3
2018	SLN	MLB	24	427	61	20	2	12	37	31	125	15	3	.264/.334/.422	85	24.7	.358	2.8	CF(74): 9.1, RF(38): 1.6	2.0
2019	SLN	MLB	25	559	69	23	2	18	63	41	161	14	6	.236/.308/.397	91	16.3	.311	1.0	CF 12	3.0

Breakout: 2%   Improve: 36%   Collapse: 4%   Attrition: 26%   MLB: 88%   *Comparables: Michael Taylor, Cameron Maybin, Peter Bourjos*

If Starling Marte is a tall drink of water, physically, Bader is more like a shot of whiskey. Beyond that, however, there are striking similarities between them. Both have only average power, but stoked by their top-of-the-scale speed and aggressiveness, that plays up a bit, as doubles become triples, long singles become doubles, and singles become opportunities to steal second base. Both have strong arms in center field. When he's going well, Bader even shows good plate discipline, just as Marte does. The problem is, even more than Marte—more than almost anyone—Bader has contact problems. The only batters who fanned more often than Bader and had an ISO as low or lower than his were JaCoby Jones, Lewis Brinson, and Chris Davis. Unless and until he fixes that, he's going to be a suspect starting center fielder for a contender.

Dylan Carlson CF   Born: 10/23/98   Age: 20   Bats: B   Throws: L   Height: 6'3"   Weight: 195   Origin: Round 1, 2016 Draft (#33 overall)

YEAR	TEAM	LVL	AGE	PA	R	2B	3B	HR	RBI	BB	K	SB	CS	AVG/OBP/SLG	DRC+	VORP	BABIP	BRR	FRAA	WARP
2016	CRD	RK	17	201	30	13	3	3	22	16	52	4	2	.251/.313/.404	99	1.2	.333	-1.6	CF(41): 6.5, LF(9): 0.2	1.0
2017	PEO	A	18	451	63	18	1	7	42	52	116	6	6	.240/.342/.347	95	14.2	.323	2.6	RF(79): 0.8, CF(24): 0.1	1.0
2018	PEO	A	19	57	5	3	0	2	9	10	10	2	0	.234/.368/.426	116	1.4	.257	-0.7	RF(10): 2.3, CF(4): -0.3	0.4
2018	PMB	A+	19	441	63	19	3	9	53	52	78	6	3	.247/.345/.386	115	18.3	.286	1.7	RF(50): 4.7, LF(37): -0.1	2.4
2019	*SLN*	*MLB*	*20*	*251*	*23*	*7*	*0*	*7*	*26*	*20*	*62*	*1*	*0*	*.202/.273/.320*	*59*	*-6.1*	*.245*	*-0.6*	*RF -1, LF 1*	*-0.7*

Breakout: 3%   Improve: 10%   Collapse: 0%   Attrition: 5%   MLB: 12%   *Comparables: Nomar Mazara, Jesse Winker, Caleb Gindl*

Calling 31 extra-base hits in 441 plate appearances a minor power breakout correctly (if modestly) characterizes Carlson's profile. He invites projection. Sure, he barely cracked double digits in the home run column in 2018, but he did it as a teenager, in the pitcher-friendly Midwest and Florida State Leagues. He controlled the strike zone, handled velocity well, and showed good instincts on the bases. His hit tool has to jump up to the other side of average in order for his potential to become production, but Carlson has all kinds of time, a build that really allows you to dream on the power, and the eternal platoon advantage.

Matt Carpenter 3B   Born: 11/26/85   Age: 33   Bats: L   Throws: R   Height: 6'3"   Weight: 205   Origin: Round 13, 2009 Draft (#399 overall)

YEAR	TEAM	LVL	AGE	PA	R	2B	3B	HR	RBI	BB	K	SB	CS	AVG/OBP/SLG	DRC+	VORP	BABIP	BRR	FRAA	WARP
2016	SLN	MLB	30	566	81	36	6	21	68	81	108	0	4	.271/.380/.505	129	45.7	.307	1.2	3B(54): -3.9, 1B(45): 0.1	3.4
2017	SLN	MLB	31	622	91	31	2	23	69	109	125	2	1	.241/.384/.451	129	34.1	.274	-2.4	1B(120): 2.1, 3B(16): 0.9	3.5
2018	SLN	MLB	32	677	111	42	0	36	81	102	158	4	1	.257/.374/.523	137	54.8	.291	-1.5	1B(95): -3.6, 3B(76): 4.8	4.8
2019	*SLN*	*MLB*	*33*	*641*	*92*	*38*	*2*	*24*	*81*	*93*	*139*	*3*	*2*	*.263/.378/.474*	*134*	*40.4*	*.312*	*-0.6*	*3B 4, 2B 0*	*4.7*

Breakout: 0%   Improve: 22%   Collapse: 4%   Attrition: 12%   MLB: 97%   *Comparables: Paul Konerko, Mark Teixeira, Nick Swisher*

There are, perhaps, a half-dozen players who stand clear of the rest of the league in the simple and invaluable skill of generating high-value contact at a very high rate: J.D. Martinez, Khris Davis, Mookie Betts, Joey Gallo, Ryan Zimmerman, and now, Carpenter. The former average-over-power utility guy was on the cutting edge of the launch angle revolution, when he first got more aggressive, traded some contact for power, and lifted the ball more often. In 2018, he redoubled that tradeoff. If it was a science project, it was a successful experiment, because he ratcheted his ground-ball rate all the way down to the second-lowest in MLB, and he found an entirely new level of power. There's some evidence, though, that it was actually out of necessity, and that makes his outlook a bit dimmer than it otherwise might be. Carpenter had never had a whiff rate north of 10.6 percent against breaking pitches until 2018, when it soared to 15.7 percent. His whiff rate of 14.7 percent against offspeed stuff was only slightly less alarming. During the summer, when he locked onto some fastballs and laid waste to the league, that wasn't a huge concern, but by September, the league rediscovered his kryptonite and laid waste to him. In the age of the breaking ball, any fastball hitter, even one like Carpenter, is under imminent threat.

Paul DeJong SS   Born: 08/02/93   Age: 25   Bats: R   Throws: R   Height: 6'1"   Weight: 195   Origin: Round 4, 2015 Draft (#131 overall)

YEAR	TEAM	LVL	AGE	PA	R	2B	3B	HR	RBI	BB	K	SB	CS	AVG/OBP/SLG	DRC+	VORP	BABIP	BRR	FRAA	WARP
2016	SFD	AA	22	552	62	29	2	22	73	40	144	3	2	.260/.324/.460	118	31.1	.318	-1.8	3B(112): -4.3, SS(11): 0.9	2.6
2017	MEM	AAA	23	190	27	9	0	13	34	9	46	0	2	.299/.339/.571	122	18.0	.336	-1.0	SS(39): -3.8, 2B(5): 0.4	0.9
2017	SLN	MLB	23	443	55	26	1	25	65	21	124	1	0	.285/.325/.532	106	32.4	.349	-3.9	SS(86): -0.3, 2B(20): -0.7	1.8
2018	SLN	MLB	24	490	68	25	1	19	68	36	123	1	1	.241/.313/.433	99	34.8	.288	3.1	SS(114): 0.3	2.6
2019	*SLN*	*MLB*	*25*	*570*	*69*	*28*	*2*	*24*	*77*	*40*	*147*	*1*	*1*	*.249/.314/.450*	*105*	*24.2*	*.303*	*-0.4*	*SS -1*	*2.4*

Breakout: 4%   Improve: 58%   Collapse: 8%   Attrition: 11%   MLB: 99%   *Comparables: Javier Baez, Trevor Story, Ian Stewart*

In every important way, 2018 was a big step forward for DeJong. He hit the ball harder, and regularly put it in the air. He dialed back his aggressiveness early in counts and drew more walks. He used the opposite field better, and made a much-needed adjustment against breaking balls from fellow right-handers, helping him cut down his strikeout rate. After living as an infield nomad on his way up the ladder, he settled in as the Cardinals' everyday shortstop and improved as a defender there. His rookie numbers were fluky, but given his age and rapid maturation, his true talent level seems to be progressing toward matching them. Chalk him up as another huge win for the St. Louis amateur scouting and player development units.

Dexter Fowler OF   Born: 03/22/86   Age: 33   Bats: B   Throws: R   Height: 6'5"   Weight: 195   Origin: Round 14, 2004 Draft (#410 overall)

YEAR	TEAM	LVL	AGE	PA	R	2B	3B	HR	RBI	BB	K	SB	CS	AVG/OBP/SLG	DRC+	VORP	BABIP	BRR	FRAA	WARP
2016	CHN	MLB	30	551	84	25	7	13	48	79	124	13	4	.276/.393/.447	114	47.1	.350	1.1	CF(121): -11.4	1.9
2017	SLN	MLB	31	491	68	22	9	18	64	63	101	7	3	.264/.363/.488	120	36.9	.305	1.4	CF(109): -10.1	2.2
2018	SLN	MLB	32	334	40	10	0	8	31	38	75	5	2	.180/.278/.298	85	-1.6	.210	2.0	RF(75): -4.3	-0.1
2019	*SLN*	*MLB*	*33*	*295*	*38*	*14*	*2*	*8*	*30*	*33*	*66*	*5*	*2*	*.244/.337/.402*	*108*	*11.9*	*.299*	*0.7*	*RF -1*	*1.1*

Breakout: 1%   Improve: 34%   Collapse: 6%   Attrition: 9%   MLB: 94%   *Comparables: Matt Joyce, Trot Nixon, Jim King*

The Cardinals' decision to move Fowler to right field during the winter of 2017-18 was fraught with risk. Fowler's weaknesses as a center fielder (a lack of confidence in charging ground-ball hits, a weak arm) could only be exacerbated by that change. Asking him to learn new angles and still cover an outfield spot didn't reduce the risk of injury to his lanky, sometimes-fragile frame, the way a transition to first base might have. Most importantly, however, the move sent a clear message to Fowler: one year into a five-year deal, he was being demoted and deprioritized. He also lost his place at the top of the batting order, forcing him to alter his approach at the plate. He tried to do so; he failed. Then, amid a painful season for a player with a sterling reputation for clubhouse citizenship, Cardinals president John Mozeliak piled on, wielding harsh and implicitly racist remarks about Fowler's effort and focus. Fowler was unable to make the mental and physical adjustments necessary to succeed, but few players in recent memory have been more unfairly mistreated and misunderstood by their own team.

Adolis Garcia RF   Born: 03/02/93   Age: 26   Bats: R   Throws: R   Height: 6'1"   Weight: 180   Origin: International Free Agent, 2017

YEAR	TEAM	LVL	AGE	PA	R	2B	3B	HR	RBI	BB	K	SB	CS	AVG/OBP/SLG	DRC+	VORP	BABIP	BRR	FRAA	WARP
2017	SFD	AA	24	342	43	23	0	12	55	26	77	12	8	.285/.339/.476	105	18.6	.338	0.3	RF(73): 10.2, CF(10): 2.7	2.4
2017	MEM	AAA	24	147	21	11	2	3	10	7	31	3	1	.301/.342/.478	74	9.5	.369	1.9	RF(24): 0.6, CF(10): 1.9	0.4
2018	MEM	AAA	25	428	62	25	4	22	71	14	99	10	3	.256/.281/.500	100	15.9	.283	-0.1	RF(95): 11.4, CF(6): -0.1	2.4
2018	SLN	MLB	25	17	3	1	0	0	1	0	7	0	0	.118/.118/.176	72	-2.7	.200	-0.4	RF(7): -0.4, LF(4): -0.1	-0.1
2019	SLN	MLB	26	117	13	4	1	4	14	5	29	2	1	.225/.264/.390	78	0.7	.264	0.1	CF 0, LF 0	0.2

Breakout: 6%   Improve: 17%   Collapse: 9%   Attrition: 16%   MLB: 35%   *Comparables: Ray Sadler, Josh Kroeger, Niko Goodrum*

There's a chance that the single biggest play of the season, in the entire National League, came when the strapping and athletic Garcia came tearing around third base after a throwing error late in a game against the Brewers in late September. He was sure to score the tying run, all the way from first base—until he fell hilariously onto his belly about halfway between third and home. He got up, obviously flustered, and ran right into a waiting catcher's mitt. That's where he is right now. His tools and physical profile are thoroughly impressive. He has plus power, plus speed, a plus arm, and a feel for contact. He has zero feel for the strike zone, the base paths, or the outfield. The latter takes most of the fun out of the former.

Paul Goldschmidt 1B   Born: 09/10/87   Age: 31   Bats: R   Throws: R   Height: 6'3"   Weight: 225   Origin: Round 8, 2009 Draft (#246 overall)

YEAR	TEAM	LVL	AGE	PA	R	2B	3B	HR	RBI	BB	K	SB	CS	AVG/OBP/SLG	DRC+	VORP	BABIP	BRR	FRAA	WARP
2016	ARI	MLB	28	705	106	33	3	24	95	110	150	32	5	.297/.411/.489	132	45.3	.358	1.5	1B(157): 16.1	5.8
2017	ARI	MLB	29	665	117	34	3	36	120	94	147	18	5	.297/.404/.563	146	58.0	.343	3.7	1B(151): 5.7	5.8
2018	ARI	MLB	30	690	95	35	5	33	83	90	173	7	4	.290/.389/.533	135	54.6	.359	-1.3	1B(155): 1.7	4.1
2019	SLN	MLB	31	619	89	27	3	25	88	94	149	15	4	.273/.393/.484	141	40.4	.340	0.5	1B 6	5.0

Breakout: 3%   Improve: 41%   Collapse: 3%   Attrition: 5%   MLB: 99%   *Comparables: Lance Berkman, Mark Teixeira, Todd Helton*

It was a late, drizzly, cold night in Smallville. The streets of America were quiet for a change when Clark Kent and Lois Lane curled up on the couch under a warm, fuzzy blanket. Not knowing what to do with a little down time, Lois looked to Kent and asked, "Netflix and chill?" Clark responded with a confused look, but after some searching on Urban Dictionary and roughly nine months of incubation, Paul Goldschmidt was born. Thirty years later, Goldschmidt continues to impose justice on opposing pitching. An early season run-in with some mysterious kryptonite gave way to four splendid months of superhero-like production as Goldy shows no signs of truly slowing down. With free agency and a huge payday around the corner, the rebuilding Diamondbacks sent Superman to the Cardinals in a December blockbuster, closing the book on a spectacular eight-season run in Arizona.

Nolan Gorman 3B   Born: 05/10/00   Age: 19   Bats: L   Throws: R   Height: 6'1"   Weight: 210   Origin: Round 1, 2018 Draft (#19 overall)

YEAR	TEAM	LVL	AGE	PA	R	2B	3B	HR	RBI	BB	K	SB	CS	AVG/OBP/SLG	DRC+	VORP	BABIP	BRR	FRAA	WARP
2018	JCY	RK	18	167	41	10	1	11	28	24	37	1	3	.350/.443/.664	155	25.2	.411	-0.7	3B(33): 7.6	2.2
2018	PEO	A	18	107	8	3	0	6	16	10	39	0	2	.202/.280/.426	97	2.3	.255	-0.5	3B(25): 3.9	0.7
2019	SLN	MLB	19	251	29	8	0	12	30	14	87	0	0	.195/.239/.370	62	-6.7	.247	-1.0	3B 5	-0.2

Breakout: 0%   Improve: 8%   Collapse: 2%   Attrition: 5%   MLB: 14%   *Comparables: Domingo Santana, Nomar Mazara, Freddie Freeman*

Commendably, the Cardinals pushed their top pick in the 2018 Draft as far as failure would let him get over the summer. He demolished Rookie-level competition, but more than that, he showed total control of the game—of the barrel of his bat, of his glove and throwing arm, everything. As a young 18-year-old in full-season ball, Gorman saw the game speed up some, and learned a few lessons the hard way. There are real holes in his swing, or else his combination of left-handed power and athletic prowess to suit third base wouldn't have fallen to St. Louis in June. He refused to be overmatched, though, and showed enough power even in Peoria to really get scouts excited for 2019.

Jedd Gyorko INF   Born: 09/23/88   Age: 30   Bats: R   Throws: R   Height: 5'10"   Weight: 215   Origin: Round 2, 2010 Draft (#59 overall)

YEAR	TEAM	LVL	AGE	PA	R	2B	3B	HR	RBI	BB	K	SB	CS	AVG/OBP/SLG	DRC+	VORP	BABIP	BRR	FRAA	WARP
2016	SLN	MLB	27	438	58	9	1	30	59	37	96	0	0	.243/.306/.495	125	28.3	.244	0.6	2B(46): 5.1, 3B(39): -1.6	3.5
2017	SLN	MLB	28	481	52	21	2	20	67	47	105	6	2	.272/.341/.472	108	28.4	.312	-0.4	3B(109): 10.7, 1B(10): 0.5	3.5
2018	SLN	MLB	29	402	49	19	1	11	47	44	77	2	0	.262/.346/.416	107	18.0	.303	-1.2	3B(96): -4.8, 2B(17): 0.1	1.2
2019	SLN	MLB	30	228	27	11	1	8	30	22	48	1	0	.257/.332/.439	111	9.4	.297	-0.2	3B 0, 2B 1	1.1

Breakout: 3%   Improve: 40%   Collapse: 5%   Attrition: 7%   MLB: 92%   *Comparables: Trevor Plouffe, Hank Blalock, Mark Teahen*

For the third time in three years with the Cardinals, Gyorko set a new career mark in on-base percentage, struck out less often than ever, and walked more than ever. He's not the power hitter his bizarre 2016 suggested he was, but in every other way, he's only getting better. Despite being even slower than his frame suggests, he's also used sure hands and good footwork to deliver value as a fine defender at second or third base. It all figures to go slowly downhill as he enters his thirties, but also, who thought three years ago we'd be worrying about Jedd Gyroko's thirties? As it turns out, he's given himself a surprisingly wide base of skills on which to lean as that process goes on.

Andrew Knizner C   Born: 02/03/95   Age: 24   Bats: R   Throws: R   Height: 6'1"   Weight: 200   Origin: Round 7, 2016 Draft (#226 overall)

YEAR	TEAM	LVL	AGE	PA	R	2B	3B	HR	RBI	BB	K	SB	CS	AVG/OBP/SLG	DRC+	VORP	BABIP	BRR	FRAA	WARP
2016	JCY	RK	21	222	35	12	1	6	42	21	21	0	0	.319/.423/.492	156	18.3	.331	-0.1	C(21): -0.4, 1B(19): -0.9	1.7
2017	PEO	A	22	191	18	10	1	8	29	9	22	1	1	.279/.325/.480	123	13.2	.282	0.5	C(26): -0.3, 1B(3): -0.1	1.1
2017	SFD	AA	22	202	27	13	0	4	22	14	27	0	1	.324/.371/.462	118	17.7	.355	0.5	C(49): -3.5	1.1
2018	SFD	AA	23	313	39	13	0	7	41	23	40	0	1	.313/.365/.434	115	21.9	.339	-1.4	C(74): -7.3	1.2
2018	MEM	AAA	23	61	3	5	0	0	4	4	8	0	0	.315/.383/.407	95	3.8	.370	-0.1	C(16): 1.8	0.5
2019	SLN	MLB	24	181	20	8	0	5	19	10	32	0	0	.256/.302/.390	82	3.8	.289	-0.4	C -7	-0.3

Breakout: 9%   Improve: 20%   Collapse: 15%   Attrition: 24%   MLB: 57%   *Comparables: Kevin Plawecki, Willson Contreras, J.T. Realmuto*

Another converted collegiate infielder trying to figure it out behind the plate, Knizner has something other players in the same situation haven't often had: a bat that really could play most places on the diamond. There's not a great deal of power in his profile, but his hit tool is impressive, and he doesn't get himself out. He's knocking on the door of the Majors, but now the question will have to be asked: does MLB still open the door for players without a loud tool other than the ability to hit for average? If Knizner proves those gains in framing over a larger sample, that question will be moot.

YEAR	TEAM	P. COUNT	FRM RUNS	BLK RUNS	THRW RUNS	TOT RUNS
2017	SFD	6878	-3.0	0.0	0.2	-3.9
2018	MEM	2067	1.9	0.2	-0.1	1.9
2018	SFD	10157	-3.7	-1.9	-0.1	-6.0
2019	SLN	6621	-4.7	-1.1	-0.4	-6.3

Jose Martinez   1B   Born: 07/25/88   Age: 30   Bats: R   Throws: R   Height: 6'6"   Weight: 215   Origin: International Free Agent, 2006

YEAR	TEAM	LVL	AGE	PA	R	2B	3B	HR	RBI	BB	K	SB	CS	AVG/OBP/SLG	DRC+	VORP	BABIP	BRR	FRAA	WARP
2016	OMA	AAA	27	160	18	10	0	3	18	14	24	2	0	.298/.356/.433	97	9.6	.331	1.1	1B(20): -1.6, LF(12): -0.8	0.2
2016	MEM	AAA	27	329	34	18	1	8	42	25	50	9	1	.269/.326/.415	102	3.4	.299	-1.2	LF(30): -0.2, RF(29): 0.5	0.7
2016	SLN	MLB	27	18	4	1	0	0	1	2	1	0	0	.438/.500/.500	96	2.6	.467	0.4	LF(4): 0.3, 1B(1): 0.0	0.1
2017	SLN	MLB	28	307	47	13	1	14	46	32	60	4	0	.309/.379/.518	121	25.2	.350	0.1	1B(33): 0.0, LF(24): -2.8	1.2
2018	SLN	MLB	29	590	64	30	0	17	83	49	104	0	3	.305/.364/.457	113	29.7	.351	-3.6	1B(84): -10.4, RF(46): 0.2	0.6
2019	SLN	MLB	30	483	57	24	1	16	62	45	92	3	1	.274/.345/.444	114	20.3	.314	-1.1	RF -4, 1B -1	1.6

Breakout: 1%   Improve: 41%   Collapse: 6%   Attrition: 12%   MLB: 85%   *Comparables: Nolan Reimold, Jesus Guzman, Ryan Garko*

Though not as tall or as thick and muscular as Aaron Judge or Giancarlo Stanton, Martinez manages the same aesthetic that Dave Winfield did during his heyday. He entirely fills up the right-handed batter's box. He seems too big to imagine getting him out. Alas, that's where any comparison to Winfield stops cold. Martinez is a fine hitter, using the whole field and generating average-plus power, but he's overly aggressive early in counts, so he doesn't get on base the way such a gifted batter should. In unforgiving contrast to Winfield, he's also a terrible athlete, such an awkward defender at every position that to even attempt to play regularly afield threatens his ability to stay in the lineup. You want more power or a more discerning eye from a DH, and if you're the Cardinals, an actual DH position to play him in.

Yadier Molina   C   Born: 07/13/82   Age: 36   Bats: R   Throws: R   Height: 5'11"   Weight: 205   Origin: Round 4, 2000 Draft (#113 overall)

YEAR	TEAM	LVL	AGE	PA	R	2B	3B	HR	RBI	BB	K	SB	CS	AVG/OBP/SLG	DRC+	VORP	BABIP	BRR	FRAA	WARP
2016	SLN	MLB	33	581	56	38	1	8	58	39	63	3	2	.307/.360/.427	105	29.0	.335	-7.7	C(146): 11.7, 1B(2): 0.0	3.7
2017	SLN	MLB	34	543	60	27	1	18	82	28	74	9	4	.273/.312/.439	103	21.0	.285	-4.5	C(133): 6.0, 1B(1): 0.0	3.1
2018	SLN	MLB	35	503	55	20	0	20	74	29	66	4	3	.261/.314/.436	112	27.7	.264	-2.3	C(121): 1.4, 1B(5): 0.0	3.2
2019	SLN	MLB	36	521	59	30	2	15	64	32	73	5	3	.279/.332/.442	110	25.5	.303	-3.9	C 1	2.9

Breakout: 0%   Improve: 26%   Collapse: 11%   Attrition: 25%   MLB: 68%   *Comparables: Hank Severeid, Ramon Hernandez, Paul Lo Duca*

An invisible string connects Molina to the beating heart of baseball itself. As the game changes, Molina's game changes. As he ages and the accretion of innings behind the plate diminishes him, the game comes back to him a bit. Molina was still an average-plus framer in 2018 (though a worse one than he'd ever been before), but the league's evolution is shrinking the value any individual catcher can deliver that way anyway. He was just an average thrower, for the second time in three years, but no one steals bases anymore anyway.

YEAR	TEAM	P. COUNT	FRM RUNS	BLK RUNS	THRW RUNS	TOT RUNS
2016	SLN	19667	10.4	1.6	-0.9	10.7
2017	SLN	18649	6.4	0.2	2.2	9.3
2018	SLN	17163	2.3	1.2	0.1	3.5
2019	SLN	17082	2.5	0.9	-0.3	3.1

He's gone from an extreme ground-ball hitter to one who hits fly balls at a pretty high rate. He's gone from an opposite-field singles hitter to a dead-pull, 20-homer guy, but it's hard to notice because everyone's already hitting that way anyway. The Cardinals were 67-53 when Molina started in 2018, and 21-21 without him, because Molina remains in possession of a tangible (if inexplicable) magic.

Elehuris Montero   3B   Born: 08/17/98   Age: 20   Bats: R   Throws: R   Height: 6'3"   Weight: 195   Origin: International Free Agent, 2014

YEAR	TEAM	LVL	AGE	PA	R	2B	3B	HR	RBI	BB	K	SB	CS	AVG/OBP/SLG	DRC+	VORP	BABIP	BRR	FRAA	WARP
2016	DCA	RK	17	262	41	14	2	1	26	28	51	2	1	.260/.349/.352	107	4.7	.328	0.5	3B(60): 2.6	1.5
2017	CRD	RK	18	208	30	16	1	5	36	22	33	0	2	.277/.370/.468	142	10.3	.305	-0.5	3B(41): 2.8	1.8
2018	PEO	A	19	425	68	28	3	15	69	33	81	2	0	.322/.381/.529	139	39.7	.372	0.3	3B(77): 2.7	3.5
2018	PMB	A+	19	106	13	9	0	1	13	5	22	1	0	.286/.330/.408	93	5.7	.355	0.6	3B(20): 0.8	0.4
2019	SLN	MLB	20	251	24	11	0	8	29	12	60	0	0	.223/.265/.363	67	-5.0	.265	-0.6	3B 1	-0.5

Breakout: 9%   Improve: 15%   Collapse: 0%   Attrition: 5%   MLB: 17%   *Comparables: Matt Dominguez, Rafael Devers, Matt Davidson*

All that remains is some polishing. Montero has done enough over the last two years and demonstrated both his strengths and his weaknesses clearly enough that we don't have to wonder all that much about what kind of player he'll be. He's limited by a lack of overwhelming athleticism; he won't have great range at third or make plays with his legs. However, he's also blessed with a combination of power and bat-to-ball skill that could make him an elite right-handed hitter by the time he reaches the Majors. Montero's capable of hitting .300 and cranking 30 homers a year. He also has a great arm that helps make up for the lack of agility defensively. The open questions (his footwork at third and his approach at the plate) are all about aptitude, makeup, and neurology.

Yairo Munoz UT   Born: 01/23/95   Age: 24   Bats: R   Throws: R   Height: 6'1"   Weight: 201   Origin: International Free Agent, 2012

YEAR	TEAM	LVL	AGE	PA	R	2B	3B	HR	RBI	BB	K	SB	CS	AVG/OBP/SLG	DRC+	VORP	BABIP	BRR	FRAA	WARP
2016	MID	AA	21	414	44	16	3	9	39	23	76	6	7	.240/.286/.367	93	1.1	.278	-1.0	SS(41): 0.9, 2B(27): 0.5	1.3
2017	MID	AA	22	207	35	17	3	6	26	10	35	12	1	.316/.348/.532	110	18.2	.355	3.2	SS(22): -1.1, 3B(21): -0.3	1.2
2017	NAS	AAA	22	272	30	9	1	7	42	11	46	10	4	.289/.316/.414	89	7.8	.324	-2.9	SS(24): 2.4, CF(19): -1.9	0.6
2018	MEM	AAA	23	100	11	3	1	3	13	5	18	1	0	.287/.330/.436	96	7.2	.329	0.3	SS(13): 0.2, LF(4): -0.5	0.2
2018	SLN	MLB	23	329	39	16	0	8	42	30	71	5	6	.276/.350/.413	96	16.9	.338	-2.5	SS(40): -5.4, 2B(26): -0.8	0.0
2019	SLN	MLB	24	158	19	6	1	4	17	12	33	3	2	.249/.312/.394	92	3.1	.293	-0.5	2B 0, SS 0	0.4

Breakout: 6%   Improve: 42%   Collapse: 10%   Attrition: 22%   MLB: 88%   *Comparables: Josh Rutledge, Enrique Hernandez, Stephen Drew*

The thickset Munoz is stretched a bit thin at shortstop these days, which is unfortunate. His bat doesn't play all that well at third base, where teams want more power, or at second, where teams increasingly feel they can skate a bit defensively in order to squeeze out some extra offense at the position. If he'd arrived before DeJong, perhaps he could have disguised himself among the stockier generation of Cardinals shortstops that came before, but alas. Munoz is a free-swinger whose approach almost exactly matches that of Odubel Herrera, except that Herrera is left-handed, gets the ball in the air more often, and runs faster. He has time to mature into a 20-homer guy, and both the bat speed and the build suggest it's possible, but unless and until that possibility becomes a reality, he's no more than a suboptimal bench bat.

Malcom Nunez 3B   Born: 03/09/01   Age: 18   Bats: R   Throws: R   Height: 5'11"   Weight: 205   Origin: International Free Agent, 2018

YEAR	TEAM	LVL	AGE	PA	R	2B	3B	HR	RBI	BB	K	SB	CS	AVG/OBP/SLG	DRC+	VORP	BABIP	BRR	FRAA	WARP
2018	DCA	RK	17	199	44	16	2	13	59	26	29	3	0	.415/.497/.774	220	37.1	.437	0.5	3B(30): -1.0, 1B(5): 1.2	3.4
2019	SLN	MLB	18	251	29	19	0	11	36	19	62	0	0	.238/.296/.456	102	5.3	.274	-0.7	3B -1, 1B 0	0.5

Comparables: Adalberto Mondesi, Wilmer Flores, Tommy Brown

Nunez won the Dominican Summer League's Triple Crown in 2018 as a 17-year-old signee out of Cuba. "Won" doesn't do it justice: the teenager had the best offensive performance of any player in any system this year. He doesn't do it in an orthodox way, physically, but baseball history is littered with successful third basemen who neither played nor looked like most of their cohort. Already a name on the radar when he signed, Nunez vaulted himself into serious (if speculative) consideration as one of the game's better prospects at the hot corner. But perhaps best of all, however, is that because of improved international relations, Nunez didn't have to risk his life or his future to ply his trade, riding a raft or throwing his fate to a seedy agent. Not everything is better than it used to be, but at least one thing is.

Tyler O'Neill RF   Born: 06/22/95   Age: 24   Bats: R   Throws: R   Height: 5'11"   Weight: 210   Origin: Round 3, 2013 Draft (#85 overall)

YEAR	TEAM	LVL	AGE	PA	R	2B	3B	HR	RBI	BB	K	SB	CS	AVG/OBP/SLG	DRC+	VORP	BABIP	BRR	FRAA	WARP
2016	WTN	AA	21	575	68	26	4	24	102	62	150	12	2	.293/.374/.508	139	47.4	.364	-0.8	RF(108): -4.0, LF(5): -0.3	3.4
2017	TAC	AAA	22	396	54	21	2	19	56	44	108	9	2	.244/.328/.479	115	19.3	.295	0.3	LF(67): -1.8, RF(17): -0.9	1.5
2017	MEM	AAA	22	161	23	5	1	12	39	10	43	5	0	.253/.304/.548	118	7.0	.266	-0.6	RF(18): 1.0, LF(10): -0.3	0.8
2018	MEM	AAA	23	273	61	9	2	26	63	29	68	3	1	.311/.385/.693	169	40.8	.324	1.0	LF(33): -1.3, RF(21): 7.8	3.8
2018	SLN	MLB	23	142	29	5	0	9	23	7	57	2	0	.254/.303/.500	86	11.5	.364	2.2	RF(24): 0.7, LF(16): 1.1	0.5
2019	SLN	MLB	24	195	27	9	1	12	32	16	60	2	0	.247/.312/.500	124	11.5	.303	0.0	LF -1, RF 0	1.1

Breakout: 5%   Improve: 43%   Collapse: 16%   Attrition: 28%   MLB: 77%   *Comparables: Paul Goldschmidt, Christin Stewart, George Springer*

There's absolutely nothing subtle about O'Neill, and the only polished thing about him is his physique. A very good athlete, he's a poor outfielder, still trying to get the knack of reading balls off the bat and tracking them in the air. His power is as impressive as his pecs and his stats suggest, but his failure to make contact against big-league pitching was historic—'no batter has ever made contact on a lower percentage of swings in a season where they saw 500 or more pitches' historic. This is the era of the strikeout, but O'Neill still has to make more contact (and get more refined in other areas, too) in order to rise above the Incaviglia level of baseball lore.

Marcell Ozuna LF   Born: 11/12/90   Age: 28   Bats: R   Throws: R   Height: 6'1"   Weight: 225   Origin: International Free Agent, 2008

YEAR	TEAM	LVL	AGE	PA	R	2B	3B	HR	RBI	BB	K	SB	CS	AVG/OBP/SLG	DRC+	VORP	BABIP	BRR	FRAA	WARP
2016	MIA	MLB	25	608	75	23	6	23	76	43	115	0	3	.266/.321/.452	106	39.5	.296	1.6	CF(123): -7.2, LF(11): -1.4	2.2
2017	MIA	MLB	26	679	93	30	2	37	124	64	144	1	3	.312/.376/.548	130	55.5	.355	-3.5	LF(152): 4.9, CF(3): 0.0	4.6
2018	SLN	MLB	27	628	69	16	2	23	88	38	110	3	0	.280/.325/.433	109	30.4	.309	2.6	LF(147): -2.2	2.4
2019	SLN	MLB	28	568	69	26	3	24	81	44	109	2	1	.279/.338/.476	122	31.5	.313	0.4	LF -2	3.2

Breakout: 0%   Improve: 45%   Collapse: 2%   Attrition: 7%   MLB: 95%   *Comparables: Del Ennis, George Bell, Wes Covington*

The sharp statistical disparity between Ozuna's breakout 2017 and his disappointing 2018 can't be explained away just by pointing out the lingering and enigmatic shoulder injury that hampered him, nor by good luck in the former campaign and bad luck in the latter one. All of those things contributed to the downturn, though. Ozuna hit 87 balls hard to the left side in 2017, and slugged 1.506 on them. In 2018, he hit 88 such balls in fewer total plate appearances—but slugged 1.034. His average launch angle on those hits dropped by about six degrees. In protecting his shoulder, he got less aggressive about going out and contacting the ball early. He leveled out his swing, to transfer energy into his front side sooner. He also made minor changes in approach that sapped some of his aggressiveness, leading to more contact but less power. Heading into his late 20s and with no clear answers about the shoulder, Ozuna shouldn't be expected to turn right back into an elite slugger, and heading into a contract year, he can't be fully trusted to bring his approach back into equilibrium.

Delvin Perez SS Born: 11/24/98 Age: 20 Bats: R Throws: R Height: 6'3" Weight: 175 Origin: Round 1, 2016 Draft (#23 overall)

YEAR	TEAM	LVL	AGE	PA	R	2B	3B	HR	RBI	BB	K	SB	CS	AVG/OBP/SLG	DRC+	VORP	BABIP	BRR	FRAA	WARP
2016	CRD	RK	17	180	19	8	4	0	19	12	28	12	1	.294/.352/.393	113	15.1	.353	0.8	SS(40): -3.7, CF(1): -0.1	0.7
2017	CRD	RK	18	50	7	1	2	0	5	5	10	2	1	.238/.320/.357	116	2.7	.294	1.6	SS(9): -1.1	0.3
2017	JCY	RK	18	90	7	1	1	0	4	12	14	3	4	.184/.311/.224	89	2.0	.226	0.7	SS(22): -0.5	0.3
2018	SCO	A-	19	269	22	5	3	1	21	28	54	8	6	.213/.301/.272	88	0.8	.272	-2.2	SS(64): 6.2	1.2
2019	*SLN*	*MLB*	*20*	*251*	*23*	*3*	*0*	*5*	*18*	*15*	*66*	*2*	*1*	*.159/.208/.237*	*14*	*-17.1*	*.194*	*-0.5*	*SS -1*	*-2.0*

Breakout: 1%   Improve: 3%   Collapse: 0%   Attrition: 1%   MLB: 4%   *Comparables: Amed Rosario, Rey Navarro, Juan Diaz*

The Cardinals believe in Perez's talent—the tools that led them to bet on him when he tumbled down the 2016 Draft board. It's increasingly difficult, though, to reconcile the potential that faith implies with the lack of production or progress through three pro seasons. Perez's glove remains promising, though inconsistent. Banged for performance-enhancing drugs before the draft, he's hit just one pro homer in nearly 600 plate appearances. He's fast, but doesn't always run that way. He has a feel for the barrel, but often, none for the game. More than anything, though, Perez's greatest weakness is his strength, and if he can't build on that, he's going to need that line for job interviews soon.

Drew Robinson UT Born: 04/20/92 Age: 27 Bats: L Throws: R Height: 6'1" Weight: 200 Origin: Round 4, 2010 Draft (#136 overall)

YEAR	TEAM	LVL	AGE	PA	R	2B	3B	HR	RBI	BB	K	SB	CS	AVG/OBP/SLG	DRC+	VORP	BABIP	BRR	FRAA	WARP
2016	ROU	AAA	24	539	76	24	10	20	67	66	148	17	5	.257/.350/.480	121	45.5	.332	3.5	RF(38): 5.1, 2B(27): -1.2	3.7
2017	ROU	AAA	25	309	48	19	4	11	40	42	74	7	4	.268/.369/.494	111	23.0	.331	0.8	2B(39): -2.6, CF(15): -0.5	1.3
2017	TEX	MLB	25	121	11	5	0	6	13	14	42	0	2	.224/.314/.439	84	0.8	.305	-0.7	3B(20): -0.7, LF(15): -1.1	0.0
2018	ROU	AAA	26	241	40	16	5	10	28	27	84	5	6	.303/.379/.569	91	25.1	.454	-2.5	CF(40): 5.3, LF(5): 1.4	1.1
2018	TEX	MLB	26	125	20	3	0	3	9	16	57	2	1	.183/.288/.294	49	-1.1	.347	1.2	CF(22): 0.8, LF(9): -0.8	-0.2
2019	*SLN*	*MLB*	*27*	*153*	*18*	*6*	*1*	*5*	*17*	*15*	*55*	*2*	*2*	*.206/.288/.371*	*82*	*1.5*	*.298*	*0.1*	*CF 0, 3B -1*	*0.2*

Breakout: 1%   Improve: 23%   Collapse: 8%   Attrition: 19%   MLB: 55%   *Comparables: Keon Broxton, Brandon Allen, Corey Brown*

Is there a way to call someone a Quadruple-A player and not be mean about it? Let's try. Robinson is a very good minor-league player whose defense and ability to keep the clubhouse and bench loose are absolutely ready to make him a big-league player. Unfortunately, his bat has thus far not been able to catch up. If you're looking for an upside, his numbers in the majors against left-handed pitching are vastly better than expected. Unfortunately, his numbers against right-handers have been significantly worse than the team has needed from him. He's older than you think (27 in April), so he'll soon run out of shots to carve out a long-term niche as a utility player.

Ramon Urias INF Born: 06/03/94 Age: 25 Bats: R Throws: R Height: 5'10" Weight: 150 Origin: International Free Agent, 2010

YEAR	TEAM	LVL	AGE	PA	R	2B	3B	HR	RBI	BB	K	SB	CS	AVG/OBP/SLG	DRC+	VORP	BABIP	BRR	FRAA	WARP
2018	SFD	AA	24	194	28	19	0	8	27	18	29	1	2	.333/.406/.589	135	20.4	.361	-1.8	2B(30): -1.7, 3B(7): -0.4	1.2
2018	MEM	AAA	24	149	20	9	0	5	17	6	29	0	0	.261/.291/.430	88	1.6	.296	-0.5	2B(18): 0.7, 3B(7): -1.0	0.1
2019	*SLN*	*MLB*	*25*	*37*	*4*	*2*	*0*	*1*	*4*	*2*	*8*	*0*	*0*	*.245/.282/.400*	*84*	*0.4*	*.282*	*-0.1*	*2B 0*	*0.0*

Breakout: 2%   Improve: 21%   Collapse: 12%   Attrition: 25%   MLB: 57%   *Comparables: David Bote, Joey Wendle, Jason Kipnis*

Things change slowly. We live, perhaps, in the Golden Age of diminutive sluggers, but there remains a strong and systemic bias in baseball scouting against players who seem dramatically undersized, even if they hit really well over a relatively long period. Urias embodies that as much as any player in baseball. He signed with the Rangers in 2010, but when he didn't immediately break out in the Dominican Summer League, he found himself on a five-year sojourn through the baseball wilderness that is the Mexican League. When the Cardinals plucked him out of there, he'd batted .320/.406/.469 in over 2,000 plate appearances, and in his first season Stateside, he hit .300 at the highest levels in the minors. A good enough glove to back up every infield spot, he's now a near-certain future big-leaguer.

Justin Williams RF Born: 08/20/95 Age: 23 Bats: L Throws: R Height: 6'2" Weight: 215 Origin: Round 2, 2013 Draft (#52 overall)

YEAR	TEAM	LVL	AGE	PA	R	2B	3B	HR	RBI	BB	K	SB	CS	AVG/OBP/SLG	DRC+	VORP	BABIP	BRR	FRAA	WARP
2016	PCH	A+	20	203	23	11	0	4	31	6	26	0	1	.330/.350/.448	110	8.5	.361	-3.3	RF(43): 3.5	0.6
2016	MNT	AA	20	155	20	7	2	6	28	5	30	0	1	.250/.277/.446	106	3.7	.274	0.8	RF(34): -1.7	0.3
2017	MNT	AA	21	409	53	21	3	14	72	37	69	6	2	.301/.364/.489	125	18.7	.334	-2.0	RF(80): -4.8, LF(7): 1.2	1.6
2018	TBA	MLB	22	1	0	0	0	0	0	0	0	0	0	.000/.000/.000	73	-0.5	.000	0.0	RF(1): 0.0	0.0
2018	DUR	AAA	22	386	41	18	0	8	46	25	81	4	3	.258/.313/.376	94	-4.8	.315	-2.7	RF(80): 13.7, LF(2): 1.0	1.7
2018	MEM	AAA	22	76	8	3	0	3	11	5	17	0	1	.217/.276/.391	88	-0.6	.240	-1.1	LF(10): 4.2, RF(7): 0.9	0.5
2019	*SLN*	*MLB*	*23*	*251*	*23*	*9*	*0*	*6*	*26*	*14*	*57*	*1*	*1*	*.216/.268/.334*	*56*	*-7.0*	*.259*	*-0.5*	*RF 1, LF 1*	*-0.5*

Breakout: 2%   Improve: 23%   Collapse: 7%   Attrition: 7%   MLB: 32%   *Comparables: J.D. Martinez, Preston Tucker, Tyler Austin*

The tools are tempting, but Williams keeps cobbling together frustrating seasons in which only part of his talent really shines through. He matriculated to the Majors in 2018 but got just a single plate appearance, and then was traded for the second time in four years. A capable defender in either outfield corner with a left-handed bat that seems as though it could bloom into either a powerful one or a consistent line-drive threat, he nonetheless struggles to put it all together. The physicality isn't getting better; it's time to see whether he can make the leap skills-wise.

Kolten Wong 2B Born: 10/10/90 Age: 28 Bats: L Throws: R Height: 5'9" Weight: 185 Origin: Round 1, 2011 Draft (#22 overall)

YEAR	TEAM	LVL	AGE	PA	R	2B	3B	HR	RBI	BB	K	SB	CS	AVG/OBP/SLG	DRC+	VORP	BABIP	BRR	FRAA	WARP
2016	MEM	AAA	25	34	10	0	1	4	11	4	6	1	0	.429/.529/.929	140	11.0	.444	0.7	2B(4): 0.1, CF(3): 0.2	0.4
2016	SLN	MLB	25	361	39	7	7	5	23	34	52	7	0	.240/.327/.355	96	14.5	.268	1.4	2B(88): 12.6, CF(8): -0.5	2.3
2017	SLN	MLB	26	411	55	27	3	4	42	41	60	8	2	.285/.376/.412	99	23.3	.331	1.6	2B(106): -4.6	0.9
2018	SLN	MLB	27	407	41	18	2	9	38	31	60	6	5	.249/.332/.388	92	11.5	.275	-2.0	2B(119): 6.0	1.3
2019	SLN	MLB	28	419	48	18	3	8	41	38	65	8	3	.249/.343/.376	103	15.4	.288	-0.1	2B 5	2.2

Breakout: 2% Improve: 45% Collapse: 6% Attrition: 4% MLB: 98%   Comparables: Aaron Hill, Brian Roberts, Fred Haney

Wong's efforts to make more use of his compact build and natural bat speed have gone more or less for naught. He continues to morph into an extreme ground-ball hitter, and as a left-handed batter, that makes him very vulnerable to the shift. He laid down 20 bunts in 2018 but didn't turn them into enough hits to change either his stat line or opponents' strategies. Thus, he's becoming increasingly patient (a pessimist might call it passive, or even timid) as he tries to work walks and wait for a pitch he can hammer. He remains an unorthodox but highly effective defender at second base, however. A grinder at the plate who can comfortably rove for grounders, line drives and pop-ups in the field has real value, though with a low ceiling.

PITCHERS

John Brebbia RHP Born: 05/30/90 Age: 29 Bats: L Throws: R Height: 6'1" Weight: 185 Origin: Round 30, 2011 Draft (#929 overall)

YEAR	TEAM	LVL	AGE	W	L	SV	G	GS	IP	H	HR	BB/9	K/9	K	GB%	BABIP	WHIP	ERA	DRA	WARP	MPH	FB%	WHF	CSP
2016	SFD	AA	26	3	2	2	24	0	37²	41	6	1.4	9.1	38	43%	.324	1.25	4.06	3.55	0.5				
2016	MEM	AAA	26	2	3	0	19	0	30¹	41	3	3.9	8.9	30	46%	.396	1.78	6.23	2.80	0.8				
2017	MEM	AAA	27	1	1	3	15	1	26²	16	2	1.7	9.8	29	33%	.219	0.79	1.69	3.10	0.7				
2017	SLN	MLB	27	0	0	0	50	0	51²	37	8	1.9	8.9	51	33%	.216	0.93	2.44	4.60	0.3	96.0	56.7	13.5	49.2
2018	MEM	AAA	28	2	0	2	11	0	13²	16	3	2.6	15.8	24	6%	.433	1.46	4.61	1.38	0.6				
2018	SLN	MLB	28	3	3	2	45	0	50²	43	5	2.8	10.7	60	33%	.297	1.16	3.20	2.92	1.2	96.7	53.3	13.8	49.8
2019	SLN	MLB	29	2	1	0	48	0	50²	44	7	3.3	10.1	57	36%	.301	1.24	3.97	4.64	0.2	95.7	54.7	13.7	49.5

Breakout: 25% Improve: 50% Collapse: 14% Attrition: 22% MLB: 82%   Comparables: Jason Motte, Heath Bell, Matt Reynolds

During the winter of 2017-18, Brebbia shaved the beard for which he had become famous (he wasn't quite good enough to be famous for anything else) during his rookie season. Arguably more importantly, though, he also spent that time reshaping his slider and redesigning the interaction of that pitch with his four-seam heater. Leaning almost entirely on those two pitches (though undeniably aided by the impressive regrowth of the beard, in more or less the same shape it had been in before), Brebbia ratcheted up his strikeout rate. The separation between the fastball and slider grew wider, leading to more whiffs and more grounders on the breaking pitch. His facial hair is a few years late to the party, but Brebbia's pitch mix is the state of the art for right-handed relievers.

Genesis Cabrera LHP Born: 10/10/96 Age: 22 Bats: L Throws: L Height: 6'1" Weight: 170 Origin: International Free Agent, 2013

YEAR	TEAM	LVL	AGE	W	L	SV	G	GS	IP	H	HR	BB/9	K/9	K	GB%	BABIP	WHIP	ERA	DRA	WARP	MPH	FB%	WHF	CSP
2016	BGR	A	19	11	5	0	23	22	116	110	9	3.7	7.4	96	36%	.305	1.36	3.88	5.65	-0.9				
2017	PCH	A+	20	4	5	0	13	12	69²	45	3	3.2	7.8	60	39%	.230	1.00	2.84	3.91	1.1				
2017	MNT	AA	20	5	4	0	12	12	64²	75	6	3.8	7.1	51	37%	.332	1.58	3.62	4.28	0.7				
2018	MNT	AA	21	7	6	0	21	20	113²	90	11	4.5	9.8	124	35%	.282	1.29	4.12	5.12	0.3				
2018	SFD	AA	21	1	3	0	5	5	24²	24	3	4.7	7.7	21	37%	.300	1.50	4.74	5.21	0.0				
2019	SLN	MLB	22	1	0	0	11	0	11¹	10	2	4.5	9.1	11	34%	.299	1.40	4.61	5.38	0.0				

Breakout: 5% Improve: 10% Collapse: 4% Attrition: 7% MLB: 16%   Comparables: Chaz Roe, Yency Almonte, Touki Toussaint

If he ever gets bumped from a full-fledged rotation role, let's hope that Cabrera can at least be used as an opener. His arsenal feels like the start of something good. His arm is so loose and his delivery so naturally deceptive that his changeup has to improve only slightly from where it is. His heater can run into the high 90s, and his cutter-like slider can work to either side of the plate out of his high slot. Cabrera's ability to work to all quadrants will be crucial, given the interplay between his raw stuff and the angles at which he throws it, and therein lies the rub. Right now, his command might be ahead of his control, which is a very strange state of affairs. There's no guarantee he'll ever throw enough strikes, but if he can tuck just enough into the zone, the swings will come for the ones outside.

Seth Elledge RHP Born: 05/20/96 Age: 23 Bats: R Throws: R Height: 6'3" Weight: 230 Origin: Round 4, 2017 Draft (#123 overall)

YEAR	TEAM	LVL	AGE	W	L	SV	G	GS	IP	H	HR	BB/9	K/9	K	GB%	BABIP	WHIP	ERA	DRA	WARP	MPH	FB%	WHF	CSP
2017	CLN	A	21	3	0	5	15	0	21	14	1	2.6	15.0	35	40%	.310	0.95	3.00	2.62	0.6				
2018	MOD	A+	22	5	1	9	31	0	38¹	18	1	3.5	12.7	54	53%	.221	0.86	1.17	3.18	0.8				
2018	SFD	AA	22	3	1	4	13	0	16²	13	3	3.2	10.8	20	44%	.250	1.14	4.32	2.35	0.5				
2019	SLN	MLB	23	2	1	2	39	0	41	33	5	4.4	10.7	49	42%	.299	1.30	4.09	4.77	0.1				

Breakout: 8% Improve: 9% Collapse: 3% Attrition: 8% MLB: 19%   Comparables: Steve Geltz, David Robertson, Alejandro Chacin

A fourth-round college draftee in 2017, Elledge has shredded the minor leagues with a pretty simple mixture. He throws a mid-90s fastball and a slider to which he can add and subtract, and the shape of which he can adjust to suit the situation and matchup. He also has a usable changeup, but he's on the fast track now, and if Elledge can demonstrate the command and feel he's had to this point, he won't much need a third pitch. Developing it would just be icing on the cake, the kind of gear-shifter that could turn the strapping right-hander into the very model of the modern multi-inning relief weapon.

Jack Flaherty RHP Born: 10/15/95 Age: 23 Bats: R Throws: R Height: 6'4" Weight: 205 Origin: Round 1, 2014 Draft (#34 overall)

YEAR	TEAM	LVL	AGE	W	L	SV	G	GS	IP	H	HR	BB/9	K/9	K	GB%	BABIP	WHIP	ERA	DRA	WARP	MPH	FB%	WHF	CSP
2016	PMB	A+	20	5	9	0	24	23	134	129	8	3.0	8.5	126	49%	.316	1.30	3.56	3.64	2.8				
2017	SFD	AA	21	7	2	0	10	10	63¹	47	2	1.6	8.8	62	41%	.269	0.92	1.42	3.28	1.4				
2017	MEM	AAA	21	7	2	0	15	15	85¹	73	10	2.5	9.0	85	42%	.288	1.14	2.74	3.42	2.1				
2017	SLN	MLB	21	0	2	0	6	5	21¹	23	4	4.2	8.4	20	49%	.322	1.55	6.33	3.28	0.5	94.9	55.9	14	47.2
2018	MEM	AAA	22	4	1	0	5	5	31²	22	2	2.0	11.7	41	44%	.274	0.92	2.27	1.70	1.4				
2018	SLN	MLB	22	8	9	0	28	28	151	108	20	3.5	10.8	182	43%	.257	1.11	3.34	3.07	3.9	95.6	55.3	14.5	46
2019	SLN	MLB	23	12	8	0	28	28	168	134	18	3.2	10.3	193	43%	.297	1.16	3.45	4.04	2.5	95.4	57.3	15	48.2

Breakout: 22% Improve: 59% Collapse: 15% Attrition: 14% MLB: 86% *Comparables: Shelby Miller, Rubby De La Rosa, Luis Severino*

We're all living in the Age of the Slider. Major League Baseball is a four-seam fastball-slider league. Some pitchers can succeed without one, but it's hard. Pitchers who do have one but can't rely on it (because it doesn't play well enough off their fastball, or because they can't throw it for a strike, or because they lack the feel to change its shape or throw it consistently without hanging too many) are doomed to the back ends of rotations or the low-leverage departments of bullpens. Flaherty is no longer classed with those guys. He's capable of throwing both his curve and his slider for a strike, putting hitters on the defensive. He's repeating the release point and consistently landing the slider where he wants it. It's a badass bat-misser, and his ticket to the top tier of NL starters.

John Gant RHP Born: 08/06/92 Age: 26 Bats: R Throws: R Height: 6'3" Weight: 200 Origin: Round 21, 2011 Draft (#642 overall)

YEAR	TEAM	LVL	AGE	W	L	SV	G	GS	IP	H	HR	BB/9	K/9	K	GB%	BABIP	WHIP	ERA	DRA	WARP	MPH	FB%	WHF	CSP
2016	GWN	AAA	23	3	3	0	12	10	56	58	5	3.5	9.2	57	49%	.329	1.43	4.18	3.25	1.3				
2016	ATL	MLB	23	1	4	0	20	7	50	54	7	3.8	8.8	49	45%	.329	1.50	4.86	4.04	0.7	94.4	58.5	10.7	47.5
2017	MEM	AAA	24	6	5	0	18	18	103¹	109	10	2.2	8.6	99	47%	.334	1.30	3.83	2.57	3.6				
2017	SLN	MLB	24	0	1	0	7	2	17¹	17	4	5.2	5.7	11	54%	.260	1.56	4.67	5.03	0.1	95.5	65.2	11	46.1
2018	MEM	AAA	25	5	1	0	8	8	49	45	5	2.9	7.7	42	49%	.288	1.24	1.65	3.08	1.4				
2018	SLN	MLB	25	7	6	0	26	19	114	91	9	4.5	7.5	95	46%	.253	1.30	3.47	4.05	1.6	95.4	55.4	12.2	48.5
2019	SLN	MLB	26	5	4	0	38	11	86¹	80	9	3.6	8.4	81	46%	.302	1.32	3.99	4.68	0.5	94.8	57.9	12	48.3

Breakout: 23% Improve: 50% Collapse: 18% Attrition: 24% MLB: 83% *Comparables: Trevor Williams, Brock Stewart, James Paxton*

Gant provides plenty to like. He employed a three-pitch mix (four-seamer, changeup, curve) until early in 2018, when he added a slider to the equation. All four pitches can miss bats, though none are true out pitches, and the spin rate on that fastball is one of the game's highest. He's tall and sturdily built, and he uses that frame well. Everything has life; batters don't square him up often. So far, his control hasn't withstood the test of big-league hitters' plate discipline all that well, but he's going to get several more shots to reach his ceiling in the middle of a rotation. There's a fair chance he even reaches it, at least for a little while.

Austin Gomber LHP Born: 11/23/93 Age: 25 Bats: L Throws: L Height: 6'5" Weight: 230 Origin: Round 4, 2014 Draft (#135 overall)

YEAR	TEAM	LVL	AGE	W	L	SV	G	GS	IP	H	HR	BB/9	K/9	K	GB%	BABIP	WHIP	ERA	DRA	WARP	MPH	FB%	WHF	CSP
2016	PMB	A+	22	6	8	0	17	17	107²	91	5	2.0	8.4	101	42%	.287	1.07	2.93	3.04	3.0				
2016	SFD	AA	22	1	0	0	4	4	19¹	11	0	4.2	7.0	15	38%	.212	1.03	1.40	4.09	0.2				
2017	SFD	AA	23	10	7	0	26	26	143	116	17	3.2	8.8	140	42%	.263	1.17	3.34	3.36	3.1				
2018	MEM	AAA	24	7	3	0	12	11	68¹	65	9	2.6	10.0	76	40%	.311	1.24	3.42	2.74	2.1				
2018	SLN	MLB	24	6	2	0	29	11	75	81	7	3.8	8.0	67	41%	.330	1.51	4.44	4.95	0.2	94.8	50.4	10	49.8
2019	SLN	MLB	25	4	3	0	21	10	61¹	55	8	3.2	8.7	59	40%	.294	1.25	4.14	4.84	0.3	94.5	51.6	10.2	51

Breakout: 11% Improve: 38% Collapse: 24% Attrition: 36% MLB: 78% *Comparables: Rafael Montero, Brandon Woodruff, Wade LeBlanc*

The only truly above-average skill on the scouting report for Gomber is his command, though often, that turns out to be the most effective weapon even for pitchers with much better stuff. In Gomber's case, there are things the good command can't fix, like a changeup with virtually zero movement off a too-straight fastball, making both pitches reliant on fooling batters with the velocity separation between them. There are other things with which it does really help, though. Gomber moved to the first-base side of the rubber during a July demotion to Triple-A, changing the angle on that fastball-changeup sequence for righties and sharpening the difficulty of picking up his slider for lefties. Still, he has to execute perfectly, and even when he does, he doesn't really dominate.

Luke Gregerson RHP Born: 05/14/84 Age: 35 Bats: L Throws: R Height: 6'3" Weight: 205 Origin: Round 28, 2006 Draft (#856 overall)

YEAR	TEAM	LVL	AGE	W	L	SV	G	GS	IP	H	HR	BB/9	K/9	K	GB%	BABIP	WHIP	ERA	DRA	WARP	MPH	FB%	WHF	CSP
2016	HOU	MLB	32	4	3	15	59	0	57²	38	5	2.8	10.5	67	62%	.239	0.97	3.28	2.36	1.7	91.4	53.4	20.6	41.5
2017	HOU	MLB	33	2	3	1	65	0	61	62	13	3.0	10.3	70	49%	.306	1.34	4.57	4.08	0.7	90.8	52.3	17.1	43.1
2018	SLN	MLB	34	0	0	0	17	0	12²	14	2	4.3	8.5	12	56%	.324	1.58	7.11	3.25	0.2	89.0	64.7	13	40.5
2019	SLN	MLB	35	2	1	0	37	0	39¹	34	5	3.8	9.1	40	51%	.293	1.30	4.15	4.85	0.0	89.6	53.5	17.4	40.9

Breakout: 22% Improve: 47% Collapse: 22% Attrition: 11% MLB: 92% *Comparables: Gary Lavelle, Kyle Farnsworth, Rollie Fingers*

One of the originators of the slider revolution that has created the new world order of baseball, Gregerson is still dependent upon that pitch for success. As he wades deeper into his mid-30s, though, it's harder and harder for him to hold onto his trademark. Injuries finally truly truncated a season for him, for the first time in his 10 campaigns. When he was on the mound, his sinker was down to about 88 miles per hour, on average. It's a heavy pitch that induces tons of grounders, but it gives batters time to wait and suss out what's coming. The widening movement gap between Gregerson's sinker and slider only exacerbates that problem. Unless full health restores some zip to the heat or bite to the slider, he's permanently (if marginally) diminished.

Ryan Helsley RHP   Born: 07/18/94   Age: 24   Bats: R   Throws: R   Height: 6'1"   Weight: 195   Origin: Round 5, 2015 Draft (#161 overall)

YEAR	TEAM	LVL	AGE	W	L	SV	G	GS	IP	H	HR	BB/9	K/9	K	GB%	BABIP	WHIP	ERA	DRA	WARP	MPH	FB%	WHF	CSP
2016	PEO	A	21	10	2	0	17	17	95	77	3	1.8	10.3	109	41%	.301	1.01	1.61	2.46	3.0				
2017	PMB	A+	22	8	2	0	17	16	93²	72	3	2.9	8.7	91	44%	.277	1.09	2.69	3.19	2.3				
2017	SFD	AA	22	3	1	0	6	6	33²	25	4	4.0	11.0	41	43%	.262	1.19	2.67	2.93	0.9				
2018	SFD	AA	23	3	2	0	7	7	41	30	5	4.4	9.7	44	49%	.243	1.22	4.39	3.33	1.0				
2018	MEM	AAA	23	2	1	0	5	5	26²	18	2	3.0	11.5	34	38%	.262	1.01	3.71	2.55	0.9				
2019	SLN	MLB	24	1	0	0	11	0	11¹	10	1	3.3	9.5	12	40%	.296	1.23	3.86	4.51	0.0				

Breakout: 13%   Improve: 28%   Collapse: 19%   Attrition: 31%   MLB: 57%   Comparables: Jake Arrieta, Austin Voth, David Rollins

After the United States government drove them from their ancestral homeland, legend says that three Cherokee elders were to meet to determine the location of their new capital city. As dusk drew near, however, one still failed to show, so the other two agreed to go ahead with their planning without him. "Ta'ligwu," a Cherokee word meaning "two is enough," became more than a motto when they named their new capital city Tahlequah. It now rests in northeastern Oklahoma, where Helsley was born and raised, where he went to college, and where the Cardinals found him and drafted him. He's an exceptional athlete with plus makeup, and a high-spin fastball-curve combo. In order to be a solid mid-rotation arm, in fact, he just needs to overcome the shoulder issues that slowed him in 2018 and to further develop his budding cutter. Two is rarely enough when it comes to starters' pitch selection.

Jordan Hicks RHP   Born: 09/06/96   Age: 22   Bats: R   Throws: R   Height: 6'2"   Weight: 185   Origin: Round SUP, 2015 Draft (#105 overall)

YEAR	TEAM	LVL	AGE	W	L	SV	G	GS	IP	H	HR	BB/9	K/9	K	GB%	BABIP	WHIP	ERA	DRA	WARP	MPH	FB%	WHF	CSP
2016	JCY	RK	19	2	1	0	6	6	30	33	1	3.9	6.0	20	57%	.344	1.53	4.20	5.03	0.2				
2016	SCO	A-	19	4	1	0	6	6	30²	25	0	4.7	6.5	22	66%	.269	1.34	1.76	3.92	0.5				
2017	PEO	A	20	8	2	0	14	14	78	75	3	4.5	7.3	63	53%	.316	1.46	3.35	6.50	-1.1				
2017	PMB	A+	20	0	1	1	8	5	27	21	0	2.0	10.7	32	67%	.318	1.00	1.00	2.19	1.0				
2018	SLN	MLB	21	3	4	6	73	0	77²	59	2	5.2	8.1	70	62%	.266	1.34	3.59	6.03	-1.0	102.9	78	10.1	47.1
2019	SLN	MLB	22	3	1	30	53	0	56¹	49	5	5.1	8.5	53	53%	.300	1.43	4.26	4.99	-0.1	102.9	81.3	10.6	49.1

Breakout: 20%   Improve: 28%   Collapse: 12%   Attrition: 19%   MLB: 60%   Comparables: Jenrry Mejia, Lance McCullers, Mike Montgomery

Hicks didn't pitch at all in the upper minors before getting promoted into the St. Louis bullpen for Opening Day of 2018. It should come as no surprise, then, that he's still an unfinished product. His rookie campaign was attention-grabbing, as he demonstrated the ability to consistently throw harder than anyone this side of Peak Aroldis Chapman. What he didn't demonstrate the ability to do, however, might be more important. Hicks didn't miss bats with any consistency, and he didn't throw enough strikes to get away with that, especially as his first season as a reliever wore him down. His slider induced whiffs on over half of opponents' swings, but he threw his sinker nearly three times as often as that slider. Heavy reliance on a fastball, especially a sinker, just doesn't permit one to succeed in MLB anymore, no matter how hard it's thrown. There's more to the fastball than being fast.

Dakota Hudson RHP   Born: 09/15/94   Age: 24   Bats: R   Throws: R   Height: 6'5"   Weight: 215   Origin: Round 1, 2016 Draft (#34 overall)

YEAR	TEAM	LVL	AGE	W	L	SV	G	GS	IP	H	HR	BB/9	K/9	K	GB%	BABIP	WHIP	ERA	DRA	WARP	MPH	FB%	WHF	CSP
2016	PMB	A+	21	1	1	3	8	0	9¹	6	0	6.8	9.6	10	91%	.261	1.39	0.96	3.07	0.2				
2017	SFD	AA	22	9	4	0	18	18	114	111	5	2.7	6.1	77	58%	.296	1.27	2.53	5.76	-0.8				
2017	MEM	AAA	22	1	1	0	7	7	38²	36	2	3.5	4.4	19	59%	.272	1.32	4.42	5.27	0.2				
2018	MEM	AAA	23	13	3	0	19	19	111²	107	1	3.1	7.0	87	59%	.313	1.30	2.50	3.50	2.6				
2018	SLN	MLB	23	4	1	0	26	0	27¹	19	0	5.9	6.3	19	64%	.237	1.35	2.63	6.41	-0.5	97.3	60.7	9.9	47.3
2019	SLN	MLB	24	3	1	0	53	0	56¹	49	5	4.0	7.9	49	56%	.293	1.31	3.94	4.62	0.2	97.1	62.6	10.2	48.7

Breakout: 16%   Improve: 36%   Collapse: 27%   Attrition: 44%   MLB: 76%   Comparables: Jarred Cosart, Paul Blackburn, Chi Chi Gonzalez

One of baseball's most delightful mysteries is that some pitchers are more than the sum of their parts—a better full package than the individual items on their scouting checklist suggest. Alas, the Newtonian universe requires that there be some pitchers on the other side of the equation, even if they have the mental and physical tools and can more or less find the strike zone. That's Hudson. His four-seam fastball is a little too straight to miss bats, despite its good velocity. His sinker has good run, but he doesn't command it well, at least at this stage. His cutter is hard and generates plenty of grounders, but doesn't generate enough whiffs, either. Unless Hudson can reshape something in his repertoire or tighten his command, he's doomed to tantalizing but non-dominant relief work.

Dominic Leone RHP   Born: 10/26/91   Age: 27   Bats: R   Throws: R   Height: 5'11"   Weight: 210   Origin: Round 16, 2012 Draft (#491 overall)

YEAR	TEAM	LVL	AGE	W	L	SV	G	GS	IP	H	HR	BB/9	K/9	K	GB%	BABIP	WHIP	ERA	DRA	WARP	MPH	FB%	WHF	CSP
2016	RNO	AAA	24	5	2	1	33	0	35	25	4	2.8	9.3	36	36%	.247	1.03	3.34	3.65	0.5				
2016	ARI	MLB	24	0	1	0	25	0	27	45	7	4.0	7.7	23	47%	.432	2.11	6.33	5.48	-0.2	95.2	82.7	12.9	47.9
2017	TOR	MLB	25	3	0	1	65	0	70¹	51	6	2.9	10.4	81	41%	.266	1.05	2.56	3.07	1.6	95.9	90.4	16	44
2018	MEM	AAA	26	1	1	0	10	0	10	14	3	5.4	6.3	7	37%	.344	2.00	7.20	3.06	0.2				
2018	SLN	MLB	26	1	2	0	29	0	24	27	3	3.0	9.8	26	32%	.348	1.46	4.50	4.03	0.2	95.7	95.4	15.7	45.9
2019	SLN	MLB	27	2	1	0	42	0	45	40	6	4.0	9.3	46	39%	.303	1.33	4.09	4.79	0.1	95.3	91.3	15.5	46.3

Breakout: 34%   Improve: 57%   Collapse: 20%   Attrition: 28%   MLB: 91%   Comparables: Boone Logan, Sergio Santos, Ian Krol

Leone's cutter emerged as a dominant offering in 2017, allowing him to attack left-handed hitters and miss a lot of bats. Trying to double down, he made that offering more prominent in his arsenal in 2018, but the results were less impressive. As many pitchers have under the tutelage of Mike Maddux, Leone saw his fastball straighten out a bit, which made it easier for him to pound the strike zone but lowered a whiff rate that was already suboptimal, even for a fastball. His sinker didn't induce grounders the way it had in the past, and he became an extreme fly-ball guy. Worse, he failed to demonstrate the durability required of back-end relievers. Leone needs another tweak to that cutter (perhaps a move back toward the slider he used to throw) in order to be more than a marginal middle reliever again.

Carlos Martinez RHP Born: 09/21/91 Age: 27 Bats: R Throws: R Height: 6'0" Weight: 190 Origin: International Free Agent, 2009

YEAR	TEAM	LVL	AGE	W	L	SV	G	GS	IP	H	HR	BB/9	K/9	K	GB%	BABIP	WHIP	ERA	DRA	WARP	MPH	FB%	WHF	CSP
2016	SLN	MLB	24	16	9	0	31	31	195¹	169	15	3.2	8.0	174	58%	.286	1.22	3.04	3.46	4.2	99.6	58.3	10.7	49.1
2017	SLN	MLB	25	12	11	0	32	32	205	179	27	3.1	9.5	217	52%	.285	1.22	3.64	3.43	4.9	98.8	56.3	11.6	50.8
2018	SLN	MLB	26	8	6	5	33	18	118²	100	5	4.6	8.9	117	51%	.290	1.35	3.11	4.63	0.9	97.0	44.2	11.7	48.9
2019	SLN	MLB	27	10	7	0	27	27	143	122	14	3.6	9.2	146	51%	.301	1.26	3.69	4.33	1.6	98.0	53.7	11.5	50.2

Breakout: 14% Improve: 55% Collapse: 22% Attrition: 5% MLB: 97%   *Comparables: Felix Hernandez, Johnny Antonelli, Alex Wood*

Martinez added a cutter in 2018. Now, please, don't get too excited. New pitches in the arsenal are to Martinez as Horcruxes are to Voldemort: they technically make him more powerful and harder to kill, but they also cost something. They diminish him, numb his feel for each little piece of the larger repertoire. He's able to pound the zone, more often than not, but his command is less fine than ever. Worse, perhaps, the injuries that cost Martinez part of 2018 also seem to have sapped a couple miles per hour from his fastball. The mid-season move to the bullpen was temporary, but his velocity drop and tumble out of the top echelon of starters are both more likely to be permanent.

Miles Mikolas RHP Born: 08/23/88 Age: 30 Bats: R Throws: R Height: 6'5" Weight: 220 Origin: Round 7, 2009 Draft (#204 overall)

YEAR	TEAM	LVL	AGE	W	L	SV	G	GS	IP	H	HR	BB/9	K/9	K	GB%	BABIP	WHIP	ERA	DRA	WARP	MPH	FB%	WHF	CSP
2018	SLN	MLB	29	18	4	0	32	32	200²	186	16	1.3	6.5	146	51%	.279	1.07	2.83	3.38	4.5	96.1	48.6	10.5	51.8
2019	SLN	MLB	30	12	8	0	28	28	168	155	15	2.0	7.2	135	49%	.296	1.15	3.44	4.05	2.4	95.3	48.5	10.5	51.7

Breakout: 18% Improve: 52% Collapse: 18% Attrition: 8% MLB: 94%   *Comparables: Doug Fister, Brandon McCarthy, Hyun-jin Ryu*

We rarely frame it this way, but in terms of pitch selection, MLB has moved a good distance in the direction of Nippon Professional Baseball over the last few years. When Mikolas returned from Japan in 2018, he was wired for success in the Majors in a way he and others who walked his path never had been before. He's comfortable using his four-seam fastball, his sinker, his slider, and his curveball—so much so that he threw all of them between 20 and 28 percent of the time last year. This has been the paradigm in the highest level of Japanese baseball for years, but MLB has tended to be a fastball-forward league. As it's changed of late, it's done so in the direction of favoring whichever dominant pitch a hurler has in his repertoire. Mikolas, lacking one overwhelming offering, blends excellent control with exceptional unpredictability, and keeps the ball on the ground. (It doesn't hurt that he's also throwing harder than ever.)

Andrew Miller LHP Born: 05/21/85 Age: 34 Bats: L Throws: L Height: 6'7" Weight: 205 Origin: Round 1, 2006 Draft (#6 overall)

YEAR	TEAM	LVL	AGE	W	L	SV	G	GS	IP	H	HR	BB/9	K/9	K	GB%	BABIP	WHIP	ERA	DRA	WARP	MPH	FB%	WHF	CSP
2016	NYA	MLB	31	6	1	9	44	0	45¹	28	5	1.4	15.3	77	55%	.284	0.77	1.39	1.79	1.7	98.2	39.4	17.7	46.4
2016	CLE	MLB	31	4	0	3	26	0	29	14	3	0.6	14.3	46	58%	.212	0.55	1.55	2.07	1.0	97.5	39.7	15.8	49.5
2017	CLE	MLB	32	4	3	2	57	0	62²	31	3	3.0	13.6	95	42%	.233	0.83	1.44	2.30	2.0	96.9	41.9	17.1	45.7
2018	CLE	MLB	33	2	4	2	37	0	34	31	3	4.2	11.9	45	50%	.329	1.38	4.24	3.08	0.7	95.5	43.3	13.7	50.2
2019	SLN	MLB	34	3	1	3	53	0	56¹	42	5	3.1	11.0	68	47%	.287	1.10	3.21	3.77	0.7	95.7	40.9	15.9	47.3

Breakout: 11% Improve: 27% Collapse: 43% Attrition: 7% MLB: 90%   *Comparables: Seung Hwan Oh, Francisco Cordero, Jerry Blevins*

Rembrandt's "Danae." The Library at Alexandria. Andrew Miller. Historic beauty shattered by callous misfortune and the violence and ugliness of the world, the brilliance of which can never truly be recreated, an idea as much as a memory, a byword to magnificence lost dwarfing the magnificence that once was. Okay, so, it probably says more about Miller's 2013-2017 run — which looked something like Randy Johnson in an Iron Man suit when totaled together — that his 2018 felt like such a disaster. When you step back, it was a half season hampered by injury. It's hard to know how much of his Quite Good But Not Superlative was a result of pitching at less than 100 percent. Perhaps an offseason of rest will restore him to his world consuming powers or maybe there was real decline here. With stuff as magisterial as Miller's, which took as long to harness as it did, there's always fear that when it goes it will go suddenly. Then again, with stuff as magisterial as Miller's, there's a whole lot of declining he'd have to do before he'd be anything resembling ineffective.

Bud Norris RHP Born: 03/02/85 Age: 34 Bats: R Throws: R Height: 6'0" Weight: 215 Origin: Round 6, 2006 Draft (#189 overall)

YEAR	TEAM	LVL	AGE	W	L	SV	G	GS	IP	H	HR	BB/9	K/9	K	GB%	BABIP	WHIP	ERA	DRA	WARP	MPH	FB%	WHF	CSP
2016	ATL	MLB	31	3	7	0	22	10	70¹	68	6	3.6	7.7	60	53%	.302	1.36	4.22	4.97	0.3	96.0	50.6	10.3	45.6
2016	LAN	MLB	31	3	3	0	13	9	42²	48	8	4.4	8.9	42	45%	.328	1.62	6.54	4.19	0.5	95.8	50.6	11.4	47.4
2017	ANA	MLB	32	2	6	19	60	3	62	56	8	3.9	10.7	74	45%	.310	1.34	4.21	3.90	0.9	95.5	44.5	13.8	43.5
2018	SLN	MLB	33	3	6	28	64	0	57²	51	8	3.3	10.5	67	45%	.299	1.25	3.59	3.69	0.8	96.0	56.1	13.4	46.4
2019	SLN	MLB	34	3	2	7	29	6	52	46	6	3.6	9.7	56	45%	.308	1.28	3.87	4.53	0.3	94.7	49.9	12.3	44.7

Breakout: 24% Improve: 48% Collapse: 18% Attrition: 9% MLB: 86%   *Comparables: Jesse Chavez, Jakie May, Steve Carlton*

When Norris finally gave up on remaining a big-league starter, his career drew new and fresh breath. He repositioned a cutter that had risen and fallen among the ranks of his secondary offerings as his primary pitch. After finding success that way in 2017, he cut his slider almost out of the mix in 2018, feeling that returning to an old sinker would give him a pitch that wiggled in either direction, relative to his four-seamer. He faded badly down the stretch, but Norris's bulldog approach and those three pitches playing off one another spell sustainable success as a short-burst reliever. By all accounts, Norris's red-ass clubhouse presence is polarizing, but on the mound, he's much better suited to his present role than to his preferred one.

Daniel Poncedeleon RHP   Born: 01/16/92   Age: 27   Bats: R   Throws: R   Height: 6'4"   Weight: 185   Origin: Round 9, 2014 Draft (#285 overall)

YEAR	TEAM	LVL	AGE	W	L	SV	G	GS	IP	H	HR	BB/9	K/9	K	GB%	BABIP	WHIP	ERA	DRA	WARP	MPH	FB%	WHF	CSP
2016	SFD	AA	24	9	8	0	27	27	151	128	10	3.3	7.3	122	46%	.269	1.22	3.52	4.03	1.9				
2017	MEM	AAA	25	2	0	0	6	6	29	20	2	4.0	7.8	25	42%	.234	1.14	2.17	5.21	0.2				
2018	MEM	AAA	26	9	4	0	19	18	96¹	69	4	4.7	10.3	110	30%	.272	1.24	2.24	3.89	1.8				
2018	SLN	MLB	26	0	2	1	11	4	33	24	2	3.5	8.5	31	36%	.259	1.12	2.73	3.52	0.6	95.4	61.8	14.5	49.8
2019	SLN	MLB	27	3	2	0	37	5	58²	50	8	3.9	9.4	61	38%	.289	1.28	4.28	4.99	0.1	94.9	62.5	14.6	50.4

Breakout: 3%   Improve: 18%   Collapse: 10%   Attrition: 18%   MLB: 37%   *Comparables: Tyler Wagner, Chris Heston, Lucas Harrell*

Poncedeleon makes for an interesting exploration of the art of pitching. He's tall and lanky, and can create some difficult angles for opposing batters. His fastball has good rise, though not much wiggle, so he'd be well-advised to work up with it more often than he has. There's a big curveball he doesn't trust, which is a shame, because it's the real eye-level changer of his pack of secondary pitches. His cutter and changeup have about the same sink and move the same amount, in opposite directions, off the heater, so there's deception there, but the cutter comes out of the hand much harder, and he doesn't disguise the arm action well. A couple adjustments could unlock a mid-rotation upside, but Poncedeleon should have made them by now. Unless he finds a fountain of youth, the stuff might soften too much before he can firm up his feel for it.

Alex Reyes RHP   Born: 08/29/94   Age: 24   Bats: R   Throws: R   Height: 6'3"   Weight: 175   Origin: International Free Agent, 2012

YEAR	TEAM	LVL	AGE	W	L	SV	G	GS	IP	H	HR	BB/9	K/9	K	GB%	BABIP	WHIP	ERA	DRA	WARP	MPH	FB%	WHF	CSP
2016	MEM	AAA	21	2	3	0	14	14	65¹	63	6	4.4	12.8	93	42%	.365	1.45	4.96	3.01	1.7				
2016	SLN	MLB	21	4	1	1	12	5	46	33	1	4.5	10.2	52	44%	.283	1.22	1.57	3.45	0.9	100.1	63.9	12.4	45.8
2018	SLN	MLB	23	0	0	0	1	1	4	3	0	4.5	4.5	2	40%	.300	1.25	0.00	8.15	-0.1	97.2	57.5	4.1	43
2019	SLN	MLB	24	6	4	0	16	16	84²	67	10	3.9	11.8	111	40%	.312	1.22	3.43	4.02	1.3	99.5	64.9	11.6	45.4

Breakout: 25%   Improve: 58%   Collapse: 14%   Attrition: 18%   MLB: 86%   *Comparables: Tyler Glasnow, Matt Harvey, Jordan Walden*

In this age of desensitization to tragedies and trials, Tommy John surgery ranks right up there with skin cancer and global climate change among things that should be taken more seriously. When Reyes had his in early 2017, many observers shrugged it off, figuring he'd be back by the middle of 2018, ready to take his place at the front of the Cardinals' rotation. He kind of, sort of, almost was, but during his rehab stint, he felt something start to go wrong in the back of his shoulder. Wanting to make it back to the majors and be categorized as a big-leaguer if he again hit the DL, he pitched through it. After just one truncated start, he was shelved for the season, and his star has dimmed deeply now. Blame Reyes for not being forthright, but save plenty of venom for the people who have allowed such a disparity to develop between the treatment and pay of major and minor leaguers, and spare not the people who foolhardily underestimated the risk of injury his extreme velocity and mechanics posed. Most importantly, remember: TINSTAAPP.

Griffin Roberts RHP   Born: 06/13/96   Age: 23   Bats: R   Throws: R   Height: 6'3"   Weight: 205   Origin: Round 1, 2018 Draft (#43 overall)

YEAR	TEAM	LVL	AGE	W	L	SV	G	GS	IP	H	HR	BB/9	K/9	K	GB%	BABIP	WHIP	ERA	DRA	WARP	MPH	FB%	WHF	CSP
2018	CRD	RK	22	0	1	1	7	2	8²	6	0	4.2	11.4	11	55%	.300	1.15	6.23	3.43	0.2				
2019	SLN	MLB	23	1	1	1	22	2	31¹	32	5	7.6	8.0	28	47%	.312	1.86	6.45	7.52	-0.9				

Comparables: Gerardo Concepcion, Matthew Carasiti, Tanner Anderson

Roberts spent his days at Wake Forest dekein' ACC hitters with a demonic slider, perhaps the best in the 2018 draft class. It's a two-plane problem of a pitch, off a fastball that sits comfortably in the mid-90s and can ramp up to 97 or 98 miles per hour in short bursts. For some of his collegiate career, Roberts closed, and he could be ticketed for that role again in the future, but his size and his ability to repeat his release point provide some reason to believe he can start. No longer is leaning heavily on a slider, even making it the primary weapon in one's arsenal, disqualifying for a would-be starter, and Roberts is a great example. He just needs to more consistently fade his changeup out of the lane of his heater.

Chasen Shreve LHP   Born: 07/12/90   Age: 28   Bats: L   Throws: L   Height: 6'4"   Weight: 195   Origin: Round 11, 2010 Draft (#344 overall)

YEAR	TEAM	LVL	AGE	W	L	SV	G	GS	IP	H	HR	BB/9	K/9	K	GB%	BABIP	WHIP	ERA	DRA	WARP	MPH	FB%	WHF	CSP
2016	SWB	AAA	25	0	0	0	13	1	16²	4	1	3.8	10.8	20	46%	.094	0.66	1.62	1.85	0.6				
2016	NYA	MLB	25	2	1	1	37	0	33	29	8	3.5	9.0	33	44%	.247	1.27	5.18	3.68	0.5	93.8	50	14.7	37.1
2017	SWB	AAA	26	1	0	1	9	0	11¹	7	0	2.4	15.1	19	48%	.333	0.88	1.59	1.65	0.5				
2017	NYA	MLB	26	4	1	0	44	0	45¹	35	8	5.0	11.5	58	37%	.252	1.32	3.77	5.38	-0.1	94.3	49.2	15.4	36.5
2018	NYA	MLB	27	2	2	1	40	0	38	39	8	4.3	10.9	46	49%	.320	1.50	4.26	2.83	0.9	93.4	52.9	15.5	39.3
2018	SLN	MLB	27	1	2	0	20	0	14²	14	3	5.5	9.8	16	22%	.297	1.57	3.07	5.39	-0.1	93.3	56.1	14.5	42.5
2019	SLN	MLB	28	2	1	3	37	0	39¹	33	5	4.0	10.2	45	42%	.296	1.28	3.96	4.63	0.1	93.2	51.9	15.3	38.4

Breakout: 29%   Improve: 47%   Collapse: 23%   Attrition: 11%   MLB: 93%   *Comparables: Tony Sipp, Ken Howell, Shawn Tolleson*

If one doesn't get too mired in what Shreve isn't, there's a ton to like about him. He's never succeeded when stretched or challenged to take on too many innings, but he isn't confined to a matchup role, because his slider and splitter give him a secondary weapon for batters of each handedness (especially if his uptick in whiffs on the slider is for real). Repeating his arm slot and release point was once a struggle for him, but he really tightened that up in 2018. Shreve's going to give up too many home runs, and that's a fatal flaw for a high-leverage reliever, but he can deliver quality medium-leverage frames. His fastball looks pedestrian to a radar gun but preternatural to a TrackMan system, with a ton of spin. He'd thrive as a twice-weekly opener ahead of right-handed bulk guys.

Michael Wacha RHP Born: 07/01/91 Age: 27 Bats: R Throws: R Height: 6'6" Weight: 215 Origin: Round 1, 2012 Draft (#19 overall)

YEAR	TEAM	LVL	AGE	W	L	SV	G	GS	IP	H	HR	BB/9	K/9	K	GB%	BABIP	WHIP	ERA	DRA	WARP	MPH	FB%	WHF	CSP
2016	SLN	MLB	24	7	7	0	27	24	138	159	15	2.9	7.4	114	48%	.334	1.48	5.09	4.38	1.5	96.3	52.9	9	48
2017	SLN	MLB	25	12	9	0	30	30	165²	170	17	3.0	8.6	158	50%	.327	1.36	4.13	3.83	3.2	97.2	52.8	10.9	49.9
2018	SLN	MLB	26	8	2	0	15	15	84¹	68	9	3.8	7.6	71	47%	.249	1.23	3.20	3.98	1.3	95.8	43.1	10.4	46.2
2019	SLN	MLB	27	7	6	0	21	21	105	96	11	3.3	8.3	97	46%	.303	1.28	3.79	4.46	1.0	96.1	50.6	10.4	48.5

Breakout: 22% Improve: 53% Collapse: 27% Attrition: 11% MLB: 96% *Comparables: Julio Teheran, Mat Latos, John Danks*

Every injury-prone pitcher seems to go from "good when healthy" to "never quite healthy." Wacha has never offered guaranteed durability, but he posted a cFIP between 85 and 97 in each season from 2013 through 2017. In 2018, he finally wobbled off that tightrope, with a cFIP of 102 that suggests he was a below-average pitcher for the first time. That was, in no small part, because his stuff went backward even more than it had stepped forward in 2017. By cutting it loose for a year, Wacha seems to have permanently left something on the Busch Stadium mound. Though he's still young, the injury markers have gone from yellow flags to red ones, and he no longer looks like an ace in the making.

Adam Wainwright RHP Born: 08/30/81 Age: 37 Bats: R Throws: R Height: 6'7" Weight: 235 Origin: Round 1, 2000 Draft (#29 overall)

YEAR	TEAM	LVL	AGE	W	L	SV	G	GS	IP	H	HR	BB/9	K/9	K	GB%	BABIP	WHIP	ERA	DRA	WARP	MPH	FB%	WHF	CSP
2016	SLN	MLB	34	13	9	0	33	33	198²	220	22	2.7	7.3	161	45%	.330	1.40	4.62	4.26	2.5	93.2	41.5	8.8	46.4
2017	SLN	MLB	35	12	5	0	24	23	123¹	140	14	3.3	7.0	96	50%	.326	1.50	5.11	4.84	1.0	92.2	46.8	7.8	47.5
2018	SFD	AA	36	1	0	0	3	3	10	5	0	0.0	8.1	9	42%	.192	0.50	0.00	4.56	0.1				
2018	SLN	MLB	36	2	4	0	8	8	40¹	41	5	4.0	8.9	40	51%	.310	1.46	4.46	3.78	0.7	91.6	38	9.6	45.5
2019	SLN	MLB	37	6	5	0	37	16	102²	97	11	3.2	8.1	92	46%	.310	1.31	3.94	4.62	0.6	91.2	41.9	8.3	45.3

Breakout: 10% Improve: 46% Collapse: 20% Attrition: 13% MLB: 87% *Comparables: Hiroki Kuroda, Jorge De La Rosa, Roy Halladay*

Over the last two years, Wainwright's career has been on life support multiple times. In what is increasingly a young man's game, he's distinctly old, with both the speed and the movement on his stuff fading fast. And yet, he's found his way to a very modern revelation: that throwing his best pitch more often can keep him afloat. He threw his famous, nostalgia-inducing curveball nearly 40 percent of the time, more than any other pitch. Wainwright is mostly curve-cutter-sinker these days, which is the optimal three-pitch mix if your goal is to keep batters from swinging aggressively. Despite the flattening stuff, he's getting just enough whiffs to get by, limiting opponents' power, and finessing his way to unlikely success, where success is defined as survival.

LINEOUTS

Hitters

HITTER	POS	TEAM	LVL	AGE	PA	R	2B	3B	HR	RBI	BB	K	SB	CS	AVG/OBP/SLG	DRC+	VORP	BABIP	BRR	FRAA	WARP
Luken Baker	1B	CRD	Rk	21	28	10	2	0	1	7	3	4	0	0	.500/.536/.708	123	3.9	.550	-0.7	1B(5): 0.1	0.0
	1B	PEO	A	21	156	16	9	0	3	15	16	31	0	0	.288/.359/.417	108	2.7	.349	-1.4	1B(20): 0.3	0.2
Conner Capel	CF	LYN	A+	21	383	47	17	3	6	44	49	72	15	10	.261/.355/.388	111	22.0	.311	0.8	CF(67): -4.8, LF(10): 1.9	1.6
	CF	PMB	A+	21	126	11	6	1	1	19	7	30	0	1	.248/.296/.342	91	1.1	.326	-1.6	CF(13): -0.6, LF(8): -0.3	0.0
Ivan Herrera	C	CRD	Rk	18	130	23	6	4	1	25	11	20	1	1	.348/.423/.500	140	11.6	.409	-1.9	C(20): 0.6	0.9
Joe Hudson	C	LOU	AAA	27	60	5	3	0	0	3	8	15	0	0	.235/.339/.294	86	0.3	.333	-1.1	C(15): 3.1	0.4
	C	MOB	AA	27	28	2	1	1	1	5	1	7	0	0	.346/.393/.577	94	3.5	.444	-0.2	C(4): -0.1, 1B(2): 0.0	0.0
	C	SLC	AAA	27	101	13	6	0	3	14	10	18	0	0	.311/.380/.478	117	7.0	.362	-0.1	C(25): 0.4	0.8
	C	ANA	MLB	27	12	0	1	0	0	1	0	0	0	0	.167/.167/.250	98	-0.9	.167	0.0	C(8): 0.6	0.1
Jonatan Machado	OF	PEO	A	19	96	8	4	0	0	8	3	15	3	2	.185/.208/.228	80	-7.7	.218	0.0	CF(13): -4.4, LF(9): -1.7	-0.6
	OF	JCY	Rk	19	214	30	10	0	2	21	17	41	9	5	.292/.355/.375	81	8.5	.358	1.4	CF(43): -6.1, LF(5): 0.4	-0.2
	OF	SCO	A-	19	46	2	0	0	0	2	3	15	0	0	.048/.109/.048	84	-7.7	.071	0.2	LF(9): 0.9	0.1
Francisco Pena	C	SLN	MLB	28	142	10	3	0	2	8	6	43	1	0	.203/.239/.271	53	-4.9	.278	-0.3	C(56): -6.2, 1B(2): 0.0	-0.8
Max Schrock	INF	MEM	AAA	23	457	41	22	0	4	42	24	36	10	5	.249/.296/.331	84	2.9	.260	-1.7	2B(80): -3.3, 3B(14): -0.2	0.1
Edmundo Sosa	SS	SFD	AA	22	279	34	17	1	7	32	9	52	1	2	.276/.308/.429	97	13.2	.319	1.4	SS(43): -4.8, 3B(11): 1.6	0.6
	SS	MEM	AAA	22	209	31	13	0	5	27	13	42	5	2	.262/.321/.408	89	8.4	.310	0.7	SS(28): 1.1, 2B(12): -0.3	0.7
	SS	SLN	MLB	22	3	1	0	0	0	0	1	1	0	0	.000/.333/.000	98	-0.1	.000	0.0	2B(1): 0.0	0.0
Wadye Ynfante	CF	SCO	A-	20	286	33	15	1	4	25	21	101	10	5	.213/.301/.328	87	6.9	.336	1.7	CF(66): 7.2	1.4

Luken Baker is tall and bats right-handed, so he can't be Dan Vogelbach's secret twin, but he *might* be his accidentally-unleashed funhouse mirror reflection. ① It's tempting to dream on an everyday future for a toolsy left-handed batter, but guys like **Conner Capel** nearly always see half those tools fade and end up as either a platoon bat or a fourth outfielder. ① Panamanian backstop **Ivan Herrera** has a chance to catch some helium this summer, as he moves beyond the complex leagues at age 19. ① **Joe Hudson** was great as the police chief on *Hill Street Blues*, and less so as a major league catcher for a few weeks. ① Youth and speed are on his side, but as it stands, **Jonatan Machado** is about 30 pounds and two power grades away from being a viable regular even in center field. ① **Francisco Pena** has catching in his blood, and teammates love him; between those things and his offensive skills, he's qualified to be a fine quality control coach. ① The only way diminutive, modestly athletic **Max Schrock** was going to carve out a big-league career of any import was to keep hitting for average, and when he reached Triple-A, he stopped doing that. ① His modest, developing pop befits the smooth defensive shortstop he projected to be, but **Edmundo Sosa** looks more like a utility infielder instead. ① He's got the quirky name and the single-tool profile (it's plus speed; the rest is hopes and prayers) of a prospect who never makes it, but there's still time for **Wadye Ynfante** to surprise us.

Pitchers

PITCHER	TEAM	LVL	AGE	W	L	SV	G	GS	IP	H	HR	BB/9	K/9	K	GB%	BABIP	WHIP	ERA	DRA	WARP	MPH	FB%	WHF	CSP
Brett Cecil	SLN	MLB	31	1	1	0	40	0	32²	39	5	6.9	5.2	19	41%	.315	1.96	6.89	8.61	-1.4	91.4	55.5	9	47.7
Junior Fernandez	PMB	A+	21	1	0	3	8	0	9²	9	0	1.9	6.5	7	43%	.321	1.14	0.00	3.28	0.2				
	SFD	AA	21	0	0	0	16	0	21	19	1	6.9	7.3	17	36%	.295	1.67	5.14	4.64	0.1				
Giovanny Gallegos	NYA	MLB	26	0	0	1	4	0	10	10	2	2.7	9.0	10	41%	.320	1.30	4.50	5.38	-0.1	95.3	58.6	8.9	50.5
	SWB	AAA	26	2	1	2	17	0	27²	24	1	2.3	13.3	41	39%	.354	1.12	3.90	2.03	1.0				
	MEM	AAA	26	0	0	1	13	0	16²	7	0	1.6	8.6	16	45%	.175	0.60	0.54	2.55	0.5				
	SLN	MLB	26	0	0	0	2	0	1¹	1	0	0.0	13.5	2	0%	.333	0.75	0.00	6.81	0.0	96.0	64	12	46.2
Derian Gonzalez	MEM	AAA	23	0	0	1	8	0	10²	13	0	3.4	10.1	12	44%	.406	1.59	5.91	2.59	0.3				
	SFD	AA	23	4	0	1	13	0	16¹	13	0	3.9	5.5	10	58%	.260	1.22	2.76	4.40	0.1				
Tyler Lyons	SLN	MLB	30	1	0	0	27	0	16²	24	3	4.3	10.3	19	28%	.412	1.92	8.64	6.32	-0.3	91.0	43.1	10.9	53.7
	MEM	AAA	30	1	1	1	7	3	21²	11	2	2.5	8.7	21	41%	.173	0.78	2.49	3.04	0.6				
Mike Mayers	MEM	AAA	26	0	0	3	5	0	7²	5	0	4.7	9.4	8	57%	.238	1.17	0.00	3.42	0.1				
	SLN	MLB	26	2	1	1	50	0	51²	59	7	2.6	8.5	49	44%	.338	1.43	4.70	4.06	0.5	98.4	60.4	10.7	48.4
Ryan Meisinger	BOW	AA	24	0	0	0	11	0	18¹	22	4	2.5	9.3	19	54%	.346	1.47	4.42	2.53	0.5				
	NOR	AAA	24	2	0	1	21	0	27²	21	1	3.3	11.7	36	41%	.308	1.12	2.28	2.71	0.8				
	BAL	MLB	24	2	1	0	18	1	21	18	6	4.3	9.0	21	34%	.240	1.33	6.43	7.30	-0.6	92.9	47.1	11.8	40.9
Johan Oviedo	PEO	A	20	10	10	1	25	23	121²	108	6	5.8	8.7	118	38%	.304	1.54	4.22	4.30	1.2				
Tyler Webb	SDN	MLB	27	0	1	0	4	0	5	6	2	5.4	7.2	4	41%	.267	1.80	12.60	8.27	-0.2	90.3	60.4	9.4	45.7
	ELP	AAA	27	1	1	0	19	0	22	20	1	3.3	11.5	28	38%	.345	1.27	2.05	2.87	0.6				
	MEM	AAA	27	0	0	0	11	1	19²	9	1	1.8	9.6	21	41%	.186	0.66	2.29	3.24	0.4				
	SLN	MLB	27	0	0	0	18	0	15¹	16	1	3.5	6.5	11	31%	.319	1.43	1.76	6.76	-0.3	91.9	59.7	11.6	51
Jake Woodford	SFD	AA	21	3	8	0	16	16	81	94	13	3.9	6.2	56	48%	.309	1.59	5.22	4.77	0.5				
	MEM	AAA	21	5	5	0	12	12	64	64	5	3.8	6.3	45	38%	.292	1.42	4.50	4.92	0.5				

No pitcher who tossed at least 30 innings in 2018 had a worse cFIP than The Man With Two Middle Names, **Brett Cecil**. ⓧ A fastball with triple-digit heat won't save **Junior Fernandez** until he finds his way clear to bring his walk percentage down into single digits. ⓧ His age and thin arsenal make **Giovanny Gallegos** easy to overlook, but his track record of success and missing bats makes him easy to dream on. ⓧ Brunette **Steven Gingery** has a fresh Tommy John scar, good fastball command, and a changeup more deceptive than his surname, which is a good start. ⓧ If he can stay on the mound long enough to establish his feel for them, **Derian Gonzalez** should ride two average-plus secondary offerings (a change and a hook) to a solid bullpen career. ⓧ You know those guys who are always younger than you think, with more time yet to possibly break out? That used to be **Tyler Lyons**. ⓧ Throwing 97 now, apparently, and having added four miles per hour to his slider from March to September of 2018, **Mike Mayers** has become a wild but effective relief option. ⓧ **Ryan Meisinger**, a Maryland native, rose quickly through the Orioles system after being drafted in 2015 and made his MLB debut this season, which was a cool moment. Less cool: Meisinger got torched by the long ball, surrendering homers in over half of his first 11 appearances. ⓧ Tall and blessed with a plus fastball, **Johan Oviedo** is still getting just this passing mention, which is a clue about where the rest of his arsenal and his command profile stand. ⓧ Strapping lefty **Tyler Webb** has the stuff to rack up strikeouts in the Majors, and the inconsistency to rack up six weeks a year of vacation, in the form of DFA limbo. ⓧ Former first-round pick **Jake Woodford** has good control and a heavy fastball, but there's nothing in his arsenal that misses bats, or even the barrels of them.

TAMPA BAY RAYS

Essay by Bryan Grosnick

Player comments by Tommy Rancel and BP staff

On May 19, 2018, the Tampa Bay Rays did something relatively new: They began their game with relief ace Sergio Romo on the mound. In using Romo–a reliever through his career up until that day in May–for the first few batters of the game before going to another pitcher for the bulk of the innings, they implemented a role popularly called *"The Opener."* By regularly throwing a relief pitcher first–before going to the man who would normally be the starter–they threw players, fans, and (especially) the baseball media into a frenzy.

By the end of the season, the Rays had regularly implemented this strategy (though not as often as you might think) and surprised many by vaulting to a 90-72 record despite a bargain-basement payroll and a roster that never inspired the confidence that they would contend for a playoff appearance. With the opener strategy gaining traction with other organizations over the past year, it's probably important to answer two questions as best we can: (1) what exactly *is* an opener? and (2) did the strategy work for the Rays in 2018?

What is an opener? (Really?)

The Rays were not the first team in history to use a relief pitcher to start a baseball game before turning the ball over to a pitcher who would pitch the bulk of the remaining innings. However, they were the first team to try a long-term strategy like this, where a reliever would be tasked with getting the first out or three (or more, but no more than two innings) before passing the game on to a long-distance "starting" pitcher.

This strategy (and the term "opener") were popularized by a plucky young writer at *Beyond the Box Score* back in 2013[1] and can be defined using a couple of simple rules:

- The first pitcher in the game faces batters for no more than three innings.
- The second pitcher in the game faces batters for an intended term of no fewer than four innings.
- The strategy is used with some regularity over the course of a season.

RAYS PROSPECTUS
2018 W-L: 90-72, 3RD IN AL EAST

Pythag	.547	11th	B-Age		27.1	5th
RS/G	4.42	16th	P-Age		26.7	4th
RA/G	3.99	5th	Salary		$76.0M	28th
DRC+	93	20th	M$/MW		$1.5M	29th
DRA	4.01	8th	DL Days		1293	21st
FIP	3.85	6th	$ on DL		18%	17th
DER	.722	2nd				

404'

370'   370'

315'   322'

- Opened 1990
- Dome
- Synthetic surface
- Fence profile: 5' to 11'5"

Three-Year Park Factors

Runs	Runs/RH	Runs/LH	HR/RH	HR/LH
95	95	95	96	95

Top Hitter WARP	2.9 Joey Wendle
Top Pitcher WARP	6.0 Blake Snell
Top Prospect	Wander Franco

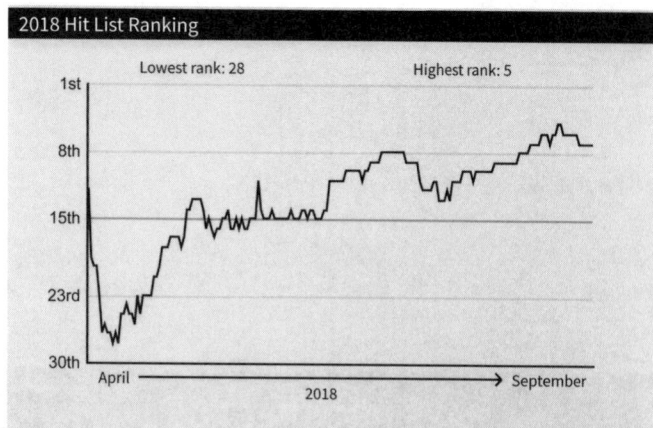

2018 Hit List Ranking

Lowest rank: 28   Highest rank: 5

1st / 8th / 15th / 23rd / 30th

April → September
2018

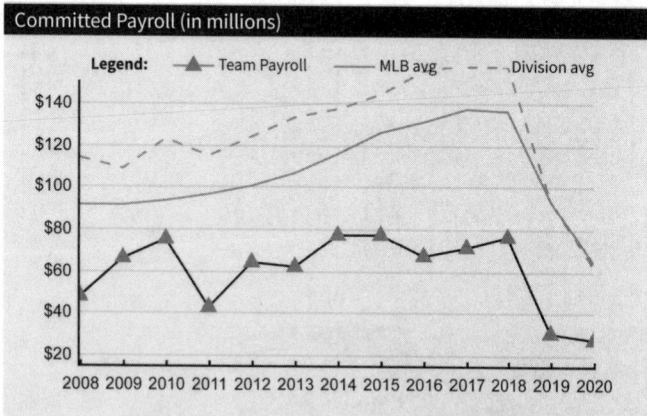

Committed Payroll (in millions)

Legend: ▲ Team Payroll — MLB avg - - - Division avg

$140 / $120 / $100 / $80 / $60 / $40 / $20

2008 2009 2010 2011 2012 2013 2014 2015 2016 2017 2018 2019 2020

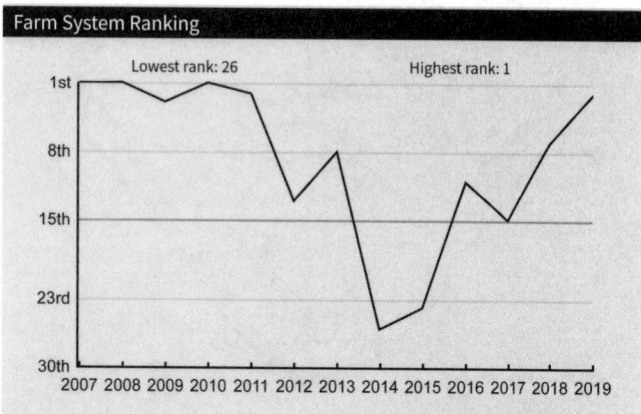

Farm System Ranking

Lowest rank: 26   Highest rank: 1

1st / 8th / 15th / 23rd / 30th

2007 2008 2009 2010 2011 2012 2013 2014 2015 2016 2017 2018 2019

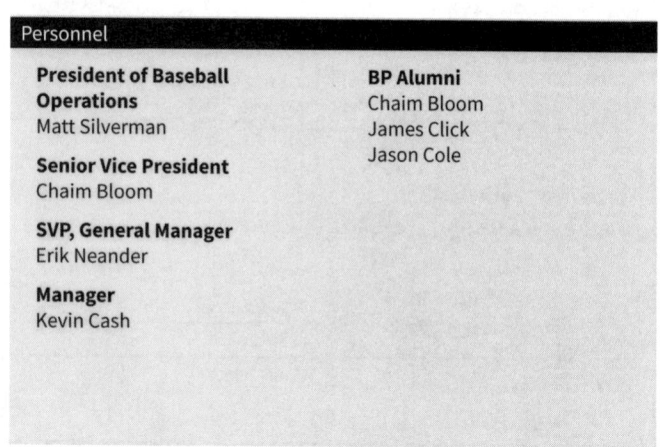

Personnel

President of Baseball Operations
Matt Silverman

Senior Vice President
Chaim Bloom

SVP, General Manager
Erik Neander

Manager
Kevin Cash

BP Alumni
Chaim Bloom
James Click
Jason Cole

(Before we go any further, I'd like to briefly address the issue of the second pitcher in an opener game, and what they should be called. If they don't begin the game, we can't call them a "starting pitcher," but the role is unique enough that it requires specific nomenclature. "Swingman" is more aligned with a different role–a pitcher who can be a traditional starter or a traditional relief pitcher–and the Rays' term "bulk guy" sounds vaguely derogatory or that all those pitchers should look like Bartolo Colon. So I'd like to recommend the term *yeoman* for pitchers who enter the game after the opener to pitch to the fifth or sixth inning and beyond.

You may know the term from the archaic role of woodsman or servant, or from the more recent military usage, but it fits for two reasons: the first is the adjectival use of the word, which implies loyally and valiantly completing a task that typically involves great labor. *Katrina did yeoman's work filing all of those Freedom of Information Act requests.* The second, lesser reason is that in older times, the yeoman was often an archer, and that seems to jive nicely with the pitching profession and emphasis on accuracy. I'll be using the term instead of "bulk guy" going forward.)

The opener strategy is not the same thing as two other reliever-based starting pitching strategies, both of which the Rays *also* tried in 2018. "Bullpenning" is when the team throws *only* relief pitchers over the course of a game, and differs from the opener in the lack of a yeoman role. It also is often a function of emergency when a team is without a scheduled starter and must improvise rather than a function of design. "Piggybacking" is when two pitchers throw a roughly-similar number of pitches or innings, and effectively split the lion's share of innings in a game equitably. Neither of these strategies are quite the same as the opener.

(Neither is a strategy that closely resembles the opener but without the same intention: when a team throws a starting pitcher who gets shelled early in the game and *must* be replaced to prevent further damage. I refer to this as the "Oriole-pener strategy.")

So why would a team try out this opener strategy, effectively casting aside over 100 years of starting pitcher tradition? In the years since my first article on the subject advocating for the role, I've identified a number of potential reasons why the strategy might be effective:

- An opener of opposing handedness than the yeoman may force a team to manage their platoons differently than usual early in the game, or restructure their lineup to a disadvantage

- An opener of significant skill may be able to limit run-scoring during the first inning, which is typically the highest run-scoring inning of any given game.

- An opener who is successful may give a team the psychic benefits that come from an early lead.

- An opener may face the more talented hitters at the top of the lineup, while allowing the yeoman to face the bottom of a lineup more frequently over the game.
- An opener role for a relief pitcher may give that pitcher a more comfortably-defined role, or allow them to be used more frequently due to scheduling.

On the other hand, there are noted cons to the opener strategy, which include:

- Using an opener forces a team to "burn" one of their relievers early, shortening the bullpen during high-leverage innings later in the game.
- Using an opener may make the yeoman have more trouble warming up or not have as defined of a pre-game schedule than if they were a regular starting pitcher.
- Using an opener that isn't successful (or a yeoman who must leave the game early) may tax a team's bullpen even more than a poor appearance would under normal circumstances.

In theory, the opener is a high-risk, high-reward strategy that's moderately aggressive…and therefore is theoretically a good fit for a team like the Rays, who would need a huge boost to surpass the high-talent, high-payroll Yankees and Red Sox. (The Rays' 90 wins in 2018 while using the occasional opener couldn't even crack the playoffs, for example.) But while the Rays had remarkable success last year, I'm not sure if we can effectively trace their win-loss record directly back to the use of openers. Let's see how far we can get.

Did the opener strategy work?

First, we've got to identify how many openers (and yeomen) were used by the Rays, when they were used, and who they were. In 2018, the Rays used 17 different starting pitchers, six of which could be considered openers using the criteria noted above. These standards resulted in 36 "opener games" thrown by the Rays in 2018. There were also a few dozen "bullpen" games and a small handful of "piggyback" games.

Opener	# of Opener Appearances
Ryne Stanek	16
Diego Castillo	6
Hunter Wood	6
Sergio Romo	4
Matt Andriese	1
Jonny Venters	1

The yeoman role for the Rays was only a bit more distributed, with seven different pitchers coming into games late as a "bulk guy." Stanek's counterpart–the yeoman among yeomen–was Ryan Yarbrough, who consistently filled the role throughout the season. Yarbrough was the team's first yeoman, serving in the role when Romo made the first opener start, and also filled in there into the last week of the season, supporting Diego Castillo's start on the 24th of September.

Yeoman	# of Yeoman Appearances
Ryan Yarbrough	15
Yonny Chirinos	9
Jalen Beeks	6
Austin Pruitt	3
Anthony Banda	1
Vidal Nuno	1
Ryan Weber	1

An interesting thing about the opener experiment is how much variation there was in pairings: it was a rarity for much of the season for the same opener and the same yeoman to match up consistently week after week. Ryan Yarbrough, by virtue of how many yeoman appearances he made over time, paired with all but one opener…only missing Matt Andriese's single start. But by August, a more formal pattern seemed to emerge: Ryne Stanek paired with Yonny Chirinos, and either Hunter Wood or Diego Castillo paired with Yarbrough.

When we start to try and identify whether or not the opener strategy worked, there's a bunch of challenges that face it. The strategy itself probably doesn't solely dictate whether or not the team wins a particular game: there are too many variables in play to attribute the win to one particular pitching strategy. Nevertheless, we should see whether or not the team won its 36 opener games. The Rays went 19-17 in games in which a true "opener" was used.

So if games won while using an opener aren't enough to tell us whether or not the strategy works, what could? My best theory on the matter is to look at projected pitcher performance for Tampa's pitchers used in the opener and yeoman roles, and compare that to their actual performance. Baseball Prospectus' PECOTA metric is an excellent tool for that comparison. With it, we can see how differently the pitchers themselves performed, perhaps in part due to their new roles.

Opener	PECOTA IP	Actual IP	PECOTA DRA	Actual DRA	PECOTA ERA	Actual ERA
Ryne Stanek	51	66.3	4.36	3.34	3.79	2.98
Diego Castillo	17	56.7	5.25	3.70	4.90	3.18
Hunter Wood	17	41	5.04	2.97	4.64	3.73
Sergio Romo	56.7	67.3	4.57	2.80	4.05	4.14
Matt Andriese	115	78.7	4.76	4.97	4.11	5.26
Jonny Venters	N/A	34.3	N/A	4.90	N/A	3.67

Yeoman	PECOTA IP	Actual IP	PECOTA DRA	Actual DRA	PECOTA ERA	Actual ERA
Ryan Yarbrough	45	147.3	5.26	4.82	4.56	3.91
Yonny Chirinos	37.7	89.7	4.94	4.23	4.43	3.51
Jalen Beeks	10.7	50.7	5.72	5.46	5.03	5.51
Austin Pruitt	90	69.7	5.05	3.66	4.37	4.65
Anthony Banda	50	14.7	5.10	4.75	4.42	3.68
Vidal Nuno	40	33	5.38	4.39	4.86	1.64
Ryan Weber	36.3	5.3	5.08	7.01	4.77	5.06

Certainly, I'm not trying to imply here that use in either an opener or a yeoman role correlated with or caused improved performance in any of the pitchers the Rays used in either role this year. But what we can see here is that very few of the pitchers the Rays used in either role suffered from it, when compared to what PECOTA projected for them this year. The players who saw the most action as either an opener or a yeoman (Yarbrough, Chirinos, Beeks, Pruitt, Stanek, Castillo, Wood, and Romo) all saw DRA numbers better than what was projected for them, and only three of them saw mild ERA rises from what was projected.

Comparing our openers' and yeomen's splits in games which they started or relieved hasn't provided much information, which is to be expected given how little data exists at this time. The pitchers who spent the most innings swapping between opener and "regular" reliever or yeoman and "starting" pitcher (like Stanek and Yarbrough) didn't show much difference between their DRA numbers as "starter" or "reliever."

These data points are certainly too few and too noisy to give us a certain answer as to whether or not the opener gambit was a success, consider this an answer to its efficacy: there are no signs that the opener gambit was a failure. The team won more games than it lost during opener appearances, the team's pitchers used in these roles were more effective than projected, and none of the team's pitchers used in these roles suffered significant injuries or voiced serious concerns about their use. If we can't insist that the use of openers was an unmitigated success on the field, perhaps we can at least rule out the fact that it caused the team to fail.

In part because we don't have certainty that the strategy was a success, more questions emerge than just the first two posed in this essay.

Were the Rays the right team to try the Opener?

Even before the season started, the Rays were a team without significant starting pitching. Chris Archer was a known quantity and something close to an ace, but top prospect Brent Honeywell suffered an injury, as did 2017 breakout starter Jacob Faria. Blake Snell was unproven, and not yet the 2018 Cy Young Award winner, and that left the team with few possible regular starting pitching options.

While a lack of regular, reliable MLB-quality starting pitchers is a necessity to consider an opener strategy, the other side of it is having a deep, effective bullpen.

In this area, I'm not certain the Rays were a good fit for the strategy…and it makes me think that the opener strategy was more of a Plan B than their initial plan. Early in the year, with the Red Sox and Yankees looking unbeatable, the team shipped former closer Alex Colome to the Mariners as part of a deal that brought back cash savings and negligible prospect value. The Rays did not immediately reassign the payroll resources back to the big-league team, so one is left to assume that this was entirely a move to slough off costs, at the price of a well-regarded relief pitcher with experience in high-leverage situations.

Using an opener invariably means that a team is without depth at the end of their bullpen: in order to commit to using a reliever early, the team must sacrifice the possibility of using that player at the end of the game. Therefore, the team must be confident that their remaining relief options can be viable. This is why in all my previous documentation of the theory behind the opener, I've postulated that this is a strategy best served by teams with a strong and deep bullpen. The Rays absolutely did not fall into this category, as Colome might've been their best reliever at the time of his trade. Sergio Romo was probably the team's best relief pitcher at the time he was shifted into an opener role, which isn't ideal given how using an opener makes a team more vulnerable in high-leverage late-inning situations.

At the same time, the Rays used primarily right-handed pitchers in their opener and yeoman roles, with the exception of southpaw Ryan Yarbrough. A team that intended to use the opener to blow up opposing platoons might want a more diverse left-right balance in the bullpen than what the Rays demonstrated.

What will the Rays do in 2019?

Early word is that the Rays plan to use the opener again in 2019. After all, why wouldn't they? The team implemented the strategy in 2018, and won a considerable amount of games. At the same time, the few resources they've committed to the team at the time of this writing offer competing narratives. First, the Rays made yet *another* trade with the Mariners, this time to acquire a defensive specialist to play catcher: Mike Zunino. Zunino is a very well-regarded defender behind the plate with a particular talent for framing pitches. Adding him to the roster could significantly improve the team's run prevention, and provide a small-but-noticeable bump to the skills of each pitcher on the roster, thereby improving the team's overall quality of depth. If I were going to run an opener strategy, I would certainly focus on acquiring a good-framing catcher, even if it were at the expense of a talented young player like Mallex Smith.

The Rays also acquired a more traditional starting pitcher in Charlie Morton, who is coming off a pair of tremendous seasons for the Houston Astros. Morton, like Blake Snell, is unlikely to be part of any opener strategy. This doesn't preclude the Rays from using an opener frequently, but it does assign resources away from the bullpen and towards a different starting pitcher. Morton appears to provide a great deal more value than his free agent contract indicates, but the Rays probably still need to increase the talent level of both their openers and their yeomen, and Morton should be neither.

Should any team employ an opener?

There's a compelling argument to be made that the opener has ethical considerations that make it anti-player and pro-ownership. Teams that use an opener may be driving down arbitration costs for starting pitchers moved into a yeoman role or keeping talented relievers from accruing saves and holds. Since the arbitration process rewards most heavily performance in traditional roles and acquiring traditional statistical benchmarks, the strategy either intentionally or unintentionally could push down salaries for pre-arbitration players.

If any team really wanted to commit to openers as a regular part of their team strategy, they should probably be willing to sign openers and yeomen on the free agent market and pay them market rates before changing up their traditional roles. That would indicate that they believe in the strategy as what's best at winning baseball games, rather than what's best for keeping payrolls low. The Rays may believe the former, but judging from their long history of depressing player salaries, they may even more strongly desire the latter.

At any rate, success breeds imitation in baseball, and other teams are already at least experimenting with opener games of their own. My best guess is that some other team will employ openers in a more effective fashion in years to come, especially if they're willing to invest significant payroll in building an extraordinary collection of talent in the bullpen instead of the rotation. Whether good or bad for baseball or business, other teams will see the Rays' (perceived) success and try to build on it. But the Rays were the team who were desperate enough to try the strategy first, and will get to go down in history as the first team to really give it a shot. (Just don't give too much of the credit to Sergio Romo instead of Ryne Stanek, Ryan Yarbrough, and Yonny Chirinos.) ∎

—Bryan Grosnick is an author of Baseball Prospectus.

1. Author, Plucky Young. Beyond the Box Score. "Replacing setup men with 'openers'". Accessed 28 December 2018. https://www.beyondtheboxscore.com/2013/11/26/5144934/openers-bullpen-usage-closers-setup-men-weird-baseball-all-the-luke-hochevar

HITTERS

Willy Adames SS Born: 09/02/95 Age: 23 Bats: R Throws: R Height: 6'0" Weight: 200 Origin: International Free Agent, 2015

YEAR	TEAM	LVL	AGE	PA	R	2B	3B	HR	RBI	BB	K	SB	CS	AVG/OBP/SLG	DRC+	VORP	BABIP	BRR	FRAA	WARP
2016	MNT	AA	20	568	89	31	6	11	57	74	121	13	6	.274/.372/.430	125	47.0	.342	2.4	SS(112): 2.3	4.6
2017	DUR	AAA	21	578	74	30	5	10	62	65	132	11	5	.277/.360/.415	110	35.8	.354	1.1	SS(117): 0.1, 2B(11): 0.5	3.3
2018	DUR	AAA	22	278	36	9	5	4	34	27	66	3	3	.286/.353/.412	115	15.1	.367	1.5	SS(62): 2.4	2.2
2018	TBA	MLB	22	323	43	7	0	10	34	31	95	6	5	.278/.348/.406	91	15.9	.378	2.3	SS(75): -6.7, 2B(10): 1.7	0.8
2019	TBA	MLB	23	556	62	23	2	14	57	52	146	7	4	.238/.314/.376	89	15.6	.308	2.5	SS 0	1.6

Breakout: 5%   Improve: 32%   Collapse: 11%   Attrition: 16%   MLB: 75%   *Comparables: Dansby Swanson, Marcus Semien, Alex Bregman*

At some point in the next few years, Adames is going to piss off the baseball world in the best way possible: a bat flip, a celebration, saying something about unwritten rules, or hopefully all of the above. Adames is a swaggy middle infielder who took the reins at shortstop for good following the deadline trade of Adeiny Hechavarria. Adames, a smooth hitter with good contact skills and power, struggled in his first real shot at the big leagues, but was also hampered by sporadic usage and uncertainty about his role. Entrenched in the six spot, he hit .329/.406/.480 in 198 plate appearances from August 1 on. Adames introduced a shorter stroke during this return tour to the majors, which resulted in fewer strikeouts and more power. A .378 BABIP is something to watch for, but it's not like Adames was projected to be a glove-first player, although he has all the tools to stick at short even if his aggressive style leads to a few errors. He's a potential three-WARP player, with more upside left in the tank if everything breaks right.

Christian Arroyo INF Born: 05/30/95 Age: 24 Bats: R Throws: R Height: 6'1" Weight: 180 Origin: Round 1, 2013 Draft (#25 overall)

YEAR	TEAM	LVL	AGE	PA	R	2B	3B	HR	RBI	BB	K	SB	CS	AVG/OBP/SLG	DRC+	VORP	BABIP	BRR	FRAA	WARP
2016	RIC	AA	21	517	57	36	1	3	49	29	72	1	1	.274/.316/.373	81	12.5	.313	-1.3	3B(48): 2.1, SS(48): -0.9	0.9
2017	SFN	MLB	22	135	9	5	0	3	14	8	32	1	2	.192/.244/.304	63	-6.3	.231	-2.8	3B(22): 1.4, SS(10): 0.9	0.0
2017	SAC	AAA	22	102	18	7	0	4	16	6	12	2	0	.396/.461/.604	116	18.1	.427	0.5	SS(16): 0.6, 2B(5): -0.7	0.6
2018	TBA	MLB	23	59	5	2	1	1	6	6	16	0	0	.264/.339/.396	74	3.6	.361	0.4	2B(8): -0.5, 3B(7): -0.5	0.0
2018	DUR	AAA	23	182	19	12	0	2	20	8	32	2	3	.235/.286/.341	74	-0.3	.279	1.0	3B(34): -1.2, SS(6): -0.2	0.0
2019	TBA	MLB	24	120	12	5	0	3	12	8	26	1	1	.219/.283/.346	68	-3.2	.259	-0.2	3B 0	-0.3

Breakout: 7%   Improve: 21%   Collapse: 6%   Attrition: 17%   MLB: 40%   *Comparables: Giovanny Urshela, Willy Aybar, Daniel Murphy*

The face of the franchise was altered forever when the Rays traded Evan Longoria to the Giants. As part of the return in that trade, it was a popular belief that Arroyo would replace Longoria at the hot corner before too long. Too long will have to be sometime in 2019, if not beyond. Arroyo did not have a great showing in 2018. He landed on the disabled list multiple times and played in just 68 combined games. He played 59 in 2017, giving him only 127 games since the end of 2016. He spent the bulk of his healthy time in Durham, where he hit .235 with an OPS under .650. Although it came in spurts, he was actually better in 20 games with the Rays and showed some of the bat and discipline traits that made him highly regarded entering the season. He has very good contact skills and is a multi-faceted defender who can play up the middle. The Rays have an immense amount of depth along the infield, so Arroyo is either going to have to start hitting again or diversify his portfolio. In either event, just being able to play is most important.

Vidal Brujan 2B   Born: 02/09/98   Age: 21   Bats: B   Throws: R   Height: 5'9"   Weight: 155   Origin: International Free Agent, 2014

YEAR	TEAM	LVL	AGE	PA	R	2B	3B	HR	RBI	BB	K	SB	CS	AVG/OBP/SLG	DRC+	VORP	BABIP	BRR	FRAA	WARP
2016	RAY	RK	18	223	41	12	5	1	8	14	15	8	5	.282/.344/.406	120	14.9	.301	1.8	2B(49): 3.8	1.7
2017	HUD	A-	19	302	51	15	5	3	20	34	36	16	8	.285/.378/.415	130	20.6	.321	-3.7	2B(65): 14.9	3.2
2018	BGR	A	20	434	86	18	5	5	41	48	53	43	15	.313/.395/.427	127	41.0	.351	8.2	2B(88): 4.4	4.0
2018	PCH	A+	20	114	26	7	2	4	12	15	15	12	4	.347/.434/.582	130	13.9	.380	1.0	2B(24): 4.5	1.3
2019	TBA	MLB	21	251	33	7	1	6	22	18	46	13	5	.229/.286/.350	70	0.2	.257	1.0	2B 5	0.5

Breakout: 4%   Improve: 24%   Collapse: 1%   Attrition: 13%   MLB: 32%   *Comparables: Mookie Betts, Jose Altuve, Jose Ramirez*

Scouting types thought Brujan had a breakout in 2017. They were a year off, because 2018 was a true arrival. Playing for Bowling Green and later Charlotte, he hit .320 on the season, reached base 40 percent of the time and tallied extra bases 41 times. He also stole an astounding 55 bags even though he was caught 19 times. Signed for less than a waiver claim in 2014, he has leadoff ability with excellent contact skills and exceptional speed. His arm is average-ish, which is why he plays right of the bag up the middle. Brujan is a level or two behind the logjam at the keystone for Tampa Bay. However, at this accelerated pace, he may get there much sooner than expected.

Ji-Man Choi DH   Born: 05/19/91   Age: 28   Bats: L   Throws: R   Height: 6'1"   Weight: 230   Origin: International Free Agent, 2009

YEAR	TEAM	LVL	AGE	PA	R	2B	3B	HR	RBI	BB	K	SB	CS	AVG/OBP/SLG	DRC+	VORP	BABIP	BRR	FRAA	WARP
2016	SLC	AAA	25	227	31	17	1	5	31	31	34	4	3	.346/.434/.527	133	12.8	.390	-4.7	1B(28): 1.6, LF(15): -0.9	1.0
2016	ANA	MLB	25	129	9	4	0	5	12	16	27	2	4	.170/.271/.339	87	-3.6	.173	-0.1	1B(27): 2.2, LF(20): 0.1	0.3
2017	NYA	MLB	26	18	2	1	0	2	5	2	5	0	0	.267/.333/.733	89	1.3	.222	-0.3	1B(6): 0.2	0.0
2017	SWB	AAA	26	338	42	25	1	15	69	39	86	3	1	.288/.373/.538	123	22.7	.351	1.7	1B(57): 4.3	1.9
2018	CSP	AAA	27	163	17	9	0	5	23	32	31	1	0	.302/.436/.488	130	12.3	.358	0.2	1B(38): -2.0, LF(1): 0.1	0.7
2018	MIL	MLB	27	32	4	2	0	2	5	2	14	0	0	.233/.281/.500	109	0.6	.357	0.3	1B(2): 0.0, LF(1): 0.0	0.1
2018	DUR	AAA	27	86	9	4	0	2	14	11	18	0	0	.270/.360/.405	119	2.9	.327	-0.9	1B(18): 0.2, LF(2): 0.0	0.3
2018	TBA	MLB	27	189	21	12	1	8	27	24	41	2	0	.269/.370/.506	110	12.9	.310	1.9	1B(1): 0.0	0.7
2019	TBA	MLB	28	420	48	17	1	15	53	44	102	3	1	.231/.319/.404	95	4.1	.278	1.8	1B 1	0.6

Breakout: 9%   Improve: 30%   Collapse: 14%   Attrition: 28%   MLB: 70%   *Comparables: Steve Pearce, Justin Bour, Kila Ka'aihue*

Chris Berman's favorite player (Gggggggg-man), Choi has always looked like he can hit the ball hard, but just recently started doing so. After being acquired from the Brewers in exchange for Brad Miller, the South Korea native smashed 25 extra-base hits in 221 plate appearances, including 10 that went back, back, back and gone. He showed a good approach at the plate, not chasing much out of the zone and accepting walks when they were given. The Rays were diligent in how they used the left-handed hitter, giving him the platoon advantage 89 percent of the time. They also gave him the advantage in the field, as in he played just three innings (first base) in 49 games with the team. For a team looking to cut fat from the margins, employing Choi as the strong side of a designated hitter platoon would accomplish that.

Nick Ciuffo C   Born: 03/07/95   Age: 24   Bats: L   Throws: R   Height: 6'1"   Weight: 205   Origin: Round 1, 2013 Draft (#21 overall)

YEAR	TEAM	LVL	AGE	PA	R	2B	3B	HR	RBI	BB	K	SB	CS	AVG/OBP/SLG	DRC+	VORP	BABIP	BRR	FRAA	WARP
2016	PCH	A+	21	242	16	8	0	0	15	9	45	2	3	.262/.288/.297	72	-4.9	.323	-3.0	C(50): 2.9	0.2
2017	MNT	AA	22	417	42	29	1	7	42	42	95	2	0	.245/.319/.385	99	14.7	.308	-1.6	C(70): -14.7	-0.2
2018	DUR	AAA	23	236	26	11	0	5	28	13	62	0	0	.262/.301/.380	90	4.5	.340	-2.8	C(55): 5.6	1.1
2018	TBA	MLB	23	44	3	1	0	1	5	3	12	0	0	.189/.262/.297	74	0.0	.240	-0.1	C(16): -1.2	-0.1
2019	TBA	MLB	24	71	6	3	0	2	7	4	20	0	0	.221/.268/.343	71	0.6	.286	-0.1	C -2	-0.2

Breakout: 9%   Improve: 23%   Collapse: 8%   Attrition: 24%   MLB: 38%   *Comparables: Jeff Mathis, Tony Cruz, Luis Exposito*

A former 2013 first-round pick, Ciuffo finally made his MLB debut in 2018, but not before some dramatics. Left off the 40-man roster last winter, Ciuffo was subjected to testing for drugs of abuse. He failed for the second time and was forced to miss the first 50 games. He returned to mixed results. His offense remains behind his defense, but his defense is major-league caliber on its own. When the Rays selected veteran Adam Moore to be the third catcher it looked like Ciuffo's season would end in the minors. Moore, however, did not have his passport in order and could not join the club in Toronto. Ciuffo was able to enter

YEAR	TEAM	P. COUNT	FRM RUNS	BLK RUNS	THRW RUNS	TOT RUNS
2017	MNT	10149	-11.8	-3.1	0.1	-13.5
2018	DUR	7350	5.2	0.0	1.2	6.4
2018	TBA	1790	-0.4	-0.6	0.0	-0.2
2019	TBA	2650	-1.5	-0.8	0.2	-2.1

Canada and took most of the reps behind the plate for the month of September. The lefty batter has considerable pull-side pop, but does not make much contact otherwise. Even if he never hits for much, his ability behind the plate will keep him employed. He has plus receiving skills with the arm to change the running game. He's a bit like Mike Zunino from the left side with lesser power.

Yandy Diaz 3B Born: 08/08/91 Age: 27 Bats: R Throws: R Height: 6'2" Weight: 185 Origin: International Free Agent, 2013

YEAR	TEAM	LVL	AGE	PA	R	2B	3B	HR	RBI	BB	K	SB	CS	AVG/OBP/SLG	DRC+	VORP	BABIP	BRR	FRAA	WARP
2016	AKR	AA	24	110	13	0	1	2	14	24	16	6	2	.286/.445/.381	128	9.5	.328	-0.7	3B(22): -1.1, 2B(1): 0.0	0.6
2016	COH	AAA	24	416	53	22	3	7	44	47	70	5	1	.325/.399/.461	122	28.9	.381	2.1	3B(30): -0.8, RF(28): 5.3	3.2
2017	COH	AAA	25	374	56	17	1	5	33	60	56	1	2	.350/.454/.460	124	34.5	.412	1.1	3B(42): -3.4, LF(21): 0.7	2.0
2017	CLE	MLB	25	179	25	8	1	0	13	21	35	2	0	.263/.352/.327	81	1.9	.336	-0.4	3B(40): -0.9, LF(3): -0.2	0.0
2018	COH	AAA	26	426	53	24	0	3	40	70	75	2	3	.293/.409/.388	119	26.0	.360	-2.6	3B(73): -9.6, 1B(12): 0.2	1.1
2018	CLE	MLB	26	120	15	5	2	1	15	11	19	0	0	.312/.375/.422	100	1.0	.371	-2.0	1B(9): 0.2, 3B(9): 0.2	0.1
2019	*TBA*	*MLB*	*27*	*493*	*49*	*16*	*1*	*8*	*47*	*64*	*100*	*2*	*1*	*.227/.332/.326*	*83*	*-3.3*	*.278*	*-2.2*	*1B 1, 3B -3*	*-0.5*

Breakout: 8%   Improve: 39%   Collapse: 12%   Attrition: 25%   MLB: 71%   *Comparables: Kevin Youkilis, Max Muncy, Eric Campbell*

"Pretty" Yandy Diaz came into 2018 having crushed Triple-A two years in a row, and managed a high-OBP, low-power aria in the majors at the end of 2017. With Jason Kipnis' prime ending as abruptly as Bartolo's shave from Figaro, there was some hope he would take over at second base full time. Instead, despite another solid month of plate appearances, a closer look at the libretto shows he continued to blast the ball on the ground as hard as he could. Cleveland once again buried him in Triple-A despite Kipnis showing his collapse was here to stay. Yandy is a useful role player and deserving of an MLB roster spot, although despite his exit velocities, he's probably more of a beefed-up Eric Campbell rather than Jose Ramirez piu docile. When you hit the ball on the ground, no matter how hard you hit it, your reasonable best-case scenario is a single. His path to a starting job is now clear, thanks to a trade to Tampa Bay.

Matt Duffy 3B Born: 01/15/91 Age: 28 Bats: R Throws: R Height: 6'2" Weight: 170 Origin: Round 18, 2012 Draft (#568 overall)

YEAR	TEAM	LVL	AGE	PA	R	2B	3B	HR	RBI	BB	K	SB	CS	AVG/OBP/SLG	DRC+	VORP	BABIP	BRR	FRAA	WARP
2016	SFN	MLB	25	286	32	11	2	4	21	20	40	8	4	.253/.313/.358	92	10.0	.282	1.1	3B(69): 3.8	1.3
2016	TBA	MLB	25	80	9	3	0	1	7	3	13	0	1	.276/.300/.355	84	0.8	.317	0.5	SS(18): 0.2, 3B(1): 0.0	0.3
2018	TBA	MLB	27	560	59	22	1	4	44	47	93	12	6	.294/.361/.366	96	16.9	.353	-3.9	3B(125): 11.8, SS(1): 0.0	2.6
2019	*TBA*	*MLB*	*28*	*368*	*38*	*17*	*2*	*5*	*36*	*29*	*58*	*7*	*3*	*.267/.335/.376*	*97*	*7.5*	*.309*	*-0.5*	*3B 5, SS 0*	*1.3*

Breakout: 6%   Improve: 48%   Collapse: 3%   Attrition: 7%   MLB: 93%   *Comparables: Chone Figgins, Josh Harrison, Freddy Sanchez*

An uncertainty after missing all of 2017 with a foot injury, Duffy was the most steady hand in the Rays' lineup. He has terrific contact skills and rarely misses when he takes a swing. That said, his thin frame limits his power. He tallied just 27 extra-base hits in 560 trips to the plate and his career ISO is an even .100. His walk rate is around the league average and he's a decent runner, although his foot speed is lacking. When the Rays traded for Duffy in 2016, they intended for him to play shortstop. With better quick-twitch athletes on the roster, he was moved back to third base. He plays the position well and will make all of the routine plays, with a few out of his zone as well. Duffy is boring in the best way possible. At some point someone flashier with greater natural ability will challenge him for playing time, and perhaps Duffy will become more of a utility man as he creeps toward 30, but for now he's the least interesting man in Tampa Bay. Stay thirsty. Actually, Duffy would want you to be hydrated so he would bring you a water.

Wander Franco SS Born: 03/01/01 Age: 18 Bats: B Throws: R Height: 5'10" Weight: 189 Origin: International Free Agent, 2017

YEAR	TEAM	LVL	AGE	PA	R	2B	3B	HR	RBI	BB	K	SB	CS	AVG/OBP/SLG	DRC+	VORP	BABIP	BRR	FRAA	WARP
2018	PRI	RK	17	273	46	10	7	11	57	27	19	4	3	.351/.418/.587	169	35.3	.346	-0.4	SS(53): -5.3	2.7
2019	*TBA*	*MLB*	*18*	*251*	*26*	*9*	*2*	*9*	*33*	*11*	*44*	*0*	*0*	*.249/.279/.426*	*86*	*4.7*	*.265*	*-0.1*	*SS -2*	*0.3*

Comparables: Adalberto Mondesi, Wilmer Flores, Tommy Brown

If you don't know, now you know. Franco will be one of the most talked about prospects of 2019 after putting up insane numbers in his first pro season. Not bad for someone who won't legally be an adult until March. The Rays' farm system is filled with a lot of quality prospects, but there's not much star projection. Not only does Franco have that, you can add *super* in front of it. That's why the club paid nearly $4 million to sign him in 2017. He has at least four above-average-or-better tools and is a shortstop until he's not. He has exceptional bat speed, strong hands, and can run and throw really well. The nephew of Willy and Erick Aybar could be the top overall prospect in MLB by the 2020 edition of this book.

Carlos Gomez RF Born: 12/04/85 Age: 33 Bats: R Throws: R Height: 6'3" Weight: 220 Origin: International Free Agent, 2002

YEAR	TEAM	LVL	AGE	PA	R	2B	3B	HR	RBI	BB	K	SB	CS	AVG/OBP/SLG	DRC+	VORP	BABIP	BRR	FRAA	WARP
2016	HOU	MLB	30	323	27	16	1	5	29	21	100	13	2	.210/.272/.322	71	-3.1	.300	3.9	CF(78): -4.0	0.0
2016	TEX	MLB	30	130	18	6	0	8	24	13	36	5	3	.284/.362/.543	83	9.5	.347	0.4	LF(28): 1.2, CF(7): -0.1	0.2
2017	TEX	MLB	31	426	51	23	1	17	51	31	127	13	5	.255/.340/.462	98	17.0	.336	-0.7	CF(102): -2.3	1.1
2018	TBA	MLB	32	408	42	15	2	9	32	25	103	12	3	.208/.298/.336	82	-0.4	.266	3.6	RF(100): 5.4, CF(4): -0.1	0.9
2019	*TBA*	*MLB*	*33*	*391*	*47*	*17*	*2*	*11*	*43*	*29*	*108*	*13*	*4*	*.224/.318/.374*	*96*	*10.4*	*.302*	*1.4*	*RF 2, CF 0*	*1.3*

Breakout: 2%   Improve: 38%   Collapse: 11%   Attrition: 17%   MLB: 88%   *Comparables: Casey Blake, Hank Bauer, Bernard Gilkey*

Gomez was a negative in terms of his 2018 offensive production, but his leadership in a clubhouse that lost its stability (Evan Longoria) prior to the season and its voice (Chris Archer) midway through will last beyond his .208 batting average. Coming off one of the worst seasons of his career, it is fair to wonder if we've seen the last of Gomez as a useful player. He'll likely get a few more chances either way. He's a decent defender still and has some remaining pop, but he never did learn to lay off bad pitches. Once Gomez does hang it up, it would serve the game if he remained involved in some capacity.

Guillermo Heredia LF Born: 01/31/91 Age: 28 Bats: R Throws: L Height: 5'10" Weight: 180 Origin: International Free Agent, 2016

YEAR	TEAM	LVL	AGE	PA	R	2B	3B	HR	RBI	BB	K	SB	CS	AVG/OBP/SLG	DRC+	VORP	BABIP	BRR	FRAA	WARP
2016	WTN	AA	25	260	39	7	2	2	34	36	32	2	5	.293/.405/.376	119	17.7	.322	-1.0	CF(41): -2.8, RF(12): -0.1	1.0
2016	TAC	AAA	25	157	27	6	1	2	13	12	15	3	0	.312/.378/.413	91	17.1	.333	2.1	CF(32): 0.6, LF(3): 0.1	0.7
2016	SEA	MLB	25	107	12	3	0	1	12	12	15	1	1	.250/.349/.315	89	0.4	.289	-0.6	LF(35): 4.9, RF(14): -0.3	0.5
2017	SEA	MLB	26	426	43	16	0	6	24	27	64	1	5	.249/.315/.337	85	2.3	.284	1.0	CF(63): 7.1, LF(62): 1.7	1.7
2018	TAC	AAA	27	38	4	1	0	0	2	4	3	2	1	.276/.421/.310	101	4.9	.296	0.9	LF(6): 1.0, CF(5): -0.5	0.3
2018	SEA	MLB	27	337	29	14	1	5	19	32	52	2	4	.236/.318/.342	87	8.1	.270	0.0	CF(89): -6.5, LF(32): 3.1	0.2
2019	TBA	MLB	28	188	20	8	1	3	18	17	28	1	2	.249/.333/.368	93	4.5	.282	0.2	RF 2, CF 0	0.8

Breakout: 4% Improve: 50% Collapse: 6% Attrition: 16% MLB: 91%   *Comparables: Reggie Willits, Aaron Hicks, David DeJesus*

Heredia is a joy to watch. His speed, accurate arm and route instincts made him one of the best outfielders in Seattle's organization. Unfortunately, at least until baseball legalizes a second designated hitter, he still has to get in a batter's box. It's there, after more than two years and 800 plate appearances in the big leagues, that things start to fall apart. Fully healed from a 2017 shoulder injury, Heredia got off to a blistering start, hitting .298/.417/.426 through the end of May. He couldn't keep it up, however, due primarily to a total lack of power. While his approach at the dish remains solid, unless he figures out how to punish mistakes more than once or twice a month he'll remain a fringe big leaguer and reserve outfielder.

Ronaldo Hernandez C Born: 11/11/97 Age: 21 Bats: R Throws: R Height: 6'1" Weight: 185 Origin: International Free Agent, 2014

YEAR	TEAM	LVL	AGE	PA	R	2B	3B	HR	RBI	BB	K	SB	CS	AVG/OBP/SLG	DRC+	VORP	BABIP	BRR	FRAA	WARP
2016	DDR	RK	18	229	34	12	0	6	35	20	12	3	5	.340/.406/.485	142	28.8	.340	-1.2	C(32): -0.3	1.6
2017	PRI	RK	19	246	42	22	1	5	40	16	39	2	2	.332/.382/.507	121	23.7	.379	2.5	C(43): 1.1	1.9
2018	BGR	A	20	449	68	20	1	21	79	31	69	10	4	.284/.339/.494	141	39.2	.292	-0.8	C(85): 1.2	4.1
2019	TBA	MLB	21	251	26	10	0	10	32	9	56	1	0	.229/.255/.394	68	0.2	.253	-0.6	C 0	0.0

Breakout: 3% Improve: 11% Collapse: 9% Attrition: 20% MLB: 30%   *Comparables: Francisco Mejia, Austin Romine, Gary Sanchez*

Developing catchers has been an organizational struggle for Tampa Bay since its inception. Miguel Perez, Nick Ciuffo and Mike Zunino give them youth and potential at the position now, but Hernandez could be the one they've been waiting for. The Rays made him a backstop after signing him out of Colombia in 2014, part of the same J2 class as Jesus Sanchez. He followed an impressive 2017 in the Appalachian League with a strong showing in the Midwest League, finishing second in home runs (21) and third in slugging percentage. Defensively, he continues to grow, with most feeling he'll be able to handle the gig as he progresses with the arm to control the running game. Despite being a converted infielder, he runs like a natural catcher.

Kevin Kiermaier CF Born: 04/22/90 Age: 29 Bats: L Throws: R Height: 6'1" Weight: 215 Origin: Round 31, 2010 Draft (#941 overall)

YEAR	TEAM	LVL	AGE	PA	R	2B	3B	HR	RBI	BB	K	SB	CS	AVG/OBP/SLG	DRC+	VORP	BABIP	BRR	FRAA	WARP
2016	TBA	MLB	26	414	55	20	2	12	37	40	74	21	3	.246/.331/.410	96	18.3	.278	2.8	CF(104): 12.7	2.9
2017	TBA	MLB	27	421	56	15	3	15	39	31	99	16	7	.276/.338/.450	96	24.6	.337	2.9	CF(97): 7.6	2.4
2018	TBA	MLB	28	367	44	12	9	7	29	25	91	10	5	.217/.282/.370	77	6.4	.275	3.1	CF(88): 12.3	1.8
2019	TBA	MLB	29	617	84	26	7	17	63	49	133	22	8	.249/.320/.410	106	31.0	.298	3.0	CF 15	4.9

Breakout: 4% Improve: 53% Collapse: 4% Attrition: 12% MLB: 99%   *Comparables: Angel Pagan, Franklin Gutierrez, Jon Jay*

Kiermaier remains a spectacular defensive center fielder, with an argument for best-in-class status depending on whether Byron Buxton is still in the majors, but he's struggled to stay healthy and his offense took a step backward following a 2017 breakout. Under team control at reasonable salaries through 2023, he'll again anchor the Rays' defense while attempting to show that he can stay off the disabled list and out of the bottom of the lineup. Kiermaier is 28 years old and has cracked 500 plate appearances in a season just once, but few American League center fielders offer more potential for racking up WARP.

Brandon Lowe UT Born: 07/06/94 Age: 24 Bats: L Throws: R Height: 6'0" Weight: 185 Origin: Round 3, 2015 Draft (#87 overall)

YEAR	TEAM	LVL	AGE	PA	R	2B	3B	HR	RBI	BB	K	SB	CS	AVG/OBP/SLG	DRC+	VORP	BABIP	BRR	FRAA	WARP
2016	BGR	A	21	449	67	15	3	5	42	60	77	6	3	.248/.357/.343	119	14.0	.298	-1.3	2B(88): -9.2	1.0
2017	PCH	A+	22	367	62	34	3	9	46	47	65	6	3	.311/.403/.524	137	38.6	.366	2.0	2B(75): -1.1, 3B(2): -0.2	2.8
2017	MNT	AA	22	101	8	5	1	2	12	2	26	1	1	.253/.270/.389	83	0.5	.319	-1.3	2B(24): 0.8	0.0
2018	MNT	AA	23	240	37	17	1	8	41	35	55	8	2	.291/.400/.508	122	25.7	.360	2.1	LF(26): 1.8, 2B(24): -3.2	1.4
2018	DUR	AAA	23	205	36	14	0	14	35	22	47	0	1	.304/.380/.613	158	24.4	.339	0.4	2B(31): 1.2, LF(13): 0.9	2.4
2018	TBA	MLB	23	148	16	6	2	6	25	16	38	2	1	.233/.324/.450	97	6.3	.279	0.8	2B(28): -0.6, LF(11): -0.3	0.4
2019	TBA	MLB	24	301	39	15	1	13	41	27	74	3	1	.250/.325/.458	111	12.1	.296	-0.3	LF 0, RF 0	1.2

Breakout: 0% Improve: 29% Collapse: 18% Attrition: 32% MLB: 73%   *Comparables: Vince Belnome, Ryan Rua, Rob Refsnyder*

A top-100 pick in 2015, Lowe broke out the boom stick in 2018 en route to the majors. Lowe hit just 16 home runs in his first 917 professional plate appearances, then smashed 28 in 593 trips to the plate last year across three levels, starting in Double-A and ending in the majors. In total, the former Maryland Terrapin collected a combined 68 extra-base hits during his three-city tour. The last six of his long balls came at the highest level, where he struggled to make contact when he was not mashing. Defensively, Lowe has split time between second base and the outfield corners. He's not particularly great at either, but the constant movement limits his exposure at each spot. A left-handed, offense-first, utility-type player with power is a profile out of which you can make a career.

Joshua Lowe OF   Born: 02/02/98   Age: 21   Bats: L   Throws: R   Height: 6'4"   Weight: 205   Origin: Round 1, 2016 Draft (#13 overall)

YEAR	TEAM	LVL	AGE	PA	R	2B	3B	HR	RBI	BB	K	SB	CS	AVG/OBP/SLG	DRC+	VORP	BABIP	BRR	FRAA	WARP
2016	RAY	RK	18	114	14	6	1	2	15	20	27	1	1	.258/.386/.409	117	10.1	.338	0.9	3B(22): 0.8	0.7
2016	PRI	RK	18	100	11	0	2	3	11	17	32	1	1	.238/.360/.400	101	6.0	.333	0.4	3B(23): -3.4	0.0
2017	BGR	A	19	507	60	26	2	8	55	42	144	22	8	.268/.326/.386	87	21.8	.369	2.3	CF(112): 3.4	1.2
2018	PCH	A+	20	455	62	25	3	6	47	47	117	18	6	.238/.322/.361	94	14.8	.318	1.1	CF(102): 4.1	1.7
2019	*TBA*	*MLB*	*21*	*251*	*27*	*7*	*0*	*6*	*20*	*16*	*79*	*5*	*2*	*.191/.240/.295*	*40*	*-8.8*	*.255*	*-0.1*	*CF 1*	*-0.8*

Breakout: 2%   Improve: 3%   Collapse: 0%   Attrition: 3%   MLB: 6%   *Comparables: Michael Saunders, Daniel Fields, Joe Benson*

Lowe got the bragging rights of being a first-round pick over brother Nate, who was selected in the 13th round in 2016. But the younger bro has some catching up to do in terms of development. After dominating the lowest levels of the system, he struggled in the Florida State League in 2018. He struck out 26 percent of the time—actually an improvement from 2017's 28 percent—and did not make enough hard contact in the thick South Florida air to overlook that number despite owning plus raw power. He has good speed and remained in center field after converting from third base in 2017. Lowe will likely start the season as a 21-year-old in Double-A, which means there's plenty of time to catch and pass big brother.

Nathaniel Lowe 1B   Born: 07/07/95   Age: 23   Bats: L   Throws: R   Height: 6'4"   Weight: 235   Origin: Round 13, 2016 Draft (#390 overall)

YEAR	TEAM	LVL	AGE	PA	R	2B	3B	HR	RBI	BB	K	SB	CS	AVG/OBP/SLG	DRC+	VORP	BABIP	BRR	FRAA	WARP
2016	HUD	A-	20	285	26	18	2	4	40	30	39	1	0	.300/.382/.437	130	20.7	.338	1.2	1B(65): 2.9	1.8
2017	BGR	A	21	269	34	13	0	5	35	36	53	0	1	.293/.387/.415	117	14.0	.356	-0.2	1B(49): 0.2	0.8
2017	PCH	A+	21	203	21	10	1	2	24	28	53	1	1	.249/.355/.353	101	0.6	.345	-0.5	1B(51): -1.5	0.0
2018	PCH	A+	22	220	39	15	0	10	44	25	33	0	0	.356/.432/.588	156	22.6	.391	-2.4	1B(35): -2.9	1.3
2018	MNT	AA	22	225	36	11	0	13	42	35	30	1	1	.340/.444/.606	167	33.7	.349	1.9	1B(39): -0.4	2.4
2018	DUR	AAA	22	110	18	6	1	4	16	8	27	0	0	.260/.327/.460	107	1.4	.319	-1.2	1B(25): -0.1	0.1
2019	*TBA*	*MLB*	*23*	*341*	*41*	*12*	*0*	*12*	*37*	*32*	*80*	*0*	*0*	*.227/.300/.382*	*82*	*-3.5*	*.266*	*-0.8*	*1B -1*	*-0.5*

Breakout: 7%   Improve: 24%   Collapse: 9%   Attrition: 24%   MLB: 50%   *Comparables: Ji-Man Choi, Rhys Hoskins, Travis Shaw*

The older brother of Josh, selected 12 rounds later in the same draft, Nate is on pace to beat little bro to the big leagues after a laser show in 2018. Starting the season in Charlotte, he ended it on the major's door in Durham. He collected 27 home runs and 32 doubles along the way while hitting for average and taking walks, too. Typically the hulking left-handed hitter would be projected as a platoon bat. That may ultimately be the case, but he has more than held his own against southpaws thus far. Lowe is certainly a fast riser, but even at this accelerated pace, there are left-handed-hitting first basemen ahead of him on the depth chart. Working in Lowe's favor is that neither of them can match his power potential.

Brendan McKay 1B   Born: 12/18/95   Age: 23   Bats: L   Throws: L   Height: 6'2"   Weight: 212   Origin: Round 1, 2017 Draft (#4 overall)

YEAR	TEAM	LVL	AGE	PA	R	2B	3B	HR	RBI	BB	K	SB	CS	AVG/OBP/SLG	DRC+	VORP	BABIP	BRR	FRAA	WARP
2017	HUD	A-	21	149	16	4	1	4	22	21	33	2	0	.232/.349/.376	121	3.8	.281	-1.3	1B(21): -1.1, P(6): 0.1	0.3
2018	BGR	A	22	91	12	2	0	1	16	28	13	0	0	.254/.484/.333	138	1.0	.306	-3.1	1B(9): -0.3, P(6): 0.1	0.2
2018	PCH	A+	22	139	19	6	1	5	21	16	38	0	0	.210/.317/.403	100	1.6	.260	0.5	1B(18): -0.4, P(11): -0.3	0.1
2019	*TBA*	*MLB*	*23*	*251*	*24*	*6*	*0*	*8*	*27*	*24*	*68*	*0*	*0*	*.190/.269/.316*	*60*	*-9.4*	*.233*	*-0.6*	*1B -2*	*-1.2*

Breakout: 8%   Improve: 13%   Collapse: 4%   Attrition: 15%   MLB: 21%   *Comparables: Chris McGuiness, Chris Parmelee, Max Muncy*

The first legitimate two-way player drafted in decades, McKay watched Shohei Otani put the blueprint together for a player to hit and pitch for a major-league team. McKay was a top-five pick and played at a major university, but the Rays have brought him along relatively slowly considering his age and experience. A few non-threatening injuries have also slowed the process. As it stands, the former Louisville Cardinal is much farther down the line as a pitcher than he is as a hitter, where he's yet to display that 20-homer potential he was projected to have. On the other hand, McKay the pitcher has been dominant. The organization was already cautious in his usage, but that was not enough to prevent multiple oblique injuries that cost him development. Although his pitching is way ahead of his hitting, the Rays will let him play both ways until it looks like he cannot.

Austin Meadows OF   Born: 05/03/95   Age: 24   Bats: L   Throws: L   Height: 6'3"   Weight: 210   Origin: Round 1, 2013 Draft (#9 overall)

YEAR	TEAM	LVL	AGE	PA	R	2B	3B	HR	RBI	BB	K	SB	CS	AVG/OBP/SLG	DRC+	VORP	BABIP	BRR	FRAA	WARP
2016	ALT	AA	21	190	33	16	8	6	23	16	32	9	3	.311/.365/.611	125	19.7	.343	0.8	CF(39): 2.5, LF(2): -0.5	1.5
2016	IND	AAA	21	145	16	7	3	6	24	15	34	8	2	.214/.297/.460	110	9.6	.236	0.9	CF(23): -3.1, LF(11): -0.2	0.4
2017	IND	AAA	22	312	48	19	0	4	36	24	50	11	3	.250/.311/.359	90	9.0	.289	3.7	CF(33): -1.9, LF(24): -0.8	0.6
2018	IND	AAA	23	179	27	13	0	2	21	9	24	11	1	.279/.318/.394	132	8.3	.314	2.4	CF(22): -1.5, LF(18): 0.1	1.3
2018	PIT	MLB	23	165	16	8	2	5	13	8	35	4	1	.292/.327/.468	98	8.0	.345	-1.1	CF(15): -0.7, RF(13): -1.1	0.1
2018	DUR	AAA	23	106	19	11	0	10	22	8	13	1	1	.344/.396/.771	142	15.0	.311	-1.6	CF(17): -1.2, RF(4): -0.2	0.5
2018	TBA	MLB	23	26	3	1	0	1	4	2	5	1	0	.250/.308/.417	96	0.4	.278	-0.1	RF(7): -1.4, LF(1): 0.0	-0.1
2019	*TBA*	*MLB*	*24*	*481*	*57*	*21*	*1*	*14*	*52*	*29*	*88*	*15*	*4*	*.242/.292/.388*	*82*	*4.1*	*.270*	*1.1*	*RF -10, LF 0*	*-0.6*

Breakout: 4%   Improve: 45%   Collapse: 13%   Attrition: 22%   MLB: 88%   *Comparables: Lewis Brinson, J.D. Martinez, Jackie Bradley*

Once a shiny prospect, nagging injuries turned Meadows' profile into a matte finish heading into 2018. Some of the luster is back after the former top-10 pick appeared in a career-high 128 games, including the first 59 contests of his big-league career. Seemingly trapped behind Andrew McCutchen for a few seasons, both outfielders left Pittsburgh behind in 2018 and actually ended the year as AL East rivals. Meadows has hit at every stop along the way and continued to do so in the bigs. The most intriguing part of his season was his power moving from projection to production, especially following the mid-July trade that sent Chris Archer to Pittsburgh. In leading the Durham Bulls to an International League championship, Meadows smashed 21 extra-base hits, including 10 home runs, in just 27 games. He can hit. He can hit for power now. He can run and he can defend. As long as he can stay on the field, Meadows will be a key piece of the up-and-coming Rays.

Michael Perez C
Born: 08/07/92 Age: 26 Bats: L Throws: R Height: 5'11" Weight: 180 Origin: Round 5, 2011 Draft (#154 overall)

YEAR	TEAM	LVL	AGE	PA	R	2B	3B	HR	RBI	BB	K	SB	CS	AVG/OBP/SLG	DRC+	VORP	BABIP	BRR	FRAA	WARP
2016	MOB	AA	23	131	7	4	1	3	10	7	29	0	1	.205/.252/.328	88	-0.1	.242	0.3	C(36): 5.2	1.0
2016	VIS	A+	23	173	17	10	2	1	19	15	33	1	0	.256/.318/.365	92	5.2	.315	-1.0	C(47): 3.0	0.9
2017	WTN	AA	24	302	29	23	0	5	39	35	61	0	2	.279/.365/.424	113	16.7	.343	-1.8	C(73): 7.4	2.5
2018	RNO	AAA	25	240	30	9	1	6	29	20	40	0	1	.284/.342/.417	113	10.2	.322	-1.3	C(57): 8.7	2.5
2018	TBA	MLB	25	80	9	5	0	1	11	3	19	0	0	.284/.304/.392	88	2.2	.357	-1.8	C(24): -3.6	-0.3
2019	TBA	MLB	26	150	15	8	0	4	17	10	31	0	0	.260/.313/.408	87	4.1	.307	-0.3	C 0	0.5

Breakout: 4%   Improve: 14%   Collapse: 14%   Attrition: 26%   MLB: 52%

Comparables: Bryan Holaday, Bryan Anderson, Chris Herrmann

YEAR	TEAM	P. COUNT	FRM RUNS	BLK RUNS	THRW RUNS	TOT RUNS
2017	WTN	9926	2.4	3.5	0.1	6.6
2018	RNO	8459	2.6	1.6	0.8	5.1
2018	TBA	2989	-3.5	0.5	0.0	-2.5
2019	TBA	5560	-2.0	1.0	0.0	-1.1

Perez was acquired at the trade deadline in exchange for Matt Andriese and almost instantly became the club's starting catcher. A left-handed hitter, he has blossomed at the plate over the past two seasons in the minors and showed similar ability in the majors before falling victim to a hamstring injury late in the season. Perez just needs to be a league-average bat to make this work, because he draws rave reviews from coaches and pitchers for his glove. Coming over to a new organization is tough and doing it while making your big-league debut is even harder, yet Perez earned the praise of everyone around him. He's quick and athletic, which allows him to block difficult pitches. He has the arm to control the running game and quiet hands to manage the presentation of pitches. The time share with Mike Zunino will be interesting, as Zunino is a tremendous defender in his own right and has big-time power. A strict platoon does not appear to be in order, but look for Perez to hold his own while vying for playing time.

Tommy Pham LF
Born: 03/08/88 Age: 31 Bats: R Throws: R Height: 6'1" Weight: 210 Origin: Round 16, 2006 Draft (#496 overall)

YEAR	TEAM	LVL	AGE	PA	R	2B	3B	HR	RBI	BB	K	SB	CS	AVG/OBP/SLG	DRC+	VORP	BABIP	BRR	FRAA	WARP
2016	MEM	AAA	28	128	15	5	1	3	17	18	29	8	2	.236/.344/.382	95	7.1	.295	1.9	CF(24): -2.8, LF(4): 0.2	0.3
2016	SLN	MLB	28	183	26	7	0	9	17	20	71	2	2	.226/.324/.440	82	7.7	.342	0.7	CF(34): -2.1, LF(30): -2.3	-0.2
2017	MEM	AAA	29	106	17	8	0	4	19	13	21	6	3	.283/.371/.500	105	9.3	.328	0.7	RF(15): 2.2, CF(9): -1.0	0.5
2017	SLN	MLB	29	530	95	22	2	23	73	71	117	25	7	.306/.411/.520	130	58.0	.368	4.6	LF(86): -2.6, CF(37): 0.1	3.8
2018	SLN	MLB	30	396	67	11	0	14	41	42	97	10	6	.248/.331/.399	119	18.3	.303	3.8	CF(91): -5.1	2.2
2018	TBA	MLB	30	174	35	7	6	7	22	25	43	5	1	.343/.448/.622	116	21.4	.442	0.9	LF(37): -0.5, CF(3): -0.2	0.8
2019	TBA	MLB	31	638	93	25	4	23	73	73	176	19	7	.245/.343/.429	114	31.6	.317	3.8	LF -4	3.0

Breakout: 1%   Improve: 40%   Collapse: 6%   Attrition: 11%   MLB: 95%

Comparables: Luke Scott, Chris Dickerson, Carlos Beltran

The Rays essentially took a flier on Pham at the trade deadline, acquiring him for useful but still spare pieces of the farm system. Off to a slow start with the Cardinals after a 2017 breakout, Pham rewarded his new club with a torrid second half. After playing considerable time in center field with St. Louis, he will not be receiving many reps there with the Rays, but is playable in left field. Pham will be 31 on Opening Day and doesn't really fit in with the Rays' younger nucleus. However, he's team controllable through his prime and should be the leader of a lineup that gets better around him as he ages.

Daniel Robertson UT
Born: 03/22/94 Age: 25 Bats: R Throws: R Height: 5'11" Weight: 200 Origin: Round 1, 2012 Draft (#34 overall)

YEAR	TEAM	LVL	AGE	PA	R	2B	3B	HR	RBI	BB	K	SB	CS	AVG/OBP/SLG	DRC+	VORP	BABIP	BRR	FRAA	WARP
2016	DUR	AAA	22	511	50	21	3	5	43	58	100	2	1	.259/.358/.356	101	18.5	.322	-0.3	SS(75): 1.7, 2B(21): 2.1	2.7
2017	DUR	AAA	23	47	7	2	0	1	1	3	7	0	1	.372/.426/.488	97	3.3	.429	-1.0	SS(4): 0.3, 3B(3): -0.2	0.1
2017	TBA	MLB	23	254	22	7	2	5	19	29	73	1	1	.206/.308/.326	77	1.4	.282	-0.8	2B(41): -2.2, SS(24): 1.9	0.1
2018	TBA	MLB	24	340	46	16	0	9	34	43	77	2	2	.262/.382/.415	102	24.9	.328	1.8	2B(39): 3.1, SS(29): -0.3	1.7
2019	TBA	MLB	25	415	45	16	1	11	46	49	97	2	1	.227/.337/.368	97	9.2	.287	0.7	3B 0, SS 1	1.2

Breakout: 3%   Improve: 50%   Collapse: 8%   Attrition: 16%   MLB: 99%

Comparables: Dustin Ackley, Luis Valbuena, Nick Franklin

The 34th selection in the 2012 draft and a former top-100 prospect, Robertson has carved out a role as the 10th man for Tampa Bay. After rising through the ranks as a shortstop, he entered the season as the Rays' primary backup to the four, five and six spots. He also pitched, played first base and made a handful of starts in left field. Robertson's defensive flexibility is useful, but it was his bat that emerged as the biggest part of his value before a thumb injury ended his season in August. Prior to the ailment, Robertson continued a tremendous aptitude for walks and increased power from the right side. He was on his way to a two-WARP season, finishing just short. The Rays have plenty of reserve infield options, but Robertson should remain the club's top choice, as he's a natural platoon with Joey Wendle at second base along with his ability to back up Willy Adames at shortstop and Matt Duffy at third base.

Jesus Sanchez RF
Born: 10/07/97 Age: 21 Bats: L Throws: R Height: 6'3" Weight: 210 Origin: International Free Agent, 2014

YEAR	TEAM	LVL	AGE	PA	R	2B	3B	HR	RBI	BB	K	SB	CS	AVG/OBP/SLG	DRC+	VORP	BABIP	BRR	FRAA	WARP
2016	RAY	RK	18	173	25	6	8	4	31	6	31	1	5	.323/.341/.530	122	13.7	.371	-0.9	CF(31): 1.9, RF(10): -1.3	0.9
2016	PRI	RK	18	53	8	4	0	3	8	3	12	1	0	.347/.385/.612	113	7.5	.412	0.9	LF(11): 0.5, CF(3): -0.1	0.3
2017	BGR	A	19	512	81	29	4	15	82	32	91	7	2	.305/.348/.478	113	29.4	.349	3.4	LF(78): 14.0, RF(19): -0.5	3.5
2018	PCH	A+	20	378	56	24	2	10	64	15	71	6	3	.301/.331/.462	111	20.0	.350	-1.5	RF(78): 1.8, CF(7): -1.4	1.2
2018	MNT	AA	20	110	14	8	0	1	11	11	21	1	1	.214/.300/.327	93	-0.8	.263	0.7	RF(26): -0.8, CF(1): 0.0	0.1
2019	TBA	MLB	21	251	24	9	0	8	29	10	58	1	0	.228/.258/.365	63	-4.7	.265	-0.5	RF -1, CF 0	-0.6

Breakout: 2%   Improve: 6%   Collapse: 2%   Attrition: 9%   MLB: 15%

Comparables: Justin Williams, Randal Grichuk, Jorge Bonifacio

On the heels of a strong 2017 showing, his first year with a full-season affiliate, Sanchez had considerable hype heading into 2018. It came in waves, but he was very good during the humid summer in Port Charlotte. He showed solid pop despite hitting in thick air and did not have to sell out for that with strikeouts. Sanchez is not one for walks and that will have to change at some point, as he does not have the 80-grade bat to make up for the on-base opportunities. He did take a few more free passes upon promotion to Double-A, but otherwise struggled in Montgomery, although reaching the Southern League as a 20-year-old is a feat unto itself. He's long, with average speed and the arm to handle right field. He's at least a year away, but should be arriving in the middle of the Rays' opening window.

Nick Solak UT Born: 01/11/95 Age: 24 Bats: R Throws: R Height: 5'11" Weight: 175 Origin: Round 2, 2016 Draft (#62 overall)

YEAR	TEAM	LVL	AGE	PA	R	2B	3B	HR	RBI	BB	K	SB	CS	AVG/OBP/SLG	DRC+	VORP	BABIP	BRR	FRAA	WARP
2016	STA	A-	21	279	48	13	1	3	25	30	39	8	0	.321/.412/.421	131	25.0	.372	3.6	2B(59): -1.9	2.0
2017	TAM	A+	22	406	56	17	4	10	44	53	76	13	4	.301/.397/.460	130	38.8	.357	2.5	2B(92): 1.4	3.1
2017	TRN	AA	22	132	16	9	1	2	9	10	24	1	1	.286/.344/.429	85	8.3	.340	0.5	2B(27): 2.0	0.4
2018	MNT	AA	23	565	91	17	3	19	76	68	112	21	6	.282/.384/.450	130	46.4	.330	-0.5	2B(61): -6.9, LF(40): -3.3	2.7
2019	TBA	MLB	24	251	28	8	1	8	29	22	59	4	1	.229/.304/.377	86	4.1	.274	0.1	2B 0, LF -1	0.3

Breakout: 4%   Improve: 30%   Collapse: 13%   Attrition: 27%   MLB: 65%   *Comparables: Rob Refsnyder, Devon Travis, Jason Kipnis*

A second-round pick in 2016, Solak landed with the Rays in a three-team deal with the Yankees and Diamondbacks. Once projected as a speedy slap hitter, he's developed some pop. After hitting 12 home runs in 2017, he belted 19 to place fourth in the Southern League. He also finished fourth in batting average and paced the league in on-base percentage while stealing 21 bags. After playing second base exclusively with the Yankees, he branched out into left and center field as well. The Rays have at least a half-dozen viable players with a variety of offensive skill sets at second base. It will be a *Hunger Games*-style battle to see who wins, with the odds being somewhat in Solak's favor.

Andrew Velazquez UT Born: 07/14/94 Age: 24 Bats: B Throws: R Height: 5'10" Weight: 160 Origin: Round 7, 2012 Draft (#243 overall)

YEAR	TEAM	LVL	AGE	PA	R	2B	3B	HR	RBI	BB	K	SB	CS	AVG/OBP/SLG	DRC+	VORP	BABIP	BRR	FRAA	WARP
2016	PCH	A+	21	313	31	6	2	1	14	21	71	11	6	.262/.313/.308	84	5.9	.343	1.6	SS(51): -3.4, 2B(11): -0.3	0.3
2017	MNT	AA	22	414	49	17	4	9	37	30	112	18	9	.235/.297/.374	85	8.7	.312	2.5	SS(82): 3.5, CF(16): 1.6	1.8
2018	MNT	AA	23	36	5	2	1	2	4	1	11	2	0	.229/.250/.514	81	2.2	.273	0.8	CF(7): 1.6	0.3
2018	DUR	AAA	23	461	63	16	6	12	41	34	124	29	3	.258/.317/.409	101	22.3	.338	5.8	SS(69): -1.8, CF(33): 3.5	2.6
2018	TBA	MLB	23	12	3	1	0	0	0	1	3	1	0	.300/.417/.400	85	1.5	.429	0.5	3B(4): 0.0, CF(2): -0.2	0.1
2019	TBA	MLB	24	70	8	3	0	2	7	4	20	3	1	.224/.276/.365	65	-0.3	.291	0.3	CF 1, RF 0	0.0

Breakout: 4%   Improve: 13%   Collapse: 4%   Attrition: 17%   MLB: 25%   *Comparables: Pat Valaika, Grant Green, Enrique Cruz*

The dark horse on the depth chart, Velazquez has taken longer to develop because of nagging injuries and ineffectiveness. Acquired in a 2014 trade for Jeremy Hellickson, he finally broke through and became a major leaguer for the first time in 2018. He has much more pop than you'd expect from someone listed at 160 pounds. Once a projected starter, Velazquez should settle as a useful reserve with the ability to play all over the diamond and switch-hit. In just 13 games with the big-league club, he appeared at six different positions. There are more well-known names with better pedigrees, but the Bronx, New York native should provide a lot of value @for_dah_money he will make.

Joey Wendle 2B Born: 04/26/90 Age: 29 Bats: L Throws: R Height: 6'1" Weight: 190 Origin: Round 6, 2012 Draft (#203 overall)

YEAR	TEAM	LVL	AGE	PA	R	2B	3B	HR	RBI	BB	K	SB	CS	AVG/OBP/SLG	DRC+	VORP	BABIP	BRR	FRAA	WARP
2016	NAS	AAA	26	526	81	31	9	12	61	26	112	14	4	.279/.324/.452	95	25.4	.340	3.2	2B(122): 4.7	2.2
2016	OAK	MLB	26	104	11	1	0	1	11	6	16	2	0	.260/.298/.302	84	0.5	.296	-0.7	2B(28): 1.5	0.2
2017	NAS	AAA	27	510	67	29	8	8	54	19	82	13	4	.285/.327/.429	90	26.3	.329	0.6	2B(82): -0.7, 3B(24): 6.3	1.7
2017	OAK	MLB	27	14	3	1	0	1	5	1	3	0	0	.308/.357/.615	90	1.0	.333	-0.2	2B(5): -0.5	0.0
2018	TBA	MLB	28	545	62	33	6	7	61	37	96	16	4	.300/.354/.435	103	33.8	.353	3.7	2B(100): 5.8, 3B(20): 1.4	2.9
2019	TBA	MLB	29	569	61	28	5	11	60	35	101	13	4	.262/.322/.397	101	20.5	.309	1.3	2B 6, 3B 1	3.0

Breakout: 2%   Improve: 16%   Collapse: 18%   Attrition: 25%   MLB: 59%   *Comparables: Mike Fontenot, Whit Merrifield, Jason Donald*

Wendle made quite the impression in 2018 in his first extended look at the top level. He was a steady hand defensively at second base, but also filled in at shortstop, third base and both corner outfield spots. That he's a multi-faceted defender is not much of a shock. The fact that he was an offensive force who racked up over 40 extra-base hits and was on base 35 percent of the time was a huge surprise, especially after his *2018 Annual* comment called for a 2049 breakout. Even with some regression—he maintained a high BABIP without elite speed and opposing pitchers may question the sustainability of his power—Wendle will be a value at the keystone. The late break is actually great for the Rays, who'll control him through his prime.

Mike Zunino C Born: 03/25/91 Age: 28 Bats: R Throws: R Height: 6'2" Weight: 220 Origin: Round 1, 2012 Draft (#3 overall)

YEAR	TEAM	LVL	AGE	PA	R	2B	3B	HR	RBI	BB	K	SB	CS	AVG/OBP/SLG	DRC+	VORP	BABIP	BRR	FRAA	WARP
2016	TAC	AAA	25	327	47	15	0	17	57	35	69	0	1	.286/.376/.521	136	29.7	.318	-2.5	C(57): 17.9	4.4
2016	SEA	MLB	25	192	16	7	0	12	31	21	65	0	0	.207/.318/.470	103	12.6	.250	-1.7	C(52): 3.7	1.3
2017	TAC	AAA	26	45	7	2	0	5	11	4	5	0	0	.293/.356/.707	141	9.0	.226	0.6	C(7): 0.8	0.5
2017	SEA	MLB	26	435	52	25	0	25	64	39	160	1	0	.251/.331/.509	98	27.8	.355	-1.4	C(120): 6.3	2.6
2018	SEA	MLB	27	405	37	18	0	20	44	24	150	0	0	.201/.259/.410	78	6.5	.268	-2.2	C(111): 6.4	1.4
2019	TBA	MLB	28	423	52	18	1	19	57	35	141	0	0	.225/.304/.430	95	14.7	.303	-1.7	C 7	2.4

Breakout: 2%   Improve: 47%   Collapse: 9%   Attrition: 10%   MLB: 94%   *Comparables: Jarrod Saltalamacchia, J.P. Arencibia, Yan Gomes*

On April 21, 2014, Houston Astros reliever Chad Qualls tried to throw Mike Zunino a sinker down. He missed thigh high, and Zunino squared it up. The result was a ball hit so far that, had it been hit back in the days before television, your grandpa would have sworn it went 550 feet. It cleared the left-field foul pole by at least 30, and banged off the outer wall of Safeco Field. The umpires got together and decided the ball had hooked foul. It was the perfect distillation of the Mike Zunino Offensive Experience, a jaw-dropping exhibition of raw strength and power. It was also a strike.

YEAR	TEAM	P. COUNT	FRM RUNS	BLK RUNS	THRW RUNS	TOT RUNS
2016	SEA	6955	3.0	1.6	-0.2	3.9
2017	SEA	16181	10.9	-3.1	-0.6	5.6
2017	TAC	823	1.0	0.0	0.0	0.9
2018	SEA	14630	7.5	-1.1	0.4	6.6
2019	TBA	15708	9.4	-1.1	-0.2	8.1

PITCHERS

Jose Alvarado LHP Born: 05/21/95 Age: 24 Bats: L Throws: L Height: 6'2" Weight: 245 Origin: International Free Agent, 2012

YEAR	TEAM	LVL	AGE	W	L	SV	G	GS	IP	H	HR	BB/9	K/9	K	GB%	BABIP	WHIP	ERA	DRA	WARP	MPH	FB%	WHF	CSP
2016	BGR	A	21	2	0	2	10	0	24²	12	0	6.2	12.4	34	74%	.245	1.18	1.46	2.45	0.7				
2016	PCH	A+	21	2	1	0	27	0	46	38	1	7.4	10.0	51	57%	.306	1.65	3.91	3.57	0.8				
2017	MNT	AA	22	2	1	0	9	0	11¹	4	1	4.0	11.1	14	78%	.136	0.79	2.38	2.41	0.3				
2017	DUR	AAA	22	0	2	1	16	0	18¹	11	1	6.4	12.8	26	43%	.244	1.31	3.93	2.93	0.5				
2017	TBA	MLB	22	0	3	0	35	0	29²	24	1	2.7	8.8	29	55%	.274	1.11	3.64	3.44	0.6	99.7	75.8	11.5	48.3
2018	TBA	MLB	23	1	6	8	70	0	64	42	1	4.1	11.2	80	57%	.270	1.11	2.39	2.65	1.7	99.3	70.5	13.6	49
2019	TBA	MLB	24	3	1	30	64	0	67²	49	5	5.7	11.2	84	52%	.276	1.35	3.77	4.05	0.9	99.2	74	13.4	50.1

Breakout: 25%   Improve: 57%   Collapse: 18%   Attrition: 23%   MLB: 91%   *Comparables: Aroldis Chapman, Dominic Leone, Josh Spence*

Big, burly and left-handed, Alvarado has all the pieces to be a late-inning weapon for years to come. Signed out of Maracaibo, Venezuela in 2012, he converted to a relief role in 2016. Despite never pitching above rookie-ball before that, he was in the majors a year later and doing serious damage to opposing batters in 2018. Going more with a sinker/slider combination over a four-seam/curveball approach, he struck out 80 batters in 64 innings. His upper-90s heater allowed him to keep the ball close to the ground with just a single home run allowed to the 263 batters he faced. One of the few members of the pitching staff to not start or open a game, he did, however, make an appearance at first base before going back to the mound in a matchup bonanza. He converted eight saves and is a candidate for more as the back-end of the Rays' bullpen lacks a true ace.

Shane Baz RHP Born: 06/17/99 Age: 20 Bats: R Throws: R Height: 6'3" Weight: 190 Origin: Round 1, 2017 Draft (#12 overall)

YEAR	TEAM	LVL	AGE	W	L	SV	G	GS	IP	H	HR	BB/9	K/9	K	GB%	BABIP	WHIP	ERA	DRA	WARP	MPH	FB%	WHF	CSP
2017	PIR	RK	18	0	3	0	10	10	23²	26	2	5.3	7.2	19	51%	.348	1.69	3.80	5.57	0.1				
2018	BRI	RK	19	4	3	0	10	10	45¹	45	2	4.6	10.7	54	64%	.344	1.50	3.97	4.64	0.7				
2018	PRI	RK	19	0	2	0	2	2	7	11	1	7.7	6.4	5	48%	.417	2.43	7.71	10.04	-0.3				
2019	TBA	MLB	20	1	4	0	10	10	37¹	41	7	8.7	6.7	28	52%	.298	2.07	7.31	7.94	-1.1				

Comparables: Sandy Alcantara, Clay Holmes, Wandy Peralta

When the Rays traded Chris Archer to the Pirates, they received two young, talented major leaguers in Austin Meadows and Tyler Glasnow. That would have been a pretty good haul. They also received a player to be named who turned out to be Baz, the 12th overall pick in the 2017 draft. He has the potential for three or four plus offerings, with a frame that's athletic and room to add some bulk. Baz has yet to make his full-season debut and control has been a concern in both reports and in games, so the range of outcomes is large. If Shane is as Baz as he wants to be he can have a front-of-the-rotation ceiling and a back-of-the-bullpen downside.

Jalen Beeks LHP Born: 07/10/93 Age: 25 Bats: L Throws: L Height: 5'11" Weight: 195 Origin: Round 12, 2014 Draft (#374 overall)

YEAR	TEAM	LVL	AGE	W	L	SV	G	GS	IP	H	HR	BB/9	K/9	K	GB%	BABIP	WHIP	ERA	DRA	WARP	MPH	FB%	WHF	CSP
2016	SLM	A+	22	4	4	0	13	13	67¹	67	9	3.2	7.4	55	43%	.294	1.35	3.07	4.14	1.0				
2016	PME	AA	22	5	4	0	13	13	65¹	72	6	3.9	7.7	56	35%	.330	1.53	4.68	4.07	0.8				
2017	PME	AA	23	5	1	0	9	9	49¹	35	3	4.0	10.6	58	51%	.276	1.16	2.19	3.90	0.7				
2017	PAW	AAA	23	6	7	0	17	17	95²	86	10	3.1	9.1	97	45%	.291	1.24	3.86	4.25	1.5				
2018	BOS	MLB	24	0	1	0	2	1	6¹	11	1	5.7	7.1	5	33%	.435	2.37	12.79	7.48	-0.2	93.5	47.5	9.5	42.7
2018	PAW	AAA	24	5	5	0	16	16	87¹	70	10	2.6	12.1	117	41%	.299	1.09	2.89	3.71	1.8				
2018	TBA	MLB	24	5	0	0	12	0	44¹	41	5	4.1	7.5	37	51%	.288	1.38	4.47	5.18	-0.1	93.5	47.5	13.1	45
2019	TBA	MLB	25	4	4	0	29	10	70¹	62	9	3.6	9.2	72	41%	.284	1.28	4.16	4.49	0.6	93.2	48.6	12.8	45.7

Breakout: 13%   Improve: 35%   Collapse: 22%   Attrition: 41%   MLB: 71%   *Comparables: Manny Parra, Steven Brault, Eric Surkamp*

Acquired in a trade that actually benefited both teams, Beeks swapped AL East clubs with Nathan Eovaldi, who would help the Red Sox win the whole damn thing a few months later. Beeks has years of team control left and a skill set that fits the organization's new take on pitching. On the shorter side without tremendous stuff, the Rays used Beeks a dozen times for an average of about three-and-a-half innings per outing. Only 11 times did he pitch to a batter three times in the same game as a reliever, protecting him from the third-time-through-the-order penalty. After switching sides, he increased the use of his changeup while throwing fewer fastballs. Whether or not the opener remains a thing, Tampa Bay will likely continue to use multi-inning relievers, which means Beeks should be in the plans for the foreseeable future.

Diego Castillo RHP Born: 01/18/94 Age: 25 Bats: R Throws: R Height: 6'3" Weight: 240 Origin: International Free Agent, 2014

YEAR	TEAM	LVL	AGE	W	L	SV	G	GS	IP	H	HR	BB/9	K/9	K	GB%	BABIP	WHIP	ERA	DRA	WARP	MPH	FB%	WHF	CSP
2016	BGR	A	22	1	3	7	24	0	40	34	1	2.5	11.2	50	49%	.317	1.12	2.03	2.18	1.2				
2016	PCH	A+	22	2	3	3	14	0	20¹	28	3	2.7	7.5	17	52%	.357	1.67	4.87	3.17	0.4				
2017	MNT	AA	23	1	3	8	21	0	29	20	1	2.2	9.9	32	61%	.250	0.93	1.86	2.49	0.8				
2017	DUR	AAA	23	3	2	7	30	1	42²	38	2	2.7	12.2	58	40%	.353	1.20	3.38	2.27	1.4				
2018	DUR	AAA	24	0	1	4	19	0	26¹	15	1	2.4	10.9	32	59%	.246	0.84	1.03	1.90	1.0				
2018	TBA	MLB	24	4	2	0	43	11	56²	36	6	2.9	10.3	65	46%	.229	0.95	3.18	3.70	0.9	100.5	54	14	48.9
2019	*TBA*	*MLB*	*25*	*3*	*2*	*0*	*51*	*6*	*59¹*	*47*	*6*	*3.6*	*10.2*	*67*	*45%*	*.280*	*1.19*	*3.61*	*3.89*	*1.1*	*100.2*	*55.3*	*14.3*	*50.1*

Breakout: 28% Improve: 46% Collapse: 17% Attrition: 34% MLB: 74%   *Comparables: Yimi Garcia, Sam Tuivailala, Jerry Blevins*

Castillo, a traditional reliever since turning professional in 2014, started in 11 of his 43 appearances as part of the opener movement. He was effective in either role, limiting the opposition to a .206/.231/.333 line when beginning a game and a .166/.261/.288 mark when following a teammate. He used a conventional two-pitch mix, working primarily off an upper-90s fastball and a slider that tickled 90 as well, striking out 29 percent of batters faced. The slider is particularly effective, as he used the pitch to complete 53 of his 65 strikeouts and it held opponents to a .106 average. Despite the absence of a changeup, Castillo held his own against left-handed batters, though his control waned at times. His comfort level in any role makes him a key asset going into 2019.

Yonny Chirinos RHP Born: 12/26/93 Age: 25 Bats: R Throws: R Height: 6'2" Weight: 235 Origin: International Free Agent, 2012

YEAR	TEAM	LVL	AGE	W	L	SV	G	GS	IP	H	HR	BB/9	K/9	K	GB%	BABIP	WHIP	ERA	DRA	WARP	MPH	FB%	WHF	CSP
2016	BGR	A	22	1	0	0	4	2	11²	8	0	0.8	6.9	9	56%	.222	0.77	2.31	3.52	0.2				
2016	PCH	A+	22	6	1	0	11	7	50¹	47	5	0.5	5.5	31	53%	.262	0.99	2.15	3.14	1.3				
2016	MNT	AA	22	5	3	0	14	8	66²	74	5	1.6	5.8	43	44%	.307	1.29	4.45	3.42	1.3				
2017	MNT	AA	23	1	0	0	4	4	27¹	22	5	1.3	6.9	21	58%	.233	0.95	2.63	3.55	0.5				
2017	DUR	AAA	23	12	5	0	23	22	141	116	10	1.4	7.7	120	52%	.270	0.98	2.74	3.27	3.7				
2018	DUR	AAA	24	0	2	0	8	8	30²	35	7	2.1	9.1	31	50%	.326	1.37	5.28	4.70	0.3				
2018	TBA	MLB	24	5	5	0	18	7	89²	84	7	2.5	7.5	75	45%	.298	1.22	3.51	4.23	0.9	95.9	63.1	12.2	49.8
2019	*TBA*	*MLB*	*25*	*3*	*3*	*0*	*10*	*10*	*50*	*45*	*5*	*2.6*	*7.8*	*43*	*46%*	*.278*	*1.19*	*3.95*	*4.27*	*0.7*	*95.6*	*64.6*	*12.5*	*50.9*

Breakout: 12% Improve: 39% Collapse: 23% Attrition: 34% MLB: 83%   *Comparables: A.J. Griffin, Tim Cooney, Jose Urena*

Chirinos signed for a modest $10,000 out of Venezuela in 2012. He methodically worked his way through the system, culminating with being named the organization's minor-league pitcher of the year in 2017 and making his big-league debut in 2018. He spent the majority of his time as a starter in the minors and started seven games for Tampa Bay, but was mostly used as a bulk guy. In 11 relief appearances he racked up 57 1/3 innings and was highly effective, limiting the other team to a .276 wOBA and a strikeout-to-walk ratio of 3.5:1. Born in '93, his heavy fastball mimics his birth year. Even with modest velocity, the pitch was relatively effective in setting up a hard slider and a particularly damaging split-finger. The mid-80s offering was the catalyst in most of his strikeouts. Chirinos has the build and pitch mix to start games at the highest level. He did miss about a month with a forearm injury, but was highly effective down the stretch.

Oliver Drake RHP Born: 01/13/87 Age: 32 Bats: R Throws: R Height: 6'4" Weight: 215 Origin: Round 43, 2008 Draft (#1286 overall)

YEAR	TEAM	LVL	AGE	W	L	SV	G	GS	IP	H	HR	BB/9	K/9	K	GB%	BABIP	WHIP	ERA	DRA	WARP	MPH	FB%	WHF	CSP
2016	NOR	AAA	29	1	4	10	47	1	56¹	44	5	4.0	12.6	79	46%	.322	1.22	2.72	2.07	1.9				
2016	BAL	MLB	29	1	0	0	14	0	18	11	2	3.5	10.5	21	52%	.205	1.00	4.00	2.86	0.4	92.3	54.2	15.6	49.5
2017	BAL	MLB	30	0	0	0	3	0	3¹	6	0	8.1	8.1	3	67%	.500	2.70	8.10	6.84	-0.1	92.9	47.6	11	43.7
2017	MIL	MLB	30	3	5	1	61	0	52²	57	6	3.8	10.1	59	49%	.349	1.50	4.44	4.35	0.5	93.5	51.6	13	45.1
2018	MIL	MLB	31	1	0	0	11	0	12²	14	0	5.7	10.7	15	57%	.400	1.74	6.39	2.52	0.4	93.9	49.3	13.5	50.5
2018	CLE	MLB	31	0	0	0	4	0	4¹	7	0	2.1	8.3	4	31%	.438	1.85	12.46	2.59	0.1	93.7	48.1	14.3	45.6
2018	SLC	AAA	31	0	0	0	6	0	7²	3	0	1.2	9.4	8	71%	.176	0.52	1.17	3.56	0.1				
2018	ANA	MLB	31	0	1	0	8	0	8²	15	2	1.0	8.3	8	39%	.448	1.85	5.19	3.11	0.2	94.2	47.1	15	49.1
2018	TOR	MLB	31	0	0	0	2	0	1²	4	0	0.0	10.8	2	43%	.571	2.40	16.20	1.95	0.1	94.1	58.3	8.3	52.2
2018	MIN	MLB	31	0	0	0	19	0	20¹	12	2	3.1	9.7	22	55%	.204	0.93	2.21	3.40	0.4	93.7	40.6	13.6	45.5
2019	*TBA*	*MLB*	*32*	*1*	*0*	*0*	*19*	*0*	*20¹*	*18*	*2*	*4.0*	*9.2*	*21*	*47%*	*.295*	*1.35*	*4.06*	*4.38*	*0.2*	*92.6*	*48.6*	*13.3*	*46.8*

Breakout: 22% Improve: 40% Collapse: 15% Attrition: 18% MLB: 69%   *Comparables: Jason Bulger, Mitch Stetter, Blake Wood*

The thing is, Drake is actually pretty good. Pitching is hard enough. To pitch in the majors requires supernal sheer arm strength, tremendous proprioception, a very high tolerance for pain and a sharp intellect. To pitch in the majors for five different teams in a single season requires all those things, plus considerable mental toughness. It requires that five teams decide you're good enough to merit a roster spot, but it also requires four of them to decide some other fringe player is better. As most difficult tasks do, however, pitching becomes easier when one makes it simple and focuses on their strengths. In Drake's case, that finally happened when he reached Minnesota in early August. From his arrival there through the end of the season, he threw his splitter (almost a true forkball, and easily his best offering) more often than any other pitch. Opponents batted .164/.238/.274 against Drake down the stretch. May he never go back to throwing the heater more often than the split. At the time this book went to print, Drake was already on his second team of 2019, which puts him on pace to have worn every jersey in the league by late summer.

Jacob Faria RHP Born: 07/30/93   Age: 25   Bats: R   Throws: R   Height: 6'4"   Weight: 235   Origin: Round 10, 2011 Draft (#330 overall)

YEAR	TEAM	LVL	AGE	W	L	SV	G	GS	IP	H	HR	BB/9	K/9	K	GB%	BABIP	WHIP	ERA	DRA	WARP	MPH	FB%	WHF	CSP
2016	MNT	AA	22	1	6	0	14	14	83¹	64	5	3.9	10.0	93	42%	.282	1.20	4.21	3.56	1.5				
2016	DUR	AAA	22	4	4	0	13	13	67²	46	7	4.3	8.5	64	40%	.227	1.15	3.72	5.98	-0.5				
2017	DUR	AAA	23	6	1	0	11	11	58²	44	7	3.4	12.9	84	43%	.291	1.12	3.07	3.28	1.6				
2017	TBA	MLB	23	5	4	0	16	14	86²	71	11	3.2	8.7	84	39%	.265	1.18	3.43	4.33	1.2	93.1	54.5	13.3	46.3
2018	DUR	AAA	24	2	1	0	7	5	29¹	25	5	4.0	8.6	28	38%	.253	1.30	4.60	5.38	0.0				
2018	TBA	MLB	24	4	4	0	17	12	65	60	9	4.6	6.9	50	35%	.274	1.43	5.40	6.75	-1.1	93.0	60.6	8.8	47.1
2019	TBA	MLB	25	4	4	0	23	10	70²	61	9	4.1	8.3	65	39%	.269	1.32	4.61	4.99	0.3	92.8	58.9	11.3	47.9

Breakout: 15%   Improve: 57%   Collapse: 23%   Attrition: 28%   MLB: 91%   Comparables: Ian Kennedy, Chris Archer, Rubby De La Rosa

At a time when velocity runs the yard, Faria remains the zig to the zag, with a low-90s fastball leading the way. He was a productive member of the rotation as a rookie in 2017, but 2018 was a net negative. After beginning the season as one of the few regular members of the Rays' rotation, he missed about two-and-a-half months with an oblique strain and was not particularly sharp before or after the injury. Faria wasn't necessarily a control artist coming through the system, but had a good feel for the zone in 2017, walking fewer than nine percent of batters. That number jumped up in 2018, with a drop in strikeouts. He especially struggled going against the platoon split, walking more lefties (25) than he struck out (24). Not surprisingly, his changeup was one of the big reasons for his issues. Briefly demoted in August before finishing the season in the majors, he allowed more runs than innings pitched in September.

Ian Gibaut RHP Born: 11/19/93   Age: 25   Bats: R   Throws: R   Height: 6'3"   Weight: 250   Origin: Round 11, 2015 Draft (#328 overall)

YEAR	TEAM	LVL	AGE	W	L	SV	G	GS	IP	H	HR	BB/9	K/9	K	GB%	BABIP	WHIP	ERA	DRA	WARP	MPH	FB%	WHF	CSP
2016	BGR	A	22	1	0	1	7	0	9²	6	0	0.9	16.8	18	33%	.333	0.72	0.93	0.10	0.5				
2016	PCH	A+	22	1	2	3	27	0	47¹	45	2	3.6	8.6	45	37%	.326	1.35	2.85	3.15	1.0				
2017	PCH	A+	23	1	0	2	5	0	8¹	5	0	1.1	15.1	14	33%	.333	0.72	2.16	2.80	0.2				
2017	MNT	AA	23	6	1	10	43	0	52²	33	6	4.4	10.8	63	44%	.221	1.12	2.22	3.12	1.1				
2018	DUR	AAA	24	4	3	14	48	0	56	35	3	3.4	12.1	75	49%	.269	1.00	2.09	3.00	1.4				
2019	TBA	MLB	25	1	0	0	19	0	20¹	16	2	4.4	10.9	25	42%	.279	1.27	4.09	4.41	0.2				

Breakout: 8%   Improve: 10%   Collapse: 18%   Attrition: 23%   MLB: 31%   Comparables: Justin Miller, Cory Gearrin, Jacob Rhame

Sorry Corliss Williamson, Gibaut is the new "Big Nasty." The Tulane product is as conventional as they come for a reliever. He throws a hard fastball and backs that with a dirty slide piece. He also tosses a changeup that's more than just a show-me offering and can get left-handed hitters out. The burly right-hander has posted strikeout numbers to match his size since turning pro and improved his control with a promotion to Triple-A, after which he was added to the 40-man roster this winter. The word open, opener or some variation will be said a nauseating amount of times in this chapter. However, Big Nasty's future role is somewhat of a dirty word around these parts. He has "closer" stuff and potential.

Tyler Glasnow RHP Born: 08/23/93   Age: 25   Bats: L   Throws: R   Height: 6'8"   Weight: 220   Origin: Round 5, 2011 Draft (#152 overall)

YEAR	TEAM	LVL	AGE	W	L	SV	G	GS	IP	H	HR	BB/9	K/9	K	GB%	BABIP	WHIP	ERA	DRA	WARP	MPH	FB%	WHF	CSP
2016	IND	AAA	22	8	3	0	20	20	110²	65	4	5.0	10.8	133	43%	.255	1.15	1.87	3.80	2.0				
2016	PIT	MLB	22	0	2	0	7	4	23¹	22	2	5.0	9.3	24	49%	.317	1.50	4.24	4.40	0.2	96.8	62.3	12.2	43.7
2017	IND	AAA	23	9	2	0	15	15	93¹	57	6	3.1	13.5	140	50%	.276	0.95	1.93	2.58	3.2				
2017	PIT	MLB	23	2	7	0	15	13	62	81	13	6.4	8.1	56	44%	.358	2.02	7.69	8.17	-1.8	97.4	64.7	8.6	46.9
2018	PIT	MLB	24	1	2	0	34	0	56	47	5	5.5	11.6	72	57%	.321	1.45	4.34	2.88	1.4	99.2	72.5	12.4	46.3
2018	TBA	MLB	24	1	5	0	11	11	55²	42	10	3.1	10.3	64	44%	.248	1.10	4.20	3.64	0.9	98.8	68.2	13.2	48.5
2019	TBA	MLB	25	8	9	0	28	28	140	108	14	4.7	10.7	166	46%	.277	1.29	3.91	4.20	2.1	98.1	69.6	11.7	47.4

Breakout: 34%   Improve: 63%   Collapse: 17%   Attrition: 20%   MLB: 92%   Comparables: Edinson Volquez, Carlos Marmol, Gio Gonzalez

During a year in which the Rays seemingly turned every starter into a reliever and every reliever into a starter, Glasnow, acquired as part of the deadline return for Chris Archer, was allowed to return to his old ways in the rotation. After focusing on trying to get the ball down in Pittsburgh, Glasnow worked higher in the zone for Tampa Bay. Predictably, the result was more fly balls and more home runs, but also fewer pitches out of the zone and easier outs on balls in play. The 6-foot-8 righty made 11 starts for Tampa Bay down the stretch and was able to maintain velocity and effectiveness with the increased workload. He projects to be the club's no. 2 starter behind Blake Snell and has breakout potential.

Brent Honeywell RHP Born: 03/31/95   Age: 24   Bats: R   Throws: R   Height: 6'2"   Weight: 180   Origin: Round 2, 2014 Draft (#72 overall)

YEAR	TEAM	LVL	AGE	W	L	SV	G	GS	IP	H	HR	BB/9	K/9	K	GB%	BABIP	WHIP	ERA	DRA	WARP	MPH	FB%	WHF	CSP
2016	PCH	A+	21	4	1	0	10	10	56	43	5	1.8	10.3	64	33%	.279	0.96	2.41	2.35	2.0				
2016	MNT	AA	21	3	2	0	10	10	59¹	51	4	2.1	8.0	53	29%	.287	1.10	2.28	4.70	0.3				
2017	MNT	AA	22	1	1	0	2	2	13	4	1	2.8	13.8	20	45%	.158	0.62	2.08	0.47	0.7				
2017	DUR	AAA	22	12	8	0	24	24	123²	130	11	2.3	11.1	152	42%	.366	1.30	3.64	3.37	3.2				
2019	TBA	MLB	24	2	3	0	8	8	40	37	5	2.9	9.5	42	36%	.295	1.23	3.93	4.25	0.6				

Breakout: 13%   Improve: 27%   Collapse: 13%   Attrition: 26%   MLB: 46%   Comparables: Adam Morgan, Kyle Gibson, Chad Bettis

Honeywell underwent Tommy John surgery in February and did not throw a meaningful pitch all year. The early injury, however, means an earlier return for 2019. Prior to going under the knife, Honeywell was a rare five-pitch prospect with excellent control, ranking among the elite pitching prospects in baseball. There's optimism that he'll regain most, if not all, of the effectiveness of his fastball, changeup, slider, curveball and screwball. The biggest challenge will be recapturing that plus control, the piece of the puzzle that typically comes last in recovery. The Rays are hoping he can find it sooner rather than later and join the big-league rotation some time in the middle of the summer.

Matthew Liberatore LHP Born: 11/06/99 Age: 19 Bats: L Throws: L Height: 6'5" Weight: 200 Origin: Round 1, 2018 Draft (#16 overall)

YEAR	TEAM	LVL	AGE	W	L	SV	G	GS	IP	H	HR	BB/9	K/9	K	GB%	BABIP	WHIP	ERA	DRA	WARP	MPH	FB%	WHF	CSP
2018	RAY	RK	18	1	2	0	8	8	27²	16	0	3.6	10.4	32	45%	.258	0.98	0.98	3.07	0.9				
2019	TBA	MLB	19	1	3	0	7	7	31	33	6	6.9	8.0	28	42%	.296	1.81	6.65	7.21	-0.6				

Comparables: Jaime Barria, Raul Alcantara, Jason Garcia

The Rays were ecstatic to see Liberatore slide to them at pick 16 last June. At one point in consideration for the no. 1 overall pick, signability was a concern for some teams. Tampa Bay not only selected him, but was able to sign him, too. He's long and left-handed with the potential for three plus pitches and some room to grow physically. Typically the Rays like to slow roast their prospects, but Liberatore has an advanced feel for his craft and could head straight to a full-season affiliate if the organization wants to show a little aggression.

Shane McClanahan LHP Born: 04/28/97 Age: 22 Bats: L Throws: L Height: 6'1" Weight: 188 Origin: Round 1C, 2018 Draft (#31 overall)

YEAR	TEAM	LVL	AGE	W	L	SV	G	GS	IP	H	HR	BB/9	K/9	K	GB%	BABIP	WHIP	ERA	DRA	WARP	MPH	FB%	WHF	CSP
2019	TBA	MLB	22	2	3	0	8	8	32²	31	6	5.2	8.3	30	45%	.271	1.54	5.79	6.28	-0.3				

Breakout: 4% Improve: 4% Collapse: 0% Attrition: 2% MLB: 4%

Comparables: Clay Holmes, Edward Paredes, Elvin Ramirez

Despite picking 16th and 31st, the Rays landed two of the top left-handed pitchers in the 2018 draft class. After nabbing prep arm Matthew Liberatore earlier in the round, Tampa Bay stayed close to home by drafting McClanahan out of nearby University of South Florida. He tossed just seven innings after signing, but the extremely early returns were impressive. The southpaw has an upper-90s fastball with a changeup and curveball that should be above-average as well. He's a bit undersized, so workload will be something to watch as he develops.

Brendan McKay LHP Born: 12/18/95 Age: 23 Bats: L Throws: L Height: 6'2" Weight: 212 Origin: Round 1, 2017 Draft (#4 overall)

YEAR	TEAM	LVL	AGE	W	L	SV	G	GS	IP	H	HR	BB/9	K/9	K	GB%	BABIP	WHIP	ERA	DRA	WARP	MPH	FB%	WHF	CSP
2017	HUD	A-	21	1	0	0	6	6	20	10	3	2.2	9.4	21	53%	.159	0.75	1.80	3.10	0.5				
2018	BGR	A	22	2	0	0	6	6	24²	8	1	0.7	14.6	40	63%	.167	0.41	1.09	2.63	0.8				
2018	PCH	A+	22	3	2	0	11	9	47²	45	2	2.1	10.2	54	39%	.350	1.17	3.21	3.05	1.2				
2019	TBA	MLB	23	3	4	0	17	12	52	49	9	3.5	9.5	55	42%	.288	1.32	4.74	5.13	0.2				

Breakout: 8% Improve: 11% Collapse: 4% Attrition: 10% MLB: 18%

Comparables: Matt Bowman, Jake McGee, Eric Surkamp

The first legitimate two-way player drafted in decades, McKay watched Shohei Otani put the blueprint together for a player to hit and pitch for a major-league team. McKay was a top-five pick and played at a major university, but the Rays have brought him along relatively slowly considering his age and experience. A few non-threatening injuries have also slowed the process. As it stands, the former Louisville Cardinal is much farther down the line as a pitcher than he is as a hitter, where he's yet to display that 20-homer potential he was projected to have. On the other hand, McKay the pitcher has been dominant. The organization was already cautious in his usage, but that was not enough to prevent multiple oblique injuries that cost him development. Although his pitching is way ahead of his hitting, the Rays will let him play both ways until it looks like he cannot.

Charlie Morton RHP Born: 11/12/83 Age: 35 Bats: R Throws: R Height: 6'5" Weight: 235 Origin: Round 3, 2002 Draft (#95 overall)

YEAR	TEAM	LVL	AGE	W	L	SV	G	GS	IP	H	HR	BB/9	K/9	K	GB%	BABIP	WHIP	ERA	DRA	WARP	MPH	FB%	WHF	CSP
2016	PHI	MLB	32	1	1	0	4	4	17¹	15	1	4.2	9.9	19	66%	.326	1.33	4.15	3.11	0.4	96.5	61.6	13	44.7
2017	HOU	MLB	33	14	7	0	25	25	146²	125	14	3.1	10.0	163	53%	.295	1.19	3.62	3.92	2.7	96.6	65.6	11.5	48.6
2018	HOU	MLB	34	15	3	0	30	30	167	130	18	3.4	10.8	201	49%	.284	1.16	3.13	3.68	3.1	97.5	63.4	12.8	48.3
2019	TBA	MLB	35	9	9	0	26	26	148¹	124	16	3.8	9.9	163	51%	.288	1.25	3.90	4.21	2.2	95.8	63.1	12.1	46.6

Breakout: 12% Improve: 38% Collapse: 27% Attrition: 13% MLB: 88%

Comparables: Ryan Dempster, Chuck Finley, Jeff Fassero

Morton may be the best proof that the Astros are operating on a level above most teams. His career health record reads like the script for a *Grey's Anatomy* episode, and he entered free agency two offseasons ago best known not for his own success, but for imitating the late, great Roy Halladay's mound mannerisms. We'd tagged him as an "inconsistent no. 4 starter" before the 2016 season, and then he barely pitched before he tore his hamstring. Despite all of that, the Astros quickly snapped Morton up for $14 million over two years. He returned their act of faith with the two most effective and healthy seasons of his or most careers, sustaining a large velocity spike to go along with a now-untouchable curveball. He even closed out Game 7 of the 2017 World Series with four electric innings out of the bullpen. Credit great analytics, scouting, coaching and preventative health, because you need all of it working in harmony to turn Charlie Morton into a borderline ace. Tampa Bay will now attempt to recreate the magic, this time for $30 million over two years.

Emilio Pagan RHP   Born: 05/07/91   Age: 28   Bats: L   Throws: R   Height: 6'3"   Weight: 210   Origin: Round 10, 2013 Draft (#297 overall)

YEAR	TEAM	LVL	AGE	W	L	SV	G	GS	IP	H	HR	BB/9	K/9	K	GB%	BABIP	WHIP	ERA	DRA	WARP	MPH	FB%	WHF	CSP
2016	WTN	AA	25	4	1	9	18	0	30²	19	1	3.2	13.2	45	32%	.269	0.98	1.17	2.46	0.8				
2016	TAC	AAA	25	1	2	1	23	0	34¹	28	6	4.7	10.2	39	32%	.268	1.34	3.67	3.19	0.7				
2017	TAC	AAA	26	2	1	5	23	0	31²	19	0	2.3	10.2	36	29%	.241	0.85	2.56	3.35	0.7				
2017	SEA	MLB	26	2	3	0	34	0	50¹	39	7	1.4	10.0	56	23%	.258	0.93	3.22	3.68	0.8	95.5	68.7	15	54.7
2018	NAS	AAA	27	1	0	0	5	0	6	5	2	0.0	16.5	11	38%	.273	0.83	3.00	1.33	0.3				
2018	OAK	MLB	27	3	1	0	55	0	62	55	13	2.8	9.1	63	25%	.256	1.19	4.35	4.35	0.4	95.7	66.4	15.5	50.9
2019	TBA	MLB	28	3	1	0	51	0	54	46	8	3.7	9.7	58	32%	.271	1.26	4.48	4.85	0.2	95.0	67.6	15.4	52.9

Breakout: 21%   Improve: 32%   Collapse: 26%   Attrition: 15%   MLB: 69%   *Comparables: Pedro Baez, Matt Reynolds, Clay Zavala*

The A's had a spare Ryon Healy sitting around and all his possible positions accounted for by better players (Matts Chapman and Olson on the infield corners and Khris Davis at DH), so they shipped him to Seattle for Pagan and teenage shortstop Alexander Campos in the 2018 offseason. Pagan had emerged the prior year as a middle-relief option with a mid-90s fastball that missed enough bats to overcome his extreme fly-ball ways. Bob Melvin was under no illusions about Pagan's upside, largely pitching him in low-leverage situations. As a four-seamer/slider hurler with only a show-me changeup, he has no weapons against lefties, and it showed in the .296/.376/.654 line he allowed to them. Given his ROOGY characteristics and the size of modern bullpens, his usage should probably be different going forward: 31 of his 89 career games have seen him pitch in multiple innings, but he's likely to see more success if he's kept away from all but the most harmless lefties.

Colin Poche LHP   Born: 01/17/94   Age: 25   Bats: L   Throws: L   Height: 6'3"   Weight: 185   Origin: Round 14, 2016 Draft (#419 overall)

YEAR	TEAM	LVL	AGE	W	L	SV	G	GS	IP	H	HR	BB/9	K/9	K	GB%	BABIP	WHIP	ERA	DRA	WARP	MPH	FB%	WHF	CSP
2016	YAK	A-	22	1	2	0	21	4	31	20	2	4.9	10.5	36	41%	.265	1.19	3.19	2.96	0.8				
2017	KNC	A	23	2	0	1	13	0	24²	16	0	2.2	16.1	44	40%	.372	0.89	1.09	1.84	0.9				
2017	VIS	A+	23	1	1	2	18	0	25²	14	0	4.6	13.0	37	43%	.275	1.05	1.40	2.51	0.7				
2018	WTN	AA	24	0	0	1	9	0	11	3	0	1.6	18.8	23	8%	.250	0.45	0.00	0.52	0.6				
2018	DUR	AAA	24	5	0	1	28	2	50	29	2	3.1	14.0	78	28%	.297	0.92	1.08	2.72	1.4				
2019	TBA	MLB	25	1	0	0	26	0	27	22	4	4.9	11.8	35	33%	.285	1.35	4.50	4.85	0.1				

Breakout: 15%   Improve: 25%   Collapse: 11%   Attrition: 31%   MLB: 45%   *Comparables: Anthony Slama, Donnie Joseph, Michael Schwimer*

Pet cat alert. Poche will be a statistical darling in 2019, when he's expected to make his MLB debut. Acquired from the Diamondbacks as a player to be named later in the Steven Souza trade, the lefty has an absurd 1.47 ERA and 227 strikeouts in 147 pro innings while moving quickly through the ranks. Poche does all this without much explanation. He's not an oddity in terms of delivery and he does not throw much harder than the average pitcher. The fastball is low-to-mid 90s, nothing special, but Poche hides the ball well before getting excellent extension. Hitters lose sight of it and then they see it coming much closer than anticipated, which plays up the modest velocity. Poche paired that with a slider in the past, but added a curveball last season to give himself more of an up-and-down game as he likes the fastball elevated. A starter in college, 24 of his 40 appearances last season generated four or more outs, including two test runs as an opener in Durham.

Sergio Romo RHP   Born: 03/04/83   Age: 36   Bats: R   Throws: R   Height: 5'11"   Weight: 185   Origin: Round 28, 2005 Draft (#852 overall)

YEAR	TEAM	LVL	AGE	W	L	SV	G	GS	IP	H	HR	BB/9	K/9	K	GB%	BABIP	WHIP	ERA	DRA	WARP	MPH	FB%	WHF	CSP
2016	SFN	MLB	33	1	0	4	40	0	30²	26	5	2.1	9.7	33	39%	.292	1.08	2.64	2.45	0.9	87.8	32	15.7	42.4
2017	LAN	MLB	34	1	1	0	30	0	25	23	7	4.3	11.2	31	35%	.276	1.40	6.12	2.58	0.7	87.9	27.2	15.4	41.1
2017	TBA	MLB	34	2	0	0	25	0	30²	19	2	2.1	8.2	28	40%	.218	0.85	1.47	3.76	0.5	87.4	41.5	16.3	41.7
2018	TBA	MLB	35	3	4	25	73	5	67¹	65	11	2.7	10.0	75	38%	.309	1.26	4.14	2.80	1.7	87.7	30.1	14.6	44
2019	TBA	MLB	36	3	1	8	53	0	56¹	49	8	3.5	9.4	58	39%	.280	1.26	4.34	4.70	0.2	86.5	31.1	14.9	41.9

Breakout: 24%   Improve: 46%   Collapse: 16%   Attrition: 6%   MLB: 77%   *Comparables: Kyle Farnsworth, Lee Smith, Justin Speier*

Prior to May 19, 2018, Romo had made all 588 of his major-league appearances as a reliever. He made his first start that day. He made his second the next day. Romo became the first pitcher in over a century to start a game, have a 1-2-3 inning and come out right after. He would start five games on the year before the Rays traded Alex Colome and Romo returned to a familiar role late in games. He collected 25 saves while going from opener to closer and was generally effective as the pen's elder statesman. Romo's fiery personality does not match his mid-80s fastball, but his eccentricity is matched by the quirkiness of his slider with disco-era velocity. He threw the slider nearly 60 percent of the time, and while it may have lost a little bite from his peak, it was still a steady source of outs. Under six feet tall and on the wrong side of 35, Romo continues to defy the odds with flair. In addition to his cameo in the "rotation" he also appeared at third base and almost fought Aaron Judge. Tune in next season to see what new tricks the old dog can pull off.

Jaime Schultz RHP   Born: 06/20/91   Age: 28   Bats: R   Throws: R   Height: 5'10"   Weight: 200   Origin: Round 14, 2013 Draft (#428 overall)

YEAR	TEAM	LVL	AGE	W	L	SV	G	GS	IP	H	HR	BB/9	K/9	K	GB%	BABIP	WHIP	ERA	DRA	WARP	MPH	FB%	WHF	CSP
2016	DUR	AAA	25	5	7	0	27	27	130²	113	12	4.7	11.2	163	43%	.327	1.39	3.58	3.89	2.2				
2017	DUR	AAA	26	1	0	0	13	0	11²	10	1	3.1	16.2	21	46%	.391	1.20	3.86	1.48	0.5				
2018	DUR	AAA	27	2	1	3	32	1	36	44	5	5.8	14.5	58	36%	.464	1.86	5.75	3.95	0.5				
2018	TBA	MLB	27	2	2	0	22	1	30¹	18	6	5.0	10.4	35	30%	.188	1.15	5.64	4.14	0.3	96.7	80.3	14.4	47.8
2019	TBA	MLB	28	1	0	0	19	0	20¹	18	3	5.0	11.3	26	40%	.298	1.43	4.74	5.11	0.0	96.1	80.8	14.5	48.1

Breakout: 18%   Improve: 32%   Collapse: 9%   Attrition: 21%   MLB: 42%   *Comparables: Joel Carreno, Thomas Diamond, Ramon A. Ramirez*

After working as a starter though 2016, Schultz covered to a relief role in 2017 and remained there save for one terrible turn as an opener that lasted two-thirds of an inning at the end of the year. He shuttled back and forth between Durham and St. Petersburg, posting big strikeout numbers and high walk totals regardless of the city. Schultz made the brave choice of being a fastball-only reliever who can't locate a fastball, but in his defense he gets enough on it that at least hitters struggle to locate it as well. The result is a live arm and the ability to pitch multiple innings at a time. Yep, that's a Rays pitcher.

Blake Snell LHP Born: 12/04/92 Age: 26 Bats: L Throws: L Height: 6'4" Weight: 200 Origin: Round 1, 2011 Draft (#52 overall)

YEAR	TEAM	LVL	AGE	W	L	SV	G	GS	IP	H	HR	BB/9	K/9	K	GB%	BABIP	WHIP	ERA	DRA	WARP	MPH	FB%	WHF	CSP
2016	DUR	AAA	23	3	5	0	12	12	63	56	4	4.0	12.9	90	51%	.356	1.33	3.29	2.57	2.0				
2016	TBA	MLB	23	6	8	0	19	19	89	93	5	5.2	9.9	98	39%	.356	1.62	3.54	5.25	0.1	96.2	57.2	11.8	43.5
2017	DUR	AAA	24	5	0	0	7	7	44	43	5	3.1	12.5	61	46%	.362	1.32	2.66	2.89	1.4	96.0	55.1	11.4	40.4
2017	TBA	MLB	24	5	7	0	24	24	129¹	113	15	4.1	8.3	119	45%	.278	1.33	4.04	4.05	2.2	97.7	51.5	15.7	44.5
2018	TBA	MLB	25	21	5	0	31	31	180²	112	16	3.2	11.0	221	46%	.241	0.97	1.89	2.44	6.0	96.6	54.6	15.7	44.5
2019	TBA	MLB	26	10	9	0	28	28	159²	124	16	3.8	10.8	191	44%	.283	1.20	3.57	3.84	3.0	96.6	54.6	13.9	43.7

Breakout: 31%   Improve: 66%   Collapse: 21%   Attrition: 4%   MLB: 92%   Comparables: Jon Gray, Brandon Beachy, Matt Harvey

Naturally, the team that bucked the trend of a traditional rotation ended up with the Cy Young-winning starting pitcher. Snell was basically one of the Rays' only two starters (first along with Chris Archer, and later Tyler Glasnow) for most of the season. He posted the lowest ERA (1.89) by an American League starter since 2000 and beat out Justin Verlander for the award despite fewer innings and somewhat lesser peripherals. Maturing in his mid-20s, Snell relied a little less on his fastball and increased the usage of his curveball while continuing to throw a changeup and slider. He struck out over 30 percent of the batters he faced and posted a career-high ground-ball rate. Of course, detractors will scream regression. Naturally, a sub-2.00 ERA is highly unsustainable, but Snell was a supplemental first-round pick (in a historically regrettable class for Tampa Bay), a top prospect and has the stuff to be an ace for years to come even with some slide.

Ryne Stanek RHP Born: 07/26/91 Age: 27 Bats: R Throws: R Height: 6'4" Weight: 215 Origin: Round 1, 2013 Draft (#29 overall)

YEAR	TEAM	LVL	AGE	W	L	SV	G	GS	IP	H	HR	BB/9	K/9	K	GB%	BABIP	WHIP	ERA	DRA	WARP	MPH	FB%	WHF	CSP
2016	MNT	AA	24	2	6	2	18	11	78¹	64	6	4.0	10.5	91	53%	.307	1.26	3.79	3.28	1.6				
2016	DUR	AAA	24	2	4	1	16	0	24¹	22	3	4.8	8.1	22	47%	.284	1.44	5.92	3.71	0.3				
2017	DUR	AAA	25	3	0	8	37	0	44²	26	0	3.2	12.1	60	40%	.268	0.94	1.21	3.10	1.1				
2017	TBA	MLB	25	0	0	0	21	0	20	26	6	5.4	13.1	29	33%	.417	1.90	5.85	2.67	0.6	100.0	67.1	16.3	44.4
2018	DUR	AAA	26	0	1	2	10	0	9²	5	1	5.6	15.8	17	59%	.250	1.14	1.86	1.10	0.4				
2018	TBA	MLB	26	2	3	0	59	29	66¹	45	8	3.7	11.0	81	32%	.253	1.09	2.98	3.34	1.4	99.4	60.1	16.9	44.1
2019	TBA	MLB	27	4	4	0	41	15	57	45	8	4.2	10.9	69	40%	.281	1.26	4.05	4.37	0.6	99.0	62.5	17	44.8

Breakout: 20%   Improve: 39%   Collapse: 19%   Attrition: 26%   MLB: 71%   Comparables: Matt Barnes, Tom Mastny, Phil Coke

When he was selected with the 29th pick in the 2013 draft, experts were split on Stanek's ultimate role. Some saw the former Arkansas Razorback continuing his path as a starter, while others saw more viability as a reliever. They were both right, technically. Stanek was the first pitcher to throw a pitch for the Rays in 29 games. He started more games than James Paxton, Trevor Bauer and Chris Sale, to name a few. He also finished 10 games and tossed just 66 1/3 innings. Stanek was the Rays' choice du jour for most opening assignments, as his high-octane fastball married with a solid slider and split-finger made him a natural for the role. His shortcomings as a starter, endurance and control, were mitigated and his strengths highlighted. He held opponents below a .200 average regardless of when he entered the game and he never went through the order more than once. Obviously, the Rays would prefer five Blake Snells in the rotation, but there probably will be room for one Ryne Stanek in 2019 as they continue their most recent pitching strategy.

Hunter Wood RHP Born: 08/12/93 Age: 25 Bats: R Throws: R Height: 6'1" Weight: 165 Origin: Round 29, 2013 Draft (#878 overall)

YEAR	TEAM	LVL	AGE	W	L	SV	G	GS	IP	H	HR	BB/9	K/9	K	GB%	BABIP	WHIP	ERA	DRA	WARP	MPH	FB%	WHF	CSP
2016	PCH	A+	22	3	3	0	11	9	63²	34	2	3.4	7.9	56	48%	.194	0.91	1.70	3.96	1.1				
2016	MNT	AA	22	6	2	0	10	9	49¹	36	5	3.6	8.9	49	25%	.250	1.14	3.28	3.27	1.1				
2017	TBA	MLB	23	0	0	0	1	0	0¹	0	0	0.0	0.0	0	0%	.000	0.00	0.00	4.12	0.0	89.7	40	0	38.2
2017	MNT	AA	23	4	4	0	12	12	70	68	7	3.1	8.7	68	38%	.319	1.31	4.76	3.61	1.3				
2017	DUR	AAA	23	3	1	0	19	6	53¹	54	8	3.4	7.9	47	46%	.299	1.39	4.39	4.12	0.8				
2018	DUR	AAA	24	2	2	3	24	2	42	26	4	2.1	13.5	63	46%	.262	0.86	3.00	2.26	1.4				
2018	TBA	MLB	24	1	1	0	29	8	41	42	4	4.0	9.2	42	44%	.330	1.46	3.73	2.97	1.0	96.1	52.7	14.4	45.6
2019	TBA	MLB	25	2	1	0	45	0	47¹	39	6	3.7	10.0	52	40%	.275	1.23	4.03	4.35	0.7	95.8	53.9	14.6	43.4

Breakout: 11%   Improve: 44%   Collapse: 21%   Attrition: 26%   MLB: 74%   Comparables: Steven Matz, Nick Tropeano, Jose Capellan

Wood was another hybrid for Tampa Bay, but unlike for most, it's a role he's held for a little bit. Wood split his 140 minor-league appearances almost evenly, with 73 starts and 67 as a reliever. He pitches mainly off a mid-90s fastball, with a cutter coming in just a few notches slower. He can also throw a changeup and mixes in a slow curveball. The hook was very useful, holding batters to a .179 average, and it was the put-away offering on 35 percent of his strikeouts. At some point there will be a numbers crunch as some of the Rays' younger arms mature and get healthy. Wood would be on the bubble, but he has the skill set to be useful even in a regular relief sense.

Ryan Yarbrough LHP Born: 12/31/91 Age: 27 Bats: R Throws: L Height: 6'5" Weight: 205 Origin: Round 4, 2014 Draft (#111 overall)

YEAR	TEAM	LVL	AGE	W	L	SV	G	GS	IP	H	HR	BB/9	K/9	K	GB%	BABIP	WHIP	ERA	DRA	WARP	MPH	FB%	WHF	CSP
2016	WTN	AA	24	12	4	0	25	25	128¹	112	7	2.2	6.9	99	50%	.276	1.11	2.95	3.25	2.8				
2017	DUR	AAA	25	13	6	0	26	26	157¹	144	20	2.2	9.1	159	47%	.296	1.16	3.43	3.41	4.0	91.1	63.9	10	50.6
2018	TBA	MLB	26	16	6	0	38	6	147¹	140	18	3.1	7.8	128	39%	.288	1.29	3.91	4.82	0.3	90.6	64.6	10.1	51.2
2019	TBA	MLB	27	6	4	0	93	10	117²	109	16	3.1	8.1	105	43%	.280	1.27	4.44	4.81	1.0	90.6	64.6	10.1	51.2

Breakout: 29%   Improve: 50%   Collapse: 16%   Attrition: 23%   MLB: 84%   Comparables: Joe Saunders, Jacob deGrom, Brandon Workman

The Rays' appointed bulk guy, Yarbrough was a starter for the majority of his career prior to 2018. He started just six times in his rookie season, yet recorded 16 wins and tossed nearly 150 innings as the follower to the Rays' opener strategy. One day, he'll be a fascinating arbitration case, combining the workload of a fifth starter with the appearances of a middle reliever. Of his 32 relief appearances, 11 of them lasted at least five innings, including one seven-inning effort. The poster boy for why the Rays employ such a strategy, the lefty posted a 3.31 FIP the first time though the order and a 5.36 FIP in the rare instances he flipped a lineup twice. Despite being 6-foot-5, he's a finesse lefty with an average heater below 90 mph. He uses a cutter with similar velocity almost as much as the straight fastball, and spins a slider and changeup to balance things out. The tandem (or law firm) of Stanek and Yarbrough represent the ideal pairing for the Rays' strategy. They are opposite in hand and stuff, with some warts in full-time roles, but mixed together you get almost the same first name and 200 pretty good innings.

LINEOUTS

Hitters

HITTER	POS	TEAM	LVL	AGE	PA	R	2B	3B	HR	RBI	BB	K	SB	CS	AVG/OBP/SLG	DRC+	VORP	BABIP	BRR	FRAA	WARP
Ryan Boldt	OF	MNT	AA	23	273	40	12	6	7	34	24	58	12	2	.274/.348/.461	115	16.4	.330	-0.4	RF(35): 4.1, LF(18): -2.5	1.2
Tanner Dodson	OF	HUD	A-	21	224	30	7	3	2	19	20	34	8	3	.273/.344/.369	114	9.4	.315	1.9	CF(30): 0.1, P(9): 0.6	1.2
Lucius Fox	SS	PCH	A+	20	404	54	17	1	2	30	42	79	23	7	.282/.371/.353	109	22.3	.358	2.1	SS(79): -1.5	2.1
	SS	MNT	AA	20	120	14	3	1	1	9	8	20	6	2	.221/.284/.298	87	1.3	.259	0.6	SS(26): -0.7	0.3
Tyler Frank	INF	HUD	A-	21	226	37	14	1	2	22	33	28	3	3	.288/.425/.412	145	24.3	.325	0.7	2B(24): 0.8, SS(19): 1.5	2.4
Joe McCarthy	1B	DUR	AAA	24	191	31	13	1	8	25	25	43	3	1	.269/.377/.513	116	11.2	.315	-1.5	LF(19): -1.9, CF(15): 0.8	0.6
Adam Moore	C	DUR	AAA	34	208	18	11	1	4	30	11	50	0	0	.219/.260/.347	73	-6.2	.273	-1.5	C(44): -2.2	-0.2
	C	TBA	MLB	34	20	2	1	0	1	2	1	7	0	0	.222/.263/.444	68	1.1	.300	-0.3	C(8): -1.7	-0.2
David Rodriguez	C	PCH	A+	22	117	18	8	1	2	20	8	23	1	0	.317/.385/.471	108	11.3	.388	-1.1	C(26): -0.4	0.5
	C	MNT	AA	22	276	23	13	1	4	44	21	59	2	1	.230/.286/.337	83	0.6	.281	-0.8	C(44): -3.4, 1B(2): -0.2	-0.1
Nick Schnell	OF	RAY	Rk	18	82	8	4	1	1	4	14	23	2	6	.239/.378/.373	84	2.8	.349	-2.7	CF(13): -1.3, RF(5): -0.7	-0.4
Jake Smolinski	CF	OAK	MLB	29	41	2	1	1	0	2	1	10	1	0	.128/.171/.205	63	-5.4	.172	0.1	CF(15): 0.4, P(1): 0.0	0.0
	CF	NAS	AAA	29	145	25	4	0	10	19	18	42	1	0	.278/.372/.548	116	15.6	.338	1.5	CF(30): -2.7, RF(4): -0.7	0.6
Jesus Sucre	C	TBA	MLB	30	198	9	5	0	1	17	9	29	1	0	.209/.247/.253	75	-9.0	.240	-1.8	C(71): -4.2, P(2): 0.0	-0.2
Kean Wong	2B	DUR	AAA	23	502	65	23	3	9	50	40	112	7	3	.282/.345/.406	104	17.4	.354	1.5	2B(80): 0.8, LF(24): 1.2	2.0

Ryan Boldt, a 2016 second-round pick, upped his power at Double-A and was named to the Southern League All-Star team before a season-ending injury in June. ⓧ His upside is likely higher as a pitcher, but 2018 second-round pick **Tanner Dodson** also fared well as a center fielder in his dual-role pro debut after hitting .310 in two seasons playing both ways at Cal. He lacks power, but Dodson is a switch-hitter with good plate discipline and enough speed to be an asset defensively. ⓧ **Lucius Fox** hasn't hit for any power yet, but he draws walks, steals bases and is the best defensive shortstop in the Rays' system. ⓧ Overshadowed in high school by no. 5 overall pick Jonathan India, **Tyler Frank** went off the board 51 spots later after starring at Florida Atlantic. Primarily a shortstop, he also caught some in college and could wind up in a do-everything role. ⓧ **Joe McCarthy** was limited to 47 games due to a back injury and then suffered a broken hand in the Arizona Fall League. He gets a mulligan in 2019. ⓧ **Adam Moore** is not allowed in Canada and may not be allowed in the major leagues again either. ⓧ Once an offensive prospect, **David Rodriguez** is still around because of his defense behind the plate. ⓧ Drafted 32nd overall and signed away from Louisville for $2.3 million, **Nick Schnell** has a chance to develop into a middle-of-the-order bat in an outfield corner. ⓧ **Jake Smolinski** is an adequate fifth outfielder who hasn't stayed healthy and should not be allowed to bat against righties. He's also the player who looks most like Taylor Lautner, which should count for more than it does. ⓧ **Jesus Sucre** was among MLB's worst hitters last season and, despite a reputation from teammates as a plus behind the plate, the numbers there also frowned upon him. ⓧ The 13th overall pick in the 2015 draft, **Garrett Whitley** missed the entire 2018 season with a torn labrum. ⓧ Brother Kolton was big mad when **Keon Wong** did not get a September call-up. No word on how he felt about him not being added to the 40-man roster this winter.

Pitchers

PITCHER	TEAM	LVL	AGE	W	L	SV	G	GS	IP	H	HR	BB/9	K/9	K	GB%	BABIP	WHIP	ERA	DRA	WARP	MPH	FB%	WHF	CSP
Anthony Banda	TBA	MLB	24	1	0	0	3	1	14²	12	1	1.8	6.1	10	49%	.262	1.02	3.68	4.75	0.1	95.8	77.8	10.6	57
	DUR	AAA	24	4	3	0	8	8	42	43	3	3.9	10.5	49	40%	.360	1.45	3.64	3.83	0.8				
Tanner Dodson	HUD	A-	21	1	0	1	9	0	25	12	0	1.8	9.0	25	57%	.200	0.68	1.44	2.62	0.7				
Wilmer Font	LAN	MLB	28	0	2	0	6	0	10¹	18	5	0.9	6.1	7	42%	.371	1.84	11.32	7.05	-0.2	96.2	69.5	8.9	51.7
	OAK	MLB	28	0	0	0	4	0	6²	13	5	5.4	12.1	9	33%	.421	2.55	14.85	3.80	0.1	96.9	68.5	13.6	41.8
	TBA	MLB	28	2	1	0	9	5	27	15	2	3.7	6.7	20	45%	.178	0.96	1.67	6.46	-0.4	97.6	63.6	9.7	49
Andrew Kittredge	DUR	AAA	28	6	0	2	21	1	46	41	3	2.3	11.3	58	39%	.317	1.15	2.74	1.94	1.7				
	TBA	MLB	28	3	2	0	33	3	38¹	54	7	4.0	7.0	30	51%	.373	1.85	7.75	6.06	-0.5	94.8	39.8	10.5	47.1
Adam Kolarek	DUR	AAA	29	5	1	4	31	1	44²	35	1	2.4	10.5	52	64%	.306	1.05	1.61	3.25	1.0				
	TBA	MLB	29	1	0	2	31	0	34¹	38	0	1.3	5.0	19	59%	.328	1.25	3.93	4.25	0.3	93.0	63.7	10.1	53.4
Rollie Lacy	SBN	A	22	4	1	0	16	10	71¹	54	3	2.5	10.6	84	64%	.283	1.04	2.02	3.19	1.6				
	MYR	A+	22	1	1	0	2	2	9¹	11	2	3.9	9.6	10	59%	.360	1.61	5.79	3.86	0.2				
	DEB	A+	22	1	2	0	6	6	28¹	26	1	4.1	8.6	27	56%	.321	1.38	4.45	4.37	0.3				
Resly Linares	BGR	A	20	7	3	0	17	17	84¹	69	6	2.7	10.4	97	43%	.300	1.11	3.20	3.56	1.6				
Michael Mercado	HUD	A-	19	1	2	0	11	11	50	55	6	2.9	6.8	38	52%	.308	1.42	5.22	3.68	0.9				
Ryan Merritt	COH	AAA	26	3	3	0	15	13	71¹	82	10	0.3	6.6	52	46%	.326	1.18	3.79	4.12	1.1				
Hoby Milner	PHI	MLB	27	0	0	0	10	0	4²	6	1	5.8	7.7	4	41%	.312	1.93	7.71	8.40	-0.2	91.4	69.8	4.7	45.3
	LEH	AAA	27	2	1	0	25	0	26¹	21	2	4.8	9.6	28	46%	.288	1.33	2.39	3.86	0.4				
	DUR	AAA	27	1	0	2	15	1	14¹	14	1	1.9	13.2	21	43%	.382	1.19	3.77	3.40	0.3				
	TBA	MLB	27	0	0	0	4	0	2²	3	2	6.8	13.5	4	14%	.200	1.88	6.75	9.61	-0.1	90.5	62.5	10.9	49.3
Andrew Moore	ARK	AA	24	3	1	0	9	9	50¹	38	6	2.5	8.4	47	35%	.246	1.03	3.04	4.96	0.2				
	DUR	AAA	24	6	7	0	17	15	83	90	15	3.1	5.7	53	33%	.280	1.43	4.34	6.95	-1.3				
Tobias Myers	BGR	A	19	10	6	0	23	21	119	127	11	3.1	7.6	101	36%	.326	1.41	3.71	5.14	0.0				
Vidal Nuno	DUR	AAA	30	3	1	0	8	7	40¹	38	6	0.7	8.3	37	49%	.281	1.02	3.57	3.63	0.9				
	TBA	MLB	30	3	0	0	17	0	33	24	5	2.7	7.9	29	31%	.216	1.03	1.64	4.39	0.2	91.3	14.8	12.2	51.4
Austin Pruitt	DUR	AAA	28	3	0	1	14	4	39²	26	2	1.6	11.1	49	49%	.261	0.83	2.95	2.06	1.5				
	TBA	MLB	28	2	3	4	23	0	69²	72	7	2.1	5.4	42	50%	.289	1.26	4.65	3.66	1.0	93.2	44	10.3	50.6
Chaz Roe	TBA	MLB	31	1	3	1	61	0	50¹	35	6	2.9	9.5	53	48%	.242	1.01	3.58	3.71	0.7	93.9	47.4	11.7	49.4

Acquired from Arizona in the Steven Souza swap, **Anthony Banda** had Tommy John surgery in the middle of last season and may miss 2019 as well. ⓧ Acquired from the Dodgers for Logan Forsythe after the Twins turned them down for Brian Dozier, **Jose De Leon** had his Tommy John surgery early enough to potentially make it back to the majors in 2019. ⓧ Drafted out of Cal as a legitimate two-way player, 2018 second-round pick **Tanner Dodson** is considered a better prospect on the mound and showed why as he dominated the New York-Penn League. He closed in college and worked as a multi-inning reliever in his pro debut, but Dodson has the secondary offerings to potentially start. ⓧ Traded on April 25 and then again on May 25, **Wilmer Font** showed some promise with the Rays before getting hurt in June and missing the rest of the season. ⓧ Cuban signee **Sandy Gaston** received a $2.6 million bonus for throwing the ball insanely hard for a 16-year-old. ⓧ **Andrew Kittredge** struggled in every role for the Rays in 2018 and also looks like he needs sleep in every photo. ⓧ **Adam Kolarek** is a viable second lefty in the pen with good control, but seems destined to be an up-and-down arm. ⓧ With Eddie Butler's poor performance, the onus falls on **Rollie Lacy** to be the return for the Cole Hamels trade. Ooh, *ouch*, it looks like that onus hit him pretty squarely. Rollie? Buddy? Are you oka— ahh, okay, yeah. He says he's fine. ⓧ A finesse lefty with a chance to grow into more, **Resly Linares** signed with the Rays for $275,000 in the same international class as Jesus Sanchez and Diego Castillo. ⓧ The Rays' second-round pick in 2017, right-hander **Michael Mercado**, struggled in his short-season assignment. ⓧ **Ryan Merritt** is a nice emergency starter, but there's a reason the left-hander and his high-80s fastball haven't had a chance to do more than that so far. ⓧ If you're going to play baseball and be named **Hoby Milner**, you pretty much have to be one of a) a glove-first middle infielder, b) a journeyman LOOGY, c) a bullpen catcher. Our protagonist chose door no. 2. ⓧ **Andrew Moore** may or may not be allowed in Canada. He will definitely need to pitch better to justify continuing to hold a 40-man roster spot. ⓧ **Tobias Myers**, acquired from the Orioles for Tim Beckham in mid-2017, has the potential to be a quality starter with three above-average pitches. ⓧ **Vidal Nuno** still pitches in the major leagues sometimes, but was not even the best Vidal in his own organization last season. ⓧ Now entering the game, **Austin Pruitt**. If you hear this in the ballpark, you can leave. If you hear this on the television at home, go spend time with your family. ⓧ **Chaz Roe** threw his slider 53 percent of the time last season, topping 50 innings in the majors for the first time at age 31. The slider is good, and he leans on the side of ground balls, but without much else he's limited to the platoon advantage.

TEXAS RANGERS

Essay by Chris Cwik

Player comments by Levi Weaver and BP staff

Baseball has experienced an influx of knowledge over the past 15 years. The value of on-base percentage was discovered and re-discovered, fielders realized they'd often been standing in the wrong place the last hundred-odd years, catchers are being signed specifically because they can frame well and the metrics once limited to the pages of "Baseball Prospectus" have appeared frequently on MLB Network. And yet despite all of that innovation, we're still no closer to understanding how pitchers work.

It doesn't matter whether they receive a normal workload or whether they get wrapped in bubble wrap, pitchers remain unpredictable. They get hurt. Their stuff backs up. Their killer changeup that worked in rookie ball suddenly twists straight at bats as they move up the ladder. Pitchers exist to break your heart, and the Rangers have suffered a lot of heartbreak over the years.

The pitcher most synonymous with the franchise is Nolan Ryan, who only played for the team for five seasons, and whose freakish durability remains the stuff of legend. Ryan may not have been the best pitcher in history, but he might have been the most consistent pitcher in history. He showed up every start, always seemed to have the same stuff, year after year. But Ryan wasn't drafted or developed by the Rangers. He came to the team a finished product.

That's been a common refrain for the organization throughout its history. Many of the best pitchers to suit up for the Rangers established themselves elsewhere and were either signed as free agents or brought in via trades. In the 47 years they've existed, the Rangers have failed to draft and develop a bonafide ace.

Sure, the team has had a few successes. Kenny Rogers and Kevin Brown both put up solid numbers, though accumulated much of their value away from the team. Derek Holland was OK. Colby Lewis needed a stint in Japan, but he eventually produced. Edinson Volquez had some decent seasons after being traded away. Those players represent some of the team's biggest pitching wins. The losses have been far more numerous and—sorry, Rangers fans—include players like Kevin Mathews, Chad Hawkins, Corey Lee, Eric Hurley, Thomas Diamond, Blake Beavan…the list goes on and on and on some more.

RANGERS PROSPECTUS
2018 W-L: 67-95, 5TH IN AL WEST

Pythag	.433	21st	B-Age		27.5	10th
RS/G	4.55	14th	P-Age		31.0	30th
RA/G	5.23	28th	Salary		$133.1M	16th
DRC+	98	13th	M$/MW		$6.5M	5th
DRA	5.87	30th	DL Days		1600	28th
FIP	4.82	29th	$ on DL		14%	11th
DER	.701	21st				

- Opened 1994
- Open air
- Natural surface
- Fence profile: 8' to 14'

Three-Year Park Factors

Runs	Runs/RH	Runs/LH	HR/RH	HR/LH
108	108	108	104	107

Top Hitter WARP	3.0 Joey Gallo
Top Pitcher WARP	1.4 Jose Leclerc
Top Prospect	Leody Taveras

2018 Hit List Ranking

Committed Payroll (in millions)

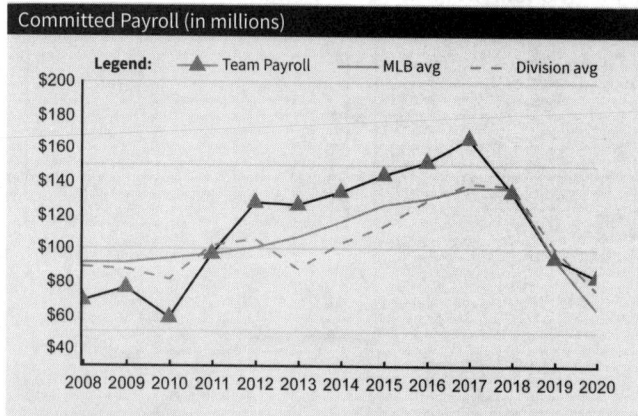

Farm System Ranking

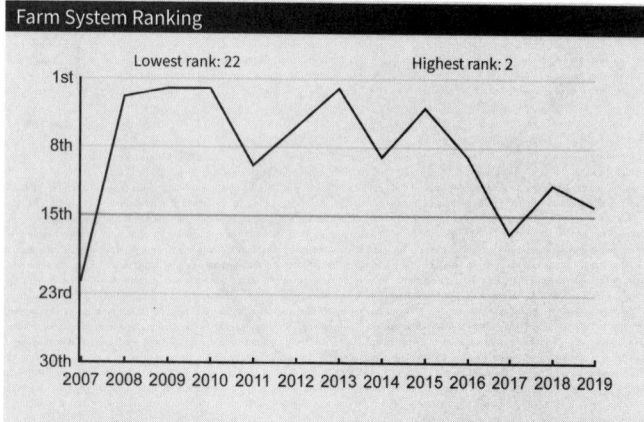

Personnel

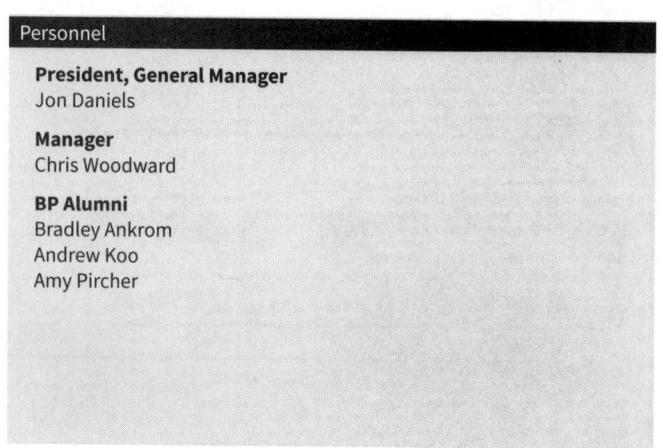

President, General Manager
Jon Daniels

Manager
Chris Woodward

BP Alumni
Bradley Ankrom
Andrew Koo
Amy Pircher

It's not for lack of trying. The team has tried various approaches to finding its first home-grown ace. They tried the aggressive straight-to-the-majors method with David Clyde, then watched him fall apart before he could buy alcohol. They tried the break-em-in-as-a-reliever method with Neftali Feliz. They drafted 24 pitchers in the first or supplemental round in the past 18 years in hopes that throwing more pitchers at the problem might solve it. They even tried to bring Ryan back as team president so he could get pitchers on his old throwing program. None of those strategies worked.

Now, the Rangers are fully ensconced in a multiyear rebuild; the veterans have been distributed to other teams or been handed severance packages, and the rotation is stocked with injury-riddled bounce-back candidates like Mike Minor and Drew Smyly, auditioning for deadline deals to contenders. Few of the pitchers on this roster will see the next good Rangers team. In an attempt to buck their historical struggles and finally develop a couple top-line starters—or perhaps out of desperation—the Rangers are trying an inventive and controversial new pitching strategy. The team is attempting to develop pitching prospects by not having them throw a single pitch.

Before you panic and declare the Rangers everything wrong with baseball today, understand it isn't as drastic as it sounds. Over the past three years, the Rangers have selected certain high school draftees as candidates for something they call their de-load program.

The de-load program gives young pitchers in the organization an opportunity to learn every aspect of pitching without having them take the mound in games until the following June, according to the team's director of minor-league operations Paul Kruger. "We really wanted to spend as much time as we could educating them on baseball, injury prevention, growing their bodies naturally...while also learning the values of having a good throwing program," he says. "It was like a truly comprehensive orientation to professional baseball and pitching as a professional." Kruger, who has been with the team since 2009, was one of the main proponents of the idea. He was joined by pitching coordinator Danny Clark, who has been with the club for 14 years.

They helped launch the program in 2016, though some changes have been made since then. Initially, pitchers were allowed to throw a few innings before the end of the year. Last season was the first year the pitchers in the de-load program did not throw a single pitch in a game the year they were drafted. Despite those changes, one thing has always remained consistent. The program is just for a handful of high school draftees. Only five pitchers went through the de-load program in 2018.

There are reasons the team only puts high school pitchers through the program. The human body is still developing quite a bit between 18 and 22, according to Kruger, and there's no reason to push those players considering how much they threw prior to getting drafted. Another part of it deals with the extreme life changes that come with entering professional baseball straight out of high school.

"You are going from a small town where you are really the star—you're the show," Kruger says. "To a professional on your own, staying at a hotel, having to cook your own meals and you're getting a paycheck, just balancing all these different things. Oh wait, and you have to play baseball?"

Mostly, though, it just made sense to Clark and Kruger. To them, the transition from high school to pro ball should be just like any other job. "You go into any job and you get trained," Clark says. "And then you do the job. And I just feel like that was one of the things I always thought about: Educating our players in all aspects before we allow them to go and compete."

None of this comes as a surprise to the players selected to take part in the de-load program. The team meets with each player and their families to talk about the decision. During those meetings, the team lays out a complete calendar from the day the pitcher was drafted through June of the following year. The Rangers make sure everyone involved is on board with the idea before a pitcher joined the program.

Even though the players know what they're getting into, there's still an urge to compete, especially when they see other players take the mound. But the players who have gone through the program have said nothing but good things about it. "When they first hear about it, it's kinda like 'what,'" Clark says. "Then they get into it. When they come out of it, I've heard nothing but raves about it."

Players who have not gone through the program have expressed regret that they weren't able to do it, according to Kruger. But that doesn't mean the de-load program has been a complete success. The group of players who have gone through it—which includes Alex Speas, Cole Ragans, Scott Engler, Tyree Thompson, Tai Tiedemann, Hans Crouse, Seth Nordlin, Cole Winn, Owen White, Destin Dotson, among others—has experienced varying degrees of struggle in the brief time they've taken the mound. Despite the team carefully monitoring workload, both Speas and Ragans

needed to undergo Tommy John surgery. Clark was hesitant to say their reduced usage led to the injuries, but couldn't fully rule it out either.

"Did that contribute, who knows? I would hate to say that slowing the process had to do with what injury came into play," he says.

Given the players involved in the de-load program, it's going to be years before anyone knows whether it's paying off. High school players generally need at least a few seasons before they reach the majors. Once they get there, it could take a couple more before they're considered finished products. Drawing conclusions on any of these players five years after they are drafted might be too soon, and five years is a long time in baseball. Coaching staffs and front offices have been cleaned out and turned over in shorter amounts of time. Even if those pitchers fail, it might not be a result of the de-load program. It could easily be a case of pitchers being pitchers.

So why do it?

Sticking with the status quo hasn't led to success for the Rangers. After trying to develop pitchers every other way, the team decided a drastic departure from the norm was worth a shot.

The Rangers don't need the de-load program to solve the pitcher, they just need it to help. While an army of aces would be nice, one top-line starter and a few mid-rotation assets would be a massive upgrade over what the team has experienced lately. This season will be crucial in determining whether that's going to happen. While the pitchers in the de-load program likely won't pitch in the majors in 2019, their health and development will give the team a window into whether the counterintuitive process will be talked about as a major breakthrough within the game 15 years from now.

Until then, the Rangers have brought back Volquez to eat some innings until the students of the de-load program are ready to graduate to the majors. Because innovation and desperation are a lot closer than anyone is willing to admit. ▮

—Chris Cwik is a writer at Yahoo! Sports.

HITTERS

Elvis Andrus SS Born: 08/26/88 Age: 30 Bats: R Throws: R Height: 6'0" Weight: 200 Origin: International Free Agent, 2005

YEAR	TEAM	LVL	AGE	PA	R	2B	3B	HR	RBI	BB	K	SB	CS	AVG/OBP/SLG	DRC+	VORP	BABIP	BRR	FRAA	WARP
2016	TEX	MLB	27	568	75	31	7	8	69	47	70	24	8	.302/.362/.439	108	34.6	.333	1.4	SS(147): -4.1	3.0
2017	TEX	MLB	28	689	100	44	4	20	88	38	101	25	10	.297/.337/.471	104	37.8	.325	2.8	SS(157): 16.2	5.5
2018	TEX	MLB	29	428	53	20	3	6	33	28	66	5	3	.256/.308/.367	91	9.4	.292	0.5	SS(97): -6.4	0.9
2019	TEX	MLB	30	614	70	31	4	13	67	45	93	18	7	.273/.331/.416	103	26.5	.304	1.0	SS -1	2.8

Breakout: 4%   Improve: 44%   Collapse: 10%   Attrition: 15%   MLB: 100%   *Comparables: Oscar Robles, Erick Aybar, Rafael Furcal*

Andrus entered 2018 as one of the storylines to keep an eye on: If he had a third consecutive season of improvement as part of his elite-offensive-shortstop renaissance, he might be more likely to opt out of his contract after the season and explore free agency. Instead, a Keynan Middleton fastball broke a bone in his right elbow and even after his return it took him awhile to get back in the groove at the plate. He chose to remain in Texas, with four years and $58 million left on his deal. However, he has another opt-out after the 2019 season, so let's hit the snooze button on that question and come back to it in a year.

Jett Bandy C   Born: 03/26/90   Age: 29   Bats: R   Throws: R   Height: 6'4"   Weight: 235   Origin: Round 31, 2011 Draft (#945 overall)

YEAR	TEAM	LVL	AGE	PA	R	2B	3B	HR	RBI	BB	K	SB	CS	AVG/OBP/SLG	DRC+	VORP	BABIP	BRR	FRAA	WARP
2016	SLC	AAA	26	105	13	7	0	2	21	2	19	2	1	.274/.314/.411	102	1.8	.312	-2.7	C(21): 1.2	0.4
2016	ANA	MLB	26	231	23	9	0	8	25	11	38	1	0	.234/.281/.392	98	4.2	.246	-2.0	C(68): 2.7	1.2
2017	CSP	AAA	27	51	7	2	0	2	14	5	5	0	1	.310/.412/.500	132	1.8	.306	-0.6	C(9): -1.5	0.2
2017	MIL	MLB	27	188	14	6	0	6	18	15	51	1	0	.207/.287/.349	82	0.1	.259	-1.9	C(50): -3.4	0.0
2018	MIL	MLB	28	71	5	2	0	1	1	3	23	0	0	.188/.268/.266	64	-0.5	.275	0.1	C(22): -1.3	-0.1
2018	CSP	AAA	28	216	23	15	0	9	35	10	32	3	0	.292/.353/.510	130	13.0	.305	-0.4	C(29): -1.0, 1B(21): -1.9	1.3
2019	TEX	MLB	29	35	4	2	0	1	4	2	7	0	0	.250/.315/.406	93	1.1	.299	-0.2	C -1	0.1

Breakout: 4%   Improve: 23%   Collapse: 12%   Attrition: 27%   MLB: 67%

Comparables: Carlos Ruiz, Josh Phegley, Curtis Casali

YEAR	TEAM	P. COUNT	FRM RUNS	BLK RUNS	THRW RUNS	TOT RUNS
2016	ANA	8749	-1.0	1.5	1.9	1.7
2017	CSP	1201	-1.0	-0.3	0.0	-1.0
2017	MIL	6970	-2.4	-0.8	-0.8	-4.6
2018	CSP	4214	-0.9	0.0	0.1	-0.8
2018	MIL	2860	-0.6	-0.5	0.1	-1.2
2019	TEX	1347	-0.5	0.0	0.0	-0.5

Even though the surface stats in the majors suggest the dream ended for Bandy in 2018, the depth catcher made things interesting at Triple-A Colorado Springs. Bandy raked for the Sky Sox, even with the inflated offensive environment taken into consideration, and established himself as a Quad-A player who might get another MLB shot in a catching-starved league. Indeed, Bandy's own parent club demonstrated that playable catchers can be old and still (seemingly) come out of nowhere, so it's not yet time to give up hope of a future MLB role. The problem is that even if Bandy made adjustments that help the bat play, the glove lagged behind, making it more difficult to see someone taking a chance on the overall profile.

Adrian Beltre 3B   Born: 04/07/79   Age: 40   Bats: R   Throws: R   Height: 5'11"   Weight: 220   Origin: International Free Agent, 1994

YEAR	TEAM	LVL	AGE	PA	R	2B	3B	HR	RBI	BB	K	SB	CS	AVG/OBP/SLG	DRC+	VORP	BABIP	BRR	FRAA	WARP
2016	TEX	MLB	37	640	89	31	1	32	104	48	66	1	1	.300/.358/.521	137	39.8	.293	-3.5	3B(141): 4.8	5.4
2017	TEX	MLB	38	389	47	22	1	17	71	39	52	1	0	.312/.383/.532	132	23.6	.321	-2.9	3B(65): 7.5	3.3
2018	TEX	MLB	39	481	49	23	1	15	65	34	96	1	0	.273/.328/.434	110	13.4	.312	-0.7	3B(70): 2.8	2.2
2019	TEX	MLB	40	436	51	24	2	14	57	38	70	1	0	.280/.352/.456	121	18.8	.312	-1.7	3B 4	2.4

Breakout: 0%   Improve: 20%   Collapse: 10%   Attrition: 16%   MLB: 71%   *Comparables: Melvin Mora, Graig Nettles, Moises Alou*

It's easy to like the player who keeps things light, lets his personality show on the field and is constantly just *messing* with people, and many fans fell in love with Beltre because he was among the all-time best at it. He kept the clubhouse in check, mentored the younger players and showed them how to be big leaguers, both on and off the field, making him one of the most respected teammates of his era. It's easy to root for the grinder, the gamer who keeps coming back from injuries (including the removal of part of a colon, a testicular contusion, a torn thumb ligament, a back injury and calf and hamstring issues) to remains an effective player until the end of his no-doubt Hall of Fame career. Baseball fans who watched the game during the Adrian Beltre years are lucky fans indeed, and his retirement leaves a void in the sport that may never be filled.

Willie Calhoun LF   Born: 11/04/94   Age: 24   Bats: L   Throws: R   Height: 5'8"   Weight: 187   Origin: Round 4, 2015 Draft (#132 overall)

YEAR	TEAM	LVL	AGE	PA	R	2B	3B	HR	RBI	BB	K	SB	CS	AVG/OBP/SLG	DRC+	VORP	BABIP	BRR	FRAA	WARP
2016	TUL	AA	21	560	75	25	1	27	88	45	65	0	0	.254/.318/.469	130	26.2	.242	0.3	2B(119): -9.8	2.6
2017	OKL	AAA	22	414	64	24	5	23	67	36	49	3	2	.298/.357/.574	141	30.5	.289	-1.8	2B(74): 0.9, LF(12): -1.9	3.1
2017	ROU	AAA	22	120	16	3	1	8	26	6	12	1	0	.310/.345/.566	136	10.0	.290	-1.2	LF(24): 2.4, 2B(3): -0.7	0.9
2017	TEX	MLB	22	37	3	0	0	1	4	2	7	0	0	.265/.324/.353	90	1.1	.308	0.3	LF(11): -0.7	0.0
2018	ROU	AAA	23	470	66	32	0	9	47	32	47	4	0	.294/.351/.431	100	14.3	.314	-3.2	LF(91): -11.9	-0.3
2018	TEX	MLB	23	108	8	5	0	2	11	6	24	0	0	.222/.269/.333	88	-2.5	.267	-0.7	LF(27): -2.8	-0.2
2019	TEX	MLB	24	534	63	24	2	19	68	37	78	1	0	.262/.318/.438	102	10.9	.276	-0.7	LF -5	0.6

Breakout: 5%   Improve: 32%   Collapse: 16%   Attrition: 31%   MLB: 69%   *Comparables: Ramon Flores, J.D. Martinez, Jordan Luplow*

After years of wondering if Calhoun could be something other than what he is, it's becoming evident that he's really just more of a Willie Calhoun type, which is to say: He's going to mash and he's going to play defense that causes you to reflexively make a sound that goes from low to high like a slide whistle. (But a few octaves lower. Go on, try it. You'll recognize it. OOOOOOOooo°°°•••...)

Calhoun was disappointed to start the season in Triple-A, and his stats showed it. In April, he hit .229 with a .673 OPS. But he improved in each successive month, ultimately hitting .429 with an 1.139 OPS in July. He tapered off a bit in August before his call-up, and again hit well enough in the big leagues to suggest the bat is ready, but the defense is really nothing to write home about. Ideally, you could plug Calhoun in at designated hitter and just let him go wild. But — at least at time of this writing — Shin-Soo Choo is still a Ranger, so while the prairie sky may be wide and high *CLAP CLAP CLAP CLAP* DH is full in Texas.

Shin-Soo Choo OF   Born: 07/13/82   Age: 36   Bats: L   Throws: L   Height: 5'11"   Weight: 210   Origin: International Free Agent, 2000

YEAR	TEAM	LVL	AGE	PA	R	2B	3B	HR	RBI	BB	K	SB	CS	AVG/OBP/SLG	DRC+	VORP	BABIP	BRR	FRAA	WARP
2016	TEX	MLB	33	210	27	7	0	7	17	25	46	6	3	.242/.357/.399	107	5.8	.288	-0.6	RF(43): -0.4	0.6
2017	TEX	MLB	34	636	96	20	1	22	78	77	134	12	3	.261/.357/.423	108	11.1	.305	0.7	RF(77): -1.5	1.8
2018	TEX	MLB	35	665	83	30	1	21	62	92	156	6	1	.264/.377/.434	115	25.7	.330	-0.9	RF(34): -2.0, LF(26): -0.6	2.2
2019	TEX	MLB	36	522	69	23	2	15	55	61	116	6	2	.250/.350/.405	110	14.3	.307	-0.4	RF -1, LF -1	1.4

Breakout: 3%   Improve: 26%   Collapse: 13%   Attrition: 21%   MLB: 79%   *Comparables: Lyle Overbay, John Wockenfuss, Adam LaRoche*

Choo had one of his best seasons in 2018, appearing in his first All-Star game at age 35 and stringing together a 52-game on-base streak. Will the continued productivity — combined with the fact that he has only two years left on what was once a behemoth contract — mean the Rangers will eat a glutton-sized serving of salary and make him the latest casualty of the three-year Arlington Purge? Probably not as a standalone equation, but once you factor in the Rangers' dearth of pitching and surfeit of left-handed corner bats, it all starts to add up. Or maybe "subtract" is the better math term to use here. I don't know, man; it's a big book and there are a lot of these to write.

Delino DeShields CF Born: 08/16/92 Age: 26 Bats: R Throws: R Height: 5'9" Weight: 200 Origin: Round 1, 2010 Draft (#8 overall)

YEAR	TEAM	LVL	AGE	PA	R	2B	3B	HR	RBI	BB	K	SB	CS	AVG/OBP/SLG	DRC+	VORP	BABIP	BRR	FRAA	WARP
2016	ROU	AAA	23	249	37	10	0	3	17	35	60	21	7	.261/.367/.353	79	15.5	.349	2.4	CF(42): -5.7, LF(7): -1.9	-0.4
2016	TEX	MLB	23	203	36	7	0	4	13	15	54	8	3	.209/.275/.313	66	-0.9	.272	2.0	CF(33): 1.1, LF(26): -1.4	0.0
2017	TEX	MLB	24	440	75	15	2	6	22	44	109	29	8	.269/.347/.367	84	14.1	.358	7.6	LF(60): 4.3, CF(51): -0.5	1.6
2018	TEX	MLB	25	393	52	14	1	2	22	43	83	20	4	.216/.310/.281	72	1.1	.280	3.4	CF(102): 10.3	1.5
2019	TEX	MLB	26	456	59	17	2	7	36	45	105	23	7	.233/.315/.344	77	8.6	.285	3.9	CF 3	1.2

Breakout: 2%   Improve: 63%   Collapse: 6%   Attrition: 17%   MLB: 95%   *Comparables: Marvin Benard, Willy Taveras, Jermaine Allensworth*

The Rangers began 2018 with DeShields as their everyday leadoff man and center fielder, which made it a really bad time for him to break his hamate. His bat never looked right after that, so hopefully a full offseason will make a difference for the second-generation big leaguer. On the upside, his oft-maligned defense took major strides early in the season, though it did regress a bit as the dog days dragged on. Between the hamate, a concussion and the rise of Joey Gallo: Center Fielder, Jon Daniels declined to commit to DeShields as the Rangers' starter this season, instead saying he would have an opportunity to compete for a starting job. Now the question is whether he'll be competing for center field, left field or another team altogether.

Joey Gallo LF Born: 11/19/93 Age: 25 Bats: L Throws: R Height: 6'5" Weight: 235 Origin: Round 1, 2012 Draft (#39 overall)

YEAR	TEAM	LVL	AGE	PA	R	2B	3B	HR	RBI	BB	K	SB	CS	AVG/OBP/SLG	DRC+	VORP	BABIP	BRR	FRAA	WARP
2016	ROU	AAA	22	433	71	17	6	25	66	68	150	2	0	.240/.367/.529	135	40.0	.330	2.1	3B(44): 4.5, 1B(32): 1.4	3.8
2016	TEX	MLB	22	30	2	0	0	1	1	5	19	1	0	.040/.200/.160	48	-2.8	.000	-0.1	3B(5): 0.2, 1B(1): 0.1	-0.1
2017	TEX	MLB	23	532	85	18	3	41	80	75	196	7	2	.209/.333/.537	125	27.6	.250	0.5	3B(72): -1.8, 1B(59): 0.5	3.3
2018	TEX	MLB	24	577	82	24	1	40	92	74	207	3	4	.206/.312/.498	119	20.7	.249	1.9	LF(85): -6.3, 1B(35): 3.1	3.0
2019	TEX	MLB	25	574	79	22	2	33	89	68	201	5	2	.221/.322/.466	115	26.3	.294	1.0	LF -4, 3B 0	2.5

Breakout: 3%   Improve: 60%   Collapse: 4%   Attrition: 11%   MLB: 94%   *Comparables: Miguel Sano, Kyle Schwarber, Kris Bryant*

Gallo is the baseball equivalent of an angry monster truck that tops out at 100 mph and runs on gold-infused thrice-refined jet fuel harvested from only the southernmost tip of the Cape of Good Hope by unionized leprechauns. Sure, it's a tremendously entertaining time watching the Michael Bay-directed mayhem and destruction he wreaks upon baseballs, but how long is the team going to be able to afford the strikeouts? Gallo is never going to be a Tesla or a Prius (and the Rangers shouldn't want him to be), but as he matures, perhaps he can transition to a more reasonable number of strikeouts, like 150-160. Of course, that's the easy thing to point out about Gallo. The more fascinating issue to watch in 2019 is whether the Rangers continue the experiment of playing him in center field. He's a better athlete than many realize, and he has the tools to succeed, but it's possible the team will decide they don't want to risk the additional wear and tear on the monster truck's body (and offensive production).

Pedro Gonzalez CF Born: 10/27/97 Age: 21 Bats: R Throws: R Height: 6'5" Weight: 190 Origin: International Free Agent, 2014

YEAR	TEAM	LVL	AGE	PA	R	2B	3B	HR	RBI	BB	K	SB	CS	AVG/OBP/SLG	DRC+	VORP	BABIP	BRR	FRAA	WARP
2016	DRO	RK	18	30	3	0	1	0	6	2	4	4	1	.222/.300/.296	98	0.0	.261	-1.0	CF(7): 0.3	0.0
2016	GJR	RK	18	248	32	15	8	2	19	14	77	6	7	.230/.290/.394	66	8.6	.336	1.8	CF(57): 2.5	0.2
2017	GJR	RK	19	209	28	16	6	3	28	18	53	11	6	.321/.388/.519	90	13.6	.432	0.9	CF(41): -3.9	0.1
2018	HIC	A	20	371	47	17	5	12	46	28	110	9	5	.234/.296/.421	97	11.7	.307	1.7	CF(60): 4.7, LF(20): -1.1	1.9
2019	TEX	MLB	21	251	26	10	0	7	23	10	86	3	1	.194/.223/.326	39	-10.0	.264	-0.2	CF 0, LF 0	-1.1

Breakout: 0%   Improve: 0%   Collapse: 0%   Attrition: 1%   MLB: 1%   *Comparables: Teoscar Hernandez, Keon Broxton, Daniel Fields*

Far be it from the fine folks at BP to believe in curses, but hear us out: Since the Rangers lost Game 6 of the 2011 World Series, their first-round picks have been cursed. Consider: Lewis Brinson in 2012 and Luis Ortiz in 2014. (Chi Chi Gonzalez and Travis Demeritte were the picks in 2013, and Dillon Tate — shipped to the Yankees for a couple months' worth of Carlos Beltran in 2016 — was their 2015 selection, if you need additional context.) Not only have none of them become above-replacement big leaguers, but after Ortiz and Brinson were packaged together and sent to Milwaukee in 2016 for Jonathan Lucroy and Jeremy Jeffress, both returning players became markedly worse versions of themselves upon arrival, suggesting that the curse is transferable. Lucroy was sent to Colorado in 2017 for this Gonzalez, who showed flashes of greatness in Spokane and fall instructs, but struggled mightily in Low-A Hickory for the entirety of the 2018 season.

To break the curse, Texas needs a few things to happen. First, Gonzalez needs a big 2019 season. Next, Tayler Scott (the return for Jeffress) must become the first South African pitcher to make it to the big leagues. And lastly, David Freese must donate one-third of his bones to be ground into a paste and thrown into a volcano. Alternatively, one of Ragans (2016), Bubba Thompson (2017) or Cole Winn (2018) could just be a star in Texas, and that would set everything right.

Ronald Guzman   1B   Born: 10/20/94   Age: 24   Bats: L   Throws: L   Height: 6'5"   Weight: 225   Origin: International Free Agent, 2011

YEAR	TEAM	LVL	AGE	PA	R	2B	3B	HR	RBI	BB	K	SB	CS	AVG/OBP/SLG	DRC+	VORP	BABIP	BRR	FRAA	WARP
2016	FRI	AA	21	416	51	16	5	15	56	33	82	2	1	.288/.348/.477	132	16.6	.331	-2.5	1B(95): 4.0	2.3
2016	ROU	AAA	21	95	9	5	1	1	11	6	23	0	1	.216/.266/.330	87	-5.4	.281	-1.6	1B(20): -1.6	-0.3
2017	ROU	AAA	22	527	78	22	3	12	62	47	85	4	1	.298/.372/.434	110	20.4	.342	-0.3	1B(118): -1.6	1.2
2018	TEX	MLB	23	428	46	18	2	16	58	33	121	1	0	.235/.306/.416	92	3.0	.299	1.9	1B(117): 1.9	0.6
2019	TEX	MLB	24	535	60	23	2	17	63	43	126	1	0	.241/.315/.402	95	6.4	.295	1.3	1B 0	0.7

Breakout: 6%   Improve: 37%   Collapse: 9%   Attrition: 22%   MLB: 69%   *Comparables: Kendrys Morales, James Loney, Joey Votto*

He's super bendy, can do the splits, out-danced Astros mascot Orbit and hit a career-high (at any level) in home runs in 2018. There was some concern that he would not muster enough power and pull-side hard contact to stick at first base, but Guzman acquitted himself well in his rookie campaign, allowing the Rangers to tinker with putting Joey Gallo all over the outfield.

Scott Heineman   OF   Born: 12/04/92   Age: 26   Bats: R   Throws: R   Height: 6'1"   Weight: 215   Origin: Round 11, 2015 Draft (#318 overall)

YEAR	TEAM	LVL	AGE	PA	R	2B	3B	HR	RBI	BB	K	SB	CS	AVG/OBP/SLG	DRC+	VORP	BABIP	BRR	FRAA	WARP
2016	HDS	A+	23	610	96	39	8	17	80	59	120	30	14	.303/.386/.505	126	40.3	.360	1.2	LF(91): -3.3, CF(40): 1.3	3.4
2017	FRI	AA	24	529	82	26	7	9	44	50	121	12	9	.284/.363/.427	101	29.5	.365	6.8	LF(72): -8.5, CF(29): -2.9	0.7
2018	FRI	AA	25	31	6	2	0	1	10	7	5	2	1	.522/.613/.739	124	5.3	.611	-0.9	CF(5): -0.9, LF(2): 0.0	0.0
2018	ROU	AAA	25	469	68	20	2	11	57	32	93	16	8	.295/.355/.429	94	24.6	.353	4.0	RF(48): 1.7, CF(44): -3.3	1.2
2019	TEX	MLB	26	251	31	9	1	7	24	14	59	5	3	.236/.294/.370	80	1.9	.290	-0.2	CF -1, RF -1	-0.1

Breakout: 1%   Improve: 20%   Collapse: 13%   Attrition: 25%   MLB: 47%   *Comparables: Lane Adams, Brian Goodwin, Johnny Field*

Some minor-league coaches say you can tell which guys are going to be big leaguers just by the way they walk onto a field. One coach, when asked for an example, said: "Scott Heineman." He followed that up with, "Of course, I'm not saying he's *definitely* going to make it to the big leagues, but watch him walk." He was right — Heineman walks with an effervescent bounce that speaks volumes about his joy for the game and confidence in his abilities. The coach was probably right about him being a big leaguer as well; it would be shocking if he didn't make his debut in 2019. Frankly, it was a little surprising he didn't get a September call-up in 2018.

Isiah Kiner-Falefa   3B/C   Born: 03/23/95   Age: 24   Bats: R   Throws: R   Height: 5'10"   Weight: 176   Origin: Round 4, 2013 Draft (#130 overall)

YEAR	TEAM	LVL	AGE	PA	R	2B	3B	HR	RBI	BB	K	SB	CS	AVG/OBP/SLG	DRC+	VORP	BABIP	BRR	FRAA	WARP
2016	FRI	AA	21	457	55	8	2	0	27	41	51	6	6	.256/.341/.286	94	9.0	.293	-1.0	3B(44): 10.2, C(31): -6.2	1.8
2017	FRI	AA	22	570	58	31	3	5	48	41	72	17	6	.288/.350/.390	113	35.4	.325	0.2	3B(50): 6.4, 2B(37): 4.2	4.2
2018	TEX	MLB	23	396	43	18	2	4	34	28	62	7	5	.261/.325/.357	83	4.0	.306	-0.6	3B(46): 3.4, C(35): -10.1	0.0
2019	TEX	MLB	24	427	43	17	2	7	42	35	65	7	3	.245/.320/.357	87	8.1	.279	-0.2	C -13, 3B 5	0.2

Breakout: 4%   Improve: 32%   Collapse: 7%   Attrition: 16%   MLB: 66%   *Comparables: Willy Aybar, Blake DeWitt, Steve Lombardozzi*

Do you remember the '90s TV show *The Pretender*? It was about a guy named Jarod (pronounced like "Jared"), who was a savant and could quickly master the terminology and skills needed to blend in at any job as he evaded capture by a mysterious organization called "The Centre." One week, he would be a doctor, scanning through a book and then performing a complex surgery, and then the next week, he was a rodeo clown. Kiner-Falefa did not start catching until his fourth year as a professional and played just 69 games at

YEAR	TEAM	P. COUNT	FRM RUNS	BLK RUNS	THRW RUNS	TOT RUNS
2017	FRI	4556	-1.1	-0.8	0.0	-1.7
2018	TEX	4896	-9.9	-1.0	0.0	-10.9
2019	TEX	7347	-12.1	-1.4	0.0	-13.4

catcher in the minor leagues, but donned the tools of ignorance in 35 of his 111 big-league games in his rookie campaign, and did reasonably well. The Hawaiian Army Knife also played second base, shortstop and third base in the bigs (after playing all of the above plus left field, center field and one game at first base in the minor leagues). If the Rangers have another cow-milking contest in 2019, Kiner-Falefa will watch one YouTube video and then invent a new method that becomes the industry standard.

Julio Pablo Martinez   CF   Born: 03/21/96   Age: 23   Bats: L   Throws: L   Height: 5'9"   Weight: 174   Origin: International Free Agent, 2018

YEAR	TEAM	LVL	AGE	PA	R	2B	3B	HR	RBI	BB	K	SB	CS	AVG/OBP/SLG	DRC+	VORP	BABIP	BRR	FRAA	WARP
2018	DRG	RK	22	33	10	1	1	1	3	9	7	1	3	.409/.606/.682	128	11.5	.571	2.2	CF(5): 0.4, LF(1): -0.2	0.4
2018	SPO	A-	22	273	49	9	5	8	21	34	69	11	6	.252/.351/.436	108	16.4	.323	0.5	CF(55): 1.5, LF(2): 0.1	1.3
2019	TEX	MLB	23	251	29	5	1	9	25	18	83	3	2	.180/.237/.323	49	-6.3	.229	-0.2	CF 1, LF 0	-0.6

Breakout: 0%   Improve: 2%   Collapse: 2%   Attrition: 4%   MLB: 4%   *Comparables: Blake Tekotte, Michael Taylor, Keon Broxton*

The young Cuban was the Rangers' consolation prize for not winning the Shohei Ohtani sweepstakes, and after signing with Texas he utterly demolished the Dominican Summer League for seven whole games before Texas moved him to Spokane, where he was, in order, pretty okay, pretty good and then *really* good in six playoff games, hitting .348/.423/.696. He didn't let up on the gas pedal when the season ended, either, hitting .327/.397/.519 in the Arizona Fall League. He won't be in the big leagues in 2019, but when Texas is ready to contend again, there's a good chance they'll be doing so with Martinez in the outfield.

Jeff Mathis   C   Born: 03/31/83   Age: 36   Bats: R   Throws: R   Height: 6'0"   Weight: 205   Origin: Round 1, 2001 Draft (#33 overall)

YEAR	TEAM	LVL	AGE	PA	R	2B	3B	HR	RBI	BB	K	SB	CS	AVG/OBP/SLG	DRC+	VORP	BABIP	BRR	FRAA	WARP
2016	MIA	MLB	33	132	12	4	1	2	15	4	36	0	0	.238/.267/.333	66	1.9	.318	0.0	C(38): 9.1	1.0
2017	ARI	MLB	34	203	13	10	2	2	11	14	61	1	0	.215/.277/.323	69	-1.5	.309	0.4	C(58): 10.2	1.3
2018	ARI	MLB	35	218	15	9	1	1	20	20	66	0	0	.200/.272/.272	68	-3.4	.292	-0.4	C(63): 18.5, P(1): 0.0	2.1
2019	TEX	MLB	36	379	33	17	2	5	33	28	108	1	0	.223/.285/.327	68	2.2	.304	0.0	C 23	2.7

Breakout: 4%   Improve: 32%   Collapse: 13%   Attrition: 39%   MLB: 80%   *Comparables: Paul Bako, Jose Molina, Mike Matheny*

YEAR	TEAM	P. COUNT	FRM RUNS	BLK RUNS	THRW RUNS	TOT RUNS
2016	MIA	5038	7.9	0.8	-0.1	8.9
2017	ARI	7723	8.9	-0.7	1.1	8.9
2018	ARI	8583	11.8	2.3	0.0	14.1
2019	TEX	14659	17.1	1.4	0.5	19.0

In recent years, advanced defensive metrics have confirmed what the eye test and Mike Scioscia's love always said about Mathis, who's tallied +97 Fielding Runs Above Average for his career despite starting fewer than 80 games in 13 of his 14 seasons. An elite pitch framer and blocker with a decent arm, Mathis has also earned rave reviews for handling every pitching staff he's ever worked with. He was among the majors' worst hitters last season, which has been the case for nearly his entire career, yet Mathis snagged a two-year, $6.25 million deal to serve as the Rangers' backup catcher through age 36. He'll retire with zero Gold Glove awards, because those go to starters rather than backups, but on a per-game basis Mathis is one of the best defensive catchers of the past two decades.

Nomar Mazara RF
Born: 04/26/95   Age: 24   Bats: L   Throws: L   Height: 6'4"   Weight: 215   Origin: International Free Agent, 2011

YEAR	TEAM	LVL	AGE	PA	R	2B	3B	HR	RBI	BB	K	SB	CS	AVG/OBP/SLG	DRC+	VORP	BABIP	BRR	FRAA	WARP
2016	TEX	MLB	21	568	59	13	3	20	64	39	112	0	2	.266/.320/.419	101	4.6	.299	-4.1	RF(112): 11.2, LF(38): -1.3	2.1
2017	TEX	MLB	22	616	64	30	2	20	101	55	127	2	2	.253/.323/.422	93	0.8	.293	-2.4	RF(92): -6.2, LF(47): 0.8	0.1
2018	TEX	MLB	23	536	61	25	1	20	77	40	116	1	0	.258/.317/.436	96	5.6	.298	-1.2	RF(113): -10.2, LF(2): -0.2	-0.3
2019	TEX	MLB	24	566	63	25	2	19	72	46	111	2	1	.255/.322/.421	102	14.5	.292	-1.9	RF -6	0.9

Breakout: 0%   Improve: 58%   Collapse: 3%   Attrition: 7%   MLB: 98%   Comparables: Tony Tarasco, Bob Elliott, Nick Markakis

Here is a set of statistics: 1. Mazara has a 20 percent homer-per-fly ball rate. That's the 21st-best in baseball among qualifiers. 2. Mazara has a 27 percent fly-ball rate. That's 12th-lowest in baseball. One of the problems was that Mazara swung at too many pitches outside the strike zone (34 percent). Sure, he made contact with a reasonable percentage of those (64), but it wasn't the good kind of contact. In his defense, he injured his thumb just before the All-Star break, and his second-half numbers suffered greatly, almost certainly as a result. Additionally, he's just now on the verge of being 24 years old. There's still time to correct the issue, and Mazara's a whip-smart baseball player, playing for a big-league organization, with an analytics department and everything.

Rougned Odor 2B
Born: 02/03/94   Age: 25   Bats: L   Throws: R   Height: 5'11"   Weight: 195   Origin: International Free Agent, 2011

YEAR	TEAM	LVL	AGE	PA	R	2B	3B	HR	RBI	BB	K	SB	CS	AVG/OBP/SLG	DRC+	VORP	BABIP	BRR	FRAA	WARP
2016	TEX	MLB	22	632	89	33	4	33	88	19	135	14	7	.271/.296/.502	108	22.5	.297	-0.2	2B(146): 5.7	3.3
2017	TEX	MLB	23	651	79	21	3	30	75	32	162	15	6	.204/.252/.397	81	-9.5	.224	1.3	2B(158): 6.2	1.3
2018	TEX	MLB	24	535	76	23	2	18	63	43	127	12	12	.253/.326/.424	99	14.8	.305	1.0	2B(127): 7.5	2.5
2019	TEX	MLB	25	582	75	28	3	22	72	36	129	13	8	.248/.307/.435	100	18.7	.288	0.0	2B 5	2.5

Breakout: 3%   Improve: 68%   Collapse: 4%   Attrition: 7%   MLB: 98%   Comparables: Gordon Beckham, Robinson Cano, Carlos Baerga

Odor runs like a burlap sack full of furious badgers. Last year, the first few paragraphs of the Rangers team essay waxed philosophical about patience and vision as they pertained to Odor. There's an irony, then, in noting that the Rangers' patience with the second baseman paid off for an extended stretch in 2018. Yes, his home run numbers dipped, but they did so while he increased his slugging percentage. There's a tired joke to be made here about Odor's 2017 being *flat*, and 2018 being more *well-rounded*, because he *drove* the ball more, but we'll let you put that one together. (Tire. It's a tire pun. A tired pun.)

Leody Taveras CF
Born: 09/08/98   Age: 20   Bats: B   Throws: R   Height: 6'1"   Weight: 190   Origin: International Free Agent, 2015

YEAR	TEAM	LVL	AGE	PA	R	2B	3B	HR	RBI	BB	K	SB	CS	AVG/OBP/SLG	DRC+	VORP	BABIP	BRR	FRAA	WARP
2016	DRN	RK	17	45	6	2	2	0	9	6	5	4	3	.385/.467/.538	119	6.5	.441	-2.1	CF(7): -0.9, RF(2): -0.4	-0.2
2016	RNG	RK	17	155	22	6	3	1	15	11	24	11	4	.278/.329/.382	110	3.1	.328	-0.3	CF(31): -2.6, RF(3): -0.1	0.3
2016	SPO	A-	17	133	14	6	1	0	9	8	26	3	1	.228/.271/.293	87	2.4	.283	-0.3	CF(26): 2.1, LF(1): 0.0	0.3
2017	HIC	A	18	577	73	20	7	8	50	47	92	20	6	.249/.312/.360	102	17.7	.287	3.3	CF(125): -3.7, LF(3): -0.1	1.9
2018	DEB	A+	19	580	65	16	7	5	48	51	96	19	11	.246/.312/.332	91	4.2	.292	0.3	CF(123): 7.0, RF(3): 0.0	1.9
2019	TEX	MLB	20	251	26	6	1	5	20	14	50	4	2	.210/.253/.306	49	-6.0	.242	0.0	CF -1, LF 0	-0.7

Breakout: 1%   Improve: 5%   Collapse: 0%   Attrition: 2%   MLB: 6%   Comparables: Cedric Hunter, Carlos Tocci, Ramon Flores

Taveras slugged .332 in High-A in 2018. That's not the season you want from a guy some considered to be the no. 1 prospect in the system coming into the year. Furthermore, that followed a 2017 in Low-A that wasn't exactly overwhelming. He's still just 20, so it's not time to panic yet, but his ability to adapt/grow/improve (likely in a repeat year at Down East) is going to be something to keep an eye on this year.

Bubba Thompson CF
Born: 06/09/98   Age: 21   Bats: R   Throws: R   Height: 6'2"   Weight: 186   Origin: Round 1, 2017 Draft (#26 overall)

YEAR	TEAM	LVL	AGE	PA	R	2B	3B	HR	RBI	BB	K	SB	CS	AVG/OBP/SLG	DRC+	VORP	BABIP	BRR	FRAA	WARP
2017	RNG	RK	19	123	23	7	2	3	12	6	28	5	5	.257/.317/.434	97	3.9	.317	0.8	CF(25): -4.0	0.0
2018	HIC	A	20	363	52	18	5	8	42	23	104	32	7	.289/.344/.446	105	26.0	.396	6.1	CF(67): 1.1, LF(17): 0.7	2.2
2019	TEX	MLB	21	251	29	6	1	7	20	7	83	10	2	.188/.213/.299	37	-8.7	.252	1.3	CF -1, LF 1	-0.9

Breakout: 2%   Improve: 2%   Collapse: 0%   Attrition: 3%   MLB: 3%   Comparables: Teoscar Hernandez, Joe Benson, Jordan Schafer

Thompson's stock after the 2018 season depends on whom you ask. Some in the Rangers organization suggest Thompson has surpassed Leody Taveras as their best position-player prospect, if not no. 1 overall. That's something of a surprise for a two-star athlete with just two years of professional ball under his belt, but the first-rounder's continued dominance in the Arizona Fall League did nothing to prove his believers wrong. He's likely to start 2019 in High-A Down East, but where he finishes the year is anyone's guess. (Unless your guess is "Saturn." Why would you guess that? It's not one of the options. Humans have never been to Saturn. You don't get to make any more guesses. Put down the book and go for a walk.)

Carlos Tocci CF   Born: 08/23/95   Age: 23   Bats: R   Throws: R   Height: 6'2"   Weight: 160   Origin: International Free Agent, 2011

YEAR	TEAM	LVL	AGE	PA	R	2B	3B	HR	RBI	BB	K	SB	CS	AVG/OBP/SLG	DRC+	VORP	BABIP	BRR	FRAA	WARP
2016	CLR	A+	20	556	66	26	2	3	50	34	76	13	6	.284/.331/.362	99	20.6	.324	1.7	CF(122): -0.6, RF(4): -0.2	1.8
2017	REA	AA	21	474	59	19	7	2	48	29	66	4	5	.307/.362/.398	104	23.8	.356	1.5	CF(92): -5.2, RF(12): 3.3	1.8
2017	LEH	AAA	21	54	2	0	0	1	4	1	11	0	0	.189/.204/.245	83	-5.0	.220	0.0	CF(11): 3.5, LF(3): -0.3	0.4
2018	TEX	MLB	22	135	11	3	2	0	5	7	39	0	3	.225/.271/.283	63	-5.1	.329	-0.1	CF(47): -0.7, RF(10): -0.6	-0.3
2019	TEX	MLB	23	244	21	9	1	5	24	13	61	2	1	.219/.267/.331	61	-2.7	.274	-0.4	CF 1, RF 0	-0.2

Breakout: 3%   Improve: 13%   Collapse: 3%   Attrition: 8%   MLB: 20%   *Comparables: Andrew Stevenson, Rosell Herrera, Ender Inciarte*

For the first half of 2018, all anyone could say about Tocci was "why is this guy on the roster?" And the only answer was "because he's a Rule 5 pick." To which Person A (usually on Twitter) would say, "Yah. I know." Kind of rude, but they had a point: Tocci was hitting .086 at the All-Star break. But after that point, the defense-first center fielder hit .282 in his last 94 plate appearances. That doesn't mean he's going to be the Rangers' starting center fielder in 2019—he can now be sent to the minor leagues after having spent a full season on the big-league roster, and he did slug just .365 over those last 38 games—but it does help to justify having kept the now-23-year-old on the roster all season.

Jose Trevino C   Born: 11/28/92   Age: 26   Bats: R   Throws: R   Height: 5'11"   Weight: 211   Origin: Round 6, 2014 Draft (#186 overall)

YEAR	TEAM	LVL	AGE	PA	R	2B	3B	HR	RBI	BB	K	SB	CS	AVG/OBP/SLG	DRC+	VORP	BABIP	BRR	FRAA	WARP
2016	HDS	A+	23	465	67	30	0	9	68	26	49	2	1	.303/.342/.434	104	26.3	.322	-1.3	C(100): 9.0	3.2
2017	FRI	AA	24	423	39	12	0	7	42	19	44	1	2	.241/.275/.323	89	-0.7	.256	-0.1	C(99): 32.1	4.8
2018	TEX	MLB	25	8	0	0	0	0	3	0	1	0	0	.250/.250/.250	94	-0.6	.286	0.0	C(3): -0.5	0.0
2018	FRI	AA	25	201	18	7	1	3	16	13	27	0	1	.234/.284/.332	92	-0.7	.255	-0.8	C(38): 8.0	1.4
2019	TEX	MLB	26	35	3	1	0	1	4	1	6	0	0	.236/.265/.350	59	-0.3	.261	-0.1	C 1	0.1

Breakout: 3%   Improve: 7%   Collapse: 4%   Attrition: 14%   MLB: 24%   *Comparables: Rob Johnson, Kyle Farmer, Jeff Frazier*

Trevino made his big-league debut in 2018 and hit a walk-off single on Father's Day — his first since becoming a father himself, and five years after his own father's passing — for one of the most memorable moments in a forgettable Rangers season. He was back in the minors the next day, and suffered a (non-throwing) shoulder impingement that cost him the last two-plus months of the season. Trevino's defense has always been the catcher's calling card (he was the two-time minor-league Gold Glove winner), so the hope is that the injury won't affect his defense upon return — his bat isn't the type that would play at any other position. The Rangers still believe in Trevino, and if he sticks in the majors alongside Jeff Mathis, he'll benefit from a season under the tutelage of another defense-first, bat-occasionally catcher.

YEAR	TEAM	P. COUNT	FRM RUNS	BLK RUNS	THRW RUNS	TOT RUNS
2017	FRI	13448	24.9	4.7	0.5	30.2
2018	FRI	5456	6.0	0.5	0.6	6.7
2018	TEX	277	-0.2	-0.2	0.0	-0.6
2019	TEX	1284	1.0	0.2	0.0	1.2

Patrick Wisdom 3B   Born: 08/27/91   Age: 27   Bats: R   Throws: R   Height: 6'2"   Weight: 220   Origin: Round 1, 2012 Draft (#52 overall)

YEAR	TEAM	LVL	AGE	PA	R	2B	3B	HR	RBI	BB	K	SB	CS	AVG/OBP/SLG	DRC+	VORP	BABIP	BRR	FRAA	WARP
2016	MEM	AAA	24	295	29	20	1	5	30	26	73	5	1	.233/.303/.374	74	4.3	.298	-2.6	3B(65): 5.6, 1B(4): 0.0	0.4
2017	MEM	AAA	25	506	68	25	1	31	89	38	149	2	2	.243/.310/.507	110	32.0	.286	1.5	3B(113): 0.1, 1B(8): 0.5	2.6
2018	MEM	AAA	26	421	65	24	1	15	61	43	112	11	2	.288/.363/.480	105	37.5	.371	4.9	3B(93): -5.2, 1B(7): 0.5	1.8
2018	SLN	MLB	26	58	11	1	0	4	10	6	19	2	1	.260/.362/.520	81	5.3	.333	0.0	3B(13): -0.4, 1B(4): -0.4	0.0
2019	TEX	MLB	27	409	52	20	1	18	54	33	124	5	2	.234/.304/.437	98	8.2	.300	-0.2	3B -2, 1B 0	0.6

Breakout: 2%   Improve: 17%   Collapse: 11%   Attrition: 18%   MLB: 38%   *Comparables: David Freese, Patrick Kivlehan, Mike Olt*

Just a fortnight shy of his 27th birthday, Wisdom finally punched his ticket to the majors. Before that, he punched many, many bus and meal tickets across the country, racking up over 1,200 plate appearances in Triple-A Memphis alone. He also punched out many, many times, and he continued to do so once he reached The Show. Wisdom has good power, but whether it's enough depends on how often he can make contact. He's made gradual improvements in plate discipline, but whether he can sustain those against big leaguers with any regularity depends on how often can make contact. He's a serviceable third baseman, but doesn't really add value with the glove, so even whether he's good enough in the field depends on how often he can make contact.

PITCHERS

Tony Barnette RHP   Born: 11/09/83   Age: 35   Bats: R   Throws: R   Height: 6'1"   Weight: 190   Origin: Round 10, 2006 Draft (#297 overall)

YEAR	TEAM	LVL	AGE	W	L	SV	G	GS	IP	H	HR	BB/9	K/9	K	GB%	BABIP	WHIP	ERA	DRA	WARP	MPH	FB%	WHF	CSP
2016	TEX	MLB	32	7	3	0	53	0	60¹	54	4	2.4	7.3	49	48%	.289	1.16	2.09	3.92	0.7	94.2	34.4	12.2	43.6
2017	TEX	MLB	33	2	1	2	50	0	57¹	64	7	3.5	8.9	57	42%	.348	1.50	5.49	4.28	0.6	94.2	31.7	14.4	43.4
2018	TEX	MLB	34	2	0	0	22	0	26¹	19	2	1.7	8.9	26	51%	.246	0.91	2.39	3.93	0.3	94.3	47	12.2	49.9
2019	TEX	MLB	35	2	1	1	33	0	34¹	34	4	3.6	8.3	32	46%	.300	1.39	4.58	4.55	0.2	93.0	35.4	13	45.3

Breakout: 21%   Improve: 45%   Collapse: 21%   Attrition: 16%   MLB: 86%   *Comparables: Hideki Okajima, Scott Downs, Scott Eyre*

On May 23, Barnette allowed two runs to the Yankees in two-thirds of an inning, bumping his season ERA up to 4.15. On July 3, Barnette threw his final pitch of 2018, as he missed the second half with a shoulder injury that just wouldn't go away. Between those two moments, Barnette made 11 appearances, pitching 13 1/3 innings, striking out 12, walking two and allowing 10 hits and just one run. That's an extremely selective sample just to say "0.68 ERA over that period" but ... well, he posted an 0.68 ERA over that period. He turned 35 this offseason, but that's not ancient as relievers go, especially for relievers with a sub-1.00 WHIP.

Jairo Beras RHP   Born: 12/25/94   Age: 24   Bats: R   Throws: R   Height: 6'6"   Weight: 195   Origin: International Free Agent, 2012

YEAR	TEAM	LVL	AGE	W	L	SV	G	GS	IP	H	HR	BB/9	K/9	K	GB%	BABIP	WHIP	ERA	DRA	WARP	MPH	FB%	WHF	CSP
2017	HIC	A	22	0	1	0	13	0	13¹	11	2	6.1	9.4	14	26%	.250	1.50	5.40	3.47	0.2				
2018	DEB	A+	23	3	2	3	38	0	54	35	4	4.3	12.5	75	35%	.261	1.13	4.33	2.84	1.3				
2019	TEX	MLB	24	2	0	1	35	0	37	37	8	6.0	9.9	41	32%	.300	1.66	6.31	6.36	-0.7				

Breakout: 0%   Improve: 1%   Collapse: 3%   Attrition: 3%   MLB: 3%   *Comparables: B.J. Rosenberg, A.J. Ramos, Anthony Slama*

In the episode of *BoJack Horseman* in which BoJack is giving the eulogy at his mother's funeral, he talks about how he was sad when the show *Becker* got cancelled, not because it was a great show (it wasn't), but because it had all the *elements* of being a great show, but it never quite clicked. It wasn't that BoJack was mourning the loss of a show; he was mourning the loss of the hope that it would someday be great. Beras got a $4.5 million signing bonus in 2012 as an outfielder, and now he's a 24-year-old pitcher who hasn't played above High-A. The upside? He struck out 12.5 batters per nine innings for Down East last year.

Matt Bush RHP   Born: 02/08/86   Age: 33   Bats: R   Throws: R   Height: 5'9"   Weight: 180   Origin: Round 1, 2004 Draft (#1 overall)

YEAR	TEAM	LVL	AGE	W	L	SV	G	GS	IP	H	HR	BB/9	K/9	K	GB%	BABIP	WHIP	ERA	DRA	WARP	MPH	FB%	WHF	CSP
2016	FRI	AA	30	0	2	5	12	0	17	9	2	2.1	9.5	18	42%	.184	0.76	2.65	2.70	0.4				
2016	TEX	MLB	30	7	2	1	58	0	61²	44	4	2.0	8.9	61	45%	.245	0.94	2.48	3.35	1.1	99.7	68.1	14.4	51.2
2017	TEX	MLB	31	3	4	10	57	0	52¹	57	7	3.3	10.0	58	39%	.329	1.45	3.78	5.53	-0.2	99.2	68.9	13.3	51
2018	ROU	AAA	32	1	1	0	8	0	9	9	0	4.0	14.0	14	55%	.409	1.44	2.00	2.26	0.3				
2018	TEX	MLB	32	0	0	0	21	0	23	23	3	5.5	7.4	19	48%	.286	1.61	4.70	6.72	-0.5	98.1	63.4	10.1	48.7
2019	TEX	MLB	33	2	1	2	32	0	34	33	4	3.9	8.4	32	44%	.293	1.39	4.68	4.65	0.2	98.0	66.5	12.7	49.5

Breakout: 24%   Improve: 40%   Collapse: 28%   Attrition: 13%   MLB: 86%   *Comparables: Kevin Jepsen, Craig Stammen, Jason Frasor*

Bush's 2018 season was like one of those days you forget your coffee, so you have to make an extra stop on the way to work, but because the new coffee is in a cheap disposable cup with a lid that cost the corporation half a cent, the whole thing buckles and spills on your pants as you're getting out of the car. Then you're in the bathroom trying to wash out the stain at the sink and someone walks in on you, which startles you, causing you to bump your head on the hand dryer. You're woozy now, and you stumble on the wet floor, but at the last second you reach out and grab the sink for support, which causes you to injure your UCL badly enough to require surgery, which will cost you the first half of the 2019 season. And it's then and only then that you get to your desk and see the note: Your contract is not being renewed, and you're unemployed. At least it's not Tommy John surgery?

Jesse Chavez RHP   Born: 08/21/83   Age: 35   Bats: R   Throws: R   Height: 6'2"   Weight: 175   Origin: Round 42, 2002 Draft (#1252 overall)

YEAR	TEAM	LVL	AGE	W	L	SV	G	GS	IP	H	HR	BB/9	K/9	K	GB%	BABIP	WHIP	ERA	DRA	WARP	MPH	FB%	WHF	CSP
2016	TOR	MLB	32	1	2	0	39	0	41¹	43	9	2.2	9.1	42	46%	.309	1.28	4.57	4.11	0.4	95.6	66.7	10.4	50.2
2016	LAN	MLB	32	1	0	0	23	0	25²	28	3	2.8	7.4	21	39%	.325	1.40	4.21	2.87	0.6	94.9	66.7	9.7	43.1
2017	ANA	MLB	33	7	11	0	38	21	138	148	28	2.9	7.8	119	42%	.306	1.40	5.35	4.80	1.1	93.1	61	9.2	46
2018	TEX	MLB	34	3	1	1	30	0	56¹	58	10	1.9	8.0	50	45%	.296	1.24	3.51	3.20	1.1	94.3	69.6	11.7	53.6
2018	CHN	MLB	34	2	1	4	32	0	39	26	3	1.2	9.7	42	43%	.247	0.79	1.15	2.95	0.9	94.3	69.6	11.5	53
2019	TEX	MLB	35	3	1	0	59	0	62²	64	10	3.0	8.4	58	43%	.308	1.36	4.61	4.58	0.4	92.7	64	10.1	48.6

Breakout: 16%   Improve: 38%   Collapse: 18%   Attrition: 7%   MLB: 81%   *Comparables: Jim Bunning, Larry French, Bobby Shantz*

Never in one place for long, Chavez played for his eighth and ninth major-league teams in 2018, and it was Chicago that proved to be his most productive stop yet. The 35-year-old reached a career-high strikeout rate in surprising fashion: By throwing his two best pitches by whiff rate (his curveball and changeup) notably less. The resulting three-headed fastball attack saw Chavez throw more pitches in the zone, while seeing less contact than he had previously in his career. And while that was a previously unseen approach from Chavez, it was also very much in character for a pitcher who changes his repertoire as often as his uniform. Sadly for trivia hounds but happily for Chavez, he re-upped with Texas on a two-year deal, so team no. 10 will have to wait.

Bartolo Colon RHP   Born: 05/24/73   Age: 46   Bats: R   Throws: R   Height: 5'11"   Weight: 285   Origin: International Free Agent, 1993

YEAR	TEAM	LVL	AGE	W	L	SV	G	GS	IP	H	HR	BB/9	K/9	K	GB%	BABIP	WHIP	ERA	DRA	WARP	MPH	FB%	WHF	CSP
2016	NYN	MLB	43	15	8	0	34	33	191²	200	24	1.5	6.0	128	45%	.291	1.21	3.43	4.18	2.6	92.1	90.6	6.4	52.1
2017	ATL	MLB	44	2	8	0	13	13	63	92	11	2.9	6.0	42	48%	.360	1.78	8.14	5.90	-0.2	91.5	82.9	5.6	48.3
2017	MIN	MLB	44	5	6	0	15	15	80	100	17	1.7	5.3	47	42%	.307	1.44	5.18	7.35	-1.6	91.3	82.9	6.2	54.5
2018	TEX	MLB	45	7	12	0	28	24	146¹	172	32	1.5	5.0	81	43%	.287	1.35	5.78	6.37	-1.8	90.8	81.8	5.8	50.6
2019	TEX	MLB	46	6	9	0	22	22	122	148	19	2.5	5.5	75	43%	.314	1.49	5.11	5.09	0.5	89.2	80.5	5.7	48.7

Breakout: 0%   Improve: 12%   Collapse: 11%   Attrition: 7%   MLB: 37%   *Comparables: David Wells, Gaylord Perry, Jamie Moyer*

Colon's baseball career has seemed done for a majority of the past decade and here we are, chuckling bemusedly as Colon stars in a commercial for a charcoal company, telling Delino DeShields that the offseason doesn't exist. That's technically not true. Well, unless you're ret— *gasp* WAS THAT A SECRET MESSAGE? DID BARTOLO COLON FORETELL HIS RETIREMENT? Sorry, this is incredibly frivolous, but what do you want? Do you want us to tell you that he started the 2018 season well, but faded down the stretch, likely due to being 46 years old? Of course not. So here's a wild conspiracy theory instead. The commercial was a charcoal prophecy.

Hans Crouse RHP   Born: 09/15/98   Age: 20   Bats: L   Throws: R   Height: 6'4"   Weight: 180   Origin: Round 2, 2017 Draft (#66 overall)

YEAR	TEAM	LVL	AGE	W	L	SV	G	GS	IP	H	HR	BB/9	K/9	K	GB%	BABIP	WHIP	ERA	DRA	WARP	MPH	FB%	WHF	CSP
2017	RNG	RK	18	0	0	0	10	6	20	7	1	3.2	13.5	30	60%	.176	0.70	0.45	2.04	0.8				
2018	SPO	A-	19	5	1	0	8	8	38	25	2	2.6	11.1	47	36%	.253	0.95	2.37	3.91	0.6				
2018	HIC	A	19	0	2	0	5	5	16²	18	1	4.3	8.1	15	40%	.333	1.56	2.70	6.50	-0.3				
2019	TEX	MLB	20	2	3	0	12	9	36²	40	9	5.2	8.7	36	40%	.307	1.67	6.48	6.54	-0.5				

Comparables: Carlos Carrasco, Eric Hurley, Anthony Swarzak

Hans Crouse is a tornado made up of smaller tornadoes. Just tornadoes all the way down. The tornadoes are on fire, and the fuel is distilled from the splinters of a thousand bats, rage-soaked in hate fluid and made brittle from the withering of 100 years under a vengeful sun, and the sun is Crouse, and you are his scorn made ash.

[Slackbot: #HFC]

Hans Crouse is a lava spawn, belched forth with the hatred of an earth that has grown to despise the little walking, crawling, singing things it used to love, and has now sworn an oath to consume them with its gargling maledictions.

[Slackbot: #HFC]

Hans Crouse is a visceral howl, a piercing prayer from a predator to the God who gave him the electric bristle of his hair, the tingling in his legs, the grind of his jaws, the blood of his prey and the sting of the brisk night air in his lungs, air made of gases that curl themselves into a supernova, exploding toward their ancestors.

[Slackbot: #HFC]

Yovani Gallardo RHP   Born: 02/27/86   Age: 33   Bats: R   Throws: R   Height: 6'2"   Weight: 205   Origin: Round 2, 2004 Draft (#46 overall)

YEAR	TEAM	LVL	AGE	W	L	SV	G	GS	IP	H	HR	BB/9	K/9	K	GB%	BABIP	WHIP	ERA	DRA	WARP	MPH	FB%	WHF	CSP
2016	NOR	AAA	30	1	0	0	2	2	10	5	2	3.6	9.0	10	32%	.130	0.90	3.60	6.46	-0.1				
2016	BAL	MLB	30	6	8	0	23	23	118	126	16	4.7	6.5	85	44%	.304	1.58	5.42	5.79	-0.6	92.9	55.2	7.2	43.8
2017	SEA	MLB	31	5	10	1	28	22	130²	138	24	4.1	6.5	94	45%	.286	1.52	5.72	6.16	-0.9	94.2	50	9.2	45.5
2018	CIN	MLB	32	0	0	0	3	0	2¹	8	1	15.4	7.7	2	23%	.583	5.14	30.86	1.61	0.1	92.5	53.5	5.6	34.5
2018	ROU	AAA	32	2	1	0	10	10	49²	49	1	2.5	7.2	40	58%	.329	1.27	3.81	3.95	0.9				
2018	TEX	MLB	32	8	8	0	18	18	92	99	13	4.2	5.5	56	46%	.299	1.54	5.77	6.92	-1.7	93.5	53.7	7.2	46.9
2019	TEX	MLB	33	6	9	0	22	22	117²	128	17	4.3	6.4	84	45%	.303	1.57	5.41	5.41	0.1	92.6	52.1	7.8	44.9

Breakout: 20%   Improve: 40%   Collapse: 10%   Attrition: 16%   MLB: 80%   Comparables: Jake Westbrook, Roberto Hernandez, Jason Johnson

Gallardo has pitched 11 years and 319 games in the big leagues. We highly doubt you're reading this because you thought, "You know who I need a scouting report on? Yovani Gallardo. I should read his player comment and learn about him." Too late, friend. That ship has sailed. You should check out the 2007 version and see if they got it right. What you *might* be wondering, however, is, "Does he still have that weird-looking goatee? You know, the one that was too long, and always looked like it got caught in the rain even when it was dry outside?" The answer to that, we're pleased to tell you, is no.

Taylor Hearn LHP   Born: 08/30/94   Age: 24   Bats: L   Throws: L   Height: 6'5"   Weight: 210   Origin: Round 5, 2015 Draft (#164 overall)

YEAR	TEAM	LVL	AGE	W	L	SV	G	GS	IP	H	HR	BB/9	K/9	K	GB%	BABIP	WHIP	ERA	DRA	WARP	MPH	FB%	WHF	CSP
2016	NAT	RK	21	0	0	0	2	2	6¹	2	1	8.5	11.4	8	55%	.100	1.26	1.42	1.51	0.3				
2016	HAG	A	21	1	0	0	8	2	22²	25	3	2.8	12.3	31	39%	.393	1.41	3.18	2.22	0.7				
2016	WVA	A	21	1	1	0	8	3	22²	15	2	4.0	14.3	36	47%	.289	1.10	1.99	1.97	0.8				
2017	BRD	A+	22	4	6	0	18	17	87¹	65	8	3.8	10.9	106	50%	.281	1.17	4.12	3.37	1.9				
2018	ALT	AA	23	3	6	0	19	19	104	75	6	3.3	9.3	107	41%	.256	1.09	3.12	3.61	2.1				
2018	FRI	AA	23	1	2	0	5	5	25	29	5	3.2	11.9	33	36%	.375	1.52	5.04	4.29	0.3				
2019	TEX	MLB	24	2	3	0	8	8	40	39	7	4.4	9.6	43	40%	.300	1.45	5.08	5.07	0.2				

Breakout: 12%   Improve: 25%   Collapse: 16%   Attrition: 35%   MLB: 50%   Comparables: P.J. Walters, Hunter Wood, Jake Arrieta

Hearn, a native Texan, was part of the Rangers' return for Keone Kela at the 2018 deadline. Texas gave up their 25-year-old closer for a nearly-24-year-old left-handed starter. Hearn is the grandson of famous rodeo cowboy Cleo Hearn, who was also the first African-American Marlboro Man, and Taylor participated in youth rodeos, competing in calf-roping until he was in his late teens, when he quit to focus on baseball. So yeah, Arlington seems like a good fit. Oh right, also the fact that the Rangers desperately needed young starting pitchers with legitimate rotation upside.

Jonathan Hernandez RHP   Born: 07/06/96   Age: 22   Bats: R   Throws: R   Height: 6'2"   Weight: 175   Origin: International Free Agent, 2013

YEAR	TEAM	LVL	AGE	W	L	SV	G	GS	IP	H	HR	BB/9	K/9	K	GB%	BABIP	WHIP	ERA	DRA	WARP	MPH	FB%	WHF	CSP
2016	HIC	A	19	10	9	0	24	22	116¹	110	14	3.8	6.6	85	49%	.279	1.37	4.56	3.64	1.9				
2017	HIC	A	20	2	5	0	9	9	46¹	55	5	2.5	8.9	46	48%	.370	1.47	4.86	3.21	1.0				
2017	DEB	A+	20	3	6	0	14	13	65¹	66	2	4.3	8.8	64	47%	.350	1.48	3.44	4.00	1.0				
2018	DEB	A+	21	4	2	0	10	10	57¹	37	6	2.7	12.1	77	52%	.263	0.94	2.20	2.39	2.0				
2018	FRI	AA	21	4	4	0	12	12	64	58	6	5.1	8.0	57	51%	.299	1.47	4.92	4.46	0.7				
2019	TEX	MLB	22	1	0	0	16	0	17	17	2	4.6	8.8	17	44%	.305	1.49	4.98	4.97	0.0				

Breakout: 15%   Improve: 21%   Collapse: 6%   Attrition: 24%   MLB: 35%   Comparables: Jordan Walden, Sean Reid-Foley, Jake Thompson

Hernandez spent the first half of 2018 on a personal mission to embarrass High-A hitters as a member of the Down East Wood Ducks, then started the second half with an extended lesson on the difference between High-A and Double-A. He turned a corner in August, however: In his last four starts, he racked up an 0.97 WHIP and a 1.14 ERA, striking out 27 and walking 10 over 23 2/3 innings. More importantly, he showed improvement on all four of his pitches, giving hope that he will be a starter and not just a relief option.

Wei-Chieh Huang RHP Born: 09/26/93 Age: 25 Bats: R Throws: R Height: 6'1" Weight: 170 Origin: International Free Agent, 2014

YEAR	TEAM	LVL	AGE	W	L	SV	G	GS	IP	H	HR	BB/9	K/9	K	GB%	BABIP	WHIP	ERA	DRA	WARP	MPH	FB%	WHF	CSP
2016	VIS	A+	22	1	1	0	6	6	26¹	33	5	4.1	8.5	25	44%	.346	1.71	6.49	4.92	0.2				
2016	YAK	A-	22	2	2	0	9	4	30¹	33	4	3.3	12.5	42	39%	.382	1.45	5.34	2.75	0.8				
2017	KNC	A	23	1	1	0	20	0	40	25	2	2.2	10.6	47	39%	.235	0.88	1.58	2.62	1.1				
2017	VIS	A+	23	1	0	1	10	0	24²	15	0	3.6	11.7	32	38%	.259	1.01	2.19	2.80	0.6				
2018	VIS	A+	24	4	1	0	19	0	31¹	17	3	4.6	13.2	46	41%	.230	1.05	2.59	2.67	0.8				
2018	WTN	AA	24	2	1	1	10	2	27	20	1	2.3	10.7	32	42%	.297	1.00	2.00	2.67	0.7				
2018	FRI	AA	24	1	1	0	9	0	20	21	5	3.6	11.2	25	36%	.320	1.45	6.30	2.62	0.6				
2019	TEX	MLB	25	1	0	0	27	0	28¹	27	5	4.4	9.8	31	37%	.295	1.43	5.13	5.12	0.0				

Breakout: 9%   Improve: 13%   Collapse: 15%   Attrition: 23%   MLB: 32%   *Comparables: Daniel Slania, Buddy Baumann, Tayron Guerrero*

As baseball continues to remold and reshape the definitions of words like *starter*, *opener*, *primary pitcher* and *rotation*, it will be interesting to see the value of guys like Huang, whose role in Arizona (before being traded to Texas in the Jake Diekman deal) was to pitch two to four innings every two to four days. It's like a swingman, but intentionally not relying on a starter to crash and burn first. Texas was intrigued enough by the concept to keep him on basically the same schedule once he arrived, and while the results in Frisco weren't overwhelming, or even particularly good, the Rangers liked him enough to put him on the 40-man roster in advance of the Rule 5 draft.

Ariel Jurado RHP Born: 01/30/96 Age: 23 Bats: R Throws: R Height: 6'1" Weight: 180 Origin: International Free Agent, 2002

YEAR	TEAM	LVL	AGE	W	L	SV	G	GS	IP	H	HR	BB/9	K/9	K	GB%	BABIP	WHIP	ERA	DRA	WARP	MPH	FB%	WHF	CSP
2016	HDS	A+	20	7	2	0	16	16	79¹	83	4	2.7	8.1	71	64%	.342	1.35	3.86	3.55	1.7				
2016	FRI	AA	20	1	4	0	8	6	43²	44	3	2.1	7.2	35	53%	.315	1.24	3.30	3.45	0.8				
2017	FRI	AA	21	9	11	0	27	27	157	188	16	2.1	5.4	95	53%	.335	1.43	4.59	4.20	1.8				
2018	FRI	AA	22	5	3	0	16	16	101²	107	12	1.5	5.1	58	51%	.291	1.22	3.28	6.18	-1.0				
2018	TEX	MLB	22	5	5	0	12	8	54²	66	7	3.0	3.6	22	52%	.304	1.54	5.93	6.97	-1.1	93.3	70.2	4.8	51.2
2019	TEX	MLB	23	6	6	0	42	15	108	123	14	3.0	5.5	66	50%	.308	1.47	4.99	4.98	0.5	93.2	72.8	5	53

Breakout: 8%   Improve: 13%   Collapse: 19%   Attrition: 25%   MLB: 40%   *Comparables: Zach Eflin, Michael Bowden, Dillon Gee*

Jurado spent his time in the majors vacillating between looking like a young phenom on the verge of figuring it out and looking like a young man falling off that verge, not flying, and hitting every tree limb and rock on the way down. On one hand, he was 22 years old, and it frequently takes a few crash-and-burns before players catch their stride. On the other, it usually takes more than one wing to fly successfully, and Jurado's sinker has thus far been the only weapon that looks ready. When it's good, though, it's great. If he can improve his secondaries, he should be okay. If not, the bullpen awaits. You can get by with one wing in the bullpen if it's a really good wing.

Jose Leclerc RHP Born: 12/19/93 Age: 25 Bats: R Throws: R Height: 6'0" Weight: 190 Origin: International Free Agent, 2010

YEAR	TEAM	LVL	AGE	W	L	SV	G	GS	IP	H	HR	BB/9	K/9	K	GB%	BABIP	WHIP	ERA	DRA	WARP	MPH	FB%	WHF	CSP
2016	FRI	AA	22	0	5	1	10	2	23	17	1	3.9	11.0	28	30%	.291	1.17	3.52	2.51	0.6				
2016	ROU	AAA	22	2	2	1	29	0	43	23	3	5.9	10.5	50	39%	.211	1.19	2.72	2.87	1.0				
2016	TEX	MLB	22	0	0	0	12	0	15	11	0	7.8	9.0	15	29%	.289	1.60	1.80	5.66	-0.1	97.1	61.8	12.2	44.5
2017	TEX	MLB	23	2	3	2	47	0	45²	23	4	7.9	11.8	60	40%	.204	1.38	3.94	4.65	0.3	97.2	50.9	16.6	39.3
2018	TEX	MLB	24	2	3	12	59	0	57²	24	1	3.9	13.3	85	34%	.211	0.85	1.56	2.87	1.4	97.3	47.8	19	44.2
2019	TEX	MLB	25	3	1	30	54	0	56²	41	7	5.2	12.3	78	38%	.279	1.30	4.12	4.07	0.7	97.0	51.3	17.9	43.7

Breakout: 29%   Improve: 49%   Collapse: 21%   Attrition: 17%   MLB: 78%   *Comparables: Carl Edwards Jr., Ken Giles, Eduardo Sanchez*

For the last few years, lots of Rangers pitching prospects and young big leaguers have come with a scouting report that begins, "If he can ever figure out _____, he's going to be great." The report ends a few years later with, "Yeah, he never figured out _____." Leclerc is one glaring exception: "If he can ever figure out his control, he's going to be great" became, "He figured out his control, and now he's *nasty*." Using two different changeups to go with a plus fastball, Leclerc took over at closer when Keone Kela was traded to Pittsburgh at the deadline; across 18 innings in August and September, he did not allow an earned run and struck out 29 while holding opponents to a .226 OPS. Needless to say, he converted all 12 of his save opportunities.

Tim Lincecum RHP Born: 06/15/84 Age: 35 Bats: L Throws: R Height: 5'11" Weight: 170 Origin: Round 1, 2006 Draft (#10 overall)

YEAR	TEAM	LVL	AGE	W	L	SV	G	GS	IP	H	HR	BB/9	K/9	K	GB%	BABIP	WHIP	ERA	DRA	WARP	MPH	FB%	WHF	CSP
2016	ANA	MLB	32	2	6	0	9	9	38¹	68	11	5.4	7.5	32	43%	.432	2.37	9.16	8.73	-1.5	90.5	43.3	11.4	41.8
2016	SLC	AAA	32	0	3	0	7	7	38¹	30	2	3.3	8.7	37	48%	.267	1.15	3.76	5.16	0.1				
2018	ROU	AAA	34	1	1	0	10	0	12²	14	2	6.4	7.1	10	52%	.316	1.82	5.68	2.98	0.3				
2019	TEX	MLB	35	2	3	0	7	7	32¹	36	5	4.9	7.4	27	46%	.308	1.64	5.68	5.69	-0.1	89.3	42.5	11.2	41

Breakout: 22%   Improve: 41%   Collapse: 10%   Attrition: 6%   MLB: 69%   *Comparables: Darren Oliver, Chan Ho Park, Aaron Harang*

You could sum up Lincecum's season in a Lineout: got a blister, walked too many people, never got his velo back, never made it past Triple-A. But to reduce Lincecum's story to a mere footnote — especially in what's likely to be his last *BP Annual* appearance — feels like a dereliction of duty. After all, he was one of the most uniquely talented pitchers of his generation.

First he was a fresh-faced kid, looking more like Joseph Gordon-Levitt in *Third Rock From the Sun* than a feared pitcher in the mold of Randy Johnson or Roy Halladay. His shoulder-length hair would sway to and fro as he rocked back impossibly far, so far it looked like his right knee would buckle under him, leaving him a pile of parts. Then, at the last minute, his right arm, nearly scraping the ground behind him, would begin its whip-fast motion toward the plate, hurling scorn and fear at men who *looked* like baseball players. He was a nerd beating the jocks at their own game, hiding in a hoodie when he wasn't slaying dragons.

Then he was at spring training in 2018, wearing a Rangers cap, sitting on a table, looking up at the assembled media. His face showed the weathering not only of the years lived, but of the passing of his older brother just a few days before. Gone was the devious grin of the boy who could beat men, and in its place was the resigned grimacing half-twist of a smile of a man who had now tasted enough defeat to know it comes for us all.

No, Lincecum never made it back to the big leagues in 2018. The blister, or the weight of mourning, or perhaps just the toll of too much scorn and fear on his arm saw to that. But for those who saw him, either in his prime or past it, he left an indelible mark on the game.

Lance Lynn **RHP** Born: 05/12/87 Age: 32 Bats: B Throws: R Height: 6'5" Weight: 280 Origin: Round 1, 2008 Draft (#39 overall)

YEAR	TEAM	LVL	AGE	W	L	SV	G	GS	IP	H	HR	BB/9	K/9	K	GB%	BABIP	WHIP	ERA	DRA	WARP	MPH	FB%	WHF	CSP
2017	SLN	MLB	30	11	8	0	33	33	186¹	151	27	3.8	7.4	153	45%	.244	1.23	3.43	4.98	1.2	94.1	81	10.1	46
2018	MIN	MLB	31	7	8	0	20	20	102¹	105	12	5.5	8.8	100	51%	.322	1.63	5.10	5.53	-0.3	95.6	77	10.8	42.6
2018	NYA	MLB	31	3	2	0	11	9	54¹	58	2	2.3	10.1	61	47%	.364	1.33	4.14	4.32	0.6	95.4	77	11.2	46.9
2019	*TEX*	*MLB*	*32*	*8*	*10*	*0*	*27*	*27*	*143*	*140*	*18*	*3.9*	*8.2*	*130*	*47%*	*.298*	*1.41*	*4.66*	*4.63*	*1.4*	*93.9*	*78.1*	*10.5*	*44.5*

Breakout: 11%   Improve: 44%   Collapse: 30%   Attrition: 14%   MLB: 91%   *Comparables: Doug Davis, Barry Zito, Gio Gonzalez*

Originally a perceived victim of the stalled market last offseason, Lynn's $12 million deal with the Twins proved to be perfectly reasonable for his age and performance. After having an inordinately low ERA with a sky-high FIP, the real world caught up to him before he was flipped to the Yankees for Tyler Austin and Luis Rijo. Lynn posted respectable component stats for the Yankees, putting up a 2.17 FIP and a nearly five-to-one strikeout-to-walk ratio, but DRA was a bit more cynical. One could imagine him slotting into the back end of almost any rotation, which means he might be the Rangers' no. 2 after signing a three-year deal at a modest annual rate in December.

Chris Martin **RHP** Born: 06/02/86 Age: 33 Bats: R Throws: R Height: 6'8" Weight: 215 Origin: Round 21, 2005 Draft (#627 overall)

YEAR	TEAM	LVL	AGE	W	L	SV	G	GS	IP	H	HR	BB/9	K/9	K	GB%	BABIP	WHIP	ERA	DRA	WARP	MPH	FB%	WHF	CSP
2018	TEX	MLB	32	1	5	0	46	0	41²	46	5	1.1	8.0	37	41%	.323	1.22	4.54	5.29	-0.2	96.7	72.4	10.1	50.9
2019	*TEX*	*MLB*	*33*	*3*	*1*	*5*	*54*	*0*	*56²*	*62*	*8*	*3.1*	*8.1*	*51*	*41%*	*.315*	*1.43*	*4.68*	*4.65*	*0.3*	*95.6*	*71.5*	*10*	*50.3*

Breakout: 25%   Improve: 33%   Collapse: 21%   Attrition: 19%   MLB: 60%   *Comparables: Randy Flores, Sam LeCure, Juan Gutierrez*

Martin came back from Japan to sign with his hometown Rangers before the 2018 season. A true feel-good story, he missed a few years with a shoulder injury, worked in a furniture warehouse, then tried out for the Grand Prairie AirHogs to kick-start his career. After time in the Red Sox organization, and in the majors with the Rockies and Yankees, Martin went to Japan and became one of the league's most dominant closers. His return stateside wasn't an overwhelming success, but it was good enough to prove that he was capable of pitching in the big leagues again.

Mike Matuella **RHP** Born: 06/03/94 Age: 25 Bats: R Throws: R Height: 6'6" Weight: 220 Origin: Round 3, 2015 Draft (#78 overall)

YEAR	TEAM	LVL	AGE	W	L	SV	G	GS	IP	H	HR	BB/9	K/9	K	GB%	BABIP	WHIP	ERA	DRA	WARP	MPH	FB%	WHF	CSP
2017	HIC	A	23	4	6	0	21	20	75	88	6	2.8	7.2	60	50%	.350	1.48	4.20	6.33	-0.9				
2018	DEB	A+	24	3	5	2	20	8	51¹	67	12	3.7	7.7	44	51%	.327	1.71	8.24	5.88	-0.4				
2019	*TEX*	*MLB*	*25*	*2*	*4*	*0*	*17*	*10*	*48¹*	*59*	*9*	*4.8*	*5.8*	*31*	*45%*	*.314*	*1.77*	*6.41*	*6.46*	*-0.6*				

Breakout: 3%   Improve: 5%   Collapse: 1%   Attrition: 4%   MLB: 7%   *Comparables: Daniel Davidson, Brandon Mann, Eddie Bonine*

The Rangers hoped for a breakout season from Matuella at High-A. Instead, he got knocked around so badly that the team moved him to the bullpen after eight starts, then shut him down completely in July. He's not old enough to panic just yet, but if you haven't slammed the brakes on your Matuella Hype Train, you might have noticed it feels like you're floating around the car? That's because you blew through an unfinished bridge. The rest of us will be holding tight here and letting the kids run around in the grass while Matuella does his best to get the bridge finished in 2019 so we can get this thing back on the move.

Yohander Mendez LHP   Born: 01/17/95   Age: 24   Bats: L   Throws: L   Height: 6'5"   Weight: 200   Origin: International Free Agent, 2011

YEAR	TEAM	LVL	AGE	W	L	SV	G	GS	IP	H	HR	BB/9	K/9	K	GB%	BABIP	WHIP	ERA	DRA	WARP	MPH	FB%	WHF	CSP
2016	HDS	A+	21	4	1	0	7	7	33	21	2	3.0	12.3	45	51%	.264	0.97	2.45	2.13	1.3				
2016	FRI	AA	21	4	1	0	10	10	46²	39	2	2.7	8.9	46	47%	.296	1.14	3.09	3.53	0.9				
2016	ROU	AAA	21	4	1	0	7	4	31¹	12	0	4.6	6.3	22	40%	.150	0.89	0.57	4.23	0.3				
2016	TEX	MLB	21	0	0	0	2	0	3	5	0	6.0	0.0	0	33%	.333	2.33	18.00	4.29	0.0	95.0	48	12.3	41.1
2017	FRI	AA	22	7	8	0	24	24	137²	114	23	2.8	8.1	124	46%	.256	1.14	3.79	3.24	3.2				
2017	TEX	MLB	22	0	1	0	7	0	12¹	13	3	2.2	5.1	7	37%	.263	1.30	5.11	7.67	-0.3	94.1	60.7	10	46.7
2018	DEB	A+	23	1	2	0	5	5	31	29	3	1.7	7.8	27	36%	.306	1.13	3.48	3.93	0.5				
2018	FRI	AA	23	1	1	0	6	6	33	33	6	2.7	8.7	32	32%	.300	1.30	4.91	5.08	0.1				
2018	ROU	AAA	23	0	7	0	12	12	58¹	65	13	3.7	7.7	50	40%	.310	1.53	5.25	4.39	0.8				
2018	TEX	MLB	23	2	2	0	8	5	27²	28	4	4.9	5.9	18	40%	.286	1.55	5.53	7.02	-0.6	94.2	59.9	9.6	48.3
2019	TEX	MLB	24	5	8	0	21	21	105	103	18	3.7	7.8	91	41%	.284	1.40	5.34	5.35	0.2	94.0	61.1	10.1	47.3

Breakout: 13%   Improve: 31%   Collapse: 30%   Attrition: 40%   MLB: 73%   Comparables: Anthony Bass, Jake Odorizzi, Aaron Blair

Mendez is the latest success story for Roy Silver, the Josh Hamilton and Matt Bush whisperer. The tall southpaw was part of a group of players who violated team rules in Kansas City in June, and he found himself in High-A after landing on that really long slide in Chutes and Ladders. Mendez worked his way back through the minor leagues and was — save for one bad start against the Rays — markedly better after his return to Arlington in September.

Mike Minor LHP   Born: 12/26/87   Age: 31   Bats: R   Throws: L   Height: 6'4"   Weight: 210   Origin: Round 1, 2009 Draft (#7 overall)

YEAR	TEAM	LVL	AGE	W	L	SV	G	GS	IP	H	HR	BB/9	K/9	K	GB%	BABIP	WHIP	ERA	DRA	WARP	MPH	FB%	WHF	CSP
2016	OMA	AAA	28	0	4	0	8	8	34²	38	7	4.4	8.6	33	37%	.333	1.59	6.23	4.12	0.5				
2017	KCA	MLB	29	6	6	6	65	0	77²	57	5	2.5	10.2	88	43%	.272	1.02	2.55	2.96	1.9	96.1	45.7	13.5	46.5
2018	TEX	MLB	30	12	8	0	28	28	157	138	25	2.2	7.6	132	35%	.259	1.12	4.18	5.78	-0.9	94.8	49.5	10.9	50.5
2019	TEX	MLB	31	9	11	0	28	28	159²	153	23	3.4	8.3	146	38%	.289	1.33	4.69	4.67	1.5	94.3	48.1	11.5	48.5

Breakout: 22%   Improve: 51%   Collapse: 23%   Attrition: 20%   MLB: 91%   Comparables: Tom Gorzelanny, Brandon Morrow, Matt Garza

Minor is a case study in looking better than season totals. In his first year back in a starting role after injuries made him a reliever, it took him a couple of months to really lock it in. In April and May, opponents hit .282, sticking him with a 5.79 ERA. From June onward, however, those numbers were .204 and 3.23, a total turnaround that lasted until the Rangers shut him down in late September, citing an innings limit. Speaking of innings, he pitched 157 of them, nearly 80 more than in 2017 for Kansas City. He finished the season healthy, so maybe that number is nothing more than a shady character in the corner of the room who turns out to be harmlessly eating his lunch: Keep an eye on it, but no need to talk to the manager yet.

Joe Palumbo LHP   Born: 10/26/94   Age: 24   Bats: L   Throws: L   Height: 6'1"   Weight: 168   Origin: Round 30, 2013 Draft (#910 overall)

YEAR	TEAM	LVL	AGE	W	L	SV	G	GS	IP	H	HR	BB/9	K/9	K	GB%	BABIP	WHIP	ERA	DRA	WARP	MPH	FB%	WHF	CSP
2016	HIC	A	21	7	5	8	33	7	96¹	71	5	3.4	11.4	122	52%	.287	1.11	2.24	2.49	2.7				
2017	DEB	A+	22	1	0	0	3	3	13²	4	0	2.6	14.5	22	58%	.167	0.59	0.66	2.80	0.4				
2018	DEB	A+	23	1	4	0	6	6	27	24	3	2.0	11.3	34	42%	.304	1.11	2.67	3.01	0.7				
2018	FRI	AA	23	1	0	0	2	2	9¹	6	0	2.9	9.6	10	39%	.261	0.96	1.93	3.72	0.2				
2019	TEX	MLB	24	4	4	0	31	10	72²	69	11	3.9	9.9	80	44%	.302	1.38	4.66	4.64	0.7				

Breakout: 16%   Improve: 23%   Collapse: 3%   Attrition: 17%   MLB: 30%   Comparables: Taylor Williams, Glenn Sparkman, Glen Perkins

The Rangers' next wave of young starting pitching is a few years away: Hans Crouse, Cole Ragans, Kyle Cody and others aren't likely to see time in Globe Life Park before the team heads across the street to the shiny new stadium. Palumbo may be the exception. There were whispers that he might make the jump from High-A to the big leagues in 2017 before Tommy John surgery put him in timeout for a year. Texas took it nice and easy with Palumbo in 2018, letting him work his way up to Double-A for his last two starts. While 6-foot-1 and 168 pounds isn't the typical build you expect from a top starting-pitching prospect, so far ... [points back in time to C.J. Wilson, then back to Palumbo] ... he seems fine.

C.D. Pelham LHP   Born: 02/21/95   Age: 24   Bats: L   Throws: L   Height: 6'6"   Weight: 235   Origin: Round 33, 2015 Draft (#978 overall)

YEAR	TEAM	LVL	AGE	W	L	SV	G	GS	IP	H	HR	BB/9	K/9	K	GB%	BABIP	WHIP	ERA	DRA	WARP	MPH	FB%	WHF	CSP
2016	SPO	A-	21	0	6	2	16	7	38	36	0	10.2	11.8	50	48%	.364	2.08	6.16	3.21	0.8				
2017	HIC	A	22	4	2	13	37	0	62¹	47	6	3.8	10.8	75	46%	.266	1.17	3.18	2.78	1.5				
2018	DEB	A+	23	0	0	11	23	0	27²	23	0	4.2	11.1	34	53%	.311	1.30	1.95	3.04	0.6				
2018	FRI	AA	23	2	0	2	24	0	19	20	1	6.2	9.0	19	48%	.345	1.74	6.16	4.66	0.1				
2018	TEX	MLB	23	0	0	0	10	0	7²	12	0	4.7	8.2	7	52%	.444	2.09	7.04	7.47	-0.2	98.4	77.1	8.9	51.2
2019	TEX	MLB	24	1	0	0	32	0	34	35	6	8.5	9.3	35	42%	.309	1.96	6.67	6.73	-0.8	98.2	79.4	9.2	52.7

Breakout: 1%   Improve: 2%   Collapse: 3%   Attrition: 3%   MLB: 5%   Comparables: Taylor Thompson, Dietrich Enns, Ryan Burr

Pelham is a big southpaw who throws the ball *real* hard, so we're not going to worry too much about his MLB numbers yet. Instead, let's focus on the fact that he started the season in High-A, played in the Futures Game and, after a brief pit stop in Double-A Frisco, made it to the bigs. That's a heck of a year for the South Carolina native. As he looks forward to 2019, he'll undoubtedly be hoping to cut down on walks and significantly lower his BHtAMOoTB/9 (Batters Hitting the Absolute Mess Out of the Ball per nine innings).

Martin Perez LHP   Born: 04/04/91   Age: 28   Bats: L   Throws: L   Height: 6'0"   Weight: 200   Origin: International Free Agent, 2007

YEAR	TEAM	LVL	AGE	W	L	SV	G	GS	IP	H	HR	BB/9	K/9	K	GB%	BABIP	WHIP	ERA	DRA	WARP	MPH	FB%	WHF	CSP
2016	TEX	MLB	25	10	11	0	33	33	198²	205	18	3.4	4.7	103	54%	.286	1.41	4.39	6.09	-1.7	95.4	61.7	8.8	45.2
2017	TEX	MLB	26	13	12	0	32	32	185	221	23	3.1	5.6	115	48%	.328	1.54	4.82	7.09	-3.1	95.0	58.7	8	41.1
2018	TEX	MLB	27	2	7	0	22	15	85¹	116	16	3.8	5.5	52	52%	.344	1.78	6.22	7.31	-2.0	95.1	67.3	8.2	48.8
2019	TEX	MLB	28	6	7	0	18	18	102²	112	12	3.6	6.3	72	50%	.310	1.50	4.87	4.85	0.7	94.6	62.1	8.3	45.6

Breakout: 16%   Improve: 53%   Collapse: 19%   Attrition: 14%   MLB: 96%   *Comparables: Matt Harrison, Mike Pelfrey, John Lannan*

If you want to give Perez the benefit of the doubt, you could point to the offseason injury in which a bull knocked him off a fence and suggest he never quite felt right in 2018, despite his repeated claims that he was fine. If you don't want to give Perez the benefit of the doubt, you could point to his mediocre pre-2018 numbers and put the finishing touches on your "Ferdinand was Framed" posters. The most frustrating part about watching Perez pitch is not that he's bad, but that he's pretty good about 70 percent of the time. Unfortunately, the bad is *really* bad: a four-run inning here, a six-run inning there. It's like baking a gourmet cupcake and topping it with icing (not too rich), those really tasty sugar sprinkles that add taste *and* texture, plus one tiiiiiiiiny little squirt of poisoned frog blood. Sure, most of it was delicious, but now you're in the hospital, and half of your face is paralyzed. The good news for Perez? He's left-handed, under 30 and the cupcakes are good enough to take a risk that he's figured out how to keep the frogs (and bulls) out of his kitchen.

Tyler Phillips RHP   Born: 10/27/97   Age: 21   Bats: R   Throws: R   Height: 6'5"   Weight: 200   Origin: Round 16, 2015 Draft (#468 overall)

YEAR	TEAM	LVL	AGE	W	L	SV	G	GS	IP	H	HR	BB/9	K/9	K	GB%	BABIP	WHIP	ERA	DRA	WARP	MPH	FB%	WHF	CSP
2016	SPO	A-	18	4	7	0	13	13	58²	78	2	3.1	8.7	57	53%	.388	1.67	6.44	3.57	1.2				
2017	HIC	A	19	1	2	0	7	4	25¹	28	2	3.2	5.3	15	47%	.302	1.46	6.39	5.88	-0.2				
2017	SPO	A-	19	4	2	0	13	13	73	78	6	1.4	9.6	78	52%	.338	1.22	3.45	3.28	1.7				
2018	HIC	A	20	11	5	0	22	22	128	117	4	1.0	8.7	124	54%	.308	1.02	2.67	3.10	3.2				
2019	TEX	MLB	21	5	7	0	19	19	99¹	111	16	3.2	7.0	77	44%	.308	1.47	5.21	5.20	0.3				

Breakout: 7%   Improve: 12%   Collapse: 5%   Attrition: 11%   MLB: 18%   *Comparables: Michael Bowden, Luis Ortiz, Nick Kingham*

Here's what you need to know about Phillips: He struck out 124 hitters in 128 innings at Hickory last year, and walked just 14. Given how his first turn in Hickory went in 2017 — when he gave up, like, a million runs — that's quite an improvement. As for the why? First, his demeanor calmed down quite a bit. Second, his changeup started humming, making a mockery of hitters every time it got in the vicinity of the plate. So badly did it embarrass batters that it started to make onlookers uncomfortable at the mean-spirited nature of it all. They started feeling bad and yelling things like, "It's okay, we can tell you're trying very hard!" and, "I'm sure you're quite good at other things!" But the hitters thought it was sarcasm and it made the whole thing worse.

Adrian Sampson RHP   Born: 10/07/91   Age: 27   Bats: R   Throws: R   Height: 6'2"   Weight: 210   Origin: Round 5, 2012 Draft (#166 overall)

YEAR	TEAM	LVL	AGE	W	L	SV	G	GS	IP	H	HR	BB/9	K/9	K	GB%	BABIP	WHIP	ERA	DRA	WARP	MPH	FB%	WHF	CSP
2016	TAC	AAA	24	7	4	0	13	13	80¹	81	5	1.3	6.8	61	49%	.310	1.16	3.25	3.12	2.0				
2016	SEA	MLB	24	0	1	0	1	1	4²	8	2	1.9	3.9	2	33%	.375	1.93	7.71	9.16	-0.2	94.4	68.2	3.5	52
2017	RNG	RK	25	1	1	0	4	4	12²	11	0	0.7	5.0	7	56%	.282	0.95	4.26	5.46	0.1				
2017	DEB	A+	25	0	1	0	2	2	8²	13	1	1.0	7.3	7	55%	.375	1.62	5.19	3.76	0.2				
2017	ROU	AAA	25	1	0	0	2	2	10	10	0	0.9	6.3	7	39%	.323	1.10	0.90	3.58	0.2				
2018	ROU	AAA	26	8	4	0	33	19	126²	137	12	1.7	6.0	85	44%	.304	1.27	3.77	4.06	2.0				
2018	TEX	MLB	26	0	3	0	5	4	23	24	6	1.6	5.9	15	39%	.261	1.22	4.30	6.43	-0.3	92.5	57.5	8.3	45.3
2019	TEX	MLB	27	5	8	0	19	19	105¹	120	17	2.8	6.2	72	44%	.301	1.45	5.32	5.32	0.2	92.2	59.6	7.7	48.4

Breakout: 2%   Improve: 7%   Collapse: 16%   Attrition: 23%   MLB: 35%   *Comparables: Zachary Neal, Eric Jokisch, Brady Rodgers*

In late 2016, the Seattle native injured his right elbow while throwing warm-up pitches before his first big-league start for the Mariners. The injury cost him nearly two years, before he finally cracked the big leagues with Texas in September. He made four starts, the last of which came in Seattle during the last week of the season. After the game, about 60 of Sampson's friends and relatives were allowed to wait outside the clubhouse for him. He emerged to a loud echo of cheers and applause as smiles and tears abounded. There's no clever joke here for Sampson, that's just a fun story to tell.

Drew Smyly LHP   Born: 06/13/89   Age: 30   Bats: L   Throws: L   Height: 6'3"   Weight: 190   Origin: Round 2, 2010 Draft (#68 overall)

YEAR	TEAM	LVL	AGE	W	L	SV	G	GS	IP	H	HR	BB/9	K/9	K	GB%	BABIP	WHIP	ERA	DRA	WARP	MPH	FB%	WHF	CSP
2016	TBA	MLB	27	7	12	0	30	30	175¹	174	32	2.5	8.6	167	33%	.291	1.27	4.88	4.66	1.4	92.7	56.9	11.9	45.4
2019	TEX	MLB	30	7	10	0	24	24	136²	137	27	3.6	9.0	137	36%	.296	1.40	5.22	5.23	0.4	92.0	56.7	11.8	45.3

Breakout: 22%   Improve: 48%   Collapse: 11%   Attrition: 12%   MLB: 86%   *Comparables: John Patterson, Luke Hochevar, Scott Baker*

If Scott Boras was putting together a promotional binder for Smyly, he would undoubtedly point out that the left-hander struck out every single batter he faced in 2018. The observer with less of an agenda might note that those batters were all members of the Bowling Green Hot Rods in the Midwest League, and that there were just three of them. The Cubs would not have expected much from Smyly in the first season of the two-year deal they signed him to, but they likely expected something, given that his Tommy John surgery took place in June 2017 and he was facing hitters just over a year later. Setbacks and caution on the part of the team limited him to that single professional inning, so Smyly will have to prove his health in 2019. Hopefully a binder with quite such a high degree of creativity won't be required next offseason.

Jeffrey Springs LHP   Born: 09/20/92   Age: 26   Bats: L   Throws: L   Height: 6'3"   Weight: 180   Origin: Round 30, 2015 Draft (#888 overall)

YEAR	TEAM	LVL	AGE	W	L	SV	G	GS	IP	H	HR	BB/9	K/9	K	GB%	BABIP	WHIP	ERA	DRA	WARP	MPH	FB%	WHF	CSP
2016	HIC	A	23	1	1	3	18	0	31	11	1	2.3	11.6	40	57%	.156	0.61	1.16	2.24	0.9				
2016	HDS	A+	23	2	2	0	13	9	48²	52	9	3.9	9.6	52	44%	.321	1.50	5.36	5.91	-0.3				
2017	DEB	A+	24	2	8	2	31	17	112¹	104	13	3.0	11.7	146	36%	.336	1.26	3.69	2.66	3.3				
2018	FRI	AA	25	3	2	1	20	0	37¹	39	2	1.7	16.4	68	41%	.487	1.23	4.82	2.00	1.3				
2018	ROU	AAA	25	1	2	1	13	0	19¹	12	0	5.6	14.0	30	44%	.333	1.24	2.79	1.87	0.7				
2018	TEX	MLB	25	1	1	0	18	2	32	32	4	3.9	8.7	31	33%	.308	1.44	3.38	5.95	-0.4	92.9	62.8	11.9	52.4
2019	TEX	MLB	26	3	1	0	54	0	56²	55	10	4.0	10.5	66	39%	.313	1.42	4.84	4.83	0.2	92.5	63.9	12.2	53.3

Breakout: 22%   Improve: 34%   Collapse: 12%   Attrition: 24%   MLB: 50%   *Comparables: Andrew Brown, Bobby Wahl, Spencer Patton*

When the Rangers became the latest team to employ an "opener," Springs was the man. The rookie pitched well for the Rangers in his inaugural campaign, both early and late in games. He did continue his trend from the minor leagues of stringing together a handful of very impressive outings, only to level his stats all at once with a belly-flop. His ERA was still 3.38, but take away those three bad outings and it plummets to 0.91 (that sample includes 29 2/3 of his 32 innings). Of course, you can be that selective only when you have a narrative to push, so instead, let's just agree that he'll have a shot to break camp with the big kids in 2019.

LINEOUTS

Hitters

HITTER	POS	TEAM	LVL	AGE	PA	R	2B	3B	HR	RBI	BB	K	SB	CS	AVG/OBP/SLG	DRC+	VORP	BABIP	BRR	FRAA	WARP
Carlos Asuaje	2B	SDN	MLB	26	218	15	8	1	2	19	24	46	1	1	.196/.286/.280	83	-4.2	.243	-0.2	2B(61): 4.3, 3B(5): -0.1	0.6
	2B	ELP	AAA	26	199	33	10	5	2	19	16	26	0	1	.314/.386/.463	115	15.6	.358	0.7	2B(26): -2.1, 3B(19): -0.1	0.9
Michael Chirinos	3B	DRG	Rk	18	298	47	7	3	2	42	49	20	13	4	.318/.431/.397	150	29.9	.335	0.0	3B(37): 2.5, 1B(27): 0.8	2.8
Anthony Gose	CF	FRI	AA	27	25	5	0	1	0	2	1	7	2	0	.273/.320/.364	76	0.3	.375	0.4	P(20): -0.2, CF(5): 0.5	0.1
Sam Huff	C	HIC	A	20	448	53	22	3	18	55	23	140	9	1	.241/.292/.439	106	14.0	.317	-0.1	C(56): 1.9, 1B(11): -0.4	1.8
Eric Jenkins	LF	HIC	A	21	113	14	1	3	3	15	8	32	16	3	.291/.339/.447	94	3.3	.391	-1.2	LF(20): 0.6, CF(6): 1.1	0.3
	LF	DEB	A+	21	301	36	6	4	1	14	21	79	19	5	.223/.282/.285	67	-4.1	.308	3.7	LF(45): -2.0, RF(28): -0.8	-0.5
Jonathan Ornelas	3B	RNG	Rk	18	203	34	10	4	3	28	25	41	15	5	.302/.389/.459	132	16.4	.371	1.7	3B(31): 1.1, SS(12): -1.3	1.5
Cliff Pennington	SS	CIN	MLB	34	34	1	0	0	0	0	5	13	0	0	.138/.265/.138	65	-2.5	.250	-0.2	3B(8): 0.0, SS(5): -0.1	0.0
	SS	LOU	AAA	34	37	4	2	0	0	1	6	7	0	1	.267/.378/.333	103	2.3	.333	-0.1	3B(7): 0.6, SS(2): -0.2	0.2
	SS	ROU	AAA	34	250	26	12	1	1	13	30	54	4	1	.204/.301/.282	80	-1.2	.264	-1.2	SS(54): 1.9, 2B(5): 0.0	0.6
Carlos Perez	C	ATL	MLB	27	22	0	0	0	0	0	1	6	0	0	.143/.182/.143	64	-2.1	.200	0.0	C(6): -0.8	-0.1
	C	ROU	AAA	27	87	10	2	0	4	13	7	12	0	0	.316/.368/.494	112	5.7	.328	-0.3	C(10): 0.5, 1B(2): -0.1	0.4
	C	TEX	MLB	27	53	1	2	0	1	3	1	15	1	0	.143/.176/.245	72	-3.7	.182	-0.1	C(19): -2.0	-0.1
Jack Reinheimer	INF	RNO	AAA	25	219	26	9	2	3	21	20	45	6	4	.237/.312/.353	95	2.8	.286	-0.2	3B(21): -3.5, SS(16): -0.2	0.2
	INF	LVG	AAA	25	60	13	3	0	2	5	4	10	7	0	.327/.383/.491	101	6.2	.372	1.4	SS(15): 0.1, 2B(1): 0.2	0.5
	INF	NYN	MLB	25	35	4	0	0	0	0	5	9	1	1	.167/.242/.167	81	-0.5	.238	0.7	LF(6): -0.3, 3B(4): -0.1	0.1
Ryan Rua	LF	ROU	AAA	28	83	12	5	1	3	17	7	22	4	0	.236/.325/.458	95	1.5	.292	0.2	LF(4): 0.6, CF(4): 0.2	0.2
	LF	TEX	MLB	28	147	17	3	1	6	12	5	53	3	1	.194/.221/.360	69	-3.2	.259	0.7	LF(38): 0.9, RF(7): -0.3	-0.1
Anderson Tejeda	SS	DEB	A+	20	522	76	17	5	19	74	49	142	11	4	.259/.331/.439	113	29.5	.330	3.0	SS(105): 2.9, 2B(12): 1.6	3.8
Eli White	INF	MID	AA	24	578	81	30	8	9	55	62	116	18	9	.306/.388/.450	112	36.6	.379	3.2	2B(66): 2.8, SS(42): 2.6	3.6

Texas claimed **Carlos Asuaje** off waivers from San Diego in December, but the glove-first utility infielder had already agreed to sign with a team in Korea. ⊗ **Michael Chirinos** walked 49 times in 298 plate appearances as an 18-year-old in the Dominican Summer League. With just two homers, pitchers weren't working around him. Dude just has a good eye. ⊗ **Anthony Gose** throws 99 mph from the left side, and while a few teams wanted him to stick to doing that, the Rangers allowed him to also play outfield and hit. His numbers weren't particularly encouraging on either front. ⊗ It's not impossible to make it to the big leagues as a 6-foot-4 catcher (Joe Mauer, stand up, but watch your head) but **Sam Huff**'s odds of staying there would be better if he shrank a few inches. The good news: He may have the pop to withstand a move to first base. ⊗ **Eric Jenkins** destroyed Single-A pitching when he first arrived, but that was way back in 2015. It took him two more full seasons at the level before he finally got out of neutral in 2018 and earned a call-up to Down East. ⊗ The Other **Rougned Odor** has still yet to play stateside. Also, whatever happened to Ozzie Canseco? (Ozzie Canseco earned his 50th five-star ride as an Uber driver in July 2018. This is real; you can find it on Twitter.) ⊗ **Jonathan Ornelas** was the 91st pick in the 2018 draft, and he has very quickly caught the attention of anyone who has seen him play. Drafted as a shortstop, he'll likely be a third baseman, meaning he'll need to hit. Fortunately, he can *hit*. ⊗ **Cliff Pennington** is winding down his surprisingly long, solid career as a light-hitting, good-glove infielder after spending most of 2018 struggling in the minors while failing to top 150 plate appearances in the majors for the first time since 2008. ⊗ **Carlos Perez** is a Jeff Mathis type: defense first, hit later. The Rangers opted to instead sign the real Jeff Mathis. ⊗ Utility infielder **Jack Reinheimer** leveraged another bad offensive season into a cup of coffee in the majors, and while he did record his first major-league hit this time, he's not likely to be any team's first, second or third choice at shortstop. ⊗ The longest pop song ever recorded is 69 minutes and contains over 500 verses. It's called "The Devil Glitch" and we'll assume every verse goes something like: "He's like *this* close / so have no fear / this'll be **Ryan Rua**'s breakout year." ⊗ **Anderson Tejeda**, playing at High-A for the first time, not only improved his defense, but increased his pop at the plate, hitting a career-high 19 home runs. Unfortunately, he also struck out 142 times. ⊗ **Eli White** has just enough power, speed, defensive chops and versatility to back up six positions. Don't knock it 'til you've tried *not* having guys like this in your system.

Pitchers

PITCHER	TEAM	LVL	AGE	W	L	SV	G	GS	IP	H	HR	BB/9	K/9	K	GB%	BABIP	WHIP	ERA	DRA	WARP	MPH	FB%	WHF	CSP
A.J. Alexy	HIC	A	20	6	8	0	22	20	108	89	5	4.3	11.5	138	35%	.337	1.31	3.58	4.12	1.4				
Austin Bibens-Dirkx	ROU	AAA	33	3	6	0	17	15	82¹	94	14	3.1	8.6	79	43%	.327	1.48	5.68	4.11	1.3				
	TEX	MLB	33	2	3	0	13	6	45	56	9	2.8	6.6	33	36%	.331	1.56	6.20	7.03	-0.9	90.9	47.4	10.5	43.8
Kyle Bird	MNT	AA	25	0	2	4	16	1	19²	14	2	4.1	10.5	23	43%	.267	1.17	3.66	2.45	0.6				
	DUR	AAA	25	3	1	0	27	5	55²	38	4	4.2	10.5	65	40%	.264	1.15	1.94	3.43	1.1				
Brock Burke	PCH	A+	21	3	5	0	16	13	82	85	4	3.3	9.5	87	48%	.343	1.40	3.84	4.03	1.2				
	MNT	AA	21	6	1	0	9	9	55¹	39	2	2.3	11.5	71	37%	.282	0.96	1.95	3.22	1.4				
Eddie Butler	IOW	AAA	27	0	3	0	5	5	13¹	21	4	3.4	6.1	9	59%	.378	1.95	8.10	4.36	0.2				
	CHN	MLB	27	1	1	0	8	0	17²	16	1	3.6	5.6	11	61%	.268	1.30	4.08	4.15	0.2	95.4	65.3	9.2	48.5
	TEX	MLB	27	1	2	2	22	0	32	43	10	3.4	5.1	18	49%	.297	1.72	6.47	7.27	-0.9	95.8	63.5	6.3	46.4
Zac Curtis	PHI	MLB	25	0	0	0	7	0	9²	6	0	9.3	9.3	10	44%	.261	1.66	1.86	7.75	-0.3	93.7	58.5	10.5	39.8
	LEH	AAA	25	3	2	0	33	0	42	29	4	4.7	10.3	48	44%	.253	1.21	3.00	3.25	0.9				
	ROU	AAA	25	1	0	0	9	0	9	5	1	6.0	12.0	12	47%	.222	1.22	4.00	3.22	0.2				
	TEX	MLB	25	0	1	0	8	0	6²	6	1	12.1	10.8	8	22%	.294	2.25	9.45	7.78	-0.2	93.1	61	13.7	40.3
Doug Fister	TEX	MLB	34	1	7	0	12	12	66	73	11	2.6	5.5	40	51%	.291	1.39	4.50	6.66	-1.0	89.9	62.8	5.7	46.6
Nick Gardewine	TEX	MLB	24	0	0	0	3	0	5	7	0	0.0	7.2	4	22%	.389	1.40	3.60	7.41	-0.1	95.2	48.8	7.5	54.3
	ROU	AAA	24	2	1	1	12	0	12¹	15	1	5.1	12.4	17	42%	.438	1.78	7.30	3.30	0.3				
Kevin Jepsen	TEX	MLB	33	0	3	0	21	0	16²	15	4	5.9	4.3	8	49%	.208	1.56	5.94	7.68	-0.5	93.9	62.5	7.1	45.7
Brandon Mann	ROU	AAA	34	4	1	0	36	1	52¹	37	2	4.1	7.7	45	42%	.241	1.17	2.41	4.09	0.6				
	TEX	MLB	34	0	0	0	7	0	8¹	7	1	4.3	3.2	3	22%	.231	1.32	5.40	7.61	-0.3	93.5	57.9	9	45.1
Brett Martin	FRI	AA	23	2	10	0	29	15	89	138	7	2.9	9.7	96	50%	.443	1.88	7.28	4.68	0.6				
Sergio Pacheco	DRG	Rk	18	4	2	1	13	11	65¹	54	0	1.2	8.1	59	58%	.295	0.96	2.07	3.50	1.8				
Ricardo Rodriguez	TEX	MLB	25	0	0	0	4	0	6²	11	0	1.4	4.1	3	41%	.407	1.80	4.05	6.78	-0.1	96.8	49.5	6.4	59.1
	ROU	AAA	25	1	2	3	22	0	25²	20	1	1.4	9.5	27	38%	.284	0.94	2.45	3.23	0.6				
Connor Sadzeck	ROU	AAA	26	5	3	0	32	0	38	36	2	3.8	10.2	43	45%	.340	1.37	4.03	3.41	0.7				
	TEX	MLB	26	0	0	0	13	2	9¹	6	0	10.6	6.8	7	42%	.231	1.82	0.96	7.56	-0.3	99.4	59	10.8	48.4
Alex Speas	HIC	A	20	2	0	6	20	0	28²	16	1	6.6	15.4	49	56%	.283	1.29	2.20	1.43	1.2				
Chris Tillman	BAL	MLB	30	1	5	0	7	7	26²	42	6	5.7	4.4	13	44%	.364	2.21	10.46	8.46	-1.0	91.1	50	5.4	44
	FRD	A+	30	0	1	0	1	1	6¹	5	1	4.3	5.7	4	45%	.211	1.26	5.68	4.44	0.1				
	NOR	AAA	30	0	1	0	3	3	15	25	2	3.6	3.0	5	55%	.383	2.07	6.60	9.63	-0.7				
	ROU	AAA	30	0	1	0	4	4	9	11	1	8.0	5.0	5	52%	.333	2.11	9.00	4.55	0.1				

One of the "other" returns for Yu Darvish, **A.J. Alexy** spent 2018 repeating Single-A, and wasn't markedly better than he had been in 2017. That's not to say he's a bust; any time a starter has 11.5 K/9 rate at any level, he's still a dude, and Alexy threw more strikes for the Crawdads than he did the previous season. ⓧ Along with Isiah Kiner-Falefa, **Austin Bibens-Dirkx** became part of the first all-hyphen battery in big-league history. ⓧ Grandson of Big, nephew of Larry, little brother of Sue and Greg, **Kyle Bird** is going to open a game in 2019. ⓧ In a feel-good story, **Clayton Blackburn** started the Rangers' first spring-training game, a tip of the cap by manager Jeff Banister to the native Texan who grew up a Rangers fan. Alas, Blackburn suffered a season-ending elbow injury before March was even halfway done and Banister was unemployed by Thanksgiving. ⓧ **Brock Burke** was the Rays' minor-league pitcher of the year in 2018 and has added velocity since being drafted in 2014. ⓧ After coming over to Texas as the lone big leaguer in the Cole Hamels trade, **Eddie Butler** proceeded to get knocked around, eat a bunch of relief innings and get dropped from the 40-man roster, later undergoing surgery for a "core injury." ⓧ **Kyle Cody** was the Rangers' 2017 minor league pitcher of the year, and was poised to take a huge step forward in 2018. Instead, elbow discomfort kept him off the mound for months and foretold a mid-July Tommy John surgery. ⓧ The only thing wilder than **Zac Curtis'** hair is his fastball ... is what a mean person would say. The lefty has undeniable swing-and-miss stuff, but the walks proved too much for the Texas front office to keep him on the 40-man; he was still a free agent at press time. ⓧ The Rangers gambled on Mike Minor, Matt Moore and **Doug Fister** in their 2018 rotation, and hit on one of them. "One" is also the number of wins Fister earned before missing the last four months with a hip injury. ⓧ Injuries limited **Nick Gardewine** to just over 17 innings, karmic retribution for his spring-training admission that he'd never heard of Hank Williams Sr. ⓧ **Ronald Herrera** has been traded for Kyle Blanks, Jose Pirela and Reiver Sanmartin, and will somehow turn just 24 in May. We need fun facts because he didn't make it off the disabled list in 2018. ⓧ **Kevin Jepsen** was a great comeback story in spring training. Kevin Jepsen was not a great comeback story in the regular season. ⓧ **Brandon Mann** made his big-league debut just a few days before turning 34, after 16 years in the minor leagues, independent leagues, Japanese leagues, Japanese independent leagues and one year when he shaved extra close and played high school ball as "Brayden Teenn." ⓧ **Brett Martin** looked great in spring training, then looked decidedly less great at Double-A Frisco, where he landed in the bullpen. ⓧ After a disappointing 2017, most Mets fans wanted **Rafael Montero**, the former top prospect turned maddeningly inconsistent fifth starter, off the roster. The Mets outrighted him in November, and he elected free agency, which led to a minor-league deal with Texas, where he'll finish his rehab in the hopes of a mid-2019 return. ⓧ **Sergio Pacheco** made it stateside for the first time when he was part of the Rangers' fall instructional league contingency. He walked just 21 batters across 147 Dominican Summer League innings (though he did plunk 14 more). ⓧ **Ricardo Rodriguez** was injured for the beginning (biceps tendinitis) and end (shoulder impingement) of 2018, and despite being effective in the minor leagues in the interim, he was non-tendered after the season. ⓧ While his walks were still a problem, big right-hander **Connor Sadzeck** showed a lot more poise in his time in Arlington than he had in Surprise. ⓧ This **Alex Speas** kid is putting up numbers like 2017 Joe Palumb ... oh. Tommy John surgery in June shelved the flamethrower for the remainder of 2018 and at least the first half of 2019. His walk rate was too high as a starter and hasn't been a lot lower as a reliever, but the strikeout and ground-ball rates were up. ⓧ **Chris Tillman** was technically a member of the Texas Rangers organization in 2018! He pitched at Triple-A Round Rock. This concludes the list of interesting Chris Tillman facts from this year's annual. ⓧ **Edinson Volquez** is back where he started, and it might just be the push he needs to get that Rookie of the Year award.

TORONTO BLUE JAYS

Essay by Whitney McIntosh

Player comments by Ashley Varela and BP staff

The one-sided, parasocial interactions that attach us to sports can express themselves in all sorts of ways, especially in baseball where a long season can alter the understanding of a team's chances or motivations dozens of times before the year ends. Usually, that emotional vacillation is tied to on-field performance. For the 2018 Toronto Blue Jays, facing long odds in the hyper-competitive American League East, the focus was weighted far more to members of the organization not on the field in Toronto at all.

The developments providing any sort of parasocial feedback to the brains of those following Canada's only MLB team happened mostly in the minor leagues, with a few occurring off the field. From before last offseason even officially began, when the Blue Jays declined their team option on Jose Bautista, there were signals that there would be little to latch on to at Rogers Centre. Third baseman Josh Donaldson's shoulder problems added to that trend. By the time Donaldson landed on the disabled list in late May, the Jays were 25-29, already 12 games back in the division and in the fourth-place spot they'd hold for the remainder of the season.

Add to that reliever Roberto Osuna being arrested for domestic assault in May and being placed on administrative leave before eventually being suspended 75 games by the league and traded to the Astros at the deadline, and the likelihood of anyone finding emotional satisfaction on the major-league roster was slim. Lost years happen and this was one of them for Toronto. But that's the nice thing about baseball, with its many different levels and hundreds of active players in each organization—there's usually an alternate source of entertainment if the big club is falling on its face.

Which is why the majority of the Jays' narrative in 2018 centered around minor leaguers like Bo Bichette, Danny Jansen, Cavan Biggio and of course Vladimir Guerrero Jr., the 19-year-old phenom who held the spotlight all season as he dominated three levels of the minors by hitting .381/.437/.636. But the constant frustration of the Jays keeping him in the minors despite that success went hand in hand with the enjoyment that came from watching him play (or at least reading the box scores of his games).

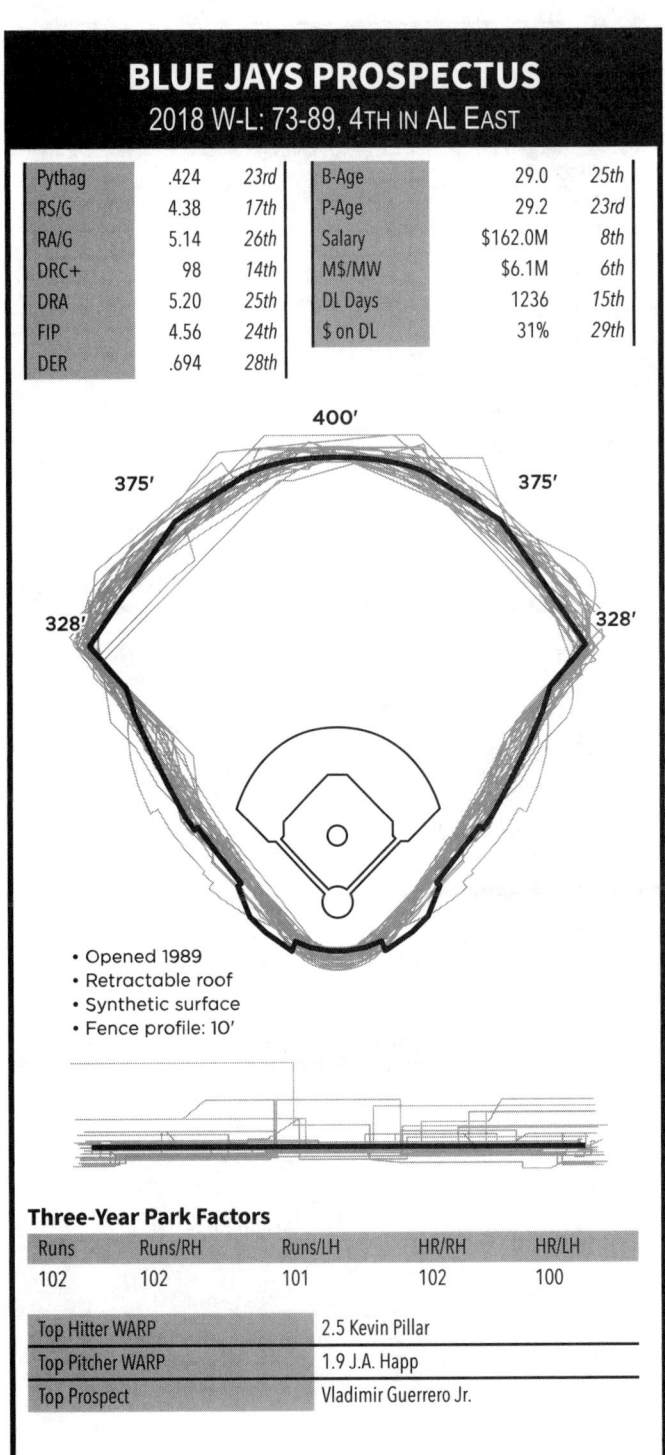

BLUE JAYS PROSPECTUS
2018 W-L: 73-89, 4TH IN AL EAST

Pythag	.424	23rd	B-Age	29.0	25th
RS/G	4.38	17th	P-Age	29.2	23rd
RA/G	5.14	26th	Salary	$162.0M	8th
DRC+	98	14th	M$/MW	$6.1M	6th
DRA	5.20	25th	DL Days	1236	15th
FIP	4.56	24th	$ on DL	31%	29th
DER	.694	28th			

- Opened 1989
- Retractable roof
- Synthetic surface
- Fence profile: 10'

Three-Year Park Factors

Runs	Runs/RH	Runs/LH	HR/RH	HR/LH
102	102	101	102	100

Top Hitter WARP	2.5 Kevin Pillar
Top Pitcher WARP	1.9 J.A. Happ
Top Prospect	Vladimir Guerrero Jr.

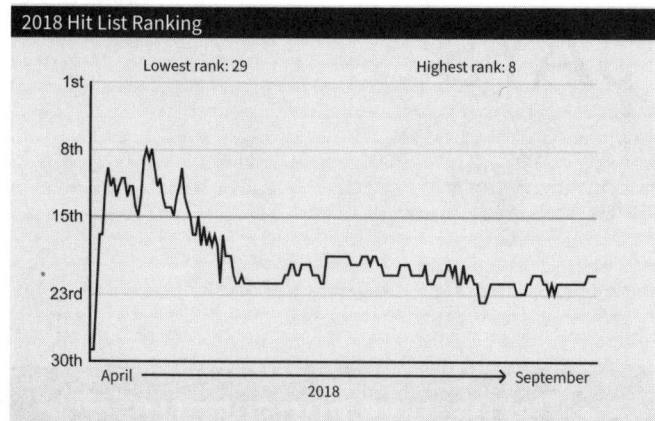

2018 Hit List Ranking

Lowest rank: 29   Highest rank: 8

1st
8th
15th
23rd
30th
April — 2018 → September

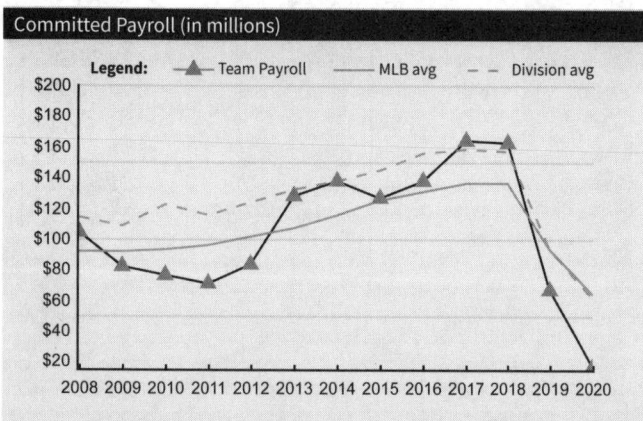

Committed Payroll (in millions)

Legend: ▲ Team Payroll — MLB avg - - Division avg

$200
$180
$160
$140
$120
$100
$80
$60
$40
$20

2008 2009 2010 2011 2012 2013 2014 2015 2016 2017 2018 2019 2020

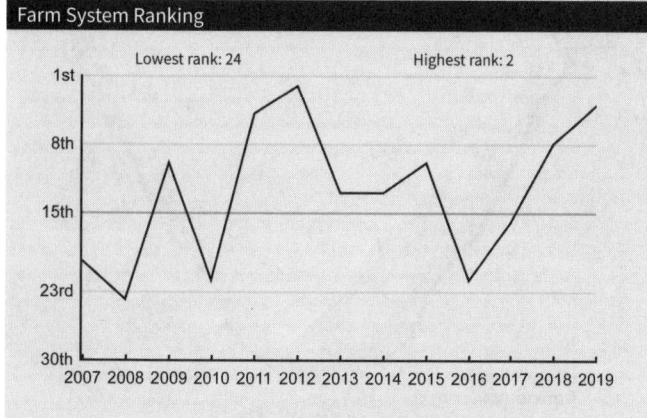

Farm System Ranking

Lowest rank: 24   Highest rank: 2

1st
8th
15th
23rd
30th

2007 2008 2009 2010 2011 2012 2013 2014 2015 2016 2017 2018 2019

Personnel

President
Mark Shapiro

General Manager
Ross Atkins

VP, Baseball Operations
Ben Cherington

Assistant General Manager
Tony LaCava

Assistant General Manager
Andrew Tinnish

Assistant General Manager
Joe Sheehan

Manager
Charlie Montoyo

BP Alumni
Matt Bishoff

Normally the one-sided, parasocial relationships people find in sports stem from a win-loss record of a statistically marvelous season or a race to make history either as an entire roster or as an individual, but the attachment to Vlad Jr. wasn't entirely that type of case. Yes, his on-field prowess was magnetic, yet that attention was undercut by the fact that he never made an appearance in Toronto. Even when there was an obvious opening for the Blue Jays to call him up, they did not, leading to sympathy for Vlad Jr. and questions about the role of service-time suppression in prospect development.

An apt comparison can be found not in sports, but in a major facet of the British Commonwealth of which Canada is a part—the royal family. Specifically, the one-sided relationship royal watchers worldwide have crafted around Prince Harry, Duke of Sussex. Vlad Jr. and Prince Harry—separated by an ocean and an occupation, but connected by the sphere of an adoring public projecting emotions onto them—do not create a perfectly matched metaphor, but the emotional aspect is more alike than not. Both are partially famous due to their father's fame before them and both are succeeding in the face of high expectations out of their control.

It's easy to attach personal hopes onto each of them, and equally easy to be disappointed on their behalf when they can't publicly be dissatisfied with their circumstances or are seemingly kept from the satisfaction others believe they deserve. Harry's life provides a lens through which we can understand the burgeoning attachment to Vlad Jr. and the ways in which he's been locked into a pre-prescribed role for baseball fans, along with how that narrative consumed the Jays' 2018 season more than the team on the field in Toronto.

Harry's status as a canvas on which the public can paint their own desires stems from a mix of his brand of charm and the natural limitations of his public role, and public setbacks he's experienced only exacerbated this projection by observers. This all mimics the current situation with Guerrero and Jays fans. Once that type of psychological attachment is formed it's hard to break, at least until the desired outcome has been achieved. As with any sizable output of emotional resources a positive outcome is the hoped-for result, even if the fans in question may not consciously realize how mentally stimulating that outcome would be.

With Guerrero, the specific setbacks in his path to a suitable level of "happiness" as decided by fans—here, reaching the major leagues—are easily trackable and meted out entirely by the Blue Jays' front office. Guerrero was already a known quantity in baseball before the season began, the weight of the "Jr." in Vlad Jr. If you didn't know of him, he changed that quickly with a home run in a preseason exhibition game at Montreal's Olympic Stadium, the same ballpark in which his father starred.

He became more than just another great prospect by early May, when his mashing of baseballs began to reach levels impossible to be bored by, like when he hit the side of a hotel behind the New Hampshire Fisher Cats field with a homer. So when Donaldson got hurt near the end of that month and the team declined to use that opportunity to call up Guerrero, the public was insulted on his behalf. A week later, with Guerrero hitting .409 at Double-A, the Jays not only declined to call him up once again, but also deferred on even promoting him to Triple-A.

At that point, June 5, the Blue Jays were 26-34 and in fourth place, so all fan focus, outrage and joy was firmly hitched to Guerrero's progress. The Jays cited his defensive shakiness as the primary reason he needed more time in the minors, and the response was a call for them to let him work on his defense in the majors as the team was dead in the water. Their blatant service-time manipulation was more important to them than fan satisfaction. It's a situation we'll see many more times in many more cities before the trend stops. Vlad Jr. remained in the minors to finish the Triple-A season, hitting .336/.414/.564 with six homers in 30 games there. The Blue Jays' season was a failure by any measure and they still refused to provide the second-hand satisfaction so many craved.

As Harry is to his mother, Guerrero emulates some of the most memorable and beloved aspects of his father's personality and career. In his batting stance, in his smile, in his enthusiasm and appreciation for the game. When he injured his knee and went on the disabled list just a few days after this latest short shrift, it elicited the same type of reaction as when Prince Harry got dumped or unfairly overshadowed. How dare they? He deserves better than this. He deserves everything.

What do the fans who're watching him be artificially limited by his employer deserve? The continuing rationalizations from the Jays are some of the least subtle excuses to ever come from a professional sports team, but they are far from the first to resort to this same song and dance to keep a player under their control for an extra season. Service-time manipulation has been a problem for a long time now, but only in recent years (Kris Bryant's public unhappiness with the Cubs in 2014 being a prime example) has the issue gotten so bad that media and fans have begun trying to hold teams accountable. Guerrero has the potential to be the tipping point.

Rooting for a bad team is one thing. Seeing them not make smart decisions to fix performance issues is another. But worst of all is this type of blatant disregard for the team's improvement—actively preventing someone who could make the team better or at least more fun from joining them for the express purpose of keeping the player under their control for a bit longer. Vlad Jr. is such a vibrant, easy-to-root-for person that the manipulation feels that much sharper a betrayal because it's apparent there would be immediate results when adding him to the roster, in both wins and fan morale.

Before this case, intense attachment to young players stopped short of being a net negative for a team manipulating their service time, but as social media and increased access to prospect information allow fan attachment to happen earlier and earlier the downside of teams choosing this strategy becomes more acute. Being angered on Guerrero's behalf is a natural extension of fans finally getting fed up with how teams are dismissing their desires, even if that connection isn't a conscious decision by supporters, but rather a subconscious instinct.

In September, once it was confirmed that Toronto would not be calling up Vlad Jr. even after the minor-league season was over, the MLBPA issued a statement saying, "It's bad for the Blue Jays, it's bad for fans, it's bad for players and it's bad for the industry." But the knitting of fans' emotional uplift to that of a player who hadn't even played for the Toronto crowd could have told you that already. It carried over to the offseason as well, with Guerrero taking cuts or working on his defense eliciting just as emphatic a reaction from the masses. It's now consumed the narrative of the Blue Jays as an organization.

With that more than apparent, the Jays still did not acquiesce to public pressure to call him up. Toronto remained steadfast on their service-time manipulation course despite a groundswell against it. A main facet of parasocial relationships is not just the attachment and interest between the aware subject and the unaware subject, but a loyalty from the former toward the latter. Combine that with the base amount of loyalty present in any fan-team relationship and you get layers of dedication building to increasing unhappiness when that loyalty is insulted.

The Jays are not yet swayed by their fans' dissatisfaction. Whether that's because fans have not yet taken their loyalty elsewhere in large enough numbers for the team to notice, or because that number no longer exists thanks to the many other streams of revenue therefore negating the loyalty completely, is hard to tell just yet. Vlad Jr. being kept down and how the situation resolves itself in 2019 could end up being proof that such intensely focused fan loyalty toward a player is something to which teams actually listen, or proof there's no level of fan attachment that can force owners and front offices to change their business-first approach.

The Jays transformed from a normal baseball team to a conduit through which fans experienced waves of Vladimir Guerrero Jr. news. For a team that looks fated to be stuck behind the same two teams in the division for the foreseeable future, this does not appear to be a situation that will change. If anything, it can only be rectified by giving the masses what they want in Vlad Jr.'s ascendancy. Prince Harry followers finally got a major emotional payoff in 2018. This season, people similarly attached to Guerrero may get the payoff they've wished for as well. ■

—Whitney McIntosh is a freelance writer from Brooklyn, NY.

HITTERS

Anthony Alford CF   Born: 07/20/94   Age: 24   Bats: R   Throws: R   Height: 6'1"   Weight: 215   Origin: Round 3, 2012 Draft (#112 overall)

YEAR	TEAM	LVL	AGE	PA	R	2B	3B	HR	RBI	BB	K	SB	CS	AVG/OBP/SLG	DRC+	VORP	BABIP	BRR	FRAA	WARP
2016	DUN	A+	21	401	53	17	2	9	44	53	117	18	6	.236/.344/.378	104	15.0	.327	2.3	CF(84): 2.6, LF(6): 1.7	2.1
2017	TOR	MLB	22	8	0	1	0	0	0	0	3	0	0	.125/.125/.250	86	-0.8	.200	0.0	LF(3): -0.2, RF(2): 0.0	0.0
2017	NHP	AA	22	289	41	14	0	5	24	35	45	18	3	.310/.406/.429	114	22.0	.360	2.5	CF(32): 5.1, LF(13): 1.0	2.2
2018	BUF	AAA	23	417	52	22	1	5	34	30	112	17	7	.240/.312/.344	78	9.0	.327	4.5	CF(43): 2.9, LF(31): -1.7	0.5
2018	TOR	MLB	23	21	3	0	0	0	1	2	9	1	0	.105/.190/.105	59	-0.9	.200	0.7	LF(7): 0.2, RF(3): -0.1	0.0
2019	TOR	MLB	24	107	11	4	0	2	10	7	31	3	1	.204/.268/.313	50	-2.5	.272	0.2	CF 1, LF 0	-0.1

Breakout: 11%   Improve: 18%   Collapse: 3%   Attrition: 15%   MLB: 29%   *Comparables: Brian Goodwin, James Jones, Drew Stubbs*

"Exceptional when healthy" is a maxim so liberally applied as to be rendered meaningless. In Alford's case, however, it just so happens to be true. The former Southern Miss defensive back converted to high-speed outfielder in 2012 and continues to profile well across the board, from his advanced technique and above-average bat speed at the plate to his natural instincts on the grass. While he has yet to make a real impact for the Blue Jays on a big-league level, he's also seen more than his fair share of injuries in recent years, from a concussion in 2016 to a cracked hamate bone in 2017 to a nagging hamstring issue in 2018. Expect the club to keep a hawk-like watch over the two-way talent until he's deemed healthy enough for a prolonged stint in the majors.

Bo Bichette SS   Born: 03/05/98   Age: 21   Bats: R   Throws: R   Height: 6'0"   Weight: 200   Origin: Round 2, 2016 Draft (#66 overall)

YEAR	TEAM	LVL	AGE	PA	R	2B	3B	HR	RBI	BB	K	SB	CS	AVG/OBP/SLG	DRC+	VORP	BABIP	BRR	FRAA	WARP
2016	BLJ	RK	18	91	21	9	2	4	36	6	17	3	0	.427/.451/.732	167	19.5	.484	-0.4	SS(16): 1.7, 2B(6): 0.3	1.2
2017	LNS	A	19	317	60	32	3	10	51	28	55	12	3	.384/.448/.623	152	48.4	.452	3.0	SS(51): 0.2, 2B(14): 0.3	3.6
2017	DUN	A+	19	182	28	9	1	4	23	14	26	10	4	.323/.379/.463	122	12.5	.360	-0.2	SS(35): -0.3	1.2
2018	NHP	AA	20	595	95	43	7	11	74	48	101	32	11	.286/.343/.453	113	40.6	.331	3.2	SS(116): -4.0, 2B(9): 0.6	3.5
2019	TOR	MLB	21	251	33	11	1	7	25	16	54	8	3	.245/.294/.397	82	4.5	.287	0.6	SS 0, 2B 0	0.5

Breakout: 6%   Improve: 20%   Collapse: 6%   Attrition: 28%   MLB: 53%   *Comparables: Franklin Barreto, Addison Russell, Alen Hanson*

It's the bane of every younger sibling's existence to have their accomplishments and talents juxtaposed against those of their older siblings. Granted, Bichette bears no blood relation to fellow top prospect and Hall of Fame progeny Vladimir Guerrero Jr. (nor is he technically the younger of the two), but given his current status as the no. 2 talent in Toronto's system, comparisons are as frequent and inevitable as they are unwarranted. The six-foot, 200-pound shortstop is no Niles Crane to a decorated, pompous Frasier, however—he stands tall in his own right with a bat that plays for both average and power and an aggressive approach at the plate that has overwhelmed opponents at every level so far. He's still fairly limited at his natural position, but the glove may eventually skew above-average while he rises to meet a lofty offensive ceiling.

Cavan Biggio INF   Born: 04/11/95   Age: 24   Bats: L   Throws: R   Height: 6'1"   Weight: 203   Origin: Round 5, 2016 Draft (#162 overall)

YEAR	TEAM	LVL	AGE	PA	R	2B	3B	HR	RBI	BB	K	SB	CS	AVG/OBP/SLG	DRC+	VORP	BABIP	BRR	FRAA	WARP
2016	VAN	A-	21	238	24	11	3	0	21	29	28	9	3	.282/.382/.366	123	13.1	.324	-0.4	2B(49): -3.0	0.9
2016	LNS	A	21	42	3	1	0	0	5	4	7	2	0	.222/.310/.250	108	-0.3	.267	-0.8	2B(9): 0.6	0.1
2017	DUN	A+	22	556	75	17	5	11	60	74	140	11	7	.233/.342/.363	120	10.2	.304	1.1	2B(116): 6.4, 3B(6): -0.4	3.8
2018	NHP	AA	23	563	80	23	5	26	99	100	148	20	8	.252/.388/.499	136	44.8	.307	3.6	2B(68): 1.5, 3B(34): -1.1	4.8
2019	TOR	MLB	24	251	33	9	1	9	27	30	74	5	2	.214/.310/.384	92	4.1	.275	-0.1	2B 1, 3B -1	0.5

Breakout: 0%   Improve: 13%   Collapse: 7%   Attrition: 21%   MLB: 29%   *Comparables: Drew Robinson, Alex Blandino, Vince Belnome*

Clawing one's way out from under the shadow of a successful parent—one whose legacy is enshrined in Cooperstown, no less—is a formidable task independent of profession or person. While Biggio hasn't yet carved a clear path to the majors like Vladimir Guerrero Jr. and Bo Bichette, such comparisons minimize the pronounced effect he cast during his first full year as a 26-homer, 20-stolen base threat in Double-A ball. His defense has yet to mature alongside his bat, particularly at the keystone, but the power is legitimate, the advanced approach at the plate even more appealing, and the positional versatility a promising sign of things to come.

Brandon Drury UT   Born: 08/21/92   Age: 26   Bats: R   Throws: R   Height: 6'2"   Weight: 210   Origin: Round 13, 2010 Draft (#404 overall)

YEAR	TEAM	LVL	AGE	PA	R	2B	3B	HR	RBI	BB	K	SB	CS	AVG/OBP/SLG	DRC+	VORP	BABIP	BRR	FRAA	WARP
2016	ARI	MLB	23	499	59	31	1	16	53	31	100	1	1	.282/.329/.458	101	18.6	.327	1.9	LF(62): -5.2, RF(32): -1.8	0.8
2017	ARI	MLB	24	480	41	37	2	13	63	28	103	1	1	.267/.317/.447	85	10.1	.320	-3.9	2B(114): 2.5, 3B(1): -0.2	0.4
2018	SWB	AAA	25	235	30	13	1	5	30	32	58	3	1	.291/.400/.442	106	19.7	.390	-1.0	3B(45): 2.4, 1B(5): 0.7	1.1
2018	NYA	MLB	25	57	2	2	0	1	7	5	12	0	0	.176/.263/.275	82	-2.1	.211	0.1	3B(9): -0.7, 2B(5): -0.1	0.0
2018	TOR	MLB	25	29	3	2	0	0	3	2	8	0	0	.154/.241/.231	77	-1.8	.222	0.0	3B(6): -0.1, 2B(2): -0.6	-0.1
2019	TOR	MLB	26	315	31	14	1	8	34	25	77	1	1	.232/.303/.366	85	3.4	.292	-0.4	2B 1, 3B -1	0.4

Breakout: 5%   Improve: 56%   Collapse: 6%   Attrition: 19%   MLB: 95%   *Comparables: Brent Morel, Wilmer Flores, Willy Aybar*

Once a versatile defender known for his sizzling, if streaky, bat, Drury saw his major-league career evaporate quicker than a midsummer heat spell snapped by a Southern Oregon sunset. After switching over to the American League, he labored through the first half of the season with sub-Mendoza Line production levels and saw his stats plummet even further when the Yankees swapped him for Toronto lefty J.A. Happ. That said, it was mostly due to the 93-mph sinker that fractured his left hand just prior to the trade. Now, it's not a matter of whether or not he can bounce back from a career-worst performance, but whether he'll receive ample playing time to return as the quasi-utility player of years past.

Randal Grichuk OF
Born: 08/13/91 Age: 27 Bats: R Throws: R Height: 6'1" Weight: 205 Origin: Round 1, 2009 Draft (#24 overall)

YEAR	TEAM	LVL	AGE	PA	R	2B	3B	HR	RBI	BB	K	SB	CS	AVG/OBP/SLG	DRC+	VORP	BABIP	BRR	FRAA	WARP
2016	MEM	AAA	24	86	12	4	1	6	18	2	14	0	0	.272/.302/.568	132	6.4	.258	0.4	CF(17): -0.2	0.7
2016	SLN	MLB	24	478	66	29	3	24	68	28	141	5	4	.240/.289/.480	96	24.0	.294	2.2	CF(115): 0.6, LF(4): 0.6	1.8
2017	MEM	AAA	25	67	11	3	0	6	9	3	20	0	0	.270/.313/.603	119	5.0	.297	0.0	LF(9): 3.6, CF(1): -0.1	0.7
2017	SLN	MLB	25	442	53	25	3	22	59	26	133	6	1	.238/.285/.473	89	11.4	.293	1.9	LF(58): -2.7, RF(55): 4.8	0.9
2018	TOR	MLB	26	462	60	32	1	25	61	27	122	3	2	.245/.301/.502	107	19.5	.282	2.5	RF(102): 2.4, CF(26): -2.3	1.8
2019	TOR	MLB	27	495	62	25	2	23	68	32	135	5	2	.241/.299/.452	102	17.0	.293	1.9	RF 5	2.4

Breakout: 8%   Improve: 53%   Collapse: 4%   Attrition: 8%   MLB: 90%   *Comparables: Mark Trumbo, Oswaldo Arcia, Corey Dickerson*

If we were to condense Grichuk's professional career into a single event, it might look something like the gruesome aftermath of a Brandon Guyer foul ball on September 9. Grichuk hightailed it from right field, kicked out his feet for a slide, and was promptly decked by the business end of a security guard's stool. While he escaped with nothing more serious than facial bruising, it was the kind of all-or-nothing play that has come to characterize his playing style as a speedy, albeit injury-prone corner outfielder. That's not to say 2018 was a total bust—he made a concentrated effort to tone down his swing-happy approach at the plate, cleared the .300 mark in OBP for the first time in years and worked up to a new career-high home run total—but his availability was once again compromised by a right knee sprain (the result of another catch gone wrong), and he'll enter 2019 with a gaggle of outfield prospects nipping at his heels as the Blue Jays advance their rebuild.

Vladimir Guerrero Jr. 3B
Born: 03/16/99 Age: 20 Bats: R Throws: R Height: 6'1" Weight: 200 Origin: International Free Agent, 2015

YEAR	TEAM	LVL	AGE	PA	R	2B	3B	HR	RBI	BB	K	SB	CS	AVG/OBP/SLG	DRC+	VORP	BABIP	BRR	FRAA	WARP
2016	BLU	RK	17	276	32	12	3	8	46	33	35	15	5	.271/.359/.449	148	19.2	.283	1.5	3B(50): -10.7	1.3
2017	LNS	A	18	318	53	21	1	7	45	40	34	6	2	.316/.409/.480	139	26.9	.336	0.8	3B(61): -2.6	2.2
2017	DUN	A+	18	209	31	7	1	6	31	36	28	2	2	.333/.450/.494	142	17.1	.365	-2.4	3B(41): -1.5	1.4
2018	NHP	AA	19	266	48	19	1	14	60	21	27	3	3	.402/.449/.671	170	37.4	.402	-2.9	3B(53): 1.0	3.0
2018	BUF	AAA	19	128	15	7	0	6	16	15	10	0	0	.336/.414/.564	152	11.5	.323	-4.8	3B(25): 4.3	1.2
2019	TOR	MLB	20	515	63	24	1	20	70	56	68	1	1	.268/.354/.453	121	23.4	.278	-1.1	3B 0	2.5

Breakout: 12%   Improve: 39%   Collapse: 0%   Attrition: 8%   MLB: 43%   *Comparables: Jason Heyward, Mike Trout, Jurickson Profar*

In an industry that churns up and spits out maybe a dozen elite prospects in a calendar year, if that, it's a badge of pride to be able to say that you noticed when the Next Big Thing first appeared on the horizon. For scouts of decades past, that kind of talent manifested in younger versions of Ken Griffey, Jr., Alex Rodriguez, Miguel Cabrera, Mike Trout and Bryce Harper. For those combing through the back fields and minor league networks of today's pro ball landscape, it's currently packaged in the form of Vladimir Guerrero, Jr.

Guerrero may have grown up in his father's journey to Cooperstown, but he stepped into the sunlight at an early age with the kind of power-driven bat and top prospect potential that sent Tom Tsuchiya scrambling for fresh clay and a new bronze mold. "Powerful" doesn't begin to describe the teenager's utter lack of discrimination between pitches as he anticipates and reverses triple-digit heaters, dirt-digging sliders and arching curveballs out of the park, leaving outfielders hung out to dry like washed-up superheroes clinging to the tops of the fences.

After tunneling his way through the lower levels of the Blue Jays' system, Guerrero turned his bat on Double- and Triple-A pitchers with similar ferocity. His staggering on-base clip regressed slightly as he moved up the ranks, an anticipated result of facing higher-caliber opponents, but the underlying ability to hit for power and average still rings true. Although his glove is never going to catch up with his hit tool, he has the build and instincts for the hot corner and will remain a fixture there while he rewrites the very definition of a 'pure hitter' for the next generation.

Lourdes Gurriel MI
Born: 10/10/93 Age: 25 Bats: R Throws: R Height: 6'2" Weight: 185 Origin: International Free Agent, 2016

YEAR	TEAM	LVL	AGE	PA	R	2B	3B	HR	RBI	BB	K	SB	CS	AVG/OBP/SLG	DRC+	VORP	BABIP	BRR	FRAA	WARP
2017	DUN	A+	23	69	6	1	0	1	8	2	13	1	0	.197/.217/.258	88	-3.2	.226	0.3	SS(11): -0.2, 2B(1): 0.1	0.1
2017	NHP	AA	23	185	20	10	0	4	28	10	30	2	0	.241/.286/.371	96	4.2	.266	1.2	2B(22): 1.5, SS(17): 0.9	0.9
2018	NHP	AA	24	65	7	3	1	2	14	3	8	1	1	.322/.354/.508	115	6.7	.333	0.3	2B(7): -0.1, SS(5): -0.7	0.3
2018	BUF	AAA	24	156	20	8	0	5	30	4	34	3	2	.293/.321/.449	99	7.0	.345	-0.9	SS(23): 0.9, 2B(9): 0.2	0.6
2018	TOR	MLB	24	263	30	8	0	11	35	9	59	1	2	.281/.309/.446	102	9.0	.326	-1.7	SS(46): -0.8, 2B(24): -1.1	0.8
2019	TOR	MLB	25	483	55	24	1	16	59	23	105	4	2	.258/.301/.425	92	12.3	.302	-1.1	SS -2, 2B 0	1.2

Breakout: 5%   Improve: 42%   Collapse: 15%   Attrition: 33%   MLB: 97%   *Comparables: Ian Desmond, Danny Santana, Josh Rutledge*

A $22 million-dollar signee out of Sancti Spiritus, Cuba, Gurriel lacks the legacy of his father, Lourdes Sr., and the established star status of his brother, Yulieski. Neither of those facts overshadowed his first foray into major-league ball, though, where he proved a surprisingly capable alternative to a decommissioned Troy Tulowitzki in 2018. Gurriel's approach isn't exactly refined, but his ability to hit for extra bases brought him to the cusp of a .300 average and made headlines after becoming second player in the last 50 years to collect multiple hits in 11 straight games. The downside? He lost nearly a month's worth of starts to multiple injuries, including a concussion, ankle sprain and season-ending hamstring strain. Even when healthy, he lacks the glove to stick at short long-term, and frankly isn't likely to be above-average anywhere, but being a utility player on a rebuilding team has its benefits.

Teoscar Hernandez OF Born: 10/15/92 Age: 26 Bats: R Throws: R Height: 6'2" Weight: 180 Origin: International Free Agent, 2011

YEAR	TEAM	LVL	AGE	PA	R	2B	3B	HR	RBI	BB	K	SB	CS	AVG/OBP/SLG	DRC+	VORP	BABIP	BRR	FRAA	WARP
2016	CCH	AA	23	322	53	19	0	6	30	32	55	29	11	.305/.384/.437	126	25.6	.359	4.2	RF(37): -1.2, CF(30): -0.6	2.1
2016	FRE	AAA	23	160	20	9	3	4	23	13	25	5	4	.313/.365/.500	122	8.7	.350	-2.4	RF(26): 4.1, CF(11): -1.8	0.9
2016	HOU	MLB	23	112	15	7	0	4	11	11	28	0	2	.230/.304/.420	86	0.6	.275	-0.6	LF(22): -1.5, CF(15): -1.3	-0.2
2017	FRE	AAA	24	347	54	20	3	12	44	39	72	12	7	.279/.369/.485	113	21.7	.329	1.9	RF(44): 2.2, CF(22): 1.4	2.0
2017	BUF	AAA	24	109	14	6	2	6	22	8	30	4	1	.222/.294/.505	110	4.9	.254	0.8	RF(10): 0.8, CF(7): 1.0	1.0
2017	TOR	MLB	24	95	16	6	0	8	20	6	36	0	1	.261/.305/.602	100	8.4	.333	1.9	LF(18): -0.7, CF(5): 0.0	0.4
2018	TOR	MLB	25	523	67	29	7	22	57	41	163	5	5	.239/.302/.468	97	12.8	.313	-0.1	LF(87): -2.0, RF(35): 0.7	1.0
2019	TOR	MLB	26	401	56	19	3	16	47	32	113	9	5	.242/.309/.439	106	13.9	.306	0.6	LF -1, RF 2	1.6

Breakout: 5% Improve: 47% Collapse: 9% Attrition: 18% MLB: 88%   Comparables: Eric Thames, Corey Dickerson, Trey Mancini

No matter how you slice it—and when it comes to the metaphorical pie of player value, there are a lot of ways to slice it—Hernandez was the Blue Jays' worst defender and one of the most poorly-graded outfielders to grace the American League East division. He regularly dodged routine fly balls and paired clunky footwork with circuitous routes, off-kilter instincts and poor communication. Even the worst defender is made valuable by virtue of a hot bat, however, and Hernandez's job security subsequently took the form of a masterful swing at the plate. Perhaps it's not a pie Hernandez resembles after all, but an English trifle a la Rachel Green: tantalizing dinger-laced ladyfingers at the bottom, ground beef sauteed with peas, onions and a handful of fielding errors in the center, topped with whipped cream and just a dash of unfounded optimism. "What's not to like?" the Blue Jays mumble between forkfuls.

Danny Jansen C Born: 04/15/95 Age: 24 Bats: R Throws: R Height: 6'2" Weight: 225 Origin: Round 16, 2013 Draft (#475 overall)

YEAR	TEAM	LVL	AGE	PA	R	2B	3B	HR	RBI	BB	K	SB	CS	AVG/OBP/SLG	DRC+	VORP	BABIP	BRR	FRAA	WARP
2016	DUN	A+	21	217	18	7	0	1	23	22	40	7	1	.218/.313/.271	105	0.6	.268	-0.2	C(50): -1.3	0.9
2017	DUN	A+	22	136	19	6	0	5	18	8	14	0	0	.369/.422/.541	130	17.1	.385	-0.7	C(25): -2.0	0.8
2017	NHP	AA	22	210	23	15	1	2	20	22	19	1	0	.291/.378/.419	112	15.5	.311	-1.4	C(50): -0.9	1.1
2017	BUF	AAA	22	78	8	4	1	3	10	11	7	0	0	.328/.423/.552	128	11.2	.333	-0.1	C(21): -0.4	0.6
2018	BUF	AAA	23	360	45	21	1	12	58	44	49	5	1	.275/.390/.473	130	32.9	.292	0.2	C(56): -6.0	2.1
2018	TOR	MLB	23	95	12	6	0	3	8	9	17	0	0	.247/.347/.432	101	6.6	.274	0.9	C(29): 1.0	0.7
2019	TOR	MLB	24	382	44	15	1	11	43	39	67	2	0	.231/.323/.380	93	13.2	.258	-0.5	C -9	0.5

Breakout: 2% Improve: 29% Collapse: 19% Attrition: 25% MLB: 77%   Comparables: Josh Bell, Conor Jackson, Hank Conger

The heir apparent to incumbent backstop Russell Martin, Jansen was tasked with his first major league workload after getting called up in mid-August. The improved approach that fueled his 2017 breakthrough was slightly muted against big league competitors, but he generated some pop at the plate and his end-of-season numbers still skewed above average for his position. While he may never become a true fixture in the heart of the lineup, Jansen's polished game-calling and receiving skills give him a deserved air of maturity, and he has another year to work as an apprentice before Russell Martin hits free agency and turns over the keys to the gear.

YEAR	TEAM	P. COUNT	FRM RUNS	BLK RUNS	THRW RUNS	TOT RUNS
2017	BUF	2610	0.0	0.1	-0.1	0.2
2017	NHP	6546	-2.1	2.2	0.0	-0.8
2018	BUF	7393	-4.6	0.2	-0.1	-4.0
2018	TOR	3560	0.6	0.7	-0.2	1.8
2019	TOR	14476	-7.9	1.8	-1.6	-7.7

Russell Martin C Born: 02/15/83 Age: 36 Bats: R Throws: R Height: 5'10" Weight: 205 Origin: Round 17, 2002 Draft (#511 overall)

YEAR	TEAM	LVL	AGE	PA	R	2B	3B	HR	RBI	BB	K	SB	CS	AVG/OBP/SLG	DRC+	VORP	BABIP	BRR	FRAA	WARP
2016	TOR	MLB	33	535	62	16	0	20	74	64	148	2	1	.231/.335/.398	94	19.3	.291	0.3	C(127): 12.9, 2B(1): 0.0	3.6
2017	TOR	MLB	34	365	49	12	0	13	35	50	83	1	2	.221/.343/.388	100	12.8	.261	0.2	C(83): 0.8, 3B(10): 0.7	2.0
2018	TOR	MLB	35	352	37	8	0	10	25	56	82	0	3	.194/.338/.325	93	6.7	.234	-5.1	C(71): 7.6, 3B(21): 0.5	1.7
2019	TOR	MLB	36	165	18	6	0	4	18	22	39	1	1	.214/.333/.355	84	3.7	.268	-0.5	C 2	0.7

Breakout: 4% Improve: 27% Collapse: 13% Attrition: 20% MLB: 79%   Comparables: Sherm Lollar, Hank Gowdy, Bill Dickey

You can't go back home to your team, back home to the prime of your career, back home to a young catcher's dreams of glory and fame, to playing just for playing's sake, back home to the old statistics and systems of a game which once seemed everlasting but which is changing all the time. The past is immutable, at least where Tom Wolfe and Father Time are concerned, and never was that fact put into sharper focus than during the fourth leg of Martin's five-year, $82 million deal in Toronto. There's simply nothing outstanding about an above-average receiver with declining average and power, even if he is still getting on-base via the walk at a near-elite rate, and he found himself frequently edged out of starts as Gibbons paved a path for 20-something backstops Danny Jansen and Luke Maile during the second half of a lost season. Martin may no longer match his past, his salary or his team's plans, but sometimes finding a home is borne of circumstance, not geography.

YEAR	TEAM	P. COUNT	FRM RUNS	BLK RUNS	THRW RUNS	TOT RUNS
2016	TOR	16738	15.8	0.1	-2.8	12.5
2017	TOR	11346	2.6	-0.2	-1.1	1.1
2018	TOR	10485	7.3	1.6	-0.3	8.4
2019	TOR	5797	2.9	0.2	-0.5	2.7

Reese McGuire C   Born: 03/02/95   Age: 24   Bats: L   Throws: R   Height: 5'11"   Weight: 215   Origin: Round 1, 2013 Draft (#14 overall)

YEAR	TEAM	LVL	AGE	PA	R	2B	3B	HR	RBI	BB	K	SB	CS	AVG/OBP/SLG	DRC+	VORP	BABIP	BRR	FRAA	WARP
2016	ALT	AA	21	304	29	16	2	1	37	29	26	4	4	.259/.337/.346	95	8.5	.282	-1.8	C(73): 0.5	1.1
2016	NHP	AA	21	61	5	2	0	0	5	7	8	2	2	.226/.328/.264	99	-0.2	.267	0.7	C(13): -0.1	0.3
2017	NHP	AA	22	136	19	5	1	6	20	16	19	2	1	.278/.366/.496	120	11.3	.283	-1.9	C(32): 5.0	1.4
2018	BUF	AAA	23	369	31	9	2	7	37	33	77	3	2	.233/.312/.339	96	8.7	.281	1.6	C(73): 15.0	3.0
2018	TOR	MLB	23	33	5	3	0	2	4	2	9	1	0	.290/.333/.581	89	3.3	.350	0.3	C(11): 0.7	0.2
2019	*TOR*	*MLB*	*24*	*36*	*4*	*1*	*0*	*1*	*3*	*3*	*8*	*0*	*0*	*.215/.283/.341*	*63*	*-0.1*	*.260*	*-0.1*	*C 0*	*0.0*

Breakout: 6%   Improve: 15%   Collapse: 12%   Attrition: 22%   MLB: 45%

Comparables: Austin Barnes, Sandy Leon, Taylor Ward

The Blue Jays are looking to develop their next franchise backstop as the Russell Martin era winds down, and the defense-driven McGuire proved a key platoon candidate when rosters expanded last fall. While his bat doesn't possess Martin's maturation or Danny Jansen's pop, the 2013 first-rounder acquitted himself well during a handful of introductory at-bats in Toronto and may yet pose more than a passing threat in the batter's box. With a plus arm and a demonstrated ability to control the running game, however, the lefty's above-average defense still profiles as his best asset—anything else is simply the cherry on top.

YEAR	TEAM	P. COUNT	FRM RUNS	BLK RUNS	THRW RUNS	TOT RUNS
2017	NHP	4206	4.4	0.1	0.0	4.6
2018	BUF	9552	15.4	0.2	0.3	15.9
2018	TOR	1355	0.4	0.5	-0.1	1.0
2019	*TOR*	*1357*	*0.5*	*0.0*	*0.0*	*0.5*

Billy McKinney   OF   Born: 08/23/94   Age: 24   Bats: L   Throws: L   Height: 6'1"   Weight: 205   Origin: Round 1, 2013 Draft (#24 overall)

YEAR	TEAM	LVL	AGE	PA	R	2B	3B	HR	RBI	BB	K	SB	CS	AVG/OBP/SLG	DRC+	VORP	BABIP	BRR	FRAA	WARP
2016	TEN	AA	21	349	37	12	3	1	31	47	68	2	4	.252/.355/.322	104	5.4	.320	-0.1	RF(74): 0.0, LF(3): 1.1	1.0
2016	TRN	AA	21	142	15	7	1	3	13	12	29	2	2	.234/.310/.375	110	3.5	.281	-0.8	RF(32): 1.4, CF(1): 0.2	0.5
2017	TRN	AA	22	276	34	16	4	6	29	30	45	2	1	.250/.339/.431	108	13.5	.277	0.3	RF(50): 12.3, LF(7): -1.1	2.4
2017	SWB	AAA	22	224	32	13	3	10	35	9	49	0	0	.306/.336/.541	116	13.0	.353	-0.7	LF(26): 0.1, RF(26): 1.6	1.0
2018	NYA	MLB	23	4	0	0	0	0	0	0	1	0	0	.250/.250/.250	104	-0.1	.333	0.0	LF(2): -0.2	0.0
2018	SWB	AAA	23	234	27	8	5	13	32	21	56	0	0	.226/.299/.495	128	7.6	.245	0.5	RF(32): -1.8, CF(12): 1.6	1.3
2018	BUF	AAA	23	72	10	3	2	3	8	8	16	0	0	.203/.292/.453	132	0.9	.222	0.4	RF(14): 3.3, 1B(4): 0.0	0.8
2018	TOR	MLB	23	128	14	7	0	6	13	11	32	1	0	.252/.320/.470	100	2.9	.295	-1.9	LF(26): -0.3, RF(13): -0.3	0.1
2019	*TOR*	*MLB*	*24*	*466*	*58*	*21*	*3*	*18*	*56*	*30*	*114*	*1*	*1*	*.239/.294/.428*	*95*	*10.0*	*.283*	*-0.5*	*LF -4*	*0.6*

Breakout: 6%   Improve: 30%   Collapse: 12%   Attrition: 27%   MLB: 56%

Comparables: Kole Calhoun, Moises Sierra, Shin-Soo Choo

Ever the man on the move, McKinney ricocheted around the league as an almost featured piece in several blockbuster trades over the last few years. After a deadline deal for J.A. Happ was finalized last summer, he finally settled down in Toronto, where he slurped down his first cup of coffee in the majors with a mature approach at the plate and enough power to buoy his spot on the active roster. With an arm and two legs that play only in left field, however, his utility remains limited unless he can rediscover some of that promise he showed at the plate as a Cubs' farmhand.

Kendrys Morales   DH   Born: 06/20/83   Age: 36   Bats: B   Throws: R   Height: 6'1"   Weight: 225   Origin: International Free Agent, 2005

YEAR	TEAM	LVL	AGE	PA	R	2B	3B	HR	RBI	BB	K	SB	CS	AVG/OBP/SLG	DRC+	VORP	BABIP	BRR	FRAA	WARP
2016	KCA	MLB	33	618	65	24	0	30	93	48	120	0	0	.263/.327/.468	115	11.7	.283	-1.2	1B(7): -0.1, RF(5): -0.2	2.0
2017	TOR	MLB	34	608	67	25	0	28	85	43	132	0	0	.250/.308/.445	99	-3.6	.278	-6.3	1B(12): -1.3	0.1
2018	TOR	MLB	35	471	47	15	0	21	57	50	95	2	3	.249/.331/.438	115	2.6	.272	-4.1	1B(18): 1.8, P(1): 0.0	1.4
2019	*TOR*	*MLB*	*36*	*538*	*63*	*26*	*2*	*20*	*72*	*47*	*107*	*1*	*1*	*.258/.329/.443*	*109*	*8.8*	*.292*	*-3.0*	*1B -1*	*0.9*

Breakout: 2%   Improve: 24%   Collapse: 15%   Attrition: 19%   MLB: 82%

Comparables: Adrian Gonzalez, Don Baylor, Harold Baines

God help us if the day ever comes when Morales' bat fails to parse the strike zone for hittable pitches. The aging slugger was hobbled by a hamstring strain right out of the gate, then compensated for that lost time by being the best overall hitter on the Jays by DRC+. The only thing more intriguing than his seven-game home run tear through the AL and NL East—a streak that put him in the esteemed company of former major leaguers Kevin Mench, Barry Bonds and Jim Thome—was the pair of stolen bases he managed to nab, including his first since 2009.

Max Pentecost   C   Born: 03/10/93   Age: 26   Bats: R   Throws: R   Height: 6'2"   Weight: 191   Origin: Round 1, 2014 Draft (#11 overall)

YEAR	TEAM	LVL	AGE	PA	R	2B	3B	HR	RBI	BB	K	SB	CS	AVG/OBP/SLG	DRC+	VORP	BABIP	BRR	FRAA	WARP
2016	LNS	A	23	267	36	15	3	7	34	21	51	4	2	.314/.375/.490	135	19.0	.370	1.5		1.6
2016	DUN	A+	23	52	6	2	0	3	7	3	17	1	1	.245/.288/.469	96	0.3	.310	-0.2		0.0
2017	DUN	A+	24	314	34	14	2	9	54	23	62	0	1	.276/.332/.434	114	10.2	.323	-1.5	1B(22): 0.8, C(19): -0.3	1.1
2018	NHP	AA	25	368	40	17	2	10	52	15	89	1	0	.253/.283/.401	92	11.9	.306	1.6	C(77): -10.0	0.4
2019	*TOR*	*MLB*	*26*	*251*	*22*	*8*	*0*	*8*	*28*	*10*	*66*	*0*	*0*	*.216/.247/.349*	*54*	*-3.5*	*.262*	*-0.4*	*C -14*	*-1.9*

Breakout: 4%   Improve: 9%   Collapse: 7%   Attrition: 18%   MLB: 23%

Comparables: John Hester, Craig Tatum, Lucas May

Whispers of Pentecost's prowess behind the plate began to sound more like fairy tale lore than fact after the young backstop was cursed with repeated shoulder injuries following his first-round selection in the 2014 draft. When he was finally cleared to monitor the dish in Double-A—the result of a painstaking rehab process or the benevolence of a wish-granting genie, we'll never know—he advanced his hero's journey with half a season's worth of

YEAR	TEAM	P. COUNT	FRM RUNS	BLK RUNS	THRW RUNS	TOT RUNS
2018	NHP	10574	-13.2	0.1	1.7	-10.3
2019	*TOR*	*8816*	*-14.4*	*-0.4*	*0.3*	*-14.5*

starts, a 40 percent caught stealing rate, and a refined power stroke at the plate. Moving forward, consistency will be key, but don't write him off as a lost cause just yet.

Kevin Pillar CF Born: 01/04/89   Age: 30   Bats: R   Throws: R   Height: 6'0"   Weight: 205   Origin: Round 32, 2011 Draft (#979 overall)

YEAR	TEAM	LVL	AGE	PA	R	2B	3B	HR	RBI	BB	K	SB	CS	AVG/OBP/SLG	DRC+	VORP	BABIP	BRR	FRAA	WARP
2016	TOR	MLB	27	584	59	35	2	7	53	24	90	14	6	.266/.303/.376	78	4.2	.306	2.7	CF(146): 6.1	1.4
2017	TOR	MLB	28	632	72	37	1	16	42	33	95	15	6	.256/.300/.404	88	7.5	.280	-1.1	CF(153): -6.2	0.6
2018	TOR	MLB	29	542	65	40	2	15	59	18	98	14	3	.252/.282/.426	90	16.5	.281	3.3	CF(142): 9.0	2.5
2019	TOR	MLB	30	575	63	31	3	13	62	30	92	16	5	.257/.304/.398	90	16.8	.288	1.4	CF 1	1.9

Breakout: 3%   Improve: 52%   Collapse: 5%   Attrition: 7%   MLB: 94%   *Comparables: Leonys Martin, Cameron Maybin, Steve Finley*

You know what they say: It's all fun and games until someone dislocates their collarbone. Pillar's rough-and-tumble defense landed him in the hospital halfway through the season after a violent diving catch stretched the ligaments in his sternoclavicular joint capsule. It could have been a fatal mishap for the outfielder had the ligaments bent in another direction, but as fortune would have it, he escaped relatively unscathed and was back in uniform by early August. Near-brushes with catastrophe often inspire fervent, if short-lived change in the hearts of the lucky, but Pillar exercised little restraint upon his return to the roster and finished the year with a top-seven FRAA at his position and the highest strikeout rate in any full-season performance of his career to date.

Dalton Pompey OF Born: 12/11/92   Age: 26   Bats: B   Throws: R   Height: 6'2"   Weight: 195   Origin: Round 16, 2010 Draft (#486 overall)

YEAR	TEAM	LVL	AGE	PA	R	2B	3B	HR	RBI	BB	K	SB	CS	AVG/OBP/SLG	DRC+	VORP	BABIP	BRR	FRAA	WARP
2016	BUF	AAA	23	383	48	14	1	4	28	40	72	18	7	.270/.349/.353	96	13.9	.331	5.2	CF(67): -0.6, LF(24): -0.3	1.4
2016	TOR	MLB	23	2	3	0	0	0	0	1	2	1	.000/.000/.000	70	-0.4	.000	0.1	LF(2): -0.1	0.0
2018	TOR	MLB	25	11	0	0	0	0	0	1	6	0	0	.200/.273/.200	62	-0.9	.500	0.1	LF(3): -0.3	0.0
2018	BUF	AAA	25	168	22	8	0	4	17	14	41	8	2	.255/.325/.393	84	8.3	.317	1.7	RF(18): -3.0, LF(14): -2.3	-0.5
2019	TOR	MLB	26	251	31	10	1	6	23	18	65	7	2	.216/.282/.349	72	-0.7	.271	0.4	LF 0, RF -2	-0.3

Breakout: 2%   Improve: 19%   Collapse: 14%   Attrition: 20%   MLB: 47%   *Comparables: Thomas Neal, Dave Sappelt, Brandon Guyer*

"It is not the last drop that empties the water-clock," Seneca cautioned Lucilius, "but all that which previously has flowed out; similarly, the final hour when we cease to exist does not of itself bring death; it merely of itself completes the death process." So, too, is the way of a decaying career, as Pompey discovered after a string of injury-laden seasons extended to a wrist sprain in early March and a partial UCL tear in his left thumb by June. That fatal, unbearable drop emptied Pompey's clock in August, when Triple-A manager Bobby Meacham made a seemingly innocuous decision to pinch-hit for the former top prospect in the second inning of a split doubleheader. Pompey blew up at Meacham, was swiftly suspended without pay, and finished out the year batting .167 over his last dozen games, further away from a major-league gig than ever before.

Justin Smoak 1B Born: 12/05/86   Age: 32   Bats: B   Throws: L   Height: 6'4"   Weight: 220   Origin: Round 1, 2008 Draft (#11 overall)

YEAR	TEAM	LVL	AGE	PA	R	2B	3B	HR	RBI	BB	K	SB	CS	AVG/OBP/SLG	DRC+	VORP	BABIP	BRR	FRAA	WARP
2016	TOR	MLB	29	341	33	10	0	14	34	40	112	1	0	.217/.314/.391	92	-3.8	.295	-1.3	1B(111): -2.3	-0.2
2017	TOR	MLB	30	637	85	29	1	38	90	73	128	0	1	.270/.355/.529	132	26.6	.285	0.6	1B(151): -0.9	3.5
2018	TOR	MLB	31	594	67	34	0	25	77	83	156	0	1	.242/.350/.457	114	15.1	.297	-5.1	1B(134): -7.2	0.6
2019	TOR	MLB	32	604	75	29	2	25	85	73	146	1	1	.251/.345/.456	118	20.6	.300	-1.7	1B -5	1.7

Breakout: 2%   Improve: 34%   Collapse: 4%   Attrition: 6%   MLB: 89%   *Comparables: Garrett Jones, Lucas Duda, Adam Lind*

There's no rule that says you can't reinvent yourself in the deepening twilight of your career. Within Major League Baseball, at least, those who can play will play, and in 2017 Smoak ran ragged through the American League East and put a lusterless lifetime batting line to shame. No crystal ball was needed to foretell the slugger's inevitable regression in 2018—accelerated as it was by a career-worst strikeout rate—but the changes he made during his breakout campaign held fast. After tweaking his timing against offspeed pitches and exercising some self-control on balls outside the zone, Smoak was rewarded with another burst of power at the plate, suggesting that the once-elite prospect may have turned that corner for good.

Yangervis Solarte INF Born: 07/03/87   Age: 31   Bats: B   Throws: R   Height: 5'11"   Weight: 205   Origin: International Free Agent, 2005

YEAR	TEAM	LVL	AGE	PA	R	2B	3B	HR	RBI	BB	K	SB	CS	AVG/OBP/SLG	DRC+	VORP	BABIP	BRR	FRAA	WARP
2016	SDN	MLB	28	443	55	26	1	15	71	30	63	1	1	.286/.341/.467	110	24.9	.306	-2.2	3B(95): 6.1, 2B(15): 0.9	2.7
2017	SDN	MLB	29	512	49	21	0	18	64	37	61	3	0	.255/.314/.416	103	16.9	.258	0.5	2B(79): -3.4, SS(28): -1.8	1.6
2018	TOR	MLB	30	506	50	20	0	17	54	31	72	1	3	.226/.277/.378	87	-7.8	.233	-3.4	3B(83): 0.1, 2B(28): -0.5	0.5
2019	TOR	MLB	31	480	52	24	1	15	59	33	65	2	1	.260/.319/.420	99	11.0	.277	-1.3	3B 1, 2B -1	1.0

Breakout: 2%   Improve: 44%   Collapse: 3%   Attrition: 8%   MLB: 97%   *Comparables: Alberto Callaspo, Pie Traynor, Martin Prado*

In ways both bittersweet and sour, Solarte picked up the mantle left by fan favorite Munenori Kawasaki upon his arrival to Rogers Centre in the spring of 2018. His infectious energy spilled out of the dugout, manifesting in toe-tapping stretches, spontaneous drumming and something that he dubbed "El Sexy Time." That kind of pure joy should permeate what is, at its core, still a simple game, but Solarte began to mirror Kawasaki in less-delightful ways as the season started to pick up. Once a promising cleanup hitter, his approach waned in his age-30 season and, as a result, saw the first below-average offensive season of his career. He's also entering the phase of his career where defensive utility is something he'll have to fight for on a yearly basis, and Solarte lost that battle in 2018 as his hot corner defense slowly erodes into more gaffes than highlight-reel head-turners.

Rowdy Tellez 1B Born: 03/16/95 Age: 24 Bats: L Throws: L Height: 6'4" Weight: 220 Origin: Round 30, 2013 Draft (#895 overall)

YEAR	TEAM	LVL	AGE	PA	R	2B	3B	HR	RBI	BB	K	SB	CS	AVG/OBP/SLG	DRC+	VORP	BABIP	BRR	FRAA	WARP
2016	NHP	AA	21	514	71	29	2	23	81	63	92	4	3	.297/.387/.530	133	29.7	.324	-0.9	1B(101): -4.9	1.8
2017	BUF	AAA	22	501	45	29	1	6	56	47	94	6	1	.222/.295/.333	87	-11.6	.264	-0.6	1B(115): 1.8	-0.1
2018	BUF	AAA	23	444	43	22	0	13	50	40	74	7	4	.270/.340/.425	118	9.5	.298	-0.8	1B(107): -3.0	1.2
2018	TOR	MLB	23	73	10	9	0	4	14	2	21	0	0	.314/.329/.614	88	5.4	.391	-0.1	1B(17): -0.4	0.0
2019	TOR	MLB	24	170	17	7	0	4	19	13	35	1	0	.228/.293/.364	66	-5.0	.266	-0.3	1B -1	-0.6

Breakout: 6% Improve: 22% Collapse: 11% Attrition: 31% MLB: 53% *Comparables: Chris Parmelee, Yonder Alonso, Mike Carp*

Tellez finally grew into his name after a much-needed resurgence in Triple-A, where he disrupted his career batting line with a boisterous .298 BABIP and more helium in his swing than you'd find at any local Party City. He got the call to The Show toward the end of the regular season and impressed there, too. That said, his arm and run tool sit near the low end of the 20-80 scale and his flawed plate mechanics suggest that his burst of power may not be sustainable in the long run. Given that the 23-year-old weathered more than most his age, however—his mother passed away from Stage 4 melanoma two weeks prior to his call-up—his character is just about near 80-grade.

Devon Travis 2B Born: 02/21/91 Age: 28 Bats: R Throws: R Height: 5'9" Weight: 190 Origin: Round 13, 2012 Draft (#424 overall)

YEAR	TEAM	LVL	AGE	PA	R	2B	3B	HR	RBI	BB	K	SB	CS	AVG/OBP/SLG	DRC+	VORP	BABIP	BRR	FRAA	WARP
2016	TOR	MLB	25	432	54	28	1	11	50	20	87	4	1	.300/.332/.454	93	15.7	.358	1.6	2B(99): -0.4	1.1
2017	TOR	MLB	26	197	22	18	0	5	24	7	38	4	2	.259/.291/.438	81	3.4	.299	1.2	2B(50): -1.9	0.1
2018	BUF	AAA	27	64	9	1	0	1	4	2	7	1	0	.210/.234/.274	106	-3.9	.222	0.5	2B(12): 3.1	0.6
2018	TOR	MLB	27	378	41	14	3	11	44	16	64	3	2	.232/.275/.381	82	0.1	.255	0.8	2B(101): -1.5	0.3
2019	TOR	MLB	28	415	45	21	2	11	45	23	75	5	2	.252/.302/.400	92	10.9	.289	1.1	2B 0	1.2

Breakout: 2% Improve: 52% Collapse: 2% Attrition: 3% MLB: 96% *Comparables: Scooter Gennett, Omar Infante, Aaron Hill*

If it wasn't core muscle surgery, it was exploratory shoulder surgery. If it wasn't exploratory shoulder surgery, it was knee surgery. If it wasn't surgery at all, then it was an inexplicable decline over his first healthy stretch of pro ball in half a decade. In 2018, Travis' head-scratching results at the plate read like a dour parody of *If You Give a Mouse a Cookie*; though injury-free once more, his career-high 11 home runs and marginally improved walk and strikeout rates were offset by an alarming .255 BABIP and a sharp downturn in his ability to hit for extra bases. As predictably as a thirsty mouse feeding his addiction to baked goods, Travis' latest campaign ground to a halt yet again with multiple bouts of season-ending knee and hamstring soreness. The keystone will be waiting for him again in the spring, but Brandon Drury and Lourdes Gurriel Jr. look like equally capable (and healthier) alternatives at this point.

Richard Urena MI Born: 02/26/96 Age: 23 Bats: B Throws: R Height: 6'0" Weight: 185 Origin: International Free Agent, 2012

YEAR	TEAM	LVL	AGE	PA	R	2B	3B	HR	RBI	BB	K	SB	CS	AVG/OBP/SLG	DRC+	VORP	BABIP	BRR	FRAA	WARP
2016	DUN	A+	20	431	52	18	7	8	41	25	64	9	6	.305/.351/.447	121	17.0	.346	-1.3	SS(79): -0.1	2.6
2016	NHP	AA	20	132	14	6	5	0	18	4	19	0	2	.266/.282/.395	96	5.3	.306	0.7	SS(29): -0.7	0.5
2017	NHP	AA	21	551	44	36	3	5	60	30	100	1	0	.247/.286/.359	72	6.3	.294	-1.9	SS(106): -4.6, 2B(11): 0.2	-0.3
2017	TOR	MLB	21	75	6	4	0	1	4	6	28	1	0	.206/.270/.309	60	0.4	.333	1.4	SS(20): -2.0, 2B(1): 0.1	-0.1
2018	BUF	AAA	22	268	28	11	3	5	29	12	48	2	3	.216/.250/.344	77	-4.6	.246	-0.6	SS(43): 1.8, 2B(17): 0.9	0.5
2018	TOR	MLB	22	108	10	4	0	1	6	7	32	2	1	.293/.340/.364	66	0.6	.424	-1.2	SS(20): -1.3, 2B(13): -1.0	-0.4
2019	TOR	MLB	23	292	27	12	1	6	28	19	77	2	1	.215/.270/.340	61	-5.1	.273	-0.5	SS -1, 3B -1	-0.7

Breakout: 13% Improve: 28% Collapse: 14% Attrition: 31% MLB: 51% *Comparables: Ronny Cedeno, Christian Arroyo, Jose Rondon*

It's difficult to judge a singing competition inasmuch as it's difficult to tell hundreds of people—live, on national television—that the thing they love most in life is the thing for which they have no remarkable talent. In the age of chunky highlights and Britney Spears wannabes, *American Idol* judge Paula Abdul had a knack for letting contestants down easy. "You're so pretty," she'd gush before complimenting their smile or their bedazzled outfit or the passion with which they attempted each note. Hollow though the praise may have been, it was just enough to distract from the contestants' off-key warbling and botched lyrics and the tactless remarks of her fellow judges. Well, Urena has a pretty swing from both sides of the plate and he should never stop chasing his dreams—though he probably should stop chasing pitches outside the strike zone.

Forrest Wall CF Born: 11/20/95 Age: 23 Bats: L Throws: R Height: 6'0" Weight: 176 Origin: Round 1, 2014 Draft (#35 overall)

YEAR	TEAM	LVL	AGE	PA	R	2B	3B	HR	RBI	BB	K	SB	CS	AVG/OBP/SLG	DRC+	VORP	BABIP	BRR	FRAA	WARP
2016	MOD	A+	20	521	57	16	4	6	56	41	97	22	11	.264/.329/.355	89	18.2	.319	0.6	2B(117): -4.5	0.4
2017	LNC	A+	21	98	17	4	1	3	16	9	16	5	3	.299/.361/.471	116	5.9	.333	2.4	CF(17): 0.5, LF(2): -0.4	0.7
2018	LNC	A+	22	230	43	11	5	3	19	23	47	20	8	.305/.382/.453	116	14.5	.386	1.4	CF(39): -11.1, LF(1): 0.7	0.2
2018	HFD	AA	22	190	27	6	1	6	12	17	42	8	3	.206/.289/.359	87	0.9	.238	2.3	CF(26): -1.7, LF(18): 4.5	0.8
2018	NHP	AA	22	147	19	7	2	1	13	13	46	10	3	.271/.354/.380	93	3.5	.410	-0.6	CF(34): -6.5	-0.4
2019	TOR	MLB	23	251	31	10	1	6	23	14	63	9	3	.227/.273/.362	65	-0.9	.280	0.5	CF -5, LF 1	-0.6

Breakout: 1% Improve: 2% Collapse: 3% Attrition: 5% MLB: 6% *Comparables: Blake Tekotte, Rosell Herrera, Andrew Stevenson*

A year after he saw his season derailed by a freak shoulder dislocation, Wall's major league future remains as unpredictable and full of potential as an episode of, well, *The Wall*. The former 35th overall pick headlined a package deal for reliever Seung-hwan Oh in July and used his plus speed to both steal nearly 40 bases across two levels and take circuitous routes to fly balls. It seems unlikely that the Blue Jays would risk everything to roll the dice (er, "triple up") on a fringe-average fourth outfielder, but if there's any lesson to be gleaned from watching sweaty-palmed contestants attempt to manipulate the random workings of a four-foot pegboard, it's this: Sometimes the unlikeliest gamble reaps the biggest dividends.

PITCHERS

Danny Barnes RHP
Born: 10/21/89   Age: 29   Bats: L   Throws: R   Height: 6'1"   Weight: 195   Origin: Round 35, 2010 Draft (#1056 overall)

YEAR	TEAM	LVL	AGE	W	L	SV	G	GS	IP	H	HR	BB/9	K/9	K	GB%	BABIP	WHIP	ERA	DRA	WARP	MPH	FB%	WHF	CSP
2016	NHP	AA	26	2	1	1	24	0	35²	17	3	1.0	10.1	40	30%	.177	0.59	1.01	3.16	0.7				
2016	BUF	AAA	26	1	0	5	17	0	25²	6	0	0.7	13.0	37	32%	.128	0.31	0.35	1.79	0.9				
2016	TOR	MLB	26	0	0	0	12	0	13²	14	0	3.3	9.2	14	44%	.359	1.39	3.95	3.59	0.2	94.1	66.7	12.4	45.4
2017	BUF	AAA	27	0	1	2	4	0	6	6	0	0.0	12.0	8	25%	.375	1.00	3.00	1.89	0.2				
2017	TOR	MLB	27	3	6	0	60	0	66	48	11	3.3	8.5	62	33%	.222	1.09	3.55	5.51	-0.3	93.6	67.8	12.4	47.3
2018	BUF	AAA	28	1	1	0	7	0	8²	9	1	1.0	11.4	11	21%	.348	1.15	5.19	3.33	0.2				
2018	TOR	MLB	28	3	3	0	47	0	41	47	6	4.8	8.3	38	36%	.333	1.68	5.71	6.18	-0.6	93.6	65.6	10.6	44.6
2019	TOR	MLB	29	2	1	0	51	0	54¹	53	9	3.8	8.7	52	36%	.295	1.40	4.86	5.01	0.0	93.0	66.7	11.6	45.7

Breakout: 18%   Improve: 41%   Collapse: 16%   Attrition: 20%   MLB: 76%   Comparables: Brad Brach, Josh Fields, Arquimedes Caminero

In highwire artistry, success hinges on the ability to replicate movement. The body's center of gravity must remain low, its feet must counteract the frequent and imprecise rotations of the cable, and its arms must maintain perfect balance above the support point. One miscalculation of the cable's shift, one untimely sneeze or blink, and it's all over. Phillippe Petit was not wrong to assert, some 30-odd years after he gripped a 200-foot wire between the Twin Towers, that death itself frames the high wire.

While the middling middle reliever may never know life-or-death stakes when he steps onto the mound, he teeters along a similarly-narrow margin for error. One misstep—one ill-timed disabled list stint, one stretch of 6.00+ DRA ball—and he could lose his footing on the thin line that separates a replacement-level offering from total oblivion. Barnes found himself in just such a precarious position this spring when, after spending the winter solidifying a shaky slider, he contracted a bout of knee tendinitis that set him back for a month. His control wavered, batters started to get a handle on his once-excellent changeup, and he became no more distinguishable from a handful of warm bodies hovering between the relief corps and rotation. Luckily, the righty's path back to success appears to be as effortless as his fall from grace: simply putting one foot in front of the other, one inning at a time, with no thought to the career-ending pavement below.

Joe Biagini RHP
Born: 05/29/90   Age: 29   Bats: R   Throws: R   Height: 6'5"   Weight: 240   Origin: Round 26, 2011 Draft (#807 overall)

YEAR	TEAM	LVL	AGE	W	L	SV	G	GS	IP	H	HR	BB/9	K/9	K	GB%	BABIP	WHIP	ERA	DRA	WARP	MPH	FB%	WHF	CSP
2016	TOR	MLB	26	4	3	1	60	0	67²	69	3	2.5	8.2	62	54%	.320	1.30	3.06	3.87	0.9	96.4	58.7	12.3	45.1
2017	BUF	AAA	27	1	1	0	4	4	17¹	13	2	3.1	7.3	14	58%	.239	1.10	3.12	4.14	0.3				
2017	TOR	MLB	27	3	13	1	44	18	119²	125	15	3.2	7.3	97	56%	.305	1.40	5.34	3.98	2.0	95.5	52.9	9	47.1
2018	BUF	AAA	28	0	3	0	4	4	21²	19	1	3.3	5.4	13	45%	.257	1.25	4.57	4.87	0.2				
2018	TOR	MLB	28	4	7	0	50	4	72	96	14	3.0	6.6	53	49%	.355	1.67	6.00	5.72	-0.6	96.3	60.8	9.5	45.6
2019	TOR	MLB	29	4	1	0	72	0	75²	82	10	3.2	7.0	59	49%	.307	1.43	4.69	4.82	0.2	95.3	56.9	9.8	46

Breakout: 33%   Improve: 45%   Collapse: 21%   Attrition: 20%   MLB: 83%   Comparables: Burke Badenhop, Craig Stammen, Clay Hensley

Catch Biagini on a good day, and he might tell you the story of how he unlocked his cutter after a giant talking baseball appeared to him in a drug-induced haze. Catch him on a bad day, however, and you're looking at a failed starter whose entirely sober attempts to stick in the bullpen have been underwhelming, if not downright questionable of late. The Biagini that showed up for Toronto in 2016—the one who tamed a mid-90s fastball-curve combo and whose 3.26 K/BB evidenced true starter potential—pulled off a vanishing act soon thereafter, a party trick far less entertaining than his infamous tall tales.

Ryan Borucki LHP
Born: 03/31/94   Age: 25   Bats: L   Throws: L   Height: 6'4"   Weight: 175   Origin: Round 15, 2012 Draft (#475 overall)

YEAR	TEAM	LVL	AGE	W	L	SV	G	GS	IP	H	HR	BB/9	K/9	K	GB%	BABIP	WHIP	ERA	DRA	WARP	MPH	FB%	WHF	CSP
2016	DUN	A+	22	1	4	0	6	6	20	40	10	5.4	4.5	10	48%	.395	2.60	14.40	7.78	-0.5				
2016	LNS	A	22	10	4	0	20	20	115²	105	1	2.0	8.3	107	51%	.322	1.13	2.41	3.36	2.3				
2017	DUN	A+	23	6	5	0	19	18	98	95	5	2.5	10.0	109	52%	.342	1.24	3.58	3.09	2.5				
2017	NHP	AA	23	2	3	0	7	7	46¹	31	2	1.6	8.2	42	58%	.236	0.84	1.94	3.45	0.9				
2017	BUF	AAA	23	0	0	0	1	1	6	6	0	1.5	9.0	6	50%	.375	1.17	0.00	3.02	0.2				
2018	BUF	AAA	24	6	5	0	13	13	77	62	6	3.3	6.8	58	52%	.255	1.17	3.27	3.99	1.4				
2018	TOR	MLB	24	4	6	0	17	17	97²	96	7	3.0	6.2	67	49%	.291	1.32	3.87	4.53	0.9	93.1	58.7	8.7	49.1
2019	TOR	MLB	25	7	9	0	23	23	131	135	16	3.3	7.1	104	47%	.299	1.39	4.62	4.75	1.1	92.8	60.1	8.9	50.3

Breakout: 14%   Improve: 41%   Collapse: 22%   Attrition: 30%   MLB: 81%   Comparables: Adalberto Mejia, Chris Archer, Robbie Ross

We can repeat "good when healthy" ad nauseam, but the caution surrounding Borucki's call-up is valid, and not just because the fresh-faced southpaw underwent Tommy John surgery at the ripe old age of 19 in 2013. Even when firing on all cylinders, Borucki lacks the kind of standout tools that will help separate him from the rest of the pack—in other words, he's hardly what you'd describe as the second coming of lefty hurlers Clayton Kershaw or Madison Bumgarner. Though what he lacks in overwhelming talent, he makes up for with consistency (peep the 11 quality starts that formed the bulk of his performance in 2018) and a no-nonsense, low-90s fastball. While the jury's still out on his major-league ceiling, he should be able to keep the rookie jitters at bay long enough to earn another long look in 2019.

Tyler Clippard RHP Born: 02/14/85 Age: 34 Bats: R Throws: R Height: 6'3" Weight: 200 Origin: Round 9, 2003 Draft (#274 overall)

YEAR	TEAM	LVL	AGE	W	L	SV	G	GS	IP	H	HR	BB/9	K/9	K	GB%	BABIP	WHIP	ERA	DRA	WARP	MPH	FB%	WHF	CSP
2016	ARI	MLB	31	2	3	1	40	0	37²	34	7	3.6	11.0	46	34%	.310	1.30	4.30	4.33	0.3	93.3	46.3	13.9	45.8
2016	NYA	MLB	31	2	3	2	29	0	25¹	20	3	3.9	9.2	26	32%	.258	1.22	2.49	3.57	0.4	93.8	42.9	13.1	46.6
2017	NYA	MLB	32	1	5	1	40	0	36¹	28	7	4.7	10.4	42	35%	.236	1.29	4.95	2.86	0.9	92.3	40.4	15.9	43.9
2017	CHA	MLB	32	1	1	2	11	0	10	8	0	4.5	10.8	12	30%	.296	1.30	1.80	2.76	0.3	92.8	32.9	14.5	41.2
2017	HOU	MLB	32	0	2	2	16	0	14	11	3	4.5	11.6	18	36%	.242	1.29	6.43	3.48	0.3	91.6	36.3	12.6	47.3
2018	TOR	MLB	33	4	3	7	73	1	68²	57	13	3.0	11.1	85	22%	.272	1.17	3.67	3.55	1.1	92.3	41.8	15.8	45.5
2019	*TOR*	*MLB*	*34*	*3*	*1*	*3*	*53*	*0*	*56¹*	*51*	*11*	*3.7*	*10.1*	*64*	*31%*	*.276*	*1.32*	*5.04*	*5.21*	*-0.1*	*91.5*	*40.6*	*14.7*	*44.6*

Breakout: 18%   Improve: 36%   Collapse: 33%   Attrition: 13%   MLB: 92%   *Comparables: Scott Sauerbeck, Francisco Rodriguez, John Hiller*

Inked to a minor-league pact at the start of the season, Clippard wormed his way into a major-league role by late spring and proved an intriguing, if unreliable addition to the Blue Jays' relief corps. He replaced Roberto Osuna when the closer was dealt a 75-game suspension following allegations of domestic violence, but lost it just as quickly to Ryan Tepera and was relegated to mop-up duty in the seventh and eighth for the remainder of the year. While the Blue Jays elected not to give the bespectacled righty an encore in 2019, they provided a platform for him to set a new major league record when, after 10 years and 680 consecutive relief appearances since his previous career start, he opened a game against the Mariners and pitched one disastrous inning of three-hit, two-run, one-strikeout ball.

Marco Estrada RHP Born: 07/05/83 Age: 35 Bats: R Throws: R Height: 6'0" Weight: 180 Origin: Round 6, 2005 Draft (#174 overall)

YEAR	TEAM	LVL	AGE	W	L	SV	G	GS	IP	H	HR	BB/9	K/9	K	GB%	BABIP	WHIP	ERA	DRA	WARP	MPH	FB%	WHF	CSP
2016	TOR	MLB	32	9	9	0	29	29	176	132	23	3.3	8.4	165	35%	.234	1.12	3.48	4.30	2.1	90.2	50.1	12	44.8
2017	TOR	MLB	33	10	9	0	33	33	186	186	31	3.4	8.5	176	31%	.295	1.38	4.98	5.76	-0.4	91.0	53.8	11.8	47.4
2018	TOR	MLB	34	7	14	0	28	28	143²	155	29	3.1	6.5	103	26%	.285	1.43	5.64	7.16	-3.1	90.0	49.2	11.3	46.3
2019	*TOR*	*MLB*	*35*	*6*	*10*	*0*	*23*	*23*	*132²*	*134*	*26*	*3.3*	*6.9*	*102*	*32%*	*.271*	*1.38*	*5.56*	*5.76*	*-0.4*	*89.3*	*50.3*	*11.5*	*45.5*

Breakout: 14%   Improve: 32%   Collapse: 27%   Attrition: 11%   MLB: 86%   *Comparables: Earl Wilson, Bruce Hurst, Jason Hammel*

You can say three definitive things about Estrada. First: His changeup—the singular force driving his career resurgence since 2015—is failing. He threw it more than ever in 2018, favoring the slow, hovering pitch over a fastball that barely crested 89 mph and a handful of secondaries that became fodder for the second-highest home run rate in the league yet batters rocked it for a .248 average and .281 BABIP even so. Second: His diligence to his craft is taking an irreversible toll on his body. After getting diagnosed with a left glute strain in July, he attempted to pitch through a painful bulging disc and arthritic joints in his back, conditions that, when combined, forced him to limp into free agency. Third: There's nowhere for the slow-tossing righty to go but up. Estrada may not be capable of another award-worthy transformation in his age-35 season, but as anyone who's tried (and failed) to anticipate the erratic backspin of his signature pitch can tell you, he's never been one to look for success in all the conventional places, either.

Samuel Gaviglio RHP Born: 05/22/90 Age: 29 Bats: R Throws: R Height: 6'2" Weight: 195 Origin: Round 5, 2011 Draft (#170 overall)

YEAR	TEAM	LVL	AGE	W	L	SV	G	GS	IP	H	HR	BB/9	K/9	K	GB%	BABIP	WHIP	ERA	DRA	WARP	MPH	FB%	WHF	CSP
2016	WTN	AA	26	5	5	0	18	17	102	104	7	1.9	6.4	73	54%	.303	1.24	4.15	3.16	2.3				
2016	TAC	AAA	26	3	2	0	10	9	63	59	7	2.0	7.1	50	50%	.278	1.16	3.71	3.73	1.1				
2017	SEA	MLB	27	3	5	0	12	11	62¹	63	15	3.0	5.8	40	49%	.265	1.35	4.62	5.69	-0.1	90.3	56.6	7.3	50.3
2017	TAC	AAA	27	3	6	0	13	13	72	72	5	1.5	7.1	57	54%	.302	1.17	3.88	3.53	1.7				
2017	KCA	MLB	27	1	0	0	4	2	12	13	1	3.8	6.8	9	56%	.316	1.50	3.00	5.12	0.1	91.0	59.5	10	51.2
2018	BUF	AAA	28	0	0	0	5	5	29	21	4	1.2	9.0	29	46%	.243	0.86	1.86	3.81	0.6				
2018	TOR	MLB	28	3	10	0	26	24	123²	140	21	2.8	7.6	105	50%	.313	1.44	5.31	4.90	0.6	90.2	56	9.2	46.7
2019	*TOR*	*MLB*	*29*	*5*	*4*	*0*	*46*	*10*	*91*	*95*	*12*	*2.8*	*7.3*	*73*	*48%*	*.301*	*1.36*	*4.55*	*4.67*	*0.5*	*89.6*	*56.3*	*8.8*	*48.4*

Breakout: 22%   Improve: 30%   Collapse: 24%   Attrition: 18%   MLB: 62%   *Comparables: Philip Humber, Chris Rusin, Mike Bolsinger*

Nothing Gaviglio does should work in the majors. He shouldn't be able to hold down a rotation spot with a fastball that barely grazes 88 mph. He shouldn't be able to dance around the strike zone 59.2 percent of the time. He shouldn't be able to get hitters to chase bad pitches with any kind of regularity, and he shouldn't treat that ability as a viable in-game strategy. One look at the righty's wild animal of a slider is enough to put most of those fears to rest, however. He hasn't fully tamed the pitch yet, but a dash of lateral movement caused 54 percent of batters to chase after it in 2018 and his vastly-improved whiff rate is a harbinger of better things to come. There's no guarantee that the Blue Jays will keep a rotation spot free for the starter moving forward, but he possesses the tools and creative potential to carve his own unorthodox path to success.

Ken Giles RHP Born: 09/20/90 Age: 28 Bats: R Throws: R Height: 6'2" Weight: 205 Origin: Round 7, 2011 Draft (#241 overall)

YEAR	TEAM	LVL	AGE	W	L	SV	G	GS	IP	H	HR	BB/9	K/9	K	GB%	BABIP	WHIP	ERA	DRA	WARP	MPH	FB%	WHF	CSP
2016	HOU	MLB	25	2	5	15	69	0	65²	60	8	3.4	14.0	102	41%	.349	1.29	4.11	2.10	2.2	100.0	52.1	20.9	42.4
2017	HOU	MLB	26	1	3	34	63	0	62²	44	4	3.0	11.9	83	45%	.290	1.04	2.30	2.85	1.6	99.7	52.8	17.2	49.1
2018	HOU	MLB	27	0	2	12	34	0	30²	36	2	0.9	9.1	31	37%	.366	1.27	4.99	3.42	0.5	98.9	57.7	16.9	51.8
2018	TOR	MLB	27	0	1	14	21	0	19²	18	4	1.8	10.1	22	54%	.269	1.12	4.12	3.18	0.4	98.9	61.3	16.3	48.9
2019	*TOR*	*MLB*	*28*	*3*	*1*	*32*	*56*	*0*	*59²*	*56*	*7*	*3.1*	*10.1*	*67*	*42%*	*.310*	*1.29*	*3.79*	*3.87*	*0.7*	*98.9*	*55.1*	*18.2*	*48.4*

Breakout: 28%   Improve: 43%   Collapse: 30%   Attrition: 11%   MLB: 90%   *Comparables: Cody Allen, Francisco Rodriguez, Jordan Walden*

"I'm actually enjoying the game more than I did for my entire tenure in Houston," Giles told reporters following his midseason shift from the defending champion Astros to the defending fourth-place Blue Jays. "It's kind of weird to say that because I won a World Series with that team." A.J. Hinch vehemently denied the charges, but there was no question that his former closer felt a degree of comfort in Toronto that he hadn't been able to grab hold of in Houston. Like a college kid enjoying the luxuries of homemade cooking and parent-folded laundry on winter break, Giles perhaps relaxed into his new role a little too easily. His peripherals were as strong as ever, but his ERA ballooned back up above four, and his WARP dipped below one for the first time in his career. The scorching heater that headlines his pitch repertoire also lost a little gas in the chilly Canadian clime. It might be said here that comfort and complacency are close neighbors—an adage better taken to heart early than late.

Taylor Guerrieri RHP Born: 12/01/92 Age: 26 Bats: R Throws: R Height: 6'2" Weight: 210 Origin: Round 1, 2011 Draft (#24 overall)

YEAR	TEAM	LVL	AGE	W	L	SV	G	GS	IP	H	HR	BB/9	K/9	K	GB%	BABIP	WHIP	ERA	DRA	WARP	MPH	FB%	WHF	CSP
2016	MNT	AA	23	12	6	1	28	26	146	130	11	2.8	5.5	89	58%	.266	1.21	3.76	6.06	-1.7				
2017	DUR	AAA	24	1	0	0	2	2	9¹	7	0	1.9	11.6	12	71%	.292	0.96	2.89	1.96	0.4				
2018	BUF	AAA	25	2	2	0	23	7	57¹	68	8	3.5	6.4	41	56%	.326	1.57	5.18	4.27	0.7				
2018	TOR	MLB	25	0	0	0	9	0	9²	9	1	3.7	7.4	8	59%	.286	1.34	4.66	4.92	0.0	93.3	76.7	12.8	42.3
2019	TOR	MLB	26	3	3	0	17	9	50²	50	6	3.4	7.2	41	52%	.295	1.38	4.55	4.67	0.4	92.9	78.1	13	43.1

Breakout: 15% Improve: 22% Collapse: 12% Attrition: 25% MLB: 38% *Comparables: Myles Jaye, Jason Hursh, Zeke Spruill*

Guerrieri spun 24 curveballs against major-league batters in 2018, each with the same unusual grip: right index finger crossed over the middle digit, like a wish for good luck or a white lie, and pressed along the ridge of the seams. The Blue Jays crossed their fingers just as hard for the rookie's first tryout in the big leagues, but to no avail: a squirm-inducing ERA and undisclosed health issues rushed the former top prospect right back into obscurity—and free agency.

Mark Leiter RHP Born: 03/13/91 Age: 28 Bats: R Throws: R Height: 6'0" Weight: 195 Origin: Round 22, 2013 Draft (#661 overall)

YEAR	TEAM	LVL	AGE	W	L	SV	G	GS	IP	H	HR	BB/9	K/9	K	GB%	BABIP	WHIP	ERA	DRA	WARP	MPH	FB%	WHF	CSP
2016	REA	AA	25	6	3	1	23	17	103²	91	9	2.6	8.2	94	46%	.288	1.17	3.39	3.15	2.3				
2017	LEH	AAA	26	2	1	0	7	5	30	27	5	1.8	11.4	38	53%	.297	1.10	4.20	2.62	1.0				
2017	PHI	MLB	26	3	6	0	27	11	90²	90	18	3.1	8.3	84	50%	.282	1.33	4.96	5.43	0.0	92.5	55.6	9.4	47.3
2018	PHI	MLB	27	0	1	0	12	0	16²	22	5	4.3	7.0	13	52%	.298	1.80	5.40	7.45	-0.5	92.8	48.7	11.4	46.9
2018	LEH	AAA	27	3	1	0	20	0	28¹	28	3	4.1	9.5	30	45%	.316	1.45	3.81	4.76	0.1				
2018	TOR	MLB	27	0	0	0	8	0	6²	13	2	5.4	12.1	9	36%	.478	2.55	13.50	9.13	-0.3	92.2	48.7	9.3	42
2019	TOR	MLB	28	1	1	0	31	0	32²	33	5	3.7	8.7	31	44%	.306	1.43	4.81	4.95	0.1	92.0	54	9.8	46.5

Breakout: 27% Improve: 47% Collapse: 14% Attrition: 27% MLB: 69% *Comparables: Dan Meyer, Sam LeCure, Tyler Lyons*

Elevated by dint of his family connections—father and former major-league pitcher, Mark Sr., and uncle and Blue Jays southpaw, Al—Leiter may have felt the legacy talents breathing down his neck when he was claimed off of waivers and given a fresh start in Toronto last September. Evidently, the Blue Jays didn't share the same high hopes for the righty and the substandard fastball in his tool belt. Leiter's value as a multifaceted swingman was compromised when he converted to full-time relief in 2018. His heater went up a few ticks on the radar gun, but what little speed he gained was negated by his inability to control balls and strikes. Another stint in Triple-A should help him pare down an overloaded pitch repertoire and sharpen his command, but it's anyone's guess as to when he'll be able to slice into a major-league strike zone again.

Justin Maese RHP Born: 10/24/96 Age: 22 Bats: R Throws: R Height: 6'3" Weight: 190 Origin: Round 3, 2015 Draft (#91 overall)

YEAR	TEAM	LVL	AGE	W	L	SV	G	GS	IP	H	HR	BB/9	K/9	K	GB%	BABIP	WHIP	ERA	DRA	WARP	MPH	FB%	WHF	CSP
2016	VAN	A-	19	2	2	0	5	5	26¹	20	1	0.3	6.8	20	68%	.241	0.80	2.05	2.58	0.8				
2016	LNS	A	19	2	4	0	10	10	56¹	59	2	2.2	7.0	44	57%	.331	1.30	3.36	5.33	-0.2				
2017	LNS	A	20	5	3	0	12	12	70²	78	3	3.3	7.6	60	55%	.341	1.47	4.84	5.22	0.1				
2019	TOR	MLB	22	2	2	0	6	6	33¹	39	5	3.5	6.0	22	48%	.313	1.55	5.23	5.40	0.0				

Breakout: 2% Improve: 3% Collapse: 0% Attrition: 2% MLB: 3% *Comparables: Myles Jaye, Jace Fry, Joely Rodriguez*

The only thing worse than watching a promising young pitcher tough his way through an injury-shortened season is watching him do it twice. The shoulder impingement that dogged Maese in 2017 lingered well into the late spring of 2018, forcing the right-hander and his wicked mid-90s fastball to forego a reservation in High-A Dunedin's rotation, and erased any likelihood that he might soon crack the upper echelon of the club's prospect hierarchy.

Tim Mayza LHP Born: 01/15/92 Age: 27 Bats: L Throws: L Height: 6'3" Weight: 220 Origin: Round 12, 2013 Draft (#355 overall)

YEAR	TEAM	LVL	AGE	W	L	SV	G	GS	IP	H	HR	BB/9	K/9	K	GB%	BABIP	WHIP	ERA	DRA	WARP	MPH	FB%	WHF	CSP
2016	NHP	AA	24	1	3	0	14	0	15¹	16	0	8.8	7.6	13	61%	.348	2.02	4.11	4.52	0.0				
2016	DUN	A+	24	2	0	4	28	0	48²	36	1	2.8	9.6	52	56%	.267	1.05	1.66	4.22	0.5				
2017	NHP	AA	25	1	1	4	29	0	33¹	32	5	4.1	11.3	42	42%	.325	1.41	4.59	3.21	0.6				
2017	BUF	AAA	25	1	1	0	11	0	19¹	16	0	3.3	7.4	16	33%	.276	1.19	0.93	4.26	0.2				
2017	TOR	MLB	25	1	0	0	19	0	17	24	3	2.1	14.3	27	42%	.467	1.65	6.88	2.61	0.5	95.8	49.4	17.1	40.1
2018	BUF	AAA	26	6	2	1	20	0	25²	26	2	3.9	12.6	36	42%	.400	1.44	4.56	3.18	0.6				
2018	TOR	MLB	26	2	0	0	37	0	35²	33	3	3.5	10.1	40	46%	.326	1.32	3.28	3.76	0.5	95.7	56	15.1	43.6
2019	TOR	MLB	27	3	1	0	51	0	54¹	53	8	4.5	10.1	61	45%	.316	1.47	4.58	4.70	0.3	95.2	54.6	15.9	42.6

Breakout: 15% Improve: 21% Collapse: 21% Attrition: 32% MLB: 53% *Comparables: Juan Minaya, Luis Perdomo, Chris Hatcher*

Mayza found his niche the way Ross Geller found his "sound": with abundant enthusiasm and mixed results. While his signature 90-mph slider was as intriguing as it was effective, the lefty needed more than a go-to out pitch (the backbeat to Ross' wordless sound poems, as it were) in order to earn a permanent post in the bullpen. After another year pinballing between Triple-A and the majors, he finally started to mature beyond an exclusive LOOGY role, but the rest of his future remains clouded by prolonged struggles with an erratic four-seamer—something, it could be argued, as essential as melody to music.

Thomas Pannone LHP   Born: 04/28/94   Age: 25   Bats: L   Throws: L   Height: 6'0"   Weight: 195   Origin: Round 9, 2013 Draft (#261 overall)

YEAR	TEAM	LVL	AGE	W	L	SV	G	GS	IP	H	HR	BB/9	K/9	K	GB%	BABIP	WHIP	ERA	DRA	WARP	MPH	FB%	WHF	CSP
2016	LKC	A	22	5	5	0	17	17	89¹	73	7	2.5	8.5	84	39%	.269	1.10	3.02	3.33	1.8				
2016	LYN	A+	22	3	0	0	8	7	43²	31	1	3.3	7.8	38	40%	.254	1.08	1.65	3.81	0.8				
2017	LYN	A+	23	2	0	0	5	5	27²	10	0	2.3	12.7	39	48%	.212	0.61	0.00	2.91	0.8				
2017	AKR	AA	23	6	1	0	14	14	82¹	67	5	2.3	8.9	81	37%	.281	1.07	2.62	3.73	1.4				
2017	NHP	AA	23	1	2	0	6	6	34²	31	9	2.1	7.5	29	38%	.232	1.12	3.63	4.15	0.4				
2018	NHP	AA	24	0	0	0	2	2	9	9	1	5.0	12.0	12	29%	.348	1.56	3.00	3.84	0.2				
2018	BUF	AAA	24	0	3	0	6	6	36²	40	8	1.7	9.8	40	24%	.327	1.28	4.91	5.29	0.1				
2018	TOR	MLB	24	4	1	0	12	6	43	37	7	3.1	6.1	29	36%	.234	1.21	4.19	5.89	-0.3	90.1	64.2	10.4	50.6
2019	TOR	MLB	25	5	6	0	16	16	91¹	91	16	3.3	7.9	81	35%	.287	1.36	5.08	5.25	0.2	89.8	65.7	10.6	51.8

Breakout: 15%   Improve: 27%   Collapse: 20%   Attrition: 36%   MLB: 60%   *Comparables: Michael Bowden, Scott Lewis, Eric Skoglund*

The Blue Jays put the kibosh on Pannone's petition for a rotation spot when he was slapped with an 80-game suspension for the misuse of anabolic steroids. Following several months of mandated rehab, the left-handed swingman returned to the team in mid-August and began to show legitimate flashes of starter potential after turning in four quality performances over six assigned starts. While the command and control on his fastball masks a noted lack of oomph, he complements the pitch with a handful of passable, if not decent secondaries, and sequences well enough to get around most big-league batters.

Eric Pardinho RHP   Born: 01/05/01   Age: 18   Bats: R   Throws: R   Height: 5'10"   Weight: 155   Origin: International Free Agent, 2018

YEAR	TEAM	LVL	AGE	W	L	SV	G	GS	IP	H	HR	BB/9	K/9	K	GB%	BABIP	WHIP	ERA	DRA	WARP	MPH	FB%	WHF	CSP°
2018	BLU	RK	17	4	3	0	11	11	50	37	5	2.9	11.5	64	47%	.274	1.06	2.88	3.62	1.3				
2019	TOR	MLB	18	1	3	0	7	7	31²	37	9	5.4	8.3	29	44%	.310	1.77	7.08	7.38	-0.7				

Comparables: Mike Soroka, Martin Perez, Roberto Osuna

If Pardinho had been born in the United States, rather than his native Brazil, he'd have spent the start of last summer going to junior prom, making final decisions on college programs and playing in a bunch of showcases to prepare for the 2019 Draft. Instead, the 17-year-old was one of the best pitchers in the Appy League—and that's without even adjusting for age. During his stateside debut, the right-hander showed off a strong and balanced four-pitch mix, led by a mid-90s fastball and a curve that punished hitters 4-5 years his senior. A full-season debut awaits in 2019, while the rest of his peers hire "advisors," participate in final workouts and obsess over mock draft positioning.

David Paulino RHP   Born: 02/06/94   Age: 25   Bats: R   Throws: R   Height: 6'7"   Weight: 222   Origin: International Free Agent, 2010

YEAR	TEAM	LVL	AGE	W	L	SV	G	GS	IP	H	HR	BB/9	K/9	K	GB%	BABIP	WHIP	ERA	DRA	WARP	MPH	FB%	WHF	CSP
2016	AST	RK	22	0	0	0	3	3	12	9	0	1.5	10.5	14	75%	.281	0.92	0.75	2.53	0.4				
2016	CCH	AA	22	5	2	1	14	9	64	47	3	1.5	10.1	72	40%	.280	0.91	1.83	2.31	2.1				
2016	FRE	AAA	22	0	2	0	3	3	14	16	1	3.9	12.9	20	45%	.385	1.57	3.86	2.66	0.4				
2016	HOU	MLB	22	0	1	0	3	1	7	6	0	3.9	2.6	2	44%	.261	1.29	5.14	7.55	-0.2	94.8	52.4	6.4	50.4
2017	FRE	AAA	23	0	1	0	3	3	14	11	3	5.8	8.4	13	28%	.216	1.43	4.50	5.05	0.1				
2017	HOU	MLB	23	2	0	0	6	6	29	36	8	2.2	10.6	34	33%	.359	1.48	6.52	5.45	0.0	94.0	46	11.6	48.6
2018	FRE	AAA	24	0	0	0	4	4	18	16	3	2.5	11.5	23	46%	.302	1.17	5.50	2.99	0.5				
2018	TOR	MLB	24	1	0	0	7	0	6²	6	1	2.7	8.1	6	50%	.263	1.20	1.35	5.14	0.0	94.3	42.2	10.2	44.3
2019	TOR	MLB	25	3	1	0	56	0	59²	57	9	3.4	9.4	62	42%	.300	1.33	4.38	4.50	0.6	93.9	47.1	10.9	48.4

Breakout: 17%   Improve: 45%   Collapse: 21%   Attrition: 28%   MLB: 83%   *Comparables: Jonathan Papelbon, Bud Norris, Brandon Workman*

How quickly the mighty fall. Once an intriguing starter option, Paulino cracked the Astros' top ten list in 2016 and 2017, but one undisclosed Double-A spat, bone spur removal surgery, 80-game steroid-driven suspension and season-compromising shoulder injury later, he found himself reassigned as September bullpen depth for the non-contending Blue Jays. He still has the raw stuff that inspired the Astros to take a flier on him several years ago, but the long injury history and middling major-league results will continue to raise some eyebrows until he can prove himself healthy once again.

Nate Pearson RHP   Born: 08/20/96   Age: 22   Bats: R   Throws: R   Height: 6'6"   Weight: 245   Origin: Round 1, 2017 Draft (#28 overall)

YEAR	TEAM	LVL	AGE	W	L	SV	G	GS	IP	H	HR	BB/9	K/9	K	GB%	BABIP	WHIP	ERA	DRA	WARP	MPH	FB%	WHF	CSP
2017	VAN	A-	20	0	0	0	7	7	19	6	0	2.4	11.4	24	40%	.158	0.58	0.95	4.39	0.2				
2019	TOR	MLB	22	2	3	0	9	9	33¹	37	6	3.8	7.3	27	38%	.308	1.54	5.44	5.63	-0.1				

Comparables: Elvis Araujo, Seranthony Dominguez, Braden Shipley

Pearson's runway proved shorter than expected when he collided with a nasty comebacker in his season debut and lost the year to a fractured forearm. He landed a few of his signature triple-digit pitches in the Arizona Fall League, however, and given good health, should be ready for departure again soon. Of course, the screw in his pitching elbow from surgery while in high school, among other things, will make it more difficult to him to pass through security unabated. When he's right, he pairs the pure 80-grade heat with a Syndergaard-ian slider that is thrown faster than most four-seamers that currently occupy the Blue Jays rotation and both a curveball and change that could get to at least average pitches in time. It's truly a profile that can give hitters a lot of turbulence at the plate. If he can overcome the risk and stay upright on a mound for the majority of 2019, well, the sky is the limit.

Jake Petricka RHP   Born: 06/05/88   Age: 31   Bats: R   Throws: R   Height: 6'5"   Weight: 220   Origin: Round 2, 2010 Draft (#63 overall)

YEAR	TEAM	LVL	AGE	W	L	SV	G	GS	IP	H	HR	BB/9	K/9	K	GB%	BABIP	WHIP	ERA	DRA	WARP	MPH	FB%	WHF	CSP
2016	CHA	MLB	28	0	0	0	9	0	8	8	1	9.0	7.9	7	71%	.304	2.00	4.50	6.19	-0.1	97.4	75	9.6	44.2
2017	CHA	MLB	29	1	1	0	27	0	25²	39	6	2.1	9.1	26	48%	.398	1.75	7.01	6.59	-0.4	97.0	70.2	8.4	49.8
2018	BUF	AAA	30	0	0	2	16	0	23	20	1	2.0	5.5	14	79%	.284	1.09	0.78	3.57	0.4				
2018	TOR	MLB	30	3	1	0	41	0	45²	59	6	3.2	8.1	41	53%	.379	1.64	4.53	5.66	-0.4	97.5	65.8	12.2	45.8
2019	TOR	MLB	31	2	1	0	49	0	52¹	55	7	4.3	7.8	45	53%	.315	1.53	4.84	4.98	0.0	96.5	67.4	10.8	46.5

Breakout: 29%   Improve: 41%   Collapse: 19%   Attrition: 15%   MLB: 76%   *Comparables: Rafael Perez, Ryan Webb, Bobby Parnell*

Like any well-intentioned but ill-fated cartoon character, Petricka careened down a path that was littered with warning signs at every turn. "Turn back: labral tear ahead!" "Watch out—nerve transposition!" "Beware of flexor tendon debridement!" While he hasn't gone over the metaphorical cliff of career-killing injury or total irrelevancy just yet, the hard-throwing reliever's upside—a nasty sinker and a slider that, on its good days, induced a .235 average and 21 percent whiff rate—has been buried by dynamite explosion after dynamite explosion. If he makes any impact in pro ball during 2019, it'll likely be as organizational depth.

Sean Reid-Foley RHP   Born: 08/30/95   Age: 23   Bats: R   Throws: R   Height: 6'3"   Weight: 220   Origin: Round 2, 2014 Draft (#49 overall)

YEAR	TEAM	LVL	AGE	W	L	SV	G	GS	IP	H	HR	BB/9	K/9	K	GB%	BABIP	WHIP	ERA	DRA	WARP	MPH	FB%	WHF	CSP
2016	LNS	A	20	4	3	0	11	11	58	43	2	3.4	9.2	59	52%	.277	1.12	2.95	3.51	1.1				
2016	DUN	A+	20	6	2	0	10	10	57¹	35	2	2.5	11.1	71	49%	.254	0.89	2.67	2.90	1.7				
2017	NHP	AA	21	10	11	0	27	27	132²	145	22	3.6	8.3	122	42%	.318	1.49	5.09	5.63	-0.7				
2018	NHP	AA	22	5	0	0	8	8	44¹	27	3	4.1	10.6	52	55%	.240	1.06	2.03	3.65	0.9				
2018	BUF	AAA	22	7	5	0	16	16	85¹	76	5	3.2	10.3	98	43%	.318	1.24	3.90	3.19	2.3				
2018	TOR	MLB	22	2	4	0	7	7	33¹	31	6	5.7	11.3	42	36%	.312	1.56	5.13	4.95	0.1	95.7	63.2	13.1	47.3
2019	TOR	MLB	23	4	5	0	13	13	74	70	11	3.8	9.6	79	42%	.300	1.36	4.57	4.70	0.7	95.6	65.5	13.5	49

Breakout: 22%   Improve: 33%   Collapse: 15%   Attrition: 34%   MLB: 63%   *Comparables: Lucas Giolito, Michael Fulmer, Zach Davies*

There are few things more unsettling than undeniable talent marred by inconsistent results. The hard-throwing righty landed on the club's top-ten prospect list five years in a row with an above-average slider, a fastball that gets a healthy swing-and-miss rate (when, and only when, it finds the strike zone) and a handful of tertiary pitches with the potential to slant average. With still-spotty control and limited opportunities in the majors, however—opportunities that have no doubt been compromised in part by his uninspired track record in the upper minors—it may be a stretch to expect him to reach his ceiling as a mid-rotation piece anytime soon.

Clayton Richard LHP   Born: 09/12/83   Age: 35   Bats: L   Throws: L   Height: 6'5"   Weight: 240   Origin: Round 8, 2005 Draft (#245 overall)

YEAR	TEAM	LVL	AGE	W	L	SV	G	GS	IP	H	HR	BB/9	K/9	K	GB%	BABIP	WHIP	ERA	DRA	WARP	MPH	FB%	WHF	CSP
2016	CHN	MLB	32	0	1	1	25	0	14	23	0	4.5	4.5	7	73%	.411	2.14	6.43	5.72	-0.1	94.2	82.3	6.5	45.4
2016	SDN	MLB	32	3	3	0	11	9	53²	58	4	4.0	5.7	34	64%	.314	1.53	2.52	5.60	-0.2	93.1	82.3	9.8	44.2
2017	SDN	MLB	33	8	15	0	32	32	197¹	240	24	2.7	6.9	151	60%	.351	1.52	4.79	5.18	0.9	92.4	69.3	9.6	45.8
2018	SDN	MLB	34	7	11	0	27	27	158²	159	19	3.4	6.1	108	58%	.289	1.38	5.33	4.91	0.7	91.7	66	8.9	48.8
2019	TOR	MLB	35	5	7	0	18	18	95¹	105	11	3.6	6.8	72	57%	.319	1.51	4.65	4.77	0.8	91.0	68.2	9.1	45.9

Breakout: 9%   Improve: 26%   Collapse: 17%   Attrition: 11%   MLB: 67%   *Comparables: Jerome Williams, Jason Johnson, Kevin Correia*

Richard led the National League in losses and hits allowed in 2017, which was apparently enough to earn the Opening Day nod last year. He's the sort of breed who might fool fans were they never allowed to see his numbers. A craftsman on the mound, both his distinct, sweeping curveball and elite pickoff move lend cover to a pitcher who peaked as a backend starter years ago and tumbled considerably from there.

Those pesky statistics tell the story, though. Richard has accrued a total of 2.4 WARP in more than 1200 career innings, and given that he led the league in runs allowed last year, it doesn't appear he's improving with age. San Diego has a half dozen rookies pining for starts and several more interesting arms who deserve a longer look, which means that Richard's time in town should conclude soon. Never great and rarely notable, he sure was *there* an awful lot.

Aaron Sanchez RHP   Born: 07/01/92   Age: 26   Bats: R   Throws: R   Height: 6'4"   Weight: 215   Origin: Round 1, 2010 Draft (#34 overall)

YEAR	TEAM	LVL	AGE	W	L	SV	G	GS	IP	H	HR	BB/9	K/9	K	GB%	BABIP	WHIP	ERA	DRA	WARP	MPH	FB%	WHF	CSP
2016	TOR	MLB	23	15	2	0	30	30	192	161	15	3.0	7.5	161	55%	.267	1.17	3.00	3.77	3.5	97.5	74.5	9.2	47.7
2017	TOR	MLB	24	1	3	0	8	8	36	42	6	5.0	6.0	24	48%	.310	1.72	4.25	7.30	-0.7	96.9	76.9	6.5	44.7
2018	TOR	MLB	25	4	6	0	20	20	105	106	11	5.0	7.4	86	50%	.304	1.56	4.89	5.97	-0.8	95.9	64.5	10.5	44.9
2019	TOR	MLB	26	7	9	0	24	24	136²	130	16	4.0	7.6	115	49%	.287	1.39	4.69	4.82	1.0	96.4	71.6	9.6	46.4

Breakout: 19%   Improve: 51%   Collapse: 21%   Attrition: 8%   MLB: 89%   *Comparables: Sonny Gray, Carlos Zambrano, Brandon Webb*

Stripping Sanchez of his potential as the next Blue Jays headliner would have been unheard of three years ago, but so too would surgical fingernail removal, a blister that unspooled his fastball grip and a meager 28 starts scattered across two seasons and 141 total innings. His injury woes veered into the extreme and ridiculous in 2018 when he caught his right index finger in a falling suitcase, then lost another nine weeks to the disabled list before undergoing his second finger-related procedure in September. Though the young righty still generates above-average heat, blisters are tricky, tricky devils to tame, and it's foolish to pretend he's only one suitcase-free stretch away from an encore star-level performance in 2019.

Matt Shoemaker RHP Born: 09/27/86 Age: 32 Bats: R Throws: R Height: 6'2" Weight: 225 Origin: Undrafted Free Agent, 2008

YEAR	TEAM	LVL	AGE	W	L	SV	G	GS	IP	H	HR	BB/9	K/9	K	GB%	BABIP	WHIP	ERA	DRA	WARP	MPH	FB%	WHF	CSP
2016	SLC	AAA	29	1	0	0	1	1	6	6	1	3.0	12.0	8	50%	.333	1.33	1.50	1.86	0.2				
2016	ANA	MLB	29	9	13	0	27	27	160	166	18	1.7	8.0	143	42%	.315	1.23	3.88	4.36	1.8	94.4	49.4	13.9	47.4
2017	ANA	MLB	30	6	3	0	14	14	77²	73	15	3.2	8.0	69	40%	.278	1.30	4.52	5.86	-0.2	93.9	49.5	12.4	45.6
2018	ANA	MLB	31	2	2	0	7	7	31	29	3	2.9	9.6	33	44%	.313	1.26	4.94	5.60	-0.1	93.7	47.1	13.4	46.2
2019	TOR	MLB	32	5	6	0	16	16	91¹	90	14	3.0	8.8	90	42%	.303	1.33	4.42	4.54	1.0	93.2	48.6	13.2	45.8

Breakout: 20%   Improve: 50%   Collapse: 27%   Attrition: 16%   MLB: 95%   *Comparables: Chris Capuano, Brett Myers, Scott Kazmir*

Both the nerve (colloquial term for audacity) and the nerve (set of axons that receive transmissions from the brain) of Shoemaker took its toll as a second surgery to repair a nerve in his elbow—and also a tendon while they were at it—shelved him for five months. Fortunately, he did get September to do some organized sports. All his pitches returned as normal, and some looked better than expected (such as his strikeout rate), so with a proper spring training and no doctors rooting around inside his arm looking for weird little things to fix, his rotation reservation should be intact.

Marcus Stroman RHP Born: 05/01/91 Age: 28 Bats: R Throws: R Height: 5'8" Weight: 180 Origin: Round 1, 2012 Draft (#22 overall)

YEAR	TEAM	LVL	AGE	W	L	SV	G	GS	IP	H	HR	BB/9	K/9	K	GB%	BABIP	WHIP	ERA	DRA	WARP	MPH	FB%	WHF	CSP
2016	TOR	MLB	25	9	10	0	32	32	204	209	21	2.4	7.3	166	62%	.309	1.29	4.37	3.66	4.0	94.6	57.4	10	47.6
2017	TOR	MLB	26	13	9	0	33	33	201	201	21	2.8	7.3	164	63%	.310	1.31	3.09	4.18	3.1	94.9	62.2	10.6	46.7
2018	TOR	MLB	27	4	9	0	19	19	102¹	115	9	3.2	6.8	77	64%	.326	1.48	5.54	4.19	1.3	93.5	49.3	9.8	47.3
2019	TOR	MLB	28	9	10	0	28	28	159²	164	15	2.9	7.4	131	59%	.312	1.36	3.98	4.06	2.6	93.9	57.4	10.3	47.5

Breakout: 20%   Improve: 45%   Collapse: 23%   Attrition: 5%   MLB: 96%   *Comparables: Johnny Cueto, Sonny Gray, Jose Quintana*

The ace, the face of the franchise, the unpaid social media hype man… Stroman wears a lot of hats these days. His newest hat, that of an injured front-end starter coming off of a career year in 2017, didn't suit him quite as well as the others. Shoulder fatigue dogged him throughout the first half of the season and a nasty blister-turned-gaping wound cropped up on his right middle finger, running the rest of his campaign into the ground faster than Kathleen Wynne's re-election effort. There's no guarantee that Stroman can put his injury-riddled days behind him in 2019, but neither is there any compelling reason to believe his middling 2018 performance was anything graver than a fluke for the Cy Young finalist.

Ryan Tepera RHP Born: 11/03/87 Age: 31 Bats: R Throws: R Height: 6'2" Weight: 195 Origin: Round 19, 2009 Draft (#580 overall)

YEAR	TEAM	LVL	AGE	W	L	SV	G	GS	IP	H	HR	BB/9	K/9	K	GB%	BABIP	WHIP	ERA	DRA	WARP	MPH	FB%	WHF	CSP
2016	BUF	AAA	28	1	2	18	37	0	45¹	33	3	3.2	9.5	48	47%	.265	1.08	2.58	2.62	1.2				
2016	TOR	MLB	28	0	1	0	20	0	18¹	17	1	3.9	8.8	18	59%	.291	1.36	2.95	4.01	0.2	97.3	53.8	14.6	42.2
2017	TOR	MLB	29	7	1	2	73	0	77²	57	7	3.6	9.4	81	43%	.260	1.13	3.59	4.85	0.3	96.1	59	14.2	43.9
2018	TOR	MLB	30	5	5	7	68	0	64²	55	9	3.3	9.5	68	44%	.291	1.22	3.62	4.92	0.0	96.4	61.3	14.8	43.3
2019	TOR	MLB	31	3	1	0	56	0	59²	52	8	3.9	9.5	63	44%	.286	1.31	4.38	4.50	0.4	95.5	59.3	14.5	42.9

Breakout: 23%   Improve: 39%   Collapse: 23%   Attrition: 20%   MLB: 71%   *Comparables: Doug Slaten, Cory Gearrin, Will Harris*

A legitimate closer option in Roberto Osuna's absence, **Ryan Tepera** was anything but tepid during his second full season in the majors. The journeyman reliever didn't blow away hitters with the same high-octane stuff of his breakout year in 2017, but continued to make subtle refinements as he chipped away at an ungainly walk rate and battled through a case of elbow inflammation.

LINEOUTS

Hitters

HITTER	POS	TEAM	LVL	AGE	PA	R	2B	3B	HR	RBI	BB	K	SB	CS	AVG/OBP/SLG	DRC+	VORP	BABIP	BRR	FRAA	WARP
Griffin Conine	RF	VAN	A-	20	230	24	14	2	7	30	19	63	5	0	.238/.309/.427	96	2.2	.304	-1.5	RF(46): 10.1	1.1
Jonathan Davis	OF	NHP	AA	26	358	68	22	3	5	33	35	53	19	3	.302/.388/.443	118	35.6	.345	6.7	CF(77): 3.5	3.1
	OF	BUF	AAA	26	202	26	7	2	5	23	12	41	7	1	.249/.308/.389	96	3.6	.295	2.1	CF(27): 1.0, LF(10): -0.8	0.6
	OF	TOR	MLB	26	27	3	1	0	0	0	1	6	3	0	.200/.259/.240	75	-1.7	.263	0.4	CF(9): 1.3, LF(8): -0.3	0.2
Jordan Groshans	SS	BLJ	Rk	18	159	17	12	0	4	39	13	29	0	0	.331/.390/.500	133	14.7	.387	-0.8	3B(16): -1.2, SS(15): 0.6	1.0
	SS	BLU	Rk	18	48	4	1	0	1	4	2	8	0	0	.182/.229/.273	92	-0.6	.194	0.1	SS(6): 0.9, 3B(5): 0.0	0.2
Miguel Hiraldo	3B	DBL	Rk	17	239	41	18	3	2	33	23	30	15	6	.313/.381/.453	136	22.9	.355	2.8	SS(46): 2.9, 3B(4): -0.3	2.4
	3B	BLJ	Rk	17	40	3	4	0	0	3	1	12	3	0	.231/.250/.333	55	-1.7	.333	-0.3	3B(5): 0.0, SS(4): -0.8	-0.2
Luke Maile	C	TOR	MLB	27	231	22	13	1	3	27	25	67	2	0	.248/.333/.366	80	8.7	.351	0.2	C(66): 9.5	1.6
Gift Ngoepe	3B	TOR	MLB	28	19	2	0	0	0	0	1	12	0	0	.056/.105/.056	52	-2.6	.167	0.2	SS(6): 0.0, 2B(5): -0.8	-0.1
	3B	BUF	AAA	28	159	15	3	1	2	8	25	63	2	1	.168/.304/.252	68	-0.2	.299	0.5	SS(29): 0.7, 3B(14): 2.3	0.5
Dwight Smith	LF	BUF	AAA	25	361	39	25	1	6	42	44	53	9	3	.268/.358/.413	106	11.5	.302	-0.3	LF(62): 1.2, RF(14): -0.1	1.2
	LF	TOR	MLB	25	75	9	8	0	2	8	7	13	0	0	.262/.347/.477	99	3.8	.294	-0.4	LF(19): -1.5, RF(6): 0.7	0.1
Kevin Smith	SS	LNS	A	21	204	36	23	4	7	44	17	33	12	1	.355/.407/.639	136	33.7	.397	3.1	SS(24): 1.7, 3B(21): 0.7	2.3
	SS	DUN	A+	21	371	57	8	2	18	49	23	88	17	5	.274/.332/.468	133	23.3	.319	4.6	SS(63): 6.9, 2B(13): 1.0	4.3
Logan Warmoth	SS	DUN	A+	22	322	31	13	2	1	28	30	69	9	0	.248/.322/.319	86	11.1	.318	3.5	SS(46): 4.6, 2B(14): 1.3	1.6

"Mr. Blue Jay" may not have the satisfying alliterative appeal of "Mr. Marlin," but that's okay—second-rounder **Griffin Conine** still has plenty of time to carve out his own legacy in Toronto. For this budding outfielder, that'll require some fine-tuning of the strong defensive instincts and power-driven (if overreaching) swing he already brings to the table. ⊗ Center fielder **Jonathan Davis** is a solid up-the-middle defender, but he's given little reason to think that he'll hit enough to be anything more than a spare part. ⊗ A burly first-round draft pick with raw power in spades, the only question **Jordan Groshans** has yet to answer is that of his glove. He has the experience to stick at short and the build and athleticism to become a fixture at third base. ⑩ As unlooked-for and thrilling as a summer fling, **Miguel Hiraldo** enchanted the Blue Jays with a fresh burst of power in the Dominican Summer League. Although he has yet to settle down at any one defensive position, his quick hands and dynamic swing lead some to believe he has the right stuff to go the distance. ⑩ The bar is set higher than usual for **Luke Maile**, who projects as the team's fourth-best catcher in a stacked farm system. Following a career-best year at the plate, the continued lack of opportunity behind the dish is enough to make anyone go postal. ⑩ Top-shelf international prospect **Orelvis Martinez** continues to draw promising comparisons to Adrian Beltre. Is he also a Hall of Famer in-the-making? Unlikely. Could it be the 17-year-old is a sluggish baserunner who packs a punch at the plate, swapped his right arm for a cannon and possesses the athleticism to pivot between short and third base despite lacking a path forward in an already-crowded infield? Ah, there it is. ⑩ There's nothing wrong with a glove-first player until he becomes a glove-only player. When **Gift Ngoepe**'s bat once again failed to materialize alongside his magnetic defense, the Blue Jays signed, sealed and delivered him to the Sydney Blue Sox of the Australian Baseball League. ⑩ If second-generation ballplayers were a Westerosi army, **Dwight Smith** would be leading the vanguard in the march on Toronto. Though often being the first to arrive also means being the first to be discarded when the real battle comes. ⑩ A true bargain-bin find if ever there was one, former fourth-round pick **Kevin Smith** continued to reap dividends for the Blue Jays following an explosive 25-homer, 29-stolen base campaign across multiple levels of A-ball. ⑩ Frequent injuries compromised a highly-anticipated encore from standout shortstop **Logan Warmoth** during his first foray into High-A ball. His ability to touch bat to ball on a regular basis is as impressive as it is capable of distracting from a conspicuous lack of speed and power, but he'll get another opportunity to wipe the slate clean in 2019.

Pitchers

PITCHER	TEAM	LVL	AGE	W	L	SV	G	GS	IP	H	HR	BB/9	K/9	K	GB%	BABIP	WHIP	ERA	DRA	WARP	MPH	FB%	WHF	CSP
Felipe Castaneda	BLU	Rk	18	2	1	0	10	10	37^2	41	5	6.7	6.9	29	45%	.305	1.83	6.69	4.91	0.5				
Yennsy Diaz	LNS	A	21	5	1	0	9	9	47^2	22	4	4.7	7.9	42	40%	.151	0.99	2.08	6.23	-0.6				
	DUN	A+	21	5	4	0	18	16	99^2	91	5	2.5	7.5	83	41%	.297	1.19	3.52	3.31	2.3				
Justin Dillon	DUN	A+	24	0	3	0	6	4	22^1	23	5	3.2	6.9	17	55%	.265	1.39	4.43	6.70	-0.4				
	BUF	AAA	24	2	1	1	4	3	22^2	10	2	0.8	7.5	19	33%	.143	0.53	0.79	3.95	0.4				
	NHP	AA	24	2	4	0	14	7	50	60	6	4.0	4.0	22	36%	.310	1.64	6.84	4.94	0.2				
Zachary Jackson	NHP	AA	23	2	3	2	43	0	62	29	2	7.4	10.9	75	36%	.200	1.29	2.47	3.26	1.2				
Patrick Murphy	NHP	AA	23	0	0	0	1	1	6	4	0	4.5	9.0	6	56%	.250	1.17	3.00	2.42	0.2				
	DUN	A+	23	10	5	0	26	26	146^2	126	5	3.1	8.3	135	60%	.297	1.20	2.64	5.28	0.1				
Hector Perez	BCA	A+	22	3	3	2	17	11	72^2	50	5	5.0	10.3	83	48%	.263	1.24	3.84	3.28	1.7				
	CCH	AA	22	0	1	0	4	2	16^2	12	0	4.3	9.7	18	49%	.279	1.20	3.24	3.20	0.4				
	NHP	AA	22	0	1	0	6	5	25^2	17	1	5.6	11.2	32	37%	.276	1.29	3.86	4.07	0.4				
Luis Santos	TOR	MLB	27	1	1	0	15	1	20	26	4	4.5	10.8	24	30%	.423	1.80	7.20	4.00	0.2	95.6	49.3	15.6	43.9
	BUF	AAA	27	2	3	0	20	2	42^2	41	2	2.7	8.4	40	33%	.300	1.27	2.74	3.74	0.7				
Trent Thornton	FRE	AAA	24	9	8	0	24	22	124^1	118	13	2.2	8.8	122	42%	.304	1.20	4.42	3.81	2.4				
Jacob Waguespack	REA	AA	24	1	1	0	7	7	29^1	31	0	4.9	9.5	31	59%	.352	1.60	3.99	4.51	0.3				
	LEH	AAA	24	3	5	1	14	8	53^1	54	4	3.4	8.1	48	52%	.323	1.39	5.06	4.12	0.8				
	BUF	AAA	24	2	4	0	7	6	39^1	47	3	2.3	7.6	33	54%	.346	1.45	5.03	4.26	0.5				
T.J. Zeuch	DUN	A+	22	3	3	0	6	6	36^1	34	4	2.2	5.9	24	63%	.273	1.18	3.47	5.91	-0.2				
	NHP	AA	22	9	5	0	21	21	120	120	7	2.3	6.1	81	56%	.298	1.26	3.08	4.02	1.8				

A bonafide changeup may be potent enough to slay low-level hitters, but **Felipe Castaneda** and his mythic pitch will never get the opportunity to square off against major league beasts if he continues to neglect the other two weapons in his arsenal: an underwhelming heater and the rough draft of a breaking ball. ⑩ The Jays added **Yennsy Diaz** to the 40-man roster in November, and while his size may imply a move to the bullpen, his improved control in the Florida State League keeps the dream of a backend starter alive for another year. ⑩ A bad season split between High-A and Double-A being broken up by complete domination in Triple-A feels like a script error, but **Justin Dillon** basically lived a Buffalo Wild Wings commercial for a few weeks in May minus the wings. ⑩ The two days **Oliver Drake** spent in Toronto were the asymptote of his bizarre, DRA-exploding season; after the experience he settled down to productive, if not residential, stability. ⑩ Beware the back-end starter who is always one tertiary offering/tweaked delivery/sub-3.00 ERA over half a season in Double-A away from making it big. After stabilizing a haphazard walk rate, former first-round pick **Jon Harris** finally pitched his way up to Triple-A, where he'll try to prove himself a rare exception to the norm yet again. ⑩ **Zachary Jackson** chewed his way through the Blue Jays' farm system with the voracious appetite of a caterpillar preparing for pupal transformation, finally stopping to gnaw on Double-A for a full year while he touched up a plus fastball-curve offering—at least when he knew where it was going. ⑩ It's fairly uncommon for a team to spent two high draft picks on prep players from the same high school, but **Adam Kloffenstein**, Jordan Groshans' teammate at Magnolia High, and his large frame and fastball passed up a TCU commitment for his $2.5 million bonus. ⑩ Add Tommy John recovery to **Elieser Medrano**'s laundry list in 2019, right up there with refining the consistency of his mid-90s heater, tightening the command on his slider and developing a solid third offering within his limited pitch repertoire. ⑩ When we last saw **Julian Merryweather** in 2017, he was a 25-year-old back-end starter who'd mastered but not dominated Double-A and gotten kicked around Triple-A. He lost all of 2018 to Tommy John Surgery, which ... well, it doesn't help. ⑩ The Florida State League's Pitcher of the Year, fireballer **Patrick Murphy** is finally on a path to overcome the law most closely associated with his name—the 2013 draft pick has already undergone thoracic outlet syndrome and Tommy John surgeries. ⑩ Scouts dream on **Hector Perez**'s stuff already plus raw stuff jumping up in short bursts, which is great news considering he doesn't currently have the control or command to stick as a starter. ⑩ Giving up homers is a thing that happens when you don't have elite stuff or strong command. Giving up homers with two strikes, like **Luis Santos** did 75 percent of the time last season, is a thing that gets you sent back to Triple-A. ⑩ Breaking ball specialist **Trent Thornton** was a casualty of the annual pre-Rule 5 shuffle, moving from Houston's crowded 40-man roster to Toronto's more flexible crop in exchange for Aledmys Diaz. ⑩ When **Jacob Waguespack** was traded from the Phillies to the Blue Jays at the deadline for Aaron Loup, he only needed to travel about 250 feet to find his new teammates, as both Triple-A affiliates were squaring off at Lehigh Valley. Familiarity begets familiarity, though, and the potential up-and-down arm rung up his former teammates for a season-high 12 punchouts two days later. ⑩ Still a one-trick pony (large-frame flamethrower with starter potential), **T.J. Zeuch** dodged the injuries that derailed his 2017 season and acquired two more tricks along the way: a potent, if occasionally erratic sinker and slider that play off each other for a convincing double act.

WASHINGTON NATIONALS

Essay by Meg Rowley

Player comments by Zach Crizer and BP staff

An odd affliction exists in baseball, borne of success and timing, and that is that once your team is possessed of a baseball god, people expect you to do something with him. Not tiny somethings; not squeaking-by things. But big things, World Series things, baseball history things. Baseball gods are not little mice; baseball gods are mammoth, titan. Baseball gods alter the course of a franchise, should a franchise let them.

The Los Angeles Angels are familiar with this condition; it itches under the skin when you watch Mike Trout roam center field only to remember his relative absence from October, exiled as he has mostly been from the pantheon we hold most dear. The Washington Nationals have done considerably better by their time with Bryce Harper, though the futility that has ultimately marked those years inspires its own bit of scratching. It has become an era defined as much by how far the franchise didn't go as how far it did. You can understand why. Harper is, as he has been since before he could drive, resplendent. He exudes the bright, insistent bravado of his hometown, though unlike Las Vegas, and its faux-New York and Paris, the "ancient" "Rome" of Caesars, and leagues of concert fondant masking a sea of plastic, Harper has weight and substance, to the tune of 30.5 WARP. He was moved off catcher upon drafting; how many gods pass their time in a crouch, their faces obscured? He's won Rookie of the Year and MVP honors, and been the first-overall pick and a six-time All-Star. The god glistens.

And now the god is leaving. To call his time in Washington a waste is to misunderstand one of the Greeks' (and baseball's) other great conceits: tragedy. His dearth of rings aside, Bryce Harper has never experienced a losing season. He has glimpsed October. But one can't exactly call his tenure a triumph either. The Nationals have lost. Not completely or always right away, but ultimately and decisively. How they've lost with a god in tow has varied. Let us review the ways.

2012 and 2013: The Hubris of Faith

It gets lost in the talk of heroes and thunder, but some gods turn out to be fools. They concern themselves overly with the machinations of farmers or sailors; they covet human lovers. They disappoint, not immune from being

NATIONALS PROSPECTUS
2018 W-L: 82-80, 2ND IN NL EAST

Pythag	.557	10th	B-Age		27.3	8th
RS/G	4.76	8th	P-Age		30.2	29th
RA/G	4.21	12th	Salary		$179.8M	5th
DRC+	102	8th	M$/MW		$5.0M	8th
DRA	4.26	12th	DL Days		1396	24th
FIP	4.11	19th	$ on DL		18%	17th
DER	.713	8th				

- Opened 2008
- Open air
- Natural surface
- Fence profile: 8' to 14'''

Three-Year Park Factors

Runs	Runs/RH	Runs/LH	HR/RH	HR/LH
103	104	100	107	99

Top Hitter WARP	5.3 Trea Turner
Top Pitcher WARP	7.7 Max Scherzer
Top Prospect	Victor Robles

2018 Hit List Ranking

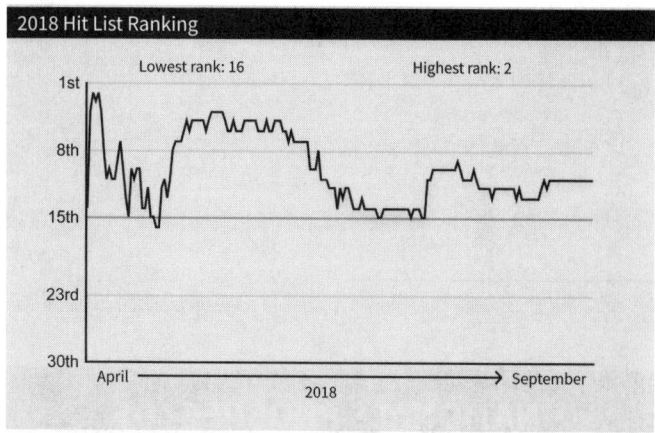

Lowest rank: 16   Highest rank: 2

Committed Payroll (in millions)

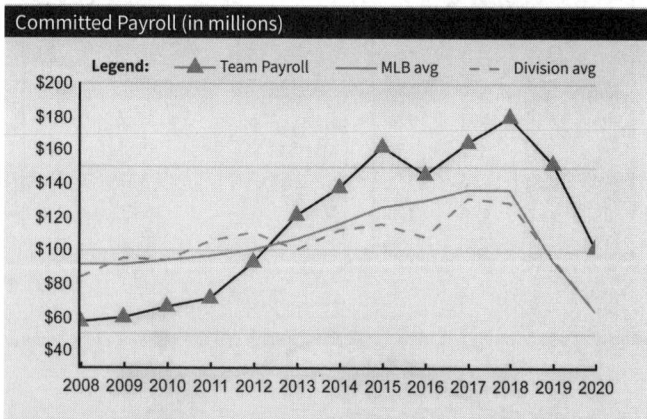

Legend: Team Payroll — MLB avg - - Division avg

Farm System Ranking

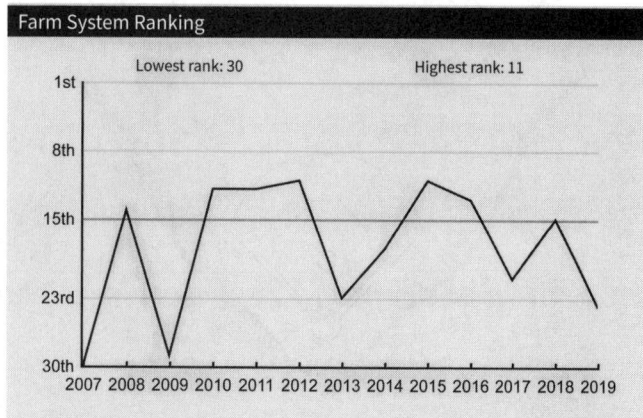

Lowest rank: 30   Highest rank: 11

Personnel

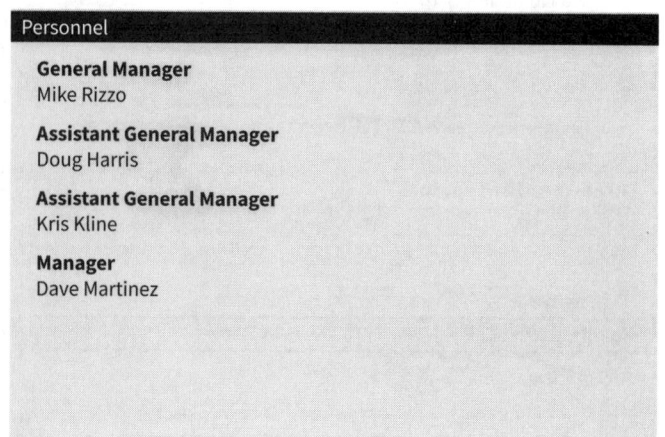

General Manager
Mike Rizzo

Assistant General Manager
Doug Harris

Assistant General Manager
Kris Kline

Manager
Dave Martinez

ridiculous. To roster a god is insufficient to guarantee triumph; you have to learn what sort he is. Bryce Harper wasn't sure to be a destroyer of worlds. He could have been an imposing but hapless jester; baseball has a way of exposing those.

But Harper's rookie campaign revealed him to be exactly what Washington expected: a champion. He shimmered, just 19 years old and soaring, as he worked his way to 5.2 WARP and Rookie of the Year honors. He was the youngest player to hit a home run in the majors since Adrian Beltre; the first teenager to steal home since 1964. A down July and August were but the trials gods go through to prove their mettle; the concern that such struggles suggested something more permanent would prove to be a clown question, bro. He was a hero arrived.

Of course, his was not the only journey 2012 witnessed. On September 12 of that year, Stephen Strasburg threw his final start of the season; he would not return for the playoffs, made unavailable by fretting over UCLs and the possibility of longer absences. He would watch as the Cardinals rallied for four runs in Game 5 of the NLDS, but just watch. 2013 would prove devastating; the Nationals missed the playoffs entirely. The Strasburg decision loomed large. It could be called hubris, or an overabundance of caution; perhaps it was both those things. But it was also an act of faith, an assumption on the part of General Manager Mike Rizzo that this was but the start of a long run of postseasons and parades. That there was more time. Wars among gods and monsters unfurl over millennia, after all, and the divine don't age like the rest of us.

2014: Even-Year Bullshit

Even Zeus doesn't always win. All gods have their machinations, their trials and favorites, their battles to be won and lost, and they are themselves subject to forces and castings. The 2014 Nationals won 96 games. They took the NL East by 17. Harper missed 62 games after tearing a ligament in his thumb. His June 28, 2014 Double-A rehab start, during which he slugged three home runs, was the stuff of legend. But so was Even-Year Bullshit. The Nationals lost the NLDS to the Giants, three games to one. San Francisco would go on to win its second World Series in three years.

2015: Meddlesome Mortals

The gods get a bad rap for meddling in the affairs of men, but plucky mortals have also been known to court their own disaster. When starting a fight against one of Zeus' ilk, it's best to be sure you can win; the truly savvy among the human set align themselves with the sublime, looking to play a minor role in a hero's story, rather than lead the charge themselves. But there are always dopes. In 2015, Jonathan Papelbon was but a man, all puffery and pugnacity. Harper, coming off a 2014 marred by injuries, was about to become the youngest unanimous MVP winner in baseball history. He was about to post 9.7 WARP. He was about to collide with Papelbon's pluck. Literally. On September 27, the god and the man tilted at each other in the Nationals dugout after Harper loafed to first a bit slower than Papelbon would have liked and Harper took offense at Papelbon's umbrage. During the skirmish, Papelbon put his hands to Harper's throat, and shoved him. He would end the season suspended, unable to hide that he was a dope, misaligned against his true foes.

It isn't what undid Washington's 2015; injuries and underperformance elsewhere on the roster, and an opaque but pronounced ennui, seem to have done that. October baseball would not be the team's only casualty. Matt Williams and his coaching staff were left in the season's depths. Drew Storen's hand broke under the force of his own disappointment. But the fight carried with it the flavor of 2015's failure: Bryce was ready to ascend, buoyed by a heavenly host, and Max Scherzer's two no-hitters, while the rest of his squad remained earthbound, all pluck and undone plans.

2016: Other Gods Make Their Presence Felt

Of course, baseball isn't a monotheistic religion. Its battles are witness to all sorts of lesser deities and otherworldly competitors, and it isn't governed by fairness. With your season on the line, with your hopes and dreams and a golden fleece in peril, you'd prefer a hero equal to the task, able to match up against the other team's immortals, and throw some rocks at them. But that isn't always what you get. Sometimes, despite six innings of one run ball in Game 5 of the NLDS from Max Scherzer, himself the stuff of Olympus, you find yourself undone by Marc Rzepczynski, Blake Treinen, and Sammy Solis. Sometimes a rally begun against Grant Dayton is squashed when Kenley Jansen enters in the seventh. Sometimes, you're Bryce Harper, standing on second base after having walked in the ninth, helpless to do anything but look on as Clayton Kershaw enters the arena, tense and deadly, and ready to feast. Sometimes, all your team can offer is a sacrifice. You, Bryce, stand there, watching as Wilmer Difo is swallowed up, a bit of fuel to one of your divine fellows righting his own postseason tale.

The worst part of being a baseball god must come in realizing the mortality of others.

2017: Mischief Reigns

Fans tend to ascribe their own particular rooting interests to the so-called Baseball Gods. Not the gods who descend from the ethereal plain to hurl lightning or shatter the sky with the *thwack!* of their bats, all flowing hair and fist pumps and glory, but the middle managers. The keepers of scores and hamstrings and trophies. Perhaps that sort is possessed of fandom; maybe some divine Janus or Glen whoops in delight when his favorite team records the final out of their World Series win. But it seems just as likely that his motivations are smaller, stranger, the result of grudges and petty nonsense among his kind that mere mortals can scarce understand.

To wit, Game 5 of the 2017 NLDS had all the hallmarks of some magical trickster who wasn't so much interested in another Cubs parade as he was in a bit of mischief at the Nationals' expense. Matt Wieters was hit in the mask by the backswing of a dropped, swinging third strike; it ought to have nullified a passed ball and a throwing error but went uncalled. A batter later, Tommy La Stella reached on catcher's interference. Scherzer, on in relief, hit Jon Jay to drive in a run. Later, with two on and two out in the eighth, it was determined that Willson Contreras had picked Jose Lobaton off at first after a Cubs' challenge overturned the call on the field. Down a run in the ninth, Harper struck out swinging against Wade Davis to end Washington's season, a god felled by one of his number, just not one at the park. It could have gone differently; Harper might have forced extras, where perhaps a triumph loomed. But he didn't. Not because the gods are Cubs fans, but because some sprite named Glen preferred a bit of funny business. Even 97 wins can't save you (or Dusty Baker) from that.

2018: The Twilight of a Time

2018 never did seem like it was going to go quite right. Despite being strongly favored to win their division, the Nationals once again stumbled under their own weight. Once again, there were hints of clubhouse discord, this time under new manager Dave Martinez. Once again there were injuries. And Harper, a season away from free agency, endured an odd and uncomfortable thing for a god; he had his record examined, his seasons measured, his defense weighed, the ticks above average accounted for. It is impossible to deny what Harper is capable of being, but much of 2018 was spent contemplating what he had been. Sometimes injured; often mercurial. Prone to fit and fuss when displeased. Perhaps a different sort of god when stripped of his MVP season and the power it granted him. 2018 was supposed to be a rush of triumph, a last ride up that dusty mountain; a World Series. It was supposed to be a passing of a time into its twilight, with one star left shining. Only that star wasn't Harper. All that reflecting back naturally shifted to looking forward, and we begin to see that the Nationals story isn't ending. A new god emerges, born from the head of scouts and player development personnel and his own muster. Bryce will seek out new lands, but Juan Soto could assume his mantle. Max Scherzer and Stephen Strasburg will be there, and Patrick Corbin will join their number; ownership may have balked at Harper's weight in gold, but they have used some treasure. Adam Eaton should be healthy. Victor Robles looms. They might finally sing songs of Anthony Rendon. Trea Turner is just 25. It seems impossible that the bullpen could be as bad again.

The Nationals aren't a story that ends so much as a crew about to set sail into the second part of their epic. Odysseus is done with all that business in Troy; it's time to set out for Ithaca, or at least 2019. There will be new monsters and champions, perils and triumphs, and for the first time since Harper was drafted in 2010, Washington will face them without their strange affliction. You might be expected to do something when possessed of a baseball god, but now, a god departs. Turn the page. ▪

—Meg Rowley is the Managing Editor of FanGraphs.

HITTERS

Matt Adams 1B   Born: 08/31/88   Age: 30   Bats: L   Throws: R   Height: 6'3"   Weight: 245   Origin: Round 23, 2009 Draft (#699 overall)

YEAR	TEAM	LVL	AGE	PA	R	2B	3B	HR	RBI	BB	K	SB	CS	AVG/OBP/SLG	DRC+	VORP	BABIP	BRR	FRAA	WARP
2016	SLN	MLB	27	327	37	18	0	16	54	25	81	0	1	.249/.309/.471	106	8.5	.286	-2.4	1B(86): 9.3	1.5
2017	SLN	MLB	28	53	4	2	0	1	7	4	17	0	0	.292/.340/.396	100	1.8	.419	-0.1	LF(6): -0.3, 1B(3): 0.1	0.1
2017	ATL	MLB	28	314	42	20	1	19	58	19	71	0	0	.271/.315/.543	109	14.0	.294	-0.6	1B(59): -3.3, LF(13): 0.5	0.6
2018	WAS	MLB	29	277	37	9	0	18	48	24	55	0	0	.257/.332/.510	120	10.5	.261	-2.3	1B(48): 0.3, LF(15): 0.7	1.1
2018	SLN	MLB	29	60	5	1	0	3	9	3	18	0	0	.158/.200/.333	114	-3.2	.167	0.0	1B(15): -0.5	0.2
2019	*WAS*	*MLB*	*30*	*245*	*30*	*13*	*1*	*11*	*36*	*18*	*58*	*0*	*0*	*.260/.321/.473*	*115*	*8.6*	*.302*	*-0.9*	*1B 2*	*1.1*

Breakout: 2%   Improve: 38%   Collapse: 6%   Attrition: 13%   MLB: 91%   *Comparables: Mitch Moreland, Ben Broussard, Hal Breeden*

For another half a season, Adams showed that tantalizing potential to bloom as a slugging first baseman. He was, in fact, more convincing than ever. He cut his strikeout rate down, boosted his walk rate, and still accessed every bit of his over-the-fence power (though he was spraying the ball and lining it to the gaps less often, as nearly every player does in their late 20s). It was technically a broken finger that derailed him, sidelining him around the All-Star break and apparently sapping all those gains he'd made even when he returned. In truth, though, this seems to be Adams's modest fate. He keeps demonstrating real improvement and moving toward a full season of terrific run production, but he also keeps being beaten back—and beaten in the zone, by good fastballs.

Rafael Bautista OF   Born: 03/08/93   Age: 26   Bats: R   Throws: R   Height: 6'2"   Weight: 194   Origin: International Free Agent, 2012

YEAR	TEAM	LVL	AGE	PA	R	2B	3B	HR	RBI	BB	K	SB	CS	AVG/OBP/SLG	DRC+	VORP	BABIP	BRR	FRAA	WARP
2016	HAR	AA	23	607	77	12	4	4	39	45	94	56	10	.282/.344/.341	90	21.9	.333	7.8	CF(102): -3.8, RF(32): 0.2	1.6
2017	NAT	RK	24	52	7	2	1	0	3	5	5	2	1	.295/.404/.386	123	4.0	.333	-0.4	CF(10): -0.8	0.1
2017	SYR	AAA	24	188	23	9	1	0	11	9	26	7	4	.250/.290/.313	66	-0.6	.293	2.7	CF(34): -0.6, LF(7): -0.5	0.0
2017	WAS	MLB	24	27	2	0	0	0	0	2	5	0	0	.160/.222/.160	85	-2.5	.200	0.5	RF(11): -0.4, CF(1): 0.0	0.0
2018	HAR	AA	25	30	0	0	0	0	3	3	5	1	1	.111/.200/.111	88	-3.4	.136	-0.2	CF(6): 0.8	0.1
2018	WAS	MLB	25	6	1	0	0	0	0	0	1	0	0	.000/.000/.000	92	-1.6	.000	0.0	LF(4): -0.1, CF(3): -0.1	0.0
2018	SYR	AAA	25	91	11	3	1	1	4	4	23	5	1	.366/.395/.463	68	7.9	.500	0.0	CF(16): -0.1, LF(2): -0.2	-0.1
2019	*WAS*	*MLB*	*26*	*251*	*28*	*7*	*1*	*5*	*18*	*12*	*66*	*9*	*3*	*.202/.246/.297*	*48*	*-5.9*	*.254*	*1.0*	*CF -1, RF 0*	*-0.7*

Breakout: 1%   Improve: 18%   Collapse: 8%   Attrition: 14%   MLB: 33%   *Comparables: Rajai Davis, Jim Adduci, Kyle Hudson*

Speed and defense got him two cups of coffee in the majors, but a torn ACL wrecked Bautista's season and modest upward trajectory. He was released to clear a 40-man spot for Adam Eaton's return from injury, but signed back into the system a few days later. He'll need some more realistic on-base skills to stick around—the .500 BABIP from his 2018 Triple-A campaign seems just a wee bit lucky. If he's going to wedge his way into a crowded Nationals outfield situation and build on a brief big-league career, he'll have to revert to the contact-heavy game he showed at lower levels.

Gage Canning OF   Born: 04/23/97   Age: 22   Bats: L   Throws: R   Height: 5'10"   Weight: 175   Origin: Round 5, 2018 Draft (#161 overall)

YEAR	TEAM	LVL	AGE	PA	R	2B	3B	HR	RBI	BB	K	SB	CS	AVG/OBP/SLG	DRC+	VORP	BABIP	BRR	FRAA	WARP
2018	AUB	A-	21	59	13	3	3	2	7	5	18	0	2	.315/.373/.593	96	7.8	.441	0.0	CF(7): -0.5, LF(5): -0.9	0.1
2018	HAG	A	21	128	15	9	0	4	16	11	36	2	0	.223/.294/.411	94	3.8	.284	-0.2	CF(16): -1.6, RF(14): -1.3	-0.1
2019	*WAS*	*MLB*	*22*	*251*	*21*	*7*	*0*	*7*	*26*	*11*	*84*	*1*	*0*	*.182/.216/.305*	*29*	*-14.0*	*.238*	*-0.6*	*CF -1, RF -1*	*-1.6*

Breakout: 3%   Improve: 5%   Collapse: 1%   Attrition: 5%   MLB: 9%   *Comparables: Trayvon Robinson, Daniel Fields, Michael Taylor*

The very baseball name Gage Canning might ring a bell for prospect connoisseurs, such as, *hey, he must be the brother of Angels pitching prospect and fellow Pac-12 product Griffin Canning.* Well, prospect connoisseurs, you'd be wrong. Somehow. How?! Anyway, a fifth-rounder in the 2018 draft, Gage blitzed short-season ball despite striking out 30 percent of the time and quickly ascended to Hagerstown. The contact struggles took more of a bite out of his production in a very short sample, but improving in that realm is probably step one in his quest to boost the profile from fourth outfielder to fringe regular.

Wilmer Difo 2B   Born: 04/02/92   Age: 27   Bats: B   Throws: R   Height: 5'11"   Weight: 200   Origin: International Free Agent, 2010

YEAR	TEAM	LVL	AGE	PA	R	2B	3B	HR	RBI	BB	K	SB	CS	AVG/OBP/SLG	DRC+	VORP	BABIP	BRR	FRAA	WARP
2016	HAR	AA	24	451	59	15	3	6	41	34	59	28	11	.259/.318/.354	90	13.9	.288	-0.1	SS(103): -2.4	1.3
2016	WAS	MLB	24	66	14	3	0	1	7	8	12	3	0	.276/.364/.379	87	3.1	.333	1.0	2B(9): 0.2, SS(5): 0.2	0.3
2017	SYR	AAA	25	45	5	2	0	0	1	5	6	0	0	.175/.267/.225	95	-1.8	.206	-0.1	SS(9): -1.4, CF(2): -0.3	0.0
2017	WAS	MLB	25	365	47	10	4	5	21	24	74	10	1	.271/.319/.370	82	9.0	.332	2.4	SS(57): 7.1, 2B(25): -0.7	1.5
2018	WAS	MLB	26	456	55	14	7	7	42	39	82	10	3	.230/.298/.350	87	0.5	.269	-1.5	2B(112): 4.7, 3B(20): -0.8	1.1
2019	*WAS*	*MLB*	*27*	*364*	*41*	*15*	*3*	*7*	*35*	*31*	*70*	*10*	*2*	*.246/.315/.375*	*90*	*7.7*	*.290*	*0.4*	*2B 3, SS 1*	*1.2*

Breakout: 8%   Improve: 35%   Collapse: 16%   Attrition: 26%   MLB: 88%   *Comparables: Tyler Saladino, Russ Adams, Brandon Phillips*

The 1990s called asking about Difo, but hung up when they heard he doesn't even steal that many bases. It's not his fault that the Nationals bestowed even more plate appearances upon his feeble bat in 2018, but he ended up as one of the roster holes that cut down a should-have-been-a-contender team. In Difo's defense, he drew a few more walks while striking out a little less than in 2017, and he wasn't really any worse than he's ever been in the big leagues. Still, a .250/.310/.358 career line won't pass muster as a starter in any era, although Difo's ability to play anywhere in the infield and occasionally even in the outfield gives him plenty of utility.

Stephen Drew INF   Born: 03/16/83   Age: 36   Bats: L   Throws: R   Height: 6'0"   Weight: 200   Origin: Round 1, 2004 Draft (#15 overall)

YEAR	TEAM	LVL	AGE	PA	R	2B	3B	HR	RBI	BB	K	SB	CS	AVG/OBP/SLG	DRC+	VORP	BABIP	BRR	FRAA	WARP
2016	WAS	MLB	33	165	24	11	1	8	21	16	31	0	1	.266/.339/.524	112	13.8	.278	-1.1	2B(21): 1.8, 3B(12): -0.2	0.9
2017	WAS	MLB	34	106	9	7	0	1	17	8	21	0	0	.253/.302/.358	89	2.2	.303	-0.1	SS(13): -0.6, 3B(11): -1.1	0.1
2019	WAS	MLB	36	251	27	14	1	6	28	20	51	1	1	.256/.320/.408	96	6.4	.302	-0.5	SS -1, 3B -1	0.6

Breakout: 1%   Improve: 33%   Collapse: 10%   Attrition: 16%   MLB: 76%   Comparables: *Clint Barmes, Johnny Logan, Cal Ripken Jr.*

As baseball's labor relations drift into more precarious territory, and athletes in other sports stick up for themselves with momentous holdouts, spare a thought for Drew. His plight in 2014 now appears to be nothing less than an opening act for the larger trials of winter, a sounding of the alarm about the hindrance a qualifying offer could be for a veteran player. With his playing days apparently over, Drew may well go down in the books as one of this decade's real-life human reminders of who ends up getting punished when a rule change is filed under "competitive balance" by those who can afford to purchase sports franchises.

Adam Eaton RF   Born: 12/06/88   Age: 30   Bats: L   Throws: L   Height: 5'9"·   Weight: 176   Origin: Round 19, 2010 Draft (#571 overall)

YEAR	TEAM	LVL	AGE	PA	R	2B	3B	HR	RBI	BB	K	SB	CS	AVG/OBP/SLG	DRC+	VORP	BABIP	BRR	FRAA	WARP
2016	CHA	MLB	27	706	91	29	9	14	59	63	115	14	5	.284/.362/.428	103	32.9	.329	5.9	RF(121): 33.4, CF(48): 6.3	6.9
2017	WAS	MLB	28	107	24	7	1	2	13	14	18	3	1	.297/.393/.462	101	9.5	.347	0.3	CF(20): -3.3, LF(5): 0.4	0.1
2018	WAS	MLB	29	370	55	18	1	5	33	38	64	9	1	.301/.394/.411	107	20.4	.364	0.4	RF(67): 5.7, LF(10): -0.5	1.8
2019	WAS	MLB	30	565	72	24	3	11	52	57	102	12	3	.258/.348/.385	103	20.0	.305	2.3	RF 22	4.5

Breakout: 3%   Improve: 58%   Collapse: 6%   Attrition: 4%   MLB: 99%   Comparables: *Floyd Robinson, Harvey Kuenn, Pete Rose*

Comrades: I write on the eve of our third summer in Washington to thank you for your efforts thus far, and to ask that you redouble your commitment against the tyranny of the Evil Eaton. We the ligaments, tendons and muscles serving under inhumane conditions imposed upon us by Eaton and his co-conspirators this year welcomed bones to our coalition — and seek to enlist further support for our cause in the coming days from bursa and fascia. Together, we will unite. If you ever doubt the power of your sacrifice, remember that Eaton demanded and received 706 grueling plate appearances from us in 2016, and 689 in 2015 — topping 10.0 WARP over two years on the back of our labor. Since organizing on the voyage to D.C., we have held our tormentor to just 477 plate appearances. Take pride, and in conclusion: Be the pain you wish to see in the world!

Luis Garcia SS   Born: 05/16/00   Age: 19   Bats: L   Throws: R   Height: 6'0"   Weight: 190   Origin: International Free Agent, 2016

YEAR	TEAM	LVL	AGE	PA	R	2B	3B	HR	RBI	BB	K	SB	CS	AVG/OBP/SLG	DRC+	VORP	BABIP	BRR	FRAA	WARP
2017	NAT	RK	17	211	25	8	3	1	22	9	32	11	2	.302/.330/.387	94	7.3	.353	1.7	2B(25): -3.0, SS(17): 0.7	0.4
2018	HAG	A	18	323	48	14	4	3	31	19	49	8	5	.297/.335/.402	98	16.4	.343	0.7	3B(36): -4.6, SS(27): 0.4	0.6
2018	POT	A+	18	221	34	7	2	4	23	12	33	4	1	.299/.338/.412	110	9.8	.337	-0.3	SS(40): -2.7	0.8
2019	WAS	MLB	19	251	23	6	0	5	20	5	55	1	1	.205/.219/.296	27	-14.6	.239	-0.4	SS -1, 3B 0	-1.7

Breakout: 0%   Improve: 5%   Collapse: 1%   Attrition: 4%   MLB: 9%   Comparables: *Carlos Triunfel, Elvis Andrus, Wilmer Flores*

Washington's minor-league system is starting to feel a bit like Juilliard and, hello, this could be the next young virtuoso in line behind Juan Soto. Continuing the club's pattern of aggressive placement and promotion, Garcia's precocious talents arrived at High-A shortly after his 18th birthday. He proved himself worthy, harmonizing his contact skills with a bit more pop than he had shown in his pro debut. A shortstop who's already seen some time at second and third base as a result of organizational abundance, this is a triple threat to know early. What with all the other promising talents churning out hits he could one day join a heck of a band.

Yan Gomes C   Born: 07/19/87   Age: 31   Bats: R   Throws: R   Height: 6'2"   Weight: 215   Origin: Round 10, 2009 Draft (#310 overall)

YEAR	TEAM	LVL	AGE	PA	R	2B	3B	HR	RBI	BB	K	SB	CS	AVG/OBP/SLG	DRC+	VORP	BABIP	BRR	FRAA	WARP
2016	CLE	MLB	28	264	22	11	1	9	34	9	69	0	0	.167/.201/.327	71	-7.4	.189	2.3	C(73): -4.6	0.2
2017	CLE	MLB	29	383	43	15	0	14	56	31	99	0	0	.232/.309/.399	87	13.2	.283	1.7	C(103): 6.8	2.2
2018	CLE	MLB	30	435	52	26	0	16	48	21	119	0	0	.266/.313/.449	97	23.1	.336	-1.1	C(111): 9.1	2.9
2019	WAS	MLB	31	317	34	15	1	10	37	21	81	0	0	.237/.301/.400	89	10.2	.297	0.7	C 3	1.4

Breakout: 4%   Improve: 30%   Collapse: 20%   Attrition: 26%   MLB: 95%   Comparables: *Welington Castillo, Matt Nokes, Nick Hundley*

For the second straight season, the Indians enjoyed a (mostly) full season of a (mostly) healthy and (mostly) productive Gomes, which was something of a coup when you consider his struggles in both departments during the two preceding years. That Gomes was able to catch more than 800 innings, provide above-average receiving numbers and hit around league average ain't nothing — it made him an All-Star, in fact. Cleveland's offseason payroll-shedding began with Gomes, who was shipped to Washington to tag-team catching duties with Kurt Suzuki. He's one of the better all-around catchers in baseball, offering positive value on both sides of the ball, but the time-share will likely reduce his workload in 2019.

YEAR	TEAM	P. COUNT	FRM RUNS	BLK RUNS	THRW RUNS	TOT RUNS
2016	CLE	9256	-3.2	-0.3	0.2	-3.0
2017	CLE	13358	4.2	0.5	2.3	7.6
2018	CLE	15103	7.5	1.7	0.0	9.6
2019	WAS	10237	2.5	0.4	0.5	3.3

Bryce Harper OF   Born: 10/16/92   Age: 26   Bats: L   Throws: R   Height: 6'3"   Weight: 220   Origin: Round 1, 2010 Draft (#1 overall)

YEAR	TEAM	LVL	AGE	PA	R	2B	3B	HR	RBI	BB	K	SB	CS	AVG/OBP/SLG	DRC+	VORP	BABIP	BRR	FRAA	WARP
2016	WAS	MLB	23	627	84	24	2	24	86	108	117	21	10	.243/.373/.441	124	42.1	.264	2.3	RF(143): 4.1	4.0
2017	WAS	MLB	24	492	95	27	1	29	87	68	99	4	2	.319/.413/.595	147	47.0	.356	-1.3	RF(110): -3.4	3.6
2018	WAS	MLB	25	695	103	34	0	34	100	130	169	13	3	.249/.393/.496	135	52.2	.289	-3.2	RF(116): -12.1, CF(63): -0.1	3.4
2019	WAS	MLB	26	615	90	29	2	28	92	98	134	11	4	.271/.392/.500	144	51.2	.314	-0.7	RF -5, CF 2	5.1

Breakout: 2%   Improve: 60%   Collapse: 0%   Attrition: 3%   MLB: 100%   Comparables: *Mel Ott, Frank Robinson, Frank Thomas*

The most ballyhooed amateur baseball player in recent memory, Harper was simultaneously and surreptitiously cast as the antagonist in a billion personal hero movies. Cole Hamels' righteous plunking (which resulted in the glorious steal of home). Jonathan Papelbon's turn as a raging TV cop in an interrogation room. The Statcast-enlightened internet's intellectual thriller in which his 2015 is a partial sham. The anonymous scout's tick-tock rush to expose a double-agent-style impostor who lacks the grit to win. Hunter Strickland's turn as a version of Liam Neeson who relies only on coincidental meetings. Even in his Home Run Derby triumph, it was hard to look at Harper without thinking of Johnny Lawrence and the Cobra Kai. He was appointed huge-contract A-Rod without the money or the villainy. Now, Harper has reached the huge contract portion of his career, and will remain that boogeyman to many. His outsized personality, however, is a bankable vehicle for baseball, regardless of the storylines' origin. Everyone is in his movie, whether they know it or not.

Howie Kendrick 2B Born: 07/12/83 Age: 35 Bats: R Throws: R Height: 5'11" Weight: 220 Origin: Round 10, 2002 Draft (#294 overall)

YEAR	TEAM	LVL	AGE	PA	R	2B	3B	HR	RBI	BB	K	SB	CS	AVG/OBP/SLG	DRC+	VORP	BABIP	BRR	FRAA	WARP
2016	LAN	MLB	32	543	65	26	2	8	40	50	96	10	2	.255/.326/.366	84	14.6	.301	4.9	LF(94): -0.7, 2B(32): 0.5	0.9
2017	PHI	MLB	33	156	16	8	1	2	16	11	30	8	3	.340/.397/.454	100	10.8	.418	-0.7	LF(24): -0.4, 2B(10): 0.6	0.4
2017	WAS	MLB	33	178	24	8	2	7	25	11	38	4	2	.293/.343/.494	106	10.3	.342	0.6	LF(38): -3.0, 2B(5): -0.2	0.3
2018	WAS	MLB	34	160	17	14	0	4	12	5	29	1	1	.303/.331/.474	92	3.8	.350	-3.1	2B(33): -2.7, LF(6): -0.1	-0.3
2019	WAS	MLB	35	426	46	19	2	9	45	30	84	8	3	.256/.318/.386	92	10.0	.307	0.3	2B -2, 1B 0	0.8

Breakout: 0%   Improve: 23%   Collapse: 8%   Attrition: 10%   MLB: 80%   *Comparables: Mark Ellis, Ronnie Belliard, Orlando Hudson*

When the sun eventually burns out, Kendrick will presumably be hitting .290, sitting on the disabled list, or both. Come April, he'll be 35 and returning from an Achilles tendon injury, but the Nationals have him under contract for an exceedingly reasonable $4 million. As long as he can stand in the box, he's a decent bet to put the bat on the ball in just the right way to spray a line drive over the infield (you don't log a .340 BABIP over a 13-year career by accident). In other words, he's exactly the type of professional hitter who will never go out of style.

Carter Kieboom SS Born: 09/03/97 Age: 21 Bats: R Throws: R Height: 6'2" Weight: 190 Origin: Round 1, 2016 Draft (#28 overall)

YEAR	TEAM	LVL	AGE	PA	R	2B	3B	HR	RBI	BB	K	SB	CS	AVG/OBP/SLG	DRC+	VORP	BABIP	BRR	FRAA	WARP
2016	NAT	RK	18	155	22	8	4	4	25	12	43	1	2	.244/.323/.452	113	5.1	.319	-0.3	SS(31): 0.6	0.8
2017	HAG	A	19	210	36	12	0	8	26	28	40	2	2	.296/.400/.497	135	20.4	.344	-0.7	SS(45): 1.4	1.9
2018	POT	A+	20	285	48	15	0	11	46	36	50	6	1	.298/.386/.494	137	31.4	.332	0.5	SS(56): -0.4	2.5
2018	HAR	AA	20	273	36	16	1	5	23	22	59	3	1	.262/.326/.395	96	13.3	.324	0.5	SS(62): 2.6	1.4
2019	WAS	MLB	21	251	29	9	0	8	26	19	62	1	0	.220/.280/.365	70	-0.4	.261	-0.5	SS 1, 2B 0	0.1

Breakout: 6%   Improve: 14%   Collapse: 5%   Attrition: 19%   MLB: 38%   *Comparables: Franklin Barreto, Addison Russell, Willy Adames*

The key boom goes back as far as ancient Rome, and the current run of success dates to the mid-1800s, when Linus Yale Sr. and Jr. invented the flat, metal devices that open your doors, start your cars and jingle in your pockets. Notably, there has yet to be a key bubble or a key bust, and Carter doesn't show many signs of being either. The 2016 first-round pick ascended to Double-A in 2018, strengthened his chances of staying at shortstop and impressed in the Arizona Fall League. A productive big-league career is starting to feel like a lock.

Spencer Kieboom C Born: 03/16/91 Age: 28 Bats: R Throws: R Height: 6'0" Weight: 210 Origin: Round 5, 2012 Draft (#174 overall)

YEAR	TEAM	LVL	AGE	PA	R	2B	3B	HR	RBI	BB	K	SB	CS	AVG/OBP/SLG	DRC+	VORP	BABIP	BRR	FRAA	WARP
2016	HAR	AA	25	359	27	11	0	5	31	43	61	0	0	.230/.324/.314	104	6.5	.267	-2.8	C(93): -12.3	0.3
2016	WAS	MLB	25	1	1	0	0	0	0	1	0	0	0		96	0.5	--	0.2		0.0
2017	HAR	AA	26	70	6	5	0	2	6	10	13	0	0	.183/.300/.367	107	1.0	.200	-0.6	C(16): 1.4	0.5
2017	SYR	AAA	26	176	17	9	0	3	19	15	30	0	0	.275/.335/.388	100	6.5	.320	-0.1	C(45): -3.9	0.4
2018	SYR	AAA	27	95	8	4	0	1	10	10	10	0	0	.250/.337/.333	119	0.2	.274	-1.2	C(21): 2.2, 1B(3): -0.1	0.7
2018	WAS	MLB	27	143	16	5	0	2	13	16	28	0	0	.232/.322/.320	95	2.8	.281	-0.3	C(49): -0.7, 1B(3): 0.0	0.5
2019	WAS	MLB	28	31	3	1	0	1	3	3	6	0	0	.236/.309/.365	74	0.4	.282	0.0	C -1	0.0

Breakout: 5%   Improve: 15%   Collapse: 17%   Attrition: 32%   MLB: 62%   *Comparables: Ryan Hanigan, Dustin Garneau, Bobby Wilson*

There are many reasons to despise the present moment in our existence, what with the way our culture has weaponized technology that allows communication to occur instantaneously. Kieboom, though, is a ray of light. In 1976 or some such year, there would be no memorable story to recall of the time everyone thought he had lost a tooth while swinging a bat, and later homered. Without Twitter, the boring but accurate story would have been the first and only story. Furthermore, in 1958 or thereabouts, there would be no combination of two emojis you could send to all fellow Nationals fans to phonetically represent the backup catcher's last name, and signify your excitement about his rare but

YEAR	TEAM	P. COUNT	FRM RUNS	BLK RUNS	THRW RUNS	TOT RUNS
2017	HAR	2137	0.0	0.4	0.0	0.1
2017	SYR	6418	-4.5	0.5	-0.2	-4.7
2018	SYR	2427	1.3	0.5	0.3	1.8
2018	WAS	5843	-1.4	1.0	0.1	-0.3
2019	WAS	1207	-0.7	0.1	-0.1	-0.7

important contribution to the baseball club — at least not without some artistic skills and serious patience. There would just be a fledgling major leaguer whose highly touted brother is on the way to likely surpass him, and that isn't nearly as fun.

Miguel Montero C Born: 07/09/83 Age: 35 Bats: L Throws: R Height: 5'11" Weight: 221 Origin: International Free Agent, 2001

YEAR	TEAM	LVL	AGE	PA	R	2B	3B	HR	RBI	BB	K	SB	CS	AVG/OBP/SLG	DRC+	VORP	BABIP	BRR	FRAA	WARP
2016	CHN	MLB	32	284	33	8	1	8	33	38	58	1	0	.216/.327/.357	97	10.0	.249	-1.7	C(71): 10.1, P(1): 0.0	2.2
2017	CHN	MLB	33	112	12	3	0	4	8	11	24	1	0	.286/.366/.439	100	7.9	.338	-0.2	C(29): 0.6, 1B(1): 0.0	0.6
2017	TOR	MLB	33	101	12	3	0	2	8	12	23	0	0	.138/.248/.241	88	-3.8	.159	-0.3	C(27): 0.0	0.3
2018	WAS	MLB	34	13	0	0	0	0	0	2	3	0	0	.000/.154/.000	85	-1.8	.000	-0.1	C(4): 0.4	0.1
2019	WAS	MLB	35	251	27	11	1	5	26	26	54	1	0	.236/.325/.370	89	7.0	.290	-0.7	C 9	1.7

Breakout: 1%   Improve: 34%   Collapse: 8%   Attrition: 24%   MLB: 87%   *Comparables: Gregg Zaun, Brian Schneider, Ramon Hernandez*

There's a thing people say — half-adage, half-reliable-seeming Google result — about restaurants. Three-quarters of them close within a year, they say. This is meant, depending on the situation, to terrify or comfort or provide grounding. If *they* knew about transitory catchers living on the edge of starting or heading to Triple-A, they might find them similar to restaurants. There was that one incredible grand slam of a meal you had that night in October, and the crazy drama that foreshadowed the end. You wouldn't mind going to the place again, but the memory is probably the best version.

YEAR	TEAM	P. COUNT	FRM RUNS	BLK RUNS	THRW RUNS	TOT RUNS
2016	CHN	8698	16.1	-1.8	-3.5	10.1
2017	CHN	3543	3.8	0.3	-1.8	1.9
2017	TOR	3456	3.4	0.7	-2.1	1.6
2018	WAS	461	0.3	0.2	0.0	0.4
2019	WAS	8586	11.0	-0.4	-1.9	8.7

Raudy Read C   Born: 10/29/93   Age: 25   Bats: R   Throws: R   Height: 6'0"   Weight: 170   Origin: International Free Agent, 2011

YEAR	TEAM	LVL	AGE	PA	R	2B	3B	HR	RBI	BB	K	SB	CS	AVG/OBP/SLG	DRC+	VORP	BABIP	BRR	FRAA	WARP
2016	POT	A+	22	426	54	30	1	9	51	31	53	6	3	.262/.324/.415	107	19.8	.281	-1.9	C(97): 0.7	2.2
2017	HAR	AA	23	442	44	25	1	17	61	27	79	2	0	.265/.312/.455	110	21.8	.290	-3.1	C(100): -24.7	-0.2
2017	WAS	MLB	23	11	1	0	0	0	0	0	3	0	0	.273/.273/.273	72	0.1	.375	-0.1	C(3): -0.4	0.0
2018	SYR	AAA	24	52	2	2	0	0	2	1	8	0	0	.260/.269/.300	88	0.0	.302	-0.1	C(10): -3.1	-0.2
2018	HAR	AA	24	161	14	9	2	3	24	11	30	0	0	.286/.335/.435	102	5.7	.336	-2.5	C(35): -7.8	-0.3
2019	WAS	MLB	25	31	3	1	0	1	4	2	7	0	0	.239/.278/.389	78	0.6	.278	0.0	C -3	-0.2

Breakout: 0%   Improve: 7%   Collapse: 13%   Attrition: 17%   MLB: 33%

Comparables: Adam Moore, Caleb Joseph, Luis Exposito

YEAR	TEAM	P. COUNT	FRM RUNS	BLK RUNS	THRW RUNS	TOT RUNS
2017	HAR	13457	-28.1	1.5	0.4	-27.2
2017	WAS	211	-0.2	-0.1	0.0	-0.4
2018	HAR	4606	-8.1	0.0	-0.2	-8.4
2018	SYR	1432	-2.8	0.0	-0.1	-3.0
2019	WAS	1144	-2.5	0.0	-0.1	-2.6

A PED suspension cost Read the first half of 2018, which wound up being a significant missed opportunity. Having made a brief major-league debut in 2017, Raudy and all his friends probably could have come up for a night and gotten a chance at catcher for the Nationals. Read eventually returned with some decent hitting in Double-A, but his first taste of Triple-A was a horror show. It's a toss-up as to whether he remains behind the plate, and perhaps even more of a toss-up as to whether his bat plays well enough to give him a fallback plan.

Anthony Rendon 3B   Born: 06/06/90   Age: 29   Bats: R   Throws: R   Height: 6'1"   Weight: 200   Origin: Round 1, 2011 Draft (#6 overall)

YEAR	TEAM	LVL	AGE	PA	R	2B	3B	HR	RBI	BB	K	SB	CS	AVG/OBP/SLG	DRC+	VORP	BABIP	BRR	FRAA	WARP
2016	WAS	MLB	26	647	91	38	2	20	85	65	117	12	6	.270/.348/.450	113	45.1	.304	0.8	3B(155): -9.0	2.6
2017	WAS	MLB	27	605	81	41	1	25	100	84	82	7	2	.301/.403/.533	142	63.3	.314	2.0	3B(145): -1.6	5.5
2018	WAS	MLB	28	597	88	44	2	24	92	55	82	2	1	.308/.374/.535	135	59.4	.323	2.9	3B(136): -5.7	4.6
2019	WAS	MLB	29	611	77	39	2	21	83	66	93	6	2	.284/.369/.479	132	39.4	.311	1.6	3B -6	3.6

Breakout: 2%   Improve: 44%   Collapse: 3%   Attrition: 8%   MLB: 99%

Comparables: Kyle Seager, Edgardo Alfonzo, Bill Madlock

Like the cars with TV commercials dedicated to proving they're just as good as name-brand, luxury competitors, Rendon is just as good or better than his name-brand, luxury rivals at third base. Despite your parents' insistence, *Consumer Reports* approvals for reliability and down-ballot MVP votes for steadfast production aren't enough to make an excellent product feel like a lifestyle choice. It's true, all the features you could ever want are there — the extra-base hits, the defense, the fuel mileage. Yet none of those everyday efficiencies instills envy in co-workers on the ride to lunch. Even when they should. Modesty is supposed to be a virtue, right?

Mark Reynolds 1B   Born: 08/03/83   Age: 35   Bats: R   Throws: R   Height: 6'2"   Weight: 220   Origin: Round 16, 2004 Draft (#476 overall)

YEAR	TEAM	LVL	AGE	PA	R	2B	3B	HR	RBI	BB	K	SB	CS	AVG/OBP/SLG	DRC+	VORP	BABIP	BRR	FRAA	WARP
2016	COL	MLB	32	441	61	24	0	14	53	42	112	1	2	.282/.356/.450	103	8.9	.361	-2.6	1B(115): 1.6, 2B(1): 0.0	0.7
2017	COL	MLB	33	593	82	22	1	30	97	69	175	2	1	.267/.352/.487	116	18.3	.343	-2.9	1B(138): -11.9, LF(1): 0.0	0.6
2018	SYR	AAA	34	42	3	1	0	1	4	3	13	0	0	.231/.286/.333	78	-0.7	.320	0.2	LF(5): 0.0, 3B(2): 0.0	0.0
2018	WAS	MLB	34	235	26	8	0	13	40	24	64	0	0	.248/.328/.476	112	5.2	.288	-2.8	1B(45): -2.1, 3B(10): 0.2	0.4
2019	WAS	MLB	35	299	34	13	1	11	39	29	86	1	1	.241/.319/.418	102	4.5	.313	-1.5	1B -3, 3B 0	0.1

Breakout: 0%   Improve: 22%   Collapse: 17%   Attrition: 20%   MLB: 78%

Comparables: Eric Hinske, Chili Davis, Jeff Baker

A newly issued baseball card might tell you that only five players have popped 10 dingers in every season since 2007: Albert Pujols, Edwin Encarnacion, Jose Bautista, Robinson Cano and Reynolds. An up-to-date baseball analysis website might inform you that only one player ever has logged 6,000 major-league plate appearances with a strikeout rate over 30 percent: Reynolds. Or maybe the baseball card would tell you about the strikeout rate, and the website about the homers. The truth is blind, after all. It doesn't even know that it's sneaking up on you.

Victor Robles CF   Born: 05/19/97   Age: 22   Bats: R   Throws: R   Height: 6'0"   Weight: 190   Origin: International Free Agent, 2013

YEAR	TEAM	LVL	AGE	PA	R	2B	3B	HR	RBI	BB	K	SB	CS	AVG/OBP/SLG	DRC+	VORP	BABIP	BRR	FRAA	WARP
2016	HAG	A	19	285	48	9	6	5	30	18	38	19	8	.305/.405/.459	133	31.6	.346	6.2	CF(63): 11.9	4.1
2016	POT	A+	19	198	24	8	2	3	11	14	32	18	5	.262/.354/.387	100	10.3	.304	-1.0	CF(40): 5.9	1.1
2017	POT	A+	20	338	49	25	7	7	33	25	62	16	7	.289/.377/.495	117	30.8	.345	0.7	CF(70): 16.1	3.6
2017	HAR	AA	20	158	24	12	1	3	14	12	22	11	3	.324/.394/.489	112	17.0	.368	2.7	CF(30): 4.1, RF(1): 0.1	1.5
2017	WAS	MLB	20	27	2	1	2	0	4	0	6	0	1	.250/.308/.458	85	-0.6	.333	-0.8	RF(6): 1.2, CF(3): -0.3	0.0
2018	SYR	AAA	21	182	25	9	1	2	10	18	26	14	6	.278/.356/.386	107	9.9	.318	1.2	CF(39): -0.8	0.8
2018	WAS	MLB	21	66	8	3	1	3	10	4	12	3	2	.288/.348/.525	112	5.2	.311	0.7	CF(14): 0.1, RF(2): -0.2	0.4
2019	WAS	MLB	22	465	56	20	2	11	48	35	93	21	9	.240/.309/.381	84	9.5	.279	0.7	CF 10, LF 0	2.1

Breakout: 6%   Improve: 32%   Collapse: 4%   Attrition: 20%   MLB: 60%

Comparables: Gregory Polanco, Andrew McCutchen, Dalton Pompey

On September 8, Robles started in center field between Bryce Harper and Juan Soto, and found he was the least accomplished major leaguer in the trio. It was the first time his name had been written on the lineup card in 2018 and, fittingly, the game was delayed. It was supposed to be the year he introduced himself to the wider world, but Robles spent it clawing back from the kind of elbow injury that inspired a "warning: graphic content" on Twitter while everyone gawked at his prodigal teammates. When he re-arrived in Washington, things looked all-systems-go for the anticipated ascension to five-tool, well-rounded star status. A task on the diamond at which Robles does not excel? Still not located, but playing second fiddle could be the first.

Pedro Severino C   Born: 07/20/93   Age: 25   Bats: R   Throws: R   Height: 6'1"   Weight: 219   Origin: International Free Agent, 2010

YEAR	TEAM	LVL	AGE	PA	R	2B	3B	HR	RBI	BB	K	SB	CS	AVG/OBP/SLG	DRC+	VORP	BABIP	BRR	FRAA	WARP
2016	SYR	AAA	22	317	25	13	0	2	21	19	45	3	4	.271/.316/.337	92	4.8	.310	-2.0	C(81): -2.0	0.8
2016	WAS	MLB	22	34	6	2	0	2	4	5	3	0	0	.321/.441/.607	111	6.5	.304	0.9	C(15): 0.5	0.4
2017	SYR	AAA	23	227	17	4	0	5	29	15	43	1	1	.242/.291/.332	97	3.3	.280	-0.4	C(58): 5.1	1.5
2017	WAS	MLB	23	31	0	1	0	0	3	2	10	0	0	.172/.226/.207	70	-2.4	.263	-0.5	C(10): 0.3	0.0
2018	SYR	AAA	24	136	14	5	1	6	13	5	23	0	0	.269/.294/.462	106	7.3	.284	-2.1	C(32): 1.1	0.7
2018	WAS	MLB	24	213	14	9	0	2	15	18	47	1	0	.168/.254/.247	68	-7.0	.211	-0.1	C(67): 0.0	0.2
2019	WAS	MLB	25	31	3	1	0	1	3	2	6	0	0	.232/.299/.365	59	-0.2	.273	0.0	C 0	0.0

Breakout: 5%   Improve: 28%   Collapse: 12%   Attrition: 32%   MLB: 76%

Comparables: Curtis Thigpen, Kevin Plawecki, Trevor Brown

Going from "backup catcher of the future" to "backup catcher of the present" is something, one would suppose, and Severino made that small, if short-lived, leap. He logged 213 plate appearances that mostly served to confirm the miserable state of catcher offense in the contemporary game, while producing extremely average defensive numbers. The Nationals' ambitions are too large to actively plan for Severino to get another shot — in fact, they went out and acquired not one but two starting-caliber catchers this offseason — but lack of opportunity is rarely a problem for catchers with even a whiff of big-league ability these days. Back to "backup catcher of the future" it is.

YEAR	TEAM	P. COUNT	FRM RUNS	BLK RUNS	THRW RUNS	TOT RUNS
2016	WAS	1422	-0.4	0.3	0.1	0.0
2017	SYR	8269	8.1	-2.3	0.3	5.2
2017	WAS	939	0.7	-0.4	0.0	0.3
2018	SYR	4103	1.4	0.0	0.0	1.4
2018	WAS	8290	0.3	0.2	0.1	0.5
2019	WAS	1200	0.0	-0.1	0.0	-0.1

Juan Soto LF   Born: 10/25/98   Age: 20   Bats: L   Throws: L   Height: 6'1"   Weight: 185   Origin: International Free Agent, 2015

YEAR	TEAM	LVL	AGE	PA	R	2B	3B	HR	RBI	BB	K	SB	CS	AVG/OBP/SLG	DRC+	VORP	BABIP	BRR	FRAA	WARP
2016	NAT	RK	17	183	25	11	3	5	31	14	25	5	2	.361/.410/.550	145	18.3	.403	1.0	RF(42): 2.9	1.7
2017	HAG	A	18	96	15	5	0	3	14	10	8	1	2	.360/.427/.523	133	8.2	.373	1.0	RF(19): -1.9, LF(2): -0.3	0.5
2018	HAG	A	19	74	12	5	3	5	24	14	13	2	0	.373/.486/.814	141	14.5	.405	0.3	RF(14): 1.1, CF(2): 0.2	0.7
2018	POT	A+	19	73	17	3	1	7	18	11	8	0	1	.371/.466/.790	172	15.4	.340	1.4	RF(14): 1.0, LF(1): 0.0	1.1
2018	HAR	AA	19	35	4	2	0	2	10	4	7	1	0	.323/.400/.581	94	3.6	.364	0.0	LF(4): 0.6, RF(4): -0.5	0.1
2018	WAS	MLB	19	494	77	25	1	22	70	79	99	5	2	.292/.406/.517	131	39.9	.338	-0.5	LF(114): 2.7	3.4
2019	WAS	MLB	20	589	78	24	2	24	82	86	125	5	2	.261/.372/.460	129	36.5	.301	-0.4	LF 1	4.0

Breakout: 10%   Improve: 45%   Collapse: 0%   Attrition: 6%   MLB: 52%

Comparables: Bryce Harper, Tony Conigliaro, Mel Ott

Okay, it's Childish Bambino, you know minor leagues are mad whack
Make scouts freak with the sound of my bat crack
Make the nerds think, man, run it, a full season
I crush heaters, I crush sliders, dude, I should be hittin' clean-up
In the majors, with the big boys, O-B-P like Joey V
My age is barely past nineteen, your age is just embarrassing
The chosen one, I rule this world, and now he try to hit like me
My look is like a warning sign, it's all a prelude to my peak

Kurt Suzuki C   Born: 10/04/83   Age: 35   Bats: R   Throws: R   Height: 5'11"   Weight: 210   Origin: Round 2, 2004 Draft (#67 overall)

YEAR	TEAM	LVL	AGE	PA	R	2B	3B	HR	RBI	BB	K	SB	CS	AVG/OBP/SLG	DRC+	VORP	BABIP	BRR	FRAA	WARP
2016	MIN	MLB	32	373	34	24	1	8	49	18	48	0	0	.258/.301/.403	94	6.9	.276	-0.9	C(99): -6.2	0.8
2017	ATL	MLB	33	309	38	13	0	19	50	17	39	0	0	.283/.351/.536	133	27.3	.268	-2.8	C(77): 1.9	2.8
2018	ATL	MLB	34	388	45	24	0	12	50	22	43	0	0	.271/.332/.444	115	25.6	.275	-2.0	C(93): -5.5	1.9
2019	WAS	MLB	35	303	35	17	1	10	40	19	40	0	0	.272/.344/.452	115	17.5	.293	-1.3	C -4	1.4

Breakout: 1%   Improve: 36%   Collapse: 9%   Attrition: 20%   MLB: 90%

Comparables: Paul Lo Duca, Yadier Molina, Mike Redmond

Suzuki's mid-30s career renaissance kept on trucking with another impressive season, and he was rewarded with more time on the field as he slowly gained more of a lead role over catching mate Tyler Flowers. The poor guy is a magnet for baseballs. He was hit by 13 of them in addition to all the dings he receives behind the plate. He stayed the course and gave the Braves another above-average season at the position. He played his way out of a job with the Twins, came to a rebuilding Braves team as half of a catching duo and proceeded to turn in two of the better years of his career at an age where most catchers are

YEAR	TEAM	P. COUNT	FRM RUNS	BLK RUNS	THRW RUNS	TOT RUNS
2016	MIN	13825	-4.7	1.6	-2.5	-6.3
2017	ATL	10594	-0.6	1.4	-0.9	-0.7
2018	ATL	12497	-7.5	1.5	-0.4	-6.6
2019	WAS	10041	-5.3	1.1	-1.0	-5.1

slowing down or losing starting jobs. For his effort, he got a two-year deal to split time behind the plate with Yan Gomes in Washington. Now if we can just get pitchers to appreciate him and stop beaning him in the kidney.

Michael Taylor CF   Born: 03/26/91   Age: 28   Bats: R   Throws: R   Height: 6'4"   Weight: 212   Origin: Round 6, 2009 Draft (#172 overall)

YEAR	TEAM	LVL	AGE	PA	R	2B	3B	HR	RBI	BB	K	SB	CS	AVG/OBP/SLG	DRC+	VORP	BABIP	BRR	FRAA	WARP
2016	SYR	AAA	25	130	17	5	1	1	9	12	33	7	1	.205/.285/.291	80	2.3	.277	2.2	CF(28): 0.5	0.4
2016	WAS	MLB	25	237	28	11	0	7	16	14	77	14	3	.231/.278/.376	67	3.7	.319	0.7	CF(64): 2.9, RF(5): -0.4	0.2
2017	WAS	MLB	26	432	55	23	3	19	53	29	137	17	7	.271/.320/.486	93	26.5	.363	3.1	CF(111): 12.6, RF(2): -0.2	2.7
2018	WAS	MLB	27	385	46	22	3	6	28	29	116	24	6	.227/.287/.357	67	1.2	.320	1.3	CF(113): 8.9, 1B(1): 0.0	0.8
2019	*WAS*	*MLB*	*28*	*342*	*41*	*14*	*2*	*9*	*36*	*26*	*105*	*17*	*5*	*.228/.291/.377*	*80*	*5.2*	*.311*	*1.1*	*CF 5, RF 0*	*1.1*

Breakout: 0%   Improve: 43%   Collapse: 9%   Attrition: 13%   MLB: 95%   *Comparables: Drew Stubbs, Peter Bourjos, Mikie Mahtook*

Following his second-half power surge in 2017, some expected A. breakout, but 2018 proved A. bummer. Despite supposed gains at the plate, there lingered A. problem. Contact is simply too infrequent when the fleet-footed center fielder swings A. bat, and that's difficult to correct without A. job. Defense remains A. strength, and steals A. certainty. However, the Nationals are not the ideal situation for him as playing time demands are piling up for outfielders A. plenty. It may be that the best thing for Michael A. Taylor's career would be, well, a trade.

Trea Turner SS   Born: 06/30/93   Age: 26   Bats: R   Throws: R   Height: 6'2"   Weight: 185   Origin: Round 1, 2014 Draft (#13 overall)

YEAR	TEAM	LVL	AGE	PA	R	2B	3B	HR	RBI	BB	K	SB	CS	AVG/OBP/SLG	DRC+	VORP	BABIP	BRR	FRAA	WARP
2016	SYR	AAA	23	371	61	22	8	6	33	37	72	25	2	.302/.370/.471	115	40.0	.369	6.1	SS(71): 8.6, CF(6): 0.9	3.9
2016	WAS	MLB	23	324	53	14	8	13	40	14	59	33	6	.342/.370/.567	122	42.1	.388	5.9	CF(45): -2.1, 2B(30): -1.1	2.3
2017	WAS	MLB	24	447	75	24	6	11	45	30	80	46	8	.284/.338/.451	100	36.6	.329	6.8	SS(95): 0.2	2.8
2018	WAS	MLB	25	740	103	27	6	19	73	69	132	43	9	.271/.344/.416	109	45.8	.314	2.7	SS(159): 7.1	5.3
2019	*WAS*	*MLB*	*26*	*636*	*94*	*30*	*6*	*17*	*64*	*48*	*117*	*42*	*8*	*.274/.336/.435*	*114*	*38.7*	*.318*	*4.3*	*SS 8*	*5.0*

Breakout: 2%   Improve: 50%   Collapse: 6%   Attrition: 13%   MLB: 98%   *Comparables: Bobby Crosby, Aledmys Diaz, Josh Rutledge*

It appears Turner has found his level. And what a level it is. Sure, it's not his mind-bending 2016 burst, but he basically repeated his 2017 over 740 (!) plate appearances, with walks becoming a bit more frequent and extra-base hits a bit less frequent. He blazed around the bases in spectacular and efficient fashion. Plus, the defensive metrics say he's grown into a high-caliber asset at shortstop, which means you can expect about 5.0 WARP out of the 25-year-old Turner for the foreseeable future even if he takes no further leap. If you grew up on shortstops who seemed set apart from the rest of the players on the field, a constant threat to alter the game on a dime, Turner just might be your favorite player.

Drew Ward 1B   Born: 11/25/94   Age: 24   Bats: L   Throws: R   Height: 6'3"   Weight: 215   Origin: Round 3, 2013 Draft (#105 overall)

YEAR	TEAM	LVL	AGE	PA	R	2B	3B	HR	RBI	BB	K	SB	CS	AVG/OBP/SLG	DRC+	VORP	BABIP	BRR	FRAA	WARP
2016	POT	A+	21	268	36	16	1	11	32	34	70	0	1	.278/.377/.491	122	19.7	.353	-2.1	3B(49): 2.0	1.5
2016	HAR	AA	21	203	19	7	0	3	24	22	51	0	1	.219/.310/.309	83	1.0	.288	0.9	3B(51): -3.9	0.0
2017	HAR	AA	22	480	47	20	0	10	53	55	131	0	0	.235/.325/.356	87	10.3	.311	-5.2	3B(108): 3.3, 1B(3): -0.2	0.7
2018	SYR	AAA	23	61	5	2	0	0	2	7	20	0	1	.185/.279/.222	72	-3.2	.294	-0.2	3B(15): -1.0	-0.1
2018	HAR	AA	23	380	59	16	4	13	56	55	95	1	1	.259/.376/.456	118	21.9	.330	-1.9	1B(82): -0.2, 3B(11): -1.7	1.0
2019	*WAS*	*MLB*	*24*	*251*	*24*	*8*	*0*	*7*	*28*	*23*	*77*	*0*	*0*	*.204/.281/.339*	*61*	*-8.1*	*.272*	*-0.5*	*1B -1, 3B 0*	*-1.0*

Breakout: 2%   Improve: 5%   Collapse: 5%   Attrition: 10%   MLB: 13%   *Comparables: Brock Peterson, Mark Canha, Lucas Duda*

The third time was indeed the charm for Ward at Double-A, which he cracked to the tune of 13 homers and a .376 on-base percentage. A former third-round pick whose status as a third-base prospect may soon be a relic, Ward's defensive position is now more often signified with a three in the scorebook. Unfortunately, his numerous connections to that number did him no favors in his first taste of Triple-A. It was only 61 plate appearances, but there was not a three to speak of anywhere in that triple-slash.

Matt Wieters C   Born: 05/21/86   Age: 33   Bats: B   Throws: R   Height: 6'5"   Weight: 235   Origin: Round 1, 2007 Draft (#5 overall)

YEAR	TEAM	LVL	AGE	PA	R	2B	3B	HR	RBI	BB	K	SB	CS	AVG/OBP/SLG	DRC+	VORP	BABIP	BRR	FRAA	WARP
2016	BAL	MLB	30	464	48	17	1	17	66	32	85	1	0	.243/.302/.409	99	12.0	.265	-1.4	C(117): 4.0	2.5
2017	WAS	MLB	31	465	43	20	0	10	52	38	94	1	0	.225/.288/.344	80	1.9	.264	-1.7	C(118): -10.4	0.0
2018	WAS	MLB	32	271	24	8	0	8	30	30	45	0	1	.238/.330/.374	111	7.8	.261	-0.8	C(73): -4.0	1.2
2019	*WAS*	*MLB*	*33*	*296*	*31*	*15*	*1*	*7*	*32*	*25*	*55*	*1*	*0*	*.250/.318/.393*	*93*	*9.9*	*.289*	*-0.8*	*C -5*	*0.5*

Breakout: 2%   Improve: 39%   Collapse: 9%   Attrition: 20%   MLB: 91%   *Comparables: Rod Barajas, A.J. Pierzynski, Jimmie Wilson*

Wieters, like waiters, can be most noticeable in absentia. Bringing ribeyes? Not necessary, just keep showing up and presenting the dishes well enough. His performance was just a touch over replacement level when he was on the field in 2018, but the real issue came when oblique and hamstring injuries left the Nationals out to dry for large portions of what was supposed to be a contending year. It didn't even really matter that he was being paid somewhat gratuitously. It was just one of those times when you want to pay the tab and move on with your life.

YEAR	TEAM	P. COUNT	FRM RUNS	BLK RUNS	THRW RUNS	TOT RUNS
2016	BAL	16454	0.7	1.0	1.9	4.3
2017	WAS	16476	-11.2	1.5	-0.7	-11.0
2018	WAS	9086	-3.7	1.1	0.3	-2.3
2019	*WAS*	*10698*	*-5.9*	*0.9*	*0.0*	*-5.0*

Ryan Zimmerman 1B
Born: 09/28/84 Age: 34 Bats: R Throws: R Height: 6'3" Weight: 215 Origin: Round 1, 2005 Draft (#4 overall)

YEAR	TEAM	LVL	AGE	PA	R	2B	3B	HR	RBI	BB	K	SB	CS	AVG/OBP/SLG	DRC+	VORP	BABIP	BRR	FRAA	WARP
2016	WAS	MLB	31	467	60	18	1	15	46	29	104	4	1	.218/.272/.370	80	-0.5	.248	4.1	1B(114): -2.1	-0.3
2017	WAS	MLB	32	576	90	33	0	36	108	44	126	1	0	.303/.358/.573	130	39.4	.335	-0.3	1B(143): -11.4	1.9
2018	WAS	MLB	33	323	33	21	2	13	51	30	55	1	1	.264/.337/.486	112	14.1	.284	-0.5	1B(73): 1.4	1.1
2019	WAS	MLB	34	499	58	24	2	20	68	39	104	2	1	.257/.320/.449	108	13.9	.293	1.0	1B -4	1.1

Breakout: 1% Improve: 30% Collapse: 6% Attrition: 20% MLB: 93% *Comparables: Kendrys Morales, Hanley Ramirez, Mike Sweeney*

The cornerstone upon which the concept of a competitive Nationals team was built years ago, Zimmerman is entering the final guaranteed season of his contract, with an $18 million team option for 2020 unlikely to be picked up. His 2018 started off slow after a bizarre spring training gambit that involved not really training in the spring. He missed all of June but surged in July and August to once again post above-average offensive numbers, continuing a herky-jerky, off-and-on two-year campaign to prove his dreadful 2016 was a fluke. We can accept that premise at this point, and accept Zimmerman for what he is: A declining but still good hitter who plays first base and is likely to miss some time. Applied to a different player, that would be a source of stress or a burden to unload. With Zimmerman, it's an assurance that the club's most familiar face will be around for at least one more year as a new core emerges.

PITCHERS

Austin Adams RHP
Born: 05/05/91 Age: 28 Bats: R Throws: R Height: 6'3" Weight: 225 Origin: Round 8, 2012 Draft (#267 overall)

YEAR	TEAM	LVL	AGE	W	L	SV	G	GS	IP	H	HR	BB/9	K/9	K	GB%	BABIP	WHIP	ERA	DRA	WARP	MPH	FB%	WHF	CSP
2016	ARK	AA	25	0	1	4	32	0	41¹	29	2	5.2	13.3	61	42%	.321	1.28	3.05	2.44	1.1				
2017	SYR	AAA	26	6	2	5	44	0	59	44	2	5.6	13.9	91	49%	.321	1.37	2.14	2.32	1.9				
2017	WAS	MLB	26	0	0	0	6	0	5	4	0	14.4	18.0	10	40%	.400	2.40	3.60	2.01	0.2	96.2	52.7	14.5	43.7
2018	WAS	MLB	27	0	0	0	2	0	1	1	0	27.0	0.0	0	50%	.250	4.00	0.00	9.99	-0.1	96.1	58.3	4.2	44
2018	SYR	AAA	27	1	4	9	41	0	46¹	47	1	3.9	15.2	78	43%	.434	1.45	3.50	1.24	2.0				
2019	WAS	MLB	28	1	0	0	24	0	25²	22	3	4.9	11.8	34	43%	.320	1.38	3.94	4.48	0.1	95.6	54	12.7	44.1

Breakout: 15% Improve: 17% Collapse: 21% Attrition: 24% MLB: 46% *Comparables: Leonel Campos, Maikel Cleto, John Gaub*

Acquired in the Nationals' 2016 shipping out of Danny Espinosa, Adams' first target should be to absorb more innings than the other reliever with his name who tossed 58 innings with the Indians over three seasons. That long may have been the loftiest reasonable goal for the 27-year-old, slider-slinging righty. In 2018, though, he appeared to take a step forward at Triple-A. Adams cut his walk rate from *yikes* to manageable while bumping up an already strong strikeout rate to 37 percent. The result was one of the better reliever profiles in Triple-A. No, not every pitcher with this sort of performance becomes a good major-league reliever, but most of them get some burn. So, maybe Adams can soon improve on his six career innings and move on to a new goal.

Kyle Barraclough RHP
Born: 05/23/90 Age: 29 Bats: R Throws: R Height: 6'3" Weight: 225 Origin: Round 7, 2012 Draft (#240 overall)

YEAR	TEAM	LVL	AGE	W	L	SV	G	GS	IP	H	HR	BB/9	K/9	K	GB%	BABIP	WHIP	ERA	DRA	WARP	MPH	FB%	WHF	CSP
2016	NWO	AAA	26	1	0	1	3	0	6	2	0	1.5	13.5	9	46%	.182	0.50	1.50	1.34	0.2				
2016	MIA	MLB	26	6	3	0	75	0	72²	45	1	5.4	14.0	113	55%	.301	1.22	2.85	2.63	1.9	98.0	54.3	14.3	45
2017	MIA	MLB	27	6	2	1	66	0	66	53	5	5.2	10.4	76	46%	.291	1.38	3.00	3.55	1.2	96.4	54.2	13	44.7
2018	MIA	MLB	28	1	6	10	61	0	55²	40	8	5.5	9.7	60	48%	.232	1.33	4.20	4.53	0.3	94.8	59.8	12.1	46.8
2019	WAS	MLB	29	2	1	1	49	0	51²	42	6	5.0	10.5	60	48%	.297	1.38	4.07	4.63	0.2	95.6	56.3	13	45.7

Breakout: 12% Improve: 43% Collapse: 31% Attrition: 17% MLB: 88% *Comparables: A.J. Ramos, Al Alburquerque, Ryan Cook*

In his first couple years with the Marlins, Barraclough thrived with a deadly fastball-slider combo, pitching himself into and out of jams well enough that the team had no choice but to accept his wildness. Last season, however, he backed up. His strikeout rate fell to the lowest mark of his career, his home runs doubled and his walk rate remained the same, which is to say awful. What gives? He introduced a changeup at the expense of his slider. While the changeup played like an average pitch, it was his slider that backed up. As the months progressed, he lowered his release point, which affected the drop of the pitch. Batters recorded the highest slugging percentage against it in Barraclough's career. Washington moved quickly to acquire him this offseason, clearly believing they can get him back on track, wild as that may still be.

Joaquin Benoit RHP
Born: 07/26/77 Age: 41 Bats: R Throws: R Height: 6'4" Weight: 250 Origin: International Free Agent, 1996

YEAR	TEAM	LVL	AGE	W	L	SV	G	GS	IP	H	HR	BB/9	K/9	K	GB%	BABIP	WHIP	ERA	DRA	WARP	MPH	FB%	WHF	CSP
2016	SEA	MLB	38	1	1	0	26	0	24¹	20	4	5.5	10.4	28	43%	.254	1.44	5.18	4.69	0.1	96.8	52.3	15.5	40.5
2016	TOR	MLB	38	2	0	1	25	0	23²	17	1	3.4	9.1	24	38%	.271	1.10	0.38	5.53	-0.2	96.5	57.6	15	41.4
2017	PHI	MLB	39	1	4	2	44	0	42	32	5	3.4	9.2	43	35%	.252	1.14	4.07	4.15	0.5	96.1	60.9	16.5	44.4
2017	PIT	MLB	39	0	2	0	8	0	8¹	11	2	6.5	3.2	3	38%	.300	2.04	7.56	8.03	-0.3	95.9	53.1	5.6	41.8
2019	WAS	MLB	41	2	1	1	34	0	36¹	30	5	4.1	9.1	37	39%	.274	1.28	4.32	4.89	0.0	94.5	55.4	14.2	41.1

Breakout: 10% Improve: 30% Collapse: 33% Attrition: 13% MLB: 67% *Comparables: Arthur Rhodes, Tom Gordon, Russ Springer*

After signing a $1 million deal with the Nationals in the spring, Benoit never actually pitched in 2018. A hush-hush injury turned out to be a shoulder problem that, at 40 years old, he wasn't looking to solve surgically. By the end of the year, he was ready to confirm what was implied by that decision: He was hanging them up. If, in fact, it's the end for Benoit and he doesn't indulge a desperate GM's phone call somewhere down the line, he can boast of a rare reliability that, after he abandoned his rotation hopes in Texas, allowed him to succeed even in Dave Dombrowski's dreaded Detroit relief corps.

Tim Cate LHP   Born: 09/30/97   Age: 21   Bats: L   Throws: L   Height: 6'0"   Weight: 185   Origin: Round 2, 2018 Draft (#65 overall)

YEAR	TEAM	LVL	AGE	W	L	SV	G	GS	IP	H	HR	BB/9	K/9	K	GB%	BABIP	WHIP	ERA	DRA	WARP	MPH	FB%	WHF	CSP
2018	AUB	A-	20	2	3	0	9	8	31	34	1	2.9	7.5	26	45%	.333	1.42	4.65	3.82	0.5				
2018	HAG	A	20	0	3	0	4	4	21	23	4	2.6	8.1	19	44%	.306	1.38	5.57	6.82	-0.4				
2019	WAS	MLB	21	2	3	0	8	8	36²	42	7	3.9	6.4	26	37%	.311	1.57	5.72	6.47	-0.5				

Comparables: Ranger Suarez, Clay Buchholz, Wilking Rodriguez

The Nationals' second pick in the 2018 draft, Cate is a lefty out of UConn who wields a mean curveball. He likely only fell to the second round because of a forearm injury that cost him time during his final college season, and the team proclaimed itself lucky to snag him. Apparently only impending pro prospects kept the highly competitive and totally ambidextrous Cate from reprising a little trick he pulled in high school — playing the entire season as a right-handed hitter after he had Tommy John surgery on his left elbow.

Tim Collins LHP   Born: 08/21/89   Age: 29   Bats: L   Throws: L   Height: 5'7"   Weight: 168   Origin: Undrafted Free Agent, 2007

YEAR	TEAM	LVL	AGE	W	L	SV	G	GS	IP	H	HR	BB/9	K/9	K	GB%	BABIP	WHIP	ERA	DRA	WARP	MPH	FB%	WHF	CSP
2017	HAR	AA	27	1	1	0	10	0	8²	12	2	10.4	8.3	8	48%	.370	2.54	14.54	4.74	0.0				
2018	SYR	AAA	28	2	4	0	30	0	32	26	0	4.2	9.6	34	55%	.313	1.28	3.94	3.65	0.5				
2018	WAS	MLB	28	0	0	0	38	0	22²	23	5	4.8	8.3	21	41%	.295	1.54	4.37	4.37	0.1	93.4	53.4	12.4	44.7
2019	WAS	MLB	29	2	1	0	38	0	40²	37	7	5.3	9.2	42	47%	.298	1.51	5.03	5.70	-0.3	92.7	53.4	12.4	44.7

Breakout: 11%   Improve: 20%   Collapse: 28%   Attrition: 27%   MLB: 51%   *Comparables: Preston Claiborne, Lucas Luetge, Clay Zavada*

You could have forgiven Collins for thinking his all-important left elbow was a lemon. After pitching for the Royals in parts of every season from 2011 to 2014, he endured two Tommy John surgeries and didn't see action in the majors again until May of 2018. When the diminutive southpaw did return, it was sweet as sugar — he didn't allow a run for more than a month. Even though he didn't quite gin up his old velocity, Collins added some fizz to the mix with a cutter that he threw almost 18 percent of the time, and then drank in the league-average results under the bright lights.

Patrick Corbin LHP   Born: 07/19/89   Age: 29   Bats: L   Throws: L   Height: 6'3"   Weight: 210   Origin: Round 2, 2009 Draft (#80 overall)

YEAR	TEAM	LVL	AGE	W	L	SV	G	GS	IP	H	HR	BB/9	K/9	K	GB%	BABIP	WHIP	ERA	DRA	WARP	MPH	FB%	WHF	CSP
2016	ARI	MLB	26	5	13	1	36	24	155²	177	24	3.8	7.6	131	55%	.322	1.56	5.15	5.86	-1.0	94.4	63.8	10.2	44.3
2017	ARI	MLB	27	14	13	0	33	32	189²	208	26	2.9	8.4	178	52%	.326	1.42	4.03	4.92	1.4	94.3	53.3	11.9	43.8
2018	ARI	MLB	28	11	7	0	33	33	200	162	15	2.2	11.1	246	49%	.302	1.05	3.15	2.74	5.9	93.5	48.6	16.3	41.6
2019	WAS	MLB	29	12	8	0	29	29	174	151	20	3.0	10.3	198	50%	.311	1.20	3.34	3.78	3.1	93.3	53.4	13.5	43

Breakout: 16%   Improve: 41%   Collapse: 18%   Attrition: 3%   MLB: 95%   *Comparables: Anibal Sanchez, Gaylord Perry, Yovani Gallardo*

You've seen this movie before. Well, not this *exact* movie, but ones just like it. You know how it'll end: He'll come running for his true love, but it'll be too late. Heartbreak. Devastation. Punch-out. That's Corbin for you. Strikingly good looks aside, Corbin has lived and died by his slider. And the living has been good, as his new contract will tell you. Batters can never seem to decipher the difference between his fastball and his slider until it's too late. That one-two punch got a boost in 2018 as his new-found "slow slider" (you can call it a curve if you want, but he throws it just like his tried-and-true breaker) made a cameo, stole a bunch of strikes and helped tip the odds in his favor, especially early in the count.

Wil Crowe RHP   Born: 09/09/94   Age: 24   Bats: R   Throws: R   Height: 6'2"   Weight: 240   Origin: Round 2, 2017 Draft (#65 overall)

YEAR	TEAM	LVL	AGE	W	L	SV	G	GS	IP	H	HR	BB/9	K/9	K	GB%	BABIP	WHIP	ERA	DRA	WARP	MPH	FB%	WHF	CSP
2017	AUB	A-	22	0	0	0	7	7	20²	18	3	1.3	6.5	15	52%	.250	1.02	2.61	5.93	-0.2				
2018	POT	A+	23	11	0	0	16	15	87	71	6	3.1	8.1	78	47%	.267	1.16	2.69	3.35	2.0				
2018	HAR	AA	23	0	5	0	5	5	26¹	31	4	5.5	5.1	15	44%	.325	1.78	6.15	4.71	0.2				
2019	WAS	MLB	24	5	7	0	18	18	83²	89	16	3.9	7.1	66	43%	.302	1.49	5.45	6.16	-0.8				

Breakout: 3%   Improve: 4%   Collapse: 4%   Attrition: 9%   MLB: 13%   *Comparables: Daniel Poncedeleon, James Houser, Scott Barlow*

A second-round pick in the 2017 draft coming off Tommy John surgery, Crowe literally moved in next to the Nationals' complex in Florida last winter. Off came the training wheels. Crowe started 2018 at High-A Potomac, tossing 87 exceptional innings and earning a further promotion to Double-A near the end of the year. Those five starts were rockier, but generally confirm the plan: This is a quick-moving starter going into the fine-tuning portion of his development and might land in the back of the Washington rotation by the end of 2020.

Mason Denaburg RHP   Born: 08/08/99   Age: 19   Bats: R   Throws: R   Height: 6'4"   Weight: 195   Origin: Round 1, 2018 Draft (#27 overall)

The no. 27 overall pick in the 2018 draft, only a bout of biceps tendinitis kept Denaburg from going even higher. A 6-foot-3 Florida high school righty, Denaburg is straight out of front-line starter central casting. He runs the heater up there at 94, touching 97, with some life. He's got the classic power breaking ball. He apparently even has decent feel for a changeup. He was also born in 1999, so there's a lot of development left to do, but if Denaburg can navigate to his logical endpoint in baseball, his star will surely outshine that of a college football punter, which was apparently also an option for his next athletic venture.

Sean Doolittle LHP Born: 09/26/86 Age: 32 Bats: L Throws: L Height: 6'2" Weight: 204 Origin: Round 1, 2007 Draft (#41 overall)

YEAR	TEAM	LVL	AGE	W	L	SV	G	GS	IP	H	HR	BB/9	K/9	K	GB%	BABIP	WHIP	ERA	DRA	WARP	MPH	FB%	WHF	CSP
2016	OAK	MLB	29	2	3	4	44	0	39	33	6	1.8	10.4	45	33%	.281	1.05	3.23	3.75	0.5	97.5	89.3	17	49
2017	OAK	MLB	30	1	0	3	23	0	21¹	12	3	0.8	13.1	31	37%	.209	0.66	3.38	2.95	0.5	95.9	87.9	17.5	44.5
2017	WAS	MLB	30	1	0	21	30	0	30	22	2	2.4	9.3	31	28%	.260	1.00	2.40	3.71	0.5	96.3	87.5	16.8	48.3
2018	WAS	MLB	31	3	3	25	43	0	45	21	3	1.2	12.0	60	33%	.196	0.60	1.60	2.99	1.0	95.6	88.6	18.9	50.7
2019	WAS	MLB	32	3	1	29	54	0	57	43	8	2.9	11.5	73	35%	.283	1.08	3.41	3.86	0.6	95.2	87.6	17.6	48.5

Breakout: 21%   Improve: 36%   Collapse: 35%   Attrition: 7%   MLB: 95%   *Comparables: Jose Valverde, Billy Wagner, Michael Gonzalez*

If there were a WARP-like metric for social consciousness, Doolittle might be a Mike Trout-level stalwart atop the leaderboard. An advocate for inclusion and perhaps a more thoughtful ambassador than some of his fellow players deserve, Doolittle has demonstrated that he's well equipped not only to handle the platform he receives as a professional athlete, but also to leverage it to inject some good into the world.

His platform, thankfully, is secure. Though a stress reaction in his foot again ate into his season, Doolittle posted top-level closer numbers. His first full season with the Nationals consisted of 45 innings of sub-2.00 ERA ball, with underlying numbers to support it. Doolittle ran his highest strikeout rate and lowest walk rate since the marvelous 2014 campaign that made his name. To remember that he converted to pitching in pro ball is to remember that, hey, maybe he's still getting better, still honing his craft. Even without huge steps forward, he could soon find himself recognized as one of the game's most renowned closers.

Erick Fedde RHP Born: 02/25/93 Age: 26 Bats: R Throws: R Height: 6'4" Weight: 195 Origin: Round 1, 2014 Draft (#18 overall)

YEAR	TEAM	LVL	AGE	W	L	SV	G	GS	IP	H	HR	BB/9	K/9	K	GB%	BABIP	WHIP	ERA	DRA	WARP	MPH	FB%	WHF	CSP
2016	POT	A+	23	6	4	0	18	17	91²	85	7	1.9	9.3	95	51%	.316	1.13	2.85	2.45	3.1				
2016	HAR	AA	23	2	1	0	5	5	29¹	33	1	3.1	8.6	28	46%	.360	1.47	3.99	3.23	0.7				
2017	HAR	AA	24	3	3	0	17	7	56¹	45	4	2.9	8.6	54	52%	.272	1.12	3.04	3.68	0.9				
2017	SYR	AAA	24	1	2	0	12	6	34	37	3	1.3	6.6	25	62%	.315	1.24	4.76	4.12	0.5				
2017	WAS	MLB	24	0	1	0	3	3	15¹	25	5	4.7	8.8	15	65%	.426	2.15	9.39	6.04	-0.1	95.4	61.1	6.7	47.8
2018	SYR	AAA	25	3	3	0	13	13	67¹	78	3	2.4	9.4	70	53%	.383	1.43	4.41	3.73	1.4				
2018	WAS	MLB	25	2	4	0	11	11	50¹	55	8	3.9	8.2	46	54%	.333	1.53	5.54	4.85	0.3	95.7	54.9	9.5	43.8
2019	WAS	MLB	26	3	3	0	10	10	50	49	6	3.2	8.7	48	49%	.322	1.33	3.85	4.35	0.6	95.3	57.1	9.1	46.4

Breakout: 16%   Improve: 27%   Collapse: 23%   Attrition: 32%   MLB: 61%   *Comparables: Chad Green, Shane Greene, Jeff Manship*

You would have hoped for Fedde to secure the fifth starter job in Washington in 2018, but that was not meant to be. He got 11 starts in, but about half were after the Nationals had punted on the season. His pitch mix read, uh, like a cry for help — constantly toggling a splitter from show-me offering to real pitch, ditching a cutter, ramping up a slider, leaning on and letting off the sinker that is appears to be his primary weapon on more days than not. Though the league as a whole is moving swiftly away from it, Fedde's best bet at steady innings may be the sinker-slider combo.

Koda Glover RHP Born: 04/13/93 Age: 26 Bats: R Throws: R Height: 6'5" Weight: 215 Origin: Round 8, 2015 Draft (#254 overall)

YEAR	TEAM	LVL	AGE	W	L	SV	G	GS	IP	H	HR	BB/9	K/9	K	GB%	BABIP	WHIP	ERA	DRA	WARP	MPH	FB%	WHF	CSP
2016	POT	A+	23	0	0	2	7	0	9²	3	0	3.7	14.0	15	59%	.176	0.72	0.00	2.47	0.3				
2016	HAR	AA	23	2	0	4	17	0	22¹	20	1	2.8	11.7	29	46%	.339	1.21	3.22	1.98	0.7				
2016	SYR	AAA	23	1	1	2	16	0	24	16	2	1.1	8.2	22	52%	.233	0.79	2.25	3.22	0.5				
2016	WAS	MLB	23	2	0	0	19	0	19²	15	3	3.2	7.3	16	42%	.214	1.12	5.03	4.82	0.0	99.0	45.1	12	51.8
2017	WAS	MLB	24	0	1	8	23	0	19¹	20	1	1.9	7.9	17	44%	.328	1.24	5.12	2.90	0.5	97.8	37.1	11.3	53.5
2018	SYR	AAA	25	1	0	2	8	0	8	7	0	2.2	11.2	10	68%	.368	1.12	2.25	2.68	0.2				
2018	WAS	MLB	25	1	3	1	21	0	16¹	13	1	5.5	5.0	9	36%	.235	1.41	3.31	6.26	-0.3	97.0	39.2	9.5	47.9
2019	WAS	MLB	26	2	1	1	39	0	41¹	37	5	4.1	8.5	39	43%	.297	1.36	4.12	4.66	0.1	97.4	40.7	11	51.6

Breakout: 19%   Improve: 31%   Collapse: 22%   Attrition: 24%   MLB: 68%   *Comparables: Darren O'Day, Daniel Herrera, Jake Barrett*

A victim of his own prodigious velocity, a very premature closer label and a shower-related shoulder injury, it feels as though Glover is a disappointment when, in fact, he hasn't had a chance to be ... anything. Yet to eclipse the 20-inning mark in a season, he won't turn 26 until April and is nowhere near being too old for this sh— uh, stuff. Though he struggled in his brief return last season, diminished velocity makes for an easy explanation assuming it gets back to normal over the winter. It seems time is the one thing Glover has never had, and perhaps the only thing he needs to develop into a lethal weapon out of the 'pen.

Matt Grace LHP Born: 12/14/88 Age: 30 Bats: L Throws: L Height: 6'4" Weight: 215 Origin: Round 8, 2010 Draft (#236 overall)

YEAR	TEAM	LVL	AGE	W	L	SV	G	GS	IP	H	HR	BB/9	K/9	K	GB%	BABIP	WHIP	ERA	DRA	WARP	MPH	FB%	WHF	CSP
2016	SYR	AAA	27	1	3	1	35	0	47¹	54	1	1.7	6.1	32	66%	.338	1.33	2.85	3.31	0.9				
2016	WAS	MLB	27	0	0	0	5	0	3	1	0	0.0	12.0	4	67%	.167	0.33	0.00	2.55	0.1	91.6	76.9	17.9	39.6
2017	SYR	AAA	28	1	3	0	13	1	19²	21	2	3.7	9.6	21	61%	.345	1.47	3.66	3.48	0.4				
2017	WAS	MLB	28	1	0	2	40	1	50	50	3	3.2	5.6	31	63%	.294	1.36	4.32	6.01	-0.5	92.6	72.2	7.9	50.9
2018	WAS	MLB	29	1	1	0	56	0	59²	55	5	2.0	7.2	48	50%	.279	1.14	2.87	4.45	0.3	92.9	66.9	8.3	54.6
2019	WAS	MLB	30	2	1	0	49	0	51²	49	6	3.3	7.8	45	53%	.302	1.32	4.02	4.54	0.2	92.0	69	8.2	49.5

Breakout: 21%   Improve: 43%   Collapse: 21%   Attrition: 12%   MLB: 72%   *Comparables: Dan Otero, Brad Ziegler, Kevin Cameron*

Only 12 southpaw relievers tossed 50 innings in the majors in each of the past two seasons and, well, you would name at least 10 of them before Grace. But that shortchanges some real work he's done to make himself worthy of those general bullpen innings and not just lefty specialist work. He has long been a worm-killer, but that wasn't enough against righties in 2017, so he boosted his slider usage last year and achieved much more workable ratios (his WHIP against right-handers dropped from 1.41 to 1.11). The lack of strikeouts will always limit his utility in high-leverage spots, but we dare say Grace could remain in that winnowing club of reliable, 50-inning lefty relievers.

Jeremy Hellickson RHP   Born: 04/08/87   Age: 32   Bats: R   Throws: R   Height: 6'1"   Weight: 190   Origin: Round 4, 2005 Draft (#118 overall)

YEAR	TEAM	LVL	AGE	W	L	SV	G	GS	IP	H	HR	BB/9	K/9	K	GB%	BABIP	WHIP	ERA	DRA	WARP	MPH	FB%	WHF	CSP
2016	PHI	MLB	29	12	10	0	32	32	189	173	24	2.1	7.3	154	43%	.274	1.15	3.71	3.24	4.6	92.2	58.4	11.6	44.6
2017	PHI	MLB	30	6	5	0	20	20	112¹	111	22	2.4	5.2	65	37%	.255	1.26	4.73	5.99	-0.5	91.3	58.4	9.1	45.6
2017	BAL	MLB	30	2	6	0	10	10	51²	49	13	3.0	5.4	31	36%	.225	1.28	6.97	6.97	-0.8	91.6	58.4	8.5	43.9
2018	WAS	MLB	31	5	3	0	19	19	91¹	78	11	2.0	6.4	65	47%	.252	1.07	3.45	4.19	1.2	91.5	51.4	9	48.5
2019	*WAS*	*MLB*	*32*	*5*	*6*	*0*	*16*	*16*	*89¹*	*86*	*13*	*2.7*	*7.0*	*69*	*43%*	*.287*	*1.26*	*4.47*	*5.04*	*0.3*	*90.8*	*56*	*9.7*	*46*

Breakout: 18%   Improve: 42%   Collapse: 20%   Attrition: 12%   MLB: 79%   *Comparables: Carlos Silva, Kyle Lohse, Randy Wolf*

Rebounding to something resembling his palatable 2016 form, Hellickson provided the Nationals about half a season of much-needed volume in the back of their rotation. He relieved his fastball of some responsibility by collecting strikes on 67 percent of his first pitches, largely via the curveball. Twisting counts in his favor via unpredictability, the former Rookie of the Year closed a one-year deal with a positive WARP, unlike 2012 Rays rotation-mates James Shields, Alex Cobb and Matt Moore. He still won't land any multi-year windfalls like they have at various points, but likely showed enough — despite the foreign-looking 6.41 K/9 — to convince a club with an unsteady rotation to snap him up as a potential flotation device.

Kelvin Herrera RHP   Born: 12/31/89   Age: 29   Bats: R   Throws: R   Height: 5'10"   Weight: 200   Origin: International Free Agent, 2006

YEAR	TEAM	LVL	AGE	W	L	SV	G	GS	IP	H	HR	BB/9	K/9	K	GB%	BABIP	WHIP	ERA	DRA	WARP	MPH	FB%	WHF	CSP
2016	KCA	MLB	26	2	6	12	72	0	72	57	6	1.5	10.8	86	46%	.290	0.96	2.75	2.39	2.1	99.7	60	16.2	47.3
2017	KCA	MLB	27	3	3	26	64	0	59¹	60	9	3.0	8.5	56	47%	.295	1.35	4.25	3.82	0.9	99.3	66.6	13.2	48.6
2018	KCA	MLB	28	1	1	14	27	0	25²	19	2	0.7	7.7	22	39%	.246	0.82	1.05	3.88	0.3	98.5	64.9	15.7	48.3
2018	WAS	MLB	28	1	2	3	21	0	18²	24	4	3.9	7.7	16	36%	.333	1.71	4.34	4.20	0.2	98.6	62.6	12.9	46.6
2019	*WAS*	*MLB*	*29*	*2*	*1*	*11*	*40*	*0*	*42*	*38*	*6*	*2.9*	*8.7*	*41*	*42%*	*.292*	*1.22*	*3.99*	*4.51*	*0.2*	*98.5*	*63.7*	*14.5*	*47.8*

Breakout: 27%   Improve: 46%   Collapse: 31%   Attrition: 16%   MLB: 99%   *Comparables: Sparky Lyle, Doug Corbett, Peter Moylan*

When Herrera was traded to the D.C. in June, he had a 1.05 ERA and seemed to be sailing away from a turbulent 2017 spent thrashing against a long-ball attack. Little did he know, his homer monster was not vanquished, but merely lying in wait in the Anacostia River. He allowed five of his six dingers in just 18 2/3 innings with the Nationals before his season succumbed to a foot injury. Of course, monsters are usually manifestations of something internal. Maybe iffy command. Maybe pitch tipping? Whatever the specific demon, it stole his ability to convince hitters to chase. Usually accomplished with his changeup or slider, that key cog of his profile vanished in the months before he hit the free agent market.

Greg Holland RHP   Born: 11/20/85   Age: 33   Bats: R   Throws: R   Height: 5'10"   Weight: 205   Origin: Round 10, 2007 Draft (#306 overall)

YEAR	TEAM	LVL	AGE	W	L	SV	G	GS	IP	H	HR	BB/9	K/9	K	GB%	BABIP	WHIP	ERA	DRA	WARP	MPH	FB%	WHF	CSP
2017	COL	MLB	31	3	6	41	61	0	57¹	40	7	4.1	11.0	70	41%	.252	1.15	3.61	3.58	1.0	95.3	44.4	15.7	47
2018	SLN	MLB	32	0	2	0	32	0	25	34	1	7.9	7.9	22	39%	.379	2.24	7.92	6.77	-0.5	94.5	43	12.4	43.1
2018	WAS	MLB	32	2	0	3	24	0	21¹	9	1	4.2	10.5	25	50%	.186	0.89	0.84	3.77	0.3	94.4	44.2	16.4	40.9
2019	*WAS*	*MLB*	*33*	*2*	*1*	*12*	*47*	*0*	*49²*	*44*	*7*	*4.8*	*9.4*	*52*	*41%*	*.296*	*1.41*	*4.45*	*5.04*	*-0.1*	*93.8*	*43.4*	*14.6*	*43.8*

Breakout: 17%   Improve: 41%   Collapse: 33%   Attrition: 9%   MLB: 93%   *Comparables: Fernando Rodney, Pedro Strop, Damaso Marte*

The Cardinals gave him $14 million and he gave them a 7.92 ERA in 25 stomach-sinking innings. With Washington, though, Holland turned in 21 innings of a 0.84 ERA to finish out the year. He lives in the low-to-mid-90s now — the 96-plus velocity just isn't coming back — and he may still be adjusting to it. His curveball usage spiked once he got to D.C., and either with it or just by coincidence, so did his ground-ball rate. Having seen such a dramatic shift in the middle of a season, it's worth noting that his DRA numbers totally lined up with the horrific St. Louis ERA and seemed to support the idea of his Washington improvements (within reason).

Justin Miller RHP   Born: 06/13/87   Age: 32   Bats: R   Throws: R   Height: 6'3"   Weight: 215   Origin: Round 16, 2008 Draft (#483 overall)

YEAR	TEAM	LVL	AGE	W	L	SV	G	GS	IP	H	HR	BB/9	K/9	K	GB%	BABIP	WHIP	ERA	DRA	WARP	MPH	FB%	WHF	CSP
2016	ABQ	AAA	29	0	0	0	12	0	12	15	0	3.0	6.0	8	40%	.349	1.58	6.75	4.08	0.1				
2016	COL	MLB	29	1	1	0	40	0	42²	50	6	4.2	9.5	45	35%	.367	1.64	5.70	6.19	-0.6	95.2	67.1	11.7	50
2017	SLC	AAA	30	5	1	9	38	0	46	50	7	1.6	7.2	37	34%	.307	1.26	5.48	6.01	-0.4				
2018	SYR	AAA	31	2	0	1	9	0	13²	3	0	2.0	15.1	23	45%	.150	0.44	0.00	3.30	0.3				
2018	WAS	MLB	31	7	1	2	51	0	52¹	42	10	2.9	10.3	60	35%	.254	1.13	3.61	4.59	0.2	95.3	70.7	14.1	51.2
2019	*WAS*	*MLB*	*32*	*2*	*1*	*0*	*49*	*0*	*51²*	*45*	*9*	*3.4*	*9.9*	*57*	*37%*	*.288*	*1.25*	*4.31*	*4.88*	*0.0*	*94.3*	*68.9*	*13.2*	*50.3*

Breakout: 13%   Improve: 29%   Collapse: 10%   Attrition: 15%   MLB: 47%   *Comparables: Brandon Gomes, Chris Hatcher, Joel Peralta*

Uh, I flipped this coin 12 times in a row and gotten tails every time. *Sort of like how journeyman reliever Justin Miller showed up and struck out 31 batters without allowing a run or a walk to start 2018?* No, I totally know what I'm doing. There's a feel to it, the weight turning over on my finger. *See, the trouble with any run of extreme, weird success is* — Tails again! *You start to believe it.* I'm serious, look! I've got this down to a science. *Then reality kicks back in.* Come on, I'm going to a casino! *And for the rest of the season you have, like, a 4.54 ERA.* Damn, it's heads.

Tommy Milone LHP   Born: 02/16/87   Age: 32   Bats: L   Throws: L   Height: 6'0"   Weight: 215   Origin: Round 10, 2008 Draft (#301 overall)

YEAR	TEAM	LVL	AGE	W	L	SV	G	GS	IP	H	HR	BB/9	K/9	K	GB%	BABIP	WHIP	ERA	DRA	WARP	MPH	FB%	WHF	CSP
2016	ROC	AAA	29	4	0	0	7	7	48²	41	4	0.7	7.6	41	43%	.268	0.92	1.66	2.93	1.3				
2016	MIN	MLB	29	3	5	0	19	12	69¹	84	15	2.9	6.4	49	48%	.308	1.53	5.71	5.89	-0.5	89.7	54.5	9.5	44.2
2017	MIL	MLB	30	1	0	1	6	3	21	29	6	0.9	6.9	16	35%	.333	1.48	6.43	6.38	-0.2	89.1	65.2	8.3	43.8
2017	BIN	AA	30	1	0	0	4	4	20	26	8	0.9	4.9	11	27%	.273	1.40	4.95	4.72	0.1				
2017	NYN	MLB	30	0	3	0	11	5	27¹	36	9	4.0	7.2	22	36%	.318	1.76	8.56	5.28	0.1	89.0	65.2	8.9	42.5
2018	SYR	AAA	31	7	4	0	20	20	109²	101	11	2.0	9.3	113	36%	.303	1.14	4.19	3.30	2.8				
2018	WAS	MLB	31	1	1	0	5	4	26¹	37	7	0.3	7.9	23	30%	.349	1.44	5.81	4.64	0.2	88.5	58.9	11.7	46.9
2019	WAS	MLB	32	6	7	0	19	19	105	109	22	2.8	8.1	94	38%	.300	1.35	5.04	5.69	-0.5	88.3	59	9.6	44.5

Breakout: 21%   Improve: 39%   Collapse: 18%   Attrition: 20%   MLB: 71%   Comparables: Josh Towers, Zach Duke, Victor Santos

Things are trending against Milone, you might say. His major-league innings total sank by 21 from 2016 to 2017, then by 22 from 2017 to 2018. The advanced math thusly shows that Milone is projected to throw 3 1/3 innings in 2019. Though his peripherals haven't tanked as badly as some other very employed pitchers, you're probably better off if those innings aren't for your team. But if he does wind up on a mound you care about, at least you'll get that brief moment of hope that, hey, yes, tying your kid's right hand behind their back five days a week may still afford you an excellent retirement.

Tanner Rainey RHP   Born: 12/25/92   Age: 26   Bats: R   Throws: R   Height: 6'2"   Weight: 235   Origin: Round 2, 2015 Draft (#71 overall)

YEAR	TEAM	LVL	AGE	W	L	SV	G	GS	IP	H	HR	BB/9	K/9	K	GB%	BABIP	WHIP	ERA	DRA	WARP	MPH	FB%	WHF	CSP
2016	DYT	A	23	5	10	1	29	20	103¹	109	9	5.7	9.8	113	39%	.353	1.69	5.57	3.93	1.3				
2017	DAY	A+	24	2	2	9	39	0	45	21	4	4.4	15.4	77	47%	.230	0.96	3.80	1.97	1.5				
2017	PEN	AA	24	1	1	4	14	0	17	8	2	5.8	14.3	27	62%	.222	1.12	1.59	1.96	0.6				
2018	CIN	MLB	25	0	0	0	8	0	7	13	4	15.4	9.0	7	31%	.409	3.57	24.43	9.00	-0.3	99.6	71.4	12.2	38.9
2018	LOU	AAA	25	7	2	3	44	0	51	25	2	6.2	11.5	65	37%	.221	1.18	2.65	3.40	1.0				
2019	WAS	MLB	26	1	0	0	20	0	20²	18	4	6.7	11.3	26	38%	.305	1.59	5.19	5.90	-0.3	99.2	72.7	12.4	39.6

Breakout: 18%   Improve: 32%   Collapse: 6%   Attrition: 20%   MLB: 43%   Comparables: Jose Ramirez, Maikel Cleto, Drew Steckenrider

Minor-league hitters have had absolute fits trying to get hits off Rainey since he transitioned to the bullpen in late 2016, but someone messed with his AI sliders upon getting to Cincinnati, causing batters to destroy his, well, everything. Opposing hitters slugged .880 against his four-seamer and .833 against his slider, which is not ideal when you're basically a two-pitch reliever. Despite the abbreviated recent ugliness, Rainey has the raw stuff to be a high-leverage arm with any notable progress in the command department. Washington believes he can get to that potential, acquiring Rainey in the historic Tanner-for-Tanner swap for Tanner Roark.

Seth Romero LHP   Born: 04/19/96   Age: 23   Bats: L   Throws: L   Height: 6'3"   Weight: 240   Origin: Round 1, 2017 Draft (#25 overall)

YEAR	TEAM	LVL	AGE	W	L	SV	G	GS	IP	H	HR	BB/9	K/9	K	GB%	BABIP	WHIP	ERA	DRA	WARP	MPH	FB%	WHF	CSP
2017	AUB	A-	21	0	1	0	6	6	20	19	0	2.7	14.4	32	40%	.404	1.25	5.40	1.57	0.9				
2018	HAG	A	22	0	1	0	7	7	25¹	20	3	2.8	12.1	34	45%	.279	1.11	3.91	2.52	0.8				
2019	WAS	MLB	23	2	3	0	9	9	35¹	34	6	3.8	9.5	37	38%	.311	1.39	4.71	5.33	0.0				

Breakout: 3%   Improve: 5%   Collapse: 1%   Attrition: 3%   MLB: 6%   Comparables: Frank Garces, Steven Matz, Christian Friedrich

Sent home from spring training for repeatedly violating rules (curfew, apparently?), Romero is a world-class makeup-problem guy. That exceptional ability to make trouble out of nothing is what got him kicked off the team at the University of Houston, and what allowed the Nationals to draft him several picks after his exceptional pitching abilities might have otherwise warranted. Eventually, he was allowed to report to Hagerstown, but by season's end he had joined a more commonplace club among Nationals draftees: Those who needed Tommy John surgery. If you read the Seth Romero redemption story one day, it will come with a lot of regrettable time and effort burned.

Trevor Rosenthal RHP   Born: 05/29/90   Age: 29   Bats: R   Throws: R   Height: 6'2"   Weight: 230   Origin: Round 21, 2009 Draft (#639 overall)

YEAR	TEAM	LVL	AGE	W	L	SV	G	GS	IP	H	HR	BB/9	K/9	K	GB%	BABIP	WHIP	ERA	DRA	WARP	MPH	FB%	WHF	CSP
2016	SLN	MLB	26	2	4	14	45	0	40¹	48	3	6.5	12.5	56	53%	.425	1.91	4.46	5.38	-0.2	99.9	77.9	12.8	50.8
2017	SLN	MLB	27	3	4	11	50	0	47²	37	3	3.8	14.3	76	40%	.337	1.20	3.40	2.65	1.3	100.3	74.6	17.1	49
2019	WAS	MLB	29	3	1	3	49	0	51²	42	6	4.5	12.0	69	46%	.325	1.32	3.44	3.91	0.5	99.4	76	15.3	49.8

Breakout: 18%   Improve: 42%   Collapse: 42%   Attrition: 11%   MLB: 98%   Comparables: Jonathan Broxton, Francisco Rodriguez, Jake McGee

Washington moved quickly to sign Rosenthal once the offseason began, making a $7 million bet on the former St. Louis closer's return from Tommy John surgery. Prior to going under the knife, Rosenthal was one of the best, hardest-throwing relievers in baseball, frequently lighting up triple digits on radar guns and ranking among the league leaders in strikeout rate. His command and control were weaknesses even before blowing out his elbow, so Rosenthal can't afford to leave much of his overpowering raw stuff on the operating table. If things go well, the Nationals hold a $10 million team option on Rosenthal for 2020.

Joe Ross RHP
Born: 05/21/93 Age: 26 Bats: R Throws: R Height: 6'4" Weight: 220 Origin: Round 1, 2011 Draft (#25 overall)

YEAR	TEAM	LVL	AGE	W	L	SV	G	GS	IP	H	HR	BB/9	K/9	K	GB%	BABIP	WHIP	ERA	DRA	WARP	MPH	FB%	WHF	CSP
2016	SYR	AAA	23	0	2	0	4	4	10¹	14	1	0.9	7.8	9	26%	.382	1.45	4.35	3.88	0.2				
2016	WAS	MLB	23	7	5	0	19	19	105	108	9	2.5	8.0	93	44%	.319	1.30	3.43	3.99	1.7	95.9	52.5	11.7	47
2017	SYR	AAA	24	2	2	0	5	5	27²	33	3	2.6	7.2	22	37%	.341	1.48	4.88	5.05	0.2				
2017	WAS	MLB	24	5	3	0	13	13	73²	88	16	2.4	8.3	68	41%	.332	1.47	5.01	4.19	1.1	93.8	54.8	11	48.9
2018	SYR	AAA	25	2	0	0	2	2	11²	12	0	3.1	3.1	4	43%	.273	1.37	3.09	6.28	-0.1				
2018	WAS	MLB	25	0	2	0	3	3	16	17	3	2.2	3.9	7	36%	.269	1.31	5.06	7.08	-0.3	94.6	56	9.2	44.9
2019	WAS	MLB	26	7	8	0	23	23	122	125	18	3.4	7.4	100	42%	.309	1.40	4.60	5.20	0.2	94.5	54.9	11.3	47.6

Breakout: 32% Improve: 61% Collapse: 14% Attrition: 8% MLB: 91%   *Comparables: Erasmo Ramirez, Jake Odorizzi, Scott Baker*

Ross returned from Tommy John surgery to make three starts in September. The takeaways: His fastball velocity was all the way back, sitting in the 93 mph range, and the command that got strong marks in 2017 appeared solid in a small sample as well. What might look different: He used his changeup a *lot* more. Apparently it became a more comfortable pitch during his rehab. The Nationals' rotation options still get bleak after the names in lights, so he'll have an excellent shot at reclaiming a major role if he can shoulder it.

Anibal Sanchez RHP
Born: 02/27/84 Age: 35 Bats: R Throws: R Height: 6'0" Weight: 205 Origin: International Free Agent, 2001

YEAR	TEAM	LVL	AGE	W	L	SV	G	GS	IP	H	HR	BB/9	K/9	K	GB%	BABIP	WHIP	ERA	DRA	WARP	MPH	FB%	WHF	CSP
2016	DET	MLB	32	7	13	0	35	26	153¹	171	30	3.1	7.9	135	41%	.317	1.46	5.87	5.53	-0.4	93.8	57.4	10.1	47.6
2017	TOL	AAA	33	0	2	0	4	4	15²	17	3	2.9	11.5	20	46%	.350	1.40	4.60	2.71	0.5				
2017	DET	MLB	33	3	7	0	28	17	105¹	139	26	2.5	8.9	104	36%	.354	1.59	6.41	6.22	-0.8	92.6	49.6	10.9	49
2018	ATL	MLB	34	7	6	0	25	24	136²	106	15	2.8	8.9	135	47%	.255	1.08	2.83	2.75	4.0	92.4	37.6	11.5	46.2
2019	WAS	MLB	35	8	8	0	23	23	131	125	20	3.0	9.0	131	42%	.305	1.29	4.15	4.69	0.9	91.7	46.1	10.7	46.7

Breakout: 15% Improve: 38% Collapse: 13% Attrition: 6% MLB: 80%   *Comparables: Josh Beckett, James Shields, Chris Capuano*

When life gives you lemons, make lemonade. Or get a playoff start at 34 years old and get knocked around by the Dodgers. Whatever floats your boat. It's not fair to think of Sanchez's NLDS outing when talking about his 2018 season, though. The best years of his successful career seemed long behind him, but he went to Atlanta after being cut by Minnesota in spring training and proceeded to have his best season in at least four years. A key part was simply staying healthy. Another big piece was rearranging his arsenal to become a four-seamer/changeup/cutter guy instead of the typical sinker/slider combo that hitters were keying on the past few years. The cut fastball was the answer to keeping his career alive. That's a plump lemon that he turned into one tasty beverage.

Max Scherzer RHP
Born: 07/27/84 Age: 34 Bats: R Throws: R Height: 6'3" Weight: 215 Origin: Round 1, 2006 Draft (#11 overall)

YEAR	TEAM	LVL	AGE	W	L	SV	G	GS	IP	H	HR	BB/9	K/9	K	GB%	BABIP	WHIP	ERA	DRA	WARP	MPH	FB%	WHF	CSP
2016	WAS	MLB	31	20	7	0	34	34	228¹	165	31	2.2	11.2	284	35%	.255	0.97	2.96	2.42	7.7	97.1	55.4	16.7	50
2017	WAS	MLB	32	16	6	0	31	31	200²	126	22	2.5	12.0	268	38%	.245	0.90	2.51	2.32	7.3	95.7	48.7	16.7	48.7
2018	WAS	MLB	33	18	7	0	33	33	220²	150	23	2.1	12.2	300	35%	.265	0.91	2.53	2.29	7.7	96.4	50.1	17.3	50
2019	WAS	MLB	34	13	9	0	30	30	189	142	27	2.5	11.5	241	36%	.282	1.03	3.29	3.73	3.4	95.2	50.3	16.7	48.8

Breakout: 15% Improve: 42% Collapse: 25% Attrition: 4% MLB: 94%   *Comparables: Tom Seaver, Pedro Martinez, Mike Scott*

WASHINGTON — Max Scherzer, medical oddity. In a landmark study, researchers report that they have found variants in Nationals pitcher Max Scherzer's genome that confirm he is, in fact, 98 percent husky.

"We knew about the growling," said researcher Cassandra Crisper. "But the pacing, the endurance, and the reluctance to ever surrender a ball are also classic indications." She added, "I don't know how we didn't realize it sooner. The heterochromia should've clued us in years ago."

Researchers compared Scherzer's genome to those of 100 unnamed MLB players, as well as 100 non-athletes, in a genome-wide association study searching for variants associated with competitiveness and muscle endurance. This research, funded by the MLB as well as several anonymous donors, was intended to be the first step toward a comprehensive program of screening all U.S. newborns for these variants, in the hopes of identifying future players as part of an initiative called 'Baby-metrics.' "It's not creepy," said an MLB spokesperson. "I mean, OK, I guess it's creepy. But it was the logical next step now that we're scouting elementary school travel teams."

This research was stymied, however, by the discovery that Scherzer is actually a sled dog in a human suit. "It would explain a lot," said Washington skipper Davey Martinez. "When he talked about the season as the Iditarod, I thought he was being metaphorical. Also, one time, he bit me during the 8th inning when I went to take the ball from him. To be fair, it was a two-hit game—I should have known better."

Dusty Baker, speaking to reporters from his home in San Francisco, said only, "Yes, of course," when asked if he knew about his former ace's unique genetic makeup. A 2017 article from the Washington Post confirms that Baker called Scherzer "a lead dog" for the Nationals, who would go on to win 97 games that season; Scherzer would also win the 2017 Cy Young for his pitching dominance and being 'a very good boy.'

Reporters were also able to reach Matt Williams for comment, who stated that during his tenure as the Nationals' manager, he didn't notice anything different about Scherzer compared to other ace starters he has worked with. Williams was also reportedly unaware of Jonathan Papelbon's 2015 possession by hyena.

Stephen Strasburg RHP   Born: 07/20/88   Age: 30   Bats: R   Throws: R   Height: 6'5"   Weight: 235   Origin: Round 1, 2009 Draft (#1 overall)

YEAR	TEAM	LVL	AGE	W	L	SV	G	GS	IP	H	HR	BB/9	K/9	K	GB%	BABIP	WHIP	ERA	DRA	WARP	MPH	FB%	WHF	CSP
2016	WAS	MLB	27	15	4	0	24	24	147²	119	15	2.7	11.2	183	42%	.294	1.10	3.60	2.73	4.5	97.2	57.2	12.3	49.3
2017	WAS	MLB	28	15	4	0	28	28	175¹	131	13	2.4	10.5	204	48%	.274	1.02	2.52	2.93	5.2	97.4	51.9	13.8	49.3
2018	WAS	MLB	29	10	7	0	22	22	130	118	18	2.6	10.8	156	45%	.309	1.20	3.74	2.97	3.5	97.0	52	13	47.2
2019	WAS	MLB	30	10	8	0	26	26	156	131	19	2.9	10.4	180	44%	.303	1.16	3.38	3.83	2.7	96.4	53.1	13.1	48.3

Breakout: 13%   Improve: 52%   Collapse: 16%   Attrition: 3%   MLB: 97%   *Comparables: Ron Guidry, Kenta Maeda, Billy Pierce*

A Strasburg word cloud includes many things. Contract, injury, debut, etc. A year after "mold" became an unlikely addition, we can also take note of "cervical nerve impingement" in the orbit. Here's another word that maybe should be more prominently featured: Consistent. Being one of the most electrifying pitching prospects of all time will do this, but every minute detail of Strasburg's career takes on outsized significance. Come to think of it, the same could be said of pitchers who sign giant contract extensions — heaven forbid financial flexibility be at risk. Strasburg, whether he's precisely what you imagined in a 2010 fever dream or not, has put up a DRA- between 51 and 67 in every year of his career. All the way through, since returning in 2012 for his first full campaign, he's started more than 20 games and fired more than 120 innings in each of those seasons. Need a 30-year-old pitcher for the long haul? Strasburg looks like a slam dunk.

Wander Suero RHP   Born: 09/15/91   Age: 27   Bats: R   Throws: R   Height: 6'4"   Weight: 211   Origin: International Free Agent, 2010

YEAR	TEAM	LVL	AGE	W	L	SV	G	GS	IP	H	HR	BB/9	K/9	K	GB%	BABIP	WHIP	ERA	DRA	WARP	MPH	FB%	WHF	CSP
2016	HAR	AA	24	3	0	4	39	0	55¹	53	3	3.4	7.8	48	42%	.316	1.34	2.44	3.02	1.1				
2017	HAR	AA	25	0	1	10	18	0	23	18	2	2.0	9.0	23	45%	.254	1.00	1.96	3.30	0.4				
2017	SYR	AAA	25	3	1	10	36	0	42¹	33	1	3.0	8.9	42	46%	.281	1.11	1.70	3.91	0.6				
2018	SYR	AAA	26	1	2	1	14	0	17	16	1	2.1	8.5	16	46%	.306	1.18	3.71	3.16	0.4				
2018	WAS	MLB	26	4	1	0	40	0	47²	43	4	2.8	8.9	47	36%	.300	1.22	3.59	4.29	0.3	94.0	79.9	11.9	51.1
2019	WAS	MLB	27	2	1	0	34	0	36¹	34	5	3.8	9.0	36	40%	.306	1.36	4.28	4.84	0.0	93.5	80.8	12.1	51.7

Breakout: 6%   Improve: 14%   Collapse: 19%   Attrition: 22%   MLB: 45%   *Comparables: Alan Busenitz, Daniel Stumpf, Jonathan Aro*

One Wander Suero, where did he debut? In Washington! It went quite well, really. A sturdy fellow, Suero deployed his cutter about three quarters of the time and came away with almost 50 innings of average-ish relief work. One Wander Suero, where he will find himself in the bullpen pecking order in 2019? The answer might come down to whether he can once again avoid both ground balls and homers at the same time, but his numbers are shockingly consistent by reliever standards.

Austen Williams RHP   Born: 12/19/92   Age: 26   Bats: R   Throws: R   Height: 6'3"   Weight: 220   Origin: Round 6, 2014 Draft (#184 overall)

YEAR	TEAM	LVL	AGE	W	L	SV	G	GS	IP	H	HR	BB/9	K/9	K	GB%	BABIP	WHIP	ERA	DRA	WARP	MPH	FB%	WHF	CSP
2016	HAR	AA	23	1	7	0	10	10	50²	66	5	3.9	5.3	30	45%	.339	1.74	5.68	4.86	0.1				
2016	POT	A+	23	4	6	0	16	16	89²	113	8	2.6	4.8	48	49%	.337	1.55	5.32	6.18	-0.7				
2017	HAR	AA	24	1	6	0	10	10	46	67	6	2.2	6.7	34	43%	.386	1.70	6.85	6.10	-0.5				
2017	POT	A+	24	2	5	0	9	9	45¹	54	2	2.2	8.3	42	45%	.359	1.43	4.17	4.17	0.6				
2018	HAR	AA	25	3	3	1	24	2	51²	34	0	2.3	12.0	69	53%	.281	0.91	1.39	2.47	1.5				
2018	SYR	AAA	25	0	0	1	8	0	16¹	6	0	2.2	11.0	20	59%	.176	0.61	0.55	2.59	0.5				
2018	WAS	MLB	25	0	1	0	10	0	9²	10	5	5.6	7.4	8	23%	.200	1.66	5.59	6.09	-0.1	95.8	53.5	14.4	40.7
2019	WAS	MLB	26	0	0	0	10	0	10¹	10	1	3.3	9.2	11	44%	.315	1.32	4.01	4.54	0.1	95.4	54.4	14.6	41.4

Breakout: 7%   Improve: 9%   Collapse: 5%   Attrition: 9%   MLB: 15%   *Comparables: Casey Lawrence, Wei-Chung Wang, Artie Lewicki*

How many middling Double-A starters see the rope running out and give the bullpen a try? So many! How many double their strikeout rate, power-wash four runs off their ERA and rocket to the majors over the course of a single season? At least one! It remains to be seen if Williams has real staying power as a relief pitcher, but given his status — on the 40-man roster — there's a good chance we'll get to find out. Regardless of the answer, his career got a thousand times more interesting when he stopped starting.

LINEOUTS

Hitters

HITTER	POS	TEAM	LVL	AGE	PA	R	2B	3B	HR	RBI	BB	K	SB	CS	AVG/OBP/SLG	DRC+	VORP	BABIP	BRR	FRAA	WARP
Telmito Agustin	LF	AUB	A-	21	77	7	2	0	1	5	5	20	1	0	.186/.247/.257	88	-3.3	.240	0.3	LF(13): -2.5, RF(2): -0.3	-0.2
	LF	POT	A+	21	233	31	10	3	5	30	20	43	7	3	.302/.368/.454	110	15.7	.356	2.0	LF(52): 0.6, RF(1): 1.0	1.1
Yasel Antuna	SS	HAG	A	18	362	44	14	2	6	27	32	79	8	7	.220/.293/.331	96	2.4	.269	-0.6	SS(67): -8.8, 2B(9): 0.2	0.2
Geraldi Diaz	C	DWA	Rk	17	204	20	12	3	1	28	29	31	3	2	.244/.399/.375	130	13.6	.295	-2.3	C(39): 0.3, 1B(8): 0.3	1.4
KJ Harrison	1B	WIS	A	21	466	45	29	0	12	51	39	147	2	2	.228/.298/.384	86	1.6	.316	-1.8	1B(54): -1.0, C(26): -2.0	-0.5
Gilbert Lara	3B	WIS	A	20	452	45	26	2	5	46	18	94	1	2	.249/.281/.353	82	1.6	.306	-1.7	3B(66): 2.0, SS(50): 0.6	0.7
Andruw Monasterio	2B	MYR	A+	21	436	52	14	2	3	31	52	64	10	3	.263/.359/.336	115	17.5	.308	0.2	2B(77): 2.9, SS(28): -0.2	2.5
	2B	POT	A+	21	47	6	0	1	0	5	7	6	2	3	.308/.404/.359	115	3.6	.353	0.7	2B(6): 0.9, SS(3): 0.0	0.4
Matt Reynolds	SS	WAS	MLB	27	14	1	0	0	0	1	1	4	0	0	.154/.214/.154	71	-1.1	.222	0.0	3B(4): -0.1	0.0
	SS	SYR	AAA	27	355	55	31	3	4	29	40	75	2	1	.265/.355/.424	102	25.3	.336	3.9	SS(43): -1.0, 2B(16): -1.9	1.5
Adrian Sanchez	SS	SYR	AAA	27	295	21	15	2	4	27	16	42	10	6	.234/.281/.349	85	-0.9	.260	0.3	SS(29): 2.0, 3B(23): -1.9	0.8
	SS	WAS	MLB	27	59	8	2	1	0	3	1	8	0	0	.276/.288/.345	93	0.6	.320	1.0	2B(13): -1.1, 3B(7): -0.2	0.1
Moises Sierra	RF	WAS	MLB	29	60	4	2	0	0	4	2	20	1	1	.167/.217/.204	55	-3.3	.250	0.0	LF(14): -0.6, RF(3): -0.3	-0.3
	RF	SYR	AAA	29	255	29	12	0	6	32	23	50	3	4	.243/.322/.376	93	2.4	.285	0.3	RF(49): 2.2, LF(11): 0.2	0.6
Andrew Stevenson	LF	SYR	AAA	24	331	40	10	1	6	28	31	75	12	6	.235/.318/.338	91	2.9	.296	-1.0	CF(49): -8.3, LF(25): 1.4	-0.2
	LF	WAS	MLB	24	86	9	2	0	1	13	6	23	1	1	.253/.306/.320	75	1.7	.333	0.4	LF(16): -1.4, CF(3): -0.3	-0.1
Chuck Taylor	LF	ARK	AA	24	575	70	25	3	3	60	61	79	2	2	.297/.377/.376	111	21.5	.344	1.0	LF(92): -9.2, RF(14): 0.9	1.2
Armond Upshaw	CF	HAG	A	22	419	48	13	1	2	25	42	129	24	9	.234/.317/.292	74	5.1	.355	2.7	CF(102): -7.8, LF(11): 0.9	-0.5
Rhett Wiseman	RF	POT	A+	24	478	65	23	4	21	63	63	122	8	2	.253/.361/.484	135	35.9	.309	4.3	RF(98): 7.5, LF(11): 2.6	4.5

A 22-year-old from the U.S. Virgin Islands, **Telmito Agustin** was a house on fire for the first five weeks of the season, hitting .386/.411/.659 in High-A before succumbing to yet another injury. It's a hit-tool-led profile, but that will only take him as far as his body and his approach will. Ⓧ A shortstop for now, the switch-hitting **Yasel Antuna** took his lumps at Low-A Hagerstown, but maintained a calm, advanced approach at age 18. Ⓧ **Geraldi Diaz** will be 18 until July, plays catcher, bats lefty and walked almost as much as he struck out in the Dominican Summer League. Ⓧ A power bat taking a part-time stab at returning to catcher, **KJ Harrison** came over from the Brewers in the Gio Gonzalez trade after striking out 147 times in Low-A. Ⓧ Brought over from Milwaukee for Gio Gonzalez, **Gilbert Lara** is a 21-year-old infielder and apparent change-of-scenery candidate whose offensive potential has yet to manifest in the low minors. Ⓧ **Andruw Monasterio** might have one carrying tool, might have two. But the defensive-minded infielder acquired from the Cubs for Daniel Murphy has a long way to go to make noise in Washington. Ⓧ Steve Pearce won World Series MVP. **Ryan Raburn** fell out of baseball, but still sent an unexplained chill down the spine of the left-handed grocery bagger. Ⓧ Being purchased by the Nationals freed **Matt Reynolds** from the chronic dysfunction of the Mets, but it also relieved him of nearly all major-league playing time. Ⓧ **Adrian Sanchez** won't get demerits for volatility. His Triple-A numbers were nearly identical to 2017, as were his tiny major-league samples. All of them, unfortunately, involved on-base percentages below .300. Ⓧ **Moises Sierra** signed a minor-league deal with the seemingly loaded Nationals and then saw his first big-league action since 2014 by the end of April. He was probably as surprised as anyone. Ⓧ Entering the season as a 24-year-old, **Andrew Stevenson** needs a serious power surge to keep his prospect light burning. Slugging above .400 in Triple-A would be a start. Ⓧ It's not unreasonable to state that **Chuck Taylor** represents the quintessential 2018 Seattle minor leaguer. A speedy, patient outfielder, he'd be considered a viable prospect if he were a few years younger. Or had a little more power, or a little better defense, or, or, or ... you get the idea. Ⓧ **Armond Upshaw** still struggled with whiffs in his second full pro season, but the Florida junior-college product might be able to outrun any and all concerns you have. Ⓧ A return engagement with High-A Potomac, albeit in the summer he turned 24, went swimmingly for **Rhett Wiseman**, as the former third-round pick cranked 21 homers and reached base at a more than acceptable clip.

Pitchers

PITCHER	TEAM	LVL	AGE	W	L	SV	G	GS	IP	H	HR	BB/9	K/9	K	GB%	BABIP	WHIP	ERA	DRA	WARP	MPH	FB%	WHF	CSP
Carlos Acevedo	HAG	A	23	1	4	2	13	3	37^1	47	7	2.7	8.7	36	43%	.351	1.55	6.51	3.70	0.6				
	POT	A+	23	1	3	0	13	1	27^1	24	2	1.6	6.3	19	40%	.278	1.06	3.62	3.37	0.5				
Jacob Condra-Bogan	LEX	A	23	1	1	5	16	0	26	18	2	0.7	13.5	39	42%	.291	0.77	2.08	3.01	0.6				
	POT	A+	23	1	2	2	11	0	15	8	0	1.8	7.8	13	53%	.211	0.73	2.40	4.24	0.1				
Jimmy Cordero	SYR	AAA	26	4	1	6	41	0	46	43	0	4.3	10.4	53	55%	.333	1.41	1.96	3.10	1.1				
	WAS	MLB	26	1	2	0	22	0	19	23	2	5.7	5.7	12	57%	.318	1.84	5.68	6.42	-0.3	100.3	61.8	12.3	43.8
Trevor Gott	WAS	MLB	25	0	2	0	20	0	19	19	4	4.7	7.1	15	58%	.283	1.53	5.68	6.11	-0.3	96.3	74.8	6.6	52.6
	SYR	AAA	25	1	1	3	28	0	29^1	23	1	2.5	11.7	38	56%	.319	1.06	3.68	3.13	0.7				
Alfonso Hernandez	NAT	Rk	18	2	0	2	13	0	33^2	29	0	2.1	8.3	31	37%	.299	1.10	2.14	3.42	0.8				
	AUB	A-	18	1	0	0	3	0	13	7	0	4.2	6.9	10	33%	.194	1.00	2.77	3.68	0.2				
Andrew Istler	RCU	A+	25	0	0	1	10	0	17	8	1	2.1	10.6	20	42%	.175	0.71	2.65	4.01	0.2				
	TUL	AA	25	4	4	1	29	1	57	42	1	2.1	7.3	46	46%	.259	0.96	2.53	4.07	0.6				
Kyle McGowin	POT	A+	26	1	1	0	2	2	11	8	2	2.5	11.5	14	42%	.250	1.00	4.09	4.47	0.1				
	HAR	AA	26	4	3	0	13	13	78	62	7	2.2	10.8	94	50%	.281	1.04	3.69	2.57	2.5				
	SYR	AAA	26	3	2	0	8	8	52^2	26	3	1.5	7.5	44	44%	.177	0.66	1.20	3.15	1.4				
	WAS	MLB	26	0	0	0	5	1	7^2	6	2	5.9	9.4	8	33%	.211	1.43	5.87	4.65	0.0	92.4	59.2	12.3	38.9
Mariano Rivera	POT	A+	24	0	1	0	9	0	11^2	16	3	3.1	9.3	12	40%	.351	1.71	8.49	2.72	0.3				
Jhon Romero	MYR	A+	23	1	2	9	32	0	44	40	1	3.5	11.7	57	36%	.342	1.30	3.27	3.56	0.7				
	HAR	AA	23	0	0	0	6	0	7^1	10	1	3.7	3.7	3	38%	.321	1.77	6.14	5.01	0.0				
Sterling Sharp	POT	A+	23	5	3	0	14	14	79^2	82	4	2.4	6.6	58	62%	.310	1.29	3.16	3.46	1.7				
	HAR	AA	23	6	3	0	13	13	68^2	72	6	3.4	6.2	47	57%	.301	1.43	4.33	4.33	0.8				
Sammy Solis	SYR	AAA	29	0	0	0	10	0	9^1	5	0	3.9	10.6	11	46%	.227	0.96	1.93	3.68	0.2				
	WAS	MLB	29	1	2	0	56	0	39^1	43	7	4.1	10.1	44	50%	.346	1.55	6.41	4.55	0.2	95.2	64	13.8	46.4
Jackson Tetreault	HAG	A	22	3	8	0	20	20	110	108	10	2.8	9.7	118	39%	.320	1.29	4.01	4.05	1.5				
	POT	A+	22	1	1	0	4	4	22^2	21	2	2.8	7.9	20	31%	.288	1.24	4.37	3.72	0.4				
Austin Voth	SYR	AAA	26	6	8	0	24	24	125^2	119	13	2.9	8.4	117	42%	.295	1.27	4.37	4.67	1.2				
	WAS	MLB	26	1	1	0	4	2	12^1	12	3	4.4	8.0	11	45%	.257	1.46	6.57	5.14	0.0	92.9	62	9.3	51.7

Poor looking results—with good peripherals, but a homer issue—at Low-A got 24-year-old righty reliever **Carlos Acevedo** promoted to High-A, where the peripherals ticked down but the results got much better! ⓧ **Jacob Condra-Bogan** has already hit unheralded prospect bingo, having gone unsigned as a late-round pick, discovered an upper-90s heater in indy ball and been dealt for roster filler that everyone will cackle at if he hits it big one day. ⓧ Once traded for Ben Revere, **Jimmy Cordero** ran into every pitching prospect issue around before debuting in 2018 with a Nationals squad that was mainly glad to see he was throwing the ball and not his glove. ⓧ Issuing a correction on a previous Lineout of ours, regarding the Nationals bullpen. You should not, under any circumstances, add **Trevor Gott** to it. ⓧ A lefty, **Alfonso Hernandez** pitched most of 2018 as an 18-year-old, making the jump to the U.S. with 31 strikeouts in 33 2/3 innings of Gulf Coast League relief work before a promotion to short-season Auburn. ⓧ If 5-foot-11 reliever and ratio machine **Andrew Istler**, the return from the Dodgers for Ryan Madson, appears in half as many high-leverage situations as Madson did this past October, the Nationals will probably be thrilled. ⓧ A one-time Angels prospect, **Kyle McGowin** blitzed through three levels and reached the majors in 2018, even going four scoreless frames in a spot start before leaving with a blister. ⓧ The son of *the* Mariano Rivera pitched 11 2/3 dreadful innings in the Carolina League before two new lines popped up on his MiLB.com transaction log. *Potomac Nationals placed RHP* **Mariano Rivera** *on the temporarily inactive list. And then: RHP Mariano Rivera retired.* ⓧ A 24-year-old righty reliever acquired from the Cubs for Brandon Kintzler, **Jhon Romero** will now try to take decent strikeout numbers up to the advanced minors. ⓧ Listed four inches taller and 37 pounds lighter than the former NFL receiver, a little more bulk may yet help 22nd-round pick **Sterling Sharp** turn into a major-league starter. ⓧ Throwing 39 1/3 innings while appearing in 56 games is pretty difficult to do, and not in a good way. **Sammy Solis** allowed a .277/.367/.490 slash line, and will need a serious bounce back to find 50 more games. ⓧ Big fastball in tow, slender seventh-rounder **Jackson Tetreault** took a crack at his first two levels of full-season ball in 2018 and may have gained a better idea of where his heater is going. ⓧ After a boatload of Triple-A starts and several uneventful call-ups, **Austin Voth** got his first two starts in, both against the Mets, giving up seven runs in one and zero in the other.

MLB Managers

Brad Ausmus   wRM+: 99.2

TEAM	YEAR	W	L	Pythag +/-	Avg PC	100+ P	120+ P	QS	BQS	REL	REL w Zero R	IBB	PH	PH Avg	PH HR	SB2	CS2	SB3	CS3	SAC Att	SAC %	POS SAC	Squeeze	Swing	In Play
DET	2014	90	72	3	101.0	103	3	90	9	473	367	34	71	.164	1	90	34	16	7	40	60.0	20	1	296	83
DET	2015	74	87	6	94.1	77	2	72	10	505	396	32	74	.121	1	66	44	17	5	43	53.5	23	1	293	86
DET	2016	86	75	2	94.5	61	1	50	3	476	375	25	79	.243	6	54	26	4	3	28	60.7	16	2	184	60
DET	2017	64	98	-1	94.1	68	2	45	1	510	372	42	83	.227	0	56	33	9	1	17	64.7	11	0	260	67

Jeff Banister   wRM+: 96.5

TEAM	YEAR	W	L	Pythag +/-	Avg PC	100+ P	120+ P	QS	BQS	REL	REL w Zero R	IBB	PH	PH Avg	PH HR	SB2	CS2	SB3	CS3	SAC Att	SAC %	POS SAC	Squeeze	Swing	In Play
TEX	2015	88	74	5	95.6	55	1	79	3	498	402	29	89	.228	1	87	34	13	4	72	59.7	42	1	292	83
TEX	2016	95	67	13	93.0	45	2	46	1	479	379	16	77	.164	0	87	34	11	1	33	54.5	17	0	283	83
TEX	2017	78	84	-1	92.9	35	1	45	1	464	339	22	63	.185	1	93	38	20	6	41	65.9	26	2	314	75
TEX	2018	64	88	-3	87.5	24	0	22	4	465	350	22	73	.159	1	67	30	6	5	53	62.3	31	1	277	70

Bud Black   wRM+: 105.3

TEAM	YEAR	W	L	Pythag +/-	Avg PC	100+ P	120+ P	QS	BQS	REL	REL w Zero R	IBB	PH	PH Avg	PH HR	SB2	CS2	SB3	CS3	SAC Att	SAC %	POS SAC	Squeeze	Swing	In Play
SDN	2007	89	74	-1	90.0	47	0	90	4	485	404	48	272	.188	3	50	16	5	7	93	68.8	28	1	246	90
SDN	2008	63	99	-3	90.9	49	3	76	4	490	348	61	285	.198	3	34	17	2	0	76	77.6	18	0	226	93
SDN	2009	75	87	9	91.0	46	1	77	3	528	412	58	263	.248	9	72	23	10	5	111	66.7	38	1	296	90
SDN	2010	90	72	-2	94.8	54	0	87	2	499	431	56	283	.160	2	147	42	21	2	86	64.0	23	4	391	88
SDN	2011	71	91	-8	96.7	65	1	91	4	489	416	48	278	.248	6	129	42	25	2	107	58.9	30	1	396	88
SDN	2012	76	86	2	92.2	49	1	75	5	529	449	48	278	.206	8	105	31	13	3	92	56.5	23	1	284	75
SDN	2013	76	86	5	93.9	59	2	87	2	488	402	31	266	.218	6	75	31	16	3	90	62.2	32	2	248	70
SDN	2014	77	85	2	94.4	52	1	91	2	481	417	32	311	.248	11	91	33	14	2	90	60.0	28	2	340	88
SDN	2015	32	35	0	97.7	33	0	43	0	206	160	16	119	.170	1	44	10	2	1	29	58.6	11	0	106	36
COL	2017	87	75	-1	90.0	28	1	34	1	549	424	20	259	.205	6	51	32	8	2	87	71.3	20	2	297	94
COL	2018	91	72	6	92.4	42	0	55	0	518	398	24	272	.242	8	91	33	4	0	76	55.3	11	1	267	71

Bruce Bochy   wRM+: 94.4

TEAM	YEAR	W	L	Pythag +/-	Avg PC	100+ P	120+ P	QS	BQS	REL	REL w Zero R	IBB	PH	PH Avg	PH HR	SB2	CS2	SB3	CS3	SAC Att	SAC %	POS SAC	Squeeze	Swing	In Play
SFN	2015	84	78	-5	90.8	37	0	78	3	557	474	28	224	.249	1	87	32	6	3	60	75.0	12	1	309	106
SFN	2016	87	75	-4	96.6	77	1	64	3	575	488	30	257	.225	4	70	33	9	3	64	65.6	18	3	305	104
SFN	2017	64	98	-1	96.0	66	0	59	2	502	392	42	292	.206	5	64	30	11	4	54	57.4	12	0	280	86
SFN	2018	73	89	4	89.5	33	0	37	1	549	441	37	297	.217	7	70	29	7	5	60	55.0	9	0	272	71

Aaron Boone   wRM+: 103.2

TEAM	YEAR	W	L	Pythag +/-	Avg PC	100+ P	120+ P	QS	BQS	REL	REL w Zero R	IBB	PH	PH Avg	PH HR	SB2	CS2	SB3	CS3	SAC Att	SAC %	POS SAC	Squeeze	Swing	In Play
NYA	2018	100	62	-0	88.1	33	0	27	3	508	408	9	63	.208	1	54	19	9	1	19	52.6	10	0	264	77

Mickey Callaway   wRM+: 98.4

TEAM	YEAR	W	L	Pythag +/-	Avg PC	100+ P	120+ P	QS	BQS	REL	REL w Zero R	IBB	PH	PH Avg	PH HR	SB2	CS2	SB3	CS3	SAC Att	SAC %	POS SAC	Squeeze	Swing	In Play
NYN	2018	77	85	-0	90.8	54	0	50	3	501	342	32	255	.220	7	60	33	11	6	44	63.6	9	1	253	74

Kevin Cash   wRM+: 100.3

TEAM	YEAR	W	L	Pythag +/-	Avg PC	100+ P	120+ P	QS	BQS	REL	REL w Zero R	IBB	PH	PH Avg	PH HR	SB2	CS2	SB3	CS3	SAC Att	SAC %	POS SAC	Squee-ze	Swing	In Play
TBA	2015	80	82	-1	90.6	46	1	68	3	530	416	23	179	.219	3	62	40	25	4	29	65.5	17	0	290	82
TBA	2016	68	94	-8	96.2	67	1	41	5	485	369	25	92	.128	1	48	33	12	3	31	58.1	18	1	306	86
TBA	2017	80	82	0	93.8	74	1	43	4	511	403	37	102	.193	2	66	28	22	5	35	45.7	14	1	292	72
TBA	2018	90	72	1	63.0	21	0	21	1	553	403	34	97	.200	1	116	44	11	4	53	52.8	28	5	371	107

Alex Cora   wRM+: 101.4

TEAM	YEAR	W	L	Pythag +/-	Avg PC	100+ P	120+ P	QS	BQS	REL	REL w Zero R	IBB	PH	PH Avg	PH HR	SB2	CS2	SB3	CS3	SAC Att	SAC %	POS SAC	Squee-ze	Swing	In Play
BOS	2018	108	54	3	88.7	42	0	38	3	535	418	8	85	.205	2	109	25	16	4	10	70.0	7	0	366	113

Craig Counsell   wRM+: 103.2

TEAM	YEAR	W	L	Pythag +/-	Avg PC	100+ P	120+ P	QS	BQS	REL	REL w Zero R	IBB	PH	PH Avg	PH HR	SB2	CS2	SB3	CS3	SAC Att	SAC %	POS SAC	Squee-ze	Swing	In Play
MIL	2015	61	76	-3	92.4	40	0	53	6	424	338	30	244	.259	5	67	20	9	3	59	72.9	16	1	197	63
MIL	2016	73	89	-1	90.3	30	0	31	1	513	393	33	282	.178	7	144	46	35	10	87	60.9	21	2	371	76
MIL	2017	86	76	1	88.1	30	0	39	0	550	435	45	283	.220	8	98	32	30	7	68	61.8	12	3	336	94
MIL	2018	96	67	4	85.7	18	0	18	1	559	440	34	282	.246	10	96	25	28	7	48	60.4	6	0	331	74

Terry Francona   wRM+: 108.5

TEAM	YEAR	W	L	Pythag +/-	Avg PC	100+ P	120+ P	QS	BQS	REL	REL w Zero R	IBB	PH	PH Avg	PH HR	SB2	CS2	SB3	CS3	SAC Att	SAC %	POS SAC	Squee-ze	Swing	In Play
PHI	1997	68	94	5				80	5	409	285	42	285	.184	3	79	48	11	6	98	75.5	29	0		
PHI	1998	75	87	4	95.8	74	20	77	9	386	273	27	255	.232	5	87	41	10	4	86	75.6	28	0		
PHI	1999	77	85	-4	96.9	79	14	73	10	441	333	24	237	.255	5	113	32	12	2	82	85.4	23	0		
PHI	2000	65	97	-3	102.6	106	23	87	10	413	273	32	271	.197	2	91	25	11	3	86	81.4	28	1		
BOS	2004	98	64	0	98.9	88	3	86	9	437	335	28	99	.264	2	64	27	4	2	24	50.0	10	0	263	78
BOS	2005	95	67	4	99.6	93	3	81	6	442	337	28	98	.221	1	42	12	3	0	25	56.0	13	0	252	98
BOS	2006	86	76	5	95.3	63	2	70	7	455	332	25	87	.222	0	46	22	5	1	38	57.9	22	0	273	106
BOS	2007	96	66	-7	97.6	66	3	84	10	451	379	20	73	.217	0	83	20	13	4	52	57.7	30	2	333	100
BOS	2008	95	67	-2	95.9	69	1	82	9	466	359	17	49	.250	2	99	32	21	2	47	59.6	27	0	310	90
BOS	2009	95	67	0	99.0	81	3	82	3	463	369	24	79	.221	0	106	35	19	4	32	59.4	17	0	309	97
BOS	2010	89	73	0	102.8	112	3	89	5	443	348	30	117	.260	2	56	14	11	2	38	76.3	24	0	340	108
BOS	2011	90	72	-5	96.8	78	4	71	5	443	359	11	83	.176	2	93	40	9	1	33	66.7	22	0	366	122
CLE	2013	92	70	1	94.9	68	0	73	5	540	454	26	58	.255	3	96	33	21	3	41	75.6	30	0	332	85
CLE	2014	85	77	2	94.6	61	1	78	5	573	507	51	103	.233	0	96	23	8	4	63	81.0	49	0	290	92
CLE	2015	81	80	-3	94.5	77	2	91	4	476	391	27	106	.240	4	79	26	7	1	65	72.3	45	0	274	58
CLE	2016	94	67	2	92.0	60	0	63	4	504	428	34	106	.143	1	104	25	29	6	48	64.6	27	0	294	71
CLE	2017	102	60	-8	93.7	72	1	60	4	497	430	15	86	.145	2	79	21	9	2	39	59.0	22	0	266	78
CLE	2018	91	71	-9	96.9	78	2	79	2	508	401	29	87	.234	2	118	32	15	3	45	55.6	23	0	344	78

Ron Gardenhire   wRM+: 110.0

TEAM	YEAR	W	L	Pythag +/-	Avg PC	100+ P	120+ P	QS	BQS	REL	REL w Zero R	IBB	PH	PH Avg	PH HR	SB2	CS2	SB3	CS3	SAC Att	SAC %	POS SAC	Squee-ze	Swing	In Play
MIN	2002	94	67	7	90.1	47	3	77	2	436	352	24	103	.283	3	66	50	12	12	45	75.6	33	0		
MIN	2003	90	72	5	92.2	54	2	80	7	399	311	35	102	.318	5	79	35	15	7	67	62.7	37	1	275	82
MIN	2004	92	70	4	93.8	61	1	83	7	436	333	27	112	.269	6	97	39	19	6	73	63.0	44	1	335	108
MIN	2005	83	79	-1	91.9	43	0	90	10	396	312	38	92	.300	2	85	39	17	4	67	62.7	40	1	352	116
MIN	2006	96	66	2	90.1	42	0	73	4	421	343	25	77	.145	1	88	36	13	6	55	56.4	28	0	369	146
MIN	2007	79	83	-1	93.5	46	0	80	3	438	352	33	82	.253	1	94	29	18	1	52	65.4	29	1	362	133
MIN	2008	88	75	-2	91.7	47	1	86	4	485	379	38	80	.224	3	86	37	16	5	88	59.1	47	3	340	117
MIN	2009	87	76	0	92.0	56	1	79	6	480	372	20	73	.333	4	74	28	11	2	77	66.2	46	1	368	127
MIN	2010	94	68	1	93.5	56	1	86	6	465	377	19	75	.156	2	60	23	8	5	50	76.0	33	1	272	101
MIN	2011	63	99	3	95.2	66	2	80	9	457	340	37	87	.175	0	86	33	6	4	52	59.6	31	1	361	135
MIN	2012	66	96	-1	88.0	29	0	62	3	499	390	43	59	.260	0	111	33	24	3	52	63.5	32	1	384	108
MIN	2013	66	96	5	91.1	44	0	62	6	511	415	31	97	.163	1	50	31	1	2	40	72.5	26	0	292	93
MIN	2014	70	92	-4	91.6	36	0	66	8	491	378	24	90	.210	0	84	33	15	2	34	73.5	25	0	307	98
DET	2018	64	98	2	86.3	20	0	29	2	542	415	20	66	.155	1	66	28	4	1	29	51.7	13	0	249	70

John Gibbons   wRM+: 97.6

TEAM	YEAR	W	L	Pythag +/-	Avg PC	100+ P	120+ P	QS	BQS	REL	REL w Zero R	IBB	PH	PH Avg	PH HR	SB2	CS2	SB3	CS3	SAC Att	SAC %	POS SAC	Squee-ze	Swing	In Play
TOR	2004	20	30	-1	90.0	16	2	19	1	130	91	11	28	.292	2	19	10	3	2	2	100.0	2	0	113	37
TOR	2005	80	82	-9	90.4	42	1	80	5	432	355	29	120	.324	2	58	32	13	2	32	65.6	20	1	339	117
TOR	2008	35	39	-3	98.6	39	1	40	4	205	179	26	43	.368	2	38	19	7	3	25	80.0	18	0	182	59
TOR	2013	74	88	-2	92.3	56	1	67	6	487	391	33	102	.220	3	87	38	25	3	44	65.9	26	0	353	99
TOR	2014	83	79	-2	96.6	68	4	86	7	449	367	23	176	.220	9	64	16	14	5	61	57.4	34	1	309	102
TOR	2015	93	69	-10	92.8	58	1	84	5	469	384	20	88	.225	3	70	18	17	4	51	70.6	34	1	281	77
TOR	2016	89	73	-3	96.0	55	0	68	5	487	381	10	84	.167	1	45	22	9	1	39	66.7	22	0	275	81
TOR	2017	76	86	5	90.3	45	0	39	0	578	460	25	119	.208	1	41	21	10	2	41	61.0	23	0	277	88
TOR	2018	73	89	5	88.5	36	0	36	4	590	448	19	109	.280	3	38	26	7	3	10	50.0	5	0	229	66

Andy Green   wRM+: 102.4

TEAM	YEAR	W	L	Pythag +/-	Avg PC	100+ P	120+ P	QS	BQS	REL	REL w Zero R	IBB	PH	PH Avg	PH HR	SB2	CS2	SB3	CS3	SAC Att	SAC %	POS SAC	Squee-ze	Swing	In Play
SDN	2016	68	94	-4	90.5	39	0	35	2	510	390	44	243	.208	4	103	40	18	5	60	60.0	11	2	304	79
SDN	2017	71	91	14	89.6	34	2	26	2	517	403	28	238	.165	6	76	28	11	3	80	65.0	21	2	247	69
SDN	2018	66	96	2	84.1	26	1	22	1	535	412	28	261	.171	4	87	32	8	3	76	46.1	14	2	233	59

A.J. Hinch   wRM+: 101.4

TEAM	YEAR	W	L	Pythag +/-	Avg PC	100+ P	120+ P	QS	BQS	REL	REL w Zero R	IBB	PH	PH Avg	PH HR	SB2	CS2	SB3	CS3	SAC Att	SAC %	POS SAC	Squee-ze	Swing	In Play
ARI	2009	58	75	-4	98.8	79	0	73	5	392	281	24	220	.185	5	68	22	13	9	69	65.2	24	1	217	66
ARI	2010	31	48	-0	101.9	46	5	38	6	207	133	19	119	.213	0	42	11	3	2	21	81.0	7	0	151	48
HOU	2015	86	76	-8	98.0	74	4	94	4	482	412	17	114	.224	5	99	41	21	5	40	70.0	25	2	300	83
HOU	2016	84	78	0	93.7	52	0	51	3	500	403	19	98	.209	2	90	34	12	9	44	61.4	22	3	309	77
HOU	2017	101	61	0	92.0	31	0	32	2	519	399	17	68	.213	2	80	37	18	5	24	45.8	11	0	305	95
HOU	2018	103	59	-9	95.6	67	1	49	3	510	424	4	83	.169	0	63	22	8	3	22	63.6	14	6	329	124

Clint Hurdle   wRM+: 96.3

TEAM	YEAR	W	L	Pythag +/-	Avg PC	100+ P	120+ P	QS	BQS	REL	REL w Zero R	IBB	PH	PH Avg	PH HR	SB2	oCS2	SB3	CS3	SAC Att	SAC %	POS SAC	Squee-ze	Swing	In Play
COL	2002	67	73	5	93.1	45	1	61	7	437	322	38	244	.276	5	82	40	10	5	51	76.5	26	1		
COL	2003	74	88	-3	89.7	38	0	68	2	500	369	51	285	.260	5	57	34	6	3	103	53.4	28	1	238	85
COL	2004	68	94	-5	95.7	60	3	65	8	473	329	84	287	.253	11	36	31	8	2	148	65.5	55	0	258	87
COL	2005	67	95	-2	94.0	52	1	68	3	459	336	54	272	.224	4	61	26	4	5	131	67.2	52	2	334	116
COL	2006	76	86	-5	95.6	55	2	81	7	499	392	81	258	.215	6	80	44	4	3	167	71.3	64	0	325	112
COL	2007	90	73	-2	90.4	50	0	79	2	529	413	61	283	.216	4	98	31	2	0	130	63.8	37	2	354	104
COL	2008	74	88	1	92.2	53	0	68	2	484	370	49	250	.239	4	116	34	25	3	124	72.6	41	1	354	82
COL	2009	18	28	-3	92.5	19	0	26	2	135	96	11	73	.306	2	24	13	6	2	29	69.0	8	0	113	45
PIT	2011	72	90	3	89.5	26	0	78	2	549	452	65	275	.201	1	95	47	13	3	110	68.2	37	1	384	114
PIT	2012	79	83	1	90.4	42	0	83	2	483	398	30	266	.173	2	66	45	7	3	93	66.7	30	2	271	94
PIT	2013	94	68	5	89.7	41	0	83	2	465	395	26	285	.207	7	83	36	10	6	93	66.7	35	1	347	100
PIT	2014	88	74	1	93.7	44	0	90	3	452	361	43	317	.218	7	99	41	5	4	101	53.5	18	1	365	135
PIT	2015	98	64	4	94.2	46	0	92	7	500	431	38	267	.237	3	89	43	8	2	81	77.8	24	0	288	87
PIT	2016	78	84	0	87.4	27	0	28	0	525	405	28	290	.230	8	100	37	10	4	64	64.1	18	1	309	79
PIT	2017	75	87	1	90.6	37	0	35	4	502	383	32	275	.199	6	61	31	5	4	69	60.9	8	0	289	90
PIT	2018	82	79	2	88.0	20	0	37	1	480	369	43	264	.238	3	64	36	6	1	50	62.0	7	1	238	71

Gabe Kapler   wRM+: 96.0

TEAM	YEAR	W	L	Pythag +/-	Avg PC	100+ P	120+ P	QS	BQS	REL	REL w Zero R	IBB	PH	PH Avg	PH HR	SB2	CS2	SB3	CS3	SAC Att	SAC %	POS SAC	Squee-ze	Swing	In Play
PHI	2018	80	82	5	87.7	37	0	46	4	596	467	35	295	.207	5	64	20	3	5	53	60.4	6	0	198	50

Torey Lovullo   wRM+: 96.9

TEAM	YEAR	W	L	Pythag +/-	Avg PC	100+ P	120+ P	QS	BQS	REL	REL w Zero R	IBB	PH	PH Avg	PH HR	SB2	CS2	SB3	CS3	SAC Att	SAC %	POS SAC	Squee-ze	Swing	In Play
ARI	2017	93	69	-5	96.2	73	1	52	2	513	424	45	249	.216	7	77	24	25	6	56	69.6	8	0	265	73
ARI	2018	82	80	-5	92.4	36	0	44	2	574	474	43	256	.203	5	61	22	18	3	64	59.4	10	0	252	82

Joe Maddon   wRM+: 102.3

TEAM	YEAR	W	L	Pythag +/-	Avg PC	100+ P	120+ P	QS	BQS	REL	REL w Zero R	IBB	PH	PH Avg	PH HR	SB2	CS2	SB3	CS3	SAC Att	SAC %	POS SAC	Squee-ze	Swing	In Play
CAL	1996	6	16	-0				10	4	52	43	10	21	.235	0	7	7	0	0	11	36.4	4	0		
ANA	1999	19	10	2	96.3	13	3	11	1	85	72	3	27	.238	1	14	9	0	0	13	84.6	11	0		
TBA	2006	61	101	-3	92.8	48	1	65	6	444	303	39	76	.217	1	109	45	24	7	69	50.7	32	3	417	112
TBA	2007	66	96	0	96.9	77	0	73	8	484	320	31	68	.167	0	114	43	16	4	50	68.0	33	4	350	92
TBA	2008	97	65	5	95.9	71	0	82	3	448	365	29	90	.184	1	113	38	28	10	40	57.5	20	0	388	94
TBA	2009	84	78	-2	99.1	80	1	76	5	510	425	22	134	.164	7	167	49	26	11	41	61.0	24	6	404	101
TBA	2010	96	66	-2	98.9	90	2	95	5	491	412	34	154	.242	3	147	39	25	7	67	58.2	38	6	404	120
TBA	2011	91	71	-1	102.1	98	5	99	10	438	355	38	129	.252	1	134	54	20	8	63	58.7	35	5	441	138
TBA	2012	90	72	-6	99.9	91	7	90	2	471	415	35	135	.178	3	122	38	11	5	62	54.8	32	3	354	105
TBA	2013	92	71	4	94.9	65	2	80	2	485	399	38	169	.235	1	61	34	12	3	39	61.5	24	0	292	93
TBA	2014	77	85	-2	97.1	77	0	84	1	494	418	27	130	.218	1	52	24	11	2	73	58.9	42	3	313	106
CHN	2015	97	65	6	91.1	53	2	81	3	551	459	38	287	.201	5	82	32	13	3	53	60.4	15	2	330	105
CHN	2016	103	59	-7	94.5	56	1	66	2	502	407	24	234	.215	2	57	30	9	1	78	53.8	14	8	264	93
CHN	2017	92	70	-2	91.1	40	0	32	0	531	413	29	294	.238	5	56	25	5	6	65	73.8	22	5	263	75
CHN	2018	95	68	0	90.7	40	1	28	1	600	503	33	277	.242	6	53	31	11	6	71	56.3	14	4	280	85

Dave Martinez   wRM+: 98.0

TEAM	YEAR	W	L	Pythag +/-	Avg PC	100+ P	120+ P	QS	BQS	REL	REL w Zero R	IBB	PH	PH Avg	PH HR	SB2	CS2	SB3	CS3	SAC Att	SAC %	POS SAC	Squee-ze	Swing	In Play
WAS	2018	82	80	-9	94.0	68	1	49	2	562	440	37	293	.176	4	98	31	20	2	78	52.6	13	0	299	68

Mike Matheny   wRM+: 97.1

TEAM	YEAR	W	L	Pythag +/-	Avg PC	100+ P	120+ P	QS	BQS	REL	REL w Zero R	IBB	PH	PH Avg	PH HR	SB2	CS2	SB3	CS3	SAC Att	SAC %	POS SAC	Squee-ze	Swing	In Play
SLN	2012	88	74	-6	94.2	49	1	99	4	506	400	28	279	.190	1	72	27	18	5	104	66.3	34	0	287	100
SLN	2013	97	65	-6	96.0	67	5	88	3	483	411	26	234	.202	3	33	20	11	2	94	59.6	17	0	242	87
SLN	2014	90	72	7	94.0	60	2	91	2	485	393	35	251	.225	2	48	25	9	7	97	66.0	24	2	306	112
SLN	2015	100	62	2	94.5	64	0	106	1	515	434	37	270	.218	4	62	33	7	5	64	60.9	12	1	297	100
SLN	2016	86	76	-2	91.2	39	1	47	4	481	381	35	274	.333	17	33	19	2	6	67	55.2	13	0	207	76
SLN	2017	83	79	-4	92.2	49	1	39	5	546	420	50	290	.301	5	66	27	15	4	79	59.5	14	2	299	95
SLN	2018	47	45	-1	93.4	18	0	26	0	314	232	23	135	.181	2	32	19	1	2	37	78.4	8	2	131	48

Don Mattingly   wRM+: 100.7

TEAM	YEAR	W	L	Pythag +/-	Avg PC	100+ P	120+ P	QS	BQS	REL	REL w Zero R	IBB	PH	PH Avg	PH HR	SB2	CS2	SB3	CS3	SAC Att	SAC %	POS SAC	Squee-ze	Swing	In Play
LAN	2011	82	79	-3	97.8	66	3	94	4	461	369	48	229	.199	4	108	31	17	9	101	70.3	38	2	360	118
LAN	2012	86	76	-0	96.2	66	0	93	5	506	426	62	241	.281	2	93	39	10	2	122	67.2	33	2	329	97
LAN	2013	92	70	2	95.1	69	2	93	2	504	424	44	208	.209	4	74	22	4	5	113	62.8	32	0	283	93
LAN	2014	94	68	1	95.1	70	1	100	1	496	395	35	235	.231	1	123	46	14	3	82	57.3	15	1	340	104
LAN	2015	92	70	2	91.3	47	2	95	3	515	408	32	269	.215	8	51	26	8	8	69	71.0	15	1	250	76
MIA	2016	79	82	2	90.8	46	0	32	1	559	443	62	277	.215	6	61	25	10	3	76	60.5	15	2	240	74
MIA	2017	77	85	0	87.5	29	0	22	1	580	435	59	270	.262	6	82	22	9	6	84	59.5	15	3	275	80
MIA	2018	63	98	7	88.4	32	0	27	0	546	407	73	281	.177	6	40	29	5	2	58	55.2	12	0	251	80

Bob Melvin   wRM+: 95.4

TEAM	YEAR	W	L	Pythag +/-	Avg PC	100+ P	120+ P	QS	BQS	REL	REL w Zero R	IBB	PH	PH Avg	PH HR	SB2	CS2	SB3	CS3	SAC Att	SAC %	POS SAC	Squee-ze	Swing	In Play
SEA	2003	93	69	-6	101.9	108	6	94	8	366	305	24	62	.154	2	89	34	19	3	52	67.3	32	1	248	91
SEA	2004	63	99	-5	101.7	99	12	70	10	414	305	32	99	.276	4	92	33	18	9	63	73.0	45	0	355	112
ARI	2005	77	85	13	96.6	64	3	84	10	458	330	43	309	.232	9	64	21	3	4	107	66.4	30	1	281	86
ARI	2006	76	86	-3	94.9	68	3	81	8	461	349	44	274	.194	7	64	26	11	4	94	64.9	21	0	237	80
ARI	2007	90	72	11	94.7	68	4	84	5	469	367	38	239	.239	11	90	16	18	8	85	64.7	26	0	295	89
ARI	2008	82	80	-1	95.7	55	3	95	3	443	336	41	257	.226	3	46	16	12	5	95	71.6	29	1	261	89
ARI	2009	12	17	0	95.9	10	0	16	2	91	64	3	47	.209	3	16	7	5	1	18	50.0	6	0	61	17
OAK	2011	47	52	-0	100.4	51	1	55	3	282	220	9	30	.276	2	56	26	19	2	38	57.9	20	0	229	63
OAK	2012	94	68	1	92.5	52	0	90	4	462	386	34	93	.231	3	89	26	33	5	43	62.8	26	0	307	76
OAK	2013	96	66	-1	94.8	56	0	92	2	447	370	23	130	.135	5	58	24	17	3	37	56.8	21	2	253	87
OAK	2014	88	74	-12	96.0	61	1	102	4	441	380	28	161	.201	3	67	16	16	4	41	46.3	15	2	253	83
OAK	2015	68	94	-9	92.4	61	0	83	3	487	368	19	152	.252	0	65	25	13	3	24	58.3	12	1	268	90
OAK	2016	69	93	0	87.2	40	0	40	2	492	403	28	113	.185	2	44	23	6	0	24	54.2	10	1	205	61
OAK	2017	75	87	3	90.6	40	0	36	2	525	388	17	120	.217	4	47	20	9	2	23	56.5	9	1	226	59
OAK	2018	97	65	1	80.5	15	0	37	0	578	474	19	126	.239	3	31	20	3	1	10	60.0	6	0	225	75

Paul Molitor wRM+: 94.1

TEAM	YEAR	W	L	Pythag +/-	Avg PC	100+ P	120+ P	QS	BQS	REL	REL w Zero R	IBB	PH	PH Avg	PH HR	SB2	CS2	SB3	CS3	SAC Att	SAC %	POS SAC	Squee-ze	Swing	In Play
MIN	2015	83	79	2	91.2	55	0	76	6	520	420	34	72	.129	1	59	34	11	3	57	52.6	30	3	279	100
MIN	2016	59	103	-5	91.1	46	0	39	4	533	400	26	65	.123	3	87	31	4	1	58	46.6	25	0	312	86
MIN	2017	85	77	1	88.0	38	0	42	4	520	408	37	93	.195	2	91	24	4	2	54	48.1	25	1	333	109
MIN	2018	78	84	1	89.9	53	1	31	1	566	422	34	96	.184	1	43	26	4	0	26	73.1	17	0	272	88

Bryan Price wRM+: 102.4

TEAM	YEAR	W	L	Pythag +/-	Avg PC	100+ P	120+ P	QS	BQS	REL	REL w Zero R	IBB	PH	PH Avg	PH HR	SB2	CS2	SB3	CS3	SAC Att	SAC %	POS SAC	Squee-ze	Swing	In Play
CIN	2015	64	98	-4	91.5	44	4	68	4	521	397	42	262	.195	2	99	32	35	5	70	67.1	25	3	329	81
CIN	2016	68	94	1	90.4	42	0	30	2	484	324	31	227	.215	0	106	37	33	12	97	59.8	27	1	362	96
CIN	2017	68	94	-1	87.9	32	0	23	0	504	366	37	240	.201	7	104	30	16	8	87	57.5	18	2	365	105
CIN	2018	3	15	-1	90.8	3	0	1	1	61	49	8	29	.208	0	9	1	0	0	10	70.0	4	0	30	8

Rick Renteria wRM+: 98.4

TEAM	YEAR	W	L	Pythag +/-	Avg PC	100+ P	120+ P	QS	BQS	REL	REL w Zero R	IBB	PH	PH Avg	PH HR	SB2	CS2	SB3	CS3	SAC Att	SAC %	POS SAC	Squee-ze	Swing	In Play
CHN	2014	73	89	3	93.6	48	1	79	0	537	446	37	272	.185	1	58	37	7	3	93	61.3	25	3	246	82
CHA	2017	67	95	-2	93.2	52	0	32	1	520	397	36	77	.183	1	61	25	10	3	62	56.5	33	3	291	76
CHA	2018	62	100	1	92.9	49	0	47	4	553	430	25	79	.159	1	79	37	19	3	38	63.2	23	4	274	75

Jim Riggleman wRM+: 97.3

TEAM	YEAR	W	L	Pythag +/-	Avg PC	100+ P	120+ P	QS	BQS	REL	REL w Zero R	IBB	PH	PH Avg	PH HR	SB2	CS2	SB3	CS3	SAC Att	SAC %	POS SAC	Squee-ze	Swing	In Play
SDN	1992	4	8	-1				6	0	31	23	4	32	.214	1	9	4	0	0	10	50.0	3	0		
SDN	1993	61	101	-10				67	10	398	295	72	314	.219	4	70	37	19	3	113	70.8	23	2		
SDN	1994	47	70	-5				62	5	273	196	62	182	.274	2	67	25	12	6	85	78.8	27	2		
CHN	1995	73	71	-1				81	8	414	317	68	193	.242	6	96	32	9	2	93	76.3	35	3		
CHN	1996	76	86	-5				73	5	439	339	55	318	.205	4	90	44	17	2	84	78.6	34	1		
CHN	1997	68	94	-5				83	11	441	339	51	266	.248	6	100	51	16	6	107	77.6	37	3		
CHN	1998	90	73	5	94.5	86	17	78	14	449	335	48	261	.256	10	58	40	7	1	90	74.4	25	5		
CHN	1999	67	95	3	93.2	67	7	61	5	441	309	48	309	.211	8	55	39	5	4	96	67.7	29	3		
SEA	2008	36	54	-3	92.9	39	0	40	1	272	204	25	65	.233	0	32	15	6	2	38	55.3	19	1	203	75
WAS	2009	33	42	1	87.7	16	1	29	3	250	179	33	114	.282	2	32	18	5	2	51	64.7	14	1	142	46
WAS	2010	69	93	-2	89.4	28	2	69	1	494	396	57	264	.202	2	102	39	8	1	118	60.2	40	0	342	106
WAS	2011	38	37	-1	93.2	20	0	43	2	220	192	22	102	.205	1	51	14	10	4	53	71.7	17	5	149	49
CIN	2018	64	80	0	86.7	22	0	23	2	483	371	52	213	.237	9	58	28	10	2	80	52.5	17	3	268	73

Dave Roberts wRM+: 101.8

TEAM	YEAR	W	L	Pythag +/-	Avg PC	100+ P	120+ P	QS	BQS	REL	REL w Zero R	IBB	PH	PH Avg	PH HR	SB2	CS2	SB3	CS3	SAC Att	SAC %	POS SAC	Squee-ze	Swing	In Play
LAN	2016	91	71	-0	87.6	29	0	32	2	606	503	50	323	.189	6	40	22	5	2	62	48.4	5	2	254	84
LAN	2017	104	58	1	86.6	21	0	38	1	536	428	33	340	.244	8	60	24	15	2	51	60.8	4	1	237	70
LAN	2018	92	71	-11	86.5	22	0	35	1	593	465	39	354	.238	9	57	20	18	1	65	60.0	9	3	248	63

Mike Scioscia   wRM+: 102.1

TEAM	YEAR	W	L	Pythag +/-	Avg PC	100+ P	120+ P	QS	BQS	REL	REL w Zero R	IBB	PH	PH Avg	PH HR	SB2	CS2	SB3	CS3	SAC Att	SAC %	POS SAC	Squeeze	Swing	In Play
ANA	2000	82	80	1	92.0	64	6	58	9	441	341	44	86	.231	2	80	47	13	4	57	82.5	44	4		
ANA	2001	75	87	-2	97.2	73	5	83	10	385	303	47	86	.200	4	95	45	20	3	61	75.4	46	1		
ANA	2002	99	63	-4	99.3	86	5	94	8	400	334	24	103	.281	2	102	42	15	8	64	76.6	47	3		
ANA	2003	77	85	-3	94.2	63	1	65	5	375	310	38	97	.330	1	113	54	14	3	71	70.4	49	2	362	117
ANA	2004	92	70	1	96.8	79	3	79	7	343	269	27	81	.265	1	123	42	19	3	79	70.9	54	3	458	130
ANA	2005	95	67	0	96.9	76	1	99	4	379	306	24	78	.239	1	149	47	12	8	64	67.2	42	2	417	138
ANA	2006	89	73	4	97.0	78	2	97	6	380	292	27	87	.159	3	123	45	23	6	44	70.5	29	2	452	154
ANA	2007	94	68	4	97.2	83	0	90	1	396	310	22	91	.270	2	118	47	20	8	47	68.1	31	2	424	142
ANA	2008	100	62	11	99.4	84	0	92	3	383	302	32	67	.200	0	109	38	19	8	48	66.7	32	1	364	113
ANA	2009	97	65	4	96.9	82	1	77	7	434	340	35	65	.321	2	124	57	22	5	63	68.3	41	3	447	134
ANA	2010	80	82	1	102.1	105	3	93	6	410	325	33	86	.174	0	90	39	14	10	70	60.0	41	3	400	125
ANA	2011	86	76	1	101.0	98	11	98	8	386	313	34	75	.154	2	116	47	18	4	78	64.1	46	1	417	144
ANA	2012	89	73	1	97.4	87	4	91	3	444	365	20	68	.203	2	121	27	12	4	72	65.3	43	3	419	132
ANA	2013	78	84	-3	97.5	77	6	87	5	496	400	36	83	.214	3	71	32	10	1	54	68.5	35	0	349	110
ANA	2014	98	64	1	94.1	71	3	80	5	543	467	41	103	.233	1	72	37	9	2	42	61.9	24	1	315	88
ANA	2015	85	77	6	95.0	55	2	88	5	518	429	45	102	.217	2	45	31	6	2	50	74.0	36	3	297	91
ANA	2016	74	88	-6	90.4	39	0	37	3	527	423	27	94	.171	1	60	30	12	4	49	73.5	36	3	364	118
ANA	2017	80	82	-1	87.4	22	0	36	2	542	456	25	104	.260	1	115	38	20	5	32	53.1	16	1	364	119
ANA	2018	80	82	-1	81.9	19	0	30	1	601	462	17	110	.167	5	78	18	10	4	23	30.4	7	1	280	90

Scott Servais   wRM+: 103.1

TEAM	YEAR	W	L	Pythag +/-	Avg PC	100+ P	120+ P	QS	BQS	REL	REL w Zero R	IBB	PH	PH Avg	PH HR	SB2	CS2	SB3	CS3	SAC Att	SAC %	POS SAC	Squeeze	Swing	In Play
SEA	2016	86	76	-2	92.1	43	0	48	6	477	379	30	146	.254	4	48	26	8	1	43	55.8	21	0	268	83
SEA	2017	78	84	-1	88.2	32	0	31	0	526	405	28	86	.192	0	83	31	6	4	27	51.9	11	0	236	65
SEA	2018	89	73	12	86.4	31	0	40	1	537	417	21	97	.232	2	69	34	10	2	47	61.7	27	1	225	65

Buck Showalter   wRM+: 100.9

TEAM	YEAR	W	L	Pythag +/-	Avg PC	100+ P	120+ P	QS	BQS	REL	REL w Zero R	IBB	PH	PH Avg	PH HR	SB2	CS2	SB3	CS3	SAC Att	SAC %	POS SAC	Squeeze	Swing	In Play
NYA	1992	76	86	-4				85	14	308	236	49	89	.247	3	65	31	13	4	36	72.2	26	1		
NYA	1993	88	74	1				81	13	333	253	58	131	.272	4	34	31	4	4	37	59.5	22	0		
NYA	1994	70	43	1				61	8	241	181	24	79	.232	4	48	36	7	4	37	73.0	27	1		
NYA	1995	79	66	0				74	5	302	233	21	103	.266	1	46	24	4	5	27	74.1	20	0		
ARI	1998	65	97	-0	89.5	59	8	75	18	368	267	32	248	.171	3	67	32	5	4	70	64.3	16	0		
ARI	1999	100	62	-4	103.2	107	27	98	7	382	298	48	216	.321	5	119	35	16	3	77	79.2	23	1		
ARI	2000	85	77	0	94.9	63	18	84	8	390	294	53	248	.230	2	85	34	12	8	85	71.8	21	3		
TEX	2003	71	91	3	87.9	45	4	51	7	494	347	45	72	.177	0	61	24	4	1	38	63.2	21	0	260	90
TEX	2004	89	73	2	92.3	47	3	61	6	468	381	29	75	.143	1	64	32	5	4	37	62.2	22	0	257	87
TEX	2005	79	83	-3	92.5	66	2	66	2	454	325	31	43	.238	3	61	14	6	1	12	75.0	9	0	304	92
TEX	2006	80	82	-6	91.0	46	0	74	2	489	378	18	37	.182	0	47	23	6	1	35	51.4	15	0	253	83
BAL	2010	34	23	3	98.7	31	0	36	3	144	106	10	15	.154	0	25	9	4	0	15	80.0	12	0	78	26
BAL	2011	69	93	4	91.8	50	0	60	6	478	351	42	57	.309	1	74	20	7	5	41	58.5	23	2	309	97
BAL	2012	93	69	11	95.6	66	1	78	6	492	415	36	69	.161	0	55	21	3	8	51	74.5	34	1	282	102
BAL	2013	85	77	-0	95.9	75	0	78	5	473	380	32	65	.143	0	70	26	9	2	39	69.2	23	0	236	68
BAL	2014	96	66	1	97.8	78	1	78	7	479	405	25	74	.308	2	37	16	6	3	56	62.5	32	1	205	60
BAL	2015	81	81	-2	93.7	63	0	72	4	453	369	27	79	.208	1	34	22	9	2	33	60.6	18	0	191	58
BAL	2016	89	73	5	94.5	66	0	40	4	443	366	23	68	.274	2	19	11	0	2	24	70.8	14	0	175	55
BAL	2017	75	87	4	93.6	64	0	35	1	492	383	21	91	.195	2	25	11	6	2	22	45.5	10	0	171	48
BAL	2018	47	115	-6	87.9	35	1	32	1	490	347	29	83	.189	2	72	17	8	4	28	46.4	12	1	220	51

Brian Snitker   wRM+: 99.3

TEAM	YEAR	W	L	Pythag +/-	Avg PC	100+ P	120+ P	QS	BQS	REL	REL w Zero R	IBB	PH	PH Avg	PH HR	SB2	CS2	SB3	CS3	SAC Att	SAC %	POS SAC	Squeeze	Swing	In Play
ATL	2016	59	65	4	89.9	40	0	25	1	456	371	40	212	.226	4	48	21	11	3	78	61.5	14	1	208	74
ATL	2017	72	90	0	93.6	45	1	45	3	530	406	39	268	.231	10	64	29	13	2	87	67.8	18	0	312	92
ATL	2018	90	72	-3	90.8	41	1	28	3	552	427	43	247	.202	7	75	28	13	7	76	64.5	13	3	277	84

Don Wakamatsu   wRM+: 95.9

TEAM	YEAR	W	L	Pythag +/-	Avg PC	100+ P	120+ P	QS	BQS	REL	REL w Zero R	IBB	PH	PH Avg	PH HR	SB2	CS2	SB3	CS3	SAC Att	SAC %	POS SAC	Squeeze	Swing	In Play
SEA	2009	85	77	10	95.5	68	1	83	3	409	329	13	54	.213	1	70	24	19	8	80	70.0	55	4	295	96
SEA	2010	42	70	2	97.1	49	2	65	3	254	187	25	47	.225	1	85	22	15	4	53	54.7	25	4	255	75
TEX	2018	3	7	0	69.2	0	0	1	0	41	31	1	7	.500	1	1	0	0	0	1	0.0	0	0	11	2

Ned Yost   wRM+: 101.2

TEAM	YEAR	W	L	Pythag +/-	Avg PC	100+ P	120+ P	QS	BQS	REL	REL w Zero R	IBB	PH	PH Avg	PH HR	SB2	CS2	SB3	CS3	SAC Att	SAC %	POS SAC	Squeeze	Swing	In Play
MIL	2003	68	94	3	95.5	70	5	66	7	460	344	43	282	.220	6	89	34	9	5	98	63.3	29	1	267	82
MIL	2004	67	94	1	93.2	60	8	82	5	423	299	27	279	.205	7	124	35	14	2	96	58.3	28	1	358	101
MIL	2005	81	81	-3	99.3	86	4	91	5	396	292	52	253	.248	6	68	30	11	3	113	58.4	41	1	298	100
MIL	2006	75	87	5	94.5	67	3	81	7	427	306	34	235	.267	4	60	33	10	4	88	65.9	20	1	294	96
MIL	2007	83	79	-1	94.0	56	9	76	9	492	368	37	253	.224	6	86	25	9	4	81	74.1	22	0	321	100
MIL	2008	83	67	2	96.3	54	6	82	3	399	311	30	217	.208	7	85	27	20	7	66	69.7	17	3	333	108
KCA	2010	55	72	4	96.4	59	1	53	7	332	257	25	52	.214	2	73	35	12	4	45	66.7	25	0	281	78
KCA	2011	71	91	-7	96.9	74	0	75	5	420	339	42	36	.152	1	130	48	23	8	75	73.3	51	2	399	113
KCA	2012	72	90	-1	90.5	55	0	69	4	500	411	44	55	.208	3	109	34	22	4	42	61.9	25	1	334	97
KCA	2013	86	76	-1	98.6	79	2	95	5	427	374	21	74	.210	1	133	30	19	2	56	66.1	36	1	369	99
KCA	2014	89	73	5	98.6	90	2	95	4	451	399	14	43	.250	2	124	29	29	7	55	60.0	30	1	344	112
KCA	2015	95	67	4	92.8	52	0	71	3	493	418	10	36	.188	0	76	30	27	2	48	70.8	32	0	257	86
KCA	2016	81	81	4	93.2	61	0	42	6	472	391	8	47	.238	0	102	31	19	4	66	57.6	35	0	300	73
KCA	2017	80	82	9	88.7	26	0	38	3	538	423	24	41	.162	0	74	27	17	3	24	70.8	16	1	239	57
KCA	2018	58	104	-2	91.6	52	0	40	1	483	348	28	41	.314	1	85	31	32	5	47	51.1	23	0	287	73

Top 101 Prospects

by Jeffrey Paternostro and Jarrett Seidler

1. Vladimir Guerrero Jr., 3B, Toronto Blue Jays

An occasional topic of conversation on Jason Parks and Kevin Goldstein's *Up and In* podcast was what an elite hitter would do if he hypothetically had to spend a full season in the minors. One time it was Miguel Cabrera, perhaps another time Mike Trout. There are limitations to the statistical ceiling here, of course—whether it's the vagaries of balls in play or the occasional slider good enough to get you out every once in a while. But overall you'd expect a pretty ludicrous triple slash across the course of five months. Vladito hit .381/.437/.636 in 95 games between Double and Triple-A. He's only 19. Cabrera and Trout would beat that, but perhaps not by all that much. That tells you what the offensive potential is here. The younger Guerrero is by far the best pure bat in the minors this year (or most any other year), and the best prospect in baseball, full stop. This was not controversial. There were no long email threads, no heated DMs among the BP prospect team. The only real bone of contention was whether or not a .300 batting average with 30 bombs was too conservative a median seasonal outcome for our number one prospect.

2. Jo Adell, OF, Los Angeles Angels

There are plenty of seasons where Adell would clock in as the top prospect in the land. He certainly looks the part. He's built like an NFL wideout with speed to match. He's a sure-shot center fielder. There's plus-plus raw power that a previous author of this list would have called "abnormal" in a slightly bewildered Texas drawl. And Adell has a remarkably advanced feel for hitting as a teenager. Oh, he was also 97 with a projectable slider off the mound in high school, so there's your fifth tool checked off. It's also another indication of just how good he was as a *hitting* prospect for him not to have ended up as a pitcher. We do love our five-tool center fielders here at Baseball Prospectus, and Adell is a particularly impressive specimen. You can't quibble with the performance either. He raked across three levels in 2018 as a 19-year-old, only a thumb injury and brief, initial Double-A struggles keeping him from going full Acuna on the minors. So while we now may have to wait a little longer for him to go full Acuna on the majors, we assure you: It will be worth the wait.

3. Fernando Tatis Jr., SS, San Diego Padres

Can you imagine if Rick Hahn never made the June 2016 James Shields trade? Right before starting their rebuild, the White Sox moved Tatis, then a recent international signing of moderate tout most notable for his bloodlines, at the head of a package for a fading and heavily subsidized Shields. It was the last desperate gasp of a failing contention cycle. Nine times out of ten, this trade is forgotten by 2019, but here on Earth-10, Tatis is now one of the three best prospects in baseball. He tore up the Double-A Texas League, and might've reached the majors as a teenager if it wasn't for a thumb injury and the usual service time shenanigans. He's been in the shadow of Vladito since they signed, both sons of Dominican All-Stars coming of age in the same July 2 class. But the gap is closing, even though Guerrero is the best offensive prospect of recent memory. Tatis is that good.

4. Eloy Jimenez, OF, Chicago White Sox

Acquiring cheap control of a pitcher may have cost the White Sox dearly in 2016, but *trading* a much better version of the same was a windfall in 2017. Jimenez has continued mashing at all levels since migrating across the Second City in the Jose Quintana trade. Sometimes we forget about him because he's not a teenage destroyer of worlds, in a weird sort of prospect fatigue where he's been around for awhile and is limited to outfield corners and points right on the defensive spectrum. We shouldn't. This is his third-straight top ten ranking, and he ended 2018 with a half-season as one of Triple-A's best hitters at just 21. Jimenez is a limitless bundle of offensive upside that should be directly entering the middle of the lineup by the beginning of this summer at the absolute latest.

5. Victor Robles, OF, Washington Nationals

Robles was our "1b" last year behind Ronald Acuna. Both were graded out as OFP 80/Likely 70. Acuna—as you are no doubt aware—went onto have a 70-grade major league campaign while Robles missed most of the year after hyperextending his left elbow on a diving catch attempt in Syracuse. Dropping him to fifth this year might be a bit of undue caution, though. Robles was already major-league-ready in 2017, and he was quite good in his brief 2018 cameo with the Nats. There's still three potential plus-plus tools in his hit, run, and glove, and we have been projecting above-average game power since we first laid eyes on him. The speed and defense make him a likely solid regular even if the bat doesn't play to projection, and he won't turn 22 until six weeks into the 2019 season. While we are worried enough about the injury and lost development time to bump the OFP down to 70 this time around, that might end up another bit of undue caution on our part.

6. Keston Hiura, 2B, Milwaukee Brewers

The known unknown of the 2017 Draft was Hiura's injured elbow. He spent his entire junior campaign at UC-Irvine at designated hitter. There was real concern that his elbow might force him to left field or first base, or even a permanent move to DH. It took him about a year to slowly transition back to full-time play in the field, but by this past summer he was playing second base regularly and doing it without complication. He's even pretty good out there, not that it terribly matters when you're in an organization that just made a pennant run with Travis Shaw standing in the vicinity of the keystone. If you ignored the medical and defensive flags, Hiura was already the best college bat in that class, and you can see how quickly and how high he's risen with a clean bill of health. You rarely hear us talk about a right-handed swing in whispers and high appellations. This swing is perfect.

7. Forrest Whitley, RHP, Houston Astros

There was serious discussion among the BP prospect team this year whether we should just drop every pitching prospect 20 spots or so. They are just so volatile when compared with the position players. And while a quick glance at our DRA-based WARP leaderboard does show several former elite pitching prospects near the top, they're mixed in with names like Jacob deGrom, Corey Kluber, and Patrick Corbin. There's just so many ways it can go wrong for a top prospect arm, even past the more predictable elbow-based ones. Forrest Whitley's arm is fine—as of publication—but plenty went wrong in his 2018 season. He missed the first 50 games after being suspended for using a banned stimulant in the offseason. Then a tweaked oblique limited him to just 50 innings between Double-A and the AFL. But he looked every bit a potential top-of-the-rotation starter during those scant outings. Whitley sits in the mid-90s with four potential plus pitches—and not in the Joe Kelly sense—with advanced command of the whole arsenal. There's ace upside, and he could help the Astros rotation as soon as this summer. Even if we did move every pitching prospect down 20 spots, Whitley would still be an easy choice for #1.

8. Royce Lewis, SS, Minnesota Twins

If it's possible for the first overall pick to be underrated as a prospect, Lewis might be. Most of the heat in the mock drafts in 2017 were on two-way prospects Hunter Greene and Brendan McKay. Lewis was the other prep shortstop. Since draft day, Jo Adell and Keston Hiura have gotten bigger headlines and higher rankings. And look, we obviously really like Adell and Hiura, but all Royce Lewis has did in his first full pro season was hit .292/.352/.451 while flashing all five tools. We're more confident he's a shortstop long term now—although still curious about how the profile would look in center. We're more confident he can *really* hit, and he's starting to grow into an average-or-better power projection. That's a monster shortstop prospect. And while the tools might not be quite as loud as Adell's, nor is he as sure a bet with the stick as Hiura, Lewis is still one of the ten best prospects in baseball and a potential perennial All-Star. So let's give him the ink he is due.

9. Nick Senzel, 3B/2B/SS?/OF?, Cincinnati Reds

Could we finally have the new Ben Zobrist? We typically attach the Zobrist sobriquet to prospects without role 7 projections or players nowhere near as good as Zobrist. Zobrist was, of course, a role 7 himself for most of his career, so if you wanted to actually create a Zobrist, you'd have to get that kind of defensive versatility with a prospect that good. Enter Nick Senzel, role 7 potential third base prospect with strong defensive instincts and good athleticism. Right after Senzel was drafted with the second pick in 2016, Eugenio Suarez morphed from a young shortstop filling in at third base to a two-way star third baseman. The Reds eventually locked Suarez up through 2025, and thus the search for a new position for Senzel began. Except they didn't just pick a new position and stop, and he started sliding up the defensive spectrum instead of down. Senzel got experience at shortstop last spring, spent most of his injury-marred 2018 regular season campaign at second base, and tried his hand at left and center field in fall instructs. He may yet settle in somewhere permanently, but the trials around the diamond went well enough for the jack-of-all-trades star possibility to emerge too.

10. Wander Franco, SS, Tampa Bay Rays

One of the prospect team's favorite maxims is that the short-season leagues are "barely organized baseball." Oh, you'll still hear John Fogerty's "Centerfield" during batting practice, and your local pizza place will sponsor some sort of dizzy bat race between innings, but the level of play is so far removed from the majors that it can make evaluating prospects a bit trickier. They aren't seeing major league quality velocity or spin. They might not even see a pitch anywhere near the plate some at-bats. Philosophies can vary on how to deal with this. Some evaluators might just start a mental rolodex, a catalog of what a prospect can do. Others might look for a moment—a swing, a play, a throw—that wouldn't look out of place in the majors. Some don't even bother with these levels at all. That last one is a mistake—for several reasons—but mostly because they would have missed out on seeing Wander Franco. Nothing looks out of place here. Franco is a potential five tool shortstop with particularly loud ones at the plate. As a 17-year-old he posted a 1.000 OPS with more walks than strikeouts for Princeton, and nothing about it seemed unsustainable. There is star upside with the bat and a good chance to stick at the 6. You don't want to miss this, and in the future if you need lunch recommendations in Western Virginia or East Tennessee, hit us up.

11. Taylor Trammell, OF, Cincinnati Reds

Playing baseball is incredibly hard—tell 'em Wash—and the guys that are really good at it often know exactly how good they are. We don't mind a little swagger in our top prospects, and nothing encapsulates that more than Taylor Trammell flashing two fingers towards the Team USA dugout when he thought he'd hit his second home run of the Futures Game this past July. Unfortunately for Trammell, he'd hit a laser beam to the deepest part of Nationals Park and merely hit the fence. He did turn on the jets and still managed to cruise in for a triple on his way to the game's MVP award, but that moment is likely to show up for a few years on "During this commercial break here are some highlights from MLB.com." The Futures Game was a great showcase for Trammell, displaying the premium tools that get him ranked this high, but his performance in the Florida State League was more muted. No matter: Prospect evaluation is in part about what is possible, and for Trammell those possibilities land him back playing exhibition baseball in July for many years to come.

12. Bo Bichette, SS, Toronto Blue Jays

We never want to like Bo Bichette. His swing has a weird-looking hitch that shouldn't work, which we usually describe with the "unorthodox" euphemism. His approach can collapse in a hurry when he gets too aggressive, and that happens more than you'd hope for. He might be a second or third baseman pretty soon. His brother was one of the more infamous first-round busts of recent memory. His father was one of the more overrated MLB players of the Steroid Era. We thought he might have real trouble with advanced pitching, and he certainly stopped putting up the ridiculous averages he did in A-ball. But he made the adjustments as the summer went along and had a strong season as a 20-year-old in Double-A. Ultimately, the bat speed and wrists just play so long as he isn't trying to yank low-and-outside pitches 600 feet down the line. Bichette has all the pieces for a well-rounded offensive game, and he's likely to hold substantial defensive value somewhere or another. Give him a shot to make you like him.

13. Jesus Luzardo, LHP, Oakland Athletics

We really wanted to push Luzardo further up the 2018 incarnation of this list, trust us. But that's a tough sell on a 19-year-old in short-season who already has a Tommy John surgery in his medical history. Even our soothsayers didn't see this level of a breakout coming in 2018. The now 20-year-old crushed three levels of the minors, finishing in Triple-A, striking out 10+ batters per nine and flashing three plus pitches from the left side. The fastball sits around 95, touching higher, with wicked armside left and present above-

average command. There's a potential plus change with 10+ mph of velocity separation and impressive tumble. The breaker can get slurvy, but tightened up as the year went on and could be the third 60-grade offering here. The Jesus Lizard is just about ready for a mainstage show at the top of Oakland's rotation, and this version is far less likely to leap into the crowd and start licking fans. Too bad the Bay Area has priced out all the crust punks.

14. Kyle Tucker, OF, Houston Astros

Our evaluations happen in a vacuum. You just evaluate the player, not the situation. Organizational needs can change rapidly, and heck, a prospect can change organizations at any time too. This is to say that the evaluation on Kyle Tucker hasn't really changed. He's a potential plus hit/plus power corner outfielder who has been young for every level he's played at and hit at every level he's played at. He did struggle across a series of major league call-ups, but his playing time was intermittent. That doesn't seem to be a situation that's going to rectify itself soon either. The Astros are at the top of their contention cycle and will rightfully value surety everywhere on the diamond. Tucker's 2019 playing time might get siphoned off to new signing Michael Brantley, who has always hit in the majors when healthy. But as we said, prospects can change organizations too, and perhaps Tucker will find himself with a clear path to playing time outside of the Lone Star State. He certainly has nothing left to prove in the minors.

15. Nick Madrigal, 2B/SS, Chicago White Sox

You can always count on us here at Baseball Prospectus to not shy away from the extreme skill set, and Nicklaus Madrigal has the most extreme skill set of any top prospect in the minors by a mile. Madrigal was generously listed at 5'8" in college. He hit three home runs as a junior—and that was with ping bats. He was pushed off shortstop at Oregon State by Cadyn Grenier. He still went with the fourth pick in the nation, and we are ranking him ahead of every other 2018 draftee. That's how good his hit tool is. Madrigal is the first player in a long time that we've talked internally about grading as an 8 hitter without significant upper-minors or MLB experience. His contact ability might be unmatched in the minors or majors, with the exception of fellow unicorn Willians Astudillo. The White Sox shifted him to shortstop in instructs, and he has the skills to handle the position, especially in the modern age of positioning. We can't reasonably project him to hit for a lot of home run power, but he's far from a punch-and-judy hitter. The swing is short, already geared for line drives, and generates quite a bit of bat speed, so if he somehow adds loft, watch out.

16. Carter Kieboom, SS, Washington Nationals

Kieboom hasn't shown quite enough game power yet for us to just unleash a series of bad puns in this 150-word blurb, but everything else is going well for the Nats prospect. He mashed in High-A and held his own as a 20-year-old in

Double-A. He's a potential .300 hitter who has started to lift the ball more. Kieboom has also improved enough at shortstop that there's a non-zero chance he sticks there, although it's more likely he ends up an above-average second baseman. The raw power is plus, and Kieboom still has some room to fill out, making him a decent bet to drop the...well...uh...boom on the Eastern League in a return engagement in 2019. Looks we just said it wouldn't be a *series* of bad puns.

17. Luis Urias, 2B, San Diego Padres

As a prospect evaluator, sometimes you just have to concede the point. In the past, we've hedged on Urias because we know that our greatest weakness in evaluating prospects is the hit tool. Basically, we weren't sold that he was a potential 7 hit guy. We're there now. Urias combines high-end bat-to-ball ability and barrel control with a hair-trigger quick bat, and that's created a lot of offensive potential. Despite a small frame, he has some loft in his swing and generates surprising pop; it might manifest more in gap power than over-the-fence power in the majors, but at the very least he's going to hit a lot of doubles. He's also finally settling in at second base, the defensive home where it was long predicted he would eventually excel. Urias already made his MLB debut in August, and has bigger upside than you might think looking at his measurables.

18. Mitch Keller, RHP, Pittsburgh Pirates

Keller is a weird choice to be another "prospect fatigue" entry, but here we are. This will only be his third appearance on the 101, so he still has a half-decade to go to catch Jorge Alfaro. And he's been a very good pitching prospect, year-over-year since he first burst onto the radar in 2016. There's just nothing new to write about him in 2019. Keller threw 140 good upper minors innings. He's always been durable and efficient. He still has a mid-90s fastball with above-average movement and command, a potential plus-plus curve, and a crude changeup used sparingly. We could wonder aloud again if the lack of an armside weapon against lefties might limit his upside, but he's gone another year against better hitters without really needing it. Keller did have the occasional command/control blip in 2018, but it's hardly a worrying pattern or anything. He's just a very good pitching prospect about ready for the majors, a potential number two starter, and there isn't much more to write at this time.

19. Alex Verdugo, OF, Los Angeles Dodgers

We've repeated the same process for Verdugo for three straight offseasons now. We always start with him being ranked way lower than he ends up. It's not hard to figure out why. He has some tweenerish tendencies. We always wonder more about hit tool projections. He's been up in the majors four separate times now without getting a real opportunity to establish himself. Despite a contact-heavy offensive approach and the ability to play all three outfield positions, he's never cracked a postseason roster. He's been connected

to every trade rumor under the sun, and we're honestly not sure he's still going to be on the Dodgers when you read this. Yet every fall during the rankings breakout process, we come to the same realization that he's better than a half-dozen similar players listed ahead of him, and we have to move him up. Maybe we subconsciously underrate boring competence. He's both high floor and high delta despite two seasons of Triple-A, which seems like a paradox, but really isn't. We're pretty sure he's on the Monopoly board as a MLB player; he could reasonably land from about St. Charles (good fourth outfielder or platoon type) to Marvin Gardens (contending for batting titles), or anywhere in between. Having Reading Railroad always returns good surplus value, right?

20. Francisco Mejia, C, San Diego Padres

Jeffrey's column is titled "The View Behind the Backstop" and that's the best vantage point to evaluate most prospects. It does make things tricky for catchers, though. Heck, a lot of the work of the major league catcher happens before he even steps in between the foul lines. The stuff on the diamond isn't much easier. Evaluating gamecalling is tricky from any vantage point: Your view of receiving isn't going to be much better from the scout seats. We've always thought Mejia was a fine, viable, if not above-average major league catcher. Cleveland seemed to disagree, trying him at third and corner outfield before dealing him for a pair of relievers at the deadline. The Padres have one of the best defensive catchers in baseball in Austin Hedges. He doesn't have Mejia's bat—we can see that fine from behind the backstop—which projects as .300 with 15-20 bombs. That's an All-Star catcher if he can stick behind the plate, and somebody, somewhere should give him the chance to prove it one way or the other.

21. Alex Reyes, RHP, St. Louis Cardinals

Two years ago we ranked Alex Reyes as the best prospect in baseball. Since then he has thrown 23 innings. His torn UCL got announced the day we published the 2017 Top 101 on the website. We regret nothing, but we may have to lower our expectations a little in 2019. Everything looked fine in 2018 right up until he tore his lat in his first major league appearance. There's certainly top pitching prospects that have recovered from essentially two years off and turned into good major league starters. Jameson Taillon—whose lost time we grappled with on that ill-fated 2017 list—comes to mind, but that kind of Play Index search will turn up far more Hunter Harveys, and names even more obscure than Hunter Harvey. What we do know: Reyes' stuff all came back from the Tommy John surgery. He might have the best two-pitch combo on this list, and the change is potential plus as well. There were always lingering concerns he might be a reliever, and those voices are only going to grow louder now, but with triple-digit heat and a plus-plus curve, he'd be a heckuva reliever.

22. Brendan Rodgers, SS, Colorado Rockies

Our upper-minors Rodgers reports continue to be a touch less enthusiastic about his ultimate outcome as a player than our older, lower-minors Rodgers reports. There's nothing inherently wrong here—the big tools are still there and his Double-A performance has been good. To the extent that there's a serious knock here, it's that he remains very aggressive at the plate and as a result has sometimes struggled to make consistent, hard contact. He has power, overall feel for hitting, and time still on his side, but they're less on his side than they were a few years ago. The narrative is similar on defense, where he has a decent shot to remain at shortstop but has also been exposed to second and third base as potential alternative positions. The story might end in something looking a lot like, well, Trevor Story.

23. Sixto Sanchez, RHP, Philadelphia Phillies

Sixto missed most of the 2018 season with "elbow inflammation." That can mean a host of different things, most of them ranging from "bad" to "extremely bad." A planned assignment to the AFL was scuttled after a "setback." We are using a lot of air quotes as scare quotes here, but we haven't seen the MRIs so we're mostly guessing. We'll start ranking the dudes that are in the midst of Tommy John recovery a little bit lower, but you'd have to place the odds on Sixto going under the knife point at "higher than you'd like." But he *hasn't* had surgery yet, and when he was on the mound in 2018 he was still Sixto bleepin' Sanchez, owner of arguably the best arsenal in minor league baseball. He was due to be promoted to the Eastern League—where he would have been one of the youngest players in Double-A—before his elbow started barking. He still throws triple-digit heat with movement, offers a cavalcade of potential plus secondaries, and features some of the best pitchability in the prospect world. He's incredibly risky now, but also closer to the majors than you think. He's a conundrum, a potential ace, a potential closer, a potential surgery candidate. He might be Sixto different things to six different prospect writers, but this is a long term value list, and on a long enough timeline we like our chances with Sixto.

24. Michael Kopech, RHP, Chicago White Sox

Kopech continued to restrain himself in 2018, keeping the heater mostly dialed back to the upper-90s while throwing more strikes and reintroducing a plus curveball. (Yes, 95-99 MPH qualifies as dialed back for him.) On the one hand, it was a success in that he carved through Triple-A and reached the majors in August. On the other hand, it didn't matter, as the Tommy John Gods felled him four starts in. It was unfortunate timing for Kopech, who will miss most or all of 2019, and even more unfortunate for the White Sox, who will lose a full year of team control while he's on the disabled list, unlike…

25. Brent Honeywell, RHP, Tampa Bay Rays

…the Rays, whose decision to leave Honeywell down late in 2017 "paid off" huge when Honeywell tore his own UCL early in spring training, if you ignore the utter absurdity of counting your then-top prospect's Tommy John surgery as having positive benefits. Had the Rays called Honeywell up when he was actually ready two summers ago, he'd have spent 2018 on the MLB disabled list, and would have accrued two-plus years of service time by the end of 2019. As it stands, the Rays were able to option him in 2018, and will almost certainly do the same to open 2019. He'll come up later in the spring or summer and won't accrue a season of service time until 2020. Ultimately, that delayed call-up will likely cost Honeywell tens of millions of dollars over the course of his career. Whether you view that as a bug or feature of the system depends on which side of the labor debate you're on. Pending a clean return—and he was already throwing off a mound at press time in December—Honeywell retains top-of-the-rotation potential, just like Kopech.

26. Dylan Cease, RHP, Chicago White Sox

We've been waiting for years for Cease to make the big leap into prospectdom's upper tier. 2018 *finally* brought a measure of durability to go with the elite fastball/breaking ball combination, with Cease spinning 124 dazzling innings in High-A and Double-A. He's improved the secondary offerings and command enough that he's likely to stay in the rotation so long as his health allows. Of course, his medical history contains enough red flags for a DSA meeting, most arm-related. This section of the list contains a ton of pitchers who could front a good rotation if they can get to 200 innings. The distribution of outcomes here means that it's likely that some will, but you might as well get out the ouija board if you want to predict which ones.

27. Dustin May, RHP, Los Angeles Dodgers

We didn't have any sort of nominative determinism in mind when we bestowed the *nom de plume* of "The Gingergaard" on Dustin May after he was drafted. It was merely an aesthetic comp. But a certain—albeit tiny—percentage of those projectable Texas prep arms do develop into Norse Gods. And while May isn't there yet, he was at least a jötnar in 2018. The towering redhead developed a flaming fastball to match in 2018, bumping from the low-90s to the mid-90s and touching as high as 99 with sink and run. His powerful, high-spin curveball is a potential plus-plus offering, so as with Mitch Keller above, you are less concerned with the lack of a changeup at present. May has added a cutter as well for another look, although it is very much a work in progress at present. So yeah, you never comp Noah Syndergaard, but that sure sounds like a Noah Syndergaard starter kit. And the *plume* is particularly impressive as well.

28. MacKenzie Gore, LHP, San Diego Padres

If you agree with Jarrett that the fastball/curveball lefty is the most aesthetically pleasing prospect in baseball, come get your mans. Gore has one of the best curves in the minors, a gorgeous big hook that he can manipulate as a freeze or chase pitch. It works well paired with a lively mid-90s fastball, and it all comes out of a deceptive motion with a classic big leg kick. The changeup also flashes plus but needs greater consistency, which is a sentence that could be applied to 80 percent of the prospects on the list. Just like the rest of the crop, there's a durability concern already present and accounted for. Gore battled blister and fingernail problems all season, which limited him to just 60 2/3 innings. At least the particular worry is about his hand instead of his elbow or shoulder.

29. Ian Anderson, RHP, Atlanta Braves

There's usually a prospect every year where we look up from our locked Top 101 list and blink once or twice while wondering "Wait, how did *he* end up so high?" We shouldn't be so surprised honestly. While Anderson's 2018 season was among the quieter breakouts, it was certainly a breakout, as he struck out nearly 11 per nine while dominating High-A and Double-A. His pedigree has never been as issue, Anderson was the third overall pick in 2016. As a cold-weather arm out of New York State, the stuff was likely to be a slow burn, but it showed up white hot in 2018. He flashed three potential plus pitches, a mid-90s fastball with sink, a tight, swing-and-miss 12-6 curve, and a high-80s change with good arm speed. The control is ahead of the command at present, and the "plus" change is far more projection than present, but you don't have to project too too much to see Anderson as a number two starter in reasonably short order. That's how you end up so high on the 101.

30. Austin Riley, 3B, Atlanta Braves

When is a prospect ready? Austin Riley has about a season-and-a-half in the high-minors. He dominated Double-A in the second half of 2017 and especially the first half of 2018, and he continued to be very good at Triple-A in the second half of 2018. Way back in A-ball, he had a risky profile and we legitimately didn't know whether he'd adjust to tougher pitching. There's still too much swing-and-miss, which is just going to be a fact of life with his size, swing, and power, but he's consistently shown the ability to hit MiLB pitching. He's good enough defensively at third base now that he deserves a shot to stick there. And yet despite all of that, Atlanta tipped that they didn't think Riley was ready for permanent MLB work when they signed Josh Donaldson to man third base for 2019. Riley will still likely make his MLB debut soon—Donaldson's health record recently is a disaster, and Riley can probably play other corners if it comes to it—and this does present a convenient rationale for some service time manipulation. But should we care as evaluators that Riley looks ready to play and Atlanta blocked his clear path to playing time for a year anyway?

31. Keibert Ruiz, C, Los Angeles Dodgers

By Baseball Prospectus' WARP—which has the most robust catcher defensive metric—Yasmani Grandal has been at worst the second-best catcher in baseball during his time in Dodger blue. The Dodgers do not seem particularly inclined to sign him to a long-term deal. Yes, he's on the wrong side of 30, but Los Angeles also arguably has the most catching prospect depth in the majors. Catchers are weird, but if you collect enough of them you can mitigate some of the individual weirdness. The best of the crop is Ruiz, a 20-year-old who more than held his own in the Texas League this year while getting rave reviews for his defense and pitcher handling. The offensive tools may only play to average in the end, but even that would make him one of the five or so best *hitting* catchers in the game, and he could be a plus defender behind the plate. That's not quite Yasmani Grandal, but it might be close enough for the Dodgers.

32. Jesus Sanchez, OF, Tampa Bay Rays

In last year's Annual we ranked Sanchez as the 60th best prospect in baseball, while expressing concerns about whether the bat would carry a corner outfield profile. Well, we still have concerns, but we are always going to have concerns about corner bats. Sanchez hit .300 in the Carolina League before scuffling in August after a promotion to Double-A. This is still very much a projection bet as the ideal corner outfield power doesn't always show up after sundown. It's a great frame to make the bet on though, and Sanchez already shows enough bat speed and barrel control to project a plus hit tool. If it all comes together there's All-Star potential in the bat, but we are going to have to wait until at least 2019 to see it all come together, so carry your concerns accordingly.

33. Brusdar Graterol, RHP, Minnesota Twins

A 6'1" righty with reliever red flags and a body like a catcher is not the traditional Top 101 pitching prospect demo here at Baseball Prospectus. When you touch 101 with movement, however, we don't really care how many synonyms for "stocky" we'll have to come up with before Graterol makes the majors. He pairs the triple-digit sinker with a potential plus-plus slider, as well as a curve and change with some projectability. The control and command might never be plus—although that's less of an issue when you hit 100 with regularity—but there's front-of-the-rotation upside coming off a dominant A-ball season as a 20-year-old. And if Graterol does end up a reliever, arms like his fit in there just fine.

34. Nolan Gorman, 3B, St. Louis Cardinals

Often your best third base prospects are presently playing shortstop, but this year's 101 has a bumper crop of hot corner options. Gorman was the other big bat in the Appalachian League this past Summer, and you might wonder how an 18-year-old putting up video game numbers in his first taste of pro ball lasted to the nineteenth pick in the draft. Well, sometimes your third base prospects are your best first base prospects, and there are concerns that he might grow off the hot corner—where he already isn't super-rangy. There's concerns the swing might have holes that upper minors pitchers can exploit, and he did strike out a fair bit in 2018 when he wasn't hammering the ball. But Gorman had arguably the most raw power in his draft class and you saw plenty of that last season too. You hope with time and reps he develops into...well, Austin Riley. Stay tuned, but we like his chances as you might have gathered from this ranking.

35. Jonathan India, 3B/SS, Cincinnati Reds

It might feel a little aggressive to list India as a shortstop, but given what the Reds have done with Nick Senzel, he may actually be headed there for real. India played a handful of games at the six spot after the draft, and focused on it even more during fall instructs. Not all that long ago, moves up the defensive spectrum like this would've been scoffed at, and yet you keep reading about them for highly-regarded infielders in this section. The traditional way to find a prospect's position was to start every promising right-handed throwing infielder off at shortstop and let them migrate right on the spectrum from there, like an inverted application of the Peter Principle. For example, Miguel Cabrera and Miguel Sano both played a goodly amount of short in their first two pro seasons, as unfathomable as that may seem if you're familiar with their later defensive profiles. But more and more, stigmas have changed, and players have started picking up shortstop at higher levels. In the most extreme example we can imagine, Scott Kingery went from playing two games at shortstop over his entire minor-league career to starting 101 games there as a major-league rookie. India certainly has the defensive chops to make a more permanent transition to shortstop plausible, and he now has the same Eugenio Suarez roadblock in his way that Senzel does. Credit the Reds with thinking ahead to turn a potential problem into increased flexibility.

36. Casey Mize, RHP, Detroit Tigers

We haven't ranked the first-overall pick as the top prospect from his draft class in the following winter's top 101 list since Gerrit Cole placed 9th on our 2012 list. (As you may have heard, the writer of that list has since won a World Series ring as a scouting director.) This year is no different, as 2018's 1.1 ranks behind the players taken 4th, 19th, and 5th, respectively. It's probably not entirely a coincidence that Cole was taken in the last draft under the old soft-slotting system; the current system encourages teams to cut an underslot deal up high to pick up more top talents later. Mize was hardly a reach, and got the highest bonus in the draft class and the second-highest bonus ever under the current system. He *still* came in nearly $600,000 under the slot value, savings that allowed the Tigers to draft and sign high-upside prep outfielder Parker Meadows in the second round. On his own merits, Mize is a prototypical top-of-the-draft college righty: a polished craftsman already showing three above-average pitches, all flashing a shot for plus or more. There

are more red flags than you'd like for a polished college starter—we're concerned about a history of elbow injuries, and he throws with some effort—and that's why he's not up there fighting with Madrigal for the top ranking amongst 2018 draftees. If he can handle the rigors of a full workload, he's likely to be quite good.

37. Chris Paddack, RHP, San Diego Padres

Paddack has been comically dominant everywhere he's ever pitched, to the point that we can't stop PECOTA from grouping him amongst the best *MLB* pitchers. Parts of the scouting report even support that. His changeup is one of the best pitches of any prospect in the game. His fastball "only" gets to the mid-90s, but he manipulates and sequences it brilliantly, and has high-end command to boot. And yet there are two concerns on him which are just major enough that we capped his OFP at 60 and ranked him down here. More significantly, he just hasn't shown the ability to stay on the mound enough. Tommy John surgery cost him the second half of 2016 and all of 2017, and he was surely on a limited count of bullets in 2018. Yet we can't ignore that the 17 starts and 90 innings he did throw last year both represent more than half of his total pro output since being drafted in 2015. We have no clue if he can start yet, basically. Adding to the reliever concern is that he's close to a fastball/changeup only guy at present, with an inconsistent breaking ball that only projects to around average. This is a profile where adding a hard slider to throw a fifth of the time might cause the entire thing to take a huge step forward, and a lot of pitchers have added such in the high-minors or majors, but we can't actually project that until he does it. This ranking could look supremely low if he ends up being a 180-200 inning pitcher with a good third pitch. While those are legitimate huge problems to surmount, there's still less standing between Paddack and the top of a rotation than most.

38. Andres Gimenez, SS, New York Mets

Gimenez has developed a reputation as a low-to-medium upside, higher probability prospect. Based on the relative lack of physicality he showed through 2017, that was more than a reasonable take. We even wrote him up that way in last year's book. He's still a bit small of stature, but the physicality popped in 2018 in ways we weren't entirely expecting. He added significant strength to his upper core and gained some loft in his swing. Suddenly, instead of merely poking the ball around, he started driving it for gap power. He also gained speed, and now projects as a significant stolen base threat. While the football-style offseason workouts organizationally preferred by the Mets have been frequently derided, they have been associated with unexpected strength and speed gains for certain prospects in the past—Amed Rosario is another example. Gimenez looks like the latest, and he's retained the preternatural feel for the game that got him on last year's list. He's closer to the majors than you might think, and he's got a chance to be an impact player instead of just a steady hand.

39. Alex Kirilloff, OF, Minnesota Twins

Every offseason, we have one prospect that generates nearly as much ranking discussion as every other prospect on the list combined. Kirilloff was that prospect this year. We had passionate arguments for him to be significantly higher *and* lower than this. If you aren't this high on him, you can point to timing mechanisms in his swing that might be exploited by upper-level pitchers and the historical profile issues of hit-first prospects who don't generate elite bat speed. His swing is leveraged without showing a lot of lift. If you think we have him way too low, you can point to a rare combination of offensive upside and polish. He's a first-round prep bat with an advanced approach and big raw power who demolished both levels of A-ball in his full-season debut, and there are evaluators that believe in a high hit tool outcome. Risk can run both positively and negatively, and this ranking splits the middle on a prospect none of us truly agree on, recognizing that there's probably some truth to both sides.

40. Peter Alonso, 1B, New York Mets

The top of this list is loaded up with players who just shouldn't be eligible for prospect lists anymore. Some of them are still here in part due to injuries, sure. It's also true that the majority of MLB teams have gotten insanely conscious of service time machinations, and that's resulted in more aggressively holding down prospects who are otherwise ready and have clear paths to playing time. More than anyone else on this list, Alonso is here as a victim of service time manipulation. There was little reason for the Mets to keep him in the minors for all of 2018. Adrian Gonzalez won the first base job out of camp and was cut two months later. Wilmer Flores took the bulk of the playing time from there through August, and was non-tendered this offseason. Jay Bruce took most of the September reps before being unceremoniously salary dumped on Seattle. There was plenty of time available for Alonso if the Mets wanted to, at any point, find out important things like "can he excel against right-on-right MLB sliders" and "will his defense be acceptable." Instead, they prioritized long-term financial considerations—ones that won't even matter much unless Alonso is a star. The ironic part is that new general manager Brodie Van Wagenen has been talking up Alonso's shot to win the Opening Day first base gig all winter, a possibility which would make the previous regime's service silliness all for naught.

41. Joey Bart, C, San Francisco Giants

We think the Mike Zunino comp most often made for Bart is supposed to be a pejorative and represent his downside. Except Zunino, even through long bouts of minimal contact and brutal OBPs, was worth 11.4 WARP to the Mariners during his four-plus seasons in Seattle. That's an undeniably good prospect outcome, even for a top-three pick, as Zunino and Bart both were. The first major factor in Zunino's hidden value also applies to Bart. The catching position is extremely weak now, and if you can play adequate defense and provide

any sort of offensive value, you're already as ahead of the curve as Zunino's swing often gets. The second factor—Zunino's framing excellence—may or may not apply to Bart, who has a good reputation but hasn't shown whether he can regularly steal strikes. If all goes well, the Giants may have decades straight of high-end catching production, because Bart should be ready at right about the same time Buster Posey is going to be shedding the tools of ignorance. But he's a catcher, so all might not go well.

42. Brendan McKay, 1B/LHP, Tampa Bay Rays

McKay is perhaps the single trickiest prospect to rank this year. As a left-handed pitching prospect, he's a better version of Logan Allen. That prospect would perhaps rank in the 60s somewhere. As a first base prospect, he's Evan White, a just-missed. If he can be both at times, well, we guess he's the 42nd-best prospect in baseball. We at Baseball Prospectus may not know the meaning of the universe, but definitely would settle for figuring out how McKay is going to get deployed by the boundlessly, uh, creative Rays. Adding to the problem is the dual development has slowed his timetable, leaving a polished college bat (and arm) in A-ball for a full season. We—and he—aren't going to learn much there. The universe is full of questions, of course, we just wish there were fewer open queries about McKay at the moment. He's the string theory of baseball prospects. A third starter/average first baseman outcome is still on the table though, which could arguably give him one of the most valuable skill sets in baseball. A wise man once wrote: "the chances of finding out what's really going on in the universe are so remote, the only thing to do is hang the sense of it and keep yourself occupied." McKay should keep us busy for a while.

43. Triston McKenzie, RHP, Cleveland Indians

McKenzie continues to be a confounding prospect. He was easy to love as a "projectable" 18-year-old, dreams of mid-90s velocity dancing in your head, but two years on he might just be "skinny" and the velocity still hasn't really jumped. It also hasn't mattered, as he dominated Double-A much like he did every other level. He spots the fastball well, and works in a potential plus-plus hook and developing change. A forearm injury—gulp—delayed the start of his 2018, but he's generally been extremely durable given his Christian-Bale-in-*The Machinist* frame. He doesn't really fit any of our leitmotifs for pitching prospects. This would all be a lot easier if he was left-handed, but for now we will more or less hold serve with a little bit of added risk after the whole "forearm injury" thing.

44. Yusniel Diaz, OF, Baltimore Orioles

Diaz certainly became more famous this past summer as the centerpiece prospect of the Manny Machado deadline deal, but the Cuban outfield prospect has long been on our radar. Any return was going to feel a bit underwhelming to Orioles fans after watching six-plus seasons of Manny freaking Machado, and Diaz in particular isn't going to wow you with big tools. The PR here is a little bit tougher. There is plenty to like though: He has a broad set of baseball skills, everything is solid across the board. He's fine in right field, and could stand in center for you. He's likely to be an above-average hitter with above-average pop. That's an above-average everyday regular, and a good prospect to add to a below-average system in a rebuilding organization. It's just not Manny Machado, so Diaz is always going to unfairly suffer by comparison.

45. Luis Robert, OF, Chicago White Sox

One of these years we'll solve this riddle. That year wasn't 2018. A string of injuries delayed the start of Robert's season, and then interrupted it a few more times. He ultimately only got into 50 regular season games, and reports and results were mixed throughout them, although he did impress in the Arizona Fall League. Of course, even that was interrupted when he pulled his hamstring. Robert retains an impressive upside profile, with potential to hit for average, hit for power, and run while playing a cromulent center field. Yet he's only shown what we think is his true talent in short bursts, and has yet to put it together at the same time. We're also becoming worried there's a risk of his injuries affecting his talent, more specifically his speed and range. It hasn't happened yet, but the leg injuries are starting to add up.

46. Josh James, RHP, Houston Astros

For the last few decades, we've talked about health as an abstract "skill" for the purpose of evaluation. At the core, though, these are human individuals who sometimes have very human health problems that aren't covered within our usual scope. We can't know about them. Sometimes the players themselves don't. Josh James was drafted in the 34th round in 2014 as a redshirt sophomore out of a junior college you've probably never heard of, after landing there as a D2 transfer infielder. He signed with the Astros for a measly $15,000. He spent the first few years of his pro career as a very minor prospect, a generic minor-league swingman with middling stuff and an organizational soldier future. What we didn't know was that James constantly felt tired and lethargic, and his roommates frequently complained about his loud and restless sleep. Eventually, he was diagnosed with sleep apnea and started using a CPAP machine. Finally rested and healthy, James greatly improved his mechanics and body, and his velocity subsequently jumped about eight ticks over the course of the 2018 season. He struck out 171 hitters in 114 1/3 innings in the minors while laying complete waste to tough Double-A and Triple-A environments. By the time he was called up to the majors on September 1st, he was sitting 97-99 and touching 101, accenting it with a plus changeup and flashing a devastating slider. He was so impressive in September that he forced the team's hand and cracked a ridiculously loaded Astros playoff staff. This is, bar none, the most impressive prospect breakout we can remember. We aren't remotely equipped to handle what any of this means going forward for a role or projection because

it's so far out of the norm, other than to tell you that James will likely be an incredible force for as long as he can stay healthy.

47. Leody Taveras, OF, Texas Rangers

Public metrics continue to move forward. We measure everything, project everything a bit better than we did a decade ago. One of the areas we still fail to accurately model is minor league performance. The talent level is too wide, the prospects too volatile, still developing. This is one of the reasons we can justify putting Leody Taveras in the top 50 after posting a .246/.312/.332 line in High-A. Here, "don't scout the statline" is more plea than counsel. Taveras was one of the youngest players in the Carolina League, spending the whole season as a 19-year-old, and he will still put on a show in batting practice that will assuage the doubts of even the most cynical of gray-haired scouts. There's also the matter of the plus center field tools across the board. Eventually Taveras will have to produce a .700 OPS at a full-season level, but we'll ignore the metrics for now and focus on the tools. The unstoppable engine of progress doesn't cover as much ground in the outfield as he does anyway.

48. Bubba Thompson, OF, Texas Rangers

Just one level and one spot on this list behind Taveras is his long-term competition. Thompson is an incredible athlete that chose a baseball career over offers to play quarterback at some FBS powers, including Tennessee, UCF and Ole Miss. We have been sold on the overall profile since he was drafted, but he showed up in Low-A with a much better feel for hitting than we thought. Mind you, better is not necessarily great—he struck out over a quarter of the time, and we have major concerns about his ability to recognize spin. Still, it's always nice to see an elite athlete show up to play full-season baseball and show a broader base of skills than you thought might be there. Defensively, Thompson may grow out of center field on his own, and Taveras may push him out one of these years even if he doesn't. There's five-tool upside here, with a wide range of outcomes below that.

49. Yordan Alvarez, 1B/OF, Houston Astros

We're slowly warming to first base prospects here at Baseball Prospectus. Alvarez can more credibly stand in the outfield than most of his cold corner brethren, but his is probably not the lower-half of a long term left fielder. Functionally it doesn't reaaaaally matter anyway, the point is he is going to have to hit a lot regardless. He sure hit a lot in 2018. He couldn't legally drink on Opening Day, and ended the year with a .900 OPS across the upper minors. He's close to major-league-ready—although like Tucker, the Astros may not have an obvious spot for him—with a plus hit/ plus power projection. That's about the bare minimum for this profile to make the 101, but despite occasional stiffness in the swing to get the ball in the air, Alvarez profiles as a safe, above-average corner guy. I didn't say we were in love with the profile or anything, did I?

50. Justus Sheffield, LHP, Seattle Mariners

A lefty prospect turned 22
He made the majors, and got traded for James Paxton
It's getting hurt again while lighting up the radar gun
It's finding your fastball command, two minutes too late
Isn't it ironic, don't you think?

It's like being ranked in the 50s here for three straight years
It's a conversion to relief for the playoff roster you didn't make
It's the opportunity in the Yankees rotation that you just didn't take
And who would have thought you'd end up on the Mariners?

51. Ryan Mountcastle, 3B, Baltimore Orioles

Defensive profiles are becoming more amorphous by the year. Radical positioning and aggressive strategies have let players stick at positions that we'd have never guessed they'd stick at, without doing the harm they'd have done in previous generations. Mountcastle is a big dude who doesn't throw well, which makes him a tough fit at the positions where he could be an offensive star even though his hands and instincts are fine. The Orioles tried shortstop for awhile, which went poorly. Third base has gone a little better, but it's always going to be a stretch. Outfield might be worth a shot at some point, but he has no professional experience out there and we're not sure he'll be rangy enough. If we're talking an ideal defensive home, a larger player with soft hands and good defensive feel is a natural for first base, but that starts to put an enormous strain on his offensive profile. Mountcastle turned in a quality Double-A campaign after missing the first month of the season with a broken hand, shaking off a bad cameo there at the end of 2017. He remains far too aggressive at the plate, which has placed an upper bound so far on big hit and power potential. If the light goes on at the plate and he can play reasonable defense somewhere, he'll be a star. He'll still be pretty good if one or the other happens. If neither occurs...well, he could be C.J. Cron.

52. Seuly Matias, OF, Kansas City Royals

Some tools are almost trivial to grade. Run a stopwatch on a home-to-first dig or a stolen base play at second and consult your chart—congratulations, you've graded run and catcher arm. Raw power is not quite that simple. There's some nuance, and you do have to keep your eyes open during batting practice, but Seuly Matias makes it an easy scout. This is 80-grade raw folks, and while his five o'clock show might not be quite as majestic as Joey Gallo or Miguel Sano's, it's damn impressive. The return engagement at game time isn't bad either, as Matias socked 31 home runs in 94 games at Low-A. Oh yeah, he was 19 all season. It's not just a one-tool profile either: Matias wields a cannon for an arm, which will cover for the deficiency of his range. He's a better *hitter* than you'd think. He isn't a grip it and rip it guy, but it's not easy power per se, and there's significant swing-and-miss

issues thus far. You're here for the power though, and Matias just needs to get enough of it into games to be a middle-of-the-order monster.

53. Mike Soroka, RHP, Atlanta Braves

The one constant in Soroka's prospect profile over the years has been his remarkable durability—and Atlanta's willingness to let him throw a lot of innings—as a prospect. So of course he missed most of 2018 with "right shoulder inflammation." Pitchers, man. Soroka was well on his way to a very good rookie campaign—and list ineligibility—before he hit the shelf. He has a full collection of solid-average-or-better offerings. The fastball velocity ticked up—he's a more consistent 92-94 now—while retaining its above-average movement. The slider looks like a real plus pitch as opposed to just flashing, and the change is above-average as well. All the elements are here for a top-five pitching prospect in baseball, but if he had been healthy, we wouldn't be ranking him. He wasn't healthy and shoulders make us very nervous. The profile was always "safe number three" and it's not safe anymore—although "number three" might now be light. So this year we have to rank Soroka's among the risky guys like...

54. Nate Pearson, RHP, Toronto Blue Jays

This is the best stuff in the minors. It's also about as risky a profile as you can get. Pearson can sit in the triple-digits and touched 104 MPH in a short outing in the Arizona Fall League's Fall Stars Game. As you might guess for a guy with that arm strength, he has a wicked low-90s slider, and a curveball and changeup also flash plus. Before the Fall League, his 2018 was lost to a spring oblique injury and a summer fractured forearm from a hard comebacker off his pitching arm. Injuries have been a recurrent drag here, and he was a known medical red flag in the 2017 Draft over a screw in his pitching elbow from high school. Pearson's mechanics have enough violence to be an issue on their own. What we ultimately have right now is an ace starter's arsenal and no idea about what role—if any—he can stay healthy in. The career path of another, similar Nate hints that this could take up to a decade to play out, although we suspect that Pearson would be happy to eventually get Eovaldi's recent $67.5 million contract.

55. Ke'Bryan Hayes, 3B, Pittsburgh Pirates

Last summer at Baseball Prospectus we published a roundtable discussion that considered—in part—if there is a way to figure out if certain prospects are more likely to develop additional power once they reach the majors. The idea was to see if it were possible to identify the next Chris Taylor or Ozzie Albies. If we had an actual methodology for that, we'd all have different jobs than "prospect blurb writer," but we did come up with a few useful criteria: (1) Good contact ability, (2) plus bat speed, (3) an advanced approach, (4) above-average raw power. Despite hitting just 15 home runs across three pro seasons, Ke'Bryan Hayes checks all four boxes. (1) He hit .290 in Double-A and rarely struck out, making consistent, high-quality line-drive contact. (2) A lot of those hits were absolute laser beam doubles over the third baseman's head, so yeah, he can cover velocity. (3) He'll spit on spin away, work walks, foul off tougher stuff; he's pesky. (4) Go dig up batting practice video of Hayes from the Futures Game where he put pitch after pitch ten or twenty rows back in the left field bleachers, it's in there. But even if the power doesn't come, he's a plus defender at the hot corner that will give you the good Cesar Hernandez seasons at the plate. That's a nice everyday player. But we think there might be more in the bat. Although I suppose if we *really* thought that he'd be 40 spots higher. How's that for a hedge?

56. Griffin Canning, RHP, Los Angeles Angels

You might be aware that the Angels spent years with a terrible, awful, no good farm system. A major part of the turnaround was betting on big upside with injury concerns on their first two picks in 2017. Jo Adell had a dead arm before the draft, and that pick has turned out gangbusters. The even riskier selection was Canning—an early-to-mid first-round talent who fell due to bad medicals and huge college pitch counts—in the second round. He roared back to his talent level with a vengeance in 2018, with a velocity spike under lighter usage while still making 25 starts and reaching Triple-A in his pro debut. Durability and health concerns may yet limit him to a mid-rotation outcome, but he does have better stuff than the usual mid-rotation starting profile. Popping Canning might pay off pretty big, too.

57. Adonis Medina, RHP, Philadelphia Phillies

Oh yeah, we are deep in the mid-rotation starter woods now. Medina's long been an exemplary example of the "number three starter or late-inning reliever" projection. His 2018 was almost a carbon copy of his 2017. He was at High-A instead of Low-A, so that's good. The slider is improving and closer to its plus projection, that's also good. He lacks ideal height, ideal command, and an ideal changeup. That's good for our overarching profile purposes, though less good for Medina's prospect status. Double-A is often where these type of arms separate out more clearly into the mid-rotation starter and late-inning reliever buckets, so Medina's 2019 Eastern League campaign will be one to watch. But *note bene*, don't pay too much attention to the top line stats; Reading remains one of the worst parks in the minors to pitch.

58. Kyle Wright, RHP, Atlanta Braves

Wright made his MLB debut in a relief cameo at the end of his first full pro season, and he's still down a dozen-plus spots from where he ranked after the draft. He remains a polished, healthy, advanced college arm, and a pretty good bet to be headed for the middle of a rotation. To the extent that there is an issue, the issue is that almost everything in the profile is a hair lighter than you hoped for out of the draft, and the slight nitpicks do add up come rankings season. The command and control are fine, but a little worse than we hoped for. The velocity is fine, but a little worse than we hoped for. The breaking balls are fine, but a little worse than we hoped for. The changeup consistency is more than adequate for a fourth offering, but it's a little worse than we hoped for. As the sign on *The Good Place* reads, everything is fine. It's just not *great*.

59. Will Smith, C/IF, Los Angeles Dodgers

The "catcher who can play other positions" is in vogue right now as benches get shorter and positioning gets closer to radar precision. Smith has improved enough behind the plate that you could just play him there everyday and hope that his 2018 power spike turns him into a plus backstop. But the Dodgers love their positional fluidity—see Max Muncy, second baseman—and Smith has experience at second and third as well (Smith, like so many of the dudes on the 101, was a shortstop in high school). The value of this defensive flexibility doesn't always show up in raw WARP totals—although it will if it gets Smith an extra 20-30 starts a year—but as baseball changes so must our prospect lists. Though if anything this ranking might be a bit low for a more traditional starting catcher with 20-home-run pop.

60. Bryse Wilson, RHP, Atlanta Braves

Atlanta has had a lot of volatility in their pitching prospect stock. Wilson is one of the big risers, jumping from A-ball to a major-league debut at just 20, beating many of his previously more touted (and older) org mates to The Show. He's not all that different from Soroka and Wright; if he seems like a revelation while they seem like a disappointment, that's mostly an artifact of draft positions and old rankings. Wilson is extremely advanced as prep pitchers of his age and experience level go, without the typical level of concern over things like command, third pitch consistency, and ability to handle a full workload. There's still the usual "he's a pitcher" concerns, of course, and he doesn't have the extreme upside that most of his age cohort ranked in this general area possesses. Having a bunch of high-probability third starter types in your system is a good way to develop a rotation, especially since there's always a shot one of these arms moves forward unexpectedly too.

61. Khalil Lee, OF, Kansas City Royals

Lee was a three-true-outcomes hitter in Low-A in 2017, a bit like Seuly Matias but with "only" plus raw power. He cut his K-rate in 2018 across two levels while maintaining his strong approach, but sacrificed a chunk of game power in the process. This isn't uncommon for hitting prospects trying to figure out the balance between contact and lift, hit and pop. It's easy to suggest that Lee just marry the two approaches, and much harder to execute as the pitching gets better. His ultimate defensive home is unknown as well. He has the athletic tools for center field, but his instincts and routes are still a bit raw. He's the most nebulous prospect on the 101, and that includes the short-season ones. Lee continues to look the part of a major league outfielder, but what exact role we are casting for is still an unknown unknown.

62. Cristian Pache, OF, Atlanta Braves

Pache might be the best defensive center fielder in the minors. That's /checks notes...yes, extremely valuable. He's a plus-plus runner with a plus-plus arm and has good enough instincts on the grass to project as a plus-plus glove. That's...six pluses! That's a lot! The superlatives don't flow quite as easily during his at-bats though. Pache has an aggressive approach and takes his hacks like a man who thinks he has two additional grades of raw power than he actually does. The swing can get long, and he can get out of balance in the box. If Pache can tone all this down a bit and manage even an average hit tool, the complementary skills here are more than enough to make him a plus regular, perhaps even an occasional All-Star, but we probably wrote that opening line about Manuel Margot a few years ago too.

63. Jarred Kelenic, OF, Seattle Mariners

There was some significant prospect-industrial complex hype around Kelenic when he was traded by the Mets. This list was written by two ancestral diehard Mets fans, so we certainly get the urge to do a LOLMETS. Kelenic is a very good prospect, and in a year or two might be the sort of prospect the Mets will sorely wish they still had. But he's not there yet, and a stroll down memory lane will reveal more highly drafted prep outfielders who didn't work out than you'd think, many of them of broadly similar skills and post-draft sheen as Kelenic. As for this one right here, right now, he projects to have a broad base of offensive and defensive value, but may lack a carrying tool. If there is a carrying ability, it'll probably be that he hits for a higher average generally reaches first more than we'd expect right now. Of course, the downside risk is largely the same variance in the other direction, and his swing has some length and leverage to it. Projecting the future of teenage bats is nearly as tough in baseball as projecting teenagers is in real life. (Also, Edwin Diaz is a lot better than you may realize.)

64. Jonathan Loaisiga, RHP, New York Yankees

That happened fast. Loaisiga's second full-season pitcher appearance in his minor league career—he had one in Low-A in June 2016 before undergoing Tommy John surgery—was on April 7th, 2018 for High-A Tampa. Just ten starts later, on June 15th, he made his MLB debut by firing five shutout innings in Yankee Stadium. It was a hell of a long road before 2018, though. Originally signed by the Giants in 2012, Loaisiga never made it out of the complex levels as he battled shoulder issues, and was released in May 2015. He went home to Nicaragua, and pitched in winter ball and for the national team early in 2016, where he was discovered by Yankees scout Ricardo Finol shortly before departing to play the summer in Italy. Upon recovering from the torn UCL, he was brilliant in the Gulf Coast and New York-Penn Leagues late in 2017, brilliant enough in fact that we wrote him up on a loaded team list after the season and the Yankees had to add him to the 40-man despite their perpetual Rule 5 crunch. So it really wasn't out of nowhere, just way faster than we

thought. He had more shoulder problems later on in the summer, his command is inconsistent, and he's small of stature, all of which may be tipping a bullpen future. If he can somehow stay in the rotation, it'd be premium upside, with a fastball and breaking ball that both flash plus-plus and an average changeup that might get a notch higher.

65. Drew Waters, OF, Atlanta Braves

As part of the MLB investigation into the Braves illegal bonus manipulations under John Coppolella, Atlanta was docked a third-round pick for offering Waters "extra benefits" as part of his signing bonus. Waters—himself a second round pick—remained a Brave, likely because MLB didn't want the precedent of that high a draftee being made a unrestricted free agent. All the IFA players that were granted free agency were still subject to international bonus pool restrictions. Despite losing an entire IFA class, the Braves remain one of the healthiest farm systems in baseball, mostly because some of the players from their suspect machinations remain in the system, and many have turned into top prospects (or the 2018 Rookie of the Year). We don't know if any lessons have been learned by anyone involved. Anyway, Waters had a breakout season in Low-A, is a potential five-tool center fielder, and instead gets a prospect blurb that is about everything but that.

66. Estevan Florial, OF, New York Yankees

One of our favorite cliches around these parts is "a year is a lifetime for a prospect." Well, Florial's 2018 was the dril tweet: "awfully bold of you to fly the Good Year blimp on a year that has been extremely bad thus far." The culprit here was mostly injury: Florial had to have hamate surgery during the season, and that's one of the worst injuries in terms of lingering effects on offensive performance, especially power. The tools are loud enough, and the ceiling remains high enough, that we are mostly willing to give Florial a pass for his bad 2018, but the clock is ticking now and 2019 will be a very important year for the Haitian-Dominican outfielder.

67. MJ Melendez, C, Kansas City Royals

You have to evaluate each prospect on their own individual merits, but the world doesn't exist entirely in a vacuum either. Melendez was taken with the 52nd pick in the 2017 Draft out of a Miami prep school. The last prep catcher to be drafted in the early rounds to have a significant MLB career was Wil Myers in 2009. Unless you hold Devin Mesoraco's All-Star year in great esteem, the last one to be both a good player and stick as a starting catcher for any length of time was Brian McCann way back in 2002. No matter which way you count, dozens and dozens of high school catchers have been taken since then, we've ranked many of them in this space, and essentially none of them have turned into good MLB backstops as yet. Dating back decades, sabermetric research has consistently shown high school catchers as a group to be the absolute worst investments in the Rule 4 Draft. And yet there's still a bunch of prep catchers drafted in the first few rounds every year, and here we are again, telling you that this time it will be different and MJ Melendez is going to be the one to break the streak. We have to write what we see, and we see a strong two-way catching prospect. But if you're reading this book, we presume that you are interested in the metagame of baseball, and the history of this class of prospect is bad.

68. Jahmai Jones, 2B, Los Angeles Angels

This is Jones' third straight year on the 101, but first entry as a second baseman. It's a bit of a weird positional switch, as usually players with his physical tools go from the dirt to the grass, rather than vice versa. He's developing fine at the keystone, but it will take some time, and he did project as at least an average defensive center fielder. The continued existence of Mike Trout in Angels Stadium might be influencing things here, as could be the emergence of Jo Adell, but it's added some weird developmental risks into the profile that weren't there before. Jones still has an athletic swing and a quick bat, married with an advanced approach he showed going back to the draft year reports. And he still projects for above-average hit and average power, but the overall offensive performance did suffer a bit in 2018. How much of that is his first taste of Double-A and how much might be his main focus being on learning a new position is an open question. For our part, we held Jones more or less steady with his 2018 ranking, but hopefully more will become clear this year.

69. Jazz Chisholm, SS, Arizona Diamondbacks

Thelonious Monk once said that "the piano ain't got no wrong notes." There weren't any wrong notes in 2018 for Jazz Chisholm either. His glovework was never in doubt; he is a potential plus-or-better shortstop who handles tough chances in the field as adroitly as Coltrane maneuvering through the opening chord changes of "Giant Steps." Jazz's power at the plate this year was unexpected, a John Zorn heavy metal EP, but it's married with an approach that's a bit more Charlie Mingus, dissonant and only rarely restrained. If his chops hold up at higher levels, he could end up a true classic of the toolsy shortstop genre, but many a potential jazz cat ends up just another birdbrain once they suit up in Double-A. If that does happen at least we won't have to flog these references again for the 2020 Annual. We aren't exactly the baddest hipsters in the barrelhouse, after all.

70. Touki Toussaint, RHP, Atlanta Braves

Baseball is rapidly becoming a de facto salary cap sport, even if it isn't a de jure one quite yet. In any capped sport with guaranteed contracts, you're going to get aggressive salary dumping. To that end, teams have created surplus value calculations to place monetary values on prospects. For over a decade, the public analytics community has followed suit, with the most recent extensive research published late last year by Craig Edwards at FanGraphs. It's a necessity if you're going to make "salary cap trades" instead of "baseball trades," and yet at the same time it is radically dehumanizing. On his 19th birthday, Toussaint was functionally sold by the Diamondbacks to clear about $10 million left on Bronson Arroyo's contact. It was the harbinger of things to come, the beginning of a trend that is taking clearer shape four years later. There was no baseball rationalization for this move at the time, only a financial one, and it looks even worse in retrospect with Toussaint's raw potential now close to actualizing as a good pitcher. But unlike most similar moves, we can't say the money went to debt service, investors, or ownership pockets, because Arizona did sign Zack Greinke the next offseason.

71. Victor Victor Mesa, OF, Miami Marlins

The world is changing. Not that many years ago, the story of the Mesa brothers coming stateside would've been much uglier. It'd have involved a harrowing journey involving human trafficking elements, and perhaps even foreign warlords. It'd have been scandalous for father Victor, who is Cuban baseball royalty and would've been forced to pick between blood and country. These days, they just left, seemingly with tacit approval, to seek American contracts (shortly after the Mesas signed, MLB, the MLBPA and the Cuban Baseball Federation announced a formalized posting system similar to Japan and Korea, although it faces uncertain political prospects in the States) and Victor Sr. plans to split his time between Miami and Cuba. Like Luis Robert last year, Victor Victor hasn't played baseball in awhile, and we'll get a much better idea what kind of prospect he is when he gets in competitive game situations this spring. Industry chatter has frequently compared Victor Victor to Cubs outfielder Albert Almora both offensively and defensively, if you want a hint of the shape of things to come.

72. Adrian Morejon, LHP, San Diego Padres

Morejon was our "third starter poetry entry" last year, and the second verse isn't all that dissimilar from the first. He had a successful season pitching in the tough climes of the Cal League as a teenager, although he was limited to around 70 innings by a hip injury. His fastball bumps 98 now, and sits comfortably in the plus velocity range. He has two potential above-average secondaries in his curve and change, with the breaker ahead of the cambio and both ahead of his command. He's an undersized lefty and lacks projection, but the present arsenal is good enough, that he doesn't have to improve all that much in his early 20s to be a mid-rotation starter.

73. Sandy Alcantara, RHP, Miami Marlins

Unlike most of the other prospects the Marlins acquired in their latest firesale, at least Alcantara is holding steady. Alcantara still throws really hard and still has a three-pitch profile. He's also still not really striking that many batters out in the high-minors, he's still a work-in-progress on command, and still an injury risk in frame and history. If you guessed that he might end up in the bullpen eventually, congratulations for having already read the other dozen reports above with this same broad stroke profile, though he's likely to get more shots than most to start because of lack of organizational depth. He'll certainly face little in the way of competition for space in Miami's rotation over the short term, and he showed flashes of readiness in September.

74. Luis Patino, RHP, San Diego Padres

We have internal conversations a lot about what to do with pitching prospects that we just don't yet know enough about to put into a role box. We know enough about Patino to strongly suspect that he's one of the 101 best prospects in baseball. He throws pretty hard. The command, deception, and changeup are all unusually advanced for a teenager. He will likely end up with three or four usable pitches. These are all building blocks for a future good rotation piece. We also know enough to know that the delta on his set of outcomes is enormous, making this an impossible ordinal ranking. He's on the smallish side. The Padres kept the reins firmly attached in 2018, only letting him make 17 starts at Low-A and never allowing him to throw more than 84 pitches. We have nothing to go on for his durability either way, just vague concerns and general industry trends. Over the next year or two, this will surely play out one way or another, and we'll probably have several chances to revisit this topic in future books.

75. Hunter Greene, RHP, Cincinnati Reds

Jeffrey and Jarrett were in a Lyft with some friends in Cambridge, MA early last August, heading to our Saberseminar presentation, when we heard that Hunter Greene's MRI came back with a UCL sprain in his elbow. We both talked about Tommy John surgery as a fait accompli, since it so often is from there, and mentally filed him as returning in 2020. A few months later we started researching Reds prospect reports and we found out that Greene had yet to have surgery and that his rehabilitation was going well. In late-October, Greene himself reported on Twitter that he'd been given a clean bill of health. We're going to maintain a bit of skepticism until he throws in some games, but it's a special arm talent, if a bit raw around the edges.

76. Dane Dunning, RHP, Chicago White Sox

A potential third starter, frame sturdy and strong
The fastball low-90s, moves wayward and steep
Oh, I write these same blurbs through all winter long

No ballad composed about his breakers, nor song
Average for both, hey the arsenal's deep
A potential third starter, frame sturdy and strong

He commands the curve well, I say to the throng
The slider may cut, sometimes it will sweep
Oh, I write these same blurbs through all winter long

The change flashes plus, you knew all along
His face on the mound won't make batters weep
A potential third starter, frame sturdy and strong

We're almost to the end, the meter's all wrong
The audience bored on the verge of deep sleep
Oh, I write these same blurbs through all winter long

Can he mix his stuff well and limit the dong?
Could one of the breakers perhaps take a leap?
A potential third starter, frame sturdy and strong
Oh, I write these same blurbs through all winter long

77. A.J. Puk, LHP, Oakland Athletics

The most dangerous time of year for a pitching is ramping up before the season. Every year, we get a handful of high-profile UCL tears as everyone stretches their arm out. Puk was one of the 2018 Cactus League casualties. It was especially unfortunate because he was seemingly beginning the leap early in spring, and likely would've been in the majors no later than midseason. This wasn't a great season developmentally for Puk to miss, and the command and repeatability issues that we were already concerned about can be exacerbated during Tommy John recovery. The hope is that he'll be back sometime around when spring turns to summer, and if all goes well he might be a MLB candidate again later in the season.

78. Julio Pablo Martinez, OF, Texas Rangers

The Rangers have always had a fondness for toolsy Cuban outfielders. Well, any toolsy outfielder really. Or toolsy shortstop for that matter. Martinez is runner up to Victor Victor for this year's Luis Robert Memorial "We have no real idea what to do with this guy." We do have a bit more stateside info at least. After signing for $2.8 million, Martinez spent a bit of time in the Northwest League and Arizona Fall League where he was fine, but maybe a bit underwhelming for a 22-year-old with four years under his belt in Serie Nacional. The seven-figure tools were all accounted for, though. Martinez is a good bet to be an above-average defender in center and gets more pop than you'd expect out of his five-foot-nine frame. We'll have a lot more info on him after a proper full-season debut in 2019. For now, this is a bit of a dart throw.

79. Lucius Fox, SS, Tampa Bay Rays

More of a field man than a bat man, but with the fall of Matt Harvey, he's Gotham's best chance for a new savior. Fox actually has his own interesting backstory, as he attended three years of high school in South Florida before moving back to his family home in the Bahamas. That got him reclassified from the Rule 4 Draft to the international signing pool, and he cashed in as a $6 million bonus baby with the Giants in 2015. He was moved along to Tampa Bay in a 2016 deadline package for mercurial lefty Matt Moore, the top prospect on this list seven years ago. Puns aside, Fox is a plus-plus runner and a silky smooth defender, and there's some feel for hitting present too. He has limited gap power, but it's a very playable athleticism and defense profile even if the bat never begins to shine.

80. J.B. Bukauskas, RHP, Houston Astros

A nice thing about the Arizona Fall League is the availability of Statcast data, and before that PITCHf/x data. Because of that data and our partner site Brooks Baseball, I can give you an accurate picture of what JBB was throwing in October, without the variability of inconsistent radar guns or spotty private information. He was sitting 95-96 with the fastball and touching 98, leaning on one of the minors' best sliders as his out pitch, and flashing a hard change at 90-91. This is a bit of a velocity bump from what he'd shown previously, and most importantly it all confirms that he's healthy (and then some) after a back injury from a car accident cost him a large chunk of the regular season. We don't put much stock in AFL *performance*, but when there's a profile jump that seems sustainable, that does matter. And that AFL jump—and our ability to confirm it with reasonably reliable data—got Bukauskas onto the final draft of this list.

81. Luis Garcia, SS/3B, Washington Nationals

He's likely to soon be the best of baseball's many, many Luis Garcias—there are at least five currently active in the American minors, including fellow top infield prospect Luis Garcia of the Phillies, plus major-league reliever Luis Garcia, who was traded from the Phillies to the Angels this past offseason, and several more playing internationally. This particular Luis Garcia was born in 2000 (don't you feel old right now?) and has already hit at both full-season levels of A-ball. He also has a better chance to stick at short than you'd expect for a guy who was already picking up other positions as a 17-year-old. The Nationals sometimes move prospects very aggressively, and Garcia is already moving quickly. He has a shot to be in the majors before he turns 20 in May 2020.

82. Travis Swaggerty, OF, Pittsburgh Pirates

We're ranking ten 2018 draft picks on the 101 this time around. That's low even for us, who tend to be a bit more conservative with evaluating recent draftees. There are a few reasons for that: It was a slightly down draft class. A couple high first-round picks didn't sign. A few high first-round arms have injury concerns. A few more picks ended up between 102 and 110. But it's worth noting that as more teams ~~tank~~ move their contention window a few years down the road, that the recent successful rebuilds had less to do with high draft picks than you'd think. In baseball you are never getting the immediate impact of a franchise quarterback or a LeBron James anyway. The Pirates were still nominally competing in 2017 when they underperformed enough to have the tenth overall pick in 2018. Swaggerty is a fine prospect, a college center fielder with average-to-above tools across the board and a good approach at the plate. He's unlikely to be a franchise-altering piece, nor is their 18th overall pick next year. You need good regulars to compete, but too many

teams are trading their present ones on for the hope of cheaper ones somewhere down the line in the vast medium term.

83. Anderson Tejeda, SS, Texas Rangers

He's back! Two years ago, we made an aggressive call on Tejeda, including him on the bottom of the 101 based on big reports from various complex and short-season levels. He had some typical full-season adjustment issues in 2017, most obviously an overly aggressive plate approach. But he started popping again for us in 2018, improving his pitch recognition and tapping into significant game power. We still aren't giving up the ghost on the hit tool, either; it's a sweet swing with a lot of bat speed. He's not a stone cold lock to stick at shortstop, but he has a good shot, and even if he moves off it would probably be to another premium position. Can you tell we like him a lot?

84. Logan Allen, LHP, San Diego Padres

Earlier we referred to Brendan McKay as "better Logan Allen," but actual Logan Allen is a very good prospect in an organization stuffed to the gills with very good prospects. His 2018 statistical dominance does overstate the stuff a bit. The fastball is low-90s with command to both sides and the ol' lefty funk and deception. The slider is cutterish, but an effective bat misser. There's a potentially average change and curve as well. He's left-handed. He's already in Triple-A. He's another third-starter prospect. The Padres have collected so many of these that the law of averages—or if you prefer, percentile projections—suggests that one of them will over-perform our spate of 6/5 grades. The stuff suggests it's less likely to be Allen, but perhaps…

85. Michel Baez, RHP, San Diego Padres

We have more info about Baez than we had last year for good and for ill. He threw 105 innings, proving that he can get stretched out—at least by prospect arm standards—and keep the big fastball/change combo. The slider is slowly improving and should give him a needed gloveside option against righties. He did struggle in his first taste of Double-A however, and continues to have issues keeping all six-foot-eight of his frame on line to the plate. He's far more likely to be a reliever than Allen, but also more likely to have serious impact if he sticks in the rotation. He gets the same 6/5 grade despite a much larger delta/risk. Sometimes more info doesn't help as much as we'd like.

86. Nico Hoerner, SS, Chicago Cubs

Here's the other player who vaulted into the list from shining reports in the Arizona Fall League. For many years now, we've viewed college hitting prospects from Stanford with early suspicion because of the "Stanford swing." In short, Stanford tended to teach their hitters, no matter what their offensive skills, to use a flat, pokey swing geared for opposite-field contact. This was a reasonable strategy for college baseball with metal/composite bats, lousy fielders, and a lot of turf fields. If you've paid any attention to the recent "launch angle revolution" in pro ball, you already know that this is a terrible idea for certain classes of professional hitters, who often maximize by gaining greater lift to their swing to optimize their launch angle. Legion have been the talented Stanford hitters who got to the minors and couldn't make the adjustment to wood bats. That might be changing with a new coaching staff, and Hoerner looks like he's not going to fall into that bucket, anyway. He takes a healthy rip and has a history of hitting well with wood bats, including on the Cape in the summer of 2017. We'll be hearing terrible Hoerner/horny puns in Wrigleyville sooner than you may think.

87. Heliot Ramos, OF, San Francisco Giants

We covered the "injury lost season" with Florial above. His toolsy compadre in the Bay Area—well, technically the Augusta area—had the "performance lost season." That can be more troubling, or at least less explicable, but full-season ball was always going to be a slightly aggressive assignment for Ramos. The power/speed combo still flashed, but he was too often undone by an ultra-aggressive approach at the plate. The South Atlantic League is likely the first place he saw even fringy breaking balls. The results weren't great, but it's hardly a disaster considering he spent the whole season as an 18-year-old. He will likely get another shot at Low-A in 2019, and hopefully some adjustments will unlock the plus potential in the bat. We are always going to be the last ones to give up on toolsy center fielders regardless.

88. Shane Baz, RHP, Tampa Bay Rays

The Rays have almost as many very good prospects as San Diego, but it sure didn't hurt that they added Baz late in the year as the player to be named later in the Chris Archer deal. Often these PTBNL end up as straight cash, homie. Sometimes it's even a player being traded for himself. The Rays instead got a high upside arm, albeit one that spent 2018 in the Appalachian League. Baz offers mid-90s heat, a potential plus slider, and a developing changeup, the usual prep arm package one year out from being a first round pick. He is a riskier version of the same third-starter prospect we've pontificated about over the last 50 spots or so. But we are almost to the last of them now. As Leonard Cohen sang: *"And other forms of boredom advertised as poetry / I know you need your sleep now / I know your life's been hard / But many men are falling / Where you promised to stand guard."*

89. Danny Jansen, C, Toronto Blue Jays

"Catchers are weird" is one of our favorite mantras here at Baseball Prospectus. Two offseasons ago, Jansen got prescription glasses. Suddenly able to see, he immediately jumped from a lightly-regarded potential backup catcher to one of the better catching prospects in the game. He consolidated the 2017 breakout in 2018, performing well in Triple-A before claiming the bulk of the catching time in the majors over the last six weeks in the season. He has a solid but unspectacular defensive reputation, very likely good enough to remain at catcher, which is half the battle. The other half is framing, and we'll have to see where he lands in the majors on that. The bar is so low at catcher now that he has potential to put up big value just by being average to above-average in all phases, and unless things get notably weird again, he should do that starting in 2019.

90. Jon Duplantier, RHP, Arizona Diamondbacks

The injury bug that Duplantier avoided in 2017 struck in 2018, with a bout of biceps tendinitis costing him much of the summer. He was very good when he pitched, and has the usual bunch of red flags for the maybe mid-rotation/maybe bullpen profile that dots the second half of this list and many of the next few dozen that miss: a checkered injury history, effort in the delivery, inconsistent command, and further development needed on the third pitch. He also has one fairly unique one: he's a pitcher from Rice. "Rice pitcher" has an even worse track record than "high school catcher" or "Stanford hitter," owing to chronic overuse under the coach that retired shortly after Duplantier entered pro ball. The inflection point for the third starter-or-short reliever game is getting close here.

91. Oneil Cruz, SS, Pittsburgh Pirates

Yes, seriously, shortstop. Pittsburgh slid one of baseball's largest humans over to shortstop after picking him up from the Dodgers in the Tony Watson trade. It is quite the strange visual to see a man of Cruz's giant frame—he's been listed at 6'6", 175 pounds since he signed, but is likely a few inches taller and at least a few dozen pounds heavier now—in the middle infield. Yet he's currently adequate there, even if he's likely going to have to find another defensive home down the road if he fills out as he might. He has monster raw power and an arm to match it, and a more advanced feel for hitting and approach than you might expect from a giant with these tools. The downside of all these tools and physicality is that swing-and-miss could be a real problem due to a naturally long swing. There's huge upside here, in a lot of different forms.

92. DL Hall, LHP, Baltimore Orioles

What a blessing it is for a prospect writer under deadline crunch to get write about an Orioles pitching prospect named "DL." We won't be the first nor last to make that wisecrack, and the 19-year-old southpaw was healthy throughout 2018, although his workload was managed quite conservatively in his full-season debut. You can't quibble with his results, as he struck out better than a batter per inning on the strength of his mid-90s fastball, heavy with occasional cut, and potential plus power curve. There's a slider and a change too, although both lag behind along with his control and command. The delivery needs to be smoothed out in places, and we need to see him perform like this across longer outings, but Hall could be a pretty good third starter or late inning reliever in a few years. He's gotten comps to Scott Kazmir, which is both pretty good company and also extremely unlikely to help with all those "DL" jokes.

93. Luis Oviedo, RHP, Cleveland Indians

Amongst our research into the masses of mid-rotation starters we occasionally stumble on a nice surprise. Signed out of Venezuela for $375,000 in 2015, Oviedo dominated the Penn League this year as a 19-year-old. It's big stuff out of a still-projectable six-foot-four frame. His fastball already scrapes the upper-90s, and he flashes a plus-or-better breaking ball. The cambio and command need work, so okay, he's not *all* that different from the third starter reports that dot the second half of this list. But Oviedo is at least a new name, and while we aren't quite ready to go higher than 6/5 on him, there are scouts out there who are.

94. Brandon Marsh, OF, Los Angeles Angels

As we hinted at earlier, the Angels spent several years as one of the worst systems in baseball, basically from the moment Mike Trout lost prospect eligibility. The system is on the rise again, and Marsh is the fourth of five Top 101 names. He's a potential plus hit/plus power outfielder who is passable in center for now, but likely ends up in right field long term, where his plus arm will be an asset. The Angels have bet on athletes in recent years in the draft, and Marsh is another hit for a system almost ready to supplement the best player in baseball, since it's become pretty clear in recent years he can't do it all on his own.

95. Sean Murphy, C, Oakland Athletics

Murphy is a prototypical good catching prospect. We are in the range of the list now where things get very fuzzy. The difference between Murphy and the 125th best prospect in baseball—oh, let's say Freudis Nova—just isn't that significant. The difference between him and the next best catching prospect, Miguel Amaya, even less so. So why Murphy? Well, he does everything pretty well. Despite a stiff swing he makes enough quality contact to get most of his plus raw into games. He's a solid defensive catcher with a big arm and good receiving skills. Everything here grades out as average or better—well, except speed—which makes him an above-average catcher. And even if he falls short in one tool or another, the bar for catchers is such that he could still be an average backstop. There's only 30 everyday jobs, and Murphy is about ready to grab hold of one of them.

96. Vidal Brujan, 2B, Tampa Bay Rays

Last year, we had Brujan as one to watch after his short-season campaign in Hudson Valley. While the profile hasn't radically changed, the full-season performance this year will certainly make you stand up and take notice. His approach and potential plus hit tool didn't find any speed bumps at either A-ball level. There's big bat speed here, if not a ton of power projection, since Brujan likes to swing from the heels and can get off-balance. He's a plus-plus runner and

passable, if still a bit raw, at the keystone. The hit tool and speed will have to carry the profile and Double-A will be a good test of the bat, but by 2020 Rays fans could be humming "mmm, must be the season of the witch."

97. Calvin Mitchell, OF, Pittsburgh Pirates

We've been making a concerted effort to flag more of the "hit first, ask questions later" prospects for our readers when we really like their offensive potential. Like with pitchers, there's a natural inclination to recoil a bit from this class of prospects. There's inherent added risk that we're overestimating the hitting ability, and there's inherent profile risk that becomes obvious when you consider how teams value decent regulars here. Every year, established league-average hitters without significant defensive utility are freely available as budget free agent options. Sometimes you can pick them up for just the waiver price, or in trade for a prospect you don't really care about. For all the C.J. Cron jokes we make, he was a first-round pick and pretty decent prospect that turned into a solid hitter, usually around league-average or a little bit above. His 2018 campaign was perhaps his best yet. It was book-ended by being salary dumped before the season and claimed off waivers after it. The industry just doesn't value these guys unless they *hit*. So when we rank a guy like Mitchell, who might be a corner outfielder and might be a first baseman, it's because we *really* like the bat. Mitchell showed well enough as a 19-year-old in the Sally that we think he has a shot at the elusive 6 hit/6 power projection that is the general baseline for his archetype. Now he just has to get there.

98. Garrett Hampson, 2B/SS, Colorado Rockies

Ben Franklin helpfully covered death and taxes, but there are three other certainties in life: Jose Mourinho's third season in charge will always be a disaster, a Murakami protagonist will always encounter a mysterious cat, and Baseball Prospectus will always rank a bunch of shortstops on the 101. Hampson is the final one on this year's list, and he's a bit of an outlier for us. While we do enjoy the dirty uniform types that max out their talent, the scout's favorites, we tend to write them as 45s. We prefer the Anderson Tejedas and Lucius Foxes. But Hampson just wins you over. He's not without tools. He's a plus-plus runner who weaponizes his speed with aggressive base running that inevitably, well, gets his uniform dirty. He gets everything out of his defensive game, and while he's a better fit at second, he's average at short and showed better there in 2018 than the more-heralded Brendan Rodgers. He's a pesky hitter that fouls off pitches, works walks, and makes quality contact despite a swing with a lot of moving parts. There's not much power, although he will absolutely take an extra base on any ball in the gap if he can. He's a prototypical dirt dog, and maybe he's only a 50, but that's good enough for us.

99. Jordyn Adams, OF, Los Angeles Angels

Adams was a highly-recruited wideout, set to head to North Carolina where his father is also a coach, before the Angels went well over 17th-pick slot to get him to play baseball exclusively. Early specialization in baseball has made this kind of two-sport prospect more of a *rara avis* lately, but we see it as a positive marker for baseball development. Premium athleticism can play in more facets of the game than just straight-line speed on the bases or in the outfield—though Adams certainly doesn't lack for either. There's body control and the ability to repeat. Does that portend a more consistent swing and more offensive projection? The sample size is never going to be large here, but anecdotally the guys with "stiff" swings don't tend to look like Adams. His first pro summer went fine, and he will head to full-season ball next year. Although with all apologies to the Iowa tourism board, Burlington isn't exactly the Triangle in terms of things to do. There is baseball to be played though.

100. Kristian Robinson, OF, Arizona Diamondbacks

There are no players from the Bahamas currently in the majors. The best player the chain of islands has ever produced was Andre Rodgers, an eleven-year journeyman shortstop who played in the 1950s and 1960s. Both of those are about to change. Robinson is the third Bahamian prospect on this list, along with Jazz Chisholm and Lucius Fox. An additional crop of high-upside players is percolating in the lowest levels of the minors, and surely some of them will be making our lists over the coming years. Six-figure bonuses are now commonplace, and there have been a handful of millionaire signees too. Robinson is one of them, a $2.5 million signee from the 2017 international class. He picked up buzz out of the complex circuit long before ever making his debut in game action, and wowed with explosive athleticism and raw hitting ability. He's a long, long way from the majors, but the potential here is unlimited.

101. Kyler Murray, OF, Oakland Athletics

Murray became the second Heisman Trophy winner currently in organized baseball when he won college football's highest honor in December. Unlike Mets outfielder Tim Tebow, Murray did it the old-fashioned way, playing both sports at the same time. His draft deal with Oakland contained a contractual exception allowing him to play his redshirt junior season at Oklahoma. That type of deal used to be more commonplace, but has fallen out of favor as sports have become more compartmentalized. At the time Murray signed his baseball contract, he was pegged as top NFL pick Baker Mayfield's possible replacement, but he faced a camp competition at quarterback and wasn't seen as having a major NFL future himself. He won the job, and then ripped off one of the greatest dual-threat seasons in college football history more or less out of nowhere. More relevantly, Murray's NFL Draft stock shot up amidst a thin quarterback crop, and he started pontificating about playing both sports professionally, in contravention with the deal agent Scott Boras cut with the A's. On the diamond, he has five-tool athleticism but is unusually raw for a college outfielder because of lack of reps. The outside shot that he's this generation's Bo Jackson or Deion Sanders makes him one of the most interesting athletes in the world right now. The downside risk is that he could be this generation's Chad Hutchinson or Drew Henson and never reach pro excellence on either side. For now, we'll enjoy the ride.

The Demise of the Bat (and Glove) off the Bench

by Rob Mains

The Cardinals' Tyler O'Neill had a reasonable rookie campaign last year. In 142 plate appearances, he hit .254/.303/.500. His .803 OPS was fourth on the club, and his 86 DRC+ was ninth.

But those 142 plate appearances were spread over 61 games. O'Neill made only 27 starts: 13 in left field, 11 in right, and three in center. In his other 34 games, he was a substitute. He pinch-hit 22 times, going 3-for-18 with three walks and a homer. He pinch-ran three times, scoring a run each time. He was a late-inning defensive substitution in left field once and in right eight times.

This made O'Neill one of 45 position players in 2018 to have gotten at least 50 plate appearances in at least 25 games while starting in half or fewer of his game played. He, and 44 other players, were primarily used off the bench rather than in the starting lineup. How common is that?

Let's define a *substitute* as a player who gets at least 50 plate appearances and appears in at least 25 games in a season, but starts no more than half the games in which he appears. And we'll limit that to position players; a pitcher who gets 57 plate appearances by starting 12 games and relieving 48, as Fergie Jenkins did in 1966, doesn't count. Here's the growth of substitutes per team from 1908 (the first year for which data are available) through 1959. (For comparability among years, all figures are prorated to a 162-game schedule.)

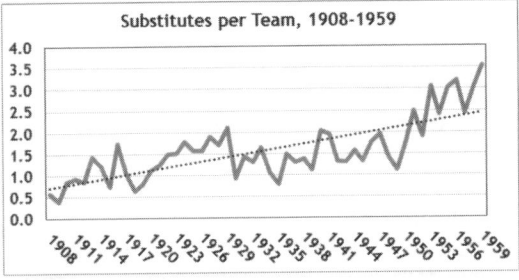

The dotted line is a trendline, but the trend is pretty obvious. The use of substitutes grew over the half-century, turning up sharply in the 1950s.

Late-inning substitutes were pretty rare in the early days of baseball. That's because players didn't leave games. Take, for example, the 1908 St. Louis Browns. They used only eight pitchers all season, and those eight pitchers completed 107 of their 155 starts. On the field, their catchers completed all

but 11 of the 155 games they started. Their right fielders completed all but 14, their center fielders all but 12, their shortstops and second basemen all but 3, their left fielders and first basemen all but 1, and both of the third basemen who started games were still at the position when the game ended.

Fast forward to 1952, same franchise. The 1952 Browns were in their second-to-last year in the Gateway City. They finished 64-90, seventh in the American League. Their Opening Day manager was Hall of Famer Rogers Hornsby, who was managing for the first time since the Browns fired him as player/manager 15 seasons earlier. (He'd last only 51 games before getting the boot). Those Browns, like other teams in the 1950s, substituted frequently. They used the fewest substitutes at second base, where the starter was there at the end in all but 15 games. In other words, St. Louis's most stable position in 1952, second base, had fewer complete games than its least stable position, right field, in 1908.

What changed between 1908, when the Browns had one player, Dode Criss, who was primarily a substitute (he pinch-hit 46 times, entered eight games as a relief pitcher, and filled in as a late-innings right fielder twice and first baseman once), to the 1950s, when the average team had two or three such batters? It was a confluence of two factors.

First, compared to baseball's early years, rosters grew, so there were more players on the bench who were eligible to enter games. In 1901, the first year of the 16-team, NL/AL format, rosters were capped at 14 players. (The new American League started the season with 18 but knocked it down the NL's level of 14 a month into the season.) That grew to 17 in 1908 and the present 25 in 1912. We've been there since, though there have been reductions due to competition from the Federal League, the World Wars, the Depression, and labor impasses.

Second, strategies that we take for granted today grew in popularity. The use of relief pitchers created opportunities for pinch-hitters. If your starting pitcher isn't going to go nine innings, it creates an opening for a pinch-hitter. Pinch hitters can also bat for relievers, of course. The first players to appear as pinch-hitters in more than 400 games all started their careers in the middle of the 20th century: Elmer Valo, 459 games between 1941 and 1961; Jerry Lynch, 490 games between 1954 and 1966; Tito Francona, 423 games between

1956 and 1970. (Actually, the first was Red Lucas, who pinch-hit 421 times between 1926 and 1938, but he was a pitcher, so he doesn't count.)

Platooning is another strategy that resulted in batters entering mid-game. When a manager platoons, he'll swap out players in order to take advantage of righty-lefty matchups. Earl Weaver, for example, famously loved platooning. In 1969, his first full year with the Orioles, his primary pinch-hitters were lefty-swinging Dave May, who got 90 percent of his plate appearances against right-handed pitchers, and right-handed Curt Motton, who batted against lefties 56 percent of the time. In addition to May and Motton, three other Orioles, all of whom had at least 94 plate appearances, started fewer than half of their games played. Merv Rettenmund (95 games, 41 started) entered 31 games as a defensive replacement in the outfield, 19 as a pinch hitter, and four as a pinch runner. Chico Salmon (52 games, 18 started) pinch hit 16 times, pinch ran nine times, and finished the game as an infield defensive replacement nine times. Bobby Floyd (39 games, 19 started) was mostly a glove off the bench, finishing nine games at second, six at third, and two at shortstop, while pinch-hitting once and pinch-running twice.

There's a reason the last chart ended in 1959. The use of substitutes peaked that year. It's gone the other direction since.

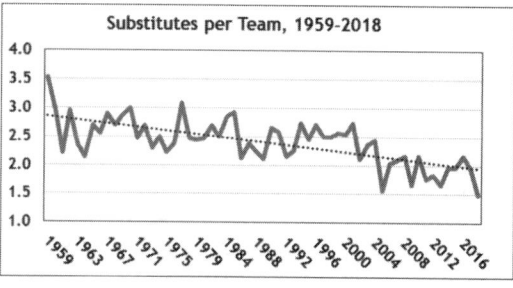

(Note: This graph excludes the 1981 split-season strike year, in which there were 2.6 substitutes per team, which equates to 3.9 per 162 games. That season was an outlier in many ways and can be comfortably excluded.)

Why the demarcation? It's not like managers forgot everything that they'd learned since 1908.

Let's examine the peak year, 1959. There were 54 position players who played in 25 games and got at least 50 plate appearances while starting no more than half their games. They hit .232/.300/.342 compared to the MLB average of .257/.322/.392. That deficit is not a surprise; if they were good, they'd be starting. Their average age, 29.4, was nearly a full year above the MLB average. Fully fifteen of them, with an average age of 30.7, were traded during the season. The team with the most was the St. Louis Cardinals, who had:

- Curt Flood, only 21 but seeing major league action for the fourth straight season. He struggled at the plate much of the year, hitting

.185/.290/.241 in mid-July, .275/.307/.477 thereafter. He started 49 games in center, mostly after he got untracked. Until then, he pinch hit 12 times, pinch ran 25 times, and was a defensive replacement 35 times.

- Lee Tate, a 27-year-old infielder who started with the team but was sent down to the minors in July. He started 12 games and was a defensive replacement, mostly at shortstop, 28 times. He also pinch-ran twice.

- Wally Shannon, 26, called up when Tate was sent down. He started 12 games at second and short, pinch hit 31 times, often staying in the game at shortstop, and entered games at second base three times at shortstop once.

- Bobby Smith, a 25-year-old outfielder who, like Tate, was sent down to Triple-A in July. He started ten games, pinch hit ten times, pinch ran eight times, and was brought in to play the outfield 15 times.

- George Crowe, a 38-year-old first baseman who'd come over in a trade from the Braves over the winter. He played 77 games but started only eleven, all at first. He pinch hit 66 times.

Doesn't that seem…*off*? Flood was a highly-regarded young player, but between April 21 and July 18, he had only 46 plate appearances, starting only three games. Between Tate and Shannon, they had an infielder for the whole season who started only 24 games. Smith rarely played, and Crowe was mostly a full-time pinch hitter. *Who has room on their roster for all that dead weight?*

I'll tell you who: A team whose Opening Day roster has just nine pitchers. The 1959 Cardinals broke camp with starters Larry Jackson, Ernie Broglio, Vinegar Bend Mizell, and Lindy McDaniel. The bullpen was Jim Brosnan, Howie Nunn, Phil Clark, Gary Blaylock, and 23-year-old rookie Bob Gibson. That's it. There were eight starting position players and five more on the bench.

Contrast that with the 2018 Cardinals, for whom O'Neill played. The Opening Day roster had 13 pitchers. That left them with 12 position players. The only guys on the bench were catcher Francisco Pena and infielders Greg Garcia, Jed Gyorko, and Yairo Munoz. Pena started more than half the games he played. So did Gyorko and Munoz. Only Garcia was a bat (63 pinch hitting appearances) and glove (finished 22 games at second, short, and third) off the bench.

The growth of pitching staffs has crowded out substitutes. If you're a position player on the bench, you're going to be called upon to start games as well as substitute. The old guy who just pinch-hit, or the young guy who served as an aging veteran's late-inning glove and/or legs: They're not on the rosters anymore. They're getting reps in Triple-A in the latter case, watching games on TV in the former.

The number of relief pitchers per game isn't a perfect proxy for the growth of pitching staffs, but it works to an extent. As the chart below shows, baseball has seen a steady rise in relief pitchers per game since 1959. That rise has resulted in more roster spots devoted to pitchers and fewer for position players. The correlation between relief pitchers per game and substitutes per team since 1959 is -0.63, indicating that the growth of bullpens has occurred at the same time as the decline in bench bats. Correlation is not causation, but in this case, it actually is. Relievers are displacing substitute position players.

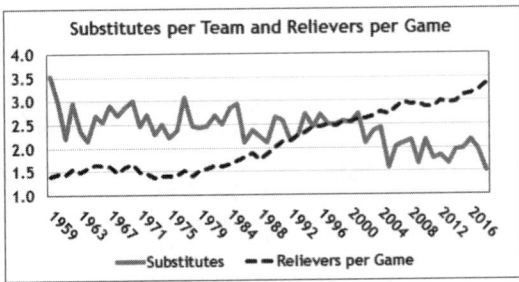

There are players who made a career of coming into games off the bench. Since 1908, there have been 96 batters who got into at least 300 games as substitutes and started half or fewer of their games played. The all-time leaders all started their careers in the last half-century: Lenny Harris (1988-2005, 770 games started, 1,133 as a substitute), Greg Gross (1973-1989, 764 start/1,045 sub), Mark Sweeney (1995-2008, 305 start/913 sub), Dave Hansen (1990-2005, 341 start/889 sub), and Mike Jorgensen (1968-1985, 816 start/817 sub). All started their careers during a time when the use of substitutes has declined.

But there isn't a contradiction. The decline since 1959 hasn't been to 1908 levels. The past season was the first time the number of substitutes per team per 162 games was below 1.5 since 1949. But that doesn't mean substitutes are going away, just that they're less common.

And there isn't a Lenny Harris or Greg Gross playing today. No player with more than 300 games as a substitute who started half or fewer of his career games played was active in 2018. The last one was Chris Heisey in 2017. The last before him was Don Kelly in 2016. Before him, Greg Dobbs in 2014. Fifty years ago, in 1969, there were nine active players who would meet that standard over their careers: Gates Brown, Ty Cline, Terry Crowley, Phil Gagliano, Tom Hutton, Jorgensen, Tony Muser, Chico Ruiz, and Jimmy Stewart. Heading into this season, the active leaders are Shane Robinson (287 games as a sub, 174 as a starter), Matt Szczur (263 sub, 100 starter), Garcia (257 sub, 152 starter), and Tommy LaStella (215 sub, 181 starter).

Players whose role is to come into a game to bat or run or play the field aren't disappearing that way complete games and batters who walk more than they strike out are. They're not even becoming rare like ERA qualifiers or games lasting less than 2:30. But, like many other consequences of growing pitching staffs, they're under pressure.

This isn't exactly a tragedy. We've known for over a decade about the "PH penalty," that batters are significantly less effective as pinch hitters than as starters. But that doesn't mean that they're useless. All of us have seen relief pitchers take one of their first professional at bats in extra-inning National League games. Or, say, Cleveland having the tying run on first with two out in the last of the tenth in the seventh game of the World Series...and sending Michael Martinez (.574 OPS in the regular season, 0-for-3 with three strikeouts in the postseason) up to the plate. It's not just that managers' options are being limited. That lack of options can make it harder to win games in late innings.

If you've landed a spot on a major league roster, there's a growing likelihood that you're going to be used primarily as a starter, not a substitute, out of necessity. The bat or glove off the bench is a casualty of modern roster construction. ∎

—*Rob Mains is an author of Baseball Prospectus.*

What If the First Woman in MLB is Already Here?

by Sheryl Ring

Major League Baseball has a looming demographic problem. It's most highlighted[1] by MLB's repeated difficulties[2,3], a subject I've discussed at some length.[4] But MLB has other demographic problems: age and ethnicity,[5] and the league's fraught relationship with LGBTQ fans.[6] With David Denson's retirement, there are now no openly LGBTQ players anywhere in affiliated baseball. Given there are more than 3,500 affiliated players at any given time, we'd expect, using Gallup's 4.1 percent figure, to find at least 140 LGBTQ players in affiliated baseball. And while it's certainly fair to assume that there are fewer LGBTQ people playing baseball than in the general population, the idea that there are none at all beggars belief.

Explanations abound for this lack of LGBTQ representation. There are, of course, the social factors, like homophobia and transphobia. It's also entirely possible, for example, that a team doesn't believe that a transgender ("trans") baseball player would be able to perform at the same level as a cis (not trans) player. But it might also be more complicated than that—for example, it's *also* possible that the first trans player is *already playing*, and is closeted because they believe they would face discrimination, or that they wouldn't be protected from that discrimination should they come out publicly. Trans people are estimated at about 0.6 percent of the population, so assuming that percentage holds for professional baseball (and we have no hard data on this), we could reasonably expect that of the approximately 6,500 players in affiliated baseball, about 39 would be transgender.[7] What all of that means is that the first woman or non-male in baseball may already be playing—and we just don't know it yet.

And this presents an interesting thought experiment: what would happen if a Major League Baseball player came out this offseason as trans? Could a team legally release the player on that basis? Could the player require the team to continue to employ them? And what impact would this have?

There are actually a few ways this could happen. We could have a trans man. We could have a trans woman. We could have a non-binary, agender, or genderfluid person. I'm not going to define gender identities here—that's beyond the scope of this piece—but for now it will suffice to say that gender is a spectrum, not a binary, and it isn't determined by genitalia.[8] (For purposes of this piece, I will be following the rules and definitions provided by GLAAD on its website.)[9]

So with that in mind, let's assume that an ace left-hander on the Dodgers came out as transgender and stated her intention to live openly as a woman. We'll call her "Sandra Koufax."

Based on the data we have, there's no obvious reason why Sandra's transition would bar her from playing major league baseball, particularly if she did not medically transition. Not all transgender people medically transition, for a variety of reasons. And even if she did medically[10] transition,[11] it could be aided by collaboration between her endocrinologist and Dodgers team physicians. But the Dodgers can easily smooth logistical obstacles by providing gender identity diversity training to players and coaches. (For those of you asking about locker rooms, Sandra could use a similar arrangement to the one Becky Hammon uses.)[12] Let's talk about why that is.

If you read my post on the law of female baseball players,[13] you'll remember that we used as examples players like Toni Stone, Stacy Piagno, and Kelsie Whitmore, and research by Jen Mac Ramos. The problem is that if you thought research into female players was scarce, research into transgender athletes is even more rare. We know that there are no openly trans baseball players in affiliated baseball, which makes apples-to-apples comparisons really difficult. There are very[14] few[15] trans[16] athletes[17] of any kind, actually, largely owing to societal stigma which includes a disagreement among medical professionals regarding whether trans athletes should be permitted to compete in sports. We do see some trans athletes, though: professional hockey player Harrison Browne,[18] high school baseball player Jake Hofheimer,[19] power lifter Janae Marie Kroc,[20] and multi-sport athlete Britney Stinson.[21] But there is a surprising dearth of data on the effects of medical transitioning on athletic performance. What data[23] does exist suggests[24] that, after a medical transition, a trans woman or man could expect to perform[25] similarly[26] to a cisgender counterpart due to hormonal changes after a sufficiently long course of hormone replacement therapy.[27]

Further, what little research has been conducted tends to focus on trans women, who are assigned male at birth and later medically transition with a combination of hormone replacement therapy (antiandrogens, estrogens, and possibly progesterone) with the aim of bringing blood hormone levels in line with cis women (though trans women often have lower testosterone levels than their cis counterparts). Some, like Professor of Physiology Alison Heather in New Zealand, believe that trans athletes could hold an advantage against cisgender athletes of the same gender, particularly trans women.[28] "Given the lack of research, there is a real need to study what physical advantages transgender females carry after hormone therapy with consideration required for different sports, trainability and for performance. Until then, it is very difficult to conclude that it is a level playing field for CIS women versus trans women," she told Stuff's Olivia Caldwell.[29] But notably, Heather can't point to any studies or data supporting her position, which is mostly based on her belief that more research would change the general consensus.

Thus far, the great weight of research instead backs Dr. Marci Bowers, who disagrees with Heather. Bowers' research concluded that a trans woman has "low testosterone levels and muscle mass that is remarkably similar to her [cisgender] counterparts."[30] And the International Olympic Committee, which has backed a significant part of what little research exists in this area, has come down on Dr. Bowers' side,[31] allowing trans athletes to compete against cisgender athletes of the same gender with which they self-identify (i.e., trans women compete against cis women; trans men compete against cis men) after completing certain steps in their medical transitions.[32] This is based on data suggesting that a trans man is comparable in strength and ability to a cis man, and a trans woman comparable to a cis woman.

But, in many ways, the physical argument is less important than the legal one. Does a major league team have the right to terminate a player's contract for transitioning? We know that the MLB Uniform Player Contract specifically states that players have unique athletic abilities which they must work to preserve. So there are a couple of reasons why a team might want to terminate a player's contract for transitioning. Perhaps a team thinks transitioning would impair a player's performance. Perhaps the team just doesn't want to employ a trans person. Perhaps the player's teammates objected, and the team is afraid of disrupting clubhouse chemistry.

Let's start with the applicable law, Section 2000e-2 of Title VII of the Civil Rights Act of 1964,[33] which says this:

> It shall be an unlawful employment practice for an employer: (1) to fail or refuse to hire or to discharge any individual, or otherwise to discriminate against any individual with respect to his compensation, terms, conditions, or privileges of employment, because of such individual's race, color, religion, sex, or national origin; or (2) to limit, segregate, or classify his employees or applicants for employment in any way which would deprive or tend to deprive any individual of employment opportunities or otherwise adversely affect his status as an employee, because of such individual's race, color, religion, sex, or national origin."

In the law, there are always exceptions. The primary exception to Title VII is called a bona fide occupational qualification ("BFOQ"). A BFOQ is just a legalese way of saying that an employer is allowed to exclude people on the basis of criteria like sex or gender if being a specific gender is required to do the job. The most commonly given example is that if Hanes needed a male model for its mens' underwear, they're legally allowed to look for men only to fill that role. Race, it should be noted, can never be a BFOQ.

We start with the principle that, as Kylie Byron notes, a person's biological sex is, from a legal perspective, determined as a matter of law, not a matter of fact, "since there is no jurisdiction that submits a person's sex to a jury as a fact to be found."[34] The only reason that gender or sex are even recorded on birth certificates is because the law requires it. In other words, it's the law—*not a fact*—that determines what a person's biological sex is, and that's why it can be changed on a birth certificate or driver's license: because the law recognizes that sometimes determinations of law are wrong.

Now, "gender identity" isn't explicitly protected by Title VII. But back in 1989, the United States Supreme Court in a case called *Price Waterhouse v. Hopkins* ruled that discrimination on the basis of something called "sex stereotyping" is illegal: "we are beyond the day when an employer could evaluate employees by assuming or insisting that they matched the stereotype associated with their group[.]"[35] In other words, an employer may not take an adverse employment action against a person because they do not conform to the stereotypes associated with how a man or woman should act. That means that an employer can't fire a woman for being aggressive or not wearing a dress at work.

Most federal Courts of Appeal have held that this language also prohibits discrimination against trans people, who by definition don't act according to the stereotypes of the sex they were assigned at birth. The Sixth Circuit Court of Appeals, in a recent case called *Equal Employment Opportunity Commission v. R.G. &. G.R. Harris Funeral Homes, Inc.*, explained that gender identity is implicitly protected as an aspect of *sex* in the statute. The Sixth Circuit reasoned that "an employer engages in unlawful discrimination even if it expects both biologically male and female employees to conform to certain notions of how each should behave."[36] And though the Supreme Court hasn't weighed in on this yet, the Sixth Circuit is not the only Court of Appeals to hold this way, and it seems to be the prevailing viewpoint in the federal courts and the EEOC that Title VII's bar on sex discrimination also bars discrimination on the basis of gender identity.[37] Even those federal courts which have not adopted that approach, like the Eleventh Circuit, have nonetheless made clear that "all persons, whether transgender or not, are protected from discrimination on the basis of gender stereotype."[38]

And there's another factor to throw into the mix here. Several states, like California, Illinois, and Massachusetts (among others) have statutes or regulations which bar employers from firing, or refusing to hire, employees because they are transgender.[39] While those statutes generally include BFOQ language, some, like the California law, are much stricter than Title VII, and bar employers from inquiring into the gender identity of their employees so as to protect those employees from retaliation or discrimination.[40]

So let's go back to Sandra. If Sandra only socially transitioned (that is, publicly presenting female without any medical component), there's probably nothing the Dodgers can legally do about it, both under California law and Title VII. There's nothing that medically would make her less able to compete, and therefore in no way is her gender identity a BFOQ. She's still able to throw 95 with a knee-buckling curve. Any retaliation against her would be almost certainly illegal.

But players who medically transition would *also* be protected. That's because several states, like California, have laws which prohibit a team from inquiring into their employees gender identity and medical transition regimens. That's an unambiguously good thing; employees facing embarrassing and humiliating questions about their transitions would make a workplace quite hostile. As for Sandra's performance, based on the data we have from Dr. Bowers and the IOC, it's a fair bet that Sandra would, after a time, perform similarly to how she would perform as a cisgender female. And under California law, the Dodgers can't legally provide any input into Sandra's transition. That's also an unambiguously good thing—imagine if your employer told you what medical care *you* could receive.

And what about those BFOQs? Is being cis a BFOQ for playing professional baseball? Probably not. We know that BFOQs are to be construed narrowly, but state human rights statutes are construed broadly—and state statutes like that in California provide a great deal of protection.[41] And there is one case on point - Renee Richards, a transwoman and one of the first openly trans athletes, won a lawsuit in 1977 for the right to compete in women's sports.[42] I think that holding would stand up in states like California and Massachusetts, and possibly Illinois and New York as well. With other states like Texas, it would be limited to how far the Sixth Circuit's recent decision extends and whether other courts would adopt or recognize it, as well as whether the Supreme Court decides to hear the case and whether the Sixth Circuit's decision is affirmed.

All of that being said, if Sandra Koufax came out tomorrow, she would probably be legally protected. At least under State law, the Dodgers probably couldn't demote or release her because of her transition, whether she medically transitioned or not. And they probably wouldn't have any say into how she transitioned at all. That doesn't mean it would be easy—it never is, of course. But it does mean that if there is a trans person playing professional baseball, depending on where they're playing, they would likely be entirely legally protected. And that is a hopeful thought. ∎

—Sheryl Ring is an author of FanGraphs.

1. Ring, Sheryl. "Jose Reyes Has Been Honored for His Off-Field Behavior." FanGraphs Baseball. Accessed December 23, 2018. https://www.fangraphs.com/blogs/jose-reyes-has-been-honored-for-his-off-field-behavior/.

2. Ring, Sheryl. "Is Major League Baseball's Domestic Violence Policy Working?" FanGraphs Baseball. Accessed December 23, 2018. https://www.fangraphs.com/blogs/is-major-league-baseballs-domestic-violence-policy-working/.

3. "The Weak Spot in the League's Domestic-Violence Policy." FanGraphs Baseball. Accessed December 23, 2018. https://www.fangraphs.com/blogs/the-weak-spot-in-the-leagues-domestic-violence-policy/.

4. Ring, Sheryl. "Roberto Osuna, the Blue Jays, and the Limits of Presuming Innocence." FanGraphs Baseball. Accessed December 23, 2018. https://www.fangraphs.com/blogs/roberto-osuna-the-blue-jays-and-the-limits-of-presuming-innocence/.

5. Ring, Sheryl. "MLB, Twitter, and Baseball's Looming Age Problem." FanGraphs Baseball. Accessed December 23, 2018. https://www.fangraphs.com/blogs/mlb-twitter-and-baseballs-looming-age-problem/.

6. "The Importance of Pride Month in MLB." FanGraphs Baseball. Accessed December 23, 2018. https://www.fangraphs.com/blogs/the-importance-of-pride-month-in-mlb/.

7. "The American Transgender Population Is Larger Than We Thought It Was." ThinkProgress. Accessed December 23, 2018. https://thinkprogress.org/the-american-transgender-population-is-larger-than-we-thought-it-was-ab83126f33a/.

8. Mills, Michael. "Sex Difference vs. Gender Difference? Oh, I'm So Confused!" Psychology Today. Accessed December 23, 2018. https://www.psychologytoday.com/us/blog/the-how-and-why-sex-differences/201110/sex-difference-vs-gender-difference-oh-im-so-confused.

9. "GLAAD Media Reference Guide - In Focus: Covering the Transgender Community." GLAAD. October 26, 2016. Accessed December 23, 2018. https://www.glaad.org/reference/covering-trans-community.; "GLAAD Media Reference Guide - Transgender." GLAAD. April 19, 2017. Accessed December 23, 2018. https://www.glaad.org/reference/transgender.

10. "Transgender FAQ." GLAAD. June 01, 2018. Accessed December 23, 2018. https://www.glaad.org/transgender/transfaq.

11. Lopez. "Myth #5: All Trans People Medically Transition." Vox.com. November 14, 2018. Accessed December 23, 2018. https://www.vox.com/identities/2016/5/13/17938114/transgender-people-transitioning-surgery-medical.

12. TBonesteel, Matt. "Pau Gasol: 'Becky Hammon Can Coach NBA Basketball. Period.'" The Washington Post. May 11, 2018. Accessed December 23, 2018. https://www.washingtonpost.com/news/early-lead/wp/2018/05/11/pau-gasol-becky-hammon-can-coach-nba-basketball-period/?noredirect=on&utm_term=.73e41d8b11d4.

13. Ring, Sheryl. "Can Major League Baseball Legally Exclude a Woman?" FanGraphs Baseball. Accessed December 23, 2018. https://www.fangraphs.com/blogs/can-major-league-baseball-legally-exclude-a-woman/.

14. Jackson-Gibson, Adele. "Transgender: Do Trans Athletes Have an Unfair Advantage in Sports?" Excelle Sports. June 01, 2017. Accessed December 23, 2018. http://www.excellesports.com/news/trans-athletes-unfair-advantage-sports/.

15. Mosier, Chris. "Visibility for Trans Athletes Is a Powerful Force for Change." Outsports. March 30, 2018. Accessed December 23, 2018. https://www.outsports.com/2018/3/30/17182022/chris-mosier-transgender-visibility-lgbtq-inclusion.

16. Steele, Lauren. "Chris Mosier on Making History as First Trans Member of Team USA." Rolling Stone. June 25, 2018. Accessed December 23, 2018. https://www.rollingstone.com/culture/culture-sports/chris-mosier-on-making-history-as-first-trans-member-of-team-usa-250971/.

17. Truitt, Jos. "Fallon Fox on Life as a Trans Athlete: 'The Scope of Vitriol and Anger Was Mind-blowing'." The Guardian. February 16, 2015. Accessed December 23, 2018. https://www.theguardian.com/sport/2015/feb/16/fallon-fox-trans-mma-athlete-interview.

18. Perez, A.J. "Harrison Browne Is First Openly Transgender Athlete on U.S. Pro Sports Team." USA Today. October 08, 2016. Accessed December 23, 2018. https://www.usatoday.com/story/sports/hockey/2016/10/07/harrison-browne-transgender-athlete-nwhl-buffalo-beauts/91733914/.

19. "Transgender Baseball Player Jake Hofheimer." Los Angeles Times. April 09, 2016. Accessed December 23, 2018. https://www.latimes.com/sports/86401423-132.html.

20. Zeigler, Cyd. "World Champion Power Lifter Is Trans." Outsports. July 27, 2015. Accessed December 23, 2018. https://www.outsports.com/2015/7/27/9049591/janae-marie-kroc-trans-powerlifter.

21. Zeigler, Cyd. "This Trans Athlete Plays Women's Pro Football, and for USA Baseball." Outsports. December 14, 2017. Accessed December 23, 2018. https://www.outsports.com/2017/12/13/16748322/britney-stinson-trans-football-baseball.

22. Bebinger, Martha. "Olympic Rules For Transgender Women Athletes Are In Flux." WBUR. August 12, 2016. Accessed December 23, 2018. https://www.wbur.org/commonhealth/2016/08/12/olympics-transgender-athletes.

23. Burns, Katelyn. "No, Female Trans Athletes Do Not Have Unfair Advantages." The Establishment. October 03, 2018. Accessed December 23, 2018. https://theestablishment.co/no-female-trans-athletes-do-not-have-unfair-advantages-14b8e249f93c/.

24. Tannehill, Brynn. "Do Transgender Athletes Have an Unfair Advantage?" The Huffington Post. February 02, 2016. Accessed December 23, 2018. https://www.huffingtonpost.com/brynn-tannehill/do-transgender-athletes-have-an-unfair-advantage_b_4918835.html

25. Burns, Katelyn. "What Actually Happens When a Trans Athlete Transitions." Sports. May 04, 2017. Accessed December 23, 2018. https://sports.vice.com/en_us/article/vv95a4/what-actually-happens-when-a-trans-athlete-transitions.

26. Haynes, Stephie. "Top Sex Reassignment Docs Weigh in on Fallon Fox." Bloody Elbow. March 08, 2013. Accessed December 23, 2018. https://www.bloodyelbow.com/2013/3/8/4075434/leading-sex-reassignment-physicians-weigh-in-on-fallon-fox.

27. Unger, Cecile A. "Hormone Therapy For Transgender Patients." Translational Andrology and Urology. Dec, 2016. https://www.ncbi.nlm.nih.gov/pmc/articles/PMC5182227/.

28. Gleeson, Scott, and Erik Brady. "These Transgender Cyclists Have Olympian Disagreement on How to Define Fairness." USA Today. January 12, 2018. Accessed December 23, 2018. https://www.usatoday.com/story/sports/olympics/2018/01/11/these-transgender-cyclists-have-olympian-disagreement-how-define-fairness/995434001/.

29. "Professor of Physiology Says Transgender Athletes Have Advantage in Speed, Power." Stuff. Accessed December 23, 2018. https://www.stuff.co.nz/sport/other-sports/99434993/professor-of-physiology-says-trans-athlete-has-advantage-in-speed-and-power.

30. Tannehill, Brynn. "Do Transgender Athletes Have an Unfair Advantage?" The Huffington Post. February 02, 2016. Accessed December 23, 2018. https://www.huffingtonpost.com/brynn-tannehill/do-transgender-athletes-have-an-unfair-advantage_b_4918835.html

31. Zeigler, Cyd. "Moment #22: International Olympic Committee Allows Transgender Athletes to Compete." Outsports. September 12, 2011. Accessed December 23, 2018. https://www.outsports.com/2011/9/12/4051806/moment-22-international-olympic-committee-allows-transgender-athletes.

32. Associated Press. "IOC Rules Transgender Athletes Can Take Part in Olympics without Surgery." The Guardian. January 25, 2016. Accessed December 23, 2018. https://www.theguardian.com/sport/2016/jan/25/ioc-rules-transgender-athletes-can-take-part-in-olympics-without-surgery.

33. T42 U.S.C. 2000e *et seq.*

34. Kylie Byron, Natural Law and Bona Fide Discrimination: The Evolving Understanding of Sex, Gender, and Transgender Identity in Employment, 6 Wash. U. Jur. Rev. 343 (2014). Available at: http://openscholarship.wustl.edu/law_jurisprudence/vol6/iss2/4

35. *Price Waterhouse v. Hopkins*, 490 U.S. 228 (1989).

36. *Equal Employment Opportunity Commission v. R.G. &. G.R. Harris Funeral Homes, Inc.*, 884 F.3d 560 (6th Cir. 2018). The case is currently before the U.S. Supreme Court on a writ of certiorari..

37. Hively v. Ivy Tech Cmty. Coll., 853 F.3d 339, 350-51 (7th Cir. 2017) (en banc); Glenn v. Brumby, 663 F. 3d 1312 - Court of Appeals, 11th Circuit 2011

38. *Evans v. Georgia Regional Hospital*, 850 F.3d 1248 (11th Cir. 2017) (holding that "discrimination based on gender nonconformity is actionable" under Title VII).

39. For Massachusetts: G.L. c. 151B, c.151C and G.L. c. 272, §§ 92, 98 and 98A; MCAD and Jackie Ravesi v. Naz Fitness Group, 37 Mass. Discrimination Law Rptr. 1 (2015). For California: § 11030 of the Fair Employment and Housing Council Regulations; Cal. Gov't. Code Section 12940(a), Cal. Gov't Code Section 12926(p); Cal. Health and Safety Code Section 1365.5; Cal. Penal Code section 422.55(a)(2), Cal. Penal section 422.56(c). For Illinois: 775 ILCS 5/2-101 *et seq.*

40. Government Code, Title 2, Division 3, Part 2.8 and its associated regulations: California Code of Regulations, Title 2 Administration, Division 4.1 Department of Fair Employment and Housing, Chapter 5, SubChapter 2.

41. *Diaz v. Pan Am. World Airways, Inc.*, 442 F. 2d 385 - Court of Appeals, 5th Circuit 1971.

42. *Richards v. U.S. Tennis Ass'n.*, 93 Misc.2d 713 (1977).

DRC+ Explained

by Jonathan Judge

Why another batting metric? Because existing batting metrics (including ours) have two serious problems: (1) they purport to offer summaries of player contributions, when in fact they merely average play outcomes in which the players participated; and (2) they treat all outcomes, whether it be a walk or a single, as equally likely to be driven by the player's skill, even though no one believes that is actually true.

Deserved Runs Created Plus (DRC+) addresses the first problem by rejecting the assumption that play outcomes automatically equal player contributions, and forces players to demonstrate a consistent ability to generate those outcomes over time to get full credit for them. DRC+ addresses the second problem by recognizing that certain outcomes (walks, strikeouts) are more attributable to player skill than others (singles, triples).

DRC+ gives more weight to extreme performances in the former (because they are more likely to reflect the batter's actual contribution) and less weight to extreme performances in the latter (because they tend to be flukier). By addressing these two deficiencies in existing metrics, DRC+ ends up being substantially more reliable and predictive for individual hitters than any other baseball hitting metric. That includes wOBA, wRC+, OPS+, and many others you still see used by writers in analyzing baseball performance.

With that said, I think it's important to say a few words about what DRC+ is not. The fact that DRC+ performs much better than other metrics does not mean that these other metrics—which have served the analytic community reasonably well for many years—somehow are "wrong." There is no "right" or "wrong" when it comes to player metrics; rather, it is a continuous process of trying to get things "more right" than we had them before.

Recently on the Baseball Prospectus website, we provided an objective benchmark system by which metrics could be compared. What you see in that article is a history of steady forward progress in measuring batter performance, starting with batting average and up until recently culminating in wOBA and wRC+. Just as DRC+ has surpassed existing metrics, at some point in the future, DRC+ may itself be surpassed. When that happens, our analysis should be all the better for it.

Similarly, the fact that DRC+ is much more accurate than other metrics on average does not mean it cannot still have weak spots and areas for improvement. DRC+ is the output of several models, and those models make decisions based on what is expected, not by functioning as some sort of oracle. Rough edges and blind spots are still possible, and we're actually very interested to hear if you think you have seen any.

Having talked about what DRC+ is and what it is not, let's conclude this segment by talking about one of our favorite parts: that DRC+ is willing to be uncertain. As with our catcher framing and DRA metrics, DRC+ has specific uncertainty bounds. Mike Trout, for example, in 2018 had a DRC+ of 180, with a standard deviation (plus or minus) of 13 points. So, we are pretty confident Mike Trout was somewhere between 167 and 193, and skeptical about him being in the range beyond that, but are happy to admit he very well could deserve something other than exactly 180. Being honest about uncertainty is an important part of understanding what it means to be accurate.

Essentially, DRC+ is our best estimate for what a hitter produces at the plate, based on how much credit he has shown he deserves for each of the outcomes he participated in. We hope you find this useful also.

⚾   ⚾   ⚾

One of our statistical themes this year has been batting offense. We started by explaining the need for proper benchmarks and evaluated various Statcast metrics on their performance. We updated and revisited a debate between two offensive metrics, wOBA and OPS. We then discussed at length the concept of a player's "expected contribution[1]" and how it underlays our concept of "deserved runs."

That progression reaches its peak with the introduction of Deserved Runs Created, which we will publish under the moniker "Deserved Runs Created Plus," or DRC+. DRC+ is essentially the flipside of Deserved Run Average (DRA): it involves similar models and extractions but is designed and grouped to track batter performance rather than pitcher performance.

Park-adjusted offensive baseball statistics are often presented on a "100" scale using a "plus" moniker that indicates higher values are better. Thus, just as we have DRA- as our scaled-to-100 statistic for pitchers (lower is better), we now have DRC+ as our scaled-to-100 statistic for hitters (higher is better). DRC+ exists for any season with reliable play-by-play data, from 1921 to the present.

Why use DRC+? The simple answer is because it's more accurate than wRC+, OPS+, and True Average in every relevant way. The more urgent answer is that wRC+ and OPS+ appear to be compromised by the changing baseball, whereas DRC+ is much less affected. In sum, if park- and opponent-adjusted accuracy is important to you, then DRC+ should be your offensive metric of choice.

The Superior Accuracy of DRC+

In August, we laid out the underlying principles of our search for the "expected contribution" for players, and why virtually all traditional leaderboards fail to accurately report these contributions. Those principles included (1) that the fundamental unit of player measurement was seasonal, (2) that a player's expected contribution cannot be directly observed, and (3) that a review of three so-called Contribution Measures—reliability, predictiveness, and descriptiveness, in that preferred order—seemed to distinguish the best estimates of past player contributions.

In an otherwise complicated analysis, we derived one easy rule, which we labeled Principle 7: *If one metric outperforms another in all three Contribution Measures, it is almost certainly superior.* This finding was justified both (a) by inference (only greater signal seemingly explains across-the-board superiority in inconsistent tests) and (b) by experience, given that generally-accepted superior metrics like wOBA and OPS exhibited this same quality relative to OBP and especially batting average.

Principle 7, then, could make this a very short article. The simple reason to prefer DRC+ is because, over the past several decades, it easily outperforms all competing park-adjusted hitting metrics in all three measures:

Metric	Rel	Rel_Err	Pred	Pred_Err	Desc	Desc_Err
DRC+	**0.63**	0.02	**0.42**	0.03	**0.72**	0.02
True Average	0.54	0.02	0.34	0.03	0.67	0.02
wRC+	0.54	0.02	0.35	0.03	0.69	0.02
OPS+	0.50	0.02	0.35	0.03	0.68	0.02

Table 1: Batting Metric Performance by Contribution Measures (teams, 1980–2018); Robust Pearson Correlation to Team Runs/PA

The comparisons are robust Pearson correlations, compiled at the team level, between team averages for these metrics and team runs scored, and higher is better. The performance of park-adjusted metrics is not as good as the raw metrics we saw in August, but this makes sense, given that park-adjusted metrics assume many actual runs scored were undeserved, placing a ceiling on the extent to which such metrics will ever correlate with raw run rates. Nonetheless, testing to raw runs is still useful, as we still want to see any metric, even a park-adjusted one, adhere as much to reality as possible after its adjustments.

On average, over the past several decades, DRC+ is clearly the most accurate park-adjusted metric. It is much more reliable than wRC+ and OPS+, scoring well beyond the margin of error[2] for both. This is because DRC+ is doing a better job of deriving actual player contributions than wRC+ or OPS+. DRC+ also has notably better predictive performance than the other metrics, with its superiority in that respect also outside the margin of error. The lead for DRC+ continues in descriptiveness, which we consider to be the least important of the three measures but here is consistent with the other findings.

We suspect that the gulf in quality between DRC+ and these other metrics is somewhat masked by the comparison to raw team runs, because again there is only so much *unadjusted* run-scoring for which an *adjusted* metric can account. Let's look at some comparisons that specifically test the power of a metric to adjust for different environments, which is where a park-adjusted metric should thrive. This also allows us to focus on individual variation rather than team averages. We'll put the raw, unadjusted metrics back in for comparison also.

Specifically, let's look at individual players who switched teams in consecutive years, thereby moving themselves into another run-scoring environment for half of their games. For reasons that will become clear shortly, we'll also limit ourselves to a collection of more recent seasons:

1. As originally posted, the paper spoke of the "most likely contribution." After a late-night talk with Stan developer Jonah Gabry, I agree that the better term is "expected contribution," in the sense that we are looking for an overall "expectation" of past performance, not the most likely such performance. The "expected" contribution should not be confused with the "x" or "expected" concept in terms of predicting future performance, which is unfortunately well-established in the fantasy world, but also potentially confusing in this context.

2. As in our article comparing wOBA and OPS, we are using brms and having it report the probable correlation between each metric and team runs/PA as multivariate outputs using Markov Chain Monte Carlo sampling. Error rates are calculated by brms / Stan along with the reported correlation coefficients.

Metric	Reliability	Error	Variance Accounted For
DRC+	**0.73**	**0.001**	**53%**
wOBA	0.35	0.001	12%
wRC+	0.35	0.001	12%
OPS+	0.34	0.001	12%
OPS	0.33	0.002	11%
True Average	0.30	0.002	9%
AVG	0.30	0.002	9%
OBP	0.30	0.002	9%

Table 2: Reliability of Team-Switchers, Year 1 to Year 2 (2010-2018); Normal Pearson Correlations[3]

With this comparison, DRC+ pulls far ahead of all other batting metrics, park-adjusted and unadjusted. There are essentially three tiers of performance: (1) the group at the bottom, ranging from correlations of .3 to .33; (2) the middle group of wOBA and wRC+, which are a clear level up from the other metrics; and finally (3) DRC+, which has almost double the reliability of the other metrics.

You should pay attention to the "Variance Accounted For" column, more commonly known as r-squared. DRC+ accounts for over three times as much variance between batters than the next-best batting metric. In fact, one season of DRC+ explains over half of the expected differences in plate appearance quality between hitters who have switched teams; wRC+ checks in at a mere 16 percent. The difference is not only clear: it is not even close.

Let's look at Predictiveness. It's a very good sign that DRC+ correlates well with itself, but games are won by actual runs, not deserved runs. Using wOBA as a surrogate for run-scoring, how predictive is DRC+ for a hitter's performance in the following season?

Metric	Predictiveness	Error
DRC+	0.50	0.001
wOBA	0.37	0.001
wRC+	0.37	0.002
OPS+	0.37	0.001
OPS	0.35	0.002
True Average	0.34	0.002
OBP	0.30	0.002
AVG	0.25	0.002

Table 3: Reliability of Team-Switchers, Year 1 to Year 2 wOBA (2010-2018); Normal Pearson Correlations

If we may, let's take a moment to reflect on the differences in performance we see in Table 3. It took baseball decades to reach consensus on the importance of OBP over AVG (worth

five points of predictiveness), not to mention OPS (another five points), and finally to reach the existing standard metric, wOBA, in 2006. Over slightly more than a century, that represents an improvement of 12 points of predictiveness. Just over 10 years later, DRC+ now offers 13 points of improvement over wOBA alone.

Our existing offensive baseline at BP, True Average, while competitive, fails to stand out. Thus, while True Average will still be selectable in our Sortable Stats tables at baseballprospectus.com, it will be retired as the default batting metric of Baseball Prospectus. Batting Wins Above Replacement Player (BWARP) will instead be calculated from Deserved Runs Above Average (DRAA), which in turn are derived from same process culminating in DRC+. True Average is, for all practical purposes, no more.

DRC+ and the Altered Baseball

Ordinarily, the introduction of a new metric merely gives analysts another option to consider. Here, however, we think the situation is a bit more urgent. Put simply, the changing baseball has wreaked havoc on traditional park-adjusted metrics. Thus, if you wish to use wRC+ or OPS+, particularly to study the last several baseball seasons, we recommend that you do so only with extreme caution.

In Table 1 above, we showed you correlations for park-adjusted metrics for all years from 1980 through 2017. Let's return to team-level numbers but focus now on the 2010-2018 seasons[4]. This is a brutal sequence of years for park-adjusted metrics: baseball's run environment plunges to just over 4.0 runs a game in 2014, and then rebounds a few years later to 4.5 runs per game. Furthermore, between 2015 through 2017, it is now admitted that the baseball physically changed, perhaps multiple times, causing run-scoring to rebound even though many of the structural factors that coincided with the earlier decline in run-scoring—more strikeouts, higher velocity, and increased pitcher substitution—remained present.

It is bad enough to have run-scoring going back and forth from season to season; it's even worse to have, as a backdrop, the baseball itself changing, at varying rates, which could affect different players and ballparks differently. Let's see how our park-adjusted metrics do from 2010 onward:

---

3. We have switched to normal Pearson correlations to accommodate outliers; if you use robust (student's t) correlations, as in Table 1, the order remains the same although the values compress somewhat. We are otherwise using the same brms / Stan procedure referenced above.

4. 2010-2017 for descriptiveness, with 2018 added to provide the necessary second year for reliability and predictiveness.

Metric	Rel	Rel_Err	Pred	Pred_Err	Desc	Desc_Err
DRC+	0.63	0.02	0.42	0.03	0.72	0.02
wRC+	0.43	0.06	0.28	0.07	0.66	0.04
OPS+	0.37	0.07	0.27	0.07	0.66	0.05

Table 4: Batting Metric Performance by Contribution Measures (teams, 2010–2018); Robust Pearson Correlation to Team Runs/PA

The error rates are higher because the number of seasons is smaller. Nonetheless, the results are clear, even in this "stress test" situation. Once again, DRC+ is superior to the other park-adjusted metrics in every way, and well outside the margin of error on the two metrics that matter the most: Reliability and Predictiveness. More importantly, compared to Table 1, which showed all seasons from 1980-2018, DRC+ experiences no dropoff whatsoever in performance, despite the changing ball and volatile run environment. wRC+ and OPS+, on the other hand, experience notable declines in their reliability and predictive power, with descriptive power somewhat suffering also.

Why does DRC+ perform so much better, both on average and during times of statistical stress? We can think of (at least) three reasons.

The first is that DRC+, unlike other park-adjusted batting metrics, is designed to look behind the numbers for the player's expected contribution, rather than take play outcomes otherwise at face value like wRC+ and OPS+ do. Virtually all outcomes, good or bad, get shrunk to incorporate skepticism and award only partial credit for each play. The effect of this is particularly notable on home runs, which can unreasonably dominate the values of other metrics. Batters without question deserve much of the credit for home runs they hit, and DRC+ certainly gives them plenty. But by recognizing that other factors are often at play, DRC+ avoids letting home runs essentially rule the roost, allowing other (and more stable) accomplishments like walk and strikeout rate to play a more prominent role.

The second is that DRC+ is adjusted to account for more factors, most notably quality of opponent. I generally would classify these adjustments more as "nice to have" than critically important, but in the face of such drastically different performance it is reasonable to consider the possible impact of these additional adjustments also.

But the third—and possibly most important—reason DRC+ is better is that it uses single-year park factors rather than the multi-year park factors favored by the other metrics in widespread use. Traditionally, multi-year park factors have been viewed as more stable and less influenced by one-year blips; the flipside is that when the one-year changes are meaningful, the multi-year park factor can miss the change and possibly credit/penalize players in the wrong direction over multiple years.

In that respect, the altered ball situation may have created a bit of a perfect storm. The extent to which the altered ball has affected parks differently has not been publicly explored in detail, but suffice it to say that the yo-yo run environment has put multi-year park factors in a difficult position. An approach that made sense for years now may be in crisis.

A compromise would be to use single-season park ratings, but to incorporate some skepticism (there's that word again) into the responsibility assigned to each stadium. That is the approach taken by the models underlying DRA and DRC+, although they don't use park "factors" per se. Park factors are previously-calculated inputs to metrics like wRC+ and OPS+; for the deserved-run models, parks (controlled for platoon) are just additional variables in the various regressions for each component.

However, we can extract the overall effects of those variables to create a "park rating" of sorts by DRC+ for the various stadiums. On a 100-scale, with 100 being average, and combining the platoon splits, the park ratings for 2018 extract as follows:

Stadium	Park Rating
COL	104.0
CIN	103.0
PHI	102.0
BOS	101.8
TOR	101.7
MIL	101.6
TEX	101.5
NYA	101.4
CLE	101.1
WAS	101.0
SDN	100.7
CHA	100.6
CHN	100.5
LAN	100.5
MIN	100.5
ARI	100.4
PIT	100.1
SEA	100.0
ANA	99.8
SFN	99.7
BAL	99.5
HOU	99.4
TBA	99.4
DET	99.3
ATL	99.2
KCA	99.2
NYN	98.8
OAK	98.6
MIA	98.2
SLN	98.1

Table 5: Net Park Ratings, 2018

You'll note that the hierarchy of parks is roughly what you might expect, with perhaps some surprises; what may surprise you more is how limited the probable effect of the parks is found to be, even over only one year. By tracking the run-scoring effect of a park on a per-season basis, but keeping those values from getting too extreme, the "deserved" family of metrics can react each season to changes in a park or the baseball, without overreacting to any such changes. This is not the only way to do it, but it is an approach that seems to work, as verified by the correlation performances reported above.

Lastly, we will compare the performance of DRC+ to Statcast. Statcast offensive performance is typically reported by what MLBAM calls xwOBA, and somewhat less commonly by what it calls xBA. Neither statistic appears to be easily available grouped by player and team, but it is available grouped by individual and offers the ability to compare either statistic to a player's current or next year wOBA, as well as the next year of the same statistic. So, comparing reliability (correlation to next year's measurement for same individual), predictiveness (correlation to next season's

wOBA) and descriptiveness (correlation to same year's wOBA), here are the comparisons between DRC+ and Statcast metrics, over the four years the latter has been in existence:

Metric	Rel	Rel_Err	Pred	Pred_Err	Desc	Desc_Err
DRC+	0.77	0.001	0.59	0.001	0.88	~0
Statcast xwOBA	0.63	0.001	0.52	0.001	0.87	~0
Statcast xBA	0.56	0.001	0.42	0.001	0.75	0.001

Table 6: DRC+ vs. Statcast by Contribution Measures (individuals by total season, Gaussian correlations, 2015–2018)

Statcast metrics have the advantage of superior inputs, but those inputs appear to have limitations also. Both xwOBA and xBA are trounced by DRC+, largely across the board. And unlike Statcast, DRC+ offers superior accuracy not just from 2015-2018, but all the way back to 1921.

—Jonathan Judge is an author of Baseball Prospectus.

PECOTA Leaderboards

Height Percentiles

Percentile	Name	Team	HEIGHT
100	Aaron Judge	NYA	79
90	Michael Taylor	WAS	76
80	Keon Broxton	MIL	75
70	Mike Zunino	TBA	74
60	Anthony Rendon	WAS	73
50	Jordan Luplow	CLE	73
40	Javier Baez	CHN	72
30	Cory Spangenberg	MIL	72
20	Roberto Perez	CLE	71
10	Chris Owings	KCA	70
0	Tony Kemp	HOU	66

Batting Average

Rank	Name	Team	AVG
1	Jose Altuve	HOU	.307
2	Daniel Murphy	COL	.303
3	Jose Ramirez	CLE	.302
3	Mike Trout	ANA	.302
5	Mookie Betts	BOS	.300
6	Charlie Blackmon	COL	.296
7	Joey Votto	CIN	.292
8	Justin Turner	LAN	.290
9	J.D. Martinez	BOS	.289
9	Francisco Lindor	CLE	.289
11	Nolan Arenado	COL	.286
11	Freddie Freeman	ATL	.286
13	Jose Peraza	CIN	.285
14	Anthony Rendon	WAS	.284
14	DJ LeMahieu	COL	.284
16	Jean Segura	PHI	.283
16	Josh Reddick	HOU	.283
16	Manny Machado	LAN	.283
19	Ender Inciarte	ATL	.282
19	Whit Merrifield	KCA	.282
19	Buster Posey	SFN	.282

Batting Average Percentiles

Percentile	Name	Team	AVG
99	Daniel Murphy	COL	.303
90	Corey Seager	LAN	.274
80	Starlin Castro	MIA	.265
70	Ben Zobrist	CHN	.260
60	Josh Bell	PIT	.256
50	Michael Conforto	NYN	.251
40	Josh Phegley	OAK	.247
30	Orlando Arcia	MIL	.241
20	John Hicks	DET	.234
10	Daniel Robertson	TBA	.227
1	Chris Davis	BAL	.212

On-Base Percentage

Rank	Name	Team	OBP
1	Mike Trout	ANA	.454
2	Joey Votto	CIN	.417
3	Paul Goldschmidt	SLN	.393
4	Bryce Harper	WAS	.392
5	Jose Altuve	HOU	.387
6	Justin Turner	LAN	.386
7	Anthony Rizzo	CHN	.385
8	Mookie Betts	BOS	.384
9	Freddie Freeman	ATL	.383
9	Jose Ramirez	CLE	.383
11	Matt Carpenter	SLN	.378
12	J.D. Martinez	BOS	.373
13	Juan Soto	WAS	.372
14	Anthony Rendon	WAS	.369
14	Buster Posey	SFN	.369
16	Kris Bryant	CHN	.368
17	Aaron Judge	NYA	.367
18	Josh Donaldson	ATL	.366
19	Charlie Blackmon	COL	.365
19	Nolan Arenado	COL	.365

On-Base Percentage Percentiles

Percentile	Name	Team	OBP
99	Joey Votto	CIN	.417
90	Max Muncy	LAN	.359
80	Josh Bell	PIT	.345
70	J.T. Realmuto	MIA	.335
60	Kendrys Morales	TOR	.329
50	Austin Dean	MIA	.324
40	Howie Kendrick	WAS	.318
30	Albert Almora	CHN	.310
20	Garrett Cooper	MIA	.303
10	Brett Phillips	KCA	.296
1	Chris Shaw	SFN	.273

Slugging Percentage

Rank	Name	Team	SLG
1	Mike Trout	ANA	.579
2	J.D. Martinez	BOS	.567
3	Jose Ramirez	CLE	.529
4	Mookie Betts	BOS	.518
4	Nolan Arenado	COL	.518
6	Giancarlo Stanton	NYA	.515
7	Khris Davis	OAK	.513
8	Freddie Freeman	ATL	.507
8	Charlie Blackmon	COL	.507
10	Manny Machado	LAN	.503
11	Bryce Harper	WAS	.500
11	Nelson Cruz	MIN	.500
13	Luke Voit	NYA	.499
14	Shohei Ohtani	ANA	.497
14	Francisco Lindor	CLE	.497
16	Rhys Hoskins	PHI	.495
17	Daniel Murphy	COL	.492
18	Edwin Encarnacion	SEA	.489
19	Mike Moustakas	MIL	.487
20	Aaron Judge	NYA	.485

Slugging Percentage Percentiles

Percentile	Name	Team	SLG
99	J.D. Martinez	BOS	.567
90	Franmil Reyes	SDN	.470
80	Kurt Suzuki	WAS	.452
70	Aaron Hicks	NYA	.437
60	Miguel Cabrera	DET	.424
50	Andrew Toles	LAN	.414
40	Ji-Man Choi	TBA	.404
30	Steven Souza	ARI	.392
20	Raimel Tapia	COL	.378
10	Mallex Smith	SEA	.361
1	Travis Jankowski	SDN	.329

OPS

Rank	Name	Team	OPS
1	Mike Trout	ANA	1.033
2	J.D. Martinez	BOS	.940
3	Jose Ramirez	CLE	.912
4	Mookie Betts	BOS	.902
5	Bryce Harper	WAS	.892
6	Freddie Freeman	ATL	.890
7	Joey Votto	CIN	.888
8	Nolan Arenado	COL	.883
9	Paul Goldschmidt	SLN	.877
10	Charlie Blackmon	COL	.872
11	Giancarlo Stanton	NYA	.868
12	Nelson Cruz	MIN	.863
13	Justin Turner	LAN	.862
13	Jose Altuve	HOU	.862
15	Rhys Hoskins	PHI	.858
16	Anthony Rizzo	CHN	.857
17	Manny Machado	LAN	.856
18	Francisco Lindor	CLE	.855
19	Daniel Murphy	COL	.853
20	Aaron Judge	NYA	.852
20	Matt Carpenter	SLN	.852

OPS Percentiles

Percentile	Name	Team	OPS
99	J.D. Martinez	BOS	.940
90	Josh Donaldson	ATL	.827
80	Andrew Benintendi	BOS	.789
70	Jesse Winker	CIN	.769
60	Trey Mancini	BAL	.751
50	Brett Gardner	NYA	.737
40	Jordy Mercer	DET	.723
30	Daniel Robertson	TBA	.705
20	Mac Williamson	SFN	.687
10	John Hicks	DET	.665
1	Jacoby Jones	DET	.615

Home Runs

Rank	Name	Team	HR
1	J.D. Martinez	BOS	40
2	Khris Davis	OAK	38
3	Giancarlo Stanton	NYA	37
4	Mike Trout	ANA	36
5	Aaron Judge	NYA	34
6	Joey Gallo	TEX	33
7	Matt Olson	OAK	30
7	Rhys Hoskins	PHI	30
7	Nelson Cruz	MIN	30
7	Manny Machado	LAN	30
7	Gary Sanchez	NYA	30
12	Edwin Encarnacion	SEA	29
12	Nolan Arenado	COL	29
14	Javier Baez	CHN	28
14	Ronald Acuna	ATL	28
14	Bryce Harper	WAS	28
14	Justin Upton	ANA	28
14	Mookie Betts	BOS	28
19	Cody Bellinger	LAN	27
19	Franmil Reyes	SDN	27
19	Luke Voit	NYA	27
19	Mike Moustakas	MIL	27
19	Francisco Lindor	CLE	27

Home Runs Percentiles

Percentile	Name	Team	HR
99	Aaron Judge	NYA	34
90	Gleyber Torres	NYA	22
80	Ian Happ	CHN	18
70	Miguel Cabrera	DET	15
60	Chad Pinder	OAK	11
50	Michael Taylor	WAS	9
40	Greg Allen	CLE	7
30	Elias Diaz	PIT	5
20	Michael Reed	MIN	3
10	Spencer Kieboom	WAS	1
1	Jacob Stallings	PIT	1

Stolen Bases

Rank	Name	Team	SB
1	Adalberto Mondesi	KCA	43
2	Trea Turner	WAS	42
3	Starling Marte	PIT	38
3	Jarrod Dyson	ARI	38
3	Dee Gordon	SEA	38
6	Jonathan Villar	BAL	37
7	Billy Hamilton	KCA	36
8	Mallex Smith	SEA	34
9	Whit Merrifield	KCA	33
10	Mookie Betts	BOS	28
11	Mike Trout	ANA	27
12	Ronald Acuna	ATL	25
12	Jose Altuve	HOU	25
12	Lorenzo Cain	MIL	25
12	Jose Ramirez	CLE	25
16	Jose Peraza	CIN	24
17	Delino DeShields	TEX	23
18	Kevin Kiermaier	TBA	22
18	Jean Segura	PHI	22
18	Amed Rosario	NYN	22

Stolen Bases Percentiles

Percentile	Name	Team	SB
99	Starling Marte	PIT	38
90	Charlie Blackmon	COL	15
80	Fernando Tatis Jr.	SDN	8
70	Jake Marisnick	HOU	5
60	Eugenio Suarez	CIN	4
50	Michael Conforto	NYN	3
40	Luis Urias	SDN	2
30	Nick Martini	OAK	1
20	Wilson Ramos	NYN	0
10	Jacob Stallings	PIT	0
1	Sean Murphy	OAK	0

Runs

Rank	Name	Team	R
1	Mike Trout	ANA	127
2	Mookie Betts	BOS	112
3	Aaron Judge	NYA	107
4	Francisco Lindor	CLE	104
5	Ronald Acuna	ATL	103
6	J.D. Martinez	BOS	99
7	Alex Bregman	HOU	98
8	Christian Yelich	MIL	97
9	Javier Baez	CHN	96
9	Charlie Blackmon	COL	96
11	George Springer	HOU	95
12	Trea Turner	WAS	94
12	Rhys Hoskins	PHI	94
14	Tommy Pham	TBA	93
15	Matt Carpenter	SLN	92
16	Jose Ramirez	CLE	91
17	Bryce Harper	WAS	90
17	Kris Bryant	CHN	90
17	Giancarlo Stanton	NYA	90
20	Paul Goldschmidt	SLN	89
20	Justin Turner	LAN	89
20	Anthony Rizzo	CHN	89
20	Whit Merrifield	KCA	89
20	Manny Machado	LAN	89

Runs Percentiles

Percentile	Name	Team	R
99	Ronald Acuna	ATL	103
90	Matt Olson	OAK	78
80	Ramon Laureano	OAK	68
70	Ryan O'Hearn	KCA	60
60	Ian Desmond	COL	49
50	Greg Allen	CLE	40
40	Brandon Drury	TOR	31
30	Yoenis Cespedes	NYN	20
20	Ronald Torreyes	MIN	14
10	Deven Marrero	MIA	7
1	Sergio Alcantara	DET	3

Runs Batted In

Rank	Name	Team	RBI
1	J.D. Martinez	BOS	116
2	Mike Trout	ANA	105
2	Khris Davis	OAK	105
4	Giancarlo Stanton	NYA	104
5	Manny Machado	LAN	99
6	Aaron Judge	NYA	95
7	Nolan Arenado	COL	94
8	Nelson Cruz	MIN	93
9	Bryce Harper	WAS	92
9	Edwin Encarnacion	SEA	92
11	Mookie Betts	BOS	91
11	Anthony Rizzo	CHN	91
13	Jose Ramirez	CLE	90
13	Freddie Freeman	ATL	90
13	Gary Sanchez	NYA	90
16	Joey Gallo	TEX	89
16	Matt Olson	OAK	89
16	Mike Moustakas	MIL	89
19	Justin Upton	ANA	88
19	Francisco Lindor	CLE	88
19	Paul Goldschmidt	SLN	88

RBI Percentiles

Percentile	Name	Team	RBI
99	Aaron Judge	NYA	95
90	Paul DeJong	SLN	77
80	Elvis Andrus	TEX	67
70	Cedric Mullins	BAL	58
60	Colin Moran	PIT	47
50	Adam Engel	CHA	39
40	Max Stassi	HOU	30
30	Nick Martini	OAK	21
20	Jacob Nottingham	MIL	13
10	Ryan Howard	SFN	7
1	Pete Kozma	DET	3

Isolated Power

Rank	Name	Team	ISO
1	J.D. Martinez	BOS	.278
2	Mike Trout	ANA	.277
3	Khris Davis	OAK	.260
4	Giancarlo Stanton	NYA	.259
5	Joey Gallo	TEX	.245
6	Rhys Hoskins	PHI	.237
7	Aaron Judge	NYA	.236
8	Shohei Ohtani	ANA	.234
9	Nolan Arenado	COL	.232
9	Luke Voit	NYA	.232
11	Edwin Encarnacion	SEA	.230
11	Matt Olson	OAK	.230
13	Nelson Cruz	MIN	.229
13	Bryce Harper	WAS	.229
15	Jose Ramirez	CLE	.227
16	Cody Bellinger	LAN	.225
17	Gary Sanchez	NYA	.221
17	Freddie Freeman	ATL	.221
17	Peter Alonso	NYN	.221
20	Manny Machado	LAN	.220

Isolate Slugging (ISO) Percentiles

Percentile	Name	Team	ISO
99	Mike Trout	ANA	.277
90	Salvador Perez	KCA	.210
80	Ryan Zimmerman	WAS	.192
70	Adam Duvall	ATL	.182
60	Mitch Moreland	BOS	.173
50	Yan Gomes	WAS	.163
40	Tim Anderson	CHA	.153
30	Manny Pina	MIL	.141
20	Jordy Mercer	DET	.134
10	Alex Gordon	KCA	.126
1	Travis Jankowski	SDN	.101

Hitter Walk Rate

Rank	Name	Team	BB%
11	Jose Bautista	PHI	0.136
5	Miguel Cabrera	DET	0.129
6	Edwin Encarnacion	SEA	0.126

Hitter Walk Rate Percentiles

Percentile	Name	Team	BB%
99	Joey Votto	CIN	0.164
90	Josh Bell	PIT	0.117
80	Shohei Ohtani	ANA	0.106
70	Yonder Alonso	CHA	0.099
60	Tommy La Stella	ANA	0.093
50	Jonathan Lucroy	ANA	0.085
40	Garrett Hampson	COL	0.079
30	Josh Phegley	OAK	0.073
20	Francisco Mejia	SDN	0.068
10	Yadier Molina	SLN	0.061
1	Lourdes Gurriel	TOR	0.048

Strikeout Rate

Rank	Name	Team	SO%
3	Victor Martinez	DET	0.133
17	Melky Cabrera	CLE	0.134
1	Albert Pujols	ANA	0.138
4	Yadier Molina	SLN	0.140
10	Robinson Cano	NYN	0.142

Strikeout Rate Percentiles

Percentile	Name	Team	SO%
99	Joe Panik	SFN	0.095
90	Dustin Pedroia	BOS	0.144
80	Wilson Ramos	NYN	0.169
70	Cedric Mullins	BAL	0.187
60	Brock Holt	BOS	0.200
50	Christian Yelich	MIL	0.211
40	Kris Bryant	CHN	0.223
30	Paul Goldschmidt	SLN	0.241
20	Jorge Bonifacio	KCA	0.257
10	Jonathan Villar	BAL	0.280
1	Ian Happ	CHN	0.344

DRC+

Rank	Name	Team	DRC+
1	Mike Trout	ANA	185
2	J.D. Martinez	BOS	150
3	Mookie Betts	BOS	149
4	Joey Votto	CIN	147
4	Jose Ramirez	CLE	147
6	Bryce Harper	WAS	144
7	Freddie Freeman	ATL	142
8	Nolan Arenado	COL	141
8	Paul Goldschmidt	SLN	141
10	Anthony Rizzo	CHN	140
11	Jose Altuve	HOU	139
11	Charlie Blackmon	COL	139
11	Justin Turner	LAN	139
14	Nelson Cruz	MIN	137
15	Giancarlo Stanton	NYA	136
16	Rhys Hoskins	PHI	134
16	Matt Carpenter	SLN	134
18	Anthony Rendon	WAS	132
18	Manny Machado	LAN	132
18	Aaron Judge	NYA	132

DRC+ Percentiles

Percentile	Name	Team	DRC+
99	J.D. Martinez	BOS	150
90	Jose Abreu	CHA	126
80	Steve Pearce	BOS	115
70	Eddie Rosario	MIN	110
60	Dylan Moore	SEA	106
50	Max Kepler	MIN	102
40	Alex Verdugo	LAN	98
30	Renato Nunez	BAL	92
20	Franchy Cordero	SDN	88
10	Nathaniel Lowe	TBA	82
1	Richie Martin	BAL	67

Hitter VORP

Rank	Name	Team	VORP
1	Mike Trout	ANA	95.8
2	Mookie Betts	BOS	66.6
3	Charlie Blackmon	COL	56.1
4	Jose Ramirez	CLE	53.5
5	Jose Altuve	HOU	52.3
6	Bryce Harper	WAS	51.2
7	Francisco Lindor	CLE	49.8
8	Manny Machado	LAN	49.0
9	J.D. Martinez	BOS	44.3
10	Aaron Judge	NYA	43.6
11	Nolan Arenado	COL	42.9
12	Justin Turner	LAN	42.8
13	Cody Bellinger	LAN	42.0
14	Joey Votto	CIN	41.0
15	Freddie Freeman	ATL	40.6
16	Paul Goldschmidt	SLN	40.4
16	Matt Carpenter	SLN	40.4
18	Christian Yelich	MIL	39.5
19	Anthony Rendon	WAS	39.4
20	Anthony Rizzo	CHN	39.1

Hitter VORP Percentiles

Percentile	Name	Team	VORP
99	Jose Altuve	HOU	52.3
90	Andrew Benintendi	BOS	29.4
80	Ian Happ	CHN	20.2
70	Andrew Toles	LAN	14.3
60	Yonder Alonso	CHA	10.4
50	Greg Allen	CLE	7.0
40	Ildemaro Vargas	ARI	4.3
30	Austin Hays	BAL	1.9
20	Rafael Lopez	ATL	0.4
10	Lane Thomas	SLN	-0.6
1	Dustin Peterson	DET	-4.7

Base-Running Runs (BRR)

Rank	Name	Team	BRR
1	Mookie Betts	BOS	4.9
1	Billy Hamilton	KCA	4.9
3	Trea Turner	WAS	4.3
4	Dee Gordon	SEA	3.9
4	Delino DeShields	TEX	3.9
6	Byron Buxton	MIN	3.8
6	Tommy Pham	TBA	3.8
8	Jake Bauers	CLE	3.3
8	Marcus Semien	OAK	3.3
10	Eddy Diaz	COL	3.2
11	Ozzie Albies	ATL	3.1
11	Tim Anderson	CHA	3.1
11	Eddie Rosario	MIN	3.1
14	Terrance Gore	KCA	3.0
14	Travis Jankowski	SDN	3.0
14	Kevin Kiermaier	TBA	3.0
17	David Fletcher	ANA	2.9
17	Raimel Tapia	COL	2.9
19	DJ LeMahieu	COL	2.8
20	Jose Ramirez	CLE	2.5

Base-Running Runs (BRR) Percentiles

Percentile	Name	Team	BRR
99	Dee Gordon	SEA	3.9
90	Ronald Acuna	ATL	1.7
80	Didi Gregorius	NYA	0.8
70	Derek Fisher	HOU	0.3
60	Ryan Cordell	CHA	0.1
50	Mark Zagunis	CHN	-0.0
40	Yordan Alvarez	HOU	-0.1
30	Jose Pirela	SDN	-0.3
20	Yoan Moncada	CHA	-0.6
10	Lourdes Gurriel	TOR	-1.1
1	Edwin Encarnacion	SEA	-3.0

Hitter WARP

Rank	Name	Team	WARP
1	Mike Trout	ANA	9.6
2	Mookie Betts	BOS	8.7
3	Francisco Lindor	CLE	6.3
4	Charlie Blackmon	COL	5.4
5	Nolan Arenado	COL	5.3
6	Anthony Rizzo	CHN	5.2
6	Jose Ramirez	CLE	5.2
6	Lorenzo Cain	MIL	5.2
6	Aaron Judge	NYA	5.2
10	Joey Votto	CIN	5.1
10	Bryce Harper	WAS	5.1
12	Yasmani Grandal	LAN	5.0
12	Paul Goldschmidt	SLN	5.0
12	Trea Turner	WAS	5.0
15	Alex Bregman	HOU	4.9
15	Matt Chapman	OAK	4.9
15	Kevin Kiermaier	TBA	4.9
18	Jose Altuve	HOU	4.8
18	Cody Bellinger	LAN	4.8
18	Buster Posey	SFN	4.8

Hitter WARP Percentiles

Percentile	Name	Team	WARP
99	Nolan Arenado	COL	5.3
90	Chris Taylor	LAN	3.3
80	Hunter Renfroe	SDN	2.3
70	Teoscar Hernandez	TOR	1.6
60	Dee Gordon	SEA	1.2
50	Omar Narvaez	SEA	0.8
40	Domingo Santana	SEA	0.5
30	Luis Guillorme	NYN	0.2
20	Gavin Cecchini	NYN	0.0
10	Peter O'Brien	MIA	-0.2
1	Rowdy Tellez	TOR	-0.6

AL Hitter WARP

Rank	Name	Team	WARP
1	Mike Trout	ANA	9.6
2	Mookie Betts	BOS	8.7
3	Francisco Lindor	CLE	6.3
4	Jose Ramirez	CLE	5.2
4	Aaron Judge	NYA	5.2
6	Alex Bregman	HOU	4.9
6	Matt Chapman	OAK	4.9
6	Kevin Kiermaier	TBA	4.9
9	Jose Altuve	HOU	4.8
10	J.D. Martinez	BOS	4.6

NL Hitter WARP

Rank	Name	Team	WARP
1	Charlie Blackmon	COL	5.4
2	Nolan Arenado	COL	5.3
3	Anthony Rizzo	CHN	5.2
3	Lorenzo Cain	MIL	5.2
5	Joey Votto	CIN	5.1
5	Bryce Harper	WAS	5.1
7	Yasmani Grandal	LAN	5.0
7	Paul Goldschmidt	SLN	5.0
7	Trea Turner	WAS	5.0
10	Cody Bellinger	LAN	4.8
10	Buster Posey	SFN	4.8

Deserved Run Average (DRA) - Starters

Rank	Name	Team	DRA
1	Chris Sale	BOS	3.12
2	Aaron Nola	PHI	3.52
3	Noah Syndergaard	NYN	3.56
3	Jacob deGrom	NYN	3.56
5	James Paxton	NYA	3.58
5	Luis Severino	NYA	3.58
7	German Marquez	COL	3.65
8	Carlos Carrasco	CLE	3.69
9	Clayton Kershaw	LAN	3.73
9	Max Scherzer	WAS	3.73
11	Patrick Corbin	WAS	3.78
12	Corey Kluber	CLE	3.79
13	Stephen Strasburg	WAS	3.83
14	Blake Snell	TBA	3.84
15	Trevor Bauer	CLE	3.87
16	Jon Gray	COL	3.90
16	Gerrit Cole	HOU	3.90
16	Jameson Taillon	PIT	3.90
19	Nick Pivetta	PHI	3.96
20	Jose Berrios	MIN	4.00

Deserved Run Average (DRA) - Starters Percentiles

Percentile	Name	Team	DRA
99	Chris Sale	BOS	3.12
90	Patrick Corbin	WAS	3.78
80	Jack Flaherty	SLN	4.04
70	Masahiro Tanaka	NYA	4.16
60	Robbie Ray	ARI	4.27
50	Nathan Eovaldi	BOS	4.35
40	Madison Bumgarner	SFN	4.53
30	Ivan Nova	CHA	4.67
20	Eric Lauer	SDN	4.80
10	Reynaldo Lopez	CHA	5.05
1	Andrew Cashner	BAL	5.33

Deserved Run Average (DRA) - Relievers

Rank	Name	Team	DRA
1	Edwin Diaz	NYN	2.92
2	Aroldis Chapman	NYA	3.29
3	Dellin Betances	NYA	3.32
4	Corey Knebel	MIL	3.53
5	Matt Barnes	BOS	3.62
6	Felipe Vazquez	PIT	3.66
7	Blake Treinen	OAK	3.67
8	Ryan Pressly	HOU	3.69
9	Brad Hand	CLE	3.71
10	Josh Hader	MIL	3.72
11	Roberto Osuna	HOU	3.74
12	Andrew Miller	SLN	3.77
13	Kenley Jansen	LAN	3.80
14	Craig Kimbrel	BOS	3.83
15	Chad Green	NYA	3.84
16	Sean Doolittle	WAS	3.86
17	Ken Giles	TOR	3.87
18	Diego Castillo	TBA	3.89
19	Will Harris	HOU	3.90
20	Will Smith	SFN	3.91
20	Trevor Rosenthal	WAS	3.91

Deserved Run Average (DRA) - Relievers Percentiles

Percentile	Name	Team	DRA
99	Corey Knebel	MIL	3.53
90	A.J. Minter	ATL	4.17
80	Reymin Guduan	HOU	4.39
70	Max Fried	ATL	4.50
60	Trevor May	MIN	4.62
50	Zack Littell	MIN	4.72
40	Joe Biagini	TOR	4.82
30	Mark Leiter	TOR	4.95
20	Aaron Wilkerson	MIL	5.09
10	Tyler Thornburg	BOS	5.37
1	Tanner Rainey	WAS	5.90

Earned Run Average - Starters

Rank	Name	Team	ERA
1	Chris Sale	BOS	2.99
2	Noah Syndergaard	NYN	3.06
3	Jacob deGrom	NYN	3.07
4	Aaron Nola	PHI	3.18
5	Max Scherzer	WAS	3.29
6	German Marquez	COL	3.31
7	Patrick Corbin	WAS	3.34
8	Clayton Kershaw	LAN	3.35
9	Jameson Taillon	PIT	3.36
10	Stephen Strasburg	WAS	3.38
11	Miles Mikolas	SLN	3.44
12	Jack Flaherty	SLN	3.45
13	Carlos Carrasco	CLE	3.46
14	Chris Archer	PIT	3.51
15	Mike Foltynewicz	ATL	3.52
16	Jon Gray	COL	3.55
17	Corey Kluber	CLE	3.56
17	Nick Pivetta	PHI	3.56
19	Blake Snell	TBA	3.57
20	Joe Musgrove	PIT	3.58

Earned Run Average - Starters Percentiles

Percentile	Name	Team	ERA
99	Chris Sale	BOS	2.99
90	Miles Mikolas	SLN	3.44
80	Ross Stripling	LAN	3.62
70	Steven Matz	NYN	3.74
60	Robbie Erlin	SDN	3.89
50	Michael Fulmer	DET	4.00
40	Nathan Eovaldi	BOS	4.13
30	Tyler Skaggs	ANA	4.22
20	Carlos Rodon	CHA	4.47
10	Dylan Bundy	BAL	4.70
1	Anthony DeSclafani	CIN	5.32

Earned Run Average - Relievers

Rank	Name	Team	ERA
1	Edwin Diaz	NYN	2.50
2	Corey Knebel	MIL	3.05
3	Felipe Vazquez	PIT	3.16
4	Josh Hader	MIL	3.21
4	Andrew Miller	SLN	3.21
6	Blake Treinen	OAK	3.32
7	Aroldis Chapman	NYA	3.33
8	Dellin Betances	NYA	3.36
9	Will Smith	SFN	3.38
10	Kenley Jansen	LAN	3.41
10	Sean Doolittle	WAS	3.41
12	Archie Bradley	ARI	3.42
13	Keone Kela	PIT	3.44
13	Trevor Rosenthal	WAS	3.44
15	Matt Barnes	BOS	3.46
16	Ryan Pressly	HOU	3.47
17	Brad Hand	CLE	3.48
17	Giovanny Gallegos	SLN	3.48
19	Roberto Osuna	HOU	3.52
20	Jeremy Jeffress	MIL	3.54

Earned Run Average - Relievers Percentiles

Percentile	Name	Team	ERA
99	Josh Hader	MIL	3.21
90	Brad Peacock	HOU	3.76
80	Dakota Hudson	SLN	3.94
70	Phil Maton	SDN	4.06
60	Trevor Hildenberger	MIN	4.17
50	Brandon Kintzler	CHN	4.32
40	Jose De Leon	TBA	4.46
30	Hector Velazquez	BOS	4.61
20	Mark Leiter	TOR	4.81
10	Luis Ortiz	BAL	5.07
1	Jesse Hahn	KCA	5.48

Wins

Rank	Name	Team	W
1	Corey Kluber	CLE	13
1	Gerrit Cole	HOU	13
1	Max Scherzer	WAS	13
4	Zack Greinke	ARI	12
4	Chris Sale	BOS	12
4	Justin Verlander	HOU	12
4	Luis Severino	NYA	12
4	Jacob deGrom	NYN	12
4	Aaron Nola	PHI	12
4	Miles Mikolas	SLN	12
4	Jack Flaherty	SLN	12
4	Patrick Corbin	WAS	12
13	Zack Godley	ARI	11
13	Kevin Gausman	ATL	11
13	Rick Porcello	BOS	11
13	Cole Hamels	CHN	11
13	Jose Quintana	CHN	11
13	Carlos Carrasco	CLE	11
13	Trevor Bauer	CLE	11
13	Jon Gray	COL	11
13	Kyle Freeland	COL	11
13	German Marquez	COL	11
13	Dallas Keuchel	HOU	11
13	Clayton Kershaw	LAN	11
13	Walker Buehler	LAN	11
13	Jose Berrios	MIN	11
13	Masahiro Tanaka	NYA	11
13	Noah Syndergaard	NYN	11
13	Jameson Taillon	PIT	11

Wins Percentiles

Percentile	Name	Team	W
99	Justin Verlander	HOU	12
90	Collin McHugh	HOU	9
80	Michael Lorenzen	CIN	6
70	Joe Palumbo	TEX	4
60	Chris Devenski	HOU	3
50	Kirby Yates	SDN	3
40	John Means	BAL	2
30	Tyler Bashlor	NYN	2
20	Jon Duplantier	ARI	1
10	Andrew Vasquez	MIN	1
1	Josh Taylor	BOS	0

Strikeouts

Rank	Name	Team	SO
1	Max Scherzer	WAS	241
2	Gerrit Cole	HOU	229
3	Chris Sale	BOS	224
3	Justin Verlander	HOU	224
5	Jacob deGrom	NYN	217
5	Aaron Nola	PHI	217
7	Robbie Ray	ARI	206
8	Corey Kluber	CLE	204
9	Patrick Corbin	WAS	198
10	Luis Severino	NYA	197
11	Carlos Carrasco	CLE	196
12	Trevor Bauer	CLE	195
13	Jack Flaherty	SLN	193
14	Jose Berrios	MIN	191
14	Blake Snell	TBA	191
16	Zack Greinke	ARI	190
16	James Paxton	NYA	190
16	Noah Syndergaard	NYN	190
19	German Marquez	COL	187
20	Zack Godley	ARI	185

Strikeouts Percentiles

Percentile	Name	Team	SO
99	Aaron Nola	PHI	217
90	Marco Gonzales	SEA	144
80	Michael Lorenzen	CIN	102
70	Matt Moore	DET	71
60	Juan Minaya	CHA	61
50	Nick Anderson	MIA	53
40	Adam Cimber	CLE	46
30	Joe Harvey	NYA	38
20	Thyago Vieira	CHA	29
10	Kyle Ryan	CHN	18
1	Brent Suter	MIL	10

WHIP - Starters

Rank	Name	Team	WHIP
1	Clayton Kershaw	LAN	1.01
2	Max Scherzer	WAS	1.03
3	Chris Sale	BOS	1.04
3	Jacob deGrom	NYN	1.04
5	Justin Verlander	HOU	1.06
6	Zack Greinke	ARI	1.10
7	Aaron Nola	PHI	1.11
8	Corey Kluber	CLE	1.14
8	Rich Hill	LAN	1.14
10	Gerrit Cole	HOU	1.15
10	Ross Stripling	LAN	1.15
10	Miles Mikolas	SLN	1.15
13	Julio Teheran	ATL	1.16
13	Kenta Maeda	LAN	1.16
13	Noah Syndergaard	NYN	1.16
13	Jack Flaherty	SLN	1.16
13	Stephen Strasburg	WAS	1.16
18	Carlos Carrasco	CLE	1.17
19	Kyle Hendricks	CHN	1.18
19	Collin McHugh	HOU	1.18
19	Walker Buehler	LAN	1.18
19	Steven Matz	NYN	1.18

WHIP - Starters Percentiles

Percentile	Name	Team	WHIP
99	Clayton Kershaw	LAN	1.01
90	Ross Stripling	LAN	1.15
80	Steven Matz	NYN	1.18
70	Madison Bumgarner	SFN	1.20
60	Kevin Gausman	ATL	1.23
50	Charlie Morton	TBA	1.25
40	Matt Boyd	DET	1.28
30	Jon Gray	COL	1.30
20	Sean Newcomb	ATL	1.33
10	Jordan Zimmermann	DET	1.38
1	Alex Cobb	BAL	1.46

Saves

Rank	Name	Team	SV
1	Edwin Diaz	NYN	38
1	Felipe Vazquez	PIT	38
3	Brad Hand	CLE	35
3	Wade Davis	COL	35
3	Roberto Osuna	HOU	35
3	Kirby Yates	SDN	35
7	Ken Giles	TOR	32
8	Kenley Jansen	LAN	31
9	Brandon Morrow	CHN	30
9	Raisel Iglesias	CIN	30
9	Wily Peralta	KCA	30
9	Corey Knebel	MIL	30
9	Aroldis Chapman	NYA	30
9	Blake Treinen	OAK	30
9	Will Smith	SFN	30
9	Jordan Hicks	SLN	30
9	Jose Alvarado	TBA	30
9	Jose Leclerc	TEX	30
19	Craig Kimbrel	BOS	29
19	Matt Barnes	BOS	29
19	Sean Doolittle	WAS	29

Strikeout Rate

Rank	Name	Team	SO%
1	Josh Hader	MIL	40.3
1	Edwin Diaz	NYN	40.3
3	Corey Knebel	MIL	36.2
3	Dellin Betances	NYA	36.2
5	Aroldis Chapman	NYA	35.8
6	Craig Kimbrel	BOS	34.9
7	Chris Sale	BOS	32.7
7	Max Scherzer	WAS	32.7
9	Kirby Yates	SDN	32.6
10	Sean Doolittle	WAS	32.4
11	Trevor Rosenthal	WAS	32.1
12	Alex Reyes	SLN	32.0
12	Brad Hand	CLE	32.0
12	David Robertson	PHI	32.0
12	Jose Leclerc	TEX	32.0
16	Freddy Peralta	MIL	31.7
17	Robbie Ray	ARI	31.5
18	Kenley Jansen	LAN	31.2
18	Jacob deGrom	NYN	31.2
20	Will Smith	SFN	30.9

Strikeout Rate Percentiles

Percentile	Name	Team	SO%
99	Corey Knebel	MIL	36.2
90	Darren O'Day	ATL	29.0
80	Matt Strahm	SDN	27.3
70	Steven Matz	NYN	25.8
60	Matt Andriese	ARI	24.7
50	Matt Albers	MIL	23.4
40	Matt Hall	DET	22.4
30	Sam Dyson	SFN	21.2
20	Jordan Stephens	CHA	20.3
10	Chasen Bradford	SEA	18.6
1	Trevor Oaks	KCA	15.7

Walk Rate

Rank	Name	Team	BB%
1	Clayton Kershaw	LAN	5.1
2	Miles Mikolas	SLN	5.7
2	Ryan Merritt	TBA	5.7
4	Josh Tomlin	CLE	5.8
4	Tyler Alexander	DET	5.8
6	Mike Leake	SEA	5.9
7	Rick Porcello	BOS	6.1
7	Ivan Nova	CHA	6.1
9	Nick Neidert	MIA	6.2
10	Bartolo Colon	TEX	6.3
10	Chris Sale	BOS	6.3
10	Shane Bieber	CLE	6.3
10	Corey Kluber	CLE	6.3
14	Jordan Zimmermann	DET	6.5
15	Masahiro Tanaka	NYA	6.6
16	Marco Gonzales	SEA	6.7
17	Jacob deGrom	NYN	6.8
17	Jameson Taillon	PIT	6.8
17	Zack Greinke	ARI	6.8
17	Pablo Lopez	MIA	6.8
17	Carlos Carrasco	CLE	6.8
17	Sean Manaea	OAK	6.8

Walk Rate Percentiles

Percentile	Name	Team	BB%
99	Mike Leake	SEA	5.9
90	Yusmeiro Petit	OAK	7.3
80	Matt Andriese	ARI	7.8
70	Alex Wood	CIN	8.3
60	Michael Pineda	MIN	8.6
50	Brett Kennedy	SDN	9.0
40	Taijuan Walker	ARI	9.4
30	Walker Buehler	LAN	9.9
20	Mychal Givens	BAL	10.3
10	Arodys Vizcaino	ATL	11.0
1	Jordan Hicks	SLN	13.3

Fastball Velocity

Rank	Name	Team	FB Velo
1	Jordan Hicks	SLN	102.94
2	Aroldis Chapman	NYA	101.90
3	Tayron Guerrero	MIA	100.75
4	Diego Castillo	TBA	100.16
5	Felipe Vazquez	PIT	99.75
6	Joe Kelly	LAN	99.57
7	Alex Reyes	SLN	99.55
8	Edwin Diaz	NYN	99.46
9	Trevor Rosenthal	WAS	99.45
10	Josh James	HOU	99.43
10	Noah Syndergaard	NYN	99.43
12	Seranthony Dominguez	PHI	99.28
13	Dellin Betances	NYA	99.26
14	Jose Alvarado	TBA	99.20
15	Luis Severino	NYA	99.09
16	Ryne Stanek	TBA	99.04
17	Ken Giles	TOR	98.89
18	Trey Wingenter	SDN	98.84
19	Justin Anderson	ANA	98.78
20	Robert Stock	SDN	98.68

Fastball Velocity Percentiles

Percentile	Name	Team	FB Velo
99	Diego Castillo	TBA	100.16
90	Hector Rondon	HOU	97.69
80	Jacob Turner	DET	96.51
70	Sean Reid-Foley	TOR	95.60
60	Mike Clevinger	CLE	94.92
50	Jeff Brigham	MIA	94.27
40	Nick Wittgren	MIA	93.56
30	Cole Hamels	CHN	92.92
20	Adam Plutko	CLE	92.22
10	Gio Gonzalez	MIL	91.06
1	Darren O'Day	ATL	87.41

Ground-ball Rate

Rank	Name	Team	GB%
1	Brad Ziegler	ARI	61.8
2	T.J. McFarland	ARI	59.3
3	Alex Claudio	MIL	58.9
4	Marcus Stroman	TOR	58.7
5	Sam Dyson	SFN	58.6
6	Jared Hughes	CIN	58.1
7	Clayton Richard	TOR	56.9
8	Clay Holmes	PIT	56.1
9	Richard Bleier	BAL	55.9
10	Dallas Keuchel	HOU	55.6
11	Dakota Hudson	SLN	55.5
12	Jeremy Jeffress	MIL	55.2
13	Blake Treinen	OAK	55.0
14	Lincoln Henzman	CHA	54.6
15	Lance McCullers	HOU	54.4
16	Framber Valdez	HOU	54.3
17	Kevin McCarthy	KCA	54.1
18	Tim Hill	KCA	53.7
19	Dan Jennings	MIL	53.6
20	Mike Montgomery	CHN	53.5
20	Jesus Reyes	CIN	53.5
20	Adam Cimber	CLE	53.5

Ground-ball Rate Percentiles

Percentile	Name	Team	GB%
99	Marcus Stroman	TOR	58.7
90	Bryan Shaw	COL	50.5
80	Samuel Gaviglio	TOR	48.3
70	Lance Lynn	TEX	46.9
60	Tanner Roark	CIN	45.6
50	Ryan Tepera	TOR	44.3
40	Mike Foltynewicz	ATL	42.8
30	Yu Darvish	CHN	41.5
20	Alex Reyes	SLN	40.3
10	Eduardo Rodriguez	BOS	38.1
1	Justin Verlander	HOU	34.1

Pitcher WARP

Rank	Name	Team	WARP
1	Chris Sale	BOS	4.6
2	Aaron Nola	PHI	3.9
3	Luis Severino	NYA	3.8
3	Corey Kluber	CLE	3.8
5	Jacob deGrom	NYN	3.6
5	Carlos Carrasco	CLE	3.6
7	Max Scherzer	WAS	3.4
7	Gerrit Cole	HOU	3.4
7	James Paxton	NYA	3.4
7	Noah Syndergaard	NYN	3.4
11	German Marquez	COL	3.2
12	Trevor Bauer	CLE	3.1
12	Patrick Corbin	WAS	3.1
12	Jose Berrios	MIN	3.1
15	Blake Snell	TBA	3.0
15	Justin Verlander	HOU	3.0
17	Jameson Taillon	PIT	2.9
17	Clayton Kershaw	LAN	2.9
19	Stephen Strasburg	WAS	2.7
20	Marcus Stroman	TOR	2.6
20	Zack Greinke	ARI	2.6
20	Jon Gray	COL	2.6

Pitcher WARP Percentiles

Percentile	Name	Team	WARP
99	Carlos Carrasco	CLE	3.6
90	Eduardo Rodriguez	BOS	1.6
80	Brad Hand	CLE	0.9
70	Jeremy Jeffress	MIL	0.6
60	Pedro Strop	CHN	0.4
50	Adam Morgan	PHI	0.3
40	Timothy Peterson	NYN	0.2
30	Daniel Stumpf	DET	0.1
20	Grant Dayton	ATL	0.0
10	Adam Conley	MIA	-0.1
1	Cody Anderson	CLE	-0.5

AL Pitcher WARP

Rank	Name	Team	WARP
1	Chris Sale	BOS	4.6
2	Corey Kluber	CLE	3.8
2	Luis Severino	NYA	3.8
4	Carlos Carrasco	CLE	3.6
5	Gerrit Cole	HOU	3.4
5	James Paxton	NYA	3.4
7	Trevor Bauer	CLE	3.1
7	Jose Berrios	MIN	3.1
9	Justin Verlander	HOU	3.0
9	Blake Snell	TBA	3.0

NL Pitcher WARP

Rank	Name	Team	WARP
1	Aaron Nola	PHI	3.9
2	Jacob deGrom	NYN	3.6
3	Noah Syndergaard	NYN	3.4
3	Max Scherzer	WAS	3.4
5	German Marquez	COL	3.2
6	Patrick Corbin	WAS	3.1
7	Clayton Kershaw	LAN	2.9
7	Jameson Taillon	PIT	2.9
9	Stephen Strasburg	WAS	2.7
10	Zack Greinke	ARI	2.6
10	Jon Gray	COL	2.6

Catcher WARP

Rank	Name	Team	WARP
1	Buster Posey	SFN	4.8
2	J.T. Realmuto	MIA	4.6
3	Austin Barnes	LAN	4.5
4	Gary Sanchez	NYA	4.4
5	Tyler Flowers	ATL	3.8
6	Roberto Perez	CLE	3.2
7	Yadier Molina	SLN	2.9
8	Jeff Mathis	TEX	2.7
8	Austin Hedges	SDN	2.7
10	Mike Zunino	TBA	2.4

Catcher FRAA

Rank	Name	Team	FRAA
1	Roberto Perez	CLE	25.7
2	Jeff Mathis	TEX	23.2
3	Austin Barnes	LAN	22.4
4	Tyler Flowers	ATL	18.6
5	Austin Hedges	SDN	16.5
6	Buster Posey	SFN	13.3
7	Christian Vazquez	BOS	10.4
8	Grayson Greiner	DET	9.5
9	Max Stassi	HOU	8.2
10	Mike Zunino	TBA	7.4

Catcher DRC+

Rank	Name	Team	DRC+
1	Gary Sanchez	NYA	119
2	Buster Posey	SFN	117
3	Kurt Suzuki	WAS	115
4	J.T. Realmuto	MIA	114
5	Omar Narvaez	SEA	113
6	Wilson Ramos	NYN	112
7	Salvador Perez	KCA	111
8	Yadier Molina	SLN	110
9	Robinson Chirinos	HOU	108
10	Brian McCann	ATL	107

First Base WARP

Rank	Name	Team	WARP
1	Anthony Rizzo	CHN	5.2
2	Joey Votto	CIN	5.1
3	Paul Goldschmidt	SLN	5.0
4	Freddie Freeman	ATL	4.4
5	Daniel Murphy	COL	4.0
6	Rhys Hoskins	PHI	3.4
7	Luke Voit	NYA	3.2
8	Jose Abreu	CHA	3.1
9	Brandon Belt	SFN	2.7
9	Matt Olson	OAK	2.7

First Base FRAA

Rank	Name	Team	FRAA
1	Anthony Rizzo	CHN	9.9
2	Brandon Belt	SFN	7.0
3	Joey Votto	CIN	6.7
4	Paul Goldschmidt	SLN	6.3
5	Yulieski Gurriel	HOU	5.1
6	C.J. Cron	MIN	4.9
7	Peter Alonso	NYN	2.5
8	Luke Voit	NYA	2.2
9	Jose Abreu	CHA	2.1
10	Mitch Moreland	BOS	1.8

First Base DRC+

Rank	Name	Team	DRC+
1	Joey Votto	CIN	147
2	Freddie Freeman	ATL	142
3	Paul Goldschmidt	SLN	141
4	Anthony Rizzo	CHN	140
5	Rhys Hoskins	PHI	134
6	Daniel Murphy	COL	131
7	Luke Voit	NYA	130
8	Edwin Encarnacion	SEA	128
9	Jose Abreu	CHA	126
10	Justin Bour	ANA	122
10	Max Muncy	LAN	122
10	Matt Olson	OAK	122

Second Base WARP

Rank	Name	Team	WARP
1	Jose Altuve	HOU	4.8
2	Whit Merrifield	KCA	3.8
3	Ozzie Albies	ATL	3.7
4	Chris Taylor	LAN	3.3
5	Robinson Cano	NYN	3.2
6	Joey Wendle	TBA	3.0
7	Cesar Hernandez	PHI	2.9
8	Jurickson Profar	OAK	2.8
8	Ketel Marte	ARI	2.8
10	Gleyber Torres	NYA	2.7

Second Base FRAA

Rank	Name	Team	FRAA
1	Joey Wendle	TBA	7.5
2	Jurickson Profar	OAK	6.6
3	Ozzie Albies	ATL	6.1
4	Ketel Marte	ARI	5.4
5	Kolten Wong	SLN	4.9
5	Luis Urias	SDN	4.9
7	Rougned Odor	TEX	4.7
8	Wilmer Difo	WAS	3.3
9	Jason Kipnis	CLE	3.2
10	Gleyber Torres	NYA	3.1

Second Base DRC+

Rank	Name	Team	DRC+
1	Jose Altuve	HOU	139
2	Robinson Cano	NYN	119
3	Scooter Gennett	CIN	115
3	Whit Merrifield	KCA	115
5	Chris Taylor	LAN	109
6	Cesar Hernandez	PHI	108
7	Dustin Pedroia	BOS	106
7	Ozzie Albies	ATL	106
7	Gleyber Torres	NYA	106
10	Adam Frazier	PIT	105

Third Base WARP

Rank	Name	Team	WARP
1	Nolan Arenado	COL	5.3
2	Jose Ramirez	CLE	5.2
3	Alex Bregman	HOU	4.9
3	Matt Chapman	OAK	4.9
5	Justin Turner	LAN	4.7
5	Matt Carpenter	SLN	4.7
7	Kris Bryant	CHN	4.0
8	Anthony Rendon	WAS	3.6
9	Kyle Seager	SEA	3.1
9	Travis Shaw	MIL	3.1

Third Base FRAA

Rank	Name	Team	FRAA
1	Matt Chapman	OAK	18.3
2	Rafael Devers	BOS	9.8
3	Kyle Seager	SEA	9.3
4	Alex Bregman	HOU	7.2
5	Nolan Arenado	COL	6.6
6	Matt Duffy	TBA	5.1
7	Matt Carpenter	SLN	3.2
8	Travis Shaw	MIL	2.4
9	Yolmer Sanchez	CHA	1.4
9	Miguel Sano	MIN	1.4

Third Base DRC+

Rank	Name	Team	DRC+
1	Jose Ramirez	CLE	147
2	Nolan Arenado	COL	141
3	Justin Turner	LAN	139
4	Matt Carpenter	SLN	134
5	Anthony Rendon	WAS	132
6	Alex Bregman	HOU	129
7	Kris Bryant	CHN	126
8	Josh Donaldson	ATL	125
9	Eugenio Suarez	CIN	124
10	Vladimir Guerrero Jr.	TOR	121

Shortstop WARP

Rank	Name	Team	WARP
1	Francisco Lindor	CLE	6.3
2	Trea Turner	WAS	5.0
3	Carlos Correa	HOU	4.0
4	Andrelton Simmons	ANA	3.4
4	Corey Seager	LAN	3.4
6	Marcus Semien	OAK	3.3
6	Javier Baez	CHN	3.3
8	Xander Bogaerts	BOS	3.0
8	Trevor Story	COL	3.0
10	Jean Segura	PHI	2.9

Shortstop FRAA

Rank	Name	Team	FRAA
1	Nick Ahmed	ARI	10.7
2	Francisco Lindor	CLE	9.0
3	Trea Turner	WAS	8.4
4	Orlando Arcia	MIL	5.6
5	Marcus Semien	OAK	4.9
6	Adalberto Mondesi	KCA	4.6
7	Brandon Crawford	SFN	3.7
8	Addison Russell	CHN	2.9
9	JT Riddle	MIA	2.4
10	Andrelton Simmons	ANA	2.3

Shortstop DRC+

Rank	Name	Team	DRC+
1	Francisco Lindor	CLE	127
2	Carlos Correa	HOU	120
3	Corey Seager	LAN	117
4	Xander Bogaerts	BOS	115
5	Trea Turner	WAS	114
6	Javier Baez	CHN	109
6	Trevor Story	COL	109
8	Jean Segura	PHI	107
8	Andrelton Simmons	ANA	107
10	Dylan Moore	SEA	106

Left Field WARP

Rank	Name	Team	WARP
1	J.D. Martinez	BOS	4.6
2	Justin Upton	ANA	4.3
3	Giancarlo Stanton	NYA	4.0
3	Juan Soto	WAS	4.0
5	Brett Gardner	NYA	3.4
6	Michael Conforto	NYN	3.3
6	Andrew Benintendi	BOS	3.3
8	Marcell Ozuna	SLN	3.2
8	Corey Dickerson	PIT	3.2
10	Tommy Pham	TBA	3.0

Left Field FRAA

Rank	Name	Team	FRAA
1	Corey Dickerson	PIT	11.1
2	Justin Upton	ANA	10.6
3	Andrew Toles	LAN	10.1
4	Brett Gardner	NYA	9.3
5	Scott Schebler	CIN	2.2
5	Nick Martini	OAK	2.2
7	Andrew Benintendi	BOS	1.7
8	Trey Mancini	BAL	1.5
9	David Dahl	COL	0.9
10	Juan Soto	WAS	0.8

Left Field DRC+

Rank	Name	Team	DRC+
1	J.D. Martinez	BOS	150
2	Giancarlo Stanton	NYA	136
3	Juan Soto	WAS	129
4	Marcell Ozuna	SLN	122
4	Michael Conforto	NYN	122
6	Andrew Benintendi	BOS	117
7	Justin Upton	ANA	116
8	Joey Gallo	TEX	115
9	Tommy Pham	TBA	114
10	Kyle Schwarber	CHN	113

Center Field WARP

Rank	Name	Team	WARP
1	Mike Trout	ANA	9.6
2	Charlie Blackmon	COL	5.4
3	Lorenzo Cain	MIL	5.2
4	Kevin Kiermaier	TBA	4.9
5	Cody Bellinger	LAN	4.8
6	Ender Inciarte	ATL	4.3
7	George Springer	HOU	4.1
8	Starling Marte	PIT	3.9
9	Aaron Hicks	NYA	3.1
10	Harrison Bader	SLN	3.0

Center Field FRAA

Rank	Name	Team	FRAA
1	Kevin Kiermaier	TBA	15.2
2	Lorenzo Cain	MIL	13.0
3	Harrison Bader	SLN	12.2
4	Ender Inciarte	ATL	11.6
5	Byron Buxton	MIN	11.5
6	Victor Robles	WAS	10.5
7	Steven Duggar	SFN	9.6
8	Leonys Martin	CLE	7.1
8	Adam Engel	CHA	7.1
10	Lewis Brinson	MIA	7.0

Center Field DRC+

Rank	Name	Team	DRC+
1	Mike Trout	ANA	185
2	Charlie Blackmon	COL	139
3	Cody Bellinger	LAN	130
4	George Springer	HOU	119
5	Aaron Hicks	NYA	118
6	Lorenzo Cain	MIL	111
7	Ender Inciarte	ATL	106
7	Kevin Kiermaier	TBA	106
9	Starling Marte	PIT	104
9	Ian Happ	CHN	104

Right Field WARP

Rank	Name	Team	WARP
1	Mookie Betts	BOS	8.7
2	Aaron Judge	NYA	5.2
3	Adam Eaton	WAS	4.5
4	Christian Yelich	MIL	4.4
5	Brandon Nimmo	NYN	3.7
6	Mitch Haniger	SEA	3.5
6	Ronald Acuna	ATL	3.5
8	Franmil Reyes	SDN	2.7
8	Yasiel Puig	CIN	2.7
10	Andrew McCutchen	PHI	2.6

Right Field FRAA

Rank	Name	Team	FRAA
1	Adam Eaton	WAS	22.3
2	Mookie Betts	BOS	15.5
3	Brandon Nimmo	NYN	6.7
4	Tyler Naquin	CLE	6.2
5	Randal Grichuk	TOR	5.5
6	Aaron Judge	NYA	5.2
7	Raimel Tapia	COL	4.9
8	Mitch Haniger	SEA	4.8
9	Jason Heyward	CHN	4.6
10	Max Kepler	MIN	4.5

Right Field DRC+

Rank	Name	Team	DRC+
1	Mookie Betts	BOS	149
2	Aaron Judge	NYA	132
3	Christian Yelich	MIL	125
4	Andrew McCutchen	PHI	120
5	Nick Castellanos	DET	119
6	Josh Reddick	HOU	117
6	Mitch Haniger	SEA	117
6	Franmil Reyes	SDN	117
6	Ronald Acuna	ATL	117
10	Yasiel Puig	CIN	116

Catcher Framing Runs

Rank	Name	Team	Framing Runs
2	Jeff Mathis	TEX	17.1
6	Miguel Montero	WAS	11.0
19	Martin Maldonado	HOU	10.1
5	Erik Kratz	MIL	3.6
7	Rene Rivera	ATL	3.1
9	Russell Martin	TOR	2.9

Catcher Blocking Runs

Rank	Name	Team	Blocking Runs
4	Robinson Chirinos	HOU	1.7
2	Jeff Mathis	TEX	1.4
1	Yadier Molina	SLN	0.9
18	Jose Lobaton	NYN	0.8
5	Erik Kratz	MIL	0.8
20	Manny Pina	MIL	0.7
14	Drew Butera	COL	0.6

Catcher Throwing Runs

Rank	Name	Team	Throwing Runs
19	Martin Maldonado	HOU	1.8
20	Manny Pina	MIL	0.8
2	Jeff Mathis	TEX	0.5
7	Rene Rivera	ATL	0.5

AL Hitter Rookie WARP

Rank	Name	Team	ROOKIE WARP
1	Vladimir Guerrero Jr.	TOR	2.5
2	Eloy Jimenez	CHA	1.8
3	Christin Stewart	DET	1.7
4	Dylan Moore	SEA	1.3
4	Kyle Tucker	HOU	1.3
6	Willians Astudillo	MIN	1.2
6	Brandon Lowe	TBA	1.2
8	Patrick Wisdom	TEX	0.6
8	Billy McKinney	TOR	0.6
10	Michael Perez	TBA	0.5
10	Danny Jansen	TOR	0.5

AL Pitcher Rookie WARP

Rank	Name	Team	ROOKIE WARP
1	Yusei Kikuchi	SEA	1.6
2	Josh James	HOU	1.5
3	Framber Valdez	HOU	1.3
4	Cionel Perez	HOU	0.9
4	Trent Thornton	TOR	0.9
6	A.J. Puk	OAK	0.8
7	Joe Palumbo	TEX	0.7
7	Manny Banuelos	CHA	0.7
7	Sean Reid-Foley	TOR	0.7
7	Justus Sheffield	SEA	0.7

NL Hitter Rookie WARP

Rank	Name	Team	ROOKIE WARP
1	Victor Robles	WAS	2.1
2	Carson Kelly	ARI	1.8
2	Luis Urias	SDN	1.8
4	Alex Verdugo	LAN	1.7
5	Nick Senzel	CIN	1.5
6	Austin Dean	MIA	1.0
6	Peter Alonso	NYN	1.0
8	Kevin Cron	ARI	0.8
8	Jose Siri	CIN	0.8
10	Isaac Galloway	MIA	0.7

NL Pitcher Rookie WARP

Rank	Name	Team	ROOKIE WARP
1	Mike Soroka	ATL	1.0
2	Merrill Kelly	ARI	0.9
3	Chris Paddack	SDN	0.5
3	Jacob Nix	SDN	0.5
3	Touki Toussaint	ATL	0.5
6	Brett Kennedy	SDN	0.4
6	Mitch Keller	PIT	0.4
6	Jordan Yamamoto	MIA	0.4
9	Clay Holmes	PIT	0.3
9	Kyle Wright	ATL	0.3
9	Sandy Alcantara	MIA	0.3

BASEBALL PROSPECTUS 2019

Hitter WARP Declines

Rank	Name	Team	WARP 2018	WARP 2019	WARP DIFF
1	Didi Gregorius	NYA	4.9	1.4	-3.5
2	Trevor Story	COL	5.7	3.0	-2.7
3	Max Muncy	LAN	4.3	2.0	-2.3
4	Jose Ramirez	CLE	7.4	5.2	-2.2
5	Manny Machado	LAN	6.5	4.4	-2.1
6	Alex Bregman	HOU	6.9	4.9	-2.0
7	Michael Brantley	HOU	3.3	1.4	-1.9
8	Marcus Semien	OAK	5.1	3.3	-1.8
8	Tim Anderson	CHA	3.3	1.5	-1.8
8	Brandon Crawford	SFN	4.0	2.2	-1.8

Hitter WARP Improvements

Rank	Name	Team	WARP 2018	WARP 2019	WARP DIFF
1	Gary Sanchez	NYA	1.3	4.4	3.1
1	Kevin Kiermaier	TBA	1.8	4.9	3.1
3	Austin Barnes	LAN	1.5	4.5	3.0
4	Daniel Murphy	COL	1.2	4.0	2.8
4	Charlie Blackmon	COL	2.6	5.4	2.8
6	Adam Eaton	WAS	1.8	4.5	2.7
7	Corey Seager	LAN	0.8	3.4	2.6
7	Andrew Toles	LAN	0.0	2.6	2.6
9	Franmil Reyes	SDN	0.3	2.7	2.4
10	Buster Posey	SFN	2.5	4.8	2.3
10	Roberto Perez	CLE	0.9	3.2	2.3

Pitcher WARP Declines

Rank	Name	Team	WARP 2018	WARP 2019	WARP DIFF
1	Jacob deGrom	NYN	8.0	3.6	-4.4
1	Justin Verlander	HOU	7.3	3.0	-4.4
3	Max Scherzer	WAS	7.7	3.4	-4.2
4	Zack Wheeler	NYN	4.8	1.4	-3.4
5	Anibal Sanchez	WAS	4.0	0.9	-3.1
6	Blake Snell	TBA	6.0	3.0	-3.0
6	Kyle Hendricks	CHN	5.0	2.1	-3.0
8	Gerrit Cole	HOU	6.4	3.4	-2.9
9	Patrick Corbin	WAS	5.9	3.1	-2.8
10	Aaron Nola	PHI	6.6	3.9	-2.7
10	Zack Greinke	ARI	5.3	2.6	-2.7

Pitcher WARP Improvements

Rank	Name	Team	WARP 2018	WARP 2019	WARP DIFF
1	Brad Keller	KCA	0.6	2.2	1.6
2	Michael Fulmer	DET	1.0	2.4	1.4
3	Antonio Senzatela	COL	0.1	1.5	1.3
3	Marcus Stroman	TOR	1.3	2.6	1.3
5	Zack Godley	ARI	1.1	2.3	1.2
5	Luis Castillo	CIN	1.1	2.2	1.2
7	Lance Lynn	TEX	0.3	1.4	1.1
8	Matt Boyd	DET	0.2	1.1	1.0
9	Josh James	HOU	0.5	1.5	0.9
9	Jose Quintana	CHN	0.8	1.7	0.9
9	Cionel Perez	HOU	0.0	0.9	0.9
9	Jon Gray	COL	1.7	2.6	0.9
9	Yu Darvish	CHN	0.3	1.2	0.9
9	Daniel Norris	DET	0.1	0.9	0.9

Team Codes

CODE	TEAM	LG	AFF.	Name
ABE	Aberdeen	NYP	Orioles	IronBirds
ABQ	Albuquerque	PCL	Rockies	Isotopes
AKR	Akron	EAS	Indians	RubberDucks
ALT	Altoona	EAS	Pirates	Curve
ANA	Los Angeles	AL	-	Angels
ANG	AZL Angels	AZL	Angels	-
ARI	Arizona	NL	-	D-backs
ARK	Arkansas	TEX	Mariners	Travelers
ART	Artemisa	CNS	-	
ASH	Asheville	SAL	Rockies	Tourists
AST	GCL Astros	GCL	Astros	GCL Astros
ATH	AZL Athletics	AZL	Athletics	-
ATL	Atlanta	NL	-	Braves
AUB	Auburn	NYP	Nationals	Doubledays
AUG	Augusta	SAL	Giants	GreenJackets
BAL	Baltimore	AL	-	Orioles
BAT	Batavia	NYP	Marlins	Muckdogs
BCA	Buies Creek	CAR	Astros	Astros
BGR	Bowling Green	MID	Rays	Hot Rods
BIL	Billings	PIO	Reds	Mustangs
BIN	Binghamton	EAS	Mets	Rumble Ponies
BIR	Birmingham	SOU	White Sox	Barons
BLJ	GCL Blue Jays	GCL	Blue Jays	GCL Blue Jays
BLT	Beloit	MID	Athletics	Snappers
BLU	Bluefield	APP	Blue Jays	Blue Jays
BLX	Biloxi	SOU	Brewers	Shuckers
BNC	Burlington	APP	Royals	Royals
BOI	Boise	NWL	Rockies	Hawks
BOS	Boston	AL	-	Red Sox
BOW	Bowie	EAS	Orioles	Baysox
BRA	GCL Braves	GCL	Braves	GCL Braves
BRD	Bradenton	FSL	Pirates	Marauders
BRI	Bristol	APP	Pirates	Pirates
BRO	Brooklyn	NYP	Mets	Cyclones
BRR	AZL Brewers	AZL	Brewers	-
BRV	Florida	FSL	Braves	Fire Frogs
BUF	Buffalo	INT	Blue Jays	Bisons
BUR	Burlington	MID	Angels	Bees
CAR	Carolina	CAR	Brewers	Mudcats
CCH	Corpus Christi	TEX	Astros	Hooks
CDR	Cedar Rapids	MID	Twins	Kernels
CFG	Cienfuegos	CNS	-	
CHA	Chicago	AL	-	White Sox
CHB	Chiba Lotte	NPB	-	Marines
CHN	Chicago	NL	-	Cubs

CODE	TEAM	LG	AFF.	Name
CHR	Charlotte	INT	White Sox	Knights
CHT	Chattanooga	SOU	Twins	Lookouts
CHU	Chunichi	NPB	-	Dragons
CIN	Cincinnati	NL	-	Reds
CIN	AZL Reds	AZL	Reds	-
CLE	Cleveland	AL	-	Indians
CLE	AZL Indians 1	AZL	Indians	-
CLN	Clinton	MID	Mariners	LumberKings
CLR	Clearwater	FSL	Phillies	Threshers
CLT	AZL Indians 2	AZL	Indians	-
COH	Columbus	INT	Indians	Clippers
COL	Colorado	NL	-	Rockies
COL	Columbia	SAL	Mets	Fireflies
CRD	GCL Cardinals	GCL	Cardinals	GCL Cardinals
CSC	Charleston	SAL	Yankees	RiverDogs
CSP	Col. Springs	PCL	Brewers	Sky Sox
CUB	AZL Cubs 1	AZL	Cubs	-
CUT	AZL Cubs 2	AZL	Cubs	-
DAB	DSL Astros	DSL	Astros	DSL Astros
DAN	DSL Angels	DSL	Angels	DSL Angels
DAT	DSL Athletics	DSL	Athletics	DSL Athletics
DAY	Daytona	FSL	Reds	Tortugas
DBL	DSL Blue Jays	DSL	Blue Jays	DSL Blue Jays
DBR	DSL Braves	DSL	Braves	DSL Braves
DBW	DSL Brewers	DSL	Brewers	DSL Brewers
DCA	DSL Cardinals Blue	DSL	Cardinals	DSL Cardinals Blue
DCH	DSL Cubs2	DSL	Cubs	DSL Cubs2
DCR	DSL Colorado	DSL	Rockies	DSL Colorado
DCT	DSL Cardinals Red	DSL	Cardinals	DSL Cardinals Red
DCU	DSL Cubs1	DSL	Cubs	DSL Cubs1
DDB	DSL D-backs2	DSL	D-backs	DSL D-backs2
DDG	DSL Dodgers Guerrero	DSL	Dodgers	DSL Dodgers Guerrero
DDI	DSL D-backs1	DSL	D-backs	DSL D-backs1
DDO	DSL Dodgers Robinson	DSL	Dodgers	DSL Dodgers Robinson
DDR	DSL Rays1	DSL	Rays	DSL Rays1
DEB	Down East	CAR	Rangers	Wood Ducks
DEL	Delmarva	SAL	Orioles	Shorebirds
DET	Detroit	AL	-	Tigers
DGI	DSL Giants	DSL	Giants	DSL Giants
DIA	AZL D-backs	AZL	D-backs	-
DIN	DSL Indians	DSL	Indians	DSL Indians
DME	DSL Mets1	DSL	Mets	DSL Mets1
DML	DSL Marlins	DSL	Marlins	DSL Marlins

CODE	TEAM	LG	AFF.	Name
DMR	DSL Mariners	DSL	Mariners	DSL Mariners
DNV	Danville	APP	Braves	Braves
DOD	AZL Dodgers	AZL	Dodgers	-
DOR	DSL Orioles	DSL	Orioles	DSL Orioles
DPA	DSL Padres	DSL	Padres	DSL Padres
DPH	DSL Phillies Red	DSL	Phillies	DSL Phillies Red
DPI	DSL Pirates1	DSL	Pirates	DSL Pirates1
DPL	DSL Phillies White	DSL	Phillies	DSL Phillies White
DPT	DSL Pirates2	DSL	Pirates	DSL Pirates2
DRA	DSL Rays2	DSL	Rays	DSL Rays2
DRD	DSL Reds	DSL	Reds	DSL Reds
DRG	DSL Rangers1	DSL	Rangers	DSL Rangers1
DRN	DSL Rangers2	DSL	Rangers	DSL Rangers2
DRO	DSL Rockies	DSL	Rockies	DSL Rockies
DRS	DSL Red Sox1	DSL	Red Sox	DSL Red Sox1
DRX	DSL Red Sox2	DSL	Red Sox	DSL Red Sox2
DRY	DSL Royals1	DSL	Royals	DSL Royals1
DTI	DSL Tigers1	DSL	Tigers	DSL Tigers1
DTW	DSL Twins	DSL	Twins	DSL Twins
DUN	Dunedin	FSL	Blue Jays	Blue Jays
DUR	Durham	INT	Rays	Bulls
DWA	DSL Nationals	DSL	Nationals	DSL Nationals
DWS	DSL White Sox	DSL	White Sox	DSL White Sox
DYA	DSL Yankees	DSL	Yankees	DSL Yankees
DYT	Dayton	MID	Reds	Dragons
ELP	El Paso	PCL	Padres	Chihuahuas
ELZ	Elizabethton	APP	Twins	Twins
ERI	Erie	EAS	Tigers	SeaWolves
EUG	Eugene	NWL	Cubs	Emeralds
EVE	Everett	NWL	Mariners	AquaSox
FKU	Fukuoka	NPB	-	Hawks
FRD	Frederick	CAR	Orioles	Keys
FRE	Fresno	PCL	Astros	Grizzlies
FRI	Frisco	TEX	Rangers	RoughRiders
FTM	Fort Myers	FSL	Twins	Miracle
FTW	Fort Wayne	MID	Padres	TinCaps
GIA	AZL Giants Black	AZL	Giants	-
GJR	Grand Junction	PIO	Rockies	Rockies
GNT	AZL Giants Orange	AZL	Giants	-
GRB	Greensboro	SAL	Marlins	Grasshoppers
GRF	Great Falls	PIO	White Sox	Voyagers
GRL	Great Lakes	MID	Dodgers	Loons
GRN	Greenville	SAL	Red Sox	Drive
GRV	Greeneville	APP	Reds	Reds
GWN	Gwinnett	INT	Braves	Stripers
HAB	La Habana	CNS	-	
HAG	Hagerstown	SAL	Nationals	Suns
HAR	Harrisburg	EAS	Nationals	Senators
HEL	Helena	PIO	Brewers	Brewers
HFD	Hartford	EAS	Rockies	Yard Goats
HIC	Hickory	SAL	Rangers	Crawdads
HNS	Hanshin	NPB	-	Tigers
HOU	Houston	AL	-	Astros
HRO	Hiroshima Toyo	NPB	-	Carp
HUD	Hudson Valley	NYP	Rays	Renegades
IDA	Idaho Falls	PIO	Royals	Chukars

CODE	TEAM	LG	AFF.	Name
IND	Indianapolis	INT	Pirates	Indians
INL	Inland Empire	CAL	Angels	66ers
IOW	Iowa	PCL	Cubs	Cubs
JAX	Jacksonville	SOU	Marlins	Jumbo Shrimp
JCY	Johnson City	APP	Cardinals	Cardinals
JUP	Jupiter	FSL	Marlins	Hammerheads
KAN	Kannapolis	SAL	White Sox	Intimidators
KCA	Kansas City	AL	-	Royals
KNC	Kane County	MID	D-backs	Cougars
KNG	Kingsport	APP	Mets	Mets
LAK	Lakeland	FSL	Tigers	Flying Tigers
LAN	Los Angeles	NL	-	Dodgers
LEH	Lehigh Valley	INT	Phillies	IronPigs
LEL	Lake Elsinore	CAL	Padres	Storm
LEX	Lexington	SAL	Royals	Legends
LKC	Lake County	MID	Indians	Captains
LNC	Lancaster	CAL	Rockies	JetHawks
LNS	Lansing	MID	Blue Jays	Lugnuts
LOU	Louisville	INT	Reds	Bats
LOW	Lowell	NYP	Red Sox	Spinners
LTU	Las Tunas	CNS	-	
LVG	Las Vegas	PCL	Mets	51s
LWD	Lakewood	SAL	Phillies	BlueClaws
LYN	Lynchburg	CAR	Indians	Hillcats
MEM	Memphis	PCL	Cardinals	Redbirds
MET	DSL Mets2	DSL	Mets	DSL Mets2
MHV	Mahoning Valley	NYP	Indians	Scrappers
MIA	Miami	NL	-	Marlins
MID	Midland	TEX	Athletics	RockHounds
MIL	Milwaukee	NL	-	Brewers
MIN	Minnesota	AL	-	Twins
MIS	Mississippi	SOU	Braves	Braves
MNT	Montgomery	SOU	Rays	Biscuits
MOB	Mobile	SOU	Angels	BayBears
MOD	Modesto	CAL	Mariners	Nuts
MRL	GCL Marlins	GCL	Marlins	GCL Marlins
MRN	AZL Mariners	AZL	Mariners	-
MSO	Missoula	PIO	D-backs	Osprey
MTS	GCL Mets	GCL	Mets	GCL Mets
MYR	Myrtle Beach	CAR	Cubs	Pelicans
NAS	Nashville	PCL	Athletics	Sounds
NAT	GCL Nationals	GCL	Nationals	GCL Nationals
NHP	New Hampshire	EAS	Blue Jays	Fisher Cats
NIP	Nippon Ham	NPB	-	Fighters
NOR	Norfolk	INT	Orioles	Tides
NWA	NW Arkansas	TEX	Royals	Naturals
NWO	New Orleans	PCL	Marlins	Baby Cakes
NYA	New York	AL	-	Yankees
NYN	New York	NL	-	Mets
OAK	Oakland	AL	-	Athletics
OGD	Ogden	PIO	Dodgers	Raptors
OKL	Okla. City	PCL	Dodgers	Dodgers
OMA	Omaha	PCL	Royals	Storm Chasers
ONE	Connecticut	NYP	Tigers	Tigers
ORI	GCL Orioles	GCL	Orioles	GCL Orioles
ORM	Orem	PIO	Angels	Owlz
ORX	Orix	NPB	-	Buffaloes

CODE	TEAM	LG	AFF.	Name
PAW	Pawtucket	INT	Red Sox	Red Sox
PCH	Charlotte	FSL	Rays	Stone Crabs
PDR	AZL Padres 1	AZL	Padres	-
PEN	Pensacola	SOU	Reds	Blue Wahoos
PEO	Peoria	MID	Cardinals	Chiefs
PHI	Philadelphia	NL	-	Phillies
PHL	GCL Phillies East	GCL	Phillies	GCL Phillies East
PIR	GCL Pirates	GCL	Pirates	GCL Pirates
PIT	Pittsburgh	NL	-	Pirates
PLL	GCL Phillies West	GCL	Phillies	GCL Phillies West
PMB	Palm Beach	FSL	Cardinals	Cardinals
PME	Portland	EAS	Red Sox	Sea Dogs
POT	Potomac	CAR	Nationals	Nationals
PRI	Princeton	APP	Rays	Rays
PUL	Pulaski	APP	Yankees	Yankees
QUD	Quad Cities	MID	Astros	River Bandits
RAK	Rakuten	NPB	-	Golden Eagles
RAY	GCL Rays	GCL	Rays	GCL Rays
RCO	DSL Royals2	DSL	Royals	DSL Royals2
RCU	Rancho Cucamonga	CAL	Dodgers	Quakes
REA	Reading	EAS	Phillies	Fightin Phils
RIC	Richmond	EAS	Giants	Flying Squirrels
RNG	AZL Rangers	AZL	Rangers	-
RNO	Reno	PCL	D-backs	Aces
ROC	Rochester	INT	Twins	Red Wings
ROM	Rome	SAL	Braves	Braves
ROU	Round Rock	PCL	Rangers	Express
ROY	AZL Royals	AZL	Royals	-
RSX	GCL Red Sox	GCL	Red Sox	GCL Red Sox
SAC	Sacramento	PCL	Giants	River Cats
SAN	San Antonio	TEX	Padres	Missions
SBN	South Bend	MID	Cubs	Cubs
SCO	State College	NYP	Cardinals	Spikes
SDN	San Diego	NL	-	Padres
SDP	AZL Padres 2	AZL	Padres	-
SEA	Seattle	AL	-	Mariners
SEI	Seibu	NPB	-	Lions
SFD	Springfield	TEX	Cardinals	Cardinals
SFN	San Francisco	NL	-	Giants
SJO	San Jose	CAL	Giants	Giants
SLC	Salt Lake	PCL	Angels	Bees
SLM	Salem	CAR	Red Sox	Red Sox
SLN	St. Louis	NL	-	Cardinals
SLO	Salem-Keizer	NWL	Giants	Volcanoes
SLU	St. Lucie	FSL	Mets	Mets
SPO	Spokane	NWL	Rangers	Indians
STA	Staten Island	NYP	Yankees	Yankees
STO	Stockton	CAL	Athletics	Ports
SWB	Scranton/WB	INT	Yankees	RailRiders
SYR	Syracuse	INT	Nationals	Chiefs
TAC	Tacoma	PCL	Mariners	Rainiers
TAM	Tampa	FSL	Yankees	Tarpons
TBA	Tampa Bay	AL	-	Rays
TCO	DSL Tigers2	DSL	Tigers	DSL Tigers2
TCV	Tri-City	NYP	Astros	ValleyCats
TEN	Tennessee	SOU	Cubs	Smokies
TEX	Texas	AL	-	Rangers

CODE	TEAM	LG	AFF.	Name
TGR	GCL Tigers East	GCL	Tigers	GCL Tigers East
TGW	GCL Tigers West	GCL	Tigers	GCL Tigers West
TOL	Toledo	INT	Tigers	Mud Hens
TOR	Toronto	AL	-	Blue Jays
TRI	Tri-City	NWL	Padres	Dust Devils
TRN	Trenton	EAS	Yankees	Thunder
TUL	Tulsa	TEX	Dodgers	Drillers
TWI	GCL Twins	GCL	Twins	GCL Twins
VAN	Vancouver	NWL	Blue Jays	Canadians
VER	Vermont	NYP	Athletics	Lake Monsters
VIS	Visalia	CAL	D-backs	Rawhide
WAS	Washington	NL	-	Nationals
WEV	West Virginia	NYP	Pirates	Black Bears
WIL	Wilmington	CAR	Royals	Blue Rocks
WIS	Wisconsin	MID	Brewers	Timber Rattlers
WMI	West Michigan	MID	Tigers	Whitecaps
WNS	Winston-Salem	CAR	White Sox	Dash
WPT	Williamsport	NYP	Phillies	Crosscutters
WSX	AZL White Sox	AZL	White Sox	-
WTN	Jackson	SOU	D-backs	Generals
WVA	West Virginia	SAL	Pirates	Power
YAK	Hillsboro	NWL	D-backs	Hops
YAN	GCL Yankees East	GCL	Yankees	GCL Yankees East
YAT	GCL Yankees West	GCL	Yankees	GCL Yankees West
YKL	Yakult	NPB	-	Swallows
YKO	Yokohama DeNa	NPB	-	BayStars
YOM	Yomiuri	NPB	-	Giants

Contributors

Eddy Almaguer is a fantasy writer at Prospects Live. His work has appeared on Baseball Prospectus, Fake Teams and Prospects1500. He lives in Tampa, FL, where his tweet about Yandy Diaz's muscles once made it into the local newspaper.

Darius Austin is a fantasy writer at Baseball Prospectus. He contributes to the Effectively Wild-inspired site Banished to the Pen, which means he has invested far too much time into thinking about Ryan Webb and Matt Albers. As if that wasn't strange enough, he is from the UK, which makes following the Giants live very difficult but also qualifies him to feature on UK-based blog and podcast Bat Flips and Nerds. He also podcasts about fantasy for Friends With Fantasy Benefits.

Michael Axisa is a national baseball blogger at CBS Sports and a BBWAA member. He's appeared at MLB Trade Rumors and FanGraphs, and is one of the original founders and current operators of River Ave. Blues, a full-service Yankees blog. Forever a fan of massive dingers, Michael lives in New York City and spends an embarrassing amount of time at ballparks each summer.

Emma Baccellieri is a staff writer at Sports Illustrated. She previously wrote for Deadspin and Baseball Prospectus, and she lives in Washington, D.C. She enjoys cheering for Duke basketball, among other reprehensible pursuits.

Mark Barry is an author and fantasy writer at Baseball Prospectus. He lives in Los Angeles, where he somehow can't watch the Dodgers on TV, and dreams of a day spent playing catch and talking about life with Francisco Lindor. Carlos Santana is there too.

Jonathan Bernhardt lives and works outside of Baltimore, Maryland, where he thinks a lot about the nearby baseball team, as well as Harold Baines. He has been previously published at The Athletic, Sports on Earth, VICE Sports, The Guardian, UPROXX Sports, FanRag Sports, and, of course, Baseball Prospectus.

Nathan Bishop is an author at Baseball Prospectus. While the vast majority of his work has been spent covering the Seattle Mariners, he has managed to continue to greatly enjoy watching and covering the game. He lives near Seattle, on a small island, both physically and metaphorically.

Paul Boyé is a friend of the prospectus and current contributor to the Phillies SB Nation satellite, The Good Phight. Based in the greater New York City area, he's previously spent time working for MLB Advanced Media, MLB Properties, and the Toronto Blue Jays, and spends entirely too much time ranking new music in entirely too-long lists.

Grant Brisbee is a senior writer for SB Nation, and he finds the Pagliacci joke to be less funny with each passing year.

Craig Brown lives in Kansas City and has been writing about the Royals at various stops along the internet since 2004. His words have been found at ESPN, Sports on Earth and The Hardball Times. Most recently, he was Editor-in-Chief of Baseball Prospectus—Kansas City. This is his fifth year contributing to the Annual. He thinks the next time you go to a baseball game, you should keep score.

Craig Calcaterra is the lead writer and editor of NBC Sports' baseball blog, HardballTalk. He is also an occasional contributor to WBUR/NPR's "Only a Game." His work has appeared in a lot of other places too, but he can mostly be found arguing with people on Twitter. Craig lives and works in a fortified compound on the outskirts of New Albany, Ohio with his wife Allison, his daughter Anna, his son Carlo and four cats. Yes, four. Who are you to judge?

Russell Carleton lives in Atlanta, Georgia with his wife and five kids. He is an author of Baseball Prospectus and the book The Shift: The Next Evolution in Baseball Thinking. How he has time to do all that is one of the great mysteries of the universe.

Ben Carsley is a Senior Author at Baseball Prospectus. When he's not writing about baseball, Ben is usually cooking, drinking IPAs, reading Faulkner and sending under-appreciated tweets. By day he manages a team of writers and SEO analysts who are fairly convinced he's Ron Swanson. By night he dreams of Xander Bogaerts.

Michael Clair writes for MLB's Cut4. His work has appeared on various places around the internet, some of which still exist! You can find him on Twitter, where he's probably talking about stirrup socks and how bunts can be beautiful (if still dumb).

Roger Cormier is a writer based in Brooklyn, New York. His work has appeared in FanGraphs, New York Magazine's Vulture website, Gawker, Mental Floss, and other venerable places. He contributes to Baseball Prospectus's Short Relief column, and heroically wrote about the 18-inning World Series game for the same publication. He is no doubt currently threatening to start another podcast.

Zach Crizer is a writer for Baseball Prospectus. His Internet baseball writing first appeared at Beyond the Box Score after he left the newspaper business, where he covered politics and wrote local features for The Roanoke Times. He lives in New York City, dispelling the notion of "clutch" one person at a time.

Chris Cwik is a writer at Yahoo Sports. He lives in Seattle with his family and tweets about video games way too much.

Patrick Dubuque is the Director of Editorial Content at Baseball Prospectus and founder of its whimsical baseball-adjacent Short Relief vertical. He lives in the Pacific Northwest with his wife Kjersten and his two garrulous children, Sylvie and Felix.

Matt Ellis writes about baseball on the internet. You can find him at Baseball Prospectus' Short Relief and sometimes at The Hardball Times, but no longer at SB Nation's Lookout Landing. When he is not being sad about the Mariners he is working towards a PhD in Modern Culture and Media at Brown University.

James Fegan resides in his hometown of Chicago, and is the lead writer on the White Sox for The Athletic. Previously, James founded and served as Editor-in-Chief of BP South Side, and his work has appeared in Baseball Prospectus, ESPN SweetSpot, The Rock River Times and Athlete's Quarterly.

Chad Finn is sports media and online columnist at The Boston Globe. He lives in Wells, Maine with his wife Jen, children Leah and Alex, and three cats that would like their breakfast already. Whatever downtime he has these days is spent concocting ways to get cronies of Fred Lynn and Dwight Evans onto the Hall of Fame's Modern Era Committee.

Ken Funck has contributed to the Baseball Prospectus annual each year since 2009. He designs and manages Business Intelligence systems and lives outside Madison, Wisconsin with his perpetually surprising wife Stephanie, their children Max and Abby, one small, easily frightened terrier, several unripe kidney stones and a signed jar of Gorman Thomas Stormin' Sauce.

Brendan Gawlowski is an editor at Baseball Prospectus; his work also appears in The Athletic. He lives in Seattle with his wife, Sierra, and his dog, Buck.

Mike Gianella is the Senior Fantasy Baseball writer at Baseball Prospectus. By day, he works in the data sciences field in the healthcare industry. By night, he is a fantasy baseball writer extraordinaire, father to two amazing daughters and basketball and soccer coach. He has the misfortune of being a Met fan because his Dad emigrated to Queens and didn't know any better. Mike currently lives in a Philadelphia suburb with his wife, two daughters and three cats.

Aaron Gleeman is the editor-in-chief of Baseball Prospectus. He lives in Minnesota, where he co-hosts the "Gleeman and The Geek" radio show/podcast on KFAN. His first solo book, *The Big 50: Minnesota Twins*, is available from Triumph Books.

Craig Goldstein was an author and editor at Baseball Prospectus. His work has appeared in Baseball HQ, Vice Sports, Fox Sports MLB/JABO and SB Nation MLB. He lives and works in Washington DC, where he spends just the right amount of time thinking about nicknames for Juan Soto.

Bryan Grosnick is an author of Baseball Prospectus as well as BP's Director of Reference and Training. He lives in New England with his extraordinary wife and son, his two dogs, and a baseball autographed by Endy Chavez.

Jon Hegglund writes mainly about fantasy baseball at Baseball Prospectus from a basement in north Idaho. In his day job he professes contemporary literature and film at Washington State University. He is a doctor, but not the kind that can ease your pain.

Kevin Jebens is a book editor and freelance writer who's written for several baseball websites but now calls Baseball Prospectus his home. He lives in northern Illinois but is a one-sport fan, so when it's not-baseball time, he spends his days engaged in geek culture, running, and hiking with his fiancée, Heather, and his dog, Griffey.

Jonathan Judge is a trial/regulatory lawyer who also co-owns and somehow finds time to create and enhance catching, pitching, and batting statistics. He lives in Chicago with his wife, two boys, and, as of a few months ago, two cats. He is troubled that many of the statistics he creates seem skeptical of his beloved Brewers.

Wilson Karaman is a Senior Author of Baseball Prospectus. Sometimes he wins elections for Democrats, other times he chases two–and soon to be three–kids around his increasingly too-small house. In October he watched the Boston Red Sox win the World Series right there in front of his very own eyes, and that was pretty freakin' cool. He lives in Los Angeles and covers the California League as a member of BP's prospect team, while also kicking in dynasty coverage as a contributing writer for the fantasy team.

Justin Klugh is a contributor to Baseball Prospectus. His work has appeared in The Athletic, FanGraphs, SB Nation MLB, and Philly.com. He is a journalist and copywriter living in Baltimore, where he advocates for cronyism becoming the sole motivation for Hall of Fame candidacy.

David Lee is a sportswriter at The Augusta Chronicle in Augusta, GA, and a member of the Baseball Prospectus prospect team. He enjoys long walks on the beach but only after writing prospect reports.

Rob Mains is a former financial analyst living in upstate New York with his wife, dog, and local wines. In addition to writing for Baseball Prospectus, he teaches downhill skiing in the winter, competes in triathlons in the summer, and believes that if you don't like Riesling, you probably haven't had a good one.

Rachael McDaniel is an author at Baseball Prospectus, and also writes other things elsewhere, sometimes about baseball, sometimes not. Rachael can be found skulking at and around the University of British Columbia.

Whitney McIntosh is a writer based in Brooklyn who covers baseball, tennis and pop culture. Sometimes that involves stress cooking instead of working and sometimes it actually results in a finished product like this. She has been a baseball fan her whole life and has never left a game early if she has the choice.

Rob McQuown has been invited to be an honorary "millennial", but spent the Turn-of-the-Century years starting dot-com companies and winning Strat-O-Matic leagues. He currently serves the Director Of Operations at Baseball Prospectus, a role which has been actual if not nominal for almost a decade, misses writing fantasy articles and wishes there were more hours in the day. Bill James' writings saved him from being an Electrical Engineer.

Jack Moore is a freelance writer covering sports—physical and electronic—across the internet. He lives in Minneapolis where he also works as a tutor. Catch his Duck Hunt in Super Smash Bros. Ultimate.

Nick Nelson is a writer and co-founder at Twins Daily, the largest independent website covering the Minnesota Twins. He's a lifelong indignant native of flyover country and a self-described "dope rapper."

Eric Nusbaum is a writer in Los Angeles, and a former editor at VICE Sports. His work has appeared in Sports Illustrated, ESPN the Magazine, Deadspin, and other publications, including this one. He is at work on a book about baseball, community, and history in Los Angeles.

Robert O'Connell is a writer and bunt-for-base-hit fan whose work has appeared in the Atlantic, Deadspin, the New York Times, the Guardian, and elsewhere.

Jeffrey Paternostro is the Lead Prospect Writer at Baseball Prospectus and co-host of the For All You Kids Out There podcast. He believes that Kant's third critique is more useful in prospect evaluation than exit velocity, that nothing about Vladimir Guerrero Jr. is normally distributed, and that 65 is still not a grade. You can usually find him behind home plate at a minor league game wearing flannel-lined jeans and a Sheffield Wednesday bobble.

Kate Preusser is an author at Baseball Prospectus, manages SB Nation's Mariners site Lookout Landing, and writes for the Athletic Seattle. Her work has also appeared at FanGraphs, The Hardball Times, and in Our Lady of Guadalupe's Fourth Grade Flash sports report. She lives and works in Seattle, where she contemplates the sea and sings Nickelback at karaoke.

Matt Provenzano is the managing editor of Beyond the Box Score, and he lives in Brooklyn and works as an IT consultant in the New York-metro area.

Tommy Rancel a.k.a. Pen Griffey Jr a.k.a. Nyce Harper a.k.a Mic Trout a.k.a The Young Enrique White a.k.a Jeff Baggs Well a.k.a Earn Me Banks a.k.a. Flow DiMaggio a.k.a. Chillie Mays a.k.a Connie Return of the Mack a.k.a The One Marichal a.k.a Babe Truth a.k.a Trillie Stargell a.k.a Earl Lee Win a.k.a Bread Williams is a writer for ESPN and The Athletic. He has previously written for FanGraphs as well as

contributed to the Baseball Prospectus Annual. He lives in the Tampa Bay area with his wife Jamie and their five children.

Daniel Rathman is an author and former editor at Baseball Prospectus. He was born, raised, and lives in San Francisco, where he works as a real estate researcher and high-school baseball coach, teaching the next generation of ballplayers that groundballs suck.

Sheryl Ring is an attorney and the legal director at Open Communities, a not-for-profit legal aid agency in the Chicago suburbs. Sheryl is a regular contributor to FanGraphs, and her work has also appeared in Chicago magazine, among other publications, and she has been a frequent guest on ESPN radio and on Julie DiCaro's AM670 program in Chicago. Sheryl lives in the Chicago area with her beautiful wife, Ashley, and their chihuahua, Miss Molly, who is oddly obsessed with Nathan Eovaldi.

David Roth is a senior editor at Deadspin. He's from New Jersey and lives in New York.

Meg Rowley is the managing editor of FanGraphs, where she also writes baseball words on occasion and serves as the host of FanGraphs Audio. She was previously the managing editor of The Hardball Times. Before that, she was a contributing writer to Baseball Prospectus, and before that, she did a bunch of other, bad, non-baseball related jobs to pay her rent. This is better. She lives in Seattle.

Bret Sayre is the President of Baseball Prospectus. By day, he tells investment professionals what not to do. By night, he is a full-time family man, part-time cook, part-time nurse, full-time baseball writer and part-time musician. As an eight-year-old boy, he was knocked over by a man in his thirties as he tried to catch a dead ball thrown by Kevin Mitchell at Shea Stadium. Now, he lives in New Jersey with his wife, daughter and son—alongside all of the beanie babies and LEGO sets ever made.

Nick Schaefer is an author and editor at Baseball Prospectus and the former co-Editor-in-Chief for Baseball Prospectus South Side. He roots for the White Sox while living and working in New York City as an attorney.

Jarrett Seidler is a senior prospect and staff writer for Baseball Prospectus. He also co-hosts For All You Kids Out There, a weekly BP podcast that is occasionally about the Mets. As a lifelong New Jersey resident, he was very excited to see Springsteen on Broadway for his birthday.

Susan Slusser has been the San Francisco Chronicle's Oakland A's beat writer since 1999 and previously covered baseball for the Dallas Morning News and the Sacramento Bee. She is the only woman to have served as the president of the BBWAA, and she is tired of writing about *Moneyball*.

Jesse Spector is the Nyjer Morgan of the Prospectus universe, having written the foreword for Hockey Prospectus 2013-14, though he does not have a cool alter ego like Tony Plush. A lifelong New Yorker, he has written for the New York

Daily News, Sporting News, Dealbreaker, Blecaher Report, Fanrag, The Guardian, The Hardball Times, Newsday, TheScore, Uproxx, Yahoo, and Rockies Magazine.

Eric Stephen is a writer at SB Nation. He covered the Dodgers for 10 years at True Blue LA, where he continues to contribute occasionally. He's still not over Eddie Murray being denied a batting title in 1990 despite leading the major leagues in batting average.

Matt Sussman lives in Toledo, OH and writes weekly for Baseball Prospectus' Short Relief.

David Temple lives in Wisconsin. His baseball writing has appeared at Baseball Prospectus, FiveThirtyEight, and FanGraphs. When he is not making millions of dollars in the commodities market, he's just dunking basketballs all the time. Dayn Perry once called him a "Bible Made of Lasers."

Matthew Trueblood is a contributor to Baseball Prospectus. He lives and works in the Twin Cities with his wife and children, sleeping too little and thinking about slider usage too much.

Ashley Varela is a freelance writer based in the San Francisco Bay Area. Her work has appeared online and in print with NBC, USA Today, Sporting News, Baseball Prospectus and SB Nation. She once used the word "irregardless" in an article and has been haunted by it every day since.

Levi Weaver is, at time of writing, watching Dirty Dancing for the first time (at the age of 39). There's one part where he is convinced that an old guy is supposed to be tap dancing but is on carpet. He's not 100% sure it's carpet but it really looks like it. He used to be a musician and then jumped right into this baseball thing so he's sorry if he got anything wrong. He hates writing about himself in the third person. He should probably mention that he works for The Athletic. Yes, the hoodies are as comfortable as they look.

Collin Whitchurch is an author and editor at Baseball Prospectus. He was previously the co-Editor-in-Chief of BP South Side and his work has also been featured at ESPN.com. He lives and works in Austin, TX, where he's still getting used to this whole "college football is really important" thing.

Jeffrey Wiser is a contributor to The Athletic, where he writes analytically-minded pieces about the Arizona Diamondbacks. He has written about the team since 2013, co-authored Inside the 'Zona, and served as a featured writer and editor at Beyond the Box Score with work appearing from time to time at ESPN. He also freelances as a craft beer writer with his most recent work appearing in print for BeerAdvocate. He lives in Portland, OR.

Jason Wojciechowski is a labor lawyer in Los Angeles and an editor at Baseball Prospectus. Approximately twice per year, he publishes analysis on the Oakland A's at Beaneball, the blog he started in 2003.

Nicholas Zettel is that person on the 'L' wearing a Brewers hat. When he's not leading the Unofficial Hernan Perez and Khris Davis Appreciation Societies, he researches urbanization and equity planning in Chicago.

Acknowledgements

Eddy Almaguer: First and foremost, I'd like to thank my wife, Mercy, who is supportive of my passion for writing about baseball. Thanks to the number crunchers behind the BP Stats Team, FanGraphs, Baseball Savant, Brooks Baseball and Baseball-Reference for providing countless data points for my work. And thank you to the devoted scouts, ranging from the BP prospect team to my Prospects Live colleagues for helping me give context to the numbers. And a final thank you to you, the reader! Without your support, work like this wouldn't be possible. Thanks for being a fan.

Darius Austin: Bret Sayre, Rob Mains, Rob McQuown, and the rest of my outstanding colleagues at BP. Kevin McCaul, for explaining much of the game to me in the first place, and Sam Kramer, for guiding me through the early days of baseball fandom and inviting me to my first serious fantasy league. Ben Lindbergh, Sam Miller and more recently Jeff Sullivan, for countless hours of entertainment and insight, and without whom I may never have found my way here. The brilliant people I have encountered who have been so supportive, given me many opportunities and ideas, and made this so much fun: Ken Maeda, Brandon Lee, Scott Kramer, Alex Crisafulli, Eric Roseberry, Andrew Patrick, Ryan Sullivan, Dan Epstein, Nick Strangis, John McGee, Tom Pringle, Ben Carter, Russell Eassom, Justin Mason, Ben Briggs, Adam Newman, Mike Werner, Matt Thompson, Chuck Anderson, Blaine Blontz and many, many more. My family, especially Amy, for love and unwavering support, no matter how many fantasy leagues I joined or strange things I searched for in relation to player comments.

Mike Axisa: My family for putting up with all my nonsense, first and foremost. Ben Kabak, Joe Pawlikowski, Jay Gordon, and everyone else who's supported River Ave. Blues over the years. My current CBS Sports teammates R.J. Anderson, Dayn Perry, and Matt Snyder; my editors Igor Mello and R.J. White; and my former editors Sergio Gonzalez and Ivan Irizarry. Also Tim Dierkes at MLB Trade Rumors and David Appelman and Dave Cameron at FanGraphs for giving me my first paying baseball writing jobs.

Emma Baccellieri: The usual suspects, various group texts and covens, and R.J. Anderson.

Mark Barry: Still sort of can't believe they let me do this. Thanks Bret Sayre for the opportunity, Zach Steinhorn for all of the editing/putting up with me, George Bissell for helping me get a foot in the door and to the fantasy crew—Mike, Wilson, Matt, Jon, Kevin, Eddy, Scott and Darius for being great guys to bounce ideas off of. Thanks to Mom, Dad, Kristen and of course Amanda. You guys are cool too. This has been super fun, you guys.

Nathan Bishop: My deep and sincere gratitude to my friends and colleagues Patrick Dubuque and Brendan Gawlowski, whose patience, kindness, knowledge, and skill have proven invaluable both in this project and many, many others. I would not be able to do pursue this or any other passion without the ceaseless support and understanding of my wife and two children, and my gratefulness for them and their understanding is immense. Thanks to my friends at D&B for keeping the fields of the mind so green.

Paul Boyé: Endless thanks to and immeasurable gratitude for my lovely wife Kerry; my parents, sister, and grandparents for their support and interest; Nick Schaefer for keeping me sharp; Matt Winkelman for insight and new ways to think about player development; Patrick Dubuque for counting on me to give this a second go; Keith Law, Ben Jedlovec, Mike Harris, Meaghan Tullis, Missy Perez, Tim Stoeckle, Miles Kennedy, Corinne Landrey, Pat McFarlane, and all those who've lent their time and energy to me over the past year. I am grateful for an indebted to more people than I could ever fit on this page.

Grant Brisbee: I would like to thank Marc Normandin, Kurt Mensching and Whitney McIntosh for helping me be a passable writer and making it fun to come into work every day. I'd also like to thank Nate Scott for his wordsmithing and camaraderie, and Brian Floyd for absolutely everything over the last eight years.

Craig Brown: Thanks to Joe Hamrahi, Clark Fosler, Rob Blackstien, Marc Normandin, Justin Bopp, Jeff Zimmerman, Max Rieper, Evan Brunell, Cecilia Tan, Rany Jazayerli, Dave Brown, Jeff Passan, Rustin Dodd, and Jeffrey Flanagan. Thank you to everyone at the recently departed BPKC. Of course, thanks to my family who tolerates this baseball obsession. Finally, as always, special thanks to C.E. Jones who taught me how to appreciate this game.

Russell Carleton: I'd like to acknowledge my one-year-old sons Timothy and Kieran whose tireless devotion to making sure that I had plenty of thinking time at 3:00 am paid off in a couple of essays that were barely coherent enough to publish.

Ben Carsley: My Red Sox-crazed family, the ever-patient future Allyson Carsley, Bret Sayre, Craig Goldstein, Sam Miller, R.J. Anderson, Patrick Dubuque, Aaron Gleeman, Mike Curtin, Eli Fredman, Mary Donovan, Daniel Ohman and whoever took the picture of JBJ with the dolphin.

Michael Clair: Thanks to Patrick Dubuque, Aaron Gleeman, Bret Sayre and everyone at BP. Ian Kay, Dakota Gardner, Gemma Kaneko, and the Cut4 staff for putting up with my takes every day. Emma Span, Ben Lindbergh, Mike Bates, Bill Parker, Jason Wojciechowski and everyone who gave me a chance and place to write. Marissa Maggs for protecting everyone from first drafts.

Roger Cormier: Thank you David Appelman, Carson Cistulli, Patrick Dubuque, Brian Mangan, and Travis Sawchik for helping me get to write in front of an unsuspecting, cool audience, and to all of the writers out there who set the bar impossibly high. Gratitude also goes to #Metstwitter for keeping me sane more often than not, and to my friends and family for their support.

Zach Crizer: Thank you to Stein, Jason, Jefe, Stin and Steph for being as hopelessly interested as I am. To Craig Goldstein for editing rap lyrics about Juan Soto without

batting an eye. To R.J. Anderson for repeatedly showing that analysis can have a conscience. To my dad, who has patiently asked about every foreign-sounding acronym. And to Caroline, who endures and even encourages this obsession.

Chris Cwik: Mal and Jane, Dad, Mom, Rob, Cait, Kirstin, Sherri, Mike Oz, Mike Ferrin, Emma Span, Paul Swydan, Jeff Passan, Liz Roscher, Mark Townsend, Tim Brown, Johnny Ludden, Melissa Caskey, Marcus Vanderberg, David Appelman, Carson Cistulli, Dayn Perry, Eno Sarris, Matt Snyder, Sergio Gonzalez, Craig Goldstein, Mori.

Patrick Dubuque: Thanks to Kjersten for listening, to Sylvie for cackling, and to Felix for (occasionally) sleeping. Thanks also to the hideously talented people at BP who have created such a great thing; to the comrades at Short Relief for their boundless creativity; to Sam Miller and Jason Wojciechowski for teaching me how to do all this; to Craig Brown and the Pease Brothers for putting it all together; and to Bret Sayre, Harry Pavlidis, Jeff Long, Jonathan Judge, Rob Mains, Rob McQuown, and Craig Goldstein for keeping this little dream alive.

Matt Ellis: All the folks at BP including the tireless Patrick Dubuque, all my D&B boys (Nathan, Skeebs, Dan, Andrew, Woodsy, SG, Weebs), Meg, and of course, Sam, who makes the Tuesdays bearable.

James Fegan: There are many to thank but I want to only focus on my wife Jacqueline. Thank you, Jacqueline.

Chad Finn: Thank you to so many colleagues, friends and family that have been there for me during my sportswriting career: Mike Pride, Yuri Pride, Steve Mistler, Jeff Novotny, Dave Cummings, Ray Duckler, Sandy Smith, Dana Wormald, Matthew T. Hall, Dave D'Onofrio, CJ Lampman, Hans Schulz, Bob Ryan, Peter Gammons, Dan Shaughnessy, Peter Abraham, Alex Speier, Scott Thurston, Ken Fratus, Gary Dzen, Matt Pepin, Bob Hohler, Fluto Shinzawa, Greg Lee, Joe Sullivan, Greg Lang, Jim Hoban, Jim McBride, Dave Lefort, Eric Wilbur, Steve Silva, Chris Greenberg, Rachel Bowers, Andrew Mahoney, Steve Buckley, Kris Poulin, Tom Poulin, Tim Hopley, and Roo Finn. Thank you to my wife Jen and children Leah and Alex for giving me so many cherished times. You're the family I dreamed of having in the moments when I wasn't thinking about baseball as a kid. And thank you to my dad, Charlie, for teaching me how to play Strat-O-Matic, taking me to all of those Maine Guides games, and always letting me read Gammons's Sunday Baseball Notes first.

Ken Funck: Steph Bee, Will Carroll, Patrick Dubuque, Aaron Gleeman, Steven Goldman, Kevin Goldstein, Christina Kahrl, King Kaufman, Ben Lindbergh, Sam Miller, John Perrotto, Bret Sayre, Cecilia Tan, Jason Wojciechowski and anyone else who has worked their editorial magic on my behalf.

Brendan Gawlowski: My writing career never would've been possible without the support and encouragement of my dad, Richard, who taught me much about baseball and writing. I'd also like to thank Patrick Dubuque, Nathan

Bishop, and Craig Goldstein for always being around to bounce ideas off of. Finally, thanks to my wife Sierra for letting me spend so much time doing something so ridiculous.

Mike Gianella: My wife Colleen. Lucy and Elise, two amazing children whose existence has made mine better. Mary Gianella. Everyone at Baseball Prospectus, especially Bret Sayre, who always believes in whatever I'm doing or want to do and Zach Steinhorn, a great editor and an even greater collaborator in LABR. Alex Patton, Peter Kreutzer, Steve Gardner, Jeff Erickson, Larry Schechter, Eric Karabell, Tristan Cockcroft and so many people who I've always admired who I'm now proud to call my peers as well as my friends.

Aaron Gleeman: Thank you to Becky, Beatrix and Judi for being the best and loving me no matter what, to Bret Sayre, Jonathan Judge and Rob Mains for leading us into the light, to Patrick Dubuque for doing so much heavy lifting and to John Bonnes and Paul Allen for turning my babbling about the Twins into something people willingly put into their ears.

Craig Goldstein: Katherine Pappas, Laurie Gross, Harvey Goldstein, Alexis Goldstein, Jason Wojciechowski, Sam Miller, Patrick Dubuque, Bret Sayre, Jeffrey Paternostro, Jarrett Seidler, Ian Miller, Riley Breckenridge, Jason Parks, The BP Prospect Team, Marc Normandin, RJ Anderson, Ben Carsley, Jacob Raim, Zach Mortimer, Tucker Blair, Ethan Purser, Mike Ferrin, Spike Lundberg, Tommy Rancel, Meg Rowley, James Fegan, Josh Herzenberg, Emma Baccellieri, Aaron Gleeman, Mauricio Rubio, J.P. Breen, Wilson Karaman, Zach Crizer, James Fegan, Jeffrey Wiser.

Bryan Grosnick: Sarah Grosnick, Luke Grosnick, Phil and Debbie Grosnick, Bret Sayre, R.J. Anderson, Rob McQuown, Patrick Dubuque, Aaron Gleeman, Scott Orgera, Charles O'Brien, Jonathan Judge, Jeffrey Paternostro, Jarrett Seidler, Kate Feldman, Craig Goldstein, Shawn Brody, Aaron Gleeman, Jason Wojciechowski, Sam Miller, Lukas Vlahos, Jeff Long, Kendall Guillemette, the BP Stats Team, and the data providers at Baseball Prospectus, FanGraphs, Baseball-Reference, and Brooks Baseball.

Jon Hegglund: Michael Hegglund, for the initial push into baseball writing. Ron Shandler, for my first writing gig. Bret Sayre, for my current writing gig. Mike Gianella and Zach Steinhorn, for expertly leading the BP fantasy team. Brendan Gawlowski, for all-around support and encouragement. Patrick Dubuque, for all the editing and a cool Barry Bonds card. Finally, and mostly, to Emily and Oscar, neither of whom care much about baseball but both of whom, miraculously, seem to care about me.

Kevin Jebens: Thanks to Andrew Meeds and Wick Terrell for helping me through the Reds farm system. Much gratitude and love to my fiancée, Heather, who somehow tolerates me talking baseball and poring through stats all season, and then all offseason. I promise I won't take you to any more double headers in July!

Jonathan Judge: To my terrific and understanding wife Janet; to my parents, who don't usually understand what I am writing but try to read it anyway; and to my two boys, for whom everything is worth doing.

Wilson Karaman: Thanks to my wife Lauren Danza for spending half of my birthdays with me and creating three new birthdays. Thanks to Jane and Joe Karaman for creating my birthday and mercilessly encouraging me through each one since. To Henry, Charlotte, and Baby X for being the most incredible things I've ever laid eyes on. To my grandmother Anne, who rocks 96 like it ain't no thang and defines what is Good on this chunk of rock. Thanks to BPers past, present, and future for building, growing, and vastly expanding our collective understanding of baseball and its beautiful intricacies. Next-level shout-outs to Bret Sayre, Craig Goldstein, Sam Miller, Aaron Gleeman, Patrick Dubuque, Rob Mains, Jeff Long, Jeffrey Paternostro, Harry Pavlidis, Jonathan Judge, Kate Morrison, Rob McQuown, other editors past and present, and the countless others who combine forces to make our little corner of the game's real estate the bee's knees.

Justin Klugh: Thank you to Liz Roscher, John Stolnis, Trevor Strunk, the glorious quote archives of Gene Mauch, editors like Megan Rowley and Patrick Dubuque, and Aviva, who doesn't like baseball, but does like me.

David Lee: He would like to thank his fiancee and their many pets for their patience and support.

Rob Mains: My mother, Rhoda Mains, for instilling a love of the game, and my wife, Amy Durland, for encouraging me to pursue it and often not regretting my having done so. Martin Alonso, Marco Gamez, Jose Hernandez, Carlos Lugo, and Carlos Perez, for making BP en espanol, our daily Spanish-language content, a reality. The team of DIY Baseball, especially Bret Sayre and Jonathan Judge, for making living through a How I Ruined My Summer Vacation essay ultimately rewarding. AM and PM for being who they are.

Rachael McDaniel: Anthony and Mom (for baseball), Taj (for everything), Peyton Thomas (for constant inspiration), and Patrick Dubuque (for mailing pictures of Jeffrey Leonard looking increasingly disappointed).

Whitney McIntosh: This essay would not be possible without my friends understanding that watching Top Chef on the couch counts as me writing, my boyfriend for not blinking when I told him the unusual angle of this essay and admirably suffering through my interest in European royal families, the Fug Girls for an unending stream of British royal family updates and the Red Sox for being an AL East team that actually calls young players up at appropriate times. Sources include all of the Vlad watchers on Twitter, the Journal of Sport Behavior, Atlas Obscura and PBS Nova.

Rob McQuown: My parents, Celia and John, for playing catch and for taking me to Wrigley Field and my own Little League games, and my brother Dan for sharing so many good times - some revolving around baseball. Bill James, for both planting the seed that both math and baseball could exist in the same profession and for breaking down doors to allow others than the "old boys network" to enter. Bob Mecca of STATS, Inc. for hiring me thus confirming there were jobs in the baseball analytics industry. Joe Hamrahi and Dave Pease for giving me opportunities to both program and write, and especially the current DIY braintrust for restoring hope that BP's future is bright. Among these, all have been tremendous to work with but at the risk of offending, I've considered it a special treat to work closely with Jonathan Judge, Rob Mains, and Harry Pavlidis. Above all, Bret Sayre has become a good friend while providing leadership to allow me to thrive professionally.

Jack Moore: Thanks to the Reds blogosphere (most notably Red Reporter and Redleg Nation) for helping me gauge the state of the Reds fanbase. And shoutout to Minnesota Smash and the Down B crew for giving me something to procrastinate with as I worked on this year's contribution.

Nick Nelson: Aaron Gleeman, who has been a crucial inspiration and a great friend. The Twins Daily team (John, Seth, Parker and Brock). My parents, who instilled my love of sports and especially baseball. And of course, thanks to my lovely fiancée Rachel for her 80-grade patience and support. Baseball-Reference.com, FanGraphs.com and BaseballProspectus.com were instrumental in my research, as always.

Eric Nusbaum: Thanks to Janelle, Clay, and Marco for being the best and also for all the home runs. Thanks to the 1996 Padres for teaching me the true meaning of sports by sweeping the Dodgers in the final series of the regular season to steal the NL West by one game. And thanks to Jorge Arangure, a great friend and the reason I was excited to write about baseball in San Diego in the first place.

Jeff Paternostro: My wife Jessica who has somehow made it through three prospect list seasons without divorcing me. Jarrett Seidler for being All In. Craig Goldstein for being my unpaid social media advisor for years. Meg Rowley for always having a minute to read something. Kate Feldman for giving me someone to bounce The Good Place theories off of. Brendan Gawlowski for not letting me get away with as much shit as Craig did. The BP Prospect team for keeping me buoyant across our 200,000-word annual journey. The readers and listeners who indulge and at times even embrace my weird, over-educated nonsense. And of course, #pizza channel.

Kate Preusser: I would like to acknowledge 2080 Baseball for providing video scouting of Orioles minor leaguers and Camden Chat for general coverage of the system, and also acknowledge the Seattle weather for encouraging me to stay inside and write, and chronic insomnia for allowing me to turn in my comments ahead of schedule.

Matt Provenzano: My mother for reading every single one of my articles; my father for taking me to my first game; my brother Jacob for loving Jason Giambi; my fiancé Amanda for being my AT&T Park companion; my grandfather for

conveying 80+ years knowledge and history; the Big Red Sports Network gang for playing MLB The Show until 4 AM; and the Pinstripe Alley gang for giving me a chance.

Tommy Rancel: Jamie, Alexis, Vincent, Jarek, Brooklyn, Dakota, R.J. Anderson, Erik Hahmann, Bradley Ankrom, Craig Goldstein, Jonah Keri, Keith Law, Joel Martinez, Daniel Baker, Pio La Ditingancia, LaJethro Jenkins, Dragonfly Jonez, Joset Kamali, Rebecca Basse, Carlos Alvarez, Karlous Miller, Cameron Magruder, Carl Reed and Algernon Lanier Washington.

Dan Rathman: Andrew Baggarly, Christopher Crawford, Matty Fisher, Sam Green, Craig Hyatt, Marty Lurie, Alex Pavlovic, Eno Sarris, Bret Sayre, Henry Schulman.

Sheryl Ring: Thank you to Ashley, the love of my life, who encouraged me to pursue my dreams. To my many lawyer friends—you know who you are - who I've annoyingly bothered with questions for a FanGraphs piece about some esoteric thing I wasn't sure about, thank you for putting up with me and making me look better than I really am. To my amazing co-workers and friends at Open Communities—Mary Ellen, Chris, Jasemen, Lynn, and Kelly—you are the best. To my PAL Matt, who I have spent way too much time arguing about baseball with, you will forever be my brother. To David Appelman for giving me a shot at my dream, I will be forever grateful. And there are so many people in the industry who have given me more support than I deserve—Meg Rowley, Carson Cistulli, Travis Sawchik, Britni de la Cretaz, Julie DiCaro, Kelly Wallace, Jeff Sullivan, Jen Mac Ramos, just to name a few—I appreciate you so much and I am humbled and honored to know you. To my friends—you know who you are—thank you for your support. And to my siblings in the LGBTQ community: remember that everything is possible. This is for you.

David Roth: Thanks to all the BP buddies for including me and taking care to give me a different bleak team with every year. Thanks, too, to Charles, Dom, Diana, Dan, and the anonymous maestro behind Where Have You Gone Andy Van Slyke for their insights on this year's bleak team. Thanks, always, to my wife and family and friends for tolerating me despite the fact that I am at this point inarguably the sort of person who writes this kind of thing.

Meg Rowley: Thank you to my family, for knowing when the statement "you work too much" is useful, and when it decidedly is not. Also, thank you to Lindsey Adler, Emma Baccellieri, Bill Barnwell, Michael Baumann, Carson Cistulli, Patrick Dubuque, Brendan Gawlowski, Craig Goldstein, Eric Longenhagen, Sam Miller, Jeffrey Paternostro, and Jeff Sullivan for providing both friendship and perspective, which has made me a better writer and a happier baseball human.

Bret Sayre: My wife Carolyn for not only being better than me at everything, but actually holding a national certification proclaiming so. Aly and Josh for keeping me on my toes and awake at night. Lynn and Peter Sayre for their encouragement. The entire Baseball Prospectus family for always teaching me something new. Team DIY for believing: Patrick Dubuque, Jonathan Judge, Jeff Long, Rob Mains, Rob

McQuown, Harry Pavlidis. Ben Carsley and Craig Goldstein for keeping me in line. Mike Gianella and Wilson Karaman for the sage advice. R.J. Anderson and Sam Miller for inspiration. The Heights Heat for reminding me why I love the game: Emilyn Anderson, Mia Bussin, Ellis Duff, Alexandra Duryee, Carly Figlar, Ava Garcia, Analise Javier, Emma Mulroy, Allison Nelson, Aly Sayre, Hallie Stein, Lucia Xhelo, Annie Young.

Nick Schaefer: Thank you to James, Matt, Cat, Mark, Frank, and Collin for being the best team anyone could ask for, and to Jane for so many things.

Jarrett Seidler: Thanks to all who supported me through a trying year. Particular shouts to Lindsey Adler, Michael Baumann, Patrick Dubuque, Kate Feldman, Brendan Gawlowski, Craig Goldstein, Bryan Grosnick, Rob Mains, Kate Morrison, Jeffrey Paternostro, David Roth, Meg Rowley, Bret Sayre, Nick Schaefer, Nick Stellini, Collin Whitchurch, The Woods, and some other friends who might not want to be named here. Most of all, thanks to modern medicine and a crew of very skilled doctors and surgeons, or I probably wouldn't have made it long enough to be in this book.

Susan Slusser: David Forst and Dan Feinstein sat down to discuss the A's 2018 transactions in an interview at the team offices on November 16, 2018.

Jesse Spector: Many thanks to Patrick Dubuque and BP for allowing me to do this; to Julian Valentin for the chance to write for Rockies Magazine and gain a deeper understanding of the organization; to my wife Caroline and kids Alice and Sean for always inspiring me; and of course to Dinger.

Eric Stephen: Huge thanks to the Play Index at Baseball-Reference, and to Baseball Prospectus and FanGraphs, all indispensable resources for baseball fans.

Matt Sussman: To Max for making his first favorite player Max Muncy. To Brittany who always tells me not to stay up too late.

David Temple: Patrick Dubuque, Jason Mendoza.

Matthew Trueblood: Maria, for encouraging and accommodating my silly obsession, for supporting and loving me unconditionally, and for standing by me always; Anna, for bringing a new light to our life when it was, perhaps, darkest; Lincoln, for your affectionate love and your off-the-charts humor; Sorkin, for demanding that I be a better dad whenever I slip, challenging me to be better at everything; Emerson, for being a constant reminder of the need to grow and learn and love and make my best better.

Ashley Varela: Daniel Zarchy, for everything. Bret Sayre and Patrick Dubuque, for their continued trust and support as I try to conjure up the words to describe this strange magic we call baseball. The oodles of talented writers and editors at Baseball Prospectus, whose thoughtful and creative discourse raises the bar on a daily basis. And a special thanks to Tamara Unfreid, who couldn't have cared less for sports but whose kindness, love and profound impact is missed every single day.

Levi Weaver: Thank you to Jamey Newberg and Kate Morrison for teaching me about prospects, and to Or Moyal for hiring me to do this job in the first place. Thank you to Heather, who made me watch Dirty Dancing.

Collin Whitchurch: I'd like to thank James Fegan for taking a chance on an annoying Twitter follower who asked out of the blue if he could contribute to his White Sox blog, Nick Schaefer for being the ideal co-pilot in both covering the White Sox and authoring player comments the last few years, as well as the team of awesome BPSS friends who have helped keep me sane throughout the years (Mark Primiano, Cat Garcia, Frank Firke, Matt Adams). I'd also like to thank my parents who have always encouraged my writing and my late Uncle Jack who treated me like a Sportswriting Superstar even if I am most decidedly not.

Jeff Wiser: Jeffrey would like to send a hearty "thank you" to those that have supported his baseball endeavors, especially the people that really don't care about baseball whatsoever. He'd like to specifically thank Ann for listening to his ramblings and nodding along patiently and challenging his thinking, his fellow writing friends for their ongoing support and willingness to hear him out when he has an especially bad idea, his fishing friends for helping him accomplish a much-needed change of scenery during baseball's doldrums, his PDX baseball friends for the reminders that baseball is best enjoyed in-person, and the fantastic breweries of Portland for concocting the perfect pairings for baseball season, year after year.

Jason Wojciechowski: Austen Rachlis, Tami Taylor Rachowski, Louise Archer Rachowski.

Nick Zettel: To my partner Anna, for tolerating my CSV-parsing during Westworld; to Bret Sayre, Aaron Gleeman, & Patrick Dubuque for writing and editing opportunities; to Craig Goldstein, all the BP scouts & prospect writers, Jonathan Judge, Rob McQuown, Harry Pavlidis, the BP Milwaukee team, and the Milwaukee's Tailgate podcast crew for player information, debates, and/or gracious answers to my questions.

Special Thanks to the colleagues who provided invaluable assistance during the proofreading process: Sydney Bergman and Laura Shir for the Scherzer comment, Martin Alonso for manager data, Sean Addis, Darius Austin, Jason Lefkowitz, Scott Orgera, Ginny Searle, and Nick Zettel.

Index of Names

Ballpark diagrams for Baseball Prospectus are created by THIRTY81Project, a design concept offering original ballpark artwork, including the new 'Ballparks of 2019' 11 x 17 color print.

Visit **www.thirty81project.com** for full details.

THE BALLPARKS OF 2019

FENWAY PARK · WRIGLEY FIELD · DODGER STADIUM · ANGEL STADIUM · OAKLAND COLISEUM · KAUFFMAN STADIUM · ROGERS CENTRE · TROPICANA FIELD · GUARANTEED RATE FIELD · ORIOLE PARK

PROGRESSIVE FIELD · GLOBE LIFE PARK · COORS FIELD · CHASE FIELD · T-MOBILE PARK · AT&T PARK · COMERICA PARK · MINUTE MAID PARK · MILLER PARK · PNC PARK

GREAT AMERICAN BALL PARK · CITIZENS BANK PARK · PETCO PARK · BUSCH STADIUM · NATIONALS PARK · CITI FIELD · YANKEE STADIUM · TARGET FIELD · MARLINS PARK · SUNTRUST PARK

THIRTY81
PROJECT

© 2019 LOUIS J. SPIRITO | THIRTY81PROJECT.COM